The grass withers, the flowers fade, but the Word of our God shall stand forever.

ISAIAH 40:8

This Bible belongs to the
James Spitters' FAMILY

DATE   12-25-'97

From the very first he made man and woman to be joined together permanently in marriage. MARK 10:6-7

Marriage

James Allen Spitters
AND Julie Nicole Book
WERE UNITED IN MARRIAGE ON June , 1997
AT First Church of God, St. Joseph
BY Pastor Bob Moss

WITNESSED BY

MAID OF HONOR Jennifer Book
BEST MAN Chris Spitters
ATTENDANTS Kim Book, Brenda Rasen, Julie Sanders, Michael Spitters, Tom Spitters, John Book, Scott Spitters

Children are a gift from God; they are his reward.

PSALM 127:3

Births

NAME _____

DATE _____ BIRTHPLACE _____

NAME _____

DATE _____ BIRTHPLACE _____

NAME _____

DATE _____ BIRTHPLACE _____

NAME _____

DATE _____ BIRTHPLACE _____

NAME _____

DATE _____ BIRTHPLACE _____

There is only one Lord,

one faith, one baptism.

EPHESIANS 4:5

Baptisms

_____ WAS BAPTIZED ON _____

AT _____ BY _____

_____ WAS BAPTIZED ON _____

AT _____ BY _____

_____ WAS BAPTIZED ON _____

AT _____ BY _____

_____ WAS BAPTIZED ON _____

AT _____ BY _____

_____ WAS BAPTIZED ON _____

AT _____ BY _____

God is going to raise our bodies from the dead by his power just as he raised up the Lord Jesus Christ. 1 CORINTHIANS 6:14

NAME _____

DATE _____

NAME _____

DATE _____

NAME _____

DATE _____

NAME _____

DATE _____

NAME _____

DATE _____

THE FAMILY

Husband

NAME _____ BIRTHPLACE _____ DATE _____

BROTHERS AND SISTERS _____

PARENTS

FATHER

NAME _____

BIRTHPLACE _____ DATES _____

MOTHER

NAME _____

BIRTHPLACE _____ DATES _____

GRANDPARENTS

PATERNAL

GRANDFATHER: Frank Spitters, Sr.

BIRTHPLACE _____ DATES _____

GRANDMOTHER: Dorothea

BIRTHPLACE _____ DATES _____

MATERNAL

GRANDFATHER: Rev. Eldon Curtis Watterworth

BIRTHPLACE _____ DATES _____

GRANDMOTHER: Olga Pauline Ginter Watterworth

BIRTHPLACE: Elkton, MI. DATES _____

GREAT-GRANDPARENTS

PATERNAL

GRANDFATHER'S FATHER _____

BIRTHPLACE _____ DATES _____

GRANDFATHER'S MOTHER _____

BIRTHPLACE _____ DATES _____

GRANDMOTHER'S FATHER _____

BIRTHPLACE _____ DATES _____

GRANDMOTHER'S MOTHER _____

BIRTHPLACE _____ DATES _____

MATERNAL

GRANDFATHER'S FATHER: Maitland Watterworth

BIRTHPLACE _____ DATES _____

GRANDFATHER'S MOTHER _____

BIRTHPLACE _____ DATES _____

GRANDMOTHER'S FATHER: Henry Ginter

BIRTHPLACE _____ DATES _____

GRANDMOTHER'S MOTHER: Della

BIRTHPLACE _____ DATES _____

NAME   **BIRTHPLACE**   **DATE**

BROTHERS AND SISTERS

PARENTS

FATHER   *MOTHER*

NAME   NAME

BIRTHPLACE   DATES   BIRTHPLACE   DATES

GRANDPARENTS

PATERNAL   *MATERNAL*

GRANDFATHER   **GRANDFATHER**

BIRTHPLACE   DATES   BIRTHPLACE   DATES

GRANDMOTHER   **GRANDMOTHER**

BIRTHPLACE   DATES   BIRTHPLACE   DATES

GREAT-GRANDPARENTS

PATERNAL   *MATERNAL*

GRANDFATHER'S FATHER   **GRANDFATHER'S FATHER**

BIRTHPLACE   DATES   BIRTHPLACE   DATES

GRANDFATHER'S MOTHER   **GRANDFATHER'S MOTHER**

BIRTHPLACE   DATES   BIRTHPLACE   DATES

GRANDMOTHER'S FATHER   **GRANDMOTHER'S FATHER**

BIRTHPLACE   DATES   BIRTHPLACE   DATES

GRANDMOTHER'S MOTHER   **GRANDMOTHER'S MOTHER**

BIRTHPLACE   DATES   BIRTHPLACE   DATES

Oh, give thanks to the Lord, for he is so good! For his loving-kindness is forever.

PSALM 118:29

Special Memories

EVENT _____

PLACE _____ DATE _____

EVENT _____

PLACE _____ DATE _____

EVENT _____

PLACE _____ DATE _____

EVENT _____

PLACE _____ DATE _____

EVENT _____

PLACE _____ DATE _____

The Family Devotions Bible

THE LIVING BIBLE

Tyndale House Publishers, Inc.
Wheaton, Illinois

The Family Devotions Bible
© 1993 Tyndale House Publishers, Inc.
All rights reserved.

Cover and interior artwork copyright © 1993 by Carolyn Vibbert

Devotional stories are taken from issues of *Keys for Kids,* published bimonthly by the "Children's Bible Hour," Box 1, Grand Rapids, MI 49501.

Notes are adapted from the *Life Application Bible,* © 1988, 1989, 1990, 1991 by Tyndale House Publishers, Inc.

The Bible text used in this edition of *The Family Devotions Bible* is *The Living Bible,* copyright © 1971 owned by assignment by KNT Charitable Trust. All rights reserved.

The Living Bible text may be quoted up to and inclusive of two hundred fifty (250) verses without express written permission of the publisher, provided that the verses quoted do not account for more than 20 percent of the total work in which they are quoted. This credit line will be used:

> Verses marked TLB are taken from *The Living Bible,* copyright © 1971. Used by permission of Tyndale House Publishers, Inc., Wheaton, Illinois 60189. All rights reserved.

Quotations in excess of two hundred fifty (250) verses, or other permission requests, must be directed to and approved in writing by Tyndale House Publishers, Inc., 351 Executive Dr., P.O. Box 80, Wheaton, IL 60189.

Library of Congress Cataloging-in-Publication Data

Bible. English. Living Bible. date
  The family devotions Bible : the Living Bible.
    p. cm.
  Includes index.
  ISBN 0-8423-1223-4. — ISBN 0-8423-1224-2 (softcover)
  1. Family—Prayer-books and devotions—English. 2. Devotional calendars. I. Tyndale House Publishers. II. Title.
BS195.L58 1993   92-21145
220.5'208—dc20

Printed in the United States of America

99 98 97 96 95 94 93
7   6   5   4   3   2

Contributors

The devotional stories included in this Bible are written by

Katherine Ruth Adams
Esther M. Bailey
Brenda Benedict
Judi Boogaart
David C. Carson
V. Louise Cunningham
Brenda Decker
Harriet A. Durrell
Donna Edinger
Carolyn J. Gaston
Judy A. Gillispie
Jorlyn Grasser
Jonnye R. Griffin
Ruth M. Hamel
Jan Hansen
Alicia Heckman
Ruth Jay
Gail L. Jenner
Pamela G. Jones
Beverly Kenniston
Nance E. Keyes
Phyllis Klomparens
Daryl Knauer
Linda E. Knight
Sherry Kuyt
Donna L. Lawless
Joyce Lee
Dolores A. Lemieux
Amy E. Linde
Agnes G. Livezey
April Lymer
Dawn E. Maloney
Deborah S. Marett
Hazel Marett
Lorna B. Marlowe
Patricia A. McCarthy
Ruth McQuilkin
Valerae C. Murphy
Sara Nelson
Matilda Nordtvedt
Miriam K. Nowak
Mary Rose Pearson
Raelene Phillips
Victoria L. Reinhardt
Phyllis Robinson
Deana Rogers
Catherine Runyon
Lynn Stamm Rex
Sam L. Sullivan
Lois A. Teufel
Trudy Vander Veen
Charlie VanderMeer
Lyndel Walker
Linda M. Weddle
Barbara Westberg
Lola M. Williams
Carolyn Yost

The author's initials appear at the end of each story. Bible book introductions were written by Judy A. Gillispie.

Contents

ix The Books of the Bible

xi Alphabetical Book Listing

xiii Introduction

xv User's Guide

xvii List of Topics

1 Old Testament

893 New Testament

1273 Complete List of Memory Verses

1275 List of Memory Verses by Topic

1281 Topical Index

Books of the Bible

The Old Testament

Genesis 3
Exodus 61
Leviticus 113
Numbers 147
Deuteronomy 189
Joshua 229
Judges 257
Ruth 281
1 Samuel 287
2 Samuel 325
1 Kings 353
2 Kings 381
1 Chronicles 409
2 Chronicles 439
Ezra 471
Nehemiah 481
Esther 497
Job 505
Psalms 531
Proverbs 613
Ecclesiastes 643
Song of Solomon 655
Isaiah 661
Jeremiah 719
Lamentations 769
Ezekiel 775
Daniel 817
Hosea 833
Joel 841
Amos 845
Obadiah 853
Jonah 855
Micah 859
Nahum 865
Habakkuk 869
Zephaniah 873
Haggai 877
Zechariah 879
Malachi 889

The New Testament

Matthew 895
Mark 933
Luke 959
John 1001
Acts 1035
Romans 1073
1 Corinthians 1095
2 Corinthians 1119
Galatians 1135
Ephesians 1145
Philippians 1155
Colossians 1161
1 Thessalonians 1167
2 Thessalonians 1173
1 Timothy 1177
2 Timothy 1185
Titus 1191
Philemon 1195
Hebrews 1197
James 1215
1 Peter 1223
2 Peter 1231
1 John 1235
2 John 1241
3 John 1243
Jude 1247
Revelation 1249

Alphabetical Book Listing

Acts 1035
Amos 845

1 Chronicles 409
2 Chronicles 439
Colossians 1161
1 Corinthians 1095
2 Corinthians 1119

Daniel 817
Deuteronomy 189

Ecclesiastes 643
Ephesians 1145
Esther 497
Exodus 61
Ezekiel 775
Ezra 471

Galatians 1135
Genesis 3

Habakkuk 869
Haggai 877
Hebrews 1197
Hosea 833

Isaiah 661

James 1215
Jeremiah 719
Job 505
Joel 841
John 1001
1 John 1235
2 John 1241
3 John 1243
Jonah 855
Joshua 229
Jude 1247
Judges 257

1 Kings 353
2 Kings 381

Lamentations 769
Leviticus 113
Luke 959

Malachi 889
Mark 933
Matthew 895
Micah 859

Nahum 865
Nehemiah 481
Numbers 147

Obadiah 853

1 Peter 1223
2 Peter 1231
Philemon 1195
Philippians 1155
Proverbs 613
Psalms 531

Revelation 1249
Romans 1073
Ruth 281

1 Samuel 287
2 Samuel 325
Song of Solomon 655

1 Thessalonians 1167
2 Thessalonians 1173
1 Timothy 1177
2 Timothy 1185
Titus 1191

Zechariah 879
Zephaniah 873

Introduction

Welcome to *The Family Devotions Bible*. God gave us his Word to tell us about himself and his plan for our life. When we read the Bible, we see God's love in action and we learn about what he wants us to do. "The whole Bible was given to us by inspiration from God and is useful to teach us what is true and to make us realize what is wrong in our lives; it straightens us out and helps us do what is right. It is God's way of making us well prepared at every point, fully equipped to do good to everyone" (2 Timothy 3:16-17).

You can see that reading the Bible is very important. As we read, however, we need to look for ways the Bible's teaching can apply to our own lives—specific examples of how God's Word can make a difference in the way we live. That's what makes *The Family Devotions Bible* unique. Throughout the Bible, you'll find notes on selected verses, memory verses, and 365 devotional stories to help children and adults alike make the Bible's valuable teaching a part of everyday life.

The delightful stories are taken from *Keys for Kids,* a bimonthly publication of the "Children's Bible Hour." They are simple, direct, and concrete, and, like Jesus' parables, they speak to all of us in terms we can easily understand. And like all good stories, they are made for sharing, so look upon them as the basis for family sharing and growth.

User's Guide

The Family Devotions Bible contains several special features to aid in your family devotional reading.

- **Book introductions** preceding each book of the Bible give interesting information about the book. Designed to be read aloud at family devotions, the introductions help focus children's attention on key themes or stories they will be hearing in the book you're about to read.

- **Devotional stories,** each printed near the Scripture reading to which it refers, provide contemporary illustrations of the day's Scripture reading. Each story includes a "How about you?" section that asks children to apply the story to their own lives.

- Two **chain-reference systems** give you several options for using the devotionals. The first chain-reference at the end of each story directs you to the next consecutive story. Using this system, you will read the devotionals in biblical order, from Genesis through Revelation. The first story appears on page 5.

- The stories are divided into **forty-five categories**—aspects of Christian growth or character traits to be developed—and a second chain-reference system directs you to the next story on the same topic. If you follow this series of references, you will be able to focus on a particular topic for several days in a row. To use the topical approach, you may begin with the first story on the first topic, *Accepting Others,* which is found on page 207. Or you may begin with the topic of your choice from the list on the next page.

- **Memory verses** are listed with each devotional—one for each topic. A complete list of the memory verses appears on page 1273. The verses are listed with their topics on page 1275, to aid in memorizing and reviewing.

- **Notes for parents** on selected verses give additional commentary and application information. Each topic has three to five notes, and their locations are included in the topical index on page 1281.

List of Topics

The devotionals and notes in this Bible are divided into forty-five categories to enable you to focus on a particular topic for several days in a row, if you like.

You may begin with any topic from the list below. The page number following each topic indicates the location of the first devotional in that category. At the end of each story, there is a chain-reference that will direct you to the next story on that topic.

ACCEPTING OTHERS 207
(7 Devotionals)
AVOIDING SIN 195
(14 Devotionals)
BECOMING MORE LIKE
  JESUS 131
(14 Devotionals)
CONFESSING SIN 41
(14 Devotionals)
CONTENTMENT 89
(7 Devotionals)
CULTIVATING GODLY
  ATTITUDES 121
(14 Devotionals)
DEALING WITH CHANGE 15
(7 Devotionals)
ENCOURAGING OTHERS 705
(7 Devotionals)
FAITH IN ACTION 141
(7 Devotionals)
FORGIVING OTHERS 39
(7 Devotionals)
GIVING THANKS 169
(7 Devotionals)
GIVING TO GOD 105
(7 Devotionals)
GOING TO CHURCH 193
(7 Devotionals)
HONESTY 33
(7 Devotionals)
HUMILITY 449
(7 Devotionals)

KEEPING YOUR PROMISES 181
(7 Devotionals)
KNOWING GOD 197
(7 Devotionals)
KNOWING YOU'RE SPECIAL TO
  GOD 307
(7 Devotionals)
LEAVING THE FUTURE IN GOD'S
  HANDS 75
(7 Devotionals)
LOVING OTHERS 313
(7 Devotionals)
MAKING THE BEST CHOICES 275
(7 Devotionals)
OBEDIENCE 25
(7 Devotionals)
OPTIMISM 19
(7 Devotionals)
OVERCOMING ANGER 133
(7 Devotionals)
OVERCOMING FEAR 13
(7 Devotionals)
PATIENCE 549
(7 Devotionals)
PERSEVERANCE 37
(7 Devotionals)
PRAYING AT ALL TIMES 45
(7 Devotionals)
PUTTING GOD FIRST 115
(7 Devotionals)
RECEIVING CHRIST AS SAVIOR 235
(14 Devotionals)

RESISTING TEMPTATION 7
(7 Devotionals)
RESPECTING AUTHORITY 225
(7 Devotionals)
**RESPECTING GOD'S
WARNINGS** 21
(7 Devotionals)
RESPECTING GOD'S WORD 11
(7 Devotionals)
RESPECTING OTHERS 5
(14 Devotionals)
SERVING GOD BOLDLY 17
(7 Devotionals)
SERVING GOD WILLINGLY 291
(7 Devotionals)
SHARING YOUR FAITH 427
(14 Devotionals)

SHOWING COMPASSION 569
(7 Devotionals)
SHOWING KINDNESS 81
(7 Devotionals)
**STANDING FOR
RIGHTEOUSNESS** 139
(7 Devotionals)
TRUE JOY 83
(7 Devotionals)
**TRUSTING GOD FOR
GUIDANCE** 27
(7 Devotionals)
TRUSTING GOD FOR HELP 29
(7 Devotionals)
TRUSTING GOD'S PLAN 9
(7 Devotionals)

OLD TESTAMENT

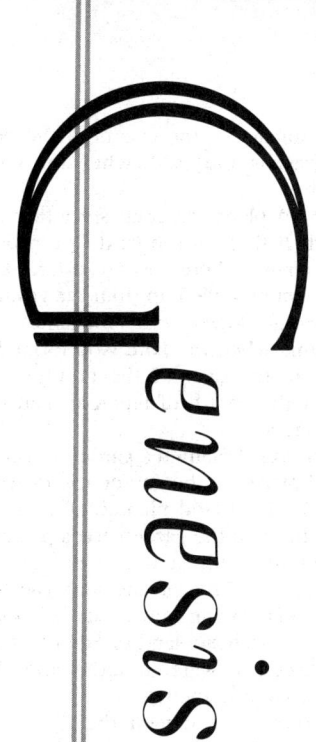

Genesis

WHAT'S THE longest book you've ever read? Did you read the whole thing because it was a great story?

Genesis is called a book, but it's really only the first chapter of a long and exciting story. The whole Old Testament tells about the Israelites—God's chosen people—and their travels, their battles, their worship, their mistakes, their songs, and the lessons they learned. But the story of the whole nation of Israel begins with just one person—Abraham—and we find his story in Genesis.

Abraham had faith in God, and that is why God chose him. Abraham wasn't a superstar or a genius or from a royal family. He was just ordinary Abraham, and he trusted God.

God's reward for Abraham's faith and obedience was incredible. God made a contract with Abraham. Through Abraham's son Isaac, his grandson Jacob, and his twelve great-grandsons, Abraham's family grew into thousands of people and became a nation.

Before Abraham's story begins, Genesis answers some important questions. How did the earth begin? Where did people come from? Why is there sin in the world? What kind of relationship does God want with people? Genesis doesn't provide all the scientific details, but it does tell what God wants us to know.

The word *Genesis* means "beginning." As you read, you'll learn about the beginning of the earth and also the beginning of God's relationship with people.

God Makes Everything

When God began creating the heavens and the earth, ²the earth was a shapeless, chaotic mass, with the Spirit of God brooding over the dark vapors.

³Then God said, "Let there be light." And light appeared. ⁴,⁵And God was pleased with it and divided the light from the darkness. He called the light "daytime," and the darkness "nighttime." Together they formed the first day.

⁶And God said, "Let the vapors separate to form the sky above and the oceans below." ⁷,⁸So God made the sky, dividing the vapor above from the water below. This all happened on the second day.

⁹,¹⁰Then God said, "Let the water beneath the sky be gathered into oceans so that the dry land will emerge." And so it was. Then God named the dry land "earth," and the water "seas." And God was pleased. ¹¹,¹²And he said, "Let the earth burst forth with every sort of grass and seed-bearing plant, and fruit trees with seeds inside the fruit, so

that these seeds will produce the kinds of plants and fruits they came from." And so it was, and God was pleased. [13]This all occurred on the third day.

[14,15]Then God said, "Let bright lights appear in the sky to give light to the earth and to identify the day and the night; they shall bring about the seasons on the earth, and mark the days and years." And so it was. [16]For God had made two huge lights, the sun and moon, to shine down upon the earth—the larger one, the sun, to preside over the day and the smaller one, the moon, to preside through the night; he had also made the stars. [17]And God set them in the sky to light the earth, [18]and to preside over the day and night, and to divide the light from the darkness. And God was pleased. [19]This all happened on the fourth day.

[20]Then God said, "Let the waters teem with fish and other life, and let the skies be filled with birds of every kind." [21,22]So God created great sea animals, and every sort of fish and every kind of bird. And God looked at them with pleasure, and blessed them all. "Multiply and stock the oceans," he told them, and to the birds he said, "Let your numbers increase. Fill the earth!" [23]That ended the fifth day.

[24]And God said, "Let the earth bring forth every kind of animal—cattle and reptiles and wildlife of every kind." And so it was. [25]God made all sorts of wild animals and cattle and reptiles. And God was pleased with what he had done.

[26]Then God said, "Let us make a man—someone like ourselves, to be the master of all life upon the earth and in the skies and in the seas."

[27]So God made man like his Maker.
Like God did God make man;
Man and maid did he make them.

[28]And God blessed them and told them, "Multiply and fill the earth and subdue it; you are masters of the fish and birds and all the animals. [29]And look! I have given you the seed-bearing plants throughout the earth and all the fruit trees for your food. [30]And I've given all the grass and plants to the animals and birds for their food." [31]Then God looked over all that he had made, and it was excellent in every way. This ended the sixth day.

2 God Makes Adam and Eve

Now at last the heavens and earth were successfully completed, with all that they contained. [2]So on the seventh day, having finished his task, God ceased from this work he had been doing, [3]and God blessed the seventh day and declared it holy, because it was the day when he ceased this work of creation.

[4]Here is a summary of the events in the creation of the heavens and earth when the Lord God made them.

[5]There were no plants or grain sprouting up across the earth at first, for the Lord God hadn't sent any rain; nor was there anyone to farm the soil. [6](However, water welled up from the ground at certain places and flowed across the land.)

[7]The time came when the Lord God formed a man's body from the dust of the ground and breathed into it the breath of life. And man became a living person.

[8]Then the Lord God planted a garden in Eden, to the east, and placed in the garden the man he had formed. [9]The Lord God planted all sorts of beautiful trees there in the garden, trees producing the choicest of fruit. At the center of the garden he placed the Tree of Life, and also the Tree of Conscience, giving knowledge of Good and Bad. [10]A river from the land of Eden flowed through the garden to water it; afterwards the river divided into four branches.

[11,12]One of these was named the Pishon; it winds across the entire length of the land of Havilah, where nuggets of pure gold are found, also beautiful bdellium and even lapis lazuli. [13]The second branch is called the Gihon, crossing the entire length of the land of Cush. [14]The third branch is the Tigris, which flows to the east of the city of Asher. And the fourth is the Euphrates.

[15]The Lord God placed the man in the Garden of Eden as its gardener, to tend and care for it. [16,17]But the Lord God gave the man this warning: "You may eat any fruit in the garden except fruit from the Tree of Conscience—for its fruit will open your eyes to make you aware of right and wrong, good and bad. If you eat its fruit, you will be doomed to die."

[18]And the Lord God said, "It isn't good for man to be alone; I will make a companion for him, a helper suited to his needs." [19,20]So the Lord God formed from the soil every kind of animal and bird, and brought them to the man to see what he would call them; and whatever he called them, that was their name. But still there was no proper helper for the man. [21]Then the Lord God caused the man to fall into a deep sleep, and took one of his ribs and closed up the place from which he had removed it, [22]and made the rib into a woman, and brought her to the man.

[23]"This is it!" Adam exclaimed. "She is part of my own bone and flesh! Her name is 'woman' because she was taken out of a man." [24]This explains why a man leaves his father and mother and is joined to his wife in such a way that the two become one person. [25]Now although the man and his wife were both naked, neither of them was embarrassed or ashamed.

Family Devotions

☐ **Devotion 1**
Respecting Others

Read Genesis 1:28-31

"I hope we don't have to have the Cookes over here again for a long time," grumbled Katie. "Those little kids messed up my whole room this afternoon."

"Just remember you used to be little yourself," Mom reminded her. "I'll give you a hand straightening up so we can get going to pick up Dad at the airport." Soon the job was finished.

After meeting Dad, they each had a soda pop while they waited for his luggage. Katie finished her pop just as they left the building. When they reached the car, she looked around the parking lot and then casually dropped the can on a clump of grass near a lightpost. She also unwrapped a stick of gum and left the wrapper beside the pop can.

"You can't leave your trash out here on the ground!" exclaimed Mom.

Katie shrugged. "Everybody does it," she said.

"Pick that up right now and put it in the car," ordered Dad. "You know we return the cans for recycling, and you can put the paper in the wastebasket at home." Katie frowned, but she did as she was told and climbed into the car without a word.

"The Cookes visited this afternoon," Mom told Dad as he started the engine.

"And their kids terrorized my room," Katie blurted out.

"Toddlers really can trash something in a hurry," agreed Mom. "They don't take proper care of others' property."

"Yes, but it's even worse when older kids or adults do that kind of thing. They ought to know better," said Dad looking back at Katie in the rearview mirror. "God created this beautiful earth, but we sometimes don't take proper care of his property. We mess it up by polluting." Katie got the point.

Respecting Others Memory Verse

Don't be selfish; don't live to make a good impression on others. Be humble, thinking of others as better than yourself.
Philippians 2:3

How About You?

Do you take time to find a wastebasket—even for small things like candy wrappers? Part of respecting others is doing your part to keep the earth—which we all share—clean.
N. E. K.

• For the next devotional, turn to page 7. • For the next devotional on *Respecting Others*, turn to page 73.
• For notes on *Respecting Others*, see pages 322, 382, 1088, and 1218.

3 Adam and Eve Are Tempted

The serpent was the craftiest of all the creatures the Lord God had made. So the serpent came to the woman. "Really?" he asked. *"None* of the fruit in the garden? God says you mustn't eat *any* of it?"

²,³"Of course we may eat it," the woman told him. "It's only the fruit from the tree at the *center* of the garden that we are not to eat. God says we mustn't eat it or even touch it, or we will die."

⁴"That's a lie!" the serpent hissed. "You'll not die! ⁵God knows very well that the instant you eat it you will become like him, for your eyes will be opened—you will be able to distinguish good from evil!"

⁶The woman was convinced. How lovely and fresh looking it was! And it would make her so wise! So she ate some of the fruit and gave some to her husband, and he ate it too. ⁷And as they ate it, suddenly they became aware of their nakedness, and were embarrassed. So they strung fig leaves together to cover themselves around the hips.

⁸That evening they heard the sound of the Lord God walking in the garden; and they hid themselves among the trees. ⁹The Lord God called to Adam, "Why are you hiding?"

¹⁰And Adam replied, "I heard you coming and didn't want you to see me naked. So I hid."

¹¹"Who told you you were naked?" the Lord God asked. "Have you eaten fruit from the tree I warned you about?"

¹²"Yes," Adam admitted, "but it was the woman you gave me who brought me some, and I ate it."

¹³Then the Lord God asked the woman, "How could you do such a thing?"

"The serpent tricked me," she replied.

¹⁴So the Lord God said to the serpent, "This is your punishment: You are singled out from among all the domestic and wild animals of the whole earth—to be cursed. You shall grovel in the dust as long as you live, crawling along on your belly. ¹⁵From now on you and the woman will be enemies, as will your offspring and hers. You will strike his heel, but he will crush your head."

¹⁶Then God said to the woman, "You shall bear children in intense pain and suffering; yet even so, you shall welcome your husband's affections, and he shall be your master."

¹⁷And to Adam, God said, "Because you listened to your wife and ate the fruit when I told you not to, I have placed a curse upon the soil. All your life you will struggle to extract a living from it. ¹⁸It will grow thorns and thistles for you, and you shall eat its grasses. ¹⁹All your life you will sweat to master it, until your dying day. Then you will return to the ground from which you came. For you were made from the ground, and to the ground you will return."

²⁰The man named his wife Eve (meaning "The life-giving one"), for he said, "She shall become the mother of all mankind"; ²¹and the Lord God clothed Adam and his wife with garments made from skins of animals.

²²Then the Lord said, "Now that the man has become as we are, knowing good from bad, what if he eats the fruit of the Tree of Life and lives forever?" ²³So the Lord God banished him forever from the Garden of Eden, and sent him out to farm the ground from which he had been taken. ²⁴Thus God expelled him, and placed mighty angels at the east of the Garden of Eden, with a flaming sword to guard the entrance to the Tree of Life.

4 Cain Kills Abel

Then Adam had sexual intercourse with Eve his wife, and she conceived and gave birth to a son, Cain (meaning "I have created"). For, as she said, "With God's help, I have created a man!" ²Her next child was his brother, Abel.

Abel became a shepherd, while Cain was a farmer. ³At harvest time Cain brought the Lord a gift of his farm produce, ⁴and Abel brought the fatty cuts of meat from his best lambs, and presented them to the Lord. And the Lord accepted Abel's offering, ⁵but not Cain's. This made Cain both dejected and very angry, and his face grew dark with fury.

⁶"Why are you angry?" the Lord asked him. "Why is your face so dark with rage? ⁷It can be bright with joy if you will do what you should! But if you refuse to obey, watch out. Sin is waiting to attack you, longing to destroy you. But you can conquer it!"

⁸One day Cain suggested to his brother, "Let's go out into the fields." And while they were together there, Cain attacked and killed his brother.

⁹But afterwards the Lord asked Cain, "Where is your brother? Where is Abel?"

"How should I know?" Cain retorted. "Am I supposed to keep track of him wherever he goes?"

¹⁰But the Lord said, "Your brother's blood calls to me from the ground. What have you done? ¹¹You are hereby banished from this ground which you have defiled with your brother's blood. ¹²No longer will it yield crops for you, even if you toil on it forever! From now on you will be a fugitive and a tramp upon the earth, wandering from place to place."

¹³Cain replied to the Lord, "My punishment is greater than I can bear. ¹⁴For you have banished me from my farm and from you, and made me a fugitive and a tramp; and everyone who sees me will try to kill me."

¹⁵The Lord replied, "They won't kill you, for I will give seven times your punishment to anyone who does." Then the Lord put an identifying mark on Cain as a warning not to kill him. ¹⁶So Cain

Family Devotions

☐ **Devotion 2**
Resisting Temptation

Read Genesis 3:1-7

Resisting Temptation Memory Verse

For since he himself has now been through suffering and temptation, he knows what it is like when we suffer and are tempted, and he is wonderfully able to help us.
Hebrews 2:18

"Dad, my fishing line is pulling!" shouted Ron.

Dad laughed. "That's because there's a fish on the end. Start reeling him in."

Soon the little sunfish was lying on the sand, but it was too small to keep. Reluctantly Ron put it back into the water. It flipped its tail, and in a moment it had disappeared.

"Whoa!" said Dad as Ron tossed his line back into the lake. "Aren't you forgetting something?"

Ron looked at him with a question in his eyes.

"The bait," Dad explained.

Ron laughed. "Oh, yeah," he said, pulling his line back in. "I guess no fish would be dumb enough to bite on the bare hook, would he? I'll disguise it and make it look good with this juicy worm. The fish won't know there's any danger, and he'll open his big mouth and swallow the hook. Then I'll have him!" With a grin he returned the line to the water once more.

"This reminds me of the way Satan works," Dad mused.

Ron was curious. "What do you mean, Dad?"

"Well, Satan tries to make sin look attractive," explained Dad. "Sometimes we're uneasy about something, or maybe we've been warned that it's wrong. Yet it looks good. Or it feels good. Or our friends are doing it, and we're tempted to try it, too. Satan is a master at disguising sin. He knows how to make bad things look good to us. So when you're tempted by a questionable activity, remember the fish. He wouldn't have gotten caught if he had stayed away from the hook."

How About You?

Does Satan use an interesting story on TV to get you accustomed to hearing bad language so that it doesn't bother you anymore? Does he catch your attention with a "good" movie so that you become careless about what you watch? Does he make playing games at the arcade so much fun that you do it even if you know you're spending too much money? What other methods does he use? Be careful. Ask God daily to help you stay away from the attractive bait Satan uses. *P. R.*

• For the next devotional, turn to page 9.   • For the next devotional o*n Resisting Temptation*, turn to page 47.
• For notes on *Resisting Temptation*, see pages 268, 448, 964, and 1258.

went out from the presence of the Lord and settled in the land of Nod, east of Eden.

[17]Then Cain's wife conceived and presented him with a baby son named Enoch; so when Cain founded a city, he named it Enoch, after his son.

[18]Enoch was the father of Irad; Irad was the father of Mehujael; Mehujael was the father of Methusael; Methusael was the father of Lamech;

[19]Lamech married two wives—Adah and Zillah. [20]To Adah was born a baby named Jabal. He became the first of the cattlemen and those living in tents. [21]His brother's name was Jubal, the first musician—the inventor of the harp and flute. [22]To Lamech's other wife, Zillah, was born Tubal-cain. He opened the first foundry forging instruments of bronze and iron.

[23]One day Lamech said to Adah and Zillah, "Listen to me, my wives. I have killed a youth who attacked and wounded me. [24]If anyone who kills Cain will be punished seven times, anyone taking revenge against me for killing that youth should be punished seventy-seven times!"

[25]Later on Eve gave birth to another son and named him Seth (meaning "Granted"); for, as Eve put it, "God has granted me another son for the one Cain killed." [26]When Seth grew up, he had a son and named him Enosh. It was during his lifetime that men first began to call themselves "the Lord's people."

5 Adam's Family

Here is a list of some of the descendants of Adam—the man who was like God from the day of his creation. [2]God created man and woman and blessed them, and called them Man from the start.

[3-5]*Adam:* Adam was 130 years old when his son Seth was born, the very image of his father in every way. After Seth was born, Adam lived another 800 years, producing sons and daughters, and died at the age of 930.

[6-8]*Seth:* Seth was 105 years old when his son Enosh was born. Afterwards he lived another 807 years, producing sons and daughters, and died at the age of 912.

[9-11]*Enosh:* Enosh was ninety years old when his son Kenan was born. Afterwards he lived another 815 years, producing sons and daughters, and died at the age of 905.

[12-14]*Kenan:* Kenan was seventy years old when his son Mahalalel was born. Afterwards he lived another 840 years, producing sons and daughters, and died at the age of 910.

[15-17]*Mahalalel:* Mahalalel was sixty-five years old when his son Jared was born. Afterwards he lived 830 years, producing sons and daughters, and died at the age of 895.

[18-20]*Jared:* Jared was 162 years old when his son Enoch was born. Afterwards he lived another 800 years, producing sons and daughters, and died at the age of 962.

[21-24]*Enoch:* Enoch was sixty-five years old when his son Methuselah was born. Afterwards he lived another 300 years in fellowship with God, and produced sons and daughters; then, when he was 365, and in constant touch with God, he disappeared, for God took him!

[25-27]*Methuselah:* Methuselah was 187 years old when his son Lamech was born; afterwards he lived another 782 years, producing sons and daughters, and died at the age of 969.

[28-31]*Lamech:* Lamech was 182 years old when his son Noah was born. Lamech named him Noah (meaning "Relief") because he said, "He will bring us relief from the hard work of farming this ground which God has cursed." Afterwards Lamech lived 595 years, producing sons and daughters, and died at the age of 777.

[32]*Noah:* Noah was 500 years old and had three sons, Shem, Ham, and Japheth.

6 Noah Builds the Ark

Now a population explosion took place upon the earth. It was at this time that beings from the spirit world looked upon the beautiful earth women and took any they desired to be their wives. [3]Then Jehovah said, "My Spirit must not forever be disgraced in man, wholly evil as he is. I will give him 120 years to mend his ways."

[4]In those days, and even afterwards, when the evil beings from the spirit world were sexually involved with human women, their children became giants, of whom so many legends are told. [5]When the Lord God saw the extent of human wickedness, and that the trend and direction of men's lives were only towards evil, [6]he was sorry he had made them. It broke his heart.

[7]And he said, "I will blot out from the face of the earth all mankind that I created. Yes, and the animals too, and the reptiles and the birds. For I am sorry I made them."

[8]But Noah was a pleasure to the Lord. Here is the story of Noah:[9,10]He was the only truly righteous man living on the earth at that time. He tried always to conduct his affairs according to God's will. And he had three sons—Shem, Ham, and Japheth.

[11]Meanwhile, the crime rate was rising rapidly across the earth, and, as seen by God, the world was rotten to the core.

[12,13]As God observed how bad it was, and saw that all mankind was vicious and depraved, he said to Noah, "I have decided to destroy all mankind; for the earth is filled with crime because of man. Yes, I will destroy mankind from the earth. [14]Make a boat from resinous wood, sealing it with tar; and

FAMILY DEVOTIONS

☐ DEVOTION 3
TRUSTING GOD'S PLAN

Read Genesis 4:6-7

One look at Randy's flushed face told Mom something was wrong. "What is it, honey?" she asked.

"If Jeff doesn't leave me alone on the bus, I'm going to have to fight him!" Randy blurted out.

"Oh?" Mom responded. "If you do, you had better be prepared to take the consequences."

Randy looked up. "Will you whip me?"

"No," Mom said, "but Jeff might. There must be a better solution than a fight. Does Jeff bother you at school?"

"No. He knows Miss Jenkins won't allow it," Randy answered, "but it's different on the bus."

"Well, let's pray about it, Randy," Mom said. "The Lord will help you find a solution."

The next day Randy came home from school grinning from ear to ear. Before Mom could ask, he told her, "Jeff left me alone today."

"What did you do?" Mom asked.

Randy chuckled. "I sat in the front seat of the bus," he said. "With the driver right there, Jeff didn't dare make trouble." Together Randy and Mom celebrated with cookies and milk.

Randy was surprised when Mom came over and hugged him a little later. "You've taught me a lesson today, Randy. I've been having a little trouble with my temper lately," she confessed. "There are a couple of people I've been tempted to tell off. I think the devil has been encouraging me to really give them a piece of my mind. But now I know how to keep Satan from bothering me."

Randy looked surprised. "How?"

"By getting just as close to Jesus as I can," Mom answered. "I've been sitting in the 'back of the bus.' I need to move up."

Trusting God's Plan Memory Verses

This plan of mine is not what you would work out, neither are my thoughts the same as yours! For just as the heavens are higher than the earth, so are my ways higher than yours, and my thoughts than yours.
Isaiah 55:8-9

How About You?
Are you tempted to go to "fist city" to solve your problems? Think again. Don't let anger destroy you. Get close to Jesus through reading his Word, praying, and keeping your thoughts on him. Trust his plan for solving your problems peaceably. *B. W.*

- For the next devotional, turn to page 11. • For the next devotional on *TRUSTING GOD'S PLAN*, turn to page 149.
- For notes on *TRUSTING GOD'S PLAN*, see pages 252, 296, 731, and 870.

construct decks and stalls throughout the ship. [15]Make it 450 feet long, 75 feet wide, and 45 feet high. [16]Construct a skylight all the way around the ship, eighteen inches below the roof; and make three decks inside the boat—a bottom, middle, and upper deck—and put a door in the side.

[17]"Look! I am going to cover the earth with a flood and destroy every living being—everything in which there is the breath of life. All will die. [18]But I promise to keep you safe in the ship, with your wife and your sons and their wives. [19,20]Bring a pair of every animal—a male and a female—into the boat with you, to keep them alive through the flood. Bring in a pair of each kind of bird and animal and reptile. [21]Store away in the boat all the food that they and you will need." [22]And Noah did everything as God commanded him.

7 God Sends the Great Flood

Finally the day came when the Lord said to Noah, "Go into the boat with all your family, for among all the people of the earth, I consider you alone to be righteous. [2]Bring in the animals, too—a pair of each, except those kinds I have chosen for eating and for sacrifice: take seven pairs of each of them, [3]and seven pairs of every kind of bird. Thus there will be every kind of life reproducing again after the flood has ended. [4]One week from today I will begin forty days and nights of rain; and all the animals and birds and reptiles I have made will die."

[5]So Noah did everything the Lord commanded him. [6]He was 600 years old when the flood came. [7]He boarded the boat with his wife and sons and their wives, to escape the flood. [8,9]With him were all the various kinds of animals—those for eating and sacrifice, and those that were not, and the birds and reptiles. They came into the boat in pairs, male and female, just as God commanded Noah.

[10-12]One week later, when Noah was 600 years, two months, and seventeen days old, the rain came down in mighty torrents from the sky, and the subterranean waters burst forth upon the earth for forty days and nights. [13]But Noah had gone into the boat that very day with his wife and his sons, Shem, Ham, and Japheth, and their wives. [14,15]With them in the boat were pairs of every kind of animal—domestic and wild—and reptiles and birds of every sort. [16]Two by two they came, male and female, just as God had commanded. Then the Lord God closed the door and shut them in.

[17]For forty days the roaring floods prevailed, covering the ground and lifting the boat high above the earth. [18]As the water rose higher and higher above the ground, the boat floated safely upon it; [19]until finally the water covered all the high mountains under the whole heaven, [20]standing twenty-two feet and more above the highest peaks. [21]And all living things upon the earth perished—birds, domestic and wild animals, and reptiles and all mankind—[22]everything that breathed and lived upon dry land. [23]All existence on the earth was blotted out—man and animals alike, and reptiles and birds. God destroyed them all, leaving only Noah alive, and those with him in the boat. [24]And the water covered the earth 150 days.

8

God didn't forget about Noah and all the animals in the boat! He sent a wind to blow across the waters, and the floods began to disappear, [2]for the subterranean water sources ceased their gushing, and the torrential rains subsided. [3,4]So the flood gradually receded until, 150 days after it began, the boat came to rest upon the mountains of Ararat. [5]Three months later, as the waters continued to go down, other mountain peaks appeared.

[6]After another forty days, Noah opened a porthole [7]and released a raven that flew back and forth until the earth was dry. [8]Meanwhile he sent out a dove to see if it could find dry ground, [9]but the dove found no place to light, and returned to Noah, for the water was still too high. So Noah held out his hand and drew the dove back into the boat.

[10]Seven days later Noah released the dove again, [11]and this time, toward evening, the bird returned to him with an olive leaf in her beak. So Noah knew that the water was almost gone. [12]A week later he released the dove again, and this time she didn't come back.

[13]Twenty-nine days after that, Noah opened the door to look, and the water was gone. [14]Eight more weeks went by. Then at last the earth was dry. [15,16]Then God told Noah, "You may all go out. [17]Release all the animals, birds, and reptiles, so that they will breed abundantly and reproduce in great numbers." [18,19]So the boat was soon empty. Noah, his wife, and his sons and their wives all disembarked, along with all the animals, reptiles, and birds—all left the ark in pairs and groups.

[20]Then Noah built an altar and sacrificed on it some of the animals and birds God had designated for that purpose. [21]And Jehovah was pleased with the sacrifice and said to himself, "I will never do it again—I will never again curse the earth, destroying all living things, even though man's bent is always toward evil from his earliest youth, and even though he does such wicked things. [22]As long as the earth remains, there will be springtime and harvest, cold and heat, winter and summer, day and night."

9

God blessed Noah and his sons and told them to have many children and to repopulate the earth.

[2,3]"All wild animals and birds and fish will be afraid of you," God told him; "for I have placed them in

Family Devotions

☐ DEVOTION 4

RESPECTING GOD'S WORD

Read Genesis 6:1-21

Respecting God's Word Memory Verse

Your words are what sustain me; they are food to my hungry soul. They bring joy to my sorrowing heart and delight me. How proud I am to bear your name, O Lord.

Jeremiah 15:16

"You can't do that!" exclaimed Larry as his friend Dennis moved his marker on the game board. "Don't you know the rules?"

Dennis looked up. "Yeah, but we always play it this way at home," he said as Mark, another friend, took a turn.

Then Dale took a turn. He landed on a space that said "You lose ten points." Dale shrugged. "We just skip those penalty points."

"This is no fun!" declared Larry. "Everybody plays by his own rules. We might as well quit."

"Or play by the rules of the person who made up the game in the first place," suggested Mom, who had just come in. "There's a rule sheet right there in the box."

Larry and his friends looked at one another. "Good idea," they agreed.

When Larry's father came home, he greeted Larry with a grin. "Well, what did you do today, Son?" he asked.

Larry explained what had happened that afternoon. "I learned," he said, "that it's important to play by the rules."

"Well, that's a good lesson to learn," Dad said approvingly. "I wish everybody would learn that."

"Not everybody plays games," Larry pointed out.

Dad raised his eyebrows. "Well, in a way they do," he said. "Everybody plays the 'game' of life. If we'd all follow the rules of the one who invented it, this would be a happier world. Do you know who I'm talking about?"

Larry nodded. "God," he said. "He gave his rules in the Bible. Everybody ought to follow them."

How About You?

Do you know God's rules? Do you follow them, or do you change them to suit yourself? You need to refer to his "rule sheet," the Bible, so you'll know what he says. But just knowing isn't enough. You need to follow his rules—to do what he says—as well. *H. M.*

- For the next devotional, turn to page 13. • For the next devotional on RESPECTING GOD'S WORD, turn to page 93.
- For notes on RESPECTING GOD'S WORD, see pages 208, 369, 1188, and 1248.

your power, and they are yours to use for food, in addition to grain and vegetables. ⁴But never eat animals unless their life-blood has been drained off. ⁵,⁶And murder is forbidden. Man-killing animals must die, and any man who murders shall be killed; for to kill a man is to kill one made like God. ⁷Yes, have many children and repopulate the earth and subdue it."

⁸Then God told Noah and his sons, ⁹⁻¹¹"I solemnly promise you and your children and the animals you brought with you—all these birds and cattle and wild animals—that I will never again send another flood to destroy the earth. ¹²And I seal this promise with this sign: ¹³I have placed my rainbow in the clouds as a sign of my promise until the end of time, to you and to all the earth. ¹⁴When I send clouds over the earth, the rainbow will be seen in the clouds, ¹⁵and I will remember my promise to you and to every being, that never again will the floods come and destroy all life. ¹⁶,¹⁷For I will see the rainbow in the cloud and remember my eternal promise to every living being on the earth."

¹⁸The names of Noah's three sons were Shem, Ham, and Japheth. (Ham is the ancestor of the Canaanites.) ¹⁹From these three sons of Noah came all the nations of the earth.

²⁰,²¹Noah became a farmer and planted a vineyard, and he made wine. One day as he was drunk and lay naked in his tent, ²²Ham, the father of Canaan, saw his father's nakedness and went outside and told his two brothers. ²³Then Shem and Japheth took a robe and held it over their shoulders and, walking backwards into the tent, let it fall across their father to cover his nakedness as they looked the other way. ²⁴,²⁵When Noah awoke from his drunken stupor, and learned what had happened and what Ham, his younger son, had done, he cursed Ham's descendants:

"A curse upon the Canaanites," he swore.
"May they be the lowest of slaves
To the descendants of Shem and Japheth."

²⁶,²⁷Then he said,

"God bless Shem,
And may Canaan be his slave.
God bless Japheth,
And let him share the prosperity of Shem,
And let Canaan be his slave."

²⁸Noah lived another 350 years after the flood ²⁹and was 950 years old at his death.

10 Noah's Family

These are the families of Shem, Ham, and Japheth, who were the three sons of Noah; for sons were born to them after the flood.

²The sons of Japheth were: Gomer, Magog, Madai, Javan, Tubal, Meshech, Tiras.

³The sons of Gomer: Ashkenaz, Riphath, Togarmah.

⁴The sons of Javan: Elishah, Tarshish, Kittim, Dodanim.

⁵Their descendants became the maritime nations in various lands, each with a separate language.

⁶The sons of Ham were: Cush, Mizraim, Put, Canaan.

⁷The sons of Cush were: Seba, Havilah, Sabtah, Raamah, Sabteca.

The sons of Raamah were: Sheba, Dedan.

⁸One of the descendants of Cush was Nimrod, who became the first of the kings. ⁹He was a mighty hunter, blessed of God, and his name became proverbial. People would speak of someone as being "like Nimrod—a mighty hunter, blessed of God." ¹⁰The heart of his empire included Babel, Erech, Accad, and Calneh in the land of Shinar. ¹¹,¹²From there he extended his reign to Assyria. He built Nineveh, Rehoboth-Ir, Calah, and Resen (which is located between Nineveh and Calah), the main city of the empire.

¹³,¹⁴Mizraim was the ancestor of the people inhabiting these areas: Ludim, Anamim, Lehabim, Naphtuhim, Pathrusim, Casluhim (from whom came the Philistines), and Caphtorim.

¹⁵⁻¹⁹Canaan's oldest son was Sidon, and he was also the father of Heth; from Canaan descended these nations: Jebusites, Amorites, Girgashites, Hivites, Arkites, Sinites, Arvadites, Zemarites, Hamathites. Eventually the descendants of Canaan spread from Sidon all the way to Gerar, in the Gaza strip; and to Sodom, Gomorrah, Admah, and Zeboiim, near Lasha.

²⁰These, then, were the descendants of Ham, spread abroad in many lands and nations, with many languages.

²¹Eber descended from Shem, the oldest brother of Japheth. ²²Here is a list of Shem's other descendants: Elam, Asshur, Arpachshad, Lud, Aram.

²³Aram's sons were: Uz, Hul, Gether, Mash.

²⁴Arpachshad's son was Shelah, and Shelah's son was Eber.

²⁵Two sons were born to Eber: Peleg (meaning "Division," for during his lifetime the people of the world were separated and dispersed), and Joktan (Peleg's brother).

²⁶⁻³⁰Joktan was the father of Almodad, Sheleph, Hazarmaveth, Jerah, Hadoram, Uzal, Diklah, Obal, Abima-el, Sheba, Ophir, Havi-lah, Jobab.

These descendants of Joktan lived all the way from Mesha to the eastern hills of Sephar.

³¹These, then, were the descendants of Shem, classified according to their political groupings, languages, and geographical locations.

☐ DEVOTION 5
OVERCOMING FEAR

Read Genesis 7:17-20; 8:1; 9:8-17

Overcoming Fear Memory Verse

Fear not, for I am with you. Do not be dismayed. I am your God. I will strengthen you; I will help you; I will uphold you with my victorious right hand.
Isaiah 41:10

With thumping heart, Kim waited in dread of the next flash of lightning and loud crash of thunder. It wasn't long before it came. The piercing lightning cracked the black darkness, and a frightening boom almost made her heart stop. Shaking, Kim reached for her bedside lamp, but when she pushed the switch, nothing happened. Dad came in with a flashlight. "The power is out," he said. "Come in the living room until the storm is over."

Mom lit some candles, and the three of them sat on the couch waiting for the worst of the storm to pass. "Why does it have to be so dark and the lightning so bright and the thunder so loud?" moaned Kim.

Dad gave her a hug. "I was just thinking," he said, "about God's promise to never again destroy the earth with a flood. No matter how frightening a storm gets, we can count on that promise. We know that God is in charge of the thunder and lightning and rain. You know, one of the best things to do when you're afraid is to talk to God. Let's do that right now."

Mom and Dad each prayed a short prayer, and then Kim prayed. "Dear God," she said, "I know you're right here in the stormy darkness with me. Please help me remember that, so I won't be so afraid." After her prayer, she suggested in a brave voice, "Why don't we have some milk and cookies while we're waiting for the storm to pass?"

"Great idea," agreed Mom. And they all headed for the kitchen guided by the flashlight's beam.

How About You?
Are you afraid of thunder and lightning? Many people of all ages and in all countries have been—and are—afraid of storms. But God is in the stormy darkness and the thunder and lightning just as he's in the sunshine. He'll take care of you. Talk with him and tell him about your fears. Praise him for his care for you during the storms. C. Y.

• For the next devotional, turn to page 15. • For the next devotional on OVERCOMING FEAR, turn to page 79.
• For notes on OVERCOMING FEAR, see pages 191, 482, 554, 592, and 912.

All of the men listed above descended from Noah, through many generations, living in the various nations that developed after the flood.

11 Building a Tower to the Sky

At that time all mankind spoke a single language. ²As the population grew and spread eastward, a plain was discovered in the land of Babylon and was soon thickly populated. ³,⁴The people who lived there began to talk about building a great city, with a temple-tower reaching to the skies—a proud, eternal monument to themselves.

"This will weld us together," they said, "and keep us from scattering all over the world." So they made great piles of hardburned brick, and collected bitumen to use as mortar.

⁵But when God came down to see the city and the tower mankind was making, ⁶he said, "Look! If they are able to accomplish all this when they have just *begun* to exploit their linguistic and political unity, just think of what they will do later! Nothing will be unattainable for them! ⁷Come, let us go down and give them different languages, so that they won't understand each other's words!"

⁸So, in that way, God scattered them all over the earth; and that ended the building of the city. ⁹That is why the city was called Babel (meaning "confusion"), because it was there that Jehovah confused them by giving them many languages, thus widely scattering them across the face of the earth.

¹⁰,¹¹Shem's line of descendants included Arpachshad, born two years after the flood when Shem was 100 years old; after that he lived another 500 years and had many sons and daughters.

¹²,¹³When Arpachshad was thirty-five years old, his son Shelah was born, and after that he lived another 403 years and had many sons and daughters.

¹⁴,¹⁵Shelah was thirty years old when his son Eber was born, living 403 years after that, and had many sons and daughters.

¹⁶,¹⁷Eber was thirty-four years old when his son Peleg was born. He lived another 430 years afterwards and had many sons and daughters.

¹⁸,¹⁹Peleg was thirty years old when his son Reu was born. He lived another 209 years afterwards and had many sons and daughters.

²⁰,²¹Reu was thirty-two years old when Serug was born. He lived 207 years after that, with many sons and daughters.

²²,²³Serug was thirty years old when his son Nahor was born. He lived 200 years afterwards, with many sons and daughters.

²⁴,²⁵Nahor was twenty-nine years old at the birth of his son Terah. He lived 119 years afterwards and had sons and daughters.

²⁶By the time Terah was seventy years old, he had three sons, Abram, Nahor, and Haran.

²⁷And Haran had a son named Lot. ²⁸But Haran died young, in the land where he was born (in Ur of the Chaldeans), and was survived by his father.

²⁹Meanwhile, Abram married his half-sister Sarai, while his brother Nahor married their orphaned niece, Milcah, who was the daughter of their brother Haran; and she had a sister named Iscah. ³⁰But Sarai was barren; she had no children. ³¹Then Terah took his son Abram, his grandson Lot (his son Haran's child), and his daughter-in-law Sarai, and left Ur of the Chaldeans to go to the land of Canaan; but they stopped instead at the city of Haran and settled there. ³²And there Terah died at the age of 205.

12 Abram Moves to New Lands

God had told Abram, "Leave your own country behind you, and your own people, and go to the land I will guide you to. ²If you do, I will cause you to become the father of a great nation; I will bless you and make your name famous, and you will be a blessing to many others. ³I will bless those who bless you and curse those who curse you; and the entire world will be blessed because of you."

⁴So Abram departed as the Lord had instructed him, and Lot went too; Abram was seventy-five years old at that time. ⁵He took his wife Sarai, his nephew Lot, and all his wealth—the cattle and slaves he had gotten in Haran—and finally arrived in Canaan. ⁶Traveling through Canaan, they came to a place near Shechem, and set up camp beside the oak at Moreh. (This area was inhabited by Canaanites at that time.)

⁷Then Jehovah appeared to Abram and said, "I am going to give this land to your descendants." And Abram built an altar there to commemorate Jehovah's visit. ⁸Afterwards Abram left that place and traveled southward to the hilly country between Bethel on the west and Ai on the east. There he made camp, and made an altar to the Lord and prayed to him. ⁹Thus he continued slowly southward to the Negeb, pausing frequently.

¹⁰There was at that time a terrible famine in the land: and so Abram went on down to Egypt to live. ¹¹⁻¹³But as he was approaching the borders of Egypt, he asked Sarai his wife to tell everyone that she was his sister! "You are very beautiful," he told her, "and when the Egyptians see you they will say, 'This is his wife. Let's kill him and then we can have her!' But if you say you are my sister, then the Egyptians will treat me well because of you, and spare my life!" ¹⁴And sure enough, when they arrived in Egypt everyone spoke of her beauty. ¹⁵When the palace aides saw her, they praised her to their king, the Pharaoh, and she

Family Devotions

☐ Devotion 6
Dealing with Change

Read Genesis 12:1-5

Dealing with Change
Memory Verse

We know that all that happens to us is working for our good if we love God and are fitting into his plans.
Romans 8:28

Nathan hadn't been very happy lately. His father's job had moved the family from the Midwest to the South, and Nathan missed his friends and the happy times they'd had together. He was sure he never could be happy here. There was just no use in trying.

One day, the family took a trip to the beach. They all went swimming, but Nathan refused to admit it was fun. Later, the family hunted for shells on the beach. Nathan found a starfish, but two of its arms were broken off. He was about to throw it away when Dad spoke up. "Let me see it," Dad said, holding out his hand. Nathan handed the starfish to him, and Dad turned it over. "See the little moving feet?"

"You mean it's alive?" Nathan asked in surprise. Dad nodded. "But it's gonna die," continued Nathan. "It only has three arms instead of five."

Dad nodded. "Yes, but it will survive. Starfish can regenerate."

"What does that mean?"

"In time, the starfish will grow new arms to replace the old ones," Dad explained.

"And I thought it was useless," Nathan said thoughtfully.

"Nathan, right now you're something like that starfish. You've been cut off from your old friends and you're hurting. It's scary to begin again, but with God's help, you can make new friends and develop new interests," encouraged Dad.

Nathan looked at the starfish and smiled. "If he can begin again, I guess I can, too."

How About You?

How do you face new situations? Do you accept them as a challenge to learn and grow? Or do you look at them with discouragement and refuse to try again? Perhaps someone close to you has died, a friend has moved away, or you've gained a new stepparent and things seem so uncertain for you. Ask God for strength to accept your new situation. Then look for ways you can reach out and be friendly to those around you. *J. H.*

- For the next devotional, turn to page 17. • For the next devotional on *Dealing with Change*, turn to page 155.
- For notes on *Dealing with Change*, see pages 56, 156, 288, 1186, and 1198.

was taken into his harem. ¹⁶Then Pharaoh gave Abram many gifts because of her—sheep, oxen, donkeys, men and women slaves, and camels.

¹⁷But the Lord sent a terrible plague upon Pharaoh's household on account of her being there. ¹⁸Then Pharaoh called Abram before him and accused him sharply. "What is this you have done to me?" he demanded. "Why didn't you tell me she was your wife? ¹⁹Why were you willing to let me marry her, saying she was your sister? Here, take her and be gone!" ²⁰And Pharaoh sent them out of the country under armed escort—Abram, his wife, and all his household and possessions.

13 Lot Leaves Abram

So they left Egypt and traveled north into the Negeb—Abram with his wife, and Lot, and all that they owned, for Abram was very rich in livestock, silver, and gold. ³,⁴Then they continued northward toward Bethel where he had camped before, between Bethel and Ai—to the place where he had built the altar. And there he again worshiped the Lord.

⁵Lot too was very wealthy, with sheep and cattle and many servants. ⁶But the land could not support both Abram and Lot with all their flocks and herds. There were too many animals for the available pasture. ⁷So fights broke out between the herdsmen of Abram and Lot, despite the danger they all faced from the tribes of Canaanites and Perizzites present in the land. ⁸Then Abram talked it over with Lot. "This fighting between our men has got to stop," he said. "We can't afford to let a rift develop between our clans. Close relatives such as we are must present a united front! ⁹I'll tell you what we'll do. Take your choice of any section of the land you want, and we will separate. If you want that part over there to the east, then I'll stay here in the western section. Or, if you want the west, then I'll go over there to the east."

¹⁰Lot took a long look at the fertile plains of the Jordan River, well watered everywhere (this was before Jehovah destroyed Sodom and Gomorrah); the whole section was like the Garden of Eden, or like the beautiful countryside around Zoar in Egypt. ¹¹So that is what Lot chose—the Jordan valley to the east of them. He went there with his flocks and servants, and thus he and Abram parted company. ¹²For Abram stayed in the land of Canaan, while Lot lived among the cities of the plain, settling at a place near the city of Sodom. ¹³The men of this area were unusually wicked, and sinned greatly against Jehovah.

¹⁴After Lot was gone, the Lord said to Abram, "Look as far as you can see in every direction, ¹⁵for I am going to give it all to you and your descendants. ¹⁶And I am going to give you so many descendants that, like dust, they can't be counted! ¹⁷Hike in all directions and explore the new possessions I am giving you." ¹⁸Then Abram moved his tent to the oaks of Mamre, near Hebron, and built an altar to Jehovah there.

14 Abram Rescues Lot

Now war filled the land—Amraphel, king of Shinar, Arioch, king of Ellasar, Ched-or-laomer, king of Elam, and Tidal, king of Goiim ²fought against: Bera, king of Sodom, Birsha, king of Gomorrah, Shinab, king of Admah, Shemeber, king of Zeboiim, and the king of Bela (later called Zoar).

³These kings (of Sodom, Gomorrah, Admah, Zeboiim, and Bela) mobilized their armies in Siddim Valley (that is, the valley of the Dead Sea). ⁴For twelve years they had all been subject to King Ched-or-laomer, but now in the thirteenth year, they rebelled.

⁵,⁶One year later, Ched-or-laomer and his allies arrived and the slaughter began. For they were victorious over the following tribes at the places indicated: the Rephaim in Ashteroth-karnaim; the Zuzim in Ham; the Emim in the plain of Kiriathaim; the Horites in Mount Seir, as far as El-paran at the edge of the desert.

⁷Then they swung around to Enmishpat (later called Kadesh) and destroyed the Amalekites, and also the Amorites living in Hazazan-tamar.

⁸,⁹But now the other army, that of the kings of Sodom, Gomorrah, Admah, Zeboiim, and Bela (Zoar), unsuccessfully attacked Ched-or-laomer and his allies as they were in the Dead Sea Valley (four kings against five). ¹⁰As it happened, the valley was full of asphalt pits. And as the army of the kings of Sodom and Gomorrah fled, some slipped into the pits, and the remainder fled to the mountains. ¹¹Then the victors plundered Sodom and Gomorrah and carried off all their wealth and food, and went on their homeward way, ¹²taking with them Lot—Abram's nephew who lived in Sodom—and all he owned. ¹³One of the men who escaped came and told Abram the Hebrew, who was camping among the oaks belonging to Mamre the Amorite (brother of Eshcol and Aner, Abram's allies).

¹⁴When Abram learned that Lot had been captured, he called together the men born into his household, 318 of them in all, and chased after the retiring army as far as Dan. ¹⁵He divided his men and attacked during the night from several directions, and pursued the fleeing army to Hobah, north of Damascus, ¹⁶and recovered everything—the loot that had been taken, his relative Lot, and all of Lot's possessions, including the women and other captives.

¹⁷As Abram returned from his strike against Ched-or-laomer and the other kings at the Valley of Shaveh (later called King's Valley), the king of

Family Devotions

☐ DEVOTION 7
SERVING GOD BOLDLY

Read Genesis 14:11-20

Serving God Boldly
Memory Verse

Yes, be bold and strong!
Banish fear and doubt!
For remember, the Lord
your God is with you
wherever you go.
Joshua 1:9

"Hi, Grandma," called Karen as her grandmother drove up after choir practice.

Karen climbed into the front seat of Grandma's car. She put her books beside her and buckled up. Then she sighed deeply. "Oh, Grandma," she said. "I don't know how Sandy and I will ever be ready to sing in church next week. I've memorized the song, but I still keep forgetting the words. I don't think I can sing in front of so many people."

"Sounds like butterflies to me," said Grandma, "but God has given you a lovely voice, and I'm sure you'll do fine."

"I'm too scared," Karen insisted. Her voice trembled.

Grandma stopped at a red light. She looked at Karen. "You're a Christian, honey," she said, "and you can do whatever God gives you to do." She turned her eyes back to the flow of traffic and moved forward as she continued, "Do you remember when Grandpa died? I was all alone and lived miles from anyone—and I had never driven a car."

"You hadn't?" asked Karen. "I didn't know that. You drive all the time now."

"Yes," said Grandma, "but at first I was so terrified of driving that I thought I'd never learn. Then one day I realized that the Lord was right there with me. I began to trust him to help me, and after that it became easier and easier. Even now, I never get into this car without first thanking God that he's here with me in the driver's seat." She paused, then added, "With him behind the wheel—in any area of my life—I can go anywhere. And so can you."

Grandma pulled up to the curb in front of Karen's house. Karen smiled at her grandmother before opening the car door. "I guess I haven't been asking for God's help," she admitted, "but when we practice again, I will. And when we get up to sing, I especially will. Maybe I'm too scared to sing, but if God helps me, I know I can do it."

How About You?
Is it hard for you to pray in public? To meet new people? To give your testimony? When you have to do something you find hard to do, who is "behind the wheel"? Do you turn to God and seek his help? Just as he delivered Abram's enemies over to him, God will help you do anything he wants you to do. Simply ask him. *G. L. J.*

• For the next devotional, turn to page 19.   • For the next devotional on SERVING GOD BOLDLY, turn to page 65.
• For notes on SERVING GOD BOLDLY, see pages 327, 404, 501, 720, and 856.

...ut to meet him, ¹⁸and Melchizedek, ...lem (Jerusalem), who was a priest of ... Highest Heaven, brought him bread ... ¹⁹,²⁰Then Melchizedek blessed Abram with this blessing:

"The blessing of the supreme God, Creator of heaven and earth, be upon you, Abram; and blessed be God, who has delivered your enemies over to you."

Then Abram gave Melchizedek a tenth of all the loot.

²¹The king of Sodom told him, "Just give me back my people who were captured; keep for yourself the booty stolen from my city."

²²But Abram replied, "I have solemnly promised Jehovah, the supreme God, Creator of heaven and earth, ²³that I will not take so much as a single thread from you, lest you say, 'Abram is rich because of what I gave him!' ²⁴All I'll accept is what these young men of mine have eaten; but give a share of the loot to Aner, Eshcol, and Mamre, my allies."

15 God Makes a Promise to Abram

Afterwards Jehovah spoke to Abram in a vision, and this is what he told him: "Don't be fearful, Abram, for I will defend you. And I will give you great blessings."

²,³But Abram replied, "O Lord Jehovah, what good are all your blessings when I have no son? For without a son, some other member of my household will inherit all my wealth."

⁴Then Jehovah told him, "No, no one else will be your heir, for you will have a son to inherit everything you own."

⁵Then God brought Abram outside beneath the nighttime sky and told him, "Look up into the heavens and count the stars if you can. Your descendants will be like that—too many to count!" ⁶And Abram believed God; then God considered him righteous on account of his faith.

⁷And he told him, "I am Jehovah who brought you out of the city of Ur of the Chaldeans, to give you this land."

⁸But Abram replied, "O Lord Jehovah, how can I be sure that you will give it to me?" ⁹Then Jehovah told him to take a three-year-old heifer, a three-year-old female goat, a three-year-old ram, a turtledove and a young pigeon, ¹⁰and to slay them and to cut them apart down the middle, and to separate the halves, but not to divide the birds. ¹¹And when the vultures came down upon the carcasses, Abram shooed them away.

¹²That evening as the sun was going down, a deep sleep fell upon Abram, and a vision of terrible foreboding, darkness, and horror.

¹³Then Jehovah told Abram, "Your descendants will be oppressed as slaves in a foreign land for 400 years. ¹⁴But I will punish the nation that enslaves them, and at the end they will come away with great wealth. ¹⁵(But you will die in peace, at a ripe old age.) ¹⁶After four generations they will return here to this land; for the wickedness of the Amorite nations living here now will not be ready for punishment until then."

¹⁷As the sun went down and it was dark, Abram saw a smoking firepot and a flaming torch that passed between the halves of the carcasses. ¹⁸So that day Jehovah made this covenant with Abram: "I have given this land to your descendants from the Wadi-el-Arish to the Euphrates River. ¹⁹⁻²¹And I give to them these nations: Kenites, Kenizzites, Kadmonites, Hittites, Perizzites, Rephaim, Amorites, Canaanites, Girgashites, Jebusites."

16 Sarai Becomes Jealous

But Sarai and Abram had no children. So Sarai took her maid, an Egyptian girl named Hagar, ²,³and gave her to Abram to be his second wife.

"Since the Lord has given me no children," Sarai said, "you may sleep with my servant girl, and her children shall be mine."

And Abram agreed. (This took place ten years after Abram had first arrived in the land of Canaan.) ⁴So he slept with Hagar, and she conceived; and when she realized she was pregnant, she became very proud and arrogant toward her mistress Sarai.

⁵Then Sarai said to Abram, "It's all your fault. For now this servant girl of mine despises me, though I myself gave her the privilege of being your wife. May the Lord judge you for doing this to me!"

⁶"You have my permission to punish the girl as you see fit," Abram replied. So Sarai beat her and she ran away.

⁷The Angel of the Lord found her beside a desert spring along the road to Shur.

⁸*The Angel:* "Hagar, Sarai's maid, where have you come from, and where are you going?"

Hagar: "I am running away from my mistress."

⁹⁻¹²*The Angel:* "Return to your mistress and act as you should, for I will make you into a great nation. Yes, you are pregnant and your baby will be a son, and you are to name him Ishmael ('God hears'), because God has heard your woes. This son of yours will be a wild one—free and untamed as a wild ass! He will be against everyone, and everyone will feel the same toward him. But he will live near the rest of his kin."

¹³Thereafter Hagar spoke of Jehovah—for it was he who appeared to her—as "the God who

Family Devotions

☐ **Devotion 8**
Optimism

Read Genesis 17:1-8

Ned carefully made his bed, then swept his bedroom floor. "Company's coming," he explained to his dog, Rags, who was watching every move he made.

Ned and his family had moved to a new town a year ago, and he had missed his friends very much. But now they had moved back to their hometown, and he had invited his old friend Dan to come for the weekend. Ned had a big time planned. "I can hardly wait until Dan gets here," he told Rags, reaching down to ruffle the fur on the dog's neck. Rags pushed his cool, damp nose into Ned's hand—his special way of showing his love.

The lonely year would have been worse without Rags. Ned remembered the time Rags had been hot and dry with fever. Ned had been afraid his dog would die, and he'd prayed that God would make Rags well again. When Rags got better, Ned had thanked God over and over. Since then, his dog's cool, wet nose always made Ned think of God's faithfulness. "Great is your faithfulness," quoted Ned. "It's just like the Bible says, Rags." The dog wagged his tail as though he fully agreed, nuzzling Ned's hand again with his nose.

Ned jumped at the sound of the telephone and ran to answer it. "Oh, hi, Dan," he said. "You're not coming? Why? . . . Your uncle got tickets to the football game? Oh . . . uh, sure. I . . . I understand. Well, OK. Bye."

Ned ran into his room with Rags at his heels. He flung himself on his bed. Hot tears streamed down his face. He cried for a long time. Then as he grew quiet, he felt a cool, wet nose push into his hand. He put his arm around the dear, old dog, and he thought of God's love.

"It's true, Rags. God is faithful," he murmured. "My friend disappointed me, but God is here with me just as sure as you are. I didn't get what I wanted this time, but I know God loves me and cares for me just the same."

Optimism Memory Verse

Fix your thoughts on what is true and good and right. Think about things that are pure and lovely, and dwell on the fine, good things in others. Think about all you can praise God for and be glad about.
Philippians 4:8

How About You?

Has a friend or relative disappointed you? Have you been lonely, sick, or had other trouble? Remember that God is faithful and will never leave you. When you're feeling sad, remember God loves you and faithfully cares for you—in good times and in bad. When he makes a promise, it's forever. C. Y.

• For the next devotional, turn to page 21. • For the next devotional on Optimism, turn to page 55. • For notes on Optimism, see pages 143, 536, 677, and 940.

looked upon me," for she thought, "I saw God and lived to tell it."

¹⁴Later that well was named "The Well of the Living One Who Sees Me." It lies between Kadesh and Bered.

¹⁵So Hagar gave Abram a son, and Abram named him Ishmael. ¹⁶(Abram was eighty-six years old at this time.)

17 God's Contract with Abram

When Abram was ninety-nine years old, God appeared to him and told him, "I am the Almighty; obey me and live as you should. ²⁻⁴I will prepare a contract between us, guaranteeing to make you into a mighty nation. In fact you shall be the father of not only one nation, but a multitude of nations!" Abram fell face downward in the dust as God talked with him.

⁵"What's more," God told him, "I am changing your name. It is no longer 'Abram' ('Exalted Father'), but 'Abraham' ('Father of Nations')—for that is what you will be. I have declared it. ⁶I will give you millions of descendants who will form many nations! Kings shall be among your descendants! ⁷,⁸And I will continue this agreement between us generation after generation, forever, for it shall be between me and your children as well. It is a contract that I shall be your God and the God of your posterity. And I will give all this land of Canaan to you and them, forever. And I will be your God.

⁹,¹⁰"Your part of the contract," God told him, "is to obey its terms. You personally and all your posterity have this continual responsibility: that every male among you shall be circumcised; ¹¹the foreskin of his penis shall be cut off. This will be the proof that you and they accept this covenant. ¹²Every male shall be circumcised on the eighth day after birth. This applies to every foreign-born slave as well as to everyone born in your household. This is a permanent part of this contract, and it applies to all your posterity. ¹³All must be circumcised. Your bodies will thus be marked as participants in my everlasting covenant. ¹⁴Anyone who refuses these terms shall be cut off from his people; for he has violated my contract."

¹⁵Then God added, "Regarding Sarai your wife—her name is no longer 'Sarai' but 'Sarah' ('Princess'). ¹⁶And I will bless her and give you a son from her! Yes, I will bless her richly, and make her the mother of nations! Many kings shall be among your posterity."

¹⁷Then Abraham threw himself down in worship before the Lord, but inside he was laughing in disbelief! "Me, be a father?" he said in amusement. "Me—100 years old? And Sarah, to have a baby at 90?"

¹⁸And Abraham said to God, "Yes, do bless Ishmael!"

¹⁹"No," God replied, "that isn't what I said. *Sarah* shall bear you a son; and you are to name him Isaac ('Laughter'), and I will sign my covenant with him forever, and with his descendants. ²⁰As for Ishmael, all right, I will bless him also, just as you have asked me to. I will cause him to multiply and become a great nation. Twelve princes shall be among his posterity. ²¹But my contract is with Isaac, who will be born to you and Sarah next year at about this time."

²²That ended the conversation and God left. ²³Then, that very day, Abraham took Ishmael his son and every other male—born in his household or bought from outside—and cut off their foreskins, just as God had told him to. ²⁴⁻²⁷Abraham was ninety-nine years old at that time, and Ishmael was thirteen. Both were circumcised the same day, along with all the other men and boys of the household, whether born there or bought as slaves.

18 Angels Visit Abraham

The Lord appeared again to Abraham while he was living in the oak grove at Mamre. This is the way it happened: One hot summer afternoon as he was sitting in the opening of his tent, ²he suddenly noticed three men coming toward him. He sprang up and ran to meet them and welcomed them.

³,⁴"Sirs," he said, "please don't go any farther. Stop awhile and rest here in the shade of this tree while I get water to refresh your feet, ⁵and a bite to eat to strengthen you. Do stay awhile before continuing your journey."

"All right," they said, "do as you have said."

⁶Then Abraham ran back to the tent and said to Sarah, "Quick! Mix up some pancakes! Use your best flour, and make enough for the three of them!" ⁷Then he ran out to the herd and selected a fat calf and told a servant to hurry and butcher it. ⁸Soon, taking them cheese and milk and the roast veal, he set it before the men and stood beneath the trees beside them as they ate.

⁹"Where is Sarah, your wife?" they asked him.

"In the tent," Abraham replied.

¹⁰Then the Lord said, "Next year I will give you and Sarah a son!" (Sarah was listening from the tent door behind him.) ¹¹Now Abraham and Sarah were both very old, and Sarah was long since past the time when she could have a baby.

¹²So Sarah laughed silently. "A woman my age have a baby?" she scoffed to herself. "And with a husband as old as mine?"

¹³Then God said to Abraham, "Why did Sarah laugh? Why did she say 'Can an old woman like me have a baby?' ¹⁴Is anything too hard for God?

Family Devotions

☐ Devotion 9
Respecting God's Warnings

Read Genesis 19:1, 12-17, 24-26

Steve glanced uneasily at the danger signs posted around the old mine shaft. "Come on," urged his older brother, John, as he climbed over the fence and dropped down inside the enclosure.

"What if someone finds out we came here?" protested Steve. "We're supposed to be gathering wood for the fire."

John shrugged and walked away. Then a horrible, crashing sound filled Steve's ears as John disappeared. "John!" cried Steve. "Where are you?"

"Down here," came the muffled reply. "I can't . . . move."

Steve gulped. "Hang on," he called. "I'll go get Dad." Frantically he ran to the site of the church retreat where the men were setting up camp. As soon as Steve saw the tents, he started shouting, "Help! Help! John's trapped in an old mine."

The rest of the evening was a blur to Steve. He dimly remembered Pastor Jack calling for help on his ham radio, waiting for the rangers to come in the helicopter, and then waiting for his father to return with news from the hospital. How Steve wished he and John had obeyed the instructions to stay within sight of camp! How he wished they had paid attention to the danger signs!

When Dad returned, Steve was relieved to hear that John would be all right. He told his father how sorry he was that he had disobeyed. Dad nodded. "I hope you've learned a lesson from what happened," he said. "What did the signs at the mine say?"

"They said, 'Danger, Keep Out!'" replied Steve.

"Exactly," said Dad, "and when you and John didn't obey them, you had to pay the consequences. God's Word also says, 'Danger. Keep out of sin, or you will have to pay the consequences.' Not in those exact words. But one verse says, 'You may be sure that your sin will catch up with you.' Don't ignore God's warning. When you're faced with temptation, run away from it, and ask God to help you."

Respecting God's Warnings Memory Verse

If my people will humble themselves and pray, and search for me, and turn from their wicked ways, I will hear them from heaven and forgive their sins and heal their land.
2 Chronicles 7:14

How About You?

Do you think you can disobey, cheat, or lie—"just once"—and it won't matter? Do you think nobody will ever find out? God already knows, and very often other people find out, too. Sin is dangerous and has serious consequences. *J. B.*

• For the next devotional, turn to page 25. • For the next devotional on *Respecting God's Warnings*, turn to page 525. • For notes on *Respecting God's Warnings*, see pages 219, 874, and 1126.

Next year, just as I told you, I will certainly see to it that Sarah has a son."

¹⁵But Sarah denied it. "I didn't laugh," she lied, for she was afraid.

¹⁶Then the men stood up from their meal and started on toward Sodom; and Abraham went with them part of the way.

¹⁷"Should I hide my plan from Abraham?" God asked. ¹⁸"For Abraham shall become a mighty nation, and he will be a source of blessing for all the nations of the earth. ¹⁹And I have picked him out to have godly descendants and a godly household—men who are just and good—so that I can do for him all I have promised."

²⁰So the Lord told Abraham, "I have heard that the people of Sodom and Gomorrah are utterly evil, and that everything they do is wicked. ²¹I am going down to see whether these reports are true or not. Then I will know."

²²,²³So the other two went on toward Sodom, but the Lord remained with Abraham a while. Then Abraham approached him and said, "Will you kill good and bad alike? ²⁴Suppose you find fifty godly people there within the city—will you destroy it, and not spare it for their sakes? ²⁵That wouldn't be right! Surely you wouldn't do such a thing, to kill the godly with the wicked! Why, you would be treating godly and wicked exactly the same! Surely you wouldn't do that! Should not the Judge of all the earth be fair?"

²⁶And God replied, "If I find fifty godly people there, I will spare the entire city for their sake."

²⁷Then Abraham spoke again. "Since I have begun, let me go on and speak further to the Lord, though I am but dust and ashes. ²⁸*Suppose there are only forty-five?* Will you destroy the city for lack of five?"

And God said, "I will not destroy it if I find forty-five."

²⁹Then Abraham went further with his request. *"Suppose there are only forty?"*

And God replied, "I won't destroy it if there are forty."

³⁰"Please don't be angry," Abraham pleaded. "Let me speak: *suppose only thirty are found there?"*

And God replied, "I won't do it if there are thirty there."

³¹Then Abraham said, "Since I have dared to speak to God, let me continue—*suppose there are only twenty?"*

And God said, "Then I won't destroy it for the sake of the twenty."

³²Finally, Abraham said, "Oh, let not the Lord be angry; I will speak but this once more! *Suppose only ten are found?"*

And God said, "Then, for the sake of the ten, I won't destroy it."

³³And the Lord went on his way when he had finished his conversation with Abraham. And Abraham returned to his tent.

19 God Destroys Sodom

That evening the two angels came to the entrance of the city of Sodom, and Lot was sitting there as they arrived. When he saw them he stood up to meet them, and welcomed them.

²"Sirs," he said, "come to my home as my guests for the night; you can get up as early as you like and be on your way again."

"Oh, no thanks," they said, "we'll just stretch out here along the street."

³But he was very urgent, until at last they went home with him, and he set a great feast before them, complete with freshly baked unleavened bread. After the meal, ⁴as they were preparing to retire for the night, the men of the city—yes, Sodomites, young and old from all over the city—surrounded the house ⁵and shouted to Lot, "Bring out those men to us so we can rape them."

⁶Lot stepped outside to talk to them, shutting the door behind him. ⁷"Please, fellows," he begged, "don't do such a wicked thing. ⁸Look—I have two virgin daughters, and I'll surrender them to you to do with as you wish. But leave these men alone, for they are under my protection."

⁹"Stand back," they yelled. "Who do you think you are? We let this fellow settle among us and now he tries to tell us what to do! We'll deal with you far worse than with those other men." And they lunged at Lot and began breaking down the door.

¹⁰But the two men reached out and pulled Lot in and bolted the door ¹¹and temporarily blinded the men of Sodom so that they couldn't find the door.

¹²"What relatives do you have here in the city?" the men asked. "Get them out of this place—sons-in-law, sons, daughters, or anyone else. ¹³For we will destroy the city completely. The stench of the place has reached to heaven and God has sent us to destroy it."

¹⁴So Lot rushed out to tell his daughters' fiancés, "Quick, get out of the city, for the Lord is going to destroy it." But the young men looked at him as though he had lost his senses.

¹⁵At dawn the next morning the angels became urgent. "Hurry," they said to Lot, "take your wife and your two daughters who are here and get out while you can, or you will be caught in the destruction of the city."

¹⁶When Lot still hesitated, the angels seized his hand and the hands of his wife and two daughters and rushed them to safety, outside the city, for the Lord was merciful.

¹⁷"Flee for your lives," the angels told him. *"And don't look back.* Escape to the mountains. Don't stay down here on the plain or you will die."

¹⁸⁻²⁰"Oh no, sirs, please," Lot begged, "since you've been so kind to me and saved my life, and

you've granted me such mercy, let me flee to that little village over there instead of into the mountains, for I fear disaster in the mountain. See, the village is close by and it is just a small one. Please, please, let me go there instead. Don't you see how small it is? And my life will be saved."

21"All right," the angel said, "I accept your proposition and won't destroy that little city. 22But hurry! For I can do nothing until you are there." (From that time on that village was named Zoar, meaning "Little City.")

23The sun was rising as Lot reached the village. 24Then the Lord rained down fire and flaming tar from heaven upon Sodom and Gomorrah, 25and utterly destroyed them, along with the other cities and villages of the plain, eliminating all life—people, plants, and animals alike. 26But Lot's wife looked back as she was following along behind him and became a pillar of salt.

27That morning Abraham was up early and hurried out to the place where he had stood before the Lord. 28He looked out across the plain to Sodom and Gomorrah and saw columns of smoke and fumes, as from a furnace, rising from the cities there. 29So God heeded Abraham's plea and kept Lot safe, removing him from the maelstrom of death that engulfed the cities.

30Afterwards Lot left Zoar, fearful of the people there, and went to live in a cave in the mountains with his two daughters. 31One day the older girl said to her sister, "There isn't a man anywhere in this entire area that our father would let us marry. And our father will soon be too old for having children. 32Come, let's fill him with wine and then we will sleep with him, so that our clan will not come to an end." 33So they got him drunk that night, and the older girl went in and had sexual intercourse with her father; but he was unaware of her lying down or getting up again.

34The next morning she said to her younger sister, "I slept with my father last night. Let's fill him with wine again tonight, and you go in and lie with him, so that our family line will continue." 35So they got him drunk again that night, and the younger girl went in and lay with him, and, as before, he didn't know that anyone was there. 36And so it was that both girls became pregnant from their father. 37The older girl's baby was named Moab; he became the ancestor of the nation of the Moabites. 38The name of the younger girl's baby was Benammi; he became the ancestor of the nation of the Ammonites.

20 Abraham Tricks the King

Now Abraham moved south to the Negeb and settled between Kadesh and Shur. One day, when visiting the city of Gerar, 2he declared that Sarah was his sister! Then King Abimelech sent for her, and had her brought to him at his palace.

3But that night God came to him in a dream and told him, "You are a dead man, for that woman you took is married."

4But Abimelech hadn't slept with her yet, so he said, "Lord, will you slay an innocent man? 5He told me, 'She is my sister,' and she herself said, 'Yes, he is my brother.' I hadn't the slightest intention of doing anything wrong."

6"Yes, I know," the Lord replied. "That is why I held you back from sinning against me; that is why I didn't let you touch her. 7Now restore her to her husband, and he will pray for you (for he is a prophet) and you shall live. But if you don't return her to him, you are doomed to death along with all your household."

8The king was up early the next morning, and hastily called a meeting of all the palace personnel and told them what had happened. And great fear swept through the crowd.

9,10Then the king called for Abraham. "What is this you've done to us?" he demanded. "What have I done that deserves treatment like this, to make me and my kingdom guilty of this great sin? Who would suspect that you would do a thing like this to me? Whatever made you think of this vile deed?"

11,12"Well," Abraham said, "I figured this to be a godless place. 'They will want my wife and will kill me to get her,' I thought. And besides, she *is* my sister—or at least a half-sister (we both have the same father)—and I married her. 13And when God sent me traveling far from my childhood home, I told her, 'Have the kindness to mention, wherever we come, that you are my sister.'"

14Then King Abimelech took sheep and oxen and servants—both men and women—and gave them to Abraham, and returned Sarah his wife to him.

15"Look my kingdom over, and choose the place where you want to live," the king told him. 16Then he turned to Sarah. "Look," he said, "I am giving your 'brother' a thousand silver pieces as damages for what I did, to compensate for any embarrassment and to settle any claim against me regarding this matter. Now justice has been done."

17Then Abraham prayed, asking God to cure the king and queen and the other women of the household, so that they could have children; 18for God had stricken all the women with barrenness to punish Abimelech for taking Abraham's wife.

21 Isaac Is Born

Then God did as he had promised, and Sarah became pregnant and gave Abraham a baby son in his old age, at the time God had said; 3and

Abraham named him Isaac (meaning "Laughter!"). ⁴,⁵Eight days after he was born, Abraham circumcised him, as God required. (Abraham was 100 years old at that time.)

⁶And Sarah declared, "God has brought me laughter! All who hear about this shall rejoice with me. ⁷For who would have dreamed that I would ever have a baby? Yet I have given Abraham a child in his old age!"

⁸Time went by and the child grew and was weaned; and Abraham gave a party to celebrate the happy occasion. ⁹But when Sarah noticed Ishmael—the son of Abraham and the Egyptian girl Hagar—teasing Isaac, ¹⁰she turned upon Abraham and demanded, "Get rid of that slave girl and her son. He is not going to share your property with my son. I won't have it."

¹¹This upset Abraham very much, for after all, Ishmael too was his son.

¹²But God told Abraham, "Don't be upset over the boy or your slave-girl wife; do as Sarah says, for Isaac is the son through whom my promise will be fulfilled. ¹³And I will make a nation of the descendants of the slave-girl's son, too, because he also is yours."

¹⁴So Abraham got up early the next morning, prepared food for the journey, and strapped a canteen of water to Hagar's shoulders and sent her away with their son. She walked out into the wilderness of Beersheba, wandering aimlessly.

¹⁵When the water was gone she left the youth in the shade of a bush ¹⁶and went off and sat down a hundred yards or so away. "I don't want to watch him die," she said, and burst into tears, sobbing wildly.

¹⁷Then God heard the boy crying, and the Angel of God called to Hagar from the sky, "Hagar, what's wrong? Don't be afraid! For God has heard the lad's cries as he is lying there. ¹⁸Go and get him and comfort him, for I will make a great nation from his descendants."

¹⁹Then God opened her eyes and she saw a well; so she refilled the canteen and gave the lad a drink. ²⁰,²¹And God blessed the boy and he grew up in the wilderness of Paran, and became an expert archer. And his mother arranged a marriage for him with a girl from Egypt.

²²About this time King Abimelech and Phicol, commander of his troops, came to Abraham and said to him, "It is evident that God helps you in everything you do; ²³swear to me by God's name that you won't defraud me or my son or my grandson, but that you will be on friendly terms with my country, as I have been toward you."

²⁴Abraham replied, "All right, I swear to it!" ²⁵Then Abraham complained to the king about a well the king's servants had taken violently away from Abraham's servants.

²⁶"This is the first I've heard of it," the king exclaimed, "and I have no idea who is responsible. Why didn't you tell me before?"

²⁷Then Abraham gave sheep and oxen to the king, as sacrifices to seal their pact.

²⁸,²⁹But when he took seven ewe lambs and set them off by themselves, the king inquired, "Why are you doing that?"

³⁰And Abraham replied, "They are my gift to you as a public confirmation that this well is mine."

³¹So from that time on the well was called Beersheba ("Well of the Oath"), because that was the place where they made their covenant. ³²Then King Abimelech and Phicol, commander of his army, returned home again. ³³And Abraham planted a tamarisk tree beside the well and prayed there to the Lord, calling upon the Eternal God. ³⁴And Abraham lived in the Philistine country for a long time.

22 Abraham Offers Isaac

Later on, God tested Abraham's [faith and obedience].

"Abraham!" God called.

"Yes, Lord?" he replied.

²"Take with you your only son—yes, Isaac whom you love so much—and go to the land of Moriah and sacrifice him there as a burnt offering upon one of the mountains which I'll point out to you!"

³The next morning Abraham got up early, chopped wood for a fire upon the altar, saddled his donkey, and took with him his son Isaac and two young men who were his servants, and started off to the place where God had told him to go. ⁴On the third day of the journey Abraham saw the place in the distance.

⁵"Stay here with the donkey," Abraham told the young men, "and the lad and I will travel yonder and worship, and then come right back."

⁶Abraham placed the wood for the burnt offering upon Isaac's shoulders, while he himself carried the knife and the flint for striking a fire. So the two of them went on together.

⁷"Father," Isaac asked, "we have the wood and the flint to make the fire, but where is the lamb for the sacrifice?"

⁸"God will see to it, my son," Abraham replied. And they went on.

⁹When they arrived at the place where God had told Abraham to go, he built an altar and placed the wood in order, ready for the fire, and then tied Isaac and laid him on the altar over the wood. ¹⁰And Abraham took the knife and lifted it up to plunge it into his son, to slay him.

¹¹At that moment the Angel of God shouted to him from heaven, "Abraham! Abraham!"

Family Devotions

☐ DEVOTION 10
OBEDIENCE

Read Genesis 22:1-12

Sara overheard Mom telling Dad that she had failed to clean out her closet. "I even gave her a box to put the outgrown clothes into," said Mom.

Sara didn't listen to the rest of her parents' conversation. She went outside, feeling dejected, and sat on one of her swings. Her collie, Jinx, came over to her, but Sara ignored her pet. She thought of all the things she did do right. She considered herself to be a very obedient daughter. She made her bed before school. She set the table for dinner each afternoon. And she dried the dishes her mother washed each evening. Why was Mom now complaining to Dad? What was it her parents wanted from her anyway? She would clean that closet later. Why did it have to be done right now?

Soon Dad came out and sat on the other swing. "Sara, what about cleaning your closet?" he asked.

"I'm going to do it, Dad," replied Sara. "I wanted to see that special on TV first."

Dad picked up a stick and threw it. "Get it, Jinx," he said. The dog was off with a bound to retrieve the stick. Dad turned his attention back to Sara. "Now, that is immediate obedience. Jinx didn't say, 'I'll do it when I get around to it.' He just obeyed." After a pause, Dad added, "A truck collecting clothing for needy people stopped here today, Sara. None of your outgrown clothes got put on it because you didn't obey Mom immediately."

Now Sara felt bad. "Why didn't Mom tell me the truck was coming?" she asked. "I would've cleaned the closet right away if I'd known."

"We want you to be willing to obey us without always asking for reasons," said Dad quietly. "God didn't say, 'Children, obey your parents when you understand why.' He said, 'Children, obey your parents.' To be truly obedient, you must be *immediately* obedient."

"Like Jinx," murmured Sara, giving her dog a hug.

Obedience Memory Verse

Oh, that they would always have such a heart for me, wanting to obey my commandments. Then all would go well with them in the future, and with their children throughout all generations!
Deuteronomy 5:29

How About You?

When your parents tell you to do something, do you put them off? Do you demand reasons? Or do you try to argue that you will do it later when you've nothing else to do? The only true obedience is immediate obedience. *R. P.*

• For the next devotional, turn to page 27. • For the next devotional on OBEDIENCE, turn to page 63. • For notes on OBEDIENCE, see pages 319, 425, 500, 510, and 757.

"Yes, Lord!" he answered.

[12] "Lay down the knife; don't hurt the lad in any way," the Angel said, "for I know that God is first in your life—you have not withheld even your beloved son from me."

[13] Then Abraham noticed a ram caught by its horns in a bush. So he took the ram and sacrificed it, instead of his son, as a burnt offering on the altar. [14] Abraham named the place "Jehovah provides"—and it still goes by that name to this day.

[15] Then the Angel of God called again to Abraham from heaven. [16] "I, the Lord, have sworn by myself that because you have obeyed me and have not withheld even your beloved son from me, [17] I will bless you with incredible blessings and multiply your descendants into countless thousands and millions, like the stars above you in the sky, and like the sands along the seashore. They will conquer their enemies, [18] and your offspring will be a blessing to all the nations of the earth—all because you have obeyed me."

[19] So they returned to his young men and traveled home again to Beer-sheba.

[20-23] After this, a message arrived that Milcah, the wife of Abraham's brother Nahor, had borne him eight sons. Their names were: Uz, the oldest, Buz, the next oldest, Kemuel (father of Aram), Chesed, Hazo, Pildash, Jidlaph, Bethuel (father of Rebekah).

[24] He also had four other children from his concubine, Reumah: Tebah, Gaham, Tahash, Maacah.

23 Sarah Dies

When Sarah was 127 years old, she died in Hebron in the land of Canaan; there Abraham mourned and wept for her. [3] Then, standing beside her body, he said to the men of Heth:

[4] "Here I am, a visitor in a foreign land, with no place to bury my wife. Please sell me a piece of ground for this purpose."

[5,6] "Certainly," the men replied, "for you are an honored prince of God among us; it will be a privilege to have you choose the finest of our sepulchres, so that you can bury her there."

[7] Then Abraham bowed low before them and said, [8] "Since this is your feeling in the matter, be so kind as to ask Ephron, Zohar's son, [9] to sell me the cave of Mach-pelah, down at the end of his field. I will of course pay the full price for it, whatever is publicly agreed upon, and it will become a permanent cemetery for my family."

[10] Ephron was sitting there among the others, and now he spoke up, answering Abraham as the others listened, speaking publicly before all the citizens of the town: [11] "Sir," he said to Abraham, "please listen to me. I will give you the cave and the field without any charge. Here in the presence of my people, I give it to you free. Go and bury your dead."

[12] Abraham bowed again to the men of Heth, [13] and replied to Ephron, as all listened: "No, let me buy it from you. Let me pay the full price of the field, and then I will bury my dead."

[14,15] "Well, the land is worth 400 pieces of silver," Ephron said, "but what is that between friends? Go ahead and bury your dead."

[16] So Abraham paid Ephron the price he had suggested—400 pieces of silver, as publicly agreed. [17,18] This is the land he bought: Ephron's field at Mach-pelah, near Mamre, and the cave at the end of the field, and all the trees in the field. They became his permanent possession, by agreement in the presence of the men of Heth at the city gate. [19,20] So Abraham buried Sarah there, in the field and cave deeded to him by the men of Heth as a burial plot.

24 Isaac Gets Married

Abraham was now a very old man, and God blessed him in every way. [2] One day Abraham said to his household administrator, who was his oldest servant,

[3] "Swear by Jehovah, the God of heaven and earth, that you will not let my son marry one of these local girls, these Canaanites. [4] Go instead to my homeland, to my relatives, and find a wife for him there."

[5] "But suppose I can't find a girl who will come so far from home?" the servant asked. "Then shall I take Isaac there, to live among your relatives?"

[6] "No!" Abraham warned. "Be careful that you don't do that under any circumstance. [7] For the Lord God of heaven told me to leave that land and my people, and promised to give me and my children this land. He will send his angel on ahead of you, and he will see to it that you find a girl from there to be my son's wife. [8] But if you don't succeed, then you are free from this oath; but under no circumstances are you to take my son there."

[9] So the servant vowed to follow Abraham's instructions.

[10] He took with him ten of Abraham's camels loaded with samples of the best of everything his master owned and journeyed to Iraq, to Nahor's village. [11] There he made the camels kneel down outside the town, beside a spring. It was evening, and the women of the village were coming to draw water.

[12] "O Jehovah, the God of my master," he prayed, "show kindness to my master Abraham and help me to accomplish the purpose of my journey. [13] See, here I am, standing beside this spring, and the girls of the village are coming out

FAMILY DEVOTIONS

☐ *DEVOTION 11*

TRUSTING GOD FOR GUIDANCE

Read Genesis 24:1-9

Trusting God for Guidance Memory Verse

I will instruct you (says the Lord) and guide you along the best pathway for your life; I will advise you and watch your progress.
Psalm 32:8

Dan hurried to Brown's Garden Store. He had heard that they were hiring boys to help with the Christmas trees. In the manager's office, a tall, smiling man greeted Dan. "Well, we can use you after school next Monday," he said. "I'm not sure about after that. Be sure to wear old clothes and boots—the work is dirty."

On Monday, Dan joined several boys who were listening to a man in brown coveralls. "See those trucks?" said the man. "We'll be taking them out to the field. Your job is to help load trees—but be careful! No broken branches! Lopsided Christmas trees don't sell!"

The boys headed for the trucks, and Dan suddenly noticed that they were all wearing old clothes. He had forgotten. Did he feel dumb! "Mister," Dan yelled to the retreating brown coveralls, "I forgot about the clothes, but I can hurry home and be right back!"

"We can't wait," the man replied gruffly. "You better go inside and report to the manager."

After hearing his embarrassed explanation, Mr. Davis, the tall, smiling manager, spoke kindly to him. "I was your age once, Dan," he said, "and someone told me about the importance of listening and being reliable. It made a big difference in my life." Then he unexpectedly asked, "Do you attend Sunday school, Dan?" Surprised by the question, Dan shook his head. "I'd like to invite you to join my class of boys if you have no other plans on Sunday," said Mr. Davis. "Toby Sanders, one of the boys working for us, is in my class. You know him, don't you?"

Dan nodded. He thought for a minute. "I guess I could make it," he said.

"Good! I'll call your folks and clear it with them," said Mr. Davis with a big smile. "I'll look for you on Sunday, Dan—and maybe we'll have another work opening soon. Next time I know you'll remember to dress properly."

How About You?
Are you careful to listen to instructions and follow orders when they're given? If not, you may miss out on something good. Ask God for his guidance for your life, too. Follow his directions as best you can—don't miss out on his best for you. *P. K.*

• For the next devotional, turn to page 29. • For the next devotional on *TRUSTING GOD FOR GUIDANCE*, turn to page 77. • For notes on *TRUSTING GOD FOR GUIDANCE*, see pages 522, 553, 614, 676, and 1056.

to draw water. ¹⁴This is my request: When I ask one of them for a drink and she says, 'Yes, certainly, and I will water your camels too!'—let her be the one you have appointed as Isaac's wife. That is how I will know."

¹⁵,¹⁶As he was still speaking to the Lord about this, a beautiful young girl named Rebekah arrived with a water jug on her shoulder and filled it at the spring. (Her father was Bethuel the son of Nahor and his wife Milcah.) ¹⁷Running over to her, the servant asked her for a drink.

¹⁸"Certainly, sir," she said, and quickly lowered the jug for him to drink. ¹⁹Then she said, "I'll draw water for your camels, too, until they have enough!"

²⁰So she emptied the jug into the watering trough and ran down to the spring again and kept carrying water to the camels until they had enough. ²¹The servant said no more, but watched her carefully to see if she would finish the job, so that he would know whether she was the one. ²²Then at last, when the camels had finished drinking, he produced a quarter-ounce gold earring and two five-ounce gold bracelets for her wrists.

²³"Whose daughter are you, miss?" he asked. "Would your father have any room to put us up for the night?"

²⁴"My father is Bethuel," she replied. "My grandparents are Milcah and Nahor. ²⁵Yes, we have plenty of straw and food for the camels, and a guest room."

²⁶The man stood there a moment with head bowed, worshiping Jehovah. ²⁷"Thank you, Lord God of my master Abraham," he prayed; "thank you for being so kind and true to him, and for leading me straight to the family of my master's relatives."

²⁸The girl ran home to tell her folks, ²⁹,³⁰and when her brother Laban saw the ring, and the bracelets on his sister's wrists, and heard her story, he rushed out to the spring where the man was still standing beside his camels, and said to him, ³¹"Come and stay with us, friend; why stand here outside the city when we have a room all ready for you, and a place prepared for the camels!"

³²So the man went home with Laban, and Laban gave him straw to bed down the camels, and feed for them, and water for the camel drivers to wash their feet. ³³Then supper was served. But the old man said, "I don't want to eat until I have told you why I am here."

"All right," Laban said, "tell us your errand."

³⁴"I am Abraham's servant," he explained. ³⁵"And Jehovah has overwhelmed my master with blessings so that he is a great man among the people of his land. God has given him flocks of sheep and herds of cattle, and a fortune in silver and gold, and many slaves and camels and donkeys.

³⁶"Now when Sarah, my master's wife, was very old, she gave birth to my master's son, and my master has given him everything he owns. ³⁷And my master made me promise not to let Isaac marry one of the local girls, ³⁸but to come to his relatives here in this far-off land, to his brother's family, and to bring back a girl from here to marry his son. ³⁹'But suppose I can't find a girl who will come?' I asked him. ⁴⁰'She will,' he told me—'for my Lord, in whose presence I have walked, will send his angel with you and make your mission successful. Yes, find a girl from among my relatives, from my brother's family. ⁴¹You are under oath to go and ask. If they won't send anyone, then you are freed from your promise.'

⁴²"Well, this afternoon when I came to the spring I prayed this prayer: 'O Jehovah, the God of my master Abraham, if you are planning to make my mission a success, please guide me in this way: ⁴³Here I am, standing beside this spring. I will say to some girl who comes out to draw water, "Please give me a drink of water!" ⁴⁴And she will reply, "Certainly! And I'll water your camels too!" Let that girl be the one you have selected to be the wife of my master's son.'

⁴⁵"Well, while I was still speaking these words, Rebekah was coming along with her water jug upon her shoulder; and she went down to the spring and drew water and filled the jug. I said to her, 'Please give me a drink.' ⁴⁶She quickly lifted the jug down from her shoulder so that I could drink, and told me, 'Certainly, sir, and I will water your camels too!' So she did! ⁴⁷Then I asked her, 'Whose family are you from?' And she told me, 'Nahor's. My father is Bethuel, the son of Nahor and his wife Milcah.' So I gave her the ring and the bracelets. ⁴⁸Then I bowed my head and worshiped and blessed Jehovah, the God of my master Abraham, because he had led me along just the right path to find a girl from the family of my master's brother. ⁴⁹So tell me, yes or no. Will you or won't you be kind to my master and do what is right? When you tell me, then I'll know what my next step should be, whether to move this way or that."

⁵⁰Then Laban and Bethuel replied, "The Lord has obviously brought you here, so what can we say? ⁵¹Take her and go! Yes, let her be the wife of your master's son, as Jehovah has directed."

⁵²At this reply, Abraham's servant fell to his knees before Jehovah. ⁵³Then he brought out jewels set in solid gold and silver for Rebekah, and lovely clothing; and he gave many valuable presents to her mother and brother. ⁵⁴Then they had supper, and the servant and the men with

Family Devotions

☐ DEVOTION 12
TRUSTING GOD FOR HELP

Read Genesis 25:27-34

It was lunchtime, and Karen watched in amusement as her baby brother, Kyle, sat stubbornly shaking his head, refusing to eat the strained peas Mom was offering him on a spoon.

"Maybe you should give him some applesauce," suggested Karen. "He always likes that."

"No," responded Mom, "he has to learn to eat what we give him and what he needs." Mom took Kyle out of his chair and set him on the floor. "Maybe he'll get more reasonable if we let him get good and hungry before we try feeding him again."

A short time later, Karen heard a rustling noise coming from behind the kitchen door. There was Kyle, rummaging in the trash bag. Paper towels and empty cans were strewn about, and clenched between his teeth was an old banana peel. "Oh, Mom! Look at this!" laughed Karen as she cleaned up the mess.

Mom rushed to the rescue, but Kyle cried when she took the banana peel out of his mouth. "Shame on you, rooting around in the garbage after refusing the good lunch I made for you!" Mom scolded. But little Kyle just didn't understand. He kept trying to get back into the trash, and finally Mom put him in his playpen.

"Wasn't that silly, Mom?" asked Karen. "Kyle sure doesn't know what's good for him, does he?"

"No," Mom replied, "he doesn't." She paused, then added, "Very often older people don't, either. We neglect the things God has provided for our happiness and growth, and then try to fulfill our needs our own way. But the things we come up with are just like garbage compared with the things of the Lord. They are 'peelings,' not 'peas.'"

"You're right, we are like that," Karen agreed, turning away from the TV. "I think I'll watch that Christian video Grandma gave me instead of this program."

Trusting God for Help
Memory Verse

God is our refuge and strength, a tested help in times of trouble.
Psalm 46:1

How About You?
Do you have a need in your life? A need for fellowship? For spiritual growth? For emotional fulfillment? For a sense of achievement? The things of this world will never satisfy those needs. Let God do it. Read his Word. Talk to him. Sing his praises with other Christians. Whatever your need, trust God to meet it. S. K.

• For the next devotional, turn to page 33. • For the next devotional on TRUSTING GOD FOR HELP, turn to page 67.
• For notes on TRUSTING GOD FOR HELP, see pages 240, 249, 464, 539, and 751.

him stayed there overnight. But early the next morning he said, "Send me back to my master!"

⁵⁵"But we want Rebekah here at least another ten days or so!" her mother and brother exclaimed. "Then she can go."

⁵⁶But he pleaded, "Don't hinder my return; the Lord has made my mission successful, and I want to report back to my master."

⁵⁷"Well," they said, "we'll call the girl and ask her what she thinks."

⁵⁸So they called Rebekah. "Are you willing to go with this man?" they asked her.

And she replied, "Yes, I will go."

⁵⁹So they told her good-bye, sending along the woman who had been her childhood nurse, ⁶⁰and blessed her with this blessing as they parted:

"Our sister,
May you become
The mother of many millions!
May your descendants
Overcome all your enemies."

⁶¹So Rebekah and her servant girls mounted the camels and went with him.

⁶²Meanwhile, Isaac, whose home was in the Negeb, had returned to Beer-lahai-roi. ⁶³One evening as he was taking a walk out in the fields, meditating, he looked up and saw the camels coming. ⁶⁴Rebekah noticed him and quickly dismounted.

⁶⁵"Who is that man walking through the fields to meet us?" she asked the servant.

And he replied, "It is my master's son!" So she covered her face with her veil. ⁶⁶Then the servant told Isaac the whole story.

⁶⁷And Isaac brought Rebekah into his mother's tent, and she became his wife. He loved her very much, and she was a special comfort to him after the loss of his mother.

25 Abraham Dies

Now Abraham married again. Keturah was his new wife, and she bore him several children: Zimran, Jokshan, Medan, Midian, Ishbak, Shuah. ³Jokshan's two sons were Sheba and Dedan. Dedan's sons were Asshurim, Letushim, and Leummim. ⁴Midian's sons were Ephah, Epher, Hanoch, Abida, and Eldaah.

⁵Abraham deeded everything he owned to Isaac; ⁶however, he gave gifts to the sons of his concubines and sent them off into the east, away from Isaac.

⁷,⁸Then Abraham died, at the ripe old age of 175, ⁹,¹⁰and his sons Isaac and Ishmael buried him in the cave of Mach-pelah near Mamre, in the field Abraham had purchased from Ephron the son of Zohar, the Hethite, where Sarah, Abraham's wife, was buried.

¹¹After Abraham's death, God poured out rich blessings upon Isaac. (Isaac had now moved south to Beer-lahai-roi in the Negeb.)

¹²⁻¹⁵Here is a list, in the order of their births, of the descendants of Ishmael, who was the son of Abraham and Hagar the Egyptian, Sarah's slave girl: Nebaioth, Kedar, Adbeel, Mibsam, Mishma, Dumah, Massa, Hadad, Tema, Jetur, Naphish, Kedemah. ¹⁶These twelve sons of his became the founders of twelve tribes that bore their names. ¹⁷Ishmael finally died at the age of 137, and joined his ancestors. ¹⁸These descendants of Ishmael were scattered across the country from Havilah to Shur (which is a little way to the northeast of the Egyptian border in the direction of Assyria). And they were constantly at war with one another.

¹⁹This is the story of Isaac's children: ²⁰Isaac was forty years old when he married Rebekah, the daughter of Bethuel the Aramean from Paddam-aram. Rebekah was the sister of Laban. ²¹Isaac pleaded with Jehovah to give Rebekah a child, for even after many years of marriage she had no children. Then at last she became pregnant. ²²And it seemed as though children were fighting each other inside her!

"I can't endure this," she exclaimed. So she asked the Lord about it.

²³And he told her, "The sons in your womb shall become two rival nations. One will be stronger than the other; and the older shall be a servant of the younger!"

²⁴And sure enough, she had twins. ²⁵The first was born so covered with reddish hair that one would think he was wearing a fur coat! So they called him "Esau." ²⁶Then the other twin was born with his hand on Esau's heel! So they called him Jacob (meaning "Grabber"). Isaac was sixty years old when the twins were born.

²⁷As the boys grew, Esau became a skillful hunter, while Jacob was a quiet sort who liked to stay at home. ²⁸Isaac's favorite was Esau, because of the venison he brought home, and Rebekah's favorite was Jacob.

²⁹One day Jacob was cooking stew when Esau arrived home exhausted from the hunt.

³⁰*Esau:* "Boy, am I starved! Give me a bite of that red stuff there!" (From this came his nickname "Edom," which means "Red Stuff.")

³¹*Jacob:* "All right, trade me your birthright for it!"

³²*Esau:* "When a man is dying of starvation, what good is his birthright?"

³³*Jacob:* "Well then, vow to God that it is mine!"

And Esau vowed, thereby selling all his eldest-son rights to his younger brother. ³⁴Then Jacob gave Esau bread, peas, and stew; so he ate and drank and went on about his business, indifferent to the loss of the rights he had thrown away.

26 Isaac Tricks the King

Now a severe famine overshadowed the land, as had happened before, in Abraham's time, and so Isaac moved to the city of Gerar where Abimelech, king of the Philistines, lived.

²Jehovah appeared to him there and told him, "Don't go to Egypt. ³Do as I say and stay here in this land. If you do, I will be with you and bless you, and I will give all this land to you and to your descendants, just as I promised Abraham your father. ⁴And I will cause your descendants to become as numerous as the stars! And I will give them all of these lands; and they shall be a blessing to all the nations of the earth. ⁵I will do this because Abraham obeyed my commandments and laws."

⁶So Isaac stayed in Gerar. ⁷And when the men there asked him about Rebekah, he said, "She is my sister!" For he feared for his life if he told them she was his wife; he was afraid they would kill him to get her, for she was very attractive. ⁸But sometime later, King Abimelech, king of the Philistines, looked out of a window and saw Isaac and Rebekah making love.

⁹Abimelech called for Isaac and exclaimed, "She is your wife! Why did you say she is your sister?"

"Because I was afraid I would be murdered," Isaac replied. "I thought someone would kill me to get her from me."

¹⁰"How could you treat us this way?" Abimelech exclaimed. "Someone might carelessly have raped her, and we would be doomed." ¹¹Then Abimelech made a public proclamation: "Anyone harming this man or his wife shall die."

¹²That year Isaac's crops were tremendous—100 times the grain he sowed. For Jehovah blessed him. ¹³He was soon a man of great wealth and became richer and richer. ¹⁴He had large flocks of sheep and goats, great herds of cattle, and many servants. And the Philistines became jealous of him. ¹⁵So they filled up his wells with earth—all those dug by the servants of his father Abraham.

¹⁶And King Abimelech asked Isaac to leave the country. "Go somewhere else," he said, "for you have become too rich and powerful for us."

¹⁷So Isaac moved to Gerar Valley and lived there instead. ¹⁸And Isaac redug the wells of his father Abraham, the ones the Philistines had filled after his father's death, and gave them the same names they had had before, when his father had named them. ¹⁹His shepherds also dug a new well in Gerar Valley, and found a gushing underground spring.

²⁰Then the local shepherds came and claimed it. "This is our land and our well," they said, and argued over it with Isaac's herdsmen. So he named the well, "The Well of Argument!" ²¹Isaac's men then dug another well, but again there was a fight over it. So he called it, "The Well of Anger." ²²Abandoning that one, he dug again, and the local residents finally left him alone. So he called it, "The Well of Room Enough for Us at Last!" "For now at last," he said, "the Lord has made room for us and we shall thrive."

²³When he went to Beer-sheba, ²⁴Jehovah appeared to him on the night of his arrival. "I am the God of Abraham your father," he said. "Fear not, for I am with you and will bless you, and will give you so many descendants that they will become a great nation—because of my promise to Abraham, who obeyed me." ²⁵Then Isaac built an altar and worshiped Jehovah; and he settled there, and his servants dug a well.

²⁶One day Isaac had visitors from Gerar. King Abimelech arrived with his advisor, Ahuzzath, and also Phicol, his army commander.

²⁷"Why have you come?" Isaac asked them. "This is obviously no friendly visit, since you kicked me out in a most uncivil way."

²⁸"Well," they said, "we can plainly see that Jehovah is blessing you. We've decided to ask for a treaty between us. ²⁹Promise that you will not harm us, just as we have not harmed you, and in fact, have done only good to you and have sent you away in peace; we bless you in the name of the Lord."

³⁰So Isaac prepared a great feast for them, and they ate and drank in preparation for the treaty ceremonies. ³¹In the morning, as soon as they were up, they each took solemn oaths to seal a nonaggression pact. Then Isaac sent them happily home again.

³²That very same day Isaac's servants came to tell him, "We have found water"—in the well they had been digging. ³³So he named the well, "The Well of the Oath," and the city that grew up there was named "Oath," and is called that to this day.

³⁴Esau, at the age of forty, married a girl named Judith, daughter of Be-eri the Hethite; and he also married Basemath, daughter of Elon the Hethite. ³⁵But Isaac and Rebekah were bitter about his marrying them.

27 Jacob Deceives Isaac

One day, in Isaac's old age when he was almost blind, he called for Esau his oldest son.

Isaac: "My son?"
Esau: "Yes, father?"
²⁻⁴*Isaac:* "I am an old man now, and expect every day to be my last. Take your bow and arrows out into the fields and get me some venison, and prepare it just the way I like it—savory and

good—and bring it here for me to eat, and I will give you the blessings that belong to you, my first-born son, before I die."

[5] But Rebekah overheard the conversation. So when Esau left for the field to hunt for the venison, [6,7] she called her son Jacob and told him what his father had said to his brother.

[8-10] *Rebekah:* "Now do exactly as I tell you. Go out to the flocks and bring me two young goats, and I'll prepare your father's favorite dish from them. Then take it to your father, and after he has enjoyed it he will bless *you* before his death, instead of Esau!"

[11,12] *Jacob:* "But mother! He won't be fooled that easily. Think how hairy Esau is, and how smooth my skin is! What if my father feels me? He'll think I'm making a fool of him and curse me instead of blessing me!"

[13] *Rebekah:* "Let his curses be on me, dear son. Just do what I tell you. Go out and get the goats."

[14] So Jacob followed his mother's instructions, bringing the dressed kids, which she prepared in his father's favorite way. [15] Then she took Esau's best clothes—they were there in the house—and instructed Jacob to put them on. [16] And she made him a pair of gloves from the hairy skin of the young goats, and fastened a strip of the hide around his neck; [17] then she gave him the meat, with its rich aroma, and some fresh-baked bread.

[18] Jacob carried the platter of food into the room where his father was lying.

Jacob: "Father?"
Isaac: "Yes? Who is it, my son—Esau or Jacob?"
[19] *Jacob:* "It's Esau, your oldest son. I've done as you told me to. Here is the delicious venison you wanted. Sit up and eat it, so that you will bless me with all your heart!"
[20] *Isaac:* "How were you able to find it so quickly, my son?"
Jacob: "Because Jehovah your God put it in my path!"
[21] *Isaac:* "Come over here. I want to feel you and be sure it really is Esau!"

[22] (Jacob goes over to his father. He feels him!)

Isaac: (to himself) "The voice is Jacob's, but the hands are Esau's!"

[23] (The ruse convinces Isaac and he gives Jacob his blessings):

[24] *Isaac:* "Are you really Esau?"
Jacob: "Yes, of course."

[25] *Isaac:* "Then bring me the venison, and I will eat it and bless you with all my heart."

(Jacob takes it over to him and Isaac eats; he also drinks the wine Jacob brings him.)

[26] *Isaac:* "Come here and kiss me, my son!"
(Jacob goes over and kisses him on the cheek. Isaac sniffs his clothes, and finally seems convinced.)

[27-29] *Isaac:* "The smell of my son is the good smell of the earth and fields that Jehovah has blessed. May God always give you plenty of rain for your crops, and good harvests and grapes. May many nations be your slaves. Be the master of your brothers. May all your relatives bow low before you. Cursed are all who curse you, and blessed are all who bless you."

[30] (As soon as Isaac has blessed Jacob, and almost before Jacob leaves the room, Esau arrives, coming in from his hunting. [31] He also has prepared his father's favorite dish and brings it to him.)

Esau: "Here I am, father, with the venison. Sit up and eat it so that you can give me your finest blessings!"
[32] *Isaac:* "Who is it?"
Esau: "Why, it's me, of course! Esau, your oldest son!"

[33] (Isaac begins to tremble noticeably.)

Isaac: "Then who is it who was just here with venison, and I have already eaten it and blessed him with irrevocable blessing?"

[34] (Esau begins to sob with deep and bitter sobs.)

Esau: "O my father, bless me, bless me too!"
[35] *Isaac:* "Your brother was here and tricked me and has carried away your blessing."
[36] *Esau:* (bitterly) "No wonder they call him 'The Cheater.' For he took my birthright, and now he has stolen my blessing. Oh, haven't you saved even one blessing for me?"
[37] *Isaac:* "I have made him your master, and have given him yourself and all of his relatives as his servants. I have guaranteed him abundance of grain and wine—what is there left to give?"
[38] *Esau:* "Not one blessing left for me? O my father, bless me too."

(Isaac says nothing as Esau weeps.)

[39,40] *Isaac:* "Yours will be no life of ease and luxury, but you shall hew your way with your sword.

Family Devotions

☐ DEVOTION 13
HONESTY

Read Genesis 27:1-18, 23-25

"The time is 6:21," announced Tim as he got up from the table.

"Well, thanks heaps for keeping us informed," said his sister, Meg. "I'll be glad when that digital watch of yours isn't so new. I don't need to know the exact time every minute of the day." She got up to answer the phone. "For you, Tim," she said.

Tim took the phone. "Hello? . . . Oh, hi, George. No, I can't play tonight. See ya later."

"Why did you tell George you can't play tonight?" asked Mom. "I thought you and some of your friends were going to the gym to play basketball."

"Yeah, well. George is such a klutz," said Tim. "The time is now—"

"Don't change the subject," said Dad. "You lied to George, didn't you?"

"Oh, Dad, it was such a little thing," protested Tim. "I mean it's no big deal—just a little white lie." But Mom and Dad explained to Tim that God didn't see it that way, and though he refused to admit they were right, he agreed to call George back and invite him to join the game. "No answer," he said a few minutes later. "Well, at least I tried." He put on his jacket and left for the gym.

When Tim returned home, he looked unhappy. "What's the problem?" asked Dad.

"I fell," replied Tim, holding out his arm. Dad saw a small scratch across the face of Tim's new watch.

"Oh, that's too bad," sympathized Dad. "But at least it's just a little scratch."

"Yeah," said Tim, "but it goes right across the numbers."

Mom had come to look. "A little scratch ruins a watch," she murmured, "and a 'little' sin ruins a testimony for the Lord. It matters."

Tim knew what she meant. After thinking about it a minute, he admitted, "I guess you're right. I'll apologize to George tomorrow."

Honesty Memory Verse

Stop lying to each other; tell the truth, for we are parts of each other and when we lie to each other we are hurting ourselves.
Ephesians 4:25

How About You?

Have you told a little lie? Been a little unkind? Do you think a "little" sin doesn't matter? It does. It hurts your testimony for the Lord. Confess even sins you think are small, and ask the Lord to help you overcome them. H. M.

• For the next devotional, turn to page 37. • For the next devotional on *HONESTY*, turn to page 51. • For notes on *HONESTY*, see pages 304, 813, and 863.

For a time you will serve your brother, but you will finally shake loose from him and be free."

[41] So Esau hated Jacob because of what he had done to him. He said to himself, "My father will soon be gone, and then I will kill Jacob." [42] But someone got wind of what he was planning and reported it to Rebekah. She sent for Jacob and told him that his life was being threatened by Esau.

[43] "This is what to do," she said. "Flee to your Uncle Laban in Haran. [44] Stay there with him awhile until your brother's fury is spent, [45] and he forgets what you have done. Then I will send for you. For why should I be bereaved of both of you in one day?"

[46] Then Rebekah said to Isaac, "I'm sick and tired of these local girls. I'd rather die than see Jacob marry one of them."

28 Jacob Is Sent to Find a Wife

So Isaac called for Jacob and blessed him and said to him, "Don't marry one of these Canaanite girls. [2] Instead, go at once to Paddan-aram, to the house of your grandfather Bethuel, and marry one of your cousins—your Uncle Laban's daughters. [3] God Almighty bless you and give you many children; may you become a great nation of many tribes! [4] May God pass on to you and to your descendants the mighty blessings promised to Abraham. May you own this land where we now are foreigners, for God has given it to Abraham."

[5] So Isaac sent Jacob away, and he went to Paddan-aram to visit his Uncle Laban, his mother's brother—the son of Bethuel the Aramean.

[6-8] Esau realized that his father despised the local girls, and that his father and mother had sent Jacob to Paddan-aram, with his father's blessing, to get a wife from there, and that they had strictly warned him against marrying a Canaanite girl, and that Jacob had agreed and had left for Paddan-aram. [9] So Esau went to his Uncle Ishmael's family and married another wife from there, besides the wives he already had. Her name was Mahalath, the sister of Nebaioth, and daughter of Ishmael, Abraham's son.

[10] So Jacob left Beer-sheba and journeyed toward Haran. [11] That night, when he stopped to camp at sundown, he found a rock for a headrest and lay down to sleep, [12] and dreamed that a staircase reached from earth to heaven, and he saw the angels of God going up and down upon it.

[13] At the top of the stairs stood the Lord. "I am Jehovah," he said, "the God of Abraham, and of your father, Isaac. The ground you are lying on is yours! I will give it to you and to your descendants. [14] For you will have descendants as many as dust! They will cover the land from east to west and from north to south; and all the nations of the earth will be blessed through you and your descendants. [15] What's more, I am with you, and will protect you wherever you go, and will bring you back safely to this land; I will be with you constantly until I have finished giving you all I am promising."

[16,17] Then Jacob woke up. "God lives here!" he exclaimed in terror. "I've stumbled into his home! This is the awesome entrance to heaven!" [18] The next morning he got up very early and set his stone headrest upright as a memorial pillar, and poured olive oil over it. [19] He named the place Bethel ("House of God"), though the previous name of the nearest village was Luz.

[20] And Jacob vowed this vow to God: "If God will help and protect me on this journey and give me food and clothes, [21] and will bring me back safely to my father, then I will choose Jehovah as my God! [22] And this memorial pillar shall become a place for worship; and I will give you back a tenth of everything you give me!"

29 Jacob Meets Rachel

Jacob traveled on, finally arriving in the land of the East. [2] He saw in the distance three flocks of sheep lying beside a well in an open field, waiting to be watered. But a heavy stone covered the mouth of the well. [3] (The custom was that the stone was not removed until all the flocks were there. After watering them, the stone was rolled back over the mouth of the well again.) [4] Jacob went over to the shepherds and asked them where they lived.

"At Haran," they said.

[5] "Do you know a fellow there named Laban, the son of Nahor?"

"We sure do."

[6] "How is he?"

"He's well and prosperous. Look, there comes his daughter Rachel with the sheep."

[7] "Why don't you water the flocks so they can get back to grazing?" Jacob asked. "They'll be hungry if you stop so early in the day!"

[8] "We don't roll away the stone and begin the watering until all the flocks and shepherds are here," they replied.

[9] As this conversation was going on, Rachel arrived with her father's sheep, for she was a shepherdess. [10] And because she was his cousin—the daughter of his mother's brother—and because the sheep were his uncle's, Jacob went over to the well and rolled away the stone and watered his uncle's flock. [11] Then Jacob kissed Rachel and started crying! [12,13] He explained about being her cousin on her father's side, and that he was her Aunt Rebekah's son. She quickly ran and told her father, Laban, and as soon as he heard of Jacob's arrival, he rushed out to meet him and greeted

The Family Devotions Bible

him warmly and brought him home. Then Jacob told him his story.

¹⁴"Just think, my very own flesh and blood," Laban exclaimed.

After Jacob had been there about a month, ¹⁵Laban said to him one day, "Just because we are relatives is no reason for you to work for me without pay. How much do you want?" ¹⁶Now Laban had two daughters, Leah, the older, and her younger sister, Rachel. ¹⁷Leah had lovely eyes, but Rachel was shapely, and in every way a beauty. ¹⁸Well, Jacob was in love with Rachel. So he told her father, "I'll work for you seven years if you'll give me Rachel as my wife."

¹⁹"Agreed!" Laban replied. "I'd rather give her to you than to someone outside the family."

²⁰So Jacob spent the next seven years working to pay for Rachel. But they seemed to him but a few days, he was so much in love. ²¹Finally the time came for him to marry her.

"I have fulfilled my contract," Jacob said to Laban. "Now give me my wife, so that I can sleep with her."

²²So Laban invited all the men of the settlement to celebrate with Jacob at a big party. ²³Afterwards, that night, when it was dark, Laban took Leah to Jacob, and he slept with her. ²⁴(And Laban gave to Leah a servant girl, Zilpah, to be her maid.) ²⁵But in the morning—it was Leah!

"What sort of trick is this?" Jacob raged at Laban. "I worked for seven years for Rachel. What do you mean by this trickery?"

²⁶"It's not our custom to marry off a younger daughter ahead of her sister," Laban replied smoothly. ²⁷"Wait until the bridal week is over and you can have Rachel too—if you promise to work for me another seven years!"

²⁸So Jacob agreed to work seven more years. Then Laban gave him Rachel, too. ²⁹And Laban gave to Rachel a servant girl, Bilhah, to be her maid. ³⁰So Jacob slept with Rachel, too, and he loved her more than Leah, and stayed and worked the additional seven years.

³¹But because Jacob was slighting Leah, Jehovah let her have a child, while Rachel was barren. ³²So Leah became pregnant and had a son, Reuben (meaning "God has noticed my trouble"), for she said, "Jehovah has noticed my trouble—now my husband will love me." ³³She soon became pregnant again and had another son and named him Simeon (meaning "Jehovah heard"), for she said, "Jehovah heard that I was unloved, and so he has given me another son." ³⁴Again she became pregnant and had a son, and named him Levi (meaning "Attachment") for she said, "Surely now my husband will feel affection for me, since I have given him three sons!" ³⁵Once again she was pregnant and had a son and named him Judah (meaning "Praise"), for she said, "Now I will praise Jehovah!" And then she stopped having children.

30

Rachel, realizing she was barren, became envious of her sister. "Give me children or I'll die," she exclaimed to Jacob.

²Jacob flew into a rage. "Am I God?" he flared. "He is the one who is responsible for your barrenness."

³Then Rachel told him, "Sleep with my servant-girl Bilhah, and her children will be mine." ⁴So she gave him Bilhah to be his wife, and he slept with her, ⁵and she became pregnant and presented him with a son. ⁶Rachel named him Dan (meaning "Justice"), for she said, "God has given me justice, and heard my plea and given me a son." ⁷Then Bilhah, Rachel's servant-girl, became pregnant again and gave Jacob a second son. ⁸Rachel named him Naphtali (meaning "Wrestling"), for she said, "I am in a fierce contest with my sister and I am winning!"

⁹Meanwhile, when Leah realized that she wasn't getting pregnant anymore, she gave her servant-girl Zilpah to Jacob, to be his wife, ¹⁰and soon Zilpah presented him with a son. ¹¹Leah named him Gad (meaning "My luck has turned!").

¹²Then Zilpah produced a second son, ¹³and Leah named him Asher (meaning "Happy"), for she said, "What joy is mine! The other women will think me blessed indeed!"

¹⁴One day during the wheat harvest, Reuben found some mandrakes growing in a field and brought them to his mother Leah. Rachel begged Leah to give some of them to her.

¹⁵But Leah angrily replied, "Wasn't it enough to steal my husband? And now will you steal my son's mandrakes too?"

Rachel said sadly, "He will sleep with you tonight because of the mandrakes."

¹⁶That evening as Jacob was coming home from the fields, Leah went out to meet him. "You must sleep with me tonight!" she said; "for I am hiring you with some mandrakes my son has found!" So he did. ¹⁷And God answered her prayers and she became pregnant again, and gave birth to her fifth son. ¹⁸She named him Issachar

---

PATIENCE 29:20-28 People often wonder if waiting a long time for something they desire is worth it. Jacob waited seven years to marry Rachel. After being tricked, he agreed to work seven more years for her! The most important goals and desires are worth waiting and paying for. Movies and TV have created the illusion that people have to wait only about an hour to solve their problems or get what they want. Don't be trapped into thinking the same is true in real life. Patience is hardest when we need it the most, but it is the key to achieving our goals. **To begin the series of devotionals on PATIENCE, turn to page 549.**

(meaning "Wages"), for she said, "God has repaid me for giving my slave-girl to my husband." ¹⁹Then once again she became pregnant, with a sixth son. ²⁰She named him Zebulun (meaning "Gifts"), for she said, "God has given me good gifts for my husband. Now he will honor me, for I have given him six sons." ²¹Afterwards she gave birth to a daughter and named her Dinah.

²²Then God remembered about Rachel's plight, and answered her prayers by giving her a child. ²³,²⁴For she became pregnant and gave birth to a son. "God has removed the dark slur against my name," she said. And she named him Joseph (meaning "May I also have another!"), for she said, "May Jehovah give me another son."

²⁵Soon after the birth of Joseph to Rachel, Jacob said to Laban, "I want to go back home. ²⁶Let me take my wives and children—for I earned them from you—and be gone, for you know how fully I have paid for them with my service to you."

²⁷"Please don't leave me," Laban replied, "for a fortune-teller that I consulted told me that the many blessings I've been enjoying are all because of your being here. ²⁸How much of a raise do you need to get you to stay? Whatever it is, I'll pay it."

²⁹Jacob replied, "You know how faithfully I've served you through these many years, and how your flocks and herds have grown. ³⁰For it was little indeed you had before I came, and your wealth has increased enormously; Jehovah has blessed you from everything I do! But now, what about me? When should I provide for my own family?"

³¹,³²"What wages do you want?" Laban asked again.

Jacob replied, "If you will do one thing, I'll go back to work for you. Let me go out among your flocks today and remove all the goats that are speckled or spotted, and all the black sheep. Give them to me as my wages. ³³Then if you ever find any white goats or sheep in my flock, you will know that I have stolen them from you!"

³⁴"All right!" Laban replied. "It shall be as you have said!"

³⁵,³⁶So that very day Laban went out and formed a flock for Jacob of all the male goats that were ringed and spotted, and the females that were speckled and spotted with any white patches, and all of the black sheep. He gave them to Jacob's sons to take them three days' distance, and Jacob stayed and cared for Laban's flock. ³⁷Then Jacob took fresh shoots from poplar, almond, and sycamore trees, and peeled white streaks in them, ³⁸and placed these rods beside the watering troughs so that Laban's flocks would see them when they came to drink; for that is when they mated. ³⁹,⁴⁰So the flocks mated before the white-streaked rods, and their offspring were streaked and spotted, and Jacob added them to his flock. Then he divided out the ewes from Laban's flock and segregated them from the rams, and let them mate only with Jacob's black rams. Thus he built his flocks from Laban's. ⁴¹Moreover, he watched for the stronger animals to mate, and placed the peeled branches before them, ⁴²but didn't with the feebler ones. So the less healthy lambs were Laban's and the stronger ones were Jacob's! ⁴³As a result, Jacob's flocks increased rapidly and he became very wealthy, with many servants, camels, and donkeys.

31 Jacob Leaves Laban

But Jacob learned that Laban's sons were grumbling, "He owes everything he owns to our father. All his wealth is at our father's expense." ²Soon Jacob noticed a considerable cooling in Laban's attitude toward him.

³Jehovah now spoke to Jacob and told him, "Return to the land of your fathers, and to your relatives there; and I will be with you."

⁴So one day Jacob sent for Rachel and Leah to come out to the field where he was with the flocks, ⁵to talk things over with them.

"Your father has turned against me," he told them, "and now the God of my fathers has come and spoken to me. ⁶You know how hard I've worked for your father, ⁷but he has been completely unscrupulous and has broken his wage contract with me again and again and again. But God has not permitted him to do me any harm! ⁸For if he said the speckled animals would be mine, then all the flock produced speckled; and when he changed and said I could have the streaked ones, then all the lambs were streaked! ⁹In this way God has made me wealthy at your father's expense.

¹⁰"And at the mating season, I had a dream, and saw that the he-goats mating with the flock were streaked, speckled, and mottled. ¹¹Then, in my dream, the Angel of God called to me ¹²and told me that I should mate the white female goats with streaked, speckled, and mottled male goats. 'For I have seen all that Laban has done to you,' the Angel said. ¹³'I am the God you met at Bethel,' he continued, 'the place where you anointed the pillar and made a vow to serve me. Now leave this country and return to the land of your birth.'"

¹⁴Rachel and Leah replied, "That's fine with us! There's nothing for us here—none of our father's wealth will come to us anyway! ¹⁵He has reduced our rights to those of foreign women; he sold us, and what he received for us has disappeared. ¹⁶The riches God has given you from our father were legally ours and our children's to begin with! So go ahead and do whatever God has told you to."

¹⁷⁻²⁰So one day while Laban was out shearing sheep, Jacob set his wives and sons on camels, and

FAMILY DEVOTIONS

☐ DEVOTION 14
PERSEVERANCE

Read Genesis 32:22-29

Perseverance Memory Verse

Be strong and courageous and get to work. Don't be frightened by the size of the task, for the Lord my God is with you; he will not forsake you. He will see to it that everything is finished correctly.
1 Chronicles 28:20

"That was Arnie again," Bill complained as he hung up the phone. "I wish he'd quit calling me. I don't want to help him with his model airplane!"

The following day Arnie called again—and the day after that, and the day after that. Finally Bill agreed to help. "If nothing else, we'll get the dumb plane done so Arnie won't keep bugging me," Bill told his mother. Mom nodded and Bill was out the door.

"Well, persistence scored again," observed Mom when Bill returned home. "Just like Jacob wrestling with God."

Bill frowned. "What are you talking about?"

Mom laughed. "Jacob wrestled all night just to be blessed. He was persistent," she explained. "That reminds me of Arnie. He kept calling and calling until you finally agreed to help him. In the same way, we should keep asking—keep praying in God's will, and he'll answer our persistent prayers of faith."

"I gave in even though I didn't really want to," said Bill thoughtfully. "What if I'd keep begging for something God doesn't want? Would he give in, like I gave in to Arnie?"

"No," replied Mom, "but if you're persistent in prayer, God will answer by showing you a better way."

Just then the phone rang. It was Arnie again! "It was fun making the airplane today," said Arnie. Bill cringed—he was afraid Arnie might have another model ready to build. But all Arnie said was, "I just wanted to say thanks for your help, Bill."

As Bill hung up the receiver, he felt good. *It was nice of Arnie to call and say thanks,* he thought. Then he thought of one more thing—it was important to say thanks when God answered, too.

How About You?
Do you pray and pray and pray? Or do you give up when you don't get instant answers? Be persistent. God will answer in his special time and perfect way when you remain faithful in your prayers. And then be sure to thank him. *N. E. K.*

• For the next devotional, turn to page 39. • For the next devotional on *PERSEVERANCE,* turn to page 69.
• For notes on *PERSEVERANCE,* see pages 326, 461, 503, 760, and 1174.

fled without telling Laban his intentions. He drove the flocks before him—Jacob's flocks he had gotten there at Paddan-aram—and took everything he owned and started out to return to his father Isaac in the land of Canaan. ²¹So he fled with all of his possessions (and Rachel stole her father's household gods and took them with her) and crossed the Euphrates River and headed for the territory of Gilead.

²²Laban didn't learn of their flight for three days. ²³Then, taking several men with him, he set out in hot pursuit and caught up with them seven days later, at Mount Gilead. ²⁴That night God appeared to Laban in a dream.

"Watch out what you say to Jacob," he was told. "Don't give him your blessing and don't curse him." ²⁵Laban finally caught up with Jacob as he was camped at the top of a ridge; Laban, meanwhile, camped below him in the mountains.

²⁶"What do you mean by sneaking off like this?" Laban demanded. "Are my daughters prisoners, captured in a battle, that you have rushed them away like this? ²⁷Why didn't you give me a chance to have a farewell party, with singing and orchestra and harp? ²⁸Why didn't you let me kiss my grandchildren and tell them good-bye? This is a strange way to act. ²⁹I could crush you, but the God of your father appeared to me last night and told me, 'Be careful not to be too hard on Jacob!' ³⁰But see here—though you feel you must go, and long so intensely for your childhood home—why have you stolen my idols?"

³¹"I sneaked away because I was afraid," Jacob answered. "I said to myself, 'He'll take his daughters from me by force.' ³²But as for your household idols, a curse upon anyone who took them. Let him die! If you find a single thing we've stolen from you, I swear before all these men, I'll give it back without question." For Jacob didn't know that Rachel had taken them.

³³Laban went first into Jacob's tent to search there, then into Leah's, and then searched the two tents of the concubines, but didn't find them. Finally he went into Rachel's tent. ³⁴Rachel, remember, was the one who had stolen the idols; she had stuffed them into her camel saddle and now was sitting on them! So although Laban searched the tents thoroughly, he didn't find them.

³⁵"Forgive my not getting up, father," Rachel explained, "but I'm having my monthly period." So Laban didn't find them.

³⁶,³⁷Now Jacob got mad. "What did you find?" he demanded of Laban. "What is my crime? You have come rushing after me as though you were chasing a criminal and have searched through everything. Now put everything I stole out here in front of us, before your men and mine, for all to see and to decide whose it is! ³⁸Twenty years I've been with you, and all that time I cared for your ewes and goats so that they produced healthy offspring, and I never touched one ram of yours for food. ³⁹If any were attacked and killed by wild animals, did I show them to you and ask you to reduce the count of your flock? No, I took the loss. You made me pay for every animal stolen from the flocks, whether I could help it or not. ⁴⁰I worked for you through the scorching heat of the day, and through the cold and sleepless nights. ⁴¹Yes, twenty years—fourteen of them earning your two daughters, and six years to get the flock! And you have reduced my wages ten times! ⁴²In fact, except for the grace of God—the God of my grandfather Abraham, even the glorious God of Isaac, my father—you would have sent me off without a penny to my name. But God has seen your cruelty and my hard work, and that is why he appeared to you last night."

⁴³Laban replied, "These women are my daughters, and these children are mine, and these flocks and all that you have—all are mine. So how could I harm my own daughters and grandchildren? ⁴⁴Come now and we will sign a peace pact, you and I, and will live by its terms."

⁴⁵So Jacob took a stone and set it up as a monument, ⁴⁶and told his men to gather stones and make a heap, and Jacob and Laban ate together beside the pile of rocks. ⁴⁷,⁴⁸They named it "The Witness Pile"—"Jegar-sahadutha," in Laban's language, and "Galeed" in Jacob's.

"This pile of stones will stand as a witness against us [if either of us trespasses across this line]," Laban said. ⁴⁹So it was also called "The Watchtower" (Mizpah). For Laban said, "May the Lord see to it that we keep this bargain when we are out of each other's sight. ⁵⁰And if you are harsh to my daughters, or take other wives, I won't know, but God will see it. ⁵¹,⁵²This heap," Laban continued, "stands between us as a witness of our vows that I will not cross this line to attack you and you will not cross it to attack me. ⁵³I call upon the God of Abraham and Nahor, and of their father, to destroy either one of us who does."

So Jacob took oath before the mighty God of his father, Isaac, to respect the boundary line. ⁵⁴Then Jacob presented a sacrifice to God there at the top of the mountain, and invited his companions to a feast, and afterwards spent the night with them on the mountain. ⁵⁵Laban was up early the next morning and kissed his daughters and grandchildren, and blessed them, and returned home.

32 Jacob Meets Esau

So Jacob and his household started on again. And the angels of God came to meet him. When he saw them he exclaimed, "God lives here!" So he named the place "God's territory!"

³Jacob now sent messengers to his brother,

Family Devotions

☐ **Devotion 15**
Forgiving Others

Read Genesis 27:41; 33:1-11

"I'm never going to speak to Michelle again!" Tonya cried, storming into the house. "I told her so, too!"

Mom frowned. "Never is a long time."

"I don't care how long it is," Tonya snapped. "Michelle is so selfish! She won't share. . . ." Tonya's words faded as she ran down the hall to her room.

"Tonya!" Mom called after her. "Get your sweater. It's time to go visit my aunt Margaret."

A short trip across town brought Tonya and her mother to the Colonial Plaza Nursing Home. As she walked beside her mother down the hall, Tonya's mind was still churning with angry thoughts about Michelle.

"Why, Aunt Margaret, what's the matter?" Mom's startled cry brought Tonya back to reality. Mom was kneeling beside the old lady's wheelchair.

In Aunt Margaret's hand was a crumpled letter. Tears were streaming down her cheeks. "Oh, Betty," she sobbed. "It's too late."

"Too late for what?" Mom questioned.

"Too late to say I'm sorry." Aunt Margaret's voice quavered.

It was some time before Tonya and her mother made sense out of what Aunt Margaret was saying. When they finally left, Tonya was wiping her eyes. In the car she turned to her mother. "You mean Aunt Margaret and Aunt Sarah had not spoken to each other for twenty years?"

Mom nodded sadly. "Yes, and now Aunt Sarah is dead. Aunt Margaret can't even remember why they quarreled. Each was too proud and stubborn to say I'm sorry. So the wall between them grew and grew." She looked at her silent daughter. "One day Aunt Margaret said to Aunt Sarah, 'I'll never speak to you again!' Little did she realize what she was saying."

Tonya gulped. "When we get home, I'd better call Michelle. Never is a long time—too long."

Forgiving Others Memory Verse

Be gentle and ready to forgive; never hold grudges. Remember, the Lord forgave you, so you must forgive others.
Colossians 3:13

How About You?

Do you sometimes say things you don't really mean? Is there someone to whom you need to apologize? It will never be any easier than it is right now. So do it. You will always be glad you did. B. W.

• For the next devotional, turn to page 41. • For the next devotional on *Forgiving Others*, turn to page 59.
• For notes on *Forgiving Others*, see pages 273, 356, 586, and 822.

Esau, in Edom, in the land of Seir, ⁴with this message: "Hello from Jacob! I have been living with Uncle Laban until recently, ⁵and now I own oxen, donkeys, sheep, goats, and many servants, both men and women. I have sent these messengers to inform you of my coming, hoping that you will be friendly to us."

⁶The messengers returned with the news that Esau was on the way to meet Jacob—with an army of 400 men! ⁷Jacob was frantic with fear. He divided his household, along with the flocks and herds and camels, into two groups; ⁸for he said, "If Esau attacks one group, perhaps the other can escape."

⁹Then Jacob prayed, "O God of Abraham my grandfather, and of my father Isaac—O Jehovah who told me to return to the land of my relatives, and said that you would do me good— ¹⁰I am not worthy of the least of all your loving-kindnesses shown me again and again just as you promised me. For when I left home I owned nothing except a walking stick! And now I am two armies! ¹¹O Lord, please deliver me from destruction at the hand of my brother Esau, for I am frightened—terribly afraid that he is coming to kill me and these mothers and my children. ¹²But you promised to do me good, and to multiply my descendants until they become as the sands along the shores—too many to count."

¹³⁻¹⁵Jacob stayed where he was for the night, and prepared a present for his brother Esau: 200 female goats, 20 male goats, 200 ewes, 20 rams, 30 milk camels, with their colts, 40 cows, 10 bulls, 20 female donkeys, 10 male donkeys.

¹⁶He instructed his servants to drive them on ahead, each group of animals by itself, separated by a distance between. ¹⁷He told the men driving the first group that when they met Esau and he asked, "Where are you going? Whose servants are you? Whose animals are these?"— ¹⁸they should reply: "These belong to your servant Jacob. They are a present for his master Esau! He is coming right behind us!"

¹⁹Jacob gave the same instructions to each driver, with the same message. ²⁰Jacob's strategy was to appease Esau with the presents before meeting him face to face! "Perhaps," Jacob hoped, "he will be friendly to us." ²¹So the presents were sent on ahead, and Jacob spent that night in the camp.

²²⁻²⁴But during the night he got up and wakened his two wives and his two concubines and eleven sons, and sent them across the Jordan River at the Jabbok ford with all his possessions, then returned again to the camp and was there alone; and a Man wrestled with him until dawn. ²⁵And when the Man saw that he couldn't win the match, he struck Jacob's hip and knocked it out of joint at the socket.

²⁶Then the Man said, "Let me go, for it is dawn."

But Jacob panted, "I will not let you go until you bless me."

²⁷"What is your name?" the Man asked.

"Jacob," was the reply.

²⁸"It isn't anymore!" the Man told him. "It is Israel—one who has power with God. Because you have been strong with God, you shall prevail with men."

²⁹"What is *your* name?" Jacob asked him.

"No, you mustn't ask," the Man told him. And he blessed him there.

³⁰Jacob named the place "Peniel" ("The Face of God"), for he said, "I have seen God face to face, and yet my life is spared." ³¹The sun rose as he started on, and he was limping because of his hip. ³²(That is why even today the people of Israel don't eat meat from near the hip, in memory of what happened that night.)

33

Then, far in the distance, Jacob saw Esau coming with his 400 men. ²Jacob now arranged his family into a column, with his two concubines and their children at the head, Leah and her children next, and Rachel and Joseph last. ³Then Jacob went on ahead. As he approached his brother he bowed low seven times before him. ⁴And then Esau ran to meet him and embraced him affectionately and kissed him; and both of them were in tears!

⁵Then Esau looked at the women and children and asked, "Who are these people with you?"

"My children," Jacob replied. ⁶Then the concubines came forward with their children, and bowed low before him. ⁷Next came Leah with her children, and bowed, and finally Rachel and Joseph came and made their bows.

⁸"And what were all the flocks and herds I met as I came?" Esau asked.

And Jacob replied, "They are my gifts, to curry your favor!"

⁹"Brother, I have plenty," Esau laughed. "Keep what you have."

¹⁰"No, but please accept them," Jacob said, "for what a relief it is to see your friendly smile! I was as frightened of you as though approaching God! ¹¹Please take my gifts. For God has been very generous to me and I have enough." So Jacob insisted, and finally Esau accepted them.

¹²"Well, let's be going," Esau said. "My men and I will stay with you and lead the way."

¹³But Jacob replied, "As you can see, some of the children are small, and the flocks and herds have their young, and if they are driven too hard, they will die. ¹⁴So you go on ahead of us and we'll follow at our own pace and meet you at Seir."

¹⁵"Well," Esau said, "at least let me leave you

FAMILY DEVOTIONS

☐ **DEVOTION 16**
CONFESSING SIN

Read Genesis 35:1-4, 9-12

"Just think, Dad—we get to stay up till two o'clock!" Steve exclaimed as he told his dad about the New Year's Eve party his Sunday school class would be having.

"Sounds great," Dad said. Then, with a twinkle in his eye, he added, "Have I ever told you about the New Year's Eve celebrations we had when I was a boy back in Italy?"

"Did you have a parade or something?" Steve asked.

"Yes, and fireworks, too," Dad said. "But what happened later that night was the most interesting part of the whole celebration. As midnight approached, people gathered up all their trash, old clothing, boxes, and whatever else they wanted to get rid of. There was a New Year's Eve custom of 'out with the old to make way for the new,' so they simply tossed it all out the windows."

"I'd sure hate to be the street cleaner the next day," laughed Steve.

Dad began to look thoughtful. "I think that we, as Christians, could learn a lesson from that strange custom," he said. "The Bible says 'When someone becomes a Christian, he becomes a brand-new person inside. He is not the same anymore. A new life has begun!' But we sometimes try to develop Christian habits—prayer, attending church, witnessing—without giving up our sinful habits. God cannot bless us and help us to grow until we get rid of the old junk in our lives."

Steve looked thoughtful. "I think you're telling me that even though I've made a resolution to get better grades, God won't help me do it unless I first throw out my sin of laziness."

"Exactly." Dad smiled. "Let's both make a list of some of the junk we need to get rid of."

Confessing Sin
Memory Verse

But if we confess our sins to him, he can be depended on to forgive us and to cleanse us from every wrong. [And it is perfectly proper for God to do this for us because Christ died to wash away our sins.]
1 John 1:9

How About You?

Do you sometimes wonder why it's so hard to do the right things, to form good habits, or to grow as a Christian? Perhaps there's some junk in your life that needs to be thrown out. It might be something like a tape or CD collection that is not pleasing to God, immodest clothing, or questionable books and magazines. It might be cigarettes or drugs. Or maybe it's a sin like anger or envy. Whatever it is, get rid of it. God will give you something new and much better to take its place! S. K.

- For the next devotional, turn to page 45.
- For the next devotional on CONFESSING SIN, turn to page 117.
- For notes on CONFESSING SIN, see pages 429, 479, 836, 881, and 1220.

some of my men to assist you and be your guides."

"No," Jacob insisted, "we'll get along just fine. Please do as I suggest."

[16] So Esau started back to Seir that same day. [17] Meanwhile Jacob and his household went as far as Succoth. There he built himself a camp, with pens for his flocks and herds. (That is why the place is called Succoth, meaning "huts.") [18] Then they arrived safely at Shechem, in Canaan, and camped outside the city. [19] (He bought the land he camped on from the family of Hamor, Shechem's father, for 100 pieces of silver. [20] And there he erected an altar and called it "El-Elohe-Israel," "The Altar to the God of Israel.")

34 Jacob's Sons Take Revenge

One day Dinah, Leah's daughter, went out to visit some of the neighborhood girls, [2] but when Shechem, son of King Hamor the Hivite, saw her, he took her and raped her. [3] He fell deeply in love with her, and tried to win her affection.

[4] Then he spoke to his father about it. "Get this girl for me," he demanded. "I want to marry her."

[5] Word soon reached Jacob of what had happened, but his sons were out in the fields herding cattle, so he did nothing until their return. [6,7] Meanwhile King Hamor, Shechem's father, went to talk with Jacob, arriving just as Jacob's sons came in from the fields, too shocked and angry to overlook the insult, for it was an outrage against all of them.

[8] Hamor told Jacob, "My son Shechem is truly in love with your daughter, and longs for her to be his wife. Please let him marry her. [9,10] Moreover, we invite you folks to live here among us and to let your daughters marry our sons, and we will give our daughters as wives for your young men. And you shall live among us wherever you wish and carry on your business among us and become rich!"

[11] Then Shechem addressed Dinah's father and brothers. "Please be kind to me and let me have her as my wife," he begged. "I will give whatever you require. [12] No matter what dowry or gift you demand, I will pay it—only give me the girl as my wife."

[13] Her brothers then lied to Shechem and Hamor, acting dishonorably because of what Shechem had done to their sister. [14] They said, "We couldn't possibly. For you are not circumcised. It would be a disgrace for her to marry such a man. [15] I'll tell you what we'll do—if every man of you will be circumcised, [16] then we will intermarry with you and live here and unite with you to become one people. [17] Otherwise we will take her and be on our way."

[18,19] Hamor and Shechem gladly agreed, and lost no time in acting upon this request, for Shechem was very much in love with Dinah, and could, he felt sure, sell the idea to the other men of the city—for he was highly respected and very popular. [20] So Hamor and Shechem appeared before the city council and presented their request.

[21] "Those men are our friends," they said. "Let's invite them to live here among us and ply their trade. For the land is large enough to hold them, and we can intermarry with them. [22] But they will only consider staying here on one condition—that every one of us men be circumcised, the same as they are. [23] But if we do this, then all they have will become ours and the land will be enriched. Come on, let's agree to this so that they will settle here among us."

[24] So all the men agreed, and all were circumcised. [25] But three days later, when their wounds were sore and sensitive to every move they made, two of Dinah's brothers, Simeon and Levi, took their swords, entered the city without opposition, and slaughtered every man there, [26] including Hamor and Shechem. They rescued Dinah from Shechem's house and returned to their camp again. [27] Then all of Jacob's sons went over and plundered the city because their sister had been dishonored there. [28] They confiscated all the flocks and herds and donkeys—everything they could lay their hands on, both inside the city and outside in the fields, [29] and took all the women and children, and wealth of every kind.

[30] Then Jacob said to Levi and Simeon, "You have made me stink among all the people of this land—all the Canaanites and Perizzites. We are so few that they will come and crush us, and we will all be killed."

[31] "Should he treat our sister like a prostitute?" they retorted.

35 Rachel and Isaac Die

"Move on to Bethel now, and settle there," God said to Jacob, "and build an altar to worship me—the God who appeared to you when you fled from your brother Esau."

[2] So Jacob instructed all those in his household to destroy the idols they had brought with them, and to wash themselves and to put on fresh clothing. [3] "For we are going to Bethel," he told them, "and I will build an altar there to the God who answered my prayers in the day of my distress, and was with me on my journey."

[4] So they gave Jacob all their idols and their earrings, and he buried them beneath the oak tree near Shechem. [5] Then they started on again. And the terror of God was upon all the cities they journeyed through, so that they were not attacked. [6] Finally they arrived at Luz (also called Bethel), in Canaan. [7] And Jacob erected an altar there and named it "The altar to the God who met me here at Bethel" because it was there at

Bethel that God appeared to him when he was fleeing from Esau.

⁸Soon after this Rebekah's old nurse, Deborah, died and was buried beneath the oak tree in the valley below Bethel. And ever after it was called "The Oak of Weeping."

⁹Upon Jacob's arrival at Bethel, en route from Paddan-aram, God appeared to him once again and blessed him. ¹⁰And God said to him, "You shall no longer be called Jacob ('Grabber'), but Israel ('One who prevails with God'). ¹¹I am God Almighty," the Lord said to him, "and I will cause you to be fertile and to multiply and to become a great nation, yes, many nations; many kings shall be among your descendants. ¹²And I will pass on to you the land I gave to Abraham and Isaac. Yes, I will give it to you and to your descendants."

¹³,¹⁴Afterwards Jacob built a stone pillar at the place where God had appeared to him; and he poured wine over it as an offering to God and then anointed the pillar with olive oil. ¹⁵Jacob named the spot Bethel ("House of God"), because God had spoken to him there.

¹⁶Leaving Bethel, he and his household traveled on toward Ephrath (Bethlehem). But Rachel's pains of childbirth began while they were still a long way away. ¹⁷After a very hard delivery, the midwife finally exclaimed, "Wonderful—another boy!" ¹⁸And with Rachel's last breath (for she died) she named him "Ben-oni" ("Son of my sorrow"); but his father called him "Benjamin" ("Son of my right hand").

¹⁹So Rachel died, and was buried near the road to Ephrath (also called Bethlehem). ²⁰And Jacob set up a monument of stones upon her grave, and it is there to this day.

²¹Then Israel journeyed on and camped beyond the Tower of Eder. ²²It was while he was there that Reuben slept with Bilhah, his father's concubine, and someone told Israel about it.

Here are the names of the twelve sons of Jacob:

²³The sons of Leah: Reuben, Jacob's oldest child, Simeon, Levi, Judah, Issachar, Zebulun.

²⁴The sons of Rachel: Joseph, Benjamin.

²⁵The sons of Bilhah, Rachel's servant-girl: Dan, Naphtali.

²⁶The sons of Zilpah, Leah's servant-girl: Gad, Asher.

All these were born to him at Paddan-aram.

²⁷So Jacob came at last to Isaac his father at Mamre in Kiriath-arba (now called Hebron), where Abraham too had lived. ²⁸,²⁹Isaac died soon afterwards, at the ripe old age of 180. And his sons Esau and Jacob buried him.

36 Esau's Family

Here is a list of the descendants of Esau (also called Edom): ²,³Esau married three local girls from Canaan: Adah (daughter of Elon the Hethite), Oholibamah (daughter of Anah and granddaughter of Zibeon the Hivite), Basemath (his cousin—she was a daughter of Ishmael—the sister of Nebaioth).

⁴Esau and Adah had a son named Eliphaz. Esau and Basemath had a son named Reuel.

⁵Esau and Oholibamah had sons named Jeush, Jalam, and Korah. All these sons were born to Esau in the land of Canaan.

⁶⁻⁸Then Esau took his wives, children, household servants, cattle and flocks—all the wealth he had gained in the land of Canaan—and moved away from his brother Jacob to Mount Seir. (For there was not land enough to support them both because of all their cattle.)

⁹Here are the names of Esau's descendants, the Edomites, born to him in Mount Seir:

¹⁰⁻¹²Descended from his wife Adah, born to her son Eliphaz were: Teman, Omar, Zepho, Gatam, Kenaz, Amalek (born to Timna, Eliphaz' concubine).

¹³,¹⁴Esau also had grandchildren from his wife Basemath. Born to her son Reuel were: Nahath, Zerah, Shammah, Mizzah.

¹⁵,¹⁶Esau's grandchildren became the heads of clans, as listed here: the clan of Teman, the clan of Omar, the clan of Zepho, the clan of Kenaz, the clan of Korah, the clan of Gatam, the clan of Amalek.

The above clans were the descendants of Eliphaz, the oldest son of Esau and Adah.

¹⁷The following clans were the descendants of Reuel, born to Esau and his wife Basemath while they lived in Canaan: the clan of Nahath, the clan of Zerah, the clan of Shammah, the clan of Mizzah.

¹⁸,¹⁹And these are the clans named after the sons of Esau and his wife Oholibamah (daughter of Anah): the clan of Jeush, the clan of Jalam, the clan of Korah.

²⁰,²¹These are the names of the tribes that descended from Seir, the Horite—one of the native families of the land of Seir: the tribe of Lotan, the tribe of Shobal, the tribe of Zibeon, the tribe of Anah, the tribe of Dishon, the tribe of Ezer, the tribe of Dishan.

²²The children of Lotan (the son of Seir) were Hori and Heman. (Lotan had a sister, Timna.)

²³The children of Shobal: Alvan, Manahath, Ebal, Shepho, Onam.

²⁴The children of Zibeon: Aiah, Anah. (This is the boy who discovered a hot springs in the wasteland while he was grazing his father's donkeys.)

²⁵The children of Anah: Dishon, Oholibamah.

²⁶The children of Dishon: Hemdan, Eshban, Ithran, Cheran.

²⁷The children of Ezer: Bilhan, Zaavan, Akan.

²⁸⁻³⁰The children of Dishan: Uz, Aran.

³¹⁻³⁹These are the names of the kings of Edom (before Israel had her first king):

of Beor), from Dinhabah in

...y: King Jobab (son of BoZerah), ...he city of Bozrah.

...d by: King Husham, from the land of Temanites.

Succeeded by: King Hadad (son of Bedad), the leader of the forces that defeated the army of Midian when it invaded Moab. His city was Avith.

Succeeded by: King Samlah, from Masrekah.

Succeeded by: King Shaul, from Rehoboth-by-the-River.

Succeeded by: King Baal-hanan (son of Achbor).

Succeeded by: King Hadad, from the city of Pau.

King Hadad's wife was Mehetabel, daughter of Matred and granddaughter of Mezahab.

40-43Here are the names of the sub-tribes of Esau, living in the localities named after themselves: the clan of Timna, the clan of Alvah, the clan of Jetheth, the clan of Oholibamah, the clan of Elah, the clan of Pinon, the clan of Kenaz, the clan of Teman, the clan of Mibzar, the clan of Magdiel, the clan of Iram.

These, then, are the names of the subtribes of Edom, each giving its name to the area it occupied. (All were Edomites, descendants of Esau.)

37 Joseph's Strange Dreams

So Jacob settled again in the land of Canaan, where his father had lived.

²Jacob's son Joseph was now seventeen years old. His job, along with his half-brothers, the sons of his father's wives Bilhah and Zilpah, was to shepherd his father's flocks. But Joseph reported to his father some of the bad things they were doing. ³Now as it happened, Israel loved Joseph more than any of his other children, because Joseph was born to him in his old age. So one day Jacob gave him a special gift—a brightly colored coat. ⁴His brothers of course noticed their father's partiality, and consequently hated Joseph; they couldn't say a kind word to him. ⁵One night Joseph had a dream and promptly reported the details to his brothers, causing even deeper hatred.

⁶"Listen to this," he proudly announced. ⁷"We were out in the field binding sheaves, and my sheaf stood up, and your sheaves all gathered around it and bowed low before it!"

⁸"So you want to be our king, do you?" his brothers derided. And they hated him both for the dream and for his cocky attitude.

⁹Then he had another dream and told it to his brothers. "Listen to my latest dream," he boasted. "The sun, moon, and eleven stars bowed low before me!" ¹⁰This time he told his father as well as his brothers; but his father rebuked him. "What is this?" he asked. "Shall I indeed, and your mother and brothers come and bow before you?" ¹¹His brothers were fit to be tied concerning this affair, but his father gave it quite a bit of thought and wondered what it all meant.

¹²One day Joseph's brothers took their father's flocks to Shechem to graze them there. ¹³,¹⁴A few days later Israel called for Joseph, and told him, "Your brothers are over in Shechem grazing the flocks. Go and see how they are getting along, and how it is with the flocks, and bring me word."

"Very good," Joseph replied. So he traveled to Shechem from his home at Hebron Valley. ¹⁵A man noticed him wandering in the fields.

"Who are you looking for?" he asked.

¹⁶"For my brothers and their flocks," Joseph replied. "Have you seen them?"

¹⁷"Yes," the man told him, "they are no longer here. I heard your brothers say they were going to Dothan." So Joseph followed them to Dothan and found them there. ¹⁸But when they saw him coming, recognizing him in the distance, they decided to kill him!

¹⁹,²⁰"Here comes that master-dreamer," they exclaimed. "Come on, let's kill him and toss him into a well and tell Father that a wild animal has eaten him. Then we'll see what will become of all his dreams!"

²¹,²²But Reuben hoped to spare Joseph's life. "Let's not kill him," he said; "we'll shed no blood—let's throw him alive into this well here; that way he'll die without our touching him!" (Reuben was planning to get him out later and return him to his father.) ²³So when Joseph got there, they pulled off his brightly-colored robe, ²⁴and threw him into an empty well—there was no water in it. ²⁵Then they sat down for supper. Suddenly they noticed a string of camels coming towards them in the distance, probably Ishmaelite traders who were taking gum, spices, and herbs from Gilead to Egypt.

²⁶,²⁷"Look there," Judah said to the others. "Here come some Ishmaelites. Let's sell Joseph to them! Why kill him and have a guilty conscience? Let's not be responsible for his death, for, after all, he is our brother!" And his brothers agreed. ²⁸So when the traders came by, his brothers pulled Joseph out of the well and sold him to them for twenty pieces of silver, and they took him along to Egypt. ²⁹Some time later, Reuben (who was away when the traders came by) returned to get Joseph out of the well. When Joseph wasn't there, he ripped at his clothes in anguish and frustration.

³⁰"The child is gone; and I, where shall I go

FAMILY DEVOTIONS

☐ **DEVOTION 17**
PRAYING AT ALL TIMES

Read Genesis 37:5-9, 18-28

Praying at All Times
Memory Verse

Don't worry about anything; instead, pray about everything; tell God your needs, and don't forget to thank him for his answers.
Philippians 4:6

"Doesn't Justin ever quit talking?" complained Joanne. "He's always bothering me. I wish he'd leave me alone."

"We've talked about this before," said Mom. "Why don't you pray about it and then confront your brother?"

"Oh, Mom," grumbled Joanne, "you always want to pray about everything! I have an idea that will work better."

When Justin ran into the house a little later, Joanne retreated to her room. Soon Justin banged on her door and called out to her, but she turned the volume on her radio up so she couldn't hear what he said. After several attempts to get her attention, Justin gave up and walked away.

At dinnertime, Joanne went to the kitchen. She noticed that Justin had changed clothes. "Are you going somewhere, Justin?" asked Dad, who had just arrived home.

Justin nodded. "I'm going with the Kehoes on a pizza and skating outing," he said. "They got discount tickets."

"Sounds like fun," said Dad. He looked at Joanne. "Why aren't you going?" he asked.

"I wasn't invited," Joanne answered crossly.

"You were too!" said Justin as the Kehoes' car came up the driveway. "I tried to tell you, but you wouldn't listen."

Joanne stormed to her room. A little later, Mom went to talk to her. "Well, how do you feel now about giving Justin the silent treatment?" asked Mom.

"I wanted to teach him a lesson and make him feel bad," said Joanne with a sigh, "but I'm the one who feels bad."

"I think you're also the one learning the lesson," said Mom. "It concerns me that you not only cut off communication from your brother, but you're trying to cut off communication with God, too. By trying to work this out your own way, you missed out on a blessing God wanted to give you."

How About You?
Do you keep open communication with the Lord? Don't ignore God and try to work things out in your own way, especially when you're angry with someone. Seek the Lord's help in everything. *N. E. K.*

• For the next devotional, turn to page 47. • For the next devotional on PRAYING AT ALL TIMES, turn to page 101.
• For notes on PRAYING AT ALL TIMES, see pages 363, 442, 945, 1040, and 1051.

now?" he wept to his brothers. ³¹Then the brothers killed a goat and spattered its blood on Joseph's coat, ³²and took the coat to their father and asked him to identify it.

"We found this in the field," they told him. "Is it Joseph's coat or not?" ³³Their father recognized it at once.

"Yes," he sobbed, "it is my son's coat. A wild animal has eaten him. Joseph is without doubt torn in pieces."

³⁴Then Israel tore his garments and put on sackcloth and mourned for his son in deepest mourning for many weeks. ³⁵His family all tried to comfort him, but it was no use.

"I will die in mourning for my son," he would say, and then break down and cry.

³⁶Meanwhile, in Egypt, the traders sold Joseph to Potiphar, an officer of the Pharaoh—the king of Egypt. Potiphar was captain of the palace guard, the chief executioner.

38 Judah and Tamar

About this time, Judah left home and moved to Adullam and lived there with a man named Hirah. ²There he met and married a Canaanite girl—the daughter of Shua. ³⁻⁵They lived at Chezib and had three sons, Er, Onan, and Shelah. These names were given to them by their mother, except for Er, who was named by his father.

⁶When his oldest son, Er, grew up, Judah arranged for him to marry a girl named Tamar. ⁷But Er was a wicked man, and so the Lord killed him.

⁸Then Judah said to Er's brother, Onan, "You must marry Tamar, as our law requires of a dead man's brother; so that her sons from you will be your brother's heirs."

⁹But Onan was not willing to have a child who would not be counted as his own, and so, although he married her, whenever he went in to sleep with her, he spilled the sperm on the bed to prevent her from having a baby which would be his brother's. ¹⁰So far as the Lord was concerned, it was very wrong of him [to deny a child to his deceased brother], so he killed him, too. ¹¹Then Judah told Tamar, his daughter-in-law, not to marry again at that time, but to return to her childhood home and to her parents, and to remain a widow there until his youngest son, Shelah, was old enough to marry her. (But he didn't really intend for Shelah to do this, for fear God would kill him, too, just as he had his two brothers.) So Tamar went home to her parents.

¹²In the process of time Judah's wife died. After the time of mourning was over, Judah and his friend Hirah, the Adullamite, went to Timnah to supervise the shearing of his sheep. ¹³When someone told Tamar that her father-in-law had left for the sheep-shearing at Timnah, ¹⁴and realizing by now that she was not going to be permitted to marry Shelah, though he was fully grown, she laid aside her widow's clothing and covered herself with a veil to disguise herself, and sat beside the road at the entrance to the village of Enaim, which is on the way to Timnah. ¹⁵Judah noticed her as he went by and thought she was a prostitute, since her face was veiled. ¹⁶So he stopped and propositioned her to sleep with him, not realizing of course that she was his own daughter-in-law.

"How much will you pay me?" she asked.

¹⁷"I'll send you a young goat from my flock," he promised.

"What pledge will you give me, so that I can be sure you will send it?" she asked.

¹⁸"Well, what do you want?" he inquired.

"Your identification seal and your walking stick," she replied. So he gave them to her and she let him come and sleep with her; and she became pregnant as a result. ¹⁹Afterwards she resumed wearing her widow's clothing as usual. ²⁰Judah asked his friend Hirah the Adullamite to take the young goat back to her, and to pick up the pledges he had given her, but Hirah couldn't find her!

²¹So he asked around of the men of the city, "Where does the prostitute live who was soliciting out beside the road at the entrance of the village?"

"But we've never had a public prostitute here," they replied. ²²So he returned to Judah and told him he couldn't find her anywhere, and what the men of the place had told him.

²³"Then let her keep them!" Judah exclaimed. "We tried our best. We'd be the laughingstock of the town to go back again."

²⁴About three months later word reached Judah that Tamar, his daughter-in-law, was pregnant, obviously as a result of prostitution.

"Bring her out and burn her," Judah shouted.

²⁵But as they were taking her out to kill her she sent this message to her father-in-law: "The man who owns this identification seal and walking stick is the father of my child. Do you recognize them?"

²⁶Judah admitted that they were his and said, "She is more in the right than I am, because I refused to keep my promise to give her to my son Shelah." But he did not marry her.

²⁷In due season the time of her delivery arrived and she had twin sons. ²⁸As they were being born, the midwife tied a scarlet thread around the wrist of the child who appeared first, ²⁹but he drew back his hand and the other baby was actually the first to be born. "Where did *you* come from!" she exclaimed. And ever after he was called Perez (meaning "Bursting Out"). ³⁰Then, soon afterwards, the baby with the scarlet thread on his wrist was born, and he was named Zerah.

Family Devotions

☐ **Devotion 18**
Resisting Temptation

Read Genesis 39:7-23

Resisting Temptation Memory Verse

For since he himself has now been through suffering and temptation, he knows what it is like when we suffer and are tempted, and he is wonderfully able to help us.
Hebrews 2:18

As Michelle carefully counted out the money she had taken from her drawer, her sister, Rachel, watched from a comfortable spot on the bed. "If we go around the neighborhood and ask if there are any odd jobs we can do, we just might make enough money to get Mom that Bible we looked at!" Michelle exclaimed. The girls had decided to pool their money and get Mom a special Mother's Day gift.

"Mrs. Stowe is always looking for someone to mow her lawn. Let's try her house," suggested Rachel eagerly.

Soon the girls were busy mowing and raking Mrs. Stowe's yard. It was a very hot day, and they were dripping with sweat by the time they were finished. Wiping her forehead, Michelle gratefully took the money Mrs. Stowe gave them and put it in her pocket. "I'd give anything for a nice bottle of pop right now!" she said as they started down the street.

"A cold bottle of orange soda sure would taste great!" agreed Rachel.

Just then both girls noticed a sign in the window of the 7-Eleven store across the street. *Ice Cold Pop!* it said in big letters.

Michelle and Rachel looked at each other. "Oh, this is so tempting, Rachel. What should we do?" asked Michelle.

"Run!" shouted Rachel.

And that's exactly what they did! They ran right in the direction of home to get a nice cold glass of water before looking for more work.

Later, Michelle turned to Rachel as she counted out their earnings. "Now we have just enough to get that Bible," she said happily. "Good thing we didn't spend any on pop."

Rachel nodded. "My Sunday school teacher says the best way to keep from giving in to temptation is to run from it," she said. "I'm glad we did that. It really works!"

H o w A b o u t Y o u ?

Do you sometimes find it hard to overcome temptation? When you're tempted to cheat, lie, disobey, try drugs, be unkind—or commit any sin—remember that God always provides a way for you to escape. But you have to do your part, too. Often that involves getting out of situations that could bring about defeat. In fact, you should run from them. *L. E. K.*

• For the next devotional, turn to page 51. • For the next devotional on *Resisting Temptation*, turn to page 103.
• For notes on *Resisting Temptation*, see pages 268, 448, 964, and 1258.

39 Potiphar Buys Joseph

When Joseph arrived in Egypt as a captive of the Ishmaelite traders, he was purchased from them by Potiphar, a member of the personal staff of Pharaoh, the king of Egypt. Now this man Potiphar was the captain of the king's bodyguard and his chief executioner. [2]The Lord greatly blessed Joseph there in the home of his master, so that everything he did succeeded. [3]Potiphar noticed this and realized that the Lord was with Joseph in a very special way. [4]So Joseph naturally became quite a favorite with him. Soon he was put in charge of the administration of Potiphar's household, and all of his business affairs. [5]At once the Lord began blessing Potiphar for Joseph's sake. All his household affairs began to run smoothly, his crops flourished and his flocks multiplied. [6]So Potiphar gave Joseph the complete administrative responsibility over everything he owned. He hadn't a worry in the world with Joseph there, except to decide what he wanted to eat! Joseph, by the way, was a very handsome young man.

[7]One day at about this time Potiphar's wife began making eyes at Joseph, and suggested that he come and sleep with her.

[8]Joseph refused. "Look," he told her, "my master trusts me with everything in the entire household; [9]he himself has no more authority here than I have! He has held back nothing from me except you yourself because you are his wife. How can I do such a wicked thing as this? It would be a great sin against God."

[10]But she kept on with her suggestions day after day, even though he refused to listen, and kept out of her way as much as possible. [11]Then one day as he was in the house going about his work—as it happened, no one else was around at the time—[12]she came and grabbed him by the sleeve demanding, "Sleep with me." He tore himself away, but as he did, his jacket slipped off and she was left holding it as he fled from the house. [13]When she saw that she had his jacket, and that he had fled, [14,15]she began screaming; and when the other men around the place came running in to see what had happened, she was crying hysterically. "My husband had to bring in this Hebrew slave to insult us!" she sobbed. "He tried to rape me, but when I screamed, he ran, and forgot to take his jacket."

[16]She kept the jacket, and when her husband came home that night, [17]she told him her story.

"That Hebrew slave you've had around here tried to rape me, [18]and I was only saved by my screams. He fled, leaving his jacket behind!"

[19]Well, when her husband heard his wife's story, he was furious. [20]He threw Joseph into prison, where the king's prisoners were kept in chains. [21]But the Lord was with Joseph there, too, and was kind to him by granting him favor with the chief jailer. [22]In fact, the jailer soon handed over the entire prison administration to Joseph, so that all the other prisoners were responsible to him. [23]The chief jailer had no more worries after that, for Joseph took care of everything, and the Lord was with him so that everything ran smoothly and well.

40 Joseph Explains Two Dreams

Some time later it so happened that the king of Egypt became angry with both his chief baker and his chief butler, so he jailed them both in the prison where Joseph was, in the castle of Potiphar, the captain of the guard, who was the chief executioner. [4]They remained under arrest there for quite some time, and Potiphar assigned Joseph to wait on them. [5]One night each of them had a dream. [6]The next morning Joseph noticed that they looked dejected and sad.

[7]"What in the world is the matter?" he asked.

[8]And they replied, "We both had dreams last night, but there is no one here to tell us what they mean."

"Interpreting dreams is God's business," Joseph replied. "Tell me what you saw."

[9,10]The butler told his dream first. "In my dream," he said, "I saw a vine with three branches that began to bud and blossom, and soon there were clusters of ripe grapes. [11]I was holding Pharaoh's wine cup in my hand, so I took the grapes and squeezed the juice into it, and gave it to him to drink."

[12]"I know what the dream means," Joseph said. "The three branches mean three days! [13]Within three days Pharaoh is going to take you out of prison and give you back your job again as his chief butler. [14]And please have some pity on me when you are back in his favor, and mention me to Pharaoh, and ask him to let me out of here. [15]For I was kidnapped from my homeland among the Hebrews, and now this—here I am in jail when I did nothing to deserve it."

[16]When the chief baker saw that the first dream had such a good meaning, he told his dream to Joseph, too.

"In my dream," he said, "there were three baskets of pastries on my head. [17]In the top basket were all kinds of bakery goods for Pharaoh, but the birds came and ate them."

[18,19]"The three baskets mean three days," Joseph told him. "Three days from now Pharaoh will take off your head and impale your body on a pole, and the birds will come and pick off your flesh!"

[20]Pharaoh's birthday came three days later, and he held a party for all of his officials and household staff. He sent for his chief butler and chief baker, and they were brought to him from the

prison. ²¹Then he restored the chief butler to his former position; ²²but he sentenced the chief baker to be impaled, just as Joseph had predicted. ²³Pharaoh's wine taster, however, promptly forgot all about Joseph, never giving him a thought.

41 Joseph Becomes the Ruler

One night two years later, Pharaoh dreamed that he was standing on the bank of the Nile River, ²when suddenly, seven sleek, fat cows came up out of the river and began grazing in the grass. ³Then seven other cows came up from the river, but they were very skinny and all their ribs stood out. They went over and stood beside the fat cows. ⁴Then the skinny cows ate the fat ones! At which point, Pharaoh woke up!

⁵Soon he fell asleep again and had a second dream. This time he saw seven heads of grain on one stalk, with every kernel well formed and plump. ⁶Then, suddenly, seven more heads appeared on the stalk, but these were shriveled and withered by the east wind. ⁷And these thin heads swallowed up the seven plump, well-formed heads! Then Pharaoh woke up again and realized it was all a dream. ⁸Next morning, as he thought about it, he became very concerned as to what the dreams might mean; he called for all the magicians and sages of Egypt and told them about it, but not one of them could suggest what his dreams meant. ⁹Then the king's wine taster spoke up. "Today I remember my sin!" he said. ¹⁰"Some time ago when you were angry with a couple of us and put me and the chief baker in jail in the castle of the captain of the guard, ¹¹the chief baker and I each had a dream one night. ¹²We told the dreams to a young Hebrew fellow there who was a slave of the captain of the guard, and he told us what our dreams meant. ¹³And everything happened just as he said: I was restored to my position of wine taster, and the chief baker was executed, and impaled on a pole."

¹⁴Pharaoh sent at once for Joseph. He was brought hastily from the dungeon, and after a quick shave and change of clothes, came in before Pharaoh.

¹⁵"I had a dream last night," Pharaoh told him, "and none of these men can tell me what it means. But I have heard that you can interpret dreams, and that is why I have called for you."

¹⁶"I can't do it by myself," Joseph replied, "but God will tell you what it means!"

¹⁷So Pharaoh told him the dream. "I was standing upon the bank of the Nile River," he said, ¹⁸"when suddenly, seven fat, healthy-looking cows came up out of the river and began grazing along the river bank. ¹⁹But then seven other cows came up from the river, very skinny and bony—in fact, I've never seen such poor-looking specimens in all the land of Egypt. ²⁰And these skinny cattle ate up the seven fat ones that had come out first, ²¹and afterwards they were still as skinny as before! Then I woke up.

²²"A little later I had another dream. This time there were seven heads of grain on one stalk, and all seven heads were plump and full. ²³Then, out of the same stalk, came seven withered, thin heads. ²⁴And the thin heads swallowed up the fat ones! I told all this to my magicians, but not one of them could tell me the meaning."

²⁵"Both dreams mean the same thing," Joseph told Pharaoh. "God was telling you what he is going to do here in the land of Egypt. ²⁶The seven fat cows (and also the seven fat, well-formed heads of grain) mean that there are seven years of prosperity ahead. ²⁷The seven skinny cows (and also the seven thin and withered heads of grain) indicate that there will be seven years of famine following the seven years of prosperity.

²⁸"So God has showed you what he is about to do: ²⁹The next seven years will be a period of great prosperity throughout all the land of Egypt; ³⁰but afterwards there will be seven years of famine so great that all the prosperity will be forgotten and wiped out; famine will consume the land. ³¹The famine will be so terrible that even the memory of the good years will be erased. ³²The double dream gives double impact, showing that what I have told you is certainly going to happen, for God has decreed it, and it is going to happen soon. ³³My suggestion is that you find the wisest man in Egypt and put him in charge of administering a nationwide farm program. ³⁴,³⁵Let Pharaoh divide Egypt into five administrative districts, and let the officials of these districts gather into the royal storehouses all the excess crops of the next seven years, ³⁶so that there will be enough to eat when the seven years of famine come. Otherwise, disaster will surely strike."

³⁷Joseph's suggestions were well received by Pharaoh and his assistants. ³⁸As they discussed who should be appointed for the job, Pharaoh said, "Who could do it better than Joseph? For he is a man who is obviously filled with the Spirit of God." ³⁹Turning to Joseph, Pharaoh said to him, "Since God has revealed the meaning of the dreams to you, you are the wisest man in the country! ⁴⁰I am hereby appointing you to be in charge of this entire project. What you say goes, throughout all the land of Egypt. I alone will outrank you."

SERVING GOD WILLINGLY 41:38-40 Joseph rose quickly to the top, from prison walls to Pharaoh's palace. His training for this important position involved being first a slave and then a prisoner. In each situation he learned the importance of serving God and others. Whatever your situation, no matter how undesirable, consider it part of your training program for serving God. **To begin the series of devotionals on SERVING GOD WILLINGLY, turn to page 291.**

41,42Then Pharaoh placed his own signet ring on Joseph's finger as a token of his authority, and dressed him in beautiful clothing and placed the royal gold chain about his neck and declared, "See, I have placed you in charge of all the land of Egypt."

43Pharaoh also gave Joseph the chariot of his second-in-command, and wherever he went the shout arose, "Kneel down!" 44And Pharaoh declared to Joseph, "I, the king of Egypt, swear that you shall have complete charge over all the land of Egypt."

45Pharaoh gave him a name meaning "He has the godlike power of life and death!" And he gave him a wife, a girl named Asenath, daughter of Potiphera, priest of Heliopolis. So Joseph became famous throughout the land of Egypt. 46He was thirty years old as he entered the service of the king. Joseph went out from the presence of Pharaoh and began traveling all across the land.

47And sure enough, for the next seven years there were bumper crops everywhere. 48During those years, Joseph requisitioned for the government a portion of all the crops grown throughout Egypt, storing them in nearby cities. 49After seven years of this, the granaries were full to overflowing, and there was so much that no one kept track of the amount.

50During this time before the arrival of the first of the famine years, two sons were born to Joseph by Asenath, the daughter of Potiphera, priest of the sun god Re of Heliopolis. 51Joseph named his oldest son Manasseh (meaning "Made to Forget"—what he meant was that God had made up to him for all the anguish of his youth, and for the loss of his father's home). 52The second boy was named Ephraim (meaning "Fruitful"—"For God has made me fruitful in this land of my slavery," he said).

53So at last the seven years of plenty came to an end. 54Then the seven years of famine began, just as Joseph had predicted. There were crop failures in all the surrounding countries, too, but in Egypt there was plenty of grain in the storehouses. 55The people began to starve. They pleaded with Pharaoh for food, and he sent them to Joseph. "Do whatever he tells you to," he instructed them.

56,57So now, with severe famine all over the world, Joseph opened up the storehouses and sold grain to the Egyptians and to those from other lands who came to Egypt to buy grain from Joseph.

42 Joseph's Brothers Buy Grain

When Jacob heard that there was grain available in Egypt he said to his sons, "Why are you standing around looking at one another? 2I have heard that there is grain available in Egypt. Go down and buy some for us before we all starve to death."

3So Joseph's ten older brothers went down to Egypt to buy grain. 4However, Jacob wouldn't let Joseph's younger brother Benjamin go with them, for fear some harm might happen to him [as it had to his brother Joseph]. 5So it was that Israel's sons arrived in Egypt along with many others from many lands to buy food, for the famine was as severe in Canaan as it was everywhere else.

6Since Joseph was governor of all Egypt, and in charge of the sale of the grain, it was to him that his brothers came, and bowed low before him, with their faces to the earth. 7Joseph recognized them instantly, but pretended he didn't.

"Where are you from?" he demanded roughly.

"From the land of Canaan," they replied. "We have come to buy grain."

8,9Then Joseph remembered the dreams of long ago! But he said to them, "You are spies. You have come to see how destitute the famine has made our land."

10"No, no," they exclaimed. "We have come to buy food. 11We are all brothers and honest men, sir! We are not spies!"

12"Yes, you are," he insisted. "You have come to see how weak we are."

13"Sir," they said, "there are twelve of us brothers, and our father is in the land of Canaan. Our youngest brother is there with our father, and one of our brothers is dead."

14"So?" Joseph asked. "What does that prove? You are spies. 15This is the way I will test your story: I swear by the life of Pharaoh that you are not going to leave Egypt until this youngest brother comes here. 16One of you go and get your brother! I'll keep the rest of you here, bound in prison. Then we'll find out whether your story is true or not. If it turns out that you don't have a younger brother, then I'll know you are spies."

17So he threw them all into jail for three days.

18The third day Joseph said to them, "I am a God-fearing man and I'm going to give you an opportunity to prove yourselves. 19I'm going to take a chance that you are honorable; only one of you shall remain in chains in jail, and the rest of you may go on home with grain for your families; 20but bring your youngest brother back to me. In this way I will know whether you are telling me the truth; and if you are, I will spare you." To this they agreed.

21Speaking among themselves, they said, "This has all happened because of what we did to Joseph long ago. We saw his terror and anguish and heard his pleadings, but we wouldn't listen."

22"Didn't I tell you not to do it?" Reuben asked.

FAMILY DEVOTIONS

☐ **DEVOTION 19**
HONESTY

Read Genesis 43:19-23

"Here's ten dollars. That should be enough," said Mom as she put money and a shopping list into Joey's hand. "You may keep the change."

After Joey finished getting the items for his mother, he headed for his favorite candy shop. *The clerk said my change was a dollar and twenty-seven cents,* he mused as he pulled out the change, *but it's five dollars and twenty-seven cents! She gave me the wrong amount. Great! I'll buy some candy and save the rest for Saturday when I go to the amusement park with Steve.*

After Joey got home, he worked on his model car while his mother ironed and listened to her favorite radio preacher. "I'd like to close my message today with a true story about integrity," said the speaker. Then he told about a pastor who noticed that he had been given too much change by a bus driver. As he rode along, he was tempted to put the extra money in his wallet without saying anything. But he knew that would be wrong. So, as he left the bus, he returned the extra money to the driver. "You made a mistake on my change," he said.

"That was no mistake," replied the bus driver. "That was a test. You see, I visited your church last Sunday when you were preaching on honesty, and I wanted to see if you practice what you preach. I think I'll come to hear you again."

Wow, thought Joey. *Maybe God is giving me a test, too. I'm going to take that extra money back to the store right now!*

Honesty Memory Verse

Stop lying to each other; tell the truth, for we are parts of each other and when we lie to each other we are hurting ourselves.
Ephesians 4:25

How About You?

Have you ever had the idea that no one would know when you did something dishonest? Be careful. You never know who may be watching you, perhaps even testing you. When you cheat, lie, neglect your work, or do other wrong things, you displease God, and you are a poor testimony for him. *P. R.*

• For the next devotional, turn to page 55. • For the next devotional on *HONESTY,* turn to page 71. • For notes on *HONESTY,* see pages 304, 813, and 863.

"But you wouldn't listen. And now we are going to die because we murdered him."

[23] Of course they didn't know that Joseph understood them as he was standing there, for he had been speaking to them through an interpreter. [24] Now he left the room and found a place where he could weep. Returning, he selected Simeon from among them and had him bound before their eyes. [25] Joseph then ordered his servants to fill the men's sacks with grain, but also gave secret instructions to put each brother's payment at the top of his sack! He also gave them provisions for their journey. [26] So they loaded up their donkeys with the grain and started for home. [27] But when they stopped for the night and one of them opened his sack to get some grain to feed the donkeys, there was his money in the mouth of the sack!

[28] "Look," he exclaimed to his brothers, "my money is here in my sack." They were filled with terror. Trembling, they exclaimed to each other. "What is this that God has done to us?" [29] So they came to their father, Jacob, in the land of Canaan and told him all that had happened.

[30] "The king's chief assistant spoke very roughly to us," they told him, "and took us for spies. [31] 'No, no,' we said, 'we are honest men, not spies. [32] We are twelve brothers, sons of one father; one is dead, and the youngest is with our father in the land of Canaan.' [33] Then the man told us, 'This is the way I will find out if you are what you claim to be. Leave one of your brothers here with me and take grain for your families and go on home, [34] but bring your youngest brother back to me. Then I shall know whether you are spies or honest men; if you prove to be what you say, then I will give you back your brother and you can come as often as you like to purchase grain.'"

[35] As they emptied out the sacks, there at the top of each was the money paid for the grain! Terror gripped them, as it did their father.

[36] Then Jacob exclaimed, "You have bereaved me of my children—Joseph didn't come back, Simeon is gone, and now you want to take Benjamin too! Everything has been against me."

[37] Then Reuben said to his father, "Kill my two sons if I don't bring Benjamin back to you. I'll be responsible for him."

[38] But Jacob replied, "My son shall not go down with you, for his brother Joseph is dead and he alone is left of his mother's children. If anything should happen to him, I would die."

43 Joseph's Brothers Return

But there was no relief from the terrible famine throughout the land. [2] When the grain they had brought from Egypt was almost gone, their father said to them, "Go again and buy us a little food."

[3-5] But Judah told him, "The man wasn't fooling one bit when he said, 'Don't ever come back again unless your brother is with you.' We cannot go unless you let Benjamin go with us."

[6] "Why did you ever tell him you had another brother?" Israel moaned. "Why did you have to treat me like that?"

[7] "But the man specifically asked us about our family," they told him. "He wanted to know whether our father was still living and he asked us if we had another brother, so we told him. How could we know that he was going to say, 'Bring me your brother'?"

[8] Judah said to his father, "Send the lad with me and we will be on our way; otherwise we will all die of starvation—and not only we, but you and all our little ones. [9] I guarantee his safety. If I don't bring him back to you, then let me bear the blame forever. [10] For we could have gone and returned by this time if you had let him come."

[11] So their father Israel finally said to them, "If it can't be avoided, then at least do this. Load your donkeys with the best products of the land. Take them to the man as gifts—balm, honey, spices, myrrh, pistachio nuts, and almonds. [12] Take double money so that you can pay back what was in the mouths of your sacks, as it was probably someone's mistake, [13] and take your brother and go. [14] May God Almighty give you mercy before the man, so that he will release Simeon and return Benjamin. And if I must bear the anguish of their deaths, then so be it."

[15] So they took the gifts and double money and went to Egypt, and stood before Joseph. [16] When Joseph saw that Benjamin was with them, he said to the manager of his household, "These men will eat with me this noon. Take them home and prepare a big feast." [17] So the man did as he was told and took them to Joseph's palace. [18] They were badly frightened when they saw where they were being taken.

"It's because of the money returned to us in our sacks," they said. "He wants to pretend we stole it and seize us as slaves, with our donkeys."

[19] As they arrived at the entrance to the palace, they went over to Joseph's household manager, [20] and said to him, "O sir, after our first trip to Egypt to buy food, [21] as we were returning home, we stopped for the night and opened our sacks, and the money was there that we had paid for the grain. Here it is; we have brought it back again, [22] along with additional money to buy more grain. We have no idea how the money got into our sacks."

[23] "Don't worry about it," the household manager told them; "your God, even the God of your

fathers, must have put it there, for we collected your money all right."

Then he released Simeon and brought him out to them. ²⁴They were then conducted into the palace and given water to refresh their feet; and their donkeys were fed. ²⁵Then they got their presents ready for Joseph's arrival at noon, for they were told that they would be eating there. ²⁶When Joseph came home they gave him their presents, bowing low before him.

²⁷He asked how they had been getting along. "And how is your father—the old man you spoke about? Is he still alive?"

²⁸"Yes," they replied. "He is alive and well." Then again they bowed before him.

²⁹Looking at his brother Benjamin, he asked, "Is this your youngest brother, the one you told me about? How are you, my son? God be gracious to you." ³⁰Then Joseph made a hasty exit, for he was overcome with love for his brother and had to go out and cry. Going into his bedroom, he wept there. ³¹Then he washed his face and came out, keeping himself under control. "Let's eat," he said.

³²Joseph ate by himself, his brothers were served at a separate table, and the Egyptians at still another; for Egyptians despise Hebrews and never eat with them. ³³He told each of them where to sit, and seated them in the order of their ages, from the oldest to the youngest, much to their amazement! ³⁴Their food was served to them from his own table. He gave the largest serving to Benjamin—five times as much as to any of the others! They had a wonderful time bantering back and forth, and the wine flowed freely!

44 Joseph Tests His Brothers

When his brothers were ready to leave, Joseph ordered his household manager to fill each of their sacks with as much grain as they could carry—and to put into the mouth of each man's sack the money he had paid! ²He was also told to put Joseph's own silver cup at the top of Benjamin's sack, along with the grain money. So the household manager did as he was told. ³The brothers were up at dawn and on their way with their loaded donkeys.

⁴But when they were barely out of the city, Joseph said to his household manager, "Chase after them and stop them and ask them why they are acting like this when their benefactor has been so kind to them? ⁵Ask them, 'What do you mean by stealing my lord's personal silver drinking cup, which he uses for fortune telling? What a wicked thing you have done!'" ⁶So he caught up with them and spoke to them along the lines he had been instructed.

⁷"What in the world are you talking about?" they demanded. "What kind of people do you think we are, that you accuse us of such a terrible thing as that? ⁸Didn't we bring back the money we found in the mouth of our sacks? Why would we steal silver or gold from your master's house? ⁹If you find his cup with any one of us, let that one die. And all the rest of us will be slaves forever to your master."

¹⁰"Fair enough," the man replied, "except that only the one who stole it will be a slave, and the rest of you can go free."

¹¹They quickly took down their sacks from the backs of their donkeys and opened them. ¹²He began searching the oldest brother's sack, going on down the line to the youngest. And the cup was found in Benjamin's! ¹³They ripped their clothing in despair, loaded the donkeys again, and returned to the city. ¹⁴Joseph was still home when Judah and his brothers arrived, and they fell to the ground before him.

¹⁵"What were you trying to do?" Joseph demanded. "Didn't you know such a man as I would know who stole it?"

¹⁶And Judah said, "Oh, what shall we say to my lord? How can we plead? How can we prove our innocence? God is punishing us for our sins. Sir, we have all returned to be your slaves, both we and he in whose sack the cup was found."

¹⁷"No," Joseph said. "Only the man who stole the cup, he shall be my slave. The rest of you can go on home to your father."

¹⁸Then Judah stepped forward and said, "O sir, let me say just this one word to you. Be patient with me for a moment, for I know you can doom me in an instant, as though you were Pharaoh himself.

¹⁹"Sir, you asked us if we had a father or a brother, ²⁰and we said, 'Yes, we have a father, an old man, and a child of his old age, a little one. And his brother is dead, and he alone is left of his mother's children, and his father loves him very much.' ²¹And you said to us, 'Bring him here so that I can see him.' ²²But we said to you, 'Sir, the lad cannot leave his father, for his father would die.' ²³But you told us, 'Don't come back here unless your youngest brother is with you.' ²⁴So we returned to our father and told him what you had said. ²⁵And when he said, 'Go back again and buy us a little food,' ²⁶we replied, 'We can't, unless you let our youngest brother go with us. Only then may we come.'

²⁷"Then my father said to us, 'You know that my wife had two sons, ²⁸and that one of them went away and never returned—doubtless torn to pieces by some wild animal; I have never seen him since. ²⁹And if you take away his brother from me also, and any harm befalls him, I shall die with sorrow.' ³⁰And now, sir, if I go back to my father and the lad is not with us—seeing that our father's life is bound up in the lad's life— ³¹when he sees that the boy is not with us, our father will die; and we will be responsible for

bringing down his gray hairs with sorrow to the grave. ³²Sir, I pledged my father that I would take care of the lad. I told him, 'If I don't bring him back to you, I shall bear the blame forever.' ³³Please sir, let me stay here as a slave instead of the lad, and let the lad return with his brothers. ³⁴For how shall I return to my father if the lad is not with me? I cannot bear to see what this would do to him."

45 Joseph Forgives His Brothers

Joseph could stand it no longer.

"Out, all of you," he cried out to his attendants, and he was left alone with his brothers. ²Then he wept aloud. His sobs could be heard throughout the palace, and the news was quickly carried to Pharaoh's palace.

³"I am Joseph!" he said to his brothers. "Is my father still alive?" But his brothers couldn't say a word, they were so stunned with surprise.

⁴"Come over here," he said. So they came closer. And he said again, "I am Joseph, your brother whom you sold into Egypt! ⁵But don't be angry with yourselves that you did this to me, for God did it! He sent me here ahead of you to preserve your lives. ⁶These two years of famine will grow to seven, during which there will be neither plowing nor harvest. ⁷God has sent me here to keep you and your families alive, so that you will become a great nation. ⁸Yes, it was God who sent me here, not you! And he has made me a counselor to Pharaoh, and manager of this entire nation, ruler of all the land of Egypt.

⁹"Hurry, return to my father and tell him, 'Your son Joseph says, "God has made me chief of all the land of Egypt. Come down to me right away! ¹⁰You shall live in the land of Goshen so that you can be near me with all your children, your grandchildren, your flocks and herds, and all that you have. ¹¹,¹²I will take care of you there'" (you men are witnesses of my promise, and my brother Benjamin has heard me say it) "'for there are still five years of famine ahead of us. Otherwise you will come to utter poverty along with all your household.'" ¹³Tell our father about all my power here in Egypt, and how everyone obeys me. And bring him to me quickly."

¹⁴Then, weeping with joy, he embraced Benjamin and Benjamin began weeping too. ¹⁵And he did the same with each of his brothers, who finally found their tongues! ¹⁶The news soon reached Pharaoh—"Joseph's brothers have come"; and Pharaoh was very happy to hear it, as were his officials.

¹⁷Then Pharaoh said to Joseph, "Tell your brothers to load their pack animals and return quickly to their homes in Canaan, ¹⁸and to bring your father and all of your families and come here to Egypt to live. Tell them, 'Pharaoh will assign to you the very best territory in the land of Egypt. You shall live off the fat of the land!' ¹⁹And tell your brothers to take wagons from Egypt to carry their wives and little ones, and to bring your father here. ²⁰Don't worry about your property, for the best of all the land of Egypt is yours."

²¹So Joseph gave them wagons, as Pharaoh had commanded, and provisions for the journey, ²²and he gave each of them new clothes—but to Benjamin he gave five changes of clothes and three hundred pieces of silver! ²³He sent his father ten donkey-loads of the good things of Egypt, and ten donkeys loaded with grain and all kinds of other food, to eat on his journey. ²⁴So he sent his brothers off.

"Don't quarrel along the way!" was his parting shot! ²⁵And leaving, they returned to the land of Canaan, to Jacob their father.

²⁶"Joseph is alive," they shouted to him. "And he is ruler over all the land of Egypt!" But Jacob's heart was like a stone; he couldn't take it in. ²⁷But when they had given him Joseph's messages, and when he saw the wagons filled with food that Joseph had sent him, his spirit revived.

²⁸And he said, "It must be true! Joseph my son is alive! I will go and see him before I die."

46 Jacob Moves to Egypt

So Israel set out with all his possessions, and came to Beer-sheba, and offered sacrifices there to the God of his father, Isaac. ²During the night God spoke to him in a vision.

"Jacob! Jacob!" he called.

"Yes?" Jacob answered.

³,⁴"I am God," the voice replied, "the God of your father. Don't be afraid to go down to Egypt, for I will see to it that you become a great nation there. And I will go down with you into Egypt and I will bring your descendants back again; but you shall die in Egypt with Joseph at your side."

⁵So Jacob left Beer-sheba, and his sons brought him to Egypt, along with their little ones and their wives, in the wagons Pharaoh had provided for them. ⁶They brought their livestock, too, and all their belongings accumulated in the land of Canaan, and came to Egypt—Jacob and all his children, ⁷sons and daughters, grandsons and granddaughters—all his loved ones.

⁸⁻¹⁴Here are the names of his sons and grandchildren who went with him into Egypt:

Reuben, his oldest son;
Reuben's sons: Hanoch, Pallu, Hezron, and Carmi.
Simeon and his sons: Jemuel, Jamin, Ohad,
    Jachin, Zohar, and Shaul (Shaul's mother
    was a girl from Canaan).
Levi and his sons: Gershon, Kohath, Merari.
Judah and his sons: Er, Onan, Shelah, Perez, Zerah
    (however, Er and Onan died while still in
    Canaan, before Israel went to Egypt).

Family Devotions

☐ DEVOTION 20
OPTIMISM

Read Genesis 45:4-8; 50:18-20

*Optimism
Memory Verse*

Fix your thoughts on what is true and good and right. Think about things that are pure and lovely, and dwell on the fine, good things in others. Think about all you can praise God for and be glad about.
Philippians 4:8

Rodney hated riding the late bus home, but since he stayed after school for track practice, it was necessary. "Those guys are so mean to me—just because they know I go to church," he complained when he arrived home one day. "I feel like punching them out!"

"And what would that do for your Christian testimony?" asked Mom. "Be patient, Son. Be true to God and he'll use this for his good purpose."

Rodney wasn't so sure. "It's been a couple of weeks already, and I don't see anything good about it," he said with a sigh.

After the evening meal, Rodney got up stiffly from the table. "You're walking around like you feel awfully sore and tired," Dad observed. "Are you sure being on the team isn't too much for you, Son?"

"I feel pretty sore," Rodney agreed. He stretched his body, slowly collapsing onto the couch. "But I don't mind aching," he added quickly. "It's for a good cause. Coach says we're strengthening our bodies so we'll be ready when we go against tough competition."

"So I guess what seems bad now will be turned around for good, eh?" asked Dad.

Rodney grinned. "Now you sound like Mom," he said. "That's what she tells me when I complain about the problem I'm having on the late bus. But I don't see anything good about that."

"I heard that!" Mom called from the kitchen.

Rodney and Dad grinned. "Mom's right," said Dad. "Just as the hard workouts are for a good cause and prepare your track team for success later, difficult situations we face as Christians build us up for whatever the future holds. So when circumstances seem unbearable, think of them as being for a good cause, too—even if you can't see it right away. God will eventually turn those negative experiences into something for his good."

How About You?
Do you get discouraged and angry when you're treated unfairly or when bad things happen? Ask God to turn these difficult experiences into something good. *N. E. K.*

• For the next devotional, turn to page 59. • For the next devotional on *OPTIMISM*, turn to page 161. • For notes on *OPTIMISM*, see pages 143, 536, 677, and 940.

The sons of Perez were Hezron and Hamul.
Issachar and his sons: Tola, Puvah, Iob, Shimron.
Zebulun and his sons: Sered, Elon, Jahleel.

15So these descendants of Jacob and Leah, not including their daughter Dinah, born to Jacob in Paddan-aram, were thirty-three in all.

16,17Also accompanying him were:

Gad and his sons: Ziphion, Haggi, Shuni, Ezbon, Eri, Arodi, and Areli.
Asher and his sons: Imnah, Ishvah, Ishvi, Beriah, and a sister, Serah.
Beriah's sons were Heber and Malchiel.

18These sixteen persons were the sons of Jacob and Zilpah, the slave-girl given to Leah by her father, Laban.

19-22Also in the total of Jacob's household were these fourteen sons and descendants of Jacob and Rachel:

Joseph and Benjamin;
Joseph's sons, born in the land of Egypt, were Manasseh and Ephraim (their mother was Asenath, the daughter of Potiphera, priest of Heliopolis);
Benjamin's sons: Bela, Becher, Ashbel, Gera, Naaman, Ehi, Rosh, Muppim, Huppim, and Ard.

23-25Also in the group were these seven sons and descendants of Jacob and Bilhah, the slave-girl given to Rachel by her father, Laban:

Dan and his son: Hushim.
Naphtali and his sons: Jahzeel, Guni, Jezer, and Shillem.

26So the total number of those going to Egypt, of his own descendants, not counting the wives of Jacob's sons, was sixty-six. 27With Joseph and his two sons included, this total of Jacob's household there in Egypt totaled seventy.

28Jacob sent Judah on ahead to tell Joseph that they were on the way, and would soon arrive in Goshen—which they did. 29Joseph jumped into his chariot and journeyed to Goshen to meet his father and they fell into each other's arms and wept a long while.

30Then Israel said to Joseph, "Now let me die, for I have seen you again and know you are alive."

31And Joseph said to his brothers and to all their households, "I'll go and tell Pharaoh that you are here, and that you have come from the land of Canaan to join me. 32And I will tell him, 'These men are shepherds. They have brought with them their flocks and herds and everything they own.' 33So when Pharaoh calls for you and asks you about your occupation, 34tell him, 'We have been shepherds from our youth, as our fathers have been for many generations.' When you tell him this, he will let you live here in the land of Goshen." For shepherds were despised and hated in other parts of Egypt.

47

Upon their arrival, Joseph went in to see Pharaoh.

"My father and my brothers are here from Canaan," he reported, "with all their flocks and herds and possessions. They wish to settle in the land of Goshen."

2He took five of his brothers with him, and presented them to Pharaoh.

3Pharaoh asked them, "What is your occupation?"

And they replied, "We are shepherds like our ancestors. 4We have come to live here in Egypt, for there is no pasture for our flocks in Canaan—the famine is very bitter there. We request permission to live in the land of Goshen."

5,6And Pharaoh said to Joseph, "Choose anywhere you like for them to live. Give them the best land of Egypt. The land of Goshen will be fine. And if any of them are capable, put them in charge of my flocks, too."

7Then Joseph brought his father Jacob to Pharaoh. And Jacob blessed Pharaoh.

8"How old are you?" Pharaoh asked him.

9Jacob replied, "I have lived 130 long, hard years, and I am not nearly as old as many of my ancestors."

10Then Jacob blessed Pharaoh again before he left.

11So Joseph assigned the best land of Egypt—the land of Rameses—to his father and brothers, just as Pharaoh had commanded. 12And Joseph furnished food to them in accordance with the number of their dependents.

13The famine became worse and worse, so that all the land of Egypt and Canaan was starving. 14Joseph collected all the money in Egypt and Canaan in exchange for grain, and he brought the money to Pharaoh's treasure-houses. 15When the people were out of money, they came to Joseph crying again for food.

"Our money is gone," they said, "but give us bread; for why should we die?"

16"Well then," Joseph replied, "give me your livestock. I will trade you food in exchange."

17So they brought their cattle to

DEALING WITH CHANGE 46:3-4 God told Jacob to leave his home and travel to a strange and faraway land. But God reassured him by promising to go with him and take care of him. When new situations or surroundings frighten you, recognize that experiencing fear in the face of change is normal. To be paralyzed by the fear, however, is an indication that you question God's ability to take care of you. **To begin the series of devotionals on DEALING WITH CHANGE, turn to page 15.**

Joseph in exchange for food. Soon all the horses, flocks, herds, and donkeys of Egypt were in Pharaoh's possession.

¹⁸The next year they came again and said, "Our money is gone, and our cattle are yours, and there is nothing left but our bodies and land. ¹⁹Why should we die? Buy us and our land and we will be serfs to Pharaoh. We will trade ourselves for food, then we will live, and the land won't be abandoned."

²⁰So Joseph bought all the land of Egypt for Pharaoh; all the Egyptians sold him their fields because the famine was so severe. And the land became Pharaoh's. ²¹Thus all the people of Egypt became Pharaoh's serfs. ²²The only land he didn't buy was that belonging to the priests, for they were assigned food from Pharaoh and didn't need to sell.

²³Then Joseph said to the people, "See, I have bought you and your land for Pharaoh. Here is grain. Go and sow the land. ²⁴And when you harvest it, a fifth of everything you get belongs to Pharaoh. Keep four parts for yourselves to be used for next year's seed, and as food for yourselves and for your households and little ones."

²⁵"You have saved our lives," they said. "We will gladly be the serfs of Pharaoh."

²⁶So Joseph made it a law throughout the land of Egypt—and it is still the law—that Pharaoh should have as his tax 20 percent of all the crops except those produced on the land owned by the temples.

²⁷So Israel lived in the land of Goshen in Egypt, and soon the people of Israel began to prosper, and there was a veritable population explosion among them. ²⁸Jacob lived seventeen years after his arrival, so that he was 147 years old at the time of his death. ²⁹As the time drew near for him to die, he called for his son Joseph and said to him, "Swear to me most solemnly that you will honor this, my last request: do not bury me in Egypt. ³⁰But when I am dead, take me out of Egypt and bury me beside my ancestors." And Joseph promised. ³¹"Swear that you will do it," Jacob insisted. And Joseph did. Soon afterwards Jacob took to his bed.

48 Jacob Blesses Joseph's Sons

One day not long after this, word came to Joseph that his father was failing rapidly. So, taking with him his two sons, Manasseh and Ephraim, he went to visit him. ²When Jacob heard that Joseph had arrived, he gathered his strength and sat up in the bed to greet him, ³and said to him,

"God Almighty appeared to me at Luz in the land of Canaan and blessed me, ⁴and said to me, 'I will make you a great nation and I will give this land of Canaan to you and to your children's children, for an everlasting possession.' ⁵And now, as to these two sons of yours, Ephraim and Manasseh, born here in the land of Egypt before I arrived, I am adopting them as my own, and they will inherit from me just as Reuben and Simeon will. ⁶But any other children born to you shall be your own, and shall inherit Ephraim's and Manasseh's portion from you. ⁷For your mother, Rachel, died after only two children when I came from Paddan-aram, as we were just a short distance from Ephrath, and I buried her beside the road to Bethlehem." ⁸Then Israel looked over at the two boys. "Are these the ones?" he asked.

⁹"Yes," Joseph told him, "these are my sons whom God has given me here in Egypt."

And Israel said, "Bring them over to me and I will bless them."

¹⁰Israel was half blind with age, so that he could hardly see. So Joseph brought the boys close to him and he kissed and embraced them.

¹¹And Israel said to Joseph, "I never thought that I would see you again, but now God has let me see your children too."

¹²,¹³Joseph took the boys by the hand, bowed deeply to him, and led the boys to their grandfather's knees—Ephraim at Israel's left hand and Manasseh at his right. ¹⁴But Israel crossed his arms as he stretched them out to lay his hands upon the boys' heads, so that his right hand was upon the head of Ephraim, the younger boy, and his left hand was upon the head of Manasseh, the older. He did this purposely.

¹⁵Then he blessed Joseph with this blessing: "May God, the God of my fathers Abraham and Isaac, the God who has shepherded me all my life, wonderfully bless these boys. ¹⁶He is the Angel who has kept me from all harm. May these boys be an honor to my name and to the names of my fathers Abraham and Isaac; and may they become a mighty nation."

¹⁷But Joseph was upset and displeased when he saw that his father had laid his right hand on Ephraim's head; so he lifted it to place it on Manasseh's head instead.

¹⁸"No, Father," he said. "You've got your right hand on the wrong head! This one over here is the older. Put your right hand on him!"

¹⁹But his father refused. "I know what I'm doing, my son," he said. "Manasseh too shall become a great nation, but his younger brother shall become even greater."

²⁰So Jacob blessed the boys that day with this

HUMILITY 49:18 In the middle of his prophecy to Dan, Jacob exclaimed, "I trust in your salvation, Lord." He was emphasizing to Dan that he would be a strong leader only if his trust was in God, not in his natural strength or ability. Those who are strong, attractive, or talented often find it easier to trust in themselves than in God, who gave them their gifts. Remember to thank God for what you are and have, so your trust does not become misplaced. **To begin the series of devotionals on HUMILITY, turn to page 449.**

blessing: "May the people of Israel bless each other by saying, 'God make you as prosperous as Ephraim and Manasseh.'" (Note that he put Ephraim before Manasseh.)

²¹Then Israel said to Joseph, "I am about to die, but God will be with you and will bring you again to Canaan, the land of your fathers. ²²And I have given the choice land of Shekem to you instead of to your brothers, as your portion of that land which I took from the Amorites with my sword and with my bow."

49 Jacob Talks about His Sons

Then Jacob called together all his sons and said, "Gather around me and I will tell you what is going to happen to you in the days to come. ²Listen to me, O sons of Jacob; listen to Israel your father.

³"Reuben, you are my oldest son, the child of my vigorous youth. You are the head of the list in rank and in honor. ⁴But you are unruly as the wild waves of the sea, and you shall be first no longer. I am demoting you, for you slept with one of my wives and thus dishonored me.

⁵"Simeon and Levi are two of a kind. They are men of violence and injustice. ⁶O my soul, stay away from them. May I never be a party to their wicked plans. For in their anger they murdered a man, and maimed oxen just for fun. ⁷Cursed be their anger, for it is fierce and cruel. Therefore, I will scatter their descendants throughout Israel.

⁸"Judah, your brothers shall praise you. You shall destroy your enemies. Your father's sons shall bow before you. ⁹Judah is a young lion that has finished eating its prey. He has settled down as a lion—who will dare to rouse him? ¹⁰The scepter shall not depart from Judah until Shiloh comes, whom all people shall obey. ¹¹He has chained his steed to the choicest vine and washed his clothes in wine. ¹²His eyes are darker than wine and his teeth are whiter than milk.

¹³"Zebulun shall dwell on the shores of the sea and shall be a harbor for ships, with his borders extending to Sidon.

¹⁴"Issachar is a strong beast of burden resting among the saddlebags. ¹⁵When he saw how good the countryside was, how pleasant the land, he willingly bent his shoulder to the task and served his masters with vigor.

¹⁶"Dan shall govern his people like any other tribe in Israel. ¹⁷He shall be a serpent in the path that bites the horses' heels, so that the rider falls off. ¹⁸I trust in your salvation, Lord.

¹⁹"A marauding band shall stamp upon Gad, but he shall rob and pursue them!

²⁰"Asher shall produce rich foods, fit for kings!

²¹"Naphtali is a deer let loose, producing lovely fawns.

²²"Joseph is a fruitful tree beside a fountain. His branches shade the wall. ²³He has been severely injured by those who shot at him and persecuted him, ²⁴but their weapons were shattered by the Mighty One of Jacob, the Shepherd, the Rock of Israel. ²⁵May the God of your fathers, the Almighty, bless you with blessings of heaven above and of the earth beneath—blessings of the breasts and of the womb, ²⁶blessings of the grain and flowers, blessings reaching to the utmost bounds of the everlasting hills. These shall be the blessings upon the head of Joseph who was exiled from his brothers.

²⁷"Benjamin is a wolf that prowls. He devours his enemies in the morning, and in the evening divides the loot."

²⁸So these are the blessings that Israel, their father, blessed his twelve sons with.

²⁹,³⁰Then he told them, "Soon I will die. You must bury me with my fathers in the land of Canaan, in the cave in the field of Mach-pelah, facing Mamre—the field Abraham bought from Ephron the Hethite for a burial ground. ³¹There they buried Abraham and Sarah, his wife; there they buried Isaac and Rebekah, his wife; and there I buried Leah. ³²It is the cave which my grandfather Abraham purchased from the sons of Heth." ³³Then, when Jacob had finished his prophecies to his sons, he lay back in the bed, breathed his last, and died.

50 Jacob Dies and Is Buried

Joseph threw himself upon his father's body and wept over him and kissed him. ²Afterwards he commanded his morticians to embalm the body. ³The embalming process required forty days, with a period of national mourning of seventy days. ⁴Then, when at last the mourning was over, Joseph approached Pharaoh's staff and requested them to speak to Pharaoh on his behalf.

⁵"Tell His Majesty," he requested them, "that Joseph's father made Joseph swear to take his body back to the land of Canaan, to bury him there. Ask His Majesty to permit me to go and bury my father; assure him that I will return promptly."

⁶Pharaoh agreed. "Go and bury your father, as you promised," he said.

⁷So Joseph went, and a great number of Pharaoh's counselors and assistants—all the senior officers of the land, ⁸as well as all of Joseph's people—his brothers and their families. But they left their little children and flocks and herds in the land of Goshen. ⁹So a very great number of chariots, cavalry, and people accompanied Joseph.

¹⁰When they arrived at Atad (meaning "Threshing Place of Brambles"), beyond the Jordan River, they held a very great and solemn funeral service, with a

Family Devotions

☐ **Devotion 21**
Forgiving Others

Read Genesis 50:14-21

"Tests! Tests! Tests!" grumbled Steve and Sheila to Gramps Wilson one day. "We hate tests!"

Gramps smiled. "I reckon we all do," he agreed, "but tests are a part of life. Everybody has 'em."

"*You* don't," protested the children. "You're out of school."

But before long Steve and Sheila learned that not all tests are on paper, and not all lessons are learned from a book. The next time Gramps saw them they looked very unhappy. He asked what was wrong. "We found out last night our folks are getting a divorce," Steve mumbled.

"Oh, Gramps, why did this have to happen?" sobbed Sheila. "If they loved us, they wouldn't do this to us."

"Oh, they do love you," Gramps assured her, "and I don't know just why this happened. It's a test life is giving you."

"Well, it's not fair!" declared Steve. "Why are they doing this to us?"

As the children talked with Gramps, he reminded them of Joseph, who had been sold into Egypt by his brothers. Joseph faced many lonely hours and difficult situations, but he didn't become bitter. Although he didn't know why things happened as they did, he realized that God allowed them for a reason. He stayed sweet and kind and even forgave his brothers.

"That's what we're going to have to do," Sheila said thoughtfully. "We'll have to try to be patient and kind. We don't know why this divorce is happening, but we'll just have to make the best of it."

"Yeah, I guess so," agreed Steve. "Mom and Dad must be pretty unhappy, too."

Gramps nodded. "I'm sure they are," he said. "Try not to be bitter or angry. Look for ways to make things easier for everyone. Ask the Lord to help you pass this test."

Forgiving Others Memory Verse

Be gentle and ready to forgive; never hold grudges. Remember, the Lord forgave you, so you must forgive others.
Colossians 3:13

How About You?

Are you facing one of life's tests? A divorce in your family? Loss of Dad's job? Mom going to work? Whatever it is, trust the Lord. Wait to see what he is working out for you. Meanwhile, be patient, sweet, and kind. Help those around you pass their tests, too. B. W.

- For the next devotional, turn to page 63. • For the next devotional on *Forgiving Others*, turn to page 251.
- For notes on *Forgiving Others*, see pages 273, 356, 586, and 822.

seven-day period of lamentation for Joseph's father. ¹¹The local residents, the Canaanites, renamed the place Abel-mizraim (meaning "Egyptian Mourners") for they said, "It is a place of very deep mourning by these Egyptians." ¹²,¹³So his sons did as Israel commanded them, and carried his body into the land of Canaan and buried it there in the cave of Machpelah—the cave Abraham had bought in the field of Ephron the Hethite, close to Mamre.

¹⁴Then Joseph returned to Egypt with his brothers and all who had accompanied him to the funeral of his father. ¹⁵But now that their father was dead, Joseph's brothers were frightened.

"Now Joseph will pay us back for all the evil we did to him," they said. ¹⁶,¹⁷So they sent him this message: "Before he died, your father instructed us to tell you to forgive us for the great evil we did to you. We servants of the God of your father beg you to forgive us." When Joseph read the message, he broke down and cried.

¹⁸Then his brothers came and fell down before him and said, "We are your slaves."

¹⁹But Joseph told them, "Don't be afraid of me. Am I God, to judge and punish you? ²⁰As far as I am concerned, God turned into good what you meant for evil, for he brought me to this high position I have today so that I could save the lives of many people. ²¹No, don't be afraid. Indeed, I myself will take care of you and your families." And he spoke very kindly to them, reassuring them.

²²So Joseph and his brothers and their families continued to live in Egypt. Joseph was 110 years old when he died. ²³He lived to see the birth of his son Ephraim's children, and the children of Machir, Manasseh's son, who played at his feet.

²⁴"Soon I will die," Joseph told his brothers, "but God will surely come and get you, and bring you out of this land of Egypt and take you back to the land he promised to the descendants of Abraham, Isaac and Jacob." ²⁵Then Joseph made his brothers promise with an oath that they would take his body back with them when they returned to Canaan. ²⁶So Joseph died at the age of 110, and they embalmed him, and his body was placed in a coffin in Egypt.

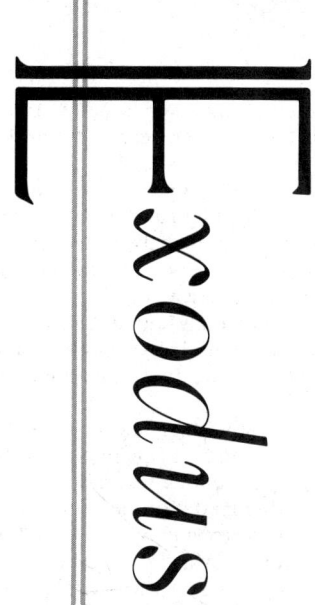

Exodus

DO YOU like to watch movies with death-defying stunts and heart-stopping action? The book of Exodus can top them all. It's filled with incredible conflicts and amazing miracles. It's a book in which God shows off his power and cleverness.

Abraham's twelve great-grandsons had moved to Egypt to avoid a famine. They settled in and had families. Now, four hundred years later, there were thousands of Israelites.

God wanted the Israelites to move back to the Promised Land, but they were made slaves in Egypt. That wasn't a problem for God because now the miracles could begin: a burning bush, sticks that turned into snakes, pitch darkness during the day, an invasion of frogs, and the Passover. The Egyptians let the Israelites go free.

What was next for the Israelites? God gave them the Ten Commandments, instructions on worship, and commands to have celebrations. God wanted the people to remember that they were his chosen people.

God wants to remind us, too, that we are his because of our faith in Jesus Christ. As you read Exodus, look for ways God cared about his people—big ways and small ways.

The Hebrews Become Slaves

This is the list of the sons of Jacob who accompanied him to Egypt, with their families: Reuben, Simeon, Levi, Judah, Issachar, Zebulun, Benjamin, Dan, Naphta'i, Gad, Asher. 5So the total number who went with him was seventy (for Joseph was already there). 6In due season Joseph and each of his brothers died, ending that generation. 7Meanwhile, their descendants were very fertile, increasing rapidly in numbers; there was a veritable population explosion so that they soon became a large nation, and they filled the land of Goshen.

8Then, eventually, a new king came to the throne of Egypt who felt no obligation to the descendants of Joseph.

9He told his people, "These Israelis are becoming dangerous to us because there are so many of them. 10Let's figure out a way to put an end to this. If we don't, and war breaks out, they will join our enemies and fight against us and escape out of the country."

11So the Egyptians made slaves of them and put

...skmasters over them to wear them down ...er heavy burdens while building the cities of Pithom and Rameses as supply centers for the king. ¹²But the more the Egyptians mistreated and oppressed them, the more the Israelis seemed to multiply! The Egyptians became alarmed ¹³,¹⁴and made the Hebrew slavery more bitter still, forcing them to toil long and hard in the fields and to carry heavy loads of mortar and brick.

¹⁵,¹⁶Then Pharaoh, the king of Egypt, instructed the Hebrew midwives (their names were Shiphrah and Puah) to kill all Hebrew boys as soon as they were born, but to let the girls live. ¹⁷But the midwives feared God and didn't obey the king—they let the boys live too.

¹⁸The king summoned them before him and demanded, "Why have you disobeyed my command and let the baby boys live?"

¹⁹"Sir," they told him, "the Hebrew women have their babies so quickly that we can't get there in time! They are not slow like the Egyptian women!"

²⁰And God blessed the midwives [because they were God-fearing women]. So the people of Israel continued to multiply and to become a mighty nation. ²¹And because the midwives revered God, he gave them children of their own. ²²Then Pharaoh commanded all of his people to throw the newborn Hebrew boys into the Nile River. But the girls, he said, could live.

2 Moses Is Born

There were at this time a Hebrew fellow and girl of the tribe of Levi who married and had a family, and a baby son was born to them. When the baby's mother saw that he was an unusually beautiful baby, she hid him at home for three months. ³Then, when she could no longer hide him, she made a little boat from papyrus reeds, waterproofed it with tar, put the baby in it, and laid it among the reeds along the river's edge. ⁴The baby's sister watched from a distance to see what would happen to him.

⁵Well, this is what happened: A princess, one of Pharaoh's daughters, came down to bathe in the river, and as she and her maids were walking along the riverbank, she spied the little boat among the reeds and sent one of the maids to bring it to her. ⁶When she opened it, there was a baby! And he was crying. This touched her heart. "He must be one of the Hebrew children!" she said.

⁷Then the baby's sister approached the princess and asked her, "Shall I go and find one of the Hebrew women to nurse the baby for you?"

⁸"Yes, do!" the princess replied. So the little girl rushed home and called her mother!

⁹"Take this child home and nurse him for me," the princess instructed the baby's mother, "and I will pay you well!" So she took him home and nursed him.

¹⁰Later, when he was older, she brought him back to the princess and he became her son. She named him Moses (meaning "to draw out") because she had drawn him out of the water.

¹¹One day, many years later when Moses had grown up and become a man, he went out to visit his fellow Hebrews and saw the terrible conditions they were under. During his visit he saw an Egyptian knock a Hebrew to the ground—one of his own Hebrew brothers! ¹²Moses looked this way and that to be sure no one was watching, then killed the Egyptian and hid his body in the sand.

¹³The next day as he was out visiting among the Hebrews again, he saw two of them fighting. "What are you doing, hitting your own Hebrew brother like that?" he said to the one in the wrong.

¹⁴"And who are you?" the man demanded. "I suppose you think you are *our* prince and judge! And do you plan to kill me as you did that Egyptian yesterday?" When Moses realized that his deed was known, he was frightened. ¹⁵And sure enough, when Pharaoh heard about it he ordered Moses arrested and executed. But Moses ran away into the land of Midian. As he was sitting there beside a well, ¹⁶seven girls who were daughters of the priest of Midian came to draw water and fill the water troughs for their father's flocks. ¹⁷But the shepherds chased the girls away. Moses then came to their aid and rescued them from the shepherds and watered their flocks.

¹⁸When they returned to their father, Reuel, he asked, "How did you get the flocks watered so quickly today?"

¹⁹"An Egyptian defended us against the shepherds," they told him; "he drew water for us and watered the flocks."

²⁰"Well, where is he?" their father demanded. "Did you just leave him there? Invite him home for supper."

²¹Moses eventually decided to accept Reuel's invitation to live with them, and Reuel gave him one of the girls, Zipporah, as his wife. ²²They had a baby named

---

STANDING FOR RIGHTEOUSNESS 2:3ff. Moses' mother knew how wrong it would be to destroy her child. But there was little she could do to change Pharaoh's new law. Her only alternative was to hide the child and later place him in a tiny reed basket on the river. God used her small but courageous act to place her son, the Hebrew of his choice, in the house of Pharaoh. Do you sometimes feel surrounded by evil and frustrated by how little you can do about it? What seems a small and futile act to you may be just what God will use to change a situation. When faced with evil, look for ways to act against it. Then trust God to use your act, however small, in his war against evil. **To begin the series of devotionals on STANDING FOR RIGHTEOUSNESS, turn to page 139.**

Family Devotions

☐ **Devotion 22**
Obedience

Read Exodus 1:15-21

Obedience Memory Verse

Oh, that they would always have such a heart for me, wanting to obey my commandments. Then all would go well with them in the future, and with their children throughout all generations!
Deuteronomy 5:29

"Sit, Rex! Sit." Rex sat, and Jenny gave the big black dog a pat on his head. "Good boy! Here's a treat for obeying." She gave Rex a dog biscuit.

"Rex is getting good at obeying you," Dad called to Jenny. He was watching from the porch as Jenny worked with Rex in the backyard.

Jenny grinned and nodded. "Stay," she said firmly to Rex. "Stay." Jenny walked a few steps away just as her cousin Brian came up the walk.

"Hi, Rex!" called Brian. "Come here, boy. C'mon, Rex. Come here."

Rex perked up his ears and looked at Brian. Then he looked back at Jenny and whined, but he stayed where he was. "Good boy!" Jenny gave him another dog treat.

"Rex reminds me of the Hebrew midwives we read about during devotions last night," said Dad.

Brian laughed. "What on earth do you mean by that?"

"We read about some women named Shiphrah and Puah," explained Dad. "The Hebrew midwives were told by the king to kill all the boy babies born to the Israelites. But they knew it was better to obey God than man, so they decided not to do it. Because of that God blessed them. Even though they disobeyed the king, they still were blessed by God."

"I know what you're getting at." Jenny put her arm around Rex as he lay beside her on the floor. "Rex had to disobey Brian in order to obey me, but he did it."

"Yes, he did." Dad gave Rex a pat on the head. "We must always obey our master. In Rex's case, his master—or mistress—is Jenny. Our master is God. If we obey God, he will bless us."

"Like when I gave Rex a good treat for obeying me," Jenny said. Smiling, Dad nodded.

How About You?
Would you steal if your friends encouraged you to do so? Would you cheat on a test because your friend wanted the answers? Or do you obey God rather than people? When you're tempted to sin, ask God to give you strength to obey him. Then do it—he'll bless you for it. A. L.

• For the next devotional, turn to page 65. • For the next devotional on *Obedience*, turn to page 199. • For notes on *Obedience*, see pages 319, 425, 500, 510, and 757.

...meaning "foreigner"), for he said, "I ...ger in a foreign land."

...ral years later the king of Egypt died. The ...s were groaning beneath their burdens, in ...p trouble because of their slavery, and weeping ...tterly before the Lord. He heard their cries from heaven, 24and remembered his promise to Abraham, Isaac, and Jacob [to bring their descendants back into the land of Canaan]. 25Looking down upon them, he knew that the time had come for their rescue.

3 The Burning Bush

One day as Moses was tending the flock of his father-in-law, Jethro, the priest of Midian, out at the edge of the desert near Horeb, the mountain of God, 2suddenly the Angel of Jehovah appeared to him as a flame of fire in a bush. When Moses saw that the bush was on fire and that it didn't burn up, 3,4he went over to investigate. Then God called out to him,

"Moses! Moses!"

"Who is it?" Moses asked.

5"Don't come any closer," God told him. "Take off your shoes, for you are standing on holy ground. 6I am the God of your fathers—the God of Abraham, Isaac, and Jacob." (Moses covered his face with his hands, for he was afraid to look at God.)

7Then the Lord told him, "I have seen the deep sorrows of my people in Egypt and have heard their pleas for freedom from their harsh taskmasters. 8I have come to deliver them from the Egyptians and to take them out of Egypt into a good land, a large land, a land 'flowing with milk and honey'—the land where the Canaanites, Hittites, Amorites, Perizzites, Hivites, and Jebusites live. 9Yes, the wail of the people of Israel has risen to me in heaven, and I have seen the heavy tasks the Egyptians have oppressed them with. 10Now I am going to send you to Pharaoh, to demand that he let you lead my people out of Egypt."

11"But I'm not the person for a job like that!" Moses exclaimed.

12Then God told him, "I will certainly be with you, and this is the proof that I am the one who is sending you: When you have led the people out of Egypt, you shall worship God here upon this mountain!"

13But Moses asked, "If I go to the people of Israel and tell them that their fathers' God has sent me, they will ask, 'Which God are you talking about?' What shall I tell them?"

14"'The Sovereign God,'" was the reply. "Just say, 'I Am has sent me!' 15Yes, tell them, 'Jehovah, the God of your ancestors Abraham, Isaac, and Jacob, has sent me to you.' (This is my eternal name, to be used throughout all generations.)

16"Call together all the elders of Israel," God instructed him, "and tell them about Jehovah appearing to you here in this burning bush and that he said to you, 'I have visited my people and have seen what is happening to them there in Egypt. 17I promise to rescue them from the drudgery and humiliation they are undergoing, and to take them to the land now occupied by the Canaanites, Hittites, Amorites, Perizzites, Hivites, and Jebusites, a land "flowing with milk and honey."' 18The elders of the people of Israel will accept your message. They must go with you to the king of Egypt and tell him, 'Jehovah, the God of the Hebrews, has met with us and instructed us to go three days' journey into the desert to sacrifice to him. Give us your permission.'

19"But I know that the king of Egypt will not let you go except under heavy pressure. 20So I will give him all the pressure he needs! I will destroy Egypt with my miracles, and then at last he will let you go. 21And I will see to it that the Egyptians load you down with gifts when you leave, so that you will by no means go out empty-handed! 22Every woman will ask for jewels, silver, gold, and the finest of clothes from her Egyptian master's wife and neighbors. You will clothe your sons and daughters with the best of Egypt!"

4

But Moses said, "They won't believe me! They won't do what I tell them to. They'll say, 'Jehovah never appeared to you!'"

2"What do you have there in your hand?" the Lord asked him.

And he replied, "A shepherd's rod."

3"Throw it down on the ground," the Lord told him. So he threw it down—and it became a serpent, and Moses ran from it!

4Then the Lord told him, "Grab it by the tail!" He did, and it became a rod in his hand again!

5"Do that and they will believe you!" the Lord told him. "Then they will realize that Jehovah, the God of their ancestors Abraham, Isaac, and Jacob, has really appeared to you. 6Now reach your hand inside your robe, next to your chest." And when he did, and took it out again, it was white with leprosy! 7"Now put it in again," Jehovah said. And when he did, and took it out again, it was normal, just as before!

8"If they don't believe the first miracle, they will the second," the Lord said, 9"and if they don't accept you after these two signs, then take water from the Nile River and pour it upon the dry land, and it will turn to blood."

10But Moses pleaded, "O Lord, I'm just not a good speaker. I never have been, and I'm not now, even after you have spoken to me, for I have a speech impediment."

11"Who makes mouths?" Jehovah asked him. "Isn't it I, the Lord? Who makes a man so that he can speak

FAMILY DEVOTIONS

☐ **DEVOTION 23**
SERVING GOD BOLDLY

Read Exodus 3:1-11; 4:10-12

Serving God Boldly
Memory Verse

Yes, be bold and strong!
Banish fear and doubt!
For remember, the Lord
your God is with you
wherever you go.
Joshua 1:9

How About You?
Do you let God guide you into situations where he can use you? Are you using your talents to serve him? Do you speak up for Jesus whenever you get a chance? Remember to ask God to help. He will give you strength and will help you to speak well, just as he did for Moses. *J. H.*

It was youth night at Centerville Church, and the young people were in charge of the entire evening service. They used their talents to serve the Lord as they sang, played instruments, worked in the nursery, put on a skit, ushered, took up the offering, and even preached.

After the special program, Mr. Jenkins approached Connie. "You did a fine job on your ventriloquism," he complimented her. "Your skit was cute, and it had a good message, too. I'm in charge of a special program that we're planning where I work. Would you do a skit there?"

Connie was pleased with Mr. Jenkins's comments and readily agreed. But when she thought about it later, she became apprehensive about what she had done. "I forgot that Mr. Jenkins works at that center for children who've been in trouble with the law," she told her mother. "I can't give a talk there!"

"Why not, dear?" asked Mom. "Those children need to hear the gospel, too."

"But they're so tough," explained Connie. "They aren't church kids. They'll laugh at me. I can't do it—I just can't!"

To Connie's surprise, Mom agreed with her. "You're right, Connie," she said. "They're too tough! Just send your dummy with Mr. Jenkins. Let the dummy handle those kids."

Connie glanced at her mother in surprise. "Mom," she protested, "you know he can't talk without me! I put the words in his mouth. He can't do anything without me."

Mom smiled and nodded. "That's how God works, too," she reminded Connie. "You are his mouthpiece. Without him your words will be meaningless. It's his power that reaches people and meets their needs. He'll give you his power and the words to say if you ask him."

"Are you saying I'm God's 'dummy'?" Connie grinned. "You're right, Mom. I will ask for his help. I want to be his mouthpiece. I know that without him I can do nothing."

• For the next devotional, turn to page 67. • For the next devotional on *SERVING GOD BOLDLY,* turn to page 309.
• For notes on *SERVING GOD BOLDLY,* see pages 327, 404, 501, 720, and 856.

or not speak, see or not see, hear or not hear? ¹²Now go ahead and do as I tell you, for I will help you to speak well, and I will tell you what to say."

¹³But Moses said, "Lord, please! Send someone else."

¹⁴Then the Lord became angry. "All right," he said, "your brother, Aaron, is a good speaker. And he is coming here to look for you and will be very happy when he finds you. ¹⁵So I will tell you what to tell him, and I will help both of you to speak well, and I will tell you what to do. ¹⁶He will be your spokesman to the people. And you will be as God to him, telling him what to say. ¹⁷And be sure to take your rod along so that you can perform the miracles I have shown you."

¹⁸Moses returned home and talked it over with Jethro, his father-in-law. "With your permission," Moses said, "I will go back to Egypt and visit my relatives. I don't even know whether they are still alive."

"Go with my blessing," Jethro replied.

¹⁹Before Moses left Midian, Jehovah said to him, "Don't be afraid to return to Egypt, for all those who wanted to kill you are dead."

²⁰So Moses took his wife and sons and put them on a donkey, and returned to the land of Egypt, holding tightly to the "rod of God"!

²¹Jehovah told him, "When you arrive back in Egypt you are to go to Pharaoh and do the miracles I have shown you, but I will make him stubborn so that he will not let the people go. ²²Then you are to tell him, 'Jehovah says, "Israel is my eldest son, ²³and I have commanded you to let him go away and worship me, but you have refused: and now see, I will slay your eldest son."'"

²⁴As Moses and his family were traveling along and had stopped for the night, Jehovah appeared to Moses and threatened to kill him. ²⁵,²⁶Then Zipporah his wife took a flint knife and cut off the foreskin of her young son's penis, and threw it against Moses' feet, remarking disgustedly, "What a blood-smeared husband you've turned out to be!"

Then God let him alone.

²⁷Now Jehovah said to Aaron, "Go into the wilderness to meet Moses." So Aaron traveled to Mount Horeb, the mountain of God, and met Moses there, and they greeted each other warmly. ²⁸Moses told Aaron what God had said they must do, and what they were to say, and told him about the miracles they must do before Pharaoh.

²⁹So Moses and Aaron returned to Egypt and summoned the elders of the people of Israel to a council meeting. ³⁰Aaron told them what Jehovah had said to Moses, and Moses performed the miracles as they watched. ³¹Then the elders believed that God had sent them, and when they heard that Jehovah had visited them and had seen their sorrows, and had decided to rescue them, they all rejoiced and bowed their heads and worshiped.

5 Making Bricks without Straw

After this presentation to the elders, Moses and Aaron went to see Pharaoh. They told him, "We bring you a message from Jehovah, the God of Israel. He says, 'Let my people go, for they must make a holy pilgrimage out into the wilderness, for a religious feast, to worship me there.'"

²"Is that so?" retorted Pharaoh. "And who is Jehovah, that I should listen to him, and let Israel go? I don't know Jehovah and I will not let Israel go."

³But Aaron and Moses persisted. "The God of the Hebrews has met with us," they declared. "We must take a three days' trip into the wilderness and sacrifice there to Jehovah our God; if we don't obey him, we face death by plague or sword."

⁴,⁵"Who do you think you are," Pharaoh shouted, "distracting the people from their work? Get back to your jobs!" ⁶That same day Pharaoh sent this order to the taskmasters and officers he had set over the people of Israel: ⁷,⁸"Don't give the people any more straw for making bricks! However, don't reduce their production quotas by a single brick, for they obviously don't have enough to do or else they wouldn't be talking about going out into the wilderness and sacrificing to their God. ⁹Load them with work and make them sweat; that will teach them to listen to Moses' and Aaron's lies!"

¹⁰,¹¹So the taskmasters and officers informed the people: "Pharaoh has given orders to furnish you with no more straw. Go and find it wherever you can; but you must produce just as many bricks as before!" ¹²So the people scattered everywhere to gather straw.

¹³The taskmasters were brutal. "Fulfill your daily quota just as before," they kept demanding. ¹⁴Then they whipped the Israeli work-crew bosses. "Why haven't you fulfilled your quotas either yesterday or today?" they roared.

¹⁵These foremen went to Pharaoh and pleaded with him. "Don't treat us like this," they begged. ¹⁶"We are given no straw and told to make as many bricks as before, and we are beaten for something that isn't our fault—it is the fault of your taskmasters for making such unreasonable demands."

¹⁷But Pharaoh replied, "You don't have enough work, or else you wouldn't be saying, 'Let us go and sacrifice to Jehovah.' ¹⁸Get back to work. No straw will be given you, and you must deliver the regular quota of bricks."

¹⁹Then the foremen saw that they were indeed in a bad situation. ²⁰When they met Moses and Aaron waiting for them outside the palace, as they came out from their meeting with Pharaoh, ²¹they swore at them. "May God judge you for making us

FAMILY DEVOTIONS

☐ *DEVOTION 24*
TRUSTING GOD FOR HELP

Read Exodus 4:10-15

Trusting God for Help
Memory Verse

God is our refuge and strength, a tested help in times of trouble.
Psalm 46:1

Carrie could hardly believe what her English teacher was saying. "We're going to give speeches next week," said Miss Thompson. "Pick any topic in which you're interested, and be prepared to talk about it for three minutes."

Carrie was so upset she could hardly wait to speak to her teacher about it after class. As soon as the other students had left, she approached Miss Thompson. "Please don't make me give a speech, Miss Thompson," she pleaded in a shaking voice. "I just can't talk in front of people! I know I'll make a mistake, and the other kids will laugh at me!"

Her teacher smiled kindly. "Part of being a good speaker is learning to forget about yourself and to concentrate on your subject matter. Don't worry so much about what others will think. Just be yourself. I'm sure you'll do fine."

During the next few days, Carrie often thought and prayed about her speech. She found a verse in her Bible that really helped her—Philippians 4:13: "I can do everything God asks me to with the help of Christ who gives me the strength and power."

When her turn finally came, she swallowed hard and walked up to the front of the room. "My topic for today," she said in a nervous, squeaky voice, "is stage fright. It's something I really feel like an expert on." The kids laughed, and Carrie began to feel better. She talked about the causes of stage fright and about some famous people who had problems with it. She also shared some of what she had learned from Miss Thompson.

As Carrie went back to her seat after her speech, she thought, *That wasn't so bad after all. I don't think I'd want to make another speech right away, but if I had to, I'm sure God would help me again!*

How About You?

Does it make you nervous to have to talk in front of a group of people? It will help if you are honest about your nervousness and if you stop worrying about what others will think of you. Pick a subject about which you feel strongly, and remember that God will help you. If he wants you to speak, either privately or publicly, he will help you find the right words to say. *S. K.*

• For the next devotional, turn to page 69.   • For the next devotional on *TRUSTING GOD FOR HELP*, turn to page 575.
• For notes on *TRUSTING GOD FOR HELP*, see pages 240, 249, 464, 539, and 751.

stink before Pharaoh and his people," they said, "and for giving them an excuse to kill us."

²²Then Moses went back to the Lord. "Lord," he protested, "how can you mistreat your own people like this? Why did you ever send me if you were going to do this to them? ²³Ever since I gave Pharaoh your message, he has only been more and more brutal to them, and you have not delivered them at all!"

6 The Hebrews Won't Listen

"Now you will see what I shall do to Pharaoh," the Lord told Moses. "For he must be forced to let my people go; he will not only let them go, but will *drive them out of his land!* ²,³I am Jehovah, the Almighty God who appeared to Abraham, Isaac, and Jacob—though I did not reveal my name, Jehovah, to them. ⁴And I entered into a solemn covenant with them; under its terms I promised to give them and their descendants the land of Canaan where they were living. ⁵And now I have heard the groanings of the people of Israel, in slavery now to the Egyptians, and I remember my promise.

⁶"Therefore tell the descendants of Israel that I will use my mighty power and perform great miracles to deliver them from slavery and make them free. ⁷And I will accept them as my people and be their God. And they shall know that I am Jehovah their God who has rescued them from the Egyptians. ⁸,⁹I will bring them into the land I promised to give to Abraham, Isaac, and Jacob. It shall belong to my people."

So Moses told the people what God had said, but they wouldn't listen any more because they were too dispirited after the tragic consequence of what he had said before.

¹⁰Now the Lord spoke to Moses again and told him, ¹¹"Go back again to Pharaoh and tell him that he *must* let the people of Israel go."

¹²"But look," Moses objected, "my own people won't even listen to me any more; how can I expect Pharaoh to? I'm no orator!"

¹³Then the Lord ordered Moses and Aaron to return to the people of Israel and to Pharaoh, king of Egypt, demanding that the people be permitted to leave.

¹⁴These are the names of the heads of the clans of the various tribes of Israel:

The sons of Reuben, Israel's oldest son: Hanoch, Pallu, Hezron, Carmi.

¹⁵The heads of the clans of the tribe of Simeon: Jemuel, Jamin, Ohad, Jachin, Zohar, Shaul (whose mother was a Canaanite).

¹⁶These are the names of the heads of the clans of the tribe of Levi, in the order of their ages: Gershon, Kohath, Merari. (Levi lived 137 years.)

¹⁷The sons of Gershon were: Libni, Shime-i (and their clans).

¹⁸The sons of Kohath: Amram, Izhar, Hebron, Uzziel. (Kohath lived 133 years.)

¹⁹The sons of Merari: Mahli, Mushi.

The above are the families of the Levites, listed according to their ages.

²⁰And Amram married Jochebed, his father's sister; and Aaron and Moses were their sons.

Amram lived to the age of 137.

²¹The sons of Izhar: Korah, Nepheg, Zichri.

²²The sons of Uzziel: Misha-el, Elzaphan, Sithri.

²³Aaron married Elisheba, the daughter of Amminadab and sister of Nahshon. Their children were: Nadab, Abihu, Eleazar, Ithamar.

²⁴The sons of Korah: Assir, Elkanah, Abiasaph.

These are the families within the clan of Korah.

²⁵Aaron's son Eleazar married one of the daughters of Puti-el, and Phinehas was one of his children. These are all the names of the heads of the clans of the Levites and the families within the clans.

²⁶Aaron and Moses, included in that list, are the same Aaron and Moses to whom Jehovah said, "Lead all the people of Israel out of the land of Egypt," ²⁷and who went to Pharaoh to ask permission to lead the people from the land, ²⁸,²⁹and to whom the Lord said, "I am Jehovah. Go in and give Pharaoh the message I have given you."

³⁰This is that Moses who argued with the Lord, "I can't do it; I'm no speaker—why should Pharaoh listen to *me?*"

7 Aaron's Rod Becomes a Snake

Then the Lord said to Moses, "See, I have appointed you as my ambassador to Pharaoh, and your brother, Aaron, shall be your spokesman. ²Tell Aaron everything I say to you, and he will announce it to Pharaoh, demanding that the people of Israel be allowed to leave Egypt. ³But I will cause Pharaoh to stubbornly refuse, and I will multiply my miracles in the land of Egypt. ⁴Yet even then Pharaoh won't listen to you; so I will crush Egypt with a final major disaster and then lead my people out. ⁵The Egyptians will find out that I am indeed God when I show them my power and force them to let my people go."

⁶So Moses and Aaron did as the Lord commanded them. ⁷Moses was eighty years old and Aaron eighty-three at this time of their confrontation with Pharaoh.

⁸Then the Lord said to Moses and Aaron, ⁹"Pharaoh will demand that you show him a miracle to prove that God has sent you; when he does, Aaron is to throw down his rod, and it will become a serpent."

¹⁰So Moses and Aaron went in to see Pharaoh,

FAMILY DEVOTIONS

☐ **DEVOTION 25**
PERSEVERANCE

Read Exodus 5:1-9; 6:1-13

Perseverance
Memory Verse

Be strong and courageous and get to work. Don't be frightened by the size of the task, for the Lord my God is with you; he will not forsake you. He will see to it that everything is finished correctly.
1 Chronicles 28:20

"Stop, Brad!" Mom's cries were drowned out by the roar of the lawn mower. "Oh no!" she moaned. "He's cut down my rosebush."

When Brad apologized later, Mom sighed. "It was a small bush, and I know you didn't see it," she said. "Let's forget it."

A few weeks later, when Brad came in from mowing Mr. Johnson's lawn, he had tears in his eyes. "Why, Brad, what's the matter? Did you hurt yourself?" Mom asked.

"No . . ." Brad choked down a sob. "But Mr. Johnson is so hateful!"

"Didn't your work please him?" Mom handed Brad a Kleenex.

"I do my best, but it's never good enough." Brad blew his nose loudly. "He's always cutting me down, saying I'm too slow or too sloppy or I charge too much. Said in his day folks did things for their neighbors without charging. Said he could be dead a week and wouldn't even be missed until someone came wanting some money!"

"Poor old man," Mom said softly.

"He's not poor!" Brad snorted. "He's got more money than anyone I know."

"I feel sorry for him. It's sad to be old and lonely and rich. Even when people try to help him, he thinks they're just after his money. Don't let what he says get to you," Mom said comfortingly. "Now, how about mowing our lawn?"

Several minutes later Brad called, "Mom, come out here. I want to show you something." Mom found him pointing at the ground. "Remember the rosebush I cut down? There it is, sprouting out again from the roots."

Mom smiled as she knelt and pulled grass from around the bush. "You know, Brad, we can do the same thing. When people cut us down, we can sprout again. If our roots are in the Word of God, his love will cause us to spring up."

How About You?
Do you know someone who seems to delight in cutting you down? Don't stay down, no matter how dismal your circumstances are. Get up! You can do this by: (1) praying for those who have hurt you, (2) refusing to think about what they did or said, and (3) meditating on the Word of God. *B. W.*

• For the next devotional, turn to page 71.   • For the next devotional on *PERSEVERANCE*, turn to page 245.
• For notes on *PERSEVERANCE*, see pages 326, 461, 503, 760, and 1174.

and performed the miracle, as Jehovah had instructed them—Aaron threw down his rod before Pharaoh and his court, and it became a serpent. ¹¹Then Pharaoh called in his sorcerers—the magicians of Egypt—and they were able to do the same thing with their magical arts! ¹²Their rods became serpents, too! But Aaron's serpent swallowed their serpents! ¹³Pharaoh's heart was still hard and stubborn, and he wouldn't listen, just as the Lord had predicted. ¹⁴The Lord pointed this out to Moses, that Pharaoh's heart had been unmoved, and that he would continue to refuse to let the people go.

¹⁵"Nevertheless," the Lord said, "go back to Pharaoh in the morning, to be there as he goes down to the river. Stand beside the riverbank and meet him there, holding in your hand the rod that turned into a serpent. ¹⁶Say to him, 'Jehovah, the God of the Hebrews, has sent me back to demand that you let his people go to worship him in the wilderness. You wouldn't listen before, ¹⁷and now the Lord says this: "You are going to find out that I am God. For I have instructed Moses to hit the water of the Nile with his rod, and the river will turn to blood! ¹⁸The fish will die and the river will stink, so that the Egyptians will be unwilling to drink it."'"

¹⁹Then the Lord instructed Moses: "Tell Aaron to point his rod toward the waters of Egypt: all its rivers, canals, marshes, and reservoirs, and even the water stored in bowls and pots in the homes will turn to blood."

²⁰So Moses and Aaron did as the Lord commanded them. As Pharaoh and all of his officials watched, Aaron hit the surface of the Nile with the rod, and the river turned to blood. ²¹The fish died and the water became so foul that the Egyptians couldn't drink it; and there was blood throughout the land of Egypt. ²²But then the magicians of Egypt used their secret arts and they, too, turned water into blood; so Pharaoh's heart remained hard and stubborn, and he wouldn't listen to Moses and Aaron, just as the Lord had predicted, ²³and he returned to his palace, unimpressed. ²⁴Then the Egyptians dug wells along the riverbank to get drinking water, for they couldn't drink from the river.

²⁵A week went by.

8 Pharaoh Learns about God's Power

Then the Lord said to Moses, "Go in again to Pharaoh and tell him, 'Jehovah says, "Let my people go and worship me. ²If you refuse, I will send vast hordes of frogs across your land from one border to the other. ³,⁴The Nile River will swarm with them, and they will come out into your houses, even into your bedrooms and right into your beds! Every home in Egypt will be filled with them. They will fill your ovens and your kneading bowls; you and your people will be immersed in them!"'"

⁵Then the Lord said to Moses, "Instruct Aaron to point the rod toward all the rivers, streams, and pools of Egypt, so that there will be frogs in every corner of the land." ⁶Aaron did, and frogs covered the nation. ⁷But the magicians did the same with their secret arts, and they, too, caused frogs to come up upon the land.

⁸Then Pharaoh summoned Moses and Aaron and begged, "Plead with God to take the frogs away, and I will let the people go and sacrifice to him."

⁹"Be so kind as to tell me when you want them to go," Moses said, "and I will pray that the frogs will die at the time you specify, everywhere except in the river."

¹⁰"Do it tomorrow," Pharaoh said.

"All right," Moses replied, "it shall be as you have said; then you will know that there is no one like the Lord our God. ¹¹All the frogs will be destroyed, except those in the river."

¹²So Moses and Aaron went out from the presence of Pharaoh, and Moses pleaded with the Lord concerning the frogs he had sent. ¹³And the Lord did as Moses promised—dead frogs covered the countryside and filled the nation's homes. ¹⁴They were piled into great heaps, making a terrible stench throughout the land. ¹⁵But when Pharaoh saw that the frogs were gone, he hardened his heart and refused to let the people go, just as the Lord had predicted.

¹⁶Then the Lord said to Moses, "Tell Aaron to strike the dust with his rod, and it will become lice, throughout all the land of Egypt." ¹⁷So Moses and Aaron did as God commanded, and suddenly lice infested the entire nation, covering the Egyptians and their animals. ¹⁸Then the magicians tried to do the same thing with their secret arts, but this time they failed.

¹⁹"This is the finger of God," they exclaimed to Pharaoh. But Pharaoh's heart was hard and stubborn, and he wouldn't listen to them, just as the Lord had predicted.

²⁰Next the Lord told Moses, "Get up early in the morning and meet Pharaoh as he comes out to the river to bathe, and say to him, 'Jehovah says, "Let my people go and worship me. ²¹If you refuse I will send swarms of flies throughout Egypt. Your homes will be filled with them and the ground will be covered with them. ²²But it will be very different in the land of Goshen where the Israelis live. No flies will be there; thus you will know that I am the Lord God of all the earth, ²³for I will make a distinction between your people and my people. All this will happen tomorrow."'"

Family Devotions

☐ Devotion 26
Honesty

Read Exodus 8:8, 15, 24-32

"There!" Pete exclaimed as he finished pounding a nail. "This is the best tree house I've ever seen! I can hardly wait to sleep here. We'll be rocked to sleep, the way this tree sways. It's like being in a swaying castle!"

Vern nodded in agreement. "Let's ask if we can sleep out here tonight," he suggested.

"I know my dad won't let me," said Pete. "He wants to check it out first to be sure it's safe, and I know he won't have time to do that today."

"My dad said the same thing," Vern admitted. "Hey! I know! Let's each ask our folks for permission to spend the night with each other. They'll think we're at each other's houses, but we'll really be sleeping in the tree house."

"I don't know...." Pete sounded doubtful, but with Vern's coaxing, he agreed to try it.

Their plan worked, but in the middle of the night they were awakened by a loud crack of thunder! "Hey! I'm getting wet!" yelled Pete. "It's pouring and the roof is leaking. Come on! Let's get over to my house."

The storm had awakened Pete's parents, too, and they were very surprised when the boys stumbled into the kitchen. "Where have you been?" Pete's dad asked.

"We . . . ah . . . we were sleeping in the tree house, Dad," answered Pete.

"The tree house? You asked if you could stay at Vern's house overnight."

"Not really," replied Pete. "I just asked if I could spend the night with Vern."

"I see," said Dad. "You used the correct words, but what about your intentions? You deceived us in order to sleep in the tree house, which is really the same as lying. Do you see that?"

"Yes," admitted the boys together, and both apologized.

"I'm thankful God protected you tonight," said Dad, "but I'm afraid the tree house will be off-limits until you show us that we can trust you again."

Honesty Memory Verse

Stop lying to each other; tell the truth, for we are parts of each other and when we lie to each other we are hurting ourselves.
Ephesians 4:25

How About You?
Are you guilty of giving false impressions or of telling fibs or white lies? God hates every form of lying and deception. He is pleased only when our intentions as well as our words are pure. A. G. L.

• For the next devotional, turn to page 73. • For the next devotional on *Honesty*, turn to page 521. • For notes on *Honesty*, see pages 304, 813, and 863.

24And Jehovah did as he had said, so that there were terrible swarms of flies in Pharaoh's palace and in every home in Egypt.

25Pharaoh hastily summoned Moses and Aaron and said, "All right, go ahead and sacrifice to your God, but do it here in the land. Don't go out into the wilderness."

26But Moses replied, "That won't do! Our sacrifices to God are hated by the Egyptians, and if we do this right here before their eyes, they will kill us. 27We must take a three-day trip into the wilderness and sacrifice there to Jehovah our God, as he commanded us."

28"All right, go ahead," Pharaoh replied, "but don't go too far away. Now, hurry and plead with God for me."

29"Yes," Moses said, "I will ask him to cause the swarms of flies to disappear. But I am warning you that you must never again lie to us by promising to let the people go and then changing your mind."

30So Moses went out from Pharaoh and asked the Lord to get rid of the flies. 31,32And the Lord did as Moses asked and caused the swarms to disappear, so that not one remained. But Pharaoh hardened his heart again and did not let the people go!

9 The Longest Night

"Go back to Pharaoh," the Lord commanded Moses, "and tell him, 'Jehovah, the God of the Hebrews, demands that you let his people go to sacrifice to him. 2If you refuse, 3the power of God will send a deadly plague to destroy your cattle, horses, donkeys, camels, flocks, and herds. 4But the plague will affect only the cattle of Egypt; none of the Israeli herds and flocks will even be touched!'"

5The Lord announced that the plague would begin the very next day, 6and it did. The next morning all the cattle of the Egyptians began dying, but not one of the Israeli herds was even sick. 7Pharaoh sent to see whether it was true that none of the Israeli cattle were dead, yet when he found out that it was so, even then his mind remained unchanged and he refused to let the people go.

8Then Jehovah said to Moses and Aaron, "Take ashes from the kiln and have Moses toss them into the sky as Pharaoh watches. 9They will spread like fine dust over all the land of Egypt and cause boils to break out upon people and animals alike, throughout the land."

10So they took ashes from the kiln and went to Pharaoh; as he watched, Moses tossed them toward the sky, and they became boils that broke out on men and animals alike throughout all Egypt. 11And the magicians couldn't stand before Moses because of the boils, for the boils appeared upon them too. 12But Jehovah hardened Pharaoh in his stubbornness, so that he refused to listen, just as the Lord had predicted to Moses.

13Then the Lord said to Moses, "Get up early in the morning and stand before Pharaoh and tell him, 'Jehovah the God of the Hebrews says, "Let my people go to worship me. 14This time I am going to send a plague that will really speak to you and to your servants and to all the Egyptian people, and prove to you there is no other God in all the earth. 15I could have killed you all by now, 16but I didn't, for I wanted to demonstrate my power to you and to all the earth. 17So you still think you are so great, do you, and defy my power, and refuse to let my people go? 18Well, tomorrow about this time I will send a hailstorm across the nation such as there has never been since Egypt was founded! 19Quick! Bring in your cattle from the fields, for every man and animal left out in the fields will die beneath the hail!"'"

20Some of the Egyptians, terrified by this threat, brought their cattle and slaves in from the fields; 21but those who had no regard for the word of Jehovah left them out in the storm.

22Then Jehovah said to Moses, "Point your hand toward heaven and cause the hail to fall throughout all Egypt, upon the people, animals, and trees."

23So Moses held out his hand, and the Lord sent thunder and hail and lightning. 24It was terrible beyond description. Never in all the history of Egypt had there been a storm like that. 25All Egypt lay in ruins. Everything left in the fields, men and animals alike, was killed, and the trees were shattered and the crops were destroyed. 26The only spot in all Egypt without hail that day was the land of Goshen where the people of Israel lived.

27Then Pharaoh sent for Moses and Aaron. "I finally see my fault," he confessed. "Jehovah is right, and I and my people have been wrong all along. 28Beg God to end this terrifying thunder and hail, and I will let you go at once."

29"All right," Moses replied, "as soon as I have left the city I will spread out my hands to the Lord, and the thunder and hail will stop. This will prove to you that the earth is controlled by Jehovah. 30But as for you and your officials, I know that even yet you will not obey him." 31All the flax and barley were knocked down and destroyed (for the barley was ripe, and the flax was in bloom), 32but the wheat and the emmer were not destroyed, for they were not yet out of the ground.

33So Moses left Pharaoh and went out of the city and lifted his hands to heaven to the Lord, and the thunder and hail stopped, and the rain

FAMILY DEVOTIONS

☐ **DEVOTION 27**
RESPECTING OTHERS

Read Exodus 10:16-29

"I'm tired of being preached at all the time!" Matt complained one day. "I get preached at in Sunday school and in church and even at home. It's always 'Do this,' or 'Don't do that.' 'Love your brother.' 'Obey your mother.' 'Pray every day.'"

Dad raised his eyebrows. "Son, God gives us teachers, pastors, and parents to teach and help us," he said.

Matt shrugged. "Maybe so. But it gets to me the way my Sunday school teacher and Pastor Ensey are always telling everyone how to live. Who are they to lay down the laws?"

"They don't lay down the laws," answered Dad. "They're God's messengers. They simply tell us about his laws."

Matt jumped to his feet. "Well, I don't like messengers! Think I'll go for a bike ride." Dad sighed.

The next evening when Matt came in from his newspaper route, his face was as red as his hair. "Some people make me so mad!" he fumed, throwing his cap on the table. "I tried to collect today from old Mrs. Carrington. Mr. Bentley told me not to deliver any more papers to her until she paid her bill. And would you believe that old lady bawled me out? She called me a smart-aleck teenager. Why should she yell at me? I don't make the rules! Why doesn't she yell at Mr. Bentley? I'm just the delivery boy. I just took her the message."

A funny look crossed Matt's face when his dad smiled and said, "Well, I seem to remember that you don't like messengers either." Dad paused, then added, "If you don't like the messages your pastor and teachers are giving you, Matt, you should tell God, not the messengers. Right?"

Matt ran his fingers through his hair and said thoughtfully, "I guess I'm just like old Mrs. Carrington. I guess it's not the message or the messengers that are wrong, it's me. I don't know if Mrs. Carrington will ever change, but I'm going to—starting right now!"

Respecting Others
Memory Verse

You must love the Lord your God with all your heart, and with all your soul, and with all your strength, and with all your mind. And you must love your neighbor just as much as you love yourself.
Luke 10:27

How About You?
Do you gripe and grumble when the preaching convicts you? Or when the teaching applies to you? When others bring you God's message, you had better listen. Don't get mad and pout at them. They are simply the messengers. Listen to them. B. W.

• For the next devotional, turn to page 75. • For the next devotional on *RESPECTING OTHERS*, turn to page 87. • For notes on *RESPECTING OTHERS*, see pages 322, 382, 1088, and 1218.

ceased pouring down. 34When Pharaoh saw this, he and his officials sinned yet more by their stubborn refusal to do what they had promised; 35so Pharaoh refused to let the people leave, just as the Lord had predicted to Moses.

10 Then the Lord said to Moses, "Go back again and make your demand upon Pharaoh; but I have hardened him and his officials, so that I can do more miracles demonstrating my power. 2What stories you can tell your children and grandchildren about the incredible things I am doing in Egypt! Tell them what fools I made of the Egyptians, and how I proved to you that I am Jehovah."

3So Moses and Aaron requested another audience with Pharaoh and told him: "Jehovah, the God of the Hebrews, asks, 'How long will you refuse to submit to me? Let my people go so they can worship me. 4,5If you refuse, tomorrow I will cover the entire nation with a thick layer of locusts so that you won't even be able to see the ground, and they will finish destroying everything that escaped the hail. 6They will fill your palace, and the homes of your officials, and all the houses of Egypt. Never in the history of Egypt has there been a plague like this will be!'" Then Moses stalked out.

7The court officials now came to Pharaoh and asked him, "Are you going to destroy us completely? Don't you know even yet that all Egypt lies in ruins? Let the *men* go and serve Jehovah their God!"

8So Moses and Aaron were brought back to Pharaoh. "All right, go and serve Jehovah your God!" he said. "But just who is it you want to go?"

9"We will go with our sons and daughters, flocks and herds," Moses replied. "We will take everything with us; for we must all join in the holy pilgrimage."

10"In the name of God I will not let you take your little ones!" Pharaoh retorted. "I can see your plot! 11Never! You that are men, go and serve Jehovah, for that is what you asked for." And they were driven out from Pharaoh's presence.

12Then the Lord said to Moses, "Hold out your hand over the land of Egypt to bring locusts—they will cover the land and eat everything the hail has left."

13So Moses lifted his rod and Jehovah caused an east wind to blow all that day and night; and when it was morning, the east wind had brought the locusts. 14And the locusts covered the land of Egypt from border to border; it was the worst locust plague in all Egyptian history; and there will never again be another like it. 15For the locusts covered the face of the earth and blotted out the sun so that the land was darkened; and they ate every bit of vegetation the hail had left; there remained not one green thing—not a tree, not a plant throughout all the land of Egypt.

16Then Pharaoh sent an urgent call for Moses and Aaron and said to them, "I confess my sin against Jehovah your God and against you. 17Forgive my sin only this once, and beg Jehovah your God to take away this deadly plague. I solemnly promise that I will let you go as soon as the locusts are gone."

18So Moses went out from Pharaoh and entreated the Lord, 19and he sent a very strong west wind that blew the locusts out into the Red Sea, so that there remained not one locust in all the land of Egypt! 20But the Lord hardened Pharaoh's heart and he did not let the people go.

21Then Jehovah said to Moses, "Lift your hands to heaven, and darkness without a ray of light will descend upon the land of Egypt." 22So Moses did, and there was thick darkness over all the land for three days. 23During all that time the people scarcely moved—but all the people of Israel had light as usual.

24Then Pharaoh called for Moses and said, "Go and worship Jehovah—but let your flocks and herds stay here; you can even take your children with you."

25"No," Moses said, "we must take our flocks and herds for sacrifices and burnt offerings to Jehovah our God. 26Not a hoof shall be left behind; for we must have sacrifices for the Lord our God, and we do not know what he will choose until we get there."

27So the Lord hardened Pharaoh's heart and he would not let them go.

28"Get out of here and don't let me ever see you again," Pharaoh shouted at Moses. "The day you do, you shall die."

29"Very well," Moses replied. "I will never see you again."

Egypt's Firstborn Will Die

11 Then the Lord said to Moses, "I will send just one more disaster on Pharaoh and his land, and after that he will let you go; in fact, he will be so anxious to get rid of you that he will practically throw you out of the country. 2Tell all the men and women of Israel to ask their Egyptian neighbors for gold and silver jewelry."

3(For God caused the Egyptians to be very favorable to the people of Israel, and Moses was a very great man in the land of Egypt and was revered by Pharaoh's officials and the Egyptian people alike.)

4Now Moses announced to Pharaoh, "Jehovah says, 'About midnight I will pass through Egypt. 5And all the oldest sons shall die in every family in Egypt, from the oldest child of Pharaoh, heir to his

Family Devotions

☐ DEVOTION 28

LEAVING THE FUTURE IN GOD'S HANDS

Read Exodus 12:1-13

Lesa tore open the screen door and stumbled down the hallway. "Mom! Mom!" she cried. "Is it true?"

"Whoa! Settle down there, Lesa." Dad met her and put his arms around her tightly. "What's wrong?"

"Oh, Daddy, David said his mom doesn't have a job anymore, and that all the plant workers have been laid off," exclaimed Lesa.

"Yes, honey, it's true," Dad said, nodding.

"Daddy, if you don't have your job anymore, how will we pay for Kari's doctor bills?"

Just then, Mom came down the steps with baby Kari. Kari's eyes lit up when she saw Lesa, and she eagerly reached out her hands. Dad let Lesa out of his bear hug so that she could take Kari.

Lesa couldn't help remembering the time when Kari was sick and had to go to the hospital so often. Lesa squeezed her little sister even tighter in her arms.

Dad saw the tight hug Lesa gave Kari. "Lesa, who's holding Kari?" he asked.

"I am," Lesa said. "Why did you ask that?"

"Well," said Dad, "is she really safe in your arms? Maybe I should take her."

Lesa gave Dad a very puzzled look. "But, Dad, you and Mom have taught me to be very careful with Kari. I'm in fourth grade, you know. Why don't you trust me with Kari now?"

Dad smiled. "Actually, I do," he said. "I'll leave her with you. But think about this—a few minutes ago, you were all worried because I'm out of work. I know it's a scary thought, and I'll admit that Mom and I feel a little shaky about it, too. But we reminded each other that we're safe in the arms that are holding us."

Lesa stared blankly at her father for a minute, and then she smiled. "God's arms," she said simply. Yes, it was true. God's arms were underneath her family. He would hold them tightly, no matter what happened with Dad's job!

Leaving the Future in God's Hands Memory Verse

For I know the plans I have for you, says the Lord. They are plans for good and not for evil, to give you a future and a hope.
Jeremiah 29:11

How About You?

Are you worried about your future? Do you know someone who's been laid off or lost his job? Remember, God knew it was going to happen before you did, and he knows what to do about it. Trust him. P.J.

• For the next devotional, turn to page 77. • For the next devotional on LEAVING THE FUTURE IN GOD'S HANDS, turn to page 321. • For notes on LEAVING THE FUTURE IN GOD'S HANDS, see pages 405, 452, 831, and 1061.

throne, to the oldest child of his lowliest slave; and even the firstborn of the animals. ⁶The wail of death will resound throughout the entire land of Egypt; never before has there been such anguish, and it will never be again.

⁷"'But not a dog shall move his tongue against any of the people of Israel, nor shall any of their animals die. Then you will know that Jehovah makes a distinction between Egyptians and Israelis.' ⁸All these officials of yours will come running to me, bowing low and begging, 'Please leave at once, and take all your people with you.' Only then will I go!" Then, red-faced with anger, Moses stomped from the palace.

⁹The Lord had told Moses, "Pharaoh won't listen, and this will give me the opportunity of doing mighty miracles to demonstrate my power." ¹⁰So, although Moses and Aaron did these miracles right before Pharaoh's eyes, the Lord hardened his heart so that he wouldn't let the people leave the land.

12 The First Passover

Then the Lord said to Moses and Aaron, ²"From now on, this month will be the first and most important of the entire year. ³,⁴Annually, on the tenth day of this month (announce this to all the people of Israel) each family shall get a lamb (or, if a family is small, let it share the lamb with another small family in the neighborhood; whether to share in this way depends on the size of the families). ⁵This animal shall be a year-old male, either a sheep or a goat, without any defects.

⁶"On the evening of the fourteenth day of this month, all these lambs shall be killed, ⁷and their blood shall be placed on the two side-frames of the door of every home and on the panel above the door. Use the blood of the lamb eaten in that home. ⁸Everyone shall eat roast lamb that night, with unleavened bread and bitter herbs. ⁹The meat must not be eaten raw or boiled, but roasted, including the head, legs, heart, and liver. ¹⁰Don't eat any of it the next day; if all is not eaten that night, burn what is left.

¹¹"Eat it with your traveling clothes on, prepared for a long journey, wearing your walking shoes and carrying your walking sticks in your hands; eat it hurriedly. This observance shall be called the Lord's Passover. ¹²For I will pass through the land of Egypt tonight and kill all the oldest sons and firstborn male animals in all the land of Egypt, and execute judgment upon all the gods of Egypt—for I am Jehovah. ¹³The blood you have placed on the doorposts will be proof that you obey me, and when I see the blood I will pass over you and I will not destroy your firstborn children when I smite the land of Egypt.

¹⁴"You shall celebrate this event each year (this is a permanent law) to remind you of this fatal night. ¹⁵The celebration shall last seven days. For that entire period you are to eat only bread made without yeast. Anyone who disobeys this rule at any time during the seven days of the celebration shall be excommunicated from Israel. ¹⁶On the first day of the celebration, and again on the seventh day, there will be special religious services for the entire congregation, and no work of any kind may be done on those days except the preparation of food.

¹⁷"This annual 'Celebration with Unleavened Bread' will cause you always to remember today as the day when I brought you out of the land of Egypt; so it is a law that you must celebrate this day annually, generation after generation. ¹⁸Only bread without yeast may be eaten from the evening of the fourteenth day of the month until the evening of the twenty-first day of the month. ¹⁹For these seven days there must be no trace of yeast in your homes; during that time anyone who eats anything that has yeast in it shall be excommunicated from the congregation of Israel. These same rules apply to foreigners who are living among you just as much as to those born in the land. ²⁰Again I repeat, during those days you must not eat anything made with yeast; serve only yeastless bread."

²¹Then Moses called for all the elders of Israel and said to them, "Go and get lambs from your flocks, a lamb for one or more families depending upon the number of persons in the families, and kill the lamb so that God will pass over you and not destroy you. ²²Drain the lamb's blood into a basin, and then take a cluster of hyssop branches and dip them into the lamb's blood, and strike the hyssop against the lintel above the door and against the two side panels, so that there will be blood upon them, and none of you shall go outside all night.

²³"For Jehovah will pass through the land and kill the Egyptians; but when he sees the blood upon the panel at the top of the door and on the two side pieces, he will pass over that home and not permit the Destroyer to enter and kill your firstborn. ²⁴And remember, this is a permanent law for you and your posterity. ²⁵And when you come into the land that the Lord will give you, just as he promised, and when you are celebrating the Passover, ²⁶and your children ask, 'What does all this mean? What is this ceremony about?' ²⁷you will reply, 'It is the celebration of Jehovah's passing over us, for he passed over the homes of the people of Israel, though he killed the Egyptians; he passed over our houses and did not come in to

FAMILY DEVOTIONS

☐ *DEVOTION 29*
***TRUSTING GOD
FOR GUIDANCE***

Read Exodus 13:17-22

*Trusting God
for Guidance
Memory Verse*

I will instruct you
(says the Lord) and
guide you along the best
pathway for your life;
I will advise you and
watch your progress.
Psalm 32:8

Nine-year-old Tim watched as his father guided the aluminum fishing boat across the lake. The wind was strong, and the waves were high. Dad had to fight to keep the small boat on course, and Tim was intrigued by it all.

"This is fun!" he cried out. "Can I steer for a while?"

"The lake is pretty rough," Dad said, raising his voice to be heard above the motor. "I'm afraid you can't handle it alone."

"You can help me," Tim insisted. He still wanted to guide the boat across the lake to the spot where he and his father were to spend the day fishing. "When you see I'm not doing it right, you can help me."

Carefully Tim and his dad changed places, and Tim began to guide the boat across the rough water. "This is easy!" he called out. Suddenly a big wave stood before them, and Tim turned the boat with a jerk. The boat began to zigzag back and forth until Dad came to the rescue. Placing his hand over Tim's, he guided the fishing craft until things were once again under control.

"Boy," Tim said with relief in his voice, "I guess it's a good thing you were there to take over."

His father smiled and nodded. "This is a good example of our Christian life, Son. We sometimes think we can handle the problems of the world by ourselves, and God lets us try. Then just about the time things seem to be completely out of hand, God puts his hand over ours and guides us through the situation."

How About You?

When things seem to be going well, do you forget that you need God? Do you think you can handle that math test alone? That you don't need help with your paper route? When you try to get along without God's help, sooner or later you'll run into trouble. God wants to help you and show you the best path to take. Let him. R. J.

• For the next devotional, turn to page 79. • For the next devotional on *TRUSTING GOD FOR GUIDANCE,* turn to page 239. • For notes on *TRUSTING GOD FOR GUIDANCE,* see pages 522, 553, 614, 676, and 1056.

destroy us.'" And all the people bowed their heads and worshiped.

²⁸So the people of Israel did as Moses and Aaron had commanded. ²⁹And that night, at midnight, Jehovah killed all the firstborn sons in the land of Egypt, from Pharaoh's oldest son to the oldest son of the captive in the dungeon; also all the firstborn of the cattle. ³⁰Then Pharaoh and his officials and all the people of Egypt got up in the night; and there was bitter crying throughout all the land of Egypt, for there was not a house where there was not one dead.

³¹And Pharaoh summoned Moses and Aaron during the night and said, "Leave us; please go away, all of you; go and serve Jehovah as you said. ³²Take your flocks and herds and be gone; and oh, give me a blessing as you go." ³³And the Egyptians were urgent upon the people of Israel, to get them out of the land as quickly as possible. For they said, "We are as good as dead."

³⁴The Israelis took with them their bread dough without yeast, and bound their kneading troughs into their spare clothes, and carried them on their shoulders. ³⁵And the people of Israel did as Moses said and asked the Egyptians for silver and gold jewelry and for clothing. ³⁶And the Lord gave the Israelis favor with the Egyptians, so that they gave them whatever they wanted. And the Egyptians were practically stripped of everything they owned!

³⁷That night the people of Israel left Rameses and started for Succoth; there were six hundred thousand of them, besides all the women and children, going on foot. ³⁸People of various sorts went with them; and there were flocks and herds—a vast exodus of cattle. ³⁹When they stopped to eat, they baked bread from the yeastless dough they had brought along. It was yeastless because the people were pushed out of Egypt and didn't have time to wait for bread to rise to take with them on the trip.

⁴⁰,⁴¹The sons of Jacob and their descendants had lived in Egypt 430 years, and it was on the last day of the 430th year that all of Jehovah's people left the land. ⁴²This night was selected by the Lord to bring his people out from the land of Egypt; so the same night was selected as the date of the annual celebration of God's deliverance.

⁴³Then Jehovah said to Moses and Aaron, "These are the rules concerning the observance of the Passover. No foreigners shall eat the lamb, ⁴⁴but any slave who has been purchased may eat it if he has been circumcised. ⁴⁵A hired servant or a visiting foreigner may not eat of it. ⁴⁶You shall, all of you who eat each lamb, eat it together in one house, and not carry it outside; and you shall not break any of its bones. ⁴⁷All the congregation of Israel shall observe this memorial at the same time.

⁴⁸"As to foreigners, if they are living with you and want to observe the Passover with you, let all the males be circumcised, and then they may come and celebrate with you—then they shall be just as though they had been born among you; but no uncircumcised person shall ever eat the lamb. ⁴⁹The same law applies to those born in Israel and to foreigners living among you."

⁵⁰So the people of Israel followed all of Jehovah's instructions to Moses and Aaron. ⁵¹That very day the Lord brought out the people of Israel from the land of Egypt, wave after wave of them crossing the border.

13 Firstborn Dedicated to God

The Lord instructed Moses, "Dedicate to me all of the firstborn sons of Israel, and every firstborn male animal; they are mine!"

³Then Moses said to the people, "This is a day to remember forever—the day of leaving Egypt and your slavery; for the Lord has brought you out with mighty miracles. Now remember, during the annual celebration of this event you are to use no yeast; don't even have any in your homes. ⁴,⁵Celebrate this day of your exodus, at the end of March each year, when Jehovah brings you into the land of the Canaanites, Hittites, Amorites, Hivites, and Jebusites—the land he promised your fathers, a land 'flowing with milk and honey.' ⁶,⁷For seven days you shall eat only bread without yeast, and there must be no yeast in your homes or anywhere within the borders of your land! Then, on the seventh day, a great feast to the Lord shall be held.

⁸"During those celebration days each year you must explain to your children why you are celebrating—it is a celebration of what the Lord did for you when you left Egypt. ⁹This annual memorial week will brand you as his own unique people, just as though he had branded his mark of ownership upon your hands or your forehead.

¹⁰"So celebrate the event annually in late March. ¹¹And remember, when the Lord brings you into the land he promised to your ancestors long ago, where the Canaanites are now living, ¹²all firstborn sons and firstborn male animals belong to the Lord, and you shall give them to him. ¹³A firstborn donkey may be purchased back from the Lord in exchange for a lamb or baby goat; but if you decide not to trade, the donkey shall be killed. However, you *must* buy back your firstborn sons.

¹⁴"And in the future, when your children ask you, 'What is this all about?' you shall tell them, 'With mighty miracles Jehovah brought us out of Egypt from our slavery. ¹⁵Pharaoh wouldn't let us go, so Jehovah killed all the firstborn males throughout the land of Egypt, both of men and

Family Devotions

☐ **Devotion 30**

Overcoming Fear

Read Exodus 14:13-22

Overcoming Fear
Memory Verse

Fear not, for I am with you. Do not be dismayed. I am your God. I will strengthen you; I will help you; I will uphold you with my victorious right hand.
Isaiah 41:10

Little Kelsey climbed from the pool. Then she eagerly walked along the edge to the side where her father was standing in waist deep water. "Catch me again, Daddy!" she called. She leaped toward her father almost before he could get his arms up to catch her.

"Whee!" called Daddy, as he pulled her around in the water and then took her to the shallow end where she could touch the bottom. Soon Kelsey was back up the steps and heading toward her jumping spot.

"Kelsey sure does trust Dad to catch her," observed her older sister, Linda. "And I can't believe how many times Dad keeps doing it. You'd think he'd get tired of it."

Mom smiled. "It makes your father happy that Kelsey trusts him enough to jump into his arms again and again. And because he caught her the first few times, she learned to trust him more and more—she jumped almost before he was ready the last time. You know," she said, "I think this is a good picture of our faith in God."

Linda was perplexed. "How is that like us and God?"

"Well, I think God is pleased, too, when his children trust him," explained Mom. "And the more often we trust him, the easier it is to trust him the next time."

Linda nodded. "I think I'm starting to find that out for myself," she said.

"Good," said Mom. "The more we use our faith, the more it grows. When Kelsey jumps into the pool, she doesn't think, 'I hope Dad will catch me.' She *knows* he will. That's the kind of faith that pleases God."

How About You?
Do you have enough faith to trust God to help you with your problems? Trust him to help you walk calmly past that yard where a dog barks fiercely. Trust him to care for you in the middle of a thunderstorm. Exercise your faith by speaking up for the Lord, even when someone might tease you for it. Trust God to take care of each problem you have. Then watch your faith grow. *L. W.*

- For the next devotional, turn to page 81. • For the next devotional on *Overcoming Fear*, turn to page 581.
- For notes on *Overcoming Fear*, see pages 191, 482, 554, 592, and 912.

animals; that is why we now give all the firstborn males to the Lord—except that all the eldest sons are always bought back.' ¹⁶Again I say, this celebration shall identify you as God's people, just as much as if his brand of ownership were placed upon your foreheads. It is a reminder that the Lord brought us out of Egypt with great power."

¹⁷,¹⁸So at last Pharaoh let the people go.

God did not lead them through the land of the Philistines, although that was the most direct route from Egypt to the Promised Land. The reason was that God felt the people might become discouraged by having to fight their way through, even though they had left Egypt armed; he thought they might return to Egypt. Instead, God led them along a route through the Red Sea wilderness.

¹⁹Moses took the bones of Joseph with them, for Joseph had made the sons of Israel vow before God that they would take his bones with them when God led them out of Egypt—as he was sure God would.

²⁰Leaving Succoth, they camped in Etham at the edge of the wilderness. ²¹The Lord guided them by a pillar of cloud during the daytime and by a pillar of fire at night. So they could travel either by day or night. ²²The cloud and fire were never out of sight.

14 Crossing the Red Sea

Jehovah now instructed Moses, ²"Tell the people to turn toward Piha-hiroth between Migdol and the sea, opposite Baal-zephon, and to camp there along the shore. ³For Pharaoh will think, 'Those Israelites are trapped now, between the desert and the sea!' ⁴And once again I will harden Pharaoh's heart and he will chase after you. I have planned this to gain great honor and glory over Pharaoh and all his armies, and the Egyptians shall know that I am the Lord."

So they camped where they were told.

⁵When word reached the king of Egypt that the Israelis were not planning to return to Egypt after three days, but to keep on going, Pharaoh and his staff became bold again. "What is this we have done, letting all these slaves get away?" they asked. ⁶So Pharaoh led the chase in his chariot, ⁷followed by the pick of Egypt's chariot corps—600 chariots in all—and other chariots driven by Egyptian officers. ⁸He pursued the people of Israel, for they had taken much of the wealth of Egypt with them. ⁹Pharaoh's entire cavalry—horses, chariots, and charioteers—was used in the chase; and the Egyptian army overtook the people of Israel as they were camped beside the shore near Piha-hiroth, across from Baal-zephon.

¹⁰As the Egyptian army approached, the people of Israel saw them far in the distance, speeding after them, and they were terribly frightened and cried out to the Lord to help them.

¹¹And they turned against Moses, whining, "Have you brought us out here to die in the desert because there were not enough graves for us in Egypt? Why did you make us leave Egypt? ¹²Isn't this what we told you, while we were slaves, to leave us alone? We said it would be better to be slaves to the Egyptians than dead in the wilderness."

¹³But Moses told the people, "Don't be afraid. Just stand where you are and watch, and you will see the wonderful way the Lord will rescue you today. The Egyptians you are looking at—you will never see them again. ¹⁴The Lord will fight for you, and you won't need to lift a finger!"

¹⁵Then the Lord said to Moses, "Quit praying and get the people moving! Forward, march! ¹⁶Use your rod—hold it out over the water, and the sea will open up a path before you, and all the people of Israel shall walk through on dry ground! ¹⁷I will harden the hearts of the Egyptians, and they will go in after you and you will see the honor I will get in defeating Pharaoh and all his armies, chariots, and horsemen. ¹⁸And all Egypt shall know that I am Jehovah."

¹⁹Then the Angel of God, who was leading the people of Israel, moved the cloud around behind them, ²⁰and it stood between the people of Israel and the Egyptians. And that night, as it changed to a pillar of fire, it gave darkness to the Egyptians but light to the people of Israel! So the Egyptians couldn't find the Israelis!

²¹Meanwhile, Moses stretched his rod over the sea, and the Lord opened up a path through the sea, with walls of water on each side; and a strong east wind blew all that night, drying the sea bottom. ²²So the people of Israel walked through the sea on dry ground! ²³Then the Egyptians followed them between the walls of water along the bottom of the sea—all of Pharaoh's horses, chariots, and horsemen. ²⁴But in the early morning Jehovah looked down from the cloud of fire upon the array of the Egyptians, and began to harass them. ²⁵Their chariot wheels began coming off, so that their chariots scraped along the dry ground. "Let's get out of here," the Egyptians yelled. "Jehovah is fighting for them and against us."

²⁶When all the Israelites were on the other side, the Lord said to Moses, "Stretch out your hand again over the sea, so that the waters will come back over the Egyptians and their chariots and horsemen." ²⁷Moses did, and the sea returned to normal beneath the morning light. The Egyptians tried to flee, but the Lord drowned them in the sea. ²⁸The water covered the path and the chariots and horsemen. And of all the army of Pharaoh

FAMILY DEVOTIONS

☐ **DEVOTION 31**
SHOWING KINDNESS

Read Exodus 16:1-6

Showing Kindness Memory Verse

That's why whenever we can we should always be kind to everyone, and especially to our Christian brothers.
Galatians 6:10

The sign read: Camp Joy—Christ-Centered Fun for Girls and Boys.

Wow, Nicholas said to himself as he scuffed into the dining hall, *if this is fun, I'd hate to see something that isn't fun!*

Nicholas didn't like camp. He didn't like the kids in his cabin, and he didn't like the food. He usually ate, though, because he wouldn't have to talk to anyone if his mouth was full of food. During rest time, he stretched out on his bunk and ignored the talking that went on around him.

Dave, his counselor, stopped Nicholas as he walked reluctantly toward the softball field one afternoon. "Nicholas, you don't look as if you're having much fun."

"I'm not," grumbled Nicholas. "I don't like this camp. None of the kids are friendly to me."

"Oh, I see," murmured Dave. "Have you been friendly to them?"

"Well . . ."

"The Bible tells us that if we show friendliness to others, they will be friendly to us," encouraged Dave. "We have to make that effort, though. Go over there and get involved in that ball game. Talk to the other kids. You might be surprised at how much fun you can have."

Nicholas didn't really believe his counselor, but he supposed he could give it a try. He ran over to the backstop where the camp director was assigning teams. He laughed at a joke told by one of the campers, and then surprised himself by telling a joke of his own. When he was up to bat and later playing in right field, he did his very best. Suddenly he realized that what his counselor had said was right—he *was* having fun!

H o w   A b o u t   Y o u ?

When you're in a new situation, do you wait for others to be friendly to you, or do you make an effort to talk to those around you? Complaining all the time is a good way to miss the blessings God wants to give you, just like the Israelites did. Instead of pouting and complaining that you aren't having fun, do your best to enter into the activities and show kindness to others. *L. M. W.*

• For the next devotional, turn to page 83.   • For the next devotional on *SHOWING KINDNESS,* turn to page 91.
• For notes on *SHOWING KINDNESS,* see pages 664, 880, 1038, and 1244.

that chased after Israel through the sea, not one remained alive. ²⁹The people of Israel had walked through on dry land, and the waters had been walled up on either side of them. ³⁰Thus Jehovah saved Israel that day from the Egyptians; and the people of Israel saw the Egyptians dead, washed up on the seashore. ³¹When the people of Israel saw the mighty miracle the Lord had done for them against the Egyptians, they were afraid and revered the Lord, and believed in him and in his servant Moses.

15 Songs to the Lord

Then Moses and the people of Israel sang this song to the Lord:

I will sing to the Lord, for he has triumphed gloriously;
He has thrown both horse and rider into the sea.
²The Lord is my strength, my song, and my salvation.
He is my God, and I will praise him.
He is my father's God—I will exalt him.
³The Lord is a warrior—
Yes, Jehovah is his name.
⁴He has overthrown Pharaoh's chariots and armies,
Drowning them in the sea.
The famous Egyptian captains are dead beneath the waves.
⁵The water covers them.
They went down into the depths like a stone.
⁶Your right hand, O Lord, is glorious in power;
It dashes the enemy to pieces.
⁷In the greatness of your majesty
You overthrew all those who rose against you.
You sent forth your anger, and it consumed them as fire consumes straw.
⁸At the blast of your breath
The waters divided!
They stood as solid walls to hold the seas apart.
⁹The enemy said, "I will chase after them,
Catch up with them, destroy them.
I will cut them apart with my sword
And divide the captured booty."
¹⁰But God blew with his wind, and the sea covered them.
They sank as lead in the mighty waters.
¹¹Who else is like the Lord among the gods?
Who is glorious in holiness like him?
Who is so awesome in splendor,
A wonder-working God?
¹²You reached out your hand and the earth swallowed them.
¹³You have led the people you redeemed.
But in your loving-kindness
You have guided them wonderfully
To your holy land.
¹⁴The nations heard what happened, and they trembled.
Fear has gripped the people of Philistia.
¹⁵The leaders of Edom are appalled,
The mighty men of Moab tremble;
All the people of Canaan melt with fear.
¹⁶Terror and dread have overcome them.
O Lord, because of your great power they won't attack us!
Your people whom you purchased
Will pass by them in safety.
¹⁷You will bring them in and plant them on your mountain,
Your own homeland, Lord—
The sanctuary you made for them to live in.
¹⁸Jehovah shall reign forever and forever.
¹⁹The horses of Pharaoh, his horsemen, and his chariots
Tried to follow through the sea;
But the Lord let down the walls of water on them
While the people of Israel walked through on dry land.

²⁰Then Miriam the prophetess, the sister of Aaron, took a tambourine and led the women in dances. ²¹And Miriam sang this song:

Sing to the Lord, for he has triumphed gloriously.
The horse and rider have been drowned in the sea.

²²Then Moses led the people of Israel on from the Red Sea, and they moved out into the wilderness of Shur and were there three days without water. ²³Arriving at Marah, they couldn't drink the water because it was bitter (that is why the place was called Marah, meaning "bitter"). ²⁴Then the people turned against Moses. "Must we die of thirst?" they demanded. ²⁵Moses pleaded with the Lord to help them, and the Lord showed him a tree to throw into the water, and the water became sweet.

It was there at Marah that the Lord laid before them the following conditions, to test their commitment to him: ²⁶"If you will listen to the voice of the Lord your God, and obey it, and do what is right, then I will not make you suffer the diseases I sent on the Egyptians, for I am the Lord who heals you." ²⁷And they came to Elim where there were twelve springs and seventy palm trees; and they camped there beside the springs.

FAMILY DEVOTIONS

☐ *DEVOTION 32*
TRUE JOY

Read Exodus 16:7-12

True Joy
Memory Verse

Always be full of joy in the Lord; I say it again, rejoice!
Philippians 4:4

Julie felt grouchy as she sat on the couch at the home of her Sunday school teacher, Mrs. Watson. She didn't really want to be on what she called "this stupid old parents' night planning committee." Maria and Danny, the other committee members, seemed to be enjoying it, however—or at least they *had* been. They had made several suggestions, but Julie just scowled about all of them. Now the others seemed to be losing a lot of their enthusiasm, too.

"Julie," said Mrs. Watson finally, "why don't you help me prepare the snacks? Maria and Danny, I like your ideas. Keep thinking."

Glumly, Julie followed Mrs. Watson into the kitchen and arranged cookies on a plate while Mrs. Watson prepared hot chocolate. "Maybe I'll add just a little lemon juice to this chocolate," Mrs. Watson said.

"Lemon juice?" Julie was surprised. "That'll make it sour!"

Mrs. Watson looked at the bottle of lemon juice she held in her hand. "You're right, of course," she agreed. "And you know, Julie, just like a little lemon juice can ruin this hot chocolate, so, too, a bad attitude from just one person can ruin the special night we're planning. We want this to be a good parents' night, especially since we know there will be unsaved dads and moms attending. Maria and Danny have come up with some good ideas, but you've soured them all."

Julie bit her lip and stared at the floor. "I'm sorry," she said at last, and she really was. "I'll apologize to Maria and Danny. I really do like their ideas. Oh, and Mrs. Watson?"

"Yes, Julie?"

Julie grinned. "Please put the lemon juice away."

How About You?
Are you a complainer? Do you often get moody and cranky if things don't go the way you want? You might be surprised how quickly your bad mood can spread. The Lord wants you to be joyful and get along with others. *L. M. W.*

• For the next devotional, turn to page 87.   • For the next devotional on *TRUE JOY,* turn to page 203.
• For notes on *TRUE JOY,* see pages 532, 1024, and 1160.

16 God Sends Manna and Quail

Now they left Elim and journeyed on into the Sihn Wilderness, between Elim and Mt. Sinai, arriving there on the fifteenth day of the second month after leaving Egypt. ²There, too, the people spoke bitterly against Moses and Aaron.

³"Oh, that we were back in Egypt," they moaned, "and that the Lord had killed us there! For there we had plenty to eat. But now you have brought us into this wilderness to kill us with starvation."

⁴Then the Lord said to Moses, "Look, I'm going to rain down food from heaven for them. Everyone can go out each day and gather as much food as he needs. And I will test them in this, to see whether they will follow my instructions or not. ⁵Tell them to gather twice as much as usual on the sixth day of each week."

⁶Then Moses and Aaron called a meeting of all the people of Israel and told them, "This evening you will realize that it was the Lord who brought you out of the land of Egypt. ⁷⁻⁹In the morning you will see more of his glory; for he has heard your complaints against him (for you aren't really complaining against *us*—who are *we?*). The Lord will give you meat to eat in the evening, and bread in the morning. Come now before Jehovah and hear his reply to your complaints."

¹⁰So Aaron called them together and suddenly, out toward the wilderness, from within the guiding cloud, there appeared the awesome glory of Jehovah.

¹¹,¹²And Jehovah said to Moses, "I have heard their complaints. Tell them, 'In the evening you will have meat and in the morning you will be stuffed with bread, and you shall know that I am Jehovah your God.'"

¹³That evening vast numbers of quail arrived and covered the camp, and in the morning the desert all around the camp was wet with dew; ¹⁴and when the dew disappeared later in the morning it left thin white flakes that covered the ground like frost. ¹⁵When the people of Israel saw it they asked each other, "What is it?"

And Moses told them, "It is the food Jehovah has given you. ¹⁶Jehovah has said for everyone to gather as much as is needed for his household—about two quarts for each person."

¹⁷So the people of Israel went out and gathered it—some getting more and some less before it melted on the ground, ¹⁸and there was just enough for everyone. Those who gathered more had nothing left over and those who gathered little had no lack! Each home had just enough.

¹⁹And Moses told them, "Don't leave it overnight."

²⁰But of course some of them wouldn't listen, and left it until morning; and when they looked, it was full of maggots and had a terrible odor; and Moses was very angry with them. ²¹So they gathered the food morning by morning, each home according to its need; and when the sun became hot upon the ground, the food melted and disappeared. ²²On the sixth day there was twice as much as usual on the ground—four quarts instead of two; the leaders of the people came and asked Moses why this had happened.

²³And he told them, "Because the Lord has appointed tomorrow as a day of seriousness and rest, a holy Sabbath to the Lord when we must refrain from doing our daily tasks. So cook as much as you want to today, and keep what is left for tomorrow."

²⁴And the next morning the food was wholesome and good, without maggots or odor. ²⁵Moses said, "This is your food for today, for today is the Sabbath to Jehovah and there will be no food on the ground today. ²⁶Gather the food for six days, but the seventh is a Sabbath, and there will be none there for you on that day."

²⁷But some of the people went out anyway to gather food, even though it was the Sabbath, but there wasn't any.

²⁸,²⁹"How long will these people refuse to obey?" the Lord asked Moses. "Don't they realize that I am giving them twice as much on the sixth day, so that there will be enough for two days? For the Lord has given you the seventh day as a day of Sabbath rest; stay in your tents and don't go out to pick up food from the ground that day." ³⁰So the people rested on the seventh day.

³¹And the food became known as "manna" (meaning "What is it?"); it was white, like coriander seed, and flat, and tasted like honey bread.

³²Then Moses gave them this further instruction from the Lord: they were to take two quarts of it to be kept as a museum specimen forever, so that later generations could see the bread the Lord had fed them with in the wilderness, when he brought them from Egypt. ³³Moses told Aaron to get a container and put two quarts of manna in it and to keep it in a sacred place from generation to generation. ³⁴Aaron did this, just as the Lord had instructed Moses, and eventually it was kept in the Ark in the Tabernacle.

³⁵So the people of Israel ate the manna forty years until they arrived in the land of Canaan, where there were crops to eat. ³⁶The omer—the container used to measure the manna—held about two quarts; it is approximately a tenth of a bushel.

17 Water from a Rock

Now, at God's command, the people of Israel left the Sihn desert, going by easy stages to Rephidim. But upon arrival, there was no water!

²So once more the people growled and complained to Moses. "Give us water!" they wailed.

"Quiet!" Moses commanded. "Are you trying to test God's patience with you?"

³But, tormented by thirst, they cried out, "Why did you ever take us out of Egypt? Why did you bring us here to die, with our children and cattle too?"

⁴Then Moses pleaded with Jehovah. "What shall I do? For they are almost ready to stone me."

⁵,⁶Then Jehovah said to Moses, "Take the elders of Israel with you and lead the people out to Mt. Horeb. I will meet you there at the rock. Strike it with your rod—the same one you struck the Nile with—and water will come pouring out, enough for everyone!" Moses did as he was told, and the water gushed out! ⁷Moses named the place Massah (meaning "tempting Jehovah to slay us"), and sometimes they referred to it as Meribah (meaning "argument" and "strife!")—for it was there that the people of Israel argued against God and tempted him to slay them by saying, "Is Jehovah going to take care of us or not?"

⁸But now the warriors of Amalek came to fight against the people of Israel at Rephidim. ⁹Moses instructed Joshua to issue a call to arms to the Israelites, to fight the army of Amalek.

"Tomorrow," Moses told him, "I will stand at the top of the hill, with the rod of God in my hand!"

¹⁰So Joshua and his men went out to fight the army of Amalek. Meanwhile Moses, Aaron, and Hur went to the top of the hill. ¹¹And as long as Moses held up the rod in his hands, Israel was winning; but whenever he rested his arms at his sides, the soldiers of Amalek were winning. ¹²Moses' arms finally became too tired to hold up the rod any longer; so Aaron and Hur rolled a stone for him to sit on, and they stood on each side, holding up his hands until sunset. ¹³As a result, Joshua and his troops crushed the army of Amalek, putting them to the sword.

¹⁴Then the Lord instructed Moses, "Write this into a permanent record, to be remembered forever, and announce to Joshua that I will utterly blot out every trace of Amalek." ¹⁵,¹⁶Moses built an altar there and called it "Jehovah-nissi" (meaning "Jehovah is my flag").

"Raise the banner of the Lord!" Moses said. "For the Lord will be at war with Amalek generation after generation."

18 Jethro Visits Moses

Word soon reached Jethro, Moses' father-in-law, the priest of Midian, about all the wonderful things God had done for his people and for Moses, and how the Lord had brought them out of Egypt.

²Then Jethro took Moses' wife, Zipporah, to him (for he had sent her home), ³along with Moses' two sons, Gershom (meaning "foreigner," for Moses said when he was born, "I have been wandering in a foreign land") ⁴and Eliezer (meaning "God is my help," for Moses said at his birth, "The God of my fathers was my helper and delivered me from the sword of Pharaoh"). ⁵,⁶They arrived while Moses and the people were camped at Mt. Sinai.

"Jethro, your father-in-law, has come to visit you," Moses was told, "and he has brought your wife and your two sons."

⁷Moses went out to meet his father-in-law and greeted him warmly; they asked about each other's health and then went into Moses' tent to talk further. ⁸Moses related to his father-in-law all that had been happening and what the Lord had done to Pharaoh and the Egyptians in order to deliver Israel, and all the problems there had been along the way, and how the Lord had delivered his people from all of them. ⁹Jethro was very happy about everything the Lord had done for Israel, and about his bringing them out of Egypt.

¹⁰"Bless the Lord," Jethro said, "for he has saved you from the Egyptians and from Pharaoh, and has rescued Israel. ¹¹I know now that the Lord is greater than any other god because he delivered his people from the proud and cruel Egyptians."

¹²Jethro offered sacrifices to God, and afterwards Aaron and the leaders of Israel came to meet Jethro, and they all ate the sacrificial meal together before the Lord.

¹³The next day Moses sat as usual to hear the people's complaints against each other, from morning to evening.

¹⁴When Moses' father-in-law saw how much time this was taking, he said, "Why are you trying to do all this alone, with people standing here all day long to get your help?"

¹⁵,¹⁶"Well, because the people come to me with their disputes, to ask for God's decisions," Moses told him. "I am their judge, deciding who is right and who is wrong, and instructing them in God's ways. I apply the laws of God to their particular disputes."

¹⁷"It's not right!" his father-in-law exclaimed. ¹⁸"You're going to wear yourself out—and if you do, what will happen to the people? Moses, this job is too heavy a burden for you to try to handle all by yourself. ¹⁹,²⁰Now listen, and let me give you a word of advice, and God will bless you: Be these people's lawyer—their representative before God—bringing him their questions to decide; you will tell them his decisions, teaching them God's

laws, and showing them the principles of godly living.

²¹"Find some capable, godly, honest men who hate bribes, and appoint them as judges, one judge for each 1000 people; he in turn will have ten judges under him, each in charge of a hundred; and under each of them will be two judges, each responsible for the affairs of fifty people; and each of these will have five judges beneath him, each counseling ten persons. ²²Let these men be responsible to serve the people with justice at all times. Anything that is too important or complicated can be brought to you. But the smaller matters they can take care of themselves. That way it will be easier for you because you will share the burden with them. ²³If you follow this advice, and if the Lord agrees, you will be able to endure the pressures, and there will be peace and harmony in the camp."

²⁴Moses listened to his father-in-law's advice and followed this suggestion. ²⁵He chose able men from all over Israel and made them judges over the people—thousands, hundreds, fifties, and tens. ²⁶They were constantly available to administer justice. They brought the hard cases to Moses but judged the smaller matters themselves.

²⁷Soon afterwards Moses let his father-in-law return to his own land.

19 God Talks to Moses

The Israelis arrived in the Sinai peninsula three months after the night of their departure from Egypt. ²,³After breaking camp at Rephidim, they came to the base of Mt. Sinai and set up camp there. Moses climbed the rugged mountain to meet with God, and from somewhere in the mountain God called to him and said,

"Give these instructions to the people of Israel. Tell them, ⁴'You have seen what I did to the Egyptians, and how I brought you to myself as though on eagles' wings. ⁵Now if you will obey me and keep your part of my contract with you, you shall be my own little flock from among all the nations of the earth; for all the earth is mine. ⁶And you shall be a kingdom of priests to God, a holy nation.'"

⁷Moses returned from the mountain and called together the leaders of the people and told them what the Lord had said.

⁸They all responded in unison, "We will certainly do everything he asks of us." Moses reported the words of the people to the Lord.

⁹Then he said to Moses, "I am going to come to you in the form of a dark cloud, so that the people themselves can hear me when I talk with you, and then they will always believe you. ¹⁰Go down now and see that the people are ready for my visit. Sanctify them today and tomorrow, and have them wash their clothes. ¹¹Then, the day after tomorrow, I will come down upon Mt. Sinai as all the people watch. ¹²Set boundary lines the people may not pass, and tell them, 'Beware! Do not go up into the mountain or even touch its boundaries; whoever does shall die— ¹³no hand shall touch him, but he shall be stoned or shot to death with arrows, whether man or animal.' Stay away from the mountain entirely until you hear a ram's horn sounding one long blast; then gather at the foot of the mountain!"

¹⁴So Moses went down to the people and sanctified them and they washed their clothing.

¹⁵He told them, "Get ready for God's appearance two days from now, and do not have sexual intercourse with your wives."

¹⁶On the morning of the third day there was a terrific thunder and lightning storm, and a huge cloud came down upon the mountain, and there was a long, loud blast as from a ram's horn; and all the people trembled. ¹⁷Moses led them out from the camp to meet God, and they stood at the foot of the mountain. ¹⁸All Mt. Sinai was covered with smoke because Jehovah descended upon it in the form of fire; the smoke billowed into the sky as from a furnace, and the whole mountain shook with a violent earthquake. ¹⁹As the trumpet blast grew louder and louder, Moses spoke and God thundered his reply. ²⁰So the Lord came down upon the top of Mt. Sinai and called Moses up to the top of the mountain, and Moses ascended to God.

²¹But the Lord told Moses, "Go back down and warn the people not to cross the boundaries. They must not come up here to try to see God, for if they do, many of them will die. ²²Even the priests on duty must sanctify themselves, or else I will destroy them."

²³"But the people won't come up into the mountain!" Moses protested. "You told them not to! You told me to set boundaries around the mountain and to declare it off limits because it is reserved for God."

²⁴But Jehovah said, "Go down and bring Aaron back with you, and don't let the priests and the people break across the boundaries to try to come up here, or I will punish them."

²⁵So Moses went down to the people and told them what God had said.

20 The Ten Commandments

Then God issued this edict:
²"I am Jehovah your God who liberated you from your slavery in Egypt.

³"You may worship no other god than me.

⁴"You shall not make yourselves any idols: no

Family Devotions

☐ DEVOTION 33
RESPECTING OTHERS

Read Exodus 20:12

Before Sunday school class began, all the sixth-grade boys gathered in a group outside. They didn't realize that a window was open near them, and their teacher was overhearing every remark they made.

Mark opened the conversation. "What did you guys do yesterday?"

"My old man made me help him paint our basement. I wanted to play football," Kyle grumbled.

"Well, my old lady had her parents over all day," said Terry, "and the Grams are both deaf. I spent the whole day saying things louder after they said, 'huh?'"

Mark had a complaint, too. "Karen and Jim made me wash their car. I told them I wasn't the one who got it dirty."

The others laughed. Then Kyle said, "Mark, how do you get away with calling your parents by their first names?"

Mark laughed. "Are you kidding? If I ever did that to their face, they'd skin me alive!"

Just then a buzzer sounded and the boys filed into class. Mr. Beach asked, "How many of you know the Ten Commandments?" A few hands went up, and at Mr. Beach's nod, Mark recited them rapidly.

"Good," said Mr. Beach. "Now, how many of you realize you broke one of those commandments just a few minutes ago?" This time no hands went up, but there were many puzzled looks.

"Think about the fifth commandment," said Mr. Beach. "It says, 'Honor your father and mother.' Now think about your conversation before class." The boys began to look ashamed. They really did love their parents, but had thoughtlessly been disrespectful. After discussing it, Mr. Beach gave them a homework assignment for the next week. It was to put into practice the fifth commandment.

Respecting Others Memory Verse

Don't be selfish; don't live to make a good impression on others. Be humble, thinking of others as better than yourself.
Philippians 2:3

How About You?

When you're away from your parents, do you call them the "old man" or "old lady?" Do you honor them to their face and make fun of them behind their back? If so, you're guilty of breaking the fifth commandment. Ask God to forgive you and to help you to truly honor your parents! R. P.

• For the next devotional, turn to page 89. • For the next devotional on *RESPECTING OTHERS*, turn to page 97.
• For notes on *RESPECTING OTHERS*, see pages 322, 382, 1088, and 1218.

images of animals, birds, or fish. ⁵You must never bow or worship it in any way; for I, the Lord your God, am very possessive. I will not share my affection with any other god!

"And when I punish people for their sins, the punishment continues upon the children, grandchildren, and great-grandchildren of those who hate me; ⁶but I lavish my love upon thousands of those who love me and obey my commandments.

⁷"You shall not use the name of Jehovah your God irreverently, nor use it to swear to a falsehood. You will not escape punishment if you do.

⁸"Remember to observe the Sabbath as a holy day. ⁹Six days a week are for your daily duties and your regular work, ¹⁰but the seventh day is a day of Sabbath rest before the Lord your God. On that day you are to do no work of any kind, nor shall your son, daughter, or slaves—whether men or women—or your cattle or your house guests. ¹¹For in six days the Lord made the heaven, earth, and sea, and everything in them, and rested the seventh day; so he blessed the Sabbath day and set it aside for rest.

¹²"Honor your father and mother, that you may have a long, good life in the land the Lord your God will give you.

¹³"You must not murder.

¹⁴"You must not commit adultery.

¹⁵"You must not steal.

¹⁶"You must not lie.

¹⁷"You must not be envious of your neighbor's house, or want to sleep with his wife, or want to own his slaves, oxen, donkeys, or anything else he has."

¹⁸All the people saw the lightning and the smoke billowing from the mountain, and heard the thunder and the long, frightening trumpet blast; and they stood at a distance, shaking with fear.

¹⁹They said to Moses, "You tell us what God says and we will obey, but don't let God speak directly to us, or it will kill us."

²⁰"Don't be afraid," Moses told them, "for God has come in this way to show you his awesome power, so that from now on you will be afraid to sin against him!"

²¹As the people stood in the distance, Moses entered into the deep darkness where God was.

²²And the Lord told Moses to be his spokesman to the people of Israel. "You are witnesses to the fact that I have made known my will to you from heaven. ²³Remember, you must not make or worship idols made of silver or gold or of anything else!

²⁴"The altars you make for me must be simple altars of earth. Offer upon them your sacrifices to me—your burnt offerings and peace offerings of sheep and oxen. Build altars only where I tell you to, and I will come and bless you there. ²⁵You may also build altars from stone, but if you do, then use only uncut stones and boulders. Don't chip or shape the stones with a tool, for that would make them unfit for my altar. ²⁶And don't make steps for the altar, or someone might look up beneath the skirts of your clothing and see your nakedness.

21 Laws about People

"Here are other laws you must obey:

²"If you buy a Hebrew slave, he shall serve only six years and be freed in the seventh year, and need pay nothing to regain his freedom.

³"If he sold himself as a slave before he married, then if he married afterwards, only he shall be freed; but if he was married before he became a slave, then his wife shall be freed with him at the same time. ⁴But if his master gave him a wife while he was a slave, and they have sons or daughters, the wife and children shall still belong to the master, and he shall go out by himself free.

⁵"But if the man shall plainly declare, 'I prefer my master, my wife, and my children, and I would rather not go free,' ⁶then his master shall bring him before the judges and shall publicly bore his ear with an awl, and after that he will be a slave forever.

⁷"If a man sells his daughter as a slave, she shall not be freed at the end of six years as the men are. ⁸If she does not please the man who bought her, then he shall let her be bought back again; but he has no power to sell her to foreigners, since he has wronged her by no longer wanting her after marrying her. ⁹And if he arranges an engagement between a Hebrew slave-girl and his son, then he may no longer treat her as a slave-girl, but must treat her as a daughter. ¹⁰If he himself marries her and then takes another wife, he may not reduce her food or clothing, or fail to sleep with her as his wife. ¹¹If he fails in any of these three things, then she may leave freely without any payment.

¹²"Anyone who hits a man so hard that he dies shall surely be put to death. ¹³But if it is accidental—an act of God—and not intentional, I will appoint a place where he can run and get protection. ¹⁴However, if a man deliberately attacks another, intending to kill him, drag him even from my altar, and kill him.

¹⁵"Anyone who strikes his father or mother shall surely be put to death.

¹⁶"A kidnapper must be killed, whether he is caught in possession of his victim or has already sold him as a slave.

¹⁷"Anyone who reviles or curses his mother or father shall surely be put to death.

¹⁸"If two men are fighting, and one hits the other with a stone or with his fist and injures him so that he must be confined to bed, but doesn't die, ¹⁹if later he is able to walk again, even with a limp, the

FAMILY DEVOTIONS

☐ DEVOTION 34
CONTENTMENT

Read Exodus 20:15-17

At the discount store, Scott met his friends, Jerry and Ken. "Hi," he said. "Whatcha doin'?"

"We're playing five-finger discount," Jerry announced, holding up a small pocket knife.

"What?" asked Scott.

"You find something in the store that you can pick up with five fingers, you hide it in your hand, and you walk out of the store without paying for it."

"That's stealing," gasped Scott.

"Shhh," Ken said. "It's just a game. Sometimes you can't get what you want any other way."

Scott cupped his hand around a little car he had been looking at. For a long time he had wanted a car like that for his collection. It would be so easy to get the five-finger discount.

"Go on," his friends urged him. "It's easy."

Scott looked longingly at the car. "I'd better go," he said, putting down the car.

"Well, think about it," said Jerry. "You can come back for it tomorrow."

Dessert that night was Scott's favorite—chocolate fudge cake. Mother sat down and looked at her piece. Suddenly she got up and put it back on the cake plate. "When I take the dessert, I take it because it tastes so good," she said. "Then when the doctor weighs me at the end of the week, I get upset that my diet isn't working. Sometimes it's hard to resist immediate pleasure regardless of what it will cost me in the long run."

Scott knew just what she meant. He had been tempted to do something wrong just for the immediate pleasure of having the little car. Even if he hadn't gotten caught, the car would have cost him a guilty conscience. It would have cost him many uncomfortable moments. He was glad he had resisted.

Contentment Memory Verse

I know how to live on almost nothing or with everything. I have learned the secret of contentment in every situation, whether it be a full stomach or hunger, plenty or want.
Philippians 4:12

How About You?
Are there things you think you need right away just to please yourself? The immediate pleasure you'd receive isn't worth the long-term results. Trust God to meet your needs in his own good time. N. E. K.

- For the next devotional, turn to page 91.   • For the next devotional on CONTENTMENT, turn to page 159.
- For notes on CONTENTMENT, see pages 542, 547, 902, and 1063.

man who hit him will be innocent except that he must pay for the loss of his time until he is thoroughly healed, and pay any medical expenses.

20"If a man beats his slave to death—whether the slave is male or female—that man shall surely be punished. 21However, if the slave does not die for a couple of days, then the man shall not be punished—for the slave is his property.

22"If two men are fighting, and in the process hurt a pregnant woman so that she has a miscarriage, but she lives, then the man who injured her shall be fined whatever amount the woman's husband shall demand, and as the judges approve. 23But if any harm comes to the woman and she dies, he shall be executed.

24"If her eye is injured, injure his; if her tooth is knocked out, knock out his; and so on—hand for hand, foot for foot, 25burn for burn, wound for wound, lash for lash.

26"If a man hits his slave in the eye, whether man or woman, and the eye is blinded, then the slave shall go free because of his eye. 27And if a master knocks out his slave's tooth, he shall let him go free to pay for the tooth.

28"If an ox gores a man or woman to death, the ox shall be stoned and its flesh not eaten, but the owner shall not be held—29unless the ox was known to gore people in the past, and the owner had been notified and still the ox was not kept under control; in that case, if it kills someone, the ox shall be stoned and the owner also shall be killed. 30But the dead man's relatives may accept a fine instead, if they wish. The judges will determine the amount.

31"The same law holds if the ox gores a boy or a girl. 32But if the ox gores a slave, whether male or female, the slave's master shall be given thirty pieces of silver, and the ox shall be stoned.

33"If a man digs a well and doesn't cover it, and an ox or a donkey falls into it, 34the owner of the well shall pay full damages to the owner of the animal, and the dead animal shall belong to him.

35"If a man's ox injures another, and it dies, then the two owners shall sell the live ox and divide the price between them—and each shall also own half of the dead ox. 36But if the ox was known from past experience to gore, and its owner has not kept it under control, then there will not be a division of the income; but the owner of the living ox shall pay in full for the dead ox, and the dead one shall be his.

22 Laws about Property

"If a man steals an ox or sheep and then kills or sells it, he shall pay a fine of five to one—five oxen shall be returned for each stolen ox. For sheep, the fine shall be four to one—four sheep returned for each sheep stolen.

2"If a thief is caught in the act of breaking into a house and is killed, the one who killed him is not guilty. 3But if it happens in the daylight, it must be presumed to be murder and the man who kills him is guilty.

"If a thief is captured, he must make full restitution; if he can't, then he must be sold as a slave for his debt.

4"If he is caught in the act of stealing a live ox or donkey or sheep or whatever it is, he shall pay double value as his fine.

5"If someone deliberately lets his animal loose and it gets into another man's vineyard; or if he turns it into another man's field to graze, he must pay for all damages by giving the owner of the field or vineyard an equal amount of the best of his own crop.

6"If the field is being burned off and the fire gets out of control and goes into another field so that the shocks of grain, or the standing grain, are destroyed, the one who started the fire shall make full restitution.

7"If someone gives money or goods to anyone to keep for him, and it is stolen, the thief shall pay double if he is found. 8But if no thief is found, then the man to whom the valuables were entrusted shall be brought before God to determine whether or not he himself has stolen his neighbor's property.

9"In every case in which an ox, donkey, sheep, clothing, or anything else is lost, and the owner believes he has found it in the possession of someone else who denies it, both parties to the dispute shall come before God for a decision, and the one whom God declares guilty shall pay double to the other.

10"If a man asks his neighbor to keep a donkey, ox, sheep, or any other animal for him, and it dies, or is hurt, or gets away, and there is no eyewitness to report just what happened to it, 11then the neighbor must take an oath that he has not stolen it, and the owner must accept his word, and no restitution shall be made for it. 12But if the animal or property has been stolen, the neighbor caring for it must repay the owner. 13If it was attacked by some wild animal, he shall bring the torn carcass to confirm the fact, and shall not be required to make restitution.

14"If a man borrows an animal (or anything else) from a neighbor, and it is injured or killed, and the owner is not there at the time, then the man who borrowed it must pay for it. 15But if the owner is there, he need not pay; and if it was rented, then he need not pay, because this possibility was included in the original rental fee.

16"If a man seduces a girl who is not engaged to

Family Devotions

☐ **Devotion 35**
Showing Kindness

Read Exodus 22:21; 23:9

Pete noticed an Asian boy sitting by himself in the school cafeteria. *He's new here, and he must be lonely,* thought Pete, remembering how he had felt last year when he was the new boy at school. Pete started to go out to play with his friends, but at the door, he stopped and turned around.

Sliding onto the bench across from the new boy, Pete said, "Hi. I'm Pete. What's your name?"

"My name is Kim," said the boy.

"Where are you from?" asked Pete.

"Korea," answered the boy.

Pete wasn't sure what made him do it, but as they walked to class together, he invited Kim to come home with him after school. Kim looked pleased.

Playing with Kim turned out to be more fun than Pete expected. The boys played Ping-Pong, darts, and marbles.

When Kim invited Pete over to meet his family, Pete went. They served him Korean food and taught him to eat with chopsticks. He also learned about Korea. Before long, Pete and Kim became good friends.

"I'm so glad I got to know Kim," Pete confided to his father one day. "I feel like I've had a trip to Korea every time I visit his home."

"The liberal man shall be rich! By watering others, he waters himself," quoted Dad with a smile.

"What does that mean?" asked Pete.

"It's from the Bible, and it means that your actions often work like a boomerang—they come back to you," replied Dad. "Kindness comes right back to the one who practices it. When you are kind to others, you are blessed yourself."

Showing Kindness Memory Verse

That's why whenever we can we should always be kind to everyone, and especially to our Christian brothers. **Galatians 6:10**

How About You?

Are you kind to everyone, even those who may be different from you? Kindness always pays. Even if the person to whom you are kind should fail to respond in gratitude, God sees all, and he will repay you. But he also works things out so that if you are kind to someone, you will not only make that person happy but you will become happy yourself! M. N.

- For the next devotional, turn to page 93. • For the next devotional on *Showing Kindness*, turn to page 137.
- For notes on *Showing Kindness*, see pages 664, 880, 1038, and 1244.

anyone and sleeps with her, he must pay the usual dowry and accept her as his wife. [17]But if her father utterly refuses to let her marry him, then he shall pay the money anyway.

[18]"A sorceress shall be put to death.

[19]"Anyone having sexual relations with an animal shall certainly be executed.

[20]"Anyone sacrificing to any other god than Jehovah shall be executed.

[21]"You must not oppress a stranger in any way; remember, you yourselves were foreigners in the land of Egypt.

[22]"You must not exploit widows or orphans; [23]if you do so in any way, and they cry to me for my help, I will surely give it. [24]And my anger shall flame out against you, and I will kill you with enemy armies, so that your wives will be widows and your children fatherless.

[25]"If you lend money to a needy fellow-Hebrew, you are not to handle the transaction in an ordinary way, with interest. [26]If you take his clothing as a pledge at his repayment, you must let him have it back at night. [27]For it is probably his only warmth; how can he sleep without it? If you don't return it, and he cries to me for help, I will hear and be very gracious to him [at your expense], for I am very compassionate.

[28]"You shall not blaspheme God, nor curse government officials—your judges and your rulers.

[29]"You must be prompt in giving me the tithe of your crops and your wine, and the redemption payment for your oldest son.

[30]"As to the firstborn of the oxen and the sheep, give it to me on the eighth day, after leaving it with its mother for seven days.

[31]"And since you yourselves are holy—my special people—do not eat any animal that has been attacked and killed by a wild animal. Leave its carcass for the dogs to eat.

23

"Do not pass along untrue reports. Do not cooperate with an evil man by affirming on the witness stand something you know is false.

[2,3]"Don't join mobs intent on evil. When on the witness stand, don't be swayed in your testimony by the mood of the majority present, and do not slant your testimony in favor of a man just because he is poor.

[4]"If you come upon an enemy's ox or donkey that has strayed away, you must take it back to its owner. [5]If you see your enemy trying to get his donkey onto its feet beneath a heavy load, you must not go on by but must help him.

[6]"A man's poverty is no excuse for twisting justice against him.

[7]"Keep far away from falsely charging anyone with evil; never let an innocent person be put to death. I will not stand for this.

[8]"Take no bribes, for a bribe makes you unaware of what you clearly see! A bribe hurts the cause of the person who is right.

[9]"Do not oppress foreigners; you know what it's like to be a foreigner; remember your own experience in the land of Egypt.

[10]"Sow and reap your crops for six years, [11]but let the land rest and lie fallow during the seventh year, and let the poor among the people harvest any volunteer crop that may come up; leave the rest for the animals to enjoy. The same rule applies to your vineyards and your olive groves.

[12]"Work six days only, and rest the seventh; this is to give your oxen and donkeys a rest, as well as the people of your household—your slaves and visitors.

[13]"Be sure to obey all of these instructions; and remember—never mention the name of any other god.

[14]"There are three annual religious pilgrimages you must make.

[15]"The first is the Pilgrimage of Unleavened Bread, when for seven days you are not to eat bread with yeast, just as I commanded you before. This celebration is to be an annual event at the regular time in March, the month you left Egypt; everyone must bring me a sacrifice at that time. [16]Then there is the Harvest Pilgrimage, when you must bring to me the first of your crops. And, finally, the Pilgrimage of Ingathering at the end of the harvest season. [17]At these three times each year, every man in Israel shall appear before the Lord God.

[18]"No sacrificial blood shall be offered with leavened bread; no sacrificial fat shall be left unoffered until the next morning.

[19]"As you reap each of your crops, bring me the choicest sample of the first day's harvest; it shall be offered to the Lord your God.

"Do not boil a young goat in its mother's milk.

[20]"See, I am sending an Angel before you to lead you safely to the land I have prepared for you. [21]Reverence him and obey all of his instructions; do not rebel against him, for he will not pardon your transgression; he is my representative—he bears my name. [22]But if you are careful to obey him, following all my instructions, then I will be an enemy to your enemies. [23]For my Angel shall go before you and bring you into the land of the Amorites, Hittites, Perizzites, Canaanites, Hivites, and Jebusites, to live there. And I will destroy those people before you.

[24]"You must not worship the gods of these other nations, nor sacrifice to them in any way, and you must not follow the evil example of

Family Devotions

☐ DEVOTION 36
RESPECTING GOD'S WORD

Read Exodus 24:1-7

Dave excitedly helped Dad unpack the big box. He thought they were the last family on earth to buy a VCR. "I know how to hook up this baby," he told his father. "I helped Tony get his hooked up last Christmas." Dad smiled and let Dave work.

After plugging in the various cords to the TV and the antenna hookup, he turned it on and slipped in the video they'd picked up at the store. Nothing happened.

"Are you sure you've got it hooked up right?" his father asked, offering to check it out.

Dave pushed his father's hand away. "Sure," he said. "This model is practically the same as Tony's, and we got it together OK. There's got to be something wrong with this one."

"Read the instruction sheet," Dad suggested. "This one could be different from Tony's."

Dave picked up the instructions that had come with the VCR and began to read them. Then he went back to the set and switched two of the cords. This time when he started the tape, it played perfectly.

"If all else fails," Dave said, embarrassed, "read the directions."

"Better yet," said Dad, "read the instructions *first*. That principle is true in our Christian lives, too. God's instruction book, the Bible, not only tells us how to accept Jesus Christ as our personal Savior, it also tells us how to live the Christian life. And we need to read it *before* we try doing things our own way and mess them up."

Respecting God's Word
Memory Verse

Your words are what sustain me; they are food to my hungry soul. They bring joy to my sorrowing heart and delight me. How proud I am to bear your name, O Lord.
Jeremiah 15:16

How About You?

Are you a Christian? Then God's Word, the Bible, should be your guide, your instruction book. It explains what a Christian should do if he falls into sin. It commands every believer to love, to give, to witness, and many other things. God's book is very important. But if it's going to be helpful, it has to be read. R.J.

• For the next devotional, turn to page 97.   • For the next devotional on RESPECTING GOD'S WORD, turn to page 109.
• For notes on RESPECTING GOD'S WORD, see pages 208, 369, 1188, and 1248.

these heathen people; you must utterly conquer them and break down their shameful idols.

 25 "You shall serve the Lord your God only; then I will bless you with food and with water, and I will take away sickness from among you. 26There will be no miscarriages nor barrenness throughout your land, and you will live out the full quota of the days of your life.

 27"The terror of the Lord shall fall upon all the people whose land you invade, and they will flee before you; 28and I will send hornets to drive out the Hivites, Canaanites, and Hittites from before you. 29I will not do it all in one year, for the land would become a wilderness, and the wild animals would become too many to control. 30But I will drive them out a little at a time, until your population has increased enough to fill the land. 31And I will set your enlarged boundaries from the Red Sea to the Philistine coast, and from the southern deserts as far as the Euphrates River; and I will cause you to defeat the people now living in the land, and you will drive them out ahead of you.

 32"You must make no covenant with them, nor have anything to do with their gods. 33Don't let them live among you! For I know that they will infect you with their sin of worshiping false gods, and that would be an utter disaster to you."

24 The People Promise to Obey

The Lord now instructed Moses, "Come up here with Aaron, Nadab, Abihu, and seventy of the elders of Israel. All of you except Moses are to worship at a distance. 2Moses alone shall come near to the Lord; and remember, none of the ordinary people are permitted to come up into the mountain at all."

3Then Moses announced to the people all the laws and regulations God had given him; and the people answered in unison, "We will obey them all."

4Moses wrote down the laws; and early the next morning he built an altar at the foot of the mountain, with twelve pillars around the altar because there were twelve tribes of Israel. 5Then he sent some of the young men to sacrifice the burnt offerings and peace offerings to the Lord. 6Moses took half of the blood of these animals and drew it off into basins. The other half he splashed against the altar.

7And he read to the people the Book he had written—the Book of the Covenant—containing God's directions and laws. And the people said again, "We solemnly promise to obey every one of these rules."

8Then Moses threw the blood from the basins toward the people and said, "This blood confirms and seals the covenant the Lord has made with you in giving you these laws."

9Then Moses, Aaron, Nadab, Abihu, and seventy of the elders of Israel went up into the mountain. 10And they saw the God of Israel; under his feet there seemed to be a pavement of brilliant sapphire stones, as clear as the heavens.

11Yet, even though the elders saw God, he did not destroy them; and they had a meal together before the Lord.

12And the Lord said to Moses, "Come up to me into the mountain, and remain until I give you the laws and commandments I have written on tablets of stone, so that you can teach the people from them." 13So Moses and Joshua, his assistant, went up into the mountain of God.

14He told the elders, "Stay here and wait for us until we come back; if there are any problems while I am gone, consult with Aaron and Hur."

15Then Moses went up the mountain and disappeared into the cloud at the top. 16And the glory of the Lord rested upon Mt. Sinai, and the cloud covered it six days; the seventh day he called to Moses from the cloud. 17Those at the bottom of the mountain saw the awesome sight: the glory of the Lord on the mountaintop looked like a raging fire. 18And Moses disappeared into the cloud-covered mountaintop, and was there for forty days and forty nights.

25 How to Build the Tabernacle

Jehovah said to Moses, "Tell the people of Israel that everyone who wants to may bring me an offering from this list: gold, silver, bronze, blue cloth, purple cloth, scarlet cloth, fine linen, goats' hair, red-dyed rams' skins, goatskins, acacia wood, olive oil for the lamps, spices for the anointing oil and for the fragrant incense, onyx stones, stones to be set in the ephod and in the breastplate.

8"For I want the people of Israel to make me a sacred Temple where I can live among them.

9"This home of mine shall be a tent pavilion—a Tabernacle. I will give you a drawing of the construction plan and the details of each furnishing.

10"Using acacia wood, make an Ark 3¾ feet long, 2¼ feet wide, and 2¼ feet high. 11Overlay it inside and outside with pure gold, with a molding of gold all around it. 12Cast four rings of gold for it and attach them to the four lower corners, two rings on each side. 13,14Make poles from acacia wood overlaid with gold, and fit the poles into the rings at the sides of the Ark to carry it. 15These carrying poles shall never be taken from the rings, but are to be left there permanently. 16When the Ark is finished, place inside it the tablets of stone I will give you, with the Ten Commandments engraved on them.

17"And make a lid of pure gold, 3¾ feet long and 2¼ feet wide. This is the place of mercy for your sins.

[18]Then make two statues of Guardian Angels using beaten gold, and place them at the two ends of the lid of the Ark. [19]They shall be one piece with the mercy place, one at each end. [20]The Guardian Angels shall be facing each other, looking down upon the place of mercy, and shall have wings spread out above the gold lid. [21]Install the lid upon the Ark, and place within the Ark the tablets of stone I shall give you. [22]And I will meet with you there and talk with you from above the place of mercy between the Guardian Angels; and the Ark will contain the laws of my covenant. There I will tell you my commandments for the people of Israel.

[23]"Then make a table of acacia wood 3 feet long, 1½ feet wide, and 2¼ feet high. [24]Overlay it with pure gold, and run a rib of gold around it. [25]Put a molding four inches wide around the edge of the top, and a gold ridge along the molding, all around. [26,27]Make four gold rings and put the rings at the outside corner of the four legs, close to the top; these are rings for the poles that will be used to carry the table. [28]Make the poles from acacia wood overlaid with gold. [29]And make gold dishes, spoons, pitchers, and flagons; [30]and always keep the special Bread of the Presence on the table before me.

[31]"Make a lampstand of pure, beaten gold. The entire lampstand and its decorations shall be one piece—the base, shaft, lamps, and blossoms. [32,33]It will have three branches going out from each side of the center shaft, each branch decorated with three almond flowers. [34,35]The central shaft itself will be decorated with four almond flowers—one placed between each set of branches; also, there will be one flower above the top set of branches and one below the bottom set. [36]These decorations and branches and the shaft are all to be one piece of pure, beaten gold. [37]Then make seven lamps for the lampstand, and set them so that they reflect their light forward. [38]The snuffers and trays are to be made of pure gold. [39]You will need about 107 pounds of pure gold for the lampstand and its accessories.

[40]"Be sure that everything you make follows the pattern I am showing you here on the mountain.

26 The Tent

"Make the tabernacle-tent from ten colored sheets of fine linen, 42 feet long and 6 feet wide, dyed blue, purple, and scarlet, with figures of Guardian Angels embroidered on them. [3]Join five sheets end to end for each side of the tent, forming two long pieces, one for each side. [4,5]Use loops at the edges to join these two long pieces together side by side. There are to be fifty loops on each side, opposite each other. [6]Then make fifty gold clasps to fasten the loops together, so that the Tabernacle, the dwelling place of God, becomes a single unit.

[7,8]"The roof of the Tabernacle is made of goats' hair tarpaulins. There are to be eleven of these tarpaulins, each 45 feet across and 6 feet wide. [9]Connect five of these tarpaulins into one wide section; and use the other six for another wide section. (The sixth tarpaulin will hang down to form a curtain across the front of the sacred tent.) [10,11]Use fifty loops along the edges of each of these two wide pieces, to join them together with fifty bronze clasps. Thus the two widths become one. [12]There will be a 1½-foot length of this roof-covering hanging down from the back of the tent, [13]and a 1½-foot length at the front. [14]On top of these blankets is placed a layer of rams' skins, dyed red, and over them a top layer of goatskins. This completes the roof-covering.

[15,16]"The framework of the sacred tent shall be made from acacia wood, each frame-piece being 15 feet high and 2¼ feet wide, standing upright, [17]with grooves on each side to mortise into the next upright piece. [18,19]Twenty of these frames will form the south side of the sacred tent, with forty silver bases for the frames to fit into—two bases under each piece of the frame. [20]On the north side there will also be twenty of these frames, [21]with their forty silver bases, two bases for each frame, one under each edge. [22]On the west side there will be six frames, [23]and two frames at each corner. [24]These corner frames will be connected at the bottom and top with clasps. [25]So, in all, there will be eight frames on that end of the building with sixteen silver bases for the frames—two bases under each frame.

[26,27]"Make bars of acacia wood to run across the frames, five bars on each side of the Tabernacle. Also five bars for the rear of the building, facing westward. [28]The middle bar, halfway up the frames, runs all the way from end to end of the Tabernacle. [29]Overlay the frames with gold, and make gold rings to hold the bars; and also overlay the bars with gold. [30]Set up this Tabernacle-tent in the manner I showed you on the mountain.

[31]"[Inside the Tabernacle], make a curtain from fine linen, with blue, purple, and scarlet Guardian Angels embroidered into the cloth. [32]Hang this curtain on gold hooks set into four pillars made from acacia wood overlaid with gold. The pillars are to be set in silver bases. [33]Behind this curtain place the Ark containing the stone tablets engraved with God's laws. The curtain will separate the Holy Place and the Most Holy Place.

[34]"Now install the mercy place—the golden lid of the Ark—in the Most Holy Place. [35]Place the table and lampstand across the room from each other on the outer side of the veil, the lampstand on the south and the table on the north.

36"As a screen for the door of the sacred tent, make another curtain from fine linen, skillfully embroidered in blue, purple, and scarlet. 37Hang this curtain on gold hooks set into posts made from acacia wood overlaid with gold. The posts are to rest on bronze bases.

27 The Altar

"Using acacia wood, make a square altar 7½ feet wide, and 4½ feet high. 2Make horns for the four corners of the altar, attach them firmly, and overlay everything with bronze. 3The ash buckets, shovels, basins, carcass-hooks, and fire pans are all to be made of bronze. 4Make a bronze grating, with a metal ring at each corner, 5and fit the grating halfway down into the firebox, resting it upon the ledge built there. 6For moving the altar, make poles from acacia wood overlaid with bronze. 7To carry it, put the poles into the rings at each side of the altar. 8The altar is to be hollow, made from planks, just as was shown you on the mountain.

9,10"Then make a courtyard for the Tabernacle, enclosed with curtains made from fine-twined linen. On the south side the curtains will stretch for 150 feet, and be held up by twenty posts, fitting into twenty bronze post holders. The curtains will be held up with silver hooks attached to silver rods, attached to the posts. 11It will be the same on the north side of the court—150 feet of curtains held up by twenty posts fitted into bronze sockets, with silver hooks and rods. 12The west side of the court will be 75 feet wide, with ten posts and ten sockets. 13The east side will also be 75 feet. 14,15On each side of the entrance there will be 22½ feet of curtain, held up by three posts imbedded in three sockets.

16"The entrance to the court will be a 30-foot-wide curtain, made of beautifully embroidered blue, purple, and scarlet fine-twined linen, and attached to four posts imbedded in their four sockets. 17All the posts around the court are to be connected by silver rods, using silver hooks, the posts being imbedded in solid bronze bases. 18So the entire court will be 150 feet long and 75 feet wide, with curtain walls 7½ feet high, made from fine-twined linen.

19"All utensils used in the work of the Tabernacle, including all the pins and pegs for hanging the utensils on the walls, will be made of bronze.

20"Instruct the people of Israel to bring you pure olive oil to use in the lamps of the Tabernacle, to burn there continually. 21Aaron and his sons shall place this eternal flame in the outer holy room, tending it day and night before the Lord, so that it never goes out. This is a permanent rule for the people of Israel.

28 Clothes for the Priests

"Consecrate Aaron your brother, and his sons Nadab, Abihu, Eleazar, and Ithamar, to be priests, to minister to me. 2Make special clothes for Aaron, to indicate his separation to God—beautiful garments that will lend dignity to his work. 3Instruct those to whom I have given special skill as tailors to make the garments that will set him apart from others, so that he may minister to me in the priest's office. 4This is the wardrobe they shall make: a chestpiece, an ephod, a robe, an embroidered shirt, a turban, and a sash. They shall also make special garments for Aaron's sons.

5,6"The ephod shall be made by the most skilled of the workmen, using gold, blue, purple, and scarlet threads of fine linen. 7It will consist of two pieces, front and back, joined at the shoulders. 8And the sash shall be made of the same material—threads of gold, blue, purple, and scarlet fine-twined linen. 9Take two onyx stones and engrave on them the names of the tribes of Israel. 10Six names shall be on each stone, so that all the tribes are named in the order of their births. 11When engraving these names, use the same technique as in making a seal; and mount the stones in gold settings. 12Fasten the two stones upon the shoulders of the ephod, as memorial stones for the people of Israel: Aaron will carry their names before the Lord as a constant reminder. 13,14Two chains of pure, twisted gold shall be made and attached to gold clasps on the shoulder of the ephod.

15"Then, using the most careful workmanship, make a chestpiece to be used as God's oracle; use the same gold, blue, purple, and scarlet threads of fine-twined linen as you did in the ephod. 16This chestpiece is to be of two folds of cloth, forming a pouch nine inches square. 17Attach to it four rows of stones: A ruby, a topaz, and an emerald shall be in the first row. 18The second row will be carbuncle, a sapphire, and a diamond. 19The third row will be an amber, an agate, and an amethyst. 20The fourth row will be an onyx, a beryl, and a jasper—all set in gold settings. 21Each stone will represent one of the tribes of Israel and the name of that tribe will be engraved upon it like a seal.

22-24"Attach the top of the chestpiece to the ephod by means of two twisted cords of pure gold. One end of each cord is attached to gold rings placed at the outer top edge of the chestpiece. 25The other ends of the two cords are attached to the front edges of the two settings of the onyx stones on the shoulder of the ephod. 26Then make two more gold rings and place them on the two lower, inside edges of the chestpiece; 27also make two other gold rings for the bottom front edge of the ephod at the sash. 28Now attach the bottom of the chestpiece to the bottom rings of the ephod by

Family Devotions

☐ **Devotion 37**
Respecting Others

Read Exodus 28:33-35, 40-43

Respecting Others
Memory Verse

You must love the Lord your God with all your heart, and with all your soul, and with all your strength, and with all your mind. And you must love your neighbor just as much as you love yourself.
Luke 10:27

"Praise the Lord," sang Erin as she wrote a note to her friend Bethany, who was sitting beside her in the Sunday morning worship service. "Ask your mom if you can come home with me," the note read. Bethany nodded.

As the service went on, Erin's mind was busy planning what she and Bethany could do together in the afternoon. She did feel a twinge of guilt because she knew she should be paying more attention to the service. *The Lord will understand. He knows I'm excited about Bethany coming,* she told herself.

Bethany did go home with Erin. After dinner, she noticed a book on Erin's dresser. "Oh!" she exclaimed. "Have you finished this? Could I borrow it?"

"Sure," agreed Erin, thinking that Bethany would take the book home with her. But Bethany sat down and began to leaf through it. Although she continued to murmur replies to what Erin said, she was soon engrossed in the book. She wasn't interested in any of the things Erin wanted to do together. "I really want to read this. You understand, don't you?" said Bethany. Erin felt hurt and disappointed.

That evening, Erin again went to church with her family. Once more, she had Bethany on her mind. *She said she wanted to come over, but she didn't act like she wanted to be with me,* Erin thought. As she pouted over the events of the day, she again felt some guilt for not paying attention to the worship service. *Oh, well. I'm upset about Bethany,* she thought. *The Lord understands.* Then she remembered Bethany's words, "You understand, don't you?"

The Lord must feel as disappointed with me as I felt with Bethany, thought Erin.

Erin decided to put Bethany out of her mind. She sang praises with the rest of the congregation, and this time she put her whole heart into it.

How About You?

Following God's detailed instructions for their clothing was one way the priests showed that they took their worship responsibilities seriously. God wants you to take worship seriously, too, though you show it in different ways than the Old Testament priests did. Do you worship God in church? Or do you write notes, whisper to friends, or think about what someone is wearing that day? Put such things out of your mind and give the Lord your wholehearted worship. *K. R. A.*

• For the next devotional, turn to page 101.   • For the next devotional on *Respecting Others,* turn to page 135.
• For notes on *Respecting Others,* see pages 322, 382, 1088, and 1218.

means of blue ribbons; this will prevent the chestpiece from coming loose from the ephod. ²⁹In this way Aaron shall carry the names of the tribes of Israel on the chestpiece over his heart (it is God's oracle) when he goes into the Holy Place; thus Jehovah will be reminded of them continually. ³⁰,³¹Insert into the pocket of the chestpiece the Urim and Thummim, to be carried over Aaron's heart when he goes in before Jehovah. Thus Aaron shall always be carrying the oracle over his heart when he goes in before the Lord.

"The ephod shall be made of blue cloth, ³²with an opening for Aaron's head. It shall have a woven band around this opening, just as on the neck of a coat of mail, so that it will not fray. ³³,³⁴The bottom edge of the ephod shall be embroidered with blue, purple, and scarlet pomegranates, alternated with gold bells. ³⁵Aaron shall wear the ephod whenever he goes in to minister to the Lord; the bells will tinkle as he goes in and out of the presence of the Lord in the Holy Place, so that he will not die.

³⁶"Next, make a plate of pure gold and engrave on it, just as you would upon a seal, 'Consecrated to Jehovah.' ³⁷,³⁸This plate is to be attached by means of a blue ribbon to the front of Aaron's turban. In this way Aaron will be wearing it upon his forehead, and thus bear the guilt connected with any errors regarding the offerings of the people of Israel. It shall always be worn when he goes into the presence of the Lord, so that the people will be accepted and forgiven.

³⁹"Weave Aaron's embroidered shirt from fine-twined linen, using a checkerboard pattern; make the turban, too, of this linen; and make him an embroidered sash.

⁴⁰"Then, for Aaron's sons, make robes, sashes, and turbans to give them honor and respect. ⁴¹Clothe Aaron and his sons with these garments, and then dedicate these men to their ministry by anointing their heads with olive oil, thus sanctifying them as the priests, my ministers. ⁴²Also make linen undershorts for them, to be worn beneath their robes next to their bodies, reaching from hips to knees. ⁴³These are to be worn whenever Aaron and his sons go into the Tabernacle or to the altar in the Holy Place, lest they be guilty and die. This is a permanent ordinance for Aaron and his sons.

29 How to Dedicate the Priests

"This is the ceremony for the dedication of Aaron and his sons as priests: get a young bull and two rams with no defects, ²and bread made without yeast, and thin sheets of sweetened bread mingled with oil, and unleavened wafers with oil poured over them. (The various kinds of bread shall be made with finely ground wheat flour.) ³,⁴Place the bread in a basket and bring it to the entrance of the Tabernacle, along with the young bull and the two rams.

"Bathe Aaron and his sons there at the entrance. ⁵Then put Aaron's robe on him, and the embroidered shirt, ephod, chestpiece, and sash, ⁶and place on his head the turban with the gold plate. ⁷Then take the anointing oil and pour it upon his head. ⁸Next, dress his sons in their robes, ⁹with their woven sashes, and place caps on their heads. They will then be priests forever; thus you shall consecrate Aaron and his sons.

¹⁰"Then bring the young bull to the Tabernacle, and Aaron and his sons shall lay their hands upon its head; ¹¹and you shall kill it before the Lord, at the entrance of the Tabernacle. ¹²Place its blood upon the horns of the altar, smearing it on with your finger, and pour the rest at the base of the altar. ¹³Then take all the fat that covers the inner parts, also the gall bladder and two kidneys, and the fat on them, and burn them upon the altar. ¹⁴Then take the body, including the skin and the dung, outside the camp and burn it as a sin offering.

¹⁵,¹⁶"Next, Aaron and his sons shall lay their hands upon the head of one of the rams as it is killed. Its blood shall also be collected and sprinkled upon the altar. ¹⁷Cut up the ram and wash off the entrails and the legs; place them with the head and the other pieces of the body, ¹⁸and burn it all upon the altar; it is a burnt offering to the Lord, and very pleasant to him.

¹⁹,²⁰"Now take the other ram, and Aaron and his sons shall lay their hands upon its head as it is killed. Collect the blood and place some of it upon the tip of the right ear of Aaron and his sons, and upon their right thumbs and the big toes of their right feet; sprinkle the rest of the blood over the altar. ²¹Then scrape off some of the blood from the altar and mix it with some of the anointing oil and sprinkle it upon Aaron and his sons and upon their clothes; and they and their clothing shall be sanctified to the Lord.

²²"Then take the fat of the ram, including the fat tail and the fat that covers the insides, also the gall bladder and the two kidneys and the fat surrounding them, and the right thigh—for this is the ram for ordination of Aaron and his sons— ²³and one loaf of bread, one cake of shortening bread, and one wafer from the basket of unleavened bread that was placed before the Lord: ²⁴Place these in the hands of Aaron and his sons, to wave them in a gesture of offering to the Lord. ²⁵Afterwards, take them from their hands and burn them on the altar as a fragrant burnt offering to him. ²⁶Then take the breast of Aaron's ordination ram and wave it before the Lord in a gesture of offering; afterwards, keep it for yourself.

²⁷"Give the breast and thigh of the consecration ram ²⁸to Aaron and his sons. The people of

Israel must always contribute this portion of their sacrifices—whether peace offerings or thanksgiving offerings—as their contribution to the Lord.

[29] "These sacred garments of Aaron shall be preserved for the consecration of his son who succeeds him, from generation to generation, for his anointing ceremony. [30] Whoever is the next High Priest after Aaron shall wear these clothes for seven days before beginning to minister in the Tabernacle and the Holy Place.

[31] "Take the ram of consecration—the ram used in the ordination ceremony—and boil its meat in a sacred area. [32] Aaron and his sons shall eat the meat, also the bread in the basket, at the door of the Tabernacle. [33] They alone shall eat those items used in their atonement (that is, in their consecration ceremony). The ordinary people shall not eat them, for these things are set apart and holy. [34] If any of the meat or bread remains until the morning, burn it; it shall not be eaten, for it is holy.

[35] "This, then, is the way you shall ordain Aaron and his sons to their offices. This ordination shall go on for seven days. [36] Every day you shall sacrifice a young bull as a sin offering for atonement; afterwards, purge the altar by making atonement for it; pour olive oil upon it to sanctify it. [37] Make atonement for the altar and consecrate it to God every day for seven days. After this the altar shall be exceedingly holy, so that whatever touches it shall be set apart for God.

[38] "Each day offer two yearling lambs upon the altar, [39] one in the morning and the other in the evening. [40] With one of them offer 3 quarts of finely ground flour mixed with 2½ pints of oil, pressed from olives; also 2½ pints of wine, as an offering.

[41] Offer the other lamb in the evening, along with the flour and the wine as in the morning, for a fragrant offering to the Lord, an offering made to the Lord by fire.

[42] "This shall be a perpetual daily offering at the door of the Tabernacle before the Lord, where I will meet with you and speak with you. [43] And I will meet with the people of Israel there, and the Tabernacle shall be sanctified by my glory. [44] Yes, I will sanctify the Tabernacle and the altar and Aaron and his sons who are my ministers, the priests. [45] And I will live among the people of Israel and be their God, [46] and they shall know that I am the Lord their God. I brought them out of Egypt so that I could live among them. I am Jehovah their God.

30 Preparations for Worship

"Then make a small altar for burning incense. It shall be made from acacia wood. [2] It is to be eighteen inches square and three feet high, with horns carved from the wood of the altar—they are not to be merely separate parts that are attached. [3] Overlay the top, sides, and horns of the altar with pure gold, and run a gold molding around the entire altar. [4] Beneath the molding, on each of two sides, construct two gold rings to hold the carrying poles. [5] The poles are to be made of acacia wood overlaid with gold. [6] Place the altar just outside the veil, near the place of mercy that is above the Ark containing the Ten Commandments. I will meet with you there.

[7] "Every morning when Aaron trims the lamps, he shall burn sweet spices on the altar, [8] and each evening when he lights the lamps he shall burn the incense before the Lord, and this shall go on from generation to generation. [9] Offer no unauthorized incense, burnt offerings, meal offerings, or wine offerings.

[10] "Once a year Aaron must sanctify the altar, placing upon its horns the blood of the sin offering for atonement. This shall be a regular, annual event from generation to generation, for this is the Lord's supremely holy altar."

[11,12] And Jehovah said to Moses, "Whenever you take a census of the people of Israel, each man who is numbered shall give a ransom to the Lord for his soul, so that there will be no plague among the people when you number them. [13] His payment shall be half a dollar. [14] All who have reached their twentieth birthday shall give this offering. [15] The rich shall not give more and the poor shall not give less, for it is an offering to the Lord to make atonement for yourselves. [16] Use this money for the care of the Tabernacle; it is to bring you, the people of Israel, to the Lord's attention, and to make atonement for you."

[17,18] And the Lord said to Moses, "Make a bronze basin with a bronze pedestal. Put it between the Tabernacle and the altar, and fill it with water. [19] Aaron and his sons shall wash their hands and feet there, [20] when they go into the Tabernacle to appear before the Lord, or when they approach the altar to burn offerings to the Lord. They must always wash before doing so, or they will die. [21] These are instructions to Aaron and his sons from generation to generation."

[22,23] Then the Lord told Moses to collect the choicest of spices—eighteen pounds of pure myrrh; half as much of cinnamon and of sweet cane; [24] the same amount of cassia as of myrrh; and 1½ gallons of olive oil. [25] The Lord instructed skilled perfumemakers to compound all this into a holy anointing oil.

[26,27] "Use this," he said, "to anoint the Tabernacle, the Ark, the table and all its instruments, the lampstand and all its utensils, the incense altar, [28] the burnt offering altar with all its instruments, and the washbasin and its pedestal. [29] Sanctify

them, to make them holy; whatever touches them shall become holy. ³⁰Use it to anoint Aaron and his sons, sanctifying them so that they can minister to me as priests. ³¹And say to the people of Israel, 'This shall always be my holy anointing oil. ³²It must never be poured upon an ordinary person, and you shall never make any of it yourselves, for it is holy, and it shall be treated by you as holy. ³³Anyone who compounds any incense like it or puts any of it upon someone who is not a priest shall be excommunicated.'"

³⁴These were the Lord's directions to Moses concerning the incense: "Use sweet spices—stacte, onycha, galbanum, and pure frankincense, weighing out the same amounts of each, ³⁵using the usual techniques of the incensemaker, and seasoning it with salt; it shall be a pure and holy incense. ³⁶Beat some of it very fine and put some of it in front of the Ark where I meet with you in the Tabernacle; this incense is most holy. ³⁷Never make it for yourselves, for it is reserved for the Lord and you must treat it as holy. ³⁸Anyone making it for himself shall be excommunicated."

31 Workmen Given Special Skill

The Lord also said to Moses, "See, I have appointed Bezalel (son of Uri, and grandson of Hur, of the tribe of Judah), ³and have filled him with the Spirit of God, giving him great wisdom, ability, and skill in constructing the Tabernacle and everything it contains. ⁴He is highly capable as an artistic designer of objects made of gold, silver, and bronze. ⁵He is skilled, too, as a jeweler and in carving wood.

⁶"And I have appointed Oholiab (son of Ahisamach of the tribe of Dan) to be his assistant; moreover, I have given special skill to all who are known as experts, so that they can make all the things I have instructed you to make: ⁷the Tabernacle; the Ark with the place of mercy upon it; all the furnishings of the Tabernacle; ⁸the table and its instruments; the pure gold lampstand with its instruments; the altar of incense; ⁹the burnt offering altar with its instruments; the laver and its pedestal; ¹⁰the beautifully made, holy garments for Aaron the priest, and the garments for his sons, so that they can minister as priests; ¹¹the anointing oil; and the sweet-spice incense for the Holy Place. They are to follow exactly the directions I gave you."

¹²,¹³The Lord then gave these further instructions to Moses: "Tell the people of Israel to rest on my Sabbath day, for the Sabbath is a reminder of the covenant between me and you forever; it helps you to remember that I am Jehovah who makes you holy. ¹⁴,¹⁵Yes, rest on the Sabbath, for it is holy. Anyone who does not obey this command must die; anyone who does any work on that day shall be killed. ¹⁶,¹⁷Work six days only, for the seventh day is a special day to remind you of my covenant—a weekly reminder forever of my promises to the people of Israel. For in six days the Lord made heaven and earth, and rested on the seventh day, and was refreshed."

¹⁸Then, as God finished speaking with Moses on Mount Sinai, he gave him the two tablets of stone on which the Ten Commandments were written with the finger of God.

32 The Golden Calf

When Moses didn't come back down the mountain right away, the people went to Aaron. "Look," they said, "make us a god to lead us, for this fellow Moses who brought us here from Egypt has disappeared; something must have happened to him."

²,³"Give me your gold earrings," Aaron replied.

So they all did—men and women, boys and girls. ⁴Aaron melted the gold, then molded and tooled it into the form of a calf. The people exclaimed, "O Israel, this is the god that brought you out of Egypt!"

⁵When Aaron saw how happy the people were about it, he built an altar before the calf and announced, "Tomorrow there will be a feast to Jehovah!"

⁶So they were up early the next morning and began offering burnt offerings and peace offerings to the calf idol; afterwards they sat down to feast and drink at a wild party, followed by sexual immorality.

⁷Then the Lord told Moses, "Quick! Go on down, for your people that you brought from Egypt have defiled themselves, ⁸and have quickly abandoned all my laws. They have molded themselves a calf, and worshiped it, and sacrificed to it, and said, 'This is your god, O Israel, that brought you out of Egypt.'"

⁹Then the Lord said, "I have seen what a stubborn, rebellious lot these people are. ¹⁰Now let me alone and my anger shall blaze out against them and destroy them all; and I will make you, Moses, into a great nation instead of them."

¹¹But Moses begged God not to do it. "Lord," he pleaded, "why is your anger so hot against your own people whom you brought from the land of Egypt with such great power and mighty miracles? ¹²Do you want the Egyptians to say, 'God tricked them into coming to the mountains so that he could slay them, destroying them from off the face of the earth'? Turn back from your fierce wrath. Turn away from this terrible evil you are planning against your people! ¹³Remember your promise to your servants—to Abraham, Isaac, and

Family Devotions

☐ DEVOTION 38
PRAYING AT ALL TIMES

Read Exodus 33:17-18

*Praying at
All Times
Memory Verse*

Don't worry about anything; instead, pray about everything; tell God your needs, and don't forget to thank him for his answers.
Philippians 4:6

Brenda hung up the phone. "We're trying to figure out what to do about Gerry," she told her mother. "She's being a sometimes friend. She only wants to be our friend when she needs help with homework. She ignores us when she's doing something that's fun."

As Brenda crawled into bed a little later, Mom appeared at her door. "Have you had your quiet time with the Lord today?" asked Mom.

Brenda yawned and glanced at the Bible on the nightstand. "I'll read it in the morning," she said. "I'm too tired tonight." Mom prayed with her briefly, tucked her in, and left the room.

The next morning Brenda overslept. As she hurried downstairs, she tripped. "Mom!" she wailed. "My ankle!" Mom hurried to help. *Dear God,* prayed Brenda silently while Mom wrapped her ankle and put ice packs on it, *please take this pain away. Make my ankle better.*

Unable to walk, Brenda stayed home from school. "Honey," said Mom after making her comfortable on the couch, "you told me about the problem with your friend Gerry. How does it feel when she asks for your help but doesn't include you in her fun times?"

Brenda sighed. "It bugs me, and it hurts, too. Friends should be friends *all* the time."

"Well," Mom continued, "last night I thought about how you talked so long to your friends on the phone but were too tired to talk to God."

Brenda squeezed her hands around the ice pack. "I prayed this morning," she defended herself.

"Did you?" asked Mom. "About what?"

"My ankle," said Brenda quietly.

Mom nodded. "You prayed because you needed help," she said. "God is an all-the-time friend. Don't you think it hurts him when you're a sometimes friend?"

How About You?
Do you talk to God as you do to a friend, or do you pray only when you have a need? You can chat with your heavenly Father anytime, not just in a crisis. Thank him for the things you see on your way to school. Share your thoughts about people and things that happen. Live in an attitude of prayer all the time. *N. E. K.*

• For the next devotional, turn to page 103.   • For the next devotional on *PRAYING AT ALL TIMES,* turn to page 171.
• For notes on *PRAYING AT ALL TIMES,* see pages 363, 442, 945, 1040, and 1051.

Israel. For you swore by your own self, 'I will multiply your posterity as the stars of heaven, and I will give them all of this land I have promised to your descendants, and they shall inherit it forever.'"

14So the Lord changed his mind and spared them.

15Then Moses went down the mountain, holding in his hands the Ten Commandments written on both sides of two stone tablets. 16(God himself had written the commandments on the tablets.)

17When Joshua heard the noise below them, of all the people shouting, he exclaimed to Moses, "It sounds as if they are preparing for war!"

18But Moses replied, "No, it's not a cry of victory or defeat, but singing."

19When they came near the camp, Moses saw the calf and the dancing, and in terrible anger he threw the tablets to the ground, and they lay broken at the foot of the mountain. 20He took the calf and melted it in the fire, and when the metal cooled, he ground it into powder and spread it upon the water and made the people drink it.

21Then he turned to Aaron. "What in the world did the people do to you," he demanded, "to make you bring such a terrible sin upon them?"

22"Don't get so upset," Aaron replied. "You know these people and what a wicked bunch they are. 23They said to me, 'Make us a god to lead us, for something has happened to this fellow Moses who led us out of Egypt.' 24Well, I told them, 'Bring me your gold earrings.' So they brought them to me and I threw them into the fire, and ... well ... this calf came out!"

25When Moses saw that the people had been committing adultery—at Aaron's encouragement, and much to the amusement of their enemies—26he stood at the camp entrance and shouted, "All of you who are on the Lord's side, come over here and join me." And all the Levites came.

27He told them, "Jehovah the God of Israel says, 'Get your swords and go back and forth from one end of the camp to the other and kill even your brothers, friends, and neighbors.'" 28So they did, and about three thousand men died that day.

29Then Moses told the Levites, "Today you have ordained yourselves for the service of the Lord, for you obeyed him even though it meant killing your own sons and brothers; now he will give you a great blessing."

30The next day Moses said to the people, "You have sinned a great sin, but I will return to the Lord on the mountain—perhaps I will be able to obtain his forgiveness for you."

31So Moses returned to the Lord and said, "Oh, these people have sinned a great sin and have made themselves gods of gold. 32Yet now if you will only forgive their sin—and if not, then blot *me* out of the book you have written."

33And the Lord replied to Moses, "Whoever has sinned against me will be blotted out of my book. 34And now go, lead the people to the place I told you about, and I assure you that my Angel shall travel on ahead of you; however, when I come to visit these people, I will punish them for their sins."

35And the Lord sent a great plague upon the people because they had worshiped Aaron's calf.

33 The People Are Sorry

The Lord said to Moses, "Lead these people you brought from Egypt to the land I promised Abraham, Isaac, and Jacob; for I said, 'I will give this land to your descendants.' 2I will send an Angel before you to drive out the Canaanites, Amorites, Hittites, Perizzites, Hivites, and Jebusites. 3It is a land 'flowing with milk and honey'; but I will not travel among you, for you are a stubborn, unruly people, and I would be tempted to destroy you along the way."

4When the people heard these stern words, they went into mourning and stripped themselves of their jewelry and ornaments.

5For the Lord had told Moses to tell them, "You are an unruly, stubborn people. If I were there among you for even a moment, I would exterminate you. Remove your jewelry and ornaments until I decide what to do with you." 6So, after that, they wore no jewelry.

7Moses always erected the sacred tent (the "Tent for Meeting with God," he called it) far outside the camp, and everyone who wanted to consult with Jehovah went out there.

8Whenever Moses went to the Tabernacle, all the people, when they saw it, stood and would rise and stand in their tent doors. 9As he entered, the pillar of cloud would come down and stand at the door while the Lord spoke with Moses. 10Then all the people worshiped from their tent doors, bowing low to the pillar of cloud. 11Inside the tent the Lord spoke to Moses face to face, as a man speaks to his friend. Afterwards Moses would return to the camp, but the young man who assisted him, Joshua (son of Nun), stayed behind in the Tabernacle.

12Moses talked there with the Lord and said to him, "You have been telling me, 'Take these people to the Promised Land,' but you haven't told me whom you will send with me. You say you are my friend, and that I have found favor before you; 13please, if this is really so, guide me clearly along the way you want me to travel so that I will understand you and walk acceptably before you. For don't forget that this nation is your people."

Family Devotions

☐ **Devotion 39**
Resisting Temptation

Read Exodus 34:10-17

Resisting Temptation Memory Verse

For since he himself has now been through suffering and temptation, he knows what it is like when we suffer and are tempted, and he is wonderfully able to help us.
Hebrews 2:18

"Just because the guys on that show use bad language, it doesn't mean I'm going to," complained Tony when his mother made him turn off the TV set.

As Tony headed outdoors, he considered asking his mother if he could have some candy from a plate he spied on the counter. But she had gone upstairs, and he was sure she'd say no anyway. He walked closer. *I'll just take a peek*, he thought. *Ummmmm! It looks so good.* He reached out and picked up a green piece. *I wonder if this one's mint.* He broke off a tiny corner and tasted it. He nibbled another corner. Soon the whole thing was gone. *Guess I'll try a little piece of fudge.* The fudge was delicious, too, and when that was gone, he tried some peanut brittle.

After dinner that evening, Mother said, "Wait till you see what Mrs. Anders gave me." She got the plate of candies, but Tony noticed she looked a little puzzled. "I thought this plate was more full," she said. "But isn't it lovely? Everyone can choose a couple of pieces for dessert."

Tony felt so guilty! All evening he tried to forget it, but he couldn't. "What's the trouble, Son?" Mother asked when she noticed how unhappy he appeared.

Tears filled Tony's eyes. "I did it," he blurted out. "I ate the candy." And the story spilled out. "I'm sorry," he finished.

"Do you see how, little by little, you gave in to temptation?" asked Mother. "How one small peek led to handling and smelling and tasting and eating? That's how Satan works. He gets you to give in, just a little at a time, so it doesn't seem so bad."

Tony nodded. He thought of the TV show he had wanted to watch. Now he could see why it wasn't a good idea.

How About You?

When you're not allowed to watch a certain TV show, do you like to see just the beginning to find out how it starts? When you're at the store, do you like to peek at the pictures in some magazines that you would never actually buy? Would you like to take just one puff on a cigarette to see how it tastes or just one sip of alcohol? Satan wants you to try "just a little." He knows that next time you might try a little more. Follow God's advice. Say no right from the start. *H. M.*

• For the next devotional, turn to page 105.   • For the next devotional on *Resisting Temptation*, turn to page 533.
• For notes on *Resisting Temptation*, see pages 268, 448, 964, and 1258.

¹⁴And the Lord replied, "I myself will go with you and give you success."

¹⁵For Moses had said, "If you aren't going with us, don't let us move a step from this place. ¹⁶If you don't go with us, who will ever know that I and my people have found favor with you, and that we are different from any other people upon the face of the earth?"

¹⁷And the Lord had replied to Moses, "Yes, I will do what you have asked, for you have certainly found favor with me, and you are my friend."

¹⁸Then Moses asked to see God's glory.

¹⁹The Lord replied, "I will make my goodness pass before you, and I will announce to you the meaning of my name Jehovah, the Lord. I show kindness and mercy to anyone I want to. ²⁰But you may not see the glory of my face, for man may not see me and live. ²¹However, stand here on this rock beside me. ²²And when my glory goes by, I will put you in the cleft of the rock and cover you with my hand until I have passed. ²³Then I will remove my hand, and you shall see my back but not my face."

34 Moses Talks with God

The Lord told Moses, "Prepare two stone tablets like the first ones, and I will write upon them the same commands that were on the tablets you broke. ²Be ready in the morning to come up into Mount Sinai and present yourself to me on the top of the mountain. ³No one shall come with you and no one must be anywhere on the mountain. Do not let the flocks or herds feed close to the mountain."

⁴So Moses took two tablets of stone like the first ones, and was up early and climbed Mount Sinai, as the Lord had told him to, taking the two stone tablets in his hands.

⁵,⁶Then the Lord descended in the form of a pillar of cloud and stood there with him, and passed in front of him and announced the meaning of his name. "I am Jehovah, the merciful and gracious God," he said, "slow to anger and rich in steadfast love and truth. ⁷I, Jehovah, show this steadfast love to many thousands by forgiving their sins; or else I refuse to clear the guilty, and require that a father's sins be punished in the sons and grandsons, and even later generations."

⁸Moses fell down before the Lord and worshiped. ⁹And he said, "If it is true that I have found favor in your sight, O Lord, then please go with us to the Promised Land; yes, it is an unruly, stubborn people, but pardon our iniquity and our sins, and accept us as your own."

¹⁰The Lord replied, "All right, this is the contract I am going to make with you. I will do miracles such as have never been done before anywhere in all the earth, and all the people of Israel shall see the power of the Lord—the terrible power I will display through you. ¹¹Your part of the agreement is to obey all of my commandments; then I will drive out from before you the Amorites, Canaanites, Hittites, Perizzites, Hivites, and Jebusites.

¹²"Be very, very careful never to compromise with the people there in the land where you are going, for if you do, you will soon be following their evil ways. ¹³Instead, you must break down their heathen altars, smash the obelisks they worship, and cut down their shameful idols. ¹⁴For you must worship no other gods, but only Jehovah, for he is a God who claims absolute loyalty and exclusive devotion.

¹⁵"No, do not make a peace treaty of any kind with the people living in the land, for they are spiritual prostitutes, committing adultery against me by sacrificing to their gods. If you become friendly with them and one of them invites you to go with him and worship his idol, you are apt to do it. ¹⁶And you would accept their daughters, who worship other gods, as wives for your sons—and then your sons would commit adultery against me by worshiping their wives' gods. ¹⁷You must have nothing to do with idols.

¹⁸"Be sure to celebrate the Feast of Unleavened Bread for seven days, just as I instructed you, at the dates appointed each year in March; that was the month you left Egypt.

¹⁹"Every firstborn male is mine—cattle, sheep, and goats. ²⁰The firstborn colt of a donkey may be redeemed by giving a lamb in its place. If you decide not to redeem it, then its neck must be broken. But your sons must all be redeemed. And no one shall appear before me without a gift.

²¹"Even during plowing and harvest times, work only six days, and rest on the seventh.

²²"And you must remember to celebrate these three annual religious festivals: the Festival of Weeks, the Festival of the First Wheat, and the Harvest Festival. ²³On each of these three occasions all the men and boys of Israel shall appear before the Lord. ²⁴No one will attack and conquer your land when you go up to appear before the Lord your God those three times each year. For I will drive out the nations from before you and enlarge your boundaries.

²⁵"You must not use leavened bread with your sacrifices to me, and none of the meat of the Passover lamb may be kept over until the following morning. ²⁶And you must bring the best of the first of each year's crop to the Tabernacle of the Lord your God. You must not cook a young goat in its mother's milk."

²⁷And the Lord said to Moses, "Write down these laws that I have given you, for they represent the terms of my covenant with you and with Israel."

FAMILY DEVOTIONS

☐ DEVOTION 40
GIVING TO GOD

Read Exodus 35:20-29

Giving to God
Memory Verse

Bring all the tithes into the storehouse so that there will be food enough in my Temple; if you do, I will open up the windows of heaven for you and pour out a blessing so great you won't have room enough to take it in! Try it! Let me prove it to you!
Malachi 3:10

"Camping is fun, but it's sure easier to do the washing at home, isn't it?" observed Jody. She continued to slosh the clothes around in a bucket.

"Yes," agreed Mom as she wrung out a shirt, twisting it tightly. "Would you hang this up for me, please?"

"Sure." Jody hung the shirt on the clothesline. "Can I wring out this sweater now?" she asked.

"Oh, don't wring that," said Mom. "Just squeeze it gently and then roll it in a towel. Wringing wouldn't be good for that material." She turned to a third bucket. "Now these," she said, "are drip-dry. We'll hang them up dripping wet. The water will just drip right off of them and leave them almost wrinkle-free."

"Sounds great," said Jody. "Wrinkle-free and work-free!"

Later that day Dad gave Jody her allowance. She looked at the money in her hand. "Would it be OK if I put all of this in the special missionary offering in church tomorrow?" she asked suddenly. "Since we're camping, I don't really need any of it this week."

Mom smiled. "You've come a long way in your giving."

"What do you mean?" asked Jody.

"Remember when you first started getting an allowance? We insisted that you give a tenth to the Lord, so you did. But you weren't happy about it," Mom reminded her. "It was kind of 'wrung' out of you, like I wrung the water out of the cotton shirt this morning. Later, you gave your tenth willingly, but that's all you'd give. It was as though you were 'gently squeezed' into giving that much. I know that now you often give extra money. That reminds me of the drip-dry clothes where the water freely runs off. And which clothes did we decide we preferred?"

"The drip-dry ones." Jody smiled.

"Right," agreed Mom. "That's the kind of giver God prefers, too."

How About You?
What kind of giver are you? Do you give only because you have to? Or do you gladly give just a small portion of your money to the Lord? Or best of all, do you give generously and cheerfully? That's the kind of giver God loves! *H. M.*

• For the next devotional, turn to page 109. • For the next devotional on *GIVING TO GOD*, turn to page 349.
• For notes on *GIVING TO GOD*, see pages 182, 433, and 1128.

[28]Moses was up on the mountain with the Lord for forty days and forty nights, and in all that time he neither ate nor drank. At that time God wrote out the Covenant—the Ten Commandments—on the stone tablets.

[29]Moses didn't realize as he came back down the mountain with the tablets that his face glowed from being in the presence of God. [30]Because of this radiance upon his face, Aaron and the people of Israel were afraid to come near him.

[31]But Moses called them over to him, and Aaron and the leaders of the congregation came and talked with him. [32]Afterwards, all the people came to him, and he gave them the commandments the Lord had given him upon the mountain. [33]When Moses had finished speaking with them, he put a veil over his face; [34]but whenever he went into the Tabernacle to speak with the Lord, he removed the veil until he came out again; then he would pass on to the people whatever instructions God had given him, [35]and the people would see his face aglow. Afterwards he would put the veil on again until he returned to speak with God.

35 Gifts for the Tabernacle

Now Moses called a meeting of all the people and told them, "These are the laws of Jehovah you must obey.

[2]"Work six days only; the seventh day is a day of solemn rest, a holy day to be used to worship Jehovah; anyone working on that day must die. [3]Don't even light the fires in your homes that day."

[4]Then Moses said to all the people, "This is what the Lord has commanded: [5-9]All of you who wish to, all those with generous hearts, may bring these offerings to Jehovah:

Gold, silver, and bronze;
Blue, purple, and scarlet cloth, made of fine-twined linen or of goats' hair;
Tanned rams' skins and specially treated goatskins;
Acacia wood;
Olive oil for the lamps;
Spices for the anointing oil and for the incense;
Onyx stones and stones to be used for the ephod and chestpiece.

[10-19]"Come, all of you who are skilled craftsmen having special talents, and construct what God has commanded us:

The Tabernacle tent, and its coverings, clasps, frames, bars, pillars, and bases;
The Ark and its poles;
The place of mercy;
The curtain to enclose the Holy Place;
The table, its carrying poles, and all of its utensils;
The Bread of the Presence;
Lamp holders, with lamps and oil;
The incense altar and its carrying poles;
The anointing oil and sweet incense;
The curtain for the door of the Tabernacle;
The altar for the burnt offerings;
The bronze grating of the altar, and its carrying poles and utensils;
The basin with its pedestal;
The drapes for the walls of the court;
The pillars and their bases;
Drapes for the entrance to the court;
The posts of the Tabernacle court, and their cords;
The beautiful clothing for the priests, to be used when ministering in the Holy Place;
The holy garments for Aaron the priest, and for his sons."

[20]So all the people went to their tents to prepare their gifts. [21]Those whose hearts were stirred by God's Spirit returned with their offerings of materials for the Tabernacle, its equipment, and for the holy garments. [22]Both men and women came, all who were willing-hearted. They brought to the Lord their offerings of gold, jewelry—earrings, rings from their fingers, necklaces—and gold objects of every kind. [23]Others brought blue, purple, and scarlet cloth made from the fine-twined linen or goats' hair; and rams' skins dyed red, and specially treated goatskins. [24]Others brought silver and bronze as their offering to the Lord; and some brought the acacia wood needed in the construction.

[25]The women skilled in sewing and spinning prepared blue, purple, and scarlet thread and cloth, and fine-twined linen, and brought them in. [26]Some other women gladly used their special skill to spin the goats' hair into cloth. [27]The leaders brought onyx stones to be used for the ephod and the chestpiece; [28]and spices, and oil—for the light, and for compounding the anointing oil and the sweet incense. [29]So the people of Israel—every man and woman who wanted to assist in the work given to them by the Lord's command to Moses—brought their freewill offerings to him.

[30,31]And Moses told them, "Jehovah has specifically appointed Bezalel (the son of Uri and grandson of Hur of the tribe of Judah) as general superintendent of the project. [32]He will be able to

create beautiful workmanship from gold, silver, and bronze; ³³he can cut and set stones like a jeweler and can do beautiful carving; in fact, he has every needed skill. ³⁴And God has made him and Oholiab gifted teachers of their skills to others. (Oholiab is the son of Ahisamach, of the tribe of Dan.) ³⁵God has filled them both with unusual skills as jewelers, carpenters, embroidery designers in blue, purple, and scarlet on linen backgrounds, and as weavers—they excel in all the crafts we will be needing in the work.

36 Building the Tabernacle

"All the other craftsmen with God-given abilities are to assist Bezalel and Oholiab in constructing and furnishing the Tabernacle." So Moses told Bezalel and Oholiab and all others who felt called to the work to begin. ³Moses gave them the materials donated by the people and additional gifts were received each morning.

⁴⁻⁷But finally the workmen all left their task to meet with Moses and told him, "We have more than enough materials on hand now to complete the job!" So Moses sent a message throughout the camp announcing that no more donations were needed. Then at last the people were restrained from bringing more!

⁸,⁹The skilled weavers first made ten sheets from fine linen, then embroidered into them blue, purple, and scarlet Guardian Angels. Each sheet was 42 feet long and 6 feet wide. ¹⁰Five of these sheets were attached end to end, then five others similarly attached, forming two long roofsheets. ¹¹,¹²Fifty blue ribbons were looped along the edges of these two long sheets, each loop being opposite its mate on the other long sheet. ¹³Then fifty clasps of gold were made to connect the loops, thus tying the two long sheets together to form the ceiling of the Tabernacle.

¹⁴,¹⁵Above the ceiling was a second layer formed by eleven draperies made of goats' hair (uniformly 45 feet long and 6 feet wide). ¹⁶Bezalel coupled five of these draperies together to make one long piece, and six others to make another long piece. ¹⁷Then he made fifty loops along the end of each ¹⁸and fifty small bronze clasps to couple the loops so that the draperies were firmly attached to each other.

¹⁹The top layer of the roof was made of rams' skins, dyed red, and tanned goatskins.

²⁰For the sides of the Tabernacle he used frames of acacia wood standing on end. ²¹The height of each frame was 15 feet and the width 2¼ feet. ²²Each frame had two clasps joining it to the next. ²³There were twenty frames on the south side, ²⁴with the bottoms fitting into forty silver bases. Each frame was connected to its base by two clasps. ²⁵,²⁶There were also twenty frames on the north side of the Tabernacle, with forty silver bases, two for each frame. ²⁷The west side of the Tabernacle, which was its rear, was made from six frames, ²⁸plus another at each corner. ²⁹These frames, including those at the corners, were linked to each other at both top and bottom by rings. ³⁰So, on the west side, there were a total of eight frames with sixteen silver bases beneath them, two for each frame.

³¹,³²Then he made five sets of bars from acacia wood to tie the frames together along the sides, five for each side of the Tabernacle. ³³The middle bar of the five was halfway up the frames, along each side, running from one end to the other. ³⁴The frames and bars were all overlaid with gold, and the rings were pure gold.

³⁵The blue, purple, and scarlet inner curtain was made from woven linen, with Guardian Angels skillfully embroidered into it. ³⁶The curtain was then attached to four gold hooks set into four posts of acacia wood, overlaid with gold and set into four silver bases.

³⁷Then he made a drapery for the entrance to the Tabernacle; it was woven from finespun linen, embroidered with blue, purple, and scarlet. ³⁸This drapery was connected by five hooks to five posts. The posts and their capitals and rods were overlaid with gold; their five bases were molded from bronze.

37 Making the Ark

Next Bezalel made the Ark. This was constructed of acacia wood and was 3¾ feet long, 2¼ feet wide, and 2¼ feet high. ²It was plated with pure gold inside and out, and had a molding of gold all the way around the sides. ³There were four gold rings fastened into its four feet, two rings at each end. ⁴Then he made poles from acacia wood, and overlaid them with gold, ⁵and put the poles into the rings at the sides of the Ark, to carry it.

⁶Then, from pure gold, he made a lid called "the place of mercy"; it was 3¾ feet long and 2¼ feet wide. ⁷He made two statues of Guardian Angels of beaten gold and placed them at the two ends of the gold lid. ⁸They were molded so that they were actually a part of the gold lid—it was all one piece. ⁹The Guardian Angels faced each other, with outstretched wings that overshadowed the place of mercy, looking down upon it.

¹⁰Then he made a table, using acacia wood, 3 feet long, 1½ feet wide, and 2¼ feet high. ¹¹It was overlaid with pure gold, with a gold molding all around the edge. ¹²A rim 4 inches high was constructed around the edges of the table, with a gold molding along the rim. ¹³Then he cast four

rings of gold and placed them into the four table legs, ¹⁴close to the molding, to hold the carrying poles in place. ¹⁵He made the carrying poles of acacia wood covered with gold. ¹⁶Next, using pure gold, he made the bowls, flagons, dishes, and spoons to be placed upon this table.

¹⁷Then he made the lampstand, again using pure, beaten gold. Its base, shaft, lamp-holders, and decorations of almond flowers were all of one piece. ¹⁸The lampstand had six branches, three from each side. ¹⁹Each of the branches was decorated with identical carvings of blossoms. ²⁰,²¹The main stem of the lampstand was similarly decorated with almond blossoms, a flower on the stem beneath each pair of branches; also a flower below the bottom pair and above the top pair, four in all. ²²The decorations and branches were all one piece of pure, beaten gold. ²³,²⁴Then he made the seven lamps at the ends of the branches, the snuffers, and the ashtrays, all of pure gold. The entire lampstand weighed 107 pounds, all pure gold.

²⁵The incense altar was made of acacia wood. It was 18 inches square and 3 feet high, with its corner-horns made as part of the altar so that it was all one piece. ²⁶He overlaid it all with pure gold and ran a gold molding around the edge. ²⁷Two gold rings were placed on each side, beneath this molding, to hold the carrying poles. ²⁸The carrying poles were gold-plated acacia wood.

²⁹Then, from sweet spices, he made the sacred oil for anointing the priests, and the pure incense, using the techniques of the most skilled perfumers.

38 Making the Burnt Offering Altar

The burnt-offering altar was also constructed of acacia wood; it was 7½ feet square at the top, and 4½ feet high. ²There were four horns at the four corners, all of one piece with the rest. This altar was overlaid with bronze. ³Then he made bronze utensils to be used with the altar—the pots, shovels, basins, meat hooks, and fire pans. ⁴Next he made a bronze grating that rested upon a ledge about halfway up [in the firebox]. ⁵Four rings were cast for each side of the grating, to insert the carrying poles. ⁶The carrying poles themselves were made of acacia wood, overlaid with bronze. ⁷The carrying poles were inserted into the rings at the side of the altar. The altar was hollow, with plank siding.

⁸The bronze washbasin and its bronze pedestal were cast from the solid bronze mirrors donated by the women who assembled at the entrance to the Tabernacle.

⁹Then he constructed the courtyard. The south wall was 150 feet long; it consisted of drapes woven from fine-twined linen thread. ¹⁰There were twenty posts to hold drapes, with bases of bronze and with silver hooks and rods. ¹¹The north wall was also 150 feet long, with twenty bronze posts and bases and with silver hooks and rods. ¹²The west side was 75 feet wide; the walls were made from drapes supported by ten posts and bases, and with silver hooks and rods. ¹³The east side was also 75 feet wide.

¹⁴,¹⁵The drapes at either side of the entrance were 22½ feet wide, each with three posts and three bases. ¹⁶All the drapes making up the walls of the court were woven of fine-twined linen. ¹⁷Each post had a bronze base, and all the hooks and rods were silver; the tops of the posts were overlaid with silver, and the rods to hold up the drapes were solid silver.

¹⁸The drapery covering the entrance to the court was made of fine-twined linen, beautifully embroidered with blue, purple, and scarlet thread.

It was 30 feet long and 7½ feet wide, just the same as the drapes composing the walls of the court. ¹⁹It was supported by four posts, with four bronze bases and with silver hooks and rods; the tops of the posts were also silver.

²⁰All the nails used in constructing the Tabernacle and court were bronze.

²¹This summarizes the various steps in building the Tabernacle to house the Ark, so that the Levites could carry on their ministry. All was done in the order designated by Moses and was supervised by Ithamar, son of Aaron the priest. ²²Bezalel (son of Uri and grandson of Hur, of the tribe of Judah) was the master craftsman, ²³assisted by Oholiab (son of Ahisamach of the tribe of Dan); he too was a skilled craftsman and also an expert at engraving, weaving, and at embroidering blue, purple, and scarlet threads into fine linen cloth.

²⁴The people brought gifts of 3,140 pounds of gold, all of which was used throughout the Tabernacle.

²⁵,²⁶The amount of silver used was 9,575 pounds, which came from the fifty-cent head tax collected from all those registered in the census who were twenty years old or older, a total of 603,550 men. ²⁷The bases for the frames of the sanctuary walls and for the posts supporting the veil required 9,500 pounds of silver, 95 pounds for each socket. ²⁸The silver left over was used for the posts

---

ENCOURAGING OTHERS 39:43 Moses inspected the finished work, saw that it was done the way God wanted, and then blessed the people. A good leader follows up on assigned tasks and gives rewards for good work. In whatever responsible position you find yourself, follow up to make sure tasks are completed as intended, and show your appreciation to the people who have helped. **To begin the series of devotionals on ENCOURAGING OTHERS, turn to page 705.**

Family Devotions

☐ DEVOTION 41
RESPECTING GOD'S WORD

Read Exodus 40:16, 21, 23, 32

Joanna slipped quietly through the kitchen and tried to sneak to her bedroom, but Mom appeared in the doorway. "Hi, honey," Mom greeted cheerfully. "I didn't hear you come in. How did you do on that math test?" Mom asked.

Joanna gulped. "Not so hot," she answered. "And I studied so hard!" She choked on her words. Taking the test from her notebook, she handed it to her mother.

"You didn't follow the directions," Mom said. "Joanna, when are you going to learn to read the directions first?"

"I don't know," Joanna mumbled.

"Yesterday you tried to make cupcakes. You didn't follow the directions in the recipe, and what happened?"

"I blew it," admitted Joanna, head down.

"And what about last week when you helped me do laundry?" Mom reminded her. "I told you exactly what to do, but you didn't follow my directions."

Joanna giggled this time. "Yeah, and Dad ended up with pink underwear."

Mom smiled, too, but only briefly. "You know, Joanna," she sighed, "learning to follow directions is extremely important. Failure to follow directions could harm you—both physically and spiritually."

"What do you mean?" Joanna asked.

"God's Word is full of instructions for us. Often we neglect to follow those instructions, and we cause ourselves a lot of grief," Mom explained.

"Or sometimes we don't even bother to read the instructions at all," Joanna added thoughtfully. She couldn't remember the last time that she had read the Bible.

"Right," Mom agreed, "and unless you read them, you can't possibly obey them—on math tests or in life."

"Mom, I'm going to make a real effort to do better from now on. I don't want to fail any more tests!" Joanna said with determination.

Respecting God's Word Memory Verse

Your words are what sustain me; they are food to my hungry soul. They bring joy to my sorrowing heart and delight me. How proud I am to bear your name, O Lord.
Jeremiah 15:16

How About You?
When was the last time you read God's Word? The Bible contains many specific directions and many principles that you should follow in your daily life. Read it and follow the instructions God gives. *B. D.*

- For the next devotional, turn to page 115. • For the next devotional on *RESPECTING GOD'S WORD,* turn to page 123.
- For notes on *RESPECTING GOD'S WORD,* see pages 208, 369, 1188, and 1248.

and to overlay their tops, and for the rods and hooks.

²⁹⁻³¹The people brought 7,540 pounds of bronze, which was used for casting the bases for the posts at the entrance to the Tabernacle, and for the bronze altar, the bronze grating, the altar utensils, the bases for the posts supporting the drapes enclosing the court, and for all the nails used in the construction of the Tabernacle and the court.

39 Making the Priest's Clothing

Then, for the priests, the people made beautiful garments of blue, purple, and scarlet cloth—garments to be used while ministering in the Holy Place. This same cloth was used for Aaron's sacred garments, in accordance with the Lord's instructions to Moses. ²The ephod was made from this cloth too, woven from fine-twined linen thread. ³Bezalel beat gold into thin plates and cut it into wire threads, to work into the blue, purple, and scarlet linen; it was a skillful and beautiful piece of workmanship when finished.

⁴,⁵The ephod was held together by shoulder straps at the top and was tied down by an elaborate one-piece woven sash made of the same gold, blue, purple, and scarlet cloth cut from fine-twined linen thread, just as God had directed Moses. ⁶,⁷The [two] onyx stones, attached to the [two] shoulder straps of the ephod, were set in gold, and the stones were engraved with the names of the tribes of Israel, just as initials are engraved upon a ring. These stones were reminders to Jehovah concerning the people of Israel; all this was done in accordance with the Lord's instructions to Moses.

⁸The chestpiece was a beautiful piece of work, just like the ephod, made from the finest gold, blue, purple, and scarlet linen. ⁹It was a piece nine inches square, doubled over to form a pouch; ¹⁰there were four rows of stones across it. In the first row were a sardius, a topaz, and a carbuncle; ¹¹in the second row were an emerald, a sapphire, and a diamond. ¹²In the third row were a jacinth, an agate, and an amethyst. ¹³In the fourth row, a beryl, an onyx, and a jasper—all set in gold filigree. ¹⁴The stones were engraved like a seal, with the names of the twelve tribes of Israel.

¹⁵⁻¹⁸[To attach the chestpiece to the ephod], a gold ring was placed at the top of each shoulder strap of the ephod, and from these gold rings, two strands of twined gold attached to gold clasps on the top corners of the chestpiece. ¹⁹Two gold rings were also set at the lower edge of the chestpiece, on the under side, next to the ephod. ²⁰Two other gold rings were placed low on the shoulder straps of the ephod, close to where the ephod joined its beautifully woven sash. ²¹The chestpiece was held securely above the beautifully woven sash of the ephod by tying the rings of the chestpiece to the rings of the ephod with a blue ribbon.

All this was commanded to Moses by the Lord.

²²The main part of the ephod was woven, all of blue, ²³and there was a hole at the center, just as in a coat of mail, for the head to go through, reinforced around the edge so that it would not tear. ²⁴Pomegranates were attached to the bottom edge of the robe; these were made of linen cloth, embroidered with blue, purple, and scarlet. ²⁵,²⁶Bells of pure gold were placed between the pomegranates along the bottom edge of the skirt, with bells and pomegranates alternating all around the edge. This robe was worn when Aaron ministered to the Lord, just as the Lord had commanded Moses.

²⁷Robes were now made for Aaron and his sons from fine-twined linen thread. ²⁸,²⁹The chestpiece, the beautiful turbans, and the caps and the underclothes were all made of this linen, and the linen belt was beautifully embroidered with blue, purple, and scarlet threads, just as Jehovah had commanded Moses. ³⁰Finally, they made the holy plate of pure gold to wear on the front of the turban, engraved with the words, "Consecrated to Jehovah." ³¹It was tied to the turban with a blue cord, just as the Lord had instructed.

³²And so at last the Tabernacle was finished, following all of the Lord's instructions to Moses.

³³⁻⁴⁰Then they brought the entire Tabernacle to Moses:

Furniture; clasps; frames; bars;
Posts; bases; layers of covering for the roof and sides—the rams' skins dyed red, the specially tanned goatskins, and the entrance drape; the Ark with the Ten Commandments in it;
The carrying poles;
The place of mercy;
The table and all its utensils;
The Bread of the Presence;
The pure [gold] lampstand with its lamps, utensils, and oil;
The gold altar;
The anointing oil;
The sweet incense;
The curtain-door of the Tabernacle;
The bronze altar;
The bronze grating;
The poles and the utensils;
The washbasin and its base;
The drapes for the walls of the court and the posts holding them up;

The bases and the drapes at the gate of the court;
The cords and nails;
All the utensils used there in the work of the Tabernacle.

⁴¹They also brought for his inspection the beautifully tailored garments to be worn while ministering in the Holy Place and the holy garments for Aaron the priest, and those for his sons, to be worn when on duty. ⁴²So the people of Israel followed all the Lord's instructions to Moses. ⁴³And Moses inspected all their work and blessed them because it was all as the Lord had instructed him.

40   The Tabernacle Is Built

The Lord now said to Moses, ²"Put together the Tabernacle on the first day of the first month. ³In it place the Ark containing the Ten Commandments; and install the veil to enclose the Ark within the Holy of Holies. ⁴Then bring in the table and place the utensils on it, and bring in the lampstand and light the lamps.

⁵"Place the gold altar for the incense in front of the Ark. Set up the drapes at the entrance of the Tabernacle, ⁶and place the altar for burnt offerings in front of the entrance. ⁷Set the washbasin between the Tabernacle-tent and the altar, and fill it with water. ⁸Then make the courtyard around the outside of the tent, and hang the curtain-door at the entrance to the courtyard.

⁹"Take the anointing oil and sprinkle it here and there upon the Tabernacle and everything in it, upon all of its utensils and parts, and all the furniture, to hallow it; and it shall become holy. ¹⁰Sprinkle the anointing oil upon the altar of burnt offering and its utensils, sanctifying it; for the altar shall then become most holy. ¹¹Then anoint the washbasin and its pedestal, sanctifying it.

¹²"Now bring Aaron and his sons to the entrance of the Tabernacle and wash them with water; ¹³and clothe Aaron with the holy garments and anoint him, sanctifying him to minister to me as a priest. ¹⁴Then bring his sons and put their robes upon them, ¹⁵and anoint them as you did their father, that they may minister to me as priests; their anointing shall be permanent from generation to generation: all their children and children's children shall forever be my priests."

¹⁶So Moses proceeded to do all as the Lord had commanded him. ¹⁷On the first day of the first month, in the second year, the Tabernacle was put together. ¹⁸Moses erected it by setting its frames into their bases and attaching the bars. ¹⁹Then he spread the coverings over the framework and put on the top layers, just as the Lord had commanded him.

²⁰Inside the Ark he placed the stones with the Ten Commandments engraved on them, and attached the carrying poles to the Ark and installed the gold lid, the place of mercy. ²¹Then he brought the Ark into the Tabernacle and set up the curtain to screen it, just as the Lord had commanded.

²²Next he placed the table at the north side of the room outside the curtain ²³and set the Bread of the Presence upon the table before the Lord, just as the Lord had commanded.

²⁴And he placed the lampstand next to the table, on the south side of the Tabernacle. ²⁵Then he lighted the lamps before the Lord, following all the instructions, ²⁶and placed the gold altar in the Tabernacle next to the curtain, ²⁷and burned upon it the incense made from sweet spices, just as the Lord had commanded.

²⁸He attached the curtain at the entrance of the Tabernacle, ²⁹and placed the outside altar for the burnt offerings near the entrance, and offered upon it a burnt offering and a meal offering, just as the Lord had commanded him.

³⁰Next he placed the washbasin between the tent and the altar and filled it with water so that the priests could use it for washing. ³¹Moses and Aaron and Aaron's sons washed their hands and feet there. ³²Whenever they walked past the altar to enter the Tabernacle, they stopped and washed, just as the Lord had commanded Moses.

³³Then he erected the enclosure surrounding the tent and the altar, and set up the curtain-door at the entrance of the enclosure. So at last Moses finished the work.

³⁴Then the cloud covered the Tabernacle and the glory of the Lord filled it. ³⁵Moses was not able to enter because the cloud was standing there, and the glory of the Lord filled the Tabernacle. ³⁶Whenever the cloud lifted and moved, the people of Israel journeyed onward, following it. ³⁷But if the cloud stayed, they stayed until it moved. ³⁸The cloud rested upon the Tabernacle during the daytime, and at night there was fire in the cloud so that all the people of Israel could see it.

This continued throughout all their journeys.

Leviticus

EVERYWHERE WE go we find rules and laws. Leviticus is full of rules. But these rules have a special purpose: to help us know that God is holy, and to help us to be holy, too. Leviticus also promises great results for obeying God: peace, safety, provision, freedom, and best of all, a growing relationship with God.

It might seem that God is getting nit-picky with all the details in Leviticus. But that is his way of showing that he is concerned about the details of our lives. He cares about the smallest things that we care about.

The rules in Leviticus were given to Moses by God when the Israelites were in the desert at Mount Sinai. Look for the variety of rules God gave—rules about offerings, food, parenting, health, forgiveness, relationships, and celebrations.

As you read these rules, look for how often God reminds us that he is God. He is holy, and there is no other god. Through obeying God, we become holy—like him. This is our motive for obeying all the rules in the Bible.

How to Give a Burnt Offering

1 The Lord now spoke to Moses from the Tabernacle, 2,3and commanded him to give the following instructions to the people of Israel: "When you sacrifice to the Lord, use animals from your herds and flocks.

"If your sacrifice is to be an ox given as a burnt offering, use only a bull with no physical defects. Bring the animal to the entrance of the Tabernacle where the priests will accept your gift for the Lord. 4The person bringing it is to lay his hand upon its head, and it then becomes his substitute: the death of the animal will be accepted by God instead of the death of the man who brings it, as the penalty for his sins. 5The man shall then kill the animal there before the Lord, and Aaron's sons, the priests, will present the blood before the Lord, sprinkling it upon all sides of the altar at the entrance of the Tabernacle. 6,7Then the priests will skin the animal and quarter it, and build a wood fire upon the altar, 8and put the sections of the animal and its head and fat upon the wood.

⁹The internal organs and the legs are to be washed, then the priests will burn them upon the altar, and they will be an acceptable burnt offering with which the Lord is pleased.

¹⁰"If the animal used as a burnt offering is a sheep or a goat, it too must be a male, and without any blemishes. ¹¹The man who brings it will kill it before the Lord on the north side of the altar, and Aaron's sons, the priests, will sprinkle its blood back and forth upon the altar. ¹²Then the man will quarter it, and the priests will lay the pieces, with the head and the fat, on top of the wood on the altar. ¹³But the internal organs and the legs shall first be washed with water. Then the priests shall burn it all upon the altar as an offering to the Lord; for burnt offerings give much pleasure to the Lord.

¹⁴"If anyone wishes to use a bird as his burnt offering, he may choose either turtledoves or young pigeons. ¹⁵⁻¹⁷A priest will take the bird to the altar and wring off its head, and the blood shall be drained out at the side of the altar. Then the priest will remove the crop and the feathers and throw them on the east side of the altar with the ashes. Then, grasping it by the wings, he shall tear it apart, but not completely. And the priest shall burn it upon the altar, and the Lord will have pleasure in this sacrifice.

2 How to Give a Grain Offering

"Anyone who wishes to sacrifice a grain offering to the Lord is to bring fine flour and is to pour olive oil and incense upon it. ²Then he is to take a handful, representing the entire amount, to one of the priests to burn, and the Lord will be fully pleased. ³The remainder of the flour is to be given to Aaron and his sons as their food; but all of it is counted as a holy burnt offering to the Lord.

⁴"If bread baked in the oven is brought as an offering to the Lord, it must be made from finely ground flour, baked with olive oil but without yeast. Wafers made without yeast and spread with olive oil may also be used as an offering. ⁵If the offering is something from the griddle, it shall be made of finely ground flour without yeast, and mingled with olive oil. ⁶Break it into pieces and pour oil upon it—it is a form of grain offering. ⁷If your offering is cooked in a pan, it too shall be made of fine flour mixed with olive oil.

⁸"However it is prepared—whether baked, fried, or grilled—you are to bring this grain offering to the priest and he shall take it to the altar to present it to the Lord.

⁹"The priests are to burn only a representative portion of the offering, but all of it will be fully appreciated by the Lord. ¹⁰The remainder belongs to the priests for their own use, but it is all counted as a holy burnt offering to the Lord.

¹¹"Use no yeast with your offerings of flour; for no yeast or honey is permitted in burnt offerings to the Lord. ¹²You may offer yeast bread and honey as thanksgiving offerings at harvest time, but not as burnt offerings.

¹³"Every offering must be seasoned with salt, because the salt is a reminder of God's covenant.

¹⁴"If you are offering from the first of your harvest, remove the kernels from a fresh ear, crush and roast them, then offer them to the Lord. ¹⁵Put olive oil and incense on the offering, for it is a grain offering. ¹⁶Then the priests shall burn part of the bruised grain mixed with oil and all of the incense as a representative portion before the Lord.

3 How to Give a Peace Offering

"When anyone wants to give an offering of thanksgiving to the Lord, he may use either a bull or a cow, but the animal must be entirely without defect if it is to be offered to the Lord! ²The man who brings the animal shall lay his hand upon its head and kill it at the door of the Tabernacle. Then Aaron's sons shall throw the blood against the sides of the altar ³⁻⁵and shall burn before the Lord the fat that covers the inward parts, the two kidneys and the loin-fat on them, and the gall bladder. And it will give the Lord much pleasure.

⁶"If a goat or sheep is used as a thank-offering to the Lord, it must have no defect and may be either a male or female.

⁷,⁸"If it is a lamb, the man who brings it shall lay his hand upon its head and kill it at the entrance of the Tabernacle; the priests shall throw the blood against the sides of the altar, ⁹⁻¹¹and shall offer upon the altar the fat, the tail removed close to the backbone, the fat covering the internal organs, the two kidneys with the loin-fat on them, and the gall bladder, as a burnt offering to the Lord.

¹²"If anyone brings a goat as his offering to the Lord, ¹³he shall lay his hand upon its head and kill it at the entrance of the Tabernacle. The priest shall throw its blood against the sides of the altar, ¹⁴and shall offer upon the altar, as a burnt offering to the Lord, the fat that covers the insides, ¹⁵,¹⁶the two kidneys and the loin-fat on them, and the gall bladder. This burnt offering is very pleasing to the Lord. All the fat is Jehovah's. ¹⁷This is a permanent law throughout your land, that you shall eat neither fat nor blood."

4 How to Give a Sin Offering

Then the Lord gave these further instructions to Moses:

FAMILY DEVOTIONS

☐ **DEVOTION 42**
PUTTING GOD FIRST

Read Leviticus 1:1-4

Carol sighed as she looked at her memory verse. "Grandma, in Bible times people had to sacrifice an animal as payment for sins, didn't they?" she asked. "Didn't the sacrifice have to be killed and placed on an altar?"

Grandma nodded as she looked up from her knitting. "That's right," she agreed, "but when Jesus died for our sins, he became the perfect sacrifice, and animal sacrifices were no longer needed."

"Then what does this verse mean?" asked Carol. "It says we're to give our bodies to God as 'a living sacrifice.' It's so confusing. How can I be a living sacrifice when a sacrifice is something that's killed? I can't do much if I'm dead."

"To be a living sacrifice means to give your all—your whole life—to God so he can use it," replied Grandma, reaching down for a piece of yarn. "Pretend this yarn is my life," she continued. "It's my love, my family, my time, my actions. Here, I give it to you." She handed one end of the yarn to Carol while she held the other end. "There—it's all yours now, right? I'm sacrificing it to you."

"Well, if it's all mine, why are you still holding on to it?" Carol asked with a giggle.

"Good point," approved Grandma. "You see, sometimes people say they give everything to God's control—that they've made their lives a living sacrifice to serve him. But they leave a string attached to an area like music, friends, recreation, or something else. Then . . ." Grandma slid the string out of Carol's grasp, ". . . they pull it back out of God's hands. That's not a sacrifice. When an Israelite took a sacrifice to the priest, he left it there."

"So a living sacrifice means giving your whole life to God and leaving it there, without any strings to pull it back," said Carol.

"That's right," agreed Grandma. "Once a sacrifice is given, there's no taking it back."

Putting God First
Memory Verse

In everything you do, put God first, and he will direct you and crown your efforts with success.
Proverbs 3:6

How About You?
Have you given God control of every part of your life? Does your choice of friends please him? Do your school activities and study habits please the Lord? Would he approve of the music you listen to? Sacrifice every area of your life to God—no strings attached. Be willing to do whatever he wants you to do. *J. B.*

• For the next devotional, turn to page 117. • For the next devotional on *PUTTING GOD FIRST*, turn to page 211.
• For notes on *PUTTING GOD FIRST*, see pages 397, 492, 644, 791, and 982.

² "Tell the people of Israel that these are the laws concerning anyone who unintentionally breaks any of my commandments. ³If a priest sins unintentionally and so brings guilt upon the people, he must offer a young bull without defect as a sin offering to the Lord. ⁴He shall bring it to the door of the Tabernacle, and shall lay his hand upon its head and kill it there before Jehovah. ⁵Then the priest shall take the animal's blood into the Tabernacle, ⁶and shall dip his finger in the blood and sprinkle it seven times before the Lord in front of the veil that bars the way to the Holy of Holies. ⁷Then the priest shall put some of the blood upon the horns of the incense altar before the Lord in the Tabernacle; the remainder of the blood shall be poured out at the base of the altar for burnt offerings, at the entrance to the Tabernacle. ⁸Then he shall take all the fat on the entrails, ⁹the two kidneys and the loin-fat on them, and the gall bladder, ¹⁰and shall burn them on the altar of burnt offering, just as in the case of a bull or cow sacrificed as a thank-offering. ¹¹,¹²But the remainder of the young bull—the skin, meat, head, legs, internal organs, and intestines—shall be carried to a ceremonially clean place outside the camp—a place where the ashes are brought from the altar—and burned there on a wood fire.

¹³"If the entire nation of Israel sins without realizing it and does something that Jehovah has said not to do, all the people are guilty. ¹⁴When they realize it, they shall offer a young bull for a sin offering, bringing it to the Tabernacle ¹⁵where the leaders of the nation shall lay their hands upon the animal's head and kill it before the Lord. ¹⁶Then the priest shall bring its blood into the Tabernacle, ¹⁷and shall dip his finger in the blood and sprinkle it seven times before the Lord, in front of the veil. ¹⁸Then he shall put blood upon the horns of the altar there in the Tabernacle before the Lord, and all the remainder of the blood shall be poured out at the base of the burnt offering altar, at the entrance to the Tabernacle. ¹⁹All the fat shall be removed and burned upon the altar. ²⁰He shall follow the same procedure as for a sin offering; in this way the priest shall make atonement for the nation, and everyone will be forgiven. ²¹The priest shall then cart the young bull outside the camp and burn it there, just as though it were a sin offering for an individual, only this time it is a sin offering for the entire nation.

²²"If one of the leaders sins without realizing it and is guilty of disobeying one of God's laws, ²³as soon as it is called to his attention he must bring as his sacrifice a male goat without any physical defect. ²⁴He shall lay his hand upon its head and kill it at the place where the burnt offerings are killed, and present it to the Lord. This is his sin offering. ²⁵Then the priest shall take some of the blood of this sin offering and place it with his finger upon the horns of the altar of burnt offerings, and the rest of the blood shall be poured out at the base of the altar. ²⁶All the fat shall be burned upon the altar, just as if it were the fat of the sacrifice of a thank-offering; thus the priest shall make atonement for the leader concerning his sin, and he shall be forgiven.

²⁷"If any one of the common people sins and doesn't realize it, he is guilty. ²⁸But as soon as he does realize it, he is to bring as his sacrifice a female goat without defect to atone for his sin. ²⁹He shall bring it to the place where the animals for burnt offerings are killed, and there lay his hand upon the head of the sin offering and kill it. ³⁰And the priest shall take some of the blood with his finger and smear it upon the horns of the burnt offering altar. Then the priest shall pour out the remainder of the blood at the base of the altar. ³¹All the fat shall be taken off, just as in the procedure for the thank-offering sacrifice, and the priest shall burn it upon the altar; and the Lord will appreciate it. Thus the priest shall make atonement for that man, and he shall be forgiven.

³²"However, if he chooses to bring a lamb as his sin offering, it must be a female without physical defect. ³³He shall bring it to the place where the burnt offerings are killed, and lay his hand upon its head and kill it there as a sin offering. ³⁴The priest shall take some of the blood with his finger and smear it upon the horns of the burnt offering altar, and all the rest of the blood shall be poured out at the base of the altar. ³⁵The fat shall be used just as in the case of a thank-offering lamb—the priest shall burn the fat on the altar as in any other sacrifice made to Jehovah by fire; and the priest shall make atonement for the man, and his sin shall be forgiven.

5 What to Give If One Is Poor

"Anyone refusing to give testimony concerning what he knows about a crime is guilty.

²"Anyone touching anything ceremonially unclean—such as the dead body of an animal forbidden for food, wild or domesticated, or the dead body of some forbidden insect—is guilty, even though he wasn't aware of touching it. ³Or if he touches human discharge of any kind, he becomes guilty as soon as he realizes that he has touched it.

⁴"If anyone makes a rash vow, whether the vow is good or bad, when he realizes what a foolish vow he has taken, he is guilty.

⁵"In any of these cases, he shall confess his sin

☐ **DEVOTION 43**
CONFESSING SIN

Read Leviticus 4:13-14, 27-28

Confessing Sin
Memory Verse

Create in me a new, clean heart, O God, filled with clean thoughts and right desires.
Psalm 51:10

Karen had looked forward to spending part of her summer vacation with her favorite aunt. One afternoon, Aunt Dee announced that they were going to have company that night. "Please take out the good silver and set the table," she said to Karen.

Karen went to the closet where she knew her aunt kept the good silverware tray and took it out carefully. A look of surprise came over her face when she opened the box. "Aunt Dee," she called in concern, "it's all black and ugly looking."

Aunt Dee came into the dining room and looked at the silverware. "Oh, of course," she said. "It hasn't been used for some time. We'll have to clean it before we can use it. I'll help you."

Karen and her aunt began to polish the tarnished silverware. "If silver is such a precious metal, how come it turns black like this?" Karen asked.

"I don't know exactly why it does that," answered Aunt Dee, "but I do know that the longer it sits around in a box or drawer without being used, the more likely it is to tarnish. Fortunately, it can be polished again."

"Sort of like Christians," Karen said softly. She recalled a sermon about how Christians should be kept clean and shining, ready for the Lord to use. She mentioned the illustration to her aunt.

"That is so right," Aunt Dee agreed "When we allow sinful things to stain our lives, we can hardly expect God to use us in his service. We should be careful to keep ourselves from becoming soiled by the things of this world. And we should go daily to the Lord, confessing our sin and asking him to help us keep from becoming tarnished."

How About You?
Are you fit for the Master's use? If God wants you to do something for him, are you clean and ready for his work? Don't allow sin to come into your life and stay there. You need to confess your sin and receive God's forgiveness. Then you're ready to witness to a friend, to sing in the choir, to help in the nursery, or to be used in whatever task God has for you. R. J.

• For the next devotional, turn to page 121. • For the next devotional on CONFESSING SIN, turn to page 153.
• For notes on CONFESSING SIN, see pages 429, 479, 836, 881, and 1220.

⁶and bring his guilt offering to the Lord, a female lamb or goat, and the priest shall make atonement for him, and he shall be freed from his sin, and need not fulfill the vow.

⁷"If he is too poor to bring a lamb to the Lord, then he shall bring two turtledoves or two young pigeons as his guilt offering; one of the birds shall be his sin offering and the other his burnt offering. ⁸The priest shall offer as the sin sacrifice whichever bird is handed to him first, breaking its neck, but not severing its head from its body. ⁹Then he shall sprinkle some of the blood at the side of the altar and the rest shall be drained out at the base of the altar; this is the sin offering. ¹⁰He shall offer the second bird as a burnt offering, following the customary procedures that have been set forth; so the priest shall make atonement for him concerning his sin, and he shall be forgiven.

¹¹"If he is too poor to bring turtledoves or young pigeons as his sin offering, then he shall bring a tenth of a bushel of fine flour. He must not mix it with olive oil or put any incense on it because it is a sin offering. ¹²He shall bring it to the priest, and the priest shall take out a handful as a representative portion and burn it on the altar just as any other offering to Jehovah made by fire; this shall be his sin offering. ¹³In this way the priest shall make atonement for him for any sin of this kind, and he shall be forgiven. The rest of the flour shall belong to the priest, just as was the case with the grain offering."

¹⁴And the Lord said to Moses, ¹⁵"If anyone sins by unintentionally defiling what is holy, then he shall bring a ram without defect, worth whatever fine you charge against him, as his guilt offering to the Lord. ¹⁶And he shall make restitution for the holy thing he has defiled, or the tithe omitted, by paying for the loss, plus a 20 percent penalty; he shall bring it to the priest, and the priest shall make atonement for him with the ram of the guilt offering, and he shall be forgiven.

¹⁷,¹⁸"Anyone who disobeys some law of God without realizing it is guilty anyway, and must bring his sacrifice of a value determined by Moses. This sacrifice shall be a ram without blemish taken to the priest as a guilt offering; with it the priest shall make atonement for him, so that he will be forgiven for whatever it is he has done without realizing it. ¹⁹It must be offered as a guilt offering, for he is certainly guilty before the Lord."

6 Burnt and Grain Offerings

And the Lord said to Moses, ²"If anyone sins against me by refusing to return a deposit on something borrowed or rented, or by refusing to return something entrusted to him, or by robbery, or by oppressing his neighbor, ³or by finding a lost article and lying about it, swearing that he doesn't have it— ⁴,⁵on the day he is found guilty of any such sin, he shall restore what he took, adding a 20 percent fine, and give it to the one he has harmed; and on the same day he shall bring his guilt offering to the Tabernacle. ⁶His guilt offering shall be a ram without defect, and must be worth whatever value you demand. He shall bring it to the priest, ⁷and the priest shall make atonement for him before the Lord, and he shall be forgiven."

⁸Then the Lord said to Moses, ⁹*"Give Aaron and his sons these regulations concerning the burnt offering:*

"The burnt offering shall be left upon the hearth of the altar all night, with the altar fire kept burning. ¹⁰(The next morning) the priest shall put on his linen undergarments and his linen outer garments, and clean out the ashes of the burnt offering, and put them beside the altar. ¹¹Then he shall change his clothes and carry the ashes outside the camp to a place that is ceremonially clean. ¹²Meanwhile, the fire on the altar must be kept burning—it must not go out. The priest shall put on fresh wood each morning, and lay the daily burnt offering on it, and burn the fat of the daily peace offering. ¹³The fire must be kept burning upon the altar continually. It must never go out.

¹⁴*"These are the regulations concerning the grain offering:*

"Aaron's sons shall stand in front of the altar to offer it before the Lord. ¹⁵The priest shall then take out a handful of the finely ground flour, with the olive oil and the incense mixed into it, and burn it upon the altar as a representative portion for the Lord; and it will be received with pleasure by the Lord. ¹⁶After taking out this handful, the remainder of the flour will belong to Aaron and his sons for their food; it shall be eaten without yeast in the courtyard of the Tabernacle. ¹⁷(Stress this instruction, that if it is baked, it must be without yeast.) I have given to the priests this part of the burnt offerings made to me. However, all of it is most holy, just as is the entire sin offering and the entire guilt offering. ¹⁸It may be eaten by any male descendant of Aaron, any priest, generation after generation. But only the priests may eat these offerings made by fire to the Lord."

¹⁹,²⁰And Jehovah said to Moses, "On the day Aaron and his sons are anointed and inducted into the priesthood, they shall bring to the Lord a regular grain offering—a tenth of a bushel of fine flour, half to be offered in the morning and half in the evening. ²¹It shall be cooked on a griddle, using olive oil, and should be well cooked, then brought to the Lord as an offering that pleases him very much. ²²,²³As the sons of the priests

replace their fathers, they shall be inducted into office by offering this same sacrifice on the day of their anointing. This is a perpetual law. These offerings shall be entirely burned up before the Lord; none of it shall be eaten."

24Then the Lord said to Moses, 25*"Tell Aaron and his sons that these are the instructions concerning the sin offering:*

"This sacrifice is most holy, and shall be killed before the Lord at the place where the burnt offerings are killed. 26The priest who performs the ceremony shall eat it in the courtyard of the Tabernacle. 27Only those who are sanctified—the priests—may touch this meat; if any blood sprinkles onto their clothing, it must be washed in a holy place. 28Then the clay pot in which the clothing is boiled shall be broken; or if a bronze kettle is used, it must be scoured and rinsed out thoroughly. 29Every male among the priests may eat this offering, but only they, for it is most holy. 30No sin offering may be eaten by the priests if any of its blood is taken into the Tabernacle to make atonement in the Holy Place. That carcass must be entirely burned with fire before the Lord.

7 Guilt and Peace Offerings

"Here are the instructions concerning the most holy offering for guilt:

2"The sacrificial animal shall be killed at the place where the burnt offering sacrifices are slain, and its blood shall be sprinkled back and forth upon the altar. 3The priest will offer upon the altar all its fat, including the tail, the fat that covers the insides, 4the two kidneys and the loin-fat, and the gall bladder—all shall be set aside for sacrificing. 5The priests will burn them upon the altar as a guilt offering to the Lord. 6Only males among the priests may then eat the carcass, and it must be eaten in a holy place, for this is a most holy sacrifice.

7"The same instructions apply to both the sin offering and the guilt offering—the carcass shall be given to the priest who is in charge of the atonement ceremony, for his food. 8(When the offering is a burnt sacrifice, the priest who is in charge shall also be given the animal's hide.) 9The priests who present the people's grain offerings to the Lord shall be given whatever remains of the sacrifice after the ceremony is completed. This rule applies whether the sacrifice is baked, fried, or grilled. 10All other grain offerings, whether mixed with olive oil or dry, are the common property of all sons of Aaron.

11*"Here are the instructions concerning the sacrifices given to the Lord as special peace offerings:*

12"If it is an offering of thanksgiving, unleavened short bread shall be included with the sacrifice, along with unleavened wafers spread with olive oil and loaves from a batter of flour mixed with olive oil. 13This thanksgiving peace offering shall be accompanied with loaves of leavened bread. 14Part of this sacrifice shall be presented to the Lord by a gesture of waving it before the altar, then it shall be given to the assisting priest, the one who sprinkles the blood of the animal presented for the sacrifice. 15After the animal has been sacrificed and presented to the Lord as a peace offering to show special appreciation and thanksgiving to him, its meat is to be eaten that same day, and none left to be eaten the next day.

16"However, if someone brings a sacrifice that is not for thanksgiving, but is because of a vow or is simply a voluntary offering to the Lord, any portion of the sacrifice that is not eaten the day it is sacrificed may be eaten the next day. 17,18But anything left over until the third day shall be burned. For if any of it is eaten on the third day, the Lord will not accept it; it will have no value as a sacrifice, and there will be no credit to the one who brought it to be offered; and the priest who eats it shall be guilty, for it is detestable to the Lord, and the person who eats it must answer for his sin.

19"Any meat that comes into contact with anything that is ceremonially unclean shall not be eaten, but burned; and as for the meat that may be eaten, it may be eaten only by a person who is ceremonially clean. 20Any priest who is ceremonially unclean but eats the thanksgiving offering anyway, shall be cut off from his people, for he has defiled what is sacred. 21Anyone who touches anything that is ceremonially unclean, whether it is uncleanness from man or beast, and then eats the peace offering, shall be cut off from his people, for he has defiled what is holy."

22Then the Lord said to Moses, 23"Tell the people of Israel never to eat fat, whether from oxen, sheep, or goats. 24The fat of an animal that dies of disease, or is attacked and killed by wild animals, may be used for other purposes, but never eaten. 25Anyone who eats fat from an offering sacrificed by fire to the Lord shall be outlawed from his people.

26,27"Never eat blood, whether of birds or animals. Anyone who does shall be excommunicated from his people."

28And the Lord said to Moses, 29"Tell the people of Israel that anyone bringing a thanksgiving offering to the Lord must bring it personally with his own hands. 30He shall bring the offering of the fat and breast, which is to be presented to the Lord by waving it before the altar. 31Then the priest shall burn the fat upon the altar, but the breast shall belong to Aaron and his sons, 32,33while the right thigh shall be given to the officiating priest. 34For I have designated the breast and thigh as donations from the people of Israel to the sons of Aaron. Aaron and his sons must always be given this portion of the sacrifice. ³⁵This is their pay! It is to be set apart from the burnt offerings, and given to all who have been appointed to minister to the Lord as priests—to Aaron and to his sons. ³⁶For on the day the Lord anointed them, he commanded that the people of Israel give these portions to them; it is their right forever throughout all their generations."

³⁷These were the instructions concerning the burnt offering, grain offering, sin offering, and guilt offering, and concerning the consecration offering and the peace offering; ³⁸these instructions were given to Moses by the Lord on Mount Sinai, to be passed on to the people of Israel so that they would know how to offer their sacrifices to God in the Sinai desert.

8 Aaron and His Sons

The Lord said to Moses, "Now bring Aaron and his sons to the entrance of the Tabernacle, together with their garments, the anointing oil, the young bull for the sin offering, the two rams, and the basket of bread made without yeast; and summon all Israel to a meeting there."

⁴So all the people assembled, ⁵and Moses said to them, "What I am now going to do has been commanded by Jehovah."

⁶Then he took Aaron and his sons and washed them with water, ⁷and he clothed Aaron with the special coat, sash, robe, and the ephod-jacket with its beautifully woven belt. ⁸Then he put on him the chestpiece and deposited the Urim and the Thummim inside its pouch; ⁹and placed on Aaron's head the turban with the sacred gold plate at its front—the holy crown—as the Lord had commanded Moses.

¹⁰Then Moses took the anointing oil and sprinkled it upon the Tabernacle itself and on each item in it, sanctifying them. ¹¹When he came to the altar he sprinkled it seven times, and also sprinkled the utensils of the altar and the washbasin and its pedestal, to sanctify them. ¹²Then he poured the anointing oil upon Aaron's head, thus setting him apart for his work. ¹³Next Moses placed the robes on Aaron's sons, with the belts and caps, as the Lord had commanded him.

¹⁴Then he took the young bull for the sin offering, and Aaron and his sons laid their hands upon its head ¹⁵,¹⁶as Moses killed it. He smeared some of the blood with his finger upon the four horns of the altar and upon the altar itself, to sanctify it, and poured out the rest of the blood at the base of the altar; thus he sanctified the altar, making atonement for it. He took all the fat covering the entrails, the fatty mass above the liver, and the two kidneys and their fat, and burned them all on the altar. ¹⁷The carcass of the young bull, with its hide and dung, was burned outside the camp, as the Lord had commanded Moses.

¹⁸Then he presented to the Lord the ram for the burnt offering. Aaron and his sons laid their hands upon its head, ¹⁹and Moses killed it and sprinkled the blood back and forth upon the altar. ²⁰Next he quartered the ram and burned the pieces, the head and the fat. ²¹He then washed the insides and the legs with water, and burned them upon the altar, so that the entire ram was consumed before the Lord; it was a burnt offering that pleased the Lord very much, for Jehovah's directions to Moses were followed in every detail.

²²Then Moses presented the other ram, the ram of consecration; Aaron and his sons laid their hands upon its head. ²³Moses killed it and took some of its blood and smeared it upon the lobe of Aaron's right ear and the thumb of his right hand and upon the big toe of his right foot. ²⁴Next he smeared some of the blood upon Aaron's sons—upon the lobes of their right ears, upon their right thumbs, and upon the big toes of their right feet. The rest of the blood he sprinkled back and forth upon the altar.

²⁵Then he took the fat, the tail, the fat upon the inner organs, the gall bladder, the two kidneys with their fat, and the right shoulder, ²⁶and placed on top of these one unleavened wafer, one wafer spread with olive oil, and a slice of bread, all taken from the basket that had been placed there before the Lord. ²⁷All this was placed in the hands of Aaron and his sons to present to the Lord by a gesture of waving them before the altar. ²⁸Moses then took it all back from them and burned it upon the altar, along with the burnt offering to the Lord; and Jehovah was pleased by the offering. ²⁹Now Moses took the breast and presented it to the Lord by waving it before the altar; this was Moses' portion of the ram of consecration, just as the Lord had instructed him.

³⁰Next he took some of the anointing oil and some of the blood that had been sprinkled upon the altar, and sprinkled it upon Aaron and upon his clothes and upon his sons and upon their clothes, thus consecrating to the Lord's use Aaron and his sons and their clothes.

³¹Then Moses said to Aaron and his sons, "Boil the meat at the entrance of the Tabernacle, and eat it along with the bread that is in the basket of consecration, just as I instructed you to do. ³²Anything left of the meat and bread must be burned."

³³Next he told them not to leave the Tabernacle entrance for seven days, after which time their consecration would be completed—for it takes seven days. ³⁴Then Moses stated again that all he had done that day had been commanded by the

Family Devotions

☐ DEVOTION 44

CULTIVATING GODLY ATTITUDES

Read Leviticus 7:11-15, 28-29

Cultivating Godly Attitudes
Memory Verse

Your attitude should be the kind that was shown us by Jesus Christ.
Philippians 2:5

Josh frowned when his little brother asked to take some eggs to school for show-and-tell. "You mean the blue eggs from my Araucana hens?" Josh asked. "I'm selling those eggs to earn money for wilderness camp. But I guess you can take a couple."

"Oh, goody!" exclaimed Nathan. "I've told all the kids about your blue eggs, but they don't believe me. Now I can show them!"

After school, Josh got a call from his friend Paul. "Going to the football game tonight?" Paul wanted to know.

"No, we're having a special meeting at our church, and I'm going there. Want to come?"

"No way! Not me! I can't see that church really makes any difference anyway," said Paul.

That night, the pastor mentioned the spring dinner in two weeks when they would be collecting food and money for the needy. "We all have something we can give," said Pastor Allen. "Even boys and girls do. Think about it."

Josh did think about it. He was thankful, but he had nothing to give. Suddenly he remembered his eggs! Oh, no! He couldn't give them up! That was his camp money!

The night of the dinner, Josh thought about the fun he'd have at camp, but he also thought about the many people out of work and facing hard times. He saw all the gifts others had brought, and he had nothing. Suddenly he knew what to do. He would give his egg money to help the needy. Wilderness camp could wait for another year.

Later, Josh told Paul about it. "Why did you do a crazy thing like that?" Paul asked.

"Well, it's kind of like my little brother's show-and-tell," Josh explained. "I always *tell* God I'm thankful, but I decided it was time I *showed* him that I meant it. So to show thanks for all I have, I gave money to help those who have less than I do."

Paul was quiet. Finally he said, "I never thought believing in God made much difference. You've told me before, but now you've showed me, too. Guess maybe I'll go to church with you sometime."

How About You?
Do you just tell God you're thankful, or do you also show thanks? By obeying his Word, doing things with a right attitude, and helping others, you show your thanks to God—and you tell the world he's great! *J. H.*

• For the next devotional, turn to page 123. • For the next devotional on CULTIVATING GODLY ATTITUDES, turn to page 125. • For notes on CULTIVATING GODLY ATTITUDES, see pages 337, 383, 472, 622, and 1216.

Lord in order to make atonement for them. ³⁵And again he warned Aaron and his sons to stay at the entrance of the Tabernacle day and night for seven days. "If you leave," he told them, "you will die—this is what the Lord has said."

³⁶So Aaron and his sons did all that the Lord had commanded Moses.

9 The Priests Begin Their Work

On the eighth day (of the consecration ceremonies), Moses summoned Aaron and Aaron's sons and the elders of Israel, ²and told Aaron to take a bull calf from the herd for a sin offering, and a ram without bodily defect for a burnt offering, and to offer them before the Lord.

³"And tell the people of Israel," Moses instructed, "to select a male goat for their sin offering, also a yearling calf and a yearling lamb, all without bodily defect, for their burnt offering. ⁴In addition, the people are to bring to the Lord a peace offering sacrifice—an ox and a ram, and a grain offering—flour mingled with olive oil. For today," Moses said, "Jehovah will appear to them."

⁵So they brought all these things to the entrance of the Tabernacle, as Moses had commanded, and the people came and stood there before the Lord.

⁶Moses told them, "When you have followed the Lord's instructions, his glory will appear to you."

⁷Moses then told Aaron to proceed to the altar and to offer the sin offering and the burnt offering, making atonement for himself first, and then for the people, as the Lord had commanded. ⁸So Aaron went up to the altar and killed the calf as a sacrifice for his own sin; ⁹his sons caught the blood for him, and he dipped his finger in it and smeared it upon the horns of the altar, and poured out the rest at the base of the altar. ¹⁰Then he burned upon the altar the fat, kidneys, and gall bladder from this sin offering, as the Lord had commanded Moses, ¹¹but he burned the meat and hide outside the camp.

¹²Next he killed the burnt offering animal, and his sons caught the blood, and he sprinkled it back and forth upon the altar; ¹³they brought the animal to him piece by piece, including the head, and he burned each part upon the altar. ¹⁴Then he washed the insides and the legs, and offered these also upon the altar as a burnt offering.

¹⁵Next he sacrificed the people's offering; he killed the goat and offered it in just the same way as he had the sin offering for himself. ¹⁶Thus he sacrificed their burnt offering to the Lord, in accordance with the instructions God had given.

¹⁷Then he presented the grain offering, taking a handful and burning it upon the altar in addition to the regular morning offering.

¹⁸Next he killed the ox and ram—the people's peace offering sacrifice; and Aaron's sons brought the blood to him, and he sprinkled it back and forth upon the altar. ¹⁹Then he collected the fat of the ox and the ram—the fat from their tails and the fat covering the inner organs—and the kidneys and gall bladders. ²⁰The fat was placed upon the breasts of these animals, and Aaron burned it upon the altar; ²¹but he waved the breasts and right shoulders slowly before the Lord as a gesture of offering it to him, just as Moses had commanded.

²²Then, with hands spread out toward the people, Aaron blessed them and came down from the altar. ²³Moses and Aaron went into the Tabernacle, and when they came out again they blessed the people; and the glory of the Lord appeared to the whole assembly. ²⁴Then fire came from the Lord and consumed the burnt offering and fat on the altar; and when the people saw it, they all shouted and fell flat upon the ground before the Lord.

10 Two Priests Are Killed by Fire

But Nadab and Abihu, the sons of Aaron, placed unholy fire in their censers, laid incense on the fire, and offered the incense before the Lord—contrary to what the Lord had just commanded them! ²So fire blazed forth from the presence of the Lord and destroyed them.

³Then Moses said to Aaron, "This is what the Lord meant when he said, 'I will show myself holy among those who approach me, and I will be glorified before all the people.'" And Aaron was speechless.

⁴Then Moses called for Mishael and Elzaphon, Aaron's cousins, the sons of Uzziel, and told them, "Go and get the charred bodies from before the Tabernacle, and carry them outside the camp."

⁵So they went over and got them, and carried them out in their coats as Moses had told them to.

⁶Then Moses said to Aaron and his sons Eleazar and Ithamar, "Do not mourn—do not let your hair hang loose as a sign of your mourning, and do not tear your clothes. If you do, God will strike you dead too, and his wrath will come upon all the people of Israel. But the rest of the people of Israel may lament the death of Nadab and Abihu, and mourn because of the terrible fire the Lord has sent. ⁷But you are not to leave the Tabernacle under penalty of death, for the anointing oil of Jehovah is upon you." And they did as Moses commanded.

⁸,⁹Now the Lord instructed Aaron, "Never drink wine or strong drink when you go into the Tabernacle, lest you die; and this rule applies to your sons and to all your descendants from generation to generation. ¹⁰ Your duties will be to arbitrate for the people, to teach them the difference between what is holy and what is ordinary, what is

FAMILY DEVOTIONS

☐ DEVOTION 45

RESPECTING GOD'S WORD

Read Leviticus 10:8-11

Every Sunday morning Keith grumbled about going to church. He complained about his clothes, about having to get up early, and about anything else he could think of. "Why can't we stay home once in a while?" he whined. "Why do we always have to go to church and Sunday school?"

Dad rumpled Keith's hair as he walked by. "It's good for you," he said, "and it pleases the Lord."

That afternoon Keith and his dad decided to take a bike ride. "My tires are a little soft," said Keith as they started out. "I meant to pump them up at the gas station yesterday, but I forgot. I think they'll be fine though."

"We could pump them up before we go," suggested Dad.

"I don't feel like bothering," replied Keith. "They'll be fine. Let's go."

Before long, Keith began to get tired. "Whew, it's hard to peddle with soft tires," he exclaimed. He was glad when they finally reached home. He ran and got the tire pump. After the tires were filled, Keith tried the bike again. "It pedals easy as pie now," he said.

Dad nodded. "That's good. But now it's time to put your bike away and get ready for church."

"Aw, Dad," whined Keith, "seems like we just got back from church. I was thinking of taking another spin on my bike."

"I was thinking, too," said Dad. "Just as it's hard work to ride a bike with soft tires, it's hard work to live for God without the things we learn in church and Sunday school. It's hard work to live without the encouragement we get from other Christians. We need to get 'pumped up' regularly with God's Word and with Christian fellowship. It pays to take time to do that."

Respecting God's Word Memory Verse

Your words are what sustain me; they are food to my hungry soul. They bring joy to my sorrowing heart and delight me. How proud I am to bear your name, O Lord.
Jeremiah 15:16

How About You?
Do you sometimes complain about having to go to church or Sunday school? Having family devotions? God's Word can teach you how to live as God wants you to, and you need to take time to learn about it. *C. Y.*

• For the next devotional, turn to page 125. • For the next devotional on RESPECTING GOD'S WORD, turn to page 597. • For notes on RESPECTING GOD'S WORD, see pages 208, 369, 1188, and 1248.

pure and what is impure; ¹¹and to teach them all the laws Jehovah has given through Moses."

¹²Then Moses said to Aaron and to his sons who were left, Eleazar and Ithamar, "Take the grain offering—the food that remains after the handful has been offered to the Lord by burning it on the altar—make sure there is no leaven in it, and eat it beside the altar. The offering is most holy; ¹³therefore, you must eat it in the sanctuary, in a holy place. It belongs to you and to your sons, from the offerings to Jehovah made by fire; for so I am commanded. ¹⁴But the breast and the thigh, which have been offered to the Lord by the gesture of waving it before him, may be eaten in any holy place. It belongs to you and to your sons and daughters for your food. It is your portion of the peace offering sacrifices of the people of Israel.

¹⁵The people are to bring the thigh that was set aside, along with the breast that was offered when the fat was burned, and they shall be presented before the Lord by the gesture of waving them. And afterwards they shall belong to you and your family, for the Lord has commanded this."

¹⁶Then Moses searched everywhere for the goat of the sin offering and discovered that it had been burned! He was very angry about this with Eleazar and Ithamar, the remaining sons of Aaron.

¹⁷"Why haven't you eaten the sin offering in the sanctuary, since it is most holy, and God has given it to you to take away the iniquity and guilt of the people, to make atonement for them before the Lord?" he demanded. ¹⁸"Since its blood was not taken inside the sanctuary, you should certainly have eaten it there, as I ordered you."

¹⁹But Aaron interceded with Moses. "They offered their sin offering and burnt offering before the Lord," he said, "but if I had eaten the sin offering on such a day as this, would it have pleased the Lord?" ²⁰And when Moses heard that, he was satisfied.

Clean and Unclean Animals

Then the Lord said to Moses and Aaron, ²,³"Tell the people of Israel that the animals which may be used for food include any animal with cloven hooves which chews its cud. ⁴⁻⁷This means that the following may *not* be eaten:

The camel (it chews the cud but does not have cloven hooves);
The coney, or rock badger (because although it chews the cud, it does not have cloven hooves);
The hare (because although it chews the cud, it does not have cloven hooves);
The swine (because although it has cloven hooves, it does not chew the cud).

⁸You may not eat their meat or even touch their dead bodies; they are forbidden foods for you.

⁹"As to fish, you may eat whatever has fins and scales, whether taken from rivers or from the sea; ¹⁰but all other water creatures are strictly forbidden to you. ¹¹You mustn't eat their meat or even touch their dead bodies. ¹²I'll repeat it again—any water creature that does not have fins or scales is forbidden to you.

¹³⁻¹⁹"Among the birds, these are the ones you may *not* eat: the eagle, the metire, the osprey, the falcon (all kinds), the kite, the raven (all kinds), the ostrich, the nighthawk, the seagull, the hawk (all kinds), the owl, the cormorant, the ibis, the marsh hen, the pelican, the vulture, the stork, the heron (all kinds), the hoopoe, the bat.

²⁰"No insects may be eaten, ²¹,²²with the exception of those that jump; locusts of all varieties—ordinary locusts, bald locusts, crickets, and grasshoppers—may be eaten. ²³All insects that fly and walk or crawl are forbidden to you.

²⁴"Anyone touching their dead bodies shall be defiled until the evening ²⁵and must wash his clothes immediately. He must also quarantine himself until nightfall, as being ceremonially defiled.

²⁶"You are also defiled by touching any animal with only semiparted hoofs, or any animal that does not chew the cud. ²⁷Any animal that walks on paws is forbidden to you as food. Anyone touching the dead body of such an animal shall be defiled until evening. ²⁸Anyone carrying away the carcass shall wash his clothes and be ceremonially defiled until evening; for it is forbidden to you.

²⁹,³⁰"These are the forbidden small animals which scurry about your feet or crawl upon the ground: the mole, the rat, the great lizard, the gecko, the mouse, the lizard, the snail, the chameleon.

³¹Anyone touching their dead bodies shall be defiled until evening, ³²and anything upon which the carcass falls shall be defiled—any article of wood, or of clothing, a rug, or a sack; anything it touches must be put into water and is defiled until evening. After that it may be used again. ³³If it falls into a pottery bowl, anything in the bowl is defiled, and you shall smash the bowl. ³⁴If the water used to cleanse the defiled article touches any food, all of it is defiled. Any drink which is in the defiled bowl is also contaminated.

³⁵"If the dead body of such an animal touches any clay oven, it is defiled and must be smashed. ³⁶If the body falls into a spring or cistern where there is water, that water is not defiled; yet anyone who pulls out the carcass is defiled. ³⁷And if the carcass touches grain to be sown in the field, it is not contaminated; ³⁸but if the seeds are wet and the carcass falls upon it, the seed is defiled.

FAMILY DEVOTIONS

☐ **DEVOTION 46**
CULTIVATING GODLY ATTITUDES

Read Leviticus 11:44-45

"Mom, look at this old mirror!" Carrie exclaimed, her voice echoing off the attic ceiling. She giggled at her short, squat reflection. "It makes me look so funny."

Mom came up behind her and looked. "That's very old," she said with a laugh. "It was your great-grandmother's."

"Can we take it down to show everybody?" asked Carrie.

"Sure," agreed Mom, "they'd like to see it, too. But first let's take the things for the garage sale downstairs."

That evening, the Stevens family laughed together over their reflections in the antique mirror. "It's fun to look in that old mirror, but I sure am glad we have better ones to use now," said Carrie as they ate their supper.

"Oh?" asked Dad. "Why is that?"

Carrie giggled. "Because that old one doesn't reflect me the way I really am," she said. "It makes me look all squashed."

"Yeah," agreed her brother, Gary. "A good mirror shows you just as you are."

"I wonder how well all our mirrors are working," said Mom as she cut the apple pie.

"What do you mean?" asked Carrie. "They're fine."

Mom smiled. "I don't mean the mirrors on the walls or dressers," she explained. "I mean us."

"Us! We're people, not mirrors," said Gary.

"We are also mirrors," said Mom. "As Christians we should reflect Christ in everything we say and do."

"And when we do, we should reflect a true image," added Dad. "People should see Christ living in us, the way he really is—not a 'squashed' reflection."

Cultivating Godly Attitudes Memory Verse

Whatever you do or say, let it be as a representative of the Lord Jesus, and come with him into the presence of God the Father to give him your thanks.
Colossians 3:17

How About You?

God wants us to be holy, or pure, because he is holy. Do you reflect Christ's love in your life when you talk with your friends or when you play? Or is your reflection of him marred by mean and hateful actions? Yield to Christ each moment of the day so your life can be a true reflection of his love. *J. B.*

• For the next devotional, turn to page 131. • For the next devotional on CULTIVATING GODLY ATTITUDES, turn to page 163. • For notes on CULTIVATING GODLY ATTITUDES, see pages 337, 383, 472, 622, and 1216.

39"If an animal which you are permitted to eat dies of disease, anyone touching the carcass shall be defiled until evening. 40Also, anyone eating its meat or carrying away its carcass shall wash his clothes and be defiled until evening.

41,42"Animals that crawl shall not be eaten. This includes all reptiles that slither along upon their bellies as well as those that have legs. No crawling thing with many feet may be eaten, for it is defiled. 43Do not defile yourselves by touching it.

44"I am the Lord your God. Keep yourselves pure concerning these things, and be holy, for I am holy; therefore do not defile yourselves by touching any of these things that crawl upon the earth. 45For I am the Lord who brought you out of the land of Egypt to be your God. You must therefore be holy, for I am holy." 46These are the laws concerning animals, birds, and whatever swims in the water or crawls upon the ground. 47These are the distinctions between what is ceremonially clean and may be eaten, and what is ceremonially defiled and may not be eaten, among all animal life upon the earth.

12 Mothers and Childbirth

The Lord told Moses to give these instructions to the people of Israel:

2"When a baby boy is born, the mother shall be ceremonially defiled for seven days, and under the same restrictions as during her monthly menstrual periods. 3On the eighth day, her son must be circumcised. 4Then, for the next thirty-three days, while she is recovering from her ceremonial impurity, she must not touch anything sacred nor enter the Tabernacle.

5"When a baby girl is born, the mother's ceremonial impurity shall last two weeks, during which time she will be under the same restrictions as during menstruation. Then for a further sixty-six days she shall continue her recovery.

6"When these days of purification are ended (the following instructions are applicable whether her baby is a boy or girl), she must bring a yearling lamb as a burnt offering, and a young pigeon or a turtledove for a sin offering.

She must take them to the door of the Tabernacle to the priest; 7and the priest will offer them before the Lord and make atonement for her; then she will be ceremonially clean again after her bleeding at childbirth.

"These then, are the procedures after childbirth. 8But if she is too poor to bring a lamb, then she must bring two turtledoves or two young pigeons. One will be for a burnt offering and the other for a sin offering. The priest will make atonement for her with these, so that she will be ceremonially pure again."

13 Rules about Leprosy

The Lord said to Moses and Aaron, "If anyone notices a swelling in his skin, or a scab or boil or pimple with transparent skin, leprosy is to be suspected. He must be brought to Aaron the priest or to one of his sons 3for the spot to be examined. If the hair in this spot turns white, and if the spot looks to be more than skin-deep, it is leprosy, and the priest must declare him a leper.

4"But if the white spot in the skin does not seem to be deeper than the skin and the hair in the spot has not turned white, the priest shall quarantine him for seven days. 5At the end of that time, on the seventh day, the priest will examine him again, and if the spot has not changed and has not spread in the skin, then the priest must quarantine him seven days more. 6Again on the seventh day the priest will examine him, and if the marks of the disease have become fainter and have not spread, then the priest shall pronounce him cured; it was only a scab, and the man need only wash his clothes and everything will be normal again. 7But if the spot spreads in the skin after he has come to the priest to be examined, he must come back to the priest again, 8and the priest shall look again, and if the spot has spread, then the priest must pronounce him a leper.

9,10"When anyone suspected of having leprosy is brought to the priest, the priest is to look to see if there is a white swelling in the skin with white hairs in the spot, and an ulcer developing. 11If he finds these symptoms, it is an established case of leprosy, and the priest must pronounce him defiled. The man is not to be quarantined for further observation, for he is definitely diseased. 12But if the priest sees that the leprosy has erupted and spread all over his body from head to foot wherever he looks, 13then the priest shall pronounce him cured of leprosy, for it has all turned white; he is cured. 14,15But if there is raw flesh anywhere, the man shall be declared a leper. It is proved by the raw flesh. 16,17But if the raw flesh later changes to white, the leper will return to the priest to be examined again. If the spot has indeed turned completely white, then the priest will pronounce him cured.

18"In the case of a man who has a boil in his skin which heals, 19but which leaves a white swelling or a bright spot, sort of reddish white, the man must go to the priest for examination. 20If the priest sees that the trouble seems to be down under the skin, and if the hair at the spot has turned white, then the priest shall declare him defiled, for leprosy has broken out from the boil. 21But if the priest sees that there are no white hairs in this spot, and the spot does not appear to be deeper than the skin, and if the color is gray, then the priest shall quarantine him for seven days. ²²If during that time the spot spreads, the priest must declare him a leper. ²³But if the bright spot grows no larger and does not spread, it is merely the scar from the boil, and the priest shall declare that all is well.

²⁴"If a man is burned in some way, and the burned place becomes bright reddish white or white, ²⁵then the priest must examine the spot. If the hair in the bright spot turns white and the problem seems to be more than skin-deep, it is leprosy that has broken out from the burn, and the priest must pronounce him a leper. ²⁶But if the priest sees that there are no white hairs in the bright spot and the brightness appears to be no deeper than the skin and is fading, the priest shall quarantine him for seven days ²⁷and examine him again the seventh day. If the spot spreads in the skin, the priest must pronounce him a leper. ²⁸But if the bright spot does not move or spread in the skin, and is fading, it is simply a scar from the burn, and the priest shall declare that he does not have leprosy.

²⁹,³⁰"If a man or woman has a sore on the head or chin, the priest must examine him; if the infection seems to be below the skin and yellow hair is found in the sore, the priest must pronounce him a leper. ³¹But if the priest's examination reveals that the spot seems to be only in the skin but there is healthy hair in it, then he shall be quarantined for seven days, ³²and examined again on the seventh day. If the spot has not spread and no yellow hair has appeared, and if the infection does not seem to be deeper than the skin, ³³he shall shave off all the hair around the spot (but not on the spot itself) and the priest shall quarantine him for another seven days. ³⁴He shall be examined again on the seventh day, and if the spot has not spread, and it appears to be no deeper than the skin, the priest shall pronounce him well, and after washing his clothes, he is free. ³⁵But if, later on, this spot begins to spread, ³⁶then the priest must examine him again and, without waiting to see if any yellow hair develops, declare him a leper. ³⁷But if it appears that the spreading has stopped and black hairs are found in the spot, then he is healed and is not a leper, and the priest shall declare him healed.

³⁸"If a man or a woman has white, transparent areas in the skin, ³⁹but these spots are growing dimmer, this is not leprosy, but an ordinary infection that has broken out in the skin.

⁴⁰"If a man's hair is gone, this does not make him a leper even though he is bald! ⁴¹If the hair is gone from the front part of his head, he simply has a bald forehead, but this is not leprosy. ⁴²However, if in the baldness there is a reddish white spot, it may be leprosy breaking out. ⁴³In that case the priest shall examine him, and if there is a reddish white lump that looks like leprosy, ⁴⁴then he is a leper, and the priest must pronounce him such.

⁴⁵"Anyone who is discovered to have leprosy must tear his clothes and let his hair grow in wild disarray, and cover his upper lip and call out as he goes, "I am a leper, I am a leper." ⁴⁶As long as the disease lasts, he is defiled and must live outside the camp.

⁴⁷,⁴⁸"If leprosy is suspected in a woolen or linen garment or fabric, or in a piece of leather or leatherwork, ⁴⁹and there is a greenish or a reddish spot in it, it is probably leprosy, and must be taken to the priest to be examined. ⁵⁰The priest will put it away for seven days ⁵¹and look at it again on the seventh day. If the spot has spread, it is a contagious leprosy, ⁵²and he must burn the clothing, fabric, linen or woolen covering, or leather article, for it is contagious and must be destroyed by fire.

⁵³"But if when he examines it again on the seventh day the spot has not spread, ⁵⁴the priest shall order the suspected article to be washed, then isolated for seven more days. ⁵⁵If after that time the spot has not changed its color, even though it has not spread, it is leprosy and shall be burned, for the article is infected through and through. ⁵⁶But if the priest sees that the spot has faded after the washing, then he shall cut it out from the garment or leather goods or whatever it is in. ⁵⁷However, if it then reappears, it is leprosy and he must burn it. ⁵⁸But if after washing it there is no further trouble, it can be put back into service after another washing."

⁵⁹These are the regulations concerning leprosy in a garment or anything made of skin or leather, indicating whether to pronounce it leprous or not.

14 And the Lord gave Moses these regulations concerning a person whose leprosy disappears:

³"The priest shall go out of the camp to examine him. If the priest sees that the leprosy is gone, ⁴he shall require two living birds of a kind permitted for food, and shall take some cedar wood, a scarlet string, and some hyssop branches, to be used for the purification ceremony of the one who is healed. ⁵The priest shall then order one of the birds killed in an earthenware pot held above running water. ⁶The other bird, still living, shall be dipped in the blood, along with the cedar wood, the scarlet thread, and the hyssop branch. ⁷Then the priest shall sprinkle the blood seven times upon the man cured of his leprosy, and the priest shall pronounce him cured, and shall let the living bird fly into the open field.

⁸"Then the man who is cured shall wash his clothes, shave off all his hair, and bathe himself, and return to live inside the camp; however, he must stay outside his tent for seven days. ⁹The seventh day he

shall again shave all the hair from his head, beard, and eyebrows, and wash his clothes and bathe, and shall then be declared fully cured of his leprosy.

¹⁰"The next day, the eighth day, he shall take two male lambs without physical defect, one yearling ewe-lamb without physical defect, ten quarts of finely ground flour mixed with olive oil, and a pint of olive oil; ¹¹then the priest who examines him shall place the man and his offerings before the Lord at the entrance of the Tabernacle. ¹²The priest shall take one of the lambs and the pint of olive oil and offer them to the Lord as a guilt offering by the gesture of waving them before the altar. ¹³Then he shall kill the lamb at the place where sin offerings and burnt offerings are killed, there at the Tabernacle; this guilt offering shall then be given to the priest for food, as in the case of a sin offering. It is a most holy offering. ¹⁴The priest shall take the blood from this guilt offering and smear some of it upon the tip of the right ear of the man being cleansed, and upon the thumb of his right hand, and upon the big toe of his right foot.

¹⁵"Then the priest shall take the olive oil and pour it into the palm of his left hand, ¹⁶and dip his right finger into it, and sprinkle it with his finger seven times before the Lord. ¹⁷Some of the oil remaining in his left hand shall then be placed by the priest upon the tip of the man's right ear and the thumb of his right hand and the big toe of his right foot—just as he did with the blood of the guilt offering. ¹⁸The remainder of the oil in his hand shall be used to anoint the man's head. Thus the priest shall make atonement for him before the Lord.

¹⁹"Then the priest must offer the sin offering and again perform the rite of atonement for the person being cleansed from his leprosy; and afterwards the priest shall kill the burnt offering, ²⁰and offer it along with the grain offering upon the altar, making atonement for the man, who shall then be pronounced finally cleansed.

²¹"If he is so poor that he cannot afford two lambs, then he shall bring only one, a male lamb for the guilt offering, to be presented to the Lord in the rite of atonement by waving it before the altar; and only three quarts of fine white flour, mixed with olive oil, for a grain offering, and a pint of olive oil. ²²"He shall also bring two turtledoves or two young pigeons—whichever he is able to afford— and use one of the pair for a sin offering and the other for a burnt offering. ²³He shall bring them to the priest at the entrance of the Tabernacle on the eighth day, for his ceremony of cleansing before the Lord. ²⁴The priest shall take the lamb for the guilt offering, and the pint of oil, and wave them before the altar as a gesture of offering to the Lord. ²⁵Then he shall kill the lamb for the guilt offering and smear some of its blood upon the tip of the man's right ear—the man on whose behalf the ceremony is being performed—and upon the thumb of his right hand and upon the big toe of his right foot. ²⁶"The priest shall then pour the olive oil into the palm of his own left hand, ²⁷and with his right finger he is to sprinkle some of it seven times before the Lord. ²⁸Then he must put some of the olive oil from his hand upon the tip of the man's right ear, and upon the thumb of his right hand, and upon the big toe of his right foot, just as he did with the blood of the guilt offering. ²⁹The remaining oil in his hand shall be placed upon the head of the man being cleansed, to make atonement for him before the Lord.

³⁰"Then he must offer the two turtledoves or two young pigeons (whichever pair he is able to afford). ³¹One of the pair is for a sin offering and the other for a burnt offering, to be sacrificed along with the grain offering; and the priest shall make atonement for the man before the Lord."

³²These, then, are the laws concerning those who are cleansed of leprosy but are not able to bring the sacrifices normally required for the ceremony of cleansing.

³³,³⁴Then the Lord said to Moses and Aaron, "When you arrive in the land of Canaan which I have given you, and I place leprosy in some house there, ³⁵then the owner of the house shall come and report to the priest, 'It seems to me that there may be leprosy in my house!'

³⁶"The priest shall order the house to be emptied before he examines it, so that everything in the house will not be declared contaminated if he decides that there is leprosy there. ³⁷If he finds greenish or reddish streaks in the walls of the house which seem to be beneath the surface of the wall, ³⁸he shall close up the house for seven days, ³⁹and return the seventh day to look at it again. If the spots have spread in the wall, ⁴⁰then the priest shall order the removal of the spotted section of wall, and the material must be thrown into a defiled place outside the city. ⁴¹Then he shall order the inside walls of the house scraped thoroughly and the scrapings dumped in a defiled place outside the city. ⁴²Other stones shall be brought to replace those that have been removed, new mortar used, and the house replastered.

⁴³"But if the spots appear again, ⁴⁴the priest shall come again and look, and if he sees that the spots have spread, it is leprosy, and the house is defiled. ⁴⁵Then he shall order the destruction of the house—all its stones, timbers, and mortar shall be carried out of the city to a defiled place. ⁴⁶Anyone entering the house while it is closed shall be defiled until evening. ⁴⁷Anyone who lies down or eats in the house shall wash his clothing.

⁴⁸"But if, when the priest comes again to look, the spots have not reappeared after the fresh plastering, then he will pronounce the house cleansed and

declare the leprosy gone. ⁴⁹He shall also perform the ceremony of cleansing, using two birds, cedar wood, scarlet thread, and hyssop branches. ⁵⁰He shall kill one of the birds over fresh water in an earthenware bowl, ⁵¹,⁵²and dip the cedar wood, hyssop branch, and scarlet thread, as well as the living bird, into the blood of the bird that was killed over the fresh water, and shall sprinkle the house seven times. In this way the house shall be cleansed. ⁵³Then he shall let the live bird fly away into an open field outside the city. This is the method for making atonement for the house and cleansing it."

⁵⁴These, then, are the laws concerning the various places where leprosy may appear: ⁵⁵in a garment or in a house, ⁵⁶or in any swelling in one's skin, or a scab from a burn, or a bright spot. ⁵⁷In this way you will know whether or not it is actually leprosy. That is why these laws are given.

15 Rules of Health for Men and Women

The Lord told Moses and Aaron to give the people of Israel these further instructions:

"Any man who has a genital discharge is ceremonially defiled. ³This applies not only while the discharge is active, but also for a time after it heals. ⁴Any bed he lies on and anything he sits on is contaminated: ⁵so anyone touching the man's bed is ceremonially defiled until evening, and must wash his clothes and bathe himself. ⁶Anyone sitting on a seat the man has sat upon while defiled is himself ceremonially impure until evening, and must wash his clothes and bathe himself. ⁷The same instructions apply to anyone touching him. ⁸Anyone he spits on is ceremonially impure until evening, and must wash his clothes and bathe himself. ⁹Any saddle he rides on is defiled. ¹⁰Anyone touching or carrying anything else that was beneath him shall be defiled until evening, and must wash his clothes and bathe himself. ¹¹If the defiled man touches anyone without first rinsing his hands, that person must wash his clothes and bathe himself and be defiled until evening. ¹²Any earthen pot touched by the defiled man must be broken, and every wooden utensil must be rinsed in water.

¹³"When the discharge stops, he shall begin a seven-day cleansing ceremony by washing his clothes and bathing in running water. ¹⁴On the eighth day he shall take two turtledoves or two young pigeons and come before the Lord at the entrance of the Tabernacle, and give them to the priest. ¹⁵The priest shall sacrifice them there, one for a sin offering and the other for a burnt offering; thus the priest shall make atonement before the Lord for the man because of his discharge.

¹⁶"Whenever a man's semen goes out from him, he shall take a complete bath and be ceremonially impure until the evening. ¹⁷Any clothing or bedding the semen spills on must be washed and remain ceremonially defiled until evening. ¹⁸After sexual intercourse, the woman as well as the man must bathe, and they are ceremonially defiled until the next evening.

¹⁹"Whenever a woman menstruates, she shall be in a state of ceremonial defilement for seven days afterwards, and during that time anyone touching her shall be defiled until evening. ²⁰Anything she lies on or sits on during that time shall be defiled. ²¹⁻²³Anyone touching her bed or anything she sits upon shall wash his clothes and bathe himself and be ceremonially defiled until evening. ²⁴A man having sexual intercourse with her during this time is ceremonially defiled for seven days, and every bed he lies upon shall be defiled.

²⁵"If the menstrual flow continues after the normal time, or at some irregular time during the month, the same rules apply as indicated above, ²⁶so that anything she lies upon during that time is defiled, just as it would be during her normal menstrual period, and everything she sits on is in a similar state of defilement. ²⁷Anyone touching her bed or anything she sits on shall be defiled, and shall wash his clothes and bathe and be defiled until evening. ²⁸Seven days after the menstruating stops, she is no longer ceremonially defiled.

²⁹"On the eighth day, she shall take two turtledoves or two young pigeons and bring them to the priest at the entrance of the Tabernacle, ³⁰and the priest shall offer one for a sin offering and the other for a burnt offering, and make atonement for her before the Lord for her menstrual defilement. ³¹In this way you shall cleanse the people of Israel from their defilement, lest they die because of defiling my Tabernacle that is among them."

³²This, then, is the law for the man who is defiled by a genital disease or by a seminal emission; ³³and for a woman's menstrual period; and for anyone who has sexual intercourse with her while she is in her period of defilement afterwards.

16 The Day of Atonement

After Aaron's two sons died before the Lord, the Lord said to Moses, "Warn your brother Aaron not to enter into the Holy Place behind the

---

KNOWING GOD 16:1-25 Aaron had to spend hours preparing himself to meet God. But we can approach God anytime (Hebrews 4:16). What a privilege! We are offered easier access to God than the High Priests of Old Testament times! Still, we must never forget that God is holy nor let this privilege cause us to approach God thoughtlessly. The way to God has been opened to us by Christ. But easy access to God does not eliminate our need to prepare our hearts as we draw near in prayer. **To begin the series of devotionals on KNOWING GOD, turn to page 197.**

veil, where the Ark and the place of mercy are, just whenever he chooses. The penalty for intrusion is death. For I myself am present in the cloud above the place of mercy.

³"Here are the conditions for his entering there: He must bring a young bull for a sin offering, and a ram for a burnt offering. ⁴He must bathe himself and put on the sacred linen coat, shorts, belt, and turban. ⁵The people of Israel shall then bring him two male goats for their sin offering, and a ram for their burnt offering. ⁶First he shall present to the Lord the young bull as a sin offering for himself, making atonement for himself and his family. ⁷Then he shall bring the two goats before the Lord at the entrance of the Tabernacle, ⁸and cast lots to determine which is the Lord's and which is to be sent away. ⁹The goat allotted to the Lord shall then be sacrificed by Aaron as a sin offering. ¹⁰The other goat shall be kept alive and placed before the Lord. The rite of atonement shall be performed over it, and it shall then be sent out into the desert as a scapegoat.

¹¹"After Aaron has sacrificed the young bull as a sin offering for himself and his family, ¹²he shall take a censer full of live coals from the altar of the Lord, and fill his hands with sweet incense beaten into fine powder, and bring it inside the veil. ¹³There before the Lord he shall put the incense upon the coals, so that a cloud of incense will cover the mercy place above the Ark (containing the stone tablets of the Ten Commandments); thus he will not die. ¹⁴And he shall bring some of the blood of the young bull and sprinkle it with his finger upon the east side of the mercy place, and then seven times in front of it.

¹⁵"Then he must go out and sacrifice the people's sin offering goat, and bring its blood within the veil, and sprinkle it upon the place of mercy and in front of it, just as he did with the blood of the young bull. ¹⁶Thus he shall make atonement for the holy place because it is defiled by the sins of the people of Israel, and for the Tabernacle, located right among them and surrounded by their defilement. ¹⁷Not another soul shall be inside the Tabernacle when Aaron enters to make atonement in the Holy Place—not until after he comes out again and has made atonement for himself and his household and for all the people of Israel. ¹⁸Then he shall go out to the altar before the Lord and make atonement for it. He must smear the blood of the young bull and the goat on the horns of the altar, ¹⁹and sprinkle blood upon the altar seven times with his finger, thus cleansing it from the sinfulness of Israel and making it holy.

²⁰"When he has completed the rite of atonement for the Holy Place, the entire Tabernacle, and the altar, he shall bring the live goat and, ²¹laying both hands upon its head, confess over it all the sins of the people of Israel. He shall lay all their sins upon the head of the goat and send it into the desert, led by a man appointed for the task. ²²So the goat shall carry all the sins of the people into a land where no one lives, and the man shall let it loose in the wilderness.

²³"Then Aaron shall go into the Tabernacle again and take off the linen garments he wore when he went behind the veil, and leave them there in the Tabernacle. ²⁴ Then he shall bathe in a sacred place, put on his clothes again, and go out and sacrifice his own burnt offering for the people, making atonement for himself and for them. ²⁵He shall also burn upon the altar the fat for the sin offering.

²⁶"(The man who took the goat out into the desert shall afterwards wash his clothes and bathe himself and then come back into the camp.) ²⁷And the young bull and the goat used for the sin offering (their blood was taken into the Holy Place by Aaron, to make atonement) shall be carried outside the camp and burned, including the hides and internal organs. ²⁸Afterwards, the person doing the burning shall wash his clothes and bathe himself and then return to camp.

²⁹,³⁰"This is a permanent law: You must do no work on the twenty-fifth day of September, but must spend the day in self-examination and humility. This applies whether you are born in the land or are a foreigner living among the people of Israel; for this is the day commemorating the atonement, cleansing you in the Lord's eyes from all of your sins. ³¹It is a Sabbath of solemn rest for you, and you shall spend the day in quiet humility; this is a permanent law. ³²This ceremony, in later generations, shall be performed by the anointed High Priest, consecrated in place of his ancestor Aaron; he shall be the one to put on the holy linen garments, ³³and make atonement for the holy sanctuary, the Tabernacle, the altar, the priests, and the people. ³⁴This shall be an everlasting law for you, to make atonement for the people of Israel once each year, because of their sins."

And Aaron followed all these instructions that the Lord gave to Moses.

17 Warning Against Sacrificing Wrongly

The Lord gave to Moses these additional instructions for Aaron and the priests and for all the people of Israel:

³,⁴"Any Israelite who sacrifices an ox, lamb, or goat anywhere except at the Tabernacle is guilty of murder and shall be excommunicated from his nation. ⁵ The purpose of this law is to stop the people of Israel from sacrificing in the open fields, and to cause them to bring their sacrifices

Family Devotions

☐ DEVOTION 47
BECOMING MORE LIKE JESUS

Read Leviticus 19:16

Mindy and her mother watched in horror as fire swept through the wheat field on their farm. "How did it start, Mother?" Mindy sobbed.

"We can't be certain, Mindy," answered Mother. "It could have been someone driving by who was careless with a cigarette, or it could have been started by a spark from the combine. A little spark is all it takes to start a fire."

The wheat crop was lost. "I'm just thankful we were able to keep the fire from spreading to any other fields or buildings," said Dad that evening.

Just then the phone rang, and Mindy answered it. It was her friend Rachel, and the girls talked for a while. After Mindy had hung up, Mother looked at her thoughtfully.

"The fire this afternoon was not nearly as destructive as some of those fires you just started," she said.

"What?" Mindy was shocked. "I never in my whole life started a fire. What are you talking about?"

"I'm talking about the rumors I heard you sharing with Rachel about the new girl in school," Mother replied.

"Rhonda? Well, if she didn't cheat, how could she get such a good grade on her first day at school?" Mindy defended herself. "Stacy told me some things about Rhonda. I was only warning Rachel."

"Mindy, you said some very unkind things about a girl you don't even know. You had no right to do that," scolded Mother. "You can't be certain that any of those rumors are true, but they'll spread like a fire and ruin that girl's reputation. I think you ought to have the courage to stop the fire instead of spreading it."

"But, Mom," Mindy protested. "I was just—"

"You were just starting a fire," Mother finished. "I hope you'll call Rachel and make an effort to put out the fire you helped start. Be more cautious from now on."

Becoming More Like Jesus Memory Verse

No, he has told you what he wants, and this is all it is: *to be fair, just, merciful, and to walk humbly with your God.*
Micah 6:8

How About You?
Do you ever say unkind words? Do you help spread gossip and rumors that will hurt other people? God says that a mouth which is used to bless and praise him should not be used to hurt others. How will you use your tongue? B. D.

• For the next devotional, turn to page 133. • For the next devotional on BECOMING MORE LIKE JESUS, turn to page 215. • For notes on BECOMING MORE LIKE JESUS, see pages 234, 983, 1105, and 1164.

to the priest at the entrance of the Tabernacle, and to burn the fat as a savor the Lord will appreciate and enjoy— ⁶for in this way the priest will be able to sprinkle the blood upon the altar of the Lord at the entrance of the Tabernacle, and to burn the fat as a savor the Lord will appreciate and enjoy— ⁷instead of the people's sacrificing to evil spirits out in the fields. This shall be a permanent law for you, from generation to generation. ^{8,9}I repeat: Anyone, whether an Israelite or a foreigner living among you who offers a burnt offering or a sacrifice anywhere other than at the entrance of the Tabernacle, where it will be sacrificed to the Lord, shall be excommunicated.

¹⁰"And I will turn my face against anyone, whether an Israelite or a foreigner living among you, who eats blood in any form. I will excommunicate him from his people. ¹¹For the life of the flesh is in the blood, and I have given you the blood to sprinkle upon the altar as an atonement for your souls; it is the blood that makes atonement because it is the life. ¹²That is the reasoning behind my decree to the people of Israel, that neither they, nor any foreigner living among them, may eat blood. ¹³Anyone, whether an Israelite or a foreigner living among you, who goes hunting and kills an animal or bird of a kind permitted for food, must pour out the blood and cover it with dust, ¹⁴for the blood is the life. That is why I told the people of Israel never to eat it, for the life of every bird and animal is its blood. Therefore, anyone who eats blood must be excommunicated.

¹⁵"And anyone—native born or foreigner—who eats the dead body of an animal that dies a natural death, or is killed by wild animals, must wash his clothes and bathe himself and be defiled until evening; after that he shall be declared cleansed. ¹⁶But if he does not wash his clothes and bathe, he shall suffer the consequence."

18 Wrong Sexual Relationships

The Lord then told Moses to tell the people of Israel,

"I am Jehovah your God, ³so don't act like heathen—like the people of Egypt where you lived so long, or the people of Canaan where I am going to take you. ^{4,5}You must obey only my laws, and you must carry them out in detail, for I am the Lord your God. If you obey them, you shall live. I am the Lord.

⁶"None of you shall marry a near relative, for I am the Lord. ⁷Do not disgrace your father by having intercourse with your mother, ⁸nor any other of your father's wives. ⁹Do not have intercourse with your sister or half-sister, whether the daughter of your father or your mother, whether brought up in the same household or elsewhere.

¹⁰"You shall not have intercourse with your granddaughter—the daughter of either your son or your daughter—for she is a close relative. ¹¹You may not have intercourse with a half-sister—your father's wife's daughter; ¹²nor your aunt—your father's sister—because she is so closely related to your father; ¹³nor your aunt—your mother's sister—because she is a close relative of your mother; ¹⁴nor your aunt—the wife of your father's brother.

¹⁵"You may not marry your daughter-in-law—your son's wife; ¹⁶nor your brother's wife, for she is your brother's. ¹⁷You may not marry both a woman and her daughter or granddaughter, for they are near relatives, and to do so is horrible wickedness. ¹⁸You shall not marry two sisters, for they will be rivals. However, if your wife dies, then it is all right to marry her sister.

¹⁹"There must be no sexual relationship with a woman who is menstruating; ²⁰nor with anyone else's wife, to defile yourself with her.

²¹"You shall not give any of your children to Molech, burning them upon his altar; never profane the name of your God, for I am Jehovah.

²²"Homosexuality is absolutely forbidden, for it is an enormous sin. ²³A man shall have no sexual intercourse with any female animal, thus defiling himself; and a woman must never give herself to a male animal, to mate with it; this is a terrible perversion.

²⁴"Do not defile yourselves in any of these ways, for these are the things the heathen do; and because they do them, I am going to cast them out from the land into which you are going. ²⁵That entire country is defiled with this kind of activity; that is why I am punishing the people living there, and will throw them out of the land. ²⁶You must strictly obey all of my laws and ordinances, and you must not do any of these abominable things; these laws apply both to you who are born in the nation of Israel and to foreigners living among you.

²⁷"Yes, all these abominations have been done continually by the people of the land where I am taking you, and the land is defiled. ²⁸Do not do these things or I will throw you out of the land, just as I will throw out the nations that live there now. ^{29,30}Whoever does any of these terrible deeds shall be excommunicated from this nation. So be very sure to obey my laws, and do not practice any of these horrible customs. Do not defile yourselves with the evil deeds of those living in the land where you are going. For I am Jehovah your God."

19 Commands for Daily Life

The Lord also told Moses to tell the people of Israel, "You must be holy because I, the Lord your God, am holy. You must respect your

FAMILY DEVOTIONS

☐ **DEVOTION 48**
OVERCOMING ANGER

Read Leviticus 19:17-18

Overcoming Anger Memory Verses:

Dear brothers, don't ever forget that it is best to listen much, speak little, and not become angry; for anger doesn't make us good, as God demands that we must be.
James 1:19-20

Mom and Patty were working together on cleaning the refrigerator—the last thing they had to finish before they could go shopping. As they worked, Mom asked, "Would you like to invite Melissa to go shopping with us?"

"No," Patty answered shortly as she unloaded the refrigerator shelves.

Mom looked surprised. "Why not?"

Patty shrugged. "She's probably doing something with Amy today. Melissa is Amy's friend now."

"Can't Melissa have more than one friend?" Mom asked. "You could invite Amy, too."

"No!" snapped Patty. After a long silence, she added, "Melissa knows I can't stand Amy. Last year Amy said some really hateful things about me, and she—*phew!* What do I smell?"

Mom grimaced. "You must have uncovered something spoiled," she said.

Patty gingerly picked up a bowl. "It's this old tuna casserole. *Phewweeee!*"

After the casserole was disposed of and the kitchen was sprayed with air freshener, Mom said, "Patty, sometimes we keep old things in our hearts until they spoil and cause our attitudes to stink. For a year you have been carrying a grudge against Amy. It's beginning to stink."

"But, Mom," began Patty, "she said—"

"I know. You've told me what she said at least twenty times. Don't you think it's time to throw that stinking grudge out?" Mom asked gently.

Patty took a deep breath. A few minutes later, she went to the telephone. Mom smiled as she heard Patty say, "Amy, would you and Melissa like to go shopping with my mom and me today?"

How About You?
Are you carrying a nasty, stinking grudge? Ask God to help you get rid of it today. Ask him to give you a sweet and forgiving spirit. *B. W.*

• For the next devotional, turn to page 135.   • For the next devotional on OVERCOMING ANGER, turn to page 625.
• For notes on OVERCOMING ANGER, see pages 176, 511, 936, and 1003.

mothers and fathers, and obey my Sabbath law, for I am the Lord your God. ³,⁴Do not make or worship idols, for I am Jehovah your God.

⁵"When you sacrifice a peace offering to the Lord, offer it correctly so that it will be accepted: ⁶Eat it the same day you offer it, or the next day at the latest; any remaining until the third day must be burned. ⁷For any of it eaten on the third day is repulsive to me and will not be accepted. ⁸If you eat it on the third, day you are guilty, for you profane the holiness of Jehovah, and you shall be excommunicated from Jehovah's people.

⁹"When you harvest your crops, don't reap the corners of your fields, and don't pick up stray grains of wheat from the ground. ¹⁰It is the same with your grape crop—don't strip every last piece of fruit from the vines, and don't pick up the grapes that fall to the ground. Leave them for the poor and for those traveling through, for I am Jehovah your God.

¹¹"You must not steal nor lie nor defraud. ¹²You must not swear to a falsehood, thus bringing reproach upon the name of your God, for I am Jehovah.

¹³"You shall not rob nor oppress anyone, and you shall pay your hired workers promptly. If something is due them, don't even keep it overnight.

¹⁴"You must not curse the deaf nor trip up a blind man as he walks. Fear your God; I am Jehovah!

¹⁵"Judges must always be just in their sentences, not noticing whether a person is poor or rich; they must always be perfectly fair.

¹⁶"Don't gossip. Don't falsely accuse your neighbor of some crime, for I am Jehovah.

¹⁷"Don't hate your brother. Rebuke anyone who sins; don't let him get away with it, or you will be equally guilty. ¹⁸Don't seek vengeance. Don't bear a grudge; but love your neighbor as yourself, for I am Jehovah.

¹⁹"Obey my laws: Do not mate your cattle with a different kind; don't sow your field with two kinds of seed; don't wear clothes made of half wool and half linen.

²⁰"If a man seduces a slave girl who is engaged to be married, they shall be tried in a court but not put to death, because she is not free. ²¹The man involved shall bring his guilt offering to the Lord at the entrance of the Tabernacle; the offering shall be a ram. ²²The priest shall make atonement with the ram for the sin the man has committed, and it shall be forgiven him.

²³"When you enter the land and have planted all kinds of fruit trees, do not eat the first three crops, for they are considered ceremonially defiled. ²⁴And the fourth year the entire crop shall be devoted to the Lord, and shall be given to the Lord in praise to him. ²⁵Finally, in the fifth year, the crop is yours.

²⁶"I am Jehovah your God! You must not eat meat with undrained blood nor use fortune telling or witchcraft.

²⁷"You must not trim off your hair on your temples or clip the edges of your beard, as the heathen do. ²⁸You shall not cut yourselves nor put tattoo marks upon yourselves in connection with funeral rites; I am the Lord.

²⁹"Do not violate your daughter's sanctity by making her a prostitute, lest the land become full of enormous wickedness.

³⁰"Keep my Sabbath laws and reverence my Tabernacle, for I am the Lord.

³¹"Do not defile yourselves by consulting mediums and wizards, for I am Jehovah your God.

³²"You shall give due honor and respect to the elderly, in the fear of God. I am Jehovah.

³³"Do not take advantage of foreigners in your land; do not wrong them. ³⁴They must be treated like any other citizen; love them as yourself, for remember that you too were foreigners in the land of Egypt. I am Jehovah your God.

³⁵,³⁶"You must be impartial in judgment. Use accurate measurements—lengths, weights, and volumes—and give full measure, for I am Jehovah your God who brought you from the land of Egypt. ³⁷You must heed all of my commandments and ordinances, carefully obeying them, for I am Jehovah."

20 Punishments for Sin

The Lord gave Moses these further instructions for the people of Israel:

"Anyone—whether an Israelite or a foreigner living among you—who sacrifices his child as a burnt offering to Molech shall without fail be stoned by his peers. ³And I myself will turn against that man and cut him off from all his people, because he has given his child to Molech, thus making my Tabernacle unfit for me to live in, and insulting my holy name. ⁴And if the people of the land pretend they do not know what the man has done and refuse to put him to death, ⁵then I myself will set my face against that man and his family and cut him off, along with all others who turn to other gods than me.

⁶"I will set my face against anyone who consults mediums and wizards instead of me and I will cut that person off from his people. ⁷So sanctify yourselves and be holy, for I am the Lord your God. ⁸You must obey all of my commandments, for I am the Lord who sanctifies you.

⁹"Anyone who curses his father or mother shall surely be put to death—for he has cursed his own flesh and blood.

FAMILY DEVOTIONS

☐ **DEVOTION 49**
RESPECTING OTHERS

Read Leviticus 19:32

Respecting Others
Memory Verse

Don't be selfish; don't live to make a good impression on others. Be humble, thinking of others as better than yourself.
Philippians 2:3

As Janet walked into the nursing home with her mother, she wrinkled her nose. "What's that awful smell?" she asked. She had not really wanted to come here in the first place, and the smell of medication and illness didn't do anything to change her mind!

"These people are old and sick," Mother replied, "and a sickroom often has an unpleasant odor. But I think you'll be glad you came after you've visited Grandma Harper and some of the other people here. They're always such a blessing to me."

Janet could not imagine getting a blessing from being around these old people. But she had promised to give a report next Sunday on her nursing home visit, so she just sighed and followed her mother down the hall.

They had hardly entered the room when Grandma Harper called out cheerily, "Oh, you brought your precious daughter!" She held out her hands to Janet. "Honey, around here we seldom see young and beautiful girls like you. Most of us have so many wrinkles we've forgotten what it was like to be young." She laughed pleasantly as she spoke, and Janet began to smile, too. Before long, she was telling the elderly woman about her school activities, her Sunday school class, and even about her birthday party. By this time there were several other people in the room, and at their urging, she sang a song for them. When they asked for another, Mother suggested that she sing an old, familiar one. Janet did, and soon several quavering, old voices joined the clear, young one in some well-loved hymns.

When they were ready to leave, Janet promised to bring other members of her class with her the next time. "You should hear them sing," she said with a smile.

Back in the car, Janet turned to her mother. "You were right, Mom," she said. "I'm the one who got the blessing."

How About You?
Are there some elderly people in your hometown who would enjoy a visit from a group of young people? Many of the sick and elderly are not able to go to church. Will you visit them and share some of God's blessings with them? Remember, you, too, will be blessed. *R. J.*

• For the next devotional, turn to page 137.   • For the next devotional on *RESPECTING OTHERS*, turn to page 165.
• For notes on *RESPECTING OTHERS*, see pages 322, 382, 1088, and 1218.

10"If a man commits adultery with another man's wife, both the man and woman shall be put to death. 11If a man sleeps with his father's wife, he has defiled what is his father's; both the man and the woman must die, for it is their own fault. 12And if a man has sexual intercourse with his daughter-in-law, both shall be executed: they have brought it upon themselves by defiling each other. 13The penalty for homosexual acts is death to both parties. They have brought it upon themselves. 14If a man has sexual intercourse with a woman and with her mother, it is a great evil. All three shall be burned alive to wipe out wickedness from among you.

15"If a man has sexual intercourse with an animal, he shall be executed and the animal killed. 16If a woman has sexual intercourse with an animal, kill the woman and the animal, for they deserve their punishment.

17"If a man has sexual intercourse with his sister, whether the daughter of his father or of his mother, it is a shameful thing, and they shall publicly be cut off from the people of Israel. He shall bear his guilt. 18If a man has sexual intercourse with a woman during her period of menstruation, both shall be excommunicated, for he has uncovered the source of her flow, and she has permitted it.

19"Sexual intercourse is outlawed between a man and his maiden aunt—whether the sister of his mother or of his father—for they are near of kin; they shall bear their guilt. 20If a man has intercourse with his uncle's wife, he has taken what belongs to his uncle; their punishment is that they shall bear their sin and die childless. 21If a man marries his brother's wife, this is impurity; for he has taken what belongs to his brother, and they shall be childless.

22"You must obey all of my laws and ordinances so that I will not throw you out of your new land. 23You must not follow the customs of the nations I cast out before you, for they do all these things I have warned you against; that is the reason I abhor them. 24I have promised you their land; I will give it to you to possess it. It is a land 'flowing with milk and honey.' I am the Lord your God who has made a distinction between you and the people of other nations.

25"You shall therefore make a distinction between the birds and animals I have given you permission to eat and those you may not eat. You shall not contaminate yourselves and make yourselves hateful to me by eating any animal or bird which I have forbidden, though the land teem with them. 26You shall be holy to me, for I the Lord am holy, and I have set you apart from all other peoples to be mine.

27"A medium or a wizard—whether man or woman—shall surely be stoned to death. They have caused their own doom."

21 Rules for the Priests

The Lord said to Moses: "Tell the priests never to defile themselves by touching a dead person, 2,3unless it is a near relative—a mother, father, son, daughter, brother, or unmarried sister for whom he has special responsibility since she has no husband. 4For the priest is a leader among his people, and he may not ceremonially defile himself as an ordinary person can.

5"The priests shall not clip bald spots in their hair or beards, nor cut their flesh. 6They shall be holy unto their God and shall not dishonor and profane his name; otherwise they will be unfit to make food offerings by fire to the Lord their God. 7A priest shall not marry a prostitute, nor a woman of another tribe, and he shall not marry a divorced woman, for he is a holy man of God. 8The priest is set apart to offer the sacrifices of your God; he is holy, for I, the Lord who sanctifies you, am holy. 9The daughter of any priest who becomes a prostitute, thus violating her father's holiness as well as her own, shall be burned alive.

10"The High Priest—anointed with the special anointing oil and wearing the special garments—must not let his hair hang loose in mourning, nor tear his clothing, 11nor be in the presence of any dead person—not even his father or mother. 12He shall not leave the sanctuary [when on duty], nor treat my Tabernacle like an ordinary house, for the consecration of the anointing oil of his God is upon him; I am Jehovah. 13He must marry a virgin. 14,15He may not marry a widow, nor a woman who is divorced, nor a prostitute. She must be a virgin from his own tribe, for he must not be the father of children of mixed blood—half priestly and half ordinary."

16,17And the Lord said to Moses, "Tell Aaron that any of his descendants from generation to generation who have any bodily defect may not offer the sacrifices to God. 18For instance, if a man is blind or lame, or has a broken nose or any extra fingers or toes, 19or has a broken foot or hand, 20or has a humped back, or is a dwarf, or has a defect in his eye, or has pimples or scabby skin, or has imperfect testicles—21although he is a descendant of Aaron—he is not permitted to offer the fire sacrifices to the Lord because of his physical defect. 22However, he shall be fed with the food of the priests from the offerings sacrificed to God, both from the holy and most holy offerings. 23But he shall not go in behind the veil, nor come near the altar, because of the physical defect; this would defile my sanctuary, for it is Jehovah who sanctifies it."

FAMILY DEVOTIONS

☐ *DEVOTION 50*
SHOWING KINDNESS

Read Leviticus 19:33-34

Showing Kindness Memory Verse

That's why whenever we can we should always be kind to everyone, and especially to our Christian brothers.
Galatians 6:10

"Timothy! I'm here in the garden," called Mom as she saw Timothy coming home from kindergarten.

Timothy raced around to the side of the house, laughing excitedly. He found his mother on her knees, pulling weeds from a bed of brightly colored flowers. "Want to hear a joke Tommy told me on the way home?" he asked.

Mom smiled as she stood up and walked a few feet to a stone bench. "Come sit with me, Timothy," she invited. "Let's hear that joke. I bet it's a good one."

Timothy sat on the ground beside the bench and started to tell his mother a story that made fun of Dutch people. She laughed at the silly joke. Then she said, "I have a surprise for you, Timothy. You're Dutch—your great-grandparents came from Holland. So when you make fun of Dutch people, you're making fun of yourself." Timothy's mouth dropped open in surprise. "Laughing at yourself is one thing," continued Mom, "but laughing at others is something else. You need to be very careful about telling jokes that poke fun at people who are different from you."

"Do you think they might get mad?" asked Timothy.

"Well, lots of people don't mind," replied Mom, "but others might feel hurt or angry. So unless you know such a joke won't hurt anyone's feelings, it's better not to tell it at all. Always remember that people are different from each other because that's the way God meant them to be. What do you notice about these flowers?" she asked.

Timothy considered them for a minute. "Well, they're all different colors," he said. "I like 'em that way."

"So do I," agreed Mom. "Some are red, and some are yellow, and some are purple. God didn't make all flowers the same color, and he didn't give all people the same color skin and hair and eyes. God likes variety, and we should, too." She smiled at Timothy as she added, "I hope, Son, that you'll be a person who appreciates everyone God has created."

How About You?
Are you considerate of people who are different from you? It's interesting to learn about different races and cultures. God created each one for his own pleasure and in his own image. Learn to see others as God sees them. *A. E. L.*

• For the next devotional, turn to page 139.   • For the next devotional on *SHOWING KINDNESS,* turn to page 541.
• For notes on *SHOWING KINDNESS,* see pages 664, 880, 1038, and 1244.

138 Leviticus

²⁴So Moses gave these instructions to Aaron and his sons and to all the people of Israel.

22

The Lord told Moses, "Instruct Aaron and his sons to be very careful not to defile my holy name by desecrating the people's sacred gifts; for I am Jehovah. ³From now on and forever, if a priest who is ceremonially defiled sacrifices the animals brought by the people or handles the gifts dedicated to Jehovah, he shall be discharged from the priesthood. For I am Jehovah!

⁴"No priest who is a leper or who has a running sore may eat the holy sacrifices until healed. And any priest who touches a dead person, or who is defiled by a seminal emission, ⁵or who touches any reptile or other forbidden thing, or who touches anyone who is ceremonially defiled for any reason—⁶that priest shall be defiled until evening and shall not eat of the holy sacrifices until after he has bathed that evening. ⁷When the sun is down, then he shall be purified again and may eat the holy food, for it is his source of life. ⁸He may not eat any animal that dies of itself or is torn by wild animals, for this will defile him. I am Jehovah. ⁹Warn the priests to follow these instructions carefully, lest they be declared guilty and die for violating these rules. I am the Lord who sanctifies them.

¹⁰"No one may eat of the holy sacrifices unless he is a priest; no one visiting the priest, for instance, nor a hired servant, may eat this food. ¹¹However, there is one exception—if the priest buys a slave with his own money, that slave may eat it, and any slave children born in his household may eat it. ¹²If a priest's daughter is married outside the tribe, she may not eat the sacred offerings. ¹³But if she is a widow or divorced and has no son to support her, and has returned home to her father's household, she may eat of her father's food again. But otherwise, no one who is not in the priestly families may eat this food.

¹⁴"If someone should eat of the holy sacrifices without realizing it, he shall return to the priest the amount he has used, with 20 percent added; ¹⁵for the holy sacrifices brought by the people of Israel must not be defiled by being eaten by unauthorized persons, for these sacrifices have been offered to the Lord. ¹⁶Anyone who violates this law is guilty and is in great danger because he has eaten the sacred offerings; for I am Jehovah who sanctifies the offerings."

¹⁷,¹⁸And the Lord said to Moses, "Tell Aaron and his sons and all the people of Israel that if an Israelite or other person living among you offers a burnt offering sacrifice to the Lord—whether it is to fulfill a promise or is a spontaneous free will offering—¹⁹it will only be acceptable to the Lord if it is a male animal without defect; it must be a young bull or a sheep or a goat. ²⁰Anything that has a defect must not be offered, for it will not be accepted.

²¹"Anyone sacrificing a peace offering to the Lord from the herd or flock, whether to fulfill a vow or as a voluntary offering, must sacrifice an animal that has no defect, or it will not be accepted: ²²An animal that is blind or disabled or mutilated, or which has sores or itch or any other skin disease, must not be offered to the Lord; it is not a fit burnt offering for the altar of the Lord. ²³If the young bull or lamb presented to the Lord has anything superfluous or lacking in its body parts, it may be offered as a free will offering, but not for a vow. ²⁴An animal that has injured genitals—crushed or castrated—shall not be offered to the Lord at any time. ²⁵This restriction applies to the sacrifices made by foreigners among you as well as those made by yourselves, for no defective animal is acceptable for this sacrifice."

²⁶,²⁷And the Lord said to Moses, "When a bullock, sheep, or goat is born, it shall be left with its mother for seven days, but from the eighth day onward it is acceptable as a sacrifice by fire to the Lord. ²⁸You shall not slaughter a mother animal and her offspring the same day, whether she is a cow or ewe. ²⁹,³⁰When you offer the Lord a sacrifice of thanksgiving, you must do it in the right way, eating the sacrificial animal the same day it is slain. Leave none of it for the following day. I am the Lord.

³¹"You must keep all of my commandments, for I am the Lord. ³²,³³You must not treat me as common and ordinary. Revere me and hallow me, for I, the Lord, made you holy to myself and rescued you from Egypt to be my own people! I am Jehovah!"

23

Special Days

The Lord said to Moses, "Announce to the people of Israel that they are to celebrate several annual festivals of the Lord—times when all Israel will assemble and worship me. ³(These are in addition to your Sabbaths—the seventh day of every week—which are always days of rest in every home, times for assembling to worship, and for resting from the normal business of the week.)

⁴These are the holy festivals which are to be observed each year:

⁵"*The Passover of the Lord:* This is to be celebrated on the first day of April, beginning at sundown.

⁶"*The Festival of Unleavened Bread:* This is to be celebrated beginning the day following the

FAMILY DEVOTIONS

☐ *DEVOTION 51*
STANDING FOR RIGHTEOUSNESS

Read Leviticus 22:31-32

Derek was watching his favorite TV program as Mom worked on her knitting and Dad read the paper. The program was a comedy show about a family similar to their own. Derek laughed when an embarrassing incident took place in the story, and the star of the show said, "Oh, my God!"

Hearing this, Dad looked up from his paper. "Derek, how can you laugh when people use God's name in vain like that?" he asked. "You claim to love God and say he is your heavenly Father. Yet you seem to have forgotten that his name is holy."

"I know, Dad," Derek replied soberly. "I wish they didn't swear on TV so much, too, but what can I do about it?"

"You can turn off the program," said Mom, "and then you could inform the TV station and those who sponsor the program that you turned it off, and tell them why."

"Good suggestion," agreed Dad. "Maybe you and your friends can do something about it."

Derek thought a lot about that. He discussed it with his friends and his youth leader at church. Soon Derek was heading up a campaign for cleaner TV. Through their local library they got the sponsors' addresses, and they wrote letters complaining about the program's foul language. They said if the companies continued to sponsor such programs, they and their families would quit buying the products. They also contacted the station they were watching to say how they felt.

They didn't always feel that their campaign was doing any good. But they knew they were right to stand up for what they believed in. And it helped them remember that God will not stand for his name being used in vain!

Standing for Righteousness Memory Verse

For the eyes of the Lord search back and forth across the whole earth, looking for people whose hearts are perfect toward him, so that he can show his great power in helping them.
2 Chronicles 16:9

How About You?
Have you heard people say, "Oh, God!" or "Oh, my Lord!" so much that it doesn't even bother you anymore? It still bothers God! When you're talking with friends and they use God's name in vain, do you ask them not to? Perhaps you could begin a campaign of your own to promote cleaner language on TV. R. P.

• For the next devotional, turn to page 141.   • For the next devotional on STANDING FOR RIGHTEOUSNESS, turn to page 175.   • For notes on STANDING FOR RIGHTEOUSNESS, see pages 62, 298, 371, 678, and 948.

Passover, and for seven days you must not eat any bread made with yeast. ⁷On the first day of this festival, you shall gather the people for worship, and all ordinary work shall cease. ⁸You shall do the same on the seventh day of the festival. On each of the intervening days you shall make an offering by fire to the Lord.

⁹⁻¹¹"*The Festival of First Fruits:* When you arrive in the land I will give you and you reap your first harvest, bring the first sheaf of the harvest to the priest on the day after the Sabbath. He shall wave it before the Lord in a gesture of offering, and it will be accepted by the Lord as your gift. ¹²That same day you shall sacrifice to the Lord a male yearling lamb without defect as a burnt offering. ¹³A grain offering shall accompany it, consisting of a fifth of a bushel of finely ground flour mixed with olive oil, to be offered by fire to the Lord; this will be very pleasant to him. Also offer a drink offering consisting of three pints of wine. ¹⁴Until this is done you must not eat any of the harvest for yourselves—neither fresh kernels nor bread nor parched grain. This is a permanent law throughout your nation.

¹⁵,¹⁶"*The Harvest Festival (Festival of Pentecost):* Fifty days later you shall bring to the Lord an offering of a sample of the new grain of your later crops. ¹⁷This shall consist of two loaves of bread from your homes to be waved before the Lord in a gesture of offering. Bake this bread from a fifth of a bushel of fine flour containing yeast. It is an offering to the Lord of the first sampling of your later crops. ¹⁸Along with the bread and the wine, you shall sacrifice as burnt offerings to the Lord seven yearling lambs without defects, one young bull, and two rams. All are fire offerings, very acceptable to Jehovah. ¹⁹And you shall offer one male goat for a sin offering and two male yearling lambs for a peace offering.

²⁰"The priests shall wave these offerings before the Lord along with the loaves representing the first sampling of your later crops. They are holy to the Lord and will be given to the priests as food. ²¹That day shall be announced as a time of sacred convocation of all the people; don't do any work that day. This is a law to be honored from generation to generation. ²²(When you reap your harvests, you must not thoroughly reap all the corners of the fields, nor pick up the fallen grain; leave it for the poor and for foreigners living among you who have no land of their own; I am Jehovah your God!)

²³,²⁴"*The Festival of Trumpets:* Mid-September is a time for all the people to meet together for worship; it is a time of remembrance, and is to be announced by loud blowing of trumpets. ²⁵Don't do any hard work on that day, but offer a sacrifice by fire to the Lord.

²⁶,²⁷"*The Day of Atonement* follows nine days later: All the people are to come together before the Lord, saddened by their sin; and they shall offer sacrifices by fire to the Lord. ²⁸Don't do any work that day, for it is a special day for making atonement before the Lord your God. ²⁹Anyone who does not spend the day in repentance and sorrow for sin shall be excommunicated from his people. ³⁰,³¹And I will put to death anyone who does any kind of work that day. This is a law of Israel from generation to generation. ³²For this is a Sabbath of rest, and in it you shall go without food and be filled with sorrow; this time for atonement begins in the evening and continues through the next day.

³³,³⁴"*The Festival of Shelters:* Five days later, on the last day of September, is the Festival of Shelters to be celebrated before the Lord for seven days. ³⁵On the first day there will be a sacred assembly of all the people; don't do any hard work that day. ³⁶On each of the seven days of the festival you are to sacrifice an offering by fire to the Lord. The eighth day requires another sacred convocation of all the people, at which time there will again be an offering by fire to the Lord. It is the closing assembly, and no regular work is permitted.

³⁷"(These, then, are the regular annual festivals—sacred convocations of all people—when offerings to the Lord are to be made by fire. ³⁸These annual festivals are in addition to your regular Sabbaths—the weekly days of holy rest. The sacrifices made during the festivals are to be in addition to your regular giving and normal fulfillment of your vows.)

³⁹"This last day of September, at the end of your harvesting, is the time to begin to celebrate this seven-day festival before the Lord. Remember that the first and last days of the festival are special days of rest. ⁴⁰On the first day, take boughs of fruit trees laden with fruit, and palm fronds, and the boughs of leafy trees—such as willows that grow by the brooks—and [build shelters with them], rejoicing before the Lord your God for seven days. ⁴¹This seven-day annual feast is a law from generation to generation. ⁴²During those seven days, all of you who are native Israelites are to live in these shelters. ⁴³The purpose of this is to remind the people of Israel, generation after generation, that I rescued you from Egypt, and caused you to live in shelters. I am Jehovah your God."

⁴⁴So Moses announced these annual festivals of the Lord to the people of Israel.

24 The Memorial Offering

The Lord said to Moses, "Tell the people of Israel to bring you pure olive oil for an eternal

FAMILY DEVOTIONS

☐ DEVOTION 52
FAITH IN ACTION

Read Leviticus 23:22

Faith in Action Memory Verse

In response to all he has done for us, let us outdo each other in being helpful and kind to each other and in doing good.
Hebrews 10:24

Tony liked to hang around his father's small hardware store and watch as Dad worked on repair jobs. One Saturday he sat in the back room while Dad fiddled with a broken toaster. Finally Dad set the toaster down with a grin. "All finished," he said. On a small card he wrote, "Labor, one hour." Then he took several minutes to clean and shine the toaster.

Tony frowned. "Dad you counted wrong," he said. "I know you worked on that thing for at least an hour and ten minutes, besides the time you spent cleaning it." When his father just smiled, Tony continued, "And another thing, a lot of times I've seen you round off the amount somebody owes you. But you always make it lower, not higher. How are you ever going to make money that way?"

"Oh, I'm managing," Dad replied cheerfully. "I believe that if I give my customers good service and try not to charge any more than I have to, they'll keep coming back to my store. Besides, the Bible teaches we shouldn't reap the corners."

Tony looked confused. "Huh? I don't get it."

"Well, in Leviticus, God told farmers to leave some of their crop behind when they harvested it, so that needy people could take what they wanted. I don't have a farm, but I figure that the principle applies to my business, too. It means that I shouldn't try to squeeze every nickel I can out of my customers. I should leave the corners for them."

"If the farmer did all the work, he should get to keep all the harvest," objected Tony.

"But it's God who gives us the strength to work, and he blesses our efforts," Dad reminded him. "You've got a good head for business, Son, but you need to learn to be more generous. Even if nobody else notices, God will!"

How About You?

Do you cheat others in little ways—working on your chores for twenty-five minutes instead of thirty, skipping chores when you think Mom won't notice, doing a sloppy job on your schoolwork because you know the teacher will accept it anyway? You should begin making an effort to do a little more than what is required of you. God will certainly reward your extra efforts, and it will earn you a good reputation in the eyes of others as well. *S. K.*

• For the next devotional, turn to page 149. • For the next devotional on *FAITH IN ACTION*, turn to page 395. • For notes on *FAITH IN ACTION*, see pages 583, 846, 1068, and 1232.

flame ³,⁴in the lampstand of pure gold which stands outside the veil that secludes the Holy of Holies. Each morning and evening Aaron shall supply it with fresh oil and trim the wicks. It will be an eternal flame before the Lord from generation to generation.

⁵⁻⁸"Every Sabbath day the High Priest shall place twelve loaves of bread in two rows upon the gold table that stands before the Lord. These loaves shall be baked from finely ground flour, using a fifth of a bushel for each. Pure frankincense shall be sprinkled along each row. This will be a memorial offering made by fire to the Lord, in memory of his everlasting covenant with the people of Israel. ⁹The bread shall be eaten by Aaron and his sons, in a place set apart for the purpose. For these are offerings made by fire to the Lord under a permanent law of God and are most holy."

¹⁰Out in the camp one day, a young man whose mother was an Israelite and whose father was an Egyptian, got into a fight with one of the men of Israel. ¹¹During the fight the Egyptian man's son cursed God, and was brought to Moses for judgment. (His mother's name was Shelomith, daughter of Dibri of the tribe of Dan.) ¹²He was put in jail until the Lord would indicate what to do with him.

¹³,¹⁴And the Lord said to Moses, "Take him outside the camp and tell all who heard him to lay their hands upon his head; then all the people are to execute him by stoning. ¹⁵,¹⁶And tell the people of Israel that anyone who curses his God must pay the penalty: he must die. All the congregation shall stone him; this law applies to the foreigner as well as to the Israelite who blasphemes the name of Jehovah. He must die.

¹⁷"Also, all murderers must be executed. ¹⁸Anyone who kills an animal [that isn't his] shall replace it. ¹⁹The penalty for injuring anyone is to be injured in exactly the same way: ²⁰fracture for fracture, eye for eye, tooth for tooth. Whatever anyone does to another shall be done to him.

²¹"To repeat, whoever kills an animal must replace it, and whoever kills a man must die. ²²You shall have the same law for the foreigner as for the home-born citizen, for I am Jehovah your God."

²³So they took the youth out of the camp and stoned him until he died, as Jehovah had commanded Moses.

25 Rest for the Land

While Moses was on Mount Sinai, the Lord gave him these instructions for the people of Israel:

"When you come into the land I am going to give you, you must let the land rest before the Lord every seventh year. ³For six years you may sow your field and prune your vineyards and harvest your crops, ⁴but during the seventh year the land is to lie fallow before the Lord, uncultivated. Don't sow your crops and don't prune your vineyards during that entire year. ⁵Don't even reap for yourself the volunteer crops that come up, and don't gather the grapes for yourself; for it is a year of rest for the land. ⁶,⁷Any crops that do grow that year shall be free to all—for you, your servants, your slaves, and any foreigners living among you. Cattle and wild animals alike shall be allowed to graze there.

⁸"Every fiftieth year, ⁹on the Day of Atonement, let the trumpets blow loud and long throughout the land. ¹⁰For the fiftieth year shall be holy, a time to proclaim liberty throughout the land to all enslaved debtors, and a time for the canceling of all public and private debts. It shall be a year when all the family estates sold to others shall be returned to the original owners or their heirs.

¹¹"What a happy year it will be! In it you shall not sow, nor gather crops nor grapes; ¹²for it is a holy Year of Jubilee for you. That year your food shall be the volunteer crops that grow wild in the fields. ¹³Yes, during the Year of Jubilee everyone shall return home to his original family possession; if he has sold it, it shall be his again! ¹⁴⁻¹⁶Because of this, if the land is sold or bought during the preceding forty-nine years, a fair price shall be arrived at by counting the number of years until the Jubilee. If the Jubilee is many years away, the price will be high; if few years, the price will be low; for what you are really doing is selling the number of crops the new owner will get from the land before it is returned to you.

¹⁷,¹⁸"You must fear your God and not overcharge! For I am Jehovah. Obey my laws if you want to live safely in the land. ¹⁹When you obey, the land will yield bumper crops and you can eat your fill in safety. ²⁰But you will ask, 'What shall we eat the seventh year, since we are not allowed to plant or harvest crops that year?' ²¹,²²The answer is, 'I will bless you with bumper crops the sixth year that will last you until the crops of the eighth year are harvested!' ²³And remember, the land is mine, so you may not sell it permanently. You are merely my tenants and sharecroppers!

²⁴"In every contract of sale there must be a stipulation that the land can be redeemed at any time by the seller. ²⁵If anyone becomes poor and sells some of his land, then his nearest relatives may redeem it. ²⁶If there is no one else to redeem it, and he himself gets together enough money, ²⁷then he may always buy it back at a price proportionate to the number of harvests until the Jubilee, and the owner must accept the money

and return the land to him. ²⁸But if the original owner is not able to redeem it, then it shall belong to the new owner until the Year of Jubilee; but at the Jubilee year it must be returned again.

²⁹"If a man sells a house in the city, he has up to one year to redeem it, with full right of redemption during that time. ³⁰But if it is not redeemed within the year, then it will belong permanently to the new owner—it does not return to the original owner in the Year of Jubilee. ³¹But village houses—a village is a settlement without fortifying walls around it—are like farmland, redeemable at any time, and are always returned to the original owner in the Year of Jubilee.

³²"There is one exception: The homes of the Levites, even though in walled cities, may be redeemed at any time, ³³and must be returned to the original owners in the Year of Jubilee; for the Levites will not be given farmland like the other tribes, but will receive only houses in their cities, and the surrounding fields. ³⁴The Levites are not permitted to sell the fields of common land surrounding their cities, for these are their permanent possession, and they must belong to no one else.

³⁵"If your brother becomes poor, you are responsible to help him; invite him to live with you as a guest in your home. ³⁶Fear your God and let your brother live with you; and don't charge him interest on the money you lend him. ³⁷Remember—no interest; and give him what he needs, at your cost: don't try to make a profit! ³⁸For I, the Lord your God, brought you out of the land of Egypt to *give* you the land of Canaan, and to be your God.

³⁹"If a fellow Israelite becomes poor and sells himself to you, you must not treat him as an ordinary slave, ⁴⁰but rather as a hired servant or as a guest; and he shall serve you only until the Year of Jubilee. ⁴¹At that time he can leave with his children and return to his own family and possessions. ⁴²For I brought you from the land of Egypt, and you are my servants; so you may not be sold as ordinary slaves ⁴³or treated harshly; fear your God.

⁴⁴"However, you may purchase slaves from the foreign nations living around you, ⁴⁵and you may purchase the children of the foreigners living among you, even though they have been born in your land. ⁴⁶They will be permanent slaves for you to pass on to your children after you; but your brothers, the people of Israel, shall not be treated so.

⁴⁷"If a foreigner living among you becomes rich, and an Israelite becomes poor and sells himself to the foreigner or to the foreigner's family, ⁴⁸he may be redeemed by one of his brothers, ⁴⁹his uncle, nephew, or anyone else who is a near relative. He may also redeem himself if he can find the money. ⁵⁰The price of his freedom shall be in proportion to the number of years left before the Year of Jubilee—whatever it would cost to hire a servant for that number of years. ⁵¹If there are still many years until the Jubilee, he shall pay almost the amount he received when he sold himself; ⁵²if the years have passed and only a few remain until the Jubilee, then he will repay only a small part of the amount he received when he sold himself. ⁵³If he sells himself to a foreigner, the foreigner must treat him as a hired servant rather than as a slave or as property. ⁵⁴If he has not been redeemed by the time the Year of Jubilee arrives, then he and his children shall be freed at that time. ⁵⁵For the people of Israel are *my* servants; I brought them from the land of Egypt; I am the Lord your God.

26 Rewards for Obedience

"You must have no idols; you must never worship carved images, obelisks, or shaped stones, for I am the Lord your God. ²You must obey my Sabbath laws of rest, and reverence my Tabernacle, for I am the Lord.

³"If you obey all of my commandments, ⁴,⁵I will give you regular rains, and the land will yield bumper crops, and the trees will be loaded with fruit long after the normal time! And grapes will still be ripening when sowing time comes again. You shall eat your fill, and live safely in the land, ⁶for I will give you peace, and you will go to sleep without fear. I will chase away the dangerous animals. ⁷You will chase your enemies; they will die beneath your swords. ⁸Five of you will chase a hundred, and a hundred of you, ten thousand! You will defeat all of your enemies. ⁹I will look after you, and multiply you, and fulfill my covenant with you. ¹⁰You will have such a surplus of crops that you won't know what to do with them when the new harvest is ready! ¹¹And I will live among you and not despise you. ¹²I will walk among you and be your God, and you shall be my people. ¹³For I am the Lord your God who brought you out of the land of Egypt, so that you would be slaves no longer; I have broken your chains so that you can walk with dignity.

¹⁴"But if you will not listen to me or obey me,

OPTIMISM 26:40-45 When the people of Israel faced suffering, God offered them hope. One key to holding on to hope in God is to maintain his perspective on all of life while looking at our present experiences. The hope we need is best expressed in Jeremiah 29:11: "For I know the plans I have for you, says the Lord. They are plans for good and not for evil, to give you a future and a hope." To retain hope in the midst of suffering shows we have an eternal perspective on our present difficulties. **To begin the series of devotionals on OPTIMISM, turn to page 19.**

¹⁵but reject my laws, ¹⁶this is what I will do to you: I will punish you with sudden terrors and panic, and with tuberculosis and burning fever; your eyes shall be consumed and your life shall ebb away; you will sow your crops in vain, for your enemies will eat them. ¹⁷I will set my face against you and you will flee before your attackers; those who hate you will rule you; you will even run when no one is chasing you!

¹⁸"And if you still disobey me, I will punish you seven times more severely for your sins. ¹⁹I will break your proud power and make your heavens as iron and your earth as bronze. ²⁰Your strength shall be spent in vain; for your land shall not yield its crops, nor your trees their fruit.

²¹"And if even then you will not obey me and listen to me, I will send you seven times more plagues because of your sins. ²²I will send wild animals to kill your children and destroy your cattle and reduce your numbers so that your roads will be deserted.

²³"And if even this will not reform you, but you continue to walk against my wishes, ²⁴then I will walk against your wishes, and I, even I, will personally smite you seven times for your sin. ²⁵I will revenge the breaking of my covenant by bringing war against you. You will flee to your cities, and I will send a plague among you there; and you will be conquered by your enemies. ²⁶I will destroy your food supply so that one oven will be large enough to bake all the bread available for ten entire families; and you will still be hungry after your pittance has been doled out to you.

²⁷"And if you still won't listen to me or obey me, ²⁸then I will let loose my great anger and send you seven times greater punishment for your sins. ²⁹You shall eat your own sons and daughters, ³⁰and I will destroy the altars on the hills where you worship your idols, and I will cut down your incense altars, leaving your dead bodies to rot among your idols; and I will abhor you. ³¹I will make your cities desolate, and destroy your places of worship, and will not respond to your incense offerings. ³²Yes, I will desolate your land; your enemies shall live in it, utterly amazed at what I have done to you.

³³"I will scatter you out among the nations, destroying you with war as you go. Your land shall be desolate and your cities destroyed. ³⁴,³⁵Then at last the land will rest and make up for the many years you refused to let it lie idle; for it will lie desolate all the years that you are captives in enemy lands. Yes, then the land will rest and enjoy its Sabbaths! It will make up for the rest you didn't give it every seventh year when you lived upon it.

³⁶"And for those who are left alive, I will cause them to be dragged away to distant lands as prisoners of war and slaves. There they will live in constant fear. The sound of a leaf driven in the wind will send them fleeing as though chased by a man with a sword; they shall fall when no one is pursuing them. ³⁷Yes, though none pursue they shall stumble over each other in flight, as though fleeing in battle, with no power to stand before their enemies. ³⁸You shall perish among the nations and be destroyed among your enemies. ³⁹Those left shall pine away in enemy lands because of their sins, the same sins as those of their fathers.

⁴⁰,⁴¹"But at last they shall confess their sins and their fathers' sins of treachery against me. (Because they were against me, I was against them, and brought them into the land of their enemies.) When at last their evil hearts are humbled and they accept the punishment I send them for their sins, ⁴²then I will remember again my promises to Abraham, Isaac, and Jacob, and I will remember the land (and its desolation). ⁴³For the land shall enjoy its Sabbaths as it lies desolate. But then at last they shall accept their punishment for rejecting my laws and for despising my rule. ⁴⁴But despite all they have done, I will not utterly destroy them and my covenant with them, for I am Jehovah their God. ⁴⁵For their sakes I will remember my promises to their ancestors to be their God. For I brought their forefathers out of Egypt as all the nations watched in wonder. I am Jehovah."

⁴⁶These were the laws, ordinances, and instructions that Jehovah gave to the people of Israel, through Moses, on Mount Sinai.

27 Payments to the Lord

The Lord said to Moses, "Tell the people of Israel that when a person makes a special vow to give himself to the Lord, he shall give these payments instead: ³A man from the age of twenty to sixty shall pay twenty-five dollars; ⁴a woman from the age of twenty to sixty shall pay fifteen dollars; ⁵a boy from five to twenty shall pay ten dollars; a girl, five dollars. ⁶A boy one month to five years old shall have paid for him two and a half dollars; a girl, one and a half dollars. ⁷A man over sixty shall pay seven and a half dollars; a woman, five dollars. ⁸But if the person is too poor to pay this amount, he shall be brought to the priest, and the priest shall talk it over with him, and he shall pay as the priest shall decide.

⁹"But if it is an animal that is vowed to be given to the Lord as a sacrifice, it must be given. ¹⁰The vow may not be changed; the donor may neither change his mind about giving it to the Lord, nor substitute good for bad or bad for good; if he does, both the first and the second shall belong to

the Lord! ¹¹,¹²But if the animal given to the Lord is not a kind that is permitted as a sacrifice, the owner shall bring it to the priest to value it, and he shall be told how much to pay instead. ¹³If the animal is a kind that may be offered as a sacrifice, but the man wants to redeem it, then he shall pay 20 percent more than the value set by the priest.

¹⁴,¹⁵"If someone donates his home to the Lord and then wishes to redeem it, the priest will decide its value, and the man shall pay that amount plus 20 percent, and the house will be his again.

¹⁶"If a man dedicates any part of his field to the Lord, value it in proportion to its size, as indicated by the amount of seed required to sow it. A section of land that requires ten bushels of barley seed for sowing is valued at twenty-five dollars. ¹⁷If a man dedicates his field in the Year of Jubilee, then the whole estimate shall stand; ¹⁸but if it is after the Year of Jubilee, then the value shall be in proportion to the number of years remaining until the next Year of Jubilee. ¹⁹If the man decides to redeem the field, he shall pay 20 percent in addition to the priest's valuation, and the field will be his again. ²⁰But if he decides not to redeem the field, or if he has sold the field to someone else [and has given to the Lord his rights to it at the Year of Jubilee], it shall not be returned to him again. ²¹When it is freed in the Year of Jubilee, it shall belong to the Lord as a field devoted to him, and it shall be given to the priests.

²²"If a man dedicates to the Lord a field he has bought, but which is not part of his family possession, ²³the priest shall estimate the value until the Year of Jubilee, and he shall immediately give that estimated value to the Lord, ²⁴and in the Year of Jubilee the field shall return to the original owner from whom it was bought. ²⁵All the valuations shall be stated in standard money.

²⁶"You may not dedicate to the Lord the firstborn of any ox or sheep, for it is already his. ²⁷But if it is the firstborn of an animal that cannot be sacrificed because it is not on the list of those acceptable to the Lord, then the owner shall pay the priest's estimate of its worth, plus 20 percent; or if the owner does not redeem it, the priest may sell it to someone else. ²⁸However, anything utterly devoted to the Lord—people, animals, or inherited fields—shall not be sold or redeemed, for they are most holy to the Lord. ²⁹No one sentenced by the courts to die may pay a fine instead; he shall surely be put to death.

³⁰"A tenth of the produce of the land, whether grain or fruit, is the Lord's, and is holy. ³¹If anyone wants to buy back this fruit or grain, he must add a fifth to its value. ³²And the Lord owns every tenth animal of your herds and flocks and other domestic animals, as they pass by for counting. ³³The tenth given to the Lord shall not be selected on the basis of whether it is good or bad, and there shall be no substitutions; for if there is any change made, then both the original and the substitution shall belong to the Lord, and may not be bought back!"

³⁴These are the commandments the Lord gave to Moses for the people of Israel on Mount Sinai.

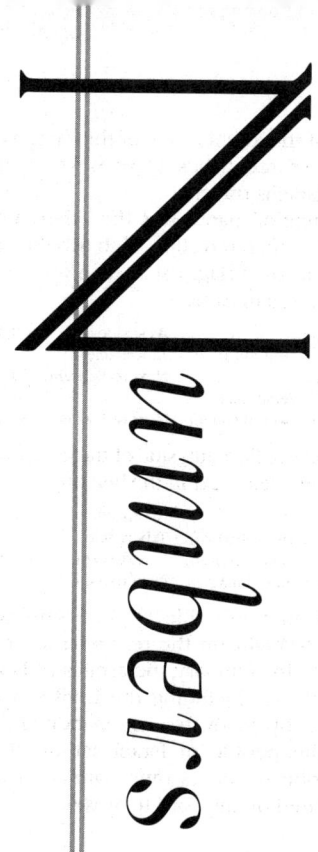

Numbers

SOMETIMES THINGS don't turn out the way we expect them to. This happened to the Israelites, too.

They expected a quick and easy trip from Egypt to Canaan, their Promised Land. God had led them to Mount Sinai, and now, after nearly two years, they were still camped there. What was God waiting for?

First, God had Moses take a census to count the number of people in all twelve tribes. This is how the book of Numbers got its name. Then God chose one special tribe, the Levites, to be the priests—or ministers—and teach the people about him. The Levites had to learn their job.

Finally the Israelites could leave for Canaan. They were seeing God's great power every day. Were they trusting God now? No! As they traveled, they grumbled and complained and were afraid that God didn't know what he was doing. Their complaining showed that they did not trust God to take care of them. Because they refused to trust him, God decided that the Israelites would have to wander in the desert for forty years. During that time, God took care of them every day.

Things didn't turn out the way the Israelites had expected, and things don't always turn out the way we expect, either. But we can always trust that God has a plan and that he's taking care of us. As you read Numbers, look for signs of God's care when unexpected things happen.

The People Are Counted

It was on the fifteenth day of April of the second year after the Israelis left Egypt that the Lord issued the following instructions to Moses. (He was in the Tabernacle at the camp of Israel on the Sinai peninsula at the time.)

$^{2-15}$"Take a census of all the men twenty years old and older who are able to go to war, indicating their tribe and family. You and Aaron are to direct the project, assisted by these leaders from each tribe:"

Tribe	Leader
Reuben	Elizur (son of Shedeur)
Simeon	Shelumiel (son of Zurishaddai)
Judah	Nahshon (son of Amminadab)
Issachar	Nethanel (son of Zuar)
Zebulun	Eliab (son of Helon)
Ephraim (son of Joseph)	Elishama (son of Ammihud)
Manasseh (son of Joseph)	Gamaliel (son of Pedahzur)
Benjamin	Abidan (son of Gideoni)
Dan	Ahiezer (son of Ammishaddai)
Asher	Pagiel (son of Ochran)
Gad	Eliasaph (son of Deuel)
Naphtali	Ahira (son of Enan)

¹⁶These were the tribal leaders elected from among the people.

¹⁷⁻¹⁹ On the same day Moses and Aaron and the above-named leaders summoned all the men of Israel who were twenty years old or older to come and register, each man indicating his tribe and family, as the Lord had commanded Moses. ²⁰⁻⁴⁶Here is the final tabulation:

Tribe	Total
Reuben (the oldest son of Jacob)	46,500
Simeon	59,300
Gad	45,650
Judah	74,600
Issachar	54,400
Zebulun	57,400
Joseph: Ephraim (son of Joseph)	40,500
Joseph: Manasseh (son of Joseph)	32,200
Benjamin	35,400
Dan	62,700
Asher	41,500
Naphtali	53,400
Grand Total:	603,550

⁴⁷⁻⁴⁹This total does not include the Levites, for the Lord had said to Moses, "Exempt the entire tribe of Levi from the draft, and do not include their number in the census. ⁵⁰For the Levites are assigned for the work connected with the Tabernacle and its transportation. They are to live near the Tabernacle, ⁵¹and whenever the Tabernacle is moved, the Levites are to take it down and set it up again; anyone else touching it shall be executed. ⁵²Each tribe of Israel shall have a separate camping area with its own flag. ⁵³The Levites' tents shall be clustered around the Tabernacle as a wall between the people of Israel and God's wrath—to protect them from his fierce anger against their sins."

⁵⁴So all these instructions of the Lord to Moses were put into effect.

2 Where the Tribes Camped

The Lord gave these further instructions to Moses and Aaron: "Each tribe will have its own tent area, with its flagpole and tribal banner; and at the center of these tribal compounds will be the Tabernacle." ³⁻³¹Here are the tribal locations:

Tribe:	Leader:	Location:	Census:
Judah	Nahshon (son of Amminadab)	East side of Tabernacle	74,600
Issachar	Nethanel (son of Zuar)	Next to Judah	54,400
Zebulun	Eliab (son of Helon)	Next to Issachar	57,400

So the total of all those on Judah's side of the camp was 186,400. These three tribes led the way whenever the Israelites traveled to a new campsite.

Reuben	Elizur (son of Shedeur)	South side of Tabernacle	46,500
Simeon	Shelumiel (son of Zurishaddai)	Next to Reuben	59,300
Gad	Eliasaph (son of Reuel)	Next to Simeon	45,650

So the total of the Reuben side of the camp was 151,450. These three tribes were next in line whenever the Israelis traveled.

Next in the line of march was the Tabernacle, with the Levites. When traveling, each tribe stayed together under its own flag, just as each was separate from the others in camp.

Ephraim	Elishama (son of Ammihud)	West side of Tabernacle	40,500
Manasseh	Gamaliel (son of Pedahzur)	Next to Ephraim	32,200
Benjamin	Abidan (son of Gideoni)	Next to Manasseh	35,400

So the total on the Ephraim side of the camp was 108,100, and they were next in the line of march.

Dan	Ahiezer (son of Ammishaddai)	North side of Tabernacle	62,700
Asher	Pagiel (son of Ochran)	Next to Dan	41,500
Naphtali	Ahira (son of Enan)	Next to Asher	53,400

So the total on Dan's side of the camp was 157,600. They brought up the rear whenever Israel traveled. ³²,³³In summary, the armies of Israel totaled 603,550 (not including the Levites, who were exempted by Jehovah's commandment to Moses). ³⁴So the people of Israel set up their camps, each tribe under its own banner, in the locations indicated by the Lord to Moses.

3 What the Levites Did

At the time when the Lord spoke to Moses on Mount Sinai, ²Aaron's sons were: Nadab (his oldest), Abihu, Eleazar, Ithamar. ³All were anointed as priests and set apart to minister at the Tabernacle. ⁴But Nadab and Abihu died before the Lord in the wilderness of Sinai when they used unholy fire. And since they had no children, this left only Eleazar and Ithamar to assist their father, Aaron.

⁵Then the Lord said to Moses, ⁶"Summon the tribe of Levi and present them to Aaron as his assistants. ⁷⁻⁹They will follow his instructions and perform the sacred duties at the Tabernacle on behalf of all the people of Israel. For they are assigned to him as representatives of all the people of Israel. They are in charge of all the furnishings and maintenance of the Tabernacle. ¹⁰However, only Aaron and his sons may carry out the duties of the priesthood; anyone else who presumes to assume this office shall be executed."

¹¹,¹²And the Lord said to Moses, "I have accepted the Levites in substitution for all the oldest sons of the people of Israel. The Levites are mine ¹³in exchange for all the oldest sons. From the day I killed all the oldest sons of the Egyptians, I took for myself all the firstborn in Israel of both men and animals! They are mine; I am Jehovah."

¹⁴,¹⁵The Lord now spoke again to Moses at the Sinai peninsula, telling him, "Take a census of the

FAMILY DEVOTIONS

☐ DEVOTION 53
TRUSTING GOD'S PLAN

Read Numbers 3:14-37

Trusting God's Plan Memory Verses:

This plan of mine is not what you would work out, neither are my thoughts the same as yours! For just as the heavens are higher than the earth, so are my ways higher than yours, and my thoughts than yours.
Isaiah 55:8-9

"There were lots of kids at vacation Bible school today," observed Linda as she left the church with her parents.

"Yes, it was a good morning," agreed her father, who was pastor of the church.

"The teachers surely were busy," added Mother. She looked at Linda. "I appreciate all your help, honey."

"I wish I could do more," said Linda as they walked home. "I only do little things—like pick up the paper after the kids are gone or show the new kids where they have to go. Nothing exciting or important like teaching."

After Linda climbed into bed that evening, Mom handed her a note. "This is from your dad and me," she said, sitting on the bed.

Linda began reading it out loud, but very slowly. "Thank you linda for your help at vbs each day the little things you do really are important and were proud youre our daughter we love you very much."

Linda was quiet a moment. "Thanks for the note," she said, wrinkling her brow. "It was hard to read, though."

"Oh?" asked Mom, looking surprised. "Why was that?"

"Well, you didn't capitalize words or put any punctuation in the note," Linda answered.

"Oh," Mom said with a twinkle in her eye, "do you think those little things are important?"

"Of course!" Linda laughed.

"You're right," Mom agreed. "And guess what? It's the same with little jobs—especially those done for the Lord. Any time you begin thinking the little things you do aren't important, just think about this note."

How About You?

Do you sometimes feel as though the jobs you do aren't important? Try to remember that in God's sight it doesn't matter whether a job is big or little, exciting or boring. He needs small things done, too; that's why he assigned the care of the Tabernacle and its utensils to certain tribes. The most important thing is that you faithfully do whatever he calls you to do. Whether it's washing dishes, mowing the lawn, or even closing a door for someone, do it in such a way that God himself would say to you, "Well done." *S. N.*

• For the next devotional, turn to page 153. • For the next devotional on *TRUSTING GOD'S PLAN*, turn to page 217.
• For notes on *TRUSTING GOD'S PLAN*, see page 252, 296, 731, and 870.

tribe of Levi, indicating each person's clan; count every male down to one month old." ¹⁶⁻²⁴So Moses did:

Levi's son	Levi's grandsons (clan names)	Census	Leader	Camp Location
Gershon	Libni Shimei	7,500	Elisaph (son of Lael)	West side of Tabernacle

²⁵⁻³⁰*Responsibilities:*

The responsibility of these two clans of Levites was the care of the Tabernacle: its coverings, its entry drapes, the drapes covering the fence surrounding the courtyard, the screen at the entrance of the courtyard surrounding the Tabernacle, the altar, and all the ropes used in tying the Tabernacle together.

Levi's son	Levi's grandsons (clan names)	Census	Leader	Camp Location
Kohath	Amram Izhar Hebron Uzziel	8,600	Elizaphan (son of Uzziel)	South side of Tabernacle

³¹⁻³⁵*Responsibilities:*

The responsibility of these four clans of Levites was the care of the Ark, the table, the lampstand, the altars, the various utensils used in the Tabernacle, the veil, and any repairs needed on any of these items. (Note: Eleazar, Aaron's son, shall be the chief administrator over the leaders of the Levites, with special responsibility for the oversight of the sanctuary.)

Levi's son	Levi's grandsons (clan names)	Census	Leader	Camp Location
Merari	Mahli Mushi	6,200	Zuriel (son of Abihail)	North side of Tabernacle

³⁶,³⁷*Responsibilities:*

The responsibility of these two clans was the care of the frames of the Tabernacle building; the posts; the bases for the posts, and all of the equipment needed for their use; the posts around the courtyard and their bases, pegs, and ropes.

³⁸The area east of the Tabernacle was reserved for the tents of Moses and of Aaron and his sons, who had the final responsibility for the Tabernacle on behalf of the people of Israel. (Anyone who was not a priest or Levite, but came into the Tabernacle, was to be executed.)

³⁹So all the Levites, as numbered by Moses and Aaron at the command of the Lord, were 22,000 males one month old and older.

⁴⁰Then the Lord said to Moses, "Now take a census of all the eldest sons in Israel who are one month old and older, and register each name. ⁴¹The Levites shall be mine (I am Jehovah) as substitutes for the eldest sons of Israel; and the Levites' cattle are mine as substitutes for the firstborn cattle of the whole nation."

⁴²So Moses took a census of the eldest sons of the people of Israel, as the Lord had commanded, ⁴³and found the total number of eldest sons one month old and older to be 22,273.

⁴⁴Now the Lord said to Moses, ⁴⁵"Give me the Levites instead of the eldest sons of the people of Israel; and give me the cattle of the Levites instead of the firstborn cattle of the people of Israel; yes, the Levites shall be mine; I am Jehovah. ⁴⁶To redeem the 273 eldest sons in excess of the number of Levites, ⁴⁷,⁴⁸pay five dollars for each one to Aaron and his sons."

⁴⁹So Moses received redemption money for the 273 eldest sons of Israel who were in excess of the number of Levites. (All the others were redeemed because the Levites had been given to the Lord in their place.) ⁵⁰The money collected came to a total of $1,365. ⁵¹And Moses gave it to Aaron and his sons as the Lord had commanded.

4 Jobs for the Kohath Clan

Then the Lord said to Moses and Aaron, "Take a census of the Kohath division of the Levite tribe. ³This census will be of all males from ages thirty to fifty who are able to work in the Tabernacle. ⁴These are their sacred duties:

⁵"When the camp moves, Aaron and his sons will enter the Tabernacle first and take down the veil and cover the Ark with it. ⁶Then they will cover the veil with goatskin leather, cover the goatskins with a blue cloth, and place the carrying poles of the Ark in their rings.

⁷"Next they must spread a blue cloth over the table where the Bread of the Presence is displayed, and place the dishes, spoons, bowls, cups, and the Bread upon the cloth. ⁸They will spread a scarlet cloth over that, and finally a covering of goatskin leather on top of the scarlet cloth. Then they shall insert the carrying poles into the table.

⁹"Next they must cover with a blue cloth the lampstand, the lamps, snuffers, trays, and the reservoir of olive oil. ¹⁰This entire group of objects shall then be covered with goatskin leather, and the bundle shall be placed upon a carrying frame.

¹¹"They must then spread a blue cloth over the gold altar, cover it with a covering of goatskin leather, and insert the carrying poles into the altar. ¹²All of the remaining utensils of the Tabernacle are to be wrapped in a blue cloth, covered with goatskin leather, and placed on the carrying frame.

¹³"The ashes are to be removed from the altar, and the altar shall be covered with a purple cloth. ¹⁴All of the altar utensils are to be placed upon the cloth—the firepans, hooks, shovels, basins,

and other containers—and a cover of goatskin leather will be spread over them. Finally, the carrying poles are to be put in place. ¹⁵When Aaron and his sons have finished packing the sanctuary and all the utensils, the clan of Kohath shall come and carry the units to wherever the camp is traveling; but they must not touch the holy items, lest they die. This, then, is the sacred work of the sons of Kohath.

¹⁶"Aaron's son Eleazar shall be responsible for the oil for the light, the sweet incense, the daily grain offering, and the anointing oil—in fact, the supervision of the entire Tabernacle and everything in it will be his responsibility."

¹⁷⁻¹⁹Then the Lord said to Moses and Aaron, "Don't let the families of Kohath destroy themselves! This is what you must do so that they will not die when they carry the most holy things: Aaron and his sons shall go in with them and point out what each is to carry. ²⁰Otherwise they must never enter the sanctuary for even a moment, lest they look at the sacred objects there and die."

²¹⁻²³And the Lord said to Moses, "Take a census of the Gershonite division of the tribe of Levi, all of the men between the ages of thirty and fifty who are eligible for the sacred work of the Tabernacle. ²⁴These will be their duties:

²⁵"They will carry the curtains of the Tabernacle, the Tabernacle itself with its coverings, the goatskin leather roof, and the curtain for the Tabernacle entrance. ²⁶They are also to carry the drapes covering the courtyard fence, and the curtain across the entrance to the courtyard that surrounds the altar and the Tabernacle. They will also carry the altar, the ropes, and all of the accessories. They are fully responsible for the transportation of these items. ²⁷Aaron or any of his sons may assign the Gershonites' tasks to them, ²⁸but the Gershonites will be directly responsible to Aaron's son Ithamar.

²⁹"Now take a census of the Merari division of the Levite tribe, all of the men from thirty to fifty who are eligible for the Tabernacle service. ³⁰,³¹When the Tabernacle is moved, they are to carry the frames of the Tabernacle, the bars, the bases, ³²the frames for the courtyard fence with their bases, pegs, cords, and everything else connected with their use and repair.

"Assign duties to each man by name. ³³The Merari division will also report to Aaron's son Ithamar."

³⁴So Moses and Aaron and the other leaders took a census of the Kohath division, ³⁵including all of the men thirty to fifty years of age who were eligible for the Tabernacle service, ³⁶and found that the total number was 2,750. ³⁷All this was done to carry out the Lord's instructions to Moses. ³⁸⁻⁴¹A similar census of the Gershon division totaled 2,630. ⁴²⁻⁴⁵And of the Merari division, 3,200. ⁴⁶⁻⁴⁸Thus Moses and Aaron and the leaders of Israel found that the total of all the Levites who were thirty to fifty years old and who were eligible for the Tabernacle service and transportation was 8,580. ⁴⁹This census was taken in response to the Lord's instructions to Moses.

5 Lepers Must Leave Camp

These are further instructions from the Lord to Moses: "Inform the people of Israel that they must expel all lepers from the camp, and all who have open sores, or who have been defiled by touching a dead person. ³This applies to men and women alike. Remove them so that they will not defile the camp where I live among you." ⁴These instructions were put into effect.

⁵,⁶Then the Lord said to Moses, "Tell the people of Israel that when anyone, man or woman, betrays the Lord by betraying a trust, it is sin. ⁷He must confess his sin and make full repayment for what he has stolen, adding 20 percent and returning it to the person he took it from. ⁸But if the person he wronged is dead, and there is no near relative to whom the payment can be made, it must be given to the priest, along with a lamb for atonement. ⁹,¹⁰When the people of Israel bring a gift to the Lord it shall go to the priests."

¹¹,¹²And the Lord said to Moses, "Tell the people of Israel that if a man's wife commits adultery, ¹³but there is no proof, there being no witness, ¹⁴and he is jealous and suspicious, ¹⁵the man shall bring his wife to the priest with an offering for her of a tenth of a bushel of barley meal without oil or frankincense mingled with it—for it is a suspicion offering—to bring out the truth as to whether or not she is guilty.

¹⁶"The priest shall bring her before the Lord, ¹⁷and take holy water in a clay jar and mix into it dust from the floor of the Tabernacle. ¹⁸He shall unbind her hair and place the suspicion offering in her hands to determine whether or not her husband's suspicions are justified. The priest shall stand before her holding the jar of bitter water that brings a curse. ¹⁹He shall require her to swear that she is innocent, and then he shall say to her, 'If no man has slept with you except your husband, be free from the effects of this bitter water that causes the curse. ²⁰But if you have committed adultery, ²¹,²²then Jehovah shall make you a curse among your people, for he will make your thigh rot away and your body swell.' And the woman shall be required to say, 'Yes, let it be so.' ²³Then the priest shall write these curses in a book and wash them off into the bitter water. ²⁴(When he

requires the woman to drink the water, it becomes bitter within her [if she is guilty].)

25"Then the priest shall take the suspicion offering from the woman's hand and wave it before Jehovah, and carry it to the altar. 26He shall take a handful, representing all of it, and burn the handful upon the altar, and then require the woman to drink the water. 27If she has been defiled, having committed adultery against her husband, the water will become bitter within her, and her body will swell and her thigh will rot, and she shall be a curse among her people. 28But if she is pure and has not committed adultery, she shall be unharmed and will soon become pregnant.

29"This, then, is the law concerning a wayward wife—or a husband's suspicions against his wife—30to determine whether or not she has been unfaithful to him. He shall bring her before the Lord and the priest shall handle the situation as outlined above. 31Her husband shall not be brought to trial for causing her horrible disease, for she is responsible."

6 The Nazirite

The Lord gave Moses these further instructions for the people of Israel: "When either a man or a woman takes the special vow of a Nazirite, consecrating himself to the Lord in a special way, 3,4he must not thereafter, during the entire period of his special consecration to the Lord, taste strong drink or wine or even fresh wine, grape juice, grapes, or raisins! He may eat nothing that comes from grape vines, not even the seeds or skins!

5"Throughout that time he must never cut his hair, for he is holy and consecrated to the Lord; that is why he must let his hair grow.

6,7"And he may not go near any dead body during the entire period of his vow, even if it is the body of his father, mother, brother, or sister; for his vow of consecration remains in effect, 8and he is consecrated to the Lord throughout the entire period. 9If he is defiled by having someone fall dead beside him, then seven days later he shall shave his defiled head; he will then be cleansed from the contamination of being in the presence of death. 10The next day, the eighth day, he must bring two turtledoves or two young pigeons to the priest at the entrance of the Tabernacle. 11The priest shall offer one of the birds for a sin offering, and the other for a burnt offering, and make atonement for his defilement. And he must renew his vows that day and let his hair begin to grow again. 12The days of his vow that were fulfilled before his defilement no longer count. He must begin all over again with a new vow, and must bring a male lamb a year old for a guilt offering.

13"At the conclusion of the period of his vow of separation to the Lord, he must go to the entrance of the Tabernacle 14and offer a burnt sacrifice to the Lord, a year-old lamb without defect. He must also offer a sin offering, a yearling ewe lamb without defect; a peace offering, a ram without defect; 15a basket of bread made without yeast; pancakes made of fine flour mixed with olive oil; unleavened wafers spread with oil; and the accompanying grain offering and drink offerings. 16The priest shall present these offerings before the Lord: first the sin offering and the burnt offering; 17then the ram for a peace offering, along with the basket of bread made without yeast; and finally the grain offering along with the drink offering.

18"Then the Nazirite shall shave his long hair—the sign of his vow of separation. This shall be done at the entrance of the Tabernacle, after which the hair shall be put in the fire under the peace offering sacrifice. 19After the man's head has been shaved, the priest shall take the roasted shoulder of the lamb, one of the pancakes (made without yeast), and one of the wafers (also made without yeast), and put them all into the man's hands. 20The priest shall then wave it all back and forth before the Lord in a gesture of offering; all of it is a holy portion for the priest, as are the rib piece and shoulder that were waved before the Lord. After that the Nazirite may again drink wine, for he is freed from his vow.

21"These are the regulations concerning a Nazirite and his sacrifices at the conclusion of his period of special dedication. In addition to these sacrifices he must bring any further offering he promised at the time he took his vow to become a Nazirite."

22,23Now the Lord said to Moses, "Tell Aaron and his sons that they are to give this special blessing to the people of Israel: 24-26'May the Lord bless and protect you; may the Lord's face radiate with joy because of you; may he be gracious to you, show you his favor, and give you his peace.' 27This is how Aaron and his sons shall call down my blessings upon the people of Israel; and I myself will personally bless them."

7 Gifts for the Tabernacle

Moses anointed and sanctified each part of the Tabernacle, including the altar and its utensils, on the day he finished setting it up. 2Then the leaders of Israel—the chiefs of the tribes, the men who had organized the census—brought their offerings. 3They brought six covered wagons, each drawn by two oxen—a wagon for every two leaders and an ox for each one; and they presented them to the Lord in front of the Tabernacle.

4,5"Accept their gifts," the Lord told Moses, "and use these wagons for the work of the Tabernacle.

Family Devotions

☐ DEVOTION 54
CONFESSING SIN

Read Numbers 5:5-10

The numbers on the watch flashed eerily in the darkness. Carl sighed and stuffed it under his pillow. Oh, why had he ever stolen it?

Carl had never owned a watch, and when he saw this one displayed on the store counter, it seemed he couldn't resist slipping it into his pocket. Now he realized what a foolish thing he had done. He couldn't wear the watch for fear his folks would notice it. Already he had begun to wonder if anyone at the store had seen him steal it.

Maybe things will seem better today, he thought, as he climbed out of bed the next morning. But twice on the way to school, he was sure he saw someone following him. At lunchtime he noticed several teachers talking together, and one of them seemed to glance in Carl's direction.

That night as he lay in his bed, Carl heard footsteps in the hallway. "Who's there?" he whispered hoarsely.

The door swung open, and Carl's father stepped in. "I just got up for a drink of water, Son. Is everything all right?"

Something inside Carl seemed to snap. "It's in my top drawer, so go ahead and take it," he sobbed.

Carl poured out the whole story; ending with his impression that everybody seemed to know what he had done. Dad nodded. "I think I know what you mean," he said. "Actually, someone did witness your theft of that watch, and he has been bothering you about it ever since."

"But who, Dad?" Carl wondered.

"The Holy Spirit," explained Dad. "When the Spirit begins to convict people of sin, they often have the miserable feeling that someone is chasing them. You'll have no rest until you stop running from God and do the right thing."

So, on his knees, Carl asked for God's forgiveness. He would take the watch back the very next day and accept the consequences.

Confessing Sin Memory Verse

But if we confess our sins to him, he can be depended on to forgive us and to cleanse us from every wrong. [And it is perfectly proper for God to do this for us because Christ died to wash away our sins.]
1 John 1:9

How About You?

Whenever you do something wrong, it's really God you're sinning against. Perhaps there is some sin in your heart about which God's Spirit is convicting you. Stop running from him. Seek the perfect peace of his forgiveness. *S. K.*

• For the next devotional, turn to page 155.   • For the next devotional on CONFESSING SIN, turn to page 185.
• For notes on CONFESSING SIN, see pages 429, 479, 836, 881, and 1220.

Give them to the Levites for whatever needs they may have."

⁶So Moses presented the wagons and the oxen to the Levites. ⁷Two wagons and four oxen were given to the Gershon division for their use, ⁸and four wagons and eight oxen were given to the Merari division, which was under the leadership of Ithamar, Aaron's son. ⁹None of the wagons or teams was given to the Kohath division, for they were required to carry their portion of the Tabernacle upon their shoulders.

¹⁰The leaders also presented dedication gifts on the day the altar was anointed, placing them before the altar. ¹¹The Lord said to Moses, "Let each of them bring his gift on a different day for the dedication of the altar."

¹²So Nahshon, the son of Amminadab of the tribe of Judah, brought his gift the first day. ¹³It consisted of a silver platter weighing three pounds and a silver bowl of about two pounds, both filled with grain offerings of fine flour mixed with oil. ¹⁴He also brought a tiny gold box of incense which weighed only about four ounces. ¹⁵He brought a young bull, a ram, and a male yearling lamb as burnt offerings; ¹⁶a male goat for a sin offering; ¹⁷and for the peace offerings two oxen, five rams, five male goats, and five male yearling lambs.

¹⁸⁻²³The next day Nethanel, the son of Zuar, chief of the tribe of Issachar, brought his gifts and offerings. They were exactly the same as Nahshon had presented on the previous day.

²⁴⁻²⁹On the third day Eliab, the son of Helon, chief of the tribe of Zebulun, came with his offerings—the same as those presented on the previous days.

³⁰⁻³⁵On the fourth day the gifts were presented by Elizur, son of Shedeur, chief of the tribe of Reuben; his gifts and offerings were the same as those given on the previous days.

³⁶⁻⁴¹On the fifth day came Shelumiel, the son of Zurishaddai, chief of the tribe of Simeon, with the same gifts.

⁴²⁻⁴⁷The next day it was Eliasaph's turn, son of Deuel, chief of the tribe of Gad. He, too, offered the same gifts and sacrifices.

⁴⁸⁻⁵³On the seventh day, Elishama, the son of Ammihud, chief of the tribe of Ephraim, brought his gifts, the same as those presented on the previous days.

⁵⁴⁻⁵⁹Gamaliel, son of Pedahzur, prince of the tribe of Manasseh, came the eighth day with the same offerings.

⁶⁰⁻⁶⁵ On the ninth day it was Abidan the son of Gideoni, chief of the tribe of Benjamin, with his gifts, the same as those offered by the others.

⁶⁶⁻⁷¹Ahiezer, the son of Ammishaddai, brought his gifts on the tenth day. He was the chief of the tribe of Dan and his offerings were the same as those on the previous days.

⁷²⁻⁷⁷Pagiel, son of Ochran, chief of the tribe of Asher, brought his gifts on the eleventh day—the same gifts and offerings as the others.

⁷⁸⁻⁸³On the twelfth day came Ahira, son of Enan, chief of the tribe of Naphtali, with his offerings; they were identical to those brought by the others.

⁸⁴⁻⁸⁶So, beginning the day the altar was anointed, it was dedicated by these gifts from the chiefs of the tribes of Israel. Their combined offerings were as follows:

12 silver platters (each weighing about three pounds);
12 silver bowls (each weighing about two pounds); (so the total weight of the silver was about sixty pounds);
12 gold trays (the trays weighing about four ounces apiece); (so the total weight of gold was about three pounds).

⁸⁷For the burnt offerings they brought:

12 bulls, 12 rams,
12 yearling male goats (with the grain offerings that accompanied them).

For sin offerings they brought:

12 male goats.

⁸⁸For the peace offerings they brought:

24 young bulls,
60 rams, 60 male goats,
60 male lambs one year old.

⁸⁹When Moses went into the Tabernacle to speak with God, he heard the Voice speaking to him from above the place of mercy over the Ark, between the statues of the two Guardian Angels.

8 Setting Up the Lamps

The Lord said to Moses, ²"Tell Aaron that when he lights the seven lamps in the lampstand, he is to set them so that they will throw their light forward."

³So Aaron did this. ⁴The lampstand, including the floral decorations on the base and branches, was made entirely of beaten gold. It was constructed according to the exact design the Lord had shown Moses.

⁵,⁶Then the Lord said to Moses, "Now set apart the Levites from the other people of Israel. ⁷Do this by sprinkling water of purification upon them, then having them shave their entire bodies and wash their clothing and themselves. ⁸Have them bring a young bull and a grain offering of fine flour

Family Devotions

☐ DEVOTION 55
Dealing with Change

Read Numbers 9:15-23

Ooooh! I don't feel good," moaned Shelly as she came to the breakfast table. "Can't I just stay home today?" She sat down and clutched her stomach.

"I don't believe you have a fever," said Mom as she felt her daughter's forehead, "but if you really don't feel well, I suppose you should stay home."

Later that morning Mom was making cookies and Shelly joined her in the kitchen. "Oh, let me help!" she exclaimed. Putting on one of Mom's aprons, Shelly squealed as one of the eggs broke and slid down her arm and onto the floor. "Oh, I never will learn to do this right! It's a good thing I have a big apron on."

"It certainly is!" agreed Mom, laughing as she helped clean up the mess. Looking at Shelly thoughtfully, she said, "The stomachache seems to have disappeared." As Shelly nodded, Mom continued, "Do you think you really were sick, honey, or were you just nervous about going to a new school?"

"Oh, Mom," Shelly burst out, "I wish we had never moved! I feel so strange in this school, and I don't have any friends. I don't know *anybody.*"

"It will get better," Mom assured her. "You know, you were glad you had the protection of that apron as we made cookies. But are you aware that you also have protection as you go to school?" Shelly looked surprised as Mom continued, "You're a Christian, a child of God, and he is your protection. When the people of Israel were moving about in the wilderness, the Lord went with them as a cloud of protection. You can't see him like they could, but he's with you just the same. God will take care of you, even in a new school and among many new faces. Remember, he is with you always."

Shelly nodded slowly. "Ann and Barb were really friendly yesterday. I guess I'll go this afternoon and take them a cookie," she decided. "It shouldn't be so bad if I just remember I'm well protected."

Dealing with Change Memory Verse

We know that all that happens to us is working for our good if we love God and are fitting into his plans.
Romans 8:28

How About You?

What are you afraid of? A new school? A difficult class? A school bully? The dark? If you're a Christian, God is your protection in whatever situation you face. Trust him. H.M.

• For the next devotional, turn to page 159. • For the next devotional on DEALING WITH CHANGE, turn to page 223.
• For notes on DEALING WITH CHANGE, see pages 56, 156, 288, 1186, and 1198.

mingled with oil, along with another young bull for a sin offering. ⁹Then bring the Levites to the door of the Tabernacle as all the people watch. ¹⁰There the leaders of the tribes shall lay their hands upon them, ¹¹and Aaron, with a gesture of offering, shall present them to the Lord as a gift from the entire nation of Israel. The Levites will represent all the people in serving the Lord.

¹²"Next, the Levite leaders shall lay their hands upon the heads of the young bulls and offer them before the Lord; one for a sin offering and the other for a burnt offering, to make atonement for the Levites. ¹³Then the Levites are to be presented to Aaron and his sons, just as any other gift to the Lord is given to the priests! ¹⁴In this way you will dedicate the Levites from among the rest of the people of Israel, and the Levites shall be mine. ¹⁵After you have sanctified them and presented them in this way, they shall go in and out of the Tabernacle to do their work.

¹⁶"They are mine from among all the people of Israel, and I have accepted them in place of all the firstborn children of the Israelites: I have taken the Levites as their substitutes. ¹⁷For all the firstborn among the people of Israel are mine, both men and animals; I claimed them for myself the night I killed all the firstborn Egyptians. ¹⁸Yes, I have accepted the Levites in place of all the eldest sons of Israel. ¹⁹And I will give the Levites as a gift to Aaron and his sons. The Levites will carry out the sacred duties required of the people of Israel in the Tabernacle, and will offer the people's sacrifices, making atonement for them. There will be no plague among the Israelites—as there would be if the ordinary people entered the Tabernacle."

²⁰So Moses and Aaron and all the people of Israel dedicated the Levites, carefully following Jehovah's instructions to Moses. ²¹The Levites purified themselves and washed their clothes, and Aaron presented them to the Lord in a gesture of offering. He then performed the rite of atonement over them to purify them. ²²After that they went into the Tabernacle as assistants to Aaron and his sons; everything was done just as the Lord had commanded Moses.

²³,²⁴The Lord also instructed Moses, "The Levites are to begin serving in the Tabernacle at the age of twenty-five, and are to retire at the age of fifty. ²⁵,²⁶After retirement they can assist with various light duties in the Tabernacle, but will have no regular responsibilities."

9 Passover Is Celebrated Again

Jehovah gave these instructions to Moses while he and the rest of the Israelis were on the Sinai peninsula, during the first month of the second year after leaving Egypt:

²,³"The people of Israel must celebrate the Passover annually on April first, beginning in the evening. Be sure to follow all of my instructions concerning this celebration."

⁴,⁵So Moses announced that the Passover celebration would begin on the evening of April first, there in the Sinai peninsula, just as the Lord had commanded. ⁶,⁷But as it happened, some of the men had just attended a funeral and were ceremonially defiled by having touched the dead, so they couldn't eat the Passover lamb that night. They came to Moses and Aaron and explained their problem and protested at being forbidden from offering their sacrifice to the Lord at the time he had appointed.

⁸Moses said he would ask the Lord about it, ⁹and this was God's reply:

¹⁰"If any of the people of Israel, now or in the generations to come, are defiled at Passover time because of touching a dead body, or if they are on a journey and cannot be present, they may still celebrate the Passover, but one month later, ¹¹on May first, beginning in the evening. They are to eat the lamb at that time, with unleavened bread and bitter herbs. ¹²They must not leave any of it until the next morning, and must not break a bone of it, and must follow all the regular instructions concerning the Passover.

¹³"But anyone who is not defiled, and anyone who is not away on a trip, and yet refuses to celebrate the Passover at the regular time, shall be excommunicated from the people of Israel for refusing to sacrifice to Jehovah at the proper time; he must bear his guilt. ¹⁴And if a foreigner is living among you and wants to celebrate the Passover to the Lord, he shall follow all these same instructions. There is one law for all."

¹⁵On the day the Tabernacle was raised the Cloud covered it; and that evening the Cloud changed to the appearance of fire, and stayed that way throughout the night. ¹⁶It was always so—the daytime Cloud changing to the appearance of fire at night. ¹⁷When the Cloud lifted, the people of Israel moved on to wherever it stopped, and camped there. ¹⁸In this way they journeyed at the command of the Lord and stopped where he

---

DEALING WITH CHANGE 10:21 Those who travel, move, or face new challenges know what it is to be uprooted. Life is full of changes, and few things remain stable. The people of Israel were constantly moving through the desert. They were able to handle change only because God's presence in the Tabernacle was always with them. The portable Tabernacle signified God and his people moving together. For us, stability does not mean lack of change, but moving with God in every circumstance. **To begin the series of devotionals on DEALING WITH CHANGE, turn to page 15.**

told them to, then remained there as long as the Cloud stayed. ¹⁹If it stayed a long time, then they stayed a long time. But if it stayed only a few days, then they remained only a few days; for so the Lord had instructed them. ²⁰,²¹Sometimes the fire-cloud stayed only during the night and moved on the next morning. But day or night, when it moved, the people broke camp and followed. ²²If the Cloud stayed above the Tabernacle two days, a month, or a year, that is how long the people of Israel stayed; but as soon as it moved, they moved. ²³So it was that they camped or traveled at the commandment of the Lord; and whatever the Lord told Moses they should do, they did.

10 The Silver Trumpets

Now the Lord said to Moses, "Make two trumpets of beaten silver to be used for summoning the people to assemble and for signaling the breaking of camp. ³When both trumpets are blown, the people will know that they are to gather at the entrance of the Tabernacle. ⁴But if only one is blown, then only the chiefs of the tribes of Israel shall come to you.

⁵⁻⁷"Different trumpet blasts will be necessary to distinguish between the summons to assemble and the signal to break camp and move onward. When the travel signal is blown, the tribes camped on the east side of the Tabernacle shall leave first; at the second signal, the tribes on the south shall go. ⁸Only the priests are permitted to blow the trumpets. This is a permanent instruction to be followed from generation to generation.

⁹"When you arrive in the Promised Land and go to war against your enemies, God will hear you and save you from your enemies when you sound the alarm with these trumpets. ¹⁰Use the trumpets in times of gladness, too, blowing them at your annual festivals and at the beginning of each month to rejoice over your burnt offerings and peace offerings. And God will be reminded of his covenant with you. For I am Jehovah, your God."

¹¹The Cloud lifted from the Tabernacle on the twentieth day of the second month of the second year of Israel's leaving Egypt; ¹²so the Israelites left the Sinai wilderness, and followed the Cloud until it stopped in the wilderness of Paran. ¹³This was their first journey after having received the Lord's travel instructions to Moses.

¹⁴At the head of the march was the tribe of Judah grouped behind its flag and led by Nahshon, the son of Amminadab. ¹⁵Next came the tribe of Issachar, led by Nethanel, the son of Zuar, ¹⁶and the tribe of Zebulun, led by Eliab, the son of Helon.

¹⁷The Tabernacle was taken down and the men of the Gershon and Merari divisions of the tribe of Levi were next in the line of march, carrying the Tabernacle upon their shoulders. ¹⁸Then came the flag of the camp of Reuben, with Elizur the son of Shedeur leading his people. ¹⁹Next was the tribe of Simeon headed by Shelumiel, the son of Zurishaddai; ²⁰and the tribe of Gad led by Eliasaph, the son of Deuel.

²¹Next came the Kohathites carrying the items from the inner sanctuary. (The Tabernacle was already erected in its new location by the time they arrived.) ²²Next in line was the tribe of Ephraim behind its flag, led by Elishama, the son of Ammihud; ²³and the tribe of Manasseh led by Gamaliel the son of Pedahzur; ²⁴and the tribe of Benjamin, led by Abidan the son of Gideoni. ²⁵Last of all were the tribes headed by the flag of the tribe of Dan under the leadership of Ahiezer, the son of Ammishaddai; ²⁶the tribe of Asher, led by Pagiel, the son of Ochran; ²⁷and the tribe of Naphtali, led by Ahira, the son of Enan. ²⁸That was the order in which the tribes traveled.

²⁹One day Moses said to his brother-in-law, Hobab (son of Reuel, the Midianite), "At last we are on our way to the Promised Land. Come with us and we will do you good; for the Lord has given wonderful promises to Israel!"

³⁰But his brother-in-law replied, "No, I must return to my own land and kinfolk."

³¹"Stay with us," Moses pleaded, "for you know the ways of the wilderness and will be a great help to us. ³²If you come, you will share in all the good things the Lord does for us."

³³They traveled for three days after leaving Mount Sinai, with the Ark at the front of the column to choose a place for them to stop. ³⁴It was daytime when they left, with the Cloud moving along ahead of them as they began their march. ³⁵As the Ark was carried forward, Moses cried out, "Arise, O Lord, and scatter your enemies; let them flee before you." ³⁶And when the Ark was set down he said, "Return, O Lord, to the millions of Israel."

11 Someone to Help Moses

The people were soon complaining about all their misfortunes, and the Lord heard them. His anger flared out against them because of their complaints, so the fire of the Lord began destroying those at the far end of the camp. ²They

ENCOURAGING OTHERS 10:29-32 By complimenting his wilderness skills, Moses let Hobab know he was needed. Others cannot know you appreciate them if you do not tell them they are important to you. Complimenting those who deserve it builds lasting relationships and helps others know they are valued. Think about those who have helped you this month. What can you do to let them know how much you need and appreciate them? **To begin the series of devotionals on ENCOURAGING OTHERS, turn to page 705.**

screamed to Moses for help, and when he prayed for them the fire stopped. ³Ever after, the area was known as "The Place of Burning," because the fire from the Lord burned among them there.

⁴,⁵Then the Egyptians who had come with them began to long for the good things of Egypt. This added to the discontent of the people of Israel and they wept, "Oh, for a few bites of meat! Oh, that we had some of the delicious fish we enjoyed so much in Egypt, and the wonderful cucumbers and melons, leeks, onions, and garlic! ⁶But now our strength is gone, and day after day we have to face this manna!"

⁷The manna was the size of small seeds, whitish yellow in color. ⁸The people gathered it from the ground and pounded it into flour, then boiled it, and then made pancakes from it—they tasted like pancakes fried in vegetable oil. ⁹The manna fell with the dew during the night.

¹⁰Moses heard all the families standing around their tent doors weeping, and the anger of the Lord grew hot; Moses too was highly displeased.

¹¹Moses said to the Lord, "Why pick on me, to give me the burden of a people like this? ¹²Are they *my* children? Am I their father? Is that why you have given me the job of nursing them along like babies until we get to the land you promised their ancestors? ¹³Where am I supposed to get meat for all these people? For they weep to me saying, 'Give us meat!' ¹⁴I can't carry this nation by myself! The load is far too heavy! ¹⁵If you are going to treat me like this, please kill me right now; it will be a kindness! Let me out of this impossible situation!"

¹⁶Then the Lord said to Moses, "Summon before me seventy of the leaders of Israel; bring them to the Tabernacle, to stand there with you. ¹⁷I will come down and talk with you there, and I will take of the Spirit which is on you and will put it upon them also; they shall bear the burden of the people along with you, so that you will not have the task alone.

¹⁸"And tell the people to purify themselves, for tomorrow they shall have meat to eat. Tell them, 'The Lord has heard your tearful complaints about all you left behind in Egypt, and he is going to give you meat. You shall eat it, ¹⁹,²⁰not for just a day or two, or five or ten or even twenty! For one whole month you will have meat until you vomit it from your noses; for you have rejected the Lord who is here among you, and you have wept for Egypt.'"

²¹But Moses said, "There are 600,000 men alone [besides all the women and children], and yet you promise them meat for a whole month! ²²If we butcher all our flocks and herds it won't be enough! We would have to catch every fish in the ocean to fulfill your promise!"

²³Then the Lord said to Moses, "When did I become weak? Now you shall see whether my word comes true or not!"

²⁴So Moses left the Tabernacle and reported Jehovah's words to the people; and he gathered the seventy elders and placed them around the Tabernacle. ²⁵And the Lord came down in the Cloud and talked with Moses, and the Lord took of the Spirit that was upon Moses and put it upon the seventy elders; and when the Spirit rested upon them, they prophesied for some time.

²⁶But two of the seventy—Eldad and Medad—were still in the camp, and when the Spirit rested upon them, they prophesied there. ²⁷Some young men ran and told Moses what was happening, ²⁸and Joshua (the son of Nun), one of Moses' personally chosen assistants, protested, "Sir, make them stop!"

²⁹But Moses replied, "Are you jealous for my sake? I only wish that all of the Lord's people were prophets, and that the Lord would put his Spirit upon them all!" ³⁰Then Moses returned to the camp with the elders of Israel.

³¹The Lord sent a wind that brought quail from the sea and let them fall into the camp and all around it! As far as one could walk in a day in any direction, there were quail flying three or four feet above the ground. ³²So the people caught and killed quail all that day and through the night and all the next day too! The least anyone gathered was 100 bushels! Quail were spread out all around the camp. ³³But as everyone began eating the meat, the anger of the Lord rose against the people and he killed large numbers of them with a plague. ³⁴So the name of that place was called, "The Place of the Graves Caused by Lust," because they buried the people there who had lusted for meat and for Egypt. ³⁵And from that place they journeyed to Hazeroth, where they stayed awhile.

12 Miriam Gets Leprosy

One day Miriam and Aaron were criticizing Moses because his wife was a Cushite woman, ²and they said, "Has the Lord spoken only through Moses? Hasn't he spoken through us, too?"

But the Lord heard them. ³,⁴Immediately he summoned Moses, Aaron, and Miriam to the Tabernacle: "Come here, you three," he commanded. So they stood before the Lord. (Now Moses was the humblest man on earth.)

⁵Then the Lord descended in the Cloud and stood at the entrance of the Tabernacle. "Aaron and Miriam, step forward," he commanded; and they did. ⁶And the Lord said to them, "Even with a prophet, I would communicate by visions and

Family Devotions

☐ *Devotion 56*
Contentment

Read Numbers 11:4-10

Contentment Memory Verse

I know how to live on almost nothing or with everything. I have learned the secret of contentment in every situation, whether it be a full stomach or hunger, plenty or want.
Philippians 4:12

"It's so cold! I can't stand it a minute longer." Jessie pulled her coat tightly around her.

"Oh, Jessie," said Mom, "you were just as excited about coming downtown to see the Christmas lights as the rest of us! Now you're complaining and we've only been here ten minutes."

"But I'll freeze to death!" chattered Jessie.

"You will not freeze to death," replied Mother. "I can guarantee that!" She laughed. "Seems to me, I remember a day last July when you complained for an entire morning about the heat. You wished for winter, remember? You put Christmas music on the stereo. Now it's cold for real, and you're wishing for hot weather! Aren't you ever satisfied?"

"But, Mom . . . ," Jessie protested.

"It's not that cold, honey," said Mother firmly. "I think you should listen to yourself sometimes. You never seem to be happy. If it's hot, you want it cold. If it's cold, you want it hot. The Bible says we're to be content in every situation, no matter what it is."

Jessie did remember that day in July when she had complained about the heat! In fact, there had been more than one summer day when she had wished for winter. Suddenly she remembered how the people of Israel had complained about the manna God had provided for them. She sure didn't want to be like that! Smiling, she walked on ahead and called out, "Come on! Let's go see the rest of the Christmas lights. If it were hot, all the beautiful snow would melt."

H o w   A b o u t   Y o u ?
Do you often wish for something you don't have? Or wish you could be doing something that you can't do? Instead of wishing for what you don't have, be thankful for what you do have. Listen to yourself talk. Are you a complainer, or are you content? *L. M. W.*

• For the next devotional, turn to page 161. • For the next devotional on Contentment, turn to page 263.
• For notes on Contentment, see pages 542, 547, 902, and 1063.

dreams; ⁷,⁸but that is not how I communicate with my servant Moses. He is completely at home in my house! With him I speak face to face! And he shall see the very form of God! Why then were you not afraid to criticize him?"

⁹Then the anger of the Lord grew hot against them, and he departed. ¹⁰As the Cloud moved from above the Tabernacle, Miriam suddenly became white with leprosy. When Aaron saw what had happened, ¹¹he cried out to Moses, "Oh, sir, do not punish us for this sin; we were fools to do such a thing. ¹²Don't let her be as one dead, whose body is half rotted away at birth."

¹³And Moses cried out to the Lord, "Heal her, O God, I beg you!"

¹⁴And the Lord said to Moses, "If her father had but spit in her face she would be defiled seven days. Let her be banished from the camp for seven days, and after that she can come back again."

¹⁵So Miriam was excluded from the camp for seven days, and the people waited until she was brought back in before they traveled again. ¹⁶Afterwards they left Hazeroth and camped in the wilderness of Paran.

13 The Twelve Spies

Jehovah now instructed Moses, ²"Send spies into the land of Canaan—the land I am giving to Israel; send one leader from each tribe."

³⁻¹⁵(The Israelis were camped in the wilderness of Paran at the time.) Moses did as the Lord had commanded and sent these twelve tribal leaders:

Shammua, son of Zaccur, from the tribe of Reuben;
Shaphat, son of Hori, from the tribe of Simeon;
Caleb, son of Jephunneh, from the tribe of Judah;
Igal, son of Joseph, from the tribe of Issachar;
Hoshea, son of Nun, from the half-tribe of Ephraim;
Palti, son of Raphu, from the tribe of Benjamin;
Gaddiel, son of Sodi, from the tribe of Zebulun;
Gaddi, son of Susi, from the tribe of Joseph (actually, the half-tribe of Manasseh);
Ammiel, son of Gemalli, from the tribe of Dan;
Sethur, son of Michael, from the tribe of Asher;
Nahbi, son of Vophsi, from the tribe of Naphtali;
Geuel, son of Machi, from the tribe of Gad.

¹⁶It was at this time that Moses changed Hoshea's name to Joshua.

¹⁷Moses sent them out with these instructions: "Go northward into the hill country of the Negeb, ¹⁸and see what the land is like; see also what the people are like who live there, whether they are strong or weak, many or few; ¹⁹and whether the land is fertile or not; and what cities there are, and whether they are villages or are fortified; ²⁰whether the land is rich or poor, and whether there are many trees. Don't be afraid, and bring back some samples of the crops you see." (The first of the grapes were being harvested at that time.)

²¹So they spied out the land all the way from the wilderness of Zin to Rehob near Hamath. ²²Going northward, they passed first through the Negeb and arrived at Hebron. There they saw the Ahimanites, Sheshites, and Talmites, all families descended from Anak. (By the way, Hebron was very ancient, having been founded seven years before Tanis in Egypt.) ²³Then they came to what is now known as the Valley of Eshcol where they cut down a single cluster of grapes so large that it took two of them to carry it on a pole between them! They also took some samples of the pomegranates and figs. ²⁴The Israelis named the valley "Eshcol" at that time (meaning "Cluster") because of the cluster of grapes they found!

²⁵After forty days of exploration they returned from their tour. ²⁶They made their report to Moses, Aaron, and all the people of Israel in the wilderness of Paran at Kadesh, and they showed the fruit they had brought with them.

²⁷This was their report: "We arrived in the land you sent us to see, and it is indeed a magnificent country—a land 'flowing with milk and honey.' Here is some fruit we have brought as proof. ²⁸But the people living there are powerful, and their cities are fortified and very large; and what's more, we saw Anakim giants there! ²⁹The Amalekites live in the south, while in the hill country there are the Hittites, Jebusites, and Amorites; down along the coast of the Mediterranean Sea and in the Jordan River valley are the Canaanites."

³⁰But Caleb reassured the people as they stood before Moses. "Let us go up at once and possess it," he said, "for we are well able to conquer it!"

³¹"Not against people as strong as they are!" the other spies said. "They would crush us!"

³²So the majority report of the spies was negative: "The land is full of warriors, the people are powerfully built, ³³and we saw some of the Anakim there, descendants of the ancient race of giants. We felt like grasshoppers before them, they were so tall!"

14 Forty Years in the Wilderness

Then all the people began weeping aloud, and they carried on all night. ²Their voices rose in a great chorus of complaint against Moses and Aaron.

FAMILY DEVOTIONS

☐ **DEVOTION 57**
OPTIMISM

Read Numbers 13:25-33

"Cindi is a real pain in the neck," Quentin complained to his grandparents one day as they were riding in the car. "She's always bugging me. Mom makes me take her everywhere I go."

Grandma looked around. "Cindi?" she called. "Where are you?"

Quentin grinned. "Well, *almost* everywhere," he said.

"Cindi told me that you're the 'bestest big brother in the world,'" Grandma quoted.

Quentin looked ashamed. "Well, I mean she . . . she . . ."

"Look!" Grandpa slowed down. "See that deer?"

"Where?" Grandma and Quentin asked.

Grandpa pointed. "Over there . . . in those trees."

Quentin squinted. He and Grandma didn't see it. "Well, it's too late now," said Grandpa as they rounded a curve.

Grandma turned to face Quentin. "Isn't it strange how we see what we're looking for?" she asked. "Grandpa likes to watch for wild animals, so he saw a deer."

Grandpa's eyes met Quentin's in the rearview mirror. "When we look for bad things, we find them," he said. "When we look for good, we find that."

"The Lord has given you a wonderful family, Quentin," Grandma said softly. "You should look for good in them. When you do, you'll find it. They—"

"Look!" Grandpa cried. "See that covey of quail in the grass along the highway?"

"I see!" Quentin exclaimed. "I see."

Optimism Memory Verse

Fix your thoughts on what is true and good and right. Think about things that are pure and lovely, and dwell on the fine, good things in others. Think about all you can praise God for and be glad about.
Philippians 4:8

How About You?

Do you look for good or bad in others? Listen to yourself. Are your remarks positive or negative? God wants his children to be gentle and courteous, not harsh and judgmental. So start looking for good and talking about it. Your day will be brighter, you'll be better company for others, and you'll be a better testimony for the Lord. B. W.

• For the next devotional, turn to page 163. • For the next devotional on *OPTIMISM*, turn to page 571. • For notes on *OPTIMISM*, see pages 143, 536, 677, and 940.

"We wish we had died in Egypt," they wailed, "or even here in the wilderness, ³rather than be taken into this country ahead of us. Jehovah will kill us there, and our wives and little ones will become slaves. Let's get out of here and return to Egypt!" ⁴The idea swept the camp. "Let's elect a leader to take us back to Egypt!" they shouted.

⁵Then Moses and Aaron fell face downward on the ground before the people of Israel. ⁶Two of the spies, Joshua (the son of Nun), and Caleb (the son of Jephunneh), ripped their clothing ⁷and said to all the people, "It is a wonderful country ahead, ⁸and the Lord loves us. He will bring us safely into the land and give it to us. It is *very* fertile, a land 'flowing with milk and honey'! ⁹Oh, do not rebel against the Lord, and do not fear the people of the land. For they are but bread for us to eat! The Lord is with us and he has removed his protection from them! Don't be afraid of them!"

¹⁰,¹¹But the only response of the people was to talk of stoning them. Then the glory of the Lord appeared, and the Lord said to Moses, "How long will these people despise me? Will they *never* believe me, even after all the miracles I have done among them? ¹²I will disinherit them and destroy them with a plague, and I will make you into a nation far greater and mightier than they are!"

¹³"But what will the Egyptians think when they hear about it?" Moses pleaded with the Lord. "They know full well the power you displayed in rescuing your people. ¹⁴They have told this to the inhabitants of this land, who are well aware that you are with Israel and that you talk with her face to face. They see the pillar of cloud and fire standing above us, and they know that you lead and protect us day and night. ¹⁵Now if you kill all your people, the nations that have heard your fame will say, ¹⁶'The Lord had to kill them because he wasn't able to take care of them in the wilderness. He wasn't strong enough to bring them into the land he swore he would give them.'

¹⁷,¹⁸"Oh, please, show the great power [of your patience] by forgiving our sins and showing us your steadfast love. Forgive us, even though you have said that you don't let sin go unpunished, and that you punish the father's fault in the children to the third and fourth generation. ¹⁹Oh, I plead with you, pardon the sins of this people because of your magnificent, steadfast love, just as you have forgiven them all the time from when we left Egypt until now."

²⁰,²¹Then the Lord said, "All right, I will pardon them as you have requested. But I vow by my own name that just as it is true that all the earth shall be filled with the glory of the Lord, ²²so it is true that not one of the men who has seen my glory and the miracles I did both in Egypt and in the wilderness—and ten times refused to trust me and obey me— ²³shall even see the land I promised to this people's ancestors. ²⁴But my servant Caleb is a different kind of man—he has obeyed me fully. I will bring him into the land he entered as a spy, and his descendants shall have their full share in it. ²⁵But now, since the people of Israel are so afraid of the Amalekites and the Canaanites living in the valleys, tomorrow you must turn back into the wilderness in the direction of the Red Sea."

²⁶,²⁷Then the Lord said to Moses and to Aaron, "How long will this wicked nation complain about me? For I have heard all that they have been saying. ²⁸Tell them, 'The Lord vows to do to you what you feared: ²⁹You will all die here in this wilderness! Not a single one of you twenty years old and older, who has complained against me, ³⁰shall enter the Promised Land. Only Caleb (son of Jephunneh) and Joshua (son of Nun) are permitted to enter it.

³¹"'You said your children would become slaves of the people of the land. Well, instead I will bring *them* safely into the land and they shall inherit what you have despised. ³²But as for you, your dead bodies shall fall in this wilderness. ³³You must wander in the desert like nomads for forty years. In this way you will pay for your faithlessness, until the last of you lies dead in the desert.

³⁴,³⁵"'Since the spies were in the land for forty days, you must wander in the wilderness for forty years—a year for each day, bearing the burden of your sins. I will teach you what it means to reject me. I, Jehovah, have spoken. Every one of you who has conspired against me shall die here in this wilderness.'"

³⁶⁻³⁸Then the ten spies who had incited the rebellion against Jehovah by striking fear into the hearts of the people were struck dead before the Lord. Of all the spies, only Joshua and Caleb remained alive. ³⁹What sorrow there was throughout the camp when Moses reported God's words to the people!

⁴⁰They were up early the next morning and started toward the Promised Land.

"Here we are!" they said. "We realize that we have sinned, but now we are ready to go on into the land the Lord has promised us."

⁴¹But Moses said, "It's too late. Now you are disobeying the Lord's orders to return to the wilderness. ⁴²Don't go ahead with your plan or you will be crushed by your enemies, for the Lord is not with you. ⁴³Don't you remember? The Amalekites and the Canaanites are there! You have deserted the Lord, and now he will desert you."

⁴⁴But they went ahead into the hill country, despite the fact that neither the Ark nor Moses left the camp. ⁴⁵Then the Amalekites and the Canaanites

Family Devotions

☐ **Devotion 58**

Cultivating Godly Attitudes

Read Numbers 14:26-30

Cultivating Godly Attitudes
Memory Verse

Your attitude should be the kind that was shown us by Jesus Christ.
Philippians 2:5

Billy was pouting in the backseat of the car. When Mom asked why, his sister, Mary, laughed. "He's just mad because Dad wouldn't let him buy that set of Indian arrowheads he saw at the gift shop," she said.

"I don't see why I couldn't have it," Billy scowled. "It was only six dollars. I never get to buy anything."

Dad raised his eyebrows. "Sounds like you're having a pity party," he said. "That's what we call it when someone feels so sorry for himself that he doesn't even want to be cheered up."

"Well," Billy grumbled, "you've only let me buy one souvenir, and we've already been on vacation four days! Besides, I always have to sit in the backseat."

"I've had to sit in the backseat, too." Mary pouted. "It's so hot, and you know I get carsick sometimes."

Dad and Mom exchanged glances. Mom's eyes twinkled. "Well, how about me?" she whined. "That mattress last night was so hard, I couldn't sleep, and the fried eggs I got for breakfast were cold and overdone. And I've got—"

"You think you've got it bad?" interrupted Dad in a complaining tone. "I've spent a whole lot more on this trip than I planned because the rain kept us from camping out the last two nights, and we had to stay in a motel."

The children stared. It surely seemed strange to have their parents whining! Dad and Mom laughed at the expression on their faces. "Look at that magnificent view," Dad said, pulling into a scenic turnoff. "We've been so busy with our pity party that we've been forgetting about the good things around us."

"Yeah," Billy admitted. "I guess you're right."

Mary said quietly, "Maybe we should try to think of all the things we're thankful for."

"That's a great idea!" agreed Dad. "A praise party is more fun than a pity party, any day!"

How About You?
Do you sometimes complain and feel sorry for yourself? God was very unhappy with the people of Israel when they grumbled and complained. Having this attitude makes you blind to the blessings of God and to the needs of others. Stop being selfish. Be thankful instead. Change your pity party into a praise party. *S. K.*

• For the next devotional, turn to page 165. • For the next devotional on *Cultivating Godly Attitudes*, turn to page 415. • For notes on *Cultivating Godly Attitudes*, see pages 337, 383, 472, 622, and 1216.

who lived in the hills came down and attacked them and chased them to Hormah.

15 More Rules about Offerings

The Lord told Moses to give these instructions to the people of Israel: "When your children finally live in the land I am going to give them, 3,4and they want to please the Lord with a burnt offering or any other offering by fire, their sacrifice must be an animal from their flocks of sheep and goats, or from their herds of cattle. Each sacrifice—whether an ordinary one, or a sacrifice to fulfill a vow, or a free-will offering, or a special sacrifice at any of the annual festivals—must be accompanied by a grain offering. If a lamb is being sacrificed, use three quarts of fine flour mixed with three pints of oil, 5accompanied by three pints of wine for a drink offering.

6"If the sacrifice is a ram, use six quarts of fine flour mixed with four pints of oil,7and four pints of wine for a drink offering. This will be a sacrifice that is a pleasing fragrance to the Lord.

8,9"If the sacrifice is a young bull, then the grain offering accompanying it must consist of nine quarts of fine flour mixed with three quarts of oil, 10plus three quarts of wine for the drink offering. This shall be offered by fire as a pleasing fragrance to the Lord.

11,12"These are the instructions for what is to accompany each sacrificial bull, ram, lamb, or young goat. 13,14These instructions apply both to native-born Israelis and to foreigners living among you who want to please the Lord with sacrifices offered by fire; 15,16for there is the same law for all, native-born or foreigner, and this shall be true forever from generation to generation; all are the same before the Lord. Yes, one law for all!"

17,18The Lord also said to Moses at this time, "Instruct the people of Israel that when they arrive in the land that I am going to give them, 19-21they must present to the Lord a sample of each year's new crops by making a loaf, using coarse flour from the first grain that is cut each year. This loaf must be waved back and forth before the altar in a gesture of offering to the Lord. It is an annual offering from your threshing floor and must be observed from generation to generation.

22"If by mistake you or future generations fail to carry out all of these regulations that the Lord has given you over the years through Moses, 23,24then when the people realize their error, they must offer one young bull for a burnt offering. It will be a pleasant odor before the Lord, and must be offered along with the usual grain offering and drink offering, and one male goat for a sin offering. 25And the priest shall make atonement for all of the people of Israel and they shall be forgiven; for it was an error, and they have corrected it with their sacrifice made by fire before the Lord, and by their sin offering. 26All the people shall be forgiven, including the foreigners living among them, for the entire population is involved in such error and forgiveness.

27"If the error is made by a single individual, then he shall sacrifice a one-year-old female goat for a sin offering, 28and the priest shall make atonement for him before the Lord, and he shall be forgiven. 29This same law applies to individual foreigners who are living among you.

30"But anyone who deliberately makes the 'mistake,' whether he is a native Israeli or a foreigner, is blaspheming Jehovah, and shall be cut off from among his people. 31For he has despised the commandment of the Lord and deliberately failed to obey his law; he must be executed and die in his sin."

32One day while the people of Israel were in the wilderness, one of them was caught gathering wood on the Sabbath day. 33He was arrested and taken before Moses and Aaron and the other judges. 34They jailed him until they could find out the Lord's mind concerning him.

35Then the Lord said to Moses, "The man must die—all the people shall stone him to death outside the camp."

36So they took him outside the camp and killed him as the Lord had commanded.

37,38The Lord said to Moses, "Tell the people of Israel to make tassels for the hems of their clothes (this is a permanent regulation from generation to generation) and to attach the tassels to their clothes with a blue cord. 39The purpose of this regulation is to remind you, whenever you notice the tassels, of the commandments of the Lord, and that you are to obey his laws instead of following your own desires and going your own ways, as you used to do in serving other gods. 40It will remind you to be holy to your God. 41For I am Jehovah your God who brought you out of the land of Egypt; yes, I am the Lord, your God."

16 Korah Rebels

One day Korah (son of Izhar, grandson of Kohath, and a descendant of Levi) conspired with Dathan and Abiram (the sons of Eliab) and On (the son of Peleth), all three from the tribe of Reuben, 2to incite a rebellion against Moses. Two hundred and fifty popular leaders, all members of the Assembly, were involved.

3They went to Moses and Aaron and said, "We have had enough of your presumption; you are no better than anyone else; everyone in Israel has been chosen of the Lord, and he is with all of us. What right do you have to put yourselves forward,

FAMILY DEVOTIONS

☐ **DEVOTION 59**
RESPECTING OTHERS

Read Numbers 16:1-3, 28-32

"No!" cried Marianne, as her little brother reached for a cookie fresh from the oven. Peter howled and kicked furiously.

"What's going on here?" asked Mother, coming into the kitchen.

"Peter's mad because I stopped him from picking up the hot cookies," said Marianne. Just then the phone rang and Marianne went to answer it.

A few minutes later, Marianne returned to the kitchen and slumped down on a chair as Mother took more cookies from the oven. "That was Leslie," said Marianne. "She was telling me about all the rules Pastor Dan has made up for our ski trip. Leslie says there'll be room-cleaning requirements, chaperons, and even a curfew! It sounds like he's trying to ruin all our fun!"

"Hmmmm. . . ." Mother sounded thoughtful. "Just like you were trying to ruin Peter's fun when you wouldn't let him touch the hot cookies?" she asked.

Marianne looked surprised. "I don't mind if he has some cookies," she said. "I just didn't want him to get burned."

"And Pastor Dan doesn't mind if you have fun," said Mother, "but he doesn't want you to get hurt. Pastor Dan is head of the youth group; therefore, God holds him accountable for every young person in the group. That's why he sets up guidelines whenever you're under his care."

Marianne sighed. "I suppose," she said as the oven timer buzzed. She grinned at Peter, who was sitting quietly, staring at the cookies. "Come on, little brother," she said. "Let's have cookies and milk. They've cooled down, and they'll be great now—you'll see. And I'll try to remember how good the ski trip will be if I follow the rules."

Respecting Others Memory Verse

You must love the Lord your God with all your heart, and with all your soul, and with all your strength, and with all your mind. And you must love your neighbor just as much as you love yourself.
Luke 10:27

How About You?

Do you sometimes balk at rules? God says you are to obey those who have authority over you. When you choose to do that, it will not only benefit you, it will also delight your heavenly Father. *J. R. G.*

• For the next devotional, turn to page 169.   • For the next devotional on *RESPECTING OTHERS*, turn to page 315.
• For notes on *RESPECTING OTHERS*, see pages 322, 382, 1088, and 1218.

claiming that we must obey you, and acting as though you were greater than anyone else among all these people of the Lord?"

⁴When Moses heard what they were saying he fell face downward to the ground. ⁵Then he said to Korah and to those who were with him, "In the morning the Lord will show you who are his, and who is holy, and whom he has chosen as his priest. ⁶,⁷Do this: You, Korah, and all those with you, take censers tomorrow and light them, and put incense upon them before the Lord, and we will find out whom the Lord has chosen. You are the presumptuous ones, you sons of Levi."

⁸,⁹Then Moses spoke again to Korah: "Does it seem a small thing to you that the God of Israel has chosen you from among all the people of Israel to be near to himself as you work in the Tabernacle of Jehovah, and to stand before the people to minister to them? ¹⁰Is it nothing to you that he has given this task to only you Levites? And now are you demanding the priesthood also? ¹¹,¹²That is what you are really after! That is why you are revolting against Jehovah. And what has Aaron done, that you are dissatisfied with him?" Then Moses summoned Dathan and Abiram (the sons of Eliab), but they refused to come.

¹³"Is it a small thing," they mimicked, "that you brought us out of lovely Egypt to kill us here in this terrible wilderness, and that now you want to make yourself our king? ¹⁴What's more, you haven't brought us into the wonderful country you promised, nor given us fields and vineyards. Whom are you trying to fool? We refuse to come."

¹⁵Then Moses was very angry and said to the Lord, "Do not accept their sacrifices! I have never stolen so much as a donkey from them and have not hurt one of them."

¹⁶And Moses said to Korah, "Come here tomorrow before the Lord with all your friends; Aaron will be here too. ¹⁷Be sure to bring your censers with incense on them; a censer for each man, 250 in all; and Aaron will also be here with his."

¹⁸So they did. They came with their censers and lit them and placed the incense on them, and stood at the entrance of the Tabernacle with Moses and Aaron. ¹⁹Meanwhile, Korah had stirred up the entire nation against Moses and Aaron, and they all assembled to watch. Then the glory of Jehovah appeared to all the people, ²⁰and Jehovah said to Moses and Aaron, ²¹"Get away from these people so that I may instantly destroy them."

²²But Moses and Aaron fell face downward to the ground before the Lord. "O God, the God of all mankind," they pleaded, "must you be angry with all the people when one man sins?"

²³,²⁴And the Lord said to Moses, "Then tell the people to get away from the tents of Korah, Dathan, and Abiram."

²⁵So Moses rushed over to the tents of Dathan and Abiram, followed closely by the 250 Israeli leaders. ²⁶"Quick!" he told the people, "get away from the tents of these wicked men, and don't touch anything that belongs to them, lest you be included in their sins [and be destroyed with them]."

²⁷So all the people stood back from the tents of Korah, Dathan, and Abiram. And Dathan and Abiram came out and stood at the entrances of their tents with their wives and sons and little ones.

²⁸And Moses said, "By this you shall know that Jehovah has sent me to do all these things that I have done—for I have not done them on my own. ²⁹If these men die a natural death or from some ordinary accident or disease, then Jehovah has not sent me. ³⁰But if the Lord does a miracle and the ground opens up and swallows them and everything that belongs to them, and they go down alive into Sheol, then you will know that these men have despised the Lord."

³¹He had hardly finished speaking the words when the ground suddenly split open beneath them, ³²and a great fissure swallowed them up, along with their tents and families and the friends who were standing with them, and everything they owned. ³³So they went down alive into Sheol and the earth closed upon them, and they perished. ³⁴All of the people of Israel fled at their screams, fearing that the earth would swallow them too. ³⁵Then fire came from Jehovah and burned up the 250 men who were offering incense.

³⁶,³⁷And the Lord said to Moses, "Tell Eleazar the son of Aaron the priest to pull those censers from the fire; for they are holy, dedicated to the Lord. He must also scatter the burning incense ³⁸from the censers of these men who have sinned at the cost of their lives. He shall then beat the metal into a sheet as a covering for the altar, for these censers are holy because they were used before the Lord; and the altar sheet shall be a reminder to the people of Israel."

³⁹So Eleazar the priest took the 250 bronze censers and beat them out into a sheet of metal to cover the altar, ⁴⁰to be a reminder to the people of Israel that no unauthorized person—no one who is not a descendant of Aaron—may come before the Lord to burn incense, lest the same thing happen to him as happened to Korah and his associates. Thus the Lord's directions to Moses were carried out.

⁴¹But the very next morning all the people began muttering again against Moses and Aaron, saying, "You have killed the Lord's people."

⁴²Soon a great, sullen mob formed; suddenly, as they looked toward the Tabernacle, the Cloud appeared and the awesome glory of the Lord was seen. ⁴³,⁴⁴Moses and Aaron came and stood at the entrance of the Tabernacle, and the Lord said to Moses,

⁴⁵"Get away from these people so that I can instantly destroy them." But Moses and Aaron fell face downward to the earth before the Lord.

⁴⁶And Moses said to Aaron, "Quick, take a censer and place fire in it from the altar; lay incense on it, and carry it quickly among the people and make atonement for them; for God's anger has gone out among them—the plague has already begun."

⁴⁷Aaron did as Moses had told him to, and ran among the people, for the plague had indeed already begun; and he put on the incense and made atonement for them. ⁴⁸And he stood between the living and the dead, and the plague was stopped, ⁴⁹but not before 14,700 people had died (in addition to those who had died the previous day with Korah). ⁵⁰Then Aaron returned to Moses at the entrance of the Tabernacle; and so the plague was stopped.

17 A Rod like a Fruit Tree

Then the Lord said to Moses, "Tell the people of Israel that each of their tribal chiefs is to bring you a wooden rod with his name inscribed upon it. Aaron's name is to be on the rod of the tribe of Levi. ⁴Put these rods in the inner room of the Tabernacle where I meet with you, in front of the Ark. ⁵I will use these rods to identify the man I have chosen: for buds will grow on his rod! Then at last this murmuring and complaining against you will stop!"

⁶So Moses gave the instructions to the people, and each of the twelve chiefs (including Aaron) brought him a rod. ⁷He put them before the Lord in the inner room of the Tabernacle, ⁸and when he went in the next day, he found that Aaron's rod, representing the tribe of Levi, had budded and was blossoming, and had ripe almonds hanging from it! ⁹When Moses brought them out to show the others, they stared in disbelief! Then each man except Aaron claimed his rod. ¹⁰The Lord told Moses to place Aaron's rod permanently beside the Ark as a reminder of this rebellion. He was to [bring it out and show it to the people again] if there were any further complaints about Aaron's authority; this would ward off further catastrophe to the people. ¹¹So Moses did as the Lord commanded him.

¹²,¹³But the people of Israel only grumbled the more. "We are as good as dead," they whined. "Everyone who even comes close to the Tabernacle dies. Must we all perish?"

18 The Priests' and Levites' Duties

The Lord now spoke to Aaron: "You and your sons and your family are responsible for any desecration of the sanctuary," he said, "and will be held liable for any impropriety in your priestly work.

²,³"Your kinsmen, the tribe of Levi, are your assistants; but only you and your sons may perform the sacred duties in the Tabernacle itself. The Levites must be careful not to touch any of the sacred articles or the altar, lest I destroy both them and you. ⁴No one who is not a member of the tribe of Levi shall assist you in any way. ⁵Remember, only the priests are to perform the sacred duties within the sanctuary and at the altar. If you follow these instructions, the wrath of God will never again fall upon any of the people of Israel for violating this law. ⁶I say it again—your kinsmen the Levites are your assistants for the work of the Tabernacle. They are a gift to you from the Lord. ⁷But you and your sons, the priests, shall personally handle all the sacred service, including the altar and all that is within the veil, for the priesthood is your special gift of service. Anyone else who attempts to perform these duties shall die."

⁸The Lord gave these further instructions to Aaron: "I have given the priests all the gifts which are brought to the Lord by the people; all these offerings presented to the Lord by the gesture of waving them before the altar belong to you and your sons, by permanent law. ⁹The grain offerings, the sin offerings, and the guilt offerings are yours, except for the sample presented to the Lord by burning upon the altar. All these are most holy offerings. ¹⁰They are to be eaten only in a most holy place, and only by males. ¹¹All other gifts presented to me by the gesture of waving them before the altar are for you and your families, sons and daughters alike. For all the members of your families may eat these unless anyone is ceremonially impure at the time.

¹²"Yours also are the first-of-the-harvest gifts the people bring as offerings to the Lord—the best of the olive oil, wine, grain, ¹³and every other crop. Your families may eat these unless they are ceremonially defiled at the time. ¹⁴,¹⁵So everything that is dedicated to the Lord shall be yours, including the firstborn sons of the people of Israel, and the firstborn of their animals. ¹⁶However, you may never accept the firstborn sons, nor the firstborn of any animals that I do not permit for food. Instead, there must be a payment of two and a half dollars made for each firstborn child. It is to be brought when he is one month old.

¹⁷"However, the firstborn of cows, sheep, or goats may not be bought back; they must be sacrificed to the Lord. Their blood is to be sprinkled upon the altar, and their fat shall be burned as a fire offering; it is very pleasant to the Lord. ¹⁸The meat of these animals shall be yours, including the breast and right thigh that are presented to the Lord by the gesture of waving before the altar. ¹⁹Yes, I have given to you all of these 'wave offerings' brought by the people of Israel to the Lord; they are for you and your families

as food; this is a permanent contract between the Lord and you and your descendants.

[20] "You priests may own no property nor have any other income, for I am all that you need.

[21] As for the tribe of Levi, your relatives, they shall be paid for their service with the tithes from the entire land of Israel.

[22] "From now on, Israelites other than the priests and Levites shall not enter the sanctuary lest they be judged guilty and die. [23] Only the Levites shall do the work there, and they shall be guilty if they fail. This is a permanent law among you, that the Levites shall own no property in Israel, [24] for the people's tithes, offered to the Lord by the gesture of waving before the altar, shall belong to the Levites; these are their inheritance, and so they have no need for property."

[25,26] The Lord also said to Moses, "Tell the Levites to give to the Lord a tenth of the tithes they receive—a tithe of the tithe, to be presented to the Lord by the gesture of waving before the altar. [27] The Lord will consider this as your first-of-the-harvest offering to him of grain and wine, as though it were from your own property. [28,29] This tithe of the tithe shall be selected from the choicest part of the tithes you receive as the Lord's portion, and shall be given to Aaron the priest. [30] It shall be credited to you just as though it were from your own threshing floor and wine press. [31] Aaron and his sons and their families may eat it in their homes or anywhere they wish, for it is their compensation for their service in the Tabernacle. [32] You Levites will not be held guilty for accepting the Lord's tithes if you then give the best tenth to the priests. But beware that you do not treat the holy gifts of the people of Israel as though they were common, lest you die."

19 What to Do when Defiled

The Lord said to Moses and Aaron, "Here is another of my laws:

"Tell the people of Israel to bring you a red heifer without defect, one that has never been yoked. Give her to Eleazar the priest and he shall take her outside the camp and someone shall kill her as he watches. [4] Eleazar shall take some of her blood upon his finger and sprinkle it seven times toward the front of the Tabernacle. [5] Then someone shall burn the heifer as he watches—her hide, meat, blood, and dung. [6] Eleazar shall take cedar wood and hyssop branches and scarlet thread, and throw them into the burning pile.

[7] "Then he must wash his clothes, and bathe, and afterwards return to the camp and be ceremonially defiled until the evening. [8] And the one who burns the animal must wash his clothes and bathe, and he too shall be defiled until evening. [9] Then someone who is not ceremonially defiled shall gather up the ashes of the heifer and place them in some purified place outside the camp, where they shall be kept for the people of Israel as a source of water for the purification ceremonies, for removal of sin. [10] And the one who gathers up the ashes of the heifer must wash his clothes and be defiled until evening; this is a permanent law for the benefit of the people of Israel and any foreigners living among them.

[11] "Anyone who touches a dead human body shall be defiled for seven days, [12] and must purify himself the third and seventh days with water [run through the ashes of the red heifer]; then he will be purified; but if he does not do this on the third day, he will continue to be defiled even after the seventh day. [13] Anyone who touches a dead person and does not purify himself in the manner specified has defiled the Tabernacle of the Lord, and shall be excommunicated from Israel. The cleansing water was not sprinkled upon him, so the defilement continues.

[14] "When a man dies in a tent, these are the various regulations: Everyone who enters the tent, and those who are in it at the time, shall be defiled seven days. [15] Any container in the tent without a lid over it is defiled.

[16] "If someone out in a field touches the corpse of someone who has been killed in battle or who has died in any other way, or if he even touches a bone or a grave, he shall be defiled seven days. [17] To become purified again, ashes from the red heifer sin offering are to be added to spring water in a kettle. [18] Then a person who is not defiled shall take hyssop branches and dip them into the water and sprinkle the water upon the tent and upon all the pots and pans in the tent, and upon anyone who has been defiled by being in the tent, or by touching a bone, or touching someone who has been killed or is otherwise dead, or has touched a grave. [19] This shall take place on the third and seventh days; then the defiled person must wash his clothes and bathe himself, and that evening he will be out from under the defilement.

[20] "But anyone who is defiled and doesn't purify himself shall be excommunicated, for he has defiled the sanctuary of the Lord, and the water to cleanse him has not been sprinkled upon him; so he remains defiled. [21] This is a permanent law. The man who sprinkles the water must afterwards wash his clothes; and anyone touching the water shall be defiled until evening. [22] And anything a defiled person touches shall be defiled until evening."

20 Moses Disobeys God

The people of Israel arrived in the wilderness of Zin in April and camped at Kadesh,

FAMILY DEVOTIONS

☐ **DEVOTION 60**
GIVING THANKS

Read Numbers 21:4-6

"M*mmmmm*, this roast beef is delicious!" exclaimed Troy.

"I'm glad you like it," replied Mom. "Too bad your dad isn't here to enjoy it with us. I'm glad he got called back to work, but I wish he didn't have to work second shift."

"Me, too," agreed Bud. "He's had to miss all my basketball games. It's not fair!"

The next evening, the family lingered over supper, glad to have Dad with them. "I really miss our family devotions now that I'm only home for dinner on Saturday and Sunday evenings," Dad said. "Troy, did you choose something for tonight?"

Troy grinned as he replied, "Yep! I read this story this week and it made me think of us." Troy took the Bible and read from Numbers. Then he looked up and grinned. "Today is an anniversary," he announced. "Anybody know what of?"

"I do," responded Dad promptly. "It was just three months ago that I got called back to work."

"Oh, that's right!" said Mom. "I remember how thrilled we were." She paused, then slowly added, "I see your point, Troy. I guess we've been like the Israelites, haven't we? At first they were thrilled with manna, just like we were thrilled with Dad's job. But then they began to get tired of it. I'm afraid we've been doing that, too, and I confess that I was probably the first to complain. I hope you'll all forgive me."

"Yeah," Bud agreed. "I really am thankful that you have a job, Dad, even though I wish you could come to my games. I'm sorry I've been such a baby about it."

Dad looked around the table at all of them. "You guys know how hard it is for me to miss so many evenings with you, but for right now this is the way God is providing for us. I've probably done my share of complaining, too. Let's all ask God to forgive us, and then let's make some plans for the next few weekends to spend some extra time together as a family."

Giving Thanks Memory Verse

Is anyone among you suffering? He should keep on praying about it. And those who have reason to be thankful should continually be singing praises to the Lord.
James 5:13

How About You?

Is there some blessing in your life that you've begun to despise? Perhaps you prayed for a brother or sister, but now that you have one you sometimes wish you didn't. Or maybe you prayed that your Sunday school class would grow, and now that it has, you don't like it because a new member does better than you. Be careful. Never despise God's blessings. R. P.

• For the next devotional, turn to page 171. • For the next devotional on GIVING THANKS, turn to page 293. • For notes on GIVING THANKS, see pages 582, 608, and 834.

where Miriam died and was buried. ²There was not enough water to drink at that place, so the people again rebelled against Moses and Aaron. A great mob formed, ³and they held a protest meeting.

"Would that we too had died with our dear brothers the Lord killed!" they shouted at Moses. ⁴"You have deliberately brought us into this wilderness to get rid of us, along with our flocks and herds. ⁵Why did you ever make us leave Egypt and bring us here to this evil place? Where is the fertile land of wonderful crops—the figs, vines, and pomegranates you told us about? Why, there isn't even water enough to drink!"

⁶Moses and Aaron turned away and went to the entrance of the Tabernacle, where they fell face downward before the Lord; and the glory of Jehovah appeared to them.

⁷And he said to Moses, ⁸"Get Aaron's rod; then you and Aaron must summon the people. As they watch, speak to that rock over there and tell it to pour out its water! You will give them water from a rock, enough for all the people and all their cattle!"

⁹So Moses did as instructed. He took the rod from the place where it was kept before the Lord; ¹⁰then Moses and Aaron summoned the people to come and gather at the rock; and he said to them, "Listen, you rebels! Must we bring you water from this rock?"

¹¹Then Moses lifted the rod and struck the rock twice, and water gushed out; and the people and their cattle drank.

¹²But the Lord said to Moses and Aaron, "Because you did not believe me and did not sanctify me in the eyes of the people of Israel, you shall not bring them into the land I have promised them!"

¹³This place was named Meribah (meaning "Rebel Waters"), because it was where the people of Israel fought against Jehovah, and where he showed himself to be holy before them.

¹⁴While Moses was at Kadesh he sent messengers to the king of Edom: "We are the descendants of your brother, Israel," he declared. "You know our sad history, ¹⁵how our ancestors went down to visit Egypt and stayed there so long, and became slaves of the Egyptians. ¹⁶But when we cried to the Lord he heard us and sent an Angel who brought us out of Egypt, and now we are here at Kadesh, encamped on the borders of your land. ¹⁷Please let us pass through your country. We will be careful not to go through your planted fields, nor through your vineyards; we won't even drink water from your wells, but will stay on the main road and not leave it until we have crossed your border on the other side."

¹⁸But the king of Edom said, "Stay out! If you attempt to enter my land, I will meet you with an army!"

¹⁹"But, sir," protested the Israeli ambassadors, "we will stay on the main road and will not even drink your water unless we pay whatever you demand for it. We only want to pass through and nothing else."

²⁰But the king of Edom was adamant. "Stay out!" he warned, and, mobilizing his army, he marched to the frontier with a great force. ²¹,²²Because Edom refused to allow Israel to pass through their country, Israel turned back and journeyed from Kadesh to Mount Hor.

²³Then the Lord said to Moses and Aaron at the border of the land of Edom, ²⁴"The time has come for Aaron to die—for he shall not enter the land I have given the people of Israel, for the two of you rebelled against my instructions concerning the water at Meribah. ²⁵Now take Aaron and his son Eleazar and lead them up onto Mount Hor. ²⁶There you shall remove Aaron's priestly garments from him and put them on Eleazar his son; and Aaron shall die there."

²⁷So Moses did as the Lord commanded him. The three of them went up together into Mount Hor as all the people watched. ²⁸When they reached the summit, Moses removed the priestly garments from Aaron and put them on his son Eleazar; and Aaron died on the top of the mountain. Moses and Eleazar returned, ²⁹and when the people were informed of Aaron's death, they mourned for him for thirty days.

21 Israelites Defeat King of Arad

When the king of Arad heard that the Israelis were approaching (for they were traveling the same route as the spies), he mobilized his army and attacked Israel, taking some of the men as prisoners. ²Then the people of Israel vowed to the Lord that if he would help them conquer the king of Arad and his people, they would completely annihilate all the cities of that area. ³The Lord heeded their request and defeated the Canaanites; and the Israelis completely destroyed them and their cities. The name of the region was thereafter called Hormah (meaning "Utterly Destroyed").

⁴Then the people of Israel returned to Mount Hor, and from there continued southward along the road to the Red Sea in order to go around the land of Edom. The people were very discouraged; ⁵they began to murmur against God and to complain against Moses. "Why have you brought us out of Egypt to die here in the wilderness?" they whined. "There is nothing to eat here, and nothing to drink, and we hate this insipid manna."

⁶So the Lord sent poisonous snakes among them to punish them, and many of them were bitten and died.

⁷Then the people came to Moses and cried out, "We have sinned, for we have spoken against

Family Devotions

☐ **Devotion 61**
Praying at All Times

Read Numbers 21:7

"Tracy hates me!" Ann sobbed. Her hand trembled as she held the Christmas card out to her mother. "Look what she sent me!"

Mom took the card and looked at it. The cover had a picture of an angel announcing the message of "Peace on earth, good will toward men!" Then she opened it and read aloud, "Merry Christmas from your ex-friend." Mom's face turned grim. "Oh, that's too bad," she said. "Tracy shouldn't have sent this to you."

"I told you she hates me!" cried Ann. "We were best friends until Sara moved next door to her. Now she only likes Sara—she won't play with me anymore." Ann burst into tears, and Mom held her tightly until she calmed down.

"What Tracy did was wrong," Mom said quietly. "It makes me angry, too. But, honey, you can't change other people; you can only pray for them. Do you think you could pray for Tracy?"

"Pray for her?" Ann asked stonily. "I don't ever want to see her again! Why should I pray for her?"

"Look out the window," suggested Mom. "Do you see how the snow is beginning to fall?" Tracy nodded. "The ground is dark and frozen—like the feelings you and Tracy have for each other just now," continued Mom, "but it will soon have a blanket of snow to cover it and make it beautiful again. Prayer works something like that. When you pray and tell God about your angry feelings, he understands. He sends his blanket of peace to cover your pain. In fact, Jesus is called the Prince of Peace—he brings the gift of 'peace on earth, good will toward men.' Wouldn't you like to have it?" Solemnly, Ann nodded her head. "Good," said Mom. "God also gives you wisdom about how you should act. When you bless those who hurt you, God can change their feelings, too."

Praying at All Times Memory Verse

Don't worry about anything; instead, pray about everything; tell God your needs, and don't forget to thank him for his answers.
Philippians 4:6

How About You?
Are you hurt because someone has spoken against you? Do you find it hard to forgive and forget? You can choose to pray for the people who have hurt you, just as Moses did. Then God will help you find peace. *A. E. L.*

• For the next devotional, turn to page 175.   • For the next devotional on *Praying at All Times*, turn to page 483.
• For notes on *Praying at All Times*, see pages 363, 442, 945, 1040, and 1051.

Jehovah and against you. Pray to him to take away the snakes." So Moses prayed for the people.

⁸Then the Lord told him, "Make a bronze replica of one of these snakes and attach it to the top of a pole; anyone who is bitten shall live if he simply looks at it!"

⁹So Moses made the replica, and whenever anyone who had been bitten looked at the bronze snake, he recovered!

¹⁰Israel journeyed next to Oboth and camped there. ¹¹Then they went on to Iyeabarim, in the wilderness, a short distance east of Moab, ¹²and from there they traveled to the valley of the brook Zared and set up camp. ¹³Then they moved to the far side of the Arnon River, near the borders of the Amorites. (The Arnon River is the boundary line between the Moabites and the Amorites. ¹⁴This fact is mentioned in *The Book of the Wars of Jehovah*, where it is stated that the valley of the Arnon River and the city of Waheb ¹⁵lie between the Amorites and the people of Moab.)

¹⁶Then Israel traveled to Beer (meaning "A Well"). This is the place where the Lord told Moses, "Summon the people, and I will give them water." ¹⁷,¹⁸What happened is described in this song the people sang:

Spring up, O well!
Sing of the water!
This is a well
The leaders dug.
It was hollowed
With their staves
And shovels.

Then they left the desert and proceeded on through Mattanah, ¹⁹Nahaliel, and Bamoth; ²⁰then to the valley in the plateau of Moab, which overlooks the desert with Mount Pisgah in the distance.

²¹Israel now sent ambassadors to King Sihon of the Amorites.

²²"Let us travel through your land," they requested. "We will not leave the road until we have passed beyond your borders. We won't trample your fields or touch your vineyards or drink your water."

²³But King Sihon refused. Instead he mobilized his army and attacked Israel in the wilderness, battling them at Jahaz. ²⁴But Israel slaughtered them and occupied their land from the Arnon River to the Jabbok River, as far as the borders of the Ammonites; but they were stopped there by the rugged terrain.

²⁵,²⁶So Israel captured all the cities of the Amorites and lived in them, including the city of Heshbon, which had been King Sihon's capital. ²⁷⁻³⁰The ancient poets had referred to King Sihon in this poem:

Come to Heshbon,
King Sihon's capital,
For a fire has flamed forth
And devoured
The city of Ar in Moab,
On the heights of the Arnon River.
Woe to Moab!
You are finished,
O people of Chemosh;
Your sons have fled,
And your daughters are captured
By King Sihon of the Amorites.
He has destroyed
The little children
And the men and women
As far as Dibon, Nophah, and Medeba.

³¹,³²While Israel was there in the Amorite country, Moses sent spies to look over the Jazer area; he followed up with an armed attack, capturing all of the towns and driving out the Amorites. ³³They next turned their attention to the city of Bashan, but King Og of Bashan met them with his army at Edrei. ³⁴The Lord told Moses not to fear—that the enemy was already conquered! "The same thing will happen to King Og as happened to King Sihon at Heshbon," the Lord assured him. ³⁵And sure enough, Israel was victorious and killed King Og, his sons, and his subjects, so that not a single survivor remained; and Israel occupied the land.

22 King Balak Offers Money to Balaam

The people of Israel now traveled to the plains of Moab and camped east of the Jordan River opposite Jericho. ²,³When King Balak of Moab (the son of Zippor) realized how many of them there were, and when he learned what they had done to the Amorites, he and his people were terrified. ⁴They quickly consulted with the leaders of Midian.

"This mob will eat us like an ox eats grass," they exclaimed.

So King Balak ⁵,⁶sent messengers to Balaam (son of Beor) who was living in his native land of Pethor, near the Euphrates River. He begged Balaam to come and help him.

"A vast horde of people has arrived from Egypt, and they cover the face of the earth and are headed toward me," he frantically explained. "Please come and curse them for me, so that I can drive them out of my land; for I know what fantastic blessings fall on those whom you bless, and I also know that those whom you curse are doomed."

⁷The messengers he sent were some of the top leaders of Moab and Midian. They went to Balaam

with money in hand and urgently explained to him what Balak wanted.

⁸"Stay here overnight," Balaam said, "and I'll tell you in the morning whatever the Lord directs me to say." So they did.

⁹That night God came to Balaam and asked him, "Who are these men?"

¹⁰"They have come from King Balak of Moab," he replied. ¹¹"The king says that a vast horde of people from Egypt has arrived at his border, and he wants me to go at once and curse them, in the hope that he can battle them successfully."

¹²"Don't do it!" God told him. "You are not to curse them, for I have blessed them!"

¹³The next morning Balaam told the men, "Go on home! The Lord won't let me do it."

¹⁴So King Balak's ambassadors returned without him and reported his refusal. ¹⁵Balak tried again. This time he sent a larger number of even more distinguished ambassadors than the former group. ¹⁶,¹⁷They came to Balaam with this message:

"King Balak pleads with you to come. He promises you great honors plus any payment you ask. Name your own figure! Only come and curse these people for us."

¹⁸But Balaam replied, "If he were to give me a palace filled with silver and gold, I could do nothing contrary to the command of the Lord my God. ¹⁹However, stay here tonight so that I can find out whether the Lord will add anything to what he said before."

²⁰That night God told Balaam, "You may get up and go with these men, but be sure to say only what I tell you to."

²¹So the next morning he saddled his donkey and started off with them. ²²,²³But God was angry about Balaam's eager attitude, so he sent an angel to stand in the road to kill him. As Balaam and two servants were riding along, Balaam's donkey suddenly saw the angel of the Lord standing in the road with a drawn sword. She bolted off the road into a field, but Balaam beat her back onto the road. ²⁴Now the angel of the Lord stood at a place where the road went between two vineyard walls. ²⁵When the donkey saw him standing there, she squirmed past by pressing against the wall, crushing Balaam's foot in the process. So he beat her again. ²⁶Then the angel of the Lord moved farther down the road and stood in a place so narrow that the donkey couldn't get by at all.

²⁷So she lay down in the road! In a great fit of temper Balaam beat her again with his staff.

²⁸Then the Lord caused the donkey to speak! "What have I done that deserves your beating me these three times?" she asked.

²⁹"Because you have made me look like a fool!" Balaam shouted. "I wish I had a sword with me, for I would kill you."

³⁰"Have I ever done anything like this before in my entire life?" the donkey asked.

"No," he admitted.

³¹Then the Lord opened Balaam's eyes and he saw the angel standing in the roadway with drawn sword, and he fell flat on the ground before him.

³²"Why did you beat your donkey those three times?" the angel demanded. "I have come to stop you because you are headed for destruction. ³³Three times the donkey saw me and shied away from me; otherwise I would certainly have killed you by now and spared her."

³⁴Then Balaam confessed, "I have sinned. I didn't realize you were there. I will go back home if you don't want me to go on."

³⁵But the angel told him, "Go with the men, but say only what I tell you to say." So Balaam went on with them. ³⁶When King Balak heard that Balaam was on the way, he left the capital and went out to meet him at the Arnon River, at the border of his land.

³⁷"Why did you delay so long?" he asked Balaam. "Didn't you believe me when I said I would give you great honors?"

³⁸Balaam replied, "I have come, but I have no power to say anything except what God tells me to say; and that is what I shall speak." ³⁹Balaam accompanied the king to Kiriathhuzoth, ⁴⁰where King Balak sacrificed oxen and sheep, and gave animals to Balaam and the ambassadors for their sacrifices. ⁴¹The next morning Balak took Balaam to the top of Mount Bamoth-baal, from which he could see the people of Israel spread out before him.

23 Who Will Balaam Obey?

Balaam said to the king, "Build seven altars here, and prepare seven young bulls and seven rams for sacrifice."

²Balak followed his instructions, and a young bull and a ram were sacrificed on each altar.

³,⁴Then Balaam said to the king, "Stand here by your burnt offerings and I will see if the Lord will meet me; and I will tell you what he says to me." So he went up to a barren height, and God met him there. Balaam told the Lord, "I have prepared seven altars and have sacrificed a young bull and a ram on each." ⁵Then the Lord gave Balaam a message for King Balak.

⁶When Balaam returned, the king was standing beside the burnt offerings with all the princes of Moab. ⁷⁻¹⁰This was Balaam's message:

"King Balak, king of Moab, has brought me
From the land of Aram,
From the eastern mountains.
'Come,' he told me, 'curse Jacob for me!
Let your anger rise on Israel.'

But how can I curse
What God has not cursed?
How can I denounce
A people God has not denounced?
I see them from the cliff tops,
I watch them from the hills.
They live alone,
And prefer to remain distinct
From every other nation.
They are as numerous as dust!
They are beyond numbering.
If only I could die as happy as an Israelite!
Oh, that my end might be like theirs!"

[11] "What have you done to me?" demanded King Balak. "I told you to curse my enemies, and now you have blessed them!"

[12] But Balaam replied, "Can I say anything except what Jehovah tells me to?"

[13] Then Balak told him, "Come with me to another place; there you will see only a portion of the nation of Israel. Curse at least that many!"

[14] So King Balak took Balaam into the fields of Zophim at the top of Mount Pisgah, and built seven altars there; and he offered up a young bull and a ram on each altar.

[15] Then Balaam said to the king, "Stand here by your burnt offering while I go to meet the Lord." [16] And the Lord met Balaam and told him what to say. [17] So he returned to where the king and the princes of Moab were standing beside their burnt offerings.

"What has Jehovah said?" the king eagerly inquired.

[18-24] And he replied,

"Rise up, Balak, and hear:
Listen to me, you son of Zippor.
God is not a man, that he should lie;
He doesn't change his mind like humans do.
Has he ever promised,
Without doing what he said?
Look! I have received a command to bless them,
For God has blessed them,
And I cannot reverse it!
He has not seen sin in Jacob.
He will not trouble Israel!
Jehovah their God is with them.
He is their king!
God has brought them out of Egypt.
Israel has the strength of a wild ox.
No curse can be placed on Jacob,
And no magic shall be done against him.
For now it shall be said of Israel,
'What wonders God has done for them!'
These people rise up as a lion;
They shall not lie down
Until they have eaten what they capture
And have drunk the blood of the slain!"

[25] "If you aren't going to curse them, at least don't *bless* them!" the king exclaimed to Balaam.

[26] But Balaam replied, "Didn't I tell you that I must say whatever Jehovah tells me to?"

[27] Then the king said to Balaam, "I will take you to yet another place. Perhaps it will please God to let you curse them from there."

[28] So King Balak took Balaam to the top of Mount Peor, overlooking the desert. [29] Balaam again told the king to build seven altars, and to prepare seven young bulls and seven rams for the sacrifice. [30] The king did as Balaam said, and offered a young bull and ram on every altar.

24

Balaam realized by now that Jehovah planned to bless Israel, so he didn't even go to meet the Lord as he had earlier. Instead, he went at once and looked out toward the camp of Israel [2] which stretched away across the plains, divided by tribal areas.

Then the Spirit of God came upon him, [3-9] and he spoke this prophecy concerning them:

"Balaam the son of Beor says—
The man whose eyes are open says—
'I have listened to the word of God,
I have seen what God Almighty showed me;
I fell, and my eyes were opened:
Oh, the joys awaiting Israel,
Joys in the homes of Jacob.
I see them spread before me as green valleys,
And fruitful gardens by the riverside;
As aloes planted by the Lord himself;
As cedar trees beside the waters.
They shall be blessed with an abundance of water,
And they shall live in many places.
Their king will be greater than Agag;
Their kingdom is exalted.
God has brought them from Egypt.
Israel has the strength of a wild ox,
And shall eat up the nations that oppose him;
He shall break their bones in pieces,
And shall shoot them with many arrows.
Israel sleeps as a lion or a lioness—
Who dares arouse him?
Blessed is everyone who blesses you, O Israel,
And curses shall fall upon everyone who curses you.'"

[10] King Balak was livid with rage by now. Striking his hands together in anger and disgust he shouted, "I called you to curse my enemies and instead you have blessed them three times. [11] Get

FAMILY DEVOTIONS

☐ DEVOTION 62
STANDING FOR RIGHTEOUSNESS

Read Numbers 25:1-3

Standing for Righteousness Memory Verse

For the eyes of the Lord search back and forth across the whole earth, looking for people whose hearts are perfect toward him, so that he can show his great power in helping them.

2 Chronicles 16:9

"But I don't see how it will hurt me to go to one party!" Marla continued her argument. "How can I win them to the Lord if I don't run around with them?"

"Being friendly is one thing, Marla. Being best friends is another." Mom looked at the clock. "Please go call the twins for me. It's time for them to come inside."

Minutes later Marla and the young twins came into the kitchen. "Oh no! Look at you!" Mom scolded the twins. "You're filthy!"

"We played with Buffy," Shawn explained with a grin.

"Buffy was dirty. He rolled over and over in the mud," Shelly added.

Mom groaned. "You clean Shelly, Marla. I'll take Shawn."

Later at the dinner table the family shared a laugh over the twins' antics that afternoon. As they were finishing dessert, Marla asked Dad if she could go to the party at Patti's house. Dad raised one eyebrow. "Is Patti the girl who was over here last week? The one with the loud mouth who was carrying the blaring radio?"

Marla nodded. "She's OK, Dad. Maybe I can win her to the Lord."

"Marla, when the twins went out to play, they were clean. By playing with Buffy, did they clean him up any?" Dad asked.

Marla looked puzzled. "What do you mean?"

"They didn't get him clean because it's dirt that rubs off, not cleanliness. Instead of the twins getting their puppy clean, he got them dirty." Dad said. "We want you to win Patti and her friends to the Lord, but you can't do it by 'playing in the dirt' with them. You can't influence Patti by doing what she does or going where she goes. Your life needs to be different—a clean, godly life."

"It's easy to get dirty, but it takes work to stay clean," Mom added, as she stood up. "Now how about helping me? We have some dirty dishes here that will take some work to clean, too."

How About You?
Do you try to witness by going along with the crowd? That is not God's way. The Bible says in Romans 12, "Don't copy the behavior and customs of this world, but be a new and different person." *You witness best by showing how good it is to be a Christian.* B. W.

• For the next devotional, turn to page 181. • For the next devotional on STANDING FOR RIGHTEOUSNESS, turn to page 237. • For notes on STANDING FOR RIGHTEOUSNESS, see pages 62, 298, 371, 678, and 948.

out of here! Go back home! I had planned to promote you to great honor, but Jehovah has kept you from it!"

¹²Balaam replied, "Didn't I tell your messengers ¹³that even if you gave me a palace filled with silver and gold, I could not go beyond the words of Jehovah, and could not say a word of my own? I said that I would say only what Jehovah says! ¹⁴Yes, I shall return now to my own people. But first, let me tell you what the Israelites are going to do to your people!"

¹⁵⁻¹⁹So he spoke this prophecy to him:

"Balaam the son of Beor is the man
Whose eyes are open!
He hears the words of God
And has knowledge from the Most High;
He sees what Almighty God has shown him;
He fell, and his eyes were opened:
I see in the future of Israel,
Far down the distant trail,
That there shall come a star from Jacob!
This ruler of Israel
Shall smite the people of Moab,
And destroy the sons of Sheth.
Israel shall possess all Edom and Seir.
They shall overcome their enemies.
Jacob shall arise in power
And shall destroy many cities."

²⁰Then Balaam looked over at the homes of the people of Amalek and prophesied:

"Amalek was the first of the nations,
But its destiny is destruction!"

²¹,²²Then he looked over at the Kenites:

"Yes, you are strongly situated,
Your nest is set in the rocks!
But the Kenites shall be destroyed,
And the mighty army of the king of Assyria
     shall deport you from this land!"

²³,²⁴He concluded his prophecies by saying:

"Alas, who can live when God does this?
Ships shall come from the coasts of Cyprus,
And shall oppress both Eber and Assyria.
They too must be destroyed."

²⁵So Balaam and Balak returned to their homes.

25 The Israelites Worship Baal

While Israel was camped at Acacia, some of the young men began going to wild parties with the local Moabite girls. ²These girls also invited them to attend the sacrifices to their gods, and soon the men were not only attending the feasts, but also bowing down and worshiping the idols. ³Before long all Israel was joining freely in the worship of Baal, the god of Moab; and the anger of the Lord was hot against his people.

⁴He issued the following command to Moses:

"Execute all the tribal leaders of Israel. Hang them up before the Lord in broad daylight, so that his fierce anger will turn away from the people."

⁵So Moses ordered the judges to execute all who had worshiped Baal.

⁶But one of the Israeli men insolently brought a Midianite girl into the camp, right before the eyes of Moses and all the people, as they were weeping at the door of the Tabernacle. ⁷When Phinehas (son of Eleazar and grandson of Aaron the priest) saw this, he jumped up, grabbed a spear, ⁸and rushed after the man into his tent, where he had taken the girl. He thrust the spear all the way through the man's body and into her stomach. So the plague was stopped, ⁹but only after 24,000 people had already died.

¹⁰,¹¹Then the Lord said to Moses, "Phinehas (son of Eleazar and grandson of Aaron the priest) has turned away my anger for he was angry with my anger, and would not tolerate the worship of any God but me. So I have stopped destroying all Israel as I had intended. ¹²,¹³Now because of what he has done—because of his zeal for his God, and because he has made atonement for the people of Israel by what he did—I promise that he and his descendants shall be priests forever."

¹⁴The name of the man who was killed with the Midianite girl was Zimri, son of Salu, a leader of the tribe of Simeon. ¹⁵The girl's name was Cozbi, daughter of Zur, a Midianite prince.

¹⁶,¹⁷Then the Lord said to Moses, "Destroy the Midianites, ¹⁸for they are destroying you with their wiles. They are causing you to worship Baal, and they are leading you astray, as you have just seen by the death of Cozbi."

OVERCOMING ANGER 25:10-11 It is clear from Phinehas's story that some anger is proper and justified. But how can we know when our anger is appropriate and when it should be restrained? Ask these questions when you become angry: (1) Why am I angry? (2) Whose rights are being violated (mine or another's)? (3) Is the truth (a principle of God) being violated? If only your rights are at stake, it may be wiser to keep angry feelings under control. But if the truth is at stake, anger is often justified, although violence and retaliation are usually the wrong way to express it (Phinehas's case was unique). If we are becoming more and more like God, we should be angered by sin. **To begin the series of devotionals on OVERCOMING ANGER, turn to page 133.**

26 People Counted Again

After the plague had ended, Jehovah said to Moses and to Eleazar (son of Aaron the priest), ²"Take a census of all the men of Israel who are twenty years old or older, to find out how many of each tribe and clan are able to go to war."

³,⁴So Moses and Eleazar issued census instructions to the leaders of Israel. (The entire nation was camped in the plains of Moab beside the Jordan River, opposite Jericho.) Here are the results of the census:

⁵⁻¹¹*The tribe of Reuben:* 43,730.

(Reuben was Israel's oldest son.) In this tribe were the following clans, named after Reuben's sons:

The Hanochites, named after their ancestor Hanoch.
The Palluites, named after their ancestor Pallu. (In the subclan of Eliab—who was one of the sons of Pallu—were the families of Nemuel, Abiram, and Dathan. This Dathan and Abiram were the two leaders who conspired with Korah against Moses and Aaron, and in fact challenged the very authority of God! But the earth opened and swallowed them; and 250 men were destroyed by fire from the Lord that day, as a warning to the entire nation.)
The Hezronites, named after their ancestor Hezron.
The Carmites, named after their ancestor Carmi.

¹²⁻¹⁴*The tribe of Simeon:* 22,200.

In this tribe were the following clans, founded by Simeon's sons:

The Nemuelites, named after their ancestor Nemuel.
The Jaminites, named after their ancestor Jamin.
The Jachinites, named after their ancestor Jachin.
The Zerahites, named after their ancestor Zerah.
The Shaulites, named after their ancestor Shaul.

¹⁵⁻¹⁸*The tribe of Gad:* 40,500.

In this tribe were the following clans founded by the sons of Gad:

The Zephonites, named after their ancestor Zephon.
The Haggites, named after their ancestor Haggi.
The Shunites, named after their ancestor Shuni.
The Oznites, named after their ancestor Ozni.
The Erites, named after their ancestor Eri.
The Arodites, named after their ancestor Arod.
The Arelites, named after their ancestor Areli.

¹⁹⁻²²*The tribe of Judah:* 76,500

In this tribe were the following clans named after the sons of Judah—but not including Er and Onan who died in the land of Canaan:

The Shelanites, named after their ancestor Shelah.
The Perezites, named after their ancestor Perez.
The Zerahites, named after their ancestor Zerah.
This census also included the subclans of Perez:
  The Hezronites, named after their ancestor Hezron.
  The Hamulites, named after their ancestor Hamul.

²³⁻²⁵*The tribe of Issachar:* 64,300.

In this tribe were the following clans named after the sons of Issachar:

The Tolaites, named after their ancestor Tola.
The Punites, named after their ancestor Puvah.
The Jashubites, named after their ancestor Jashub.
The Shimronites, named after their ancestor Shimron.

²⁶,²⁷*The tribe of Zebulun:* 60,500.

In this tribe were the following clans named after the sons of Zebulun:

The Seredites, named after their ancestor Sered.
The Elonites, named after their ancestor Elon.
The Jahleelites, named after their ancestor Jahleel.

²⁸⁻³⁷*The tribe of Joseph:* 32,500 *in the half-tribe of Ephraim; and* 52,700 *in the half-tribe of Manasseh.*

In the half-tribe of Manasseh was the clan of Machirites, named after their ancestor Machir.

The subclan of the Machirites was the Gileadites, named after their ancestor Gilead.
The tribes of the Gileadites:
  The Jezerites, named after their ancestor Jezer.
  The Helekites, named after their ancestor Helek.
  The Asrielites, named after their ancestor Asriel.
  The Shechemites, named after their ancestor Shechem.
  The Shemidaites, named after their ancestor Shemida.
  The Hepherites, named after their ancestor Hepher. (Hepher's son, Zelophehad, had no sons. Here are the names of his daughters: Mahlah, Noah, Hoglah, Milcah, Tirzah.

The 32,500 registered in the half-tribe of Ephraim included the following clans, named after the sons of Ephraim:

The Shuthelahites, named after their ancestor Shuthelah. (A subclan of the Shuthelahites was the Eranites, named after their ancestor Eran, a son of Shuthelah.)

The Becherites, named after their ancestor Becher.

The Tahanites, named after their ancestor Tahan.

38-41 *The tribe of Benjamin:* 45,600.

In this tribe were the following clans named after the sons of Benjamin:

The Belaites, named after their ancestor Bela.
Subclans named after sons of Bela were:
   The Ardites, named after their ancestor Ard.
   The Naamites, named after their ancestor Naaman.
The Ashbelites, named after their ancestor Ashbel.
The Ahiramites, named after their ancestor Ahiram.
The Shuphamites, named after their ancestor Shephupham.
The Huphamites, named after their ancestor Hupham.

42,43 *The tribe of Dan:* 64,400.

In this tribe was the clan of the Shuhamites, named after Shuham, the son of Dan.

44-47 *The tribe of Asher:* 53,400.

In this tribe were the following clans named after the sons of Asher:

The Imnites, named after their ancestor Imnah.
The Ishvites, named after their ancestor Ishvi.
The Beriites, named after their ancestor Beriah.
Subclans named after the sons of Beriah were:
   The Heberites, named after their ancestor Heber.
   The Malchielites, named after their ancestor Malchiel.

Asher also had a daughter named Serah.

48-50 *The tribe of Naphtali:* 45,400.

In this tribe were the following clans, named after the sons of Naphtali:

The Jahzeelites, named after their ancestor Jahzeel.
The Gunites, named after their ancestor Guni.
The Jezerites, named after their ancestor Jezer.
The Shillemites, named after their ancestor Shillem.

51 So the total number of the men of draft age throughout Israel was 601,730.

52,53 Then the Lord told Moses to divide the land among the tribes in proportion to their population, as indicated by the census— 54 the larger tribes to be given more land, the smaller tribes less land.

55,56 "Let the representatives of the larger tribes have a lottery, drawing for the larger sections," the Lord instructed, "and let the smaller tribes draw for the smaller sections."

57 These are the clans of the Levites numbered in the census:

The Gershonites, named after their ancestor Gershon.
The Kohathites, named after their ancestor Kohath.
The Merarites, named after their ancestor Merari.

58,59 These are the families of the tribe of Levi: the Libnites, the Hebronites, the Mahlites, the Mushites, the Korahites.

While Levi was in Egypt, a daughter, Jochebed, was born to him and she became the wife of Amram, son of Kohath. They were the parents of Aaron, Moses, and Miriam. 60 To Aaron were born Nadab, Abihu, Eleazar, and Ithamar. 61 But Nadab and Abihu died when they offered unauthorized incense before the Lord.

62 *The total number of Levites in the census* was 23,000, counting all the males a month old and upward. But the Levites were not included in the total census figure of the people of Israel, for the Levites were given no land when it was divided among the tribes.

63 So these are the census figures as prepared by Moses and Eleazar the priest, in the plains of Moab beside the Jordan River, across from Jericho. 64,65 Not one person in this entire census had been counted in the previous census taken in the wilderness of Sinai! For all who had been counted then had died, as the Lord had decreed when he said of them, "They shall die in the wilderness." The only exceptions were Caleb (son of Jephunneh) and Joshua (son of Nun).

27 Zelophehad's Daughters

One day the daughters of Zelophehad came to the entrance of the Tabernacle to give a petition to Moses, Eleazar the priest, the tribal leaders, and others who were there. The names of these women were Mahlah, Noah, Hoglah, Milcah, and Tirzah. They were members of the half-tribe of Manasseh (a son of Joseph). Their ancestor was Machir, son of Manasseh. Manasseh's son Gilead was their great-grandfather, his son Hepher was their grandfather, and his son Zelophehad was their father.

3,4 "Our father died in the wilderness," they said,

"and he was not one of those who perished in Korah's revolt against the Lord—it was a natural death, but he had no sons. Why should the name of our father disappear just because he had no son? We feel that we should be given property along with our father's brothers."

⁵So Moses brought their case before the Lord.

⁶,⁷And the Lord replied to Moses, "The daughters of Zelophehad are correct. Give them land along with their uncles; give them the property that would have been given to their father if he had lived. ⁸Moreover, this is a general law among you, that if a man dies and has no sons, then his inheritance shall be passed on to his daughters. ⁹And if he has no daughter, it shall belong to his brothers. ¹⁰And if he has no brother, then it shall go to his uncles. ¹¹But if he has no uncles, then it shall go to the nearest relative."

¹²One day the Lord said to Moses, "Go up into Mount Abarim and look across the river to the land I have given to the people of Israel. ¹³After you have seen it, you shall die as Aaron your brother did, ¹⁴for you rebelled against my instructions in the wilderness of Zin. When the people of Israel rebelled, you did not glorify me before them by following my instructions to order water to come out of the rock." He was referring to the incident at the waters of Meribah ("Place of Strife") in Kadesh, in the wilderness of Zin.

¹⁵Then Moses said to the Lord, ¹⁶"O Jehovah, the God of the spirits of all mankind, [before I am taken away] please appoint a new leader for the people, ¹⁷a man who will lead them into battle and care for them, so that the people of the Lord will not be as sheep without a shepherd."

¹⁸The Lord replied, "Go and get Joshua (son of Nun), who has the Spirit in him, ¹⁹and take him to Eleazar the priest, and as all the people watch, charge him with the responsibility of leading the people. ²⁰Publicly give him your authority so that all the people of Israel will obey him ²¹He shall be the one to consult with Eleazar the priest in order to get directions from the Lord. The Lord will speak to Eleazar through the use of the Urim, and Eleazar will pass on these instructions to Joshua and the people. In this way the Lord will continue to give them guidance."

²²So Moses did as Jehovah commanded and took Joshua to Eleazar the priest. As the people watched, ²³Moses laid his hands upon him and dedicated him to his responsibilities, as the Lord had commanded.

28 Daily Offerings

The Lord gave Moses these instructions to give to the people of Israel: "The offerings which you burn on the altar for me are my food, and are a pleasure to me; so see to it that they are brought regularly and are offered as I have instructed you.

³"When you make offerings by fire, you shall use yearling male lambs—each without defect. Two of them shall be offered each day as a regular burnt offering. ⁴One lamb shall be sacrificed in the morning, the other in the evening. ⁵With them shall be offered a grain offering of three quarts of finely ground flour mixed with three pints of oil. ⁶This is the burnt offering ordained at Mount Sinai, to be regularly offered as a fragrant odor, an offering made by fire to the Lord. ⁷Along with it shall be the drink offering, consisting of three pints of strong wine with each lamb, poured out in the holy place before the Lord. ⁸Offer the second lamb in the evening with the same grain offering and drink offering. It too is a fragrant odor to the Lord, an offering made by fire.

⁹,¹⁰"On the Sabbath day, sacrifice two yearling male lambs—both without defect—in addition to the regular offerings. They are to be accompanied by a grain offering of six quarts of fine flour mixed with oil, and the usual drink offering.

¹¹"Also, on the first day of each month there shall be an extra burnt offering to the Lord of two young bulls, one ram, and seven male yearling lambs—all without defect. ¹²Accompany them with nine quarts of finely ground flour mixed with oil as a grain offering with each bull; and six quarts of finely ground flour mixed with oil as a grain offering for the ram; ¹³and for each lamb, three quarts of finely ground flour mixed with oil for a grain offering. This burnt offering shall be presented by fire and will please the Lord very much. ¹⁴Along with each sacrifice shall be a drink offering—six pints of wine with each bull, four pints for a ram, and three pints for a lamb. This, then, will be the burnt offering each month throughout the year.

¹⁵"Also on the first day of each month you shall offer one male goat for a sin offering to the Lord. This is in addition to the regular daily burnt offering and its drink offering.

¹⁶"On April first you shall celebrate the Passover—[when the death angel passed over the oldest sons of the Israelites in Egypt, leaving them unharmed]. ¹⁷On the following day a great, joyous seven-day festival will begin, but no leavened bread shall be served. ¹⁸On the first day of the festival all the people shall be called together before the Lord. No hard work shall be done on that day. ¹⁹You shall offer as burnt sacrifices to the Lord two young bulls, one ram, and seven yearling male lambs—all without defect. ²⁰,²¹With each bull there shall be a grain offering of nine quarts of fine flour mixed with oil; with the ram there

shall be six quarts; and with each of the seven lambs there shall be three quarts of fine flour. ²²You must also offer a male goat as a sin offering, to make atonement for yourselves. ²³These offerings shall be in addition to the usual daily sacrifices. ²⁴This same sacrifice shall be offered on each of the seven days of the feast; they will be very pleasant to the Lord. ²⁵On the seventh day there shall again be a holy and solemn assembly of all the people, and during that day you may do no hard work.

²⁶"On the first day of the Harvest Festival all the people must come before the Lord for a special, solemn assembly to celebrate the new harvest. On that day you are to present the first of the new crop of grain as a grain offering to the Lord; there is to be no regular work by anyone on that day. ²⁷A special burnt offering, very pleasant to the Lord, shall be offered that day. It shall consist of two young bulls, one ram, and seven yearling male lambs. ²⁸,²⁹These shall be accompanied by your grain offering of nine quarts of fine flour mixed with oil with each bull, six quarts with the ram, and three quarts with each of the seven lambs. ³⁰ Also offer one male goat to make atonement for yourselves. ³¹These special offerings are in addition to the regular daily burnt offerings and grain offerings and drink offerings. Make sure that the animals you sacrifice are without defect.

29 Festival of Trumpets

"The Festival of Trumpets shall be celebrated on the fifteenth day of September each year; there shall be a solemn assembly of all the people on that day, and no hard work may be done. ²On that day you shall offer a burnt sacrifice consisting of one young bull, one ram, and seven yearling male lambs—all without defect. These are sacrifices which the Lord will appreciate and enjoy. ³,⁴ A grain offering of nine quarts of fine flour mingled with oil shall be offered with the bull, six quarts with the ram, and three quarts with each of the seven lambs. ⁵In addition, there shall be a male goat sacrificed as a sin offering, to make atonement for you. ⁶These special sacrifices are in addition to the regular monthly burnt offering for that day, and also in addition to the regular daily burnt sacrifices, which are to be offered with the respective grain offerings and drink offerings, as specified by the ordinances governing them.

⁷"Ten days later another convocation of all the people shall be held. This will be a day of solemn humility before the Lord, and no work of any kind may be done. ⁸On that day you shall offer a burnt sacrifice to the Lord—it will be very pleasant to him—of one young bull, one ram, seven yearling male lambs—each without defect—⁹,¹⁰and their accompanying grain offerings. Nine quarts of fine flour mixed with oil are to be offered with the bull, six with the ram, and three with each of the seven lambs. ¹¹You are also to sacrifice one male goat for a sin offering. This is in addition to the sin offering of the Day of Atonement [offered annually on that day], and in addition to the regular daily burnt sacrifices, grain offerings, and drink offerings.

¹²"Five days later there shall be yet another assembly of all the people, and on that day no hard work shall be done; it is the beginning of a seven-day festival before the Lord. ¹³Your special burnt sacrifice that day, which will give much pleasure to the Lord, shall be thirteen young bulls, two rams, and fourteen male yearling lambs—each without defect—¹⁴accompanied by the usual grain offerings—nine quarts of fine flour mingled with oil for each of the thirteen young bulls; six quarts for each of the two rams; ¹⁵and three quarts for each of the fourteen lambs. ¹⁶There must also be a male goat sacrificed for a sin offering, in addition to the regular daily burnt sacrifice with its accompanying grain offerings and drink offerings.

¹⁷"On the second day of this seven-day festival you shall sacrifice twelve young bulls, two rams, and fourteen male yearling lambs—each without defect—¹⁸ accompanied by the usual grain offerings and drink offerings. ¹⁹Also, in addition to the regular daily burnt sacrifice, you are to sacrifice a male goat with its accompanying grain offering and drink offering for a sin offering.

²⁰"On the third day of the festival, offer eleven young bulls, two rams, fourteen male yearling lambs—each without defect—²¹and the usual grain offering and drink offering with each sacrifice. ²²And in addition to the regular daily burnt sacrifices, sacrifice a male goat for a sin offering, with its accompanying grain offering and drink offering.

²³"On the fourth day of the festival, you are to sacrifice ten young bulls, two rams, and fourteen male yearling lambs—each without defect—²⁴each with its accompanying grain offering and drink offering; ²⁵also a male goat as a sin offering (along with the usual grain and drink offerings) in addition to the regular daily sacrifices.

²⁶,²⁷"On the fifth day of the festival, sacrifice nine young bulls, two rams, and fourteen male yearling lambs—each without defect—accompanied by the usual grain offerings and drink offerings; ²⁸also sacrifice a male goat with the usual grain and drink offerings, as a special sin offering, in addition to the usual daily sacrifices.

²⁹"On the sixth day of the festival, you must sacrifice eight young bulls, two rams, and fourteen male yearling lambs—each without defect—

Family Devotions

☐ **Devotion 63**
Keeping Your Promises

Read Numbers 30:1-2

Keeping Your Promises
Memory Verse

God delights in those who keep their promises and abhors those who don't.
Proverbs 12:22

When Mrs. Brown asked Paul to distribute invitations to the after-school Bible club in her home, he agreed readily. "I'd like these passed out today," explained Mrs. Brown. "The club starts the day after tomorrow."

"No problem," said Paul, and he took several invitations. "I can easily do it tonight."

Mrs. Brown looked grateful. "This really helps me out."

"I'm going to pass these out for Mrs. Brown," Paul told his mother when he got home. Then he laid the invitations on an end table and went out to play. After supper he did his homework and worked on his model car, completely forgetting about the invitations. The next day, while dusting the furniture, Mom found them.

After school that day, Paul came bursting into the house. Not noticing the stern look on Mom's face, he began to tell her his problem. "That Rick!" he exploded angrily. "He told me he'd return a book to the library for me, and he didn't do it! Now I have to pay a fine. I think he should . . ." His voice trailed off when he saw the invitations in Mom's hand. Before she could say a word, he murmured, "Oh, Mom, I forgot."

"Paul, I'm disappointed that you didn't do the job you said you'd do," said Mom. "I think your experience with Rick today is a good lesson on the importance of doing what you promise. If you can't or don't want to help, say so right away. Don't say you'll do something, letting someone depend on you, and then fail him or her."

"I know it's late, but I'll still run around the neighborhood with these right now—before I have a snack," said Paul. "I'm really sorry, and I'll apologize to Mrs. Brown, too. Be back soon, Mom."

How About You?
Are you faithful to do whatever you said you'd do? It's easy to make quick promises, but not so easy to carry them out. Make sure you follow through on promises made to others. God always keeps his promises, and he wants us to be like him. *C. Y.*

• For the next devotional, turn to page 185. • For the next devotional on *Keeping Your Promises*, turn to page 213.
• For notes on *Keeping Your Promises*, see pages 183, 284, and 838.

³⁰along with their usual grain and drink offerings. ³¹In addition to the usual daily sacrifices, sacrifice a male goat and the usual grain and drink offerings as a sin offering.

³²"On the seventh day of the festival, sacrifice seven young bulls, two rams, and fourteen male yearling lambs—each without defect—³³each with its customary grain and drink offerings; ³⁴also sacrifice an extra sin offering of one male goat, with the usual grain and drink offerings, in addition to the regular daily sacrifices.

³⁵"On the eighth day summon the people to another solemn assembly; you must do no hard work that day. ³⁶Sacrifice a burnt offering—they are very pleasant to the Lord—of one young bull, one ram, seven male yearling lambs—each without defect—³⁷and the customary grain and drink offerings. ³⁸Sacrifice also one male goat with the usual grain and drink offerings for a sin offering, in addition to the regular daily sacrifices. ³⁹These offerings are compulsory at the times of your annual feasts, and are in addition to sacrifices and offerings you present in connection with vows, or as free-will offerings, burnt sacrifices, grain offerings, drink offerings, or peace offerings."

⁴⁰So Moses gave all of these instructions to the people of Israel.

30 Rules about Vows

Now Moses summoned the leaders of the tribes and told them, "The Lord has commanded that when anyone makes a promise to the Lord, either to do something or to quit doing something, that vow must not be broken: the person making the vow must do exactly as he has promised.

³"If a woman promises the Lord to do or not do something, and she is still a girl at home in her father's home, ⁴and her father hears that she has made a vow with penalties, but says nothing, then her vow shall stand. ⁵But if her father refuses to let her make the vow, or feels that the penalties she has agreed to are too harsh, then her promise will automatically become invalid. Her father must state his disagreement on the first day he hears about it; and then Jehovah will forgive her because her father would not let her do it.

⁶"If she takes a vow or makes a foolish pledge, and later marries, ⁷and her husband learns of her vow and says nothing on the day he hears of it, her vow shall stand. ⁸But if her husband refuses to accept her vow or foolish pledge, his disagreement makes it void, and Jehovah will forgive her.

⁹"But if the woman is a widow or is divorced, she must fulfill her vow.

¹⁰"If she is married and living in her husband's home when she makes the vow, ¹¹and her husband hears of it and does nothing, the vow shall stand; ¹²but if he refuses to allow it on the first day he hears of it, her vow is void and Jehovah will forgive her. ¹³So her husband may either confirm or nullify her vow, ¹⁴but if he says nothing for a day, then he has already agreed to it. ¹⁵If he waits more than a day and then refuses to permit the vow, whatever penalties to which she agreed shall come upon him—he shall be responsible."

¹⁶These, then, are the commandments the Lord gave Moses concerning relationships between a man and his wife and between a father and his daughter who is living at home.

31 The War Against Midian

Then the Lord said to Moses, "Take vengeance on the Midianites for leading you into idolatry, and then you must die."

³Moses said to the people, "Some of you must take arms to wage Jehovah's war against Midian. ⁴,⁵Conscript 1,000 men from each tribe." So this was done; and out of the many thousands of Israel, 12,000 armed men were sent to battle by Moses. ⁶Phinehas (son of Eleazar the priest) led them into battle, accompanied by the Ark, with trumpets blaring. ⁷And every man of Midian was killed. ⁸Among those killed were all five of the Midianite kings—Evi, Rekem, Zur, Hur, and Reba. Balaam, the son of Beor, was also killed.

⁹⁻¹¹Then the Israeli army took as captives all the women and children, and seized the cattle and flocks and a lot of miscellaneous booty. All of the cities, towns, and villages of Midian were then burned. ¹²The captives and other war loot were brought to Moses and Eleazar the priest, and to the rest of the people of Israel who were camped on the plains of Moab beside the Jordan River, across from Jericho. ¹³Moses and Eleazar the priest and all the leaders of the people went out to meet the victorious army, ¹⁴but Moses was very angry with the army officers and battalion leaders.

¹⁵"Why have you let all the women live?" he demanded. ¹⁶"These are the very ones who followed Balaam's advice and caused the people of Israel to worship idols on Mount Peor, and they are the cause of the plague that destroyed us. ¹⁷Now kill all the boys and all the women who have had sexual intercourse. ¹⁸Only the little girls may live; you may keep them for

---

GIVING TO GOD **31:28-30** Moses told the people of Israel to give a portion of the war spoils to God. Another portion was to go to the people who remained behind. Similarly, the money we earn is not ours alone. Everything we possess comes directly or indirectly from God and ultimately belongs to him. We should return a portion to him and also share what we have been given with those in need. **To begin the series of devotionals on GIVING TO GOD, turn to page 105.**

yourselves. ¹⁹Now stay outside of the camp for seven days, all of you who have killed anyone or touched a dead body. Then purify yourselves and your captives on the third and seventh days. ²⁰Remember also to purify all your garments and everything made of leather, goat's hair, or wood."

²¹Then Eleazar the priest said to the men who were in the battle, "This is the commandment Jehovah has given Moses: ²²'Anything that will stand heat—such as gold, silver, bronze, iron, tin, or lead—²³shall be passed through fire in order to be made ceremonially pure; it must then be further purified with the purification water. But anything that won't stand heat shall be purified by the water alone.' ²⁴On the seventh day you must wash your clothes and be purified, and then you may come back into the camp."

²⁵And the Lord said to Moses, ²⁶"You and Eleazar the priest and the leaders of the tribes are to make a list of all the loot, including the people and animals; ²⁷then divide it into two parts. Half of it is for the men who were in the battle, and the other half is to be given to the people of Israel. ²⁸But first, the Lord gets a share of all the captives, oxen, donkeys, and flocks kept by the army. His share is one out of every five hundred. ²⁹Give this share to Eleazar the priest to be presented to the Lord by the gesture of waving before the altar. ³⁰Also levy a 2 percent tribute of all the captives, flocks, and cattle that are given to the people of Israel. Present this to the Levites in charge of the Tabernacle, for it is the Lord's portion."

³¹So Moses and Eleazar the priest did as the Lord commanded. ³²⁻³⁵The total booty (besides the jewelry, clothing, etc., which the soldiers kept for themselves) was 675,000 sheep; 72,000 oxen; 61,000 donkeys; and 32,000 young girls. ³⁶⁻⁴⁰So the half given to the army totaled: 337,500 sheep (of which 675 were given to the Lord); 36,000 oxen (of which 72 were given to the Lord); 30,500 donkeys (of which 61 were given to the Lord); 16,000 girls (of whom 32 went to the Levites).

⁴¹All of the Lord's portion was given to Eleazar the priest, as the Lord had directed Moses.

⁴²⁻⁴⁶The half of the booty assigned to the people of Israel—Moses had separated it from the half belonging to the warriors—amounted to: 337,500 sheep, 36,000 oxen, 30,500 donkeys, and 16,000 girls.

⁴⁷In accordance with the Lord's directions, Moses gave 2 percent of these to the Levites.

⁴⁸,⁴⁹Then the officers and battalion leaders came to Moses and said, "We have accounted for all the men who went out to battle, and not one of us is missing! ⁵⁰So we have brought a special thank-offering to the Lord from our loot—gold jewelry, bracelets, anklets, rings, earrings, and necklaces. This is to make atonement for our souls before the Lord."

⁵¹,⁵²Moses and Eleazar the priest received this special offering from the captains and battalion leaders and company commanders, and found its total value to be more than $300,000. ⁵³(The soldiers had also kept personal loot for themselves.) ⁵⁴The offering was taken into the Tabernacle and kept there before the Lord as a memorial of the people of Israel.

32 Some Tribes Get Their Land

When Israel arrived in the land of Jazar and Gilead, the tribes of Reuben and Gad (who had large flocks of sheep) noticed what wonderful sheep country it was. ²So they came to Moses and Eleazar the priest and the other tribal leaders and said, ³,⁴"The Lord has used Israel to destroy the population of this whole countryside—Ataroth, Dibon, Jazer, Nimrah, Heshbon, Elealeh, Sebam, Nebo, and Beon. And it is all wonderful sheep country, ideal for our flocks. ⁵Please let us have this land as our portion instead of the land on the other side of the Jordan River."

⁶"You mean you want to sit here while your brothers go across and do all the fighting?" Moses demanded. ⁷"Are you trying to discourage the rest of the people from going across to the land that the Lord has given them? ⁸This is the same kind of thing your fathers did! I sent them from Kadesh-barnea to spy out the land, ⁹but when they finished their survey and returned from the valley of Eshcol, they discouraged the people from going on into the Promised Land. ¹⁰,¹¹And the Lord's anger was hot against them, and he swore that of all those he had rescued from Egypt, no one over twenty years of age would ever see the land he promised Abraham, Isaac, and Jacob, for they had refused to do what he wanted them to.

¹²"The only exceptions were Caleb (son of Jephunneh the Kenizzite) and Joshua (son of Nun)—for they wholeheartedly followed the Lord and urged the people to go on into the Promised Land.

¹³"The Lord made us wander back and forth in the wilderness for forty years until all that evil generation died. ¹⁴But here you are, a brood of

---

KEEPING YOUR PROMISES 32:16-19 The land on the east side of the Jordan had been conquered. The hard work was done by all of the tribes together. But the tribes of Reuben and Gad and the half-tribe of Manasseh did not stop after their land was cleared. They promised to keep working with the others until everyone's land was conquered. After others have helped you, do you find excuses for being unable to help them? Finish the whole job, even those parts that may not benefit you directly. **To begin the series of devotionals on KEEPING YOUR PROMISES, turn to page 181.**

sinners doing exactly the same thing! Only there are more of you, so Jehovah's anger against Israel will be even fiercer this time. ¹⁵If you turn away from God like this, he will make the people stay even longer in the wilderness, and you will be responsible for destroying his people and bringing disaster to this entire nation!"

¹⁶"Not at all!" they explained. "We will build sheepfolds for our flocks and cities for our little ones, ¹⁷but we ourselves will go over armed, ahead of the rest of the people of Israel, until we have brought them safely to their inheritance. But first we will need to build walled cities here for our families, to keep them safe from attack by the local inhabitants. ¹⁸We will not settle down here until all the people of Israel have received their inheritance. ¹⁹We don't want land on the other side of the Jordan; we would rather have it on this side, on the east."

²⁰Then Moses said, "All right, if you will do what you have said and arm yourselves for Jehovah's war, ²¹and keep your troops across the Jordan until the Lord has driven out his enemies, ²²then, when the land is finally subdued before the Lord, you may return. Then you will have discharged your duty to the Lord and to the rest of the people of Israel. And the land on the eastern side shall be your possession from the Lord. ²³But if you don't do as you have said, then you will have sinned against the Lord, and you may be sure that your sin will catch up with you. ²⁴Go ahead and build cities for your families and sheepfolds for your sheep, and do all you have said."

²⁵"We will follow your instructions exactly," the people of Gad and Reuben replied. ²⁶"Our children, wives, flocks, and cattle shall stay here in the cities of Gilead. ²⁷But all of us who are conscripted will go over to battle for the Lord, just as you have said."

²⁸So Moses gave his approval by saying to Eleazar, Joshua, and the tribal leaders of Israel, ²⁹"If all the men of the tribes of Gad and Reuben who are conscripted for the Lord's battles go with you over Jordan, then, when the land is conquered, you must give them the land of Gilead; ³⁰but if they refuse, then they must accept land among the rest of you in the land of Canaan."

³¹The tribes of Gad and Reuben said again, "As the Lord has commanded, so we will do— ³²we will follow the Lord fully armed into Canaan, but our own land shall be here on this side of the Jordan."

³³So Moses assigned the territory of King Sihon of the Amorites, and of King Og of Bashan—all the land and cities—to the tribes of Gad, Reuben, and the half-tribe of Manasseh (son of Joseph).

³⁴⁻³⁶The people of Gad built these cities: Dibon, Ataroth, Aroer, Atroth-shophan, Jazer, Jogbehah, Beth-nimrah, Beth-haran. They were all fortified cities with sheepfolds.

³⁷,³⁸The children of Reuben built the following cities: Heshbon, Elealeh, Kiriathaim, Nebo, Baal-meon, Sibmah. (The Israelites later changed the names of some of these cities they had conquered and rebuilt.)

³⁹Then the clan of Machir of the tribe of Manasseh went to Gilead and conquered it, and drove out the Amorites who were living there. ⁴⁰So Moses gave Gilead to the Machirites, and they lived there. ⁴¹The men of Jair, another clan of the tribe of Manasseh, occupied many of the towns in Gilead, and changed the name of their area to Havroth-jair. ⁴²Meanwhile, a man named Nobah led an army to Kenath and its surrounding villages, and occupied them, and he called the area Nobah, after his own name.

33 The Promised Land

This is the itinerary of the nation of Israel from the time Moses and Aaron led them out of Egypt. ²Moses had written down their movements as the Lord had instructed him. ³,⁴They left the city of Rameses, Egypt, on the first day of April, the day after the night of the Passover. They left proudly, hurried along by the Egyptians who were burying all their eldest sons, killed by the Lord the night before. The Lord had certainly defeated all the gods of Egypt that night!

⁵,⁶After leaving Rameses, they stayed in Succoth, Etham (at the edge of the wilderness), and ⁷Pihahiroth (near Baal-zephon, where they camped at the foot of Mount Migdol). ⁸From there they went through the middle of the Red Sea and on for three days into the Etham wilderness, camping at Marah.

⁹Leaving Marah, they came to Elim, where there are twelve springs of water and seventy palm trees; they stayed there for quite a long time.

¹⁰Leaving Elim, they camped beside the Red Sea, ¹¹and then in the wilderness of Sihn.

¹²Next was Dophkah, ¹³and then Alush; ¹⁴then on to Rephidim (where there was no water for the people to drink).

¹⁵⁻³⁷From Rephidim they went to the wilderness of Sinai; from the wilderness of Sinai to Kibroth-hattaavah;

From Kibroth-hattaavah to Hazeroth;
From Hazeroth to Rithmah;
From Rithmah to Rimmon-parez;
From Rimmon-parez to Libnah;
From Libnah to Rissah;
From Rissah to Kehelathah;
From Kehelathah to Mount Shepher;
From Mount Shepher to Haradah;

Family Devotions

☐ **Devotion 64**
Confessing Sin

Read Numbers 32:23

Confessing Sin Memory Verse

Create in me a new, clean heart, O God, filled with clean thoughts and right desires.
Psalm 51:10

Time passed quickly the day Staci and her family visited her grandparents' farm. As they were preparing to leave, Grandma Walker handed Staci's father a paper sack. "Victor, will you fill this with potatoes from the smokehouse? I'll send some home with you. Get some onions, too. But be careful. Last week Grandpa killed a black widow spider out there."

The following week Staci spent a lot of time in her room reading some magazines her friend Denise had loaned her. She was very careful to keep them hidden in her notebook, for she knew her parents would not approve of them. Friday afternoon, just as she reached for a magazine, her mother screamed. Staci dropped her notebook and ran to the kitchen.

Mom was leaning against the cupboard. "There's a black widow spider in there!" She pointed at the open potato bin. "I was reaching in to get potatoes for dinner when I saw it!"

At that moment, Dad walked through the door. How glad they were to see him! When the spider was dead and the potato bin had been emptied, searched, and refilled, Mom took a deep breath. "Just think, I've put my hand in there several times this week."

Dad grinned wryly. "And I put the potatoes, spider and all, in the sack." Staci shivered.

After dinner and devotions, she excused herself—to do homework, she said. As she shut the door and reached for the magazine in her notebook, she remembered the hidden spider. Sharply, she drew back her hand. She could no more touch that magazine than she could have touched the spider. No one had said a word, but Staci knew the Spirit of the Lord was convicting her. *Tomorrow,* she promised herself, *I'll return it, and I'll tell Denise not to bring me any more.*

H o w   A b o u t   Y o u ?
Is there hidden sin in your life? Confess it and get rid of it. Don't play with sin. It's far more dangerous than spiders. *B. W.*

• For the next devotional, turn to page 193.   • For the next devotional on *Confessing Sin*, turn to page 277.
• For notes on *Confessing Sin*, see pages 429, 479, 836, 881, and 1220.

From Haradah to Makheloth;
From Makheloth to Tahath;
From Tahath to Terah;
From Terah to Mithkah;
From Mithkah to Hashmonah;
From Hashmonah to Moseroth;
From Moseroth to Bene-jaakan;
From Bene-jaakan to Hor-haggidgad;
From Hor-haggidgad to Jotbathah;
From Jotbathah to Abronah;
From Abronah to Ezion-geber;
From Ezion-geber to Kadesh (in the wilderness of Zin);
From Kadesh to Mount Hor (at the edge of the land of Edom).

38,39 While they were at the foot of Mount Hor, Aaron the priest was directed by the Lord to go up into the mountain, and there he died. This occurred during the fortieth year after the people of Israel had left Egypt. The date of his death was July 15, when he was 123 years old.

40 It was then that the Canaanite king of Arad, who lived in the Negeb, in the land of Canaan, heard that the people of Israel were approaching his land. 41 After dealing with him, the Israelis journeyed from Mount Hor and camped in Zalmonah, 42 then at Punon, 43 then at Oboth, 44 then Iyeabarim (at the border of Moab). 45 From there they went to Dibon-gad, 46 and then to Almon-diblathaim, 47 and on into the mountains of Abarim, near Mount Nebo, 48 and finally to the plains of Moab beside the river Jordan, opposite Jericho. 49 While in that area they camped at various places along the Jordan River, from Bethjeshimoth as far as Abel-shittim, on the plains of Moab.

50,51 It was while they were camped there that the Lord told Moses to tell the people of Israel, "When you pass across the Jordan River into the land of Canaan, 52 you must drive out all the people living there and destroy all their idols—their carved stones, molten images, and the open-air sanctuaries in the hills where they worship their idols. 53 I have given the land to you; take it and live there. 54 You will be given land in proportion to the size of your tribes. The larger sections of land will be divided by lot among the larger tribes, and the smaller sections will be allotted to the smaller tribes. 55 But if you refuse to drive out the people living there, those who remain will be as cinders in your eyes and thorns in your sides. 56 And I will destroy you as I had planned for you to destroy them."

34 Borders of the New Land

The Lord told Moses to tell the people of Israel, "When you come into the land of Canaan (I am giving you the entire land as your homeland), 3 the southern portion of the country will be the wilderness of Zin, along the edge of Edom. The southern boundary will begin at the Dead Sea, 4 and will continue south past Scorpion Pass in the direction of Zin. Its southernmost point will be Kadesh-barnea, from which it will go to Hazaraddar, and on to Azmon. 5 From Azmon the boundary will follow the Brook of Egypt down to the Mediterranean Sea.

6 "Your western boundary will be the coastline of the Mediterranean Sea.

7-9 "Your northern border will begin at the Mediterranean Sea and will proceed eastward to Mount Hor, then to Lebo-Hamath, and on through Zedad and Ziphron to Hazar-enan.

10,11 "The eastern border will be from Hazar-enan south to Shepham, then on to Riblah at the east side of Ain. From there it will make a large half-circle, first going south and then westward until it touches the southernmost tip of the Sea of Galilee, 12 and then along the Jordan River, ending at the Dead Sea."

13 "This is the territory you are to apportion among yourselves by lot," Moses said. "It is to be divided up among the nine and one-half tribes, 14,15 for the tribes of Reuben and Gad and the half-tribe of Manasseh have already been assigned land on the east side of the Jordan, opposite Jericho."

16-28 And the Lord said to Moses, "These are the names of the men I have appointed to handle the dividing up of the land: Eleazar the priest, Joshua (son of Nun), and one leader from each tribe, as listed below:

Tribe	Leader
Judah	Caleb (son of Jephunneh)
Simeon	Shemuel (son of Ammihud)
Benjamin	Elidad (son of Chislon)
Dan	Bukki (son of Jogli)
Manasseh	Hanniel (son of Ephod)
Ephraim	Kemuel (son of Shiphtan)
Zebulun	Elizaphan (son of Parnach)
Issachar	Paltiel (son of Azzan)
Asher	Ahihud (son of Shelomi)
Naphtali	Pedahel (son of Ammihud)

29 These are the names of the men I have appointed to oversee the dividing of the land among the tribes."

35 Cities for the Levites

While Israel was camped beside the Jordan on the plains of Moab, opposite Jericho, the Lord said to Moses,

2 "Instruct the people of Israel to give to the Levites as their inheritance certain cities and surrounding pasture lands. 3 These cities are for their homes, and the surrounding lands for their cattle, flocks, and other livestock. 4,5 Their gardens and

vineyards shall extend 1500 feet out from the city walls in each direction, with an additional 1500 feet beyond that for pastureland.

⁶"You shall give the Levites the six Cities of Refuge, where a person who has accidentally killed someone can run and be safe, and forty-two other cities besides. ⁷In all, there shall be forty-eight cities with the surrounding pastureland given to the Levites. ⁸These cities shall be in various parts of the nation; the larger tribes with many cities will give several to the Levites, while the smaller tribes will give fewer."

⁹,¹⁰And the Lord said to Moses, "Tell the people that when they arrive in the land, ¹¹Cities of Refuge shall be designated for anyone to flee into if he has killed someone accidentally. ¹²These cities will be places of protection from the dead man's relatives who want to avenge his death; for the slayer must not be killed unless a fair trial establishes his guilt. ¹³,¹⁴Three of these six Cities of Refuge are to be located in the land of Canaan, and three on the east side of the Jordan River. ¹⁵These are not only for the protection of Israelites, but also for foreigners and travelers.

¹⁶"But if someone is struck and killed by a piece of iron, it must be presumed to be murder, and the murderer must be executed. ¹⁷Or if the slain man was struck down with a large stone, it is murder, and the murderer shall die. ¹⁸The same is true if he is killed with a wooden weapon. ¹⁹The avenger of his death shall personally kill the murderer when he meets him. ²⁰So if anyone kills another out of hatred by throwing something at him, or ambushing him, ²¹or angrily striking him with his fist so that he dies, he is a murderer; and the murderer shall be executed by the avenger.

²²,²³"But if it is an accident—a case in which something is thrown unintentionally, or in which a stone is thrown without anger, without realizing it will hit anyone, and without wanting to harm an enemy—yet the man dies, ²⁴then the people shall judge whether or not it was an accident, and whether or not to hand the killer over to the avenger of the dead man. ²⁵If it is decided that it was accidental, then the people shall save the killer from the avenger; the killer shall be permitted to stay in the City of Refuge; and he must live there until the death of the High Priest.

²⁶"If the slayer leaves the city, ²⁷and the avenger finds him outside and kills him, it is not murder, ²⁸for the man should have stayed inside the city until the death of the High Priest. But after the death of the High Priest, the man may return to his own land and home. ²⁹These are permanent laws for all Israel from generation to generation.

³⁰"All murderers must be executed, but only if there is more than one witness; no man shall die with only one person testifying against him. ³¹Whenever anyone is judged guilty of murder, he must die—no ransom may be accepted for him. ³²Nor may a payment be accepted from a refugee in a City of Refuge, permitting him to return to his home before the death of the High Priest. ³³In this way the land will not be polluted, for murder pollutes the land, and no atonement can be made for murder except by the execution of the murderer. ³⁴You shall not defile the land where you are going to live, for I, Jehovah, will be living there."

36 Each Tribe's Land to Remain Secure

Then the heads of the subclan of Gilead (of the clan of Machir, of the tribe of Manasseh, one of the sons of Joseph) came to Moses and the leaders of Israel with a petition: "The Lord instructed you to divide the land by lot among the people of Israel," they reminded Moses, "and to give the inheritance of our brother Zelophehad to his daughters. ³But if they marry into another tribe, their land will go with them to the tribe into which they marry. In this way the total area of our tribe will be reduced ⁴and will not be returned at the Year of Jubilee."

⁵Then Moses replied publicly, giving them these instructions from the Lord: "The men of the tribe of Joseph have a proper complaint. ⁶This is what the Lord has further commanded concerning the daughters of Zelophehad: 'Let them be married to anyone they like, so long as it is within their own tribe. ⁷In this way none of the land of the tribe will shift to any other tribe, for the inheritance of every tribe is to remain permanently as it was first allotted. ⁸The girls throughout the tribes of Israel who are heiresses must marry within their own tribe, so that their land won't leave the tribe. ⁹In this way no inheritance shall move from one tribe to another.'"

¹⁰The daughters of Zelophehad did as the Lord commanded Moses. ¹¹,¹²These girls, Mahlah, Tirzah, Hoglah, Milcah, and Noah, were married to men in their own tribe of Manasseh (son of Joseph); so their inheritance remained in their tribe.

¹³These are the commandments and ordinances that the Lord gave to the people of Israel through Moses, while they were camped on the plains of Moab beside the Jordan River, across from Jericho.

Deuteronomy

IN THE past four books of the Bible, we've been reading how God brought his people to their Promised Land. We can read through it pretty quickly compared to the forty years it took the Israelites to live it!

As the Israelites stood on the border of their new country, Moses reminded them of all they had been through and what God had taught them. Deuteronomy is mostly a speech by Moses reviewing what had happened. And he had good reason to remind the people. They had short memories when it came to remembering God's miracles, care, and forgiveness!

Moses knew that loving and obeying God should be as natural as breathing and walking and talking. Moses taught the people that they can love God because he loved and chose them first.

Before the people entered their next stage of life—in the new land—Moses made sure they knew who had brought them there.

As you read Deuteronomy, look for reasons for following God and the blessings that will come from obeying him. God still gives blessings for following him.

Moses Talks to the People

1 This book records Moses' address to the people of Israel when they were camped in the valley of the Arabah in the wilderness of Moab, east of the Jordan River. (Cities in the area included Suph, Paran, Tophel, Laban, Hazeroth, and Dizahab.) The speech was given on February 15, forty years after the people of Israel left Mount Horeb—though it takes only eleven days to travel by foot from Mount Horeb to Kadesh-barnea, going by way of Mount Seir! At the time of this address, King Sihon of the Amorites had already been defeated at Heshbon, and King Og of Bashan had been defeated at Ashtaroth, near Edre-i. Here, then, is Moses' address to Israel, stating all the laws God had commanded him to pass on to them:

⁶"It was forty years ago, at Mount Horeb, that Jehovah our God told us, 'You have stayed here long enough. ⁷Now go and occupy the hill country of the Amorites, the valley of the Arabah, and the Negeb, and all the land of Canaan and Lebanon—the entire area from the shores of the Mediterranean Sea to the

Euphrates River. ⁸I am giving all of it to you! Go in and possess it, for it is the land the Lord promised to your ancestors Abraham, Isaac, and Jacob, and all of their descendants.'

⁹"At that time I told the people, 'I need help! You are a great burden for me to carry all by myself, ¹⁰for the Lord has multiplied you to become as many as the stars! ¹¹And may he multiply you a thousand times more and bless you as he promised, ¹²but what can one man do to settle all your quarrels and problems? ¹³So choose some men from each tribe who are wise, experienced, and understanding, and I will appoint them as your leaders.'

¹⁴"They agreed to this; ¹⁵I took the men they selected, some from every tribe, and appointed them as administrative assistants in charge of thousands, hundreds, fifties, and tens to decide their quarrels and assist them in every way. ¹⁶I instructed them to be perfectly fair at all times, even to foreigners. ¹⁷'When giving your decisions,' I told them, 'never favor a man because he is rich; be fair to great and small alike. Don't fear their displeasure, for you are judging in the place of God. Bring me any cases too difficult for you, and I will handle them.' ¹⁸And I gave them other instructions at that time also.

¹⁹⁻²¹"Then we left Mount Horeb and traveled through the great and terrible desert, finally arriving among the Amorite hills to which the Lord our God had directed us. We were then at Kadesh-barnea [on the border of the Promised Land] and I said to the people, 'The Lord God has given us this land. Go and possess it as he told us to. Don't be afraid! Don't even doubt!'

²²"But they replied, 'First let's send out spies to discover the best route of entry, and to decide which cities we should capture first.'

²³"This seemed like a good idea, so I chose twelve spies, one from each tribe. ²⁴,²⁵They crossed into the hills and came to the Valley of Eshcol, and returned with samples of the local fruit. One look was enough to convince us that it was indeed a good land the Lord our God had given us. ²⁶But the people refused to go in and rebelled against the Lord's command.

²⁷"They murmured and complained in their tents and said, 'The Lord must hate us, bringing us here from Egypt to be slaughtered by these Amorites. ²⁸What are we getting into? Our brothers who spied out the land have frightened us with their report. They say that the people of the land are tall and powerful, and that the walls of their cities rise high into the sky! They have even seen giants there—the descendants of the Anakim!'

²⁹"But I said to them, 'Don't be afraid! ³⁰The Lord God is your leader, and he will fight for you with his mighty miracles, just as you saw him do in Egypt. ³¹And you know how he has cared for you again and again here in the wilderness, just as a father cares for his child!' ³²But nothing I said did any good.

"They refused to believe the Lord our God ³³who had led them all the way, and had selected the best places for them to camp, and had guided them by a pillar of fire at night and a pillar of cloud during the day.

³⁴,³⁵"Well, the Lord heard their complaining and was very angry. He vowed that not one person in that entire generation would live to see the good land he had promised their fathers, ³⁶except Caleb (the son of Jephunneh), who, because he had wholly followed the Lord, would receive as his personal inheritance some of the land he had walked over.

³⁷"And the Lord was even angry with me because of them and said to me, 'You shall not enter the Promised Land! ³⁸Instead, your assistant, Joshua (the son of Nun), shall lead the people. Encourage him as he prepares to take over the leadership. ³⁹I will give the land to the children they said would die in the wilderness. ⁴⁰But as for you of the older generation, turn around now and go on back across the desert toward the Red Sea.'

⁴¹"Then they confessed, 'We have sinned! We will go into the land and fight for it as the Lord our God has told us to.' So they strapped on their weapons and thought it would be easy to conquer the whole area.

⁴²"But the Lord said to me, 'Tell them not to do it, for I will not go with them; they will be struck down before their enemies.'

⁴³"I told them, but they wouldn't listen. Instead, they rebelled again against the Lord's commandment and went on up into the hill country to fight. ⁴⁴But the Amorites who lived there came out against them and chased them like bees and killed them from Seir to Hormah. ⁴⁵Then they returned and wept before the Lord, but he wouldn't listen. ⁴⁶So they stayed there at Kadesh for a long time.

2 Stuck in the Wilderness

"Then we turned back across the wilderness toward the Red Sea, for so the Lord had instructed me. For many years we wandered around in the area of Mount Seir. ²Then at last the Lord said,

³"'You have stayed here long enough. Turn northward. ⁴Inform the people that they will be passing through the country belonging to their brothers the Edomites, the descendants of Esau who live in Seir; the Edomites will be nervous, so be careful. ⁵Don't start a fight! For I have given them all the Mount Seir hill country as their permanent possession, and I will not give you even a tiny piece of their land. ⁶Pay them for whatever food or water you use. ⁷The Lord your God has watched over you and blessed you every step of

the way for all these forty years as you have wandered around in this great wilderness; and you have lacked nothing in all that time.'

⁸"So we passed through Edom where our brothers lived, crossing the Arabah Road that goes south to Elath and Ezion-geber, and traveling northward toward the Moab desert.

⁹"Then the Lord warned us, 'Don't attack the Moabites either, for I will not give you any of their land; I have given it to the descendants of Lot.'

¹⁰"(The Emim used to live in that area, a very large tribe, tall as the giants of Anakim; ¹¹both the Emim and the Anakim are often referred to as the Rephaim, but the Moabites call them Emim. ¹²In earlier days the Horites lived in Seir, but they were driven out and displaced by the Edomites, the descendants of Esau, just as Israel would displace the peoples of Canaan, whose land had been assigned to Israel by the Lord.)

¹³"'Now cross Zered Brook,' the Lord said; and we did.

¹⁴,¹⁵"So it took us thirty-eight years to finally get across Zered Brook from Kadesh! For the Lord had decreed that this could not happen until all the men, who thirty-eight years earlier were old enough to bear arms, had died. Yes, the hand of the Lord was against them until finally all were dead.

¹⁶,¹⁷"Then at last the Lord said to me,

¹⁸"'Today Israel shall cross the borders of Moab at Ar, ¹⁹into the land of the Ammonites. But do not attack them, for I will not give you any of their land. I have given it to the descendants of Lot.'

²⁰"(That area, too, used to be inhabited by the Rephaim, called 'Zamzummim' by the Ammonites. ²¹They were a large and powerful tribe, as tall as the Anakim; but Jehovah destroyed them as the Ammonites came in, and the Ammonites lived there in their place. ²²The Lord had similarly helped the descendants of Esau at Mount Seir, for he destroyed the Horites who were living there before them. ²³Another similar situation occurred when the people of Caphtor invaded and destroyed the tribe of Avvim living in villages scattered across the countryside as far away as Gaza.)

²⁴"Then the Lord said, 'Cross the Arnon River into the land of King Sihon the Amorite, king of Heshbon. War against him and begin to take possession of his land. ²⁵Beginning today I will make people throughout the whole earth tremble with fear because of you, and dread your arrival.'

²⁶"Then from the wilderness of Kedemoth I sent ambassadors to King Sihon of Heshbon with a proposal of peace. ²⁷'Let us pass through your land,' we said. 'We will stay on the main road and won't turn off into the fields on either side. ²⁸We will not steal food as we go, but will purchase every bite we eat and everything we drink; all we want is permission to pass through. ²⁹The Edomites at Seir allowed us to go through their country, and so did the Moabites, whose capital is at Ar. We are on our way across the Jordan into the land the Lord our God has given us.'

³⁰"But King Sihon refused because Jehovah your God made him obstinate, so that he could destroy Sihon by the hands of Israel, as has now been done.

³¹"Then the Lord said to me, 'I have begun to give you the land of King Sihon; when you possess it, it shall belong to Israel forever.'

³²"King Sihon then declared war on us and mobilized his forces at Jahaz. ³³,³⁴ But the Lord our God crushed him, and we conquered all his cities and utterly destroyed everything, including the women and babies. We left nothing alive ³⁵,³⁶except the cattle, which we took as our reward, along with the booty gained from ransacking the cities we had taken. We conquered everything from Aroer to Gilead—from the edge of the Arnon River valley, and including all the cities in the valley. Not one city was too strong for us, for the Lord our God gave all of them to us. ³⁷However, we stayed away from the people of Ammon and from the Jabbok River and the hill country cities, the places Jehovah our God had forbidden us to enter.

3 Dividing the Land

"Next we turned toward King Og's land of Bashan. He immediately mobilized his army and attacked us at Edre-i. But the Lord told me not to be afraid of him. 'All his people and his land are yours,' the Lord told me. 'You will do to him as you did to King Sihon of the Amorites at Heshbon.' ³So the Lord helped us fight against King Og and his people, and we killed them all. ⁴We conquered all sixty of his cities, the entire Argob region of Bashan. ⁵These were well-fortified cities with high walls and barred gates. Of course we also took all of the unwalled towns. ⁶We utterly destroyed the kingdom of Bashan just as we had destroyed King Sihon's kingdom at Heshbon, killing the entire population—men, women, and children alike. ⁷But we kept the cattle and loot for ourselves.

⁸"We now possessed all the land of the two kings of the Amorites east of the Jordan River—all the land from the valley of the Arnon to Mount

---

OVERCOMING FEAR 3:21-22 "Don't be afraid . . . God will fight for you." What encouraging news for Joshua, who was to lead his men against the persistent forces of evil occupying the Promised Land. And God promised to help him win every battle. Our battles may not be against godless armies, but they are just as real. Whether we are resisting temptation or battling fear, God has promised to fight with and for us as we obey him. **To begin the series of devotionals on OVERCOMING FEAR, turn to page 13.**

Hermon. ⁹(The Sidonians called Mount Hermon 'Sirion,' while the Amorites called it 'Senir.') ¹⁰We had now conquered all the cities on the plateau, and all of Gilead and Bashan as far as the cities of Salecah and Edre-i.

¹¹"Incidentally, King Og of Bashan was the last of the giant Rephaim. His iron bedstead is kept in a museum at Rabbah, one of the cities of the Ammonites, and measures thirteen and a half feet long by six feet wide.

¹²"At that time I gave the conquered land to the tribes of Reuben, Gad, and the half-tribe of Manasseh. To the tribes of Reuben and Gad I gave the area beginning at Aroer on the Arnon River, plus half of Mount Gilead, including its cities. ¹³The half-tribe of Manasseh received the remainder of Gilead and all of the former kingdom of King Og, the Argob region. (Bashan is sometimes called 'The Land of the Rephaim.') ¹⁴The clan of Jair, of the tribe of Manasseh, took over the whole Argob region (Bashan) to the borders of the Geshurites and Maacathites. They renamed their country after themselves, calling it Havvoth-jair (meaning 'Jair's Villages') as it is still known today. ¹⁵Then I gave Gilead to the clan of Machir. ¹⁶The tribes of Reuben and Gad received the area extending from the Jabbok River in Gilead (which was the Ammonite frontier) to the middle of the valley of the Arnon River. ¹⁷They also received the Arabah (or wasteland), bounded by the Jordan River on the west, from Chinnereth to Mount Pisgah and the Dead Sea (also called the Sea of the Arabah).

¹⁸"At that time I reminded the tribes of Reuben and Gad and the half-tribe of Manasseh that, although the Lord had given them the land, they could not begin settling down until their armed men led the other tribes across the Jordan to the land the Lord was giving them.

¹⁹"'But your wives and children,' I told them, 'may live here in the cities the Lord has given you, caring for your many cattle ²⁰until you return after the Lord has given victory to the other tribes too. When they conquer the land the Lord your God has given across the Jordan River, then you may return here to your own land.'

²¹"Then I said to Joshua, 'You have seen what the Lord your God has done to those two kings. You will do the same to all the kingdoms on the other side of the Jordan. ²²Don't be afraid of the nations there, for the Lord your God will fight for you.'

²³⁻²⁵"At that time I made this plea to God: 'O Lord God, please let me cross over into the Promised Land—the good land beyond the Jordan River with its rolling hills—and Lebanon. I want to see the result of all the greatness and power you have been showing us; for what God in all of heaven or earth can do what you have done for us?'

²⁶"But the Lord was angry with me because of you and would not let me cross over. 'Speak of it no more,' he ordered, ²⁷'but go to the top of Mount Pisgah where you can look out in every direction, and there you will see the land in the distance. But you shall not cross the Jordan River. ²⁸Commission Joshua to replace you, and then encourage him, for he shall lead the people across to conquer the land you will see from the mountaintop.'

²⁹"So we remained in the valley near Beth-peor.

4 Obey God

"And now, O Israel, listen carefully to these laws I teach you, and obey them if you want to live and enter into and possess the land given you by the Lord God of your ancestors. ²Do not add other laws or subtract from these; just obey them, for they are from the Lord your God. ³You have seen what the Lord did to you at Baalpeor, where he destroyed many people for worshiping idols. ⁴But all of you who were faithful to the Lord your God are still alive today.

⁵"These are the laws for you to obey when you arrive in the land where you will live. They are from the Lord our God. He has given them to me to pass on to you. ⁶If you obey them, they will give you a reputation for wisdom and intelligence. When the surrounding nations hear these laws, they will exclaim, 'What other nation is as wise and prudent as Israel!' ⁷For what other nation, great or small, has God among them, as the Lord our God is here among us whenever we call upon him? ⁸And what nation, no matter how great, has laws as fair as these I am giving you today?

⁹"But watch out! Be very careful never to forget what you have seen God doing for you. May his miracles have a deep and permanent effect upon your lives! Tell your children and your grandchildren about the glorious miracles he did. ¹⁰Tell them especially about the day you stood before the Lord at Mount Horeb, and he told me, 'Summon the people before me and I will instruct them, so that they will learn always to reverence me, and so that they can teach my laws to their children.' ¹¹You stood at the foot of the mountain, and the mountain burned with fire; flames shot far into the sky, surrounded by black clouds and deep darkness. ¹²And the Lord spoke to you from the fire; you heard his words but didn't see him. ¹³He proclaimed the laws you must obey—the Ten Commandments—and wrote them on two stone tablets. ¹⁴Yes, it was at that time that the Lord commanded me to issue the laws you must obey when you arrive in the Promised Land.

¹⁵"But beware! You didn't see the form of God that day as he spoke to you from the fire at Mount Horeb, ¹⁶,¹⁷so do not defile yourselves by trying to make a statue of God—an idol in any form, whether

FAMILY DEVOTIONS

☐ **DEVOTION 65**
GOING TO CHURCH

Read Deuteronomy 4:9-14

Stacy rolled over in bed when her clock radio went on Sunday morning. "Morning already?" she said with a yawn. "It seems like I just got home from baby-sitting a little while ago." She got up and staggered down the hall, pulling on her bathrobe. "Morning," she murmured to her mom. "Would you please turn on the iron? I have to press my dress."

"Has anyone seen my blue socks?" yelled Steve. Then he scanned his room for his Sunday school book. "I still have to learn my verse. I hope it's a short one this week."

The Langs made it to church almost on time. They really enjoyed the morning, although Stacy had a little trouble keeping her eyes open during the sermon. Dad commented about their hectic morning as they rode home from church. "I'm embarrassed about being late for Sunday school so often," he said. "Our Sunday mornings seem to be getting more and more disorganized, and they definitely don't prepare our hearts for worship. Does anyone have any suggestions?"

"Well, for one thing, we should get our clothes ready on Saturday," said Mom.

"I guess I should do my Sunday school lesson earlier in the week," admitted Steve.

"I feel badly about being so tired," remarked Stacy. "I think I'm going to tell people that I can only baby-sit until ten o'clock on Saturday nights."

Dad nodded his approval. "And let's try starting Sunday morning by playing some good Christian music on the stereo. Waking up to that kind of music may help to prepare us to really worship the Lord with our whole hearts."

Going to Church Memory Verse

Let us not neglect our church meetings, as some people do, but encourage and warn each other, especially now that the day of his coming back again is drawing near.
Hebrews 10:25

How About You?

What was it like at your house last Sunday morning? Were you prepared to worship God and learn from him when you walked into church? Why not follow the suggestions given in the story? Have your clothes ready on Saturday, learn your memory verse early, and get a good night's sleep. Then you should be ready to reverence God and to learn from his Word. D. R.

• For the next devotional, turn to page 195. • For the next devotional on GOING TO CHURCH, turn to page 201.
• For notes on GOING TO CHURCH, see pages 770, 965, and 1002.

of a man, woman, animal, bird, ¹⁸ a small animal that runs along the ground, or a fish. ¹⁹And do not look up into the sky to worship the sun, moon, or stars. The Lord may permit other nations to get away with this, but not you. ²⁰The Lord has rescued you from prison—Egypt—to be his special people, his own inheritance; this is what you are today. ²¹,²²But he was angry with me because of you; he vowed that I could not go over the Jordan River into the good land he has given you as your inheritance. I must die here on this side of the river. ²³Beware lest you break the contract the Lord your God has made with you! You will break it if you make any idols, for the Lord your God has utterly forbidden this. ²⁴He is a devouring fire, a jealous God.

²⁵"In the future, when your children and grandchildren are born and you have been in the land a long time, and you have defiled yourselves by making idols, and the Lord your God is very angry because of your sin, ²⁶heaven and earth are witnesses that you shall be quickly destroyed from the land. Soon now you will cross the Jordan River and conquer that land. But your days there will be brief; you will then be utterly destroyed. ²⁷For the Lord will scatter you among the nations, and you will be but few in number. ²⁸There, far away, you will worship idols made from wood and stone, idols that neither see nor hear nor eat nor smell.

²⁹"But you will also begin to search again for Jehovah your God, and you will find him when you search for him with all your heart and soul. ³⁰When those bitter days have come upon you in the latter times, you will finally return to the Lord your God and listen to what he tells you. ³¹For the Lord your God is merciful—he will not abandon you nor destroy you nor forget the promises he has made to your ancestors.

³²"In all history, going back to the time when God created man upon the earth, search from one end of the heavens to the other to see if you can find anything like this: ³³An entire nation heard the voice of God speaking to it from fire, as you did, and lived! ³⁴Where else will you ever find another example of God's removing a nation from its slavery by sending terrible plagues, mighty miracles, war, and terror? Yet that is what the Lord your God did for you in Egypt, right before your very eyes. ³⁵He did these things so you would realize that Jehovah is God, and that there is no one else like him. ³⁶He let you hear his voice instructing you from heaven, and he let you see his great pillar of fire upon the earth; you even heard his words from the center of the fire.

³⁷"It was because he loved your ancestors and chose to bless their descendants that he personally brought you out from Egypt with a great display of power. ³⁸He drove away other nations greater by far than you and gave you their land as an inheritance, as it is today. ³⁹This is your wonderful thought for the day: Jehovah is God both in heaven and down here upon the earth; and there is no God other than him! ⁴⁰You must obey these laws that I will tell you today, so that all will be well with you and your children, and so that you will live forever in the land the Lord your God is giving you."

⁴¹Then Moses instructed the people of Israel to set apart three cities east of the Jordan River, ⁴²where anyone who accidentally killed someone could flee for safety. ⁴³These cities were Bezer, on the plateau in the wilderness, for the tribe of Reuben; Ramoth, in Gilead, for the tribe of Gad; and Golan, in Bashan, for the tribe of Manasseh.

⁴⁴⁻⁴⁶Listed below are the laws Moses issued to the people of Israel when they left Egypt, and as they were camped east of the Jordan River near the city of Beth-peor. (This was the land formerly occupied by the Amorites under King Sihon, whose capital was Heshbon; he and his people were destroyed by Moses and the Israelis. ⁴⁷Israel conquered his land and that of King Og of Bashan—they were two Amorite kings east of the Jordan. ⁴⁸Israel also conquered all the area from Aroer at the edge of the Arnon River valley to Mount Sirion, or Mount Hermon, as it is sometimes called; ⁴⁹and all the Arabah east of the Jordan River over to the Dead Sea, below the slopes of Mount Pisgah.)

5 The Ten Commandments

Moses continued speaking to the people of Israel and said, "Listen carefully now to all these laws God has given you; learn them, and be sure to obey them!

²,³"The Lord our God made a contract with you at Mount Horeb—*not with your ancestors, but with you who are here alive today.* ⁴He spoke with you face to face from the center of the fire, there at the mountain. ⁵I stood as an intermediary between you and Jehovah, for you were afraid of the fire and did not go up to him on the mountain. He spoke to me and I passed on his laws to you. This is what he said:

⁶"'I am Jehovah your God who rescued you from slavery in Egypt.

⁷"'Never worship any god but me.

⁸"'Never make idols; don't worship images, whether of birds, animals, or fish. ⁹,¹⁰You shall not bow down to any images nor worship them in any way, for I am the Lord your God. I am a jealous God, and I will bring the curse of a father's sins upon even the third and fourth generation of the children of those who hate me; but I will show kindness to a thousand generations of those who love me and keep my commandments.

¹¹"'You must never use my name to make a vow you don't intend to keep. I will not overlook that.

Family Devotions

☐ **Devotion 66**
Avoiding Sin

Read Deuteronomy 5:18

Hey, Carl, did you see that girl lying on the beach back there?" asked Brad. He was on a fishing outing with his friend Carl and Carl's dad. Mr. Stone had gone back to the car for more bait, and the boys were alone for a few minutes.

"D'ya mean the one in the pink bikini?" replied Carl. "She sure has a tan!"

"Who cares about the tan? Get a look at that body! If she looks that good in a bikini, I wonder what she'd look like with nothing on!" Brad snickered.

"Shh! Here comes Dad," answered Carl.

Mr. Stone was very concerned about the conversation he'd caught a snatch of, and he prayed silently that God would show him how to handle the situation. On the way home, he began, "Boys, do you know the Ten Commandments?"

"Most of them!" answered Brad. Between the two of them, he and Carl got off to a good start reciting them.

When they got to the seventh, Mr. Stone stopped them. "Do you know what that one means?" he asked.

"Our Sunday school teacher said *adultery* means sexual sin with someone you're not married to," answered Carl.

"That's right, Carl," replied his father. "But Jesus said in the New Testament that if a boy looks on a girl with lust in his eye, it's just as bad as committing the act of sex with her. It's important to ask God to help us keep our minds and bodies pure for him."

Carl and Brad wondered how Mr. Stone knew what they had been talking about on the pier. They were a little embarrassed to think he might have overheard them, but they decided they were glad for his reminder.

Avoiding Sin Memory Verse

How can a young man stay pure? By reading your Word and following its rules.
Psalm 119:9

How About You?

Do you ever wish you could have sexual contact with some boy or girl? Remember that God has reserved your body for the one person you will marry someday. The only time it is right to share sexual love with that person is after you are married. Ask God to keep your mind and body pure. Don't ever break the seventh commandment. *R. P.*

- For the next devotional, turn to page 197.   • For the next devotional on *Avoiding Sin*, turn to page 265.
- For notes on *Avoiding Sin*, see pages 220, 332, 392, and 657.

¹²"Keep the Sabbath day holy. This is my command. ¹³Work the other six days, ¹⁴but the seventh day is the Sabbath of the Lord your God; no work shall be done that day by you or by any of your household—your sons, daughters, servants, oxen, donkeys, or cattle; even foreigners living among you must obey this law. Everybody must rest as you do. ¹⁵Why should you keep the Sabbath? It is because you were slaves in Egypt, and the Lord your God brought you out with a great display of miracles.

¹⁶"'Honor your father and mother (remember, this is a commandment of the Lord your God); if you do so, you shall have a long, prosperous life in the land he is giving you.

¹⁷"'You must not murder.

¹⁸"'You must not commit adultery.

¹⁹"'You must not steal.

²⁰"'You must not tell lies.

²¹"'You must not burn with desire for another man's wife, nor envy him for his home, land, servants, oxen, donkeys, nor anything else he owns.'

²²"The Lord has given these laws to each one of you from the heart of the fire, surrounded by the clouds and thick darkness that engulfed Mount Sinai. Those were the only commandments he gave you at that time, and he wrote them out on two stone tablets and gave them to me. ²³But when you heard the loud voice from the darkness and saw the terrible fire at the top of the mountain, all your tribal leaders came to me ²⁴and pleaded, 'Today the Lord our God has shown us his glory and greatness; we have even heard his voice from the heart of the fire. Now we know that a man may speak to God and not die; ²⁵but we will surely die if he speaks to us again. This awesome fire will consume us. ²⁶,²⁷What man can hear, as we have, the voice of the living God speaking from the heart of the fire, and live? You go and listen to all that God says, then come and tell us, and we will listen and obey.'

²⁸"And the Lord agreed to your request and said to me, 'I have heard what the people have said to you, and I agree. ²⁹Oh, that they would always have such a heart for me, wanting to obey my commandments. Then all would go well with them in the future, and with their children throughout all generations! ³⁰Go and tell them to return to their tents. ³¹Then you come back and stand here beside me, and I will give you all my commandments, and you shall teach them to the people; and they will obey them in the land I am giving to them.'"

³²So Moses told the people, "You must obey all the commandments of the Lord your God, following his directions in every detail, going the whole way he has laid out for you; ³³only then will you live long and prosperous lives in the land you are to enter and possess.

6 Love God and Obey Him

"The Lord your God told me to give you all these commandments which you are to obey in the land you will soon be entering, where you will live. ²The purpose of these laws is to cause you, your sons, and your grandsons to reverence the Lord your God by obeying all of his instructions as long as you live; if you do, you will have long, prosperous years ahead of you. ³Therefore, O Israel, listen closely to each command and be careful to obey it, so that all will go well with you, and so that you will have many children. If you obey these commands, you will become a great nation in a glorious land 'flowing with milk and honey,' even as the God of your fathers promised you.

⁴"O Israel, listen: Jehovah is our God, Jehovah alone. ⁵You must love him with *all* your heart, soul, and might. ⁶And you must think constantly about these commandments I am giving you today. ⁷You must teach them to your children and talk about them when you are at home or out for a walk; at bedtime and the first thing in the morning. ⁸Tie them on your finger, wear them on your forehead, ⁹and write them on the doorposts of your house!

¹⁰⁻¹²"When the Lord your God has brought you into the land he promised your ancestors, Abraham, Isaac, and Jacob, and when he has given you great cities full of good things—cities you didn't build, wells you didn't dig, and vineyards and olive trees you didn't plant—and when you have eaten until you can hold no more, then beware lest you forget the Lord who brought you out of the land of Egypt, the land of slavery. ¹³When you are full, don't forget to be reverent to him and to serve him and to use *his* name alone to endorse your promises.

¹⁴"You must not worship the gods of the neighboring nations, ¹⁵for Jehovah your God who lives among you is a jealous God, and his anger may rise quickly against you, and wipe you off the face of the earth. ¹⁶You must not provoke him and try his patience as you did when you complained against him at Massah. ¹⁷You must actively obey him in everything he commands. ¹⁸Only then will you be doing what is right and good in the Lord's eyes. If you obey him, all will go well for you, and you will be able to go in and possess the good land that the Lord promised your ancestors. ¹⁹You will also be able to throw out all the enemies living in your land, as the Lord agreed to help you do.

²⁰"In the years to come when your son asks you, 'What is the purpose of these laws which the Lord our God has given us?' ²¹you must tell him,

FAMILY DEVOTIONS

☐ **DEVOTION 67**
KNOWING GOD

Read Deuteronomy 6:4-8

Knowing God
Memory Verse

Oh, that we might know the Lord! Let us press on to know him, and he will respond to us as surely as the coming of dawn or the rain of early spring.
Hosea 6:3

"Son, come here, please," Mom called from Pete's room.

"What is it, Mom?" Pete asked as he skidded to a halt in front of her.

"This." Mom was holding up Pete's Bible. "It's all covered with dust."

"Sorry, Mom," said Pete. "I keep forgetting to dust that shelf by the bed."

"That's not what I meant," explained Mom. "Pete, how long has it been since you've read your Bible?"

Pete shrugged carelessly. "I need a Bible for Sunday school, but then I use the one from the den downstairs. Anyhow, since we go to church on Sundays—twice—I hear enough about God then to last me through the week."

Mom followed Pete to his room at bedtime, switched on the light, and then shut it right back off. "Mom!" exclaimed Pete as the room once again became dark. "I can't see!"

"But the light was on for a minute," said Mom, "and I'm sure you can remember where things are. Can't you just make do with the light you got then?"

"Mom . . . ," grumbled Peter as he reached for the switch and turned the light back on. "Once it's off, it doesn't do anything for me."

"But, Pete," said Mom softly, "isn't that what you've been trying to do with God? You told me that by going to church twice on Sundays, you learn enough about God to remember all week. But it doesn't work that way. Just like you need to leave the light on to see in your room, you need to make constant use of God's Word in order to grow as a Christian."

"By not reading my Bible, I 'turn off the light' on myself, huh?" asked Pete. "Well, can I leave my light on extra long tonight? I guess I need to turn on my other light, too."

How About You?
Do you think that if you go to church you can get through the rest of the week without bothering with daily devotions? That isn't true. Every day you need to turn on the light of God's Word for spiritual direction. *D. M.*

• For the next devotional, turn to page 199. • For the next devotional on KNOWING GOD, turn to page 333.
• For notes on KNOWING GOD, see pages 129, 610, 815, and 1208.

'We were Pharaoh's slaves in Egypt, and the Lord brought us out of Egypt with great power ²²and mighty miracles—with terrible blows against Egypt and Pharaoh and all his people. We saw it all with our own eyes. ²³He brought us out of Egypt so that he could give us this land he had promised to our ancestors. ²⁴And he has commanded us to obey all of these laws and to reverence him so that he can preserve us alive as he has until now. ²⁵For it always goes well with us when we obey all the laws of the Lord our God.'

7 Defeat the Enemy Nations

"When the Lord brings you into the Promised Land, as he soon will, he will destroy the following seven nations, all greater and mightier than you are: the Hittites, the Girgashites, the Amorites, the Canaanites, the Perizzites, the Hivites, the Jebusites.

²"When the Lord your God delivers them over to you to be destroyed, do a complete job of it—don't make any treaties or show them mercy; utterly wipe them out. ³Do not intermarry with them, nor let your sons and daughters marry their sons and daughters. ⁴That would surely result in your young people's beginning to worship their gods. Then the anger of the Lord would be hot against you, and he would surely destroy you.

⁵"You must break down the heathen altars and shatter the obelisks and cut up the shameful images and burn the idols.

⁶"For you are a holy people, dedicated to the Lord your God. He has chosen you from all the people on the face of the whole earth to be his own chosen ones. ⁷He didn't choose you and pour out his love upon you because you were a larger nation than any other, for you were the smallest of all! ⁸It was just because he loves you, and because he kept his promise to your ancestors. That is why he brought you out of slavery in Egypt with such amazing power and mighty miracles.

⁹"Understand, therefore, that the Lord your God is the faithful God who for a thousand generations keeps his promises and constantly loves those who love him and who obey his commands. ¹⁰But those who hate him shall be punished publicly and destroyed. He will deal with them personally. ¹¹Therefore, obey all these commandments I am giving you today. ¹²Because of your obedience, the Lord your God will keep his part of the contract which, in his tender love, he made with your fathers. ¹³And he will love you and bless you and make you into a great nation. He will make you fertile and give fertility to your ground and to your animals, so that you will have large crops of grain, grapes, and olives, and great flocks of cattle, sheep, and goats when you arrive in the land he promised your fathers to give you. ¹⁴You will be blessed above all the nations of the earth; not one of you, whether male or female, shall be barren, not even your cattle. ¹⁵And the Lord will take away all your sickness and will not let you suffer any of the diseases of Egypt you remember so well; he will give them all to your enemies!

¹⁶"You must destroy all the nations the Lord your God delivers into your hands. Have no pity, and do not worship their gods; if you do, it will be a sad day for you. ¹⁷Perhaps you will think to yourself, 'How can we ever conquer these nations that are so much more powerful than we are?' ¹⁸But don't be afraid of them! Just remember what the Lord your God did to Pharaoh and to all the land of Egypt. ¹⁹Do you remember the terrors the Lord sent upon them—your parents saw it with their own eyes—and the mighty miracles and wonders, and the power and strength of Almighty God that he used to bring you out of Egypt? Well, the Lord your God will use this same might against the people you fear. ²⁰Moreover, the Lord your God will send hornets to drive out those who hide from you!

²¹"No, do not be afraid of those nations, for the Lord your God is among you, and he is a great and awesome God. ²²He will cast them out a little at a time; he will not do it all at once, for if he did, the wild animals would multiply too quickly and become dangerous. ²³He will do it gradually, and you will move in against those nations and destroy them. ²⁴He will deliver their kings into your hands, and you will erase their names from the face of the earth. No one will be able to stand against you.

²⁵"Burn their idols and do not touch the silver or gold they are made of. Do not take it or it will be a snare to you, for it is horrible to the Lord your God. ²⁶Do not bring an idol into your home and worship it, for then your doom is sealed. Utterly detest it, for it is a cursed thing.

8 Do Not Forget God

"You must obey all the commandments I give you today. If you do, you will not only live, you will multiply and will go in and take over the land promised to your fathers by the Lord. ²Do you remember how the Lord led you through the wilderness for all those forty years, humbling you and testing you to find out how you would respond, and whether or not you would really obey him? ³Yes, he humbled you by letting you go hungry and then feeding you with manna, a food previously unknown to both you and your ancestors. He did it to help you realize that food isn't

FAMILY DEVOTIONS

☐ DEVOTION 68
OBEDIENCE

Read Deuteronomy 8:1-10

Obedience Memory Verse

Oh, that they would always have such a heart for me, wanting to obey my commandments. Then all would go well with them in the future, and with their children throughout all generations! *Deuteronomy 5:29*

Dawn was delighted when her parents gave her a puppy for her birthday. He wriggled in her arms as she hugged him tight. "I'll call him Duke!" she announced.

"Well, Duke has lots of things to learn," her father said. "You'll need to reward him when he's good and spank him when he does something bad, so he'll learn right away which things he's not supposed to do."

Dawn frowned. "He won't be bad, Daddy. I'll love him so much that he'll want to be really good. Duke's going to be the best dog in the world!"

But Duke was not a good dog. He dug up the flower bed and chewed on shoes. He ran away when he was called. Dawn scolded and spanked until she was tired of it, but it seemed to do no good. Duke went right on getting into places where he wasn't supposed to be.

One day Dawn came into the living room looking very sad. "Why is Duke so bad?" she burst out. "I scold him and scold him, and he acts like he's sorry. He licks my face and wags his tail, so I pet him and hug him. And then he turns right around and is bad all over again. I love him so much. Why does he keep on being bad?"

Dad put down his paper and pulled Dawn onto his lap. "Sometimes it takes a long time to train a puppy," he said. "What you just told me reminds me an awful lot of what happens between us and God."

"What do you mean?" asked Dawn.

"Well, remember when you got Duke? You said you would love him so much that he'd want to be good to please you, but instead he's been a lot of trouble," replied Dad. "Very often we're the same way with God. He loves us so much that we should all want to be good to please him, but instead we want to do things our own way."

How About You?
Are you an obedient child of God? He loves you so much and wants only the very best for you. Listen to his Word and do what it says. God will be pleased, and you will be happy, too. *D. S. M.*

• For the next devotional, turn to page 201. • For the next devotional on OBEDIENCE, turn to page 727. • For notes on OBEDIENCE, see pages 319, 425, 500, 510, and 757.

everything, and that real life comes by obeying every command of God. ⁴For all these forty years your clothes haven't grown old, and your feet haven't been blistered or swollen. ⁵So you should realize that, as a man punishes his son, the Lord punishes you to help you.

⁶"Obey the laws of the Lord your God. Walk in his ways and fear him. ⁷For the Lord your God is bringing you into a good land of brooks, pools, gushing springs, valleys, and hills; ⁸it is a land of wheat and barley, of grape vines, fig trees, pomegranates, olives, and honey; ⁹it is a land where food is plentiful, and nothing is lacking; it is a land where iron is as common as stone, and copper is abundant in the hills. ¹⁰When you have eaten your fill, bless the Lord your God for the good land he has given you.

¹¹"But that is the time to be careful! Beware that in your plenty you don't forget the Lord your God and begin to disobey him. ¹²,¹³For when you have become full and prosperous and have built fine homes to live in, and when your flocks and herds have become very large, and your silver and gold have multiplied, ¹⁴that is the time to watch out that you don't become proud and forget the Lord your God who brought you out of your slavery in the land of Egypt. ¹⁵Beware that you don't forget the God who led you through the great and terrible wilderness with the dangerous snakes and scorpions, where it was so hot and dry. He gave you water from the rock! ¹⁶He fed you with manna in the wilderness (it was a kind of bread unknown before) so that you would become humble and so that your trust in him would grow, and he could do you good. ¹⁷He did it so that you would never feel that it was your own power and might that made you wealthy. ¹⁸Always remember that it is the Lord your God who gives you power to become rich, and he does it to fulfill his promise to your ancestors.

¹⁹"But if you forget about the Lord your God and worship other gods instead, and follow evil ways, you shall certainly perish, ²⁰just as the Lord has caused other nations in the past to perish. That will be your fate, too, if you don't obey the Lord your God.

9 Do Not Forget God's Mercy

"O Israel, listen! Today you are to cross the Jordan River and begin to dispossess the nations on the other side. Those nations are much greater and more powerful than you are! They live in high walled cities. Among them are the famed Anak giants, against whom none can stand! ³But the Lord your God will go before you as a devouring fire to destroy them, so that you will quickly conquer them and drive them out.

⁴"Then, when the Lord has done this for you, don't say to yourselves, 'The Lord has helped us because we are so good!' No, it is because of the wickedness of the other nations that he is doing it. ⁵It is not at all because you are such fine, upright people that the Lord will drive them out from before you! I say it again, it is only because of the wickedness of the other nations, and because of his promises to your ancestors, Abraham, Isaac, and Jacob, that he will do it. ⁶I say it yet again: *Jehovah your God is not giving you this good land because you are good, for you are not*—you are a wicked, stubborn people.

⁷"Don't you remember (oh, never forget it!) how continually angry you made the Lord your God out in the wilderness, from the day you left Egypt until now? For all this time you have constantly rebelled against him.

⁸"Don't you remember how angry you made him at Mount Horeb? He was ready to destroy you. ⁹I was on the mountain at the time, receiving the contract which Jehovah had made with you—the stone tablets with the laws inscribed upon them. I was there for forty days and forty nights, and all that time I ate nothing. I didn't even take a drink of water. ¹⁰,¹¹At the end of those forty days and nights the Lord gave me the contract, the tablets on which he had written the commandments he had spoken from the fire-covered mountain while the people had watched below. ¹²He told me to go down quickly because the people I had led out of Egypt had defiled themselves, quickly turning away from the laws of God, and had made an idol from molten metal.

¹³,¹⁴"'Let me alone that I may destroy this evil, stubborn people!' the Lord told me, 'and I will blot out their name from under heaven, and I will make a mighty nation of you, mightier and greater than they are.'

¹⁵"I came down from the burning mountain, holding in my hands the two tablets inscribed with the laws of God. ¹⁶There below me I could see the calf you had made in your terrible sin against the Lord your God. How quickly you turned away from him! ¹⁷I lifted the tablets high above my head and dashed them to the ground! I smashed them before your eyes! ¹⁸Then, for another forty days and nights I lay before the Lord, neither eating bread nor drinking water, for you had done what the Lord hated most, thus provoking him to great anger. ¹⁹How I feared for you—for the Lord was ready to destroy you. But that time, too, he listened to me. ²⁰Aaron was in great danger because the Lord was so angry with him; but I prayed, and the Lord spared him. ²¹I took your sin—the calf you had made—and burned it and ground it into fine dust, and threw it into the stream that cascaded out of the mountain.

²²"Again at Taberah and once again at Massah you angered the Lord, and yet again at Kibroth-hattaavah.

Family Devotions

☐ **Devotion 69**
Going to Church

Read Deuteronomy 10:12-21

"I heard some sad news at the church board meeting last night," Mr. Lansing told his son, Gary.

"You did?" Gary looked up. "What was it, Dad?"

"It involves the family who moved into the yellow brick house on Elm Street," Dad told him. "Their name is Peterson. A couple of weeks ago they attended our church, and on Monday night Pastor Helms visited them." That didn't sound sad to Gary. That sounded happy! It was neat to see new people come to church. Gary listened as Dad went on. "They said they liked Pastor Helms's message, at least what they heard of it. The sad part is that they said three boys were sitting behind them, talking and laughing during the entire service, making it difficult for them to concentrate. The Petersons told Pastor Helms they didn't think they'd come back to our church."

"That's too bad," Gary said. And then he remembered that some new people had been sitting in front of him and his friends in church a couple of weeks ago! He slowly realized why his dad was telling him about the Petersons. He was one of those who had been talking. He looked up at his dad, embarrassed.

"Son, we've told you before that it's not only important to listen for what you can get out of the message, but it is just plain bad manners to disturb those around you! For the next month you will sit with Mom and me. If you do sit with your friends again after that, you will sit farther up than Mom and I do, not behind us."

Gary nodded numbly. "Yes, Dad." For the rest of the day he thought about what had happened. He knew what he'd have to do. He'd have to go to the Petersons' house and apologize to them for making so much noise. He'd also invite them to come to church again.

Going to Church Memory Verse

Let us not neglect our church meetings, as some people do, but encourage and warn each other, especially now that the day of his coming back again is drawing near.
Hebrews 10:25

How About You?

Do you listen quietly during church? There have been many occasions when people haven't come back to a church because of the whispering during the service. Sit still. Be polite to those who are around you. Welcome new people instead of being rude to them!
L. M. W.

• For the next devotional, turn to page 203. • For the next devotional on *Going to Church*, turn to page 489.
• For notes on *Going to Church*, see pages 770, 965, and 1002.

²³At Kadesh-barnea, when the Lord told you to enter the land he had given you, you rebelled and wouldn't believe that he would help you; you refused to obey him. ²⁴Yes, you have been rebellious against the Lord from the first day I knew you. ²⁵That is why I fell down before him for forty days and nights when the Lord was ready to destroy you.

²⁶"I prayed to him, 'O Lord God, don't destroy your own people. They are your inheritance saved from Egypt by your mighty power and glorious strength. ²⁷Don't notice the rebellion and stubbornness of these people, but remember instead your promises to your servants Abraham, Isaac, and Jacob. Oh, please overlook the awful wickedness and sin of these people. ²⁸For if you destroy them, the Egyptians will say, "It is because the Lord wasn't able to bring them to the land he promised them," or "He destroyed them because he hated them: he brought them into the wilderness to slay them." ²⁹They are your people and your inheritance that you brought from Egypt by your great power and your mighty arm.'

10 Ten Commandments Rewritten

"At that time the Lord told me to cut two more stone tablets like the first ones, and to make a wooden Ark to keep them in, and to return to God on the mountain. ²He said he would rewrite on the tablets the same commandments that were on the tablets I had smashed, and that I should place them in the Ark. ³So I made an Ark of acacia wood and hewed out two stone tablets like the first two, and took the tablets up on the mountain to God. ⁴He again wrote the Ten Commandments on them and gave them to me. (They were the same commandments he had given you from the heart of the fire on the mountain as you all watched below.) ⁵Then I came down and placed the tablets in the Ark I had made, where they are to this day, just as the Lord commanded me.

⁶"The people of Israel then journeyed from Beeroth of Bene-jaakan to Moserah, where Aaron died and was buried. His son Eleazar became the next priest.

⁷"Then they journeyed to Gudgodah, and from there to Jotbathah, a land of brooks and water. ⁸It was there that Jehovah set apart the tribe of Levi to carry the Ark containing the Ten Commandments of Jehovah, and to stand before the Lord and to do his work and to bless his name, just as is done today. ⁹(That is why the tribe of Levi does not have a portion of land reserved for it in the Promised Land, as their brother tribes do; for as the Lord told them, he himself is their inheritance.)

¹⁰"As I said before, I stayed on the mountain before the Lord for forty days and nights the second time, just as I had the first, and the Lord again yielded to my pleas and didn't destroy you.

¹¹"But he said to me, 'Arise and lead the people to the land I promised their fathers. It is time to go in and possess it.'

¹²,¹³"And now, Israel, what does the Lord your God require of you except to listen carefully to all he says to you, and to obey for your own good the commandments I am giving you today, and to love him, and to worship him with all your hearts and souls? ¹⁴Earth and highest heaven belong to the Lord your God. ¹⁵And yet he rejoiced in your fathers and loved them so much that he chose you, their children, to be above every other nation, as is evident today. ¹⁶Therefore, cleanse your sinful hearts and stop your stubbornness.

¹⁷"Jehovah your God is God of gods and Lord of lords. He is the great and mighty God, the God of terror who shows no partiality and takes no bribes. ¹⁸He gives justice to the fatherless and widows. He loves foreigners and gives them food and clothing. ¹⁹(You too must love foreigners, for you yourselves were foreigners in the land of Egypt.) ²⁰You must fear the Lord your God and worship him and cling to him, and take oaths by his name alone. ²¹He is your praise and he is your God, the one who has done mighty miracles you yourselves have seen. ²²When your ancestors went down into Egypt there were only seventy of them, but now the Lord your God has made you as many as the stars in the sky!

11

"You must love the Lord your God and obey every one of his commands. ²Listen! I am not talking now to your children who have never experienced the Lord's punishments or seen his greatness and his awesome power. ³They weren't there to see the miracles he did in Egypt against Pharaoh and all his land. ⁴They didn't see what God did to the armies of Egypt and to their horses and chariots—how he drowned them in the Red Sea as they were chasing you, and how the Lord has kept them powerless against you until this very day! ⁵They didn't see how the Lord cared for you time and again through all the years you were wandering in the wilderness, until your arrival here. ⁶They weren't there when Dathan and Abiram (the sons of Eliab, descendants of Reuben) sinned, and the earth opened up and swallowed them, with their households and tents and all their belongings, as all Israel watched!

⁷"But *you* have seen these mighty miracles! ⁸How carefully, then, you should obey these commandments I am going to give you today, so that you may have the strength to go in and possess the land you are about to enter. ⁹If you obey the commandments, you will have a long and good

FAMILY DEVOTIONS

☐ DEVOTION 70
TRUE JOY

Read Deuteronomy 12:18

"Dad, may I use your oilcan?" Bill's father looked up at his eager young son. "I want to unsqueak the cupboard doors for Mom. She says the hinges need a little oil and that I can be the oilman. She says pretty soon they're going to drive her wild with their squeaking."

Dad laughed as he took the oilcan from the workbench and handed it to Bill. "Then by all means, take it away!"

At dinner that evening Bill shared the neighborhood news. "Todd and Jim are mad at each other again," he said. "They're always fighting. Did you know Mrs. Gentry broke her arm? She fell down her basement stairs. Mr. Snell—that old man at the corner—stood at his window for half an hour and watched us sliding. He's probably got nothing better to do." Bill paused to nibble at his salad.

"I guess the people in our neighborhood could use some oil," observed Dad.

"Oil?" asked Bill. "What do you mean?"

"When I was little," Dad explained, "I learned a Bible verse about the 'oil of gladness.' The Bible often talks about rejoicing in everything. It sounds to me like some of our neighbors could use a little gladness—kind of like Mom's cupboards needed a little oil," said Dad. "Since you're the oilman today, I think you should be the one to spread it around the neighborhood."

"Yeah? How do I do that?" Bill looked thoughtful. "I know what I can do," he said a moment later, eyeing the dessert on the counter. "I can take a piece of pie to Mr. Snell. And I can offer to run errands for Mrs. Gentry. What can I do about Todd and Jim?"

"I don't know," said Mom. "But you're off to a good start. I'm sure you'll think of something."

True Joy Memory Verse

Always be full of joy in the Lord; I say it again, rejoice!
Philippians 4:4

How About You?

Do you spread gladness? God's Word says you should "rejoice before the Lord your God in everything you do." Will you share that joy with others? Offer a cheerful smile to help someone feel better. Take time to chat a few minutes with a lonely person. Lend a helping hand. Do it for Jesus. *H. M.*

life in the land the Lord promised to your ancestors and to you, their descendants—a wonderful land 'flowing with milk and honey'! ¹⁰For the land you are about to enter and possess is not like the land of Egypt where you have come from, where irrigation is necessary. ¹¹It is a land of hills and valleys with plenty of rain— ¹²a land that the Lord your God personally cares for! His eyes are always upon it, day after day throughout the year!

¹³"And if you will carefully obey all of his commandments that I am going to give you today, and if you will love the Lord your God with all your hearts and souls and will worship him, ¹⁴then he will continue to send both the early and late rains that will produce wonderful crops of grain, grapes for your wine, and olive oil. ¹⁵He will give you lush pastureland for your cattle to graze in, and you yourselves shall have plenty to eat and be fully content.

¹⁶"But beware that your hearts do not turn from God to worship other gods. ¹⁷For if you do, the anger of the Lord will be hot against you, and he will shut the heavens—there will be no rain and no harvest, and you will quickly perish from the good land the Lord has given you. ¹⁸So keep these commandments carefully in mind. Tie them to your hand to remind you to obey them, and tie them to your forehead between your eyes! ¹⁹Teach them to your children. Talk about them when you are sitting at home, when you are out walking, at bedtime, and before breakfast! ²⁰Write them upon the doors of your houses and upon your gates, ²¹so that as long as there is sky above the earth, you and your children will enjoy the good life awaiting you in the land the Lord has promised you.

²²"If you carefully obey all the commandments I give you, loving the Lord your God, walking in all his ways, and clinging to him, ²³then the Lord will drive out all the nations in your land, no matter how much greater and stronger than you they might be. ²⁴Wherever you go, the land is yours. Your frontiers will stretch from the southern Negeb to Lebanon, and from the Euphrates River to the Mediterranean Sea. ²⁵No one will be able to stand against you, for the Lord your God will send fear and dread ahead of you wherever you go, just as he has promised.

²⁶"I am giving you the choice today between God's blessing or God's curse! ²⁷There will be blessing if you obey the commandments of the Lord your God that I am giving you today, ²⁸and a curse if you refuse them and worship the gods of these other nations. ²⁹When the Lord your God brings you into the land to possess it, a blessing shall be proclaimed from Mount Gerizim and a curse from Mount Ebal! ³⁰(Gerizim and Ebal are mountains west of the Jordan River, where the Canaanites live, in the wasteland near Gilgal, where the oaks of Moreh are.) ³¹For you are to cross the Jordan and live in the land the Lord is giving you. ³²But you must obey all the laws I am giving you today.

12 Only One Altar for Sacrifices

"These are the laws you must obey when you arrive in the land that Jehovah, the God of your fathers, has given you forever:

²"You must destroy all the heathen altars wherever you find them—high in the mountains, up in the hills, or under the trees. ³Break the altars, smash the obelisks, burn the shameful images, cut down the metal idols, and leave nothing even to remind you of them!

⁴,⁵"You must not make sacrifices to your God just anywhere, as the heathen sacrifice to their gods. Rather, you must build a sanctuary for him at a place he himself will select as his home. ⁶There you shall bring to the Lord your burnt offerings and other sacrifices—your tithes, your offerings presented by the gesture of waving before the altar, your offerings to fulfill your vows, your free-will offerings, and your offerings of the firstborn animals of your flocks and herds. ⁷There you and your families shall feast before the Lord your God and shall rejoice in all he has done for you.

⁸"You will no longer go your own way as you do now, everyone doing whatever he thinks is right; ⁹(for these laws don't go into effect until you arrive in the place of rest the Lord will give to you). ¹⁰But when you cross the Jordan River and live in the Promised Land, and the Lord gives you rest and keeps you safe from all your enemies, ¹¹then you must bring all your burnt sacrifices and other offerings to his sanctuary, the place he will choose as his home. ¹²You shall rejoice there before the Lord with your sons and daughters and servants; and remember to invite the Levites to feast with you, for they have no land of their own.

¹³"You are not to sacrifice your burnt offerings just anywhere; ¹⁴you may only do so in the place the Lord will choose. He will pick a place in the territory allotted to one of the tribes. Only there may you offer your sacrifices and bring your offerings. ¹⁵However, the meat you eat may be butchered anywhere, just as you do now with gazelle and deer. Eat as much of this meat as you wish and as often as you are able to obtain it, because the Lord has prospered you. Those who are ceremonially defiled may eat it too. ¹⁶The only restriction is that you are not to eat the blood—pour it out on the ground, like water.

¹⁷"But none of the offerings may be eaten at home. Neither the tithe of your grain and new

wine and olive oil, nor the firstborn of your flocks and herds, nor anything you have vowed to give the Lord, nor your freewill offerings, nor the offerings to be presented to the Lord by waving them before his altar. [18]All these must be brought to the central altar where you, your children, and the Levites shall eat them before the Lord your God. He will tell you where this altar must be located. Rejoice before the Lord your God in everything you do. [19](By the way, be very careful not to forget about the Levites. Share with them.)

[20-23]"If, when the Lord enlarges your borders, the central altar is too far away from you, then your flocks and herds may be butchered on your own farms, just as you do now with gazelle and deer. And even persons who are ceremonially defiled may eat them. The only restriction is never to eat the blood, for the blood is the life, and you shall not eat the life with the meat. [24,25]Instead, pour the blood out upon the earth. If you do, all will be well with you and your children. [26,27]Only your gifts to the Lord, and the offerings you have promised in your vows, and your burnt offerings need be taken to the central altar. These may only be sacrificed upon the altar of the Lord your God. The blood will be poured out upon the altar, and you will eat the meat.

[28]"Be careful to obey all of these commandments. If you do what is right in the eyes of the Lord your God, all will go well with you and your children forever. [29]When he destroys the nations in the land where you will live, [30]don't follow their example in worshiping their gods. Do not ask, 'How do these nations worship their gods?' and then go and worship as they do! [31]You must not insult the Lord your God like that! These nations have done horrible things that he hates, all in the name of their religion. They have even roasted their sons and daughters in front of their gods. [32]Obey all the commandments I give you. Do not add to or subtract from them.

13 Don't Listen to False Prophets

"If there is a prophet among you, or one who claims to foretell the future by dreams, [2]and if his predictions come true but he says, 'Come, let us worship the gods of the other nations,' [3]don't listen to him. For the Lord is testing you to find out whether or not you really love him with all your heart and soul. [4]You must *never* worship any God but Jehovah; obey only his commands and cling to him.

[5]"The prophet who tries to lead you astray must be executed, for he has attempted to foment rebellion against the Lord your God who brought you out of slavery in the land of Egypt. By executing him you will clear out the evil from among you.

[6,7]If your nearest relative or closest friend, even a brother, son, daughter, or beloved wife whispers to you to come and worship these foreign gods, [8]do not consent or listen, and have no pity: Do not spare that person from the penalty; don't conceal his horrible suggestion. [9]Execute him! Your own hand shall be the first upon him to put him to death, then the hands of all the people. [10]Stone him to death because he has tried to draw you away from the Lord your God who brought you from the land of Egypt, the place of slavery. [11]Then all Israel will hear about his evil deed and will fear such wickedness as this among you.

[12-14]"If you ever hear it said about one of the cities of Israel that some worthless rabble have led their fellow citizens astray with the suggestion that they worship foreign gods, first check the facts to see if the rumor is true. If you find that it is, that it is certain that such a horrible thing is happening among you in one of the cities the Lord has given you, [15]you must without fail declare war against that city and utterly destroy all of its inhabitants, and even all of the cattle. [16]Afterwards you must pile all the booty into the middle of the street and burn it, then put the entire city to the torch, as a burnt offering to Jehovah your God. That city shall forever remain a lifeless mound and may never be rebuilt. [17]Keep none of the booty! Then the Lord will turn from his fierce anger and be merciful to you, and have compassion upon you, and make you a great nation just as he promised your ancestors.

[18]"Of course, the Lord your God will be merciful only if you have been obedient to him and to his commandments that I am giving you today, and if you have been doing that which is right in the eyes of the Lord.

14 What to Eat and Not Eat

"Since you are the people of God, never cut yourselves [as the heathen do when they worship their idols] nor shave the front halves of your heads for funerals. [2]You belong exclusively to the Lord your God, and he has chosen you to be his own possession, more so than any other nation on the face of the earth.

[3-5]"You are not to eat any animal I have declared to be ceremonially defiled. These are the animals you may eat: the ox, the sheep, the goat, the deer, the gazelle, the roebuck, the wild goat, the ibex, the antelope, and the mountain sheep.

[6]"Any animal that has cloven hooves and chews the cud may be eaten, [7]but if the animal doesn't have both, it may not be eaten. So you may not eat the camel, the hare, or the coney. They chew the cud but do not have cloven hooves. [8]Pigs may not be eaten because, although they have cloven

hooves, they don't chew the cud. You may not even touch the dead bodies of such animals.

9"Only sea animals with fins and scales may be eaten; 10all other kinds are ceremonially defiled.

11-18"You may eat any bird except the following: the eagle, the vulture, the osprey, the buzzard, the falcon (any variety), the raven (any variety), the ostrich, the nighthawk, the sea gull, the hawk (any variety), the screech owl, the great owl, the horned owl, the pelican, the vulture, the cormorant, the stork, the heron (any variety), the hoopoe, the bat.

19,20"With certain exceptions, insects are a defilement to you and may not be eaten.

21"Don't eat anything that has died a natural death. However, a foreigner among you may eat it. You may give it or sell it to him, but don't eat it yourself, for you are holy to the Lord your God.

"You must not boil a young goat in its mother's milk.

22"You must tithe all of your crops every year. 23Bring this tithe to eat before the Lord your God at the place he shall choose as his sanctuary; this applies to your tithes of grain, new wine, olive oil, and the firstborn of your flocks and herds. The purpose of tithing is to teach you always to put God first in your lives. 24If the place the Lord chooses for his sanctuary is so far away that it isn't convenient to carry your tithes to that place, 25then you may sell the tithe portion of your crops and herds and take the money to the Lord's sanctuary. 26When you arrive, use the money to buy an ox, a sheep, some wine, or beer, to feast there before the Lord your God, and to rejoice with your household.

27"Don't forget to share your income with the Levites in your community, for they have no property or crops as you do.

28"Every third year you are to use your entire tithe for local welfare programs: 29Give it to the Levites who have no inheritance among you, or to foreigners, or to widows and orphans within your city, so that they can eat and be satisfied; and then Jehovah your God will bless you and your work.

15 Lending Money

"At the end of every seventh year there is to be a canceling of all debts! 2Every creditor shall write 'Paid in full' on any promissory note he holds against a fellow Israelite, for the Lord has released everyone from his obligation. 3(This release does not apply to foreigners.) 4,5No one will become poor because of this, for the Lord will greatly bless you in the land he is giving you if you obey this command. The only prerequisite for his blessing is that you carefully heed all the commands of the Lord your God that I am giving you today. 6He will bless you as he has promised. You shall lend money to many nations but will never need to borrow! You shall rule many nations, but they shall not rule over you!

7"But if, when you arrive in the land the Lord will give you, there are any among you who are poor, you must not shut your heart or hand against them; 8you must lend them as much as they need. 9Beware! Don't refuse a loan because the year of debt cancellation is close at hand! If you refuse to make the loan and the needy man cries out to the Lord, it will be counted against you as a sin. 10You must lend him what he needs, and don't moan about it either! For the Lord will prosper you in everything you do because of this! 11There will always be some among you who are poor; that is why this commandment is necessary. You must lend to them liberally.

12"If you buy a Hebrew slave, whether a man or woman, you must free him at the end of the sixth year you have owned him, 13 and don't send him away empty-handed! 14Give him a large farewell present from your flock, your olive press, and your wine press. Share with him in proportion as the Lord your God has blessed you. 15Remember that you were slaves in the land of Egypt and the Lord your God rescued you! That is why I am giving you this command.

16"But if your Hebrew slave doesn't want to leave—if he says he loves you and enjoys your pleasant home and gets along well with you—17then take an awl and pierce his ear into the door, and after that he shall be your slave forever. Do the same with your women slaves. 18But when you free a slave you must not feel bad, for remember that for six years he has cost you less than half the price of a hired hand! And the Lord your God will prosper all you do because you have released him!

19"You shall set aside for God all the firstborn males from your flocks and herds. Do not use the firstborn of your herds to work your fields, and do not shear the firstborn of your flocks of sheep and goats. 20Instead, you and your family shall eat these animals before the Lord your God each year at his sanctuary. 21However, if this firstborn animal has any defect such as being lame or blind, or if anything else is wrong with it, you shall

---

SHOWING COMPASSION 15:7-11 God told the people of Israel to help the poor among them when they arrived in the Promised Land. This was an important part of possessing the land. Many people conclude that people are poor through some fault of their own. This kind of reasoning makes it easy to shut our hearts and hands against them. But we are not to invent reasons for not helping the poor. We are to respond to the needs of the poor no matter who or what was responsible for their condition. Who are the poor in your commmunity? How could your family help them? **To begin the series of devotionals on SHOWING COMPASSION, turn to page 569.**

FAMILY DEVOTIONS

☐ **DEVOTION 71**
ACCEPTING OTHERS

Read Deuteronomy 16:9-14

Accepting Others
Memory Verse

How wonderful it is,
how pleasant,
when brothers live
in harmony!
Psalm 133:1

Frank and his friend Marc looked at the creek which ran through the field near their homes. They were trying to figure out how to build a bridge over it. "I bet my dad has a board we could use," said Marc.

The two boys ran to the shed in Marc's backyard and found a wide board. They carried it to the creek, lifted it high, and gave it a heave, hoping it would land with both ends on dry ground. *Splash!* One end missed.

"I don't think this board will work," said Frank. "Look how it sags in the middle." He looked at his watch. "Mom expects me home soon," he added. "Let's work on this some more tomorrow. I'll ask my parents for suggestions on bridge building." The boys set the board against the outside of the shed to dry, and Frank headed home.

Mom greeted Frank at the door. "I'm glad you're home a little early," she said. "We're having the Habibs over for dinner tonight."

"Not them!" groaned Frank. He didn't like these new neighbors. They didn't speak English very well, and the boy his age didn't act like the other boys. Frank still couldn't pronounce his name. "Maybe I can eat at Marc's," he said. "We're building a bridge."

"You're eating here," Mom said firmly. "We're building a bridge, too."

"What do you mean?"

"The Habibs may seem strange to us, just like we're strange to them—but it's just because we come from different cultures. Having them over for dinner to learn about each other is like building a bridge between us."

"I don't think the Habibs believe in God," said Frank. He thought for sure he had one up on Mom with that comment.

"Perhaps not," said Mom, "but they'll have a better chance to get to know him if we share his love with them tonight. Now go wash up for dinner."

How About You?
When you see people who are different from you, do you stay away or do you "build a bridge" with Jesus' love? He loves all the people of the world. He wants to show that love through you. *N. E. K.*

• For the next devotional, turn to page 211. • For the next devotional on ACCEPTING OTHERS, turn to page 289.
• For notes on ACCEPTING OTHERS, see pages 270, 1140, 1196, and 1254.

not sacrifice it. ²²Instead, use it for food for your family at home. Anyone, even if ceremonially defiled at the time, may eat it, just as anyone may eat a gazelle or deer. ²³But don't eat the blood; pour it out upon the ground like water.

16 Special Holidays

"Always remember to celebrate the Passover during the month of April, for that was when Jehovah your God brought you out of Egypt by night. ²Your Passover sacrifice shall be either a lamb or an ox, sacrificed to the Lord your God at his sanctuary. ³Eat the sacrifice with unleavened bread. Eat unleavened bread for seven days as a reminder of the bread you ate as you escaped from Egypt. This is to remind you that you left Egypt in such a hurry that there was no time for the bread to rise. Remember that day all the rest of your lives! ⁴For seven days no trace of yeast shall be in your homes, and none of the Passover lamb shall be left until the next morning.

⁵"The Passover is not to be eaten in your homes. ⁶It must be eaten at the place the Lord shall choose as his sanctuary. Sacrifice it there on the anniversary evening just as the sun goes down. ⁷Roast the lamb and eat it, then start back to your homes the next morning. ⁸For the following six days you shall eat no bread made with yeast. On the seventh day there shall be a quiet gathering of the people of each city before the Lord your God. Don't do any work that day.

⁹"Seven weeks after the harvest begins, ¹⁰there shall be another festival before the Lord your God called the Festival of Weeks. At that time bring to him a free-will offering proportionate in size to his blessing upon you as judged by the amount of your harvest. ¹¹It is a time to rejoice before the Lord with your family and household. And don't forget to include the local Levites, foreigners, widows, and orphans. Invite them to accompany you to the celebration at the sanctuary. ¹²Remember! You were a slave in Egypt, so be sure to carry out this command.

¹³"Another celebration, the Festival of Shelters, must be observed for seven days at the end of the harvest season, after the grain is threshed and the grapes have been pressed. ¹⁴This will be a happy time of rejoicing together with your family and servants. And don't forget to include the Levites, foreigners, orphans, and widows of your town.

¹⁵"This feast will be held at the sanctuary, which will be located at the place the Lord will designate. It is a time of deep thanksgiving to the Lord for blessing you with a good harvest and in so many other ways; it shall be a time of great joy.

¹⁶"Every man in Israel shall appear before the Lord your God three times a year at the sanctuary for these festivals:

The Festival of Unleavened Bread,
The Festival of Weeks,
The Festival of Shelters.

"On each of these occasions bring a gift to the Lord. ¹⁷Give as you are able, according as the Lord has blessed you.

¹⁸"Appoint judges and administrative officials for all the cities the Lord your God is giving you. They will administer justice in every part of the land. ¹⁹Never twist justice to benefit a rich man, and never accept bribes. For bribes blind the eyes of the wisest and corrupt their decisions. ²⁰Justice must prevail.

"That is the only way you will be successful in the land that the Lord your God is giving you.

²¹"Never, under any circumstances, are you to erect shameful images beside the altar of the Lord your God. ²²And never set up stone pillars to worship them, for the Lord hates them!

17

"Never sacrifice a sick or defective ox or sheep to the Lord your God. He doesn't feel honored by such gifts!

²,³"If anyone, whether man or woman, in any village throughout your land violates your covenant with God by worshiping other gods, the sun, moon, or stars—which I have strictly forbidden—⁴first check the rumor very carefully; if there is no doubt it is true, ⁵then that man or woman shall be taken outside the city and shall be stoned to death. ⁶However, never put a man to death on the testimony of only one witness; there must be at least two or three. ⁷The witnesses shall throw the first stones, and then all the people shall join in. In this way you will purge all evil from among you.

⁸"If a case arises that is too hard for you to decide—for instance, whether someone is guilty of murder when there is insufficient evidence, or whether someone's rights have been violated—you shall take the case to the sanctuary of the Lord your God, ⁹to the priests and Levites, and the chief judge on duty at the time will make the decision.

RESPECTING GOD'S WORD 17:18-20 The king was to be a man of God's Word. He was to (1) have a copy of the law made for his personal use, (2) keep it with him all the time, (3) read from it every day, and (4) obey it completely. By this process he would learn respect for God, keep himself from feeling more important than others, and avoid neglecting God in times of prosperity. We can't know what God wants unless we read his Word, and his Word won't affect our lives unless we read and think about it regularly. **To begin the series of devotionals on** RESPECTING GOD'S WORD, **turn to page 11.**

¹⁰His decision is without appeal and is to be followed to the letter. ¹¹The sentence he imposes is to be fully executed. ¹²If the defendant refuses to accept the decision of the priest or judge appointed by God for this purpose, the penalty is death. Such sinners must be purged from Israel. ¹³Then everyone will hear about what happened to the man who refused God's verdict, and they will be afraid to defy a court's judgment.

¹⁴"When you arrive in the land the Lord your God will give you, and have conquered it, and begin to think, 'We ought to have a king like the other nations around us'—¹⁵be sure that you select as king the man the Lord your God shall choose. He must be an Israelite, not a foreigner. ¹⁶Be sure that he doesn't build up a large stable of horses for himself, nor send his men to Egypt to raise horses for him there, for the Lord has told you, 'Never return to Egypt again.' ¹⁷He must not have too many wives, lest his heart be turned away from the Lord, neither shall he be excessively rich.

¹⁸"And when he has been crowned and sits upon his throne as king, then he must copy these laws from the book kept by the Levite-priests. ¹⁹That copy of the laws shall be his constant companion. He must read from it every day of his life so that he will learn to respect the Lord his God by obeying all of his commands. ²⁰This regular reading of God's laws will prevent him from feeling that he is better than his fellow citizens. It will also prevent him from turning away from God's laws in the slightest respect and will ensure his having a long, good reign. His sons will then follow him upon the throne.

18 Giving to the Priests and Levites

"Remember that the priests and all the other members of the Levite tribe will not be given property like the other tribes. So the priests and Levites are to be supported by the sacrifices brought to the altar of the Lord and by the other offerings the people bring to him. ²They don't need to own property, for the Lord is their property! That is what he promised them! ³The shoulder, the cheeks, and the stomach of every ox or sheep brought for sacrifice must be given to the priests. ⁴In addition, the priests shall receive the harvest samples brought in thanksgiving to the Lord—the first of the grain, the new wine, the olive oil, and of the fleece at shearing time. ⁵For the Lord your God has chosen the tribe of Levi, of all the tribes, to minister to the Lord from generation to generation.

⁶,⁷"Any Levite, no matter where he lives in the land of Israel, has the right to come to the sanctuary at any time and minister in the name of the Lord, just like his brother Levites who work there regularly. ⁸He shall be given his share of the sacrifices and offerings as his right, not just if he is in need.

⁹"When you arrive in the Promised Land you must be very careful lest you be corrupted by the horrible customs of the nations now living there. ¹⁰For example, any Israeli who presents his child to be burned to death as a sacrifice to heathen gods must be killed. No Israeli may practice black magic, or call on the evil spirits for aid, or be a fortune teller, ¹¹or be a serpent charmer, medium, or wizard, or call forth the spirits of the dead. ¹²Anyone doing these things is an object of horror and disgust to the Lord, and it is because the nations do these things that the Lord your God will displace them. ¹³You must walk blamelessly before the Lord your God. ¹⁴The nations you replace all do these evil things, but the Lord your God will not permit you to do such things.

¹⁵"Instead, he will raise up for you a Prophet like me, an Israeli, a man to whom you must listen and whom you must obey. ¹⁶For this is what you yourselves begged of God at Mount Horeb. There at the foot of the mountain you begged that you might not have to listen to the terrifying voice of God again, or see the awesome fire on the mountain, lest you die.

¹⁷"'All right,' the Lord said to me, 'I will do as they have requested. ¹⁸I will raise up from among them a Prophet, an Israeli like you. I will tell him what to say, and he shall be my spokesman to the people. ¹⁹I will personally deal with anyone who will not listen to him and heed his messages from me. ²⁰But any prophet who falsely claims that his message is from me, shall die. And any prophet who claims to give a message from other gods must die.' ²¹If you wonder, 'How shall we know whether the prophecy is from the Lord or not?' ²²this is the way to know: If the thing he prophesies doesn't happen, it is not the Lord who has given him the message; he has made it up himself. You have nothing to fear from him.

19 Cities of Refuge

"When the Lord your God has destroyed the nations you will displace, and when you are living in their cities and homes, ²,³you must set apart three Cities of Refuge so that anyone who accidentally kills someone may flee to safety. Divide the country into three districts, with one of these cities in each district; and keep the roads to these cities in good repair.

⁴"Here is an example of the purpose of these cities: ⁵If a man goes into the forest with his neighbor to chop wood, and the axe head flies off the handle and kills the man's neighbor, he may

flee to one of those cities and be safe. 6,7Anyone seeking to avenge the death will not be able to. These cities must be scattered so that one of them will be reasonably close to everyone; otherwise the angry avenger might catch and kill the innocent slayer, even though he should not have died since he had not killed deliberately.

8"If the Lord enlarges your boundaries as he promised your ancestors, and gives you all the land he promised 9(whether he does this depends on your obedience to all these commandments I am giving you today—loving the Lord your God and walking his paths), then you must designate three additional Cities of Refuge. 10In this way you will be able to avoid the death of innocent people, and you will not be held responsible for unjustified bloodshed.

11"But if anyone hates his neighbor and springs out of hiding and kills him, and then flees into one of the Cities of Refuge, 12the elders of his hometown shall send for him and shall bring him home and deliver him over to the dead man's avenger, to kill him. 13Don't pity him! Purge all murderers from Israel! Only then will all go well with you.

14"When you arrive in the land the Lord your God is giving you, remember that you must never steal a man's land by moving the boundary marker.

15"Never convict anyone on the testimony of one witness. There must be at least two, and three is even better. 16If anyone gives false witness, claiming he has seen someone do wrong when he hasn't, 17both men shall be brought before the priests and judges on duty before the Lord at the time. 18They must be closely questioned, and if the witness is lying, 19his penalty shall be the punishment he thought the other man would get. In this way you will purge out evil from among you. 20Then those who hear about it will be afraid to tell lies on the witness stand. 21You shall not show pity to a false witness. Life for life, eye for eye, tooth for tooth, hand for hand, foot for foot; this is your rule in such cases.

20 Rules about War

"When you go to war and see before you vast numbers of horses and chariots, an army far greater than yours, don't be frightened! The Lord your God is with you—the same God who brought you safely out of Egypt! 2Before you begin the battle, a priest shall stand before the Israeli army and say,

3"'Listen to me, all you men of Israel! Don't be afraid as you go out to fight today! 4For the Lord your God is going with you! He will fight for you against your enemies, and he will give you the victory!'

5"Then the officers of the army shall address the men in this manner: 'Has anyone just built a new house but not yet dedicated it? If so, go home! For you might be killed in the battle, and someone else would dedicate it! 6Has anyone just planted a vineyard but not yet eaten any of its fruit? If so, go home! You might die in battle and someone else would eat it! 7Has anyone just become engaged? Well, go home and get married! For you might die in the battle, and someone else would marry your fiancée. 8And now, is anyone afraid? If you are, go home before you frighten the rest of us!' 9When the officers have finished saying this to their men, they will announce the names of the battalion leaders.

10"As you approach a city to fight against it, first offer it a truce. 11If it accepts the truce and opens its gates to you, then all its people shall become your servants. 12But if it refuses and won't make peace with you, you must besiege it. 13When the Lord your God has given it to you, kill every male in the city; 14but you may keep for yourselves all the women, children, cattle, and booty. 15These instructions apply only to distant cities, not to those in the Promised Land itself.

16"For in the cities within the boundaries of the Promised Land you are to save no one; destroy every living thing. 17Utterly destroy the Hittites, the Amorites, the Canaanites, the Perizzites, the Hivites, and the Jebusites. This is the commandment of the Lord your God. 18The purpose of this command is to prevent the people of the land from luring you into idol worship and into participation in their loathsome customs, thus sinning deeply against the Lord your God.

19"When you besiege a city, don't destroy the fruit trees. Eat all the fruit you wish; just don't cut down the trees. They aren't enemies who need to be slaughtered! 20But you may cut down trees that aren't valuable for food. Use them for the siege [to make ladders, portable towers, and battering rams].

21 An Unsolved Murder

"If, when you arrive in the Promised Land, a murder victim is found lying in a field and no one has seen the murder, 2the elders and judges shall measure from the body to the nearest city. 3Then the elders of that city shall take a heifer that has never been yoked, 4and lead it to a valley where there is running water—a valley neither plowed nor sowed—and there break its neck.

5"Then the priests shall come (for the Lord your God has chosen them to minister before him and to pronounce his blessings and decide lawsuits and punishments), 6and shall wash their hands over the heifer, 7and say, 'Our hands have

FAMILY DEVOTIONS

☐ DEVOTION 72
PUTTING GOD FIRST

Read Deuteronomy 18:9-14

Putting God First
Memory Verse

In everything you do, put God first, and he will direct you and crown your efforts with success.
Proverbs 3:6

"You know my friend Sammy?" asked Joshua one evening. "The kids at school are starting to call him Sammy Squirrel. Every day his mom packs him a nice lunch, but he always wants to have something from everybody else's lunch, too."

"Huh?" snorted Joshua's brother, Mark. "What's that got to do with squirrels?"

"Well, you know how that squirrel stole the birdseed from our bird feeder even though it had plenty of its own food," explained Joshua. "Sammy's just like that! He's never satisfied with what he has."

"Well, that's no reason for you to call him names," Mom scolded mildly.

Later that evening, Joshua was looking through a book on witchcraft that he had borrowed from the library. *This is wild,* he thought. *They do real magic! It would be fun to see it.*

Joshua closed the book quickly when Dad came into the room. "What do you have there?" asked Dad.

"Just a book," said Joshua, feeling a little uneasy.

"The Magic in Witchcraft?" asked Dad, noticing the title. "Isn't one Sammy Squirrel enough, Son?"

"What?" asked Joshua. "Sammy doesn't have anything to do with this."

"You wanted to call him Sammy Squirrel because he had everything he needed right in front of his face, but he still reached out for more—and for things that don't rightfully belong to him," Dad reminded Joshua. "As a Christian, you have everything you need for living. You have the Bible as your guide. You have our loving Lord Jesus for the forgiveness of sins. You have the Holy Spirit to work in your life." Dad paused, then added, "may I ask why you are reaching out for more—and for things that don't belong to you, but to the devil?"

"I just thought I'd take a look," said Joshua sheepishly.

"Don't even dabble in it," said Dad sternly. "God has filled you to overflowing. You don't need anything else."

How About You?
Are you satisfied with all the wisdom and knowledge God has displayed in his Word? Or do you dabble in things of the world? Don't be a Sammy Squirrel Christian. Be content with the Christian life that God has given you. *N. E. K.*

• For the next devotional, turn to page 213. • For the next devotional on *PUTTING GOD FIRST,* turn to page 253.
• For notes on *PUTTING GOD FIRST,* see pages 397, 492, 644, 791, and 982.

not shed this blood, neither have our eyes seen it. ⁸O Lord, forgive your people Israel whom you have redeemed, and do not charge them with murdering an innocent man. Forgive us the guilt of this man's blood.' ⁹In this way you will put away the guilt from among you by following the Lord's directions.

¹⁰"When you go to war and the Lord your God delivers your enemies to you, ¹¹and you see among the captives a beautiful girl you want as your wife, ¹²take her home with you. She must shave her head and pare her nails ¹³and change her clothing, laying aside that which she was wearing when she was captured, then remain in your home in mourning for her father and mother for a full month. After that you may marry her. ¹⁴However, if after marrying her you decide you don't like her, you must let her go free—you may not sell her or treat her as a slave, for you have humiliated her.

¹⁵"If a man has two wives but loves one and not the other, and both have borne him children, and the mother of his oldest son is the wife he doesn't love, ¹⁶he may not give a larger inheritance to his younger son, the son of the wife he loves. ¹⁷He must give the customary double portion to his oldest son, who is the beginning of his strength and who owns the rights of a firstborn son, even though he is the son of the wife his father doesn't love.

¹⁸"If a man has a stubborn, rebellious son who will not obey his father or mother, even though they punish him, ¹⁹then his father and mother shall take him before the elders of the city ²⁰and declare, 'This son of ours is stubborn and rebellious and won't obey; he is a worthless drunkard.' ²¹Then the men of the city shall stone him to death. In this way you shall put away this evil from among you, and all the young men of Israel will hear about what happened and will be afraid.

²²"If a man has committed a crime worthy of death, and is executed and then hanged on a tree, ²³his body shall not remain on the tree overnight. You must bury him the same day, for anyone hanging on a tree is cursed of God. Don't defile the land the Lord your God has given you.

22 Helping Neighbors

"If you see someone's ox or sheep wandering away, don't pretend you didn't see it; take it back to its owner. ²If you don't know who the owner is, take it to your farm and keep it there until the owner comes looking for it, and then give it to him. ³The same applies to donkeys, clothing, or anything else you find. Keep it for its owner.

⁴"If you see someone trying to get an ox or donkey onto its feet when it has slipped beneath its load, don't look the other way. Go and help!

⁵"A woman must not wear men's clothing, and a man must not wear women's clothing. This is abhorrent to the Lord your God.

⁶"If a bird's nest is lying on the ground, or if you spy one in a tree, and there are young ones or eggs in it with the mother sitting in the nest, don't take the mother with the young. ⁷Let her go, and take only the young. The Lord will bless you for it.

⁸"Every new house must have a guardrail around the edge of the flat rooftop to prevent anyone from falling off and bring guilt to both the house and its owner.

⁹"Do not sow other crops in the rows of your vineyard. If you do, both the crops and the grapes shall be confiscated by the priests.

¹⁰"Don't plow with an ox and a donkey harnessed together.

¹¹"Don't wear clothing woven from two kinds of thread: for instance, wool and linen.

¹²"You must sew tassels on the four corners of your cloaks.

¹³,¹⁴"If a man marries a girl, then after sleeping with her accuses her of having had premarital intercourse with another man, saying, 'She was not a virgin when I married her,' ¹⁵then the girl's father and mother shall bring the proof of her virginity to the city judges.

¹⁶"Her father shall tell them, 'I gave my daughter to this man to be his wife, and now he despises her ¹⁷,¹⁸and has accused her of shameful things, claiming that she was not a virgin when she married; yet here is the proof.' And they shall spread before the judges the blood-stained sheet from her marriage bed. The judges shall sentence the man to be whipped, ¹⁹and fine him one hundred dollars to be given to the girl's father, for he has falsely accused a virgin of Israel. She shall remain his wife and he may never divorce her. ²⁰But if the man's accusations are true, and she was not a virgin, ²¹the judges shall take the girl to the door of her father's home where the men of the city shall stone her to death. She has defiled Israel by flagrant crime, being a prostitute while living at home with her parents; and such evil must be cleansed from among you.

²²"If a man is discovered committing adultery, both he and the other man's wife must be killed; in this way evil will be cleansed from Israel. ²³,²⁴If a girl who is engaged is seduced within the walls of a city, both she and the man who seduced her shall be taken outside the gates and stoned to death—the girl because she didn't scream for help, and the man because he has violated the virginity of another man's fiancée. ²⁵⁻²⁷In this way you will reduce crime among you. But if this deed

FAMILY DEVOTIONS

☐ DEVOTION 73
KEEPING YOUR PROMISES

Read Deuteronomy 23:21-23

Chad liked the missionary who was speaking in his church. Mr. Rathbun had told them thrilling stories of his ministry in a foreign land.

"In that country there are many orphaned children," Mr. Rathbun was saying. "If we could build a home for them, we could show them love, and it would give us the opportunity to teach them about Jesus and win them to Christ. We are asking Christians to pray earnestly about this home and to give up just one cup of coffee or one bottle of pop each week and give the money to the Lord for this home. Can I see the hands of people who'd be willing to help in this way?" Chad's hand shot right up. He was glad to see many hands raised, including those of his friends Greg and Gary.

One Saturday a few weeks later the three boys were biking home after ball practice. "I'm hot," said Greg. "Let's get some pop at the gas station."

As they were getting out their coins, Chad exclaimed, "Hey, wait! We promised to give up one pop a week. It's Saturday already, and I haven't given one up this week yet, have you?"

"Nah," said Greg. "I'll give up two next week."

"Yeah," agreed Gary. "I'm too thirsty now."

Chad felt hurt as the boys drank their pop. He didn't even want a sip of theirs when they offered it. "I don't see how you can break your promise," he told them.

That evening Chad was very quiet. "Something wrong?" asked Dad.

"Yeah," Chad said. He told his father about his friends and then added, "I was mad all the way home until I remembered I was just as bad as they were. I promised to pray for Mr. Rathbun and the orphanage, but I haven't done it much."

"I'm glad you see your own faults, Chad," Dad told him. "You see, promises aren't to be taken lightly. The Lord says it's better not to make a promise than to make one and not keep it. You can pray that God will work in your friends' hearts so they will see this, too."

Keeping Your Promises Memory Verse

God delights in those who keep their promises and abhors those who don't.
Proverbs 12:22

How About You?

Have you made promises to God that you haven't kept? God keeps all his promises and he expects you to keep yours. Be careful about making promises. Ask God to help you keep the ones you make. A. G. L.

• For the next devotional, turn to page 215.   • For the next devotional on *Keeping Your Promises*, turn to page 283.
• For notes on *Keeping Your Promises*, see pages 183, 284, and 838.

takes place out in the country, only the man shall die. The girl is as innocent as a murder victim; for it must be assumed that she screamed, but there was no one to hear and rescue her out in the field. ²⁸,²⁹If a man rapes a girl who is not engaged and is caught in the act, he must pay a fine to the girl's father and marry her; he may never divorce her. ³⁰A man shall not sleep with his father's widow since she belonged to his father.

23 Rules about the Sanctuary

"If a man's testicles are crushed or his penis cut off, he shall not enter the sanctuary. ²A bastard may not enter the sanctuary, nor any of his descendants for ten generations.

³"No Ammonite or Moabite may ever enter the sanctuary, even after the tenth generation. ⁴The reason for this law is that these nations did not welcome you with food and water when you came out of Egypt; they even tried to hire Balaam, the son of Beor from Pethor, Mesopotamia, to curse you. ⁵But the Lord wouldn't listen to Balaam; instead, he turned the intended curse into a blessing for you because the Lord loves you. ⁶You must never, as long as you live, try to help the Ammonites or the Moabites in any way. ⁷But don't look down on the Edomites and the Egyptians; the Edomites are your brothers and you lived among the Egyptians. ⁸The grandchildren of the Egyptians who came with you from Egypt may enter the sanctuary of the Lord.

⁹,¹⁰"When you are at war, the men in the camps must stay away from all evil. Any man who becomes ceremonially defiled because of a seminal emission during the night must leave the camp ¹¹and stay outside until the evening; then he shall bathe himself and return at sunset. ¹²The toilet area shall be outside the camp. ¹³Each man must have a spade as part of his equipment; after every bowel movement he must dig a hole with the spade and cover the excrement. ¹⁴The camp must be holy, for the Lord walks among you to protect you and to cause your enemies to fall before you; and the Lord does not want to see anything indecent lest he turn away from you.

¹⁵,¹⁶"If a slave escapes from his master, you must not force him to return; let him live among you in whatever town he shall choose, and do not oppress him.

¹⁷,¹⁸"No prostitutes are permitted in Israel, either men or women; you must not bring to the Lord any offering from the earnings of a prostitute or a homosexual, for both are detestable to the Lord your God.

¹⁹"Don't demand interest on loans you make to a brother Israelite, whether it is in the form of money, food, or anything else. ²⁰You may take interest from a foreigner, but not from an Israeli. For if you take interest from a brother, an Israeli, the Lord your God won't bless you when you arrive in the Promised Land.

²¹"When you make a vow to the Lord, be prompt in doing whatever it is you promised him, for the Lord demands that you promptly fulfill your vows; it is a sin if you don't. ²²(But it is not a sin if you refrain from vowing!) ²³ Once you make the vow, you must be careful to do as you have said, for it was your own choice, and you have vowed to the Lord your God.

²⁴"You may eat your fill of the grapes from another man's vineyard, but do not take any away in a container. ²⁵It is the same with someone else's grain—you may eat a few handfuls of it, but don't use a sickle.

24

"If a man doesn't like something about his wife, he may write a letter stating that he has divorced her, give her the letter, and send her away. ²If she then remarries ³and the second husband also divorces her or dies, ⁴the former husband may not marry her again, for she has been defiled; this would bring guilt upon the land the Lord your God is giving you.

⁵"A newly married man is not to be drafted into the army nor given any other special responsibilities; for a year he shall be free to be at home, happy with his wife.

⁶"It is illegal to take a millstone as a pledge, for it is a tool by which its owner gains his livelihood. ⁷If anyone kidnaps a brother Israelite and treats him as a slave or sells him, the kidnapper must die, in order to purge the evil from among you.

⁸"Be very careful to follow the instructions of the priest in cases of leprosy, for I have given him rules and guidelines you must obey to the letter: ⁹Remember what the Lord your God did to Miriam as you were coming from Egypt.

¹⁰"If you lend anything to another man, you must not enter his house to get his security. ¹¹Stand outside! The owner will bring it out to you. ¹²,¹³If the man is poor and gives you his cloak as security, you are not to sleep in it. Take it back to him at sundown so that he can use it through the night and bless you; and the Lord your God will count it as righteousness for you.

¹⁴,¹⁵"Never oppress a poor hired man, whether a fellow Israelite or a foreigner living in your town. Pay him his wage each day before sunset, for since he is poor he needs it right away; otherwise he may cry out to the Lord against you and it would be counted as a sin against you.

¹⁶"Fathers shall not be put to death for the sins of their sons nor the sons for the sins of their

Family Devotions

☐ DEVOTION 74
BECOMING MORE LIKE JESUS

Read Deuteronomy 26:12-13

Becoming More Like Jesus Memory Verse

Let everything you do reflect your love of the truth and the fact that you are in dead earnest about it.
Titus 2:7

"Christie," said Mom, "Mrs. Jamison called, and she wondered if you could watch Matt and Stevie tonight while she's at her class." Christie gladly agreed.

That evening, Christie discovered that baby-sitting the Jamison boys was quite a challenge. She was glad when she finally saw the boys' mother pull into the driveway. Soon they were all piled into the car to take Christie home.

All the way home, Christie kept wondering how much she would get paid. But when they arrived at her house, Mrs. Jamison said, "Since Rick died, our budget has been really tight—I'm sorry I can't pay you right now. I hope I'll have a little extra next week."

"Sure, that's OK," Christie heard herself say, but she walked into the house feeling very cheated. "Mom, Mrs. Jamison didn't even pay me!" she complained loudly. "And the boys were terrible!"

Mom looked up from her sewing. "I'm sorry, dear, but I'm sure they don't have much money." Then she added, "Maybe you could do this for Jesus. If you're doing it for him, you'll get a reward in heaven; isn't that enough?" Christie could scarcely believe what she heard! But as she went down the hall to her room, her mother's words kept ringing in her ears, and she knew God was speaking to her heart.

During the following weeks, Mrs. Jamison often asked Christie to baby-sit. And although it always meant she was in for an eventful evening, Christie chose to continue helping in this way. One day Mrs. Jamison turned to her before taking her home. "I appreciate your patience in waiting for this," Mrs. Jamison said as she held out a check.

Christie shook her head. "There's no charge," she told Mrs. Jamison. "I just want to do this for you." Christie could hardly believe she had said it, but she found that it was true. She really did want to do this as a gift to the Lord!

How About You?
Do you always expect people to pay you when you help them? It's nice to be paid for what you do, but any pay you may receive now cannot compare with what the Lord will give you when you serve him through serving others. And he especially wants us to help widows and children who have lost a parent. Don't always expect to be paid for being helpful. Be willing to wait for the reward God will give. A. H.

• For the next devotional, turn to page 217. • For the next devotional on BECOMING MORE LIKE JESUS, turn to page 317. • For notes on BECOMING MORE LIKE JESUS, see pages 234, 983, 1105, and 1164.

fathers; every man worthy of death shall be executed for his own crime.

17"Justice must be given to migrants and orphans, and you must never accept a widow's garment in pledge of her debt. 18Always remember that you were slaves in Egypt and that the Lord your God rescued you; that is why I have given you this command. 19If, when reaping your harvest, you forget to bring in a sheaf from the field, don't go back after it. Leave it for the migrants, orphans, and widows; then the Lord your God will bless and prosper all you do. 20When you beat the olives from your olive trees, don't go over the boughs twice; leave anything remaining for the migrants, orphans, and widows. 21It is the same for the grapes in your vineyard; don't glean the vines after they are picked, but leave what's left for those in need. 22Remember that you were slaves in the land of Egypt—that is why I am giving you this command.

25

"If a man is guilty of a crime and the penalty is a beating, the judge shall command him to lie down and be beaten in his presence with up to forty stripes in proportion to the seriousness of the crime; but no more than forty stripes may be given lest the punishment seem too severe, and your brother be degraded in your eyes.

4"Don't muzzle an ox as it treads out the grain.

5"If a man's brother dies without a son, his widow must not marry outside the family; instead, her husband's brother must marry her and sleep with her. 6The first son she bears to him shall be counted as the son of the dead brother, so that his name will not be forgotten. 7But if the dead man's brother refuses to do his duty in this matter, refusing to marry the widow, then she shall go to the city elders and say to them, 'My husband's brother refuses to let his brother's name continue—he refuses to marry me.' 8The elders of the city will then summon him and talk it over with him, and if he still refuses, 9the widow shall walk over to him in the presence of the elders, pull his sandal from his foot and spit in his face. She shall then say, 'This is what happens to a man who refuses to build his brother's house.' 10And ever afterwards his house shall be referred to as 'the home of the man who had his sandal pulled off.'

11"If two men are fighting and the wife of one intervenes to help her husband by grabbing the testicles of the other man, 12her hand shall be cut off without pity.

13-15"In all your transactions you must use accurate scales and honest measurements, so that you will have a long, good life in the land the Lord your God is giving you. 16All who cheat with unjust weights and measurements are detestable to the Lord your God.

17"You must never forget what the people of Amalek did to you as you came from Egypt. 18Remember that they fought with you and struck down those who were faint and weary and lagging behind, with no respect or fear of God. 19Therefore, when the Lord your God has given you rest from all your enemies in the Promised Land, you are utterly to destroy the name of Amalek from under heaven. Never forget this.

26 Giving God the First and Best

"When you arrive in the land and have conquered it and are living there, 2,3you must present to the Lord at his sanctuary the first sample from each annual harvest. Bring it in a basket and hand it to the priest on duty and say to him, 'This gift is my acknowledgment that the Lord my God has brought me to the land he promised our ancestors.' 4The priest will then take the basket from your hand and set it before the altar. 5You shall then say before the Lord your God, 'My ancestors were migrant Arameans who went to Egypt for refuge. They were few in number, but in Egypt they became a mighty nation. 6,7The Egyptians mistreated us and we cried to the Lord God. He heard us and saw our hardship, toil, and oppression, 8and brought us out of Egypt with mighty miracles and a powerful hand. He did great and awesome miracles before the Egyptians 9and has brought us to this place and given us this land "flowing with milk and honey!" 10And now, O Lord, see, I have brought you a token of the first of the crops from the ground you have given me.' Then place the samples before the Lord your God, and worship him. 11Afterwards, go and feast on all the good things he has given you. Celebrate with your family and with any Levites or migrants living among you.

12"Every third year is a year of special tithing. That year you are to give all your tithes to the Levites, migrants, orphans, and widows, so that they will be well fed. 13Then you shall declare before the Lord your God, 'I have given all of my tithes to the Levites, the migrants, the orphans, and the widows, just as you commanded me; I have not violated or forgotten any of your rules. 14I have not touched the tithe while I was ceremonially defiled (for instance, while I was in mourning), nor have I offered any of it to the dead. I have obeyed the Lord my God and have done everything you commanded me. 15Look down from your holy home in heaven and bless your people and the land you have given us, as you promised our ancestors; make it a land "flowing with milk and honey"!'

16"You must wholeheartedly obey all of these commandments and ordinances that the Lord your God is giving you today. 17You have declared today that he is your God, and you have promised to obey and keep his laws and ordinances, and to heed all he

FAMILY DEVOTIONS

☐ **DEVOTION 75**
TRUSTING GOD'S PLAN

Read Deuteronomy 26:16-18

Trusting God's Plan
Memory Verses:

This plan of mine is not what you would work out, neither are my thoughts the same as yours! For just as the heavens are higher than the earth, so are my ways higher than yours, and my thoughts than yours.
Isaiah 55:8-9

It was Saturday afternoon, and Mandy was slumped in the rocker, trying to read. Her mom was sitting on the floor, surrounded by fabric, pattern pieces, tape measure, scissors, and pins. She was cutting out a blouse to sew for herself. After watching her mom for a few minutes, Mandy laid down her book and said, "I don't know how you do it, Mom. How do you turn all that confusion into the pretty blouse on the pattern envelope? It doesn't look anything like it right now!"

"That's true," Mom replied. "But I'll bet you could do it, too, if you wanted to."

"Oh, sure!" grunted Mandy.

"Really. You just need to follow the instructions." Mom held up a printed paper. "See, this paper says which pieces to use and how to cut and fit them together. If I do what it says, my blouse will turn out like the one in the picture."

"That's because you're good at sewing," Mandy answered. After a bit, she looked up again. "I wonder if that's what my teacher was talking about in Sunday school last week."

"What's that, Mandy?" asked Mom.

"She told us how God has in mind a plan of the wonderful person each of us could be—like the picture of the finished blouse on the pattern," explained Mandy. "Then she said that to become the person God wants us to be, we need to obey him and do what he tells us in the Bible. That's like following the instructions in the pattern."

"That's right!" exclaimed Mom. "God is fashioning us into something special. Even when things look confusing or impossible—like this blouse does to you just now—we have to keep obeying him, and he will make us into a beautiful finished product. That's a wonderful illustration, Mandy. You're a smart girl. Why, I'll bet you're even smart enough to figure out how to sew a blouse yourself."

"Maybe I am," said Mandy, "but I think I'll tackle something easier first—like finishing my book!"

How About You?
Are you letting God fashion you into the person you could be? Do you look for his instructions in his Word and ask him to help you follow them? A quiet and obedient spirit makes you beautiful to God. He has a wonderful plan for your life—trust him. J. B.

- For the next devotional, turn to page 223.   • For the next devotional on TRUSTING GOD'S PLAN, turn to page 399.
- For notes on TRUSTING GOD'S PLAN, see page 252, 296, 731, and 870.

tells you to do. ¹⁸And the Lord has declared today that you are his very own people, just as he promised, and that you must obey all of his laws. ¹⁹If you do, he will make you greater than any other nation, allowing you to receive praise, honor, and renown; but to attain this honor and renown you must be a holy people to the Lord your God, as he requires."

27 The Altar on Mount Ebal

Then Moses and the elders of Israel gave the people these further instructions to obey:

²⁻⁴"When you cross the Jordan River and go into the Promised Land—a land 'flowing with milk and honey'—take out boulders from the river bottom and immediately pile them into a monument on the other side, at Mount Ebal. Face the stones with a coating of lime and then write the laws of God in the lime. ⁵,⁶And build an altar there to the Lord your God. Use uncut boulders, and on the altar offer burnt offerings to the Lord your God. ⁷Sacrifice peace offerings upon it also, and feast there with great joy before the Lord your God. ⁸Write all of these laws plainly [upon the monument]."

⁹Then Moses and the Levite-priests addressed all Israel as follows: "O Israel, listen! Today you have become the people of the Lord your God, ¹⁰so today you must begin to obey all of these commandments I have given you."

¹¹That same day Moses gave this charge to the people:

¹²"When you cross into the Promised Land, the tribes of Simeon, Levi, Judah, Issachar, Joseph, and Benjamin shall stand upon Mount Gerizim to proclaim a blessing, ¹³and the tribes of Reuben, Gad, Asher, Zebulun, Dan, and Naphtali shall stand upon Mount Ebal to proclaim a curse. ¹⁴Then the Levites standing between them shall shout to all Israel,

¹⁵"'The curse of God be upon anyone who makes and worships an idol, even in secret, whether carved of wood or made from molten metal—for these handmade gods are hated by the Lord.' And all the people shall reply, 'Amen.'

¹⁶"'Cursed is anyone who despises his father or mother.' And all the people shall reply, 'Amen.'

¹⁷"'Cursed is he who moves the boundary marker between his land and his neighbor's.' And all the people shall reply, 'Amen.'

¹⁸"'Cursed is he who takes advantage of a blind man.' And all the people shall reply, 'Amen.'

¹⁹"'Cursed is he who is unjust to the foreigner, the orphan, and the widow.' And all the people shall reply, 'Amen.'

²⁰"'Cursed is he who commits adultery with one of his father's wives, for she belongs to his father.' And all the people shall reply, 'Amen.'

²¹"'Cursed is he who has sexual intercourse with an animal.' And all the people shall reply, 'Amen.'

²²"'Cursed is he who has sexual intercourse with his sister, whether she be a full sister or a half-sister.' And all the people shall reply, 'Amen.'

²³"'Cursed is he who has sexual intercourse with his widowed mother-in-law.' And all the people shall reply, 'Amen.'

²⁴"'Cursed is he who secretly slays another.' And all the people shall reply, 'Amen.'

²⁵"'Cursed is he who accepts a bribe to kill an innocent person.' And all the people shall reply, 'Amen.'

²⁶"'Cursed is anyone who does not obey these laws.' And all the people shall reply, 'Amen.'

28 Obedience Brings Blessing

"If you fully obey all of these commandments of the Lord your God, the laws I am declaring to you today, God will transform you into the greatest nation in the world. ²⁻⁶These are the blessings that will come upon you:

Blessings in the city,
Blessings in the field;
Many children,
Ample crops,
Large flocks and herds;
Blessings of fruit and bread;
Blessings when you come in,
Blessings when you go out.

⁷"The Lord will defeat your enemies before you; they will march out together against you but scatter before you in seven directions! ⁸The Lord will bless you with good crops and healthy cattle, and prosper everything you do when you arrive in the land the Lord your God is giving you. ⁹He will change you into a holy people dedicated to himself; this he has promised to do if you will only obey him and walk in his ways. ¹⁰All the nations in the world shall see that you belong to the Lord, and they will stand in awe.

¹¹"The Lord will give you an abundance of good things in the land, just as he promised: many children, many cattle, and abundant crops. ¹²He will open to you his wonderful treasury of rain in the heavens, to give you fine crops every season. He will bless everything you do; and you shall lend to many nations, but shall not borrow from them. ¹³If you will only listen and obey the commandments of the Lord your God that I am giving you today, he will make you the head and not the tail, and you shall always have the upper hand. ¹⁴But each of these blessings depends on your not turning aside in any way from the laws I have given you; and you must never worship other gods.

15-19"If you won't listen to the Lord your God and won't obey these laws I am giving you today, then all of these curses shall come upon you:

Curses in the city,
Curses in the fields,
Curses on your fruit and bread,
The curse of barren wombs,
Curses upon your crops,
Curses upon the fertility of your cattle and flocks,
Curses when you come in,
Curses when you go out.

20"For the Lord himself will send his personal curse upon you. You will be confused and a failure in everything you do, until at last you are destroyed because of the sin of forsaking him. 21He will send disease among you until you are destroyed from the face of the land you are about to enter and possess. 22He will send tuberculosis, fever, infections, plague, and war. He will blight your crops, covering them with mildew. All these devastations shall pursue you until you perish.

23"The heavens above you will be as unyielding as bronze, and the earth beneath will be as iron. 24The land will become as dry as dust for lack of rain, and dust storms shall destroy you.

25"The Lord will cause you to be defeated by your enemies. You will march out to battle gloriously, but flee before your enemies in utter confusion; and you will be tossed to and fro among all the nations of the earth. 26Your dead bodies will be food to the birds and wild animals, and no one will be there to chase them away.

27"He will send upon you Egyptian boils, tumors, scurvy, and itch, for none of which will there be a remedy. 28He will send madness, blindness, fear, and panic upon you. 29You shall grope in the bright sunlight just as the blind man gropes in darkness. You shall not prosper in anything you do; you will be oppressed and robbed continually, and nothing will save you.

30"Someone else will marry your fiancée; someone else will live in the house you build; someone else will eat the fruit of the vineyard you plant. 31Your oxen shall be butchered before your eyes, but you won't get a single bite of the meat. Your donkeys will be driven away as you watch and will never return to you again. Your sheep will be given to your enemies. And there will be no one to protect you. 32You will watch as your sons and daughters are taken away as slaves. Your heart will break with longing for them, but you will not be able to help them. 33A foreign nation you have not even heard of will eat the crops you will have worked so hard to grow. You will always be oppressed and crushed. 34You will go mad because of all the tragedy you see around you. 35The Lord will cover you with boils from head to foot.

36"He will exile you and the king you will choose to a nation to whom neither you nor your ancestors gave a second thought; and while in exile you shall worship gods of wood and stone! 37You will become an object of horror, a proverb and a byword among all the nations, for the Lord will thrust you away.

38"You will sow much but reap little, for the locusts will eat your crops. 39You will plant vineyards and care for them, but you won't eat the grapes or drink the wine, for worms will destroy the vines. 40Olive trees will be growing everywhere, but there won't be enough olive oil to anoint yourselves! For the trees will drop their fruit before it is matured. 41Your sons and daughters will be snatched away from you as slaves. 42The locusts shall destroy your trees and vines. 43Foreigners living among you shall become richer and richer while you become poorer and poorer. 44They shall lend to you, not you to them! They shall be the head and you shall be the tail!

45"All these curses shall pursue and overtake you until you are destroyed—all because you refuse to listen to the Lord your God. 46These horrors shall befall you and your descendants as a warning: 47,48You will become slaves to your enemies because of your failure to praise God for all that he has given you. The Lord will send your enemies against you, and you will be hungry, thirsty, naked, and in want of everything. A yoke of iron shall be placed around your neck until you are destroyed!

49"The Lord will bring a distant nation against you, swooping down upon you like an eagle; a nation whose language you don't understand—

RESPECTING GOD'S WARNINGS 27:15-26 These curses were a series of oaths, spoken by the priests and affirmed by the people, by which the people promised to stay away from wrong actions. By saying Amen, "So be it," the people took responsibility for their actions. Sometimes looking at a list of curses like this gives us the idea that God has a bad temper and is out to crush anyone who steps out of line. But we need to see these restrictions not as threats, but as loving warnings about the plain facts of life. Just as parents warn children to stay away from hot stoves and busy streets, God warns us to stay away from dangerous actions. Motivated by love and not anger, his strong words help us avoid the serious consequences that naturally result from neglecting God or wronging others. But God does not leave us with only curses or consequences. Immediately following these curses, we discover the great blessings (positive consequences) that come from living for God (28:1-14). These give us extra incentive to obey God's laws. While all these blessings may not come in our lifetime on earth, those who obey God will experience the fullness of his blessing when he establishes the new heaven and the new earth. **To begin the series of devotionals on RESPECTING GOD'S WARNINGS, turn to page 21.**

⁵⁰a nation of fierce and angry men who will have no mercy upon young or old. ⁵¹They will eat you out of house and home until your cattle and crops are gone. Your grain, new wine, olive oil, calves, and lambs will all disappear. ⁵²That nation will lay siege to your cities and knock down your highest walls—the walls you will trust to protect you. ⁵³You will even eat the flesh of your own sons and daughters in the terrible days of siege that lie ahead. ⁵⁴The most tenderhearted man among you will be utterly callous toward his own brother and his beloved wife and his children who are still alive. ⁵⁵He will refuse to give them a share of the flesh he is devouring—the flesh of his own children—because he is starving in the midst of the siege of your cities. ⁵⁶,⁵⁷The most tender and delicate woman among you—the one who would not so much as touch her feet to the ground—will refuse to share with her beloved husband, son, and daughter. She will hide from them the afterbirth and the new baby she has borne, so that she herself can eat them: so terrible will be the hunger during the siege and the awful distress caused by your enemies at your gates.

⁵⁸,⁵⁹"If you refuse to obey all the laws written in this book, thus refusing reverence to the glorious and fearful name of Jehovah your God, then Jehovah will send perpetual plagues upon you and upon your children. ⁶⁰He will bring upon you all the diseases of Egypt that you feared so much, and they shall plague the land. ⁶¹And that is not all! The Lord will bring upon you every sickness and plague there is, even those not mentioned in this book, until you are destroyed. ⁶²There will be few of you left, though before you were as numerous as stars. All this if you do not listen to the Lord your God.

⁶³"Just as the Lord has rejoiced over you and has done such wonderful things for you and has multiplied you, so the Lord at that time will rejoice in destroying you; and you shall disappear from the land. ⁶⁴For the Lord will scatter you among all the nations from one end of the earth to the other. There you will worship heathen gods that neither you nor your ancestors have known, gods made of wood and stone! ⁶⁵There among those nations you shall find no rest, but the Lord will give you trembling hearts, darkness, and bodies wasted from sorrow and fear. ⁶⁶Your lives will hang in doubt. You will live night and day in fear, and will have no reason to believe that you will see the morning light. ⁶⁷In the morning you will say, 'Oh, that night were here!' And in the evening you will say, 'Oh, that morning were here!' You will say this because of the awesome horrors surrounding you. ⁶⁸Then the Lord will send you back to Egypt in ships, a journey I promised you would never need to make again; and there you will offer to sell yourselves to your enemies as slaves—but no one will even want to buy you."

29 God's Covenant Reviewed

It was on the plains of Moab that Moses restated the covenant that the Lord had made with the people of Israel at Mount Horeb. ²,³He summoned all Israel before him and told them,

"You have seen with your own eyes the great plagues and mighty miracles that the Lord brought upon Pharaoh and his people in the land of Egypt. ⁴But even yet the Lord hasn't given you hearts that understand or eyes that see or ears that hear! ⁵For forty years God has led you through the wilderness, yet your clothes haven't become old, and your shoes haven't worn out! ⁶The reason he hasn't let you settle down to grow grain for bread or grapes for wine and strong drink is so that you would realize that it is the Lord your God who has been caring for you.

⁷"When we came here, King Sihon of Heshbon and King Og of Bashan came out against us in battle, but we destroyed them, ⁸and took their land and gave it to the tribes of Reuben and Gad and to the half-tribe of Manasseh as their inheritance. ⁹Therefore, obey the terms of this covenant so that you will prosper in everything you do. ¹⁰All of you—your leaders, the people, your judges, and your administrative officers—are standing today before the Lord your God, ¹¹along with your little ones and your wives and the foreigners that are among you—those who chop your wood and carry your water. ¹²You are standing here to enter into a contract with Jehovah your God, a contract he is making with you today. ¹³He wants to confirm you today as his people, and to confirm that he is your God, just as he promised your ancestors, Abraham, Isaac, and Jacob. ¹⁴,¹⁵This contract is not with you alone as you stand before him today, but with all future generations of Israel as well.

¹⁶"Surely you remember how we lived in the land of Egypt, and how as we left, we came safely through the territory of enemy nations. ¹⁷And you have seen their heathen idols made of wood, stone, silver, and gold.

AVOIDING SIN 29:18 Moses cautioned that the day the Hebrews chose to turn from God, a root would be planted that would produce bitter fruit. When we decide to do what we know is wrong, we plant an evil seed that begins to grow out of control, eventually producing a crop of sorrow and pain. But we can prevent those seeds of sin from taking root. If you have done something wrong, confess it to God and others immediately. If the seed never finds fertile soil, its bitter fruit will never ripen. **To begin the series of devotionals on AVOIDING SIN, turn to page 195.**

¹⁸The day that any of you—man or woman, family or tribe of Israel—begins to turn away from the Lord our God and desires to worship these gods of other nations, that day a root will be planted that will grow bitter and poisonous fruit.

¹⁹"Let no one blithely think, when he hears the warnings of this curse, 'I shall prosper even though I walk in my own stubborn way!' ²⁰For the Lord will not pardon! His anger and jealousy will be hot against that man. And all the curses written in this book shall lie heavily upon him, and the Lord will blot out his name from under heaven. ²¹The Lord will separate that man from all the tribes of Israel, to pour out upon him all the curses (which are recorded in this book) that befall those who break this contract. ²²Then your children and the generations to come and the foreigners that pass by from distant lands shall see the devastation of the land and the diseases the Lord will have sent upon it. ²³They will see that the whole land is alkali and salt, a burned over wasteland, unsown, without crops, without a shred of vegetation—just like Sodom and Gomorrah and Admah and Zeboiim, destroyed by the Lord in his anger.

²⁴"'Why has the Lord done this to his land?' the nations will ask. 'Why was he so angry?'

²⁵"And they will be told, 'Because the people of the land broke the contract made with them by Jehovah, the God of their ancestors, when he brought them out of the land of Egypt. ²⁶For they worshiped other gods, violating his express command. ²⁷That is why the anger of the Lord was hot against this land, so that all his curses (which are recorded in this book) broke forth upon them. ²⁸In great anger the Lord rooted them out of their land and threw them away into another land, where they still live today!'

²⁹"There are secrets the Lord your God has not revealed to us, but these words that he has revealed are for us and our children to obey forever.

30 Coming Back to God

"When all these things have happened to you—the blessings and the curses I have listed—you will meditate upon them as you are living among the nations where the Lord your God will have driven you. ²If at that time you want to return to the Lord your God, and you and your children have begun wholeheartedly to obey all of the commandments I have given you today, ³then the Lord your God will rescue you from your captivity! He will have mercy upon you and come and gather you out of all the nations where he will have scattered you. ⁴Though you are at the ends of the earth, he will go and find you and bring you back again ⁵ to the land of your ancestors. You shall possess the land again, and he will do you good and bless you even more than he did your ancestors! ⁶He will cleanse your hearts and the hearts of your children and of your children's children so that you will love the Lord your God with all your hearts and souls, and Israel shall come alive again!

⁷,⁸"If you return to the Lord and obey all the commandments that I command you today, the Lord your God will take his curses and turn them against your enemies—against those who hate you and persecute you. ⁹The Lord your God will prosper everything you do and give you many children and much cattle and wonderful crops; for the Lord will again rejoice over you as he did over your fathers. ¹⁰He will rejoice if you but obey the commandments written in this book of the law, and if you turn to the Lord your God with all your hearts and souls.

¹¹"Obeying these commandments is not something beyond your strength and reach; ¹²for these laws are not in the far heavens, so distant that you can't hear and obey them, and with no one to bring them down to you; ¹³nor are they beyond the ocean, so far that no one can bring you their message; ¹⁴but they are very close at hand—in your hearts and on your lips—so obey them.

¹⁵"Look, today I have set before you life and death, depending on whether you obey or disobey. ¹⁶I have commanded you today to love the Lord your God and to follow his paths and to keep his laws, so that you will live and become a great nation, and so that the Lord your God will bless you and the land you are about to possess. ¹⁷But if your hearts turn away and you won't listen—if you are drawn away to worship other gods— ¹⁸then I declare to you this day that you shall surely perish; you will not have a long, good life in the land you are going in to possess.

¹⁹"I call heaven and earth to witness against you that today I have set before you life or death, blessing or curse. Oh, that you would choose life; that you and your children might live! ²⁰Choose to love the Lord your God and to obey him and to cling to him, for he is your life and the length of your days. You will then be able to live safely in the land the Lord promised your ancestors, Abraham, Isaac, and Jacob."

31 Joshua Appointed Leader

After Moses had said all these things to the people of Israel, ²he told them, "I am now 120 years old! I am no longer able to lead you, for the Lord has told me that I shall not cross the Jordan River. ³But the Lord himself will lead you and will destroy the nations living there, and you shall overcome them. Joshua is your new commander, as the Lord has instructed. ⁴The Lord will destroy the nations living in the land, just as he destroyed Sihon and Og, the kings of the Amorites. ⁵The Lord will deliver over to you the people living there, and you shall destroy them as I have commanded you. ⁶Be strong! Be courageous! Do not be afraid of them! For the Lord your God will be with you. He will neither fail you nor forsake you."

⁷Then Moses called for Joshua and said to him, as all Israel watched, "Be strong! Be courageous! For you shall lead these people into the land promised by the Lord to their ancestors; see to it that they conquer it. ⁸Don't be afraid, for the Lord will go before you and will be with you; he will not fail nor forsake you."

⁹Then Moses wrote out the laws he had already delivered to the people and gave them to the priests, the sons of Levi, who carried the Ark containing the Ten Commandments of the Lord. Moses also gave copies of the laws to the elders of Israel. ¹⁰,¹¹The Lord commanded that these laws be read to all the people at the end of every seventh year—the Year of Release—at the Festival of Tabernacles, when all Israel would assemble before the Lord at the sanctuary.

¹²"Call them all together," the Lord instructed, "—men, women, children, and foreigners living among you—to hear the laws of God and to learn his will, so that you will reverence the Lord your God and obey his laws. ¹³Do this so that your little children who have not known these laws will hear them and learn how to revere the Lord your God as long as you live in the Promised Land."

¹⁴Then the Lord said to Moses, "The time has come when you must die. Summon Joshua and come into the Tabernacle where I can give him his instructions." So Moses and Joshua came and stood before the Lord.

¹⁵He appeared to them in a great cloud at the Tabernacle entrance, ¹⁶and said to Moses, "You shall die and join your ancestors. After you are gone, these people will begin worshiping foreign gods in the Promised Land. They will forget about me and break the contract I have made with them. ¹⁷Then my anger will flame out against them and I will abandon them, hiding my face from them, and they shall be destroyed. Terrible trouble will come upon them, so that they will say, 'God is no longer among us!' ¹⁸I will turn away from them because of their sins in worshiping other gods.

¹⁹"Now write down the words of this song, and teach it to the people of Israel as my warning to them. ²⁰When I have brought them into the land I promised their ancestors—a land 'flowing with milk and honey'—and when they have become fat and prosperous, and worship other gods and despise me and break my contract, ²¹and great disasters come upon them, then this song will remind them of the reason for their woes. (For this song will live from generation to generation.) I know now, even before they enter the land, what these people are like."

²²So, on that very day, Moses wrote down the words of the song and taught it to the Israelites. ²³Then he charged Joshua (son of Nun) to be strong and courageous and said to him, "You must bring the people of Israel into the land the Lord promised them; for the Lord says, 'I will be with you.'"

²⁴When Moses had finished writing down all the laws that are recorded in this book, ²⁵he instructed the Levites who carried the Ark containing the Ten Commandments ²⁶to put this book of the law beside the Ark, as a solemn warning to the people of Israel.

²⁷"For I know how rebellious and stubborn you are," Moses told them. "If even today, while I am still here with you, you are defiant rebels against the Lord, how much more rebellious will you be after my death! ²⁸Now summon all the elders and officers of your tribes so that I can speak to them, and call heaven and earth to witness against them. ²⁹I know that after my death you will utterly defile yourselves and turn away from God and his commands; and in the days to come evil will crush you for you will do what the Lord says is evil, making him very angry."

³⁰So Moses recited this entire song to the whole assembly of Israel:

32 Moses' Song

"Listen, O heavens and earth!
Listen to what I say!
²My words shall fall upon you
Like the gentle rain and dew,
Like rain upon the tender grass,
Like showers on the hillside.
³I will proclaim the greatness of the Lord.
How glorious he is! ⁴He is the Rock. His work
  is perfect.
Everything he does is just and fair.
He is faithful, without sin.
⁵But Israel has become corrupt,
Smeared with sin. They are no longer his;
They are a stubborn, twisted generation.
⁶Is this the way you treat Jehovah?
O foolish people,
Is not God your Father?
Has he not created you?
Has he not established you and made you
  strong?
⁷Remember the days of long ago!
(Ask your father and the aged men;

Family Devotions

☐ **DEVOTION 76**
DEALING WITH CHANGE

Read Deuteronomy 31:6-8

Dealing with Change
Memory Verse

We know that all that happens to us is working for our good if we love God and are fitting into his plans.
Romans 8:28

"Wish I were a plant," grumbled Billy as he helped his grandfather water the garden. "These plants are lucky. They get to stay here in the same place their whole lives."

"Not looking forward to moving, are you, Billy?" said Grandpa sympathetically. Billy's father had taken a new job in another state.

Billy poked his toe at a weed. "I'll have to make all new friends. Plus I'll have to get used to a new school." He sighed as he emptied the watering can.

"Let me show you something," said Grandpa. He led the way to some shelves beside the garage. "See these plants?" he said, pointing to some pots on the shelves.

Billy nodded. "They're all tomato plants," he observed. "But why are they all in different sized pots?"

"As they grow, I move them into larger containers," explained Grandpa. "A lot of people don't realize that the tomato plant is one of the few plants—if not the only plant—that is improved by transplanting. I transplant them two or three times, and it makes them stronger. The roots are better, and the whole plant is more fruitful." Grandpa paused, then he added, "Maybe the Lord is transplanting you to make you stronger, too."

"I'm not a plant!" protested Billy.

Grandpa chuckled. "No," he agreed, "but the Lord knows that we often grow stronger in difficult situations. They cause us to sink our roots deeper in him, and then we can be more fruitful for him." Grandpa squeezed Billy's shoulder. "Don't wilt from transplanting," he encouraged. "Let God strengthen you through it."

How About You?
Do you allow tough situations to make you stronger? Do you sink your roots deeper in the Lord? Or do you wilt? No matter where God has planted you, he'll make you strong if you'll let him. Why not thank God right now for the strength he has available for you, and determine to do good things for him! D. E. M.

• For the next devotional, turn to page 225. • For the next devotional on DEALING WITH CHANGE, turn to page 231.
• For notes on DEALING WITH CHANGE, see pages 56, 156, 288, 1186, and 1198.

They will tell you all about it.)
⁸When God divided up the world among the nations,
He gave each of them a supervising angel!
⁹But he appointed none for Israel;
For Israel was God's own personal possession!
¹⁰God protected them in the howling wilderness
As though they were the apple of his eye.
¹¹He spreads his wings over them,
Even as an eagle overspreads her young.
She carries them upon her wings—
As does the Lord his people!
¹²When the Lord alone was leading them,
And they lived without foreign gods,
¹³God gave them fertile hilltops,
Rolling, fertile fields,
Honey from the rock,
And olive oil from stony ground!
¹⁴He gave them milk and meat—
Choice Bashan rams, and goats—
And the finest of the wheat;
They drank the sparkling wine.
¹⁵But Israel was soon overfed;
Yes, fat and bloated;
Then, in plenty, they forsook their God.
They shrugged away the Rock of their salvation.
¹⁶Israel began to follow foreign gods,
And Jehovah was very angry;
He was jealous of his people.
¹⁷They sacrificed to heathen gods,
To new gods never before worshiped.
¹⁸They spurned the Rock who had made them,
Forgetting it was God who had given them birth.
¹⁹God saw what they were doing,
And detested them!
His sons and daughters were insulting him.
²⁰He said, 'I will abandon them;
See what happens to them then!
For they are a stubborn, faithless generation.
²¹They have made me very jealous of their idols,
Which are not gods at all.
Now I, in turn, will make them jealous
By giving my affections
To the foolish Gentile nations of the world.
²²For my anger has kindled a fire
That burns to the depths of the underworld,
Consuming the earth and all of its crops,
And setting its mountains on fire.
²³I will heap evils upon them
And shoot them down with my arrows.
²⁴I will waste them with hunger,
Burning fever, and fatal disease.
I will devour them! I will set wild beasts upon them,
To rip them apart with their teeth;
And deadly serpents
Crawling in the dust.
²⁵Outside, the enemies' sword—
Inside, the plague—
Shall terrorize young men and girls alike;
The baby nursing at the breast,
And aged men.
²⁶I had decided to scatter them to distant lands,
So that even the memory of them
Would disappear.
²⁷But then I thought,
"My enemies will boast,
'Israel is destroyed by our own might;
It was not the Lord
Who did it!'"
²⁸Israel is a stupid nation;
Foolish, without understanding.
²⁹Oh, that they were wise!
Oh, that they could understand!
Oh, that they would know what they are getting into!
³⁰How could one single enemy chase a thousand of them,
And two put ten thousand to flight,
Unless their Rock had abandoned them,
Unless the Lord had destroyed them?
³¹But the rock of other nations
Is not like our Rock;
Prayers to their gods are valueless.
³²They act like men of Sodom and Gomorrah:
Their deeds are bitter with poison;
³³They drink the wine of serpent venom.
³⁴But Israel is my special people,
Sealed as jewels within my treasury.
³⁵Vengeance is mine,
And I decree the punishment of all her enemies:
Their doom is sealed.
³⁶The Lord will see his people righted,
And will have compassion on them when they slip.
He will watch their power ebb away,
Both slave and free.
³⁷Then God will ask,
'Where are their gods—
The rocks they claimed to be their refuge?
³⁸Where are these gods now,
To whom they sacrificed their fat and wine?
Let those gods arise,
And help them!
³⁹Don't you see that I alone am God?
I kill and make live.
I wound and heal—
No one delivers from my power.
⁴⁰,⁴¹I raise my hand to heaven
And vow by my existence,

Family Devotions

☐ **Devotion 77**
Respecting Authority

Read Deuteronomy 31:12-13

Respecting Authority
Memory Verse

Children, obey your parents; this is the right thing to do because God has placed them in authority over you.
Ephesians 6:1

Christina ran into her bedroom and slammed the door. How unreasonable her mother could be! Christina wanted to go to the slumber party at Sarah's house, but her mother wouldn't let her go. "You know Sarah's family are not Christians," Mom had said, "and the girls are much older than you are and rather wild."

But Christina wouldn't listen. "You never give me any freedom," she had stormed. "You don't want me to have any fun!"

She was still sniffling when she heard a sound at her window. Looking up, she saw a bird beating its wings against the glass. It seemed to be trying to get inside. As she watched, her mother knocked on the door. "I have some clean laundry, Christina."

As Mom set the clothes on the dresser, she saw the bird beating at the glass. "Christina," Mom said softly, "open the window and let the poor bird in. It's cruel to keep him out when he desperately wants to get in."

"Mom, you've got to be kidding! He wouldn't know what to do once he got inside. He'd be trapped and frightened and wouldn't know how to get out again! He might get hurt."

"But, don't you want him to have his freedom?"

"He's got more space and freedom outside," Christina said grumpily.

Mom smiled and nodded. "So by saying no, you're really giving him freedom and protecting him," she said. "I know it doesn't make a lot of sense to you right now that I said no to the party, but God gave me the responsibility of protecting you. I don't want you to get caught in a situation where you might get hurt."

Christina looked at the foolish bird. "I still wish I could go to the party," she admitted, "but I know you said no because you love me. Even though I don't agree with you, I'll accept your decision."

"I do love you, Christina," Mom said as she came over and gave her daughter a hug.

How About You?
Do you feel that your parents are restricting your freedom by giving you rules and expecting you to obey? In love, they are actually protecting you from situations or things that could harm you. Trust their judgment and obey their decisions. True freedom includes living within bounds set up by God. *J. H.*

• For the next devotional, turn to page 231.   • For the next devotional on *Respecting Authority*, turn to page 247.
• For notes on *Respecting Authority*, see pages 311, 420, and 1182.

That I will whet the lightning of my sword!
And hurl my punishments upon my enemies!
⁴²My arrows shall be drunk with blood!
My sword devours the flesh and blood
Of all the slain and captives.
The heads of the enemy
Are gory with blood.'
⁴³Praise his people,
Gentile nations,
For he will avenge his people,
Taking vengeance on his enemies,
Purifying his land
And his people."

⁴⁴,⁴⁵When Moses and Joshua had recited all the words of this song to the people, ⁴⁶Moses made these comments:

"Meditate upon all the laws I have given you today, and pass them on to your children. ⁴⁷These laws are not mere words—they are your life! Through obeying them you will live long, plentiful lives in the land you are going to possess across the Jordan River."

⁴⁸That same day, the Lord said to Moses, ⁴⁹"Go to Mount Nebo in the Abarim mountains, in the land of Moab across from Jericho. Climb to its heights and look out across the land of Canaan, the land I am giving to the people of Israel. ⁵⁰After you see the land, you must die and join your ancestors, just as Aaron, your brother, died in Mount Hor and joined them. ⁵¹For you dishonored me among the people of Israel at the springs of Meribah-kadesh, in the wilderness of Zin. ⁵²You will see spread out before you the land I am giving the people of Israel, but you will not enter it."

33 Moses Blesses All the People

This is the blessing Moses, the man of God, gave to the people of Israel before his death:

²"The Lord came to us at Mount Sinai,
And dawned upon us from Mount Seir;
He shone from Mount Paran,
Surrounded by ten thousands of holy angels,
And with flaming fire at his right hand.
³How he loves his people—
His holy ones are in his hands.
They followed in your steps, O Lord.
They have received their directions from you.
⁴The laws I have given
Are your precious possession.
⁵The Lord became king in Jerusalem,
Elected by a convocation of the leaders of the tribes!
⁶Let Reuben live forever
And may his tribe increase!"

⁷And Moses said of Judah:

"O Lord, hear the cry of Judah
And unite him with Israel;
Fight for him against his enemies."

⁸Then Moses said concerning the tribe of Levi:

"Give to godly Levi
Your Urim and your Thummim.
You tested Levi at Massah and at Meribah;
⁹He obeyed your instructions
[and destroyed many sinners],
Even his own children, brothers, fathers, and mothers.
¹⁰The Levites shall teach God's laws to Israel
And shall work before you at the incense altar
And the altar of burnt offering.
¹¹O Lord, prosper the Levites
And accept the work they do for you.
Crush those who are their enemies;
Don't let them rise again."

¹²Concerning the tribe of Benjamin, Moses said:

"He is beloved of God
And lives in safety beside him.
God surrounds him with his loving care,
And preserves him from every harm."

¹³Concerning the tribe of Joseph, he said:

"May his land be blessed by God
With the choicest gifts of heaven
And of the earth that lies below.
¹⁴May he be blessed
With the best of what the sun makes grow;
Growing richly month by month,
¹⁵With the finest of mountain crops
And of the everlasting hills.
¹⁶May he be blessed with the best gifts
Of the earth and its fullness,
And with the favor of God who appeared
In the burning bush.
Let all these blessings come upon Joseph,
The prince among his brothers.
¹⁷He is a young bull in strength and splendor,
With the strong horns of a wild ox
To push against the nations everywhere;
This is my blessing on the multitudes of Ephraim
And the thousands of Manasseh."

¹⁸Of the tribe of Zebulun, Moses said:

"Rejoice, O Zebulun, you outdoorsmen,
And Issachar, you lovers of your tents;
¹⁹They shall summon the people

To celebrate their sacrifices with them.
Lo, they taste the riches of the sea
And the treasures of the sand."

[20] Concerning the tribe of Gad, Moses said:

"A blessing upon those who help Gad.
He crouches like a lion,
With savage arm and face and head.
[21] He chose the best of the land for himself
Because it is reserved for a leader.
He led the people
Because he carried out God's penalties for
    Israel."

[22] Of the tribe of Dan, Moses said:

"Dan is like a lion's cub
Leaping out from Bashan."

[23] Of the tribe of Naphtali, Moses said:

"O Naphtali, you are satisfied
With all the blessings of the Lord;
The Mediterranean coast and the Negeb
Are your home."

[24] Of the tribe of Asher:

"Asher is a favorite son,
Esteemed above his brothers;
He bathes his feet in oil.
[25] May you be protected with strong bolts
Of iron and bronze,
And may your strength match the length of
    your days!
[26] There is none like the God of Jerusalem—
He descends from the heavens
In majestic splendor to help you.
[27] The eternal God is your Refuge,
And underneath are the everlasting arms.
He thrusts out your enemies before you;
It is he who cries, 'Destroy them!'

[28] So Israel dwells safely,
Prospering in a land of corn and wine,
While the gentle rains descend from heaven.
[29] What blessings are yours, O Israel!
Who else has been saved by the Lord?
He is your shield and your helper!
He is your excellent sword!
Your enemies shall bow low before you,
And you shall trample on their backs!"

34 Moses Dies

Then Moses climbed from the plains of Moab to Pisgah Peak in Mount Nebo, across from Jericho. And the Lord pointed out to him the Promised Land, as they gazed out across Gilead as far as Dan:

[2] "There is Naphtali; and there is Ephraim and Manasseh; and across there, Judah, extending to the Mediterranean Sea; [3] there is the Negeb; and the Jordan Valley; and Jericho, the city of palm trees; and Zoar," the Lord told him.

[4] "It is the Promised Land," the Lord told Moses. "I promised Abraham, Isaac, and Jacob that I would give it to their descendants. Now you have seen it, but you will not enter it."

[5] So Moses, the disciple of the Lord, died in the land of Moab as the Lord had said. [6] The Lord buried him in a valley near Beth-peor in Moab, but no one knows the exact place.

[7] Moses was 120 years old when he died, yet his eyesight was perfect and he was as strong as a young man. [8] The people of Israel mourned for him for thirty days on the plains of Moab.

[9] Joshua (son of Nun) was full of the spirit of wisdom, for Moses had laid his hands upon him; so the people of Israel obeyed him and followed the commandments the Lord had given to Moses.

[10] There has never been another prophet like Moses, for the Lord talked to him face to face. [11,12] And at God's command he performed amazing miracles that have never been equaled.

Joshua

DURING ALL the years the Israelites traveled in the desert, Joshua had been Moses' right-hand man. Now Moses was dead, and God chose Joshua to lead the hundreds of thousands of Israelites.

The book of Joshua shows how God keeps his promises. He promised the Israelites a country of their own. He promised to keep them safe through forty years in the desert. He promised to fight for them in each city so they could see his power.

To keep these promises, God made the sun stand still. He made the walls of Jericho fall down. He used an unlikely person—a woman in an enemy city—to help the Israelite spies.

Joshua and the Israelites tried to keep their promises to God, too. They had promised to follow God and obey him. As a symbol of their trust in God, they set up a monument of stones when they crossed into their new country. They trusted God in most of their battles. They renewed their covenant with God to serve only him.

God still wants his people to trust him and serve him only. Let's learn from Joshua how faithful and strong God is.

"Be Brave, Joshua!"

After the death of Moses, the Lord's disciple, God spoke to Moses' assistant, whose name was Joshua (the son of Nun), and said to him,

²"Now that my disciple is dead, [you are the new leader of Israel]. Lead my people across the Jordan River into the Promised Land. ³I say to you what I said to Moses: 'Wherever you go will be part of the land of Israel—⁴all the way from the Negeb desert in the south to the Lebanon mountains in the north, and from the Mediterranean Sea in the west to the Euphrates River in the east, including all the land of the Hittites.' ⁵No one will be able to oppose you as long as you live, for I will be with you just as I was with Moses; I will not abandon you or fail to help you.

⁶"Be strong and brave, for you will be a successful leader of my people; and they shall conquer all the land I promised to their ancestors. ⁷You need only to be strong and courageous and to obey to the letter every law Moses gave you, for if you are careful to obey every one of them, you will be

successful in everything you do. ⁸Constantly remind the people about these laws, and you yourself must think about them every day and every night so that you will be sure to obey all of them. For only then will you succeed. ⁹Yes, be bold and strong! Banish fear and doubt! For remember, the Lord your God is with you wherever you go."

¹⁰,¹¹Then Joshua issued instructions to the leaders of Israel to tell the people to get ready to cross the Jordan River. "In three days we will go across and conquer and live in the land which God has given us!" he told them.

¹²,¹³Then he summoned the leaders of the tribes of Reuben, Gad, and the half-tribe of Manasseh and reminded them of their agreement with Moses: "The Lord your God has given you a homeland here on the east side of the Jordan River," Moses had told them, ¹⁴so your wives and children and cattle may remain here, but your troops, fully armed, must lead the other tribes across the Jordan River to help them conquer their territory on the other side; ¹⁵stay with them until they complete the conquest. Only then may you settle down here on the east side of the Jordan."

¹⁶To this they fully agreed and pledged themselves to obey Joshua as their commander-in-chief.

¹⁷,¹⁸"We will obey you just as we obeyed Moses," they assured him, "and may the Lord your God be with you as he was with Moses. If anyone, no matter who, rebels against your commands, he shall die. So lead on with courage and strength!"

2 Spies Visit Jericho

Then Joshua sent two spies from the Israeli camp at Acacia to cross the river and check out the situation on the other side, especially at Jericho. They arrived at an inn operated by a woman named Rahab, who was a prostitute. They were planning to spend the night there, ²but someone informed the king of Jericho that two Israelis who were suspected of being spies had arrived in the city that evening. ³He dispatched a police squadron to Rahab's home, demanding that she surrender them.

"They are spies," he explained. "They have been sent by the Israeli leaders to discover the best way to attack us."

⁴But she had hidden them, so she told the officer in charge, "The men were here earlier, but I didn't know they were spies. ⁵They left the city at dusk as the city gates were about to close, and I don't know where they went. If you hurry, you can probably catch up with them!"

⁶But actually she had taken them up to the roof and hidden them beneath piles of flax that were drying there. ⁷So the constable and his men went all the way to the Jordan River looking for them; meanwhile, the city gates were kept shut. ⁸Rahab went up to talk to the men before they retired for the night.

⁹"I know perfectly well that your God is going to give my country to you," she told them. "We are all afraid of you; everyone is terrified if the word *Israel* is even mentioned. ¹⁰For we have heard how the Lord made a path through the Red Sea for you when you left Egypt! And we know what you did to Sihon and Og, the two Amorite kings east of the Jordan, and how you ruined their land and completely destroyed their people. ¹¹No wonder we are afraid of you! No one has any fight left in him after hearing things like that, for your God is the supreme God of heaven, not just an ordinary god. ¹²,¹³Now I beg for this one thing: Swear to me by the sacred name of your God that when Jericho is conquered you will let me live, along with my father and mother, my brothers and sisters, and all their families. This is only fair after the way I have helped you."

¹⁴The men agreed. "If you won't betray us, we'll see to it that you and your family aren't harmed," they promised. ¹⁵"We'll defend you with our lives." Then, since her house was on top of the city wall, she let them down by a rope from a window.

¹⁶"Escape to the mountains," she told them. "Hide there for three days until the men who are searching for you have returned; then go on your way."

¹⁷,¹⁸But before they left, the men had said to her, "We cannot be responsible for what happens to you unless this rope is hanging from this window and unless all your relatives—your father, mother, brothers, and anyone else—are here inside the house. ¹⁹If they go out into the street, we assume no responsibility whatsoever; but we swear that no one inside this house will be killed or injured. ²⁰However, if you betray us, then this oath will no longer bind us in any way."

²¹"I accept your terms," she replied. And she left the scarlet rope hanging from the window.

²²The spies went up into the mountains and stayed there three days, until the men who were chasing them had returned to the city after searching everywhere along the road without success. ²³Then the two spies came down from the mountain and crossed the river and reported to Joshua all that had happened to them.

²⁴"The Lord will certainly give us the entire land," they said, "for all the people over there are scared to death of us."

3 Crossing the Jordan River

Early the next morning Joshua and all the people of Israel left Acacia and arrived that evening at the banks of the Jordan River, where they camped for a few days before crossing.

²⁻⁴On the third day officers went through the

FAMILY DEVOTIONS

☐ DEVOTION 78
DEALING WITH CHANGE

Read Joshua 1:1-5

Dealing with Change
Memory Verse

We know that all that happens to us is working for our good if we love God and are fitting into his plans.
Romans 8:28

At the close of the church service, Carrie listened in disbelief as Pastor Allen said, "After much prayer, we feel the Lord is calling our family to serve him at an Indian reservation. We will be leaving in a month." Carrie was horrified at the news. That meant Becky would move, too. The pastor's daughter, Becky, was her best friend.

When the service ended, Carrie dashed out to the car. She was too upset to even speak to Becky. "How could Pastor Allen do this?" Carrie sobbed on the way home.

"He must obey the Lord's leading," Dad said gently.

"But I don't want him to leave," Carrie wailed. "Becky's my best friend. They belong here!"

"Not if the Lord is calling them somewhere else," Dad replied.

Carrie was upset all day. At bedtime Mom gave her a hug. "Honey," she said, "your old crib is set up in the guest room. Why don't you sleep in it tonight?" Carrie stared at her mother. "I remember how you fought against the idea of moving out of it when you got your first bed," Mom continued, "so I thought maybe it would make you feel better to sleep in it again tonight."

Carrie laughed. "You can't be serious, Mom! I don't want to sleep in a crib anymore. Besides, I wouldn't fit."

Mom smiled. "That's true," she agreed. "Part of growing up means leaving behind old things and adjusting to new ways. People may change or move away, but God is still with us, planning things for our good. And keeping the Allens here apparently doesn't fit into God's plan."

"Right," said Dad. "Let's thank God for the good years we've had with them and then try to make their last days at our church extra special."

"I guess you're right," Carrie said slowly. "It won't be easy for Becky, either, but I'll help her all I can."

How About You?
Are you faced with a move, a new family member, or a new church or school? Are you angry about changes or new circumstances in your life? It isn't easy to let the familiar go, but God will still be with you in your new situation, just as he promised to be with Joshua. *J. H.*

• For the next devotional, turn to page 233. • For the next devotional on *DEALING WITH CHANGE*, turn to page 233.
• For notes on *DEALING WITH CHANGE*, see pages 56, 156, 288, 1186, and 1198.

camp giving these instructions: "When you see the priests carrying the Ark of God, follow them. You have never before been where we are going now, so they will guide you. However, stay about a half mile behind, with a clear space between you and the Ark; be sure that you don't get any closer."

⁵Then Joshua told the people to purify themselves. "For tomorrow," he said, "the Lord will do a great miracle."

⁶In the morning Joshua ordered the priests, "Take up the Ark and lead us across the river!" And so they started out.

⁷"Today," the Lord told Joshua, "I will give you great honor, so that all Israel will know that I am with you just as I was with Moses. ⁸Instruct the priests who are carrying the Ark to stop at the edge of the river."

⁹Then Joshua summoned all the people and told them, "Come and listen to what the Lord your God has said. ¹⁰Today you are going to know for sure that the living God is among you and that he will, without fail, drive out the Canaanites, Hittites, Hivites, Perizzites, Girgashites, Amorites, and Jebusites—all the people who now live in the land you will soon occupy. ¹¹Think of it! The Ark of God, who is Lord of the whole earth, will lead you across the river!

¹²"Now select twelve men, one from each tribe, for a special task. ¹³,¹⁴When the priests who are carrying the Ark touch the water with their feet, the river will stop flowing as though held back by a dam, and will pile up as though against an invisible wall!" Now it was the harvest season and the Jordan was overflowing all its banks; but as the people set out to cross the river and as the feet of the priests who were carrying the Ark touched the water at the river's edge, ¹⁵,¹⁶suddenly, far up the river at the city of Adam, near Zarethan, the water began piling up as though against a dam! And the water below that point flowed on to the Dead Sea until the riverbed was empty. Then all the people crossed at a spot where the river was close to the city of Jericho, ¹⁷and the priests who were carrying the Ark stood on dry ground in the middle of the Jordan and waited as all the people passed by.

4

When all the people were safely across, the Lord said to Joshua,

²,³"Tell the twelve men chosen for a special task, one from each tribe, each to take a stone from where the priests are standing in the middle of the Jordan, and to carry them out and pile them up as a monument at the place where you camp tonight."

⁴So Joshua summoned the twelve men ⁵and told them, "Go out into the middle of the Jordan where the Ark is. Each of you is to carry out a stone on your shoulder—twelve stones in all, one for each of the twelve tribes. ⁶We will use them to build a monument so that in the future, when your children ask, 'What is this monument for?' ⁷you can tell them, 'It is to remind us that the Jordan River stopped flowing when the Ark of God went across!' The monument will be a permanent reminder to the people of Israel of this amazing miracle."

⁸So the men did as Joshua told them. They took twelve stones from the middle of the Jordan river—one for each tribe, just as the Lord had commanded Joshua. They carried them to the place where they were camped for the night and constructed a monument there. ⁹Joshua also built another monument of twelve stones in the middle of the river, at the place where the priests were standing; and it is there to this day. ¹⁰The priests who were carrying the Ark stood in the middle of the river until all these instructions of the Lord, which had been given to Joshua by Moses, had been carried out. Meanwhile, the people had hurried across the riverbed, ¹¹and when everyone was over, the people watched the priests carry the Ark up out of the riverbed.

¹²,¹³The troops of Reuben, Gad, and the half-tribe of Manasseh—fully armed as Moses had instructed, and forty thousand strong—led the other tribes of the Lord's army across to the plains of Jericho.

¹⁴It was a tremendous day for Joshua! The Lord made him great in the eyes of all the people of Israel, and they revered him as much as they had Moses and respected him deeply all the rest of his life. ¹⁵,¹⁶For it was Joshua who, at the Lord's command, issued the orders to the priests carrying the Ark.

"Come up from the riverbed," the Lord now told him to command them.

¹⁷So Joshua issued the order. ¹⁸And as soon as the priests came out, the water poured down again as usual and overflowed the banks of the river as before! ¹⁹This miracle occurred on the 25th of March. That day the entire nation crossed the Jordan River and camped in Gilgal at the eastern edge of the city of Jericho; ²⁰and there the twelve stones from the Jordan were piled up as a monument.

²¹Then Joshua explained again the purpose of the stones: "In the future," he said, "when your children ask you why these stones are here and what they mean, ²²you are to tell them that these stones are a reminder of this amazing miracle—that the nation of Israel crossed the Jordan River on dry ground! ²³Tell them how the Lord our God dried up the river right before our eyes and then kept it dry until we were all across! It is the same

Family Devotions

☐ DEVOTION 79

DEALING WITH CHANGE

Read Joshua 3:1-5, 12-17

Dealing with Change
Memory Verse

We know that all that happens to us is working for our good if we love God and are fitting into his plans.
Romans 8:28

Jan clasped her hands together nervously as the plane taxied down the runway. She had always wanted to fly, and here she was—flying with her brother, Don, to visit their grandmother. But now she was nervous.

After they were airborne, Jan didn't relax at all. "Do the engines sound funny?" she asked several times. "Should we be flying so high? We're not going to go through clouds again, are we? What if there's another plane in the clouds? Won't we crash?"

"Would you feel better if *you* were flying the plane?" Don finally asked in disgust. "I think the pilot knows what he's doing. I'm having fun."

"Me, too," said Jan, but she was very glad when they were finally back on solid ground.

"Did you have a good flight?" asked Grandma when she met them at the gate.

Don nodded. "I did. But Jan was nervous as a cat. I told her she should take over for the pilot. I'm glad she didn't, though, because then I'd have been nervous."

"I guess so!" exclaimed Grandma, putting an arm around Jan's shoulders. "I'm afraid we all lack trust in our pilot from time to time."

Jan looked at Grandma in surprise. "Are you afraid of flying too, Grandma?"

Grandma smiled. "Not really," she said. "I was thinking of how we sometimes fail to trust our pilot through life. Do you know who I mean?"

Jan nodded. "God," she said.

"Yes," said Grandma. "Of course, the airplane pilot wouldn't have let you take over the flight because it would have meant disaster. God does give us the choice—but it's foolish for us to try to take over."

How About You?
Are you enjoying your trip through life? Or do you fret about things that happen over which you have no control? Trust God. Think about how much he loves you. Whatever he leads you into will be best for you! H. M.

• For the next devotional, turn to page 235. • For the next devotional on DEALING WITH CHANGE, turn to page 673.
• For notes on DEALING WITH CHANGE, see pages 56, 156, 288, 1186, and 1198.

thing the Lord did forty years ago at the Red Sea! ²⁴He did this so that all the nations of the earth will realize that Jehovah is the mighty God, and so that all of you will worship him forever."

5 Joshua Circumcises the Men

When the nations west of the Jordan River—the Amorites and Canaanites who lived along the Mediterranean coast—heard that the Lord had dried up the Jordan River so the people of Israel could cross, their courage melted away completely and they were paralyzed with fear.

²,³The Lord then told Joshua to set aside a day to circumcise the entire male population of Israel. (It was the second time in Israel's history that this was done.) The Lord instructed them to manufacture flint knives for this purpose. The place where the circumcision rite took place was named "The Hill of the Foreskins." ⁴,⁵The reason for this second circumcision ceremony was that although when Israel left Egypt all of the men who had been old enough to bear arms had been circumcised, that entire generation had died during the years in the wilderness, and none of the boys born since that time had been circumcised. ⁶For the nation of Israel had traveled back and forth across the wilderness for forty years until all the men who had been old enough to bear arms when they left Egypt were dead; they had not obeyed the Lord, and he vowed that he wouldn't let them enter the land he had promised to Israel—a land that "flowed with milk and honey." ⁷So now Joshua circumcised their children—the men who had grown up to take their fathers' places.

⁸,⁹And the Lord said to Joshua, "Today I have ended your shame of not being circumcised." So the place where this was done was called Gilgal (meaning, "to end"), and is still called that today. After the ceremony the entire nation rested in camp until the raw flesh of their wounds had been healed.

¹⁰While they were camped at Gilgal on the plains of Jericho, they celebrated the Passover during the evening of April first. ¹¹,¹²The next day they began to eat from the gardens and grain fields which they invaded, and they made unleavened bread. The following day no manna fell, and it was never seen again! So from that time on they lived on the crops of Canaan.

¹³As Joshua was sizing up the city of Jericho, a man appeared nearby with a drawn sword. Joshua strode over to him and demanded, "Are you friend or foe?"

¹⁴"I am the Commander-in-Chief of the Lord's army," he replied.

Joshua fell to the ground before him and worshiped him and said, "Give me your commands."

¹⁵"Take off your shoes," the Commander told him, "for this is holy ground." And Joshua did.

6 The Battle for Jericho

The gates of Jericho were kept tightly shut because the people were afraid of the Israelis; no one was allowed to go in or out.

²But the Lord said to Joshua, "Jericho and its king and all its mighty warriors are already defeated, for I have given them to you! ³,⁴Your entire army is to walk around the city once a day for six days, followed by seven priests walking ahead of the Ark, each carrying a trumpet made from a ram's horn. On the seventh day you are to walk around the city seven times, with the priests blowing their trumpets. ⁵Then, when they give one long, loud blast, all the people are to give a mighty shout, and the walls of the city will fall down; then move in upon the city from every direction."

⁶⁻⁹So Joshua summoned the priests and gave them their instructions: the armed men would lead the procession, followed by seven priests blowing continually on their trumpets. Behind them would come the priests carrying the Ark, followed by a rear guard.

¹⁰"Let there be complete silence except for the trumpets," Joshua commanded. "Not a single word from any of you until I tell you to shout; then *shout!*"

¹¹The Ark was carried around the city once that day, after which everyone returned to the camp again and spent the night there. ¹²⁻¹⁴At dawn the next morning they went around again and returned again to the camp. They followed this pattern for six days.

¹⁵At dawn of the seventh day they started out again, but this time they went around the city not once, but seven times. ¹⁶The

---

BECOMING MORE LIKE JESUS 6:21 Why did God demand that the people of Israel destroy almost everyone and everything in Jericho? He was carrying out severe judgment against the wickedness of the Canaanites. This judgment, or "ban," usually required that everything be destroyed (Deuteronomy 12:2-3; 13:12-18). Because of their evil practices and their idolatry, the Canaanites were a stronghold of rebellion against God. If this threat was not removed, it would affect all Israel like a cancerous growth (which is the sad story of the book of Judges).

God's purpose in all this was to keep the people's faith and religion pure. He did not want the loot to cause Israel to be reminded of Canaanite practices. God desires purity in each of us as well. He wants us to clean up our lives and begin to reflect Christ when we begin a new life with him. We must not let the desire for personal gain distract us from our spiritual purpose. We must also reject any objects that commemorate a life lived in rebellion to God. **To begin the series of devotionals on BECOMING MORE LIKE JESUS, turn to page 131.**

Family Devotions

☐ DEVOTION 80
RECEIVING CHRIST AS SAVIOR

Read Joshua 2:1-15; 6:22-25

Receiving Christ as Savior
Memory Verse

For God loved the world so much that he gave his only Son so that anyone who believes in him shall not perish but have eternal life.
John 3:16

One Sunday morning at the church Jeremy attended, the pastor made an announcement. "We have a visitor with us today—Mr. Peter Black," he said. "Mr. Black would like to share his testimony of what the Lord has done in his life."

As the man stood up and began to speak, Jeremy could hardly believe his ears. Why, this man had been a criminal—in and out of prison for about twenty years! Now he was a Christian and spent most of his free time telling other people about Jesus. *How exciting!* thought Jeremy. *I wish I had a testimony like that!*

After church Jeremy's parents invited Mr. Black to their home for dinner. As they sat at the table, the guest smiled at Jeremy and said, "Your mother tells me that you're a Christian, too."

"That's right," said Jeremy, feeling embarrassed. "I was only five when I asked Jesus into my heart. I didn't have any really big sins in my life, so I don't have an exciting story to tell like you do."

A sad look came over Mr. Black's face. "Son, let me tell you something," he said. "I am forty-two years old. I have spent nearly half of my life in jail. Because of my prison record, I have a hard time finding a job. I have been married and divorced twice and have three children who hardly even know me. My health is poor because of all the drinking I did over the years. You see," he continued, "although I finally did accept the Lord, that didn't undo all the terrible consequences of the sins in my life. Be thankful that you came to know him early!"

I do thank you, Lord, Jeremy prayed silently. *Thank you for saving me as a little boy—so that I have a whole life ahead to use for you!*

How About You?
It's wonderful when someone like the man in this story or Rahab, whom you read about in today's Scripture, comes to know the Lord, but it's even better when you accept Christ as your Savior at a young age. If you have, take time to thank him now, and determine to live your whole life in his service. If you've put off accepting the Lord, don't wait any longer. Accept him today. S. K.

• For the next devotional, turn to page 237. • For the next devotional on RECEIVING CHRIST AS SAVIOR, turn to page 301. • For notes on RECEIVING CHRIST AS SAVIOR, see pages 839, 842, 1146, 1234, and 1240.

seventh time, as the priests blew a long, loud trumpet blast, Joshua yelled to the people, *"Shout!* The Lord has given us the city!"

17(He had told them previously, "Kill everyone except Rahab the prostitute and anyone in her house, for she protected our spies. 18Don't take any loot, for everything is to be destroyed. If it isn't, disaster will fall upon the entire nation of Israel. 19But all the silver and gold and the utensils of bronze and iron will be dedicated to the Lord and must be brought into his treasury.")

20So when the people heard the trumpet blast, they shouted as loud as they could. And suddenly the walls of Jericho crumbled and fell before them, and the people of Israel poured into the city from every side and captured it! 21They destroyed everything in it—men and women, young and old; oxen; sheep; donkeys—everything.

22Meanwhile Joshua had said to the two spies, "Keep your promise. Go and rescue the prostitute and everyone with her."

23The young men found her and rescued her, along with her father, mother, brothers, and other relatives who were with her. Arrangements were made for them to live outside the camp of Israel. 24Then the Israelis burned the city and everything in it except that the silver and gold and the bronze and iron utensils were kept for the Lord's treasury. 25Thus Joshua saved Rahab the prostitute and her relatives who were with her in the house, and they still live among the Israelites because she hid the spies sent to Jericho by Joshua.

26Then Joshua declared a terrible curse upon anyone who might rebuild Jericho, warning that when the foundation was laid, the builder's oldest son would die, and when the gates were set up, his youngest son would die.

27So the Lord was with Joshua, and his name became famous everywhere.

7 Achan Disobeys God

But there was sin among the Israelis. God's command to destroy everything except that which was reserved for the Lord's treasury was disobeyed. For Achan (the son of Carmi, grandson of Zabdi, and great-grandson of Zerah, of the tribe of Judah) took some loot for himself, and the Lord was very angry with the entire nation of Israel because of this.

2Soon after Jericho's defeat, Joshua sent some of his men to spy on the city of Ai, east of Bethel.

3Upon their return they told Joshua, "It's a small city and it won't take more than two or three thousand of us to destroy it; there's no point in all of us going there."

4So approximately three thousand soldiers were sent—and they were soundly defeated. 5About thirty-six of the Israelis were killed during the attack, and many others died while being chased by the men of Ai as far as the quarries. The Israeli army was paralyzed with fear at this turn of events. 6Joshua and the elders of Israel tore their clothing and lay prostrate before the Ark of the Lord until evening, with dust on their heads.

7Joshua cried out to the Lord, "O Jehovah, why have you brought us over the Jordan River if you are going to let the Amorites kill us? Why weren't we content with what we had? Why didn't we stay on the other side? 8O Lord, what am I to do now that Israel has fled from her enemies! 9For when the Canaanites and the other nearby nations hear about it, they will surround us and attack us and wipe us out. And then what will happen to the honor of your great name?"

10,11But the Lord said to Joshua, "Get up off your face! Israel has sinned and disobeyed my commandment and has taken loot when I said it was not to be taken; and they have not only taken it, they have lied about it and have hidden it among their belongings. 12That is why the people of Israel are being defeated. That is why your men are running from their enemies—for they are cursed. I will not stay with you any longer unless you completely rid yourselves of this sin.

13"Get up! Tell the people, 'Each of you must undergo purification rites in preparation for tomorrow, for the Lord your God of Israel says that someone has stolen from him, and you cannot defeat your enemies until you deal with this sin. 14In the morning you must come by tribes, and the Lord will point out the tribe to which the guilty man belongs. And that tribe must come by its clans and the Lord will point out the guilty clan; and the clan must come by its families, and then each member of the guilty family must come one by one. 15And the one who has stolen that which belongs to the Lord shall be burned with fire, along with everything he has, for he has violated the covenant of the Lord and has brought calamity upon all of Israel.'"

16So, early the next morning, Joshua brought the tribes of Israel before the Lord, and the tribe of Judah was indicated. 17Then he brought the clans of Judah, and the clan of Zerah was singled out. Then the families of that clan were brought before the Lord and the family of Zabdi was indicated. 18Zabdi's family was brought man by man, and his grandson Achan was found to be the guilty one.

19Joshua said to Achan, "My son, give glory to the God of Israel and make your confession. Tell me what you have done."

20Achan replied, "I have sinned against the Lord, the God of Israel. 21For I saw a beautiful robe imported from Babylon, and some silver

FAMILY DEVOTIONS

☐ DEVOTION 81

STANDING FOR RIGHTEOUSNESS

Read Joshua 7:1-12

"You didn't say much at supper tonight, Kev," said Travis, a high schooler, to his younger brother.

Kevin scowled. "I'm ticked at Mom. She blew up at me in front of my friends today."

"Boy, that's hard," said Travis. "What did you do?"

"Nothin'. We were *helping* Mr. Gomez clean his yard."

"Are you sure you weren't just messing around in Mr. Gomez's stuff?" asked Travis gently.

"You sound like Mom," said Kevin. "Mr. Gomez asked my friends and me if we could do some straightening up for him out back. But later when Mom saw us, she started yelling at us to leave Mr. Gomez's yard alone—she didn't even give me a chance to explain."

"Kev, it's hard when we take punches for something we didn't do. But you're throwing some punches, too. You're holding a grudge against Mom."

"That's not as bad as what she did," interrupted Kevin.

"Look, I helped you with your Sunday school take-home paper yesterday. What was the lesson in the puzzle?"

Kevin thought and then said slowly, "To forgive people who hurt us—because that pleases God."

"That's right. Kevin, we all do things that hurt each other sometimes—even in our family," explained Travis. "Wouldn't it be awful if we all held grudges for everything we did wrong? You need to forgive Mom."

Kevin looked thoughtful. "I guess you're right."

There was a knock at the bedroom door. Mom stuck her head in.

"Travis, could I talk to Kevin alone, please?" she asked.

"Sure, Mom," said Travis, getting up. As he started to close the door, he heard his mom saying, "Kevin, I was already feeling bad about losing my temper with you this afternoon when Mr. Gomez called just now. Can you forgive me—"

Travis smiled as he shut the door.

Standing for Righteousness Memory Verse

For the eyes of the Lord search back and forth across the whole earth, looking for people whose hearts are perfect toward him, so that he can show his great power in helping them.
2 Chronicles 16:9

How About You?
Do the wrong things you do seem small compared to the "big sins" of people around you? Achan thought the loot he took and the lies he told were small, but to God they were important. What are some ways you can please God even in the little things? J. A. G.

• For the next devotional, turn to page 239. • For the next devotional on STANDING FOR RIGHTEOUSNESS, turn to page 567. • For notes on STANDING FOR RIGHTEOUSNESS, see pages 62, 298, 371, 678, and 1948.

worth $200, and a bar of gold worth $500. I wanted them so much that I took them, and they are hidden in the ground beneath my tent, with the silver buried deeper than the rest."

²²So Joshua sent some men to search for the loot. They ran to the tent and found the stolen goods hidden there just as Achan had said, with the silver buried beneath the rest. ²³They brought it all to Joshua and laid it on the ground in front of him. ²⁴Then Joshua and all the Israelites took Achan, the silver, the robe, the wedge of gold, his sons, his daughters, his oxen, donkeys, sheep, his tent, and everything he had, and brought them to the valley of Achor.

²⁵Then Joshua said to Achan, "Why have you brought calamity upon us? The Lord will now bring calamity upon you."

And the men of Israel stoned them to death and burned their bodies, ²⁶and piled a great heap of stones upon them. The stones are still there to this day, and even today that place is called "The Valley of Calamity." And so the fierce anger of the Lord was ended.

8 The Israelites Attack Ai

Then the Lord said to Joshua, "Don't be afraid or discouraged; take the entire army and go to Ai, for it is now yours to conquer. I have given the king of Ai and all of his people to you. ²You shall do to them as you did to Jericho and her king; but this time you may keep the loot and the cattle for yourselves. Set an ambush behind the city."

^{3,4}Before the main army left for Ai, Joshua sent thirty thousand of his bravest troops to hide in ambush close behind the city, alert for action.

⁵"This is the plan," he explained to them. "When our main army attacks, the men of Ai will come out to fight as they did before, and we will run away. ⁶We will let them chase us until they have all left the city; for they will say, 'The Israelis are running away again just as they did before!' ⁷Then you will jump up from your ambush and enter the city, for the Lord will give it to you. ⁸Set the city on fire, as the Lord has commanded. You now have your instructions."

⁹So they left that night and lay in ambush between Bethel and the west side of Ai; but Joshua and the rest of the army remained in the camp at Jericho. ¹⁰Early the next morning Joshua roused his men and started toward Ai, accompanied by the elders of Israel, ¹¹⁻¹³and stopped at the edge of a valley north of the city. That night Joshua sent another five thousand men to join the troops in ambush on the west side of the city. He himself spent the night in the valley.

¹⁴The King of Ai, seeing the Israelis across the valley, went out early the next morning and attacked at the Plain of Arabah. But of course he didn't realize that there was an ambush behind the city. ¹⁵Joshua and the Israeli army fled across the wilderness as though badly beaten, ¹⁶and all the soldiers in the city were called out to chase after them; so the city was left defenseless; ¹⁷there was not a soldier left in Ai or Bethel, and the city gates were left wide open.

¹⁸Then the Lord said to Joshua, "Point your spear toward Ai, for I will give you the city." Joshua did. ¹⁹And when the men in ambush saw his signal, they jumped up and poured into the city and set it on fire. ^{20,21}When the men of Ai looked behind them, smoke from the city was filling the sky, and they had nowhere to go. When Joshua and the troops who were with him saw the smoke, they knew that their men who had been in ambush were inside the city, so they turned upon their pursuers and began killing them. ²²Then the Israelis who were inside the city came out and began destroying the enemy from the rear. So the men of Ai were caught in a trap and all of them died; not one man survived or escaped, ²³except for the king of Ai, who was captured and brought to Joshua.

²⁴When the army of Israel had finished slaughtering all the men outside the city, they went back and finished off everyone left inside. ²⁵So the entire population of Ai, twelve thousand in all, was wiped out that day. ²⁶For Joshua kept his spear pointed toward Ai until the last person was dead. ²⁷Only the cattle and the loot were not destroyed, for the armies of Israel kept these for themselves. (The Lord had told Joshua they could.) ²⁸So Ai became a desolate mound of refuse, as it still is today.

²⁹Joshua hanged the king of Ai on a tree until evening, but as the sun was going down, he took down the body and threw it in front of the city gate. There he piled a great heap of stones over it, which can still be seen.

³⁰Then Joshua built an altar to the Lord God of Israel at Mount Ebal, ³¹as Moses had commanded in the book of his laws: "Make me an altar of boulders that have neither been broken nor carved," the Lord had said concerning Mount Ebal. Then the priests offered burnt sacrifices and peace offerings to the Lord on the altar. ³²And as the people of Israel watched, Joshua carved upon the stones of the altar each of the Ten Commandments.

³³Then all the people of Israel—including the elders, officers, judges, and the foreigners living among them—divided into two groups, half of them standing at the foot of Mount Gerizim and half at the foot of Mount Ebal. Between them stood the priests with the Ark, ready to pronounce their blessing. (This was all done in accordance with the instructions given long before by Moses.) ³⁴Joshua then read to them all of the

FAMILY DEVOTIONS

☐ **DEVOTION 82**
TRUSTING GOD FOR GUIDANCE

Read Joshua 9:3-18

Trusting God for Guidance
Memory Verse

I will instruct you (says the Lord) and guide you along the best pathway for your life; I will advise you and watch your progress.
Psalm 32:8

Lynn had a tough decision to make. Should she go on her class hayride, or should she go to the church party being held the same night? She had prayed about it and really knew in her heart that she should support her church youth group. But the hayride would be Lynn's first class party since attending her new school. She really wanted to go! *I know,* she thought. *I'll ask Connie what she thinks.*

"I think you should go on the hayride," advised her older sister, Connie. "The kids might think you're a snob if you don't show up. Besides, you might be able to be a testimony for the Lord there." Lynn was easily convinced. She would go to the school party.

The hayride was rowdy from the start. The kids were keyed up, and some of them carried things too far, roughly pushing each other off the wagon as it moved slowly down the dark country road. One time Lynn fell with a *thump* to the road. In spite of a bruised knee, she had to jump up quickly and run hard to catch up and climb back on the wagon. She was surprised that the parents who were along to supervise didn't do more to calm things down. Fun was fun, but this was just too rough!

"Hey, look!" shouted one of the boys as he flicked a piece of gravel off his finger. "I have a lethal weapon!" Before anyone could stop them, several kids began pelting each other with stones from the roadside. Ping! A stone hit Lynn's glasses, shattering them.

Much later, Lynn lay in bed, giving careful thought to the past evening. *Oh, why did I ever ask for Connie's advice,* she thought, *when I knew all the time what the Lord wanted me to do!* Before going to sleep she silently asked him to forgive her and to help her obey him.

How About You?

Has there ever been a time when you knew what God wanted you to do, but you kept hoping someone would advise you to do what you really wanted to do? Do you know what God wants you to do about that student who doesn't seem to have friends? About showing kindness to that older person? About missing church on Sunday? When you know God's will, do it. *P. R.*

• For the next devotional, turn to page 245. • For the next devotional on *TRUSTING GOD FOR GUIDANCE,* turn to page 445. • For notes on *TRUSTING GOD FOR GUIDANCE,* see pages 522, 553, 614, 676, and 1056.

statements of blessing and curses that Moses had written in the book of God's laws. ³⁵Every commandment Moses had ever given was read before the entire assembly, including the women and children and the foreigners who lived among the Israelis.

9 Gibeonites Trick Joshua

When the kings of the surrounding area heard what had happened to Jericho, they quickly combined their armies to fight for their lives against Joshua and the Israelis. These were the kings of the nations west of the Jordan River, along the shores of the Mediterranean as far north as the Lebanon mountains—the Hittites, Amorites, Canaanites, Perizzites, Hivites, and Jebusites.

³⁻⁵But when the people of Gibeon heard what had happened to Jericho and Ai, they resorted to trickery to save themselves. They sent ambassadors to Joshua wearing worn-out clothing, as though from a long journey, with patched shoes, weatherworn saddlebags on their donkeys, old, patched wineskins and dry, moldy bread. ⁶When they arrived at the camp of Israel at Gilgal, they told Joshua and the men of Israel, "We have come from a distant land to ask for a peace treaty with you."

⁷The Israelis replied to these Hivites, "How do we know you don't live nearby? For if you do, we cannot make a treaty with you."

⁸They replied, "We will be your slaves."

"But who are you?" Joshua demanded. "Where do you come from?"

⁹And they told him, "We are from a very distant country; we have heard of the might of the Lord your God and of all that he did in Egypt, ¹⁰and what you did to the two kings of the Amorites—Sihon, king of Heshbon, and Og, king of Bashan. ¹¹So our elders and our people instructed us, 'Prepare for a long journey; go to the people of Israel and declare our nation to be their servants, and ask for peace.' ¹²This bread was hot from the ovens when we left, but now as you see, it is dry and moldy; ¹³these wineskins were new, but now they are old and cracked; our clothing and shoes have become worn out from our long, hard trip."

¹⁴,¹⁵Joshua and the other leaders finally believed them. They did not bother to ask the Lord but went ahead and signed a peace treaty. And the leaders of Israel ratified the agreement with a binding oath.

¹⁶Three days later the facts came out—these men were close neighbors. ¹⁷The Israeli army set out at once to investigate and reached their cities in three days. (The names of the cities were Gibeon, Chephirah, Beeroth, and Kiriath-jearim.) ¹⁸But the cities were not harmed because of the vow which the leaders of Israel had made before the Lord God. The people of Israel were angry with their leaders because of the peace treaty.

¹⁹But the leaders replied, "We have sworn before the Lord God of Israel that we will not touch them, and we won't. ²⁰We must let them live, for if we break our oath, the wrath of Jehovah will be upon us."

²¹So they became servants of the Israelis, chopping their wood and carrying their water.

²²Joshua summoned their leaders and demanded, "Why have you lied to us by saying that you lived in a distant land, when you were actually living right here among us? ²³Now a curse shall be upon you! From this moment you must always furnish us with servants to chop wood and carry water for the service of our God."

²⁴They replied, "We did it because we were told that Jehovah instructed his disciple Moses to conquer this entire land and destroy all the people living in it. So we feared for our lives because of you; that is why we have done it. ²⁵But now we are in your hands; you may do with us as you wish."

²⁶So Joshua would not allow the people of Israel to kill them, ²⁷but they became woodchoppers and water-carriers for the people of Israel and for the altar of the Lord—wherever it would be built (for the Lord hadn't yet told them where to build it). This arrangement is still in force at the time of this writing.

10 The Sun and Moon Stand Still

When Adoni-zedek, the king of Jerusalem, heard how Joshua had captured and destroyed Ai and had killed its king, the same as he had done at Jericho, and how the people of Gibeon had made peace with Israel and were now their allies, ²he was very frightened. For Gibeon was a great city—as great as the royal cities and much larger than Ai—and its men were known as hard fighters. ³So King Adoni-zedek of Jerusalem sent messengers to several other kings: King Hoham of Hebron, King Piram of Jarmuth, King Japhia of Lachish, King Debir of Eglon.

TRUSTING GOD FOR HELP 10:25 With God's help, Israel won the battle against five armies without losing a single soldier. Such a triumph was part of God's daily business as he worked with his people for victory. Joshua told his men never to be afraid because God would give them similar victories over all their enemies. God has often protected us and won victories in our lives. The same God who empowered Joshua and who has led us in the past will help us with our present and future needs. Reminding ourselves of his help in the past will give us hope for the struggles that lie ahead. **To begin the series of devotionals on TRUSTING GOD FOR HELP, turn to page 29.**

⁴"Come and help me destroy Gibeon," he urged them, "for they have made peace with Joshua and the people of Israel."

⁵So these five Amorite kings combined their armies for a united attack on Gibeon. ⁶The men of Gibeon hurriedly sent messengers to Joshua at Gilgal.

"Come and help your servants!" they demanded. "Come quickly and save us! For all the kings of the Amorites who live in the hills are here with their armies."

⁷So Joshua and the Israeli army left Gilgal and went to rescue Gibeon.

⁸"Don't be afraid of them," the Lord said to Joshua, "for they are already defeated! I have given them to you to destroy. Not a single one of them will be able to stand up to you."

⁹Joshua traveled all night from Gilgal and took the enemy armies by surprise. ¹⁰Then the Lord threw them into a panic so that the army of Israel slaughtered great numbers of them at Gibeon and chased the others all the way to Beth-horon and Azekah and Makkedah, killing them along the way. ¹¹And as the enemy was racing down the hill to Beth-horon, the Lord destroyed them with a great hailstorm that continued all the way to Azekah; in fact, more men died from the hail than by the swords of the Israelites.

¹²As the men of Israel were pursuing and harassing the foe, Joshua prayed aloud, "Let the sun stand still over Gibeon, and let the moon stand in its place over the valley of Aijalon!"

¹³And the sun and the moon didn't move until the Israeli army had finished the destruction of its enemies! This is described in greater detail in *The Book of Jashar.* So the sun stopped in the heavens and stayed there for almost twenty-four hours! ¹⁴There had never been such a day before, and there has never been another since, when the Lord stopped the sun and moon—all because of the prayer of one man. But the Lord was fighting for Israel. ¹⁵(Afterwards Joshua and the Israeli army returned to Gilgal.)

¹⁶During the battle the five kings escaped and hid in a cave at Makkedah. ¹⁷When the news was brought to Joshua that they had been found, ¹⁸he issued a command that a great stone be rolled against the mouth of the cave and that guards be placed there to keep the kings inside.

¹⁹Then Joshua commanded the rest of the army, "Go on chasing the enemy and cut them down from the rear. Don't let them get back to their cities, for the Lord will help you to completely destroy them."

²⁰So Joshua and the Israeli army continued the slaughter and wiped out the five armies except for a tiny remnant that managed to reach their fortified cities. ²¹Then the Israelis returned to their camp at Makkedah without having lost a single man! And after that no one dared to attack Israel.

²²,²³Joshua now instructed his men to remove the stone from the mouth of the cave and to bring out the five kings—of Jerusalem, Hebron, Jarmuth, Lachish, and Eglon. ²⁴Joshua told the captains of his army to put their feet on the kings' necks.

²⁵"Don't ever be afraid or discouraged," Joshua said to his men. "Be strong and courageous, for the Lord is going to do this to all of your enemies."

²⁶With that, Joshua plunged his sword into each of the five kings, killing them. He then hanged them on five trees until evening.

²⁷As the sun was going down, Joshua instructed that their bodies be taken down and thrown into the cave where they had been hiding; and a great pile of stones was placed at the mouth of the cave. (The pile is still there today.)

²⁸On that same day Joshua destroyed the city of Makkedah and killed its king and everyone in it. Not one person in the entire city was left alive. ²⁹Then the Israelis went to Libnah. ³⁰There, too, the Lord gave them the city and its king. Every last person was slaughtered, just as at Jericho.

³¹From Libnah they went to Lachish and attacked it. ³²And the Lord gave it to them on the second day; here, too, the entire population was slaughtered, just as at Libnah.

³³During the attack on Lachish, King Horam of Gezer arrived with his army to try to help defend the city, but Joshua's men killed him and destroyed his entire army.

³⁴,³⁵The Israeli army then captured Eglon on the first day and, as at Lachish, they killed everyone in the city. ³⁶After leaving Eglon they went to Hebron ³⁷and captured it and all of its surrounding villages, slaughtering the entire population. Not one person was left alive. ³⁸Then they turned back to Debir, ³⁹which they quickly captured with all of its outlying villages. And they killed everyone just as they had at Libnah.

⁴⁰So Joshua and his army conquered the whole country—the nations and kings of the hill country, the Negeb, the lowlands, and the mountain slopes. They destroyed everyone in the land, just as the Lord God of Israel had commanded, ⁴¹slaughtering them from Kadesh-barnea to Gaza, and from Goshen to Gibeon. ⁴²This was all accomplished in one campaign, for the Lord God of Israel was fighting for his people. ⁴³Then Joshua and his army returned to their camp at Gilgal.

The Surprise Attack

When King Jabin of Hazor heard what had happened, he sent urgent messages to the following kings:

King Jobab of Madon;
The king of Shimron;
The king of Achshaph;
All the kings of the northern hill country;
The kings in the Arabah, south of Chinneroth;
Those in the lowland;
The kings in the mountain areas of Dor, on the west;
The kings of Canaan, both east and west;
The kings of the Amorites;
The kings of the Hittites;
The kings of the Perizzites;
The kings in the Jebusite hill country;
The Hivite kings in the cities on the slopes of Mount Hermon, in the land of Mizpah.

4All these kings responded by mobilizing their armies and uniting to crush Israel. Their combined troops, along with a vast array of horses and chariots, covered the landscape around the Springs of Merom as far as one could see; 5for they established their camp at the Springs of Merom.

6But the Lord said to Joshua, "Don't be afraid of them, for by this time tomorrow they will all be dead! Hamstring their horses and burn their chariots." 7Joshua and his troops arrived suddenly at the Springs of Merom and attacked. 8And the Lord gave all that vast army to the Israelis, who chased them as far as Great Sidon and a place called the Salt Pits, and eastward into the valley of Mizpah; so not one enemy troop survived the battle. 9Then Joshua and his men did as the Lord had instructed, for they hamstrung the horses and burned all the chariots.

10On the way back, Joshua captured Hazor and killed its king. (Hazor had at one time been the capital of the federation of all those kingdoms.) 11Every person there was killed and the city was burned.

12Then he attacked and destroyed all the other cities of those kings. All the people were slaughtered, just as Moses had commanded long before. 13(However, Joshua did not burn any of the cities built on mounds except for Hazor.) 14All the loot and cattle of the ravaged cities were taken by the Israelis for themselves, but they killed all the people. 15For so the Lord had commanded his disciple Moses; and Moses had passed the commandment on to Joshua, who did as he had been told: he carefully obeyed all of the Lord's instructions to Moses.

16So Joshua conquered the entire land—the hill country, the Negeb, the land of Goshen, the lowlands, the Arabah, and the hills and lowlands of Israel. 17The Israeli territory now extended all the way from Mount Halak, near Seir, to Baal-gad in the valley of Lebanon, at the foot of Mount Hermon. And Joshua killed all the kings of those territories. 18It took seven years of war to accomplish all of this. 19None of the cities was given a peace treaty except the Hivites of Gibeon; all of the others were destroyed. 20For the Lord made the enemy kings want to fight the Israelis instead of asking for peace; so they were mercilessly killed, as the Lord had commanded Moses.

21During this period Joshua routed all of the giants—the descendants of Anak who lived in the hill country in Hebron, Debir, Anab, Judah, and Israel; he killed them all and completely destroyed their cities. 22None was left in all the land of Israel, though some still remained in Gaza, Gath, and Ashdod.

23So Joshua took the entire land just as the Lord had instructed Moses; and he gave it to the people of Israel as their inheritance, dividing the land among the tribes. So the land finally rested from its war.

12 A List of Conquered Kings

Here is the list of the kings on the east side of the Jordan River whose cities were destroyed by the Israelis: (The area involved stretched all the way from the valley of the Arnon River to Mount Hermon, including the cities of the eastern desert.)

2King Sihon of the Amorites, who lived in Heshbon. His kingdom extended from Aroer, on the edge of the Arnon Valley, and from the middle of the valley of the Arnon River to the Jabbok River, which is the boundary of the Ammonites. This includes half of the present area of Gilead, which lies north of the Jabbok River. 3Sihon also controlled the Jordan River valley as far north as the western shores of the Lake of Galilee; and as far south as the Dead Sea and the slopes of Mount Pisgah.

4King Og of Bashan, the last of the Rephaim, who lived at Ashtaroth and Edrei: 5He ruled a territory stretching from Mount Hermon in the north to Salecah on Mount Bashan in the east, and on the west, extending to the boundary of the kingdoms of Geshur and Maacah. His kingdom also stretched south to include the northern half of Gilead

---

PATIENCE 11:18 The conquest of Canaan seems to have happened quickly (we can read about it in one sitting), but it actually took seven years. We often expect quick changes in our lives and quick victories over sin. But our journey with God is a lifelong process, and the changes and victories may take time. It is easy to grow impatient with God and feel like giving up hope because things are moving too slowly. When we are close to a situation, it is difficult to see progress. But when we look back we can see that God never stopped working. **To begin the series of devotionals on PATIENCE, turn to page 549.**

where the boundary touched the border of the kingdom of Sihon, king of Heshbon. ⁶Moses and the people of Israel had destroyed these people, and Moses gave the land to the tribes of Reuben and the half-tribe of Manasseh.

⁷Here is a list of the kings destroyed by Joshua and the armies of Israel on the west side of the Jordan. (This land which lay between Baal-gad in the Valley of Lebanon and Mount Halak, west of Mount Seir, was allotted by Joshua to the other tribes of Israel. ⁸⁻²⁴The area included the hill country, the lowlands, the Arabah, the mountain slopes, the Judean Desert, and the Negeb.

The people who lived there were the Hittites, the Amorites, the Canaanites, the Perizzites, the Hivites, and the Jebusites): the king of Jericho; the king of Ai, near Bethel; the king of Jerusalem; the king of Hebron; the king of Jarmuth; the king of Lachish; the king of Eglon; the king of Gezer; the king of Debir; the king of Geder; the king of Hormah; the king of Arad; the king of Libnah; the king of Adullam; the king of Makkedah; the king of Bethel; the king of Tappuah; the king of Hepher; the king of Aphek; the king of Lasharon; the king of Madon; the king of Hazor; the king of Shimron-meron; the king of Achshaph; the king of Taanach; the king of Megiddo; the king of Kedesh; the king of Jokneam, in Carmel; the king of Dor in the city of Naphathdor; the king of Goiim in Gilgal; the king of Tirzah. So in all, thirty-one kings and their cities were destroyed.

13 Joshua Divides Up the Land

Joshua was now an old man. "You are growing old," the Lord said to him, "and there are still many nations to be conquered. ²⁻⁷Here is a list of the areas still to be occupied:

All the land of the Philistines;
The land of the Geshurites;
The territory now belonging to the Canaanites from the brook of Egypt to the southern boundary of Ekron;
Five cities of the Philistines: Gaza, Ashdod, Ashkelon, Gath, Ekron;
The land of the Avvim in the south;
In the north, all the land of the Canaanites, including Mearah (which belongs to the Sidonians), stretching northward to Aphek at the boundary of the Amorites;
The land of the Gebalites on the coast and all of the Lebanon mountain area from Baal-gad beneath Mount Hermon in the south to the entrance of Hamath in the north;
All the hill country from Lebanon to Misrephoth-maim, including all the land of the Sidonians.

I am ready to drive these people out from before the nation of Israel, so include all this territory when you divide the land among the nine tribes and the half-tribe of Manasseh as I have commanded you."

⁸The other half of the tribe of Manasseh and the tribes of Reuben and Gad had already received their inheritance on the east side of the Jordan, for Moses had previously assigned this land to them. ⁹Their territory ran from Aroer, on the edge of the valley of the Arnon River, included the city in the valley, and crossed the tableland of Medeba to Dibon; ¹⁰it also included all the cities of King Sihon of the Amorites, who reigned in Heshbon, and extended as far as the borders of Ammon. ¹¹It included Gilead; the territory of the Geshurites and the Maacathites; all of Mount Hermon; Mount Bashan with its city of Salecah; ¹²and all the territory of King Og of Bashan, who had reigned in Ashtaroth and Edrei. (He was the last of the Rephaim, for Moses had attacked them and driven them out. ¹³However, the people of Israel had not driven out the Geshurites or the Maacathites, who still live there among the Israelites to this day.)

¹⁴The Territorial Assignments

The Land Given to the Tribe of Levi: Moses hadn't assigned any land to the tribe of Levi: instead, they were given the offerings brought to the Lord.

¹⁵*The Land Given to the Tribe of Reuben:* Fitting the size of its territory to its size of population, Moses had assigned the following area to the tribe of Reuben: ¹⁶Their land extended from Aroer on the edge of the valley of the Arnon River, past the city of Arnon in the middle of the valley, to beyond the tableland near Medeba. ¹⁷It included Heshbon and the other cities on the plain—Dibon, Bamoth-baal, Beth-baal-meon, ¹⁸Jahaz, Kedemoth, Mephaath, ¹⁹Kiriathaim, Sibmah, Zereth-shahar on the mountain above the valley, ²⁰Beth-peor, Beth-jeshimoth, and the slopes of Mount Pisgah.

²¹The land of Reuben also included the cities of the tableland and the kingdom of Sihon. Sihon was the king who had lived in Heshbon and was killed by Moses along with the other chiefs of Midian—Evi, Rekem, Zur, Hur, and Reba. ²²The people of Israel also killed Balaam the magician, the son of Beor. ²³The Jordan River was the western boundary of the tribe of Reuben.

²⁴*The Land Given to the Tribe of Gad:* Moses also assigned land to the tribe of Gad in proportion to its population. ²⁵This territory included Jazer, all the cities of Gilead, and half of the land of Ammon as far as Aroer near Rabbah. ²⁶It also extended from Heshbon to Ramath-mizpeh and Betonim, and from

Mahanaim to Lodebar. ²⁷,²⁸In the valley were Beth-haram, and Beth-nimrah, Succoth, Zaphon, and the rest of the kingdom of King Sihon of Heshbon. The Jordan River was the western border, extending as far as the Lake of Galilee; then the border turned east from the Jordan River.

²⁹*The Land Given to the Half-Tribe of Manasseh: Moses had assigned the following territory to the half-tribe of Manasseh in proportion to its needs:* ³⁰Their territory extended north from Mahanaim, included all of Bashan, the former kingdom of King Og, and the sixty cities of Jair in Bashan. ³¹Half of Gilead and King Og's royal cities of Ashtaroth and Edrei were given to half of the clan Machir, who was Manasseh's son.

³²That was how Moses divided the land east of the Jordan River where the people were camped at that time across from Jericho. ³³But Moses had given no land to the tribe of Levi for, as he had explained to them, the Lord God was their inheritance. He was all they needed. He would take care of them in other ways.

14 West of the Jordan River

The conquered lands of Canaan were allotted to the remaining nine and a half tribes of Israel. The decision as to which tribe would receive which area was decided by throwing dice before the Lord, and he caused them to turn up in the ways he wanted. Eleazar the priest, Joshua, and the tribal leaders supervised the lottery.

³,⁴(Moses had already given land to the two and a half tribes on the east side of the Jordan River. The tribe of Joseph had become two separate tribes, Manasseh and Ephraim, and the Levites were given no land at all, except cities in which to live and the surrounding pasturelands for their cattle. ⁵So the distribution of the land was in strict accordance with the Lord's directions to Moses.)

⁶*The Land Given to Caleb:* A delegation from the tribe of Judah, led by Caleb, came to Joshua in Gilgal.

"Remember what the Lord said to Moses about you and me when we were at Kadesh-barnea?" Caleb asked Joshua. ⁷"I was forty years old at the time, and Moses had sent us from Kadesh-barnea to spy out the land of Canaan. I reported what I felt was the truth, ⁸but our brothers who went with us frightened the people and discouraged them from entering the Promised Land. But since I had followed the Lord my God, ⁹Moses told me, 'The section of Canaan you were just in shall belong to you and your descendants forever.'

¹⁰"Now, as you see, from that time until now the Lord has kept me alive and well for all these forty-five years since crisscrossing the wilderness, and today I am eighty-five years old. ¹¹I am as strong now as I was when Moses sent us on that journey, and I can still travel and fight as well as I could then! ¹²So I'm asking that you give me the hill country that the Lord promised me. You will remember that as spies we found the Anakim living there in great, walled cities, but if the Lord is with me, I shall drive them out of the land."

¹³,¹⁴So Joshua blessed him and gave him Hebron as a permanent inheritance because he had followed the Lord God of Israel. ¹⁵(Before that time Hebron had been called Kiriath-arba, after a great hero of the Anakim.)

And there was no resistance from the local populations as the Israelis resettled the land.

15 Land for Judah

The land given *to the Tribe of Judah* (as assigned by sacred lot): Judah's southern boundary began at the northern border of Edom, crossed the Wilderness of Zin, and ended at the northern edge of the Negeb. ²⁻⁴More specifically, this boundary began at the south bay of the Dead Sea, ran along the road going south of Mount Akrabbim, on into the Wilderness of Zin to Hezron (south of Kadesh-barnea), and then up through Karka and Azmon, until it finally reached the Brook of Egypt, and along that to the Mediterranean Sea.

⁵The eastern boundary extended along the Dead Sea to the mouth of the Jordan River.

The northern boundary began at the bay where the Jordan River empties into the Salt Sea, ⁶crossed to Beth-hoglah, then proceeded north of Beth-arabah to the stone of Bohan (son of Reuben). ⁷From that point it went through the Valley of Achor to Debir, where it turned northwest toward Gilgal, opposite the slopes of Adummim on the south side of the valley. From there the border extended to the springs at En-shemesh and on to En-rogel. ⁸The boundary then passed through the Valley of Hinnom, along the southern shoulder of Jebus (where the city of Jerusalem is located), then west to the top of the mountain above the Valley of Hinnom, and on up to the northern end of the Valley of Rephaim. ⁹From there the border extended from the top of the mountain to the spring of Nephtoah, and from there to the cities of Mount Ephron before it turned northward to circle around Baalah (which is another name for Kiriath-jearim). ¹⁰,¹¹Then the border circled west of Baalah to Mount Seir, passed along to the town of Chesalon on the northern shoulder of Mount Jearim, and went down to Beth-shemesh. Turning northwest again, the boundary line proceeded past the south of Timnah to the shoulder of the hill north of Ekron, where it bent to the left, passing south of Shikkeron and Mount Baalah. Turning

FAMILY DEVOTIONS

☐ DEVOTION 83
PERSEVERANCE

Read Joshua 14:6-14

*Perseverance
Memory Verse*

Be strong and courageous and get to work. Don't be frightened by the size of the task, for the Lord my God is with you; he will not forsake you. He will see to it that everything is finished correctly.
1 Chronicles 28:20

Just as Lindsey finished dialing the phone, her mother walked into the living room. "Are you still on the phone?" asked Mom. "Hang up now, please. I have to call the dentist."

Lindsey shook her head. "Just a second, Mom!" she said. "I might get it this time!" As Mom was about to reply, Lindsey frowned and hung up the phone. "Awww—busy again," she muttered.

Mom folded her arms crossly. "What's going on, anyway?" she asked.

"I thought you knew," said Lindsey. "Radio station WHUM is having a contest this week. Every now and then, they play a certain song, and whoever is the third person to call wins fifty dollars." She sighed. "They've played it four times today, and every time I call, I get a busy signal."

"Well, I need to make a dental appointment," said Mom. "Don't you have anything more constructive to do? How about studying your Sunday school lesson?"

Lindsey frowned. "Oh, Mom, that's boring," she said. "What's the use of doing it, if I don't get anything out of it?"

Mom looked concerned. "Well," she said, "what's the use of continuing to call that radio station number? You don't get anything out of that, either."

"But one of these times, I'm going to get through!" exclaimed Lindsey. "Then my persistence will pay off—I'll have some more money for my bicycle fund."

Mom gave Lindsey a hug. "Persistence is a good quality, honey," she agreed, "and if you apply it to studying God's Word, you'll find it pays off there as well. Keep reading your Bible. Keep on doing your Sunday school lesson. One of these times you'll 'get through.' You'll get something important out of it. Be as persistent in your spiritual life as you are with that contest, and you'll find that a close relationship with God is worth much more than a bike."

How About You?
What should you do when the Bible seems boring and your prayers seem to bounce back? First, make sure you know Christ as your personal Savior. Then, ask God to show you any areas of sin in your life and deal with them. If you still feel out of fellowship with him, just keep trusting and obeying him. Like Caleb, you'll be rewarded if you don't give up! *S. K.*

• For the next devotional, turn to page 247.   • For the next devotional on *PERSEVERANCE*, turn to page 259.
• For notes on *PERSEVERANCE*, see pages 326, 461, 503, 760, and 1174.

again to the north, it passed Jabneel and ended at the Mediterranean Sea.

¹²The western border was the shoreline of the Mediterranean.

¹³*The Land Given to Caleb:* The Lord instructed Joshua to assign some of Judah's territory to Caleb (son of Jephunneh), so he was given the city of Arba (also called Hebron), which had been named after Anak's father. ¹⁴Caleb drove out the descendants of the three sons of Anak: Talmai, Sheshai, and Ahiman. ¹⁵Then he fought against the people living in the city of Debir (formerly called Kiriath-sepher).

¹⁶Caleb said that he would give his daughter Achsah to be the wife of anyone who would go and capture Kiriath-sepher. ¹⁷Othniel (son of Kenaz), Caleb's nephew, was the one who conquered it, so Achsah became Othniel's wife. ¹⁸,¹⁹As she was leaving with him, she urged him to ask her father for an additional field as a wedding present. She got off her donkey to speak to Caleb about this.

"What is it? What can I do for you?" he asked.

And she replied, "Give me another present! For the land you gave me is a desert. Give us some springs too!" Then he gave her the upper and lower springs.

²⁰So this was the assignment of land to the tribe of Judah:

²¹⁻³²The cities of Judah which were situated along the borders of Edom in the Negeb, namely: Kabzeel, Eder, Jagur, Kinah, Dimonah, Adadah, Kedesh, Hazor, Ithnan, Ziph, Telem, Bealoth, Hazor-hadattah, Kerioth-hezron (or, Hazor), Amam, Shema, Moladah, Hazar-gaddah, Heshmon, Beth-pelet, Hazar-shual, Beer-sheba, Biziothiah, Baalah, Iim, Ezem, Eltolad, Chesil, Hormah, Ziklag, Madmannah, Sansannah, Lebaoth, Shilhim, Ain, and Rimmon. In all, there were twenty-nine of these cities with their surrounding villages.

³³⁻³⁶The following cities situated in the lowlands were also given to Judah: Eshtaol, Zorah, Ashnah, Zanoah, En-gannim, Tappuah, Enam, Jarmuth, Adullam, Socoh, Azekah, Shaaraim, Adithaim, Gederah, and Gederothaim. In all, there were fourteen of these cities with their surrounding villages.

³⁷⁻⁴⁴The tribe of Judah also inherited twenty-five other cities with their villages: Zenan, Hadashah, Migdal-gad, Dilean, Mizpeh, Joktheel, Lachish, Bozkath, Eglon, Cabbon, Lahmam, Chitlish, Gederoth, Beth-dagon, Naamah, Makkedah, Libnah, Ether, Ashan, Iphtah, Ashnah, Nezib, Keilah, Achzib, and Mareshah.

⁴⁵The territory of the tribe of Judah also included all the towns and villages of Ekron. ⁴⁶From Ekron the boundary extended to the Mediterranean and included the cities along the borders of Ashdod with their nearby villages; ⁴⁷also the city of Ashdod with its villages, and Gaza with its villages as far as the Brook of Egypt; also the entire Mediterranean coast from the mouth of the Brook of Egypt on the south to Tyre on the north.

⁴⁸⁻⁶²Judah also received these forty-four cities in the hill country with their surrounding villages: Shamir, Jattir, Socoh, Dannah, Kiriath-sannah (or Debir), Anab, Eshtemoh, Anim, Goshen, Holon, Giloh, Arab, Dumah, Eshan, Janim, Beth-tappuah, Aphekah, Humtah, Kiriath-arba (or, Hebron), Zior, Maon, Carmel, Ziph, Juttah, Jezreel, Jokdeam, Zanoah, Kain, Gibeah, Timnah, Halhul, Beth-zur, Gedor, Maarath, Beth-anoth, Eltekon, Kiriath-baal (also known as Kiriath-jearim), Rabbah, Beth-arabah, Middin, Secacah, Nibshan, The City of Salt, and En-gedi.

⁶³But the tribe of Judah could not drive out the Jebusites who lived in the city of Jerusalem, so the Jebusites live there among the people of Judah to this day.

16 Land for Ephraim

The southern boundary *of the Tribes of Joseph* (Ephraim and the half-tribe of Manasseh): This boundary extended from the Jordan River at Jericho through the wilderness and the hill country to Bethel. It then went from Bethel to Luz, then on to Ataroth, in the territory of the Archites; and west to the border of the Japhletites as far as Lower Beth-horon, then to Gezer and on over to the Mediterranean.

⁵,⁶*The Land Given to the Tribe of Ephraim:* The eastern boundary began at Ataroth-addar. From there it ran to Upper Beth-horon, then on to the Mediterranean Sea. The northern boundary began at the Sea, ran east past Michmethath, then continued on past Taanath-shiloh and Janoah. ⁷From Janoah it turned southward to Ataroth and Naarah, touched Jericho, and ended at the Jordan River. ⁸[The western half of the northern boundary] went from Tappuah and followed along Kanah Brook to the Mediterranean Sea. ⁹Ephraim was also given some of the cities in the territory of the half-tribe of Manasseh. ¹⁰The Canaanites living in Gezer were never driven out, so they still live as slaves among the people of Ephraim.

17 Land for Manasseh

The land given *to the Half-tribe of Manasseh* (Joseph's oldest son): The clan of Machir (Manasseh's oldest son who was the father of Gilead) had already been given the land of Gilead and Bashan [on the east side of the Jordan River], for they were great warriors. ²So now, land on the west side of the Jordan was given to the clans of Abiezer, Helek, Asriel, Shechem, Shemida, and Hepher.

FAMILY DEVOTIONS

☐ **DEVOTION 84**
RESPECTING AUTHORITY

Read Joshua 17:14–18:3

Aimee was having a wonderful time at her aunt and uncle's farm. Every day she went for a ride on her favorite pony, Socks. She loved to trot through the fields and wander through the shady woods. However, she did not like all the work that went along with riding Socks.

"Did you remember to clean out your pony's stall this morning, Aimee?" asked Uncle Rob at lunch one day.

Aimee frowned. "Well, I did it yesterday, and it really didn't look very dirty yet," she explained.

"I see." Uncle Rob didn't look very pleased. "Does Socks have plenty of hay and water?"

"She has water, but she needs some hay," said Aimee.

"Aimee," said Uncle Rob thoughtfully, "God has given us animals to enjoy, but it's also our responsibility to make sure they are well taken care of. Tell me, why do you like to ride Socks so much?"

"Because she does what I tell her to without fussing," replied Aimee promptly. "I don't have to pull hard on the reins to get her to stop or turn—she listens really good."

Uncle Rob nodded. "You know," he said, "in some ways, we're like horses. Nobody likes a horse that doesn't listen well. In the same way, a Christian who doesn't listen well to God's instructions is not a Christian he can use." Aimee looked at her uncle uncertainly, not sure what he was getting at. "Part of God's instructions are to obey those in authority over us," added Uncle Rob. "When you came to spend the week with us, we gave you both the pleasure *and* the responsibility of having a horse."

"You mean I should take better care of Socks?" Aimee asked.

"Yes," said Uncle Rob. "When you only do the things you want to do, you're being selfish instead of obeying instructions—you're fighting the 'reins' God has given."

"I'm sorry, Uncle Rob," apologized Aimee. "I'll go feed Socks right now!"

Respecting Authority
Memory Verse

Children, obey your parents; this is the right thing to do because God has placed them in authority over you.
Ephesians 6:1

How About You?
Do you listen well and quickly obey those whom God has placed over you? Or do you listen to some instructions and ignore others? You need to obey in all areas. Remember, God is pleased with Christians who listen well and obey quickly. *D. M.*

• For the next devotional, turn to page 251.   • For the next devotional on *RESPECTING AUTHORITY*, turn to page 355.
• For notes on *RESPECTING AUTHORITY*, see pages 311, 420, and 1182.

³However, Hepher's son Zelophehad (grandson of Gilead, great-grandson of Machir, and great-great-grandson of Manasseh) had no sons. He had only five daughters whose names were Mahlah, Noah, Hoglah, Milcah, and Tirzah. ⁴These women came to Eleazar the priest and to Joshua and the Israeli leaders and reminded them,

"The Lord told Moses that we were to receive as much property as the men of our tribe."

⁵,⁶So, as the Lord had commanded through Moses, these five women were given an inheritance along with their five great-uncles, and the total inheritance came to ten sections of land (in addition to the land of Gilead and Bashan across the Jordan River).

⁷The northern boundary of the tribe of Manasseh extended southward from the border of Asher to Michmethath, which is east of Shechem. On the south the boundary went from Michmethath to the Spring of Tappuah. ⁸(The land of Tappuah belonged to Manasseh, but the city of Tappuah, on the border of Manasseh's land, belonged to the tribe of Ephraim.) ⁹From the spring of Tappuah the border of Manasseh followed the north bank of the Brook of Kanah to the Mediterranean Sea. (Several cities south of the brook belonged to the tribe of Ephraim, though they were located in Manasseh's territory.) ¹⁰The land south of the brook and as far west as the Mediterranean Sea was assigned to Ephraim, and the land north of the brook and east of the sea went to Manasseh. Manasseh's northern boundary was the territory of Asher, and the eastern boundary was the territory of Issachar.

¹¹The half-tribe of Manasseh was also given the following cities, which were situated in the areas assigned to Issachar and Asher: Beth-shean, Ibleam, Dor, En-dor, Taanach, Megiddo (where are the three cliffs), with their respective villages. ¹²But since the descendants of Manasseh could not drive out the people who lived in those cities, the Canaanites remained. ¹³Later on, however, when the Israelis became strong enough, they forced the Canaanites to work as slaves.

¹⁴Then the two tribes of Joseph came to Joshua and asked, "Why have you given us only one portion of land when the Lord has given us such large populations?"

¹⁵"If the hill country of Ephraim is not large enough for you," Joshua replied, "and if you are able to do it, you may clear out the forest land where the Perizzites and Rephaim live."

¹⁶⁻¹⁸"Fine," said the tribes of Joseph, "for the Canaanites in the lowlands around Beth-shean and the Valley of Jezreel have iron chariots and are too strong for us."

"Then you shall have the mountain forests," Joshua replied, "and since you are such a large, strong tribe you will surely be able to clear it all and live there. And I'm sure you can drive out the Canaanites from the valleys, too, even though they are strong and have iron chariots."

18 Joshua Assigns the Rest

After the conquest—although seven of the tribes of Israel had not yet entered and conquered the land God had given them—all Israel gathered at Shiloh to set up the Tabernacle.

³Then Joshua asked them, "How long are you going to wait before clearing out the people living in the land that the Lord your God has given to you? ⁴Select three men from each tribe, and I will send them to scout the unconquered territory and bring back a report of its size and natural divisions so that I can divide it for you. ⁵,⁶The scouts will map it into seven sections, and then I will throw the sacred dice to decide which section will be assigned to each tribe. ⁷However, remember that the Levites won't receive any land; they are priests of the Lord. That is their wonderful heritage. And of course the tribes of Gad and Reuben and the half-tribe of Manasseh won't receive any more, for they already have land on the east side of the Jordan where Moses promised them that they could settle."

⁸So the scouts went out to map the country and to bring back their report to Joshua. Then the Lord could assign the sections of land to the tribes by the throw of the sacred dice. ⁹The men did as they were told and divided the entire territory into seven sections, listing the cities in each section. Then they returned to Joshua and the camp at Shiloh. ¹⁰There at the Tabernacle at Shiloh the Lord showed Joshua by the sacred lottery which tribe should have each section:

¹¹*The Land Given to the Tribe of Benjamin:*

The section of land assigned to the families of the tribe of Benjamin lay between the territory previously assigned to the tribes of Judah and Joseph.

¹²The northern boundary began at the Jordan River, went north of Jericho, then west through the hill country and the Wilderness of Beth-aven. ¹³From there the boundary went south to Luz (also called Bethel) and proceeded down to Ataroth-addar in the hill country south of Lower Beth-horon. ¹⁴There the border turned south, passing the mountain near Beth-horon and ending at the village of Kiriath-baal (sometimes called Kiriath-jearim), one of the cities of the tribe of Judah. This was the western boundary.

¹⁵The southern border ran from the edge of Kiriath-baal, over Mount Ephron to the spring of Naphtoah, ¹⁶and down to the base of the mountain beside the valley of Hinnom, north of the

valley of Rephaim. From there it continued across the valley of Hinnom, crossed south of the old city of Jerusalem where the Jebusites lived, and continued down to En-rogel. [17]From En-rogel the boundary proceeded northeast to En-shemesh and on to Geliloth (which is opposite the slope of Adummim). Then it went down to the Stone of Bohan (who was a son of Reuben), [18]where it passed along the north edge of the Arabah. The border then went down into the Arabah, [19]ran south past Beth-hoglah, and ended at the north bay of the Dead Sea—which is the southern end of the Jordan River.

[20]The eastern border was the Jordan River. This was the land assigned to the tribe of Benjamin. [21-28]These twenty-six cities were included in the land given to the tribe of Benjamin: Jericho, Beth-hoglah, Emek-keziz, Beth-arabah, Zimaraim, Bethel, Avvim, Parah, Ophrah, Chephar-ammoni, Ophni, Geba, Gibeon, Ramah, Beeroth, Mizpeh, Chephirah, Mozah, Rekem, Irpeel, Taralah, Zela, Haeleph, Jebus (or Jerusalem), Gibeah, and Kiriath-jearim. All of these cities and their surrounding villages were given to the tribe of Benjamin.

19 Land for Simeon

The land given *to the Tribe of Simeon:* The tribe of Simeon received the next assignment of land—including part of the land previously assigned to Judah. [2-7]Their inheritance included these seventeen cities with their respective villages: Beer-sheba, Sheba, Moladah, Hazar-shual, Balah, Ezem, Eltolad, Bethul, Hormah, Ziklag, Beth-marcaboth, Hazar-susah, Beth-lebaoth, Sharuhen, En-rimmon, Ether, and Ashan. [8]The cities as far south as Baalath-beer (also known as Ramah-in-the-Negeb) were also given to the tribe of Simeon. [9]So the Simeon tribe's inheritance came from what had earlier been given to Judah, for Judah's section had been too large for them.

[10]*The Land Given to the Tribe of Zebulun:* The third tribe to receive its assignment of land was Zebulun. Its boundary started on the south side of Sarid. [11]From there it circled to the west, going near Mareal and Dabbesheth until it reached the brook east of Jokneam. [12]In the other direction, the boundary line went east to the border of Chisloth-tabor, and from there to Daberath and Japhia; [13]then it continued east of Gath-hepher, Ethkazin, and Rimmon and turned toward Neah. [14]The northern boundary of Zebulun passed Hannathon and ended at the Valley of Iphtahel. [15,16]The cities in these areas, besides those already mentioned, included Kattath, Nahalal, Shimron, Idalah, Bethlehem, and each of their surrounding villages. Altogether there were twelve of these cities.

[17-23]*The Land Given to the Tribe of Issachar:* The fourth tribe to be assigned its land was Issachar. Its boundaries included the following cities: Jezreel, Chesulloth, Shunem, Hapharaim, Shion, Anaharath, Rabbith, Kishion, Ebez, Remeth, En-gannim, En-haddah, Beth-pazzez, Tabor, Shahazumah, and Beth-shemesh—sixteen cities in all, each with its surrounding villages. The boundary of Issachar ended at the Jordan River.

[24-26]*The Land Given to the Tribe of Asher:* The fifth tribe to be assigned its land was Asher. The boundaries included these cities: Helkath, Hali, Beten, Achshaph, Allammelech, Amad, and Mishal.

The boundary on the west side went from Carmel to Shihor-libnath, [27]turned east toward Beth-dagon, and ran as far as Zebulun in the Valley of Iphtahel, running north of Beth-emek and Neiel. It then passed to the east of Kabul, [28]Ebron, Rehob, Hammon, Kanah, and Greater Sidon. [29]Then the boundary turned toward Ramah and the fortified city of Tyre and came to the Mediterranean Sea at Hosah. The territory also included Mahalab, Achzib, [30,31]Ummah, Aphek, and Rehob—an overall total of twenty-two cities and their surrounding villages.

[32]*The Land Given to the Tribe of Naphtali:* The sixth tribe to receive its assignment was the tribe of Naphtali. [33]Its boundary began at Judah, at the oak in Zaanannim, and extended across to Adami-nekeb, Jabneel, and Lakkum, ending at the Jordan River. [34]The western boundary began near Heleph and ran past Aznoth-tabor, then to Hukkok, and coincided with the Zebulun boundary in the south, and with the boundary of Asher on the west, and with the Jordan River at the east. [35-39]The fortified cities included in this territory were: Ziddim, Zer, Hammath, Rakkath, Chinnereth, Adamah, Ramah, Hazor, Kedesh, Edrei, Enhazor, Yiron, Migdal-el, Horem, Beth-anath, and Beth-shemesh.

So altogether the territory included nineteen cities with their surrounding villages.

[40]*The Land Given to the Tribe of Dan:* The last tribe to be assigned its land was Dan. [41-46]The cities within its area included: Zorah, Eshtaol, Ir-shemesh, Shaalabbin, Aijalon, Ithlah, Elon, Timnah, Ekron, Eltekeh, Gibbethon, Baalath, Jehud, Bene-berak, Gath-rimmon, Me-jarkon, and Rakkon, also the territory near Joppa. [47,48]But some of this territory proved impossible to conquer, so the tribe

---

TRUSTING GOD FOR HELP **19:47-48** Some of the land looked impossible to conquer for the tribe of Dan. They were not familiar with the territory, and the local inhabitants were fierce. Although God had given Israel victory in even worse situations, the tribe of Dan chose to migrate north to avoid the intense opposition. Anyone can trust God when the going is easy. It is when everything looks impossible that our faith and courage are put to the test. Have faith that God is great enough to tackle your most difficult situations. **To begin the series of devotionals on** *TRUSTING GOD FOR HELP,* **turn to page 29.**

of Dan captured the city of Leshem, slaughtered its people, and lived there; and they called the city "Dan," naming it after their ancestor.

⁴⁹So all the land was divided among the tribes, with the boundaries indicated; and the nation of Israel gave a special piece of land to Joshua, ⁵⁰for the Lord had said that he could have any city he wanted. He chose Timnath-serah in the hill country of Ephraim; he rebuilt it and lived there.

⁵¹Eleazar the priest, Joshua, and the leaders of the tribes of Israel supervised the sacred lottery to divide the land among the tribes. This was done in the Lord's presence at the entrance of the Tabernacle at Shiloh.

20 Cities of Refuge

The Lord said to Joshua, ²"Tell the people of Israel to designate now the Cities of Refuge, as I instructed Moses. ³If a man is guilty of killing someone unintentionally, he can run to one of these cities and be protected from the relatives of the dead man, who may try to kill him in revenge. ⁴When the innocent killer reaches any of these cities, he will meet with the city council and explain what happened, and they must let him come in and must give him a place to live among them. ⁵If a relative of the dead man comes to kill him in revenge, the innocent slayer must not be released to him for the death was accidental. ⁶The man who caused the accidental death must stay in that city until he has been tried by the judges and found innocent, and must live there until the death of the High Priest who was in office at the time of the accident. But then he is free to return to his own city and home."

⁷The cities chosen as Cities of Refuge were Kedesh of Galilee in the hill country of Naphtali; Shechem, in the hill country of Ephraim; and Kiriath-arba (also known as Hebron) in the hill country of Judah. ⁸The Lord also instructed that three cities be set aside for this purpose on the east side of the Jordan River, across from Jericho. They were Bezer, in the wilderness of the land of the tribe of Reuben; Ramoth of Gilead, in the territory of the tribe of Gad; and Golan of Bashan, in the land of the tribe of Manasseh. ⁹These Cities of Refuge were for foreigners living in Israel as well as for the Israelis themselves, so that anyone who accidentally killed another man could run to that place for a trial and not be killed in revenge.

21 Towns for the Levites

Then the leaders of the tribe of Levi came to Shiloh to consult with Eleazar the priest and with Joshua and the leaders of the various tribes.

²"The Lord instructed Moses to give cities to us Levites for our homes, and pastureland for our cattle," they said.

³So they were given some of the recently conquered cities with their pasturelands. ⁴Thirteen of these cities had been assigned originally to the tribes of Judah, Simeon, and Benjamin. These were given to some of the priests of the Kohath division (of the tribe of Levi, descendants of Aaron). ⁵The other families of the Kohath division were given ten cities from the territories of Ephraim, Dan, and the half-tribe of Manasseh. ⁶The Gershon division received thirteen cities, selected by sacred lot in the area of Bashan. These cities were given by the tribes of Issachar, Asher, Naphtali, and the half-tribe of Manasseh. ⁷The Merari division received twelve cities from the tribes of Reuben, Gad, and Zebulun. ⁸So the Lord's command to Moses was obeyed, and the cities and pasturelands were assigned by the toss of the sacred dice.

⁹⁻¹⁶First to receive their assignment were the priests—the descendants of Aaron, who was a member of the Kohath division of the Levites. The tribes of Judah and Simeon gave them the nine cities listed below, with their surrounding pasturelands:

Hebron, in the Judean hills, as a City of Refuge—it was also called Kiriath-arba (Arba was the father of Anak)—although the fields beyond the city and the surrounding villages were given to Caleb, the son of Jephunneh; Libnah, Jattir, Eshtemoa, Holon, Debir, Ain, Juttah, and Beth-shemesh.

¹⁷,¹⁸The tribe of Benjamin gave them these four cities and their pasturelands: Gibeon, Gaba, Anathoth, and Almon. ¹⁹So in all, thirteen cities were given to the priests—the descendants of Aaron.

²⁰⁻²²The other families of the Kohath division received four cities and pasturelands from the tribe of Ephraim: Shechem (a City of Refuge), Gezer, Kibza-im, and Beth-horon.

²³,²⁴The following four cities and pasturelands were given by the tribe of Dan: Elteke, Gibbethon, Aijalon, and Gath-rimmon.

²⁵The half-tribe of Manasseh gave the cities of Taanach and Gath-rimmon with their surrounding pasturelands. ²⁶So the total number of cities and pasturelands given to the remainder of the Kohath division was ten.

²⁷The descendants of Gershon, another division of the Levites, received two cities and pasturelands from the half-tribe of Manasseh: Golan, in Bashan (a City of Refuge), and Be-eshterah.

²⁸,²⁹The tribe of Issachar gave four cities: Kishion, Daberath, Jarmuth, and Engannim.

³⁰,³¹The tribe of Asher gave four cities and pasturelands: Mishal, Abdon, Helkath, and Rehob.

³²The tribe of Naphtali gave: Kedesh, in Galilee (a City of Refuge), Hammoth-dor, and Kartan.

Family Devotions

☐ **Devotion 85**
Forgiving Others

Read Joshua 20:1-6

Forgiving Others
Memory Verse

Be gentle and ready to forgive; never hold grudges. Remember, the Lord forgave you, so you must forgive others.
Colossians 3:13

"That dumb old Debbie!" cried Glenna, slamming the kitchen door. "I'll never play with her again."

"What's the matter?" Mom asked. "I thought Debbie was your best friend."

"Some friend!" exclaimed Glenna. "She broke the shell beads Grandma sent me from Florida. Look!" She opened her hands to show her mother the pile of tiny shells.

"Hmmm," murmured Mom. "The shells don't seem to be broken—only the cord they were on. We can restring them good as new. Was Debbie angry about something?"

"No," admitted Glenna. "I just let her try them on, and when she straightened them, they broke. The shells went all over the floor. She should have been more careful!"

"I see," said Mom. After a moment she added, "Maybe we shouldn't go to Faith Church anymore, either."

"Why not?" asked Glenna in surprise. "We've gone to that church as long as I can remember! I have lots of friends there—I like going there."

"But look at this." Mom held up a broken cup. "Pastor and Mrs. Howard stopped by, and I gave them a cup of coffee. When Pastor set the cup down, the handle came off. Of course, I can glue it back on, only—"

"But, Mom, that's silly," protested Glenna. "He didn't mean to break it. It was an accident. Why would—oh!" She stopped as she saw the slight smile her mother wore and the twinkle in her eye. "I guess you're trying to say I'm being unfair to Debbie," she finally said. "I guess the broken beads were an accident, too."

Mom smiled as she commented, "It's funny how much easier it is to see that someone else is acting foolishly than it is to see that you are. Next time you begin to feel angry toward someone, think about how it looks to other people—and more important, how it looks to God."

How About You?
Has someone made you angry by ruining something of yours? Did you stop being friends because of it or say mean things about that person? Think carefully now—are you being foolish? Why not ask God to forgive you for your unloving attitude, and then make things right with your friend, too. *L. M. W.*

- For the next devotional, turn to page 253.   • For the next devotional on *Forgiving Others*, turn to page 343.
- For notes on *Forgiving Others*, see pages 273, 356, 586, and 822.

33So thirteen cities with their pasturelands were assigned to the division of Gershon.

34,35The remainder of the Levites—the Merari division—were given four cities by the tribe of Zebulun: Jokneam, Kartah, Dimnah, and Nahalal.

36,37Reuben gave them: Bezer, Jahaz, Kedemoth, and Mephaath. 38,39Gad gave them four cities with pasturelands: Ramoth (a City of Refuge), Mahanaim, Heshbon, and Jazer.

40So the Merari division of the Levites was given twelve cities in all.

41,42The total number of cities and pasturelands given to the Levites came to forty-eight.

43So in this way the Lord gave to Israel all the land he had promised to their ancestors, and they went in and conquered it and lived there. 44And the Lord gave them peace, just as he had promised, and no one could stand against them; the Lord helped them destroy all their enemies. 45Every good thing the Lord had promised them came true.

22 The Eastern Tribes Settle Down

Joshua now called together the troops from the tribes of Reuben, Gad, and the half-tribe of Manasseh, 2,3and addressed them as follows:

"You have done as the Lord's disciple Moses commanded you, and have obeyed every order I have given you—every order of the Lord your God. You have not deserted your brother tribes, even though the campaign has lasted for such a long time. 4And now the Lord our God has given us success and rest as he promised he would. So go home now to the land given you by the Lord's servant Moses, on the other side of the Jordan River. 5Be sure to continue to obey all of the commandments Moses gave you. Love the Lord and follow his plan for your lives. Cling to him and serve him enthusiastically."

6So Joshua blessed them and sent them home. 7,8(Moses had assigned the land of Bashan to the half-tribe of Manasseh, although the other half of the tribe was given land on the west side of the Jordan.) As Joshua sent away these troops, he blessed them and told them to share their great wealth with their relatives back home—their loot of cattle, silver, gold, bronze, iron, and clothing.

9So the troops of Reuben, Gad, and the half-tribe of Manasseh left the army of Israel at Shiloh in Canaan and crossed the Jordan River to their own homeland of Gilead. 10Before they went across, while they were still in Canaan, they built a large monument for everyone to see, in the shape of an altar.

11But when the rest of Israel heard about what they had done, 12they mustered an army at Shiloh and prepared to go to war against their brother tribes. 13First, however, they sent a delegation led by Phinehas, the son of Eleazar the priest. They crossed the river and talked to the tribes of Reuben, Gad, and Manasseh. 14In this delegation were ten high officials of Israel, one from each of the ten tribes, and each a clan leader. 15When they arrived in the land of Gilead they said to the tribes of Reuben, Gad, and the half-tribe of Manasseh,

16"The whole congregation of the Lord demands to know why you are sinning against the God of Israel by turning away from him and building an altar of rebellion against the Lord. 17,18Was our guilt at Peor—from which we have not even yet been cleansed despite the plague that tormented us—so little that you must rebel again? For you know that if you rebel today the Lord will be angry with all of us tomorrow. 19If you need the altar because your land is defiled, then join us on our side of the river where the Lord lives among us in his Tabernacle, and we will share our land with you. But do not rebel against the Lord by building another altar in addition to the only true altar of our God. 20Don't you remember that when Achan, the son of Zerah, sinned against the Lord, the entire nation was punished in addition to the one man who had sinned?"

21This was the reply of the people of Reuben, Gad, and the half-tribe of Manasseh to these high officials:

22,23"We swear by Jehovah, the God of gods, that we have not built the altar in rebellion against the Lord. He knows (and let all Israel know it too) that we have not built the altar to sacrifice burnt offerings or grain offerings or peace offerings—may the curse of God be on us if we did. 24,25We have done it because we love the Lord and because we fear that in the future your children will say to ours, 'What right do you have to worship the Lord God of Israel? The Lord has placed the Jordan River as a barrier between our people and your people! You have no part in the Lord.' And your children may make our children stop worshiping him. 26,27So we decided to build the altar as a symbol to show our children and your children that we, too, may worship the Lord with our burnt offerings and peace offerings and sacrifices, and your children will not be able to say to ours, 'You have

---

TRUSTING GOD'S PLAN **21:43-45** God proved faithful in fulfilling every promise he had given to Israel. Fulfillment of some promises took several years, but "every good thing the Lord had promised them came true" (21:45). His promises will be fulfilled according to his timetable, not ours, but we know that his Word is sure. The more we learn of those promises God has fulfilled and continues to fulfill, the easier it is to hope for those yet to come. **To begin the series of devotionals on TRUSTING GOD'S PLAN, turn to page 9.**

Family Devotions

☐ **Devotion 86**
Putting God First

Read Joshua 24:14-15

Putting God First Memory Verse

In everything you do, put God first, and he will direct you and crown your efforts with success.
Proverbs 3:6

"Mr. Henry sure rushed out after the service this morning!" observed Dennis one Sunday noon.

"He was having some trouble at the farm," said Dad. "Thousands of baby chicks arrived yesterday, and last night the heaters in his chicken house went on the blink. I heard he actually slept in the chicken house last night."

"Talk about dedication!" exclaimed Dennis, making a face at the idea. Then he excused himself from the table.

"Where are you headed, Son?" asked Mom.

"Over to Bob's," replied Dennis. "The guys are all going sledding on his hill."

When Dennis arrived home, his face was cold and his clothes were soaked. "Take those boots off before you walk through the house!" ordered Mom. "And hurry and get changed—it's almost time for church."

"May I please stay home tonight? The guys are going back to Bob's to play round-robin Ping-Pong." He could see Dad shaking his head. "You're the one who said my friends need my Christian influence," Dennis argued. "If that's the case, I need to be with them."

"Wasn't it you who marveled at Mr. Henry's dedication when you heard he'd slept in the chicken house last night?" Mom asked. "Mr. Henry didn't say a word to you, but his actions impressed you quite a bit."

"Well . . . yeah." Dennis wasn't sure where this conversation was leading.

"People who watch Mr. Henry can tell he's committed to farming. Because of that commitment, many people find it easy to trust him for advice," explained Dad.

"That principle holds true in regard to Christians, too. Telling others about being a Christian is good, but it has more impact when they can see your commitment to God."

"And that commitment to God shows in your faithful church attendance," added Mom, "so . . . go get ready for church."

How About You?

Are you committed to God? Can others see that commitment by the way you live and by what takes first place in your life? Others will see the Lord through your actions as well as your words. N. E. K.

- For the next devotional, turn to page 259.   • For the next devotional on *Putting God First*, turn to page 295.
- For notes on *Putting God First*, see pages 397, 492, 644, 791, and 982.

no part in the Lord our God.' ²⁸If they say this, our children can reply, 'Look at the altar of the Lord that our fathers made, patterned after the altar of Jehovah. It is not for burnt offerings or sacrifices but is a symbol of the relationship with God that both of us have.' ²⁹Far be it from us to turn away from the Lord or to rebel against him by building our own altar for burnt offerings, grain offerings, or sacrifices. Only the altar in front of the Tabernacle may be used for that."

³⁰When Phinehas the priest and the high officials heard this from the tribes of Reuben, Gad, and Manasseh, they were very happy. ³¹Phinehas replied to them, "Today we know that the Lord is among us because you have not sinned against the Lord as we thought; instead, you have saved us from destruction!"

³²Then Phinehas and the ten ambassadors went back to the people of Israel and told them what had happened, ³³and all Israel rejoiced and praised God and spoke no more of war against Reuben and Gad. ³⁴The people of Reuben and Gad named the altar "The Altar of Witness," for they said, "It is a witness between us and them that Jehovah is our God too."

23 Joshua's Final Orders

Long after this, when the Lord had given success to the people of Israel against their enemies and when Joshua was very old, ²he called for the leaders of Israel—the elders, judges, and officers—and said to them, "I am an old man now, ³and you have seen all that the Lord your God has done for you during my lifetime. He has fought for you against your enemies and has given you their land. ⁴,⁵And I have divided to you the land of the nations yet unconquered as well as the land of those you have already destroyed. All the land from the Jordan River to the Mediterranean Sea shall be yours, for the Lord your God will drive out all the people living there now, and you will live there instead, just as he has promised you.

⁶"But be very sure to follow all the instructions written in the book of the laws of Moses; do not deviate from them the least little bit. ⁷Be sure that you do not mix with the heathen people still remaining in the land; do not even mention the names of their gods, much less swear by them or worship them. ⁸But follow the Lord your God just as you have until now. ⁹He has driven out great, strong nations from before you, and no one has been able to defeat you. ¹⁰Each one of you has put to flight a thousand of the enemy, for the Lord your God fights for you, just as he has promised. ¹¹So be very careful to keep on loving him.

¹²"If you don't, and if you begin to intermarry with the nations around you, ¹³ then know for a certainty that the Lord your God will no longer chase those nations from your land. Instead, they will be a snare and a trap to you, a pain in your side and a thorn in your eyes, and you will disappear from this good land which the Lord your God has given you.

¹⁴"Soon I will be going the way of all the earth—I am going to die.

"You know very well that God's promises to you have all come true. ¹⁵,¹⁶But as certainly as the Lord has given you the good things he promised, just as certainly he will bring evil upon you if you disobey him. For if you worship other gods, he will completely wipe you out from this good land that the Lord has given you. His anger will rise hot against you, and you will quickly perish."

24 Joshua's Good-bye Speech

Then Joshua summoned all the people of Israel to him at Shechem, along with their leaders—the elders, officers, and judges. So they came and presented themselves before God.

²Then Joshua addressed them as follows: "The Lord God of Israel says, 'Your ancestors, including Terah the father of Abraham and Nahor, lived east of the Euphrates River; and they worshiped other gods. ³But I took your father Abraham from that land across the river and led him into the land of Canaan and gave him many descendants through Isaac, his son. ⁴Isaac's children, whom I gave him, were Jacob and Esau. To Esau I gave the area around Mount Seir while Jacob and his children went into Egypt.

⁵"Then I sent Moses and Aaron to bring terrible plagues upon Egypt; and afterwards I brought my people out as free men. ⁶But when they arrived at the Red Sea, the Egyptians chased after them with chariots and cavalry. ⁷Then Israel cried out to me and I put darkness between them and the Egyptians; and I brought the sea crashing in upon the Egyptians, drowning them. You saw what I did. Then Israel lived in the wilderness for many years.

⁸"Finally I brought you into the land of the Amorites on the other side of the Jordan; and they fought against you, but I destroyed them and gave you their land. ⁹Then King Balak of Moab started a war against Israel, and he asked Balaam, the son of Beor, to curse you. ¹⁰But I wouldn't listen to him. Instead I made him bless you; and so I delivered Israel from him.

¹¹"Then you crossed the Jordan River and came to Jericho. The men of Jericho fought against you, and so did many others—the Perizzites, the Canaanites, the Hittites, the Girgashites, the Hivites, and the Jebusites. Each in turn fought against you, but I destroyed them all. ¹²And I sent hornets

ahead of you to drive out the two kings of the Amorites and their people. It was not your swords or bows that brought you victory! ¹³I gave you land you had not worked for and cities you did not build—these cities where you are now living. I gave you vineyards and olive groves for food, though you did not plant them.'

¹⁴"So revere Jehovah and serve him in sincerity and truth. Put away forever the idols your ancestors worshiped when they lived beyond the Euphrates River and in Egypt. Worship the Lord alone. ¹⁵But if you are unwilling to obey the Lord, then decide today whom you will obey. Will it be the gods of your ancestors beyond the Euphrates or the gods of the Amorites here in this land? But as for me and my family, we will serve the Lord." ¹⁶And the people replied, "We would never forsake the Lord and worship other gods! ¹⁷For the Lord our God is the one who rescued our fathers from their slavery in the land of Egypt. He is the God who did mighty miracles before the eyes of Israel, as we traveled through the wilderness, and preserved us from our enemies when we passed through their land. ¹⁸It was the Lord who drove out the Amorites and the other nations living here in the land. Yes, we choose the Lord, for he alone is our God."

¹⁹But Joshua replied to the people, "You can't worship the Lord God, for he is holy and jealous; he will not forgive your rebellion and sins. ²⁰If you forsake him and worship other gods, he will turn upon you and destroy you, even though he has taken care of you for such a long time."

²¹But the people answered, "We choose the Lord!"

²²"You have heard yourselves say it," Joshua said. "You have chosen to obey the Lord."

"Yes," they replied, "we are witnesses."

²³"All right," he said, "then you must destroy all the idols you now own, and you must obey the Lord God of Israel."

²⁴The people replied to Joshua, "Yes, we will worship and obey the Lord alone."

²⁵So Joshua made a covenant with them that day at Shechem, committing them to a permanent and binding contract between themselves and God. ²⁶Joshua recorded the people's reply in the book of the laws of God and took a huge stone as a reminder and rolled it beneath the oak tree that was beside the Tabernacle.

²⁷Then Joshua said to all the people, "This stone has heard everything the Lord said, so it will be a witness to testify against you if you go back on your word."

²⁸Then Joshua sent the people away to their own sections of the country.

²⁹Soon after this he died at the age of 110. ³⁰He was buried on his own estate at Timnath-serah, in the hill country of Ephraim, on the north side of the mountains of Gaash.

³¹Israel obeyed the Lord throughout the lifetimes of Joshua and the other old men who had personally witnessed the amazing deeds the Lord had done for Israel.

³²The bones of Joseph, the people of Israel had brought them along when they left Egypt—were buried in Shechem, in the parcel of ground Jacob had bought from the sons of Hamor. (The land was located in the territory assigned to the tribes of Joseph.)

³³Eleazar, the son of Aaron, also died; he was buried in the hill country of Ephraim, at Gibeah, the city that had been given to his son Phinehas.

Judges

HOW DOES God feel when we disobey him? The book of Judges gives us a clue.

The Israelites were getting settled in their land. They didn't have a king or president because they wanted God to be their leader. But families stopped teaching their children about God. Soon everyone started worshiping other gods.

How did God respond? He wanted his people back! First God showed the Israelites that following other gods isn't worth it. False gods have no power to protect or care for people. The Israelites were attacked by enemies and defeated. Then the Israelites realized they were wrong and called to the Living God for help. God forgave them and sent them leaders—called judges—to help them defeat their enemies and guide them back to God. While the Israelites followed God, things went well. But each time a judge died, they turned away from God again. This happened over and over.

How often does God forgive the wrong things we do? Every time we ask him! As you read Judges, look for how God responded to Israel's sin.

God Gives Victory

After Joshua died, the nation of Israel went to the Lord to receive his instructions.

"Which of our tribes should be the first to go to war against the Canaanites?" they inquired.

²God's answer came, "Judah. And I will give them a great victory."

³The leaders of the tribe of Judah, however, asked help from the tribe of Simeon. "Join us in clearing out the people living in the territory allotted to us," they said, "and then we will help you conquer yours." So the army of Simeon went with the army of Judah. ⁴⁻⁶And the Lord helped them defeat the Canaanites and Perizzites, so that ten thousand of the enemy were slain at Bezek. King Adoni-bezek escaped, but the Israeli army soon captured him and cut off his thumbs and big toes.

⁷"I have treated seventy kings in this same manner and have fed them the scraps under my table!" King Adoni-bezek said. "Now God has paid me back." He was taken to Jerusalem and died there.

8(Judah had conquered Jerusalem and massacred its people, setting the city on fire.) 9Afterward the army of Judah fought the Canaanites in the hill country and in the Negeb, as well as on the coastal plains. 10Then Judah marched against the Canaanites in Hebron (formerly called Kiriath-arba), destroying the cities of Sheshai, Ahiman, and Talmai. 11Later they attacked the city of Debir (formerly called Kiriath-sepher).

12"Who will lead the attack against Debir?" Caleb challenged them. "Whoever conquers it shall have my daughter Achsah as his wife!"

13Caleb's nephew, Othniel, son of his younger brother Kenaz, volunteered to lead the attack; and he conquered the city and won Achsah as his bride. 14As they were leaving for their new home, she urged him to ask her father for an additional piece of land. She dismounted from her donkey to speak to Caleb about it.

"What do you wish?" he asked.

15And she replied, "You have been kind enough to give me land in the Negeb, but please give us springs of water too."

So Caleb gave her the upper and lower springs.

16When the tribe of Judah moved into its new land in the Negeb wilderness south of Arad, the descendants of Moses' father-in-law—members of the Kenite tribe—accompanied them. They left their homes in Jericho, "The City of Palm Trees," and the two tribes lived together after that. 17Afterwards the army of Judah joined Simeon's, and they fought the Canaanites at the city of Zephath and massacred all its people. So now the city is named Hormah (meaning, "massacred"). 18The army of Judah also conquered the cities of Gaza, Ashkelon, and Ekron, with their surrounding villages. 19The Lord helped the tribe of Judah exterminate the people of the hill country, though they failed in their attempt to conquer the people of the valley, who had iron chariots.

20The city of Hebron was given to Caleb as the Lord had promised; so Caleb drove out the inhabitants of the city; they were descendants of the three sons of Anak.

21The tribe of Benjamin failed to exterminate the Jebusites living in their part of the city of Jerusalem, so they still live there today, mingled with the Israelis.

22,23As for the tribe of Joseph, they attacked the city of Bethel, formerly known as Luz, and the Lord was with them. First they sent scouts, 24who captured a man coming out of the city. They offered to spare his life and that of his family if he would show them the entrance passage through the wall. 25So he showed them how to get in, and they massacred the entire population except for this man and his family. 26Later the man moved to Syria and founded a city there, naming it Luz, too, as it is still known today.

27The tribe of Manasseh failed to drive out the people living in Beth-shean, Taanach, Dor, Ibleam, Megiddo, with their surrounding towns; so the Canaanites stayed there. 28In later years when the Israelis were stronger, they put the Canaanites to work as slaves, but never did force them to leave the country. 29This was also true of the Canaanites living in Gezer; they still live among the tribe of Ephraim.

30And the tribe of Zebulun did not massacre the people of Kitron or Nahalol, but made them their slaves; 31,32nor did the tribe of Asher drive out the residents of Acco, Sidon, Ahlab, Achzib, Helbah, Aphik, or Rehob; so the Israelis still live among the Canaanites, who were the original people of that land. 33And the tribe of Naphtali did not drive out the people of Beth-shemesh or of Beth-anath, so these people continue to live among them as servants.

34As for the tribe of Dan, the Amorites forced them into the hill country and wouldn't let them come down into the valley; 35but when the Amorites later spread into Mount Heres, Aijalon, and Shaalbim, the tribe of Joseph conquered them and made them their slaves. 36The boundary of the Amorites begins at the ascent of Scorpion Pass, runs to a spot called The Rock, and continues upward from there.

2 Covenant Is Broken

One day the Angel of the Lord arrived at Bochim, coming from Gilgal, and announced to the people of Israel, "I brought you out of Egypt into this land that I promised to your ancestors, and I said that I would never break my covenant with you, 2if you, on your part, would make no peace treaties with the people living in this land; I told you to destroy their heathen altars. Why have you not obeyed? 3And now since you have broken the contract, it is no longer in effect, and I no longer promise to destroy the nations living in your land; rather, they shall be thorns in your sides, and their gods will be a constant temptation to you."

4The people broke into tears as the Angel finished speaking; 5so the name of that place was called "Bochim" (meaning, "the place where people wept"). Then they offered sacrifices to the Lord.

6When Joshua finally disbanded the armies of Israel, the tribes moved into their new territories and took possession of the land. 7-9Joshua, the man of God, died at the age of 110 and was buried at the edge of his property in Timnath-heres, in the hill country of Ephraim, north of Mount Gaash. The people had remained true to the Lord

FAMILY DEVOTIONS

☐ **DEVOTION 87**
PERSEVERANCE

Read Judges 1:16–2:5

Carl and his friend Jay burst into the living room. "Look, Dad, I've got a new model." Carl held up the box so his father could see the picture of the fighter plane.

"Nice!" approved Dad. "You must have quite a collection. You've brought home several models lately."

"Right! I've got a Tiger, and a Hornet, and a B-52—"

"Can I see them?" interrupted Jay.

Carl hesitated. "Well, I haven't finished them yet. But I've got 'em all started. I'll finish them someday."

Dad looked up, frowning. "In that case I think I'd better hold this one for you until the others are done. Leaving things unfinished is a waste of time and effort."

"Aw, Dad," protested Carl, "it's just a model."

"Yes," agreed Dad, "but I'm afraid you're developing lifelong habits that will hurt you, Carl. Remember the garden last spring? You got the ground all prepared, but you never got it planted. And then there was the doghouse you started to build."

"Don't remind me," groaned Carl. "But don't worry. I'll do it tomorrow."

Jay laughed. "My dad always says, 'Tomorrow never comes.'"

"He's right," agreed Dad. "God tells us we are to be faithful in the things we have to do, big or small. Good work habits will help you serve the Lord better. If you can't finish the things you start for your own pleasure, you probably won't finish the things you start for him, either."

Carl looked at the model he was holding. Then he handed it to Dad. "Here, don't put this too far away. I'll need it soon," he said. He looked at Jay. "I've got some models I need to get to work on. Want to give me a hand?"

Perseverance
Memory Verse

Be strong and courageous and get to work. Don't be frightened by the size of the task, for the Lord my God is with you; he will not forsake you. He will see to it that everything is finished correctly.
1 Chronicles 28:20

How About You?

Do you lose interest in projects before you finish them? Have you ever promised the Lord you would be faithful in a certain area, such as praying or Bible reading, and then failed to do so? God has the power to help you keep on working when the job may seem uninteresting or difficult. Ask him to give you his strength to complete any service you begin. Make up your mind not to quit before a job is finished as the people of Israel did. *C. R.*

• For the next devotional, turn to page 263. • For the next devotional on PERSEVERANCE, turn to page 551.
• For notes on PERSEVERANCE, see pages 326, 461, 503, 760, and 1174.

throughout Joshua's lifetime, and as long afterward as the old men of his generation were still living—those who had seen the mighty miracles the Lord had done for Israel.

[10]But finally all that generation died; and the next generation did not worship Jehovah as their God and did not care about the mighty miracles he had done for Israel. [11]They did many things that the Lord had expressly forbidden, including the worshiping of heathen gods. [12-14]They abandoned Jehovah, the God loved and worshiped by their ancestors—the God who had brought them out of Egypt. Instead, they were worshiping and bowing low before the idols of the neighboring nations. So the anger of the Lord flamed out against all Israel. He left them to the mercy of their enemies, for they had departed from Jehovah and were worshiping Baal and the Ashtaroth idols.

[15]So now when the nation of Israel went out to battle against its enemies, the Lord blocked their path. He had warned them about this, and in fact had vowed that he would do it. But when the people were in this terrible plight, [16]the Lord raised up judges to save them from their enemies.

[17]Yet even then Israel would not listen to the judges, but broke faith with Jehovah by worshiping other gods instead. How quickly they turned away from the true faith of their ancestors, for they refused to obey God's commands. [18]Each judge rescued the people of Israel from their enemies throughout his lifetime, for the Lord was moved to pity by the groaning of his people under their crushing oppressions; so he helped them as long as that judge lived. [19]But when the judge died, the people turned from doing right and behaved even worse than their ancestors had. They prayed to heathen gods again, throwing themselves to the ground in humble worship. They stubbornly returned to the evil customs of the nations around them.

[20]Then the anger of the Lord would flame out against Israel again. He declared, "Because these people have violated the treaty I made with their ancestors, [21]I will no longer drive out the nations left unconquered by Joshua when he died. [22]Instead, I will use these nations to test my people, to see whether or not they will obey the Lord as their ancestors did."

[23]So the Lord left those nations in the land and did not drive them out, nor let Israel destroy them.

3 Canaanites Left in the Land

Here is a list of the nations the Lord left in the land to test the new generation of Israel who had not experienced the wars of Canaan. For God wanted to give opportunity to the youth of Israel to exercise faith and obedience in conquering their enemies: the Philistines (five cities), the Canaanites, the Sidonians, the Hivites living in Mount Lebanon, from Baal-hermon to the entrance of Hamath. [4]These people were a test to the new generation of Israel, to see whether they would obey the commandments the Lord had given to them through Moses.

[5]So Israel lived among the Canaanites, Hittites, Hivites, Perizzites, Amorites, and Jebusites. [6]But instead of destroying them, the people of Israel intermarried with them. The young men of Israel took their girls as wives, and the Israeli girls married their men. And soon Israel was worshiping their gods. [7]So the people of Israel were very evil in God's sight, for they turned against Jehovah their God and worshiped Baal and the Asheroth idols.

[8]Then the anger of the Lord flamed out against Israel, and he let King Cushan-rishathaim of eastern Syria conquer them. They were under his rule for eight years. [9]But when Israel cried out to the Lord, he gave them Caleb's nephew, Othniel (son of Kenaz, Caleb's younger brother) to save them. [10]The Spirit of the Lord took control of him, and he reformed and purged Israel so that when he led the forces of Israel against the army of King Cushan-rishathaim, the Lord helped Israel conquer him completely.

[11]Then, for forty years under Othniel, there was peace in the land. But when Othniel died, [12]the people of Israel turned once again to their sinful ways, so God helped King Eglon of Moab to conquer part of Israel at that time. [13]Allied with him were the armies of the Ammonites and the Amalekites. These forces defeated the Israelis and took possession of Jericho, often called "The City of Palm Trees." [14]For the next eighteen years the people of Israel were required to pay crushing taxes to King Eglon.

[15]But when they cried to the Lord, he sent them a savior, Ehud (son of Gera, a Benjaminite), who was left-handed. Ehud was the man chosen to carry Israel's annual tax money to the Moabite capital. [16]Before he went on this journey, he made himself a double-edged dagger eighteen inches long and hid it in his clothing, strapped against his right thigh. [17-19]After delivering the money to King Eglon (who, by the way, was very fat!), he started home again. But outside

---

KNOWING YOU'RE SPECIAL TO GOD   3:15-21 This is a strange story, but it teaches us that God can use us just the way he made us. Being left-handed in Ehud's day was considered a handicap or, at best, an abnormality. But Ehud's perceived weakness was used by God to give Israel victory. Let God use you the way you are to accomplish his work. **To begin the series of devotionals on KNOWING YOU'RE SPECIAL TO GOD, turn to page 307.**

the city, at the quarries of Gilgal, he sent his companions on and returned alone to the king.

"I have a secret message for you," he told him.

The king immediately dismissed all those who were with him so that he could have a private interview. [20]Ehud walked over to him as he was sitting in a cool upstairs room and said to him, "It is a message from God!"

King Eglon stood up at once to receive it, [21]whereupon Ehud reached beneath his robe with his strong left hand, pulled out the double-bladed dagger strapped against his right thigh, and plunged it deep into the king's belly. [22,23]The hilt of the dagger disappeared beneath the flesh, and the fat closed over it as the entrails oozed out. Leaving the dagger there, Ehud locked the doors behind him and escaped across an upstairs porch.

[24]When the king's servants returned and saw that the doors were locked, they waited, thinking that perhaps he was using the bathroom. [25]But when, after a long time, he still didn't come out, they became concerned and got a key. And when they opened the door, they found their master dead on the floor.

[26]Meanwhile Ehud had escaped past the quarries to Seirah. [27]When he arrived in the hill country of Ephraim, he blew a trumpet as a call to arms and mustered an army under his own command.

[28]"Follow me," he told them, "for the Lord has put your enemies, the Moabites, at your mercy!"

The army then proceeded to seize the fords of the Jordan River near Moab, preventing anyone from crossing. [29]Then they attacked the Moabites and killed about ten thousand of the strongest and most skillful of their fighting men, letting not one escape. [30]So Moab was conquered by Israel that day, and the land was at peace for the next eighty years.

[31]The next judge after Ehud was Shamgar (son of Anath). He once killed six hundred Philistines with an ox goad, thereby saving Israel from disaster.

4 Deborah and Barak

After Ehud's death the people of Israel again sinned against the Lord, [2,3]so the Lord let them be conquered by King Jabin of Hazor, in Canaan. The commander-in-chief of his army was Sisera, who lived in Harosheth-hagoiim. He had nine hundred iron chariots and made life unbearable for the Israelis for twenty years. But finally they begged the Lord for help.

[4]Israel's leader at that time, the one who was responsible for bringing the people back to God, was Deborah, a prophetess, the wife of Lappidoth. [5]She held court at a place now called "Deborah's Palm Tree," between Ramah and Bethel, in the hill country of Ephraim; and the Israelites came to her to decide their disputes.

[6]One day she summoned Barak (son of Abinoam), who lived in Kedesh, in the land of Naphtali, and said to him, "The Lord God of Israel has commanded you to mobilize ten thousand men from the tribes of Naphtali and Zebulun. Lead them to Mount Tabor [7]to fight King Jabin's mighty army with all his chariots, under General Sisera's command. The Lord says, 'I will draw them to the Kishon River, and you will defeat them there.'"

[8]"I'll go, but only if you go with me!" Barak told her.

[9]"All right," she replied, "I'll go with you; but I'm warning you now that the honor of conquering Sisera will go to a woman instead of to you!" So she went with him to Kedesh.

[10]When Barak summoned the men of Zebulun and Naphtali to mobilize at Kedesh, ten thousand men volunteered. And Deborah marched with them. [11] (Heber, the Kenite—the Kenites were the descendants of Moses' father-in-law Hobab—had moved away from the rest of his clan, and had been living in various places as far away as the Oak of Zaanannim, near Kedesh.) [12]When General Sisera was told that Barak and his army were camped at Mount Tabor, [13]he mobilized his entire army, including the nine hundred iron chariots, and marched from Harosheth-hagoiim to the Kishon River.

[14]Then Deborah said to Barak, "Now is the time for action! The Lord leads on! He has already delivered Sisera into your hand!"

So Barak led his ten thousand men down the slopes of Mount Tabor into battle.

[15]Then the Lord threw the enemy into a panic, both the soldiers and the charioteers, and Sisera leaped from his chariot and escaped on foot. [16]Barak and his men chased the enemy and the chariots as far as Harosheth-hagoiim, until all of Sisera's army was destroyed; not one man was left alive. [17]Meanwhile, Sisera had escaped to the tent of Jael, the wife of Heber the Kenite, for there was a mutual-assistance agreement between King Jabin of Hazor and the clan of Heber.

[18]Jael went out to meet Sisera and said to him, "Come into my tent, sir. You will be safe here in our protection. Don't be afraid." So he went into her tent, and she covered him with a blanket.

[19]"Please give me some water," he said, "for I am very thirsty." So she gave him some milk and covered him again.

[20]"Stand in the door of the tent," he told her, "and if anyone comes by, looking for me, tell them that no one is here."

[21]Then Jael took a sharp tent peg and a hammer and, quietly creeping up to him as he slept,

she drove the peg through his temples and into the ground; and so he died, for he was fast asleep from weariness.

²²When Barak came by looking for Sisera, Jael went out to meet him and said, "Come, and I will show you the man you are looking for."

So he followed her into the tent and found Sisera lying there dead, with the tent peg through his temples. ²³So that day the Lord used Israel to subdue King Jabin of Canaan. ²⁴And from that time on Israel became stronger and stronger against King Jabin, until he and all his people were destroyed.

5 Deborah and Barak's Song

Then Deborah and Barak sang this song about the wonderful victory:

²"Praise the Lord!
Israel's leaders bravely led;
The people gladly followed!
Yes, bless the Lord!
³Listen, O you kings and princes,
For I shall sing about the Lord,
The God of Israel.
⁴When you led us out from Seir,
Out across the fields of Edom,
The earth trembled
And the sky poured down its rain.
⁵Yes, even Mount Sinai quaked
At the presence of the God of Israel!
⁶In the days of Shamgar and of Jael,
The main roads were deserted.
Travelers used the narrow, crooked side paths.
⁷Israel's population dwindled,
Until Deborah became a mother to Israel.
⁸When Israel chose new gods,
Everything collapsed.
Our masters would not let us have
A shield or spear.
Among forty thousand men of Israel,
Not a weapon could be found!
⁹How I rejoice
In the leaders of Israel
Who offered themselves so willingly!
Praise the Lord!
¹⁰Let all Israel, rich and poor,
Join in his praises—
Those who ride on white donkeys
And sit on rich carpets,
And those who are poor and must walk.
¹¹The village musicians
Gather at the village well
To sing of the triumphs of the Lord.
Again and again they sing the ballad
Of how the Lord saved Israel
With an army of peasants!
The people of the Lord
Marched through the gates!
¹²Awake, O Deborah, and sing!
Arise, O Barak!
O son of Abinoam, lead away your captives!
¹³,¹⁴Down from Mount Tabor marched the noble remnant.
The people of the Lord
Marched down against great odds.
They came from Ephraim and Benjamin,
From Machir and from Zebulun.
¹⁵Down into the valley
Went the princes of Issachar
With Deborah and Barak.
At God's command they rushed into the valley.
(But the tribe of Reuben didn't go.
¹⁶Why did you sit at home among the sheepfolds,
Playing your shepherd pipes?
Yes, the tribe of Reuben has an uneasy conscience.
¹⁷Why did Gilead remain across the Jordan,
And why did Dan remain with his ships?
And why did Asher sit unmoved
Upon the seashore,
At ease beside his harbors?)
¹⁸But the tribes of Zebulun and Naphtali
Dared to die upon the fields of battle.
¹⁹The kings of Canaan fought in Taanach
By Megiddo's springs,
But did not win the victory.
²⁰The very stars of heaven
Fought Sisera.
²¹The rushing Kishon River
Swept them away.
March on, my soul, with strength!
²²Hear the stamping
Of the horsehoofs of the enemy!
See the prancing of his steeds!
²³But the Angel of Jehovah
Put a curse on Meroz.
'Curse them bitterly,' he said,
'Because they did not come to help the Lord
Against his enemies.'
²⁴Blessed be Jael,
The wife of Heber the Kenite—
Yes, may she be blessed
Above all women who live in tents.
²⁵He asked for water
And she gave him milk in a beautiful cup!
²⁶Then she took a tent pin and a workman's hammer
And pierced Sisera's temples,
Crushing his head.
She pounded the tent pin through his head.
²⁷He sank, he fell, he lay dead at her feet.
²⁸The mother of Sisera watched through the window

FAMILY DEVOTIONS

☐ **DEVOTION 88**
CONTENTMENT

Read Judges 3:30–4:3

Contentment
Memory Verse

I know how to live on almost nothing or with everything. I have learned the secret of contentment in every situation, whether it be a full stomach or hunger, plenty or want.
Philippians 4:12

The Murrays were concluding their family devotions by reading from an exciting missionary book. "The jungle closed in around Pedro," read Dad. "He knew his enemies were looking for him. Since Pedro had become a Christian, other members of his tribe were determined to kill him. There seemed no escape. Pedro prayed as he ran."

"This is so scary," Mary whispered.

Dad continued reading. "Suddenly a dark-skinned man stepped out of the bushes just ahead. He motioned for Pedro to follow him and started moving deeper into the jungle. *Should I follow him?* Pedro thought. *Is this man an enemy, too? I've never seen him before.* Pedro didn't know what to do." Dad looked up, put a marker in the book and closed it. "End of chapter," he said. "Bedtime!"

"Oh no!" groaned Kurt.

"Just one more page?" pleaded Mary.

Mom shook her head. "There's school tomorrow."

Kurt stretched. "Boy, some people live such exciting lives, and mine is so ordinary. School, practicing trumpet, studying, eating, sleeping, and school again."

"Well, I suspect Pedro was glad when his life became somewhat ordinary after he escaped from his enemies," Dad said.

"Then he does get away!" Kurt laughed heartily at his unexpected discovery. "Well, I still think my days are pretty dull."

"God planned for ordinary days in our lives," said Dad. "He knows we need them to grow and learn about him. Even men of the Bible had ordinary days. Daniel didn't face lions every day. He also worked in the king's court doing many ordinary jobs. And Paul was a tentmaker. He no doubt spent many days sewing, measuring, and cutting. We need to see all those ordinary days as gifts from God."

With a yawn Kurt stood up. "Yeah. Now I better get to bed, so I can be rested for another ordinary day."

How About You?
Do you sometimes feel all the exciting things are happening to everyone else? These days of school, eating, sleeping, and more school are a part of God's plan to prepare you for the future. See each day as a gift from God. *J. G.*

- For the next devotional, turn to page 265. • For the next devotional on *CONTENTMENT*, turn to page 339.
- For notes on *CONTENTMENT*, see pages 542, 547, 902, and 1063.

For his return.
'Why is his chariot so long in coming?
Why don't we hear the sound of the wheels?'
29But her ladies-in-waiting—and she herself—replied,
30"There is much loot to be divided,
And it takes time.
Each man receives a girl or two;
And Sisera will get gorgeous robes,
And he will bring home
Many gifts for me.'
31O Lord, may all your enemies
Perish as Sisera did,
But may those who love the Lord
Shine as the sun!"

After that there was peace in the land for forty years.

6 God Calls Gideon to Lead Israel

Then the people of Israel began once again to worship other gods, and once again the Lord let their enemies harass them. This time it was by the people of Midian, for seven years. 2The Midianites were so cruel that the Israelis took to the mountains, living in caves and dens. 3,4When they planted their seed, marauders from Midian, Amalek, and other neighboring nations came and destroyed their crops and plundered the countryside as far away as Gaza, leaving nothing to eat and taking away all their sheep, oxen, and donkeys. 5These enemy hordes arrived on droves of camels too numerous to count and stayed until the land was completely stripped and devastated. 6,7So Israel was reduced to abject poverty because of the Midianites. Then at last the people of Israel began to cry out to the Lord for help.

8However, the Lord's reply through the prophet he sent to them was this: "The Lord God of Israel brought you out of slavery in Egypt, 9and rescued you from the Egyptians and from all who were cruel to you, and drove out your enemies before you, and gave you their land. 10He told you he is the Lord your God, and you must not worship the gods of the Amorites who live around you on every side. But you have not listened to him."

11But one day the Angel of the Lord came and sat beneath the oak tree at Ophrah, on the farm of Joash the Abiezrite. Joash's son, Gideon, had been threshing wheat by hand in the bottom of a grape press—a pit where grapes were pressed to make wine—for he was hiding from the Midianites.

12The Angel of the Lord appeared to him and said, "Mighty soldier, the Lord is with you!"

13"Stranger," Gideon replied, "if the Lord is with us, why has all this happened to us? And where are all the miracles our ancestors have told us about—such as when God brought them out of Egypt? Now the Lord has thrown us away and has let the Midianites completely ruin us."

14Then the Lord turned to him and said, "I will make you strong! Go and save Israel from the Midianites! I am sending you!"

15But Gideon replied, "Sir, how can *I* save Israel? My family is the poorest in the whole tribe of Manasseh, and I am the least thought of in the entire family!"

16Whereupon the Lord said to him, "But I, Jehovah, will be with you! And you shall quickly destroy the Midianite hordes!"

17Gideon replied, "If it is really true that you are going to help me like that, then do some miracle to prove it! Prove that it is really Jehovah who is talking to me! 18But stay here until I go and get a present for you."

"All right," the Angel agreed. "I'll stay here until you return."

19Gideon hurried home and roasted a young goat and baked some unleavened bread from a bushel of flour. Then, carrying the meat in a basket and broth in a pot, he took it out to the Angel, who was beneath the oak tree, and presented it to him.

20The Angel said to him, "Place the meat and the bread upon that rock over there, and pour the broth over it."

When Gideon had followed these instructions, 21the Angel touched the meat and bread with his staff, and fire flamed up from the rock and consumed them! And suddenly the Angel was gone!

22When Gideon realized that it had indeed been the Angel of the Lord, he cried out, "Alas, O Lord God, for I have seen the Angel of the Lord face to face!"

23"It's all right," the Lord replied. "Don't be afraid! You shall not die."

24And Gideon built an altar there and named it "The Altar of Peace with Jehovah." (The altar is still there in Ophrah in the land of the Abiezrites.) 25That night the Lord told Gideon to hitch his father's best ox to the family altar of Baal and pull it down, and to cut down the wooden idol of the goddess Asherah that stood nearby.

26"Replace it with an altar for the Lord your God, built here on this hill, laying the stones carefully. Then sacrifice the ox as a burnt offering to the Lord, using the wooden idol as wood for the fire on the altar."

27So Gideon took ten of his servants and did as the Lord had commanded. But he did it at night for fear of the other members of his father's household, and for fear of the men of the city; for he knew what would happen if they found out who did it! 28Early the next morning, as the city

FAMILY DEVOTIONS

☐ **DEVOTION 89**
AVOIDING SIN

Read Judges 7:1-22

Zack plopped down on the couch. "Oh, Dad, I'm just sick of school," he complained. "You ought to hear those kids talk. They cuss and cut people down and tell filthy jokes. Then they call me a dweeb because I don't act like they do. I'd like to punch those guys in the nose!"

Dad had just begun to reply when they heard a loud snarl near the back door, followed by some sharp yips. *Arf-arf! Grrrowwwl! Yap-yap!* "That sounds like Cuddles," cried Zack, jumping to his feet. "It must be a dogfight." He ran out of the house, followed by his father. Cuddles, Zack's cocker spaniel puppy, was on the bottom of the dog pile. "They're going to kill her!" Zack screamed.

Dad ran toward the garage. "I'll get the baseball bat."

Grrroowwl! An extra-loud growl chilled the air as Pete, the neighbor's chow, jumped into the fight. Dogs scattered. "Look, Dad!" Zack yelled. "Pete is fighting Cuddles's battle."

The big dog stood protectively over the little one. Dad shook his head in amazement. When Zack knelt beside his whimpering puppy, Pete turned and walked proudly down the street. Zack chuckled. "You've got yourself some friend, Cuddles," he said.

Zack felt a hand on his shoulder. He looked up. "So do you, Son," said Dad. "You may be outnumbered at school—there may be a lot more unbelievers than believers, and they may pick on you. But you've got a friend who makes up the difference."

Zack stood up with Cuddles in his arms. "Guess I do, don't I?" he said. "Thanks, Dad, for reminding me." He started up the steps. "Sure helps to have a big friend, huh, Cuddles?"

Avoiding Sin
Memory Verse

Dear brothers, you are only visitors here. Since your real home is in heaven, I beg you to keep away from the evil pleasures of this world; they are not for you, for they fight against your very souls.
1 Peter 2:11

How About You?
Do you get teased when you refuse to join the crowd in doing wrong? Do you feel like you're outnumbered? Are the problems in your life too big for you? Give them to Jesus. He'll fight your battles for you and help you to do what's right. *B. W.*

• For the next devotional, turn to page 275. • For the next devotional on *AVOIDING SIN,* turn to page 387.
• For notes on *AVOIDING SIN,* see pages 220, 332, 392, and 657.

began to stir, someone discovered that the altar of Baal was knocked apart, the idol beside it was gone, and a new altar had been built instead, with the remains of a sacrifice on it.

29"Who did this?" everyone demanded. Finally they learned that it was Gideon, the son of Joash.

30"Bring out your son," they shouted to Joash. "He must die for insulting the altar of Baal and for cutting down the Asherah idol."

31But Joash retorted to the whole mob, "Does Baal need *your* help? What an insult to a god! You are the ones who should die for insulting Baal! If Baal is really a god, let him take care of himself and destroy the one who broke apart his altar!"

32From then on Gideon was called "Jerubbaal," a nickname meaning "Let Baal take care of himself!"

33Soon afterward the armies of Midian, Amalek, and other neighboring nations united in one vast alliance against Israel. They crossed the Jordan and camped in the valley of Jezreel. 34Then the Spirit of the Lord came upon Gideon, and he blew a trumpet as a call to arms, and the men of Abiezer came to him. 35 He also sent messengers throughout Manasseh, Asher, Zebulun, and Naphtali, summoning their fighting forces, and all of them responded.

36Then Gideon said to God, "If you are really going to use me to save Israel as you promised, 37prove it to me in this way: I'll put some wool on the threshing floor tonight, and if, in the morning, the fleece is wet and the ground is dry, I will know you are going to help me!"

38And it happened just that way! When he got up the next morning, he pressed the fleece together and wrung out a whole bowlful of water!

39Then Gideon said to the Lord, "Please don't be angry with me, but let me make one more test: this time let the fleece remain dry while the ground around it is wet!"

40So the Lord did as he asked; that night the fleece stayed dry, but the ground was covered with dew!

7 Gideon's Army of 300

Jerubbaal (that is, Gideon—his other name) and his army got an early start and went as far as the spring of Harod. The armies of Midian were camped north of them, down in the valley beside the hill of Moreh.

2The Lord then said to Gideon, "There are too many of you! I can't let all of you fight the Midianites, for then the people of Israel will boast to me that they saved themselves by their own strength! 3Send home any of your men who are timid and frightened."

So twenty-two thousand of them left, and only ten thousand remained who were willing to fight.

4But the Lord told Gideon, "There are still too many! Bring them down to the spring and I'll show you which ones shall go with you and which ones shall not."

5,6So Gideon assembled them at the water. There the Lord told him, "Divide them into two groups decided by the way they drink. In Group 1 will be all the men who cup the water in their hands to get it to their mouths and lap it like dogs. In Group 2 will be those who kneel, with their mouths in the stream."

Only three hundred of the men drank from their hands; all the others drank with their mouths to the stream.

7"I'll conquer the Midianites with these three hundred!" the Lord told Gideon. "Send all the others home!"

8,9So after Gideon had collected all the clay jars and trumpets they had among them, he sent them home, leaving only three hundred men with him.

During the night, with the Midianites camped in the valley just below, the Lord said to Gideon, "Get up! Take your troops and attack the Midianites, for I will cause you to defeat them! 10But if you are afraid, first go down to the camp alone—take along your servant Purah if you like— 11and listen to what they are saying down there! You will be greatly encouraged and be eager to attack!"

So he took Purah and crept down through the darkness to the outposts of the enemy camp. 12,13The vast armies of Midian, Amalek, and the other nations of the Mideast were crowded across the valley like locusts—yes, like the sand upon the seashore—and there were too many camels even to count! Gideon crept up to one of the tents just as a man inside had wakened from a nightmare and was telling his tent-mate about it.

"I had this strange dream," he was saying, "and there was this huge loaf of barley bread that came tumbling down into our camp. It hit our tent and knocked it flat!"

14The other soldier replied, "Your dream can mean only one thing! Gideon, the son of Joash, the Israeli, is going to come and massacre all the allied forces of Midian!"

15When Gideon heard the dream and the interpretation, all he could do was just stand there worshiping God! Then he returned to his men and shouted, "Get up! For the Lord is going to use you to conquer all the vast armies of Midian!"

16He divided the three hundred men into three groups and gave each man a trumpet and a clay jar with a torch in it. 17Then he explained his plan.

"When we arrive at the outer guardposts of the

camp," he told them, "do just as I do. ¹⁸As soon as I and the men in my group blow our trumpets, you blow yours on all sides of the camp and shout, 'We fight for God and for Gideon!'"

¹⁹,²⁰It was just after midnight and the change of guards when Gideon and the hundred men with him crept to the outer edge of the camp of Midian.

Suddenly they blew their trumpets and broke their clay jars so that their torches blazed into the night. Then the other two hundred of his men did the same, blowing the trumpets in their right hands, and holding the flaming torches in their left hands, all shouting, "For the Lord and for Gideon!"

²¹Then they just stood and watched as the whole vast enemy army began rushing around in a panic, shouting and running away. ²²For in the confusion the Lord caused the enemy troops to begin fighting and killing each other from one end of the camp to the other, and they fled into the night to places as far away as Beth-shittah near Zererah, and to the border of Abel-meholah near Tabbath.

²³Then Gideon sent for the troops of Naphtali, Asher, and Manasseh and told them to come and chase and destroy the fleeing army of Midian. ²⁴Gideon also sent messengers throughout the hill country of Ephraim summoning troops who seized the fords of the Jordan River at Beth-barah, thus preventing the Midianites from escaping by going across. ²⁵Oreb and Zeeb, the two generals of Midian, were captured. Oreb was killed at the rock now known by his name, and Zeeb at the winepress of Zeeb, as it is now called; and the Israelis took the heads of Oreb and Zeeb across the Jordan to Gideon.

8 Gideon's Wise Answer

But the tribal leaders of Ephraim were violently angry with Gideon.

"Why didn't you send for us when you first went out to fight the Midianites?" they demanded.

²,³But Gideon replied, "God let you capture Oreb and Zeeb, the generals of the army of Midian! What have I done in comparison with that? Your actions at the end of the battle were more important than ours at the beginning!" So they calmed down.

⁴Gideon now crossed the Jordan River with his three hundred men. They were very tired, but still chasing the enemy. ⁵He asked the men of Succoth for food. "We are weary from chasing after Zebah and Zalmunna, the kings of Midian," he said.

⁶But the leaders of Succoth replied, "You haven't caught them yet! If we feed you and you fail, they'll return and destroy us."

⁷Then Gideon warned them, "When the Lord has delivered them to us, I will return and tear your flesh with the thorns and briars of the wilderness."

⁸Then he went up to Penuel and asked for food there, but got the same answer. ⁹And he said to them also, "When this is all over, I will return and break down this tower."

¹⁰By this time King Zebah and King Zalmunna with a remnant of fifteen thousand troops were in Karkor. That was all that was left of the allied armies of the east; for one hundred twenty thousand had already been killed. ¹¹Then Gideon circled around by the caravan route east of Nobah and Jogbehah, striking at the Midianite army in surprise raids. ¹²The two kings fled, but Gideon chased and captured them, routing their entire force. ¹³Later, Gideon returned by way of Heres Pass. ¹⁴There he captured a young fellow from Succoth and demanded that he write down the names of all the seventy-seven political and religious leaders of the city.

¹⁵He then returned to Succoth. "You taunted me that I would never catch King Zebah and King Zalmunna, and you refused to give us food when we were tired and hungry," he said. "Well, here they are!"

¹⁶Then he took the leaders of the city and scraped them to death with wild thorns and briars. ¹⁷He also went to Penuel and knocked down the city tower and killed the entire male population.

¹⁸Then Gideon asked King Zebah and King Zalmunna, "The men you killed at Tabor—what were they like?"

They replied, "They were dressed just like you—like sons of kings!"

¹⁹"They must have been my brothers!" Gideon exclaimed. "I swear that if you hadn't killed them I wouldn't kill you."

²⁰Then, turning to Jether, his oldest son, he instructed them to kill them. But the boy was only a lad and was afraid to.

²¹Then Zebah and Zalmunna said to Gideon, "You do it; we'd rather be killed by a man!" So Gideon killed them and took the ornaments from their camels' necks.

²²Now the men of Israel said to Gideon, "Be our king! You and your sons and all your descendants shall be our rulers, for you have saved us from Midian."

²³,²⁴But Gideon replied, "I will not be your king, nor shall my son; the Lord is your King! However, I have one request. Give me all the earrings collected from your fallen foes"—for the troops of Midian, being Ishmaelites, all wore gold earrings.

²⁵"Gladly!" they replied, and spread out a sheet for everyone to throw in the gold earrings he had gathered. ²⁶Their value was estimated at $25,000, not including the crescents and pendants, or the

royal clothing of the kings, or the chains around the camels' necks. ²⁷Gideon made an ephod from the gold and put it in Ophrah, his hometown. But all Israel soon began worshiping it, so it became an evil deed that Gideon and his family did.

²⁸That is the true account of how Midian was subdued by Israel. Midian never recovered, and the land was at peace for forty years—all during Gideon's lifetime. ²⁹He returned home ³⁰and eventually had seventy sons, for he married many wives. ³¹He also had a concubine in Shechem, who presented him with a son named Abimelech. ³²Gideon finally died, an old, old man, and was buried in the sepulcher of his father, Joash, in Ophrah, in the land of the Abiezrites.

³³But as soon as Gideon was dead, the Israelis began to worship the idols Baal and Baal-berith. ³⁴They no longer considered the Lord as their God, though he had rescued them from all their enemies on every side. ³⁵Nor did they show any kindness to the family of Gideon despite all he had done for them.

9 Abimelech Tries to Become King

One day Gideon's son Abimelech visited his uncles—his mother's brothers—in Shechem. ²"Go and talk to the leaders of Shechem," he requested, "and ask them whether they want to be ruled by seventy kings—Gideon's seventy sons—or by one man—meaning me, your own flesh and blood!"

³So his uncles went to the leaders of the city and proposed Abimelech's scheme; and they decided that since his mother was a native of their town they would go along with it. ⁴They gave him money from the temple offerings of the idol Baal-berith, which he used to hire some worthless loafers who agreed to do whatever he told them to. ⁵He took them to his father's home at Ophrah and there, upon one stone, they slaughtered all seventy of his half brothers, except for the youngest, Jotham, who escaped and hid. ⁶Then the citizens of Shechem and Beth-millo called a meeting under the oak beside the garrison at Shechem, and Abimelech was acclaimed king of Israel.

⁷When Jotham heard about this, he stood at the top of Mount Gerizim and shouted across to the men of Shechem, "If you want God's blessing, listen to me! ⁸Once upon a time the trees decided to elect a king. First they asked the olive tree, ⁹but it refused.

"'Should I quit producing the olive oil that blesses God and man, just to wave to and fro over the other trees?' it asked.

¹⁰"Then they said to the fig tree, 'You be our king!'

¹¹"But the fig tree also refused. 'Should I quit producing sweetness and fruit just to lift my head above all the other trees?' it asked.

¹²"Then they said to the grapevine, 'You reign over us!'

¹³"But the grapevine replied, 'Shall I quit producing the wine that cheers both God and man, just to be mightier than all the other trees?'

¹⁴"Then all the trees finally turned to the thorn bush. 'You be our king!' they explained.

¹⁵"And the thorn bush replied, 'If you really want me, come and humble yourselves beneath my shade! If you refuse, let fire flame forth from me and burn down the great cedars of Lebanon!'

¹⁶"Now make sure that you have done the right thing in making Abimelech your king, that you have done right by Gideon and all of his descendants. ¹⁷For my father fought for you and risked his life and delivered you from the Midianites, ¹⁸yet you have revolted against him and killed his seventy sons upon one stone. And now you have chosen his slave girl's son, Abimelech, to be your king just because he is your relative. ¹⁹If you are sure that you have done right by Gideon and his descendants, then may you and Abimelech have a long and happy life together. ²⁰But if you have not been fair to Gideon, then may Abimelech destroy the citizens of Shechem and Beth-millo; and may they destroy Abimelech!"

²¹Then Jotham escaped and lived in Beer for fear of his brother, Abimelech. ²²,²³Three years later God stirred up trouble between King Abimelech and the citizens of Shechem, and they revolted. ²⁴In the events that followed, both Abimelech and the citizens of Shechem who aided him in butchering Gideon's seventy sons were given their just punishment for these murders. ²⁵For the men of Shechem set an ambush for Abimelech along the trail at the top of the mountain. (While they were waiting for him to come along, they robbed everyone else who passed that way.) But someone warned Abimelech about their plot.

²⁶At that time Gaal (the son of Ebed) moved to Shechem with his brothers, and he became one of the leading citizens. ²⁷During the harvest feast at Shechem that year, held in the temple of the local god, the wine flowed freely and everyone began cursing Abimelech.

²⁸"Who is Abimelech," Gaal

RESISTING TEMPTATION 8:31 This relationship between Gideon and a concubine produced a son who tore apart Gideon's family and caused tragedy for the nation. Gideon's life illustrates the fact that heroes in battle are not always heroic in day-to-day living. Gideon led the nation but could not lead his family. No matter who you are, moral laxness will cause problems. Just because you have won a single battle with temptation does not mean you will automatically overcome the next. We need to be constantly watchful against temptation. **To begin the series of devotionals on RESISTING TEMPTATION, turn to page 7.**

shouted, "and why should he be our king? Why should we be his servants? He and his friend Zebul should be *our* servants. Down with Abimelech! ²⁹Make me your king and you'll soon see what happens to Abimelech! I'll tell Abimelech, 'Get up an army and come on out and fight!'"

³⁰But when Zebul, the mayor of the city, heard what Gaal was saying, he was furious. ³¹He sent messengers to Abimelech in Arumah telling him, "Gaal, son of Ebed, and his relatives have come to live in Shechem, and now they are arousing the city to rebellion against you. ³²Come by night with an army and hide out in the fields; ³³and in the morning, as soon as it is daylight, storm the city. When he and those who are with him come out against you, you can do with them as you wish!"

³⁴So Abimelech and his men marched through the night and split into four groups, stationing themselves around the city. ³⁵The next morning as Gaal sat at the city gates, discussing various issues with the local leaders, Abimelech and his men began their march upon the city.

³⁶When Gaal saw them, he exclaimed to Zebul, "Look over at that mountain! Doesn't it look like people coming down?"

"No!" Zebul said. "You're just seeing shadows that look like men!"

³⁷"No, look over there," Gaal said. "I'm sure I see people coming toward us. And look! There are others coming along the road past the oak of Meonenim!"

³⁸Then Zebul turned on him triumphantly. "Now where is that big mouth of yours?" he demanded. "Who was it who said, 'Who is Abimelech, and why should he be our king?' The men you taunted and cursed are right outside the city! Go on out and fight!"

³⁹So Gaal led the men of Shechem into the battle and fought with Abimelech, ⁴⁰but was defeated, and many of the men of Shechem were left wounded all the way to the city gate. ⁴¹Abimelech was living at Arumah at this time, and Zebul drove Gaal and his relatives out of Shechem and wouldn't let them live there any longer.

⁴²The next day the men of Shechem went out to battle again. However, someone had told Abimelech about their plans, ⁴³so he had divided his men into three groups hiding in the fields. And when the men of the city went out to attack, he and his men jumped up from their hiding places and began killing them. ⁴⁴Abimelech stormed the city gate to keep the men of Shechem from getting back in, while his other two groups cut them down in the fields. ⁴⁵The battle went on all day before Abimelech finally captured the city, killed its people, and leveled it to the ground. ⁴⁶The people at the nearby town of Migdal saw what was happening and took refuge in the fort next to the temple of Baal-berith.

⁴⁷,⁴⁸When Abimelech learned of this, he led his forces to Mount Zalmon where he began chopping a bundle of firewood, and placed it upon his shoulder. "Do as I have done," he told his men. ⁴⁹So each of them quickly cut a bundle and carried it back to the town where, following Abimelech's example, the bundles were piled against the walls of the fort and set on fire. So all the people inside died, about a thousand men and women.

⁵⁰Abimelech next attacked the city of Thebez, and captured it. ⁵¹However, there was a fort inside the city and the entire population fled into it, barricaded the gates, and climbed to the top of the roof to watch. ⁵²But as Abimelech was preparing to burn it, ⁵³a woman on the roof threw down a millstone. It landed on Abimelech's head, crushing his skull.

⁵⁴"Kill me!" he groaned to his youthful armor-bearer. "Never let it be said that a woman killed Abimelech!"

So the young man pierced him with his sword, and he died. ⁵⁵When his men saw that he was dead, they disbanded and returned to their homes. ⁵⁶,⁵⁷Thus God punished both Abimelech and the men of Shechem for their sin of murdering Gideon's seventy sons. So the curse of Jotham, Gideon's son, came true.

10 Tola and Jair

After Abimelech's death, the next judge of Israel was Tola (son of Puah and grandson of Dodo). He was from the tribe of Issachar, but lived in the city of Shamir in the hill country of Ephraim. ²He was Israel's judge for twenty-three years. When he died, he was buried in Shamir, ³and was succeeded by Jair, a man from Gilead, who judged Israel for twenty-two years. ⁴His thirty sons rode around together on thirty donkeys, and they owned thirty cities in the land of Gilead which are still called "The Cities of Jair." ⁵When Jair died he was buried in Kamon.

⁶Then the people of Israel turned away from the Lord again and worshiped the heathen gods Baal and Ashtaroth, and the gods of Syria, Sidon, Moab, Ammon, and Philistia. Not only this, but they no longer worshiped Jehovah at all. ⁷,⁸This made Jehovah very angry with his people, so he immediately permitted the Philistines and the Ammonites to begin tormenting them. These attacks took place east of the Jordan River in the land of the Amorites (that is, in Gilead), ⁹and also in Judah, Benjamin, and Ephraim. For the Ammonites crossed the Jordan to attack the Israelis. This

went on for eighteen years. [10]Finally the Israelis turned to Jehovah again and begged him to save them.

"We have sinned against you and have forsaken you as our God and have worshiped idols," they confessed.

[11]But the Lord replied, "Didn't I save you from the Egyptians, the Amorites, the Ammonites, the Philistines, [12]the Sidonians, the Amalekites, and the Maonites? Has there ever been a time when you cried out to me that I haven't rescued you? [13]Yet you continue to abandon me and to worship other gods. So go away; I won't save you any more. [14]Go and cry to the new gods you have chosen! Let them save you in your hour of distress!"

[15]But they pleaded with him again and said, "We have sinned. Punish us in any way you think best, only save us once more from our enemies."

[16]Then they destroyed their foreign gods and worshiped only the Lord; and he was grieved by their misery. [17]The armies of Ammon were mobilized in Gilead at that time, preparing to attack Israel's army at Mizpah.

[18]"Who will lead our forces against the Ammonites?" the leaders of Gilead asked each other. "Whoever volunteers shall be our king!"

Jephthah's Foolish Vow

Now Jephthah was a great warrior from the land of Gilead, but his mother was a prostitute. His father (whose name was Gilead) had several other sons by his legitimate wife, and when these half brothers grew up, they chased Jephthah out of the country.

"You son of a whore!" they said. "You'll not get any of our father's estate."

[3]So Jephthah fled from his father's home and lived in the land of Tob. Soon he had quite a band of malcontents as his followers, living off the land as bandits. [4]It was about this time that the Ammonites began their war against Israel. [5]The leaders of Gilead sent for Jephthah, [6]begging him to come and lead their army against the Ammonites.

[7]But Jephthah said to them, "Why do you come to me when you hate me and have driven me out of my father's house? Why come now when you're in trouble?"

[8]"Because we need you," they replied. "If you will be our commander-in-chief against the Ammonites, we will make you the king of Gilead."

[9]"Sure!" Jephthah exclaimed. "Do you expect me to believe that?"

[10]"We swear it," they replied. "We promise with a solemn oath."

[11]So Jephthah accepted the commission and was made commander-in-chief and king. The contract was ratified before the Lord in Mizpah at a general assembly of all the people. [12]Then Jephthah sent messengers to the king of Ammon, demanding to know why Israel was being attacked. [13]The king of Ammon replied that the land belonged to the people of Ammon; it had been stolen from them, he said, when the Israelis came from Egypt; the whole territory from the Arnon River to the Jabbok and the Jordan was his, he claimed.

"Give us back our land peaceably," he demanded.

[14,15]Jephthah replied, "Israel did not steal the land. [16]What happened was this: When the people of Israel arrived at Kadesh, on their journey from Egypt after crossing the Red Sea, [17]they sent a message to the king of Edom asking permission to pass through his land. But their petition was denied. Then they asked the king of Moab for similar permission. It was the same story there, so the people of Israel stayed in Kadesh.

[18]"Finally they went around Edom and Moab through the wilderness, and traveled along the eastern border until at last they arrived beyond the boundary of Moab at the Arnon River; but they never once crossed into Moab. [19]Then Israel sent messengers to King Sihon of the Amorites, who lived in Heshbon, and asked permission to cross through his land to get to their destination.

[20]"But King Sihon didn't trust Israel, so he mobilized an army at Jahaz and attacked them. [21,22]But the Lord our God helped Israel defeat King Sihon and all your people, so Israel took over all of your land from the Arnon River to the Jabbok, and from the wilderness to the Jordan River.

[23]"So you see, it was the Lord God of Israel who took away the land from the Amorites and gave it to Israel. Why, then, should we return it to you? [24]You keep whatever your god Chemosh gives you, and we will keep whatever Jehovah our God gives us! [25]And besides, just who do you think you are? Are you better than King Balak, the king of Moab? Did he try to recover his land after Israel defeated him? No, of course not. [26]But now after three hundred years you make an issue of this!

ACCEPTING OTHERS 11:3 Circumstances beyond his control forced Jephthah away from his people and into life as an outcast. Today, both believers and nonbelievers may drive away those who fail to meet the standards we set up. Often, as in Jephthah's case, great potential is wasted because of prejudice—refusing to look beyond stereotypes that have no real basis. Look around you to see if there are Jephthahs being rejected due to things beyond their control. As a Christian you know that everyone can have a place in God's family. Is there anything you can do to help these people to be accepted? **To begin the series of devotionals on ACCEPTING OTHERS, turn to page 207.**

Israel has been living here for all that time, spread across the land from Heshbon to Aroer, and all along the Arnon River. Why have you made no effort to recover it before now? ²⁷No, I have not sinned against you; rather, you have wronged me by coming to war against me; but Jehovah the Judge will soon show which of us is right—Israel or Ammon."

²⁸But the king of Ammon paid no attention to Jephthah's message.

²⁹At that time the Spirit of the Lord came upon Jephthah, and he led his army across the land of Gilead and Manasseh, past Mizpah in Gilead, and attacked the army of Ammon. ³⁰,³¹Meanwhile Jephthah had vowed to the Lord that if God would help Israel conquer the Ammonites, then when he returned home in peace, the first person coming out of his house to meet him would be sacrificed as a burnt offering to the Lord!

³²So Jephthah led his army against the Ammonites, and the Lord gave him the victory. ³³He destroyed the Ammonites with a terrible slaughter all the way from Aroer to Minnith, including twenty cities, and as far away as Vineyard Meadow. Thus the Ammonites were subdued by the people of Israel.

³⁴When Jephthah returned home his daughter—his only child—ran out to meet him, playing on a tambourine and dancing for joy. ³⁵When he saw her, he tore his clothes in anguish.

"Alas, my daughter!" he cried out. "You have brought me to the dust. For I have made a vow to the Lord and I cannot take it back."

³⁶And she said, "Father, you must do whatever you promised the Lord, for he has given you a great victory over your enemies, the Ammonites. ³⁷But first let me go up into the hills and roam with my girlfriends for two months, weeping because I'll never marry."

³⁸"Yes," he said. "Go."

And so she did, bewailing her fate with her friends for two months. ³⁹Then she returned to her father, who did as he had vowed. So she was never married. And after that it became a custom in Israel ⁴⁰that the young girls went away for four days each year to lament the fate of Jephthah's daughter.

12 Jephthah Attacks Ephraim

Then the tribe of Ephraim mobilized its army at Zaphon and sent this message to Jephthah: "Why didn't you call for us to help you fight against Ammon? We are going to burn down your house, with you in it!"

²"I summoned you, but you refused to come!" Jephthah retorted. "You failed to help us in our time of need, ³so I risked my life and went to battle without you, and the Lord helped me to conquer the enemy. Is that anything for you to fight us about?"

⁴Then Jephthah, furious at the taunt of Ephraim that the men of Gilead were mere outcasts and the scum of the earth, mobilized his army and attacked the army of Ephraim. ⁵He captured the fords of the Jordan behind the army of Ephraim, and whenever a fugitive from Ephraim tried to cross the river, the Gilead guards challenged him.

"Are you a member of the tribe of Ephraim?" they asked. If the man replied that he was not, ⁶then they demanded, "Say 'Shibboleth.'" But if he couldn't pronounce the *H* and said, "Sibboleth" instead of "Shibboleth," he was dragged away and killed. So forty-two thousand people of Ephraim died there at that time.

⁷Jephthah was Israel's judge for six years. At his death he was buried in one of the cities of Gilead.

⁸The next judge was Ibzan, who lived in Bethlehem. ⁹,¹⁰He had thirty sons and thirty daughters. He married his daughters to men outside his clan and brought in thirty girls to marry his sons. He judged Israel for seven years before he died, and was buried at Bethlehem.

¹¹,¹²The next judge was Elon from Zebulun. He judged Israel for ten years and was buried at Aijalon in Zebulun.

¹³Next was Abdon (son of Hillel) from Pirathon. ¹⁴He had forty sons and thirty grandsons, who rode on seventy donkeys. He was Israel's judge for eight years. ¹⁵Then he died and was buried in Pirathon, in Ephraim, in the hill country of the Amalekites.

13 Samson Is Born

Once again Israel sinned by worshiping other gods, so the Lord let them be conquered by the Philistines, who kept them in subjection for forty years.

²,³Then one day the Angel of the Lord appeared to the wife of Manoah, of the tribe of Dan, who lived in the city of Zorah. She had no children, but the Angel said to her, "Even though you have been barren so long, you will soon conceive and have a son! ⁴Don't drink any wine or beer and don't eat any food that isn't kosher. ⁵Your son's hair must never be cut, for he shall be a Nazirite, a special servant of God from the time of his birth; and he will begin to rescue Israel from the Philistines."

⁶The woman ran and told her husband, "A man from God appeared to me and I think he must be the Angel of the Lord, for he was almost too glorious to look at. I didn't ask where he was from, and he didn't tell me his name, ⁷but he told me, 'You are going to have a baby boy!' And he told me not to drink any wine or beer and not to eat food that

isn't kosher, for the baby is going to be a Nazirite—he will be dedicated to God from the moment of his birth until the day of his death!"

⁸Then Manoah prayed, "O Lord, please let the man from God come back to us again and give us more instructions about the child you are going to give us." ⁹The Lord answered his prayer, and the Angel of God appeared once again to his wife as she was sitting in the field. But again she was alone—Manoah was not with her— ¹⁰so she quickly ran and found her husband and told him, "The same man is here again!"

¹¹Manoah ran back with his wife and asked, "Are you the man who talked to my wife the other day?"

"Yes," he replied, "I am."

¹²So Manoah asked him, "Can you give us any special instructions about how we should raise the baby after he is born?"

¹³,¹⁴And the Angel replied, "Be sure that your wife follows the instructions I gave her. She must not eat grapes or raisins, or drink any wine or beer, or eat anything that isn't kosher."

¹⁵Then Manoah said to the Angel, "Please stay here until we can get you something to eat."

¹⁶"I'll stay," the Angel replied, "but I'll not eat anything. However, if you wish to bring something, bring an offering to sacrifice to the Lord." (Manoah didn't yet realize that he was the Angel of the Lord.)

¹⁷Then Manoah asked him for his name. "When all this comes true and the baby is born," he said to the Angel, "we will certainly want to tell everyone that you predicted it!"

¹⁸"Don't even ask my name," the Angel replied, "for it is a secret."

¹⁹Then Manoah took a young goat and a grain offering and offered it as a sacrifice to the Lord; and the Angel did a strange and wonderful thing, ²⁰for as the flames from the altar were leaping up toward the sky, and as Manoah and his wife watched, the Angel ascended in the fire! Manoah and his wife fell face downward to the ground, ²¹and that was the last they ever saw of him. It was then that Manoah finally realized that it had been the Angel of the Lord.

²²"We will die," Manoah cried out to his wife, "for we have seen God!"

²³But his wife said, "If the Lord were going to kill us, he wouldn't have accepted our burnt offerings and wouldn't have appeared to us and told us this wonderful thing and done these miracles."

²⁴When her son was born they named him Samson, and the Lord blessed him as he grew up. ²⁵And the Spirit of the Lord began to excite him whenever he visited the parade grounds of the army of the tribe of Dan, located between the cities of Zorah and Eshtaol.

14 Samson Gets Married

One day when Samson was in Timnah he noticed a certain Philistine girl, ²and when he got home he told his father and mother that he wanted to marry her. ³They objected strenuously.

"Why don't you marry a Jewish girl?" they asked. "Why must you go and get a wife from these heathen Philistines? Isn't there one girl among all the people of Israel you could marry?"

But Samson told his father, "She is the one I want. Get her for me."

⁴His father and mother didn't realize that the Lord was behind the request, for God was setting a trap for the Philistines, who at that time were the rulers of Israel.

⁵As Samson and his parents were going to Timnah, a young lion attacked Samson in the vineyards on the outskirts of the town. ⁶At that moment the Spirit of the Lord came mightily upon him and since he had no weapon, he ripped the lion's jaws apart and did it as easily as though it were a young goat! But he didn't tell his father or mother about it. ⁷Upon arriving at Timnah, he talked with the girl and found her to be just what he wanted, so the arrangements were made.

⁸When he returned for the wedding, he turned off the path to look at the carcass of the lion. And he found a swarm of bees in it and some honey! ⁹He took some of the honey with him, eating as he went, and gave some of it to his father and mother. But he didn't tell them where he had gotten it.

¹⁰,¹¹As his father was making final arrangements for the marriage, Samson threw a party for thirty young men of the village, as was the custom of the day. ¹²When Samson asked if they would like to hear a riddle, they replied that they would.

"If you solve my riddle during these seven days of the celebration," he said, "I'll give you thirty plain robes and thirty fancy robes. ¹³But if you can't solve it, then you must give the robes to me!"

"All right," they agreed, "let's hear it."

¹⁴This was his riddle: "Food came out of the eater, and sweetness from the strong!" Three days later they were still trying to figure it out.

¹⁵On the fourth day they said to his new wife, "Get the answer from your husband, or we'll burn down your father's house with you in it. Were we invited to this party just to make us poor?"

¹⁶So Samson's wife broke down in tears before him and said, "You don't love me at all; you hate me, for you have told a riddle to my people and haven't told me the answer!"

"I haven't even told it to my father or mother; why should I tell you?" he replied.

¹⁷So she cried whenever she was with him and kept it up for the remainder of the celebration. At last, on the seventh day, he told her the answer and she, of course, gave the answer to the young men. ¹⁸So before sunset of the seventh day they gave him their reply.

"What is sweeter than honey?" they asked, "and what is stronger than a lion?"

"If you hadn't plowed with my heifer, you wouldn't have found the answer to my riddle!" he retorted.

¹⁹Then the Spirit of the Lord came upon him and he went to the city of Ashkelon, killed thirty men, took their clothing, and gave it to the young men who had told him the answer to his riddle. But he was furious about it and abandoned his wife and went back home to live with his father and mother. ²⁰So his wife was married instead to the fellow who had been best man at Samson's wedding.

15 Samson Kills Many Enemies

Later on, during the wheat harvest, Samson took a young goat as a present to his wife, intending to sleep with her; but her father wouldn't let him in.

²"I really thought you hated her," he explained, "so I married her to your best man. But look, her sister is prettier than she is. Marry her instead."

³Samson was furious. "You can't blame me for whatever happens now," he shouted.

⁴So he went out and caught three hundred foxes and tied their tails together in pairs, with a torch between each pair. ⁵Then he lit the torches and let the foxes run through the fields of the Philistines, burning the grain to the ground along with all the sheaves and shocks of grain, and destroying the olive trees.

⁶"Who did this?" the Philistines demanded.

"Samson," was the reply, "because his wife's father gave her to another man." So the Philistines came and got the girl and her father and burned them alive.

⁷"Now my vengeance will strike again!" Samson vowed. ⁸So he attacked them with great fury and killed many of them. Then he went to live in a cave in the rock of Etam. ⁹The Philistines in turn sent a huge posse into Judah and raided Lehi.

¹⁰"Why have you come here?" the men of Judah asked.

And the Philistines replied, "To capture Samson and do to him as he has done to us."

¹¹So three thousand men of Judah went down to get Samson at the cave in the rock of Etam.

"What are you doing to us?" they demanded of him. "Don't you realize that the Philistines are our rulers?"

But Samson replied, "I only paid them back for what they did to me."

¹²,¹³"We have come to capture you and take you to the Philistines," the men of Judah told him.

"All right," Samson said, "but promise me that you won't kill me yourselves."

"No," they replied, "we won't do that."

So they tied him with two new ropes and led him away. ¹⁴As Samson and his captors arrived at Lehi, the Philistines shouted with glee; but then the strength of the Lord came upon Samson, and the ropes with which he was tied snapped like thread and fell from his wrists! ¹⁵Then he picked up a donkey's jawbone that was lying on the ground and killed a thousand Philistines with it. ¹⁶,¹⁷Tossing away the jawbone, he remarked,

> "Heaps upon heaps,
> All with a donkey's jaw!
> I've killed a thousand men,
> All with a donkey's jaw!"

(The place has been called "Jawbone Hill" ever since.)

¹⁸But now he was very thirsty and he prayed to the Lord and said, "You have given Israel such a wonderful deliverance through me today! Must I now die of thirst and fall to the mercy of these heathen?" ¹⁹So the Lord caused water to gush out from a hollow in the ground, and Samson's spirit was revived as he drank. Then he named the place "The Spring of the Man Who Prayed," and the spring is still there today.

²⁰Samson was Israel's leader for the next twenty years, but the Philistines still controlled the land.

16 Samson's Foolish Choices

One day Samson went to the Philistine city of Gaza and spent the night with a prostitute. ²Word soon spread that he had been seen in the city, so the police were alerted and many men of the city lay in wait all night at the city gate to capture him if he tried to leave.

"In the morning," they thought, "when there is enough light, we'll find him and kill him."

FORGIVING OTHERS 15:1ff. Samson's reply in 15:11 tells the story of this chapter: "I only paid them back for what they did to me." It is a tale of action, reaction, and chain reaction based on anger, hatred, hurt, and revenge. Revenge is an uncontrollable monster. Each vengeful act of retaliation brings another. It is a boomerang which cannot be thrown without cost to the thrower. Don't allow revenge to get your life in its grasp. The revenge cycle can be broken only by forgiveness. **To begin the series of devotionals on FORGIVING OTHERS, turn to page 39.**

³Samson stayed in bed with the girl until midnight, then went out to the city gates and lifted them, with the two gateposts, right out of the ground. He put them on his shoulders and carried them to the top of the mountain across from Hebron!

⁴Later on he fell in love with a girl named Delilah over in the valley of Sorek. ⁵The five heads of the Philistine nation went personally to her and demanded that she find out from Samson what made him so strong, so that they would know how to overpower and subdue him and put him in chains.

"Each of us will give you a thousand dollars for this job," they promised.

⁶So Delilah begged Samson to tell her his secret. *"Please* tell me, Samson, why you are so strong," she pleaded. "I don't think anyone could ever capture you!"

⁷"Well," Samson replied, "if I were tied with seven raw-leather bowstrings, I would become as weak as anyone else."

⁸So they brought her the seven bowstrings, and while he slept she tied him with them. ⁹Some men were hiding in the next room, so as soon as she had tied him up she exclaimed,

"Samson! The Philistines are here!"

Then he snapped the bowstrings like cotton thread, and so his secret was not discovered.

¹⁰Afterward Delilah said to him, "You are making fun of me! You told me a lie! *Please* tell me how you can be captured!"

¹¹"Well," he said, "if I am tied with brand new ropes which have never been used, I will be as weak as other men."

¹²So that time, as he slept, Delilah took new ropes and tied him with them. The men were hiding in the next room, as before. Again Delilah exclaimed,

"Samson! The Philistines have come to capture you!"

But he broke the ropes from his arms like spiderwebs!

¹³"You have mocked me again and told me more lies!" Delilah complained. "Now tell me how you can *really* be captured."

"Well," he said, "if you weave my hair into your loom . . . !"

¹⁴So while he slept, she did just that and then screamed, "The Philistines have come, Samson!" And he woke up and yanked his hair away, breaking the loom.

¹⁵"How can you say you love me when you don't confide in me?" she whined. "You've made fun of me three times now, and you still haven't told me what makes you so strong!"

¹⁶,¹⁷She nagged at him every day until he couldn't stand it any longer and finally told her his secret.

"My hair has never been cut," he confessed, "for I've been a Nazirite to God since before my birth. If my hair were cut, my strength would leave me, and I would become as weak as anyone else."

¹⁸Delilah realized that he had finally told her the truth, so she sent for the five Philistine leaders.

"Come just this once more," she said, "for this time he has told me everything."

So they brought the money with them. ¹⁹She lulled him to sleep with his head in her lap, and they brought in a barber and cut off his hair. Delilah began to hit him, but she could see that his strength was leaving him.

²⁰Then she screamed, "The Philistines are here to capture you, Samson!" And he woke up and thought, "I will do as before; I'll just shake myself free." But he didn't realize that the Lord had left him. ²¹So the Philistines captured him and gouged out his eyes and took him to Gaza, where he was bound with bronze chains and made to grind grain in the prison. ²²But before long his hair began to grow again.

²³,²⁴The Philistine leaders declared a great festival to celebrate the capture of Samson. The people made sacrifices to their god Dagon and excitedly praised him.

"Our god has delivered our enemy Samson to us!" they gloated as they saw him there in chains. "The scourge of our nation who killed so many of us is now in our power!" ²⁵,²⁶Half drunk by now, the people demanded, "Bring out Samson so we can have some fun with him!"

So he was brought from the prison and made to stand at the center of the temple, between the two pillars supporting the roof. Samson said to the boy who was leading him by the hand, "Place my hands against the two pillars. I want to rest against them."

²⁷By then the temple was completely filled with people. The five Philistine leaders were there as well as three thousand people in the balconies who were watching Samson and making fun of him.

²⁸Then Samson prayed to the Lord and said, "O Lord Jehovah, remember me again—please strengthen me one more time, so that I may pay back the Philistines for the loss of at least one of my eyes."

²⁹Then Samson pushed against the pillars with all his might.

³⁰"Let me die with the Philistines," he prayed.

And the temple crashed down upon the Philistine leaders and all the people. So those he killed at the moment of his death were more than those he had killed during his entire lifetime. ³¹Later, his brothers and other relatives came down to get his

Family Devotions

☐ DEVOTION 90

MAKING THE BEST CHOICES

Read Judges 16:1-5, 16-31

Making the Best Choices Memory Verse

He will always give you all you need from day to day if you will make the Kingdom of God your primary concern.
Luke 12:31

"The junior choir is giving a Christmas program at the nursing home today. Mrs. Wilson wants me to play the piano, but I said no. I need to get some notebooks for school," Jolene explained.

Mother raised her eyebrows. "Couldn't you play and still have time to get the notebooks?" she asked. "Playing would be a real service to the Lord."

Jolene shrugged in annoyance. "Oh, Mother! Someone else can do it just as well." She picked up her books and headed for the door.

When Jolene arrived home that afternoon, she not only had two new notebooks, but a small stuffed dog as well. "I've named him Orville," she giggled as she showed Mother. "Isn't he cute? Would you believe he cost only a dollar? I didn't have that much left, but then I remembered that the silver dollar Aunt Jo sent me was still in my purse."

Mother was shocked. "But I thought you knew that coin was actually worth more than a dollar!"

Jolene looked ashamed. "Well, yeah," she admitted, "but Orville was on sale!"

The following Saturday, Jolene went shopping with her mother. They passed a coin shop, and in the window display were several silver dollars, each worth a lot of money. "I don't suppose my dollar was worth nearly that much," sighed Jolene, "but I still wish I had it back."

"It's spent, and you may as well forget it," answered Mother. "I remember the day you spent your dollar. It was the same day you refused to play at the nursing home. You know, honey, your life is a lot like a coin—you can spend it any way you want to, but you can spend it only once. You need to make sure you spend it wisely."

Soberly, Jolene nodded. "I didn't spend either my dollar or my life wisely that day, did I? I'm going to rename Orville. I'll call him Silver Dollar, and he'll remind me that I need to be careful how I spend my money and my life."

How About You?
Are you "buying" the most you can with your life? Be careful to make wise choices in what you do. *H. M.*

• For the next devotional, turn to page 277. • For the next devotional on MAKING THE BEST CHOICES, turn to page 367. • For notes on MAKING THE BEST CHOICES, see pages 358, 652, and 944.

body, and they brought him back home and buried him between Zorah and Eshtaol, where his father, Manoah, was buried. He had led Israel for twenty years.

17 Micah's Idol Collection

In the hill country of Ephraim lived a man named Micah.

²One day he said to his mother, "That thousand dollars you thought was stolen from you, and you were cursing about—well, I stole it!"

"God bless you for confessing it," his mother replied. ³So he returned the money to her.

"I am going to give it to the Lord as a credit for your account," she declared. "I'll have an idol carved for you and plate it with the silver."

⁴,⁵So his mother took a fifth of it to a silversmith, and the idol he made from it was placed in Micah's shrine. Micah had many idols in his collection, also an ephod and some teraphim, and he installed one of his sons as the priest. ⁶(For in those days Israel had no king, so everyone did whatever he wanted to—whatever seemed right in his own eyes.)

⁷,⁸One day a young priest from the town of Bethlehem, in Judah, arrived in that area of Ephraim, looking for a good place to live. He happened to stop at Micah's house as he was traveling through.

⁹"Where are you from?" Micah asked him.

And he replied, "I am a priest from Bethlehem, in Judah, and I am looking for a place to live."

¹⁰,¹¹"Well, stay here with me," Micah said, "and you can be my priest. I will give you one hundred dollars a year plus a new suit and your board and room." The young man agreed to this and became as one of Micah's sons. ¹²So Micah consecrated him as his personal priest.

¹³"I know the Lord will really bless me now," Micah exclaimed, "because now I have a genuine priest working for me!"

18 The Danites Steal Micah's Idols

As has already been stated, there was no king in Israel at that time. The tribe of Dan was trying to find a place to settle, for they had not yet driven out the people living in the land assigned to them. ²So the men of Dan chose five army heroes from the cities of Zorah and Eshtaol as scouts to go and spy out the land they were supposed to settle in. Arriving in the hill country of Ephraim, they stayed at Micah's home. ³Noticing the young Levite's accent, they took him aside and asked him, "What are you doing here? Why did you come?" ⁴He told them about his contract with Micah, and that he was his personal priest.

⁵"Well, then," they said, "ask God whether or not our trip will be successful."

⁶"Yes," the priest replied, "all is well. The Lord is taking care of you."

⁷So the five men went on to the town of Laish and noticed how secure everyone felt. Their manner of life was Phoenician, and they were wealthy. They lived quietly and were unprepared for an attack, for there were no tribes in the area strong enough to try it. They lived a great distance from their relatives in Sidon, and had little or no contact with the nearby villages. ⁸So the spies returned to their people in Zorah and Eshtaol.

"What about it?" they were asked. "What did you find?"

⁹,¹⁰And the men replied, "Let's attack! We have seen the land and it is ours for the taking—a broad, fertile, wonderful place—a real paradise. The people aren't even prepared to defend themselves! Come on, let's go! For God has given it to us!"

¹¹So six hundred armed troops of the tribe of Dan set out from Zorah and Eshtaol. ¹²They camped first at a place west of Kiriath-jearim in Judah (which is still called "The Camp of Dan"), ¹³then they went on up into the hill country of Ephraim.

As they passed the home of Micah, ¹⁴the five spies told the others. "There is a shrine in there with an ephod, some teraphim, and many plated idols. It's obvious what we ought to do!"

¹⁵,¹⁶So the five men went over to the house and with all of the armed men standing just outside the gate, they talked to the young priest and asked him how he was getting along. ¹⁷Then the five spies entered the shrine and took the idols, the ephod, and the teraphim.

¹⁸"What are you doing?" the young priest demanded when he saw them carrying them out.

¹⁹"Be quiet and come with us," they said. "Be a priest to all of us. Isn't it better for you to be a priest to a whole tribe in Israel instead of just to one man in his private home?"

²⁰The young priest was then quite happy to go with them, and he took along the ephod, the teraphim, and the idols. ²¹They started on their way again, placing their children, cattle, and household goods at the front of the column. ²²When they were quite a distance from Micah's home, Micah and some of his neighbors came chasing after them, ²³yelling at them to stop.

"What do you want, chasing after us like this?" the men of Dan demanded.

²⁴"What do you mean, 'What do I want'!" Micah retorted. "You've taken away all my gods and my priest, and I have nothing left!"

²⁵"Be careful how you talk, mister," the men of

FAMILY DEVOTIONS

☐ DEVOTION 91
CONFESSING SIN

Read Judges 17:1-6

Jack and Wendy were hungry, but Mom was gone. "Hey, there's candy up in the cupboard," said Wendy. "Let's sneak some. Mom will never know."

Jack looked uncertain. "Doesn't that make you feel guilty?" he asked.

Wendy shook her head. "Nah. Not anymore."

Jack still hesitated, but when he saw his sister eating a chocolate bar, he just couldn't resist. The two finished their candy, carefully threw away the wrappers, and went outside to play in the snow.

After a while their feet were wet and cold, but they wanted to finish the snow fort they were building. They refused to give in and go back indoors. For some time they kept on working. When Mom arrived home, she called them inside. She was shocked when she saw how wet and cold their feet were. "Why didn't you come inside when your feet got cold?" she scolded.

"We wanted to finish our fort," Wendy replied. "Besides, they didn't feel so cold after a while, Mom!"

Mom looked grim. "That sensation of cold was meant to be a warning to you. If you had stayed out much longer, you might have gotten frostbite. The most dangerous time is not when you feel cold, but when you stop feeling it." She rubbed their feet gently and added, "It reminds me of sin. We're in danger if our conscience stops bothering us when we do something wrong."

When Mom left the room, the children looked at each other, remembering the candy they had eaten.

"I sure feel my feet now," commented Jack. "Now that they're getting warmed up, they hurt. And my conscience hurts, too."

"Mine, too," agreed Wendy. "And it's going to hurt more when we tell Mom about the candy we took. But I'm sure we'll feel better afterward!"

Confessing Sin Memory Verse

But if we confess our sins to him, he can be depended on to forgive us and to cleanse us from every wrong. [And it is perfectly proper for God to do this for us because Christ died to wash away our sins.]
1 John 1:9

How About You?
Are there habits or activities in your life that made you feel guilty in the past but not anymore? You may have changed, but God's standards of right and wrong haven't. We should never become like the people of Israel, who did whatever seemed right in their own eyes. Don't let yourself become numb to sin! S. K.

• For the next devotional, turn to page 283. • For the next devotional on CONFESSING SIN, turn to page 335. • For notes on CONFESSING SIN, see pages 429, 479, 836, 881, and 1220.

Dan replied. "Somebody's apt to get angry and kill every one of you."

²⁶So the men of Dan kept going. When Micah saw that there were too many of them for him to handle, he turned back home.

²⁷Then, with Micah's idols and the priest, the men of Dan arrived at the city of Laish. There weren't even any guards, so they went in and slaughtered all the people and burned the city to the ground. ²⁸There was no one to help the inhabitants, for they were too far away from Sidon, and they had no local allies, for they had no dealings with anyone. This happened in the valley next to Beth-rehob. Then the people of the tribe of Dan rebuilt the city and lived there. ²⁹The city was named "Dan" after their ancestor, Israel's son, but it had originally been called Laish.

³⁰Then they set up the idols and appointed a man named Jonathan (son of Gershom and grandson of Moses!) and his sons as their priests. This family continued as priests until the city was finally conquered by its enemies. ³¹So Micah's idols were worshiped by the tribe of Dan as long as the Tabernacle remained at Shiloh.

19 A Horrible Crime

At this time before Israel had a king, there was a man of the tribe of Levi living on the far side of the hill country of Ephraim, who brought home a girl from Bethlehem in Judah to be his concubine. ²But she became angry with him and ran away, and returned to her father's home in Bethlehem, and was there about four months. ³Then her husband, taking along a servant and an extra donkey, went to see her to try to win her back again. When he arrived at her home, she let him in and introduced him to her father, who was delighted to meet him. ⁴Her father urged him to stay awhile, so he stayed three days, and they all had a very pleasant time.

⁵On the fourth day they were up early, ready to leave, but the girl's father insisted on their having breakfast first. ⁶Then he pleaded with him to stay one more day, as they were having such a good time. ⁷At first the man refused, but his father-in-law kept urging him until finally he gave in. ⁸The next morning they were up early again, and again the girl's father pleaded, "Stay just today and leave sometime this evening." So they had another day of feasting.

⁹That afternoon as he and his wife and servant were preparing to leave, his father-in-law said, "Look, it's getting late. Stay just tonight, and we will have a pleasant evening together and tomorrow you can get up early and be on your way."

¹⁰But this time the man was adamant, so they left, getting as far as Jerusalem (also called Jebus) before dark.

¹¹His servant said to him, "It's getting too late to travel; let's stay here tonight."

¹²,¹³"No," his master said, "we can't stay in this heathen city where there are no Israelites—we will go on to Gibeah, or possibly Ramah."

¹⁴So they went on. The sun was setting just as they came to Gibeah, a village of the tribe of Benjamin, ¹⁵so they went there for the night. But as no one invited them in, they camped in the village square. ¹⁶Just then an old man came by on his way home from his work in the fields. (He was originally from the hill country of Ephraim, but was living now in Gibeah, even though it was in the territory of Benjamin.) ¹⁷When he saw the travelers camped in the square, he asked them where they were from and where they were going.

¹⁸"We're on the way home from Bethlehem, in Judah," the man replied. "I live on the far edge of the Ephraim hill country, near Shiloh. But no one has taken us in for the night, ¹⁹even though we have fodder for our donkeys and plenty of food and wine for ourselves."

²⁰"Don't worry," the old man said, "be my guests; for you mustn't stay here in the square. It's too dangerous."

²¹So he took them home with him. He fed their donkeys while they rested, and afterward they had supper together. ²²Just as they were beginning to warm to the occasion, a gang of sex perverts gathered around the house and began beating at the door and yelling at the old man to bring out the man who was staying with him, so they could rape him. ²³The old man stepped outside to talk to them.

"No, my brothers, don't do such a dastardly act," he begged, "for he is my guest. ²⁴Here, take my virgin daughter and this man's wife. I'll bring them out and you can do whatever you like to them—but don't do such a thing to this man."

²⁵But they wouldn't listen to him. Then the girl's husband pushed her out to them, and they abused her all night, taking turns raping her until morning. Finally, just at dawn, they let her go. ²⁶She fell down at the door of the house and lay there until it was light. ²⁷When her husband opened the door to be on his way, he found her there, fallen down in front of the door with her hands digging into the threshold.

²⁸"Well, come on," he said. "Let's get going."

But there was no answer, for she was dead; so he threw her across the donkey's back and took her home. ²⁹When he got there he took a knife and cut her body into twelve parts and sent one piece to each tribe of Israel. ³⁰Then the entire nation was roused to action against the men of Benjamin because of this awful deed.

"There hasn't been such a horrible crime since Israel left Egypt," everyone said. "We've got to do something about it."

20 Israel Attacks Benjamin

Then the entire nation of Israel sent their leaders and 450,000 troops to assemble with one mind before the Lord at Mizpah. They came from as far away as Dan and Beersheba, and everywhere between, and from across the Jordan in the land of Gilead. [3](Word of the mobilization of the Israeli forces at Mizpah soon reached the land of Benjamin.) The chiefs of Israel now called for the murdered woman's husband and asked him just what had happened.

[4]"We arrived one evening at Gibeah, a village in Benjamin," he began. [5]"That night the men of Gibeah surrounded the house, planning to kill me, and they raped my wife until she was dead. [6]So I cut her body into twelve pieces and sent the pieces throughout the land of Israel, for these men have committed a terrible crime. [7]Now then, sons of Israel, express your mind and give me your counsel!"

[8-10]And as one man they replied, "Not one of us will return home until we have punished the village of Gibeah. A tenth of the army will be selected by lot as a supply line to bring us food, and the rest of us will destroy Gibeah for this horrible deed."

[11]So the whole nation united in this task.

[12]Then messengers were sent to the tribe of Benjamin, asking, "Did you know about the terrible thing that was done among you? [13]Give up these evil men from the city of Gibeah so that we can execute them and purge Israel of her evil." But the people of Benjamin wouldn't listen. [14,15]Instead, 26,000 of them arrived in Gibeah to join the 700 local men in their defense against the rest of Israel. [16](Among all these there were 700 men who were left-handed sharpshooters. They could hit a target within a hair's breadth, never missing!) [17]The army of Israel, not counting the men of Benjamin, numbered 400,000 men.

[18]Before the battle the Israeli army went to Bethel first to ask counsel from God. "Which tribe shall lead us against the people of Benjamin?" they asked.

And the Lord replied, "Judah shall go first."

[19,20]So the entire army left early the next morning to go to Gibeah, to attack the men of Benjamin. [21]But the men defending the village stormed out and killed 22,000 Israelis that day. [22-24]Then the Israeli army wept before the Lord until evening and asked him, "Shall we fight further against our brother Benjamin?"

And the Lord said, "Yes." So the men of Israel took courage and went out again the next day to fight at the same place. [25]And that day they lost another 18,000 men, all experienced swordsmen.

[26]Then the entire army went up to Bethel and wept before the Lord and fasted until evening, offering burnt sacrifices and peace offerings. [27,28](The Ark of God was in Bethel in those days. Phinehas, the son of Eleazar and grandson of Aaron, was the priest.)

The men of Israel asked the Lord, "Shall we go out again and fight against our brother Benjamin, or shall we stop?"

And the Lord said, "Go, for tomorrow I will see to it that you defeat the men of Benjamin."

[29]So the Israeli army set an ambush all around the village, [30]and went out again on the third day and set themselves in their usual battle formation. [31]When the army of Benjamin came out of the town to attack, the Israeli forces retreated and Benjamin was drawn away from the town as they chased after Israel. And as they had done previously, Benjamin began to kill the men of Israel along the roadway running between Bethel and Gibeah, so that about thirty of them died.

[32]Then the army of Benjamin shouted, "We're defeating them again!" But the armies of Israel had agreed in advance to run away so that the army of Benjamin would chase them and be drawn away from the town. [33]But when the main army of Israel reached Baal-tamar, it turned and attacked, and the 10,000 men in ambush west of Geba jumped up from where they were [34]and advanced against the rear of the army of Benjamin, who still didn't realize the impending disaster. [35-39]So the Lord helped Israel defeat Benjamin, and the Israeli army killed 25,100 men of Benjamin that day, leaving but a tiny remnant of their forces.

Summary of the Battle: The army of Israel retreated from the men of Benjamin in order to give the ambush more room for maneuvering. When the men of Benjamin had killed about thirty of the Israelis, they were confident of a massive slaughter just as on the previous days. But then the men in ambush rushed into the village and slaughtered everyone in it, and set it on fire. The great cloud of smoke pouring into the sky was the signal for the Israeli army to turn around and attack the army of Benjamin, [40,41]who now looked behind them and were terrified to discover that their city was on fire, and that they were in serious trouble. [42]So they ran toward the wilderness, but the Israelis chased after them, and the men who had set the ambush came out and joined the slaughter from the rear. [43]They encircled the army of Benjamin east of Gibeah, and killed most of them there. ⁴⁴Eighteen thousand of the Benjamin troops died in that day's battle. ⁴⁵The rest of the army fled into the wilderness toward the rock of Rimmon, but 5,000 were killed along the way, and 2,000 more near Gidom.

⁴⁶,⁴⁷So the tribe of Benjamin lost 25,000 thousand brave warriors that day, leaving only 600 men who escaped to the rock of Rimmon, where they lived for four months. ⁴⁸Then the Israeli army returned and slaughtered the entire population of the tribe of Benjamin—men, women, children, and cattle—and burned down every city and village in the entire land.

21 Wives for the Men of Benjamin

The leaders of Israel had vowed at Mizpah never to let their daughters marry a man from the tribe of Benjamin. ²And now the Israeli leaders met at Bethel and sat before God until evening, weeping bitterly.

³"O Lord God of Israel," they cried out, "why has this happened, that now one of our tribes is missing?"

⁴The next morning they were up early and built an altar, and offered sacrifices and peace offerings on it. ⁵And they said among themselves, "Was any tribe of Israel not represented when we held our council before the Lord at Mizpah?" For at that time it was agreed by solemn oath that anyone who refused to come must die. ⁶There was deep sadness throughout all Israel for the loss of their brother tribe, Benjamin.

"Gone," they kept saying to themselves, "gone—an entire tribe of Israel has been cut off and is gone. ⁷And how shall we get wives for the few who remain, since we have sworn by the Lord that we will not give them our daughters?"

⁸,⁹Then they thought again of their oath to kill anyone who refused to come to Mizpah and discovered that no one had attended from Jabesh-gilead. ¹⁰⁻¹²So they sent 12,000 of their best soldiers to destroy the people of Jabesh-gilead. All the men, married women, and children were slain, but the young virgins of marriageable age were saved. There were 400 of these, and they were brought to the camp at Shiloh.

¹³Then Israel sent a peace delegation to the little remnant of the men of Benjamin at Rimmon Rock. ¹⁴The 400 girls were given to them as wives, and they returned to their homes; but there were not enough of these girls for all of them. ¹⁵(What a sad time it was in Israel in those days because the Lord had made a breach in the tribes of Israel.)

¹⁶"What shall we do for wives for the others, since all the women of the tribe of Benjamin are dead?" the leaders of Israel asked. ¹⁷"There must be some way to get wives for them, so that an entire tribe of Israel will not be lost forever. ¹⁸But we can't give them our own daughters. We have sworn with a solemn oath that anyone who does this shall be cursed of God."

¹⁹Suddenly someone thought of the annual religious festival held in the fields of Shiloh, between Lebonah and Bethel, along the east side of the road that goes from Bethel to Shechem.

²⁰They told the men of Benjamin who still needed wives, "Go and hide in the vineyards, ²¹and when the girls of Shiloh come out for their dances, rush out and catch them and take them home with you to be your wives! ²²And when their fathers and brothers come to us in protest, we will tell them, 'Please be understanding and let them have your daughters, for we didn't find enough wives for them when we destroyed Jabesh-gilead, and you couldn't have given your daughters to them without being guilty.'"

²³So the men of Benjamin did as they were told and kidnapped the girls who took part in the celebration, and carried them off to their own land. Then they rebuilt their cities and lived in them. ²⁴So the people of Israel returned to their homes.

²⁵(There was no king in Israel in those days, and every man did whatever he thought was right.)

Ruth

WHEN YOU want to get a close look at something, you put it under a microscope. That's what the book of Ruth is like. We've been reading about the whole nation of Israel. Now we get to look very closely at just one Israelite family.

Naomi's family lived during the time of the judges. She and her husband and two sons worshiped and obeyed God. After a sad turn of events, Naomi was left in a foreign country with only her two daughters-in-law.

This was scary for Naomi because she had no one to take care of her. But God provided two people to help her. In order to help, they had to focus on what was truly important, make choices, and keep promises.

One of these people was Ruth, Naomi's daughter-in-law. She promised to move to Israel and take care of Naomi. Ruth knew what was important, and she kept her promises to Naomi.

The other person was Boaz, a close relative of Naomi. He knew what God expected of him. He made promises to Ruth and kept them.

As you read, look for examples of how Naomi, Ruth, and Boaz made the right choices, and think of ways to follow their examples.

Ruth Goes Home with Naomi

Long ago when judges ruled in Israel, a man named Elimelech, from Bethlehem, left the country because of a famine and moved to the land of Moab. With him were his wife, Naomi, and his two sons, Mahlon and Chilion. ³During the time of their residence there, Elimelech died and Naomi was left with her two sons.

⁴,⁵These young men, Mahlon and Chilion, married girls of Moab, Orpah and Ruth. But later, both men died, so that Naomi was left alone, without her husband or sons. ⁶,⁷She decided to return to Israel with her daughters-in-law, for she had heard that the Lord had blessed his people by giving them good crops again.

⁸But after they had begun their homeward journey, she changed her mind and said to her two daughters-in-law, "Why don't you return to your parents' homes instead of coming with me? And may the Lord reward you for your faithfulness to your husbands and to me. ⁹And may he bless you with another happy marriage." Then

she kissed them, and they all broke down and cried.

[10]"No," they said. "We want to go with you to your people."

[11]But Naomi replied, "It is better for you to return to your own people. Do I have younger sons who could grow up to be your husbands? [12]No, my daughters, return to your parents' homes, for I am too old to have a husband. And even if that were possible, and I became pregnant tonight, and bore sons [13] would you wait for them to grow up? No, of course not, my daughters; oh, how I grieve for you that the Lord has punished me in a way that injures you."

[14]And again they cried together, and Orpah kissed her mother-in-law good-bye, and returned to her childhood home; but Ruth insisted on staying with Naomi.

[15]"See," Naomi said to her, "your sister-in-law has gone back to her people and to her gods; you should do the same."

[16]But Ruth replied, "Don't make me leave you, for I want to go wherever you go and to live wherever you live; your people shall be my people, and your God shall be my God; [17]I want to die where you die and be buried there. May the Lord do terrible things to me if I allow anything but death to separate us."

[18]And when Naomi saw that Ruth had made up her mind and could not be persuaded otherwise, she stopped urging her. [19]So they both came to Bethlehem, and the entire village was stirred by their arrival.

"Is it really Naomi?" the women asked.

[20]But she told them, "Don't call me Naomi. Call me Mara," (Naomi means "pleasant"; Mara means "bitter") "for Almighty God has dealt me bitter blows. [21]I went out full and the Lord has brought me home empty; why should you call me Naomi when the Lord has turned his back on me and sent such calamity!"

[22](Their return from Moab and arrival in Bethlehem was at the beginning of the barley harvest.)

Ruth Gleans in the Fields

2 Now Naomi had an in-law there in Bethlehem who was a very wealthy man. His name was Boaz.

[2]One day Ruth said to Naomi, "Perhaps I can go out into the fields of some kind man to glean the free grain behind his reapers."

And Naomi said, "All right, dear daughter. Go ahead."

[3]So she did. And as it happened, the field where she found herself belonged to Boaz, this relative of Naomi's husband.

[4,5]Boaz arrived from the city while she was there. After exchanging greetings with the reapers he said to his foreman, "Hey, who's that girl over there?"

[6]And the foreman replied, "It's that girl from the land of Moab who came back with Naomi. [7]She asked me this morning if she could pick up the grains dropped by the reapers, and she has been at it ever since except for a few minutes' rest over there in the shade."

[8,9]Boaz went over and talked to her. "Listen, my child," he said to her. "Stay right here with us to glean; don't think of going to any other fields. Stay right behind my women workers; I have warned the young men not to bother you; when you are thirsty, go and help yourself to the water."

[10,11]She thanked him warmly. "How can you be so kind to me?" she asked. "You must know I am only a foreigner."

"Yes, I know," Boaz replied, "and I also know about all the love and kindness you have shown your mother-in-law since the death of your husband, and how you left your father and mother in your own land and have come here to live among strangers. [12]May the Lord God of Israel, under whose wings you have come to take refuge, bless you for it."

[13]"Oh, thank you, sir," she replied. "You are so good to me, and I'm not even one of your workers!"

[14]At lunch time Boaz called to her, "Come and eat with us."

So she sat with his reapers and he gave her food, more than she could eat. [15]And when she went back to work again, Boaz told his young men to let her glean right among the sheaves without stopping her, [16]and to snap off some heads of barley and drop them on purpose for her to glean, and not to make any remarks. [17]So she worked there all day, and in the evening when she had beaten out the barley she had gleaned, it came to a whole bushel! [18]She carried it back into the city and gave it to her mother-in-law, with what was left of her lunch.

[19]"So much!" Naomi exclaimed. "Where in the world did you glean today? Praise the Lord for whoever was so kind to you." So Ruth told her mother-in-law all about it and mentioned that the owner of the field was Boaz.

[20]"Praise the Lord for a man like that! God has continued his kindness to us as well as to your dead husband!" Naomi cried excitedly. "Why, that man is one of our closest relatives!"

[21]"Well," Ruth told her, "he said to come back and stay close behind his reapers until the entire field is harvested."

[22]"This is wonderful!" Naomi exclaimed. "Do as he has said. Stay with his girls right through the

Family Devotions

☐ DEVOTION 92
KEEPING YOUR PROMISES

Read Ruth 3:18–4:1

Keeping Your Promises Memory Verse

God delights in those who keep their promises and abhors those who don't.
Proverbs 12:22

Cindy was excited. It was Sunday morning, the day she and her two friends, Shannon and Jill, were to sing in church. They had practiced their song several times the past two weeks. Now Cindy stood at the church door waiting for her friends. She hoped this would be the first of many times that the three girls would sing. She had also invited her aunt, who was not a Christian, to come to church that day.

"Are you nervous?" Jill asked as she ran up the church steps. "I could hardly sleep last night because I was so excited."

"Kind of," Cindy agreed.

Just then Shannon's brother, Dave, walked by. "Where's Shannon?" both girls asked at once.

"Oh, didn't you know?" Dave seemed surprised. "Our neighbors called last night, and Shannon went camping with them. She won't be back until tomorrow."

Cindy and Jill looked at each other in shock! How could Shannon do this? They hurried to find the pianist, who assured them that they could sing anyhow.

Well, the girls did sing, and they did a good job. Even Cindy's aunt said so, but Cindy and Jill both knew that it would have sounded better if Shannon had been there. They were still upset by what had happened.

"This won't be the last time someone lets you down," Cindy's mother told her on the way home. "There are many people who just don't have a sense of responsibility. Remember this experience whenever you're tempted to back out of something at the last minute. God expects faithfulness from his servants. We owe it to him and we owe it to others as well. If one person doesn't do his or her job, it hinders everyone."

"I guess there are times we all let other people down," Cindy admitted. "Maybe it's actually a good thing this happened. I know it will make me think twice before I break a promise to do something."

How About You?
Do you take your responsibilities seriously? Or do you just not show up at the last minute if something better comes along? Like Boaz, we need to follow through on our commitments promptly and responsibly. Faithfulness is important in being a witness for Christ. L. M. W.

• For the next devotional, turn to page 289. • For the next devotional on KEEPING YOUR PROMISES, turn to page 637.
• For notes on KEEPING YOUR PROMISES, see pages 183, 284, and 838.

whole harvest; you will be safer there than in any other field!"

²³So Ruth did and gleaned with them until the end of the barley harvest, and then the wheat harvest too.

3 Ruth Marries Boaz

One day Naomi said to Ruth, "My dear, isn't it time that I try to find a husband for you and get you happily married again? ²The man I'm thinking of is Boaz! He has been so kind to us and is a close relative. I happen to know that he will be winnowing barley tonight out on the threshing-floor. ³Now do what I tell you—bathe and put on some perfume and some nice clothes and go on down to the threshing-floor, but don't let him see you until he has finished his supper. ⁴Notice where he lies down to sleep; then go and lift the cover off his feet and lie down there, and he will tell you what to do concerning marriage."

⁵And Ruth replied, "All right. I'll do whatever you say."

⁶,⁷So she went down to the threshing-floor that night and followed her mother-in-law's instructions. After Boaz had finished a good meal, he lay down very contentedly beside a heap of grain and went to sleep. Then Ruth came quietly and lifted the covering off his feet and lay there. ⁸Suddenly, around midnight, he wakened and sat up, startled. There was a woman lying at his feet!

⁹"Who are you?" he demanded.

"It's I, sir—Ruth," she replied. "Make me your wife according to God's law, for you are my close relative."

¹⁰"Thank God for a girl like you!" he exclaimed. "For you are being even kinder to Naomi now than before. Naturally you'd prefer a younger man, even though poor. But you have put aside your personal desires. ¹¹Now don't worry about a thing, my child; I'll handle all the details, for everyone knows what a wonderful person you are. ¹²But there is one problem. It's true that I am a close relative, but there is someone else who is more closely related to you than I am. ¹³Stay here tonight, and in the morning I'll talk to him, and if he will marry you, fine; let him do his duty; but if he won't, then I will, I swear by Jehovah; lie down until the morning."

¹⁴So she lay at his feet until the morning and was up early, before daybreak, for he had said to her, "Don't let it be known that a woman was here at the threshing-floor."

¹⁵⁻¹⁸"Bring your shawl," he told her. Then he tied up a bushel and a half of barley in it as a present for her mother-in-law and laid it on her back. Then she returned to the city.

"Well, what happened, dear?" Naomi asked her when she arrived home. She told Naomi everything and gave her the barley from Boaz, and mentioned his remark that she mustn't go home without a present.

Then Naomi said to her, "Just be patient until we hear what happens, for Boaz won't rest until he has followed through on this. He'll settle it today."

4

So Boaz went down to the marketplace and found the relative he had mentioned.

"Say, come over here," he called to him. "I want to talk to you a minute."

So they sat down together. ²Then Boaz called for ten of the chief men of the village and asked them to sit as witnesses.

³Boaz said to his relative, "You know Naomi, who came back to us from Moab. She is selling our brother Elimelech's property. ⁴I felt that I should speak to you about it so that you can buy it if you wish, with these respected men as witnesses. If you want it, let me know right away, for if you don't take it, I will. You have the first right to purchase it and I am next."

The man replied, "All right, I'll buy it."

⁵Then Boaz told him, "Your purchase of the land from Naomi requires your marriage to Ruth so that she can have children to carry on her husband's name and to inherit the land."

⁶"Then I can't do it," the man replied. "For her son would become an heir to my property too; you buy it."

⁷In those days it was the custom in Israel for a man transferring a right of purchase to pull off his sandal and hand it to the other party; this publicly validated the transaction. ⁸So, as the man said to Boaz, "You buy it for yourself," he drew off his sandal.

⁹Then Boaz said to the witnesses and to the crowd standing around, "You have seen that today I have bought all the property of Elimelech, Chilion, and Mahlon, from Naomi, ¹⁰and that with it I have purchased Ruth the Moabitess, the widow of Mahlon, to be my wife, so that she can have a son to carry on the family name of her dead husband."

¹¹And all the people standing

KEEPING YOUR PROMISES 3:18–4:1 Naomi said Boaz would follow through with his promise at once. He obviously had a reputation for keeping his word. He did not rest until his task was completed. Such reliable people stand out in any age and culture. Do others regard you as one who will do what you say? Keeping your word and following through on assignments should be high on anyone's priority list. Building a reputation for integrity, however, must be done one brick at a time. **To begin the series of devotionals on KEEPING YOUR PROMISES, turn to page 181.**

there and the witnesses replied, "We are witnesses. May the Lord make this woman, who has now come into your home, as fertile as Rachel and Leah, from whom all the nation of Israel descended! May you be a great and successful man in Bethlehem, ¹²and may the descendants the Lord will give you from this young woman be as numerous and honorable as those of our ancestor Perez, the son of Tamar and Judah."

¹³So Boaz married Ruth, and when he slept with her, the Lord gave her a son.

¹⁴And the women of the city said to Naomi, "Bless the Lord who has given you this little grandson; may he be famous in Israel. ¹⁵May he restore your youth and take care of you in your old age; for he is the son of your daughter-in-law who loves you so much, and who has been kinder to you than seven sons!"

¹⁶,¹⁷Naomi took care of the baby, and the neighbor women said, "Now at last Naomi has a son again!"

And they named him Obed. He was the father of Jesse and grandfather of King David.

¹⁸⁻²²This is the family tree of Boaz, beginning with his ancestor Perez: Perez, Hezron, Ram, Amminadab, Nashon, Salmon, Boaz, Obed, Jesse, David.

1 Samuel

HAVE YOU ever wanted something badly, and then, once you got it, you were sorry you asked for it? The Israelites were in this situation.

All the nations surrounding Israel had kings. Even though God himself was their ruler, Israel wanted a human king so they could be like everybody else. Samuel warned the people that this was a mistake, but they insisted. God decided to give the people what they wanted and let them learn a lesson.

The king he gave them, Saul, looked like a great king, but deep down he was afraid to trust God. Eventually God rejected Saul as king.

God knew that what a person looked like on the outside wasn't as important as what he was like on the inside. So God told Samuel to pick David, who loved God, to be the next king. David had to wait until Saul died to become king, even though he knew God had chosen him. Unlike the Israelites, David waited patiently for God's timing and did not demand his own way.

We have the choice of following Saul's example or David's example when it comes to trusting and obeying God. Look for what happens when you obey or disobey God as you read 1 Samuel.

Samuel Is Born

This is the story of Elkanah, a man of the tribe of Ephraim who lived in Ramathaim-zophim, in the hills of Ephraim.

His father's name was Jeroham,
His grandfather was Elihu,
His great-grandfather was Tohu,
His great-great-grandfather was Zuph.

²He had two wives, Hannah and Peninnah. Peninnah had some children, but Hannah didn't.

³Each year Elkanah and his families journeyed to the Tabernacle at Shiloh to worship the Lord of the heavens and to sacrifice to him. (The priests on duty at that time were the two sons of Eli—Hophni and Phinehas.) ⁴On the day he presented his sacrifice, Elkanah would celebrate the happy occasion by giving presents to Peninnah and her

children; ⁵but although he loved Hannah very much, he could give her only one present, for the Lord had sealed her womb; so she had no children to give presents to. ⁶Peninnah made matters worse by taunting Hannah because of her barrenness. ⁷Every year it was the same—Peninnah scoffing and laughing at her as they went to Shiloh, making her cry so much she couldn't eat.

⁸"What's the matter, Hannah?" Elkanah would exclaim. "Why aren't you eating? Why make such a fuss over having no children? Isn't having me better than having ten sons?"

⁹One evening after supper, when they were at Shiloh, Hannah went over to the Tabernacle. Eli the priest was sitting at his customary place beside the entrance. ¹⁰She was in deep anguish and was crying bitterly as she prayed to the Lord.

¹¹And she made this vow: "O Lord of heaven, if you will look down upon my sorrow and answer my prayer and give me a son, then I will give him back to you, and he'll be yours for his entire lifetime, and his hair shall never be cut."

¹²,¹³Eli noticed her mouth moving as she was praying silently and, hearing no sound, thought she had been drinking.

¹⁴"Must you come here drunk?" he demanded. "Throw away your bottle."

¹⁵,¹⁶"Oh no, sir!" she replied, "I'm not drunk! But I am very sad and I was pouring out my heart to the Lord. Please don't think that I am just some drunken bum!"

¹⁷"In that case," Eli said, "cheer up! May the Lord of Israel grant you your petition, whatever it is!"

¹⁸"Oh, thank you, sir!" she exclaimed, and went happily back, and began to take her meals again.

¹⁹,²⁰The entire family was up early the next morning and went to the Tabernacle to worship the Lord once more. Then they returned home to Ramah, and when Elkanah slept with Hannah, the Lord remembered her petition; in the process of time, a baby boy was born to her. She named him Samuel (meaning "asked of God") because, as she said, "I asked the Lord for him."

²¹,²²The next year Elkanah and Peninnah and her children went on the annual trip to the Tabernacle without Hannah, for she told her husband, "Wait until the baby is weaned, and then I will take him to the Tabernacle and leave him there."

²³"Well, whatever you think best," Elkanah agreed. "May the Lord's will be done."

So she stayed home until the baby was weaned. ²⁴Then, though he was still so small, they took him to the Tabernacle in Shiloh, along with a three-year-old bull for the sacrifice, and a bushel of flour and some wine. ²⁵After the sacrifice they took the child to Eli.

²⁶"Sir, do you remember me?" Hannah asked him. "I am the woman who stood here that time praying to the Lord! ²⁷I asked him to give me this child, and he has given me my request; ²⁸and now I am giving him to the Lord for as long as he lives." So she left him there at the Tabernacle for the Lord to use.

2 Hannah's Prayer of Thanks

This was Hannah's prayer:

"How I rejoice in the Lord!
How he has blessed me!
Now I have an answer for my enemies,
For the Lord has solved my problem.
How I rejoice!
²No one is as holy as the Lord!
There is no other God,
Nor any Rock like our God.
³Quit acting so proud and arrogant!
The Lord knows what you have done,
And he will judge your deeds.
⁴Those who were mighty are mighty no more!
Those who were weak are now strong.
⁵Those who were well are now starving;
Those who were starving are fed.
The barren woman now has seven children;
She with many children has no more!
⁶The Lord kills,
The Lord gives life.
⁷Some he causes to be poor
And others to be rich.
He cuts one down
And lifts another up.
⁸He lifts the poor from the dust—
Yes, from a pile of ashes—
And treats them as princes
Sitting in the seats of honor.
For all the earth is the Lord's
And he has set the world in order.
⁹He will protect his godly ones,
But the wicked shall be silenced in darkness.
No one shall succeed by strength alone.
¹⁰Those who fight against the Lord shall be broken;
He thunders against them from heaven.

DEALING WITH CHANGE 2:2 Hannah praised God for being a Rock—firm, strong, and unchanging. In our fast-paced world, friends come and go and circumstances change. It's difficult to find a solid foundation that will not change. Those who devote their lives to achievements, causes, or possessions have as their security that which is finite and changeable. The possessions that we work so hard to obtain will all pass away. But God is always present. Hope in him. He will never fail. **To begin the series of devotionals on DEALING WITH CHANGE, turn to page 15.**

FAMILY DEVOTIONS

☐ DEVOTION 93
ACCEPTING OTHERS

Read 1 Samuel 1:9-17

Accepting Others
Memory Verse

How wonderful it is, how pleasant, when brothers live in harmony!
Psalm 133:1

"There was a new girl in our class today," Mary Ellen announced at the dinner table. "I don't like her, though. She's a snob. She sits just like this." Mary Ellen turned her nose up, pushed her shoulders back, and sat very erect. "When Debi asked her if she wanted to jump rope with us, she said, 'No, thank you,' so prissy."

"Hmmm," murmured Mother as she passed the chicken casserole. "Aren't you judging a little prematurely? God says we shouldn't do that."

Dad peered at the casserole. "What is this?"

"A new casserole," said Mother.

"I don't want any," stated five-year-old Matthew. "I don't like it."

Mary Ellen laughed. "You've never tasted it," she said.

"I know I won't like it," Matthew repeated.

"Well, I want you to try it," said Dad. "Take two bites, Matthew."

Matthew looked pleadingly at Mother. "You heard your dad," she said. "Two bites." Matthew put a tiny bit on the edge of his spoon. "That's not even enough to taste," Mother said as she filled his spoon. "Now taste it."

Matthew grimaced as he put the spoon to his mouth. He swallowed, then slowly grinned. "It *is* good!" he exclaimed.

When the laughter had died down, Mother looked at Mary Ellen. "You are acting about the new girl just like Matthew did about the new casserole. You haven't given her a fair chance."

The next day Mary Ellen came bouncing in from school. "Guess what, Mother? I do like Jolene," she said. "She's nice. She sits like she does because she wears a back brace. That's why she couldn't jump rope. She just hated to tell anybody."

Mother smiled. "I'm glad you gave her a fair chance," she said. "I'm sure the Lord is, too."

How About You?
Are you afraid to try new things or meet new people? If you judge them on the basis of first impressions, as Eli judged Hannah, you may miss some wonderful experiences. Determine now to give everyone you meet a fair chance to be your friend. God warns about judging unfairly. B. W.

• For the next devotional, turn to page 291. • For the next devotional on *ACCEPTING OTHERS*, turn to page 299.
• For notes on *ACCEPTING OTHERS*, see pages 270, 1140, 1196, and 1254.

He judges throughout the earth.
He gives mighty strength to his King,
And gives great glory to his anointed one."

¹¹So they returned home to Ramah without Samuel; and the child became the Lord's helper, for he assisted Eli the priest.

¹²Now the sons of Eli were evil men who didn't love the Lord. ¹³,¹⁴It was their regular practice to send out a servant whenever anyone was offering a sacrifice, and while the flesh of the sacrificed animal was boiling, the servant would put a three-pronged fleshhook into the pot and demand that whatever it brought up be given to Eli's sons. They treated all of the Israelites in this way when they came to Shiloh to worship. ¹⁵Sometimes the servant would come even before the rite of burning the fat on the altar had been performed, and he would demand raw meat before it was boiled, so that it could be used for roasting.

¹⁶If the man offering the sacrifice replied, "Take as much as you want, but the fat must first be burned" [as the law requires], then the servant would say,

"No, give it to me now or I'll take it by force."

¹⁷So the sin of these young men was very great in the eyes of the Lord; for they treated the people's offerings to the Lord with contempt.

¹⁸Samuel, though only a child, was the Lord's helper and wore a little linen robe just like the priest's. ¹⁹Each year his mother made a little coat for him and brought it to him when she came with her husband for the sacrifice. ²⁰Before they returned home Eli would bless Elkanah and Hannah and ask God to give them other children to take the place of this one they had given to the Lord. ²¹ And the Lord gave Hannah three sons and two daughters. Meanwhile Samuel grew up in the service of the Lord.

²²Eli was now very old, but he was aware of what was going on around him. He knew, for instance, that his sons were seducing the young women who assisted at the entrance of the Tabernacle.

²³⁻²⁵"I have been hearing terrible reports from the Lord's people about what you are doing," Eli told his sons. "It is an awful thing to make the Lord's people sin. Ordinary sin receives heavy punishment, but how much more this sin of yours that has been committed against the Lord!" But they wouldn't listen to their father, for the Lord was already planning to kill them.

²⁶Little Samuel was growing in two ways—he was getting taller, and he was becoming everyone's favorite (and he was a favorite of the Lord's, too!).

²⁷One day a prophet came to Eli and gave him this message from the Lord: "Didn't I demonstrate my power when the people of Israel were slaves in Egypt? ²⁸Didn't I choose your ancestor Levi from among all his brothers to be my priest, and to sacrifice upon my altar, and to burn incense, and to wear a priestly robe as he served me? And didn't I assign the sacrificial offerings to you priests? ²⁹Then why are you so greedy for all the other offerings which are brought to me? Why have you honored your sons more than me—for you and they have become fat from the best of the offerings of my people!

³⁰"Therefore, I, the Lord God of Israel, declare that although I promised that your branch of the tribe of Levi could always be my priests, it is ridiculous to think that what you are doing can continue. I will honor only those who honor me, and I will despise those who despise me. ³¹I will put an end to your family, so that it will no longer serve as priests. Every member will die before his time. None shall live to be old. ³²You will envy the prosperity I will give my people, but you and your family will be in distress and need. Not one of them will live out his days. ³³Those who are left alive will live in sadness and grief; and their children shall die by the sword. ³⁴And to prove that what I have said will come true, I will cause your two sons, Hophni and Phinehas, to die on the same day!

³⁵"Then I will raise up a faithful priest who will serve me and do whatever I tell him to do. I will bless his descendants, and his family shall be priests to my kings forever. ³⁶Then all of your descendants shall bow before him, begging for money and food. 'Please,' they will say, 'give me a job among the priests so that I will have enough to eat.'"

3 God Speaks to Samuel

Meanwhile little Samuel was helping the Lord by assisting Eli. Messages from the Lord were very rare in those days, ²,³but one night after Eli had gone to bed (he was almost blind with age by now), and Samuel was sleeping in the Temple near the Ark, ⁴,⁵the Lord called out, "Samuel! Samuel!"

"Yes?" Samuel replied. "What is it?" He jumped up and ran to Eli. "Here I am. What do you want?" he asked.

"I didn't call you," Eli said. "Go on back to bed." So he did. ⁶Then the Lord called again, "Samuel!" And again Samuel jumped up and ran to Eli.

"Yes?" he asked. "What do you need?"

"No, I didn't call you, my son," Eli said. "Go on back to bed."

⁷(Samuel had never had a message from Jehovah before.) ⁸So now the Lord called the third time, and once more Samuel jumped up and ran to Eli.

"Yes?" he asked. "What do you need?"

Then Eli realized it was the Lord who had spoken to the child. ⁹So he said to Samuel, "Go and lie down

Family Devotions

☐ **DEVOTION 94**

SERVING GOD WILLINGLY

Read 1 Samuel 2:18; 3:1-21

Serving God Willingly
Memory Verse

Anyone who takes care of a little child like this is caring for me! And whoever cares for me is caring for God who sent me. Your care for others is the measure of your greatness.
Luke 9:48

"Today was Pastor Wilson's birthday, and we had a party for him," announced Jonathan on the way home from Sunday school. "It would be fun to be a minister. That's what I'm going to be when I grow up."

"I don't know how much fun it would be, but I'm sure it's rewarding," Dad said.

"Could we stop by Grannie Nelson's and check on her?" asked Mom.

"Do we have to?" groaned Jonathan. "I'm starved, and you know how she talks and talks."

"She's lonely," replied Mom. "She needs someone to minister to her."

"Minister to her?" Jonathan echoed. "If she needs a preacher, tell Pastor Wilson."

"I didn't say she needs a preacher," Mom said, smiling. "What I said is that Grannie Nelson needs a *minister*. We can't all be preachers, but we can all be ministers—even you, Jonathan!"

"Well, I am going to be one when I grow up, if I don't starve to death first," Jonathan complained.

"You can be one now," Mom insisted. "A minister is simply a servant. You can minister to Grannie Nelson."

"Aw, you're just kidding. Pastor Wilson isn't a servant!" said Jonathan.

"He certainly is," Dad corrected. "He is God's servant."

"If you're not willing to serve others, you cannot be a minister," added Mom.

"Do you know how the child Samuel ministered to the Lord?" Dad asked as they turned into Grannie Nelson's driveway. "He ministered to the Lord by serving Eli. He lit the lamp in the Tabernacle, swept the floors, and ran errands."

Jonathan took a deep breath. "Well, that isn't exactly how I had it pictured, but I guess I'd better start now."

How About You?
Did you know that Christians are to be ministers? As a servant of God, your job is to serve others. Look around you. Find one person today that you can serve. You'll be surprised how much fun it is! And as you serve people, you are actually ministering to the Lord. *B. W.*

• For the next devotional, turn to page 293. • For the next devotional on *SERVING GOD WILLINGLY*, turn to page 385.
• For notes on *SERVING GOD WILLINGLY*, see pages 49, 419, 890, 920, and 922.

again, and if he calls again, say, 'Yes, Lord, I'm listening.'" So Samuel went back to bed.

[10] And the Lord came and called as before, "Samuel! Samuel!"

And Samuel replied, "Yes, I'm listening."

[11] Then the Lord said to Samuel, "I am going to do a shocking thing in Israel. [12] I am going to do all of the dreadful things I warned Eli about. [13] I have continually threatened him and his entire family with punishment because his sons are blaspheming God, and he doesn't stop them. [14] So I have vowed that the sins of Eli and of his sons shall never be forgiven by sacrifices and offerings."

[15] Samuel stayed in bed until morning, then opened the doors of the Temple as usual, for he was afraid to tell Eli what the Lord had said to him. [16,17] But Eli called him.

"My son," he said, "what did the Lord say to you? Tell me everything. And may God punish you if you hide anything from me!"

[18] So Samuel told him what the Lord had said.

"It is the Lord's will," Eli replied; "let him do what he thinks best."

[19] As Samuel grew, the Lord was with him and people listened carefully to his advice. [20] And all Israel from one end of the land to the other knew that Samuel was going to be a prophet of the Lord. [21, 4:1] Then the Lord began to give messages to him there at the Tabernacle in Shiloh, and he passed them on to the people of Israel.

4 The Ark Is Stolen

At that time Israel was at war with the Philistines. The Israeli army was camped near Ebenezer, the Philistines at Aphek. [2] And the Philistines defeated Israel, killing four thousand of them. [3] After the battle was over, the army of Israel returned to their camp and their leaders discussed why the Lord had let them be defeated.

"Let's bring the Ark here from Shiloh," they said. "If we carry it into battle with us, the Lord will be among us and he will surely save us from our enemies."

[4] So they sent for the Ark of the Lord of heaven who is enthroned above the angels. Hophni and Phinehas, the sons of Eli, accompanied it into the battle. [5] When the Israelis saw the Ark coming, their shout of joy was so loud that it almost made the ground shake!

[6] "What's going on?" the Philistines asked. "What's all the shouting about over in the camp of the Hebrews?"

When they were told it was because the Ark of the Lord had arrived, [7] they panicked.

"God has come into their camp!" they cried out. "Woe upon us, for we have never had to face anything like this before! [8] Who can save us from these mighty gods of Israel? They are the same gods who destroyed the Egyptians with plagues when Israel was in the wilderness. [9] Fight as you never have before, O Philistines, or we will become their slaves just as they have been ours."

[10] So the Philistines fought desperately and Israel was defeated again. Thirty thousand men of Israel died that day, and the remainder fled to their tents. [11] And the Ark of God was captured, and Hophni and Phinehas were killed.

[12] A man from the tribe of Benjamin ran from the battle and arrived at Shiloh the same day with his clothes torn and dirt on his head. [13] Eli was waiting beside the road to hear the news of the battle, for his heart trembled for the safety of the Ark of God. As the messenger from the battlefront arrived and told what had happened, a great cry arose throughout the city.

[14] "What is all the noise about?" Eli asked. And the messenger rushed over to Eli and told him what had happened. [15] (Eli was ninety-eight years old and was blind.)

[16] "I have just come from the battle—I was there today," he told Eli, [17] "and Israel has been defeated and thousands of the Israeli troops are dead on the battlefield. Hophni and Phinehas were killed too, and the Ark has been captured."

[18] When the messenger mentioned what had happened to the Ark, Eli fell backward from his seat beside the gate and his neck was broken by the fall, and he died (for he was old and fat). He had judged Israel for forty years.

[19] When Eli's daughter-in-law, Phinehas' wife, who was pregnant, heard that the Ark had been captured and that her husband and father-in-law were dead, her labor pains suddenly began. [20] Just before she died, the women who were attending her told her that everything was all right and that the baby was a boy. But she did not reply or respond in any way. [21,22] Then she murmured, "Name the child 'Ichabod,' for Israel's glory is gone." (Ichabod means "there is no glory." She named him this because the Ark of God had been captured and because her husband and her father-in-law were dead.)

5 Philistines Are Punished

The Philistines took the captured Ark of God from the battleground at Ebenezer to the temple of their idol Dagon in the city of Ashdod. [3] But when the local citizens went to see it the next morning, Dagon had fallen with his face to the ground before the Ark of Jehovah! They set him up again, [4] but the next morning the same thing had happened—the idol had fallen face down before the Ark of the Lord again. This time his head and hands had been cut off and were lying in the

Family Devotions

☐ DEVOTION 95
GIVING THANKS

Read 1 Samuel 7:7-12

The Johnson family stood looking at the big oak tree lying across their yard. During the night, a fierce storm had blown the tree down. Mark was the first to speak. "God sure did take good care of us, didn't he, Dad?"

"He surely did," Dad replied placing his hand on Mark's shoulder. "That really makes me stop and praise him."

Mark looked at their house standing just a short distance from the fallen tree, yet not harmed at all. "Yeah," he said in awe. "I hope I never forget all the things God has done for us. Whenever I'm scared of something, it helps to remember how God took care of me in the past."

"We had a story in Bible club about how Samuel once set up a stone as a memorial of how God had won a battle for Israel," commented Susan. "It had kind of a funny name, but it meant something like 'God has helped us.'"

"You're thinking of the name *Ebenezer,*" said Mom. "Were you thinking of setting up a memorial rock of your own?"

Susan laughed. "Well, not exactly, but I thought maybe we could make a notebook of all the times God helps us. We could add to it whenever we get the chance."

"Hey, that's a good idea," agreed Mark. "Maybe we could put in a picture of all of us standing in front of this big tree. Whenever we see the picture we'll be reminded of God's help."

Mom and Dad both smiled approvingly. "We can call it our Ebenezer book," suggested Dad. "What a good way to remember all that God has done for us."

Giving Thanks Memory Verse

Is anyone among you suffering? He should keep on praying about it. And those who have reason to be thankful should continually be singing praises to the Lord.
James 5:13

How About You?

Do you have a way of remembering the things the Lord has done for you? Have you received some special answers to prayer, or has God protected you in a dangerous situation? Maybe he's helped you through a hard class at school. Why don't you try to keep a record of what God has done for you? Don't do it to dwell on the past, but do it to be reminded of God's great help when you're faced with a difficult situation. D. R.

doorway; only the trunk of his body was left intact. ⁵(That is why to this day neither the priests of Dagon nor his worshipers will walk on the threshold of the temple of Dagon in Ashdod.)

⁶Then the Lord began to destroy the people of Ashdod and the nearby villages with bubonic plague. ⁷When the people realized what was happening, they exclaimed, "We can't keep the Ark of the God of Israel here any longer. We will all perish along with our god Dagon."

⁸So they called a conference of the mayors of the five cities of the Philistines to decide how to dispose of the Ark. The decision was to take it to Gath. ⁹But when the Ark arrived at Gath, the Lord began destroying its people, young and old, with the plague, and there was a great panic. ¹⁰So they sent the Ark to Ekron, but when the people of Ekron saw it coming they cried out, "They are bringing the Ark of the God of Israel here to kill us too!"

¹¹So they summoned the mayors again and begged them to send the Ark back to its own country, lest the entire city die. For the plague had already begun, and great fear was sweeping across the city. ¹²Those who didn't die were deathly ill; and there was weeping everywhere.

6 The Ark Comes Back

The Ark remained in the Philistine country for seven months in all. ²Then the Philistines called for their priests and diviners and asked them, "What shall we do about the Ark of God? What sort of gift shall we send with it when we return it to its own land?"

³"Yes, send it back with a gift," they were told. "Send a guilt offering so that the plague will stop. Then, if it doesn't, you will know God didn't send the plague upon you after all."

⁴,⁵"What guilt offering shall we send?" they asked.

And they were told, "Send five gold models of the tumor caused by the plague, and five gold models of the rats that have ravaged the whole land—the capital cities and villages alike. If you send these gifts and then praise the God of Israel, perhaps he will stop persecuting you and your god. ⁶Don't be stubborn and rebellious as Pharaoh and the Egyptians were. They wouldn't let Israel go until God had destroyed them with dreadful plagues. ⁷Now build a new cart and hitch to it two cows that have just had calves—cows that never before have been yoked—and shut their calves away from them in the barn. ⁸Place the Ark of God on the cart beside a chest containing the gold models of the rats and tumors, and let the cows go wherever they want to. ⁹If they cross the border of our land and go into Beth-shemesh, then you will know that it was God who brought this great evil upon us; if they don't [but return to their calves], then we will know that the plague was simply a coincidence and was not sent by God at all."

¹⁰So these instructions were carried out. Two cows with newborn calves were hitched to the cart and their calves were shut up in the barn. ¹¹Then the Ark of the Lord and the chest containing the gold rats and tumors were placed upon the cart. ¹²And sure enough, the cows went straight along the road toward Beth-shemesh, lowing as they went; and the Philistine mayors followed them as far as the border of Beth-shemesh. ¹³The people of Beth-shemesh were reaping wheat in the valley, and when they saw the Ark, they went wild with joy!

¹⁴The cart came into the field of a man named Joshua and stopped beside a large rock. So the people broke up the wood of the cart for a fire and killed the cows and sacrificed them to the Lord as a burnt offering. ¹⁵Several men of the tribe of Levi lifted the Ark and the chest containing the gold rats and tumors from the cart and laid them on the rock. And many burnt offerings and sacrifices were offered to the Lord that day by the men of Beth-shemesh.

¹⁶After the five Philistine mayors had watched for awhile, they returned to Ekron that same day. ¹⁷The five gold models of tumors which had been sent by the Philistines as a guilt offering to the Lord were gifts from the mayors of the capital cities, Ashdod, Gaza, Ashkelon, Gath, and Ekron. ¹⁸The gold rats were to placate God for the other Philistine cities, both the fortified cities and the country villages controlled by the five capitals. (By the way, that large rock at Beth-shemesh can still be seen in the field of Joshua.) ¹⁹But the Lord killed seventy of the men of Beth-shemesh because they looked into the Ark. And the people mourned because of the many people whom the Lord had killed.

²⁰"Who is able to stand before Jehovah, this holy God?" they cried out. "Where can we send the Ark from here?"

²¹So they sent messengers to the people at Kiriath-jearim and told them that the Philistines had brought back the Ark of the Lord.

"Come and get it!" they begged.

7 God Sends Thunder

So the men of Kiriath-jearim came and took the Ark to the hillside home of Abinadab and installed his son Eleazar to be in charge of it. ²The Ark remained there for twenty years, and during that time all Israel was in sorrow because the Lord had seemingly abandoned them.

Family Devotions

☐ **Devotion 96**
Putting God First

Read 1 Samuel 8:4-22

"Did you see the way Gary hit that last ball?" asked Chad excitedly as his father started the car. "It went so far I bet the other team hasn't found it yet! I want to be just like him when I get to high school."

"Me, too! Gary's the best player we have." Chad's friend Travis continued the hero worship.

"Can we stop at this next restaurant, Dad?" asked Chad. "The team's going to eat here."

The three of them were just starting to enjoy their food when the team burst loudly through the restaurant entrance. Chad and Travis were delighted when Gary and three of the other players took a table near their booth. But as the boys watched, they saw the team members—led by Gary—blow the paper from their straws onto the floor, throw food at the busboy, and shout rude statements until the coach threatened to make them get back on the bus. They heard Gary swear. They saw him behave rudely toward the waitress. Both Chad and Travis felt disappointed as they realized their hero's behavior was not something to be admired.

As the boys returned silently to the car, they tried to forget what they'd heard, but it was impossible. "How can such a neat ball player be such a rotten person?" asked Chad.

"You can still admire Gary's athletic ability," Dad said, "but it's not a good idea to make people into idols. Sooner or later they always let you down. Jesus is the one you should choose for your role model. He'll never let you down."

Putting God First
Memory Verse

In everything you do, put God first, and he will direct you and crown your efforts with success.
Proverbs 3:6

How About You?
Has that sports figure you admire been found guilty of bribery or taking drugs? Does the television personality you like use foul language and brag about an immoral life-style? Beware of making people into idols. The nation of Israel thought a king would be a great hero, but God warned them of what would really happen. Only Jesus is perfect. Choose him for your hero. *R. M.*

• For the next devotional, turn to page 299. • For the next devotional on *Putting God First,* turn to page 561.
• For notes on *Putting God First,* see pages 397, 492, 644, 791, and 982.

³At that time Samuel said to them, "If you are really serious about wanting to return to the Lord, get rid of your foreign gods and your Ashtaroth idols. Determine to obey only the Lord; then he will rescue you from the Philistines."

⁴So they destroyed their idols of Baal and Ashtaroth and worshiped only the Lord.

⁵Then Samuel told them, "Come to Mizpah, all of you, and I will pray to the Lord for you."

⁶So they gathered there and, in a great ceremony, drew water from the well and poured it out before the Lord. They also went without food all day as a sign of sorrow for their sins. So it was at Mizpah that Samuel became Israel's judge.

⁷When the Philistine leaders heard about the great crowds at Mizpah, they mobilized their army and advanced. The Israelis were badly frightened when they learned that the Philistines were approaching.

⁸"Plead with God to save us!" they begged Samuel.

⁹So Samuel took a suckling lamb and offered it to the Lord as a whole burnt offering and pleaded with him to help Israel. And the Lord responded. ¹⁰Just as Samuel was sacrificing the burnt offering, the Philistines arrived for battle, but the Lord spoke with a mighty voice of thunder from heaven, and they were thrown into confusion, and the Israelis routed them ¹¹and chased them from Mizpah to Beth-car, killing them all along the way. ¹²Samuel then took a stone and placed it between Mizpah and Jeshanah and named it Ebenezer (meaning, "the Stone of Help"), for he said, "The Lord has certainly helped us!" ¹³So the Philistines were subdued and didn't invade Israel again at that time because the Lord was against them throughout the remainder of Samuel's lifetime. ¹⁴The Israeli cities between Ekron and Gath, which had been conquered by the Philistines, were now returned to Israel, for the Israeli army rescued them from their Philistine captors. And there was peace between Israel and the Amorites in those days.

¹⁵Samuel continued as Israel's judge for the remainder of his life. ¹⁶He rode circuit annually, setting up his court first at Bethel, then Gilgal, and then Mizpah, and cases of dispute were brought to him in each of those three cities from all the surrounding territory. ¹⁷Then he would come back to Ramah, for his home was there, and he would hear cases there too. And he built an altar to the Lord at Ramah.

8 Israel Demands a King

In his old age, Samuel retired and appointed his sons as judges in his place. ²Joel and Abijah, his oldest sons, held court in Beersheba; ³but they were not like their father, for they were greedy for money. They accepted bribes and were very corrupt in the administration of justice. ⁴Finally the leaders of Israel met in Ramah to discuss the matter with Samuel. ⁵They told him that since his retirement things hadn't been the same, for his sons were not good men.

"Give us a king like all the other nations have," they pleaded. ⁶Samuel was terribly upset and went to the Lord for advice.

⁷"Do as they say," the Lord replied, "for I am the one they are rejecting, not you—they don't want me to be their king any longer. ⁸Ever since I brought them from Egypt they have continually forsaken me and followed other gods. And now they are giving you the same treatment. ⁹Do as they ask, but warn them about what it will be like to have a king!"

¹⁰So Samuel told the people what the Lord had said:

¹¹"If you insist on having a king, he will conscript your sons and make them run before his chariots; ¹²some will be made to lead his troops into battle, while others will be slave laborers; they will be forced to plow in the royal fields and harvest his crops without pay, and make his weapons and chariot equipment. ¹³He will take your daughters from you and force them to cook and bake and make perfumes for him. ¹⁴He will take away the best of your fields and vineyards and olive groves and give them to his friends. ¹⁵He will take a tenth of your harvest and distribute it to his favorites. ¹⁶He will demand your slaves and the finest of your youth and will use your animals for his personal gain. ¹⁷He will demand a tenth of your flocks, and you shall be his slaves. ¹⁸You will shed bitter tears because of this king you are demanding, but the Lord will not help you."

¹⁹But the people refused to listen to Samuel's warning.

"Even so, we still want a king," they said, ²⁰"for we want to be like the nations around us. He will govern us and lead us to battle."

²¹So Samuel told the Lord what the people had said, ²²and the Lord replied again, "Then do as they say and give them a king."

So Samuel agreed and sent the men home again.

TRUSTING GOD'S PLAN 9:3ff. Often we think that events just happen to us, but as we learn from this story about Saul, God often uses common occurences to lead us where he wants. It is important to evaluate all situations as potential "divine appointments" designed to shape our lives. Think of all the good and bad circumstances that have affected you lately. Can you see God's purpose in them? Perhaps he is building a certain quality in your life or leading you to serve him in a new area. **To begin the series of devotionals on TRUSTING GOD'S PLAN, turn to page 9.**

9 Saul Becomes King

Kish was a rich, influential man from the tribe of Benjamin. He was the son of Abiel, grandson of Zeror, great-grandson of Becorath, and great-great-grandson of Aphiah. ²His son Saul was the most handsome man in Israel. And he was head and shoulders taller than anyone else in the land!

³One day Kish's donkeys strayed away, so he sent Saul and a servant to look for them. ⁴They traveled all through the hill country of Ephraim, the land of Shalisha, the Shaalim area, and the entire land of Benjamin, but couldn't find them anywhere. ⁵Finally, after searching in the land of Zuph, Saul said to the servant, "Let's go home; by now my father will be more worried about us than about the donkeys!"

⁶But the servant said, "I've just thought of something! There is a prophet who lives here in this city; he is held in high honor by all the people because everything he says comes true; let's go and find him, and perhaps he can tell us where the donkeys are."

⁷"But we don't have anything to pay him with," Saul replied. "Even our food is gone, and we don't have a thing to give him."

⁸"Well," the servant said, "I have a dollar! We can at least offer it to him and see what happens!"

⁹⁻¹¹"All right," Saul agreed, "let's try it!"

So they started into the city where the prophet lived. As they were climbing a hill toward the city, they saw some young girls going out to draw water and asked them if they knew whether the seer was in town. (In those days prophets were called seers. "Let's go and ask the seer," people would say, rather than, "Let's go and ask the prophet," as we would say now.)

¹²,¹³"Yes," they replied, "stay right on this road. He lives just inside the city gates. He has just arrived back from a trip to take part in a public sacrifice up on the hill. So hurry, because he'll probably be leaving about the time you get there; the guests can't eat until he arrives and blesses the food."

¹⁴So they went into the city, and as they were entering the gates they saw Samuel coming out toward them to go up the hill. ¹⁵The Lord had told Samuel the previous day,

¹⁶"About this time tomorrow I will send you a man from the land of Benjamin. You are to anoint him as the leader of my people. He will save them from the Philistines, for I have looked down on them in mercy and have heard their cry."

¹⁷When Samuel saw Saul the Lord said, "That's the man I told you about! He will rule my people."

¹⁸Just then Saul approached Samuel and asked, "Can you please tell me where the seer's house is?"

¹⁹"I am the seer!" Samuel replied. "Go on up the hill ahead of me and we'll eat together; in the morning I will tell you what you want to know and send you on your way. ²⁰And don't worry about those donkeys that were lost three days ago, for they have been found. And anyway, you own all the wealth of Israel now!"

²¹"Pardon me, sir," Saul replied. "I'm from the tribe of Benjamin, the smallest in Israel, and my family is the least important of all the families of the tribe! You must have the wrong man!"

²²Then Samuel took Saul and his servant into the great hall and placed them at the head of the table, honoring them above the thirty special guests. ²³Samuel then instructed the chef to bring Saul the choicest cut of meat, the piece that had been set aside for the guest of honor. ²⁴So the chef brought it in and placed it before Saul.

"Go ahead and eat it," Samuel said, "for I was saving it for you, even before I invited these others!"

So Saul ate with Samuel. ²⁵After the feast, when they had returned to the city, Samuel took Saul up to the porch on the roof and talked with him there. ²⁶,²⁷At daybreak the next morning, Samuel called up to him, "Get up; it's time you were on your way!"

So Saul got up, and Samuel accompanied him to the edge of the city. When they reached the city walls, Samuel told Saul to send the servant on ahead. Then he told him, "I have received a special message for you from the Lord."

10

Then Samuel took a flask of olive oil and poured it over Saul's head, and kissed him on the cheek and said,

"I am doing this because the Lord has appointed you to be the king of his people, Israel! ²When you leave me, you will see two men beside Rachel's tomb at Zelzah, in the land of Benjamin; they will tell you that the donkeys have been found and that your father is worried about you and is asking, 'How am I to find my son?' ³And when you get to the oak of Tabor, you will see three men coming toward you who are on their way to worship God at the altar at Bethel; one will be bringing three young goats, another will have three loaves of bread, and the third will have a bottle of wine. ⁴They will greet you and offer you two of the loaves, which you are to accept. ⁵After that you will come to Gibeath-elohim, also known as "God's Hill," where the garrison of the Philistines is. As you arrive there you will meet a band of prophets coming down the hill playing a psaltery, a timbrel, a flute, and a harp, and prophesying as they come.

⁶"At that time the Spirit of the Lord will come

mightily upon you and you will prophesy with them, and you will feel and act like a different person. 7From that time on your decisions should be based on whatever seems best under the circumstances, for the Lord will guide you. 8Go to Gilgal and wait there seven days for me, for I will be coming to sacrifice burnt offerings and peace offerings. I will give you further instructions when I arrive."

9As Saul said good-bye and started to go, God gave him a new attitude, and all of Samuel's prophecies came true that day. 10When Saul and the servant arrived at the Hill of God, they saw the prophets coming toward them, and the Spirit of God came upon him, and he too began to prophesy.

11When his friends heard about it, they exclaimed, "What? Saul a prophet?" 12And one of the neighbors added, "With a father like his?" So that is the origin of the proverb, "Is Saul a prophet too?"

13When Saul had finished prophesying he climbed the hill to the altar.

14"Where in the world did you go?" Saul's uncle asked him.

And Saul replied, "We went to look for the donkeys, but we couldn't find them; so we went to the prophet Samuel to ask him where they were."

15"Oh? And what did he say?" his uncle asked.

16"He said the donkeys had been found!" Saul replied. (But he didn't tell him that he had been anointed as king!)

17Samuel now called a convocation of all Israel at Mizpah 18,19and gave them this message from the Lord God: "I brought you from Egypt and rescued you from the Egyptians and from all of the nations that were torturing you. But although I have done so much for you, you have rejected me and have said, 'We want a king instead!' All right, then, present yourselves before the Lord by tribes and clans."

20So Samuel called the tribal leaders together before the Lord, and the tribe of Benjamin was chosen by sacred lot. 21Then he brought each family of the tribe of Benjamin before the Lord, and the family of the Matrites was chosen. And finally the sacred lot selected Saul, the son of Kish. But when they looked for him, he had disappeared!

22So they asked the Lord, "Where is he? Is he here among us?"

And the Lord replied, "He is hiding in the baggage."

23So they found him and brought him out, and he stood head and shoulders above anyone else.

24Then Samuel said to all the people, "This is the man the Lord has chosen as your king. There isn't his equal in all of Israel!"

And all the people shouted, "Long live the king!"

25Then Samuel told the people again what the rights and duties of a king were; he wrote them in a book and put it in a special place before the Lord. Then Samuel sent the people home again.

26When Saul returned to his home at Gibeah, a band of men whose hearts the Lord had touched became his constant companions. 27There were, however, some bums and loafers who exclaimed, "How can this man save us?" And they despised him and refused to bring him presents, but he took no notice.

A Surprise Attack

At this time Nahash led the army of the Ammonites against the Israeli city of Jabesh-gilead. But the citizens of Jabesh asked for peace. "Leave us alone and we will be your servants," they pleaded.

2"All right," Nahash said, "but only on one condition: I will gouge out the right eye of every one of you as a disgrace upon all Israel!"

3"Give us seven days to see if we can get some help!" replied the elders of Jabesh. "If none of our brothers will come and save us, we will agree to your terms."

4When a messenger came to Gibeah, Saul's hometown, and told the people about their plight, everyone broke into tears.

5Saul was plowing in the field, and when he returned to town he asked, "What's the matter? Why is everyone crying?"

So they told him about the message from Jabesh. 6Then the Spirit of God came strongly upon Saul and he became very angry. 7He took two oxen and cut them into pieces and sent messengers to carry them throughout all Israel.

"This is what will happen to the oxen of anyone who refuses to follow Saul and Samuel to battle!" he announced. And God caused the people to be afraid of Saul's anger, and they came to him as one man.

8He counted them in Bezek and found that there were three hundred thousand of them in addition to thirty thousand from Judah.

9So he sent the messengers back to Jabesh-gilead to say, "We will rescue you before tomorrow noon!" What joy there was

---

STANDING FOR RIGHTEOUSNESS 11:6 Anger is a powerful emotion. Often it is used wrongly to hurt others with words or physical violence. But anger directed at sin and the mistreatment of others is not wrong. Saul was angered by the Ammonites' threat to humiliate and mistreat his countrymen. God used Saul's anger to bring justice and freedom. When injustice or sin makes you angry, ask God how you can channel that anger in constructive ways to help bring about a positive change. **To begin the series of devotionals on STANDING FOR RIGHTEOUSNESS, turn to page 139.**

Family Devotions

☐ **Devotion 97**
Accepting Others

Read 1 Samuel 10:26-27

Accepting Others
Memory Verse

How wonderful it is, how pleasant, when brothers live in harmony!
Psalm 133:1

"Cal Gordon thinks our gym class should go to a high-school football game for a field trip!" exclaimed Greg. He was sitting on the back-porch steps with his friend Kirk, watching the clouds float lazily by.

"Oh no!" groaned Kirk. "It would be lots more fun to go to Sportland, U.S.A. I suppose he'll go around trying to get everybody to vote for the dumb football game. That makes me mad! I can't stand that guy!"

"Me, neither," agreed Greg. He pointed up at one of the clouds. "Speaking of footballs, that big cloud up there looks just like a foot kicking a football."

Kirk looked where Greg was pointing. "I don't see a football. I see a dog with a bone."

"How about that one?" Greg pointed again. "That's a dragon with big teeth and a long tail."

"Naw, that's an alligator," said Kirk with a grin. "You'd better get glasses." The boys spent the next few minutes pointing out various pictures they saw in the cloud formations. Sometimes they agreed on what the clouds looked like; sometimes they didn't.

"You know, it's fun that we see different things in the clouds," Greg said thoughtfully. "It doesn't make us mad that we don't look at them in the same way. Maybe I shouldn't get so mad when people look at other things differently from the way I do, either."

Kirk looked at his friend. "You mean Cal, don't you?" he asked. He sighed. "I suppose you're right. I guess there's no law that says he has to like the same things we like. OK, but I'm still going to try to get kids to vote for Sportland, and may the best man win!"

How About You?
Do you get angry if people disagree with you? You shouldn't. As long as they're not in opposition to Scripture, you need to be tolerant of the opinions of others. People look at many things in different ways. Sometimes there is no definite right or wrong, and you need to agree to disagree. Love people and accept them even if they don't see things exactly as you do. *H. M.*

- For the next devotional, turn to page 301. • For the next devotional on *Accepting Others,* turn to page 305.
- For notes on *Accepting Others,* see pages 270, 1140, 1196, and 1254.

throughout the city when that message arrived!

¹⁰The men of Jabesh then told their enemies, "We surrender. Tomorrow we will come out to you and you can do to us as you wish."

¹¹But early the next morning Saul arrived, having divided his army into three detachments, and launched a surprise attack against the Ammonites and slaughtered them all morning. The remnant of their army was so badly scattered that no two of them were left together.

¹²Then the people exclaimed to Samuel, "Where are those men who said that Saul shouldn't be our king? Bring them here and we will kill them!"

¹³But Saul replied, "No one will be executed today; for today the Lord has rescued Israel!"

¹⁴Then Samuel said to the people, "Come, let us all go to Gilgal and reconfirm Saul as our king."

¹⁵So they went to Gilgal and in a solemn ceremony before the Lord they crowned him king. Then they offered peace offerings to the Lord, and Saul and all Israel were very happy.

12 Samuel Reminds the People

Then Samuel addressed the people again: "Look," he said, "I have done as you asked. I have given you a king. ²I have selected him ahead of my own sons and now I stand here, an old, gray-haired man who has been in public service from the time he was a lad. ³Now tell me as I stand before the Lord and before his anointed king—whose ox or donkey have I stolen? Have I ever defrauded you? Have I ever oppressed you? Have I ever taken a bribe? Tell me and I will make right whatever I have done wrong."

⁴"No," they replied, "you have never defrauded or oppressed us in any way and you have never taken even one single bribe."

⁵"The Lord and his anointed king are my witnesses," Samuel declared, "that you can never accuse me of robbing you."

"Yes, it is true," they replied.

⁶"It was the Lord who appointed Moses and Aaron," Samuel continued. "He brought your ancestors out of the land of Egypt.

⁷"Now stand here quietly before the Lord as I remind you of all the good things he has done for you and for your ancestors:

⁸"When the Israelites were in Egypt and cried out to the Lord, he sent Moses and Aaron to bring them into this land. ⁹But they soon forgot about the Lord their God, so he let them be conquered by Sisera, the general of King Hazor's army, and by the Philistines and the king of Moab.

¹⁰"Then they cried to the Lord again and confessed that they had sinned by turning away from him and worshiping the Baal and Ashtaroth idols. And they pleaded, 'We will worship you and you alone if you will only rescue us from our enemies.' ¹¹Then the Lord sent Gideon, Barak, Jephthah, and Samuel to save you, and you lived in safety.

¹²"But when you were afraid of Nahash, the king of Ammon, you came to me and said that you wanted a king to reign over you. But the Lord your God was already your King, for he has always been your King. ¹³All right, here is the king you have chosen. Look him over. You have asked for him, and the Lord has answered your request.

¹⁴"Now if you will fear and worship the Lord, and listen to his commandments and not rebel against the Lord, and if both you and your king follow the Lord your God, then all will be well. ¹⁵But if you rebel against the Lord's commandments and refuse to listen to him, then his hand will be as heavy upon you as it was upon your ancestors.

¹⁶"Now watch as the Lord does great miracles. ¹⁷You know that it does not rain at this time of the year, during the wheat harvest; I will pray for the Lord to send thunder and rain today, so that you will realize the extent of your wickedness in asking for a king!"

¹⁸So Samuel called to the Lord, and the Lord sent thunder and rain; and all the people were very much afraid of the Lord and of Samuel.

¹⁹"Pray for us lest we die!" they cried out to Samuel. "For now we have added to all our other sins by asking for a king."

²⁰"Don't be frightened," Samuel reassured them. "You have certainly done wrong, but make sure now that you worship the Lord with true enthusiasm, and that you don't turn your back on him in any way. ²¹Other gods can't help you. ²²The Lord will not abandon his chosen people, for that would dishonor his great name. He made you a special nation for himself—just because he wanted to!

²³"As for me, I will certainly not sin against the Lord by ending my prayers for you; and I will continue to teach you those things which are good and right.

²⁴"Trust the Lord and sincerely worship him; think of all the tremendous things he has done for you. ²⁵But if you continue to sin, you and your king will be destroyed."

13 Saul's Mistake

By this time Saul had reigned for one year. In the second year of his reign, ²he selected three thousand special troops and took two thousand of them with him to Michmash and Mount Bethel while the other thousand remained with Jonathan, Saul's son, in Gibeah in the land of Benjamin. The rest of the army was sent home. ³,⁴Then Jonathan attacked and destroyed the garrison of the Philistines at Geba. The news spread quickly

Family Devotions

☐ **Devotion 98**
Receiving Christ as Savior

Read 1 Samuel 9:2; 13:1-14

When Tony arrived at Sunday school, he was surprised to see a beautiful radio on the table in front of his teacher, Mr. Brock. In fact, it was more than just a radio. It also contained a cassette and CD player. *"Whew!"* whistled Tony. "That's really neat. What's it for?"

Mr. Brock smiled. "It is pretty nice-looking, isn't it?" he agreed. The boys all crowded around as he pointed out various attractive features of the set. He showed them how the cassettes and CDs were inserted and which buttons controlled them. He pointed out that they could either listen or record; he showed them where the speakers were located. He indicated the controls for the radio and demonstrated how the antenna was used. When one of the boys suggested that they listen to it, Mr. Brock nodded agreeably and turned the radio on. But all remained silent. Mr. Brock looked at the class.

"Say, can anyone tell me why there is no sound coming from the radio?" he asked.

"Is it plugged in?" asked one of the boys.

"Aha!" said Mr. Brock, "that's exactly the problem. It needs to be plugged in." He took the plug and inserted it into the electrical outlet behind him. Immediately the room was filled with music.

"I brought the radio for an object lesson, boys," said Mr. Brock. "Our lives are much like this radio. We may look good to those who see us. We may even look good to ourselves. But no matter how good we may look on the outside, without God our lives are hollow. We have no power. Before we can amount to anything, we have to be plugged in to the right source of power. That power is God himself, and we come to God only through Jesus Christ, God's Son. I want to challenge each of you boys to accept Jesus as your Savior."

Receiving Christ as Savior Memory Verse

If you tell others with your own mouth that Jesus Christ is your Lord and believe in your own heart that God has raised him from the dead, you will be saved.
Romans 10:9

How About You?

Do you read the Bible? Pray? Go to church? Do good deeds? All these are fine things to do, but by themselves, they accomplish nothing. You must first be plugged in to the source of power. You must trust Christ as your own personal Savior. Have you done that? Why not do it right now? C. V. M.

• For the next devotional, turn to page 305. • For the next devotional on *Receiving Christ as Savior*, turn to page 347. • For notes on *Receiving Christ as Savior*, see pages 839, 842, 1146, 1234, and 1240.

throughout the land of the Philistines, and Saul sounded the call to arms throughout Israel. He announced that he had destroyed the Philistine garrison and warned his men that the army of Israel stank to high heaven as far as the Philistines were concerned. So the entire Israeli army mobilized again and joined at Gilgal. ⁵The Philistines recruited a mighty army of three thousand chariots, six thousand horsemen, and so many soldiers that they were as thick as sand along the seashore; and they camped at Michmash east of Beth-aven.

⁶When the men of Israel saw the vast mass of enemy troops, they lost their nerve entirely and tried to hide in caves, thickets, coverts, among the rocks, and even in tombs and cisterns. ⁷Some of them crossed the Jordan River and escaped to the land of Gad and Gilead. Meanwhile, Saul stayed at Gilgal, and those who were with him trembled with fear at what awaited them. ⁸Samuel had told Saul earlier to wait seven days for his arrival, but when he still didn't come, and Saul's troops were rapidly slipping away, ⁹he decided to sacrifice the burnt offering and the peace offerings himself. ¹⁰But just as he was finishing, Samuel arrived. Saul went out to meet him and to receive his blessing, ¹¹but Samuel said, "What is this you have done?"

"Well," Saul replied, "when I saw that my men were scattering from me, and that you hadn't arrived by the time you said you would, and that the Philistines were at Michmash, ready for battle, ¹²I said, 'The Philistines are ready to march against us and I haven't even asked for the Lord's help!' So I reluctantly offered the burnt offering without waiting for you to arrive."

¹³"You fool!" Samuel exclaimed. "You have disobeyed the commandment of the Lord your God. He was planning to make you and your descendants kings of Israel forever, ¹⁴but now your dynasty must end; for the Lord wants a man who will obey him. And he has discovered the man he wants and has already appointed him as king over his people; for you have not obeyed the Lord's commandment."

¹⁵Samuel then left Gilgal and went to Gibeah in the land of Benjamin.

When Saul counted the soldiers who were still with him, he found only six hundred left! ¹⁶Saul and Jonathan and these six hundred men set up their camp in Geba in the land of Benjamin; but the Philistines stayed at Michmash. ¹⁷Three companies of raiders soon left the camp of the Philistines; one went toward Ophrah in the land of Shual, ¹⁸another went to Beth-horon, and the third moved toward the border above the valley of Zeboim near the desert.

¹⁹There were no blacksmiths at all in the land of Israel in those days, for the Philistines wouldn't allow them for fear of their making swords and spears for the Hebrews. ²⁰So whenever the Israelites needed to sharpen their plowshares, discs, axes, or sickles, they had to take them to a Philistine blacksmith. ²¹The schedule of charges was as follows:

For sharpening a plow point, 60¢
For sharpening a disc, 60¢
For sharpening an axe, 30¢
For sharpening a sickle, 30¢
For sharpening an ox goad, 30¢

²²So there was not a single sword or spear in the entire "army" of Israel that day, except for Saul's and Jonathan's. ²³The mountain pass at Michmash had meanwhile been secured by a contingent of the Philistine army.

14 Jonathan's Brave Fight

A day or so later, Prince Jonathan said to his young bodyguard, "Come on, let's cross the valley to the garrison of the Philistines." But he didn't tell his father that he was leaving.

²Saul and his six hundred men were camped at the edge of Gibeah, around the pomegranate tree at Migron. ³Among his men was Ahijah the priest (the son of Ahitub, Ichabod's brother; Ahitub was the son of Phinehas and the grandson of Eli, the priest of the Lord in Shiloh).

No one realized that Jonathan had gone. ⁴To reach the Philistine garrison, Jonathan had to go over a narrow pass between two rocky crags which had been named Bozez and Seneh. ⁵The crag on the north was in front of Michmash and the southern one was in front of Geba.

⁶"Yes, let's go across to those heathen," Jonathan had said to his bodyguard. "Perhaps the Lord will do a miracle for us. For it makes no difference to him how many enemy troops there are!"

⁷"Fine!" the youth replied. "Do as you think best; I'm with you heart and soul, whatever you decide."

⁸"All right, then this is what we'll do," Jonathan told him. ⁹"When they see us, if they say, 'Stay where you are or we'll kill you!' then we will stop and wait for them. ¹⁰But if they say, 'Come on up and fight!' then we will do just that; for it will be God's signal that he will help us defeat them!"

¹¹When the Philistines saw them coming they shouted, "Look! The Israelis are crawling out of their holes!" ¹²Then they shouted to Jonathan, "Come on up here and we'll show you how to fight!"

"Come on, climb right behind me," Jonathan exclaimed to his bodyguard, "for the Lord will help us defeat them!"

¹³So they clambered up on their hands and knees, and the Philistines fell back as Jonathan and the lad killed them right and left, ¹⁴about twenty men in all, and their bodies were scattered over about half an acre of land. ¹⁵Suddenly panic broke out throughout the entire Philistine army, and even among the raiders. And just then there was a great earthquake, increasing the terror.

¹⁶Saul's lookouts in Gibeah saw a strange sight—the vast army of the Philistines began to melt away in all directions.

¹⁷"Find out who isn't here," Saul ordered. And when they had checked, they found that Jonathan and his bodyguard were gone. ¹⁸"Bring the Ark of God," Saul shouted to Ahijah. (For the Ark was among the people of Israel at that time.) ¹⁹But while Saul was talking to the priest, the shouting and the tumult in the camp of the Philistines grew louder and louder. "Quick! What does God say?" Saul demanded.

²⁰Then Saul and his six hundred men rushed out to the battle and found the Philistines killing each other, and there was terrible confusion everywhere. ²¹And now the Hebrews who had been drafted into the Philistine army revolted and joined with the Israelis. ²²Finally even the men hiding in the hills joined the chase when they saw that the Philistines were running away. ²³So the Lord saved Israel that day, and the battle continued out beyond Beth-aven.

²⁴,²⁵Saul had declared, "A curse upon anyone who eats anything before evening—before I have full revenge on my enemies." So no one ate anything all day, even though they found honeycomb on the ground in the forest, ²⁶for they all feared Saul's curse. ²⁷Jonathan, however, had not heard his father's command; so he dipped a stick into a honeycomb, and when he had eaten the honey he felt much better. ²⁸Then someone told him that his father had laid a curse upon anyone who ate food that day, and everyone was weary and faint as a result.

²⁹"That's ridiculous!" Jonathan exclaimed. "A command like that only hurts us. See how much better I feel now that I have eaten this little bit of honey. ³⁰If the people had been allowed to eat freely from the food they found among our enemies, think how many more we could have slaughtered!"

³¹But hungry as they were, they chased and killed the Philistines all day from Michmash to Aijalon, growing more and more faint. ³²That evening they flew upon the battle loot and butchered the sheep, oxen, and calves, and ate the raw, bloody meat. ³³Someone reported to Saul what was happening, that the people were sinning against the Lord by eating blood.

"That is very wrong," Saul said. "Roll a great stone over here, ³⁴and go out among the troops and tell them to bring the oxen and sheep here to kill and drain them, and not to sin against the Lord by eating the blood." So that is what they did.

³⁵And Saul built an altar to the Lord—his first.

³⁶Afterwards Saul said, "Let's chase the Philistines all night and destroy every last one of them."

"Fine!" his men replied. "Do as you think best."

But the priest said, "Let's ask God first."

³⁷So Saul asked God, "Shall we go after the Philistines? Will you help us defeat them?" But the Lord made no reply all night.

³⁸Then Saul said to the leaders, "Something's wrong! We must find out what sin was committed today. ³⁹I vow by the name of the God who saved Israel that though the sinner be my own son Jonathan, he shall surely die!" But no one would tell him what the trouble was.

⁴⁰Then Saul proposed, "Jonathan and I will stand over here, and all of you stand over there." And the people agreed.

⁴¹Then Saul said, "O Lord God of Israel, why haven't you answered my question? What is wrong? Are Jonathan and I guilty, or is the sin among the others? O Lord God, show us who is guilty." And Jonathan and Saul were chosen by sacred lot as the guilty ones, and the people were declared innocent.

⁴²Then Saul said, "Now draw lots between me and Jonathan." And Jonathan was chosen as the guilty one.

⁴³"Tell me what you've done," Saul demanded of Jonathan.

"I tasted a little honey," Jonathan admitted. "It was only a little bit on the end of a stick; but now I must die."

⁴⁴"Yes, Jonathan," Saul said, "you must die; may God strike me dead if you are not executed for this."

⁴⁵But the troops retorted, "Jonathan, who saved Israel today, shall die? Far from it! We vow by the life of God that not one hair on his head will be touched, for he has been used of God to do a mighty miracle today." So the people rescued Jonathan.

⁴⁶Then Saul called back the army, and the Philistines returned home. ⁴⁷And now, since he was securely in the saddle as king of Israel, Saul sent the Israeli army out in every direction against Moab, Ammon, Edom, the kings of Zobah, and the Philistines. And wherever he turned, he was successful. ⁴⁸He did great deeds and conquered the Amalekites and saved Israel from all those who had been their conquerors.

⁴⁹Saul had three sons, Jonathan, Ishvi, and Malchishua; and two daughters, Merab and Michal.

⁵⁰,⁵¹Saul's wife was Ahinoam, the daughter of Ahimaaz. And the general-in-chief of his army was his cousin Abner, his uncle Ner's son. (Abner's father, Ner, and Saul's father, Kish, were brothers; both were the sons of Abiel.)

⁵²The Israelis fought constantly with the Philistines throughout Saul's lifetime. And whenever Saul saw any brave, strong young man, he conscripted him into his army.

15 Saul Fails to Obey

One day Samuel said to Saul, "I crowned you king of Israel because God told me to. Now be sure that you obey him. ²Here is his commandment to you: 'I have decided to settle accounts with the nation of Amalek for refusing to allow my people to cross their territory when Israel came from Egypt. ³Now go and completely destroy the entire Amalek nation—men, women, babies, little children, oxen, sheep, camels, and donkeys.'"

⁴So Saul mobilized his army at Telaim. There were two hundred thousand troops in addition to ten thousand men from Judah. ⁵The Amalekites were camped in the valley below them. ⁶Saul sent a message to the Kenites, telling them to get out from among the Amalekites or else die with them. "For you were kind to the people of Israel when they came out of the land of Egypt," he explained. So the Kenites packed up and left.

⁷Then Saul butchered the Amalekites from Havilah all the way to Shur, east of Egypt. ⁸He captured Agag, the king of the Amalekites, but killed everyone else. ⁹However, Saul and his men kept the best of the sheep and oxen and the fattest of the lambs—everything, in fact, that appealed to them. They destroyed only what was worthless or of poor quality.

¹⁰Then the Lord said to Samuel, ¹¹"I am sorry that I ever made Saul king, for he has again refused to obey me."

Samuel was so deeply moved when he heard what God was saying, that he cried to the Lord all night. ¹²Early the next morning he went out to find Saul. Someone said that he had gone to Mount Carmel to erect a monument to himself and had then gone on to Gilgal. ¹³When Samuel finally found him, Saul greeted him cheerfully. "Hello there," he said. "Well, I have carried out the Lord's command!"

¹⁴"Then what was all the bleating of sheep and lowing of oxen I heard?" Samuel demanded.

¹⁵"It's true that the army spared the best of the sheep and oxen," Saul admitted, "but they are going to sacrifice them to the Lord your God; and we have destroyed everything else."

¹⁶Then Samuel said to Saul, "Stop! Listen to what the Lord told me last night!"

"What was it?" Saul asked.

¹⁷And Samuel told him, "When you didn't think much of yourself, God made you king of Israel. ¹⁸And he sent you on an errand and told you, 'Go and completely destroy the sinners, the Amalekites, until they are all dead.' ¹⁹Then why didn't you obey the Lord? Why did you rush for the loot and do exactly what God said not to?"

²⁰"But I *have* obeyed the Lord," Saul insisted. "I did what he told me to; and I brought King Agag but killed everyone else. ²¹And it was only when my troops demanded it that I let them keep the best of the sheep and oxen and loot to sacrifice to the Lord."

²²Samuel replied, "Has the Lord as much pleasure in your burnt offerings and sacrifices as in your obedience? Obedience is far better than sacrifice. He is much more interested in your listening to him than in your offering the fat of rams to him. ²³For rebellion is as bad as the sin of witchcraft, and stubbornness is as bad as worshiping idols. And now because you have rejected the word of Jehovah, he has rejected you from being king."

²⁴"I have sinned," Saul finally admitted. "Yes, I have disobeyed your instructions and the command of the Lord, for I was afraid of the people and did what they demanded. ²⁵Oh, please pardon my sin now and go with me to worship the Lord."

²⁶But Samuel replied, "It's no use! Since you have rejected the commandment of the Lord, he has rejected you from being the king of Israel."

²⁷As Samuel turned to go, Saul grabbed at him to try to hold him back and tore his robe.

²⁸And Samuel said to him, "See? The Lord has torn the kingdom of Israel from you today and has given it to a countryman of yours who is better than you are. ²⁹And he who is the glory of Israel is not lying, nor will he change his mind, for he is not a man!"

³⁰Then Saul pleaded again, "I have sinned; but oh, at least honor me before the leaders and before my people by going with me to worship the Lord your God."

³¹So Samuel finally agreed and went with him.

HONESTY 15:13-14 Saul thought he had won a great victory over the Amalekites, but God saw it as a great failure because Saul had disobeyed him and then lied to Samuel about the results of the battle. Saul may have thought his lie wouldn't be detected, or that what he did was OK. Saul was wrong.

Dishonest people soon begin to believe the lies they construct around themselves. Then they lose the ability to tell the difference between telling the truth and lying. By believing your own lies, you will begin a life of alienation from God. That is why honesty is so important in our relationships, both with God and with others. **To begin the series of devotionals on HONESTY, turn to page 33.**

Family Devotions

☐ *Devotion 99*
ACCEPTING OTHERS

Read 1 Samuel 16:1-7

Keith nudged Jerry and pointed to the lady coming down the walk. She had a lovely face, but she was wearing dark glasses and was accompanied by a large dog in a special harness. "Did you ever in your life see such an ugly mutt?" Keith said with scorn.

But Jerry, who loved dogs, just shrugged. He realized that the lady was blind, and he knew this must be a Seeing Eye dog. "I think he's neat," Jerry said. "He takes that lady wherever she wants to go."

To the boys' surprise, the lady stopped and spoke to them. "I heard you discussing my dog," she said. "This is Shawnee, and he's been taking me places for six years now. He's saved my life twice that I know of, and probably more times that I don't know about. He's always there when I need him, and he's a good listener, too."

"Wow," murmured Jerry.

The lady smiled. "I've been told that Shawnee is not a pretty dog," she said, "but even if he's the ugliest thing in the world to look at, he's still beautiful to me."

"I can see why you think that," agreed Keith.

The lady nodded. "Yes, the accident that took away my physical sight gave me a different kind of sight. I no longer judge animals or people on what they look like. I'm blind to all that. Instead, I look at what they're like on the inside. That's what counts, not the outside."

After chatting a few minutes longer, the boys headed homeward. "That lady sure was nice," said Jerry, "and so was her dog. I'm going to try not to make fun of the way another person looks after this."

"Me, too," agreed Keith. He grinned and added, "I won't even make fun of how a dog looks."

Accepting Others
Memory Verse

How wonderful it is, how pleasant, when brothers live in harmony!
Psalm 133:1

How About You?
Do you ever laugh at people because they don't look as nice as you do? Do you look down on them because of scars or other physical handicaps? In a sense, God is blind to outward appearances. He cares about what is on the inside. That should be your concern, too. Never laugh at anyone for what he looks like. He may be more beautiful than you on the inside. *D.M.*

• For the next devotional, turn to page 307. • For the next devotional on *Accepting Others*, turn to page 671.
• For notes on *Accepting Others*, see pages 270, 1140, 1196, and 1254.

[32] Then Samuel said, "Bring King Agag to me." Agag arrived all full of smiles, for he thought, "Surely the worst is over and I have been spared!" [33] But Samuel said, "As your sword has killed the sons of many mothers, now your mother shall be childless." And Samuel chopped him in pieces before the Lord at Gilgal. [34] Then Samuel went home to Ramah, and Saul returned to Gibeah. [35] Samuel never saw Saul again, but he mourned constantly for him; and the Lord was sorry that he had ever made Saul king of Israel.

16 Samuel Anoints David

Finally the Lord said to Samuel, "You have mourned long enough for Saul, for I have rejected him as king of Israel. Now take a vial of olive oil and go to Bethlehem and find a man named Jesse, for I have selected one of his sons to be the new king."

[2] But Samuel asked, "How can I do that? If Saul hears about it, he will kill me."

"Take a heifer with you," the Lord replied, "and say that you have come to make a sacrifice to the Lord. [3] Then call Jesse to the sacrifice, and I will show you which of his sons to anoint."

[4] So Samuel did as the Lord had told him to. When he arrived at Bethlehem, the elders of the city came trembling to meet him.

"What is wrong?" they asked. "Why have you come?"

[5] But he replied, "All is well. I have come to sacrifice to the Lord. Purify yourselves and come with me to the sacrifice."

And he performed the purification rite on Jesse and his sons, and invited them too. [6] When they arrived, Samuel took one look at Eliab and thought, "Surely this is the man the Lord has chosen!"

[7] But the Lord said to Samuel, "Don't judge by a man's face or height, for this is not the one. I don't make decisions the way you do! Men judge by outward appearance, but I look at a man's thoughts and intentions."

[8] Then Jesse told his son Abinadab to step forward and walk in front of Samuel. But the Lord said, "This is not the right man either."

[9] Next Jesse summoned Shammah, but the Lord said, "No, this is not the one." In the same way all seven of his sons presented themselves to Samuel and were rejected.

[10,11] "The Lord has not chosen any of them," Samuel told Jesse. "Are these all there are?"

"Well, there is the youngest," Jesse replied. "But he's out in the fields watching the sheep."

"Send for him at once," Samuel said, "for we will not sit down to eat until he arrives."

[12] So Jesse sent for him. He was a fine looking boy, ruddy-faced, and with pleasant eyes. And the Lord said, "This is the one; anoint him."

[13] So as David stood there among his brothers, Samuel took the olive oil he had brought and poured it upon David's head; and the Spirit of Jehovah came upon him and gave him great power from that day onward. Then Samuel returned to Ramah.

[14] But the Spirit of the Lord had left Saul, and instead, the Lord had sent a tormenting spirit that filled him with depression and fear. [15,16] Some of Saul's aides suggested a cure.

"We'll find a good harpist to play for you whenever the tormenting spirit is bothering you," they said. "The harp music will quiet you and you'll soon be well again."

[17] "All right," Saul said. "Find me a harpist."

[18] One of them said he knew a young fellow in Bethlehem, the son of a man named Jesse, who was not only a talented harp player, but was handsome, brave, and strong, and had good, solid judgment. "What's more," he added, "the Lord is with him."

[19] So Saul sent messengers to Jesse, asking that he send his son David the shepherd. [20] Jesse responded by sending not only David but a young goat and a donkey carrying a load of food and wine. [21] From the instant he saw David, Saul admired and loved him; and David became his bodyguard.

[22] Then Saul wrote to Jesse, "Please let David join my staff, for I am very fond of him."

[23] And whenever the tormenting spirit from God troubled Saul, David would play the harp and Saul would feel better, and the evil spirit would go away.

17 David Fights Goliath

The Philistines now mustered their army for battle and camped between Socoh in Judah and Azekah in Ephes-dammim. [2] Saul countered with a buildup of forces at Elah Valley. [3] So the Philistines and Israelis faced each other on opposite hills, with the valley between them.

[4-7] Then Goliath, a Philistine champion from Gath, came out of the Philistine ranks to face the forces of Israel. He was a giant of a man, measuring over nine feet tall! He wore a bronze helmet, a two-hundred-pound coat of mail, bronze leggings, and carried a bronze javelin several inches thick, tipped with a twenty-five-pound iron spearhead, and his armor-bearer walked ahead of him with a huge shield.

[8] He stood and shouted across to the Israelis, "Do you need a whole army to settle this? I will represent the Philistines, and you choose someone to represent you, and we will settle this in

Family Devotions

☐ DEVOTION 100
KNOWING YOU'RE SPECIAL TO GOD

Read 1 Samuel 16:4-13

"Mother, why am I so little?" asked Todd. He put down his pencil and scowled in disgust at his small hands.

"Well, Todd, you're only ten," his mother called from the kitchen. "You've got a lot of growing to do yet."

"I know, Mom, but while I'm growing, all my friends will be growing, too. They'll always be bigger than I am!" Todd grumbled. "Whenever we play baseball or football or anything, I'm the worst. I always get knocked over because I'm so small. Nobody ever wants me on their team."

"So you think that God made a mistake when he made you," observed Mother.

"Mother!" exclaimed Todd. "I never said anything like that!"

"Didn't you?" asked Mother. "You just said you didn't like being small. Isn't that the same as saying that God didn't make you to your liking?"

"Well," said Todd thoughtfully, "I hadn't thought about it that way."

"You should never be ashamed of the way you're made, Todd. God made you the way you are for a reason, and he loves you just as you are. It's how you look on the inside that counts, not the outside."

Todd sighed. "I suppose you're right, Mom." Suddenly he grinned. "I'll give up trying to be big on the outside and start trying to be big on the inside."

"How will you do that?" asked Mother, puzzled.

"I can work hard in school and get good grades," explained Todd. "And I can learn Bible verses and Bible stories so I'll know more about God, too."

"Todd," said Mother, smiling, "you've already got a good start on being grown up. And don't forget that your dad and I will always love you, no matter how small you are."

"Small?" said Todd. "Right now I feel about ten feet tall!"

Knowing You're Special to God Memory Verse

But now the Lord who created you, O Israel, says, Don't be afraid, for I have ransomed you; I have called you by name; you are mine.
Isaiah 43:1

How About You?

Have you ever wished you were taller? Or prettier? Or had brown eyes instead of green or blue? God made you the way you are because he wanted you that way. He never makes mistakes. Don't worry so much about how you look on the outside. Work on growing and being beautiful on the inside. D. M.

• For the next devotional, turn to page 309. • For the next devotional on KNOWING YOU'RE SPECIAL TO GOD, turn to page 411. • For notes on KNOWING YOU'RE SPECIAL TO GOD, see pages 260, 878, 908, and 960.

single combat! ⁹If your man is able to kill me, then we will be your slaves. But if I kill him, then you must be our slaves! ¹⁰I defy the armies of Israel! Send me a man who will fight with me!"

¹¹When Saul and the Israeli army heard this, they were dismayed and frightened. ¹²David (the son of aging Jesse, a member of the tribe of Judah who lived in Bethlehem) had seven older brothers. ¹³The three oldest—Eliab, Abinadab, and Shammah—had already volunteered for Saul's army to fight the Philistines. ¹⁴,¹⁵David was the youngest son and was on Saul's staff on a part-time basis. He went back and forth to Bethlehem to help his father with the sheep. ¹⁶For forty days, twice a day, morning and evening the Philistine giant strutted before the armies of Israel.

¹⁷One day Jesse said to David, "Take this bushel of roasted grain and these ten loaves of bread to your brothers. ¹⁸Give this cheese to their captain and see how the boys are getting along; and bring us back a letter from them!"

¹⁹(Saul and the Israeli army were camped at the valley of Elah.)

²⁰So David left the sheep with another shepherd and took off early the next morning with the gifts. He arrived at the outskirts of the camp just as the Israeli army was leaving for the battlefield with shouts and battle cries. ²¹Soon the Israeli and Philistine forces stood facing each other, army against army. ²²David left his luggage with a baggage officer and hurried out to the ranks to find his brothers. ²³As he was talking with them, he saw Goliath the giant step out from the Philistine troops and shout his challenge to the army of Israel. ²⁴As soon as they saw him the Israeli army began to run away in fright.

²⁵"Have you seen the giant?" the soldiers were asking. "He has insulted the entire army of Israel. And have you heard about the huge reward the king has offered to anyone who kills him? And the king will give him one of his daughters for a wife, and his whole family will be exempted from paying taxes!"

²⁶David talked to some others standing there to verify the report. "What will a man get for killing this Philistine and ending his insults to Israel?" he asked them. "Who is this heathen Philistine, anyway, that he is allowed to defy the armies of the living God?" ²⁷And he received the same reply as before.

²⁸But when David's oldest brother, Eliab, heard David talking like that, he was angry. "What are you doing around here, anyway?" he demanded. "What about the sheep you're supposed to be taking care of? I know what a cocky brat you are; you just want to see the battle!"

²⁹"What have I done now?" David replied. "I was only asking a question!"

³⁰And he walked over to some others and asked them the same thing and received the same answer. ³¹When it was finally realized what David meant, someone told King Saul, and the king sent for him.

³²"Don't worry about a thing," David told him. "I'll take care of this Philistine!"

³³"Don't be ridiculous!" Saul replied. "How can a kid like you fight with a man like him? You are only a boy, and he has been in the army *since* he was a boy!"

³⁴But David persisted. "When I am taking care of my father's sheep," he said, "and a lion or a bear comes and grabs a lamb from the flock, ³⁵I go after it with a club and take the lamb from its mouth. If it turns on me, I catch it by the jaw and club it to death. ³⁶I have done this to both lions and bears, and I'll do it to this heathen Philistine too, for he has defied the armies of the living God! ³⁷The Lord who saved me from the claws and teeth of the lion and the bear will save me from this Philistine!"

Saul finally consented, "All right, go ahead," he said, "and may the Lord be with you!"

³⁸,³⁹Then Saul gave David his own armor—a bronze helmet and a coat of mail. David put it on, strapped the sword over it, and took a step or two to see what it was like, for he had never worn such things before. "I can hardly move!" he exclaimed, and took them off again. ⁴⁰Then he picked up five smooth stones from a stream and put them in his shepherd's bag and, armed only with his shepherd's staff and sling, started across to Goliath. ⁴¹,⁴²Goliath walked out toward David with his shield-bearer ahead of him, sneering in contempt at this nice little red-cheeked boy!

⁴³"Am I a dog," he roared at David, "that you come at me with a stick?" And he cursed David by the names of his gods. ⁴⁴"Come over here and I'll give your flesh to the birds and wild animals," Goliath yelled.

⁴⁵David shouted in reply, "You come to me with a sword and a spear, but I come to you in the name of the Lord of the armies of heaven and of Israel—the very God whom you have defied. ⁴⁶Today the Lord will conquer you, and I will kill you and cut off your head; and then I will give the dead bodies of *your* men to the birds and wild animals, and the whole world will know that there is a God in Israel! ⁴⁷And Israel will learn that the Lord does not depend on weapons to fulfill his plans—he works without regard to human means! He will give you to us!"

⁴⁸,⁴⁹As Goliath approached, David ran out to meet him and, reaching into his shepherd's bag, took out a stone, hurled it from his sling, and hit the Philistine in the forehead. The stone sank in, and the man fell on his face to the ground. ⁵⁰,⁵¹So

Family Devotions

☐ *Devotion 101*
Serving God Boldly

Read 1 Samuel 17:45-51

"I can't do this," Randy said, wadding up another sheet of paper and tossing it toward the wastebasket. "I can't draw. And I don't know what to write, either."

"I've got my cards all finished," said his big sister, Ella. "They were fun to make. I can't wait to go with the youth group to take them to the people at the nursing home."

Randy rested his head on the table. "You're older," he said, "so you can draw better, and you know what to say to old people. I'm just a kid." He stood up. "I'm not going!" *Why would those old people listen when we tell them about God anyway?* he said to himself. *We're just kids.* "Forget it," he added with a sigh, and he started to walk away from the table.

Just then, his little sister danced in through the door singing a song about David. "Just think! David was just a kid, but he conquered that huge giant!" she said. "All he had was a sling and a stone."

"He had more than that," argued her playmate, chasing in behind her. "He had the power of God. David could do anything God wanted him to do. Anyone can when they go to God for help."

Randy's little sister looked at him. "What are you doing?" she asked, reaching for a crayon.

Randy shrugged. "Drawing a card for our youth project."

"You?" both girls giggled.

At first Randy felt angry. "Sure," he said, after a quick thought. Sitting down, he reached for a sheet of paper and folded it into a card. "And I can do this because I'm going to ask God to help me. He helped David and he'll help me, too."

Serving God Boldly
Memory Verse

Yes, be bold and strong! Banish fear and doubt! For remember, the Lord your God is with you wherever you go.
Joshua 1:9

How About You?

Do you have trouble witnessing to others or serving the Lord in some way? The next time you feel like you can't do something for the Lord because you're just a kid, remember David, and ask for the Lord's strength. *N. E. K.*

• For the next devotional, turn to page 313.   • For the next devotional on *Serving God Boldly*, turn to page 901.
• For notes on *Serving God Boldly*, see pages 327, 404, 501, 720, and 856.

David conquered the Philistine giant with a sling and a stone. Since he had no sword, he ran over and pulled Goliath's from its sheath and killed him with it, and then cut off his head. When the Philistines saw that their champion was dead, they turned and ran.

52 Then the Israelis gave a great shout of triumph and rushed after the Philistines, chasing them as far as Gath and the gates of Ekron. The bodies of the dead and wounded Philistines were strewn all along the road to Shaaraim. 53 Then the Israeli army returned and plundered the deserted Philistine camp.

54 (Later David took Goliath's head to Jerusalem, but stored his armor in his tent.)

55 As Saul was watching David go out to fight Goliath, he asked Abner, the general of his army, "Abner, what sort of family does this young fellow come from?"

"I really don't know," Abner said.

56 "Well, find out!" the king told him.

57 After David had killed Goliath, Abner brought him to Saul with the Philistine's head still in his hand.

58 "Tell me about your father, my boy," Saul said.

And David replied, "His name is Jesse and we live in Bethlehem."

18 David and Jonathan

After King Saul had finished his conversation with David, David met Jonathan, the king's son, and there was an immediate bond of love between them. Jonathan swore to be his blood brother, 4 and sealed the pact by giving him his robe, sword, bow, and belt.

King Saul now kept David with him and wouldn't let him return home any more. 5 He was Saul's special assistant, and he always carried out his assignments successfully. So Saul made him commander of his troops, an appointment that was applauded by the army and general public alike. 6 But something had happened when the victorious Israeli army was returning home after David had killed Goliath. Women came out from all the towns along the way to celebrate and to cheer for King Saul, and were singing and dancing for joy with tambourines and cymbals.

7 However, this was their song: "Saul has slain his thousands, and David his ten thousands!"

8 Of course Saul was very angry. "What's this?" he said to himself. "They credit David with ten thousands and me with only thousands. Next they'll be making him their king!"

9 So from that time on King Saul kept a jealous watch on David. 10 The very next day, in fact, a tormenting spirit from God overwhelmed Saul, and he began to rave like a madman. David began to soothe him by playing the harp, as he did whenever this happened. But Saul, who was fiddling with his spear, 11,12 suddenly hurled it at David, intending to pin him to the wall. But David jumped aside and escaped. This happened another time, too, for Saul was afraid of him and jealous because the Lord had left him and was now with David. 13 Finally Saul banned him from his presence and demoted him to the rank of captain. But the controversy put David more than ever in the public eye.

14 David continued to succeed in everything he undertook, for the Lord was with him. 15,16 When King Saul saw this, he became even more afraid of him; but all Israel and Judah loved him, for he was as one of them.

17 One day Saul said to David, "I am ready to give you my oldest daughter Merab as your wife. But first you must prove yourself to be a real soldier by fighting the Lord's battles." For Saul thought to himself, "I'll send him out against the Philistines and let them kill him rather than doing it myself."

18 "Who am I that I should be the king's son-in-law?" David exclaimed. "My father's family is nothing!"

19 But when the time arrived for the wedding, Saul married her to Adriel, a man from Meholath, instead. 20 In the meantime Saul's daughter Michal had fallen in love with David, and Saul was delighted when he heard about it.

21 "Here's another opportunity to see him killed by the Philistines!" Saul said to himself. But to David he said, "You can be my son-in-law after all, for I will give you my youngest daughter."

22 Then Saul instructed his men to say confidentially to David that the king really liked him a lot, and that they all loved him and thought he should accept the king's proposition and become his son-in-law.

23 But David replied, "How can a poor man like me from an unknown family find enough dowry to marry the daughter of a king?"

24 When Saul's men reported this back to him, 25 he told them, "Tell David that the only dowry I need is one hundred dead Philistines! Vengeance on my enemies is all I want." But what Saul had in mind was that David would be killed in the fight.

26 David was delighted to accept the offer. So, before the time limit expired, 27 he and his men went out and killed two hundred Philistines and presented their foreskins to King Saul. So Saul gave Michal to him.

28 When the king realized how much the Lord was with David and how immensely popular he was with all the people, 29 he became even more

afraid of him and grew to hate him more with every passing day. ³⁰Whenever the Philistine army attacked, David was more successful against them than all the rest of Saul's officers. So David's name became very famous throughout the land.

19 Saul Tries to Kill David

Saul now urged his aides and his son Jonathan to assassinate David. But Jonathan, because of his close friendship with David, ²told him what his father was planning. "Tomorrow morning," he warned him, "you must find a hiding place out in the fields. ³I'll ask my father to go out there with me, and I'll talk to him about you; then I'll tell you everything I can find out."

⁴The next morning as Jonathan and his father were talking together, he spoke well of David and begged him not to be against David.

"He's never done anything to harm you," Jonathan pleaded. "He has always helped you in any way he could. ⁵Have you forgotten about the time he risked his life to kill Goliath, and how the Lord brought a great victory to Israel as a result? You were certainly happy about it then. Why should you now murder an innocent man? There is no reason for it at all!"

⁶Finally Saul agreed and vowed, "As the Lord lives, he shall not be killed."

⁷Afterwards Jonathan called David and told him what had happened. Then he took David to Saul and everything was as it had been before. ⁸War broke out shortly after that, and David led his troops against the Philistines and slaughtered many of them, and put to flight their entire army.

⁹,¹⁰But one day as Saul was sitting at home, listening to David playing the harp, suddenly the tormenting spirit from the Lord attacked him. He had his spear in his hand and hurled it at David in an attempt to kill him. But David dodged out of the way and fled into the night, leaving the spear imbedded in the timber of the wall. ¹¹Saul sent troops to watch David's house and kill him when he came out in the morning.

"If you don't get away tonight," Michal warned him, "you'll be dead by morning."

¹²So she helped him get down to the ground through a window. ¹³Then she took an idol and put it in his bed, and covered it with blankets, with its head on a pillow of goat's hair. ¹⁴When the soldiers came to arrest David and take him to Saul, she told them he was sick and couldn't get out of bed. ¹⁵Saul said to bring him in his bed, then, so that he could kill him. ¹⁶But when they came to carry him out, they discovered that it was only an idol!

¹⁷"Why have you deceived me and let my enemy escape?" Saul demanded of Michal.

"I had to," Michal replied. "He threatened to kill me if I didn't help him."

¹⁸In that way David got away and went to Ramah to see Samuel, and told him all that Saul had done to him. So Samuel took David with him to live at Naioth. ¹⁹When the report reached Saul that David was at Naioth in Ramah, ²⁰he sent soldiers to capture him; but when they arrived and saw Samuel and the other prophets prophesying, the Spirit of God came upon them and they also began to prophesy. ²¹When Saul heard what had happened, he sent other soldiers, but they too prophesied! The same thing happened a third time! ²²Then Saul himself went to Ramah and arrived at the great well in Secu.

"Where are Samuel and David?" he demanded.

Someone told him they were at Naioth. ²³But on the way to Naioth the Spirit of God came upon Saul, and he too began to prophesy! ²⁴He tore off his clothes and lay naked all day and all night, prophesying with Samuel's prophets. Saul's men were incredulous!

"What!" they exclaimed. "Is Saul a prophet too?"

20 Jonathan Warns David

David now fled from Naioth in Ramah and found Jonathan.

"What have I done?" he exclaimed. "Why is your father so determined to kill me?"

²"That's not true!" Jonathan protested. "I'm sure he's not planning any such thing, for he always tells me everything he's going to do, even little things, and I know he wouldn't hide something like this from me. It just isn't so."

³"Of course you don't know about it!" David fumed. "Your father knows perfectly well about our friendship, so he has said to himself, 'I'll not tell Jonathan—why should I hurt him?' But the truth is that I am only a step away from death! I swear it by the Lord and by your own soul!"

⁴"Tell me what I can do," Jonathan begged.

⁵And David replied, "Tomorrow is the beginning of the celebration of the new moon. Always before, I've been with your father for this occasion, but tomorrow I'll hide in the field and stay there until the evening of the third day. ⁶If your

---

RESPECTING AUTHORITY 19:1-2 Is it ever right to disobey your father, as Jonathan did here? It is clearly a principle of Scripture that when a father instructs a son to break God's laws, the son should obey God rather than man. This principle assumes that the son is old enough to be accountable and to see through any deception. A son's role is to be respectful, helpful, and obedient to his father (Ephesians 6:1-3), but not to follow commands or advice that violate God's laws. **To begin the series of devotionals on RESPECTING AUTHORITY, turn to page 225.**

father asks where I am, tell him that I asked permission to go home to Bethlehem for an annual family reunion. ⁷If he says, 'Fine!' then I'll know that all is well. But if he is angry, then I'll know that he is planning to kill me. ⁸Do this for me as my sworn brother. Or else kill me yourself if I have sinned against your father, but don't betray me to him!"

⁹"Of course not!" Jonathan exclaimed. "Look, wouldn't I say so if I knew that my father was planning to kill you?"

¹⁰Then David asked, "How will I know whether or not your father is angry?"

¹¹"Come out to the field with me," Jonathan replied. And they went out there together.

¹²Then Jonathan told David, "I promise by the Lord God of Israel that about this time tomorrow, or the next day at the latest, I will talk to my father about you and let you know at once how he feels about you. ¹³If he is angry and wants you killed, then may the Lord kill me if I don't tell you, so you can escape and live. May the Lord be with you as he used to be with my father. ¹⁴And remember, you must demonstrate the love and kindness of the Lord not only to me during my own lifetime, ¹⁵but also to my children after the Lord has destroyed all of your enemies."

¹⁶So Jonathan made a covenant with the family of David, and David swore to it with a terrible curse against himself and his descendants, should he be unfaithful to his promise. ¹⁷But Jonathan made David swear to it again, this time by his love for him, for he loved him as much as he loved himself.

¹⁸Then Jonathan said, "Yes, they will miss you tomorrow when your place at the table is empty. ¹⁹By the day after tomorrow, everyone will be asking about you, so be at the hideout where you were before, over by the stone pile. ²⁰I will come out and shoot three arrows in front of the pile as though I were shooting at a target. ²¹Then I'll send a lad to bring the arrows back. If you hear me tell him, 'They're on this side,' then you will know that all is well and that there is no trouble. ²²But if I tell him, 'Go farther—the arrows are still ahead of you,' then it will mean that you must leave immediately. ²³And may the Lord make us keep our promises to each other, for he has witnessed them."

²⁴,²⁵So David hid himself in the field.

When the new moon celebration began, the king sat down to eat at his usual place against the wall. Jonathan sat opposite him and Abner was sitting beside Saul, but David's place was empty. ²⁶Saul didn't say anything about it that day, for he supposed that something had happened so that David was ceremonially impure. Yes, surely that must be it! ²⁷But when his place was still empty the next day, Saul asked Jonathan, "Why hasn't David been here for dinner either yesterday or today?"

²⁸,²⁹"He asked me if he could go to Bethlehem to take part in a family celebration," Jonathan replied. "His brother demanded that he be there, so I told him to go ahead."

³⁰Saul boiled with rage. "You fool!" he yelled at him. "Do you think I don't know that you want this son of a nobody to be king in your place, shaming yourself and your mother? ³¹As long as that fellow is alive, you'll never be king. Now go and get him so I can kill him!"

³²"But what has he done?" Jonathan demanded. "Why should he be put to death?"

³³Then Saul hurled his spear at Jonathan, intending to kill him; so at last Jonathan realized that his father really meant it when he said David must die. ³⁴Jonathan left the table in fierce anger and refused to eat all that day, for he was crushed by his father's shameful behavior toward David.

³⁵The next morning, as agreed, Jonathan went out into the field and took a young boy with him to gather his arrows.

³⁶"Start running," he told the boy, "so that you can find the arrows as I shoot them." So the boy ran and Jonathan shot an arrow beyond him. ³⁷When the boy had almost reached the arrow, Jonathan shouted, "The arrow is still ahead of you. ³⁸Hurry, hurry, don't wait." So the boy quickly gathered up the arrows and ran back to his master. ³⁹He, of course, didn't understand what Jonathan meant; only Jonathan and David knew. ⁴⁰Then Jonathan gave his bow and arrows to the boy and told him to take them back to the city.

⁴¹As soon as he was gone, David came out from where he had been hiding near the south edge of the field. Both of them were crying as they said goodbye, especially David. ⁴²At last Jonathan said to David, "Cheer up, for we have entrusted each other and each other's children into God's hands forever." So they parted, David going away and Jonathan returning to the city.

21 David Eats the Holy Bread

David went to the city of Nob to see Ahimelech, the priest. Ahimelech trembled when he saw him.

"Why are you alone?" he asked. "Why is no one with you?"

²"The king has sent me on a private matter," David lied. "He told me not to tell anybody why I am here. I have told my men where to meet me later. ³Now, what is there to eat? Give me five loaves of bread or anything else you can."

⁴"We don't have any regular bread," the priest replied, "but there is the holy bread, which I guess you can have if only your young men have not slept with any women for awhile."

⁵"Rest assured," David replied. "I never let my

FAMILY DEVOTIONS

☐ DEVOTION 102
LOVING OTHERS

Read 1 Samuel 18:1-3; 20:12-17

Loving Others
Memory Verse

Little children, let us stop just *saying* we love people; let us *really* love them, and *show it* by our *actions*.
1 John 3:18

Danny had tried to be a good friend to Ho, but the boy did not seem to appreciate anything. When the other kids started calling Ho *Slant-eyes*, it was Danny who came to his aid. And when the kids at church failed to include Ho in their plans, Danny was the one who had stood up for him. And now look what was happening! Ho seemed to forget that Danny even existed. Now that the kids had finally accepted him, Ho seemed to spend all his spare time with them.

"I'm through helping him," Danny told his dad. "I'll give him a taste of his own medicine. I'm going to ignore him."

At that moment the telephone rang, and Danny hurried to answer it. "Hello, Danny," came a familiar voice on the other end of the line. "This is Ho."

Danny wanted to hang up, but he thought he'd better not be that rude. "Yeah, Ho," he said. "You calling about something special?" After listening a few minutes, Danny said shortly, "I'll see. Can't promise." Then he hung up.

"Was that Ho?" Dad asked.

Danny nodded. "Yeah. He wants me to help him get on the volleyball team. Well, he can just forget that idea. He only calls when he needs something."

Danny's father was quiet for a long time. Finally he spoke. "I wonder if God feels that way when we come to him," he said soberly. "He probably wants us to come and simply have a friendly talk with him now and then, but we only seem to call on him when we need something."

How About You?
Do you have friends who seem to use you—who talk to you only when they want something? That isn't a nice feeling, is it? Do you ever treat others that way? Don't be a sometimes friend. Don't use people to get things you want. Be the kind of friend Jonathan was to David. R.J.

Danny got the message. He wanted to ignore Ho's requests because Ho so often ignored him. But as he thought more, he realized it was a good thing God didn't act that way. God was always there to hear, no matter how much he had been ignored. Danny decided he was going to be more faithful about talking to God. And if he wanted to be like Jesus, he guessed he'd better see what he could do to help Ho, too.

For the next devotional, turn to page 315. • For the next devotional on LOVING OTHERS, turn to page 373.
For notes on LOVING OTHERS, see pages 658, 951, 967, and 1242.

men run wild when they are on an expedition, and since they stay clean even on ordinary trips, how much more so on this one!"

⁶So, since there was no other food available, the priest gave him the holy bread—the Bread of the Presence that was placed before the Lord in the Tabernacle. It had just been replaced that day with fresh bread.

⁷(Incidentally, Doeg the Edomite, Saul's chief herdsman, was there at that time for ceremonial purification.)

⁸David asked Ahimelech if he had a spear or sword he could use. "The king's business required such haste, and I left in such a rush that I came away without a weapon!" David explained.

⁹"Well," the priest replied, "I have the sword of Goliath, the Philistine—the fellow you killed in the valley of Elah. It is wrapped in a cloth in the clothes closet. Take that if you want it, for there is nothing else here."

"Just the thing!" David replied. "Give it to me!"

¹⁰Then David hurried on, for he was fearful of Saul, and went to King Achish of Gath. ¹¹But Achish's officers weren't happy about his being there. "Isn't he the top leader of Israel?" they asked. "Isn't he the one the people honor at their dances, singing, 'Saul has slain his thousands and David his ten thousands'?"

¹²David heard these comments and was afraid of what King Achish might do to him, ¹³so he pretended to be insane! He scratched on doors and let his spittle flow down his beard, ¹⁴,¹⁵until finally King Achish said to his men, "Must you bring me a madman? We already have enough of them around here! Should such a fellow as this be my guest?"

22 David Hides in a Cave

So David left Gath and escaped to the cave of Adullam, where his brothers and other relatives soon joined him. ²Then others began coming—those who were in any kind of trouble, such as being in debt, or merely discontented—until David was the leader of about four hundred men.

³(Later David went to Mizpeh in Moab to ask permission of the king for his father and mother to live there under royal protection until David knew what God was going to do for him. ⁴They stayed in Moab during the entire period when David was living in the cave.)

⁵One day the prophet Gad told David to leave the cave and return to the land of Judah. So David went to the forest of Hereth. ⁶The news of his arrival in Judah soon reached Saul. He was in Gibeah at the time, sitting beneath an oak tree playing with his spear, surrounded by his officers.

⁷"Listen here, you men of Benjamin!" Saul exclaimed when he heard the news. "Has David promised you fields and vineyards and commissions in his army? ⁸Is that why you are against me? For not one of you has ever told me that my own son is on David's side. You're not even sorry for me. Think of it! My own son—encouraging David to come and kill me!"

⁹,¹⁰Then Doeg the Edomite, who was standing there with Saul's men, spoke up. "When I was at Nob," he said, "I saw David talking to Ahimelech the priest. Ahimelech consulted the Lord to find out what David should do, and then gave him food and the sword of Goliath the Philistine."

¹¹,¹²King Saul immediately summoned Ahimelech and all his family and all the other priests at Nob. When they arrived Saul shouted at him, "Listen to me, you son of Ahitub!"

"What is it?" quavered Ahimelech.

¹³"Why have you and David conspired against me?" Saul demanded. "Why did you give him food and a sword and talk to God for him? Why did you encourage him to revolt against me and to come here and attack me?"

¹⁴"But sir," Ahimelech replied, "is there anyone among all your servants who is as faithful as David your son-in-law? Why, he is the captain of your bodyguard and a highly honored member of your own household! ¹⁵This was certainly not the first time I had consulted God for him! It's unfair for you to accuse me and my family in this matter, for we knew nothing of any plot against you."

¹⁶"You shall die, Ahimelech, along with your entire family!" the king shouted. ¹⁷He ordered his bodyguards, "Kill these priests, for they are allies and conspirators with David; they knew he was running away from me, but they didn't tell me!"

But the soldiers refused to harm the clergy.

¹⁸Then the king said to Doeg, "You do it."

So Doeg turned on them and killed them, eighty-five priests in all, all wearing their priestly robes. ¹⁹Then he went to Nob, the city of the priests, and killed the priests' families—men, women, children, and babies, and also all the oxen, donkeys, and sheep. ²⁰Only Abiathar, one of the sons of Ahimelech, escaped and fled to David.

²¹When he told him what Saul had done, ²²David exclaimed, "I knew it! When I saw Doeg there, I knew he would tell Saul. Now I have caused the death of all of your father's family. ²³Stay here with me, and I'll protect you with my own life. Any harm to you will be over my dead body."

23 David Protects Keilah

One day news came to David that the Philistines were at Keilah robbing the threshing floors.

²David asked the Lord, "Shall I go and attack them?"

Family Devotions

☐ *Devotion 103*
Respecting Others

Read 1 Samuel 24:1-11

Respecting Others
Memory Verse

Don't be selfish; don't live to make a good impression on others. Be humble, thinking of others as better than yourself.
Philippians 2:3

"Mom, we had a substitute teacher today. It was so funny!" Jane laughed as she came into the house. "Todd, Mike, and John all switched seats. So all day long she was calling them the wrong names. Then some of the kids told her that our teacher always let us out for recess early, so we got out fifteen minutes before everyone else! What a dummy!"

Mom frowned. "How was your substitute supposed to know you weren't supposed to be let out early? Has she taught your class before?" she asked.

"No," answered Jane. "I guess she couldn't have known, could she?"

"And how would she know if the boys were in the right seats or not?" asked Mom.

Jane shrugged. "I suppose our teacher left a seating chart for her."

"But she didn't know who the kids were, did she?" said Mom. "It really wasn't very nice, or funny, to fool her and laugh at her."

"Well, she's just a sub," said Jane with a shrug. "It doesn't matter."

"Oh yes, it does matter!" exclaimed Mom. "You are under her authority while she's in your class, and you must respect and obey her. It's not only common courtesy. It's a command from God."

Jane's eyes widened. "It is? I thought the Bible just said to obey your parents."

"It also tells us to obey anyone who is in authority over us," said Mom, "and that includes substitute teachers."

"I suppose she must have felt really bad," said Jane thoughtfully. Suddenly she had an idea. "Mom, will you drive me back to school? I heard our sub say she'd be correcting papers after school, so she should still be there. I could apologize to her."

"That's a great idea!" said Mom. "Let's go now."

How About You?
Have you or any of your classmates ever had a little fun with a substitute teacher? Have you played tricks and given the substitute a bad day? Did you think it was funny? God doesn't. He tells us that we must not only obey our parents, but we must also respect and obey anyone who has authority over us. *D. M.*

• For the next devotional, turn to page 317. • For the next devotional on *Respecting Others*, turn to page 507.
• For notes on *Respecting Others*, see pages 322, 382, 1088, and 1218.

"Yes, go and save Keilah," the Lord told him.

³But David's men said, "We're afraid even here in Judah; we certainly don't want to go to Keilah to fight the whole Philistine army!"

⁴David asked the Lord again, and the Lord again replied, "Go down to Keilah, for I will help you conquer the Philistines."

⁵They went to Keilah and slaughtered the Philistines and confiscated their cattle, and so the people of Keilah were saved. ⁶(Abiathar the priest went to Keilah with David, taking his ephod with him to get answers for David from the Lord.) ⁷Saul soon learned that David was at Keilah.

"Good!" he exclaimed. "We've got him now! God has delivered him to me, for he has trapped himself in a walled city!"

⁸So Saul mobilized his entire army to march to Keilah and besiege David and his men. ⁹But David learned of Saul's plan and told Abiathar the priest to bring the ephod and to ask the Lord what he should do.

¹⁰"O Lord God of Israel," David said, "I have heard that Saul is planning to come and destroy Keilah because I am here. ¹¹Will the men of Keilah surrender me to him? And will Saul actually come, as I have heard? O Lord God of Israel, please tell me."

And the Lord said, "He will come."

¹²"And will these men of Keilah betray me to Saul?" David persisted.

And the Lord replied, "Yes, they will betray you."

¹³So David and his men—about six hundred of them now—left Keilah and began roaming the countryside. Word soon reached Saul that David had escaped, so he didn't go there after all. ¹⁴,¹⁵David now lived in the wilderness caves in the hill country of Ziph. One day near Horesh he received the news that Saul was on the way to Ziph to search for him and kill him. Saul hunted him day after day, but the Lord didn't let him find him.

¹⁶(Prince Jonathan now went to find David; he met him at Horesh and encouraged him in his faith in God.

¹⁷"Don't be afraid," Jonathan reassured him. "My father will never find you! You are going to be the king of Israel and I will be next to you, as my father is well aware." ¹⁸So the two of them renewed their pact of friendship; and David stayed at Horesh while Jonathan returned home.)

¹⁹But now the men of Ziph went to Saul in Gibeah and betrayed David to him.

"We know where he is hiding," they said. "He is in the caves of Horesh on Hachilah Hill, down in the southern part of the wilderness. ²⁰Come on down, sir, and we will catch him for you and your fondest wish will be fulfilled!"

²¹"Well, praise the Lord!" Saul said. "At last someone has had pity on me! ²²Go and check again to be sure of where he is staying and who has seen him there, for I know that he is very crafty. ²³Discover his hiding places and then come back and give me a more definite report. Then I'll go with you. And if he is in the area at all, I'll find him if I have to search every inch of the entire land!"

²⁴,²⁵So the men of Ziph returned home. But when David heard that Saul was on his way to Ziph, he and his men went even further into the wilderness of Maon in the south of the desert. But Saul followed them there. ²⁶He and David were now on opposite sides of a mountain. As Saul and his men began to close in, David tried his best to escape, but it was no use. ²⁷But just then a message reached Saul that the Philistines were raiding Israel again, ²⁸so Saul quit the chase and returned to fight the Philistines. Ever since that time the place where David was camped has been called, "The Rock of Escape!" ²⁹David then went to live in the caves of Engedi.

24 David Refuses to Get Even

After Saul's return from his battle with the Philistines, he was told that David had gone into the wilderness of Engedi; ²so he took three thousand special troops and went to search for him among the rocks and wild goats of the desert. ³At the place where the road passes some sheepfolds, Saul went into a cave to go to the bathroom, but as it happened, David and his men were hiding in the cave!

⁴"Now's your time!" David's men whispered to him. "Today is the day the Lord was talking about when he said, 'I will certainly put Saul into your power, to do with as you wish'!" Then David crept forward and quietly slit off the bottom of Saul's robe! ⁵But then his conscience began bothering him.

⁶"I shouldn't have done it," he said to his men. "It is a serious sin to attack God's chosen king in any way."

⁷,⁸These words of David persuaded his men not to kill Saul.

After Saul had left the cave and gone on his way, David came out and shouted after him, "My lord the king!" And when Saul looked around, David bowed low before him.

⁹,¹⁰Then he shouted to Saul, "Why do you listen to the people who say I am trying to harm you? This very day you have seen it isn't true. For the Lord placed you at my mercy back there in the cave, and some of my men told me to kill you, but I spared you. For I said, 'I will never harm him—he is the Lord's chosen king.' ¹¹See what I have in my hand? It is the hem of your robe! I cut it off, but I didn't kill you! Doesn't this convince you that I am not trying to harm you and that I have not sinned against you, even though you have been hunting for my life?

Family Devotions

☐ **DEVOTION 104**

BECOMING MORE LIKE JESUS

Read 1 Samuel 25:1-31

"'Scuse me." Dave reached right across his sister's plate to get the salt.

"The next time you do that," scolded Nancy, "I'll wipe my knife on your shirt."

"Children!" exclaimed Mom. "Watch your manners! Dave, if you want something, please ask to have it passed."

"But it's quicker to get it myself," Dave retorted.

"It might be quicker, but it's not good manners," said Mom.

As Nancy started to leave the table, Dad stopped her. "Before you leave the table, Nancy, you should ask to be excused."

"Tell you what—let's make a game to help you," Mom suggested. "Each time you use good manners, you get a check mark beside your name. And each time you use bad manners—like reaching in front of someone or interrupting someone when they're talking—we'll erase a check mark. At the end of each week, the winner gets a special treat."

The plan worked well. At the end of the first week, Dave was only a few points behind Nancy.

"Hey, this is kinda fun," said Dave after receiving a check mark the next week. "I'll beat you this time, Nancy. I'm getting gooder and gooder at remem—"

"Better and better, not gooder and gooder," Nancy interrupted sarcastically.

"Oops!" Mom erased a mark behind Nancy's name. "You forgot the rule—don't interrupt."

The next day Dave's friend, Bill Jones, invited him to stay overnight. A few days after that, Mrs. Jones met Dave's mother at the supermarket. "I just want to tell you how well Dave behaved," Mrs. Jones said.

"I felt very proud of you, Dave," Mom said that evening at the dinner table. "You see, good manners can become a habit that others admire."

Becoming More Like Jesus Memory Verse

No, he has told you what he wants, and this is all it is: *to be fair, just, merciful, and to walk humbly with your God.*
Micah 6:8

How About You?

Do you usually use your worst manners on your own family? Practicing good manners is important, and the place to begin is at home. Be thoughtful and courteous. Ask the Lord to help you overcome the weaknesses in your manners. *C. V. M.*

• For the next devotional, turn to page 321.   • For the next devotional on BECOMING MORE LIKE JESUS, turn to page 499.   • For notes on BECOMING MORE LIKE JESUS, see pages 234, 983, 1105, and 1164.

[12] "The Lord will decide between us. Perhaps he will kill you for what you are trying to do to me, but I will never harm you. [13] As that old proverb says, 'Wicked is as wicked does,' but despite your wickedness, I'll not touch you. [14] And who is the king of Israel trying to catch, anyway? Should he spend his time chasing one who is as worthless as a dead dog or a flea? [15] May the Lord judge as to which of us is right and punish whichever one of us is guilty. He is my lawyer and defender, and he will rescue me from your power!"

[16] Saul called back, "Is it really you, my son David?" Then he began to cry. [17] And he said to David, "You are a better man than I am, for you have repaid me good for evil. [18] Yes, you have been wonderfully kind to me today, for when the Lord delivered me into your hand, you didn't kill me. [19] Who else in all the world would let his enemy get away when he had him in his power? May the Lord reward you well for the kindness you have shown me today. [20] And now I realize that you are surely going to be king, and Israel shall be yours to rule. [21] Oh, swear to me by the Lord that when that happens you will not kill my family and destroy my line of descendants!"

[22] So David promised, and Saul went home, but David and his men went back to their cave.

25 Abigail Stops a Fight

Shortly afterwards Samuel died, and all Israel gathered for his funeral and buried him in his family plot at Ramah.

Meanwhile David went down to the wilderness of Paran. [2] A wealthy man from Maon owned a sheep ranch there, near the village of Carmel. He had three thousand sheep and a thousand goats, and was at his ranch at this time for the sheep shearing. [3] His name was Nabal and his wife, a beautiful and very intelligent woman, was named Abigail. But the man, who was a descendant of Caleb, was uncouth, churlish, stubborn, and ill-mannered.

[4] When David heard that Nabal was shearing his sheep, [5] he sent ten of his young men to Carmel to give him this message: [6] "May God prosper you and your family and multiply everything you own. [7] I am told that you are shearing your sheep and goats. While your shepherds have lived among us, we have never harmed them, nor stolen anything from them the whole time they have been in Carmel. [8] Ask your young men and they will tell you whether or not this is true. Now I have sent my men to ask for a little contribution from you, for we have come at a happy time of holiday. Please give us a present of whatever is at hand."

[9] The young men gave David's message to Nabal and waited for his reply.

[10] "Who is this fellow David?" he sneered. "Who does this son of Jesse think he is? There are lots of servants these days who run away from their masters. [11] Should I take my bread and my water and my meat that I've slaughtered for my shearers and give it to a gang who comes from God knows where?"

[12] So David's messengers returned and told him what Nabal had said.

[13] "Get your swords!" was David's reply as he strapped on his own. Four hundred of them started off with David and two hundred remained behind to guard their gear.

[14] Meanwhile, one of Nabal's men went and told Abigail, "David sent men from the wilderness to talk to our master, but he insulted them and railed at them. [15,16] But David's men were very good to us and we never suffered any harm from them; in fact, day and night they were like a wall of protection to us and the sheep, and nothing was stolen from us the whole time they were with us. [17] You'd better think fast, for there is going to be trouble for our master and his whole family—he's such a stubborn lout that no one can even talk to him!"

[18] Then Abigail hurriedly took two hundred loaves of bread, two barrels of wine, five dressed sheep, two bushels of roasted grain, one hundred raisin cakes, and two hundred fig cakes, and packed them onto donkeys.

[19] "Go on ahead," she said to her young men, "and I will follow." But she didn't tell her husband what she was doing. [20] As she was riding down the trail on her donkey, she met David coming toward her.

[21] David had been saying to himself, "A lot of good it did us to help this fellow. We protected his flocks in the wilderness so that not one thing was lost or stolen, but he has repaid me bad for good. All that I get for my trouble is insults. [22] May God curse me if even one of his men remains alive by tomorrow morning!"

[23] When Abigail saw David, she quickly dismounted and bowed low before him.

[24] "I accept all blame in this matter, my lord," she said. "Please listen to what I want to say. [25] Nabal is a bad-tempered boor, but please don't pay any attention to what he said. He is a fool—just like his name means. But I didn't see the messengers you sent. [26] Sir, since the Lord has kept you from murdering and taking vengeance into your own hands, I pray by the life of God, and by your own life too, that all your enemies shall be as cursed as Nabal is. [27] And now, here is a present I have brought to you and your young men. [28] Forgive me for my boldness in coming out here. The Lord will surely reward you with eternal royalty for your descendants, for you are fighting his battles; and you will never do wrong throughout your entire life. [29] Even when you are chased by those who seek your life, you are safe in the care of the Lord your God, just as though you were

safe inside his purse! But the lives of your enemies shall disappear like stones from a sling! ³⁰,³¹When the Lord has done all the good things he promised you and has made you king of Israel, you won't want the conscience of a murderer who took the law into his own hands! And when the Lord has done these great things for you, please remember me!"

³²David replied to Abigail, "Bless the Lord God of Israel who has sent you to meet me today! ³³Thank God for your good sense! Bless you for keeping me from murdering the man and carrying out vengeance with my own hands. ³⁴For I swear by the Lord, the God of Israel who has kept me from hurting you, that if you had not come out to meet me, not one of Nabal's men would be alive tomorrow morning."

³⁵Then David accepted her gifts and told her to return home without fear, for he would not kill her husband. ³⁶When she arrived home she found that Nabal had thrown a big party. He was roaring drunk, so she didn't tell him anything about her meeting with David until the next morning. ³⁷,³⁸By that time he was sober, and when his wife told him what had happened, he had a stroke and lay paralyzed for about ten days, then died, for the Lord killed him.

³⁹When David heard that Nabal was dead, he said, "Praise the Lord! God has paid back Nabal and kept me from doing it myself; he has received his punishment for his sin."

Then David wasted no time in sending messengers to Abigail to ask her to become his wife. ⁴⁰When the messengers arrived at Carmel and told her why they had come, ⁴¹she readily agreed to his request. ⁴²Quickly getting ready, she took along five of her serving girls as attendants, mounted her donkey, and followed the men back to David. So she became his wife.

⁴³David also married Ahinoam from Jezreel. ⁴⁴King Saul, meanwhile, had forced David's wife Michal, Saul's daughter, to marry a man from Gallim named Palti (the son of Laish).

26 David Sneaks into Camp

Now the men from Ziph came back to Saul at Gibeah to tell him that David had returned to the wilderness and was hiding on Hachilah Hill. ²So Saul took his elite corps of three thousand troops and went to hunt him down. ³,⁴Saul camped along the road at the edge of the wilderness where David was hiding, but David knew of Saul's arrival and sent out spies to watch his movements.

⁵⁻⁷David slipped over to Saul's camp one night to look around. King Saul and General Abner were sleeping inside a ring formed by the slumbering soldiers.

"Any volunteers to go down there with me?" David asked Ahimelech (the Hittite) and Abishai (Joab's brother and the son of Zeruiah).

"I'll go with you," Abishai replied. So David and Abishai went to Saul's camp and found him asleep, with his spear in the ground beside his head.

⁸"God has put your enemy within your power this time for sure," Abishai whispered to David. "Let me go and put that spear through him. I'll pin him to the earth with it—I'll not need to strike a second time!"

⁹"No," David said. "Don't kill him, for who can remain innocent after attacking the Lord's chosen king? ¹⁰Surely God will strike him down some day, or he will die in battle or of old age. ¹¹But God forbid that I should kill the man he has chosen to be king! But I'll tell you what—we'll take his spear and his jug of water and then get out of here!"

¹²So David took the spear and jug of water, and they got away without anyone seeing them or even waking up, because the Lord had put them sound asleep. ¹³They climbed the mountain slope opposite the camp until they were at a safe distance.

¹⁴Then David shouted down to Abner and Saul, "Wake up, Abner!"

"Who is it?" Abner demanded.

¹⁵"Well, Abner, you're a great fellow, aren't you?" David taunted. "Where in all Israel is there anyone as wonderful? So why haven't you guarded your master the king when someone came to kill him? ¹⁶This isn't good at all! I swear by the Lord that you ought to die for your carelessness. Where is the king's spear and the jug of water that was beside his head? Look and see!"

¹⁷,¹⁸Saul recognized David's voice and said, "Is that you, my son David?"

And David replied, "Yes, sir, it is. Why are you chasing me? What have I done? What is my crime? ¹⁹If the Lord has stirred you up against me, then let him accept my peace offering. But if this is simply the scheme of a man, then may he be cursed by God. For you have driven me out of my home so that I can't be with the Lord's people, and you have sent me away to worship heathen gods. ²⁰Must I die on foreign soil, far from the

---

OBEDIENCE 26:8ff. The strongest moral decisions are the ones we make before temptation strikes. David was determined to follow God, and this carried over into his decision not to murder God's anointed king, Saul, even when his men and the circumstances seemed to make it a feasible option. Who would you have been like in such a situation—David or David's men? To be like David and follow God, we must realize that we can't do wrong in order to execute justice. Even when our closest friends counsel us to a certain action that seems right, we must always put God's commands first. **To begin the series of devotionals on OBEDIENCE, turn to page 25.**

presence of Jehovah? Why should the king of Israel come out to hunt my life like a partridge on the mountains?"

²¹Then Saul confessed, "I have done wrong. Come back home, my son, and I'll no longer try to harm you; for you saved my life today. I have been a fool, and very, very wrong."

²²"Here is your spear, sir," David replied. "Let one of your young men come over and get it. ²³The Lord gives his own reward for doing good and for being loyal, and I refused to kill you even when the Lord placed you in my power. ²⁴Now may the Lord save my life, even as I have saved yours today. May he rescue me from all my troubles."

²⁵And Saul said to David, "Blessings on you, my son David. You shall do heroic deeds and be a great conqueror."

Then David went away and Saul returned home.

27 David Among the Philistines

But David kept thinking to himself, "Some day Saul is going to get me. I'll try my luck among the Philistines until Saul gives up and quits hunting for me; then I will finally be safe again."

²,³So David took his six hundred men and their families to live at Gath under the protection of King Achish. He had his two wives with him—Ahinoam of Jezreel and Abigail of Carmel, Nabal's widow. ⁴Word soon reached Saul that David had fled to Gath, so he quit hunting for him.

⁵One day David said to Achish, "My lord, if it is all right with you, we would rather live in one of the country towns instead of here in the royal city."

⁶So Achish gave him Ziklag (which still belongs to the kings of Judah to this day), ⁷and they lived there among the Philistines for a year and four months. ⁸He and his men spent their time raiding the Geshurites, the Girzites, and the Amalekites—people who had lived near Shur along the road to Egypt ever since ancient times. ⁹They didn't leave one person alive in the villages they hit and took for themselves the sheep, oxen, donkeys, camels, and clothing before returning to their homes.

¹⁰"Where did you make your raid today?" Achish would ask.

And David would reply, "Against the south of Judah and the people of Jerahmeel and the Kenites."

¹¹No one was left alive to come to Gath and tell where he had really been. This happened again and again while he was living among the Philistines. ¹²Achish believed David and thought that the people of Israel must hate him bitterly by now. "Now he will have to stay here and serve me forever!" the king thought.

28 Saul Visits a Witch

About that time the Philistines mustered their armies for another war with Israel.

"Come and help us fight," King Achish said to David and his men.

²"Good," David agreed. "You will soon see what a help we can be to you."

"If you are, you shall be my personal bodyguard for life," Achish told him.

³(Meanwhile, Samuel had died and all Israel had mourned for him. He was buried in Ramah, his hometown. King Saul had banned all mediums and wizards from the land of Israel.)

⁴The Philistines set up their camp at Shunem, and Saul and the armies of Israel were at Gilboa. ⁵,⁶When Saul saw the vast army of the Philistines, he was frantic with fear and asked the Lord what he should do. But the Lord refused to answer him, either by dreams, or by Urim, or by the prophets. ⁷,⁸Saul then instructed his aides to try to find a medium so that he could ask her what to do, and they found one at Endor. Saul disguised himself by wearing ordinary clothing instead of his royal robes. He went to the woman's home at night, accompanied by two of his men.

"I've got to talk to a dead man," he pleaded. "Will you bring his spirit up?"

⁹"Are you trying to get me killed?" the woman demanded. "You know that Saul has had all of the mediums and fortune-tellers executed. You are spying on me."

¹⁰But Saul took a solemn oath that he wouldn't betray her.

¹¹Finally the woman said, "Well, whom do you want me to bring up?"

"Bring me Samuel," Saul replied.

¹²When the woman saw Samuel, she screamed, "You've deceived me! You are Saul!"

¹³"Don't be frightened!" the king told her. "What do you see?"

"I see a specter coming up out of the earth," she said.

¹⁴"What does he look like?"

"He is an old man wrapped in a robe."

Saul realized that it was Samuel and bowed low before him.

¹⁵"Why have you disturbed me by bringing me back?" Samuel asked Saul.

"Because I am in deep trouble," he replied. "The Philistines are at war with us, and God has left me and won't reply by prophets or dreams; so I have called for you to ask you what to do."

¹⁶But Samuel replied, "Why ask me if the Lord has left you and has become your enemy? ¹⁷He

Family Devotions

☐ DEVOTION 105
LEAVING THE FUTURE IN GOD'S HANDS

Read 1 Samuel 28:1-20

"Where are we going, Dad?" asked Kevin as his father turned at the intersection.

"Wait and see," Dad said with a wink.

"Madame Margarite, Spiritualist, Reader," Sarah read as they drove past a sign on Main Street. "Have your fortune told here."

"I'd sure like to know the future," Laura sighed. "Like, will Brad ask me to the youth banquet?"

"How much does it cost to have your fortune told, Dad?" Kevin asked.

"I don't know," Dad answered, "and I may never find out. God's Word warns against going to fortune-tellers."

"Why?" Sarah, Laura, and Kevin spoke in unison.

"It would be fun to know the future," Kevin argued.

"Suppose we had known last Christmas that Grandma Snider was going to have a stroke the next week. Would we have enjoyed Christmas?" Dad asked.

"No, I guess not," answered Laura slowly.

"One young man was told by a fortune-teller that he would die when he was sixty-five," Dad said. "He began living very dangerously, thinking nothing could kill him. He took crazy risks. At the age of twenty-eight, he drowned."

"Then the fortune-teller was wrong!" Kevin exclaimed.

"Very often they are, but many people base their lives on those false predictions. That's dangerous," Dad warned.

"Going to a fortune-teller is 'following evil men's advice.' That's in a psalm I learned," said Laura.

Dad pulled the car into the parking lot of a new ice cream store. "The future is God's secret. He wants us to trust him, just as you trusted me today even though you didn't know where we were going. God wisely hides sorrows from us, and he provides many beautiful surprises."

"All we have to do is wait and see." Laura laughed.

Leaving the Future in God's Hands
Memory Verse

For I know the plans I have for you, says the Lord. They are plans for good and not for evil, to give you a future and a hope.
Jeremiah 29:11

How About You?

Do you worry about the future? Worry is unbelief and is not pleasing to God. Make up your mind to stop worrying about tomorrow. Trust God. He has everything under control. B. W.

• For the next devotional, turn to page 333. • For the next devotional on LEAVING THE FUTURE IN GOD'S HANDS, turn to page 403. • For notes on LEAVING THE FUTURE IN GOD'S HANDS, see pages 405, 452, 831, and 1061.

has done just as he said he would and has taken the kingdom from you and given it to your rival, David. ¹⁸All this has come upon you because you did not obey the Lord's instructions when he was so angry with Amalek. ¹⁹What's more, the entire Israeli army will be routed and destroyed by the Philistines tomorrow, and you and your sons will be here with me."

²⁰Saul now fell full length upon the ground, paralyzed with fright because of Samuel's words. He was also faint with hunger, for he had eaten nothing all day. ²¹When the woman saw how distraught he was, she said, "Sir, I obeyed your command at the risk of my life. ²²Now do what I say, and let me give you something to eat so you'll regain your strength for the trip back."

²³But he refused. The men who were with him added their pleas to that of the woman until he finally yielded and got up and sat on the bed. ²⁴The woman had been fattening a calf, so she hurried out and killed it and kneaded dough and baked unleavened bread. ²⁵She brought the meal to the king and his men, and they ate it. Then they went out into the night.

29 David Leaves the Philistines

The Philistine army now mobilized at Aphek, and the Israelis camped at the springs in Jezreel. ²As the Philistine captains were leading out their troops by battalions and companies, David and his men marched at the rear with King Achish.

³But the Philistine commanders demanded, "What are these Israelis doing here?"

And King Achish told them, "This is David, the runaway servant of King Saul of Israel. He's been with me for years, and I've never found one fault in him since he arrived."

⁴But the Philistine leaders were angry. "Send them back!" they demanded. "They aren't going into the battle with us—they'll turn against us. Is there any better way for him to reconcile himself with his master than by turning against us in the battle? ⁵This is the same man the women of Israel sang about in their dances: 'Saul has slain his thousands and David his ten thousands!'"

⁶So Achish finally summoned David and his men.

"I swear by the Lord," he told them, "you are some of the finest men I've ever met, and I think you should go with us, but my commanders say no. ⁷Please don't upset them, but go back quietly."

⁸"What have I done to deserve this treatment?" David demanded. "Why can't I fight your enemies?"

⁹But Achish insisted, "As far as I'm concerned, you're as perfect as an angel of God. But my commanders are afraid to have you with them in the battle. ¹⁰Now get up early in the morning and leave as soon as it is light."

¹¹So David headed back into the land of the Philistines while the Philistine army went on to Jezreel.

30

Three days later, when David and his men arrived home at their city of Ziklag, they found that the Amalekites had raided the city and burned it to the ground, ²carrying off all the women and children. ³As David and his men looked at the ruins and realized what had happened to their families, ⁴they wept until they could weep no more. ⁵(David's two wives, Ahinoam and Abigail, were among those who had been captured.) ⁶David was seriously worried, for in their bitter grief for their children, his men began talking of killing him. But David took strength from the Lord.

⁷Then he said to Abiathar the priest, "Bring me the oracle!" So Abiathar brought it.

⁸David asked the Lord, "Shall I chase them? Will I catch them?"

And the Lord told him, "Yes, go after them; you will recover everything that was taken from you!"

⁹,¹⁰So David and his six hundred men set out after the Amalekites. When they reached Besor Brook, two hundred of the men were too exhausted to cross, but the other four hundred kept going. ¹¹,¹²Along the way they found an Egyptian youth in a field and brought him to David. He had not had anything to eat or drink for three days and nights, so they gave him part of a fig cake, two clusters of raisins, and some water, and his strength soon returned.

¹³"Who are you and where do you come from?" David asked him.

"I am an Egyptian—the servant of an Amalekite," he replied. "My master left me behind three days ago because I was sick. ¹⁴We were on our way back from raiding the Cherethites in the Negeb, and had raided the south of Judah and the land of Caleb, and had burned Ziklag."

¹⁵"Can you tell me where they went?" David asked.

The young man replied, "If you swear by God's name that

RESPECTING OTHERS 30:11-15 The Amalekites cruelly left this slave to die, but God used him to lead David and his men to the Amalekite camp. David and his men treated the young man kindly, and he returned the kindness by leading them to the enemy. Treat those you meet with respect and dignity no matter how insignificant they may seem. You never know how God will use them to help you or haunt you, depending upon your response to them. **To begin the series of devotionals on RESPECTING OTHERS, turn to page 5.**

you will not kill me or give me back to my master, then I will guide you to them."

¹⁶So he led them to the Amalekite encampment. They were spread out across the fields, eating and drinking and dancing with joy because of the vast amount of loot they had taken from the Philistines and from the men of Judah. ¹⁷David and his men rushed in among them and slaughtered them all that night and the entire next day until evening. No one escaped except four hundred young men who fled on camels. ¹⁸,¹⁹David got back everything they had taken. The men recovered their families and all of their belongings, and David rescued his two wives. ²⁰His troops rounded up all the flocks and herds and drove them on ahead of them. "These are all yours personally, as your reward!" they told David.

²¹When they reached Besor Brook and the two hundred men who had been too exhausted to go on, David greeted them joyfully. ²²But some of the ruffians among David's men declared, "They didn't go with us, so they can't have any of the loot. Give them their wives and their children and tell them to be gone."

²³But David said, "No, my brothers! The Lord has kept us safe and helped us defeat the enemy. ²⁴Do you think that anyone will listen to you when you talk like this? We share and share alike—those who go to battle and those who guard the equipment."

²⁵From then on David made this a law for all of Israel, and it is still followed.

²⁶When he arrived at Ziklag, he sent part of the loot to the elders of Judah. "Here is a present for you, taken from the Lord's enemies," he wrote them. ²⁷⁻³¹The gifts were sent to the elders in the following cities where David and his men had been: Bethel, South Ramoth, Jattir, Aroer, Siphmoth, Eshtemoa, Racal, the cities of the Jerahmeelites, the cities of the Kenites, Hormah, Borashan, Athach, Hebron.

31 Saul Dies in Battle

Meanwhile the Philistines had begun the battle against Israel, and the Israelis fled from them and were slaughtered wholesale on Mount Gilboa. ²The Philistines closed in on Saul and killed his sons Jonathan, Abinidab, and Malchishua.

³,⁴Then the archers overtook Saul and wounded him badly. He groaned to his armor-bearer, "Kill me with your sword before these heathen Philistines capture me and torture me." But his armor-bearer was afraid to, so Saul took his own sword and fell upon the point of the blade, and it pierced him through. ⁵When his armor-bearer saw that he was dead, he also fell upon his sword and died with him. ⁶So Saul, his armor-bearer, his three sons, and his troops died together that same day.

⁷When the Israelis on the other side of the valley and beyond the Jordan heard that their comrades had fled and that Saul and his sons were dead, they abandoned their cities; and the Philistines lived in them.

⁸The next day when the Philistines went out to strip the dead, they found the bodies of Saul and his three sons on Mount Gilboa. ⁹They cut off Saul's head and stripped off his armor and sent the wonderful news of Saul's death to their idols and to the people throughout their land.

¹⁰His armor was placed in the temple of Ashtaroth, and his body was fastened to the wall of Beth-shan.

¹¹But when the people of Jabesh-gilead heard what the Philistines had done, ¹²warriors from that town traveled all night to Beth-shan and took down the bodies of Saul and his sons from the wall and brought them to Jabesh, where they cremated them. ¹³Then they buried their remains beneath the oak tree at Jabesh and fasted for seven days.

2 Samuel

THE BOOK of 2 Samuel could be named "The Nonstop Adventures of David." There's fast action throughout David's whole reign.

David became king after Saul and his sons died in battle. David's adventures began right away as he tried to win over Saul's followers. The adventure continued with the prophet Nathan, who always told David the truth whether he liked it or not. Adventure also came with David's many children, whose lives read like a soap opera.

But through all his adventures, David never lost his love for God. In his kindness to Saul's family, in his urgency to build the Temple, in his conflicts with his children, David's motive was clearly his love for the Lord.

David wasn't perfect—his sins were terrible. But his sadness over his sin was equally strong. He was heartbroken when he hurt the God he loved.

Because David obeyed God, God promised him that his kingdom would last forever. God kept his promise when he sent Jesus, a descendant of David, who will reign as king forever.

David was just like you and me, and we can follow his example. Let your love for God grow as you read 2 Samuel.

Saul was dead and David had returned to Ziklag after slaughtering the Amalekites. Three days later a man arrived from the Israeli army with his clothes torn and with dirt on his head as a sign of mourning. He fell to the ground before David in deep respect.

³"Where do you come from?" David asked.

"From the Israeli army," he replied.

⁴"What happened?" David demanded. "Tell me how the battle went."

And the man replied, "Our entire army fled. Thousands of men are dead and wounded on the field, and Saul and his son Jonathan have been killed."

⁵"How do you know they are dead?"

⁶"Because I was on Mount Gilboa and saw Saul leaning against his spear with the enemy chariots closing in upon him. ⁷When he saw me he cried out for me to come to him.

⁸"'Who are you?' he asked.

"'An Amalekite,' I replied.

⁹"'Come and put me out of my misery,' he begged, 'for I am in terrible pain but life lingers on.'

[10]"So I killed him, for I knew he couldn't live. Then I took his crown and one of his bracelets to bring to you, my lord."

[11]David and his men tore their clothes in sorrow when they heard the news. [12]They mourned and wept and fasted all day for Saul and his son Jonathan, and for the Lord's people, and for the men of Israel who had died that day.

[13]Then David said to the young man who had brought the news, "Where are you from?"

And he replied, "I am an Amalekite."

[14]"Why did you kill God's chosen king?" David demanded.

[15]Then he said to one of his young men, "Kill him!" So he ran him through with his sword and he died.

[16]"You die self-condemned," David said, "for you yourself confessed that you killed God's appointed king."

[17,18]Then David composed a dirge for Saul and Jonathan and afterward commanded that it be sung throughout Israel. It is quoted here from the book, *Heroic Ballads*.

[19]O Israel, your pride and joy lies dead upon the hills;
Mighty heroes have fallen.
[20]Don't tell the Philistines, lest they rejoice.
Hide it from the cities of Gath and Ashkelon,
Lest the heathen nations laugh in triumph.
[21]O Mount Gilboa,
Let there be no dew nor rain upon you,
Let no crops of grain grow on your slopes.
For there the mighty Saul has died;
He is God's appointed king no more.
[22]Both Saul and Jonathan slew their strongest foes,
And did not return from battle empty-handed.
[23]How much they were loved, how wonderful they were—
Both Saul and Jonathan!
They were together in life and in death.
They were swifter than eagles, stronger than lions.
[24]But now, O women of Israel, weep for Saul;
He enriched you
With fine clothing and gold ornaments.
[25]These mighty heroes have fallen in the midst of the battle.
Jonathan is slain upon the hills.
[26]How I weep for you, my brother Jonathan;
How much I loved you!
And your love for me was deeper
Than the love of women!
[27]The mighty ones have fallen,
Stripped of their weapons, and dead.

2 Judah Crowns David King

David then asked the Lord, "Shall I move back to Judah?"

And the Lord replied, "Yes."

"Which city shall I go to?"

And the Lord replied, "Hebron."

[2]So David and his wives—Ahinoam from Jezreel and Abigail the widow of Nabal from Carmel— [3]and his men and their families all moved to Hebron. [4]Then the leaders of Judah came to David and crowned him king of the Judean confederacy.

When David heard that the men of Jabesh-gilead had buried Saul, [5]he sent them this message: "May the Lord bless you for being so loyal to your king and giving him a decent burial. [6]May the Lord be loyal to you in return and reward you with many demonstrations of his love! And I too will be kind to you because of what you have done. [7]And now I ask you to be my strong and loyal subjects, now that Saul is dead. Be like the tribe of Judah who have appointed me as their new king."

[8]But Abner, Saul's commander-in-chief, had gone to Mahanaim to crown Saul's son Ish-bosheth as king. [9]His territory included Gilead, Ashuri, Jezreel, Ephraim, the tribe of Benjamin, and all the rest of Israel. [10,11]Ish-bosheth was forty years old at the time. He reigned in Mahanaim for two years; meanwhile, David was reigning in Hebron and was king of the Judean confederacy for seven and one-half years.

[12]One day General Abner led some of Ish-bosheth's troops to Gibeon from Mahanaim, [13]and General Joab (the son of Zeruiah) led David's troops out to meet them. They met at the pool of Gibeon, where they sat facing each other on opposite sides of the pool. [14]Then Abner suggested to Joab, "Let's watch some sword play between our young men!"

Joab agreed, [15]so twelve men were chosen from each side to fight in mortal combat. [16]Each one grabbed his opponent by the hair and thrust his sword into the other's side, so that all of them died. The place has been known ever since as Sword Field.

[17]The two armies then began to fight each other, and by the end of the day Abner and the men of Israel had been defeated by Joab and the forces of David. [18]Joab's brothers, Abishai and Asahel, were also in the

---

PERSEVERANCE 2:21-23 Abner repeatedly warned Asahel to turn back or risk losing his life, but Asahel refused to turn from his self-imposed duty. Perseverance is a good trait if it is for a worthy cause. But if the goal is only personal honor or gain, perseverance may be no more than stubbornness. Asahel's stubbornness not only cost his life, but also spurred unfortunate disunity in David's army for years to come (3:26-27; 1 Kings 2:28-35). Before you decide to pursue a goal, make sure it is worthy of your devotion. **To begin the series of devotionals on PERSEVERANCE, turn to page 37.**

battle. Asahel could run like a deer, ¹⁹and he began chasing Abner. He wouldn't stop for anything, but kept on, singleminded, after Abner alone.

²⁰When Abner looked behind and saw him coming, he called out to him, "Is that you, Asahel?"

"Yes," he called back, "it is."

²¹"Go after someone else!" Abner warned. But Asahel refused and kept on coming.

²²Again Abner shouted to him, "Get away from here. I could never face your brother Joab if I have to kill you!"

²³But he refused to turn away, so Abner pierced him through the belly with the butt end of his spear. It went right through his body and came out his back. He stumbled to the ground and died there, and everyone stopped when they came to the place where he lay.

²⁴Now Joab and Abishai set out after Abner. The sun was just going down as they arrived at Ammah Hill near Giah, along the road into the Gibeon desert. ²⁵Abner's troops from the tribe of Benjamin regrouped there at the top of the hill, ²⁶and Abner shouted down to Joab, "Must our swords continue to kill each other forever? How long will it be before you call off your people from chasing their brothers?"

²⁷Joab shouted back, "I swear by God that even if you hadn't spoken, we would all have gone home tomorrow morning." ²⁸Then he blew his trumpet and his men stopped chasing the troops of Israel.

²⁹That night Abner and his men retreated across the Jordan Valley, crossed the river, and traveled all the next morning until they arrived at Mahanaim. ³⁰Joab and the men who were with him returned home, too, and when he counted his casualties, he learned that only nineteen men were missing, in addition to Asahel. ³¹But three hundred and sixty of Abner's men (all from the tribe of Benjamin) were dead. ³²Joab and his men took Asahel's body to Bethlehem and buried him beside his father; then they traveled all night and reached Hebron at daybreak.

3 David Becomes Stronger

That was the beginning of a long war between the followers of Saul and of David. David's position now became stronger and stronger, while Saul's dynasty became weaker and weaker.

²Several sons were born to David while he was at Hebron. The oldest was Amnon, born to his wife Ahinoam. ³His second son, Chileab, was born to Abigail, the widow of Nabal of Carmel. The third was Absalom, born to Maacah, the daughter of King Talmai of Geshur. ⁴The fourth was Adonijah, who was born to Haggith. Then Shephatiah was born to Abital, and ⁵Ithream was born to Eglah.

⁶As the war went on, Abner became a very powerful political leader among the followers of Saul. ⁷He took advantage of his position by sleeping with one of Saul's concubines, a girl named Rizpah. But when Ish-bosheth accused Abner of this, ⁸Abner was furious.

"Am I a Judean dog to be kicked around like this?" he shouted. "After all I have done for you and for your father by not betraying you to David, is this my reward—to find fault with me about some woman? ⁹,¹⁰May God curse me if I don't do everything I can to take away the entire kingdom from you, all the way from Dan to Beersheba, and give it to David, just as the Lord predicted."

¹¹Ish-bosheth made no reply, for he was afraid of Abner.

¹²Then Abner sent messengers to David to discuss a deal—to surrender the kingdom of Israel to him in exchange for becoming commander-in-chief of the combined armies of Israel and Judah.

¹³"All right," David replied, "but I will not negotiate with you unless you bring me my wife Michal, Saul's daughter." ¹⁴David then sent this message to Ish-bosheth: "Give me back my wife Michal, for I bought her with the lives of one hundred Philistines."

¹⁵So Ish-bosheth took her away from her husband Palti. ¹⁶He followed along behind her as far as Behurim, weeping as he went. Then Abner told him, "Go on home now." So he returned.

¹⁷Meanwhile, Abner consulted with the leaders of Israel and reminded them that for a long time they had wanted David as their king.

¹⁸"Now is the time!" he told them. "For the Lord has said, 'It is David by whom I will save my people from the Philistines and from all their other enemies.'"

¹⁹Abner also talked to the leaders of the tribe of Benjamin; then he went to Hebron and reported to David his progress with the people of Israel and Benjamin. ²⁰Twenty men accompanied him, and David entertained them with a feast.

²¹As Abner left, he promised David, "When I get back I will call a convention of all the people of Israel, and they will elect you as their king, as you've so long desired." So David let Abner return in safety.

²²But just after Abner left, Joab and some of

SERVING GOD BOLDLY 3:7 Ish-bosheth was right to speak out against Abner's behavior, but he didn't have the strength to maintain his authority (3:11). Lack of moral backbone became the root of Israel's troubles over the next four centuries. Only four of the next forty kings of Israel were called "good." It takes courage and strength to stand firm in your convictions to confront wrongdoing in the face of opposition. When you believe something is wrong, do not let yourself be talked out of your position. Firmly attack the wrong and uphold the right. **To begin the series of devotionals on SERVING GOD BOLDLY, turn to page 17.**

David's troops returned from a raid, bringing much loot with them. ²³When Joab was told that Abner had just been there visiting the king and had been sent away in peace, ²⁴,²⁵he rushed to the king, demanding, "What have you done? What do you mean by letting him get away? You know perfectly well that he came to spy on us and that he plans to return and attack us!"

²⁶Then Joab sent messengers to catch up with Abner and tell him to come back. They found him at the well of Sirah and he returned with them; but David knew nothing about it. ²⁷When Abner arrived at Hebron, Joab took him aside at the city gate as if to speak with him privately; but then he pulled out a dagger and killed him in revenge for the death of his brother Asahel.

²⁸When David heard about it he declared, "I vow by the Lord that I and my people are innocent of this crime against Abner. ²⁹Joab and his family are the guilty ones. May each of his children be victims of cancer, or be lepers, or be sterile, or die of starvation, or be killed by the sword!"

³⁰So Joab and his brother, Abishai, killed Abner because of the death of their brother, Asahel, at the battle of Gibeon.

³¹Then David said to Joab and to all those who were with him, "Go into deep mourning for Abner." And King David accompanied the bier to the cemetery. ³²They buried Abner in Hebron. And the king and all the people wept at the graveside.

³³,³⁴"Should Abner have died like a fool?" the king lamented.

"Your hands were not bound,
Your feet were not tied—
You were murdered—
The victim of a wicked plot."

And all the people wept again for him. ³⁵,³⁶David had refused to eat anything the day of the funeral, and now everyone begged him to take a bite of supper. But David vowed that he would eat nothing until sundown. This pleased his people, just as everything else he did pleased them! ³⁷Thus the whole nation, both Judah and Israel, understood from David's actions that he was in no way responsible for Abner's death.

³⁸And David said to his people, "A great leader and a great man has fallen today in Israel; ³⁹and even though I am God's chosen king, I can do nothing with these two sons of Zeruiah. May the Lord repay wicked men for their wicked deeds."

4 King Ish-bosheth Is Murdered

When King Ish-bosheth heard about Abner's death at Hebron, he was paralyzed with fear, and his people too were badly frightened. ²,³The command of the Israeli troops then fell to two brothers, Baanah and Rechab, who were captains of King Ish-bosheth's raiding bands. They were the sons of Rimmon, who was from Beeroth in Benjamin. (People from Beeroth are counted as Benjaminites even though they fled to Gittaim, where they now live.)

⁴(There was a little lame grandson of King Saul's named Mephibosheth, who was the son of Prince Jonathan. He was five years old at the time Saul and Jonathan were killed at the battle of Jezreel. When the news of the outcome of the battle reached the capital, the child's nurse grabbed him and fled, but she fell and dropped him as she was running, and he became lame.)

⁵Rechab and Baanah arrived at King Ish-bosheth's home one noon as he was taking a nap. ⁶,⁷They walked into the kitchen as though to get a sack of wheat, but then sneaked into his bedroom and murdered him and cut off his head. Taking his head with them, they fled across the desert that night and escaped. ⁸They presented the head to David at Hebron.

"Look!" they exclaimed. "Here is the head of Ish-bosheth, the son of your enemy Saul who tried to kill you. Today the Lord has given your revenge upon Saul and upon his entire family!"

⁹But David replied, "I swear by the Lord who saved me from my enemies, ¹⁰ that when someone told me, 'Saul is dead,' thinking he was bringing me good news, I killed him; that is how I rewarded him for his 'glad tidings.' ¹¹And how much more shall I do to wicked men who kill a good man in his own house and on his bed! Shall I not demand your lives?"

¹²So David ordered his young men to kill them, and they did. They cut off their hands and feet and hanged their bodies beside the pool in Hebron. And they took Ish-bosheth's head and buried it in Abner's tomb in Hebron.

5 David Becomes King

Representatives of all the tribes of Israel now came to David at Hebron and gave him their pledge of loyalty.

"We are your blood brothers," they said. ²"And even when Saul was our king you were our real leader. The Lord has said that you should be the shepherd and leader of his people."

³So David made a contract before the Lord with the leaders of Israel there at Hebron, and they crowned him king of Israel. ⁴,⁵(He had already been the king of Judah for seven years, since the age of thirty. He then ruled thirty-three years in Jerusalem as king of both Israel and Judah; so he reigned for forty years altogether.)

⁶David now led his troops to Jerusalem to fight against the Jebusites who lived there. "You'll never come in here," they told him. "Even the blind and lame could keep you out!" For they thought they were safe. ⁷But David and his troops defeated them and captured the stronghold of Zion, now called the City of David.

⁸When the insulting message from the defenders of the city reached David, he told his troops, "Go up through the water tunnel into the city and destroy those 'lame' and 'blind' Jebusites. How I hate them." (That is the origin of the saying, "Even the blind and the lame could conquer you!")

⁹So David made the stronghold of Zion (also called the City of David) his headquarters. Then, beginning at the old Millo section of the city, he built northward toward the present city center. ¹⁰So David became greater and greater, for the Lord God of heaven was with him.

¹¹Then King Hiram of Tyre sent cedar lumber, carpenters, and masons to build a palace for David. ¹²David now realized why the Lord had made him the king and blessed his kingdom so greatly—it was because God wanted to pour out his kindness on Israel, his chosen people.

¹³After moving from Hebron to Jerusalem, David married additional wives and concubines, and had many sons and daughters. ¹⁴⁻¹⁶These are his children who were born at Jerusalem: Shammua, Shobab, Nathan, Solomon, Ibhar, Elishua, Nepheg, Japhia, Elishama, Eliada, Eliphelet.

¹⁷When the Philistines heard that David had been crowned king of Israel, they tried to capture him; but David was told that they were coming and went into the stronghold. ¹⁸The Philistines arrived and spread out across the valley of Rephaim.

¹⁹Then David asked the Lord, "Shall I go out and fight against them? Will you defeat them for me?"

And the Lord replied, "Yes, go ahead, for I will give them to you."

²⁰So David went out and fought with them at Baal-perazim and defeated them. "The Lord did it!" he exclaimed. "He burst through my enemies like a raging flood." So he named the place "Bursting." ²¹At that time David and his troops confiscated many idols that had been abandoned by the Philistines. ²²But the Philistines returned and again spread out across the valley of Rephaim.

²³When David asked the Lord what to do, he replied, "Don't make a frontal attack. Go behind them and come out by the balsam trees. ²⁴When you hear a sound like marching feet in the tops of the balsam trees, attack! For it will signify that the Lord has prepared the way for you and will destroy them."

²⁵So David did as the Lord had instructed him and destroyed the Philistines all the way from Geba to Gezer.

6 David Brings the Ark Home

Then David mobilized thirty thousand special troops and led them to Baal-judah to bring home the Ark of the Lord of heaven who is enthroned above the Guardian Angels. ³The Ark was placed upon a new cart and taken from the hillside home of Abinadab. It was driven by Abinadab's sons, Uzzah and Ahio. ⁴Ahio was walking in front ⁵and was followed by David and the other leaders of Israel, who were joyously waving branches of juniper trees and playing every sort of musical instrument before the Lord—lyres, harps, tambourines, castanets, and cymbals.

⁶But when they arrived at the threshing floor of Nacon, the oxen stumbled and Uzzah put out his hand to steady the Ark. ⁷Then the anger of the Lord flared out against Uzzah and he killed him for doing this, so he died there beside the Ark. ⁸David was angry at what the Lord had done, and named the spot "The Place of Wrath upon Uzzah" (which it is still called to this day).

⁹David was now afraid of the Lord and asked, "How can I ever bring the Ark home?" ¹⁰So he decided against taking it into the City of David, but carried it instead to the home of Obed-edom, who had come from Gath. ¹¹It remained there for three months, and the Lord blessed Obed-edom and all his household.

¹²When David heard this, he brought the Ark to the City of David with a great celebration. ¹³After the men who were carrying it had gone six paces, they stopped and waited so that he could sacrifice an ox and a fat lamb. ¹⁴And David danced before the Lord with all his might and was wearing priests' clothing. ¹⁵So Israel brought home the Ark of the Lord with much shouting and blowing of trumpets.

¹⁶(But as the procession came into the city, Michal, Saul's daughter, watched from a window and saw King David leaping and dancing before the Lord; and she was filled with contempt for him.)

¹⁷The Ark was placed inside the tent that David

PATIENCE 5:4-5 David did not become king of all Israel until he was thirty-seven years old, although he had been promised the kingship many years earlier (1 Samuel 16:13). During those years, David had to wait patiently for the fulfillment of God's promise. If you feel pressured to achieve instant results and success, remember David's patience. Just as his time of waiting prepared him for his important task, a waiting period may help prepare you by strengthening your spiritual character. **To begin the series of devotionals on PATIENCE, turn to page 549.**

had prepared for it; and he sacrificed burnt offerings and peace offerings to the Lord. ¹⁸Then he blessed the people in the name of the Lord of heaven ¹⁹and gave a present to everyone—men and women alike—of a loaf of bread, some wine, and a cake of raisins. When it was all over, and everyone had gone home, ²⁰David returned to bless his family.

But Michal came out to meet him and exclaimed in disgust, "How glorious the king of Israel looked today! He exposed himself to the girls along the street like a common pervert!"

²¹David retorted, "I was dancing before the Lord who chose me above your father and his family and who appointed me as leader of Israel, the people of the Lord! So I am willing to act like a fool in order to show my joy in the Lord. ²²Yes, and I am willing to look even more foolish than this, but I will be respected by the girls of whom you spoke!"

²³So Michal was childless throughout her life.

7 When the Lord finally sent peace upon the land, and Israel was no longer at war with the surrounding nations, ²David said to Nathan the prophet, "Look! Here I am living in this beautiful cedar palace while the Ark of God is out in a tent!"

³"Go ahead with what you have in mind," Nathan replied, "for the Lord is with you."

⁴But that night the Lord said to Nathan, ⁵"Tell my servant David not to do it! ⁶For I have never lived in a temple. My home has been a tent ever since the time I brought Israel out of Egypt. ⁷And I have never once complained to Israel's leaders, the shepherds of my people. Have I ever asked them, 'Why haven't you built me a beautiful cedar temple?'

⁸"Now go and give this message to David from the Lord of heaven: 'I chose you to be the leader of my people Israel when you were a mere shepherd, tending your sheep in the pastureland. ⁹I have been with you wherever you have gone and have destroyed your enemies. And I will make your name greater yet, so that you will be one of the most famous men in the world! ¹⁰,¹¹I have selected a homeland for my people from which they will never have to move. It will be their own land where the heathen nations won't bother them as they did when the judges ruled my people. There will be no more wars against you; and your descendants shall rule this land for generations to come! ¹²For when you die, I will put one of your sons upon your throne, and I will make his kingdom strong. ¹³He is the one who shall build me a temple. And I will continue his kingdom into eternity. ¹⁴I will be his father and he shall be my son. If he sins, I will use other nations to punish him, ¹⁵but my love and kindness shall not leave him as I took it from Saul, your predecessor. ¹⁶Your family shall rule my kingdom forever.'"

¹⁷So Nathan went back to David and told him everything the Lord had said.

¹⁸Then David went into the Tabernacle and sat before the Lord and prayed, "O Lord God, why have you showered your blessings on such an insignificant person as I am? ¹⁹And now, in addition to everything else, you speak of giving me an eternal dynasty! Such generosity is far beyond any human standard! O Lord God! ²⁰What can I say? For you know what I am like! ²¹You are doing all these things just because you promised to and because you want to! ²²How great you are, Lord God! We have never heard of any other god like you. And there is no other god. ²³What other nation in all the earth has received such blessings as Israel, your people? For you have rescued your chosen nation in order to bring glory to your name. You have done great miracles to destroy Egypt and its gods. ²⁴You chose Israel to be your people forever, and you became our God.

²⁵"And now, Lord God, do as you have promised concerning me and my family. ²⁶And may you be eternally honored when you have established Israel as your people and have established my dynasty before you. ²⁷For you have revealed to me, O Lord of heaven, God of Israel, that I am the first of a dynasty which will rule your people forever; that is why I have been bold enough to pray this prayer of acceptance. ²⁸For you are indeed God, and your words are truth; and you have promised me these good things— ²⁹so do as you have promised! Bless me and my family forever! May our dynasty continue on and on before you; for you, Lord God, have promised it."

8 **David Strengthens His Kingdom**
After this David subdued and humbled the Philistines by conquering Gath, their largest city. ²He also devastated the land of Moab. He divided his victims by making them lie down side by side in rows. Two-thirds of each row, as measured with a tape, were butchered, and one-third were spared to become David's servants—they paid him tribute each year.

³He also destroyed the forces of King Hadadezer (son of Rehob) of Zobah in a battle at the Euphrates River, for Hadadezer had attempted to regain his power. ⁴David captured seventeen hundred cavalry and twenty thousand infantry; then he lamed all of the chariot horses except for one hundred teams. ⁵He also slaughtered twenty-two thousand Syrians from Damascus when they

came to help Hadadezer. ⁶David placed several army garrisons in Damascus, and the Syrians became David's subjects and brought him annual tribute money. So the Lord gave him victories wherever he turned. ⁷David brought the gold shields to Jerusalem which King Hadadezer's officers had used. ⁸He also carried back to Jerusalem a very large amount of bronze from Hadadezer's cities of Betah and Berothai.

⁹When King Toi of Hamath heard about David's victory over the army of Hadadezer, ¹⁰he sent his son Joram to congratulate him, for Hadadezer and Toi were enemies. He gave David presents made from silver, gold, and bronze. ¹¹,¹²David dedicated all of these to the Lord, along with the silver and gold he had taken from Syria, Moab, Ammon, the Philistines, Amalek, and King Hadadezer.

¹³So David became very famous. After his return he destroyed eighteen thousand Edomites at the Valley of Salt, ¹⁴and then placed garrisons throughout Edom, so that the entire nation was forced to pay tribute to Israel—another example of the way the Lord made him victorious wherever he went.

¹⁵David reigned with justice over Israel and was fair to everyone. ¹⁶The general of his army was Joab (son of Zeruiah), and his secretary of state was Jehoshaphat (son of Ahilud). ¹⁷Zadok (son of Ahitub) and Ahimelech (son of Abiathar) were the High Priests, and Seraiah was the king's private secretary. ¹⁸Benaiah (son of Jehoiada) was captain of his bodyguard, and David's sons were his assistants.

9 David Is Kind to Mephibosheth

One day David began wondering if any of Saul's family was still living, for he wanted to be kind to them, as he had promised Prince Jonathan. ²He heard about a man named Ziba, who had been one of Saul's servants, and summoned him.

"Are you Ziba?" the king asked.

"Yes, sir, I am," he replied.

³The king then asked him, "Is anyone left from Saul's family? If so, I want to fulfill a sacred vow by being kind to him."

"Yes," Ziba replied, "Jonathan's lame son is still alive."

⁴"Where is he?" the king asked.

"In Lo-debar," Ziba told him. "At the home of Machir."

⁵,⁶So King David sent for Mephibosheth—Jonathan's son and Saul's grandson. Mephibosheth arrived in great fear and greeted the king in deep humility, bowing low before him.

⁷But David said, "Don't be afraid! I've asked you to come so that I can be kind to you because of my vow to your father Jonathan. I will restore to you all the land of your grandfather Saul, and you shall live here at the palace!"

⁸Mephibosheth fell to the ground before the king. "Should the king show kindness to a dead dog like me?" he exclaimed.

⁹Then the king summoned Saul's servant Ziba. "I have given your master's grandson everything that belonged to Saul and his family," he said. ¹⁰,¹¹"You and your sons and servants are to farm the land for him, to produce food for his family; but he will live here with me."

Ziba, who had fifteen sons and twenty servants, replied, "Sir, I will do all you have commanded."

And from that time on, Mephibosheth ate regularly with King David, as though he were one of his own sons. ¹²Mephibosheth had a young son, Mica. All the household of Ziba became Mephibosheth's servants, ¹³but Mephibosheth (who was lame in both feet) moved to Jerusalem to live at the palace.

10 A King Mocks David's Men

Some time after this the Ammonite king died and his son Hanun replaced him.

²"I am going to show special respect for him," David said, "because his father Nahash was always so loyal and kind to me." So David sent ambassadors to express regrets to Hanun about his father's death.

³But Hanun's officers told him, "These men aren't here to honor your father! David has sent them to spy out the city before attacking it!"

⁴So Hanun took David's men and shaved off half their beards and cut their robes off at the buttocks and sent them home half naked. ⁵When David heard what had happened he told them to stay at Jericho until their beards grew out; for the men were very embarrassed over their appearance.

⁶Now the people of Ammon realized how seriously they had angered David, so they hired twenty thousand Syrian mercenaries from the lands of Rehob and Zobah, one thousand from the king of Maacah, and ten thousand from the land of Tob. ⁷,⁸When David heard about this, he sent Joab and the entire Israeli army to attack them. The Ammonites defended the gates of their city while the Syrians from Zobah, Rehob, Tob, and Maacah fought in the fields. ⁹When Joab realized that he would have to fight on two fronts, he selected the best fighters in his army, placed them under his personal command, and took them out to fight the Syrians in the fields. ¹⁰He left the rest of the army to his brother Abishai, who was to attack the city.

¹¹"If I need assistance against the Syrians, come

out and help me," Joab instructed him. "And if the Ammonites are too strong for you, I will come and help you. ¹²Courage! We must really act like men today if we are going to save our people and the cities of our God. May the Lord's will be done."

¹³And when Joab and his troops attacked, the Syrians began to run away. ¹⁴Then, when the Ammonites saw the Syrians running, they ran too, and retreated into the city. Afterwards Joab returned to Jerusalem. ¹⁵,¹⁶The Syrians now realized that they were no match for Israel. So when they regrouped, they were joined by additional Syrian troops summoned by Hadadezer from the other side of the Euphrates River. These troops arrived at Helam under the command of Shobach, the commander-in-chief of all of Hadadezer's forces.

¹⁷When David heard what was happening, he personally led the Israeli army to Helam, where the Syrians attacked him. ¹⁸But again the Syrians fled from the Israelis, this time leaving seven hundred charioteers dead on the field, also forty thousand cavalrymen, including General Shobach. ¹⁹When Hadadezer's allies saw that the Syrians had been defeated, they surrendered to David and became his servants. And the Syrians were afraid to help the Ammonites anymore after that.

David and Bathsheba

In the spring of the following year, at the time when wars begin, David sent Joab and the Israeli army to destroy the Ammonites. They began by laying siege to the city of Rabbah. But David stayed in Jerusalem.

²One night he couldn't get to sleep and went for a stroll on the roof of the palace. As he looked out over the city, he noticed a woman of unusual beauty taking her evening bath. ³He sent to find out who she was and was told that she was Bathsheba, the daughter of Eliam and the wife of Uriah. ⁴Then David sent for her and when she came he slept with her. (She had just completed the purification rites after menstruation.) Then she returned home. ⁵When she found that he had gotten her pregnant she sent a message to inform him.

⁶So David dispatched a memo to Joab: "Send me Uriah the Hittite." ⁷When he arrived, David asked him how Joab and the army were getting along and how the war was prospering. ⁸Then he told him to go home and relax, and he sent a present to him at his home. ⁹But Uriah didn't go there. He stayed that night at the gateway of the palace with the other servants of the king.

¹⁰When David heard what Uriah had done, he summoned him and asked him, "What's the matter with you? Why didn't you go home to your wife last night after being away for so long?"

¹¹Uriah replied, "The Ark and the armies and the general and his officers are camping out in open fields, and should I go home to wine and dine and sleep with my wife? I swear that I will never be guilty of acting like that."

¹²"Well, stay here tonight," David told him, "and tomorrow you may return to the army."

So Uriah stayed around the palace. ¹³David invited him to dinner and got him drunk; but even so he didn't go home that night, but again he slept at the entry to the palace.

¹⁴Finally the next morning David wrote a letter to Joab and gave it to Uriah to deliver. ¹⁵The letter instructed Joab to put Uriah at the front of the hottest part of the battle—and then pull back and leave him there to die! ¹⁶So Joab assigned Uriah to a spot close to the besieged city where he knew that the enemies' best men were fighting; ¹⁷and Uriah was killed along with several other Israeli soldiers.

¹⁸When Joab sent a report to David of how the battle was going, ¹⁹⁻²¹he told his messenger, "If the king is angry and asks, 'Why did the troops go so close to the city? Didn't they know there would be shooting from the walls? Wasn't Abimelech killed at Thebez by a woman who threw down a millstone on him?'—then tell him, 'Uriah was killed too.'"

²²So the messenger arrived at Jerusalem and gave the report to David.

²³"The enemy came out against us," he said, "and as we chased them back to the city gates, ²⁴the men on the wall attacked us; and some of our men were killed, and Uriah the Hittite is dead too."

²⁵"Well, tell Joab not to be discouraged," David said. "The sword kills one as well as another! Fight harder next time, and conquer the city; tell him he is doing well."

²⁶When Bathsheba heard that her husband was dead, she mourned for him; ²⁷then, when the period of mourning was over, David sent for her and

---

AVOIDING SIN **11:1ff.** In the episode with Bathsheba, David allowed himself to fall deeper and deeper into sin. (1) David abandoned his purpose by staying home from battle (11:1). (2) He focused on his own desires (11:3). (3) When temptation came he looked into it instead of turning away from it (11:4). (4) He sinned deliberately (11:4). (5) He tried to cover up his sin by deceiving others (11:6-15). (6) He committed murder to continue the cover-up (11:15, 17). (7) His sin was exposed (12:9). (8) His sin was punished (12:10-14). (9) The consequences of his sin affected many others (12:11, 14-15).

David could have chosen to stop and turn from evil at any stage along the way. But once the progression of sin gets started it is difficult to stop (James 1:14-15). The deeper the mess, the less we want to admit having caused it. It's much easier to stop sliding down a hill when you are near the top rather than halfway down. The best solution is to stop sin before it starts. **To begin the series of devotionals on *AVOIDING SIN*, turn to page 195.**

Family Devotions

☐ **Devotion 106**
Knowing God

Read 2 Samuel 12:1-11

It was Kurt's and Kristen's responsibility to see that the swimming pool got the proper amount of chlorine and other chemicals, but they hadn't done their job. Now the water was green. This meant they couldn't swim for two whole days.

"I'll bet these two days are going to be the hottest ones all summer," moaned Kurt, as he wiped the sweat off his forehead. "I can't believe that the water turned green so fast. It didn't look that bad yesterday."

"You're right," sighed Kristen, fanning herself. "We should have used the water tester. By the time we could see that the algae was growing, it was too late to prevent it with chemicals."

"Did you say you haven't been using the water tester to see whether or not you needed to add chemicals?" Mom asked.

"Yeah," replied Kurt. "We thought we'd be able to tell if the water was getting dirty just by looking at it."

"How could all of that green stuff get in the pool overnight?"

"You didn't *see* it yesterday," responded Mom. "The algae was there all right, but you needed to use the water tester so that you would know that it was there. That reminds me of some sins," she remarked. "Some little actions hardly seem like sin at all, but given a chance to grow, they can become very ugly."

"Too bad we don't have a guide to tell us when there's a problem—like we have the water tester for the pool," observed Kristen.

"We do!" exclaimed Kurt. "We can use the Bible. It's our guide to help us know when our actions aren't right, so we can change them."

"Well, I think you two have learned some good lessons from this experience," said Mom.

Both children nodded, and Kurt grinned as he said, "C'mon, Kristen. No need to use the water tester for the pool today, but let's go use our other guide—the Bible."

Knowing God Memory Verse

Oh, that we might know the Lord! Let us press on to know him, and he will respond to us as surely as the coming of dawn or the rain of early spring.
Hosea 6:3

How About You?

Do you ever have trouble with little sins getting out of control? Do your actions measure up to God's standards? Do you know what God says about lying? Cheating? Loving? Forgiving? The Bible is the guide to test your actions. Use it daily. *D. R.*

- For the next devotional, turn to page 335. • For the next devotional on *Knowing God*, turn to page 595.
- For notes on *Knowing God*, see pages 129, 610, 815, and 1208.

brought her to the palace and she became one of his wives; and she gave birth to his son. But the Lord was very displeased with what David had done.

12 Nathan Scolds David

So the Lord sent the prophet Nathan to tell David this story:

"There were two men in a certain city, one very rich, owning many flocks of sheep and herds of goats; ³and the other very poor, owning nothing but a little lamb he had managed to buy. It was his children's pet, and he fed it from his own plate and let it drink from his own cup; he cuddled it in his arms like a baby daughter. ⁴Recently a guest arrived at the home of the rich man. But instead of killing a lamb from his own flocks for food for the traveler, he took the poor man's lamb and roasted it and served it."

⁵David was furious. "I swear by the living God," he vowed, "any man who would do a thing like that should be put to death; ⁶he shall repay four lambs to the poor man for the one he stole and for having no pity."

⁷Then Nathan said to David, *"You* are that rich man! The Lord God of Israel says, 'I made you king of Israel and saved you from the power of Saul. ⁸I gave you his palace and his wives and the kingdoms of Israel and Judah; and if that had not been enough, I would have given you much, much more. ⁹Why, then, have you despised the laws of God and done this horrible deed? For you have murdered Uriah and stolen his wife. ¹⁰Therefore murder shall be a constant threat in your family from this time on because you have insulted me by taking Uriah's wife. ¹¹I vow that because of what you have done, I will cause your own household to rebel against you. I will give your wives to another man, and he will go to bed with them in public view. ¹²You did it secretly, but I will do this to you openly, in the sight of all Israel.'"

¹³"I have sinned against the Lord," David confessed to Nathan.

Then Nathan replied, "Yes, but the Lord has forgiven you, and you won't die for this sin. ¹⁴But you have given great opportunity to the enemies of the Lord to despise and blaspheme him, so your child shall die."

¹⁵Then Nathan returned to his home. And the Lord made Bathsheba's baby deathly sick. ¹⁶David begged him to spare the child and went without food, and lay all night before the Lord on the bare earth. ¹⁷The leaders of the nation pleaded with him to get up and eat with them, but he refused. ¹⁸Then, on the seventh day, the baby died. David's aides were afraid to tell him.

"He was so broken up about the baby being sick," they said, "what will he do to himself when we tell him the child is dead?"

¹⁹But when David saw them whispering, he realized what had happened.

"Is the baby dead?" he asked.

"Yes," they replied, "he is." ²⁰Then David got up off the ground, washed himself, brushed his hair, changed his clothes, and went into the Tabernacle and worshiped the Lord. Then he returned to the palace and ate. ²¹His aides were amazed.

"We don't understand you," they told him. "While the baby was still living, you wept and refused to eat; but now that the baby is dead, you have stopped your mourning and are eating again."

²²David replied, "I fasted and wept while the child was alive, for I said, 'Perhaps the Lord will be gracious to me and let the child live.' ²³But why should I fast when he is dead? Can I bring him back again? I shall go to him, but he shall not return to me."

²⁴Then David comforted Bathsheba; and when he slept with her, she conceived and gave birth to a son and named him Solomon. And the Lord loved the baby, ²⁵and sent congratulations and blessings through Nathan the prophet. David nicknamed the baby Jedidiah (meaning, "Beloved of Jehovah") because of the Lord's interest. ²⁶,²⁷Meanwhile Joab and the Israeli army were successfully ending their siege of Rabbah the capital of Ammon. Joab sent messengers to tell David, "Rabbah and its beautiful harbor are ours! ²⁸Now bring the rest of the army and finish the job, so that you will get the credit for the victory instead of me."

²⁹,³⁰So David led his army to Rabbah and captured it. Tremendous amounts of loot were carried back to Jerusalem, and David took the king of Rabbah's crown—a $50,000 treasure made from solid gold set with gems—and placed it on his own head. ³¹He made slaves of the people of the city and made them labor with saws, picks, and axes and work in the brick kilns; that is the way he treated all of the cities of the Ammonites. Then David and the army returned to Jerusalem.

13 Amnon Rapes Tamar

Prince Absalom, David's son, had a beautiful sister named Tamar. And Prince Amnon (her half brother) fell desperately in love with her. ²Amnon became so tormented by his love for her that he became ill. He had no way of talking to her, for the girls and young men were kept strictly apart. ³But Amnon had a very crafty

Family Devotions

☐ **DEVOTION 107**
CONFESSING SIN

Read 2 Samuel 12:13-20

Confessing Sin
Memory Verse

Create in me a new, clean heart, O God, filled with clean thoughts and right desires.
Psalm 51:10

This is so boring, Brenda thought as she trudged along behind her mother at the grocery store. "May I walk around while you wait in line for cold cuts?" she asked. "I'll obey our shopping rules." Mother hesitated, but then agreed to let Brenda walk off some of her excess energy.

I'll see how many times I can circle up this aisle and down the next one before the man at the delicatessen calls the number on Mom's ticket, Brenda thought. She set the goal to complete her route five times. "Oh no!" Brenda murmured as she finished her fourth round. "Mom's up next!" She increased her speed, forgetting the no running rule. She raced around the bend, her arm swung out, and *splat!* Two large jars of applesauce smashed to the floor.

Mother came quickly, and Brenda dragged her feet as Mother propelled her to the service desk. Brenda could hardly hold back tears as she told the assistant manager what happened. "Someone will clean up the mess right away," the man assured her.

"And Brenda will pay for the jars," said Mother firmly. As they walked to the checkout, Mother added, "I'll pay for the broken jars now, but you'll have to pay me back with your own money."

"But I don't have very much money. And I am sorry for what I did," whined Brenda. She sighed. "I wish I could make those jars go back up on the shelf, unsmashed."

"But you can't, can you?" said Mother. She wrapped her arm around Brenda. "I know you're sorry; but the jars are still broken, and you still need to pay for them." She paused. "That's the way it is with sin," she added. "When we're sorry and confess our sin, God forgives us. But sin still has consequences. When you're tempted to sin, it's good to remember that."

How About You?
Do you find yourself doing things you know you shouldn't do? When that happens, it's your responsibility to tell God what you've done and to ask him to remove the sin. But don't forget that even though you've been forgiven, there may still be a price to pay. Today's Scripture gives an example of that. *N. E. K.*

• For the next devotional, turn to page 339.   • For the next devotional on CONFESSING SIN, turn to page 457.
• For notes on CONFESSING SIN, see pages 429, 479, 836, 881, and 1220.

friend—his cousin Jonadab (the son of David's brother Shimeah).

⁴One day Jonadab said to Amnon, "What's the trouble? Why should the son of a king look so haggard morning after morning?"

So Amnon told him, "I am in love with Tamar, my half sister."

⁵"Well," Jonadab said, "I'll tell you what to do. Go back to bed and pretend you are sick; when your father comes to see you, ask him to let Tamar come and prepare some food for you. Tell him you'll feel better if she feeds you."

⁶So Amnon did. And when the king came to see him, Amnon asked him for this favor—that his sister Tamar be permitted to come and cook a little something for him to eat. ⁷David agreed and sent word to Tamar to go to Amnon's quarters and prepare some food for him. ⁸So she did and went into his bedroom so that he could watch her mix some dough; then she baked some special bread for him. ⁹But when she set the serving tray before him, he refused to eat!

"Everyone get out of here," he told his servants; so they all left the apartment.

¹⁰Then he said to Tamar, "Now bring me the food again here in my bedroom and feed it to me." So Tamar took it to him. ¹¹But as she was standing there before him, he grabbed her and demanded, "Come to bed with me, my darling."

¹²"Oh, Amnon," she cried. "Don't be foolish! Don't do this to me! You know what a serious crime it is in Israel. ¹³Where could I go in my shame? And you would be called one of the greatest fools in Israel. Please, just speak to the king about it, for he will let you marry me."

¹⁴But he wouldn't listen to her; and since he was stronger than she, he forced her. ¹⁵Then suddenly his love turned to hate, and now he hated her more than he had loved her.

"Get out of here!" he snarled at her.

¹⁶"No, no!" she cried. "To reject me now is a greater crime than the other you did to me."

But he wouldn't listen to her. ¹⁷,¹⁸He shouted for his valet and demanded, "Throw this woman out and lock the door behind her."

So he put her out. She was wearing a long robe with sleeves, as was the custom in those days for virgin daughters of the king. ¹⁹Now she tore the robe and put ashes on her head and with her head in her hands went away crying.

²⁰Her brother Absalom asked her, "Is it true that Amnon raped you? Don't be so upset, since it's all in the family anyway. It's not anything to worry about!"

So Tamar lived as a desolate woman in her brother Absalom's quarters.

²¹⁻²⁴When King David heard what had happened, he was very angry, but Absalom said nothing one way or the other about this to Amnon. However, he hated him with a deep hatred because of what he had done to his sister. Then, two years later, when Absalom's sheep were being sheared at Baal-hazor in Ephraim, Absalom invited his father and all his brothers to come to a feast to celebrate the occasion.

²⁵The king replied, "No, my boy; if we all came, we would be too much of a burden on you."

Absalom pressed him, but he wouldn't come, though he sent his thanks.

²⁶"Well, then," Absalom said, "if you can't come, how about sending my brother Amnon instead?"

"Why Amnon?" the king asked.

²⁷Absalom kept on urging the matter until finally the king agreed and let all of his sons attend, including Amnon.

²⁸Absalom told his men, "Wait until Amnon gets drunk, then, at my signal, kill him! Don't be afraid. I'm the one who gives the orders around here, and this is a command. Take courage and do it!"

²⁹,³⁰So they murdered Amnon. Then the other sons of the king jumped on their mules and fled. As they were on the way back to Jerusalem, the report reached David: "Absalom has killed all of your sons, and not one is left alive!"

³¹The king jumped up, ripped off his robe, and fell prostrate to the ground. His aides also tore their clothes in horror and sorrow.

³²,³³But just then Jonadab (the son of David's brother Shimeah) arrived and said, "No, not all have been killed! It was only Amnon! Absalom has been plotting this ever since Amnon raped Tamar. No, no! Your sons aren't all dead! It was only Amnon."

³⁴Meanwhile Absalom escaped. Now the watchman on the Jerusalem wall saw a great crowd coming toward the city along the road at the side of the hill.

³⁵"See!" Jonadab told the king. "There they are now! Your sons are coming, just as I said."

³⁶They soon arrived, weeping and sobbing, and the king and his officials wept with them. ³⁷⁻³⁹Absalom fled to King Talmai of Geshur (the son of Ammihud) and stayed there three years. Meanwhile David, now reconciled to Amnon's death, longed day after day for fellowship with his son Absalom.

14 A Widow Asks for Help

When General Joab realized how much the king was longing to see Absalom, ²,³he sent for a woman of Tekoa who had a reputation for great wisdom and told her to ask for an appointment with the king. He told her what to say to him.

"Pretend you are in mourning," Joab instructed her. "Wear mourning clothes, and dishevel your hair as though you have been in deep sorrow for a long time."

⁴When the woman approached the king, she fell face downward on the floor in front of him, and cried out, "O king! Help me!"

⁵,⁶"What's the trouble?" he asked.

"I am a widow," she replied, "and my two sons had a fight out in the field, and since no one was there to part them, one of them was killed. ⁷Now the rest of the family is demanding that I surrender my other son to them to be executed for murdering his brother. But if I do that, I will have no one left, and my husband's name will be destroyed from the face of the earth."

⁸"Leave it with me," the king told her. "I'll see to it that no one touches him."

⁹"Oh, thank you, my lord," she replied. "And I'll take the responsibility if you are criticized for helping me like this."

¹⁰"Don't worry about that!" the king replied. "If anyone objects, bring him to me; I can assure you he will never complain again!"

¹¹Then she said, "Please swear to me by God that you won't let anyone harm my son. I want no more bloodshed."

"I vow by God," he replied, "that not a hair of your son's head shall be disturbed!"

¹²"Please let me ask one more thing of you!" she said.

"Go ahead," he replied. "Speak!"

¹³"Why don't you do as much for all the people of God as you have promised to do for me?" she asked. "You have convicted yourself in making this decision, because you have refused to bring home your own banished son. ¹⁴All of us must die eventually; our lives are like water that is poured out on the ground—it can't be gathered up again. But God will bless you with a longer life if you will find a way to bring your son back from his exile. ¹⁵,¹⁶But I have come to plead with you for my son because my life and my son's life have been threatened, and I said to myself, 'Perhaps the king will listen to me and rescue us from those who would end our existence in Israel. ¹⁷Yes, the king will give us peace again.' I know that you are like the angel of God and can discern good from evil. May God be with you."

¹⁸"I want to know one thing," the king replied.

"Yes, my lord?" she asked.

¹⁹"Did Joab send you here?"

And the woman replied, "How can I deny it? Yes, Joab sent me and told me what to say. ²⁰He did it in order to place the matter before you in a different light. But you are as wise as an angel of God, and you know everything that happens!"

²¹So the king sent for Joab and told him, "All right, go and bring back Absalom."

²²Joab fell to the ground before the king and blessed him and said, "At last I know that you like me! For you have granted me this request!"

²³Then Joab went to Geshur and brought Absalom back to Jerusalem.

²⁴"He may go to his own quarters," the king ordered, "but he must never come here. I refuse to see him."

²⁵Now no one in Israel was such a handsome specimen of manhood as Absalom, and no one else received such praise. ²⁶He cut his hair only once a year—and then only because it weighed three pounds and was too much of a load to carry around! ²⁷He had three sons and one daughter, Tamar, who was a very beautiful girl.

²⁸After Absalom had been in Jerusalem for two years and had not yet seen the king, ²⁹he sent for Joab to ask him to intercede for him; but Joab wouldn't come. Absalom sent for him again, but again he refused to come.

³⁰So Absalom said to his servants, "Go and set fire to that barley field of Joab's next to mine," and they did.

³¹Then Joab came to Absalom and demanded, "Why did your servants set my field on fire?"

³²And Absalom replied, "Because I wanted you to ask the king why he brought me back from Geshur if he didn't intend to see me. I might as well have stayed there. Let me have an interview with the king; then if he finds that I am guilty of murder, let him execute me."

³³So Joab told the king what Absalom had said. Then at last David summoned Absalom, and he came and bowed low before the king, and David kissed him.

15 Absalom Rebels

Absalom then bought a magnificent chariot and chariot horses, and hired fifty footmen to run ahead of him. ²He got up early every morning and went out to the gate of the city; and when anyone came to bring a case to the king for trial, Absalom called him over and expressed interest in his problem.

³He would say, "I can see that you are right in this matter; it's unfortunate that the king doesn't have anyone to assist him in hearing these cases.

CULTIVATING GODLY ATTITUDES 15:14 If David had not escaped from Jerusalem, there might have been a fight that would have destroyed both him and the innocent inhabitants of the city. Some fights that we think are necessary may be costly and destructive to those around us. When you're involved in a conflict, seek what is best for everyone involved, not just what you want to do. **To begin the series of devotionals on CULTIVATING GODLY ATTITUDES, turn to page 121.**

4"I surely wish I were the judge; then anyone with a lawsuit could come to me, and I would give him justice!"

5And when anyone came to bow to him, Absalom wouldn't let him, but shook his hand instead! 6So in this way Absalom stole the hearts of all the people of Israel.

7,8After four years, Absalom said to the king, "Let me go to Hebron to sacrifice to the Lord in fulfillment of a vow I made to him while I was at Geshur—that if he would bring me back to Jerusalem, I would sacrifice to him."

9"All right," the king told him, "go and fulfill your vow."

So Absalom went to Hebron. 10But while he was there, he sent spies to every part of Israel to incite rebellion against the king. "As soon as you hear the trumpets," his message read, "you will know that Absalom has been crowned in Hebron." 11He took two hundred men from Jerusalem with him as guests, but they knew nothing of his intentions. 12While he was offering the sacrifice, he sent for Ahithophel, one of David's counselors who lived in Giloh. Ahithophel declared for Absalom, as did more and more others. So the conspiracy became very strong.

13A messenger soon arrived in Jerusalem to tell King David, "All Israel has joined Absalom in a conspiracy against you!"

14"Then we must flee at once or it will be too late!" was David's instant response to his men. "If we get out of the city before he arrives, both we and the city of Jerusalem will be saved."

15"We are with you," his aides replied. "Do as you think best."

16So the king and his household set out at once. He left no one behind except ten of his young wives to keep the palace in order. 17,18David paused at the edge of the city to let his troops move past him to lead the way—six hundred Gittites who had come with him from Gath, and the Cherethites and Pelethites.

19,20But suddenly the king turned to Ittai, the captain of the six hundred Gittites, and said to him, "What are you doing here? Go on back with your men to Jerusalem, to your king, for you are a guest in Israel, a foreigner in exile. It seems but yesterday that you arrived, and now today should I force you to wander with us, who knows where? Go on back and take your troops with you, and may the Lord be merciful to you."

21But Ittai replied, "I vow by God and by your own life that wherever you go, I will go, no matter what happens—whether it means life or death."

22So David replied, "All right, come with us." Then Ittai and his six hundred men and their families went along.

23There was deep sadness throughout the city as the king and his retinue passed by, crossed Kidron Brook, and went out into the country. 24Abiathar and Zadok and the Levites took the Ark of the Covenant of God and set it down beside the road until everyone had passed. 25,26Then, following David's instructions, Zadok took the Ark back into the city. "If the Lord sees fit," David said, "he will bring me back to see the Ark and the Tabernacle again. But if he is through with me, well, let him do what seems best to him."

27Then the king told Zadok, "Look, here is my plan. Return quietly to the city with your son Ahimaaz and Abiathar's son Jonathan. 28I will stop at the ford of the Jordan River and wait there for a message from you. Let me know what happens in Jerusalem before I disappear into the wilderness."

29So Zadok and Abiathar carried the Ark of God back into the city and stayed there.

30David walked up the road that led to the Mount of Olives, weeping as he went. His head was covered and his feet were bare as a sign of mourning. And the people who were with him covered their heads and wept as they climbed the mountain. 31When someone told David that Ahithophel, his advisor, was backing Absalom, David prayed, "O Lord, please make Ahithophel give Absalom foolish advice!" 32As they reached the spot at the top of the Mount of Olives where people worshiped God, David found Hushai the Archite waiting for him with torn clothing and earth upon his head.

33,34But David told him, "If you go with me, you will only be a burden; return to Jerusalem and tell Absalom, 'I will counsel you as I did your father.' Then you can frustrate and counter Ahithophel's advice. 35,36Zadok and Abiathar, the priests, are there. Tell them the plans that are being made to capture me, and they will send their sons Ahimaaz and Jonathan to find me and tell me what is going on."

37So David's friend Hushai returned to the city, getting there just as Absalom arrived.

16 Ziba Joins David

David was just past the top of the hill when Ziba, the manager of Mephibosheth's household, caught up with him. He was leading two donkeys loaded with two hundred loaves of bread, one hundred clusters of raisins, one hundred bunches of grapes, and a small barrel of wine.

2"What are these for?" the king asked Ziba.

And Ziba replied, "The donkeys are for your people to ride on, and the bread and summer fruit are for the young men to eat; the wine is to be

FAMILY DEVOTIONS

☐ **DEVOTION 108**
CONTENTMENT

Read 2 Samuel 16:1-4; 19:24-30

David frowned when he looked outside. "It can't rain today," he grumbled. "It will spoil everything!" It was David's birthday and his grandparents were coming for a picnic.

Just then the phone rang, and Mom went to the kitchen to answer it. "Grandma wants to talk to you, David," she called a little later.

"Some birthday," David muttered when he finished talking with his grandmother. "Grandpa hurt his back and has to stay in bed. They'll try to come next week instead of today. It's going to be a lonely day!"

Mom hugged David. "I'm sorry things aren't working out the way we planned. But we'll do something else today, and we'll celebrate your birthday next week."

"I have an idea," said Dad. "Who else might be lonely today?"

"Maybe Jeff," said David. "His father died a couple of months ago."

"Call him up," suggested Dad, "and see if he can come over."

Jeff was delighted with the invitation, and he and David had a great time together. David was surprised to find that the two of them had many things in common.

Before bedtime, David and his dad had a talk. "I expected my birthday to be perfect," David said, "and then everything went wrong. But I found out that things don't have to happen just one certain way in order to have a good time. I'm really glad I had a chance to spend the day with Jeff."

Contentment Memory Verse

I know how to live on almost nothing or with everything. I have learned the secret of contentment in every situation, whether it be a full stomach or hunger, plenty or want.
Philippians 4:12

How About You?

Have you found that things don't always work out the way you hope? Mephibosheth certainly had reason to be angry when he found that his servant had lied about him to King David. But instead of being angry and trying to work things out himself, Mephibosheth was content with whatever David thought was fair. In the same way, we need to be content with whatever God plans for us—even when it's different from what we would plan for ourselves. J. H.

• For the next devotional, turn to page 343.   • For the next devotional on CONTENTMENT, turn to page 1159.
• For notes on CONTENTMENT, see pages 542, 547, 902, and 1063.

taken with you into the wilderness for any who become faint."

³"And where is Mephibosheth?" the king asked him.

"He stayed at Jerusalem," Ziba replied. "He said, 'Now I'll get to be king! Today I will get back the kingdom of my father, Saul.'"

⁴"In that case," the king told Ziba, "I give you everything he owns."

"Thank you, thank you, sir," Ziba replied.

⁵As David and his party passed Bahurim, a man came out of the village cursing them. It was Shimei, the son of Gera, a member of Saul's family. ⁶He threw stones at the king and the king's officers and all the mighty warriors who surrounded them!

⁷,⁸"Get out of here, you murderer, you scoundrel!" he shouted at David. "The Lord is paying you back for murdering King Saul and his family; you stole his throne and now the Lord has given it to your son Absalom! At last you will taste some of your own medicine, you murderer!"

⁹"Why should this dead dog curse my lord the king?" Abishai demanded. "Let me go over and strike off his head!"

¹⁰"No!" the king said. "If the Lord has told him to curse me, who am I to say no? ¹¹My own son is trying to kill me, and this Benjaminite is merely cursing me. Let him alone, for no doubt the Lord has told him to do it. ¹²And perhaps the Lord will see that I am being wronged and will bless me because of these curses."

¹³So David and his men continued on, and Shimei kept pace with them on a nearby hillside, cursing as he went and throwing stones at David and tossing dust into the air. ¹⁴The king and all those who were with him were weary by the time they reached Bahurim, so they stayed there awhile and rested.

¹⁵Meanwhile, Absalom and his men arrived at Jerusalem, accompanied by Ahithophel. ¹⁶When David's friend, Hushai the Archite, arrived, he went immediately to see Absalom.

"Long live the king!" he exclaimed. "Long live the king!"

¹⁷"Is this the way to treat your friend David?" Absalom asked him. "Why aren't you with him?"

¹⁸"Because I work for the man who is chosen by the Lord and by Israel," Hushai replied. ¹⁹"And anyway, why shouldn't I? I helped your father and now I will help you!"

²⁰Then Absalom turned to Ahithophel and asked him, "What shall I do next?"

²¹Ahithophel told him, "Go and sleep with your father's wives, for he has left them here to keep the house. Then all Israel will know that you have insulted him beyond the possibility of reconciliation, and they will all close ranks behind you."

²²So a tent was erected on the roof of the palace where everybody could see it, and Absalom went into the tent to lie with his father's wives. ²³(Absalom did whatever Ahithophel told him to, just as David had; for every word Ahithophel spoke seemed as wise as though it had come directly from the mouth of God.)

17 Absalom Follows Bad Advice

"Now," Ahithophel said, "give me twelve thousand men to start out after David tonight. ²,³I will come upon him while he is weary and discouraged, and he and his troops will be thrown into a panic and everyone will run away; and I will kill only the king and let all those who are with him live, and restore them to you."

⁴Absalom and all the elders of Israel approved of the plan, ⁵but Absalom said, "Ask Hushai the Archite what he thinks about this."

⁶When Hushai arrived, Absalom told him what Ahithophel had said.

"What is your opinion?" Absalom asked him. "Should we follow Ahithophel's advice? If not, speak up."

⁷"Well," Hushai replied, "this time I think Ahithophel has made a mistake. ⁸You know your father and his men; they are mighty warriors and are probably as upset as a mother bear who has been robbed of her cubs. And your father is an old soldier and isn't going to be spending the night among the troops; ⁹he has probably already hidden in some pit or cave. And when he comes out and attacks and a few of your men fall, there will be panic among your troops and everyone will start shouting that your men are being slaughtered. ¹⁰Then even the bravest of them, though they have hearts of lions, will be paralyzed with fear; for all Israel knows what a mighty man your father is and how courageous his soldiers are.

¹¹"What I suggest is that you mobilize the entire army of Israel, bringing them from as far away as Dan and Beersheba, so that you will have a huge force. And I think that you should personally lead the troops. ¹²Then when we find him we can destroy his entire army so that not one of them is left alive. ¹³And if David has escaped into some city, you will have the entire army of Israel there at your command, and we can take ropes and drag the walls of the city into the nearest valley until every stone is torn down."

¹⁴Then Absalom and all the men of Israel said, "Hushai's advice is better than Ahithophel's." For the Lord had arranged to defeat the counsel of Ahithophel, which really was the better plan, so that he could bring disaster upon Absalom! ¹⁵Then Hushai reported to Zadok and Abiathar, the priests, what Ahithophel had said and what he himself had suggested instead.

¹⁶"Quick!" he told them. "Find David and urge him not to stay at the ford of the Jordan River tonight. He must go across at once into the wilderness beyond; otherwise he will die, and his entire army with him."

¹⁷Jonathan and Ahimaaz had been staying at En-rogel so as not to be seen entering and leaving the city. Arrangements had been made for a servant girl to carry to them the messages they were to take to King David. ¹⁸But a boy saw them leaving En-rogel to go to David, and he told Absalom about it. Meanwhile, they escaped to Bahurim where a man hid them inside a well in his backyard. ¹⁹The man's wife put a cloth over the top of the well with grain on it to dry in the sun; so no one suspected they were there.

²⁰When Absalom's men arrived and asked her if she had seen Ahimaaz and Jonathan, she said they had crossed the brook and were gone. They looked for them without success and returned to Jerusalem. ²¹Then the two men crawled out of the well and hurried on to King David. "Quick!" they told him, "cross the Jordan tonight!" And they told him how Ahithophel had advised that he be captured and killed. ²²So David and all the people with him went across during the night and were all on the other bank before dawn.

²³Meanwhile, Ahithophel—publicly disgraced when Absalom refused his advice—saddled his donkey, went to his hometown, set his affairs in order, and hanged himself; so he died and was buried beside his father.

²⁴David soon arrived at Mahanaim. Meanwhile, Absalom had mobilized the entire army of Israel and was leading the men across the Jordan River. ²⁵Absalom had appointed Amasa as general of the army, replacing Joab. (Amasa was Joab's second cousin; his father was Ithra, an Ishmaelite, and his mother was Abigail, the daughter of Nahash, who was the sister of Joab's mother, Zeruiah.) ²⁶Absalom and the Israeli army now camped in the land of Gilead.

²⁷When David arrived at Mahanaim, he was warmly greeted by Shobi (son of Nahash of Rabbah, an Ammonite) and Machir (son of Ammiel of Lodebar) and Barzillai (a Gileadite of Rogelim). ²⁸,²⁹They brought him and those who were with him mats to sleep on, cooking pots, serving bowls, wheat and barley flour, parched grain, beans, lentils, honey, butter, and cheese. For they said, "You must be very tired and hungry and thirsty after your long march through the wilderness."

18 Absalom Is Defeated

David now appointed regimental colonels and company commanders over his troops. ²A third were placed under Joab's brother, Abishai (the son of Zeruiah); and a third under Ittai, the Gittite. The king planned to lead the army himself, but his men objected strongly.

³"You mustn't do it," they said, "for if we have to turn and run, and half of us die, it will make no difference to them—they will be looking only for you. You are worth ten thousand of us, and it is better that you stay here in the city and send us help if we need it."

⁴"Well, whatever you think best," the king finally replied. So he stood at the gate of the city as all the troops passed by.

⁵And the king commanded Joab, Abishai, and Ittai, "For my sake, deal gently with young Absalom." And all the troops heard the king give them this charge.

⁶So the battle began in the forest of Ephraim, ⁷and the Israeli troops were beaten back by David's men. There was a great slaughter and twenty thousand men laid down their lives that day. ⁸The battle raged all across the countryside, and more men disappeared in the forest than were killed. ⁹During the battle Absalom came upon some of David's men and as he fled on his mule, it went beneath the thick boughs of a great oak tree, and his hair caught in the branches. His mule went on, leaving him dangling in the air. ¹⁰One of David's men saw him and told Joab.

¹¹"What? You saw him there and didn't kill him?" Joab demanded. "I would have rewarded you handsomely and made you a commissioned officer."

¹²"For a million dollars I wouldn't do it," the man replied. "We all heard the king say to you and Abishai and Ittai, 'For my sake, please don't harm young Absalom.' ¹³And if I had betrayed the king by killing his son (and the king would certainly find out who did it), you yourself would be the first to accuse me."

¹⁴"Enough of this nonsense," Joab said. Then he took three daggers and plunged them into the heart of Absalom as he dangled alive from the oak. ¹⁵Ten of Joab's young armor-bearers then surrounded Absalom and finished him off. ¹⁶Then Joab blew the trumpet, and his men returned from chasing the army of Israel. ¹⁷They threw Absalom's body into a deep pit in the forest and piled a great heap of stones over it. And the army of Israel fled to their homes.

¹⁸(Absalom had built a monument to himself in the King's Valley, for he said, "I have no sons to carry on my name." He called it "Absalom's Monument," as it is still known today.)

¹⁹Then Zadok's son Ahimaaz said, "Let me run to King David with the good news that the Lord has saved him from his enemy Absalom."

²⁰"No," Joab told him, "it wouldn't be good news to the king that his son is dead. You can be my messenger some other time."

²¹Then Joab said to a man from Cush, "Go tell the king what you have seen." The man bowed and ran off.

²²But Ahimaaz pleaded with Joab, "Please let me go too."

"No, we don't need you now, my boy." Joab replied. "There is no further news to send."

²³"Yes, but let me go anyway," he begged.

And Joab finally said, "All right, go ahead." Then Ahimaaz took a shortcut across the plain and got there ahead of the man from Cush. ²⁴David was sitting at the gate of the city. When the watchman climbed the stairs to his post at the top of the wall, he saw a lone man running toward them.

²⁵He shouted the news down to David, and the king replied, "If he is alone, he has news."

As the messenger came closer, ²⁶the watchman saw another man running toward them. He shouted down, "Here comes another one."

And the king replied, "He will have more news."

²⁷"The first man looks like Ahimaaz, the son of Zadok," the watchman said.

"He is a good man and comes with good news," the king replied.

²⁸Then Ahimaaz cried out to the king, "All is well!" He bowed low with his face to the ground and said, "Blessed be the Lord your God who has destroyed the rebels who dared to stand against you."

²⁹"What of young Absalom?" the king demanded. "Is he all right?"

"When Joab told me to come, there was a lot of shouting; but I didn't know what was happening," Ahimaaz answered.

³⁰"Wait here," the king told him. So Ahimaaz stepped aside.

³¹Then the man from Cush arrived and said, "I have good news for my lord the king. Today Jehovah has rescued you from all those who rebelled against you."

³²"What about young Absalom? Is he all right?" the king demanded.

And the man replied, "May all of your enemies be as that young man is!"

³³Then the king broke into tears, and went up to his room over the gate, crying as he went. "O my son Absalom, my son, my son Absalom. If only I could have died for you! O Absalom, my son, my son."

19 David Returns to Jerusalem

Word soon reached Joab that the king was weeping and mourning for Absalom. ²As the people heard of the king's deep grief for his son, the joy of that day's wonderful victory was turned into deep sadness. ³The entire army crept back into the city as though they were ashamed and had been beaten in battle.

⁴The king covered his face with his hands and kept on weeping, "O my son Absalom! O Absalom my son, my son!"

⁵Then Joab went to the king's room and said to him, "We saved your life today and the lives of your sons, your daughters, your wives, and concubines; and yet you act like this, making us feel ashamed, as though we had done something wrong. ⁶You seem to love those who hate you, and hate those who love you. Apparently we don't mean anything to you; if Absalom had lived and all of us had died, you would be happy. ⁷Now go out there and congratulate the troops, for I swear by Jehovah that if you don't, not a single one of them will remain here during the night; then you will be worse off than you have ever been in your entire life."

⁸⁻¹⁰So the king went out and sat at the city gates, and as the news spread throughout the city that he was there, everyone went to him.

Meanwhile, there was much discussion and argument going on all across the nation: "Why aren't we talking about bringing the king back?" was the great topic everywhere. "For he saved us from our enemies, the Philistines; and Absalom, whom we made our king instead, chased him out of the country, but now Absalom is dead. Let's ask David to return and be our king again."

¹¹,¹²Then David sent Zadok and Abiathar the priests to say to the elders of Judah, "Why are you the last ones to reinstate the king? For all Israel is ready, and only you are holding out. Yet you are my own brothers, my own tribe, my own flesh and blood!"

¹³And he told them to tell Amasa, "Since you are my nephew, may God strike me dead if I do not appoint you as commander-in-chief of my army in place of Joab." ¹⁴Then Amasa convinced all the leaders of Judah, and they responded as one man. They sent word to the king, "Return to us and bring back all those who are with you."

¹⁵So the king started back to Jerusalem. And when he arrived at the Jordan River, it seemed as if everyone in Judah had come to Gilgal to meet him and escort him across the river! ¹⁶Then Shimei (the son of Gera the Benjaminite), the man from Bahurim, hurried across with the men of Judah to welcome King David. ¹⁷A thousand men from the tribe of Benjamin were with him, including Ziba, the servant of Saul, and Ziba's fifteen sons and twenty servants; they rushed down to the Jordan to arrive ahead of the king. ¹⁸They all worked hard ferrying the king's household and troops across, and helped them in every way they could.

As the king was crossing, Shimei fell down be-

FAMILY DEVOTIONS

☐ **DEVOTION 109**
FORGIVING OTHERS

Read 2 Samuel 19:15-23

Forgiving Others Memory Verse

Be gentle and ready to forgive; never hold grudges. Remember, the Lord forgave you, so you must forgive others.
Colossians 3:13

"Oooohhhh! I just can't get this checkbook to balance with the bank statement," moaned Mom.

Dad looked over her shoulder. "Last week I wrote a check for twenty dollars to Hanson Hardware," he said. "Is it listed in the checkbook?"

Mom quickly scanned the check register. "No, it's not. That helps, but it still doesn't balance."

"Mom! Mom!" Stephen burst into the room. "Melissa hit me!"

"But he hit me first," yelled Melissa.

"Well, I owed you one from last time," Stephen roared. "The Bible says if someone hits you, you have the right to hit him back!"

Mom gasped. "Why, Son! That's not what the Bible teaches at all."

"Yes, it is," replied Stephen firmly. "The Old Testament says, 'An eye for an eye, and a tooth for a tooth.'"

"Sit down," ordered Dad. "That passage isn't talking about personal vengeance. It was meant as a civil law, to insure justice in the nation of Israel. People who return blow for blow find the score is never settled. Someone always owes someone else a blow."

Mom sighed. "That sounds like my checkbook. The account never balances."

Dad nodded. "Jesus did away with the law of revenge. He told us to return good for evil. That's the only way to settle the score."

"You mean when Stephen hits me, I'm supposed to do something good for him?" Melissa asked. "That's not fair!"

Dad nodded. "God says to overcome evil with good."

Stephen and Melissa looked at each other. "We'll try," they said in unison. "Hey, this might be fun," added Stephen. "It'll sure be different."

Mom smiled. "Great. That balances one account. Now, if I could just get this checkbook to balance."

How About You?
Are you keeping score of the wrongs others do to you? Are you figuring out how you can get back at them? God's way to settle the score is to do something good for them. Try it. You'll feel a lot better when the account is balanced that way. B. W.

For the next devotional, turn to page 347. • For the next devotional on *FORGIVING OTHERS*, turn to page 917.
For notes on *FORGIVING OTHERS*, see pages 273, 356, 586, and 822.

fore him, ¹⁹and pleaded, "My lord the king, please forgive me and forget the terrible thing I did when you left Jerusalem; ²⁰for I know very well how much I sinned. That is why I have come here today, the very first person in all the tribe of Joseph to greet you."

²¹Abishai asked, "Shall not Shimei die, for he cursed the Lord's chosen king!"

²²"Don't talk to me like that!" David exclaimed. "This is not a day for execution but for celebration! I am once more king of Israel!"

²³Then, turning to Shimei, he vowed, "Your life is spared."

²⁴,²⁵Now Mephibosheth, Saul's grandson, arrived from Jerusalem to meet the king. He had not washed his feet or clothes nor trimmed his beard since the day the king left Jerusalem.

"Why didn't you come with me, Mephibosheth?" the king asked him.

²⁶And he replied, "My lord, O king, my servant Ziba deceived me. I told him, 'Saddle my donkey so that I can go with the king.' For as you know I am lame. ²⁷But Ziba has slandered me by saying that I refused to come. But I know that you are as an angel of God, so do what you think best. ²⁸I and all my relatives could expect only death from you, but instead you have honored me among all those who eat at your own table! So how can I complain?"

²⁹"All right," David replied. "My decision is that you and Ziba will divide the land equally between you."

³⁰"Give him all of it," Mephibosheth said. "I am content just to have you back again!"

³¹,³²Barzillai, who had fed the king and his army during their exile in Mahanaim, arrived from Rogelim to conduct the king across the river. He was very old now, about eighty, and very wealthy.

³³"Come across with me and live in Jerusalem," the king said to Barzillai. "I will take care of you there."

³⁴"No," he replied, "I am far too old for that. ³⁵I am eighty years old today, and life has lost its excitement. Food and wine are no longer tasty, and entertainment is not much fun; I would only be a burden to my lord the king. ³⁶Just to go across the river with you is all the honor I need! ³⁷Then let me return again to die in my own city, where my father and mother are buried. But here is Chimham. Let him go with you and receive whatever good things you want to give him."

³⁸"Good," the king agreed. "Chimham shall go with me, and I will do for him whatever I would have done for you."

³⁹So all the people crossed the Jordan with the king; and after David had kissed and blessed Barzillai, he returned home. ⁴⁰The king then went on to Gilgal, taking Chimham with him. And most of Judah and half of Israel were there to greet him. ⁴¹But the men of Israel complained to the king because only men from Judah had ferried him and his household across the Jordan.

⁴²"Why not?" the men of Judah replied. "The king is one of our own tribe. Why should this make you angry? We have charged him nothing—he hasn't fed us or given us gifts!"

⁴³"But there are ten tribes in Israel," the others replied, "so we have ten times as much right in the king as you do; why didn't you invite the rest of us? And, remember, we were the first to speak of bringing him back to be our king again."

The argument continued back and forth, and the men of Judah were very rough in their replies.

20 Sheba Rebels Against David

Then a hothead whose name was Sheba (son of Bichri, a Benjaminite) blew a trumpet and yelled, "We want nothing to do with David. Come on, you men of Israel, let's get out of here. He's not our king!"

²So all except Judah and Benjamin turned around and deserted David and followed Sheba! But the men of Judah stayed with their king, accompanying him from the Jordan to Jerusalem. ³When he arrived at his palace in Jerusalem, the king instructed that his ten wives he had left to keep house should be placed in seclusion. Their needs were to be cared for, he said, but he would no longer sleep with them as his wives. So they remained in virtual widowhood until their deaths.

⁴Then the king instructed Amasa to mobilize the army of Judah within three days and to report back at that time. ⁵So Amasa went out to notify the troops, but it took him longer than the three days he had been given.

⁶Then David said to Abishai, "That fellow Sheba is going to hurt us more than Absalom did. Quick, take my bodyguard and chase after him before he gets into a fortified city where we can't reach him."

⁷So Abishai and Joab set out after Sheba with an elite guard from Joab's army and the king's own bodyguard. ⁸⁻¹⁰As they arrived at the great stone in Gibeon, they came face to face with Amasa. Joab was wearing his uniform with a dagger strapped to his side. As he stepped forward to greet Amasa, he stealthily slipped the dagger from its sheath. "I'm glad to see you, my brother," Joab said, and took him by the beard with his right hand as though to kiss him. Amasa didn't notice the dagger in his left hand, and Joab stabbed him in the stomach with it, so that his bowels gushed out onto the ground. He did not need to strike again,

and he died there. Joab and his brother, Abishai, left him lying there and continued after Sheba.

¹¹One of Joab's young officers shouted to Amasa's troops, "If you are for David, come and follow Joab."

¹²But Amasa lay in his blood in the middle of the road, and when Joab's young officers saw that a crowd was gathering around to stare at him, they dragged him off the road into a field and threw a garment over him. ¹³With the body out of the way, everyone went on with Joab to capture Sheba.

¹⁴Meanwhile Sheba had traveled across Israel to mobilize his own clan of Bichri at the city of Abel in Beth-maacah. ¹⁵When Joab's forces arrived, they besieged Abel and built a mound to the top of the city wall and began battering it down.

¹⁶But a wise woman in the city called out to Joab, "Listen to me, Joab. Come over here so I can talk to you."

¹⁷As he approached, the woman asked, "Are you Joab?"

And he replied, "I am."

¹⁸So she told him, "There used to be a saying, 'If you want to settle an argument, ask advice at Abel.' For we always give wise counsel. ¹⁹You are destroying an ancient, peace-loving city, loyal to Israel. Should you destroy what is the Lord's?"

²⁰And Joab replied, "That isn't it at all. ²¹All I want is a man named Sheba from the hill country of Ephraim, who has revolted against King David. If you will deliver him to me, we will leave the city in peace."

"All right," the woman replied, "we will throw his head over the wall to you."

²²Then the woman went to the people with her wise advice, and they cut off Sheba's head and threw it out to Joab. And he blew the trumpet and called his troops back from the attack, and they returned to the king at Jerusalem.

²³Joab was commander-in-chief of the army, and Benaiah was in charge of the king's bodyguard. ²⁴Adoram was in charge of the forced labor battalions, and Jehoshaphat was the historian who kept the records. ²⁵Sheva was the secretary, and Zadok and Abiathar were the chief priests. ²⁶Ira the Jairite was David's personal chaplain.

21 Saul's Sons Are Executed

There was a famine during David's reign that lasted year after year for three years, and David spent much time in prayer about it. Then the Lord said, "The famine is because of the guilt of Saul and his family, for they murdered the Gibeonites."

²So King David summoned the Gibeonites. They were not part of Israel but were what was left of the nation of the Amorites. Israel had sworn not to kill them; but Saul, in his nationalistic zeal, had tried to wipe them out.

³David asked them, "What can I do for you to rid ourselves of this guilt and to induce you to ask God to bless us?"

⁴"Well, money won't do it," the Gibeonites replied, "and we don't want to see Israelites executed in revenge."

"What can I do, then?" David asked. "Just tell me and I will do it for you."

⁵,⁶"Well, then," they replied, "give us seven of Saul's sons—the sons of the man who did his best to destroy us. We will hang them before the Lord in Gibeon, the city of King Saul."

"All right," the king said, "I will do it."

⁷He spared Jonathan's son Mephibosheth, who was Saul's grandson, because of the oath between himself and Jonathan. ⁸But he gave them Saul's two sons Armoni and Mephibosheth, whose mother was Rizpah, the daughter of Aiah. He also gave them the five adopted sons of Michal that she brought up for Saul's daughter Merab, the wife of Adriel. ⁹The men of Gibeon impaled them in the mountain before the Lord. So all seven of them died together at the beginning of the barley harvest.

¹⁰Then Rizpah, the mother of two of the men, spread sackcloth upon a rock and stayed there through the entire harvest season to prevent the vultures from tearing at their bodies during the day and the wild animals from eating them at night. ¹¹When David learned what she had done, ¹²⁻¹⁴he arranged for the men's bones to be buried in the grave of Saul's father, Kish. At the same time he sent a request to the men of Jabesh-gilead, asking them to bring him the bones of Saul and Jonathan. They had stolen their bodies from the public square at Beth-shan where the Philistines had impaled them after they had died in battle on Mount Gilboa. So their bones were brought to him. Then at last God answered prayer and ended the famine.

¹⁵Once when the Philistines were at war with Israel, and David and his men were in the thick of the battle, David became weak and exhausted. ¹⁶Ishbi-benob, a giant whose speartip weighed more than twelve pounds and who was sporting a new suit of armor, closed in on David and was about to kill him. ¹⁷But Abishai, the son of Zeruiah, came to his rescue and killed the Philistine. After that David's men declared, "You are not going out to battle again! Why should we risk snuffing out the light of Israel?"

¹⁸Later, during a war with the Philistines at Gob, Sibbecai the Hushathite killed Saph, another giant. ¹⁹At still another time and at the same place, Elhanan killed the brother of Goliath the Gittite,

whose spearhandle was as huge as a weaver's beam! ²⁰,²¹And once when the Philistines and the Israelis were fighting at Gath, a giant with six fingers on each hand and six toes on each foot defied Israel, and David's nephew Jonathan—the son of David's brother Shimei—killed him. ²²These four were from the tribe of giants in Gath and were killed by David's troops.

22 David's Song of Praise

David sang this song to the Lord after he had rescued him from Saul and from all his other enemies:

²"Jehovah is my rock,
My fortress and my Savior.
³I will hide in God,
Who is my rock and my refuge.
He is my shield
And my salvation,
My refuge and high tower.
Thank you, O my Savior,
For saving me from all my enemies.
⁴I will call upon the Lord,
Who is worthy to be praised;
He will save me from all my enemies.
⁵The waves of death surrounded me;
Floods of evil burst upon me;
⁶I was trapped and bound
By hell and death;
⁷But I called upon the Lord in my distress,
And he heard me from his Temple.
My cry reached his ears.
⁸Then the earth shook and trembled;
The foundations of the heavens quaked
Because of his wrath.
⁹Smoke poured from his nostrils;
Fire leaped from his mouth
And burned up all before him,
Setting fire to the world.
¹⁰He bent the heavens down and came to earth;
He walked upon dark clouds.
¹¹He rode upon the glorious—
On the wings of the wind.
¹²Darkness surrounded him,
And clouds were thick around him;
¹³The earth was radiant with his brightness.
¹⁴The Lord thundered from heaven;
The God above all gods gave out a mighty shout.
¹⁵He shot forth his arrows of lightning
And routed his enemies.
¹⁶By the blast of his breath
Was the sea split in two.
The bottom of the sea appeared.
¹⁷From above, he rescued me.
He drew me out from the waters;
¹⁸He saved me from powerful enemies,
From those who hated me
And from those who were too strong for me.
¹⁹They came upon me
In the day of my calamity,
But the Lord was my salvation.
²⁰He set me free and rescued me,
For I was his delight.
²¹The Lord rewarded me for my goodness,
For my hands were clean;
²²And I have not departed from my God.
²³I knew his laws,
And I obeyed them.
²⁴I was perfect in obedience
And kept myself from sin.
²⁵That is why the Lord has done so much for me,
For he sees that I am clean.
²⁶You are merciful to the merciful;
You show your perfections
To the blameless.
²⁷To those who are pure,
You show yourself pure;
But you destroy those who are evil.
²⁸You will save those in trouble,
But you bring down the haughty;
For you watch their every move.
²⁹O Lord, you are my light!
You make my darkness bright.
³⁰By your power I can crush an army;
By your strength I leap over a wall.
³¹As for God, his way is perfect;
The word of the Lord is true.
He shields all who hide behind him.
³²Our Lord alone is God;
We have no other Savior.
³³God is my strong fortress;
He has made me safe.
³⁴He causes the good to walk a steady tread
Like mountain goats upon the rocks.
³⁵He gives me skill in war
And strength to bend a bow of bronze.
³⁶You have given me the shield of your salvation;
Your gentleness has made me great.
³⁷You have made wide steps for my feet,
To keep them from slipping.
³⁸I have chased my enemies
And destroyed them.
I did not stop till all were gone.
³⁹I have destroyed them
So that none can rise again.
They have fallen beneath my feet.
⁴⁰For you have given me strength for the battle
And have caused me to subdue
All those who rose against me.
⁴¹You have made my enemies

Family Devotions

☐ **Devotion 110**
Receiving Christ as Savior

Read 2 Samuel 22:21-27

Receiving Christ as Savior
Memory Verse

For God loved the world so much that he gave his only Son so that anyone who believes in him shall not perish but have eternal life.
John 3:16

"Half of these nuts aren't any good," complained Kathy, who had been cracking nuts for the dessert her mother was making. "They're black and dried up on the inside, even though they look fine on the outside!" She picked up a nut and showed it to Mother.

"I bet I can tell which ones are good," insisted her brother, Karl, shaking one. "This one's good." Kathy took it and cracked it open. Sure enough, it was good. "See," said Karl gleefully. "I'll pick them for you." He chose another one. "This one's good too." Kathy cracked it open. No, it was dried up. Karl frowned and handed her another nut. It, too, was no good.

"You can't tell any better than I can," declared Kathy, cracking one Karl had rejected. It was good.

As the family ate dessert that evening, Kathy told Dad about the trouble with the nuts. "They sound like some people I know," observed Dad.

Karl's eyes twinkled. "You know some nutty people?"

Dad smiled. "I know some people who look good on the outside, but I'm not sure what we'd see if we could look on the inside—at their hearts," he said. "Jesus said the scribes and Pharisees were like that. They appeared to be good, but they really were hypocrites."

"I wonder how many people are like that today—even among church members," added Mother. "They all look good to us. We really can't tell for sure who has accepted Jesus as Savior, but God knows. He sees through the shell and knows what each person is like on the inside."

Kathy nodded. "We can't fool God, can we?" she said.

How About You?
Are you fooling people? Do you go to church, say your memory verses, and look good to others? Looking good on the outside isn't enough. Have you truly trusted Jesus as Savior? If you haven't done so, accept him today. Be clean and whole inside as well as outside. H. M.

• For the next devotional, turn to page 349. • For the next devotional on *Receiving Christ as Savior*, turn to page 703. • For notes on *Receiving Christ as Savior*, see pages 839, 842, 1146, 1234, and 1240.

Turn and run away;
I have destroyed them all.
⁴²They looked in vain for help;
They cried to God,
But he refused to answer.
⁴³I beat them into dust;
I crushed and scattered them
Like dust along the streets.
⁴⁴You have preserved me
From the rebels of my people;
You have preserved me
As the head of the nations.
Foreigners shall serve me
⁴⁵And shall quickly submit to me
When they hear of my power.
⁴⁶They shall lose heart
And come, trembling,
From their hiding places.
⁴⁷The Lord lives.
Blessed be my Rock.
Praise to him—
The Rock of my salvation.
⁴⁸Blessed be God
Who destroys those who oppose me
⁴⁹And rescues me from my enemies.
Yes, you hold me safe above their heads.
You deliver me from violence.
⁵⁰No wonder I give thanks to you, O Lord,
   among the nations,
And sing praises to your name.
⁵¹He gives wonderful deliverance to his king
And shows mercy to his anointed—
To David and his family,
Forever."

23 David's Last Words

These are the last words of David:

"David, the son of Jesse, speaks.
David, the man to whom God gave such wonderful success;
David, the anointed of the God of Jacob;
David, sweet psalmist of Israel:
²The Spirit of the Lord spoke by me,
And his word was on my tongue.
³The Rock of Israel said to me:
'One shall come who rules righteously,
Who rules in the fear of God.
⁴He shall be as the light of the morning;
A cloudless sunrise
When the tender grass
Springs forth upon the earth;
As sunshine after rain.'
⁵And it is my family
He has chosen!
Yes, God has made
An everlasting covenant with me;
His agreement is eternal, final, sealed.
He will constantly look after
My safety and success.
⁶But the godless are as thorns to be thrown away,
For they tear the hand that touches them.
⁷One must be armed to chop them down;
They shall be burned."

⁸These are the names of the Top Three—the most heroic men in David's army: the first was Josheb-basshebeth from Tah-chemon, known also as Adino, the Eznite. He once killed eight hundred men in one battle.

⁹Next in rank was Eleazar, the son of Dodo and grandson of Ahohi. He was one of the three men who, with David, held back the Philistines that time when the rest of the Israeli army fled. ¹⁰He killed the Philistines until his hand was too tired to hold his sword; and the Lord gave him a great victory. (The rest of the army did not return until it was time to collect the loot!)

¹¹,¹²After him was Shammah, the son of Agee from Harar. Once during a Philistine attack, when all his men deserted him and fled, he stood alone at the center of a field of lentils and beat back the Philistines; and God gave him a great victory.

¹³One time when David was living in the cave of Adullam and the invading Philistines were at the valley of Rephaim, three of The Thirty—the top-ranking officers of the Israeli army—went down at harvest time to visit him. ¹⁴David was in the stronghold at the time, for Philistine marauders had occupied the nearby city of Bethlehem. ¹⁵David remarked, "How thirsty I am for some of that good water in the city well!" (The well was near the city gate.)

¹⁶So the three men broke through the Philistine ranks and drew water from the well and brought it to David. But he refused to drink it! Instead, he poured it out before the Lord.

¹⁷"No, my God," he exclaimed, "I cannot do it! This is the blood of these men who have risked their lives."

¹⁸,¹⁹Of those three men, Abishai, the brother of Joab (son of Zeruiah), was the greatest. Once he took on three hundred of the enemy single-handed and killed them all. It was by such feats that he earned a reputation equal to The Three, though he was not actually one of them. But he was the greatest of The Thirty—the top-ranking officers of the army—and was their leader.

²⁰There was also Benaiah (son of Jehoiada), a heroic soldier from Kabzeel. Benaiah killed two giants, sons of Ariel of Moab. Another time he went down into a pit and, despite the slippery snow on the ground, took on a lion that was

Family Devotions

☐ DEVOTION 111
GIVING TO GOD

Read 2 Samuel 24:18-24

"Do you have your offerings to put in the collection plate?" Mom asked Joanne and Betsy.

Joanne nodded, but Betsy shook her head. "I spent all my allowance," she confessed. "Will you give me some money for the offering, Mom?" Mom frowned, but she reached into her wallet, took out some quarters, and handed them to Betsy.

That afternoon, Betsy had a suggestion for her mother. "If you can't think of anything to get me for my birthday, I have some ideas," she said.

"I've been thinking about that," replied Mom, "and I've decided to see if Joanne has any extra socks in her drawer that I can give you." She smiled brightly at Betsy. "Or maybe she has something else she wouldn't mind giving up."

"Mom!" said Betsy. "I'm serious."

"What's wrong with that idea?" Mom asked, pretending to be surprised.

"It's . . . it's leftovers," said Betsy. "Besides, it wouldn't really be from you if you gave me something that belonged to Joanne." Betsy frowned. Then she added, "It seems like a thoughtless present."

"You're right," agreed Mom. "It wouldn't truly be giving if I wrapped something that didn't belong to me in the first place—something I didn't put any thought, effort, or money into—now would it?" Betsy shook her head. "This morning at church you were satisfied to offer God a gift that wasn't really from you," Mom reminded her.

"But you used to always give us money for church," argued Betsy.

"When you were too young to have your own money, I gave you some so you'd get in the habit of giving to God," Mom said. "Now that you have a little of your own cash, it's up to you to willingly give some of that to the Lord. Then you'll be giving a real offering instead of simply dropping some of my money in the plate."

Giving to God Memory Verse

Bring all the tithes into the storehouse so that there will be food enough in my Temple; if you do, I will open up the windows of heaven for you and pour out a blessing so great you won't have room enough to take it in! Try it! Let me prove it to you!
Malachi 3:10

How About You?

Do you give back to the Lord a portion of the money you receive? David said he didn't want to give the Lord an offering that cost him nothing. When you give, give from your heart and from your own blessings, rather than from your parents'. *N. E. K.*

• For the next devotional, turn to page 355.   • For the next devotional on GIVING TO GOD, turn to page 621.
• For notes on GIVING TO GOD, see pages 182, 433, and 1128.

caught there and killed it. ²¹Another time, armed only with a staff, he killed an Egyptian warrior who was armed with a spear; he wrenched the spear from the Egyptian's hand and killed him with it. ²²These were some of the deeds that gave Benaiah almost as much renown as the Top Three. ²³He was one of the greatest of The Thirty, but was not actually one of the Top Three. And David made him chief of his bodyguard.

²⁴⁻³⁹Asahel, the brother of Joab, was also one of The Thirty. Others were:

Elhanan (son of Dodo) from Bethlehem;
Shammah from Harod;
Elika from Harod;
Helez from Palti;
Ira (son of Ikkesh) from Tekoa;
Abiezer from Anathoth;
Mebunnai from Hushath;
Zalmon from Ahoh;
Maharai from Netophah;
Heleb (son of Baanah) from Netophah;
Ittai (son of Ribai) from Gibeah, of the tribe of Benjamin;
Benaiah of Pirathon;
Hiddai from the brooks of Gaash;
Abi-albon from Arbath;
Azmaveth from Bahurim;
Eliahba from Shaalbon;
The sons of Jashen;
Jonathan;
Shammah from Harar;
Ahiam (the son of Sharar) from Harar;
Eliphelet (son of Ahasbai) from Maacah;
Eliam (the son of Ahithophel) from Gilo;
Hezro from Carmel;
Paarai from Arba;
Igal (son of Nathan) from Zobah;
Bani from Gad;
Zelek from Ammon;
Naharai from Beeroth, the armor-bearer of Joab (son of Zeruiah);
Ira from Ithra;
Gareb from Ithra;
Uriah the Hittite—thirty-seven in all.

24 David's Threshing Floor

Once again the anger of the Lord flared against Israel, and he caused David to harm them by taking a national census. "Go and count the people of Israel and Judah," the Lord told him.

²So the king said to Joab, commander-in-chief of his army, "Take a census of all the people from one end of the nation to the other, so that I will know how many of them there are."

³But Joab replied, "God grant that you will live to see the day when there will be a hundred times as many people in your kingdom as there are now! But you have no right to rejoice in their strength."

⁴But the king's command overcame Joab's remonstrance; so Joab and the other army officers went out to count the people of Israel. ⁵First they crossed the Jordan and camped at Aroer, south of the city that lies in the middle of the valley of Gad, near Jazer; ⁶then they went to Gilead in the land of Tahtim-hodshi and to Dan-jaan and around to Sidon; ⁷and then to the stronghold of Tyre, and all the cities of the Hivites and Canaanites, and south to Judah as far as Beersheba. ⁸Having gone through the entire land, they completed their task in nine months and twenty days. ⁹And Joab reported the number of the people to the king—800,000 men of conscription age in Israel and 500,000 in Judah.

¹⁰But after he had taken the census, David's conscience began to bother him, and he said to the Lord, "What I did was very wrong. Please forgive this foolish wickedness of mine."

¹¹The next morning the word of the Lord came to the prophet Gad, who was David's contact with God.

The Lord said to Gad, ¹²"Tell David that I will give him three choices."

¹³So Gad came to David and asked him, "Will you choose seven years of famine across the land, or to flee for three months before your enemies, or to submit to three days of plague? Think this over and let me know what answer to give to God."

¹⁴"This is a hard decision," David replied, "but it is better to fall into the hand of the Lord (for his mercy is great) than into the hands of men."

¹⁵So the Lord sent a plague upon Israel that morning, and it lasted for three days; and seventy thousand men died throughout the nation. ¹⁶But as the death angel was preparing to destroy Jerusalem, the Lord was sorry for what was happening and told him to stop. He was by the threshing floor of Araunah the Jebusite at the time.

¹⁷When David saw the angel, he said to the Lord, "Look, I am the one who has sinned! What have these sheep done? Let your anger be only against me and my family."

¹⁸That day Gad came to David and said to him, "Go and build an altar to the Lord on the threshing floor of Araunah the Jebusite." ¹⁹So David went to do what the Lord had commanded him. ²⁰When Araunah saw the king and his men coming toward him, he came forward and fell flat on the ground with his face in the dust.

²¹"Why have you come?" Araunah asked.

And David replied, "To buy your threshing

floor, so that I can build an altar to the Lord, and he will stop the plague."

²²"Use anything you like," Araunah told the king. "Here are oxen for the burnt offering, and you can use the threshing instruments and ox yokes for wood to build a fire on the altar. ²³I will give it all to you, and may the Lord God accept your sacrifice."

²⁴But the king said to Araunah, "No, I will not have it as a gift. I will buy it, for I don't want to offer to the Lord my God burnt offerings that have cost me nothing."

So David paid him for the threshing floor and the oxen. ²⁵And David built an altar there to the Lord and offered burnt offerings and peace offerings. And the Lord answered his prayer, and the plague was stopped.

1 Kings

WHAT WAS the best advice you ever got? Did you follow it? Good advice can only help us if we act on it. This is what Solomon learned in 1 Kings.

King David was very old and about to die. He appointed his son Solomon to be king. David knew a lot of important things he could have advised Solomon about—treaties, advisors, local disturbances, laws. But David gave Solomon only one piece of advice for leadership, more important than everything else: Follow God's ways.

How did Solomon respond to David's good advice? The first thing he asked God for was *wisdom* to lead the people in God's ways. God rewarded him by making him the wisest person who ever lived!

But after many years as king, Solomon stopped following God's wisdom and ways. Then problems started in his kingdom. The problems got so bad that after Solomon died, the northern tribes and the southern tribes split and formed two countries with two kings. God's people had divided themselves, all because their leaders forgot to follow God's ways.

If you were to follow David's advice, how would your life be different? As you read 1 Kings, look for examples that show that following God's way is the best way.

Solomon Becomes King

In his old age King David was confined to his bed; but no matter how many blankets were heaped upon him, he was always cold. ²"The cure for this," his aides told him, "is to find a young virgin to be your concubine and nurse. She will lie in your arms and keep you warm."

³,⁴So they searched the country from one end to the other to find the most beautiful girl in all the land. Abishag, from Shunam, was finally selected. They brought her to the king, and she lay in his arms to warm him (but he had no sexual relations with her).

⁵At about that time, David's son Adonijah (his mother was Haggith) decided to crown himself king in place of his aged father. So he hired chariots and drivers and recruited fifty men to run down the streets before him as royal footmen. ⁶Now his father, King David, had never disciplined him at any time—not so much as by a single scolding! He was a very handsome man

and was Absalom's younger brother. ⁷He took General Joab and Abiathar the priest into his confidence, and they agreed to help him become king. ⁸But among those who remained loyal to King David and refused to endorse Adonijah were the priests Zadok and Benaiah, the prophet Nathan, Shimei, Rei, and David's army chiefs.

⁹Adonijah went to En-rogel where he sacrificed sheep, oxen, and fat young goats at the Serpent's Stone. Then he summoned all of his brothers—the other sons of King David—and all the royal officials of Judah, requesting that they come to his coronation. ¹⁰But he didn't invite Nathan the prophet, Benaiah, the loyal army officers, or his brother Solomon.

¹¹Then Nathan the prophet went to Bathsheba, Solomon's mother, and asked her, "Do you realize that Haggith's son, Adonijah, is now the king and that our lord David doesn't even know about it? ¹²If you want to save your own life and the life of your son Solomon—do exactly as I say! ¹³Go at once to King David and ask him, 'My lord, didn't you promise me that my son Solomon would be the next king and would sit upon your throne? Then why is Adonijah reigning?' ¹⁴And while you are still talking with him, I'll come and confirm everything you've said."

¹⁵So Bathsheba went into the king's bedroom. He was an old, old man now, and Abishag was caring for him. ¹⁶Bathsheba bowed low before him.

"What do you want?" he asked her.

¹⁷She replied, "My lord, you vowed to me by the Lord your God that my son Solomon would be the next king and would sit upon your throne. ¹⁸But instead, Adonijah is the new king, and you don't even know about it. ¹⁹He has celebrated his coronation by sacrificing oxen, fat goats, and many sheep and has invited all your sons and Abiathar the priest and General Joab. But he didn't invite Solomon. ²⁰And now, my lord the king, all Israel is waiting for your decision as to whether Adonijah is the one you have chosen to succeed you. ²¹If you don't act, my son Solomon and I will be arrested and executed as criminals as soon as you are dead."

²²,²³While she was speaking, the king's aides told him, "Nathan the prophet is here to see you."

Nathan came in and bowed low before the king, ²⁴and asked, "My lord, have you appointed Adonijah to be the next king? Is he the one you have selected to sit upon your throne? ²⁵Today he celebrated his coronation by sacrificing oxen, fat goats, and many sheep, and has invited your sons to attend the festivities. He also invited General Joab and Abiathar the priest; and they are feasting and drinking with him and shouting, 'Long live King Adonijah!' ²⁶But Zadok the priest and Benaiah and Solomon and I weren't invited. ²⁷Has this been done with your knowledge? For you haven't said a word as to which of your sons you have chosen to be the next king."

²⁸"Call Bathsheba," David said. So she came back in and stood before the king.

²⁹And the king vowed, "As the Lord lives who has rescued me from every danger, ³⁰I decree that your son Solomon shall be the next king and shall sit upon my throne, just as I swore to you before by the Lord God of Israel."

³¹Then Bathsheba bowed low before him again and exclaimed, "Oh, thank you, sir. May my lord the king live forever!"

³²"Call Zadok the priest," the king ordered, "and Nathan the prophet, and Benaiah."

When they arrived, ³³he said to them, "Take Solomon and my officers to Gihon. Solomon is to ride on my personal mule, ³⁴and Zadok the priest and Nathan the prophet are to anoint him there as king of Israel. Then blow the trumpets and shout, 'Long live King Solomon!' ³⁵When you bring him back here, place him upon my throne as the new king; for I have appointed him king of Israel and Judah."

³⁶"Amen! Praise God!" replied Benaiah, and added, ³⁷"May the Lord be with Solomon as he has been with you, and may God make Solomon's reign even greater than yours!"

³⁸So Zadok the priest, Nathan the prophet, Benaiah, and David's bodyguard took Solomon to Gihon, riding on King David's own mule. ³⁹At Gihon, Zadok took a flask of sacred oil from the Tabernacle and poured it over Solomon; and the trumpets were blown and all the people shouted, "Long live King Solomon!"

⁴⁰Then they all returned with him to Jerusalem, making a joyous and noisy celebration all along the way.

⁴¹Adonijah and his guests heard the commotion and shouting just as they were finishing their banquet.

"What's going on?" Joab demanded. "Why is the city in such an uproar?"

⁴²And while he was still speaking, Jonathan, the son of Abiathar the priest, rushed in.

"Come in," Adonijah said to him, "for you are a good man; you must have good news."

⁴³"Our lord King David has declared Solomon as king!" Jonathan shouted. ⁴⁴,⁴⁵"The king sent him to Gihon with Zadok the priest and Nathan the prophet and Benaiah, protected by the king's own bodyguard; and he rode on the king's own mule. And Zadok and Nathan have anointed him as the new king! They have just returned, and the whole city is celebrating and rejoicing. That's what all the noise is. ⁴⁶,⁴⁷Solomon is sitting on the throne, and all the people are congratulating King

Family Devotions

☐ DEVOTION 112
RESPECTING AUTHORITY

Read 1 Kings 1:5-8, 43-45

"Oh!" yelled Danny. "Oh, ouch! That hurts!"

"I know, Son," said Dad. "Spankings do hurt, but that's the point. Maybe this will help you remember to obey next time." He patted Danny's shoulder. "We don't enjoy spanking you. We do it because we love you."

Later that day, Danny came down with a cough. It grew worse and worse, until finally Mom called the doctor's office. Soon Dad was on his way to pick up a prescription at the pharmacy. When he returned with a big bottle of dark brown medicine, Danny eyed the bottle warily. "Do I really have to take that stuff?" he asked. Mom nodded and poured out a big spoonful. Danny gulped it down. "Oh, yuck! It tastes terrible! I'm sure not going to take any more!" But that night, Danny woke up coughing again. His throat hurt, and he was glad when Mom came in, bringing the medicine bottle.

The next morning Danny felt better. "That medicine really helped," he admitted at breakfast. "It tasted awful, but I'm glad I took it."

"Good," said Dad, "because you'll need to take another dose after breakfast. Neither spankings nor bad-tasting medicines are enjoyable. But both produce good results. It reminds me that God sometimes has to use unpleasant things to bring about good results in his children, too."

"That's right," agreed Mom. "Even when you're grown up, the Lord will sometimes use difficult circumstances to convict you of sin and help you grow in him. Times of chastening are always hard, whether from parents or from God, but the results are worth it. Try to remember that and even be thankful for discipline." Danny nodded as he watched Mom pour out another spoonful of medicine.

Respecting Authority Memory Verse

Children, obey your parents; this is the right thing to do because God has placed them in authority over you.
Ephesians 6:1

How About You?
Do you enjoy being disciplined? No one does! But the discipline you receive from your parents helps you grow into a mature, responsible adult. Even if you think your parents aren't always fair in their discipline, remember that God is in control, and his chastening is always just right. Don't resent discipline—be glad someone cares. S. K.

• For the next devotional, turn to page 357. • For the next devotional on RESPECTING AUTHORITY, turn to page 357.
• For notes on RESPECTING AUTHORITY, see pages 311, 420, and 1182.

David, saying, 'May God bless you even more through Solomon than he has blessed you personally! May God make Solomon's reign even greater than yours!' And the king is lying in bed, acknowledging their blessings. ⁴⁸He is saying, 'Blessed be the Lord God of Israel who has selected one of my sons to sit upon my throne while I am still alive to see it.'"

⁴⁹,⁵⁰Then Adonijah and his guests jumped up from the banquet table and fled in panic; for they were fearful for their lives. Adonijah rushed into the Tabernacle and caught hold of the horns of the sacred altar. ⁵¹When word reached Solomon that Adonijah was claiming sanctuary in the Tabernacle, and pleading for clemency, ⁵²Solomon replied, "If he behaves himself, he will not be harmed; but if he does not, he shall die." ⁵³So King Solomon summoned him, and they brought him down from the altar. He came to bow low before the king; and then Solomon curtly dismissed him.

"Go on home," he said.

2 Instructions for Solomon

As the time of King David's death approached, he gave this charge to his son Solomon: ²"I am going where every man on earth must some day go. I am counting on you to be a strong and worthy successor. ³Obey the laws of God and follow all his ways; keep each of his commands written in the law of Moses so that you will prosper in everything you do, wherever you turn. ⁴If you do this, then the Lord will fulfill the promise he gave me, that if my children and their descendants watch their step and are faithful to God, one of them shall always be the king of Israel—my dynasty will never end.

⁵"Now listen to my instructions. You know that Joab murdered my two generals, Abner and Amasa. He pretended that it was an act of war, but it was done in a time of peace. ⁶You are a wise man and will know what to do—don't let him die in peace. ⁷But be kind to the sons of Barzillai the Gileadite. Make them permanent guests of the king, for they took care of me when I fled from your brother Absalom. ⁸And do you remember Shimei, the son of Gera the Benjaminite from Bahurim? He cursed me with a terrible curse as I was going to Mahanaim; but when he came down to meet me at the Jordan River, I promised I wouldn't kill him. ⁹But that promise doesn't bind you! You are a wise man, and you will know how to arrange a bloody death for him."

¹⁰Then David died and was buried in Jerusalem. ¹¹He had reigned over Israel for forty years, seven of them in Hebron and thirty-three in Jerusalem. ¹²And Solomon became the new king, replacing his father David; and his kingdom prospered.

¹³One day Adonijah, the son of Haggith, came to see Solomon's mother, Bathsheba.

"Have you come to make trouble?" she asked him.

"No," he replied, "I come in peace. ¹⁴As a matter of fact, I have a favor to ask of you."

"What is it?" she asked.

¹⁵"Everything was going well for me," he said, "and the kingdom was mine: everyone expected me to be the next king. But the tables are turned, and everything went to my brother instead; for that is the way the Lord wanted it. ¹⁶But now I have just a small favor to ask of you; please don't turn me down."

"What is it?" she asked.

¹⁷He replied, "Speak to King Solomon on my behalf (for I know he will do anything you request) and ask him to give me Abishag, the Shunammite, as my wife."

¹⁸"All right," Bathsheba replied, "I'll ask him."

¹⁹So she went to ask the favor of King Solomon. The king stood up from his throne as she entered and bowed low to her. He ordered that a throne for his mother be placed beside his; so she sat at his right hand.

²⁰"I have one small request to make of you," she said. "I hope you won't turn me down."

"What is it, my mother?" he asked. "You know I won't refuse you."

²¹"Then let your brother Adonijah marry Abishag," she replied.

²²"Are you crazy?" he demanded. "If I were to give him Abishag, I would be giving him the kingdom too! For he is my older brother! He and Abiathar the priest and General Joab would take over!" ²³,²⁴Then King Solomon swore with a great oath, "May God strike me dead if Adonijah does not die this very day for this plot against me! I swear it by the living God who has given me the throne of my father David and this kingdom he promised me."

²⁵So King Solomon sent Benaiah to execute him, and he killed him with a sword.

²⁶Then the king said to Abiathar the priest, "Go back to your home in Anathoth. You should be killed, too, but I won't do it now. For you carried the Ark of the

---

FORGIVING OTHERS 1:52-53 While Adonijah feared for his life and expected the severest punishment, Solomon simply dismissed his brother and sent him home. As a new king, Solomon had the power to kill his rivals, something Adonijah would have done had his conspiracy succeeded. But Solomon acted as if he had nothing to prove, thus showing his authority and power. Trying to prove one's power and authority often proves only one's fear and self-doubt. Sometimes forgiving a personal attack shows more strength than lashing out in revenge. **To begin the series of devotionals on FORGIVING OTHERS, turn to page 39.**

FAMILY DEVOTIONS

☐ DEVOTION 113
RESPECTING AUTHORITY

Read 1 Kings 2:1-4

Rich watched his father pull out the stake that had been wired to a small tree ever since it had been planted.

"A small tree often doesn't have the strength or ability to stand alone," Dad said. "This stake acted as a support, but now I believe the tree is big enough to take any winds that may come along." He stood back and looked at the tree. It was growing tall and straight because it had been held in that position by the supporting stake. "That's pretty much like life," added Dad thoughtfully.

"What do you mean?" Rich asked.

"When you were small, your mother and I held on to your hand every time you took a step," Dad explained. "We didn't want you to fall and get hurt. Then as you began to grow and get control of your walk, we let you go by yourself, but we still watched you."

Rich nodded as he thought about it. Even now there were many times that he needed his parents' advice and help. He guessed maybe he would always depend on them. He mentioned that to his father.

"We'll be glad to help whenever you call on us," Dad replied, smiling. "When the time comes that we are no longer here, you'll be ready to go on without us. There's a verse in the Bible that your mother and I try to follow as we raise you."

"Which one?" Rich asked.

"It's Proverbs 22:6," replied Dad. "Teach a child to choose the right path, and when he is older, he will remain upon it."

"Sort of like the tree, isn't it?" Rich asked. "When it was small and frail, you had to keep an eye on it all the time so it didn't grow wrong. But now that it's old enough, it will keep growing straight without the supporting stake."

Dad smiled broadly. "That's it," he agreed. "Exactly!"

Respecting Authority Memory Verse

Children, obey your parents; this is the right thing to do because God has placed them in authority over you.
Ephesians 6:1

How About You?
How do you feel when you are restricted in some way by your parents' rules and guidance? Don't get angry. Every young tree needs help to grow big and strong and straight. Thank God for your supporting stake—your parents. *R.J.*

• For the next devotional, turn to page 367. • For the next devotional on RESPECTING AUTHORITY, turn to page 377.
• For notes on RESPECTING AUTHORITY, see pages 311, 420, and 1182.

Lord during my father's reign, and you suffered right along with him in all of his troubles."

²⁷So Solomon forced Abiathar to give up his position as the priest of the Lord, thereby fulfilling the decree of Jehovah at Shiloh concerning the descendants of Eli.

²⁸When Joab heard about Adonijah's death (Joab had joined Adonijah's revolt, though not Absalom's) he ran to the Tabernacle for sanctuary and caught hold of the horns of the altar. ²⁹When news of this reached King Solomon, he sent Benaiah to execute him.

³⁰Benaiah went into the Tabernacle and said to Joab, "The king says to come out!"

"No," he said, "I'll die here."

So Benaiah returned to the king for further instructions.

³¹"Do as he says," the king replied. "Kill him there beside the altar and bury him. This will remove the guilt of his senseless murders from me and from my father's family. ³²Then Jehovah will hold him personally responsible for the murders of two men who were better than he. For my father was no party to the deaths of General Abner, commander-in-chief of the army of Israel, and General Amasa, commander-in-chief of the army of Judah. ³³May Joab and his descendants be forever guilty of these murders, and may the Lord declare David and his descendants guiltless concerning their deaths."

³⁴So Benaiah returned to the Tabernacle and killed Joab; and he was buried beside his house in the desert.

³⁵Then the king appointed Benaiah as commander-in-chief, and Zadok as priest instead of Abiathar.

³⁶,³⁷The king now sent for Shimei and told him, "Build a house here in Jerusalem, and don't step outside the city on pain of death. The moment you go beyond Kidron Brook, you die; and it will be your own fault."

³⁸"All right," Shimei replied, "whatever you say." So he lived in Jerusalem for a long time.

³⁹But three years later two of Shimei's slaves escaped to King Achish of Gath. When Shimei learned where they were, ⁴⁰he saddled a donkey and went to Gath to visit the king. And when he had found his slaves, he took them back to Jerusalem.

⁴¹When Solomon heard that Shimei had left Jerusalem and had gone to Gath and returned, ⁴²he sent for him and demanded, "Didn't I command you in the name of God to stay in Jerusalem or die? You replied, 'Very well, I will do as you say.' ⁴³Then why have you not kept your agreement and obeyed my commandment? ⁴⁴And what about all the wicked things you did to my father, King David? May the Lord take revenge on you, ⁴⁵but may I receive God's rich blessings, and may one of David's descendants always sit upon this throne."

⁴⁶Then, at the king's command, Benaiah took Shimei outside and killed him.

So Solomon's grip upon the kingdom became secure.

3 Solomon Asks for Wisdom

Solomon made an alliance with Pharaoh, the king of Egypt, and married one of his daughters. He brought her to Jerusalem to live in the City of David until he could finish building his palace and the Temple and the wall around the city.

²At that time the people of Israel sacrificed their offerings on altars in the hills, for the Temple of the Lord hadn't yet been built.

³(Solomon loved the Lord and followed all of his father David's instructions except that he continued to sacrifice in the hills and to offer incense there.) ⁴The most famous of the hilltop altars was at Gibeon, and now the king went there and sacrificed one thousand burnt offerings! ⁵The Lord appeared to him in a dream that night and told him to ask for anything he wanted, and it would be given to him!

⁶Solomon replied, "You were wonderfully kind to my father David because he was honest and true and faithful to you, and obeyed your commands. And you have continued your kindness to him by giving him a son to succeed him. ⁷O Lord my God, now you have made me the king instead of my father David, but I am as a little child who doesn't know his way around. ⁸And here I am among your own chosen people, a nation so great that there are almost too many people to count! ⁹Give me an understanding mind so that I can govern your people well and know the difference between what is right and what is wrong. For who by himself is able to carry such a heavy responsibility?"

¹⁰The Lord was pleased with his reply and was glad that Solomon had asked for wisdom. ¹¹So he replied, "Because you have asked for wisdom in governing my people and haven't asked for a long life, or riches for yourself, or the defeat of your enemies—¹²yes, I'll give you what you asked for! I will

---

MAKING THE BEST CHOICES 3:6-9 When given a chance to have anything in the world, Solomon asked for wisdom in order to lead well and to make right decisions. We can ask God for this same wisdom (James 1:5). Notice that Solomon asked for wisdom to carry out his job. He did not ask God to do the job for him. We should not ask God to do *for* us what he wants to do *through* us. Instead we should ask God to give us the wisdom to know what to do and how to do it. **To begin the series of devotionals on MAKING THE BEST CHOICES, turn to page 275.**

give you a wiser mind than anyone else has ever had or ever will have! ¹³And I will also give you what you didn't ask for—riches and honor! And no one in all the world will be as rich and famous as you for the rest of your life! ¹⁴And I will give you a long life if you follow me and obey my laws as your father David did."

¹⁵Then Solomon woke up and realized it had been a dream. He returned to Jerusalem and went into the Tabernacle. And as he stood before the Ark of the Covenant of the Lord, he sacrificed burnt offerings and peace offerings. Then he invited all of his officials to a great banquet.

¹⁶Soon afterwards two young prostitutes came to the king to have an argument settled.

¹⁷,¹⁸"Sir," one of them began, "we live in the same house, just the two of us, and recently I had a baby. When it was three days old, this woman's baby was born too. ¹⁹But her baby died during the night when she rolled over on it in her sleep and smothered it. ²⁰Then she got up in the night and took my son from beside me while I was asleep, and laid her dead child in my arms and took mine to sleep beside her. ²¹And in the morning when I tried to feed my baby it was dead! But when it became light outside, I saw that it wasn't my son at all."

²²Then the other woman interrupted, "It certainly was her son, and the living child is mine."

"No," the first woman said, "the dead one is yours and the living one is mine." And so they argued back and forth before the king.

²³Then the king said, "Let's get the facts straight: both of you claim the living child, and each says that the dead child belongs to the other. ²⁴All right, bring me a sword." So a sword was brought to the king. ²⁵Then he said, "Divide the living child in two and give half to each of these women!"

²⁶Then the woman who really was the mother of the child, and who loved him very much, cried out, "Oh no, sir! Give her the child—don't kill him!"

But the other woman said, "All right, it will be neither yours nor mine; divide it between us!"

²⁷Then the king said, "Give the baby to the woman who wants him to live, for she is the mother!"

²⁸Word of the king's decision spread quickly throughout the entire nation, and all the people were awed as they realized the great wisdom God had given him.

4 Solomon's Cabinet Members

Here is a list of King Solomon's cabinet members:

Azariah (son of Zadok) was the High Priest;
Elihoreph and Ahijah (sons of Shisha) were secretaries;
Jehoshaphat (son of Ahilud) was the official historian and in charge of the archives;
Benaiah (son of Jehoiada) was commander-in-chief of the army;
Zadok and Abiathar were priests;
Azariah (son of Nathan) was secretary of state;
Zabud (son of Nathan) was the king's personal priest and special friend;
Ahishar was manager of palace affairs;
Adoniram (son of Abda) was superintendent of public works.

⁷There were also twelve officials of Solomon's court—one man from each tribe—responsible for requisitioning food from the people for the king's household. Each of them arranged provisions for one month of the year.

⁸⁻¹⁹The names of these twelve officers were:

Ben-hur, whose area for this taxation was the hill country of Ephraim;
Ben-deker, whose area was Makaz, Shaalbim, Beth-shemesh, and Elon-beth-hanan;
Ben-hesed, whose area was Arubboth, including Socoh and all the land of Hepher;
Ben-abinadab (who married Solomon's daughter, the princess Taphath), whose area was the highlands of Dor;
Baana (son of Ahilud), whose area was Taanach and Megiddo, all of Beth-shean near Zarethan below Jezreel, and all the territory from Beth-shean to Abel-meholah and over to Jokmeam;
Ben-geber, whose area was Ramoth-gilead, including the villages of Jair (the son of Manasseh) in Gilead; and the region of Argob in Bashan, including sixty walled cities with bronze gates;
Ahinadab (the son of Iddo), whose area was Mahanaim;
Ahimaaz (who married Princess Basemath, another of Solomon's daughters), whose area was Naphtali;
Baana (son of Hushai), whose areas were Asher and Bealoth;
Jehoshaphat (son of Paruah), whose area was Issachar;
Shimei (son of Ela), whose area was Benjamin;
Geber (son of Uri), whose area was Gilead, including the territories of King Sihon of the Amorites and King Og of Bashan.

A general manager supervised these officials and their work.

²⁰Israel and Judah were a wealthy, populous, contented nation at this time. ²¹King Solomon ruled the whole area from the Euphrates River to the land of the Philistines and down to the borders of Egypt.

The conquered peoples of those lands sent taxes to Solomon and continued to serve him throughout his lifetime.

22The daily food requirements for the palace were 195 bushels of fine flour, 390 bushels of meal, 23 10 oxen from the fattening pens, 20 pasture-fed cattle, 100 sheep, and, from time to time, deer, gazelles, roebucks, and plump fowl.

24His dominion extended over all the kingdoms west of the Euphrates River, from Tiphsah to Gaza. And there was peace throughout the land. 25Throughout the lifetime of Solomon, all of Judah and Israel lived in peace and safety; and each family had its own home and garden.

26Solomon owned forty thousand chariot horses and employed twelve thousand charioteers. 27Each month the tax officials provided food for King Solomon and his court, 28also the barley and straw for the royal horses in the stables.

29God gave Solomon great wisdom and understanding, and a mind with broad interests. 30In fact, his wisdom excelled that of any of the wise men of the East, including those in Egypt. 31He was wiser than Ethan the Ezrahite and Heman, Calcol, and Darda, the sons of Mahol; and he was famous among all the surrounding nations. 32He was the author of 3,000 proverbs and wrote 1,005 songs. 33He was a great naturalist, with interest in animals, birds, snakes, fish, and trees—from the great cedars of Lebanon down to the tiny hyssop which grows in cracks in the wall. 34And kings from many lands sent their ambassadors to him for his advice.

5 Solomon Builds the Temple

King Hiram of Tyre had always been a great admirer of David, so when he learned that David's son Solomon was the new king of Israel, he sent ambassadors to extend congratulations and good wishes. 2,3Solomon replied with a proposal about the Temple of the Lord he wanted to build. His father David, Solomon pointed out to Hiram, had not been able to build it because of the numerous wars going on, and he had been waiting for the Lord to give him peace.

4"But now," Solomon said to Hiram, "the Lord my God has given Israel peace on every side; I have no foreign enemies or internal rebellions. 5So I am planning to build a Temple for the Lord my God, just as he instructed my father that I should do. For the Lord told him, 'Your son, whom I will place upon your throne, shall build me a Temple.' 6Now please assist me with this project. Send your woodsmen to the mountains of Lebanon to cut cedar timber for me, and I will send my men to work beside them, and I will pay your men whatever wages you ask; for as you know, no one in Israel can cut timber like you Sidonians!"

7Hiram was very pleased with the message from Solomon. "Praise God for giving David a wise son to be king of the great nation of Israel," he said. 8Then he sent this reply to Solomon: "I have received your message and I will do as you have asked concerning the timber. I can supply both cedar and cypress. 9My men will bring the logs from the Lebanon mountains to the Mediterranean Sea and build them into rafts. We will float them along the coast to wherever you need them; then we will break the rafts apart and deliver the timber to you. You can pay me with food for my household."

10So Hiram produced for Solomon as much cedar and cypress timber as he desired, 11and in return Solomon sent him an annual payment of 125,000 bushels of wheat for his household and 96 gallons of pure olive oil. 12So the Lord gave great wisdom to Solomon just as he had promised. And Hiram and Solomon made a formal alliance of peace.

13Then Solomon drafted thirty thousand laborers from all over Israel, 14and rotated them to Lebanon, ten thousand a month, so that each man was a month in Lebanon and two months at home. Adoniram was the general superintendent of this labor camp. 15Solomon also had seventy thousand additional laborers, eighty thousand stonecutters in the hill country, 16and thirty-three hundred foremen. 17The stonecutters quarried and shaped huge blocks of stone—a very expensive job—for the foundation of the Temple. 18Men from Gebal helped Solomon's and Hiram's builders in cutting the timber and making the boards, and in preparing the stone for the Temple.

6

It was in the spring of the fourth year of Solomon's reign that he began the actual construction of the Temple. (This was 480 years after the people of Israel left their slavery in Egypt.) 2The Temple was ninety feet long, thirty feet wide, and forty-five feet high. 3All along the front of the Temple was a porch thirty feet long and fifteen feet deep. 4Narrow windows were used throughout.

5An annex of rooms was built along the full length of both sides of the Temple against the outer walls. 6These rooms were three stories high, the lower floor being $7\frac{1}{2}$ feet wide, the second floor 9 feet wide, and the upper floor $10\frac{1}{2}$ feet wide. The rooms were connected to the walls of the Temple by beams resting on blocks built out from the wall—so the beams were not inserted into the walls themselves.

7The stones used in the construction of the

Temple were prefinished at the quarry, so the entire structure was built without the sound of hammer, axe, or any other tool at the building site.

⁸The bottom floor of the side rooms was entered from the right side of the Temple, and there were winding stairs going up to the second floor; another flight of stairs led from the second to the third. ⁹After completing the Temple, Solomon paneled it all, including the beams and pillars, with cedar. ¹⁰As already stated, there was an annex on each side of the building, attached to the Temple walls by cedar timbers. Each story of the annex was 7½ feet high.

¹¹,¹²Then the Lord sent this message to Solomon concerning the Temple he was building: "If you do as I tell you to and follow all of my commandments and instructions, I will do what I told your father David I would do: ¹³I will live among the people of Israel and never forsake them."

¹⁴At last the Temple was finished. ¹⁵The entire inside, from floor to ceiling, was paneled with cedar, and the floors were made of cypress boards. ¹⁶The thirty-foot inner room at the far end of the Temple—the Most Holy Place—was also paneled from the floor to the ceiling with cedar boards. ¹⁷The remainder of the Temple—other than the Most Holy Place—was sixty feet long. ¹⁸Throughout the Temple the cedar paneling laid over the stone walls was carved with designs of rosebuds and open flowers.

¹⁹The inner room was where the Ark of the Covenant of the Lord was placed. ²⁰This inner sanctuary was thirty feet long, thirty feet wide, and thirty feet high. Its walls and ceiling were overlaid with pure gold, and Solomon made a cedar-wood altar for this room. ²¹,²²Then he overlaid the interior of the remainder of the Temple—including the cedar altar—with pure gold; and he made gold chains to protect the entrance to the Most Holy Place.

²³⁻²⁸Within the inner sanctuary Solomon placed two statues of Guardian Angels made from olive wood, each fifteen feet high. They were placed so that their outspread wings reached from wall to wall, while their inner wings touched each other at the center of the room; each wing was 7½ feet long, so each angel measured fifteen feet from wing tip to wing tip. The two angels were identical in all dimensions, and each was overlaid with gold.

²⁹Figures of angels, palm trees, and open flowers were carved on all the walls of both rooms of the Temple, ³⁰and the floor of both rooms was overlaid with gold.

³¹The doorway to the inner sanctuary was a five-sided opening, ³²and its two olive-wood doors were carved with Guardian Angels, palm trees, and open flowers, all overlaid with gold.

³³Then he made square doorposts of olive wood for the entrance to the Temple. ³⁴There were two folding doors of cypress wood, and each door was hinged to fold back upon itself. ³⁵Angels, palm trees, and open flowers were carved on these doors and carefully overlaid with gold.

³⁶The wall of the inner court had three layers of hewn stone and one layer of cedar beams.

³⁷The foundation of the Temple was laid in the month of May in the fourth year of Solomon's reign, ³⁸and the entire building was completed in every detail in November of the eleventh year of his reign. So it took seven years to build.

7 Solomon Builds His Palace

Then Solomon built his own palace, which took thirteen years to construct.

²One of the rooms in the palace was called the Hall of the Forest of Lebanon. It was huge—measuring 150 feet long, 75 feet wide, and 45 feet high. The great cedar ceiling beams rested upon four rows of cedar pillars. ³,⁴There were forty-five windows in the hall, set in three tiers, one tier above the other, five to a tier, facing each other from three walls. ⁵Each of the doorways and windows had a square frame.

⁶Another room was called the Hall of Pillars. It was seventy-five feet long and forty-five feet wide, with a porch in front covered by a canopy that was supported by pillars.

⁷There was also the Throne Room or Judgment Hall, where Solomon sat to hear legal matters; it was paneled with cedar from the floor to the rafters.

⁸His cedar-paneled living quarters surrounded a courtyard behind this hall. (He designed similar living quarters, the same size, in the palace that he built for Pharaoh's daughter—one of his wives.) ⁹These buildings were constructed entirely from huge, expensive stones, cut to measure. ¹⁰The foundation stones were twelve to fifteen feet across. ¹¹The huge stones in the walls were also cut to measure and were topped with cedar beams. ¹²The Great Court had three courses of hewn stone in its walls, topped with cedar beams, just like the inner court of the Temple and the porch of the palace.

¹³King Solomon then asked for a man named Hiram to come from Tyre, for he was a skilled craftsman in bronze work. ¹⁴He was half Jewish, being the son of a widow of the tribe of Naphtali, and his father had been a foundry worker from Tyre. So he came to work for King Solomon.

¹⁵He cast two hollow bronze pillars, each twenty-seven feet high and eighteen feet around, with three-inch-thick walls. ¹⁶⁻²²At the tops of the

pillars he made two lily-shaped capitals from molten bronze, each 7½ feet high. The upper part of each capital was shaped like a lily, six feet high. Each capital was decorated with seven sets of bronze, chain-designed lattices and four hundred pomegranates in two rows. Hiram set these pillars at the entrance of the Temple. The one on the south was named the Jachin Pillar, and the one on the north, the Boaz Pillar.

²³Then Hiram cast a round bronze tank, 7½ feet high and 15 feet from brim to brim; 45 feet in circumference. ²⁴On the underside of the rim were two rows of ornaments an inch or two apart, which were cast along with the tank. ²⁵It rested on twelve bronze oxen standing tail to tail, three facing north, three west, three south, and three east. ²⁶The sides of the tank were four inches thick; its brim was shaped like a goblet, and it had a twelve thousand gallon capacity.

²⁷⁻³⁰Then he made ten four-wheeled movable stands, each 6 feet square and 4½ feet high. They were constructed with undercarriages braced with square crosspieces. These crosspieces were decorated with carved lions, oxen, and angels. Above and below the lions and oxen were wreath decorations. Each of these movable stands had four bronze wheels and bronze axles, and at each corner of the stands were supporting posts made of bronze and decorated with wreaths on each side. ³¹The top of each stand was a round piece 1½ feet high. Its center was concave, 2¼ feet deep, decorated on the outside with wreaths. Its panels were square, not round.

³²The stands rode on four wheels which were connected to axles that had been cast as part of the stands. The wheels were twenty-seven inches high ³³and were similar to chariot wheels. All the parts of the stands were cast from molten bronze, including the axles, spokes, rims, and hubs. ³⁴There were supports at each of the four corners of the stands, and these, too, were cast with the stands. ³⁵A nine-inch rim surrounded the tip of each stand, banded with lugs. All was cast as one unit with the stand. ³⁶Guardian Angels, lions, and palm trees surrounded by wreaths were engraved on the borders of the band wherever there was room. ³⁷All ten stands were the same size and were made alike, for each was cast from the same mold.

³⁸Then he made ten brass vats, and placed them on the stands. Each vat was six feet square and contained 240 gallons of water. ³⁹Five of these vats were arranged on the left and five on the right-hand side of the room. The tank was in the southeast corner, on the right-hand side of the room. ⁴⁰Hiram also made the necessary pots, shovels, and basins and at last completed the work in the Temple of the Lord that had been assigned to him by King Solomon.

⁴¹⁻⁴⁶Here is a list of the items he made:

Two pillars;
A capital at the top of each pillar;
Latticework covering the bases of the capitals of each pillar;
Four hundred pomegranates in two rows on the latticework, to cover the bases of the two capitals;
Ten movable stands holding ten vats;
One large tank and twelve oxen supporting it;
Pots;
Shovels;
Basins.

All these items were made of burnished bronze and were cast at the plains of the Jordan River between Succoth and Zarethan. ⁴⁷The total weight of these pieces was not known because they were too heavy to weigh!

⁴⁸All the utensils and furniture used in the Temple were made of solid gold. This included the altar, the table where the Bread of the Presence of God was displayed, ⁴⁹the lampstands (five on the right-hand side and five on the left, in front of the Most Holy Place), the flowers, lamps, tongs, ⁵⁰cups, snuffers, basins, spoons, firepans, the hinges of the doors to the Most Holy Place, and the main entrance doors of the Temple. Each of these was made of solid gold.

⁵¹When the Temple was finally finished, Solomon took into the treasury of the Temple the silver, the gold, and all the vessels dedicated for that purpose by his father David.

8 The Ark and the Temple

Then Solomon called a convocation at Jerusalem of all the leaders of Israel—the heads of the tribes and clans—to observe the transferring of the Ark of the Covenant of the Lord from the Tabernacle in Zion, the City of David, to the Temple. ²This celebration occurred at the time of the Tabernacle Festival in the month of October. ³,⁴During the festivities the priests carried the Ark to the Temple, along with all the sacred vessels that had previously been in the Tabernacle. ⁵King Solomon and all the people gathered before the Ark, sacrificing uncounted sheep and oxen.

⁶Then the priests took the Ark into the inner sanctuary of the Temple—the Most Holy Place—and placed it under the wings of the statues of the mighty angels. ⁷The angels had been constructed in such a manner that their wings spread out over the spot where the Ark would be placed; so now their wings overshadowed the Ark and its carrying poles. ⁸The poles were so long that they stuck out past the angels and

could be seen from the next room, but not from the outer court; and they remain there to this day. ⁹There was nothing in the Ark at that time except the two stone tablets that Moses had placed there at Mount Horeb at the time the Lord made his covenant with the people of Israel after they left Egypt.

¹⁰*Look! As the priests are returning from the inner sanctuary, a bright cloud fills the Temple!* ¹¹*The priests have to go outside because the glory of the Lord is filling the entire building!*

¹²,¹³Now King Solomon prayed this invocation:

"The Lord has said that he would live in the
    thick darkness;
But, O Lord, I have built you a lovely home on
    earth, a place for you to live forever."

¹⁴Then the king turned around and faced the people as they stood before him, and blessed them. ¹⁵"Blessed be the Lord God of Israel," he said, "who has done today what he promised my father David: ¹⁶for he said to him, 'When I brought my people from Egypt, I didn't appoint a place for my Temple, but I appointed a man to be my people's leader.' ¹⁷This man was my father David. He wanted to build a Temple for the Lord God of Israel, ¹⁸but the Lord told him not to. 'I am glad you want to do it,' he said, ¹⁹'but your son is the one who shall build my Temple.' ²⁰And now the Lord has done what he promised; for I have followed my father as king of Israel, and now this Temple has been built for the Lord God of Israel. ²¹And I have prepared a place in the Temple for the Ark that contains the covenant made by the Lord with our fathers, at the time that he brought them out of the land of Egypt."

²²,²³Then, as all the people watched, Solomon stood before the altar of the Lord with his hands spread out toward heaven and said, "O Lord God of Israel, there is no god like you in heaven or earth, for you are loving and kind and you keep your promises to your people if they do their best to do your will. ²⁴Today you have fulfilled your promise to my father David, who was your servant; ²⁵and now, O Lord God of Israel, fulfill your further promise to him: that if his descendants follow your ways and try to do your will as he did, one of them shall always sit upon the throne of Israel. ²⁶Yes, O God of Israel, fulfill this promise too.

²⁷"But is it possible that God would really live on earth? Why, even the skies and the highest heavens cannot contain you, much less this Temple I have built! ²⁸And yet, O Lord my God, you have heard and answered my request: ²⁹Please watch over this Temple night and day—this place you have promised to live in—and as I face toward the Temple and pray, whether by night or by day, please listen to me and answer my requests. ³⁰Listen to every plea of the people of Israel whenever they face this place to pray; yes, hear in heaven where you live, and when you hear, forgive.

³¹"If a man is accused of doing something wrong and then, standing here before your altar, swears that he didn't do it, ³²hear him in heaven and do what is right; judge whether or not he did it.

³³,³⁴"And when your people sin and their enemies defeat them, hear them from heaven and forgive them if they turn to you again and confess that you are their God. Bring them back again to this land which you have given to their fathers.

³⁵,³⁶"And when the skies are shut up and there is no rain because of their sin, hear them from heaven and forgive them when they pray toward this place and confess your name. And after you have punished them, help them to follow the good ways in which they should walk, and send rain upon the land that you have given your people.

³⁷"If there is a famine in the land caused by plant disease or locusts or caterpillars, or if Israel's enemies besiege one of her cities, or if the people are struck by an epidemic or plague—or whatever the problem is—³⁸then when the people realize their sin and pray toward this Temple, ³⁹hear them from heaven and forgive and answer all who have made an honest confession; for you know each heart. ⁴⁰In this way they will always learn to reverence you as they continue to live in this land that you have given their fathers.

⁴¹,⁴²"And when foreigners hear of your great name and come from distant lands to worship you (for they shall hear of your great name and mighty miracles) and pray toward this Temple, ⁴³hear them from heaven and answer their prayers. And all the nations of the earth will know and fear your name just as your own people Israel do; and all the earth will know that this is your Temple.

⁴⁴"When you send your people out to battle against their enemies and they pray to you, looking toward your chosen city of Jerusalem and

---

PRAYING AT ALL TIMES **8:56-61** Solomon blessed the people and prayed for them. His prayer can be a pattern for our prayers. He had five basic requests: (1) for God's presence (8:57); (2) for the desire to do God's will in everything (8:58); (3) for help with daily needs (8:59); (4) for the desire to live good and perfect lives (8:61); (5) for the ability to obey God's laws and commandments (8:61). These prayer requests are just as applicable today as in Solomon's time. **To begin the series of devotionals on PRAYING AT ALL TIMES, turn to page 45.**

toward this Temple that I have built in your name, ⁴⁵hear their prayer and help them.

⁴⁶"If they sin against you (and who doesn't?) and you become angry with them and let their enemies lead them away as captives to some foreign land, whether far or near, ⁴⁷and they come to their senses and turn to you and cry to you saying, 'We have sinned, we have done wrong'; ⁴⁸if they honestly return to you and pray toward this land that you have given their fathers, and toward this city of Jerusalem that you have chosen, and toward this Temple that I have built for your name, ⁴⁹hear their prayers and pleadings from heaven where you live, and come to their assistance.

⁵⁰"Forgive your people for all of their evil deeds, and make their captors merciful to them; ⁵¹for they are your people—your inheritance that you brought out from the Egyptian furnace. ⁵²May your eyes be open and your ears listening to their pleas. O Lord, hear and answer them whenever they cry out to you, ⁵³for when you brought our fathers out of the land of Egypt, you told your servant Moses that you had chosen Israel from among all the nations of the earth to be your own special people."

⁵⁴,⁵⁵Solomon had been kneeling with his hands outstretched toward heaven. As he finished this prayer, he rose from before the altar of Jehovah and cried out this blessing upon all the people of Israel:

⁵⁶"Blessed be the Lord who has fulfilled his promise and given rest to his people Israel; not one word has failed of all the wonderful promises proclaimed by his servant Moses. ⁵⁷May the Lord our God be with us as he was with our fathers; may he never forsake us. ⁵⁸May he give us the desire to do his will in everything, and to obey all the commandments and instructions he has given our ancestors. ⁵⁹And may these words of my prayer be constantly before him day and night, so that he helps me and all of Israel in accordance with our daily needs. ⁶⁰May people all over the earth know that the Lord is God and that there is no other god at all. ⁶¹O my people, may you live good and perfect lives before the Lord our God; may you always obey his laws and commandments, just as you are doing today."

⁶²,⁶³Then the king and all the people dedicated the Temple by sacrificing peace offerings to the Lord—a total of 22,000 oxen and 120,000 sheep and goats! ⁶⁴As a temporary measure the king sanctified the court in front of the Temple for the burnt offerings, grain offerings, and the fat of the peace offerings: for the bronze altar was too small to handle so much. ⁶⁵The celebration lasted for fourteen days, and a great crowd came from one end of the land to the other. ⁶⁶Afterwards Solomon sent the people home, happy for all the goodness that the Lord had shown to his servant David and to his people Israel. And they blessed the king.

9 God's Warning to Solomon

When Solomon had finished building the Temple and the palace and all the other buildings he had always wanted, ²,³the Lord appeared to him the second time (the first time had been at Gibeon) and said to him,

"I have heard your prayer. I have hallowed this Temple that you have built and have put my name here forever. I will constantly watch over it and rejoice in it. ⁴And if you live in honesty and truth as your father David did, always obeying me, ⁵then I will cause your descendants to be the kings of Israel forever, just as I promised your father David when I told him, 'One of your sons shall always be upon the throne of Israel.'

⁶"However, if you or your children turn away from me and worship other gods and do not obey my laws, ⁷then I will take away the people of Israel from this land that have given them. I will take them from this Temple which I have hallowed for my name, and I will cast them out of my sight; and Israel will become a joke to the nations and an example and proverb of sudden disaster. ⁸This Temple will become a heap of ruins, and everyone passing by will be amazed and will whistle with astonishment, asking, 'Why has the Lord done such things to this land and this Temple?' ⁹And the answer will be, 'The people of Israel abandoned the Lord their God who brought them out of the land of Egypt; they worshiped other gods instead. That is why the Lord has brought this evil upon them.'"

¹⁰At the end of the twenty years during which Solomon built the Temple and the palace, ¹¹,¹²he gave twenty cities in the land of Galilee to King Hiram of Tyre as payment for all the cedar and cypress lumber and gold he had furnished for the construction of the palace and Temple. Hiram came from Tyre to see the cities, but he wasn't at all pleased with them.

¹³"What sort of deal is this, my brother?" he asked. "These cities are a wasteland!" (And they are still known as "The Wasteland" today.) ¹⁴For Hiram had sent gold to Solomon valued at $3,500,000!

¹⁵Solomon had conscripted forced labor to build the Temple, his palace, Fort Millo, the wall of Jerusalem, and the cities of Hazor, Megiddo, and Gezer. ¹⁶ Gezer was the city the king of Egypt conquered and burned, killing the Israeli population; later he had given the city to his daughter as a dowry—she was one of Solomon's wives. ¹⁷,¹⁸So now Solomon rebuilt Gezer along with Lower

Beth-horon, Baalath, and Tamar, a desert city. ¹⁹He also built cities for grain storage, cities in which to keep his chariots, cities for homes for his cavalry and chariot drivers, and resort cities near Jerusalem and in the Lebanon mountains and elsewhere throughout the land.

²⁰,²¹Solomon conscripted his labor forces from those who survived in the nations he conquered—the Amorites, Hittites, Perizzites, Hivites, and Jebusites. For the people of Israel had not been able to wipe them out completely at the time of the invasion and conquest of Israel, and they continue as slaves even today. ²²Solomon didn't conscript any Israelis for this work, although they became soldiers, officials, army officers, chariot commanders, and cavalrymen. ²³And there were 550 men of Israel who were overseers of the labor forces.

Miscellaneous Notes:

²⁴King Solomon moved Pharaoh's daughter from the City of David—the old sector of Jerusalem—to the new quarters he had built for her in the palace. Then he built Fort Millo.

²⁵After the Temple was completed, Solomon offered burnt offerings and peace offerings three times a year on the altar he had built. And he also burned incense upon it.

²⁶King Solomon had a shipyard in Ezion-geber near Eloth on the Red Sea in the land of Edom, where he built a fleet of ships.

²⁷,²⁸King Hiram supplied experienced sailors to accompany Solomon's crews. They used to sail back and forth from Ophir, bringing gold to King Solomon, the total value of which was several million dollars each trip.

10 The Queen of Sheba Visits

When the queen of Sheba heard how wonderfully the Lord had blessed Solomon with wisdom, she decided to test him with some hard questions. ²She arrived in Jerusalem with a long train of camels carrying spices, gold, and jewels; and she told him all her problems. ³Solomon answered all her questions; nothing was too difficult for him, for the Lord gave him the right answers every time. ⁴She soon realized that everything she had ever heard about his great wisdom was true. She also saw the beautiful palace he had built, ⁵and when she saw the wonderful foods on his table, the great number of servants and aides who stood around in splendid uniforms, his cupbearers, and the many offerings he sacrificed by fire to the Lord—well, there was no more spirit in her!

⁶She exclaimed to him, "Everything I heard in my own country about your wisdom and about the wonderful things going on here is all true. ⁷I didn't believe it until I came, but now I have seen it for myself! And really! The half had not been told me! Your wisdom and prosperity are far greater than anything I've ever heard of! ⁸Your people are happy and your palace aides are content—but how could it be otherwise, for they stand here day after day listening to your wisdom! ⁹Blessed be the Lord your God who chose you and set you on the throne of Israel. How the Lord must love Israel—for he gave you to them as their king! And you give your people a just, good government!"

¹⁰Then she gave the king a gift of $3,500,000 in gold, along with a huge quantity of spices and precious gems; in fact, it was the largest single gift of spices King Solomon had ever received.

¹¹(And when King Hiram's ships brought gold to Solomon from Ophir, they also brought along a great supply of algum trees and gems. ¹²Solomon used the algum wood to make pillars for the Temple and the palace, and for harps and harpsichords for his choirs. Never before or since has there been such a supply of beautiful wood.)

¹³In exchange for the gifts from the queen of Sheba, King Solomon gave her everything she asked him for, besides the presents he had already planned. Then she and her servants returned to their own land.

¹⁴Each year Solomon received gold worth a quarter of a billion dollars, ¹⁵besides sales taxes and profits from trade with the kings of Arabia and the other surrounding territories. ¹⁶,¹⁷Solomon had some of the gold beaten into two hundred pieces of armor (gold worth $6,000 went into each piece) and three hundred shields ($1,800 worth of gold in each). And he kept them in his palace in the Hall of the Forest of Lebanon.

¹⁸He also made a huge ivory throne and overlaid it with pure gold. ¹⁹It had six steps and a rounded back, with arm rests; and a lion standing on each side. ²⁰And there were two lions on each step—twelve in all. There was no other throne in all the world so splendid as that one.

²¹All of King Solomon's cups were of solid gold, and in the Hall of the Forest of Lebanon his entire dining service was made of solid gold. (Silver wasn't used because it wasn't considered to be of much value!)

²²King Solomon's merchant fleet was in partnership with King Hiram's, and once every three years a great load of gold, silver, ivory, apes, and peacocks arrived at the Israeli ports.

²³So King Solomon was richer and wiser than all the kings of the earth. ²⁴Great men from many lands came to interview him and listen to his God-given wisdom. ²⁵They brought him annual tribute of silver and gold dishes, beautiful cloth, myrrh, spices, horses, and mules.

²⁶Solomon built up a great stable of horses

with a vast number of chariots and cavalry—1,400 chariots in all and 12,000 cavalrymen, who lived in the chariot cities and with the king at Jerusalem. ²⁷Silver was as common as stones in Jerusalem in those days, and cedar was of no greater value than the common sycamore! ²⁸Solomon's horses were brought to him from Egypt and southern Turkey, where his agents purchased them at wholesale prices. ²⁹An Egyptian chariot delivered to Jerusalem cost $400, and the horses were valued at $150 each. Many of these were then resold to the Hittite and Syrian kings.

Solomon Turns from God

King Solomon married many other girls besides the Egyptian princess. Many of them came from nations where idols were worshiped—Moab, Ammon, Edom, Sidon, and from the Hittites—²even though the Lord had clearly instructed his people not to marry into those nations, because the women they married would get them started worshiping their gods. Yet Solomon did it anyway. ³He had seven hundred wives and three hundred concubines; and sure enough, they turned his heart away from the Lord, ⁴especially in his old age. They encouraged him to worship their gods instead of trusting completely in the Lord as his father David had done. ⁵Solomon worshiped Ashtoreth, the goddess of the Sidonians, and Milcom, the horrible god of the Ammonites. ⁶Thus Solomon did what was clearly wrong and refused to follow the Lord as his father David did. ⁷He even built a temple on the Mount of Olives, across the valley from Jerusalem, for Chemosh, the depraved god of Moab, and another for Molech, the unutterably vile god of the Ammonites. ⁸Solomon built temples for these foreign wives to use for burning incense and sacrificing to their gods.

⁹,¹⁰Jehovah was very angry with Solomon about this, for now Solomon was no longer interested in the Lord God of Israel who had appeared to him twice to warn him specifically against worshiping other gods. But he hadn't listened, ¹¹so now the Lord said to him, "Since you have not kept our agreement and have not obeyed my laws, I will tear the kingdom away from you and your family and give it to someone else. ¹²,¹³However, for the sake of your father David, I won't do this while you are still alive. I will take the kingdom away from your son. And even so I will let him be king of one tribe, for David's sake and for the sake of Jerusalem, my chosen city."

¹⁴So the Lord caused Hadad the Edomite to grow in power. And Solomon became apprehensive, for Hadad was a member of the royal family of Edom. ¹⁵Years before, when David had been in Edom with Joab to arrange for the burial of some Israeli soldiers who had died in battle, the Israeli army had killed nearly every male in the entire country. ¹⁶⁻¹⁸It took six months to accomplish this, but they finally killed all except Hadad and a few royal officials who took him to Egypt (he was a very small child at the time). They slipped out of Midian and went to Paran, where others joined them and accompanied them to Egypt, and Pharaoh had given them homes and food.

¹⁹Hadad became one of Pharaoh's closest friends, and he gave him a wife—the sister of Queen Tahpenes. ²⁰She presented him with a son, Genubath, who was brought up in Pharaoh's palace among Pharaoh's own sons. ²¹When Hadad, there in Egypt, heard that David and Joab were both dead, he asked Pharaoh for permission to return to Edom.

²²"Why?" Pharaoh asked him. "What do you lack here? How have we disappointed you?"

"Everything is wonderful," he replied "but even so, I'd like to go back home."

²³Another of Solomon's enemies whom God raised to power was Rezon, one of the officials of King Hadadezer of Zobah who had deserted his post and fled the country. ²⁴He had become the leader of a gang of bandits—men who fled with him to Damascus (where he later became king) when David destroyed Zobah. ²⁵During Solomon's entire lifetime, Rezon and Hadad were his enemies, for they hated Israel intensely.

²⁶Another rebel leader was Jeroboam (the son of Nebat), who came from the city of Zeredah in Ephraim; his mother was Zeruah, a widow. ²⁷,²⁸Here is the story back of his rebellion: Solomon was rebuilding Fort Millo, repairing the walls of this city his father had built. Jeroboam was very able, and when Solomon saw how industrious he was, he put him in charge of his labor battalions from the tribe of Joseph.

²⁹One day as Jeroboam was leaving Jerusalem, the prophet Ahijah from Shiloh (who had put on a new robe for the occasion) met him and called him aside to talk to him. And as the two of them were alone in the field, ³⁰Ahijah tore his new robe into twelve parts ³¹and said to Jeroboam, "Take ten of these pieces, for the Lord God of Israel says, 'I will tear the kingdom from the hand of Solomon and give ten of the tribes to you! ³²But I will leave him one tribe for the sake of my servant David and for the sake of Jerusalem, which I have chosen above all the other cities of Israel. ³³For Solomon has forsaken me and worships Ashtoreth, the goddess of the Sidonians; and Chemosh, the god of Moab; and Milcom, the god of the Ammonites. He has not followed my paths and has not done what I consider right; he has not kept my laws and instructions as his father David

Family Devotions

☐ DEVOTION 114

MAKING THE BEST CHOICES

Read 1 Kings 11:1-13

"Pam, it's time to leave for the missionary meeting at church," called Mother. "Are you ready?" When Pam didn't respond, Mother headed for her room. Hearing her mother's footsteps approaching, Pam slipped a book under her pillow and quickly changed the dial on her radio. "What were you listening to?" Mother asked. "I called and called, and you didn't seem to hear me."

"Oh, I was just looking for some good music," said Pam.

"Well, are you ready to leave for church?" asked Mother.

Pam reluctantly stood up. "I suppose," she muttered. But she was grouchy all the way to church because she really wanted to stay home and watch her favorite television program.

Pam expected to be bored, but when the missionary showed slides, she watched intently. "Many of our people worship idols, practice black magic, and dabble in the spirit world," the missionary said. "When they accept Christ as Savior and become new creatures in him, they no longer want to do many of the things they did before. This last slide shows a big bonfire where they're burning their idols, magic books, and special potions. They're getting rid of anything that would keep them from living for God. They're often persecuted for their stand, but Jesus means more to them than worldly possessions or popularity." He turned off the projector and waited for the lights to come on. Then he asked, "Is there anything you need to burn? Anything you need to get rid of so that it won't keep you from living for God?"

Pam thought about the heavy metal music she had listened to before her mom had come to her room. She remembered the book she didn't want her mom to see and the way she had wanted to put a television program above church attendance.

Pam bowed her head to pray. Just like those natives in Africa, she, too, had some idols to destroy in her life.

Making the Best Choices
Memory Verse

He will always give you all you need from day to day if you will make the Kingdom of God your primary concern.
Luke 12:31

How About You?

Does Jesus have first place in your life, or are you letting TV, video games, a new bicycle, or friends control your thinking and actions? Are they coming before God? Examine your life. If there are some idols you need to put away, take care of it today. J. H.

• For the next devotional, turn to page 373. • For the next devotional on *MAKING THE BEST CHOICES*, turn to page 467. • For notes on *MAKING THE BEST CHOICES*, see pages 358, 652, and 944.

did. ³⁴I will not take the kingdom from him now, however; for the sake of my servant David, my chosen one who obeyed my commandments, I will let Solomon reign for the rest of his life.

³⁵"But I will take away the kingdom from his son and give ten of the tribes to you. ³⁶His son shall have the other one so that the descendants of David will continue to reign in Jerusalem, the city I have chosen to be the place for my name to be enshrined. ³⁷And I will place you on the throne of Israel and give you absolute power. ³⁸If you listen to what I tell you and walk in my path and do whatever I consider right, obeying my commandments as my servant David did, then I will bless you; and your descendants shall rule Israel forever. (I once made this same promise to David. ³⁹But because of Solomon's sin, I will punish the descendants of David—though not forever.)'"

⁴⁰Solomon tried to kill Jeroboam, but he fled to King Shishak of Egypt and stayed there until the death of Solomon.

⁴¹The rest of what Solomon did and said is written in the book *The Acts of Solomon*. ⁴²He ruled in Jerusalem for forty years, ⁴³and then died and was buried in the city of his father David; and his son Rehoboam reigned in his place.

12 The Kingdom Splits in Two

Rehoboam's inauguration was at Shechem, and all Israel came for the coronation ceremony. ²⁻⁴Jeroboam, who was still in Egypt where he had fled from King Solomon, heard about the plans from his friends. They urged him to attend, so he joined the rest of Israel at Shechem and was the ringleader in getting the people to make certain demands upon Rehoboam.

"Your father was a hard master," they told Rehoboam. "We don't want you as our king unless you promise to treat us better than he did."

⁵"Give me three days to think this over," Rehoboam replied. "Come back then for my answer." So the people left.

⁶Rehoboam talked it over with the old men who had counseled his father Solomon.

"What do you think I should do?" he asked them.

⁷And they replied, "If you give them a pleasant reply and agree to be good to them and serve them well, you can be their king forever."

⁸But Rehoboam refused the old men's counsel and called in the young men with whom he had grown up.

⁹"What do you think I should do?" he asked them.

¹⁰And the young men replied, "Tell them, 'If you think my father was hard on you, well, I'll be harder! ¹¹Yes, my father was harsh, but I'll be even harsher! My father used whips on you, but I'll use scorpions!'"

¹²So when Jeroboam and the people returned three days later, ¹³,¹⁴the new king answered them roughly. He ignored the old men's advice and followed that of the young men; ¹⁵so the king refused the people's demands. (But the Lord's hand was in it—he caused the new king to do this in order to fulfill his promise to Jeroboam, made through Ahijah, the prophet from Shiloh.)

¹⁶,¹⁷When the people realized that the king meant what he said and was refusing to listen to them, they began shouting, "Down with David and all his relatives! Let's go home! Let Rehoboam be king of his own family!"

And they all deserted him except for the tribe of Judah, who remained loyal and accepted Rehoboam as their king. ¹⁸When King Rehoboam sent Adoram (who was in charge of the draft) to conscript men from the other tribes, a great mob stoned him to death. But King Rehoboam escaped by chariot and fled to Jerusalem. ¹⁹And Israel has been in rebellion against the dynasty of David to this day.

²⁰When the people of Israel learned of Jeroboam's return from Egypt, he was asked to come before an open meeting of all the people; and there he was made king of Israel. Only the tribe of Judah continued under the kingship of the family of David.

²¹When King Rehoboam arrived in Jerusalem, he summoned his army—all the able-bodied men of Judah and Benjamin: 180,000 special troops—to force the rest of Israel to acknowledge him as their king. ²²But God sent this message to Shemaiah, the prophet:

²³,²⁴"Tell Rehoboam the son of Solomon, king of Judah, and all the people of Judah and Benjamin that they must not fight against their brothers, the people of Israel. Tell them to disband and go home, for what has happened to Rehoboam is according to my wish." So the army went home as the Lord had commanded.

²⁵Jeroboam now built the city of Shechem in the hill country of Ephraim, and it became his capital. Later he built Penuel. ²⁶Jeroboam thought, "Unless I'm careful, the people will want a descendant of David as their king. ²⁷When they go to Jerusalem to offer sacrifices at the Temple, they will become friendly with King Rehoboam; then they will kill me and ask him to be their king instead."

²⁸So on the advice of his counselors, the king had two golden calf idols made and told the people, "It's too much trouble to go to Jerusalem to worship; from now on these will be your

gods—they rescued you from your captivity in Egypt!"

²⁹One of these calf idols was placed in Bethel and the other in Dan. ³⁰This was of course a great sin, for the people worshiped them. ³¹He also made shrines on the hills and ordained priests from the rank and file of the people—even those who were not from the priest-tribe of Levi. ³²,³³Jeroboam also announced that the annual Tabernacle Festival would be held at Bethel on the first of November (a date he decided upon himself), similar to the annual festival at Jerusalem; he himself offered sacrifices upon the altar to the calves at Bethel and burned incense to them. And it was there at Bethel that he ordained priests for the shrines on the hills.

13 Jeroboam Makes Two Golden Calves

As Jeroboam approached the altar to burn incense to the golden calf idol, a prophet of the Lord from Judah walked up to him. ²Then, at the Lord's command, the prophet shouted, "O altar, the Lord says that a child named Josiah shall be born into the family line of David, and he shall sacrifice upon you the priests from the shrines on the hills who come here to burn incense; and men's bones shall be burned upon you."

³Then he gave this proof that his message was from the Lord: "This altar will split apart, and the ashes on it will spill to the ground."

⁴The king was very angry with the prophet for saying this. He shouted to his guards, "Arrest that man!" and shook his fist at him. Instantly the king's arm became paralyzed in that position; he couldn't pull it back again! ⁵At the same moment a wide crack appeared in the altar and the ashes poured out, just as the prophet had said would happen. For this was the prophet's proof that God had been speaking through him.

⁶"Oh, please, please," the king cried out to the prophet, "beg the Lord your God to restore my arm again."

So he prayed to the Lord, and the king's arm became normal again.

⁷Then the king said to the prophet, "Come to the palace with me and rest awhile and have some food; and I'll give you a reward because you healed my arm."

⁸But the prophet said to the king, "Even if you gave me half your palace, I wouldn't go into it; nor would I eat or drink even water in this place! ⁹For the Lord has given me strict orders not to eat anything or drink any water while I'm here, and not to return to Judah by the road I came on."

¹⁰So he went back another way.

¹¹As it happened, there was an old prophet living in Bethel, and his sons went home and told him what the prophet from Judah had done and what he had said to the king.

¹²"Which way did he go?" the old prophet asked. So they told him.

¹³"Quick, saddle the donkey," the old man said. And when they had saddled the donkey for him, ¹⁴he rode after the prophet and found him sitting under an oak tree.

"Are you the prophet who came from Judah?" he asked him.

"Yes," he replied, "I am."

¹⁵Then the old man said to the prophet, "Come home with me and eat."

¹⁶,¹⁷"No," he replied, "I can't; for I am not allowed to eat anything or to drink any water at Bethel. The Lord strictly warned me against it; and he also told me not to return home by the same road I came on."

¹⁸But the old man said, "I am a prophet too, just as you are; and an angel gave me a message from the Lord. I am to take you home with me and give you food and water."

But the old man was lying to him. ¹⁹So they went back together, and the prophet ate some food and drank some water at the old man's home.

²⁰Then, suddenly, while they were sitting at the table, a message from the Lord came to the old man, ²¹,²²and he shouted at the prophet from Judah, "The Lord says that because you have been disobedient to his clear command and have come here, and have eaten and drunk water in the place he told you not to, therefore your body shall not be buried in the grave of your fathers."

²³After finishing the meal, the old man saddled the prophet's donkey, ²⁴,²⁵and the prophet started off again. But as he was traveling along, a lion came out and killed him. His body lay there on the road, with the donkey and the lion standing beside it. Those who came by and saw the body lying in the road and the lion standing quietly beside it, reported it in Bethel where the old prophet lived.

²⁶When he heard what had happened he exclaimed, "It is the prophet who disobeyed the Lord's command; the Lord fulfilled his warning by causing the lion to kill him."

RESPECTING GOD'S WORD 13:7-31 This prophet had been given strict orders from God not to eat or drink anything while on his mission (13:9). He died because he listened to a man who claimed to have a message from God, rather than to God himself. This prophet should have followed God's Word instead of hearsay. Trust what Scripture says rather than what someone claims is true. And disregard what others claim to be messages from God if their words contradict the Bible. **To begin the series of devotionals on RESPECTING GOD'S WORD, turn to page 11.**

²⁷Then he said to his sons, "Saddle my donkey!" And they did.

²⁸He found the prophet's body lying in the road; and the donkey and lion were still standing there beside it, for the lion had not eaten the body nor attacked the donkey. ²⁹So the prophet laid the body upon the donkey and took it back to the city to mourn over it and bury it.

³⁰He laid the body in his own grave, exclaiming, "Alas, my brother!"

³¹Afterwards he said to his sons, "When I die, bury me in the grave where the prophet is buried. Lay my bones beside his bones. ³²For the Lord told him to shout against the altar in Bethel, and his curse against the shrines in the cities of Samaria shall surely be fulfilled."

³³Despite the prophet's warning, Jeroboam did not turn away from his evil ways; instead, he made more priests than ever from the common people, to offer sacrifices to idols in the shrines on the hills. Anyone who wanted to could be a priest. ³⁴This was a great sin and resulted in the destruction of Jeroboam's kingdom and the death of all of his family.

14 Jeroboam's Son Dies

Jeroboam's son Abijah now became very sick. ²Jeroboam told his wife, "Disguise yourself so that no one will recognize you as the queen, and go to Ahijah the prophet at Shiloh—the man who told me that I would become king. ³Take him a gift of ten loaves of bread, some fig bars, and a jar of honey, and ask him whether the boy will recover."

⁴So his wife went to Ahijah's home at Shiloh. He was an old man now and could no longer see. ⁵But the Lord told him that the queen, pretending to be someone else, would come to ask about her son, for he was very sick. And the Lord told him what to tell her.

⁶So when Ahijah heard her at the door, he called out, "Come in, wife of Jeroboam! Why are you pretending to be someone else?" Then he told her, "I have sad news for you. ⁷Give your husband this message from the Lord God of Israel: 'I promoted you from the ranks of the common people and made you king of Israel. ⁸I ripped the kingdom away from the family of David and gave it to you, but you have not obeyed my commandments as my servant David did. His heart's desire was always to obey me and to do whatever I wanted him to. ⁹But you have done more evil than all the other kings before you; you have made other gods and have made me furious with your gold calves. And since you have refused to acknowledge me, ¹⁰I will bring disaster upon your home and will destroy all of your sons—this boy who is sick and all those who are well. I will sweep away your family as a stable hand shovels out manure. ¹¹I vow that those of your family who die in the city shall be eaten by dogs, and those who die in the field shall be eaten by birds.'"

¹²Then Ahijah said to Jeroboam's wife, "Go on home, and when you step into the city, the child will die. ¹³All of Israel will mourn for him and bury him, but he is the only member of your family who will come to a quiet end. For this child is the only good thing that the Lord God of Israel sees in the entire family of Jeroboam. ¹⁴And the Lord will raise up a king over Israel who will destroy the family of Jeroboam. ¹⁵Then the Lord will shake Israel like a reed whipped about in a stream; he will uproot the people of Israel from this good land of their fathers and scatter them beyond the Euphrates River, for they have angered the Lord by worshiping idol-gods. ¹⁶He will abandon Israel because Jeroboam sinned and made all of Israel sin along with him."

¹⁷So Jeroboam's wife returned to Tirzah; and the child died just as she walked through the door of her home. ¹⁸And there was mourning for him throughout the land, just as the Lord had predicted through Ahijah.

¹⁹The rest of Jeroboam's activities—his wars and the other events of his reign—are recorded in *The Annals of the Kings of Israel*. ²⁰Jeroboam reigned twenty-two years, and when he died, his son Nadab took the throne.

²¹Meanwhile, Rehoboam the son of Solomon was king in Judah. He was forty-one years old when he began to reign, and he was on the throne seventeen years in Jerusalem, the city which, among all the cities of Israel, the Lord had chosen to live in. (Rehoboam's mother was Naamah, an Ammonite woman.) ²²During his reign the people of Judah, like those in Israel, did wrong and angered the Lord with their sin, for it was even worse than that of their ancestors. ²³They built shrines and obelisks and idols on every high hill and under every green tree. ²⁴There was homosexuality throughout the land, and the people of Judah became as depraved as the heathen nations which the Lord drove out to make room for his people.

²⁵In the fifth year of Rehoboam's reign, King Shishak of Egypt attacked and conquered Jerusalem. ²⁶He ransacked the Temple and the palace and stole everything, including all the gold shields Solomon had made. ²⁷Afterwards Rehoboam made bronze shields as substitutes, and the palace guards used these instead. ²⁸Whenever the king went to the Temple, the guards paraded before him and then took the shields back to the guard chamber.

²⁹The other events in Rehoboam's reign are

written in *The Annals of the Kings of Judah.* ³⁰There was constant war between Rehoboam and Jeroboam. ³¹When Rehoboam died—his mother was Naamah the Ammonitess—he was buried among his ancestors in Jerusalem, and his son Abijam took the throne.

15 Abijam Rules Judah

Abijam began his three-year reign as king of Judah in Jerusalem during the eighteenth year of Jeroboam's reign in Israel. (Abijam's mother was Maacah, the daughter of Abishalom.) ³He was as great a sinner as his father was, and his heart was not right with God, as King David's was. ⁴But despite Abijam's sin, the Lord remembered David's love and did not end the line of David's royal descendants. ⁵For David had obeyed God during his entire life except for the affair concerning Uriah the Hittite. ⁶During Abijam's reign there was constant war between Israel and Judah. ⁷The rest of Abijam's history is recorded in *The Annals of the Kings of Judah.* ⁸When he died he was buried in Jerusalem, and his son Asa reigned in his place.

⁹Asa became king of Judah, in Jerusalem, in the twentieth year of the reign of Jeroboam over Israel, ¹⁰and reigned forty-one years. (His grandmother was Maacah, the daughter of Abishalom.) ¹¹He pleased the Lord like his ancestor King David. ¹²He executed the male prostitutes and removed all the idols his father had made. ¹³He deposed his grandmother Maacah as queen-mother because she had made an idol—which he cut down and burned at Kidron Brook. ¹⁴However, the shrines on the hills were not removed, for Asa did not realize that these were wrong. ¹⁵He made permanent exhibits in the Temple of the bronze shields his grandfather had dedicated, along with the silver and gold vessels he himself had donated.

¹⁶There was lifelong war between King Asa of Judah and King Baasha of Israel. ¹⁷King Baasha built the fortress city of Ramah in an attempt to cut off all trade with Jerusalem. ¹⁸Then Asa took all the silver and gold left in the Temple treasury and all the treasures of the palace, and gave them to his officials to take to Damascus, to King Ben-hadad of Syria, with this message:

¹⁹"Let us be allies just as our fathers were. I am sending you a present of gold and silver. Now break your alliance with King Baasha of Israel so that he will leave me alone."

²⁰Ben-hadad agreed and sent his armies against some of the cities of Israel; and he destroyed Ijon, Dan, Abel-beth-maacah, all of Chinneroth, and all the cities in the land of Naphtali. ²¹When Baasha received word of the attack, he discontinued building the city of Ramah and returned to Tirzah. ²²Then King Asa made a proclamation to all Judah, asking every able-bodied man to help demolish Ramah and haul away its stones and timbers. And King Asa used these materials to build the city of Geba in Benjamin and the city of Mizpah.

²³The rest of Asa's biography—his conquests and deeds and the names of the cities he built—is found in *The Annals of the Kings of Judah.* In his old age his feet became diseased, ²⁴and when he died, he was buried in the royal cemetery in Jerusalem. Then his son Jehoshaphat became the new king of Judah.

²⁵Meanwhile over in Israel, Nadab, the son of Jeroboam, had become king. He reigned two years, beginning in the second year of the reign of King Asa of Judah. ²⁶But he was not a good king; like his father, he worshiped many idols and led all of Israel into sin.

²⁷Then Baasha (the son of Ahijah, from the tribe of Issachar) plotted against him and assassinated him while he was with the Israeli army laying siege to the Philistine city of Gibbethon. ²⁸So Baasha replaced Nadab as the king of Israel in Tirzah during the third year of the reign of King Asa of Judah. ²⁹He immediately killed all of the descendants of King Jeroboam, so that not one of the royal family was left, just as the Lord had said would happen when he spoke through Ahijah, the prophet from Shiloh. ³⁰This was done because Jeroboam had angered the Lord God of Israel by sinning and leading the rest of Israel into sin.

³¹Further details of Baasha's reign are recorded in *The Annals of the Kings of Israel.*

³²,³³There was continuous warfare between King Asa of Judah and King Baasha of Israel. Baasha reigned for twenty-four years, ³⁴but all that time he continually disobeyed the Lord. He followed the evil paths of Jeroboam, for he led the people of Israel into the sin of worshiping idols.

16 Baasha Rules Israel

A message of condemnation from the Lord was delivered to King Baasha at this time by the prophet Jehu:

²"I lifted you out of the dust," the message said, "to make you king of my people Israel; but you have

---

STANDING FOR RIGHTEOUSNESS 15:30 All the descendants of Jeroboam were killed because he led Israel into sin. Sin is always judged harshly, but the worst sinners are those who lead others into sin. Jesus said it would be better if such people had a millstone tied around their necks and were thrown into the sea (Mark 9:42). If you ever take the responsibility of leading others, remember the consequences of leading them astray. Teaching the truth is a responsibility that goes hand in hand with the privilege of leadership. **To begin the series of devotionals on STANDING FOR RIGHTEOUSNESS, turn to page 139.**

walked in the evil paths of Jeroboam. You have made my people sin, and I am angry! ³So now I will destroy you and your family, just as I did the descendants of Jeroboam. ⁴⁻⁷Those of your family who die in the city will be eaten by dogs, and those who die in the fields will be eaten by the birds."

The message was sent to Baasha and his family because he had angered the Lord by all his evil deeds. He was as evil as Jeroboam despite the fact that the Lord had destroyed all of Jeroboam's descendants for their sins.

The rest of Baasha's biography—his deeds and conquests—are written in *The Annals of the Kings of Israel.*

⁸Elah, Baasha's son, began reigning during the twenty-sixth year of the reign of King Asa of Judah, but he reigned only two years. ⁹Then General Zimri, who had charge of half the royal chariot troops, plotted against him. One day King Elah was half drunk at the home of Arza, the superintendent of the palace, in the capital city of Tirzah. ¹⁰Zimri simply walked in and struck him down and killed him. (This occurred during the twenty-seventh year of the reign of King Asa of Judah.) Then Zimri declared himself to be the new king of Israel.

¹¹He immediately killed the entire royal family—leaving not a single male child. He even destroyed distant relatives and friends. ¹²This destruction of the descendants of Baasha was in line with what the Lord had predicted through the prophet Jehu. ¹³The tragedy occurred because of the sins of Baasha and his son Elah; for they had led Israel into worshiping idols, and the Lord was very angry about it. ¹⁴The rest of the history of Elah's reign is written in *The Annals of the Kings of Israel.*

¹⁵,¹⁶But Zimri lasted only seven days; for when the army of Israel, which was then engaged in attacking the Philistine city of Gibbethon, heard that Zimri had assassinated the king, they decided on General Omri, commander-in-chief of the army, as their new ruler. ¹⁷So Omri led the army of Gibbethon to besiege Tirzah, Israel's capital. ¹⁸When Zimri saw that the city had been taken, he went into the palace and burned it over him and died in the flames. ¹⁹For he, too, had sinned like Jeroboam; he had worshiped idols and had led the people of Israel to sin with him. ²⁰The rest of the story of Zimri and his treason are written in *The Annals of the Kings of Israel.*

²¹But now the kingdom of Israel was split in two; half the people were loyal to General Omri, and the other half followed Tibni, the son of Ginath. ²²But General Omri won and Tibni was killed; so Omri reigned without opposition.

²³King Asa of Judah had been on the throne thirty-one years when Omri began his reign over Israel, which lasted twelve years, six of them in Tirzah. ²⁴Then Omri bought the hill now known as Samaria from its owner, Shemer, for $4,000 and built a city on it, calling it Samaria in honor of Shemer. ²⁵But Omri was worse than any of the kings before him; ²⁶he worshiped idols as Jeroboam had and led Israel into this same sin. So God was very angry. ²⁷The rest of Omri's history is recorded in *The Annals of the Kings of Israel.* ²⁸When Omri died he was buried in Samaria, and his son Ahab became king in his place.

²⁹King Asa of Judah had been on the throne thirty-eight years when Ahab became the king of Israel; and Ahab reigned for twenty-two years. ³⁰But he was even more wicked than his father Omri; he was worse than any other king of Israel! ³¹And as though that were not enough, he married Jezebel, the daughter of King Ethbaal of the Sidonians, and then began worshiping Baal. ³²First he built a temple and an altar for Baal in Samaria. ³³Then he made other idols and did more to anger the Lord God of Israel than any of the other kings of Israel before him.

³⁴(It was during his reign that Hiel, a man from Bethel, rebuilt Jericho. When he laid the foundations, his oldest son, Abiram, died; and when he finally completed it by setting up the gates, his youngest son, Segub, died. For this was the Lord's curse upon Jericho as declared by Joshua, the son of Nun.)

17 Ravens Feed Elijah

Then Elijah, the prophet from Tishbe in Gilead, told King Ahab, "As surely as the Lord God of Israel lives—the God whom I worship and serve—there won't be any dew or rain for several years until I say the word!"

²Then the Lord said to Elijah, ³"Go to the east and hide by Cherith Brook at a place east of where it enters the Jordan River. ⁴Drink from the brook and eat what the ravens bring you, for I have commanded them to feed you."

⁵So he did as the Lord had told him to and camped beside the brook. ⁶The ravens brought him bread and meat each morning and evening, and he drank from the brook. ⁷But after awhile the brook dried up, for there was no rainfall anywhere in the land.

⁸,⁹Then the Lord said to him, "Go and live in the village of Zarephath, near the city of Sidon. There is a widow there who will feed you. I have given her my instructions."

¹⁰So he went to Zarephath. As he arrived at the gates of the city he saw a widow gathering sticks; and he asked her for a cup of water.

¹¹As she was going to get it, he called to her, "Bring me a bite of bread too."

¹²But she said, "I swear by the Lord your God that I haven't a single piece of bread in the house. And I have only a handful of flour left and a little

Family Devotions

☐ DEVOTION 115
LOVING OTHERS

Read 1 Kings 18:3-4

Loving Others
Memory Verse

Little children, let us stop just *saying* we love people; let us *really* love them, and *show it* by our *actions*.
1 John 3:18

"Guess what?" Lisa bounded into the room, followed by Amy. "Amy and I are going to give a demonstration at the next 4-H Club meeting."

"Great," said Mom. "What will you demonstrate?"

Both girls looked at her with a blank stare, and then burst into peals of laughter. "We hadn't thought about that." All was quiet as they thought. Then Lisa snapped her fingers. "I know. Let's give a demonstration on flower arranging. Mom has a book that will show us how, and we have lots of flowers in our garden."

All afternoon the girls studied and practiced arranging flowers. Finally, they came into the living room, carrying a bouquet. "Beautiful!" Mom exclaimed. "I'm amazed at what you've done."

"We're still working on our speech. We have three weeks to practice," Lisa said. "May I go with Amy to her Aunt Clara's house tomorrow morning? We want to give this arrangement to her. She's crippled and can't even get out of bed now." Mom smiled her approval, and the next morning the girls took the flowers to the elderly lady and spent an hour talking with her.

"How did your demonstration go?" Mom asked when Lisa returned home.

"That's not for a few weeks yet," Lisa replied. She was surprised that Mom had forgotten.

Mom smiled. "I'm talking about the demonstration you performed this morning," she said. "The flowers you arranged are beautiful, but not nearly as beautiful as the love you girls showed by taking the flowers to Amy's aunt and spending time with her. I'm sure it meant a lot to her. You girls are demonstrating something far more important than flower arranging."

Lisa raised her eyebrows. "We are?"

Mom smiled. "Yes. A lot of people talk about God's love, but you're demonstrating it by your thoughtfulness."

How About You?
Obadiah demonstrated his love for God by helping the prophets when Queen Jezebel wanted to kill them. You probably won't be able to do something that dramatic, but you can still show the world the love of God by your actions. Are you kind and thoughtful? Do you help whenever you can? Demonstrate God's love to someone today. *B. W.*

• For the next devotional, turn to page 377.   • For the next devotional on LOVING OTHERS, turn to page 529.
• For notes on LOVING OTHERS, see pages 658, 951, 967, and 1242.

cooking oil in the bottom of the jar. I was just gathering a few sticks to cook this last meal, and then my son and I must die of starvation."

¹³But Elijah said to her, "Don't be afraid! Go ahead and cook that 'last meal,' but bake me a little loaf of bread first; and afterwards there will still be enough food for you and your son. ¹⁴For the Lord God of Israel says that there will always be plenty of flour and oil left in your containers until the time when the Lord sends rain and the crops grow again!"

¹⁵So she did as Elijah said, and she and Elijah and her son continued to eat from her supply of flour and oil as long as it was needed. ¹⁶For no matter how much they used, there was always plenty left in the containers, just as the Lord had promised through Elijah!

¹⁷But one day the woman's son became sick and died.

¹⁸"O man of God," she cried, "what have you done to me? Have you come here to punish my sins by killing my son?"

¹⁹"Give him to me," Elijah replied. And he took the boy's body from her and carried it upstairs to the guest room where he lived, and laid the body on his bed, ²⁰and then cried out to the Lord, "O Lord my God, why have you killed the son of this widow with whom I am staying?"

²¹And he stretched himself upon the child three times and cried out to the Lord, "O Lord my God, please let this child's spirit return to him."

²²And the Lord heard Elijah's prayer; and the spirit of the child returned, and he became alive again! ²³Then Elijah took him downstairs and gave him to his mother.

"See! He's alive!" he beamed.

²⁴"Now I know for sure that you are a prophet," she told him afterward, "and that whatever you say is from the Lord!"

18 Elijah Defeats Baal's Prophets

It was three years later that the Lord said to Elijah, "Go and tell King Ahab that I will soon send rain again!"

²So Elijah went to tell him. Meanwhile the famine had become very severe in Samaria.

³,⁴The man in charge of Ahab's household affairs was Obadiah, who was a devoted follower of the Lord. Once when Queen Jezebel had tried to kill all of the Lord's prophets, Obadiah had hidden one hundred of them in two caves—fifty in each—and had fed them with bread and water.

⁵That same day, while Elijah was on the way to see King Ahab, the king said to Obadiah, "We must check every stream and brook to see if we can find enough grass to save at least some of my horses and mules. You go one way and I'll go the other, and we will search the entire land."

⁶So they did, each going alone. ⁷Suddenly Obadiah saw Elijah coming toward him! Obadiah recognized him at once and fell to the ground before him.

"Is it really you, my lord Elijah?" he asked.

⁸"Yes, it is," Elijah replied. "Now go and tell the king I am here."

⁹"Oh, sir," Obadiah protested, "what harm have I done to you that you are sending me to my death? ¹⁰For I swear by God that the king has searched every nation and kingdom on earth from end to end to find you. And each time when he was told 'Elijah isn't here,' King Ahab forced the king of that nation to swear to the truth of his claim. ¹¹And now you say, 'Go and tell him Elijah is here'! ¹²But as soon as I leave you, the Spirit of the Lord will carry you away, who knows where, and when Ahab comes and can't find you, he will kill me; yet I have been a true servant of the Lord all my life. ¹³Has no one told you about the time when Queen Jezebel was trying to kill the Lord's prophets, and I hid a hundred of them in two caves and fed them with bread and water? ¹⁴And now you say, 'Go tell the king that Elijah is here'! Sir, if I do that, I'm dead!"

¹⁵But Elijah said, "I swear by the Lord God of the armies of heaven, in whose presence I stand, that I will present myself to Ahab today."

¹⁶So Obadiah went to tell Ahab that Elijah had come; and Ahab went out to meet him.

¹⁷"So it's you, is it?—the man who brought this disaster upon Israel!" Ahab exclaimed when he saw him.

¹⁸"You're talking about yourself," Elijah answered. "For you and your family have refused to obey the Lord and have worshiped Baal instead. ¹⁹Now bring all the people of Israel to Mount Carmel, with all 450 prophets of Baal and the 400 prophets of Asherah who are supported by Jezebel."

²⁰So Ahab summoned all the people and the prophets to Mount Carmel.

²¹Then Elijah talked to them. "How long are you going to waver between two opinions?" he asked the people. "If the Lord is God, *follow* him! But if Baal is God, then follow *him!*"

²²Then Elijah spoke again. "I am the only prophet of the Lord who is left," he told them, "but Baal has 450 prophets. ²³Now bring two young bulls. The prophets of Baal may choose whichever one they wish and cut it into pieces and lay it on the wood of their altar, but without putting any fire under the wood; and I will prepare the other young bull and lay it on the wood on the Lord's altar, with no fire under it. ²⁴Then pray to your god, and I will pray to the Lord; and the god who answers by sending fire to light the

wood is the true God!" And all the people agreed to this test.

²⁵Then Elijah turned to the prophets of Baal. "You first," he said, "for there are many of you; choose one of the bulls and prepare it and call to your god; but don't put any fire under the wood."

²⁶So they prepared one of the young bulls and placed it on the altar; and they called to Baal all morning, shouting, "O Baal, hear us!" But there was no reply of any kind. Then they began to dance around the altar. ²⁷About noontime, Elijah began mocking them.

"You'll have to shout louder than that," he scoffed, "to catch the attention of your god! Perhaps he is talking to someone, or is out sitting on the toilet, or maybe he is away on a trip, or is asleep and needs to be wakened!"

²⁸So they shouted louder and, as was their custom, cut themselves with knives and swords until the blood gushed out. ²⁹They raved all afternoon until the time of the evening sacrifice, but there was no reply, no voice, no answer.

³⁰Then Elijah called to the people, "Come over here."

And they all crowded around him as he repaired the altar of the Lord that had been torn down. ³¹He took twelve stones, one to represent each of the tribes of Israel, ³²and used the stones to rebuild the Lord's altar. Then he dug a trench about three feet wide around the altar. ³³He piled wood upon the altar and cut the young bull into pieces and laid the pieces on the wood.

"Fill four barrels with water," he said, "and pour the water over the carcass and the wood."

After they had done this he said, ³⁴"Do it again." And they did.

"Now, do it once more!" And they did; ³⁵and the water ran off the altar and filled the trench.

³⁶At the customary time for offering the evening sacrifice, Elijah walked up to the altar and prayed, "O Lord God of Abraham, Isaac, and Israel, prove today that you are the God of Israel and that I am your servant; prove that I have done all this at your command. ³⁷O Lord, answer me! Answer me so these people will know that you are God and that you have brought them back to yourself."

³⁸Then, suddenly, fire flashed down from heaven and burned up the young bull, the wood, the stones, the dust, and even evaporated all the water in the ditch!

³⁹And when the people saw it, they fell to their faces upon the ground shouting, "Jehovah is God! Jehovah is God!"

⁴⁰Then Elijah told them to grab the prophets of Baal. "Don't let a single one escape," he commanded.

So they seized them all, and Elijah took them to Kishon Brook and killed them there.

⁴¹Then Elijah said to Ahab, "Go and enjoy a good meal! For I hear a mighty rainstorm coming!"

⁴²So Ahab prepared a feast. But Elijah climbed to the top of Mount Carmel and got down on his knees, with his face between his knees, ⁴³and said to his servant, "Go and look out toward the sea."

He did, but returned to Elijah and told him, "I didn't see anything."

Then Elijah told him, "Go again, and again, and again, seven times!"

⁴⁴Finally, the seventh time, his servant told him, "I saw a little cloud about the size of a man's hand rising from the sea."

Then Elijah shouted, "Hurry to Ahab and tell him to get into his chariot and get down the mountain, or he'll be stopped by the rain!"

⁴⁵And sure enough, the sky was soon black with clouds, and a heavy wind brought a terrific rainstorm. Ahab left hastily for Jezreel, ⁴⁶and the Lord gave special strength to Elijah so that he was able to run ahead of Ahab's chariot to the entrance of the city!

19 God Whispers to Elijah

When Ahab told Queen Jezebel what Elijah had done, and that he had slaughtered the prophets of Baal, ²she sent this message to Elijah: "You killed my prophets, and now I swear by the gods that I am going to kill you by this time tomorrow night."

³So Elijah fled for his life; he went to Beersheba, a city of Judah, and left his servant there. ⁴Then he went on alone into the wilderness, traveling all day, and sat down under a broom bush and prayed that he might die.

"I've had enough," he told the Lord. "Take away my life. I've got to die sometime, and it might as well be now."

⁵Then he lay down and slept beneath the broom bush. But as he was sleeping, an angel touched him and told him to get up and eat! ⁶He looked around and saw some bread baking on hot stones and a jar of water! So he ate and drank and lay down again.

⁷Then the angel of the Lord came again and touched him and said, "Get up and eat some more, for there is a long journey ahead of you."

⁸So he got up and ate and drank, and the food gave him enough strength to travel forty days and forty nights to Mount Horeb, the mountain of God, ⁹where he lived in a cave.

But the Lord said to him, "What are you doing here, Elijah?"

¹⁰He replied, "I have worked very hard for the

Lord God of the heavens; but the people of Israel have broken their covenant with you and torn down your altars and killed your prophets, and only I am left; and now they are trying to kill me too."

[11] "Go out and stand before me on the mountain," the Lord told him. And as Elijah stood there the Lord passed by, and a mighty windstorm hit the mountain; it was such a terrible blast that the rocks were torn loose, but the Lord was not in the wind. After the wind, there was an earthquake, but the Lord was not in the earthquake. [12] And after the earthquake, there was a fire, but the Lord was not in the fire. And after the fire, there was the sound of a gentle whisper. [13] When Elijah heard it, he wrapped his face in his scarf and went out and stood at the entrance of the cave.

And a voice said, "Why are you here, Elijah?"

[14] He replied again, "I have been working very hard for the Lord God of the armies of heaven, but the people have broken their covenant and have torn down your altars; they have killed every one of your prophets except me; and now they are trying to kill me too."

[15] Then the Lord told him, "Go back by the desert road to Damascus, and when you arrive, anoint Hazael to be king of Syria. [16] Then anoint Jehu (son of Nimshi) to be king of Israel, and anoint Elisha (the son of Shaphat of Abel-meholah) to replace you as my prophet. [17] Anyone who escapes from Hazael shall be killed by Jehu, and those who escape Jehu shall be killed by Elisha! [18] And incidentally, there are 7,000 men in Israel who have never bowed to Baal nor kissed him!"

[19] So Elijah went and found Elisha who was plowing a field with eleven other teams ahead of him; he was at the end of the line with the last team. Elijah went over to him and threw his coat across his shoulders and walked away again.

[20] Elisha left the oxen standing there and ran after Elijah and said to him, "First let me go and say good-bye to my father and mother, and then I'll go with you!"

Elijah replied, "Go on back! Why all the excitement?"

[21] Elisha then returned to his oxen, killed them, and used wood from the plow to build a fire to roast their flesh. He passed around the meat to the other plowmen, and they all had a great feast. Then he went with Elijah, as his assistant.

20 God Gives Israel Victory

King Ben-hadad of Syria now mobilized his army and, with thirty-two allied nations and their hordes of chariots and horses, besieged Samaria, the Israeli capital. [2,3] He sent this message into the city to King Ahab of Israel: "Your silver and gold are mine, as are your prettiest wives and the best of your children!"

[4] "All right, my lord," Ahab replied. "All that I have is yours!"

[5,6] Soon Ben-hadad's messengers returned again with another message: "You must not only give me your silver, gold, wives, and children, but about this time tomorrow I will send my men to search your palace and the homes of your people, and they will take away whatever they like!"

[7] Then Ahab summoned his advisors. "Look what this man is doing," he complained to them. "He is stirring up trouble despite the fact that I have already told him he could have my wives and children and silver and gold, just as he demanded."

[8] "Don't give him anything more," the elders advised.

[9] So he told the messengers from Ben-hadad, "Tell my lord the king, 'I will give you everything you asked for the first time, but your men may not search the palace and the homes of the people.'" So the messengers returned to Ben-hadad.

[10] Then the Syrian king sent this message to Ahab: "May the gods do more to me than I am going to do to you if I don't turn Samaria into handfuls of dust!"

[11] The king of Israel retorted, "Don't count your chickens before they hatch!"

[12] This reply of Ahab's reached Ben-hadad and the other kings as they were drinking in their tents.

"Prepare to attack!" Ben-hadad commanded his officers.

[13] Then a prophet came to see King Ahab and gave him this message from the Lord: "Do you see all these enemy forces? I will deliver them all to you today. Then at last you will know that I am the Lord."

[14] Ahab asked, "How will he do it?"

And the prophet replied, "The Lord says, 'By the troops from the provinces.'"

"Shall we attack first?" Ahab asked.

"Yes," the prophet answered.

[15] So he mustered the troops from the provinces, 232 of them, then the rest of his army of 7,000 men. [16] About noontime, as Ben-hadad and the thirty-two allied kings were still drinking themselves drunk, the first of Ahab's troops marched out of the city.

[17] As they approached, Ben-hadad's scouts reported to him, "Some troops are coming!"

[18] "Take them alive," Ben-hadad commanded, "whether they have come for truce or for war."

[19] By now Ahab's entire army had joined the attack. [20] Each one killed a Syrian soldier, and suddenly the entire Syrian army panicked and fled. The Israelis chased them, but King Ben-hadad and

FAMILY DEVOTIONS

☐ *DEVOTION 116*
RESPECTING AUTHORITY

Read 1 Kings 21:4-10

There was something about the Bible story that made Tami uncomfortable. Her Sunday school teacher was telling about an Old Testament king who acted like a spoiled child. When he didn't get his own way, he refused to eat, ran to his bedroom, threw himself on his bed, and began to pout.

Tami squirmed uneasily in her seat as she remembered what happened at home just that morning. She had wanted to wear her new jeans to Sunday school, but her mother insisted that she wear a dress. Like the king, Tami had thrown herself on the bed. She had waited for her mother to come up and tell her she could wear anything she wanted, but that didn't happen. Tami had grudgingly put on a dress, but she continued to pout all the way to church and avoided even speaking to her mother.

Although pouting didn't work for her, it had seemed to work for King Ahab. His wife, wicked Queen Jezebel, thought since he was the king he should be able to have anything he wanted. She arranged for the man who had displeased the king to be killed, so Ahab could have the thing he had wanted! But wait! Tami's teacher was now pointing out verses from the Bible that said God was displeased with Jezebel and Ahab. He told them he would punish both of them. King Ahab's pouting had not paid off after all.

As Tami left the Sunday school room that morning, she made a very important decision. She would tell her mother that she was sorry for the way she had acted. Then she would try, with God's help, to accept her parents' decisions even when it meant she would not get her own way.

Respecting Authority Memory Verse

Children, obey your parents; this is the right thing to do because God has placed them in authority over you.
Ephesians 6:1

How About You?

Do you pout when parents or teachers don't allow you to have your own way? When your friends don't want to play what you want to play? If you allow yourself to pout in self-pity, it may result in unkind actions against the person you're mad at. God is not pleased when you pout. Don't insist on your own way. Please God by pleasing others. *R. J.*

• For the next devotional, turn to page 385.   • For the next devotional on *RESPECTING AUTHORITY*, turn to page 653.
• For notes on *RESPECTING AUTHORITY*, see pages 311, 420, and 1182.

a few others escaped on horses. ²¹ However, the great bulk of the horses and chariots were captured, and most of the Syrian army was killed in a great slaughter.

²²Then the prophet approached King Ahab and said, "Get ready for another attack by the king of Syria."

²³For after their defeat, Ben-hadad's officers said to him, "The Israeli God is a god of the hills; that is why they won. But we can beat them easily on the plains. ²⁴Only this time replace the kings with generals! ²⁵Recruit another army like the one you lost; give us the same number of horses, chariots, and men, and we will fight against them in the plains; there's not a shadow of a doubt that we will beat them." So King Ben-hadad did as they suggested. ²⁶The following year he called up the Syrian army and marched out against Israel again, this time at Aphek. ²⁷Israel then mustered its army, set up supply lines, and moved into the battle; but the Israeli army looked like two little flocks of baby goats in comparison to the vast Syrian forces that filled the countryside!

²⁸Then a prophet went to the king of Israel with this message from the Lord: "Because the Syrians have declared, 'The Lord is a God of the hills and not of the plains,' I will help you defeat this vast army, and you shall know that I am indeed the Lord."

²⁹The two armies camped opposite each other for seven days, and on the seventh day the battle began. And the Israelis killed 100,000 Syrian infantrymen that first day. ³⁰The rest fled behind the walls of Aphek, but the wall fell on them and killed another 27,000. Ben-hadad fled into the city and hid in the inner room of one of the houses.

³¹"Sir," his officers said to him, "we have heard that the kings of Israel are very merciful. Let us wear sackcloth and put ropes on our heads and go out to King Ahab to see if he will let you live."

³²So they went to the king of Israel and begged, "Your servant Ben-hadad pleads, 'Let me live!'"

"Oh, is he still alive?" the king of Israel asked. "He is my brother!"

³³The men were quick to grab this straw of hope and hurried to clinch the matter by exclaiming, "Yes, your brother Ben-hadad!"

"Go and get him," the king of Israel told them. And when Ben-hadad arrived, he invited him up into his chariot!

³⁴Ben-hadad told him, "I will restore the cities my father took from your father, and you may establish trading posts in Damascus, as my father did in Samaria."

³⁵Meanwhile, the Lord instructed one of the prophets to say to another man, "Strike me with your sword!" But the man refused.

³⁶Then the prophet told him, "Because you have not obeyed the voice of the Lord, a lion shall kill you as soon as you leave me." And sure enough, as he turned to go a lion attacked and killed him.

³⁷Then the prophet turned to another man and said, "Strike me with your sword." And he did, wounding him.

³⁸The prophet waited for the king beside the road, having placed a bandage over his eyes to disguise himself.

³⁹As the king passed by, the prophet called out to him, "Sir, I was in the battle, and a man brought me a prisoner and said, 'Keep this man; if he gets away, you must die, or else pay me $2,000!' ⁴⁰But while I was busy doing something else, the prisoner disappeared!"

"Well, it's your own fault," the king replied. "You'll have to pay."

⁴¹Then the prophet yanked off the bandage from his eyes, and the king recognized him as one of the prophets. ⁴²Then the prophet told him, "The Lord says, 'Because you have spared the man I said must die, now you must die in his place, and your people shall perish instead of his.'"

⁴³So the king of Israel went home to Samaria angry and sullen.

21 Ahab Steals a Vineyard

Naboth, a man from Jezreel, had a vineyard on the outskirts of the city near King Ahab's palace. ²One day the king talked to him about selling him this land.

"I want it for a garden," the king explained, "because it's so convenient to the palace." He offered cash or, if Naboth preferred, a piece of better land in trade.

³But Naboth replied, "Not on your life! That land has been in my family for generations."

⁴So Ahab went back to the palace angry and sullen. He refused to eat and went to bed with his face to the wall!

⁵"What in the world is the matter?" his wife, Jezebel, asked him. "Why aren't you eating? What has made you so upset and angry?"

⁶"I asked Naboth to sell me his vineyard or to trade it, and he refused!" Ahab told her.

⁷"Are you the king of Israel or not?" Jezebel demanded. "Get up and eat and don't worry about it. I'll get you Naboth's vineyard!"

⁸So she wrote letters in Ahab's name, sealed them with his seal, and addressed them to the civic leaders of Jezreel, where Naboth lived. ⁹In her letter she commanded: "Call the citizens together for fasting and prayer. Then summon Naboth, ¹⁰and find two scoundrels who will accuse him of cursing God and the king. Then take him out and execute him."

[11]The city fathers followed the queen's instructions. [12]They called the meeting and put Naboth on trial. [13]Then two men who had no conscience accused him of cursing God and the king; and he was dragged outside the city and stoned to death. [14]The city officials then sent word to Jezebel that Naboth was dead.

[15]When Jezebel heard the news, she said to Ahab, "You know the vineyard Naboth wouldn't sell you? Well, you can have it now! He's dead!"

[16]So Ahab went down to the vineyard to claim it.

[17]But the Lord said to Elijah, [18]"Go to Samaria to meet King Ahab. He will be at Naboth's vineyard, taking possession of it. [19]Give him this message from me: 'Isn't killing Naboth bad enough? Must you rob him too? Because you have done this, dogs shall lick your blood outside the city just as they licked the blood of Naboth!'"

[20]"So my enemy has found me!" Ahab exclaimed to Elijah.

"Yes," Elijah answered, "I have come to place God's curse upon you because you have sold yourself to the devil. [21]The Lord is going to bring great harm to you and sweep you away; he will not let a single one of your male descendants survive! [22]He is going to destroy your family as he did the family of King Jeroboam and the family of King Baasha, for you have made him very angry and have led all of Israel into sin. [23]The Lord has also told me that the dogs of Jezreel shall tear apart the body of your wife, Jezebel. [24]The members of your family who die in the city shall be eaten by dogs, and those who die in the country shall be eaten by vultures."

[25]No one else was so completely sold out to the devil as Ahab, for his wife, Jezebel, encouraged him to do every sort of evil. [26]He was especially guilty because he worshiped idols just as the Amorites did—the people whom the Lord had chased out of the land to make room for the people of Israel. [27]When Ahab heard these prophecies, he tore his clothing, put on rags, fasted, slept in sackcloth, and went about in deep humility.

[28]Then another message came to Elijah: [29]"Do you see how Ahab has humbled himself before me? Because he has done this, I will not do what I promised during his lifetime; it will happen to his sons; I will destroy his descendants."

22 Ahab Dies in Battle

For three years there was no war between Syria and Israel. [2]But during the third year, while King Jehoshaphat of Judah was visiting King Ahab of Israel, [3]Ahab said to his officials, "Do you realize that the Syrians are still occupying our city of Ramoth-gilead? And we're sitting here without doing a thing about it!"

[4]Then he turned to Jehoshaphat and asked him, "Will you send your army with mine to recover Ramoth-gilead?"

And King Jehoshaphat of Judah replied, "Of course! You and I are brothers; my people are yours to command, and my horses are at your service. [5]But," he added, "we should ask the Lord first, to be sure of what he wants us to do."

[6]So King Ahab summoned his 400 heathen prophets and asked them, "Shall I attack Ramoth-gilead, or not?"

And they all said, "Yes, go ahead, for God will help you conquer it."

[7]But Jehoshaphat asked, "Isn't there a prophet of the Lord here? I'd like to ask him too."

[8]"Well, there's one," King Ahab replied, "but I hate him, for he never prophesies anything good. He always has something gloomy to say. His name is Micaiah, the son of Imlah."

"Oh, come now!" Jehoshaphat replied. "Don't talk like that!"

[9]So King Ahab called to one of his aides, "Go get Micaiah. Hurry!"

[10]Meanwhile, all the prophets continued prophesying before the two kings, who were dressed in their royal robes and were sitting on thrones placed on the threshing floor near the city gate. [11]One of the prophets, Zedekiah (son of Chenaanah), made some iron horns and declared, "The Lord promises that you will push the Syrians around with these horns until they are destroyed."

[12]And all the others agreed. "Go ahead and attack Ramoth-gilead," they said, "for the Lord will cause you to triumph!"

[13]The messenger who went to get Micaiah told him what the other prophets were saying and urged him to say the same thing.

[14]But Micaiah told him, "This I vow, that I will say only what the Lord tells me to!"

[15]When he arrived, the king asked him, "Micaiah, shall we attack Ramoth-gilead, or not?"

"Why, of course! Go right ahead!" Micaiah told him. "You will have a great victory, for the Lord will cause you to conquer!"

[16]"How many times must I tell you to speak only what the Lord tells you to?" the king demanded.

[17]Then Micaiah told him, "I saw all Israel scattered upon the mountains as sheep without a shepherd. And the Lord said, 'Their king is dead; send them to their homes.'"

[18]Turning to Jehoshaphat, Ahab complained, "Didn't I tell you this would happen? He *never* tells me anything good. It's *always* bad."

[19]Then Micaiah said, "Listen to this further

word from the Lord. I saw the Lord sitting on his throne, and the armies of heaven stood around him.

[20]"Then the Lord said, 'Who will entice Ahab to go and die at Ramoth-gilead?'

"Various suggestions were made, [21]until one angel approached the Lord and said, 'I'll do it!'

[22]"'How?' the Lord asked.

"And he replied, 'I will go as a lying spirit in the mouths of all his prophets.'

"And the Lord said, 'That will do it; you will succeed. Go ahead.'

[23]"Don't you see? The Lord has put a lying spirit in the mouths of all these prophets, but the fact of the matter is that the Lord has decreed disaster upon you."

[24]Then Zedekiah (son of Chenaanah) walked over and slapped Micaiah on the face.

"When did the Spirit of the Lord leave me and speak to you?" he demanded.

[25]And Micaiah replied, "You will have the answer to your question when you find yourself hiding in an inner room."

[26]Then King Ahab ordered Micaiah's arrest.

"Take him to Amon, the mayor of the city, and to my son Joash. [27]Tell them, 'The king says to put this fellow in jail and feed him with bread and water—and only enough to keep him alive—until I return in peace.'"

[28]"If you return in peace," Micaiah replied, "it will prove that the Lord has not spoken through me." Then he turned to the people standing nearby and said, "Take note of what I've said."

[29]So King Ahab of Israel and King Jehoshaphat of Judah led their armies to Ramoth-gilead.

[30]Ahab said to Jehoshaphat, "You wear your royal robes, but I'll not wear mine!"

So Ahab went into the battle disguised in an ordinary soldier's uniform. [31]For the king of Syria had commanded his thirty-two chariot captains to fight no one except King Ahab himself. [32,33]When they saw King Jehoshaphat in his royal robes, they thought, "That's the man we're after." So they wheeled around to attack him. But when Jehoshaphat shouted out to identify himself, they turned back! [34]However, someone shot an arrow at random and it struck King Ahab between the joints of his armor.

"Take me out of the battle, for I am badly wounded," he groaned to his chariot driver.

[35]The battle became more and more intense as the day wore on, and King Ahab went back in, propped up in his chariot with the blood from his wound running down onto the floorboards. Finally, toward evening, he died. [36,37]Just as the sun was going down the cry ran through his troops. "It's all over—return home! The king is dead!"

And his body was taken to Samaria and buried there. [38]When his chariot and armor were washed beside the pool of Samaria, where the prostitutes bathed, dogs came and licked the king's blood just as the Lord had said would happen.

[39]The rest of Ahab's history—including the story of the ivory palace and the cities he built—is written in *The Annals of the Kings of Israel*. [40]So Ahab was buried among his ancestors, and Ahaziah, his son, became the new king of Israel.

[41]Meanwhile, over in Judah, Jehoshaphat the son of Asa had become king during the fourth year of the reign of King Ahab of Israel. [42]Jehoshaphat was thirty-five years old when he ascended the throne, and he reigned in Jerusalem for twenty-five years. His mother was Azubah, the daughter of Shilhi. [43]He did as his father Asa had done, obeying the Lord in all but one thing: he did not destroy the shrines on the hills, so the people sacrificed and burned incense there. [44]He also made peace with Ahab, the king of Israel. [45]The rest of the deeds of Jehoshaphat and his heroic achievements and his wars are described in *The Annals of the Kings of Judah*.

[46]He also closed all the houses of male prostitution that still continued from the days of his father Asa. [47](There was no king in Edom at that time, only a deputy.)

[48]King Jehoshaphat built great freighters to sail to Ophir for gold; but they never arrived, for they were wrecked at Ezion-geber. [49]Ahaziah, King Ahab's son and successor, had proposed to Jehoshaphat that his men go, too, but Jehoshaphat had refused the offer.

[50]When King Jehoshaphat died he was buried with his ancestors in Jerusalem, the city of his forefather David; and his son Jehoram took the throne. [51]It was during the seventeenth year of the reign of King Jehoshaphat of Judah that Ahaziah, Ahab's son, began to reign over Israel in Samaria; and he reigned two years. [52,53]But he was not a good king, for he followed in the footsteps of his father and mother and of Jeroboam, who had led Israel into the sin of worshiping idols. So Ahaziah made the Lord God of Israel very angry.

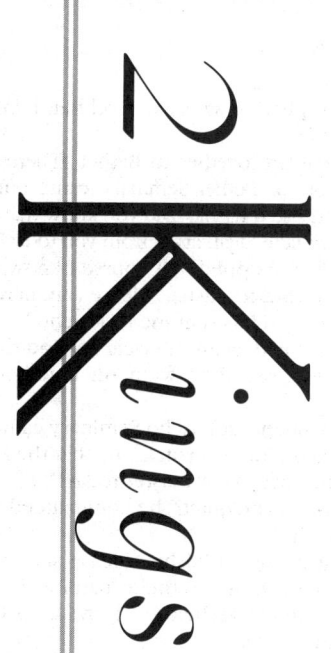

2 Kings

HAVE YOU ever been compared to your brother or sister, or to a classmate? Sometimes people say they hope you do as well as your brother. Sometimes they hope you're *not* like your brother!

Second Kings does a lot of comparing. David had been a very good king who loved God and led well. Good kings are compared to David, and that is a great compliment. Jeroboam had been a very bad king who disobeyed God and led the people to do wrong. Bad kings are compared to Jeroboam, and he is an awful person to be like.

As you read about the kings of Israel and Judah, figure out from their actions which king they were like—David or Jeroboam. Decide if you would want them to be *your* king.

There's another person in 2 Kings who wanted to be compared to someone good—not King David, but the prophet Elijah. Elisha was a prophet who followed and learned from Elijah. He respected Elijah's relationship with God and wanted to follow his example.

It's not bad to be compared to someone if that person loves and obeys God. As you read, decide which people you want to be like.

King Ahaziah Dies for His Sin

After King Ahab's death the nation of Moab declared its independence and refused to pay tribute to Israel any longer.

²Israel's new king, Ahaziah, had fallen off the upstairs porch of his palace at Samaria and was seriously injured. He sent messengers to the temple of the god Baal-zebub at Ekron to ask whether he would recover.

³But an angel of the Lord told Elijah the prophet, "Go and meet the messengers and ask them, 'Is it true that there is no God in Israel? Is that why you are going to Baal-zebub, the god of Ekron, to ask whether the king will get well? ⁴,⁵Because King Ahaziah has done this, the Lord says that he will never leave the bed he is lying on; he will surely die.'"

When Elijah told the messengers this, they returned immediately to the king.

"Why have you returned so soon?" he asked them.

⁶"A man came up to us," they said, "and told us to go back to the king and tell him, 'The Lord wants to

know why you are asking questions of Baal-zebub, the god of Ekron. Is it because there is no God in Israel? Now, since you have done this, you will not leave the bed you are lying on; you will surely die.'"

⁷"Who was this fellow?" the king demanded. "What did he look like?"

⁸"He was a hairy man," they replied, "with a wide leather belt."

"It was Elijah the prophet!" the king exclaimed. ⁹Then he sent an army captain with fifty soldiers to arrest him. They found him sitting on top of a hill. The captain said to him, "O man of God, the king has commanded you to come along with us."

¹⁰But Elijah replied, "If I am a man of God, let fire come down from heaven and destroy you and your fifty men!" Then lightning struck them and killed them all!

¹¹So the king sent another captain with fifty men to demand, "O man of God, the king says that you must come down right away."

¹²Elijah replied, "If I am a man of God, let fire come down from heaven and destroy you and your fifty men." And again the fire from God burned them up.

¹³Once more the king sent fifty men, but this time the captain fell to his knees before Elijah and pleaded with him, "O man of God, please spare my life and the lives of these, your fifty servants. ¹⁴Have mercy on us! Don't destroy us as you did the others."

¹⁵Then the angel of the Lord said to Elijah, "Don't be afraid. Go with him." So Elijah went to the king.

¹⁶"Why did you send messengers to Baal-zebub, the god of Ekron, to ask about your sickness?" Elijah demanded. "Is it because there is no God in Israel to ask? Because you have done this, you shall not leave this bed; you will surely die."

¹⁷So Ahaziah died as the Lord had predicted through Elijah, and his brother Joram became the new king—for Ahaziah did not have a son to succeed him. This occurred in the second year of the reign of King Jehoram (son of Jehoshaphat) of Judah. ¹⁸The rest of the history of Ahaziah's reign is recorded in *The Annals of the Kings of Israel.*

2 A Whirlwind Takes Elijah Away

Now the time came for the Lord to take Elijah to heaven—by means of a whirlwind! Elijah said to Elisha as they left Gilgal, "Stay here, for the Lord has told me to go to Bethel."

But Elisha replied, "I swear to God that I won't leave you!"

So they went on together to Bethel. ³There the young prophets of Bethel Seminary came out to meet them and asked Elisha, "Did you know that the Lord is going to take Elijah away from you today?"

"Quiet!" Elisha snapped. "Of course I know it."

⁴Then Elijah said to Elisha, "Please stay here in Bethel, for the Lord has sent me to Jericho."

But Elisha replied again, "I swear to God that I won't leave you." So they went on together to Jericho.

⁵Then the students at Jericho Seminary came to Elisha and asked him, "Do you know that the Lord is going to take away your master today?"

"Will you please be quiet?" he commanded. "Of course I know it!"

⁶,⁷Then Elijah said to Elisha, "Please stay here, for the Lord has sent me to the Jordan River."

But Elisha replied as before, "I swear to God that I won't leave you."

So they went on together and stood beside the Jordan River as fifty of the young prophets watched from a distance. ⁸Then Elijah folded his cloak together and struck the water with it; and the river divided and they went across on dry ground!

⁹When they arrived on the other side Elijah said to Elisha, "What wish shall I grant you before I am taken away?"

And Elisha replied, "Please grant me twice as much prophetic power as you have had."

¹⁰"You have asked a hard thing," Elijah replied. "If you see me when I am taken from you, then you will get your request. But if not, then you won't."

¹¹As they were walking along, talking, suddenly a chariot of fire, drawn by horses of fire, appeared and drove between them, separating them, and Elijah was carried by a whirlwind into heaven.

¹²Elisha saw it and cried out, "My father! My father! The Chariot of Israel and the charioteers!"

As they disappeared from sight he tore his robe. ¹³,¹⁴Then he picked up Elijah's cloak and returned to the bank of the Jordan River, and struck the water with it.

"Where is the Lord God of Elijah?" he cried out. And the water parted and Elisha went across!

¹⁵When the young prophets of Jericho saw what had happened, they exclaimed, "The spirit of Elijah rests upon Elisha!" And they went to meet him and greeted him respectfully.

¹⁶"Sir," they said, "just say the word and fifty of our best athletes will search the wilderness for your master; perhaps the Spirit of the Lord has left him on some mountain or in some ravine."

RESPECTING OTHERS 1:13-15 Notice how the third captain went to Elijah. Although the first two captains called Elijah "man of God," they were not being genuine. The third captain also called him "man of God," but he humbly begged for mercy. His attitude, which showed respect for God and his power, saved the lives of his men. Effective living begins with a right attitude toward God. Let respect characterize your attitude toward God and others. **To begin the series of devotionals on RESPECTING OTHERS, turn to page 5.**

"No," Elisha said, "don't bother."

[17] But they kept urging until he was embarrassed and finally said, "All right, go ahead." Then fifty men searched for three days, but didn't find him.

[18] Elisha was still at Jericho when they returned. "Didn't I tell you not to go?" he growled.

[19] Now a delegation of the city officials of Jericho visited Elisha. "We have a problem," they told him. "This city is located in beautiful natural surroundings, as you can see; but the water is bad and causes our women to have miscarriages."

[20] "Well," he said, "bring me a new bowl filled with salt." So they brought it to him.

[21] Then he went out to the city well and threw the salt in and declared, "The Lord has healed these waters. They shall no longer cause death or miscarriage."

[22] And sure enough! The water was purified, just as Elisha had said.

[23] From Jericho he went to Bethel. As he was walking along the road, a gang of young men from the city began mocking and making fun of him because of his bald head. [24] He turned around and cursed them in the name of the Lord; and two female bears came out of the woods and tore forty-two of them. [25] Then he went to Mount Carmel and finally returned to Samaria.

3 Elisha Helps King Jehoshaphat

Ahab's son Joram began his reign over Israel during the eighteenth year of the reign of King Jehoshaphat of Judah; and he reigned twelve years. His capital was Samaria. [2] He was a very evil man, but not as wicked as his father and mother had been, for he at least tore down the pillar to Baal that his father had made. [3] Nevertheless he still clung to the great sin of Jeroboam (the son of Nebat), who had led the people of Israel into the worship of idols.

[4] King Mesha of Moab and his people were sheep ranchers. They paid Israel an annual tribute of 100,000 lambs and the wool of 100,000 rams; [5] but after Ahab's death, the king of Moab rebelled against Israel. [6-8] So King Joram mustered the Israeli army and sent this message to King Jehoshaphat of Judah:

"The king of Moab has rebelled against me. Will you help me fight him?"

"Of course I will," Jehoshaphat replied. "My people and horses are yours to command. What are your battle plans?"

"We'll attack from the wilderness of Edom," Joram replied.

[9] So their two armies, now joined also by troops from Edom, moved along a roundabout route through the wilderness for seven days; but there was no water for the men or their pack animals.

[10] "Oh, what shall we do?" the king of Israel cried out. "The Lord has brought us here to let the king of Moab defeat us."

[11] But Jehoshaphat, the king of Judah, asked, "Isn't there a prophet of the Lord with us? If so, we can find out what to do!"

"Elisha is here," one of the king of Israel's officers replied. Then he added, "He was Elijah's assistant."

[12] "Fine," Jehoshaphat said. "He's just the man we want." So the kings of Israel, Judah, and Edom went to consult Elisha.

[13] "I want no part of you," Elisha snarled at King Joram of Israel. "Go to the false prophets of your father and mother!"

But King Joram replied, "No! For it is the Lord who has called us here to be destroyed by the king of Moab!"

[14] "I swear by the Lord God that I wouldn't bother with you except for the presence of King Jehoshaphat of Judah," Elisha replied. [15] "Now bring me someone to play the lute." And as the lute was played, the message of the Lord came to Elisha:

[16] "The Lord says to fill this dry valley with trenches to hold the water he will send. [17] You won't see wind nor rain, but this valley will be filled with water, and you will have plenty for yourselves and for your animals! [18] But this is only the beginning, for the Lord will make you victorious over the army of Moab. [19] You will conquer the best of their cities—even those that are fortified—and ruin all the good land with stones."

[20] And sure enough, the next day at about the time when the morning sacrifice was offered—look! Water! It was flowing from the direction of Edom, and soon there was water everywhere.

[21] Meanwhile, when the people of Moab heard about the three armies marching against them, they mobilized every man who could fight, old and young, and stationed themselves along their frontier. [22] But early the next morning the sun looked red as it shone across the water!

[23] "Blood!" they exclaimed. "The three armies have attacked and killed each other! Let's go and collect the loot!"

[24] But when they arrived at the Israeli camp, the

CULTIVATING GODLY ATTITUDES **2:9** Elisha asked for twice as much power as Elijah had. This was a bold request, but God granted it. Why? Because Elisha's motives were pure. His main goal was not to be better or more powerful than Elijah, but to accomplish more for God. If our motives are pure, we don't have to be afraid to ask great things from God. When we ask God for great power or ability, we need to examine our desires and get rid of any selfishness we find. **To begin the series of devotionals on *CULTIVATING GODLY ATTITUDES*, turn to page 121.**

army of Israel rushed out and began killing them; and the army of Moab fled. Then the men of Israel moved forward into the land of Moab, destroying everything as they went. 25They destroyed the cities, threw stones on every good piece of land, stopped up the wells, and felled the fruit trees; finally, only Fort Kir-haraseth was left, but even that finally fell to them.

26When the king of Moab saw that the battle had been lost, he led 700 of his swordsmen in a last desperate attempt to break through to the king of Edom; but he failed. 27Then he took his oldest son, who was to have been the next king, and to the horror of the Israeli army, killed him and sacrificed him as a burnt offering upon the wall. So the army of Israel turned back in disgust to their own land.

4 Elisha Helps a Poor Widow

One day the wife of one of the seminary students came to Elisha to tell him of her husband's death. He was a man who had loved God, she said. But he had owed some money when he died, and now the creditor was demanding it back. If she didn't pay, he said he would take her two sons as his slaves.

2"What shall I do?" Elisha asked. "How much food do you have in the house?"

"Nothing at all, except a jar of olive oil," she replied.

3"Then borrow many pots and pans from your friends and neighbors!" he instructed. 4"Go into your house with your sons and shut the door behind you. Then pour olive oil from your jar into the pots and pans, setting them aside as they are filled!"

5So she did. Her sons brought the pots and pans to her, and she filled one after another! 6Soon every container was full to the brim!

"Bring me another jar," she said to her sons.

"There aren't any more!" they told her. And then the oil stopped flowing!

7When she told the prophet what had happened, he said to her, "Go and sell the oil and pay your debt, and there will be enough money left for you and your sons to live on!"

8One day Elisha went to Shunem. A prominent woman of the city invited him in to eat, and afterwards, whenever he passed that way, he stopped for dinner.

9She said to her husband, "I'm sure this man who stops in from time to time is a holy prophet. 10Let's make a little room for him on the roof; we can put in a bed, a table, a chair, and a lamp, and he will have a place to stay whenever he comes by."

11,12Once when he was resting in the room he said to his servant Gehazi, "Tell the woman I want to speak to her."

When she came, 13he said to Gehazi, "Tell her that we appreciate her kindness to us. Now ask her what we can do for her. Does she want me to put in a good word for her to the king or to the general of the army?"

"No," she replied, "I am perfectly content."

14"What can we do for her?" he asked Gehazi afterwards.

He suggested, "She doesn't have a son, and her husband is an old man."

15,16"Call her back again," Elisha told him.

When she returned, he talked to her as she stood in the doorway. "Next year at about this time you shall have a son!"

"O man of God," she exclaimed, "don't lie to me like that!"

17But it was true; the woman soon conceived and had a baby boy the following year, just as Elisha had predicted.

18One day when her child was older, he went out to visit his father, who was working with the reapers. 19He complained about a headache and soon was moaning in pain. His father said to one of the servants, "Carry him home to his mother."

20So he took him home, and his mother held him on her lap; but around noontime he died. 21She carried him up to the bed of the prophet and shut the door; 22then she sent a message to her husband: "Send one of the servants and a donkey so that I can hurry to the prophet and come right back."

23"Why today?" he asked. "This isn't a religious holiday."

But she said, "It's important. I must go."

24So she saddled the donkey and said to the servant, "Hurry! Don't slow down for my comfort unless I tell you to."

25As she approached Mount Carmel, Elisha saw her in the distance and said to Gehazi, "Look, that woman from Shunem is coming. 26Run and meet her and ask her what the trouble is. See if her husband is all right and if the child is well."

"Yes," she told Gehazi, "everything is fine."

27But when she came to Elisha at the mountain she fell to the ground before him and caught hold of his feet. Gehazi began to push her away, but the prophet said, "Let her alone; something is deeply troubling her and the Lord hasn't told me what it is."

28Then she said, "It was you who said I'd have a son. And I begged you not to lie to me!"

29Then he said to Gehazi, "Quick, take my staff! Don't talk to anyone along the way. Hurry! Lay the staff upon the child's face."

30But the boy's mother said, "I swear to God

FAMILY DEVOTIONS

☐ DEVOTION 117
SERVING GOD WILLINGLY

Read 2 Kings 5:1-5

Melinda lay across her bed as she read an exciting missionary story. *Wow*, she thought. *I wish I could serve God, but there's not much a kid can do.*

"Melinda, come here please," Mom called from the kitchen. "Mrs. Nelson is sick and I want you to take this stew over there." Melinda sighed but did as Mom asked.

At the Nelsons' Melinda noticed that the breakfast and lunch dishes were still on the table. So she loaded them into the dishwasher and set the table for dinner.

When Melinda got back home, Mom asked her to run some magazines over to Grannie Wilson. Grannie was so pleased to see her that Melinda sat down and visited awhile. "You're a sweet girl, Melinda," Grannie said. "Most young people these days don't have time for us old folks."

At dinner that night Melinda's mood became heavy. "I wish I could grow up fast so I could serve the Lord," she said, "like the missionary I've been reading about."

Mom looked up in amazement. "Why, Melinda, you've been doing things for the Lord all afternoon."

"Me? For the Lord?" Melinda asked.

"You helped Mrs. Nelson," Mom pointed out. "You visited with Grannie Wilson."

"But, Mom, that was for *people*," sighed Melinda. "I want to do something for the *Lord*."

"How do you think missionaries serve the Lord?" asked Mom. "They do it by doing things for people. We serve God by serving others. And that's what you've been doing."

"Really?" A big smile slowly spread over Melinda's face. "Well, in that case, would you like some help with the dishes?"

Serving God Willingly Memory Verse

Anyone who takes care of a little child like this is caring for me! And whoever cares for me is caring for God who sent me. Your care for others is the measure of your greatness.
Luke 9:48

How About You?

What have you done to serve God lately? You serve him by serving others. Just like the little girl who was given to Naaman's wife as a maid, you can find ways to help others wherever you are right now. Make a list of two or three things you can do today to help others. Then check at the end of the day to see if you've done them. B. W.

• For the next devotional, turn to page 387. • For the next devotional on SERVING GOD WILLINGLY, turn to page 421.
• For notes on SERVING GOD WILLINGLY, see pages 49, 419, 890, 920, and 922.

that I won't go home without you." So Elisha returned with her.

³¹Gehazi went on ahead and laid the staff upon the child's face, but nothing happened. There was no sign of life. He returned to meet Elisha and told him, "The child is still dead."

³²When Elisha arrived, the child was indeed dead, lying there upon the prophet's bed. ³³He went in and shut the door behind him and prayed to the Lord. ³⁴Then he lay upon the child's body, placing his mouth upon the child's mouth, and his eyes upon the child's eyes, and his hands upon the child's hands. And the child's body began to grow warm again! ³⁵Then the prophet went down and walked back and forth in the house a few times; returning upstairs, he stretched himself again upon the child. This time the little boy sneezed seven times and opened his eyes!

³⁶Then the prophet summoned Gehazi. "Call her!" he said. And when she came in, he said, "Here's your son!"

³⁷She fell to the floor at his feet and then picked up her son and went out.

³⁸Elisha now returned to Gilgal, but there was a famine in the land. One day as he was teaching the young prophets, he said to Gehazi, "Make some stew for supper for these men."

³⁹One of the young men went out into the field to gather vegetables and came back with some wild gourds. He shredded them and put them into a kettle without realizing that they were poisonous. ⁴⁰But after the men had eaten a bite or two they cried out, "Oh, sir, there's poison in this stew!"

⁴¹"Bring me some meal," Elisha said. He threw it into the kettle and said, "Now it's all right! Go ahead and eat!" And then it didn't harm them.

⁴²One day a man from Baal-shalishah brought Elisha a sack of fresh corn and twenty individual loaves of barley bread made from the first grain of his harvest. Elisha told Gehazi to use it to feed the young prophets.

⁴³"What?" Gehazi exclaimed. "Feed one hundred men with only this?"

But Elisha said, "Go ahead, for the Lord says there will be plenty for all, and some will even be left over!"

⁴⁴And sure enough, there was, just as the Lord had said!

5 Naaman Is Healed

The king of Syria had high admiration for Naaman, the commander-in-chief of his army, for he had led his troops to many glorious victories. So he was a great hero, but he was a leper. ²Bands of Syrians had invaded the land of Israel, and among their captives was a little girl who had been given to Naaman's wife as a maid.

³One day the little girl said to her mistress, "I wish my master would go to see the prophet in Samaria. He would heal him of his leprosy!"

⁴Naaman told the king what the little girl had said.

⁵"Go and visit the prophet," the king told him. "I will send a letter of introduction for you to carry to the king of Israel."

So Naaman started out, taking gifts of $20,000 in silver, $60,000 in gold, and ten suits of clothing. ⁶The letter to the king of Israel said: "The man bringing this letter is my servant Naaman; I want you to heal him of his leprosy."

⁷When the king of Israel read it, he tore his clothes and said, "This man sends me a leper to heal! Am I God, that I can kill and give life? He is only trying to get an excuse to invade us again."

⁸But when Elisha the prophet heard about the king of Israel's plight, he sent this message to him: "Why are you so upset? Send Naaman to me, and he will learn that there is a true prophet of God here in Israel."

⁹So Naaman arrived with his horses and chariots and stood at the door of Elisha's home. ¹⁰Elisha sent a messenger out to tell him to go and wash in the Jordan River seven times and he would be healed of every trace of his leprosy! ¹¹But Naaman was angry and stalked away.

"Look," he said, "I thought at least he would come out and talk to me! I expected him to wave his hand over the leprosy and call upon the name of the Lord his God and heal me! ¹²Aren't the Abana River and Pharpar River of Damascus better than all the rivers of Israel put together? If it's rivers I need, I'll wash at home and get rid of my leprosy." So he went away in a rage.

¹³But his officers tried to reason with him and said, "If the prophet had told you to do some great thing, wouldn't you have done it? So you should certainly obey him when he says simply to go and wash and be cured!"

¹⁴So Naaman went down to the Jordan River and dipped himself seven times, as the prophet had told him to. And his flesh became as healthy as a little child's, and he was healed! ¹⁵Then he and his entire party went back to find the prophet; they stood humbly before him and Naaman said, "I know at last that there is no God in all the world except in Israel; now please accept my gifts."

¹⁶But Elisha replied, "I swear by Jehovah my God that I will not accept them."

Naaman urged him to take them, but he absolutely refused. ¹⁷"Well," Naaman said, "all right. But please give me two muleloads of earth to take back with me, for from now on I will never again

Family Devotions

☐ DEVOTION 118
AVOIDING SIN

Read 2 Kings 5:20-27

"Quick! Someone's coming." David's friend Brian whispered the warning, and David punched the button on the VCR remote control just in time.

"There it is," said Mom, coming into the den. She walked to the desk, picked up the dictionary, and left.

David knew he shouldn't turn the VCR back on. The movie Brian had brought over had violent scenes and bad language.

After supper, David's younger sister Carolyn was contentedly sucking her thumb. "What's that in your mouth?" Dad asked. Carolyn quickly took her thumb out of her mouth. Later that evening David noticed Carolyn lying on the couch, her head buried under a pillow. He sneaked over and pulled the pillow off his sister's head. Carolyn was again sucking away on her thumb!

"Sucking your thumb may damage your teeth whether anyone sees you do it or not," Dad told her gently.

"That's right," said Mom. "Hiding while you do it won't make the damage any less." She paused, then added, "Hiding any damaging activity from others never lessens the damage done to your body—or to your mind and spirit."

It seemed to David that Mom looked right at him while she spoke. He didn't think she knew about the movie, but the damage was done anyway. He couldn't forget the violence he had seen or the bad language he had heard.

As David prayed later that night, he confessed what he had done. He also asked God to give him courage to say no the next time he was tempted to do wrong things in secret.

The test came a few days later. "My dad has this great R-rated movie," Brian told him one day. "We can watch it before my folks get home."

"No, thanks," said David. "I don't care if our parents don't know. I don't want to watch it."

Avoiding Sin Memory Verse

How can a young man stay pure? By reading your Word and following its rules.
Psalm 119:9

How About You?

Do you read magazines, watch movies, or listen to music in secret? If so, is it because you know it's wrong? You can't keep a wrong activity from hurting you by hiding it from others. And you can't hide what you do from God—he will hold you responsible, even for things others don't know about. K. R. A.

• For the next devotional, turn to page 395. • For the next devotional on AVOIDING SIN, turn to page 617. • For notes on AVOIDING SIN, see pages 220, 332, 392, and 657.

offer any burnt offerings or sacrifices to any other god except the Lord. ¹⁸However, may the Lord pardon me this one thing—when my master the king goes into the temple of the god Rimmon to worship there and leans on my arm, may the Lord pardon me when I bow too."

¹⁹"All right," Elisha said. So Naaman started home again.

²⁰But Gehazi, Elisha's servant, said to himself, "My master shouldn't have let this fellow get away without taking his gifts. I will chase after him and get something from him."

²¹So Gehazi caught up with him. When Naaman saw him coming, he jumped down from his chariot and ran to meet him.

"Is everything all right?" he asked.

²²"Yes," he said, "but my master has sent me to tell you that two young prophets from the hills of Ephraim have just arrived, and he would like $2,000 in silver and two suits to give to them."

²³"Take $4,000," Naaman insisted. He gave him two expensive robes, tied up the money in two bags, and gave them to two of his servants to carry back with Gehazi. ²⁴But when they arrived at the hill where Elisha lived, Gehazi took the bags from the servants and sent the men back. Then he hid the money in his house.

²⁵When he went in to his master, Elisha asked him, "Where have you been, Gehazi?"

"I haven't been anywhere," he replied.

²⁶But Elisha asked him, "Don't you realize that I was there in thought when Naaman stepped down from his chariot to meet you? Is this the time to receive money and clothing and olive farms and vineyards and sheep and oxen and servants? ²⁷Because you have done this, Naaman's leprosy shall be upon you and upon your children and your children's children forever."

And Gehazi walked from the room a leper, his skin as white as snow.

6 A Servant Sees a Fiery Army

One day the seminary students came to Elisha and told him, "As you can see, our dormitory is too small. Tell us, as our president, whether we can build a new one down beside the Jordan River, where there are plenty of logs."

"All right," he told them, "go ahead."

³"Please, sir, come with us," someone suggested.

"I will," he said.

⁴When they arrived at the Jordan, they began cutting down trees; ⁵but as one of them was chopping, his axhead fell into the river.

"Oh, sir," he cried, "it was borrowed!"

⁶"Where did it fall?" the prophet asked. The youth showed him the place, and Elisha cut a stick and threw it into the water; and the axhead rose to the surface and floated! ⁷"Grab it," Elisha said to him; and he did.

⁸Once when the king of Syria was at war with Israel, he said to his officers, "We will mobilize our forces at ____" (naming the place).

⁹Immediately Elisha warned the king of Israel, "Don't go near ____" (naming the same place) "for the Syrians are planning to mobilize their troops there!"

¹⁰The king sent a scout to see if Elisha was right, and sure enough, he had saved him from disaster. This happened several times.

¹¹The king of Syria was puzzled. He called together his officers and demanded, "Which of you is the traitor? Who has been informing the king of Israel about my plans?"

¹²"It's not us, sir," one of the officers replied. "Elisha, the prophet, tells the king of Israel even the words you speak in the privacy of your bedroom!"

¹³"Go and find out where he is, and we'll send troops to seize him," the king exclaimed.

And the report came back, "Elisha is at Dothan."

¹⁴So one night the king of Syria sent a great army with many chariots and horses to surround the city. ¹⁵When the prophet's servant got up early the next morning and went outside, there were troops, horses, and chariots everywhere.

"Alas, my master, what shall we do now?" he cried out to Elisha.

¹⁶"Don't be afraid!" Elisha told him. "For our army is bigger than theirs!"

¹⁷Then Elisha prayed, "Lord, open his eyes and let him see!" And the Lord opened the young man's eyes so that he could see horses of fire and chariots of fire everywhere upon the mountain!

¹⁸As the Syrian army advanced upon them, Elisha prayed, "Lord, please make them blind." And he did.

¹⁹Then Elisha went out and told them, "You've come the wrong way! This isn't the right city! Follow me and I will take you to the man you're looking for." And he led them to Samaria!

²⁰As soon as they arrived Elisha prayed, "Lord, now open their eyes and let them see." And the Lord did, and they discovered that they were in Samaria, the capital city of Israel!

²¹When the king of Israel saw them, he shouted to Elisha, "Oh, sir, shall I kill them? Shall I kill them?"

²²"Of course not!" Elisha told him. "Do we kill prisoners of war? Give them food and drink and send them home again."

²³So the king made a great feast for them and then sent them home to their king. And after that

the Syrian raiders stayed away from the land of Israel.

²⁴Later on, however, King Ben-hadad of Syria mustered his entire army and besieged Samaria. ²⁵As a result there was a great famine in the city, and after a long while even a donkey's head sold for fifty dollars and a pint of dove's dung brought three dollars!

²⁶⁻³⁰One day as the king of Israel was walking along the wall of the city, a woman called to him, "Help, my lord the king!"

"If the Lord doesn't help you, what can I do?" he retorted. "I have neither food nor wine to give you. However, what's the matter?"

She replied, "This woman proposed that we eat my son one day and her son the next. So we boiled my son and ate him, but the next day when I said, 'Kill your son so we can eat him,' she hid him."

When the king heard this he tore his clothes. (The people watching noticed through the rip he tore in them that he was wearing an inner robe made of sackcloth next to his flesh.)

³¹"May God kill me if I don't execute Elisha this very day," the king vowed.

³²Elisha was sitting in his house at a meeting with the elders of Israel when the king sent a messenger to summon him. But before the messenger arrived Elisha said to the elders, "This murderer has sent a man to kill me. When he arrives, shut the door and keep him out, for his master will soon follow him."

³³While Elisha was still saying this, the messenger arrived [followed by the king].

"The Lord has caused this mess," the king stormed. "Why should I expect any help from him?"

7
Four Lepers Visit an Enemy Camp

Elisha replied, "The Lord says that by this time tomorrow two gallons of flour or four gallons of barley grain will be sold in the markets of Samaria for a dollar!"

²The officer assisting the king said, "That couldn't happen if the Lord made windows in the sky!"

But Elisha replied, "You will see it happen, but you won't be able to buy any of it!"

³Now there were four lepers sitting outside the city gates.

"Why sit here until we die?" they asked each other. ⁴"We will starve if we stay here and we will starve if we go back into the city; so we might as well go out and surrender to the Syrian army. If they let us live, so much the better; but if they kill us, we would have died anyway."

⁵So that evening they went out to the camp of the Syrians, but there was no one there! ⁶(For the Lord had made the whole Syrian army hear the clatter of speeding chariots and a loud galloping of horses and the sounds of a great army approaching. "The king of Israel has hired the Hittites and Egyptians to attack us," they cried out. ⁷So they panicked and fled into the night, abandoning their tents, horses, donkeys, and everything else.)

⁸When the lepers arrived at the edge of the camp they went into one tent after another, eating, drinking wine, and carrying out silver and gold and clothing and hiding it. ⁹Finally they said to each other, "This isn't right. This is wonderful news, and we aren't sharing it with anyone! Even if we wait until morning, some terrible calamity will certainly fall upon us; come on, let's go back and tell the people at the palace."

¹⁰So they went back to the city and told the watchmen what had happened—they had gone out to the Syrian camp and no one was there! The horses and donkeys were tethered and the tents were all in order, but there was not a soul around. ¹¹Then the watchmen shouted the news to those in the palace.

¹²The king got out of bed and told his officers, "I know what has happened. The Syrians know we are starving, so they have left their camp and have hidden in the fields, thinking that we will be lured out of the city. Then they will attack us and make slaves of us and get in."

¹³One of his officers replied, "We'd better send out scouts to see. Let them take five of the remaining horses—if something happens to the animals it won't be any greater loss than if they stay here and die with the rest of us!"

¹⁴Four chariot-horses were found and the king sent out two charioteers to see where the Syrians had gone. ¹⁵They followed a trail of clothing and equipment all the way to the Jordan River—thrown away by the Syrians in their haste. The scouts returned and told the king, ¹⁶and the people of Samaria rushed out and plundered the camp of the Syrians. So it was true that two gallons of flour and four gallons of barley were sold that day for one dollar, just as the Lord had said!

¹⁷The king appointed his special assistant to control the traffic at the gate, but he was knocked down and trampled and killed as the people rushed out. This is what Elisha had predicted on the previous day when the king had come to arrest him, ¹⁸and the prophet had told the king that flour and barley would sell for so little on the following day.

¹⁹The king's officer had replied, "That couldn't happen even if the Lord opened the windows of heaven!"

And the prophet had said, "You will see it happen, but you won't be able to buy any of it!" ²⁰And he couldn't, for the people trampled him to death at the gate!

8 A Woman Gets Her Land Back

Elisha had told the woman whose son he had brought back to life, "Take your family and move to some other country, for the Lord has called down a famine on Israel that will last for seven years."

²So the woman took her family and lived in the land of the Philistines for seven years. ³After the famine ended, she returned to the land of Israel and went to see the king about getting back her house and land. ⁴Just as she came in, the king was talking with Gehazi, Elisha's servant, and saying, "Tell me some stories of the great things Elisha has done." ⁵And Gehazi was telling the king about the time when Elisha brought a little boy back to life. At that very moment, the mother of the boy walked in!

"Oh, sir!" Gehazi exclaimed. "Here is the woman now, and this is her son—the very one Elisha brought back to life!"

⁶"Is this true?" the king asked her. And she told him that it was. So he directed one of his officials to see to it that everything she had owned was restored to her, plus the value of any crops that had been harvested during her absence.

⁷Afterwards Elisha went to Damascus (the capital of Syria), where King Ben-hadad lay sick. Someone told the king that the prophet had come.

⁸,⁹When the king heard the news, he said to Hazael, "Take a present to the man of God and tell him to ask the Lord whether I will get well again."

So Hazael took forty camel-loads of the best produce of the land as presents for Elisha and said to him, "Your son Ben-hadad, the king of Syria, has sent me to ask you whether he will recover."

¹⁰And Elisha replied, "Tell him, 'Yes.' But the Lord has shown me that he will surely die!"

¹¹Elisha stared at Hazael until he became embarrassed, and then Elisha started crying.

¹²"What's the matter, sir?" Hazael asked him.

Elisha replied, "I know the terrible things you will do to the people of Israel: you will burn their forts, kill the young men, dash their babies against the rocks, and rip open the bellies of the pregnant women!"

¹³"Am I a dog?" Hazael asked him. "I would *never* do that sort of thing."

But Elisha replied, "The Lord has shown me that you are going to be the king of Syria."

¹⁴When Hazael went back, the king asked him, "What did he tell you?"

And Hazael replied, "He told me that you would recover."

¹⁵But the next day Hazael took a blanket and dipped it in water and held it over the king's face until he smothered to death. And Hazael became king instead.

¹⁶King Jehoram, the son of King Jehoshaphat of Judah, began his reign during the fifth year of the reign of King Joram of Israel, the son of Ahab. ¹⁷Jehoram was thirty-two years old when he became king, and he reigned in Jerusalem for eight years. ¹⁸But he was as wicked as Ahab and the other kings of Israel; he even married one of Ahab's daughters. ¹⁹Nevertheless, because God had promised his servant David that he would watch over and guide his descendants, he did not destroy Judah.

²⁰During Jehoram's reign, the people in Edom revolted from Judah and appointed their own king. ²¹King Jehoram tried unsuccessfully to crush the rebellion: he crossed the Jordan River and attacked the city of Zair, but was quickly surrounded by the army of Edom. Under cover of night he broke through their ranks, but his army deserted him and fled. ²²So Edom has maintained its independence to this day. Libnah also rebelled at that time.

²³The rest of the history of King Jehoram is written in *The Annals of the Kings of Judah*. ²⁴,²⁵He died and was buried in the royal cemetery in the City of David—the old section of Jerusalem.

Then his son Ahaziah became the new king during the twelfth year of the reign of King Joram of Israel, the son of Ahab. ²⁶Ahaziah was twenty-two years old when he began to reign, but he reigned only one year, in Jerusalem. His mother was Athaliah, the granddaughter of King Omri of Israel. ²⁷He was an evil king, just as all of King Ahab's descendants were—for he was related to Ahab by marriage.

²⁸He joined King Joram of Israel (son of Ahab) in his war against Hazael, the king of Syria, at Ramoth-gilead. King Joram was wounded in the battle, ²⁹so he went to Jezreel to rest and recover from his wounds. While he was there, King Ahaziah of Judah (son of Jehoram) came to visit him.

HUMILITY **8:12-13** Elisha told Hazael he would sin greatly. Hazael protested, "I would *never* do that sort of thing." He did not acknowledge his personal potential for evil. In our "enlightened" society, it is easy to think we are above gross sin and can control our actions. We think that we would never sink so low. Instead, we should take a more biblical and realistic look at ourselves and admit our sinful potential. Then we will ask for God's strength to resist such evil. **To begin the series of devotionals on HUMILITY, turn to page 449.**

9 Jehu Will Be King

Meanwhile Elisha had summoned one of the young prophets.

"Get ready to go to Ramoth-gilead," he told him. "Take this vial of oil with you ²and find Jehu (the son of Jehoshaphat, the son of Nimshi). Call him into a private room away from his friends, ³and pour the oil over his head. Tell him that the Lord has anointed him to be the king of Israel; then run for your life!"

⁴So the young prophet did as he was told. When he arrived in Ramoth-gilead, ⁵he found Jehu sitting around with the other army officers.

"I have a message for you, sir," he said.

"For which one of us?" Jehu asked.

"For you," he replied.

⁶So Jehu left the others and went into the house, and the young man poured the oil over his head and said, "The Lord God of Israel says, 'I anoint you king of the Lord's people, Israel. ⁷You are to destroy the family of Ahab; you will avenge the murder of my prophets and of all my other people who were killed by Jezebel. ⁸The entire family of Ahab must be wiped out—every male, no matter who. ⁹I will destroy the family of Ahab as I destroyed the families of Jeroboam (son of Nebat) and of Baasha (son of Ahijah). ¹⁰Dogs shall eat Ahab's wife Jezebel at Jezreel, and no one will bury her.'"

Then he opened the door and ran.

¹¹Jehu went back to his friends and one of them asked him, "What did that crazy fellow want? Is everything all right?"

"You know very well who he was and what he wanted," Jehu replied.

¹²"No, we don't," they said. "Tell us."

So he told them what the man had said and that he had been anointed king of Israel!

¹³They quickly carpeted the bare steps with their coats and blew a trumpet, shouting, "Jehu is king!"

¹⁴That is how Jehu (son of Jehoshaphat, son of Nimshi) rebelled against King Joram. (King Joram had been with the army at Ramoth-gilead, defending Israel against the forces of King Hazael of Syria. ¹⁵But he had returned to Jezreel to recover from his wounds.)

"Since you want me to be king," Jehu told the men who were with him, "don't let anyone escape to Jezreel to report what we have done."

¹⁶Then Jehu jumped into a chariot and rode to Jezreel himself to find King Joram, who was lying there wounded. (King Ahaziah of Judah was there too, for he had gone to visit him.) ¹⁷The watchman on the Tower of Jezreel saw Jehu and his company approaching and shouted, "Someone is coming."

"Send out a rider and find out if he is friend or foe," King Joram shouted back. ¹⁸So a soldier rode out to meet Jehu.

"The king wants to know whether you are friend or foe," he demanded. "Do you come in peace?"

Jehu replied, "What do you know about peace? Get behind me!"

The watchman called out to the king that the messenger had met them but was not returning. ¹⁹So the king sent out a second rider. He rode up to them and demanded in the name of the king to know whether their intentions were friendly or not.

Jehu answered, "What do you know about friendliness? Get behind me!"

²⁰"He isn't returning either!" the watchman exclaimed. "It must be Jehu, for he is driving so furiously."

²¹"Quick! Get my chariot ready!" King Joram commanded.

Then he and King Ahaziah of Judah rode out to meet Jehu. They met him at the field of Naboth, ²²and King Joram demanded, "Do you come as a friend, Jehu?"

Jehu replied, "How can there be friendship as long as the evils of your mother Jezebel are all around us?"

²³Then King Joram reined the chariot-horses around and fled, shouting to King Ahaziah, "There is treachery, Ahaziah! Treason!"

²⁴Then Jehu drew his bow with his full strength and shot Joram between the shoulders; and the arrow pierced his heart, and he sank down dead in his chariot.

²⁵Jehu said to Bidkar, his assistant, "Throw him into the field of Naboth, for once when you and I were riding along behind his father Ahab, the Lord revealed this prophecy to me: ²⁶'I will repay him here on Naboth's property for the murder of Naboth and his sons.' So throw him out on Naboth's field, just as the Lord said."

²⁷Meanwhile, King Ahaziah of Judah had fled along the road to Beth-haggan. Jehu rode after him, shouting, "Shoot him too."

So they shot him in his chariot at the place where the road climbs to Gur, near Ibleam. He was able to go on as far as Megiddo, but died there. ²⁸His officials took him by chariot to Jerusalem where they buried him in the royal cemetery. ²⁹(Ahaziah's reign over Judah had begun in the twelfth year of the reign of King Joram of Israel.)

³⁰When Jezebel heard that Jehu had come to Jezreel, she painted her eyelids and fixed her hair and sat at a window. ³¹When Jehu entered the gate of the palace, she shouted at him, "How are you today, you murderer! You son of a Zimri who murdered his master!"

32He looked up and saw her at the window and shouted, "Who is on my side?" And two or three eunuchs looked out at him.

33"Throw her down!" he yelled.

So they threw her out the window, and her blood spattered against the wall and on the horses; and she was trampled by the horses' hoofs.

34Then Jehu went into the palace for lunch. Afterwards he said, "Someone go and bury this cursed woman, for she is the daughter of a king."

35But when they went out to bury her, they found only her skull, her feet, and her hands.

36When they returned and told him, he remarked, "That is just what the Lord said would happen. He told Elijah the prophet that dogs would eat her flesh 37and that her body would be scattered like manure upon the field, so that no one could tell whose it was."

10 Jehu Kills Ahab's Family

Then Jehu wrote a letter to the city council of Samaria and to the guardians of Ahab's seventy sons—all of whom were living there.

2,3"Upon receipt of this letter, select the best one of Ahab's sons to be your king, and prepare to fight for his throne. For you have chariots and horses and a fortified city and an armory."

4But they were too frightened to do it. "Two kings couldn't stand against this man! What can we do?" they said.

5So the manager of palace affairs and the city manager, together with the city council and the guardians of Ahab's sons, sent him this message:

"Jehu, we are your servants and will do anything you tell us to. We have decided that you should be our king instead of one of Ahab's sons."

6Jehu responded with this message: "If you are on my side and are going to obey me, bring the heads of your master's sons to me at Jezreel at about this time tomorrow."

(These seventy sons of King Ahab were living in the homes of the chief men of the city, where they had been raised since childhood.) 7When the letter arrived, all seventy of them were murdered, and their heads were packed into baskets and presented to Jehu at Jezreel. 8When a messenger told Jehu that the heads of the king's sons had arrived, he said to pile them in two heaps at the entrance of the city gate, and to leave them there until the next morning.

9,10In the morning he went out and spoke to the crowd that had gathered around them. "You aren't to blame," he told them. "I conspired against my master and killed him, but I didn't kill his sons! The Lord has done that, for everything he says comes true. He declared through his servant Elijah that this would happen to Ahab's descendants."

11Jehu then killed all the rest of the members of the family of Ahab who were in Jezreel, as well as all of his important officials, personal friends, and private chaplains. Finally, no one was left who had been close to him in any way. 12Then he set out for Samaria and stayed overnight at a shepherd's inn along the way. 13While he was there he met the brothers of King Ahaziah of Judah.

"Who are you?" he asked them.

And they replied, "We are brothers of King Ahaziah. We are going to Samaria to visit the sons of King Ahab and of the Queen Mother, Jezebel."

14"Grab them!" Jehu shouted to his men. And he took them out to the cistern and killed all forty-two of them.

15As he left the inn, he met Jehonadab, the son of Rechab, who was coming to meet him. After they had greeted each other, Jehu said to him, "Are you as loyal to me as I am to you?"

"Yes," Jehonadab replied.

"Then give me your hand," Jehu said, and he helped him into the royal chariot.

16"Now come along with me," Jehu said, "and see how much I have done for the Lord." So Jehonadab rode along with him. 17When he arrived in Samaria he butchered all of Ahab's friends and relatives, just as Elijah, speaking for the Lord, had predicted.

Then Jehu called a meeting of all the people of the city and said to them, "Ahab hardly worshiped Baal at all in comparison to the way I am going to! 18,19Summon all the prophets and priests of Baal, and call together all his worshipers. See to it that every one of them comes, for we worshipers of Baal are going to have a great celebration to praise him. Any of Baal's worshipers who don't come will be put to death."

But Jehu's plan was to exterminate them. 20,21He sent messengers throughout all Israel summoning those who worshiped Baal; and they all came and filled the temple of Baal from one end to the other. 22He instructed the head of the robing room, "Be sure that every worshiper wears one of the special robes."

23Then Jehu and Jehonadab (son of Rechab) went into the temple to address the people: "Check to be sure that only those who worship Baal are here; don't let anyone in who worships the Lord!"

24As the priests of Baal began offering sacrifices and burnt offer-

---

AVOIDING SIN **10:24** Israel was supposed to be intolerant of the religions of surrounding nations, which were evil and corrupt. Israel was God's special nation, chosen to be an example of what was right, true, and fair. But Israel's kings, priests, and elders, contaminated by surrounding pagan beliefs, had become tolerant and apathetic. We are to be completely intolerant of sin and remove it from our lives. **To begin the series of devotionals on *AVOIDING SIN*, turn to page 195.**

ings, Jehu surrounded the building with eighty of his men and told them, "If you let anyone escape, you'll pay for it with your own life."

²⁵As soon as he had finished sacrificing the burnt offering, Jehu went out and told his officers and men, "Go in and kill the whole bunch of them. Don't let a single one escape."

So they slaughtered them all and dragged their bodies outside. Then Jehu's men went into the inner temple, ²⁶dragged out the pillar used for the worship of Baal, and burned it. ²⁷They wrecked the temple and converted it into a public toilet, which it still is today. ²⁸Thus Jehu destroyed every trace of Baal from Israel. ²⁹However, he didn't destroy the gold calves at Bethel and Dan—this was the great sin of Jeroboam (son of Nebat), for it resulted in all Israel sinning.

³⁰Afterwards the Lord said to Jehu, "You have done well in following my instructions to destroy the dynasty of Ahab. Because of this I will cause your son, your grandson, and your great-grandson to be the kings of Israel."

³¹But Jehu didn't follow the Lord God of Israel with all his heart, for he continued to worship Jeroboam's gold calves that had been the cause of such great sin in Israel.

^{32,33}At about that time the Lord began to whittle down the size of Israel. King Hazael conquered several sections of the country east of the Jordan River, as well as all of Gilead, Gad, and Reuben; he also conquered parts of Manasseh from the Aroer River in the valley of the Arnon as far as Gilead and Bashan.

³⁴The rest of Jehu's activities are recorded in *The Annals of the Kings of Israel*. ³⁵When Jehu died, he was buried in Samaria; and his son Jehoahaz became the new king. ³⁶In all, Jehu reigned as king of Israel, in Samaria, for twenty-eight years.

11 Joash Becomes King

When Athaliah, the mother of King Ahaziah of Judah, learned that her son was dead, she killed all of his children, ^{2,3}except for his year-old son Joash. Joash was rescued by his Aunt Jehosheba, who was a sister of King Ahaziah (for she was a daughter of King Jehoram, Ahaziah's father). She stole him away from among the rest of the king's children who were waiting to be slain and hid him and his nurse in a storeroom of the Temple. They lived there for six years while Athaliah reigned as queen.

⁴In the seventh year of Queen Athaliah's reign, Jehoiada the priest summoned the officers of the palace guard and the queen's bodyguard. He met them in the Temple, swore them to secrecy, and showed them the king's son.

⁵Then he gave them their instructions: "A third of those who are on duty on the Sabbath are to guard the palace. ⁶⁻⁸The other two-thirds shall stand guard at the Temple; surround the king, weapons in hand, and kill anyone who tries to break through. Stay with the king at all times."

⁹So the officers followed Jehoiada's instructions. They brought to Jehoiada the men who were going off duty on the Sabbath and those who were coming on duty, ¹⁰and he armed them from the Temple's supply of spears and shields that had belonged to King David. ¹¹The guards, with weapons ready, stood across the front of the sanctuary and surrounded the altar, which was near Joash's hideaway.

¹²Then Jehoiada brought out the young prince and put the crown upon his head and gave him a copy of the Ten Commandments, and anointed him as king. Then everyone clapped and shouted, "Long live the king!"

^{13,14}When Athaliah heard all the noise, she ran into the Temple and saw the new king standing beside the pillar, as was the custom at times of coronation, surrounded by her bodyguard and many trumpeters; and everyone was rejoicing and blowing trumpets.

"Treason! Treason!" she screamed, and began to tear her clothes.

¹⁵"Get her out of here," shouted Jehoiada to the officers of the guard. "Don't kill her here in the Temple. But kill anyone who tries to come to her rescue."

¹⁶So they dragged her to the palace stables and killed her there.

¹⁷Jehoiada made a treaty between the Lord, the king, and the people, that they would be the Lord's people. He also made a contract between the king and the people. ¹⁸Everyone went over to the temple of Baal and tore it down, breaking the altars and images and killing Mattan, the priest of Baal, in front of the altar. And Jehoiada set guards at the Temple of the Lord. ¹⁹Then he and the officers and the guard and all the people led the king from the Temple, past the guardhouse, and into the palace. And he sat upon the king's throne.

²⁰So everyone was happy, and the city settled back into quietness after Athaliah's death. ²¹Joash was seven years old when he became king.

12 Joash Rules Judah

It was seven years after Jehu had become the king of Israel that Joash became king of Judah. He reigned in Jerusalem for forty years. (His mother was Zibiah, from Beersheba.) ²All his life Joash did what was right because Jehoiada the High Priest instructed him. ³Yet even so he didn't destroy the shrines on the hills—the people still sacrificed and burned incense there.

^{4,5}One day King Joash said to Jehoiada, "The Temple building needs repairing. Whenever any-

one brings a contribution to the Lord, whether it is a regular assessment or some special gift, use it to pay for whatever repairs are needed."

⁶But in the twenty-third year of his reign the Temple was still in disrepair. ⁷So Joash called for Jehoiada and the other priests and asked them, "Why haven't you done anything about the Temple? Now don't use any more money for your own needs; from now on it must all be spent on getting the Temple into good condition."

⁸So the priests agreed to set up a special repair fund that would not go through their hands, lest it be diverted to care for their personal needs. ⁹Jehoiada the priest bored a hole in the lid of a large chest and set it on the right-hand side of the altar at the Temple entrance. The doorkeepers put all of the people's contributions into it. ¹⁰Whenever the chest became full, the king's financial secretary and the High Priest counted it, put it into bags, ¹¹,¹²and gave it to the construction superintendents to pay the carpenters, stonemasons, quarrymen, timber dealers, and stone merchants, and to buy the other materials needed to repair the Temple of the Lord. ¹³,¹⁴It was not used to buy silver cups, gold snuffers, bowls, trumpets, or similar articles, but only for repairs to the building. ¹⁵No accounting was required from the construction superintendents, for they were honest and faithful men. ¹⁶However, the money that was contributed for guilt offerings and sin offerings was given to the priests for their own use. It was not put into the chest.

¹⁷About this time, King Hazael of Syria went to war against Gath and captured it; then he moved on toward Jerusalem to attack it. ¹⁸King Joash took all the sacred objects that his ancestors—Jehoshaphat, Jehoram, and Ahaziah, the kings of Judah—had dedicated, along with what he himself had dedicated, and all the gold in the treasuries of the Temple and the palace, and sent it to Hazael. So Hazael called off the attack.

¹⁹The rest of the history of Joash is recorded in *The Annals of the Kings of Judah*. ²⁰But his officers plotted against him and assassinated him in his royal residence at Millo on the road to Silla. ²¹The assassins were Jozachar, the son of Shimeath, and Jehozabad, the son of Shomer—both trusted aides. He was buried in the royal cemetery in Jerusalem, and his son Amaziah became the new king.

13 Jehoahaz Rules Israel

Jehoahaz (the son of Jehu) began a seventeen-year reign over Israel during the twenty-third year of the reign of King Joash of Judah. ²But he was an evil king, and he followed the wicked paths of Jeroboam, who had caused Israel to sin.

³So the Lord was very angry with Israel, and he continually allowed King Hazael of Syria and his son Ben-hadad to conquer them.

⁴But Jehoahaz prayed for the Lord's help, and the Lord listened to him; for the Lord saw how terribly the king of Syria was oppressing Israel. ⁵So the Lord raised up leaders among the Israelis to rescue them from the tyranny of the Syrians; and then Israel lived in safety again as they had in former days. ⁶But they continued to sin, following the evil ways of Jeroboam; and they continued to worship the goddess Asherah at Samaria. ⁷Finally the Lord reduced Jehoahaz's army to fifty mounted troops, ten chariots, and ten thousand infantry; for the king of Syria had destroyed the others as though they were dust beneath his feet.

⁸The rest of the history of Jehoahaz is recorded in *The Annals of the Kings of Israel*.

⁹,¹⁰Jehoahaz died and was buried in Samaria, and his son Joash reigned in Samaria for sixteen years. He came to the throne in the thirty-seventh year of the reign of King Joash of Judah. ¹¹But he was an evil man, for, like Jeroboam, he encouraged the people to worship idols and led them into sin. ¹²The rest of the history of the reign of Joash, including his wars against King Amaziah of Judah, are written in *The Annals of the Kings of Israel*. ¹³Joash died and was buried in Samaria with the other kings of Israel; and Jeroboam II became the new king.

¹⁴When Elisha was in his last illness, King Joash visited him and wept over him.

"My father! My father! You are the strength of Israel!" he cried.

¹⁵Elisha told him, "Get a bow and some arrows," and he did.

¹⁶,¹⁷"Open that eastern window," he instructed. Then he told the king to put his hand upon the bow, and Elisha laid his own hands upon the king's hands.

"Shoot!" Elisha commanded, and he did.

Then Elisha proclaimed, "This is the Lord's arrow, full of victory over Syria; for you will completely conquer the Syrians at Aphek. ¹⁸Now pick up the other arrows and strike them against the floor."

So the king picked them up and struck the floor three times. ¹⁹But the prophet was angry with him. "You should have struck the floor five or six times," he exclaimed, "for then you would have beaten Syria until they were entirely destroyed; now you will be victorious only three times."

²⁰,²¹So Elisha died and was buried.

In those days bandit gangs of Moabites used to invade the land each spring. Once some men who were burying a friend spied these marauders so they hastily threw his body into the tomb of Elisha.

Family Devotions

☐ **Devotion 119**

Faith in Action

Read 2 Kings 12:15

Faith in Action Memory Verse

In response to all he has done for us, let us outdo each other in being helpful and kind to each other and in doing good.
Hebrews 10:24

Susan flicked the dust cloth over the windowsill, took another quick swipe at the bedside table, and tugged the curtains so they hung neatly. She glanced approvingly around her room. Then she saw a telltale scrap of paper sticking out from under the edge of the ruffled bedskirt. Susan slid the offending piece out of sight with her toe.

"Dear Mom," she wrote on a notepad, "I finished my room. I'm at Julie's. Love ya." She signed her name, almost unable to believe she'd done that room in less than ten minutes.

When Susan returned home, Mom greeted her with a question. "Did you really clean your room?"

"Sure, Mom," Susan replied uneasily.

"It looked fine until I looked under the bed," Mom said. "Then I wondered about your integrity."

"My what?" asked Susan.

Mom answered with a question of her own. "Just suppose I swept all the dirt and crumbs under the table, piled last month's newspapers on top of them, and pretended they weren't there. What would you think?"

"We'd all see the mess," said Susan with a laugh, "so we'd know better."

"Well, what if I covered them up so you couldn't see them?" asked Mom. "Would it be dishonest to try to persuade you that the kitchen was clean?"

"Well, I guess so," said Susan hesitantly.

"I agree," said Mom. "Hiding the mess and pretending it's all cleaned up is like telling a lie about your work. When I ask you to do something, I expect you to do a good job. It will take longer, but you'll be happier with yourself, and I'll be able to trust you to accept responsibility honestly. That's integrity."

"I'll go finish my room right now—with integrity," said Susan.

How About You?
Do you always act with integrity—with honesty? See how well you can do a job, rather than how quickly you can get it done. It pleases God when you respond to authority with integrity. It means you are responding to him. P. K.

• For the next devotional, turn to page 399. • For the next devotional on *Faith in Action*, turn to page 537.
• For notes on *Faith in Action*, see pages 583, 846, 1068, and 1232.

And as soon as the body touched Elisha's bones, the dead man revived and jumped to his feet!

²²King Hazael of Syria had oppressed Israel during the entire reign of King Jehoahaz. ²³But the Lord was gracious to the people of Israel, and they were not totally destroyed. For God pitied them, and also he was honoring his contract with Abraham, Isaac, and Jacob. And this is still true. ²⁴Then King Hazael of Syria died, and his son Ben-hadad reigned in his place.

²⁵King Joash of Israel (the son of Jehoahaz) was successful on three occasions in reconquering the cities that his father had lost to Ben-hadad.

14 Amaziah Rules Judah

During the second year of the reign of King Joash of Israel, King Amaziah began his reign over Judah. ²Amaziah was twenty-five years old at the time, and he reigned in Jerusalem for twenty-nine years. (His mother was Jehoaddin, a native of Jerusalem.) ³He was a good king in the Lord's sight, though not quite like his ancestor David; but he was as good a king as his father Joash. ⁴However, he didn't destroy the shrines on the hills, so the people still sacrificed and burned incense there.

⁵As soon as he had a firm grip on the kingdom, he killed the men who had assassinated his father; ⁶but he didn't kill their children, for the Lord had commanded through the law of Moses that fathers shall not be killed for their children, nor children for the sins of their fathers: everyone must pay the penalty for his own sins. ⁷Once Amaziah killed ten thousand Edomites in Salt Valley; he also conquered Sela and changed its name to Joktheel, as it is called to this day.

⁸One day he sent a message to King Joash of Israel (the son of Jehoahaz and the grandson of Jehu), daring him to mobilize his army and come out and fight.

⁹But King Joash replied, "The thistle of Lebanon demanded of the mighty cedar tree, 'Give your daughter to be a wife for my son.' But just then a wild animal passed by and stepped on the thistle and trod it into the ground! ¹⁰You have destroyed Edom and are very proud about it; but my advice to you is, be content with your glory and stay home! Why provoke disaster for both yourself and Judah?"

¹¹But Amaziah refused to listen, so King Joash of Israel mustered his army. The battle began at Bethshemesh, one of the cities of Judah, ¹²and Judah was defeated and the army fled home. ¹³King Amaziah was captured, and the army of Israel marched on Jerusalem and broke down its wall from the Gate of Ephraim to the Corner Gate, a distance of about six hundred feet. ¹⁴King Joash took many hostages and all the gold and silver from the Temple and palace treasury, also the gold cups. Then he returned to Samaria.

¹⁵The rest of the history of Joash and his war with King Amaziah of Judah are recorded in *The Annals of the Kings of Israel*. ¹⁶When Joash died, he was buried in Samaria with the other kings of Israel. And his son Jeroboam became the new king.

¹⁷Amaziah lived fifteen years longer than Joash, ¹⁸and the rest of his biography is recorded in *The Annals of the Kings of Judah*. ¹⁹There was a plot against his life in Jerusalem, and he fled to Lachish; but his enemies sent assassins and killed him there. ²⁰His body was returned on horses, and he was buried in the royal cemetery, in the City of David section of Jerusalem.

²¹Then his son Azariah became the new king at the age of sixteen. ²²After his father's death, he built Elath and restored it to Judah.

²³Meanwhile, over in Israel, Jeroboam II had become king during the fifteenth year of the reign of King Amaziah of Judah. Jeroboam's reign lasted forty-one years. ²⁴But he was as evil as Jeroboam I (the son of Nebat), who had led Israel into the sin of worshiping idols. ²⁵Jeroboam II recovered the lost territories of Israel between Hamath and the Dead Sea, just as the Lord God of Israel had predicted through Jonah (son of Amittai) the prophet from Gathhepher. ²⁶For the Lord saw the bitter plight of Israel—she had no one to help her. ²⁷And he had not said that he would blot out the name of Israel, so he used King Jeroboam II to save her.

²⁸The rest of Jeroboam's biography—all that he did, and his great power, and his wars, and how he recovered Damascus and Hamath (which had been captured by Judah)—is recorded in *The Annals of the Kings of Israel*. ²⁹When Jeroboam II, died he was buried with the other kings of Israel, and his son Zechariah became the new king of Israel.

15 Azariah Rules Judah

New king of Judah: Azariah
Father's name: Amaziah, the former king
His age at the beginning of his reign: 16 years old
Length of reign: 52 years, in Jerusalem
Mother's name: Jecoliah of Jerusalem
Reigning in Israel at that time: King Jeroboam, who had been the king there for 27 years

³Azariah was a good king, and he pleased the Lord just as his father Amaziah had. ⁴But like his predecessors, he didn't destroy the shrines on the hills where the people sacrificed and burned incense. ⁵Because of this the Lord struck him with leprosy, which lasted until the day of his death; so he lived in a house by himself. And his son Jotham was the acting king. ⁶The rest of the history of

Azariah is recorded in *The Annals of the Kings of Judah.* ⁷When Azariah died, he was buried with his ancestors in the City of David, and his son Jotham became king.

⁸New king of Israel: Zechariah
Father's name: Jeroboam
Length of reign: 6 months, in Samaria
Reigning in Judah at that time: King Azariah,
    who had been the king there for 38 years

⁹But Zechariah was an evil king in the Lord's sight, just like his ancestors. Like Jeroboam I (the son of Nebat), he encouraged Israel in the sin of worshiping idols. ¹⁰Then Shallum (the son of Jabesh) conspired against him and assassinated him at Ibleam and took the crown himself. ¹¹The rest of the history of Zechariah's reign is found in *The Annals of the Kings of Israel.* ¹²(So the Lord's statement to Jehu came true, that Jehu's son, grandson, and great-grandson would be kings of Israel.)

¹³New king of Israel: Shallum
Father's name: Jabesh
Length of reign: 1 month, in Samaria
Reigning in Judah at that time: King Uzziah,
    who had been the king there for 39 years

¹⁴One month after Shallum became king, Menahem (the son of Gadi) came to Samaria from Tirzah and assassinated him and took the throne. ¹⁵Additional details about King Shallum and his conspiracy are recorded in *The Annals of the Kings of Israel.*

¹⁶Menahem destroyed the city of Tappuah and the surrounding countryside, for its citizens refused to accept him as their king; he killed the entire population and ripped open the pregnant women.

¹⁷New king of Israel: Menahem
Length of reign: 10 years, in Samaria
Reigning in Judah at that time: King Azariah,
    who had been the king there for 39 years

¹⁸But Menahem was an evil king. He worshiped idols, as King Jeroboam I had done so long before, and he led the people of Israel into grievous sin. ¹⁹,²⁰Then King Pul of Assyria invaded the land; but King Menahem bought him off with a gift of $2,000,000, so he turned around and returned home. Menahem extorted the money from the rich, assessing each one $2,000 in the form of a special tax. ²¹The rest of the history of King Menahem is written in *The Annals of the Kings of Israel.* ²²When he died, his son Pekahiah became the new king.

²³New king of Israel: Pekahiah
Father's name: King Menahem
Length of reign: 2 years, in Samaria
Reigning in Judah at that time: King Azariah,
    who had been the king there for 50 years

²⁴But Pekahiah was an evil king, and he continued the idol-worship begun by Jeroboam I (son of Nebat) who led Israel down that evil trail. ²⁵Then Pekah (son of Remaliah), the commanding general of his army, conspired against him with fifty men from Gilead and assassinated him in the palace at Samaria (Argob and Arieh were also slain in the revolt). So Pekah became the new king. ²⁶The rest of the history of King Pekahiah is recorded in *The Annals of the Kings of Israel.*

²⁷New king of Israel: Pekah
Father's name: Remaliah
Length of reign: 20 years, in Samaria
Reigning in Judah at that time: King Azariah,
    who had been the king there for 52 years

²⁸Pekah, too, was an evil king, and he continued in the example of Jeroboam I (son of Nebat), who led all of Israel into the sin of worshiping idols. ²⁹It was during his reign that King Tiglath-pileser led an attack against Israel. He captured the cities of Ijon, Abel-beth-maacah, Janoah, Kedesh, Hazor, Gilead, Galilee, and all the land of Naphtali; and he took the people away to Assyria as captives. ³⁰Then Hoshea (the son of Elah) plotted against Pekah and assassinated him; and he took the throne for himself.

New king of Israel: Hoshea
Reigning in Judah at that time: King Jotham
    (son of Uzziah), who had been the king
    there for 20 years

³¹The rest of the history of Pekah's reign is recorded in *The Annals of the Kings of Israel.*

³²,³³New king of Judah: Jotham
Father's name: King Uzziah
His age at the beginning of his reign: 25 years old
Length of reign: 16 years, in Jerusalem
Mother's name: Jerusha (daughter of Zadok)

PUTTING GOD FIRST 15:34-35 "Jotham was a good king . . . but." Much good can be said of Jotham and his reign as king of Judah, but he failed in a most critical area: he didn't destroy the shrines to the false gods, although leaving them clearly violated the first commandment (Exodus 20:3). Like Jotham, we may live basically good lives and yet miss doing what is most important. A lifetime of doing good is not enough if we make the crucial mistake of not following God with all our hearts. A true follower of God puts him first in all areas of life. **To begin the series of devotionals on PUTTING GOD FIRST, turn to page 115.**

Reigning in Israel at that time: King Pekah
(son of Remaliah), who had been the king there for 2 years

³⁴,³⁵Generally speaking, Jotham was a good king. Like his father Uzziah, he followed the Lord. But he didn't destroy the shrines on the hills where the people sacrificed and burned incense. It was during King Jotham's reign that the upper gate of the Temple of the Lord was built. ³⁶The rest of Jotham's history is written in *The Annals of the Kings of Judah.* ³⁷In those days the Lord caused King Rezin of Syria and King Pekah of Israel to attack Judah. ³⁸When Jotham died he was buried with the other kings of Judah in the royal cemetery, in the City of David section of Jerusalem. Then his son Ahaz became the new king.

16 Ahaz Rules Judah

New king of Judah: Ahaz
Father's name: Jotham
His age at the beginning of his reign: 20 years old
Length of reign: 16 years, in Jerusalem
Character of his reign: evil
Reigning in Israel at that time: King Pekah
(son of Remaliah), who had been the king there for 17 years

²But he did not follow the Lord as his ancestor David had; ³he was as wicked as the kings of Israel. He even killed his own son by offering him as a burnt sacrifice to the gods, following the heathen customs of the nations around Judah—nations that the Lord destroyed when the people of Israel entered the land. ⁴He also sacrificed and burned incense at the shrines on the hills and at the numerous altars in the groves of trees.

⁵Then King Rezin of Syria and King Pekah (son of Remaliah) of Israel declared war on Ahaz and besieged Jerusalem; but they did not conquer it. ⁶However, at that time King Rezin of Syria recovered the city of Elath for Syria; he drove out the Jews and sent Syrians to live there, as they do to this day. ⁷King Ahaz sent a messenger to King Tiglath-pileser of Assyria, begging him to help him fight the attacking armies of Syria and Israel. ⁸Ahaz took the silver and gold from the Temple and from the royal vaults and sent it as a payment to the Assyrian king. ⁹So the Assyrians attacked Damascus, the capital of Syria. They took away the population of the city as captives, resettling them in Kir, and King Rezin of Syria was killed.

¹⁰King Ahaz now went to Damascus to meet with King Tiglath-pileser, and while he was there he noticed an unusual altar in a heathen temple. He jotted down its dimensions and made a sketch and sent it back to Uriah the priest with a detailed description. ¹¹,¹²Uriah built one just like it by following these directions and had it ready for the king, who, upon his return from Damascus, inaugurated it with an offering. ¹³The king presented a burnt offering and a grain offering, poured a drink offering over it, and sprinkled the blood of peace offerings upon it. ¹⁴Then he removed the old bronze altar from the front of the Temple (it had stood between the Temple entrance and the new altar), and placed it on the north side of the new altar. ¹⁵He instructed Uriah the priest to use the new altar for the sacrifices of burnt offering, the evening grain offering, the king's burnt offering and grain offering, and the offerings of the people, including their drink offerings. The blood from the burnt offerings and sacrifices was also to be sprinkled over the new altar. So the old altar was used only for purposes of divination.

"The old bronze altar," he said, "will be only for my personal use."

¹⁶Uriah the priest did as King Ahaz instructed him. ¹⁷Then the king dismantled the wheeled stands in the Temple, removed their crosspieces and the water vats they supported, and removed the great tank from the backs of the bronze oxen and placed it upon the stone pavement. ¹⁸In deference to the king of Assyria he also removed the festive passageway he had constructed between the palace and the Temple.

¹⁹The rest of the history of the reign of King Ahaz is recorded in *The Annals of the Kings of Judah.* ²⁰When Ahaz died he was buried in the royal cemetery, in the City of David sector of Jerusalem, and his son Hezekiah became the new king.

17 Israel Is Taken into Captivity

New king of Israel: Hoshea
Father's name: Elah
Length of reign: 9 years, in Samaria
Character of his reign: evil—but not as bad as some of the other kings of Israel
Reigning in Judah at that time: King Ahaz, who had been the king there for 12 years

³King Shalmaneser of Assyria attacked and defeated King Hoshea, so Israel had to pay heavy annual taxes to Assyria. ⁴Then Hoshea conspired against the king of Assyria by asking King So of Egypt to help him shake free of Assyria's power, but this treachery was discovered. At the same time he refused to pay the annual tribute to Assyria. So the king of Assyria put him in prison and in chains for his rebellion.

⁵Now the land of Israel was filled with Assyrian troops for three years besieging Samaria, the capital city of Israel. ⁶Finally, in the ninth year of King

FAMILY DEVOTIONS

☐ **DEVOTION 120**
TRUSTING GOD'S PLAN

Read 2 Kings 17:5-14

Trusting God's Plan
Memory Verses:

This plan of mine is not what you would work out, neither are my thoughts the same as yours! For just as the heavens are higher than the earth, so are my ways higher than yours, and my thoughts than yours.
Isaiah 55:8-9

Bobby shrieked in protest as his mother got up to lead him into the doctor's examining room. Bobby's sister, Lisa, looked at him sympathetically. "Don't cry yet, Bobby!" she said. "You haven't even gotten your shot yet!"

"I don't wanna get shot!" screeched the little boy.

While the nurse swabbed Bobby's arm with antiseptic, he screamed and wiggled. "This will prick a little bit," she said kindly, "but it will be over soon." Sure enough, almost before Bobby could draw a breath to give another yell, the nurse had finished. As they walked out to their car, Bobby wore a big smile and admired the little toy car the nurse had given him.

"That wasn't so bad, was it?" asked Lisa.

Bobby shook his head. "Not so bad," he murmured, "but I still don't like shots. They hurt!"

"We know, honey," said Mom soothingly, "but the hurt lasts only a little while, and the medicine in the shot helps you stay healthy. If you didn't get shots, you might get a sickness that would hurt far worse than a shot."

"Bobby's too little to understand," remarked Lisa as she watched her brother play with his car. "But someday he'll be glad he got hurt today, won't he, Mom?"

"I'm sure he will," smiled Mom. "And you know, that could serve as a lesson for you and me. When we're going through hard times, we may wonder whether or not God really cares about us. But everything he allows us to experience—even moments of pain and sadness—are for our good and his glory. If we could see things from his point of view, we'd think about our earthly trials in a completely different way."

How About You?
Is it hard to be patient when you're not feeling well? When you have to go to a new school? When things just aren't going well? Perhaps God wants to teach you something, as he was trying to teach Israel and Judah to turn back to him. Maybe he wants to allow you to be an example of his grace. Maybe he wants to cleanse you of some sin in your life, or to protect you from an even greater danger in the future. Whatever his purposes are, you will find peace and joy when you fully submit to him. He knows best! *S. K.*

• For the next devotional, turn to page 403.   • For the next devotional on *TRUSTING GOD'S PLAN*, turn to page 519.
• For notes on *TRUSTING GOD'S PLAN*, see pages 252, 296, 731, and 870.

Hoshea's reign, Samaria fell and the people of Israel were exiled to Assyria. They were placed in colonies in the city of Halah and along the banks of the Habor River in Gozan, and among the cities of the Medes.

⁷This disaster came upon the nation of Israel because the people worshiped other gods, thus sinning against the Lord their God who had brought them safely out of their slavery in Egypt. ⁸They had followed the evil customs of the nations which the Lord had cast out from before them. ⁹The people of Israel had also secretly done many things that were wrong, and they had built altars to other gods throughout the land. ¹⁰They had placed obelisks and idols at the top of every hill and under every green tree; ¹¹and they had burned incense to the gods of the very nations which the Lord had cleared out of the land when Israel came in. So the people of Israel had done many evil things, and the Lord was very angry. ¹²Yes, they worshiped idols, despite the Lord's specific and repeated warnings.

¹³Again and again the Lord had sent prophets to warn both Israel and Judah to turn from their evil ways; he had warned them to obey his commandments which he had given to their ancestors through these prophets, ¹⁴but Israel wouldn't listen. The people were as stubborn as their ancestors and refused to believe in the Lord their God. ¹⁵They rejected his laws and the covenant he had made with their ancestors, and despised all his warnings. In their foolishness they worshiped heathen idols despite the Lord's stern warnings. ¹⁶They defied all the commandments of the Lord their God and made two calves from molten gold. They made detestable, shameful idols and worshiped Baal and the sun, moon, and stars. ¹⁷They even burned their own sons and daughters to death on the altars of Molech; they consulted fortune-tellers and used magic and sold themselves to evil. So the Lord was very angry. ¹⁸He swept them from his sight until only the tribe of Judah remained in the land.

¹⁹But even Judah refused to obey the commandments of the Lord their God; they too walked in the same evil paths as Israel had. ²⁰So the Lord rejected all the descendants of Jacob. He punished them by delivering them to their attackers until they were destroyed. ²¹For Israel split off from the kingdom of David and chose Jeroboam I (the son of Nebat) as its king. Then Jeroboam drew Israel away from following the Lord. He made them sin a great sin, ²²and the people of Israel never quit doing the evil things that Jeroboam led them into, ²³until the Lord finally swept them away, just as all his prophets had warned would happen. So Israel was carried off to the land of Assyria where they remain to this day.

²⁴And the king of Assyria transported colonies of people from Babylon, Cuthah, Avva, Hamath, and Sepharvaim and resettled them in the cities of Samaria, replacing the people of Israel. So the Assyrians took over Samaria and the other cities of Israel. ²⁵But since these Assyrian colonists did not worship the Lord when they first arrived, the Lord sent lions among them to kill some of them.

²⁶Then they sent a message to the king of Assyria: "We colonists here in Israel don't know the laws of the god of the land, and he has sent lions among us to destroy us because we have not worshiped him."

²⁷,²⁸The king of Assyria then decreed that one of the exiled priests from Samaria should return to Israel and teach the new residents the laws of the god of the land. So one of them returned to Bethel and taught the colonists from Babylon how to worship the Lord.

²⁹But these foreigners also worshiped their own gods. They placed them in the shrines on the hills near their cities. ³⁰Those from Babylon worshiped idols of their god Succoth-benoth; those from Cuth worshiped their god Nergal; and the men of Hamath worshiped Ashima. ³¹The gods Nibhaz and Tartak were worshiped by the Avvites, and the people from Sephar even burned their own children on the altars of their gods Adrammelech and Anammelech.

³²They also worshiped the Lord, and they appointed from among themselves priests to sacrifice to the Lord on the hilltop altars. ³³But they continued to follow the religious customs of the nations from which they came. ³⁴And this is still going on among them today—they follow their former practices instead of truly worshiping the Lord or obeying the laws he gave to the descendants of Jacob (whose name was later changed to Israel). ³⁵,³⁶For the Lord had made a contract with them—that they were never to worship or make sacrifices to any heathen gods. They were to worship only the Lord who had brought them out of the land of Egypt with such tremendous miracles and power. ³⁷The descendants of Jacob were to obey all of God's laws and *never* worship other gods.

³⁸For God had said, *"You must never forget the covenant I made with you; never worship other gods.* ³⁹*You must worship only the Lord; he will save you from all your enemies."*

⁴⁰But Israel didn't listen, and the people continued to worship other gods. ⁴¹These colonists from Babylon worshiped the Lord, yes—but they also worshiped their idols. And to this day their descendants do the same thing.

 Hezekiah Rules Judah
New king of Judah: Hezekiah
Father's name: Ahaz
His age at the beginning of his reign: 25 years old
Length of reign: 29 years, in Jerusalem

Mother's name: Abi (daughter of Zechariah)
Character of his reign: good (similar to that of his ancestor David)
Reigning in Israel at that time: King Hoshea (son of Elah), who had been the king there for 3 years

⁴He removed the shrines on the hills, broke down the obelisks, knocked down the shameful idols of Asherah, and broke up the bronze serpent that Moses had made, because the people of Israel had begun to worship it by burning incense to it; even though, as King Hezekiah pointed out to them, it was merely a piece of bronze. ⁵He trusted very strongly in the Lord God of Israel. In fact, none of the kings before or after him were as close to God as he was. ⁶For he followed the Lord in everything, and carefully obeyed all of God's commands to Moses. ⁷So the Lord was with him and prospered everything he did. Then he rebelled against the king of Assyria and refused to pay tribute any longer. ⁸He also conquered the Philistines as far distant as Gaza and its suburbs, destroying cities both large and small.

⁹It was during the fourth year of his reign (which was the seventh year of the reign of King Hoshea in Israel) that King Shalmaneser of Assyria attacked Israel and began a siege on the city of Samaria. ¹⁰Three years later (during the sixth year of the reign of King Hezekiah and the ninth year of the reign of King Hoshea of Israel) Samaria fell. ¹¹It was at that time that the king of Assyria transported the Israelis to Assyria and put them in colonies in the city of Halath and along the banks of the Habor River in Gozan, and in the cities of the Medes. ¹²For they had refused to listen to the Lord their God or to do what he wanted them to do. Instead, they had transgressed his covenant and disobeyed all the laws given to them by Moses the servant of the Lord.

¹³Later, during the fourteenth year of the reign of King Hezekiah, King Sennacherib of Assyria besieged and captured all the fortified cities of Judah. ¹⁴King Hezekiah sued for peace and sent this message to the king of Assyria at Lachish: "I have done wrong. I will pay whatever tribute you demand if you will only go away." The king of Assyria then demanded a settlement of $1,500,000. ¹⁵To gather this amount, King Hezekiah used all the silver stored in the Temple and in the palace treasury. ¹⁶He even stripped off the gold from the Temple doors, and from the doorposts he had overlaid with gold, and gave it all to the Assyrian king.

¹⁷Nevertheless the king of Assyria sent his field marshal, his chief treasurer, and his chief of staff from Lachish with a great army; and they camped along the highway beside the field where cloth was bleached, near the conduit of the upper pool. ¹⁸They demanded that King Hezekiah come out to speak to them, but instead he sent a truce delegation of the following men: Eliakim, his business manager; Shebnah, his secretary; and Joah, his royal historian.

¹⁹Then the Assyrian general sent this message to King Hezekiah: "The great king of Assyria says, 'No one can save you from my power! ²⁰,²¹You need more than mere promises of help before rebelling against me. But which of your allies will give you more than words? Egypt? If you lean on Egypt, you will find her to be a stick that breaks beneath your weight and pierces your hand. The Egyptian Pharaoh is totally unreliable! ²²And if you say, "We're trusting the Lord to rescue us"—just remember that he is the very one whose hilltop altars you've destroyed. For you require everyone to worship at the altar in Jerusalem!' ²³I'll tell you what: Make a bet with my master, the king of Assyria! If you have two thousand men left who can ride horses, we'll furnish the horses! ²⁴And with an army as small as yours, you are no threat to even the least lieutenant in charge of the smallest contingent in my master's army. Even if Egypt supplies you with horses and chariots, it will do no good. ²⁵And do you think we have come here on our own? No! The Lord sent us and told us, 'Go and destroy this nation!'"

²⁶Then Eliakim, Shebnah, and Joah said to them, "Please speak in Aramaic, for we understand it. Don't use Hebrew, for the people standing on the walls will hear you."

²⁷But the Assyrian general replied, "Has my master sent me to speak only to you and to your master? Hasn't he sent me to the people on the walls too? For they are doomed with you to eat their own excrement and drink their own urine!"

²⁸Then the Assyrian ambassador shouted in Hebrew to the people on the wall, "Listen to the great king of Assyria! ²⁹'Don't let King Hezekiah fool you. He will never be able to save you from my power. ³⁰Don't let him fool you into trusting in the Lord to rescue you. ³¹,³²Don't listen to King Hezekiah. Surrender! You can live in peace here in your own land until I take you to another land just like this one—with plentiful crops, grain, grapes, olive trees, and honey. All of this instead of death! Don't listen to King Hezekiah when he tries to persuade you that the Lord will deliver you. ³³Have any of the gods of the other nations ever delivered their people from the king of Assyria? ³⁴What happened to the gods of Hamath, Arpad, Sepharvaim, Hena, and Ivvah? Did they rescue Samaria? ³⁵What god has ever been able to save any nation from my power? So what makes you think the Lord can save Jerusalem?'"

³⁶But the people on the wall remained silent,

for the king had instructed them to say nothing. ³⁷Then Eliakim (son of Hilkiah) the business manager, and Shebnah the king's secretary, and Joah (son of Asaph) the historian went to King Hezekiah with their clothes torn and told him what the Assyrian general had said.

19 Isaiah Tells of God's Plan

When King Hezekiah heard their report, he tore his clothes and put on sackcloth and went into the Temple to pray. ²Then he told Eliakim, Shebnah, and some of the older priests to clothe themselves in sackcloth and to go to Isaiah (son of Amoz), the prophet, with this message:

³"King Hezekiah says, 'This is a day of trouble, insult, and dishonor. It is as when a child is ready to be born, but the mother has no strength to deliver it. ⁴Yet perhaps the Lord your God has heard the Assyrian general defying the living God and will rebuke him. Oh, pray for the few of us who are left.'"

⁵,⁶Isaiah replied, "The Lord says, 'Tell your master not to be troubled by the sneers these Assyrians have made against me.' ⁷For the king of Assyria will receive bad news from home and will decide to return; and the Lord will see to it that he is killed when he arrives there."

⁸Then the Assyrian general returned to his king at Libnah (for he received word that he had left Lachish). ⁹Soon afterwards news reached the king that King Tirhakah of Ethiopia was coming to attack him. Before leaving to meet the attack, he sent back this message to King Hezekiah:

¹⁰"Don't be fooled by that god you trust in. Don't believe it when he says that I won't conquer Jerusalem. ¹¹You know perfectly well what the kings of Assyria have done wherever they have gone; they have completely destroyed everything. Why would you be any different? ¹²Have the gods of the other nations delivered them—such nations as Gozan, Haran, Rezeph, and Eden in the land of Telassar? The former kings of Assyria destroyed them all! ¹³What happened to the king of Hamoth and the king of Arpad? What happened to the kings of Sepharvaim, Hena, and Ivvah?"

¹⁴Hezekiah took the letter from the messengers, read it, and went over to the Temple and spread it out before the Lord. ¹⁵Then he prayed this prayer:

"O Lord God of Israel, sitting on your throne high above the angels, you alone are the God of all the kingdoms of the earth. You created the heavens and the earth. ¹⁶Bend low, O Lord, and listen. Open your eyes, O Lord, and see. Listen to this man's defiance of the living God. ¹⁷Lord, it is true that the kings of Assyria have destroyed all those nations ¹⁸and have burned their idol-gods. But they weren't gods at all; they were destroyed because they were only things that men had made of wood and stone. ¹⁹O Lord our God, we plead with you to save us from his power; then all the kingdoms of the earth will know that you alone are God."

²⁰Then Isaiah sent this message to Hezekiah: "The Lord God of Israel says, 'I have heard you! ²¹And this is my reply to King Sennacherib: The virgin daughter of Zion isn't afraid of you! The daughter of Jerusalem scorns and mocks at you. ²²Whom have you defied and blasphemed? And toward whom have you felt so cocky? It is the Holy One of Israel!

²³"'You have boasted, "My chariots have conquered the highest mountains, yes, the peaks of Lebanon. I have cut down the tallest cedars and choicest cypress trees and have conquered the farthest borders. ²⁴I have been refreshed at many conquered wells, and I destroyed the strength of Egypt just by walking by!"

²⁵"'Why haven't you realized long before this that it is I, the Lord, who lets you do these things? I decreed your conquest of all those fortified cities! ²⁶So of course the nations you conquered had no power against you! They were like grass shriveling beneath the hot sun, and like grain blighted before it is half grown. ²⁷I know everything about you. I know all your plans and where you are going next; and I also know the evil things you have said about me. ²⁸And because of your arrogance against me, I am going to put a hook in your nose and a bridle in your mouth and turn you back on the road by which you came. ²⁹And this is the proof that I will do as I have promised: This year my people will eat the volunteer wheat and use it as seed for next year's crop; and in the third year they will have a bountiful harvest.

³⁰"'O my people Judah, those of you who have escaped the ravages of the siege shall become a great nation again; you shall be rooted deeply in the soil and bear fruit for God. ³¹A remnant of my people shall become strong in Jerusalem. The Lord is eager to cause this to happen.

³²"'And my command concerning the king of Assyria is that he shall not enter this city. He shall not stand before it with a shield, nor build a ramp against its wall, nor even shoot an arrow into it. ³³He shall return by the road he came, ³⁴for I will defend and save this city for the sake of my own name and for the sake of my servant David.'"

³⁵That very night the angel of the Lord killed 185,000 Assyrian troops, and dead bodies were seen all across the landscape in the morning.

³⁶Then King Sennacherib returned to Nineveh; ³⁷and as he was worshiping in the temple of his

Family Devotions

☐ **Devotion 121**

Leaving the Future in God's Hands

Read 2 Kings 19:9-22, 30-37

Calvin stumbled into the water. The rolling waves cooled his warm body and relaxed his troubled mind. Because it felt so good and soothing to him, he swam out to deeper water. "I wish I could stay here forever," he sighed, "and not think about anything."

But Calvin had a lot to think about. He had a tumor on his left leg, and in two more days he would be admitted to a hospital where a specialist would perform surgery. It wasn't known yet whether the doctor could remove just the tumor or if Calvin's leg would have to be amputated. Calvin's mind was filled with questions. How would the operation go? What if he lost his leg? Would he ever be able to play ball and run on the track team again?

The shrieks of his little sister, Cindy, interrupted his thoughts. "Daddy, I can't go swimming here!" she squealed. "The waves are too big! I don't like this ocean. It's scary!"

"Look," Dad said. "The waves aren't too rough for me. They aren't moving me. Here! Take my hand, and we'll swim together. You'll be safe."

Cindy was hesitant. She wanted to swim, but the waves were so big. Then she looked at her dad. He was strong! He would protect her! Cindy put her little hand into her daddy's big hand. Soon she was enjoying the water as it splashed about her.

Calvin swam back to Cindy. "See, Cal," she shouted. "I'm not afraid now. Daddy's holding my hand. He won't let me go."

Calvin smiled at Cindy and at himself. Little Cindy had just taught him a lesson. If she could trust their father in the rolling waves, he could trust his heavenly Father.

The days ahead might be rough, but God would hold him and give him strength. That's all he needed to know to give him peace.

Leaving the Future in God's Hands Memory Verse

For I know the plans I have for you, says the Lord. They are plans for good and not for evil, to give you a future and a hope.
Jeremiah 29:11

How About You?

Are you facing a difficult time in your life? Are you ready to give up? Don't! Tell God about your struggles, like Hezekiah did. Ask him for wisdom and strength and courage. Ask him to hold you safely through it all. He will. J. H.

god Nisroch, his sons Adrammelech and Sharezer killed him. They escaped into eastern Turkey—the land of Ararat—and his son Esarhaddon became the new king.

20 Hezekiah Gets Sick

Hezekiah now became deathly sick, and Isaiah the prophet went to visit him.

"Set your affairs in order and prepare to die," Isaiah told him. "The Lord says you won't recover."

[2] Hezekiah turned his face to the wall.

[3] "O Lord," he pleaded, "remember how I've always tried to obey you and to please you in everything I do...." Then he broke down and cried.

[4] So before Isaiah had left the courtyard, the Lord spoke to him again.

[5] "Go back to Hezekiah, the leader of my people, and tell him that the Lord God of his ancestor David has heard his prayer and seen his tears. I will heal him, and three days from now he will be out of bed and at the Temple! [6] I will add fifteen years to his life and save him and this city from the king of Assyria. And it will all be done for the glory of my own name and for the sake of my servant David."

[7] Isaiah then instructed Hezekiah to boil some dried figs and to make a paste of them and spread it on the boil. And he recovered!

[8] Meanwhile, King Hezekiah had said to Isaiah, "Do a miracle to prove to me that the Lord will heal me and that I will be able to go to the Temple again three days from now."

[9] "All right, the Lord will give you a proof," Isaiah told him. "Do you want the shadow on the sundial to go forward ten points or backward ten points?"

[10] "The shadow always moves forward," Hezekiah replied; "make it go backward."

[11] So Isaiah asked the Lord to do this, and he caused the shadow to move ten points backward on the sundial of Ahaz!

[12] At that time Merodach-baladan (the son of King Baladan of Babylon) sent ambassadors with greetings and a present to Hezekiah, for he had learned of his sickness. [13] Hezekiah welcomed them and showed them all his treasures—the silver, gold, spices, aromatic oils, the armory—everything.

[14] Then Isaiah went to King Hezekiah and asked him, "What did these men want? Where are they from?"

"From far away in Babylon," Hezekiah replied.

[15] "What have they seen in your palace?" Isaiah asked.

And Hezekiah replied, "Everything. I showed them all my treasures."

[16] Then Isaiah said to Hezekiah, "Listen to the word of the Lord: [17] The time will come when everything in this palace shall be carried to Babylon. All the treasures of your ancestors will be taken—nothing shall be left. [18] Some of your own sons will be taken away and made into eunuchs who will serve in the palace of the king of Babylon."

[19] "All right," Hezekiah replied, "if this is what the Lord wants, it is good." But he was really thinking, "At least there will be peace and security during the remainder of my own life!"

[20] The rest of the history of Hezekiah and his great deeds—including the pool and conduit he made and how he brought water into the city—are recorded in *The Annals of the Kings of Judah*. [21] When he died, his son Manasseh became the new king.

21 Manasseh Rules Judah

New king of Judah: Manasseh
His age at the beginning of his reign: 12 years old
Length of reign: 55 years, in Jerusalem
Mother's name: Hephzibah
Character of his reign: evil; he did the same things the nations had done that were thrown out of the land to make room for the people of Israel

[3-5] He rebuilt the hilltop shrines that his father Hezekiah had destroyed. He built altars for Baal and made a shameful Asherah idol, just as Ahab the king of Israel had done. Heathen altars to the sun god, moon god, and the gods of the stars were placed even in the Temple of the Lord—in the very city and building that the Lord had selected to honor his own name. [6] And he sacrificed one of his sons as a burnt offering on a heathen altar. He practiced black magic and used fortune-telling, and patronized mediums and wizards. So the Lord was very angry, for Manasseh was an evil man, in God's sight. [7] Manasseh even set up a shameful Asherah idol in the Temple—the very place that the Lord had spoken to David and Solomon about when he said, "I will place my name forever in this Temple, and in Jerusalem—the city I have chosen from among all the cities

---

SERVING GOD BOLDLY 20:5-6 Over a hundred-year period of Judah's history (732–640 B.C.), Hezekiah was the only faithful king; but what a difference he made! Because of Hezekiah's faith and prayer, God healed him and saved his city from the Assyrians. You can make a difference too, even if your faith puts you in the minority. Faith and prayer, if they are sincere and directed toward the one true God, can bring about change in any situation. **To begin the series of devotionals on SERVING GOD BOLDLY, turn to page 17.**

of the tribes of Israel. ⁸If the people of Israel will only follow the instructions I gave them through Moses, I will never again expel them from this land of their fathers."

⁹But the people did not listen to the Lord, and Manasseh enticed them to do even more evil than the surrounding nations had done, even though Jehovah had destroyed those nations for their evil ways when the people of Israel entered the land.

¹⁰Then the Lord declared through the prophets,

¹¹"Because King Manasseh has done these evil things and is even more wicked than the Amorites who were in this land long ago, and because he has led the people of Judah into idolatry: ¹²I will bring such evil upon Jerusalem and Judah that the ears of those who hear about it will tingle with horror. ¹³I will punish Jerusalem as I did Samaria, and as I did King Ahab of Israel and his descendants. I will wipe away the people of Jerusalem as a man wipes a dish and turns it upside down to dry. ¹⁴Then I will reject even those few of my people who are left, and I will hand them over to their enemies. ¹⁵For they have done great evil and have angered me ever since I brought their ancestors from Egypt."

¹⁶In addition to the idolatry which God hated and into which Manasseh led the people of Judah, he murdered great numbers of innocent people. And Jerusalem was filled from one end to the other with the bodies of his victims.

¹⁷The rest of the history of Manasseh's sinful reign is recorded in *The Annals of the Kings of Judah*. ¹⁸When he died he was buried in the garden of his palace at Uzza, and his son Amon became the new king.

¹⁹,²⁰New king of Judah: Amon
His age at the beginning of his reign: 22 years old
Length of reign: 2 years, in Jerusalem
Mother's name: Meshullemeth (daughter of Haruz, of Jotbah)
Character of his reign: evil

²¹He did all the evil things his father had done: he worshiped the same idols ²²and turned his back on the Lord God of his ancestors. He refused to listen to God's instructions. ²³But his aides conspired against him and killed him in the palace. ²⁴Then a posse of civilians killed all the assassins and placed Amon's son Josiah upon the throne. ²⁵The rest of Amon's biography is recorded in *The Annals of the Kings of Judah*. ²⁶He was buried in a crypt in the garden of Uzza, and his son Josiah became the new king.

22 Josiah Becomes King

New king of Judah: Josiah
His age at the beginning of his reign: 8 years old
Length of reign: 31 years, in Jerusalem
Mother's name: Jedidah (daughter of Adaiah of Bozkath)
Character of his reign: good; he followed in the steps of his ancestor King David, obeying the Lord completely

³,⁴In the eighteenth year of his reign, King Josiah sent his secretary Shaphan (son of Azaliah, son of Meshullam) to the Temple to give instruction to Hilkiah, the High Priest:

"Collect the money given to the priests at the door of the Temple when the people come to worship. ⁵,⁶Give this money to the building superintendents so that they can hire carpenters and masons to repair the Temple, and to buy lumber and stone."

⁷(The building superintendents were not required to keep account of their expenditures, for they were honest men.)

⁸One day Hilkiah the High Priest went to Shaphan the secretary and exclaimed, "I have discovered a scroll in the Temple, with God's laws written on it!"

He gave the scroll to Shaphan to read. ⁹,¹⁰When Shaphan reported to the king about the progress of the repairs at the Temple, he also mentioned the scroll found by Hilkiah. Then Shaphan read it to the king. ¹¹When the king heard what was written in it, he tore his clothes in terror. ¹²,¹³He commanded Hilkiah the priest, and Shaphan, and Asaiah, the king's assistant, and Ahikam (Shaphan's son), and Achbor (Michaiah's son) to ask the Lord, "What shall we do? For we have not been following the instructions of this book: you must be very angry with us, for neither we nor our ancestors have followed your commands."

¹⁴So Hilkiah the priest, and Ahikam, and Achbor, and Shaphan, and Asaiah went to the Mishneh section of Jerusalem to find Huldah the prophetess. (She was the wife of Shallum—son of Tikvah, son of Harhas—who was in charge of the palace

---

LEAVING THE FUTURE IN GOD'S HANDS 21:6 Manasseh was an evil king, and he angered God with his sin. Listed among his sins are occult practices—black magic and fortune-telling, and consulting mediums and wizards. These acts were strictly forbidden by God (Leviticus 19:31; Deuteronomy 18:9-13) because they demonstrate a lack of faith in him, involve sinful actions, and open the door to demonic influences. Today, many books, TV shows, and games emphasize fortune-telling, séances, and other occult practices. Don't let desire to know the future or the belief that superstition is harmless lead you into condoning occult practices. They are counterfeits of God's power and have at their root a system of beliefs totally opposed to God. **To begin the series of devotionals on LEAVING THE FUTURE IN GOD'S HANDS, turn to page 75.**

tailor shop.) ¹⁵,¹⁶She gave them this message from the Lord God of Israel:

"Tell the man who sent you to me that I am going to destroy this city and its people, just as I stated in that book you read. ¹⁷For the people of Judah have thrown me aside and have worshiped other gods and have made me very angry; and my anger can't be stopped. ¹⁸,¹⁹But because you were sorry and concerned and humbled yourself before the Lord when you read the book and its warnings that this land would be cursed and become desolate, and because you have torn your clothing and wept before me in contrition, I will listen to your plea. ²⁰The death of this nation will not occur until after you die—you will not see the evil that I will bring upon this place."

So they took the message to the king.

23 Josiah Obeys God's Law

Then the king sent for the elders and other leaders of Judah and Jerusalem to go to the Temple with him. So all the priests and prophets and the people, small and great, of Jerusalem and Judah gathered there at the Temple so that the king could read to them the entire book of God's laws which had been discovered in the Temple. ³He stood beside the pillar in front of the people, and he and they made a solemn promise to the Lord to obey him at all times and to do everything the book commanded.

⁴Then the king instructed Hilkiah the High Priest and the rest of the priests and the guards of the Temple to destroy all the equipment used in the worship of Baal, Asherah, and the sun, moon, and stars. The king had it all burned in the fields of the Kidron Valley outside Jerusalem, and he carried the ashes to Bethel. ⁵He killed the heathen priests who had been appointed by the previous kings of Judah, for they had burned incense in the shrines on the hills throughout Judah and even in Jerusalem. They had also offered incense to Baal and to the sun, moon, stars, and planets. ⁶He removed the shameful idol of Asherah from the Temple and took it outside Jerusalem to Kidron Brook; there he burned it and beat it to dust and threw the dust on the graves of the common people. ⁷He also tore down the houses of male prostitution around the Temple, where the women wove robes for the Asherah idol.

⁸He brought back to Jerusalem the priests of the Lord, who were living in other cities of Judah, and tore down all the shrines on the hills where they had burned incense, even those as far away as Geba and Beersheba. He also destroyed the shrines at the entrance of the palace of Joshua, the former mayor of Jerusalem, located on the left side as one enters the city gate. ⁹However, these priests did not serve at the altar of the Lord in Jerusalem, even though they ate with the other priests.

¹⁰Then the king destroyed the altar of Topheth in the Valley of the Sons of Hinnom, so that no one could ever again use it to burn his son or daughter to death as a sacrifice to Molech. ¹¹He tore down the statues of horses and chariots located near the entrance of the Temple, next to the quarters of Nathan-melech the eunuch. These had been dedicated by former kings of Judah to the sun god. ¹²Then he tore down the altars that the kings of Judah had built on the palace roof above the Ahaz Room. He also destroyed the altars that Manasseh had built in the two courts of the Temple; he smashed them to bits and scattered the pieces in Kidron Valley.

¹³Next he removed the shrines on the hills east of Jerusalem and south of Destruction Mountain. (Solomon had built these shrines for Ashtoreth, the evil goddess of the Sidonians; and for Chemosh, the evil god of Moab; and for Milcom, the evil god of the Ammonites.) ¹⁴He smashed the obelisks and cut down the shameful idols of Asherah; then he defiled these places by scattering human bones over them. ¹⁵He also tore down the altar and shrine at Bethel that Jeroboam I had made when he led Israel into sin. He crushed the stones to dust and burned the shameful idol of Asherah.

¹⁶As Josiah was looking around, he noticed several graves in the side of the mountain. He ordered his men to bring out the bones in them and to burn them there upon the altar at Bethel to defile it, just as the Lord's prophet had declared would happen to Jeroboam's altar.

¹⁷"What is that monument over there?" he asked.

And the men of the city told him, "It is the grave of the prophet who came from Judah and proclaimed that what you have just done would happen here at the altar at Bethel!"

¹⁸So King Josiah replied, "Leave it alone. Don't disturb his bones."

So they didn't burn his bones or those of the prophet from Samaria.

¹⁹Josiah demolished the shrines on the hills in all of Samaria. They had been built by the various kings of Israel and had made the Lord very angry. But now he crushed them into dust, just as he had done at Bethel. ²⁰He executed the priests of the heathen shrines upon their own altars, and he burned human bones upon the altars to defile them. Finally he returned to Jerusalem.

²¹The king then issued orders for his people to observe the Passover ceremonies as recorded by the Lord their God in *The Book of the Covenant*. ²²There had not been a Passover celebration like

that since the days of the judges of Israel, and there was never another like it in all the years of the kings of Israel and Judah. ²³This Passover was in the eighteenth year of the reign of King Josiah, and it was celebrated in Jerusalem.

²⁴Josiah also exterminated the mediums and wizards, and every kind of idol worship, both in Jerusalem and throughout the land. For Josiah wanted to follow all the laws that were written in the book that Hilkiah the priest had found in the Temple. ²⁵There was no other king who so completely turned to the Lord and followed all the laws of Moses; and no king since the time of Josiah has approached his record of obedience.

²⁶But the Lord still did not hold back his great anger against Judah, caused by the evils of King Manasseh. ²⁷For the Lord had said, "I will destroy Judah just as I have destroyed Israel; and I will discard my chosen city of Jerusalem and the Temple that I said was mine."

²⁸The rest of the biography of Josiah is written in *The Annals of the Kings of Judah*. ²⁹In those days King Neco of Egypt went out to help the king of Assyria at the Euphrates River. Then King Josiah went out with his troops to fight King Neco; but King Neco withstood him at Megiddo and killed him. ³⁰His officers took his body back in a chariot from Megiddo to Jerusalem and buried him in the grave he had selected. And his son Jehoahaz was chosen by the nation as its new king.

³¹,³²New king of Judah: Jehoahaz
His age at the beginning of his reign: 23 years old
Length of reign: 3 months, in Jerusalem
Mother's name: Hamutal (the daughter of Jeremiah of Libnah)
Character of his reign: evil, like the other kings who had preceded him

³³Pharaoh-Neco jailed him at Riblah in Hamath to prevent his reigning in Jerusalem, and he levied a tax against Judah totaling $230,000. ³⁴The Egyptian king then chose Eliakim, another of Josiah's sons, to reign in Jerusalem; and he changed his name to Jehoiakim. Then he took King Jehoahaz to Egypt, where he died. ³⁵Jehoiakim taxed the people to get the money that the Pharaoh had demanded.

³⁶,³⁷New king of Judah: Jehoiakim
His age at the beginning of his reign: 25 years old
Length of reign: 11 years, in Jerusalem
Mother's name: Zebidah (daughter of Pedaiah of Rumah)
Character of his reign: evil, like the other kings who had preceded him

24 Jehoiachin and Babylon

During the reign of King Jehoiakim, King Nebuchadnezzar of Babylon attacked Jerusalem. Jehoiakim surrendered and paid him tribute for three years, but then rebelled. ²And the Lord sent bands of Chaldeans, Syrians, Moabites, and Ammonites against Judah in order to destroy the nation, just as the Lord had warned through his prophets that he would. ³,⁴It is clear that these disasters befell Judah at the direct command of the Lord. He had decided to wipe Judah out of his sight because of the many sins of Manasseh, for he had filled Jerusalem with blood, and the Lord would not pardon it.

⁵The rest of the history of the life of Jehoiakim is recorded in *The Annals of the Kings of Judah*. ⁶When he died, his son Jehoiachin became the new king. ⁷(The Egyptian Pharaoh never returned after that, for the king of Babylon occupied the entire area claimed by Egypt—all of Judah from the Brook of Egypt to the Euphrates River.)

⁸,⁹New king of Judah: Jehoiachin
His age at the beginning of his reign: 18 years old
Length of reign: 3 months, in Jerusalem
Mother's name: Nehushta (daughter of Elnathan, a citizen of Jerusalem)

¹⁰During his reign the armies of King Nebuchadnezzar of Babylon besieged the city of Jerusalem. ¹¹Nebuchadnezzar himself arrived during the siege, ¹²and King Jehoiachin, all of his officials, and the queen mother surrendered to him. The surrender was accepted, and Jehoiachin was imprisoned in Babylon during the eighth year of Nebuchadnezzar's reign.

¹³The Babylonians carried home all the treasures from the Temple and the royal palace; and they cut apart all the gold bowls which King Solomon of Israel had placed in the Temple at the Lord's directions. ¹⁴King Nebuchadnezzar took ten thousand captives from Jerusalem, including all the princes and the best of the soldiers, craftsmen, and smiths. So only the poorest and least skilled people were left in the land. ¹⁵Nebuchadnezzar took King Jehoiachin, his wives and officials, and the queen mother, to Babylon. ¹⁶He also took seven thousand of the best troops and one thousand craftsmen and smiths, all of whom were strong and fit for war. ¹⁷Then the king of Babylon appointed King Jehoiachin's great-uncle, Mattaniah, to be the next king; and he changed his name to Zedekiah.

18,19 New king of Judah: Zedekiah
His age at the beginning of his reign: 21 years old
Length of reign: 11 years, in Jerusalem
Mother's name: Hamutal (daughter of Jeremiah of Libnah)
Character of his reign: evil, like that of Jehoiakim

20 So the Lord finally, in his anger, destroyed the people of Jerusalem and Judah. But now King Zedekiah rebelled against the king of Babylon.

25 Jerusalem Gets Demolished

Then King Nebuchadnezzar of Babylon mobilized his entire army and laid siege to Jerusalem, arriving on March 25 of the ninth year of the reign of King Zedekiah of Judah. 2 The siege continued into the eleventh year of his reign.

3 The last food in the city was eaten on July 24, 4,5 and that night the king and his troops made a hole in the inner wall and fled out toward the Arabah through a gate that lay between the double walls near the king's garden. The Babylonian troops surrounding the city took out after him and captured him in the plains of Jericho, and all his men scattered. 6 He was taken to Riblah, where he was tried and sentenced before the king of Babylon. 7 He was forced to watch as his sons were killed before his eyes; then his eyes were put out, and he was bound with chains and taken away to Babylon.

8 General Nebuzaradan, the captain of the royal bodyguard, arrived at Jerusalem from Babylon on July 22 of the nineteenth year of the reign of King Nebuchadnezzar. 9 He burned down the Temple, the palace, and all the other houses of any worth. 10 He then supervised the Babylonian army in tearing down the walls of Jerusalem. 11 The remainder of the people in the city and the Jewish deserters who had declared their allegiance to the king of Babylon were all taken as exiles to Babylon. 12 But the poorest of the people were left to farm the land.

13 The Babylonians broke up the bronze pillars of the Temple and the bronze tank and its bases and carried all the bronze to Babylon. 14,15 They also took all the pots, shovels, firepans, snuffers, spoons, and other bronze instruments used for the sacrifices. The gold and silver bowls, with all the rest of the gold and silver, were melted down to bullion. 16 It was impossible to estimate the weight of the two pillars and the great tank and its bases—all made for the Temple by King Solomon—because they were so heavy. 17 Each pillar was 27 feet high, with an intricate bronze network of pomegranates decorating the 4 1/2-foot capitals at the tops of the pillars.

18 The general took Seraiah, the chief priest, his assistant Zephaniah, and the three Temple guards to Babylon as captives. 19 A commander of the army of Judah, the chief recruiting officer, five of the king's counselors, and sixty farmers, all of whom were discovered hiding in the city, 20 were taken by General Nebuzaradan to the king of Babylon at Riblah, 21 where they were put to the sword and died.

So Judah was exiled from its land.

22 Then King Nebuchadnezzar appointed Gedaliah (the son of Ahikam and grandson of Shaphan) as governor over the people left in Judah. 23 When the Israeli guerrilla forces learned that the king of Babylon had appointed Gedaliah as governor, some of these underground leaders and their men joined him at Mizpah. These included Ishmael, the son of Nethaniah; Johanan, the son of Kareah; Seraiah, the son of Tanhumeth the Netophathite; and Jaazaniah, son of Maachathite, and their men.

24 Gedaliah vowed that if they would give themselves up and submit to the Babylonians, they would be allowed to live in the land and would not be exiled. 25 But seven months later, Ishmael, who was a member of the royal line, went to Mizpah with ten men and killed Gedaliah and his court—both the Jews and the Babylonians.

26 Then all the men of Judah and the guerrilla leaders fled in panic to Egypt, for they were afraid of what the Babylonians would do to them.

27 King Jehoiachin was released from prison on the twenty-seventh day of the last month of the thirty-seventh year of his captivity.

This occurred during the first year of the reign of King Evil-merodach of Babylon. 28 He treated Jehoiachin kindly and gave him preferential treatment over all the other kings who were being held as prisoners in Babylon. 29 Jehoiachin was given civilian clothing to replace his prison garb, and for as long as he lived, he ate regularly at the king's table. 30 The king also gave him a daily cash allowance for the rest of his life.

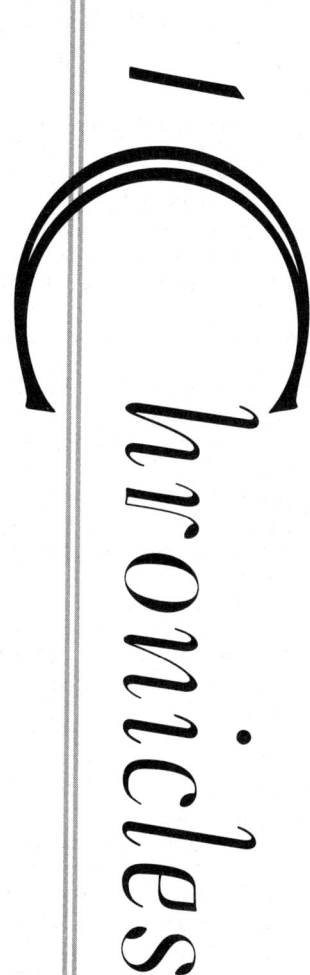

1 Chronicles

HOW MUCH does God know about you? Everything, right? First Chronicles is a book that will help you know how true this is.

The two books of Chronicles review everything that's happened in the Bible from Adam through the kings. First Chronicles starts by naming every person who had a part in important events. Why did God have all these people listed in the Bible? There are several reasons, but one is that God cared about them all. Each person is important to God. God knows every individual who ever lived, by name. And he knows each of us by name, too.

First Chronicles goes on to review the kingship of David. You read about it once in 1 and 2 Samuel, but Chronicles talks about it in a different way. The books of Samuel pointed out how much David loved God. The books of Chronicles point out how much God was involved with what happened in David's life and in Israel. God shows clearly that he is ruler over all—from whole nations to individuals.

It's great to know that God knows us and is involved in our lives. As you read 1 Chronicles, look for the people God thought were important—their names are listed. Also look for God's action in people's lives.

Adam's Descendants

These are the earliest generations of mankind: Adam, Seth, Enosh, Kenan, Mahalalel, Jared, Enoch, Methuselah, Lamech, Noah, Shem, Ham, and Japheth.

5-9The sons of *Japheth* were: Gomer, Magog, Madai, Javan, Tubal, Meshech, and Tiras.

The sons of *Gomer:* Ashkenaz, Diphath, and Togarmah.

The sons of Javan: Elishah, Tarshish, Kittim, and Rodanim.

The sons of *Ham:* Cush, Mizraim, Canaan, and Put.

The sons of *Cush* were: Seba, Havilah, Sabta, Raama, and Sabteca.

The sons of Raama were Sheba and Dedan.

10Another of the sons of *Cush* was Nimrod, who became a great hero.

11,12The clans named after the sons of *Mizraim* were: the Ludim, the Anamim, the Lehabim, the Naphtuhim, the Pathrusim, the Caphtorim, and the Casluhim (the ancestors of the Philistines).

13-16 Among *Canaan's* sons were: Sidon (his firstborn) and Heth.

Canaan was also the ancestor of the Jebusites, Amorites, Girgashites, Hivites, Arkites, Sinites, Arvadites, Zemarites, and Hamathites.

17 The sons of *Shem:* Elam, Asshur, Arpachshad, Lud, Aram, Uz, Hul, Gether, and Meshech.

18 *Arpachshad's* son was Shelah, and *Shelah's* son was Eber.

19 *Eber* had two sons: Peleg (which means "Divided," for it was during his lifetime that the people of the earth were divided into different language groups) and Joktan.

20-23 The sons of Joktan: Almodad, Sheleph, Hazarmaveth, Jerah, Hadoram, Uzal, Diklah, Ebal, Abimael, Sheba, Ophir, Havilah, and Jobab.

24-27 So the son of *Shem* was Arpachshad, the son of Arpachshad was Shelah, the son of Shelah was Eber, the son of Eber was Peleg, the son of Peleg was Reu, the son of Reu was Serug, the son of Serug was Nahor, the son of Nahor was Terah, the son of Terah was Abram (later known as Abraham).

28-31 Abraham's sons were Isaac and Ishmael.

The sons of *Ishmael:* Nebaioth (the oldest), Kedar, Adbeel, Mibsam, Mishma, Dumah, Massa, Hadad, Tema, Jetur, Naphish, and Kedemah.

32 Abraham also had sons by his concubine Keturah: Zimram, Jokshan, Medan, Midian, Ishbak, and Shuah.

Jokshan's sons were Sheba and Dedan.

33 The sons of *Midian:* Ephah, Epher, Hanoch, Abida, and Eldaah. These were the descendants of Abraham by his concubine Keturah.

34 Abraham's son *Isaac* had two sons, Esau and Israel.

35 The sons of *Esau:* Eliphaz, Reuel, Jeush, Jalam, and Korah.

36 The sons of *Eliphaz:* Teman, Omar, Zephi, Gatam, Kenaz, Timna, and Amalek.

37 The sons of *Reuel:* Nahath, Zerah, Shammah, and Mizzah.

38,39 The sons of *Esau* also included Lotan, Shobal, Zibeon, Anah, Dishon, Ezer, and Dishan; and Esau's daughter was named Timna. *Lotan's* sons: Hori and Homam.

40 The sons of *Shobal:* Alian, Manahath, Ebal, Shephi, and Onam. *Zibeon's* sons were Aiah and Anah.

41 *Anah's* son was Dishon. The sons of *Dishon:* Hamran, Eshban, Ithran, and Cheran.

42 The sons of *Ezer:* Bilhan, Zaavan, and Jaakan. *Dishan's* sons were Uz and Aran.

43 Here is a list of the names of the kings of Edom who reigned before the kingdom of Israel began:

Bela (the son of Beor), who lived in the city of Dinhabah.

44 When Bela died, Jobab the son of Zerah from Bozrah became the new king.

45 When Jobab died, Husham from the country of the Temanites became the king.

46 When Husham died, Hadad the son of Bedad—the one who destroyed the army of Midian in the fields of Moab—became king and ruled from the city of Avith.

47 When Hadad died, Samlah from the city of Masrekah came to the throne.

48 When Samlah died, Shaul from the river town of Rehoboth became the new king.

49 When Shaul died, Baal-hanan the son of Achbor became king.

50 When Baal-hanan died, Hadad became king and ruled from the city of Pai (his wife was Mehetabel, the daughter of Matred and granddaughter of Mezahab).

51-54 At the time of Hadad's death, the kings of Edom were: Chief Timna, Chief Aliah, Chief Jetheth, Chief Oholibamah, Chief Elah, Chief Pinon, Chief Kenaz, Chief Teman, Chief Mibzar, Chief Magdiel, Chief Iram.

2 Jacob's Descendants

The sons of Israel were:

Reuben, Simeon, Levi, Judah, Issachar, Zebulun, Dan, Joseph, Benjamin, Naphtali, Gad, Asher.

3 Judah had three sons by Bathshua, a girl from Canaan: Er, Onan, and Shelah. But the oldest son, Er, was so wicked that the Lord killed him.

4 Then Er's widow, Tamar, and her father-in-law, Judah, became the parents of twin sons, Perez and Zerah. So Judah had five sons.

5 The sons of *Perez* were Hezron and Hamul.

6 The sons of *Zerah* were: Zimri, Ethan, Heman, Calcol, and Dara.

7 (Achan, the son of Carmi, was the man who robbed God and was such a troublemaker for his nation.)

8 *Ethan's* son was Azariah.

9 The sons of *Hezron* were Jerahmeel, Ram, and Chelubai.

10 Ram was the father of Amminadab, and Amminadab was the father of Nahshon, a leader of Israel.

11 Nahshon was the father of Salma, and Salma was the father of Boaz.

12 Boaz was the father of Obed, and Obed was the father of Jesse.

13 *Jesse's* first son was Eliab, his second was Abinadab, his third was Shimea, 14 his fourth was Nethanel, his fifth was Raddai, 15 his sixth was Ozem, and his seventh was David. 16 He also had two girls (by the same wife) named Zeruiah and Abigail.

Zeruiah's sons were Abishai, Joab, and Asahel.

Family Devotions

☐ DEVOTION 122
KNOWING YOU'RE SPECIAL TO GOD

Read 1 Chronicles 1:1-10

"Danny, while you were gone, Michael called," Danny's mother told him. "He wants you to call him back."

Danny went to phone his friend. There was no answer. Then he remembered that Michael was out of town for the weekend. "Are you sure it was Michael *Burk*?" he asked.

"Oh, no, it was Michael *White*," said Mom.

Just then Danny's older sister burst into the room. "Guess what! I'm finally going out with Michael!"

Danny and Mom looked at each other and burst out laughing. *"Which* Michael?" they said together.

That night, Danny looked at his list of prayer requests. One name on it was that of a boy at church who needed surgery for a serious heart condition. "Dear Lord, please bless Michael," Danny began. Then he paused. "You know, the one who needs heart surgery."

Suddenly, Danny thought about how many Michaels there were in the world and how many Dannys. There must be plenty of Joes and Janes and Pauls, too. Danny had always thought of God as his personal friend, but suddenly he felt small and unimportant and lonely.

A few days later, Dad, who was a doctor, called from the hospital. "Michael had his surgery today, and he's doing fine," he told Danny. "Guess what? There are three other Michaels on this floor! But don't worry. *Our* Michael's mother is the head nurse on this floor. Believe me, she knows which Michael belongs to her."

When Danny prayed for his friend that night, he knew he didn't have to remind God which Michael was being prayed for, or which Danny was doing the asking. Just as a mother knows her son, God knows each of his children.

Knowing You're Special to God Memory Verse

But now the Lord who created you, O Israel, says, Don't be afraid, for I have ransomed you; I have called you by name; you are mine.
Isaiah 43:1

How About You?
Do you think God ever gets tired of caring for so many people? Do you ever wonder if he is too busy to hear your requests, fears, or problems? Don't worry! God knows each of his children, and each one is special to him. *C. R.*

• For the next devotional, turn to page 415. • For the next devotional on KNOWING YOU'RE SPECIAL TO GOD, turn to page 535. • For notes on KNOWING YOU'RE SPECIAL TO GOD, see pages 260, 878, 908, and 960.

¹⁷*Abigail*, whose husband was Jether from the land of Ishmael, had a son named Amasa.

¹⁸Caleb (the son of Hezron) had two wives, Azubah and Jerioth. These are the children of *Azubah:* Jesher, Shobab, and Ardon.

¹⁹After Azubah's death, Caleb married Ephrath, who presented him with a son, Hur.

²⁰*Hur's* son was Uri, and *Uri's* son was Bezalel.

²¹Hezron married Machir's daughter at the age of sixty, and she presented him with a son, Segub. (Machir was also the father of Gilead.)

²²*Segub* was the father of Jair, who ruled twenty-three cities in the land of Gilead. ²³But Geshur and Aram wrested these cities from him and also took Kenath and its sixty surrounding villages.

²⁴Soon after his father *Hezron's* death, Caleb married Ephrathah, his father's widow, and she gave birth to Ashhur, the father of Tekoa.

²⁵These are the sons of Jerahmeel (the oldest son of *Hezron*): Ram (the oldest), Bunah, Oren, Ozem, and Ahijah.

²⁶*Jerahmeel's* second wife Atarah was the mother of Onam.

²⁷The sons of *Ram:* Maaz, Jamin, and Eker.

²⁸*Onam's* sons were Shammai and Jada. *Shammai's* sons were Nadab and Abishur.

²⁹The sons of *Abishur* and his wife Abihail were Ahban and Molid.

³⁰*Nadab's* sons were Seled and Appaim. *Seled* died without children, ³¹but *Appaim* had a son named Ishi; *Ishi's* son was Sheshan; and *Sheshan's* son was Ahlai.

³²*Shammai's* brother Jada had two sons, Jether and Jonathan. *Jether* died without children, ³³but *Jonathan* had two sons named Peleth and Zaza.

³⁴,³⁵*Sheshan* had no sons, although he had several daughters. He gave one of his daughters to be the wife of Jarha, his Egyptian servant. And they had a son whom they named Attai.

³⁶*Attai's* son was Nathan; Nathan's son was Zabad; ³⁷Zabad's son was Ephlal; Ephlal's son was Obed; ³⁸Obed's son was Jehu; Jehu's son was Azariah; ³⁹Azariah's son was Helez; Helez's son was Eleasah; ⁴⁰Eleasah's son was Sismai; Sismai's son was Shallum; ⁴¹Shallum's son was Jekamiah; Jekamiah's son was Elishama.

⁴²The oldest son of Caleb (Jerahmeel's brother) was Mesha; he was the father of Ziph, who was father of Mareshah, who was the father of Hebron.

⁴³The sons of *Hebron:* Korah, Tappuah, Rekem, and Shema.

⁴⁴*Shema* was the father of Raham, who was the father of Jorkeam. *Rekem* was the father of Shammai.

⁴⁵*Shammai's* son was Maon, the father of Bethzur.

⁴⁶*Caleb's* concubine Ephah bore him Haran, Moza, and Gazez; *Haran* had a son named Gazez.

⁴⁷The sons of Jahdai: Regem, Jotham, Geshan, Pelet, Ephah, and Shaaph.

⁴⁸,⁴⁹Another of *Caleb's* concubines, Maacah, bore him Sheber, Tirhanah, Shaaph (the father of Madmannah), and Sheva (the father of Machbenah and of Gibea). *Caleb* also had a daughter, whose name was Achsah.

⁵⁰The sons of Hur (who was the oldest son of *Caleb* and Ephrathah) were Shobal (the father of Kiriath-jearim), ⁵¹Salma (the father of Bethlehem), and Hareph (the father of Beth-gader).

⁵²Shobal's sons included Kiriath-jearim and Haroeh, the ancestor of half of the Menuhoth tribe.

⁵³The families of *Kiriath-jearim* were the Ithrites, the Puthites, the Shumathites, and the Mishraites (from whom descended the Zorathites and Eshtaolites).

⁵⁴The descendants of Salma were his son Bethlehem, the Netophathites, Atrothbeth-joab, half the Manahathites, and the Zorites; ⁵⁵they also included the families of the writers living at Jabez—the Tirathites, Shimeathites, and Sucathites. All these are Kenites who descended from Hammath, the founder of the family of Rechab.

3 David's Descendants

King David's oldest son was Amnon, who was born to his wife, Ahinoam of Jezreel.

The second was Daniel, whose mother was Abigail from Carmel.

²The third was Absalom, the son of his wife Maacah, who was the daughter of King Talmai of Geshur.

The fourth was Adonijah, the son of Haggith.

³The fifth was Shephatiah, the son of Abital.

The sixth was Ithream, the son of his wife Eglah.

⁴These six were born to him in Hebron, where he reigned seven and a half years. Then he moved the capital to Jerusalem, where he reigned another thirty-three years.

⁵While he was in Jerusalem, his wife Bathsheba (the daughter of Ammiel) became the mother of his sons Shimea, Shobab, Nathan, and Solomon.

⁶⁻⁸David also had nine other sons: Ibhar, Elishama, Eliphelet, Nogah, Nepheg, Japhia, Elishama, Eliada, and Eliphelet.

⁹(This list does not include the sons of his concubines.) David also had a daughter Tamar.

¹⁰⁻¹⁴These are the descendants of King *Solomon:* Rehoboam, Abijah, Asa, Jehoshaphat, Jehoram, Ahaziah, Joash, Amaziah, Azariah, Jotham, Ahaz, Hezekiah, Manasseh, Amon, Josiah.

¹⁵The sons of *Josiah* were: Johanan, Jehoiakim, Zedekiah, Shallum.

[16] The sons of *Jehoiakim:* Jeconiah, Zedekiah.

[17,18] These are the sons who were born to King *Jeconiah* during the years that he was under house arrest: Shealtiel, Malchiram, Pedaiah, Shenazzar, Jekamiah, Hoshama, Nedabiah.

[19,20] *Pedaiah* was the father of Zerubbabel and Shimei.

Zerubbabel's children were: Meshullam, Hananiah, Hashubah, Ohel, Berechiah, Hasadiah, Jushab-hesed, Shelomith (a daughter).

[21,22] *Hananiah's* sons were Pelatiah and Jeshaiah; Jeshaiah's son was Rephaiah; Rephaiah's son was Arnan; Arnan's son was Obadiah; Obadiah's son was Shecaniah. Shecaniah's son was Shemaiah; Shemaiah had six sons, including Hattush, Igal, Bariah, Neariah, and Shaphat.

[23] *Neariah* had three sons: Elioenai, Hizkiah, Azrikam.

[24] *Elioenai* had seven sons: Hodaviah, Eliashib, Pelaiah, Akkub, Johanan, Delaiah, Anani.

4 Judah's Descendants

These are the sons of Judah: Perez, Hezron, Carmi, Hur, Shobal.

[2] *Shobal's* son Reaiah was the father of Jahath, the ancestor of Ahumai and Lahad. These were known as the Zorathite clans.

[3,4] The descendants of Etam: Jezreel, Ishma, Idbash, Hazzelelponi (his daughter), Penuel (the ancestor of Gedor), Ezer (the ancestor of Hushah), the son of Hur, the oldest son of Ephrathah, who was the father of Bethlehem.

[5] Ashhur, the father of Tekoa, had two wives—Helah, and Naarah.

[6] *Naarah* bore him Ahuzzam, Hepher, Temeni, and Haahashtari; [7] and *Helah* bore him Zereth, Izhar, and Ethnan.

[8] Koz was the father of Anub and Zobebah; he was also the ancestor of the clan named after Aharhel, the son of Harum.

[9] Jabez was more distinguished than any of his brothers. His mother named him Jabez because she had such a hard time at his birth (Jabez means "Distress").

[10] He was the one who prayed to the God of Israel, "Oh, that you would wonderfully bless me and help me in my work; please be with me in all that I do, and keep me from all evil and disaster!" And God granted him his request.

[11,12] The descendants of Recah were:

Chelub (the brother of Shuhah), whose son was Mahir, the father of Eshton;
Eshton was the father of Bethrapha, Paseah, and Tehinnah;
Tehinnah was the father of Irnahash.

[13] The sons of Kenaz were Othniel and Seraiah.

Othniel's sons were Hathath and Meonothai;

[14] *Meonothai* was the father of Ophrah;

Seraiah was the father of Joab, the ancestor of the inhabitants of Craftsman Valley (called that because many craftsmen lived there).

[15] The sons of Caleb (the son of Jephunneh): Iru, Elah, Naam.

The sons of *Elah* included Kenaz.

[16] Jehallelel's sons were: Ziph, Ziphah, Tiria, Asarel.

[17] Ezrah's sons were: Jether, Mered, Epher, Jalon.

Mered married Bithiah, an Egyptian princess. She was the mother of Miriam, Shammai, and Ishbah—an ancestor of Eshtemoa.

[18] *Eshtemoa's* wife was a Jewess; she was the mother of Jered, Heber, and Jekuthiel, who were, respectively, the ancestors of the Gedorites, Socoites, and Zanoahites.

[19] Hodiah's wife was the sister of Naham. One of her sons was the father of Keilah the Garmite, and another was the father of Eshtemoa the Maacathite.

[20] The sons of Shimon: Amnon, Rinnah, Ben-hanan, Tilon.

The sons of Ishi: Zoheth, Ben-zoheth.

[21,22] The sons of Shelah (the son of Judah):

Er (the father of Lecah),
Laadah (the father of Mareshah),
The families of the linen workers who worked at Beth-ashbea,
Jokim,
The clans of Cozeba,
Joash,
Saraph (who was a ruler in Moab before he returned to Lehem).

These names all come from very ancient records.

[23] These clans were noted for their pottery, gardening, and planting; they all worked for the king:

[24] The sons of Simeon: Nemuel, Jamin, Jarib, Zerah, Shaul.

[25] *Shaul's* son was Shallum, his grandson was Mibsam, and his great-grandson was Mishma.

[26] *Mishma's* sons included Hammuel (the father of Zaccur and grandfather of Shimei).

[27] *Shimei* had sixteen sons and six daughters, but none of his brothers had large families—they all had fewer children than was normal in Judah.

[28] They lived at Beersheba, Moladah, Hazarshual, [29] Bilhah, Ezem, Tolad, [30] Bethuel, Hormah,

Ziklag, ³¹Beth-marcaboth, Hazar-susim, Beth-biri, and Shaaraim. These cities were under their control until the time of David.

³²,³³Their descendants also lived in or near Etam, Ain, Rimmon, Tochen, and Ashan; some were as far away as Baal. (These facts are recorded in their genealogies.)

³⁴⁻³⁹These are the names of some of the princes of wealthy clans who traveled to the east side of Gedor Valley in search of pasture for their flocks: Meshobab, Jamlech, Joshah, Joel, Jehu, Elioenai, Jaakobah, Jeshohaiah, Asaiah, Adiel, Jesimiel, Benaiah, Ziza (the son of Shiphi, son of Allon, son of Jedaiah, son of Shimri, son of Shemaiah).

⁴⁰,⁴¹They found good pastures, and everything was quiet and peaceful; but the land belonged to the descendants of Ham.

So during the reign of King Hezekiah of Judah these princes invaded the land and struck down the tents and houses of the descendants of Ham; they killed the inhabitants of the land and took possession of it for themselves.

⁴²Later, five hundred of these invaders from the tribe of Simeon went to Mount Seir. (Their leaders were Pelatiah, Neariah, Rephaiah, and Uzziel—all sons of Ishi.)

⁴³There they destroyed the few surviving members of the tribe of Amalek. And they have lived there ever since.

5 Reuben's Descendants

The oldest son of Israel was Reuben, but since he dishonored his father by sleeping with one of his father's wives, his birthright was given to his half brother, Joseph. So the official genealogy doesn't name Reuben as the oldest son.

²Although Joseph received the birthright, yet Judah was a powerful and influential tribe in Israel, and from Judah came a Prince.

³The sons of Reuben, Israel's son, were: Hanoch, Pallu, Hezron, Carmi.

⁴Joel's descendants were his son Shemaiah, his grandson Gog, and his great-grandson Shimei.

⁵*Shimei's* son was Micah; his grandson was Reaiah; and his great-grandson was Baal.

⁶*Baal's* son was Beerah. He was a prince of the tribe of Reuben and was taken into captivity by King Tilgath-pilneser of Assyria.

⁷,⁸His relatives became heads of clans and were included in the official genealogy: Jeiel, Zechariah, Bela (the son of Azaz, grandson of Shema, and great-grandson of Joel).

These Reubenites lived in Aroer and as far distant as Mount Nebo and Baal-meon.

⁹Joel was a cattleman, and he pastured his animals eastward to the edge of the desert and to the Euphrates River, for there were many cattle in the land of Gilead.

¹⁰During the reign of King Saul, the men of Reuben defeated the Hagrites in war and moved into their tents on the eastern edge of Gilead. ¹¹Across from them, in the land of Bashan, lived the descendants of Gad, who were spread as far as Salecah.

¹²Joel was the greatest and was followed by Shapham, also Janai and Shaphat. ¹³Their relatives, the heads of the seven clans, were Michael, Meshullam, Sheba, Jorai, Jacan, Zia, and Eber.

¹⁴The descendants of Buz, in the order of their generations, were: Jahdo, Jeshishai, Michael, Gilead, Jaroah, Huri, Abihail.

¹⁵Ahi, the son of Abdiel and grandson of Guni, was the leader of the clan. ¹⁶The clan lived in and around Gilead (in the land of Bashan) and throughout the entire pasture country of Sharon. ¹⁷All were included in the official genealogy at the time of King Jotham of Judah and King Jeroboam of Israel.

¹⁸There were 44,760 armed, trained, and brave troops in the army of Reuben, Gad, and the half-tribe of Manasseh. ¹⁹They declared war on the Hagrites, the Jeturites, the Naphishites, and the Nodabites. ²⁰They cried out to God to help them, and he did, for they trusted in him. So the Hagrites and all their allies were defeated. ²¹The booty included 50,000 camels, 250,000 sheep, 2,000 donkeys, and 100,000 captives. ²²A great number of the enemy also died in the battle, for God was fighting against them. So the Reubenites lived in the territory of the Hagrites until the time of the exile.

²³The half-tribe of Manasseh spread through the land from Bashan to Baal-hermon, Senir, and Mount Hermon. They too were very numerous.

²⁴The chiefs of their clans were the following: Epher, Ishi, Eliel, Azriel, Jeremiah, Hodaviah, Jahdiel.

Each of these men had a great reputation as a warrior and leader. ²⁵But they were not true to the God of their fathers; instead they worshiped the idols of the people whom God had destroyed. ²⁶So God caused King Pul of Assyria (also known as Tilgath-pilneser III) to invade the land and deport the men of Reuben, Gad, and the half-tribe of Manasseh. They took them to Halah, Habor, Hara, and the Gozan River, where they remain to this day.

6 Levi's Descendants

These are the names of the sons of Levi: Gershom, Kohath, Merari.

²*Kohath's* sons were: Amram, Izhar, Hebron, Uzziel.

Family Devotions

☐ **Devotion 123**
Cultivating Godly Attitudes

Read 1 Chronicles 4:9-10

Cultivating Godly Attitudes
Memory Verse

Whatever you do or say, let it be as a representative of the Lord Jesus, and come with him into the presence of God the Father to give him your thanks.
Colossians 3:17

David Carlson had never been to a funeral, but now his grandfather had died. He felt nervous about attending the service. "Just keep remembering all the wonderful things Grandfather taught you," his mother said, "and keep in mind that this is only his body in the casket. He is with the Lord in heaven."

David nodded. He knew that everyone would die someday unless Jesus came back first. And he knew that when Christians die, they go to be with Jesus.

"Death is not to be feared if we are part of God's family," his mother was saying now. "Of course, we'll miss Grandfather, and that makes us feel sad. But we can be happy for him, and we can be thankful for the wonderful memories we have of him."

David's father put down his newspaper and joined the conversation. "David, what do you remember most about Grandfather?" he asked.

David thought for a minute. "I remember how nice he was to me and how he helped other people and . . ." David paused, then added, "And the way he prayed for me."

"Your grandfather would be so pleased to know he was remembered for those things," said Dad with a smile. "When the time comes for me to die, I want to leave good memories, too."

Those words stayed with David the rest of the day. When he went to bed, he prayed, thanking God for the years he had had with a godly grandfather and asking the Lord Jesus to help him be the kind of Christian who would leave good memories when his life was over.

How About You?
When the time comes for God to call you home, what memories will you leave behind? If someone were recording your family tree, like the list here in 1 Chronicles, what special thing could be said about you? Would it be recorded that you were honest, kind, helpful, and loving? That you prayed for others and served the Lord? Live in such a way that you will be happy to have your deeds remembered by others and by God. *R.J.*

• For the next devotional, turn to page 421. • For the next devotional on *Cultivating Godly Attitudes*, turn to page 455. • For notes on *Cultivating Godly Attitudes*, see pages 337, 383, 472, 622, and 1216.

³*Amram's* descendants included: Aaron, Moses, Miriam.

Aaron's sons were: Nadab, Abihu, Eleazar, Ithamar.

⁴⁻¹⁵The oldest sons of the successive generations of Aaron were as follows:

Eleazar, the father of
Phinehas, the father of
Abishua, the father of
Bukki, the father of
Uzzi, the father of
Zerahiah, the father of
Meraioth, the father of
Amariah, the father of
Ahitub, the father of
Zadok, the father of
Ahimaaz, the father of
Azariah, the father of
Johanan, the father of
Azariah (the High Priest in Solomon's Temple at Jerusalem), the father of
Amariah, the father of
Ahitub, the father of
Zadok, the father of
Shallum, the father of
Hilkiah, the father of
Azariah, the father of
Seraiah, the father of
Jehozadak (who went into exile when the Lord sent the people of Judah and Jerusalem into captivity under Nebuchadnezzar).

¹⁶As previously stated, the sons of Levi were: Gershom, Kohath, Merari.

¹⁷The sons of *Gershom* were: Libni, Shimei.

¹⁸The sons of *Kohath* were: Amram, Izhar, Hebron, Uzziel.

¹⁹⁻²¹The sons of *Merari* were: Mahli, Mushi. The subclans of the Levites were:

In the Gershom clan: Libni, Jahath, Zimmah, Joah, Iddo, Zerah, Jeatherai.

²²⁻²⁴In the Kohath clan: Amminadab, Korah, Assir, Elkanah, Ebiasaph, Assir, Tahath, Uriel, Uzziah, Shaul.

²⁵⁻²⁷The subclan of *Elkanah* was further divided into the families of his sons: Amasai, Ahimoth, Elkanah, Zophai, Nahath, Eliab, Jeroham, Elkanah.

²⁸The families of the subclan of Samuel were headed by Samuel's sons: Joel, the oldest; Abijah, the second.

²⁹,³⁰The subclans of the clan of Merari were headed by his sons: Mahli, Libni, Shimei, Uzzah, Shimea, Haggiah, Asaiah.

³¹King David appointed songleaders and choirs to praise God in the Tabernacle after he had placed the Ark in it. ³²Then, when Solomon built the Temple at Jerusalem, the choirs carried on their work there.

³³⁻³⁸These are the names and ancestries of choir leaders: Heman the Cantor was from the clan of Kohath; his genealogy was traced back through: Joel, Samuel, Elkanah III, Jeroham, Eliel, Toah, Zuph, Elkanah II, Mahath, Amasai, Elkanah I, Joel, Azariah, Zephaniah, Tahath, Assir, Ebiasaph, Korah, Izhar, Kohath, Levi, Israel.

³⁹⁻⁴³Heman's assistant was his colleague Asaph, whose genealogy was traced back through: Berechiah, Shimea, Michael, Baaseiah, Malchijah, Ethni, Zerah, Adaiah, Ethan, Zimmah, Shimei, Jahath, Gershom, Levi.

⁴⁴⁻⁴⁷Heman's second assistant was Ethan, a representative from the clan of Merari, who stood on his left. Merari's ancestry was traced back through: Kishi, Abdi, Malluch, Hashabiah, Amaziah, Hilkiah, Amzi, Bani, Shemer, Mahli, Mushi, Merari, Levi.

⁴⁸Their relatives—all the other Levites—were appointed to various other tasks in the Tabernacle. ⁴⁹But only Aaron and his descendants were the priests. Their duties included sacrificing burnt offerings and incense, handling all the tasks relating to the inner sanctuary—the Holy of Holies—and the tasks relating to the annual Day of Atonement for Israel. They saw to it that all the details commanded by Moses the servant of God were strictly followed.

⁵⁰⁻⁵³The descendants of Aaron were: Eleazar, Phinehas, Abishua, Bukki, Uzzi, Zerahiah, Meraioth, Amariah, Ahitub, Zadok, Ahimaaz.

⁵⁴This is a record of the cities and land assigned by lot to the descendants of Aaron, all of whom were members of the Kohath clan:

⁵⁵⁻⁵⁷Hebron and its surrounding pasturelands in Judah (although the fields and suburbs were given to Caleb the son of Jephunneh), ⁵⁸,⁵⁹and the following Cities of Refuge with their surrounding pasturelands: Libnah, Jattir, Eshtemoa, Hilen, Debir, Ashan, Beth-shemesh.

⁶⁰Thirteen other cities with surrounding pastures—including Geba, Alemeth, and Anathoth—were given to the priests by the tribe of Benjamin. ⁶¹Lots were then drawn to assign land to the remaining descendants of Kohath, and they received ten cities in the territory of the half-tribe of Manasseh.

⁶²The subclans of the Gershom clan received by lot thirteen cities in the Bashan area from the tribes of Issachar, Asher, Naphtali, and Manasseh.

⁶³The subclans of Merari received by lot twelve cities from the tribes of Reuben, Gad, and Zebulun.

⁶⁴,⁶⁵Cities and pasturelands were also assigned

by lot to the Levites (and then renamed) from the tribes of Judah, Simeon, and Benjamin.

66-69 The tribe of Ephraim gave these Cities of Refuge with the surrounding pasturelands to the subclans of Kohath: Shechem in Mount Ephraim, Gezer, Jokme-am, Beth-horon, Aijalon, Gath-rimmon.

70 The following Cities of Refuge and their pasturelands were given to the subclans of the Kohathites by the half-tribe of Manasseh: Aner, Bileam.

71 Cities of Refuge and pastureland given to the clan of Gershom by the half-tribe of Manasseh were: Golan, in Bashan; Ashtaroth.

72 The tribe of Issachar gave them Kedesh, Daberath, 73 Ramoth, and Anem, and the surrounding pastureland of each.

74 The tribe of Asher gave them Abdon, Mashal, 75 Hukok, and Rehob, with their pasturelands.

76 The tribe of Naphtali gave them Kedesh in Galilee, Hammon, and Kiriathaim with pasturelands.

77 The tribe of Zebulun gave Rimmono and Tabor to the Merari clan as Cities of Refuge.

78,79 And across the Jordan River, opposite Jericho, the tribe of Reuben gave them Bezer (a desert town), Jahzah, Kedemoth and Mephaath, along with their pasturelands.

80 The tribe of Gad gave them Ramoth in Gilead, Mahanaim, 81 Heshbon, and Jazer, each with their surrounding pasturelands.

7 Issachar's Descendants

The sons of Issachar: Tola, Puah, Jashub, Shimron.

2 The sons of *Tola*, each of whom was the head of a subclan: Uzzi, Rephaiah, Jeriel, Jahmai, Ibsam, Shemuel.

At the time of King David, the total number of men of war from these families totaled 22,600.

3 *Uzzi's* son was Izrahiah among whose five sons were Michael, Obadiah, Joel, and Isshiah, all chiefs of subclans. 4 Their descendants, at the time of King David, numbered 36,000 troops; for all five of them had several wives and many sons. 5 The total number of men available for military service from all the clans of the tribe of Issachar numbered 87,000 stouthearted warriors, all included in the official genealogy.

6 The sons of Benjamin were: Bela, Becher, Jediael.

7 The sons of *Bela:* Ezbon, Uzzi, Uzziel, Jerimoth, Iri.

These five mighty warriors were chiefs of subclans and were the leaders of 22,034 troops (all of whom were recorded in the official genealogies).

8 The sons of *Becher* were: Zemirah, Joash, Eliezer, Elioenai, Omri, Jeremoth, Abijah, Anathoth, Alemeth.

9 At the time of David there were 20,200 mighty warriors among their descendants; and they were led by their clan chiefs.

10 The son of *Jediael* was Bilhan.

The sons of *Bilhan* were: Jeush, Benjamin, Ehud, Chenaanah, Zethan, Tarshish, Ahishahar.

11 They were the chiefs of the subclans of *Jediael,* and their descendants included 17,200 warriors at the time of King David.

12 The sons of Ir were Shuppim and Huppim. Hushim was one of the sons of Aher.

13 The sons of Naphtali (descendants of Jacob's wife Bilhah) were: Jahziel, Guni, Jezer, Shallum.

14 The sons of Manasseh, born to his Aramaean concubine, were Asriel and Machir (who became the father of Gilead).

15 It was Machir who found wives for Huppim and Shuppim. Machir's sister was Maacah. Another descendant was Zelophehad, who had only daughters.

16 Machir's wife, also named Maacah, bore him a son whom she named Peresh; his brother's name was Sheresh, and he had sons named Ulam and Rakem.

17 Ulam's son was Bedan. So these were the sons of Gilead, the grandsons of Machir, and the great-grandsons of Manasseh.

18 Hammolecheth, Machir's sister, bore Ishhod, Abiezer, and Mahlah.

19 The sons of Shemida were Ahian, Shechem, Likhi, and Aniam.

20,21 The sons of Ephraim: Shuthelah, Bered, Tahath, Eleadah, Tahath, Zabad, Shuthelah, Ezer, Elead.

Elead and *Ezer* attempted to rustle cattle at Gath, but they were killed by the local farmers. 22 Their father Ephraim mourned for them a long time, and his brothers tried to comfort him. 23 Afterwards his wife conceived and bore a son whom he called Beriah (meaning "a tragedy") because of what had happened.

24 Ephraim's daughter's name was Sheerah. She built Lower and Upper Beth-horon and Uzzensheerah.

25-27 This is Ephraim's line of descent:

Rephah, the father of
Resheph, the father of
Telah, the father of
Tahan, the father of
Ladan, the father of
Ammihud, the father of
Elishama, the father of
Nun, the father of
Joshua.

²⁸They lived in an area bounded on one side by Bethel and its surrounding towns, on the east by Naaran, on the west by Gezer and its villages, and finally by Shechem and its surrounding villages as far as Ayyah and its towns.

²⁹The tribe of Manasseh, descendants of Joseph the son of Israel, controlled the following cities and their surrounding areas: Beth-shean, Taanach, Megiddo, and Dor.

³⁰The children of Asher: Imnah, Ishvah, Ishvi, Beriah, Serah (their sister).

³¹The sons of *Beriah* were: Heber, Malchiel (the father of Birzaith).

³²*Heber's* children were: Japhlet, Shomer, Hotham, Shua (their sister).

³³*Japhlet's* sons were: Pasach, Bimhal, Ashvath.

³⁴His brother *Shomer's* sons were: Rohgah, Jehubbah, Aram.

³⁵The sons of his brother *Hotham* were: Zophah, Imna, Shelesh, Amal.

³⁶,³⁷The sons of *Zophah* were: Suah, Harnepher, Shual, Beri, Imrah, Bezer, Hod, Shamma, Shilshah, Ithran, Beera.

³⁸The sons of *Ithran* were: Jephunneh, Pispa, Ara.

³⁹The sons of Ulla were: Arah, Hanniel, Rizia.

⁴⁰These descendants of Asher were heads of subclans and were all skilled warriors and chiefs. Their descendants in the official genealogy numbered 36,000 men of war.

8 Benjamin's Descendants

The sons of Benjamin, according to age, were: Bela, the first, Ashbel, the second, Aharah, the third, Nohah, the fourth, Rapha, the fifth.

³⁻⁵The sons of *Bela* were: Addar, Gera, Abihud, Abishua, Naaman, Ahoah, Gera, Shephuphan, Huram.

⁶,⁷The sons of Ehud, chiefs of the subclans living at Geba, were captured in war and exiled to Manahath. They were: Naaman, Ahijah, Gera (also called Heglam), the father of Uzza and Ahihud.

⁸⁻¹⁰Shaharaim divorced his wives Hushim and Baara, but he had children in the land of Moab by Hodesh, his new wife: Jobab, Zibia, Mesha, Malcam, Jeuz, Sachia, Mirmah.

These sons all became chiefs of subclans.

¹¹His wife *Hushim* had borne him Abitub and Elpaal.

¹²The sons of *Elpaal* were: Eber, Misham, Shemed (who built Ono and Lod and their surrounding villages).

¹³His other sons were Beriah and Shema, chiefs of subclans living in Aijalon; they chased out the inhabitants of Gath.

¹⁴*Elpaal's* sons also included: Ahio, Shashak, Jeremoth.

¹⁵,¹⁶The sons of *Beriah* were: Zebadiah, Arad, Eder, Michael, Ishpah, Joha.

¹⁷,¹⁸The sons of *Elpaal* also included: Zebadiah, Meshullam, Hizki, Heber, Ishmerai, Izliah, Jobab.

¹⁹⁻²¹The sons of Shimei were: Jakim, Zichri, Zabdi, Elienai, Zillethai, Eliel, Adaiah, Beraiah, Shimrath.

²²⁻²⁵The sons of *Shashak* were: Ishpan, Eber, Eliel, Abdon, Zichri, Hanan, Hananiah, Elam, Anthothijah, Iphdeiah, Penuel.

²⁶,²⁷The sons of Jeroham were: Shamsherai, Shehariah, Athaliah, Jaareshiah, Elijah, Zichri.

²⁸These were the chiefs of the subclans living at Jerusalem.

²⁹Jeiel, the father of Gibeon, lived at Gibeon; and his wife's name was Maacah. ³⁰⁻³²His oldest son was named Abdon, followed by: Zur, Kish, Baal, Nadab, Gedor, Ahio, Zecher, Mikloth who was the father of Shimeah.

All of these families lived together near Jerusalem.

³³Ner was the father of Kish, and Kish was the father of Saul;

Saul's sons included: Jonathan, Malchi-shua, Abinadab, Eshbaal.

³⁴The son of *Jonathan* was Mephibosheth;

The son of Mephibosheth was Micah.

³⁵The sons of Micah: Pithon, Melech, Tarea, Ahaz.

³⁶Ahaz was the father of Jehoaddah, Jehoaddah was the father of: Alemeth, Azmaveth, Zimri. Zimri's son was Moza.

³⁷Moza was the father of Binea, whose sons were: Raphah, Eleasah, Azel.

³⁸Azel had six sons: Azrikam, Bocheru, Ishmael, Sheariah, Obadiah, Hanan.

³⁹Azel's brother Eshek had three sons: Ulam, the first, Jeush, the second, Eliphelet, the third.

⁴⁰*Ulam's* sons were prominent warriors who were expert marksmen with their bows. These men had 150 sons and grandsons, and they were all from the tribe of Benjamin.

9 The Exiled People Return Home

The family tree of every person in Israel was carefully recorded in *The Annals of the Kings of Israel*.

Judah was exiled to Babylon because the people worshiped idols.

²The first to return and live again in their former cities were families from the tribes of Israel and also the priests, the Levites, and the Temple assistants.

³Then some families from the tribes of Judah, Benjamin, Ephraim, and Manasseh arrived in Jerusalem:

⁴One family was that of Uthai (the son of Ammi-

hud, son of Omri, son of Imri, son of Bani) of the clan of Perez (son of Judah).

⁵The Shilonites were another family to return, including Asaiah (Shilon's oldest son) and his sons; ⁶there were also the sons of Zerah, including Jeuel and his relatives: 690 in all.

⁷,⁸Among the members of the tribe of Benjamin who returned were these:

Sallu (the son of Meshullam, the son of Hodaviah, the son of Hassenuah);
Ibneiah (the son of Jeroham);
Elah (the son of Uzzi, the son of Michri);
Meshullam (the son of Shephatiah, the son of Reuel, the son of Ibnijah).

⁹These men were all chiefs of subclans. A total of 956 Benjaminites returned.

¹⁰,¹¹The priests who returned were:

Jedaiah, Jehoiarib, Jachin,
Azariah (the son of Hilkiah, son of Meshullam, son of Zadok, son of Meraioth, son of Ahitub). He was the chief custodian of the Temple.

¹²Another of the returning priests was Adaiah (son of Jeroham, son of Pashhur, son of Malchijah).
Another priest was Maasai (son of Adiel, son of Jahzerah, son of Meshullam, son of Meshillemith, son of Immer).

¹³In all, 1,760 priests returned.

¹⁴Among the Levites who returned was Shemaiah (son of Hasshub, son of Azrikam, son of Hashabiah, who was a descendant of Merari).

¹⁵,¹⁶Other Levites who returned included:

Bakbakkar, Heresh, Galal,
Mattaniah (the son of Mica, who was the son of Zichri, who was the son of Asaph),
Obadiah (the son of Shemaiah, son of Galal, son of Jeduthun),
Berechiah (the son of Asa, son of Elkanah, who lived in the area of the Netophathites).

¹⁷,¹⁸The gatekeepers were Shallum (the chief gatekeeper), Akkub, Talmon, and Ahiman—all Levites. They are still responsible for the eastern royal gate. ¹⁹Shallum's ancestry went back through Kore and Ebiasaph to Korah. He and his close relatives the Korahites were in charge of the sacrifices and the protection of the sanctuary, just as their ancestors had supervised and guarded the Tabernacle. ²⁰Phinehas, the son of Eleazar, was the first director of this division in ancient times. And the Lord was with him.

²¹At that time Zechariah, the son of Meshelemiah, had been responsible for the protection of the entrance to the Tabernacle. ²²There were 212 doorkeepers in those days. They were chosen from their villages on the basis of their genealogies, and they were appointed by David and Samuel because of their reliability. ²³They and their descendants were in charge of the Lord's Tabernacle. ²⁴They were assigned to each of the four sides: east, west, north, and south. ²⁵And their relatives in the villages were assigned to help them from time to time, for seven days at a time.

²⁶The four head gatekeepers, all Levites, were in an office of great trust, for they were responsible for the rooms and treasuries in the Tabernacle of God. ²⁷Because of their important positions, they lived near the Tabernacle, and they opened the gates each morning. ²⁸Some of them were assigned to care for the various vessels used in the sacrifices and worship; they checked them in and out to avoid loss. ²⁹Others were responsible for the furniture, the items in the sanctuary, and the supplies such as fine flour, wine, incense, and spices.

³⁰Other priests prepared the spices and incense.

³¹And Mattithiah (a Levite and the oldest son of Shallum the Korahite) was entrusted with making the flat cakes for grain offerings.

³²Some members of the Kohath clan were in charge of the preparation of the special bread each Sabbath.

³³,³⁴The cantors were all prominent Levites. They lived in Jerusalem at the Temple and were on duty at all hours. They were free from other responsibilities and were selected by their genealogies.

³⁵-³⁷Jeiel (whose wife was Maacah) lived in Gibeon. He had many sons, including: Gibeon, Abdon (the oldest), Zur, Kish, Baal, Ner, Nadab, Gedor, Ahio, Zechariah, Mikloth.

³⁸Mikloth lived with his son Shimeam in Jerusalem near his relatives.

³⁹Ner was the father of Kish, Kish was the father of Saul, Saul was the father of Jonathan, Malchi-shua, Abinadab, and Eshbaal.

SERVING GOD WILLINGLY 9:17-18 Gatekeepers guarded the four main entrances to the Temple and opened the gates each morning for those who wanted to worship. In addition, they did other day-to-day chores to keep the Temple running smoothly—cleaning, preparing the offerings for sacrifice, and accounting for the gifts that were given to the Temple (9:22-32). Gatekeepers had to be reliable, honest, and trustworthy (9:26). Any jobs that you have in your family or in your church, no matter how small or unimportant they may seem, should be done responsibly. The gatekeepers at the Temple were responsible in their jobs; be responsible in yours. **To begin the series of devotionals on SERVING GOD WILLINGLY, turn to page 291.**

1 Chronicles

⁴⁰Jonathan was the father of Mephibosheth;
Mephibosheth was the father of Micah;
⁴¹Micah was the father of Pithon, Melech, Tahrea, and Ahaz;
⁴²Ahaz was the father of Jarah;
Jarah was the father of Alemeth, Azmaveth, and Zimri;
Zimri was the father of Moza.
⁴³Moza was the father of Binea, Rephaiah, Eleasah, and Azel.
⁴⁴Azel had six sons: Azrikam, Bocheru, Ishmael, Sheariah, Obadiah, Hanan.

10 Saul Dies; David Becomes King

The Philistines attacked and defeated the Israeli troops, who turned and fled and were slaughtered on the slopes of Mount Gilboa. ²They caught up with Saul and his three sons, Jonathan, Abinadab, and Malchi-shua, and killed them all. ³Saul had been hard pressed with heavy fighting all around him, when the Philistine archers shot and wounded him.

⁴He cried out to his bodyguard, "Quick, kill me with your sword before these uncircumcised heathen capture and torture me."

But the man was afraid to do it, so Saul took his own sword and fell against its point; and it pierced his body. ⁵Then his bodyguard, seeing that Saul was dead, killed himself in the same way. ⁶So Saul and his three sons died together; the entire family was wiped out in one day.

⁷When the Israelis in the valley below the mountain heard that their troops had been routed and that Saul and his sons were dead, they abandoned their cities and fled. And the Philistines came and lived in them. ⁸When the Philistines went back the next day to strip the bodies of the men killed in action and to gather the booty from the battlefield, they found the bodies of Saul and his sons. ⁹So they stripped off Saul's armor and cut off his head; then they displayed them throughout the nation and celebrated the wonderful news before their idols. ¹⁰They fastened his armor to the walls of the Temple of the Gods and nailed his head to the wall of Dagon's temple.

¹¹But when the people of Jabesh-gilead heard what the Philistines had done to Saul, ¹²their heroic warriors went out to the battlefield and brought back his body and the bodies of his three sons. Then they buried them beneath the oak tree at Jabesh and mourned and fasted for seven days.

¹³Saul died for his disobedience to the Lord and because he had consulted a medium, ¹⁴and did not ask the Lord for guidance. So the Lord killed him and gave the kingdom to David, the son of Jesse.

11 David Conquers Jerusalem

Then the leaders of Israel went to David at Hebron and told him, "We are your relatives, ²and even when Saul was king, you were the one who led our armies to battle and brought them safely back again. And the Lord your God has told you, 'You shall be the shepherd of my people Israel. You shall be their king.'"

³So David made a contract with them before the Lord, and they anointed him as king of Israel, just as the Lord had told Samuel. ⁴Then David and the leaders went to Jerusalem (or Jebus, as it used to be called) where the Jebusites—the original inhabitants of the land—lived. ⁵,⁶But the people of Jebus refused to let them enter the city. So David captured the fortress of Zion, later called the City of David, and said to his men, "The first man to kill a Jebusite shall be made commander-in-chief!" Joab, the son of Zeruiah, was the first, so he became the general of David's army. ⁷David lived in the fortress and that is why that area of Jerusalem is called the City of David. ⁸He extended the city out around the fortress while Joab rebuilt the rest of Jerusalem. ⁹And David became more and more famous and powerful, for the Lord of the heavens was with him.

¹⁰These are the names of some of the bravest of David's warriors (who also encouraged the leaders of Israel to make David their king, as the Lord had said would happen):

¹¹Jashobeam (the son of a man from Hachmon) was the leader of The Top Three—the three greatest heroes among David's men. He once killed 300 men with his spear.

¹²The second of The Top Three was Eleazar, the son of Dodo, a member of the subclan of Ahoh. ¹³He was with David in the battle against the Philistines at Pasdammim. The Israeli army was in a barley field and had begun to run away, ¹⁴but he held his ground in the middle of the field, and recovered it and slaughtered the Philistines; and the Lord saved them with a great victory.

¹⁵Another time, three of The Thirty went to David while he was hiding in the cave of Adullam. The Philistines were camped

---

RESPECTING AUTHORITY 10:11-12 The actions of the heroic warriors who brought back and buried the bodies of King Saul and his sons should encourage us to respect our God-given leaders. How easy it is to be critical of those in authority over us, focusing only on their weaknesses. We cannot excuse sin, but we should respect the positions of those in authority, whether at work, at church, or in government. First Thessalonians 5:12-13 gives instructions for honoring church leaders. Romans 13:1ff. gives instructions for relating to government leaders. **To begin the series of devotionals on RESPECTING AUTHORITY, turn to page 225.**

Family Devotions

☐ DEVOTION 124
SERVING GOD WILLINGLY

Read 1 Chronicles 11:10-14

Jason pointed a long stick at a clump of bushes. The imaginary enemy was just behind it, ready to take over Jason's territory!

"Winning the war again?" asked Dad, who had been in a real war. "You know I don't like you to even pretend to shoot anyone, Son."

"I hope I get to be a real hero some day," said Jason.

"I know how you feel," said Dad, "but I hope you get to be a hero some other way than by being in a war. Tell me, what would you like to be when you get older?"

"Somebody important," said Jason promptly. "Like David in the Bible. He killed Goliath and got to be king."

"How about being as important as Eleazar of Ahoh?" asked Dad. Jason looked puzzled, and Dad laughed. "We'll talk about him later," he promised as he walked into the house.

That night at family devotions Dad said, "We're going to read about Eleazar of Ahoh, one of David's bravest warriors."

"He was only famous because he served with King David," observed Jason when Dad had finished reading the passage.

"Think so?" asked Dad. "Or could it be possible that King David was famous because of great heroes like Eleazar?" Dad closed his Bible and looked at his family. "For every general, there are thousands of soldiers. They carry out his plans, and he becomes famous. We have one Lord—Jesus Christ—and it's our responsibility to glorify him, not to make a name for ourselves. I'd be happy to be an Eleazar of Ahoh in God's army."

Serving God Willingly
Memory Verse

Anyone who takes care of a little child like this is caring for me! And whoever cares for me is caring for God who sent me. Your care for others is the measure of your greatness.
Luke 9:48

How About You?
Does serving Jesus and others seem dull? Do you perform your chores routinely, just waiting for the time when you can be independent and not have to take orders anymore? Jesus instructed his people to serve. Forget about your own dreams of fame and get busy serving the Lord. That's the way to true greatness. *C. R.*

• For the next devotional, turn to page 427. • For the next devotional on SERVING GOD WILLINGLY, turn to page 435.
• For notes on SERVING GOD WILLINGLY, see pages 49, 419, 890, 920, and 922.

in the Valley of Rephaim, ¹⁶and David was in the stronghold at the time; an outpost of the Philistines had occupied Bethlehem. ¹⁷David wanted a drink from the Bethlehem well beside the gate, and when he mentioned this to his men, ¹⁸,¹⁹these three broke through to the Philistine camp, drew some water from the well, and brought it back to David. But he refused to drink it! Instead he poured it out as an offering to the Lord and said, "God forbid that I should drink it! It is the very blood of these men who risked their lives to get it."

²⁰Abishai, Joab's brother, was commander of The Thirty. He had gained his place among The Thirty by killing 300 men at one time with his spear. ²¹He was the chief and the most famous of The Thirty, but he was not as great as The Three.

²²Benaiah, whose father was a mighty warrior from Kabzeel, killed the two famous giants from Moab. He also killed a lion in a slippery pit when there was snow on the ground. ²³Once he killed an Egyptian who was seven and a half feet tall, whose spear was as thick as a weaver's beam. But Benaiah went up to him with only a club in his hand, and pulled the spear away from him and used it to kill him. ²⁴,²⁵He was nearly as great as The Three, and he was very famous among The Thirty. David made him captain of his bodyguard.

²⁶⁻⁴⁷Other famous warriors among David's men were:

Asahel (Joab's brother);
Elhanan, the son of Dodo from Bethlehem;
Shammoth from Harod;
Helez from Pelon;
Ira (son of Ikkesh) from Tekoa;
Abiezer from Anathoth;
Sibbecai from Hushath;
Ilai from Ahoh;
Maharai from Netophah;
Heled (son of Baanah) from Netophah;
Ithai (son of Ribai) a Benjaminite from Gibeah;
Benaiah from Pirathon;
Hurai from near the brooks of Gaash;
Abiel from Arbath;
Azmaveth from Baharum;
Eliahba from Shaalbon;
The sons of Hashem from Gizon;
Jonathan (son of Shagee) from Harar;
Ahiam (son of Sacher) from Harar;
Eliphal (son of Ur);
Hepher from Mecherath;
Ahijah from Pelon;
Hezro from Carmel;
Naarai (son of Ezbai);
Joel (brother of Nathan);
Mibhar (son of Hagri);
Zelek from Ammon;
Naharai from Beeroth—he was General Joab's armorbearer;
Ira from Ithra;
Gareb from Ithra;
Uriah the Hittite;
Zabad (son of Ahlai);
Adina (son of Shiza) from the tribe of Reuben—he was among the thirty-one leaders of the tribe of Reuben;
Hanan (son of Maacah);
Joshaphat from Mithna;
Uzzia from Ashterath;
Shama and Jeiel (sons of Hotham) from Aroer;
Jediael (son of Shimri);
Joha (his brother) from Tiza;
Eliel from Mahavi;
Jeribai and Joshaviah (sons of Elnaam);
Ithmah from Moab;
Eliel; Obed; Jaasiel from Mezoba.

12 More Warriors Join David

These are the names of the famous warriors who joined David at Ziklag while he was hiding from King Saul. ²All of them were expert archers and slingers, and they could use their left hands as readily as their right! Like King Saul, they were all of the tribe of Benjamin.

³⁻⁷Their chief was Ahiezer, son of Shemaah from Gibeah. The others were:

His brother Joash; Jeziel and Pelet, sons of Azmaveth; Beracah; Jehu from Anathoth; Ishmaiah from Gibeon (a brave warrior rated as high or higher than The Thirty); Jeremiah; Jahaziel; Johanan; Jozabad from Gederah; Eluzai; Jerimoth; Bealiah; Shemariah; Shephatiah from Haruph; Elkanah, Isshiah, Azarel, Joezer, Jashobeam—all Korahites; Joelah and Zebadiah (sons of Jeroham from Gedor).

⁸⁻¹³Great and brave warriors from the tribe of Gad also went to David in the wilderness. They were experts with both shield and spear and were "lion-faced men, swift as deer upon the mountains."

Ezer was the chief;
Obadiah was second in command;
Eliab was third in command;
Mishmannah was fourth in command;
Jeremiah was fifth in command;
Attai was sixth in command;
Eliel was seventh in command;
Johanan was eighth in command;
Elzabad was ninth in command;

Jeremiah was tenth in command;
Machbannai was eleventh in command.

¹⁴These men were army officers; the weakest was worth a hundred normal troops, and the greatest was worth a thousand! ¹⁵They crossed the Jordan River during its seasonal flooding and conquered the lowlands on both the east and west banks.

¹⁶Others came to David from Benjamin and Judah. ¹⁷David went out to meet them and said, "If you have come to help me, we are friends; but if you have come to betray me to my enemies when I am innocent, then may the God of our fathers see and judge you."

¹⁸Then the Holy Spirit came upon them, and Amasai, a leader of The Thirty, replied,

"We are yours, David;
We are on your side, son of Jesse.
Peace, peace be unto you,
And peace to all who aid you;
For your God is with you."

So David let them join him, and he made them captains of his army.

¹⁹Some men from Manasseh deserted the Israeli army and joined David just as he was going into battle with the Philistines against King Saul. But as it turned out, the Philistine generals refused to let David and his men go with them. After much discussion they sent them back, for they were afraid that David and his men would imperil them by deserting to King Saul.

²⁰Here is a list of the men from Manasseh who deserted to David as he was en route to Ziklag: Adnah, Jozabad, Jediael, Michael, Jozabad, Elihu, Zillethai.

Each was a high-ranking officer of Manasseh's troops. ²¹They were brave and able warriors, and they assisted David when he fought against the Amalek raiders at Ziklag.

²²More men joined David almost every day until he had a tremendous army—the army of God. ²³Here is the registry of recruits who joined David at Hebron. They were all anxious to see David become king instead of Saul, just as the Lord had said would happen.

²⁴⁻³⁷From Judah, 6,800 troops armed with shields and spears.

From the tribe of Simeon, 7,100 outstanding warriors.

From the Levites, 4,600.

From the priests—descendants of Aaron—there were 3,700 troops under the command of Zadok, a young man of unusual courage, and Jehoiada. (He and twenty-two members of his family were officers of the fighting priests.)

From the tribe of Benjamin, the same tribe Saul was from, there were 3,000. (Most of that tribe retained its allegiance to Saul.)

From the tribe of Ephraim, 20,800 mighty warriors, each famous in his respective clan.

From the half-tribe of Manasseh, 18,000 were sent for the express purpose of helping David become king.

From the tribe of Issachar there were 200 leaders of the tribe with their relatives—all men who understood the temper of the times and knew the best course for Israel to take.

From the tribe of Zebulun there were 50,000 trained warriors; they were fully armed and totally loyal to David.

From Naphtali there were 1,000 officers and 37,000 troops equipped with shields and spears.

From the tribe of Dan there were 28,600 troops, all of them prepared for war.

From the tribe of Asher, there were 40,000 trained and ready troops.

From the other side of the Jordan River—where the tribes of Reuben and Gad and the half-tribe of Manasseh lived—there were 120,000 troops equipped with every kind of weapon.

³⁸All these men came in battle array to Hebron with the single purpose of making David the king of Israel. In fact, all of Israel was ready for this change. ³⁹They feasted and drank with David for three days, for preparations had been made for their arrival. ⁴⁰People from nearby and from as far away as Issachar, Zebulun, and Naphtali brought food on donkeys, camels, mules, and oxen. Vast supplies of flour, fig cakes, raisins, wine, oil, cattle, and sheep were brought to the celebration, for joy had spread throughout the land.

13 David Celebrates but Uzza Dies

After David had consulted with all of his army officers, ²he addressed the assembled men of Israel as follows:

"Since you think that I should be your king, and since the Lord our God has given his approval, let us send messages to our brothers throughout the land of Israel, including the priests and Levites, inviting them to come and join us. ³And let us bring back the Ark of our God, for we have been neglecting it ever since Saul became king."

⁴There was unanimous consent, for everyone agreed with him. ⁵So David summoned the people of Israel from all across the nation so that

they could be present when the Ark of God was brought from Kiriath-jearim.

⁶Then David and all Israel went to Baalah (i.e., Kiriath-jearim) in Judah to bring back the Ark of the Lord God enthroned above the angels. ⁷It was taken from the house of Abinadab on a new cart. Uzza and Ahio drove the oxen. ⁸Then David and all the people danced before the Lord with great enthusiasm, accompanied by singing and by zithers, harps, tambourines, cymbals, and trumpets. ⁹But as they arrived at the threshing-floor of Chidon, the oxen stumbled and Uzza reached out his hand to steady the Ark. ¹⁰Then the anger of the Lord blazed out against Uzza, and killed him because he had touched the Ark. And so he died there before God. ¹¹David was angry at the Lord for what he had done to Uzza and he named the place "The Outbreak Against Uzza." And it is still called that today.

¹²Now David was afraid of God and asked, "How shall I ever get the Ark of God home?"

¹³Finally he decided to take it to the home of Obed-edom the Gittite instead of bringing it to the City of David. ¹⁴The Ark remained there with the family of Obed-edom for three months, and the Lord blessed him and his family.

14 God Blesses David

King Hiram of Tyre sent masons and carpenters to help build David's palace and he supplied him with much cedar lumber. ²David now realized why the Lord had made him king and why he had made his kingdom so great; it was for a special reason—to give joy to God's people!

³After David moved to Jerusalem, he married additional wives and became the father of many sons and daughters.

⁴⁻⁷These are the names of the sons born to him in Jerusalem: Shammua, Shobab, Nathan, Solomon, Ibhar, Elishua, Elpelet, Nogah, Nepheg, Japhia, Elishama, Beeliada, Eliphelet.

⁸When the Philistines heard that David was Israel's new king, they mobilized their forces to capture him. But David learned that they were on the way, so he called together his army. ⁹The Philistines were raiding the Valley of Rephaim, ¹⁰and David asked the Lord, "If I go out and fight them, will you give me the victory?"

And the Lord replied, "Yes, I will."

¹¹So he attacked them at Baal-perazim and wiped them out. He exulted, "God has used me to sweep away my enemies like water bursting through a dam!" That is why the place has been known as Baal-perazim ever since (meaning, "The Place of Breaking Through").

¹²After the battle the Israelis picked up many idols left by the Philistines, but David ordered them burned.

¹³Later the Philistines raided the valley again, ¹⁴and again David asked God what to do.

The Lord replied, "Go around by the mulberry trees and attack from there. ¹⁵When you hear a sound like marching in the tops of the mulberry trees, that is your signal to attack, for God will go before you and destroy the enemy."

¹⁶So David did as the Lord commanded him; and he cut down the army of the Philistines all the way from Gibeon to Gezer. ¹⁷David's fame spread everywhere, and the Lord caused all the nations to fear him.

15 The Ark Comes Back

David now built several palaces for himself in Jerusalem, and he also built a new Tabernacle to house the Ark of God, ²and issued these instructions: "[When we transfer the Ark to its new home], no one except the Levites may carry it, for God has chosen them for this purpose; they are to minister to him forever."

³Then David summoned all Israel to Jerusalem to celebrate the bringing of the Ark into the new Tabernacle. ⁴⁻¹⁰These were the priests and Levites present:

120 from the clan of Kohath; with Uriel as their leader;

220 from the clan of Merari; with Asaiah as their leader;

130 from the clan of Gershom; with Joel as their leader;

200 from the subclan of Elizaphan; with Shemaiah as their leader;

80 from the subclan of Hebron; with Eliel as their leader;

112 from the subclan of Uzziel; with Amminadab as their leader.

¹¹Then David called for Zadok and Abiathar, the High Priests, and for the Levite leaders: Uriel, Asaiah, Joel, Shemaiah, Eliel, and Amminadab.

¹²"You are the leaders of the clans of the Levites," he told them. "Now sanctify yourselves with all your brothers so that you may bring the Ark of Jehovah, the God of Israel, to the place I have prepared for it. ¹³The Lord destroyed us before because we handled the matter improperly—you were not carrying it."

¹⁴So the priests and the Levites underwent the ceremonies of sanctification in preparation for bringing home the Ark of Jehovah, the God of Israel. ¹⁵Then the Levites carried the Ark on their shoulders with its carrying poles, just as the Lord had instructed Moses.

[16] King David also ordered the Levite leaders to organize the singers into an orchestra, and they played loudly and joyously upon psaltries, harps, and cymbals. [17] Heman (son of Joel), Asaph (son of Berechiah), and Ethan (son of Kushaiah) from the clan of Merari were the heads of the musicians.

[18] The following men were chosen as their assistants: Zechariah, Jaaziel, Shemiramoth, Jehiel, Unni, Eliab, Benaiah, Maaseiah, Mattithiah, Eliphelehu, Mikneiah, Obed-edom and Jeiel, the doorkeepers.

[19] Heman, Asaph, and Ethan were chosen to sound the bronze cymbals; [20] and Zechariah, Aziel, Shemiramoth, Jehiel, Unni, Eliab, Maaseiah, and Benaiah comprised an octet accompanied by harps. [21] Mattithiah, Eliphelehu, Mikneiah, Obed-edom, Jeiel, and Azaziah were the harpists. [22] The song leader was Chenaniah, the chief of the Levites, who was selected for his skill. [23] Berechiah and Elkanah were guards for the Ark. [24] Shebaniah, Joshaphat, Nethanel, Amasai, Zechariah, Benaiah, and Eliezer—all of whom were priests—formed a bugle corps to march at the head of the procession. And Obed-edom and Jehiah guarded the Ark.

[25] Then David and the elders of Israel and the high officers of the army went with great joy to the home of Obed-edom to take the Ark to Jerusalem. [26] And because God didn't destroy the Levites who were carrying the Ark, they sacrificed seven bulls and seven lambs. [27] David, the Levites carrying the Ark, the singers, and Chenaniah the song leader were all dressed in linen robes. David also wore a linen ephod. [28] So the leaders of Israel took the Ark to Jerusalem with shouts of joy, the blowing of horns and trumpets, the crashing of cymbals, and loud playing on the harps and zithers.

[29] (But as the Ark arrived in Jerusalem, David's wife Michal, the daughter of King Saul, felt a deep disgust for David as she watched from the window and saw him dancing like a madman.)

16 David Praises God

So they brought the Ark of God into the special tent that David had prepared for it, and the leaders of Israel sacrificed burnt offerings and peace offerings before God. [2] At the conclusion of these offerings David blessed the people in the name of the Lord; [3] then he gave every person present (men and women alike) a loaf of bread, some wine, and a cake of raisins.

[4] He appointed certain of the Levites to minister before the Ark by giving constant praise and thanks to the Lord God of Israel and by asking for his blessings upon his people. These are the names of those given this assignment: [5] Asaph, the leader of this detail, sounded the cymbals. His associates were Zechariah, Jeiel, Shemiramoth, Jehiel, Mattithiah, Eliab, Benaiah, Obed-edom, and Jeiel; they played the harps and zithers. [6] The priests Benaiah and Jahaziel played their trumpets regularly before the Ark.

[7] At that time David began the custom of using choirs in the Tabernacle to sing thanksgiving to the Lord. Asaph was the director of this choral group of priests.

[8] "Oh, give thanks to the Lord and pray to
him," they sang.
"Tell the peoples of the world
About his mighty doings.
[9] Sing to him; yes, sing his praises
And tell of his marvelous works.
[10] Glory in his holy name;
Let all rejoice who seek the Lord.
[11] Seek the Lord; yes, seek his strength
And seek his face untiringly.
[12,13] O descendants of his servant Abraham,
O chosen sons of Jacob,
Remember his mighty miracles
And his marvelous miracles
And his authority:
[14] He is the Lord our God!
His authority is seen throughout the earth.
[15] Remember his covenant forever—
The words he commanded
To a thousand generations:
[16] His agreement with Abraham,
And his oath to Isaac,
[17] And his confirmation to Jacob.
He promised Israel
With an everlasting promise:
[18] 'I will give you the land of Canaan
As your inheritance.'
[19] When Israel was few in number—oh, so
few—
And merely strangers in the Promised Land;
[20] When they wandered from country to country,
From one kingdom to another—
[21] God didn't let anyone harm them.
Even kings were killed who sought to hurt
them.
[22] 'Don't harm my chosen people,' he declared.

OBEDIENCE 15:13-15 When David's first attempt to move the Ark failed (1 Chronicles 13:8-14), he learned an important lesson: when God gives specific instructions, it is wise to follow them precisely. This time David saw to it that the Levites carried the Ark (Numbers 4:5-15). The way we can know God's instructions is to know his Word. We may not fully understand the reasons behind God's instructions, but we can know that his wisdom is complete and his judgment infallible. Just as children may not understand the reasons for all their parents' instructions, we may not understand all of God's instructions. But in both cases, we must obey whether we understand or not. **To begin the series of devotionals on OBEDIENCE, turn to page 25.**

'These are my prophets—touch them not.'
²³Sing to the Lord, O earth,
Declare each day that he is the one who saves!
²⁴Show his glory to the nations!
Tell everyone about his miracles.
²⁵For the Lord is great and should be highly praised;
He is to be held in awe above all gods.
²⁶The other so-called gods are demons,
But the Lord made the heavens.
²⁷Majesty and honor march before him,
Strength and gladness walk beside him.
²⁸O people of all nations of the earth,
Ascribe great strength and glory to his name!
²⁹Yes, ascribe to the Lord
The glory due his name!
Bring an offering and come before him;
Worship the Lord when clothed with holiness!
³⁰Tremble before him, all the earth!
The world stands unmoved.
³¹Let the heavens be glad, the earth rejoice;
Let all the nations say, 'It is the Lord who reigns.'
³²Let the vast seas roar,
Let the countryside and everything in it rejoice!
³³Let the trees in the woods sing for joy before the Lord,
For he comes to judge the earth.
³⁴Oh, give thanks to the Lord, for he is good;
His love and his kindness go on forever.
³⁵Cry out to him, 'Oh, save us, God of our salvation;
Bring us safely back from among the nations.
Then we will thank your holy name,
And triumph in your praise.'
³⁶Blessed be Jehovah, God of Israel,
Forever and forevermore."

And all the people shouted "Amen!" and praised the Lord.

³⁷David arranged for Asaph and his fellow Levites to minister regularly at the Tabernacle, doing each day whatever needed to be done. ³⁸This group included Obed-edom (the son of Jeduthun), Hosah and sixty-eight of their colleagues as guards.

³⁹Meanwhile the old Tabernacle of the Lord on the hill of Gibeon continued to be active. David left Zadok the priest and his fellow-priests to minister to the Lord there. ⁴⁰They sacrificed burnt offerings to the Lord each morning and evening upon the altar set aside for that purpose, just as the Lord had commanded Israel. ⁴¹David also appointed Heman, Jeduthun, and several others who were chosen by name to give thanks to the Lord for his constant love and mercy. ⁴²They used their trumpets and cymbals to accompany the singers with loud praises to God. And Jeduthun's sons were appointed as guards.

⁴³At last the celebration ended and the people returned to their homes, and David returned to bless his own household.

17 God Makes a Promise to David

After David had been living in his new palace for some time he said to Nathan the prophet, "Look! I'm living here in a cedar-paneled home while the Ark of the Covenant of God is out there in a tent!"

²And Nathan replied, "Carry out your plan in every detail, for it is the will of the Lord."

³But that same night God said to Nathan, ⁴"Go and give my servant David this message: 'You are not to build my temple! ⁵I've gone from tent to tent as my home from the time I brought Israel out of Egypt. ⁶In all that time I never suggested to any of the leaders of Israel—the shepherds I appointed to care for my people—that they should build me a cedar-lined temple.'

⁷"Tell my servant David, 'The Lord of heaven says to you, I took you from being a shepherd and made you the king of my people. ⁸And I have been with you everywhere you've gone; I have destroyed your enemies, and I will make your name as great as the greatest of the earth. ⁹And I will give a permanent home to my people Israel and will plant them in their land. They will not be disturbed again; the wicked nations won't conquer them as they did before ¹⁰when the judges ruled them. I will subdue all of your enemies. And I now declare that I will cause your descendants to be kings of Israel just as you are.

¹¹"'When your time here on earth is over and you die, I will place one of your sons upon your throne; and I will make his kingdom strong. ¹²He is the one who shall build me a temple, and I will establish his royal line of descent forever. ¹³I will be his father, and he shall be my son; I will never remove my mercy and love from him as I did from Saul. ¹⁴I will place him over my people and over the kingdom of Israel forever—and his descendants will always be kings.'"

¹⁵So Nathan told King David everything the Lord had said.

¹⁶Then King David went in and sat before the Lord and said, "Who am I, O Lord God, and what is my family that you have given me all this? ¹⁷For all the great things you have already done for me are nothing in comparison to what you have promised to do in the future! For now, O Lord God, you are speaking of future generations of my children being kings too! You speak as though I were someone very great. ¹⁸What else can I say? You know that I am but a dog, yet you have

Family Devotions

☐ **Devotion 125**
Sharing Your Faith

Read 1 Chronicles 16:23-31

When Jeff's parents had announced that they were moving to Taiwan to help the missionaries, Jeff hadn't realized that everything would be so strange. He was glad he had at least one friend who spoke English. George was his age, and he attended English classes at the mission. He had even taken an American name.

"I show you town," the friendly black-haired boy said one day in his best English. The boys hopped on their bikes. Dodging people, other bikes, and trucks on the narrow streets, they pedaled around the small town. "Come," said George as he parked his bike in front of a large building.

When George pushed open the door, Jeff gasped at what he saw. "God factory," explained George waving his hand at the rows and rows of half-made idols stacked on the floor of the warehouse. "My father makes. He paints faces. Very nice. Many people buy."

Jeff got a sick feeling in his stomach. He could not believe that people would make their own gods. How could man-made gods help anybody, when they were only pieces of wood? "Your father makes gods?" asked George.

Jeff shook his head slowly. Trying to make George understand, he found himself talking just like him. "No, George," he said, "we not make gods. Our God make us!"

Jeff had always known that God had made him, but he had never thought that was anything so special before. Now he realized what a wonderful God he had! He was so glad he knew the true God. Silently he prayed, *Thank you, God, for making me. Help me tell George and other people about you so they won't have to worship a man-made god who can't even hear their prayers.*

Sharing Your Faith Memory Verse

And I assure you of this: I, the Messiah, will publicly honor you in the presence of God's angels if you publicly acknowledge me here on earth as your Friend.
Luke 12:8

How About You?

Aren't you glad you can know the living God? He's the Creator of the whole universe. But there are still many people who don't know that. Will you share this knowledge with them? Begin in your own neighborhood. Maybe someday God will even allow you to carry his message to other lands. M. N.

• For the next devotional, turn to page 435.   • For the next devotional on *Sharing Your Faith*, turn to page 545.
• For notes on *Sharing Your Faith*, see pages 462, 776, 1015, and 1074.

decided to honor me! ¹⁹O Lord, you have given me these wonderful promises just because you want to be kind to me, because of your own great heart. ²⁰O Lord, there is no one like you—there is no other God. In fact, we have never even heard of another god like you!

²¹"And what other nation in all the earth is like Israel? You have made a unique nation and have redeemed it from Egypt so that the people could be your people. And you made a great name for yourself when you did glorious miracles in driving out the nations from before your people. ²²You have declared that your people Israel belong to you forever, and you have become their God.

²³"And now I accept your promise, Lord, that I and my children will always rule this nation. ²⁴And may this bring eternal honor to your name as everyone realizes that you always do what you say. They will exclaim, 'The Lord of heaven is indeed the God of Israel!' And Israel shall always be ruled by my children and their posterity! ²⁵Now I have the courage to pray to you, for you have revealed this to me. ²⁶God himself has promised this good thing to me! ²⁷May this blessing rest upon my children forever, for when you grant a blessing, Lord, it is an eternal blessing!"

18 David Conquers Many Enemies

David finally subdued the Philistines and conquered Gath and its surrounding towns. ²He also conquered Moab and required its people to send him a large sum of money every year. ³He conquered the dominion of King Hadadezer of Zobah (as far as Hamath) at the time Hadadezer went to tighten his grip along the Euphrates River. ⁴David captured a thousand of his chariots, seven thousand cavalry, and twenty thousand troops. He crippled all the chariot teams except a hundred that he kept for his own use.

⁵When the Syrians arrived from Damascus to help King Hadadezer, David killed twenty-two thousand of them; ⁶then he placed a garrison of his troops in Damascus, the Syrian capital. So the Syrians, too, were forced to send him large amounts of money every year. And the Lord gave David victory everywhere he went. ⁷He brought the gold shields of King Hadadezer's officers to Jerusalem, ⁸as well as a great amount of bronze from Hadadezer's cities of Tibhath and Cun. (King Solomon later melted the bronze and used it for the Temple. He molded it into the bronze tank, the pillars, and the instruments used in offering sacrifices on the altar.)

⁹When King Tou of Hamath learned that King David had destroyed Hadadezer's army, ¹⁰he sent his son Hadoram to greet and congratulate King David on his success and to present him with many gifts of gold, silver, and bronze, seeking an alliance. For Hadadezer and Tou had been enemies and there had been many wars between them. ¹¹King David dedicated these gifts to the Lord, as he did the silver and gold he took from the nations of Edom, Moab, Ammon, Amalek, and the Philistines.

¹²Abishai (son of Zeruiah) then destroyed eighteen thousand Edomites in the Valley of Salt. ¹³He put garrisons in Edom and forced the Edomites to pay large sums of money annually to David. This is just another example of how the Lord gave David victory after victory. ¹⁴David reigned over all of Israel and was a just ruler.

¹⁵Joab (son of Zeruiah) was commander-in-chief of the army; Jehoshaphat (son of Ahilud) was the historian; ¹⁶Zadok (son of Ahitub) and Ahimelech (son of Abiathar) were the head priests; Shavsha was the king's special assistant; ¹⁷Benaiah (son of Jehoiada) was in charge of the king's bodyguard—the Cherethites and Pelethites—and David's sons were his chief aides.

19 David Defends His People

When King Nahash of Ammon died, his son Hanun became the new king.

²,³Then David declared, "I am going to show friendship to Hanun because of all the kind things his father did for me."

So David sent a message of sympathy to Hanun for the death of his father. But when David's ambassadors arrived, King Hanun's counselors warned him, "Don't fool yourself that David has sent these men to honor your father! They are here to spy out the land so that they can come in and conquer it!"

⁴So King Hanun insulted King David's ambassadors by shaving their beards and cutting their robes off at the middle to expose their buttocks; then he sent them back to David in shame. ⁵When David heard what had happened, he sent a message to his embarrassed emissaries, telling them to stay at Jericho until their beards had grown out again. ⁶When King Hanun realized his mistake

---

HUMILITY 17:16-20 David responded to God's answer and promises with deep humility, not resentment. This king who had conquered his enemies and was loved by his people said, "Who am I . . . that you have given me all this?" David recognized that God was the *true* king. God has done just as much for us, and he plans to do even more! Like David, we should humble ourselves and give glory to God, saying, "O Lord, there is no one like you—there is no other God." When God chooses another person to do something you wanted to do, can you respond with such humility? **To begin the series of devotionals on HUMILITY, turn to page 449.**

he sent $2,000,000 to enlist mercenary troops, chariots, and cavalry from Mesopotamia, Aram-maacah, and Zobah. ⁷He hired thirty-two thousand chariots, as well as the support of the king of Maacah and his entire army. These forces camped at Medeba where they were joined by the troops King Hanun had recruited from his cities.

⁸When David learned of this, he sent Joab and the mightiest warriors of Israel. ⁹The army of Ammon went out to meet them and began the battle at the gates of the city of Medeba. Meanwhile, the mercenary forces were out in the field. ¹⁰When Joab realized that the enemy forces were both in front and behind him, he divided his army and sent one group to engage the Syrians. ¹¹The other group, under the command of his brother Abishai, moved against the Ammonites.

¹²"If the Syrians are too strong for me, come and help me," Joab told his brother; "and if the Ammonites are too strong for you, I'll come and help you. ¹³Be courageous and let us act like men to save our people and the cities of our God. And may the Lord do what is best."

¹⁴So Joab and his troops attacked the Syrians, and the Syrians turned and fled. ¹⁵When the Ammonites, under attack by Abishai's troops, saw that the Syrians were retreating, they fled into the city. Then Joab returned to Jerusalem.

¹⁶After their defeat, the Syrians summoned additional troops from east of the Euphrates River, led personally by Shophach, King Hadadezer's commander-in-chief. ¹⁷,¹⁸When this news reached David, he mobilized all Israel, crossed the Jordan River, and engaged the enemy troops in battle. But the Syrians again fled from David, and he killed seven thousand charioteers and forty thousand of their troops. He also killed Shophach, the commander-in-chief of the Syrian army. ¹⁹Then King Hadadezer's troops surrendered to King David and became his subjects. And never again did the Syrians aid the Ammonites in their battles.

20 David Defeats the Ammonites

The following spring (spring was the season when wars usually began) Joab led the Israeli army in successful attacks against the cities and villages of the people of Ammon. After destroying them, he laid siege to Rabbah and conquered it. Meanwhile, David had stayed in Jerusalem. ²When David arrived on the scene, he removed the crown from the head of King Milcom of Rabbah and placed it upon his own head. It was made of gold inlaid with gems and weighed seventy-five pounds! David also took great amounts of plunder from the city. ³He drove the people from the city and set them to work with saws, iron picks, and axes, as was his custom with all the conquered Ammonite peoples. Then David and all his army returned to Jerusalem.

⁴The next war was against the Philistines again, at Gezer. But Sibbecai, a man from Hushath, killed one of the sons of the giant, Sippai, and so the Philistines surrendered. ⁵During another war with the Philistines, Elhanan (the son of Jair) killed Lahmi, the brother of Goliath the giant; the handle of his spear was like a weaver's beam! ⁶,⁷During another battle, at Gath, a giant with six fingers on each hand and six toes on each foot (his father was also a giant) defied and taunted Israel; but he was killed by David's nephew Jonathan, the son of David's brother Shimea. ⁸These giants were descendants of the giants of Gath, and they were killed by David and his soldiers.

21 David Counts the People

Then Satan brought disaster upon Israel, for he made David decide to take a census.

²"Take a complete census throughout the land and bring me the totals," he told Joab and the other leaders.

³But Joab objected. "If the Lord were to multiply his people a hundred times, would they not all be yours? So why are you asking us to do this? Why must you cause Israel to sin?"

⁴But the king won the argument, and Joab did as he was told; he traveled all through Israel and returned to Jerusalem. ⁵The total population figure which he gave came to 1,100,000 men of military age in Israel and 470,000 in Judah. ⁶But he didn't include the tribes of Levi and Benjamin in his figures because he was so distressed at what the king had made him do.

⁷And God, too, was displeased with the census and punished Israel for it.

⁸But David said to God, "I am the one who has sinned. Please forgive me, for I realize now how wrong I was to do this."

⁹Then the Lord said to Gad, David's personal prophet, ¹⁰,¹¹"Go and tell David, 'The Lord has offered you three choices. Which will you choose? ¹²You may have three years of famine, or three months of destruction by the enemies of Israel, or three days of deadly plague as the angel

---

CONFESSING SIN 21:8 When David realized his sin, he took full responsibility, admitted he was wrong, and asked God to forgive him. Many people want to add God and his blessings to their lives without acknowledging their personal sin and guilt. But confession and repentance must come before receiving forgiveness. Like David, we must take full responsibility for our actions and confess them to God before we can expect him to forgive us and continue his work in our lives. **To begin the series of devotionals on CONFESSING SIN, turn to page 41.**

of the Lord brings destruction to the land. Think it over and let me know what answer to return to the one who sent me.'"

¹³"This is a terrible decision to make," David replied, "but let me fall into the hands of the Lord rather than into the power of men, for God's mercies are very great."

¹⁴So the Lord sent a plague upon Israel and 70,000 men died as a result. ¹⁵During the plague God sent an angel to destroy Jerusalem; but then he felt such compassion that he changed his mind and commanded the destroying angel, "Stop! It is enough!" (The angel of the Lord was standing at the time by the threshing-floor of Ornan the Jebusite.) ¹⁶When David saw the angel of the Lord standing between heaven and earth with his sword drawn, pointing toward Jerusalem, he and the elders of Israel clothed themselves in sackcloth and fell to the ground before the Lord.

¹⁷And David said to God, "I am the one who sinned by ordering the census. But what have these sheep done? O Lord my God, destroy me and my family, but do not destroy your people."

¹⁸Then the angel of the Lord told Gad to instruct David to build an altar to the Lord at the threshing-floor of Ornan the Jebusite. ¹⁹,²⁰So David went to see Ornan, who was threshing wheat at the time. Ornan saw the angel as he turned, and his four sons ran and hid. ²¹Then Ornan saw the king approaching. So he left the threshing-floor and bowed to the ground before King David.

²²David said to Ornan, "Let me buy this threshing-floor from you at its full price; then I will build an altar to the Lord and the plague will stop."

²³"Take it, my lord, and use it as you wish," Ornan said to David. "Take the oxen, too, for burnt offerings; use the threshing instruments for wood for the fire and use the wheat for the grain offering. I give it all to you."

²⁴"No," the king replied, "I will buy it for the full price; I cannot take what is yours and give it to the Lord. I will not offer a burnt offering that has cost me nothing!"

²⁵So David paid Ornan $4,300 in gold ²⁶and built an altar to the Lord there, and sacrificed burnt offerings and peace offerings upon it; and he called out to the Lord, who answered by sending down fire from heaven to burn up the offering on the altar. ²⁷Then the Lord commanded the angel to put back his sword into its sheath; ²⁸and when David saw that the Lord had answered his plea, he sacrificed to him again. ²⁹The Tabernacle and altar made by Moses in the wilderness were on the hill of Gibeon, ³⁰but David didn't have time to go there to plead before the Lord, for he was terrified by the drawn sword of the angel of Jehovah.

22 The Temple Materials

Then David said, "Right here at Ornan's threshing-floor is the place where I'll build the Temple of the Lord and construct the altar for Israel's burnt offering!"

²David now drafted all the resident aliens in Israel to prepare blocks of squared stone for the Temple. ³They also manufactured iron into the great quantity of nails needed for the doors in the gates and for the clamps; and they smelted so much bronze that it was too much to weigh. ⁴The men of Tyre and Sidon brought great rafts of cedar logs to David.

⁵"Solomon my son is young and tender," David said, "and the Temple of the Lord must be a marvelous structure, famous and glorious throughout the world; so I will begin the preparations for it now."

So David collected the construction materials before his death. ⁶He now commanded his son Solomon to build a temple for the Lord God of Israel.

⁷"I wanted to build it myself," David told him, ⁸"but the Lord said not to do it. 'You have killed too many men in great wars,' he told me. 'You have reddened the ground before me with blood: so you are not to build my Temple. ⁹But I will give you a son,' he told me, 'who will be a man of peace, for I will give him peace with his enemies in the surrounding lands. His name shall be Solomon (meaning "Peaceful"), and I will give peace and quietness to Israel during his reign. ¹⁰He shall build my Temple, and he shall be as my own son and I will be his father; and I will cause his sons and his descendants to reign over every generation of Israel.'

¹¹"So now, my son, may the Lord be with you and prosper you as you do what he told you to do and build the Temple of the Lord. ¹²And may the Lord give you the good judgment to follow all his laws when he makes you king of Israel. ¹³For if you carefully obey the rules and regulations that he gave to Israel through Moses, you will prosper. Be strong and courageous, fearless and enthusiastic!

¹⁴"By hard work I have collected several billion dollars worth of gold bullion, millions in silver, and so much iron and bronze that I haven't even weighed it; I have also gathered timber and stone for the walls. This is at least a beginning, something with which to start. ¹⁵And you have many skilled stonemasons and carpenters and craftsmen of every kind. ¹⁶They are expert gold and silver smiths and bronze and iron workers. So get to work, and may the Lord be with you!"

¹⁷Then David ordered all the leaders of Israel to assist his son in this project.

18"The Lord your God is with you," he declared. "He has given you peace with the surrounding nations, for I have conquered them in the name of the Lord and for his people. 19Now try with every fiber of your being to obey the Lord your God, and you will soon be bringing the Ark and the other holy articles of worship into the Temple of the Lord!"

23 David Gives the Levites Jobs

By this time David was an old, old man, so he stepped down from the throne and appointed his son Solomon as the new king of Israel. 2He summoned all the political and religious leaders of Israel for the coronation ceremony. 3At this time a census was taken of the men of the tribe of Levi who were thirty years or older. The total came to 38,000.

4,5"Twenty-four thousand of them will supervise the work at the Temple," David instructed, "6,000 are to be bailiffs and judges, 4,000 will be temple guards, and 4,000 will praise the Lord with the musical instruments I have made."

6Then David divided them into three main divisions named after the sons of Levi—the Gershom division, the Kohath division, and the Merari division.

7Subdivisions of the *Gershom* corps were named after his sons Ladan and Shimei. 8,9These subdivisions were still further divided into six groups named after the sons of *Ladan:* Jehiel the leader, Zetham, Joel; and the sons of *Shimei* — Shelomoth, Haziel, and Haran.

10,11The subclans of *Shimei* were named after his four sons: Jahath was greatest, Zizah was next, and Jeush and Beriah were combined into a single subclan because neither had many sons.

12The division of Kohath was subdivided into four groups named after his sons Amram, Izhar, Hebron, and Uzziel.

13*Amram* was the ancestor of Aaron and Moses. Aaron and his sons were set apart for the holy service of sacrificing the people's offerings to the Lord. He served the Lord constantly and pronounced blessings in his name at all times.

14,15As for Moses, the man of God, his sons, Gershom and Eliezer, were included with the tribe of Levi. 16*Gershom's* sons were led by Shebuel, 17and *Eliezer's* only son, Rehabiah, was the leader of his clan, for he had many children.

18The sons of *Izhar* were led by Shelomith.

19The sons of *Hebron* were led by Jeriah. Amariah was second in command, Jahaziel was third, and Jekameam was fourth.

20The sons of *Uzziel* were led by Micah, and Isshiah was the second in command.

21The sons of *Merari* were Mahli and Mushi. The sons of *Mahli* were Eleazar and Kish. 22*Eleazar* died without any sons, and his daughters were married to their cousins, the sons of *Kish*. 23*Mushi's* sons were Mahli, Eder, and Jeremoth.

24In the census, all the men of Levi who were twenty years old or older were classified under the names of these clans and subclans; and they were all assigned to the ministry at the Temple. 25For David said, "The Lord God of Israel has given us peace, and he will always live in Jerusalem. 26Now the Levites will no longer need to carry the Tabernacle and its instruments from place to place."

27(This census of the tribe of Levi was one of the last things David did before his death.) 28The work of the Levites was to assist the priests—the descendants of Aaron—in the sacrifices at the Temple; they also did the custodial work and helped perform the ceremonies of purification. 29They provided the Bread of the Presence, the flour for the grain offerings, and the wafers made without yeast (either fried or mixed with olive oil); they also checked all the weights and measures. 30Each morning and evening they stood before the Lord to sing thanks and praise to him. 31They assisted in the special sacrifices of burnt offerings, the Sabbath sacrifices, the new moon celebrations, and at all the festivals. There were always as many Levites present as were required for the occasion. 32And they took care of the Tabernacle and the Temple and assisted the priests in whatever way they were needed.

24 David Divides the Priests

The priests (the descendants of Aaron) were placed into two divisions named after Aaron's sons, Eleazar and Ithamar.

Nadab and Abihu were also sons of Aaron, but they died before their father did and had no children; so only Eleazar and Ithamar were left to carry on. 3David consulted with Zadok, who represented the Eleazar clan, and with Ahimelech, who represented the Ithamar clan; then he divided Aaron's descendants into many groups to serve at various times. 4*Eleazar's* descendants were divided into sixteen groups and *Ithamar's* into eight (for there was more leadership ability among the descendants of Eleazar).

5All tasks were assigned to the various groups by coin-toss so that there would be no preference, for there were many famous men and high officials of the Temple in each division. 6Shemaiah, a Levite and the son of Nethanel, acted as recording secretary and wrote down the names and assignments in the presence of the king and of these leaders: Zadok the priest, Ahimelech the son of Abiathar, and the heads of the priests and

Levites. Two groups from the division of Eleazar and one from the division of Ithamar were assigned to each task.

⁷⁻¹⁸The work was assigned (by coin-toss) in this order:

First, the group led by Jehoiarib;
Second, the group led by Jedaiah;
Third, the group led by Harim;
Fourth, the group led by Seorim;
Fifth, the group led by Malchijah;
Sixth, the group led by Mijamin;
Seventh, the group led by Hakkoz;
Eighth, the group led by Ahijah;
Ninth, the group led by Jeshua;
Tenth, the group led by Shecaniah;
Eleventh, the group led by Eliashib;
Twelfth, the group led by Jakim;
Thirteenth, the group led by Huppah;
Fourteenth, the group led by Jeshebeab;
Fifteenth, the group led by Bilgah;
Sixteenth, the group led by Immer;
Seventeenth, the group led by Hezir;
Eighteenth, the group led by Happizzez;
Nineteenth, the group led by Pethahiah;
Twentieth, the group led by Jehezkel;
Twenty-first, the group led by Jachin;
Twenty-second, the group led by Gamul;
Twenty-third, the group led by Delaiah;
Twenty-fourth, the group led by Maaziah.

¹⁹Each group carried out the Temple duties as originally assigned by God through their ancestor Aaron.

²⁰These were the other descendants of Levi: Amram; his descendant Shubael; and Shubael's descendant Jehdeiah; ²¹the Rehabiah group, led by his oldest son Isshiah; ²²the Izhar group, consisting of Shelamoth and his descendant Jahath. ²³The Hebron group: Jeriah, Hebron's oldest son; Amariah, his second son; Jahaziel, his third son; Jekameam, his fourth son.

²⁴,²⁵The Uzziel group was led by his son Micah and his grandsons Shamir and Isshiah, and by Isshiah's son Zechariah.

²⁶,²⁷The Merari group was led by his sons: Mahli and Mushi. (Jaaziah's group, led by his son Beno, included his brothers Shoham, Zaccur, and Ibri.) ²⁸*Mahli's* descendants were Eleazar, who had no sons, ²⁹and Kish, among whose sons was Jerahmeel. ³⁰The sons of *Mushi* were Mahli, Eder, and Jerimoth.

These were the descendants of Levi in their various clans. ³¹Like the descendants of Aaron, they were assigned to their duties by coin-toss without distinction as to age or rank. It was done in the presence of King David, Zadok, Ahimelech, and the leaders of the priests and the Levites.

25 The Musicians' Duties

David and the officials of the Tabernacle then appointed men to prophesy to the accompaniment of zithers, harps, and cymbals. These men were from the groups of Asaph, Heman, and Jeduthun. Here is a list of their names and their work:

²Under the leadership of Asaph, the king's private prophet, were his sons Zaccur, Joseph, Nethaniah, and Asharelah.

³Under Jeduthun, who led in giving thanks and praising the Lord (while accompanied by the zither), were his six sons: Gedaliah, Zeri, Jeshaiah, Shimei, Hashabiah, and Mattithiah.

⁴,⁵Under the direction of Heman, the king's private chaplain, were his sons: Bukkiah, Mattaniah, Uzziel, Shebuel, Jerimoth, Hananiah, Hanani, Eliathah, Geddalti, Romamti-ezer, Joshbekashah, Mallothi, Hothir, and Mahazioth. (For God had honored him with fourteen sons and three daughters.) ⁶,⁷Their music ministry included the playing of cymbals, harps, and zithers; all were under the direction of their father as they performed this ministry in the Tabernacle.

Asaph, Jeduthun, and Heman reported directly to the king. They and their families were all trained in singing praises to the Lord; each one—288 of them in all—was a master musician. ⁸The singers were appointed to their particular term of service by coin-toss, without regard to age or reputation.

⁹⁻³¹The first toss indicated Joseph of the Asaph clan;
The second, Gedaliah, along with twelve of his sons and brothers;
The third, Zaccur and twelve of his sons and brothers;
The fourth, Izri and twelve of his sons and brothers;
Fifth, Nethaniah and twelve of his sons and brothers;
Sixth, Bukkiah and twelve of his sons and brothers;
Seventh, Jesharelah and twelve of his sons and brothers;
Eighth, Jeshaiah and twelve of his sons and brothers;
Ninth, Mattaniah and twelve of his sons and brothers;
Tenth, Shimei and twelve of his sons and brothers;
Eleventh, Azarel and twelve of his sons and brothers;
Twelfth, Hashabiah and twelve of his sons and brothers;
Thirteenth, Shubael and twelve of his sons and brothers;

Fourteenth, Mattithiah and twelve of his sons and brothers;
Fifteenth, Jeremoth and twelve of his sons and brothers;
Sixteenth, Hananiah and twelve of his sons and brothers;
Seventeenth, Joshbekasha and twelve of his sons and brothers;
Eighteenth, Hanani and twelve of his sons and brothers;
Nineteenth, Mallothi and twelve of his sons and brothers;
Twentieth, Eliathah and twelve of his sons and brothers;
Twenty-first, Hothir and twelve of his sons and brothers;
Twenty-second, Giddalti and twelve of his sons and brothers;
Twenty-third, Mahazioth and twelve of his sons and brothers;
Twenty-fourth, Romamti-ezer and twelve of his sons and brothers.

26 The Temple Guards' Duties

The temple guards were from the Asaph division of the Korah clan. The captain of the guard was Meshelemiah, the son of Kore.

2,3 His sergeants were his sons: Zechariah (the oldest), Jediael (the second), Zebadiah (the third), Jathniel (the fourth), Elam (the fifth), Jehohanan (the sixth), Eliehoenai (the seventh).

4,5 The sons of Obed-edom were also appointed as Temple guards: Shemaiah (the oldest), Jehozabad (the second), Joah (the third), Sacar (the fourth), Nethanel (the fifth), Ammiel (the sixth), Issachar (the seventh), Peullethai (the eighth).

What a blessing God gave him with all those sons!

6,7 Shemaiah's sons were all outstanding men and had positions of great authority in their clan. Their names were: Othni, Rephael, Obed, Elzabad.

Their brave brothers, Elihu and Semachiah, were also very able men.

8 All of these sons and grandsons of Obed-edom—all sixty-two of them—were outstanding men who were particularly well qualified for their work. 9 Meshelemiah's eighteen sons and brothers, too, were real leaders. 10 Hosah, one of the Merari group, appointed Shimri as the leader among his sons, though he was not the oldest. 11 The names of some of his other sons were: Hilkiah, the second; Tebaliah, the third; Zechariah, the fourth.

Hosah's sons and brothers numbered thirteen in all.

12 The divisions of the Temple guards were named after the leaders. Like the other Levites, they were responsible to minister at the Temple. 13 They were assigned guard duty at the various gates without regard to the reputation of their families, for it was all done by coin-toss. 14,15 The responsibility of the east gate went to Shelemiah and his group; of the north gate to his son Zechariah, a man of unusual wisdom; of the south gate to Obed-edom and his group (his sons were given charge of the storehouses); 16 of the west gate and the Shallecheth Gate on the upper road, to Shuppim and Hosah. 17 Six guards were assigned daily to the east gate, four to the north gate, four to the south gate, and two to each of the storehouses. 18 Six guards were assigned each day to the west gate, four to the upper road, and two to the nearby areas. 19 The Temple guards were chosen from the clans of Korah and Merari.

20-22 Other Levites, led by Ahijah, were given the care of the gifts brought to the Lord and placed in the Temple treasury. These men of the Ladan subclan from the clan of Gershom included Zetham and Joel, the sons of Jehieli. 23,24 Shebuel, son of Gershom and grandson of Moses, was the chief officer of the treasury. He was in charge of the divisions named after Amram, Izhar, Hebron, and Uzziel.

25 The line of descendants from Eliezer went through Rehabiah, Jeshaiah, Joram, Zichri, and Shelomoth. 26 Shelomoth and his brothers were appointed to care for the gifts given to the Lord by King David and the other leaders of the nation such as the officers and generals of the army. 27 For these men dedicated their war loot to support the operating expenses of the Temple. 28 Shelomoth and his brothers were also responsible for the care of the items dedicated to the Lord by Samuel the prophet, Saul the son of Kish, Abner the son of Ner, Joab the son of Zeruiah, and anyone else of distinction who brought gifts to the Lord.

29 Chenaniah and his sons (from the subclan of Izhar) were appointed public administrators and judges. 30 Hashabiah and 1,700 of his clansmen from Hebron, all outstanding men, were placed in charge of the territory of Israel west of the Jordan River; they were responsible for the religious affairs and public administration of that area. 31,32 Twenty-seven hundred outstanding men of

---

GIVING TO GOD 26:27 War loot rightfully belonged to the victorious army. These soldiers, however, gave their portion of all the battle spoils to the Temple to express their dedication to God. Like these soldiers, we should think of what we *can* give, rather than what we are obligated to give. Is your giving a matter of rejoicing rather than duty? Give as a response of joy and love for God and others. **To begin the series of devotionals on GIVING TO GOD, turn to page 105.**

the clan of the Hebronites, under the supervision of Jerijah, were appointed to control the religious and public affairs of the tribes of Reuben, Gad, and the half-tribe of Manasseh. These men, all of whom had excellent qualifications, were appointed on the basis of their ancestry and ability at Jazer in Gilead in the fortieth year of King David's reign.

27 The Commanders of the Army

The Israeli army was divided into twelve regiments, each with 24,000 troops, including officers and administrative staff. These units were called up for active duty one month each year. Here is the list of the units and their regimental commanders:

2,3 The commander of the First Division was Jashobeam. He had charge of 24,000 troops who were on duty the first month of each year.

4 The commander of the Second Division was Dodai (a descendant of Ahohi). He had charge of 24,000 troops who were on duty the second month of each year. Mikloth was his executive officer.

5,6 The commander of the Third Division was Benaiah. His 24,000 men were on duty the third month of each year. (He was the son of Jehoiada the High Priest and was the chief of the thirty highest-ranking officers in David's army.) His son Ammizabad succeeded him as division commander.

7 The commander of the Fourth Division was Asahel (the brother of Joab), who was later replaced by his son Zebadiah. He had 24,000 men on duty the fourth month of each year.

8 The commander of the Fifth Division was Shamuth from Izrah, with 24,000 men on duty the fifth month of each year.

9 The commander of the Sixth Division was Ira, the son of Ikkesh from Tekoa; he had 24,000 men on duty the sixth month of each year.

10 The commander of the Seventh Division was Helez from Pelona in Ephraim, with 24,000 men on duty the seventh month of each year.

11 The commander of the Eighth Division was Sibbecai of the Hushite subclan from Zerah, who had 24,000 men on duty the eighth month of each year.

12 The commander of the Ninth Division was Abiezer (from Anathoth in the tribe of Benjamin), who commanded 24,000 troops during the ninth month of each year.

13 The commander of the Tenth Division was Maharai from Netophah in Zerah, with 24,000 men on duty the tenth month of each year.

14 The commander of the Eleventh Division was Benaiah from Pirathon in Ephraim, with 24,000 men on duty during the eleventh month of each year.

15 The commander of the Twelfth Division was Heldai from Netophah in the area of Othniel, who commanded 24,000 men on duty during the twelfth month of each year.

16-22 The top political officers of the tribes of Israel were as follows:

Over Reuben, Eliezer (son of Zichri);
Over Simeon, Shephatiah (son of Maacah);
Over Levi, Hashabiah (son of Kemuel);
Over the descendants of Aaron, Zadok;
Over Judah, Elihu (a brother of King David);
Over Issachar, Omri (son of Michael);
Over Zebulun, Ishmaiah (son of Obadiah);
Over Naphtali, Jeremoth (son of Azriel);
Over Ephraim, Hoshea (son of Azaziah);
Over the half-tribe of Manasseh, Joel (son of Pedaiah);
Over the other half of Manasseh, in Gilead, Iddo (son of Zechariah);
Over Benjamin, Jaasiel (son of Abner);
Over Dan, Azarel (son of Jeroham).

23 When David took his census, he didn't include the twenty-year-olds or those younger, for the Lord had promised a population explosion for his people. 24 Joab began the census, but he never finished it, for the anger of God broke out upon Israel; the final total was never put into the annals of King David.

25 Azmaveth (son of Adiel) was the chief financial officer in charge of the palace treasuries, and Jonathan (son of Uzziah) was chief of the regional treasuries throughout the cities, villages, and fortresses of Israel.

26 Ezri (son of Chelub) was manager of the laborers on the king's estates. 27 And Shimei from Ramath had the oversight of the king's vineyards; and Zabdi from Shiphma was responsible for his wine production and storage. 28 Baal-hanan from Gedera was responsible for the king's olive yards and sycamore trees in the lowlands bordering Philistine territory, while Joash had charge of the supplies of olive oil.

29 Shitrai from Sharon was in charge of the cattle on the Plains of Sharon, and Shaphat (son of Adlai) had charge of those in the valleys. 30 Obil, from the territory of Ishmael, had charge of the camels, and Jehdeiah from Meronoth had charge of the donkeys. 31 The sheep were under the care of Jaziz the Hagrite. These men were King David's overseers.

32 The attendant to the king's sons was Jonathan, David's uncle, a wise counselor and an educated man. Jehiel (the son of Hachmoni) was their tutor.

Family Devotions

☐ **Devotion 126**

Serving God Willingly

Read 1 Chronicles 28:8-20

Christa enjoyed occasionally playing the piano for the opening exercises in Sunday school. But then Ken asked her to accompany his trumpet solo at Bible club. "I suppose I can," she agreed reluctantly.

During the next few months, Mom noticed that Christa was often invited to play for various groups. She usually agreed to play, but she did so without much enthusiasm. Her face often looked gloomy, and she grumbled about how busy it made her.

Then one evening Christa spoke to her older brother, Bill, as he left the dinner table. "Would you help me with my math? I just don't understand it."

"I've got things to do," Bill replied. "Call one of your friends to help you."

"I'm sure you can take a little time to help your sister," suggested Mom.

"Oh, all right," Bill growled. "I'll be in my room. Call when you need me." He stomped out.

"Oh, Mom!" wailed Christa. "When he's so grouchy about it, I don't even feel like having him help me. But I do need help. Why can't he be nice about it?"

"Are you always pleasant when people ask you to do something?" asked Mom gently.

Christa blushed as she remembered how unhappily she had promised to play for someone just that afternoon. "Well, I never thought about how it would make them feel," she admitted. "I guess other people don't like my attitude any more than I like Bill's. I'll try to help out a little more cheerfully from now on!"

Serving God Willingly
Memory Verse

Anyone who takes care of a little child like this is caring for me! And whoever cares for me is caring for God who sent me. Your care for others is the measure of your greatness.
Luke 9:48

How About You?
Are you grumpy when you are asked to serve in some way? Solomon was told to serve God with a "clean heart and a willing mind." That's good advice for Christians, too. You should be happy to serve the Lord who has done so much for you. H.M.

- For the next devotional, turn to page 437.   • For the next devotional on *Serving God Willingly*, turn to page 667.
- For notes on *Serving God Willingly*, see pages 49, 419, 890, 920, and 922.

³³Ahithophel was the king's official counselor, and Hushai the Archite was his personal advisor. ³⁴Ahithophel was assisted by Jehoiada (the son of Benaiah) and by Abiathar. Joab was commander-in-chief of the Israeli army.

28 Plans for the Temple

David now summoned all of his officials to Jerusalem—the political leaders, the commanders of the twelve army divisions, the other army officers, those in charge of his property and livestock, and all the other men of authority in his kingdom. ²He rose and stood before them and addressed them as follows:

"My brothers and my people! It was my desire to build a temple in which the Ark of the Covenant of the Lord could rest—a place for our God to live in. I have now collected everything that is necessary for the building, ³but God has told me, 'You are not to build my temple, for you are a warrior and have shed much blood.'

⁴"Nevertheless, the Lord God of Israel has chosen me from among all my father's family to begin a dynasty that will rule Israel forever; he has chosen the tribe of Judah, and from among the families of Judah, my father's family; and from among his sons, the Lord took pleasure in me and has made me king over all Israel. ⁵And from among my sons—the Lord has given me many children—he has chosen Solomon to succeed me on the throne of his Kingdom of Israel. ⁶He has told me, 'Your son Solomon shall build my Temple; for I have chosen him as my son and I will be his father. ⁷And if he continues to obey my commandments and instructions as he has until now, I will make his kingdom last forever.'"

⁸Then David turned to Solomon and said:

"Here before the leaders of Israel, the people of God, and in the sight of our God, I am instructing you to search out every commandment of the Lord so that you may continue to rule this good land and leave it to your children to rule forever. ⁹Solomon, my son, get to know the God of your fathers. Worship and serve him with a clean heart and a willing mind, for the Lord sees every heart and understands and knows every thought. If you seek him, you will find him; but if you forsake him, he will permanently throw you aside. ¹⁰So be very careful, for the Lord has chosen you to build his holy Temple. Be strong and do as he commands."

¹¹Then David gave Solomon the blueprint of the Temple and its surroundings—the treasuries, the upstairs rooms, the inside rooms, and the sanctuary for the place of mercy. ¹²He also gave Solomon his plans for the outer court, the outside rooms, the Temple storage areas, and the treasuries for the gifts dedicated by famous persons. For the Holy Spirit had given David all these plans. ¹³ The king also passed on to Solomon the instructions concerning the work of the various groups of priests and Levites; and he gave specifications for each item in the Temple which was to be used for worship and sacrifice.

¹⁴David weighed out enough gold and silver to make these various items, ¹⁵as well as the specific amount of gold needed for the lampstands and lamps. He also weighed out enough silver for the silver candlesticks and lamps, each according to its use. ¹⁶He weighed out the gold for the table on which the Bread of the Presence would be placed and for the other gold tables, and he weighed the silver for the silver tables. ¹⁷Then he weighed out the gold for the solid gold hooks used in handling the sacrificial meat and for the basins, cups, and bowls of gold and silver. ¹⁸Finally, he weighed out the refined gold for the altar of incense and for the gold angels whose wings were stretched over the Ark of the Covenant of the Lord.

¹⁹"Every part of this blueprint," David told Solomon, "was given to me in writing from the hand of the Lord." ²⁰Then he continued, "Be strong and courageous and get to work. Don't be frightened by the size of the task, for the Lord my God is with you; he will not forsake you. He will see to it that everything is finished correctly. ²¹And these various groups of priests and Levites will serve in the Temple. Others with skills of every kind will volunteer, and the army and the entire nation are at your command."

29 The People Bring Gifts

Then King David turned to the entire assembly and said: "My son Solomon, whom God has chosen to be the next king of Israel, is still young and inexperienced, and the work ahead of him is enormous; for the temple he will build is not just another building—it is for the Lord God himself! ²Using every resource at my command, I have gathered as much as I could for building it—enough gold, silver, bronze, iron, wood, and great quantities of onyx, other precious stones, costly jewels, and marble. ³And now, because of my devotion to the Temple of God, I am giving all of my own private treasures to aid in the construction. This is in addition to the building materials I have already collected. ⁴,⁵These personal contributions consist of millions of dollars of gold from Ophir and huge amounts of silver to be used for overlaying the walls of the buildings. It will also be used for the articles made of gold and silver and for the artistic decorations. Now then, who will follow my example? Who will give himself and all that he has to the Lord?"

Family Devotions

☐ DEVOTION 127
GIVING THANKS

Read 1 Chronicles 29:10-20

Tim began eating his cereal. "You didn't pray," his sister reminded him.

Tim shrugged. "I'm in a hurry."

It was Tim's turn to stack the breakfast dishes. Usually Mom thanked him for his help, but today she didn't say anything, even though Tim had done a good job.

On the way to school, Tim saw a younger child fall and drop several books. Tim hurried to help him. The child grabbed the books and ran off without even looking at Tim. *What an ungrateful kid!* thought Tim.

At recess, Tim offered to pass out papers. Up and down the rows he went, putting the papers on the desks. When he was finished, his teacher glanced up. "You can go now," she said absently. Didn't she even appreciate his help?

On Tim's paper route, there was an old man crippled with arthritis. Since it was hard for him to bend over, Tim always rang his doorbell and handed the paper to him. Today the man grumbled, "I've been looking for you. You're late!"

I don't mind the extra trouble of waiting for him to answer his door, Tim thought, *but it sure would be nice to know he liked what I do for him.*

"Why the sad face, Tim?" asked Mrs. Brown, a nice lady who lived on his street.

"Oh, nothing big. But it just seems as though everyone takes me for granted," complained Tim.

"I've felt that way myself," said Mrs. Brown. "And I'm sure God must feel that way often."

"Why would he feel that way?"

"Well, I appreciate all he does for me," said Mrs. Brown, "but so often I neglect to tell him. And I want to tell you, Tim, I appreciate having you for a friend and neighbor."

Tim smiled and felt better, but he was thoughtful as he walked home. The next morning he quietly thanked God for his food before he began to eat.

Giving Thanks Memory Verse

Is anyone among you suffering? He should keep on praying about it. And those who have reason to be thankful should continually be singing praises to the Lord.
James 5:13

How About You?
Do you get tired of thanking God for your food at every meal? How about all your other blessings? Maybe you do appreciate them, but do you thank God in your own words for all he gives you? God enjoys hearing you say thank you. *C. Y.*

• For the next devotional, turn to page 445.   • For the next devotional on GIVING THANKS, turn to page 559.
• For notes on GIVING THANKS, see pages 582, 608, and 834.

6,7 Then the clan leaders, the heads of the tribes, the army officers, and the administrative officers of the king pledged huge sums of gold, silver and foreign currency, also 675 tons of bronze and 3,750 tons of iron. 8 They also contributed great amounts of jewelry, which were deposited at the Temple treasury with Jehiel (a descendant of Gershom). 9 Everyone was excited and happy for this opportunity of service, and King David was moved with deep joy.

10 While still in the presence of the whole assembly, David expressed his praises to the Lord: "O Lord God of our father Israel, praise your name for ever and ever! 11 Yours is the mighty power and glory and victory and majesty. Everything in the heavens and earth is yours, O Lord, and this is your kingdom. We adore you as being in control of everything. 12 Riches and honor come from you alone, and you are the Ruler of all mankind; your hand controls power and might, and it is at your discretion that men are made great and given strength. 13 O our God, we thank you and praise your glorious name, 14 but who am I and who are my people that we should be permitted to give anything to you? Everything we have has come from you, and we only give you what is yours already! 15 For we are here for but a moment, strangers in the land as our fathers were before us; our days on earth are like a shadow, gone so soon, without a trace. 16 O Lord our God, all of this material that we have gathered to build a temple for your holy name comes from you! It all belongs to you! 17 I know, my God, that you test men to see if they are good; for you enjoy good men. I have done all this with good motives, and I have watched your people offer their gifts willingly and joyously.

18 "O Lord, God of our fathers Abraham, Isaac, and Israel! Make your people always want to obey you, and see to it that their love for you never changes. 19 Give my son Solomon a good heart toward God, so that he will want to obey you in the smallest detail and will look forward eagerly to finishing the building of your temple, for which I have made all of these preparations."

20 Then David said to all the people, "Give praise to the Lord your God!" And they did, bowing low before the Lord and the king.

21 The next day they brought a thousand young bulls, a thousand rams, and a thousand lambs as burnt offerings to the Lord; they also offered drink offerings and many other sacrifices on behalf of all Israel. 22 Then they feasted and drank before the Lord with great joy.

And again they crowned King David's son Solomon as their king. They anointed him before the Lord as their leader, and they anointed Zadok as their priest. 23 So God appointed Solomon to take the throne of his father David; and he prospered greatly, and all Israel obeyed him. 24 The national leaders, the army officers, and his brothers all pledged their allegiance to King Solomon. 25 And the Lord gave him great popularity with all the people of Israel, and he amassed even greater wealth and honor than his father.

26,27 David was king of the land of Israel for forty years; seven of them during his reign in Hebron and thirty-three in Jerusalem. 28 He died at an old age, wealthy and honored; and his son Solomon reigned in his place. 29 Detailed biographies of King David have been written in the history of Samuel the prophet, the history written by Nathan the prophet, and in the history written by the prophet Gad. 30 These accounts tell of his reign and of his might and all that happened to him and to Israel and to the kings of the nearby nations.

2 Chronicles

HOW DO you feel when you see God answer your prayers? You'll see a lot of answered prayers in 2 Chronicles.

This book tells the story of the kings again, from Solomon's reign to the fall of Jerusalem. It brings out the relationship the kings had with God. It focuses on their spiritual decisions as much as their governing decisions.

When the kings prayed, God answered. They prayed to dedicate themselves to God. They cried out to God when huge armies came against them. They prayed for the people they ruled, asking God to forgive them for sinning. God answered these prayers in amazing ways.

The kings who *didn't* pray saw God in action, too. They didn't ask God to help them or protect them, so he didn't. They told God to go away and leave them alone, so he did. They learned that life without God's friendship is awful. God sent many prophets to tell the kings and people to turn back to him, but the people didn't listen.

Second Chronicles shows us that God responds to our prayers—and to our lack of prayers. Look for reasons to stick close to God as you read this book.

Solomon Asks God for Wisdom

King David's son Solomon was now the undisputed ruler of Israel, for the Lord his God had made him a powerful monarch. 2,3He summoned all the army officers and judges to Gibeon as well as all the political and religious leaders of Israel. He led them up to the hill to the old Tabernacle constructed by Moses, the Lord's assistant, while he was in the wilderness. 4(There was a later Tabernacle in Jerusalem, built by King David for the Ark of God when he removed it from Kiriath-jearim.) 5,6The bronze altar made by Bezalel (son of Uri, son of Hur) still stood in front of the old Tabernacle, and now Solomon and those he had invited assembled themselves before it, as he sacrificed upon it 1,000 burnt offerings to the Lord.

7That night God appeared to Solomon and told him, "Ask me for anything, and I will give it to you!"

8Solomon replied, "O God, you have been so kind and good to my father David, and now you have given me the kingdom—9this is all I want!

For you have fulfilled your promise to David my father and have made me king over a nation as full of people as the earth is full of dust! ¹⁰Now give me wisdom and knowledge to rule them properly, for who is able to govern by himself such a great nation as this one of yours?"

¹¹God replied, "Because your greatest desire is to help your people, and you haven't asked for personal wealth and honor, and you haven't asked me to curse your enemies, and you haven't asked for a long life, but for wisdom and knowledge to properly guide my people—¹²yes, I am giving you the wisdom and knowledge you asked for! And I am also giving you riches, wealth, and honor such as no other king has ever had before you! And there will never again be so great a king in all the world!"

¹³Solomon then left the Tabernacle, returned down the hill, and went back to Jerusalem to rule Israel. ¹⁴He built up a huge force of 1,400 chariots and recruited 12,000 cavalry to guard the cities where the chariots were garaged, though some, of course, were stationed at Jerusalem near the king. ¹⁵During Solomon's reign, silver and gold were as plentiful in Jerusalem as rocks on the road! And expensive cedar lumber was used like common sycamore! ¹⁶Solomon sent horse-traders to Egypt to purchase entire herds at wholesale prices. ¹⁷At that time Egyptian chariots sold for $400 each and horses for $100, delivered at Jerusalem. Many of these were then resold to the kings of the Hittites and Syria.

2 Solomon Makes Plans

Solomon now decided that the time had come to build a temple for the Lord and a palace for himself. ²This required a force of 70,000 laborers, 80,000 stonecutters in the hills, and 3,600 foremen. ³Solomon sent an ambassador to King Hiram at Tyre, requesting shipments of cedar lumber such as Hiram had supplied to David when he was building his palace.

⁴"I am about to build a temple for the Lord my God," Solomon told Hiram. "It will be a place where I can burn incense and sweet spices before God, and display the special sacrificial bread, and sacrifice burnt offerings each morning and evening, and on the Sabbaths, and at the new moon celebration and other regular festivals of the Lord our God. For God wants Israel always to celebrate these special occasions. ⁵It is going to be a wonderful temple because he is a great God, greater than any other. ⁶But who can ever build him a worthy home? Not even the highest heaven would be beautiful enough! And who am I to be allowed to build a temple for God? But it will be a place to worship him.

⁷"So send me skilled craftsmen—goldsmiths and silversmiths, brass and iron workers; and send me weavers to make purple, crimson, and blue cloth; and skilled engravers to work beside the craftsmen of Judah and Jerusalem who were selected by my father David. ⁸Also send me cedar trees, fir trees, and algum trees from the Forests of Lebanon, for your men are without equal as lumbermen, and I will send my men to help them. ⁹An immense amount of lumber will be needed, for the temple I am going to build will be large and incredibly beautiful. ¹⁰As to the financial arrangements, I will pay your men 20,000 sacks of crushed wheat, 20,000 barrels of barley, 20,000 barrels of wine, and 20,000 barrels of olive oil."

¹¹King Hiram replied to King Solomon: "It is because the Lord loves his people that he has made you their king! ¹²Blessed be the Lord God of Israel who made the heavens and the earth and who has given to David such a wise, intelligent, and understanding son to build God's Temple and a royal palace for himself.

¹³"I am sending you a master craftsman—my famous Huramabi! He is a brilliant man, ¹⁴the son of a Jewish woman from Dan in Israel; his father is from here in Tyre. He is a skillful goldsmith and silversmith, and also does exquisite work with brass and iron and knows all about stonework, carpentry, and weaving; and he is an expert in the dyeing of purple and blue linen and crimson cloth. He is an engraver besides, and an inventor! He will work with your craftsmen and those appointed by my lord David, your father. ¹⁵So send along the wheat, barley, olive oil, and wine you mentioned, ¹⁶and we will begin cutting wood from the Lebanon mountains, as much as you need, and bring it to you in log floats across the sea to Joppa, and from there you can take them inland to Jerusalem."

¹⁷Solomon now took a census of all foreigners in the country (just as his father David had done) and found that there were 153,600 of them. ¹⁸He indentured 70,000 as common laborers, 80,000 as loggers, and 3,600 as foremen.

3 The Construction Begins

Finally the actual construction of the Temple began. Its location was in Jerusalem at the top of Mount Moriah, where the Lord had appeared to Solomon's father, King David, and where the threshing-floor of Ornan the Jebusite had been. David had selected it as the site for the Temple. ²The actual construction began on the seventeenth day of April in the fourth year of King Solomon's reign.

³The foundation was ninety feet long and thirty feet wide. ⁴A covered porch ran along the entire

thirty-foot width of the Temple, with the inner walls and ceiling overlaid with pure gold! The roof was 180 feet high.

⁵The main part of the Temple was paneled with cypress wood, plated with pure gold, and engraved with palm trees and chains. ⁶Beautiful jewels were inlaid into the walls to add to the beauty; the gold, by the way, was of the best, from Parvaim. ⁷All the walls, beams, doors, and thresholds throughout the Temple were plated with gold, with angels engraved on the walls.

⁸Within the Temple, at one end, was the most sacred room—the Holy of Holies—thirty feet square. This too was overlaid with the finest gold, valued at millions of dollars. ⁹Twenty-six-ounce gold nails were used. The upper rooms were also plated with pure gold.

¹⁰Within the innermost room, the Holy of Holies, Solomon placed two sculptured statues of angels and plated them with gold. ¹¹⁻¹³They stood on the floor facing the outer room, with wings stretched wingtip to wingtip across the room, from wall to wall. ¹⁴Across the entrance to this room he placed a veil of blue and crimson finespun linen, decorated with angels.

¹⁵At the front of the Temple were two pillars 52½ feet high, topped by a 7½-foot capital flaring out to the roof. ¹⁶He made chains and placed them on top of the pillars, with 100 pomegranates attached to the chains. ¹⁷Then he set up the pillars at the front of the Temple, one on the right and the other on the left. And he gave them names: Jachin (the one on the right), and Boaz (the one on the left).

4 Huramabi's Skillful Work

He also made a bronze altar 30 feet long, 30 feet wide, and 15 feet high. ²Then he forged a huge round tank 15 feet across from rim to rim. The rim stood 7½ feet above the floor, and was 45 feet around. ³The tank was encircled at its base by two rows of gourd designs, cast as part of the tank. ⁴The tank stood on twelve metal oxen facing outward; three faced north, three faced west, three faced south, and three faced east. ⁵The walls of the tank were five inches thick, flaring out like the cup of a lily. It held 3,000 barrels of water.

⁶He also constructed ten vats for water to wash the offerings, five to the right of the huge tank and five to the left. The priests used the tank, and not the vats, for their own washing.

⁷Carefully following God's instructions, he then cast ten gold lampstands and placed them in the Temple, five against each wall; ⁸he also built ten tables and placed five against each wall on the right and left. And he molded 100 solid gold bowls. ⁹Then he constructed a court for the priests, also the public court, and overlaid the doors of these courts with bronze. ¹⁰The huge tank was in the southeast corner of the outer room of the Temple. ¹¹Huramabi also made the necessary pots, shovels, and basins for use in connection with the sacrifices.

So at last he completed the work assigned to him by King Solomon:

¹²⁻¹⁶The construction of the two pillars,
The two flared capitals on the tops of the pillars,
The two sets of chains on the capitals,
The 400 pomegranates hanging from the two sets of chains on the capitals,
The bases for the vats and the vats themselves,
The huge tank and the twelve oxen under it,
The pots, shovels, and fleshhooks.

This skillful craftsman, Huramabi, made all of the above-mentioned items for King Solomon using polished bronze. ¹⁷,¹⁸The king did the casting at the claybanks of the Jordan valley between Succoth and Zeredah. Great quantities of bronze were used, too heavy to weigh.

¹⁹Solomon commanded that all of the furnishings of the Temple—the utensils, the altar, and the table for the Bread of the Presence must be made of gold; ²⁰also the lamps and lampstands, ²¹the floral decorations, tongs, ²²lamp snuffers, basins, spoons, and firepans—all were made of solid gold. Even the doorway of the Temple, the main door, and the inner doors to the Holy of Holies were overlaid with gold.

5 The Ark and the Temple

So the Temple was finally finished. Then Solomon brought in the gifts dedicated to the Lord by his father, King David. They were stored in the Temple treasuries.

²Solomon now summoned to Jerusalem all of the leaders of Israel—the heads of the tribes and clans—for the ceremony of transferring the Ark from the [Tabernacle in the] City of David, also known as Zion, [to its new home in the Temple]. ³This celebration took place in October at the annual Festival of Tabernacles. ⁴,⁵As the leaders of Israel watched, the Levites lifted the Ark and carried it out of the Tabernacle, along with all the other sacred vessels. ⁶King Solomon and the others sacrificed sheep and oxen before the Ark in such numbers that no one tried to keep count!

⁷,⁸Then the priests carried the Ark into the inner room of the Temple—the Holy of Holies—and placed it beneath the angels' wings; their wings spread over the Ark and its carrying poles. ⁹These carrying poles were so long that their

ends could be seen from the outer room, but not from the outside doorway.

The Ark is still there at the time of this writing. [10]Nothing was in the Ark except the two stone tablets that Moses had put there at Mount Horeb, when the Lord made a covenant with the people of Israel as they were leaving Egypt.

[11,12]When the priests had undergone the purification rites for themselves, they all took part in the ceremonies without regard to their normal duties. And how the Levites were praising the Lord as the priests came out of the Holy of Holies! The singers were Asaph, Heman, Jeduthun, and all their sons and brothers, dressed in fine-spun linen robes and standing at the east side of the altar. The choir was accompanied by 120 priests who were trumpeters, while others played the cymbals, lyres, and harps. [13,14]The band and chorus united as one to praise and thank the Lord; their selections were interspersed with trumpet obbligatos, the clashing of cymbals, and the loud playing of other musical instruments—all praising and thanking the Lord. Their theme was "He is so good! His loving-kindness lasts forever!"

And at that moment the glory of the Lord, coming as a bright cloud, filled the Temple so that the priests could not continue their work.

6 Solomon Blesses the People

This is the prayer prayed by Solomon on that occasion:

"The Lord has said that he would live in the
  thick darkness,
But I have made a Temple for you, O Lord, to
  live in forever!"

[3]Then the king turned around to the people and they stood to receive his blessing:

[4]"Blessed be the Lord God of Israel," he said to them, "the God who talked personally to my father David and has now fulfilled the promise he made to him. For he told him, [5,6]'I have never before, since bringing my people from the land of Egypt, chosen a city anywhere in Israel as the location of my Temple where my name will be glorified; and never before have I chosen a king for my people Israel. But now I have chosen Jerusalem as that city, and David as that king.'

[7]"My father David wanted to build this Temple, [8]but the Lord said not to. It was good to have the desire, the Lord told him, [9]but he was not the one to build it: his son was chosen for that task. [10]And now the Lord has done what he promised, for I have become king in my father's place, and I have built the Temple for the Name of the Lord God of Israel [11]and placed the Ark there. And in the Ark is the Covenant between the Lord and his people Israel."

[12,13]As he spoke, Solomon was standing before the people on a platform in the center of the outer court, in front of the altar of the Lord. The platform was made of bronze, $7\frac{1}{2}$ feet square and $4\frac{1}{2}$ feet high. Now, as all the people watched, he knelt down, reached out his arms toward heaven, and prayed this prayer:

[14]"O Lord God of Israel, there is no God like you in all of heaven and earth. You are the God who keeps his kind promises to all those who obey you and who are anxious to do your will. [15]And you have kept your promise to my father David, as is evident today. [16]And now, O God of Israel, carry out your further promise to him that 'your descendants shall always reign over Israel if they will obey my laws as you have.' [17]Yes, Lord God of Israel, please fulfill this promise too. [18]But will God really live upon the earth with men? Why, even the heaven and the heaven of heavens cannot contain you—how much less this Temple I have built!

[19]"How I pray that you will heed my prayers, O Lord my God! Listen to my prayer that I am praying to you now! [20,21]Look down with favor day and night upon this Temple—upon this place where you have said that you would put your name. May you always hear and answer the prayers I will pray to you as I face toward this place. Listen to my prayers and to those of your people Israel when they pray toward this Temple; yes, hear us from heaven, and when you hear, forgive.

[22]"Whenever someone commits a crime and is required to swear to his innocence before this altar, [23]then hear from heaven and punish him if he is lying, or else declare him innocent.

[24]"If your people Israel are destroyed before their enemies because they have sinned against you, and if they turn to you and call themselves your people, and pray to you here in this Temple, [25]then listen to them from heaven and forgive their sins and give them back this land you gave to their fathers.

[26]"When the skies are shut and there is no rain because of our sins, and then we pray toward this Temple and claim you as our God, and turn from our sins because you have punished us, [27]then

---

PRAYING AT ALL TIMES 6:30 Have you ever felt far from God, separated by feelings of failure and personal problems? In his prayer, Solomon underscores the fact that God stands ready to hear us, to forgive our sins, and to restore our relationship to him. God is waiting and listening for our confessions of guilt and willingness to obey him. He is ready to forgive us and restore us to fellowship with him. Don't wait to experience this loving forgiveness. **To begin the series of devotionals on PRAYING AT ALL TIMES, turn to page 45.**

listen from heaven and forgive the sins of your people, and teach them what is right; and send rain upon this land that you have given to your people as their own property.

[28] "If there is a famine in the land, or plagues, or crop disease, or attacks of locusts or caterpillars, or if your people's enemies are in the land besieging our cities—whatever the trouble is— [29] listen to every individual's prayer concerning his private sorrow, as well as all the public prayers. [30] Hear from heaven where you live and forgive, and give each one whatever he deserves, for you know the hearts of all mankind. [31] Then they will reverence you forever and will continually walk where you tell them to go.

[32] "And when foreigners hear of your power, and come from distant lands to worship your great name, and to pray toward this Temple, [33] hear them from heaven where you live, and do what they request of you. Then all the peoples of the earth will hear of your fame and will reverence you, just as your people Israel do; and they too will know that this Temple I have built is truly yours.

[34] "If your people go out at your command to fight their enemies, and they pray toward this city of Jerusalem that you have chosen, and this Temple that I have built for your name, [35] then hear their prayers from heaven and give them success.

[36] "If they sin against you (and who has never sinned?) and you become angry with them, and you let their enemies defeat them and take them away as captives to some foreign nation near or far; [37,38] and if in that land of exile they turn to you again, and face toward this land you gave their fathers and this city and your Temple I have built, and plead with you with all their hearts to forgive them, [39] then hear from heaven where you live and help them, and forgive your people who have sinned against you.

[40] "Yes, O my God, be wide awake and attentive to all the prayers made to you in this place. [41] And now, O Lord God, arise and enter this resting place of yours where the Ark of your strength has been placed. Let your priests, O Lord God, be clothed with salvation, and let your people rejoice in your kind deeds. [42] O Lord God, do not ignore me—do not turn your face away from me, your anointed one. Oh, remember your love for David and your kindness to him."

7

God's Glory Fills the Temple

As Solomon finished praying, fire flashed down from heaven and burned up the sacrifices! And the glory of the Lord filled the Temple, so that the priests couldn't enter! [3] All the people had been watching, and now they fell flat on the pavement and worshiped and thanked the Lord.

"How good he is!" they exclaimed. "He is always so loving and kind."

[4,5] Then the king and all the people dedicated the Temple by sacrificing burnt offerings to the Lord. King Solomon's contribution for this purpose was 22,000 oxen and 120,000 sheep. [6] The priests were standing at their posts of duty, and the Levites were playing their thanksgiving song, "His Loving-kindness Is Forever," using the musical instruments King David himself had made and had used to praise the Lord. Then, when the priests blew the trumpets, all the people stood again. [7] Solomon consecrated the inner court of the Temple for use that day as a place of sacrifice because there were too many sacrifices for the bronze altar to accommodate.

[8] For the next seven days they celebrated the Tabernacle Festival, with large crowds coming in from all over Israel; they arrived from as far away as Hamath at one end of the country to the brook of Egypt at the other. [9] A final religious service was held on the eighth day. [10] Then on October 7 he sent the people home, joyful and happy because the Lord had been so good to David and Solomon and to his people Israel.

[11] So Solomon finished building the Temple as well as his own palace. He completed what he had planned to do.

[12] One night the Lord appeared to Solomon and told him, "I have heard your prayer and have chosen this Temple as the place where I want you to sacrifice to me. [13] If I shut up the heavens so that there is no rain, or if I command the locust swarms to eat up all of your crops, or if I send an epidemic among you, [14] then if my people will humble themselves and pray, and search for me, and turn from their wicked ways, I will hear them from heaven and forgive their sins and heal their land. [15] I will listen, wide awake, to every prayer made in this place. [16] For I have chosen this Temple and sanctified it to be my home forever; my eyes and my heart shall always be here.

[17] "As for yourself, if you follow me as your father David did, [18] then I will see to it that you and your descendants will always be the kings of Israel; [19] but if you don't follow me, if you refuse the laws I have given you and worship idols, [20] then I will destroy my people from this land of mine that I have given them, and this Temple shall be destroyed even though I have sanctified it for myself. Instead, I will make it a public horror and disgrace. [21] Instead of its being famous, all who pass by will be incredulous.

"'Why has the Lord done such a terrible thing to this land and to this Temple?' they will ask.

[22] "And the answer will be, 'Because his people

abandoned the Lord God of their fathers, the God who brought them out of the land of Egypt, and they worshiped other gods instead. That is why he has done all this to them.'"

8 Solomon's Building Activities

It was now twenty years since Solomon had become king, and the great building projects of the Lord's Temple and his own royal palace were completed. ²He now turned his energies to rebuilding the cities that King Hiram of Tyre had given to him, and he relocated some of the people of Israel into them. ³It was at this time, too, that Solomon fought against the city of Hamath-zobah and conquered it. ⁴He built Tadmor in the desert and built cities in Hamath as supply centers. ⁵He fortified the cities of upper Beth-horon and lower Beth-horon, both being supply centers, building their walls and installing barred gates. ⁶He also built Baalath and other supply centers at this time and constructed cities where his chariots and horses were kept. He built to his heart's desire in Jerusalem and Lebanon and throughout the entire realm.

⁷,⁸He began the practice that still continues of conscripting as slave laborers the Hittites, Amorites, Perizzites, Hivites, and Jebusites—the descendants of those nations that the Israelis had not completely wiped out. ⁹However, he didn't make slaves of any of the Israeli citizens, but used them as soldiers, officers, charioteers, and cavalrymen; ¹⁰also, 250 of them were government officials who administered all public affairs.

¹¹Solomon now moved his wife (she was Pharaoh's daughter) from the City of David sector of Jerusalem to the new palace he had built for her. For he said, "She must not live in King David's palace for the Ark of the Lord was there, and it is holy ground."

¹²Then Solomon sacrificed burnt offerings to the Lord on the altar he had built in front of the porch of the Temple. ¹³The number of sacrifices differed from day to day in accordance with the instructions Moses had given; there were extra sacrifices on the Sabbaths, on new moon festivals, and at the three annual festivals—the Passover celebration, the Festival of Weeks, and the Festival of Tabernacles. ¹⁴In assigning the priests to their posts of duty he followed the organizational chart prepared by his father David; he also assigned the Levites to their work of praise and of helping the priests in each day's duties; and he assigned the gatekeepers to their gates. ¹⁵Solomon did not deviate in any way from David's instructions concerning these matters and concerning the treasury personnel. ¹⁶Thus Solomon successfully completed the construction of the Temple.

¹⁷,¹⁸Then he went to the seaport towns of Ezion-geber and Eloth, in Edom, to launch a fleet presented to him by King Hiram. These ships, with King Hiram's experienced crews working alongside Solomon's men, went to Ophir and brought back to him several million dollars worth of gold on each trip!

9 The Queen of Sheba Visits

When the queen of Sheba heard of Solomon's fabled wisdom, she came to Jerusalem to test him with hard questions. A very great retinue of aides and servants accompanied her, including camel-loads of spices, gold, and jewels. ²And Solomon answered all her problems. Nothing was hidden from him; he could explain everything to her. ³When she discovered how wise he really was, and how breathtaking the beauty of his palace, ⁴and how wonderful the food at his tables, and how many servants and aides he had, and when she saw their spectacular uniforms and his stewards in full regalia, and saw the size of the men in his bodyguard, she could scarcely believe it!

⁵Finally she exclaimed to the king, "Everything I heard about you in my own country is true! ⁶I didn't believe it until I got here and saw it with my own eyes. Your wisdom is far greater than I could ever have imagined. ⁷What a privilege for these men of yours to stand here and listen to you talk! ⁸Blessed be the Lord your God! How he must love Israel to give them a just king like you! He wants them to be a great, strong nation forever."

⁹She gave the king a gift of over a million dollars in gold, and great quantities of spices of incomparable quality, and many, many jewels.

¹⁰King Hiram's and King Solomon's crews brought gold from Ophir, also sandalwood and jewels. ¹¹The king used the sandalwood to make terraced steps for the Temple and the palace and to construct harps and lyres for the choir. Never before had there been such beautiful instruments in all the land of Judah.

¹²King Solomon gave the queen of Sheba gifts of the same value as she had brought to him, plus everything else she asked for! Then she and her retinue returned to their own land.

¹³,¹⁴Solomon received a quarter of a billion dollars worth of gold each year from the kings of Arabia and many other lands that paid annual tribute to him. In addition, there was a trade balance from the exports of his merchants. ¹⁵He used some of the gold to make 200 large shields, each worth $100,000, ¹⁶and 300 smaller shields, each worth $50,000. The king placed these in the Forest of Lebanon Room in his palace. ¹⁷He also made a huge ivory throne overlaid with pure

Family Devotions

☐ DEVOTION 128
TRUSTING GOD FOR GUIDANCE

Read 2 Chronicles 7:14

Ron's radio-controlled car zipped down the driveway. Just as it reached the road, Ron pushed the lever on the control box to the right, guiding the car back up the driveway. "Ready, Dad?" he asked as his father stepped out the front door, with another car in his hand. "Let's hit the parking lot!"

When they reached the nearby parking lot, Ron and his father found a couple of boys already there. "That's OK. There's room for all of us," said Dad as he and Ron went to the far end.

They had a good time. Dad made his Chevy model jump off the curb, flipping it back onto its tires. Ron skidded his Turbo through some sand, turning it sharply to catch up with Dad's car. "Look! My car is going crazy!" Ron exclaimed. "It won't follow my directions!"

Dad watched for a moment. "I think it's too far away to receive your signals," he observed. "Look—it's too close to those other boys and must be on the same frequency as one of their cars. I think it's following the directions one of them is giving."

Just then one of the boys looked up. He laughed and waved. "I'll send it back to you," he called.

Soon Ron's car was again under his control.

On the way home, Ron and Dad talked about what had happened. "It reminds me of how important it is for us, as Christians, to stay close to the right source to guide us," Dad said. "If we get too far away—for example, if we skip Bible reading and prayer or miss Christian fellowship at church—we may not get the spiritual guidance we need. We also place ourselves in a position to be easily influenced in the wrong direction by unbelieving friends." Ron looked at his car. "I'll remember that," he said. "I don't want to be controlled by wrong influences."

Trusting God for Guidance Memory Verse

I will instruct you (says the Lord) and guide you along the best pathway for your life; I will advise you and watch your progress.
Psalm 32:8

How About You?
Do you find yourself going along with the crowd? Are you easily influenced to join in when friends are trying to get you to do something that isn't right? Perhaps it's because you've gotten too far from the Lord. Remember that he promises to hear you whenever you pray. Ask him for strength against the influence of the world. *N. E. K.*

• For the next devotional, turn to page 449. • For the next devotional on TRUSTING GOD FOR GUIDANCE, turn to page 543. • For notes on TRUSTING GOD FOR GUIDANCE, see pages 522, 553, 614, 676, and 1056.

gold. ¹⁸It had six gold steps and a footstool of gold; also gold armrests, each flanked by a gold lion. ¹⁹Gold lions also stood at each side of each step. No other throne in all the world could be compared with it! ²⁰All of King Solomon's cups were solid gold, as were all the furnishings in the Forest of Lebanon Room. Silver was too cheap to count for much in those days!

²¹Every three years the king sent his ships to Tarshish, using sailors supplied by King Hiram, to bring back gold, silver, ivory, apes, and peacocks.

²²So King Solomon was richer and wiser than any other king in all the earth. ²³Kings from every nation came to visit him and to hear the wisdom God had put into his heart. ²⁴Each brought him annual tribute of silver and gold bowls, clothing, armor, spices, horses, and mules.

²⁵In addition, Solomon had 4,000 stalls of horses and chariots, and 12,000 cavalrymen stationed in the chariot cities as well as in Jerusalem to protect the king. ²⁶He ruled over all kings and kingdoms from the Euphrates River to the land of the Philistines and as far away as the border of Egypt. ²⁷He made silver become as plentiful in Jerusalem as stones in the road! And cedar was used as though it were common sycamore. ²⁸Horses were brought to him from Egypt and other countries.

²⁹The rest of Solomon's biography is written in the history of Nathan the prophet and in the prophecy of Ahijah the Shilonite, and also in the visions of Iddo the seer concerning Jeroboam the son of Nebat.

³⁰So Solomon reigned in Jerusalem over all of Israel for forty years. ³¹Then he died and was buried in Jerusalem, and his son Rehoboam became the new king.

10 Rehoboam Takes Bad Advice

All the leaders of Israel came to Shechem for Rehoboam's coronation. ²,³Meanwhile, friends of Jeroboam (son of Nebat) sent word to him of Solomon's death. He was in Egypt at the time, where he had gone to escape from King Solomon. He now quickly returned, and was present at the coronation, and led the people's demands on Rehoboam:

⁴"Your father was a hard master," they said. "Be easier on us than he was, and we will let you be our king!"

⁵Rehoboam told them to return in three days for his decision. ⁶He discussed their demand with the old men who had counseled his father Solomon.

"What shall I tell them?" he asked.

⁷"If you want to be their king," they replied, "you will have to give them a favorable reply and treat them with kindness."

⁸,⁹But he rejected their advice and asked the opinion of the young men who had grown up with him. "What do you fellows think I should do?" he asked. "Shall I be easier on them than my father was?"

¹⁰"No!" they replied. "Tell them, 'If you think my father was hard on you, just wait and see what I'll be like!' Tell them, 'My little finger is thicker than my father's loins! ¹¹I am going to be tougher on you, not easier! My father used whips on you, but I'll use scorpions!'"

¹²So when Jeroboam and the people returned in three days to hear King Rehoboam's decision, ¹³he spoke roughly to them; for he refused the advice of the old men ¹⁴and followed the counsel of the younger ones.

"My father gave you heavy burdens, but I will give you heavier!" he told them. "My father punished you with whips, but I will punish you with scorpions!"

¹⁵So the king turned down the people's demands. (God caused him to do it in order to fulfill his prediction spoken to Jeroboam by Ahijah the Shilonite.) ¹⁶When the people realized what the king was saying, they turned their backs and deserted him.

"Forget David and his dynasty!" they shouted angrily. "We'll get someone else to be our king. Let Rehoboam rule his own tribe of Judah! Let's go home!" So they did.

¹⁷The people of the tribe of Judah, however, remained loyal to Rehoboam. ¹⁸Afterwards, when King Rehoboam sent Hadoram to draft forced labor from the other tribes of Israel, the people stoned him to death. When this news reached King Rehoboam, he jumped into his chariot and fled to Jerusalem. ¹⁹And Israel has refused to be ruled by a descendant of David to this day.

11 God Says Not to Fight

Upon arrival at Jerusalem, Rehoboam mobilized the armies of Judah and Benjamin, 180,000 strong, and declared war against the rest of Israel in an attempt to reunite the kingdom.

²But the Lord told Shemaiah the prophet,

³"Go and say to King Rehoboam of Judah, Solomon's son, and to the people of Judah and of Benjamin:

⁴"'The Lord says, Do not fight against your brothers. Go home, for I am behind their rebellion.'" So they obeyed the Lord and refused to fight against Jeroboam.

⁵⁻¹⁰Rehoboam stayed in Jerusalem and fortified these cities of Judah with walls and gates to protect himself: Bethlehem, Etam, Tekoa, Beth-zur, Soco, Adullam, Gath, Mareshah, Ziph, Adoraim, Lachish, Azekah, Zorah, Aijalon, and Hebron.

¹¹He also rebuilt and strengthened the forts, and manned them with companies of soldiers under their officers, and stored them with food, olive oil, and wine. ¹²Shields and spears were placed in armories in every city as a further safety measure. For only Judah and Benjamin remained loyal to him.

¹³,¹⁴However, the priests and Levites from the other tribes now abandoned their homes and moved to Judah and Jerusalem, for King Jeroboam had fired them, telling them to stop being priests of the Lord. ¹⁵He had appointed other priests instead who encouraged the people to worship idols instead of God and to sacrifice to carved statues of goats and calves, which he placed on the hills. ¹⁶Laymen, too, from all over Israel began moving to Jerusalem where they could freely worship the Lord God of their fathers and sacrifice to him. ¹⁷This strengthened the kingdom of Judah, so King Rehoboam survived for three years without difficulty; for during those years there was an earnest effort to obey the Lord as King David and King Solomon had done.

¹⁸Rehoboam married his cousin Mahalath. She was the daughter of David's son Jerimoth and of Abihail, the daughter of David's brother Eliab. ¹⁹Three sons were born from this marriage—Jeush, Shemariah, and Zaham.

²⁰Later he married Maacah, the daughter of Absalom. The children she bore him were Abijah, Attai, Ziza, and Shelomith. ²¹He loved Maacah more than any of his other wives and concubines (he had eighteen wives and sixty concubines—with twenty-eight sons and sixty daughters). ²²Maacah's son Abijah was his favorite, and he intended to make him the next king. ²³He very wisely scattered his other sons in the fortified cities throughout the land of Judah and Benjamin, and gave them large allowances and arranged for them to have several wives apiece.

12 Egypt Conquers Jerusalem

But just when Rehoboam was at the height of his popularity and power he abandoned the Lord, and the people followed him in this sin. ²As a result, King Shishak of Egypt attacked Jerusalem in the fifth year of King Rehoboam's reign ³with 1,200 chariots, 60,000 cavalrymen and an unnumbered host of infantrymen—Egyptians, Libyans, Sukkiim, and Ethiopians. ⁴He quickly conquered Judah's fortified cities and soon arrived at Jerusalem.

⁵The prophet Shemaiah now met with Rehoboam and the Judean leaders from every part of the nation (they had fled to Jerusalem for safety) and told them, "The Lord says, 'You have forsaken me, so I have forsaken you and abandoned you to Shishak.'"

⁶Then the king and the leaders of Israel confessed their sins and exclaimed, "The Lord is right in doing this to us!"

⁷And when the Lord saw them humble themselves, he sent Shemaiah to tell them, "Because you have humbled yourselves, I will not completely destroy you; some will escape. I will not use Shishak to pour out my anger upon Jerusalem. ⁸But you must pay annual tribute to him. Then you will realize how much better it is to serve me than to serve him!"

⁹So King Shishak of Egypt conquered Jerusalem and took away all the treasures of the Temple and of the palace, also all of Solomon's gold shields. ¹⁰King Rehoboam replaced them with bronze shields and committed them to the care of the captain of his bodyguard. ¹¹Whenever the king went to the Temple, the guards would carry them and afterwards return them to the armory. ¹²When the king humbled himself, the Lord's anger was turned aside and he didn't send total destruction; in fact, even after Shishak's invasion, the economy of Judah remained strong.

¹³King Rehoboam reigned seventeen years in Jerusalem, the city God had chosen as his residence after considering all the other cities of Israel. He had become king at the age of forty-one, and his mother's name was Naamah the Ammonitess. ¹⁴But he was an evil king, for he never did decide really to please the Lord. ¹⁵The complete biography of Rehoboam is recorded in the histories written by Shemaiah the prophet and by Iddo the seer and in *The Genealogical Register.*

There were continual wars between Rehoboam and Jeroboam. ¹⁶When Rehoboam died he was buried in Jerusalem, and his son Abijah became the new king.

13 Abijah Defeats Jeroboam

Abijah became the new king of Judah in Jerusalem in the eighteenth year of the reign of King Jeroboam of Israel. He lasted three years. His mother's name was Micaiah (daughter of Uriel of Gibeah).

Early in his reign war broke out between Judah and Israel. ³Judah, led by King Abijah, fielded 400,000 seasoned warriors against twice as many Israeli troops—strong, courageous men led by King Jeroboam. ⁴When the army of Judah arrived at Mount Zemaraim, in the hill country of Ephraim, King Abijah shouted to King Jeroboam and the Israeli army:

⁵"Listen! Don't you realize that the Lord God of Israel swore that David's descendants would always be the kings of Israel? ⁶Your King Jeroboam is a mere servant of David's son and was a traitor to his master. ⁷Then a whole gang of worthless rebels

joined him, defying Solomon's son Rehoboam, for he was young and frightened and couldn't stand up to them. ⁸Do you really think you can defeat the kingdom of the Lord that is led by a descendant of David? Your army is twice as large as mine, but you are cursed with those gold calves you have with you that Jeroboam made for you—he calls them your gods! ⁹And you have driven away the priests of the Lord and the Levites and have appointed heathen priests instead. Just like the people of other lands, you accept as priests anybody who comes along with a young bullock and seven rams for consecration. Anyone at all can be a priest of these no-gods of yours!

¹⁰"But as for us, the Lord is our God and we have not forsaken him. Only the descendants of Aaron are our priests, and the Levites alone may help them in their work. ¹¹They burn sacrifices to the Lord every morning and evening—burnt offerings and sweet incense; and they place the Bread of the Presence upon the holy table. The gold lampstand is lighted every night, for we are careful to follow the instructions of the Lord our God; but you have forsaken him. ¹²So you see, God is with us; he is our Leader. His priests, trumpeting as they go, will lead us into battle against you. O people of Israel, do not fight against the Lord God of your fathers, for you will not succeed!"

¹³,¹⁴Meanwhile, Jeroboam had secretly sent part of his army around behind the men of Judah to ambush them; so Judah was surrounded, with the enemy before and behind them. Then they cried out to the Lord for mercy, and the priests blew the trumpets. ¹⁵,¹⁶The men of Judah began to shout. And as they shouted, God used King Abijah and the men of Judah to turn the tide of battle against King Jeroboam and the army of Israel, ¹⁷and they slaughtered 500,000 elite troops of Israel that day.

¹⁸,¹⁹So Judah, depending upon the Lord God of their fathers, defeated Israel, and chased King Jeroboam's troops, and captured some of his cities—Bethel, Jeshanah, Ephron, and their suburbs. ²⁰King Jeroboam of Israel never regained his power during Abijah's lifetime, and eventually the Lord struck him and he died.

²¹Meanwhile, King Abijah of Judah became very strong. He married fourteen wives and had twenty-two sons and sixteen daughters. ²²His complete biography and speeches are recorded in the prophet Iddo's *History of Judah*.

14 Asa Rules Judah

King Abijah was buried in Jerusalem. Then his son Asa became the new king of Judah, and there was peace in the land for the first ten years of his reign, ²for Asa was careful to obey the Lord his God. ³He demolished the heathen altars on the hills, and broke down the obelisks, and chopped down the shameful Asherim idols, ⁴and demanded that the entire nation obey the commandments of the Lord God of their ancestors. ⁵Also, he removed the sun images from the hills and the incense altars from every one of Judah's cities. That is why God gave his kingdom peace. ⁶This made it possible for him to build walled cities throughout Judah.

⁷"Now is the time to do it, while the Lord is blessing us with peace because of our obedience to him," he told his people. "Let us build and fortify cities now, with walls, towers, gates, and bars." So they went ahead with these projects very successfully.

⁸King Asa's Judean army was 300,000 strong, equipped with light shields and spears. His army of Benjaminites numbered 280,000, armed with large shields and bows. Both armies were composed of well-trained, brave men.

⁹,¹⁰But now he was attacked by an army of 1,000,000 troops from Ethiopia with 300 chariots, under the leadership of General Zerah. They advanced to the city of Mareshah, in the valley of Zephathah, and King Asa sent his troops to battle with them there.

¹¹"O Lord," he cried out to God, "no one else can help us! Here we are, powerless against this mighty army. Oh, help us, Lord our God! For we trust in you alone to rescue us, and in your name we attack this vast horde. Don't let mere men defeat you!"

¹²Then the Lord defeated the Ethiopians, and Asa and the army of Judah triumphed as the Ethiopians fled. ¹³They chased them as far as Gerar, and the entire Ethiopian army was wiped out so that not one man remained; for the Lord and his army destroyed them all. Then the army of Judah carried off vast quantities of plunder. ¹⁴While they were at Gerar they attacked all the cities in that area, and terror from the Lord came upon the residents. As a result, additional vast quantities of plunder were collected from these cities too. ¹⁵They not only plundered the cities but destroyed the cattle

---

RESISTING TEMPTATION 14:7 Times of peace are not just for resting. They allow us to prepare for times of trouble. King Abijah recognized the period of peace as the right time to build his defenses. He knew that it was too late to prepare defenses at the moment of attack. It is also difficult to withstand spiritual attack unless defenses are prepared beforehand. Decisions about what to do when temptations arise must be made with a cool head in the peace of untroubled moments, long before the heat of temptation is upon us. Build your defenses now before temptation strikes. **To begin the series of devotionals on RESISTING TEMPTATION, turn to page 7.**

Family Devotions

☐ **Devotion 129**
Humility

Read 2 Chronicles 15:7

Humility Memory Verse

For everyone who tries to honor himself shall be humbled; and he who humbles himself shall be honored.
Luke 14:11

After Sunday school, Angela and Diane caught up with Allison in the hall. The three girls had just been appointed to the food committee for the class picnic, with Allison as chairman. "When shall we meet?" Diane asked.

"Not today. I'm going home with Shelly," Allison called over her shoulder as she hurried away.

Later that week, the committee finally got together. "What do we want to eat?" Allison asked.

Diane had been thinking about it, and she handed Allison a copy of the menu she had planned. Allison glanced at it. "Looks OK. Who brings what?"

Diane handed her another list. Allison glanced at it, too.

"I suppose this will do," she said. "I don't have time to plan a better one. Why don't you and Angela tell everyone what to bring?" She handed the second list back to Diane. "I'd better keep this first list so I can show Miss Wilson the menu. See you later."

The picnic was a success. "We didn't forget a thing," Angela remarked as she and Diane cleared the table. Allison was playing games.

As everyone prepared to leave, Diane saw Miss Wilson pat Allison's shoulder. "You did a great job, Allison," said the teacher. "It's nice to have someone I can depend upon."

Allison smiled sweetly. "I enjoyed helping, Miss Wilson."

A dark red flush spread over Diane's face. "Did you hear that, Angela? Allison didn't do one thing, and she's taking the credit for our hard work!"

Angela laughed, "Oh, well, I know better, and you know better. We had fun doing it, and we did a good job. That's the important thing. We may not be getting credit from Miss Wilson, but God knows how much work we put into it. I'd rather be working for him, anyway!"

How About You?

Have you ever worked hard, done a good job, and then had someone else get the credit for your work? The reward for a job well done is not always praise and honor from others. The satisfaction of knowing you've done your best is more important than praise. And God's approval is most important. B. W.

• For the next devotional, turn to page 455. • For the next devotional on *Humility*, turn to page 509. • For notes on *Humility*, see pages 57, 390, 428, 854, and 1228.

tents and captured great herds of sheep and camels before finally returning to Jerusalem.

15 Asa Rebuilds the Altar

Then the Spirit of God came upon Azariah (son of Oded), ²and he went out to meet King Asa as he was returning from the battle.

"Listen to me, Asa! Listen, armies of Judah and Benjamin!" he shouted. "The Lord will stay with you as long as you stay with him! Whenever you look for him, you will find him. But if you forsake him, he will forsake you. ³For a long time now, over in Israel, the people haven't worshiped the true God and have not had a true priest to teach them. They have lived without God's laws. ⁴But whenever they have turned again to the Lord God of Israel in their distress and searched for him he has helped them. ⁵In their times of rebellion against God there was no peace. Problems troubled the nation on every hand. Crime was on the increase everywhere. ⁶There were external wars and internal fighting of city against city, for God was plaguing them with all sorts of trouble. ⁷But you men of Judah, keep up the good work and don't get discouraged, for you will be rewarded."

⁸When King Asa heard this message from God, he took courage and destroyed all the idols in the land of Judah and Benjamin and in the cities he had captured in the hill country of Ephraim, and he rebuilt the altar of the Lord in front of the Temple.

⁹Then he summoned all the people of Judah and Benjamin and the immigrants from Israel (for many had come from the territories of Ephraim, Manasseh, and Simeon in Israel when they saw that the Lord God was with King Asa). ¹⁰They all came to Jerusalem in June of the fifteenth year of King Asa's reign ¹¹and sacrificed to the Lord seven hundred oxen and seven thousand sheep—it was part of the plunder they had captured in the battle. ¹²Then they entered into a contract to worship only the Lord God of their fathers ¹³and agreed that anyone who refused to do this must die—whether old or young, man or woman. ¹⁴They shouted out their oath of loyalty to God with trumpets blaring and horns sounding. ¹⁵All were happy for this covenant with God, for they had entered into it with all their hearts and wills and wanted him above everything else, and they found him! And he gave them peace throughout the nation.

¹⁶King Asa even removed his mother Maacah from being the queen mother because she made an Asherah idol; he cut down the idol and crushed and burned it at Kidron Brook. ¹⁷Over in Israel the idol-temples were not removed. But here in Judah and Benjamin the heart of King Asa was perfect before God throughout his lifetime. ¹⁸He brought back into the Temple the silver and gold bowls that he and his father had dedicated to the Lord. ¹⁹So there was no more war until the thirty-fifth year of King Asa's reign.

16 Asa Forgets God

In the thirty-sixth year of King Asa's reign, King Baasha of Israel declared war on him and built the fortress of Ramah in order to control the road to Judah. ²Asa's response was to take the silver and gold from the Temple and from the palace, and to send it to King Ben-hadad of Syria at Damascus with this message:

³"Let us renew the mutual security pact that there was between your father and my father. See, here is silver and gold to induce you to break your alliance with King Baasha of Israel, so that he will leave me alone."

⁴Ben-hadad agreed to King Asa's request and mobilized his armies to attack Israel. They destroyed the cities of Ijon, Dan, Abel-maim and all of the supply centers in Naphtali. ⁵As soon as King Baasha of Israel heard what was happening, he discontinued building Ramah and gave up his plan to attack Judah. ⁶Then King Asa and the people of Judah went out to Ramah and carried away the building stones and timbers and used them to build Geba and Mizpah instead.

⁷About that time the prophet Hanani came to King Asa and told him, "Because you have put your trust in the king of Syria instead of in the Lord your God, the army of the king of Syria has escaped from you. ⁸Don't you remember what happened to the Ethiopians and Libyans and their vast army, with all of their chariots and cavalrymen? But you relied then on the Lord, and he delivered them all into your hand. ⁹For the eyes of the Lord search back and forth across the whole earth, looking for people whose hearts are perfect toward him, so that he can show his great power in helping them. What a fool you have been! From now on you shall have wars."

¹⁰Asa was so angry with the prophet for saying this that he threw him into jail. And Asa oppressed all the people at that time.

¹¹The rest of the biography of Asa is written in *The Annals of the Kings of Israel and Judah.* ¹²In the thirty-ninth year of his reign, Asa became seriously diseased in his feet, but he didn't go to the Lord with the problem but to the doctors. ¹³,¹⁴So he died in the forty-first year of his reign and was buried in his own vault that he had hewn out for himself in Jerusalem. He was laid on a bed perfumed with sweet spices and ointments, and his people made a very great burning of incense for him at his funeral.

17

Jehoshaphat Rules Judah

Then his son Jehoshaphat became the king and mobilized for war against Israel. ²He placed garrisons in all of the fortified cities of Judah, in various other places throughout the country, and in the cities of Ephraim that his father had conquered.

³The Lord was with Jehoshaphat because he followed in the good footsteps of his father's early years and did not worship idols. ⁴He obeyed the commandments of his father's God—quite unlike the people across the border in the land of Israel. ⁵So the Lord strengthened his position as king of Judah. All the people of Judah cooperated by paying their taxes, so he became very wealthy as well as being very popular. ⁶He boldly followed the paths of God—even knocking down the heathen altars on the hills and destroying the Asherim idols.

⁷⁻⁹In the third year of his reign he began a nationwide religious education program. He sent out top government officials as teachers in all the cities of Judah. These men included Ben-hail, Obadiah, Zechariah, Nethanel, and Micaiah. He also used the Levites for this purpose, including Shemaiah, Nethaniah, Zebadiah, Asahel, Shemiramoth, Jehonathan, Adonijah, Tobijah, and Tobadonijah; also the priests, Elishama and Jehoram. They took copies of *The Book of the Law of the Lord* to all the cities of Judah to teach the Scriptures to the people.

¹⁰Then the fear of the Lord fell upon all the surrounding kingdoms so that none of them declared war on King Jehoshaphat.

¹¹Even some of the Philistines brought him presents and annual tribute, and the Arabs donated 7,700 rams and 7,700 male goats. ¹²So Jehoshaphat became very strong and built fortresses and supply cities throughout Judah.

¹³His public works program was also extensive, and he had a huge army stationed at Jerusalem, his capital. ¹⁴,¹⁵Three hundred thousand Judean troops were there under General Adnah. Next in command was Jehohanan with an army of 280,000 men. ¹⁶Next was Amasiah (son of Zichri), a man of unusual piety, with 200,000 troops. ¹⁷Benjamin supplied 200,000 men equipped with bows and shields under the command of Eliada, a great general. ¹⁸His second in command was Jehozabad, with 180,000 trained men. ¹⁹These were the troops in Jerusalem in addition to those placed by the king in the fortified cities throughout the nation.

18

Jehoshaphat and Ahab

But rich, popular King Jehoshaphat of Judah made a marriage alliance [for his son] with [the daughter of] King Ahab of Israel. ²A few years later he went down to Samaria to visit King Ahab, and King Ahab gave a great party for him and his aides, butchering great numbers of sheep and oxen for the feast. Then he asked King Jehoshaphat to join forces with him against Ramoth-gilead.

³⁻⁵"Why, of course!" King Jehoshaphat replied. "I'm with you all the way. My troops are at your command! However, let's check with the Lord first."

So King Ahab summoned 400 of his heathen prophets and asked them, "Shall we go to war with Ramoth-gilead or not?"

And they replied, "Go ahead, for God will give you a great victory!"

⁶,⁷But Jehoshaphat wasn't satisfied. "Isn't there some prophet of the Lord around here too?" he asked. "I'd like to ask him the same question."

"Well," Ahab told him, "there is one, but I hate him, for he never prophesies anything but evil! His name is Micaiah (son of Imlah)."

"Oh, come now, don't talk like that!" Jehoshaphat exclaimed. "Let's hear what he has to say."

⁸So the king of Israel called one of his aides. "Quick! Go and get Micaiah (son of Imlah)," he ordered.

⁹The two kings were sitting on thrones in full regalia at an open place near the Samaria gate, and all the "prophets" were prophesying before them. ¹⁰One of them, Zedekiah (son of Chenaanah), made some iron horns for the occasion and proclaimed, "The Lord says you will gore the Syrians to death with these!"

¹¹And all the others agreed. "Yes," they chorused, "go up to Ramoth-gilead and prosper, for the Lord will cause you to conquer."

¹²The man who went to get Micaiah told him what was happening and what all the prophets were saying—that the war would end in triumph for the king.

"I hope you will agree with them and give the king a favorable reading," the man ventured.

¹³But Micaiah replied, "I vow by God that whatever God says is what I will say."

¹⁴When he arrived before the king, the king asked him, "Micaiah, shall we go to war against Ramoth-gilead or not?"

And Micaiah replied, "Sure, go ahead! It will be a glorious victory!"

¹⁵"Look here," the king said sharply, "how many times must I tell you to speak nothing except what the Lord tells you to?"

¹⁶Then Micaiah told him, "In my vision I saw all Israel scattered upon the mountain as sheep without a shepherd. And the Lord said, 'Their master has been killed. Send them home.'"

¹⁷"Didn't I tell you?" the king of Israel exclaimed to Jehoshaphat. "He does it every time. He *never* prophesies *anything* but evil against me."

¹⁸"Listen to what else the Lord has told me," Micaiah continued. "I saw him upon his throne surrounded by vast throngs of angels.

¹⁹,²⁰"And the Lord said, 'Who can get King Ahab to go to battle against Ramoth-gilead and be killed there?'

"There were many suggestions, but finally a spirit stepped forward before the Lord and said, 'I can do it!'

"'How?' the Lord asked him.

²¹"He replied, 'I will be a lying spirit in the mouths of all of the king's prophets!'

"'It will work,' the Lord said; 'go and do it.'

²²"So you see, the Lord has put a lying spirit in the mouths of these prophets of yours, when actually he has determined just the opposite of what they are telling you!"

²³Then Zedekiah (son of Chenaanah) walked up to Micaiah and slapped him across the face. "You liar!" he yelled. "When did the Spirit of the Lord leave me and enter you?"

²⁴"You'll find out soon enough," Micaiah replied, "when you are hiding in an inner room!"

²⁵"Arrest this man and take him back to Governor Amon and to my son Joash," the king of Israel ordered. ²⁶"Tell them, 'The king says to put this fellow in prison and feed him with bread and water until I return safely from the battle!'"

²⁷Micaiah replied, "If you return safely, the Lord has not spoken through me." Then, turning to those around them, he remarked, "Take note of what I have said."

²⁸So the king of Israel and the king of Judah led their armies to Ramoth-gilead.

²⁹The king of Israel said to Jehoshaphat, "I'll disguise myself so that no one will recognize me, but you put on your royal robes!" So that is what they did.

³⁰Now the king of Syria had issued these instructions to his charioteers: "Ignore everyone but the king of Israel!"

³¹So when the Syrian charioteers saw King Jehoshaphat of Judah in his royal robes, they went for him, supposing that he was the man they were after. But Jehoshaphat cried out to the Lord to save him, and the Lord made the charioteers see their mistake and leave him. ³²For as soon as they realized he was not the king of Israel, they stopped chasing him. ³³But one of the Syrian soldiers shot an arrow haphazardly at the Israeli troops, and it struck the king of Israel at the opening where the lower armor and the breastplate meet. "Get me out of here," he groaned to the driver of his chariot, "for I am badly wounded." ³⁴The battle grew hotter and hotter all that day, and King Ahab went back in, propped up in his chariot, to fight the Syrians, but just as the sun sank into the western skies, he died.

19 A Message for Jehoshaphat

As King Jehoshaphat of Judah returned home, uninjured, ²the prophet Jehu (son of Hanani) went out to meet him.

"Should you be helping the wicked, and loving those who hate the Lord?" he asked him. "Because of what you have done, God's wrath is upon you. ³But there are some good things about you in that you got rid of the shameful idols throughout the land, and you have tried to be faithful to God."

⁴So Jehoshaphat made no more trips to Israel after that but remained quietly at Jerusalem. Later he went out again among the people, traveling from Beersheba to the hill country of Ephraim to encourage them to worship the God of their ancestors. ⁵He appointed judges throughout the nation in all the larger cities, ⁶and instructed them:

"Watch your step—I have not appointed you—God has; and he will stand beside you and help you give justice in each case that comes before you. ⁷Be very much afraid to give any other decision than what God tells you to. For there must be no injustice among God's judges, no partiality, no taking of bribes."

⁸Jehoshaphat set up courts in Jerusalem, too, with the Levites and priests and clan leaders and judges. ⁹These were his instructions to them: "You are to act always in the fear of God, with honest hearts. ¹⁰Whenever a case is referred to you by the judges out in the provinces, whether murder cases or other violations of the laws and ordinances of God, you are to clarify the evidence for them and help them to decide justly, lest the wrath of God come down upon you and them; if you do this, you will discharge your responsibility."

¹¹Then he appointed Amariah the High Priest to be the court of final appeal in cases involving violation of sacred affairs; and Zebadiah (son of Ishmael), a ruler in Judah, as the court of final appeal in all civil cases; with the Levites as their assistants. "Be fearless in your stand for truth and honesty. And may God use you to defend the innocent," was his final word to them.

LEAVING THE FUTURE IN GOD'S HANDS 18:22 God used the seductive influence of these false prophets to judge Ahab. These prophets, supported by Ahab, snared him in his sin. Because he listened to them instead of God, he was killed in battle. The lying spirit is a picture of the prophets' entire way of life—telling the king only what he wanted to hear, not what he needed to hear. When we want guidance about the future, we must look first to God, not to "false prophets" like fortune-tellers or astrologers. **To begin the series of devotionals on LEAVING THE FUTURE IN GOD'S HANDS, turn to page 75.**

20 God Gives a Victory

Later on the armies of the kings of Moab, Ammon, and of the Meunites declared war on Jehoshaphat and the people of Judah. ²Word reached Jehoshaphat that "a vast army is marching against you from beyond the Dead Sea from Syria. It is already at Hazazon-tamar" (also called Engedi). ³Jehoshaphat was badly shaken by this news and determined to beg for help from the Lord; so he announced that all the people of Judah should go without food for a time, in penitence and intercession before God. ⁴People from all across the nation came to Jerusalem to plead unitedly with him. ⁵Jehoshaphat stood among them as they gathered at the new court of the Temple and prayed this prayer:

⁶"O Lord God of our fathers—the only God in all the heavens, the Ruler of all the kingdoms of the earth—you are so powerful, so mighty. Who can stand against you? ⁷O our God, didn't you drive out the heathen who lived in this land when your people arrived? And didn't you give this land forever to the descendants of your friend Abraham? ⁸Your people settled here and built this Temple for you, ⁹truly believing that in a time like this—whenever we are faced with any calamity such as war, disease, or famine—we can stand here before this Temple and before you—for you are here in this Temple—and cry out to you to save us; and that you will hear us and rescue us.

¹⁰"And now see what the armies of Ammon, Moab, and Mount Seir are doing. You wouldn't let our ancestors invade those nations when Israel left Egypt, so we went around and didn't destroy them. ¹¹Now see how they reward us! For they have come to throw us out of your land which you have given us. ¹²O our God, won't you stop them? We have no way to protect ourselves against this mighty army. We don't know what to do, but we are looking to you."

¹³As the people from every part of Judah stood before the Lord with their little ones, wives, and children, ¹⁴the Spirit of the Lord came upon one of the men standing there—Jahaziel (son of Zechariah, son of Benaiah, son of Jeiel, son of Mattaniah the Levite, who was one of the sons of Asaph).

¹⁵"Listen to me, all you people of Judah and Jerusalem, and you, O king Jehoshaphat!" he exclaimed. "The Lord says, 'Don't be afraid! Don't be paralyzed by this mighty army! For the battle is not yours, but God's! ¹⁶Tomorrow, go down and attack them! You will find them coming up the slopes of Ziz at the end of the valley that opens into the wilderness of Jeruel. ¹⁷But you will not need to fight! Take your places; stand quietly and see the incredible rescue operation God will perform for you, O people of Judah and Jerusalem! Don't be afraid or discouraged! Go out there tomorrow, for the Lord is with you!'"

¹⁸Then King Jehoshaphat fell to the ground with his face to the earth, and all the people of Judah and the people of Jerusalem did the same, worshiping the Lord. ¹⁹Then the Levites of the Kohath clan and the Korah clan stood to praise the Lord God of Israel with songs of praise that rang out strong and clear.

²⁰Early the next morning the army of Judah went out into the wilderness of Tekoa. On the way Jehoshaphat stopped and called them to attention. "Listen to me, O people of Judah and Jerusalem," he said. "Believe in the Lord your God and you shall have success! Believe his prophets and everything will be all right!"

²¹After consultation with the leaders of the people, he determined that there should be a choir leading the march, clothed in sanctified garments and singing the song "His Loving-kindness Is Forever" as they walked along praising and thanking the Lord! ²²And at the moment they began to sing and to praise, the Lord caused the armies of Ammon, Moab, and Mount Seir to begin fighting among themselves, and they destroyed each other! ²³For the Ammonites and Moabites turned against their allies from Mount Seir and killed every one of them. And when they had finished that job, they turned against each other! ²⁴So, when the army of Judah arrived at the watchtower that looks out over the wilderness, as far as they could look there were dead bodies lying on the ground—not a single one of the enemy had escaped. ²⁵King Jehoshaphat and his people went out to plunder the bodies and came away loaded with money, garments, and jewels stripped from the corpses—so much that it took them three days to cart it all away! ²⁶On the fourth day they gathered in the Valley of Blessing, as it is called today, and how they praised the Lord!

²⁷Then they returned to Jerusalem, with Jehoshaphat leading them, full of joy that the Lord had given them this marvelous rescue from their enemies. ²⁸They marched into Jerusalem accompanied by a band of harps, lyres, and trumpets and proceeded to the Temple. ²⁹And as had happened before, when the surrounding kingdoms heard that the Lord himself had fought against the enemies of Israel, the fear of God fell upon them. ³⁰So Jehoshaphat's kingdom was quiet, for his God had given him rest.

³¹A thumbnail sketch of King Jehoshaphat: He became king of Judah when he was thirty-five years old and reigned twenty-five years in Jerusalem. His mother's name was Azubah, the daughter of Shilhi. ³²He was a good king, just as his father Asa was. He continually tried to follow the Lord ³³with the exception that he did not destroy the idol shrines on

the hills, nor had the people as yet really decided to follow the God of their ancestors.

³⁴The details of Jehoshaphat's reign from first to last are written in the history of Jehu the son of Hanani, which is inserted in *The Annals of the Kings of Israel.*

³⁵But at the close of his life, Jehoshaphat, king of Judah, went into partnership with Ahaziah, king of Israel, who was a very wicked man. ³⁶They made ships in Ezion-geber to sail to Tarshish. ³⁷Then Eliezer, son of Dodavahu from Mareshah, prophesied against Jehoshaphat, telling him, "Because you have allied yourself with King Ahaziah, the Lord has destroyed your work." So the ships met disaster and never arrived at Tarshish.

21 Jehoram Displeases God

When Jehoshaphat died, he was buried in the cemetery of the kings in Jerusalem, and his son Jehoram became the new ruler of Judah. ²His brothers—other sons of Jehoshaphat—were Azariah, Jehiel, Zechariah, Azariah, Michael, and Shephatiah. ³,⁴Their father had given each of them valuable gifts of money and jewels, also the ownership of some of the fortified cities of Judah. However, he gave the kingship to Jehoram because he was the oldest. But when Jehoram had become solidly established as king, he killed all of his brothers and many other leaders of Israel. ⁵He was thirty-two years old when he began to reign, and he reigned eight years in Jerusalem. ⁶But he was as wicked as the kings who were over in Israel. Yes, as wicked as Ahab, for Jehoram had married one of the daughters of Ahab, and his whole life was one constant binge of doing evil. ⁷However, the Lord was unwilling to end the dynasty of David, for he had made a covenant with David always to have one of his descendants upon the throne.

⁸At that time the king of Edom revolted, declaring his independence of Judah. ⁹Jehoram attacked him with his full army and with all of his chariots, marching by night, and almost managed to subdue him. ¹⁰But to this day Edom has been successful in throwing off the yoke of Judah. Libnah revolted too because Jehoram had turned away from the Lord God of his fathers. ¹¹What's more, Jehoram constructed idol shrines in the mountains of Judah and led the people of Jerusalem in worshiping idols; in fact, he compelled his people to worship them.

¹²Then Elijah the prophet wrote him this letter: "The Lord God of your ancestor David says that because you have not followed in the good ways of your father Jehoshaphat, nor the good ways of King Asa, ¹³but you have been as evil as the kings over in Israel and have made the people of Jerusalem and Judah worship idols just as in the times of King Ahab, and because you have killed your brothers who were better than you, ¹⁴now the Lord will destroy your nation with a great plague. You, your children, your wives, and all that you have will be struck down. ¹⁵You will be stricken with an intestinal disease and your bowels will rot away."

¹⁶Then the Lord stirred up the Philistines and the Arabs living next to the Ethiopians to attack Jehoram. ¹⁷They marched against Judah, broke across the border, and carried away everything of value in the king's palace, including his sons and his wives; only his youngest son, Jehoahaz, escaped.

¹⁸It was after this that Jehovah struck him down with the incurable bowel disease. ¹⁹In the process of time, at the end of two years, his intestines came out, and he died in terrible suffering. (The customary pomp and ceremony was omitted at his funeral.) ²⁰He was thirty-two years old when he began to reign, and he reigned in Jerusalem eight years and died unmourned. He was buried in Jerusalem, but not in the royal cemetery.

22 Ahaziah Gets Evil Advice

Then the people of Jerusalem chose Ahaziah, his youngest son, as their new king (for the marauding bands of Arabs had killed his older sons). ²Ahaziah was twenty-two years old when he began to reign, and he reigned one year in Jerusalem. His mother's name was Athaliah, granddaughter of Omri. ³He, too, walked in the evil ways of Ahab, for his mother encouraged him in doing wrong. ⁴Yes, he was as evil as Ahab, for Ahab's family became his advisors after his father's death, and they led him on to ruin.

⁵Following their evil advice, Ahaziah made an alliance with King Joram of Israel (the son of Ahab), who was at war with King Hazael of Syria at Ramoth-gilead. Ahaziah led his army there to join the battle. King Joram of Israel was wounded ⁶and returned to Jezreel to recover. Ahaziah went to visit him, ⁷but this turned out to be a fatal mistake; for God had decided to punish Ahaziah for his alliance with Joram. It was during this visit that Ahaziah went out with Joram to challenge Jehu (son of Nimshi), whom the Lord had appointed to end the dynasty of Ahab.

⁸While Jehu was hunting down and killing the family and friends of Ahab, he met King Ahaziah's nephews, the princes of Judah, and killed them. ⁹As he and his men were searching for Ahaziah, they found him hiding in the city of Samaria and brought him to Jehu, who killed him. Even so, Ahaziah was given a royal burial because he was the grandson of King Jehoshaphat—a man who enthusiastically served the Lord. None of his sons, however, except for Joash, lived to succeed him as king, ¹⁰for their grandmother Athaliah killed them when she heard the news of her son Ahaziah's death.

Family Devotions

☐ **Devotion 130**
Cultivating Godly Attitudes

Read 2 Chronicles 20:15-26

Cultivating Godly Attitudes
Memory Verse

Your attitude should be the kind that was shown us by Jesus Christ.
Philippians 2:5

With hands in his pockets, Tony stalked toward home. His teeth were clenched and his jaws tight. He was having trouble with Butch and his gang. Looking over his shoulder, he saw the four boys about half a block behind him. They were pointing at him and laughing.

Tony's heart shifted gears. What could he do? He was six blocks from home. If he ran, they would pounce on him. He knew they wanted him to run. They had been teasing him about being a sissy Christian. But how could he fight four big bullies?

He quickened his steps as the voices behind him grew closer. "O, Lord, what can I do? Help me," he pleaded. Then he remembered the Scripture his dad had read that morning. The people of Judah had been outnumbered, too. The Lord had told King Jehoshaphat not to be afraid. "Would you fight my battle, too?" Tony asked God.

Then he remembered what the people of Judah did. They sang praises. Tony gulped. "OK, Lord, I'll praise you," he whispered softly. Quietly, he started singing, "Bless the Lord, O my soul. Bless the Lord, O my soul; and all that is within me, bless his holy name."

He took a deep breath. He did feel better singing than worrying. Glancing back, he saw the bullies were getting closer. He sang louder, "And forever I will praise him. And forever I will praise him. . . ." When he looked around again, he was surprised to see that Butch and his gang had stopped. They were shouting at one another. Suddenly Butch grabbed one boy by the collar and a fight was on. Tony watched in amazement for a minute. Then with a big grin, he ran home singing, "And forget not his blessings, and forget not his blessings. . . ."

He ran into the house. "Mom," he called, "you're not going to believe this!"

How About You?
Are there times when you are outnumbered? Does it seem like everyone is against you? Don't worry. Praise the Lord. Let him fight your battles. He may not cause your enemies to fight one another, but he has a way of solving your problems when you praise him. Make an attitude of praise and thanksgiving a habit. *B. W.*

• For the next devotional, turn to page 457. • For the next devotional on *Cultivating Godly Attitudes*, turn to page 635. • For notes on *Cultivating Godly Attitudes*, see pages 337, 383, 472, 622, and 1216.

¹¹Joash was rescued by his Aunt Jehoshabeath, who was King Ahaziah's sister, and was hidden away in a storage room in the Temple. She was a daughter of King Jehoram and the wife of Jehoiada the priest. ¹²Joash remained hidden in the Temple for six years while Athaliah reigned as queen. He was cared for by his nurse and by his aunt and uncle.

23 Young Joash Becomes King

In the seventh year of the reign of Queen Athaliah, Jehoiada the priest got up his courage and took some of the army officers into his confidence: Azariah (son of Jeroham), Ishmael (son of Jehohanan), Azariah (son of Obed), Maaseiah (son of Adaiah), and Elishaphat (son of Zichri). ²,³These men traveled out across the nation secretly to tell the Levites and clan leaders about his plans and to summon them to Jerusalem. On arrival they swore allegiance to the young king, who was still in hiding at the Temple.

"At last the time has come for the king's son to reign!" Jehoiada exclaimed. "The Lord's promise—that a descendant of King David shall be our king—will be true again. ⁴This is how we'll proceed: A third of you priests and Levites who come off duty on the Sabbath will stay at the entrance as guards. ⁵,⁶Another third will go over to the palace, and a third will be at the Lower Gate. Everyone else must stay in the outer courts of the Temple, as required by God's laws. For only the priests and Levites on duty may enter the Temple itself, for they are sanctified. ⁷You Levites, form a bodyguard for the king, weapons in hand, and kill any unauthorized person entering the Temple. Stay right beside the king."

⁸So all the arrangements were made. Each of the three leaders led a third of the priests arriving for duty that Sabbath, and a third of those whose week's work was done and were going off duty—for Jehoiada the chief priest didn't release them to go home. ⁹Then Jehoiada issued spears and shields to all the army officers. These had once belonged to King David and were stored in the Temple. ¹⁰These officers, fully armed, formed a line from one side to the other in front of the Temple and around the altar in the outer court. ¹¹Then they brought out the little prince and placed the crown upon his head, and handed him a copy of the law of God, and proclaimed him king.

A great shout went up, "Long live the king!" as Jehoiada and his sons anointed him.

¹²When Queen Athaliah heard all the noise and commotion and the shouts of praise to the king, she rushed over to the Temple to see what was going on—and there stood the king by his pillar at the entrance, with the army officers and the trumpeters surrounding him, and people from all over the land rejoicing and blowing trumpets, and the singers singing, accompanied by an orchestra leading the people in a great psalm of praise.

Athaliah ripped her clothes and screamed, "Treason! Treason!"

¹³,¹⁴"Take her out and kill her," Jehoiada the priest shouted to the army officers. "Don't do it here at the Temple. And kill anyone who tries to help her."

¹⁵⁻¹⁷So the crowd opened up for them to take her out, and they killed her at the palace stables.

Then Jehoiada made a solemn contract that he and the king and the people would be the Lord's. And all the people rushed over to the temple of Baal and knocked it down, and broke up the altars, and knocked down the idols, and killed Mattan the priest of Baal before his altar. ¹⁸Jehoiada now appointed the Levite priests as guards, and to sacrifice the burnt offering to the Lord as prescribed in the law of Moses. He made the identical assignments of the Levite clans that King David had. They sang with joy as they worked. ¹⁹The guards at the Temple gates kept out everything that was not consecrated and all unauthorized personnel.

²⁰Then the army officers, nobles, governors, and all the people escorted the king from the Temple, wending their way from the Upper Gate to the palace, and seated the king upon his throne. ²¹So all the people of the land rejoiced, and the city was quiet and peaceful because Queen Athaliah was dead.

24 Joash Repairs the Temple

Joash was seven years old when he became king, and he reigned forty years in Jerusalem. His mother's name was Zibiah, from Beersheba. ²Joash tried hard to please the Lord all during the lifetime of Jehoiada the priest. ³Jehoiada arranged two marriages for him, and he had sons and daughters.

⁴Later on Joash decided to repair and recondition the Temple. ⁵He summoned the priests and Levites and gave them these instructions:

"Go to all the cities of Judah and collect offerings for the building fund so that we can maintain the Temple in good repair. Get at it right away. Don't delay." But the Levites took their time.

⁶So the king called for Jehoiada the High Priest and asked him, "Why haven't you demanded that the Levites go out and collect the Temple taxes from the cities of Judah and from Jerusalem? The tax law enacted by Moses the servant of the Lord must be enforced so that the Temple can be repaired."

⁷,⁸(The followers of wicked Athaliah had ravaged the Temple, and everything dedicated to the worship of God had been removed to the temple

FAMILY DEVOTIONS

☐ DEVOTION 131
CONFESSING SIN

Read 2 Chronicles 24:17-20

Ah-choo!" Karen sneezed as she settled down in her seat. She felt lousy, but she hadn't wanted to stay home. She was too mad. Mom had caught her copying a book report that her brother had written last year, and she had put up a big fuss. She insisted that Karen read the book herself and do her own report. Besides that, she was grounded for a whole week. "Copying is cheating and stealing," Mom said. Karen knew she should be sorry, but she wasn't.

As the hours passed, Karen continued to sneeze and sniff. Her nose was so stuffy. As she sniffed, she noticed that several of her neighbors gave her scowling looks. Her throat was sore, too, and she coughed a lot. Finally recess came. "Let's go jump rope," she suggested to Suzie, but Suzie shook her head and hurried away.

"Karen," said Miss Wilson, "don't you think you ought to go home? Your cold sounds terrible!" Reluctantly Karen agreed, so Miss Wilson arranged for Mom to pick her up.

Later, when Karen was settled at home, she let out a long sigh. "It's sure good to be here," she said. "Everybody avoided me at school."

Mom smiled. "You can't blame them," she said. "Nobody wanted to catch your cold, so they stayed away. Your cold separated you from your friends. It reminds me of sin." Karen looked at her mother in surprise. "You see," Mom went on, "sin separates us from fellowship with God. He always loves us, but he cannot fellowship with us when we refuse to do anything about our sin."

Karen knew it was true. Ever since she had gotten mad at Mom, she had felt far away from God. No, it was before that. It was ever since she decided to copy that she felt guilty and alone. "I know what you mean," she told Mom. "I need to confess some things to God, and I'm sorry I got mad at you, too."

Confessing Sin Memory Verse

But if we confess our sins to him, he can be depended on to forgive us and to cleanse us from every wrong. [And it is perfectly proper for God to do this for us because Christ died to wash away our sins.]
1 John 1:9

How About You?
Is there a sin that is separating you from God? Even if you are a Christian, you need to confess any sin in your life. *H. M.*

• For the next devotional, turn to page 467. • For the next devotional on CONFESSING SIN, turn to page 491.
• For notes on CONFESSING SIN, see pages 429, 479, 836, 881, and 1220.

of Baalim.) So now the king instructed that a chest be made and set outside the Temple gate. ⁹Then a proclamation was sent to all the cities of Judah and throughout Jerusalem telling the people to bring to the Lord the tax that Moses the servant of God had assessed upon Israel. ¹⁰And all the leaders and the people were glad, and brought the money and placed it in the chest until it was full.

¹¹Then the Levites carried the chest to the king's accounting office, where the recording secretary and the representative of the High Priest counted the money and took the chest back to the Temple again. This went on day after day, and money continued to pour in. ¹²The king and Jehoiada gave the money to the building superintendents, who hired masons and carpenters to restore the Temple, and to foundrymen, who made articles of iron and brass. ¹³So the work went forward, and finally the Temple was in much better condition than before. ¹⁴When all was finished, the remaining money was brought to the king and Jehoiada, and it was agreed to use it for making the gold and silver spoons and bowls used for incense, and for making the instruments used in the sacrifices and offerings.

Burnt offerings were sacrificed continually during the lifetime of Jehoiada the priest. ¹⁵He lived to a very old age, finally dying at 130. ¹⁶He was buried in the City of David among the kings because he had done so much good for Israel, for God, and for the Temple.

¹⁷,¹⁸But after his death, the leaders of Judah came to King Joash and induced him to abandon the Temple of the God of their ancestors and to worship shameful idols instead! So the wrath of God came down upon Judah and Jerusalem again. ¹⁹God sent prophets to bring them back to the Lord, but the people wouldn't listen.

²⁰Then the Spirit of God came upon Zechariah, Jehoiada's son. He called a meeting of all the people. Standing before them upon a platform, he said to them, "God wants to know why you are disobeying his commandments. For when you do, everything you try fails. You have forsaken the Lord, and now he has forsaken you."

²¹Then the leaders plotted to kill Zechariah, and finally King Joash himself ordered him executed in the court of the Temple. ²²That was how King Joash repaid Jehoiada for his love and loyalty—by killing his son. Zechariah's last words as he died were, "Lord, see what they are doing and pay them back."

²³A few months later the Syrian army arrived and conquered Judah and Jerusalem, killing all the leaders of the nation and sending back great quantities of booty to the king of Damascus. ²⁴It was a great triumph for the tiny Syrian army, but the Lord let the great army of Judah be conquered by them because they had forsaken the Lord God of their ancestors. In that way God executed judgment upon Joash. ²⁵When the Syrians left—leaving Joash severely wounded—his own officials decided to kill him for murdering the son of Jehoiada the priest. They assassinated him as he lay in bed, and buried him in the City of David, but not in the cemetery of the kings. ²⁶The conspirators were Zabad, whose mother was Shimeath, a woman from Ammon; and Jehozabad, whose mother was Shimrith, a woman from Moab.

²⁷If you want to read about the sons of Joash and the curses laid upon Joash, and about the restoration of the Temple, see *The Annals of the Kings*.

When Joash died, his son Amaziah became the new king.

25 Amaziah Does Good and Evil

Amaziah was twenty-five years old when he became king, and he reigned twenty-nine years in Jerusalem. His mother's name was Jehoaddan, a native of Jerusalem. ²He did what was right, but sometimes resented it! ³When he was well established as the new king, he executed the men who had assassinated his father. ⁴However, he didn't kill their children but followed the command of the Lord written in the law of Moses, that the fathers shall not die for the children's sins, nor the children for the father's sins. No, everyone must pay for his own sins.

⁵,⁶Another thing Amaziah did was to organize the army, assigning leaders to each clan from Judah and Benjamin. Then he took a census and found that he had an army of 300,000 men twenty years old and older, all trained and highly skilled in the use of spear and sword. He also paid $200,000 to hire 100,000 experienced mercenaries from Israel.

⁷But a prophet arrived with this message from the Lord: "Sir, do not hire troops from Israel, for the Lord is not with them. ⁸If you let them go with your troops to battle, you will be defeated no matter how well you fight; for God has power to help or to frustrate."

⁹"But the money!" Amaziah whined. "What shall I do about that?"

And the prophet replied, "The Lord is able to give you much more than this!"

¹⁰So Amaziah sent them home again to Ephraim, which made them very angry and insulted. ¹¹Then Amaziah took courage and led his army to the Valley of Salt and there killed 10,000 men from Seir. ¹²Another 10,000 were taken alive to the top of a cliff and thrown over so that they were crushed upon the rocks below.

¹³Meanwhile, the army of Israel that had been sent home raided several of the cities of Judah in the vicinity of Beth-horon toward Samaria, killing 3,000 people and carrying off great quantities of booty.

¹⁴When King Amaziah returned from this slaughter of the Edomites, he brought with him idols taken from the people of Seir, set them up as gods, bowed before them, and burned incense to them! ¹⁵This made the Lord very angry, and he sent a prophet to demand, "Why have you worshiped gods who couldn't even save their own people from you?"

¹⁶"Since when have I asked your advice?" the king retorted. "Be quiet now before I have you killed."

The prophet left with this parting warning: "I know that God has determined to destroy you because you have worshiped these idols and have not accepted my counsel."

¹⁷King Amaziah of Judah now took the advice of his counselors and declared war on King Joash of Israel (son of Jehoahaz, grandson of Jehu).

¹⁸King Joash replied with this parable: "Out in the Lebanon mountains a thistle demanded of a cedar tree, 'Give your daughter in marriage to my son.' Just then a wild animal came by and stepped on the thistle, crushing it! ¹⁹You are very proud about your conquest of Edom, but my advice is to stay home and don't meddle with me, lest you and all Judah get badly hurt."

²⁰But Amaziah wouldn't listen for God was arranging to destroy him for worshiping the gods of Edom. ²¹The armies met at Beth-shemesh in Judah, ²²and Judah was defeated and its army fled home. ²³King Joash of Israel captured the defeated King Amaziah of Judah and took him as a prisoner to Jerusalem. Then King Joash ordered 200 yards of the walls of Jerusalem dismantled, from the gate of Ephraim to the Corner Gate. ²⁴He carried off all the treasures and gold bowls from the Temple, as well as the treasures from the palace; and he took hostages, including Obed-edom, and returned to Samaria.

²⁵However, King Amaziah of Judah lived on for fifteen years after the death of King Joash of Israel. ²⁶The complete biography of King Amaziah is written in *The Annals of the Kings of Judah and Israel.* ²⁷This account includes a report of Amaziah's turning away from God, how his people conspired against him in Jerusalem, and how he fled to Lachish—but they went after him and killed him there. ²⁸And they brought him back on horses to Jerusalem and buried him in the royal cemetery.

26 A King Turns into a Leper

The people of Judah now crowned sixteen-year-old Uzziah as their new king. ²After his father's death, he rebuilt the city of Eloth and restored it to Judah. ³In all, he reigned fifty-two years in Jerusalem. His mother's name was Jecoliah, from Jerusalem. ⁴He followed in the footsteps of his father Amaziah and was, in general, a good king in the Lord's sight.

⁵While Zechariah was alive Uzziah was always eager to please God. Zechariah was a man who had special revelations from God. And as long as the king followed the paths of God, he prospered, for God blessed him.

⁶He declared war on the Philistines and captured the city of Gath and broke down its walls, also those of Jabneh and Ashdod. Then he built new cities in the Ashdod area and in other parts of the Philistine country. ⁷God helped him not only with his wars against the Philistines but also in his battles with the Arabs of Gur-baal and in his wars with the Meunites. ⁸The Ammonites paid annual tribute to him, and his fame spread even to Egypt, for he was very powerful.

⁹He built fortified towers in Jerusalem at the Corner Gate, and the Valley Gate, and at the turning of the wall. ¹⁰He also constructed forts in the Negeb and made many water reservoirs, for he had great herds of cattle out in the valleys and on the plains. He was a man who loved the soil and had many farms and vineyards, both on the hillsides and in the fertile valleys.

¹¹He organized his army into regiments to which men were drafted under quotas set by Jeiel, the secretary of the army, and his assistant, Maaseiah. The commander-in-chief was General Hananiah. ¹²Twenty-six hundred brave clan leaders commanded these regiments. ¹³The army consisted of 307,500 men, all elite troops. ¹⁴Uzziah issued to them shields, spears, helmets, coats of mail, bows, and slingstones. ¹⁵And he produced engines of war manufactured in Jerusalem, invented by brilliant men to shoot arrows and huge stones from the towers and battlements. So he became very famous, for the Lord helped him wonderfully until he was very powerful.

¹⁶But at that point he became proud—and corrupt. He sinned against the Lord his God by entering the forbidden sanctuary of the Temple and personally burning incense upon the altar. ¹⁷,¹⁸Azariah the High Priest went in after him with eighty other priests, all brave men, and demanded that he get out.

"It is not for you, Uzziah, to burn incense," they declared. "That is the work of the priests alone, the sons of Aaron who are consecrated to this work. Get out, for you have trespassed, and the Lord is not going to honor you for this!"

¹⁹Uzziah was furious and refused to set down the incense burner he was holding. But look! Suddenly—leprosy appeared in his forehead! ²⁰When Azariah and the others saw it, they rushed him out; in fact, he himself was as anxious to get out as

they were to get him out because the Lord had struck him.

²¹So King Uzziah was a leper until the day of his death and lived in isolation, cut off from his people and from the Temple. His son Jotham became vice-regent, in charge of the king's affairs and of the judging of the people of the land.

²²The other details of Uzziah's reign from first to last are recorded by the prophet Isaiah (son of Amoz). ²³When Uzziah died, he was buried in the royal cemetery even though he was a leper, and his son Jotham became the new king.

27 King Jotham Follows God

Jotham was twenty-five years old at the time he became king, and he reigned sixteen years in Jerusalem. His mother was Jerushah, daughter of Zadok. ²He followed the generally good example of his father Uzziah—who had, however, sinned by invading the Temple—but even so his people became very corrupt.

³He built the Upper Gate of the Temple and also did extensive rebuilding of the walls on the hill where the Temple was situated. ⁴And he built cities in the hill country of Judah and erected fortresses and towers on the wooded hills.

⁵His war against the Ammonites was successful so that for the next three years he received from them an annual tribute of $200,000 in silver, 10,000 sacks of wheat, and 10,000 sacks of barley. ⁶King Jotham became powerful because he was careful to follow the path of the Lord his God.

⁷The remainder of his history, including his wars and other activities, is written in *The Annals of the Kings of Israel and Judah*. ⁸In summary, then, he was twenty-five years old when he began to reign, and he reigned sixteen years in Jerusalem. ⁹When he died, he was buried in Jerusalem, and his son Ahaz became the new king.

28 Ahaz Angers God

Ahaz was twenty years old when he became king, and he reigned sixteen years in Jerusalem. But he was an evil king, unlike his ancestor King David. ²For he followed the example of the kings over in Israel and worshiped the idols of Baal. ³He even went out to the Valley of Hinnom, and it was not just to burn incense to the idols, for he even sacrificed his own children in the fire, just like the heathen nations that were thrown out of the land by the Lord to make room for Israel. ⁴Yes, he sacrificed and burned incense at the idol shrines on the hills and under every green tree.

⁵That is why the Lord God allowed the king of Syria to defeat him and deport large numbers of his people to Damascus. The armies from Israel also slaughtered great numbers of his troops. ⁶On a single day Pekah, the son of Remaliah, killed 120,000 of his bravest soldiers because they had turned away from the Lord God of their fathers. ⁷Then Zichri, a great warrior from Ephraim, killed the king's son Maaseiah, the king's administrator Azrikam, and the king's second-in-command Elkanah. ⁸The armies from Israel also captured 200,000 Judean women and children and tremendous amounts of booty, which they took to Samaria.

⁹But Oded, a prophet of the Lord, was there in Samaria, and he went out to meet the returning army.

"Look!" he exclaimed. "The Lord God of your fathers was angry with Judah and let you capture them, but you have butchered them without mercy, and all heaven is disturbed. ¹⁰And now are you going to make slaves of these people from Judah and Jerusalem? What about your own sins against the Lord your God? ¹¹Listen to me and return these relatives of yours to their homes, for now the fierce anger of the Lord is upon *you*."

¹²Some of the top leaders of Ephraim also added their opposition. These men were Azariah the son of Johanan, Berechiah the son of Meshillemoth, Jehizkiah the son of Shallum, and Amasa the son of Hadlai.

¹³"You must not bring the captives here!" they declared. "If you do, the Lord will be angry, and this sin will be added to our many others. We are in enough trouble with God as it is."

¹⁴So the army officers turned over the captives and booty to the political leaders to decide what to do. ¹⁵Then the four men already mentioned distributed captured stores of clothing to the women and children who needed it and gave them shoes, food, and wine, and put those who were sick and old on donkeys, and took them back to their families in Jericho, the City of Palm Trees. Then their escorts returned to Samaria.

¹⁶About that time King Ahaz of Judah asked the king of Assyria to be his ally in his war against the armies of Edom. For Edom was invading Judah and capturing many people as slaves. ¹⁷,¹⁸Meanwhile, the Philistines had invaded the lowland cities and the Negeb and had already captured Beth-shemesh, Aijalon, Gederoth, Soco, Timnah, and Gimzo with their surrounding villages, and were living there. ¹⁹For the Lord brought Judah very low on account of the evil deeds of King Ahaz of Israel, for he had destroyed the spiritual fiber of Judah and had been faithless to the Lord. ²⁰But when Tilgath-pilneser, king of Assyria, arrived, he caused trouble for King Ahaz instead of helping him. ²¹So even though Ahaz had given him the Temple gold and the palace treasures, it did no good.

²²In this time of deep trial, King Ahaz collapsed spiritually. ²³He sacrificed to the gods of the

people of Damascus who had defeated him, for he felt that since these gods had helped the kings of Syria, they would help him too if he sacrificed to them. But instead, they were his ruin, and that of all his people. ²⁴The king took the gold bowls from the Temple and slashed them to pieces, and nailed the door of the Temple shut so that no one could worship there, and made altars to the heathen gods in every corner of Jerusalem. ²⁵And he did the same in every city of Judah, thus angering the Lord God of his fathers.

²⁶The other details of his life and activities are recorded in *The Annals of the Kings of Judah and Israel.* ²⁷When King Ahaz died, he was buried in Jerusalem but not in the royal tombs, and his son Hezekiah became the new king.

29 Hezekiah Opens God's House

Hezekiah was twenty-five years old when he became the king of Judah, and he reigned twenty-nine years in Jerusalem. His mother's name was Abijah, the daughter of Zechariah. ²His reign was generally good in the Lord's sight, just as his ancestor David's had been.

³In the very first month of the first year of his reign, he reopened the doors of the Temple and repaired them. ⁴,⁵He summoned the priests and Levites to meet him at the open space east of the Temple and addressed them thus:

"Listen to me, you Levites. Sanctify yourselves and sanctify the Temple of the Lord God of your ancestors—clean all the debris from the holy place. ⁶For our fathers have committed a deep sin before the Lord our God; they abandoned the Lord and his Temple and turned their backs on it. ⁷The doors have been shut tight, the perpetual flame has been put out, and the incense and burnt offerings have not been offered. ⁸Therefore, the wrath of the Lord has been upon Judah and Jerusalem. He has caused us to be objects of horror, amazement, and contempt, as you see us today. ⁹Our fathers have been killed in war, and our sons and daughters and wives are in captivity because of this.

¹⁰"But now I want to make a covenant with the Lord God of Israel so that his fierce anger will turn away from us. ¹¹My children, don't neglect your duties any longer, for the Lord has chosen you to minister to him and to burn incense."

¹²⁻¹⁴Then the Levites went into action:

From the Kohath clan, Mahath (son of Amasai) and Joel (son of Azariah);
From the Merari clan, Kish (son of Abdi) and Azariah (son of Jehallelel);
From the Gershon clan, Joah (son of Zimmah) and Eden (son of Joah).
From the Elizaphan clan, Shimri and Jeuel;
From the Asaph clan, Zechariah and Mattaniah;
From the Hemanite clan, Jehuel and Shimei;
From the Jeduthun clan, Shemaiah and Uzziel.

¹⁵They in turn summoned their fellow Levites and sanctified themselves, and began to clean up and sanctify the Temple, as the king (who was speaking for the Lord) had commanded them. ¹⁶The priests cleaned up the inner room of the Temple and brought out into the court all the filth and decay they found there. The Levites then carted it out to the brook Kidron. ¹⁷This all began on the first day of April, and by the eighth day they had reached the outer court, which took eight days to clean up, so the entire job was completed in sixteen days.

¹⁸Then they went back to the palace and reported to King Hezekiah, "We have completed the cleansing of the Temple and of the altar of burnt offerings and of its accessories, also the table of the Bread of the Presence and its equipment. ¹⁹What's more, we have recovered and sanctified all the utensils thrown away by King Ahaz when he closed the Temple. They are beside the altar of the Lord."

²⁰Early the next morning King Hezekiah went to the Temple with the city officials, ²¹taking seven young bulls, seven rams, seven lambs, and seven male goats for a sin offering for the nation and for the Temple.

He instructed the priests, the sons of Aaron, to sacrifice them on the altar of the Lord. ²²So they killed the young bulls, and the priests took the blood and sprinkled it on the altar, and they killed the rams and sprinkled their blood upon the altar, and did the same with the lambs. ²³The male goats for the sin offering were then brought before the king and his officials, who laid their hands upon them. ²⁴Then the priests killed the animals and made a sin offering with their blood upon the altar to make atonement for all Israel, as the king had commanded—for the king had spec-

---

PERSEVERANCE 29:11 The Levites, chosen by God to serve in the Temple, had been kept from their duties by Ahaz's wickedness (28:24). But Hezekiah called them back into service, saying, "Don't neglect your duties any longer, for the Lord has chosen you to minister."

We may not have to face a wicked king, but pressures or responsibilities can render us inactive and ineffective. When you have been given a job to do, don't neglect your responsibility. If you have stopped serving God, whether by choice or by force, look for the opportunities (and listen to the "Hezekiahs") God will send your way to help you resume your responsibilities. Then, like the Levites, be ready to serve responsibly (29:12). **To begin the series of devotionals on PERSEVERANCE, turn to page 37.**

ified that the burnt offering and sin offering must be sacrificed for the entire nation.

25,26He organized Levites at the Temple into an orchestral group, using cymbals, psalteries, and harps. This was in accordance with the directions of David and the prophets Gad and Nathan, who had received their instructions from the Lord. The priests formed a trumpet corps. 27Then Hezekiah ordered the burnt offering to be placed upon the altar, and as the sacrifice began, the instruments of music began to play the songs of the Lord, accompanied by the trumpets. 28Throughout the entire ceremony everyone worshiped the Lord as the singers sang and the trumpets blew. 29Afterwards the king and his aides bowed low before the Lord in worship. 30Then King Hezekiah ordered the Levites to sing before the Lord some of the psalms of David and of the prophet Asaph, which they gladly did, and bowed their heads and worshiped.

31"The consecration ceremony is now ended," Hezekiah said. "Now bring your sacrifices and thank offerings." So the people from every part of the nation brought their sacrifices and thank offerings, and those who wished to brought burnt offerings too. 32,33In all, there were 70 young bulls for burnt offerings, 100 rams, and 200 lambs. In addition, 600 oxen and 3,000 sheep were brought as holy gifts. 34But there were too few priests to prepare the burnt offerings, so their brothers the Levites helped them until the work was finished—and until more priests had reported to work—for the Levites were much more ready to sanctify themselves than the priests were. 35There was an abundance of burnt offerings, and the usual drink offering with each, and many peace offerings. So it was that the Temple was restored to service, and the sacrifices offered again. 36And Hezekiah and all the people were very happy because of what God had accomplished so quickly.

30 Passover—Happy Again

King Hezekiah now sent letters throughout all of Israel, Judah, Ephraim, and Manasseh, inviting everyone to come to the Temple at Jerusalem for the annual Passover celebration. 2,3The king, his aides, and all the assembly of Jerusalem had voted to celebrate the Passover in May this time, rather than at the normal time in April, because not enough priests were sanctified at the earlier date, and there wasn't enough time to get notices out. 4The king and his advisors were in complete agreement in this matter, 5so they sent a Passover proclamation throughout Israel, from Dan to Beersheba, inviting everyone. They had not kept it in great numbers as prescribed.

6"Come back to the Lord God of Abraham, Isaac, and Israel," the king's letter said, "so that he will return to us who have escaped from the power of the kings of Assyria. 7Do not be like your fathers and brothers who sinned against the Lord God of their fathers and were destroyed. 8Do not be stubborn, as they were, but yield yourselves to the Lord and come to his Temple which he has sanctified forever, and worship the Lord your God so that his fierce anger will turn away from you. 9For if you turn to the Lord again, your brothers and your children will be treated mercifully by their captors, and they will be able to return to this land. For the Lord your God is full of kindness and mercy and will not continue to turn away his face from you if you return to him."

10So the messengers went from city to city throughout Ephraim and Manasseh and as far as Zebulun. But for the most part they were received with laughter and scorn! 11However, some from the tribes of Asher, Manasseh, and Zebulun turned to God and came to Jerusalem. 12But in Judah the entire nation felt a strong, God-given desire to obey the Lord's direction as commanded by the king and his officers. 13And so it was that a very large crowd assembled at Jerusalem in the month of May for the Passover celebration. 14They set to work and destroyed the heathen altars in Jerusalem, and knocked down all the incense altars, and threw them into Kidron Brook.

15On the first day of May the people killed their Passover lambs. Then the priests and Levites became ashamed of themselves for not taking a more active part, so they sanctified themselves and brought burnt offerings into the Temple. 16They stood at their posts as instructed by the law of Moses the man of God; and the priests sprinkled the blood received from the Levites.

17-19Since many of the people arriving from Ephraim, Manasseh, Issachar, and Zebulun were ceremonially impure because they had not undergone the purification rites, the Levites killed their Passover lambs for them, to sanctify them. Then King Hezekiah prayed for them, and they were permitted to eat the Passover anyway, even though this was contrary to God's rules. But

---

SHARING YOUR FAITH 30:11 In most places, Hezekiah's messengers were scorned when they invited people to the Passover, but some accepted the invitation. Our efforts to tell others about God often meet with similar reactions. Many people will not accept the invitation to accept Christ. But this must not stop us from reaching out. If you know and understand that rejection of the gospel is common, it can help you guard against feelings of personal rejection. Remember that the Holy Spirit convicts and convinces. Our task is to invite others to consider God's actions, his claims, and his promises. **To begin the series of devotionals on SHARING YOUR FAITH, turn to page 427.**

Hezekiah said, "May the good Lord pardon everyone who determines to follow the Lord God of his fathers, even though he is not properly sanctified for the ceremony." [20]And the Lord listened to Hezekiah's prayer and did not destroy them.

[21]So the people of Israel celebrated the Passover at Jerusalem for seven days with great joy.

Meanwhile the Levites and priests praised the Lord with music and cymbals day after day. [22](King Hezekiah spoke very appreciatively to the Levites of their excellent music.)

So for seven days the observance continued, and peace offerings were sacrificed, and the people confessed their sins to the Lord God of their fathers. [23]The enthusiasm continued, so it was unanimously decided to continue the observance for another seven days. [24]King Hezekiah gave the people 1,000 young bulls for offerings and 7,000 sheep; and the princes donated 1,000 young bulls and 10,000 sheep. And at this time another large group of priests stepped forward and sanctified themselves.

[25]Then the people of Judah, together with the priests, the Levites, the foreign residents, and the visitors from Israel, were filled with deep joy. [26]For Jerusalem hadn't seen a celebration like this one since the days of King David's son Solomon. [27]Then the priests and Levites stood and blessed the people, and the Lord heard their prayers from his holy temple in heaven.

31 The People Worship Again

Afterwards a massive campaign against idol worship was begun. Those who were at Jerusalem for the Passover went out to the cities of Judah, Benjamin, Ephraim, and Manasseh and tore down the idol altars, the obelisks, the shameful images, and other heathen centers of worship. Then the people who had come to the Passover from the northern tribes returned again to their own homes.

[2]Hezekiah now organized the priests and Levites into service corps to offer the burnt offerings and peace offerings, and to worship and give thanks and praise to the Lord. [3]He also made a personal contribution of animals for the daily morning and evening burnt offerings, as well as for the weekly Sabbath and monthly new moon festivals, and for the other annual feasts as required in the law of God.

[4]In addition, he required the people in Jerusalem to bring their tithes to the priests and Levites so that they wouldn't need other employment but could apply themselves fully to their duties as required in the law of God. [5,6]The people responded immediately and generously with the first of their crops and grain, new wine, olive oil, money, and everything else—a tithe of all they owned, as required by law to be given to the Lord their God. Everything was laid out in great piles. The people who had moved to Judah from the northern tribes and the people of Judah living in the provinces also brought in the tithes of their cattle and sheep, and brought a tithe of the dedicated things to give to the Lord, and piled them up in great heaps. [7,8]The first of these tithes arrived in June, and the piles continued to grow until October. When Hezekiah and his officials came and saw these huge piles, how they blessed the Lord and praised his people!

[9]"Where did all this come from?" Hezekiah asked the priests and Levites.

[10]And Azariah the High Priest from the clan of Zadok replied, "These are tithes! We have been eating from these stores of food for many weeks, but all this is left over, for the Lord has blessed his people."

[11]Hezekiah decided to prepare storerooms in the Temple. [12,13]All the dedicated supplies were brought into the Lord's house. Conaniah the Levite was put in charge, assisted by his brother Shimei and the following aides: Jehiel, Azaziah, Nahath, Asahel, Jerimoth, Jozabad, Eliel, Ismachiah, Mahath, Benaiah.

These appointments were made by King Hezekiah and Azariah the High Priest.

[14,15]Kore (son of Imnah, the Levite), who was the gatekeeper at the East Gate, was put in charge of distributing the offerings to the priests. His faithful assistants were Eden, Miniamin, Jeshua, Shemaiah, Amariah, and Shecaniah. They distributed the gifts to the clans of priests in their cities, dividing them to young and old alike. [16]However, the priests on duty at the Temple and their families were supplied directly from there, so they were not included in this distribution. [17,18]The priests were listed in the genealogical register by clans, and the Levites twenty years old and older were listed under the names of their work corps. A regular food allotment was given to all families of properly registered priests, for they had no other source of income because their time and energies were devoted to the service of the Temple. [19]One of the priests was appointed in each of the cities of the priests to issue food and other supplies to all priests in the area and to all registered Levites.

[20]In this way King Hezekiah handled the distribution throughout all Judah, doing what was just and fair in the sight of the Lord his God. [21]He worked very hard to encourage respect for the Temple, the law, and godly living, and was very successful.

32 An Angel Fights for Judah

Some time later after this good work of King Hezekiah, King Sennacherib of Assyria invaded Judah and laid siege to the fortified cities, planning to place them under tribute. ²When it was clear that Sennacherib was intending to attack Jerusalem, ³Hezekiah summoned his princes and officers for a council of war, and it was decided to plug the springs outside the city. ⁴They organized a huge work crew to block them and to cut off the brook running through the fields.

"Why should the king of Assyria come and find water?" they asked.

⁵Then Hezekiah further strengthened his defenses by repairing the wall wherever it was broken down, and by adding to the fortifications, and constructing a second wall outside it. He also reinforced Fort Millo in the City of David and manufactured large numbers of weapons and shields. ⁶He recruited an army and appointed officers, and summoned them to the plains before the city, and encouraged them with this address:

⁷"Be strong, be brave, and do not be afraid of the king of Assyria or his mighty army, for there is someone with us who is far greater than he is! ⁸He has a great army, but they are all mere men, while we have the Lord our God to fight our battles for us!" This greatly encouraged them.

⁹Then King Sennacherib of Assyria, while still besieging the city of Lachish, sent ambassadors with this message to King Hezekiah and the citizens of Jerusalem:

¹⁰"King Sennacherib of Assyria asks, 'Do you think you can survive my siege of Jerusalem? ¹¹King Hezekiah is trying to persuade you to commit suicide by staying there—to die by famine and thirst—while he promises that "the Lord our God will deliver us from the king of Assyria"! ¹²Don't you realize that Hezekiah is the very person who destroyed all the idols, and commanded Judah and Jerusalem to use only the one altar at the Temple, and to burn incense upon it alone? ¹³Don't you realize that I and the other kings of Assyria before me have never yet failed to conquer a nation we attacked? The gods of those nations weren't able to do a thing to save their lands! ¹⁴Name just one time when anyone, anywhere, was able to resist us successfully. What makes you think your God can do any better? ¹⁵Don't let Hezekiah fool you! Don't believe him. I say it again—no god of any nation has ever yet been able to rescue his people from me or my ancestors; how much less your God!'" ¹⁶Thus the ambassador mocked the Lord God and God's servant Hezekiah, heaping up insults.

¹⁷King Sennacherib also sent letters scorning the Lord God of Israel.

"The gods of all the other nations failed to save their people from my hand, and the God of Hezekiah will fail too," he wrote.

¹⁸The messengers who brought the letters shouted threats in the Jewish language to the people gathered on the walls of the city, trying to frighten and dishearten them. ¹⁹These messengers talked about the God of Jerusalem just as though he were one of the heathen gods—a handmade idol!

²⁰Then King Hezekiah and Isaiah the prophet (son of Amoz) cried out in prayer to God in heaven, ²¹and the Lord sent an angel who destroyed the Assyrian army with all its officers and generals! So Sennacherib returned home in deep shame to his own land. And when he arrived at the temple of his god, some of his own sons killed him there. ²²That is how the Lord saved Hezekiah and the people of Jerusalem. And now there was peace at last throughout his realm.

²³From then on King Hezekiah became immensely respected among the surrounding nations, and many gifts for the Lord arrived at Jerusalem, with valuable presents for King Hezekiah too.

²⁴But about that time Hezekiah became deathly sick, and he prayed to the Lord, and the Lord replied with a miracle. ²⁵However, Hezekiah didn't respond with true thanksgiving and praise for he had become proud, and so the anger of God was upon him and upon Judah and Jerusalem. ²⁶But finally Hezekiah and the residents of Jerusalem humbled themselves, so the wrath of the Lord did not fall upon them during Hezekiah's lifetime.

²⁷So Hezekiah became very wealthy and was highly honored. He had to construct special treasury buildings for his silver, gold, precious stones, and spices, and for his shields and gold bowls. ²⁸,²⁹He also built many storehouses for his grain, new wine, and olive oil, with many stalls for his animals and folds for the great flocks of sheep and goats he purchased; and he acquired many towns, for God had given him great wealth. ³⁰He dammed up the Upper Spring of Gihon and brought the water down through an aqueduct to the west side of the City of David sector in Jerusalem. He prospered in everything he did.

³¹However, when ambassadors arrived from Babylon to find out about the miracle of his being healed, God left him to himself in order to test him and to see what he was really like.

³²The rest of the story of Hezekiah and all of the good things he

---

TRUSTING GOD FOR HELP   32:1ff. When King Hezekiah was confronted with the frightening prospect of an Assyrian invasion, he made two important decisions. He did everything he could to deal with the situation, and he trusted God for the outcome. That is exactly what we must do when faced with difficult or frightening situations. Do everything you possibly can to solve the problem or improve the situation. As you do this, commit it to God in prayer and trust him for the solution. **To begin the series of devotionals on TRUSTING GOD FOR HELP, turn to page 29.**

did are written in *The Book of Isaiah* (the prophet, the son of Amoz), and in *The Annals of the Kings of Judah and Israel*. [33]When Hezekiah died, he was buried in the royal hillside cemetery among the other kings, and all Judah and Jerusalem honored him at his death. Then his son Manasseh became the new king.

33 Manasseh's Heart Is Changed

Manasseh was only twelve years old when he became king, and he reigned fifty-five years in Jerusalem. [2]But it was an evil reign, for he encouraged his people to worship the idols of the heathen nations destroyed by the Lord when the people of Israel entered the land. [3]He rebuilt the heathen altars his father Hezekiah had destroyed—the altars of Baal, and of the shameful images, and of the sun, moon, and stars. [4,5]He even constructed heathen altars in both courts of the Temple of the Lord for worshiping the sun, moon and stars—in the very place where the Lord had said that he would be honored forever. [6]And Manasseh sacrificed his own children as burnt offerings in the Valley of Hinnom. He consulted spirit-mediums, too, and fortune-tellers and sorcerers, and encouraged every sort of evil, making the Lord very angry.

[7]Think of it! He placed an idol in the very Temple of God, where God had told David and his son Solomon, "I will be honored here in this Temple and in Jerusalem—the city I have chosen to be honored forever above all the other cities of Israel. [8]And if you will only obey my commands—all the laws and instructions given to you by Moses—I won't ever again exile Israel from this land which I gave your ancestors."

[9]But Manasseh encouraged the people of Judah and Jerusalem to do even more evil than the nations the Lord destroyed when Israel entered the land. [10]Warnings from the Lord were ignored by both Manasseh and his people. [11]So God sent the Assyrian armies, and they seized him with hooks and bound him with bronze chains and carted him away to Babylon. [12]Then at last he came to his senses and cried out humbly to God for help. [13]And the Lord listened and answered his plea by returning him to Jerusalem and to his kingdom! At that point Manasseh finally realized that the Lord was really God!

[14]It was after this that he rebuilt the outer wall of the City of David and the wall from west of the Spring of Gihon in the Kidron Valley, and then to the Fish Gate, and around Citadel Hill, where it was built very high. And he stationed his army generals in all of the fortified cities of Judah. [15]He also removed the foreign gods from the hills and took his idol from the Temple, and tore down the altars he had built on the mountain, where the Temple stood, and the altars that were in Jerusalem, and dumped them outside the city. [16]Then he rebuilt the altar of the Lord and offered sacrifices upon it—peace offerings and thanksgiving offerings—and demanded that the people of Judah worship the Lord God of Israel. [17]However, the people still sacrificed upon the altars on the hills, but only to the Lord their God.

[18]The rest of Manasseh's deeds, and his prayer to God, and God's reply through the prophets—this is all written in *The Annals of the Kings of Israel*. [19]His prayer, and the way God answered, and a frank account of his sins and errors, including a list of the locations where he built idols on the hills and set up shameful and graven images (this of course was before the great change in his attitude), are recorded in *The Annals of the Prophets*.

[20,21]When Manasseh died, he was buried beneath his own palace, and his son Amon became the new king. Amon was twenty-two years old when he began to reign in Jerusalem, but he lasted for only two years. [22]It was an evil reign like the early years of his father Manasseh; for Amon sacrificed to all the idols just as his father had. [23]But he didn't change as his father did; instead he sinned more and more. [24]At last his own officers assassinated him in his palace. [25]But some public-spirited citizens killed all of those who assassinated him and declared his son Josiah to be the new king.

34 The Book of the Law Is Found

Josiah was only eight years old when he became king. He reigned thirty-one years in Jerusalem. [2]His was a good reign, as he carefully followed the good example of his ancestor King David. [3]For when he was sixteen years old, in the eighth year of his reign, he began to search for the God of his ancestor David, and four years later he began to clean up Judah and Jerusalem, destroying the heathen altars and the shameful idols on the hills. [4]He went out personally to watch as the altars of Baal were knocked apart, the obelisks above the altars chopped down, and the shameful idols ground into dust and scattered over the graves of those who had sacrificed to them. [5]Then he burned the bones of the heathen priests upon their own altars, feeling that this action would clear the people of Judah and Jerusalem from the guilt of their sin of idol-worship.

[6]Then he went to the cities of Manasseh, Ephraim, and Simeon, even to distant Naphtali, and did the same thing there. [7]He broke down the heathen altars, ground to powder the shameful idols, and chopped down the obelisks. He did this

everywhere throughout the whole land of Israel before returning to Jerusalem.

⁸During the eighteenth year of his reign, after he had purged the land and cleaned up the situation at the Temple, he appointed Shaphan (son of Azaliah) and Maaseiah, governor of Jerusalem, and Joah (son of Joahaz), the city treasurer, to repair the Temple. ⁹They set up a collection system for gifts for the Temple. The money was collected at the Temple gates by the Levites on guard duty there. Gifts were brought by the people coming from Manasseh, Ephraim, and other parts of the remnant of Israel, as well as from the people of Jerusalem. The money was taken to Hilkiah the High Priest for accounting, ¹⁰,¹¹and then used by the Levites to pay the carpenters and stonemasons and to purchase building materials—stone building blocks, timber, lumber, and beams. He now rebuilt what earlier kings of Judah had torn down.

¹²The workmen were energetic under the leadership of Jahath and Obadiah, Levites of the subclan of Merari. Zechariah and Meshullam, of the subclan of Kohath, were the building superintendents. The Levites who were skilled musicians played background music while the work progressed. ¹³Other Levites superintended the unskilled laborers who carried in the materials to the workmen. Still others assisted as accountants, supervisors, and carriers.

¹⁴One day when Hilkiah the High Priest was at the Temple recording the money collected at the gates, he found an old scroll that turned out to be the laws of God as given to Moses!

¹⁵,¹⁶"Look!" Hilkiah exclaimed to Shaphan, the king's secretary. "See what I have found in the Temple! These are the laws of God!" Hilkiah gave the scroll to Shaphan, and Shaphan took it to the king, along with his report that there was good progress being made in the reconstruction of the Temple.

¹⁷"The money chests have been opened and counted, and the money has been put into the hand of the overseers and workmen," he said to the king.

¹⁸Then he mentioned the scroll and how Hilkiah had discovered it. So he read it to the king. ¹⁹When the king heard what these laws required of God's people, he ripped his clothing in despair ²⁰and summoned Hilkiah, Ahikam (son of Shaphan), Abdon (son of Micah), Shaphan the treasurer, and Asaiah, the king's personal aide.

²¹"Go to the Temple and plead with the Lord for me!" the king told them. "Pray for all the remnant of Israel and Judah! For this scroll says that the reason the Lord's great anger has been poured out upon us is that our ancestors have not obeyed these laws that are written here."

²²So the men went to Huldah the prophetess, the wife of Shallum (son of Tokhath, son of Hasrah). (Shallum was the king's tailor, living in the second ward.) When they told her of the king's trouble, ²³she replied, "The Lord God of Israel says, Tell the man who sent you,

²⁴'Yes, the Lord will destroy this city and its people. All the curses written in the scroll will come true. ²⁵For my people have forsaken me and have worshiped heathen gods, and I am very angry with them for their deeds. Therefore, my unquenchable wrath is poured out upon this place.'

²⁶"But the Lord also says this to the king of Judah who sent you to ask me about this: Tell him, the Lord God of Israel says, ²⁷'Because you are sorry and have humbled yourself before God when you heard my words against this city and its people, and have ripped your clothing in despair and wept before me—I have heard you, says the Lord, ²⁸and I will not send the promised evil upon this city and its people until after your death.'" So they brought back to the king this word from the Lord. ²⁹Then the king summoned all the elders of Judah and Jerusalem, ³⁰and the priests and Levites and all the people great and small, to accompany him to the Temple. There the king read the scroll to them—the covenant of God that was found in the Temple. ³¹As the king stood before them, he made a pledge to the Lord to follow his commandments with all his heart and soul and to do what was written in the scroll. ³²And he required everyone in Jerusalem and Benjamin to subscribe to this pact with God, and all of them did.

³³So Josiah removed all idols from the areas occupied by the Jews and required all of them to worship Jehovah their God. And throughout the remainder of his lifetime they continued serving Jehovah, the God of their ancestors.

35 Josiah Celebrates Passover

Then Josiah announced that the Passover would be celebrated on the first day of April in Jerusalem. The Passover lambs were slain that evening. ²He also reestablished the priests in their duties and encouraged them to begin their work at the Temple again. ³He issued this order to the sanctified Levites, the religious teachers in Israel:

"Since the Ark is now in Solomon's Temple and you don't need to carry it back and forth upon your shoulders, spend your time ministering to the Lord and to his people. ⁴,⁵Form yourselves into the traditional service corps of your ancestors, as first organized by King David of Israel and by his son Solomon. Each corps will assist particular clans of the people who bring in their offerings to the Temple. ⁶Kill the Passover lambs and

Family Devotions

☐ DEVOTION 132

MAKING THE BEST CHOICES

Read 2 Chronicles 34:14-33

Making the Best Choices
Memory Verse

He will always give you all you need from day to day if you will make the Kingdom of God your primary concern.
Luke 12:31

Jim Matthew picked up his baseball mitt and ran outside. At the same moment the mail carrier arrived and started up the porch steps. "Hey, slow down there, young fellow," he said, "and I'll give you a letter from your friend in Clarksville."

"Just leave it in the box with the rest of the mail," Jim called out and went quickly on his way. The mailman scratched his head in surprise. Not too many weeks ago Jim had stopped him every day asking if there was a letter from Clarksville. Now he hardly seemed to care at all.

Jim's mom and dad had noticed the change in him, too. All of a sudden he seemed to have found new friends and had almost no interest in his old ones. His parents were also concerned because he seemed so restless and impatient when they had family devotions. He was in a hurry to be finished and get back to his friends.

When they gathered for devotions that evening, the letter from Clarksville still lay unopened on the coffee table. Dad placed the Bible beside it. "You've been neglecting your letters lately, haven't you?" he observed.

"Letters?" asked Jim. "Oh, you mean the one that came today. I'll read it pretty soon."

"I mean that one," said Dad, picking it up, "and this one, too." He also picked up the Bible. "You used to like to discuss things you read in the Bible, but lately, your new friends seem to take all your time and attention. Letters from old friends—even God's letter to you—have had to take second place, or maybe even third or fourth place."

Jim thought about that. Yes, not only had he shoved aside his friends' letters, reading them only if it was convenient, but he had done the same with God's letter—the Bible. Silently he bowed his head and asked God to give him a new love for the Word of God and for the Lord Jesus Christ. "Thanks, Lord," he prayed, "for being such a good friend." As he finished his prayer, Jim thought about his friend in Clarksville. He would read that letter right away and answer it soon.

How About You?
If you wrote a letter to someone, you would want him to read it, wouldn't you? God does, too. Is reading his letter, the Bible, a regular part of your day's schedule? R.J.

• For the next devotional, turn to page 477. • For the next devotional on MAKING THE BEST CHOICES, turn to page 579. • For notes on MAKING THE BEST CHOICES, see pages 358, 652, and 944.

sanctify yourselves and prepare to assist the people who come. Follow all of the instructions of the Lord through Moses."

⁷Then the king contributed 30,000 lambs and young goats for the people's Passover offerings and 3,000 young bulls. ⁸The king's officials made willing contributions to the priests and Levites. Hilkiah, Zechariah, and Jehiel, the overseers of the Temple, gave the priests 2,600 sheep and goats and 300 oxen as Passover offerings. ⁹The Levite leaders—Conaniah, Shemaiah, and Nethanel, and his brothers Hashabiah, Jeiel, and Jozabad—gave 5,000 sheep and goats and 500 oxen to the Levites for their Passover offerings.

¹⁰When everything was organized and the priests were standing in their places, and the Levites were formed into service corps as the king had instructed, ¹¹then the Levites killed the Passover lambs and presented the blood to the priests, who sprinkled it upon the altar as the Levites removed the skins. ¹²They piled up the carcasses for each tribe to present its own burnt sacrifices to the Lord, as it is written in the law of Moses. They did the same with the oxen. ¹³Then, as directed by the laws of Moses, they roasted the Passover lambs and boiled the holy offerings in pots, kettles, and pans, and hurried them out to the people to eat. ¹⁴Afterwards the Levites prepared a meal for themselves and for the priests, for they had been busy from morning till night offering the fat of the burnt offerings.

¹⁵The singers (the sons of Asaph) were in their places, following directions issued centuries earlier by King David, Asaph, Heman, and Jeduthun the king's prophet. The gatekeepers guarded the gates and didn't need to leave their posts of duty, for their meals were brought to them by their Levite brothers. ¹⁶The entire Passover ceremony was completed in that one day. All the burnt offerings were sacrificed upon the altar of the Lord, as Josiah had instructed.

¹⁷Everyone present in Jerusalem took part in the Passover observance, and this was followed by the Feast of Unleavened Bread for the next seven days. ¹⁸Never since the time of Samuel the prophet had there been such a Passover—not one of the kings of Israel could vie with King Josiah in this respect, involving so many of the priests, Levites, and people from Jerusalem and from all parts of Judah, and from over in Israel. ¹⁹This all happened in the eighteenth year of the reign of Josiah.

²⁰Afterwards King Neco of Egypt led his army to Carchemish on the Euphrates River, and Josiah declared war on him.

²¹But King Neco sent ambassadors to Josiah with this message: "I don't want a fight with you, O king of Judah! I have come only to fight the power with which I am at war. Leave me alone! God has told me to hurry! Don't meddle with God or he will destroy you, for he is with me."

²²But Josiah refused to turn back. Instead he led his army into the battle at the Valley of Megiddo. (He laid aside his royal robes so that the enemy wouldn't recognize him.) Josiah refused to believe that Neco's message was from God. ²³The enemy archers struck King Josiah with their arrows and fatally wounded him.

"Take me out of the battle," he exclaimed to his aides.

²⁴,²⁵So they lifted him out of his chariot and placed him in his second chariot and brought him back to Jerusalem where he died. He was buried there in the royal cemetery. And all Judah and Jerusalem, including even Jeremiah the prophet, mourned for him, as did the Temple choirs. To this day they still sing sad songs about his death, for these songs of sorrow were recorded among the official lamentations.

²⁶The other activities of Josiah, and his good deeds, and how he followed the laws of the Lord, ²⁷all are written in *The Annals of the Kings of Israel and Judah*.

36 Jerusalem Is Destroyed

Josiah's son Jehoahaz was selected as the new king. ²He was twenty-three years old when he began to reign, but lasted only three months. ³Then he was deposed by the king of Egypt, who demanded an annual tribute from Judah of $230,000.

⁴The king of Egypt now appointed Eliakim, the brother of Jehoahaz, as the new king of Judah. (Eliakim's name was changed to Jehoiakim.) Jehoahaz was taken to Egypt as a prisoner. ⁵Jehoiakim was twenty-five years old when he became king, and he reigned eleven years in Jerusalem; but his reign was an evil one. ⁶Finally Nebuchadnezzar king of Babylon conquered Jerusalem and took away the king in chains to Babylon. ⁷Nebuchadnezzar also took some of the gold bowls and other items from the Temple, placing them in his own temple in Babylon. ⁸The rest of the deeds of Jehoiakim and all the evil he did are written in *The Annals of the Kings of Judah*; and his son Jehoiachin became the new king.

⁹Jehoiachin was eighteen years old when he ascended the throne. But he lasted only three months and ten days, and it was an evil reign as far as the Lord was concerned. ¹⁰The following spring he was summoned to Babylon by King Nebuchadnezzar. Many treasures from the Temple were taken away to Babylon at that time, and King Nebuchadnezzar appointed Jehoiachin's

brother Zedekiah as the new king of Judah and Jerusalem.

¹¹Zedekiah was twenty-one years old when he became king and he reigned eleven years in Jerusalem. ¹²His reign, too, was evil so far as the Lord was concerned, for he refused to take the counsel of Jeremiah the prophet, who gave him messages from the Lord. ¹³He rebelled against King Nebuchadnezzar, even though he had taken an oath of loyalty. Zedekiah was a hard and stubborn man so far as obeying the Lord God of Israel was concerned, for he refused to follow him.

¹⁴All the important people of the nation, including the High Priests, worshiped the heathen idols of the surrounding nations, thus polluting the Temple of the Lord in Jerusalem. ¹⁵Jehovah the God of their fathers sent his prophets again and again to warn them, for he had compassion on his people and on his Temple. ¹⁶But the people mocked these messengers of God and despised their words, scoffing at the prophets until the anger of the Lord could no longer be restrained, and there was no longer any remedy.

¹⁷Then the Lord brought the king of Babylon against them and killed their young men, even going after them right into the Temple, and had no pity upon them, killing even young girls and old men. The Lord used the king of Babylon to destroy them completely. ¹⁸He also took home with him all the items, great and small, used in the Temple, and treasures from both the Temple and the palace, and took with him all the royal princes. ¹⁹Then his army burned the Temple and broke down the walls of Jerusalem and burned all the palaces and destroyed all the valuable Temple utensils. ²⁰Those who survived were taken away to Babylon as slaves to the king and his sons until the kingdom of Persia conquered Babylon.

²¹Thus the word of the Lord spoken through Jeremiah came true, that the land must rest for seventy years to make up for the years when the people refused to observe the Sabbath.

²²,²³But in the first year of King Cyrus of Persia, the Lord stirred up the spirit of Cyrus to make this proclamation throughout his kingdom, putting it into writing:

"All the kingdoms of the earth have been given to me by the Lord God of heaven, and he has instructed me to build him a Temple in Jerusalem, in the land of Judah. All among you who are the Lord's people return to Israel for this task, and the Lord be with you."

This also fulfilled the prediction of Jeremiah the prophet.

WAITING FOR something wonderful takes a lot of patience: waiting for school to let out for the summer . . . waiting for Christmas Day . . . waiting to save money for something you really want. . . . It would take a lot of patience if you had to wait your whole life for something!

The Israelites waited *seventy years* to get back to their homeland. They had been taken captive by the Babylonians, and now the Persians ruled over them. More than anything, they wanted to go back to Israel and to worship God in his Temple again.

After seventy years, the people got to go back and rebuild the Temple. They were so happy! But just when they got started, they had to wait again. Enemies kept them from building, and the Israelites had to wait a long time before they could finish it.

Many years after the Temple was built, something was still missing. The people had a temple but no one to teach them about God! This is when Ezra comes into the story. He moved to Jerusalem to teach the people God's Word.

It took a long time, but the Israelites got what they waited for—a chance to start again with God. Waiting teaches us how much we really want or need something. Look for ways to grow in patience as you read Ezra.

The Israelites Return Home

During the first year of the reign of King Cyrus of Persia, the Lord fulfilled Jeremiah's prophecy by giving King Cyrus the desire to send this proclamation throughout his empire (he also put it into the permanent records of the realm):

²"Cyrus, king of Persia, hereby announces that Jehovah, the God of heaven who gave me my vast empire, has now given me the responsibility of building him a Temple in Jerusalem, in the land of Judah. ³All Jews throughout the kingdom may now return to Jerusalem to rebuild this Temple of Jehovah, who is the God of Israel and of Jerusalem. May his blessings rest upon you. ⁴Those Jews who do not go should contribute toward the expenses of those who do and also supply them with clothing, transportation, supplies for the journey, and a freewill offering for the Temple."

⁵Then God gave a great desire to the leaders of the tribes of Judah and Benjamin, and to the priests and Levites, to return to Jerusalem at once to rebuild the Temple. ⁶And all the Jewish exiles

who chose to remain in Persia gave them whatever assistance they could, as well as gifts for the Temple.

[7]King Cyrus himself donated the gold bowls and other valuable items, which King Nebuchadnezzar had taken from the Temple at Jerusalem and had placed in the temple of his own gods. [8]He instructed Mithredath, the treasurer of Persia, to present these gifts to Sheshbazzar, the leader of the exiles returning to Judah.

[9,10]The items Cyrus donated included: 1,000 gold trays, 1,000 silver trays, 29 censers, 30 bowls of solid gold, 2,410 silver bowls (of various designs), 1,000 miscellaneous items. [11]In all there were 5,469 gold and silver items turned over to Sheshbazzar to take back to Jerusalem.

2 Here is the list of the Jewish exiles who now returned to Jerusalem and to the other cities of Judah, from which their parents had been deported to Babylon by King Nebuchadnezzar.

[2]The leaders were: Zerubbabel, Jeshua, Nehemiah, Seraiah, Reelaiah, Mordecai, Bilshan, Mispar, Bigvai, Rehum, Baanah.

Here is a census of those who returned (listed by subclans):

[3-35]From the subclan of Parosh, 2,172;
From the subclan of Shephatiah, 372;
From the subclan of Arah, 775;
From the subclan of Pahath-moab (the descendants of Jeshua and Joab), 2,812;
From the subclan of Elam, 1,254;
From the subclan of Zattu, 945;
From the subclan of Zaccai, 760;
From the subclan of Bani, 642;
From the subclan of Bebai, 623;
From the subclan of Azgad, 1,222;
From the subclan of Adonikam, 666;
From the subclan of Bigvai, 2,056;
From the subclan of Adin, 454;
From the subclan of Ater (the descendants of Hezekiah), 98;
From the subclan of Bezai, 323;
From the subclan of Jorah, 112;
From the subclan of Hashum, 223;
From the subclan of Gibbar, 95;
From the subclan of Bethlehem, 123;
From the subclan of Netophah, 56;
From the subclan of Anathoth, 128;
From the subclan of Azmaveth, 42;
From the subclans of Kiriath-arim, Chephirah, and Beeroth, 743;
From the subclans of Ramah and Geba, 621;
From the subclan of Michmas, 122;
From the subclans of Bethel and Ai, 223;
From the subclan of Nebo, 52;
From the subclan of Magbish, 156;
From the subclan of Elam, 1,254;
From the subclan of Harim, 320;
From the subclans of Lod, Hadid, and Ono, 725;
From the subclan of Jericho, 345;
From the subclan of Senaah, 3,630.

[36-39]Here are the statistics concerning the returning priests:

From the families of Jedaiah of the subclan of Jeshua, 973;
From the subclan of Immer, 1,052;
From the subclan of Pashhur, 1,247;
From the subclan of Harim, 1,017.

[40-42]Here are the statistics concerning the Levites who returned:

From the families of Jeshua and Kadmiel of the subclan of Hodaviah, 74;
The choir members from the clan of Asaph, 128;
From the descendants of the gatekeepers (the families of Shallum, Ater, Talmon, Akkub, Hatita, and Shobai), 139.

[43-54]The following families of the Temple assistants were represented:
Ziha, Hasupha, Tabbaoth, Keros, Siaha, Padon, Lebanah, Hagabah, Akkub, Hagab, Shamlai, Hanan, Giddel, Gahar, Reaiah, Rezin, Nekoda, Gazzam, Uzza, Paseah, Besai, Asnah, Meunim, Nephisim, Bakbuk, Hakupha, Harhur, Bazluth, Mehida, Harsha, Barkos, Sisera, Temah, Neziah, Hatipha.

[55-57]Those who made the trip also included the descendants of King Solomon's officials:
Sotai, Hassophereth, Peruda, Jaalah, Darkon, Giddel, Shephatiah, Hattil, Pochereth-hazzebaim, Ami.

[58]The Temple assistants and the descendants of Solomon's officers numbered 392.

[59]Another group returned to Jerusalem at this time from the Persian cities of Tel-melah, Tel-harsha,

---

CULTIVATING GODLY ATTITUDES 1:5 God "gave a great desire" to the leaders to return to Jerusalem and rebuild the Temple. Major changes begin on the inside as God works on our attitudes, beliefs, and desires. These inner changes lead to faithful actions. After forty-eight years of captivity, the arrogant Jewish nation had been humbled. When the people's attitudes and desires changed, God ended the disciplining of his people and gave them another opportunity to go home and try again. Paul reminds us that "God is at work within you, helping you want to obey him, and then helping you do what he wants" (Philippians 2:13). Doing God's will begins with your desires. Are you willing to be humble, to be open to his opportunities, and to move at his direction? Ask God to give you the desire to follow him more closely. **To begin the series of devotionals on CULTIVATING GODLY ATTITUDES, turn to page 121.**

Cherub, Addan, and Immer. However, they had lost their genealogies and could not prove that they were really Israelites. ⁶⁰This group included the subclans of Delaiah, Tobiah, and Nekoda—a total of 652.

⁶¹Three subclans of priests—Habaiah, Hakkoz, and Barzillai (he married one of the daughters of Barzillai the Gileadite and took her family name)—also returned to Jerusalem. ⁶²,⁶³But they too had lost their genealogies, so the leaders refused to allow them to continue as priests; they would not even allow them to eat the priests' share of food from the sacrifices until the Urim and Thummim could be consulted to find out from God whether they actually were descendants of priests or not.

⁶⁴,⁶⁵So a total of 42,360 persons returned to Judah; in addition to 7,337 slaves and 200 choir members, both men and women. ⁶⁶,⁶⁷They took with them 736 horses, 245 mules, 435 camels, and 6,720 donkeys.

⁶⁸Some of the leaders were able to give generously toward the rebuilding of the Temple, ⁶⁹and each gave as much as he could. The total value of their gifts amounted to $300,000 of gold, $170,000 of silver, and 100 robes for the priests.

⁷⁰So the priests and Levites and some of the common people settled in Jerusalem and its nearby villages; and the singers, the gatekeepers, the Temple workers, and the rest of the people returned to the other cities of Judah from which they had come.

3 The New Temple

During the month of September everyone who had returned to Judah came to Jerusalem from their homes in the other towns. Then Jeshua (son of Jozadak) with his fellow priests, and Zerubbabel (son of Shealtiel) and his clan, rebuilt the altar of the God of Israel and sacrificed burnt offerings upon it, as instructed in the laws of Moses, the man of God. ³The altar was rebuilt on its old site, and it was used immediately to sacrifice morning and evening burnt offerings to the Lord; for the people were fearful of attack.

⁴And they celebrated the Feast of Tabernacles as prescribed in the laws of Moses, sacrificing the burnt offerings specified for each day of the feast. ⁵They also offered the special sacrifices required for the Sabbaths, the new moon celebrations, and the other regular annual feasts of the Lord. Voluntary offerings of the people were also sacrificed. ⁶It was on the fifteenth day of September that the priests began sacrificing the burnt offerings to the Lord. (This was before they began building the foundation of the Temple.)

⁷Then they hired masons and carpenters and bought cedar logs from the people of Tyre and Sidon, paying for them with food, wine, and olive oil. The logs were brought down from the Lebanon mountains and floated along the coast of the Mediterranean Sea to Joppa, for King Cyrus had included this provision in his grant.

⁸The actual construction of the Temple began in June of the second year of their arrival at Jerusalem. The work force was made up of all those who had returned, and they were under the direction of Zerubbabel (son of Shealtiel), Jeshua (son of Jozadak), and their fellow priests and the Levites. The Levites who were twenty years old or older were appointed to supervise the workmen. ⁹The supervision of the entire project was given to Jeshua, Kadmiel, Henadad, and their sons and relatives, all of whom were Levites.

¹⁰When the builders completed the foundation of the Temple, the priests put on their official robes and blew their trumpets; and the descendants of Asaph crashed their cymbals to praise the Lord in the manner ordained by King David. ¹¹They sang rounds of praise and thanks to God, singing this song: "He is good, and his love and mercy toward Israel will last forever." Then all the people gave a great shout, praising God because the foundation of the Temple had been laid.

¹²But many of the priests and Levites and other leaders—the old men who remembered Solomon's beautiful Temple—wept aloud, while others were shouting for joy! ¹³So the shouting and the weeping mingled together in a loud commotion that could be heard far away!

4 Enemies Try to Stop the Temple

When the enemies of Judah and Benjamin heard that the exiles had returned and were rebuilding the Temple, ²they approached Zerubbabel and the other leaders and suggested, "Let us work with you, for we are just as interested in your God as you are; we have sacrificed to him ever since King Esar-haddon of Assyria brought us here."

³But Zerubbabel and Jeshua and the other Jewish leaders replied, "No, you may have no part in this work. The Temple of the God of Israel must be built by the Israelis, just as King Cyrus has commanded."

⁴,⁵Then the local residents tried to discourage and frighten them by sending agents to tell lies about them to King Cyrus. This went on during his entire reign and lasted until King Darius took the throne.

⁶And afterwards, when King Ahasuerus began to reign, they wrote him a letter of accusation against the people of Judah and Jerusalem ⁷and did the same thing during the reign of Artaxerxes.

Bishlam, Mithredath, and Tabeel and their associates wrote a letter to him in the Aramaic language, and it was translated to him. [8,9]Others who participated were Governor Rehum, Shimshai (a scribe), several judges and other local leaders, the Persians, the Babylonians, the men of Erech and Susa, [10]and men from several other nations. (They had been taken from their own lands by the great and noble Osnappar and relocated in Jerusalem, Samaria, and throughout the neighboring lands west of the Euphrates River.)

[11]Here is the text of the letter they sent to King Artaxerxes:

"Sir: Greetings from your loyal subjects west of the Euphrates River. [12]Please be informed that the Jews sent to Jerusalem from Babylon are rebuilding this historically rebellious and evil city; they have already rebuilt its walls and have repaired the foundations of the Temple. [13]But we wish you to know that if this city is rebuilt, it will be much to your disadvantage, for the Jews will then refuse to pay their taxes to you.

[14]"Since we are grateful to you as our patron, and we do not want to see you taken advantage of and dishonored in this way, we have decided to send you this information. [15]We suggest that you search the ancient records to discover what a rebellious city this has been in the past; in fact, it was destroyed because of its long history of sedition against the kings and countries who attempted to control it. [16]We wish to declare that if this city is rebuilt and the walls finished, you might as well forget about this part of your empire beyond the Euphrates, for it will be lost to you."

[17]Then the king made this reply to Governor Rehum and Shimshai the scribe, and to their companions living in Samaria and throughout the area west of the Euphrates River:

[18]"Gentlemen: Greetings! The letter you sent has been translated and read to me. [19]I have ordered a search made of the records and have indeed found that Jerusalem has in times past been a hotbed of insurrection against many kings; in fact, rebellion and sedition are normal there! [20]I find, moreover, that there have been some very great kings in Jerusalem who have ruled the entire land beyond the Euphrates River and have received vast tribute, custom, and toll. [21]Therefore, I command that these men must stop their work until I have investigated the matter more thoroughly. [22]Do not delay, for we must not permit the situation to get out of control!"

[23]When this letter from King Artaxerxes was read to Rehum and Shimshai, they hurried to Jerusalem and forced the Jews to stop building. [24]So the work ended until the second year of the reign of King Darius of Persia.

5 The Rebuilding Continues

But there were prophets in Jerusalem and Judah at that time—Haggai, and Zechariah (the son of Iddo)—who brought messages from the God of Israel to Zerubbabel (son of Shealtiel) and Jeshua (son of Jozadak), encouraging them to begin building again! So they did and the prophets helped them.

[3]But Tattenai, the governor of the lands west of the Euphrates, and Shethar-bozenai, and their companions soon arrived in Jerusalem and demanded, "Who gave you permission to rebuild this Temple and finish these walls?"

[4]They also asked for a list of the names of all the men who were working on the Temple. [5]But because the Lord was overseeing the entire situation, our enemies did not force us to stop building, but let us continue while King Darius looked into the matter and returned his decision.

[6]Following is the letter which Governors Tattenai and Shethar-bozenai and the other officials sent to King Darius:

[7]"To King Darius:

"Greetings!

[8]"We wish to inform you that we went to the construction site of the Temple of the great God of Judah. It is being built with huge stones, and timber is being laid in the city walls. The work is going forward with great energy and success. [9]We asked the leaders, 'Who has given you permission to do this?' [10]And we demanded their names so that we could notify you. [11]Their answer was, 'We are the servants of the God of heaven and earth and we are rebuilding the Temple that was constructed here many centuries ago by a great king of Israel. [12]But afterwards our ancestors angered the God of heaven, and he abandoned them and let King Nebuchadnezzar destroy this Temple and exile the people to Babylonia.'

[13]"But they insist that King Cyrus of Babylon, during the first year of his reign, issued a decree that the Temple should be rebuilt, [14]and they say King Cyrus returned the gold and silver bowls which Nebuchadnezzar had taken from the Temple in

---

ENCOURAGING OTHERS 5:1-2 God sometimes sends prophets to encourage and strengthen his people. Haggai and Zechariah not only preached, but also got involved in the labor. In the church today, God appoints prophetic voices to help us with our work (Ephesians 4:11-13). Their ministry should have the same effect upon us as Haggai's and Zechariah's had on Israel. "One who prophesies, preaching the messages of God, is helping others grow in the Lord, encouraging and comforting them" (1 Corinthians 14:3). In turn, we should encourage those who bring God's words to us. **To begin the series of devotionals on ENCOURAGING OTHERS, turn to page 705.**

Jerusalem and had placed in the temple of Babylon. They say these items were delivered into the safekeeping of a man named Sheshbazzar, whom King Cyrus appointed as governor of Judah. ¹⁵The king instructed him to return the bowls to Jerusalem and to let the Temple of God be built there as before. ¹⁶So Sheshbazzar came and laid the foundations of the Temple at Jerusalem; and the people have been working on it ever since, though it is not yet completed. ¹⁷We request that you search in the royal library of Babylon to discover whether King Cyrus ever made such a decree; and then let us know your pleasure in this matter."

6 King Darius Approves

So King Darius issued orders that a search be made in the Babylonian archives, where documents were stored.

²Eventually the record was found in the palace at Ecbatana, in the province of Media. This is what it said:

³"In this first year of the reign of King Cyrus, a decree has been sent out concerning the Temple of God at Jerusalem where the Jews offer sacrifices. It is to be rebuilt, and the foundations are to be strongly laid. The height will be ninety feet and the width will be ninety feet. ⁴There will be three layers of huge stones in the foundation, topped with a layer of new timber. All expenses will be paid by the king. ⁵And the gold and silver bowls, which were taken from the Temple of God by Nebuchadnezzar, shall be taken back to Jerusalem and put into the Temple as they were before."

⁶So King Darius II sent this message to Governor Shethar-bozenai and the other officials west of the Euphrates:

"Do not disturb the construction of the Temple. Let it be rebuilt on its former site, ⁷and don't molest the governor of Judah and the other leaders in their work. ⁸Moreover, I decree that you are to pay the full construction costs without delay from my taxes collected in your territory. ⁹Give the priests in Jerusalem young bulls, rams, and lambs for burnt offerings to the God of heaven; and give them wheat, wine, salt, and olive oil each day without fail. ¹⁰Then they will be able to offer acceptable sacrifices to the God of heaven and pray for me and my sons. ¹¹Anyone who attempts to change this message in any way shall have the beams pulled from his house and built into a gallows on which he will be hanged; and his house shall be reduced to a pile of rubble. ¹²The God who has chosen the city of Jerusalem will destroy any king and any nation that alters this commandment and destroys this Temple. I, Darius, have issued this decree; let it be obeyed with all diligence."

¹³Governors Tattenai and Shethar-bozenai, and their companions complied at once with the command of King Darius.

¹⁴So the Jewish leaders continued in their work, and they were greatly encouraged by the preaching of the prophets Haggai and Zechariah (son of Iddo).

The Temple was finally finished, as had been commanded by God and decreed by Cyrus, Darius, and Artaxerxes, the kings of Persia. ¹⁵The completion date was February 18 in the sixth year of the reign of King Darius II.

¹⁶The Temple was then dedicated with great joy by the priests, the Levites, and all the people. ¹⁷During the dedication celebration 100 young bulls, 200 rams, and 400 lambs were sacrificed; and twelve male goats were presented as a sin offering for the twelve tribes of Israel. ¹⁸Then the priests and Levites were divided into their various service corps to do the work of God as instructed in the laws of Moses.

¹⁹The Passover was celebrated on the first day of April. ²⁰For by that time many of the priests and Levites had consecrated themselves. ²¹,²²And some of the heathen people who had been relocated in Judah turned from their immoral customs and joined the Israelis in worshiping the Lord God. They, with the entire nation, ate the Passover feast and celebrated the Feast of Unleavened Bread for seven days. There was great joy throughout the land because the Lord had caused the king of Assyria to be generous to Israel and to assist in the construction of the Temple.

7 Ezra Comes to Teach

Here is the genealogy of Ezra, who traveled from Babylon to Jerusalem during the reign of King Artaxerxes of Persia:

Ezra was the son of Seriah;
Seriah was the son of Azariah;
Azariah was the son of Hilkiah;
Hilkiah was the son of Shallum;
Shallum was the son of Zadok;
Zadok was the son of Ahitub;
Ahitub was the son of Amariah;
Amariah was the son of Meraioth;
Meraioth was the son of Zerahiah;
Zerahiah was the son of Uzzi;
Uzzi was the son of Bukki;
Bukki was the son of Abishua;
Abishua was the son of Phinehas;
Phinehas was the son of Eleazar;
Eleazar was the son of Aaron, the chief priest.

⁶As a Jewish religious leader, Ezra was well versed in Jehovah's laws, which Moses had given to the people of Israel. He asked to be allowed to return to Jerusalem, and the king granted his request; for the Lord his God was blessing him. ⁷⁻⁹Many ordinary people as well as priests, Levites, singers, gatekeepers, and Temple workers traveled with him. They left Babylon in the middle of March in the seventh year of the reign of Artaxerxes and arrived at Jerusalem in the month of August; for the Lord gave them a good trip. ¹⁰This was because Ezra had determined to study and obey the laws of the Lord and to become a Bible teacher, teaching those laws to the people of Israel.

¹¹King Artaxerxes presented this letter to Ezra the priest, the student of God's commands:

¹²"From: Artaxerxes, the king of kings.

"To: Ezra the priest, the teacher of the laws of the God of heaven.

¹³"I decree that any Jew in my realm, including the priests and Levites, may return to Jerusalem with you. ¹⁴I and my Council of Seven hereby instruct you to take a copy of God's laws to Judah and Jerusalem and to send back a report of the religious progress being made there. ¹⁵We also commission you to take with you to Jerusalem the silver and gold, which we are presenting as an offering to the God of Israel.

¹⁶"Moreover, you are to collect voluntary Temple offerings of silver and gold from the Jews and their priests in all of the provinces of Babylon. ¹⁷These funds are to be used primarily for the purchase of oxen, rams, lambs, grain offerings, and drink offerings, all of which will be offered upon the altar of your Temple when you arrive in Jerusalem. ¹⁸The money that is left over may be used in whatever way you and your brothers feel is the will of your God. ¹⁹And take with you the gold bowls and other items we are giving you for the Temple of your God at Jerusalem. ²⁰If you run short of money for the construction of the Temple or for any similar needs, you may requisition funds from the royal treasury.

²¹"I, Artaxerxes the king, send this decree to all the treasurers in the provinces west of the Euphrates River: 'You are to give Ezra whatever he requests of you (for he is a priest and teacher of the laws of the God of heaven), ²²up to $200,000 in silver; 1,225 bushels of wheat; 990 gallons of wine; any amount of salt; ²³and whatever else the God of heaven demands for his Temple; for why should we risk God's wrath against the king and his sons? ²⁴I also decree that no priest, Levite, choir member, gatekeeper, Temple attendant, or other worker in the Temple shall be required to pay taxes of any kind.'

²⁵"And you, Ezra, are to use the wisdom God has given you to select and appoint judges and other officials to govern all the people west of the Euphrates River; if they are not familiar with the laws of your God, you are to teach them. ²⁶Anyone refusing to obey the law of your God and the law of the king shall be punished immediately by death, banishment, confiscation of goods, or imprisonment."

²⁷Well, praise the Lord God of our ancestors, who made the king want to beautify the Temple of the Lord in Jerusalem! ²⁸And praise God for demonstrating such loving-kindness to me by honoring me before the king and his Council of Seven and before all of his mighty princes! I was given great status because the Lord my God was with me; and I persuaded some of the leaders of Israel to return with me to Jerusalem.

8 The Exiles Who Returned

These are the names and genealogies of the leaders who accompanied me from Babylon during the reign of King Artaxerxes:

²⁻¹⁴From the clan of Phinehas—Gershom;
From the clan of Ithamar—Daniel;
From the subclan of David of the clan of Shecaniah—Hattush;
From the clan of Parosh—Zechariah, and 150 other men;
From the clan of Pahath-moab—Eliehoenai (son of Zerahiah), and 200 other men;
From the clan of Shecaniah—the son of Jahaziel, and 300 other men;
From the clan of Adin—Ebed (son of Jonathan), and 50 other men;
From the clan of Elam—Jeshaiah (son of Athaliah), and 70 other men;
From the clan of Shephatiah—Zebadiah (son of Michael), and 80 other men;
From the clan of Joab—Obadiah (son of Jehiel), and 218 other men;
From the clan of Bani—Shelomith (son of Josiphiah), and 160 other men;
From the clan of Bebai—Zechariah (son of Bebai), and 28 other men;
From the clan of Azgad—Johanan (son of Hakkatan), and 110 other men;
From the clan of Adonikam—Eliphelet, Jeuel, Shemaiah, and 60 other men (they arrived at a later time);
From the clan of Bigvai—Uthai, Zaccur, and 70 other men.

¹⁵We assembled at the Ahava River and camped there for three days while I went over the lists of the people and the priests who had arrived; and I found that not one Levite had volunteered! ¹⁶So I sent for Eliezer, Ariel, Shemaiah, Elnathan, Jarib, Elnathan, Nathan, Zechariah, and Meshullam, the Levite leaders; I

Family Devotions

☐ **DEVOTION 133**

LEAVING THE FUTURE IN GOD'S HANDS

Read Ezra 8:21-23

Roxie sat curled up on the couch with Mittens, her cat, purring on her lap. "Mittens, things will never be the same," she told the cat sadly. "We're moving, and I'll never see my friends again."

"Mittens, you're not going to like moving." Roxie was surprised to hear Dad's voice behind her. "As far as you know, this apartment is all there is to the world, but we're going to take you out of it," continued Dad. He sat down next to Roxie. She stared at him curiously as he went on talking to the cat. "Mittens, you're going to be scared when we put you in the pet carrier and put it on the plane. You're going to think your life will never be the same." Dad paused. "Maybe we should just leave you here," he added.

"But, Dad," protested Roxie, "you said that Mittens will be able to climb trees and chase mice at our new house. She'll do lots of things she's never done before. She might not like moving, but she'll like it after she gets there."

"Think so?" asked Dad. "Well, I guess you're right. Since you're not a cat, you see things from a different point of view than Mittens does, don't you? You know that when Mittens gets to her new home in the country, she'll be happy there. And Roxie, just as you see the cat's future from a different point of view than she does, God sees your future from a different point of view than you do. And he promises to protect us and go with us into our new home."

Roxie sniffed as she stroked the cat. "Well, Mittens, maybe there's a different world out there for both of us," she said finally. "We might even find a tree to climb together." Roxie smiled as she gave the cat a squeeze.

Leaving the Future in God's Hands Memory Verse

For I know the plans I have for you, says the Lord. They are plans for good and not for evil, to give you a future and a hope.
Jeremiah 29:11

How About You?

Is there a circumstance in your life that is so hard you feel you'll never get over it? God doesn't let you see into the future, but he sees what's there. And you can trust him to protect you and help you, no matter what the future holds. K. R. A.

• For the next devotional, turn to page 483. • For the next devotional on LEAVING THE FUTURE IN GOD'S HANDS, turn to page 701. • For notes on LEAVING THE FUTURE IN GOD'S HANDS, see pages 405, 452, 831, and 1061.

also sent for Joiarib and Elnathan, who were very wise men. ¹⁷I sent them to Iddo, the leader of the Jews at Casiphia, to ask him and his brothers and the Temple attendants to send us priests for the Temple of God at Jerusalem. ¹⁸And God was good! He sent us an outstanding man named Sherebiah, along with eighteen of his sons and brothers; he was a very astute man and a descendant of Mahli, the son of Levi and grandson of Israel. ¹⁹God also sent Hashabiah; and Jeshaiah (the son of Merari), with twenty of his sons and brothers; ²⁰and 220 Temple attendants. (The Temple attendants were assistants to the Levites—a job classification of Temple employees first instituted by King David.) These 220 men were all listed by name.

²¹Then I declared a fast while we were at the Ahava River so that we would humble ourselves before our God; and we prayed that he would give us a good journey and protect us, our children, and our goods as we traveled. ²²For I was ashamed to ask the king for soldiers and cavalry to accompany us and protect us from the enemies along the way. After all, we had told the king that our God would protect all those who worshiped him, and that disaster could come only to those who had forsaken him! ²³So we fasted and begged God to take care of us. And he did.

²⁴I appointed twelve leaders of the priests—Sherebiah, Hashabiah, and ten other priests— ²⁵to be in charge of transporting the silver, gold, the gold bowls, and the other items that the king and his council and the leaders and people of Israel had presented to the Temple of God. ²⁶,²⁷I weighed the money as I gave it to them and found it to total $1,300,000 in silver; $200,000 in silver utensils; many millions in gold; and twenty gold bowls worth a total of $100,000. There were also two beautiful pieces of brass that were as precious as gold. ²⁸I consecrated these men to the Lord and then consecrated the treasures—the equipment and money and bowls that had been given as free-will offerings to the Lord God of our fathers.

²⁹"Guard these treasures well!" I told them; "present them without a penny lost to the priests and the Levite leaders and the elders of Israel at Jerusalem, where they are to be placed in the treasury of the Temple."

³⁰So the priests and the Levites accepted the responsibility of taking them to God's Temple in Jerusalem. ³¹We broke camp at the Ahava River at the end of March and started off to Jerusalem; and God protected us and saved us from enemies and bandits along the way. ³²So at last we arrived safely at Jerusalem.

³³On the fourth day after our arrival, the silver, gold, and other valuables were weighed in the Temple by Meremoth (the son of Uriah the priest), Eleazar (son of Phinehas), Jozabad (son of Jeshua), and Noadiah (son of Binnui)—all of whom were Levites. ³⁴A receipt was given for each item, and the weight of the gold and silver was noted.

³⁵Then everyone in our party sacrificed burnt offerings to the God of Israel—twelve oxen for the nation of Israel; ninety-six rams; seventy-seven lambs; and twelve goats as a sin offering. ³⁶The king's decrees were delivered to his lieutenants and the governors of all the provinces west of the Euphrates River, and of course they then cooperated in the rebuilding of the Temple of God.

9 Ezra Confesses His People's Sin

But then the Jewish leaders came to tell me that many of the Jewish people and even some of the priests and Levites had taken up the horrible customs of the heathen people who lived in the land—the Canaanites, Hittites, Perizzites, Jebusites, Ammonites, Moabites, Egyptians, and Amorites. ²The men of Israel had married girls from these heathen nations and had taken them as wives for their sons. So the holy people of God were being polluted by these mixed marriages, and the political leaders were some of the worst offenders.

³When I heard this, I tore my clothing and pulled hair from my head and beard and sat down utterly baffled. ⁴Then many who feared the God of Israel because of this sin of his people came and sat with me until the time of the evening burnt offering.

⁵Finally I stood before the Lord in great embarrassment; then I fell to my knees and lifted my hands to the Lord, ⁶and cried out, "O my God, I am ashamed; I blush to lift up my face to you, for our sins are piled higher than our heads and our guilt is as boundless as the heavens. ⁷Our whole history has been one of sin; that is why we and our kings and our priests were slain by the heathen kings—we were captured, robbed, and disgraced, just as we are today. ⁸But now we have been given a moment of peace, for you have permitted a few of us to return to Jerusalem from our exile. You have given us a moment of joy and new life in our slavery. ⁹For we were slaves, but in your love and mercy you did not abandon us to slavery; instead, you caused the kings of Persia to be favorable to us. They have even given us their assistance in rebuilding the Temple of our God and in giving us Jerusalem as a walled city in Judah.

¹⁰"And now, O God, what can we say after all of this? For once again we have abandoned you and broken your laws! ¹¹The prophets warned us that the land we would possess was totally defiled by the horrible practices of the people living there. From one end to the other it is filled with corruption.

¹²You told us not to let our daughters marry their sons, and not to let our sons marry their daughters, and not to help those nations in any way. You warned us that only if we followed this rule could we become a prosperous nation and forever leave that prosperity to our children as an inheritance. ¹³And now, even after our punishment in exile because of our wickedness (and we have been punished far less than we deserved), and even though you have let some of us return, ¹⁴we have broken your commandments again and intermarried with people who do these awful things. Surely your anger will destroy us now until not even this little remnant escapes. ¹⁵O Lord God of Israel, you are a just God; what hope can we have if you give us justice as we stand here before you in our wickedness?"

10 The People Confess Their Sin

As I lay on the ground in front of the Temple, weeping and praying and making this confession, a large crowd of men, women, and children gathered around and cried with me.

²Then Shecaniah (the son of Jehiel of the clan of Elam) said to me, "We acknowledge our sin against our God, for we have married these heathen women. But there is hope for Israel in spite of this. ³For we agree before our God to divorce our heathen wives and to send them away with our children; we will follow your commands and the commands of the others who fear our God. We will obey the laws of God. ⁴Take courage and tell us how to proceed in setting things straight, and we will fully cooperate."

⁵So I stood up and demanded that the leaders of the priests and the Levites and all the people of Israel swear that they would do as Shecaniah had said; and they all agreed. ⁶Then I went into the room of Jehohanan in the Temple and refused all food and drink, for I was mourning because of the sin of the returned exiles.

⁷,⁸Then a proclamation was made throughout Judah and Jerusalem that everyone should appear at Jerusalem within three days and that the leaders and elders had decided that anyone who refused to come would be disinherited and excommunicated from Israel. ⁹Within three days, on the fifth day of December, all the men of Judah and Benjamin had arrived and were sitting in the open space before the Temple; and they were trembling because of the seriousness of the matter and because of the heavy rainfall. ¹⁰Then I, Ezra the priest, arose and addressed them:

"You have sinned, for you have married heathen women; now we are even more deeply under God's condemnation than we were before. ¹¹Confess your sin to the Lord God of your fathers and do what he demands: separate yourselves from the heathen people about you and from these women."

¹²Then all the men spoke up and said, "We will do what you have said. ¹³ But this isn't something that can be done in a day or two, for there are many of us involved in this sinful affair. And it is raining so hard that we can't stay out here much longer. ¹⁴Let our leaders arrange trials for us. Everyone who has a heathen wife will come at the scheduled time with the elders and judges of his city; then each case will be decided and the situation will be cleared up, and the fierce wrath of our God will be turned away from us."

¹⁵Only Jonathan (son of Asahel), Jahzeiah (son of Tikvah), Meshullam, and Shabbethai the Levite opposed this course of action.

¹⁶⁻¹⁹So this was the plan that was followed: Some of the clan leaders and I were designated as judges; we began our work on December 15 and finished by March 15.

Following is the list of priests who had married heathen wives (they vowed to divorce their wives and acknowledged their guilt by offering rams as sacrifices): Maaseiah, Eliezer, Jarib, Gedaliah.

²⁰The sons of Immer: Hanani, Zebadiah.

²¹The sons of Harim: Maaseiah, Elijah, Shemaiah, Jehiel, Uzziah.

²²The sons of Pashhur: Elioenai, Maaseiah, Ishmael, Nethanel, Jozabad, Elasah.

²³The Levites who were guilty: Jozabad, Shimei, Kelaiah (also called Kelita), Pethahaiah, Judah, Eliezer.

²⁴Of the singers, there was Eliashib.

Of the gatekeepers, Shallum, Telem, and Uri.

²⁵Here is the list of ordinary citizens who were declared guilty:

From the clan of Parosh: Ramiah, Izziah, Malchijah, Mijamin, Eleazar, Hashabiah, Benaiah.

²⁶From the clan of Elam: Mattaniah, Zechariah, Jehiel, Abdi, Jeremoth, Elijah.

²⁷From the clan of Zattu: Elioenai, Eliashib, Mattaniah, Jeremoth, Zabad, Aziza.

²⁸From the clan of Bebai: Jehohanan, Hananiah, Zabbai, Athlai.

²⁹From the clan of Bani: Meshullam, Malluch, Adaiah, Jashub, Sheal, Jeremoth.

CONFESSING SIN 10:3-4, 11 Following Ezra's earnest prayer, the people admitted their sin to God. Then they asked for direction in restoring their relationship with God. True repentance does not end with words of confession—that would be mere lip service. It must lead to corrected behavior and changed attitudes. When you sin and are truly sorry, confess this to God, ask his forgiveness, and accept his grace and mercy. Then, as an act of thankfulness for your forgiveness, change your ways. **To begin the series of devotionals on CONFESSING SIN, turn to page 41.**

³⁰From the clan of Pahath-moab: Adna, Chelal, Benaiah, Maaseiah, Mattaniah, Bezalel, Binnui, Manasseh.

³¹,³²From the clan of Harim: Eliezer, Isshijah, Malchijah, Shemaiah, Shimeon, Benjamin, Malluch, Shemariah.

³³From the clan of Hashum: Mattenai, Mattattah, Zabad, Eliphelet, Jeremai, Manasseh, Shimei.

³⁴⁻⁴²From the clan of Bani: Maadai, Amram, Uel, Banaiah, Bedeiah, Cheluhi, Vaniah, Meremoth, Eliashib, Mattaniah, Mattenai, Jaasu, Bani, Binnui, Shimei, Shelemiah, Nathan, Adaiah, Machnadebai, Shashai, Sharai, Azarel, Shelemiah, Shemariah, Shallum, Amariah, Joseph.

⁴³From the clan of Nebo: Jeiel, Mattithiah, Zabad, Zebina, Jaddai, Joel, Benaiah.

⁴⁴Each of these men had heathen wives, and many had children by these wives.

Nehemiah

HAVE YOU ever wanted to know what someone was thinking? Nehemiah lets us get inside his head and hear his thoughts. We know his plans, his feelings, his motives, and his prayers. The surprising part might be how often Nehemiah prayed.

Nehemiah was a busy man. He was sent to Jerusalem to make sure the city walls were rebuilt. Without walls around Jerusalem, the newly built Temple wasn't safe.

Nehemiah always wanted God's help and advice. He turned to God when he was scared, angry, confused, or sad. He also turned to God when he was happy, eager, and thankful. He didn't always stop to pray on his knees or even sit down! He often shot up silent prayers in between sentences in a conversation. Nehemiah was in the middle of things, but he relied on God.

Nehemiah lived at the same time as Ezra. In fact, you'll meet Ezra again in this book. After Nehemiah got the city walls built, he made sure the people learned how to worship God again. Nehemiah and Ezra worked together on this.

Look for how often Nehemiah prayed as you read this book.

Nehemiah Begs to Go Home

The autobiography of *Nehemiah, the son of Hecaliah*:

In December of the twentieth year of the reign of King Artaxerxes of Persia, when I was at the palace at Shushan, ²one of my fellow Jews named Hanani came to visit me with some men who had arrived from Judah. I took the opportunity to inquire about how things were going in Jerusalem. "How are they getting along—," I asked, "the Jews who returned to Jerusalem from their exile here?"

³"Well," they replied, "things are not good; the wall of Jerusalem is still torn down, and the gates are burned."

⁴When I heard this, I sat down and cried. In fact, I refused to eat for several days, for I spent the time in prayer to the God of heaven.

⁵"O Lord God," I cried out; "O great and awesome God who keeps his promises and is so loving

and kind to those who love and obey him! Hear my prayer! ⁶,⁷Listen carefully to what I say! Look down and see me praying night and day for your people Israel. I confess that we have sinned against you; yes, I and my people have committed the horrible sin of not obeying the commandments you gave us through your servant Moses. ⁸Oh, please remember what you told Moses! You said,

"If you sin, I will scatter you among the nations; ⁹but if you return to me and obey my laws, even though you are exiled to the farthest corners of the universe, I will bring you back to Jerusalem. For Jerusalem is the place in which I have chosen to live.'

¹⁰"We are your servants, the people you rescued by your great power. ¹¹O Lord, please hear my prayer! Heed the prayers of those of us who delight to honor you. Please help me now as I go in and ask the king for a great favor—put it into his heart to be kind to me." (I was the king's cupbearer.)

2 One day in April, four months later, as I was serving the king his wine he asked me, "Why so sad? You aren't sick, are you? You look like a man with deep troubles." (For until then I had always been cheerful when I was with him.) I was badly frightened, ³but I replied, "Sir, why shouldn't I be sad? For the city where my ancestors are buried is in ruins, and the gates have been burned down."

⁴"Well, what should be done?" the king asked.

With a quick prayer to the God of heaven, I replied, "If it please Your Majesty and if you look upon me with your royal favor, send me to Judah to rebuild the city of my fathers!"

⁵,⁶The king replied, with the queen sitting beside him, "How long will you be gone? When will you return?"

So it was agreed! And I set a time for my departure!

⁷Then I added this to my request: "If it please the king, give me letters to the governors west of the Euphrates River instructing them to let me travel through their countries on my way to Judah; ⁸also a letter to Asaph, the manager of the king's forest, instructing him to give me timber for the beams and for the gates of the fortress near the Temple, and for the city walls, and for a house for myself."

And the king granted these requests, for God was being gracious to me.

⁹When I arrived in the provinces west of the Euphrates River, I delivered the king's letters to the governors there. (The king, I should add, had sent along army officers and troops to protect me!) ¹⁰But when Sanballat (the Horonite) and Tobiah (an Ammonite who was a government official) heard of my arrival, they were very angry that anyone was interested in helping Israel.

¹¹,¹²Three days after my arrival at Jerusalem I stole out during the night, taking only a few men with me; for I hadn't told a soul about the plans for Jerusalem that God had put into my heart. I was mounted on my donkey and the others were on foot, ¹³and we went out through the Valley Gate toward the Jackal's Well and over to the Dung Gate to see the broken walls and burned gates. ¹⁴,¹⁵Then we went to the Fountain Gate and to the King's Pool, but my donkey couldn't get through the rubble. So we circled the city, and I followed the brook, inspecting the wall, and entered again at the Valley Gate.

¹⁶The city officials did not know I had been out there or why, for as yet I had said nothing to anyone about my plans—not to the political or religious leaders, or even to those who would be doing the work.

¹⁷But now I told them, "You know full well the tragedy of our city; it lies in ruins and its gates are burned. Let us rebuild the wall of Jerusalem and rid ourselves of this disgrace!"

¹⁸Then I told them about the desire God had put into my heart, and of my conversation with the king, and the plan to which he had agreed.

They replied at once, "Good! Let's rebuild the wall!" And so the work began.

¹⁹But when Sanballat, Tobiah, and Geshem the Arab heard of our plan, they scoffed and said, "What are you doing, rebelling against the king like this?"

²⁰But I replied, "The God of heaven will help us, and we, his servants, will rebuild this wall; but you may have no part in this affair."

3 **The Builders of the City Wall**

Then Eliashib the High Priest and the other priests rebuilt the wall as far as the Tower of the Hundred and the Tower of Hananel; then they rebuilt the Sheep Gate, hung its doors, and dedicated it. ²Men from the city of Jericho worked next to them, and beyond them was the work crew led by Zaccur (son of Imri).

³The Fish Gate was built by the sons of Hassenaah; they did the whole thing—cut the beams,

---

OVERCOMING FEAR 2:3 Nehemiah wasn't ashamed to admit his fear, but he refused to allow fear to stop him from doing what God had called him to do. When we allow our fears to rule our lives, we make them more powerful than God. Is there a task God wants you to do, but fear is holding you back? God is greater than all our fears. To recognize your fear is the first step in committing it to God. Realize that if God has called you to a task, he will help you accomplish it. **To begin the series of devotionals on OVERCOMING FEAR, turn to page 13.**

Family Devotions

☐ DEVOTION 134
PRAYING AT ALL TIMES

Read Nehemiah 1:4-11

"God bless everyone. Amen," Darla prayed. She opened her eyes and saw a slight frown on her mother's face.

"What do you mean by 'God bless everyone'?" asked Mom. "Exactly who is everyone?"

"Well," said Darla, "I mean Grandma, Scott, my friends, my Sunday school teacher, the missionaries—everyone."

"What do you want God to do for them?" Mom asked.

"Bless them," Darla said. "You know—Grandma needs help with her eyes, and Scott's having trouble sleeping. Those kinds of things."

"Then why not tell those things to God?" asked Mom.

Darla shrugged. "I don't know," she said. "I guess it's easier to say, 'bless everyone.' God knows what I mean."

That afternoon Mom and Darla went shopping. "Would you please show my daughter something to wear?" Mom asked a clerk.

"A coat?" asked the clerk. "Jeans? Tops?"

"Just something to wear," Mom answered.

"I need a red sweater," Darla said quickly, "and I need a pair of jeans." She told the clerk what size she needed, and soon she was busy in the fitting room.

"Why did you do that?" Darla asked as she tried on the clothes. "That was so embarrassing! Why didn't you say what I needed?"

"It was so much quicker and easier not to go into detail," Mom answered. Darla looked at her suspiciously. "I thought you knew that," added Mom. Darla still looked puzzled, so Mom explained. "I'm thinking of your quick 'God bless everyone' prayers," she said, handing Darla another sweater to try on. "I wanted you to see how important complete communication is. Take your time when you talk to God, being specific about who you're praying for as well as listing their needs. That will also help you know when the specific prayers are answered.

Praying at All Times
Memory Verse

Don't worry about anything; instead, pray about everything; tell God your needs, and don't forget to thank him for his answers.
Philippians 4:6

How About You?
When you pray, are you specific with God, or do you hurry through your prayers? Take time to communicate. Be specific, just as Nehemiah was. It's true that God knows what you need before you ask, but he wants you to talk with him, telling him all about your needs as well as your blessings. *N. E. K.*

- For the next devotional, turn to page 485. • For the next devotional on PRAYING AT ALL TIMES, turn to page 485.
- For notes on PRAYING AT ALL TIMES, see pages 363, 442, 945, 1040, and 1051.

hung the doors, and made the bolts and bars. [4]Meremoth (son of Uriah, son of Hakkoz) repaired the next section of wall, and beyond him were Meshullam (son of Berechiah, son of Meshezabel) and Zadok (son of Baana). [5]Next were the men from Tekoa, but their leaders were lazy and didn't help.

[6]The Old Gate was repaired by Joiada (son of Paseah) and Meshullam (son of Besodeiah). They laid the beams, set up the doors, and installed the bolts and bars. [7]Next to them were Melatiah from Gibeon; Jadon from Meronoth; and men from Gibeon and Mizpah, who were citizens of the province. [8]Uzziel (son of Harhaiah) was a goldsmith by trade, but he too worked on the wall. Beyond him was Hananiah, a manufacturer of perfumes. Repairs were not needed from there to the Broad Wall.

[9]Rephaiah (son of Hur), the mayor of half of Jerusalem, was next down the wall from them. [10]Jedaiah (son of Harumaph) repaired the wall beside his own house, and next to him was Hattush (son of Hashabneiah). [11]Then came Malchijah (son of Harim) and Hasshub (son of Pahath-moab), who repaired the Furnace Tower in addition to a section of the wall. [12]Shallum (son of Hallohesh) and his daughters repaired the next section. He was the mayor of the other half of Jerusalem.

[13]The people from Zanoah, led by Hanun, built the Valley Gate, hung the doors, and installed the bolts and bars; then they repaired the 1,500 feet of wall to the Dung Gate.

[14]The Dung Gate was repaired by Malchijah (son of Rechab), the mayor of the Beth-haccherem area; and after building it, he hung the doors and installed the bolts and bars.

[15]Shallum (son of Col-hozeh), the mayor of the Mizpah district, repaired the Fountain Gate. He rebuilt it, roofed it, hung its doors, and installed its locks and bars. Then he repaired the wall from the Pool of Siloam to the king's garden and the stairs that descend from the City of David section of Jerusalem. [16]Next to him was Nehemiah (son of Azbuk), the mayor of half the Beth-zur district; he built as far as the royal cemetery, the water reservoir, and the old Officers' Club building. [17]Next was a group of Levites working under the supervision of Rehum (son of Bani). Then came Hashabiah, the mayor of half the Keilah district, who supervised the building of the wall in his own district. [18]Next down the line were his clan brothers led by Bavvai (son of Henadad), the mayor of the other half of the Keilah district.

[19]Next to them the workers were led by Ezer (son of Jeshua), the mayor of another part of Mizpah; they also worked on the section of wall across from the Armory where the wall turns. [20]Next to him was Baruch (son of Zabbai), who built from the turn in the wall to the home of Eliashib the High Priest. [21]Meremoth (son of Uriah, son of Hakkoz) built a section of the wall extending from a point opposite the door of Eliashib's house to the side of the house.

[22]Then came the priests from the plains outside the city. [23]Benjamin, Hasshub, and Azariah (son of Maaseiah, son of Ananiah) repaired the sections next to their own houses. [24]Next was Binnui (son of Henadad), who built the portion of the wall from Azariah's house to the corner. [25]Palal (son of Uzai) carried on the work from the corner to the foundations of the upper tower of the king's castle beside the prison yard. Next was Pedaiah (son of Parosh).

[26]The Temple attendants living in Ophel repaired the wall as far as the East Water Gate and the Projecting Tower. [27]Then came the Tekoites, who repaired the section opposite the Castle Tower and over to the wall of Ophel. [28]The priests repaired the wall beyond the Horse Gate, each one doing the section immediately opposite his own house.

[29]Zadok (son of Immer) also rebuilt the wall next to his own house, and beyond him was Shemaiah (son of Shecaniah), the gatekeeper of the East Gate. [30]Next was Hananiah (son of Shelemiah); Hanun (the sixth son of Zalaph); and Meshullam (son of Berechiah), who built next to his own house. [31]Malchijah, one of the goldsmiths, repaired as far as the Temple attendants' and merchants' Guild Hall, opposite the Muster Gate; then to the upper room at the corner. [32]The other goldsmiths and merchants completed the wall from that corner to the Sheep Gate.

4 Nehemiah Builds the Walls

Sanballat was very angry when he learned that we were rebuilding the wall. He flew into a rage, and insulted and mocked us and laughed at us, and so did his friends and the Samaritan army officers. "What does this bunch of poor, feeble Jews think they are doing?" he scoffed. "Do they think they can build the wall in a day if they offer enough sacrifices? And look at those charred stones they are pulling out of the rubbish and using again!"

[3]Tobiah, who was standing beside him, remarked, "If even a fox walked along the top of their wall, it would collapse!"

[4]Then I prayed, "Hear us, O Lord God, for we are being mocked. May their scoffing fall back upon their own heads, and may they themselves become captives in a foreign land! [5]Do not ignore their sin. Do not blot it out, for they have despised you in despising us who are building your wall."

[6]At last the wall was completed to half its original height around the entire city—for the workers worked hard.

FAMILY DEVOTIONS

☐ DEVOTION 135
PRAYING AT ALL TIMES

Read Nehemiah 4:7-9

Praying at All Times
Memory Verse

Don't worry about anything; instead, pray about everything; tell God your needs, and don't forget to thank him for his answers.
Philippians 4:6

"Shouldn't you be studying your spelling?" asked Mom.

"Yeah, I s'pose," agreed Lynn. "I'll do it as soon as this program's done."

But just as the program ended, Marcia called, and Lynn spent the next half hour chatting on the phone. After that she had a bedtime snack, and then it was time to turn in. Jumping into bed, she murmured a prayer asking for help with her spelling.

As she took the test the next day, she again asked God to help her do well. She was disappointed in the results—a D! "Doesn't the Bible say that if we lack wisdom we should ask God for it?" she asked Mom that evening.

Before Mom could answer, the phone rang. Lynn ran to answer it. "That was Marcia," she said as she returned. "May I go to town with her? And may I have some money to buy a lock for my locker? Lots of kids are getting their pencils and things ripped off at school."

"Oh, that's a shame," said Mom. She reached for her purse, then changed her mind. "I have an idea. Why don't you pray about it? Ask the Lord to protect your things."

"Mom!" exclaimed Lynn. "It's all very well to pray about it, but it only makes sense to put a lock on, too."

"In other words, even though you pray, you should also do what you can to take care of the problem? You should do your part?" asked Mom. As Lynn nodded, Mom added, "And wouldn't that be true regarding your spelling test too? You didn't study. You didn't do your part. Yet you expected God to help you remember things you never learned."

Lynn looked ashamed. "I guess I really knew better. After this I'll study harder. I'll do my part, and then I know God will help me, too."

How About You?
Do you pray about your schoolwork? About friends who need to know the Lord? About money you need for something special? Prayer is important, but it is only part of the battle. You also need to study. You need to witness. You need to look for ways to work and earn money. When the walls of Jerusalem were being built, God's people prayed *and* guarded the city. Jesus told his disciples to watch *and* pray. We, too, must pray, and we must also work. H. M.

• For the next devotional, turn to page 489. • For the next devotional on *PRAYING AT ALL TIMES,* turn to page 827.
• For notes on *PRAYING AT ALL TIMES,* see pages 363, 442, 945, 1040, and 1051.

7 But when Sanballat and Tobiah and the Arabians, Ammonites, and Ashdodites heard that the work was going right ahead and that the breaks in the wall were being repaired, they became furious. 8 They plotted to lead an army against Jerusalem to bring about riots and confusion. 9 But we prayed to our God and guarded the city day and night to protect ourselves.

10 Then some of the leaders began complaining that the workmen were becoming tired; and there was so much rubble to be removed that we could never get it done by ourselves. 11 Meanwhile, our enemies were planning to swoop down upon us and kill us, thus ending our work. 12 And whenever the workers who lived in the nearby cities went home for a visit, our enemies tried to talk them out of returning to Jerusalem. 13 So I placed armed guards from each family in the cleared spaces behind the walls.

14 Then as I looked over the situation, I called together the leaders and the people and said to them, "Don't be afraid! Remember the Lord who is great and glorious; fight for your friends, your families, and your homes!"

15 Our enemies learned that we knew of their plot, and that God had exposed and frustrated their plan. Now we all returned to our work on the wall; 16 but from then on, only half worked while the other half stood guard behind them. 17 And the masons and laborers worked with weapons within easy reach beside them 18 or with swords belted to their sides. The trumpeter stayed with me to sound the alarm.

19 "The work is so spread out," I explained to them, "and we are separated so widely from each other, that when you hear the trumpet blow, you must rush to where I am; and God will fight for us."

20,21 We worked early and late, from sunrise to sunset; and half the men were always on guard. 22 I told everyone living outside the walls to move into Jerusalem so that their servants could go on guard duty as well as work during the day. 23 During this period none of us—I, nor my brothers, nor the servants, nor the guards who were with me—ever took off our clothes except for washing. And we carried our weapons with us at all times.

5 Nehemiah Defends the Poor

About this time there was a great outcry of protest from parents against some of the rich Jews who were profiteering on them. 2-4 What was happening was that families who ran out of money for food had to sell their children or mortgage their fields, vineyards, and homes to these rich men; and some couldn't even do that, for they already had borrowed to the limit to pay their taxes.

5 "We are their brothers, and our children are just like theirs," the people protested. "Yet we must sell our children into slavery to get enough money to live. We have already sold some of our daughters, and we are helpless to redeem them, for our fields, too, are mortgaged to these men."

6 I was very angry when I heard this; 7 so after thinking about it I spoke out against these rich government officials.

"What is this you are doing?" I demanded. "How dare you demand a mortgage as a condition for helping another Israelite!"

Then I called a public trial to deal with them.

8 At the trial I shouted at them, "The rest of us are doing all we can to *help* our Jewish brothers who have returned from exile as slaves in distant lands, but you are forcing them right back into slavery again. How often must we redeem them?"

And they had nothing to say in their own defense.

9 Then I pressed further. "What you are doing is very evil," I exclaimed. "Should you not walk in the fear of our God? Don't we have enough enemies among the nations around us who are trying to destroy us? 10 The rest of us are lending money and grain to our fellow-Jews without any interest. I beg you, gentlemen, stop this business of usury. 11 Restore their fields, vineyards, oliveyards, and homes to them this very day and drop your claims against them."

12 So they agreed to do it and said that they would assist their brothers without requiring them to mortgage their lands and sell them their children. Then I summoned the priests and made these men formally vow to carry out their promises. 13 And I invoked the curse of God upon any of them who refused.

"May God destroy your homes and livelihood if you fail to keep this promise," I declared.

And all the people shouted, "Amen," and praised the Lord. And the rich men did as they had promised.

14 I would like to mention that for the entire twelve years that I was governor of Judah—from the twentieth until the thirty-second year of the reign of King Artaxerxes—my aides and I accepted no salaries or other assistance from the people of Israel. 15 This was quite a contrast to the former governors who had demanded food and wine and $100 a day in cash, and had put the population at the mercy of their aides who tyrannized them; but I obeyed God and did not act that way. 16 I stayed at work on the wall and refused to speculate in land; I also required my officials to spend time on the wall. 17 All this despite the fact that I regularly fed 150 Jewish officials at my table, besides visitors from other countries! 18 The provisions required for each day were one ox, six fat sheep, and a large number of domestic fowls; and we needed a huge supply of

all kinds of wines every ten days. Yet I refused to make a special levy against the people, for they were already having a difficult time. ¹⁹O my God, please keep in mind all that I've done for these people and bless me for it.

6 Nehemiah Finishes the Walls

When Sanballat, Tobiah, Geshem the Arab, and the rest of our enemies found out that we had almost completed the rebuilding of the wall—though we had not yet hung all the doors of the gates— ²they sent me a message asking me to meet them in one of the villages in the Plain of Ono. But I realized they were plotting to kill me, ³so I replied by sending back this message to them:

"I am doing a great work! Why should I stop to come and visit with you?"

⁴Four times they sent the same message, and each time I gave the same reply. ⁵,⁶The fifth time, Sanballat's servant came with an open letter in his hand, and this is what it said:

"Geshem tells me that everywhere he goes he hears that the Jews are planning to rebel, and that is why you are building the wall. He claims you plan to be their king—that is what is being said. ⁷He also reports that you have appointed prophets to campaign for you at Jerusalem by saying, 'Look! Nehemiah is just the man we need!'

"You can be very sure that I am going to pass along these interesting comments to King Artaxerxes! I suggest that you come and talk it over with me—for that is the only way you can save yourself!"

⁸My reply was, "You know you are lying. There isn't one bit of truth to the whole story. ⁹You're just trying to scare us into stopping our work." (O Lord God, please strengthen me!)

¹⁰A few days later I went to visit Shemaiah (son of Delaiah, who was the son of Mehetabel), for he said he was receiving a message from God.

"Let us hide in the Temple and bolt the door," he exclaimed, "for they are coming tonight to kill you."

¹¹But I replied, "Should I, the governor, run away from danger? And if I go into the Temple, not being a priest, I would forfeit my life. No, I won't do it!"

¹²,¹³Then I realized that God had not spoken to him, but Tobiah and Sanballat had hired him to scare me and make me sin by fleeing to the Temple; and then they would be able to accuse me.

¹⁴"O my God," I prayed, "don't forget all the evil of Tobiah, Sanballat, Noadiah the prophetess, and all the other prophets who have tried to discourage me."

¹⁵The wall was finally finished in early September—just fifty-two days after we had begun!

¹⁶When our enemies and the surrounding nations heard about it, they were frightened and humiliated, and they realized that the work had been done with the help of our God. ¹⁷During those fifty-two days many letters went back and forth between Tobiah and the wealthy politicians of Judah. ¹⁸For many in Judah had sworn allegiance to him because his father-in-law was Shecaniah (son of Arah) and because his son Jehohanan was married to the daughter of Meshullam (son of Berechiah). ¹⁹They all told me what a wonderful man Tobiah was, and then they told him everything I had said; and Tobiah sent many threatening letters to frighten me.

7

After the wall was finished and we had hung the doors in the gates and had appointed the gatekeepers, singers, and Levites, ²I gave the responsibility of governing Jerusalem to my brother Hanani and to Hananiah, the commander of the fortress—a very faithful man who revered God more than most people do. ³I issued instructions to them not to open the Jerusalem gates until well after sunrise, and to close and lock them while the guards were still on duty. I also directed that the guards be residents of Jerusalem, and that they must be on duty at regular times, and that each homeowner who lived near the wall must guard the section of wall next to his own home. ⁴For the city was large, but the population was small; and only a few houses were scattered throughout the city.

⁵Then the Lord told me to call together all the leaders of the city, along with the ordinary citizens, for registration. For I had found the record of the genealogies of those who had returned to Judah before, and this is what was written in it:

⁶"The following is a list of the names of the Jews who returned to Judah after being exiled by King Nebuchadnezzar of Babylon.

⁷"Their leaders were: Zerubbabel, Jeshua, Nehemiah, Azariah, Raamiah, Nahamani, Mordecai, Bilshan, Mispereth, Bigvai, Nehum, Baanah.

"The others who returned at that time were:

⁸⁻³⁸From the subclan of Parosh, 2,172;
From the subclan of Shephatiah, 372;
From the subclan of Arah, 652;
From the families of Jeshua and Joab of the
  subclan of Pahath-moab, 2,818;
From the subclan of Elam, 1,254;
From the subclan of Zattu, 845;
From the subclan of Zaccai, 760;
From the subclan of Binnui, 648;
From the subclan of Bebai, 628;
From the subclan of Azgad, 2,322;
From the subclan of Adonikam, 667;

From the subclan of Bigvai, 2,067;
From the subclan of Adin, 655;
From the family of Hezekiah of the subclan of Ater, 98;
From the subclan of Hashum, 328;
From the subclan of Bezai, 324;
From the subclan of Hariph, 112;
From the subclan of Gibeon, 95;
From the subclans of Bethlehem and Netophah, 188;
From the subclan of Anathoth, 128;
From the subclan of Beth-azmaveth, 42;
From the subclans of Kiriath-jearim, Chephirah, and Beeroth, 743;
From the subclans of Ramah and Geba, 621;
From the subclan of Michmas, 122;
From the subclans of Bethel and Ai, 123;
From the subclan of Nebo, 52;
From the subclan of Elam, 1,254;
From the subclan of Harim, 320;
From the subclan of Jericho, 345;
From the subclans of Lod, Hadid, and Ono, 721;
From the subclan of Senaah, 3,930.

39-42"Here are the statistics concerning the returning priests:

From the family of Jeshua of the subclan of Jedaiah, 973;
From the subclan of Immer, 1,052;
From the subclan of Pashhur, 1,247;
From the subclan of Harim, 1,017.

43-45"Here are the statistics concerning the Levites:

From the family of Kadmiel of the subclan of Hodevah of the clan of Jeshua, 74;
The choir members from the clan of Asaph, 148;
From the clans of Shallum, (all of whom were gatekeepers), 138.

46-56"Of the Temple assistants, the following subclans were represented: Ziha, Hasupha, Tabbaoth, Keros, Sia, Padon, Lebana, Hagaba, Shalmai, Hanan, Giddel, Gahar, Reaiah, Rezin, Nekoda, Gazzam, Uzza, Paseah, Besai, Asnah, Meunim, Nephushesim, Bakbuk, Hakupha, Harhur, Bazlith, Mehida, Harsha, Barkos, Sisera, Temah, Neziah, Hatipha.

57-59"Following is a list of the descendants of Solomon's officials who returned to Judah: Sotai, Sophereth, Perida, Jaala, Darkon, Giddel, Shephatiah, Hattil, Pochereth-hazzebaim, Amon.

60"In all, the Temple assistants and the descendants of Solomon's officers numbered 392."

61Another group returned to Jerusalem at that time from the Persian cities of Tel-melah, Tel-harsha, Cherub, Addon, and Immer. But they had lost their genealogies and could not prove their Jewish ancestry; 62these were the subclans of Delaiah, Tobiah, and Nekoda—a total of 642.

63There were also several subclans of priests named after Hobaiah, Hakkoz, and Barzillai (he married one of the daughters of Barzillai the Gileadite and took her family name), 64,65whose genealogies had been lost. So they were not allowed to continue as priests or even to receive the priests' share of food from the sacrifices until the Urim and Thummim had been consulted to find out from God whether or not they actually were descendants of priests.

66There was a total of 42,360 citizens who returned to Judah at that time; 67also, 7,337 slaves and 245 choir members, both men and women. 68,69They took with them 736 horses, 245 mules, 435 camels, and 6,720 donkeys.

70Some of their leaders gave gifts for the work. The governor gave $5,000 in gold, 50 gold bowls, and 530 sets of clothing for the priests. 71The other leaders gave a total of $100,000 in gold and $77,000 in silver; 72and the common people gave $100,000 in gold, $70,000 in silver, and sixty-seven sets of clothing for the priests.

73The priests, the Levites, the gatekeepers, the choir members, the Temple attendants, and the rest of the people now returned home to their own towns and villages throughout Judah. But during the month of September, they came back to Jerusalem.

8 Ezra Reads the Law

Now, in mid-September, all the people assembled at the plaza in front of the Water Gate and requested Ezra, their religious leader, to read to them the law of God, which he had given to Moses.

So Ezra the priest brought out to them the scroll of Moses' laws. He stood on a wooden stand made especially for the occasion so that everyone could see him as he read. He faced the square in front of the Water Gate and read from early morning until noon. Everyone stood up as he opened the scroll. And all who were old enough to understand paid close attention. To his right stood Mattithiah, Shema, Anaiah, Uriah, Hilkiah, and Maaseiah. To his left were Pedaiah, Mishael, Malchijah, Hashum, Hash-baddenah, Zechariah, and Meshullam.

6Then Ezra blessed the Lord, the great God, and all the people said, "Amen," and lifted their hands toward heaven; then they bowed and worshiped the Lord with their faces toward the ground.

7,8As Ezra read from the scroll, Jeshua, Bani, Sherebiah, Jamin, Akkub, Shabbethai, Hodiah, Maaseiah, Kelita, Azariah, Jozabad, Hanan, Pelaiah, and

Family Devotions

☐ **Devotion 136**
Going to Church

Read Nehemiah 8:1-6

After dinner one evening, Dad directed nine-year-old Phil, seven-year-old Tami, and Mom to three straight-backed chairs that stood in a row in the living room. The children looked puzzled, but followed instructions. Next, Dad took his position in front of them, holding the most sought-after book—the catalog of toys. Everyone listened attentively while Dad began describing a home computer in which Phil was especially interested.

Suddenly Mom began to kick her legs while leaning against Phil's arm. Then she nudged him gently as she turned around in her seat. Next she bent forward in front of him to pick up a fallen paper while rattling a bulletin.

Phil looked at Mom rather strangely as he tried to listen. He leaned forward so he wouldn't miss a word and so Mom's wiggling wouldn't bother him. Then Mom stood up and walked in front of him. She stopped at Tami's chair to ask her in a loud whisper if Tami's friend Nancy would like to come home with Tami after church.

"Mom! How can I concentrate on what Dad's saying with all this going on!" Phil exploded.

Tami suddenly began to giggle. "I know what you're trying to do. You're showing us how we act in church during the sermon!"

"Oh," Phil groaned, "is that what you're doing?"

"You both are quiet in church," commented Dad, "but your wiggling and moving about can be just as disturbing as talking out loud."

Phil rolled his eyes and looked at Mom. "I see what you mean." He paused, then asked, "May we still read some more about the computer?"

"How about doing it after our Bible reading and prayer time?" Dad suggested.

Going to Church Memory Verse

Let us not neglect our church meetings, as some people do, but encourage and warn each other, especially now that the day of his coming back again is drawing near.
Hebrews 10:25

H o w   A b o u t   Y o u ?

Do you wiggle, rattle papers, turn around, or whisper during church services? If you do, your mind is not concentrating on the message, and you may be keeping someone else from listening, too. Ask God to help you to be still so you can learn more about him. *J. G.*

• For the next devotional, turn to page 491. • For the next devotional on *Going to Church*, turn to page 563.
• For notes on *Going to Church*, see pages 770, 965, and 1002.

the Levites went among the people and explained the meaning of the passage that was being read. ⁹All the people began sobbing when they heard the commands of the law.

Then Ezra the priest, and I as governor, and the Levites who were assisting me, said to them, "Don't cry on such a day as this! For today is a sacred day before the Lord your God— ¹⁰it is a time to celebrate with a hearty meal and to send presents to those in need, for the joy of the Lord is your strength. You must not be dejected and sad!"

¹¹And the Levites, too, quieted the people, telling them, "That's right! Don't weep! For this is a day of holy joy, not of sadness."

¹²So the people went away to eat a festive meal and to send presents; it was a time of great and joyful celebration because they could hear and understand God's words.

¹³The next day the clan leaders and the priests and Levites met with Ezra to go over the law in greater detail. ¹⁴As they studied it, they noted that Jehovah had told Moses that the people of Israel should live in tents during the Festival of Tabernacles to be held that month. ¹⁵He had said also that a proclamation should be made throughout the cities of the land, especially in Jerusalem, telling the people to go to the hills to get branches from olive, myrtle, palm, and fig trees and to make huts in which to live for the duration of the feast.

¹⁶So the people went out and cut branches and used them to build huts on the roofs of their houses, or in their courtyards, or in the court of the Temple, or on the plaza beside the Water Gate, or at the Ephraim Gate Plaza. ¹⁷They lived in these huts for the seven days of the feast, and everyone was filled with joy! (This procedure had not been carried out since the days of Joshua.) ¹⁸Ezra read from the scroll on each of the seven days of the feast, and on the eighth day there was a solemn closing service as required by the laws of Moses.

9 Ezra Leads in Confession

On October 10 the people returned for another observance; this time they fasted and clothed themselves with sackcloth and sprinkled dirt in their hair. And the Israelis separated themselves from all foreigners. ³The laws of God were read aloud to them for two or three hours, and for several more hours they took turns confessing their own sins and those of their ancestors. And everyone worshiped the Lord their God. ⁴Some of the Levites were on the platform praising the Lord God with songs of joy. These men were Jeshua, Kadmiel, Bani, Shebaniah, Bunni, Sherebiah, Bani, and Chenani.

⁵Then the Levite leaders called out to the people, "Stand up and praise the Lord your God, for he lives from everlasting to everlasting. Praise his glorious name! It is far greater than we can think or say."

The leaders in this part of the service were Jeshua, Kadmiel, Bani, Hashabneiah, Sherebiah, Hodiah, Shebaniah, and Pethahiah.

⁶Then Ezra prayed, "You alone are God. You have made the skies and the heavens, the earth and the seas, and everything in them. You preserve it all; and all the angels of heaven worship you.

⁷"You are the Lord God who chose Abram and brought him from Ur of the Chaldeans and renamed him Abraham. ⁸When he was faithful to you, you made a contract with him to forever give him and his descendants the land of the Canaanites, Hittites, Amorites, Perizzites, Jebusites, and Girgashites; and now you have done what you promised, for you are always true to your word.

⁹"You saw the troubles and sorrows of our ancestors in Egypt, and you heard their cries from beside the Red Sea. ¹⁰You displayed great miracles against Pharaoh and his people, for you knew how brutally the Egyptians were treating them; you have a glorious reputation because of those never-to-be-forgotten deeds. ¹¹You divided the sea for your people so they could go through on dry land! And then you destroyed their enemies in the depths of the sea; they sank like stones beneath the mighty waters. ¹²You led our ancestors by a pillar of cloud during the day and a pillar of fire at night so that they could find their way.

¹³"You came down upon Mount Sinai and spoke with them from heaven and gave them good laws and true commandments, ¹⁴including the laws about the holy Sabbath; and you commanded them, through Moses your servant, to obey them all.

¹⁵"You gave them bread from heaven when they were hungry and water from the rock when they were thirsty. You commanded them to go in and conquer the land you had sworn to give them; ¹⁶but our ancestors were a proud and stubborn lot, and they refused to listen to your commandments.

¹⁷"They refused to obey and didn't pay any attention to the miracles you did for them; instead, they rebelled and appointed a leader to take them back into slavery in Egypt! But you are a God of forgiveness, always ready to pardon, gracious and merciful, slow to become angry, and full of love and mercy; you didn't abandon them, ¹⁸even though they made a calf idol and proclaimed, 'This is our God! He brought us out of Egypt!' They sinned in so many ways, ¹⁹but in your great mercy you didn't abandon them to die in the wilderness! The pillar of cloud led them forward day by day, and the pillar of fire showed them the way through the night. ²⁰You sent your good Spirit to instruct them, and you did not stop giving them bread from heaven or water for their thirst. ²¹For forty years you sustained them in the wilderness;

Family Devotions

☐ DEVOTION 137
CONFESSING SIN

Read Nehemiah 9:28-38

Confessing Sin Memory Verse

Create in me a new, clean heart, O God, filled with clean thoughts and right desires.
Psalm 51:10

"Aw, Dad, how could one cigarette hurt a guy?" pleaded Jeremy. "I only wanted to give it a try. Can't we just forget it?"

Dad shook his head. "Jeremy, remember when you asked me for a dollar the other day because you wanted to send for some CDs?" he asked.

Jeremy nodded. "Sure I remember, but what does that have to do with all this?"

"Well, after you asked for the dollar, we read the fine print in the advertisement and found that you weren't just buying ten CDs for a dollar," replied Dad. "You were also obligating yourself to purchase a certain number of CDs within a certain period of time. Once we counted the true cost of buying those first ten 'bargain CDs,' you decided you really couldn't afford them."

"Yeah—that advertisement was just a come-on to get me to spend more money," agreed Jeremy.

"Well, Son, that's the way sin can be, too," said Dad. "It can seem like one very small thing—like smoking just one cigarette. But often we're buying into so much more when we choose to sin. When you smoked that cigarette, you also made the decision to disobey and to deceive your parents. And if you had gotten away with that first cigarette, you may have decided to try it again and again. Each time, you would have more and more to hide from your parents. I love you too much, Jeremy, to let you get away with smoking 'just one cigarette.' I hope the next time you're tempted to disobey, you'll count the cost a little more carefully."

Jeremy nodded. "And don't go for the bargain, right? Are you sure I haven't learned my lesson well enough to skip the grounding?" he asked hopefully.

"I'm sure," said Dad.

How About You?

Your parents' punishment may sometimes seem unfair, but it's their way of helping you learn to avoid sin. Sin has severe consequences that can be much worse than being grounded. L. W.

For the next devotional, turn to page 499. • For the next devotional on CONFESSING SIN, turn to page 577.
For notes on CONFESSING SIN, see pages 429, 479, 836, 881, and 1220.

they lacked nothing in all that time. Their clothes didn't wear out, and their feet didn't swell!

22"Then you helped them conquer great kingdoms and many nations, and you placed your people in every corner of the land; they completely took over the land of King Sihon of Heshbon and King Og of Bashan. 23You caused a population explosion among the Israelis and brought them into the land you had promised to their ancestors. 24You subdued whole nations before them—even the kings and the people of the Canaanites were powerless! 25Your people captured fortified cities and fertile land; they took over houses full of good things, with cisterns and vineyards and oliveyards and many, many fruit trees; so they ate and were full and enjoyed themselves in all your blessings.

26"But despite all this, they were disobedient and rebelled against you. They threw away your law, killed the prophets who told them to return to you, and they did many other terrible things. 27So you gave them to their enemies. But in their time of trouble they cried to you, and you heard them from heaven, and in great mercy you sent them saviors who delivered them from their enemies. 28But when all was going well, your people turned to sin again, and once more you let their enemies conquer them. Yet whenever your people returned to you and cried to you for help, once more you listened from heaven, and in your wonderful mercy delivered them! 29You punished them in order to turn them toward your laws; but even though they should have obeyed them, they were proud and wouldn't listen, and continued to sin. 30You were patient with them for many years. You sent your prophets to warn them about their sins, but still they wouldn't listen. So once again you allowed the heathen nations to conquer them. 31But in your great mercy you did not destroy them completely or abandon them forever. What a gracious and merciful God you are!

32"And now, O great and awesome God, you who keep your promises of love and kindness—do not let all the hardships we have gone through become as nothing to you. Great trouble has come upon us and upon our kings and princes and priests and prophets and ancestors from the days when the kings of Assyria first triumphed over us until now. 33Every time you punished us you were being perfectly fair; we have sinned so greatly that you gave us only what we deserved. 34Our kings, princes, priests, and ancestors didn't obey your laws or listen to your warnings. 35They did not worship you despite the wonderful things you did for them and the great goodness you showered upon them. You gave them a large, fat land, but they refused to turn from their wickedness.

36"So now we are slaves here in the land of plenty that you gave to our ancestors! Slaves among all this abundance! 37The lush yield of this land passes into the hands of the kings whom you have allowed to conquer us because of our sins. They have power over our bodies and our cattle, and we serve them at their pleasure and are in great misery. 38Because of all this, we again promise to serve the Lord! And we and our princes and Levites and priests put our names to this covenant."

10 The People Agree to Obey

I, Nehemiah the governor, signed the covenant. The others who signed it were: Zedekiah, Seraiah, Azariah, Jeremiah, Pashhur, Amariah, Malchijah, Hattush, Shebaniah, Malluch, Harim, Meremoth, Obadiah, Daniel, Ginnethon, Baruch, Meshullam, Abijah, Mijamin, Maaziah, Bilgai, Shemaiah. (All those listed above were priests.)

9-13These were the Levites who signed: Jeshua (son of Azaniah), Binnui (son of Henadad), Kadmiel, Shebaniah, Hodiah, Kelita, Pelaiah, Hanan, Mica, Rehob, Hashabiah, Zaccur, Sherebiah, Shebaniah, Hodiah, Bani, Beninu.

14-27The political leaders who signed: Parosh, Pahath-moab, Elam, Zattu, Bani, Bunni, Azgad, Bebai, Adonijah, Bigvai, Adin, Ater, Hezekiah, Azzur, Hodiah, Hashum, Bezai, Hariph, Anathoth, Nebai, Magpiash, Meshullam, Hezir, Meshezabel, Zadok, Jaddua, Pelatiah, Hanan, Anaiah, Hoshea, Hananiah, Hasshub, Hallohesh, Pilha, Shobek, Rehum, Hashabnah, Maaseiah, Ahiah, Hanan, Anan, Malluch, Harim, Baanah.

28These men signed on behalf of the entire nation—for the common people, the priests, the Levites, the gatekeepers, the choir members, the Temple servants, and all the rest who, with their wives and sons and daughters who were old enough to understand, had separated themselves from the heathen people of the land in order to serve God. 29For we all heartily agreed to this oath and vowed to accept the curse of God unless we obeyed God's laws as issued by his servant Moses.

30We also agreed not to let our daughters marry non-Jewish men and not to let our sons marry non-Jewish girls.

31We further agreed that if the heathen people in the land should bring any grain or other produce to be sold on the Sabbath or on any other holy day, we

---

PUTTING GOD FIRST 10:28ff. The wall was completed, and the covenant God made with his people in the days of Moses was restored (Deuteronomy 8). In this covenant are principles which are important for us today. Our relationship with God goes far beyond church attendance and regular devotions. It should affect every area of our lives: our relationships (10:30), our time (10:31), and our material resources (10:32-40). **To begin the series of devotionals on PUTTING GOD FIRST, turn to page 115.**

would refuse to buy it. And we agreed not to do any work every seventh year and to forgive and cancel the debts of our brother Jews.

³²We also agreed to charge ourselves annually with a Temple tax so that there would be enough money to care for the Temple of our God; ³³for we needed supplies of the special Bread of the Presence, as well as grain offerings and burnt offerings for the Sabbaths, the new moon feasts, and the annual feasts. We also needed to purchase the other items necessary for the work of the Temple and for the atonement of Israel.

³⁴Then we tossed a coin to determine when—at regular times each year—the families of the priests, Levites, and leaders should supply the wood for the burnt offerings at the Temple as required in the law.

³⁵We also agreed always to bring the first part of every crop to the Temple—whether it be a ground crop or from our fruit and olive trees.

³⁶We agreed to give to God our oldest sons and the firstborn of all our cattle, herds, and flocks, just as the law requires; we presented them to the priests who minister in the Temple of our God. ³⁷They stored the produce in the Temple of our God—the best of our grain crops, and other contributions, the first of our fruit, and the first of the new wine and olive oil. And we promised to bring to the Levites a tenth of everything our land produced, for the Levites were responsible to collect the tithes in all our rural towns. ³⁸A priest—a descendant of Aaron—would be with the Levites as they received these tithes, and a tenth of all that was collected as tithes was delivered to the Temple and placed in the storage areas. ³⁹The people and the Levites were required by law to bring these offerings of grain, new wine, and olive oil to the Temple and place them in the sacred containers for use by the ministering priests, the gatekeepers, and the choir singers.

So we agreed together not to neglect the Temple of our God.

The Move into the New City

11 The Israeli officials were living in Jerusalem, the Holy City, at this time; but now a tenth of the people from the other cities and towns of Judah and Benjamin were selected by lot to live there too. ²Some who moved to Jerusalem at this time were volunteers, and they were highly honored.

³Following is a list of the names of the provincial officials who came to Jerusalem (though most of the leaders, the priests, the Levites, the Temple assistants, and the descendants of Solomon's servants continued to live in their own homes in the various cities of Judah).

⁴⁻⁶Leaders from the tribe of Judah:

Athaiah (son of Uzziah, son of Zechariah, son of Amariah, son of Shephatiah, son of Mahalalel, a descendant of Perez);
Maaseiah (son of Baruch, son of Col-hozeh, son of Hazaiah, son of Adaiah, son of Joiarib, son of Zechariah, son of the Shilonite).
These were the 468 stalwart descendants of Perez who lived in Jerusalem.

⁷⁻⁹Leaders from the tribe of Benjamin:

Sallu (son of Meshullam, son of Joed, son of Pedaiah, son of Kolaiah, son of Maaseiah, son of Ithiel, son of Jeshaiah).
The 968 descendants of Gabbai and Sallai. Their chief was Joel, son of Zichri, who was assisted by Judah, son of Hassenuah.

¹⁰⁻¹⁴Leaders from among the priests:

Jedaiah (son of Joiarib);
Jachin;
Seraiah (son of Hilkiah, son of Meshullam, son of Zadok, son of Meraioth, son of Ahitub the chief priest).

In all, there were 822 priests doing the work at the Temple under the leadership of these men. And there were 242 priests under the leadership of Adaiah (son of Jeroham, son of Pelaliah, son of Amzi, son of Zechariah, son of Pashhur, son of Malchijah).

There were also 128 stalwart men under the leadership of Amashsai (son of Azarel, son of Ahzai, son of Meshillemoth, son of Immer); who was assisted by Zabdiel (son of Haggedolim).

¹⁵⁻¹⁷Levite leaders:

Shemaiah (son of Hasshub, son of Azrikam, son of Hashabiah, son of Bunni);
Shabbethai and Jozabad, who were in charge of the work outside the Temple;
Mattaniah (son of Mica, son of Zabdi, son of Asaph) was the one who began the thanksgiving services with prayer;
Bakbukiah and Abda (son of Shammua, son of Galal, son of Jeduthun) were his assistants.

¹⁸In all, there were 284 Levites in Jerusalem.

¹⁹There were also 172 gatekeepers, led by Akkub, Talmon, and others of their clan. ²⁰The other priests, Levites, and people lived wherever their family inheritance was located. ²¹However, the Temple workers (whose leaders were Ziha and Gishpa) all lived in Ophel.

²²,²³The supervisor of the Levites in Jerusalem and of those serving at the Temple was Uzzi (son

of Bani, son of Hashabiah, son of Mattaniah, son of Mica), a descendant of Asaph, whose clan became the Tabernacle singers. He was appointed by King David, who also set the pay scale of the singers.

24Pethahiah (son of Meshezabel, a descendant of Zerah, a son of Judah) assisted in all matters of public administration.

25-30Some of the towns where the people of Judah lived were: Kiriath-arba, Dibon, Jekabzeel (and their surrounding villages), Jeshua, Moladah, Beth-pelet, Hazar-shual, Beersheba (and its surrounding villages), Ziklag, Meconah and its villages, En-rimmon, Zorah, Jarmuth, Zanoah, Adullam (and their surrounding villages), Lachish and its nearby fields, Azekah and its towns.

So the people spread from Beersheba to the valley of Hinnom.

31-35The people of the tribe of Benjamin lived at: Geba, Michmash, Aija, Bethel (and its surrounding villages), Anathoth, Nob, Ananiah, Hazor, Ramah, Gittaim, Hadid, Zeboim, Neballat, Lod, Ono (the Valley of the Craftsmen).

36Some of the Levites who lived in Judah were sent to live with the tribe of Benjamin.

12 The Priests and Levites

Here is a list of the priests who accompanied Zerubbabel (son of Shealtiel) and Jeshua: Seraiah, Jeremiah, Ezra, Amariah, Malluch, Hattush, Shecaniah, Rehum, Meremoth, Iddo, Ginnethoi, Abijah, Mijamin, Maadiah, Bilgah, Shemaiah, Joiarib, Jedaiah, Sallu, Amok, Hilkiah, Jedaiah.

8The Levites who went with them were: Jeshua, Binnui, Kadmiel,

Sherebiah, Judah, Mattaniah—who was the one in charge of the thanksgiving service.

9Bakbukiah and Unni, their fellow clansmen, helped them during the service.

10,11Jeshua was the father of Joiakim;
Joiakim was the father of Eliashib;
Eliashib was the father of Joiada;
Joiada was the father of Jonathan;
Jonathan was the father of Jaddua.

12-21The following were the clan leaders of the priests who served under the High Priest Joiakim:

Meraiah, leader of the Seraiah clan;
Hananiah, leader of the Jeremiah clan;
Meshullam, leader of the Ezra clan;
Jehohanan, leader of the Amariah clan;
Jonathan, leader of the Malluchi clan;
Joseph, leader of the Shebaniah clan;
Adna, leader of the Harim clan;
Helkai, leader of the Meraioth clan;
Zechariah, leader of the Iddo clan;
Meshullam, leader of the Ginnethon clan;
Zichri, leader of the Abijah clan;
Piltai, leader of the Moadiah and Miniamin clans;
Shammua, leader of the Bilgah clan;
Jehonathan, leader of the Shemaiah clan;
Mattenai, leader of the Joiarib clan;
Uzzi, leader of the Jedaiah clan;
Kallai, leader of the Sallai clan;
Eber, leader of the Amok clan;
Hashabiah, leader of the Hilkiah clan;
Nethanel, leader of the Jedaiah clan.

22A genealogical record of the heads of the clans of the priests and Levites was compiled during the reign of King Darius of Persia, in the days of Eliashib, Joiada, Johanan, and Jaddua—all of whom were Levites. 23In *The Book of the Chronicles* the Levite names were recorded down to the days of Johanan, the son of Eliashib.

24These were the chiefs of the Levites at that time: Hashabiah, Sherebiah, and Jeshua (son of Kadmiel).

Their fellow-clansmen helped them during the ceremonies of praise and thanksgiving, just as commanded by David, the man of God.

25The gatekeepers who had charge of the collection centers at the gates were: Mattaniah, Bakbukiah, Obadiah, Meshullam, Talmon, Akkub.

26These were the men who were active in the time of Joiakim (son of Jeshua, son of Jozadak), and when I was the governor, and when Ezra was the priest and teacher of religion.

27During the dedication of the new Jerusalem wall, all the Levites throughout the land came to Jerusalem to assist in the ceremonies and to take part in the joyous occasion with their thanksgiving, cymbals, psaltries, and harps. 28The choir members also came to Jerusalem from the surrounding villages and from the villages of the Netophathites; 29they also came from Beth-gilgal and the area of Geba and Azmaveth, for the singers had built their own villages as suburbs of Jerusalem. 30The priests and Levites first dedicated themselves, then the people, the gates, and the wall.

31,32I led the Judean leaders to the top of the wall and divided them into two long lines to walk in opposite directions along the top of the wall, giving thanks as they went. The group which went to the right toward the Dung Gate consisted of half of the leaders of Judah, 33including Hoshaiah, Azariah, Ezra, Meshullam, 34Judah, Benjamin, Shemaiah, and Jeremiah.

35,36The priests who played the trumpets were Zechariah (son of Jonathan, son of Shemaiah, son of Mattaniah, son of Micaiah, son of Zaccur, son of Asaph), Shemaiah, Azarel, Milalai, Gilalai, Maai,

Nethanel, Judah, and Hanani. (They used the original musical instruments of King David.) Ezra the priest led this procession. ³⁷When they arrived at the Fountain Gate they went straight ahead and climbed the stairs that go up beside the castle to the old City of David; then they went to the Water Gate on the east.

³⁸The other group, of which I was a member, went around the other way to meet them. We walked from the Tower of Furnaces to the Broad Wall, ³⁹then from the Ephraim Gate to the Old Gate, passed the Fish Gate and the Tower of Hananel, and went on to the gate of the Tower of the Hundred; then we continued on to the Sheep Gate and stopped at the Prison Gate.

⁴⁰,⁴¹Both choirs then proceeded to the Temple. Those with me were joined by the trumpet-playing priests—Eliakim, Maaseiah, Miniamin, Micaiah, Elioenai, Zechariah, and Hananiah, ⁴²and by the singers—Maaseiah, Shemaiah, Eleazar, Uzzi, Jehohanan, Malchijah, Elam, and Ezer.

They sang loudly and clearly under the direction of Jezrahiah the choirmaster.

⁴³Many sacrifices were offered on that joyous day, for God had given us cause for great joy. The women and children rejoiced, too, and the joy of the people of Jerusalem was heard far away!

⁴⁴On that day men were appointed to be in charge of the treasuries, the wave offerings, the tithes, and first-of-the-harvest offerings, and to collect these from the farms as decreed by the laws of Moses. These offerings were assigned to the priests and Levites, for the people of Judah appreciated the priests and Levites and their ministry. ⁴⁵They also appreciated the work of the singers and gatekeepers, who assisted them in worshiping God and performing the purification ceremonies as required by the laws of David and his son Solomon. ⁴⁶(It was in the days of David and Asaph that the custom began of having choir directors to lead the choirs in hymns of praise and thanks to God.) ⁴⁷So now, in the days of Zerubbabel and Nehemiah, the people brought a daily supply of food for the members of the choir, the gatekeepers, and the Levites. The Levites, in turn, gave a portion of what they received to the priests.

13 Foreigners Are Sent Away

On that same day, as the laws of Moses were being read, the people found a statement which said that the Ammonites and Moabites should never be permitted to worship at the Temple. ²For they had not been friendly to the people of Israel. Instead, they had hired Balaam to curse them—although God turned the curse into a blessing. ³When this rule was read, all the foreigners were immediately expelled from the assembly.

⁴Before this had happened, Eliashib the priest, who had been appointed as custodian of the Temple storerooms and who was also a good friend of Tobiah, ⁵had converted a storage room into a beautiful guest room for Tobiah. The room had previously been used for storing the grain offerings, frankincense, bowls, and tithes of grain, new wine, and olive oil. Moses had decreed that these offerings belonged to the priests, Levites, the members of the choir, and the gatekeepers.

⁶I was not in Jerusalem at the time, for I had returned to Babylon in the thirty-second year of the reign of King Artaxerxes (though I later received his permission to go back again to Jerusalem). ⁷When I arrived back in Jerusalem and learned of this evil deed of Eliashib—that he had prepared a guest room in the Temple for Tobiah—⁸I was very upset and threw out all of his belongings from the room. ⁹Then I demanded that the room be thoroughly cleaned, and I brought back the Temple bowls, the grain offerings, and frankincense.

¹⁰I also learned that the Levites had not been given what was due them, so they and the choir singers who were supposed to conduct the worship services had returned to their farms. ¹¹I immediately confronted the leaders and demanded, "Why has the Temple been forsaken?" Then I called all the Levites back again and restored them to their proper duties. ¹²And once more all the people of Judah began bringing their tithes of grain, new wine, and olive oil to the Temple treasury.

¹³I put Shelemiah the priest, Zadok the scribe, and Pedaiah the Levite in charge of the administration of the storehouses; and I appointed Hanan (son of Zaccur, son of Mattaniah) as their assistant. These men had an excellent reputation, and their job was to make an honest distribution to their fellow-Levites.

¹⁴O my God, remember this good deed and do not forget all that I have done for the Temple.

¹⁵One day I was on a farm and saw some men treading winepresses on the Sabbath, hauling in sheaves, and loading their donkeys with wine, grapes, figs, and all sorts of produce, which they took that day into Jerusalem. So I opposed them publicly. ¹⁶There were also some men from Tyre bringing in fish and all sorts of wares and selling them on the Sabbath to the people of Jerusalem.

¹⁷Then I asked the leaders of Judah, "Why are you profaning the Sabbath? ¹⁸Wasn't it enough that your fathers did this sort of thing and brought the present evil days upon us and upon our city? And now you are bringing more wrath

upon the people of Israel by permitting the Sabbath to be desecrated in this way."

¹⁹So from then on I commanded that the gates of the city be shut as darkness fell on Friday evenings and not be opened until the Sabbath had ended; and I sent some of my servants to guard the gates so that no merchandise could be brought in on the Sabbath day. ²⁰The merchants and tradesmen camped outside Jerusalem once or twice, ²¹but I spoke sharply to them and said, "What are you doing out here, camping around the wall? If you do this again, I will arrest you." And that was the last time they came on the Sabbath.

²²Then I commanded the Levites to purify themselves and to guard the gates in order to preserve the sanctity of the Sabbath. Remember this good deed, O my God! Have compassion upon me in accordance with your great goodness.

²³About the same time I realized that some of the Jews had married women from Ashdod, Ammon, and Moab, ²⁴and that many of their children spoke in the language of Ashdod and couldn't speak the language of Judah at all. ²⁵So I confronted these parents and cursed them and punched a few of them and knocked them around and pulled out their hair; and they vowed before God that they would not let their children intermarry with non-Jews.

²⁶"Wasn't this exactly King Solomon's problem?" I demanded. "There was no king who could compare with him, and God loved him and made him the king over all Israel; but even so he was led into idolatry by foreign women. ²⁷Do you think that we will let you get away with this sinful deed?"

²⁸One of the sons of Jehoiada (the son of Eliashib the High Priest) was a son-in-law of Sanballat the Horonite, so I chased him out of the Temple. ²⁹Remember them, O my God, for they have defiled the priesthood and the promises and vows of the priests and Levites. ³⁰So I purged out the foreigners and assigned tasks to the priests and Levites, making certain that each knew his work. ³¹They supplied wood for the altar at the proper times and cared for the sacrifices and the first offerings of every harvest. Remember me, my God, with your kindness.

Esther

DO YOU know anyone who's really bold? It's fun to watch movies or read books where the good guys bravely take big risks to do something important. In the book of Esther, you'll meet two people who took big risks. They almost lost their lives because not everyone agreed with what they were doing.

This story took place when the Israelites were captives in Persia. The king of Persia could do whatever he wanted—whenever he felt like it. You'll see some of the crazy decisions he made.

The main characters in this story are Esther, a Jewish girl; Mordecai, her uncle; and Haman, the king's nobleman. Haman came up with a plot to have all the Jewish people in the Persian kingdom put to death. When Mordecai found out, he and Esther had to act quickly and cleverly to stop the plan. They moved ahead boldly with their counterplan, even though it was dangerous. They had to do what they could to help save God's people.

Today we can still take risks for God. We don't usually risk our lives, but sometimes we risk our popularity or comfort to do what we know God wants. As you read Esther, look for examples of boldness, and think of ways you can take good risks for God.

1

Trouble in the Palace

It was the third year of the reign of King Ahasuerus, emperor of vast Media-Persia, with its 127 provinces stretching from India to Ethiopia. This was the year of the great celebration at Shushan Palace, to which the emperor invited all his governors, aides, and army officers, bringing them in from every part of Media-Persia for the occasion. ⁴The celebration lasted six months, a tremendous display of the wealth and glory of his empire.

⁵When it was all over, the king gave a special party for the palace servants and officials—janitors and cabinet officials alike—for seven days of revelry, held in the courtyard of the palace garden. ⁶The decorations were green, white, and blue, fastened with purple ribbons tied to silver rings imbedded in marble pillars. Gold and silver benches stood on pavements of black, red, white, and yellow marble. ⁷Drinks were served in gold goblets of many designs, and there was an abundance of royal wine, for the king was feeling very generous. ⁸The only restriction on the drinking

was that no one should be compelled to take more than he wanted, but those who wished could have as much as they pleased. For the king had instructed his officers to let everyone decide this matter for himself.

⁹Queen Vashti gave a party for the women of the palace at the same time.

¹⁰On the final day when the king was feeling high, half drunk from wine, he told the seven eunuchs who were his personal aides—Mehuman, Biztha, Harbona, Bigtha, Abagtha, Zethar, and Carkas—¹¹to bring Queen Vashti to him with the royal crown upon her head so that all the men could gaze upon her beauty—for she was a very beautiful woman. ¹²But when they conveyed the emperor's order to Queen Vashti, she refused to come. The king was furious ¹³⁻¹⁵but first consulted his lawyers, for he did nothing without their advice. They were men of wisdom who knew the temper of the times as well as Persian law and justice, and the king trusted their judgment. These men were Carshena, Shethar, Admatha, Tarshish, Meres, Marsena, and Memucan—seven high officials of Media-Persia. They were his personal friends as well as being the chief officers of the government.

"What shall we do about this situation?" he asked them. "What penalty does the law provide for a queen who refuses to obey the king's orders, properly sent through his aides?"

¹⁶Memucan answered for the others, "Queen Vashti has wronged not only the king but every official and citizen of your empire. ¹⁷For women everywhere will begin to disobey their husbands when they learn what Queen Vashti has done. ¹⁸And before this day is out, the wife of every one of us officials throughout your empire will hear what the queen did and will start talking to us husbands the same way, and there will be contempt and anger throughout your realm. ¹⁹We suggest that, subject to your agreement, you issue a royal edict, a law of the Medes and Persians that can never be changed, that Queen Vashti be forever banished from your presence and that you choose another queen more worthy than she. ²⁰When this decree is published throughout your great kingdom, husbands everywhere, whatever their rank, will be respected by their wives!"

²¹The king and all his aides thought this made good sense, so he followed Memucan's counsel ²²and sent letters to all of his provinces, in all the local languages, stressing that every man should rule his home and should assert his authority.

2 Esther Becomes Queen

But after King Ahasuerus' anger had cooled, he began brooding over the loss of Vashti, realizing that he would never see her again.

²So his aides suggested, "Let us go and find the most beautiful girls in the empire and bring them to the king for his pleasure. ³We will appoint agents in each province to select young lovelies for the royal harem. Hegai, the eunuch in charge, will see that they are given beauty treatments, ⁴and after that, the girl who pleases you most shall be the queen instead of Vashti."

This suggestion naturally pleased the king very much, and he put the plan into immediate effect.

⁵Now there was a certain Jew at the palace named Mordecai (son of Jair, son of Shimei, son of Kish, a Benjaminite). ⁶He had been captured when Jerusalem was destroyed by King Nebuchadnezzar and had been exiled to Babylon along with King Jeconiah of Judah and many others. ⁷This man had a beautiful and lovely young cousin, Hadassah (also called Esther), whose father and mother were dead, and whom he had adopted into his family and raised as his own daughter. ⁸So now, as a result of the king's decree, Esther was brought to the king's harem at Shushan Palace along with many other young girls. ⁹Hegai, who was responsible for the harem, was very much impressed with her and did his best to make her happy; he ordered a special menu for her, favored her for the beauty treatments, gave her seven girls from the palace as her maids, and gave her the most luxurious apartment in the harem. ¹⁰Esther hadn't told anyone that she was a Jewess, for Mordecai had said not to. ¹¹He came daily to the court of the harem to ask about Esther and to find out what was happening to her.

¹²⁻¹⁴The instructions concerning these girls were that before being taken to the king's bed, each would be given six months of beauty treatments with oil of myrrh, followed by six months with special perfumes and ointments. Then, as each girl's turn came for spending the night with King Ahasuerus, she was given her choice of clothing or jewelry she wished, to enhance her beauty. She was taken to the king's apartment in the evening and the next morning returned to the second harem where the king's wives lived. There she was under the care of Shaashgaz, another of the king's eunuchs and lived there the rest of her life, never seeing the king again unless he had especially enjoyed her and called for her by name.

¹⁵When it was Esther's turn to go to the king, she accepted the advice of Hegai, the eunuch in charge of the harem, dressing according to his instructions. And all the other girls exclaimed with delight when they saw her. ¹⁶So Esther was taken to the palace of the king in January of the seventh year of his reign. ¹⁷Well, the king loved Esther more than any of the other girls. He was so delighted with her that he set the royal crown on

Family Devotions

☐ DEVOTION 138
BECOMING MORE LIKE JESUS

Read Esther 1:7-8

Steve's eighth-grade American history class was studying the temperance movement of the early 1900s. He learned that this was the time when many people who were opposed to drinking alcohol worked to get laws making its use illegal.

As Steve was studying his Sunday school lesson a few days later, he thought about the temperance movement when he found *self-control* listed among the fruit of the Spirit. "Mom," he asked, "if the idea of self-control was in the Bible all along, why did people need to make laws about drinking? Why didn't they let everyone decide for himself?"

"Well, Steve, you've asked a very good question," Mom replied. "Supporters of the temperance movement felt laws were necessary because people often didn't use temperance, or self-control, when drinking, and they drank too much. As Christians, we should be using self-control every day, whether there are laws about it or not—and not just with drinking, but in every area of our lives."

Steve thought he knew what his mother was getting at. Right now drunkenness was not his problem, but eating was another story. Steve loved to eat—and he hated to exercise! Even though he was only in eighth grade, he was already becoming very, very chubby. Some of the kids at school even called him fat! He needed to use more self-control when eating.

His mother's words seemed to haunt him after that. Every time he wanted to eat a candy bar or drink another soda, he remembered that he was supposed to show self-control in every area of his life.

With the Lord's help, Steve reached a much better weight within six months. He had learned that the fruit of the Spirit includes self-control.

Becoming More Like Jesus Memory Verse

Let everything you do reflect your love of the truth and the fact that you are in dead earnest about it.
Titus 2:7

How About You?
Do you display self-control in every area of your life? Are you tempted to overeat, gossip, or lose your temper? Ask the Lord to help you exercise self-control and say no. R. P.

her head and declared her queen instead of Vashti. ¹⁸To celebrate the occasion, he threw another big party for all his officials and servants, giving generous gifts to everyone and making grants to the provinces in the form of remission of taxes.

¹⁹Later the king demanded a second bevy of beautiful girls. By that time Mordecai had become a government official.

²⁰Esther still hadn't told anyone she was a Jewess, for she was still following Mordecai's orders, just as she had in his home.

²¹One day as Mordecai was on duty at the palace, two of the king's eunuchs, Bigthan and Teresh—who were guards at the palace gate—became angry at the king and plotted to assassinate him. ²²Mordecai heard about it and passed on the information to Queen Esther, who told the king, crediting Mordecai with the information. ²³An investigation was made, the two men found guilty, and impaled alive. This was all duly recorded in the book of the history of King Ahasuerus' reign.

3 Haman Tricks the King

Soon afterwards King Ahasuerus appointed Haman (son of Hammedatha the Agagite) as prime minister. He was the most powerful official in the empire next to the king himself. ²Now all the king's officials bowed before him in deep reverence whenever he passed by, for so the king had commanded. But Mordecai refused to bow.

³,⁴"Why are you disobeying the king's commandment?" the others demanded day after day, but he still refused. Finally they spoke to Haman about it to see whether Mordecai could get away with it because of his being a Jew, which was the excuse he had given them. ⁵,⁶Haman was furious but decided not to lay hands on Mordecai alone, but to move against all of Mordecai's people, the Jews, and destroy all of them throughout the whole kingdom of Ahasuerus.

⁷The most propitious time for this action was determined by throwing dice. This was done in April of the twelfth year of the reign of Ahasuerus, and February of the following year was the date indicated.

⁸Haman now approached the king about the matter. "There is a certain race of people scattered through all the provinces of your kingdom," he began, "and their laws are different from those of any other nation, and they refuse to obey the king's laws; therefore, it is not in the king's interest to let them live. ⁹If it please the king, issue a decree that they be destroyed, and I will pay $20,000,000 into the royal treasury for the expenses involved in this purge."

¹⁰The king agreed, confirming his decision by removing his ring from his finger and giving it to Haman, telling him, ¹¹"Keep the money, but go ahead and do as you like with these people—whatever you think best."

¹²Two or three weeks later, Haman called in the king's secretaries and dictated letters to the governors and officials throughout the empire, to each province in its own languages and dialects; these letters were signed in the name of King Ahasuerus and sealed with his ring.

¹³They were then sent by messengers into all the provinces of the empire, decreeing that the Jews—young and old, women and children—must all be killed on the 28th day of February of the following year and their property given to those who killed them. ¹⁴"A copy of this edict," the letter stated, "must be proclaimed as law in every province and made known to all your people, so that they will be ready to do their duty on the appointed day." ¹⁵The edict went out by the king's speediest couriers, after being first proclaimed in the city of Shushan. Then the king and Haman sat down for a drinking spree as the city fell into confusion and panic.

4

When Mordecai learned what had been done, he tore his clothes, put on sackcloth and ashes, and went out into the city, crying with a loud and bitter wail. ² Then he stood outside the gate of the palace, for no one was permitted to enter in mourning clothes. ³And throughout all the provinces there was great mourning among the Jews, fasting, weeping, and despair at the king's decree; and many lay in sackcloth and ashes.

⁴When Esther's maids and eunuchs came and told her about Mordecai, she was deeply distressed and sent clothing to him to replace the sackcloth, but he refused it. ⁵Then Esther sent for Hathach, one of the king's eunuchs who had been appointed as her attendant, and told him to go out to Mordecai and find out what the trouble was and why he was acting like that. ⁶So Hathach went out to the city square and found Mordecai just outside the palace gates, ⁷and heard the whole story from him, and about the $20,000,000 Haman had promised to pay into the king's treasury for the destruction of

---

OBEDIENCE 3:2 Mordecai's faith was based on conviction. He did not first take a poll to determine the safest or most popular course of action; he had the courage to stand alone. Doing what is right is not always popular. Those who do right will be in the minority, but to obey God is more important than to obey people (Acts 5:29). **To begin the series of devotionals on OBEDIENCE, turn to page 25.**

the Jews. ⁸Mordecai also gave Hathach a copy of the king's decree dooming all Jews, and told him to show it to Esther and to tell her what was happening and that she should go to the king to plead for her people. ⁹So Hathach returned to Esther with Mordecai's message. ¹⁰Esther told Hathach to go back and say to Mordecai,

¹¹"All the world knows that anyone, whether man or woman, who goes into the king's inner court without his summons is doomed to die unless the king holds out his gold scepter; and the king has not called for me to come to him in more than a month."

¹²So Hathach gave Esther's message to Mordecai.

¹³This was Mordecai's reply to Esther: "Do you think you will escape there in the palace when all other Jews are killed? ¹⁴If you keep quiet at a time like this, God will deliver the Jews from some other source, but you and your relatives will die; what's more, who can say but that God has brought you into the palace for just such a time as this?"

¹⁵Then Esther said to tell Mordecai:

¹⁶"Go and gather together all the Jews of Shushan and fast for me; do not eat or drink for three days, night or day; and I and my maids will do the same; and then, though it is strictly forbidden, I will go in to see the king; and if I perish, I perish."

¹⁷So Mordecai did as Esther told him to.

5 Queen Esther Defeats Haman

Three days later Esther put on her royal robes and entered the inner court just beyond the royal hall of the palace, where the king was sitting upon his royal throne. ²And when he saw Queen Esther standing there in the inner court, he welcomed her, holding out the golden scepter to her. So Esther approached and touched its tip.

³Then the king asked her, "What do you wish, Queen Esther? What is your request? I will give it to you, even if it is half the kingdom!"

⁴And Esther replied, "If it please Your Majesty, I want you and Haman to come to a banquet I have prepared for you today."

⁵The king turned to his aides. "Tell Haman to hurry!" he said. So the king and Haman came to Esther's banquet.

⁶During the wine course the king said to Esther, "Now tell me what you really want, and I will give it to you, even if it is half of the kingdom!"

⁷,⁸Esther replied, "My request, my deepest wish, is that if Your Majesty loves me and wants to grant my request, that you come again with Haman tomorrow to the banquet I shall prepare for you. And tomorrow I will explain what this is all about."

⁹What a happy man was Haman as he left the banquet! But when he saw Mordecai there at the gate, not standing up or trembling before him, he was furious. ¹⁰However, he restrained himself, went on home, and gathered together his friends and Zeresh, his wife, ¹¹and boasted to them about his wealth, his many children, and promotions the king had given him, and how he had become the greatest man in the kingdom next to the king himself.

¹²Then he delivered his punch line: "Yes, and Esther the queen invited only me and the king himself to the banquet she prepared for us; and tomorrow we are invited again! ¹³But yet," he added, "all this is nothing when I see Mordecai the Jew just sitting there in front of the king's gate, refusing to bow to me."

¹⁴"Well," suggested Zeresh, his wife, and all his friends, "get ready a 75-foot-high gallows, and in the morning ask the king to let you hang Mordecai on it; and when this is done you can go on your merry way with the king to the banquet." This pleased Haman immensely, and he ordered the gallows built.

6

That night the king had trouble sleeping and decided to read awhile. He ordered the historical records of his kingdom from the library, and in them he came across the item telling how Mordecai had exposed the plot of Bigthana and Teresh, two of the king's eunuchs, watchmen at the palace gates, who had plotted to assassinate him.

³"What reward did we ever give Mordecai for this?" the king asked.

His courtiers replied, "Nothing!"

⁴"Who is on duty in the outer court?" the king inquired. Now, as it happened, Haman had just arrived in the outer court of the palace to ask the king to hang Mordecai from the gallows he was building.

⁵So the courtiers replied to the king, "Haman is out there."

"Bring him in," the king ordered. ⁶So Haman

SERVING GOD BOLDLY 4:16 *Save your own skin* and *Watch out for number one* are mottoes that reflect the world's selfish outlook on life. Esther's attitude stands in sharp contrast to this. She knew what she had to do and that it could cost her life. And yet she responded, "If I perish, I perish." We should have the same commitment to do what is right despite the possible consequences. Faith is doing what God wants and trusting him to work out the results. Do you try to save your own skin by remaining silent rather than standing up for what is right? Commit yourself to do what God wants, and trust him for the outcome. **To begin the series of devotionals on SERVING GOD BOLDLY, turn to page 17.**

came in, and the king said to him, "What should I do to honor a man who truly pleases me?"

Haman thought to himself, "Whom would he want to honor more than me?" ⁷,⁸So he replied, "Bring out some of the royal robes the king himself has worn, and the king's own horse, and the royal crown, ⁹and instruct one of the king's most noble princes to robe the man and to lead him through the streets on the king's own horse, shouting before him, 'This is the way the king honors those who truly please him!'"

¹⁰"Excellent!" the king said to Haman. "Hurry and take these robes and my horse, and do just as you have said—to Mordecai the Jew, who works at the Chancellery. Follow every detail you have suggested."

¹¹So Haman took the robes and put them on Mordecai, and mounted him on the king's own steed, and led him through the streets of the city, shouting, "This is the way the king honors those he delights in."

¹²Afterwards Mordecai returned to his job, but Haman hurried home utterly humiliated. ¹³When Haman told Zeresh his wife and all his friends what had happened, they said, "If Mordecai is a Jew, you will never succeed in your plans against him; to continue to oppose him will be fatal." ¹⁴While they were still discussing it with him, the king's messengers arrived to conduct Haman quickly to the banquet Esther had prepared.

7 So the king and Haman came to Esther's banquet. ²Again, during the wine course, the king asked her, "What is your petition, Queen Esther? What do you wish? Whatever it is, I will give it to you, even if it is half of my kingdom!"

³And at last Queen Esther replied, "If I have won your favor, O king, and if it please Your Majesty, save my life and the lives of my people. ⁴For I and my people have been sold to those who will destroy us. We are doomed to destruction and slaughter. If we were only to be sold as slaves, perhaps I could remain quiet, though even then there would be incalculable damage to the king that no amount of money could begin to cover."

⁵"What are you talking about?" King Ahasuerus demanded. "Who would dare touch you?"

⁶Esther replied, "This wicked Haman is our enemy."

Then Haman grew pale with fright before the king and queen. ⁷The king jumped to his feet and went out into the palace garden as Haman stood up to plead for his life to Queen Esther, for he knew that he was doomed. ⁸In despair he fell upon the couch where Queen Esther was reclining, just as the king returned from the palace garden.

"Will he even rape the queen right here in the palace, before my very eyes?" the king roared. Instantly the death veil was placed over Haman's face.

⁹Then Harbona, one of the king's aides, said, "Sir, Haman has just ordered a 75-foot gallows constructed, to hang Mordecai, the man who saved the king from assassination! It stands in Haman's courtyard."

"Hang Haman on it," the king ordered.

¹⁰So they did, and the king's wrath was pacified.

8 A New Law to Protect the Jews
On that same day King Ahasuerus gave the estate of Haman, the Jews' enemy, to Queen Esther. Then Mordecai was brought before the king, for Esther had told the king that he was her cousin and foster father. ²The king took off his ring—which he had taken back from Haman—and gave it to Mordecai [appointing him Prime Minister]; and Esther appointed Mordecai to be in charge of Haman's estate.

³And now once more Esther came before the king, falling down at his feet and begging him with tears to stop Haman's plot against the Jews. ⁴And again the king held out the golden scepter to Esther. So she arose and stood before him, ⁵and said, "If it please Your Majesty, and if you love me, send out a decree reversing Haman's order to destroy the Jews throughout the king's provinces. ⁶For how can I endure it, to see my people butchered and destroyed?"

⁷Then King Ahasuerus said to Queen Esther and Mordecai the Jew, "I have given Esther the palace of Haman, and he has been hanged upon the gallows because he tried to destroy you. ⁸Now go ahead and send a message to the Jews, telling them whatever you want to in the king's name, and seal it with the king's ring so that it can never be reversed."

⁹,¹⁰Immediately the king's secretaries were called in—it was now the 23rd day of the month of July—and they wrote as Mordecai dictated—a decree to the Jews and to the officials, governors, and princes of all the provinces from India to Ethiopia, 127

PATIENCE 6:10-13 Mordecai had uncovered a plot to assassinate Ahasuerus and thus saved the king's life (2:21-23). Although his good deed was recorded in the history books, Mordecai had gone unrewarded. But God was saving Mordecai's reward for the right time. Just as Haman was about to hang Mordecai unjustly, the king was ready to give the reward, and Mordecai's life was spared. Although God promises to reward our good works, we sometimes feel our "payoff" is too far away. Be patient. God steps in when it will do the most good.
To begin the series of devotionals on PATIENCE, turn to page 549.

in all: the decree was translated into the languages and dialects of all the people of the kingdom. Mordecai wrote in the name of King Ahasuerus and sealed the message with the king's ring and sent the letters by swift carriers—riders on camels, mules, and young dromedaries used in the king's service. ¹¹This decree gave the Jews everywhere permission to unite in the defense of their lives and their families, to destroy all the forces opposed to them, and to take their property. ¹²The day chosen for this throughout all the provinces of King Ahasuerus was the 28th day of February! ¹³It further stated that a copy of this decree, which must be recognized everywhere as law, must be broadcast to all the people so that the Jews would be ready and prepared to overcome their enemies. ¹⁴So the mail went out swiftly, carried by the king's couriers and speeded by the king's commandment. The same decree was also issued at Shushan Palace.

¹⁵Then Mordecai put on the royal robes of blue and white and the great crown of gold, with an outer cloak of fine linen and purple, and went out from the presence of the king through the city streets filled with shouting people. ¹⁶And the Jews had joy and gladness and were honored everywhere. ¹⁷And in every city and province, as the king's decree arrived, the Jews were filled with joy and had a great celebration and declared a holiday. And many of the people of the land pretended to be Jews, for they feared what the Jews might do to them.

9 The Jews Defeat Their Enemies

So on the 28th day of February, the day the two decrees of the king were to be put into effect—the day the Jews' enemies had hoped to vanquish them, though it turned out quite to the contrary—the Jews gathered in their cities throughout all the king's provinces to defend themselves against any who might try to harm them; but no one tried, for they were greatly feared. ³And all the rulers of the provinces—the governors, officials, and aides—helped the Jews for fear of Mordecai; ⁴for Mordecai was a mighty name in the king's palace and his fame was known throughout all the provinces, for he had become more and more powerful.

⁵But the Jews went ahead on that appointed day and slaughtered their enemies. ⁶They even killed 500 men in Shushan. ⁷⁻¹⁰They also killed the ten sons of Haman (son of Hammedatha), the Jews' enemy—Parshandatha, Dalphon, Aspatha, Poratha, Adalia, Aridatha, Parmashta, Arisai, Aridai, and Vaizatha.

But they did not try to take Haman's property. ¹¹Late that evening, when the king was informed of the number of those slain in Shushan, ¹²he called for Queen Esther. "The Jews have killed 500 men in Shushan alone," he exclaimed, "and also Haman's ten sons. If they have done that here, I wonder what has happened in the rest of the provinces! But now, what more do you want? It will be granted to you. Tell me and I will do it."

¹³And Esther said, "If it please Your Majesty, let the Jews who are here at Shushan do again tomorrow as they have done today, and let Haman's ten sons be hanged upon the gallows."

¹⁴So the king agreed, and the decree was announced at Shushan, and they hung up the bodies of Haman's ten sons. ¹⁵Then the Jews at Shushan gathered together the next day also and killed 300 more men, though again they took no property.

¹⁶Meanwhile the other Jews throughout the king's provinces had gathered together and stood for their lives and destroyed all their enemies, killing 75,000 of those who hated them; but they did not take their goods. ¹⁷Throughout the provinces this was done on the 28th day of February, and the next day they rested, celebrating their victory with feasting and gladness. ¹⁸But the Jews at Shushan went on killing their enemies the second day also and rested the next day, with feasting and gladness. ¹⁹And so it is that the Jews in the unwalled villages throughout Israel to this day have an annual celebration on the second day when they rejoice and send gifts to each other.

²⁰Mordecai wrote a history of all these events and sent letters to the Jews near and far, throughout all the king's provinces, ²¹encouraging them to declare an annual holiday on the last two days of the month, ²²to celebrate with feasting, gladness, and the giving of gifts these historic days when the Jews were saved from their enemies, when their sorrow was turned to gladness and their mourning into happiness.

²³So the Jews adopted Mordecai's suggestion and began this annual custom ²⁴,²⁵as a reminder of the time when Haman (son of Hammedatha the Agagite), the enemy of all the Jews, had plotted to destroy them at the time determined by a throw of the dice; and to remind them that when the matter came before the king, he issued a decree causing Haman's plot to boomerang, and he and his sons were hanged on the gallows. ²⁶That

---

PERSEVERANCE 8:15-17 Everyone wants to be a hero and receive praise, honor, and wealth. But few are willing to pay the price. Mordecai served the government faithfully for years, bore Haman's hatred and oppression, and risked his life for his people. The price to be paid by God's heroes is long-term commitment. Are you ready or willing to pay the price? **To begin the series of devotionals on PERSEVERANCE, turn to page 37.**

is why this celebration is called "Purim" because the word for "throwing dice" in Persian is *pur*. ²⁷All the Jews throughout the realm agreed to inaugurate this tradition and to pass it on to their descendants and to all who became Jews; they declared they would never fail to celebrate these two days at the appointed time each year. ²⁸It would be an annual event from generation to generation, celebrated by every family throughout the countryside and cities of the empire, so that the memory of what had happened would never perish from the Jewish race.

²⁹⁻³¹Meanwhile Queen Esther (daughter of Abihail and later adopted by Mordecai the Jew) had written a letter throwing her full support behind Mordecai's letter inaugurating his annual Feast of Purim. In addition, letters were sent to all the Jews throughout the 127 provinces of the kingdom of Ahasuerus with messages of good will and encouragement to confirm these two days annually as the Feast of Purim, decreed by both Mordecai the Jew and by Queen Esther; indeed, the Jews themselves had decided upon this tradition as a remembrance of the time of their national fasting and prayer. ³²So the commandment of Esther confirmed these dates, and it was recorded as law.

10 God Rewards Mordecai

King Ahasuerus not only laid tribute upon the mainland but even on the islands of the sea. ²His great deeds, and also the full account of the greatness of Mordecai and the honors given him by the king, are written in *The Book of the Chronicles of the Kings of Media and Persia*. ³Mordecai the Jew was the Prime Minister, with authority next to that of King Ahasuerus himself. He was, of course, very great among the Jews and respected by all his countrymen because he did his best for his people and was a friend at court for all of them.

WHEN BAD things happen, it's easy to start questioning God. *Why did God let it happen? Doesn't God care about us? Isn't he strong enough to stop bad things? Why do bad things happen to people who trust and obey God?*

Do you ever ask questions like these when things go wrong? Job and his friends did. Job was a man who loved and obeyed God with all of his heart. So when horrible things happened to him, he couldn't understand it. He became depressed.

Job's wife told him to give up his faith in God. But Job wouldn't do that. Then three friends who visited Job had one easy answer: They said bad things are punishment for our sins. But Job knew that wasn't right. A fourth friend told Job that God was disciplining him to keep him from future sin. Job didn't accept that either.

Even though Job didn't deny his faith in God, he did a lot of complaining and questioning. Finally God himself spoke to Job. God simply said that he is who he is. He reminded Job of all his power, wisdom, creativity, and compassion. Job realized that he needed to keep having faith in God, no matter what the circumstances.

When things go wrong for us, we need to keep our faith in God. God doesn't give us all the answers, but he does give us himself to trust.

Job Loses Everything

There lived in the land of Uz a man named Job—a good man who feared God and stayed away from evil. ²,³He had a large family of seven sons and three daughters and was immensely wealthy, for he owned 7,000 sheep, 3,000 camels, 500 teams of oxen, 500 female donkeys, and employed many servants. He was, in fact, the richest cattleman in that entire area.

⁴Every year when Job's sons had birthdays, they invited their brothers and sisters to their homes for a celebration. On these occasions they would eat and drink with great merriment. ⁵When these birthday parties ended—and sometimes they lasted several days—Job would summon his children to him and sanctify them, getting up early in the morning and offering a burnt offering for each of them. For Job said, "Perhaps my sons have sinned and turned away from God in their hearts." This was Job's regular practice.

⁶One day as the angels came to present themselves before the Lord, Satan, the Accuser, came with them.

7"Where have you come from?" the Lord asked Satan.

And Satan replied, "From Earth, where I've been watching everything that's going on."

8Then the Lord asked Satan, "Have you noticed my servant Job? He is the finest man in all the earth—a good man who fears God and will have nothing to do with evil."

9"Why shouldn't he when you pay him so well?" Satan scoffed. 10"You have always protected him and his home and his property from all harm. You have prospered everything he does—look how rich he is! No wonder he 'worships' you! 11But just take away his wealth, and you'll see him curse you to your face!"

12,13And the Lord replied to Satan, "You may do anything you like with his wealth, but don't harm him physically."

So Satan went away; and sure enough, not long afterwards when Job's sons and daughters were dining at the oldest brother's house, tragedy struck.

14,15A messenger rushed to Job's home with this news: "Your oxen were plowing, with the donkeys feeding beside them, when the Sabeans raided us, drove away the animals, and killed all the farmhands except me. I am the only one left."

16While this messenger was still speaking, another arrived with more bad news: "The fire of God has fallen from heaven and burned up your sheep and all the herdsmen, and I alone have escaped to tell you."

17Before this man finished, still another messenger rushed in: "Three bands of Chaldeans have driven off your camels and killed your servants, and I alone have escaped to tell you."

18As he was still speaking, another arrived to say, "Your sons and daughters were feasting in their oldest brother's home, 19when suddenly a mighty wind swept in from the desert and engulfed the house so that the roof fell in on them and all are dead; and I alone escaped to tell you."

20Then Job stood up and tore his robe in grief and fell down upon the ground before God. 21"I came naked from my mother's womb," he said, "and I shall have nothing when I die. The Lord gave me everything I had, and they were his to take away. Blessed be the name of the Lord."

22In all of this Job did not sin or revile God.

2 Now the angels came again to present themselves before the Lord, and Satan with them.

2"Where have you come from?" the Lord asked Satan.

"From Earth, where I've been watching everything that's going on," Satan replied.

3"Well, have you noticed my servant Job?" the Lord asked. "He is the finest man in all the earth—a good man who fears God and turns away from all evil. And he has kept his faith in me despite the fact that you persuaded me to let you harm him without any cause."

4,5"Skin for skin," Satan replied. "A man will give anything to save his life. Touch his body with sickness, and he will curse you to your face!"

6"Do with him as you please," the Lord replied; "only spare his life."

7So Satan went out from the presence of the Lord and struck Job with a terrible case of boils from head to foot. 8Then Job took a broken piece of pottery to scrape himself and sat among the ashes.

9His wife said to him, "Are you still trying to be godly when God has done all this to you? Curse him and die."

10But he replied, "You talk like some heathen woman. What? Shall we receive only pleasant things from the hand of God and never anything unpleasant?" So in all this Job said nothing wrong.

11When three of Job's friends heard of all the tragedy that had befallen him, they got in touch with each other and traveled from their homes to comfort and console him. Their names were Eliphaz the Temanite, Bildad the Shuhite, and Zophar the Naamathite. 12Job was so changed that they could scarcely recognize him. Wailing loudly in despair, they tore their robes and threw dust into the air and put earth on their heads to demonstrate their sorrow. 13Then they sat upon the ground with him silently for seven days and nights, no one speaking a word; for they saw that his suffering was too great for words.

3 Job: I Wish I Had Died at Birth

At last Job spoke and cursed the day of his birth.

2,3"Let the day of my birth be cursed," he said, "and the night when I was conceived. 4Let that day be forever forgotten. Let it be lost even to God, shrouded in eternal darkness. 5Yes, let the darkness claim it for its own, and may a black cloud overshadow it. 6May it be blotted off the calendar, never again to be counted among the

---

SHOWING COMPASSION 2:13 Why did Job's friends arrive and then just sit quietly? According to Jewish tradition, people who come to comfort someone in mourning are not to speak until the mourner speaks. Often the best response to another person's suffering is silence. Job's friends realized that his pain was too deep to be healed with mere words, so they said nothing. (If only they had continued to just sit quietly!) Often, we feel we must say something spiritual and insightful to a hurting friend. Perhaps what he or she needs most is just our presence, showing that we care. Pat answers and trite quotations say much less than empathetic silence and loving companionship. **To begin the series of devotionals on SHOWING COMPASSION, turn to page 569.**

FAMILY DEVOTIONS

☐ DEVOTION 139
RESPECTING OTHERS

Read Job 1:14-22

As part of a community awareness program in Molly's town, all the newspaper carriers checked up on the senior citizens who were on their routes. At first, Molly resented the extra time it took, especially with Mrs. Deaton, an old lady on her route who talked and talked while Molly impatiently wished she were at home, playing.

One day, Mrs. Deaton got out a faded photograph album. "Who are these kids?" Molly asked, pointing to a picture of four little girls sitting on a log.

"Oh," replied Mrs. Deaton, "those are my children."

"How come they never visit you or take care of you, now that you're old?" Molly blurted out without thinking.

"The children all died during a smallpox epidemic many years ago," Mrs. Deaton explained. "Then it was just George and me until he died about twenty years ago." Molly fidgeted when she heard that. "Now don't fret," Mrs. Deaton added. "The Lord gives, and the Lord takes away, but he never forsakes! He's been with me all these years."

One day not long after that, Mrs. Deaton didn't come to the door even though Molly pounded loudly. Peering through a window, Molly saw that Mrs. Deaton was slumped over the table. "Oh, no!" Molly cried in alarm, but just then Mrs. Deaton's head jerked up. Seeing Molly's frightened face at the window, she quickly came to the door.

"Land sakes, child," she said, "I was so busy, I didn't even hear you." She smiled as Molly looked questioningly at her. "I was praying for the missionaries from my church."

Later, Molly told her mother what had happened. "I thought Mrs. Deaton was a worthless old lady," she said, "but I was wrong. I've learned a lot from her. She really knows what it means to trust God! I hope I can be like that when I'm as old as she is."

Respecting Others Memory Verse

You must love the Lord your God with all your heart, and with all your soul, and with all your strength, and with all your mind. And you must love your neighbor just as much as you love yourself.
Luke 10:27

How About You?

How do you feel about older people? Do you respect them? Do you spend time with them and listen to what they have to say? You'll find that older Christians can teach valuable lessons from the experiences they've faced. J. H.

• For the next devotional, turn to page 509.   • For the next devotional on RESPECTING OTHERS, turn to page 601.
• For notes on RESPECTING OTHERS, see pages 322, 382, 1088, and 1218.

days of the month of that year. ⁷Let that night be bleak and joyless. ⁸Let those who are experts at cursing curse it. ⁹Let the stars of the night disappear. Let it long for light but never see it, never see the morning light. ¹⁰Curse it for its failure to shut my mother's womb, for letting me be born to come to all this trouble.

¹¹"Why didn't I die at birth? ¹²Why did the midwife let me live? Why did she nurse me at her breasts? ¹³For if only I had died at birth, then I would be quiet now, asleep and at rest, ¹⁴,¹⁵along with prime ministers and kings with all their pomp, and wealthy princes whose castles are full of rich treasures. ¹⁶Oh, to have been stillborn!—to have never breathed or seen the light. ¹⁷For there in death the wicked cease from troubling, and there the weary are at rest. ¹⁸There even prisoners are at ease, with no brutal jailer to curse them. ¹⁹Both rich and poor alike are there, and the slave is free at last from his master.

²⁰,²¹"Oh, why should light and life be given to those in misery and bitterness, who long for death, and it won't come; who search for death as others search for food or money? ²²What blessed relief when at last they die! ²³Why is a man allowed to be born if God is only going to give him a hopeless life of uselessness and frustration? ²⁴I cannot eat for sighing; my groans pour out like water. ²⁵What I always feared has happened to me. ²⁶I was not fat and lazy, yet trouble struck me down."

4 Eliphaz: Words

A reply to Job from Eliphaz the Temanite:

²"Will you let me say a word? For who could keep from speaking out? ³,⁴In the past you have told many a troubled soul to trust in God and have encouraged those who are weak or falling, or lie crushed upon the ground or are tempted to despair. ⁵But now when trouble strikes, you faint and are broken.

⁶"At such a time as this should not trust in God still be your confidence? Shouldn't you believe that God will care for those who are good? ⁷,⁸Stop and think! Have you ever known a truly good and innocent person who was punished? Experience teaches that it is those who sow sin and trouble who harvest the same. ⁹They die beneath the hand of God. ¹⁰Though they are fierce as young lions, they shall all be broken and destroyed. ¹¹Like aged, helpless lions they shall starve, and all their children shall be scattered.

¹²"This truth was given me in secret, as though whispered in my ear. ¹³It came in a nighttime vision as others slept. ¹⁴Suddenly, fear gripped me; I trembled and shook with terror, ¹⁵as a spirit passed before my face—my hair stood up on end.

¹⁶I felt the spirit's presence, but couldn't see it standing there. Then out of the dreadful silence came this voice:

¹⁷"'Is mere man more just than God? More pure than his Creator?'

¹⁸,¹⁹If God cannot trust his own messengers (for even angels make mistakes), how much less men made of dust, who are crushed to death as easily as moths! ²⁰They are alive in the morning, but by evening they are dead, gone forever with hardly a thought from anyone. ²¹Their candle of life is snuffed out. They die and no one cares.

5

"They cry for help but no one listens; they turn to their gods, but none gives them aid. ²They die in helpless frustration, overcome by their own anger. ³Those who turn from God may be successful for the moment, but then comes sudden disaster. ⁴Their children are cheated, with no one to defend them. ⁵Their harvests are stolen, and their wealth slakes the thirst of many others, not themselves! ⁶Misery comes upon them to punish them for sowing seeds of sin. ⁷Mankind heads for sin and misery as predictably as flames shoot upwards from a fire.

⁸"My advice to you is this: Go to God and confess your sins to him. ⁹For he does wonderful miracles, marvels without number. ¹⁰He sends the rain upon the earth to water the fields, ¹¹and gives prosperity to the poor and humble, and takes sufferers to safety.

¹²"He frustrates the plans of crafty men. ¹³They are caught in their own traps; he thwarts their schemes. ¹⁴They grope like blind men in the daylight; they see no better in the daytime than at night.

¹⁵"God saves the fatherless and the poor from the grasp of these oppressors. ¹⁶And so at last the poor have hope, and the fangs of the wicked are broken.

¹⁷"How enviable the man whom God corrects! Oh, do not despise the chastening of the Lord when you sin. ¹⁸For though he wounds, he binds and heals again. ¹⁹He will deliver you again and again so that no evil can touch you.

²⁰"He will keep you from death in famine and from the power of the sword in time of war.

²¹"You will be safe from slander; no need to fear the future.

²²"You shall laugh at war and famine; wild animals will leave you alone. ²³Dangerous animals will be at peace with you.

²⁴"You need not worry about your home while you are gone; nothing shall be stolen from your barns.

²⁵"Your sons shall become important men; your descendants shall be as numerous as grass! ²⁶You

Family Devotions

☐ **DEVOTION 140**
HUMILITY

Read Job 5:8-27

"I was sure I'd win the Bible quiz contest last night," said Gayle with a sigh. "I can't figure out what went wrong."

"Yeah," agreed Kristen. "You always win everything."

Miss Loveland held out some crepe streamers. "Hurry, girls," she urged. "The party begins soon. Hang up the rest of these while I blow up some balloons. Tell me about the contest while you work. I couldn't attend last night."

"I was awful," Gayle said as she fastened streamers to the ceiling. "I couldn't remember the answers, and I misquoted Bible verses."

"But she's smarter than Debbie," said Kristen.

"Sure I am," said Gayle confidently. "Besides, she just started going to church last year."

"Did you study for the contest?" asked Miss Loveland.

"Oh, I don't need to study much anymore," replied Gayle, "because I know the Bible so well."

Miss Loveland looked at the balloon she was blowing up. "Debbie told me she'd studied a great deal and had been asking the Lord to help her do well that she might honor him," she said. She blew hard on the balloon. It grew bigger and bigger. Then bang! It burst into little pieces. "Well! The balloon was puffed up so much it burst," observed Miss Loveland. "You know, Gayle, I think that's your trouble, too. You were puffed up with pride. You thought you were so smart you didn't need any help. Debbie knew she had to depend on the Lord."

Gayle picked up a fragment of the balloon and looked at it thoughtfully for a moment. "That's the difference, isn't it?" she said quietly. "My pride blew me up into little pieces. Next time I'll work harder and ask the Lord to help me."

Humility Memory Verse

For everyone who tries to honor himself shall be humbled; and he who humbles himself shall be honored.
Luke 14:11

How About You?

Are there times when you think everything's going your way and then you fall flat on your face? Could pride be the trouble? As today's Scripture reading reminds us, God promises to bless those who are humble. Humbly depend on the Lord, and then he'll lift you up again. M. R. P.

• For the next devotional, turn to page 513.   • For the next devotional on *HUMILITY*, turn to page 685.
• For notes on *HUMILITY*, see pages 57, 390, 428, 854, and 1228.

shall live a long, good life; like standing grain, you'll not be harvested until it's time! ²⁷I have found from experience that all of this is true. For your own good, listen to my counsel."

6 Job: Why Am I Suffering?
Job's reply:

²"Oh, that my sadness and troubles were weighed. ³For they are heavier than the sand of a thousand seashores. That is why I spoke so rashly. ⁴For the Lord has struck me down with his arrows; he has sent his poisoned arrows deep within my heart. All God's terrors are arrayed against me. ⁵⁻⁷When wild donkeys bray, it is because their grass is gone; oxen do not low when they have food; a man complains when there is no salt in his food. And how tasteless is the uncooked white of an egg—my appetite is gone when I look at it; I gag at the thought of eating it!

⁸,⁹"Oh, that God would grant the thing I long for most—to die beneath his hand and be freed from his painful grip. ¹⁰This, at least, gives me comfort despite all the pain—that I have not denied the words of the holy God. ¹¹Oh, why does my strength sustain me? How can I be patient till I die? ¹²Am I unfeeling, like stone? Is my flesh made of brass? ¹³For I am utterly helpless, without any hope.

¹⁴"One should be kind to a fainting friend, but you have accused me without the slightest fear of God. ¹⁵⁻¹⁸My brother, you have proved as unreliable as a brook; it floods when there is ice and snow, but in hot weather, disappears. The caravans turn aside to be refreshed, but there is nothing there to drink, and so they perish. ¹⁹⁻²¹When caravans from Tema and from Sheba stop for water there, their hopes are dashed. And so my hopes in you are dashed—you turn away from me in terror and refuse to help. ²²But why? Have I ever asked you for one slightest thing? Have I begged you for a present? ²³Have I ever asked your help? ²⁴All I want is a reasonable answer—then I will keep quiet. Tell me, what have I done wrong?

²⁵,²⁶"It is wonderful to speak the truth, but your criticisms are not based on fact. Are you going to condemn me just because I impulsively cried out in desperation? ²⁷That would be like injuring a helpless orphan, or selling a friend. ²⁸Look at me! Would I lie to your face? ²⁹Stop assuming my guilt, for I am righteous. Don't be so unjust. ³⁰Don't I know the difference between right and wrong? Would I not admit it if I had sinned?

7
"How mankind must struggle. A man's life is long and hard, like that of a slave. ²How he longs for the day to end. How he grinds on to the end of the week and his wages. ³And so to me also have been allotted months of frustration, these long and weary nights. ⁴When I go to bed I think, 'Oh, that it were morning,' and then I toss till dawn.

⁵"My skin is filled with worms and blackness. My flesh breaks open, full of pus. ⁶My life drags by—day after hopeless day. ⁷My life is but a breath, and nothing good is left. ⁸You see me now, but not for long. Soon you'll look upon me dead. ⁹As a cloud disperses and vanishes, so those who die shall go away forever—¹⁰gone forever from their family and their home—never to be seen again. ¹¹Ah, let me express my anguish. Let me be free to speak out of the bitterness of my soul.

¹²"O God, am I some monster that you never let me alone? ¹³,¹⁴Even when I try to forget my misery in sleep, you terrify with nightmares. ¹⁵I would rather die of strangulation than go on and on like this. ¹⁶I hate my life. Oh, let me alone for these few remaining days. ¹⁷What is mere man that you should spend your time persecuting him? ¹⁸Must you be his inquisitor every morning and test him every moment of the day? ¹⁹Why won't you let me alone—even long enough to spit?

²⁰"Has my sin harmed you, O God, Watcher of mankind? Why have you made me your target, and made my life so heavy a burden to me? ²¹Why not just pardon my sin and take it all away? For all too soon I'll lie down in the dust and die, and when you look for me, I shall be gone."

8 Bildad: If You Were Pure
Bildad the Shuhite replies to Job:

²"How long will you go on like this, Job, blowing words around like wind? ³Does God twist justice? ⁴If your children sinned against him, and he punished them, ⁵and you begged Almighty God for them—⁶if you were pure and good, he would hear your prayer and answer you and bless you with a happy home. ⁷And though you started with little, you would end with much.

⁸"Read the history books and

OBEDIENCE 6:29-30 Job called himself a righteous man, not because he was sinless, but because he had a right relationship with God. He was not guilty of the sins his friends accused him of (see Job 31 for his summary of the kind of life he had led). *Righteousness* is not the same as *sinlessness* (Romans 3:23). No one but Jesus Christ has ever been sinless—free from all wrong thoughts and actions. Even Job needed to make some changes in his attitude toward God, as we will see by the end of the book. Nevertheless, Job was righteous (1:8). He carefully obeyed God to the best of his ability in all aspects of his life. **To begin the series of devotionals on** OBEDIENCE, **turn to page 25.**

see—⁹for we were born but yesterday and know so little; our days here on earth are as transient as shadows. ¹⁰But the wisdom of the past will teach you. The experience of others will speak to you, reminding you that ¹¹⁻¹³those who forget God have no hope. They are like rushes without any mire to grow in; or grass without water to keep it alive. Suddenly it begins to wither, even before it is cut. ¹⁴A man without God is trusting in a spider's web. Everything he counts on will collapse. ¹⁵If he counts on his home for security, it won't last. ¹⁶At dawn he seems so strong and virile, like a green plant; his branches spread across the garden. ¹⁷His roots are in the stream, down among the stones. ¹⁸But when he disappears, he isn't even missed! ¹⁹That is all he can look forward to! And others spring up from the earth to replace him!

²⁰"But look! God will not cast away a good man, nor prosper evildoers. ²¹He will yet fill your mouth with laughter and your lips with shouts of joy. ²²Those who hate you shall be clothed with shame, and the wicked destroyed."

9 Job Has More Questions

Job's reply:

²"Yes, I know all that. You're not telling me anything new. But how can a man be truly good in the eyes of God? ³If God decides to argue with him, can a man answer even one question of a thousand he asks? ⁴For God is so wise and so mighty. Who has ever opposed him successfully?

⁵"Suddenly he moves the mountains, overturning them in his anger. ⁶He shakes the earth to its foundations. ⁷The sun won't rise, the stars won't shine, if he commands it so! ⁸Only he has stretched the heavens out and stalked along the seas. ⁹He made the Bear, Orion and the Pleiades, and the constellations of the southern Zodiac.

¹⁰"He does incredible miracles, too many to count. ¹¹He passes by, invisible; he moves along, but I don't see him go. ¹²When he sends death to snatch a man away, who can stop him? Who dares to ask him, 'What are you doing?'

¹³"And God does not abate his anger. The pride of man collapses before him. ¹⁴And who am I that I should try to argue with Almighty God, or even reason with him? ¹⁵Even if I were sinless, I wouldn't say a word. I would only plead for mercy. ¹⁶And even if my prayers were answered, I could scarce believe that he had heard my cry. ¹⁷For he is the one who destroys, and multiplies my wounds without a cause. ¹⁸He will not let me breathe, but fills me with bitter sorrows. ¹⁹He alone is strong and just.

²⁰"But I? Am I righteous? My own mouth says no. Even if I were perfect, God would prove me wicked. ²¹And even if I am utterly innocent, I dare not think of it. I despise what I am. ²²Innocent or evil, it is all the same to him, for he destroys both kinds. ²³He will laugh when calamity crushes the innocent. ²⁴The whole earth is in the hands of the wicked. God blinds the eyes of the judges and lets them be unfair. If not he, then who?

²⁵"My life passes swiftly away, filled with tragedy. ²⁶My years disappear like swift ships, like the eagle that swoops upon its prey.

²⁷"If I decided to forget my complaints against God, to end my sadness and be cheerful, ²⁸then he would pour even greater sorrows upon me. For I know that you will not hold me innocent, O God, ²⁹but will condemn me. So what's the use of trying? ³⁰Even if I were to wash myself with purest water and cleanse my hands with lye to make them utterly clean, ³¹even so you would plunge me into the ditch and mud; and even my clothing would be less filthy than you consider me to be!

³²,³³"And I cannot defend myself, for you are no mere man as I am. If you were, then we could discuss it fairly, but there is no umpire between us, no middle man, no mediator to bring us together. ³⁴Oh, let him stop beating me, so that I need no longer live in terror of his punishment. ³⁵Then I could speak without fear to him and tell him boldly that I am not guilty.

10

"I am weary of living. Let me complain freely. I will speak in my sorrow and bitterness. ²I will say to God, 'Don't just condemn me—tell me *why* you are doing it. ³Does it really seem right to you to oppress and despise me, a man you have made; and to send joy and prosperity to the wicked? ⁴⁻⁷Are you unjust like men? Is your life so short that you must hound me for sins you know full well I've not committed? Is it because you know no one can save me from your hand?

⁸"You have made me, and yet you destroy me. ⁹Oh, please remember that I'm made of dust—will you change me back again to dust so soon? ¹⁰You have already poured me from bottle to bottle like milk and curdled me like cheese. ¹¹You gave me skin and flesh and knit together bones and sinews. ¹²You gave me life and were so kind and loving to me, and I was preserved by your care.

OVERCOMING ANGER 7:11 Job felt deep anguish and bitterness, and he spoke honestly to God about it to let out his frustrations. If we express our feelings to God, we can deal with them without exploding in harsh words and actions, possibly hurting ourselves and others. The next time strong emotions threaten to overwhelm you, express them openly to God in prayer. This will help you gain an eternal perspective on the situation, giving you greater ability to deal with it constructively. **To begin the series of devotionals on OVERCOMING ANGER, turn to page 133.**

13,14 "'Yet all the time your real motive in making me was to destroy me if I sinned, and to refuse to forgive my iniquity. 15Just the slightest wickedness, and I am done for. And if I'm good, that doesn't count. I am filled with frustration. 16If I start to get up off the ground, you leap upon me like a lion and quickly finish me off. 17Again and again you witness against me and pour out an ever-increasing volume of wrath upon me and bring fresh armies against me.

18"'Why then did you even let me be born? Why didn't you let me die at birth? 19Then I would have been spared this miserable existence. I would have gone directly from the womb to the grave. 20,21Can't you see how little time I have left? Oh, let me alone that I may have a little moment of comfort before I leave for the land of darkness and the shadow of death, never to return—22a land as dark as midnight, a land of the shadow of death where only confusion reigns and where the brightest light is dark as midnight.'"

11 Zophar: See Yourself
Zophar the Naamathite replies to Job:

2"Shouldn't someone stem this torrent of words? Is a man proved right by all this talk? 3Should I remain silent while you boast? When you mock God, shouldn't someone make you ashamed? 4You claim you are pure in the eyes of God! 5Oh, that God would speak and tell you what he thinks! 6Oh, that he would make you truly see yourself, for he knows everything you've done. Listen! God is doubtless punishing you far less than you deserve!

7"Do you know the mind and purposes of God? Will long searching make them known to you? Are you qualified to judge the Almighty? 8He is as faultless as heaven is high—but who are you? His mind is fathomless—what can you know in comparison? 9His Spirit is broader than the earth and wider than the sea. 10If he rushes in and makes an arrest, and calls the court to order, who is going to stop him? 11For he knows perfectly all the faults and sins of mankind; he sees all sin without searching.

12"Mere man is as likely to be wise as a wild donkey's colt is likely to be born a man!

13,14"Before you turn to God and stretch out your hands to him, get rid of your sins and leave all iniquity behind you. 15Only then, without the spots of sin to defile you, can you walk steadily forward to God without fear. 16Only then can you forget your misery. It will all be in the past. 17And your life will be cloudless; any darkness will be as bright as morning!

18"You will have courage because you will have hope. You will take your time and rest in safety. 19You will lie down unafraid, and many will look to you for help. 20But the wicked shall find no way to escape; their only hope is death."

12 Job: I Long to Speak to God
Job's reply:

2"Yes, I realize you know everything! All wisdom will die with you! 3Well, I know a few things myself—you are no better than I am. And who doesn't know these things you've been saying? 4I, the man who begged God for help, and God answered him, have become a laughingstock to my neighbors. Yes, I, a righteous man, am now the man they scoff at. 5Meanwhile, the rich mock those in trouble and are quick to despise all those in need. 6For robbers prosper. Go ahead and provoke God—it makes no difference! He will supply your every need anyway!

7-9"Who doesn't know that the Lord does things like that? Ask the dumbest beast—he knows that it is so; ask the birds—they will tell you; or let the earth teach you, or the fish of the sea. 10For the soul of every living thing is in the hand of God, and the breath of all mankind. 11Just as my mouth can taste good food, so my mind tastes truth when I hear it. 12And as you say, older men like me are wise. They understand. 13But true wisdom and power are God's. He alone knows what we should do; he understands.

14"And how great is his might! What he destroys can't be rebuilt. When he closes in on a man, there is no escape. 15He withholds the rain, and the earth becomes a desert; he sends the storms and floods the ground. 16Yes, with him is strength and wisdom. Deceivers and deceived are both his slaves.

17"He makes fools of counselors and judges. 18He reduces kings to slaves and frees their servants. 19Priests are led away as slaves. He overthrows the mighty. 20He takes away the voice of orators and the insight of the elders. 21He pours contempt upon princes and weakens the strong. 22He floods the darkness with light, even the dark shadow of death. 23He raises up a nation and then destroys it. He makes it great, and then reduces it to nothing. 24,25He takes away the understanding of presidents and kings, and leaves them wandering, lost and groping, without a guiding light.

13
"Look, I have seen many instances such as you describe. I understand what you are saying. 2I know as much as you do. I'm not stupid. 3Oh, how I long to speak directly to the Almighty. I want to talk this over with God himself. 4For you are misinterpreting the whole thing. You are doctors who don't know what they are doing. 5Oh,

FAMILY DEVOTIONS

☐ **DEVOTION 141**
TRUE JOY

Read Job 10

"You have scoliosis, which is a curved spine, Debi," Dr. Bryant said. He turned toward Mother. "A specialist will decide how it should be treated. Exercises may help, or Debi may have to wear a brace or possibly have surgery."

In the following days Debi prayed and prayed. Oh, how she wanted God to straighten her spine. "God can heal you, Debi," Mother said one night, "but if he doesn't, it's because he loves you and wants to make you a better person."

"How can wearing an ugly brace do that?" Debi sobbed.

"By teaching you discipline and compassion," Mother answered.

To her dismay, Debi did need the brace. "This will restrict your physical activities some, but not much," Dr. Roberts told her. "You'll be able to do almost everything you've always done."

A few days later, Mother noticed that Debi had allowed her room to become messy. "Go clean your room right now!" Mother scolded.

"But my brace is so awkward," whined Debi, "I can't."

Mother frowned. "I'm sorry, honey, but you will have to adjust. Go clean your room."

Later Mother heard Debi on the telephone. "Oh, I couldn't do that, Pam. I might hurt my back," she whined.

"What can't you do?" Mother asked later.

"I can't go hiking," Debi answered.

"You certainly can," Mother insisted. "Debi, a brace on your back does not make you an invalid. Your physical problem can make you a whiner or a winner."

Debi sniffed. "How can I be a winner?"

"By having the right attitude," answered Mother. "Remember Job? Everything went wrong in his life—everything but his attitude. He came out a winner. Now, call Pam back and tell her you're going hiking."

True Joy
Memory Verse

Always be full of joy in the Lord; I say it again, rejoice!
Philippians 4:4

How About You?

The question is not, What's your problem? The question is, How's your attitude? Everyone has problems. You can become a whiner or a winner. It's up to you. What's your choice? Will you say with Job, "Blessed be the name of the Lord"? *R.J.*

- For the next devotional, turn to page 519. • For the next devotional on *TRUE JOY*, turn to page 593.
- For notes on *TRUE JOY*, see pages 532, 1024, and 1160.

please be quiet! That would be your highest wisdom.

⁶"Listen to me now, to my reasons for what I think and to my pleadings.

⁷"Must you go on 'speaking for God' when he never once has said the things that you are putting in his mouth? ⁸Does God want your help if you are going to twist the truth for him? ⁹Be careful that he doesn't find out what you are doing! Or do you think you can fool God as well as men? ¹⁰No, you will be in serious trouble with him if you use lies to try to help him out. ¹¹Doesn't his majesty strike terror to your heart? How can you do this thing? ¹²These tremendous statements you have made have about as much value as ashes. Your defense of God is as fragile as a clay vase!

¹³"Be silent now and let me alone, that I may speak—and I am willing to face the consequences. ¹⁴Yes, I will take my life in my hand and say what I really think. ¹⁵God may kill me for saying this—in fact, I expect him to. Nevertheless, I am going to argue my case with him. ¹⁶This at least will be in my favor, that I am not godless, to be rejected instantly from his presence. ¹⁷Listen closely to what I am about to say. Hear me out.

¹⁸"This is my case: *I know that I am righteous.* ¹⁹Who can argue with me over this? If you could prove me wrong, I would stop defending myself and die.

²⁰"O God, there are two things I beg you not to do to me; only then will I be able to face you. ²¹Don't abandon me. And don't terrify me with your awesome presence. ²²Call to me to come—how quickly I will answer! Or let me speak to you, and you reply. ²³Tell me, what have I done wrong? Help me! Point out my sin to me. ²⁴Why do you turn away from me? Why hand me over to my enemy? ²⁵Would you blame a leaf that is blown about by the wind? Will you chase dry, useless straws?

²⁶"You write bitter things against me and bring up all the follies of my youth. ²⁷,²⁸You send me to prison and shut me in on every side. I am like a fallen, rotten tree, like a moth-eaten coat.

14

"How frail is man, how few his days, how full of trouble! ²He blossoms for a moment like a flower—and withers; as the shadow of a passing cloud, he quickly disappears. ³Must you be so harsh with frail men and demand an accounting from them? ⁴How can you demand purity in one born impure? ⁵You have set mankind so brief a span of life—months is all you give him! Not one bit longer may he live. ⁶So give him a little rest, won't you? Turn away your angry gaze and let him have a few moments of relief before he dies.

⁷"For there is hope for a tree—if it's cut down, it sprouts again and grows tender, new branches. ⁸,⁹Though its roots have grown old in the earth, and its stump decays, it may sprout and bud again at the touch of water, like a new seedling. ¹⁰But when a man dies and is buried, where does his spirit go? ¹¹,¹²As water evaporates from a lake, as a river disappears in drought, so a man lies down for the last time and does not rise again until the heavens are no more; he shall not awaken, nor be roused from his sleep. ¹³Oh, that you would hide me with the dead and forget me there until your anger ends; but mark your calendar to think of me again!

¹⁴"If a man dies, shall he live again? This thought gives me hope, so that in all my anguish I eagerly await sweet death! ¹⁵You would call and I would come, and you would reward all I do. ¹⁶But now, instead, you give me so few steps upon the stage of life and notice every mistake I make. ¹⁷You bundle them all together as evidence against me.

¹⁸,¹⁹"Mountains wear away and disappear. Water grinds the stones to sand. Torrents tear away the soil. So every hope of man is worn away. ²⁰,²¹Always you are against him, and then he passes off the scene. You make him old and wrinkled, then send him away. He never knows it if his sons are honored; or they may fail and face disaster, but he knows it not. ²²For him there is only sorrow and pain."

15 Eliphaz: Have You No Fear?

The answer of Eliphaz the Temanite:

²"You are supposed to be a wise man, and yet you give us all this foolish talk. You are nothing but a windbag. ³It isn't right to speak so foolishly. What good do such words do? ⁴,⁵Have you no fear of God? No reverence for him? Your sins are telling your mouth what to say! Your words are based on clever deception, ⁶but why should I condemn you? Your own mouth does!

⁷,⁸"Are you the wisest man alive? Were you born before the hills were made? Have you heard the secret counsel of God? Are you called into his counsel room? Do you have a monopoly on wisdom? ⁹What do you know more than we do? What do you understand that we don't? ¹⁰On our side are aged men much older than your father! ¹¹Is God's comfort too little for you? Is his gentleness too rough?

¹²"What is this you are doing, getting carried away by your anger, with flashing eyes? ¹³And you turn against God and say all these evil things against him. ¹⁴What man in all the earth can be as

pure and righteous as you claim to be? ¹⁵Why, God doesn't even trust the angels! Even the heavens can't be absolutely pure compared with him! ¹⁶How much less someone like you, who is corrupt and sinful, drinking in sin as a sponge soaks up water!

¹⁷⁻¹⁹"Listen, and I will answer you from my own experience, confirmed by the experience of wise men who have been told this same thing from their fathers—our ancestors to whom alone the land was given—and they have passed this wisdom to us:

²⁰"A wicked man is always in trouble throughout his life. ²¹He is surrounded by terrors, and if there are good days, they will soon be gone. ²²He dares not go out into the darkness lest he be murdered. ²³,²⁴He wanders around begging for food. He lives in fear, distress, and anguish. His enemies conquer him as a king defeats his foes. ²⁵,²⁶Armed with his tin shield, he clenches his fist against God, defying the Almighty, stubbornly assaulting him.

²⁷,²⁸"This wicked man is fat and rich, and has lived in conquered cities after killing off their citizens. ²⁹But he will not continue to be rich, or to extend his possessions. ³⁰No, darkness shall overtake him forever; the breath of God shall destroy him; the flames shall burn up all he has.

³¹"Let him no longer trust in foolish riches; let him no longer deceive himself, for the money he trusts in will be his only reward. ³²Before he dies, all this futility will become evident to him. For all he counted on will disappear ³³and fall to the ground like a withered grape. How little will come of his hopes! ³⁴For the godless are barren: they can produce nothing truly good. God's fire consumes them with all their possessions. ³⁵The only thing they can 'conceive' is sin, and their hearts give birth only to wickedness."

16 Job: You Are No Help
Job's reply:

²"I have heard all this before. What miserable comforters all of you are. ³Won't you ever stop your flow of foolish words? What have I said that makes you speak so endlessly? ⁴But perhaps I'd sermonize the same as you—if you were I and I were you. I would spout off my criticisms against you and shake my head at you. ⁵But no! I would speak in such a way that it would help you. I would try to take away your grief.

⁶"But now my grief remains no matter how I defend myself; nor does it help if I refuse to speak. ⁷For God has ground me down and taken away my family. ⁸O God, you have turned me to skin and bones—as a proof, they say, of my sins. ⁹God hates me and angrily tears at my flesh; he has gnashed upon me with his teeth and watched to snuff out any sign of life. ¹⁰These 'comforters' have gaping jaws to swallow me; they slap my cheek. My enemies gather themselves against me. ¹¹And God has delivered me over to sinners, into the hands of the wicked.

¹²"I was living quietly until he broke me apart. He has taken me by the neck and dashed me to pieces, then hung me up as his target. ¹³His archers surround me, letting fly their arrows, so that the ground is wet from my blood. ¹⁴Again and again he attacks me, running upon me like a giant. ¹⁵Here I sit in sackcloth; and have laid all hope in the dust. ¹⁶My eyes are red with weeping, and on my eyelids is the shadow of death.

¹⁷"Yet I am innocent, and my prayer is pure. ¹⁸O earth, do not conceal my blood. Let it protest on my behalf.

¹⁹"Yet even now the Witness to my innocence is there in heaven; my Advocate is there on high. ²⁰My friends scoff at me, but I pour out my tears to God, ²¹pleading that he will listen as a man would listen to his neighbor. ²²For all too soon I must go down that road from which I shall never return.

17
"I am sick and near to death; the grave is ready to receive me. ²I am surrounded by mockers. I see them everywhere. ³,⁴Will no one anywhere confirm my innocence? But you, O God, have kept them back from understanding this. Oh, do not let them triumph. ⁵If they accept bribes to denounce their friends, their children shall go blind.

⁶"He has made me a mockery among the people; they spit in my face. ⁷My eyes are dim with weeping and I am but a shadow of my former self. ⁸Fair-minded men are astonished when they see me.

"Yet, finally, the innocent shall come out on top, above the godless; ⁹the righteous shall move onward and forward; those with pure hearts shall become stronger and stronger.

¹⁰"As for you—all of you please go away; for I

SHOWING COMPASSION 16:1ff. Job's friends were supposed to be comforting him in his grief. Instead they condemned him for causing his own suffering. Job began his reply to Eliphaz by calling him and his friends "miserable comforters." Job's words reveal several ways to become a better comforter to those in pain: (1) don't talk just for the sake of talking; (2) don't sermonize by giving pat answers; (3) don't criticize; (4) put yourself in the other person's place; and (5) offer help and encouragement. Try Job's suggestions, knowing that they are given by one who needed great comfort. The best comforters are those who know something about personal suffering.
To begin the series of devotionals on *SHOWING COMPASSION*, turn to page 569.

do not find a wise man among you. ¹¹My good days are in the past. My hopes have disappeared. My heart's desires are broken. ¹²They say that night is day and day is night; how they pervert the truth!

¹³,¹⁴"If I die, I go out into darkness, and call the grave my father, and the worm my mother and my sister. ¹⁵Where then is my hope? Can anyone find any? ¹⁶No, my hope will go down with me to the grave. We shall rest together in the dust!"

18 Bildad: You Are Wicked
The further reply of Bildad the Shuhite:

²"Who are you trying to fool? Speak some sense if you want us to answer! ³Have we become like animals to you, stupid and dumb? ⁴Just because you tear your clothes in anger, is this going to start an earthquake? Shall we all go and hide?

⁵"The truth remains that if you do not prosper, it is because you are wicked. And your bright flame shall be put out. ⁶There will be darkness in every home where there is wickedness.

⁷"The confident stride of the wicked man will be shortened; he will realize his failing strength. ⁸,⁹He walks into traps, and robbers will ambush him. ¹⁰There is a booby trap in every path he takes. ¹¹He has good cause for fear—his enemy is close behind him!

¹²"His vigor is depleted by hunger; calamity stands ready to pounce upon him. ¹³His skin is eaten by disease. Death shall devour him. ¹⁴The wealth he trusted in shall reject him, and he shall be brought down to the King of Terrors. ¹⁵His home shall disappear beneath a fiery barrage of brimstone. ¹⁶He shall die from the roots up, and all his branches will be lopped off.

¹⁷"All memory of his existence will perish from the earth; no one will remember him. ¹⁸He will be driven out from the kingdom of light into darkness and chased out of the world. ¹⁹He will have neither son nor grandson left, nor any other relatives. ²⁰Old and young alike will be horrified by his fate. ²¹Yes, that is what happens to sinners, to those rejecting God."

19 Job: Impatient but Trusting God
The reply of Job:

²"How long are you going to trouble me, and try to break me with your words? ³Ten times now you have declared I am a sinner. Why aren't you ashamed to deal with me so harshly? ⁴And if indeed I was wrong, you have yet to prove it. ⁵You think yourselves so great? Then prove my guilt!

⁶"The fact of the matter is that God has overthrown me and caught me in his net. ⁷I scream for help and no one hears me. I shriek, but get no justice. ⁸God has blocked my path and turned my light to darkness. ⁹He has stripped me of my glory and removed the crown from my head. ¹⁰He has broken me down on every side, and I am done for. He has destroyed all hope. ¹¹His fury burns against me; he counts me as an enemy. ¹²He sends his troops to surround my tent.

¹³"He has sent away my brothers and my friends. ¹⁴My relatives have failed me; my friends have all forsaken me. ¹⁵Those living in my home, even my servants, regard me as a stranger. I am like a foreigner to them. ¹⁶I call my servant, but he doesn't come; I even beg him! ¹⁷My own wife and brothers refuse to recognize me. ¹⁸Even young children despise me. When I stand to speak, they mock.

¹⁹"My best friends abhor me. Those I loved have turned against me. ²⁰I am skin and bones and have escaped death by the skin of my teeth.

²¹"Oh, my friends, pity me, for the angry hand of God has touched me. ²²Why must you persecute me as God does? Why aren't you satisfied with my anguish? ²³,²⁴Oh, that I could write my plea with an iron pen in the rock forever.

²⁵"But as for me, I know that my Redeemer lives, and that he will stand upon the earth at last. ²⁶And I know that after this body has decayed, this body shall see God! ²⁷Then he will be on *my* side! Yes, I shall see him, not as a stranger, but as a friend! What a glorious hope!

²⁸"How dare you go on persecuting me, as though I were proven guilty? ²⁹I warn you, you yourselves are in danger of punishment for your attitude."

20 Zophar: I Have the Answer
The speech of Zophar the Naamathite:

²"I hasten to reply, for I have the answer for you. ³You have tried to make me feel ashamed of myself for calling you a sinner, but my spirit won't let me stop.

⁴"Don't you realize that ever since man was first placed upon the earth, ⁵the triumph of the wicked has been short-lived, and the joy of the godless but for a moment? ⁶Though the godless be proud as the heavens and walk with his nose in the air, ⁷yet he shall perish forever, cast away like his own dung. Those who knew him will wonder where he is gone. ⁸He will fade like a dream. ⁹Neither his friends nor his family will ever see him again.

¹⁰"His children shall beg from the poor, their hard labor shall repay his debts. ¹¹Though still a young man, his bones shall lie in the dust.

¹²"He enjoyed the taste of his wickedness, let-

ting it melt in his mouth, [13]sipping it slowly, lest it disappear.

[14]"But suddenly the food he has eaten turns sour within him. [15]He will vomit the plunder he gorged. God won't let him keep it down. [16]It is like poison and death to him. [17]He shall not enjoy the goods he stole; they will not be butter and honey to him after all. [18]His labors shall not be rewarded; wealth will give him no joy. [19]For he has oppressed the poor and foreclosed their homes; he will never recover. [20]Though he was always greedy, now he has nothing; of all the things he dreamed of—none remain. [21]Because he stole at every opportunity, his prosperity shall not continue.

[22]"He shall run into trouble at the peak of his powers; all the wicked shall destroy him. [23]Just as he is about to fill his belly, God will rain down wrath upon him. [24]He will be chased and struck down. [25]The arrow is pulled from his body—and the glittering point comes out from his gall. The terrors of death are upon him.

[26]"His treasures will be lost in deepest darkness. A raging fire will devour his goods, consuming all he has left. [27]The heavens will reveal his sins, and the earth will give testimony against him. [28]His wealth will disappear beneath the wrath of God. [29]This is what awaits the wicked man, for God prepares it for him."

21 Job: You Do Not Understand
Job's reply:

[2,3]"Listen to me; let me speak, and afterwards, mock on.

[4]"I am complaining about God, not man; no wonder my spirit is so troubled. [5]Look at me in horror, and lay your hand upon your mouth. [6]Even I am frightened when I see myself. Horror takes hold upon me and I shudder.

[7]"The truth is that the wicked live on to a good old age and become great and powerful. [8]They live to see their children grow to maturity around them, and their grandchildren too. [9]Their homes are safe from every fear, and God does not punish them. [10]Their cattle are productive, [11]they have many happy children, [12,13]they spend their time singing and dancing. They are wealthy and need deny themselves nothing; they are prosperous to the end. [14]All this despite the fact that they ordered God away and wanted no part of him and his ways.

[15]"'Who is Almighty God?' they scoff. 'Why should we obey him? What good will it do us?'

[16]"Look, everything the wicked touch has turned to gold! But I refuse even to deal with people like that. [17]Yet the wicked get away with it every time. They never have trouble, and God skips them when he distributes his sorrows and anger. [18]Are they driven before the wind like straw? Are they carried away by the storm? Not at all!

[19]"'Well,' you say, 'at least God will punish their children!' But I say that God should punish the man who sins, not his children! Let him feel the penalty himself. [20]Yes, let him be destroyed for his iniquity. Let him drink deeply of the anger of the Almighty. [21]For when he is dead, then he will never again be able to enjoy his family.

[22]"But who can rebuke God, the supreme Judge? [23,24]He destroys those who are healthy, wealthy, fat, and prosperous; [25]God also destroys those in deep and grinding poverty who have never known anything good. [26]Both alike are buried in the same dust, both eaten by the same worms.

[27]"I know what you are going to say—[28]you will tell me of rich and wicked men who came to disaster because of their sins. [29]But I reply, Ask anyone who has been around and he can tell you the truth, [30-32]that the evil man is usually spared in the day of calamity and allowed to escape. No one rebukes him openly. No one repays him for what he has done. And an honor guard keeps watch at his grave. [33]A great funeral procession precedes and follows him as the soft earth covers him. [34]How can you comfort me when your whole premise is so wrong?"

22 Eliphaz: You Must Give In
Another address from Eliphaz:

[2]"Is mere man of any worth to God? Even the wisest is of value only to himself! [3]Is it any pleasure to the Almighty if you are righteous? Would it be any gain to him if you were perfect? [4]Is it because you are good that he is punishing you? [5]Not at all! It is because of your wickedness! Your sins are endless!

[6]"For instance, you must have refused to loan money to needy friends unless they gave you all their clothing as a pledge—yes, you must have stripped them to the bone. [7]You must have refused water to the thirsty and bread to the starving. [8]But no doubt you gave men of importance anything they wanted and let the wealthy live wherever they chose. [9]You sent widows away without helping them and broke the arms of orphans. [10,11]That is why you are now surrounded by traps and sudden fears, and darkness and waves of horror.

[12]"God is so great—higher than the heavens, higher than the stars. [13]But you reply, 'That is why he can't see what I am doing! How can he judge through the thick darkness? [14]For thick clouds

swirl about him so that he cannot see us. He is way up there, walking on the vault of heaven.'

15,16"Don't you realize that those treading the ancient paths of sin are snatched away in youth, and the foundations of their lives washed out forever? 17For they said to God, 'Go away, God! What can you do for us?' 18(God forbid that I should say a thing like that.) Yet they forgot that he had filled their homes with good things. 19And now the righteous shall see them destroyed; the innocent shall laugh the wicked to scorn. 20'See,' they will say, 'the last of our enemies have been destroyed in the fire.'

21"Quit quarreling with God! Agree with him and you will have peace at last! His favor will surround you if you will only admit that you were wrong. 22Listen to his instructions and store them in your heart. 23If you return to God and put right all the wrong in your home, then you will be restored. 24If you give up your lust for money and throw your gold away, 25then the Almighty himself shall be your treasure; he will be your precious silver!

26"Then you will delight yourself in the Lord and look up to God. 27You will pray to him, and he will hear you, and you will fulfill all your promises to him. 28Whatever you wish will happen! And the light of heaven will shine upon the road ahead of you. 29If you are attacked and knocked down, you will know that there is someone who will lift you up again. Yes, he will save the humble 30and help even sinners by your pure hands."

23 Job: I Want to Find God
The reply of Job:

2"My complaint today is still a bitter one, and my punishment far more severe than my fault deserves. 3Oh, that I knew where to find God— that I could go to his throne and talk with him there. 4,5I would tell him all about my side of this argument, and listen to his reply, and understand what he wants. 6Would he merely overpower me with his greatness? No, he would listen with sympathy. 7 Fair and honest men could reason with him and be acquitted by my Judge.

8"But I search in vain. I seek him here, I seek him there and cannot find him. 9I seek him in his workshop in the North but cannot find him there; nor can I find him in the South; there, too, he hides himself. 10But he knows every detail of what is happening to me; and when he has examined me, he will pronounce me completely innocent—as pure as solid gold!

11"I have stayed in God's paths, following his steps. I have not turned aside. 12 I have not refused his commandments but have enjoyed them more than my daily food. 13Nevertheless, his mind concerning me remains unchanged, and who can turn him from his purposes? Whatever he wants to do, he does. 14So he will do to me all he has planned, and there is more ahead.

15"No wonder I am so terrified in his presence. When I think of it, terror grips me. 16,17God has given me a fainting heart; he, the Almighty, has terrified me with darkness all around me, thick, impenetrable darkness everywhere.

24
"Why doesn't God open the court and listen to my case? Why must the godly wait for him in vain? 2For a crime wave has engulfed us—landmarks are moved, flocks of sheep are stolen, 3and even the donkeys of the poor and fatherless are taken. Poor widows must surrender the little they have as a pledge to get a loan. 4The needy are kicked aside; they must get out of the way. 5Like the wild donkeys in the desert, the poor must spend all their time just getting barely enough to keep soul and body together. They are sent into the desert to search for food for their children. 6They eat what they find that grows wild and must even glean the vineyards of the wicked. 7All night they lie naked in the cold, without clothing or covering. 8They are wet with the showers of the mountains and live in caves for want of a home.

9"The wicked snatch fatherless children from their mother's breasts, and take a poor man's baby as a pledge before they will loan him any money or grain. 10That is why they must go about naked, without clothing, and are forced to carry food while they are starving. 11They are forced to press out the olive oil without tasting it and to tread out the grape juice as they suffer from thirst. 12The bones of the dying cry from the city; the wounded cry for help; yet God does not respond to their moaning.

13"The wicked rebel against the light and are not acquainted with the right and the good. 14,15They are murderers who rise in the early dawn to kill the poor and needy; at night they are thieves and adulterers, waiting for the twilight 'when no one will see me,' they say. They mask their faces so no one will know them. 16They break into houses at night and sleep in the daytime—they are not acquainted with the light. 17The black night is their morning; they ally themselves with the terrors of the darkness.

18"But how quickly they disappear from the face of the earth. Everything they own is cursed. They leave no property for their children. 19Death consumes sinners as drought and heat consume snow. 20Even the sinner's own mother shall forget him. Worms shall feed sweetly on him. No one will remember him any more. For wicked men are broken

Family Devotions

☐ DEVOTION 142

TRUSTING GOD'S PLAN

Read Job 23:10-12

Trusting God's Plan Memory Verses:

This plan of mine is not what you would work out, neither are my thoughts the same as yours! For just as the heavens are higher than the earth, so are my ways higher than yours, and my thoughts than yours.
Isaiah 55:8-9

Martin didn't understand why his mother had to have the accident! Oh, he knew the roads were wet and slippery, but other cars had been driven safely that day. So why did God let it happen? Why did Mom have the wreck?

One day during hospital visiting hours, Mom seemed to sense Martin's feelings. "Martin," she said, "don't be angry and question why God let this happen. I really believe it's working for my good—that he's refining me to make me more like Jesus. You see, Son, I was so busy that I was drifting away from a close walk with the Lord. Now that I'm lying here flat on my back, I have to look up to God." Martin nodded, but he wasn't quite sure what she meant.

Later that week, Martin's class took a field trip to a nearby silver refining plant. The refining process was very complicated, involving the use of chemicals and all sorts of sophisticated equipment. At the end of the tour they saw a small, primitive-looking furnace. Their guide explained that they kept this old furnace to remind themselves of how far the silver industry had come. "Years ago, silver refiners heated the ore in furnaces like this, cooled it, reheated it, and so forth," he said. "It was a very long process before the impurities were finally worked out."

"How did they know when the silver was pure?" one of the children asked.

The guide smiled. "We're told that when the refiner could see a good clear image of himself in the silver, he turned off the furnace and knew his job was done."

That evening, Martin thought again about what Mom had said. Perhaps Jesus had allowed her to be put in the furnace of suffering so he could see a clearer reflection of himself in her life.

How About You?

Do you ever wonder why someone has to suffer? Sometimes God allows an experience that seems to be a tragedy just to get our attention and make us better people. If you stay in God's paths and follow his steps, he will one day pronounce you as pure as solid gold! Just as purified gold or silver shows a clear reflection of the refiner, so your life should show a clear reflection of Jesus. *R. P.*

- For the next devotional, turn to page 521. • For the next devotional on TRUSTING GOD'S PLAN, turn to page 589.
- For notes on TRUSTING GOD'S PLAN, see pages 252, 296, 731, and 870.

like a tree in the storm. ²¹For they have taken advantage of the childless who have no protecting sons. They refuse to help the needy widows.

²²,²³"Yet sometimes it seems as though God preserves the rich by his power and restores them to life when anyone else would die. God gives them confidence and strength, and helps them in many ways. ²⁴But though they are very great now, yet in a moment they shall be gone like all others, cut off like heads of grain. ²⁵Can anyone claim otherwise? Who can prove me a liar and claim that I am wrong?"

25 Bildad: Who Stands before God?

The further reply of Bildad the Shuhite:

²"God is powerful and dreadful. He enforces peace in heaven. ³Who is able to number his hosts of angels? And his light shines down on all the earth. ⁴How can mere man stand before God and claim to be righteous? Who in all the earth can boast that he is clean? ⁵God is so glorious that even the moon and stars are less than nothing as compared to him. ⁶How much less is man, who is but a worm in his sight?"

26 Job: I Will Never Agree

Job's reply:

²"What wonderful helpers you all are! And how you have encouraged me in my great need! ³How you have enlightened my stupidity! What wise things you have said! ⁴How did you ever think of all these brilliant comments?

⁵,⁶"The dead stand naked, trembling before God in the place where they go. ⁷God stretches out heaven over empty space and hangs the earth upon nothing. ⁸He wraps the rain in his thick clouds and the clouds, are not split by the weight. ⁹He shrouds his throne with his clouds. ¹⁰He sets a boundary for the ocean, yes, and a boundary for the day and for the night. ¹¹The pillars of heaven tremble at his rebuke. ¹²And by his power the sea grows calm; he is skilled at crushing its pride! ¹³The heavens are made beautiful by his Spirit; he pierces the swiftly gliding serpent.

¹⁴"These are some of the minor things he does, merely a whisper of his power. Who then can withstand his thunder?"

27 Job: Fear the Lord

Job's final defense:

²"I vow by the living God, who has taken away my rights, even the Almighty God who has embittered my soul, ³that as long as I live, while I have breath from God, ⁴my lips shall speak no evil, my tongue shall speak no lies. ⁵I will never, never agree that you are right; until I die I will vow my innocence. ⁶I am *not* a sinner—I repeat it again and again. My conscience is clear for as long as I live. ⁷Those who declare otherwise are my wicked enemies. They are evil men.

⁸"But what hope has the godless when God cuts him off and takes away his life? ⁹Will God listen to his cry when trouble comes upon him? ¹⁰For he does not delight himself in the Almighty or pay any attention to God except in times of crisis.

¹¹"I will teach you about God— ¹²but really, I don't need to, for you yourselves know as much about him as I do; yet you are saying all these useless things to me.

¹³"This is the fate awaiting the wicked from the hand of the Almighty: ¹⁴If he has a multitude of children, it is so that they will die in war or starve to death. ¹⁵Those who survive shall be brought down to the grave by disease and plague, with no one to mourn them, not even their wives.

¹⁶"The evil man may accumulate money like dust, with closets jammed full of clothing—¹⁷yes, he may order them made by his tailor, but the innocent shall wear that clothing and shall divide his silver among them. ¹⁸Every house built by the wicked is as fragile as a spider web, as full of cracks as a leafy booth!

¹⁹"He goes to bed rich but wakes up to find that all his wealth is gone. ²⁰Terror overwhelms him, and he is blown away in the storms of the night. ²¹The east wind carries him away, and he is gone. It sweeps him into eternity. ²²For God shall hurl at him unsparingly. He longs to flee from God. ²³Everyone will cheer at his death and boo him into eternity.

28

"Men know how to mine silver and refine gold, ²to dig iron from the earth and melt copper from stone. ³,⁴Men know how to put light into darkness so that a mine shaft can be sunk into the earth, and the earth searched and its deep secrets explored. Into the black rock, shadowed by death, men descend on ropes, swinging back and forth.

⁵"Men know how to obtain food from the surface of the earth, while underneath there is fire.

⁶"They know how to find sapphires and gold dust—⁷treasures that no bird of prey can see, no eagle's eye observe—⁸for they are deep within the mines. No wild animal has ever walked upon those treasures; no lion has set his paw there. ⁹Men know how to tear apart flinty rocks and how to overturn the roots of mountains. ¹⁰They drill tunnels in the rocks and lay bare precious stones. ¹¹They dam up streams of water and pan the gold.

Family Devotions

☐ DEVOTION 143
HONESTY

Read Job 27:3-4

"Hi, Dad," said Melinda as she entered her father's workshop. "Can you help me build a birdhouse now?"

Dad looked up. "Hi, Melinda," he said. "I thought you were playing with Angie."

"I was," replied Melinda, "but I wanted to do this instead, so I told her I had homework to do."

Dad took several pieces of wood from the bin of scrap wood and put them on the workbench. "You mean you lied to your friend?"

"Not really." Melinda shook her head. "I do have homework to do. I'll do it after we finish the birdhouse."

"But you purposely led her to believe you were going to do it now, and that's a form of lying, too." Dad told her.

Melinda shrugged. "Well, it was just a little lie," she said, picking up another piece of wood. "It won't hurt Angie's feelings or anything. She'll never know."

"Lies—even so-called little ones—hurt the people who tell them, too," Dad told her, holding the piece of wood Melinda had just handed him. Using both hands, he easily split the wood in half.

"How did you do that?" Melinda asked, wide-eyed.

"It was easy." Dad said. "Look at the wood."

Melinda looked closely and saw a crisscross of tunnels running through it. "What made that?" she asked.

"Probably termites or carpenter ants," Dad said. "They ate away at the wood until it was soft and easy for me to break apart." He looked serious. "They're not very big, but they do a lot of damage. Like lies. Lies eat away at your strength as a Christian. They weaken your testimony for the Lord."

Honesty Memory Verse

Stop lying to each other; tell the truth, for we are parts of each other and when we lie to each other we are hurting ourselves.
Ephesians 4:25

How About You?

Is your Christian testimony strong? Or do you weaken it with fibs and so-called little white lies . . . to your friends . . . to your parents . . . to yourself? Telling the truth is sometimes hard, but remember that God wants you to speak truthfully. D. K.

• For the next devotional, turn to page 525. • For the next devotional on *HONESTY,* turn to page 623. • For notes on *HONESTY,* see pages 304, 813, and 863.

¹²"But though men can do all these things, they don't know where to find wisdom and understanding. ¹³They not only don't know how to get it, but, in fact, it is not to be found among the living.

¹⁴"'It's not here,' the oceans say; and the seas reply, 'Nor is it here.'

¹⁵"It cannot be bought for gold or silver, ¹⁶nor for all the gold of Ophir or precious onyx stones or sapphires. ¹⁷Wisdom is far more valuable than gold and glass. It cannot be bought for jewels mounted in fine gold. ¹⁸Coral or crystal is worthless in trying to get it; its price is far above rubies. ¹⁹Topaz from Ethiopia cannot purchase it, nor even the purest gold.

²⁰"Then where can we get it? Where can it be found? ²¹For it is hid from the eyes of all mankind; even the sharp-eyed birds in the sky cannot discover it.

²²"But Destruction and Death speak of knowing something about it! ²³,²⁴And God surely knows where it is to be found, for he looks throughout the whole earth, under all the heavens. ²⁵He makes the winds blow and sets the boundaries of the oceans. ²⁶He makes the laws of the rain and a path for the lightning. ²⁷He knows where wisdom is and declares it to all who will listen. He established it and examined it thoroughly. ²⁸And this is what he says to all mankind: 'Look, to fear the Lord is true wisdom; to forsake evil is real understanding.'"

29 Job: God's Care for Me

Job continues:

²"Oh, for the years gone by when God took care of me, ³when he lighted the way before me and I walked safely through the darkness; ⁴yes, in my early years, when the friendship of God was felt in my home; ⁵when the Almighty was still with me and my children were around me; ⁶when my projects prospered and even the rock poured out streams of olive oil to me!

⁷"Those were the days when I went out to the city gate and took my place among the honored elders. ⁸The young saw me and stepped aside, and even the aged rose and stood up in respect at my coming. ⁹The princes stood in silence and laid their hands upon their mouths. ¹⁰The highest officials of the city stood in quietness. ¹¹All rejoiced in what I said. All who saw me spoke well of me.

¹²"For I, as an honest judge, helped the poor in their need and the fatherless who had no one to help them. ¹³I helped those who were ready to perish, and they blessed me. And I caused the widows' hearts to sing for joy. ¹⁴All I did was just and honest, for righteousness was my clothing! ¹⁵I served as eyes for the blind and feet for the lame. ¹⁶I was as a father to the poor and saw to it that even strangers received a fair trial. ¹⁷I knocked out the fangs of the godless oppressors and made them drop their victims.

¹⁸"I thought, 'Surely I shall die quietly in my nest after a long, good life.' ¹⁹For everything I did prospered; the dew lay all night upon my fields and watered them. ²⁰Fresh honors were constantly given me, and my abilities were constantly refreshed and renewed. ²¹Everyone listened to me and valued my advice, and was silent until I spoke. ²²And after I spoke, they spoke no more, for my counsel satisfied them. ²³They longed for me to speak as those in drought-time long for rain. They waited eagerly with open mouths. ²⁴When they were discouraged, I smiled and that encouraged them and lightened their spirits. ²⁵I told them what they should do and corrected them as their chief, or as a king instructs his army, and as one who comforts those who mourn.

30

"But now those younger than I deride me—young men whose fathers are less than my dogs. ²Oh, they have strong backs all right, but they are useless, stupid fools. ³They are gaunt with famine and have been cast out into deserts and the wastelands, desolate and gloomy. ⁴They eat roots and leaves, ⁵having been driven from civilization. Men shouted after them as after thieves. ⁶So now they live in frightening ravines, and in caves, and among the rocks. ⁷They sound like animals among the bushes, huddling together for shelter beneath the nettles. ⁸These sons of theirs have also turned out to be fools, yes, children of no name, outcasts of civilization.

⁹"And now I have become the subject of their ribald song! I am a joke among *them!* ¹⁰*They* despise me and won't come near me, and don't mind spitting in my face. ¹¹For God has placed my life in jeopardy. These young men, having humbled me, now cast off all restraint before me. ¹²This rabble trip me and lay traps in my path. ¹³They block my road and do everything they can to hasten my calamity, knowing full well that I have no one to help me.

TRUSTING GOD FOR GUIDANCE 28:13 Job stated that wisdom cannot be found among the living. It is natural for people who do not understand the importance of God's Word to seek wisdom here on earth. They look to philosophers and other leaders to give them direction for living. Yet Job said, "It is not here." No leader or group of leaders can produce enough knowledge or insight to explain who we are and where we are going. When looking for guidance, seek to know God's wisdom as made clear in the Bible. **To begin the series of devotionals on TRUSTING GOD FOR GUIDANCE, turn to page 27.**

[14]They come at me from all directions. They rush upon me when I am down.

[15]"I live in terror now. They hold me in contempt, and my prosperity has vanished as a cloud before a strong wind. [16]My heart is broken. Depression haunts my days. [17]My weary nights are filled with pain as though something were relentlessly gnawing at my bones. [18]All night long I toss and turn, and my garments bind about me. [19]God has thrown me into the mud. I have become as dust and ashes.

[20]"I cry to you, O God, but you don't answer me. I stand before you and you don't bother to look. [21]You have become cruel toward me and persecute me with great power and effect. [22]You throw me into the whirlwind and dissolve me in the storm. [23]And I know that your purpose for me is death. [24]I expected my fall to be broken, just as one who falls stretches out his hand or cries for help in his calamity.

[25]"And did I not weep for those in trouble? Wasn't I deeply grieved for the needy? [26]I therefore looked for good to come. Evil came instead. I waited for the light. Darkness came. [27]My heart is troubled and restless. Waves of affliction have come upon me. [28,29]I am black but not from sunburn. I stand up and cry to the assembly for help. [But I might as well save my breath,] for I am considered a brother to jackals and a companion to ostriches. [30]My skin is black and peeling. My bones burn with fever. [31]The voice of joy and gladness has turned to mourning.

31

"I made a covenant with my eyes not to look with lust upon a girl. [2,3]I know full well that Almighty God above sends calamity on those who do. [4]He sees everything I do and every step I take.

[5]"If I have lied and deceived— [6]but God knows that I am innocent— [7,8]or if I have stepped off God's pathway, or if my heart has lusted for what my eyes have seen, or if I am guilty of any other sin, then let someone else reap the crops I have sown and let all that I have planted be rooted out.

[9]"Or if I have longed for another man's wife, [10]then may I die, and may my wife be in another man's home and someone else become her husband. [11]For lust is a shameful sin, a crime that should be punished. [12]It is a devastating fire that destroys to hell and would root out all I have planted.

[13]"If I have been unfair to my servants, [14]how could I face God? What could I say when he questioned me about it? [15]For God made me and made my servant too. He created us both.

[16]"If I have hurt the poor, or caused widows to weep, [17]or refused food to hungry orphans— [18](but we have always cared for orphans in our home, treating them as our own children)— [19,20]or if I have seen anyone freezing and not given him clothing or fleece from my sheep to keep him warm, [21]or if I have taken advantage of an orphan because I thought I could get away with it— [22]if I have done any of these things, then let my arm be torn from its socket! Let my shoulder be wrenched out of place![23]Rather that than face the judgment sent by God; that I dread more than anything else. For if the majesty of God opposes me, what hope is there?

[24]"If I have put my trust in money, [25]if my happiness depends on wealth, [26]or if I have looked at the sun shining in the skies or the moon walking down her silver pathway [27]and my heart has been secretly enticed, and I have worshiped them by kissing my hand to them, [28]this, too, must be punished by the judges. For if I had done such things, it would mean that I denied the God of heaven.

[29]"If I have rejoiced at harm to an enemy— [30](but actually I have never cursed anyone nor asked for revenge)— [31]or if any of my servants have ever gone hungry— [32](actually I have never turned away even a stranger but have opened my doors to all)— [33]or if, like Adam, I have tried to hide my sins, [34]fearing the crowd and its contempt so that I refused to acknowledge my sin and do not go out of my way to help others— [35](oh, that there were someone who would listen to me and try to see my side of this argument. Look, I will sign my signature to my defense; now let the Almighty show me that I am wrong; let *him* approve the indictments made against me by my enemies. [36]I would treasure it like a crown. [37]Then I would tell him exactly what I have done and why, presenting my defense as one he listens to).

[38,39]"Or if my land accuses me because I stole the fruit it bears, or if I have murdered its owners to get their land for myself, [40]then let thistles grow on that land instead of wheat, and weeds instead of barley."

Job's words are ended.

32

Elihu: I Am Pent Up!

The three men refused to reply further to Job because he kept insisting on his innocence.

[2]Then Elihu (son of Barachel, the Buzite, of the Clan of Ram) became angry because Job refused to admit he had sinned and to acknowledge that God had just cause for punishing him. [3]But he was also angry with Job's three friends because they had been unable to answer Job's arguments and yet had condemned him. [4]Elihu had waited until now to speak because the others were older than he.

[5]But when he saw that they had no further reply, he spoke out angrily, [6]and said, "I am young

and you are old, so I held back and did not dare to tell you what I think, ⁷for those who are older are said to be wiser; ⁸,⁹but it is not mere age that makes men wise. Rather, it is the spirit in a man, the breath of the Almighty that makes him intelligent. ¹⁰So listen to me awhile and let me express my opinion.

¹¹,¹²"I have waited all this time, listening very carefully to your arguments, but not one of them has convinced Job that he is a sinner or has proved that he is. ¹³And don't give me that line about 'only God can convince the sinner of his sin.' ¹⁴If Job had been arguing with me, I would not answer with that kind of logic!

¹⁵"You sit there baffled, with no further replies. ¹⁶Shall I then continue to wait when you are silent? ¹⁷No, I will give my answer too. ¹⁸For I am pent up and full of words, and the spirit within me urges me on. ¹⁹I am like a wine cask without a vent! My words are ready to burst out! ²⁰I must speak to find relief, so let me give my answers. ²¹,²²Don't insist that I be cautious lest I insult someone, and don't make me flatter anyone. Let me be frank lest God should strike me dead.

33

"Please listen, Job, to what I have to say. ²I have begun to speak; now let me continue. ³I will speak the truth with all sincerity. ⁴For the Spirit of God has made me, and the breath of the Almighty gives me life. ⁵Don't hesitate to answer me if you can.

⁶"Look, I am the one you were wishing for, someone to stand between you and God and to be both his representative and yours. ⁷You need not be frightened of me. I am not some person of renown to make you nervous and afraid. I, too, am made of common clay.

⁸"You have said it in my hearing, yes, you've said it again and again— ⁹'I am pure, I am innocent; I have not sinned.' ¹⁰You say God is using a fine-toothed comb to try to find a single fault, and so to count you as his enemy. ¹¹'And he puts my feet in the stocks,' you say, 'and watches every move I make.'

¹²"All right, here is my reply: In this very thing, you have sinned by speaking of God that way. For God is greater than man. ¹³Why should you fight against him just because he does not give account to you of what he does?

¹⁴"For God speaks again and again, ¹⁵in dreams, in visions of the night when deep sleep falls on men as they lie on their beds. ¹⁶He opens their ears in times like that and gives them wisdom and instruction, ¹⁷,¹⁸causing them to change their minds, and keeping them from pride, and warning them of the penalties of sin, and keeping them from falling into some trap.

¹⁹"Or God sends sickness and pain, even though no bone is broken, ²⁰so that a man loses all taste and appetite for food and doesn't care for even the daintiest dessert. ²¹He becomes thin, mere skin and bones, ²²and draws near to death.

²³,²⁴"But if a messenger from heaven is there to intercede for him as a friend, to show him what is right, then God pities him and says, 'Set him free. Do not make him die, for I have found a substitute.' ²⁵Then his body will become as healthy as a child's, firm and youthful again. ²⁶And when he prays to God, God will hear and answer and receive him with joy, and return him to his duties. ²⁷And he will declare to his friends, 'I sinned, but God let me go. ²⁸He did not let me die. I will go on living in the realm of light.'

²⁹"Yes, God often does these things for man— ³⁰brings back his soul from the pit, so that he may live in the light of the living. ³¹Mark this well, O Job. Listen to me, and let me say more. ³²But if you have anything to say at this point, go ahead. I want to hear it, for I am anxious to justify you. ³³But if not, then listen to me. Keep silence and I will teach you wisdom!"

34

Elihu: Listen to Me
Elihu continued:

²"Listen to me, you wise men. ³We can choose the sounds we want to listen to; we can choose the taste we want in food, ⁴and we should choose to follow what is right. But first of all we must define among ourselves what is good. ⁵For Job has said, 'I am innocent, but God says I'm not. ⁶I am called a liar, even though I am innocent. I am horribly punished, even though I have not sinned.'

⁷,⁸"Who else is as arrogant as Job? He must have spent much time with evil men, ⁹for he said, 'Why waste time trying to please God?'

¹⁰"Listen to me, you with understanding. Surely everyone knows that *God doesn't sin!* ¹¹Rather, he punishes the sinners. ¹²There is no truer statement than this: *God is never wicked or unjust.* ¹³He alone has authority over the earth and dispenses justice for the world. ¹⁴If God were to withdraw his Spirit, ¹⁵all life would disappear and mankind would turn again to dust.

¹⁶"Listen now and try to understand. ¹⁷Could God govern if he hated justice? Are you going to condemn the Almighty Judge? ¹⁸Are you going to condemn this God who says to kings and nobles, 'You are wicked and unjust'? ¹⁹For he doesn't care how great a man may be, and doesn't pay any more attention to the rich than to the poor. He made them all. ²⁰In a moment they die, and at midnight great and small shall suddenly pass away, removed by no human hand.

Family Devotions

☐ DEVOTION 144
RESPECTING GOD'S WARNINGS

Read Job 34:16-28

"Hey, Rodney," whispered Max. "Look over there by the bushes."

"Wow!" Rodney whispered back. "Mr. Jones must have a new dog. He's big, but he looks harmless."

"I think we can still take our regular shortcut through his backyard," said Max a little bit louder.

"But look, Max." Rodney pointed to a sign on a tree. "It says Beware of Dog."

"Sure! Just look at that baby face!" exclaimed Max as he slowly walked toward the dog. The dog began to growl. "Nice doggy, nice doggy," repeated Max.

"Hey, Max," warned Rodney, "maybe we better not go any closer. That chain looks pretty long!"

"He's as gentle as a lamb. You'll see," Max assured him. "You just have to have a way with animals, Rodney."

Suddenly, the dog lunged towards Max. "Help!" yelled Max as he frantically tried to free his pant leg from the dog's teeth.

The boys heard a shout. "What are you doing in my backyard?" Mr. Jones asked angrily as he walked towards the snarling dog. "Come here, Dude!" Dude wagged his tail and trotted to his master. "You boys should read signs more carefully." Mr. Jones spoke firmly. "You were trespassing. See that it doesn't happen again. Dude may look gentle, and most of the time he is, but he's been known to scare a few people. Warnings are given for a reason. Obey them."

Max and Rodney were quiet as they walked home. "Max," Rodney broke the silence, "Mr. Jones sounded a lot like Rev. Parker."

Max nodded. "Yeah." They were remembering Sunday's evening message. "Sin may look attractive," Rev. Parker had said. "It may look harmless. But God warns against all sin. Heed this warning. Say no when Satan tempts you."

Respecting God's Warnings
Memory Verse

If my people will humble themselves and pray, and search for me, and turn from their wicked ways, I will hear them from heaven and forgive their sins and heal their land.
2 Chronicles 7:14

How About You?

Would you like to be like "everybody else" once in a while? Do you think it wouldn't hurt you to go where they go and do what they do, even though you know it wouldn't please the Lord? You're wrong. God warns that sin has dreadful consequences. Heed his warning and live for him. *V. R.*

• For the next devotional, turn to page 529. • For the next devotional on RESPECTING GOD'S WARNINGS, turn to page 591. • For notes on RESPECTING GOD'S WARNINGS, see page 219, 874, and 1126.

21"For God carefully watches the goings on of all mankind; he sees them all. 22 No darkness is thick enough to hide evil men from his eyes, 23so there is no need to wait for some great crime before a man is called before God in judgment. 24Without making a big issue over it, God simply shatters the greatest of men and puts others in their places. 25He watches what they do and in a single night he overturns them, destroying them, 26or openly strikes them down as wicked men. 27For they turned aside from following him, 28causing the cry of the poor to come to the attention of God. Yes, he hears the cries of those being oppressed. 29,30Yet when he chooses not to speak, who can criticize? Again, he may prevent a vile man from ruling, thus saving a nation from ruin, and he can depose an entire nation just as easily.

31"Why don't people exclaim to their God, 'We have sinned, but we will stop'? 32Or, 'We know not what evil we have done; only tell us, and we will cease at once.'

33"Must God tailor his justice to your demands? Must he change the order of the universe to suit your whims? The answer must be obvious even to you! 34,35Anyone even half bright will agree with me that you, Job, are speaking like a fool. 36You should be given the maximum penalty for the wicked way you have talked about God. 37For now you have added rebellion, arrogance, and blasphemy to your other sins."

35 *Elihu continued:*

2,3"Do you think it is right for you to claim, 'I haven't sinned, but I'm no better off before God than if I had'?

4"I will answer you and all your friends too. 5Look up there into the sky, high above you. 6If you sin, does that shake the heavens and knock God from his throne? Even if you sin again and again, what effect will it have upon him? 7Or if you are good, is this some great gift to him? 8Your sins may hurt another man, or your good deeds may profit him. 9,10The oppressed may shriek beneath their wrongs and groan beneath the power of the rich; yet none of them cry to God, asking, 'Where is God my Maker who gives songs in the night 11and makes us a little wiser than the animals and birds?'

12"But when anyone does cry out this question to him, he never replies by instant punishment of the tyrants. 13But it is false to say he doesn't hear those cries; 14,15and it is even more false to say that he doesn't see what is going on. He *does* bring about justice at last if you will only wait. But do you cry out against him because he does not instantly respond in anger? 16Job, you have spoken like a fool."

36 Elihu: I Am Defending God
Elihu continued:

2"Let me go on and I will show you the truth of what I am saying. For I have not finished defending God! 3I will give you many illustrations of the righteousness of my Maker. 4I am telling you the honest truth, for I am a man of well-rounded knowledge.

5"God is almighty and yet does not despise anyone! And he is perfect in his understanding. 6He does not reward the wicked with his blessings, but gives them their full share of punishment. 7He does not ignore the good men but honors them by placing them upon eternal, kingly thrones. 8If troubles come upon them and they are enslaved and afflicted, 9then he takes the trouble to point out to them the reason, what they have done that is wrong, or how they have behaved proudly. 10He helps them hear his instruction to turn away from their sin.

11"If they listen and obey him, then they will be blessed with prosperity throughout their lives. 12If they won't listen to him, they shall perish in battle and die because of their lack of good sense. 13But the godless reap his anger. They do not even return to him when he punishes them. 14They die young after lives of dissipation and depravity. 15He delivers by distress! This makes them listen to him!

16"How he wanted to lure you away from danger into a wide and pleasant valley and to prosper you there. 17But you are too preoccupied with your imagined grievances against others. 18Watch out! Don't let your anger at others lead you into scoffing at God! Don't let your suffering embitter you at the only one who can deliver you. 19Do you really think that if you shout loudly enough against God, he will be ashamed and repent? Will this put an end to your chastisement?

20"Do not desire the nighttime, with its opportunities for crime. 21Turn back from evil, for it was to prevent you from getting into a life of evil that God sent this suffering.

22"Look, God is all-powerful. Who is a teacher like him? 23Who can say that what he does is absurd or evil? 24Instead, glorify him for his mighty works for which he is so famous. 25Everyone has seen these things from a distance.

26"God is so great that we cannot begin to know him. No one can begin to understand eternity. 27He draws up the water vapor and then distills it into rain, 28 which the skies pour down. 29Can anyone really understand the spreading of the clouds and the thunders within? 30See how he spreads the lightning around him, and blankets the tops of the mountains. 31By his fantastic powers in nature he punishes or blesses the people, giving them food in abundance. 32He fills his hands with lightning bolts. He hurls each at its target. ³³We feel his presence in the thunder. Even the cattle know when a storm is coming.

37

"My heart trembles at this. ²Listen, listen to the thunder of his voice. ³It rolls across the heavens and his lightning flashes out in every direction. ⁴Afterwards comes the roaring of the thunder—the tremendous voice of his majesty. ⁵His voice is glorious in the thunder. We cannot comprehend the greatness of his power. ⁶For he directs the snow, the showers, and storm to fall upon the earth. ⁷Man's work stops at such a time so that all men everywhere may recognize his power. ⁸The wild animals hide in the rocks or in their dens.

⁹"From the south comes the rain; from the north, the cold. ¹⁰God blows upon the rivers, and even the widest torrents freeze. ¹¹He loads the clouds with moisture, and they send forth his lightning. ¹²The lightning bolts are directed by his hand and do whatever he commands throughout the earth. ¹³He sends the storms as punishment or, in his loving-kindness, to encourage.

¹⁴"Listen, O Job, stop and consider the wonderful miracles of God. ¹⁵Do you know how God controls all nature and causes the lightning to flash forth from the clouds? ¹⁶,¹⁷Do you understand the balancing of the clouds with wonderful perfection and skill? Do you know why you become warm when the south wind is blowing and everything is still? ¹⁸Can you spread out the gigantic mirror of the skies as he does?

¹⁹,²⁰"You who think you know so much, teach the rest of us how we should approach God. For we are too dull to know! With your wisdom, would we then dare to approach him? Well, does a man wish to be swallowed alive? ²¹For as we cannot look at the sun for its brightness when the winds have cleared away the clouds, ²²neither can we gaze at the terrible majesty of God breaking forth upon us from heaven, clothed in dazzling splendor. ²³We cannot imagine the power of the Almighty, and yet he is so just and merciful that he does not destroy us. ²⁴No wonder men everywhere fear him! For he is not impressed by the world's wisest men!"

38

The Lord Speaks to Job

Then the Lord answered Job from the whirlwind:

²"Why are you using your ignorance to deny my providence? ³Now get ready to fight, for I am going to demand some answers from you, and you must reply.

⁴"Where were you when I laid the foundations of the earth? Tell me, if you know so much. ⁵Do you know how its dimensions were determined, and who did the surveying? ⁶,⁷What supports its foundations, and who laid its cornerstone as the morning stars sang together and all the angels shouted for joy?

⁸,⁹"Who decreed the boundaries of the seas when they gushed from the depths? Who clothed them with clouds and thick darkness ¹⁰and barred them by limiting their shores, ¹¹and said, 'Thus far and no farther shall you come, and here shall your proud waves stop!'?

¹²"Have you ever once commanded the morning to appear and caused the dawn to rise in the east? ¹³Have you ever told the daylight to spread to the ends of the earth, to end the night's wickedness? ¹⁴Have you ever robed the dawn in red, ¹⁵and disturbed the haunts of wicked men, and stopped the arm raised to strike?

¹⁶"Have you explored the springs from which the seas come, or walked in the sources of their depths? ¹⁷,¹⁸Has the location of the gates of Death been revealed to you? Do you realize the extent of the earth? Tell me about it if you know! ¹⁹Where does the light come from, and how do you get there? Or tell me about the darkness. Where does it come from? ²⁰Can you find its boundaries, or go to its source? ²¹But of course you know all this! For you were born before it was all created, and you are so very experienced!

²²,²³"Have you visited the treasuries of the snow, or seen where hail is made and stored? For I have reserved it for the time when I will need it in war. ²⁴Where is the path to the distribution point of light? Where is the home of the east wind? ²⁵⁻²⁷Who dug the valleys for the torrents of rain? Who laid out the path for the lightning, causing the rain to fall upon the barren deserts, so that the parched and barren ground is satisfied with water and tender grass springs up?

²⁸"Has the rain a father? Where does dew come from? ²⁹Who is the mother of the ice and frost? ³⁰For the water changes and turns to ice as hard as rock.

³¹"Can you hold back the stars? Can you restrain Orion or Pleiades? ³²Can you ensure the proper sequence of the seasons, or guide the constellation of the Bear with her satellites across the heavens? ³³Do you know the laws of the universe and how the heavens influence the earth? ³⁴Can you shout to the clouds and make it rain? ³⁵Can you make lightning appear and cause it to strike as you direct it?

³⁶"Who gives intuition and instinct? ³⁷,³⁸Who is wise enough to number all the clouds? Who can tilt the water jars of heaven, when everything is dust and clods? ³⁹,⁴⁰Can you stalk prey like a lioness, to satisfy the young lions' appetites as they lie in their dens or lie in wait in the jungle? ⁴¹Who

provides for the ravens when their young cry out to God as they try to struggle up from their nest in hunger?

39

"Do you know how mountain goats give birth? Have you ever seen them giving birth to their young? 2,3Do you know how many months of pregnancy they have before they bow themselves to give birth to their young and carry their burden no longer? 4Their young grow up in the open field, then leave their parents and return to them no more.

5"Who makes the wild donkeys wild? 6I have placed them in the wilderness and given them salt plains to live in. 7For they hate the noise of the city and want no drivers shouting at them! 8The mountain ranges are their pastureland; there they search for every blade of grass.

9"Will the wild ox be your happy servant? Will he stay beside your feeding crib? 10Can you use a wild ox to plow with? Will he pull the harrow for you? 11Because he is so strong, will you trust him? Will you let him decide where to work? 12Can you send him out to bring in the grain from the threshing-floor?

13"The ostrich flaps her wings grandly but has no true motherly love. 14She lays her eggs on top of the earth, to warm them in the dust. 15She forgets that someone may step on them and crush them, or the wild animals destroy them. 16She ignores her young as though they weren't her own and is unconcerned though they die, 17for God has deprived her of wisdom. 18But whenever she jumps up to run, she passes the swiftest horse with its rider.

19"Have you given the horse strength or clothed his neck with a quivering mane? 20Have you made him able to leap forward like a locust? His majestic snorting is something to hear! 21-23He paws the earth and rejoices in his strength, and when he goes to war, he is unafraid and does not run away though the arrows rattle against him, or the flashing spear and javelin. 24Fiercely he paws the ground and rushes forward into battle when the trumpet blows. 25At the sound of the bugle he shouts, 'Aha!' He smells the battle when far away. He rejoices at the shouts of battle and the roar of the captain's commands.

26"Do you know how a hawk soars and spreads her wings to the south? 27Is it at your command that the eagle rises high upon the cliffs to make her nest? 28She lives upon the cliffs, making her home in her mountain fortress. 29From there she spies her prey, from a very great distance. 30Her nestlings gulp down blood, for she goes wherever the slain are."

40

Job: I Am Nothing

The Lord went on:

2"Do you still want to argue with the Almighty? Or will you yield? Do you—God's critic—have the answers?"

3*Then Job replied to God:*

4"I am nothing—how could I ever find the answers? I lay my hand upon my mouth in silence. 5I have said too much already."

6*Then the Lord spoke to Job again from the whirlwind:*

7"Stand up like a man and brace yourself for battle. Let me ask you a question, and give me the answer. 8Are you going to discredit my justice and condemn me so that you can say you are right? 9Are you as strong as God, and can you shout as loudly as he? 10All right then, put on your robes of state, your majesty and splendor. 11Give vent to your anger. Let it overflow against the proud. 12Humiliate the haughty with a glance; tread down the wicked where they stand. 13Knock them into the dust, stone-faced in death. 14If you can do that, then I'll agree with you that your own strength can save you.

15"Take a look at the hippopotamus! I made him, too, just as I made you! He eats grass like an ox. 16See his powerful loins and the muscles of his belly. 17His tail is as straight as a cedar. The sinews of his thighs are tightly knit together. 18His vertebrae lie straight as a tube of brass. His ribs are like iron bars. 19How ferocious he is among all of God's creation, so let whoever hopes to master him bring a sharp sword! 20The mountains offer their best food to him—the other wild animals on which he preys. 21He lies down under the lotus plants, hidden by the reeds, 22covered by their shade among the willows there beside the stream. 23He is not disturbed by raging rivers, not even when the swelling Jordan rushes down upon him. 24No one can catch him off guard or put a ring in his nose and lead him away.

41

"Can you catch a crocodile with a hook and line? Or put a noose around his tongue? 2Can you tie him with a rope through the nose, or pierce his jaw with a spike? 3Will he beg you to desist or try to flatter you from your intentions? 4Will he agree to let you make him your slave for life? 5Can you make a pet of him like a bird, or give him to your little girls to play with? 6Do fishing partners sell him to the fishmongers? 7Will his hide be hurt by darts, or his head with a harpoon?

8"If you lay your hands upon him, you will long remember the battle that ensues and you will never try it again! 9No, it's useless to try to capture him. It is frightening even to think about it!

Family Devotions

☐ **DEVOTION 145**
LOVING OTHERS

Read Job 42:7-10

"I hate having to be nice to Sue," said Kathy. "She's never nice to me."

"Well, it's a church picnic, so you have to do it," replied Amy. "Just pretend."

Mom frowned as she looked at her daughters in the rearview mirror. "Who said you should pretend to like someone just because you're at a church function?"

"Isn't that the Christian thing to do?" asked Amy.

"Hmmm," said Mom as she tapped her finger against the steering wheel. "Do you remember last summer, when you wanted to paint that old desk?"

"Sure," said Amy.

"Yeah. You wanted to just paint over the old paint," said Kathy, "but Dad made you sand it first."

"Right," said Mom, "and why was that?"

"He said if I didn't, the new paint would eventually chip off and the old paint would show through," replied Amy.

"Pretending to like someone is like painting over old, chipped paint," said Mom. "All the old feelings are still under the surface, and sooner or later, they'll show through."

"So should we just not bother to be nice to Sue at all then?" asked Amy.

Mom shook her head. "You didn't just *not paint* the old desk," she said. "You sanded and got rid of the rough spots. You need to get rid of the old feelings, too."

"But how?" asked Kathy.

"It isn't easy," admitted Mom, "but a good place to start is with prayer. It's hard to dislike someone you're praying for."

She handed Kathy a picnic basket. "Before we get out, shall we ask the Lord to help you love Sue as he does?" The girls nodded, and they bowed their heads.

As they got out of the car, they saw that Sue was just arriving, too. "Shall we go and talk to Sue?" asked Amy.

"Yes," said Kathy. "Let's go."

Loving Others Memory Verse

Little children, let us stop just *saying* we love people; let us *really* love them, and *show it* by our *actions.*
1 John 3:18

How About You?

Do you ever just pretend to like someone? Why not ask God right now to teach you to love somebody you find it difficult to like. He loves that person. Ask him to fill your heart with his love. *G. L. J.*

• For the next devotional, turn to page 533. • For the next devotional on LOVING OTHERS, turn to page 905.
• For notes on LOVING OTHERS, see pages 658, 951, 967, and 1242.

¹⁰No one dares to stir *him* up, let alone try to conquer him. And if no one can stand before *him*, who can stand before *me?* ¹¹I owe no one anything. Everything under the heaven is mine.

¹²"I should mention, too, the tremendous strength in his limbs and throughout his enormous frame. ¹³Who can penetrate his hide, or who dares come within reach of his jaws? ¹⁴For his teeth are terrible. ¹⁵⁻¹⁷His overlapping scales are his pride, making a tight seal so no air can get between them, and nothing can penetrate.

¹⁸"When he sneezes, the sunlight sparkles like lightning across the vapor droplets. His eyes glow like sparks. ¹⁹Fire leaps from his mouth. ²⁰Smoke flows from his nostrils, like steam from a boiling pot that is fired by dry rushes. ²¹Yes, his breath would kindle coals—flames leap from his mouth.

²²"The tremendous strength in his neck strikes terror wherever he goes. ²³His flesh is hard and firm, not soft and fat. ²⁴His heart is hard as rock, just like a millstone. ²⁵When he stands up, the strongest are afraid. Terror grips them. ²⁶No sword can stop him, nor spear nor dart nor pointed shaft. ²⁷,²⁸Iron is nothing but straw to him, and brass is rotten wood. Arrows cannot make him flee. Slingstones are as ineffective as straw. ²⁹Clubs do no good, and he laughs at the javelins hurled at him. ³⁰His belly is covered with scales as sharp as shards; they tear up the ground as he drags through the mud.

³¹,³²"He makes the water boil with his commotion. He churns the depths. He leaves a shining wake of froth behind him. One would think the sea was made of frost! ³³There is nothing else so fearless anywhere on earth. ³⁴Of all the beasts, he is the proudest—monarch of all that he sees."

42 God Gives Job Good Gifts

Then Job replied to God:

²"I know that you can do anything and that no one can stop you. ³You ask who it is who has so foolishly denied your providence. It is I. I was talking about things I knew nothing about and did not understand, things far too wonderful for me.

⁴"[You said,] 'Listen and I will speak! Let me put the questions to you! See if you can answer them!'

⁵"[But now I say,] 'I had heard about you before, but now I have seen you, ⁶and I loathe myself and repent in dust and ashes.'"

⁷*After the Lord had finished speaking with Job, he said to Eliphaz the Temanite:*

"I am angry with you and with your two friends, for you have not been right in what you have said about me, as my servant Job was. ⁸Now take seven young bulls and seven rams and go to my servant Job and offer a burnt offering for yourselves; and my servant Job will pray for you, and I will accept his prayer on your behalf, and won't destroy you as I should because of your sin, your failure to speak rightly concerning my servant Job."

⁹So Eliphaz the Temanite, and Bildad the Shuhite, and Zophar the Naamathite did as the Lord commanded them, and the Lord accepted Job's prayer on their behalf. ¹⁰Then, when Job prayed for his friends, the Lord restored his wealth and happiness! In fact, the Lord gave him twice as much as before! ¹¹Then all of his brothers, sisters, and former friends arrived and feasted with him in his home, consoling him for all his sorrow and comforting him because of all the trials the Lord had brought upon him. And each of them brought him a gift of money and a gold ring.

¹²So the Lord blessed Job at the end of his life more than at the beginning. For now he had 14,000 sheep, 6,000 camels, 1,000 teams of oxen, and 1,000 female donkeys.

¹³,¹⁴God also gave him seven more sons and three more daughters.

These were the names of his daughters: Jemima, Kezia, Keren.

¹⁵And in all the land there were no other girls as lovely as the daughters of Job; and their father put them into his will along with their brothers.

¹⁶Job lived 140 years after that, living to see his grandchildren and great-grandchildren too. ¹⁷Then at last he died, an old, old man, after living a long, good life.

Psalms

DO YOU wear a mask when you pray—not a real mask, but an invisible one you use to try to hide things from God? Are you able to tell God what you're really thinking and feeling and be completely honest with him?

The book of Psalms shows us how to take off our masks. Psalms are songs and prayers to God and about God. They were written by many people; about half were written by David. What they all have in common is their honesty.

When the psalmists felt joy, they wrote about it with powerful feelings. When they worshiped God, they dug down deep into their hearts to express their faith. When they had questions, they asked God without beating around the bush. When they were scared, they ran right to God for help. When they were sad, they let their tears fall on the pages.

God knows all about us, whether we tell him or not. He wants us to follow the example of the psalmists and be ourselves with him. As you read the Psalms, let God help you take off any masks.

Pleasing God

Oh, the joys of those who do not follow evil men's advice, who do not hang around with sinners, scoffing at the things of God. ²But they delight in doing everything God wants them to, and day and night are always meditating on his laws and thinking about ways to follow him more closely.

³They are like trees along a riverbank bearing luscious fruit each season without fail. Their leaves shall never wither, and all they do shall prosper.

⁴But for sinners, what a different story! They blow away like chaff before the wind. ⁵They are not safe on Judgment Day; they shall not stand among the godly.

⁶For the Lord watches over all the plans and paths of godly men, but the paths of the godless lead to doom.

2 Great God

What fools the nations are to rage against the Lord! How strange that men should try to outwit God! ²For a summit conference of the nations has been called to plot against the Lord and his Messiah, Christ the King. ³"Come, let us break his chains," they say, "and free ourselves from all this slavery to God."

⁴But God in heaven merely laughs! He is amused by all their puny plans. ⁵And then in fierce fury he rebukes them and fills them with fear.

⁶For the Lord declares, "This is the King of my choice, and I have enthroned him in Jerusalem, my holy city."

⁷His chosen one replies, "I will reveal the everlasting purposes of God, for the Lord has said to me, 'You are my Son. This is your Coronation Day. Today I am giving you your glory.'" ⁸"Only ask and I will give you all the nations of the world. ⁹Rule them with an iron rod; smash them like clay pots!"

¹⁰O kings and rulers of the earth, listen while there is time. ¹¹Serve the Lord with reverent fear; rejoice with trembling. ¹²Fall down before his Son and kiss his feet before his anger is roused and you perish. I am warning you—his wrath will soon begin. But oh, the joys of those who put their trust in him!

3 My Hope

A Psalm of David when he fled from his son Absalom.

O Lord, so many are against me. So many seek to harm me. I have so many enemies. ²So many say that God will never help me. ³But Lord, you are my shield, my glory, and my only hope. You alone can lift my head, now bowed in shame.

⁴I cried out to the Lord, and he heard me from his Temple in Jerusalem. ⁵Then I lay down and slept in peace and woke up safely, for the Lord was watching over me. ⁶And now, although ten thousand enemies surround me on every side, I am not afraid. ⁷I will cry to him, "Arise, O Lord! Save me, O my God!" And he will slap them in the face, insulting them and breaking off their teeth.

⁸For salvation comes from God. What joys he gives to all his people.

4 Who Can Keep Us Safe?

O God, you have declared me perfect in your eyes; you have always cared for me in my distress; now hear me as I call again. Have mercy on me. Hear my prayer.

²The Lord God asks, "Sons of men, will you forever turn my glory into shame by worshiping these silly idols, when every claim that's made for them is false?"

³Mark this well: The Lord has set apart the redeemed for himself. Therefore he will listen to me and answer when I call to him. ⁴Stand before the Lord in awe, and do not sin against him. Lie quietly upon your bed in silent meditation. ⁵Put your trust in the Lord, and offer him pleasing sacrifices.

⁶Many say that God will never help us. Prove them wrong, O Lord, by letting the light of your face shine down upon us. ⁷Yes, the gladness you have given me is far greater than their joys at harvest time as they gaze at their bountiful crops. ⁸I will lie down in peace and sleep, for though I am alone, O Lord, you will keep me safe.

5 God Hates Lies

O Lord, hear me praying; listen to my plea, O God my King, for I will never pray to anyone but you. ³Each morning I will look to you in heaven and lay my requests before you, praying earnestly.

⁴I know you get no pleasure from wickedness and cannot tolerate the slightest sin. ⁵Therefore, proud sinners will not survive your searching gaze, for how you hate their evil deeds. ⁶You will destroy them for their lies; how you abhor all murder and deception.

⁷But as for me, I will come into your Temple protected by your mercy and your love; I will worship you with deepest awe.

⁸Lord, lead me as you promised me you would; otherwise my enemies will conquer me. Tell me clearly what to do, which way to turn. ⁹For they cannot speak one truthful word. Their hearts are filled to the brim with wickedness. Their suggestions are full of the stench of sin and death. Their tongues are filled with flatteries to gain their wicked ends. ¹⁰O God, hold them responsible. Catch them in their own traps; let them fall beneath the weight of their own transgressions, for they rebel against you.

¹¹But make everyone rejoice who puts his trust in you. Keep them shouting for joy because you are defending them. Fill all who love you with your happiness. ¹²For you bless the godly man, O Lord; you protect him with your shield of love.

TRUE JOY 4:7 Two kinds of joy are contrasted here—inward joy that comes from knowing and trusting God, and happiness that comes as a result of pleasant circumstances. Inward joy is steady as long as we trust God; happiness is unpredictable. Inward joy defeats discouragement; happiness covers it up. Inward joy is lasting; happiness is temporary. It's always fun to be happy, but ask God to help you to find true joy so no matter what happens, you'll be able to stay close to him. **To begin the series of devotionals on *TRUE JOY*, turn to page 83.**

Family Devotions

☐ **Devotion 146**

Resisting Temptation

Read Psalm 1

Resisting Temptation Memory Verse

For since he himself has now been through suffering and temptation, he knows what it is like when we suffer and are tempted, and he is wonderfully able to help us.
Hebrews 2:18

Shari watched as Jamie took a cigarette out of the pack in his hand. He placed it on the picnic table along with a match. Other kids in the neighborhood had tried smoking that afternoon, but Shari had refused to join them. "You're just scared to try it," Jamie teased.

"I'm not scared," she retorted unconvincingly. "I just think it's dumb to smoke, that's all."

But her answer didn't satisfy Jamie. "I'll leave one right here," he said. "Maybe you'll want to try it when nobody's looking."

Shari watched Jamie go into his house next door, and then she looked again at the cigarette on the table. If she could just show him a partly smoked cigarette, maybe he'd quit bugging her about it. She picked it up and rolled it around in her fingers. Just then her mother came out of the back door. "Shari, what are you doing out here?"

"Nothing," Shari replied, slipping the cigarette and match into her pocket. Quickly she skipped back to the house and walked briskly into the bathroom. Nervously she pulled the cigarette out of her pocket, lit it, and took a short puff. Ugh! It was awful! Just as quickly, she put it out. Then she heard the back door open and close.

"Shari?" It was her mother's voice. "Are you smoking?"

Mom was waiting, a hurt look in her eyes. Suddenly Shari broke into tears. She explained how Jamie had tempted her and teased her until she gave in.

Shari's mother shook her head. "No, honey, Jamie's teasing isn't why you gave in. You gave in because you didn't run from temptation. You looked at the cigarette, maybe even took it in your fingers to see how it would feel, and finally gave in and smoked it. If you had turned and left it, the temptation would not have overtaken you. Temptations will come. When they do, run away from them."

How About You?

Do your friends sometimes coax you to go along to see a dirty movie? Smoke? Try drugs? Look at indecent pictures? When you are tempted by these or other sins, don't stand around and think about them. Turn and run. Ask Jesus to help you. He will. R. J.

• For the next devotional, turn to page 535.   • For the next devotional on *Resisting Temptation*, turn to page 723.
• For notes on *Resisting Temptation*, see pages 268, 448, 964, and 1258.

6 God Hears My Prayers

No, Lord! Don't punish me in the heat of your anger. ²Pity me, O Lord, for I am weak. Heal me, for my body is sick, ³and I am upset and disturbed. My mind is filled with apprehension and with gloom. Oh, restore me soon.

⁴Come, O Lord, and make me well. In your kindness save me. ⁵For if I die, I cannot give you glory by praising you before my friends. ⁶I am worn out with pain; every night my pillow is wet with tears. ⁷My eyes are growing old and dim with grief because of all my enemies.

⁸Go, leave me now, you men of evil deeds, for the Lord has heard my weeping ⁹and my pleading. He will answer all my prayers. ¹⁰All my enemies shall be suddenly dishonored, terror-stricken, and disgraced. God will turn them back in shame.

7 The Perfect Judge

I am depending on you, O Lord my God, to save me from my persecutors. ² Don't let them pounce upon me as a lion would and maul me and drag me away with no one to rescue me. ³It would be different, Lord, if I were doing evil things— ⁴if I were paying back evil for good or unjustly attacking those I dislike. ⁵Then it would be right for you to let my enemies destroy me, crush me to the ground, and trample my life in the dust.

⁶But Lord! Arise in anger against the anger of my enemies. Awake! Demand justice for me, Lord! ⁷,⁸Gather all peoples before you; sit high above them, judging their sins. But justify me publicly; establish my honor and truth before them all. ⁹End all wickedness, O Lord, and bless all who truly worship God; for you, the righteous God, look deep within the hearts of men and examine all their motives and their thoughts.

¹⁰God is my shield; he will defend me. He saves those whose hearts and lives are true and right.

¹¹God is a judge who is perfectly fair, and he is angry with the wicked every day. ¹²Unless they repent, he will sharpen his sword and slay them. He has bent and strung his bow ¹³and fitted it with deadly arrows made from shafts of fire.

¹⁴The wicked man conceives an evil plot, labors with its dark details, and brings to birth his treachery and lies; ¹⁵let him fall into his own trap. ¹⁶May the violence he plans for others boomerang upon himself; let him die.

¹⁷Oh, how grateful and thankful I am to the Lord because he is so good. I will sing praise to the name of the Lord who is above all lords.

8 Why God Made Us

O Lord our God, the majesty and glory of your name fills all the earth and overflows the heavens. ²You have taught the little children to praise you perfectly. May their example shame and silence your enemies!

³When I look up into the night skies and see the work of your fingers—the moon and the stars you have made— ⁴I cannot understand how you can bother with mere puny man, to pay any attention to him!

⁵And yet you have made him only a little lower than the angels and placed a crown of glory and honor upon his head.

⁶You have put him in charge of everything you made; everything is put under his authority: ⁷all sheep and oxen, and wild animals too, ⁸the birds and fish, and all the life in the sea. ⁹O Jehovah, our Lord, the majesty and glory of your name fills the earth.

9 God Hears Us

O Lord, I will praise you with all my heart and tell everyone about the marvelous things you do. ²I will be glad, yes, filled with joy because of you. I will sing your praises, O Lord God above all gods.

³My enemies will fall back and perish in your presence; ⁴you have vindicated me; you have endorsed my work, declaring from your throne that it is good. ⁵ You have rebuked the nations and destroyed the wicked, blotting out their names forever and ever. ⁶O enemies of mine, you are doomed forever. The Lord will destroy your cities; even the memory of them will disappear.

⁷,⁸But the Lord lives on forever; he sits upon his throne to judge justly the nations of the world. ⁹All who are oppressed may come to him. He is a refuge for them in their times of trouble. ¹⁰All those who know your mercy, Lord, will count on you for help. For you have never yet forsaken those who trust in you.

¹¹Oh, sing out your praises to the God who lives in Jerusalem. Tell the world about his unforgettable deeds. ¹²He who avenges murder has an open ear to those who cry to him for justice. He does not ignore the prayers of men in trouble when they call to him for help.

¹³And now, O Lord, have mercy on me; see how I suffer at the hands of those who hate me. Lord, snatch me back from the jaws of death. ¹⁴Save me, so that I can praise you publicly before all the people at Jerusalem's gates and rejoice that you have rescued me.

¹⁵The nations fall into the pitfalls they have dug for others; the trap they set has snapped on them.

FAMILY DEVOTIONS

☐ DEVOTION 147
KNOWING YOU'RE SPECIAL TO GOD

Read Psalm 8:3-9

Mike and his friend Steve lay in their sleeping bags, looking up at the star-filled sky. "There's something I don't understand," Mike said slowly. "I can see why God created the earth and sun and moon—maybe even the other planets in our solar system—because we might be able to visit them someday. But why did he make the rest of the universe? I mean, what's the use of making something so great and wonderful if no one's ever going to see it?"

Steve thought for a moment. "Maybe all those stars help us realize how great he really is, but it makes me feel kind of small."

The next morning, Mike and Steve told Mike's mother that they had talked about the stars and the vast universe. "It made us feel kind of small and unimportant," said Mike.

Mother smiled. "God is interested in little things, too," she said. "Mike, have you shown Steve the microscope you got for your birthday?"

"Yeah, he did. It's neat!" exclaimed Steve. "Let's go use it, Mike."

"OK," agreed Mike. "I've got something on a slide to show you." The boys hurried off.

When the boys looked at a drop of water they had taken from a puddle, they were amazed at all the tiny things they found swimming in it. "I can't believe it," said Mike, moving over so Steve could peer into the lens. "There must be millions and billions of these things all over the world, and we never even see them."

"Even though no one sees these little creatures, each of them was created by God in a special way." Mother's voice came from the doorway.

"I'm glad he's interested in little things as well as in big things," said Mike. "That means he's interested in us, too. It's nice to know we're important to God."

Knowing You're Special to God Memory Verse

But now the Lord who created you, O Israel, says, Don't be afraid, for I have ransomed you; I have called you by name; you are mine.
Isaiah 43:1

How About You?
When you think about the greatness of the universe, does it make you feel small and unimportant? Do you realize that God cares about you—that you are important to him? He created you and has a purpose for your life. You could not even live if it were not for his loving care, protecting and sustaining you every minute of every day. Don't you think you should be able to trust him completely? *S. K.*

• For the next devotional, turn to page 537.   • For the next devotional on KNOWING YOU'RE SPECIAL TO GOD, turn to page 603.   • For notes on KNOWING YOU'RE SPECIAL TO GOD, see pages 260, 878, 908, and 960.

¹⁶The Lord is famous for the way he punishes the wicked in their own snares!

¹⁷The wicked shall be sent away to hell; this is the fate of all the nations forgetting the Lord. ¹⁸For the needs of the needy shall not be ignored forever; the hopes of the poor shall not always be crushed.

¹⁹O Lord, arise and judge and punish the nations; don't let them defy you! ²⁰Make them tremble in fear; put the nations in their place until at last they know they are but puny men.

10 Will the Wicked Succeed?

Lord, why are you standing aloof and far away? Why do you hide when I need you the most?

²Come and deal with all these proud and wicked men who viciously persecute the poor. Pour upon these men the evil they planned for others! ³For these men brag of all their evil lusts; they revile God and congratulate those the Lord abhors, whose only goal in life is money.

⁴These wicked men, so proud and haughty, seem to think that God is dead. They wouldn't think of looking for him! ⁵Yet there is success in everything they do, and their enemies fall before them. They do not see your punishment awaiting them. ⁶They boast that neither God nor man can ever keep them down—somehow they'll find a way!

⁷Their mouths are full of profanity and lies and fraud. They are always boasting of their evil plans. ⁸They lurk in dark alleys of the city and murder passersby. ⁹Like lions they crouch silently, waiting to pounce upon the poor. Like hunters they catch their victims in their traps. ¹⁰The unfortunate are overwhelmed by their superior strength and fall beneath their blows. ¹¹"God isn't watching," they say to themselves; "he'll never know!"

¹²O Lord, arise! O God, crush them! Don't forget the poor or anyone else in need. ¹³Why do you let the wicked get away with this contempt for God? For they think that God will never call them to account. ¹⁴Lord, you see what they are doing. You have noted each evil act. You know what trouble and grief they have caused. Now punish them. O Lord, the poor man trusts himself to you; you are known as the helper of the helpless. ¹⁵Break the arms of these wicked men. Go after them until the last of them is destroyed.

¹⁶The Lord is King forever and forever. Those who follow other gods shall be swept from his land.

¹⁷Lord, you know the hopes of humble people. Surely you will hear their cries and comfort their hearts by helping them. ¹⁸You will be with the orphans and all who are oppressed, so that mere earthly man will terrify them no longer.

11 God Sees It All

How dare you tell me, "Flee to the mountains for safety," when I am trusting in the Lord?

²For the wicked have strung their bows, drawn their arrows tight against the bowstrings, and aimed from ambush at the people of God. ³"Law and order have collapsed," we are told. "What can the righteous do but flee?"

⁴But the Lord is still in his holy temple; he still rules from heaven. He closely watches everything that happens here on earth. ⁵He puts the righteous and the wicked to the test; he hates those loving violence. ⁶He will rain down fire and brimstone on the wicked and scorch them with his burning wind.

⁷For God is good, and he loves goodness; the godly shall see his face.

12 Can I Trust God?

Lord! Help! Godly men are fast disappearing. Where in all the world can dependable men be found? ²Everyone deceives and flatters and lies. There is no sincerity left.

³,⁴But the Lord will not deal gently with people who act like that; he will destroy those proud liars who say, "We will lie to our hearts' content. Our lips are our own; who can stop us?"

⁵The Lord replies, "I will arise and defend the oppressed, the poor, the needy. I will rescue them as they have longed for me to do." ⁶The Lord's promise is sure. He speaks no careless word; all he says is purest truth, like silver seven times refined.

⁷O Lord, we know that you will forever preserve your own from the reach of evil men, ⁸although they prowl on every side and vileness is praised throughout the land.

13 I Need Help

How long will you forget me, Lord? Forever? How long will you look the other way when I am in need? ²How long must I be hiding daily anguish in my heart? How long shall my enemy have the upper hand?

³Answer me, O Lord my God; give me light in my darkness lest I die. ⁴Don't let my enemies say, "We have conquered him!" Don't let them gloat that I am down.

⁵But I will always trust in you and in your mercy and shall rejoice

---

OPTIMISM 11:1-4 David's faith stood in dramatic contrast to the fear of his advisors. Faith in God keeps us from losing hope and helps us resist fear. David's advisors were afraid because they saw only frightening circumstances. David was comforted and optimistic because he knew God was greater than anything his enemies could bring against him (7:10; 16:1; 31:2-3). Remember that God is greater than any problem you face. He offers his presence and help so you don't need to be overwhelmed. **To begin the series of devotionals on OPTIMISM, turn to page 19.**

FAMILY DEVOTIONS

☐ DEVOTION 148
FAITH IN ACTION

Read Psalm 15

When the school bell rang, Tyson pushed past several children and hurried to the drinking fountain. He edged in at the front of the long line. "No cuts!" called several children, but Tyson took a long drink. When he went to hang up his coat, he found a coat on the hook nearest the door. He moved it to a place down the line and put his own coat in his favorite spot.

It was the start of a typical day. Tyson spent a lot of time daydreaming instead of studying. At recess he tried to be the first one out the door and the last one back in. "No fair," he grumbled when he had to stay in to finish his work during the afternoon recess. He glared at his teacher.

After school, Tyson invited Jerry over to play. "I got a new detective set," he said. "Let's see if we can lift fingerprints."

The boys played until Tyson's dad came home from work. After Jerry left, Tyson told Dad about the "detective work" they had been doing. "You leave prints on everything you touch, you know," said Tyson.

"I know, Son. I know," said Dad. "And what kind of prints have you been leaving all day?"

Tyson squinted at his dad. "The same kind as always, of course," he said. "Your fingerprints don't change."

"True," agreed Dad, "but wherever you go, you leave other prints too. Let's call them 'lifeprints.' Everything you do makes an impression—or a lifeprint—on other people. What kind of prints do you think you made today on your teacher and on the kids at school?" Tyson hadn't thought of that before! "Unlike fingerprints," Dad said, "we can change the kind of lifeprints we make. But we need God's help."

Tyson nodded slowly. Changing his work and play habits wouldn't be easy. He would have to pray about that.

Faith in Action Memory Verse

In response to all he has done for us, let us outdo each other in being helpful and kind to each other and in doing good.
Hebrews 10:24

How About You?

What kind of lifeprints are you making? Do others see selfishness and laziness in your prints, or do they see kindness, courtesy, faithfulness, and friendliness? Do they see Jesus? Ask God to help you live in such a way that the prints you leave are a good testimony for him. H. M.

- For the next devotional, turn to page 541.   • For the next devotional on FAITH IN ACTION, turn to page 557.
- For notes on FAITH IN ACTION, see pages 583, 846, 1068, and 1232.

in your salvation. ⁶I will sing to the Lord because he has blessed me so richly.

14 Foolish or Wise?

That man is a fool who says to himself, "There is no God!" Anyone who talks like that is warped and evil and cannot really be a good person at all.

²The Lord looks down from heaven on all mankind to see if there are any who are wise, who want to please God. ³But no, all have strayed away; all are rotten with sin. Not one is good, not one! ⁴They eat my people like bread and wouldn't think of praying! Don't they really know any better?

⁵Terror shall grip them, for God is with those who love him. ⁶He is the refuge of the poor and humble when evildoers are oppressing them. ⁷Oh, that the time of their rescue were already here, that God would come from Zion now to save his people. What gladness when the Lord has rescued Israel!

15 What Makes Someone Good?

Lord, who may go and find refuge and shelter in your tabernacle up on your holy hill?

²Anyone who leads a blameless life and is truly sincere. ³Anyone who refuses to slander others, does not listen to gossip, never harms his neighbor, ⁴speaks out against sin, criticizes those committing it, commends the faithful followers of the Lord, keeps a promise even if it ruins him, ⁵does not crush his debtors with high interest rates, and refuses to testify against the innocent despite the bribes offered him—such a man shall stand firm forever.

16 God's Friend

Save me, O God, because I have come to you for refuge. ²I said to him, "You are my Lord; I have no other help but yours." ³I want the company of the godly men and women in the land; they are the true nobility. ⁴Those choosing other gods shall all be filled with sorrow; I will not offer the sacrifices they do or even speak the names of their gods.

⁵The Lord himself is my inheritance, my prize. He is my food and drink, my highest joy! He guards all that is mine. ⁶He sees that I am given pleasant brooks and meadows as my share! What a wonderful inheritance! ⁷I will bless the Lord who counsels me; he gives me wisdom in the night. He tells me what to do.

⁸I am always thinking of the Lord; and because he is so near, I never need to stumble or to fall.

⁹Heart, body, and soul are filled with joy. ¹⁰For you will not leave me among the dead; you will not allow your beloved one to rot in the grave. ¹¹You have let me experience the joys of life and the exquisite pleasures of your own eternal presence.

17 Seeing God Face-to-face

I am pleading for your help, O Lord; for I have been honest and have done what is right, and you must listen to my earnest cry! ²Publicly acquit me, Lord, for you are always fair. ³You have tested me and seen that I am good. You have come even in the night and found nothing amiss and know that I have told the truth. ⁴I have followed your commands and have not gone along with cruel and evil men. ⁵My feet have not slipped from your paths.

⁶Why am I praying like this? Because I know you will answer me, O God! Yes, listen as I pray. ⁷Show me your strong love in wonderful ways, O Savior of all those seeking your help against their foes. ⁸Protect me as you would the pupil of your eye; hide me in the shadow of your wings as you hover over me.

⁹My enemies encircle me with murder in their eyes. ¹⁰They are pitiless and arrogant. Listen to their boasting. ¹¹They close in upon me and are ready to throw me to the ground. ¹²They are like lions eager to tear me apart, like young lions hiding and waiting their chance.

¹³,¹⁴Lord, arise and stand against them. Push them back! Come and save me from these men of the world whose only concern is earthly gain—these men whom you have filled with your treasures so that their children and grandchildren are rich and prosperous.

¹⁵But as for me, my contentment is not in wealth but in seeing you and knowing all is well between us. And when I awake in heaven, I will be fully satisfied, for I will see you face to face.

18 God Cares for Us

This song of David was written at a time when the Lord had delivered him from his many enemies, including Saul.

Lord, how I love you! For you have done such tremendous things for me.

²The Lord is my fort where I can enter and be safe; no one can follow me in and slay me. He is a rugged mountain where I hide; he is my Savior, a rock where none can reach me, and a tower of safety. He is my shield. He is like the strong horn of a mighty fighting bull. ³All I need to do is cry to him—oh, praise the Lord—and I am saved from all my enemies!

⁴Death bound me with chains, and the floods of ungodliness mounted a massive attack against me. ⁵Trapped and helpless, I struggled against the ropes that drew me on to death.

⁶In my distress I screamed to the Lord for his help. And he heard me from heaven; my cry reached his ears. ⁷Then the earth rocked and reeled, and mountains shook and trembled. How they quaked! For he was angry. ⁸Fierce flames leaped from his mouth, setting fire to the earth; smoke blew from his nostrils. ⁹He bent the heavens down and came to my defense; thick darkness was beneath his feet. ¹⁰Mounted on a mighty angel, he sped swiftly to my aid with wings of wind. ¹¹He enshrouded himself with darkness, veiling his approach with dense clouds dark as murky waters. ¹²Suddenly the brilliance of his presence broke through the clouds with lightning and a mighty storm of hail.

¹³The Lord thundered in the heavens; the God above all gods has spoken—oh, the hailstones; oh, the fire! ¹⁴He flashed his fearful arrows of lightning and routed all my enemies. See how they run! ¹⁵Then at your command, O Lord, the sea receded from the shore. At the blast of your breath the depths were laid bare.

¹⁶He reached down from heaven and took me and drew me out of my great trials. He rescued me from deep waters. ¹⁷He delivered me from my strong enemy, from those who hated me—I who was helpless in their hands.

¹⁸On the day when I was weakest, they attacked. But the Lord held me steady. ¹⁹He led me to a place of safety, for he delights in me.

²⁰The Lord rewarded me for doing right and being pure. ²¹For I have followed his commands and have not sinned by turning back from following him. ²²I kept close watch on all his laws; I did not refuse a single one. ²³I did my best to keep them all, holding myself back from doing wrong. ²⁴And so the Lord has paid me with his blessings, for I have done what is right, and I am pure of heart. This he knows, for he watches my every step.

²⁵Lord, how merciful you are to those who are merciful. And you do not punish those who run from evil. ²⁶You give blessings to the pure but pain to those who leave your paths. ²⁷You deliver the humble but condemn the proud and haughty ones. ²⁸You have turned on my light! The Lord my God has made my darkness turn to light. ²⁹Now in your strength I can scale any wall, attack any troop.

³⁰What a God he is! How perfect in every way! All his promises prove true. He is a shield for everyone who hides behind him. ³¹For who is God except our Lord? Who but he is as a rock?

³²He fills me with strength and protects me wherever I go. ³³He gives me the surefootedness of a mountain goat upon the crags. He leads me safely along the top of the cliffs. ³⁴He prepares me for battle and gives me strength to draw an iron bow!

³⁵You have given me your salvation as my shield. Your right hand, O Lord, supports me; your gentleness has made me great. ³⁶You have made wide steps beneath my feet so that I need never slip. ³⁷I chased my enemies; I caught up with them and did not turn back until all were conquered. ³⁸I pinned them to the ground; all were helpless before me. I placed my feet upon their necks. ³⁹For you have armed me with strong armor for the battle. My enemies quail before me and fall defeated at my feet. ⁴⁰You made them turn and run; I destroyed all who hated me. ⁴¹They shouted for help, but no one dared to rescue them; they cried to the Lord, but he refused to answer them. ⁴²So I crushed them fine as dust and cast them to the wind. I threw them away like sweepings from the floor. ⁴³⁻⁴⁵You gave me victory in every battle. The nations came and served me. Even those I didn't know before come now and bow before me. Foreigners who have never seen me submit instantly. They come trembling from their strongholds.

⁴⁶God is alive! Praise him who is the great rock of protection. ⁴⁷He is the God who pays back those who harm me and subdues the nations before me.

⁴⁸He rescues me from my enemies; he holds me safely out of their reach and saves me from these powerful opponents. ⁴⁹For this, O Lord, I will praise you among the nations. ⁵⁰Many times you have miraculously rescued me, the king you appointed. You have been loving and kind to me and will be to my descendants.

19 More Valuable than Gold

The heavens are telling the glory of God; they are a marvelous display of his craftsmanship. ²Day and night they keep on telling about God. ³,⁴Without a sound or word, silent in the skies, their message reaches out to all the world. The sun lives in the heavens where God placed it ⁵and moves out across the skies as radiant as a bridegroom going to his wedding, or as joyous as an athlete looking forward to a race! ⁶The sun crosses the heavens from end to end, and nothing can hide from its heat.

⁷,⁸God's laws are perfect. They protect us, make us wise, and give us joy and light. ⁹God's laws are pure, eternal, just. ¹⁰They are more desirable than

---

TRUSTING GOD FOR HELP 18:30 Many say belief in God is a crutch for weak people who cannot make it on their own. God is indeed a shield to protect us when we *are* too weak to face certain trials by ourselves. He strengthens, protects, and guides us in order to send us back into an evil world to fight for him. David was not a coward; he was a mighty warrior who, with all his armies and weapons, knew that only God could ultimately protect and save him. **To begin the series of devotionals on *TRUSTING GOD FOR HELP*, turn to page 29.**

gold. They are sweeter than honey dripping from a honeycomb. ¹¹For they warn us away from harm and give success to those who obey them.

¹²But how can I ever know what sins are lurking in my heart? Cleanse me from these hidden faults. ¹³And keep me from deliberate wrongs; help me to stop doing them. Only then can I be free of guilt and innocent of some great crime.

¹⁴May my spoken words and unspoken thoughts be pleasing even to you, O Lord my Rock and my Redeemer.

20 God Is with Us

In your day of trouble, may the Lord be with you! May the God of Jacob keep you from all harm. ²May he send you aid from his sanctuary in Zion. ³May he remember with pleasure the gifts you have given him, your sacrifices and burnt offerings. ⁴May he grant you your heart's desire and fulfill all your plans. ⁵May there be shouts of joy when we hear the news of your victory, flags flying with praise to God for all that he has done for you. May he answer all your prayers!

⁶"God save the king"—I know he does! He hears me from highest heaven and sends great victories. ⁷Some nations boast of armies and of weaponry, but our boast is in the Lord our God. ⁸Those nations will collapse and perish; we will arise to stand firm and sure!

⁹Give victory to our king, O Lord; oh, hear our prayer.

21 Thanking God for His Answers

How the king rejoices in your strength, O Lord! How he exults in your salvation. ²For you have given him his heart's desire, everything he asks you for!

³You welcomed him to the throne with success and prosperity. You set a royal crown of solid gold upon his head. ⁴He asked for a long, good life, and you have granted his request; the days of his life stretch on and on forever. ⁵You have given him fame and honor. You have clothed him with splendor and majesty. ⁶You have endowed him with eternal happiness. You have given him the unquenchable joy of your presence. ⁷And because the king trusts in the Lord, he will never stumble, never fall; for he depends upon the steadfast love of the God who is above all gods.

⁸Your hand, O Lord, will find your enemies, all who hate you. ⁹,¹⁰When you appear, they will be destroyed in the fierce fire of your presence. The Lord will destroy them and their children. ¹¹For these men plot against you, Lord, but they cannot possibly succeed. ¹²They will turn and flee when they see your arrows aimed straight at them.

¹³Accept our praise, O Lord, for all your glorious power. We will write songs to celebrate your mighty acts!

22 Everyone Hates Me—Does God?

My God, my God, why have you forsaken me? Why do you refuse to help me or even to listen to my groans? ²Day and night I keep on weeping, crying for your help, but there is no reply— ³,⁴for *you are holy.*

The praises of our fathers surrounded your throne; they trusted you and you delivered them. ⁵You heard their cries for help and saved them; they were never disappointed when they sought your aid.

⁶But I am a worm, not a man, scorned and despised by my own people and by all mankind. ⁷Everyone who sees me mocks and sneers and shrugs. ⁸"Is this the one who rolled his burden on the Lord?" they laugh. "Is this the one who claims the Lord delights in him? We'll believe it when we see God rescue him!"

⁹⁻¹¹Lord, how you have helped me before! You took me safely from my mother's womb and brought me through the years of infancy. I have depended upon you since birth; you have always been my God. Don't leave me now, for trouble is near and no one else can possibly help.

¹²I am surrounded by fearsome enemies, strong as the giant bulls from Bashan. ¹³They come at me with open jaws, like roaring lions attacking their prey. ¹⁴My strength has drained away like water, and all my bones are out of joint. My heart melts like wax; ¹⁵my strength has dried up like sun-baked clay; my tongue sticks to my mouth, for you have laid me in the dust of death. ¹⁶The enemy, this gang of evil men, circles me like a pack of dogs; they have pierced my hands and feet. ¹⁷I can count every bone in my body. See these men of evil gloat and stare; ¹⁸they divide my clothes among themselves by a toss of the dice.

¹⁹O Lord, don't stay away. O God my Strength, hurry to my aid. ²⁰Rescue me from death; spare my precious life from all these evil men. ²¹Save me from these lions' jaws and from the horns of these wild oxen. Yes, God will answer me and rescue me.

²²I will praise you to all my brothers; I will stand up before the congregation and testify of the wonderful things you have done. ²³"Praise the Lord, each one of you who fears him," I will say. "Each of you must fear and reverence his name. Let all Israel sing his praises, ²⁴for he has not despised my cries of deep despair; he has not turned and walked away. When I cried to him, he heard and came."

²⁵Yes, I will stand and praise you before all the people. I will publicly fulfill my vows in the presence of all who reverence your name.

Family Devotions

☐ **Devotion 149**
Showing Kindness

Read Psalm 19:12-14

"There goes Melinda—that new girl," said Dee to her friends at recess. "She wears funny clothes. And you should see her father! He has a big scar on his face and looks like a criminal."

"Do you think he's really a criminal?" asked Lois. "What do you suppose he did?"

Dee shrugged. "Who knows? Robbed a bank maybe."

As Dee slid into her seat, she heard Lois whisper to Pam, "Beware of Melinda—her dad's a bank robber."

The rumor flew and grew until everyone in the class was whispering about Melinda and avoiding her. A little voice in Dee's heart said, *Dee, what have you done?* but she tried not to listen.

Sprawling on the lawn after school to enjoy the sunshine, Dee picked a dandelion that had gone to seed. She blew on it, and the seeds floated off into the air like dozens of tiny parachutes.

"Oh dear!" said Mother, who had come out with a glass of lemonade for Dee. "Those little seeds are going to take root and become more pesky dandelions!"

"Oops!" said Dee. "Sorry, Mom."

Mother sat down in a lawn chair. "Well, if you hadn't blown them, the wind would have," she said. Then she added thoughtfully, "Those little seeds remind me of words. Those seeds are gone forever. There's no way you could gather them back. Words are like that. Once we've said them, they're gone." Dee squirmed uncomfortably as she remembered her words about Melinda and her father. "Before we speak about anyone," continued Mother, "we should ask ourselves, is what I'm about to say true? Is it kind? Would God be pleased to hear me say it?"

Dee's conscience seemed to be shouting now. Her words about Melinda's father had certainly not been kind or pleasing to God. Probably they were not even true! "Mother," she said as she started for the house, "I've got some phone calls to make."

Showing Kindness
Memory Verse

That's why whenever we can we should always be kind to everyone, and especially to our Christian brothers.
Galatians 6:10

How About You?

What sort of words do you speak? Are they true? Kind? Pleasing to God? Do they build, or do they destroy? Ask God to help you watch your words. *M. N.*

• For the next devotional, turn to page 543. • For the next devotional on *Showing Kindness*, turn to page 585.
• For notes on *Showing Kindness*, see pages 664, 880, 1038, and 1244.

²⁶The poor shall eat and be satisfied; all who seek the Lord shall find him and shall praise his name. Their hearts shall rejoice with everlasting joy. ²⁷The whole earth shall see it and return to the Lord; the people of every nation shall worship him.

²⁸For the Lord is King and rules the nations. ²⁹Both proud and humble together, all who are mortal—born to die—shall worship him. ³⁰Our children too shall serve him, for they shall hear from us about the wonders of the Lord; ³¹generations yet unborn shall hear of all the miracles he did for us.

23 The Good Shepherd

Because the Lord is my Shepherd, I have everything I need!

²,³He lets me rest in the meadow grass and leads me beside the quiet streams. He gives me new strength. He helps me do what honors him the most.

⁴Even when walking through the dark valley of death I will not be afraid, for you are close beside me, guarding, guiding all the way.

⁵You provide delicious food for me in the presence of my enemies. You have welcomed me as your guest; blessings overflow!

⁶Your goodness and unfailing kindness shall be with me all of my life, and afterwards I will live with you forever in your home.

24 Who Owns the World?

The earth belongs to God! Everything in all the world is his! ²He is the one who pushed the oceans back to let dry land appear.

³Who may climb the mountain of the Lord and enter where he lives? Who may stand before the Lord? ⁴Only those with pure hands and hearts, who do not practice dishonesty and lying. ⁵They will receive God's own goodness as their blessing from him, planted in their lives by God himself, their Savior. ⁶These are the ones who are allowed to stand before the Lord and worship the God of Jacob.

⁷Open up, O ancient gates, and let the King of Glory in. ⁸Who is this King of Glory? The Lord, strong and mighty, invincible in battle. ⁹Yes, open wide the gates and let the King of Glory in.

¹⁰Who is this King of Glory? The Commander of all of heaven's armies!

25 God Will Be My Guide

To you, O Lord, I pray. ²Don't fail me, Lord, for I am trusting you. Don't let my enemies succeed. Don't give them victory over me. ³None of those who have faith in God will ever be disgraced for trusting him. But all who harm the innocent shall be defeated.

⁴Show me the path where I should go, O Lord; point out the right road for me to walk. ⁵Lead me; teach me; for you are the God who gives me salvation. I have no hope except in you. ⁶,⁷Overlook my youthful sins, O Lord! Look at me instead through eyes of mercy and forgiveness, through eyes of everlasting love and kindness.

⁸The Lord is good and glad to teach the proper path to all who go astray; ⁹he will teach the ways that are right and best to those who humbly turn to him. ¹⁰And when we obey him, every path he guides us on is fragrant with his loving-kindness and his truth.

¹¹But Lord, my sins! How many they are. Oh, pardon them for the honor of your name.

¹²Where is the man who fears the Lord? God will teach him how to choose the best.

¹³He shall live within God's circle of blessing, and his children shall inherit the earth.

¹⁴Friendship with God is reserved for those who reverence him. With them alone he shares the secrets of his promises.

¹⁵My eyes are ever looking to the Lord for help, for he alone can rescue me. ¹⁶Come, Lord, and show me your mercy, for I am helpless, overwhelmed, in deep distress; ¹⁷my problems go from bad to worse. Oh, save me from them all! ¹⁸See my sorrows; feel my pain; forgive my sins. ¹⁹See how many enemies I have and how viciously they hate me! ²⁰Save me from them! Deliver my life from their power! Oh, let it never be said that I trusted you in vain!

²¹Assign me Godliness and Integrity as my bodyguards, for I expect you to protect me ²²and to ransom Israel from all her troubles.

26 On God's Side

Dismiss all the charges against me, Lord, for I have tried to keep your laws and have trusted you without wavering. ²Cross-examine me, O Lord, and see that this is so; test my motives and affections too. ³For I have taken your loving-kindness and your truth as my ideals. ⁴I do not have fellowship with tricky, two-faced men; they are false and hypocritical. ⁵I hate the sinners' hangouts and refuse to enter them. ⁶I wash my hands to prove

---

CONTENTMENT 23:2-3 When we allow God our shepherd to guide us, we have contentment. When we choose to sin, however, we are choosing to go our own way, and we cannot blame God for the environment in which we find ourselves. Our shepherd knows the "meadow grass" and "quiet streams" that will restore us. We will reach these places only by following him obediently. Rebelling against the shepherd's leading is actually rebelling against our own best interests for the future. We must remember this the next time we are tempted to go our own way rather than the shepherd's way. **To begin the series of devotionals on CONTENTMENT, turn to page 89.**

Family Devotions

☐ **DEVOTION 150**

TRUSTING GOD FOR GUIDANCE

Read Psalm 25:4-10

Dana and Jim were very excited about their ski trip with their father. "That rig over there that looks like a bunch of J's going up the hill is called the J-bar," said Dad when they got to the slopes. "You haven't used one of those before, but that's what we'll use today." They skied over to it. Dana grabbed the bar and headed up the hill. Next, Dad got Jim on track, and then he started up the slope himself.

Partway up the hill, Dana turned her skis and plopped into the unpacked snow. The J-bar groaned to a stop, and Dad came to rescue Dana as quickly as possible. "What happened?" he asked, as she struggled to get up with his help.

"I didn't know how long it would take to get off," she said sheepishly.

"Just wait, Dana," Dad told her. "You'll know when to get off—it'll be easy."

The J-bar began to climb again, but soon it had another stop. This time it was Jim! Dad helped Jim out of the soft snow while the other skiers grumbled.

"You're too anxious—just be patient, Jim. You'll see where to let go," Dad repeated. When they reached the top of the hill, Dana and Jim were glad to find out how easy it was to dismount the J-bar.

"Were you mad at us, Dad?" asked Dana.

Dad chuckled. "No, kids," he said. "Actually, the whole experience reminded me of myself."

"Did you jump off too soon, too?" asked Jim.

Dad shook his head. "No, but I've often jumped into other things in life before the time was right," he explained. "It's not always easy to wait for the plans the Lord has for us. We can't always see the top of the hill, but if we wait patiently for the Lord to guide us, we'll make the right move at the right time."

Trusting God for Guidance
Memory Verse

I will instruct you (says the Lord) and guide you along the best pathway for your life; I will advise you and watch your progress.
Psalm 32:8

How About You?

Are you wondering what the future holds for you? Do you want God's guidance? Read your Bible every day and pray often. God knows what tomorrow will bring, and he sees what you cannot see. Ask him to guide you. Hang on to his promises and trust him. Don't go off on your own. *D. E. M.*

• For the next devotional, turn to page 545. • For the next devotional on TRUSTING GOD FOR GUIDANCE, turn to page 555. • For notes on TRUSTING GOD FOR GUIDANCE, see pages 522, 553, 614, 676, and 1056.

my innocence and come before your altar, ⁷singing a song of thanksgiving and telling about your miracles.

⁸Lord, I love your home, this shrine where the brilliant, dazzling splendor of your presence lives.

⁹,¹⁰Don't treat me as a common sinner or murderer who plots against the innocent and demands bribes.

¹¹No, I am not like that, O Lord; I try to walk a straight and narrow path of doing what is right; therefore in mercy save me.

¹²I publicly praise the Lord for keeping me from slipping and falling.

27 Why Should I Be Afraid?

The Lord is my light and my salvation; he protects me from danger—whom shall I fear? ²When evil men come to destroy me, they will stumble and fall! ³Yes, though a mighty army marches against me, my heart shall know no fear! I am confident that God will save me.

⁴The one thing I want from God, the thing I seek most of all, is the privilege of meditating in his Temple, living in his presence every day of my life, delighting in his incomparable perfections and glory. ⁵There I'll be when troubles come. He will hide me. He will set me on a high rock ⁶out of reach of all my enemies. Then I will bring him sacrifices and sing his praises with much joy.

⁷Listen to my pleading, Lord! Be merciful and send the help I need.

⁸My heart has heard you say, "Come and talk with me, O my people." And my heart responds, "Lord, I am coming."

⁹Oh, do not hide yourself when I am trying to find you. Do not angrily reject your servant. You have been my help in all my trials before; don't leave me now. Don't forsake me, O God of my salvation. ¹⁰For if my father and mother should abandon me, you would welcome and comfort me.

¹¹Tell me what to do, O Lord, and make it plain because I am surrounded by waiting enemies. ¹²Don't let them get me, Lord! Don't let me fall into their hands! For they accuse me of things I never did, and all the while are plotting cruelty. ¹³I am expecting the Lord to rescue me again, so that once again I will see his goodness to me here in the land of the living.

¹⁴Don't be impatient. Wait for the Lord, and he will come and save you! Be brave, stouthearted, and courageous. Yes, wait and he will help you.

28 Prayer Is Powerful

I plead with you to help me, Lord, for you are my Rock of safety. If you refuse to answer me, I might as well give up and die. ²Lord, I lift my hands to heaven and implore your help. Oh, listen to my cry.

³Don't punish me with all the wicked ones who speak so sweetly to their neighbors while planning to murder them. ⁴Give them the punishment they so richly deserve! Measure it out to them in proportion to their wickedness; pay them back for all their evil deeds. ⁵They care nothing for God or what he has done or what he has made; therefore God will dismantle them like old buildings, never to be rebuilt again.

⁶Oh, praise the Lord, for he has listened to my pleadings! ⁷He is my strength, my shield from every danger. I trusted in him, and he helped me. Joy rises in my heart until I burst out in songs of praise to him. ⁸The Lord protects his people and gives victory to his anointed king.

⁹Defend your people, Lord; defend and bless your chosen ones. Lead them like a shepherd and carry them forever in your arms.

29 Nature Speaks of God

Praise the Lord, you angels of his; praise his glory and his strength. ²Praise him for his majestic glory, the glory of his name. Come before him clothed in sacred garments.

³The voice of the Lord echoes from the clouds. The God of glory thunders through the skies. ⁴So powerful is his voice; so full of majesty. ⁵,⁶It breaks down the cedars. It splits the giant trees of Lebanon. It shakes Mount Lebanon and Mount Sirion. They leap and skip before him like young calves! ⁷The voice of the Lord thunders through the lightning. ⁸It resounds through the deserts and shakes the wilderness of Kadesh. ⁹The voice of the Lord spins and topples the mighty oaks. It strips the forests bare. They whirl and sway beneath the blast. But in his temple all are praising, "Glory, glory to the Lord."

¹⁰At the Flood the Lord showed his control of all creation. Now he continues to unveil his power. ¹¹He will give his people strength. He will bless them with peace.

30 Saved from the Grave

I will praise you, Lord, for you have saved me from my enemies. You refuse to let them triumph over me. ²O Lord my God, I pleaded with you, and you gave me my health again. ³You brought me back from the brink of the grave, from death itself, and here I am alive!

⁴Oh, sing to him you saints of his; give thanks to his holy name. ⁵His anger lasts a moment; his favor lasts for life! Weeping may go on all night, but in the morning there is joy.

⁶,⁷In my prosperity I said, "This is forever; nothing can stop me now! The Lord has shown me his favor.

FAMILY DEVOTIONS

☐ DEVOTION 151
SHARING YOUR FAITH

Read Psalm 31:19-24

John liked the current-issue discussions his class held, but he was very timid about speaking out for what he believed. "What do you think about murder and capital punishment?" his teacher, Mr. Lanham, asked one day. Opinions flew back and forth. John wanted to share what he'd heard in a recent sermon on the subject, but he didn't quite dare.

During dinner that night, John told his parents about his school day. He described how he felt during current issues class. "You know, it doesn't bother me to be different from the other kids in what I believe or do," he said. "I mean . . . I'm not ever tempted very much to go along with their thinking, but I don't dare tell them what I think, either."

Dad nodded. "Remember what we talked about last time we played basketball? When I approach the basket, your defense is strong," Dad said. "You work hard to keep me from shooting for a point. But when you approach the basket to shoot, you hesitate. I think this is similar. You have a strong defense in your Christian life. It's backed up by Scripture and prayer. But now it's time to get out there with a strong offense, determined to score victories for Jesus."

The following day, when Mr. Lanham presented the topic of abortion, John thought of Dad's words. *Help me, Father,* he prayed silently, then he raised his hand. "Yesterday we talked about murder," he said boldly to the class. "Well, we're talking about the same topic today because abortion is murder. People make up all kinds of excuses to say it isn't, but that doesn't change it. It's still wrong in God's sight."

Some students agreed with John, but others poked fun at him and called him a "religious freak who thinks he knows everything." John felt hurt, yet he was glad he had spoken up. He was determined to score points boldly for Jesus.

Sharing Your Faith
Memory Verse

And let us not get tired of doing what is right, for after a while we will reap a harvest of blessing if we don't get discouraged and give up.
Galatians 6:9

How About You?
Do you keep quiet when people promote ungodly positions on issues? Develop a strong offense for God. Speak up for his law in a controlled, respectable manner. The truth needs to be heard. Ask God to help you be bold for him. *N. E. K.*

• For the next devotional, turn to page 549.   • For the next devotional on *SHARING YOUR FAITH,* turn to page 607.
• For notes on *SHARING YOUR FAITH,* see pages 462, 776, 1015, and 1074.

He has made me steady as a mountain." Then, Lord, you turned your face away from me and cut off your river of blessings. Suddenly my courage was gone; I was terrified and panic-stricken. ⁸I cried to you, O Lord; oh, how I pled: ⁹"What will you gain, O Lord, from killing me? How can I praise you then to all my friends? How can my dust in the grave speak out and tell the world about your faithfulness? ¹⁰Hear me, Lord; oh, have pity and help me." ¹¹Then he turned my sorrow into joy! He took away my clothes of mourning and clothed me with joy ¹²so that I might sing glad praises to the Lord instead of lying in silence in the grave. O Lord my God, I will keep on thanking you forever!

31 Believe, No Matter What

Lord, I trust in you alone. Don't let my enemies defeat me. Rescue me because you are the God who always does what is right. ²Answer quickly when I cry to you; bend low and hear my whispered plea. Be for me a great Rock of safety from my foes. ³Yes, you are my Rock and my fortress; honor your name by leading me out of this peril. ⁴Pull me from the trap my enemies have set for me. For you alone are strong enough. ⁵,⁶Into your hand I commit my spirit.

You have rescued me, O God who keeps his promises. I worship only you; how you hate all those who worship idols, those imitation gods. ⁷I am radiant with joy because of your mercy, for you have listened to my troubles and have seen the crisis in my soul. ⁸You have not handed me over to my enemy but have given me open ground in which to maneuver.

⁹,¹⁰O Lord, have mercy on me in my anguish. My eyes are red from weeping; my health is broken from sorrow. I am pining away with grief; my years are shortened, drained away because of sadness. My sins have sapped my strength; I stoop with sorrow and with shame. ¹¹I am scorned by all my enemies and even more by my neighbors and friends. They dread meeting me and look the other way when I go by. ¹²I am forgotten like a dead man, like a broken and discarded pot. ¹³I heard the lies about me, the slanders of my enemies. Everywhere I looked I was afraid, for they were plotting against my life.

¹⁴,¹⁵But I am trusting you, O Lord. I said, "You alone are my God; my times are in your hands. Rescue me from those who hunt me down relentlessly. ¹⁶Let your favor shine again upon your servant; save me just because you are so kind! ¹⁷Don't disgrace me, Lord, by not replying when I call to you for aid. But let the wicked be shamed by what they trust in; let them lie silently in their graves, ¹⁸their lying lips quieted at last—the lips of these arrogant men who are accusing honest men of evil deeds."

¹⁹Oh, how great is your goodness to those who publicly declare that you will rescue them. For you have stored up great blessings for those who trust and reverence you.

²⁰Hide your loved ones in the shelter of your presence, safe beneath your hand, safe from all conspiring men. ²¹Blessed is the Lord, for he has shown me that his never-failing love protects me like the walls of a fort! ²²I spoke too hastily when I said, "The Lord has deserted me," for you listened to my plea and answered me.

²³Oh, love the Lord, all of you who are his people; for the Lord protects those who are loyal to him, but harshly punishes all who haughtily reject him. ²⁴So cheer up! Take courage if you are depending on the Lord.

32 God Forgives

What happiness for those whose guilt has been forgiven! What joys when sins are covered over! What relief for those who have confessed their sins and God has cleared their record.

³There was a time when I wouldn't admit what a sinner I was. But my dishonesty made me miserable and filled my days with frustration. ⁴All day and all night your hand was heavy on me. My strength evaporated like water on a sunny day ⁵until I finally admitted all my sins to you and stopped trying to hide them. I said to myself, "I will confess them to the Lord." And you forgave me! All my guilt is gone.

⁶Now I say that each believer should confess his sins to God when he is aware of them, while there is time to be forgiven. Judgment will not touch him if he does.

⁷You are my hiding place from every storm of life; you even keep me from getting into trouble! You surround me with songs of victory. ⁸I will instruct you (says the Lord) and guide you along the best pathway for your life; I will advise you and watch your progress. ⁹Don't be like a senseless horse or mule that has to have a bit in its mouth to keep it in line!

¹⁰Many sorrows come to the wicked, but abiding love surrounds those who trust in the Lord. ¹¹So rejoice in him, all those who are his, and shout for joy, all those who try to obey him.

33 Who Is in Charge?

Let all the joys of the godly well up in praise to the Lord, for it is right to praise him. ²Play joyous melodies of praise upon the lyre and on the harp. ³Compose new songs of praise to him, accompanied skillfully on the harp; sing joyfully.

⁴For all God's words are right, and everything he does is worthy of our trust. ⁵He loves whatever is just and good; the earth is filled with his tender love. ⁶He merely spoke, and the heavens were formed and all the galaxies of stars. ⁷He made the oceans, pouring them into his vast reservoirs.

⁸Let everyone in all the world—men, women and children—fear the Lord and stand in awe of him. ⁹For when he but spoke, the world began! It appeared at his command! ¹⁰And with a breath he can scatter the plans of all the nations who oppose him, ¹¹but his own plan stands forever. His intentions are the same for every generation.

¹²Blessed is the nation whose God is the Lord, whose people he has chosen as his own. ¹³⁻¹⁵The Lord gazes down upon mankind from heaven where he lives. He has made their hearts and closely watches everything they do.

¹⁶,¹⁷The best-equipped army cannot save a king—for great strength is not enough to save anyone. A war horse is a poor risk for winning victories—it is strong, but it cannot save.

¹⁸,¹⁹But the eyes of the Lord are watching over those who fear him, who rely upon his steady love. He will keep them from death even in times of famine! ²⁰We depend upon the Lord alone to save us. Only he can help us; he protects us like a shield. ²¹No wonder we are happy in the Lord! For we are trusting him. We trust his holy name. ²²Yes, Lord, let your constant love surround us, for our hopes are in you alone.

34 How to Trust God

I will praise the Lord no matter what happens. I will constantly speak of his glories and grace. ²I will boast of all his kindness to me. Let all who are discouraged take heart. ³Let us praise the Lord together and exalt his name.

⁴For I cried to him and he answered me! He freed me from all my fears. ⁵Others too were radiant at what he did for them. Theirs was no downcast look of rejection! ⁶This poor man cried to the Lord—and the Lord heard him and saved him out of his troubles. ⁷For the Angel of the Lord guards and rescues all who reverence him.

⁸Oh, put God to the test and see how kind he is! See for yourself the way his mercies shower down on all who trust in him. ⁹If you belong to the Lord, reverence him; for everyone who does this has everything he needs. ¹⁰Even strong young lions sometimes go hungry, but those of us who reverence the Lord will never lack any good thing.

¹¹Sons and daughters, come and listen and let me teach you the importance of trusting and fearing the Lord. ¹²Do you want a long, good life? ¹³Then watch your tongue! Keep your lips from lying. ¹⁴Turn from all known sin and spend your time in doing good. Try to live in peace with everyone; work hard at it.

¹⁵For the eyes of the Lord are intently watching all who live good lives, and he gives attention when they cry to him. ¹⁶But the Lord has made up his mind to wipe out even the memory of evil men from the earth. ¹⁷Yes, the Lord hears the good man when he calls to him for help and saves him out of all his troubles.

¹⁸The Lord is close to those whose hearts are breaking; he rescues those who are humbly sorry for their sins. ¹⁹The good man does not escape all troubles—he has them too. But the Lord helps him in each and every one. ²⁰Not one of his bones is broken.

²¹Calamity will surely overtake the wicked; heavy penalties are meted out to those who hate the good. ²²But as for those who serve the Lord, he will redeem them; everyone who takes refuge in him will be freely pardoned.

35 When People Aren't Fair

O Lord, fight those fighting me; declare war on them for their attacks on me. ²Put on your armor, take your shield and protect me by standing in front. ³Lift your spear in my defense, for my pursuers are getting very close. Let me hear you say that you will save me from them. ⁴Dishonor those who are trying to kill me. Turn them back and confuse them. ⁵Blow them away like chaff in the wind—wind sent by the Angel of the Lord. ⁶Make their path dark and slippery before them, with the Angel of the Lord pursuing them. ⁷For though I did them no wrong, yet they laid a trap for me and dug a pitfall in my path. ⁸Let them be overtaken by sudden ruin, caught in their own net and destroyed.

⁹But I will rejoice in the Lord. He shall rescue me! ¹⁰From the bottom of my heart praise rises to him. Where is his equal in all of heaven and earth? Who else protects the weak and helpless from

---

CONTENTMENT 34:9-10 "Those of us who reverence the Lord will never lack any good thing." At first, we may question the truth of this statement because we lack many "good" things. This is not a blanket promise that all Christians will be rich. Instead, this is David's observation of God's goodness—all those who call upon God in their need will be answered, sometimes in unexpected ways.

Remember, our deepest needs are spiritual. David was saying that to have God is to have all that one really needs. God is enough.

If you feel you don't have something you need, ask: (1) Is this truly a need? (2) Is this really good for me? (3) Is this the best time for me to have what I desire? Even if you answer yes to all three questions, God may allow you to go without to help you learn to depend on him more. We may need to learn that we need *him* more than those things. **To begin the series of devotionals on CONTENTMENT, turn to page 89.**

the strong, and the poor and needy from those who would rob them? ¹¹These evil men swear to a lie. They accuse me of things I have never even heard about. ¹²I do them good, but they return me harm. I am sinking down to death. ¹³When they were ill, I mourned before the Lord in sackcloth, asking him to make them well; I refused to eat; I prayed for them with utmost earnestness, but God did not listen. ¹⁴I went about sadly as though it were my mother, friend, or brother who was sick and nearing death. ¹⁵But now that I am in trouble they are glad; they come together in meetings filled with slander against me—I didn't even know some of those who were there. ¹⁶For they gather with the worthless fellows of the town and spend their time cursing me.

¹⁷Lord, how long will you stand there, doing nothing? Act now and rescue me, for I have but one life and these young lions are out to get it. ¹⁸Save me, and I will thank you publicly before the entire congregation, before the largest crowd I can find.

¹⁹Don't give victory to those who fight me without any reason! Don't let them rejoice at my fall—let them die. ²⁰They don't talk of peace and doing good, but of plots against innocent men who are minding their own business. ²¹They shout that they have seen *me* doing wrong! "Aha!" they say. "With our own eyes we saw him do it." ²²Lord, you know all about it. Don't stay silent! Don't desert me now!

²³Rise up, O Lord my God; vindicate me. ²⁴Declare me "not guilty," for you are just. Don't let my enemies rejoice over me in my troubles. ²⁵Don't let them say, "Aha! Our dearest wish against him will soon be fulfilled!" and, "At last we have him!" ²⁶Shame them; let these who boast against me and who rejoice at my troubles be themselves overcome by misfortune that strips them bare of everything they own. Bare them to dishonor. ²⁷But give great joy to all who wish me well. Let them shout with delight, "Great is the Lord who enjoys helping his child!" ²⁸And I will tell everyone how great and good you are; I will praise you all day long.

36 God's Goodness Is Great

Sin lurks deep in the hearts of the wicked, forever urging them on to evil deeds. They have no fear of God to hold them back. ²Instead, in their conceit, they think they can hide their evil deeds and not get caught. ³Everything they say is crooked and deceitful; they are no longer wise and good. ⁴They lie awake at night to hatch their evil plots instead of planning how to keep away from wrong.

⁵Your steadfast love, O Lord, is as great as all the heavens. Your faithfulness reaches beyond the clouds. ⁶Your justice is as solid as God's mountains. Your decisions are as full of wisdom as the oceans are with water. You are concerned for men and animals alike. ⁷How precious is your constant love, O God! All humanity takes refuge in the shadow of your wings. ⁸You feed them with blessings from your own table and let them drink from your rivers of delight.

⁹For you are the Fountain of life; our light is from your light. ¹⁰Pour out your unfailing love on those who know you! Never stop giving your blessings to those who long to do your will.

¹¹Don't let these proud men trample me. Don't let their wicked hands push me around. ¹²Look! They have fallen. They are thrown down and will not rise again.

37 Keep Doing Good

Never envy the wicked! ²Soon they fade away like grass and disappear. ³Trust in the Lord instead. Be kind and good to others; then you will live safely here in the land and prosper, feeding in safety.

⁴Be delighted with the Lord. Then he will give you all your heart's desires. ⁵Commit everything you do to the Lord. Trust him to help you do it, and he will. ⁶Your innocence will be clear to everyone. He will vindicate you with the blazing light of justice shining down as from the noonday sun.

⁷Rest in the Lord; wait patiently for him to act. Don't be envious of evil men who prosper.

⁸Stop your anger! Turn off your wrath. Don't fret and worry—it only leads to harm. ⁹For the wicked shall be destroyed, but those who trust the Lord shall be given every blessing. ¹⁰Only a little while and the wicked shall disappear. You will look for them in vain. ¹¹But all who humble themselves before the Lord shall be given every blessing and shall have wonderful peace.

¹²,¹³The Lord is laughing at those who plot against the godly, for he knows their judgment day is coming. ¹⁴Evil men take aim to slay the poor; they are ready to butcher those who do right. ¹⁵But their swords will be plunged into their own hearts, and all their weapons will be broken.

¹⁶It is better to have little and be godly than to own an evil man's wealth; ¹⁷for the strength of evil men shall be broken, but the Lord takes care of those he has forgiven.

¹⁸Day by day the Lord observes the good deeds done by godly men, and gives them eternal rewards. ¹⁹He cares for them when times are hard; even in famine, they will have enough. ²⁰But evil men shall perish. These enemies of God will wither like grass and disappear like smoke. ²¹Evil

Family Devotions

☐ DEVOTION 152
PATIENCE

Read Psalm 37:1-9

"Are we going to set up all the trees today?" asked Gary as his father drilled a hole into the trunk of a maple tree. "This will take forever."

"Making maple syrup does take a long time, and it's hard work," agreed Dad, "but it's worth the effort."

Gary helped his father until all the maple trees had buckets hanging from the pipes, ready to collect the sap that would drip out during the week.

Back in the house, Gary slumped into a chair. "What a lot of work," he said with a sigh. "Making maple syrup takes too long. Even after we collect the sap, we still have to boil it down, and that takes forever, too! I hate waiting for it," he grumbled.

"*Hmmmmm,*" murmured Dad thoughtfully. "Do you suppose God thinks and feels like that, too?"

Gary frowned. "God?" he asked. "I've never thought about what God thinks of maple syrup."

Dad smiled. "I wasn't talking about syrup," he said, "but it occurred to me that it sometimes takes us a long time to make some very small steps toward godliness. And God waits."

Mother nodded. "It's a slow process for lives to be 'boiled down,' like the sap," she agreed. "And after all the water, or negative things in our lives, is removed, it might look like there's very little left."

"God patiently waits for us to make those little steps," added Dad, "because when the result is quality, a little means a lot."

Patience Memory Verse

Now as for you, dear brothers who are waiting for the Lord's return, be patient, like a farmer who waits until the autumn for his precious harvest to ripen.
James 5:7

How About You?

Does it seem like you're making very slow progress in your Christian walk? Trust God to turn your life into quality "syrup," patiently making you more like him. N. E. K.

• For the next devotional, turn to page 551. • For the next devotional on *PATIENCE*, turn to page 645. • For notes on *PATIENCE*, see pages 35, 242, 329, and 502.

men borrow and "cannot pay it back"! But the good man returns what he owes with some extra besides. ²²Those blessed by the Lord shall inherit the earth, but those cursed by him shall die.

²³The steps of good men are directed by the Lord. He delights in each step they take. ²⁴If they fall it isn't fatal, for the Lord holds them with his hand.

²⁵I have been young and now I am old. And in all my years I have never seen the Lord forsake a man who loves him; nor have I seen the children of the godly go hungry. ²⁶Instead, the godly are able to be generous with their gifts and loans to others, and their children are a blessing.

²⁷So if you want an eternal home, leave your evil, low-down ways and live good lives. ²⁸For the Lord loves justice and fairness; he will never abandon his people. They will be kept safe forever; but all who love wickedness shall perish.

²⁹The godly shall be firmly planted in the land and live there forever. ³⁰,³¹The godly man is a good counselor because he is just and fair and knows right from wrong.

³²Evil men spy on the godly, waiting for an excuse to accuse them and then demanding their death. ³³But the Lord will not let these evil men succeed, nor let the godly be condemned when they are brought before the judge.

³⁴Don't be impatient for the Lord to act! Keep traveling steadily along his pathway and in due season he will honor you with every blessing, and you will see the wicked destroyed. ³⁵,³⁶I myself have seen it happen: a proud and evil man, towering like a cedar of Lebanon, but when I looked again, he was gone! I searched but could not find him! ³⁷But the good man—what a different story! For the good man—the blameless, the upright, the man of peace—he has a wonderful future ahead of him. For him there is a happy ending. ³⁸But evil men shall be destroyed, and their posterity shall be cut off.

³⁹The Lord saves the godly! He is their salvation and their refuge when trouble comes. ⁴⁰Because they trust in him, he helps them and delivers them from the plots of evil men.

38 Confessing Our Sin

O Lord, don't punish me while you are angry! ²Your arrows have struck deep; your blows are crushing me. ³,⁴Because of your anger, my body is sick, my health is broken beneath my sins. They are like a flood, higher than my head; they are a burden too heavy to bear. ⁵,⁶My wounds are festering and full of pus. Because of my sins, I am bent and racked with pain. My days are filled with anguish. ⁷My loins burn with inflammation, and my whole body is diseased. ⁸I am exhausted and crushed; I groan in despair.

⁹Lord, you know how I long for my health once more. You hear my every sigh. ¹⁰My heart beats wildly, my strength fails, and I am going blind. ¹¹My loved ones and friends stay away, fearing my disease. Even my own family stands at a distance.

¹²Meanwhile my enemies are trying to kill me. They plot my ruin and spend all their waking hours planning treachery. ¹³,¹⁴But I am deaf to all their threats; I am silent before them as a man who cannot speak. I have nothing to say. ¹⁵For I am waiting for you, O Lord my God. Come and protect me. ¹⁶Put an end to their arrogance, these who gloat when I am cast down!

¹⁷How constantly I find myself upon the verge of sin; this source of sorrow always stares me in the face. ¹⁸I confess my sins; I am sorry for what I have done. ¹⁹But my enemies persecute with vigor and continue to hate me—though I have done nothing against them to deserve it. ²⁰They repay me evil for good and hate me for standing for the right.

²¹Don't leave me, Lord; don't go away! ²²Come quickly! Help me, O my Savior.

39 So What's Important?

I said to myself, I'm going to quit complaining! I'll keep quiet, especially when the ungodly are around me. ²,³But as I stood there silently the turmoil within me grew to the bursting point. The more I mused, the hotter the fires inside. Then at last I spoke and pled with God: ⁴Lord, help me to realize how brief my time on earth will be. Help me to know that I am here for but a moment more. ⁵,⁶My life is no longer than my hand! My whole lifetime is but a moment to you. Proud man! Frail as breath! A shadow! And all his busy rushing ends in nothing. He heaps up riches for someone else to spend. ⁷And so, Lord, my only hope is in you.

⁸Save me from being overpowered by my sins, for even fools will mock me then.

⁹Lord, I am speechless before you. I will not open my mouth to speak one word of complaint, for my punishment is from you.

¹⁰Lord, don't hit me anymore—I am exhausted beneath your hand. ¹¹When you punish a man for his sins, he is destroyed, for he is as fragile as a moth-infested cloth; yes, man is frail as breath.

¹²Hear my prayer, O Lord; listen to my cry! Don't sit back, unmindful of my tears. For I am your guest. I am a traveler passing through the earth, as all my fathers were.

¹³Spare me, Lord! Let me recover and be filled with happiness again before my death.

40 Obeying by Waiting

I waited patiently for God to help me; then he listened and heard my cry. ²He lifted me out of the pit of despair, out from the bog and the

Family Devotions

☐ **DEVOTION 153**
PERSEVERANCE

Read Psalm 40:1-3

Tina's face was even gloomier than the falling rain as she sat gazing out the kitchen window. "I tried so hard to make the honor roll this time. I wanted you and Dad to be proud of me," she said as a tear escaped and trickled like a raindrop down her cheek.

"Dad and I are proud of you, Tina, even if you didn't make the honor roll. We know how hard you worked," replied her mother in a soothing tone. "Besides, you can try again next time."

"No, Mom, I'm through trying," declared Tina. "It's no use anyway."

Just then Billy, a neighbor boy, ran past the house. Tina and her mother gasped as Billy stumbled and fell. He landed on both knees in a mud puddle, but in a flash he was back on his feet. "I wonder why Billy got up so quickly," said Mom. "Why didn't he just stay there in that puddle awhile?"

Tina's eyes grew almost as round as the chocolate-chip cookies her mother had just set on the table. "Mom, why would he do that?" she exclaimed. "He'd get even more wet and dirty—and maybe even sick!"

"Well, you seem to be in a puddle, too, Tina," Mom pointed out, "but instead of jumping up to get out of it you plan to stay and wallow in it."

"Whatever do you mean, Mom?" asked Tina in surprise.

"Disappointment and discouragement lead to self-pity," said Mom, "and self-pity is very much like a mud puddle. You can lie in it and soak it up until you feel even more miserable and bogged down. Or, with God's help, you can jump right out of that puddle and keep on going."

Tina was thoughtful for a minute. "You're right, Mom," she said, munching on a warm, chewy cookie. "I'm going right upstairs to do my homework. Maybe I'll never make the honor roll, but with God's help, I'll at least do the very best I can."

Perseverance Memory Verse

Be strong and courageous and get to work. Don't be frightened by the size of the task, for the Lord my God is with you; he will not forsake you. He will see to it that everything is finished correctly.
1 Chronicles 28:20

How About You?

Do you keep trying even if you don't get an A or win a contest? Don't feel sorry for yourself and spend time in a pity puddle. Keep trying, and wait patiently for God to help you. He will! *J. L.*

• For the next devotional, turn to page 555. • For the next devotional on *PERSEVERANCE*, turn to page 691.
• For notes on *PERSEVERANCE*, see pages 326, 461, 503, 760, and 1174.

mire, and set my feet on a hard, firm path, and steadied me as I walked along. ³He has given me a new song to sing, of praises to our God. Now many will hear of the glorious things he did for me, and stand in awe before the Lord, and put their trust in him. ⁴Many blessings are given to those who trust the Lord and have no confidence in those who are proud or who trust in idols.

⁵O Lord my God, many and many a time you have done great miracles for us, and we are ever in your thoughts. Who else can do such glorious things? No one else can be compared with you. There isn't time to tell of all your wonderful deeds.

⁶It isn't sacrifices and offerings that you really want from your people. Burnt animals bring no special joy to your heart. But you have accepted the offer of my life-long service. ⁷Then I said, "See, I have come, just as all the prophets foretold. ⁸And I delight to do your will, my God, for your law is written upon my heart!"

⁹I have told everyone the good news that you forgive people's sins. I have not been timid about it, as you well know, O Lord. ¹⁰I have not kept this good news hidden in my heart, but have proclaimed your loving-kindness and truth to all the congregation.

¹¹O Lord, don't hold back your tender mercies from me! My only hope is in your love and faithfulness. ¹²Otherwise I perish, for problems far too big for me to solve are piled higher than my head. Meanwhile my sins, too many to count, have all caught up with me, and I am ashamed to look up. My heart quails within me.

¹³Please, Lord, rescue me! Quick! Come and help me! ¹⁴,¹⁵Confuse them! Turn them around and send them sprawling—all these who are trying to destroy me. Disgrace these scoffers with their utter failure!

¹⁶But may the joy of the Lord be given to everyone who loves him and his salvation. May they constantly exclaim, "How great God is!"

¹⁷I am poor and weak, yet the Lord is thinking about me right now! O my God, you are my helper. You are my Savior; come quickly, and save me. Please don't delay!

41 God: The Only True Friend

God blesses those who are kind to the poor. He helps them out of their troubles. ²He protects them and keeps them alive; he publicly honors them and destroys the power of their enemies. ³He nurses them when they are sick and soothes their pains and worries.

⁴"O Lord," I prayed, "be kind and heal me, for I have confessed my sins." ⁵But my enemies say, "May he soon die and be forgotten!" ⁶They act so friendly when they come to visit me while I am sick; but all the time they hate me and are glad that I am lying there upon my bed of pain. And when they leave, they laugh and mock. ⁷They whisper together about what they will do when I am dead. ⁸"It's fatal, whatever it is," they say. "He'll never get out of that bed!"

⁹Even my best friend has turned against me—a man I completely trusted; how often we ate together. ¹⁰Lord, don't you desert me! Be gracious, Lord, and make me well again so I can pay them back! ¹¹I know you are pleased with me because you haven't let my enemies triumph over me. ¹²You have preserved me because I was honest; you have admitted me forever to your presence.

¹³Bless the Lord, the God of Israel, who exists from everlasting ages past—and on into everlasting eternity ahead. Amen and amen!

42 Why Am I So Sad?

As the deer pants for water, so I long for you, O God. ²I thirst for God, the living God. Where can I find him to come and stand before him? ³Day and night I weep for his help, and all the while my enemies taunt me. "Where is this God of yours?" they scoff.

⁴,⁵Take courage, my soul! Do you remember those times (but how could you ever forget them!) when you led a great procession to the Temple on festival days, singing with joy, praising the Lord? Why then be downcast? Why be discouraged and sad? Hope in God! I shall yet praise him again. Yes, I shall again praise him for his help.

⁶Yet I am standing here depressed and gloomy, but I will meditate upon your kindness to this lovely land where the Jordan River flows and where Mount Hermon and Mount Mizar stand. ⁷All your waves and billows have gone over me, and floods of sorrow pour upon me like a thundering cataract.

⁸Yet day by day the Lord also pours out his steadfast love upon me, and through the night I sing his songs and pray to God who gives me life.

⁹"O God my Rock," I cry, "why have you forsaken me? Why must I suffer these attacks from my enemies?" ¹⁰Their taunts pierce me like a fatal wound; again and again they scoff, "Where is that God of yours?" ¹¹But, O my soul, don't be discouraged. Don't be upset. Expect God to act! For I know that I shall again have plenty of reason to praise him for all that he will do. He is my help! He is my God!

43 God Makes Me Smile Again

O God, defend me from the charges of these merciless, deceitful men. ²For you are God, my only place of refuge. Why have you tossed me aside? Why must I mourn at the oppression of my enemies?

³Oh, send out your light and your truth—let them lead me. Let them lead me to your Temple on your holy mountain, Zion. ⁴There I will go to the altar of God, my exceeding joy, and praise him with my harp. O God—my God! ⁵O my soul, why be so gloomy and discouraged? Trust in God! I shall again praise him for his wondrous help; he will make me smile again, *for he is my God!*

44 God Alone Can Save Us

O God, we have heard of the glorious miracles you did in the days of long ago. Our forefathers have told us how you drove the heathen nations from this land and gave it all to us, spreading Israel from one end of the country to the other. ³They did not conquer by their own strength and skill, but by your mighty power and because you smiled upon them and favored them.

⁴You are my King and my God. Decree victories for your people. ⁵For it is only by your power and through your name that we tread down our enemies; ⁶I do not trust my weapons. They could never save me. ⁷Only you can give us the victory over those who hate us.

⁸My constant boast is God. I can never thank you enough! ⁹And yet for a time, O Lord, you have tossed us aside in dishonor and have not helped us in our battles. ¹⁰You have actually fought against us and defeated us before our foes. Our enemies have invaded our land and pillaged the countryside. ¹¹You have treated us like sheep in a slaughter pen and scattered us among the nations. ¹²You sold us for a pittance. You valued us at nothing at all. ¹³The neighboring nations laugh and mock at us because of all the evil you have sent. ¹⁴You have made the word *Jew* a byword of contempt and shame among the nations, disliked by all. ¹⁵,¹⁶I am constantly despised, mocked, taunted, and cursed by my vengeful enemies.

¹⁷And all this has happened, Lord, despite our loyalty to you. We have not violated your covenant. ¹⁸Our hearts have not deserted you! We have not left your path by a single step. ¹⁹If we had, we could understand your punishing us in the barren wilderness and sending us into darkness and death. ²⁰If we had turned away from worshiping our God and were worshiping idols, ²¹would God not know it? Yes, he knows the secrets of every heart. ²²But that is not our case. For we are facing death threats constantly because of serving you! We are like sheep awaiting slaughter.

²³Waken! Rouse yourself! Don't sleep, O Lord! Are we cast off forever? ²⁴Why do you look the other way? Why do you ignore our sorrows and oppression? ²⁵We lie face downward in the dust. ²⁶Rise up, O Lord, and come and help us. Save us by your constant love.

45 The King's Wedding

My heart is overflowing with a beautiful thought! I will write a lovely poem to the King, for I am as full of words as the speediest writer pouring out his story.

²You are the fairest of all;
Your words are filled with grace;
God himself is blessing you forever.
³Arm yourself, O Mighty One,
So glorious, so majestic!
⁴And in your majesty
Go on to victory,
Defending truth, humility, and justice.
Go forth to awe-inspiring deeds!
⁵Your arrows are sharp
In your enemies' hearts;
They fall before you.
⁶Your throne, O God, endures forever.
Justice is your royal scepter.
⁷You love what is good
And hate what is wrong.
Therefore God, your God,
Has given you more gladness
Than anyone else.

⁸Your robes are perfumed with myrrh, aloes, and cassia. In your palaces of inlaid ivory, lovely music is being played for your enjoyment. ⁹Kings' daughters are among your concubines. Standing beside you is the queen, wearing jewelry of finest gold from Ophir.

¹⁰,¹¹"I advise you, O daughter, not to fret about your parents in your homeland far away. Your royal husband delights in your beauty. Reverence him, for he is your lord. ¹²The people of Tyre, the richest people of our day, will shower you with gifts and entreat your favors."

¹³The bride, a princess, waits within her chamber, robed in beautiful clothing woven with gold. ¹⁴Lovely she is, led beside her maids of honor to the king! ¹⁵What a joyful, glad procession as they enter in the palace gates! ¹⁶"Your sons will some day be kings like their father. They shall sit on thrones around the world!

TRUSTING GOD FOR GUIDANCE 43:3-4 The psalmist asked God to send his light and truth to guide him to the Temple where he would meet God. God's truth (see 1 John 2:27) provides the right path to follow, and God's light (see 1 John 1:5) provides the clear vision to follow it. If you feel surrounded by darkness and uncertainty, follow God's light and truth back to him. **To begin the series of devotionals on TRUSTING GOD FOR GUIDANCE, turn to page 27.**

¹⁷"I will cause your name to be honored in all generations; the nations of the earth will praise you forever."

46 God Is on Our Side

God is our refuge and strength, a tested help in times of trouble. ²And so we need not fear even if the world blows up and the mountains crumble into the sea. ³Let the oceans roar and foam; let the mountains tremble!

⁴There is a river of joy flowing through the city of our God—the sacred home of the God above all gods. ⁵God himself is living in that city; therefore it stands unmoved despite the turmoil everywhere. He will not delay his help. ⁶The nations rant and rave in anger—but when God speaks, the earth melts in submission and kingdoms totter into ruin.

⁷The Commander of the armies of heaven is here among us. He, the God of Jacob, has come to rescue us.

⁸Come, see the glorious things that our God does, how he brings ruin upon the world ⁹and causes wars to end throughout the earth, breaking and burning every weapon. ¹⁰"Stand silent! Know that I am God! I will be honored by every nation in the world!"

¹¹The Commander of the heavenly armies is here among *us!* He, the God of Jacob, has come to rescue *us!*

47 God Is the Great King

Come, everyone, and clap for joy! Shout triumphant praises to the Lord! ²For the Lord, the God above all gods, is awesome beyond words; he is the great King of all the earth. ³He subdues the nations before us ⁴and will personally select his choicest blessings for his Jewish people—the very best for those he loves.

⁵God has ascended with a mighty shout, with trumpets blaring. ⁶,⁷Sing out your praises to our God, our King. Yes, sing your highest praises to our King, the King of all the earth. Sing thoughtful praises! ⁸He reigns above the nations, sitting on his holy throne. ⁹The Gentile rulers of the world have joined with us in praising him—praising the God of Abraham—for the battle shields of all the armies of the world are his trophies. He is highly honored everywhere.

48 God Protects Jerusalem

How great is the Lord! How much we should praise him. He lives upon Mount Zion in Jerusalem. ²What a glorious sight! See Mount Zion rising north of the city high above the plains for all to see—Mount Zion, joy of all the earth, the residence of the great King.

³God himself is the defender of Jerusalem. ⁴The kings of the earth have arrived together to inspect the city. ⁵They marvel at the sight and hurry home again, ⁶afraid of what they have seen; they are filled with panic like a woman in travail! ⁷For God destroys the mightiest warships with a breath of wind. ⁸We have heard of the city's glory—the city of our God, the Commander of the armies of heaven. And now we see it for ourselves! God has established Jerusalem forever.

⁹Lord, here in your Temple we meditate upon your kindness and your love. ¹⁰Your name is known throughout the earth, O God. You are praised everywhere for the salvation you have scattered throughout the world. ¹¹O Jerusalem, rejoice! O people of Judah, rejoice! For God will see to it that you are finally treated fairly. ¹²Go, inspect the city! Walk around and count her many towers! ¹³Note her walls and tour her palaces so that you can tell your children.

¹⁴For this great God is our God forever and ever. He will be our guide until we die.

49 Money Can't Save You

Listen, everyone! High and low, rich and poor, all around the world—listen to my words, ³for they are wise and filled with insight.

⁴I will tell in song accompanied by harps the answer to one of life's most perplexing problems:

⁵*There is no need to fear when times of trouble come,* even though surrounded by enemies! ⁶They trust in their wealth and boast about how rich they are, ⁷yet not one of them, though rich as kings, can ransom his own brother from the penalty of sin! For God's forgiveness does not come that way. ⁸,⁹For a soul is far too precious to be ransomed by mere earthly wealth. There is not enough of it in all the earth to buy eternal life for just one soul, to keep it out of hell.

¹⁰Rich man! Proud man! Wise man! You must die like all the rest! You have no greater lease on life than foolish, stupid men. You must leave your wealth to others. ¹¹You name your estates

---

OVERCOMING FEAR **46:1-3** The fear of mountains or cities suddenly crumbling into the sea from a nuclear blast haunts many people today. But the psalmist says that even if the world ends, "We need not fear!" Even in the face of utter destruction, he expressed a quiet confidence in God's ability to save him. It seems impossible to face the end of the world without fear, but the Bible is clear—God is our refuge even in the face of total destruction. He is not merely a temporary retreat; he is our eternal refuge and can provide strength even in the face of global destruction. **To begin the series of devotionals on OVERCOMING FEAR, turn to page 13.**

Family Devotions

☐ **Devotion 154**

Trusting God for Guidance

Read Psalm 48

The Johnsons—Becky, Bob, Mom, and Dad—had spent the past few days with Grandpa and Grandma Johnson. They treasured the long talks, the jokes, and the delicious food. They hated to leave. It was going to be a sad good-bye, for it would be four years before they would meet again. In less than a week, the Johnsons were going to Peru as missionaries.

As they finally prepared to go home, fog settled in. "Oh, dear," moaned Mom, "I just knew we should have left earlier." Since they had brought several items to store in the grandparents' attic, she had driven the family car while Dad drove a truck they had borrowed. "John, how will I ever see the way home?" she murmured as she and the children got into the car.

"The fog lights on this truck will pierce through the mist pretty well, so I'll lead the way," said Dad. "Just follow me and keep your eyes on my taillights. I won't go very fast. Trust me."

Mom nervously gripped the steering wheel, but as the children prayed and sang, she gradually relaxed. It seemed like the trip home would never end, and it wasn't easy, either. When they got safely home, they thanked God for his protection.

"As I was driving, I couldn't help but think that God was using this fog to prepare us for Peru," said Dad. "We couldn't see very far ahead in the fog. Because we're going to an unfamiliar country, the future seems especially foggy to us. The people, customs, and language are unknown to us, and we don't know what's ahead, but God knows all about it. He'll take care of us."

"That's right," agreed Mom. "I had your taillights to guide me, and we have the Lord to guide us as we go to Peru. We can trust him."

Trusting God for Guidance
Memory Verse

I will instruct you (says the Lord) and guide you along the best pathway for your life;
I will advise you and watch your progress.
Psalm 32:8

How About You?

Does an unknown future upset you? Do you worry about a different school, an unfamiliar town, a new family or stepparent, or a new challenge awaiting you? God knows your fear and your future. Read his Word for instruction and encouragement. Pray to him for wisdom. He'll guide you because he knows the path that you should take. *J. H.*

• For the next devotional, turn to page 557. • For the next devotional on *Trusting God for Guidance*, turn to page 1031. • For notes on *Trusting God for Guidance*, see pages 522, 553, 614, 676, and 1056.

after yourselves as though your lands could be forever yours and you could live on them eternally. ¹²But man with all his pomp must die like any animal. ¹³Such is the folly of these men, though after they die they will be quoted as having great wisdom.

¹⁴Death is the shepherd of all mankind. And "in the morning" those who are evil will be the slaves of those who are good. For the power of their wealth is gone when they die, they cannot take it with them.

¹⁵But as for me, God will redeem my soul from the power of death, for he will receive me. ¹⁶So do not be dismayed when evil men grow rich and build their lovely homes. ¹⁷For when they die, they carry nothing with them! Their honors will not follow them. ¹⁸Though a man calls himself happy all through his life—and the world loudly applauds success— ¹⁹yet in the end he dies like everyone else and enters eternal darkness.

²⁰For man with all his pomp must die like any animal.

50 God Wants Our True Thanks

The mighty God, the Lord, has summoned all mankind from east to west!

²God's glory-light shines from the beautiful Temple on Mount Zion. ³He comes with the noise of thunder, surrounded by devastating fire; a great storm rages round about him. ⁴He has come to judge his people. To heaven and earth he shouts, ⁵"Gather together my own people who by their sacrifice upon my altar have promised to obey me." ⁶God will judge them with complete fairness, for all heaven declares that he is just.

⁷O my people, listen! For I am your God. Listen! Here are my charges against you: ⁸I have no complaint about the sacrifices you bring to my altar, for you bring them regularly. ⁹But it isn't sacrificial bullocks and goats that I really want from you. ¹⁰,¹¹For all the animals of field and forest are mine! The cattle on a thousand hills! And all the birds upon the mountains! ¹²If I were hungry, I would not mention it to you—for all the world is mine and everything in it. ¹³No, I don't need your sacrifices of flesh and blood. ¹⁴,¹⁵What I want from you is your true thanks; I want your promises fulfilled. *I want you to trust me in your times of trouble, so I can rescue you and you can give me glory.*

¹⁶But God says to evil men: Recite my laws no longer and stop claiming my promises, ¹⁷for you have refused my discipline, disregarding my laws. ¹⁸You see a thief and help him, and spend your time with evil and immoral men. ¹⁹You curse and lie, and vile language streams from your mouths. ²⁰You slander your own brother. ²¹I remained silent—you thought I didn't care—but now your time of punishment has come, and I list all the above charges against you. ²²This is the last chance for all of you who have forgotten God, before I tear you apart—and no one can help you then.

²³But true praise is a worthy sacrifice; this really honors me. Those who walk my paths will receive salvation from the Lord.

51 A Prayer of Forgiveness

Written after Nathan the prophet had come to inform David of God's judgment against him because of his adultery with Bathsheba, and his murder of Uriah, her husband.

O loving and kind God, have mercy. Have pity upon me and take away the awful stain of my transgressions. ²Oh, wash me, cleanse me from this guilt. Let me be pure again. ³For I admit my shameful deed—it haunts me day and night. ⁴It is against you and you alone I sinned and did this terrible thing. You saw it all, and your sentence against me is just. ⁵But I was born a sinner, yes, from the moment my mother conceived me. ⁶You deserve honesty from the heart; yes, utter sincerity and truthfulness. Oh, give me this wisdom.

⁷Sprinkle me with the cleansing blood and I shall be clean again. Wash me and I shall be whiter than snow. ⁸And after you have punished me, give me back my joy again. ⁹Don't keep looking at my sins—erase them from your sight. ¹⁰Create in me a new, clean heart, O God, filled with clean thoughts and right desires. ¹¹Don't toss me aside, banished forever from your presence. Don't take your Holy Spirit from me. ¹²Restore to me again the joy of your salvation, and make me willing to obey you. ¹³Then I will teach your ways to other sinners, and they—guilty like me—will repent and return to you. ¹⁴,¹⁵Don't sentence me to death. O my God, you alone can rescue me. Then I will sing of your forgiveness, for my lips will be unsealed—oh, how I will praise you.

¹⁶You don't want penance; if you did, how gladly I would do it! You aren't interested in offerings burned before you on the altar. ¹⁷It is a broken spirit you want—remorse and penitence. A broken and a contrite heart, O God, you will not ignore.

¹⁸And Lord, don't punish Israel for my sins—help your people and protect Jerusalem.

¹⁹And when my heart is right, then you will rejoice in the good that I do and in the bullocks I bring to sacrifice upon your altar.

52 God Punishes the Wicked

Written by David to protest against his enemy Doeg (1 Samuel 22), who later slaughtered eighty-five priests and their families.

Family Devotions

☐ **Devotion 155**
Faith in Action

Read Psalm 51:1-13

Faith in Action Memory Verse

In response to all he has done for us, let us outdo each other in being helpful and kind to each other and in doing good.
Hebrews 10:24

"Oh, look, Tracy—a bargain rack!" exclaimed Barbara. "I'm glad Mom said I could choose my own dress. Maybe I'll find something here."

"Be careful," warned her older sister. "Did you see this?" She pointed to some small lettering on a sign above the rack. "Slightly stained—greatly reduced in price. All sales final," she read. She looked at Barbara. "You'd better look them over good."

"I will," Barbara assured her. "Oh-h-h-h! This one is just what I want for the church banquet." But sure enough—there was a small spot right on the front of the skirt. "I'll wash it out," declared Barbara. "No big deal."

Barbara bought the dress, but after two washings, the spot remained. "Good thing I didn't pay much for it," she said with a groan.

Mom nodded. "It sure is," she agreed. Then she frowned. "I saw Sandy at the store today," she added. "She said you told her there'd be no room in our car for her to ride to the banquet. Why did you tell her that? We'll have plenty of room."

"But Linda's coming with me, and we don't really want Sandy to go with us," mumbled Barbara. "It's no big deal."

Mom sighed. "Like the spot in your new dress?" she asked. "That small spot greatly reduced the value of the dress. That can happen to a Christian's testimony, too."

"What do you mean?" asked Barbara.

"Maybe what you told Sandy was no big deal to you. You might consider it only a little lie—only a small stain," said Mom. "But when Sandy finds out you lied, your Christian testimony with her will be greatly reduced. Do you think this will help her want to become a Christian?"

Barbara hung her head. She knew Mom was right. "It's not too late to do something about it," added Mom. "Why not call Sandy and tell her she can ride along with us?" Barbara nodded and headed for the phone.

How About You?

Is there some sin—some stain in your life? Even if it seems very small to you, it can greatly affect your stand as a Christian in the eyes of others. You can't get that spot out yourself, but the blood of Jesus will wash it clean when you confess your sin to him. If you wronged someone else, be sure to make things right with that person, too. M. R. P.

• For the next devotional, turn to page 559.   • For the next devotional on *Faith in Action*, turn to page 919.
• For notes on *Faith in Action*, see pages 583, 846, 1068, and 1232.

You call yourself a *hero*, do you? You *boast* about this evil deed of yours against God's people. ²You are sharp as a tack in plotting your evil tricks. ³How you love wickedness—far more than good! And lying more than truth! ⁴You love to slander—you love to say anything that will do harm, O man with the lying tongue.

⁵But God will strike you down, pull you from your home, and drag you away from the land of the living. ⁶The followers of God will see it happen. They will watch in awe. Then they will laugh and say, ⁷"See what happens to those who despise God and trust in their wealth, and become ever more bold in their wickedness."

⁸But I am like a sheltered olive tree protected by the Lord himself. I trust in the mercy of God forever and ever. ⁹O Lord, I will praise you forever and ever for your punishment. And I will wait for your mercies—for everyone knows what a merciful God you are.

53 Sin Keeps Us from God

Only a fool would say to himself, "There is no God." And why does he say it? Because of his wicked heart, his dark and evil deeds. His life is corroded with sin.

²God looks down from heaven, searching among all mankind to see if there is a single one who does right and really seeks for God. ³But all have turned their backs on him; they are filthy with sin—corrupt and rotten through and through. Not one is good, not one! ⁴How can this be? Can't they understand anything? For they devour my people like bread and refuse to come to God. ⁵But soon unheard-of terror will fall on them. God will scatter the bones of these, your enemies. They are doomed, for God has rejected them.

⁶Oh, that God would come from Zion now and save Israel! Only when the Lord himself restores them can they ever be really happy again.

54 My Keeper

Written by David at the time the men of Ziph tried to betray him to Saul.

Come with great power, O God, and save me! Defend me with your might! ²Oh, listen to my prayer. ³For violent men have risen against me—ruthless men who care nothing for God are seeking my life.

⁴But God is my helper. He is a friend of mine! ⁵He will cause the evil deeds of my enemies to boomerang upon them. Do as you promised and put an end to these wicked men, O God. ⁶Gladly I bring my sacrifices to you; I will praise your name, O Lord, for it is good.

⁷God has rescued me from all my trouble, and triumphed over my enemies.

55 When Friends Hurt Us

Listen to my prayer, O God; don't hide yourself when I cry to you. ²Hear me, Lord! Listen to me! For I groan and weep beneath my burden of woe.

³My enemies shout against me and threaten me with death. They surround me with terror and plot to kill me. Their fury and hatred rise to engulf me. ⁴My heart is in anguish within me. Stark fear overpowers me. ⁵Trembling and horror overwhelm me. ⁶Oh, for wings like a dove, to fly away and rest! ⁷I would fly to the far-off deserts and stay there. ⁸I would flee to some refuge from all this storm.

⁹O Lord, make these enemies begin to quarrel among themselves—destroy them with their own violence and strife. ¹⁰Though they patrol their walls night and day against invaders, their real problem is internal—wickedness and dishonesty are entrenched in the heart of the city. ¹¹There is murder and robbery there, and cheating in the markets and wherever you look.

¹²It was not an enemy who taunted me—then I could have borne it; I could have hidden and escaped. ¹³But it was you, a man like myself, my companion and my friend. ¹⁴What fellowship we had, what wonderful discussions as we walked together to the Temple of the Lord on holy days.

¹⁵Let death seize them and cut them down in their prime, for there is sin in their homes, and they are polluted to the depths of their souls.

¹⁶But I will call upon the Lord to save me—and he will. ¹⁷I will pray morning, noon, and night, pleading aloud with God; and he will hear and answer. ¹⁸Though the tide of battle runs strongly against me, for so many are fighting me, yet he will rescue me. ¹⁹God himself—God from everlasting ages past—will answer them! For they refuse to fear him or even honor his commands.

²⁰This friend of mine betrayed me—I who was at peace with him. He broke his promises. ²¹His words were oily smooth, but in his heart was war. His words were sweet, but underneath were daggers.

²²Give your burdens to the Lord. He will carry them. He will not permit the godly to slip or fall. ²³He will send my enemies to the pit of destruction. Murderers and liars will not live out half their days. But I am trusting you to save me.

56 God Is on My Side

Lord, have mercy on me; all day long the enemy troops press in. So many are proud to fight against me; how they long to conquer me.

³,⁴But when I am afraid, I will put my confidence

Family Devotions

☐ DEVOTION 156
GIVING THANKS

Read Psalm 57

Being a teenager isn't fair, Missi thought moodily as she gazed unseeingly at the lashing rain. *You're treated like a kid, but expected to act like an adult!*

"It's raining! It's pouring," sang five-year-old Josie as she ran into the room. She slid to a stop beside Missi's chair. "I love rain. It makes puddles to wade in."

Missi shuddered. "I hate storms! You're a strange kid. You love storms and rain and snow and cold weather—and hot weather, too."

Mom laughed as she came into the room. "To Josie there is no such thing as *bad* weather," she agreed, "just different kinds of weather."

Josie wrinkled her brow. "Do you know the seasons, Missi?" Josie counted on her fingers. "There's spring and fall and winter and . . . uhhhh . . ."

"Summer," Missi filled in.

Mom sat down beside Missi. "There are different seasons in life, too," she said. "There's childhood and adolescence. Then before we know it, we are adults, parents, and even grandparents."

"And the teen years are the worst!" Missi exploded.

Mom shook her head. "No, honey," she said. "It's true there are stormy times in teen years, but people of every age experience storms."

"Is it going to storm?" Josie asked. "I'll get the candles." She ran from the room, and Missi gave a half smile.

Mom smiled, too. "Even storms have a purpose. For example, lightning puts nitrogen into the air to help plants grow," she said. "As we trust the Lord to teach us, he'll help us grow in all kinds of life's weather, too, Missi."

Giving Thanks Memory Verse

Is anyone among you suffering? He should keep on praying about it. And those who have reason to be thankful should continually be singing praises to the Lord.
James 5:13

How About You?

Are you going through some stormy times? Remember—you don't have to think of days as good or bad—just different. Make a list of things that are happening to you. Then thank God for everything. It'll help you grow. God will teach you something as you trust him through all the experiences he allows to come your way. B. W.

• For the next devotional, turn to page 561.   • For the next devotional on GIVING THANKS, turn to page 565.
• For notes on GIVING THANKS, see pages 582, 608, and 834.

in you. Yes, I will trust the promises of God. And since I am trusting him, what can mere man do to me? ⁵They are always twisting what I say. All their thoughts are how to harm me. ⁶They meet together to perfect their plans; they hide beside the trail, listening for my steps, waiting to kill me. ⁷They expect to get away with it. Don't let them, Lord. In anger cast them to the ground.

⁸You have seen me tossing and turning through the night. You have collected all my tears and preserved them in your bottle! You have recorded every one in your book.

⁹The very day I call for help, the tide of battle turns. My enemies flee! This one thing I *know: God is for me!* ¹⁰,¹¹I am trusting God—oh, praise his promises! I am not afraid of anything mere man can do to me! Yes, praise his promises. ¹²I will surely do what I have promised, Lord, and thank you for your help. ¹³For you have saved me from death and my feet from slipping, so that I can walk before the Lord in the land of the living.

57 Greater than Heaven

O God, have pity, for I am trusting you! I will hide beneath the shadow of your wings until this storm is past. ²I will cry to the God of heaven who does such wonders for me. ³He will send down help from heaven to save me because of his love and his faithfulness. He will rescue me from these liars who are so intent upon destroying me. ⁴I am surrounded by fierce lions—hotheads whose teeth are sharp as spears and arrows. Their tongues are like swords. ⁵Lord, be exalted above the highest heavens! Show your glory high above the earth. ⁶My enemies have set a trap for me. Frantic fear grips me. They have dug a pitfall in my path. But look! They themselves have fallen into it!

⁷O God, my heart is quiet and confident. No wonder I can sing your praises! ⁸Rouse yourself, my soul! Arise, O harp and lyre! Let us greet the dawn with song! ⁹I will thank you publicly throughout the land. I will sing your praises among the nations. ¹⁰Your kindness and love are as vast as the heavens. Your faithfulness is higher than the skies.

¹¹Yes, be exalted, O God, above the heavens. May your glory shine throughout the earth.

58 God Cares

Justice? You high and mighty politicians don't even know the meaning of the word! Fairness? Which of you has any left? Not one! All your dealings are crooked: you give "justice" in exchange for bribes. ³These men are born sinners, lying from their earliest words! ⁴,⁵They are poisonous as deadly snakes, cobras that close their ears to the most expert of charmers.

⁶O God, break off their fangs. Tear out the teeth of these young lions, Lord. ⁷Let them disappear like water into thirsty ground. Make their weapons useless in their hands. ⁸Let them be as snails that dissolve into slime and as those who die at birth, who never see the sun. ⁹God will sweep away both old and young. He will destroy them more quickly than a cooking pot can feel the blazing fire of thorns beneath it.

¹⁰The godly shall rejoice in the triumph of right; they shall walk the blood-stained fields of slaughtered, wicked men. ¹¹Then at last everyone will know that good is rewarded, and that there is a God who judges justly here on earth.

59 Safety in a Wicked World

Written by David at the time King Saul set guards at his home to capture and kill him. (1 Samuel 19:11)

O my God, save me from my enemies. Protect me from these who have come to destroy me. ²Preserve me from these criminals, these murderers. ³They lurk in ambush for my life. Strong men are out there waiting. And not, O Lord, because I've done them wrong. ⁴Yet they prepare to kill me. Lord, waken! See what is happening! Help me! ⁵(And O Jehovah, God of heaven's armies, God of Israel, arise and punish the heathen nations surrounding us.) Do not spare these evil, treacherous men. ⁶At evening they come to spy, slinking around like dogs that prowl the city. ⁷I hear them shouting insults and cursing God, for "No one will hear us," they think. ⁸Lord, laugh at them! (And scoff at these surrounding nations too.)

⁹O God my Strength! I will sing your praises, for you are my place of safety. ¹⁰My God is changeless in his love for me, and he will come and help me. He will let me see my wish come true upon my enemies. ¹¹Don't kill them—for my people soon forget such lessons—but stagger them with your power and bring them to their knees. Bring them to the dust, O Lord our shield. ¹²,¹³They are proud, cursing liars. Angrily destroy them. Wipe them out. (And let the nations find out, too, that God rules in Israel and will reign throughout the world.) ¹⁴,¹⁵Let these evil men slink back at evening and prowl the city all night before they are satisfied, howling like dogs and searching for food.

¹⁶But as for me, I will sing each morning about your power and mercy. For you have been my high tower of refuge, a place of safety in the day of my distress. ¹⁷O my Strength, to you I sing my praises; for you are my high tower of safety, my God of mercy.

FAMILY DEVOTIONS

☐ DEVOTION 157
PUTTING GOD FIRST

Read Psalm 63:1-7

Putting God First Memory Verse

In everything you do, put God first, and he will direct you and crown your efforts with success.
Proverbs 3:6

It was early when Alex woke up. He could tell because it was only a little bit light outside, and the sounds were early morning sounds, like birds and cars. Alex got out of bed and looked for his mother. He looked in the kitchen, but she wasn't there. She wasn't in the living room, either. Alex peeked into his mother's bedroom. She was sitting in her rocker with her Bible on her lap. Her eyes were shut, and he knew she was praying.

Alex wanted a hug, so he crawled into his mother's lap. "Good morning," said Mother, giving him a hug. "You're up early."

"Are you praying?" asked Alex.

"Yes," said Mother.

"What about?" asked Alex.

"Oh, nothing in particular," replied Mother. "I was just sitting with Jesus."

"Sitting with Jesus?" Alex didn't understand that.

Mother nodded. "Just now you came in and got on my lap because you wanted to be with me," she told him. "I'm glad you did because I love you, and I like to be with you, too. Well, sometimes I like to be with the Lord like that. Sometimes I like to sit with him, thinking about how good he is, talking with him a little, and simply enjoying him. I think he's glad I like to be with him."

"Can I sit with him, too?" asked Alex.

"Sure you can," Mother told him. "Think about him being here with us right now." Mother closed her eyes and rocked the chair. Alex closed his eyes, too, and thought about Jesus sitting with them. He liked sitting and rocking with his mom and Jesus.

How About You?
Do you have a friend you just like to be with? Someone with whom it doesn't really matter what you're doing, as long as you're together? That's part of loving someone. Jesus wants to be your best friend. Try just being with him—sit and talk with him, think about him, think about what he has done for you, or think about what the Bible says. He may whisper something to your heart when you are quiet before him. *M. K. N.*

• For the next devotional, turn to page 563. • For the next devotional on *PUTTING GOD FIRST,* turn to page 721.
• For notes on *PUTTING GOD FIRST,* see pages 397, 492, 644, 791, and 982.

60 Real Help Comes from God

Written by David at the time he was at war with Syria, with the outcome still uncertain; this was when Joab, captain of his forces, slaughtered twelve thousand men of Edom in the Valley of Salt.

O God, you have rejected us and broken our defenses; you have become angry and deserted us. Lord, restore us again to your favor. ²You have caused this nation to tremble in fear; you have torn it apart. Lord, heal it now, for it is shaken to its depths. ³You have been very hard on us and made us reel beneath your blows.

⁴,⁵But you have given us a banner to rally to; all who love truth will rally to it; then you can deliver your beloved people. Use your strong right arm to rescue us. ⁶,⁷God has promised to help us. He has vowed it by his holiness! No wonder I exult! "Shechem, Succoth, Gilead, Manasseh—still are mine!" he says. "Judah shall continue to produce kings, and Ephraim great warriors. ⁸Moab shall become my lowly servant, and Edom my slave. And I will shout in triumph over the Philistines."

⁹,¹⁰Who will bring me in triumph into Edom's strong cities? God will! He who cast us off! He who abandoned us to our foes! ¹¹Yes, Lord, help us against our enemies, for man's help is useless. ¹²With God's help we shall do mighty things, for he will trample down our foes.

61 God Always Hears Us

O God, listen to me! Hear my prayer! ²For wherever I am, though far away at the ends of the earth, I will cry to you for help. When my heart is faint and overwhelmed, lead me to the mighty, towering Rock of safety. ³For you are my refuge, a high tower where my enemies can never reach me. ⁴I shall live forever in your tabernacle; oh, to be safe beneath the shelter of your wings! ⁵For you have heard my vows, O God, to praise you every day, and you have given me the blessings you reserve for those who reverence your name.

⁶You will give me added years of life, as rich and full as those of many generations, all packed into one. ⁷And I shall live before the Lord forever. Oh, send your loving-kindness and truth to guard and watch over me, ⁸and I will praise your name continually, fulfilling my vow of praising you each day.

62 God's Control

I stand silently before the Lord, waiting for him to rescue me. For salvation comes from him alone. ²Yes, he alone is my Rock, my rescuer, defense and fortress. Why then should I be tense with fear when troubles come?

³,⁴But what is this? They pick on me at a time when my throne is tottering; they plot my death and use lies and deceit to try to force me from the throne. They are so friendly to my face while cursing in their hearts!

⁵But I stand silently before the Lord, waiting for him to rescue me. For salvation comes from him alone. ⁶Yes, he alone is my Rock, my rescuer, defense, and fortress—why then should I be tense with fear when troubles come?

⁷My protection and success come from God alone. He is my refuge, a Rock where no enemy can reach me. ⁸O my people, trust him all the time. Pour out your longings before him, for he can help! ⁹The greatest of men or the lowest—both alike are nothing in his sight. They weigh less than air on scales.

¹⁰Don't become rich by extortion and robbery; if your riches increase, don't be proud. ¹¹,¹²God has said it many times, that power belongs to him (and also, O Lord, steadfast love belongs to you). He rewards each one of us according to what our works deserve.

63 I Want to Be Near God

A Psalm of David when he was hiding in the wilderness of Judea.

O God, my God! How I search for you! How I thirst for you in this parched and weary land where there is no water. How I long to find you! ²How I wish I could go into your sanctuary to see your strength and glory, ³for your love and kindness are better to me than life itself. How I praise you! ⁴I will bless you as long as I live, lifting up my hands to you in prayer. ⁵At last I shall be fully satisfied; I will praise you with great joy.

⁶I lie awake at night thinking of you—⁷of how much you have helped me—and how I rejoice through the night beneath the protecting shadow of your wings. ⁸I follow close behind you, protected by your strong right arm. ⁹But those plotting to destroy me shall go down to the depths of hell. ¹⁰They are doomed to die by the sword, to become the food of jackals. ¹¹But I will rejoice in God. All who trust in him exult, while liars shall be silenced.

64 When People Make Traps

Lord, listen to my complaint: Oh, preserve my life from the conspiracy of these wicked men, these gangs of criminals. ³They cut me down with sharpened tongues; they aim their bitter words like arrows straight at my heart. ⁴They shoot from ambush at the innocent. Suddenly the deed is done, yet they are not afraid. ⁵They encourage each other to do evil. They meet in secret

FAMILY DEVOTIONS

☐ **DEVOTION 158**
GOING TO CHURCH

Read Psalm 66

"Why do you and your family always go to church?" Bobby's friend Adam asked him one day.

Bobby wasn't sure what his answer should be. "Because it's Sunday," he said finally.

Adam looked at him quizzically. "That's a stupid answer," he said. "That's like saying you go to school because it's Monday or Friday."

Bobby knew his answer had not been a good one. He thought about it as he headed for home. Why *did* he go to church? Was it because his parents had taken him there as a little baby, and he had never questioned going as he grew older? Or was it because it was part of their family life, and his parents made him go? He talked with his father about it when he got home.

"That's a question you need to answer for yourself," his father said. "I go to worship the Lord."

"Can't you worship him at home or out in the field?" asked Bobby. "Or some place other than church?"

Dad nodded. "Yes, you can worship the Lord any time and any place. But if you don't go to church, you'll miss the fellowship you need to have with other Christians. The Bible tells us that we should meet together with others who believe like we do."

Bobby thought about that. When the people of his church got together, it was actually a time to praise the Lord through singing and preaching. When the pastor brought the message, Bobby almost always got something new and special from it—something he probably couldn't learn from the Bible by himself. "I'm going down to talk with Adam again," he called to his parents. "I think I can give him the right answer now."

Going to Church Memory Verse

Let us not neglect our church meetings, as some people do, but encourage and warn each other, especially now that the day of his coming back again is drawing near.
Hebrews 10:25

How About You?

Do you attend church just out of habit? It's a good habit to have, but you should also go to worship the Lord, to sing praises to him, to hear his Word, and to fellowship with other Christians. *R. J.*

• For the next devotional, turn to page 565. • For the next devotional on GOING TO CHURCH, turn to page 1125.
• For notes on GOING TO CHURCH, see pages 770, 965, and 1002.

to set their traps. "He will never notice them here," they say. ⁶They keep a sharp lookout for opportunities of crime. They spend long hours with all their endless evil thoughts and plans.

⁷But God himself will shoot them down. Suddenly his arrow will pierce them. ⁸They will stagger backward, destroyed by those they spoke against. All who see it happening will scoff at them. ⁹Then everyone shall stand in awe and confess the greatness of the miracles of God; at last they will realize what amazing things he does. ¹⁰And the godly shall rejoice in the Lord, and trust and praise him.

65 Giving Thanks to God

O God in Zion, we wait before you in silent praise, and thus fulfill our vow. And because you answer prayer, all mankind will come to you with their requests. ³Though sins fill our hearts, you forgive them all. ⁴How greatly to be envied are those you have chosen to come and live with you within the holy tabernacle courts! What joys await us among all the good things there. ⁵With dread deeds and awesome power you will defend us from our enemies, O God who saves us. You are the only hope of all mankind throughout the world and far away upon the sea.

⁶He formed the mountains by his mighty strength. ⁷He quiets the raging oceans and all the world's clamor. ⁸In the farthest corners of the earth the glorious acts of God shall startle everyone. The dawn and sunset shout for joy! ⁹He waters the earth to make it fertile. The rivers of God will not run dry! He prepares the earth for his people and sends them rich harvests of grain. ¹⁰He waters the furrows with abundant rain. Showers soften the earth, melting the clods and causing seeds to sprout across the land. ¹¹,¹² Then he crowns it all with green, lush pastures in the wilderness; hillsides blossom with joy. ¹³The pastures are filled with flocks of sheep, and the valleys are carpeted with grain. All the world shouts with joy and sings.

66 We Are in God's Hand

Sing to the Lord, all the earth! ²Sing of his glorious name! Tell the world how wonderful he is.

³How awe-inspiring are your deeds, O God! How great your power! No wonder your enemies surrender! ⁴All the earth shall worship you and sing of your glories. ⁵Come, see the glorious things God has done. What marvelous miracles happen to his people! ⁶He made a dry road through the sea for them. They went across on foot. What excitement and joy there was that day!

⁷Because of his great power he rules forever. He watches every movement of the nations. O rebel lands, he will deflate your pride.

⁸Let everyone bless God and sing his praises; ⁹for he holds our lives in his hands, and he holds our feet to the path. ¹⁰You have purified us with fire, O Lord, like silver in a crucible. ¹¹You captured us in your net and laid great burdens on our backs. ¹²You sent troops to ride across our broken bodies. We went through fire and flood. But in the end, you brought us into wealth and great abundance.

¹³Now I have come to your Temple with burnt offerings to pay my vows. ¹⁴For when I was in trouble, I promised you many offerings. ¹⁵That is why I am bringing you these fat male goats, rams, and calves. The smoke of their sacrifice shall rise before you.

¹⁶Come and hear, all of you who reverence the Lord, and I will tell you what he did for me: ¹⁷For I cried to him for help with praises ready on my tongue. ¹⁸ He would not have listened if I had not confessed my sins. ¹⁹But he listened! He heard my prayer! He paid attention to it!

²⁰Blessed be God, who didn't turn away when I was praying and didn't refuse me his kindness and love.

67 A Missionary Psalm

O God, in mercy bless us; let your face beam with joy as you look down at us.

²Send us around the world with the news of your saving power and your eternal plan for all mankind. ³How everyone throughout the earth will praise the Lord! ⁴How glad the nations will be, singing for joy because you are their King and will give true justice to their people! ⁵Praise God, O world! May all the peoples of the earth give thanks to you. ⁶,⁷For the earth has yielded abundant harvests. God, even our own God, will bless us. And peoples from remotest lands will worship him.

68 The Great Provider

Arise, O God, and scatter all your enemies! Chase them away! ²Drive them off like smoke before the wind; melt them like wax in fire! So let the wicked perish at the presence of God.

³But may the godly man exult. May he rejoice and be merry. ⁴Sing praises to the Lord! Raise your voice in song to him who rides upon the clouds! Jehovah is his name—oh, rejoice in his presence. ⁵He is a father to the fatherless; he gives justice to the widows, for he is holy. ⁶He gives families to the lonely, and releases prisoners from jail, singing with joy! But for rebels there is famine and distress.

⁷O God, when you led your people through the

FAMILY DEVOTIONS

☐ **DEVOTION 159**
GIVING THANKS

Read Psalm 68:4-10, 19-20

Giving Thanks
Memory Verse

Is anyone among you suffering? He should keep on praying about it. And those who have reason to be thankful should continually be singing praises to the Lord.
James 5:13

"Is that you, Dave?" called Brad's mother.

"Naw, it's just me," Brad called from the hall.

"I thought it might be your dad. He's gone to apply for a job." Mrs. Nelson smiled at her son.

"Won't do any good. He applied for a hundred already," Brad mumbled.

"Sooner or later he'll be sure to find one," Mom replied positively.

"Probably later, much later," Brad answered. Then he blurted out, "Why doesn't God give Dad a job? We're God's children. I thought he took care of his children."

Mom nodded. "He does. The bills are paid. We still have our home. We have each other. There may not be money for extras like summer camp, Brad, but God has given us many benefits."

"I can't see—" Brad stopped as Dad burst in.

"I got it! I got the job! The pay is good, and the benefits are great!"

"What are benefits?" Brad questioned.

"You might call them added blessings," Dad explained. "I mean things like health insurance, a retirement plan, paid holidays, and sick leave."

"What did you mean when you said God has blessed us with many benefits, Mom?" Brad looked puzzled.

"I was talking about health, love, joy, eternal life, the promise that he will supply all our needs—things like that," she explained. "Every day he gives us benefits."

How About You?
Are you so busy looking at what you do *not* have that you forget to be thankful for what God has given you? Every day we receive benefits (added blessings) from the Lord. You may not always have as much money as you want, but there are many things more important than money. Right now make a list of at least five benefits God has given to you. *B. W.*

• For the next devotional, turn to page 567. • For the next devotional on GIVING THANKS, turn to page 609.
• For notes on GIVING THANKS, see pages 582, 608, and 834.

wilderness, ⁸the earth trembled and the heavens shook. Mount Sinai quailed before you—the God of Israel. ⁹,¹⁰You sent abundant rain upon your land, O God, to refresh it in its weariness! There your people lived, for you gave them this home when they were destitute.

¹¹⁻¹³The Lord speaks. The enemy flees. The women at home cry out the happy news: "The armies that came to destroy us have fled!" Now all the women of Israel are dividing the booty. See them sparkle with jewels of silver and gold, covered all over as wings cover doves! ¹⁴God scattered their enemies like snowflakes melting in the forests of Zalmon.

¹⁵,¹⁶O mighty mountains in Bashan! O splendid many-peaked ranges! Well may you look with envy at Mount Zion, the mount where God has chosen to live forever. ¹⁷Surrounded by unnumbered chariots, the Lord moves on from Mount Sinai and comes to his holy temple high upon Mount Zion. ¹⁸He ascends the heights, leading many captives in his train. He receives gifts for men, even those who once were rebels. God will live among us here.

¹⁹What a glorious Lord! He who daily bears our burdens also gives us our salvation.

²⁰He frees us! He rescues us from death. ²¹But he will crush his enemies, for they refuse to leave their guilty, stubborn ways. ²²The Lord says, "Come," to all his people's enemies; they are hiding on Mount Hermon's highest slopes and deep within the sea! ²³His people must destroy them. Cover your feet with their blood; dogs will eat them.

²⁴The procession of God my King moves onward to the sanctuary— ²⁵ singers in front, musicians behind, girls playing the timbrels in between. ²⁶Let all the people of Israel praise the Lord, who is Israel's fountain. ²⁷The little tribe of Benjamin leads the way. The princes and elders of Judah, and the princes of Zebulun and Naphtali are right behind. ²⁸Summon your might; display your strength, O God, for you have done such mighty things for us.

²⁹The kings of the earth are bringing their gifts to your temple in Jerusalem. ³⁰Rebuke our enemies, O Lord. Bring them—submissive, tax in hand. Scatter all who delight in war. ³¹Egypt will send gifts of precious metals. Ethiopia will stretch out her hands to God in adoration. ³²Sing to the Lord, O kingdoms of the earth—sing praises to the Lord, ³³to him who rides upon the ancient heavens, whose mighty voice thunders from the sky.

³⁴Power belongs to God! His majesty shines down on Israel; his strength is mighty in the heavens. ³⁵What awe we feel, kneeling here before him in the sanctuary. The God of Israel gives strength and mighty power to his people. Blessed be God!

69 A Sea of Trouble

Save me, O my God. The floods have risen. Deeper and deeper I sink in the mire; the waters rise around me. ³I have wept until I am exhausted; my throat is dry and hoarse; my eyes are swollen with weeping, waiting for my God to act. ⁴I cannot even count all those who hate me without cause. They are influential men, these who plot to kill me though I am innocent. They demand that I be punished for what I didn't do.

⁵O God, you know so well how stupid I am, and you know all my sins. ⁶O Lord God of the armies of heaven, don't let me be a stumbling block to those who trust in you. O God of Israel, don't let me cause them to be confused, ⁷though I am mocked and cursed and shamed for your sake. ⁸Even my own brothers pretend they don't know me! ⁹My zeal for God and his work burns hot within me. And because I advocate your cause, your enemies insult me even as they insult you. ¹⁰How they scoff and mock me when I mourn and fast before the Lord! ¹¹How they talk about me when I wear sackcloth to show my humiliation and sorrow for my sins! ¹²I am the talk of the town and the song of the drunkards. ¹³But I keep right on praying to you, Lord. For now is the time—you are bending down to hear! You are ready with a plentiful supply of love and kindness. Now answer my prayer and rescue me as you promised. ¹⁴Pull me out of this mire. Don't let me sink in. Rescue me from those who hate me, and from these deep waters I am in.

¹⁵Don't let the floods overwhelm me or the ocean swallow me; save me from the pit that threatens me. ¹⁶O Jehovah, answer my prayers, for your loving-kindness is wonderful; your mercy is so plentiful, so tender and so kind. ¹⁷Don't hide from me, for I am in deep trouble. Quick! Come and save me. ¹⁸Come, Lord, and rescue me. Ransom me from all my enemies. ¹⁹You know how they talk about me, and how they so shamefully dishonor me. You see them all and know what each has said.

²⁰Their contempt has broken my heart; my spirit is heavy within me. If even one would show some pity, if even one would comfort me! ²¹For food they gave me gall; for my awful thirst they offered vinegar. ²²Let their joys turn to ashes and their peace disappear; ²³let darkness, blindness, and great feebleness be theirs. ²⁴Pour out your fury upon them; consume them with the fierceness of your anger. ²⁵Let their homes be desolate and abandoned. ²⁶For they persecute the one you have smitten and scoff at the pain of the one you have pierced. ²⁷ Pile their sins high and do not overlook them. ²⁸Let these men be blotted from the list of the living; do not give them the joys of life with the righteous.

Family Devotions

☐ **DEVOTION 160**

STANDING FOR RIGHTEOUSNESS

Read Psalm 71:15-17

Standing for Righteousness Memory Verse

For the eyes of the Lord search back and forth across the whole earth, looking for people whose hearts are perfect toward him, so that he can show his great power in helping them.
2 Chronicles 16:9

How About You?
Do you tell your friends when you've bought something you really like? Do you also tell them about what the Lord has done for you? Or do you feel it's not necessary because they have plenty of opportunity to hear about him? Businesses often report that satisfied customers are their best advertisement. You need to take a stand for God and be "advertising" for him. H. M.

"It's so easy to decide to witness when you hear a message like we heard this morning," observed Dad as the Dixon family drove home from church. "But we so often forget all about it the next day. Let's each think of one person to whom we could witness this week."

Tom hesitated. "Well, I can see why we need to go to countries where people don't know about Jesus—I might do that some day. But doesn't everybody know about God here? Anybody who wants to know how to be saved can find out easily enough."

Dad was silent, then he pointed to a picture of a bicycle on a billboard at the side of the road. "Maybe you should get a Fly-Away bike," he said. "They look really great."

"No, I want a Speedster," Tom answered promptly, a little relieved that Dad was changing the subject.

"A Fly-Away would cost less," added Mom. "I saw a full-page ad in the paper last night."

Tom shook his head. "I've seen the ads and heard them on the radio, too. But Joel's big brother had a Speedster, and now Joel's got one. He says they'll outlast any other kind, and they roll better, too."

"So you'll take the word of a satisfied customer over the word of a salesman or an advertisement," observed Dad. He paused, then added, "We need to speak to others as 'satisfied customers' of the Lord."

Tom was startled. He hadn't thought of it like that before. "I think I'll witness to Joel this week," he said after a moment.

• For the next devotional, turn to page 569. • For the next devotional on *STANDING FOR RIGHTEOUSNESS*, turn to page 783. • For notes on *STANDING FOR RIGHTEOUSNESS*, see pages 62, 298, 371, 678, and 948.

29But rescue me, O God, from my poverty and pain. 30Then I will praise God with my singing! My thanks will be his praise—31that will please him more than sacrificing a bullock or an ox. 32The humble shall see their God at work for them. No wonder they will be so glad! All who seek for God shall live in joy. 33For Jehovah hears the cries of his needy ones and does not look the other way.

34Praise him, all heaven and earth! Praise him, all the seas and everything in them! 35For God will save Jerusalem; he rebuilds the cities of Judah. His people shall live in them and not be dispossessed. 36Their children shall inherit the land; all who love his name shall live there safely.

70 A Short Prayer for Help

Rescue me, O God! Lord, hurry to my aid! 2,3They are after my life and delight in hurting me. Confuse them! Shame them! Stop them! Don't let them keep on mocking me! 4But fill the followers of God with joy. Let those who love your salvation exclaim, "What a wonderful God he is!" 5But I am in deep trouble. Rush to my aid, for only you can help and save me. O Lord, don't delay.

71 Young or Old—God Helps

Lord, you are my refuge! Don't let me down! 2Save me from my enemies, for you are just! Rescue me! Bend down your ear and listen to my plea and save me. 3Be to me a great protecting Rock, where I am always welcome, safe from all attacks. For you have issued the order to save me. 4Rescue me, O God, from these unjust and cruel men. 5O Lord, you alone are my hope; I've trusted you from childhood. 6Yes, you have been with me from birth and have helped me constantly—no wonder I am always praising you! 7My success—at which so many stand amazed—is because you are my mighty protector. 8All day long I'll praise and honor you, O God, for all that you have done for me.

9And now, in my old age, don't set me aside. Don't forsake me now when my strength is failing. 10My enemies are whispering, 11"God has forsaken him! Now we can get him. There is no one to help him now!" 12O God, don't stay away! Come quickly! Help! 13Destroy them! Cover them with failure and disgrace—these enemies of mine.

14I will keep on expecting you to help me. I praise you more and more. 15I cannot count the times when you have faithfully rescued me from danger. I will tell everyone how good you are, and of your constant, daily care. 16I walk in the strength of the Lord God. I tell everyone that you alone are just and good. 17O God, you have helped me from my earliest childhood—and I have constantly testified to others of the wonderful things you do. 18And now that I am old and gray, don't forsake me. Give me time to tell this new generation (and their children too) about all your mighty miracles. 19Your power and goodness, Lord, reach to the highest heavens. You have done such wonderful things. Where is there another God like you? 20You have let me sink down deep in desperate problems. But you will bring me back to life again, up from the depths of the earth. 21You will give me greater honor than before and turn again and comfort me.

22I will praise you with music, telling of your faithfulness to all your promises, O Holy One of Israel. 23I will shout and sing your praises for redeeming me. 24I will talk to others all day long about your justice and your goodness. For all who tried to hurt me have been disgraced and dishonored.

72 The Perfect King

O God, help the king to judge as you would, and help his son to walk in godliness. 2Help him to give justice to your people, even to the poor. 3May the mountains and hills flourish in prosperity because of his good reign. 4Help him to defend the poor and needy and to crush their oppressors. 5May the poor and needy revere you constantly, as long as sun and moon continue in the skies! Yes, forever!

6May the reign of this son of mine be as gentle and fruitful as the springtime rains upon the grass—like showers that water the earth! 7May all good men flourish in his reign with abundance of peace to the end of time.

8Let him reign from sea to sea and from the Euphrates River to the ends of the earth. 9The desert nomads shall bow before him; his enemies shall fall face downward in the dust. 10Kings along the Mediterranean coast—the kings of Tarshish and the islands—and those from Sheba and from Seba—all will bring their gifts. 11Yes, kings from everywhere! All will bow before him! All will serve him!

12He will take care of the helpless and poor when they cry to him; for they have no one else to defend them. 13He feels pity for the weak and needy and will rescue them. 14He will save them from oppression and from violence, for their lives are precious to him.

15And he shall live; and to him will be given the gold of Sheba, and there will be constant praise for him. His people will bless him all day long. 16Bless us with abundant crops throughout the

Family Devotions

☐ *Devotion 161*

Showing Compassion

Read Psalm 71:18-24

As soon as Sunday school was dismissed, Marty groaned, "Who wants to go to the nursing home? What have I got in common with those old folks?"

Natalie added, "Mrs. Kendall is the best Sunday school teacher we have ever had. But visiting a nursing home is a bum idea!"

The next Saturday afternoon, eight fifth graders met at the church. "After we sing and read the Scripture, go around and introduce yourself," Mrs. Kendall instructed.

"What will we say to them?" Natalie asked.

Mrs. Kendall smiled. "You probably won't have to say much. Your main job will be listening."

Two hours later the boys and girls again piled into Mrs. Kendall's van. "That Mr. Wilson is sharp. He used to be the mayor," Marty said. "He offered to help me with my theme on the history of our town!"

"Did you know that Mr. Rowland was once the foreman of the Flying W Ranch?" asked Adam. "He told me how the Lord saved him when he was lost in a blizzard!"

"And Mrs. Baker is going to teach me how to crochet," Natalie said. "Next time we come, I need to bring—." Natalie stopped, then asked, "We are going to come again, aren't we, Mrs. Kendall?"

Mrs. Kendall smiled as she started the van. "I'll leave that decision to you. Everyone that wants to come again say *aye*." And a chorus of *ayes* filled the air.

Showing Compassion Memory Verse

What a wonderful God we have—he is the Father of our Lord Jesus Christ, the source of every mercy, and the one who so wonderfully comforts and strengthens us in our hardships and trials.
2 Corinthians 1:3

How About You?

Have you shunned older people because you didn't know how to talk to them? Many senior citizens need someone to listen to them. And you need to hear what they have to say. Plan to spend at least ten minutes today visiting with an elderly person. It will help you both. B. W.

• For the next devotional, turn to page 571.   • For the next devotional on Showing Compassion, turn to page 629.
• For notes on Showing Compassion, see pages 206, 506, 515, 710, and 934.

land, even on the highland plains; may there be fruit like that of Lebanon; may the cities be as full of people as the fields are of grass. [17]His name will be honored forever; it will continue as the sun; and all will be blessed in him; all nations will praise him.

[18]Blessed be Jehovah God, the God of Israel, who only does wonderful things! [19]Blessed be his glorious name forever! Let the whole earth be filled with his glory. Amen and amen!

[20](This ends the psalms of David, son of Jesse.)

73 Why Are Wicked People Rich?

How good God is to Israel—to those whose hearts are pure. [2]But as for me, I came *so* close to the edge of the cliff! My feet were slipping and I was almost gone. [3]For I was envious of the prosperity of the proud and wicked. [4]Yes, all through life their road is smooth! They grow sleek and fat. [5]They aren't always in trouble and plagued with problems like everyone else, [6]so their pride sparkles like a jeweled necklace, and their clothing is woven of cruelty! [7]These fat cats have everything their hearts could ever wish for! [8]They scoff at God and threaten his people. How proudly they speak! [9]They boast against the very heavens, and their words strut through the earth.

[10]And so God's people are dismayed and confused and drink it all in. [11]"Does God realize what is going on?" they ask. [12]"Look at these men of arrogance; they never have to lift a finger—theirs is a life of ease; and all the time their riches multiply."

[13]Have I been wasting my time? Why take the trouble to be pure? [14]All I get out of it is trouble and woe—every day and all day long! [15]If I had really said that, I would have been a traitor to your people. [16]Yet it is so hard to explain it—this prosperity of those who hate the Lord. [17]Then one day I went into God's sanctuary to meditate and thought about the future of these evil men. [18]What a slippery path they are on—suddenly God will send them sliding over the edge of the cliff and down to their destruction: [19]an instant end to all their happiness, an eternity of terror. [20]Their present life is only a dream! They will awaken to the truth as one awakens from a dream of things that never really were!

[21]When I saw this, what turmoil filled my heart! [22]I saw myself so stupid and so ignorant; I must seem like an animal to you, O God. [23]But even so, you love me! You are holding my right hand! [24]You will keep on guiding me all my life with your wisdom and counsel, and afterwards receive me into the glories of heaven! [25]Whom have I in heaven but you? And I desire no one on earth as much as you! [26]My health fails; my spirits droop, yet God remains! He is the strength of my heart; he is mine forever!

[27]But those refusing to worship God will perish, for he destroys those serving other gods.

[28]But as for me, I get as close to him as I can! I have chosen him, and I will tell everyone about the wonderful ways he rescues me.

74 Recall Your Promises, O Lord

O God, why have you cast us away forever? Why is your anger hot against us—the sheep of your own pasture? [2]Remember that we are your people—the ones you chose in ancient times from slavery and made the choicest of your possessions. You chose Jerusalem as your home on earth!

[3]Walk through the awful ruins of the city and see what the enemy has done to your sanctuary. [4]There they shouted their battle cry and erected their idols to flaunt their victory. [5,6]Everything lies in shambles like a forest chopped to the ground. They came with their axes and sledgehammers and smashed and chopped the carved paneling; [7]they set the sanctuary on fire, and razed it to the ground—your sanctuary, Lord. [8]"Let's wipe out every trace of God," they said, and went through the entire country burning down the assembly places where we worshiped you.

[9,10]There is nothing left to show that we are your people. The prophets are gone, and who can say when it all will end? How long, O God, will you allow our enemies to dishonor your name? Will you let them get away with this forever? [11]Why do you delay? Why hold back your power? Unleash your fist and give them a final blow.

[12]God is my King from ages past; you have been actively helping me everywhere throughout the land. [13,14]You divided the Red Sea with your strength; you crushed the sea-god's heads! You gave him to the desert tribes to eat! [15]At your command the springs burst forth to give your people water; and then you dried a path for them across the ever-flowing Jordan. [16]Day and night alike belong to you; you made the starlight and the sun. [17]All nature is within your hands; you make the summer and the winter too. [18]Lord, see how these enemies scoff at you. O Jehovah, an arrogant nation has blasphemed your name.

[19]O Lord, save me! Protect your turtledove from the hawks. Save your beloved people from these beasts. [20]Remember your promise! For the land is full of darkness and cruel men. [21]O Lord, don't let your downtrodden people be constantly insulted. Give cause for these poor and needy ones to praise your name! [22]Arise, O God, and state your case against our enemies. Remember the insults these rebels have hurled against you all day

FAMILY DEVOTIONS

☐ DEVOTION 162
OPTIMISM

Read Psalm 78:17-22

"Oh no! It looks like rain," Ben exclaimed, looking anxiously up at the sky one Saturday morning.

"It surely does," Dad agreed. "I think we'd better postpone our picnic until next week."

Ben was most unhappy about the delay. As the raindrops began to fall, his eyebrows drew together in a frown. And when the rain poured down, he grew downright grumpy. "My whole day is spoiled," he complained over and over.

"Shhhhh. Listen." His sister Becky held up her finger. A clear, pure song came from a treetop outside. A robin was singing in the rain.

"Well, let the dumb bird sing. My day is ruined," Ben grumped. He knew grumbling didn't please God, but he was so disappointed!

"Why don't you get out one of your games, Ben? We may as well have some fun in spite of the rain," suggested Dad.

Ben grudgingly went to get a game, and soon he and Becky and Dad and Mom were all busy playing and laughing. The time flew by, and Ben forgot all about the rain spoiling his fun. Suddenly Dad looked up at the clock. "Can you believe it's nearly dinnertime?" he asked.

"We'll have a picnic right here on the floor," said Mom decisively. "Becky and I will get things ready, and you guys can clean up."

When the food was brought in, they all sat on a blanket on the floor while they ate. "This is fun!" declared Ben. "The whole day was so much fun I forgot about the rain. That robin had the right idea about singin' in the rain. I had as much fun as if I had gone on a picnic. I'm sorry I grumbled."

Dad put his arm around Ben. "You've got the right idea, Son," he said. "That robin was a good example for us. There's always cause to sing, even when it rains."

Optimism Memory Verse

Fix your thoughts on what is true and good and right. Think about things that are pure and lovely, and dwell on the fine, good things in others. Think about all you can praise God for and be glad about.
Philippians 4:8

How About You?
Do you grumble when it rains in your life—when things don't go your way? There are plenty of reasons to be happy and sing in spite of rain or other disappointments. And best of all, you please God by being cheerful even when you're disappointed. *C. Y.*

• For the next devotional, turn to page 575. • For the next devotional on OPTIMISM, turn to page 707. • For notes on OPTIMISM, see pages 143, 536, 677, and 940.

long. ²³ Don't overlook the cursing of these enemies of yours; it grows louder and louder.

75 Wicked People Will Be Judged

How we thank you, Lord! Your mighty miracles give proof that you care.

²"Yes," the Lord replies, "and when I am ready, I will punish the wicked! ³Though the earth shakes and all its people live in turmoil, yet its pillars are firm, for I have set them in place!"

⁴I warned the proud to cease their arrogance! I told the wicked to lower their insolent gaze ⁵and to stop being stubborn and proud. ⁶,⁷For promotion and power come from nowhere on earth, but only from God. He promotes one and deposes another. ⁸In Jehovah's hand there is a cup of pale and sparkling wine. It is his judgment, poured out upon the wicked of the earth. They must drain that cup to the dregs.

⁹But as for me, I shall forever declare the praises of the God of Jacob. ¹⁰"I will cut off the strength of evil men," says the Lord, "and increase the power of good men in their place."

76 God Is Great

God's reputation is very great in Judah and in Israel. ²His home is in Jerusalem. He lives upon Mount Zion. ³There he breaks the weapons of our enemies.

⁴The everlasting mountains cannot compare with you in glory! ⁵The mightiest of our enemies are conquered. They lie before us in the sleep of death; not one can lift a hand against us. ⁶When you rebuked them, God of Jacob, steeds and riders fell. ⁷ No wonder you are greatly feared! Who can stand before an angry God? ⁸You pronounce sentence on them from heaven; the earth trembles and stands silently before you. ⁹You stand up to punish the evil-doers and to defend the meek of the earth. ¹⁰Man's futile wrath will bring you glory. You will use it as an ornament!

¹¹Fulfill all your vows that you have made to Jehovah your God. Let everyone bring him presents. He should be reverenced and feared, ¹²for he cuts down princes and does awesome things to the kings of the earth.

77 God Helps in Hard Times

I cry to the Lord; I call and call to him. Oh, that he would listen. ²I am in deep trouble and I need his help so much. All night long I pray, lifting my hands to heaven, pleading. There can be no joy for me until he acts. ³I think of God and moan, overwhelmed with longing for his help. ⁴I cannot sleep until you act. I am too distressed even to pray!

⁵I keep thinking of the good old days of the past, long since ended. ⁶Then my nights were filled with joyous songs. I search my soul and meditate upon the difference now. ⁷Has the Lord rejected me forever? Will he never again be favorable? ⁸Is his loving-kindness gone forever? Has his promise failed? ⁹Has he forgotten to be kind to one so undeserving? Has he slammed the door in anger on his love? ¹⁰And I said: This is my fate, that the blessings of God have changed to hate. ¹¹I recall the many miracles he did for me so long ago. ¹²Those wonderful deeds are constantly in my thoughts. I cannot stop thinking about them.

¹³O God, your ways are holy. Where is there any other as mighty as you? ¹⁴You are the God of miracles and wonders! You still demonstrate your awesome power.

¹⁵You have redeemed us who are the sons of Jacob and of Joseph by your might. ¹⁶When the Red Sea saw you, how it feared! It trembled to its depths! ¹⁷ The clouds poured down their rain, the thunder rolled and crackled in the sky. Your lightning flashed. ¹⁸There was thunder in the whirlwind; the lightning lighted up the world! The earth trembled and shook.

¹⁹Your road led by a pathway through the sea—a pathway no one knew was there! ²⁰You led your people along that road like a flock of sheep, with Moses and Aaron as their shepherds.

78 History Teaches Us

O my people, listen to my teaching. Open your ears to what I am saying. ²,³For I will show you lessons from our history, stories handed down to us from former generations. ⁴I will reveal these truths to you so that you can describe these glorious deeds of Jehovah to your children and tell them about the mighty miracles he did. ⁵For he gave his laws to Israel and commanded our fathers to teach them to their children, ⁶so that they in turn could teach their children too. Thus his laws pass down from generation to generation. ⁷In this way each generation has been able to obey his laws and to set its hope anew on God and not forget his glorious miracles. ⁸Thus they did not need to be as their fathers were—stubborn, rebellious, unfaithful, refusing to give their hearts to God.

⁹The people of Ephraim, though fully armed, turned their backs and fled when the day of battle came ¹⁰because they didn't obey his laws. They refused to follow his ways. ¹¹,¹²And they forgot about the wonderful miracles God had done for them and for their fathers in Egypt. ¹³For he divided the sea before them and led them through! The water stood banked up along both sides of them! ¹⁴In the daytime he led them by a cloud, and at night by a pillar of fire. ¹⁵He split

open the rocks in the wilderness to give them plenty of water, as though gushing from a spring. ¹⁶Streams poured from the rock, flowing like a river!

¹⁷Yet they kept on with their rebellion, sinning against the God who is above all gods. ¹⁸They murmured and complained, demanding other food than God was giving them. ¹⁹,²⁰They even spoke against God himself. "Why can't he give us decent food as well as water?" they grumbled. ²¹Jehovah heard them and was angry; the fire of his wrath burned against Israel ²²because they didn't believe in God or trust in him to care for them, ²³even though he commanded the skies to open—he opened the windows of heaven— ²⁴and rained down manna for their food. He gave them bread from heaven! ²⁵They ate angels' food! He gave them all they could hold.

²⁶And he led forth the east wind and guided the south wind by his mighty power. ²⁷He rained down birds as thick as dust, clouds of them like sands along the shore! ²⁸He caused the birds to fall to the ground among the tents. ²⁹The people ate their fill. He gave them what they asked for. ³⁰But they had hardly finished eating, and the meat was yet in their mouths, ³¹when the anger of the Lord rose against them and killed the finest of Israel's young men. ³²Yet even so the people kept on sinning and refused to believe in miracles. ³³So he cut their lives short and gave them years of terror and disaster.

³⁴Then at last, when he had ruined them, they walked awhile behind him; how earnestly they turned around and followed him! ³⁵Then they remembered that God was their Rock—that their Savior was the God above all gods. ³⁶But it was only with their words they followed him, not with their hearts; ³⁷their hearts were far away. They did not keep their promises. ³⁸Yet he was merciful and forgave their sins and didn't destroy them all. Many and many a time he held back his anger. ³⁹For he remembered that they were merely mortal men, gone in a moment like a breath of wind.

⁴⁰Oh, how often they rebelled against him in those desert years and grieved his heart. ⁴¹Again and again they turned away and tempted God to kill them, and limited the Holy One of Israel from giving them his blessings. ⁴²They forgot his power and love and how he had rescued them from their enemies; ⁴³ they forgot the plagues he sent upon the Egyptians in Tanis—⁴⁴how he turned their rivers into blood so that no one could drink, ⁴⁵how he sent vast swarms of flies to fill the land, and how the frogs had covered all of Egypt! ⁴⁶He gave their crops to caterpillars. Their harvest was consumed by locusts. ⁴⁷He destroyed their grapevines and their sycamores with hail. ⁴⁸Their cattle died in the fields, mortally wounded by huge hailstones from heaven. Their sheep were killed by lightning. ⁴⁹He loosed on them the fierceness of his anger, sending sorrow and trouble. He dispatched against them a band of destroying angels. ⁵⁰He gave free course to his anger and did not spare the Egyptians' lives, but handed them over to plagues and sickness. ⁵¹Then he killed the eldest son in each Egyptian family—he who was the beginning of its strength and joy.

⁵²But he led forth his own people like a flock, guiding them safely through the wilderness. ⁵³He kept them safe, so they were not afraid. But the sea closed in upon their enemies and overwhelmed them. ⁵⁴He brought them to the border of his land of blessing, to this land of hills he made for them. ⁵⁵He drove out the nations occupying the land and gave each tribe of Israel its apportioned place as its home.

⁵⁶Yet though he did all this for them, they still rebelled against the God above all gods and refused to follow his commands. ⁵⁷They turned back from entering the Promised Land and disobeyed as their fathers had. Like a crooked arrow, they missed the target of God's will. ⁵⁸They made him angry by erecting idols and altars to other gods.

⁵⁹When God saw their deeds, his wrath was strong and he despised his people. ⁶⁰Then he abandoned his Tabernacle at Shiloh, where he had lived among mankind, ⁶¹and allowed his Ark to be captured; he surrendered his glory into enemy hands. ⁶²He caused his people to be butchered because his anger was intense. ⁶³Their young men were killed by fire, and their girls died before they were old enough to sing their wedding songs. ⁶⁴The priests were slaughtered, and their widows died before they could even begin their lament. ⁶⁵Then the Lord rose up as though awakening from sleep, and like a mighty man aroused by wine, ⁶⁶he routed his enemies; he drove them back and sent them to eternal shame. ⁶⁷But he rejected Joseph's family, the tribe of Ephraim, ⁶⁸and chose the tribe of Judah—and Mount Zion, which he loved. ⁶⁹There he built his towering temple, solid and enduring as the heavens and the earth. ⁷⁰He chose his servant David, taking him from feeding sheep ⁷¹,⁷²and from following the ewes with lambs; God presented David to his people as their shepherd, and he cared for them with a true heart and skillful hands.

79 Life Is Not Fair, but God Is

O God, your land has been conquered by the heathen nations. Your Temple is defiled, and Jerusalem is a heap of ruins. ²The bodies of your people lie exposed—food for birds and animals. ³The enemy has butchered the entire population of Jerusalem; blood has flowed like water. No one is left even to bury them. ⁴The nations all around us scoff. They heap contempt on us.

⁵O Jehovah, how long will you be angry with us? Forever? Will your jealousy burn till every hope is gone? ⁶Pour out your wrath upon the godless nations—not on us—on kingdoms that refuse to pray, that will not call upon your name! ⁷For they have destroyed your people Israel, invading every home. ⁸Oh, do not hold us guilty for our former sins! Let your tenderhearted mercies meet our needs, for we are brought low to the dust. ⁹Help us, God of our salvation! Help us for the honor of your name. Oh, save us and forgive our sins. ¹⁰Why should the heathen nations be allowed to scoff, "Where is their God?" Publicly avenge this slaughter of your people! ¹¹Listen to the sighing of the prisoners and those condemned to die. Demonstrate the greatness of your power by saving them. ¹²O Lord, take sevenfold vengeance on these nations scorning you.

¹³Then we your people, the sheep of your pasture, will thank you forever and forever, praising your greatness from generation to generation.

80 God Will Help Us Trust Him

O Shepherd of Israel who leads Israel like a flock; O God enthroned above the Guardian Angels, bend down your ear and listen as I plead. Display your power and radiant glory. ²Let Ephraim, Benjamin, and Manasseh see you rouse yourself and use your mighty power to rescue us.

³Turn us again to yourself, O God. Look down on us in joy and love; only then shall we be saved.

⁴O Jehovah, God of heaven's armies, how long will you be angry and reject our prayers? ⁵You have fed us with sorrow and tears ⁶and have made us the scorn of the neighboring nations. They laugh among themselves.

⁷Turn us again to yourself, O God of Hosts. Look down on us in joy and love; only then shall we be saved. ⁸You brought us from Egypt as though we were a tender vine and drove away the heathen from your land and planted us. ⁹You cleared the ground and tilled the soil, and we took root and filled the land. ¹⁰The mountains were covered with our shadow; we were like the mighty cedar trees, ¹¹covering the entire land from the Mediterranean Sea to the Euphrates River. ¹²But now you have broken down our walls, leaving us without protection. ¹³The boar from the forest roots around us, and the wild animals feed on us.

¹⁴Come back, we beg of you, O God of the armies of heaven, and bless us. Look down from heaven and see our plight and care for this your vine! ¹⁵Protect what you yourself have planted, this son you have raised for yourself. ¹⁶For we are chopped and burned by our enemies. May they perish at your frown. ¹⁷ Strengthen the man you love, the son of your choice, ¹⁸and we will never forsake you again. Revive us to trust in you.

¹⁹Turn us again to yourself, O God of the armies of heaven. Look down on us, your face aglow with joy and love—only then shall we be saved.

81 A Psalm for Special Times

The Lord makes us strong! Sing praises! Sing to Israel's God!

²Sing, accompanied by drums; pluck the sweet lyre and harp. ³Sound the trumpet! Come to the joyous celebrations at full moon, new moon, and all the other holidays. ⁴For God has given us these times of joy; they are scheduled in the laws of Israel. ⁵He gave them as reminders of his war against Egypt where we were slaves on foreign soil.

I heard an unknown voice that said, ⁶"Now I will relieve your shoulder of its burden; I will free your hands from their heavy tasks." ⁷He said, "You cried to me in trouble, and I saved you; I answered from Mount Sinai where the thunder hides. I tested your faith at Meribah, when you complained there was no water. ⁸Listen to me, O my people, while I give you stern warnings. O Israel, if you will only listen! ⁹*You must never worship any other god* nor ever have an idol in your home. ¹⁰For it was I, Jehovah your God, who brought you out of the land of Egypt. Only test me! Open your mouth wide and see if I won't fill it. You will receive every blessing you can use!

¹¹"But no, my people won't listen. Israel doesn't want me around. ¹²So I am letting them go their blind and stubborn way, living according to their own desires.

¹³"But oh, that my people would listen to me! Oh, that Israel would follow me, walking in my paths! ¹⁴How quickly then I would subdue her enemies! How soon my hands would be upon her foes! ¹⁵Those who hate the Lord would cringe before him; their desolation would last forever. ¹⁶But he would feed you with the choicest foods. He would satisfy you with honey for the taking."

82 God Will Judge

God stands up to open heaven's court. He pronounces judgment on the judges. ²How long will you judges refuse to listen to the evidence? How long will you shower special favors on the wicked? ³Give fair judgment to the poor

FAMILY DEVOTIONS

☐ DEVOTION 163
TRUSTING GOD FOR HELP

Read Psalm 86

David looked around at all the people lying on the beach. Many others were swimming in the ocean waters. It seemed that everyone was laughing and shouting and making noise of some kind. Suddenly a lifeguard jumped down from his high position and ran into the water. With quick strokes, he swam out into the deep water. In a few minutes a crowd gathered nearby and watched as the lifeguard rescued a drowning girl.

"Hey, Dad," David asked later, "how did the lifeguard know that girl was drowning? There was so much noise all around. I was standing right there, and I didn't hear her call for help."

"That's because your ears and eyes weren't tuned to hear or see that she was drowning," David's father replied.

"You mean lifeguards learn to hear and see those things?" the boy asked.

Dad nodded. "First they have to take a lifesaving course," he explained. "Once they are put on duty, they keep very alert so they can both see when someone is in trouble and hear his call for help."

David was quiet for a time. Finally he spoke. "Isn't there a verse in the Bible that tells us that God always hears us when we call?"

"Yes, there are several," replied Dad.

David began to think about some of the verses he had learned in church and Sunday school. "'When you call, the Lord will answer,'" he said aloud.

"That's one," Dad agreed. "Another one says, 'In my distress I screamed to the Lord for his help. And he heard me from heaven; my cry reached his ears.'"

On and on David and his father quoted verses that told about God's care and concern. David was glad that God was always tuned in and ready to hear him.

*Trusting God
for Help
Memory Verse*

God is our refuge and strength, a tested help in times of trouble.
Psalm 46:1

H o w   A b o u t   Y o u ?
Can you think of some verses that assure you that God is ready to help you when you call to him? See how many you can find in your Bible. Then don't forget to thank him for his love and care. *R. J.*

- For the next devotional, turn to page 577.   • For the next devotional on TRUSTING GOD FOR HELP, turn to page 605.
- For notes on TRUSTING GOD FOR HELP, see pages 240, 249, 464, 539, and 751.

man, the afflicted, the fatherless, the destitute. ⁴Rescue the poor and helpless from the grasp of evil men. ⁵But you are so foolish and so ignorant! Because you are in darkness, all the foundations of society are shaken to the core. ⁶I have called you all "gods" and "sons of the Most High." ⁷But in death you are mere men. You will fall as any prince—for all must die.

⁸Stand up, O God, and judge the earth. For all of it belongs to you. All nations are in your hands.

83 Tell the World God Is Good

O God, don't sit idly by, silent and inactive when we pray. Answer us! Deliver us!

²Don't you hear the tumult and commotion of your enemies? Don't you see what they are doing, these proud men who hate the Lord? ³They are full of craftiness and plot against your people, laying plans to slay your precious ones. ⁴"Come," they say, "and let us wipe out Israel as a nation—we will destroy the very memory of her existence." ⁵This was their unanimous decision at their summit conference—they signed a treaty to ally themselves against Almighty God— ⁶these Ishmaelites and Edomites and Moabites and Hagrites; ⁷people from the lands of Gebal, Ammon, Amalek, Philistia and Tyre; ⁸Assyria has joined them too, and is allied with the descendants of Lot.

⁹Do to them as once you did to Midian, or as you did to Sisera and Jabin at the river Kishon, ¹⁰and as you did to your enemies at Endor, whose decaying corpses fertilized the soil. ¹¹Make their mighty nobles die as Oreb did, and Zeeb; let all their princes die like Zebah and Zalmunna, ¹²who said, "Let us seize for our own use these pasturelands of God!"

¹³O my God, blow them away like dust; like chaff before the wind—¹⁴as a forest fire that roars across a mountain. ¹⁵Chase them with your fiery storms, tempests, and tornados. ¹⁶Utterly disgrace them until they recognize your power and name, O Lord. ¹⁷Make them failures in everything they do; let them be ashamed and terrified ¹⁸until they learn that you alone, Jehovah, are the God above all gods in supreme charge of all the earth.

84 Our Trust Delights God

How lovely is your Temple, O Lord of the armies of heaven.

²I long, yes, faint with longing to be able to enter your courtyard and come near to the Living God. ³Even the sparrows and swallows are welcome to come and nest among your altars and there have their young, O Lord of heaven's armies, my King and my God! ⁴How happy are those who can live in your Temple, singing your praises.

⁵Happy are those who are strong in the Lord, who want above all else to follow your steps. ⁶When they walk through the Valley of Weeping, it will become a place of springs where pools of blessing and refreshment collect after rains! ⁷They will grow constantly in strength, and each of them is invited to meet with the Lord in Zion.

⁸O Jehovah, God of the heavenly armies, hear my prayer! Listen, God of Israel. ⁹O God, our Defender and our Shield, have mercy on the one you have anointed as your king.

¹⁰A single day spent in your Temple is better than a thousand anywhere else! I would rather be a doorman of the Temple of my God than live in palaces of wickedness. ¹¹For Jehovah God is our Light and our Protector. He gives us grace and glory. No good thing will he withhold from those who walk along his paths.

¹²O Lord of the armies of heaven, blessed are those who trust in you.

85 Follow God: Find Peace

Lord, you have poured out amazing blessings on this land! You have restored the fortunes of Israel, ²and forgiven the sins of your people—yes, covered over each one, ³so that all your wrath, your blazing anger, is now ended.

⁴Now bring us back to loving you, O Lord, so that your anger will never need rise against us again. ⁵(Or will you be always angry—on and on to distant generations?) ⁶Oh, revive us! Then your people can rejoice in you again. ⁷Pour out your love and kindness on us, Lord, and grant us your salvation.

⁸I am listening carefully to all the Lord is saying—for he speaks peace to his people, his saints, if they will only stop their sinning. ⁹Surely his salvation is near to those who reverence him; our land will be filled with his glory.

¹⁰Mercy and truth have met together. Grim justice and peace have kissed! ¹¹Truth rises from the earth, and righteousness smiles down from heaven.

¹²Yes, the Lord pours down his blessings on the land, and it yields its bountiful crops. ¹³Justice goes before him to make a pathway for his steps.

86 There Is Only One True God

Bend down and hear my prayer, O Lord, and answer me, for I am deep in trouble.

²Protect me from death, for I try to follow all your laws. Save me, for I am serving you and trusting you. ³Be merciful, O Lord, for I am looking up to you in constant hope. ⁴Give me happiness,

Family Devotions

☐ **Devotion 164**
Confessing Sin

Read Psalm 89:14-18

Confessing Sin Memory Verse

But if we confess our sins to him, he can be depended on to forgive us and to cleanse us from every wrong. [And it is perfectly proper for God to do this for us because Christ died to wash away our sins.]
1 John 1:9

Oh, how Terry wished he had listened to his mother when she told him not to jump his bike over the ramp he had built with planks of wood. But jumping his bike was fun, so as soon as Mother's back was turned, Terry had done it again. The planks had flown up in his face as he hit the ramp, and then all he could remember was the pain!

"Mom, I'm so sorry," he cried after the doctor set the two broken bones in his arm. "I shouldn't have disobeyed." Terry's mother accepted his apology.

The next morning Terry felt down in the dumps. The pain in his arm had kept him awake much of the night. "I can't stand this pain," he complained to Mother. "My arm hurts so bad. I've prayed and prayed that God would take the pain away, but he doesn't. If he forgave me for disobeying, why doesn't he heal the pain?"

"Oh, Terry, God always is willing to forgive sin," explained Mother, "but he doesn't always take away the consequences of our sin. Because God is a God of justice, we usually have to face the consequences. I'm afraid your arm is a painful reminder of what it costs to disobey."

How About You?
Have you ever had to face the nasty consequences of sin? Perhaps you've had to take a zero on a test even though you confessed that you cheated. Or perhaps, like Terry, you've disobeyed your parents and suffered physical injury—even a permanent injury. God always forgives confessed sin, but he does not always remove the consequences of your sins! *R. P.*

- For the next devotional, turn to page 579.   • For the next devotional on *Confessing Sin,* turn to page 599.
- For notes on *Confessing Sin,* see pages 429, 479, 836, 881, and 1220.

O Lord, for I worship only you. ⁵O Lord, you are so good and kind, so ready to forgive, so full of mercy for all who ask your aid.

⁶Listen closely to my prayer, O God. Hear my urgent cry. ⁷I will call to you whenever trouble strikes, and you will help me.

⁸Where among the heathen gods is there a god like you? Where are their miracles? ⁹All the nations—and you made each one—will come and bow before you, Lord, and praise your great and holy name. ¹⁰For you are great and do great miracles. You alone are God.

¹¹Tell me where you want me to go and I will go there. May every fiber of my being unite in reverence to your name. ¹²With all my heart I will praise you. I will give glory to your name forever, ¹³for you love me so much! You are constantly so kind! You have rescued me from deepest hell.

¹⁴O God, proud and insolent men defy me; violent, godless men are trying to kill me. ¹⁵But you are merciful and gentle, Lord, slow in getting angry, full of constant loving-kindness and of truth; ¹⁶so look down in pity and grant strength to your servant and save me. ¹⁷Send me a sign of your favor. When those who hate me see it, they will lose face because you help and comfort me.

87 Jerusalem: A City God Loves

High on his holy mountain stands Jerusalem, the city of God, the city he loves more than any other!

³O city of God, what wondrous tales are told of you! ⁴Nowadays when I mention among my friends the names of Egypt and Babylonia, Philistia and Tyre, or even distant Ethiopia, someone boasts that he was born in one or another of those countries. ⁵But someday the highest honor will be to be a native of Jerusalem! For the God above all gods will personally bless this city. ⁶When he registers her citizens, he will place a checkmark beside the names of those who were born here. ⁷And in the festivals they'll sing, "All my heart is in Jerusalem."

88 God Understands Your Hurts

O Jehovah, God of my salvation, I have wept before you day and night. ²Now hear my prayers; oh, listen to my cry, ³for my life is full of troubles, and death draws near. ⁴They say my life is ebbing out—a hopeless case. ⁵They have left me here to die, like those slain on battlefields from whom your mercies are removed.

⁶You have thrust me down to the darkest depths. ⁷Your wrath lies heavy on me; wave after wave engulfs me. ⁸You have made my friends to loathe me, and they have gone away. I am in a trap with no way out. ⁹My eyes grow dim with weeping. Each day I beg your help; O Lord, I reach my pleading hands to you for mercy.

¹⁰Soon it will be too late! Of what use are your miracles when I am in the grave? How can I praise you then? ¹¹Can those in the grave declare your loving-kindness? Can they proclaim your faithfulness? ¹²Can the darkness speak of your miracles? Can anyone in the Land of Forgetfulness talk about your help?

¹³O Lord, I plead for my life and will keep on pleading day by day. ¹⁴O Jehovah, why have you thrown my life away? Why are you turning your face from me and looking the other way?

¹⁵From my youth I have been sickly and ready to die. I stand helpless before your terrors. ¹⁶Your fierce wrath has overwhelmed me. Your terrors have cut me off. ¹⁷They flow around me all day long. ¹⁸Lover, friend, acquaintance—all are gone. There is only darkness everywhere.

89 God Keeps Promises Forever

Forever and ever I will sing about the tender kindness of the Lord! Young and old shall hear about your blessings. ²Your love and kindness are forever; your truth is as enduring as the heavens.

³,⁴The Lord God says, "I have made a solemn agreement with my chosen servant David. I have taken an oath to establish his descendants as kings forever on his throne, from now until eternity!"

⁵All heaven shall praise your miracles, O Lord; myriads of angels will praise you for your faithfulness. ⁶For who in all of heaven can be compared with God? What mightiest angel is anything like him? ⁷The highest of angelic powers stand in dread and awe of him. Who is as revered as he by those surrounding him? ⁸O Jehovah, Commander of the heavenly armies, where is there any other Mighty One like you? Faithfulness is your very character.

⁹You rule the oceans when their waves arise in fearful storms; you speak, and they lie still. ¹⁰You have cut haughty Egypt to pieces. Your enemies are scattered by your awesome power. ¹¹The heavens are yours, the world, everything—for you created them all. ¹²You created north and south! Mount Tabor and Mount Hermon rejoice to be signed by your name as their maker! ¹³Strong is your arm! Strong is your hand! Your right hand is lifted high in glorious strength.

¹⁴,¹⁵Your throne is founded on two strong pillars—the one is Justice and the other Righteousness. Mercy and Truth walk before you as your attendants. Blessed are those who hear the joyful blast of the trumpet, for they shall walk in the light of your presence. ¹⁶They rejoice all day long in your wonderful reputation and in your perfect righteousness. ¹⁷You are their strength. What

Family Devotions

☐ DEVOTION 165
MAKING THE BEST CHOICES

Read Psalm 90:9-17

Making the Best Choices
Memory Verse

He will always give you all you need from day to day if you will make the Kingdom of God your primary concern.
Luke 12:31

"Carl!" called Dad as he hung up the phone. Carl knew by the tone of Dad's voice that there was going to be trouble.

"That was your principal," said Dad with a frown. "He told me you were sent to his office today for goofing off in class and talking disrespectfully to your teacher."

Carl look uncomfortable. "It wasn't my fault," he protested. "Jack started it. Besides, that class is boring!"

"Maybe it wouldn't be so boring if you studied your lessons more often," Dad replied sternly.

Carl shrugged. "Aw, Dad, if I studied all the time, I wouldn't have any fun!"

Dad was quiet for a moment. Then he said, "Come down to my workroom. I want to show you something."

After rummaging around in a box, Dad pulled out a small, thick piece of wood. "This belonged to Grandpa Williams," he said.

Carl looked at it curiously. "That can't be worth much," he said finally.

"Oh, but it is. It's solid cherry," said Dad. "Remember the hand-carved figure Mom has on the coffee table? Grandpa Williams used to carve those and sell them to collectors. They were made from the same kind of wood as this piece."

Carl whistled. "Wow! I guess that is valuable after all."

"On the other hand," said Dad, "if it were cut up into toothpicks, it would be worth only about fifty cents."

"That's not much," said Carl.

"No," agreed Dad. "The wood must be used properly. And the same thing is true of a human life. Life is a valuable gift from God, but it's important to use it well. Don't be careless with it and waste it. That would be even sadder than turning wood like this into toothpicks."

How About You?
Do you think the most important thing in life is having fun? Are you careless in your schoolwork or lazy about prayer and Bible reading? Life passes quickly. Don't waste it. Make sure you know Christ as your Savior. Then determine to make use of every opportunity to serve him. Fill your life with treasure instead of toothpicks. *S. K.*

• For the next devotional, turn to page 581. • For the next devotional on *MAKING THE BEST CHOICES*, turn to page 885. • For notes on *MAKING THE BEST CHOICES*, see pages 358, 652, and 944.

glory! Our power is based on your favor! ¹⁸Yes, our protection is from the Lord himself and he, the Holy One of Israel, has given us our king.

¹⁹In a vision you spoke to your prophet and said, "I have chosen a splendid young man from the common people to be the king—²⁰he is my servant David! I have anointed him with my holy oil. ²¹I will steady him and make him strong. ²²His enemies shall not outwit him, nor shall the wicked overpower him. ²³I will beat down his adversaries before him and destroy those who hate him. ²⁴I will protect and bless him constantly and surround him with my love; he will be great because of me. ²⁵He will hold sway from the Euphrates River to the Mediterranean Sea. ²⁶And he will cry to me, 'You are my Father, my God, and my Rock of Salvation.'

²⁷"I will treat him as my firstborn son and make him the mightiest king in all the earth. ²⁸I will love him forever and be kind to him always; my covenant with him will never end. ²⁹He will always have an heir; his throne will be as endless as the days of heaven. ³⁰⁻³²If his children forsake my laws and don't obey them, then I will punish them, ³³but I will never completely take away my loving-kindness from them, nor let my promise fail. ³⁴No, I will not break my covenant; I will not take back one word of what I said. ³⁵,³⁶For I have sworn to David (and a holy God can never lie) that his dynasty will go on forever, and his throne will continue to the end of time. ³⁷It shall be eternal as the moon, my faithful witness in the sky!"

³⁸Then why cast me off, rejected? Why be so angry with the one you chose as king? ³⁹Have you renounced your covenant with him? For you have thrown his crown in the dust. ⁴⁰You have broken down the walls protecting him and laid in ruins every fort defending him. ⁴¹Everyone who comes along has robbed him while his neighbors mock. ⁴²You have strengthened his enemies against him and made them rejoice. ⁴³You have struck down his sword and refused to help him in battle. ⁴⁴You have ended his splendor and overturned his throne. ⁴⁵You have made him old before his time and publicly disgraced him.

⁴⁶O Jehovah, how long will this go on? Will you hide yourself from me forever? How long will your wrath burn like fire? ⁴⁷Oh, remember how short you have made man's lifespan. Is it an empty, futile life you give the sons of men? ⁴⁸No man can live forever. All will die. Who can rescue his life from the power of the grave?

⁴⁹Lord, where is the love you used to have for me? Where is your kindness that you promised to David with a faithful pledge? ⁵⁰Lord, see how all the people are despising me. ⁵¹Your enemies joke about me, the one you anointed as their king.

⁵²And yet—blessed be the Lord forever! Amen and amen!

90 God's Eternal Kingdom
A prayer of Moses, the man of God.

Lord, through all the generations you have been our home! ²Before the mountains were created, before the earth was formed, you are God without beginning or end.

³You speak, and man turns back to dust. ⁴A thousand years are but as yesterday to you! They are like a single hour! ⁵,⁶We glide along the tides of time as swiftly as a racing river and vanish as quickly as a dream. We are like grass that is green in the morning but mowed down and withered before the evening shadows fall. ⁷We die beneath your anger; we are overwhelmed by your wrath. ⁸You spread out our sins before you—our secret sins—and see them all. ⁹No wonder the years are long and heavy here beneath your wrath. All our days are filled with sighing.

¹⁰Seventy years are given us! And some may even live to eighty. But even the best of these years are often emptiness and pain; soon they disappear, and we are gone. ¹¹Who can realize the terrors of your anger? Which of us can fear you as he should?

¹²Teach us to number our days and recognize how few they are; help us to spend them as we should.

¹³O Jehovah, come and bless us! How long will you delay? Turn away your anger from us. ¹⁴Satisfy us in our earliest youth with your loving-kindness, giving us constant joy to the end of our lives. ¹⁵Give us gladness in proportion to our former misery! Replace the evil years with good. ¹⁶Let us see your miracles again; let our children see glorious things, the kind you used to do, ¹⁷and let the Lord our God favor us and give us success. May he give permanence to all we do.

91 Safe from Danger

We live within the shadow of the Almighty, sheltered by the God who is above all gods.

²This I declare, that he alone is my refuge, my place of safety; he is my God, and I am trusting him. ³For he rescues you from every trap and protects you from the fatal plague. ⁴He will shield you with his wings! They will shelter you. His faithful promises are your armor. ⁵Now you don't need to be afraid of the dark any more, nor fear the dangers of the day; ⁶nor dread the plagues of darkness, nor disasters in the morning.

⁷Though a thousand fall at my side, though ten thousand are dying around me, the evil will not touch me. ⁸I will see how the wicked are punished,

Family Devotions

☐ **Devotion 166**
Overcoming Fear

Read Psalm 91

The Carter family lived in a two-story house with big trees surrounding it. Jill especially liked the maple tree that grew outside her bedroom window. She liked the sound of leaves gently brushing against the glass.

One spring day Jill noticed a robin busily surveying the crook of a branch. Soon a second bird flew up. Jill stood absolutely still so she wouldn't frighten the birds. As she watched, they began to build a nest. The robins made many trips back and forth to the ground, gathering twigs and bits of leaves. Jill had to laugh when she saw one of the birds use a piece of hair ribbon that she had lost in the snow sometime during the winter.

Finally the nest was finished, and each day Jill checked to see if there was anything in it. Sure enough, one morning she saw four sky-blue eggs in the straw. After that she watched even more closely, waiting for the babies to hatch. Jill felt as if she had a front-row seat when the tiny birds finally broke from their shells. After that, the parent birds were kept busy feeding them.

But one day there was a terrible thunderstorm. The branch swayed back and forth, and the nest swayed with it.

"How are the robins doing, Jill?" asked Dad, as he was passing her room.

"The branch is swaying in the wind, but the wings of the mother robin are covering the babies so they won't get hurt," Jill answered. "It's neat how God created her so she would know how to protect her babies."

"I'll tell you another neat thing," said Dad, coming in to take a look. "God uses that very picture—a mother bird spreading her wings to protect the babies—as an example of how he cares for us, his children."

"That is neat, Dad," agreed Jill. "I'm glad God cares for us, too."

Overcoming Fear
Memory Verse

Fear not, for I am with you. Do not be dismayed. I am your God. I will strengthen you; I will help you; I will uphold you with my victorious right hand.
Isaiah 41:10

How About You?
Have you ever seen a mother bird protect her young? The Bible often uses word pictures to illustrate God's love for you. Remember a mother bird's care for her babies, and you'll know how carefully and completely God protects you. Keep that in mind and don't be afraid of storms, of dogs, or of anything else. *L. M. W.*

- For the next devotional, turn to page 585. • For the next devotional on *Overcoming Fear*, turn to page 693.
- For notes on *Overcoming Fear*, see pages 191, 482, 554, 592, and 912.

but I will not share it. ⁹For Jehovah is my refuge! I choose the God above all gods to shelter me. ¹⁰How then can evil overtake me or any plague come near? ¹¹For he orders his angels to protect you wherever you go. ¹²They will steady you with their hands to keep you from stumbling against the rocks on the trail. ¹³You can safely meet a lion or step on poisonous snakes, yes, even trample them beneath your feet!

¹⁴For the Lord says, "Because he loves me, I will rescue him; I will make him great because he trusts in my name. ¹⁵When he calls on me, I will answer; I will be with him in trouble and rescue him and honor him. ¹⁶I will satisfy him with a full life and give him my salvation."

92 A Song for the Lord's Day
A song to sing on the Lord's Day.

It is good to say thank you to the Lord, to sing praises to the God who is above all gods.

²Every morning tell him, "Thank you for your kindness," and every evening rejoice in all his faithfulness. ³Sing his praises, accompanied by music from the harp and lute and lyre. ⁴You have done so much for me, O Lord. No wonder I am glad! I sing for joy.

⁵O Lord, what miracles you do! And how deep are your thoughts! ⁶Unthinking people do not understand them! No fool can comprehend this: ⁷that although the wicked flourish like weeds, there is only eternal destruction ahead of them. ⁸But the Lord continues forever, exalted in the heavens, ⁹while his enemies—all evil-doers—shall be scattered.

¹⁰But you have made me as strong as a wild bull. How refreshed I am by your blessings! ¹¹I have heard the doom of my enemies announced and seen them destroyed. ¹²But the godly shall flourish like palm trees and grow tall as the cedars of Lebanon. ¹³For they are transplanted into the Lord's own garden and are under his personal care. ¹⁴Even in old age they will still produce fruit and be vital and green. ¹⁵This honors the Lord and exhibits his faithful care. He is my shelter. There is nothing but goodness in him!

93 Our Almighty God

Jehovah is King! He is robed in majesty and strength. The world is his throne.

²O Lord, you have reigned from prehistoric times, from the everlasting past. ³The mighty oceans thunder your praise. ⁴You are mightier than all the breakers pounding on the seashores of the world! ⁵Your royal decrees cannot be changed. Holiness is forever the keynote of your reign.

94 God Will Deal with the Wicked

Lord God, to whom vengeance belongs, let your glory shine out. Arise and judge the earth; sentence the proud to the penalties they deserve. ³Lord, how long shall the wicked be allowed to triumph and exult? ⁴Hear their insolence! See their arrogance! How these men of evil boast! ⁵See them oppressing your people, O Lord, afflicting those you love. ⁶,⁷They murder widows, immigrants, and orphans, for "The Lord isn't looking," they say, "and besides, he doesn't care."

⁸Fools! ⁹Is God deaf and blind—he who makes ears and eyes? ¹⁰He punishes the nations—won't he also punish you? He knows everything—doesn't he also know what you are doing?

¹¹The Lord is fully aware of how limited and futile the thoughts of mankind are, ¹²,¹³so he helps us by punishing us. This makes us follow his paths and gives us respite from our enemies while God traps them and destroys them. ¹⁴The Lord will not forsake his people, for they are his prize. ¹⁵Judgment will again be just, and all the upright will rejoice.

¹⁶Who will protect me from the wicked? Who will be my shield? ¹⁷I would have died unless the Lord had helped me. ¹⁸I screamed, "I'm slipping, Lord!" and he was kind and saved me.

¹⁹Lord, when doubts fill my mind, when my heart is in turmoil, quiet me and give me renewed hope and cheer. ²⁰Will you permit a corrupt government to rule under your protection—a government permitting wrong to defeat right? ²¹,²²Do you approve of those who condemn the innocent to death? No! The Lord my God is my fortress—the mighty Rock where I can hide. ²³God has made the sins of evil men to boomerang upon them! He will destroy them by their own plans. Jehovah our God will cut them off.

95 Let's Worship God

Oh, come, let us sing to the Lord! Give a joyous shout in honor of the Rock of our salvation!

²Come before him with thankful hearts. Let us sing him psalms of praise. ³For the Lord is a great God, the great King of all gods. ⁴He controls the formation of the depths of the earth and the mightiest mountains; all are his.

GIVING THANKS 92:1-2 During the Thanksgiving holiday, we focus on our blessings and express our gratitude to God for them. But thanks should be on our lips daily. We can never say thank you enough to parents, friends, leaders, and especially, to God. When thanksgiving becomes an integral part of your life, you will find that your attitude toward life will change. You will become more positive, gracious, loving, and humble. **To begin the series of devotionals on GIVING THANKS, turn to page 169.**

⁵He made the sea and formed the land; they too are his. ⁶Come, kneel before the Lord our Maker, ⁷for he is our God. We are his sheep, and he is our Shepherd. Oh, that you would hear him calling you today and come to him!

⁸Don't harden your hearts as Israel did in the wilderness at Meribah and Massah. ⁹For there your fathers doubted me, though they had seen so many of my miracles before. My patience was severely tried by their complaints. ¹⁰"For forty years I watched them in disgust," the Lord God says. "They were a nation whose thoughts and heart were far away from me. They refused to accept my laws. ¹¹Therefore, in mighty wrath I swore that they would never enter the Promised Land, the place of rest I planned for them."

96 How Can I Praise God?

Sing a new song to the Lord! Sing it everywhere around the world! ²Sing out his praises! Bless his name. Each day tell someone that he saves.

³Publish his glorious acts throughout the earth. Tell everyone about the amazing things he does. ⁴For the Lord is great beyond description and greatly to be praised. Worship only him among the gods! ⁵For the gods of other nations are merely idols, but our God made the heavens! ⁶Honor and majesty surround him; strength and beauty are in his Temple.

⁷O nations of the world, confess that God alone is glorious and strong. ⁸Give him the glory he deserves! Bring your offering and come to worship him. ⁹Worship the Lord with the beauty of holy lives. Let the earth tremble before him. ¹⁰Tell the nations that Jehovah reigns! He rules the world. His power can never be overthrown. He will judge all nations fairly.

¹¹Let the heavens be glad, the earth rejoice; let the vastness of the roaring seas demonstrate his glory. ¹²Praise him for the growing fields, for they display his greatness. Let the trees of the forest rustle with praise. ¹³For the Lord is coming to judge the earth; he will judge the nations fairly and with truth!

97 God Is Awesome and Just

Jehovah is King! Let all the earth rejoice! Tell the farthest islands to be glad.

²Clouds and darkness surround him. Righteousness and justice are the foundation of his throne. ³Fire goes forth before him and burns up all his foes. ⁴His lightning flashes out across the world. The earth sees and trembles. ⁵The mountains melt like wax before the Lord of all the earth. ⁶The heavens declare his perfect righteousness; every nation sees his glory.

⁷Let those who worship idols be disgraced—all who brag about their worthless gods—for every god must bow to him! ⁸,⁹Jerusalem and all the cities of Judah have heard of your justice, Lord, and are glad that you reign in majesty over the entire earth and are far greater than these other gods.

¹⁰The Lord loves those who hate evil; he protects the lives of his people and rescues them from the wicked. ¹¹Light is sown for the godly and joy for the good. ¹²May all who are godly be happy in the Lord and crown him, our holy God.

98 A Song of Joy and Victory

Sing a new song to the Lord telling about his mighty deeds! For he has won a mighty victory by his power and holiness. ²,³He has announced this victory and revealed it to every nation by fulfilling his promise to be kind to Israel. The whole earth has seen God's salvation of his people. ⁴That is why the earth breaks out in praise to God and sings for utter joy!

⁵Sing your praise accompanied by music from the harp. ⁶Let the cornets and trumpets shout! Make a joyful symphony before the Lord, the King! ⁷Let the sea in all its vastness roar with praise! Let the earth and all those living on it shout, "Glory to the Lord."

⁸,⁹Let the waves clap their hands in glee and the hills sing out their songs of joy before the Lord, for he is coming to judge the world with perfect justice.

99 God Is Fair and Holy

Jehovah is King! Let the nations tremble! He is enthroned between the Guardian Angels. Let the whole earth shake.

²Jehovah sits in majesty in Zion, supreme above all rulers of the earth. ³Let them reverence your great and holy name.

⁴This mighty King is determined to give justice. Fairness is the touchstone of everything he does. He gives justice throughout Israel. ⁵Exalt the Lord our holy God! Bow low before his feet.

⁶When Moses and Aaron and Samuel, his prophet, cried to him for help, he answered them.

FAITH IN ACTION 99:3 Everyone, even kings and rulers, should reverence God's great and holy name. But the name of God is used so often in vulgar conversation that we have lost sight of its holiness. How easy it is to treat God lightly in everyday life. If you claim him as your father, live worthy of the family name. Reverence God's name by both your *words* and your *life*.
To begin the series of devotionals on FAITH IN ACTION, turn to page 141.

⁷He spoke to them from the pillar of cloud, and they followed his instructions. ⁸O Jehovah our God! You answered them and forgave their sins, yet punished them when they went wrong.

⁹Exalt the Lord our God and worship at his holy mountain in Jerusalem, for he is holy.

100 Come Before God with Praise

Shout with joy before the Lord, O earth! ²Obey him gladly; come before him, singing with joy.

³Try to realize what this means—the Lord is God! He made us—we are his people, the sheep of his pasture.

⁴Go through his open gates with great thanksgiving; enter his courts with praise. Give thanks to him and bless his name. ⁵For the Lord is always good. He is always loving and kind, and his faithfulness goes on and on to each succeeding generation.

101 Living a Clean Life for God

I will sing about your loving-kindness and your justice, Lord. I will sing your praises!

²I will try to walk a blameless path, but how I need your help, especially in my own home, where I long to act as I should.

³Help me to refuse the low and vulgar things; help me to abhor all crooked deals of every kind, to have no part in them. ⁴I will reject all selfishness and stay away from every evil. ⁵I will not tolerate anyone who secretly slanders his neighbors; I will not permit conceit and pride. ⁶I will make the godly of the land my heroes and invite them to my home. Only those who are truly good shall be my servants. ⁷But I will not allow those who deceive and lie to stay in my house. ⁸My daily task will be to ferret out criminals and free the city of God from their grip.

102 When We Need Help

A prayer when overwhelmed with trouble.

Lord, hear my prayer! Listen to my plea!

²Don't turn away from me in this time of my distress. Bend down your ear and give me speedy answers, ³,⁴for my days disappear like smoke. My health is broken, and my heart is sick; it is trampled like grass and is withered. My food is tasteless, and I have lost my appetite. ⁵I am reduced to skin and bones because of all my groaning and despair. ⁶I am like a vulture in a far-off wilderness or like an owl alone in the desert. ⁷I lie awake, lonely as a solitary sparrow on the roof.

⁸My enemies taunt me day after day and curse at me. ⁹,¹⁰I eat ashes instead of bread. My tears run down into my drink because of your anger against me, because of your wrath. For you have rejected me and thrown me out. ¹¹My life is passing swiftly as the evening shadows. I am withering like grass, ¹²while you, Lord, are a famous King forever. Your fame will endure to every generation.

¹³I know that you will come and have mercy on Jerusalem—and now is the time to pity her—the time you promised help. ¹⁴For your people love every stone in her walls and feel sympathy for every grain of dust in her streets. ¹⁵Now let the nations and their rulers tremble before the Lord, before his glory. ¹⁶For Jehovah will rebuild Jerusalem! He will appear in his glory!

¹⁷He will listen to the prayers of the destitute, for he is never too busy to heed their requests. ¹⁸I am recording this so that future generations will also praise the Lord for all that he has done. And a people that shall be created shall praise the Lord. ¹⁹Tell them that God looked down from his temple in heaven ²⁰and heard the groans of his people in slavery—they were children of death—and released them, ²¹,²²so that multitudes would stream to the Temple in Jerusalem to praise him, and his praises were sung throughout the city; and many rulers throughout the earth came to worship him.

²³He has cut me down in middle life, shortening my days. ²⁴But I cried to him, "O God, you live forever and forever! Don't let me die half through my years! ²⁵In ages past you laid the foundations of the earth and made the heavens with your hands! ²⁶They shall perish, but you go on forever. They will grow old like worn-out clothing, and you will change them like a man putting on a new shirt and throwing away the old one! ²⁷But you yourself never grow old. You are forever, and your years never end.

²⁸"But our families will continue; generation after generation will be preserved by your protection."

103 God's Great Love for Us

I bless the holy name of God with all my heart. ²Yes, I will bless the Lord and not forget the glorious things he does for me.

³He forgives all my sins. He heals me. ⁴He ransoms me from hell. He surrounds me with loving-kindness and tender mercies. ⁵He fills my life with good things! My youth is renewed like the eagle's! ⁶He gives justice to all who are treated unfairly. ⁷He revealed his will and nature to Moses and the people of Israel.

⁸He is merciful and tender toward those who don't deserve it; he is slow to get angry and full of

FAMILY DEVOTIONS

☐ **DEVOTION 167**
SHOWING KINDNESS

Read Psalm 101:1-2

Showing Kindness
Memory Verse

That's why whenever we can we should always be kind to everyone, and especially to our Christian brothers.
Galatians 6:10

When his mother called, John left his game reluctantly. "What do you want?" he asked irritably.

"Please sweep up the cookie crumbs you left on the floor," said Mom. "And don't help yourself to any more cookies. I have just enough for the meeting at church."

John scowled. "Well, don't leave them out in the open if you don't want them eaten!"

"John! That was rude!" exclaimed Mom.

"I'm sorry," John muttered as he got the broom. His sister, Kara, came into the room while he was sweeping. Surprised, she asked why he was doing that. "Scram!" John growled. "Who asked you to stick your nose in?"

"Excuse me!" said Kara dramatically. "I came to tell you something, but now I don't know if I will." When John punched her in the shoulder, she ran behind the table. "Mr. Williams, your coach, called today," she said. "He wants to hire you to do some yard work. Guess what? He said to be sure to tell Mom he appreciated your respectful attitude at school! What a laugh!"

"What's so funny?" John asked. "I make a real effort to show I'm a Christian at school."

"Well," retorted Kara, "don't invite any of your friends or teachers home. If they saw how you act around here, they'd know what a phony you are."

How About You?
Are you as kind to your brothers and sisters as you are to your friends? Do you speak as respectfully to your parents as you do to your teachers? Sometimes we can fool people with nice words and good deeds, but our families know whether or not we are really letting Christ's love flow through us. *C. R.*

After Kara left, John felt badly. *Could Kara be right?* he wondered. At school he tried to be an example of Christian living. But when he got home, he seemed to forget about kindness. After all, his family members knew he loved them and that he was saved. He didn't have to prove it to them. So why did he feel so guilty? He knew it was the Holy Spirit convicting him. *Lord, forgive me,* he prayed. *Help me to behave like a Christian all the time, especially with the people who love me most.* Then he went to apologize to his mother and sister.

- For the next devotional, turn to page 589. • For the next devotional on *SHOWING KINDNESS,* turn to page 631.
- For notes on *SHOWING KINDNESS,* see pages 664, 880, 1038, and 1244.

kindness and love. ⁹He never bears a grudge, nor remains angry forever. ¹⁰He has not punished us as we deserve for all our sins, ¹¹for his mercy toward those who fear and honor him is as great as the height of the heavens above the earth. ¹²He has removed our sins as far away from us as the east is from the west. ¹³He is like a father to us, tender and sympathetic to those who reverence him. ¹⁴For he knows we are but dust ¹⁵and that our days are few and brief, like grass, like flowers, ¹⁶blown by the wind and gone forever.

¹⁷,¹⁸But the loving-kindness of the Lord is from everlasting to everlasting to those who reverence him; his salvation is to children's children of those who are faithful to his covenant and remember to obey him!

¹⁹The Lord has made the heavens his throne; from there he rules over everything there is. ²⁰Bless the Lord, you mighty angels of his who carry out his orders, listening for each of his commands. ²¹Yes, bless the Lord, you armies of his angels who serve him constantly.

²²Let everything everywhere bless the Lord. And how I bless him too!

104 God Takes Care of His World

I bless the Lord: O Lord my God, how great you are! You are robed with honor and with majesty and light! You stretched out the starry curtain of the heavens, ³and hollowed out the surface of the earth to form the seas. The clouds are his chariots. He rides upon the wings of the wind. ⁴The angels are his messengers—his servants of fire!

⁵You bound the world together so that it would never fall apart. ⁶You clothed the earth with floods of waters covering up the mountains. ⁷,⁸You spoke, and at the sound of your shout the water collected into its vast ocean beds, and mountains rose and valleys sank to the levels you decreed. ⁹And then you set a boundary for the seas so that they would never again cover the earth.

¹⁰He placed springs in the valleys and streams that gush from the mountains. ¹¹They give water for all the animals to drink. There the wild donkeys quench their thirst, ¹²and the birds nest beside the streams and sing among the branches of the trees. ¹³He sends rain upon the mountains and fills the earth with fruit. ¹⁴The tender grass grows up at his command to feed the cattle, and there are fruit trees, vegetables, and grain for man to cultivate, ¹⁵and wine to make him glad, and olive oil as lotion for his skin, and bread to give him strength. ¹⁶The Lord planted the cedars of Lebanon. They are tall and flourishing. ¹⁷There the birds make their nests, the storks in the firs. ¹⁸High in the mountains are pastures for the wild goats, and rock-badgers burrow in among the rocks and find protection there.

¹⁹He assigned the moon to mark the months and the sun to mark the days. ²⁰He sends the night and darkness, when all the forest folk come out. ²¹Then the young lions roar for their food, but they are dependent on the Lord. ²²At dawn they slink back into their dens to rest, ²³and men go off to work until the evening shadows fall again. ²⁴O Lord, what a variety you have made! And in wisdom you have made them all! The earth is full of your riches.

²⁵There before me lies the mighty ocean, teeming with life of every kind, both great and small. ²⁶And look! See the ships! And over there, the whale you made to play in the sea. ²⁷Every one of these depends on you to give them daily food. ²⁸You supply it, and they gather it. You open wide your hand to feed them, and they are satisfied with all your bountiful provision.

²⁹But if you turn away from them, then all is lost. And when you gather up their breath, they die and turn again to dust.

³⁰Then you send your Spirit, and new life is born to replenish all the living of the earth. ³¹Praise God forever! How he must rejoice in all his work! ³²The earth trembles at his glance; the mountains burst into flame at his touch.

³³I will sing to the Lord as long as I live. I will praise God to my last breath! ³⁴May he be pleased by all these thoughts about him, for he is the source of all my joy. ³⁵Let all sinners perish—all who refuse to praise him. But I will praise him. Hallelujah!

105 Remember God's Miracles

Thank the Lord for all the glorious things he does; proclaim them to the nations. ²Sing his praises and tell everyone about his miracles. ³Glory in the Lord; O worshipers of God, rejoice.

⁴Search for him and for his strength, and keep on searching!

⁵,⁶Think of the mighty deeds he did for us, his chosen ones— descendants of God's servant Abraham, and of Jacob. Remember how he destroyed our enemies. ⁷He is the Lord our God. His

---

FORGIVING OTHERS   103:12 East and west can never meet. This is a symbolic portrait of God's forgiveness—when he forgives our sin, he separates it from us and doesn't even remember it. We tend to dredge up the ugly past, but God will not do this for he has wiped our record clean. If we are to follow God, we must model his forgiveness. When we forgive another, we must also forget the sin. Otherwise, we have not truly forgiven. **To begin the series of devotionals on FORGIVING OTHERS, turn to page 39.**

goodness is seen everywhere throughout the land. ⁸,⁹Though a thousand generations pass he never forgets his promise, his covenant with Abraham and Isaac ¹⁰,¹¹and confirmed with Jacob. This is his never-ending treaty with the people of Israel: *"I will give you the land of Canaan as your inheritance."* ¹²He said this when they were but few in number, very few, and were only visitors in Canaan. ¹³Later they were dispersed among the nations and were driven from one kingdom to another; ¹⁴but through it all he would not let one thing be done to them apart from his decision. He destroyed many a king who tried! ¹⁵"Touch not these chosen ones of mine," he warned, "and do not hurt my prophets."

¹⁶He called for a famine on the land of Canaan, cutting off its food supply. ¹⁷Then he sent Joseph as a slave to Egypt to save his people from starvation. ¹⁸There in prison they hurt his feet with fetters and placed his neck in an iron collar ¹⁹until God's time finally came—how God tested his patience! ²⁰Then the king sent for him and set him free. ²¹He was put in charge of all the king's possessions. ²²At his pleasure he could imprison the king's aides and teach the king's advisors.

²³Then Jacob (Israel) arrived in Egypt and lived there with his sons. ²⁴In the years that followed, the people of Israel multiplied explosively until they were a greater nation than their rulers. ²⁵At that point God turned the Egyptians against the Israelis; they hated and enslaved them.

²⁶But God sent Moses as his representative, and Aaron with him, ²⁷to call down miracles of terror upon the land of Egypt. ²⁸They followed his instructions. He sent thick darkness through the land ²⁹and turned the nation's water into blood, poisoning the fish. ³⁰Then frogs invaded in enormous numbers; they were found even in the king's private rooms. ³¹When Moses spoke, the flies and other insects swarmed in vast clouds from one end of Egypt to the other. ³²Instead of rain he sent down murderous hail, and lightning flashes overwhelmed the nation. ³³Their grape vines and fig trees were ruined; all the trees lay broken on the ground. ³⁴He spoke, and hordes of locusts came ³⁵and ate up everything green, destroying all the crops. ³⁶Then he killed the oldest child in each Egyptian home, their pride and joy—³⁷and brought his people safely out from Egypt, loaded with silver and gold; there were no sick and feeble folk among them then. ³⁸Egypt was glad when they were gone, for the dread of them was great.

³⁹He spread out a cloud above them to shield them from the burning sun and gave them a pillar of flame at night to give them light. ⁴⁰They asked for meat, and he sent them quail and gave them manna—bread from heaven. ⁴¹He opened up a rock, and water gushed out to form a river through the dry and barren land; ⁴²for he remembered his sacred promises to Abraham his servant.

⁴³So he brought his chosen ones singing into the Promised Land. ⁴⁴He gave them the lands of the Gentiles, complete with their growing crops; they ate what others planted. ⁴⁵This was done to make them faithful and obedient to his laws. Hallelujah!

106 God Always Forgives

Hallelujah! Thank you, Lord! How good you are! Your love for us continues on forever. ²Who can ever list the glorious miracles of God? Who can ever praise him half enough?

³Happiness comes to those who are fair to others and are always just and good.

⁴Remember me too, O Lord, while you are blessing and saving your people. ⁵Let me share in your chosen ones' prosperity and rejoice in all their joys, and receive the glory you give to them.

⁶Both we and our fathers have sinned so much. ⁷They weren't impressed by the wonder of your miracles in Egypt and soon forgot your many acts of kindness to them. Instead they rebelled against you at the Red Sea. ⁸Even so you saved them—to defend the honor of your name and demonstrate your power to all the world. ⁹You commanded the Red Sea to divide, forming a dry road across its bottom. Yes, as dry as any desert! ¹⁰Thus you rescued them from their enemies. ¹¹Then the water returned and covered the road and drowned their foes; not one survived.

¹²Then at last his people believed him. Then they finally sang his praise.

¹³Yet how quickly they forgot again! They wouldn't wait for him to act ¹⁴but demanded better food, testing God's patience to the breaking point. ¹⁵So he gave them their demands but sent them leanness in their souls. ¹⁶They were envious of Moses, yes, and Aaron too, the man anointed by God as his priest. ¹⁷Because of this, the earth opened and swallowed Dathan, Abiram, and his friends; ¹⁸and fire fell from heaven to consume these wicked men. ¹⁹,²⁰For they preferred a statue of an ox that eats grass to the glorious presence of God himself. ²¹,²²Thus they despised their Savior who had done such mighty miracles in Egypt and at the Sea. ²³So the Lord declared he would destroy them. But Moses, his chosen one, stepped into the breach between the people and their God and begged him to turn from his wrath and not destroy them.

²⁴They refused to enter the Promised Land, for they wouldn't believe his solemn oath to care for them. ²⁵Instead, they pouted in their tents and

mourned and despised his command. ²⁶Therefore he swore that he would kill them in the wilderness ²⁷and send their children away to distant lands as exiles. ²⁸Then our fathers joined the worshipers of Baal at Peor and even offered sacrifices to the dead! ²⁹With all these things they angered him—and so a plague broke out upon them ³⁰and continued until Phineas executed those whose sins had caused the plague to start. ³¹(For this good deed Phineas will be remembered forever.)

³²At Meribah, too, Israel angered God, causing Moses serious trouble, ³³for he became angry and spoke foolishly.

³⁴Nor did Israel destroy the nations in the land as God had told them to, ³⁵but mingled in among the heathen and learned their evil ways, ³⁶sacrificing to their idols, and were led away from God. ³⁷,³⁸They even sacrificed their little children to the demons—the idols of Canaan—shedding innocent blood and polluting the land with murder. ³⁹Their evil deeds defiled them, for their love of idols was adultery in the sight of God. ⁴⁰That is why Jehovah's anger burned against his people, and he abhorred them. ⁴¹,⁴²That is why he let the heathen nations crush them. They were ruled by those who hated them and oppressed by their enemies.

⁴³Again and again he delivered them from their slavery, but they continued to rebel against him and were finally destroyed by their sin. ⁴⁴Yet, even so, he listened to their cries and heeded their distress; ⁴⁵he remembered his promises to them and relented because of his great love, ⁴⁶and caused even their enemies who captured them to pity them.

⁴⁷O Lord God, save us! Regather us from the nations so we can thank your holy name and rejoice and praise you.

⁴⁸Blessed be the Lord, the God of Israel, from everlasting to everlasting. Let all the people say, "Amen!" Hallelujah!

107 Give Thanks Always

Say thank you to the Lord for being so good, for always being so loving and kind. ²Has the Lord redeemed you? Then speak out! Tell others he has saved you from your enemies.

³He brought the exiles back from the farthest corners of the earth. ⁴They were wandering homeless in the desert, ⁵hungry and thirsty and faint. ⁶"Lord, help!" they cried, and he did! ⁷He led them straight to safety and a place to live. ⁸Oh, that these men would praise the Lord for his loving-kindness, and for all of his wonderful deeds! ⁹For he satisfies the thirsty soul and fills the hungry soul with good.

¹⁰Who are these who sit in darkness, in the shadow of death, crushed by misery and slavery? ¹¹They rebelled against the Lord, scorning him who is the God above all gods. ¹²That is why he broke them with hard labor; they fell and none could help them rise again. ¹³Then they cried to the Lord in their troubles, and he rescued them! ¹⁴He led them from the darkness and shadow of death and snapped their chains. ¹⁵Oh, that these men would praise the Lord for his loving-kindness and for all of his wonderful deeds! ¹⁶For he broke down their prison gates of brass and cut apart their iron bars.

¹⁷Others, the fools, were ill because of their sinful ways. ¹⁸Their appetites were gone, and death was near. ¹⁹Then they cried to the Lord in their troubles, and he helped them and delivered them. ²⁰He spoke, and they were healed—snatched from the door of death. ²¹Oh, that these men would praise the Lord for his loving-kindness and for all of his wonderful deeds! ²²Let them tell him thank you as their sacrifice and sing about his glorious deeds.

²³And then there are the sailors sailing the seven seas, plying the trade routes of the world. ²⁴They, too, observe the power of God in action. ²⁵He calls to the storm winds; the waves rise high. ²⁶Their ships are tossed to the heavens and sink again to the depths; the sailors cringe in terror. ²⁷They reel and stagger like drunkards and are at their wit's end. ²⁸Then they cry to the Lord in their trouble, and he saves them. ²⁹He calms the storm and stills the waves. ³⁰What a blessing is that stillness as he brings them safely into harbor! ³¹Oh, that these men would praise the Lord for his loving-kindness and for all of his wonderful deeds! ³²Let them praise him publicly before the congregation and before the leaders of the nation.

³³He dries up rivers ³⁴and turns the good land of the wicked into deserts of salt. ³⁵Again, he turns deserts into fertile, watered valleys. ³⁶He brings the hungry to settle there and build their cities, ³⁷to sow their fields and plant their vineyards, and reap their bumper crops! ³⁸How he blesses them! They raise big families there and many cattle.

³⁹But others become poor through oppression, trouble, and sorrow. ⁴⁰For God pours contempt upon the haughty and causes princes to wander among ruins; ⁴¹but he rescues the poor who are godly and gives them many children and much prosperity. ⁴²Good men everywhere will see it and be glad, while evil men are stricken silent.

⁴³Listen, if you are wise, to what I am saying. Think about the loving-kindness of the Lord!

108 With God, We Can

O God, my heart is ready to praise you! I will sing and rejoice before you.

²Wake up, O harp and lyre! We will meet the dawn with song. ³I will praise you everywhere around the world, in every nation. ⁴For your loving-kindness is great beyond measure, high as the

Family Devotions

☐ **DEVOTION 168**

TRUSTING GOD'S PLAN

Read Psalm 107:1-8

Trusting God's Plan Memory Verses:

This plan of mine is not what you would work out, neither are my thoughts the same as yours! For just as the heavens are higher than the earth, so are my ways higher than yours, and my thoughts than yours.
Isaiah 55:8-9

"Becky, would you share your testimony next week?" Mr. Helton asked after the Bible club meeting.

"Ohhh, I don't know," Becky responded dejectedly. "I don't really have anything to share."

"Why, Becky, I thought you asked Jesus to save you at one of our meetings last year," answered the teacher.

"Yes, but every time I hear people give testimonies, they tell about all the bad things they did before Jesus came into their hearts," Becky said. "I didn't do a lot of horrid things before I was saved."

Mr. Helton smiled. He knew Becky was remembering the rally to which he had taken his Bible club. First a pro football player had told about his life as a drug addict before he'd been born again. Then a lady had shared her testimony as to how she had been in the very act of committing suicide when a friend stopped in and won her to the Lord. "Becky, perhaps you have *more* to thank God for than any of the people you've heard giving testimonies," suggested Mr. Helton. "You see, since you accepted Jesus into your heart at a young age, the Lord has protected you from ever getting involved in some of the horrible sin that might have entered your life as you grew older. You can express thanks to God for this. Psalms 107 applies to you, too, when it says, 'Has the Lord redeemed you? Then speak out!'"

"But do you think anyone is interested in hearing what I have to say?" Becky wondered aloud.

"Oh, yes," Mr. Helton assured her. "Many others in our Bible club may feel just as you do—that they have little to testify about. Hearing what you have to say may help them realize how blessed they are, too. And some who are not saved may see the value of accepting Jesus now, while they are young."

Becky smiled and nodded. "Plan on my testimony next week," she said.

How About You?

Are you one of those who accepted Jesus as Savior before you ever got deeply involved in a life of sin? If so, never be sorry that you have not experienced some of the evil in the world. Instead, thank the Lord for protecting you. His plan for you is best. R. P.

• For the next devotional, turn to page 591. • For the next devotional on TRUSTING GOD'S PLAN, turn to page 981.
• For notes on TRUSTING GOD'S PLAN, see pages 252, 296, 731, and 870.

heavens. Your faithfulness reaches the skies. ⁵His glory is far more vast than the heavens. It towers above the earth. ⁶Hear the cry of your beloved child—come with mighty power and rescue me.

⁷God has given sacred promises; no wonder I exult! He has promised to give us all the land of Shechem and also Succoth Valley. ⁸"Gilead is mine to give to you," he says, "and Manasseh as well; the land of Ephraim is the helmet on my head. Judah is my scepter. ⁹But Moab and Edom are despised; and I will shout in triumph over the Philistines."

¹⁰Who but God can give me strength to conquer these fortified cities? Who else can lead me into Edom?

¹¹Lord, have you thrown us away? Have you deserted our army? ¹²Oh, help us fight against our enemies, for men are useless allies. ¹³But with the help of God we shall do mighty acts of valor. For he treads down our foes.

109 Help Me, O Lord!

O God of my praise, don't stand silent and aloof ²while the wicked slander me and tell their lies. ³They have no reason to hate and fight me, yet they do! ⁴I love them, but even while I am praying for them, they are trying to destroy me. ⁵They return evil for good, and hatred for love.

⁶Show him how it feels! Let lies be told about him, and bring him to court before an unfair judge. ⁷When his case is called for judgment, let him be pronounced guilty. Count his prayers as sins. ⁸Let his years be few and brief; let others step forward to replace him. ⁹,¹⁰May his children become fatherless and his wife a widow; may they be evicted from the ruins of their home. ¹¹May creditors seize his entire estate and strangers take all he has earned. ¹²,¹³Let no one be kind to him; let no one pity his fatherless children. May they die. May his family name be blotted out in a single generation. ¹⁴Punish the sins of his father and mother. Don't overlook them. ¹⁵Think constantly about the evil things he has done, and cut off his name from the memory of man.

¹⁶For he refused all kindness to others, and persecuted those in need, and hounded brokenhearted ones to death. ¹⁷He loved to curse others; now you curse him. He never blessed others; now don't you bless him. ¹⁸Cursing is as much a part of him as his clothing, or as the water he drinks, or the rich food he eats.

¹⁹Now may those curses return and cling to him like his clothing or his belt. ²⁰This is the Lord's punishment upon my enemies who tell lies about me and threaten me with death.

²¹But as for me, O Lord, deal with me as your child, as one who bears your name! Because you are so kind, O Lord, deliver me.

²²,²³I am slipping down the hill to death; I am shaken off from life as easily as a man brushes a grasshopper from his arm. ²⁴My knees are weak from fasting, and I am skin and bones. ²⁵I am a symbol of failure to all mankind; when they see me they shake their heads.

²⁶Help me, O Lord my God! Save me because you are loving and kind. ²⁷Do it publicly, so all will see that you yourself have done it. ²⁸Then let them curse me if they like—I won't mind that if you are blessing me! For then all their efforts to destroy me will fail, and I shall go right on rejoicing!

²⁹Make them fail in everything they do. Clothe them with disgrace. ³⁰But I will give repeated thanks to the Lord, praising him to everyone. ³¹For he stands beside the poor and hungry to save them from their enemies.

110 Jesus Christ, the Messiah

Jehovah said to my Lord the Messiah, "Rule as my regent—I will subdue your enemies and make them bow low before you."

²Jehovah has established your throne in Jerusalem to rule over your enemies. ³In that day of your power your people shall come to you willingly, dressed in holy altar robes. And your strength shall be renewed day by day like morning dew. ⁴Jehovah has taken oath and will not rescind his vow that you are a priest forever like Melchizedek. ⁵God stands beside you to protect you. He will strike down many kings in the day of his anger. ⁶He will punish the nations and fill them with their dead. He will crush many heads. ⁷But he himself shall be refreshed from springs along the way.

111 All God Does Is Good

Hallelujah! I want to express publicly before his people my heartfelt thanks to God for his mighty miracles. All who are thankful should ponder them with me. ³For his miracles demonstrate his honor, majesty, and eternal goodness.

⁴Who can forget the wonders he performs—deeds of mercy and of grace? ⁵He gives food to those who trust him; he never forgets his promises. ⁶He has shown his great power to his people by giving them the land of Israel, though it was the home of many nations living there. ⁷All he does is just and good, and all his laws are right, ⁸for they are formed from truth and goodness and stand firm forever. ⁹He has paid a full ransom for his people; now they are always free to come to Jehovah (what a holy, awe-inspiring name that is).

¹⁰How can men be wise? The only way to begin is by reverence for God. For growth in wisdom comes from obeying his laws. Praise his name forever.

FAMILY DEVOTIONS

☐ DEVOTION 169
RESPECTING GOD'S WARNINGS

Read Psalm 111:10

"I'm going to climb the fence around the power station's transformer," Jason announced to his friend.

Michael's eyes widened. "Don't do it, Jason. Dad says it's dangerous. Why do you think the electric company put up that high fence with warning signs around it?"

"To keep out scaredy-cats like you," mocked Jason. "Well, have a good time playing with the girls."

I'd better stop him, Michael thought as he watched Jason leave. He jumped to his feet and ran toward the house. "I'll tell Mother."

As soon as Michael's mother heard about it, she called the electric company. Minutes later, she and Michael ran into the front yard when they heard sirens approaching. "Stay here," Mother ordered as she ran down the street.

When Mother returned, she looked worried. "We were almost too late. Jason touched a high-voltage wire just as the emergency squad arrived. They think he'll live, but he's badly burned. It will be a long time before he recovers."

"Jason said he wasn't afraid of anything," Michael told his mother.

Mother sighed. "It's good to fear some things," she said. "For instance, the Bible says that the way to become wise is to have reverence for—or fear—God."

"Does that mean we're supposed to be afraid of God?" asked Michael.

"We are to fear God in the sense that we respect and obey him," answered Mother.

"Like I respect and obey you and Dad?" Michael asked.

Mother nodded. "That shows wisdom. If you're smart, you fear many things, and it keeps you out of a lot of trouble."

"So that's what that verse means," Michael said.

Respecting God's Warnings Memory Verse

If my people will humble themselves and pray, and search for me, and turn from their wicked ways, I will hear them from heaven and forgive their sins and heal their land.
2 Chronicles 7:14

How About You?
Are you afraid of God? If you're a Christian, he's your heavenly Father, and you don't need to be afraid of him. He loves you. But you do need to respect and obey him. B. W.

• For the next devotional, turn to page 593. • For the next devotional on RESPECTING GOD'S WARNINGS, turn to page 801. • For notes on RESPECTING GOD'S WARNINGS, see pages 219, 874, and 1126.

112 Happy Are Those Who Obey

Praise the Lord! For all who fear God and trust in him are blessed beyond expression. Yes, happy is the man who delights in doing his commands.

²His children shall be honored everywhere, for good men's sons have a special heritage. ³He himself shall be wealthy, and his good deeds will never be forgotten. ⁴When darkness overtakes him, light will come bursting in. He is kind and merciful—⁵and all goes well for the generous man who conducts his business fairly.

⁶Such a man will not be overthrown by evil circumstances. God's constant care of him will make a deep impression on all who see it. ⁷He does not fear bad news, nor live in dread of what may happen. For he is settled in his mind that Jehovah will take care of him. ⁸That is why he is not afraid but can calmly face his foes. ⁹He gives generously to those in need. His deeds will never be forgotten. He shall have influence and honor.

¹⁰Evil-minded men will be infuriated when they see all this; they will gnash their teeth in anger and slink away, their hopes thwarted.

113 God Cares about Everyone

Hallelujah! O servants of Jehovah, praise his name. ²Blessed is his name forever and forever. ³Praise him from sunrise to sunset! ⁴For he is high above the nations; his glory is far greater than the heavens.

⁵Who can be compared with God enthroned on high? ⁶Far below him are the heavens and the earth; he stoops to look, ⁷and lifts the poor from the dirt and the hungry from the garbage dump, ⁸and sets them among princes! ⁹He gives children to the childless wife, so that she becomes a happy mother.

Hallelujah! Praise the Lord.

114 Celebrate God's Great Works

Long ago when the Israelis escaped from Egypt, from that land of foreign tongue, ²then the lands of Judah and of Israel became God's new home and kingdom.

³The Red Sea saw them coming and quickly broke apart before them. The Jordan River opened up a path for them to cross. ⁴The mountains skipped like rams, the little hills like lambs! ⁵What's wrong, Red Sea, that made you cut yourself in two? What happened, Jordan River, to your waters? Why were they held back? ⁶Why, mountains, did you skip like rams? Why, little hills, like lambs?

⁷Tremble, O earth, at the presence of the Lord, the God of Jacob. ⁸For he caused gushing streams to burst from flinty rock.

115 God Lives

Glorify your name, not ours, O Lord! Cause everyone to praise your loving-kindness and your truth. ²Why let the nations say, "Their God is dead!"

³For he is in the heavens and does as he wishes. ⁴Their gods are merely manmade things of silver and of gold. ⁵They can't talk or see, despite their eyes and mouths! ⁶Nor can they hear, nor smell, ⁷nor use their hands or feet, nor speak! ⁸And those who make and worship them are just as foolish as their idols are.

⁹O Israel, trust the Lord! He is your helper. He is your shield. ¹⁰O priests of Aaron, trust the Lord! He is your helper; he is your shield. ¹¹All of you, his people, trust in him. He is your helper; he is your shield.

¹²Jehovah is constantly thinking about us, and he will surely bless us. He will bless the people of Israel and the priests of Aaron, ¹³ and all, both great and small, who reverence him.

¹⁴May the Lord richly bless both you and your children. ¹⁵Yes, Jehovah who made heaven and earth will personally bless you! ¹⁶The heavens belong to the Lord, but he has given the earth to all mankind.

¹⁷The dead cannot sing praises to Jehovah here on earth, ¹⁸but we can! We praise him forever! Hallelujah! Praise the Lord!

116 God Saves Us; Let's Worship Him

I love the Lord because he hears my prayers and answers them. ²Because he bends down and listens, I will pray as long as I breathe!

³Death stared me in the face—I was frightened and sad. ⁴Then I cried, "Lord, save me!" ⁵How kind he is! How good he is! So merciful, this God of ours! ⁶The Lord protects the simple and the childlike; I was facing death, and then he saved me. ⁷Now I can relax. For the Lord has done this wonderful miracle for me. ⁸He has saved me from death, my eyes from tears, my feet from stumbling. ⁹I shall live! Yes, in his presence—here on earth!

¹⁰,¹¹ In my discouragement I thought, "They are lying when

OVERCOMING FEAR 112:7-8 We all want to live without fear; our heroes are fearless people who take on all dangers and overcome them. The psalmist teaches us that *fear* of God can lead to a *fearless* life. To fear God means to respect and reverence him as the almighty Lord. When we trust God completely to take care of us, we will find that our other fears—even of death itself—will subside. **To begin the series of devotionals on OVERCOMING FEAR, turn to page 13.**

Family Devotions

☐ **Devotion 170**
True Joy

Read Psalm 118:24

True Joy Memory Verse

Always be full of joy in the Lord; I say it again, rejoice!
Philippians 4:4

"Mike, get up! Time to get ready for school," called Mom. Mike pulled the covers over his head and burrowed deeper into the warm cocoon of blankets. He didn't even open his eyes. He was too busy dreaming about being the pilot of a 747. It would be exciting to travel around the world. "Mike," Mom called again. "I told you to get up, and I want you to get up now! Do you hear me?"

"Yes." Mike's voice was muffled by the pillow over his head. "Mike, I said now!"

Oh, bother! Why do my good dreams always have to be interrupted? Mike thought as he finally stumbled out of bed.

"It's raining," he moaned as he entered the kitchen a little later. "Why can't the sun ever shine?" He eyed the breakfast table. "Oh, yuck!" he said with a frown. "Oatmeal! I can't stand oatmeal!"

Just then his sister, Nancy, came to the table. She was chattering excitedly about the field trip her class would be taking that day. "We never go on field trips. I hate school," complained Mike.

"Mike, would you please give thanks before we eat?" asked Mom.

"Dear heavenly Father," prayed Mike, "thank you for the beautiful day you have given us, and thank you for the good food. In Jesus' name, amen."

"Mike, I think something is very wrong," said Mom as she passed the oatmeal.

Mike looked up in surprise. "What do you mean?"

"You thanked the Lord for the beautiful day and the good food, but all you've done so far is grumble about them," she told him.

Mike thought about that. Yes, he had been grumbling. In fact, he had been out of bed for only half an hour, and he had grumbled the entire time!

"I'm sorry, Lord," he whispered. "Help me to get a new start on this day!"

How About You?

Do you grumble when Mom calls you in the morning? Do you complain about the food and then thank the Lord for it? Sometimes boys and girls get in the habit of grumbling about everything. The Bible tells you to rejoice. Be a joyful Christian, not a grumbling Christian. *L. M. W.*

• For the next devotional, turn to page 595. • For the next devotional on *True Joy*, turn to page 647. • For notes on *True Joy*, see pages 532, 1024, and 1160.

they say I will recover." ¹²But now what can I offer Jehovah for all he has done for me? ¹³I will bring him an offering of wine and praise his name for saving me. ¹⁴I will publicly bring him the sacrifice I vowed I would. ¹⁵His loved ones are very precious to him, and he does not lightly let them die.

¹⁶O Lord, you have freed me from my bonds, and I will serve you forever. ¹⁷I will worship you and offer you a sacrifice of thanksgiving. ¹⁸,¹⁹Here in the courts of the Temple in Jerusalem, before all the people, I will pay everything I vowed to the Lord. Praise the Lord.

117 Praise God for His Love

Praise the Lord, all nations everywhere. Praise him, all the peoples of the earth. ²For he loves us very dearly, and his truth endures. Praise the Lord.

118 God's Love Never Fails

Oh, thank the Lord, for he's so good! His loving-kindness is forever.

²Let the congregation of Israel praise him with these same words: "His loving-kindness is forever." ³And let the priests of Aaron chant, "His loving-kindness is forever." ⁴Let the Gentile converts chant, "His loving-kindness is forever."

⁵In my distress I prayed to the Lord, and he answered me and rescued me. ⁶He is for me! How can I be afraid? What can mere man do to me? ⁷The Lord is on my side; he will help me. Let those who hate me beware.

⁸It is better to trust the Lord than to put confidence in men. ⁹It is better to take refuge in him than in the mightiest king!

¹⁰Though all the nations of the world attack me, I will march out behind his banner and destroy them. ¹¹Yes, they surround and attack me; but with his flag flying above me I will cut them off. ¹²They swarm around me like bees; they blaze against me like a roaring flame. Yet beneath his flag I shall destroy them. ¹³You did your best to kill me, O my enemy, but the Lord helped me. ¹⁴He is my strength and song in the heat of battle, and now he has given me the victory. ¹⁵,¹⁶Songs of joy at the news of our rescue are sung in the homes of the godly. The strong arm of the Lord has done glorious things! ¹⁷I shall not die but live to tell of all his deeds. ¹⁸The Lord has punished me but not handed me over to death.

¹⁹Open the gates of the Temple—I will go in and give him my thanks. ²⁰Those gates are the way into the presence of the Lord, and the godly enter there. ²¹O Lord, thank you so much for answering my prayer and saving me.

²²The stone rejected by the builders has now become the capstone of the arch! ²³This is the Lord's doing, and it is marvelous to see! ²⁴This is the day the Lord has made. We will rejoice and be glad in it. ²⁵O Lord, please help us. Save us. Give us success. ²⁶Blessed is the one who is coming, the one sent by the Lord. We bless you from the Temple.

²⁷,²⁸Jehovah God is our light. I present to him my sacrifice upon the altar, for you are my God, and I shall give you this thanks and this praise. ²⁹Oh, give thanks to the Lord, for he is so good! For his loving-kindness is forever.

119 Happiness Is Obeying God

Happy are all who perfectly follow the laws of God. ²Happy are all who search for God and always do his will, ³rejecting compromise with evil and walking only in his paths. ⁴You have given us your laws to obey—⁵oh, how I want to follow them consistently. ⁶Then I will not be disgraced, for I will have a clean record.

⁷After you have corrected me, I will thank you by living as I should! ⁸I *will* obey! Oh, don't forsake me and let me slip back into sin again.

⁹How can a young man stay pure? By reading your Word and following its rules. ¹⁰I have tried my best to find you—don't let me wander off from your instructions. ¹¹I have thought much about your words and stored them in my heart so that they would hold me back from sin.

¹²Blessed Lord, teach me your rules. ¹³I have recited your laws ¹⁴and rejoiced in them more than in riches. ¹⁵I will meditate upon them and give them my full respect. ¹⁶I will delight in them and not forget them.

¹⁷Bless me with life so that I can continue to obey you. ¹⁸Open my eyes to see wonderful things in your Word. ¹⁹I am but a pilgrim here on earth: how I need a map—and your commands are my chart and guide. ²⁰I long for your instructions more than I can tell.

²¹You rebuke those cursed proud ones who refuse your commands—²²don't let them scorn me for obeying you. ²³For even princes sit and talk against me, but I will continue in your plans. ²⁴Your laws are both my light and my counselors.

²⁵I am completely discouraged—I lie in the dust. Revive me by your Word. ²⁶I told you my plans and you replied. Now give me your instructions. ²⁷Make me understand what you want; for then I shall see your miracles.

²⁸I weep with grief; my heart is heavy with sorrow; encourage and cheer me with your words. ²⁹,³⁰Keep me far from every wrong; help me, undeserving as I am, to obey your laws, for I have chosen to do right. ³¹I cling to your commands and follow them as closely as I can. Lord,

FAMILY DEVOTIONS

☐ DEVOTION 171
KNOWING GOD

Read Psalm 119:43-68

Knowing God
Memory Verse

Oh, that we might know the Lord! Let us press on to know him, and he will respond to us as surely as the coming of dawn or the rain of early spring.
Hosea 6:3

Mom came to tuck Wayne in. "Wayne, you used to have your Bible propped on your lap when I'd come in to say good night," said Mom. "Don't you still have devotions before you go to sleep?"

"Oh, sure. I pray after you leave," replied Wayne as he sat on the edge of his bed. "But I don't read anymore. I can't understand the Bible anyway." As he spoke, in came Heather, his golden retriever. She tipped her head and looked fondly at her master. "Hey, Heather, old girl," he greeted her. "Nice girl, Heather." As Wayne spoke, Heather inched closer and her tongue began to lick the air, itching to slobber her affection all over Wayne's face. Suddenly she could contain herself no longer. She leaped up, and all seventy pounds of Heather landed on Wayne's lap. Wayne fell back against the pillows laughing while Mom coaxed his pet out the door.

Mom came back and closed the door. "Wayne, why do you talk to Heather?" she asked. "Do you think she understands every word you say?"

"No, but I like to talk to her anyway," replied Wayne. "She always listens. And she does understand a lot of things—like *come, sit, fetch, walk,* and *roll over*. She keeps learning new words, too."

Mom picked up Wayne's Bible. "Wayne, do you know that God talks to us through his Word?"

"Yeah . . ." Wayne wasn't sure he liked what his mother was leading up to. He looked at the Bible in his mother's hand and grinned. "I get the point, Mom. God probably likes to talk to me even if I don't understand everything, just as I like to talk to Heather. And I do understand some of God's commands, and I guess I need to keep learning new things from him."

Mom smiled, kissed Wayne good night, and handed him his Bible.

How About You?
Have you stopped reading God's Word just because you can't understand everything? The more you let God speak to you, the more you will understand. He's pleased when you listen. *P. R.*

• For the next devotional, turn to page 597.   • For the next devotional on KNOWING GOD, turn to page 825.
• For notes on KNOWING GOD, see pages 129, 610, 815, and 1208.

don't let me make a mess of things. ³²If you will only help me to want your will, then I will follow your laws even more closely.

³³,³⁴Just tell me what to do and I will do it, Lord. As long as I live I'll wholeheartedly obey. ³⁵Make me walk along the right paths, for I know how delightful they really are.

³⁶Help me to prefer obedience to making money! ³⁷Turn me away from wanting any other plan than yours. Revive my heart toward you. ³⁸Reassure me that your promises are for me, for I trust and revere you.

³⁹How I dread being mocked for obeying, for your laws are right and good. ⁴⁰⁻⁴²I long to obey them! Therefore in fairness renew my life, for this was your promise—yes, Lord, to save me! Now spare me by your kindness and your love. Then I will have an answer for those who taunt me, for I trust your promises.

⁴³May I never forget your words, for they are my only hope. ⁴⁴⁻⁴⁶Therefore I will keep on obeying you forever and forever, free within the limits of your laws. I will speak to kings about their value, and they will listen with interest and respect.

⁴⁷How I love your laws! How I enjoy your commands! ⁴⁸"Come, come to me," I call to them, for I love them and will let them fill my life.

⁴⁹,⁵⁰Never forget your promises to me your servant, for they are my only hope. They give me strength in all my troubles; how they refresh and revive me! ⁵¹ Proud men hold me in contempt for obedience to God, but I stand unmoved. ⁵²From my earliest youth I have tried to obey you; your Word has been my comfort.

⁵³I am very angry with those who spurn your commands. ⁵⁴For these laws of yours have been my source of joy and singing through all these years of my earthly pilgrimage. ⁵⁵I obey them even at night and keep my thoughts, O Lord, on you. ⁵⁶What a blessing this has been to me—to constantly obey.

⁵⁷Jehovah is mine! And I promise to obey! ⁵⁸With all my heart I want your blessings. Be merciful just as you promised. ⁵⁹,⁶⁰I thought about the wrong direction in which I was headed, and turned around and came running back to you. ⁶¹Evil men have tried to drag me into sin, but I am firmly anchored to your laws.

⁶²At midnight I will rise to give my thanks to you for your good laws. ⁶³Anyone is my brother who fears and trusts the Lord and obeys him. ⁶⁴O Lord, the earth is full of your loving-kindness! Teach me your good paths.

⁶⁵Lord, I am overflowing with your blessings, just as you promised. ⁶⁶Now teach me good judgment as well as knowledge. For your laws are my guide. ⁶⁷I used to wander off until you punished me; now I closely follow all you say. ⁶⁸You are good and do only good; make me follow your lead.

⁶⁹Proud men have made up lies about me, but the truth is that I obey your laws with all my heart. ⁷⁰Their minds are dull and stupid, but I have sense enough to follow you.

⁷¹,⁷²The punishment you gave me was the best thing that could have happened to me, for it taught me to pay attention to your laws. They are more valuable to me than millions in silver and gold!

⁷³You made my body, Lord; now give me sense to heed your laws. ⁷⁴All those who fear and trust in you will welcome me because I too am trusting in your Word.

⁷⁵⁻⁷⁷I know, O Lord, that your decisions are right and that your punishment was right and did me good. Now let your loving-kindness comfort me, just as you promised. Surround me with your tender mercies that I may live. For your law is my delight.

⁷⁸Let the proud be disgraced, for they have cut me down with all their lies. But I will concentrate my thoughts upon your laws.

⁷⁹Let all others join me who trust and fear you, and we will discuss your laws. ⁸⁰Help me to love your every wish; then I will never have to be ashamed of myself.

⁸¹I faint for your salvation; but I expect your help, for you have promised it. ⁸² My eyes are straining to see your promises come true. When will you comfort me with your help? ⁸³I am shriveled like a wineskin in the smoke, exhausted with waiting. But still I cling to your laws and obey them. ⁸⁴How long must I wait before you punish those who persecute me? ⁸⁵,⁸⁶These proud men who hate your truth and laws have dug deep pits for me to fall in. Their lies have brought me into deep trouble. Help me, for you love only truth. ⁸⁷They had almost finished me off, yet I refused to yield and disobey your laws. ⁸⁸In your kindness, spare my life; then I can continue to obey you.

⁸⁹Forever, O Lord, your Word stands firm in heaven. ⁹⁰,⁹¹Your faithfulness extends to every generation, like the earth you created; it endures by your decree, for everything serves your plans.

⁹²I would have despaired and perished unless your laws had been my deepest delight. ⁹³I will never lay aside your laws, for you have used them to restore my joy and health. ⁹⁴I am yours! Save me! For I have tried to live according to your desires. ⁹⁵Though the wicked hide along the way to kill me, I will quietly keep my mind upon your promises.

⁹⁶Nothing is perfect except your words. ⁹⁷Oh, how I love them. I think about them all day long. ⁹⁸They make me wiser than my enemies because they are my constant guide. ⁹⁹Yes, wiser than my teachers, for I am ever thinking of your rules. ¹⁰⁰They make me even wiser than the aged.

Family Devotions

☐ DEVOTION 172
RESPECTING GOD'S WORD

Read Psalm 119:97-105

It had been a busy day for Jeremy, who was on a week's camping trip with his uncle Bob and cousin Eric. As the sun went down, two tired boys stretched out beside the campfire. "That was the best fish I ever ate," declared Jeremy.

Uncle Bob nodded in agreement. "Now let's have some spiritual food before we turn in for the night," he said. "I hope you boys remembered your Bibles."

Eric nodded, but Jeremy shook his head. "I always think the Bible is something for weak people who can't think for themselves," he said. "I don't need it."

Uncle Bob raised his eyebrows questioningly. "The Word of God is a very important part of my life, Jeremy," he said. "Listen to what God says about it—he calls it a light." Taking the Bible Eric handed him, Uncle Bob turned to Psalm 119. The boys listened quietly as he read several verses and then led in prayer.

As the boys were unrolling their sleeping bags a bit later, Jeremy groaned. "The mosquitoes are terrible! Where's the insect repellent?"

"It's in the glove compartment of the car," said Uncle Bob. He picked up the flashlight. "I'll get it."

"Let's go with him, Jeremy," suggested Eric. "Maybe we'll see a bear!"

As they headed into the darkness, Jeremy stumbled over a log, and down he went. As he got to his feet, he saw Uncle Bob bump into an overhanging branch. "Why don't you turn on the flashlight, Uncle Bob?" he asked. "I can't see where I'm going."

"Flashlights are OK for weak people who can't see in the dark," Uncle Bob replied carelessly, "but I don't think I need it."

Jeremy chuckled. "OK, Uncle Bob, I get the point—we need light in the dark, and we need the Bible to give us light in our lives. Now, would you please turn on that flashlight?"

Respecting God's Word
Memory Verse

Your words are what sustain me; they are food to my hungry soul. They bring joy to my sorrowing heart and delight me. How proud I am to bear your name, O Lord.
Jeremiah 15:16

How About You?
It's foolish to stumble along and not use the light that's available, isn't it? Only the light of God's Word will keep you from stumbling into sin. Are you using it? *B. W.*

• For the next devotional, turn to page 599. • For the next devotional on RESPECTING GOD'S WORD, turn to page 619.
• For notes on RESPECTING GOD'S WORD, see pages 208, 369, 1188, and 1248.

¹⁰¹I have refused to walk the paths of evil, for I will remain obedient to your Word. ¹⁰²,¹⁰³No, I haven't turned away from what you taught me; your words are sweeter than honey. ¹⁰⁴And since only your rules can give me wisdom and understanding, no wonder I hate every false teaching.

¹⁰⁵Your words are a flashlight to light the path ahead of me and keep me from stumbling. ¹⁰⁶I've said it once and I'll say it again and again: I will obey these wonderful laws of yours.

¹⁰⁷I am close to death at the hands of my enemies; oh, give me back my life again, just as you promised me. ¹⁰⁸Accept my grateful thanks and teach me your desires. ¹⁰⁹My life hangs in the balance, but I will not give up obedience to your laws. ¹¹⁰The wicked have set their traps for me along your path, but I will not turn aside. ¹¹¹Your laws are my joyous treasure forever. ¹¹²I am determined to obey you until I die.

¹¹³I hate those who are undecided whether or not to obey you; but my choice is clear—I love your law. ¹¹⁴You are my refuge and my shield, and your promises are my only source of hope. ¹¹⁵Begone, you evil-minded men! Don't try to stop me from obeying God's commands. ¹¹⁶Lord, you promised to let me live! Never let it be said that God failed me. ¹¹⁷Hold me safe above the heads of all my enemies; then I can continue to obey your laws.

¹¹⁸But you have rejected all who reject your laws. They are only fooling themselves. ¹¹⁹The wicked are the scum you skim off and throw away; no wonder I love to obey your laws! ¹²⁰I tremble in fear of you; I fear your punishments.

¹²¹Don't leave me to the mercy of my enemies, for I have done what is right; I've been perfectly fair. ¹²²Commit yourself to bless me! Don't let the proud oppress me! ¹²³My eyes grow dim with longing for you to fulfill your wonderful promise to rescue me. ¹²⁴Lord, deal with me in loving-kindness, and teach me, your servant, to obey; ¹²⁵for I am your servant; therefore give me common sense to apply your rules to everything I do.

¹²⁶Lord, it is time for you to act. For these evil men have violated your laws, ¹²⁷while I love your commandments more than the finest gold. ¹²⁸Every law of God is right, whatever it concerns. I hate every other way.

¹²⁹Your laws are wonderful; no wonder I obey them. ¹³⁰As your plan unfolds, even the simple can understand it. ¹³¹No wonder I wait expectantly for each of your commands.

¹³²Come and have mercy on me as is your way with those who love you. ¹³³Guide me with your laws so that I will not be overcome by evil. ¹³⁴Rescue me from the oppression of evil men; then I can obey you. ¹³⁵Look down in love upon me and teach me all your laws. ¹³⁶I weep because your laws are disobeyed.

¹³⁷O Lord, you are just and your punishments are fair. ¹³⁸Your demands are just and right. ¹³⁹I am indignant and angry because of the way my enemies have disregarded your laws. ¹⁴⁰I have thoroughly tested your promises, and that is why I love them so much. ¹⁴¹I am worthless and despised, but I don't despise your laws.

¹⁴²Your justice is eternal for your laws are perfectly fair. ¹⁴³In my distress and anguish your commandments comfort me. ¹⁴⁴Your laws are always fair; help me to understand them, and I shall live.

¹⁴⁵I am praying with great earnestness; answer me, O Lord, and I will obey your laws. ¹⁴⁶"Save me," I cry, "for I am obeying." ¹⁴⁷Early in the morning before the sun is up, I am praying and pointing out how much I trust in you. ¹⁴⁸I stay awake through the night to think about your promises. ¹⁴⁹Because you are so loving and kind, listen to me and make me well again.

¹⁵⁰Here come these lawless men to attack me, ¹⁵¹but you are near, O Lord; all your commandments are based on truth. ¹⁵²I have known from earliest days that your will never changes.

¹⁵³Look down upon my sorrows and rescue me, for I am obeying your commands. ¹⁵⁴Yes, rescue me and give me back my life again just as you have promised. ¹⁵⁵The wicked are far from salvation, for they do not care for your laws. ¹⁵⁶Lord, how great is your mercy; oh, give me back my life again.

¹⁵⁷My enemies are so many. They try to make me disobey, but I have not swerved from your will. ¹⁵⁸I loathed these traitors because they care nothing for your laws. ¹⁵⁹Lord, see how much I really love your demands. Now give me back my life and health because you are so kind. ¹⁶⁰There is utter truth in all your laws; your decrees are eternal.

¹⁶¹Great men have persecuted me, though they have no reason to, but I stand in awe of only your words. ¹⁶²I rejoice in your laws like one who finds a great treasure. ¹⁶³How I hate all falsehood, but how I love your laws. ¹⁶⁴I will praise you seven times a day because of your wonderful laws.

¹⁶⁵Those who love your laws have great peace of heart and mind and do not stumble. ¹⁶⁶I long for your salvation, Lord, and so I have obeyed your laws. ¹⁶⁷I have looked for your commandments, and I love them very much; ¹⁶⁸yes, I have searched for them. You know this because everything I do is known to you.

¹⁶⁹O Lord, listen to my prayers; give me the common sense you promised. ¹⁷⁰Hear my prayers; rescue me as you said you would. ¹⁷¹I praise you for letting me learn your laws. ¹⁷²I will sing about their wonder, for each of them is just. ¹⁷³Stand

Family Devotions

☐ DEVOTION 173
CONFESSING SIN

Read Psalm 130

Jim always dreaded going to the dentist. He didn't like the loud buzzing of the drill. He clenched the arms of the chair, hoping Dr. Jones was nearly done. It was a relief when the buzzing stopped and Dr. Jones checked the tooth.

"Are you finished yet?" Jim asked anxiously.

"Just a little more drilling, Jim," replied Dr. Jones. "I know this isn't pleasant, but I have to get all of the cavity out, or it would keep on decaying underneath the new filling. Then you'd probably have a toothache and could even lose the whole tooth."

Finally Dr. Jones finished drilling and began to put in the new filling. "When I drill out a cavity, I'm reminded of how I must drill sin out of my life," said Dr. Jones. "I can't leave any decayed material in the tooth because that would cause too many problems later on. It's that way in my life, too. If I leave any sins alone, they'll cause problems later on." Jim's mouth was wide open, and he couldn't answer. He just nodded numbly. "If I find myself telling even a little lie, I try to correct it." continued Dr. Jones. "I ask God to forgive me and help me to always tell the truth."

Jim felt more relaxed now that the drilling was finished, and he thought about what Dr. Jones was saying. He thought about how he often said his homework or his chores around the house were all done when that wasn't quite true—it was almost true, but not entirely true. He thought about how he no longer used bad language very often—but he did use it occasionally. Lying in the dentist chair, Jim realized he had to make some changes.

"How do you feel?" asked Dr. Jones as he helped Jim out of the chair.

Jim looked at him soberly. "Great! I'm glad to be rid of that cavity," he answered.

"I've got a couple of other cavities I'm going to finish drilling out, too. They're getting much too big."

Confessing Sin Memory Verse

Create in me a new, clean heart, O God, filled with clean thoughts and right desires.
Psalm 51:10

How About You?

Are there some things in your life that you know aren't quite right? Maybe just a little lying, a little cheating, or a little talking back to parents or teachers? Get rid of those things completely before they grow bigger and become much harder to stop. Ask for God's forgiveness and his help to drill the sin out of your life. C. Y.

• For the next devotional, turn to page 601. • For the next devotional on CONFESSING SIN, turn to page 683.
• For notes on CONFESSING SIN, see pages 429, 479, 836, 881, and 1220.

ready to help me because I have chosen to follow your will. ¹⁷⁴O Lord, I have longed for your salvation, and your law is my delight. ¹⁷⁵ If you will let me live, I will praise you; let your laws assist me.

¹⁷⁶I have wandered away like a lost sheep; come and find me, for I have not turned away from your commandments.

120 God Will Help

In my troubles I pled with God to help me and he did!

²Deliver me, O Lord, from liars. ³O lying tongue, what shall be your fate? ⁴You shall be pierced with sharp arrows and burned with glowing coals.

⁵,⁶My troubles pile high among these haters of the Lord, these men of Meshech and Kedar. I am tired of being here among these men who hate peace. ⁷I am for peace, but they are for war, and my voice goes unheeded in their councils.

121 God Guards Us

Shall I look to the mountain gods for help? ²No! My help is from Jehovah who made the mountains! And the heavens too! ³,⁴He will never let me stumble, slip, or fall. For he is always watching, never sleeping.

⁵Jehovah himself is caring for you! He is your defender. ⁶He protects you day and night. ⁷He keeps you from all evil and preserves your life. ⁸He keeps his eye upon you as you come and go and always guards you.

122 Worshiping

I was glad for the suggestion of going to Jerusalem, to the Temple of the Lord. ²,³Now we are standing here inside the crowded city. ⁴All Israel—Jehovah's people—have come to worship as the law requires, to thank and praise the Lord. ⁵Look! There are the judges holding court beside the city gates, deciding all the people's arguments.

⁶Pray for the peace of Jerusalem. May all who love this city prosper. ⁷O Jerusalem, may there be peace within your walls and prosperity in your palaces. ⁸This I ask for the sake of all my brothers and my friends who live here; ⁹and may there be peace as a protection to the Temple of the Lord.

123 God Is Merciful

O God enthroned in heaven, I lift my eyes to you.

²We look to Jehovah our God for his mercy and kindness just as a servant keeps his eyes upon his master or a slave girl watches her mistress for the slightest signal.

³,⁴Have mercy on us, Lord, have mercy. For we have had our fill of contempt and of the scoffing of the rich and proud.

124 God Is on Our Side

If the Lord had not been on our side (let all Israel admit it), if the Lord had not been on our side, ²,³we would have been swallowed alive by our enemies, destroyed by their anger. ⁴,⁵We would have drowned beneath the flood of these men's fury and pride.

⁶Blessed be Jehovah who has not let them devour us. ⁷We have escaped with our lives as a bird from a hunter's snare. The snare is broken and we are free!

⁸Our help is from the Lord who made heaven and earth.

125 God Is Our Protector

Those who trust in the Lord are steady as Mount Zion, unmoved by any circumstance.

²Just as the mountains surround and protect Jerusalem, so the Lord surrounds and protects his people. ³For the wicked shall not rule the godly, lest the godly be forced to do wrong. ⁴O Lord, do good to those who are good, whose hearts are right with the Lord; ⁵but lead evil men to execution. And let Israel have quietness and peace.

126 Tears Turn to Joy

When Jehovah brought back his exiles to Jerusalem, it was like a dream! ²How we laughed and sang for joy. And the other nations said, "What amazing things the Lord has done for them."

³Yes, glorious things! What wonder! What joy! ⁴May we be refreshed as by streams in the desert.

⁵Those who sow tears shall reap joy. ⁶Yes, they go out weeping, carrying seed for sowing, and return singing, carrying their sheaves.

127 God Makes Life Worthwhile

Unless the Lord builds a house, the builders' work is useless. Unless the Lord protects a city, sentries do no good. ²It is senseless for you to work so hard from early morning until late at night, fearing you will starve to death; for God wants his loved ones to get their proper rest.

³Children are a gift from God; they are his reward. ⁴Children born to a young man are like sharp arrows to defend him.

⁵Happy is the man who has his quiver full of them. That man shall have the help he needs when arguing with his enemies.

FAMILY DEVOTIONS

☐ *DEVOTION 174*
RESPECTING OTHERS

Read Psalm 133

Respecting Others
Memory Verse

Don't be selfish; don't live to make a good impression on others. Be humble, thinking of others as better than yourself.
Philippians 2:3

"This is ridiculous!" exclaimed Andy. He tapped his pencil impatiently on the paper in front of him. "Whoever thought up this assignment for Sunday school certainly doesn't know Jenny! I have to write down ten reasons why I like my sister, and I can't even think of one!"

"Thanks a lot!" Jenny called from the living room. "See if I ever bake cookies for you again!"

"Oops! I forgot about that." Andy wrote it down.

"How about the time last year when you were sick, and Jenny helped you with your homework?" suggested Mom.

"And how about the times I've played catch with you before a game?" Jenny asked. "Or last week when I let you ride my bike because yours was broken?"

Andy had forgotten all those things, too. He could see that Jenny really was a nice sister. He felt kind of guilty for all the times he had called her names or had purposely been a brat to her. It was hard to admit, but Andy said, "I guess I'm really kind of glad we had this assignment. It's made me appreciate my sister!"

"I can't believe I heard you say that." Jenny laughed. "In fact, I think it calls for a celebration. How about if I, being the wonderful sister that I am, make some popcorn?"

"Sounds great to me!" Andy said. He wrote one more thing on his paper. "She makes delicious popcorn!"

How About You?

Do you appreciate the brothers or sisters the Lord has given you? Do you get along with them, or do you often create arguments just for the sake of arguing? Brother and sister conflicts are not new. They've been around since Cain and Abel! Brothers and sisters often overlook the good qualities in each other because they're so busy fighting. The Bible says that they are to help each other in times of trouble. Think about that verse, and then write down some reasons why you love your brothers and sisters! L. M. W.

• For the next devotional, turn to page 603.   • For the next devotional on *RESPECTING OTHERS*, turn to page 627.
• For notes on *RESPECTING OTHERS*, see pages 322, 382, 1088, and 1218.

128 A Family Blessing

Blessings on all who reverence and trust the Lord—on all who obey him!

²Their reward shall be prosperity and happiness. ³Your wife shall be contented in your home. And look at all those children! There they sit around the dinner table as vigorous and healthy as young olive trees. ⁴That is God's reward to those who reverence and trust him.

⁵May the Lord continually bless you with heaven's blessings as well as with human joys. ⁶May you live to enjoy your grandchildren! And may God bless Israel!

129 Leave Your Enemies to God

Persecuted from my earliest youth (Israel is speaking), ²and faced with never-ending discrimination—but not destroyed! My enemies have never been able to finish me off!

³,⁴Though my back is cut to ribbons with their whips, the Lord is good. For he has snapped the chains that evil men had bound me with.

⁵May all who hate the Jews be brought to ignominious defeat. ⁶,⁷May they be as grass in shallow soil, turning sere and yellow when half grown, ignored by the reaper, despised by the binder. ⁸And may those passing by refuse to bless them by saying, "Jehovah's blessings be upon you; we bless you in Jehovah's name."

130 God Forgives

O Lord, from the depths of despair I cry for your help: ²"Hear me! Answer! Help me!"

³,⁴Lord, if you keep in mind our sins, then who can ever get an answer to his prayers? But you forgive! What an awesome thing this is! ⁵That is why I wait expectantly, trusting God to help, for he has promised. ⁶I long for him more than sentinels long for the dawn.

⁷O Israel, hope in the Lord; for he is loving and kind and comes to us with armloads of salvation. ⁸He himself shall ransom Israel from her slavery to sin.

131 A Psalm of Contentment

Lord, I am not proud and haughty. I don't think myself better than others. I don't pretend to "know it all." ²I am quiet now before the Lord, just as a child who is weaned from the breast. Yes, my begging has been stilled.

³O Israel, you too should quietly trust in the Lord—now, and always.

132 Honor God

Lord, do you remember that time when my heart was so filled with turmoil? ²⁻⁵I couldn't rest, I couldn't sleep, thinking how I ought to build a permanent home for the Ark of the Lord, a Temple for the mighty one of Israel. Then I vowed that I would do it; I made a solemn promise to the Lord.

⁶First the Ark was in Ephrathah, then in the distant countryside of Jaar. ⁷But now it will be settled in the Temple, in God's permanent home here on earth. That is where we will go to worship him. ⁸Arise, O Lord, and enter your Temple with the Ark, the symbol of your power.

⁹We will clothe the priests in white, the symbol of all purity. May our nation shout for joy.

¹⁰Do not reject your servant David—the king you chose for your people. ¹¹For you promised me that my son would sit on my throne and succeed me. And surely you will never go back on a promise! ¹²You also promised that if my descendants will obey the terms of your contract with me, then the dynasty of David shall never end.

¹³O Lord, you have chosen Jerusalem as your home: ¹⁴"This is my permanent home where I shall live," you said, "for I have always wanted it this way. ¹⁵I will make this city prosperous and satisfy her poor with food. ¹⁶I will clothe her priests with salvation; her saints shall shout for joy. ¹⁷David's power shall grow, for I have decreed for him a mighty Son. ¹⁸I'll clothe his enemies with shame, but he shall be a glorious King."

133 Living Together in Peace

How wonderful it is, how pleasant, when brothers live in harmony! ²For harmony is as precious as the fragrant anointing oil that was poured over Aaron's head and ran down onto his beard and onto the border of his robe. ³Harmony is as refreshing as the dew on Mount Hermon, on the mountains of Israel. And God has pronounced this eternal blessing on Jerusalem, even life forevermore.

134 Worship the Lord

Oh, bless the Lord, you who serve him as watchmen in the Temple every night. ²Lift your hands in holiness and bless the Lord.

³The Lord bless you from Zion—the Lord who made heaven and earth.

135 Our God Is Real

Hallelujah! ²Yes, let his people praise him as they stand in his Temple courts. ³Praise

Family Devotions

☐ DEVOTION 175
KNOWING YOU'RE SPECIAL TO GOD

Read Psalm 139:14-18

"Nine, ten, eleven." Julie painstakingly separated tiny pieces of sand from the pile she held in her hand and dropped them, grain by grain, into her pail.

"Are you just going to sit on this beach blanket, trying to count sand?" asked her brother Rick. "You could've stayed home in the sandbox."

"There must be more sand than anything else in the whole world," Julie exclaimed, ignoring her brother's remark. Rick rolled his eyes, picked up his float, and headed toward the water.

Julie stayed on the blanket, counting sand. After a little while her father looked up from the book he was reading. "How's the counting? Do you think you'll be able to finish the whole beach this afternoon?" he teased.

Julie sprinkled the remaining sand she held over her feet. "I give up," she said. "I can't even count one handful. There's so much sand on this beach, and it goes down deep, too. How much sand is there, Dad?"

Dad laughed. "There is no way we could begin to count all the sand in the world," he said. "Isn't that wonderful?"

Julie was puzzled. "Wonderful?" she asked. "Why is that wonderful?"

Dad reached into the tote bag packed with books, towels, and lotion. He took out a small Bible and turned to Psalm 139. "It says here that God thinks about us so many times a day that we couldn't count them—just as you can't count the grains of sand," he said. "Just think of that!" He scooped up a handful of sand. "God's love for us is endless."

Julie filled her bucket to the top with sand. Then she tipped it over and watched the millions of particles pour out. "Yes," she agreed. "It is wonderful, isn't it?"

Knowing You're Special to God Memory Verse

But now the Lord who created you, O Israel, says, Don't be afraid, for I have ransomed you; I have called you by name; you are mine.
Isaiah 43:1

How About You?

Do you sometimes wonder if you matter? Do your brothers or sisters or classmates say things that leave you feeling worthless? God made each person very special to him. The next time you feel less than special, think about how much sand there is over the entire earth. Then thank God that you are so special to him that his thoughts for you are more numerous than all the grains of sand in the world. *N. E. K.*

• For the next devotional, turn to page 605. • For the next devotional on KNOWING YOU'RE SPECIAL TO GOD, turn to page 1009. • For notes on KNOWING YOU'RE SPECIAL TO GOD, see pages 260, 878, 908, and 960.

the Lord because he is so good; sing to his wonderful name. ⁴For the Lord has chosen Israel as his personal possession.

⁵I know the greatness of the Lord—that he is greater far than any other god. ⁶He does whatever pleases him throughout all of heaven and earth and in the deepest seas. ⁷He makes mists rise throughout the earth; he sends the lightning to bring down the rain and sends the winds from his treasuries. ⁸He destroyed the eldest child in each Egyptian home, along with the firstborn of the flocks. ⁹He did great miracles in Egypt before Pharaoh and all his people. ¹⁰He smote great nations, slaying mighty kings—¹¹Sihon, king of Amorites; and Og, the king of Bashan; and the kings of Canaan—¹²and gave their land as an eternal gift to his people Israel.

¹³O Jehovah, your name endures forever; your fame is known to every generation. ¹⁴For Jehovah will vindicate his people and have compassion on his servants.

¹⁵The heathen worship idols of gold and silver made by men—¹⁶idols with speechless mouths, sightless eyes, ¹⁷and ears that cannot hear; they cannot even breathe. ¹⁸Those who make them become like them! And so do all who trust in them!

¹⁹O Israel, bless Jehovah! High priests of Aaron, bless his name. ²⁰O Levite priests, bless the Lord Jehovah! Oh, bless his name, all of you who trust and reverence him. ²¹All people of Jerusalem, praise the Lord, for he lives here in Jerusalem. Hallelujah!

136 Never-ending Love

Oh, give thanks to the Lord, for he is good; his loving-kindness continues forever.

²Give thanks to the God of gods, for his loving-kindness continues forever. ³Give thanks to the Lord of lords, for his loving-kindness continues forever. ⁴Praise him who alone does mighty miracles, for his loving-kindness continues forever. ⁵Praise him who made the heavens, for his loving-kindness continues forever. ⁶Praise him who planted the water within the earth, for his loving-kindness continues forever. ⁷Praise him who made the heavenly lights, for his loving-kindness continues forever: ⁸the sun to rule the day, for his loving-kindness continues forever; ⁹and the moon and stars at night, for his loving-kindness continues forever. ¹⁰Praise the God who smote the firstborn of Egypt, for his loving-kindness to Israel continues forever.

¹¹,¹²He brought them out with mighty power and upraised fist to strike their enemies, for his loving-kindness to Israel continues forever. ¹³Praise the Lord who opened the Red Sea to make a path before them, for his loving-kindness continues forever, ¹⁴and led them safely through, for his loving-kindness continues forever—¹⁵but drowned Pharaoh's army in the sea, for his loving-kindness to Israel continues forever.

¹⁶Praise him who led his people through the wilderness, for his loving-kindness continues forever. ¹⁷Praise him who saved his people from the power of mighty kings, for his loving-kindness continues forever, ¹⁸and killed famous kings who were their enemies, for his loving-kindness to Israel continues forever: ¹⁹Sihon, king of Amorites—for God's loving-kindness to Israel continues forever—²⁰and Og, king of Bashan—for his loving-kindness to Israel continues forever. ²¹God gave the land of these kings to Israel as a gift forever, for his loving-kindness to Israel continues forever; ²²yes, a permanent gift to his servant Israel, for his loving-kindness continues forever.

²³He remembered our utter weakness, for his loving-kindness continues forever. ²⁴And saved us from our foes, for his loving-kindness continues forever.

²⁵He gives food to every living thing, for his loving-kindness continues forever. ²⁶Oh, give thanks to the God of heaven, for his loving-kindness continues forever.

137 Song of the Captives

Weeping, we sat beside the rivers of Babylon thinking of Jerusalem. ²We have put away our lyres, hanging them upon the branches of the willow trees, ³,⁴for how can we sing? Yet our captors, our tormentors, demand that we sing for them the happy songs of Zion! ⁵,⁶If I forget you, O Jerusalem, let my right hand forget its skill upon the harp. If I fail to love her more than my highest joy, let me never sing again.

⁷O Jehovah, do not forget what these Edomites did on that day when the armies of Babylon captured Jerusalem. "Raze her to the ground!" they yelled. ⁸O Babylon, evil beast, you shall be destroyed. Blessed is the man who destroys you as you have destroyed us. ⁹Blessed is the man who takes your babies and smashes them against the rocks!

138 God Hears and Answers Us

Lord, with all my heart I thank you. I will sing your praises before the armies of angels. ²I face your Temple as I worship, giving thanks to you for all your loving-kindness and your faithfulness, for your promises are backed by all the honor of your name. ³When I pray, you answer me and encourage me by giving me the strength I need.

⁴Every king in all the earth shall give you thanks, O Lord, for all of them shall hear your voice. ⁵Yes, they shall sing about Jehovah's glorious ways, for his glory is very great. ⁶Yet though he is so great, he respects the humble, but proud men must keep their distance. ⁷Though I am surrounded by

Family Devotions

☐ DEVOTION 176
TRUSTING GOD FOR HELP

Read Psalm 143:7-12

Timothy wriggled into the little thicket of shrubs behind the garage. It was his own special hiding place where he always came when he was feeling sad and wanted to be alone.

Then he heard Mother calling, "Timothy! Grandpa's here." Timothy scrambled out. He didn't want to miss his beloved grandfather's visit.

Timothy and Grandpa sat down on the porch to visit—just the two of them. "Where were you just now?" Grandpa asked.

"I was feeling bad about a ball game and went to my special hiding place," Timothy said, knowing Grandpa would never tell anyone.

"Say, that's a good idea," said Grandpa sympathetically. "I had a hiding place of my own when I was a boy. It was in the hayloft of the barn." Grandpa's face beamed as he added, "Even at my age, I still have a good hiding place."

Timothy looked surprised. "You do?" He wondered what kind of place someone Grandpa's age would use to hide out.

Grandpa nodded. "Run and get your Bible," he said, "and I'll give you a clue as to where I go."

When Timothy returned, Grandpa said, "Look up Psalm 143:9, and you'll find the answer."

They read it together: "O Lord, I run to you to hide me."

"That's right," said Grandpa. "I go to God with all my hurts and sadness. God's presence is the best hiding place of all."

"Next time I'm sad, I'm going to go to the same hiding place you do, Grandpa," Timothy said. "And I can do that right in my other secret hiding place."

Trusting God for Help
Memory Verse

God is our refuge and strength, a tested help in times of trouble.
Psalm 46:1

How About You?

Are you sometimes sad and troubled? Do you take your problems and sadness to God? He's ready and waiting to hear and to help you. He wants to hear about anything that is bothering you—trouble with schoolwork, disappointments with friends, or problems in your family. The next time you need help, go to the best hiding place of all—the Lord! C. Y.

• For the next devotional, turn to page 607. • For the next devotional on TRUSTING GOD FOR HELP, turn to page 679.
• For notes on TRUSTING GOD FOR HELP, see pages 240, 249, 464, 539, and 751.

troubles, you will bring me safely through them. You will clench your fist against my angry enemies! Your power will save me. ⁸The Lord will work out his plans for my life—for your loving-kindness, Lord, continues forever. Don't abandon me—for you made me.

139 God Knows All about You

O Lord, you have examined my heart and know everything about me. ²You know when I sit or stand. When far away you know my every thought. ³You chart the path ahead of me and tell me where to stop and rest. Every moment you know where I am. ⁴You know what I am going to say before I even say it. ⁵You both precede and follow me and place your hand of blessing on my head.

⁶This is too glorious, too wonderful to believe! ⁷I can *never* be lost to your Spirit! I can *never* get away from my God! ⁸If I go up to heaven, you are there; if I go down to the place of the dead, you are there. ⁹If I ride the morning winds to the farthest oceans, ¹⁰even there your hand will guide me, your strength will support me. ¹¹If I try to hide in the darkness, the night becomes light around me. ¹²For even darkness cannot hide from God; to you the night shines as bright as day. Darkness and light are both alike to you.

¹³You made all the delicate, inner parts of my body and knit them together in my mother's womb. ¹⁴Thank you for making me so wonderfully complex! It is amazing to think about. Your workmanship is marvelous—and how well I know it. ¹⁵You were there while I was being formed in utter seclusion! ¹⁶You saw me before I was born and scheduled each day of my life before I began to breathe. Every day was recorded in your book!

¹⁷,¹⁸How precious it is, Lord, to realize that you are thinking about me constantly! I can't even count how many times a day your thoughts turn toward me. And when I waken in the morning, you are still thinking of me!

¹⁹Surely you will slay the wicked, Lord! Away, bloodthirsty men! Begone! ²⁰They blaspheme your name and stand in arrogance against you—how silly can they be? ²¹O Lord, shouldn't I hate those who hate you? Shouldn't I be grieved with them? ²²Yes, I hate them, for your enemies are my enemies too.

²³Search me, O God, and know my heart; test my thoughts. ²⁴Point out anything you find in me that makes you sad, and lead me along the path of everlasting life.

140 Prayer for Protection

O Lord, deliver me from evil men. Preserve me from the violent, ²who plot and stir up trouble all day long. ³Their words sting like poisonous snakes. ⁴Keep me out of their power. Preserve me from their violence, for they are plotting against me. ⁵These proud men have set a trap to catch me, a noose to yank me up and leave me dangling in the air; they wait in ambush with a net to throw over and hold me helpless in its meshes.

⁶⁻⁸O Jehovah, my Lord and Savior, my God and my shield—hear me as I pray! Don't let these wicked men succeed; don't let them prosper and be proud. ⁹Let their plots boomerang! Let them be destroyed by the very evil they have planned for me. ¹⁰Let burning coals fall down upon their heads, or throw them into the fire or into deep pits from which they can't escape.

¹¹Don't let liars prosper here in our land; quickly punish them. ¹²But the Lord will surely help those they persecute; he will maintain the rights of the poor. ¹³Surely the godly are thanking you, for they shall live in your presence.

141 When Tempted and Criticized

Quick, Lord, answer me—for I have prayed. Listen when I cry to you for help! ²Regard my prayer as my evening sacrifice and as incense wafting up to you.

³Help me, Lord, to keep my mouth shut and my lips sealed. ⁴Take away my lust for evil things; don't let me want to be with sinners, doing what they do, sharing their delicacies. ⁵Let the godly smite me! It will be a kindness! If they reprove me, it is medicine! Don't let me refuse it. But I am in constant prayer against the wicked and their deeds. ⁶,⁷When their leaders are condemned, and their bones are strewn across the ground, then these men will finally listen to me and know that I am trying to help them.

⁸I look to you for help, O Lord God. You are my refuge. Don't let them slay me. ⁹Keep me out of their traps. ¹⁰Let them fall into their own snares, while I escape.

142 When You Feel Trapped

How I plead with God, how I implore his mercy, pouring out my troubles before him. ³For I am overwhelmed and desperate, and you alone know which way I ought to turn to miss the traps my enemies have set for me. ⁴(There's one—just over there to the right!) No one gives me a passing thought. No one will help me; no one cares a bit what happens to me. ⁵Then I prayed to Jehovah. "Lord," I pled, "you are my only place of refuge. Only you can keep me safe.

⁶"Hear my cry, for I am very low. Rescue me from my persecutors, for they are too strong for me. ⁷Bring me out of prison so that I can thank you. The godly will rejoice with me for all your help."

Family Devotions

☐ **Devotion 177**
Sharing Your Faith

Read Psalm 145

"A total failure, that's what I am," Tom muttered as he slowly walked home after school. "When Carl asked why I always go to church, it was a perfect chance to tell him I'm a Christian and that Jesus—not the church—saved me. But I just shrugged and changed the subject. I wish I could talk about the Lord."

That evening Tom heard someone talking in his brother's room. He went to see who was there. "What are you doing?" asked Tom when he saw his brother standing in front of the mirror, talking out loud.

Keith turned around and laughed. "I'm practicing," he said. "My speech teacher said you have to practice in order to sing or to play a musical instrument well, and you also have to practice to become a good speaker," explained Keith. "He told us to practice, practice, practice, so I do and it works. I may never be a great speaker, but at least I'm improving."

Tom watched as Keith turned back to his mirror and began his speech again. *Practice,* thought Tom as he went to his own room. *That's what I have to do, too.*

When Keith passed Tom's room a little later, Tom was standing in front of his mirror. "I'm a Christian," Tom was saying, "and you can be one, too." He cleared his throat. "I'm a Christian," he repeated, "and you can be one, too." He paused. "The Bible says . . ." Keith smiled and walked on as Tom continued to practice witnessing.

Sharing Your Faith
Memory Verse

And I assure you of this: I, the Messiah, will publicly honor you in the presence of God's angels if you publicly acknowledge me here on earth as your Friend.
Luke 12:8

How About You?
Are you afraid to speak up for the Lord? Do you have trouble knowing what to say? Practice at home first in front of a mirror. Then when you've gotten used to the sound of your own voice talking about the Lord, you may want to practice with a friend or with a parent. It will seem strange at first, but try it. And then speak up for the Lord whenever you have a chance. You can be a witness for him. H. M.

• For the next devotional, turn to page 609.   • For the next devotional on *Sharing Your Faith,* turn to page 777.
• For notes on *Sharing Your Faith,* see pages 462, 776, 1015, and 1074.

143 When Weak and Scared

Hear my prayer, O Lord; answer my plea because you are faithful to your promises. ²Don't bring me to trial! For as compared with you, no one is perfect.

³My enemies chased and caught me. They have knocked me to the ground. They force me to live in the darkness like those in the grave. ⁴I am losing all hope; I am paralyzed with fear.

⁵I remember the glorious miracles you did in days of long ago. ⁶I reach out for you. I thirst for you as parched land thirsts for rain. ⁷Come quickly, Lord, and answer me, for my depression deepens; don't turn away from me or I shall die. ⁸Let me see your kindness to me in the morning, for I am trusting you. Show me where to walk, for my prayer is sincere. ⁹Save me from my enemies. O Lord, I run to you to hide me. ¹⁰Help me to do your will, for you are my God. Lead me in good paths, for your Spirit is good.

¹¹Lord, saving me will bring glory to your name. Bring me out of all this trouble because you are true to your promises. ¹²And because you are loving and kind to me, cut off all my enemies and destroy those who are trying to harm me; for I am your servant.

144 Rejoice in God's Care

Bless the Lord who is my immovable Rock. He gives me strength and skill in battle. ²He is always kind and loving to me; he is my fortress, my tower of strength and safety, my deliverer. He stands before me as a shield. He subdues my people under me.

³O Lord, what is man that you even notice him? Why bother at all with the human race? ⁴For man is but a breath; his days are like a passing shadow.

⁵Bend down the heavens, Lord, and come. The mountains smoke beneath your touch.

⁶Let loose your lightning bolts, your arrows, Lord, upon your enemies, and scatter them.

⁷Reach down from heaven and rescue me; deliver me from deep waters, from the power of my enemies. ⁸Their mouths are filled with lies; they swear to the truth of what is false.

⁹I will sing you a new song, O God, with a ten-stringed harp. ¹⁰For you grant victory to kings! You are the one who will rescue your servant David from the fatal sword. ¹¹Save me! Deliver me from these enemies, these liars, these treacherous men.

¹²⁻¹⁵Here is my description of a truly happy land where Jehovah is God:

Sons vigorous and tall as growing plants.
Daughters of graceful beauty like the pillars of a palace wall.
Barns full to the brim with crops of every kind.
Sheep by the thousands out in our fields.
Oxen loaded down with produce.
No enemy attacking the walls, but peace everywhere.
No crime in our streets.
Yes, happy are those whose God is Jehovah.

145 A Magnificent God

I will praise you, my God and King, and bless your name each day and forever.

³Great is Jehovah! Greatly praise him! His greatness is beyond discovery! ⁴Let each generation tell its children what glorious things he does. ⁵I will meditate about your glory, splendor, majesty, and miracles. ⁶Your awe-inspiring deeds shall be on every tongue; I will proclaim your greatness. ⁷Everyone will tell about how good you are and sing about your righteousness.

⁸Jehovah is kind and merciful, slow to get angry, full of love. ⁹He is good to everyone, and his compassion is intertwined with everything he does. ¹⁰All living things shall thank you, Lord, and your people will bless you. ¹¹They will talk together about the glory of your kingdom and mention examples of your power. ¹²They will tell about your miracles and about the majesty and glory of your reign. ¹³For your kingdom never ends. You rule generation after generation.

¹⁴The Lord lifts the fallen and those bent beneath their loads. ¹⁵The eyes of all mankind look up to you for help; you give them their food as they need it. ¹⁶You constantly satisfy the hunger and thirst of every living thing.

¹⁷The Lord is fair in everything he does and full of kindness. ¹⁸He is close to all who call on him sincerely. ¹⁹He fulfills the desires of those who reverence and trust him; he hears their cries for help and rescues them. ²⁰He protects all those who love him, but destroys the wicked.

²¹I will praise the Lord and call on all men everywhere to bless his holy name forever and forever.

GIVING THANKS 146–150 These last five psalms overflow with praise. Each begins with "Hallelujah" or "Praise the Lord." They show us where, why, and how to praise God. What does praise do? (1) Praise takes our minds off our problems and shortcomings, and focuses them on God. (2) Praise takes us from individual meditation to corporate worship. (3) Praise causes us to consider and appreciate God's character. (4) Praise takes our perspective from the earthly to the heavenly. How often do you thank and praise God for who he is and all he has done for you? **To begin the series of devotionals on** GIVING THANKS, **turn to page 169.**

Family Devotions

☐ DEVOTION 178
GIVING THANKS

Read Psalm 150

Peter picked up the ballpoint pen and drew a line down the middle of the paper. His Sunday school teacher had asked the class to bring in a list of things for which they were thankful and a list of things for which they were not thankful. Well, Peter could think of a lot of things he wasn't thankful about. For example, Mother had sent him to his room yesterday because he told a lie. He sure wasn't thankful for punishment. He wrote it down on the list. Opposite, he put down the word *parents*. Yes, he was thankful for them. They took care of him every day.

Peter looked again at the words *punishment* and *parents*. It didn't seem quite right to be thankful for one and not the other when his parents were the ones who punished him. Maybe he should be thankful that they cared enough to punish him when he did wrong things. He thought about it awhile and then finally crossed out *punishment*.

On the "thankful" side, Peter wrote *church*. That was definitely something to be thankful for. It was there he had made his decision to put his faith in Jesus Christ. Suddenly he thought of the memory verse he had to learn before Sunday morning. He hated to memorize. Quickly he wrote down *memorization* on the side of things for which he was not thankful.

A Bible verse popped into Peter's mind—one he had learned way back during his primary Sunday school days. He found himself repeating it word for word. "Always give thanks for everything to our God and Father in the name of our Lord Jesus Christ." He even remembered where it was found—Ephesians 5:20.

Well, that verse sure blew the idea of listing things for which he was not thankful. He crossed out the word *memorization*. Then he crossed out the words on the other side of the paper, too. In place of them he wrote in big letters: EVERYTHING!

Giving Thanks
Memory Verse

Is anyone among you suffering? He should keep on praying about it. And those who have reason to be thankful should continually be singing praises to the Lord.
James 5:13

How About You?
Are there things you do not thank God for? Maybe you hate to study. Maybe your father lost his job. Or maybe something didn't happen when you wanted it to happen, and you grumbled about it. The Bible says to give thanks for all things. Can you do that? R.J.

• For the next devotional, turn to page 617. • For the next devotional on GIVING THANKS, turn to page 987.
• For notes on GIVING THANKS, see pages 582, 608, and 834.

146 God's Help Is All You Need

Praise the Lord! Yes, really praise him! ²I will praise him as long as I live, yes, even with my dying breath.

³Don't look to men for help; their greatest leaders fail; ⁴for every man must die. His breathing stops, life ends, and in a moment all he planned for himself is ended. ⁵But happy is the man who has the God of Jacob as his helper, whose hope is in the Lord his God—⁶the God who made both earth and heaven, the seas and everything in them. He is the God who keeps every promise, ⁷who gives justice to the poor and oppressed and food to the hungry. He frees the prisoners ⁸and opens the eyes of the blind; he lifts the burdens from those bent down beneath their loads. For the Lord loves good men. ⁹He protects the immigrants and cares for the orphans and widows. But he turns topsy-turvy the plans of the wicked.

¹⁰The Lord will reign forever. O Jerusalem, your God is King in every generation! Hallelujah! Praise the Lord!

147 Yes, Praise the Lord!

Hallelujah! Yes, praise the Lord! How good it is to sing his praises! How delightful, and how right!

²He is rebuilding Jerusalem and bringing back the exiles. ³He heals the brokenhearted, binding up their wounds. ⁴He counts the stars and calls them all by name. ⁵How great he is! His power is absolute! His understanding is unlimited. ⁶The Lord supports the humble, but brings the wicked into the dust.

⁷Sing out your thanks to him; sing praises to our God, accompanied by harps. ⁸He covers the heavens with clouds, sends down the showers, and makes the green grass grow in mountain pastures. ⁹He feeds the wild animals, and the young ravens cry to him for food. ¹⁰The speed of a horse is nothing to him. How puny in his sight is the strength of a man. ¹¹But his joy is in those who reverence him, those who expect him to be loving and kind.

¹²Praise him, O Jerusalem! Praise your God, O Zion! ¹³For he has fortified your gates against all enemies and blessed your children. ¹⁴He sends peace across your nation and fills your barns with plenty of the finest wheat. ¹⁵He sends his orders to the world. How swiftly his word flies. ¹⁶He sends the snow in all its lovely whiteness, scatters the frost upon the ground, ¹⁷and hurls the hail upon the earth. Who can stand before his freezing cold? ¹⁸But then he calls for warmer weather, and the spring winds blow and all the river ice is broken. ¹⁹He has made known his laws and ceremonies of worship to Israel—²⁰something he has not done with any other nation; they have not known his commands.

Hallelujah! Yes, praise the Lord!

148 Let All Creation Give Praise

Praise the Lord, O heavens! Praise him from the skies! ²Praise him, all his angels, all the armies of heaven. ³Praise him, sun and moon and all you twinkling stars. ⁴Praise him, skies above. Praise him, vapors high above the clouds.

⁵Let everything he has made give praise to him. For he issued his command, and they came into being; ⁶he established them forever and forever. His orders will never be revoked.

⁷And praise him down here on earth, you creatures of the ocean depths. ⁸Let fire and hail, snow, rain, wind, and weather, all obey. ⁹Let the mountains and hills, the fruit trees and cedars, ¹⁰the wild animals and cattle, the snakes and birds, ¹¹the kings and all the people with their rulers and their judges, ¹²young men and maidens, old men and children—¹³all praise the Lord together. For he alone is worthy. His glory is far greater than all of earth and heaven. ¹⁴He has made his people strong, honoring his godly ones—the people of Israel, the people closest to him.

Hallelujah! Yes, praise the Lord!

149 God Enjoys Us

Hallelujah! Yes, praise the Lord! Sing him a new song. Sing his praises, all his people.

²O Israel, rejoice in your Maker. O people of Jerusalem, exult in your King. ³Praise his name with dancing, accompanied by drums and lyre.

⁴,⁵For Jehovah enjoys his people; he will save the humble. Let his people rejoice in this honor. Let them sing for joy as they lie upon their beds.

⁶,⁷Adore him, O his people! And take a double-edged sword to execute his punishment upon the nations. ⁸Bind their kings and leaders with iron chains, ⁹and execute their sentences.

He is the glory of his people. Hallelujah! Praise him!

KNOWING GOD 147:5 Sometimes we feel as if we don't understand ourselves—what we want, how we feel, what's wrong with us, or what we should do about it. If you feel troubled and don't understand yourself, remember that God understands you perfectly. Take your mind off yourself and focus it on God. Strive to become more and more like him. The more you learn about God and his ways, the better you will understand yourself. **To begin the series of devotionals on KNOWING GOD, turn to page 197.**

150 Praise the Lord, One and All

Hallelujah! Yes, praise the Lord! Praise him in his Temple and in the heavens he made with mighty power. ²Praise him for his mighty works. Praise his unequaled greatness. ³Praise him with the trumpet and with lute and harp. ⁴Praise him with the drums and dancing. Praise him with stringed instruments and horns. ⁵Praise him with the cymbals, yes, loud clanging cymbals.

⁶Let everything alive give praises to the Lord! *You* praise him!

Hallelujah!

Proverbs

WOULDN'T IT be nice to know how to handle every situation that comes our way? That would be like having the wisdom of Solomon!

Happily, Solomon and other wise people did leave us some of their wisdom in the book of Proverbs. They tell us what God showed them about friendships, family, work, conversations, money, drinking, pride, discipline, anger, and much more. By studying Proverbs, we can learn how to better deal with many areas of life.

Most proverbs are one or two sentences. They don't go into detail. It's up to us to think about them and put them to work in our lives. Other parts of Proverbs are longer explanations of things we need to know.

Solomon not only gives us his wisdom, he also tells us where to find wisdom for ourselves. He points us to the wisest one of all—God. So even if we need wisdom about something that's not covered in Proverbs, we know where to find our answers.

As you read, pick out some proverbs that you especially like or need to learn from. Then ask God to help you grow in wisdom as you follow them.

The Reason for Proverbs

These are the proverbs of King Solomon of Israel, David's son:

²He wrote them to teach his people how to live—how to act in every circumstance, ³for he wanted them to be understanding, just and fair in everything they did. ⁴"I want to make the simple-minded wise!" he said. "I want to warn young men about some problems they will face. ⁵,⁶I want those already wise to become the wiser and become leaders by exploring the depths of meaning in these nuggets of truth."

⁷⁻⁹How does a man become wise? The first step is to trust and reverence the Lord!

Only fools refuse to be taught. Listen to your father and mother. What you learn from them will stand you in good stead; it will gain you many honors.

¹⁰If young toughs tell you, "Come and join us"—turn your back on them! ¹¹ "We'll hide and

rob and kill," they say. ¹²"Good or bad, we'll treat them all alike. ¹³And the loot we'll get! All kinds of stuff! ¹⁴Come on, throw in your lot with us; we'll split with you in equal shares."

¹⁵Don't do it, son! Stay far from men like that, ¹⁶for crime is their way of life, and murder is their specialty. ¹⁷When a bird sees a trap being set, it stays away, ¹⁸but not these men; they trap themselves! They lay a booby trap for their own lives. ¹⁹Such is the fate of all who live by violence and murder. They will die a violent death.

²⁰Wisdom shouts in the streets for a hearing. ²¹She calls out to the crowds along Main Street, and to the judges in their courts, and to everyone in all the land: ²² "You simpletons!" she cries. "How long will you go on being fools? How long will you scoff at wisdom and fight the facts? ²³Come here and listen to me! I'll pour out the spirit of wisdom upon you and make you wise. ²⁴I have called you so often, but still you won't come. I have pleaded, but all in vain. ²⁵For you have spurned my counsel and reproof. ²⁶Some day you'll be in trouble, and I'll laugh! Mock me, will you?—I'll mock you! ²⁷When a storm of terror surrounds you, and when you are engulfed by anguish and distress, ²⁸then I will not answer your cry for help. It will be too late though you search for me ever so anxiously.

²⁹"For you closed your eyes to the facts and did not choose to reverence and trust the Lord, ³⁰and you turned your back on me, spurning my advice. ³¹That is why you must eat the bitter fruit of having your own way and experience the full terrors of the pathway you have chosen. ³²For you turned away from me—to death; your own complacency will kill you. Fools! ³³But all who listen to me shall live in peace and safety, unafraid."

2 Wisdom Comes from God

Every young man who listens to me and obeys my instructions will be given wisdom and good sense. ³⁻⁵Yes, if you want better insight and discernment, and are searching for them as you would for lost money or hidden treasure, then wisdom will be given you and knowledge of God himself; you will soon learn the importance of reverence for the Lord and of trusting him.

⁶For the Lord grants wisdom! His every word is a treasure of knowledge and understanding. ⁷,⁸He grants good sense to the godly—his saints. He is their shield, protecting them and guarding their pathway. ⁹He shows how to distinguish right from wrong, how to find the right decision every time. ¹⁰For wisdom and truth will enter the very center of your being, filling your life with joy. ¹¹⁻¹³ You will be given the sense to stay away from evil men who want you to be their partners in crime—men who turn from God's ways to walk down dark and evil paths ¹⁴and exult in doing wrong, for they thoroughly enjoy their sins. ¹⁵Everything they do is crooked and wrong.

¹⁶,¹⁷Only wisdom from the Lord can save a man from the flattery of prostitutes; these girls have abandoned their husbands and flouted the laws of God. ¹⁸Their houses lie along the road to death and hell. ¹⁹The men who enter them are doomed. None of these men will ever be the same again.

²⁰Follow the steps of the godly instead, and stay on the right path, ²¹for only good men enjoy life to the full; ²²evil men lose the good things they might have had, and they themselves shall be destroyed.

3 Wisdom Is Priceless

My son, never forget the things I've taught you. If you want a long and satisfying life, closely follow my instructions. ³Never tire of loyalty and kindness. Hold these virtues tightly. Write them deep within your heart. ⁴,⁵If you want favor with both God and man, and a reputation for good judgment and common sense, then trust the Lord completely; don't ever trust yourself. ⁶In everything you do, put God first, and he will direct you and crown your efforts with success.

⁷,⁸Don't be conceited, sure of your own wisdom. Instead, trust and reverence the Lord, and turn your back on evil; when you do that, then you will be given renewed health and vitality.

⁹,¹⁰Honor the Lord by giving him the first part of all your income, and he will fill your barns with wheat and barley and overflow your wine vats with the finest wines.

¹¹,¹²Young man, do not resent it when God chastens and corrects you, for his punishment is proof of his love. Just as a father punishes a son he delights in to make him better, so the Lord corrects you.

¹³⁻¹⁵The man who knows right from wrong and has good judgment and common sense is happier than the man who is immensely rich! For such wisdom is far more valuable than precious jewels. Nothing else compares with it. ¹⁶,¹⁷Wisdom gives: a long, good life, riches, honor, pleasure, peace. ¹⁸Wisdom is a tree of life to those who eat her fruit; happy is the man who keeps on eating it.

¹⁹The Lord's wisdom founded

TRUSTING GOD FOR GUIDANCE 1:7-9 In this age of information, knowledge is plentiful, but wisdom is scarce. Wisdom means far more than simply knowing a lot. It is a basic attitude that affects every aspect of life. The first step to wisdom is to trust and respect God. Faith in God should be the foundation for your understanding of the world, your attitudes, and your actions. Trust in God and he will make you truly wise. **To begin the series of devotionals on TRUSTING GOD FOR GUIDANCE, turn to page 27.**

the earth; his understanding established all the universe and space. ²⁰The deep fountains of the earth were broken open by his knowledge, and the skies poured down rain.

²¹Have two goals: wisdom—that is, knowing and doing right—and common sense. Don't let them slip away, ²²for they fill you with living energy and bring you honor and respect. ²³They keep you safe from defeat and disaster and from stumbling off the trail. ²⁴⁻²⁶With them on guard you can sleep without fear; you need not be afraid of disaster or the plots of wicked men, for the Lord is with you; he protects you.

²⁷,²⁸Don't withhold repayment of your debts. Don't say "some other time," if you can pay now. ²⁹Don't plot against your neighbor; he is trusting you. ³⁰Don't get into needless fights. ³¹Don't envy violent men. Don't copy their ways. ³²For such men are an abomination to the Lord, but he gives his friendship to the godly.

³³The curse of God is on the wicked, but his blessing is on the upright. ³⁴The Lord mocks at mockers, but helps the humble. ³⁵The wise are promoted to honor, but fools are promoted to shame!

4 You Can Learn Wisdom

Young men, listen to me as you would to your father. Listen, and grow wise, for I speak the truth—don't turn away. ³For I, too, was once a son, tenderly loved by my mother as an only child, and the companion of my father. ⁴He told me never to forget his words. "If you follow them," he said, "you will have a long and happy life. ⁵*Learn to be wise,*" he said, *"and develop good judgment and common sense! I cannot overemphasize this point."* ⁶Cling to wisdom—she will protect you. Love her—she will guard you.

⁷Getting wisdom is the most important thing you can do! And with your wisdom, develop common sense and good judgment. ⁸,⁹If you exalt wisdom, she will exalt you. Hold her fast, and she will lead you to great honor; she will place a beautiful crown upon your head. ¹⁰My son, listen to me and do as I say, and you will have a long, good life.

¹¹I would have you learn this great fact: that a life of doing right is the wisest life there is. ¹²If you live that kind of life, you'll not limp or stumble as you run. ¹³Carry out my instructions; don't forget them, for they will lead you to real living.

¹⁴Don't do as the wicked do. ¹⁵Avoid their haunts—turn away, go somewhere else, ¹⁶for evil men can't sleep until they've done their evil deed for the day. They can't rest unless they cause someone to stumble and fall. ¹⁷They eat and drink wickedness and violence!

¹⁸But the good man walks along in the ever-brightening light of God's favor; the dawn gives way to morning splendor, ¹⁹while the evil man gropes and stumbles in the dark.

²⁰Listen, son of mine, to what I say. Listen carefully. ²¹Keep these thoughts ever in mind; let them penetrate deep within your heart, ²²for they will mean real life for you and radiant health.

²³*Above all else, guard your affections.* For they influence everything else in your life. ²⁴Spurn the careless kiss of a prostitute. Stay far from her. ²⁵ Look straight ahead; don't even turn your head to look. ²⁶Watch your step. Stick to the path and be safe. ²⁷Don't sidetrack; pull back your foot from danger.

5 Run from Sin

Listen to me, my son! I know what I am saying; *listen!* ²Watch yourself, lest you be indiscreet and betray some vital information. ³For the lips of a prostitute are as sweet as honey, and smooth flattery is her stock in trade. ⁴But afterwards only a bitter conscience is left to you, sharp as a double-edged sword. ⁵She leads you down to death and hell. ⁶For she does not know the path to life. She staggers down a crooked trail and doesn't even realize where it leads.

⁷Young men, listen to me, and never forget what I'm about to say: ⁸*Run from her! Don't go near her house,* ⁹lest you fall to her temptation and lose your honor, and give the remainder of your life to the cruel and merciless; ¹⁰lest strangers obtain your wealth, and you become a slave of foreigners. ¹¹Lest afterwards you groan in anguish and in shame when syphilis consumes your body, ¹²and you say, "Oh, if only I had listened! If only I had not demanded my own way! ¹³Oh, why wouldn't I take advice? Why was I so stupid? ¹⁴For now I must face public disgrace."

¹⁵Drink from your own well, my son—be faithful and true to your wife. ¹⁶Why should you beget children with women of the street? ¹⁷Why share your children with those outside your home? ¹⁸Be happy, yes, rejoice in the wife of your youth. ¹⁹Let her breasts and tender embrace satisfy you. Let her love alone fill you with delight. ²⁰Why delight yourself with prostitutes, embracing what isn't yours? ²¹ *For God is closely watching you,* and he weighs carefully everything you do.

²²The wicked man is doomed by his own sins; they are ropes that catch and hold him. ²³He shall die because he will not listen to the truth; he has let himself be led away into incredible folly.

6 Run from Foolishness

Son, if you endorse a note for someone you hardly know, guaranteeing his debt, you are in serious trouble. ²You may have trapped yourself by your agreement. ³Quick! Get out of it if you possibly can! Swallow your pride; don't let embarrassment stand in the way. Go and beg to have your name erased. ⁴Don't put it off. Do it now. Don't rest until you do. ⁵If you can get out of this trap you have saved yourself like a deer that escapes from a hunter or a bird from the net.

⁶Take a lesson from the ants, you lazy fellow. Learn from their ways and be wise! ⁷For though they have no king to make them work, ⁸yet they labor hard all summer, gathering food for the winter. ⁹But you—all you do is sleep. When will you wake up? ¹⁰"Let me sleep a little longer!" Sure, just a little more! ¹¹And as you sleep, poverty creeps upon you like a robber and destroys you; want attacks you in full armor.

¹²,¹³Let me describe for you a worthless and a wicked man; first, he is a constant liar; he signals his true intentions to his friends with eyes and feet and fingers. ¹⁴He is always thinking up new schemes to swindle people. He stirs up trouble everywhere. ¹⁵But he will be destroyed suddenly, broken beyond hope of healing.

¹⁶⁻¹⁹For there are six things the Lord hates—no, seven: haughtiness, lying, murdering, plotting evil, eagerness to do wrong, a false witness, sowing discord among brothers.

²⁰Young man, obey your father and your mother. ²¹Take to heart all of their advice; keep in mind everything they tell you. ²²Every day and all night long their counsel will lead you and save you from harm; when you wake up in the morning, let their instructions guide you into the new day. ²³For their advice is a beam of light directed into the dark corners of your mind to warn you of danger and to give you a good life. ²⁴Their counsel will keep you far away from prostitutes, with all their flatteries, and unfaithful wives of other men.

²⁵Don't lust for their beauty. Don't let their coyness seduce you. ²⁶For a prostitute will bring a man to poverty, and an adulteress may cost him his very life. ²⁷Can a man hold fire against his chest and not be burned? ²⁸Can he walk on hot coals and not blister his feet? ²⁹So it is with the man who commits adultery with another's wife. He shall not go unpunished for this sin. ³⁰Excuses might even be found for a thief if he steals when he is starving! ³¹But even so, he is fined seven times as much as he stole, though it may mean selling everything in his house to pay it back.

³²But the man who commits adultery is an utter fool, for he destroys his own soul. ³³Wounds and constant disgrace are his lot, ³⁴for the woman's husband will be furious in his jealousy, and he will have no mercy on you in his day of vengeance. ³⁵You won't be able to buy him off no matter what you offer.

7 Keep Yourself Pure

Follow my advice, my son; always keep it in mind and stick to it. ²Obey me and live! Guard my words as your most precious possession. ³Write them down, and also keep them deep within your heart. ⁴Love wisdom like a sweetheart; make her a beloved member of your family. ⁵Let her hold you back from affairs with other women—from listening to their flattery.

⁶I was looking out the window of my house one day ⁷and saw a simple-minded lad, a young man lacking common sense, ⁸,⁹walking at twilight down the street to the house of this wayward girl, a prostitute. ¹⁰She approached him, saucy and pert, and dressed seductively. ¹¹,¹²She was the brash, coarse type, seen often in the streets and markets, soliciting at every corner for men to be her lovers.

¹³She put her arms around him and kissed him, and with a saucy look she said, "I was just coming to look for you and here you are! ¹⁴⁻¹⁷Come home with me, and I'll fix you a wonderful dinner, and after that—well, my bed is spread with lovely, colored sheets of finest linen imported from Egypt, perfumed with myrrh, aloes, and cinnamon. ¹⁸Come on, let's take our fill of love until morning, ¹⁹for my husband is away on a long trip. ²⁰He has taken a wallet full of money with him and won't return for several days."

²¹So she seduced him with her pretty speech, her coaxing and her wheedling, until he yielded to her. He couldn't resist her flattery. ²²He followed her as an ox going to the butcher or as a stag that is trapped, ²³waiting to be killed with an arrow through its heart. He was as a bird flying into a snare, not knowing the fate awaiting it there.

²⁴Listen to me, young men, and not only listen but obey; ²⁵don't let your desires get out of hand; don't let yourself think about her. Don't go near her; stay away from where she walks, lest she tempt you and seduce you. ²⁶For she has been the ruin of multitudes—a vast host of men have been her victims. ²⁷If you want to find the road to hell, look for her house.

8 Wisdom Gives Good Advice

Can't you hear the voice of wisdom? She is standing at the city gates and at every fork in the road, and at the door of every house. Listen to what she says: ⁴,⁵"Listen, men!" she calls. "How foolish and naive you are! Let me give you understanding. O foolish ones, let me show you common sense! ⁶,⁷Listen to me! For I have important information for you. Everything I say is right and true, for I hate lies and every kind of deception.

Family Devotions

☐ DEVOTION 179
AVOIDING SIN

Read Proverbs 6:27-28

"Hi, Mom," said Tiffany as she came in the door.

"Hi," greeted Mom. "What did you do at Kay's?"

Tiffany hesitated. "Oh, nothing much."

Mom's brows creased. "You're hedging, Tiffany."

"Well . . . Kay wanted to watch a movie on TV that had a lot of violence and swearing," confessed Tiffany. "I didn't really want to, but I was her guest. But don't worry, Mom. I don't let things like that affect me."

"Fooling around with sinful things is like playing with fire," replied Mother. "I was just thinking of my cousin, Annabel. I once went with Annabel and her folks on an outing in the woods. Her father built a bonfire. When the flames died down, her father threw water over the coals. They turned gray, and the fire seemed to be gone.

"Annabel and I played a game of tag. With her bare feet, Annabel ran right over those coals, not even noticing them because they looked as gray as the sand. Oh, how she screamed! Inside, the coals were still very hot, and Annabel burned both her feet very badly."

"Oh, how awful!" exclaimed Tiffany.

"Yes," said Mom. "In Proverbs it says, 'Can [a man] walk on hot coals and not blister his feet?'"

"Oh," said Tiffany, "that's what happened to Annabel."

"Yes. But God isn't warning here about real fire," said Mother. "He's talking about sinful things."

"Like bad TV and music?" asked Tiffany. "I didn't think a little would hurt."

Mom nodded. "Yes. Like the gray coals that looked harmless, sinful things often seem innocent. But sin always harms us."

"I like Kay," said Tiffany, "but next time I'm not going to watch a movie like that with her. I don't want to step on any hot coals."

Avoiding Sin Memory Verse

Dear brothers, you are only visitors here. Since your real home is in heaven, I beg you to keep away from the evil pleasures of this world; they are not for you, for they fight against your very souls.
1 Peter 2:11

How About You?
Have you felt that a few worldly things wouldn't harm you? How much fire must you touch before you're burned? Treat every sin as though it's a red-hot coal of fire. *M. R. P.*

• For the next devotional, turn to page 619. • For the next devotional on AVOIDING SIN, turn to page 663.
• For notes on AVOIDING SIN, see pages 220, 332, 392, and 657.

⁸My advice is wholesome and good. There is nothing of evil in it. ⁹My words are plain and clear to anyone with half a mind—if it is only open! ¹⁰My instruction is far more valuable than silver or gold."

¹¹For the value of wisdom is far above rubies; nothing can be compared with it. ¹²Wisdom and good judgment live together, for wisdom knows where to discover knowledge and understanding. ¹³If anyone respects and fears God, he will hate evil. For wisdom hates pride, arrogance, corruption, and deceit of every kind.

¹⁴⁻¹⁶"I, Wisdom, give good advice and common sense. Because of my strength, kings reign in power, and rulers make just laws. ¹⁷I love all who love me. Those who search for me shall surely find me. ¹⁸Unending riches, honor, justice, and righteousness are mine to distribute. ¹⁹My gifts are better than the purest gold or sterling silver! ²⁰My paths are those of justice and right. ²¹Those who love and follow me are indeed wealthy. I fill their treasuries. ²²The Lord formed me in the beginning, before he created anything else. ²³From ages past, I am. I existed before the earth began. ²⁴I lived before the oceans were created, before the springs bubbled forth their waters onto the earth, ²⁵before the mountains and the hills were made. ²⁶Yes, I was born before God made the earth and fields and the first handfuls of soil.

²⁷⁻²⁹"I was there when he established the heavens and formed the great springs in the depths of the oceans. I was there when he set the limits of the seas and gave them his instructions not to spread beyond their boundaries. I was there when he made the blueprint for the earth and oceans. ³⁰I was the craftsman at his side. I was his constant delight, rejoicing always in his presence. ³¹And how happy I was with what he created—his wide world and all his family of mankind! ³²And so, young men, listen to me, for how happy are all who follow my instructions.

³³"Listen to my counsel—oh, don't refuse it—and be wise. ³⁴Happy is the man who is so anxious to be with me that he watches for me daily at my gates, or waits for me outside my home! ³⁵For whoever finds me finds life and wins approval from the Lord. ³⁶But the one who misses me has injured himself irreparably. Those who refuse me show that they love death."

9 Knowing God Results in Wisdom

Wisdom has built a palace supported on seven pillars, ²and has prepared a great banquet, and mixed the wines, ³and sent out her maidens inviting all to come. She calls from the busiest intersections in the city, ⁴"Come, you simple ones without good judgment; ⁵come to wisdom's banquet and drink the wines that I have mixed. ⁶Leave behind your foolishness and begin to live; learn how to be wise."

⁷,⁸If you rebuke a mocker, you will only get a smart retort; yes, he will snarl at you. So don't bother with him; he will only hate you for trying to help him. But a wise man, when rebuked, will love you all the more. ⁹Teach a wise man, and he will be the wiser; teach a good man, and he will learn more. ¹⁰*For the reverence and fear of God are basic to all wisdom. Knowing God results in every other kind of understanding.* ¹¹"I, Wisdom, will make the hours of your day more profitable and the years of your life more fruitful." ¹²Wisdom is its own reward, and if you scorn her, you hurt only yourself.

¹³A prostitute is loud and brash and never has enough of lust and shame. ¹⁴She sits at the door of her house or stands at the street corners of the city, ¹⁵whispering to men going by and to those minding their own business. ¹⁶ "Come home with me," she urges simpletons. ¹⁷"Stolen melons are the sweetest; stolen apples taste the best!" ¹⁸But they don't realize that her former guests are now citizens of hell.

10 God's Wisdom Is for Everyone

Happy is the man with a level-headed son; sad the mother of a rebel.

²Ill-gotten gain brings no lasting happiness; right living does.

³The Lord will not let a good man starve to death, nor will he let the wicked man's riches continue forever.

⁴Lazy men are soon poor; hard workers get rich.

⁵A wise youth makes hay while the sun shines, but what a shame to see a lad who sleeps away his hour of opportunity.

⁶The good man is covered with blessings from head to foot, but an evil man inwardly curses his luck.

⁷We all have happy memories of good men gone to their reward, but the names of wicked men stink after them.

⁸The wise man is glad to be instructed, but a self-sufficient fool falls flat on his face.

⁹A good man has firm footing, but a crook will slip and fall.

¹⁰Winking at sin leads to sorrow; bold reproof leads to peace.

¹¹There is living truth in what a good man says, but the mouth of the evil man is filled with curses.

¹²Hatred stirs old quarrels, but love overlooks insults.

¹³Men with common sense are admired as

Family Devotions

☐ **DEVOTION 180**
RESPECTING GOD'S WORD

Read Proverbs 3:1-6; 8:5-16

Paul laid his report card on the table and picked up the newspaper. He raced upstairs, plopped down on his bed, and hurried through each page till he found what he was searching for. It was part three of "Hidden Treasures"—a five-part article about the discovery of different treasures found in the seas. Paul eagerly read and then cut out the article. He often daydreamed about all the hidden treasures that hadn't been found yet—and what it would be like to find one and get rich!

After dinner, Paul's father picked up the paper. "What's been so interesting in the newspaper lately?" he asked. "I see that another article has been cut out."

Paul's eyes got big and dreamy as he told his dad all about the treasure articles and how he yearned to become a treasure hunter some day.

Dad smiled, but Mother raised her eyebrows and brought out Paul's report card. "It looks to me as if you've been concerned with the wrong kind of treasure lately," she observed. "Your school grades have gone down."

Paul sighed. "Oh, well, treasure hunters don't have to be so smart—just lucky!"

"The report card isn't all," said Mother. "Your Sunday school teacher says you've not done as well as usual there, either. You know, Proverbs says we must seek for wisdom with the same persistence with which a treasure hunter searches for silver. Wisdom is a treasure, Paul. The Bible says 'the value of wisdom is far above rubies.'"

"Your mother's right," agreed Dad. "The Bible also says that to become wise you must begin by reverencing God. I think you need to get your treasure-hunting priorities in order, Son. I think it's time to put a little more effort into your school work—especially your Sunday school work."

"It's OK to dream of being a treasure hunter," added Mother, "as long as you find the treasure of wisdom first."

Respecting God's Word
Memory Verse

Your words are what sustain me; they are food to my hungry soul. They bring joy to my sorrowing heart and delight me. How proud I am to bear your name, O Lord.
Jeremiah 15:16

How About You?

Do you search for wisdom? Are you growing in Bible knowledge and Christian living? Nothing can be compared to the treasure of wisdom, and it begins with learning what God wants to teach you from his Word. *V. R.*

• For the next devotional, turn to page 621. • For the next devotional on RESPECTING GOD'S WORD, turn to page 1269. • For notes on RESPECTING GOD'S WORD, see pages 208, 369, 1188, and 1248.

counselors; those without it are beaten as servants.

¹⁴A wise man holds his tongue. Only a fool blurts out everything he knows; that only leads to sorrow and trouble.

¹⁵The rich man's wealth is his only strength. The poor man's poverty is his only curse.

¹⁶The good man's earnings advance the cause of righteousness. The evil man squanders his on sin.

¹⁷Anyone willing to be corrected is on the pathway to life. Anyone refusing has lost his chance.

¹⁸To hide hatred is to be a liar; to slander is to be a fool.

¹⁹Don't talk so much. You keep putting your foot in your mouth. Be sensible and turn off the flow!

²⁰When a good man speaks, he is worth listening to, but the words of fools are a dime a dozen.

²¹A godly man gives good advice, but a rebel is destroyed by lack of common sense.

²²The Lord's blessing is our greatest wealth. All our work adds nothing to it!

²³A fool's fun is being bad; a wise man's fun is being wise!

²⁴The wicked man's fears will all come true and so will the good man's hopes.

²⁵Disaster strikes like a cyclone and the wicked are whirled away. But the good man has a strong anchor.

²⁶A lazy fellow is a pain to his employers—like smoke in their eyes or vinegar that sets the teeth on edge.

²⁷Reverence for God adds hours to each day; so how can the wicked expect a long, good life?

²⁸The hope of good men is eternal happiness; the hopes of evil men are all in vain.

²⁹God protects the upright but destroys the wicked.

³⁰The good shall never lose God's blessings, but the wicked shall lose everything.

³¹The good man gives wise advice, but the liar's counsel is shunned.

³²The upright speak what is helpful; the wicked speak rebellion.

God Hates Cheating

The Lord hates cheating and delights in honesty.

²Proud men end in shame, but the meek become wise.

³A good man is guided by his honesty; the evil man is destroyed by his dishonesty.

⁴Your riches won't help you on Judgment Day; only righteousness counts then.

⁵Good people are directed by their honesty; the wicked shall fall beneath their load of sins.

⁶The good man's goodness delivers him; the evil man's treachery is his undoing.

⁷When an evil man dies, his hopes all perish, for they are based upon this earthly life.

⁸God rescues good men from danger while letting the wicked fall into it.

⁹Evil words destroy; godly skill rebuilds.

¹⁰The whole city celebrates a good man's success—and also the godless man's death.

¹¹The good influence of godly citizens causes a city to prosper, but the moral decay of the wicked drives it downhill.

¹²To quarrel with a neighbor is foolish; a man with good sense holds his tongue.

¹³A gossip goes around spreading rumors, while a trustworthy man tries to quiet them.

¹⁴Without wise leadership, a nation is in trouble; but with good counselors there is safety.

¹⁵Be sure you know a person well before you vouch for his credit! Better refuse than suffer later.

¹⁶Honor goes to kind and gracious women, mere money to cruel men.

¹⁷Your own soul is nourished when you are kind; it is destroyed when you are cruel.

¹⁸The evil man gets rich for the moment, but the good man's reward lasts forever.

¹⁹The good man finds life; the evil man, death.

²⁰The Lord hates the stubborn but delights in those who are good.

²¹You can be very sure the evil man will not go unpunished forever. And you can also be very sure God will rescue the children of the godly.

²²A beautiful woman lacking discretion and modesty is like a fine gold ring in a pig's snout.

²³The good man can look forward to happiness, while the wicked can expect only wrath.

²⁴,²⁵It is possible to give away and become richer! It is also possible to hold on too tightly and lose everything. Yes, the liberal man shall be rich! By watering others, he waters himself.

²⁶People curse the man who holds his grain for higher prices, but they bless the man who sells it to them in their time of need.

²⁷If you search for good, you will find God's favor; if you search for evil, you will find his curse.

²⁸Trust in your money and down you go! Trust in God and flourish as a tree!

²⁹The fool who provokes his family to anger and resentment will finally have nothing worthwhile left. He shall be the servant of a wiser man.

³⁰Godly men are growing a tree that bears life-giving fruit, and all who win souls are wise.

³¹Even the godly shall be rewarded here on earth; how much more the wicked!

FAMILY DEVOTIONS

☐ DEVOTION 181
GIVING TO GOD

Read Proverbs 11:24-28

As Jill and her mother left the grocery store, they met their pastor. "I'm here to buy some food for that family whose house burned yesterday," Pastor Holt told them after they had exchanged greetings.

At once Jill's mother reached into her purse, pulled out ten dollars, and handed it to the pastor. "Here's a little bit to help out," she said.

As Jill and her mother went on their way, Jill frowned. "Mom, I wanted to buy those special cookies I like so much, and you said we couldn't afford them," she complained. "I thought I understood about that, since Dad is out of work, but then you gave away ten dollars. That doesn't make any sense. How can you afford to give away money when we don't have enough for ourselves?"

"The Lord has marvelously blessed us during this time, and we've been able to get everything we really needed," answered Mother. "Your dad and I believe we should share the good things God has given us and not just keep them for ourselves. He always repays us in one way or another." Jill didn't really look convinced, but she didn't say any more about it.

That afternoon as Jill helped prepare dinner, Mother asked her to measure out one and one-fourth cups of milk for a casserole. "Fill this cup and pour it into the bowl; then just fill it to the one-fourth line the second time," she instructed. Thoughtfully, she added, "You know, Jill, emptying the measuring cup so you could add more is a little like what I was trying to tell you about giving. If we hoard God's blessings, keeping them all for ourselves, we may have no more room to receive anything else—our 'cup' may be full. But if we generously share what we have with others, God will see to it that our needs continue to be met."

Giving to God
Memory Verse

Bring all the tithes into the storehouse so that there will be food enough in my Temple; if you do, I will open up the windows of heaven for you and pour out a blessing so great you won't have room enough to take it in! Try it! Let me prove it to you!
Malachi 3:10

H o w   A b o u t   Y o u ?
Are you saving for something you need or want? It's good to do that, but don't hoard your money and possessions, selfishly planning to keep everything you get for yourself. By holding tightly to everything, refusing to give for God's work or the needs of others, you deprive yourself of more blessings from God. He loves a cheerful giver! M. R. P.

• For the next devotional, turn to page 623.   • For the next devotional on *GIVING TO GOD,* turn to page 891.
• For notes on *GIVING TO GOD,* see pages 182, 433, and 1128.

12 Gain Wisdom: Avoid Mistakes

To learn, you must want to be taught. To refuse reproof is stupid.

²The Lord blesses good men and condemns the wicked.

³Wickedness never brings real success; only the godly have that.

⁴A worthy wife is her husband's joy and crown; the other kind corrodes his strength and tears down everything he does.

⁵A good man's mind is filled with honest thoughts; an evil man's mind is crammed with lies.

⁶The wicked accuse; the godly defend.

⁷The wicked shall perish; the godly shall stand.

⁸Everyone admires a man with good sense, but a man with a warped mind is despised.

⁹It is better to get your hands dirty—and eat, than to be too proud to work—and starve.

¹⁰A good man is concerned for the welfare of his animals, but even the kindness of godless men is cruel.

¹¹Hard work means prosperity; only a fool idles away his time.

¹²Crooks are jealous of each other's loot, while good men long to help each other.

¹³Lies will get any man into trouble, but honesty is its own defense.

¹⁴Telling the truth gives a man great satisfaction, and hard work returns many blessings to him.

¹⁵A fool thinks he needs no advice, but a wise man listens to others.

¹⁶A fool is quick-tempered; a wise man stays cool when insulted.

¹⁷A good man is known by his truthfulness; a false man by deceit and lies.

¹⁸Some people like to make cutting remarks, but the words of the wise soothe and heal.

¹⁹Truth stands the test of time; lies are soon exposed.

²⁰Deceit fills hearts that are plotting for evil; joy fills hearts that are planning for good!

²¹No real harm befalls the good, but there is constant trouble for the wicked.

²²God delights in those who keep their promises and abhors those who don't.

²³A wise man doesn't display his knowledge, but a fool displays his foolishness.

²⁴Work hard and become a leader; be lazy and never succeed.

²⁵Anxious hearts are very heavy, but a word of encouragement does wonders!

²⁶The good man asks advice from friends; the wicked plunge ahead—and fall.

²⁷A lazy man won't even dress the game he gets while hunting, but the diligent man makes good use of everything he finds.

²⁸The path of the godly leads to life. So why fear death?

13 The Way to Success

A wise youth accepts his father's rebuke; a young mocker doesn't.

²The good man wins his case by careful argument; the evil-minded only wants to fight.

³Self-control means controlling the tongue! A quick retort can ruin everything.

⁴Lazy people want much but get little, while the diligent are prospering.

⁵A good man hates lies; wicked men lie constantly and come to shame.

⁶A man's goodness helps him all through life, while evil men are being destroyed by their wickedness.

⁷Some rich people are poor, and some poor people have great wealth!

⁸Being kidnapped and held for ransom never worries the poor man!

⁹The good man's life is full of light. The sinner's road is dark and gloomy.

¹⁰Pride leads to arguments; be humble, take advice, and become wise.

¹¹Wealth from gambling quickly disappears; wealth from hard work grows.

¹²Hope deferred makes the heart sick; but when dreams come true at last, there is life and joy.

¹³Despise God's Word and find yourself in trouble. Obey it and succeed.

¹⁴The advice of a wise man refreshes like water from a mountain spring. Those accepting it become aware of the pitfalls on ahead.

¹⁵A man with good sense is appreciated. A treacherous man must walk a rocky road.

¹⁶A wise man thinks ahead; a fool doesn't and even brags about it!

¹⁷An unreliable messenger can cause a lot of trouble. Reliable communication permits progress.

¹⁸If you refuse criticism, you will end in poverty and disgrace; if you accept criticism, you are on the road to fame.

CULTIVATING GODLY ATTITUDES 13:3 You have not mastered self-discipline if you do not control what you say. Words can cut and destroy. James recognized this truth when he stated, "The tongue is a small thing, but what enormous damage it can do" (James 3:5). If you wish to be self-disciplined, begin with your tongue. Watch what you say! Be careful that your words are kind, loving, and gentle. You can be angry, express honest feelings, and point out problems, yet still speak with self-discipline and love. **To begin the series of devotionals on** CULTIVATING GODLY ATTITUDES, **turn to page 121.**

Family Devotions

☐ **Devotion 182**
Honesty

Read Proverbs 12:17-22

Geri eagerly tore open the package of candy that had come as the prize in her cereal box. She counted every piece—only twenty-six. She started to count the pieces in the picture on the cereal box. She stopped counting at one hundred, and there were still more. "I thought I would get as much candy as there was in the picture," she told Dad.

"The people who make the cereal wanted you to think that so you'd buy the cereal," explained Dad. "They deceived you."

Geri frowned. "What does *deceive* mean?"

"It means leading someone to believe something that isn't true," explained Dad, and Geri sighed.

That afternoon Geri's friend Ashley came to play. Geri had recently begun taking piano lessons, and she showed Ashley what she had been learning. "I'll be your pupil," said Ashley, so they pretended that Geri was the teacher.

Soon Beth, who lived down the street, came to the door. "Do you want to play?" Beth asked.

Geri didn't. She wanted Ashley all to herself. "We're having a piano lesson," Geri said.

"Did you tell Beth the truth?" asked Dad, who had overheard the exchange.

Geri shrugged. "I didn't lie about it," she said.

"What picture did Beth get about the piano lesson?" persisted Dad. "Do you think you deceived her?"

Geri knew Beth thought her piano teacher was there. The picture she'd given Beth was just as deceiving as the picture on the cereal box. She hurried to the front door. "Come back, Beth," she called. "You can be in on our piano lesson, too."

Honesty Memory Verse

Stop lying to each other; tell the truth, for we are parts of each other and when we lie to each other we are hurting ourselves.
Ephesians 4:25

How About You?

Do you ever deceive someone by giving him the wrong idea? Do you get out of doing something by making excuses that aren't quite accurate? You can lie in ways other than saying *something that isn't true. God is as displeased with one kind of lie as with another.* K. R. A.

• For the next devotional, turn to page 625.   • For the next devotional on *Honesty*, turn to page 639.   • For notes on *Honesty*, see pages 304, 813, and 863.

¹⁹It is pleasant to see plans develop. That is why fools refuse to give them up even when they are wrong.

²⁰Be with wise men and become wise. Be with evil men and become evil.

²¹Curses chase sinners, while blessings chase the righteous!

²²When a good man dies, he leaves an inheritance to his grandchildren; but when a sinner dies, his wealth is stored up for the godly.

²³A poor man's farm may have good soil, but injustice robs him of its riches.

²⁴If you refuse to discipline your son, it proves you don't love him; for if you love him, you will be prompt to punish him.

²⁵The good man eats to live, while the evil man lives to eat.

14 Anger Causes Mistakes

A wise woman builds her house, while a foolish woman tears hers down by her own efforts.

²To do right honors God; to sin is to despise him.

³A rebel's foolish talk should prick his own pride! But the wise man's speech is respected.

⁴An empty stable stays clean—but there is no income from an empty stable.

⁵A truthful witness never lies; a false witness always lies.

⁶A mocker never finds the wisdom he claims he is looking for, yet it comes easily to the man with common sense.

⁷If you are looking for advice, stay away from fools.

⁸The wise man looks ahead. The fool attempts to fool himself and won't face facts.

⁹The common bond of rebels is their guilt. The common bond of godly people is good will.

¹⁰Only the person involved can know his own bitterness or joy—no one else can really share it.

¹¹The work of the wicked will perish; the work of the godly will flourish.

¹²Before every man there lies a wide and pleasant road that seems right but ends in death.

¹³Laughter cannot mask a heavy heart. When the laughter ends, the grief remains.

¹⁴The backslider gets bored with himself; the godly man's life is exciting.

¹⁵Only a simpleton believes everything he's told! A prudent man understands the need for proof.

¹⁶A wise man is cautious and avoids danger; a fool plunges ahead with great confidence.

¹⁷A short-tempered man is a fool. He hates the man who is patient.

¹⁸The simpleton is crowned with folly; the wise man is crowned with knowledge.

¹⁹Evil men shall bow before the godly.

²⁰,²¹Even his own neighbors despise the poor man, while the rich have many "friends." But to despise the poor is to sin. Blessed are those who help them.

²²Those who plot evil shall wander away and be lost, but those who plan good shall be granted mercy and quietness.

²³Work brings profit; talk brings poverty!

²⁴Wise men are praised for their wisdom; fools are despised for their folly.

²⁵A witness who tells the truth saves good men from being sentenced to death, but a false witness is a traitor.

²⁶Reverence for God gives a man deep strength; his children have a place of refuge and security.

²⁷Reverence for the Lord is a fountain of life; its waters keep a man from death.

²⁸A growing population is a king's glory; a dwindling nation is his doom.

²⁹A wise man controls his temper. He knows that anger causes mistakes.

³⁰A relaxed attitude lengthens a man's life; jealousy rots it away.

³¹Anyone who oppresses the poor is insulting God who made them. To help the poor is to honor God.

³²The godly have a refuge when they die, but the wicked are crushed by their sins.

³³Wisdom is enshrined in the hearts of men of common sense, but it must shout loudly before fools will hear it.

³⁴Godliness exalts a nation, but sin is a reproach to any people.

³⁵A king rejoices in servants who know what they are doing; he is angry with those who cause trouble.

15 God Delights in Our Prayers

A gentle answer turns away wrath, but harsh words cause quarrels.

²A wise teacher makes learning a joy; a rebellious teacher spouts foolishness.

³The Lord is watching everywhere and keeps his eye on both the evil and the good.

⁴Gentle words cause life and health; griping brings discouragement.

⁵Only a fool despises his father's advice; a wise son considers each suggestion.

⁶There is treasure in being good, but trouble dogs the wicked.

⁷Only the good can give good advice. Rebels can't.

⁸The Lord hates the gifts of the wicked but delights in the prayers of his people.

FAMILY DEVOTIONS

☐ DEVOTION 183
OVERCOMING ANGER

Read Proverbs 15:1

Ding, dong! The doorbell had been ringing for several minutes, but Jane and her brother were so busy arguing that they hadn't even heard it. Loud, angry words were flying back and forth when Jane finally noticed her friend Pam tapping on the living-room window. Embarrassed, she quickly went outside and closed the door behind her. "I'm sorry, Pam," she said. "I forgot you were coming over. You see, I was kind of tied up in a—a family discussion." She paused when she saw Pam looking at her sympathetically. "Well," continued Jane, "actually, it was a fight."

"Yes, I heard," said Pam softly. "I didn't mean to eavesdrop, but I couldn't help overhearing."

Jane sighed. "I don't know why we can't get along," she said. "We're all Christians, even though none of us act like it most of the time. I don't want to argue with my parents and my brother. And I don't think they like the fighting, either. But what can I do about it?"

Just then Jane and Pam heard the squeal of brakes and a crash. They rushed out to the street and saw that a car had banged into the back of a truck at a traffic light. The drivers looked their vehicles over carefully. "I'm sorry I ran into you," said one of them.

The other smiled and said, "I don't see any damage. My rubber bumper guards cushioned the impact."

As Jane and Pam walked back toward Jane's house, Pam said thoughtfully, "That accident made me think of something. The bumper guards were like a cushion, so no damage was done. Maybe you need to be like a cushion whenever someone is grumpy with you. The Bible says, 'A gentle answer turns away wrath.' Maybe if you answer softly and kindly it will help the situation in your house."

"I'll try it," Jane decided. "Something's got to be done. Maybe if I act as a cushion, it will help to stop the chaos at our house!"

Overcoming Anger Memory Verses:

Dear brothers, don't ever forget that it is best to listen much, speak little, and not become angry; for anger doesn't make us good, as God demands that we must be.
James 1:19-20

How About You?

When someone is angry with you, do you reply sharply? Or do you keep your temper and try to answer quietly and patiently? The way you respond to anger can make a real difference in your home and in your whole life. *S K*

• For the next devotional, turn to page 627.   • For the next devotional on *OVERCOMING ANGER*, turn to page 651.
• For notes on *OVERCOMING ANGER*, see pages 176, 511, 936, and 1003.

9,10 The Lord despises the deeds of the wicked but loves those who try to be good. If they stop trying, the Lord will punish them; if they rebel against that punishment, they will die.

11 The depths of hell are open to God's knowledge. How much more the hearts of all mankind!

12 A mocker stays away from wise men because he hates to be scolded.

13 A happy face means a glad heart; a sad face means a breaking heart.

14 A wise man is hungry for truth, while the mocker feeds on trash.

15 When a man is gloomy, everything seems to go wrong; when he is cheerful, everything seems right!

16 Better a little with reverence for God than great treasure and trouble with it.

17 It is better to eat soup with someone you love than steak with someone you hate.

18 A quick-tempered man starts fights; a cool-tempered man tries to stop them.

19 A lazy fellow has trouble all through life; the good man's path is easy!

20 A sensible son gladdens his father. A rebellious son saddens his mother.

21 If a man enjoys folly, something is wrong! The sensible stay on the pathways of right.

22 Plans go wrong with too few counselors; many counselors bring success.

23 Everyone enjoys giving good advice, and how wonderful it is to be able to say the right thing at the right time!

24 The road of the godly leads upward, leaving hell behind.

25 The Lord destroys the possessions of the proud but cares for widows.

26 The Lord hates the thoughts of the wicked but delights in kind words.

27 Dishonest money brings grief to all the family, but hating bribes brings happiness.

28 A good man thinks before he speaks; the evil man pours out his evil words without a thought.

29 The Lord is far from the wicked, but he hears the prayers of the righteous.

30 Pleasant sights and good reports give happiness and health.

31,32 If you profit from constructive criticism, you will be elected to the wise men's hall of fame. But to reject criticism is to harm yourself and your own best interests.

33 Humility and reverence for the Lord will make you both wise and honored.

16 Pride Leads to Trouble

We can make our plans, but the final outcome is in God's hands.

2 We can always "prove" that we are right, but is the Lord convinced?

3 Commit your work to the Lord, then it will succeed.

4 The Lord has made everything for his own purposes—even the wicked, for punishment.

5 Pride disgusts the Lord. Take my word for it—*proud men shall be punished.*

6 Iniquity is atoned for by mercy and truth; evil is avoided by reverence for God.

7 When a man is trying to please God, God makes even his worst enemies to be at peace with him.

8 A little gained honestly is better than great wealth gotten by dishonest means.

9 We should make plans—counting on God to direct us.

10 God will help the king to judge the people fairly; there need be no mistakes.

11 The Lord demands fairness in every business deal. He established this principle.

12 It is a horrible thing for a king to do evil. His right to rule depends upon his fairness.

13 The king rejoices when his people are truthful and fair.

14 The anger of the king is a messenger of death, and a wise man will appease it.

15 Many favors are showered on those who please the king.

16 How much better is wisdom than gold, and understanding than silver!

17 The path of the godly leads away from evil; he who follows that path is safe.

18 Pride goes before destruction and haughtiness before a fall.

19 Better poor and humble than proud and rich.

20 God blesses those who obey him; happy the man who puts his trust in the Lord.

21 The wise man is known by his common sense, and a pleasant teacher is the best.

22 Wisdom is a fountain of life to those possessing it, but a fool's burden is his folly.

23 From a wise mind comes careful and persuasive speech.

24 Kind words are like honey—enjoyable and healthful.

25 Before every man there lies a wide and pleasant road he thinks is right, but it ends in death.

26 Hunger is good—if it makes you work to satisfy it!

27 Idle hands are the devil's workshop; idle lips are his mouthpiece.

28 An evil man sows strife; gossip separates the best of friends.

29 Wickedness loves company—and leads others into sin.

30 The wicked man stares into space with pursed lips, deep in thought, planning his evil deeds.

FAMILY DEVOTIONS

☐ *DEVOTION 184*
RESPECTING OTHERS

Read Proverbs 16:31

Gregory was hiding in the bushes with his friends, Tom and Alan, but he knew he shouldn't be there. "Let's get out of here before someone sees us," he urged.

"We're just gonna have some fun with old Mrs. Wilson," said Tom. "You chicken?"

"I'm not chicken," protested Gregory, "but it's not right to mistreat old folks."

"Oh, c'mon," coaxed Alan as he and Tom moved toward the porch steps. "What's it gonna hurt if we just ring the bell and then hide in these bushes and listen to Mrs. Wilson complain? She'll never know who did it. Even if she sees us, she can't see well enough to tell who we are." He tiptoed up to the door, with Tom close behind.

As Gregory hesitated, Alan punched the bell. Alan and Tom headed for the bushes, but Gregory bent down and picked up a newspaper from the sidewalk. Then he planted himself at the top of the steps and waited for Mrs. Wilson to open the door.

A moment later, the door swung open, and there stood Mrs. Wilson, squinting out of the dark hallway.

"Excuse me, Mrs. Wilson," said Gregory, holding out the paper. "You didn't pick up your newspaper this morning, so I brought it to you."

"Why, thank you," said Mrs. Wilson. "Aren't you kind! Do I know you?"

"I'm Gregory Smith, and this is Tom Newton and Alan Welch." Gregory motioned to his friends, and they stepped hesitantly forward. "We all live on this street."

"Why yes, I know all of your parents," replied Mrs. Wilson. "I'm going to have to tell them what nice boys they have. Some children aren't nice to old women anymore, you know."

"Yes ma'am," said Gregory. "We know." As he turned to go, he flashed a triumphant grin at his friends.

Respecting Others Memory Verse

You must love the Lord your God with all your heart, and with all your soul, and with all your strength, and with all your mind. And you must love your neighbor just as much as you love yourself.
Luke 10:27

How About You?

Do you treat older people with the respect God wants them to have? God loves older people just as much as he loves younger ones, and he is very specific about the way he wants us to treat them. He wants you to show them the same kindness you will expect when you are older. S. L. S.

• For the next devotional, turn to page 629. • For the next devotional on RESPECTING OTHERS, turn to page 633.
• For notes on RESPECTING OTHERS, see pages 322, 382, 1088, and 1218.

³¹White hair is a crown of glory and is seen most among the godly.

³²It is better to be slow-tempered than famous; it is better to have self-control than to control an army.

³³We toss the coin, but it is the Lord who controls its decision.

17 True Friends Are Loyal

A dry crust eaten in peace is better than steak every day along with argument and strife.

²A wise slave will rule his master's wicked sons and share their estate.

³Silver and gold are purified by fire, but God purifies hearts.

⁴The wicked enjoy fellowship with others who are wicked; liars enjoy liars.

⁵Mocking the poor is mocking the God who made them. He will punish those who rejoice at others' misfortunes.

⁶An old man's grandchildren are his crowning glory. A child's glory is his father.

⁷Truth from a rebel or lies from a king are both unexpected.

⁸A bribe works like magic. Whoever uses it will prosper!

⁹Love forgets mistakes; nagging about them parts the best of friends.

¹⁰A rebuke to a man of common sense is more effective than a hundred lashes on the back of a rebel.

¹¹The wicked live for rebellion; they shall be severely punished.

¹²It is safer to meet a bear robbed of her cubs than a fool caught in his folly.

¹³If you repay evil for good, a curse is upon your home.

¹⁴It is hard to stop a quarrel once it starts, so don't let it begin.

¹⁵The Lord despises those who say that bad is good and good is bad.

¹⁶It is senseless to pay tuition to educate a rebel who has no heart for truth.

¹⁷A true friend is always loyal, and a brother is born to help in time of need.

¹⁸It is poor judgment to countersign another's note, to become responsible for his debts.

¹⁹Sinners love to fight; boasting is looking for trouble.

²⁰An evil man is suspicious of everyone and tumbles into constant trouble.

²¹It's no fun to be a rebel's father.

²²A cheerful heart does good like medicine, but a broken spirit makes one sick.

²³It is wrong to accept a bribe to twist justice.

²⁴Wisdom is the main pursuit of sensible men, but a fool's goals are at the ends of the earth!

²⁵A rebellious son is a grief to his father and a bitter blow to his mother.

²⁶How shortsighted to fine the godly for being good! And to punish nobles for being honest!

²⁷,²⁸The man of few words and settled mind is wise; therefore, even a fool is thought to be wise when he is silent. It pays him to keep his mouth shut.

18 Get the Facts before Deciding

The selfish man quarrels against every sound principle of conduct by demanding his own way.

²A rebel doesn't care about the facts. All he wants to do is yell.

³Sin brings disgrace.

⁴A wise man's words express deep streams of thought.

⁵It is wrong for a judge to favor the wicked and condemn the innocent.

⁶,⁷A fool gets into constant fights. His mouth is his undoing! His words endanger him.

⁸What dainty morsels rumors are. They are eaten with great relish!

⁹A lazy man is brother to the saboteur.

¹⁰The Lord is a strong fortress. The godly run to him and are safe.

¹¹The rich man thinks of his wealth as an impregnable defense, a high wall of safety. What a dreamer!

¹²Pride ends in destruction; humility ends in honor.

¹³What a shame—yes, how stupid!—to decide before knowing the facts!

¹⁴A man's courage can sustain his broken body, but when courage dies, what hope is left?

¹⁵The intelligent man is always open to new ideas. In fact, he looks for them.

¹⁶A gift does wonders; it will bring you before men of importance!

¹⁷Any story sounds true until someone tells the other side and sets the record straight.

¹⁸A coin toss ends arguments and settles disputes between powerful opponents.

¹⁹It is harder to win back the friendship of an offended brother than to capture a fortified city. His anger shuts you out like iron bars.

²⁰Ability to give wise advice satisfies like a good meal!

²¹Those who love to talk will suffer the consequences. Men have died for saying the wrong thing!

²²The man who finds a wife finds a good thing; she is a blessing to him from the Lord.

²³The poor man pleads, and the rich man answers with insults.

²⁴There are "friends" who pretend to be

FAMILY DEVOTIONS

☐ DEVOTION 185
SHOWING COMPASSION

Read Proverbs 17:17

"Look behind you, Mom," said Rhonda as she and her mother picked raspberries. "Down low there are some berries you missed."

"Oh, and they're nice ones." Mother bent to pick them.

"There are more in the bush behind them," said Rhonda.

Mother looked as Rhonda pointed, but she shook her head. "No, those aren't ripe yet. But I see some in the bush you just finished."

"I guess we should pick each other's bushes," laughed Rhonda. "This is fun. Remember when Carla and her mom used to come with us?"

"Yes, I miss them." Mother sighed. "How is Carla doing since her mother left home?"

"Oh, she whines all the time about how she would rather live with her mother than with her dad. We get sick of hearing about it," said Rhonda. "After all, this way she's still in the same house and the same school. But she doesn't see that she's better off with her dad."

"I guess it all depends on your viewpoint," suggested Mother. "You see Carla's problems from a distance, so you see things she doesn't see. But don't forget that she also can see things you can't see. It's like these berries—we miss some good ones and mistake others for good, depending on how we view them."

Rhonda nodded slowly. "I see what you mean."

"As Christians, we need to be more understanding and less critical of others," added Mother. "Tell me, what bothers Carla most now that her mother's gone?"

Rhonda thought for a minute. "Well, for one thing, her father is dating. And she says she misses her mom. They were so close. She could tell her mom anything."

"God can use you to help make this change easier for her," said Mother. "Show her good things about her situation and help her with the hard ones. She needs understanding."

Showing Compassion Memory Verse

What a wonderful God we have—he is the Father of our Lord Jesus Christ, the source of every mercy, and the one who so wonderfully comforts and strengthens us in our hardships and trials.
2 Corinthians 1:3

How About You?
Are you annoyed when your friends talk about their troubles? Does it bug you because it spoils your fun when you hear about the sad things happening to them? Remember, the Bible says, "a true friend is always loyal." *A. G. L.*

• For the next devotional, turn to page 631. • For the next devotional on *SHOWING COMPASSION*, turn to page 713.
• For notes on *SHOWING COMPASSION*, see pages 206, 506, 515, 710, and 934.

friends, but there is a friend who sticks closer than a brother.

19 A Lazy Man Goes Hungry

Better be poor and honest than rich and dishonest.

² It is dangerous and sinful to rush into the unknown.

³ A man may ruin his chances by his own foolishness and then blame it on the Lord!

⁴ A wealthy man has many "friends"; the poor man has none left.

⁵ Punish false witnesses. Track down liars.

⁶ Many beg favors from a man who is generous; everyone is his friend!

⁷ A poor man's own brothers turn away from him in embarrassment; how much more his friends! He calls after them, but they are gone.

⁸ He who loves wisdom loves his own best interest and will be a success.

⁹ A false witness shall be punished, and a liar shall be caught.

¹⁰ It doesn't seem right for a fool to succeed or for a slave to rule over princes!

¹¹ A wise man restrains his anger and overlooks insults. This is to his credit.

¹² The king's anger is as dangerous as a lion's. But his approval is as refreshing as the dew on grass.

¹³ A rebellious son is a calamity to his father, and a nagging wife annoys like constant dripping.

¹⁴ A father can give his sons homes and riches, but only the Lord can give them understanding wives.

¹⁵ A lazy man sleeps soundly—and he goes hungry!

¹⁶ Keep the commandments and keep your life; despising them means death.

¹⁷ When you help the poor you are lending to the Lord—and he pays wonderful interest on your loan!

¹⁸ Discipline your son in his early years while there is hope. If you don't you will ruin his life.

¹⁹ A short-tempered man must bear his own penalty; you can't do much to help him. If you try once you must try a dozen times!

²⁰ Get all the advice you can and be wise the rest of your life.

²¹ Man proposes, but God disposes.

²² Kindness makes a man attractive. And it is better to be poor than dishonest.

²³ Reverence for God gives life, happiness, and protection from harm.

²⁴ Some men are so lazy they won't even feed themselves!

²⁵ Punish a mocker and others will learn from his example. Reprove a wise man, and he will be the wiser.

²⁶ A son who mistreats his father or mother is a public disgrace.

²⁷ Stop listening to teaching that contradicts what you know is right.

²⁸ A worthless witness cares nothing for truth—he enjoys his sinning too much.

²⁹ Mockers and rebels shall be severely punished.

20 Your Actions Tell about You

Wine gives false courage; hard liquor leads to brawls; what fools men are to let it master them, making them reel drunkenly down the street!

² The king's fury is like that of a roaring lion; to rouse his anger is to risk your life.

³ It is an honor for a man to stay out of a fight. Only fools insist on quarreling.

⁴ If you won't plow in the cold, you won't eat at the harvest.

⁵ Though good advice lies deep within a counselor's heart, the wise man will draw it out.

⁶ Most people will tell you what loyal friends they are, but are they telling the truth?

⁷ It is a wonderful heritage to have an honest father.

⁸ A king sitting as judge weighs all the evidence carefully, distinguishing the true from false.

⁹ Who can ever say, "I have cleansed my heart; I am sinless"?

¹⁰ The Lord despises every kind of cheating.

¹¹ The character of even a child can be known by the way he acts—whether what he does is pure and right.

¹² If you have good eyesight and good hearing, thank God who gave them to you.

¹³ If you love sleep, you will end in poverty. Stay awake, work hard, and there will be plenty to eat!

¹⁴ "Utterly worthless!" says the buyer as he haggles over the price. But afterwards he brags about his bargain!

¹⁵ Good sense is far more valuable than gold or precious jewels.

¹⁶ It is risky to make loans to strangers!

¹⁷ Some men enjoy cheating, but the cake they buy with such ill-gotten gain will turn to gravel in their mouths.

¹⁸ Don't go ahead with your plans without the advice of others; don't go to war until they agree.

¹⁹ Don't tell your secrets to a gossip unless you want them broadcast to the world.

²⁰ God puts out the light of the man who curses his father or mother.

²¹ Quick wealth is not a blessing in the end.

FAMILY DEVOTIONS

☐ DEVOTION 186
SHOWING KINDNESS

Read Proverbs 19:22

"Look at this trophy, Dad!" exclaimed Christopher. "I still can't believe it—I won the batting championship!"

At home, Mother had a celebration dinner waiting, but after dinner Christopher left the table without a word of thanks. And when his sister picked up his trophy, he grabbed it from her, saying, "Don't touch it! You'll get fingerprints on it."

"Christopher," said Dad sternly, "I don't like what I'm hearing. The Lord commands us to treat others as we would like to be treated, but how about the way you treated your sister just now? And I didn't hear so much as a thank-you to Mom for preparing a special meal for you, either."

Christopher looked ashamed. "I'm sorry," he said. "I forgot." He sighed. "I always forget," he added in a defeated tone.

"Well, Son, tell me something," said Dad. "You really wanted to win the batting championship, didn't you?"

Christopher nodded. "Sure," he said. "That's why I practiced so hard."

"That's my point," said Dad. "It took a lot of practice, and I think we can all learn a lesson from that. We all know we should put others ahead of ourselves. If we really want to learn to do that, what should we do?"

Christopher looked puzzled a moment. Then he grinned and said, "Oh, . . . you mean we should practice?"

"Right!" said Dad. "We don't become mature Christians the moment we're saved—we have to grow in Christ. That takes practice, and lots of it. Just as you were determined to be batting champion, you need to set your mind on treating others as Christ would have you treat them. Then work hard at it every day. We all need to do that."

"That would be sort of like becoming a champion for Jesus," added Mother. "It's something worth working for."

Showing Kindness Memory Verse

That's why whenever we can we should always be kind to everyone, and especially to our Christian brothers.
Galatians 6:10

How About You?

Are you practicing being Christ-like in your treatment of others? Being kind and loving isn't easy. It takes determination and practice. Each morning ask the Lord to help you show love and kindness to others on that very day. And then work hard at doing it. M. R. P.

- For the next devotional, turn to page 633.   • For the next devotional on SHOWING KINDNESS, turn to page 899.
- For notes on SHOWING KINDNESS, see pages 664, 880, 1038, and 1244.

²²Don't repay evil for evil. Wait for the Lord to handle the matter.

²³The Lord loathes all cheating and dishonesty.

²⁴Since the Lord is directing our steps, why try to understand everything that happens along the way?

²⁵It is foolish and rash to make a promise to the Lord before counting the cost.

²⁶A wise king stamps out crime by severe punishment.

²⁷A man's conscience is the Lord's searchlight exposing his hidden motives.

²⁸If a king is kind, honest, and fair, his kingdom stands secure.

²⁹The glory of young men is their strength; of old men, their experience.

³⁰Punishment that hurts chases evil from the heart.

21 Learn by Listening

Just as water is turned into irrigation ditches, so the Lord directs the king's thoughts. He turns them wherever he wants to.

²We can justify our every deed, but God looks at our motives.

³God is more pleased when we are just and fair than when we give him gifts.

⁴Pride, lust, and evil actions are all sin.

⁵Steady plodding brings prosperity; hasty speculation brings poverty.

⁶Dishonest gain will never last, so why take the risk?

⁷Because the wicked are unfair, their violence boomerangs and destroys them.

⁸A man is known by his actions. An evil man lives an evil life; a good man lives a godly life.

⁹It is better to live in the corner of an attic than with a crabby woman in a lovely home.

¹⁰An evil man loves to harm others; being a good neighbor is out of his line.

¹¹The wise man learns by listening; the simpleton can learn only by seeing scorners punished.

¹²God, the Righteous One, knows what is going on in the homes of the wicked and will bring the wicked to judgment.

¹³He who shuts his ears to the cries of the poor will be ignored in his own time of need.

¹⁴An angry man is silenced by giving him a gift!

¹⁵A good man loves justice, but it is a calamity to evil-doers.

¹⁶The man who strays away from common sense will end up dead!

¹⁷A man who loves pleasure becomes poor; wine and luxury are not the way to riches!

¹⁸The wicked will finally lose; the righteous will finally win.

¹⁹Better to live in the desert than with a quarrelsome, complaining woman.

²⁰The wise man saves for the future, but the foolish man spends whatever he gets.

²¹The man who tries to be good, loving, and kind finds life, righteousness, and honor.

²²The wise man conquers the strong man and levels his defenses.

²³Keep your mouth closed and you'll stay out of trouble.

²⁴Mockers are proud, haughty, and arrogant.

²⁵,²⁶The lazy man longs for many things, but his hands refuse to work. He is greedy to get, while the godly love to give!

²⁷God loathes the gifts of evil men, especially if they are trying to bribe him!

²⁸No one believes a liar, but everyone respects the words of an honest man.

²⁹An evil man is stubborn, but a godly man will reconsider.

³⁰No one, regardless of how shrewd or well-advised he is, can stand against the Lord.

³¹Go ahead and prepare for the conflict, but victory comes from God.

22 Giving Can Make You Happy

If you must choose, take a good name rather than great riches; for to be held in loving esteem is better than silver and gold.

²The rich and the poor are alike before the Lord who made them all.

³A prudent man foresees the difficulties ahead and prepares for them; the simpleton goes blindly on and suffers the consequences.

⁴True humility and respect for the Lord lead a man to riches, honor, and long life.

⁵The rebel walks a thorny, treacherous road; the man who values his soul will stay away.

⁶Teach a child to choose the right path, and when he is older, he will remain upon it.

⁷Just as the rich rule the poor, so the borrower is servant to the lender.

⁸The unjust tyrant will reap disaster, and his reign of terror shall end.

⁹Happy is the generous man, the one who feeds the poor.

¹⁰Throw out the mocker, and you will be rid of tension, fighting, and quarrels.

¹¹He who values grace and truth is the king's friend.

¹²The Lord preserves the upright but ruins the plans of the wicked.

¹³The lazy man is full of excuses. "I can't go to work!" he says. "If I go outside, I might meet a lion in the street and be killed!"

¹⁴A prostitute is a dangerous trap; those cursed of God are caught in it.

Family Devotions

☐ **Devotion 187**
Respecting Others

Read Proverbs 20:20

"Hey, Dad, I went to the eye doctor today, and he said my vision was twenty-twenty," announced David at dinner. "That's perfect, you know!"

"That's right," agreed Mother as she passed the salad. Loud voices, a slamming door, and squealing tires next door interrupted her. When it was quiet again, she murmured, "Poor Mrs. Marler."

"Yes, I'm afraid Chad is worrying her to death," Dad said with a nod.

"I don't know why everybody's on Chad's case," David protested. "I like him. He gave me a ride on his motorcycle."

"Well, you are not to get on his motorcycle again," Dad ordered.

"In some ways he's a nice boy," said Mother, "but I don't approve of the way he's been acting lately. The way he talks to his parents is disgraceful!"

"He called his mother 'stupid old woman' the other day," little Cheri reported. "That's not nice."

"It certainly isn't," agreed Dad. "It's too bad Chad doesn't have twenty-twenty vision. He seems to be going blind."

"Chad's going blind?" David was horrified.

"Well, the Bible talks about the person who curses his parents. It says God will put out his light," Dad told him. "That means he will go blind—not physically, but spiritually. And a spiritually blind person can get into lots of trouble. Incidentally, that's Proverbs 20:20."

As Mother cleared the breakfast table the next morning, she told David, "Chad wrecked his folks' car and was charged with drunken driving last night."

"Ooooooh!" David exhaled. "Maybe he is going blind like Dad said."

Respecting Others Memory Verse

Don't be selfish; don't live to make a good impression on others. Be humble, thinking of others as better than yourself.
Philippians 2:3

How About You?

How's your spiritual eyesight? One way to check it is to take a look at your attitude toward your parents. Do you honor and obey them? To curse them—to speak disrespectfully of them or to them—is a warning of serious problems. *B. W.*

• For the next devotional, turn to page 635.   • For the next devotional on *Respecting Others*, turn to page 699.
• For notes on *Respecting Others*, see pages 322, 382, 1088, and 1218.

¹⁵A youngster's heart is filled with rebellion, but punishment will drive it out of him.

¹⁶He who gains by oppressing the poor or by bribing the rich shall end in poverty.

¹⁷⁻¹⁹Listen to this wise advice; follow it closely, for it will do you good, and you can pass it on to others: *Trust in the Lord.*

²⁰,²¹In the past, haven't I been right? Then believe what I am telling you now and share it with others.

²²,²³Don't rob the poor and sick! For the Lord is their defender. If you injure them, he will punish you.

²⁴,²⁵Keep away from angry, short-tempered men, lest you learn to be like them and endanger your soul.

²⁶,²⁷Unless you have the extra cash on hand, don't countersign a note. Why risk everything you own? They'll even take your bed!

²⁸Do not move the ancient boundary marks. That is stealing.

²⁹Do you know a hard-working man? He shall be successful and stand before kings!

23 Criticism Can Help You

When dining with a rich man, be on your guard and don't stuff yourself, though it all tastes so good; for he is trying to bribe you, and no good is going to come of his invitation.

⁴,⁵Don't weary yourself trying to get rich. Why waste your time? For riches can disappear as though they had the wings of a bird!

⁶⁻⁸Don't associate with evil men; don't long for their favors and gifts. Their kindness is a trick; they want to use you as their pawn. The delicious food they serve will turn sour in your stomach, and you will vomit it and have to take back your words of appreciation for their "kindness."

⁹Don't waste your breath on a rebel. He will despise the wisest advice.

¹⁰,¹¹Don't steal the land of defenseless orphans by moving their ancient boundary marks, for their Redeemer is strong; he himself will accuse you.

¹²Don't refuse to accept criticism; get all the help you can.

¹³,¹⁴Don't fail to correct your children; discipline won't hurt them! They won't die if you use a stick on them! Punishment will keep them out of hell.

¹⁵,¹⁶My son, how I will rejoice if you become a man of common sense. Yes, my heart will thrill to your thoughtful, wise words.

¹⁷,¹⁸Don't envy evil men but continue to reverence the Lord all the time, for surely you have a wonderful future ahead of you. There is hope for you yet!

¹⁹⁻²¹O my son, be wise and stay in God's paths; don't carouse with drunkards and gluttons, for they are on their way to poverty. And remember that too much sleep clothes a man with rags.

²²Listen to your father's advice and don't despise an old mother's experience. ²³Get the facts at any price, and hold on tightly to all the good sense you can get. ²⁴,²⁵The father of a godly man has cause for joy—what pleasure a wise son is! So give your parents joy!

²⁶⁻²⁸O my son, trust my advice—stay away from prostitutes. For a prostitute is a deep and narrow grave. Like a robber, she waits for her victims as one after another become unfaithful to their wives.

²⁹,³⁰Whose heart is filled with anguish and sorrow? Who is always fighting and quarreling? Who is the man with bloodshot eyes and many wounds? It is the one who spends long hours in the taverns, trying out new mixtures. ³¹Don't let the sparkle and the smooth taste of strong wine deceive you. ³²For in the end it bites like a poisonous serpent; it stings like an adder. ³³You will see hallucinations and have delirium tremens, and you will say foolish, silly things that would embarrass you no end when sober. ³⁴You will stagger like a sailor tossed at sea, clinging to a swaying mast. ³⁵And afterwards you will say, "I didn't even know it when they beat me up. . . . Let's go and have another drink!"

24 Plans Are as Bad as Actions

Don't envy godless men; don't even enjoy their company. ²For they spend their days plotting violence and cheating.

³,⁴Any enterprise is built by wise planning, becomes strong through common sense, and profits wonderfully by keeping abreast of the facts.

⁵A wise man is mightier than a strong man. Wisdom is mightier than strength.

⁶Don't go to war without wise guidance; there is safety in many counselors.

⁷Wisdom is too much for a rebel. He'll not be chosen as a counselor!

⁸To plan evil is as wrong as doing it.

⁹The rebel's schemes are sinful, and the mocker is the scourge of all mankind.

¹⁰You are a poor specimen if you can't stand the pressure of adversity.

¹¹,¹²Rescue those who are unjustly sentenced to death; don't stand back and let them die. Don't try to disclaim responsibility by saying you didn't know about it. For God, who knows all hearts, knows yours, and he knows you knew! And he will reward everyone according to his deeds.

¹³,¹⁴My son, honey whets the appetite and so does wisdom! When you enjoy becoming wise, there is hope for you! A bright future lies ahead!

Family Devotions

☐ **Devotion 188**

Cultivating Godly Attitudes

Read Proverbs 23:22-25

Cultivating Godly Attitudes
Memory Verse

Whatever you do or say, let it be as a representative of the Lord Jesus, and come with him into the presence of God the Father to give him your thanks.
Colossians 3:17

"Dad sure looks tired lately," said Jenny to her brother, Steve. It was Saturday morning, and they were playing catch in the front yard. Just a few minutes earlier, they had watched their dad slowly walk down the road to the bus stop. Even though it was Saturday, he had to go to the office.

"Dad's tired because of that big report he's writing for the convention next month," Steve explained.

"Mom's been busy, too," Jenny continued. "It's not easy teaching Sunday school class and getting the house ready for company. Wish we could help them."

"Well, we have helped Mom with the cleaning," said Steve, "but there are some jobs kids just can't do!"

They threw the ball back and forth for a while, then Jenny spoke excitedly. "Steve, how much money do you have?"

Steve grinned. "I'm rich! All last week I helped Mr. Parker clean out the back room at his store, remember? And he said he could use me later, too. Why?"

"I've got baby-sitting money saved up," said Jenny, "and I thought maybe we could take Dad and Mom out for dinner. We don't have to go to the most expensive place in town, but it would let them know how much we appreciate them."

And that's just what Jenny and Steve did! Their parents were very surprised. "You know," said Dad as they were eating, "this is the best hamburger I've ever tasted! The psalmist sure knew what he was talking about when he said, 'Children are a gift from God.'"

"I agree." Mom smiled. "It's terrific to know that our children care about us!"

Jenny and Steve grinned at each other. They were glad they had given their parents a special treat!

How About You?
When was the last time you gave your parents joy—by doing something special for them or telling them how much you appreciate the hard work they do? Dads and moms sometimes become very busy and therefore very tired. Read 1 Corinthians 13, a chapter in which the apostle Paul talks about love. Then show that kind of love to your parents. *L. M. W.*

• For the next devotional, turn to page 637.   • For the next devotional on *Cultivating Godly Attitudes*, turn to page 737.   • For notes on *Cultivating Godly Attitudes*, see pages 337, 383, 472, 622, and 1216.

¹⁵,¹⁶O evil man, leave the upright man alone and quit trying to cheat him out of his rights. Don't you know that this good man, though you trip him up seven times, will each time rise again? But one calamity is enough to lay you low.

¹⁷Do not rejoice when your enemy meets trouble. Let there be no gladness when he falls— ¹⁸for the Lord may be displeased with you and stop punishing him!

¹⁹,²⁰Don't envy the wicked. Don't covet his riches. For the evil man has no future; his light will be snuffed out.

²¹,²²My son, watch your step before the Lord and the king, and don't associate with radicals. For you will go down with them to sudden disaster, and who knows where it all will end?

²³It is wrong to sentence the poor and let the rich go free. ²⁴He who says to the wicked, "You are innocent," shall be cursed by many people of many nations; ²⁵but blessings shall be showered on those who rebuke sin fearlessly.

²⁶It is an honor to receive a frank reply.

²⁷Develop your business first before building your house.

²⁸,²⁹Don't testify spitefully against an innocent neighbor. Why lie about him? Don't say, "Now I can pay him back for all his meanness to me!"

³⁰,³¹I walked by the field of a certain lazy fellow and saw that it was overgrown with thorns; it was covered with weeds, and its walls were broken down. ³²,³³Then, as I looked, I learned this lesson:

"A little extra sleep,
A little more slumber,
A little folding of the hands to rest"

³⁴means that poverty will break in upon you suddenly like a robber and violently like a bandit.

25 Keep Your Promises

These proverbs of Solomon were discovered and copied by the aides of King Hezekiah of Judah:

²,³It is God's privilege to conceal things, and the king's privilege to discover and invent. You cannot understand the height of heaven, the size of the earth, or all that goes on in the king's mind!

⁴,⁵When you remove dross from silver, you have sterling ready for the silversmith. When you remove corrupt men from the king's court, his reign will be just and fair.

⁶,⁷Don't demand an audience with the king as though you were some powerful prince. It is better to wait for an invitation rather than to be sent back to the end of the line, publicly disgraced!

⁸⁻¹⁰Don't be hot-headed and rush to court! You may start something you can't finish and go down before your neighbor in shameful defeat. So discuss the matter with him privately. Don't tell anyone else, lest he accuse you of slander and you can't withdraw what you said.

¹¹Timely advice is as lovely as gold apples in a silver basket.

¹²It is a badge of honor to accept valid criticism.

¹³A faithful employee is as refreshing as a cool day in the hot summertime.

¹⁴One who doesn't give the gift he promised is like a cloud blowing over a desert without dropping any rain.

¹⁵Be patient and you will finally win, for a soft tongue can break hard bones.

¹⁶Do you like honey? Don't eat too much of it, or it will make you sick!

¹⁷Don't visit your neighbor too often, or you will outwear your welcome!

¹⁸Telling lies about someone is as harmful as hitting him with an axe, or wounding him with a sword, or shooting him with a sharp arrow.

¹⁹Putting confidence in an unreliable man is like chewing with a sore tooth, or trying to run on a broken foot.

²⁰Being happy-go-lucky around a person whose heart is heavy is as bad as stealing his jacket in cold weather or rubbing salt in his wounds.

²¹,²²If your enemy is hungry, give him food! If he is thirsty, give him something to drink! This will make him feel ashamed of himself, and God will reward you.

²³As surely as a wind from the north brings cold, just as surely a retort causes anger!

²⁴It is better to live in a corner of an attic than in a beautiful home with a cranky, quarrelsome woman.

²⁵Good news from far away is like cold water to the thirsty.

²⁶If a godly man compromises with the wicked, it is like polluting a fountain or muddying a spring.

²⁷Just as it is harmful to eat too much honey, so also it is bad for men to think about all the honors they deserve!

²⁸A man without self-control is as defenseless as a city with broken-down walls.

26 Rebels Are Impossible

Honor doesn't go with fools any more than snow with summertime or rain with harvesttime!

²An undeserved curse has no effect. Its intended victim will be no more harmed by it than by a sparrow or swallow flitting through the sky.

³Guide a horse with a whip, a donkey with a bridle, and a rebel with a rod to his back!

Family Devotions

☐ DEVOTION 189
KEEPING YOUR PROMISES

Read Proverbs 25:11-15, 19

Keeping Your Promises Memory Verse

God delights in those who keep their promises and abhors those who don't. Proverbs 12:22

"Janet," said Mother one Saturday morning, "isn't your youth group doing a Community Service project this afternoon?"

Janet shrugged. "Yeah, but I don't want to go," she said. "It's too hot to mow lawns and hoe gardens today."

"I heard you tell Pastor Jim you'd be there," said Mother with a frown. "I think you should go."

"Well, I go to lots of things," replied Janet. "I can't see how it would hurt to miss once."

Later Janet decided to go along with her mother to the supermarket. "It's too bad we have to take the small car," said Mother as they went out to the garage. "I really could use more room for groceries."

"Let's take the other car then," suggested Janet.

"You mean Old Unreliable?" asked Mother with a smile. "I haven't dared to drive it since it broke down on the expressway. I'll wait till it's fixed."

"It's lots prettier than this car," observed Janet.

"Well, that doesn't mean much if it's not dependable," said Mother. Then she added, "I hope you won't be offended, honey, but in a way, you remind me of that car."

"Huh?" Janet was surprised. "How come?"

"You're a wonderful person in a lot of ways, and you have talents that could be used for the Lord," Mother told her. "However, lately you've made commitments to your youth leaders, your teachers, and your father and me, but you often haven't followed through on them. Very soon, I'm afraid, people will feel they can't count on you." Janet was silent as they rode along. "I'm going to insist that you go to help with the service project this afternoon," added Mother.

Janet nodded. "I guess I should," she said with a sigh. "After all, I don't want anybody calling me Old Unreliable."

How About You?
Do you keep the commitments you make? Faithfulness is important to the Lord as well as to people. God rewards those who are faithful in serving him. Determine now to always keep your promises and to be a reliable Christian on whom others can depend. *S. K.*

• For the next devotional, turn to page 639. • For the next devotional on KEEPING YOUR PROMISES, turn to page 649.
• For notes on KEEPING YOUR PROMISES, see pages 183, 284, and 838.

4,5 When arguing with a rebel, don't use foolish arguments as he does, or you will become as foolish as he is! Prick his conceit with silly replies!

6 To trust a rebel to convey a message is as foolish as cutting off your feet and drinking poison!

7 In the mouth of a fool a proverb becomes as useless as a paralyzed leg.

8 Honoring a rebel will backfire like a stone tied to a slingshot!

9 A rebel will misapply an illustration so that its point will no more be felt than a thorn in the hand of a drunkard.

10 The master may get better work from an untrained apprentice than from a skilled rebel!

11 As a dog returns to his vomit, so a fool repeats his folly.

12 There is one thing worse than a fool, and that is a man who is conceited.

13 The lazy man won't go out and work. "There might be a lion outside!" he says. 14 He sticks to his bed like a door to its hinges! 15 He is too tired even to lift his food from his dish to his mouth! 16 Yet in his own opinion he is smarter than seven wise men.

17 Yanking a dog's ears is no more foolish than interfering in an argument that isn't any of your business.

18,19 A man who is caught lying to his neighbor and says, "I was just fooling," is like a madman throwing around firebrands, arrows, and death!

20 Fire goes out for lack of fuel, and tensions disappear when gossip stops.

21 A quarrelsome man starts fights as easily as a match sets fire to paper.

22 Gossip is a dainty morsel eaten with great relish.

23 Pretty words may hide a wicked heart, just as a pretty glaze covers a common clay pot.

24-26 A man with hate in his heart may sound pleasant enough, but don't believe him; for he is cursing you in his heart. Though he pretends to be so kind, his hatred will finally come to light for all to see.

27 The man who sets a trap for others will get caught in it himself. Roll a boulder down on someone, and it will roll back and crush you.

28 Flattery is a form of hatred and wounds cruelly.

27 Jealousy Is Dangerous

Don't brag about your plans for tomorrow—wait and see what happens.

2 Don't praise yourself; let others do it!

3 A rebel's frustrations are heavier than sand and rocks.

4 Jealousy is more dangerous and cruel than anger.

5 Open rebuke is better than hidden love!

6 Wounds from a friend are better than kisses from an enemy!

7 Even honey seems tasteless to a man who is full; but if he is hungry, he'll eat anything!

8 A man who strays from home is like a bird that wanders from its nest.

9 Friendly suggestions are as pleasant as perfume.

10 Never abandon a friend—either yours or your father's. Then you won't need to go to a distant relative for help in your time of need.

11 My son, how happy I will be if you turn out to be sensible! It will be a public honor to me.

12 A sensible man watches for problems ahead and prepares to meet them. The simpleton never looks and suffers the consequences.

13 The world's poorest credit risk is the man who agrees to pay a stranger's debts.

14 If you shout a pleasant greeting to a friend too early in the morning, he will count it as a curse!

15 A constant dripping on a rainy day and a cranky woman are much alike! 16 You can no more stop her complaints than you can stop the wind or hold onto anything with oil-slick hands.

17 A friendly discussion is as stimulating as the sparks that fly when iron strikes iron.

18 A workman may eat from the orchard he tends; anyone should be rewarded who protects another's interests.

19 A mirror reflects a man's face, but what he is really like is shown by the kind of friends he chooses.

20 Ambition and death are alike in this: neither is ever satisfied.

21 The purity of silver and gold can be tested in a crucible, but a man is tested by his reaction to men's praise.

22 You can't separate a rebel from his foolishness though you crush him to powder.

23,24 Riches can disappear fast. And the king's crown doesn't stay in his family forever—so watch your business interests closely. Know the state of your flocks and your herds; 25-27 then there will be lambs' wool enough for clothing and goats' milk enough for food for all your household after the hay is harvested, and the new crop appears, and the mountain grasses are gathered in.

28 Admit Your Mistakes

The wicked flee when no one is chasing them! But the godly are bold as lions!

2 When there is moral rot within a nation, its

Family Devotions

☐ **Devotion 190**
Honesty

Read Proverbs 29:5

Honesty
Memory Verse

Stop lying to each other; tell the truth, for we are parts of each other and when we lie to each other we are hurting ourselves.
Ephesians 4:25

"Something kind of funny happened in Nature Club today," Katy told her mother as she set the table for supper. "I sat down in my usual seat, and Sue Brown hurried over to me like we were best friends! I hardly know her at all. Anyhow, she told me how nice I looked in my green sweater and asked if it was new."

"Really?" asked Mother. "You've had that sweater a long time, and you wear it almost every week."

"I know," nodded Katy. "Then Sue went on to say how much she admired my math grades. I really got suspicious when she told me how she always likes to be around me!"

"She must have been in a good mood today," Mother commented.

"Well, after she got done telling me all those things, she went over to another girl and gave her the same treatment!" said Katy.

Mother looked thoughtful. "Maybe she's trying to make some new friends."

"You're right," laughed Katy, "and she wanted them in a hurry. I figured it out after the club meeting started. We were electing officers, and Sue was one of the three nominated for president. She thought she could get our votes by giving us compliments. I had already decided Greg would be the best president, and I guess most of the other kids agreed, because Greg won. After club, I said good-bye to Sue, but she just ignored me!"

"I'm glad you weren't taken in by her compliments," Mother said. "It's sad when someone tries to control others through flattery. Even the Bible says that flattery is a trap."

"I'm going to be careful to really mean what I'm saying when I give someone a compliment," declared Katy.

How About You?
Have you ever complimented someone because you wanted him to do something for you? Insincere compliments are called flattery, but, actually, they are lies. God's Word refers to flattery a number of times, but never favorably. It's nice to give a compliment when you really mean it, but it's wrong to give a compliment just to make someone like you. *L. M. W.*

- For the next devotional, turn to page 645.   • For the next devotional on *Honesty,* turn to page 1067.
- For notes on *Honesty,* see pages 304, 813, and 863.

government topples easily; but with honest, sensible leaders there is stability.

³When a poor man oppresses those even poorer, he is like an unexpected flood sweeping away their last hope.

⁴To complain about the law is to praise wickedness. To obey the law is to fight evil.

⁵Evil men don't understand the importance of justice, but those who follow the Lord are much concerned about it.

⁶Better to be poor and honest than rich and a cheater.

⁷Young men who are wise obey the law; a son who is a member of a lawless gang is a shame to his father.

⁸Income from exploiting the poor will end up in the hands of someone who pities them.

⁹God doesn't listen to the prayers of those who flout the law.

¹⁰A curse on those who lead astray the godly. But men who encourage the upright to do good shall be given a worthwhile reward.

¹¹Rich men are conceited, but their real poverty is evident to the poor.

¹²When the godly are successful, everyone is glad. When the wicked succeed, everyone is sad.

¹³A man who refuses to admit his mistakes can never be successful. But if he confesses and forsakes them, he gets another chance.

¹⁴Blessed is the man who reveres God, but the man who doesn't care is headed for serious trouble.

¹⁵A wicked ruler is as dangerous to the poor as a lion or bear attacking them.

¹⁶Only a stupid prince will oppress his people, but a king will have a long reign if he hates dishonesty and bribes.

¹⁷A murderer's conscience will drive him into hell. Don't stop him!

¹⁸Good men will be rescued from harm, but cheaters will be destroyed.

¹⁹Hard work brings prosperity; playing around brings poverty.

²⁰The man who wants to do right will get a rich reward. But the man who wants to get rich quick will quickly fail.

²¹Giving preferred treatment to rich people is a clear case of selling one's soul for a piece of bread.

²²Trying to get rich quick is evil and leads to poverty.

²³In the end, people appreciate frankness more than flattery.

²⁴A man who robs his parents and says, "What's wrong with that?" is no better than a murderer.

²⁵Greed causes fighting; trusting God leads to prosperity.

²⁶A man is a fool to trust himself! But those who use God's wisdom are safe.

²⁷If you give to the poor, your needs will be supplied! But a curse upon those who close their eyes to poverty.

²⁸When the wicked prosper, good men go away; when the wicked meet disaster, good men return.

29 God Rewards Fairness

The man who is often reproved but refuses to accept criticism will suddenly be broken and never have another chance.

²With good men in authority, the people rejoice; but with the wicked in power, they groan.

³A wise son makes his father happy, but a lad who hangs around with prostitutes disgraces him.

⁴A just king gives stability to his nation, but one who demands bribes destroys it.

⁵,⁶Flattery is a trap; evil men are caught in it, but good men stay away and sing for joy.

⁷The good man knows the poor man's rights; the godless don't care.

⁸Fools start fights everywhere while wise men try to keep peace.

⁹There's no use arguing with a fool. He only rages and scoffs, and tempers flare.

¹⁰The godly pray for those who long to kill them.

¹¹A rebel shouts in anger; a wise man holds his temper in and cools it.

¹²A wicked ruler will have wicked aides on his staff.

¹³Rich and poor are alike in this: each depends on God for light.

¹⁴A king who is fair to the poor shall have a long reign.

¹⁵Scolding and spanking a child helps him to learn. Left to himself, he brings shame to his mother.

¹⁶When rulers are wicked, their people are too; but good men will live to see the tyrant's downfall.

¹⁷Discipline your son and he will give you happiness and peace of mind.

¹⁸Where there is ignorance of God, crime runs wild; but what a wonderful thing it is for a nation to know and keep his laws.

¹⁹Sometimes mere words are not enough—discipline is needed. For the words may not be heeded.

²⁰There is more hope for a fool than for a man of quick temper.

²¹Pamper a servant from childhood, and he will expect you to treat him as a son!

²²A hot-tempered man starts fights and gets into all kinds of trouble.

²³Pride ends in a fall, while humility brings honor.

²⁴A man who assists a thief must really hate himself! For he knows the consequence but does it anyway.

²⁵Fear of man is a dangerous trap, but to trust in God means safety.

²⁶Do you want justice? Don't fawn on the judge, but ask the Lord for it!

²⁷The good hate the badness of the wicked. The wicked hate the goodness of the good.

30 Wonderful Things

These are the messages of Agur, son of Jakeh, addressed to Ithiel and Ucal:

²I am tired out, O God, and ready to die. I am too stupid even to call myself a human being! ³I cannot understand man, let alone God. ⁴Who else but God goes back and forth to heaven? Who else holds the wind in his fists and wraps up the oceans in his cloak? Who but God has created the world? If there is any other, what is his name—and his Son's name—if you know it?

⁵Every word of God proves true. He defends all who come to him for protection. ⁶Do not add to his words, lest he rebuke you, and you be found a liar.

⁷O God, I beg two favors from you before I die: ⁸First, help me never to tell a lie. Second, give me neither poverty nor riches! Give me just enough to satisfy my needs! ⁹For if I grow rich, I may become content without God. And if I am too poor, I may steal and thus insult God's holy name.

¹⁰Never falsely accuse a man to his employer, lest he curse you for your sin.

¹¹,¹²There are those who curse their father and mother and feel themselves faultless despite their many sins. ¹³,¹⁴They are proud beyond description, arrogant, disdainful. They devour the poor with teeth as sharp as knives!

¹⁵,¹⁶There are two things never satisfied, like a leech forever craving more: no, three things! no, four! Hell, the barren womb, a barren desert, fire.

¹⁷A man who mocks his father and despises his mother shall have his eye plucked out by ravens and eaten by vultures.

¹⁸,¹⁹There are three things too wonderful for me to understand—no, four!

How an eagle glides through the sky.
How a serpent crawls upon a rock.
How a ship finds its way across the heaving ocean.
The growth of love between a man and a girl.

²⁰There is another thing too: how a prostitute can sin and then say, "What's wrong with that?"

²¹⁻²³There are three things that make the earth tremble—no, four it cannot stand:

A slave who becomes a king.
A rebel who prospers.
A bitter woman when she finally marries.
A servant girl who marries her mistress' husband.

²⁴⁻²⁸There are four things that are small but unusually wise:

Ants: they aren't strong, but store up food for the winter.
Cliff badgers: delicate little animals who protect themselves by living among the rocks.
The locusts: though they have no leader, they stay together in swarms.
The lizards: they are easy to catch and kill, yet are found even in king's palaces!

²⁹⁻³¹There are three stately monarchs in the earth—no, four:

The lion, king of the animals. He won't turn aside for anyone.
The peacock.
The male goat.
A king as he leads his army.

³²If you have been a fool by being proud or plotting evil, don't brag about it—cover your mouth with your hand in shame.

³³As the churning of cream yields butter, and a blow to the nose causes bleeding, so anger causes quarrels.

31

These are the wise sayings of King Lemuel of Massa, taught to him at his mother's knee:

²O my son, whom I have dedicated to the Lord, ³do not spend your time with women—the royal pathway to destruction.

⁴And it is not for kings, O Lemuel, to drink wine and whiskey. ⁵For if they drink they may forget their duties and be unable to give justice to those who are oppressed. ⁶,⁷Hard liquor is for sick men at the brink of death, and wine for those in deep depression. Let them drink to forget their poverty and misery.

⁸You should defend those who cannot help themselves. ⁹Yes, speak up for the poor and helpless, and see that they get justice.

¹⁰If you can find a truly good wife, she is worth

more than precious gems! ¹¹Her husband can trust her, and she will richly satisfy his needs. ¹²She will not hinder him but help him all her life. ¹³She finds wool and flax and busily spins it. ¹⁴She buys imported foods brought by ship from distant ports. ¹⁵She gets up before dawn to prepare breakfast for her household and plans the day's work for her servant girls. ¹⁶She goes out to inspect a field and buys it; with her own hands she plants a vineyard. ¹⁷She is energetic, a hard worker, ¹⁸and watches for bargains. She works far into the night!

¹⁹,²⁰She sews for the poor and generously helps those in need. ²¹She has no fear of winter for her household, for she has made warm clothes for all of them. ²²She also upholsters with finest tapestry; her own clothing is beautifully made—a purple gown of pure linen. ²³Her husband is well known, for he sits in the council chamber with the other civic leaders. ²⁴She makes belted linen garments to sell to the merchants.

²⁵She is a woman of strength and dignity and has no fear of old age. ²⁶When she speaks, her words are wise, and kindness is the rule for everything she says. ²⁷She watches carefully all that goes on throughout her household and is never lazy. ²⁸Her children stand and bless her; so does her husband. He praises her with these words: ²⁹"There are many fine women in the world, but you are the best of them all!"

³⁰Charm can be deceptive and beauty doesn't last, but a woman who fears and reverences God shall be greatly praised. ³¹Praise her for the many fine things she does. These good deeds of hers shall bring her honor and recognition from people of importance.

Ecclesiastes

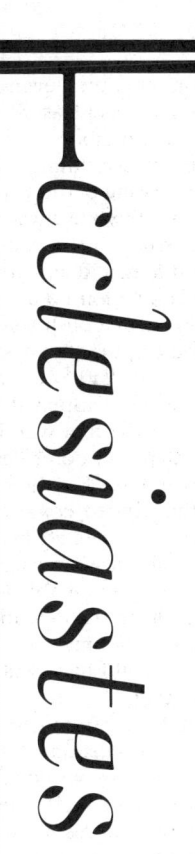

DO YOU ever get bored with life? Our daily routine can make us feel like we're stuck in a rut. It can start to feel pretty meaningless sometimes. Then we envy friends who make straight A's, pro athletes who can afford everything, and famous TV stars who can do anything they want. Which way is best?

The writer of Ecclesiastes wanted to know what the best kind of life was. He decided to go out and try *everything*. The writer of Ecclesiastes, Solomon, had enough time and money to do this.

Ecclesiastes is his journal of his search for the meaning of life. He wrote about the empty routine that got him started on his search. He wrote down each step he took and his discoveries along the way. He questioned and tested everything until he had an answer.

As you read Ecclesiastes, look for Solomon's wise and positive discoveries. Then see how your daily routine can have more meaning by following Solomon's conclusion.

Is Life Worth Living?

The author: Solomon of Jerusalem, King David's son, "The Preacher."

[2]In my opinion, nothing is worthwhile; everything is futile. [3-7]For what does a man get for all his hard work?

Generations come and go, but it makes no difference. The sun rises and sets and hurries around to rise again. The wind blows south and north, here and there, twisting back and forth, getting nowhere. The rivers run into the sea, but the sea is never full, and the water returns again to the rivers and flows again to the sea . . . [8-11]everything is unutterably weary and tiresome. No matter how much we see, we are never satisfied; no matter how much we hear, we are not content.

History merely repeats itself. Nothing is truly new; it has all been done or said before. What can you point to that is new? How do you know it didn't exist long ages ago? We don't remember what happened in those former times, and in the future generations no one will remember what we have done back here.

¹²⁻¹⁵I, the Preacher, was king of Israel, living in Jerusalem. And I applied myself to search for understanding about everything in the universe. I discovered that the lot of man, which God has dealt to him, is not a happy one. It is all foolishness, chasing the wind. What is wrong cannot be righted; it is water over the dam; and there is no use thinking of what might have been.

¹⁶⁻¹⁸I said to myself, "Look, I am better educated than any of the kings before me in Jerusalem. I have greater wisdom and knowledge." So I worked hard to be wise instead of foolish—but now I realize that even this was like chasing the wind. For the more my wisdom, the more my grief; to increase knowledge only increases distress.

2 A Good Time Isn't Everything

I said to myself, "Come now, be merry; enjoy yourself to the full." But I found that this, too, was futile. For it is silly to be laughing all the time; what good does it do?

³So after a lot of thinking, I decided to try the road of drink, while still holding steadily to my course of seeking wisdom.

Next I changed my course again and followed the path of folly, so that I could experience the only happiness most men have throughout their lives.

⁴⁻⁶Then I tried to find fulfillment by inaugurating a great public works program: homes, vineyards, gardens, parks, and orchards for myself, and reservoirs to hold the water to irrigate my plantations.

⁷,⁸Next I bought slaves, both men and women, and others were born within my household. I also bred great herds and flocks, more than any of the kings before me. I collected silver and gold as taxes from many kings and provinces.

In the cultural arts, I organized men's and women's choirs and orchestras.

And then there were my many beautiful concubines.

⁹So I became greater than any of the kings in Jerusalem before me, and with it all I remained clear-eyed, so that I could evaluate all these things. ¹⁰Anything I wanted I took and did not restrain myself from any joy. I even found great pleasure in hard work. This pleasure was, indeed, my only reward for all my labors.

¹¹But as I looked at everything I had tried, it was all so useless, a chasing of the wind, and there was nothing really worthwhile anywhere.

¹²Now I began a study of the comparative virtues of wisdom and folly, and anyone else would come to the same conclusion I did—¹³,¹⁴that wisdom is of more value than foolishness, just as light is better than darkness; for the wise man sees, while the fool is blind. And yet I noticed that there was one thing that happened to wise and foolish alike—¹⁵just as the fool will die, so will I. So of what value is all my wisdom? Then I realized that even wisdom is futile. ¹⁶For the wise and fool both die, and in the days to come both will be long forgotten. ¹⁷So now I hate life because it is all so irrational; all is foolishness, chasing the wind.

¹⁸And I am disgusted about this—that I must leave the fruits of all my hard work to others. ¹⁹And who can tell whether my son will be a wise man or a fool? And yet all I have will be given to him—how discouraging!

²⁰⁻²³So I turned in despair from hard work as the answer to my search for satisfaction. For though I spend my life searching for wisdom, knowledge, and skill, I must leave all of it to someone who hasn't done a day's work in his life; he inherits all my efforts, free of charge. This is not only foolish but unfair. So what does a man get for all his hard work? Days full of sorrow and grief, and restless, bitter nights. It is all utterly ridiculous.

²⁴⁻²⁶So I decided that there was nothing better for a man to do than to enjoy his food and drink and his job. Then I realized that even this pleasure is from the hand of God. For who can eat or enjoy apart from him? For God gives those who please him wisdom, knowledge, and joy; but if a sinner becomes wealthy, God takes the wealth away from him and gives it to those who please him. So here, too, we see an example of foolishly chasing the wind.

3 There's a Right Time for Everything

There is a right time for everything:

²A time to be born;
A time to die;
A time to plant;
A time to harvest;
³A time to kill;
A time to heal;
A time to destroy;
A time to rebuild;
⁴A time to cry;
A time to laugh;

PUTTING GOD FIRST 1:8-11 Many people feel restless and dissatisfied. They wonder (1) If I am in God's will, why am I so dissatisfied? (2) What is the meaning of life? (3) When I look back on it all, will I be happy with my accomplishments? (4) Why do I feel burned out, disillusioned, dry? (5) What is to become of me? Solomon tests our faith, challenging us to find true and lasting meaning in God alone. As you take a hard look at your life, as Solomon did his, you will see how important serving God is over all other options. Perhaps God is asking you to rethink your purpose and direction in life as Solomon did in Ecclesiastes. **To begin the series of devotionals on PUTTING GOD FIRST, turn to page 115.**

Family Devotions

☐ *Devotion 191*
Patience

Read Ecclesiastes 3:1-11

"Let me drive, Dad—please!" Craig begged as Dad turned the car onto a country road leading to Grandfather's farm. "There's not much traffic here."

Dad shook his head. "You're not old enough, Son."

"I'm fourteen. Next year I can get my permit," Craig pleaded. "Besides, Steve's dad lets him drive all the time." Immediately, Craig knew he had said the wrong thing. His father was never impressed by what Steve's dad did. When Dad did not respond, Craig knew the subject was closed. Dad was a stickler for obeying the Bible and what he called "the laws of the land."

When the family arrived at the farm, they found Grandpa in the garden, planting potatoes. Craig's little brother, Tyson, squatted down on the ground and began digging. "I wanna make a garden, too," he said.

Craig headed for the barn. "I'm going to ride Princess. At least I don't need a license to ride a horse!" he mumbled.

As they prepared to leave later that afternoon, Tyson was nowhere to be found. They searched all over, calling his name. Mom and Dad were beginning to look worried. Then Grandpa came across the yard carrying a tired little boy. "Found him in the garden sound asleep," Grandpa explained as he put Tyson in his father's arms.

Dad smiled. "What were you doing in the garden?"

"Waitin' for the 'tatoes to come up." The little boy yawned. "But it took 'em so long, I went to sleep."

Craig and his parents were still chuckling as they drove onto the freeway. "Patience is a wonderful thing," said Dad. "It's something God wants all of us to learn. In time, Craig, you'll have your driver's license, and it will have been worth the wait. And in time, Tyson, we'll have our potatoes."

Patience Memory Verse

Now as for you, dear brothers who are waiting for the Lord's return, be patient, like a farmer who waits until the autumn for his precious harvest to ripen.
James 5:7

How About You?
Do you try to take shortcuts to get what you want before the right time? God knows the best time for everything. Waiting is hard, but it is important. When you are told to wait, don't fret and fuss. Be patient. B. W.

• For the next devotional, turn to page 647. • For the next devotional on *Patience*, turn to page 709. • For notes on *Patience*, see pages 35, 242, 329, and 502.

A time to grieve;
A time to dance;
⁵A time for scattering stones;
A time for gathering stones;
A time to hug;
A time not to hug;
⁶A time to find;
A time to lose;
A time for keeping;
A time for throwing away;
⁷A time to tear;
A time to repair;
A time to be quiet;
A time to speak up;
⁸A time for loving;
A time for hating;
A time for war;
A time for peace.

⁹What does one really get from hard work? ¹⁰I have thought about this in connection with all the various kinds of work God has given to mankind. ¹¹Everything is appropriate in its own time. But though God has planted eternity in the hearts of men, even so, many cannot see the whole scope of God's work from beginning to end. ¹²So I conclude that, first, there is nothing better for a man than to be happy and to enjoy himself as long as he can; ¹³and second, that he should eat and drink and enjoy the fruits of his labors, for these are gifts from God.

¹⁴And I know this, that whatever God does is final—nothing can be added or taken from it; God's purpose in this is that man should fear the all-powerful God.

¹⁵Whatever is has been long ago; and whatever is going to be has been before; God brings to pass again what was in the distant past and disappeared.

¹⁶Moreover, I notice that throughout the earth justice is giving way to crime, and even the police courts are corrupt. ¹⁷I said to myself, "In due season God will judge everything man does, both good and bad."

¹⁸And then I realized that God is letting the world go on its sinful way so that he can test mankind, and so that men themselves will see that they are no better than beasts. ¹⁹For men and animals both breathe the same air, and both die. So mankind has no real advantage over the beasts; what an absurdity! ²⁰All go to one place—the dust from which they came and to which they must return. ²¹For who can prove that the spirit of man goes upward and the spirit of animals goes downward into dust? ²²So I saw that there is nothing better for men than that they should be happy in their work, for that is what they are here for, and no one can bring them back to life to enjoy what will be in the future, so let them enjoy it now.

4 I Would Rather Be Dead

Next I observed all the oppression and sadness throughout the earth—the tears of the oppressed, and no one helping them, while on the side of their oppressors were powerful allies. ²So I felt that the dead were better off than the living. ³And most fortunate of all are those who have never been born and have never seen all the evil and crime throughout the earth.

⁴Then I observed that the basic motive for success is the driving force of envy and jealousy! But this, too, is foolishness, chasing the wind. ⁵,⁶The fool won't work and almost starves but feels that it is better to be lazy and barely get by, than to work hard, when in the long run it is all so futile.

⁷I also observed another piece of foolishness around the earth. ⁸This is the case of a man who is quite alone, without a son or brother, yet he works hard to keep gaining more riches. And to whom will he leave it all, and why is he giving up so much now? It is all so pointless and depressing.

⁹Two can accomplish more than twice as much as one, for the results can be much better. ¹⁰If one falls, the other pulls him up; but if a man falls when he is alone, he's in trouble.

¹¹Also, on a cold night, two under the same blanket gain warmth from each other, but how can one be warm alone? ¹²And one standing alone can be attacked and defeated, but two can stand back-to-back and conquer; three is even better, for a triple-braided cord is not easily broken.

¹³It is better to be a poor but wise youth than to be an old and foolish king who refuses all advice. ¹⁴Such a lad could come from prison and succeed. He might even become king though born in poverty. ¹⁵Everyone is eager to help a youth like that, even to help him usurp the throne. ¹⁶He can become the leader of millions of people and be very popular. But, then, the younger generation grows up around him and rejects him! So again, it is all foolishness, chasing the wind.

5 Have Respect for God

As you enter the Temple, keep your ears open and your mouth shut! Don't be a fool who doesn't even realize it is sinful to make rash promises to God, for he is in heaven and you are only here on earth, so let your words be few. Just as being too busy gives you nightmares, so being a fool makes you a blabbermouth. ⁴So when you talk to God and vow to him that you will do something, don't delay in doing it, for God has no pleasure in fools. Keep your promise to him. ⁵It is far better not to say you'll do something than to

Family Devotions

☐ **Devotion 192**
True Joy

Read Ecclesiastes 3:12-13, 22

True Joy
Memory Verse

Always be full of joy in the Lord; I say it again, rejoice!
Philippians 4:4

As Mom put bread in the toaster, she sighed. "We have a lot to do today."

"We always do on Saturday," Jessica complained.

"Yeah," murmured Justin. "I hate Saturdays!"

Dad poured a cup of coffee. "I don't like them, either, because they're days of whining and grumbling," he said.

Justin scowled. "Stop the work and I'll stop grumbling."

Dad ignored him. "Please find me a shoe box, Justin. Jessica, you can bring me some paper and a pencil." When they returned, Dad said, "Let's write everything we have to do today on slips of paper and put them in this box."

"Change the sheets. Vacuum the carpet. Clean the bathrooms." Mom quickly named several tasks.

"Trim the hedge. Sweep the patio. Wash the car," added Dad. "Sweep the garage."

"Now," Dad said, "we'll take turns drawing out a slip."

"When the box is empty, we could pack a lunch and go to the park," suggested Mom.

"Yippee!" yelled the children.

"I want to draw first." Jessica reached for the box.

Dad held up his hand. "We forgot something," he said. "We need to give the Lord some time, too."

"Read a chapter in your Bible." Jessica wrote it on a slip of paper.

"Stop and give thanks for our family," wrote Justin.

"Memorize tomorrow's Bible verse," added Mom.

"Call Uncle John and invite him to church," Dad said as he wrote it down.

Then Dad held the box out to Jessica.

"This is going to be the best Saturday we've had in a long time," she said as she drew out a slip and looked at it. Then she grinned. "Even if I do have to clean the bathrooms!"

How About You?
If your tasks have become boring, make an activity box. If it won't work for your family, perhaps it will work for you. List everything you have to do today, and don't forget to include the Lord's work. Then be happy in your work! *B. W.*

• For the next devotional, turn to page 649.   • For the next devotional on *True Joy*, turn to page 715.   • For notes on *True Joy*, see pages 532, 1024, and 1160.

say you will and then not do it. ⁶,⁷In that case, your mouth is making you sin. Don't try to defend yourself by telling the messenger from God that it was all a mistake [to make the vow]. That would make God very angry; and he might destroy your prosperity. Dreaming instead of doing is foolishness, and there is ruin in a flood of empty words; fear God instead.

⁸If you see some poor man being oppressed by the rich, with miscarriage of justice anywhere throughout the land, don't be surprised! For every official is under orders from higher up, and the higher officials look up to their superiors. And so the matter is lost in red tape and bureaucracy. ⁹And over them all is the king. Oh, for a king who is devoted to his country! Only he can bring order from this chaos.

¹⁰He who loves money shall never have enough. The foolishness of thinking that wealth brings happiness! ¹¹The more you have, the more you spend, right up to the limits of your income. So what is the advantage of wealth—except perhaps to watch it as it runs through your fingers! ¹²The man who works hard sleeps well whether he eats little or much, but the rich must worry and suffer insomnia.

¹³,¹⁴There is another serious problem I have seen everywhere—savings are put into risky investments that turn sour, and soon there is nothing left to pass on to one's son. ¹⁵The man who speculates is soon back to where he began—with nothing. ¹⁶This, as I said, is a very serious problem, for all his hard work has been for nothing; he has been working for the wind. It is all swept away. ¹⁷All the rest of his life he is under a cloud—gloomy, discouraged, frustrated, and angry.

¹⁸Well, one thing, at least, is good: It is for a man to eat well, drink a good glass of wine, accept his position in life, and enjoy his work whatever his job may be, for however long the Lord may let him live. ¹⁹,²⁰And, of course, it is very good if a man has received wealth from the Lord and the good health to enjoy it. To enjoy your work and to accept your lot in life—that is indeed a gift from God. The person who does that will not need to look back with sorrow on his past, for God gives him joy.

6 Is Life Really Worth Living?

Yes, but there is a very serious evil which I have seen everywhere—²God has given to some men very great wealth and honor so that they can have everything they want, but he doesn't give them the health to enjoy it, and they die and others get it all! This is absurd, a hollow mockery, and a serious fault.

³Even if a man has a hundred sons and as many daughters and lives to be very old, but leaves so little money at his death that his children can't even give him a decent burial—I say that he would be better off born dead. ⁴For though his birth would then be futile and end in darkness, without even a name, ⁵never seeing the sun or even knowing its existence, yet that is better than to be an old, unhappy man. ⁶Though a man lives a thousand years twice over but doesn't find contentment—well, what's the use?

⁷,⁸Wise men and fools alike spend their lives scratching for food and never seem to get enough. Both have the same problem, yet the poor man who is wise lives a far better life. ⁹A bird in the hand is worth two in the bush; mere dreaming of nice things is foolish; it's chasing the wind.

¹⁰All things are decided by fate; it was known long ago what each man would be. So there's no use arguing with God about your destiny.

¹¹The more words you speak, the less they mean, so why bother to speak at all?

¹²In these few days of our empty lifetimes, who can say how one's days can best be spent? Who can know what will prove best for the future after he is gone? For who knows the future?

7 Some Tips for a Meaningful Life

A good reputation is more valuable than the most expensive perfume.

The day one dies is better than the day he is born! ²It is better to spend your time at funerals than at festivals. For you are going to die, and it is a good thing to think about it while there is still time. ³Sorrow is better than laughter, for sadness has a refining influence on us. ⁴Yes, a wise man thinks much of death, while the fool thinks only of having a good time now.

⁵It is better to be criticized by a wise man than to be praised by a fool! ⁶For a fool's compliment is as quickly gone as paper in fire, and it is silly to be impressed by it.

⁷The wise man is turned into a fool by a bribe; it destroys his understanding.

⁸Finishing is better than starting! Patience is better than pride! ⁹Don't be quick-tempered—that is being a fool.

¹⁰Don't long for "the good old days," for you don't know whether they were any better than these!

¹¹To be wise is as good as being rich; in fact, it is better. ¹²You can get anything by either wisdom or money, but being wise has many advantages.

¹³[See the way God does things and fall into line. Don't fight the facts of nature.] Who can straighten what he has made crooked? ¹⁴Enjoy prosperity whenever you can, and when hard times strike, realize that God gives one as well as

FAMILY DEVOTIONS

☐ DEVOTION 193
KEEPING YOUR PROMISES

Read Ecclesiastes 5:1-7

The church that Pete and Julie attended was going to collect a special offering for their missionaries in South America. As the family talked about it, Pete said, "I promised God I'd put half of my allowance in the missionary offering next week. That's a whole fifty cents!"

"I will, too," nodded Julie.

But when the offering plate was passed the following week, Peter put in only a dime, and Julie put in a nickel. Mother noticed, but said nothing.

Later that day, Pete's friend Jack came over with his new book about space exploration. "I want to be an astronaut when I grow up," said Jack.

"Me, too," Pete agreed. Julie overheard them and commented, "Not me. I want to be a fashion model. They make lots of money."

After Jack left, Mother spoke. "I thought you both told your Sunday school teacher that you were going to be missionaries," she said.

"Well, uh, I guess we forgot," said Pete.

"What difference does it make?" asked Julie. "Is it wrong for a Christian to be an astronaut or a model?"

"Not necessarily. And it's not necessarily wrong to put a nickel or dime in the offering plate, either," said Mother. "But if you make a promise to God and then break it, that's wrong. You both promised God half of your allowance. If you're unable to keep a promise through no fault of your own, that's one thing. But if you keep changing your mind whenever you feel like it, that's sin. It's better not to make a promise than to make one and not keep it."

Pete's face was red. "I think I'll have to be more careful about the promises I make—and about keeping them, too."

"Me, too," agreed his sister. "I'm going to put the rest of the money I promised in the offering tonight."

Keeping Your Promises Memory Verse

God delights in those who keep their promises and abhors those who don't.
Proverbs 12:22

How About You?

Are you quick to make promises to God—or to others—but reluctant to carry them out? God always does what he says he will do. You should, too. If keeping your promise means doing something hard or inconvenient, do it anyway. Think before you promise! *S. K.*

• For the next devotional, turn to page 651. • For the next devotional on KEEPING YOUR PROMISES, turn to page 925.
• For notes on KEEPING YOUR PROMISES, see pages 183, 284, and 838.

the other—so that everyone will realize that nothing is certain in this life.

¹⁵⁻¹⁷In this silly life I have seen everything, including the fact that some of the good die young and some of the wicked live on and on. So don't be too good or too wise! Why destroy yourself? On the other hand, don't be too wicked either—don't be a fool! Why should you die before your time?

¹⁸Tackle every task that comes along, and if you fear God you can expect his blessing.

¹⁹A wise man is stronger than the mayors of ten big cities! ²⁰And there is not a single man in all the earth who is always good and never sins.

²¹,²²Don't eavesdrop! You may hear your servant cursing you! For you know how often you yourself curse others!

²³I have tried my best to be wise. I declared, "I *will* be wise," but it didn't work. ²⁴Wisdom is far away and very difficult to find. ²⁵I searched everywhere, determined to find wisdom and the reason for things, . . . to prove to myself the wickedness of folly and that foolishness is madness.

²⁶A prostitute is more bitter than death. May it please God that you escape from her, but sinners don't evade her snares.

²⁷,²⁸This is my conclusion, says the Preacher. Step by step I came to this result after researching in every direction: One tenth of one percent of the men I interviewed could be said to be wise, but not one woman!

²⁹And I found that though God has made men upright, each has turned away to follow his own downward road.

8 Obey the Law

How wonderful to be wise, to understand things, to be able to analyze them and interpret them. Wisdom lights up a man's face, softening its hardness.

²,³Obey the king as you have vowed to do. Don't always be trying to get out of doing your duty, even when it's unpleasant. For the king punishes those who disobey. ⁴The king's command is backed by great power, and no one can withstand it or question it. ⁵Those who obey him will not be punished. The wise man will find a time and a way to do what he says. ⁶,⁷Yes, there is a time and a way for everything, though man's trouble lies heavy upon him; for how can he avoid what he doesn't know is going to happen?

⁸No one can hold back his spirit from departing; no one has the power to prevent his day of death, for there is no discharge from that obligation and that dark battle. Certainly a man's wickedness is not going to help him then.

⁹,¹⁰I have thought deeply about all that goes on here in the world, where people have the power of injuring each other. I have seen wicked men buried, and as their friends returned from the cemetery, having forgotten all the dead man's evil deeds, these men were praised in the very city where they had committed their many crimes! How odd! ¹¹Because God does not punish sinners instantly, people feel it is safe to do wrong. ¹²But though a man sins a hundred times and still lives, I know very well that those who fear God will be better off, ¹³unlike the wicked, who will not live long, good lives—their days shall pass away as quickly as shadows because they don't fear God.

¹⁴There is a strange thing happening here upon the earth: Providence seems to treat some good men as though they were wicked, and some wicked men as though they were good. This is all very vexing and troublesome!

¹⁵Then I decided to spend my time having fun because I felt that there was nothing better in all the earth than that a man should eat, drink, and be merry, with the hope that this happiness would stick with him in all the hard work that God gives to mankind everywhere.

¹⁶,¹⁷In my search for wisdom I observed all that was going on everywhere across the earth—ceaseless activity, day and night. (Of course, only God can see everything, and even the wisest man who says he knows everything, doesn't!)

9 Life Is Worth Living: Do It Well

This, too, I carefully explored—that godly and wise men are in God's will; no one knows whether he will favor them or not. All is chance! ²,³The same providence confronts everyone, whether good or bad, religious or irreligious, profane or godly. It seems so unfair that one fate comes to all. That is why men are not more careful to be good but instead choose their own mad course, for they have no hope—there is nothing but death ahead anyway.

⁴There is hope only for the living. "It is better to be a live dog than a dead lion!" ⁵For the living at least know that they will die! But the dead know nothing; they don't even have their memories. ⁶Whatever they did in their lifetimes—loving, hating, envying—is long gone, and they have no part in anything here on earth any more. ⁷So go ahead, eat, drink, and be merry, for it makes no difference to God! ⁸Wear fine clothes—with a dash of cologne! ⁹Live happily with the woman you love through the fleeting days of life, for the wife God gives you is your best reward down here for all your earthly toil. ¹⁰Whatever you do, do well, for in death, where you are going, there

Family Devotions

☐ **Devotion 194**
Overcoming Anger

Read Ecclesiastes 7:9

"Oh no!" Gary groaned when he opened his dresser drawer and saw he had no clean socks. It didn't help to know it was his own fault. He had failed to throw his dirty things down the clothes chute the day Mom was going to do the washing. He groaned even louder when a button popped off his shirt. As he was tying his shoe, the shoelace broke. "Everything is going wrong!" he grumbled.

When Gary was finally ready, he went to the kitchen and got a bowl of cereal and milk. While he was carrying the bowl to the table, it slipped, and the contents spilled over the floor. His face grew red with anger, and he swore.

Mom looked up, shocked. Even before she said anything, Gary felt guilty about swearing over a bowl of spilled cereal. He and his mother talked it over, and he told her about all the things that had gone wrong that morning.

"Instead of getting more and more angry each time something went wrong, what if you had stopped to pray?" Mom asked.

Gary poured a new bowl of cereal, thinking that over. "If I had prayed, I probably wouldn't have gotten so angry," he said slowly. "Swearing didn't help. In fact, I felt worse."

Mom nodded. "I'm not surprised," she said.

"I'm going to pray right now for God's forgiveness," resolved Gary. "And if anything else goes wrong today, I'm going to pray about it just as soon as it happens so I won't end up swearing again."

Overcoming Anger Memory Verses

Dear brothers, don't ever forget that it is best to listen much, speak little, and not become angry; for anger doesn't make us good, as God demands that we must be.
James 1:19-20

How About You?

Does everything seem to go wrong some days? Do you get more and more upset until finally you're tempted to swear? A better way to handle your anger is to immediately talk to God about the things bothering you. Ask him to take your anger away. Perhaps you'll even be able to laugh about some of the annoying things that happen. C. Y.

- For the next devotional, turn to page 653. • For the next devotional on *Overcoming Anger*, turn to page 857.
- For notes on *Overcoming Anger*, see pages 176, 511, 936, and 1003.

is no working or planning, or knowing, or understanding. ¹¹Again I looked throughout the earth and saw that the swiftest person does not always win the race, nor the strongest man the battle, and that wise men are often poor, and skillful men are not necessarily famous; but it is all by chance, by happening to be at the right place at the right time. ¹²A man never knows when he is going to run into bad luck. He is like a fish caught in a net, or a bird caught in a snare.

¹³Here is another thing that has made a deep impression on me as I have watched human affairs: ¹⁴There was a small city with only a few people living in it, and a great king came with his army and besieged it. ¹⁵There was in the city a wise man, very poor, and he knew what to do to save the city, and so it was rescued. But afterwards no one thought any more about him. ¹⁶Then I realized that though wisdom is better than strength, nevertheless, if the wise man is poor, he will be despised, and what he says will not be appreciated. ¹⁷But even so, the quiet words of a wise man are better than the shout of a king of fools. ¹⁸Wisdom is better than weapons of war, but one rotten apple can spoil a barrelful.

10 Behave Wisely

Dead flies will cause even a bottle of perfume to stink! Yes, a small mistake can outweigh much wisdom and honor. ²A wise man's heart leads him to do right, and a fool's heart leads him to do evil. ³You can identify a fool just by the way he walks down the street!

⁴If the boss is angry with you, don't quit! A quiet spirit will quiet his bad temper.

⁵There is another evil I have seen as I have watched the world go by, a sad situation concerning kings and rulers: ⁶For I have seen foolish men given great authority and rich men not given their rightful place of dignity! ⁷I have even seen servants riding, while princes walk like servants!

⁸,⁹Dig a well—and fall into it! Demolish an old wall—and be bitten by a snake! When working in a quarry, stones will fall and crush you! There is risk in each stroke of your axe!

¹⁰A dull axe requires great strength; be wise and sharpen the blade.

¹¹When the horse is stolen, it is too late to lock the barn.

¹²,¹³It is pleasant to listen to wise words, but a fool's speech brings him to ruin. Since he begins with a foolish premise, his conclusion is sheer madness. ¹⁴A fool knows all about the future and tells everyone in detail! But who can really know what is going to happen? ¹⁵A fool is so upset by a little work that he has no strength for the simplest matter.

¹⁶,¹⁷Woe to the land whose king is a child and whose leaders are already drunk in the morning. Happy the land whose king is a nobleman and whose leaders work hard before they feast and drink, and then only to strengthen themselves for the tasks ahead! ¹⁸Laziness lets the roof leak, and soon the rafters begin to rot. ¹⁹A party gives laughter, and wine gives happiness, and money gives everything! ²⁰Never curse the king, not even in your thoughts, nor the rich man, either; for a little bird will tell them what you've said.

11 Keep It Up: God Will Honor You

Give generously, for your gifts will return to you later. ²Divide your gifts among many, for in the days ahead you yourself may need much help.

³When the clouds are heavy, the rains come down; when a tree falls, whether south or north, the die is cast, for there it lies. ⁴If you wait for perfect conditions, you will never get anything done. ⁵God's ways are as mysterious as the pathway of the wind and as the manner in which a human spirit is infused into the little body of a baby while it is yet in its mother's womb. ⁶Keep on sowing your seed, for you never know which will grow—perhaps it all will.

⁷It is a wonderful thing to be alive! ⁸If a person lives to be very old, let him rejoice in every day of life, but let him also remember that eternity is far longer and that everything down here is futile in comparison.

⁹Young man, it's wonderful to be young! Enjoy every minute of it! Do all you want to; take in everything, but realize that you must account to God for everything you do. ¹⁰So banish grief and pain, but remember that youth, with a whole life before it, can make serious mistakes.

MAKING THE BEST CHOICES 12:1 A life without God produces a bitter, lonely, and hopeless old person. A life centered around God is fulfilling; it makes the "evil years"—when disabilities, sicknesses, and handicaps could cause barriers to enjoying life—satisfying because of the hope of eternal life. Being young is exciting. But the excitement of youth can become a barrier to closeness with God because those things that most young people live for (sports, sex, popularity) become increasingly unimportant with old age. Make your strength available to God when it is still yours—during your youthful years. Don't waste it on evil or meaningless activities that become bad habits and make you callous. Seek God now. **To begin the series of devotionals on MAKING THE BEST CHOICES, turn to page 275.**

Family Devotions

☐ DEVOTION 195
RESPECTING AUTHORITY

Read Ecclesiastes 8:5-7

"I'm sick of being ordered around!" Brad griped as he put his bike away. "Someone's always tellin' me it's time to get up, time to catch the bus, time for the bell. Just once I'd like to do what I want to do when I want to do it."

Dad looked up from his tool bench. "Just for fun, let's imagine we woke up one morning and decided everyone could do anything they wanted that day. What would you do?"

"I'd spend the day at the zoo," Brad answered.

"Well, remember, I don't have to do anything I don't want to do, and I might not want to take you to the zoo."

"Aw, you want to go," pleaded Brad.

"OK," agreed Dad, "so we go to the zoo, but we can't get in."

Brad looked startled. "Why not?"

"No schedules, so the gate attendant decided to sleep late," Dad explained.

Brad sighed. "Oh, Dad . . . I guess you're trying to tell me that if we didn't have rules and schedules, nothing would work out, right?"

"Right!" agreed Dad. "When God created the world, he organized everything. The universe is run by laws and on a schedule. Even the sun has a schedule to keep." Dad looked at his watch. "According to my schedule, it's about time for lunch. How about a hamburger and a hot-fudge sundae?"

Brad let out a *whoop* and ran for the car. "Guess not all schedules are bad," he said with a grin.

Respecting Authority Memory Verse

Children, obey your parents; this is the right thing to do because God has placed them in authority over you.
Ephesians 6:1

How About You?
Do you often complain about having to do things "on schedule"? Would you rather put things off? Working with family and friends in an organized way makes life much smoother. Make up your mind to get on schedule and stay there. B. W.

• For the next devotional, turn to page 663. • For the next devotional on RESPECTING AUTHORITY, turn to page 755.
• For notes on RESPECTING AUTHORITY, see pages 311, 420, and 1182.

12 Honor God

Don't let the excitement of being young cause you to forget about your Creator. Honor him in your youth before the evil years come—when you'll no longer enjoy living. ²It will be too late then to try to remember him when the sun and light and moon and stars are dim to your old eyes, and there is no silver lining left among your clouds. ³For there will come a time when your limbs will tremble with age, your strong legs will become weak, and your teeth will be too few to do their work, and there will be blindness too. ⁴Then let your lips be tightly closed while eating when your teeth are gone! And you will waken at dawn with the first note of the birds; but you yourself will be deaf and tuneless, with quavering voice. ⁵You will be afraid of heights and of falling—a white-haired, withered old man, dragging himself along: without sexual desire, standing at death's door, and nearing his everlasting home as the mourners go along the streets.

⁶Yes, remember your Creator now while you are young—before the silver cord of life snaps and the gold bowl is broken; before the pitcher is broken at the fountain and the wheel is broken at the cistern; ⁷then the dust returns to the earth as it was, and the spirit returns to God who gave it. ⁸ All is futile, says the Preacher; utterly futile.

⁹But then, because the Preacher was wise, he went on teaching the people all he knew; and he collected proverbs and classified them. ¹⁰For the Preacher was not only a wise man but a good teacher; he not only taught what he knew to the people, but taught them in an interesting manner. ¹¹ The wise man's words are like goads that spur to action. They nail down important truths. Students are wise who master what their teachers tell them.

¹²But, my son, be warned: there is no end of opinions ready to be expressed. Studying them can go on forever and become very exhausting!

¹³Here is my final conclusion: fear God and obey his commandments, for this is the entire duty of man. ¹⁴For God will judge us for everything we do, including every hidden thing, good or bad.

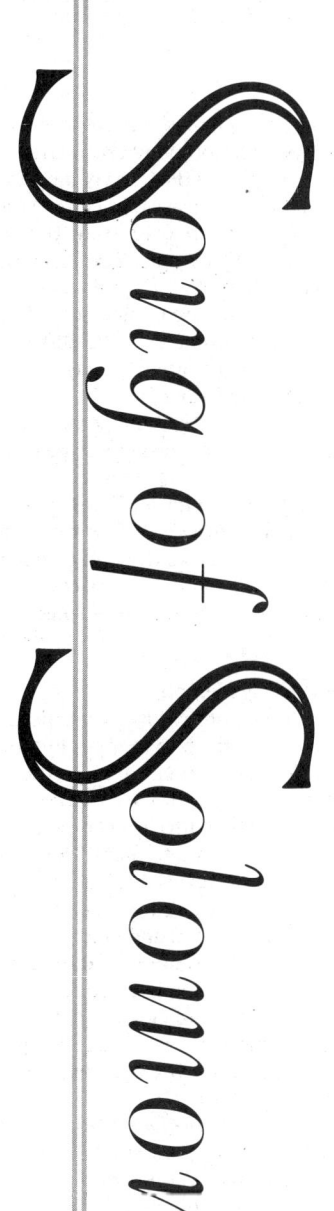

Song of Solomon

WHAT KINDS of songs do you like to listen to? Have you heard songs where the words could mean two different things?

The Song of Solomon is a song that tells a long story with an *obvious* meaning and a *hidden* meaning. It's a love song that was written by Solomon to a woman he was engaged to marry. There are three singing parts—King Solomon; the girl he loved; and their friends, the young women of Jerusalem.

The *obvious* meaning of the song might embarrass you! Solomon and his fiancée said exactly what they felt, and they were deeply in love. They expressed their feelings in poetry and drew pictures with their words.

What is a love song doing in the Bible? This is the *hidden* meaning. Solomon's song can also be a parable—a picture of God's love for us. In the New Testament, the church is called the bride of Christ. Jesus is the Bridegroom, which gives us another way to understand our relationship with him. He loves us with all his being and is committed to us forever.

As you read about Solomon's love, think about Jesus' commitment of love to you.

The Wedding Day

This song of songs, more wonderful than any other, was composed by King Solomon:

The Girl: ²"Kiss me again and again, for your love is sweeter than wine. ³ How fragrant your cologne, and how great your name! No wonder all the young girls love you! ⁴Take me with you; come, let's run!"

The Girl: "The king has brought me into his palace. How happy we will be! Your love is better than wine. No wonder all the young girls love you!"

The Girl: ⁵"I am dark but beautiful, O girls of Jerusalem, tanned as the dark tents of Kedar."

King Solomon: "But lovely as the silken tents of Solomon!"

The Girl: ⁶"Don't look down on me, you city girls, just because my complexion is so dark—the sun has tanned me. My brothers were angry with me and sent me out into the sun to tend the vineyards, but see what it has done to me!"

The Girl: [7]"Tell me, O one I love, where are you leading your flock today? Where will you be at noon? For I will come and join you there instead of wandering like a vagabond among the flocks of your companions."

King Solomon: [8]"If you don't know, O most beautiful woman in all the world, follow the trail of my flock to the shepherds' tents, and there feed your sheep and their lambs. [9]What a lovely filly you are, my love! [10]How lovely your cheeks are, with your hair falling down upon them! How stately your neck with that long string of jewels. [11]We shall make you gold earrings and silver beads."

The Girl: [12]"The king lies on his bed, enchanted by the fragrance of my perfume. [13]My beloved one is a sachet of myrrh lying between my breasts."

King Solomon: [14]"My beloved is a bouquet of flowers in the gardens of Engedi. [15]How beautiful you are, my love, how beautiful! Your eyes are soft as doves'. [16]What a lovely, pleasant thing you are, lying here upon the grass, [17]shaded by the cedar trees and firs."

2 Memories of Courtship

The Girl: "I am the rose of Sharon, the lily of the valley."

King Solomon: [2]"Yes, a lily among thorns, so is my beloved as compared with any other girls."

The Girl: [3]"My lover is an apple tree, the finest in the orchard as compared with any of the other youths. I am seated in his much-desired shade and his fruit is lovely to eat. [4]He brings me to the banquet hall, and everyone can see how much he loves me. [5]Oh, feed me with your love—your 'raisins' and your 'apples'—for I am utterly lovesick. [6]His left hand is under my head and with his right hand he embraces me. [7]O girls of Jerusalem, I adjure you by the gazelles and deer in the park, that you do not awaken my lover. Let him sleep!"

The Girl: [8]"Ah, I hear him—my beloved! Here he comes, leaping upon the mountains and bounding over the hills. [9]My beloved is like a gazelle or young deer. Look, there he is behind the wall, now looking in at the windows.

[10]"My beloved said to me, 'Rise up, my love, my fair one, and come away. [11]For the winter is past, the rain is over and gone. [12]The flowers are springing up and the time of the singing of birds has come. Yes, spring is here. [13]The leaves are coming out, and the grapevines are in blossom. How delicious they smell! Arise, my love, my fair one, and come away.'

[14]"My dove is hiding behind some rocks, behind an outcrop of the cliff. Call to me and let me hear your lovely voice and see your handsome face.

[15]"The little foxes are ruining the vineyards. Catch them, for the grapes are all in blossom.

[16]"My beloved is mine and I am his. He is feeding among the lilies! [17]Before the dawn comes and the shadows flee away, come to me, my beloved, and be like a gazelle or a young stag on the mountains of spices."

3 Memories of Engagement

The Girl: "One night my lover was missing from my bed. I got up to look for him but couldn't find him. [2]I went out into the streets of the city and the roads to seek him, but I searched in vain. [3]The police stopped me, and I said to them, 'Have you seen him anywhere, this one I love so much?' [4]It was only a little while afterwards that I found him and held him and would not let him go until I had brought him into my childhood home, into my mother's old bedroom. [5]I adjure you, O women of Jerusalem, by the gazelles and deer of the park, not to awake my lover. Let him sleep."

The Young Women of Jerusalem: [6]"Who is this sweeping in from the deserts like a cloud of smoke along the ground, smelling of myrrh and frankincense and every other spice that can be bought? [7]Look, it is the chariot of Solomon with sixty of the mightiest men of his army surrounding it. [8]They are all skilled swordsmen and experienced bodyguards. Each one has his sword upon his thigh to defend his king against any onslaught in the night. [9]For King Solomon made himself a chariot from the wood of Lebanon. [10]Its posts are silver, its canopy gold, the seat is purple; and the back is inlaid with these words: 'With love from the girls of Jerusalem!'"

The Girl: [11]"Go out and see King Solomon, O young women of Zion; see the crown with which his mother crowned him on his wedding day, his day of gladness."

4

King Solomon: "How beautiful you are, my love, how beautiful! Your eyes are those of doves. Your hair falls across your face like flocks of goats that frisk across the slopes of Gilead. ²Your teeth are white as sheep's wool, newly shorn and washed; perfectly matched, without one missing. ³Your lips are like a thread of scarlet—and how beautiful your mouth. Your cheeks are matched loveliness behind your locks. ⁴Your neck is stately as the tower of David, jeweled with a thousand heroes' shields. ⁵ Your breasts are like twin fawns of a gazelle, feeding among the lilies. ⁶ Until the morning dawns and the shadows flee away, I will go to the mountain of myrrh and to the hill of frankincense. ⁷You are so beautiful, my love, in every part of you.

⁸"Come with me from Lebanon, my bride. We will look down from the summit of the mountain, from the top of Mount Hermon, where the lions have their dens and panthers prowl. ⁹You have ravished my heart, my lovely one, my bride; I am overcome by one glance of your eyes, by a single bead of your necklace. ¹⁰How sweet is your love, my darling, my bride. How much better it is than mere wine. The perfume of your love is more fragrant than all the richest spices. ¹¹Your lips, my dear, are made of honey. Yes, honey and cream are under your tongue, and the scent of your garments is like the scent of the mountains and cedars of Lebanon.

¹²"My darling bride is like a private garden, a spring that no one else can have, a fountain of my own. ¹³,¹⁴You are like a lovely orchard bearing precious fruit, with the rarest of perfumes; nard and saffron, calamus and cinnamon, and perfume from every other incense tree, as well as myrrh and aloes, and every other lovely spice. ¹⁵You are a garden fountain, a well of living water, refreshing as the streams from the Lebanon mountains."

The Girl: ¹⁶"Come, north wind, awaken; come, south wind, blow upon my garden and waft its lovely perfume to my beloved. Let him come into his garden and eat its choicest fruits."

5

A Disturbing Dream

King Solomon: "I am here in my garden, my darling, my bride! I gather my myrrh with my spices and eat my honeycomb with my honey. I drink my wine with my milk."

The Young Women of Jerusalem: "Oh, lover and beloved, eat and drink! Yes, drink deeply!"

The Girl: ²"One night as I was sleeping, my heart awakened in a dream. I heard the voice of my beloved; he was knocking at my bedroom door. 'Open to me, my darling, my lover, my lovely dove,' he said, 'for I have been out in the night and am covered with dew.'

³"But I said, 'I have disrobed. Shall I get dressed again? I have washed my feet, and should I get them soiled?'

⁴"My beloved tried to unlatch the door, and my heart was thrilled within me. ⁵I jumped up to open it, and my hands dripped with perfume, my fingers with lovely myrrh as I pulled back the bolt. ⁶I opened to my beloved, but he was gone. My heart stopped. I searched for him but couldn't find him anywhere. I called to him, but there was no reply. ⁷The guards found me and struck and wounded me. The watchman on the wall tore off my veil. ⁸ I adjure you, O women of Jerusalem, if you find my beloved one, tell him that I am sick with love."

The Young Women of Jerusalem: ⁹"O woman of rare beauty, what is it about your loved one that is better than any other, that you command us this?"

The Girl: ¹⁰"My beloved one is tanned and handsome, better than ten thousand others! ¹¹His head is purest gold, and he has wavy, raven hair. ¹² His eyes are like doves beside the water brooks, deep and quiet. ¹³His cheeks are like sweetly scented beds of spices. His lips are perfumed lilies, his breath like myrrh. ¹⁴His arms are round bars of gold set with topaz; his body is bright ivory encrusted with jewels. ¹⁵His legs are as pillars of marble set in sockets of finest gold, like cedars of Lebanon; none can rival him. ¹⁶His mouth is altogether sweet, lovable

---

AVOIDING SIN 4:12 In comparing his bride to a private garden, Solomon was praising her virginity. Virginity, considered old-fashioned by many in today's culture, has always been God's plan for unmarried people—and with good reason. Sex without marriage is cheap. It cannot compare with the joy of giving yourself completely to the one who is totally committed to you. Ask God for his help to remain pure through the temptations that surround you. And if you need his forgiveness, know that no sin is too hard for God to forgive. Ask him for his forgiveness and help. **To begin the series of devotionals on AVOIDING SIN, turn to page 195.**

in every way. Such, O women of Jerusalem, is my beloved, my friend."

6 Wow! What a Beautiful Bride

The Young Women of Jerusalem: "O rarest of beautiful women, where has your loved one gone? We will help you find him."

The Girl: ²"He has gone down to his garden, to his spice beds, to pasture his flock and to gather the lilies. ³I am my beloved's and my beloved is mine. He pastures his flock among the lilies!"

King Solomon: ⁴"O my beloved, you are as beautiful as the lovely land of Tirzah, yes, beautiful as Jerusalem, and how you capture my heart. ⁵Look the other way, for your eyes have overcome me! Your hair, as it falls across your face, is like a flock of goats frisking down the slopes of Gilead. ⁶Your teeth are white as freshly washed ewes, perfectly matched and not one missing. ⁷Your cheeks are matched loveliness behind your hair. ⁸I have sixty other wives, all queens, and eighty concubines, and unnumbered virgins available to me; ⁹but you, my dove, my perfect one, are the only one among them all, without an equal! The women of Jerusalem were delighted when they saw you, and even the queens and concubines praise you. ¹⁰'Who is this,' they ask, 'arising as the dawn, fair as the moon, pure as the sun, so utterly captivating?'"

The Girl: ¹¹"I went down into the orchard of nuts and out to the valley to see the springtime there, to see whether the grapevines were budding or the pomegranates were blossoming yet. ¹²Before I realized it, I was stricken with terrible homesickness and wanted to be back among my own people."

The Young Women of Jerusalem: ¹³"Return, return to us, O maid of Shulam. Come back, come back, that we may see you once again."

The Girl: "Why should you seek a mere Shulammite?"

King Solomon: "Because you dance so beautifully."

7 The Bride Tells of Her Love

King Solomon: "How beautiful your tripping feet, O queenly maiden. Your rounded thighs are like jewels, the work of the most skilled of craftsmen. ²Your navel is lovely as a goblet filled with wine. Your waist is like a heap of wheat set about with lilies. ³Your two breasts are like two fawns, yes, lovely twins. ⁴Your neck is stately as an ivory tower, your eyes as limpid pools in Heshbon by the gate of Bath-rabbim. Your nose is shapely like the tower of Lebanon overlooking Damascus.

⁵"As Mount Carmel crowns the mountains, so your hair is your crown. The king is held captive in your queenly tresses.

⁶"Oh, how delightful you are; how pleasant, O love, for utter delight! ⁷You are tall and slim like a palm tree, and your breasts are like its clusters of dates. ⁸I said, I will climb up into the palm tree and take hold of its branches. Now may your breasts be like grape clusters, the scent of your breath like apples, ⁹and your kisses as exciting as the best of wine, smooth and sweet, causing the lips of those who are asleep to speak."

The Girl: ¹⁰"I am my beloved's and I am the one he desires. ¹¹Come, my beloved, let us go out into the fields and stay in the villages. ¹²Let us get up early and go out to the vineyards and see whether the vines have budded, whether the blossoms have opened, and whether the pomegranates are in flower. And there I will give you my love. ¹³There the mandrakes give forth their fragrance, and the rarest fruits are at our doors, the new as well as old, for I have stored them up for my beloved."

8 The Power of Love

The Girl: "Oh, if only you were my brother; then I could kiss you no matter who was watching, and no one would laugh at me. ²I would bring you to my childhood home, and there you would teach me. I would give you spiced wine to drink, sweet pomegranate wine. ³His left hand would be under my head and his right hand would embrace me. ⁴I adjure you, O women of Jerusalem, not to awaken him until he please."

LOVING OTHERS 8:6-7 In this final description of their love, the girl includes some of its significant characteristics (see also 1 Corinthians 13). Love is as strong as death; it cannot be killed by time or disaster; and it cannot be bought for any price because it is freely given. Love is priceless, and even the richest king cannot buy it. It must be accepted as a gift from God and then shared within the guidelines God provides. Don't let TV, magazines, or peers cheapen the meaning of love. Don't rush into a "feeling" only to discover emptiness later. True love is more than feelings. True love among people is a gift from God built over time. Let God be central in all your friendships and relationships. Only then can you discover his kind of love. **To begin the series of devotionals on LOVING OTHERS, turn to page 313.**

The Young Women of Jerusalem: ⁵"Who is this coming up from the desert, leaning on her beloved?"

King Solomon: "Under the apple tree where your mother gave birth to you in her travail, there I awakened your love."

The Girl: ⁶"Seal me in your heart with permanent betrothal, for love is strong as death, and jealousy is as cruel as Sheol. It flashes fire, the very flame of Jehovah. ⁷Many waters cannot quench the flame of love, neither can the floods drown it. If a man tried to buy it with everything he owned, he couldn't do it."

The Girl's Brothers: ⁸"We have a little sister too young for breasts. What shall we do if someone asks to marry her?"

King Solomon: ⁹"If she has no breasts, we will build upon her a battlement of silver, and if she is a door, we will enclose her with cedar boards."

The Girl: ¹⁰"I am slim, tall, and full-breasted, and I have found favor in my lover's eyes. ¹¹Solomon had a vineyard at Baal-hamon, which he rented out to some farmers there, the rent being one thousand pieces of silver from each. ¹²But as for my own vineyard, you, O Solomon, shall have my thousand pieces of silver, and I will give two hundred pieces to those who care for it. ¹³O my beloved, living in the gardens, how wonderful that your companions may listen to your voice; let me hear it too. ¹⁴Come quickly, my beloved, and be like a gazelle or young deer upon the mountains of spices."

Isaiah

ARE MOTIVES important? Does it matter *why* you do something as long as you do it? The answer to this question is the message God sent to his people through Isaiah.

The Israelites seemed to have it all together. They went to the Temple, offered the right sacrifices, and worshiped in proper form. The problem was that their hearts weren't in it. Their love for God was missing. God wanted their hearts.

Isaiah was a prophet during the reigns of Uzziah, Jotham, Ahaz, and Hezekiah, kings of Judah. God asked Isaiah to give different kinds of messages—warnings, promises, and prophecies.

God *warned* the people when they were doing wrong and told them they would be punished if they didn't stop. God *promised* that if they served only him, he would reward them. And through *prophecies,* God told them his plan to send the Messiah, who would pay the penalty for their sins and rule forever.

It does matter to God what our motives are. When we go to church, read the Bible, and pray, is our heart in it? As you read Isaiah, look for reasons to worship God with your heart.

God's Message to His People

These are the messages that came to Isaiah, son of Amoz, in the visions he saw during the reigns of King Uzziah, King Jotham, King Ahaz, and King Hezekiah—all kings of Judah. In these messages God showed him what was going to happen to Judah and Jerusalem in the days ahead.

²Listen, O heaven and earth, to what the Lord is saying:

The children I raised and cared for so long and tenderly have turned against me. ³Even the animals—the donkey and the ox—know their owner and appreciate his care for them, but not my people Israel. No matter what I do for them, they still don't care.

⁴Oh, what a sinful nation they are! They walk bent-backed beneath their load of guilt. Their fathers before them were evil too. Born to be bad, they have turned their backs upon the Lord and have despised the Holy One of Israel. They have cut themselves off from his help.

5,6 Oh, my people, haven't you had enough of punishment? Why will you force me to whip you again and again? Must you forever rebel? From head to foot you are sick and weak and faint, covered with bruises and welts and infected wounds, unanointed and unbound. 7 Your country lies in ruins; your cities are burned; while you watch, foreigners are destroying and plundering everything they see. 8 You stand there helpless and abandoned like a watchman's shanty in the field when the harvesttime is over—or when the crop is stripped and robbed.

9 *If the Lord Almighty had not stepped in to save a few of us, we would have been wiped out as Sodom and Gomorrah were.* 10 An apt comparison! Listen, you leaders of Israel, you men of Sodom and Gomorrah, as I call you now. Listen to the Lord. Hear what he is telling you! 11 I am sick of your sacrifices. Don't bring me any more of them. I don't want your fat rams; I don't want to see the blood from your offerings. 12,13 Who wants your sacrifices when you have no sorrow for your sins? The incense you bring me is a stench in my nostrils. Your holy celebrations of the new moon and the Sabbath, and your special days for fasting—even your most pious meetings—all are frauds! I want nothing more to do with them. 14 I hate them all; I can't stand the sight of them. 15 From now on, when you pray with your hands stretched out to heaven, I won't look or listen. Even though you make many prayers, I will not hear, for your hands are those of murderers; they are covered with the blood of your innocent victims.

16 Oh, wash yourselves! Be clean! Let me no longer see you doing all these wicked things; quit your evil ways. 17 Learn to do good, to be fair and to help the poor, the fatherless, and widows.

18 Come, let's talk this over! says the Lord; no matter how deep the stain of your sins, I can take it out and make you as clean as freshly fallen snow. Even if you are stained as red as crimson, I can make you white as wool! 19 If you will only let me help you, if you will only obey, then I will make you rich! 20 But if you keep on turning your backs and refusing to listen to me, you will be killed by your enemies; I, the Lord, have spoken.

21 Jerusalem, once a faithful wife! And now a prostitute! Running after other gods! Once "The City of Fair Play," but now a gang of murderers. 22 Once like sterling silver; now mixed with worthless alloy! Once so pure, but now diluted like watered-down wine! 23 Your leaders are rebels, companions of thieves; all of them take bribes and won't defend the widows and orphans. 24 Therefore the Lord, the Mighty One of Israel, says: I will pour out my anger on you, my enemies! 25 I myself will melt you in a smelting pot and skim off your slag.

26 And afterwards I will give you good judges and wise counselors like those you used to have. Then your city shall again be called "The City of Justice" and "The Faithful Town."

27 Those who return to the Lord, who are just and good, shall be redeemed. 28 (But all sinners shall utterly perish, for they refuse to come to me.) 29 Shame will cover you, and you will blush to think of all those times you sacrificed to idols in your groves of "sacred" oaks. 30 You will perish like a withered tree or a garden without water. 31 The strongest among you will disappear like burning straw; your evil deeds are the spark that sets the straw on fire, and no one will be able to put it out.

2 Walk in God's Light

This is another message to Isaiah from the Lord concerning Judah and Jerusalem:

2 In the last days Jerusalem and the Temple of the Lord will become the world's greatest attraction, and people from many lands will flow there to worship the Lord.

3 "Come," everyone will say, "let us go up the mountain of the Lord, to the Temple of the God of Israel; there he will teach us his laws, and we will obey them." For in those days the world will be ruled from Jerusalem. 4 The Lord will settle international disputes; all the nations will convert their weapons of war into implements of peace. Then at the last all wars will stop and all military training will end. 5 O Israel, come, let us walk in the light of the Lord and be obedient to his laws!

6 The Lord has rejected you because you welcome foreigners from the East who practice magic and communicate with evil spirits, as the Philistines do.

7 Israel has vast treasures of silver and gold, and great numbers of horses and chariots 8 and idols—the land is full of them! They are man-made, and yet you *worship* them! 9 Small and great, all bow before them; God will not forgive you for this sin.

10 Crawl into the caves in the rocks and hide in terror from his glorious majesty, 11 for the day is coming when your proud looks will be brought low; the Lord alone will be exalted. 12 On that day the Lord Almighty will move against the proud and haughty and bring them to the dust. 13 All the tall cedars of Lebanon and all the mighty oaks of Bashan shall bend low, 14 and all the high mountains and hills, 15 and every high tower and wall, 16 and all the proud ocean ships and trim harbor craft—*all* shall be crushed before the Lord that day. 17 All the glory of mankind will bow low; the pride of men will lie in the dust, and the Lord alone will be exalted. 18 And all idols will be utterly abolished and destroyed.

19 When the Lord stands up from his throne to shake up the earth, his enemies will crawl with

FAMILY DEVOTIONS

☐ DEVOTION 196
AVOIDING SIN

Read Isaiah 1:16-19

"Mom, whatever are you doing?" asked Tiffany as she walked in the front door. Piles of old clothes, jewelry, and broken furniture were scattered around the living room.

"It's spring cleaning time, and I decided to clean things out," Mother replied. "Why keep clothes or jewelry I never wear or furniture that I'll never get around to repairing?"

"Good point, Mom," said Tiffany as she began climbing the stairs to her bedroom.

"Hey, honey," Mother called after her, "why don't you go through some of your things, too?"

"But I use everything I have," Tiffany protested. A short time later, however, she brought a big box downstairs. "Hey, Mom, check it out," she said with a grin. She pulled out an old stuffed animal. "Look at this—hardly any stuffing left inside. And look at this old sweatshirt. It's ten sizes too small."

Mother smiled and nodded. "You know," she began thoughtfully, "this reminds me of when I was saved."

"How's that, Mom?" asked Tiffany. "Were you having a spring cleaning then, too?"

Mother laughed. "Well, in a way. After I was saved, I had to get rid of a lot of old, bad habits and replace them with new, good ones like church attendance and prayer. I had no use for my sinful garbage any longer."

"Well, I was saved when I was just a little girl," replied Tiffany. "I didn't really have any bad habits to get rid of."

"No?" Mother's brows went up. "I seem to remember that you used to tell a lot of lies."

"Oh, yeah." Tiffany blushed. "I forgot about that. I used to get mad easily, too, didn't I? I guess I did have some garbage to get rid of—I still do sometimes."

"We all need to check our lives daily to see if they please the Lord," said Mother. "The Bible says we need to wash ourselves of the bad habits we used to have and learn to do good instead."

Avoiding Sin Memory Verse

How can a young man stay pure? By reading your Word and following its rules.
Psalm 119:9

How About You?
Are there bad habits you should throw away? Smoking? Alcohol? Drugs? Cheating? Selfishness? Clean out your bad habits and learn some new, good ones instead. *V. R.*

- For the next devotional, turn to page 665.   • For the next devotional on AVOIDING SIN, turn to page 687.
- For notes on AVOIDING SIN, see pages 220, 332, 392, and 657.

fear into the holes in the rocks and into the caves because of the glory of his majesty. ²⁰Then at last they will abandon their gold and silver idols to the moles and bats ²¹and crawl into the caverns to hide among the jagged rocks at the tops of the cliffs, to try to get away from the terror of the Lord and the glory of his majesty when he rises to terrify the earth. ²²Puny man! Frail as his breath! Don't ever put your trust in him!

3 A Well-earned Punishment

The Lord will cut off Jerusalem's and Judah's food and water supplies ²and kill her leaders; he will destroy her armies, judges, prophets, elders, ³army officers, businessmen, lawyers, magicians, and politicians. ⁴Israel's kings will be like babies, ruling childishly. ⁵And the worst sort of anarchy will prevail—everyone stepping on someone else, neighbors fighting neighbors, youths revolting against authority, criminals sneering at honorable men.

⁶In those days a man will say to his brother, "You have some extra clothing, so you be our king and take care of this mess."

⁷"No!" he will reply. "I cannot be of any help! I have no extra food or clothes. Don't get me involved!"

⁸Israel's civil government will be in utter ruin because the Jews have spoken out against their Lord and will not worship him; they offend his glory. ⁹The very look on their faces gives them away and shows their guilt. And they boast that their sin is equal to the sin of Sodom; they are not even ashamed. What a catastrophe! They have doomed themselves.

¹⁰But all is well for the godly man. Tell him, "What a reward you are going to get!" ¹¹But say to the wicked, "Your doom is sure. You too shall get your just deserts. Your well-earned punishment is on the way."

¹²O my people! Can't you see what fools your rulers are? Weak as women! Foolish as little children playing king. True leaders? No, misleaders! Leading you down the garden path to destruction.

¹³The Lord stands up! He is the great Prosecuting Attorney presenting his case against his people! ¹⁴First to feel his wrath will be the elders and the princes, for they have defrauded the poor. They have filled their barns with grain extorted from the helpless peasants.

¹⁵"How dare you grind my people in the dust like that?" the Lord Almighty will demand of them.

¹⁶Next he will judge the haughty Jewish women, who mince along, noses in the air, tinkling bracelets on their ankles, with wanton eyes that rove among the crowds to catch the glances of the men. ¹⁷The Lord will send a plague of scabs to ornament their heads! He will expose their nakedness for all to see. ¹⁸No longer shall they tinkle with self-assurance as they walk. For the Lord will strip away their artful beauty and their ornaments, ¹⁹their necklaces and bracelets and veils of shimmering gauze. ²⁰Gone shall be their scarves and ankle chains, headbands, earrings, and perfumes; ²¹their rings, jewels, ²²party clothes, negligees, capes, ornate combs, and purses; ²³their mirrors, lovely lingerie, beautiful dresses, and veils. ²⁴Instead of smelling of sweet perfume, they'll stink; for sashes they'll use ropes; their well-set hair will all fall out; they'll wear sacks instead of robes.

All their beauty will be gone; all that will be left to them is shame and disgrace. ²⁵,²⁶Their husbands shall die in battle; the women, ravaged, shall sit crying on the ground.

4 God's Holy People

At that time so few men will be left alive that seven women will fight over each of them and say, "Let us all marry you! We will furnish our own food and clothing; only let us be called by your name so that we won't be mocked as old maids."

²⁻⁴Those whose names are written down to escape the destruction of Jerusalem will be washed and rinsed of all their moral filth by the horrors and the fire. They will be God's holy people. And the land will produce for them its lushest bounty and its richest fruit. ⁵Then the Lord will provide shade on all Jerusalem—over every home and all its public grounds—a canopy of smoke and cloud throughout the day, and clouds of fire at night, covering the Glorious Land, ⁶protecting it from daytime heat and from rains and storms.

5 Sour Grapes in God's Garden

Now I will sing a song about his vineyard to the one I love. *My Beloved has a vineyard on a very fertile hill.* ²He plowed it and took out all the rocks and planted his vineyard with the choicest vines. He built a watchtower and cut a winepress in the rocks. Then he waited for the harvest, but the grapes that grew were wild and sour and not at all the sweet ones he expected.

³Now, men of Jerusalem and Judah, you have heard the case! You be the judges! ⁴What more

---

SHOWING KINDNESS 3:16-26 The women of Judah had placed their emphasis on clothing and jewelry rather than on God. They dressed to be noticed, to gain approval, and to be fashionable. Instead of being concerned about the oppression around them (3:14-15), they were self-serving and self-centered. Those who abuse their possessions will end up with nothing. These verses are not an indictment against clothing and jewelry, but a judgment on those who use them lavishly while blind to the needs of others. When God blesses you, don't flaunt your wealth. Use what you have to help others. **To begin the series of devotionals on SHOWING KINDNESS, turn to page 81.**

Family Devotions

☐ DEVOTION 197
BECOMING MORE LIKE JESUS

Read Isaiah 6:5

"Listen to this, Mom!" Ruthie exclaimed as she came in from school. "Warren and Millie and I taped a radio script for our English project. It has a Christian message—we wanted to make it a testimony to all the unsaved kids in our class."

Ruthie played the tape while Mom finished preparing dinner. As the tape ended, Ruthie glanced down the hall. "What are you doing in my room?" she screamed at her brother, Pete. As Ruthie raced toward her room, Mom quickly flipped the tape over and set it to record. "You hog!" Ruthie yelled. There was a thump as she hit her brother, then pounding footsteps as he chased her back into the kitchen. "You look like a pig, and you act and smell like one, too. Oink, oink," continued Ruthie.

The arguing continued a few more minutes until Dad came in and firmly said, "Enough!"

"Can I play my English project tape for part of our devotions?" Ruthie asked after dinner. "It has a Christian message."

"Good. I'd like to hear that," agreed Dad.

Ruthie pushed the play button. "You hog! You look like a pig, and you act and smell . . ." Ruthie's face felt hot as she quickly pressed stop. "My tape!" she gasped.

"Your radio script is on the other side," Mom assured her, "but let's hear the rest of this."

"But, Mom," Ruthie whined. She could see that Mom was unyielding. "Dad?" she pleaded. At her parents' insistence, she again turned on the cassette player. Soon she pressed stop again, very embarrassed. "I said *that?*"

"Your rehearsed tape had a good Christian message," observed Mom, "but what if we could play back all your unrehearsed words and thoughts during the day? How much would be a testimony that glorifies God?"

Becoming More Like Jesus Memory Verse

No, he has told you what he wants, and this is all it is: *to be fair, just, merciful, and to walk humbly with your God.*
Micah 6:8

H o w   A b o u t   Y o u ?

Would you be more careful with your words if you knew you'd have to hear yourself over again at the end of the day? Be more careful anyway. Ask God to help you say words that glorify him. *N. E. K.*

• For the next devotional, turn to page 667. • For the next devotional on *BECOMING MORE LIKE JESUS*, turn to page 773. • For notes on *BECOMING MORE LIKE JESUS*, see pages 234, 983, 1105, and 1164.

could I have done? Why did my vineyard give me wild grapes instead of sweet? ⁵I will tear down the fences and let my vineyard go to pasture to be trampled by cattle and sheep. ⁶I won't prune it or hoe it, but let it be overgrown with briars and thorns. I will command the clouds not to rain on it any more.

⁷I have given you the story of God's people. They are the vineyard that I spoke about. Israel and Judah are his pleasant acreage! He expected them to yield a crop of justice but found bloodshed instead. He expected righteousness, but the cries of deep oppression met his ears. ⁸You buy up property so others have no place to live. Your homes are built on great estates so you can be alone in the midst of the earth! ⁹But the Lord Almighty has sworn your awful fate—with my own ears I heard him say, "Many a beautiful home will lie deserted, their owners killed or gone. ¹⁰An acre of vineyard will not produce a gallon of juice! Ten bushels of seed will yield a one-bushel crop!"

¹¹Woe to you who get up early in the morning to go on long drinking bouts that last till late at night—woe to you drunken bums. ¹²You furnish lovely music at your grand parties; the orchestras are superb! But for the Lord you have no thought or care. ¹³Therefore I will send you into exile far away because you neither know nor care that I have done so much for you. Your great and honored men will starve, and the common people will die of thirst.

¹⁴Hell is licking its chops in anticipation of this delicious morsel, Jerusalem. Her great and small shall be swallowed up, and all her drunken throngs. ¹⁵In that day the haughty shall be brought down to the dust; the proud shall be humbled; ¹⁶but the Lord Almighty is exalted above all, for he alone is holy, just, and good. ¹⁷In those days flocks will feed among the ruins. Lambs and calves and kids will pasture there!

¹⁸Woe to those who drag their sins behind them like a bullock on a rope. ¹⁹They even mock the Holy One of Israel and dare the Lord to punish them. "Hurry up and punish us, O Lord," they say. "We want to see what you can do!" ²⁰They say that what is right is wrong and what is wrong is right; that black is white and white is black; bitter is sweet and sweet is bitter.

²¹Woe to those who are wise and shrewd in their own eyes! ²²Woe to those who are "heroes" when it comes to drinking and boast about the liquor they can hold. ²³They take bribes to pervert justice, letting the wicked go free and putting innocent men in jail. ²⁴Therefore God will deal with them and burn them. They will disappear like straw on fire. Their roots will rot and their flowers wither, for they have thrown away the laws of God and despised the Word of the Holy One of Israel. ²⁵That is why the anger of the Lord is hot against his people; that is why he has reached out his hand to smash them. The hills will tremble, and the rotting bodies of his people will be thrown as refuse in the streets. But even so, his anger is not ended; his hand is heavy on them still.

²⁶He will send a signal to the nations far away, whistling to those at the ends of the earth, and they will come racing toward Jerusalem. ²⁷They never weary, never stumble, never stop; their belts are tight, their bootstraps strong; they run without stopping for rest or for sleep. ²⁸Their arrows are sharp; their bows are bent; sparks fly from their horses' hoofs, and the wheels of their chariots spin like the wind. ²⁹They roar like lions and pounce upon the prey. They seize my people and carry them off into captivity with none to rescue them. ³⁰They growl over their victims like the roaring of the sea. Over all Israel lies a pall of darkness and sorrow, and the heavens are black.

6 God Calls Isaiah

The year King Uzziah died I saw the Lord! He was sitting on a lofty throne, and the Temple was filled with his glory. ²Hovering about him were mighty, six-winged angels of fire. With two of their wings they covered their faces with two others they covered their feet, and with two they flew. ³In a great antiphonal chorus they sang, "Holy, holy, holy is the Lord Almighty; the whole earth is filled with his glory." ⁴Such singing it was! It shook the Temple to its foundations, and suddenly the entire sanctuary was filled with smoke.

⁵Then I said, "My doom is sealed, for I am a foul-mouthed sinner, a member of a sinful, foul-mouthed race; and I have looked upon the King, the Lord of heaven's armies."

⁶Then one of the mighty angels flew over to the altar and with a pair of tongs picked out a burning coal. ⁷He touched my lips with it and said, "Now you are pronounced 'not guilty' because this coal has touched your lips. Your sins are all forgiven."

⁸Then I heard the Lord asking, "Whom shall I send as a messenger to my people? Who will go?"

And I said, "Lord, I'll go! Send me."

⁹And he said, "Yes, go. But tell my people this: 'Though you hear my words repeatedly, you won't understand them. Though you watch and watch as I perform my miracles, still you won't know what they mean.' ¹⁰ Dull their understanding, close their ears, and shut their eyes. I don't want them to see or to hear or to understand, or to turn to me to heal them."

Family Devotions

☐ **Devotion 198**
Serving God Willingly

Read Isaiah 6:8

Serving God Willingly
Memory Verse

Anyone who takes care of a little child like this is caring for me! And whoever cares for me is caring for God who sent me. Your care for others is the measure of your greatness.
Luke 9:48

Jesse sat in church with his mother. He was seven years old and had never been away from home, but now they were listening to a missionary talk about a faraway land. The man, who wore a long, white robe and had a scarf wrapped around his head, turned around slowly so everyone could see his clothes. "This loose scarf keeps the sun off my head," he said.

Jesse leaned against his mother as the missionary continued. "The people are difficult to reach, but I'm happy to be there, because I know God sent me there." Jesse's eyes opened wide. He hoped God wouldn't send him to a strange land. He didn't want to leave home.

The next evening Jesse sat on the front porch. He listened to his mother working in the kitchen. He could hear the hum of his father's lawn mower in the backyard. He liked these sounds. Jesse looked down the street and saw old Mrs. Quarry, his neighbor, walking home from town with a heavy bag of groceries. She stopped in front of Jesse's house and leaned against the fence. Her groceries slipped from her arms, and an orange rolled across the lawn. A can of tomatoes clattered across the walk and into the street.

Jesse ran to help her. "I'll get your groceries, Mrs. Quarry," he said.

The old woman gave a deep sigh. "First, Jesse," she said, "please help me up my front steps. I'm so tired." She put one hand on the fence and the other on Jesse's shoulder. He hoped she wouldn't fall.

When they reached Mrs. Quarry's steps, Jesse walked beside her and held her arm. At the top of the stairs, she sat down in a porch chair. She looked up at Jesse and smiled. "God sent you, Jesse," she said. "He knew I needed help, and he sent you."

Jesse ran to pick up the groceries. He felt good. God could send him to help people, and he wouldn't even have to leave home. At least not yet.

How About You?

Are you serving God in your family? In your neighborhood? With your friends? You don't need to wait until you're older and can go to a faraway land. Ask God where he wants you to serve. Tell him, "Lord, I'll go! Send me." Then serve him by washing the dishes, mowing the lawn, helping a friend or neighbor, or doing whatever task you know God wants you to do. R. H.

• For the next devotional, turn to page 671. • For the next devotional on *Serving God Willingly,* turn to page 1203.
• For notes on *Serving God Willingly,* see pages 49, 419, 890, 920, and 922.

[11]Then I said, "Lord, how long will it be before they are ready to listen?"

And he replied, "Not until their cities are destroyed—without a person left—and the whole country is an utter wasteland, [12]and they are all taken away as slaves to other countries far away, and all the land of Israel lies deserted! [13]Yet a tenth—a remnant—will survive; and though Israel is invaded again and again and destroyed, yet Israel will be like a tree cut down, whose stump still lives to grow again."

7 Immanuel—God Is with Us

During the reign of Ahaz (the son of Jotham and grandson of Uzziah), Jerusalem was attacked by King Rezin of Syria and King Pekah of Israel (the son of Remaliah). But it was not taken; the city stood. [2]However, when the news came to the royal court, "Syria is allied with Israel against us!" the hearts of the king and his people trembled with fear as the trees of a forest shake in a storm.

[3]Then the Lord said to Isaiah, "Go out to meet King Ahaz, you and Shear-jashub, your son. You will find him at the end of the aqueduct that leads from Gihon Spring to the upper reservoir, near the road that leads down to the bleaching field. [4]Tell him to quit worrying. Tell him he needn't be frightened by the fierce anger of those two has-beens, Rezin and Pekah. [5] Yes, the kings of Syria and Israel are coming against you.

"They say, [6]'We will invade Judah and throw her people into panic. Then we'll fight our way into Jerusalem and install the son of Tabeel as their king.'

[7]"But the Lord God says, This plan will not succeed, [8]for Damascus will remain the capital of Syria alone, and King Rezin's kingdom will not increase its boundaries. And within sixty-five years Ephraim, too, will be crushed and broken. [9]Samaria is the capital of Ephraim alone, and King Pekah's power will not increase. You don't believe me? If you want me to protect you, you must learn to believe what I say."

[10]Not long after this, the Lord sent this further message to King Ahaz:

[11]"Ask me for a sign, Ahaz, to prove that I will indeed crush your enemies as I have said. Ask anything you like, in heaven or on earth."

[12]But the king refused. "No," he said, "I'll not bother the Lord with anything like that."

[13]Then Isaiah said, O House of David, you aren't satisfied to exhaust *my* patience; you exhaust the Lord's as well! [14]All right then, the Lord himself will choose the sign—a child shall be born to a virgin! And she shall call him Immanuel (meaning, "God is with us"). [15,16]By the time this child is weaned and knows right from wrong, the two kings you fear so much—the kings of Israel and Syria —will both be dead.

[17]But later on, the Lord will bring a terrible curse on you and on your nation and your family. There will be terror such as has not been known since the division of Solomon's empire into Israel and Judah—the mighty king of Assyria will come with his great army!

[18]At that time the Lord will whistle for the army of Upper Egypt, and of Assyria too, to swarm down upon you like flies and destroy you, like bees to sting and to kill. [19]They will come in vast hordes, spreading across the whole land, even into the desolate valleys, caves, and thorny parts, as well as to all your fertile acres. [20]In that day the Lord will take this "razor"—these Assyrians you have hired to save you—and use it on you to shave off everything you have: your land, your crops, your people.

[21,22]When they finally stop plundering, the whole nation will be a pastureland; whole flocks and herds will be destroyed, and a farmer will be fortunate to have a cow and two sheep left. But the abundant pastureland will yield plenty of milk, and everyone left will live on curds and wild honey. [23] At that time the lush vineyards will become patches of briars. [24]All the land will be one vast thornfield, a hunting ground overrun by wildlife. [25]No one will go to the fertile hillsides where once the gardens grew, for thorns will cover them; cattle, sheep, and goats will graze there.

8 Isaiah Predicts an Invasion

Again the Lord sent me a message: "Make a large signboard and write on it the birth announcement of the son I am going to give you. Use capital letters! His name will be Maher-shalal-hash-baz, which means 'Your enemies will soon be destroyed.'" [2]I asked Uriah the priest and Zechariah the son of Jeberechiah, both known as honest men, to watch me as I wrote so they could testify that I had written it [before the child was even on the way]. [3]Then I had sexual intercourse with my wife and she conceived and bore me a son. And the Lord said, "Call him Maher-shalal-hash-baz. [4]This name prophesies that within a couple of years, before this child is even old enough to say 'Daddy' or 'Mommy,' the king of Assyria will invade both Damascus and Samaria and carry away their riches."

[5]Then the Lord spoke to me again and said:

[6]"Since the people of Jerusalem are planning to refuse my gentle care and are enthusiastic about asking King Rezin and King Pekah to come and aid them, [7,8]therefore I will overwhelm my people with Euphrates' mighty flood; the king of Assyria and all his mighty armies will rage against them.

This flood will overflow all its channels and sweep into your land of Judah, O Immanuel, submerging it from end to end."

⁹,¹⁰Do your worst, O Syria and Israel, our enemies, but you will not succeed—you will be shattered. Listen to me, all you enemies of ours: Prepare for war against us—and perish! Yes! Perish! Call your councils of war, develop your strategies, prepare your plans of attacking us, and perish! For God is with us.

¹¹The Lord has said in strongest terms: Do not under any circumstances go along with the plans of Judah to surrender to Syria and Israel. ¹²Don't let people call you a traitor for staying true to God. Don't you panic as so many of your neighbors are doing when they think of Syria and Israel attacking you. ¹³Don't fear anything except the Lord of the armies of heaven! If you fear him, you need fear nothing else. ¹⁴,¹⁵He will be your safety; but Israel and Judah have refused his care and thereby stumbled against the Rock of their salvation and lie fallen and crushed beneath it: God's presence among them has endangered them! ¹⁶Write down all these things I am going to do, says the Lord, and seal them up for the future. Entrust them to some godly man to pass on down to godly men of future generations.

¹⁷I will wait for the Lord to help us, though he is hiding now. My only hope is in him. ¹⁸I and the children God has given me have symbolic names that reveal the plans of the Lord of heaven's armies for his people: Isaiah means "Jehovah will save (his people)," Shear-jashub means "A remnant shall return," and Maher-shalal-hash-baz means "Your enemies will soon be destroyed." ¹⁹So why are you trying to find out the future by consulting witches and mediums? Don't listen to their whisperings and mutterings. Can the living find out the future from the dead? Why not ask your God?

²⁰"Check these witches' words against the Word of God!" he says. "If their messages are different than mine, it is because I have not sent them; for they have no light or truth in them. ²¹My people will be led away captive, stumbling, weary and hungry. And because they are hungry, they will rave and shake their fists at heaven and curse their King and their God. ²²Wherever they look there will be trouble and anguish and dark despair. And they will be thrust out into the darkness."

9 The Coming Messiah

Nevertheless, that time of darkness and despair shall not go on forever. Though soon the land of Zebulun and Naphtali will be under God's contempt and judgment, yet in the future these very lands, Galilee and Northern Transjordan, where lies the road to the sea, will be filled with glory. ²The people who walk in darkness shall see a great Light—a Light that will shine on all those who live in the land of the shadow of death. ³For Israel will again be great, filled with joy like that of reapers when the harvest time has come, and like that of men dividing up the plunder they have won. ⁴For God will break the chains that bind his people and the whip that scourges them, just as he did when he destroyed the vast host of the Midianites by Gideon's little band. ⁵In that glorious day of peace there will no longer be the issuing of battle gear; no more the blood-stained uniforms of war; all such will be burned.

⁶For unto us a child is born; unto us a son is given; and the government shall be upon his shoulder. These will be his royal titles: "Wonderful," "Counselor," "The Mighty God," "The Everlasting Father," "The Prince of Peace." ⁷His ever-expanding, peaceful government will never end. He will rule with perfect fairness and justice from the throne of his father David. He will bring true justice and peace to all the nations of the world. This is going to happen because the Lord of heaven's armies has dedicated himself to do it!

⁸⁻¹⁰The Lord has spoken out against that braggart Israel who says that though our land lies in ruins now, we will rebuild it better than before. The sycamore trees are cut down, but we will replace them with cedars! ¹¹,¹²The Lord's reply to your bragging is to bring your enemies against you—the Syrians on the east and the Philistines on the west. With bared fangs they will devour Israel. And even then the Lord's anger against you will not be satisfied—his fist will still be poised to smash you. ¹³For after all this punishment you will not repent and turn to him, the Lord of heaven's armies. ¹⁴,¹⁵Therefore the Lord, in one day, will destroy the leaders of Israel and the lying prophets. ¹⁶For the leaders of his people have led them down the paths of ruin.

¹⁷That is why the Lord has no joy in their young men and no mercy upon even the widows and orphans, for they are all filthy-mouthed, wicked liars. That is why his anger is not yet satisfied, but his fist is still poised to smash them all. ¹⁸He will burn up all this wickedness, these thorns and briars, and the flames will consume the forests too, and send a vast cloud of smoke billowing up from their burning. ¹⁹,²⁰The land is blackened by that fire, by the wrath of the Lord of heaven's armies. The people are fuel for the fire. Each fights against his brother to steal his food but will never have enough. Finally they will even eat their own children! ²¹Manasseh against Ephraim and Ephraim against Manasseh—and both against Judah. Yet even after all of this, God's

anger is not yet satisfied. His hand is still heavy upon them to crush them.

10 God Will Protect His People

Woe to unjust judges and to those who issue unfair laws, says the Lord, ²so that there is no justice for the poor, the widows, and orphans. Yes, it is true that they even rob the widows and fatherless children.

³Oh, what will you do when I visit you in that day when I send desolation upon you from a distant land? To whom will you turn then for your help? Where will your treasures be safe? ⁴I will not help you; you will stumble along as prisoners or lie among the slain. And even then my anger will not be satisfied, but my fist will still be poised to strike you. ⁵,⁶Assyria is the whip of my anger; his military strength is my weapon upon this godless nation, doomed and damned; he will enslave them and plunder them and trample them like dirt beneath his feet. ⁷But the king of Assyria will not know that it is I who sent him. He will merely think he is attacking my people as part of his plan to conquer the world. ⁸He will declare that every one of his princes will soon be a king, ruling a conquered land.

⁹"We will destroy Calno just as we did Carchemish," he will say, "and Hamath will go down before us as Arpad did; and we will destroy Samaria just as we did Damascus. ¹⁰Yes, we have finished off many a kingdom whose idols were far greater than those in Jerusalem and Samaria, ¹¹so when we have defeated Samaria and her idols, we will destroy Jerusalem with hers."

¹²After the Lord has used the king of Assyria to accomplish his purpose, then he will turn upon the Assyrians and punish them too—for they are proud and haughty men.

¹³They boast, "We in our own power and wisdom have won these wars. We are great and wise. By our own strength we broke down the walls and destroyed the people and carried off their treasures. ¹⁴In our greatness we have robbed their nests of riches and gathered up kingdoms as a farmer gathers eggs, and no one can move a finger or open his mouth to peep against us!"

¹⁵But the Lord says, "Shall the axe boast greater power than the man who uses it? Is the saw greater than the man who saws? Can a rod strike unless a hand is moving it? Can a cane walk by itself?"

¹⁶Because of all your evil boasting, O king of Assyria, the Lord of Hosts will send a plague among your proud troops and strike them down. ¹⁷God, the Light and Holy One of Israel, will be the fire and flame that will destroy them. In a single night he will burn those thorns and briars, the Assyrians who destroyed the land of Israel. ¹⁸Assyria's vast army is like a glorious forest, yet it will be destroyed. The Lord will destroy them, soul and body, as when a sick man wastes away. ¹⁹Only a few from all that mighty army will be left; so few a child could count them!

²⁰Then at last those left in Israel and in Judah will trust the Lord, the Holy One of Israel, instead of fearing the Assyrians. ²¹A remnant of them will return to the mighty God. ²²But though Israel be now as many as the sands along the shore, yet only a few of them will be left to return at that time; God has rightly decided to destroy his people. ²³Yes, it has already been decided by the Lord God to consume them.

²⁴Therefore the Lord God says, "O my people in Jerusalem, don't be afraid of the Assyrians when they oppress you just as the Egyptians did long ago. ²⁵It will not last very long; in a little while my anger against you will end, and then it will rise against them to destroy them."

²⁶The Lord Almighty will send his angel to slay them in a mighty slaughter like the time when Gideon triumphed over Midian at the rock of Oreb or the time God drowned the Egyptian armies in the sea. ²⁷On that day God will end the bondage of his people. He will break the slave-yoke off their necks and destroy it as decreed.

²⁸,²⁹Look, the mighty armies of Assyria are coming! Now they are at Aiath, now at Migron; they are storing some of their equipment at Michmash and crossing over the pass; they are staying overnight at Geba. Fear strikes the city of Ramah; all the people of Gibeah—the city of Saul—are running for their lives. ³⁰Well may you scream in terror, O people of Gallim. Shout out a warning to Laish, for the mighty army comes. O poor Anathoth, what a fate is yours! ³¹There go the people of Madmenah, all fleeing, and the citizens of Gebim are preparing to run. ³²But the enemy stops at Nob for the remainder of that day. He shakes his fist at Jerusalem on Mount Zion.

³³Then, look, look! The Lord, the Lord of the armies of heaven, is chopping down the mighty tree! He is destroying all of that vast army, great and small alike, both officers and men. ³⁴He, the Mighty One, will cut down the enemy as a woodsman's axe cuts down the forest trees in Lebanon.

11 God Promises a Perfect Leader

The royal line of David will be cut off, chopped down like a tree; but from the stump will grow a Shoot—yes, a new Branch from the old root. ²And the Spirit of the Lord shall rest upon him, the Spirit of wisdom, understanding, counsel, and might; the Spirit of knowledge and of the fear of the Lord. ³His delight will be obedi-

Family Devotions

☐ **Devotion 199**
Accepting Others

Read Isaiah 11:3-5

Accepting Others
Memory Verse

How wonderful it is, how pleasant, when brothers live in harmony!
Psalm 133:1

Bobby struggled with the color chart. *Why is Mrs. Lebo making such a big deal about primary and secondary colors before letting anyone paint?* he wondered.

"Bobby, please come up front and take the red color card," Mrs. Lebo said. Bobby rose from his seat slowly. He looked at the cards resting in the chalk ledge against the board. Then he lifted a card. Everyone laughed. "That's not funny," Mrs. Lebo said sternly. "Put down that green card and pick up the red one."

Bobby frowned. "I'm color-blind," he said softly. "It's hard for me to tell red from green."

"Oh, sorry, Bobby. I didn't know that," apologized Mrs. Lebo. "You're excused." Bobby returned to his seat, feeling like everyone was looking at him.

At recess time, Bobby played with a boy of a different nationality from his own. "Hey, Bobby," one of their classmates called to him, "no wonder Ray is your best friend. You can't tell that he's a different color!"

"Ignore him," Bobby told Ray. "He's so dumb!" Bobby could never understand people who decided not to like a person based on the color of his skin.

During science, the subject of color blindness came up again. Bobby was asked several questions about it. "You mean a lot of times you don't know what color things are?" asked one girl. "Like spinach or strawberries?"

Bobby grinned. "What does it matter what color they are?" he asked. "They taste good, and Mom says they're good for me." Bobby paused. Then taking a deep breath, he added, "Color isn't what makes something good or bad. God made everything and everybody, and he gives them their value." He looked at the boys who had teased him at recess. "Especially people," he added. "I think everybody should be color-blind when it comes to seeing people."

How About You?
Do you develop opinions about others based on their color? Remember that God made everyone special, and he doesn't judge by appearance. Love people for who God made them to be—his children. *N. E. K.*

• For the next devotional, turn to page 673. • For the next devotional on *Accepting Others*, turn to page 1029.
• For notes on *Accepting Others*, see pages 270, 1140, 1196, and 1254.

ence to the Lord. He will not judge by appearance, false evidence, or hearsay, ⁴but will defend the poor and the exploited. He will rule against the wicked who oppress them. ⁵For he will be clothed with fairness and with truth.

⁶In that day the wolf and the lamb will lie down together, and the leopard and goats will be at peace. Calves and fat cattle will be safe among lions, and a little child shall lead them all. ⁷The cows will graze among bears; cubs and calves will lie down together, and lions will eat grass like the cows. ⁸Babies will crawl safely among poisonous snakes, and a little child who puts his hand in a nest of deadly adders will pull it out unharmed. ⁹Nothing will hurt or destroy in all my holy mountain, for as the waters fill the sea, so shall the earth be full of the knowledge of the Lord.

¹⁰In that day he who created the royal dynasty of David will be a banner of salvation to all the world. The nations will rally to him, for the land where he lives will be a glorious place. ¹¹At that time the Lord will bring back a remnant of his people for the second time, returning them to the land of Israel from Assyria, Upper and Lower Egypt, Ethiopia, Elam, Babylonia, Hamath, and all the distant coastal lands. ¹²He will raise a flag among the nations for them to rally to; he will gather the scattered Israelites from the ends of the earth. ¹³Then at last the jealousy between Israel and Judah will end; they will not fight each other any more. ¹⁴Together they will fly against the nations possessing their land on the east and on the west, uniting forces to destroy them, and they will occupy the nations of Edom and Moab and Ammon.

¹⁵The Lord will dry a path through the Red Sea and wave his hand over the Euphrates, sending a mighty wind to divide it into seven streams that can easily be crossed. ¹⁶He will make a highway from Assyria for the remnant there, just as he did for all of Israel long ago when they returned from Egypt.

12 Singing God's Praise

On that day you will say, "Praise the Lord! He was angry with me, but now he comforts me. ²See, God has come to save me! I will trust and not be afraid, for the Lord is my strength and song; he is my salvation. ³Oh, the joy of drinking deeply from the Fountain of Salvation!"

⁴In that wonderful day you will say, "Thank the Lord! Praise his name! Tell the world about his wondrous love. How mighty he is!" ⁵Sing to the Lord, for he has done wonderful things. Make known his praise around the world. ⁶Let all the people of Jerusalem shout his praise with joy. For great and mighty is the Holy One of Israel, who lives among you.

13 Babylon Will Be Destroyed

This is the vision God showed Isaiah (son of Amoz) concerning Babylon's doom.

²See the flags waving as their enemy attacks. Shout to them, O Israel, and wave them on as they march against Babylon to destroy the palaces of the rich and mighty. ³I, the Lord, have set apart these armies for this task; I have called those rejoicing in their strength to do this work, to satisfy my anger. ⁴Hear the tumult on the mountains! Listen as the armies march! It is the tumult and the shout of many nations. The Lord Almighty has brought them here, ⁵from countries far away. They are his weapons against you, O Babylon. They carry his anger with them and will destroy your whole land.

⁶Scream in terror, for the Lord's time has come, the time for the Almighty to crush you. ⁷Your arms lie paralyzed with fear; the strongest hearts melt ⁸and are afraid. Fear grips you with terrible pangs, like those of a woman in labor. You look at one another, helpless, as the flames of the burning city reflect upon your pallid faces. ⁹For see, the day of the Lord is coming, the terrible day of his wrath and fierce anger. The land shall be destroyed and all the sinners with it. ¹⁰The heavens will be black above them. No light will shine from stars or sun or moon.

¹¹And I will punish the world for its evil, the wicked for their sin; I will crush the arrogance of the proud man and the haughtiness of the rich. ¹² Few will live when I have finished up my work.

Men will be as scarce as gold—of greater value than the gold of Ophir. ¹³For I will shake the heavens in my wrath and fierce anger, and the earth will move from its place in the skies.

¹⁴The armies of Babylon will run until exhausted, fleeing back to their own land like deer chased by dogs, wandering like sheep deserted by their shepherd. ¹⁵Those who don't run will be butchered. ¹⁶Their little children will be dashed to death against the pavement right before their eyes; their homes will be sacked and their wives raped by the attacking hordes. ¹⁷For I will stir up the Medes against Babylon, and no amount of silver or gold will buy them off. ¹⁸The attacking armies will have no mercy on the young people of Babylon or the babies or the children.

¹⁹And so Babylon, the most glorious of kingdoms, the flower of Chaldean culture, will be as utterly destroyed as Sodom and Gomorrah were when God sent fire from heaven; ²⁰Babylon will never rise again. Generation after generation will come and go, but the land will never again be

Family Devotions

☐ Devotion 200
Dealing with Change

Read Isaiah 12

Jeremy was going on his first airplane ride, but he was not excited about it. Inside, he felt as dark and gloomy as the day around him. His parents were getting a divorce, and he was going to live with his grandparents for a while.

As they boarded the plane, Jeremy choked down the lump in his throat. Grandmother gave him a reassuring smile. "Scared?" she asked.

Jeremy shook his head. Inside, he said, *Yes, I'm scared! I'm scared of everything.* But he didn't say anything. As the plane sped down the runway, huge drops of rain splattered the windows.

Grandmother reached for his hand. "Don't be afraid, Jeremy. God loves us. He'll take care of us." Jeremy knew Grandmother was talking about more than the plane ride. He wanted to believe her, but there was so much fear in his heart. "We'll go right through these dark clouds, Jeremy," she explained. "For a few minutes, we'll be in a thick fog, because that's what clouds are—fog. But just wait until we get above the clouds."

Suddenly they were in the clouds. The interior of the plane dimmed. Then, just as suddenly, a brilliant light came streaming through the windows. Jeremy squinted as he pressed his nose to the pane. "It's beautiful," he gasped.

Grandmother nodded, "Yes. Above the clouds, the sun is always shining." The tone of her voice caused Jeremy to turn and look at her. Grandmother smiled gently. "Our family is going through a storm right now, Jeremy. Things look pretty dark. But God is still in control. One day soon we'll break through the clouds, and life will be filled with beauty and happiness again."

Jeremy brushed a tear from his cheek as he turned to look at the sea of sparkling clouds.

Dealing with Change
Memory Verse

We know that all that happens to us is working for our good if we love God and are fitting into his plans.
Romans 8:28

How About You?

Are you going through a storm in your life? Are you afraid of the future? Remember, even when you can't see the sun, it is shining. Even when you can't feel God, he is near. Trust him, and he will lift you above the clouds. B. W.

• For the next devotional, turn to page 679.   • For the next devotional on *Dealing with Change*, turn to page 1083.
• For notes on *Dealing with Change*, see pages 56, 156, 288, 1186, and 1198.

lived in. The nomads will not even camp there. The shepherds won't let their sheep stay overnight. ²¹The wild animals of the desert will make it their home. The houses will be haunted by howling creatures. Ostriches will live there, and the demons will come there to dance. ²²Hyenas and jackals will den within the palaces. Babylon's days are numbered; her time of doom will soon be here.

14 God Promises to Love His People

But the Lord will have mercy on the Israelis; they are still his special ones. He will bring them back to settle once again in the land of Israel. And many nationalities will come and join them there and be their loyal allies. ²The nations of the world will help them to return, and those coming to live in their land will serve them. Those enslaving Israel will be enslaved—Israel shall rule her enemies!

³In that wonderful day when the Lord gives his people rest from sorrow and fear, from slavery and chains, ⁴you will jeer at the king of Babylon and say, "You bully, you! At last you have what was coming to you! ⁵For the Lord has crushed your wicked power and broken your evil rule." ⁶You persecuted my people with unceasing blows of rage and held the nations in your angry grip. You were unrestrained in tyranny. ⁷But at last the whole earth is at rest and is quiet! All the world begins to sing! ⁸Even the trees of the woods—the fir trees and cedars of Lebanon—sing out this joyous song: "Your power is broken; no one will bother us now; at last we have peace."

⁹The denizens of hell crowd to meet you as you enter their domain. World leaders and earth's mightiest kings, long dead, are there to see you. ¹⁰With one voice they all cry out, "Now you are as weak as we are!" ¹¹Your might and power are gone; they are buried with you. All the pleasant music in your palace has ceased; now maggots are your sheet, worms your blanket!

¹²How you are fallen from heaven, O Lucifer, son of the morning! How you are cut down to the ground—mighty though you were against the nations of the world. ¹³For you said to yourself, "I will ascend to heaven and rule the angels. I will take the highest throne. I will preside on the Mount of Assembly far away in the north. ¹⁴I will climb to the highest heavens and be like the Most High." ¹⁵But instead, you will be brought down to the pit of hell, down to its lowest depths. ¹⁶Everyone there will stare at you and ask, "Can this be the one who shook the earth and the kingdoms of the world? ¹⁷Can this be the one who destroyed the world and made it into a shambles, who demolished its greatest cities and had no mercy on his prisoners?"

¹⁸The kings of the nations lie in stately glory in their graves, ¹⁹but your body is thrown out like a broken branch; it lies in an open grave, covered with the dead bodies of those slain in battle. It lies as a carcass in the road, trampled and mangled by horses' hoofs. ²⁰No monument will be given you, for you have destroyed your nation and slain your people. Your son will not succeed you as the king. ²¹Slay the children of this sinner. Do not let them rise and conquer the land nor rebuild the cities of the world.

²²I, myself, have risen against him, says the Lord of heaven's armies, and will cut off his children and his children's children from ever sitting on his throne. ²³I will make Babylon into a desolate land of porcupines, full of swamps and marshes. I will sweep the land with the broom of destruction, says the Lord of the armies of heaven. ²⁴He has taken an oath to do it! For this is his purpose and plan. ²⁵I have decided to break the Assyrian army when they are in Israel and to crush them on my mountains; my people shall no longer be their slaves. ²⁶This is my plan for the whole earth—I will do it by my mighty power that reaches everywhere around the world. ²⁷The Lord, the God of battle, has spoken—who can change his plans? When his hand moves, who can stop him?

²⁸This is the message that came to me the year King Ahaz died:

²⁹Don't rejoice, Philistines, that the king who smote you is dead. That rod is broken, yes; but his son will be a greater scourge to you than his father ever was! From the snake will be born an adder, a fiery serpent to destroy you! ³⁰I will shepherd the poor of my people; they shall graze in my pasture! The needy shall lie down in peace. But as for you—I will wipe you out with famine and the sword. ³¹Weep, Philistine cities—you are doomed. All your nation is doomed. For a perfectly trained army is coming down from the north against you. ³²What then shall we tell the reporters? Tell them that the Lord has founded Jerusalem and is determined that the poor of his people will find a refuge within her walls.

15 What God Will Do to Moab

Here is God's message to Moab: In one night your cities of Ar and Kir will be destroyed. ²Your people in Dibon go mourning to their temples to weep for the fate of Nebo and Medeba; they shave their heads in sorrow and cut off their beards. ³They wear sackcloth through the streets, and from every home comes the sound of weeping. ⁴The cries from the cities of Heshbon and Elealeh are heard far away, even in Jahaz. The bravest warriors of Moab cry in utter terror.

⁵My heart weeps for Moab! His people flee to Zoar and Eglath. Weeping, they climb the upward road to Luhith, and their crying will be heard all along the road to Horonaim. ⁶Even Nimrim River is desolate! The grassy banks are dried up and the tender plants are gone. ⁷The desperate refugees take only the possessions they can carry and flee across the Brook of Willows. ⁸The whole land of Moab is a land of weeping from one end to the other. ⁹The stream near Dibon will run red with blood, but I am not through with Dibon yet! Lions will hunt down the survivors, both those who escape and those who remain.

16 Moab's refugees at Sela send lambs as a token of alliance with the king of Judah. ²The women of Moab are left at the fords of the Arnon River like homeless birds. ³[The ambassadors, who accompany the gift to Jerusalem] plead for advice and help. "Give us sanctuary. Protect us. Do not turn us over to our foes. ⁴,⁵Let our outcasts stay among you; hide them from our enemies! God will reward you for your kindness to us. If you let Moab's fugitives settle among you, then when the terror is past, God will establish David's throne forever, and on that throne he will place a just and righteous King."

⁶Is this proud Moab, concerning which we heard so much? His arrogance and insolence are all gone now! ⁷Therefore all Moab weeps. Yes, Moab, you will mourn for stricken Kir-haraseth, ⁸and for the abandoned farms of Heshbon and the vineyards at Sibmah. The enemy warlords have cut down the best of the grapevines; their armies spread out as far as Jazer in the deserts, and even down to the sea. ⁹So I wail and lament for Jazer and the vineyards of Sibmah. My tears shall flow for Heshbon and Elealeh, for destruction has come upon their summer fruits and harvests. ¹⁰Gone now is the gladness, gone the joy of harvest. The happy singing in the vineyards will be heard no more; the treading out of the grapes in the wine presses has ceased forever. I have ended all their harvest joys.

¹¹I will weep, weep, weep, for Moab, and my sorrow for Kir-haraseth will be very great. ¹²The people of Moab will pray in anguish to their idols at the tops of the hills, but it will do no good; they will cry to their gods in their idol temples, but none will come to save them. ¹³,¹⁴All this concerning Moab has been said before; but now the Lord says that within three years, without fail, the glory of Moab shall be ended, and few of all its people will be left alive.

17 **What God Will Do to Syria**
This is God's message to Damascus, capital of Syria:

Look, Damascus is gone! It is no longer a city—it has become a heap of ruins! ²The cities of Aroer are deserted. Sheep pasture there, lying quiet and unafraid, with no one to chase them away. ³The strength of Israel and the power of Damascus will end, and the remnant of Syria shall be destroyed. For as Israel's glory departed, so theirs, too, will disappear, declares the Lord Almighty. ⁴Yes, the glory of Israel will be very dim when poverty stalks the land. ⁵Israel will be as abandoned as the harvested grain fields in the Valley of Rephaim. ⁶Oh, a very few of her people will be left, just as a few stray olives are left on the trees when the harvest is ended, two or three in the highest branches, four or five out on the tips of the limbs. That is how it will be in Damascus and Israel—stripped bare of people except for a few of the poor who remain.

⁷Then at last they will think of God their Creator and have respect for the Holy One of Israel. ⁸They will no longer ask their idols for help in that day, neither will they worship what their hands have made! They will no longer have respect for the images of Ashtaroth and the sun idols.

⁹Their largest cities will be as deserted as the distant wooded hills and mountaintops and become like the abandoned cities of the Amorites, deserted when the Israelites approached (so long ago). ¹⁰Why? Because you have turned from the God who can save you—the Rock who can hide you; therefore, even though you plant a wonderful, rare crop of greatest value, ¹¹and though it grows so well that it will blossom on the very morning that you plant it, yet you will never harvest it—your only harvest will be a pile of grief and incurable pain.

¹²Look, see the armies thundering toward God's land. ¹³But though they roar like breakers rolling upon a beach, God will silence them. They will flee, scattered like chaff by the wind, like whirling dust before a storm. ¹⁴In the evening Israel waits in terror, but by dawn her enemies are dead. This is the just reward of those who plunder and destroy the people of God.

18 **What God Will Do to Ethiopia**
Ah, land beyond the upper reaches of the Nile, where winged sailboats glide along the river! ²Land that sends ambassadors in fast boats down the Nile! Let swift messengers return to you, O strong and supple nation feared far and wide, a conquering, destroying nation whose land the upper Nile divides. And this is the message sent to you:

³When I raise my battle flag upon the mountain, let all the world take notice! When I blow the trumpet, listen! ⁴For the Lord has told me this: Let your mighty army now advance against the land of Israel. God will watch quietly from his Temple in Jerusalem—serene as on a pleasant summer day or a lovely autumn morning during harvesttime. ⁵But before you have begun the attack, and while your plans are ripening like grapes, he will cut you off as though with pruning shears. He will snip the spreading tendrils. ⁶Your mighty army will be left dead on the field for the mountain birds and wild animals to eat; the vultures will tear bodies all summer, and the wild animals will gnaw bones all winter. ⁷But the time will come when that strong and mighty nation, a terror to all both far and near, that conquering, destroying nation whose land the rivers divide, will bring gifts to the Lord Almighty in Jerusalem, where he has placed his name.

19 What God Will Do to Egypt

This is God's message concerning Egypt:

Look, the Lord is coming against Egypt, riding on a swift cloud; the idols of Egypt tremble; the hearts of the Egyptians melt with fear. ²I will set them to fighting against each other—brother against brother, neighbor against neighbor, city against city, province against province. ³Her wise counselors are all at their wits' end to know what to do; they plead with their idols for wisdom and call upon mediums, wizards, and witches to show them what to do. ⁴I will hand over Egypt to a hard, cruel master, to a vicious king, says the Lord Almighty.

⁵And the waters of the Nile will fail to rise and flood the fields; the ditches will be parched and dry, ⁶their channels fouled with rotting reeds. ⁷All green things along the riverbank will wither and blow away. All crops will perish; everything will die. ⁸The fishermen will weep for lack of work; those who fish with hooks and those who use the nets will all be unemployed. ⁹The weavers will have no flax or cotton, for the crops will fail. ¹⁰Great men and small—all will be crushed and broken.

¹¹What fools the counselors of Zoan are! Their best counsel to the king of Egypt is utterly stupid and wrong. Will they still boast of their wisdom? Will they dare tell Pharaoh about the long line of wise men they have come from? ¹²What has happened to your "wise counselors," O Pharaoh? Where has their wisdom gone? If they are wise, let them tell you what the Lord is going to do to Egypt. ¹³The "wise men" from Zoan are also fools, and those from Memphis are utterly deluded. They are the best you can find, but they have ruined Egypt with their foolish counsel. ¹⁴The Lord has sent a spirit of foolishness on them, so that all their suggestions are wrong; they make Egypt stagger like a sick drunkard. ¹⁵Egypt cannot be saved by anything or anybody—no one can show her the way.

¹⁶In that day the Egyptians will be as weak as women, cowering in fear beneath the udraised fist of God. ¹⁷Just to speak the name of Israel will strike deep terror in their hearts, for the Lord Almighty has laid his plans against them.

¹⁸At that time five of the cities of Egypt will follow the Lord Almighty and will begin to speak the Hebrew language. One of these will be Heliopolis, "The City of the Sun." ¹⁹And there will be an altar to the Lord in the heart of Egypt in those days and a monument to the Lord at its border. ²⁰This will be for a sign of loyalty to the Lord Almighty; then when they cry to the Lord for help against those who oppress them, he will send them a Savior—and he shall deliver them.

²¹In that day the Lord will make himself known to the Egyptians. Yes, they will know the Lord and give their sacrifices and offerings to him; they will make promises to God and keep them. ²²The Lord will smite Egypt and then restore her! For the Egyptians will turn to the Lord and he will listen to their plea and heal them.

²³In that day Egypt and Iraq will be connected by a highway, and the Egyptians and the Iraqi will move freely back and forth between their lands, and they shall worship the same God. ²⁴And Israel will be their ally; the three will be together, and Israel will be a blessing to them. ²⁵For the Lord will bless Egypt and Iraq because of their friendship with Israel. He will say, "Blessed be Egypt, my people; blessed be Iraq, the land I have made; blessed be Israel, my inheritance!"

20 Isaiah Goes Barefoot

In the year when Sargon, king of Assyria, sent the commander-in-chief of his army against the Philistine city of Ashdod and captured it, ²the Lord told Isaiah, the son of Amoz, to take off his clothing, including his shoes, and to walk around naked and barefoot. And Isaiah did as he was told.

³Then the Lord said, My ser-

TRUSTING GOD FOR GUIDANCE 19:14-15 Egypt was noted for its wisdom, but God had sent a spirit of foolishness to the "wise men" of Egypt. True wisdom can come only from God. We must ask him for wisdom in our lives, or we will also be uncertain and misdirected. Are you confused about something in your life now? Ask God for wisdom in dealing with it. **To begin the series of devotionals on TRUSTING GOD FOR GUIDANCE, turn to page 27.**

vant Isaiah, who has been walking naked and barefoot for the last three years, is a symbol of the terrible troubles I will bring upon Egypt and Ethiopia. ⁴For the king of Assyria will take away the Egyptians and Ethiopians as prisoners, making them walk naked and barefoot, both young and old, their buttocks uncovered, to the shame of Egypt. ⁵,⁶Then how dismayed the Philistines will be, who counted on "Ethiopia's power" and their "glorious ally," Egypt! And they will say, "If this can happen to Egypt, what chance have we?"

21 What God Will Do to Babylon

This is God's message concerning Babylon:

Disaster is roaring down upon you from the terrible desert, like a whirlwind sweeping from the Negeb. ²I see an awesome vision: oh, the horror of it all! God is telling me what he is going to do. I see you plundered and destroyed. Elamites and Medes will take part in the siege. Babylon will fall, and the groaning of all the nations she enslaved will end. ³My stomach constricts and burns with pain; sharp pangs of horror are upon me, like the pangs of a woman giving birth to a child. I faint when I hear what God is planning; I am terrified, blinded with dismay. ⁴My mind reels; my heart races; I am gripped by awful fear. All rest at night—so pleasant once—is gone; I lie awake, trembling.

⁵Look! They are preparing a great banquet! They load the tables with food; they pull up their chairs to eat. . . . Quick, quick, grab your shields and prepare for battle! You are being attacked!

⁶,⁷Meanwhile (in my vision) the Lord had told me, "Put a watchman on the city wall to shout out what he sees. When he sees riders in pairs on donkeys and camels, tell him, 'This is it!'"

⁸,⁹So I put the watchman on the wall, and at last he shouted, "Sir, day after day and night after night I have been here at my post. Now at last—look! Here come riders in pairs!"

Then I heard a Voice shout out, "Babylon is fallen, is fallen, and all the idols of Babylon lie broken on the ground."

¹⁰O my people, threshed and winnowed, I have told you all that the Lord Almighty, the God of Israel, has said.

¹¹This is God's message to Edom:

Someone from among you keeps calling, calling to me: "Watchman, what of the night? Watchman, what of the night? How much time is left?" ¹²The watchman replies, "Your judgment day is dawning now. Turn again to God, so that I can give you better news. Seek for him, then come and ask again!"

¹³This is God's message concerning Arabia:

O caravans from Dedan, you will hide in the deserts of Arabia. ¹⁴O people of Tema, bring food and water to these weary fugitives! ¹⁵They have fled from drawn swords and sharp arrows and the terrors of war! ¹⁶"But a long year from now," says the Lord, "the great power of their enemy, the mighty tribe of Kedar, will end. ¹⁷Only a few of its stalwart archers will survive." The Lord, the God of Israel, has spoken.

22 What God Will Do to Jerusalem

This is God's message concerning Jerusalem:

What is happening? Where is everyone going? Why are they running to the rooftops? What are they looking at? ²The whole city is in terrible uproar. What's the trouble in this busy, happy city? Bodies! Lying everywhere, slain by plague and not by sword. ³All your leaders flee; they surrender without resistance. The people slip away but they are captured too. ⁴Let me alone to weep. Don't try to comfort me—let me cry for my people as I watch them being destroyed. ⁵Oh, what a day of crushing trouble! What a day of confusion and terror from the Lord God of heaven's armies! The walls of Jerusalem are breached, and the cry of death echoes from the mountainsides. ⁶,⁷Elamites are the archers; Syrians drive the chariots; the men of Kir hold up the shields. They fill your choicest valleys and crowd against your gates.

⁸God has removed his protecting care. You run to the armory for your weapons! ⁹⁻¹¹You inspect the walls of Jerusalem to see what needs repair! You check over the houses and tear some down for stone for fixing walls. Between the city walls, you build a reservoir for water from the lower pool! But all your feverish plans will not avail, for you never ask for help from God, who lets this come upon you. He is the one who planned it long ago. ¹²The Lord God called you to repent, to weep and mourn, to shave your heads in sorrow for your sins, and to wear clothes made of sackcloth to show your remorse. ¹³But instead, you sing and dance and play, and feast and drink. "Let us eat, drink, and be merry," you say: "What's the difference, for tomorrow we die." ¹⁴The Lord Almighty has revealed to me that this sin will never be forgiven you until the day you die.

OPTIMISM 22:13-14 The people said, "Let us eat, drink, and be merry" because they had given up hope. Today, we see people giving up hope as well. There are two common responses to hopelessness: despair and self-indulgence. But this life is not all there is, so we are not to act as if we have no hope. The proper response is to turn to God and trust in his promise of a perfect and just future in the new world he will create. **To begin the series of devotionals on OPTIMISM, turn to page 19.**

15,16 Furthermore, the same Lord God of the armies of heaven has told me this: Go and say to Shebna, the palace administrator: "And who do you think you are, building this beautiful sepulchre in the rock for yourself? 17 For the Lord who allowed you to be clothed so gorgeously will hurl you away, sending you into captivity, O strong man! 18 He will wad you up in his hands like a ball and toss you away into a distant, barren land; there you will die, O glorious one—you who disgrace your nation!

19 "Yes, I will drive you out of office," says the Lord, "and pull you down from your high position. 20 And then I will call my servant Eliakim, the son of Hilkiah, to replace you. 21 He shall have your uniform and title and authority, and he will be a father to the people of Jerusalem and all Judah. 22 I will give him responsibility over all my people; whatever he says will be done; none will be able to stop him. 23,24 I will make of him a strong and steady peg to support my people; they will load him with responsibility, and he will be an honor to his family name." 25 But the Lord will pull out that other peg that seems to be so firmly fastened to the wall! It will come out and fall to the ground, and everything it supports will fall with it, for the Lord has spoken.

23 What God Will Do to Tyre

This is God's message to Tyre:

Weep, O ships of Tyre, returning home from distant lands! Weep for your harbor, for it is gone! The rumors that you heard in Cyprus are all true. 2,3 Deathly silence is everywhere. Stillness reigns where once your hustling port was full of ships from Sidon, bringing merchandise from far across the ocean, from Egypt and along the Nile. You were the merchandise mart of the world. 4 Be ashamed, O Sidon, stronghold of the sea. For you are childless now! 5 When Egypt hears the news, there will be great sorrow. 6 Flee to Tarshish, men of Tyre, weeping as you go. 7 This silent ruin is all that's left of your once joyous land. What a history was yours! Think of all the colonists you sent to distant lands!

8 Who has brought this disaster on Tyre, empire builder and top trader of the world? 9 The Commander of the armies of heaven has done it to destroy your pride and show his contempt for all the greatness of mankind. 10 Sail on, O ships of Tarshish, for your harbor is gone. 11 The Lord holds out his hand over the seas; he shakes the kingdoms of the earth; he has spoken out against this great merchant city, to destroy its strength.

12 He says, "Never again, O dishonored virgin, daughter of Sidon, will you rejoice, will you be strong. Even if you flee to Cyprus, you will find no rest."

13 It will be the Babylonians, not the Assyrians, who consign Tyre to the wild beasts. They will lay siege to it, raze its palaces, and make it a heap of ruins. 14 Wail, you ships that ply the oceans, for your home port is destroyed!

15,16 For seventy years Tyre will be forgotten. Then, in the days of another king, the city will come back to life again; she will sing sweet songs as a harlot sings who, long absent from her lovers, walks the streets to look for them again and is remembered. 17 Yes, after seventy years, the Lord will revive Tyre, but she will be no different than she was before; she will return again to all her evil ways around the world. 18 Yet [the distant time will come when] her businesses will give their profits to the Lord! They will not be hoarded but used for good food and fine clothes for the priests of the Lord!

24 Trouble Is Coming!

Look! The Lord is overturning the land of Judah and making it a vast wasteland of destruction. See how he is emptying out all its people and scattering them over the face of the earth. 2 Priests and people, servants and masters, slave girls and mistresses, buyers and sellers, lenders and borrowers, bankers and debtors—none will be spared. 3 The land will be completely emptied and looted. The Lord has spoken. 4,5 The land suffers for the sins of its people. The earth languishes, the crops wither, the skies refuse their rain. The land is defiled by crime; the people have twisted the laws of God and broken his everlasting commands. 6 Therefore the curse of God is upon them; they are left desolate, destroyed by the drought. Few will be left alive.

7 All the joys of life will go: the grape harvest will fail, the wine will be gone, the merrymakers will sigh and mourn. 8 The melodious chords of the harp and timbrel are heard no more; the happy days are ended. 9 No more are the joys of wine and song; strong drink turns bitter in the mouth.

10 The city lies in chaos; every home and shop is locked up tight to keep out looters. 11 Mobs

---

STANDING FOR RIGHTEOUSNESS 24:4-5 Not only the people suffered from their sins; even the land suffered with bad crops and crime. Today we see the results of sin in our own land—pollution, crime, poverty. Sin affects every aspect of society so extensively that even those faithful to God suffer. We cannot blame God for these conditions because human sin has brought them about. The more we who are believers renounce sin and share God's Word with others, the more we slow our society's deterioration. We must not give up: sin is rampant, but we can make a difference. **To begin the series of devotionals on** STANDING FOR RIGHTEOUSNESS, **turn to page 139.**

FAMILY DEVOTIONS

☐ DEVOTION 201
TRUSTING GOD FOR HELP

Read Isaiah 26:3-4

Trusting God for Help Memory Verse

God is our refuge and strength, a tested help in times of trouble.
Psalm 46:1

The long months in casts had finally come to an end, but Jenni's legs were still very weak. She was anxious to get started with physical therapy to strengthen them again, so she greeted Jan, her therapist, with a grin. Jan smiled back as she held out a swimsuit. "Get into this," she instructed. "Your first session will be in the pool."

"Oh, no!" Jenni cried. "I'm scared of water. And with my legs so weak, I just know my face will go under! Couldn't we do it some other way?"

But all her coaxing and pleading was useless, for working with the legs under water was the prescribed treatment. Into the pool Jenni went, but she craned her neck and kept pulling herself up high on the edge of the pool. Finally Jan spoke firmly. "Jenni, your muscles are all very tense. The therapy will be useless unless you relax. Try not to worry about the water. Look down, through the water, at your legs. Think about the good that is being accomplished in the water." Nodding fearfully, Jenni tried it. She watched Jan exercise her legs under the water. To her surprise, the therapy was much easier after that.

On the way home, Jenni told her mother how Jan's idea had calmed her. Mom smiled. "Jenni, this reminds me of the way I felt seven months ago when that drunk driver hit you," she said. "All I could think about at first was anger toward him. Then I realized that the Bible says God will keep us in perfect peace if we keep our minds on him. When I quit looking *at* the problem and looked *through* the problem to God, I found peace. Now I pray for the driver, and I thank God for how well you're doing."

Jenni grinned. "I guess it's all according to what your mind is set on," she said.

How About You?
Are there problems in your life that seem to be more than you can handle? Perhaps trouble at school, divorce in your family, illness, or even death? Look through the problem and try to see God working all things out for good. God promises peace if we keep our minds on him. R. P.

form in the streets, crying for wine; joy has reached its lowest ebb; gladness has been banished from the land. [12]The city is left in ruins; its gates are battered down. [13]Throughout the land the story is the same—only a remnant is left.

[14]But all who are left will shout and sing for joy; those in the west will praise the majesty of God, [15,16]and those in the east will respond with praise. Hear them singing to the Lord from the ends of the earth, singing glory to the Righteous One!

But my heart is heavy with grief, for evil still prevails and treachery is everywhere. [17]Terror and the captivity of hell are still your lot, O men of the world. [18]When you flee in terror, you will fall into a pit, and if you escape from the pit, you will step into a trap, for destruction falls from the heavens upon you; the world is shaken beneath you. [19]The earth has broken down in utter collapse; everything is lost, abandoned, and confused. [20]The world staggers like a drunkard; it shakes like a tent in a storm. It falls and will not rise again, for the sins of the earth are very great.

[21]On that day the Lord will punish the fallen angels in the heavens and the proud rulers of the nations on earth. [22]They will be rounded up like prisoners and imprisoned in a dungeon until they are tried and condemned. [23]Then the Lord of heaven's armies will mount his throne in Zion and rule gloriously in Jerusalem, in the sight of all the elders of his people. Such glory there will be that all the brightness of the sun and moon will seem to fade away.

25 A Day of Rejoicing

O Lord, I will honor and praise your name, for you are my God; you do such wonderful things! You planned them long ago, and now you have accomplished them, just as you said! [2]You turn mighty cities into heaps of ruins. The strongest forts are turned to rubble. Beautiful palaces in distant lands disappear and will never be rebuilt. [3]Therefore strong nations will shake with fear before you; ruthless nations will obey and glorify your name.

[4]But to the poor, O Lord, you are a refuge from the storm, a shadow from the heat, a shelter from merciless men who are like a driving rain that melts down an earthen wall. [5]As a hot, dry land is cooled by clouds, you will cool the pride of ruthless nations. [6]Here on Mount Zion in Jerusalem, the Lord Almighty will spread a wondrous feast for everyone around the world—a delicious feast of good food, with clear, well-aged wine and choice beef. [7]At that time he will remove the cloud of gloom, the pall of death that hangs over the earth; [8]he will swallow up death forever. The Lord God will wipe away all tears and take away forever all insults and mockery against his land and people. The Lord has spoken—he will surely do it!

[9]In that day the people will proclaim, "This is our God in whom we trust, for whom we waited. Now at last he is here." What a day of rejoicing! [10]For the Lord's good hand will rest upon Jerusalem, and Moab will be crushed as straw beneath his feet and left to rot. [11]God will push them down just as a swimmer pushes down the water with his hands. He will end their pride and all their evil works. [12]The high walls of Moab will be demolished and brought to dust.

26 The People Sing

Listen to them singing! In that day the whole land of Judah will sing this song:

"Our city is strong! We are surrounded by the walls of his salvation!" [2]Open the gates to everyone, for all may enter in who love the Lord. [3]He will keep in perfect peace all those who trust in him, whose thoughts turn often to the Lord! [4]Trust in the Lord God always, for in the Lord Jehovah is your everlasting strength. [5]He humbles the proud and brings the haughty city to the dust; its walls come crashing down. [6]He presents it to the poor and needy for their use.

[7]But for good men the path is not uphill and rough! God does not give them a rough and treacherous path, but smooths the road before them. [8]O Lord, we love to do your will! Our hearts' desire is to glorify your name. [9]All night long I search for you; earnestly I seek for God; for only when you come in judgment on the earth to punish it will people turn away from wickedness and do what is right.

[10]Your kindness to the wicked doesn't make them good; they keep on doing wrong and take no notice of your majesty. [11]They do not listen when you threaten; they will not look to see your upraised fist. Show them how much you love your people. Perhaps then they will be ashamed! Yes, let them be burned up by the fire reserved for your enemies.

[12]Lord, grant us peace; for all we have and are has come from you. [13]O Lord our God, once we worshiped other gods; but now we worship you alone. [14]Those we served before are dead and gone; never again will they return. You came against them and destroyed them, and they are long forgotten. [15]O praise the Lord! He has made our nation very great. He has widened the boundaries of our land!

[16]Lord, in their distress they sought for you. When your punishment was on them, they poured forth a whispered prayer. [17]How we missed your presence, Lord! We suffered as a

woman giving birth who cries and writhes in pain. ¹⁸We too have writhed in agony, but all to no avail. No deliverance has come from all our efforts. ¹⁹Yet we have this assurance: Those who belong to God shall live again. Their bodies shall rise again! Those who dwell in the dust shall awake and sing for joy! For God's light of life will fall like dew upon them!

²⁰Go home, my people, and lock the doors! Hide for a little while until the Lord's wrath against your enemies has passed. ²¹Look! The Lord is coming from the heavens to punish the people of the earth for their sins. The earth will no longer hide the murderers. The guilty will be found.

27 God Stops Feeling Angry

In that day the Lord will take his terrible, swift sword and punish leviathan, the swiftly moving serpent, the coiling, writhing serpent, the dragon of the sea.

²In that day [of Israel's freedom] let this anthem be their song:

³Israel is my vineyard; I, the Lord, will tend the fruitful vines; every day I'll water them, and day and night I'll watch to keep all enemies away. ⁴,⁵My anger against Israel is gone. If I find thorns and briars bothering her, I will burn them up, unless these enemies of mine surrender and beg for peace and my protection. ⁶The time will come when Israel will take root and bud and blossom and fill the whole earth with her fruit!

⁷,⁸Has God punished Israel as much as he has punished her enemies? No, for he has devastated her enemies, while he has punished Israel but a little, exiling her far from her own land as though blown away in a storm from the east. ⁹ And why did God do it? It was to purge away her sins, to rid her of all her idol altars and her idols. They will never be worshiped again. ¹⁰Her walled cities will be silent and empty, houses abandoned, streets grown up with grass, cows grazing through the city munching on twigs and branches.

¹¹My people are like the dead branches of a tree, broken off and used to burn beneath the pots. They are a foolish nation, a witless, stupid people, for they turn away from God. Therefore, he who made them will not have pity on them or show them his mercy. ¹²Yet the time will come when the Lord will gather them together one by one like handpicked grain, selecting them here and there from his great threshing floor that reaches all the way from the Euphrates River to the Egyptian boundary. ¹³In that day the great trumpet will be blown, and many about to perish among their enemies, Assyria and Egypt, will be rescued and brought back to Jerusalem to worship the Lord in his holy mountain.

28 A Wonderful Teacher

Woe to the city of Samaria, surrounded by her rich valley—Samaria, the pride and delight of the drunkards of Israel! Woe to her fading beauty, the crowning glory of a nation of men lying drunk in the streets! ²For the Lord will send a mighty army (the Assyrians) against you; like a mighty hailstorm he will burst upon you and dash you to the ground. ³The proud city of Samaria—yes, the joy and delight of the drunkards of Israel—will be hurled to the ground and trampled beneath the enemies' feet. ⁴Once glorious, her fading beauty surrounded by a fertile valley will suddenly be gone, greedily snatched away as an early fig is hungrily snatched and gobbled up!

⁵Then at last the Lord Almighty himself will be their crowning glory, the diadem of beauty to his people who are left. ⁶He will give a longing for justice to your judges and great courage to your soldiers who are battling to the last before your gates. ⁷But Jerusalem is now led by drunks! Her priests and prophets reel and stagger, making stupid errors and mistakes. ⁸Their tables are covered with vomit; filth is everywhere.

⁹"Who does Isaiah think he is," the people say, "to speak to us like this! Are we little children, barely old enough to talk? ¹⁰He tells us everything over and over again, a line at a time and in such simple words!"

¹¹But they won't listen; the only language they can understand is punishment! So God will punish them by sending against them foreigners who speak strange gibberish! Only then will they listen to him! ¹²They could have rest in their own land if they would obey him, if they were kind and good. He told them that, but they wouldn't listen to him. ¹³So the Lord will spell it out for them again, repeating it over and over in simple words whenever he can; yet over this simple, straightforward message they will stumble and fall and be broken, trapped and captured.

¹⁴Therefore hear the word of the Lord, you scoffing rulers in Jerusalem:

¹⁵You have struck a bargain with Death, you say, and sold yourselves to the devil in exchange for his protection against the Assyrians. "They can never touch us," you say, "for we are under the care of one who will deceive and fool them."

¹⁶But the Lord God says, "See, I am placing a Foundation Stone in Zion—a firm, tested, precious Cornerstone that is safe to build on. He who believes need never run away again. ¹⁷I will take the line and plummet of justice to check the foundation wall you built; it looks so fine, but it is so weak a storm of hail will knock it down! The enemy will come like a flood and sweep it away, and you will be drowned. ¹⁸I will cancel your

agreement of compromise with Death and the devil, so when the terrible enemy floods in, you will be trampled into the ground. ¹⁹Again and again that flood will come and carry you off, until at last the unmixed horror of the truth of my warnings will finally dawn on you."

²⁰The bed you have made is far too short to lie on; the blankets are too narrow to cover you. ²¹The Lord will come suddenly and in anger, as at Mount Perazim and Gibeon, to do a strange, unusual thing—to destroy his own people! ²²So scoff no more, lest your punishment be made even greater, for the Lord God has plainly told me that he is determined to crush you.

²³,²⁴Listen to me, listen as I plead: Does a farmer always plow and never sow? Is he forever harrowing the soil and never planting it? ²⁵Does he not finally plant his many kinds of grain, each in its own section of his land? ²⁶He knows just what to do, for God has made him see and understand. ²⁷He doesn't thresh all grains the same. A sledge is never used on dill, but it is beaten with a stick. A threshing wheel is never rolled on cummin, but it is beaten softly with a flail. ²⁸Bread grain is easily crushed, so he doesn't keep on pounding it. ²⁹The Lord Almighty is a wonderful teacher and gives the farmer wisdom.

29 No One Can Hide from God

Woe to Jerusalem, the city of David. Year after year you make your many offerings, ²but I will send heavy judgment upon you, and there will be weeping and sorrow. For Jerusalem shall become as her name "Ariel" means—an altar covered with blood. ³I will be your enemy. I will surround Jerusalem and lay siege against it, and build forts around it to destroy it. ⁴Your voice will whisper like a ghost from the earth where you lie buried.

⁵But suddenly your ruthless enemies will be driven away like chaff before the wind. ⁶In an instant, I, the Lord of Hosts, will come upon them with thunder, earthquake, whirlwind, and fire. ⁷And all the nations fighting Jerusalem will vanish like a dream! ⁸As a hungry man dreams of eating but is still hungry, and as a thirsty man dreams of drinking but is still faint from thirst when he wakes up, so your enemies will dream of victorious conquest, but all to no avail.

⁹You are amazed, incredulous? You don't believe it? Then go ahead and be blind if you must! You are stupid—and not from drinking, either! Stagger, and not from wine! ¹⁰For the Lord has poured out upon you a spirit of deep sleep. He has closed the eyes of your prophets and seers, ¹¹so all of these future events are a sealed book to them. When you give it to one who can read, he says, "I can't, for it's sealed." ¹²When you give it to another, he says, "Sorry, I can't read."

¹³And so the Lord says, "Since these people say they are mine but they do not obey me, and since their worship amounts to mere words learned by rote, ¹⁴therefore I will take awesome vengeance on these hypocrites and make their wisest counselors as fools."

¹⁵Woe to those who try to hide their plans from God, who try to keep him in the dark concerning what they do! "God can't see us," they say to themselves. "He doesn't know what is going on!" ¹⁶How stupid can they be! Isn't he, the Potter, greater than you, the jars he makes? Will you say to him, "He didn't make us"? Does a machine call its inventor dumb?

¹⁷Soon—and it will not be very long—the wilderness of Lebanon will be a fruitful field again, a lush and fertile forest. ¹⁸In that day the deaf will hear the words of a book, and out of their gloom and darkness the blind will see my plans. ¹⁹The meek will be filled with fresh joy from the Lord, and the poor shall exult in the Holy One of Israel. ²⁰Bullies will vanish and scoffers will cease, and all those plotting evil will be killed—²¹the violent man who fights at the drop of a hat, the man who waits in hiding to beat up the judge who sentenced him, and the men who use any excuse to be unfair.

²²That is why the Lord who redeemed Abraham says: "My people will no longer pale with fear or be ashamed. ²³For when they see the surging birth rate and the expanding economy, then they will fear and rejoice in my name; they will praise the Holy One of Israel and stand in awe of him. ²⁴Those in error will believe the truth, and complainers will be willing to be taught!

30 God Is Waiting

Woe to my rebellious children, says the Lord; you ask advice from everyone but me and decide to do what I don't want you to do. You yoke yourselves with unbelievers, thus piling up your sins. ²For without consulting me you have gone down to Egypt to find aid and have put your trust in Pharaoh for his protection. ³But in trusting Pharaoh, you will be disappointed, humiliated and disgraced, for he can't deliver on his promises to save you. ⁴For though his power extends to Zoan and Hanes, ⁵yet it will all turn out to your shame—he won't help one little bit!

⁶See them moving slowly across the terrible desert to Egypt—donkeys and camels laden down with treasure to pay for Egypt's aid. On through the badlands they go, where lions and swift venomous snakes live—and Egypt will give

FAMILY DEVOTIONS

☐ **DEVOTION 202**
CONFESSING SIN

Read Isaiah 29:15-16

All the way to Aunt Betty's, Kevin's conscience tormented him. *Why did you do it? You know better,* he scolded himself.

At Aunt Betty's, everyone remarked about her beautiful, spotless house—they always told her she was a wonderful housekeeper. After dinner, Aunt Betty brought out the birthday cake. "We need a picture of this," she declared. "Let's see . . . I forgot to get the camera out. It's in the hall closet."

Kevin jumped up. "I'll get it," he offered.

When Kevin opened the closet door, he stared in amazement. It was so cluttered, he was almost afraid to touch anything for fear he'd start an avalanche. "Can't you find it?" asked Aunt Betty, coming up behind him. She laughed at his expression. "Surprised? I'm a cover-up expert," she told him, "but even a cover-up expert can get away with hiding things only so long. I got caught this time, didn't I?"

That night, Kevin couldn't sleep. Finally he got up and went into his parents' room. "Dad," he whispered as he sat on the edge of the bed, "I've got a confession to make." Dad flipped on the lamp as Kevin continued. "I . . . I . . . I stole a dollar from your billfold," continued Kevin. "I . . . I'd made a bet with Joe, and I lost. I know it's wrong to steal and to bet. I'm sorry. I'll pay you back."

"You certainly will," said Dad. His face was solemn, but he sat up and slipped an arm around his son. "What made you decide to confess?" he asked.

"Aunt Betty's closet," Kevin replied promptly. "You can hide things by covering them up only so long."

Confessing Sin
Memory Verse

But if we confess our sins to him, he can be depended on to forgive us and to cleanse us from every wrong. [And it is perfectly proper for God to do this for us because Christ died to wash away our sins.]
1 John 1:9

How About You?
Is there something in your life that you are hiding? Something that needs to be confessed? Don't wait. Now is the time to clean house. Confess the matter to God and also to any person you have wronged. *B. W.*

• For the next devotional, turn to page 685. • For the next devotional on *CONFESSING SIN,* turn to page 711.
• For notes on *CONFESSING SIN,* see pages 429, 479, 836, 881, and 1220.

you nothing in return! ⁷For Egypt's promises are worthless! "The Reluctant Dragon," I call her!

⁸Now go and write down this word of mine concerning Egypt, so that it will stand until the end of time, forever and forever, as an indictment of Israel's unbelief. ⁹For if you don't write it, they will claim I never warned them. "Oh no," they'll say, "you never told us that!"

For they are stubborn rebels. ¹⁰,¹¹They tell my prophets, "Shut up—we don't want any more of your reports!" Or they say, "Don't tell us the truth; tell us nice things; tell us lies. Forget all this gloom; we've heard more than enough about your 'Holy One of Israel' and all he says."

¹²This is the reply of the Holy One of Israel:

Because you despise what I tell you and trust instead in frauds and lies and won't repent, ¹³therefore calamity will come upon you suddenly, as upon a bulging wall that bursts and falls; in one moment it comes crashing down. ¹⁴God will smash you like a broken dish; he will not act sparingly. Not a piece will be left large enough to use for carrying coals from the hearth, or a little water from the well. ¹⁵For the Lord God, the Holy One of Israel, says: Only in returning to me and waiting for me will you be saved; in quietness and confidence is your strength; but you'll have none of this.

¹⁶"No," you say. "We will get our help from Egypt; they will give us swift horses for riding to battle." But the only swiftness you are going to see is the swiftness of your enemies chasing you! ¹⁷One of them will chase a thousand of you! Five of them will scatter you until not two of you are left together. You will be like lonely trees on the distant mountaintops. ¹⁸Yet the Lord still waits for you to come to him so he can show you his love; he will conquer you to bless you, just as he said. For the Lord is faithful to his promises. Blessed are all those who wait for him to help them.

¹⁹O my people in Jerusalem, you shall weep no more, for he will surely be gracious to you at the sound of your cry. He will answer you. ²⁰Though he give you the bread of adversity and water of affliction, yet he will be with you to teach you—with your own eyes you will see your Teacher. ²¹And if you leave God's paths and go astray, you will hear a Voice behind you say, "No, this is the way; walk here." ²²And you will destroy all your silver idols and gold images and cast them out like filthy things you hate to touch. "Ugh!" you'll say to them. "Be gone!"

²³Then God will bless you with rain at planting time and with wonderful harvests and with ample pastures for your cows. ²⁴The oxen and young donkeys that till the ground will eat grain, its chaff blown away by the wind. ²⁵In that day when God steps in to destroy your enemies, he will give you streams of water flowing down each mountain and every hill. ²⁶The moon will be as bright as the sun, and the sunlight brighter than seven days! So it will be when the Lord begins to heal his people and to cure the wounds he gave them.

²⁷See, the Lord comes from afar, aflame with wrath, surrounded by thick rising smoke. His lips are filled with fury; his words consume like fire. ²⁸ His wrath pours out like floods upon them all, to sweep them all away. He will sift out the proud nations and bridle them and lead them off to their doom.

²⁹But the people of God will sing a song of solemn joy, like songs in the night when holy feasts are held; his people will have gladness of heart, as when a flutist leads a pilgrim band to Jerusalem to the Mountain of the Lord, the Rock of Israel. ³⁰And the Lord shall cause his majestic voice to be heard and shall crush down his mighty arm upon his enemies with angry indignation and devouring flames, with tornados, terrible storms, and huge hailstones. ³¹The voice of the Lord shall punish the Assyrians, who had been his rod of punishment. ³²And when the Lord smites them, his people will rejoice with music and song. ³³The funeral pyre has long been ready, prepared for Molech, the Assyrian god; it is piled high with wood. The breath of the Lord, like fire from a volcano, will set it all on fire.

31 The Sword of God

Woe to those who run to Egypt for help, trusting their mighty cavalry and chariots instead of looking to the Holy One of Israel and consulting him. ²In his wisdom, he will send great evil on his people and will not change his mind. He will rise against them for the evil they have done and crush their allies too. ³For these Egyptians are mere men, not God! Their horses are puny flesh, not mighty spirits! When the Lord clenches his fist against them, they will stumble and fall among those they are trying to help. All will fail together.

⁴,⁵But the Lord has told me this: When a lion, even a young one, kills a sheep, he pays no attention to the shepherd's shouts and noise. He goes right on and eats. In such manner the Lord will come and fight upon Mount Zion. He will not be frightened away! He, the Lord Almighty, will hover over Jerusalem as birds hover round their nests, and he will defend the city and deliver it.

⁶Therefore, O my people, though you are such wicked rebels, come, return to God. ⁷I know the glorious day will come when every one of you will throw away his gold idols and silver images—which in your sinfulness you have made.

⁸The Assyrians will be destroyed, but not by swords of men. The "sword of God" will smite

Family Devotions

☐ DEVOTION 203
HUMILITY

Read Isaiah 29:19

Rachelle threw her books on the couch and with a loud groan plopped down beside them.

"Was it that bad?" Grandma asked as she laid down her needlepoint. Grandma always had time to listen.

Glumly, Rachelle nodded. "It was a terrible day, Gram. I can't do math. I've tried and tried, but I can't understand it. I got a *D* on my last test, and I'm so ashamed."

"Have you asked your teacher for help?" asked Grandma.

"Mr. Marker?" Rachelle snorted. "No way! He explains it in class, and if we don't understand, that's our problem. I'd be embarrassed to ask him for special help."

"I think you take after your grandpa," chuckled Grandma. "He hated to ask for help, too. We could be lost in some town, and he'd wander around for an hour before he'd stop and ask for directions. He was too proud."

"I brought you a glass of iced tea, Gram," said Troy as he came into the room carrying a tray that was almost too large for him to handle. As the glass wobbled, Rachelle reached out to help. The little boy jerked the tray out of her reach. "No! I can do it all by my—"

"Oh! Look what you did!" Rachelle cried as the glass toppled and tea splattered everywhere.

"Maybe I will ask Mr. Marker for help," Rachelle said thoughtfully when things had settled down. "I guess I've been acting like Troy and Grandpa, trying to do it by myself."

Grandma nodded. "And don't forget to ask God to help you, too."

Humility
Memory Verse

For everyone who tries to honor himself shall be humbled; and he who humbles himself shall be honored.
Luke 14:11

How About You?
Is there an area in which you need help? Does a subject in school seem too difficult? Is the minister too hard to understand? Are your memory verses too hard to learn? Is there a family situation you can't handle? Don't be too proud to ask for the help you need. Pride does not please God. Ask his help first, and then ask help of parents, friends, or teachers. God has given them to you, and he wants you to use their help. *B. W.*

• For the next devotional, turn to page 687.   • For the next devotional on HUMILITY, turn to page 695.
• For notes on HUMILITY, see pages 57, 390, 428, 854, and 1228.

them. They will panic and flee, and the strong young Assyrians will be taken away as slaves. ⁹Even their generals will quake with terror and flee when they see the battle flags of Israel, says the Lord. For the flame of God burns brightly in Jerusalem.

32 A Promise of Peace

Look, a righteous King is coming, with honest princes! ²He will shelter Israel from the storm and wind. He will refresh her as a river in the desert and as the cooling shadow of a mighty rock within a hot and weary land. ³Then at last the eyes of Israel will open wide to God; his people will listen to his voice. ⁴Even the hotheads among them will be full of sense and understanding, and those who stammer in uncertainty will speak out plainly.

⁵In those days the ungodly, the atheists, will not be heroes! Wealthy cheaters will not be spoken of as generous, outstanding men! ⁶Everyone will recognize an evil man when he sees him, and hypocrites will fool no one at all. Their lies about God and their cheating of the hungry will be plain for all to see. ⁷The smooth tricks of evil men will be exposed, as will all the lies they use to oppress the poor in the courts. ⁸But good men will be generous to others and will be blessed of God for all they do.

⁹Listen, you women who loll around in lazy ease; listen to me and I will tell you your reward: ¹⁰In a short time—in just a little more than a year—suddenly you'll care, O careless ones. For the crops of fruit will fail; the harvest will not take place. ¹¹Tremble, O women of ease; throw off your unconcern. Strip off your pretty clothes—wear sackcloth for your grief. ¹²Beat your breasts in sorrow for those bountiful farms of yours that will soon be gone, and for those fruitful vines of other years. ¹³For your lands will thrive with thorns and briars; your joyous homes and happy cities will be gone. ¹⁴Palaces and mansions will all be deserted, the crowded cities empty. Wild herds of donkeys and goats will graze upon the mountains where the watchtowers are, ¹⁵until at last the Spirit is poured down on us from heaven. Then once again enormous crops will come. ¹⁶Then justice will rule through all the land, ¹⁷and out of justice, peace. Quietness and confidence will reign forever more.

¹⁸My people will live in safety, quietly at home, ¹⁹but the Assyrians will be destroyed and their cities laid low. ²⁰And God will greatly bless his people. Wherever they plant, bountiful crops will spring up, and their flocks and herds will graze in green pastures.

33 God's Great Forgiveness

Woe to you, Assyrians, who have destroyed everything around you but have never felt destruction for yourselves. You expect others to respect their promises to you, while you betray them! Now you, too, will be betrayed and destroyed.

²But to us, O Lord, be merciful, for we have waited for you. Be our strength each day and our salvation in the time of trouble. ³The enemy runs at the sound of your voice. When you stand up, the nations flee. ⁴Just as locusts strip the fields and vines, so Jerusalem will strip the fallen army of Assyria!

⁵The Lord is very great and lives in heaven. He will make Jerusalem the home of justice and goodness and righteousness. ⁶An abundance of salvation is stored up for Judah in a safe place, along with wisdom and knowledge and reverence for God.

⁷But now your ambassadors weep in bitter disappointment, for Assyria has refused their cry for peace. ⁸Your roads lie in ruins; travelers detour on back roads. The Assyrians have broken their peace pact and care nothing for the promises they made in the presence of witnesses—they have no respect for anyone. ⁹All the land of Israel is in trouble; Lebanon has been destroyed; Sharon has become a wilderness; Bashan and Carmel are plundered.

¹⁰But the Lord says, I will stand up and show my power and might. ¹¹You Assyrians will gain nothing by all your efforts. Your own breath will turn to fire and kill you. ¹²Your armies will be burned to lime, like thorns cut down and tossed in the fire. ¹³Listen to what I have done, O nations far away! And you that are near, acknowledge my might!

¹⁴The sinners among my people shake with fear. "Which one of us," they cry, "can live here in the presence of this all-consuming, Everlasting Fire?" ¹⁵I will tell you who can live here: All who are honest and fair, who reject making profit by fraud, who hold back their hands from taking bribes, who refuse to listen to those who plot murder, who shut their eyes to all enticement to do wrong. ¹⁶Such as these shall dwell on high. The rocks of the mountains will be their fortress of safety; food will be supplied to them, and they will have all the water they need.

¹⁷Your eyes will see the King in his beauty and the highlands of heaven far away. ¹⁸Your mind will think back to this time of terror when the Assyrian officers outside your walls are counting your towers and estimating how much they will get from your fallen city. ¹⁹But soon they will all be gone. These fierce, violent people with a strange, jabbering language you can't understand will disappear.

²⁰Instead you will see Jerusalem at peace, a

Family Devotions

☐ DEVOTION 204
AVOIDING SIN

Read Isaiah 33:13-16

Holly loved television! She ran to the TV and turned it on as soon as she awoke each day. When she came in from school, she watched it almost nonstop until bedtime. She didn't think TV harmed her in any way, and she wasn't very particular about what she watched either.

After school she watched a couple of soap operas that were very immoral in words and actions. The clothing was indecent, and the people were always drinking alcohol. On Tuesday night, Holly watched a comedy show in which there was a lot of swearing. When talk shows came on, Holly laughed with the audience at the dirty jokes that were told.

For the opening exercises at Sunday school one week, Holly's little sister sang, "Oh, be careful little eyes what you see. . . . For the Father up above is looking down in love, so be careful little eyes what you see!" Then the superintendent told the children they should never look at anything that they wouldn't want God to look at with them.

That week Holly didn't enjoy television so much. On one afternoon soap opera, an unmarried lady was trying to steal another lady's husband. Holly knew God wouldn't like to look at that. She tried a game show, but her favorite celebrity was wearing a T-shirt with suggestive words on the front. God wouldn't like that either. On Tuesday evening the comedy show was only half over when Holly jumped up and turned off the TV. She knew God wouldn't want to watch a program where people kept using his name in swear words. Holly felt ashamed because she suddenly realized that when she was hurt or upset, she'd been thinking dirty words. *It's because I hear them all the time on TV,* she thought to herself. *Why, those programs I watch aren't good for me. From now on I'm going to be more careful about what I let my eyes see!*

Avoiding Sin Memory Verse

Dear brothers, you are only visitors here. Since your real home is in heaven, I beg you to keep away from the evil pleasures of this world; they are not for you, for they fight against your very souls.
1 Peter 2:11

How About You?
Are you careful about what you let your eyes see on the television? You should choose programs that are clean and wholesome. And many times it is a good idea to turn the TV off! R. P.

• For the next devotional, turn to page 691. • For the next devotional on AVOIDING SIN, turn to page 805.
• For notes on AVOIDING SIN, see pages 220, 332, 392, and 657.

place where God is worshiped, a city quiet and unmoved. ²¹The glorious Lord will be to us as a wide river of protection, and no enemy can cross. ²²For the Lord is our Judge, our Lawgiver and our King; he will care for us and save us. ²³The enemies' sails hang loose on broken masts with useless tackle. Their treasure will be divided by the people of God; even the lame will win their share. ²⁴The people of Israel will no longer say, "We are sick and helpless," for the Lord will forgive them their sins and bless them.

34 Come and Listen!

Come here and listen, O nations of the earth; let the world and everything in it hear my words. ²For the Lord is enraged against the nations; his fury is against their armies. He will utterly destroy them and deliver them to slaughter. ³Their dead will be left unburied, and the stench of rotting bodies will fill the land; the mountains will flow with their blood. ⁴At that time the heavens above will melt away and disappear just like a rolled-up scroll, and the stars will fall as leaves, as ripe fruit from the trees.

⁵And when my sword has finished its work in the heavens, then watch, for it will fall upon Edom, the people I have doomed. ⁶The sword of the Lord is sated with blood; it is gorged with flesh as though used for slaying lambs and goats for sacrifice. For the Lord will slay a great sacrifice in Edom and make a mighty slaughter there. ⁷The strongest will perish, young boys and veterans too. The land will be soaked with blood, and the soil made rich with fat. ⁸For it is the day of vengeance, the year of recompense for what Edom has done to Israel. ⁹The streams of Edom will be filled with burning pitch, and the ground will be covered with fire.

¹⁰This judgment on Edom will never end. Its smoke will rise up forever. The land will lie deserted from generation to generation; no one will live there anymore. ¹¹There the hawks and porcupines will live, and owls and ravens. For God will observe that land and find it worthy of destruction. He will test its nobles and find them worthy of death. ¹²It will be called "The Land of Nothing," and its princes soon will all be gone. ¹³Thorns will overrun the palaces, nettles will grow in its forts, and it will become the haunt of jackals and a home for ostriches. ¹⁴The wild animals of the desert will mingle there with wolves and hyenas. Their howls will fill the night. There the night-monsters will scream at each other, and the demons will come there to rest. ¹⁵There the owl will make her nest and lay her eggs; she will hatch her young and nestle them beneath her wings, and the kites will come, each one with its mate.

¹⁶Search the book of the Lord and see all that he will do; not one detail will he miss; not one kite will be there without a mate, for the Lord has said it, and his Spirit will make it all come true. ¹⁷He has surveyed and subdivided the land and deeded it to those doleful creatures; they shall possess it forever, from generation to generation.

35 Streams in the Desert

Even the wilderness and desert will rejoice in those days; the desert will blossom with flowers. ²Yes, there will be an abundance of flowers and singing and joy! The deserts will become as green as the Lebanon mountains, as lovely as Mount Carmel's pastures and Sharon's meadows; for the Lord will display his glory there, the excellency of our God.

³With this news bring cheer to all discouraged ones. ⁴Encourage those who are afraid. Tell them, "Be strong, fear not, for your God is coming to destroy your enemies. He is coming to save you." ⁵And when he comes, he will open the eyes of the blind and unstop the ears of the deaf. ⁶The lame man will leap up like a deer, and those who could not speak will shout and sing! Springs will burst forth in the wilderness, and streams in the desert. ⁷The parched ground will become a pool, with springs of water in the thirsty land. Where desert jackals lived, there will be reeds and rushes!

⁸And a main road will go through that once-deserted land; it will be named "The Holy Highway." No evil-hearted men may walk upon it. God will walk there with you; even the most stupid cannot miss the way. ⁹No lion will lurk along its course, nor will there be any other dangers; only the redeemed will travel there. ¹⁰These, the ransomed of the Lord, will go home along that road to Zion, singing the songs of everlasting joy. For them all sorrow and all sighing will be gone forever; only joy and gladness will be there.

36 An Angel Destroys an Army

So in the fourteenth year of King Hezekiah's reign, Sennacherib, king of Assyria, came to fight against the walled cities of Judah and conquered them. ²Then he sent his personal representative with a great army from Lachish to confer with King Hezekiah in Jerusalem. He camped near the outlet of the upper pool, along the road going past the field where cloth is bleached.

³Then Eliakim, Hilkiah's son, who was the prime minister of Israel, and Shebna, the king's scribe, and Joah, Asaph's son, the royal secretary, formed a truce team and went out of the city to meet with him.

⁴The Assyrian ambassador told them to go and say to Hezekiah, "The mighty king of Assyria says you are a fool to think that the king of Egypt will help you. ⁵What are the Pharaoh's promises worth? Mere words won't substitute for strength, yet you rely on him for help and have rebelled against me! ⁶Egypt is a dangerous ally. She is a sharpened stick that will pierce your hand if you lean on it. That is the experience of everyone who has ever looked to her for help. ⁷But perhaps you say, 'We are trusting in the Lord our God!' Oh? Isn't he the one your king insulted, tearing down his temples and altars in the hills and making everyone in Judah worship only at the altars here in Jerusalem? ⁸,⁹My master, the king of Assyria, wants to make a little bet with you!—that you don't have 2,000 men left in your entire army! If you do, he will give you 2,000 horses for them to ride on! With that tiny army, how can you think of proceeding against even the smallest and worst contingent of my master's troops? For you'll get no help from Egypt. ¹⁰What's more, do you think I have come here without the Lord's telling me to take this land? The Lord said to me, 'Go and destroy it!'"

¹¹Then Eliakim, Shebna, and Joah said to him, "Please talk to us in Aramaic, for we understand it quite well. Don't speak in Hebrew, for the people on the wall will hear."

¹²But he replied, "My master wants everyone in Jerusalem to hear this, not just you. He wants them to know that if you don't surrender, this city will be put under siege until everyone is so hungry and thirsty that he will eat his own dung and drink his own urine."

¹³Then he shouted in Hebrew to the Jews listening on the wall, "Hear the words of the great king, the king of Assyria:

¹⁴"Don't let Hezekiah fool you—nothing he can do will save you. ¹⁵Don't let him talk you into trusting in the Lord by telling you the Lord won't let you be conquered by the king of Assyria. ¹⁶Don't listen to Hezekiah, for here is the king of Assyria's offer to you: Give me a present as a token of surrender; open the gates and come out, and I will let you each have your own farm and garden and water, ¹⁷until I can arrange to take you to a country very similar to this one—a country where there are bountiful harvests of grain and grapes, a land of plenty. ¹⁸Don't let Hezekiah deprive you of all this by saying the Lord will deliver you from my armies. Have any other nation's gods ever gained victory over the armies of the king of Assyria? ¹⁹Don't you remember what I did to Hamath and Arpad? Did their gods save them? And what about Sepharvaim and Samaria? Where are their gods now? ²⁰Of all the gods of these lands, which one has ever delivered their people from my power? Name just one! And do you think this God of yours can deliver Jerusalem from me? Don't be ridiculous!"

²¹But the people were silent and answered not a word, for Hezekiah had told them to say nothing in reply. ²²Then Eliakim (son of Hilkiah), the prime minister, and Shebna, the royal scribe, and Joah (son of Asaph), the royal secretary, went back to Hezekiah with clothes ripped to shreds as a sign of their despair and told him all that had happened.

37

When King Hezekiah heard the results of the meeting, he tore his robes and wound himself in coarse cloth used for making sacks, as a sign of humility and mourning, and went over to the Temple to pray. ²Meanwhile he sent Eliakim his prime minister, and Shebna his royal scribe, and the older priests—all dressed in sackcloth—to Isaiah the prophet, son of Amoz. ³They brought him this message from Hezekiah:

"This is a day of trouble and frustration and blasphemy; it is a serious time, as when a woman is in heavy labor trying to give birth and the child does not come. ⁴But perhaps the Lord your God heard the blasphemy of the king of Assyria's representative as he scoffed at the living God. Surely God won't let him get away with this. Surely God will rebuke him for those words. Oh, Isaiah, pray for us who are left!"

⁵So they took the king's message to Isaiah.

⁶Then Isaiah replied, "Tell King Hezekiah that the Lord says, Don't be disturbed by this speech from the servant of the king of Assyria and his blasphemy. ⁷For a report from Assyria will reach the king that he is needed at home at once, and he will return to his own land, where I will have him killed."

⁸,⁹Now the Assyrian envoy left Jerusalem and went to consult his king, who had left Lachish and was besieging Libnah. But at this point the Assyrian king received word that Tirhakah, crown prince of Ethiopia, was leading an army against him [from the south]. Upon hearing this, he sent messengers back to Jerusalem to Hezekiah with this message:

¹⁰"Don't let this God you trust in fool you by promising that Jerusalem will not be captured by the king of Assyria! ¹¹Just remember what has happened wherever the kings of Assyria have gone, for they have crushed everyone who has opposed them. Do you think you will be any different? ¹²Did their gods save the cities of Gozan, Haran, or Rezeph, or the people of Eden in Telassar? No, the Assyrian kings completely destroyed them! ¹³And don't forget what happened to the king of Hamath, to the king of Arpad, and to the kings of the cities of Sepharvaim, Hena, and Ivvah."

¹⁴As soon as King Hezekiah had read this letter, he went over to the Temple and spread it out before the Lord ¹⁵and prayed, saying, ¹⁶,¹⁷"O Lord, Almighty God of Israel enthroned between the Guardian Angels, *you alone* are God of all the kingdoms of the earth. You alone made heaven and earth. Listen as I

plead; see me as I pray. Look at this letter from King Sennacherib, for he has mocked the living God. ¹⁸It is true, O Lord, that the kings of Assyria have destroyed all those nations, just as the letter says, ¹⁹and thrown their gods into the fire; for they weren't gods at all but merely idols, carved by men from wood and stone. Of course the Assyrians could destroy them. ²⁰O Lord our God, save us so that all the kingdoms of the earth will know that you are God, and you alone."

²¹Then Isaiah, the son of Amoz, sent this message to King Hezekiah: "The Lord God of Israel says, This is my answer to your prayer against Sennacherib, Assyria's king.

²²"The Lord says to him: My people—the helpless virgin daughter of Zion—laughs at you and scoffs and shakes her head at you in scorn. ²³Who is it you scoffed against and mocked? Whom did you revile? At whom did you direct your violence and pride? It was against the Holy One of Israel! ²⁴ You have sent your messengers to mock the Lord. You boast, 'I came with my mighty army against the nations of the west. I cut down the tallest cedars and choicest cypress trees. I conquered their highest mountains and destroyed their thickest forests.'

²⁵"You boast of wells you've dug in many a conquered land, and Egypt with all its armies is no obstacle to you! ²⁶But do you not yet know that it was I who decided all this long ago? That it was I who gave you all this power from ancient times? I have caused all this to happen as I planned—that you should crush walled cities into ruined heaps. ²⁷That's why their people had so little power and were such easy prey for you. They were as helpless as the grass, as tender plants you trample down beneath your feet, as grass upon the housetops, burnt yellow by the sun. ²⁸But I know you well—your comings and goings and all you do—and the way you have raged against me. ²⁹Because of your anger against the Lord—and I heard it all!—I have put a hook in your nose and a bit in your mouth and led you back to your own land by the same road you came."

³⁰Then God said to Hezekiah, "Here is the proof that I am the one who is delivering this city from the king of Assyria: This year he will abandon his siege. Although it is too late now to plant your crops, and you will have only volunteer grain this fall, still it will give you enough seed for a small harvest next year, and two years from now you will be living in luxury again. ³¹And you who are left in Judah will take root again in your own soil and flourish and multiply. ³²For a remnant shall go out from Jerusalem to repopulate the land; the power of the Lord Almighty will cause all this to come to pass.

³³"As for the king of Assyria, his armies shall not enter Jerusalem, nor shoot their arrows there, nor march outside its gates, nor build up an earthen bank against its walls. ³⁴He will return to his own country by the road he came on and will not enter this city, says the Lord. ³⁵For my own honor I will defend it and in memory of my servant David."

³⁶That night the Angel of the Lord went out to the camp of the Assyrians and killed 185,000 soldiers; when the living wakened the next morning, all these lay dead before them. ³⁷Then Sennacherib, king of Assyria, returned to his own country, to Nineveh. ³⁸And one day while he was worshiping in the temple of Nisroch his god, his sons Adrammelech and Sharezer killed him with their swords; then they escaped into the land of Ararat, and Esar-haddon his son became king.

38 A King Asks for a Miracle

It was just before all this that Hezekiah became deathly sick, and Isaiah the prophet (Amoz' son) went to visit him and gave him this message from the Lord:

"Set your affairs in order, for you are going to die; you will not recover from this illness."

²When Hezekiah heard this, he turned his face to the wall and prayed:

³"O Lord, don't you remember how true I've been to you and how I've always tried to obey you in everything you said?" Then he broke down with great sobs.

⁴So the Lord sent another message to Isaiah:

⁵"Go and tell Hezekiah that the Lord God of your forefather David hears you praying and sees your tears and will let you live fifteen more years. ⁶ He will deliver you and this city from the king of Assyria. I will defend you, says the Lord, ⁷and here is my guarantee: ⁸I will send the sun backwards ten degrees as measured on Ahaz' sundial!"

So the sun retraced ten degrees that it had gone down!

⁹When King Hezekiah was well again, he wrote this poem about his experience:

¹⁰"My life is but half done and I must leave it all. I am robbed of my normal years, and now I must enter the gates of Sheol. ¹¹Never again will I see the Lord in the land of the living. Never again will I see my friends in this world. ¹²My life is blown away like a shepherd's tent; it is cut short as when a weaver stops his working at the loom. In one short day my life hangs by a thread.

¹³"All night I moaned; it was like being torn apart by lions. ¹⁴Delirious, I chattered like a swallow and mourned like a dove; my eyes grew weary of looking up for help. 'O God,' I cried, 'I am in trouble—help me.' ¹⁵But what can I say? For he himself has sent this sickness. All my sleep has fled because of my soul's bitterness. ¹⁶O Lord,

Family Devotions

☐ DEVOTION 205
PERSEVERANCE

Read Isaiah 40:25-31

David's mom came into his room to check on his homework. "How's your report coming?" she asked.

"It's not," David barked, "and I don't want to do it anyway!"

"You sound upset, David. Are you still fretting about yesterday?" Mom questioned.

"I wanted to be class reporter for the school paper so bad," he said. "And what did Mrs. French say? 'You have a good imagination, but you don't check facts. A reporter must be accurate. Work on it, David. Maybe you can be a reporter next year.'"

"I know you're disappointed, David, but don't give up," encouraged Mom. "Now, what school report are you working on?"

"I have to write about some famous person," David muttered. "It can be anybody."

"I know who will be a real help to you! Come with me. Let's look in the encyclopedia." David's mother helped him find some books. Then she left to fold clothes.

When Mother returned, David looked up. "I can't believe it, Mom," he said. "Abraham Lincoln was one of our greatest presidents, but this book says he lost several important political races!"

"That's right." Mom nodded. "But he's remembered for his successes, not for his failures. Often it's easy to give up when we fail, but we don't grow that way. It's not what God would have us do either. He wants us to learn from our experiences and to try harder the next time. We must learn to depend on him to help us turn failure into success."

David gave his mom a big hug. "Thanks, Mom," he said. "I'll make this report so accurate that even Mrs. French would be proud of it."

Perseverance Memory Verse

Be strong and courageous and get to work. Don't be frightened by the size of the task, for the Lord my God is with you; he will not forsake you. He will see to it that everything is finished correctly.
1 Chronicles 28:20

How About You?
What happens when you fail at something? Do you give up and quit trying? Don't get discouraged. Learn from your mistakes and realize that it takes time to learn to do things well. Depend on God to help you. *J. H.*

• For the next devotional, turn to page 693.   • For the next devotional on PERSEVERANCE, turn to page 1209.
• For notes on PERSEVERANCE, see pages 326, 461, 503, 760, and 1174.

your discipline is good and leads to life and health. Oh, heal me and make me live!

¹⁷"Yes, now I see it all—it was good for me to undergo this bitterness, for you have lovingly delivered me from death; you have forgiven all my sins. ¹⁸For dead men cannot praise you. They cannot be filled with hope and joy. ¹⁹The living, only the living, can praise you as I do today. One generation makes known your faithfulness to the next. ²⁰Think of it! The Lord healed me! Every day of my life from now on I will sing my songs of praise in the Temple, accompanied by the orchestra."

²¹(For Isaiah had told Hezekiah's servants, "Make an ointment of figs and spread it over the boil, and he will get well again."

²²And then Hezekiah had asked, "What sign will the Lord give me to prove that he will heal me?")

39 Messengers from Babylon

Soon afterwards, the king of Babylon (Merodach-baladan, the son of Baladan) sent Hezekiah a present and his best wishes, for he had heard that Hezekiah had been very sick and now was well again. ²Hezekiah appreciated this and took the envoys from Babylon on a tour of the palace, showing them his treasure house full of silver, gold, spices, and perfumes. He took them into his jewel rooms, too, and opened to them all his treasures—everything.

³Then Isaiah the prophet came to the king and said, "What did they say? Where are they from?"

"From far away in Babylon," Hezekiah replied.

⁴"How much have they seen?" asked Isaiah.

And Hezekiah replied, "I showed them everything I own, all my priceless treasures."

⁵Then Isaiah said to him, "Listen to this message from the Lord Almighty:

⁶"The time is coming when everything you have—all the treasures stored up by your fathers—will be carried off to Babylon. Nothing will be left. ⁷And some of your own sons will become slaves, yes, eunuchs, in the palace of the king of Babylon."

⁸"All right," Hezekiah replied. "Whatever the Lord says is good. At least there will be peace during my lifetime!"

40 God Will Feed His Flock

"Comfort, yes, comfort my people," says your God. ²"Speak tenderly to Jerusalem and tell her that her sad days are gone. Her sins are pardoned, and I have punished her in full for all her sins."

³Listen! I hear the voice of someone shouting, "Make a road for the Lord through the wilderness; make him a straight, smooth road through the desert. ⁴Fill the valleys; level the hills; straighten out the crooked paths, and smooth off the rough spots in the road. ⁵The glory of the Lord will be seen by all mankind together." The Lord has spoken—it shall be.

⁶The voice says, "Shout!"

"What shall I shout?" I asked.

"Shout that man is like the grass that dies away, and all his beauty fades like dying flowers. ⁷The grass withers, the flower fades beneath the breath of God. And so it is with fragile man. ⁸The grass withers, the flowers fade, but the Word of our God shall stand forever."

⁹O Crier of good news, shout to Jerusalem from the mountaintops! Shout louder—don't be afraid—tell the cities of Judah, "Your God is coming!" ¹⁰ Yes, the Lord God is coming with mighty power; he will rule with awesome strength. See, his reward is with him, to each as he has done. ¹¹ He will feed his flock like a shepherd; he will carry the lambs in his arms and gently lead the ewes with young.

¹²Who else has held the oceans in his hands and measured off the heavens with his ruler? Who else knows the weight of all the earth and weighs the mountains and the hills? ¹³Who can advise the Spirit of the Lord or be his teacher or give him counsel? ¹⁴Has he ever needed anyone's advice? Did he need instruction as to what is right and best? ¹⁵No, for all the peoples of the world are nothing in comparison with him—they are but a drop in the bucket, dust on the scales. He picks up the islands as though they had no weight at all. ¹⁶All of Lebanon's forests do not contain sufficient fuel to consume a sacrifice large enough to honor him, nor are all its animals enough to offer to our God. ¹⁷All the nations are as nothing to him; in his eyes they are less than nothing—mere emptiness and froth.

¹⁸How can we describe God? With what can we compare him? ¹⁹With an idol? An idol made from a mold, overlaid with gold, and with silver chains around its neck? ²⁰The man too poor to buy expensive gods like that will find a tree free from rot and hire a man to carve a face on it, and that's his god—a god that cannot even move!

²¹Are you so ignorant? Are you so deaf to the words of God—the words he gave before the world began? Have you never heard nor understood? ²² It is God who sits above the circle of the earth. (The people below must seem to him like grasshoppers!) He is the one who stretches out the heavens like a curtain and makes his tent from them. ²³He dooms the great men of the world and brings them all to naught. ²⁴They hardly get started, barely take root, when he blows on them and their work withers, and the wind carries them off like straw.

²⁵"With whom will you compare me? Who is my equal?" asks the Holy One.

FAMILY DEVOTIONS

☐ DEVOTION 206
OVERCOMING FEAR

Read Isaiah 41:8-10, 13

Cindy was afraid of the dark and of being alone. Sometimes her brother, Dave, would deliberately play tricks on her—tricks he knew would frighten her. *She's got to get over being afraid,* he thought, *and she will if I tease her about it.* But Cindy's continuing screams indicated that it wasn't working.

One day, after one of Dave's tricks, Dad asked him if he was afraid of anything. "Well, hornets, I guess," Dave answered.

"Do you think you'll get over your fear if someone sends hornets at you until you stop screaming?" asked Dad.

"But Dad, hornets can hurt you," David defended himself. "The dark can't."

"Then tell Cindy that the dark won't hurt her. Don't terrify her!" said Dad. He turned to Cindy. "Real courage comes from God. When we're in real danger, we must trust God to take care of us, and he will help us face it."

As Mother tucked her in bed that night, Cindy asked, "Will you stay with me for a while?"

"Yes," agreed Mother. "I will." Ten minutes after the light was turned out, Mother asked, "Are you asleep?"

"No," murmured Cindy.

"Are you afraid?" asked Mother.

"No."

"Why not?"

"Because you're here," said Cindy.

"You can't see me in the dark, so how did you know I was here?" asked Mother.

"You said you would stay," explained Cindy, "so I knew you would."

"You know, Cindy," said Mother, "God says in the Bible that we don't need to be afraid because he will never leave us. He doesn't lie. Even when we can't see him, we can believe him. We can know he is with us—just because he said he would be."

Overcoming Fear Memory Verse

Fear not, for I am with you. Do not be dismayed. I am your God. I will strengthen you; I will help you; I will uphold you with my victorious right hand.
Isaiah 41:10

How About You?
Do you trust God to take care of you? There are many verses in the Bible that tell you not to be afraid, such as the verse below. Learn some of these verses and believe them when something frightens you. *A. G. L.*

• For the next devotional, turn to page 695.   • For the next devotional on OVERCOMING FEAR, turn to page 939.
• For notes on OVERCOMING FEAR, see pages 191, 482, 554, 592, and 912.

²⁶Look up into the heavens! Who created all these stars? As a shepherd leads his sheep, calling each by its pet name, and counts them to see that none are lost or strayed, so God does with stars and planets!

²⁷O Jacob, O Israel, how can you say that the Lord doesn't see your troubles and isn't being fair? ²⁸Don't you yet understand? Don't you know by now that the everlasting God, the Creator of the farthest parts of the earth, never grows faint or weary? No one can fathom the depths of his understanding. ²⁹He gives power to the tired and worn out, and strength to the weak. ³⁰Even the youths shall be exhausted, and the young men will all give up. ³¹But they that wait upon the Lord shall renew their strength. They shall mount up with wings like eagles; they shall run and not be weary; they shall walk and not faint.

41 Don't Be Afraid, Israel!

Listen in silence before me, O lands beyond the sea. Bring your strongest arguments. Come now and speak. The court is ready for your case.

²Who has stirred up this one from the east, whom victory meets at every step? Who, indeed, but the Lord? God has given him victory over many nations and permitted him to trample kings underfoot and to put entire armies to the sword. ³He chases them away and goes on safely, though the paths he treads are new. ⁴Who has done such mighty deeds, directing the affairs of generations of mankind as they march by? It is I, the Lord, the First and Last; I alone am he.

⁵The lands beyond the sea watch in fear and wait for word of Cyrus' new campaigns. Remote lands tremble and mobilize for war. ⁶,⁷The craftsmen encourage each other as they rush to make new idols to protect them. The carver hurries the goldsmith, and the molder helps at the anvil. "Good," they say. "It's coming along fine. Now we can solder on the arms." Carefully they join the parts together and then fasten the thing in place so it won't fall over!

⁸But as for you, O Israel, you are mine, my chosen ones; for you are Abraham's family, and he was my friend. ⁹I have called you back from the ends of the earth and said that you must serve but me alone, for I have chosen you and will not throw you away. ¹⁰Fear not, for I am with you. Do not be dismayed. I am your God. I will strengthen you; I will help you; I will uphold you with my victorious right hand.

¹¹See, all your angry enemies lie confused and shattered. Anyone opposing you will die. ¹²You will look for them in vain—they will all be gone. ¹³I am holding you by your right hand—I, the Lord your God—and I say to you, Don't be afraid; I am here to help you. ¹⁴Despised though you are, fear not, O Israel; for I will help you. I am the Lord, your Redeemer; I am the Holy One of Israel. ¹⁵You shall be a new and sharp-toothed threshing instrument to tear all enemies apart, making chaff of mountains. ¹⁶You shall toss them in the air; the wind shall blow them all away; whirlwinds shall scatter them. And the joy of the Lord shall fill you full; you shall glory in the God of Israel.

¹⁷When the poor and needy seek water and there is none, and their tongues are parched from thirst, then I will answer when they cry to me. I, Israel's God, will not ever forsake them. ¹⁸I will open up rivers for them on high plateaus! I will give them fountains of water in the valleys! In the deserts will be pools of water, and rivers fed by springs shall flow across the dry, parched ground. ¹⁹I will plant trees—cedars, myrtle, olive trees, the cypress, fir and pine—on barren land. ²⁰Everyone will see this miracle and understand that it is God who did it, Israel's Holy One.

²¹Can your idols make such claims as these? Let them come and show what they can do! says God, the King of Israel. ²²Let them try to tell us what occurred in years gone by or what the future holds. ²³Yes, that's it! If you are gods, tell what will happen in the days ahead! Or do some mighty miracle that makes us stare, amazed. ²⁴But no! You are less than nothing and can do nothing at all. Anyone who chooses you needs to have his head examined!

²⁵But I have stirred up (Cyrus) from the north and east; he will come against the nations and call on my name, and I will give him victory over kings and princes. He will tread them as a potter tramples clay.

²⁶Who but I have told you this would happen? Who else predicted this, making you admit that he was right? No one else! None other said one word! ²⁷I was the first to tell Jerusalem, "Look! Look! Help is on the way!" ²⁸Not one of your idols told you this. Not one gave any answer when I asked. ²⁹See, they are all foolish, worthless things; your idols are all as empty as the wind.

42 God's Chosen One

See my servant, whom I uphold; my Chosen One in whom I delight. I have put my Spirit upon him; he will reveal justice to the nations of the world. ²He will be gentle—he will not shout nor quarrel in the streets. ³He will not break the bruised reed, nor quench the dimly burning flame. He will encourage the fainthearted, those tempted to despair. He will see full justice given to all who have been wronged. ⁴He won't be satisfied until truth and righteousness prevail throughout the earth, nor until even distant lands beyond the seas have put their trust in him.

FAMILY DEVOTIONS

☐ DEVOTION 207
HUMILITY

Read Isaiah 42:5-12

"We'll all be late for church if Beth doesn't hurry up," complained Peter. "She takes forever to fix her hair!"

Finally they were on their way. "Dad!" cried Beth, "make Peter close his window. The wind makes my hair a mess."

Before going into the church service, Beth went to comb her hair again. Peter, Mom, and Dad sat down. Mom and Dad frowned as she tiptoed into the pew during the first hymn.

After church that night, Peter got out a magnifying glass. "It's fun to look at stuff under this," he said. "It really makes everything look big."

Observing them, Dad wrote something on two small pieces of paper, which he placed on the table with some other things Peter had lined up to look at. He watched as Peter put the first paper under the magnifying glass. Peter looked at it and shrugged. Then Beth looked. "Why did you write *God* on the paper for us to see?" she asked her father.

"Because God should be magnified," explained Dad. "Whoa, there," he added as Peter picked up the second piece of paper. "Don't put that one under your glass, Son. It's not supposed to be magnified."

Peter read it and handed it to his sister. Written in small letters was the word *me*.

"You see," continued Dad, "sometimes we tend to magnify ourselves instead of God. If we do that, we might spend too much time on appearance."

"Yeah," broke in Peter with a grin, "we comb our hair all the time and make everybody late for church."

"On the other hand," said Dad, "when we magnify God instead, we try to please him in our behavior, and we don't point the finger at someone else."

Humility Memory Verse

For everyone who tries to honor himself shall be humbled; and he who humbles himself shall be honored.
Luke 14:11

How About You?
Do you spend too much time in front of your mirror? God wants you to look neat, clean, and as attractive as possible, but remember that real beauty is seen in actions more than in appearance. *H. A. D.*

- For the next devotional, turn to page 699. • For the next devotional on *HUMILITY*, turn to page 823.
- For notes on *HUMILITY*, see pages 57, 390, 428, 854, and 1228.

⁵The Lord God who created the heavens and stretched them out, who created the earth and everything in it, who gives life and breath and spirit to everyone in all the world, he is the one who says [to his Servant, the Messiah],

⁶"I the Lord have called you to demonstrate my righteousness. I will guard and support you, for I have given you to my people as the personal confirmation of my covenant with them. You shall also be a light to guide the nations unto me. ⁷You will open the eyes of the blind and release those who sit in prison darkness and despair. ⁸I am the Lord! That is my name, and I will not give my glory to anyone else; I will not share my praise with carved idols. ⁹Everything I prophesied came true, and now I will prophesy again. I will tell you the future before it happens."

¹⁰Sing a new song to the Lord; sing his praises, all you who live in earth's remotest corners! Sing, O sea! Sing, all you who live in distant lands beyond the sea! ¹¹Join in the chorus, you desert cities—Kedar and Sela! And you, too, dwellers in the mountaintops. ¹²Let the western coastlands glorify the Lord and sing his mighty power.

¹³The Lord will be a mighty warrior, full of fury toward his foes. He will give a great shout and prevail. ¹⁴Long has he been silent; he has restrained himself. But now he will give full vent to his wrath; he will groan and cry like a woman delivering her child. ¹⁵He will level the mountains and hills and blight their greenery. He will dry up the rivers and pools. ¹⁶He will bring blind Israel along a path they have not seen before. He will make the darkness bright before them and smooth and straighten out the road ahead. He will not forsake them. ¹⁷But those who trust in idols and call them gods will be greatly disappointed; they will be turned away.

¹⁸Oh, how blind and deaf you are toward God! Why won't you listen? Why won't you see? ¹⁹Who in all the world is as blind as my own people, who are designed to be my messengers of truth? Who is so blind as my "dedicated one," the "servant of the Lord"? ²⁰You see and understand what is right but won't heed nor do it; you hear, but you won't listen.

²¹The Lord has magnified his law and made it truly glorious. Through it he had planned to show the world that he is righteous. ²²But what a sight his people are—these who were to demonstrate to all the world the glory of his law; for they are robbed, enslaved, imprisoned, trapped, fair game for all, with no one to protect them. ²³Won't even one of you apply these lessons from the past and see the ruin that awaits you up ahead? ²⁴Who let Israel be robbed and hurt? Did not the Lord? It is the Lord they sinned against, for they would not go where he sent them nor listen to his laws.

²⁵That is why God poured out such fury and wrath on his people and destroyed them in battle. Yet, though set on fire and burned, they will not understand the reason why—that it is God, wanting them to repent.

43 No Other Savior

But now the Lord who created you, O Israel, says, Don't be afraid, for I have ransomed you; I have called you by name; you are mine. ²When you go through deep waters and great trouble, I will be with you. When you go through rivers of difficulty, you will not drown! When you walk through the fire of oppression, you will not be burned up—the flames will not consume you. ³For I am the Lord your God, your Savior, the Holy One of Israel. I gave Egypt and Ethiopia and Seba [to Cyrus] in exchange for your freedom, as your ransom. ⁴Others died that you might live; I traded their lives for yours because you are precious to me and honored, and I love you.

⁵Don't be afraid, for I am with you. I will gather you from east and west, ⁶from north and south. I will bring my sons and daughters back to Israel from the farthest corners of the earth. ⁷All who claim me as their God will come, for I have made them for my glory; I created them. ⁸Bring them back to me—blind as they are and deaf when I call (although they see and hear!).

⁹Gather the nations together! Which of all their idols ever has foretold such things? Which can predict a single day ahead? Where are the witnesses of anything they said? If there are no witnesses, then they must confess that only God can prophesy.

¹⁰But I have witnesses, O Israel, says the Lord! You are my witnesses and my servants, chosen to know and to believe me and to understand that I alone am God. There is no other God; there never was and never will be. ¹¹I am the Lord, and there is no other Savior. ¹²Whenever you have thrown away your idols, I have shown you my power. With one word I have saved you. You have seen me do it; you are my witnesses that it is true. ¹³From eternity to eternity I am God. No one can oppose what I do.

¹⁴The Lord, your Redeemer, the Holy One of Israel, says:

For your sakes I will send an invading army against Babylon that will walk in, almost unscathed. The boasts of the Babylonians will turn to cries of fear. ¹⁵I am the Lord, your Holy One, Israel's Creator and King. ¹⁶I am the Lord, who opened a way through the waters, making a path right through the sea. ¹⁷I called forth the mighty army of Egypt with all its chariots and horses, to lie beneath the waves, dead, their lives snuffed out like candlewicks.

18But forget all that—it is nothing compared to what I'm going to do! 19For I'm going to do a brand new thing. See, I have already begun! Don't you see it? I will make a road through the wilderness of the world for my people to go home, and create rivers for them in the desert! 20The wild animals in the fields will thank me, the jackals and ostriches too, for giving them water in the wilderness, yes, springs in the desert, so that my people, my chosen ones, can be refreshed. 21I have made Israel for myself, and these my people will some day honor me before the world.

22But O my people, you won't ask my help; you have grown tired of me! 23You have not brought me the lambs for burnt offerings; you have not honored me with sacrifices. Yet my requests for offerings and incense have been very few! I have not treated you as slaves. 24You have brought me no sweet-smelling incense nor pleased me with the sacrificial fat. No, you have presented me only with sins and wearied me with all your faults.

25I, yes, I alone am he who blots away your sins for my own sake and will never think of them again. 26Oh, remind me of this promise of forgiveness, for we must talk about your sins. Plead your case for my forgiving you. 27From the very first your ancestors sinned against me—all your forebears transgressed my law. 28That is why I have deposed your priests and destroyed Israel, leaving her to shame.

44 Idols Are False Gods

Listen to me, O my servant Israel, O my chosen ones:

2The Lord who made you, who will help you, says, O servant of mine, don't be afraid. O Jerusalem, my chosen ones, don't be afraid. 3For I will give you abundant water for your thirst and for your parched fields. And I will pour out my Spirit and my blessings on your children. 4They shall thrive like watered grass, like willows on a riverbank. 5"I am the Lord's," they'll proudly say, or, "I am a Jew," and tattoo upon their hands the name of God or the honored name of Israel.

6The Lord, the King of Israel, says—yes, it is Israel's Redeemer, the Lord Almighty, who says it—I am the First and Last; there is no other God. 7Who else can tell you what is going to happen in the days ahead? Let them tell you if they can and prove their power. Let them do as I have done since ancient times. 8Don't, don't be afraid. Haven't I proclaimed from ages past [that I would save you]? You are my witnesses—is there any other God? No! None that I know about! There is no other Rock!

9What fools they are who manufacture idols for their gods. Their hopes remain unanswered. They themselves are witnesses that this is so, for their idols neither see nor know. No wonder those who worship them are so ashamed. 10Who but a fool would make his own god—an idol that can help him not one whit! 11All that worship these will stand before the Lord in shame, along with all these carpenters—mere men—who claim that they have made a god. Together they will stand in terror. 12The metalsmith stands at his forge to make an axe, pounding on it with all his might. He grows hungry and thirsty, weak and faint. 13Then the woodcarver takes the axe and uses it to make an idol. He measures and marks out a block of wood and carves the figure of a man. Now he has a wonderful idol that can't so much as move from where it is placed. 14He cuts down cedars, he selects the cypress and the oak, he plants the ash in the forest to be nourished by the rain. 15And after his care, he uses part of the wood to make a fire to warm himself and bake his bread, and then—he really does—he takes the rest of it and makes himself a god—a god for men to worship! An idol to fall down before and praise! 16Part of the tree he burns to roast his meat and to keep him warm and fed and well content, 17and with what's left he makes his god: a carved idol! He falls down before it and worships it and prays to it. "Deliver me," he says. "You are my god!"

18Such stupidity and ignorance! God has shut their eyes so that they cannot see and closed their minds from understanding. 19The man never stops to think or figure out, "Why, it's just a block of wood! I've burned it for heat and used it to bake my bread and roast my meat. How can the rest of it be a god? Should I fall down before a chunk of wood?" 20The poor, deluded fool feeds on ashes; he is trusting what can never give him any help at all. Yet he cannot bring himself to ask, "Is this thing, this idol that I'm holding in my hand, a lie?"

21Pay attention, Israel, for you are my servant; I made you, and I will not forget to help you. 22I've blotted out your sins; they are gone like morning mist at noon! Oh, return to me, for I have paid the price to set you free.

23Sing, O heavens, for the Lord has done this wondrous thing. Shout, O earth; break forth into song, O mountains and forests, yes, and every tree; for the Lord redeemed Jacob and is glorified in Israel! 24The Lord, your Redeemer who made you, says, All things were made by me; I alone stretched out the heavens. By myself I made the earth and everything in it.

25I am the one who shows what liars all false

prophets are, by causing something else to happen than the things they say. I make wise men give opposite advice to what they should and make them into fools. ²⁶But what my prophets say, I do; when they say Jerusalem will be delivered and the cities of Judah lived in once again—it shall be done! ²⁷When I speak to the rivers and say, "Be dry!" they shall be dry. ²⁸When I say of Cyrus, "He is my shepherd," he will certainly do as I say; and Jerusalem will be rebuilt and the Temple restored, for I have spoken it.

45 The One, True God

This is Jehovah's message to Cyrus, God's anointed, whom he has chosen to conquer many lands. God shall empower his right hand, and he shall crush the strength of mighty kings. God shall open the gates of Babylon to him; the gates shall not be shut against him any more. ²I will go before you, Cyrus, and level the mountains and smash down the city gates of brass and iron bars. ³And I will give you treasures hidden in the darkness, secret riches; and you will know that I am doing this—I, the Lord, the God of Israel, the one who calls you by your name.

⁴And why have I named you for this work? For the sake of Jacob, my servant—Israel, my chosen. I called you by name when you didn't know me. ⁵I am Jehovah; there is no other God. I will strengthen you and send you out to victory even though you don't know me,⁶and all the world from east to west will know there is no other God. I am Jehovah and there is no one else. I alone am God. ⁷I form the light and make the dark. I send good times and bad. I, Jehovah, am he who does these things. ⁸Open up, O heavens. Let the skies pour out their righteousness. Let salvation and righteousness sprout up together from the earth. I, Jehovah, created them.

⁹Woe to the man who fights with his Creator. Does the pot argue with its maker? Does the clay dispute with him who forms it, saying, "Stop, you're doing it wrong!" or the pot exclaim, "How clumsy can you be!"? ¹⁰Woe to the baby just being born who squalls to his father and mother, "Why have you produced me? Can't you do anything right at all?"

¹¹Jehovah, the Holy One of Israel, Israel's Creator, says: What right have you to question what I do? Who are you to command me concerning the work of my hands? ¹²I have made the earth and created man upon it. With my hands I have stretched out the heavens and commanded all the vast myriads of stars. ¹³I have raised up Cyrus to fulfill my righteous purpose, and I will direct all his paths. He shall restore my city and free my captive people—and not for a reward!

¹⁴Jehovah says: The Egyptians, Ethiopians, and Sabeans shall be subject to you. They shall come to you with all their merchandise, and it shall all be yours. They shall follow you as prisoners in chains and fall down on their knees before you and say, "The only God there is, is your God!"

¹⁵Truly, O God of Israel, Savior, you work in strange, mysterious ways. ¹⁶All who worship idols shall be disappointed and ashamed. ¹⁷But Israel shall be saved by Jehovah with eternal salvation; they shall never be disappointed in their God through all eternity. ¹⁸For Jehovah created the heavens and earth and put everything in place, and he made the world to be lived in, not to be an empty chaos. I am Jehovah, he says, and there is no other! ¹⁹I publicly proclaim bold promises; I do not whisper obscurities in some dark corner so that no one can know what I mean. And I didn't tell Israel to ask me for what I didn't plan to give! No, for I, Jehovah, speak only truth and righteousness.

²⁰Gather together and come, you nations that escape from Cyrus' hand. What fools they are who carry around the wooden idols and pray to gods that cannot save! ²¹Consult together, argue your case and state your proofs that idol-worship pays! Who but God has said that these things concerning Cyrus would come true? What idol ever told you they would happen? For there is no other God but me—a just God and a Savior—no, not one! ²²Let all the world look to me for salvation! For I am God; there is no other. ²³I have sworn by myself, and I will never go back on my word, for it is true—that every knee in all the world shall bow to me, and every tongue shall swear allegiance to my name.

²⁴"In Jehovah is all my righteousness and strength," the people shall declare. And all who were angry with him shall come to him and be ashamed. ²⁵In Jehovah all the generations of Israel shall be justified, triumphant.

46 Who Can Compare to God?

The idols of Babylon, Bel and Nebo, are being hauled away on ox carts! But look! The beasts are stumbling! The cart is turning over! The gods are falling out onto the ground! Is that the best that they can do? If they cannot even save themselves from such a fall, how can they save their worshipers from Cyrus?

³"Listen to me, all Israel who are left; I have created you and cared for you since you were born. ⁴I will be your God through all your lifetime, yes, even when your hair is white with age. I made you and I will care for you. I will carry you along and be your Savior.

⁵"With what in all of heaven and earth do I

FAMILY DEVOTIONS

☐ DEVOTION 208
RESPECTING OTHERS

Read Isaiah 46:3-4

Charles ran into the house and slammed the front door. "Mom!" he called. "Is it true, what Betty said? Is Grandpa coming to visit again?"

"Yes, your sister is right," replied Mom. "Dad is going to get Grandpa on Saturday morning. You can probably go along if you like." She sighed. "My watch is broken, and I was hoping one of my old ones would still work. Look, Charles." She held up a small, gold wristwatch. "This is my high-school graduation present from Grandpa and Grandma. This one with the leather strap was my official nurse's watch. And this lovely one I wear now—Dad bought this for me on our first wedding anniversary. And now it won't run, either!"

Charles nodded, but he went back to the matter at hand. "I don't want to go get Grandpa," he whined. "Why does he have to come again? He spills things and talks funny. Why can't he just stay home?"

"I thought you loved Grandpa," Mom said quietly.

"I do," Charles said, "or I did before he had that stroke. He used to do stuff with me. Now he just sits around and . . . gets in the way."

Mom looked at the watches on the table. "These bring back precious memories of happy times, but none of them will run," she said. "I'm fond of them and hate to throw them out, but at least they don't have feelings. But people do." Charles looked at the floor. He knew she meant Grandpa. "My heart is full of memories of growing up with Grandpa and Grandma," added Mom. "Grandma is in heaven now, and age and illness have injured Grandpa. But he is still my father. I don't want to throw him out. I love him too much."

Charles hugged his mother. "I don't want to throw him out, either. I'll go with Dad to get him."

Respecting Others Memory Verse

You must love the Lord your God with all your heart, and with all your soul, and with all your strength, and with all your mind. And you must love your neighbor just as much as you love yourself.
Luke 10:27

How About You?

Do you value older people? Never throw them away just because they can't do all the things they once could. Use every opportunity to show them that you do love and appreciate them. As you give yourself to them, you'll be surprised to find how much you still get back in return. *B. K.*

- For the next devotional, turn to page 701.   • For the next devotional on RESPECTING OTHERS, turn to page 1137.
- For notes on RESPECTING OTHERS, see pages 322, 382, 1088, and 1218.

compare? Whom can you find who equals me? ⁶Will you compare me with an idol made lavishly with silver and with gold? They hire a goldsmith to take your wealth and make a god from it! Then they fall down and worship it! ⁷They carry it around on their shoulders, and when they set it down, it stays there, for it cannot move! And when someone prays to it, there is no answer, for it cannot get him out of his trouble.

⁸"Don't forget this, O guilty ones. ⁹And don't forget the many times I clearly told you what was going to happen in the future. For I am God—I only—and there is no other like me ¹⁰who can tell you what is going to happen. All I say will come to pass, for I do whatever I wish. ¹¹I will call that swift bird of prey from the east—that man Cyrus from far away. And he will come and do my bidding. I have said I would do it and I will. ¹²Listen to me, you stubborn, evil men! ¹³For I am offering you my deliverance; not in the distant future, but right now! I am ready to save you, and I will restore Jerusalem and Israel, who is my glory.

47 God's Revenge

"O Babylon, the unconquered, come sit in the dust; for your days of glory, pomp, and honor are ended. O daughter of Chaldea, never again will you be the lovely princess, tender and delicate. ²Take heavy millstones and grind the corn; remove your veil; strip off your robe; expose yourself to public view. ³You shall be in nakedness and shame. I will take vengeance upon you and will not repent."

⁴So speaks our Redeemer, who will save Israel from Babylon's mighty power; the Lord Almighty is his name, the Holy One of Israel.

⁵Sit in darkness and silence, O Babylon; never again will you be called "The Queen of Kingdoms." ⁶For I was angry with my people Israel and began to punish them a little by letting them fall into your hands, O Babylon. But you showed them no mercy. You have made even the old folks carry heavy burdens. ⁷You thought your reign would never end, Queen Kingdom of the world. You didn't care a whit about my people or think about the fate of those who do them harm.

⁸O pleasure-mad kingdom, living at ease, bragging as the greatest in the world—listen to the sentence of my court upon your sins. You say, "I alone am God! I'll never be a widow; I'll never lose my children." ⁹Well, those two things shall come upon you in one moment, in full measure in one day: widowhood and the loss of your children, despite all your witchcraft and magic.

¹⁰You felt secure in all your wickedness. "No one sees me," you said. Your "wisdom" and "knowledge" have caused you to turn away from me and claim that you yourself are Jehovah. ¹¹That is why disaster shall overtake you suddenly—so suddenly that you won't know where it comes from. And there will be no atonement then to cleanse away your sins.

¹²Call out the demon hordes you've worshiped all these years. Call on them to help you strike deep terror into many hearts again. ¹³You have advisors by the ton—your astrologers and stargazers, who try to tell you what the future holds. ¹⁴But they are as useless as dried grass burning in the fire. They cannot even deliver themselves! You'll get no help from them at all. Theirs is no fire to sit beside to make you warm! ¹⁵And all your friends of childhood days shall slip away and disappear, unable to help.

48 No Peace for the Wicked

Hear me, my people: you swear allegiance to the Lord without meaning a word of it when you boast of living in the Holy City and brag about depending on the God of Israel. ³Time and again I told you what was going to happen in the future. My words were scarcely spoken when suddenly I did just what I said. ⁴I knew how hard and obstinate you are. Your necks are as unbending as iron; you are as hardheaded as brass. ⁵That is why I told you ahead of time what I was going to do, so that you could never say, "My idol did it; my carved image commanded it to happen!" ⁶You have heard my predictions and seen them fulfilled, but you refuse to agree it is so. Now I will tell you new things I haven't mentioned before, secrets you haven't heard.

⁷Then you can't say, "We knew that all the time!"

⁸Yes, I'll tell you things entirely new, for I know so well what traitors you are, rebels from earliest childhood, rotten through and through. ⁹Yet for my own sake and for the honor of my name I will hold back my anger and not wipe you out. ¹⁰I refined you in the furnace of affliction, but found no silver there. You are worthless, with nothing good in you at all. ¹¹Yet for my own sake—yes, *for my own sake*—I will save you from my anger and not destroy you lest the heathen say their gods have conquered me. I will not let them have my glory.

¹²Listen to me, my people, my chosen ones! I alone am God. I am the First; I am the Last. ¹³It was my hand that laid the foundations of the earth; the palm of my right hand spread out the heavens above; I spoke and they came into being.

¹⁴Come, all of you, and listen. Among all your idols, which one has ever told you this: "The Lord loves Cyrus. He will use him to put an end to the

FAMILY DEVOTIONS

☐ DEVOTION 209

LEAVING THE FUTURE IN GOD'S HANDS

Read Isaiah 47:1-14

"Mom, Linda told me I'm a Taurus!" exclaimed Jenny as she burst through the front door. "Her mother says the stars can tell us all about ourselves and advise us about what we should do according to what day we were born. She says we can read the horoscope in the paper every day to find out what the stars say."

Jenny's mother looked up. "And does it make sense to you to believe that the stars have power over a person's life?" she asked. "Does it make sense for people to have to wait until the newspaper arrives to find out what the stars advise them to do that day?"

Jenny thought about that. She remembered a girl at summer camp who'd always worn a rabbit's foot on her belt, even to go swimming. She had believed it would bring her luck, until another little girl had asked, "How much luck can a foot bring? Look what happened to the rabbit, and he had four of them!" Believing in the power of the stars to direct her life, Jenny decided, made about as much sense as believing in a rabbit's foot.

Jenny glanced at the family Bible lying on a nearby shelf. "Linda may say I was born under the sign of Taurus," she said, "but I've been born again, haven't I?" She smiled at her mother.

"That's right, honey," her mother agreed, returning the smile. "You're a Christian, not a Taurus. You have Jesus in your life. He's more powerful than any star—he made them! And we don't have to wait for the newspaper. We have God's Word to tell us how to live."

Leaving the Future in God's Hands
Memory Verse

For I know the plans I have for you, says the Lord. They are plans for good and not for evil, to give you a future and a hope.
Jeremiah 29:11

How About You?

Do you ever find yourself avoiding the cracks in the sidewalk? Crossing the street to dodge a black cat? Reading the horoscope section of the paper? Astrology and superstition have no place in Christianity. Rid your life of these things. God hates them! L. B. M.

• For the next devotional, turn to page 703.   • For the next devotional on LEAVING THE FUTURE IN GOD'S HANDS, turn to page 747.   • For notes on LEAVING THE FUTURE IN GOD'S HANDS, see pages 405, 452, 831, and 1061.

empire of Babylonia. He will utterly rout the armies of the Chaldeans"? ¹⁵But I am saying it. I have called Cyrus; I have sent him on this errand, and I will prosper him.

¹⁶Come closer and listen. I have always told you plainly what would happen, so that you could clearly understand. And now the Lord God and his Spirit have sent me (with this message):

¹⁷The Lord, your Redeemer, the Holy One of Israel, says, I am the Lord your God, who punishes you for your own good and leads you along the paths that you should follow.

¹⁸Oh, that you had listened to my laws! Then you would have had peace flowing like a gentle river, and great waves of righteousness. ¹⁹Then you would have become as numerous as the sands along the seashores of the world, too many to count, and there would have been no need for your destruction.

²⁰Yet even now, be free from your captivity! Leave Babylon, singing as you go; shout to the ends of the earth that the Lord has redeemed his servants, the Jews. ²¹They were not thirsty when he led them through the deserts; he divided the rock, and water gushed out for them to drink. ²²But there is no peace, says the Lord, for the wicked.

49 A Light for the World

Listen to me, all of you in far-off lands: The Lord called me before my birth. From within the womb he called me by my name. ²God will make my words of judgment sharp as swords. He has hidden me in the shadow of his hand; I am like a sharp arrow in his quiver.

³He said to me: "You are my Servant, a Prince of Power with God, and you shall bring me glory."

⁴I replied, "But my work for them seems all in vain; I have spent my strength for them without response. Yet I leave it all with God for my reward."

⁵"And now," said the Lord—the Lord who formed me from my mother's womb to serve him who commissioned me to restore to him his people Israel, who has given me the strength to perform this task and honored me for doing it!— ⁶"you shall do more than restore Israel to me. I will make you a Light to the nations of the world to bring my salvation to them too."

⁷The Lord, the Redeemer and Holy One of Israel, says to the One who is despised, rejected by mankind, and kept beneath the heel of the world's rulers: "Kings shall stand at attention when you pass by; princes shall bow low because the Lord has chosen you; he, the faithful Lord, the Holy One of Israel, chooses you."

⁸,⁹The Lord says, "Your request has come at a favorable time. I will keep you from harm and give you as a token and pledge to Israel, proof that I will reestablish the land of Israel and reassign it to its own people again. Through you I am saying to the prisoners of darkness, 'Come out! I am giving you your freedom!' They will be my sheep, grazing in green pastures and on the grassy hills. ¹⁰They shall neither hunger nor thirst; the searing sun and scorching desert winds will not reach them any more. For the Lord in his mercy will lead them beside the cool waters. ¹¹And I will make my mountains into level paths for them; the highways shall be raised above the valleys. ¹²See, my people shall return from far away, from north and west and south."

¹³Sing for joy, O heavens; shout, O earth. Break forth with song, O mountains, for the Lord has comforted his people and will have compassion upon them in their sorrow.

¹⁴Yet they say, "My Lord deserted us; he has forgotten us."

¹⁵"Never! Can a mother forget her little child and not have love for her own son? Yet even if that should be, I will not forget you. ¹⁶See, I have tattooed your name upon my palm, and ever before me is a picture of Jerusalem's walls in ruins. ¹⁷Soon your rebuilders shall come and chase away all those destroying you. ¹⁸Look and see, for the Lord has vowed that all your enemies shall come and be your slaves. They will be as jewels to display, as bridal ornaments.

¹⁹"Even the most desolate parts of your abandoned land shall soon be crowded with your people, and your enemies who enslaved you shall be far away. ²⁰The generations born in exile shall return and say, 'We need more room! It's crowded here!' ²¹Then you will think to yourself, 'Who has given me all these? For most of my children were killed, and the rest were carried away into exile, leaving me here alone. Who bore these? Who raised them for me?'"

²²The Lord God says, "See, I will give a signal to the Gentiles, and they shall carry your little sons back to you in their arms, and your daughters on their shoulders. ²³Kings and queens shall serve you; they shall care for all your needs. They shall bow to the earth before you and lick the dust from off your feet; then you shall know I am the Lord. Those who wait for me shall never be ashamed."

²⁴Who can snatch the prey from the hands of a mighty man? Who can demand that a tyrant let his captives go? ²⁵But the Lord says, "Even the captives of the most mighty and most terrible shall all be freed; for I will fight those who fight you, and I will save your children. ²⁶I will feed your enemies with their own flesh, and they shall be drunk with rivers of their own blood. All the world shall

Family Devotions

☐ DEVOTION 210
RECEIVING CHRIST AS SAVIOR

Read Isaiah 49:13-16

Receiving Christ as Savior
Memory Verse

If you tell others with your own mouth that Jesus Christ is your Lord and believe in your own heart that God has raised him from the dead, you will be saved.
Romans 10:9

"Where'd you get this, Rico? Did you make it?"

Paul was holding something Rico had made at church.

Rico looked up from the model car he and Paul and Luis were building. "Yeah. At church."

"You sure go to church a lot," said Paul. "Do your parents make you?"

"Of course they make him! No one *wants* to go to church," Luis interrupted.

Rico got up his courage. "My parents want me to go, but I wanna go, too. It's fun, and I have friends there . . ." He hesitated. "And I like learning about God and how he helps me."

Paul rolled his eyes. "My parents say that God got things started but he just sits up in heaven now. He doesn't *do* anything."

"My dad says God is like a mean boss," said Luis. "He watches you every minute, waiting for you to do something wrong."

"That's not right!" said Rico.

"How do *you* know?" asked Paul.

"God tells us in the Bible what he's like," answered Rico. "You're right that God got everything started. But he doesn't ignore us now."

Rico turned to Luis. "God wants us to do what's right, but he's not waiting to pounce on us. He wants what's best for us because he cares about us."

"God *likes* us?" asked Luis.

Rico thought about how Isaiah described God. He took a deep breath. "Sometimes we think God couldn't know us. But he loves us like a parent and doesn't forget us. The Bible says God's love is like he has our names—Paul, Luis, and Rico—tattooed right on his hand. Or like he keeps a picture of us right in front of him."

"Wow, that's the kind of God I'd like to get to know," said Luis

How About You?

What's your picture of God? Is he demanding or generous? Critical or caring? Distant or close by? Find out if what you think about God is what the Bible says about God. Ask God to help you to get to know him for who he really is. *J. A. G.*

• For the next devotional, turn to page 705. • For the next devotional on *RECEIVING CHRIST AS SAVIOR*, turn to page 871. • For notes on *RECEIVING CHRIST AS SAVIOR*, see pages 839, 842, 1146, 1234, and 1240.

know that I, the Lord, am your Savior and Redeemer, the Mighty One of Israel."

50 God's Servant Obeys

The Lord asks, Did I sell you to my creditors? Is that why you aren't here? Is your mother gone because I divorced her and sent her away? No, you went away as captives because of your sins. And your mother, too, was taken in payment for your sins. ²Was I too weak to save you? Is that why the house is silent and empty when I come home? Have I no longer power to deliver? No, that is not the reason! For I can rebuke the sea and make it dry! I can turn the rivers into deserts, covered with dying fish. ³I am the one who sends the darkness out across the skies.

⁴The Lord God has given me his words of wisdom so that I may know what I should say to all these weary ones. Morning by morning he wakens me and opens my understanding to his will. ⁵The Lord God has spoken to me, and I have listened; I do not rebel nor turn away. ⁶I give my back to the whip, and my cheeks to those who pull out the beard. I do not hide from shame—they spit in my face.

⁷Because the Lord God helps me, I will not be dismayed; therefore, I have set my face like flint to do his will, and I know that I will triumph. ⁸He who gives me justice is near. Who will dare to fight against me now? Where are my enemies? Let them appear! ⁹See, the Lord God is for me! Who shall declare me guilty? All my enemies shall be destroyed like old clothes eaten up by moths!

¹⁰Who among you fears the Lord and obeys his Servant? If such men walk in darkness, without one ray of light, let them trust the Lord, let them rely upon their God. ¹¹But see here, you who live in your own light and warm yourselves from your own fires and not from God's; you will live among sorrows.

51 The People Must Fear God

Listen to me, all who hope for deliverance, who seek the Lord! Consider the quarry from which you were mined, the rock from which you were cut! Yes, think about your ancestors Abraham and Sarah, from whom you came. You worry at being so small and few, but Abraham was only *one* when I called him. But when I blessed him, he became a great nation. ³And the Lord will bless Israel again, and make her deserts blossom; her barren wilderness will become as beautiful as the Garden of Eden. Joy and gladness will be found there, thanksgiving and lovely songs.

⁴Listen to me, my people; listen, O Israel, for I will see that right prevails. ⁵My mercy and justice are coming soon; your salvation is on the way. I will rule the nations; they shall wait for me and long for me to come. ⁶Look high in the skies and watch the earth beneath, for the skies shall disappear like smoke, the earth shall wear out like a garment, and the people of the earth shall die like flies. But my salvation lasts forever; my righteous rule will never die nor end.

⁷Listen to me, you who know the right from wrong and cherish my laws in your hearts: don't be afraid of people's scorn or their slanderous talk. ⁸ For the moth shall destroy them like garments; the worm shall eat them like wool; but my justice and mercy shall last forever, and my salvation from generation to generation.

⁹Awake, O Lord! Rise up and robe yourself with strength. Rouse yourself as in the days of old when you slew Egypt, the dragon of the Nile. ¹⁰Are you not the same today, the mighty God who dried up the sea, making a path right through it for your ransomed ones?¹¹The time will come when God's redeemed will all come home again. They shall come with singing to Jerusalem, filled with joy and everlasting gladness; sorrow and mourning will all disappear.

¹²I, even I, am he who comforts you and gives you all this joy. So what right have you to fear mere mortal men, who wither like the grass and disappear? ¹³And yet you have no fear of God, your Maker—you have forgotten him, the one who spread the stars throughout the skies and made the earth. Will you be in constant dread of men's oppression, and fear their anger all day long? ¹⁴Soon, soon you slaves shall be released; dungeon, starvation and death are not your fate. ¹⁵For I am the Lord your God, the Lord Almighty, who dried a path for you right through the sea, between the roaring waves. ¹⁶And I have put my words in your mouth and hidden you safe within my hand. I planted the stars in place and molded all the earth. I am the one who says to Israel, "You are mine."

¹⁷Wake up, wake up, Jerusalem! You have drunk enough from the cup of the fury of the Lord. You have drunk to the dregs the cup of terror and squeezed out the last drops. ¹⁸Not one of her sons is left alive to help or tell her what to do. ¹⁹These two things have been your lot: desolation and destruction. Yes, famine and the sword. And who is left to sympathize? Who is left to comfort you? ²⁰For your sons have fainted and lie in the streets, helpless as wild goats caught in a net. The Lord has poured out his fury and rebuke upon them. ²¹But listen now to this, afflicted ones—full of troubles and in a stupor (but not from being drunk)— ²²this is what the Lord says, the Lord your God who cares for his people: "See, I take

FAMILY DEVOTIONS

☐ DEVOTION 211
ENCOURAGING OTHERS

Read Isaiah 51:12

Encouraging Others Memory Verse

So encourage each other to build each other up, just as you are already doing.
1 Thessalonians 5:11

"Mom," Scott asked, "why did Bobby get sick?" Scott's friend Bobby was in the hospital, seriously ill.

"Well," replied Mom, "all the bad things that happen to us are a result of sin in the world. We don't know why some people end up suffering more than others. The important thing is to remember that God cares about us and he cares about Bobby."

Several days later, Scott's mom talked to Mrs. Jonas on the phone. After she hung up she said, "Bobby is feeling a little better and would like some company. How would you like to go to the hospital to see him?"

Scott hesitated. "But Mom, what would I say?"

"Talk about the things you usually talk about—baseball, school, or hiking," suggested Mom.

Scott still looked worried. "But what if Bobby wants to talk about being sick?"

"Let him," Mom advised. "Sometimes the kindest thing to do for someone in the hospital is to listen—to let him talk about how he is feeling. Remember, you can't pretend to understand what Bobby is going through. You have never been faced with a serious illness. You can, however, remind Bobby that the Lord understands and that he loves him and cares for him very much."

Scott got his jacket. He was still scared to go, but he wanted to help Bobby. The Lord could help him know what to say when he visited his friend.

How About You?
Are you afraid to visit a sick person because you don't know what to say? Even adults are often nervous about visiting someone who is ill. But don't stay away! Let that person know you care. Share what's been happening in school and Sunday school. Share a memory verse with him. Share God's comfort with him. L. M. W.

• For the next devotional, turn to page 707. • For the next devotional on ENCOURAGING OTHERS, turn to page 995.
• For notes on ENCOURAGING OTHERS, see pages 108, 157, 474, 1156, and 1170.

from your hands the terrible cup; you shall drink no more of my fury; it is gone at last. ²³But I will put that terrible cup into the hands of those who tormented you and trampled your souls to the dust and walked upon your backs."

52 God Brings His People Home

Wake up, wake up, Jerusalem, and clothe yourselves with strength [from God]. Put on your beautiful clothes, O Zion, Holy City; for sinners—those who turn from God—will no longer enter your gates. ²Rise from the dust, Jerusalem; take off the slave bands from your neck, O captive daughter of Zion. ³For the Lord says, When I sold you into exile, I asked no fee from your oppressors; now I can take you back again and owe them not a cent! ⁴My people were tyrannized without cause by Egypt and Assyria, and I delivered them.

⁵And now, what is this? asks the Lord. Why are my people enslaved again and oppressed without excuse? Those who rule them shout in exultation, and my name is constantly blasphemed day by day. ⁶Therefore I will reveal my name to my people, and they shall know the power in that name. Then at last they will recognize that it is I, yes, I, who speaks to them.

⁷How beautiful upon the mountains are the feet of those who bring the happy news of peace and salvation, the news that the God of Israel reigns. ⁸The watchmen shout and sing with joy, for right before their eyes they see the Lord God bring his people home again. ⁹Let the ruins of Jerusalem break into joyous song, for the Lord has comforted his people; he has redeemed Jerusalem. ¹⁰The Lord has bared his holy arm before the eyes of all the nations; the ends of the earth shall see the salvation of our God.

¹¹Go now, leave your bonds and slavery. Put Babylon and all it represents far behind you—it is unclean to you. You are the holy people of the Lord; purify yourselves, all you who carry home the vessels of the Lord. ¹²You shall not leave in haste, running for your lives; for the Lord will go ahead of you, and he, the God of Israel, will protect you from behind.

¹³See, my Servant shall prosper; he shall be highly exalted. ¹⁴,¹⁵Yet many shall be amazed when they see him—yes, even far-off foreign nations and their kings; they shall stand dumbfounded, speechless in his presence. For they shall see and understand what they had not been told before. They shall see my Servant beaten and bloodied, so disfigured one would scarcely know it was a person standing there. So shall he cleanse many nations.

53

But, oh, how few believe it! Who will listen? To whom will God reveal his saving power? ²In God's eyes he was like a tender green shoot, sprouting from a root in dry and sterile ground. But in our eyes there was no attractiveness at all, nothing to make us want him. ³We despised him and rejected him—a man of sorrows, acquainted with bitterest grief. We turned our backs on him and looked the other way when he went by. He was despised, and we didn't care.

⁴Yet it was *our* grief he bore, *our* sorrows that weighed him down. And we thought his troubles were a punishment from God, for his *own* sins! ⁵But he was wounded and bruised for *our* sins. He was beaten that we might have peace; he was lashed—and we were healed! ⁶*We*—every one of us—have strayed away like sheep! *We,* who left God's paths to follow our own. Yet God laid on *him* the guilt and sins of every one of us!

⁷He was oppressed and he was afflicted, yet he never said a word. He was brought as a lamb to the slaughter; and as a sheep before her shearers is dumb, so he stood silent before the ones condemning him. ⁸From prison and trial they led him away to his death. But who among the people of that day realized it was their sins that he was dying for—that he was suffering their punishment? ⁹He was buried like a criminal, but in a rich man's grave; but he had done no wrong and had never spoken an evil word.

¹⁰But it was the Lord's good plan to bruise him and fill him with grief. However, when his soul has been made an offering for sin, then he shall have a multitude of children, many heirs. He shall live again, and God's program shall prosper in his hands. ¹¹And when he sees all that is accomplished by the anguish of his soul, he shall be satisfied; and because of what he has experienced, my righteous Servant shall make many to be counted righteous before God, for he shall bear all their sins. ¹²Therefore, I will give him the honors of one who is mighty and great because he has poured out his soul unto death. He was counted as a sinner, and he bore the sins of many, and he pled with God for sinners.

54 Everlasting Love

Sing, O childless woman! Break out into loud and joyful song, Jerusalem, for she who was abandoned has more blessings now than she whose husband stayed! ²Enlarge your house; build on additions; spread out your home! ³For you will soon be bursting at the seams! And your descendants will possess the cities left behind during the exile and rule the nations that took their lands.

⁴Fear not; you will no longer live in shame. The

FAMILY DEVOTIONS

☐ DEVOTION 212
OPTIMISM

Read Isaiah 54:4-10

Optimism
Memory Verse

Fix your thoughts on what is true and good and right. Think about things that are pure and lovely, and dwell on the fine, good things in others. Think about all you can praise God for and be glad about.
Philippians 4:8

How About You?
Is there some great sorrow in your life? Do you feel sad and lonely? Remember, God loves you and cares for you even when you can't see him. Pray about your problems, and trust him to help you through. P. K.

Amy curled up on the sofa, watching her green parakeet, who perched dejectedly in his little brass cage. Dad had given the bird to her just a few weeks before he had died and gone to be with Jesus, and she remembered Dad saying, "This little guy will keep you company." That was why Amy had named him Little Guy.

Now Dad had been gone six months. Although Amy had almost become accustomed to the emptiness of the house, she still missed little things—Dad in his place at the table, the sound of his laugh, the way he used to tap a good-night signal on her bedroom door. There was a sadness in Mom's eyes, too, and Amy knew she missed Dad a lot. But Mom had said something about picking up the pieces and going on. They had discovered some wonderful promises for widows and children as they read the Bible together each evening.

"Mom, what's wrong with Little Guy?" asked Amy. "His cage is clean and he has fresh water and seed, but he acts sick or something." Amy sounded worried. "I haven't heard him chirp lately, either," she added.

Mom came in from the kitchen and studied the little bird huddled in the sunshine. "Oh, he's just molting, Amy," she said. "Haven't you noticed all the feathers he's lost? Sometimes birds will become droopy and often stop singing during this period, but he'll be all right. He just needs a little time." Mom smiled encouragingly. Then she said, "You and I are a little like that, honey. We've lost our desire to sing, too, but God knows how we feel and he has promised to take care of us. He knows we both miss Daddy very much, but he wants us to trust him and be happy again."

"Like I want Little Guy to be happy?" Amy's words were more of a statement than a question. She gently poked a finger into the cage, touching the soft green feathers. Little Guy cocked his head and ruffled his feathers. "Chirp," he responded softly, almost as if he understood.

• For the next devotional, turn to page 709. • For the next devotional on OPTIMISM, turn to page 735. • For notes on OPTIMISM, see pages 143, 536, 677, and 940.

shame of your youth and the sorrows of widowhood will be remembered no more, ⁵for your Creator will be your "husband." The Lord Almighty is his name; he is your Redeemer, the Holy One of Israel, the God of all the earth. ⁶For the Lord has called you back from your grief—a young wife abandoned by her husband. ⁷For a brief moment I abandoned you. But with great compassion I will take you back. ⁸In a moment of anger I turned my face a little while; but with everlasting love I will have pity on you, says the Lord, your Redeemer.

⁹Just as in the time of Noah I swore that I would never again permit the waters of a flood to cover the earth and destroy its life, so now I swear that I will never again pour out my anger on you. ¹⁰For the mountains may depart and the hills disappear, but my kindness shall not leave you. My promise of peace for you will never be broken, says the Lord who has mercy upon you.

¹¹O my afflicted people, tempest-tossed and troubled, I will rebuild you on a foundation of sapphires and make the walls of your houses from precious jewels. ¹²I will make your towers of sparkling agate and your gates and walls of shining gems. ¹³And all your citizens shall be taught by me, and their prosperity shall be great. ¹⁴You will live under a government that is just and fair. Your enemies will stay far away; you will live in peace. Terror shall not come near. ¹⁵If any nation comes to fight you, it will not be sent by me to punish you. Therefore, it will be routed, for I am on your side. ¹⁶I have created the smith who blows the coals beneath the forge and makes the weapons of destruction. And I have created the armies that destroy. ¹⁷But in that coming day, no weapon turned against you shall succeed, and you will have justice against every courtroom lie. This is the heritage of the servants of the Lord. This is the blessing I have given you, says the Lord.

55 A Promise of Joy and Peace

Say there! Is anyone thirsty? Come and drink—even if you have no money! Come, take your choice of wine and milk—it's all free! ²Why spend your money on food that doesn't give you strength? Why pay for groceries that do you no good? Listen and I'll tell you where to get good food that fattens up the soul!

³Come to me with your ears wide open. Listen, for the life of your soul is at stake. I am ready to make an everlasting covenant with you, to give you all the unfailing mercies and love that I had for King David. ⁴He proved my power by conquering foreign nations. ⁵You also will command the nations, and they will come running to obey, not because of your own power or virtue, but because I, the Lord your God, have glorified you.

⁶Seek the Lord while you can find him. Call upon him now while he is near. ⁷Let men cast off their wicked deeds; let them banish from their minds the very thought of doing wrong! Let them turn to the Lord that he may have mercy upon them, and to our God, for he will abundantly pardon! ⁸This plan of mine is not what you would work out, neither are my thoughts the same as yours! ⁹For just as the heavens are higher than the earth, so are my ways higher than yours, and my thoughts than yours.

¹⁰As the rain and snow come down from heaven and stay upon the ground to water the earth, and cause the grain to grow and to produce seed for the farmer and bread for the hungry, ¹¹so also is my Word. I send it out, and it always produces fruit. It shall accomplish all I want it to and prosper everywhere I send it. ¹²You will live in joy and peace. The mountains and hills, the trees of the field—all the world around you—will rejoice. ¹³Where once were thorns, fir trees will grow; where briars grew, the myrtle trees will sprout up. This miracle will make the Lord's name very great and be an everlasting sign [of God's power and love].

56 God Will Come to the Rescue

Be just and fair to all, the Lord God says. Do what's right and good, for I am coming soon to rescue you. ²Blessed is the man who refuses to work during my Sabbath days of rest, but honors them; and blessed is the man who checks himself from doing wrong.

³And my blessings are for Gentiles, too, when they accept the Lord; don't let them think that I will make them second-class citizens. And this is for the eunuchs too. They can be as much mine as anyone. ⁴For I say this to the eunuchs who keep my Sabbaths holy, who choose the things that please me and obey my laws: ⁵I will give them—in my house, within my walls—a name far greater than the honor they would receive from having sons and daughters. For the name that I will give them is an everlasting one; it will never disappear.

⁶As for the Gentiles, the outsiders who join the people of the Lord and serve him and love his name, who are his servants and don't desecrate the Sabbath, and have accepted his covenant and promises, ⁷I will bring them also to my holy mountain of Jerusalem and make them full of joy within my House of Prayer.

I will accept their sacrifices and offerings, for my Temple shall be called "A House of Prayer for All People"! ⁸For the Lord God who brings back

Family Devotions

☐ DEVOTION 213
PATIENCE

Read Isaiah 55:6-11

"That's going to be neat when it's done," said Arlene as she watched her mother work on a patchwork quilt.

Mother smiled. "I hope so," she replied. "This project is very special to me." She picked up a few of the fabric squares. "Do you recognize these pieces of material?"

"Some of them are scraps from dresses I used to wear, aren't they?" asked Arlene.

Mother nodded. "Yes. And they remind me that God's way is best," she said. "You see, I used to become very disappointed and angry when I didn't get my way. I would even get upset with God when he didn't answer my prayers the way I wanted him to."

"Really?" asked Arlene, eager to hear her mother's story. "How do these quilt pieces remind you of that?"

"Well," said Mother, "before you came to live with us, I wanted a baby very much. I prayed that we'd be able to adopt one right away. But it didn't happen. Your father and I prayed and prayed, and we waited and waited. I sometimes felt angry at God for not giving me my way."

"But then you got me," Arlene said.

"That's just the point," said Mother with a smile. "I didn't get my way. I got God's way, and it was much better. He taught us so much during those years we were waiting. We learned a lot about patience and about trusting God to work out his best for us. And then, as you said, we adopted you."

"If you had gotten a baby earlier, you might not have gotten me," persisted Arlene.

"That's right," agreed Mother. "That's why this quilt is such a special project to me. I'm sewing together little remembrances from your life. It's my way of reminding myself how wonderful God's way was—and is—for me."

Patience Memory Verse

Now as for you, dear brothers who are waiting for the Lord's return, be patient, like a farmer who waits until the autumn for his precious harvest to ripen.
James 5:7

How About You?

Are you patient when you don't get your own way? Or do you want what you want when you want it? Ask God to help you to want and accept his ways. Trust him, knowing that his way is best. N. E. K.

the outcasts of Israel says, I will bring others too besides my people Israel.

⁹Come, wild animals of the field; come, tear apart the sheep; come, wild animals of the forest, devour my people. ¹⁰For the leaders of my people—the Lord's watchmen, his shepherds—are all blind to every danger. They are featherbrained and give no warning when danger comes. They love to lie there, love to sleep, to dream. ¹¹And they are as greedy as dogs, never satisfied; they are stupid shepherds who only look after their own interest, each trying to get as much as he can for himself from every possible source.

¹²"Come," they say. "We'll get some wine and have a party; let's all get drunk. This is really living; let it go on and on, and tomorrow will be even better!"

57 A Reward for Loving God

The good men perish; the godly die before their time, and no one seems to care or wonder why. No one seems to realize that God is taking them away from evil days ahead. ²For the godly who die shall rest in peace.

³But you—come here, you witches' sons, you offspring of adulterers and harlots! ⁴Who is it you mock, making faces and sticking out your tongues? You children of sinners and liars! ⁵You worship your idols with great zeal beneath the shade of every tree and slay your children as human sacrifices down in the valleys, under overhanging rocks. ⁶Your gods are the smooth stones in the valleys. You worship them, and they, not I, are your inheritance. Does all this make me happy? ⁷,⁸You have committed adultery on the tops of the mountains, for you worship idols there, deserting me. Behind closed doors you set your idols up and worship someone other than me. This is adultery, for you are giving these idols your love instead of loving me. ⁹ You have taken pleasant incense and perfume to Molech as your gift. You have traveled far, even to hell itself, to find new gods to love. ¹⁰You grew weary in your search, but you never gave up. You strengthened yourself and went on. ¹¹Why were you more afraid of them than of me? How is it that you gave not even a second thought to me? Is it because I've been too gentle that you have no fear of me?

¹²And then there is your "righteousness" and your "good works"—none of which will save you. ¹³Let's see if the whole collection of your idols can help you when you cry to them to save you! They are so weak that the wind can carry them off! A breath can puff them away. But he who trusts in me shall possess the land and inherit my Holy Mountain. ¹⁴I will say, Rebuild the road! Clear away the rocks and stones. Prepare a glorious highway for my people's return from captivity.

¹⁵The high and lofty One who inhabits eternity, the Holy One, says this: I live in that high and holy place where those with contrite, humble spirits dwell; and I refresh the humble and give new courage to those with repentant hearts. ¹⁶For I will not fight against you forever, nor always show my wrath; if I did, all mankind would perish—the very souls that I have made. ¹⁷I was angry and smote these greedy men. But they went right on sinning, doing everything their evil hearts desired. ¹⁸I have seen what they do, but I will heal them anyway! I will lead them and comfort them, helping them to mourn and to confess their sins. ¹⁹Peace, peace to them, both near and far, for I will heal them all. ²⁰But those who still reject me are like the restless sea, which is never still, but always churns up mire and dirt. ²¹There is no peace, says my God, for them!

58 God Tells the People to Share

Shout with the voice of a trumpet blast; tell my people of their sins! ²Yet they act so pious! They come to the Temple every day and are so delighted to hear the reading of my laws—just as though they would obey them—just as though they don't despise the commandments of their God! How anxious they are to worship correctly; oh, how they love the Temple services!

³"We have fasted before you," they say. "Why aren't you impressed? Why don't you see our sacrifices? Why don't you hear our prayers? We have done much penance, and you don't even notice it!" I'll tell you why! Because you are living in evil pleasure even while you are fasting, and you keep right on oppressing your workers. ⁴Look, what good is fasting when you keep on fighting and quarreling? This kind of fasting will never get you anywhere with me. ⁵Is this what I want—this doing of penance and bowing like reeds in the wind, putting on sackcloth and covering yourselves with ashes? Is this what you call fasting?

⁶No, the kind of fast I want is that you stop oppressing those who work for you and treat them fairly and give them what they earn. ⁷I want you to share your food with the hungry and bring right into your own homes those

---

SHOWING COMPASSION 58:1ff. True worship was more than religious ritual, going to the Temple every day, and listening to Scripture readings. These people missed the point of a living, vital relationship with God. He doesn't want us fasting or acting pious when we have unforgiven sin in our hearts and perform sinful practices with our hands. More important even than correct worship and doctrine is genuine compassion for the poor, the helpless, and the oppressed. **To begin the series of devotionals on SHOWING COMPASSION, turn to page 569.**

Family Devotions

☐ **Devotion 214**
Confessing Sin

Read Isaiah 57:15-21

"See what I bought, Mom," said Megan excitedly as she took a magic slate out of a sack. She began scribbling on it as they drove home. "Now, look," she said as she lifted the top plastic sheet. "The writing is all gone." As she talked, her brother Andy simply stared out the window. He wasn't hearing the conversation or seeing the scenery.

"Andy!" Mom raised her voice. "This is the third time I've called your name. Is something wrong?"

"No." Andy lapsed into silence again.

And now you've told another lie, his conscience said. *That makes two.*

Andy sighed deeply. *But it was such a little lie,* he argued with his conscience.

"I know something is bothering you, Andy," insisted Mom. "Do you want to talk about it?"

"I told Dad a lie yesterday," Andy blurted out.

Mom went silent for a moment. Then she nodded. "He knows that," she said softly, "but he is waiting for you to confess. He knew it would be much better if you admitted it freely."

Megan, busy with her magic slate, paid no attention to the conversation. She chuckled as she said, "I made a stupid mistake! I put a long tail on a rabbit! Oh, well! I'll just erase it and start over." Again she lifted the top plastic sheet, and like magic, her picture disappeared.

Mom smiled. "When you sin, Andy, it's something like writing the wrong thing on a magic slate," she said. "If you don't do anything about it, it remains there. But if you repent of your sins and confess them to God, he will erase them. Tell both your dad and the Lord what you told me. Let them know you're sorry, and the slate will be clean."

Megan smoothed the plastic sheet on her slate. "This time I'm going to do it right," she announced.

"Me, too, Megan," echoed Andy. "Me, too."

Confessing Sin Memory Verse

Create in me a new, clean heart, O God, filled with clean thoughts and right desires.
Psalm 51:10

How About You?

Have you told a lie? Disobeyed? Been sassy? Cheated? Right now, confess to God whatever sin you are aware of in your life, and let him wipe the slate clean. *B. W.*

- For the next devotional, turn to page 713. • For the next devotional on *Confessing Sin*, turn to page 1075.
- For notes on *Confessing Sin*, see pages 429, 479, 836, 881, and 1220.

who are helpless, poor, and destitute. Clothe those who are cold, and don't hide from relatives who need your help.

⁸If you do these things, God will shed his own glorious light upon you. He will heal you; your godliness will lead you forward, goodness will be a shield before you, and the glory of the Lord will protect you from behind. ⁹Then, when you call, the Lord will answer. "Yes, I am here," he will quickly reply. All you need to do is to stop oppressing the weak and stop making false accusations and spreading vicious rumors!

¹⁰Feed the hungry! Help those in trouble! Then your light will shine out from the darkness, and the darkness around you shall be as bright as day. ¹¹And the Lord will guide you continually, and satisfy you with all good things, and keep you healthy too; and you will be like a well-watered garden, like an ever-flowing spring. ¹²Your sons will rebuild the long-deserted ruins of your cities, and you will be known as "The People Who Rebuild Their Walls and Cities."

¹³If you keep the Sabbath holy, not having your own fun and business on that day, but enjoying the Sabbath, speaking of it with delight as the Lord's holy day, and honoring the Lord in what you do, not following your own desires and pleasure nor talking idly—¹⁴then the Lord will be your delight, and I will see to it that you ride high and get your full share of the blessings I promised to Jacob, your father. The Lord has spoken.

59 God Tells His People to Obey

Listen now! The Lord isn't too weak to save you. And he isn't getting deaf! He can hear you when you call! ²But the trouble is that your sins have cut you off from God. Because of sin he has turned his face away from you and will not listen anymore. ³For your hands are those of murderers and your fingers are filthy with sin. You lie and grumble and oppose the good. ⁴No one cares about being fair and true. Your lawsuits are based on lies; you spend your time plotting evil deeds and doing them. ⁵You spend your time and energy in spinning evil plans that end up in deadly actions. ⁶You cheat and shortchange everyone. Everything you do is filled with sin; violence is your trademark. ⁷Your feet run to do evil and rush to murder; your thoughts are only of sinning, and wherever you go you leave behind a trail of misery and death. ⁸You don't know what true peace is, nor what it means to be just and good; you continually do wrong and those who follow you won't experience any peace either.

⁹It is because of all this evil that you aren't finding God's blessings; that's why he doesn't punish those who injure you. No wonder you are in darkness when you expected light. No wonder you are walking in the gloom. ¹⁰No wonder you grope like blind men and stumble along in broad daylight, yes, even at brightest noontime, as though it were the darkest night! No wonder you are like corpses when compared with vigorous young men! ¹¹You roar like hungry bears; you moan with mournful cries like doves. You look for God to keep you, but he doesn't. He has turned away. ¹²For your sins keep piling up before the righteous God and testify against you.

Yes, we know what sinners we are. ¹³We know our disobedience; we have denied the Lord our God. We know what rebels we are and how unfair we are, for we carefully plan our lies. ¹⁴Our courts oppose the righteous man; fairness is unknown. Truth falls dead in the streets, and justice is outlawed.

¹⁵Yes, truth is gone, and anyone who tries a better life is soon attacked. The Lord saw all the evil and was displeased to find no steps taken against sin. ¹⁶He saw no one was helping you and wondered that no one intervened. Therefore he himself stepped in to save you through his mighty power and justice. ¹⁷He put on righteousness as armor and the helmet of salvation on his head. He clothed himself with robes of vengeance and of godly fury. ¹⁸He will repay his enemies for their evil deeds—fury for his foes in distant lands. ¹⁹Then at last they will reverence and glorify the name of God from west to east. For he will come like a flood tide driven by Jehovah's breath. ²⁰He will come as a Redeemer to those in Zion who have turned away from sin.

²¹"As for me, this is my promise to them," says the Lord: "My Holy Spirit shall not leave them, and they shall want the good and hate the wrong—they and their children and their children's children forever."

60 The Glory of the Lord

Arise, my people! Let your light shine for all the nations to see! For the glory of the Lord is streaming from you. ²Darkness as black as night shall cover all the peoples of the earth, but the glory of the Lord will shine from you. ³All nations will come to your light; mighty kings will come to see the glory of the Lord upon you.

⁴Lift up your eyes and see! For your sons and daughters are coming home to you from distant lands. ⁵Your eyes will shine with joy, your hearts will thrill, for merchants from around the world will flow to you, bringing you the wealth of many lands. ⁶Vast droves of camels will converge upon you, dromedaries from Midian and Sheba and Ephah too, bringing gold and incense to add to the praise of God. ⁷The flocks of Kedar shall be

FAMILY DEVOTIONS

☐ DEVOTION 215
SHOWING COMPASSION

Read Isaiah 59:3-8

"Hey, Marcia!" called Kent from the living room. "Did you see this article in the paper about the man who was killed when his car skidded off a bridge? Here's a picture. It's pretty gruesome."

"Oooh, let me see," said Marcia. "Look! Do you suppose that's blood on the ground?"

At that moment, Mom spoke up. "Don't you two have anything better to do?"

"Sure," Kent replied. "Let's watch television. They're doing a rerun of that shark movie tonight. You know, the one where that shark attacks the girl and—"

"No, let's watch boxing," said Marcia. "Last week a boxer got a cut over his eye. Wasn't that neat?"

This time, it was Dad's turn to speak up. "What's so neat about injury and suffering?"

"Oh, Dad," Kent scowled. "Why take it so seriously? After all, these things happen every day."

Dad nodded. "Yes, because of Adam's sin, sickness and injury and death are part of life. But they're not good things, and it's wrong to take pleasure in thinking about them. I've been reading a book about ancient Rome. A popular entertainment was to watch Christians being thrown to the lions. You children remind me of the Roman spectators."

Marcia was horrified. "Oh, Dad!" she exclaimed. "That would be gross!"

"I'm sure it was," Mom said, "but many people came to watch anyway. Is what you're doing so different? I don't think the Roman spectators, or you, ever really considered how terrible it was for the people involved. The hearts of the spectators had become so hard that they were fascinated by suffering instead of hating it. You children seem to like watching people suffer, too. Instead of enjoying the pain of others, we should do all we can to help them."

Showing Compassion Memory Verse

What a wonderful God we have—he is the Father of our Lord Jesus Christ, the source of every mercy, and the one who so wonderfully comforts and strengthens us in our hardships and trials.
2 Corinthians 1:3

How About You?

If you or someone you love were hurt, how would you want others to react? Would you like it if they seemed to enjoy your suffering? Or would you want them to respond with kindness and compassion? Remember, suffering isn't fun. S. K.

• For the next devotional, turn to page 715.   • For the next devotional on SHOWING COMPASSION, turn to page 837.
• For notes on SHOWING COMPASSION, see pages 206, 506, 515, 710, and 934.

given you, and the rams of Nabaioth for my altars, and I will glorify my glorious Temple in that day.

⁸And who are these who fly like a cloud to Israel, like doves to their nests? ⁹I have reserved the ships of many lands, the very best, to bring the sons of Israel home again from far away, bringing their wealth with them. For the Holy One of Israel, known around the world, has glorified you in the eyes of all.

¹⁰Foreigners will come and build your cities. Presidents and kings will send you aid. For though I destroyed you in my anger, I will have mercy on you through my grace. ¹¹Your gates will stay wide open around the clock to receive the wealth of many lands. The kings of the world will cater to you. ¹²For the nations refusing to be your allies will perish; they shall be destroyed. ¹³ The glory of Lebanon will be yours—the forests of firs, pines, and box trees—to beautify my sanctuary. My Temple will be glorious.

¹⁴The sons of anti-Semites will come and bow before you! They will kiss your feet! They will call Jerusalem "The City of the Lord" and "The Glorious Mountain of the Holy One of Israel."

¹⁵Though once despised and hated and rebuffed by all, you will be beautiful forever, a joy for all the generations of the world, for I will make you so. ¹⁶Powerful kings and mighty nations shall provide you with the choicest of their goods to satisfy your every need, and you will know at last and really understand that I, the Lord, am your Savior and Redeemer, the Mighty One of Israel. ¹⁷I will exchange your brass for gold, your iron for silver, your wood for brass, your stones for iron. Peace and righteousness shall be your taskmasters! ¹⁸Violence will disappear out of your land—all war will end. Your walls will be "Salvation" and your gates "Praise."

¹⁹No longer will you need the sun or moon to give you light, for the Lord your God will be your everlasting light, and he will be your glory. ²⁰Your sun shall never set; the moon shall not go down—for the Lord will be your everlasting light; your days of mourning all will end. ²¹All your people will be good. They will possess their land forever, for I will plant them there with my own hands; this will bring me glory. ²²The smallest family shall multiply into a clan; the tiny group shall be a mighty nation. I, the Lord, will bring it all to pass when it is time.

61 Good News

The Spirit of the Lord God is upon me, because the Lord has anointed me to bring good news to the suffering and afflicted. He has sent me to comfort the brokenhearted, to announce liberty to captives, and to open the eyes of the blind. ²He has sent me to tell those who mourn that the time of God's favor to them has come, and the day of his wrath to their enemies. ³To all who mourn in Israel he will give: beauty for ashes; joy instead of mourning; praise instead of heaviness.

For God has planted them like strong and graceful oaks for his own glory.

⁴And they shall rebuild the ancient ruins, repairing cities long ago destroyed, reviving them though they have lain there many generations. ⁵ Foreigners shall be your servants; they shall feed your flocks and plow your fields and tend your vineyards. ⁶You shall be called priests of the Lord, ministers of our God. You shall be fed with the treasures of the nations and shall glory in their riches. ⁷Instead of shame and dishonor, you shall have a double portion of prosperity and everlasting joy.

⁸For I, the Lord, love justice; I hate robbery and wrong. I will faithfully reward my people for their suffering and make an everlasting covenant with them. ⁹Their descendants shall be known and honored among the nations; all shall realize that they are a people God has blessed.

¹⁰Let me tell you how happy God has made me! For he has clothed me with garments of salvation and draped about me the robe of righteousness. I am like a bridegroom in his wedding suit or a bride with her jewels. ¹¹The Lord will show the nations of the world his justice; all will praise him. His righteousness shall be like a budding tree, or like a garden in early spring, full of young plants springing up everywhere.

62 Isaiah's Prayer

Because I love Zion, because my heart yearns for Jerusalem, I will not cease to pray for her or to cry out to God on her behalf until she shines forth in his righteousness and is glorious in his salvation. ²The nations shall see your righteousness. Kings shall be blinded by your glory; and God will confer on you a new name. ³He will hold you aloft in his hands for all to see—a splendid crown for the King of kings. ⁴Never again shall you be called "The God-forsaken Land" or the "Land That God Forgot." Your new name will be "The Land of God's Delight" and "The Bride," for the Lord delights in you and will claim you as his own. ⁵Your children will care for you, O Jerusalem, with joy like that of a young man who marries a virgin; and God will rejoice over you as a bridegroom with his bride.

⁶,⁷O Jerusalem, I have set intercessors on your walls who shall cry to God all day and all night for the fulfillment of his promises. Take no rest, all you who pray, and give God no rest until he establishes

Family Devotions

☐ DEVOTION 216
True Joy

Read Isaiah 61:3-10

True Joy
Memory Verse

Always be full of joy in the Lord; I say it again, rejoice!
Philippians 4:4

Tonya waited eagerly for Dad to get home with a Christmas tree. She pressed her nose against the window to catch the first possible glimpse of him. Finally he came into view, but his head was down, and he carried no tree. As he entered the house, he brushed past Tonya with a quick greeting. She couldn't believe it. Her father had seemed so sure that he'd be coming home with a tree, but he had let her down!

Although Tonya knew that Christmas was the time to remember the birth of Jesus, she didn't feel like celebrating. She felt more like sulking in her room, which was what she did. The sound of voices soon interrupted her thoughts.

"I feel so terrible that I can't afford to get Tonya a Christmas tree," Dad said in a voice that expressed even greater sadness than Tonya felt. She couldn't quite make out her mother's reply. Almost immediately a plan formed in Tonya's mind.

After the conversation in the kitchen ended, Tonya went to join her parents. "Dad, could we get out that little artificial Christmas tree we used in Grandma's hospital room last year?" she asked. She pretended to be thrilled at the idea. As Tonya helped her father decorate the little tree, she continued her cheerful act. "I remember when you said you took me shopping and I picked out this ornament all by myself," she said as she hung the bird in a cage on the tree.

The angel from years past overwhelmed the tiny tree, but Dad placed it on the top anyway. "Your mother and I bought this for your first Christmas," he said, as he had every year.

By the time they finished working and talking, Dad's spirits had lifted. And Tonya was surprised to discover that she no longer had to pretend to be happy. Her joy was real.

How About You?
Is there something you could do to make someone else happy? Express greater appreciation? Reduce your own requests? Hide a disappointment? Focus on God's faithfulness and how much he's done for you, then see how you can share joy with someone else. E. M. B.

• For the next devotional, turn to page 721.   • For the next devotional on *True Joy*, turn to page 1157.
• For notes on *True Joy*, see pages 532, 1024, and 1160.

Jerusalem and makes her respected and admired throughout the earth. ⁸The Lord has sworn to Jerusalem with all his integrity: "I will never again give you to your enemies; never again shall foreign soldiers come and take away your grain and wine. ⁹You raised it; you shall keep it, praising God. Within the Temple courts you yourselves shall drink the wine you pressed."

¹⁰Go out! Go out! Prepare the roadway for my people to return! Build the roads, pull out the boulders, raise the flag of Israel.

¹¹See, the Lord has sent his messengers to every land and said, "Tell my people, I, the Lord your God, am coming to save you and will bring you many gifts." ¹²And they shall be called "The Holy People" and "The Lord's Redeemed," and Jerusalem shall be called "The Land of Desire" and "The City God Has Blessed."

63 God Is Loving and Kind

Who is this who comes from Edom, from the city of Bozrah, with his magnificent garments of crimson? Who is this in royal robes, marching in the greatness of his strength?

"It is I, the Lord, announcing your salvation; I, the Lord, the one who is mighty to save!"

²"Why are your clothes so red, as from treading out the grapes?"

³"I have trodden the winepress alone. No one was there to help me. In my wrath I have trodden my enemies like grapes. In my fury I trampled my foes. It is their blood you see upon my clothes. ⁴For the time has come for me to avenge my people, to redeem them from the hands of their oppressors. ⁵I looked but no one came to help them; I was amazed and appalled. So I executed vengeance alone; unaided, I meted out judgment. ⁶I crushed the heathen nations in my anger and made them stagger and fall to the ground."

⁷I will tell of the loving-kindnesses of God. I will praise him for all he has done; I will rejoice in his great goodness to Israel, which he has granted in accordance with his mercy and love. ⁸He said, "They are my very own; surely they will not be false again." And he became their Savior. ⁹In all their affliction he was afflicted, and he personally saved them. In his love and pity he redeemed them and lifted them up and carried them through all the years.

¹⁰But they rebelled against him and grieved his Holy Spirit. That is why he became their enemy and personally fought against them. ¹¹Then they remembered those days of old when Moses, God's servant, led his people out of Egypt, and they cried out, "Where is the One who brought Israel through the sea, with Moses as their shepherd? Where is the God who sent his Holy Spirit to be among his people? ¹²Where is he whose mighty power divided the sea before them when Moses lifted up his hand, and established his reputation forever? ¹³Who led them through the bottom of the sea? Like fine stallions racing through the desert, they never stumbled. ¹⁴Like cattle grazing in the valleys, so the Spirit of the Lord gave them rest. Thus he gave himself a magnificent reputation."

¹⁵O Lord, look down from heaven and see us from your holy, glorious home; where is the love for us you used to show—your power, your mercy, and your compassion? Where are they now? ¹⁶Surely you are still our Father! Even if Abraham and Jacob would disown us, still you would be our Father, our Redeemer from ages past. ¹⁷O Lord, why have you hardened our hearts and made us sin and turn against you? Return and help us, for we who belong to you need you so. ¹⁸How briefly we possessed Jerusalem! And now our enemies have destroyed her. ¹⁹O God, why do you treat us as though we weren't your people, as though we were a heathen nation that never called you "Lord"?

64 God Is like a Potter

Oh, that you would burst forth from the skies and come down! How the mountains would quake in your presence! ²The consuming fire of your glory would burn down the forests and boil the oceans dry. The nations would tremble before you; then your enemies would learn the reason for your fame! ³So it was before when you came down, for you did awesome things beyond our highest expectations, and how the mountains quaked! ⁴For since the world began no one has seen or heard of such a God as ours, who works for those who wait for him! ⁵ You welcome those who cheerfully do good, who follow godly ways.

But we are not godly; we are constant sinners and have been all our lives. Therefore your wrath is heavy on us. How can such as we be saved? ⁶We are all infected and impure with sin. When we put on our prized robes of righteousness, we find they are but filthy rags. Like autumn leaves we fade, wither and fall. And our sins, like the wind, sweep us away. ⁷Yet no one calls upon your name or pleads with you for mercy. Therefore, you have turned away from us and turned us over to our sins.

⁸And yet, O Lord, you are our Father. We are the clay and you are the Potter. We are all formed by your hand. ⁹Oh, be not so angry with us, Lord, nor forever remember our sins. Oh, look and see that we are all your people.

¹⁰Your holy cities are destroyed; Jerusalem is a desolate wilderness. ¹¹ Our holy, beautiful Temple

where our fathers praised you is burned down, and all the things of beauty are destroyed. ¹²After all of this, must you still refuse to help us, Lord? Will you stand silent and still punish us?

65 New Heavens and New Earth

The Lord says, People who never before inquired about me are now seeking me out. Nations who never before searched for me are finding me.

²But my own people—though I have been spreading out my arms to welcome them all day long—have rebelled; they follow their own evil paths and thoughts. ³All day long they insult me to my face by worshiping idols in many gardens and burning incense on the rooftops of their homes. ⁴At night they go out among the graves and caves to worship evil spirits, and they eat pork and other forbidden foods. ⁵Yet they say to one another, "Don't come too close, you'll defile me! For I am holier than you!" They stifle me. Day in and day out they infuriate me.

⁶See, here is my decree all written out before me: *I will not stand silent; I will repay. Yes, I will repay them—* ⁷not only for their own sins but for those of their fathers too, says the Lord, for they also burned incense on the mountains and insulted me upon the hills. I will pay them back in full.

⁸But I will not destroy them all, says the Lord; for just as good grapes are found among a cluster of bad ones (and someone will say, "Don't throw them all away—there are some good grapes there!") so I will not destroy all Israel, for I have true servants there. ⁹I will preserve a remnant of my people to possess the land of Israel; those I select will inherit it and serve me there. ¹⁰As for my people who have sought me, the plains of Sharon shall again be filled with flocks, and the valley of Achor shall be a place to pasture herds.

¹¹But because the rest of you have forsaken the Lord and his Temple and worship gods of "Fate" and "Destiny," ¹²therefore I will "destine" you to the sword, and your "fate" shall be a dark one; for when I called, you didn't answer; when I spoke, you wouldn't listen. You deliberately sinned before my very eyes, choosing to do what you know I despise.

¹³Therefore, the Lord God says, You shall starve, but my servants shall eat; you shall be thirsty while they drink; you shall be sad and ashamed, but they shall rejoice. ¹⁴You shall cry in sorrow and vexation and despair, while they sing for joy. ¹⁵Your name shall be a curse word among my people, for the Lord God will slay you and call his true servants by another name.

¹⁶And yet, the days will come when all who invoke a blessing or take an oath shall swear by the God of Truth; for I will put aside my anger and forget the evil that you did. ¹⁷For see, I am creating new heavens and a new earth—so wonderful that no one will even think about the old ones anymore. ¹⁸Be glad; rejoice forever in my creation. Look! I will recreate Jerusalem as a place of happiness, and her people shall be a joy! ¹⁹And I will rejoice in Jerusalem and in my people; and the voice of weeping and crying shall not be heard there any more.

²⁰No longer will babies die when only a few days old; no longer will men be considered old at 100! Only sinners will die that young! ²¹,²²In those days, when a man builds a house, he will keep on living in it—it will not be destroyed by invading armies as in the past. My people will plant vineyards and eat the fruit themselves—their enemies will not confiscate it. For my people will live as long as trees and will long enjoy their hard-won gains. ²³Their harvests will not be eaten by their enemies; their children will not be born to be cannon fodder. For they are the children of those the Lord has blessed; and their children, too, shall be blessed. ²⁴I will answer them before they even call to me. While they are still talking to me about their needs, I will go ahead and answer their prayers! ²⁵The wolf and lamb shall feed together, the lion shall eat straw as the ox does, and poisonous snakes shall strike no more! In those days nothing and no one shall be hurt or destroyed in all my Holy Mountain, says the Lord.

66 The World Will See

Heaven is my throne and the earth is my footstool: What Temple can you build for me as good as that? ²My hand has made both earth and skies, and they are mine. Yet I will look with pity on the man who has a humble and a contrite heart, who trembles at my word.

³But those who choose their own ways, delighting in their sins, are cursed. God will not accept their offerings. When such men sacrifice an ox on the altar of God, it is no more acceptable to him than human sacrifice. If they sacrifice a lamb or bring an offering of grain, it is as loathsome to God as putting a dog or the blood of a swine on his altar! When they burn incense to him, he counts it the same as though they blessed an idol. ⁴I will send great troubles upon them—all the things they feared, for when I called them, they refused to answer, and when I spoke to them, they would not hear. Instead, they did wrong before my eyes and chose what they knew I despised.

⁵Hear the words of God, all you who fear him, and tremble at his words: Your brethren hate you and cast you out for being loyal to my name. "Glory to God," they scoff. "Be happy in the Lord!" But they shall be put to shame.

⁶What is all the commotion in the city? What is that terrible noise from the Temple? It is the voice of the Lord taking vengeance upon his enemies.

⁷,⁸Who has heard or seen anything as strange as this? For in one day, suddenly, a nation, Israel, shall be born, even before the birth pains come. In a moment, just as Israel's anguish starts, the baby is born; the nation begins. ⁹Shall I bring to the point of birth and then not deliver? asks the Lord your God. No! Never!

¹⁰Rejoice with Jerusalem; be glad with her, all you who love her, you who mourned for her. ¹¹Delight in Jerusalem; drink deep of her glory even as an infant at a mother's generous breasts. ¹²Prosperity shall overflow Jerusalem like a river, says the Lord, for I will send it; the riches of the Gentiles will flow to her. Her children shall be nursed at her breasts, carried on her hips and dandled on her knees. ¹³I will comfort you there as a little one is comforted by its mother.

¹⁴When you see Jerusalem, your heart will rejoice; vigorous health will be yours. All the world will see the good hand of God upon his people and his wrath upon his enemies. ¹⁵For see, the Lord will come with fire and with swift chariots of doom to pour out the fury of his anger and his hot rebuke with flames of fire. ¹⁶For the Lord will punish the world by fire and by his sword, and the slain of the Lord shall be many!

¹⁷Those who worship idols that are hidden behind a tree in the garden, feasting there on pork and mouse and all forbidden meat—they will come to an evil end, says Jehovah. ¹⁸I see full well what they are doing; I know what they are thinking, so I will gather together all nations and people against Jerusalem, where they shall see my glory. ¹⁹I will perform a mighty miracle against them, and I will send those who escape, as missionaries to the nations—to Tarshish, Put, Lud, Meshech, Rosh, Tubal, Javan, and to the lands beyond the sea that have not heard my fame nor seen my glory. There they shall declare my glory to the Gentiles. ²⁰And they shall bring back all your brethren from every nation as a gift to the Lord, transporting them gently on horses and in chariots, and in litters, and on mules and camels, to my holy mountain, to Jerusalem, says the Lord. It will be like offerings flowing into the Temple of the Lord at harvesttime, carried in vessels consecrated to the Lord. ²¹And I will appoint some of those returning to be my priests and Levites, says the Lord.

²²As surely as my new heavens and earth shall remain, so surely shall you always be my people, with a name that shall never disappear. ²³All mankind shall come to worship me from week to week and month to month. ²⁴And they shall go out and look at the dead bodies of those who have rebelled against me, for their worm shall never die; their fire shall not be quenched; and they shall be a disgusting sight to all mankind.

Jeremiah

DO YOU ever feel like you're too young or inexperienced to do anything important for God? Jeremiah felt that way! When God called him to be a prophet, Jeremiah said he was too young. Who would listen to him? He didn't have any experience with public speaking.

God promised to give Jeremiah the exact words he needed. One way Jeremiah got God's message across to the people was through symbols. Jeremiah would show an object to his audience and teach a lesson. He used things like a loincloth, clay, a cup of wine, a yoke, a field for sale, and a family.

Jeremiah was right about one thing—the people didn't listen to him! Jeremiah gave God's messages during the reigns of Josiah and Zedekiah. He warned the people about where they were headed—they worshiped other gods, ignored the Temple, and forgot who had given them their own country. The Israelites broke their covenant with God. But Jeremiah obeyed God, even though the people didn't.

When you think you're too young or inexperienced to do something for God, think of Jeremiah. Look for his courage as you read this book.

God Calls Jeremiah

These are God's messages to Jeremiah the priest (the son of Hilkiah) who lived in the town of Anathoth in the land of Benjamin. The first of these messages came to him in the thirteenth year of the reign of Amon's son Josiah, king of Judah. ³Others came during the reign of Josiah's son Jehoiakim, king of Judah, and at various other times until July of the eleventh year of the reign of Josiah's son Zedekiah, king of Judah, when Jerusalem was captured and the people were taken away as slaves.

⁴The Lord said to me, ⁵"I knew you before you were formed within your mother's womb; before you were born I sanctified you and appointed you as my spokesman to the world."

⁶"O Lord God," I said, "I can't do that! I'm far too young! I'm only a youth!"

⁷"Don't say that," he replied, "for you will go wherever I send you and speak whatever I tell you to. ⁸And don't be afraid of the people, for I, the Lord, will be with you and see you through."

⁹Then he touched my mouth and said, "See, I

have put my words in your mouth! ¹⁰Today your work begins, to warn the nations and the kingdoms of the world. In accord with my words spoken through your mouth I will tear down some and destroy them, and plant others, nurture them, and make them strong and great."

¹¹Then the Lord said to me, "Look, Jeremiah! What do you see?"

And I replied, "I see a whip made from the branch of an almond tree."

¹²And the Lord replied, "That's right, and it means that I will surely carry out my threats of punishment."

¹³Then the Lord asked me, "What do you see now?"

And I replied, "I see a pot of boiling water, tipping southward, spilling over Judah."

¹⁴"Yes," he said, "for terror from the north will boil out upon all the people of this land. ¹⁵I am calling the armies of the kingdoms of the north to come to Jerusalem and set their thrones at the gates of the city and all along its walls, and in all the other cities of Judah. ¹⁶This is the way I will punish my people for deserting me and for worshiping other gods—yes, idols they themselves have made! ¹⁷Get up and dress and go out and tell them whatever I tell you to say. Don't be afraid of them, or else I will make a fool of you in front of them. ¹⁸For see, today I have made you impervious to their attacks. They cannot harm you. You are strong like a fortified city that cannot be captured, like an iron pillar and heavy gates of brass. All the kings of Judah, its officers, priests, and people will not be able to prevail against you. ¹⁹They will try, but they will fail. For I am with you," says the Lord. "I will deliver you."

2 God's Rebellious People

Again the Lord spoke to me and said:

²Go and shout this in Jerusalem's streets: The Lord says, I remember how eager you were to please me as a young bride long ago, how you loved me and followed me even through the barren deserts. ³In those days Israel was a holy people, the first of my children. All who harmed them were counted deeply guilty, and great evil fell on anyone who touched them.

⁴,⁵O Israel, says the Lord, why did your fathers desert me? What sin did they find in me that turned them away and changed them into fools who worship idols? ⁶They ignore the fact that it was I, the Lord, who brought them safely out of Egypt and led them through the barren wilderness, a land of deserts and rocks, of drought and death, where no one lives or even travels. ⁷And I brought them into a fruitful land, to eat of its bounty and goodness, but they made it into a land of sin and corruption and turned my inheritance into an evil thing. ⁸Even their priests cared nothing for the Lord, and their judges ignored me; their rulers turned against me, and their prophets worshiped Baal and wasted their time on nonsense.

⁹But I will not give you up—I will plead for you to return to me and will keep on pleading; yes, even with your children's children in the years to come!

¹⁰,¹¹Look around you and see if you can find another nation anywhere that has traded in its old gods for new ones—even though their gods are nothing. Send to the west to the island of Cyprus; send to the east to the deserts of Kedar. See if anyone there has ever heard so strange a thing as this. And yet my people have given up their glorious God for silly idols! ¹²The heavens are shocked at such a thing and shrink back in horror and dismay. ¹³For my people have done two evil things: They have forsaken me, the Fountain of Life-giving Water; and they have built for themselves broken cisterns that can't hold water!

¹⁴Why has Israel become a nation of slaves? Why is she captured and led far away?

¹⁵I see great armies marching on Jerusalem with mighty shouts to destroy her and leave her cities in ruins, burned and desolate. ¹⁶I see the armies of Egypt rising against her, marching from their cities of Memphis and Tahpanhes to utterly destroy Israel's glory and power. ¹⁷And you have brought this on yourselves by rebelling against the Lord your God when he wanted to lead you and show you the way!

¹⁸What have you gained by your alliances with Egypt and with Assyria? ¹⁹Your own wickedness will punish you. You will see what an evil, bitter thing it is to rebel against the Lord your God, fearlessly forsaking him, says the Lord Almighty. ²⁰Long ago you shook off my yoke and broke away from my ties. Defiant, you would not obey me. On every hill and under every tree you've bowed low before idols.

²¹How could this happen? How could this be? For when I planted you, I chose my seed so carefully—the very best. Why have you become this degenerate race of evil men? ²²No amount of soap or lye can make you clean. You are stained with guilt that

---

SERVING GOD BOLDLY 1:6-8 Often people struggle with new challenges because they lack self-confidence. They feel they have inadequate ability, training, or experience. Jeremiah thought he was too young and inexperienced to be God's spokesman to the world. But God promised to be with him. We must never allow feelings of inadequacy to keep us from obeying God's call. He will *always* be with us. When you find yourself avoiding something you know you should do, be careful not to use lack of self-confidence as an excuse. If God gives you a job to do, he will provide all you need to do it. **To begin the series of devotionals on SERVING GOD BOLDLY, turn to page 17.**

FAMILY DEVOTIONS

☐ **DEVOTION 217**
PUTTING GOD FIRST

Read Jeremiah 2:26-32

Putting God First
Memory Verse

In everything you do, put God first, and he will direct you and crown your efforts with success.
Proverbs 3:6

"Linda Louise Lincoln, get down here!" called Mom. "Everyone is in the car waiting for you." Linda hurried out to the car.

"What's in that box you're carrying?" asked Dad.

"My new necklace. I forgot to pack it, and I want to wear it when we get dressed up for the Sunday services," said Linda, holding the box securely on her lap.

"A necklace! You made us wait all that time for a stupid piece of jewelry?" bellowed her brother Rob. "We're going camping, not to a fashion show!"

A few hours later, the Lincolns arrived at the campground. The days that followed were filled with fishing, swimming, boating, and campfires. When Sunday came, they got ready to attend the church service held at the camp pavilion. "Grab your Bibles and let's head on over," said Dad.

"Bibles?" Linda looked startled. "I didn't bring mine."

Mom, Dad, and Rob all looked at her in surprise. "But we're all doing that read through the Bible program," Rob said.

"Let's go," urged Dad. "You can look on with one of us."

When the pastor got up to speak, he said, "I'm glad you folks have not taken a vacation from God this week. You'll sense from our text how grieved God must be when we forget to spend time with him. I'm reading from Jeremiah 2. 'Can a girl forget her jewels? What bride will seek to hide her wedding dress? Yet for years on end my people have forgotten me—the most precious of their treasures.'"

Linda blushed when her brother poked her with his elbow and turned to look at her. She knew he was remembering, as she was, that she had brought her jewelry to camp but had forgotten her Bible. All week she had neglected to spend time with the Lord. Right then she made up her mind that she would copy that verse from her dad's Bible and memorize it. She didn't want to ever forget to spend time with God again.

How About You?
Have you forgotten God? Perhaps it isn't jewelry that you put ahead of the Lord, but how about TV? Or baseball? Or a bicycle? God wants you to put him first. Spend time with him daily. *P. R.*

• For the next devotional, turn to page 723.   • For the next devotional on *PUTTING GOD FIRST*, turn to page 749.
• For notes on *PUTTING GOD FIRST*, see pages 397, 492, 644, 791, and 982.

cannot ever be washed away. I see it always before me, the Lord God says. ²³You say it isn't so, that you haven't worshiped idols? How can you say a thing like that? Go and look in any valley in the land! Face the awful sins that you have done, O restless female camel, seeking for a male! ²⁴You are a wild donkey, sniffing the wind at mating time. (Who can restrain your lust?) Any jack wanting you need not search, for you come running to him! ²⁵Why don't you turn from all this weary running after other gods? But you say, "Don't waste your breath. I've fallen in love with these strangers and I can't stop loving them now!"

²⁶,²⁷Like a thief, the only shame that Israel knows is getting caught. Kings, princes, priests, and prophets—all are alike in this. They call a carved-up wooden post their father, and for their mother they have an idol chiseled out from stone. Yet in time of trouble they cry to me to save them! ²⁸Why don't you call on these gods you have made? When danger comes, let *them* go out and save you if they can! For you have as many gods as there are cities in Judah. ²⁹Don't come to me—you are all rebels, says the Lord. ³⁰I have punished your children, but it did them no good; they still will not obey. And you yourselves have killed my prophets as a lion kills its prey.

³¹O my people, listen to the words of God: Have I been unjust to Israel? Have I been to them a land of darkness and of evil? Why then do my people say, "At last we are free from God; we won't have anything to do with him again!" ³²How can you disown your God like that? Can a girl forget her jewels? What bride will seek to hide her wedding dress? Yet for years on end my people have forgotten me—the most precious of their treasures.

³³How you plot and scheme to win your lovers. The most experienced harlot could learn a lot from you! ³⁴Your clothing is stained with the blood of the innocent and the poor. Brazenly you murder without a cause. ³⁵And yet you say, "I haven't done a thing to anger God. I'm sure he isn't angry!" I will punish you severely because you say, "I haven't sinned!"

³⁶First here, then there, you flit about, going from one ally to another for their help; but it's all no good—your new friends in Egypt will forsake you as Assyria did before. ³⁷You will be left in despair and cover your face with your hands, for the Lord has rejected the ones that you trust. You will not succeed despite their aid.

3 The People Give Up God for Idols

There is a law that if a man divorces a woman who then remarries, he is not to take her back again, for she has become corrupted. But though you have left me and married many lovers, yet I have invited you to come to me again, the Lord says. ²Is there a single spot in all the land where you haven't been defiled by your adulteries—your worshiping these other gods? You sit like a prostitute beside the road waiting for a client! You sit alone like a Bedouin in the desert. You have polluted the land with your vile prostitution. ³That is why even the springtime rains have failed. For you are a prostitute and completely unashamed. ⁴,⁵And yet you say to me, "O Father, you have always been my Friend; surely you won't be angry about such a little thing! Surely you will just forget it?" So you talk and keep right on doing all the evil that you can.

⁶This message from the Lord came to me during the reign of King Josiah:

Have you seen what Israel does? Like a wanton wife who gives herself to other men at every chance, so Israel has worshiped other gods on every hill, beneath every shady tree. ⁷I thought that someday she would return to me and once again be mine; but she didn't come back. And her faithless sister Judah saw the continued rebellion of Israel. ⁸Yet she paid no attention, even though she saw that I divorced faithless Israel. But now Judah too has left me and given herself to prostitution, for she has gone to other gods to worship them. ⁹She treated it all so lightly—to her it was nothing at all that she should worship idols made of wood and stone. And so the land was greatly polluted and defiled. ¹⁰Then, afterwards, this faithless one "returned" to me, but her "sorrow" was only faked the Lord God says. ¹¹In fact, faithless Israel is less guilty than treacherous Judah!

¹²Therefore, go and say to Israel, O Israel, my sinful people, come home to me again, for I am merciful; I will not be forever angry with you. ¹³Only acknowledge your guilt; admit that you rebelled against the Lord your God and committed adultery against him by worshiping idols under every tree; confess that you refused to follow me. ¹⁴O sinful children, come home, for I am your Master, and I will bring you again to the land of Israel—one from here and two from there, wherever you are scattered. ¹⁵And I will give you leaders after my own heart, who will guide you with wisdom and understanding.

¹⁶Then, when your land is once more filled with people, says the Lord, you will no longer wish for "the good old days of long ago" when you possessed the Ark of God's covenant. Those days will not be missed or even thought about, and the Ark will not be reconstructed, for the Lord himself will be among you. ¹⁷The whole city of Jerusalem will be known as the throne of the Lord; all nations will come to him there and no longer stubbornly follow their evil desires. ¹⁸At that time the people of Judah and of Israel will return together from their exile in

Family Devotions

☐ DEVOTION 218
RESISTING TEMPTATION

Read Jeremiah 4:1-4, 14

Matt was quiet as he and his father raked the lawn one Saturday. "Dad," he said finally as he leaned on his rake, "I sometimes wonder if I'm really a Christian." Dad looked surprised. "Lately I . . . well, sometimes I have thoughts—bad thoughts—that I know a real Christian shouldn't have," added Matt, looking uncomfortable.

Dad was quiet for a moment. Then, motioning Matt to follow, he led the way to a cluster of small trees and moved back a branch to reveal a bird's nest. "I found this when I was pruning some branches," said Dad. "Do you notice anything strange about those eggs?"

"One is bigger than the others."

"That's because it wasn't laid by the bird who built this nest," explained Dad. "It was laid by a cowbird."

"A cowbird?" asked Matt. "Why would she lay her egg in another bird's nest?"

"So the other bird would think it was her own and care for the chick when it hatches," Dad replied. "The trouble is, the cowbird baby is usually bigger and stronger than the other baby birds and often takes their food or even pushes them out of the nest."

"What a mean trick!" exclaimed Matt. "Too bad the other bird can't tell that the big egg isn't her own. Then she could quick push it out before it hatches."

"That's right," Dad agreed. Then he added, "Satan is like that cowbird. He likes to put things into our minds that don't belong to us. We need to trust God to help us think and do the right things. We need to reject Satan's thoughts and push them out."

Matt nodded. "I'll watch out for thoughts like that. I'll ask God to help me push them out of my mind!"

Resisting Temptation Memory Verse

For since he himself has now been through suffering and temptation, he knows what it is like when we suffer and are tempted, and he is wonderfully able to help us.
Hebrews 2:18

How About You?

Do you sometimes have thoughts that make you doubt God, or that make you feel like doing something you shouldn't? Don't dwell on these thoughts. Reject them in Jesus' name. This is easier to do when you read the Bible regularly and cut out bad influences—dirty TV shows or magazines, and friends who use foul language. Replace bad thoughts with good ones! *S. K.*

• For the next devotional, turn to page 727.   • For the next devotional on *RESISTING TEMPTATION*, turn to page 741.
• For notes on *RESISTING TEMPTATION*, see pages 268, 448, 964, and 1258.

the north, to the land I gave their fathers as an inheritance forever. ¹⁹And I thought how wonderful it would be for you to be here among my children. I planned to give you part of this beautiful land, the finest in the world. I looked forward to your calling me "Father" and thought that you would never turn away from me again. ²⁰But you have betrayed me; you have gone off and given yourself to a host of foreign gods; you have been like a faithless wife who leaves her husband.

²¹I hear a voice high upon the windswept mountains, crying, crying. It is the sons of Israel who have turned their backs on God and wandered far away. ²²O my rebellious children, come back to me again and I will heal you from your sins.

And they reply, Yes, we will come, for you are the Lord our God. ²³We are weary of worshiping idols on the hills and of having orgies on the mountains. It is all a farce. Only in the Lord our God can Israel ever find her help and her salvation. ²⁴From our childhood we have seen everything our fathers had—flocks and herds and sons and daughters—squandered on priests and idols. ²⁵We lie in shame and in dishonor, for we and our fathers have sinned from childhood against the Lord our God; we have not obeyed him.

4 God Asks His People to Obey

O Israel, if you will truly return to me and absolutely discard your idols, ²and if you will swear by me alone, the living God, and begin to live good, honest, clean lives, then you will be a testimony to the nations of the world, and they will come to me and glorify my name.

³The Lord is saying to the men of Judah and Jerusalem, Plow up the hardness of your hearts; otherwise the good seed will be wasted among the thorns. ⁴Cleanse your minds and hearts, not just your bodies, or else my anger will burn you to a crisp because of all your sins. And no one will be able to put the fire out.

⁵Shout to Jerusalem and to all Judea, telling them to sound the alarm throughout the land. "Run for your lives! Flee to the fortified cities!" ⁶Send a signal from Jerusalem: "Flee now, don't delay!" For I the Lord am bringing vast destruction on you from the north. ⁷A lion—a destroyer of nations—stalks from his lair; and he is headed for your land. Your cities will lie in ruin without inhabitant. ⁸Put on clothes of mourning and weep with broken hearts, for the fierce anger of the Lord has not stopped yet. ⁹In that day, says the Lord, the king and the princes will tremble in fear; and the priests and the prophets will be stricken with horror.

¹⁰(Then I said, "But Lord, the people have been deceived by what you said, for you promised great blessings on Jerusalem. Yet the sword is even now poised to strike them dead!")

¹¹,¹²At that time he will send a burning wind from the desert upon them—not in little gusts but in a roaring blast—and he will pronounce their doom. ¹³The enemy shall roll down upon us like a storm wind; his chariots are like a whirlwind; his steeds are swifter than eagles. Woe, woe upon us, for we are doomed.

¹⁴O Jerusalem, cleanse your hearts while there is time. You can yet be saved by casting out your evil thoughts. ¹⁵From Dan and from Mount Ephraim your doom has been announced. ¹⁶Warn the other nations that the enemy is coming from a distant land, and they shout against Jerusalem and the cities of Judah. ¹⁷They surround Jerusalem like shepherds moving in on some wild animal! For my people have rebelled against me, says the Lord. ¹⁸Your ways have brought this down upon you; it is a bitter dose of your own medicine, striking deep within your hearts.

¹⁹My heart, my heart—I writhe in pain; my heart pounds within me. I cannot be still because I have heard, O my soul, the blast of the enemies' trumpets and the enemies' battle cries. ²⁰Wave upon wave of destruction rolls over the land, until it lies in utter ruin; suddenly, in a moment, every house is crushed. ²¹How long must this go on? How long must I see war and death surrounding me?

²²"Until my people leave their foolishness, for they refuse to listen to me; they are dull, retarded children who have no understanding. They are smart enough at doing wrong, but for doing right they have no talent, none at all."

²³I looked down upon their land, and as far as I could see in all directions everything was ruins. And all the heavens were dark. ²⁴I looked at the mountains and saw that they trembled and shook. ²⁵I looked, and mankind was gone, and the birds of the heavens had fled.

²⁶The fertile valleys were wilderness, and all the cities were broken down before the presence of the Lord, crushed by his fierce anger. ²⁷The Lord's decree of desolation covers all the land.

"Yet," he says, "there will be a little remnant of my people left. ²⁸The earth shall mourn, the heavens shall be draped with black, because of my decree against my people; I have made up my mind and will not change it."

²⁹All the cities flee in terror at the noise of marching armies coming near. The people hide in the bushes and flee to the mountains. All the cities are abandoned—all have fled in terror. ³⁰Why do you put on your most beautiful clothing and jewelry and brighten your eyes with mascara? It

will do you no good! Your allies despise you and will kill you.

³¹I have heard great crying like that of a woman giving birth to her first child; it is the cry of my people gasping for breath, pleading for help, prostrate before their murderers.

5 No Respect for God

Run up and down through every street in all Jerusalem; search high and low and see if you can find even one person who is fair and honest! Search every square, and if you find just one, I'll not destroy the city! ²Even under oath, they all lie.

³O Lord, you are looking for faithfulness. You have tried to get them to be honest, for you have punished them, but they won't change! You have destroyed them, but they refuse to turn from their sins. They are determined, with faces hard as rock, not to repent.

⁴Then I said, "But what can we expect from the poor and ignorant? They don't know the ways of God. How can they obey him?"

⁵I will go now to their leaders, the men of importance, and speak to them, for they know the ways of the Lord and the judgment that follows sin. But they too had utterly rejected their God.

⁶So I will send upon them the wild fury of the "lion from the forest"; the "desert wolves" shall pounce upon them, and a "leopard" shall lurk around their cities so that all who go out shall be torn apart. For their sins are very many; their rebellion against me is great.

⁷How can I pardon you? For even your children have turned away and worship gods that are not gods at all. I fed my people until they were fully satisfied, and their thanks was to commit adultery wholesale and to gang up at the city's brothels. ⁸They are well-fed, lusty stallions, each neighing for his neighbor's mate. ⁹Shall I not punish them for this? Shall I not send my vengeance on such a nation as this? ¹⁰Go down the rows of the vineyards and destroy them! But leave a scattered few to live. Strip the branches from each vine, for they are not the Lord's.

¹¹For the people of Israel and Judah are full of treachery against me, says the Lord. ¹²They have lied and said, "He won't bother us! No evil will come upon us! There will be neither famine nor war! ¹³God's prophets," they say, "are windbags full of words with no divine authority. Their claims of doom will fall upon themselves, not us!"

¹⁴Therefore, this is what the Lord God of Hosts says to his prophets: Because of talk like this, I'll take your words and prophecies and turn them into raging fire and burn up these people like kindling wood. ¹⁵See, I will bring a distant nation against you, O Israel, says the Lord. It is a mighty nation, an ancient nation whose language you don't understand. ¹⁶Their weapons are deadly; the men are all mighty. ¹⁷And they shall eat your harvest and your children's bread, your flocks of sheep and herds of cattle, yes, and your grapes and figs; and they shall sack your walled cities that you think are safe.

¹⁸But I will not completely blot you out. So says the Lord.

¹⁹And when your people ask, "Why is it that the Lord is doing this to us?" then you shall say, "You rejected him and gave yourselves to other gods while in your land; now you must be slaves to foreigners in their lands."

²⁰Make this announcement to Judah and to Israel:

²¹Listen, O foolish, senseless people—you with the eyes that do not see and the ears that do not listen— ²²have you no respect at all for me? the Lord God asks. How can it be that you don't even tremble in my presence? I set the shorelines of the world by perpetual decrees, so that the oceans, though they toss and roar, can never pass those bounds. Isn't such a God to be feared and worshiped?

²³,²⁴But my people have rebellious hearts; they have turned against me and gone off into idolatry. Though I am the one who gives them rain each year in spring and fall and sends the harvesttimes, yet they have no respect or fear for me. ²⁵And so I have taken away these wondrous blessings from them. This sin has robbed them of all of these good things.

²⁶Among my people are wicked men who lurk for victims like a hunter hiding in a blind. They set their traps for men. ²⁷Like a coop full of chickens their homes are full of evil plots. And the result? Now they are great and rich, ²⁸they are well fed and well groomed, and there is no limit to their wicked deeds. They refuse justice to orphans and the rights of the poor. ²⁹Should I sit back and act as though nothing is going on? the Lord God asks. Shouldn't I punish a nation such as this?

³⁰A horrible thing has happened in this land— ³¹the priests are ruled by false prophets, and my people like it so! But your doom is certain.

6 One Last Warning

Run, people of Benjamin, run for your lives! Flee from Jerusalem! Sound the alarm in Tekoa; send up a smoke signal at Beth-haccherem; warn everyone that a powerful army is on the way from the north, coming to destroy this nation! ²Helpless as a girl, you are beautiful and delicate—and doomed. ³ Evil shepherds shall surround you. They shall set up camp around the city and divide your pastures for their flocks. ⁴See them prepare for battle. At noon it has begun. All afternoon it rages until the evening shadows fall. ⁵ "Come," they say. "Let us attack by night and destroy her palaces!"

⁶For the Lord Almighty has said to them, Cut down her trees for battering rams; smash down the walls of Jerusalem. This is the city to be punished, for she is vile through and through. ⁷She spouts evil like a fountain! Her streets echo with the sounds of violence; her sickness and wounds are ever before me.

⁸This is your last warning, O Jerusalem. If you don't listen, I will empty the land. ⁹Disaster on disaster shall befall you. Even the few who remain in Israel shall be gleaned again, the Lord Almighty has said; for as a grape-gatherer checks each vine to pick what he has missed, so the remnant of my people shall be destroyed again.

¹⁰But who will listen when I warn them? Their ears are closed, and they refuse to hear. The word of God has angered them; they don't want it at all.

¹¹For all this I am full of the wrath of God against them. I am weary of holding it in. I will pour it out over Jerusalem, even upon the children playing in the streets, upon the gatherings of young men, and on husbands and wives and grandparents. ¹²Their enemies shall live in their homes and take their fields and wives. For I will punish the people of this land, the Lord has said. ¹³They are swindlers and liars, from the least of them right to the top! Yes, even my prophets and priests! ¹⁴You can't heal a wound by saying it's not there! Yet the priests and prophets give assurances of peace when all is war. ¹⁵Were my people ashamed when they worshiped idols? No, not at all—they didn't even blush. Therefore they shall lie among the slain. They shall die beneath my anger.

¹⁶Yet the Lord pleads with you still: Ask where the good road is, the godly paths you used to walk in, in the days of long ago. Travel there, and you will find rest for your souls. But you reply, "No, that is not the road we want!" ¹⁷I set watchmen over you who warned you: "Listen for the sound of the trumpet! It will let you know when trouble comes." But you said, "No! We won't pay any attention!"

¹⁸,¹⁹This, then, is my decree against my people: (Listen to it, distant lands; listen to it, O my people in Jerusalem; listen to it, all the earth!) I will bring evil upon this people; it will be the fruit of their own sin because they will not listen to me. They reject my law. ²⁰There is no use now in burning sweet incense from Sheba before me! Keep your expensive perfumes! I cannot accept your offerings; they have no sweet fragrance for me. ²¹I will make an obstacle course of the pathway of my people; fathers and sons shall be frustrated; neighbors and friends shall collapse together. ²²The Lord God says, See the armies marching from the north—a great nation is rising against you. ²³They are a cruel, merciless people, fully armed, mounted for war. The noise of their army is like a roaring sea.

²⁴We have heard the fame of their armies, and we are weak with fright. Fright and pain have gripped us like that of women in travail. ²⁵Don't go out to the fields! Don't travel the roads! For the enemy is everywhere, ready to kill; we are terrorized at every turn.

²⁶O Jerusalem, pride of my people, put on mourning clothes and sit in ashes; weep bitterly as for an only son. For suddenly the destroying armies will be upon you.

²⁷Jeremiah, I have made you an assayer of metals that you may test this my people and determine their value. Listen to what they are saying and watch what they are doing. ²⁸Are they not the worst of rebels, full of evil talk against the Lord? They are insolent as brass, hard and cruel as iron. ²⁹The bellows blow fiercely; the refining fire grows hotter, but it can never cleanse them, for there is no pureness in them to bring out. Why continue the process longer? All is dross. No matter how hot the fire, they continue in their wicked ways. ³⁰I must label them "Impure, Rejected Silver," and I have discarded them.

7 False Worship

Then the Lord said to Jeremiah:

²Go over to the entrance of the Temple of the Lord and give this message to the people: O Judah, listen to this message from God. Listen to it, all of you who worship here. ³The Lord, the God of Israel says: Even yet, if you quit your evil ways, I will let you stay in your own land. ⁴But don't be fooled by those who lie to you and say that since the Temple of the Lord is here, God will never let Jerusalem be destroyed. ⁵You may remain under these conditions only: If you stop your wicked thoughts and deeds and are fair to others; ⁶if you stop exploiting orphans, widows, and foreigners, and stop your murdering; if you stop worshiping idols as you do now to your hurt, ⁷then, and only then, will I let you stay in this land that I gave to your fathers to keep forever.

⁸You think that because the Temple is here, you will never suffer? Don't fool yourselves! ⁹Do you really think that you can steal, murder, commit adultery, lie, and worship Baal and all of those new gods of yours, ¹⁰and then come here and stand before me in my Temple and chant, "We are saved!"—only to go right back to all these evil things again? ¹¹Is my Temple but a den of robbers

Family Devotions

☐ DEVOTION 219
OBEDIENCE

Read Jeremiah 7:21-26

"Look, Dad!" Ken exclaimed one afternoon. "Smokie's playing dead, just like I taught him."

Dad laughed as he saw the dog stretched out on the porch. "I think he's just resting," he said. "Let's go for a walk and teach him to heel."

When they started out with Smokie on a leash, the dog plodded along willingly at first. Then he began to strain at the leash, trying to go out to the street. Ken scolded and tugged, but the dog paid no attention. Suddenly Smokie turned and ran in the direction Ken had been pulling. "Hey, look! He's minding me now!" Ken called.

When Smokie came to a trash can, he stopped short, sniffing at the contents. No amount of coaxing by Ken could get him to budge.

"I don't understand it," moaned Ken as Dad walked up. "Sometimes Smokie minds me, and sometimes he doesn't."

"I don't think he's obeying you at all," Dad remarked. "I think he does whatever he wants, and sometimes he just happens to want the same thing you do."

"You mean he's *accidentally* good?" asked Ken.

Dad laughed. "You could say that." Dad took the leash and showed Ken how to direct the dog, giving the leash a firm jerk every time Smokie went the wrong way.

"You know, people often behave the way Smokie did," observed Dad as they walked. "When they're in a good mood, they act kindly toward others. They go to church when they feel like it, and they contribute money or time if they feel generous. But that's not really obeying God. The true test of obedience is how we respond when we *don't* feel like obeying."

"I get it," Ken replied as he jerked the leash. "I'll try to remember that. I don't want to be just accidentally good."

Obedience Memory Verse

Oh, that they would always have such a heart for me, wanting to obey my commandments. Then all would go well with them in the future, and with their children throughout all generations!
Deuteronomy 5:29

How About You?

Do you think you're a good person because you obey God's commandments sometimes—whenever you feel like it? That's not really obeying. It's still just doing what you want to do. You need to obey him in everything, regardless of how you feel or what it might cost you. S. K.

in your eyes? For I see all the evil going on in there.

¹²Go to Shiloh, the city I first honored with my name, and see what I did to her because of all the wickedness of my people Israel. ¹³,¹⁴And now, says the Lord, I will do the same thing here because of all this evil you have done. Again and again I spoke to you about it, rising up early and calling, but you refused to hear or answer. Yes, I will destroy this Temple, as I did in Shiloh—this Temple called by my name, which you trust for help, and this place I gave to you and to your fathers. ¹⁵And I will send you into exile, just as I did your brothers, the people of Ephraim.

¹⁶Pray no more for these people, Jeremiah. Neither weep for them nor pray nor beg that I should help them, for I will not listen. ¹⁷Don't you see what they are doing throughout the cities of Judah and in the streets of Jerusalem? ¹⁸No wonder my anger is great! Watch how the children gather wood and the fathers build fires, and the women knead dough and make cakes to offer to The Queen of Heaven and to their other idol-gods! ¹⁹ Am I the one that they are hurting? asks the Lord. Most of all they hurt themselves, to their own shame. ²⁰So the Lord God says, I will pour out my anger, yes, my fury on this place—people, animals, trees, and plants will be consumed by the unquenchable fire of my anger.

²¹The Lord, the God of Israel says, Away with your offerings and sacrifices! ²²It wasn't offerings and sacrifices I wanted from your fathers when I led them out of Egypt. That was not the point of my command. ²³But what I told them was: *Obey me, and I will be your God and you shall be my people; only do as I say, and all shall be well!*

²⁴But they wouldn't listen; they kept on doing whatever they wanted to, following their own stubborn, evil thoughts. They went backward instead of forward. ²⁵Ever since the day your fathers left Egypt until now, I have kept on sending them my prophets, day after day. ²⁶But they wouldn't listen to them or even try to hear. They are hard and stubborn and rebellious—worse even than their fathers were.

²⁷Tell them everything that I will do to them, but don't expect them to listen. Cry out your warnings, but don't expect them to respond. ²⁸Say to them: This is the nation that refuses to obey the Lord its God and refuses to be taught. She continues to live a lie.

²⁹O Jerusalem, shave your head in shame and weep alone upon the mountains; for the Lord has rejected and forsaken this people of his wrath. ³⁰For the people of Judah have sinned before my very eyes, says the Lord. They have set up their idols right in my own Temple, polluting it. ³¹They have built the altar called Topheth in the Valley of Ben-hinnom, and there they burn to death their little sons and daughters as sacrifices to their gods—a deed so horrible I've never even thought of it, let alone commanded it to be done. ³² The time is coming, says the Lord, when that valley's name will be changed from Topheth, or the Valley of Ben-hinnom, to the Valley of Slaughter; for there will be so many slain to bury that there won't be room enough for all the graves, and they will dump the bodies in that valley.

³³The bodies of my people shall be food for the birds and animals, and no one shall be left to scare them away. ³⁴I will end the happy singing and laughter and the joyous voices of the bridegrooms and brides in the streets of Jerusalem and in the cities of Judah. For the land shall lie in desolation.

8 The People Believe Lies

Then, says the Lord, the enemy shall break open the graves of the kings of Judah and of the princes, and the graves of the priests, prophets, and people, ²and dig out their bones and spread them out on the ground before the sun and moon and stars—the gods of my people!—whom they have loved and worshiped. Their bones shall not be gathered up again nor buried but shall be scattered like dung upon the ground. ³And those of this evil nation who are still left alive shall long to die rather than live where I will scatter them, says the Lord Almighty.

⁴,⁵Once again give them this message from the Lord: When a person falls, he jumps up again; when he is on the wrong road and discovers his mistake, he goes back to the fork where he made the wrong turn. But these people keep on along their evil path, even though I warn them. ⁶I listen to their conversation and what do I hear? Is anyone sorry for sin? Does anyone say, "What a terrible thing I have done?" No, all are rushing pell-mell down the path of sin as swiftly as a horse rushing to the battle! ⁷The stork knows the time of her migration, as does the turtledove, the crane, and the swallow. They all return at God's appointed time each year; but not my people! They don't accept the laws of God.

⁸How can you say, "We understand his laws," when your teachers have twisted them up to mean a thing I never said? ⁹These wise teachers of yours will be shamed by exile for this sin, for they have rejected the word of the Lord. Are they then so wise? ¹⁰I will give their wives and their farms to others; for all of them, great and small, prophet and priest, have one purpose in mind—to get what isn't theirs. ¹¹They give useless medicine for my people's grievous wounds, for they assure them all is well when that isn't so at all!

¹²Are they ashamed because they worship idols? No, not in the least; they don't even know how to blush! That is why I will see to it that they lie among the fallen. I will visit them with death. ¹³Their figs and grapes will disappear, their fruit trees will die, and all the good things I prepared for them will soon be gone.

¹⁴Then the people will say, "Why should we wait here to die? Come, let us go to the walled cities and perish there. For the Lord our God has decreed our doom and given us a cup of poison to drink because of all our sins. ¹⁵We expected peace, but no peace came; we looked for health, but there was only terror."

¹⁶The noise of war resounds from the northern border. The whole land trembles at the approach of the terrible army, for the enemy is coming and is devouring the land and everything in it—the cities and people alike. ¹⁷For I will send these enemy troops among you like poisonous snakes that you cannot charm. No matter what you do, they will bite you and you shall die.

¹⁸My grief is beyond healing; my heart is broken. ¹⁹Listen to the weeping of my people all across the land.

"Where is the Lord?" they ask. "Has God deserted us?"

"Oh, why have they angered me with their carved idols and strange evil rites?" the Lord replies.

²⁰"The harvest is finished; the summer is over, and we are not saved."

²¹I weep for the hurt of my people; I stand amazed, silent, dumb with grief. ²²Is there no medicine in Gilead? Is there no physician there? Why doesn't God do something? Why doesn't he help?

9 Jeremiah Cries

Oh, that my eyes were a fountain of tears; I would weep forever; I would sob day and night for the slain of my people! ²Oh, that I could go away and forget them and live in some wayside shack in the desert, for they are all adulterous, treacherous men.

³"They bend their tongues like bows to shoot their arrows of untruth. They care nothing for right and go from bad to worse; they care nothing for me," says the Lord.

⁴Beware of your neighbor! Beware of your brother! All take advantage of one another and spread their slanderous lies. ⁵With practiced tongues they fool and defraud each other; they wear themselves out with all their sinning.

⁶"They pile evil upon evil, lie upon lie, and utterly refuse to come to me," says the Lord.

⁷Therefore, the Lord Almighty says this: "See, I will melt them in a crucible of affliction. I will refine them and test them like metal. What else can I do with them? ⁸For their tongues aim lies like poisoned spears. They speak cleverly to their neighbors while planning to kill them. ⁹Should not I punish them for such things as this?" asks the Lord. "Shall not my soul be avenged on such a nation as this?"

¹⁰Sobbing and weeping, I point to their mountains and pastures, for now they are desolate, without a living soul. Gone is the lowing of cattle, gone the birds and wild animals. All have fled.

¹¹"And I will turn Jerusalem into heaps of ruined houses where only jackals have their dens. The cities of Judah shall be ghost towns, with no one living in them."

¹²Who is wise enough to understand all this? Where is the Lord's messenger to explain it? Why is the land a wilderness so that no one dares even to travel through?

¹³"Because," the Lord replies, "my people have forsaken my commandments and not obeyed my laws. ¹⁴Instead, they have done whatever they pleased and worshiped the idols of Baal, as their fathers told them to." ¹⁵Therefore, this is what the Lord, the God of Israel, says: Look! I will feed them with bitterness and give them poison to drink. ¹⁶I will scatter them around the world, to be strangers in distant lands; and even there the sword of destruction shall chase them until I have utterly destroyed them.

¹⁷,¹⁸The Lord Almighty says: "Send for the mourners! Quick! Begin your crying! Let the tears flow from your eyes. ¹⁹Hear Jerusalem weeping in despair. 'We are ruined! Disaster has befallen us! We must leave our land and homes!'" ²⁰Listen to the words of God, O women who wail. Teach your daughters to wail and your neighbors too. ²¹For death has crept in through your windows into your homes. He has killed off the flower of your youth. Children no longer play in the streets; the young men gather no more in the squares.

²²Tell them this, says the Lord: Bodies shall be scattered across the fields like manure, like sheaves after the mower, and no one will bury them.

²³The Lord says: Let not the wise man bask in his wisdom, nor the mighty man in his might, nor the rich man in his riches. ²⁴Let them boast in this alone: That they truly know me, and understand that I am the Lord of justice and of righteousness whose love is steadfast; and that I love to be this way.

²⁵,²⁶A time is coming, says the Lord, when I will punish all those who are circumcised in body but not in spirit—the Egyptians, Edomites, Ammonites, Moabites, Arabs, and yes, even you people of Judah. For all these pagan nations also circumcise

themselves. Unless you circumcise your hearts by loving me, your circumcision is only a heathen rite like theirs, and nothing more.

10 The God of Creation

Hear the word of the Lord, O Israel:

2,3 Don't act like the people who make horoscopes and try to read their fate and future in the stars! Don't be frightened by predictions such as theirs, for it is all a pack of lies. Their ways are futile and foolish. They cut down a tree and carve an idol; 4they decorate it with gold and silver and fasten it securely in place with hammer and nails so that it won't fall over. 5And there stands their god like a helpless scarecrow in a garden! It cannot speak, and it must be carried, for it cannot walk. Don't be afraid of such a god, for it can neither harm nor help nor do you any good.

6O Lord, there is no other god like you. For you are great, and your name is full of power. 7Who would not fear you, O King of nations? (And that title belongs to you alone!) Among all the wise men of the earth and in all the kingdoms of the world there isn't anyone like you.

8The wisest of men who worship idols are altogether stupid and foolish. 9 They bring beaten sheets of silver from Tarshish and gold from Uphaz and give them to skillful goldsmiths who make their idols; then they clothe these gods in royal purple robes that expert tailors make.

10But the Lord is the only true God, the living God, the everlasting King. The whole earth shall tremble at his anger; the world shall hide before his displeasure.

11Say this to those who worship other gods: Your so-called gods, who have not made the heavens and earth, shall vanish from the earth. 12But our God formed the earth by his power and wisdom, and by his intelligence he hung the stars in space and stretched out the heavens. 13It is his voice that echoes in the thunder of the storm clouds. He causes mist to rise upon the earth; he sends the lightning and brings the rain, and from his treasuries he brings the wind.

14But foolish men without knowledge of God bow before their idols. It is a shameful business that these men are in, for what they make are frauds, gods without life or power in them. 15All are worthless, silly; they will be crushed when their makers perish. 16But the God of Jacob is not like these foolish idols. He is the Creator of all, and Israel is his chosen nation. The Lord Almighty is his name.

17Pack your bags, he says. Get ready now to leave; the siege will soon begin. 18For suddenly I'll fling you from this land and pour great troubles down; at last you shall feel my wrath.

19*Desperate is my wound. My grief is great. My sickness is incurable, but I must bear it.* 20*My home is gone; my children have been taken away, and I will never see them again. There is no one left to help me rebuild my home.* 21The shepherds of my people have lost their senses; they no longer follow God nor ask his will. Therefore they perish, and their flocks are scattered. 22Listen! Hear the terrible sound of great armies coming from the north. The cities of Judah shall become dens of jackals.

23O Lord, I know it is not within the power of man to map his life and plan his course— 24so you correct me, Lord; but please be gentle. Don't do it in your anger, for I would die. 25Pour out your fury on the nations who don't obey the Lord, for they have destroyed Israel and made a wasteland of this entire country.

11 Remember God's Promise

Then the Lord spoke to Jeremiah once again and said:

Remind the men of Judah and all the people of Jerusalem that I made a contract with their fathers—and cursed is the man who does not heed it! 4 For I told them at the time I brought them out of slavery in Egypt that if they would obey me and do whatever I commanded them, then they and all their children would be mine and I would be their God. 5And now, Israel, obey me, says the Lord, so that I can do for you the wonderful things I swore I would if you obeyed. I want to give you a land that "flows with milk and honey," as it is today.

Then I replied, "So be it, Lord!"

6Then the Lord said: Broadcast this message in Jerusalem's streets—go from city to city throughout the land and say, Remember this agreement that your fathers made with God, and do all the things they promised him they would. 7For I solemnly said to your fathers when I brought them out of Egypt—and have kept on saying it over and over again until this day: Obey my every command! 8But your fathers didn't do it. They wouldn't even listen. Each followed his own stubborn will and his proud heart. Because they refused to obey, I did to them all the evils stated in the contract.

9Again the Lord spoke to me and said: I have discovered a conspiracy against me among the men of Judah and Jerusalem. 10They have returned to the sins of their fathers, refusing to listen to me and worshiping idols. The agreement I made with their fathers is broken and canceled. 11Therefore, the Lord says, I am going to bring calamity down upon them, and they shall not escape. Though they cry for mercy, I will not listen to their pleas. ¹²Then they will pray to their idols and burn incense before them, but that cannot save them from their time of anguish and despair. ¹³O my people, you have as many gods as there are cities, and your altars of shame (your altars to burn incense to Baal) are along every street in Jerusalem.

¹⁴Therefore, Jeremiah, pray no longer for this people, neither weep nor plead for them; for I will not listen to them when they are finally desperate enough to beg me for help. ¹⁵What right do my beloved people have to come any more to my Temple? For you have been unfaithful and worshiped other gods. Can promises and sacrifices now avert your doom and give you life and joy again?

¹⁶The Lord used to call you his green olive tree, beautiful to see and full of good fruit; but now he has sent the fury of your enemies to burn you up and leave you broken and charred. ¹⁷It is because of the wickedness of Israel and Judah in offering incense to Baal that the Lord Almighty who planted the tree has ordered it destroyed.

¹⁸Then the Lord told me all about their plans and showed me their evil plots. ¹⁹I had been as unsuspecting as a lamb or ox on the way to slaughter. I didn't know that they were planning to kill me! "Let's destroy this man and all his messages," they said. "Let's kill him so that his name will be forever forgotten."

²⁰O Lord Almighty, you are just. See the hearts and motives of these men. Repay them for all that they have planned! I look to you for justice.

²¹,²²And the Lord replied, The men of the city of Anathoth shall be punished for planning to kill you. They will tell you not to prophesy in God's name on pain of death. And so their young men shall die in battle; their boys and girls shall starve. ²³Not one of these plotters of Anathoth shall survive, for I will bring a great disaster upon them. Their time has come.

12 Jeremiah Complains to God

O Lord, you always give me justice when I bring a case before you to decide. Now let me bring you this complaint: Why are the wicked so prosperous? Why are evil men so happy? ²You plant them. They take root and their business grows. Their profits multiply, and they are rich. They say, "Thank God!" But in their hearts they give no credit to you. ³But as for me—Lord, you know my heart—you know how much it longs for you. (And I am poor, O Lord!) Lord, drag them off like helpless sheep to the slaughter. Judge them, O God!

⁴How long must this land of yours put up with all their goings on? Even the grass of the field groans and weeps over their wicked deeds! The wild animals and birds have moved away, leaving the land deserted. Yet the people say, "God won't bring judgment on us. We're perfectly safe!"

⁵The Lord replied to me: If racing with mere men—these men of Anathoth—has wearied you, how will you race against horses, against the king, his court and all his evil priests? If you stumble and fall on open ground, what will you do in Jordan's jungles? ⁶Even your own brothers, your own family, have turned against you. They have plotted to call for a mob to lynch you. Don't trust them, no matter how pleasantly they speak. Don't believe them.

⁷Then the Lord said: I have abandoned my people, my inheritance; I have surrendered my dearest ones to their enemies. ⁸My people have roared at me like a lion of the forest, so I have treated them as though I hated them. ⁹My people have fallen. I will bring upon them swarms of vultures and wild animals to pick the flesh from their corpses.

¹⁰Many foreign rulers have ravaged my vineyard, trampling down the vines, and turning all its beauty into barren wilderness. ¹¹They have made it desolate; I hear its mournful cry. The whole land is desolate and no one cares. ¹²Destroying armies plunder the land; the sword of the Lord devours from one end of the nation to the other; nothing shall escape. ¹³My people have sown wheat but reaped thorns; they have worked hard, but it does them no good. They shall harvest a crop of shame, for the fierce anger of the Lord is upon them.

¹⁴And now the Lord says this to the evil nations, the nations surrounding the land God gave his people Israel: See, I will force you from your land just as Judah will be forced from hers; ¹⁵but afterwards I will return and have compassion on all of you and will bring you home to your own land again, each man to his inheritance. ¹⁶And if these heathen nations quickly learn my people's ways and claim me as their God instead of Baal (whom they taught my people to worship), then they shall be strong among my people. ¹⁷But any nation refusing to obey me will be expelled again and finished, says the Lord.

TRUSTING GOD'S PLAN 12:5-6 Life was extremely difficult for Jeremiah despite his love for and obedience to God. When he called to God for relief, God's reply in effect was, "If you think this is bad, how are you going to cope when it gets really tough?"

Not all of God's answers to prayer are nice or easy to cope with. Any Christian who has experienced war, grief, or a serious illness knows this. But we are to be committed to God even when the going gets tough and when his answers to our prayers don't bring immediate relief. **To begin the series of devotionals on TRUSTING GOD'S PLAN, turn to page 9.**

13 Good for Nothing

The Lord said to me, Go and buy a linen loincloth and wear it, but don't wash it—don't put it in water at all. ²So I bought the loincloth and put it on. ³Then the Lord's message came to me again. This time he said, ⁴Take the loincloth out to the Euphrates River and hide it in a hole in the rocks.

⁵So I did; I hid it as the Lord had told me to. ⁶Then, a long time afterwards, the Lord said: Go out to the river again and get the loincloth. ⁷And I did; I dug it out of the hole where I had hidden it. But now it was mildewed and falling apart. It was utterly useless!

⁸,⁹Then the Lord said: This illustrates the way that I will rot the pride of Judah and Jerusalem. ¹⁰This evil nation refuses to listen to me and follows its own evil desires, and worships idols; therefore, it shall become as this loincloth—good for nothing. ¹¹Even as a loincloth clings to a man's loins, so I made Judah and Israel to cling to me, says the Lord. They were my people, an honor to my name. But then they turned away.

¹²Tell them this: The Lord God of Israel says, All your wine jugs will be full of wine. And they will reply, Of course, you don't need to tell us how prosperous we will be! ¹³Then tell them: That's not what I mean. I mean that I will fill everyone living in this land with helpless bewilderment—from the king sitting on David's throne, and the priests and the prophets right on down to all the people. ¹⁴And I will smash fathers and sons against each other, says the Lord. I will not let pity nor mercy spare them from utter destruction.

¹⁵Oh, that you were not so proud and stubborn! Then you would listen to the Lord, for he has spoken. ¹⁶Give glory to the Lord your God before it is too late, before he causes deep, impenetrable darkness to fall upon you so that you stumble and fall upon the dark mountains; then, when you look for light, you will find only terrible darkness. ¹⁷Do you still refuse to listen? Then in loneliness my breaking heart shall mourn because of your pride. My eyes will overflow with tears because the Lord's flock shall be carried away as slaves.

¹⁸Say to the king and queen-mother, Come down from your thrones and sit in the dust, for your glorious crowns are removed from your heads. They are no longer yours. ¹⁹The cities of the Negeb to the south of Jerusalem have closed their gates against the enemy. They must defend themselves, for Jerusalem cannot help; and all Judah shall be taken away as slaves.

²⁰See the armies marching from the north! Where is your flock, Jerusalem, your beautiful flock he gave you to take care of? ²¹How will you feel when he sets your allies over you as your rulers? You will writhe in pain like a woman having a child. ²²And if you ask yourself, Why is all this happening to me? It is because of the grossness of your sins; that is why you have been raped and destroyed by the invading army. ²³Can the Ethiopian change the color of his skin? or a leopard take away his spots? Nor can you who are so used to doing evil now start being good.

²⁴,²⁵Because you have put me out of your mind and put your trust in false gods, I will scatter you as chaff is scattered by the fierce winds off the desert. This then is your allotment, that which is due you, which I have measured out especially for you. ²⁶I myself will expose you to utter shame. ²⁷I am keenly aware of your apostasy, your faithlessness to me, and your abominable idol worship in the fields and on the hills. Woe upon you, O Jerusalem! How long before you will be pure?

14 God Loses His Patience

This message came to Jeremiah from the Lord, explaining why he was holding back the rain:

²Judah mourns; business has ground to a halt; all the people prostrate themselves to the earth, and a great cry rises from Jerusalem. ³The nobles send servants for water from the wells, but the wells are dry. The servants return, baffled and desperate, and cover their heads in grief. ⁴The ground is parched and cracked for lack of rain; the farmers are afraid. ⁵The deer deserts her fawn because there is no grass. ⁶The wild donkeys stand upon the bare hills panting like thirsty jackals. They strain their eyes looking for grass to eat, but there is none to be found.

⁷O Lord, we have sinned against you grievously, yet help us for the sake of your own reputation! ⁸O Hope of Israel, our Savior in times of trouble, why are you as a stranger to us, as one passing through the land who is merely stopping for the night? ⁹Are you also baffled? Are you helpless to save us? O Lord, you are right here among us, and we carry your name; we are known as your people. O Lord, don't desert us now!

¹⁰But the Lord replies: You have loved to wander far from me and have not tried to follow in my paths. Now I will no longer accept you as my people; now I will remember all the evil you have done and punish your sins.

¹¹The Lord told me again: Don't ask me any more to bless this people. Don't pray for them any more. ¹²When they fast, I will not pay any attention; when they present their offerings and sacrifices to me, I will not accept them. What I

will give them in return is war and famine and disease.

¹³Then I said, O Lord God, their prophets are telling them that all is well—that no war or famine will come. They tell the people you will surely send them peace, that you will bless them.

¹⁴Then the Lord said: The prophets are telling lies in my name. I didn't send them or tell them to speak or give them any message. They prophesy of visions and revelations they have never seen nor heard; they speak foolishness concocted out of their own lying hearts. ¹⁵Therefore, the Lord says, I will punish these lying prophets who have spoken in my name though I did not send them, who say no war shall come nor famine. By war and famine they themselves shall die! ¹⁶And the people to whom they prophesy—their bodies shall be thrown out into the streets of Jerusalem, victims of famine and war; there shall be no one to bury them. Husbands, wives, sons, and daughters—all will be gone. For I will pour out terrible punishment upon them for their sins.

¹⁷Therefore, tell them this: Night and day my eyes shall overflow with tears; I cannot stop my crying, for my people have been run through with a sword and lie mortally wounded on the ground. ¹⁸If I go out in the fields, there lie the bodies of those the sword has killed; and if I walk in the streets, there lie those dead from starvation and disease. And yet the prophets and priests alike have made it their business to travel through the whole country, reassuring everyone that all is well, speaking of things they know nothing about.

¹⁹"O Lord," the people will cry, "have you completely rejected Judah? Do you abhor Jerusalem? Even after punishment, will there be no peace? We thought, Now at last he will heal us and bind our wounds. But no peace has come, and there is only trouble and terror everywhere. ²⁰O Lord, we confess our wickedness, and that of our fathers too. ²¹Do not hate us, Lord, for the sake of your own name. Do not disgrace yourself and the throne of your glory by forsaking your promise to bless us! ²²What heathen god can give us rain? Who but you alone, O Lord our God, can do such things as this? Therefore we will wait for you to help us."

15 Jerusalem, a City in Trouble

Then the Lord said to me, Even if Moses and Samuel stood before me pleading for these people, even then I wouldn't help them—away with them! Get them out of my sight! ²And if they say to you, But where can we go? tell them the Lord says: Those who are destined for death, to death; those who must die by the sword, to the sword; those doomed to starvation, to famine; and those for captivity, to captivity. ³I will appoint over them four kinds of destroyers, says the Lord: the sword to kill, the dogs to tear, and the vultures and wild animals to finish up what's left. ⁴Because of the wicked things Manasseh, son of Hezekiah, king of Judah, did in Jerusalem, I will punish you so severely that your fate will horrify the peoples of the world.

⁵Who will feel sorry for you, Jerusalem? Who will weep for you? Who will even bother to ask how you are? ⁶You have forsaken me and turned your backs upon me. Therefore, I will clench my fists against you to destroy you. I am tired of always giving you another chance. ⁷I will sift you at the gates of your cities and take from you all that you hold dear, and I will destroy my own people because they refuse to turn back to me from all their evil ways. ⁸There shall be countless widows; at noontime I will bring death to the young men and sorrow to their mothers. I will cause anguish and terror to fall upon them suddenly. ⁹The mother of seven sickens and faints, for all her sons are dead. Her sun is gone down while it is yet day. She sits childless now, disgraced, for all her children have been killed.

¹⁰Then Jeremiah said, "What sadness is mine, my mother; oh, that I had died at birth. For I am hated everywhere I go. I am neither a creditor soon to foreclose nor a debtor refusing to pay—yet they all curse me. ¹¹Well, let them curse! Lord, you know how I have pled with you on their behalf—how I have begged you to spare these enemies of mine."

¹²,¹³Can a man break bars of northern iron or bronze? This people's stubborn will can't be broken either. So, because of all your sins against me, I will deliver your wealth and treasures as loot to the enemy. ¹⁴I will have your enemies take you as slaves to a land where you have never been before, for my anger burns like fire, and it shall consume you.

¹⁵Then Jeremiah replied, "Lord, you know it is for your sake that I am suffering. They are persecuting me because I have proclaimed your word to them. Don't let them kill me! Rescue me from their clutches, and give them what they deserve! ¹⁶Your words are what sustain me; they are food to my hungry soul. They bring joy to my sorrowing heart and delight me. How proud I am to bear your name, O Lord. ¹⁷,¹⁸I have not joined the people in their merry feasts. I sit alone beneath the hand of God. I burst with indignation at their sins. Yet you have failed me in my time of need! You have let them keep right on with all their persecutions. Will they never stop hurting me? Your help is as uncertain as a seasonal mountain

brook—sometimes a flood, sometimes as dry as a bone."

¹⁹The Lord replied: "Stop this foolishness and talk some sense! Only if you return to trusting me will I let you continue as my spokesman. You are to influence *them,* not let them influence *you!* ²⁰They will fight against you like a besieging army against a high city wall. But they will not conquer you, for I am with you to protect and deliver you, says the Lord. ²¹Yes, I will certainly deliver you from these wicked men and rescue you from their ruthless hands."

16 A People Try to Run from God

On yet another occasion God spoke to me, and said:

²You must not marry and have children here. ³For the children born in this city and their mothers and fathers ⁴shall die from terrible diseases. No one shall mourn for them or bury them, but their bodies shall lie on the ground to rot and fertilize the soil. They shall die from war and famine, and their bodies shall be picked apart by vultures and wild animals. ⁵Do not mourn or weep for them, for I have removed my protection and my peace from them—taken away my lovingkindness and my mercies. ⁶Both great and small shall die in this land, unburied and unmourned, and their friends shall not cut themselves nor shave their heads as signs of sorrow (as is their heathen custom). ⁷No one shall comfort the mourners with a meal nor send them a cup of wine expressing grief for their parents' death.

⁸As a sign to them of these sad days ahead, don't you join them any more in their feasts and parties—don't even eat a meal with them. ⁹For the Lord Almighty, the God of Israel, says: In your own lifetime, before your very eyes, I will end all laughter in this land—the happy songs, the marriage feasts, the songs of bridegrooms and of brides.

¹⁰And when you tell the people all these things and they ask, "Why has the Lord decreed such terrible things against us? What have we done to merit such treatment? What is our sin against the Lord our God?" ¹¹tell them the Lord's reply is this: Because your fathers forsook me. They worshiped other gods and served them; they did not keep my laws, ¹²*and you have been worse than your fathers were!* You follow evil to your hearts' content and refuse to listen to me. ¹³Therefore, I will throw you out of this land and chase you into a foreign land where neither you nor your fathers have been before, and there you can go ahead and worship your idols all you like—and I will grant you no favors!

¹⁴,¹⁵But there will come a glorious day, says the Lord, when the whole topic of conversation will be that God is bringing his people home from a nation in the north, and from many other lands where he had scattered them. You will look back no longer to the time when I rescued you from your slavery in Egypt. That mighty miracle will scarcely be mentioned any more. Yes, I will bring you back again, says the Lord, to this same land I gave your fathers.

¹⁶Now I am sending for many fishermen to fish you from the deeps where you are hiding from my wrath. I am sending for hunters to chase you down like deer in the forests or mountain goats on inaccessible crags. Wherever you run to escape my judgment, I will find you and punish you. ¹⁷For I am closely watching you, and I see every sin. You cannot hope to hide from me.

¹⁸And I will punish you doubly for all your sins because you have defiled my land with your detestable idols and filled it up with all your evil deeds.

¹⁹O Lord, my Strength and Fortress, my Refuge in the day of trouble, nations from around the world will come to you saying, "Our fathers have been foolish, for they have worshiped worthless idols! ²⁰Can men make God? The gods they made are not real gods at all."

²¹And when they come in that spirit, I will show them my power and might and make them understand at last that I alone am God.

17 A Green and Growing Tree

My people sin as though commanded to, as though their evil were laws chiseled with an iron pen or diamond point upon their stony hearts or on the corners of their altars. ²,³Their youths do not forget to sin, worshiping idols beneath each tree, high in the mountains or in the open country down below. And so I will give all your treasures to your enemies as the price that you must pay for all your sins. ⁴And the wonderful heritage I reserved for you will slip out of your hand, and I will send you away as slaves to your enemies in distant lands. For you have kindled a fire of my anger that shall burn forever.

⁵The Lord says: Cursed is the man who puts his trust in mortal man and turns his heart away from God. ⁶He is like a stunted shrub in the desert, with no hope for the future; he lives on the salt-encrusted plains in the barren wilderness; good times pass him by forever.

⁷But blessed is the man who trusts in the Lord and has made the Lord his hope and confidence. ⁸He is like a tree planted along a riverbank, with its roots reaching deep into the water—a tree not bothered by the heat nor worried by long months

FAMILY DEVOTIONS

☐ DEVOTION 220
OPTIMISM

Read Jeremiah 17:7-8

"What a miserable day!" grumbled Adam as he and his friend Steve trudged home from school. They walked carefully, trying to sidestep the puddles that an unexpected cloudburst had produced.

"Duck weather, I call it," agreed Steve. "It's hard to believe the sun is shining up above those clouds."

Adam looked up doubtfully at the gray skies. When a raindrop hit him in the eye, he blinked and quickly looked down again. "How do you know the sun's shining up there?" he asked.

"Remember when my mom and I flew to Houston last spring?" asked Steve. Adam nodded. "It was a day just like this when we left," continued Steve, "but the plane got way up high—higher than the clouds. Then we could see the sun shining, and the clouds looked white and soft, like piles of cotton or something."

Adam thought about that as they reached his driveway. From below, the clouds looked more like the hard, sharp-edged sheet metal his dad had used to repair the roof of the toolshed. Could the sun really be shining up above the clouds? He decided to check with Mom.

After telling Steve good-bye, Adam raced up the walk. "Mom," he called as he went inside, "is it true that the sun is still shining?" Mom looked up from her work, puzzled at the question, so Adam explained what Steve had said.

Mom smiled and nodded. "Yes," she said. "Isn't that wonderful? If we could rise above the clouds, we could see the sun." She paused for a moment. "Even though we can't rise above the clouds in the sky today, we can rise above the clouds in our lives," she added. "God's light—his understanding and help—is always there for us. As we bring our problems to him in prayer, they no longer need to weigh us down like a rainy day. We can rise above them as we trust God to deal with them."

Optimism Memory Verse

Fix your thoughts on what is true and good and right. Think about things that are pure and lovely, and dwell on the fine, good things in others. Think about all you can praise God for and be glad about.
Philippians 4:8

How About You?

Do you let problems get you down, or do you quickly give them to the Lord? When you pray, do you expect an answer? You should! God is eager to bless your life and give you peace and joy. Pray every day! N. E. K.

- For the next devotional, turn to page 737. • For the next devotional on OPTIMISM, turn to page 1057.
- For notes on OPTIMISM, see pages 143, 536, 677, and 940.

of drought. Its leaves stay green, and it goes right on producing all its luscious fruit.

⁹The heart is the most deceitful thing there is and desperately wicked. No one can really know how bad it is! ¹⁰Only the Lord knows! He searches all hearts and examines deepest motives so he can give to each person his right reward, according to his deeds—how he has lived.

¹¹Like a bird that fills her nest with young she has not hatched and which will soon desert her and fly away, so is the man who gets his wealth by unjust means. Sooner or later he will lose his riches and at the end of his life become a poor old fool.

¹²But our refuge is your throne, eternal, high and glorious. ¹³O Lord, the Hope of Israel, all who turn away from you shall be disgraced and shamed; they are registered for earth and not for glory, for they have forsaken the Lord, the Fountain of living waters. ¹⁴Lord, you alone can heal me, you alone can save, and my praises are for you alone.

¹⁵Men scoff at me and say, "What is this word of the Lord you keep talking about? If these threats of yours are really from God, why don't they come true?"

¹⁶Lord, I don't want the people crushed by terrible calamity. The plan is yours, not mine. It is *your* message I've given them, not my own. I don't want them doomed! ¹⁷Lord, don't desert me now! You alone are my hope. ¹⁸Bring confusion and trouble on all who persecute me, but give me peace. Yes, bring double destruction upon them!

¹⁹Then the Lord said to me, Go and stand in the gates of Jerusalem, first at the gate where the king goes out, and then at each of the other gates, ²⁰and say to all the people: Hear the word of the Lord, kings of Judah and all the people of this nation, and all you citizens of Jerusalem. ²¹,²²The Lord says: Take warning and live; do no unnecessary work on the Sabbath day, but make it a holy day. I gave this commandment to your fathers, ²³but they didn't listen or obey. They stubbornly refused to pay attention and be taught.

²⁴But if you obey me, says the Lord, and refuse to work on the Sabbath day and keep it separate, special and holy, ²⁵then this nation shall continue forever. There shall always be descendants of David sitting on the throne here in Jerusalem; there shall always be kings and princes riding in pomp and splendor among the people, and this city shall remain forever. ²⁶And from all around Jerusalem and from the cities of Judah and Benjamin, from the Negeb and from the lowlands west of Judah, the people shall come with their burnt offerings and grain offerings and incense, bringing their sacrifices to praise the Lord in his Temple.

²⁷But if you will not listen to me, if you refuse to keep the Sabbath holy, if on the Sabbath you bring in loads of merchandise through these gates of Jerusalem, just as on other days, then I will set fire to these gates. The fire shall spread to the palaces and utterly destroy them, and no one shall be able to put out the raging flames.

18 No One Listens to Jeremiah

Here is another message to Jeremiah from the Lord:

²Go down to the shop where clay pots and jars are made, and I will talk to you there. ³I did as he told me and found the potter working at his wheel. ⁴But the jar that he was forming didn't turn out as he wished, so he kneaded it into a lump and started again.

⁵Then the Lord said: ⁶O Israel, can't I do to you as this potter has done to his clay? As the clay is in the potter's hand, so are you in my hand. ⁷Whenever I announce that a certain nation or kingdom is to be taken up and destroyed, ⁸then if that nation renounces its evil ways, I will not destroy it as I had planned. ⁹And if I announce that I will make a certain nation strong and great, ¹⁰but then that nation changes its mind, turns to evil, and refuses to obey me, then I, too, will change my mind and not bless that nation as I had said I would.

¹¹Therefore, go and warn all Judah and Jerusalem, saying: Hear the word of the Lord. I am planning evil against you now instead of good; turn back from your evil paths and do what is right.

¹²But they replied, "Don't waste your breath. We have no intention whatever of doing what God says. We will continue to live as we want to, free from any restraint, full of stubbornness and wickedness!"

¹³Then the Lord said: Even among the heathen, no one has ever heard of such a thing! My people have done something too horrible to understand. ¹⁴The snow never melts high up in the Lebanon mountains. The cold, flowing streams from the crags of Mount Hermon never run dry. ¹⁵These can be counted on. But not my people! For they have deserted me and turned to foolish idols. They have turned away from the ancient highways of good and walk the muddy paths of sin. ¹⁶Therefore, their land shall become desolate, so that all who pass by will gasp and shake their heads in amazement at its utter desolation. ¹⁷I will scatter my people before their enemies as the east wind scatters dust; and in all their trouble I will turn my back on them and refuse to notice their distress.

¹⁸Then the people said, "Come, let's get rid of Jeremiah. We have our own priests and wise men

Family Devotions

☐ **Devotion 221**
Cultivating Godly Attitudes

Read Jeremiah 17:7-10

Cultivating Godly Attitudes
Memory Verse

Your attitude should be the kind that was shown us by Jesus Christ. Philippians 2:5

Andrea glanced around the Sunday school room. "Nina brought one visitor today," she whispered to Jana, "but that makes only five for her, and I brought six. I won!"

"I'm surprised to see Maria here." Jana looked at the lone figure in the back row. "Wouldn't she feel more comfortable in the class for special children?"

Andrea shrugged. "Maybe, but then she wouldn't count for me. Remember we have to bring visitors to *our* class."

Just then Renee joined them. "Oh, Andrea, you look cute in my sweater," she gushed. "I only wore it once 'cause it never did fit me right."

At that moment the bell rang. As Andrea took a front seat, her face felt like it was on fire. She was so humiliated! She wondered how many had heard Renee's announcement that she was wearing hand-me-down clothes. *I wish she'd never given me this stupid sweater!* Andrea fumed inwardly. *I'll certainly never wear it again!*

". . . possible to do the right thing for the wrong reason." Miss Judy's words finally broke into Andrea's consciousness. "If we pray so others will think we're great Christians, our motive is wrong. If we give so others will praise us, it is wrong."

I hope Renee's listening! thought Andrea. *She just gave me her old clothes so she could act like Miss High-and-Mighty and put me down.*

". . . only invite others so we can win the contest, we should be ashamed." Miss Judy's voice broke into Andrea's thoughts again.

With a start, Andrea remembered Maria in the back row. She gulped as she realized she was no better than Renee. "I'm sorry, Lord," she whispered. "Starting now I'm going to do the right thing for the right reason." Rising quietly, she went to sit beside Maria.

How About You?
Why do you give? Pray? Go to church? Witness? Do you do it so others will say nice things about you, or because you love the Lord? Do the right things for the right reasons, and you will be blessed. B. W.

• For the next devotional, turn to page 739. • For the next devotional on *Cultivating Godly Attitudes,* turn to page 739. • For notes on *Cultivating Godly Attitudes,* see pages 337, 383, 472, 622, and 1216.

and prophets—we don't need his advice. Let's silence him that he may speak no more against us, nor bother us again."

[19]O Lord, help me! See what they are planning to do to me! [20]Should they repay evil for good? They have set a trap to kill me, yet I spoke well of them to you and tried to defend them from your anger. [21]Now, Lord, let their children starve to death and let the sword pour out their blood! Let their wives be widows and be bereft of all their children! Let their men die in epidemics and their youths die in battle! [22]Let screaming be heard from their homes as troops of soldiers come suddenly upon them, for they have dug a pit for me to fall in, and they have hidden traps along my path. [23]Lord, you know all their murderous plots against me. Don't forgive them, don't blot out their sin, but let them perish before you; deal with them in your anger.

19 Jerusalem Will Be Destroyed

The Lord said, Buy a clay jar and take it out into the valley of Ben-hinnom by the east gate of the city. Take some of the elders of the people and some of the older priests with you, and speak to them whatever words I give you.

[3]Then the Lord spoke to them and said: Listen to the word of the Lord, kings of Judah and citizens of Jerusalem! The Lord Almighty, the God of Israel, says, I will bring terrible evil upon this place, so terrible that the ears of those who hear it will prickle. [4]For Israel has forsaken me and turned this valley into a place of shame and wickedness. The people burn incense to idols—idols that neither this generation nor their forefathers nor the kings of Judah have worshiped before— and they have filled this place with the blood of innocent children. [5]They have built high altars to Baal, and there they burn their sons in sacrifice— a thing I never commanded them nor even thought of !

[6]The day is coming, says the Lord, when this valley shall no longer be called Topheth or Ben-hinnom Valley, but The Valley of Slaughter. [7]For I will upset the battle plans of Judah and Jerusalem, and I will let invading armies kill you here and leave your dead bodies for vultures and wild animals to feed upon. [8]And I will wipe Jerusalem off the earth, so that everyone going by will gasp with astonishment at all that I have done to her. [9]I will see to it that your enemies lay siege to the city until all food is gone and those trapped inside begin to eat their own children and friends.

[10]And now, Jeremiah, as these men watch, smash the jar you brought with you, [11]and say to them, This is the message to you from the Lord Almighty: As this jar lies shattered, so I will shatter the people of Jerusalem; and as this jar cannot be mended, neither can they. The slaughter shall be so great that there won't be room enough for decent burial anywhere, and their bodies shall be heaped in this valley. [12]And as it will be in this valley, so it will be in Jerusalem. For I will fill Jerusalem with dead bodies too. [13]And I will defile all the homes in Jerusalem, including the palace of the kings of Judah—wherever incense has been burned upon the roofs to your stargods, and libations poured out to them.

[14]As Jeremiah returned from Topheth where he had delivered this message, he stopped in front of the Temple of the Lord and said to all the people, [15]The Lord Almighty, the God of Israel, says: I will bring upon this city and her surrounding towns all the evil I have promised because you have stubbornly refused to listen to the Lord.

20 Jeremiah Is Arrested

Now when Pashhur (son of Immer), the priest in charge of the Temple of the Lord, heard what Jeremiah was saying, [2]he arrested Jeremiah and had him whipped and put in the stocks at Benjamin Gate near the Temple. [3]He left him there all night.

The next day when Pashhur finally released him, Jeremiah said, "Pashhur, the Lord has changed your name. He says from now on to call you 'The Man Who Lives in Terror.' [4]For the Lord will send terror on you and all your friends, and you will see them die by the swords of their enemies. I will hand over Judah to the king of Babylon, says the Lord, and he shall take away these people as slaves to Babylon and kill them. [5]And I will let your enemies loot Jerusalem. All the famed treasures of the city, with the precious jewels and gold and silver of your kings, shall be carried off to Babylon. [6]And as for you, Pashhur, you and all your family and household shall become slaves in Babylon and die there—you and those to whom you lied when you prophesied that everything would be all right."

[7]O Lord, you deceived me when you promised me your help. I have to give them your messages because you are stronger than I am, but now I am the laughingstock of the city, mocked by all. [8]You have never once let me speak a word of kindness to them; always it is disaster and horror and destruction. No wonder they scoff and mock and make my name a household joke. [9]And I can't quit! For if I say I'll never again mention the Lord—never more speak in his name—then his word in my heart is like fire that burns in my bones, and I can't hold it in any longer. [10]Yet on every side I hear their whispered threats and am afraid. "We will report," they say. Even those who

Family Devotions

☐ *Devotion 222*
Cultivating Godly Attitudes

Read Jeremiah 18:1-6

Cultivating Godly Attitudes
Memory Verse

Whatever you do or say, let it be as a representative of the Lord Jesus, and come with him into the presence of God the Father to give him your thanks.
Colossians 3:17

Joan and the others in her ceramics class watched as her mother poured a liquid into a mold. All the girls were interested in seeing how something so runny could get hard enough to become a lovely vase. Then Mom brought out a piece that had been molded a few days ago.

"Is that one done?" asked one of the girls.

"Oh, no," replied Joan's mother. "As soon as it's dry enough to handle, it needs to be rubbed and cleaned and scraped, and then it will be put into the fire."

The girls watched again as Joan's mother worked on the piece of pottery. With a knife, she scraped away the excess clay. Then, with a piece of sandpaper, she smoothed the pottery. Finally, she rubbed it with a soft sponge.

"All that work?" Joan said.

"That's just the beginning," Mom answered. "After it has gone through one firing, a colorful glaze will be applied. Then it will be put into the fire again. You know, girls, this reminds me of our lives. God works on Christians, scraping off our bad habits, smoothing us out to become more like him, and finally making us beautiful and shiny by putting us through the fire."

"But I don't think I'd like to be put through all those things," remarked one girl.

"Neither would I," Joan agreed.

"If we're not willing to let God work on us—taking away bad habits, sinful thoughts, angry words, and stubborn attitudes—then our lives will never shine for Jesus," Joan's mother replied. "It's part of his plan to make us more like him."

How About You?

Has God been scraping off the bad habits and sinful deeds in your life? Has he sent punishment when you lie, cheat, or talk back? Has he taught you patience through illness or through doing without something you really want? When he works in your life do you object? Or do you know that he cares so much about you that he wants to make you one of his shining witnesses? R. J.

• For the next devotional, turn to page 741. • For the next devotional on *Cultivating Godly Attitudes*, turn to page 1005. • For notes on *Cultivating Godly Attitudes*, see pages 337, 383, 472, 622, and 1216.

were my friends are watching me, waiting for a fatal slip. "He will trap himself," they say, "and then we will get our revenge on him."

[11] But the Lord stands beside me like a great warrior, and before him, the Mighty, Terrible One, they shall stumble. They cannot defeat me; they shall be shamed and thoroughly humiliated, and they shall have a stigma upon them forever. [12] O Lord Almighty, who knows those who are righteous and examines the deepest thoughts of hearts and minds, let me see your vengeance on them. For I have committed my cause to you. [13] Therefore, I will sing out in thanks to the Lord! Praise him! For he has delivered me, poor and needy, from my oppressors.

[14] Yet, cursed be the day that I was born! [15] Cursed be the man who brought my father the news that a son was born. [16] Let that messenger be destroyed like the cities of old which God overthrew without mercy. Terrify him all day long with battle shouts [17] because he did not kill me at my birth! Oh, that I had died within my mother's womb, that it had been my grave! [18] Why was I ever born? For my life has been but trouble and sorrow and shame.

21 God's Answer to the King Is No

Then King Zedekiah sent Pashhur (son of Malchiah) and Zephaniah the priest (son of Maaseiah) to Jeremiah and begged, "Ask the Lord to help us, for Nebuchadnezzar, king of Babylon, has declared war on us! [2] Perhaps the Lord will be gracious to us and do a mighty miracle as in olden times and force Nebuchadnezzar to withdraw his forces."

[3,4] Jeremiah replied, "Go back to King Zedekiah and tell him the Lord God of Israel says, I will make all your weapons useless against the king of Babylon and the Chaldeans besieging you. In fact, I will bring your enemies right into the heart of this city, [5] and I myself will fight against you, for I am very angry. [6] And I will send a terrible plague on this city, and both men and animals shall die. [7] And finally I will deliver King Zedekiah himself and all the remnant left in the city into the hands of King Nebuchadnezzar of Babylon, to slaughter them without pity or mercy.

[8] "Tell these people, The Lord says: Take your choice of life or death! [9] Stay here in Jerusalem and die—slaughtered by your enemies, killed by starvation and disease—or go out and surrender to the Chaldean army and live. [10] For I have set my face against this city; I will be its enemy and not its friend, says the Lord. It shall be captured by the king of Babylon and he shall reduce it to ashes.

[11] "And to the king of Judah, the Lord says: [12] I am ready to judge you because of all the evil you are doing. Quick! Give justice to these you judge! Begin doing what is right before my burning fury flashes out upon you like a fire no man can quench. [13] I will fight against this city of Jerusalem, that boasts, 'We are safe; no one can touch us here!' [14] And I myself will destroy you for your sinfulness, says the Lord. I will light a fire in the forests that will burn up everything in its path."

22 Evil Kings Will Be Judged

Then the Lord said to me: Go over and speak directly to the king of Judah and say, [2] Listen to this message from God, O king of Judah, sitting on David's throne; and let your servants and your people listen too.

[3] The Lord says: Be fair-minded. Do what is right! Help those in need of justice! Quit your evil deeds! Protect the rights of aliens and immigrants, orphans and widows; stop murdering the innocent! [4] If you put an end to all these terrible deeds you are doing, then I will deliver this nation and once more give kings to sit on David's throne, and there shall be prosperity for all. [5] But if you refuse to pay attention to this warning, I swear by my own name, says the Lord, that this palace shall become a shambles.

[6] For this is the Lord's message concerning the palace: You are as beloved to me as fruitful Gilead and the green forests of Lebanon; but I will destroy you and leave you deserted and uninhabited. [7] I will call for a wrecking crew to bring out its tools to dismantle you. They will tear out all of your fine cedar beams and throw them on the fire. [8] Men from many nations will pass by the ruins of this city and say to one another, "Why did the Lord do it? Why did he destroy such a great city?" [9] And the answer will be, "Because the people living here forgot the Lord their God and violated his agreement with them, for they worshiped idols."

[10] Don't weep for the dead! Instead weep for the captives led away! For they will never return to see their native land again. [11] For the Lord says this about Jehoahaz who succeeded his father King Josiah and was taken away as a captive: [12] He shall die in a distant land and never again see his own country.

[13] And woe to you, King Jehoiakim, for you are building your great palace with forced labor. By not paying wages you are building injustice into its walls and oppression into its doorframes and ceilings. [14] You say, "I will build a magnificent palace with huge rooms and many windows, paneled throughout with fragrant cedar and painted a lovely red." [15] But a beautiful palace does not make a great king! Why did your father Josiah

FAMILY DEVOTIONS

☐ DEVOTION 223
RESISTING TEMPTATION

Read Jeremiah 22:1-5

Amy and Carl had invited their friends to come over and play fox and geese. The children shuffled their feet into the snow to make a huge pie design. It looked like a giant wheel with eight spokes running through it.

Ken volunteered to be the first fox. "Remember, the center is the safety spot," Carl instructed. "Run into it, and you are safe. But you have to use the escape spokes to get there. If the fox catches you, you're it."

The children romped in the snow until Amy and Carl were called in for lunch. "You seemed to be having a good time out there," observed Mom. "But why didn't you take turns being the fox?"

"We did," Amy said.

Mom looked surprised. "But every time I looked out, Bryan was it," she said.

Carl laughed. "That was Bryan's own fault. He always tried to get just as close to the fox as possible before he'd run. Then he got caught."

"And he never used the escape routes until it was too late," Amy added. "That was foolish."

Mom nodded. "You know," she said, "many people do the same thing in the game of life."

"The game of life?" asked Carl.

"We face trials and temptations, but Jesus has given us escape routes," explained Mom. "We can run to him for safety. But sometimes we try to get so close to sin before we run away that we get caught by that sin. If we read God's Word, pray, and follow his commands, we'll understand the way to escape sin. We don't have to get caught."

Resisting Temptation Memory Verse

For since he himself has now been through suffering and temptation, he knows what it is like when we suffer and are tempted, and he is wonderfully able to help us.
Hebrews 2:18

How About You?
Do you run away from sin before you get involved? God demands that we do what is right, and he also promises to help us resist the temptation to do wrong. Ask Jesus for help. He will show you the way to escape. *J. H.*

• For the next devotional, turn to page 747. • For the next devotional on RESISTING TEMPTATION, turn to page 1107.
• For notes on RESISTING TEMPTATION, see pages 268, 448, 964, and 1258.

reign so long? Because he was just and fair in all his dealings. That is why God blessed him. ¹⁶He saw to it that justice and help were given the poor and the needy and all went well for him. This is how a man lives close to God. ¹⁷But you! You are full of selfish greed and all dishonesty! You murder the innocent, oppress the poor, and reign with ruthlessness.

¹⁸Therefore this is God's decree of punishment against King Jehoiakim, who succeeded his father Josiah on the throne: His family will not weep for him when he dies. His subjects will not even care that he is dead. ¹⁹He shall be buried like a dead donkey—dragged out of Jerusalem and thrown on the garbage dump beyond the gate! ²⁰Weep, for your allies are gone. Search for them in Lebanon; shout for them at Bashan; seek them at the fording points of Jordan. See, they are all destroyed. Not one is left to help you! ²¹When you were prosperous I warned you, but you replied, "Don't bother me." Since childhood you have been that way—you just won't listen! ²²And now all your allies have disappeared with a puff of wind; all your friends are taken off as slaves. Surely at last you will see your wickedness and be ashamed. ²³It's very nice to live graciously in a beautiful palace among the cedars of Lebanon, but soon you will cry and groan in anguish—anguish as of a woman in labor.

²⁴,²⁵And as for you, Coniah, son of Jehoiakim king of Judah—even if you were the signet ring on my right hand, I would pull you off and give you to those who seek to kill you, of whom you are so desperately afraid—to Nebuchadnezzar, king of Babylon, and his mighty army. ²⁶I will throw you and your mother out of this country, and you shall die in a foreign land. ²⁷You will never again return to the land of your desire. ²⁸This man Coniah is like a discarded, broken dish. He and his children will be exiled to distant lands.

²⁹O earth, earth, earth! Hear the word of the Lord! ³⁰The Lord says: Record this man Coniah as childless, for none of his children shall ever sit upon the throne of David or rule in Judah. His life will amount to nothing.

23 A Perfect King Will Come

The Lord declares:

I will send disaster upon the leaders of my people—the shepherds of my sheep—for they have destroyed and scattered the very ones they were to care for. ²Instead of leading my flock to safety, you have deserted them and driven them to destruction. And now I will pour out judgment upon you for the evil you have done to them. ³And I will gather together the remnant of my flock from wherever I have sent them and bring them back into their own fold, and they shall be fruitful and increase. ⁴And I will appoint responsible shepherds to care for them, and they shall not need to be afraid again; all of them shall be accounted for continually.

⁵,⁶For the time is coming, says the Lord, when I will place a righteous Branch upon King David's throne. He shall be a King who shall rule with wisdom and justice and cause righteousness to prevail everywhere throughout the earth. And this is his name: *The Lord Our Righteousness.* At that time Judah will be saved and Israel will live in peace.

⁷In that day people will no longer say when taking an oath, "As the Lord lives who rescued the people of Israel from the land of Egypt," ⁸but they will say, "As the Lord lives who brought the Jews back to their own land of Israel from the countries to which he had exiled them."

⁹My heart is broken for the false prophets, full of deceit. I awake with fear and stagger as a drunkard does from wine because of the awful fate awaiting them, for God has decreed holy words of judgment against them. ¹⁰For the land is full of adultery, and the curse of God is on it. The land itself is mourning—the pastures are dried up—for the prophets do evil, and their power is used wrongly.

¹¹The priests are like the prophets, all ungodly, wicked men. I have seen their despicable acts right here in my own Temple, says the Lord. ¹²Therefore, their paths will be dark and slippery; they will be chased down dark and treacherous trails and fall. For I will bring evil upon them and see to it, when their time has come, that they pay their penalty in full for all their sins.

¹³I knew the prophets of Samaria were unbelievably evil, for they prophesied by Baal and led my people Israel into sin; ¹⁴but the prophets of Jerusalem are even worse! The things they do are horrible; they commit adultery and love dishonesty. They encourage and compliment those who are doing evil instead of turning them back from their sins. These prophets are as thoroughly depraved as the men of Sodom and Gomorrah were.

¹⁵Therefore the Lord Almighty says: I will feed them with bitterness and give them poison to drink. For it is because of them that wickedness fills this land. ¹⁶This is my warning to my people, says the Lord Almighty. Don't listen to these false prophets when they prophesy to you, filling you with futile hopes. They are making up everything they say. They do not speak for me! ¹⁷They keep saying to these rebels who despise me, "Don't worry! All is well!"; and to those who live the way they want to, "The Lord has said you shall have peace!"

¹⁸But can you name even one of these prophets who lives close enough to God to hear what he is saying? Has even one of them cared enough to listen? ¹⁹See, the Lord is sending a furious whirlwind to sweep away these wicked men. ²⁰The terrible anger of the Lord will not abate until it has carried out the full penalty he decrees against them. Later, when Jerusalem has fallen, you will see what I mean.

²¹I have not sent these prophets, yet they claim to speak for me; I gave them no message, yet they say their words are mine. ²²If they were mine, they would try to turn my people from their evil ways. ²³Am I a God who is only in one place and cannot see what they are doing? ²⁴Can anyone hide from me? Am I not everywhere in all of heaven and earth?

²⁵"Listen to the dream I had from God last night," they say. And then they proceed to lie in my name. ²⁶How long will this continue? If they are "prophets," they are prophets of deceit, inventing everything they say. ²⁷By telling these false dreams they are trying to get my people to forget me in the same way as their fathers did, who turned away to the idols of Baal. ²⁸Let these false prophets tell their dreams and let my true messengers faithfully proclaim my every word. There is a difference between chaff and wheat! ²⁹Does not my word burn like fire? asks the Lord. Is it not like a mighty hammer that smashed the rock to pieces? ³⁰,³¹So I stand against these "prophets" who get their messages from each other—these smooth-tongued prophets who say, "This message is from God!" ³²Their made-up dreams are flagrant lies that lead my people into sin. I did not send them, and they have no message at all for my people, says the Lord.

³³When one of the people or one of their "prophets" or priests asks you, "Well, Jeremiah, what is the sad news from the Lord today?" you shall reply, "What sad news? You are the sad news, for the Lord has cast you away!" ³⁴And as for the false prophets and priests and people who joke about "today's sad news from God," I will punish them and their families for saying this. ³⁵You can ask each other, "What is God's message? What is he saying?" ³⁶But stop using this term, "God's sad news." For what is sad is you and your lying. You are twisting my words and inventing "messages from God" that I didn't speak. ³⁷You may respectfully ask Jeremiah, "What is the Lord's message? What has he said to you?" ³⁸,³⁹But if you ask him about "today's sad news from God," when I have warned you not to mock like that, then I, the Lord God, will unburden myself of the burden you are to me. I will cast you out of my presence, you and this city I gave to you and your fathers. ⁴⁰And I will bring reproach upon you and your name shall be infamous through the ages.

24 Good Figs, Bad Figs

After Nebuchadnezzar, king of Babylon, had captured and enslaved Jeconiah (son of Jehoiakim), king of Judah, and exiled him to Babylon along with the princes of Judah and the skilled tradesmen—the carpenters and blacksmiths—the Lord gave me this vision. ²I saw two baskets of figs placed in front of the Temple in Jerusalem. In one basket there were fresh, just-ripened figs, but in the other the figs were spoiled and moldy—too rotten to eat. ³Then the Lord said to me, "What do you see, Jeremiah?"

I replied, "Figs, some very good and some very bad."

⁴,⁵Then the Lord said: "The good figs represent the exiles sent to Babylon. I have done it for their good. ⁶I will see that they are well treated, and I will bring them back here again. I will help them and not hurt them; I will plant them and not pull them up. ⁷I will give them hearts that respond to me. They shall be my people and I will be their God, for they shall return to me with great joy.

⁸"But the rotten figs represent Zedekiah, king of Judah, his officials, and all the others of Jerusalem left here in this land; those too who live in Egypt. I will treat them like spoiled figs, too bad to use. ⁹I will make them repulsive to every nation of the earth, and they shall be mocked and taunted and cursed wherever I compel them to go. ¹⁰And I will send massacre and famine and disease among them until they are destroyed from the land of Israel, which I gave to them and to their fathers."

25 Disaster Ahead

This message for all the people of Judah came from the Lord to Jeremiah during the fourth year of the reign of King Jehoiakim of Judah (son of Josiah). This was the year Nebuchadnezzar, king of Babylon, began his reign.

²,³For the past twenty-three years, Jeremiah said, from the thirteenth year of the reign of Josiah (son of Amon) king of Judah, until now, God has been sending me his messages. I have faithfully passed them on to you, but you haven't listened. ⁴Again and again down through the years, God has sent you his prophets, but you have refused to hear. ⁵Each time the message was this: Turn from the evil road you are traveling and from the evil things you are doing. Only then can you continue to live here in this land which the Lord gave to you and to your ancestors forever. ⁶*Don't anger me by worshiping idols; but if you*

are true to me, then I'll not harm you. ⁷But you won't listen; you have gone ahead and made me furious with your idols. So you have brought upon yourselves all the evil that has come your way.

⁸,⁹And now the Lord God says, Because you have not listened to me, I will gather together all the armies of the north under Nebuchadnezzar, king of Babylon (I have appointed him as my deputy), and I will bring them all against this land and its people and against the other nations near you, and I will utterly destroy you and make you a byword of contempt forever. ¹⁰I will take away your joy, your gladness, and your wedding feasts; your businesses shall fail, and all your homes shall lie in silent darkness. ¹¹This entire land shall become a desolate wasteland; all the world will be shocked at the disaster that befalls you. Israel and her neighboring lands shall serve the king of Babylon for seventy years.

¹²Then, after these years of slavery are ended, I will punish the king of Babylon and his people for their sins; I will make the land of Chaldea an everlasting waste. ¹³I will bring upon them all the terrors I have promised in this book—all the penalties announced by Jeremiah against the nations. ¹⁴ For many nations and great kings shall enslave the Chaldeans, just as they enslaved my people; I will punish them in proportion to their treatment of my people.

¹⁵For the Lord God said to me: "Take from my hand this wine cup filled to the brim with my fury, and make all the nations to whom I send you drink from it. ¹⁶They shall drink from it and reel, crazed by the death blows I rain upon them."

¹⁷So I took the cup of fury from the Lord and made all the nations drink from it—every nation God had sent me to; ¹⁸I went to Jerusalem and to the cities of Judah, and their kings and princes drank of the cup so that from that day until this they have been desolate, hated and cursed, just as they are today. ¹⁹,²⁰I went to Egypt, and Pharaoh, his servants, the princes, and the people—they too drank from that terrible cup, along with all the foreign population living in his land. So did all the kings of the land of Uz and the kings of the Philistine cities: Ashkelon, Gaza, Ekron, and what remains of Ashdod, ²¹and I visited the nations of Edom, Moab, and Ammon; ²²and all the kings of Tyre and Sidon, and the kings of the regions across the sea; ²³ Dedan, Tema, and Buz, and the other heathen there; ²⁴and all the kings of Arabia and of the nomadic tribes of the desert; ²⁵and all the kings of Zimri, Elam, and Media; ²⁶and all the kings of the northern countries, far and near, one after the other; and all the kingdoms of the world. And finally, the king of Babylon himself drank from this cup of God's wrath.

²⁷Tell them, "The Lord of heaven's armies, the God of Israel, says, Drink from this cup of my wrath until you are drunk and vomit and fall to rise no more, for I am sending terrible wars upon you." ²⁸And if they refuse to accept the cup, tell them, "The Lord of heaven's armies says you *must* drink it! You cannot escape! ²⁹I have begun to punish my own people, so should you go free? No, you shall not evade punishment. I will call for war against all the peoples of the earth."

³⁰Therefore prophesy against them. Tell them the Lord will shout against his own from his holy temple in heaven and against all those living on the earth. He will shout as the harvesters do who tread the juice from the grapes. ³¹That cry of judgment will reach the farthest ends of the earth, for the Lord has a case against all the nations—all mankind. He will slaughter all the wicked. ³²See, declares the Lord Almighty, the punishment shall go from nation to nation—a great whirlwind of wrath shall rise against the farthest corners of the earth. ³³On that day those the Lord has slain shall fill the earth from one end to the other. No one shall mourn for them nor gather up the bodies to bury them; they shall fertilize the earth.

³⁴Weep and moan, O evil shepherds; let the leaders of mankind beat their heads upon the stones, for their time has come to be slaughtered and scattered; they shall fall like fragile women. ³⁵And you will find no place to hide, no way to escape.

³⁶Listen to the frantic cries of the shepherds and to the leaders shouting in despair, for the Lord has spoiled their pastures. ³⁷People now living undisturbed will be cut down by the fierceness of the anger of the Lord. ³⁸He has left his lair like a lion seeking prey; their land has been laid waste by warring armies—because of the fierce anger of the Lord.

26 Jeremiah Almost Dies

This message came to Jeremiah from the Lord during the first year of the reign of Jehoiakim (son of Josiah), king of Judah:

²Stand out in front of the Temple of the Lord and make an announcement to all the people who have come there to worship from many parts of Judah. Give them the entire message; don't leave out one word of all I have for them to hear. ³For perhaps they will listen and turn from their evil ways, and then I can withhold all the punishment I am ready to pour out upon them because of their evil deeds. ⁴Tell them the Lord says: If you will not listen to me and obey the laws I have given you, ⁵and if you will not listen to my servants, the prophets—for I sent them again and again to warn you, but you would not listen

to them— ⁶then I will destroy this Temple as I destroyed the Tabernacle at Shiloh, and I will make Jerusalem a curse word in every nation of the earth.

⁷,⁸When Jeremiah had finished his message, saying everything the Lord had told him to, the priests and false prophets and all the people in the Temple mobbed him, shouting, "Kill him! Kill him! ⁹What right do you have to say the Lord will destroy this Temple like the one at Shiloh?" they yelled. "What do you mean—Jerusalem destroyed and not one survivor?"

¹⁰When the high officials of Judah heard what was going on, they rushed over from the palace and sat down at the door of the Temple to hold court. ¹¹Then the priests and the false prophets presented their accusations to the officials and the people. "This man should die!" they said. "You have heard with your own ears what a traitor he is, for he has prophesied against this city."

¹²Then Jeremiah spoke in his defense. "The Lord sent me," he said, "to prophesy against this Temple and this city. He gave me every word of all that I have spoken. ¹³But if you stop your sinning and begin obeying the Lord your God, he will cancel all the punishment he has announced against you. ¹⁴As for me, I am helpless and in your power—do with me as you think best. ¹⁵But there is one thing sure, if you kill me, you will be killing an innocent man, and the responsibility will lie upon you and upon this city and upon every person living in it; for it is absolutely true that the Lord sent me to speak every word that you have heard from me."

¹⁶Then the officials and people said to the priests and false prophets, "This man does not deserve the death sentence, for he has spoken to us in the name of the Lord our God."

¹⁷Then some of the wise old men stood and spoke to all the people standing around and said: ¹⁸"The decision is right; for back in the days when Micah the Morasthite prophesied in the days of King Hezekiah of Judah, he told the people that God said: 'This hill shall be plowed like an open field and this city of Jerusalem razed into heaps of stone, and a forest shall grow at the top where the great Temple now stands!' ¹⁹But did King Hezekiah and the people kill him for saying this? No, they turned from their wickedness and worshiped the Lord and begged the Lord to have mercy upon them; and the Lord held back the terrible punishment he had pronounced against them. If we kill Jeremiah for giving us the messages of God, who knows what God will do to us!"

²⁰Another true prophet of the Lord, Uriah (son of Shemaiah) from Kiriathjearim, was also denouncing the city and the nation at the same time as Jeremiah was. ²¹But when King Jehoiakim and the army officers and officials heard what he was saying, the king sent to kill him. Uriah heard about it and fled to Egypt. ²²Then King Jehoiakim sent Elnathan (son of Achbor) to Egypt along with several other men to capture Uriah. ²³They took him prisoner and brought him back to King Jehoiakim, who butchered him with a sword and had him buried in an unmarked grave.

²⁴But Ahikam (son of Shaphan), the royal secretary, stood with Jeremiah and persuaded the court not to turn him over to the mob to kill him.

27 The People Will Be Slaves

This message came to Jeremiah from the Lord at the beginning of the reign of Jehoiakim (son of Josiah), king of Judah:

²"Make a yoke and fasten it on your neck with leather thongs as you would strap a yoke on a plow-ox. ³Then send messages to the kings of Edom, Moab, Ammon, Tyre, and Sidon, through their ambassadors in Jerusalem, ⁴saying, Tell your masters that the Lord, the God of Israel, sends you this message:

⁵"By my great power I have made the earth and all mankind and every animal; and I give these things of mine to anyone I want to. ⁶So now I have given all your countries to King Nebuchadnezzar of Babylon, who is my deputy. And I have handed over to him all your cattle for his use. ⁷All the nations shall serve him and his son and his grandson until his time is up, and then many nations and great kings shall conquer Babylon and make him their slave. ⁸Submit to him and serve him—put your neck under Babylon's yoke! I will punish any nation refusing to be his slave; I will send war, famine, and disease upon that nation until he has conquered it.

⁹"Do not listen to your false prophets, fortunetellers, dreamers, mediums, and magicians who say the king of Babylon will not enslave you. ¹⁰For they are all liars, and if you follow their advice and refuse to submit to the king of Babylon, I will drive you out of your land and send you far away to perish. ¹¹ But the people of any nation submitting to the king of Babylon will be permitted to stay in their own country and farm the land as usual."

¹²Jeremiah repeated all these prophecies to Zedekiah, king of Judah. "If you want to live, submit to the king of Babylon," he said. ¹³"Why do you insist on dying—you and your people? Why should you choose war and famine and disease, which the Lord has promised to every nation that will not submit to Babylon's king? ¹⁴Don't listen to the false prophets who keep telling you the king of Babylon will not conquer you, for they are

liars. ⁱ⁵I have not sent them, says the Lord, and they are telling you lies in my name. If you insist on heeding them, I must drive you from this land to die—you and all these 'prophets' too."

¹⁶I spoke again and again to the priests and all the people and told them: "The Lord says, Don't listen to your prophets who are telling you that soon the gold dishes taken from the Temple will be returned from Babylon. It is all a lie. ¹⁷Don't listen to them. Surrender to the king of Babylon and live, for otherwise this whole city will be destroyed. ¹⁸If they are really God's prophets, then let them pray to the Lord Almighty that the gold dishes still here in the Temple, left from before; and that those in the palace of the king of Judah and in the palaces in Jerusalem will not be carried away with you to Babylon!

¹⁹⁻²¹"For the Lord Almighty says, The pillars of bronze standing before the Temple, the great bronze basin in the Temple court, the metal stands, and all the other ceremonial articles left here by Nebuchadnezzar, king of Babylon, when he exiled all the important people of Judah and Jerusalem to Babylon, along with Jeconiah (son of Jehoiakim), king of Judah, ²²will all yet be carried away to Babylon and will stay there until I send for them. Then I will bring them all back to Jerusalem again."

28 A False Prophet

On a December day in that same year—the fourth year of the reign of Zedekiah, king of Judah—Hananiah (son of Azzur), a false prophet from Gibeon, addressed me publicly in the Temple while all the priests and people listened. He said:

²"The Lord of Hosts, the God of Israel, declares: I have removed the yoke of the king of Babylon from your necks. ³Within two years I will bring back all the Temple treasures that Nebuchadnezzar carried off to Babylon, ⁴and I will bring back King Jeconiah, son of Jehoiakim, king of Judah, and all the other captives exiled to Babylon, says the Lord. I will surely remove the yoke put on your necks by the king of Babylon."

⁵Then Jeremiah said to Hananiah, in front of all the priests and people, ⁶ "Amen! May your prophecies come true! I hope the Lord will do everything you say and bring back from Babylon the treasures of this Temple, with all our loved ones. ⁷But listen now to the solemn words I speak to you in the presence of all these people. ⁸The ancient prophets who preceded you and me spoke against many nations, always warning of *war, famine,* and *plague.* ⁹So a prophet who foretells *peace* has the burden of proof on him to prove that God has really sent him. Only when his message comes true can it be known that he really is from God."

¹⁰Then Hananiah, the false prophet, took the yoke off Jeremiah's neck and broke it. ¹¹And Hananiah said again to the crowd that had gathered, "The Lord has promised that within two years he will release all the nations now in slavery to King Nebuchadnezzar of Babylon." At that point Jeremiah walked out.

¹²Soon afterwards the Lord gave this message to Jeremiah: ¹³Go and tell Hananiah that the Lord says, You have broken a wooden yoke, but these people have yokes of iron on their necks. ¹⁴The Lord, the God of Israel, says: I have put a yoke of iron on the necks of all these nations, forcing them into slavery to Nebuchadnezzar, king of Babylon. And nothing will change this decree, for I have even given him all your flocks and herds.

¹⁵Then Jeremiah said to Hananiah, the false prophet, "Listen, Hananiah, the Lord has not sent you, and the people are believing your lies. ¹⁶Therefore the Lord says you must die. This very year your life will end because you have rebelled against the Lord."

¹⁷And sure enough, two months later Hananiah died.

29 More Warnings

After Jeconiah the king, the queen-mother, the court officials, the tribal officers, and craftsmen had been deported to Babylon by Nebuchadnezzar, Jeremiah wrote them a letter from Jerusalem, addressing it to the Jewish elders, priests, prophets, and to all the people. ³He sent the letter with Elasah (son of Shaphan) and Gemariah (son of Hilkiah) when they went to Babylon as King Zedekiah's ambassadors to Nebuchadnezzar. And this is what the letter said:

⁴The Lord Almighty, the God of Israel, sends this message to all the captives he has exiled to Babylon from Jerusalem:

⁵Build homes and plan to stay; plant vineyards, for you will be there many years. ⁶Marry and have children, and then find mates for them and have many grandchildren. Multiply! Don't dwindle away! ⁷And work for the peace and prosperity of Babylon. Pray for her, for if Babylon has peace, so will you.

⁸The Lord Almighty, the God of Israel, says: Don't let the false prophets and mediums who are there among you fool you. Don't listen to the dreams that they invent, ⁹for they prophesy lies in my name. I have not sent them, says the Lord. ¹⁰The truth is this: You will be in Babylon for seventy years. But then I will come and do for you all the good things I have promised and bring you home again. ¹¹For I know the plans I have for you,

FAMILY DEVOTIONS

☐ **DEVOTION 224**
LEAVING THE FUTURE IN GOD'S HANDS

Read Jeremiah 29:8-13

All the girls at the slumber party giggled as one of them read their horoscopes from a magazine on astrology, but Candy felt uncomfortable. People used horoscopes to try to find out what would happen in the future, and she knew that only God knows what will happen.

Next, the girl who was giving the party got out her Ouija board, and the other girls gathered around. This was another thing used for fortune-telling. Candy sat apart from the group and self-consciously leafed through a magazine.

Candy was relieved when they went on to games she could play without feeling uncomfortable. Then she had a really good time. Her favorite was the blind walk. Each girl was blindfolded while her partner led her around an obstacle course. If the blindfolded person was caught peeking, she lost points for her team. Candy found that it felt strange trusting her partner not to run her into the wall. But she really wanted to win, so she moved quickly ahead and never peeked at all. It paid off—they won.

When Candy's father picked her up the next day, she told him all about the party and the games they had played, including the activities that had bothered her. Dad nodded. "You were right to avoid those," he said. "The Bible teaches that divination, or practices that seek to foresee the future, is wrong."

"Even if it's only a game?" asked Candy.

"Yes," said Dad. "Satan can use such activities to trick you into trusting your future to something other than God." He paused. "Your future is like the blind walk game you played," he added. "God holds your hand, and you need to let him lead the way. He doesn't want you to have any part in something that encourages you to do otherwise."

Leaving the Future in God's Hands Memory Verse

For I know the plans I have for you, says the Lord. They are plans for good and not for evil, to give you a future and a hope.
Jeremiah 29:11

How About You?

Do you read your horoscope or participate in fortune-telling activities? Although these may seem like harmless fun, God's Word clearly speaks against them. When you try to find out your future in these ways, you are showing God you don't trust him. *K. R. A.*

• For the next devotional, turn to page 749.   • For the next devotional on *LEAVING THE FUTURE IN GOD'S HANDS,* turn to page 861.   • For notes on *LEAVING THE FUTURE IN GOD'S HANDS,* see pages 405, 452, 831, and 1061.

says the Lord. They are plans for good and not for evil, to give you a future and a hope. ¹²In those days when you pray, I will listen. ¹³You will find me when you seek me, if you look for me in earnest.

¹⁴Yes, says the Lord, I will be found by you, and I will end your slavery and restore your fortunes; I will gather you out of the nations where I sent you and bring you back home again to your own land.

¹⁵But now, because you accept the false prophets among you and say the Lord has sent them, ¹⁶,¹⁷I will send war, famine, and plague upon the people left here in Jerusalem—on your relatives who were not exiled to Babylon, and on the king who sits on David's throne—and make them like rotting figs, too bad to eat. ¹⁸And I will scatter them around the world. And in every nation where I place them they will be cursed and hissed and mocked, ¹⁹for they refuse to listen to me though I spoke to them again and again through my prophets.

²⁰Therefore listen to the word of God, all you Jewish captives over there in Babylon. ²¹The Lord Almighty, the God of Israel, says this about your false prophets, Ahab (son of Kolaiah) and Zedekiah (son of Maaseiah), who are declaring lies to you in my name: Look, I am turning them over to Nebuchadnezzar to execute publicly. ²²Their fate shall become proverbial of all evil, so that whenever anyone wants to curse someone he will say, "The Lord make you like Zedekiah and Ahab whom the king of Babylon burned alive!" ²³For these men have done a terrible thing among my people. They have committed adultery with their neighbors' wives and have lied in my name. I know, for I have seen everything they do, says the Lord.

²⁴And say this to Shemaiah the dreamer: ²⁵The Lord, the God of Israel, says: You have written a letter to Zephaniah (son of Maaseiah) the priest, and sent copies to all the other priests and to everyone in Jerusalem. ²⁶And in this letter you have said to Zephaniah, "The Lord has appointed you to replace Jehoiada as priest in Jerusalem. And it is your responsibility to arrest any madman who claims to be a prophet and to put him in the stocks and collar. ²⁷Why haven't you done something about this false prophet Jeremiah of Anathoth? ²⁸For he has written to us here in Babylon saying that our captivity will be long; that we should build permanent homes and plan to stay many years; that we should plant fruit trees, for we will be here to eat the fruit from them for a long time to come."

²⁹Zephaniah took the letter over to Jeremiah and read it to him! ³⁰Then the Lord gave this message to Jeremiah:

³¹Send an open letter to all the exiles in Babylon and tell them this: The Lord says that because Shemaiah the Nehelamite has "prophesied" to you when I didn't send him and has fooled you into believing his lies, ³²I will punish him and his family. None of his descendants shall see the good I have waiting for my people, for he has taught you to rebel against the Lord.

30 Bringing Back the People

This is another of the Lord's messages to Jeremiah:

²The Lord God of Israel says, Write down for the record all that I have said to you. ³For the time is coming when I will restore the fortunes of my people, Israel and Judah, and I will bring them home to this land that I gave to their fathers; they shall possess it and live here again.

⁴And write this also concerning Israel and Judah:

⁵"Where shall we find peace?" they cry. There is only fear and trembling. ⁶Do men give birth? Then why do they stand there, ashen-faced, hands pressed against their sides like women in labor?

⁷Alas, in all history when has there ever been a time of terror such as in that coming day? It is a time of trouble for my people—for Jacob—such as they have never known before. Yet God will rescue them! ⁸For on that day, says the Lord Almighty, I will break the yoke from their necks and snap their chains, and foreigners shall no longer be their masters! ⁹For they shall serve the Lord their God, and David their King, whom I will raise up for them, says the Lord.

¹⁰So don't be afraid, O Jacob my servant; don't be dismayed, O Israel; for I will bring you home again from distant lands, and your children from their exile. They shall have rest and quiet in their own land, and no one shall make them afraid. ¹¹For I am with you and I will save you, says the Lord. Even if I utterly destroy the nations where I scatter you, I will not exterminate you; I will punish you, yes—you will not go unpunished.

¹²For your sin is an incurable bruise, a terrible wound. ¹³There is no one to help you or to bind up your wound, and no medicine does any good. ¹⁴All your lovers have left you and don't care anything about you any more; for I have wounded you cruelly, as though I were your enemy; mercilessly, as though I were an implacable foe; for your sins are so many, your guilt is so great.

¹⁵Why do you protest your punishment? Your sin is so scandalous that your sorrow should never end! It is because your guilt is great that I have had to punish you so much.

¹⁶But in that coming day, all who are destroying you shall be destroyed, and all your enemies shall

Family Devotions

☐ DEVOTION 225
PUTTING GOD FIRST

Read Jeremiah 31:18-20

"Thanks for inviting me to go to church with you next Sunday, Uncle Al." Keith and his uncle were on their way to Bonny Lake. They had heard it was great fishing there. "I don't want to hurt your feelings," continued Keith, "but I'm not sure I want to get into this religious stuff."

"Oh?" asked Uncle Al in surprise. "You sounded quite interested last week. You even said the gospel was beginning to make sense to you."

"Yeah, but since then I've done a lot of thinking," Keith said slowly. "I don't think I feel like getting saved right now. The crowd I hang around with at school might not understand, and I like being with them. Someday I'll start going to church, but I think I'll just go on the way I am for a while. I know I'm not perfect, but I'm not so bad, either."

Keith's uncle drove on silently for a few minutes. "Oh, no!" he exclaimed as they passed a road sign. "I missed the turnoff. We should have gotten off this road five miles back."

"Guess we'll have to turn around and go back now, huh?" asked Keith.

But Uncle Al shook his head. "I don't feel like turning around right now," he said. "I guess we'll just keep going this way. I kinda like this road."

Keith looked at his uncle in amazement. "But we have to turn around to get to Bonny Lake," he protested, "and the longer we keep going this way, the longer it will take to get back. If we wait too long to turn around, we might not even get there in time to fish."

Uncle Al smiled at Keith as he slowed down for the next turn. "You're right," he said, "and what you said just now is exactly what I've been trying to tell you about your spiritual life—that when you're travelling down the wrong road, the sooner you turn around, the better. If you wait too long, you might never get to your goal—heaven."

Putting God First Memory Verse

In everything you do, put God first, and he will direct you and crown your efforts with success.
Proverbs 3:6

How About You?
Do you need to turn around and go in a different direction to get to heaven? You do if you've never accepted Jesus as Savior. Don't let habits, the opinions of others, or even your own feelings of laziness keep you from taking the right road. Turn to Jesus now. *S. K.*

• For the next devotional, turn to page 755. • To start the next topic, turn to page 235. • For notes on *PUTTING GOD FIRST*, see pages 397, 492, 644, 791, and 982.

be slaves. Those who rob you shall be robbed; and those attacking you shall be attacked. ¹⁷I will give you back your health again and heal your wounds. Now you are called "The Outcast" and "Jerusalem, the Place Nobody Wants."

¹⁸But, says the Lord, when I bring you home again from your captivity and restore your fortunes, Jerusalem will be rebuilt upon her ruins; the palace will be reconstructed as it was before. ¹⁹The cities will be filled with joy and great thanksgiving, and I will multiply my people and make of them a great and honored nation. ²⁰Their children shall prosper as in David's reign; their nations shall be established before me, and I will punish anyone who hurts them. ²¹They will have their own ruler again. He will not be a foreigner. And I will invite him to be a priest at my altars, and he shall approach me, for who would dare to come unless invited. ²²And you shall be my people, and I will be your God.

²³Suddenly the devastating whirlwind of the Lord roars with fury; it shall burst upon the heads of the wicked. ²⁴The Lord will not call off the fierceness of his wrath until it has finished all the terrible destruction he has planned. Later on you will understand what I am telling you.

31 God Still Loves the People

At that time, says the Lord, all the families of Israel shall recognize me as the Lord; they shall act like my people. ²I will care for them as I did those who escaped from Egypt, to whom I showed my mercies in the wilderness, when Israel sought for rest. ³For long ago the Lord had said to Israel: I have loved you, O my people, with an everlasting love; with loving-kindness I have drawn you to me. ⁴I will rebuild your nation, O virgin of Israel. You will again be happy and dance merrily with the timbrels. ⁵Again you will plant your vineyards upon the mountains of Samaria and eat from your own gardens there.

⁶The day shall come when watchmen on the hills of Ephraim will call out and say, "Arise, and let us go up to Zion to the Lord our God." ⁷For the Lord says, Sing with joy for all that I will do for Israel, the greatest of the nations! Shout out with praise and joy: The Lord has saved his people, the remnant of Israel." ⁸For I will bring them from the north and from earth's farthest ends, not forgetting their blind and lame, young mothers with their little ones, those ready to give birth. It will be a great company who comes. ⁹Tears of joy shall stream down their faces, and I will lead them home with great care. They shall walk beside the quiet streams and not stumble. For I am a Father to Israel, and Ephraim is my oldest child.

¹⁰Listen to this message from the Lord, you nations of the world, and publish it abroad: The Lord who scattered his people will gather them back together again and watch over them as a shepherd does his flock. ¹¹He will save Israel from those who are too strong for them! ¹²They shall come home and sing songs of joy upon the hills of Zion and shall be radiant over the goodness of the Lord—the good crops, the wheat, the wine, and the oil, and the healthy flocks and herds. Their life shall be like a watered garden, and all their sorrows shall be gone. ¹³The young girls will dance for joy, and menfolk—old and young—will take their part in all the fun; for I will turn their mourning into joy, and I will comfort them and make them rejoice, for their captivity with all its sorrows will be behind them. ¹⁴I will feast the priests with the abundance of offerings brought to them at the Temple; I will satisfy my people with my bounty, says the Lord.

¹⁵The Lord spoke to me again, saying: In Ramah there is bitter weeping—Rachel weeping for her children and cannot be comforted, for they are gone. ¹⁶But the Lord says: Don't cry any longer, for I have heard your prayers and you will see them again; they will come back to you from the distant land of the enemy. ¹⁷There is hope for your future, says the Lord, and your children will come again to their own land.

¹⁸I have heard Ephraim's groans: "You have punished me greatly; but I needed it all, as a calf must be trained for the yoke. Turn me again to you and restore me, for you alone are the Lord, my God. ¹⁹I turned away from God, but I was sorry afterwards. I kicked myself for my stupidity. I was thoroughly ashamed of all I did in younger days."

²⁰And the Lord replies: Ephraim is still my son, my darling child. I had to punish him, but I still love him. I long for him and surely will have mercy on him.

²¹As you travel into exile, set up road signs pointing back to Israel. Mark your pathway well. For you shall return again, O virgin Israel, to your cities here. ²²How long will you vacillate, O wayward daughter? For the Lord will cause something new and different to happen—Israel will search for God.

²³The Lord, the God of Israel, says: When I bring them back again, they shall say in Judah and her cities, "The Lord bless you, O center of righteousness, O holy hill!" ²⁴And city dwellers and farmers and shepherds alike shall live together in peace and happiness. ²⁵For I have given rest to the weary and joy to all the sorrowing.

²⁶(Then Jeremiah wakened. "Such sleep is very sweet!" he said.)

²⁷The Lord says: The time will come when I will greatly increase the population and multiply the

number of cattle here in Israel. ²⁸In the past I painstakingly destroyed the nation, but now I will carefully build it up. ²⁹The people shall no longer quote this proverb—"Children pay for their fathers' sins." ³⁰For everyone shall die for his own sins—the person eating sour grapes is the one whose teeth are set on edge.

³¹The day will come, says the Lord, when I will make a new contract with the people of Israel and Judah. ³²It won't be like the one I made with their fathers when I took them by the hand to bring them out of the land of Egypt—a contract they broke, forcing me to reject them, says the Lord. ³³But this is the new contract I will make with them: I will inscribe my laws upon their hearts, so that they shall want to honor me; then they shall truly be my people and I will be their God. ³⁴At that time it will no longer be necessary to admonish one another to know the Lord. For everyone, both great and small, shall really know me then, says the Lord, and I will forgive and forget their sins.

³⁵The Lord who gives us sunlight in the daytime and the moon and stars to light the night, and who stirs the sea to make the roaring waves—his name is Lord Almighty—says this:

³⁶I am as likely to reject my people Israel as I am to do away with these laws of nature! ³⁷Not until the heavens can be measured and the foundations of the earth explored, will I consider casting them away forever for their sins!

³⁸,³⁹For the time is coming, says the Lord, when all Jerusalem shall be rebuilt for the Lord, from the Tower of Hananel at the northeast corner, to the Corner Gate at the northwest; and from the Hill of Gareb at the southwest, across to Goah on the southeast. ⁴⁰And the entire city, including the graveyard and ash dump in the valley, and all the fields out to the brook of Kidron, and from there to the Horse Gate on the east side of the city, all shall be holy to the Lord; it shall never again be captured or destroyed.

32 Jeremiah Buys a Field

The following message came to Jeremiah from the Lord in the tenth year of the reign of Zedekiah, king of Judah (which was the eighteenth year of Nebuchadnezzar's reign). ²At this time Jeremiah was imprisoned in the dungeon beneath the palace, while the Babylonian army was besieging Jerusalem. ³King Zedekiah had put him there for continuing to prophesy that the city would be conquered by the king of Babylon, ⁴and that King Zedekiah would be caught and taken as a prisoner before the king of Babylon for trial and sentencing.

⁵"He shall take you to Babylon and imprison you there for many years until you die. Why fight the facts? You can't win! Surrender now!" Jeremiah had told him again and again.

⁶,⁷Then this message from the Lord came to Jeremiah: Your cousin Hanamel (son of Shallum) will soon arrive to ask you to buy the farm he owns in Anathoth, for by law you have a chance to buy before it is offered to anyone else.

⁸So Hanamel came, as the Lord had said he would, and visited me in the prison. "Buy my field in Anathoth, in the land of Benjamin," he said, "for the law gives you the first right to purchase it." Then I knew for sure that the message I had heard was really from the Lord.

⁹So I bought the field, paying Hanamel seventeen pieces of silver. ¹⁰I signed and sealed the deed of purchase before witnesses, weighed out the silver, and paid him. ¹¹Then I took the sealed deed containing the terms and conditions and also the unsealed copy, ¹²and publicly, in the presence of my cousin Hanamel and the witnesses who had signed the deed, and as the prison guards watched, I handed the papers to Baruch (son of Neriah, who was the son of Mahseiah). ¹³And I said to him as they all listened:

¹⁴"The Lord, God of Israel, says: Take both this sealed deed and the copy and put them into a pottery jar to preserve them for a long time. ¹⁵For the Lord, God of Israel, says, 'In the future these papers will be valuable. Someday people will again own property here in this country and will be buying and selling houses and vineyards and fields.'"

¹⁶Then after I had given the papers to Baruch I prayed:

¹⁷"O Lord God! You have made the heavens and earth by your great power; nothing is too hard for you! ¹⁸You are loving and kind to thousands, yet children suffer for their fathers' sins; you are the great and mighty God, the Lord Almighty. ¹⁹You have all wisdom and do great and mighty miracles; for your eyes are open to all the ways of men, and you reward everyone according to his life and deeds. ²⁰You have done incredible things

---

TRUSTING GOD FOR HELP 32:6-12 Trust doesn't come easy. It wasn't easy for Jeremiah to publicly buy land already captured by the enemy. But he trusted God. It wasn't easy for David to think he would become king, even after he was anointed. But he trusted God (1 Samuel 16–31). It wasn't easy for Moses to believe he and his people would escape Egypt, even after God spoke to him from a burning bush. But he trusted God (Exodus 3:1–4:20). It isn't easy for us to believe God can transform our lives when we see the mess we've made. But we must trust God. He who worked in the lives of biblical heroes is the same God who offers to work in our lives, if we will let him do it. **To begin the series of devotionals on TRUSTING GOD FOR HELP, turn to page 29.**

in the land of Egypt—things still remembered to this day. And you have continued to do great miracles in Israel and all around the world. You have made your name very great, as it is today.

21"You brought Israel out of Egypt with mighty miracles and great power and terror. 22You gave Israel this land that you promised their fathers long ago—a wonderful land that 'flows with milk and honey.' 23Our fathers came and conquered it and lived in it, but they refused to obey you or to follow your laws; they have hardly done one thing you told them to. That is why you have sent all this terrible evil upon them. 24See how the siege mounds have been built against the city walls, and the Babylonians shall conquer the city by sword, famine, and disease. Everything has happened just as you said—as you determined it should! 25And yet you say to buy the field—paying good money for it before these witnesses—even though the city will belong to our enemies."

26Then this message came to Jeremiah: 27I am the Lord, the God of all mankind; is there anything too hard for me? 28Yes, I will give this city to the Babylonians and to Nebuchadnezzar, king of Babylon; he shall conquer it. 29And the Babylonians outside the walls shall come in and set fire to the city and burn down all these houses, where the roofs have been used to offer incense to Baal and to pour out libations to other gods, causing my fury to rise! 30For Israel and Judah have done nothing but wrong since their earliest days; they have infuriated me with all their evil deeds. 31From the time this city was built until now it has done nothing but anger me; so I am determined to be rid of it.

32The sins of Israel and Judah—the sins of the people, of their kings, officers, priests and prophets—stir me up. 33They have turned their backs upon me and refused to return; day after day, year after year, I taught them right from wrong, but they would not listen or obey. 34They have even defiled my own Temple by worshiping their abominable idols there. 35And they have built high altars to Baal in the Valley of Hinnom. There they have burnt their children as sacrifices to Molech—something I never commanded and cannot imagine suggesting. What an incredible evil, causing Judah to sin so greatly!

36Now therefore the Lord God of Israel says concerning this city that it will fall to the king of Babylon through warfare, famine, and disease, 37but I will bring my people back again from all the countries where in my fury I will scatter them. I will bring them back to this very city and make them live in peace and safety. 38And they shall be my people, and I will be their God. 39And I will give them one heart and mind to worship me forever, for their own good and for the good of all their descendants.

40And I will make an everlasting covenant with them, promising never again to desert them but only to do them good. I will put a desire into their hearts to worship me, and they shall never leave me. 41I will rejoice to do them good and will replant them in this land with great joy. 42Just as I have sent all these terrors and evils upon them, so will I do all the good I have promised them.

43Fields will again be bought and sold in this land now ravaged by the Babylonians, where men and animals alike have disappeared. 44Yes, fields shall once again be bought and sold—deeds signed and sealed and witnessed—in the country of Benjamin and here in Jerusalem, in the cities of Judah and in the hill country, in the Philistine plain and in the Negeb too, for some day I will restore prosperity to them.

33 A Wonderful Promise

While Jeremiah was still in jail, the Lord sent him this second message:

2The Lord, the Maker of heaven and earth—Jehovah is his name—says this: 3Ask me and I will tell you some remarkable secrets about what is going to happen here. 4For though you have torn down the houses of this city, and the king's palace too, for materials to strengthen the walls against the siege weapons of the enemy, 5yet the Babylonians will enter, and the men of this city are already as good as dead, for I have determined to destroy them in my furious anger. I have abandoned them because of all their wickedness, and I will not pity them when they cry for help.

6Nevertheless the time will come when I will heal Jerusalem's damage and give her prosperity and peace. 7I will rebuild the cities of both Judah and Israel and restore their fortunes. 8And I will cleanse away all their sins against me and pardon them. 9Then this city will be an honor to me, and it will give me joy and be a source of praise and glory to me before all the nations of the earth! The people of the world will see the good I do for my people and will tremble with awe!

10,11The Lord declares that the happy voices of bridegrooms and of brides and the joyous song of those bringing thanksgiving offerings to the Lord will be heard again in this doomed land. The people will sing: "Praise the Lord! For he is good and his mercy endures forever!" For I will make this land happier and more prosperous than it has ever been before. 12This land—though every man and animal and city is doomed—will once more see shepherds leading sheep and lambs. 13Once again their flocks will prosper in the mountain villages and in the cities east of the Philistine plain, in all the cities of the Negeb, in the land of Benjamin, in the vicinity of Jerusalem, and in all the cities of Judah. [14]Yes, the day will come, says the Lord, when I will do for Israel and Judah all the good I promised them.

[15]At that time I will bring to the throne the true Son of David, and he shall rule justly. [16]In that day the people of Judah and Jerusalem shall live in safety and their motto will be, "The Lord is our righteousness!" [17]For the Lord declares that from then on, David shall forever have an heir sitting on the throne of Israel. [18]And there shall always be Levites to offer burnt offerings and meal offerings and sacrifices to the Lord.

[19]Then this message came to Jeremiah from the Lord: [20,21]If you can break my covenant with the day and with the night so that day and night don't come on their usual schedule, only then will my covenant with David, my servant, be broken so that he shall not have a son to reign upon his throne; and my covenant with the Levite priests, my ministers, is noncancelable. [22]And as the stars cannot be counted nor the sand upon the seashores measured, so the descendants of David my servant and the line of the Levites who minister to me will be multiplied.

[23]The Lord spoke to Jeremiah again and said: [24]Have you heard what people are saying?—that the Lord chose Judah and Israel and then abandoned them! They are sneering and saying that Israel isn't worthy to be counted as a nation. [25,26]But this is the Lord's reply: I would no more reject my people than I would change my laws of night and day, of earth and sky. I will never abandon the Jews, or David my servant, or change the plan that his child will someday rule these descendants of Abraham, Isaac, and Jacob. Instead I will restore their prosperity and have mercy on them.

34 King Zedekiah Will Be Captured

This is the message that came to Jeremiah from the Lord when Nebuchadnezzar, king of Babylon, and all his armies from all the kingdoms he ruled, came and fought against Jerusalem and the cities of Judah:

[2]Go tell Zedekiah, king of Judah, that the Lord says this: I will give this city to the king of Babylon and he shall burn it. [3]You shall not escape; you shall be captured and taken before the king of Babylon; he shall pronounce sentence against you and you shall be exiled to Babylon. [4]But listen to this, O Zedekiah, king of Judah: God says you won't be killed in war and carnage [5]but that you will die quietly among your people, and they will burn incense in your memory, just as they did for your fathers. They will weep for you and say, "Alas, our king is dead!" This I have decreed, says the Lord.

[6]So Jeremiah delivered the message to King Zedekiah. [7]At this time the Babylonian army was besieging Jerusalem, Lachish, and Azekah—the only walled cities of Judah still standing.

[8]This is the message that came to Jeremiah from the Lord after King Zedekiah of Judah had freed all the slaves in Jerusalem—[9](for King Zedekiah had ordered everyone to free his Hebrew slaves, both men and women. He had said that no Jew should be the master of another Jew for all were brothers. [10] The princes and all the people had obeyed the king's command and freed their slaves, but the action was only temporary. [11]They changed their minds and made their servants slaves again. [12]That is why the Lord gave the following message to Jerusalem.)

[13]The Lord, the God of Israel, says: I made a covenant with your fathers long ago when I brought them from their slavery in Egypt. [14]I told them that every Hebrew slave must be freed after serving six years. But this was not done. [15]Recently you began doing what was right, as I commanded you, and freed your slaves. You had solemnly promised me in my Temple that you would do it. [16]But now you refuse and have defiled my name by shrugging off your oath and have made them slaves again.

[17]Therefore, says the Lord, because you will not listen to me and release them, I will release you to the power of death by war and famine and disease. And I will scatter you over all the world as exiles. [18,19]Because you have refused the terms of our contract, I will cut you apart just as you cut apart the calf when you walked between its halves to solemnize your vows. Yes, I will butcher you, whether you are princes, court officials, priests, or people—for you have broken your oath. [20]I will give you to your enemies, and they shall kill you. I will feed your dead bodies to the vultures and wild animals. [21]And I will surrender Zedekiah, king of Judah, and his officials to the army of the king of Babylon, though he has departed from the city for a little while. [22]I will summon the Babylonian armies back again, and they will fight against it and capture this city and burn it. And I will see to it that the cities of Judah are completely destroyed and left desolate without a living soul.

35 Some Obey, Some Disobey

This is the message the Lord gave Jeremiah when Jehoiakim (son of Josiah) was the king of Judah:

[2]Go to the settlement where the families of the Rechabites live and invite them to the Temple.

Take them into one of the inner rooms and offer them a drink of wine.

³So I went over to see Jaazaniah (son of Jeremiah, who was the son of Habazziniah) and brought him and all his brothers and sons—representing all the Rechab families— ⁴to the Temple, into the room assigned for the use of the sons of Hanan the prophet (the son of Igdaliah). This room was located next to the one used by the palace official, directly above the room of Maaseiah (son of Shallum), who was the temple doorman. ⁵I set cups and jugs of wine before them and invited them to have a drink, ⁶but they refused.

"No," they said. "We don't drink, for Jonadab our father (son of Rechab) commanded that none of us should ever drink, neither we nor our children forever. ⁷He also told us not to build houses or plant crops or vineyards and not to own farms, but always to live in tents; and that if we obeyed, we would live long, good lives in our own land. ⁸And we have obeyed him in all these things. We have never had a drink of wine since then, nor have our wives or our sons or daughters either. ⁹We haven't built houses or owned farms or planted crops. ¹⁰We have lived in tents and have fully obeyed everything that Jonadab our father commanded us. ¹¹But when Nebuchadnezzar, king of Babylon, arrived in this country, we were afraid and decided to move to Jerusalem. That's why we are here."

¹²Then the Lord gave this message to Jeremiah: ¹³The Lord, the God of Israel, says: Go and say to Judah and Jerusalem, Won't you learn a lesson from the families of Rechab? ¹⁴They don't drink because their father told them not to. But I have spoken to you again and again, and you won't listen or obey. ¹⁵I have sent you prophet after prophet to tell you to turn back from your wicked ways and to stop worshiping other gods, and that if you obeyed, then I would let you live in peace here in the land I gave to you and your fathers. But you wouldn't listen or obey. ¹⁶The families of Rechab have obeyed their father completely, but you have refused to listen to me. ¹⁷Therefore, the Lord Almighty, the God of Israel, says: Because you refuse to listen or answer when I call, I will send upon Judah and Jerusalem all the evil I have ever threatened.

¹⁸,¹⁹Then Jeremiah turned to the Rechabites and said: "The Lord, the God of Israel, says that because you have obeyed your father in every respect, he shall always have descendants who will worship me."

36 Jeremiah's Scroll Burned

In the fourth year of the reign of King Jehoiakim of Judah (son of Josiah) the Lord gave this message to Jeremiah:

²"Get a scroll and write down all my messages against Israel, Judah, and the other nations. Begin with the first message back in the days of Josiah, and write down every one of them. ³Perhaps when the people of Judah see in writing all the terrible things I will do to them, they will repent. And then I can forgive them."

⁴So Jeremiah sent for Baruch (son of Neriah), and as Jeremiah dictated, Baruch wrote down all the prophecies.

⁵When all was finished, Jeremiah said to Baruch, "Since I am a prisoner here, ⁶you read the scroll in the Temple on the next day of fasting, for on that day people will be there from all over Judah. ⁷Perhaps even yet they will turn from their evil ways and ask the Lord to forgive them before it is too late, even though these curses of God have been pronounced upon them."

⁸Baruch did as Jeremiah told him to and read all these messages to the people at the Temple. ⁹This occurred on the day of fasting held in December of the fifth year of the reign of King Jehoiakim (son of Josiah). People came from all over Judah to attend the services at the Temple that day. ¹⁰Baruch went to the office of Gemariah the Scribe (son of Shaphan) to read the scroll. (This room was just off the upper assembly hall of the Temple, near the door of the New Gate.)

¹¹When Micaiah (son of Gemariah, son of Shaphan) heard the messages from God, ¹²he went down to the palace to the conference room where the administrative officials were meeting. Elishama (the scribe) was there, as well as Delaiah (son of Shamaiah), Elnathan (son of Achbor), Gemariah (son of Shaphan), Zedekiah (son of Hananiah), and all the others with similar responsibilities. ¹³When Micaiah told them about the messages Baruch was reading to the people, ¹⁴,¹⁵the officials sent Jehudi (son of Nethaniah, son of Shelemiah, son of Cushi) to ask Baruch to come and read the messages to them too, and Baruch did.

¹⁶By the time he finished they were badly frightened. "We must tell the king," they said. ¹⁷"But first, tell us how you got these messages. Did Jeremiah himself dictate them to you?" ¹⁸So Baruch explained that Jeremiah had dictated them to him word by word, and he had written them down in ink upon the scroll. ¹⁹"You and Jeremiah both hide," the officials said to Baruch. "Don't tell a soul where you are!" ²⁰Then the officials hid the scroll in the room of Elishama the scribe and went to tell the king.

²¹The king sent Jehudi to get the scroll. Jehudi brought it from Elishama the scribe and read it to the king as all his officials stood by. ²²The king was in a winterized part of the palace at the time, sitting in front of a fireplace, for it was December and cold. ²³And whenever Jehudi finished reading

FAMILY DEVOTIONS

☐ DEVOTION 226
RESPECTING AUTHORITY

Read Jeremiah 36:1-4, 21-26

Respecting Authority
Memory Verse

Children, obey your parents; this is the right thing to do because God has placed them in authority over you.
Ephesians 6:1

"I'm so tired of rules," complained Matt one evening. "When I grow up I'm going to be my own boss and do exactly as I please!"

Dad looked up from the paper with a smile. "Speaking of rules, it says here that starting next week, dogs have to be confined to their owner's property. Tag won't like that rule, will he?"

"No, but that old rabbit in Mr. Pate's garden is sure going to be relieved," Mom said, laughing. "Tag has been giving him fits lately."

Dad was right—Tag didn't like being fenced in, and time after time he dug out of the yard. One day when Matt and his mother came home from town, they discovered that Tag was missing once again. "That Tag!" exclaimed Matt. "He keeps digging out every time our backs are turned. I'll go find him."

But Tag was not to be found. A neighbor had seen the dogcatcher picking him up. Matt was in tears. "We can get him back, can't we?" he asked.

"Oh, yes," Mom said, "but he'll just get out again."

"If only he could understand that the yard is the place where he's safe!" sighed Matt. "Then he would know why we fence him in."

"You're right," agreed Mom, "and you know, Matt, we're a little like Tag. We sometimes feel fenced in, too—fenced in by rules we don't like. But God has given us parents, teachers, policemen, yes, even rules, to provide safety and protection for us."

"That makes sense," agreed Matt slowly. "I guess we do need rules and laws. But what about Tag, Mom?"

The solution to the problem was found when Dad came home. He made arrangements to pick up Tag and take him out to Uncle Frank's farm. "We'll miss him, but we can visit him," he said. "There he can run free."

How About You?
Do you rebel at having rules you must follow? You never outgrow the do's and don'ts of living. All your life there will be those who have authority over you. God says to obey them. B. W.

• For the next devotional, turn to page 773. • To start the next topic, turn to page 21. • For notes on RESPECTING AUTHORITY, see pages 311, 420, and 1182.

three or four columns, the king would take his knife, slit off the section, and throw it into the fire, until the whole scroll was destroyed. ²⁴,²⁵And no one protested except Elnathan, Delaiah, and Gemariah. They pled with the king not to burn the scroll, but he wouldn't listen to them. Not another of the king's officials showed any signs of fear or anger at what he had done.

²⁶Then the king commanded Jerahmeel (a member of the royal family) and Seraiah (son of Azriel) and Shelemiah (son of Abdeel) to arrest Baruch and Jeremiah. But the Lord hid them!

²⁷After the king had burned the scroll, the Lord said to Jeremiah: ²⁸Get another scroll and write everything again just as you did before, ²⁹and say this to the king: "The Lord says, You burned the scroll because it said the king of Babylon would destroy this country and everything in it. ³⁰And now the Lord adds this concerning you, Jehoiakim, king of Judah: He shall have no one to sit upon the throne of David. His dead body shall be thrown out to the hot sun and frosty nights, ³¹and I will punish him and his family and his officials because of their sins. I will pour out upon them all the evil I promised—upon them and upon all the people of Judah and Jerusalem, for they wouldn't listen to my warnings."

³²Then Jeremiah took another scroll and dictated again to Baruch all he had written before, only this time the Lord added a lot more!

37 Ebed-Melech Rescues Jeremiah

Nebuchadnezzar, King of Babylon, did not appoint Coniah (King Jehoiakim's son) to be the new king of Judah. Instead he chose Zedekiah (son of Josiah). ²But neither King Zedekiah nor his officials nor the people who were left in the land listened to what the Lord said through Jeremiah. ³Nevertheless, King Zedekiah sent Jehucal (son of Shelemiah) and Zephaniah the priest (son of Maaseiah) to ask Jeremiah to pray for them. ⁴(Jeremiah had not been imprisoned yet, so he could come and go as he pleased.)

⁵When the army of Pharaoh Hophra of Egypt appeared at the southern border of Judah to relieve the besieged city of Jerusalem, the Babylonian army withdrew from Jerusalem to fight the Egyptians.

⁶Then the Lord sent this message to Jeremiah: ⁷"The Lord, the God of Israel, says: Tell the king of Judah, who sent you to ask me what is going to happen, that Pharaoh's army, though it came here to help you, is about to return in flight to Egypt! The Babylonians shall defeat them and send them scurrying home. ⁸These Babylonians shall capture this city and burn it to the ground. ⁹Don't fool yourselves that the Babylonians are gone for good. They aren't! ¹⁰Even if you destroyed the entire Babylonian army until there was only a handful of survivors and they lay wounded in their tents, yet they would stagger out and defeat you and put this city to the torch!"

¹¹When the Babylonian army set out from Jerusalem to engage Pharaoh's army in battle, ¹²Jeremiah started to leave the city to go to the land of Benjamin, to see the property he had bought. ¹³But as he was walking through the Benjamin Gate, a sentry arrested him as a traitor, claiming he was defecting to the Babylonians. The guard making the arrest was Irijah (son of Shelemiah, grandson of Hananiah).

¹⁴"That's not true," Jeremiah said. "I have no intention whatever of doing any such thing!"

But Irijah wouldn't listen; he took Jeremiah before the city officials. ¹⁵,¹⁶They were incensed with Jeremiah and had him flogged and put into the dungeon under the house of Jonathan the scribe, which had been converted into a prison. Jeremiah was kept there for several days, ¹⁷but eventually King Zedekiah sent for him to come to the palace secretly. The king asked him if there was any recent message from the Lord. "Yes," said Jeremiah, "there is! You shall be defeated by the king of Babylon!"

¹⁸Then Jeremiah broached the subject of his imprisonment. "What have I ever done to deserve this?" he asked the king. "What crime have I committed? Tell me what I have done against you or your officials or the people? ¹⁹Where are those prophets now who told you that the king of Babylon would not come? ²⁰Listen, O my lord the king: I beg you, don't send me back to that dungeon, for I'll die there."

²¹Then King Zedekiah commanded that Jeremiah not be returned to the dungeon but be placed in the palace prison instead, and that he be given a small loaf of fresh bread every day as long as there was any left in the city. So Jeremiah was kept in the palace prison.

38

But when Shephatiah (son of Mattan) and Gedaliah (son of Pashhur) and Jucal (son of Shelemiah) and Pashhur (son of Malchiah) heard what Jeremiah had been telling the people— ²that everyone remaining in Jerusalem would die by sword, starvation, or disease, but anyone surrendering to the Babylonians would live, ³and that the city of Jerusalem would surely be captured by the king of Babylon— ⁴they went to the king and said: "Sir, this fellow must die. That kind of talk will undermine the morale of the few soldiers we have left, and of all the people too. This man is a traitor."

⁵So King Zedekiah agreed. "All right," he said. "Do as you like—I can't stop you."

⁶They took Jeremiah from his cell and lowered

him by ropes into an empty cistern in the prison yard. (It belonged to Malchiah, a member of the royal family.) There was no water in it, but there was a thick layer of mire at the bottom, and Jeremiah sank down into it.

⁷When Ebed-melech the Ethiopian, an important palace official, heard that Jeremiah was in the cistern, ⁸he rushed out to the Gate of Benjamin where the king was holding court.

⁹"My lord the king," he said, "these men have done a very evil thing in putting Jeremiah into the cistern. He will die of hunger, for almost all the bread in the city is gone."

¹⁰Then the king commanded Ebed-melech to take thirty men with him and pull Jeremiah out before he died. ¹¹So Ebed-melech took thirty men and went to a palace depot for discarded supplies where used clothing was kept. There he found some old rags and discarded garments which he took to the cistern and lowered to Jeremiah on a rope. ¹²Ebed-melech called down to Jeremiah, "Use these rags under your armpits to protect you from the ropes." Then, when Jeremiah was ready, ¹³they pulled him out and returned him to the palace prison, where he remained.

¹⁴One day King Zedekiah sent for Jeremiah to meet him at the side entrance of the Temple.

"I want to ask you something," the king said, "and don't try to hide the truth."

¹⁵Jeremiah said, "If I tell you the truth, you will kill me. And you won't listen to me anyway."

¹⁶So King Zedekiah swore before Almighty God his Creator that he would not kill Jeremiah or give him to the men who were after his life.

¹⁷Then Jeremiah said to Zedekiah, "The Almighty Lord, the God of Israel, says: If you will surrender to Babylon, you and your family shall live and the city will not be burned. ¹⁸If you refuse to surrender, this city shall be set afire by the Babylonian army and you will not escape."

¹⁹"But I am afraid to surrender," the king said, "for the Babylonians will hand me over to the Jews who have defected to them, and who knows what they will do to me?"

²⁰Jeremiah replied, "You won't get into their hands if only you will obey the Lord; your life will be spared, and all will go well for you. ²¹,²²But if you refuse to surrender, the Lord has said that all the women left in your palace will be brought out and given to the officers of the Babylonian army; and these women will taunt you with bitterness. 'Fine friends you have,' they'll say, 'those Egyptians. They have betrayed you and left you to your fate!' ²³All your wives and children will be led out to the Babylonians, and you will not escape. You will be seized by the king of Babylon, and this city will be burned."

²⁴Then Zedekiah said to Jeremiah, "On pain of death, don't tell anyone you told me this! ²⁵And if my officials hear that I talked with you and they threaten you with death unless you tell them what we discussed, ²⁶just say that you begged me not to send you back to the dungeon in Jonathan's house, for you would die there."

²⁷And sure enough, it wasn't long before all the city officials came to Jeremiah and asked him why the king had called for him. So he said what the king had told him to, and they left without finding out the truth, for the conversation had not been overheard by anyone. ²⁸And Jeremiah remained confined to the prison yard until the day Jerusalem was captured.

39 Jerusalem Is Captured

It was in January of the ninth year of the reign of King Zedekiah of Judah that King Nebuchadnezzar and all his army came against Jerusalem again and besieged it. ²Two years later, in the month of July, they breached the wall, and the city fell, ³and all the officers of the Babylonian army came in and sat in triumph at the middle gate. Nergal-sharezer was there, Samgar-nebo, Sarsechim, Nergal-sharezer the king's chief assistant, and many others.

⁴When King Zedekiah and his soldiers realized that the city was lost, they fled during the night, going out through the gate between the two walls back of the palace garden and across the fields toward the Jordan valley. ⁵But the Babylonians chased the king and caught him on the plains of Jericho and brought him to Nebuchadnezzar, king of Babylon who was at Riblah, in the land of Hamath, where he pronounced judgment upon him. ⁶The king of Babylon made Zedekiah watch as they killed his children and all the nobles of Judah. ⁷Then he gouged out Zedekiah's eyes and bound him in chains to send him away to Babylon as a slave.

⁸Meanwhile the army burned Jerusalem, including the palace, and tore down the walls of the city. ⁹Then Nebuzaradan, the captain of the guard, and his men sent the remnant of the population and all those who had defected to him to Babylon.

OBEDIENCE 38:9-13 Ebed-melech feared God more than man. He alone among the palace officials stood up against the murder plot. His obedience could have cost him his life. Because he obeyed, however, he was spared when Jerusalem fell (39:15-18). You can either go along with the crowd or speak up for God. When someone is treated unkindly or unjustly, for example, reach out to that person with God's love. You may be the only one who does. And, when you're being treated unkindly yourself, be sure to thank God when he sends an "Ebed-melech" your way. **To begin the series of devotionals on OBEDIENCE, turn to page 25.**

¹⁰But throughout the land of Judah he left a few people, the very poor, and gave them fields and vineyards.

¹¹,¹²Meanwhile King Nebuchadnezzar had told Nebuzaradan to find Jeremiah. "See that he isn't hurt," he said. "Look after him well and give him anything he wants." ¹³So Nebuzaradan, the captain of the guard, and Nebushazban, the chief of the eunuchs, and Nergal-sharezer, the king's advisor, and all the officials took steps to do as the king had commanded. ¹⁴They sent soldiers to bring Jeremiah out of the prison, and put him into the care of Gedaliah (son of Ahikam, son of Shaphan), to take him back to his home. And Jeremiah lived there among his people who were left in the land.

¹⁵The Lord gave the following message to Jeremiah before the Babylonians arrived, while he was still in prison: ¹⁶"Send this word to Ebed-melech the Ethiopian: The Lord, the God of Israel, says: I will do to this city everything I threatened; I will destroy it before your eyes, ¹⁷but I will deliver you. You shall not be killed by those you fear so much. ¹⁸As a reward for trusting me, I will preserve your life and keep you safe."

40 Jeremiah Is Set Free

Nebuzaradan, captain of the guard, took Jeremiah to Ramah along with all the exiled people of Jerusalem and Judah who were being sent to Babylon, but then released him.

²,³The captain called for Jeremiah and said, "The Lord your God has brought this disaster on this land, just as he said he would. For these people have sinned against the Lord. That is why it happened. ⁴Now I am going to take off your chains and let you go. If you want to come with me to Babylon, fine; I will see that you are well cared for. But if you don't want to come, don't. The world is before you—go where you like. ⁵If you decide to stay, then return to Gedaliah, who has been appointed as governor of Judah by the king of Babylon, and stay with the remnant he rules. But it's up to you; go where you like."

Then Nebuzaradan gave Jeremiah some food and money and let him go. ⁶So Jeremiah returned to Gedaliah and lived in Judah with the people left in the land.

⁷Now when the leaders of the Jewish guerrilla bands in the countryside heard that the king of Babylon had appointed Gedaliah as governor over the poor of the land who were left behind, and had not exiled everyone to Babylon, ⁸they came to see Gedaliah at Mizpah, where his headquarters were. These are the names of the leaders who came: Ishmael (son of Nethaniah), Johanan and Jonathan (sons of Kareah), Seraiah (son of Tanhumeth), the sons of Ephai (the Netophathite), Jezaniah (son of a Maacathite), and their men. ⁹And Gedaliah assured them that it would be safe to surrender to the Babylonians.

"Stay here and serve the king of Babylon," he said, "and all will go well for you. ¹⁰As for me, I will stay at Mizpah and intercede for you with the Babylonians who will come here to oversee my administration. Settle in any city you wish and live off the land. Harvest the grapes and summer fruits and olives and store them away."

¹¹When the Jews in Moab and among the Ammonites and in Edom and the other nearby countries heard that a few people were still left in Judah, and that the king of Babylon had not taken them all away, and that Gedaliah was the governor, ¹²they all began to return to Judah from the many places to which they had fled. They stopped at Mizpah to discuss their plans with Gedaliah and then went out to the deserted farms and gathered a great harvest of wine grapes and other crops.

¹³,¹⁴But soon afterwards Johanan (son of Kareah) and the other guerrilla leaders came to Mizpah to warn Gedaliah that Baalis, king of the Ammonites, had sent Ishmael (son of Nethaniah) to assassinate him. But Gedaliah wouldn't believe them. ¹⁵Then Johanan had a private conference with Gedaliah. Johanan volunteered to kill Ishmael secretly.

"Why should we let him come and murder you?" Johanan asked. "What will happen then to the Jews who have returned? Why should this remnant be scattered and lost?"

¹⁶But Gedaliah said, "I forbid you to do any such thing, for you are lying about Ishmael."

41 The Governor Dies

But in October, Ishmael (son of Nethaniah, son of Elishama), who was a member of the royal family and one of the king's top officials, arrived in Mizpah, accompanied by ten men. Gedaliah invited them to dinner. ²While they were eating, Ishmael and the ten men in league with him suddenly jumped up, pulled out their swords, and killed Gedaliah. ³Then they went out and slaughtered all the Jewish officials and Babylonian soldiers who were in Mizpah with Gedaliah.

⁴The next day, before the outside world knew what had happened, ⁵eighty men approached Mizpah from Shechem, Shiloh, and Samaria, to worship at the Temple of the Lord. They had shaved off their beards, torn their clothes, and cut themselves, and were bringing offerings and incense. ⁶Ishmael went out from the city to meet them, crying as he went. When he faced them he

said, "Oh, come and see what has happened to Gedaliah!"

⁷Then, when they were all inside the city, Ishmael and his men killed all but ten of them and threw their bodies into a cistern. ⁸The ten had talked Ishmael into letting them go by promising to bring him their treasures of wheat, barley, oil, and honey they had hidden away. ⁹The cistern where Ishmael dumped the bodies of the men he murdered was the large one constructed by King Asa when he fortified Mizpah to protect himself against Baasha, king of Israel.

¹⁰Ishmael made captives of the king's daughters and of the people who had been left under Gedaliah's care in Mizpah by Nebuzaradan, captain of the guard. Soon after, he took them with him when he headed toward the country of the Ammonites.

¹¹But when Johanan (son of Kareah) and the rest of the guerrilla leaders heard what Ishmael had done, ¹²they took all their men and set out to stop him. They caught up with him at the pool near Gibeon. ¹³,¹⁴The people with Ishmael shouted for joy when they saw Johanan and his men and ran to meet them.

¹⁵Meanwhile Ishmael escaped with eight of his men into the land of the Ammonites.

¹⁶,¹⁷Then Johanan and his men went to the village of Geruth Chimham, near Bethlehem, taking with them all those they had rescued—soldiers, women, children, and eunuchs, to prepare to leave for Egypt. ¹⁸For they were afraid of what the Babylonians would do when the news reached them that Ishmael had killed Gedaliah the governor, for he had been chosen and appointed by the Babylonian emperor.

42 Don't Go to Egypt!

Then Johanan and the army captains and all the people, great and small, came to Jeremiah ²and said, "Please pray for us to the Lord your God, for as you know so well, we are only a tiny remnant of what we were before. ³Beg the Lord your God to show us what to do and where to go."

⁴"All right," Jeremiah replied. "I will ask him and I will tell you what he says. I will hide nothing from you."

⁵Then they said to Jeremiah, "May the curse of God be on us if we refuse to obey whatever he says we should do! ⁶Whether we like it or not, we will obey the Lord our God, to whom we send you with our plea. For if we obey him, everything will turn out well for us."

⁷Ten days later the Lord gave his reply to Jeremiah. ⁸So he called for Johanan and the captains of his forces, and for all the people, great and small, ⁹and said to them: "You sent me to the Lord, the God of Israel, with your request, and this is his reply:

¹⁰"Stay here in this land. If you do, I will bless you, and no one will harm you. For I am sorry for all the punishment I have had to give to you. ¹¹Don't fear the king of Babylon any more, for I am with you to save you and to deliver you from his hand. ¹²And I will be merciful to you by making him kind so that he will not kill you or make slaves of you but will let you stay here in your land.

¹³,¹⁴"But if you refuse to obey the Lord and say, 'We will not stay here,'—and insist on going to Egypt where you think you will be free from war and hunger and alarms, ¹⁵then this is what the Lord replies, O remnant of Judah: The Lord Almighty, the God of Israel, says: If you insist on going to Egypt, ¹⁶the war and famine you fear will follow close behind you, and you will perish there. ¹⁷That is the fate awaiting every one of you who insists on going to live in Egypt. Yes, you will die from sword, famine, and disease. None of you will escape from the evil I will bring upon you there.

¹⁸"For the Lord, the God of Israel, says: Just as my anger and fury were poured out upon the people of Jerusalem, so it will be poured out on you when you enter Egypt. You will be received with disgust and with hatred—you will be cursed and reviled. And you will never again see your own land. ¹⁹For the Lord has said: O remnant of Judah, do not go to Egypt!"

Jeremiah concluded: "Never forget the warning I have given you today. ²⁰If you go, it will be at the cost of your lives. For you were deceitful when you sent me to pray for you and said, 'Just tell us what God says and we will do it!' ²¹And today I have told you exactly what he said, but you will not obey any more now than you did the other times. ²²Therefore know for a certainty that you will die by sword, famine, and disease in Egypt, where you insist on going."

43 The People Won't Believe

When Jeremiah had finished giving this message from God to all the people, ²,³Azariah (son of Hoshaiah) and Johanan (son of Kareah) and all the other proud men, said to Jeremiah, "You lie! The Lord our God hasn't told you to tell us not to go to Egypt! Baruch (son of Neriah) has plotted against us and told you to say this so that we will stay here and be killed by the Babylonians or carried off to Babylon as slaves."

⁴So Johanan and all the guerrilla leaders and all the people refused to obey the Lord and stay in Judah. ⁵All of them, including all those who had returned from the nearby countries where they had fled, now started off for Egypt with Johanan and the other captains in command. ⁶In the

crowd were men, women and children, the king's daughters, and all those whom Nebuzaradan, the captain of the guard, had left with Gedaliah. They even forced Jeremiah and Baruch to go with them too. ⁷And so they arrived in Egypt at the city of Tahpanhes, for they would not obey the Lord.

⁸Then at Tahpanhes, the Lord spoke to Jeremiah again and said: ⁹"Call together the men of Judah and, as they watch you, bury large rocks between the pavement stones at the entrance of Pharaoh's palace here in Tahpanhes, ¹⁰and tell the men of Judah this: The Lord Almighty, the God of Israel, says: I will surely bring Nebuchadnezzar, king of Babylon, here to Egypt, for he is my servant. I will set his throne upon these stones that I have hidden. He shall spread his royal canopy over them. ¹¹And when he comes, he shall destroy the land of Egypt, killing all those I want killed and capturing those I want captured, and many shall die of plague. ¹²He will set fire to the temples of the gods of Egypt and burn the idols and carry off the people as his captives. And he shall plunder the land of Egypt as a shepherd picks fleas from his cloak! And he himself shall leave unharmed. ¹³And he shall break down the obelisks standing in the city of Heliopolis and burn down the temples of the gods of Egypt."

44 God Gets Angry

This is the message God gave to Jeremiah concerning all the Jews who were living in the north of Egypt in the cities of Migdol, Tahpanhes, and Memphis, and throughout southern Egypt as well:

²,³The Lord Almighty, the God of Israel, says: You saw what I did to Jerusalem and to all the cities of Judah. Because of all their wickedness they lie in heaps and ashes, without a living soul. For my anger rose high against them for worshiping other gods—"gods" that neither they nor you nor any of your fathers have ever known.

⁴I sent my servants, the prophets, to protest over and over again and to plead with them not to do this horrible thing I hate, ⁵but they wouldn't listen and wouldn't turn back from their wicked ways; they have kept right on with their sacrifices to these "gods." ⁶And so my fury and anger boiled over and fell as fire upon the cities of Judah and into the streets of Jerusalem, and there is desolation until this day.

⁷And now the Lord, the Lord Almighty, the God of Israel, asks you: Why are you destroying yourselves? For not one of you shall live—not a man, woman or child among you who has come here from Judah, not even the babies in arms. ⁸For you are rousing my anger with the idols you have made and worshiped here in Egypt, burning incense to them, and causing me to destroy you completely and to make you a curse and a stench in the nostrils of all the nations of the earth. ⁹Have you forgotten the sins of your fathers, the sins of the kings and queens of Judah, your own sins, and the sins of your wives in Judah and Jerusalem? ¹⁰And even until this very hour there has been no apology; no one has wanted to return to me or follow the laws I gave you and your fathers before you.

¹¹Therefore the Lord, the God of Israel, says: There is fury in my face and I will destroy every one of you! ¹²I will take this remnant of Judah that insisted on coming here to Egypt, and I will consume them. They shall fall here in Egypt, killed by famine and sword; all shall die, from the least important to the greatest. They shall be despised and loathed, cursed and hated. ¹³I will punish them in Egypt just as I punished them in Jerusalem, by sword, famine, and disease. ¹⁴Not one of them shall escape from my wrath except those who repent of their coming and escape from the others by returning again to their own land.

¹⁵Then all the women present and all the men who knew that their wives had burned incense to idols (it was a great crowd of all the Jews in southern Egypt) answered Jeremiah:

¹⁶"We will not listen to your false 'Messages from God'! ¹⁷We will do whatever we want to. We will burn incense to the Queen of Heaven and sacrifice to her just as much as we like—just as we and our fathers before us, and our kings and princes have always done in the cities of Judah and in the streets of Jerusalem; for in those days we had plenty to eat, and we were well off and happy! ¹⁸But ever since we quit burning incense to the Queen of Heaven and stopped worshiping her, we have been in great trouble and have been destroyed by sword and famine."

¹⁹"And," the women added, "do you suppose that we were worshiping the Queen of Heaven and pouring out our libations to her and making cakes for her with her image on them, without our husbands knowing it and helping us? Of course not!"

²⁰Then Jeremiah said to all of them, men and women alike, who had given him that answer:

²¹"Do you think the Lord didn't know that you and your fathers, your kings and princes, and all the people were burning incense to idols in the cities of

---

PERSEVERANCE 44:9-10 When we forget a lesson or refuse to learn it, we risk repeating our mistakes. The people of Judah struggled with this same matter; to forget their former sins was to repeat them. To fail to learn from failure is to assure future failure. Your past is your school of experience. Let your past mistakes point you to God's way. **To begin the series of devotionals on PERSEVERANCE, turn to page 37.**

Judah and in the streets of Jerusalem? 22It was because he could no longer bear all the evil things you were doing that he made your land desolate, an incredible ruin, cursed, without an inhabitant, as it is today. 23The very reason all these terrible things have befallen you is because you have burned incense and sinned against the Lord and refused to obey him."

24Then Jeremiah said to them all, including the women: "Listen to the word of the Lord, all you citizens of Judah who are here in Egypt! 25The Lord, the God of Israel, says: Both you and your wives have said that you will never give up your devotion and sacrifices to the Queen of Heaven, and you have proved it by your actions. Then go ahead and carry out your promises and vows to her! 26But listen to the word of the Lord, all you Jews who are living in the land of Egypt: I have sworn by my great name,' says the Lord, that it will do you no good to seek my help and blessing any more, saying, 'O Lord our God, help us!' 27For I will watch over you, but *not* for good! I will see to it that evil befalls you, and you shall be destroyed by war and famine until all of you are dead.

28"Only those who return to Judah (it will be but a tiny remnant) shall escape my wrath, but all who refuse to go back—who insist on living in Egypt—shall find out who tells the truth, I or they! 29And this is the proof I give you that all I have threatened will happen to you and that I will punish you here: 30I will turn Pharaoh Hophra, king of Egypt, over to those who seek his life, just as I turned Zedekiah, king of Judah, over to Nebuchadnezzar, king of Babylon."

45

This is the message Jeremiah gave to Baruch in the fourth year of the reign of King Jehoiakim (son of Josiah), after Baruch had written down all God's messages as Jeremiah was dictating them to him:

2O Baruch, the Lord God of Israel says this to you: 3You have said, Woe is me! Don't I have troubles enough already? And now the Lord has added more! I am weary of my own sighing and I find no rest. 4But tell Baruch this, The Lord says: I will destroy this nation that I built; I will wipe out what I established. 5Are you seeking great things for yourself? Don't do it! For though I will bring great evil upon all these people, I will protect you wherever you go, as your reward.

46
A Message to the Egyptians

Here are the messages given to Jeremiah concerning foreign nations:

The Egyptians

2This message was given against Egypt at the occasion of the battle of Carchemish when Pharaoh Necho, king of Egypt, and his army were defeated beside the Euphrates River by Nebuchadnezzar, king of Babylon, in the fourth year of the reign of Jehoiakim (son of Josiah), king of Judah:

3Buckle on your armor, you Egyptians and advance to battle! 4Harness the horses and prepare to mount them—don your helmets, sharpen your spears, put on your armor. 5But look! The Egyptian army flees in terror; the mightiest of its soldiers run without a backward glance. Yes, terror shall surround them on every side, says the Lord. 6The swift will not escape, nor the mightiest of warriors. In the north, by the river Euphrates, they have stumbled and fallen.

7What is this mighty army, rising like the Nile at flood time, overflowing all the land? 8It is the Egyptian army, boasting that it will cover the earth like a flood, destroying every foe. 9Then come, O horses and chariots and mighty soldiers of Egypt! Come, all of you from Cush and Put and Lud who handle the shield and bend the bow! 10For this is the day of the Lord, the Lord Almighty, a day of vengeance upon his enemies. The sword shall devour until it is sated, yes, drunk with your blood, for the Lord, the Lord Almighty will receive a sacrifice today in the north country beside the river Euphrates! 11Go up to Gilead for medicine, O virgin daughter of Egypt! Yet there is no cure for your wounds. Though you have used many medicines, there is no healing for you. 12The nations have heard of your shame. The earth is filled with your cry of despair and defeat; your mightiest soldiers will stumble across each other and fall together.

13Then God gave Jeremiah this message concerning the coming of Nebuchadnezzar, king of Babylon, to attack Egypt:

14Shout it out in Egypt; publish it in the cities of Migdol, Memphis, and Tahpanhes! Mobilize for battle, for the sword of destruction shall devour all around you. 15Why has Apis, your bull god, fled in terror? Because the Lord knocked him down before your enemies. 16Vast multitudes fall in heaps. (Then the remnant of the Jews will say, "Come, let us return again to Judah where we were born and get away from all this slaughter here!")

17Rename Pharaoh Hophra and call him "The Man with No Power But with Plenty of Noise!"

18As I live, says the King, the Lord of Hosts, one is coming against Egypt who is as tall as Mount Tabor or Mount Carmel by the sea! 19Pack up; get ready to leave for exile, you citizens of Egypt, for the city of Memphis shall be utterly destroyed and left without a soul alive. 20,21Egypt is sleek as a heifer, but a gadfly sends her running—a gadfly from the north! Even her famed mercenaries have become like frightened calves. They turn and run, for it is the day of great calamity for Egypt, a time of great punishment. 22,23 Silent as a serpent gliding away, Egypt flees; the invading army marches in. The numberless soldiers cut down your people like woodsmen who clear a forest of its trees. 24Egypt is as helpless as a girl before these men from the north.

25The Lord, the God of Israel, says: I will punish Amon, god of Thebes, and all the other gods of Egypt. I will punish Pharaoh too, and all who trust in him. 26I will deliver them into the hands of those who want them killed—into the hands of Nebuchadnezzar, king of Babylon, and his army. But afterwards the land shall recover from the ravages of war.

27But don't you be afraid, O my people who return to your own land, don't be dismayed; for I will save you from far away and bring your children from a distant land. Yes, Israel shall return and be at rest, and nothing shall make her afraid. 28Fear not, O Jacob, my servant, says the Lord, for I am with you. I will destroy all the nations to which I have exiled you, but I will not destroy you. I will punish you, but only enough to correct you.

47 A Message to the Philistines
The Philistines

This is God's message to Jeremiah concerning the Philistines of Gaza, before the city was captured by the Egyptian army:

2The Lord says: A flood is coming from the north to overflow the land of the Philistines; it will destroy their cities and everything in them. Strong men will scream in terror, and all the land will weep. 3Hear the clattering hoofs and rumbling wheels as the chariots go rushing by; fathers flee without a backward glance at their helpless children, 4for the time has come when all the Philistines and their allies from Tyre and Sidon will be destroyed. For the Lord is destroying the Philistines, those colonists from Caphtor. 5The cities of Gaza and Ashkelon will be razed to the ground and lie in ruins. O descendants of the Anakim, how you will lament and mourn!

6O sword of the Lord, when will you be at rest again? Go back into your scabbard; rest and be still! 7But how can it be still when the Lord has sent it on an errand? For the city of Ashkelon and those living along the sea must be destroyed.

48 The Proud Moabites Are Doomed
The Moabites

This is the message of the Lord of Hosts, the God of Israel, against Moab:

Woe to the city of Nebo, for it shall lie in ruins. The city of Kiriathaim and its forts are overwhelmed and captured. 2-4No one will ever brag about Moab any more, for there is a plot against her life. In Heshbon plans have been completed to destroy her. "Come," they say, "we will cut her off from being a nation." In Madmen all is silent. And then the roar of battle will surge against Horonaim, for all Moab is being destroyed. Her crying will be heard as far away as Zoar. 5Her refugees will climb the hills of Luhith, weeping bitterly, while cries of terror rise from the city below. 6Flee for your lives; hide in the wilderness! 7For you trusted in your wealth and skill; therefore, you shall perish. Your god Chemosh, with his priests and princes, shall be taken away to distant lands!

8All the villages and cities, whether they be on the plateaus or in the valleys, shall be destroyed, for the Lord has said it. 9Oh, for wings for Moab that she could fly away, for her cities shall be left without a living soul. 10Cursed be those withholding their swords from your blood, refusing to do the work that God has given them!

11From her earliest history Moab has lived there undisturbed from all invasions. She is like wine that has not been poured from flask to flask and is fragrant and smooth. But now she shall have the pouring out of exile! 12The time is coming soon, the Lord has said, when he will send troublemakers to spill her out from jar to jar and then shatter the jars! 13Then at last Moab shall be ashamed of her idol Chemosh, as Israel was of her calf idol at Bethel.

14Do you remember that boast of yours: "We are heroes, mighty men of war"? 15But now Moab is to be destroyed; her destroyer is on the way; her choicest youth are doomed to slaughter, says the King, the Lord Almighty. 16Calamity is coming fast to Moab.

17O friends of Moab, weep for her and cry! See how the strong, the beautiful is shattered! 18Come down from your glory and sit in the dust, O people of Dibon, for those destroying Moab shall shatter Dibon too, and tear down all her towers. 19Those in Aroer stand anxiously beside the road to watch, and shout to those who flee from Moab, "What has happened there?"

20And they reply, "Moab lies in ruins; weep and wail. Tell it by the banks of the Arnon, that Moab is destroyed."

21All the cities of the tableland lie in ruins too, for God's judgment has been poured out upon them all—on Holon and Jahzah and Mephaath, 22and Dibon and Nebo and Beth-diblathaim, 23and Kiriathaim and Beth-gamul and Beth-meon, 24and Kerioth and Bozrah—and all the cities of the land of Moab, far and near.

²⁵The strength of Moab is ended—her horns are cut off; her arms are broken. ²⁶Let her stagger and fall like a drunkard, for she has rebelled against the Lord. Moab shall wallow in her vomit, scorned by all. ²⁷For you scorned Israel and robbed her and were happy at her fall.

²⁸O people of Moab, flee from your cities and live in the caves like doves that nest in the clefts of the rocks. ²⁹We have all heard of the pride of Moab, for it is very great. We know your loftiness, your arrogance, and your haughty heart. ³⁰I know her insolence, the Lord has said, but her boasts are false—her helplessness is great. ³¹Yes, I wail for Moab, my heart is broken for the men of Kir-heres.

³²O men of Sibmah, rich in vineyards, I weep for you even more than for Jazer. For the destroyer has cut off your spreading tendrils and harvested your grapes and summer fruits. He has plucked you bare! ³³Joy and gladness are gone from fruitful Moab. The presses yield no wine; no one treads the grapes with shouts of joy. There is shouting, yes, but not the shouting of joy. ³⁴Instead the awful cries of terror and pain rise from all over the land—from Heshbon clear across to Elealeh and to Jahaz; from Zoar to Horonaim and to Eglath-shelishiyah. The pastures of Nimrim are deserted now.

³⁵For the Lord says: I have put a stop to Moab's worshiping false gods and burning incense to idols. ³⁶Sad sings my heart for Moab and Kir-heres, for all their wealth has disappeared. ³⁷They shave their heads and beards in anguish; they slash their hands and put on clothes of sackcloth. ³⁸Crying and sorrow will be in every Moabite home and on the streets; for I have smashed and shattered Moab like an old, unwanted bottle. ³⁹How it is broken! Hear the wails! See the shame of Moab! For she is a sign of horror and of scoffing to her neighbors now.

⁴⁰A vulture circles ominously above the land of Moab, says the Lord. ⁴¹Her cities are fallen; her strongholds are seized. The hearts of her mightiest warriors fail with fear like women in the pains of giving birth. ⁴²Moab shall no longer be a nation, for she has boasted against the Lord. ⁴³Fear and traps and treachery shall be your lot, O Moab, says the Lord. ⁴⁴He who flees shall fall in a trap, and he who escapes from the trap shall run into a snare. I will see to it that you do not get away, for the time of your judgment has come. ⁴⁵They flee to Heshbon, unable to go farther. But a fire comes from Heshbon—Sihon's ancestral home—and devours the land from end to end with all its rebellious people.

⁴⁶Woe to you, O Moab; the people of the god Chemosh are destroyed, and your sons and daughters are taken away as slaves. ⁴⁷But in the latter days, says the Lord, I will reestablish Moab.

(Here the prophecy concerning Moab ends.)

49 A Message to the Ammonites

The Ammonites

What is this you are doing? Why are you living in the cities of the Jews? Aren't there Jews enough to fill them up? Didn't they inherit them from me? Why then have you, who worship Milcom, taken over Gad and all its cities? ²I will punish you for this, the Lord declares, by destroying your city of Rabbah. It shall become a desolate heap, and the neighboring towns shall be burned. Then Israel shall come and take back her land from you again. She shall dispossess those who dispossessed her, says the Lord.

³Cry out, O Heshbon, for Ai is destroyed! Weep, daughter of Rabbah! Put on garments of mourning; weep and wail, hiding in the hedges, for your god Milcom shall be exiled along with his princes and priests. ⁴You are proud of your fertile valleys, but they will soon be ruined. O wicked daughter, you trusted in your wealth and thought no one could ever harm you. ⁵But see, I will bring terror upon you, says the Lord, the Lord Almighty. For all your neighbors shall drive you from your land and none shall help your exiles as they flee. ⁶But afterward I will restore the fortunes of the Ammonites, says the Lord.

The Edomites

⁷The Lord says: Where are all your wise men of days gone by? Is there not one left in all of Teman? ⁸Flee to the remotest parts of the desert, O people of Dedan; for when I punish Edom, I will punish you! ⁹,¹⁰Those who gather grapes leave a few for the poor, and even thieves don't take everything, but I will strip bare the land of Esau, and there will be no place to hide. Her children, her brothers, her neighbors—all will be destroyed—and she herself will perish too. ¹¹(But I will preserve your fatherless children who remain, and let your widows depend upon me.)

¹²The Lord says to Edom: If the innocent must suffer, how much more must you! You shall not go unpunished! You must drink this cup of judgment! ¹³For I have sworn by my own name, says the Lord, that Bozrah shall become heaps of ruins, cursed and mocked; and her cities shall be eternal wastes.

¹⁴I have heard this message from the Lord: I have sent a messenger to call the nations to form a coalition against Edom and destroy her.

¹⁵I will make her weak among the nations and despised by all, says the Lord. ¹⁶You have been fooled by your fame and your pride, living there

in the mountains of Petra, in the clefts of the rocks. But though you live among the peaks with the eagles, I will bring you down, says the Lord.

¹⁷The fate of Edom will be horrible; all who go by will be appalled and gasp at the sight. ¹⁸Your cities will become as silent as Sodom and Gomorrah and their neighboring towns, says the Lord. No one will live there anymore. ¹⁹I will send against them one who will come like a lion from the wilds of Jordan stalking the sheep in the fold. Suddenly Edom shall be destroyed, and I will appoint over the Edomites the person of my choice. For who is like me, and who can call me to account? What shepherd can defy me?

²⁰Take note: The Lord will certainly do this to Edom and also the people of Teman—even little children will be dragged away as slaves! It will be a shocking thing to see. ²¹The earth shakes with the noise of Edom's fall; the cry of the people is heard as far away as the Red Sea. ²²The one who will come will fly as swift as a vulture and will spread his wings against Bozrah. Then the courage of the mightiest warriors will disappear like that of women in labor.

Damascus
²³The cities of Hamath and Arpad are stricken with fear, for they have heard the news of their doom. Their hearts are troubled like a wild sea in a raging storm. ²⁴Damascus has become feeble, and all her people turn to flee. Fear, anguish, and sorrow have gripped her as they do women in labor. ²⁵O famous city, city of joy, how you are forsaken now! ²⁶Your young men lie dead in the streets; your entire army shall be destroyed in one day, says the Lord Almighty. ²⁷And I will start a fire at the edge of Damascus that shall burn up the palaces of Benhadad.

Kedar and Hazor
²⁸This prophecy is about Kedar and the kingdoms of Hazor that are going to be destroyed by Nebuchadnezzar, king of Babylon, for the Lord will send him to destroy them:

²⁹Their flocks and their tents will be captured, says the Lord, with all their household goods. Their camels will be taken away, and all around will be the shouts of panic, "We are surrounded and doomed!" ³⁰Flee for your lives, says the Lord. Go deep into the deserts, O people of Hazor, for Nebuchadnezzar, king of Babylon, has plotted against you and is preparing to destroy you.

³¹"Go," said the Lord to King Nebuchadnezzar. "Attack those wealthy Bedouin tribes living alone in the desert without a care in the world, boasting that they are self-sufficient—that they need neither walls nor gates. ³²Their camels and cattle shall all be yours, and I will scatter these heathen to the winds. From all directions I will bring calamity upon them.

³³"Hazor shall be a home for wild animals of the desert. No one shall ever live there again. It shall be desolate forever."

Elam
³⁴God's message against Elam came to Jeremiah in the beginning of the reign of Zedekiah, king of Judah:

³⁵The Lord says: I will destroy the army of Elam, ³⁶and I will scatter the people of Elam to the four winds; they shall be exiled to countries throughout the world. ³⁷My fierce anger will bring great evil upon Elam, says the Lord, and I will cause her enemies to wipe her out. ³⁸And I will set my throne in Elam,' says the Lord. I will destroy her king and princes. ³⁹But in the latter days I will bring the people back, says the Lord.

50 A Message to Babylon
Babylon

This is the message from the Lord against Babylon and the Chaldeans, spoken by Jeremiah the prophet:

²Tell all the world that Babylon will be destroyed; her god Marduk will be utterly disgraced! ³For a nation shall come down upon her from the north with such destruction that no one shall live in her again; all shall be gone—both men and animals shall flee.

⁴Then the people of Israel and Judah shall join together, weeping and seeking the Lord their God. ⁵They shall ask the way to Zion and start back home again. "Come," they will say, "let us be united to the Lord with an eternal pledge that will never be broken again."

⁶My people have been lost sheep. Their shepherds led them astray and then turned them loose in the mountains. They lost their way and didn't remember how to get back to the fold. ⁷All who found them devoured them and said, "We are permitted to attack them freely, for they have sinned against the Lord, the God of justice, the hope of their fathers."

⁸But now, flee from Babylon, the land of the Chaldeans; lead my people home again. ⁹For see, I am raising up an army of great nations from the north, and I will bring them against Babylon to attack her, and she shall be destroyed. The enemies' arrows go straight to the mark; they do not miss! ¹⁰And Babylon shall be sacked until everyone is sated with loot, says the Lord.

¹¹Though you were glad, O Chaldeans, plunderers of my people, and are fat as cows that feed in lush pastures, and neigh like stallions, ¹²yet your

mother shall be overwhelmed with shame, for you shall become the least of the nations—a wilderness, a dry and desert land. ¹³Because of the anger of the Lord, Babylon shall become deserted wasteland, and all who pass by shall be appalled and shall mock at her for all her wounds.

¹⁴Yes, prepare to fight with Babylon, all you nations round about; let the archers shoot at her; spare no arrows, for she has sinned against the Lord. ¹⁵Shout against her from every side. Look! She surrenders! Her walls have fallen. The Lord has taken vengeance. Do to her as she has done! ¹⁶Let the farmhands all depart. Let them rush back to their own lands as the enemies advance.

¹⁷The Israelites are like sheep the lions chase. First the king of Assyria ate them up; then Nebuchadnezzar, the king of Babylon, crunched their bones. ¹⁸Therefore the Lord, the God of Israel, says: Now I will punish the king of Babylon and his land as I punished the king of Assyria. ¹⁹And I will bring Israel home again to her own land, to feed in the fields of Carmel and Bashan and to be happy once more on Mount Ephraim and Mount Gilead. ²⁰In those days, says the Lord, no sin shall be found in Israel or in Judah, for I will pardon the remnant I preserve.

²¹Go up, O my warriors, against the land of Merathaim and against the people of Pekod. Yes, march against Babylon, the land of rebels, a land that I will judge! Annihilate them, as I have commanded you. ²²Let there be the shout of battle in the land, a shout of great destruction. ²³Babylon, the mightiest hammer in all the earth, lies broken and shattered. Babylon is desolate among the nations! ²⁴O Babylon, I have set a trap for you and you are caught, for you have fought against the Lord.

²⁵The Lord has opened his armory and brought out weapons to explode his wrath upon his enemies. The terror that befalls Babylon will be the work of the Lord God. ²⁶Yes, come against her from distant lands; break open her granaries; knock down her walls and houses into heaps of ruins and utterly destroy her; let nothing be left. ²⁷Not even her cattle—woe to them too! Kill them all! For the time has come for Babylon to be devastated.

²⁸But my people will flee; they will escape back to their own country to tell how the Lord their God has broken forth in fury upon those who destroyed his Temple.

²⁹Send out a call for archers to come to Babylon; surround the city so that none can escape. Do to her as she has done to others, for she has haughtily defied the Lord, the Holy One of Israel. ³⁰Her young men will fall in the streets and die; her warriors will all be killed. ³¹For see, I am against you, O people so proud; and now your day of reckoning has come. ³²Land of pride, you will stumble and fall, and no one will raise you up; for the Lord will light a fire in the cities of Babylon that will burn everything around them.

³³The Lord says: The people of Israel and Judah have been wronged. Their captors hold them and refuse to let them go. ³⁴But their Redeemer is strong. His name is the Lord Almighty. He will plead for them and see that they are freed to live again in quietness in Israel.

As for the people of Babylon—there is no rest for them! ³⁵The sword of destruction shall smite the Chaldeans, says the Lord. It shall smite the people of Babylon—her princes and wise men too. ³⁶All her wise counselors shall become fools! Panic shall seize her mightiest warriors! ³⁷War shall devour her horses and chariots, and her allies from other lands shall become as weak as women. Her treasures shall all be robbed; ³⁸even her water supply will fail. And why? Because the whole land is full of images, and the people are madly in love with their idols.

³⁹Therefore this city of Babylon shall become inhabited by ostriches and jackals; it shall be a home for the wild animals of the desert. Never again shall it be lived in by human beings; it shall lie desolate forever. ⁴⁰The Lord declares that he will destroy Babylon just as he destroyed Sodom and Gomorrah and their neighboring towns. No one has lived in them since, and no one will live again in Babylon.

⁴¹See them coming! A great army from the north! It is accompanied by many kings called by God from many lands. ⁴²They are fully armed for slaughter; they are cruel and show no mercy; their battle cry roars like the surf against the shoreline. O Babylon, they ride against you fully ready for the battle.

⁴³When the king of Babylon received the dispatch, his hands fell helpless at his sides; pangs of terror gripped him like the pangs of a woman in labor.

⁴⁴*I will send against them an invader who will come upon them suddenly, like a lion from the jungles of Jordan that leaps upon the grazing sheep. I will put her defenders to flight and appoint over them whomsoever I please. For who is like me? What ruler can oppose my will? Who can call me to account?*

⁴⁵Listen to the plan of the Lord against Babylon, the land of the Chaldeans. For even little children shall be dragged away as slaves; oh, the horror; oh, the terror. ⁴⁶The whole earth shall shake at Babylon's fall, and her cry of despair shall be heard around the world.

51 Our Great and Mighty God

The Lord says: I will stir up a destroyer against Babylon, against that whole land of the Chaldeans, and destroy it. ²Winnowers shall come and winnow her and blow her away; they shall come from every side to rise against her in her day of trouble. ³The arrows of the enemy shall strike down the bowmen of Babylon and pierce her warriors in their coats of mail. No one shall be spared; both young and old alike shall be destroyed. ⁴They shall fall down slain in the land of the Chaldeans, slashed to death in her streets. ⁵For the Lord Almighty has not forsaken Israel and Judah. He is still their God, but the land of the Chaldeans is filled with sin against the Holy One of Israel.

⁶Flee from Babylon! Save yourselves! Don't get trapped! If you stay, you will be destroyed when God takes his vengeance on all of Babylon's sins. ⁷Babylon has been as a gold cup in the Lord's hands, a cup from which he made the whole earth drink and go mad. ⁸But now, suddenly Babylon too has fallen. Weep for her; give her medicine; perhaps she can yet be healed. ⁹We would help her if we could, but nothing can save her now. Let her go. Abandon her and return to your own land, for God is judging her from heaven. ¹⁰The Lord has vindicated us. Come, let us declare in Jerusalem all the Lord our God has done.

¹¹Sharpen the arrows! Lift up the shields! For the Lord has stirred up the spirit of the kings of the Medes to march on Babylon and destroy her. This is his vengeance on those who wronged his people and desecrated his Temple. ¹²Prepare your defenses, Babylon! Set many watchmen on your walls; send out an ambush, for the Lord will do all he has said he would concerning Babylon. ¹³O wealthy port, great center of commerce, your end has come; the thread of your life is cut. ¹⁴The Lord Almighty has taken this vow and sworn to it in his own name: Your cities shall be filled with enemies, like fields filled with locusts in a plague, and they shall lift to the skies their mighty shouts of victory.

¹⁵God made the earth by his power and wisdom. He stretched out the heavens by his understanding. ¹⁶When he speaks there is thunder in the heavens, and he causes the vapors to rise around the world; he brings the lightning with the rain and the winds from his treasuries. ¹⁷Compared to him, all men are stupid beasts. They have no wisdom—none at all! The silversmith is dulled by the images he makes, for in making them he lies; for he calls them gods when there is not a breath of life in them at all! ¹⁸Idols are nothing! They are lies! And the time is coming when God will come and see, and shall destroy them all. ¹⁹But the God of Israel is no idol! For he made everything there is, and Israel is his nation; the Lord Almighty is his name.

²⁰Cyrus is God's battleaxe and sword. I will use you, says the Lord, to break nations in pieces and to destroy many kingdoms. ²¹With you I will crush armies, destroying the horse and his rider, the chariot and the charioteer— ²²yes, and the civilians too, both old and young, young men and maidens, ²³shepherds and flocks, farmers and oxen, captains and rulers; ²⁴before your eyes I will repay Babylon and all the Chaldeans for all the evil they have done to my people, says the Lord.

²⁵For see, I am against you, O mighty mountain, Babylon, destroyer of the earth! I will lift my hand against you, roll you down from your heights, and leave you, a burnt-out mountain. ²⁶You shall be desolate forever; even your stones shall never be used for building again. You shall be completely wiped out.

²⁷Signal many nations to mobilize for war on Babylon. Sound the battle cry; bring out the armies of Ararat, Minni, and Ashkenaz. Appoint a leader; bring a multitude of horses! ²⁸Bring against her the armies of the kings of the Medes and their generals, and the armies of all the countries they rule.

²⁹Babylon trembles and writhes in pain, for all that the Lord has planned against her stands unchanged. Babylon will be left desolate without a living soul. ³⁰Her mightiest soldiers no longer fight; they stay in their barracks. Their courage is gone; they have become as women. The invaders have burned the houses and broken down the city gates. ³¹Messengers from every side come running to the king to tell him all is lost! ³²All the escape routes are blocked; the fortifications are burning, and the army is in panic.

³³For the Lord, the God of Israel, says: Babylon is like the wheat upon a threshing floor; in just a little while the flailing will begin.

³⁴,³⁵The Jews in Babylon say, "Nebuchadnezzar, king of Babylon, has eaten and crushed us and emptied out our strength; he has swallowed us like a great monster and filled his belly with our riches; he has cast us out of our own country. May Babylon be repaid for all she did to us! May she be paid in full for all our blood she spilled!"

³⁶And the Lord replies: I will be your lawyer; I will plead your case; I will avenge you. I will dry up her river, her water supply, ³⁷and Babylon shall become a heap of ruins, haunted by jackals, a land horrible to see, incredible, without a living soul. ³⁸In their drunken feasts, the men of Babylon roar like lions. ³⁹And while they lie inflamed with all their wine, I will prepare a different kind of feast for them and make them drink until they fall unconscious to the floor, to sleep forever, never to waken again, says the Lord. ⁴⁰I will bring them like lambs to the slaughter, like rams and goats.

⁴¹How Babylon is fallen—great Babylon, lauded by all the earth! The world can scarcely believe its

eyes at Babylon's fall! ⁴²The sea has risen upon Babylon; she is covered by its waves. ⁴³Her cities lie in ruins—she is a dry wilderness where no one lives nor even travelers pass by. ⁴⁴And I will punish Bel, the god of Babylon, and pull from his mouth what he has taken. The nations shall no longer come and worship him; the wall of Babylon has fallen.

⁴⁵O my people, flee from Babylon; save yourselves from the fierce anger of the Lord. ⁴⁶But don't panic when you hear the first rumor of approaching forces. For rumors will keep coming year by year. Then there will be a time of civil war as the governors of Babylon fight against each other. ⁴⁷For the time is surely coming when I will punish this great city and all her idols; her dead shall lie in the streets. ⁴⁸Heaven and earth shall rejoice, for out of the north shall come destroying armies against Babylon, says the Lord. ⁴⁹Just as Babylon killed the people of Israel, so must she be killed. ⁵⁰Go, you who escaped the sword! Don't stand and watch—flee while you can! Remember the Lord and return to Jerusalem far away!

⁵¹*"We are ashamed because the Temple of the Lord has been defiled by foreigners from Babylon."*

⁵²Yes, says the Lord. But the time is coming for the destruction of the idols of Babylon. All through the land will be heard the groans of the wounded. ⁵³Though Babylon be as powerful as heaven, though she increase her strength immeasurably, she shall die, says the Lord.

⁵⁴Listen! Hear the cry of great destruction out of Babylon, the land the Chaldeans rule! ⁵⁵For the Lord is destroying Babylon; her mighty voice is stilled as the waves roar in upon her. ⁵⁶Destroying armies come and slay her mighty men; all her weapons break in her hands, for the Lord God gives just punishment and is giving Babylon all her due. ⁵⁷I will make drunk her princes, wise men, rulers, captains, warriors. They shall sleep and not wake up again! So says the King, the Lord Almighty. ⁵⁸For the wide walls of Babylon shall be leveled to the ground, and her high gates shall be burned; the builders from many lands have worked in vain—their work shall be destroyed by fire!

⁵⁹During the fourth year of Zedekiah's reign, this message came to Jeremiah to give to Seraiah (son of Neriah, son of Mahseiah), concerning Seraiah's capture and exile to Babylon along with Zedekiah, king of Judah. (Seraiah was quartermaster of Zedekiah's army.) ⁶⁰Jeremiah wrote on a scroll all the terrible things God had scheduled against Babylon—all the words written above— ⁶¹,⁶²and gave the scroll to Seraiah and said to him, "When you get to Babylon, read what I have written and say, 'Lord, you have said that you will destroy Babylon so that not a living creature will remain, and it will be abandoned forever.' ⁶³Then, when you have finished reading the scroll, tie a rock to it, and throw it into the Euphrates River, ⁶⁴and say, 'So shall Babylon sink, never more to rise, because of the evil I am bringing upon her.'"

(This ends Jeremiah's messages.)

52

(Events told about in chapter 39.) Zedekiah was twenty-one years old when he became king, and he reigned eleven years in Jerusalem. His mother's name was Hamutal (daughter of Jeremiah of Libnah). ²But he was a wicked king, just as Jehoiakim had been. ³Things became so bad at last that the Lord, in his anger, saw to it that Zedekiah rebelled against the king of Babylon until he and the people of Israel were ejected from the Lord's presence in Jerusalem and Judah, and were taken away as captives to Babylon.

⁴In the ninth year of Zedekiah's reign, on the tenth day of the tenth month, Nebuchadnezzar, king of Babylon, came with all his army against Jerusalem and built forts around it, ⁵and laid siege to the city for two years. ⁶Then finally, on the ninth day of the fourth month, when the famine in the city was very serious, with the last of the food entirely gone, ⁷the people in the city tore a hole in the city wall and all the soldiers fled from the city during the night, going out by the gate between the two walls near the king's gardens (for the city was surrounded by the Chaldeans), and made a dash for it across the fields, toward Arabah.

⁸But the Chaldean soldiers chased them and caught King Zedekiah in some fields near Jericho—for all his army was scattered from him. ⁹They brought him to the king of Babylon who was staying in the city of Riblah in the kingdom of Hamath, and there judgment was passed upon him. ¹⁰He made Zedekiah watch while his sons and all the princes of Judah were killed before his eyes. ¹¹Then his eyes were gouged out, and he was taken in chains to Babylon and put in prison for the rest of his life.

¹²On the tenth day of the fifth month during the nineteenth year of the reign of Nebuchadnezzar, king of Babylon, Nebuzaradan, captain of the guard, arrived in Jerusalem, ¹³and burned the Temple and the palace and all the larger homes, ¹⁴and set the Chaldean army to work tearing down the walls of the city. ¹⁵Then he took to Babylon, as captives, some of the poorest of the people—along with those who survived the city's destruction, and those who had deserted Zedekiah and had come over to the Babylonian army, and the tradesmen who were left. ¹⁶But he left

some of the poorest people to care for the crops as vinedressers and plowmen.

[17] The Babylonians dismantled the two large bronze pillars that stood at the entrance of the Temple, and the bronze laver and bronze bulls on which it stood, and carted them off to Babylon. [18] And he took along all the bronze pots and kettles, the ash shovels used at the altar, the snuffers, spoons, bowls, and all the other items used in the Temple. [19] He also took the firepans, the solid gold and silver candlesticks, and the cups and bowls.

[20] The weight of the two enormous pillars, the laver, and twelve bulls was tremendous. They had no way of estimating it. (They had been made in the days of King Solomon.) [21] For the pillars were each 27 feet high and 18 feet in circumference, hollow, with 3-inch walls. [22] The top 7 1/2 feet of each column had bronze carvings, a network of bronze pomegranates. [23] There were 96 pomegranates on the sides, and on the network round about there were a hundred more.

[24,25] The captain of the guard took along with him as his prisoners: Seraiah the chief priest, Zephaniah his assistant, the three chief Temple guards, one of the commanding officers of the army, seven of the king's special counselors discovered in the city, the secretary of the general-in-chief of the Jewish army (who was in charge of recruitment), and sixty other men of importance found hiding. [26] He took them to the king of Babylon at Riblah, [27] where the king killed them all.

So it was that Judah's exile was accomplished.

[28] The number of captives taken to Babylon in the seventh year of Nebuchadnezzar's reign was 3,023. [29] Then, eleven years later, he took 832 more; [30] five years after that he sent Nebuzaradan, his captain of the guard, and took 745—a total of 4,600 captives in all.

[31] On February 25 of the thirty-seventh year of the imprisonment in Babylon of Jehoiachin, king of Judah, Evil-merodach, who became king of Babylon that year, was kind to King Jehoiachin and brought him out of prison. [32] He spoke pleasantly to him and gave him preference over all the other kings in Babylon; [33] he gave him new clothes and fed him from the king's kitchen as long as he lived. [34] And he was given a regular allowance to cover his daily needs until the day of his death.

Lamentations

HOW DOES it feel to hear "I told you so" after you've messed up? How does it feel when, instead, someone comforts you after you've messed up? It's better to have comfort than to have someone rub it in, isn't it?

This is the message of Lamentations. The Israelites had broken their covenant with God and were taken as prisoners to Babylon. God had warned them through prophets over and over. The people knew it would happen.

Jeremiah was one of the last prophets to warn the people, and he was rejected and persecuted. But Jeremiah wasn't happy to see the Israelites punished. Instead of saying "I told you so," he cried and asked God to forgive the people. He was very sad to see the people suffer and the great nation of Israel end.

Jeremiah also knew God's character and wrote about how trustworthy he is. Even though awful things were happening to his people, Jeremiah said there was one ray of hope: God's compassion *never* ends!

As you read Lamentations, look for God's "second chance." He never says, "I told you so." He only reminds us that he is faithful and will love us forever.

Jeremiah's Great Sadness

Jerusalem's streets, once thronged with people, are silent now. Like a widow broken with grief, she sits alone in her mourning. She, once queen of nations, is now a slave.

²She sobs through the night; tears run down her cheeks. Among all her lovers, there is none to help her. All her friends are now her enemies.

³Why is Judah led away, a slave? Because of all the wrong she did to others, making them her slaves. Now she sits in exile far away. There is no rest, for those she persecuted have turned and conquered her.

⁴The roads to Zion mourn, no longer filled with joyous throngs who come to celebrate the Temple feasts; the city gates are silent, her priests groan, her virgins have been dragged away. Bitterly she weeps.

⁵Her enemies prosper, for the Lord has punished Jerusalem for all her many sins; her young children are captured and taken far away as slaves.

⁶All her beauty and her majesty are gone; her princes are like starving deer that search for pasture—helpless game too weak to keep on running from their foes.

⁷And now in the midst of all Jerusalem's sadness she remembers happy bygone days. She thinks of all the precious joys she had before her mocking enemy struck her down—and there was no one to give her aid.

⁸For Jerusalem sinned so horribly; therefore, she is tossed away like dirty rags. All who honored her despise her now, for they have seen her stripped naked and humiliated. She groans and hides her face.

⁹She indulged herself in immorality and refused to face the fact that punishment was sure to come. Now she lies in the gutter with no one left to lift her out. "O Lord," she cries, "see my plight. The enemy has triumphed."

¹⁰Her enemies have plundered her completely, taking everything precious she owns. She has seen foreign nations violate her sacred Temple—foreigners you had forbidden even to enter.

¹¹Her people groan and cry for bread; they have sold all they have for food to give a little strength. "Look, O Lord," she prays, "and see how I'm despised."

¹²Is it nothing to you, all you who pass by? Look and see if there is any sorrow like my sorrow because of all the Lord has done to me in the day of his fierce wrath.

¹³He has sent fire from heaven that burns within my bones; he has placed a pitfall in my path and turned me back. He has left me sick and desolate the whole day through.

¹⁴He wove my sins into ropes to hitch me to a yoke of slavery. He sapped my strength and gave me to my enemies; I am helpless in their hands.

¹⁵The Lord has trampled all my mighty men. A great army has come at his command to crush the noblest youth. The Lord has trampled his beloved city as grapes in a winepress.

¹⁶For all these things I weep; tears flow down my cheeks. My Comforter is far away—he who alone could help me. My children have no future; we are a conquered land.

¹⁷Jerusalem pleads for help, but no one comforts her. For the Lord has spoken: "Let her neighbors be her foes! Let her be thrown out like filthy rags!"

¹⁸And the Lord is right, for we rebelled. And yet, O people everywhere, behold and see my anguish and despair, for my sons and daughters are taken far away as slaves to distant lands.

¹⁹I begged my allies for their help. False hope—they could not help at all. Nor could my priests and elders—they were starving in the streets while searching through the garbage dumps for bread.

²⁰*See, O Lord, my anguish;* my heart is broken and my soul despairs, for I have terribly rebelled. In the streets the sword awaits me; at home, disease and death.

²¹*Hear my groans!* And there is no one anywhere to help. All my enemies have heard my troubles, and they are glad to see what you have done. And yet, O Lord, the time will surely come—for you have promised it—when you will do to them as you have done to me.

²²Look also on their sins, O Lord, and punish them as you have punished me, for my sighs are many and my heart is faint.

2 God Hates Sin

A cloud of anger from the Lord has overcast Jerusalem; the fairest city of Israel lies in the dust of the earth, cast from the heights of heaven at his command. In his day of awesome fury he has shown no mercy even to his Temple.

²The Lord without mercy has destroyed every home in Israel. In his wrath he has broken every fortress, every wall. He has brought the kingdom to dust, with all its rulers.

³All the strength of Israel vanishes beneath his wrath. He has withdrawn his protection as the enemy attacks. God burns across the land of Israel like a raging fire.

⁴He bends his bow against his people as though he were an enemy. His strength is used against them to kill their finest youth. His fury is poured out like fire upon them.

⁵Yes, the Lord has vanquished Israel like an enemy. He has destroyed her forts and palaces. Sorrows and tears are his portion for Jerusalem.

⁶He has violently broken down his Temple as though it were a booth of leaves and branches in a garden! No longer can the people celebrate their holy feasts and Sabbaths. Kings and priests together fall before his wrath.

⁷The Lord has rejected his own altar, for he despises the false "worship" of his people; he has given their palaces to their enemies, who carouse in the Temple

---

GOING TO CHURCH   2:7   Our place of worship is not so important to God as our pattern of worship. A church may be beautiful, but if its people don't sincerely follow God, it decays from within. The people of Judah, despite their beautiful Temple, had rejected in their daily lives what they proclaimed by their worship rituals. Thus their worship turned into a mocking lie. When you worship, are you saying words you don't really mean? Do you pray for help you don't really believe will come? Do you express love for God you don't really have? Earnestly seek God, and catch a fresh vision of his love and care. Then worship him wholeheartedly. **To begin the series of devotionals on GOING TO CHURCH, turn to page 193.**

as Israel used to do on days of holy feasts!

⁸The Lord determined to destroy Jerusalem. He laid out an unalterable line of destruction. Therefore the ramparts and walls fell down before him.

⁹Jerusalem's gates are useless. All their locks and bars are broken, for he has crushed them. Her kings and princes are enslaved in far-off lands, without a temple, without a divine law to govern them or prophetic vision to guide them.

¹⁰The elders of Jerusalem sit upon the ground in silence, clothed in sackcloth; they throw dust upon their heads in sorrow and despair. The virgins of Jerusalem hang their heads in shame.

¹¹I have cried until the tears no longer come; my heart is broken, my spirit poured out, as I see what has happened to my people; little children and tiny babies are fainting and dying in the streets.

¹²"Mama, Mama, we want food," they cry, and then collapse upon their mothers' shrunken breasts. Their lives ebb away like those wounded in battle.

¹³In all the world has there ever been such sorrow? O Jerusalem, what can I compare your anguish to? How can I comfort you? For your wound is deep as the sea. Who can heal you?

¹⁴Your "prophets" have said so many foolish things, false to the core. They have not tried to hold you back from slavery by pointing out your sins. They lied and said that all was well.

¹⁵All who pass by scoff and shake their heads and say, "Is this the city called 'Most Beautiful in All the World,' and 'Joy of All the Earth'?"

¹⁶All your enemies deride you. They hiss and grind their teeth and say, "We have destroyed her at last! Long have we waited for this hour, and it is finally here! With our own eyes we've seen her fall."

¹⁷But it is the Lord who did it, just as he had warned. He has fulfilled the promises of doom he made so long ago. He has destroyed Jerusalem without mercy and caused her enemies to rejoice over her and boast of their power.

¹⁸Then the people wept before the Lord. O walls of Jerusalem, let tears fall down upon you like a river; give yourselves no rest from weeping day or night.

¹⁹Rise in the night and cry to your God. Pour out your hearts like water to the Lord; lift up your hands to him; plead for your children as they faint with hunger in the streets.

²⁰*O Lord, think! These are your own people to whom you are doing this.* Shall mothers eat their little children, those they bounced upon their knees? Shall priests and prophets die within the Temple of the Lord?

²¹See them lying in the streets—old and young, boys and girls, killed by the enemies' swords. You have killed them, Lord, in your anger; you have killed them without mercy.

²²You have deliberately called for this destruction; in the day of your anger none escaped or remained. All my little children lie dead upon the streets before the enemy.

3 One Ray of Hope

I am the man who has seen the afflictions that come from the rod of God's wrath. ²He has brought me into deepest darkness, shutting out all light. ³He has turned against me. Day and night his hand is heavy on me. ⁴He has made me old and has broken my bones.

⁵He has built forts against me and surrounded me with anguish and distress. ⁶He buried me in dark places, like those long dead. ⁷He has walled me in; I cannot escape; he has fastened me with heavy chains. ⁸And though I cry and shout, he will not hear my prayers! ⁹He has shut me into a place of high, smooth walls; he has filled my path with detours.

¹⁰He lurks like a bear, like a lion, waiting to attack me. ¹¹He has dragged me into the underbrush and torn me with his claws, leaving me bleeding and desolate.

¹²He has bent his bow and aimed it squarely at me, ¹³and sent his arrows deep within my heart.

¹⁴My own people laugh at me; all day long they sing their ribald songs.

¹⁵He has filled me with bitterness and given me a cup of deepest sorrows to drink. ¹⁶He has made me eat gravel and broken my teeth; he has rolled me in ashes and dirt. ¹⁷O Lord, all peace and all prosperity have long since gone, for you have taken them away. I have forgotten what enjoyment is. ¹⁸All hope is gone; my strength has turned to water, for the Lord has left me. ¹⁹Oh, remember the bitterness and suffering you have dealt to me! ²⁰For I can never forget these awful years; always my soul will live in utter shame.

²¹*Yet there is one ray of hope:* ²²*his compassion never ends.* It is only the Lord's mercies that have kept us from complete destruction. ²³Great is his faithfulness; his loving-kindness begins afresh each day. ²⁴My soul claims the Lord as my inheritance; therefore I will hope in him. ²⁵The Lord is wonderfully good to those who wait for him, to those who seek for him. ²⁶It is good both to hope and wait quietly for the salvation of the Lord.

²⁷It is good for a young man to be under discipline, ²⁸for it causes him to sit apart in silence beneath the Lord's demands, ²⁹to lie face downward in the dust; then at last there is hope for him. ³⁰Let him turn the other cheek to those who strike him and accept their awful insults, ³¹for the Lord will not abandon him forever. ³²Although

God gives him grief, yet he will show compassion too, according to the greatness of his loving-kindness. ³³For he does not enjoy afflicting men and causing sorrow.

³⁴⁻³⁶But you have trampled and crushed beneath your feet the lowly of the world, and deprived men of their God-given rights, and refused them justice. No wonder the Lord has had to deal with you! ³⁷For who can act against you without the Lord's permission? ³⁸It is the Lord who helps one and harms another.

³⁹Why then should we, mere humans as we are, murmur and complain when punished for our sins? ⁴⁰Let us examine ourselves instead, and let us repent and turn again to the Lord. ⁴¹Let us lift our hearts and hands to him in heaven, ⁴²for we have sinned; we have rebelled against the Lord, and he has not forgotten it.

⁴³You have engulfed us by your anger, Lord, and slain us without mercy. ⁴⁴You have veiled yourself as with a cloud so that our prayers do not reach through. ⁴⁵You have made us as refuse and garbage among the nations. ⁴⁶All our enemies have spoken out against us. ⁴⁷We are filled with fear, for we are trapped and desolate, destroyed.

⁴⁸,⁴⁹My eyes flow day and night with never-ending streams of tears because of the destruction of my people. ⁵⁰Oh, that the Lord might look down from heaven and respond to my cry! ⁵¹My heart is breaking over what is happening to the young girls of Jerusalem.

⁵²My enemies, whom I have never harmed, chased me as though I were a bird. ⁵³They threw me in a well and capped it with a rock. ⁵⁴The water flowed above my head. I thought, This is the end! ⁵⁵But I called upon your name, O Lord, from deep within the well, ⁵⁶and you heard me! You listened to my pleading; you heard my weeping! ⁵⁷Yes, you came at my despairing cry and told me not to fear.

⁵⁸O Lord, you are my lawyer! Plead my case! For you have redeemed my life. ⁵⁹You have seen the wrong they did to me; be my Judge, to prove me right. ⁶⁰You have seen the plots my foes have laid against me. ⁶¹You have heard the vile names they have called me, ⁶²and all they say about me and their whispered plans. ⁶³See how they laugh and sing with glee, preparing my doom.

⁶⁴O Lord, repay them well for all the evil they have done. ⁶⁵Harden their hearts and curse them, Lord. ⁶⁶Go after them in fierce pursuit and wipe them off the earth, beneath the heavens of the Lord.

4 God Is No Longer Angry

How the finest gold has lost its luster! For the inlaid Temple walls are scattered in the streets! ²The cream of our youth—the finest of the gold—are treated as earthenware pots. ³,⁴Even the jackals feed their young, but not my people, Israel. They are like cruel desert ostriches, heedless of their babies' cries. The children's tongues stick to the roofs of their mouths for thirst, for there is not a drop of water left. Babies cry for bread, but no one can give them any. ⁵Those who used to eat fastidiously are begging in the streets for anything at all. Those brought up in palaces now scratch in garbage pits for food. ⁶For the sin of my people is greater than that of Sodom, where utter disaster struck in a moment without the hand of man.

⁷Our princes were lean and tanned, the finest specimens of men; ⁸but now their faces are as black as soot. No one can recognize them. Their skin sticks to their bones; it is dry and hard and withered. ⁹Those killed by the sword are far better off than those who die of slow starvation. ¹⁰Tenderhearted women have cooked and eaten their own children; thus they survived the siege.

¹¹But now at last the anger of the Lord is satisfied; his fiercest anger has been poured out. He started a fire in Jerusalem that burned it down to its foundations. ¹²Not a king in all the earth—no one in all the world—would have believed an enemy could enter through Jerusalem's gates! ¹³Yet God permitted it because of the sins of her prophets and priests, who defiled the city by shedding innocent blood. ¹⁴Now these same men are blindly staggering through the streets, covered with blood, defiling everything they touch.

¹⁵"Get away!" the people shout at them. "You are defiled!" They flee to distant lands and wander there among the foreigners; but none will let them stay. ¹⁶The Lord himself has dealt with them; he no longer helps them, for they persecuted the priests and elders who stayed true to God.

¹⁷We look for our allies to come and save us, but we look in vain. The nation we expected most to help us makes no move at all.

¹⁸We can't go into the streets without danger to our lives. Our end is near—our days are numbered. We are doomed. ¹⁹Our enemies are swifter than the eagles; if we flee to the mountains they find us. If we hide in the wilderness, they are waiting for us there. ²⁰Our king—the life of our life, the Lord's anointed—was captured in their snares. Yes, even our mighty king, about whom we had boasted that under his protection we could hold our own against any nation on earth!

²¹Do you rejoice, O people of Edom, in the land of Uz? But you, too, will feel the awful anger of the Lord. ²²Israel's exile for her sins will end at last, but Edom's never.

FAMILY DEVOTIONS

☐ DEVOTION 227
BECOMING MORE LIKE JESUS

Read Lamentations 3:40

Becoming More Like Jesus Memory Verse

Let everything you do reflect your love of the truth and the fact that you are in dead earnest about it.
Titus 2:7

"Hi there, Kenny. What are you doing?" The booming voice startled Kenny, and he glanced up to find his uncle looking over his shoulder. Quickly, Kenny hid the magazine he was reading behind his back.

"Uncle Walter! I didn't hear you coming."

Uncle Walter raised his eyebrows. "So I noticed. Would you like to go with me to the construction site of the new bank? I have some business with the contractor."

"Would I ever!" Kenny jumped up. Uncle Walter turned toward the car. Kenny started to follow him, then remembered the magazine in his hand. "Uncle Walter, wait a minute. I've . . . I've . . . ahhhh, I'm thirsty." Quickly, he slipped into the house. After hiding the magazine under the pillow on his bed, he stopped by the kitchen for a drink.

Later, at the construction site, Kenny and his uncle put on hard hats. Shielding his eyes, Kenny looked up, up, up the steel frame. "Wow!" he exclaimed. "Look, Uncle Walter. See those men working on the steel beams? That looks scary!"

"It is," Uncle Walter agreed. "You'll never see a steel worker doing gymnastics on his job."

"I guess not!" Kenny couldn't keep his eyes off the men above him. "They have to watch every step."

"Watching these steel workers reminds me of the Christian life. We have to watch our step very carefully, too. One little step off the narrow road we're walking could lead to disaster."

Kenny slowly lowered his gaze and saw that Uncle Walter was watching him closely. Kenny's face turned red. "I know what's coming. You saw the magazine I was reading. I can't hide anything from you."

"Or from God," Uncle Walter reminded him.

How About You?
As a Christian, you should walk very carefully. Careless Christians stumble and fall into sin. Remember, one wrong step can get you into lots of trouble. Watch your steps—your reading material, your habits, your language, your friends, every part of your life! Take some time today to examine yourself and, if you need to, repent and turn again to the Lord. *B. W.*

• For the next devotional, turn to page 777. • For the next devotional on BECOMING MORE LIKE JESUS, turn to page 803. • For notes on BECOMING MORE LIKE JESUS, see pages 234, 983, 1105, and 1164.

5 Jeremiah Prays

O Lord, remember all that has befallen us; see what sorrows we must bear! ²Our homes, our nation, now are filled with foreigners. ³We are orphans—our fathers dead, our mothers widowed. ⁴We must even pay for water to drink; our fuel is sold to us at the highest of prices. ⁵We bow our necks beneath the victors' feet; unending work is now our lot. ⁶We beg for bread from Egypt, and Assyria too.

⁷Our fathers sinned but died before the hand of judgment fell. We have borne the blow that they deserved!

⁸Our former servants have become our masters; there is no one left to save us. ⁹We went into the wilderness to hunt for food, risking death from enemies. ¹⁰Our skin was black from famine. ¹¹They rape the women of Jerusalem and the girls in Judah's cities. ¹²Our princes are hanged by their thumbs. Even aged men are treated with contempt. ¹³They take away the young men to grind their grain, and the little children stagger beneath their heavy loads.

¹⁴The old men sit no longer in the city gates; the young no longer dance and sing. ¹⁵The joy of our hearts has ended; our dance has turned to death. ¹⁶Our glory is gone. The crown is fallen from our head. Woe upon us for our sins. ¹⁷Our hearts are faint and weary; our eyes grow dim. ¹⁸Jerusalem and the Temple of the Lord are desolate, deserted by all but wild animals lurking in the ruins.

¹⁹O Lord, forever you remain the same! Your throne continues from generation to generation. ²⁰Why do you forget us forever? Why do you forsake us for so long? ²¹Turn us around and bring us back to you again! That is our only hope! Give us back the joys we used to have! ²²*Or have you utterly rejected us? Are you angry with us still?*

AFTER YOUR mom and dad punish you, do you like reassurance that they still love you?

God's chosen people were captives in a foreign country. He wanted his people to know that he was punishing them so they would turn back to him—not to get even with them or because he wanted them to suffer. God called Ezekiel to give them his messages while they were in Babylon.

One way God communicated with Ezekiel was through visions—things that seem to happen in a dream. God spoke to Ezekiel through visions about glowing creatures, edible scrolls, dry bones, and the Temple in Jerusalem. Ezekiel reminded the people why they were in Babylon. He also wanted to reassure the people of the future hope and salvation God had planned.

In the Bible, God has promised great things for us. When we're struggling with sin or don't like the consequences of our sin, we can remember that God has something better in mind. We just have to turn back to him to find it. Look for both judgment and hope as you read Ezekiel.

A Fiery Cloud

Ezekiel was a priest (the son of Buzi) who lived with the Jewish exiles beside the Chebar Canal in Babylon.

One day late in June, when I was thirty years old, the heavens were suddenly opened to me and I saw visions from God. ⁴I saw, in this vision, a great storm coming toward me from the north, driving before it a huge cloud glowing with fire, with a mass of fire inside that flashed continually; and in the fire there was something that shone like polished brass.

⁵Then from the center of the cloud, four strange forms appeared that looked like men, ⁶except that each had four faces and two pairs of wings! ⁷ Their legs were like those of men, but their feet were cloven like calves' feet, and shone like burnished brass. ⁸And beneath each of their wings I could see human hands.

⁹The four living beings were joined wing to wing, and they flew straight forward without turning. ¹⁰Each had the face of a man [in front], with a lion's face on the right side [of his head], and the

face of an ox on the left side, and the face of an eagle at the back! ¹¹Each had two pairs of wings spreading out from the middle of his back. One pair stretched out to attach to the wings of the living beings on each side, and the other pair covered his body. ¹²Wherever their spirit went they went, going straight forward without turning.

¹³Going up and down among them were other forms that glowed like bright coals of fire or brilliant torches, and it was from these the lightning flashed. ¹⁴The living beings darted to and fro, swift as lightning.

¹⁵As I stared at all of this, I saw four wheels on the ground beneath them, one wheel belonging to each. ¹⁶The wheels looked as if they were made of polished amber, and each wheel was constructed with a second wheel crosswise inside. ¹⁷They could go in any of the four directions without having to face around. ¹⁸The four wheels had rims and spokes, and the rims were filled with eyes around their edges.

¹⁹⁻²¹When the four living beings flew forward, the wheels moved forward with them. When they flew upwards, the wheels went up too. When the living beings stopped, the wheels stopped. For the spirit of the four living beings was in the wheels; so wherever their spirit went, the wheels and the living beings went there too.

²²The sky spreading out above them looked as though it were made of crystal; it was inexpressibly beautiful.

²³The wings of each stretched straight out to touch the others' wings, and each had two wings covering his body. ²⁴And as they flew, their wings roared like waves against the shore, or like the voice of God, or like the shouting of a mighty army. When they stopped, they let down their wings. ²⁵And every time they stopped, there came a voice from the crystal sky above them.

²⁶For high in the sky above them was what looked like a throne made of beautiful blue sapphire stones, and upon it sat someone who appeared to be a Man.

²⁷,²⁸From his waist up, he seemed to be all glowing bronze, dazzling like fire; and from his waist down he seemed to be entirely flame, and there was a glowing halo like a rainbow all around him. That was the way the glory of the Lord appeared to me. And when I saw it, I fell face downward on the ground and heard the voice of someone speaking to me:

2 God Calls Ezekiel

And he said to me: "Stand up, son of dust, and I will talk to you."

²And the Spirit entered into me as he spoke, and set me on my feet.

³"Son of dust," he said, "I am sending you to the nation of Israel, to a nation rebelling against me. They and their fathers have kept on sinning against me until this very hour. ⁴For they are a hardhearted, stiff-necked people. But I am sending you to give them my messages—the messages of the Lord God. ⁵And whether they listen or not (for remember, they are rebels), they will at least know they have had a prophet among them.

⁶"Son of dust, don't be afraid of them; don't be frightened even though their threats are sharp and barbed and sting like scorpions. Don't be dismayed by their dark scowls. For remember, they are rebels! ⁷You must give them my messages whether they listen or not (but they won't, for they are utter rebels). ⁸Listen, son of dust, to what I say to you. Don't you be a rebel too! Open your mouth and eat what I give you."

⁹,¹⁰Then I looked and saw a hand holding out to me a scroll, with writing on both sides. He unrolled it, and I saw that it was full of warnings and sorrows and pronouncements of doom.

3 God Makes Ezekiel His Watchman

And he said to me: "Son of dust, eat what I am giving you—eat this scroll! Then go and give its message to the people of Israel."

²So I took the scroll.

³"Eat it all," he said. And when I ate it, it tasted sweet as honey.

⁴Then he said: "Son of dust, I am sending you to the people of Israel with my messages. ⁵I am not sending you to some far-off foreign land where you can't understand the language— ⁶no, not to tribes with strange, difficult tongues. (If I did, they would listen!) ⁷I am sending you to the people of Israel, and they won't listen to you any more than they listen to me! For the whole lot of them are hard, impudent, and stubborn. ⁸But see, I have made you hard and stubborn too—as tough as they are. ⁹I have made your forehead as hard as rock. So don't be afraid of them, or fear their sullen, angry looks, even though they are such rebels."

¹⁰Then he added: "Son of dust, let all my words sink deep into your own heart first; listen to them carefully for yourself. ¹¹Then, afterward, go to your people in exile, and whether or not they will listen, tell them: 'This is what the Lord God says!'"

¹²Then the Spirit lifted me up,

SHARING YOUR FAITH 2:6-8 Ezekiel was given the difficult responsibility of presenting God's message to the ungrateful and abusive. Sometimes we are also called to be an example or share our faith with people who may be unkind to us. Just as the Lord told Ezekiel not to give up, he tells us not to give up and join the rebels, but rather to tell the Good News "when it is convenient and when it is not" (2 Timothy 4:2). **To begin the series of devotionals on SHARING YOUR FAITH, turn to page 427.**

Family Devotions

☐ **Devotion 228**
Sharing Your Faith

Read Ezekiel 3:4-11

Some boys at school were making fun of Eric for refusing to join them in such activities as telling dirty jokes. "Baby!" they said. "Sissy!" Eric said nothing, but that night he promised himself that if the boys teased him again, he'd be brave and witness to them. It happened the very next day. "Sissy! Baby!" the boys chanted over and over when they saw Eric. Eric's knees shook. He opened his mouth, but no words came. The boys walked away, laughing.

That night Eric told his father what had happened. "Eric," Dad said thoughtfully, "you may not recall this, but one day when you were quite small, you insisted on walking by yourself on an icy sidewalk instead of letting me help you. You fell down *twice* before you finally let me hold your hand! You found you couldn't walk by yourself or even hold on to me in the icy spots. You needed my strong hand to hold you up." Dad smiled as he remembered. "I think you're trying to go it alone again—this time in your spiritual walk," he added. "You need God's help, Son. He'll hold your hand, if you'll let him."

When Eric saw the boys the next day, he prayed, *Lord, please help me to be a brave witness.* When the boys approached him and asked if he'd grown up enough to join their gang, Eric took a deep breath. "I don't want to join it," he said. "And I'd like to tell you why. I'm a Christian, and God wouldn't be pleased if I join in some of the things you do." He took another deep breath and hurried on. "Why don't you join me instead?" he asked. "I'm going to Bible club tonight—you'd like it."

The boys sneered. But as they walked away, Eric heard one boy declare, "He's odd—but he's no sissy!"

Sharing Your Faith
Memory Verse

And let us not get tired of doing what is right, for after a while we will reap a harvest of blessing if we don't get discouraged and give up.
Galatians 6:9

How About You?
Are you weak-kneed and tongue-tied when others want you to take part in wrong activities? God can make you strong enough to stand up to them! Trust him to hold your hand, then stand up and be counted for Jesus. *M. R. P.*

• For the next devotional, turn to page 779.   • For the next devotional on *Sharing Your Faith*, turn to page 779.
• For notes on *Sharing Your Faith*, see pages 462, 776, 1015, and 1074.

and the glory of the Lord began to move away, accompanied by the sound of a great earthquake. ¹³It was the noise of the wings of the living beings as they touched against each other, and the sound of their wheels beside them.

¹⁴,¹⁵The Spirit lifted me up, and took me away to Tel Abib, another colony of Jewish exiles beside the Chebar River. I went in bitterness and anger, but the hand of the Lord was strong upon me. And I sat among them, overwhelmed, for seven days.

¹⁶At the end of the seven days, the Lord said to me:

¹⁷"Son of dust, I have appointed you as a watchman for Israel; whenever I send my people a warning, pass it on to them at once. ¹⁸If you refuse to warn the wicked when I want you to tell them, 'You are under the penalty of death; therefore repent and save your life,' they will die in their sins, but I will punish you. I will demand your blood for theirs. ¹⁹But if you warn them, and they keep on sinning and refuse to repent, they will die in their sins, but you are blameless—you have done all you could. ²⁰And if a good man becomes bad, and you refuse to warn him of the consequences, and the Lord destroys him, his previous good deeds won't help him—he shall die in his sin. But I will hold you responsible for his death and punish you. ²¹But if you warn him and he repents, he shall live, and you have saved your own life too."

²²I was helpless in the hand of God, and when he said to me, "Go out into the valley and I will talk to you there"— ²³I arose and went, and oh, I saw the glory of the Lord there, just as in my first vision! And I fell to the ground on my face.

²⁴Then the Spirit entered into me and set me on my feet. He talked to me and said: "Go, imprison yourself in your house, ²⁵and I will paralyze you so you can't leave; ²⁶and I will make your tongue stick to the roof of your mouth so that you can't reprove them; for they are rebels. ²⁷But whenever I give you a message, then I will loosen your tongue and let you speak, and you shall say to them: 'The Lord God says.' Let anyone listen who wants to, and let anyone refuse who wants to, for they are rebels.

4 Ezekiel Draws a Picture

"And now, son of dust, take a large brick and lay it before you and draw a map of the city of Jerusalem on it. Draw a picture of siege mounds being built against the city, put enemy camps around it and battering rams surrounding the walls. ³And put an iron plate between you and the city, like a wall of iron. Demonstrate how an enemy army will capture Jerusalem!

"There is special meaning in each detail of what I have told you to do. For it is a warning to the people of Israel.

⁴,⁵"Now lie on your left side for 390 days, to show that Israel will be punished for 390 years by captivity and doom. Each day you lie there represents a year of punishment ahead for Israel. ⁶Afterwards, turn over and lie on your right side for forty days, to signify the years of Judah's punishment. Each day will represent one year.

⁷"Meanwhile continue your demonstration of the siege of Jerusalem; lie there with your arm bared [to signify great strength and power in the attack against her]. This will prophesy her doom. ⁸And I will paralyze you so that you can't turn over from one side to the other until you have completed all the days of your siege.

⁹"During the first 390 days eat bread made of flour mixed from wheat, barley, beans, lentils, and spelt. Mix the various kinds of flour together in a jar. ¹⁰You are to ration this out to yourself at the rate of eight ounces at a time, one meal a day. ¹¹And use one quart of water a day; don't use more than that. ¹²Each day take flour from the barrel and prepare it as you would barley cakes. While all the people are watching, bake it over a fire, using dried human dung as fuel, and eat it. ¹³For the Lord declares, Israel shall eat defiled bread in the Gentile lands to which I exile them!"

¹⁴Then I said, "O Lord God, must I be defiled by using dung? For I have never been defiled before in all my life. From the time I was a child until now I have never eaten any animal that died of sickness or that I found injured or dead; and I have never eaten any of the kinds of animals our law forbids."

¹⁵Then the Lord said, "All right, you may use cow dung instead of human dung."

¹⁶Then he told me, "Son of dust, bread will be tightly rationed in Jerusalem. It will be weighed out with great care and eaten fearfully. And the water will be portioned out in driblets, and the people will drink it with dismay. ¹⁷I will cause the people to lack both bread and water; they will look at one another in frantic terror and waste away beneath their punishment.

5 A Crazy Haircut

"Son of dust, take a sharp sword and use it as a barber's razor to shave your head and beard; use balances to weigh the hair into three equal parts. ²Place a third of it at the center of your map of Jerusalem. After your siege, burn it there. Scatter another third across your map and slash at it with a knife. Scatter the last third to the wind, for I will chase my people with the sword. ³Keep just a bit of the hair and tie it up in your robe; ⁴then

Family Devotions

☐ DEVOTION 229
SHARING YOUR FAITH

Read Ezekiel 3:16-17

"Be quiet, Daisy," murmured Ellen sleepily as she burrowed deeper into her bed. The barking continued, but Ellen scarcely heard it. Suddenly, *thump!* A hairy body landed on the bed beside her, still barking furiously. Annoyed, Ellen pushed the dog away. "Be still," she commanded again. Daisy ran down the hall toward Ellen's parents' room. Then *thump!* She was back again, pouncing on Ellen, dashing away, then pouncing again and again, all the while barking loudly. Ellen sat up, very much annoyed. "You stupid dog," she grumbled. "Let me sleep! You lie down and be still!" But the dog ran out the door, barking and looking back to see if Ellen was following.

Ellen sniffed the air. What was that smell? Smoke! It was smoke! She leaped from her bed and ran into the hall where her parents were just coming from their room. Soon they were all out in the yard, waiting for the fire trucks to arrive.

The next morning, Ellen read about the fire in the newspaper. "Dog Saves Home—Wakes Family before Much Damage Is Done," she read. She hugged Daisy. "Sorry I got mad at you," she apologized. "I'm glad you kept on pestering me even when I scolded you."

Mom looked at Ellen. "Sometimes it's good to be awakened, isn't it?" she said thoughtfully. "That will be a good thing to keep in mind when you see your friend Alicia again."

"Alicia?" asked Ellen. "What do you mean?"

"You were just telling me that you thought maybe you shouldn't invite Alicia to Sunday school or try to witness to her anymore because it seems to annoy her. In a way she's saying, 'Let me sleep.' But she needs to be awakened to her need to accept Jesus into her life," explained Mom. "Daisy loved you enough to keep after you even when you didn't like it. Maybe you need to love Alicia that way, too."

Slowly, Ellen nodded. "It's important enough to take a chance on annoying her a little, isn't it?"

Sharing Your Faith Memory Verse

And I assure you of this: I, the Messiah, will publicly honor you in the presence of God's angels if you publicly acknowledge me here on earth as your Friend.
Luke 12:8

How About You?
Are you afraid to witness to your friends because they might be annoyed or angry? Even if they are, how serious will that be? Not nearly as serious as if they never awaken to their need for Jesus. God wants you to warn them. Don't give up witnessing to them. H. M.

- For the next devotional, turn to page 783.   • For the next devotional on *SHARING YOUR FAITH*, turn to pagE 897.
- For notes on *SHARING YOUR FAITH*, see pages 462, 776, 1015, and 1074.

take a few hairs out and throw them into the fire, for a fire shall come from this remnant and destroy all Israel."

[5-7]The Lord God says, "This illustrates what will happen to Jerusalem, for she has turned away from my laws and has been even more wicked than the nations surrounding her." [8]Therefore the Lord God says, I, even I, am against you and will punish you publicly while all the nations watch. [9]Because of the terrible sins you have committed, I will punish you more terribly than I have ever done before or ever will again. [10]Fathers will eat their own sons, and sons will eat their fathers; and those who survive will be scattered into all the world.

[11]"For I promise you: Because you have defiled my Temple with idols and evil sacrifices, therefore I will not spare you nor pity you at all. [12]One-third of you will die from famine and disease; one-third will be slaughtered by the enemy; and one-third I will scatter to the winds, sending the sword of the enemy chasing after you. [13]Then at last my anger will be appeased. And all Israel will know that what I threaten I do.

[14]"So I will make a public example of you before all the surrounding nations and before everyone traveling past the ruins of your land. [15]You will become a laughingstock to the world and an awesome example to everyone, for all to see what happens when the Lord turns against an entire nation in furious rebuke. I, the Lord, have spoken it!

[16]"I will shower you with deadly arrows of famine to destroy you. The famine will become more and more serious until every bit of bread is gone. [17]And not only famine will come, but wild animals will attack and kill you and your families; disease and war will stalk your land, and the sword of the enemy will slay you; I, the Lord, have spoken it!"

6 Ezekiel Talks to the Mountains

Again a message came from the Lord:

[2]"Son of dust, look over toward the mountains of Israel and prophesy against them. [3]Say to them, 'O mountains of Israel, hear the message of the Lord God against you and against the rivers and valleys. I, even I the Lord, will bring war upon you to destroy your idols. [4-7]All your cities will be smashed and burned, and the idol altars abandoned. Your gods will be shattered; the bones of their worshipers will lie scattered among the altars. Then at last you will know I am the Lord.

[8]"But I will let a few of my people escape—to be scattered among the nations of the world. [9]Then when they are exiled among the nations, they will remember me, for I will take away their adulterous hearts—their love of idols—and I will blind their lecherous eyes that long for other gods. Then at last they will loathe themselves for all this wickedness. [10]They will realize that I alone am God and that I wasn't fooling when I told them that all this would happen to them.'"

[11]The Lord God says: "Raise your hands in horror and shake your head with deep remorse and say, 'Alas for all the evil we have done!' For you are going to perish from war and famine and disease. [12]Disease will strike down those in exile; war will destroy those in the land of Israel; and any who remain will die by famine and siege. So at last I will expend my fury on you. [13]When your slain lie scattered among your idols and altars on every hill and mountain and under every green tree and great oak where they offered incense to their gods—you will realize that I alone am God. [14]I will crush you and make your cities desolate from the wilderness in the south to Riblah in the north. Then you will know I am the Lord.'"

7 Jerusalem Will Be Punished

This further message came to me from God:

[2]"Tell Israel, 'Wherever you look—east, west, north or south—your land is finished. [3]No hope remains, for I will loose my anger on you for your worshiping of idols. [4]I will turn my eyes away and show no pity; I will repay you in full, and you shall know I am the Lord.'"

[5,6]The Lord God says: "With one blow after another I will finish you. The end has come; your final doom is waiting. [7]O Israel, the day of your damnation dawns; the time has come; the day of trouble nears. It is a day of shouts of anguish, not shouts of joy! [8,9]Soon I will pour out my fury and let it finish its work of punishing you for all your evil deeds. I will not spare nor pity you, and you will know that I, the Lord, am doing it. [10,11]The day of judgment has come; the morning dawns, for your wickedness and pride have run their course and reached their climax—none of these rich and wicked men of pride shall live. All your boasting will die away, and no one will be left to bewail your fate.

[12]"Yes, the time has come; the day draws near. There will be nothing to buy or sell, for the wrath of God is on the land. [13]And even if a merchant lives, his business will be gone, for God has spoken against all the people of Israel; all will be destroyed. Not one of those whose lives are filled with sin will recover.

[14]"The trumpets shout to Israel's army, 'Mobilize!' but no one listens, for my wrath is on them all. [15]If you go outside the walls, there stands the enemy to kill you. If you stay inside, famine and disease will devour you. [16]Any who escape will be lonely as mourning doves hiding on the mountains, each

weeping for his sins. ¹⁷All hands shall be feeble, and all knees as weak as water. ¹⁸You shall clothe yourselves with sackcloth, and horror and shame shall cover you; you shall shave your heads in sorrow and remorse.

¹⁹"Throw away your money! Toss it out like worthless rubbish, for it will have no value in that day of wrath. It will neither satisfy nor feed you, for your love of money is the reason for your sin. ²⁰I gave you gold to use in decorating the Temple, and you used it instead to make idols! Therefore, I will take it all away from you. ²¹I will give it to foreigners and to wicked men as booty. They shall defile my Temple. ²²I will not look when they defile it, nor will I stop them. Like robbers, they will loot the treasures and leave the Temple in ruins.

²³"Prepare chains for my people, for the land is full of bloody crimes. Jerusalem is filled with violence, so I will enslave her people. ²⁴I will crush your pride by bringing to Jerusalem the worst of the nations to occupy your homes, break down your fortifications you are so proud of, and defile your Temple. ²⁵For the time has come for the cutting off of Israel. You will sue for peace, but you won't get it. ²⁶,²⁷Calamity upon calamity will befall you; woe upon woe, disaster upon disaster! You will long for a prophet to guide you, but the priests and elders and the kings and princes will stand helpless, weeping in despair. The people will tremble with fear, for I will do to them the evil they have done and give them all their just deserts. They shall learn that I am the Lord."

8 The Sins of the People

Then, late in August of the sixth year of King Jehoiachin's captivity, as I was talking with the elders of Judah in my home, the power of the Lord God fell upon me. ²I saw what appeared to be a Man; from his waist down, he was made of fire; from his waist up, he was all amber-colored brightness. ³He put out what seemed to be a hand and took me by the hair. And the Spirit lifted me up into the sky and seemed to transport me to Jerusalem, to the entrance of the north gate, where the large idol was that had made the Lord so angry. ⁴Suddenly the glory of the God of Israel was there, just as I had seen it before in the valley.

⁵He said to me, "Son of dust, look toward the north." So I looked and, sure enough, north of the altar gate in the entrance stood the idol.

⁶And he said: "Son of dust, do you see what they are doing? Do you see what great sins the people of Israel are doing here, to push me from my Temple? But come, and I will show you greater sins than these!"

⁷Then he brought me to the door of the Temple court, where I could see an opening in the wall.

⁸"Now dig into the wall," he said. I did and uncovered a door to a hidden room.

⁹"Go in," he said, "and see the wickedness going on in there!"

¹⁰So I went in. The walls were covered with pictures of all kinds of snakes, lizards, and hideous creatures, besides all the various idols worshiped by the people of Israel. ¹¹Seventy elders of Israel were standing there along with Ja-azaniah (son of Shaphan) worshiping the pictures. Each of them held a censer of burning incense, so there was a thick cloud of smoke above their heads.

¹²Then the Lord said to me: "Son of dust, have you seen what the elders of Israel are doing in their minds? For they say, 'The Lord doesn't see us; he has gone away!'" ¹³Then he added, "Come, and I will show you greater sins than these!"

¹⁴He brought me to the north gate of the Temple, and there sat women weeping for Tammuz, their god.

¹⁵"Have you seen this?" he asked. "But I will show you greater evils than these!"

¹⁶Then he brought me into the inner court of the Temple, and there at the door, between the porch and the bronze altar, were about twenty-five men standing with their backs to the Temple of the Lord, facing east, worshiping the sun!

¹⁷"Have you seen this?" he asked. "Is it nothing to the people of Judah that they commit these terrible sins, leading the whole nation into idolatry, thumbing their noses at me and arousing my fury against them? ¹⁸Therefore, I will deal with them in fury. I will neither pity nor spare. And though they scream for mercy, I will not listen."

9 Some Wicked People Die

Then he thundered, "Call those to whom I have given the city! Tell them to bring their weapons with them!"

²Six men appeared at his call, coming from the upper north gate, each one with his sword. One of them wore linen clothing and carried a writer's case strapped to his side. They all went into the Temple and stood beside the bronze altar. ³And the glory of the God of Israel rose from between the Guardian Angels where it had rested and stood above the entrance to the Temple.

And the Lord called to the man with the writer's case ⁴and said to him, "Walk through the streets of Jerusalem and put a mark on the foreheads of the men who weep and sigh because of all the sins they see around them."

⁵Then I heard the Lord tell the other men: "Follow him through the city and kill everyone whose forehead isn't marked. Spare not nor pity

them—⁶kill them all—old and young, girls, women and little children; but don't touch anyone with the mark. And begin right here at the Temple." And so they began by killing the seventy elders.

⁷And he said, "Defile the Temple! Fill its courts with the bodies of those you kill! Go!" And they went out through the city and did as they were told.

⁸While they were fulfilling their orders, I was alone. I fell to the ground on my face and cried out: "O Lord God! Will your fury against Jerusalem wipe out everyone left in Israel?"

⁹But he said to me, "The sins of the people of Israel and Judah are very great and all the land is full of murder and injustice, for they say, 'The Lord doesn't see it! He has gone away!' ¹⁰And so I will not spare them nor have any pity on them, and I will fully repay them for all that they have done."

¹¹Just then the man in linen clothing, carrying the writer's case, reported back and said, "I have finished the work you gave me to do."

10 Burning Coals

Suddenly a throne of beautiful blue sapphire appeared in the sky above the heads of the Guardian Angels.

²Then the Lord spoke to the man in linen clothing and said: "Go in between the whirling wheels beneath the Guardian Angels, and take a handful of glowing coals and scatter them over the city."

He did so while I watched. ³The Guardian Angels were standing at the south end of the Temple when the man went in. And the cloud of glory filled the inner court. ⁴Then the glory of the Lord rose from above the Guardian Angels and went over to the door of the Temple. The Temple was filled with the cloud of glory, and the court of the Temple was filled with the brightness of the glory of the Lord. ⁵And the sound of the wings of the Guardian Angels was as the voice of Almighty God when he speaks and could be heard clear out in the outer court.

⁶When the Lord told the man in linen clothing to go between the Guardian Angels and take some burning coals from between the wheels, the man went in and stood beside one of the wheels, ⁷,⁸and one of the Guardian Angels reached out his hand (for each of the mighty angels had, beneath his wings, what looked like human hands) and took some live coals from the flames between the Angels and put them into the hands of the man in linen clothes, who took them and went out.

⁹⁻¹³Each of the four Guardian Angels had a wheel beside him—"The Whirl-Wheels," as I heard them called, for each one had a second wheel crosswise within—sparkling like chrysolite, giving off a greenish-yellow glow. Because of the construction of these wheels, the Angels could go straight forward in each of four directions; they did not turn when they changed direction but could go in any of the four ways their faces looked. Each of the four wheels was covered with eyes, including the rims and spokes. ¹⁴Each of the four Guardian Angels had four faces—the first was that of an ox; the second, a man's; the third, a lion's; and the fourth, an eagle's.

¹⁵,¹⁶These were the same beings I had seen beside the Chebar Canal, and when they rose into the air, the wheels rose with them and stayed beside them as they flew. ¹⁷When the Guardian Angels stood still, so did the wheels, for the spirit of the Guardian Angels was in the wheels.

¹⁸Then the glory of the Lord moved from the door of the Temple and stood above the Guardian Angels. ¹⁹And as I watched, the Guardian Angels flew with their wheels beside them to the east gate of the Temple. And the glory of the God of Israel was above them.

²⁰These were the living beings I had seen beneath the God of Israel beside the Chebar Canal. I knew they were the same, ²¹for each had four faces and four wings, with what looked like human hands under their wings. ²²Their faces too were identical to the faces of those I had seen at the Canal, and they traveled straight ahead, just as the others did.

11 God Will Bring His People Back

Then the Spirit lifted me and brought me over to the east gate of the Temple, where I saw twenty-five of the most prominent men of the city, including two officers, Jaazaniah (son of Azzur) and Pelatiah (son of Benaiah).

Then the Spirit said to me, "Son of dust, these are the men who are responsible for all of the wicked counsel being given out in this city. ³For they say to the people, 'It is time to rebuild Jerusalem, for our city is an iron shield and will protect us from all harm.' ⁴Therefore, son of dust, prophesy against them loudly and clearly."

⁵Then the Spirit of the Lord came upon me and told me to say: "The Lord says to the people of Israel: Is that what you are saying? Yes, I know it is, for I know everything you think—every thought that comes into your minds. ⁶You have murdered endlessly and filled your streets with the dead."

⁷Therefore the Lord God says: "You think this city is an iron shield? No, it isn't! It will not protect you. Your slain will lie within it, but you will be dragged out and slaughtered. ⁸I will expose you to the war you have so greatly feared, says the Lord God, ⁹and I will take you from Jerusalem and

Family Devotions

☐ **Devotion 230**
Standing for Righteousness

Read Ezekiel 11:5

Standing for Righteousness Memory Verse

For the eyes of the Lord search back and forth across the whole earth, looking for people whose hearts are perfect toward him, so that he can show his great power in helping them.
2 Chronicles 16:9

"Mom, may we buy this cereal today?" Stephanie asked. She held a brightly colored box over the grocery cart as though she were going to put it in. She giggled at Mother's raised eyebrow. "Just kidding, Mom," she said. "I know this one has too much sugar." She replaced it with a different kind. "Is this better?" she asked. Then, with a twinkle in her eye, she parroted Mom's often repeated words, "You are what you eat." Mom smiled and nodded.

When they arrived home, Stephanie flipped on the radio. Stephanie started humming along with the song that came on, but Mom reached out and changed the station. "The words of that song encourage a kind of life that isn't pleasing to God," she said with a frown.

"But it has a nice tune," protested Stephanie. "Can't we just ignore the words?"

"Listening to that kind of music is like eating food that isn't good for us. Our minds 'eat up' the words whether we pay attention to them or not," Mom explained.

Stephanie thought hard while she helped Mom put the groceries away. She thought about how she often listened to the radio at Nancy's house. She and Nancy were always busy with something else while they listened, but Stephanie knew all the words to the songs they played on Nancy's favorite station, even though she seldom paid attention to them. Something about the music made the words stick in her mind.

"We are what we think about," added Mom. "We should fill our minds with thoughts that are pleasing to God so we'll grow spiritually."

Stephanie found the box of cereal she had chosen and put it in the cupboard. "From now on I'll choose music like I choose breakfast cereals," she decided. She chuckled at the idea. "No more junk food for my mind!"

How About You?

Do you listen to music or anything else that encourages an ungodly way of life? God is pleased when you listen to things that are uplifting and that help you grow spiritually. What you hear gets into your mind whether you are aware of it or not. K. R. A.

hand you over to foreigners who will carry out my judgments against you. ¹⁰You will be slaughtered all the way to the borders of Israel, and you will know I am the Lord. ¹¹No, this city will not be an iron shield for you, and you safe within. I will chase you even to the borders of Israel, ¹²and you will know I am the Lord—you who have not obeyed me but rather have copied the nations all around you."

¹³While I was still speaking and telling them this, Pelatiah (son of Benaiah) suddenly died. Then I fell to the ground on my face and cried out: "O Lord God, are you going to kill everyone in all Israel?"

¹⁴Again a message came from the Lord:

¹⁵"Son of dust, the remnant left in Jerusalem are saying about your brother exiles: 'It is because they were so wicked that the Lord has deported them. Now the Lord has given us their land!'

¹⁶"But tell the exiles that the Lord God says: Although I have scattered you in the countries of the world, yet I will be a sanctuary to you for the time that you are there, ¹⁷and I will gather you back from the nations where you are scattered and give you the land of Israel again. ¹⁸And when you return, you will remove every trace of all this idol worship. ¹⁹I will give you one heart and a new spirit; I will take from you your hearts of stone and give you tender hearts of love for God, ²⁰so that you can obey my laws and be my people, and I will be your God. ²¹But as for those now in Jerusalem who long for idols, I will repay them fully for their sins," the Lord God says.

²²Then the Guardian Angels lifted their wings and rose into the air with their wheels beside them, and the glory of the God of Israel stood above them. ²³Then the glory of the Lord rose from over the city and stood above the mountain on the east side.

²⁴Afterwards the Spirit of God carried me back again to Babylon, to the Jews in exile there. And so ended the vision of my visit to Jerusalem. ²⁵And I told the exiles everything the Lord had shown me.

12 Ezekiel Digs a Tunnel

Again a message came to me from the Lord:

²"Son of dust," he said, "you live among rebels who could know the truth if they wanted to, but they don't want to; they could hear me if they would listen, but they won't, ³for they are rebels. So now put on a demonstration to show them what being exiled will be like. Pack whatever you can carry on your back and leave your home—go somewhere else. Go in the daylight so they can see, for perhaps even yet they will consider what this means, even though they are such rebels. ⁴Bring your baggage outside your house during the daylight so they can watch. Then leave the house at night, just as captives do when they begin their long march to distant lands. ⁵Dig a tunnel through the city wall while they are observing and carry your possessions out through the hole. ⁶As they watch, lift your pack to your shoulders and walk away into the night; muffle your face and don't gaze around. All this is a sign to the people of Israel of the evil that will come upon Jerusalem."

⁷So I did as I was told. I brought my pack outside in the daylight—all I could take into exile—and in the evening I dug through the wall with my hands. I went out into the darkness with my pack on my shoulder while the people looked on. ⁸The next morning this message came to me from the Lord:

⁹"Son of dust, these rebels, the people of Israel, have asked what all this means. ¹⁰Tell them the Lord God says it is a message to King Zedekiah in Jerusalem and to all the people of Israel. ¹¹Explain that what you did was a demonstration of what is going to happen to them, for they shall be driven out of their homes and sent away into exile.

¹²"Even King Zedekiah shall go out at night through a hole in the wall, taking only what he can carry with him, with muffled face, for he won't be able to see. ¹³I will capture him in my net and bring him to Babylon, the land of the Chaldeans; but he shall not see it, and he shall die there. ¹⁴I will scatter his servants and guards to the four winds and send the sword after them. ¹⁵And when I scatter them among the nations, then they shall know I am the Lord. ¹⁶But I will spare a few of them from death by war and famine and disease. I will save them to confess to the nations how wicked they have been, and they shall know I am the Lord."

¹⁷Then this message came to me from the Lord:

¹⁸"Son of dust, tremble as you eat your meals; ration out your water as though it were your last, ¹⁹and say to the people, the Lord God says that the people of Israel and Jerusalem shall ration their food with utmost care and sip their tiny portions of water in utter despair because of all their sins. ²⁰Your cities shall be destroyed and your farmlands deserted, and you shall know I am the Lord."

²¹Again a message came to me from the Lord:

²²"Son of dust, what is that proverb they quote in Israel—'The days as they pass make liars out of every prophet.' ²³The Lord God says, I will put an end to this proverb and they will soon stop saying it. Give them this one instead: 'The time has come for all these prophecies to be fulfilled.'

²⁴"Then you will see what becomes of all the

false predictions of safety and security for Jerusalem. ²⁵For I am the Lord! What I threaten always happens. There will be no more delays, O rebels of Israel! I will do it in your own lifetime!" says the Lord God.

²⁶Then this message came:

²⁷"Son of dust, the people of Israel say, 'His visions won't come true for a long, long time.' ²⁸Therefore say to them: 'The Lord God says, All delay has ended! I will do it now!'"

13 False Teachers Get in Trouble

Then this message came to me:

²,³"Son of dust, prophesy against the false prophets of Israel who are inventing their own visions and claiming to have messages from me when I have never told them anything at all. Woe upon them!

⁴"O Israel, these 'prophets' of yours are as useless as foxes for rebuilding your walls! ⁵O evil prophets, what have you ever done to strengthen the walls of Israel against her enemies—by strengthening Israel in the Lord? ⁶Instead you have lied when you said, 'My message is from God!' God did not send you. And yet you expect him to fulfill your prophecies. ⁷Can you deny that you have claimed to see 'visions' you never saw, and that you have said, 'This message is from God,' when I never spoke to you at all?"

⁸Therefore the Lord God says: "I will destroy you for these 'visions' and lies. ⁹My hand shall be against you, and you shall be cut off from among the leaders of Israel; I will blot out your names, and you will never see your own country again. And you shall know I am the Lord. ¹⁰For these evil men deceive my people by saying, 'God will send peace,' when that is not my plan at all! My people build a flimsy wall, and these prophets praise them for it—and cover it with whitewash!

¹¹"Tell these evil builders that their wall will fall. A heavy rainstorm will undermine it; great hailstones and mighty winds will knock it down. ¹²And when the wall falls, the people will cry out, 'Why didn't you tell us that it wasn't good enough? Why did you whitewash it and cover up its faults?' ¹³ Yes, it will surely fall." The Lord God says: "I will sweep it away with a storm of indignation, with a great flood of anger, and with hailstones of wrath. ¹⁴I will break down your whitewashed wall; it will fall on you and crush you, and you shall know I am the Lord. ¹⁵Then at last my wrath against the wall will be completed; and concerning those who praised it, I will say: The wall and its builders both are gone. ¹⁶For they were lying prophets, claiming Jerusalem will have peace when there is no peace," says the Lord God.

¹⁷"Son of dust, speak out against the women prophets too who pretend the Lord has given them his messages. ¹⁸Tell them, "The Lord God says: Woe to these women who are damning the souls of my people, of both young and old alike, by tying magic charms on their wrists, furnishing them with magic veils, and selling them indulgences. They refuse to even offer help unless they get a profit from it. ¹⁹For the sake of a few paltry handfuls of barley or a piece of bread will you turn away my people from me? You have led those to death who should not die! And you have promised life to those who should not live by lying to my people—and how they love it!'"

²⁰And so the Lord says: "I will crush you because you hunt my people's souls with all your magic charms. I will tear off the charms and set my people free like birds from cages. ²¹I will tear off the magic veils and save my people from you; they will no longer be your victims, and you shall know I am the Lord. ²²Your lies have discouraged the righteous when I didn't want it so. And you have encouraged the wicked by promising life, though they continue in their sins. ²³But you will lie no more; no longer will you talk of seeing 'visions' that you never saw nor practice your magic, for I will deliver my people out of your hands by destroying you, and you shall know I am the Lord."

14 God Hates Idols

Then some of the elders of Israel visited me to ask me for a message from the Lord, ²and this is the message that came to me to give to them:

³"Son of dust, these men worship idols in their hearts—should I let them ask me anything? ⁴Tell them, 'The Lord God says: I the Lord will personally deal with anyone in Israel who worships idols and then comes to ask my help. ⁵For I will punish the minds and hearts of those who turn from me to idols.'

⁶,⁷"Therefore, warn them that the Lord God says: 'Repent and destroy your idols, and stop worshiping them in your hearts. I the Lord will personally punish everyone, whether people of Israel or the foreigners living among you, who rejects me for idols and then comes to a prophet to ask for my help and advice. ⁸I will turn upon him and make a terrible example of him, destroying him; and you shall know I am the Lord. ⁹And if one of the false prophets gives him a message anyway, it is a lie. His prophecy will not come true, and I will stand against that 'prophet' and destroy him from among my people Israel. ¹⁰False prophets and hypocrites—evil people who say they want my words—all will be punished for their sins, ¹¹so

that the people of Israel will learn not to desert me and not to be polluted any longer with sin. They will be my people and I their God.' So says the Lord."

¹²Then this message of the Lord came to me:

¹³"Son of dust, if the people of a land sin against me, then I will crush them with my fist, break off their food supply, and send famine to destroy both man and beast. ¹⁴Even if Noah, Daniel, and Job were in it, they alone would be saved by their righteousness, and I would destroy the remainder of Israel," says the Lord God.

¹⁵"If I send an invasion of dangerous wild animals into the land to devastate the land, ¹⁶even if these three men were there, the Lord God swears that it would do no good—it would not save the people from their doom. Those three only would be saved, but the land would be devastated.

¹⁷"Or if I bring war against that land and tell the armies of the enemy to come and destroy everything, ¹⁸even if these three men were in the land, the Lord God declares that they alone would be saved.

¹⁹"And if I pour out my fury by sending an epidemic of disease into the land, and the plague kills man and beast alike, ²⁰though Noah, Daniel, and Job were living there, the Lord God says that only they would be saved because of their righteousness."

²¹And the Lord says: "Four great punishments await Jerusalem to destroy all life: war, famine, ferocious beasts, plague. ²²If there are survivors and they come here to join you as exiles in Babylon, you will see with your own eyes how wicked they are, and you will know it was right for me to destroy Jerusalem. ²³You will agree, when you meet them, that it is not without cause that all these things are being done to Israel."

15 A Useless Vine

Then this message came to me from the Lord:

²"Son of dust, what good are vines from the forest? Are they as useful as trees? Are they even as valuable as a single branch? ³No, for vines can't be used even for making pegs to hang up pots and pans! ⁴All they are good for is fuel—and even so, they burn but poorly! ⁵,⁶So they are useless both before and after being put in the fire!

"This is what I mean," the Lord God says: "The people of Jerusalem are like the vines of the forest—useless before being burned and certainly useless afterwards! ⁷And I will set myself against them to see to it that if they escape from one fire, they will fall into another; and then you shall know I am the Lord. ⁸And I will make the land desolate because they worship idols," says the Lord God.

16 Terrible Sins

Then again a message came to me from the Lord.

²"Son of dust," he said, "speak to Jerusalem about her loathsome sins. ³Tell her, 'The Lord God says: You are no better than the people of Canaan—your father must have been an Amorite and your mother a Hittite! ⁴When you were born, no one cared for you. When I first saw you, your umbilical cord was uncut, and you had been neither washed nor rubbed with salt nor clothed. ⁵No one had the slightest interest in you; no one pitied you or cared for you. On that day when you were born, you were dumped out into a field and left to die, unwanted.

⁶,⁷"But I came by and saw you there, covered with your own blood, and I said, 'Live! Thrive like a plant in the field!' And you did! You grew up and became tall, slender and supple, a jewel among jewels. And when you reached the age of maidenhood, your breasts were full-formed and your pubic hair had grown; yet you were naked.

⁸"'Later, when I passed by and saw you again, you were old enough for marriage; and I wrapped my cloak around you to legally declare my marriage vow. I signed a covenant with you, and you became mine. ⁹,¹⁰Then, when the marriage had taken place, I gave you beautiful clothes of linens and silk, embroidered, and sandals made of dolphin hide. ¹¹I gave you lovely ornaments, bracelets, and beautiful necklaces, ¹²a ring for your nose and two more for your ears, and a lovely tiara for your head. ¹³And so you were made beautiful with gold and silver, and your clothes were silk and linen and beautifully embroidered. You ate the finest foods and became more beautiful than ever. You looked like a queen, and so you were! ¹⁴Your reputation was great among the nations for your beauty; it was perfect because of all the gifts I gave you,'" says the Lord God.

¹⁵"'But you thought you could get along without me—you trusted in your beauty instead; and you gave yourself as a prostitute to every man who came along. Your beauty was his for the asking. ¹⁶You used the lovely things I gave you for making idol shrines and to decorate your bed of prostitution. Unbelievable! There has never been anything like it before! ¹⁷You took the very jewels and gold and silver ornaments I gave to you and made statues of men and worshiped them, which is adultery against me. ¹⁸You used the beautifully embroidered clothes I gave you—to cover your idols! And used my oil and incense to worship *them!* ¹⁹You set before *them* as a lovely sacrifice—imagine it—the fine flour and oil and honey I gave you! ²⁰And you took my sons and daughters you had borne to me and sacrificed

them to your gods; and they are gone. Wasn't it enough that you should be a prostitute? ²¹Must you also slay my children by sacrificing them to idols?

²²"And in all these years of adultery and sin you have not thought of those days long ago when you were naked and covered with blood.

²³"And then, in addition to all your other wickedness—woe, woe upon you, says the Lord God—²⁴you built a spacious brothel for your lovers and idol altars on every street, ²⁵and there you offered your beauty to every man who came by, in an endless stream of prostitution. ²⁶And you added lustful Egypt to your prostitutions by your alliance with her. My anger is great.

²⁷"'Therefore I have crushed you with my fist; I have reduced your boundaries and delivered you into the hands of those who hate you—the Philistines—and even they are ashamed of you.

²⁸"You have committed adultery with the Assyrians too [by making them your allies and worshiping their gods]; it seems that you can never find enough new gods. After your adultery there, you still weren't satisfied, ²⁹so you worshiped the gods of that great merchant land of Babylon—and you still weren't satisfied. ³⁰What a filthy heart you have, says the Lord God, to do such things as these; you are a brazen prostitute, ³¹building your idol altars, your brothels, on every street. You have been worse than a prostitute, so eager for sin that you have not even charged for your love! ³²Yes, you are an adulterous wife who lives with other men instead of her own husband. ³³,³⁴Prostitutes charge for their services—men pay with many gifts. But not you, you give *them* gifts, bribing them to come to you! So you are different from other prostitutes. But you had to pay them, for no one wanted you.

³⁵"'O prostitute, hear the word of the Lord: ³⁶The Lord God says: Because I see your filthy sins, your adultery with your lovers—your worshiping of idols—and the slaying of your children as sacrifices to your gods, ³⁷this is what I am going to do: I will gather together all your allies—these lovers of yours you have sinned with, both those you loved and those you hated—and I will make you naked before them that they may see you. ³⁸I will punish you as a murderess is punished and as a woman breaking wedlock living with other men. ³⁹I will give you to your lovers—these many nations—to destroy, and they will knock down your brothels and idol altars. They will strip you, take your beautiful jewels, and leave you naked and ashamed. ⁴⁰,⁴¹They will burn your homes, punishing you before the eyes of many women. And I will see to it that you stop your adulteries with other gods and end your payments to your allies for their love.

⁴²"Then at last my fury against you will die away; my jealousy against you will end, and I will be quiet and not be angry with you anymore. ⁴³But first, because you have not remembered your youth but have angered me by all these evil things you do, I will fully repay you for all of your sins,'" says the Lord. "'For you are thankless in addition to all your other faults.

⁴⁴"'Like mother, like daughter"—that is what everyone will say of you. ⁴⁵For your mother loathed her husband and her children, and you do too. And you are exactly like your sisters, for they despised their husbands and their children. Truly, your mother must have been a Hittite and your father an Amorite.

⁴⁶"'Your older sister is Samaria, living with her daughters north of you; your younger sister is Sodom and her daughters, in the south. ⁴⁷You have not merely sinned as they do—no, that was nothing to you; in a very short time you far surpassed them.

⁴⁸"'As I live, the Lord God says, Sodom and her daughters have never been as wicked as you and your daughters. ⁴⁹Your sister Sodom's sins were pride, laziness, and too much food, while the poor and needy suffered outside her door. ⁵⁰She insolently worshiped many idols as I watched. Therefore I crushed her.

⁵¹"Even Samaria has not committed half your sins. You have worshiped idols far more than your sisters have; they seem almost righteous in comparison with you! ⁵²Don't be surprised then by the lighter punishment they get. For your sins are so awful that in comparison with you, your sisters seem innocent! ⁵³(But someday I will restore the fortunes of Sodom and Samaria again, and those of Judah too.) ⁵⁴Your terrible punishment will be a consolation to them, for it will be greater than theirs.

⁵⁵"'Yes, your sisters, Sodom and Samaria, and all their people will be restored again, and Judah, too, will prosper in that day. ⁵⁶In your proud days you held Sodom in unspeakable contempt. ⁵⁷But now your greater wickedness has been exposed to all the world, and you are the one who is scorned—by Edom and all her neighbors and by all the Philistines. ⁵⁸This is part of your punishment for all your sins,'" says the Lord.

⁵⁹,⁶⁰For the Lord God says: "I will repay you for your broken promises. You lightly broke your solemn vows to me, yet I will keep the pledge I made to you when you were young. I will establish an everlasting covenant with you forever, ⁶¹and you will remember with shame all the evil you have done; and you will be overcome by my favor when I take your sisters, Samaria and Sodom, and make them your daughters, for you to rule over. You will know you don't deserve this

gracious act, for you did not keep my covenant. ⁶²I will reaffirm my covenant with you, and you will know I am the Lord. ⁶³ Despite all you have done, I will be kind to you again; you will cover your mouth in silence and in shame when I forgive you all that you have done," says the Lord God.

17 The Great Eagle

Then this message came to me from the Lord:

²"Son of dust, give this riddle to the people of Israel:

³,⁴"A great eagle with broad wings full of many-colored feathers came to Lebanon and plucked off the shoot at the top of the tallest cedar tree and carried it into a city filled with merchants. ⁵There he planted it in fertile ground beside a broad river, where it would grow as quickly as a willow tree. ⁶It took root and grew and became a low but spreading vine that turned toward the eagle and produced strong branches and luxuriant leaves. ⁷But when another great, broad-winged, full-feathered eagle came along, this tree sent its roots and branches out toward him instead, ⁸even though it was already in good soil with plenty of water to become a splendid vine, producing leaves and fruit.

⁹The Lord God asks: "Shall I let this tree grow and prosper? No! I will pull it out, roots and all! I will cut off its branches and let its leaves wither and die. It will pull out easily enough—it won't take a big crew or a lot of equipment to do that. ¹⁰Though the vine began so well, will it thrive? No, it will wither away completely when the east wind touches it, dying in the same choice soil where it had grown so well."

¹¹Then this message came to me from the Lord:

¹²,¹³"Ask these rebels of Israel: Don't you understand what this riddle of the eagles means? I will tell you. Nebuchadnezzar, king of Babylon [the first of the two eagles], came to Jerusalem, took away her king and princes [her topmost buds and shoots], and brought them to Babylon. Nebuchadnezzar made a covenant with a member of the royal family [Zedekiah], and made him take an oath of loyalty. He took a seedling and planted it in fertile ground beside a broad river. He also exiled the top men of Israel's government, ¹⁴so that Israel would not be strong again and revolt. But by keeping her promises, Israel could be respected and maintain her identity.

¹⁵"Nevertheless, Zedekiah rebelled against Babylon, sending ambassadors to Egypt to seek for a great army and many horses to fight against Nebuchadnezzar. But will Israel prosper after breaking all her promises like that? Will she succeed? ¹⁶No! For as I live," says the Lord, "the king of Israel shall die. (Nebuchadnezzar will pull out the tree, roots and all!) Zedekiah shall die in Babylon, where the king lives who gave him his power, and whose covenant he despised and broke. ¹⁷Pharaoh and all his mighty army shall fail to help Israel when the king of Babylon lays siege to Jerusalem again and slaughters many lives. ¹⁸For the king of Israel broke his promise after swearing to obey; therefore he shall not escape."

¹⁹The Lord God says: "As I live, surely I will punish him for despising the solemn oath he made in my name. ²⁰I will throw my net over him, and he shall be captured in my snare; I will bring him to Babylon and deal with him there for this treason against me. ²¹And all the best soldiers of Israel will be killed by the sword, and those remaining in the city will be scattered to the four winds. Then you will know that I, the Lord, have spoken these words."

²²,²³The Lord God says: "I will take a tender sprout from the top of a tall cedar, and I will plant it on the top of Israel's highest mountain. It shall become a noble cedar, bringing forth branches and bearing seed. Animals of every sort will gather under it; its branches will shelter every kind of bird. ²⁴And everyone shall know that it is I, the Lord, who cuts down the high trees and exalts the low, that I make the green tree wither and the dead tree grow. I, the Lord, have said that I would do it, and I will."

18 Turn and Live!

Then the Lord's message came to me again.

²"Why do people use this proverb about the land of Israel: The children are punished for their fathers' sins? ³As I live," says the Lord God, "you will not use this proverb any more in Israel, ⁴for all souls are mine to judge—fathers and sons alike—and my rule is this: It is for a man's own sins that he will die.

⁵"But if a man is just and does what is lawful and right, ⁶and has not gone out to the mountains to feast before the idols of Israel and worship them, and does not commit adultery nor lie with any woman during the time of her menstruation; ⁷if he is a merciful creditor, not holding onto the items given to him in pledge by poor debtors, and is no robber but gives food to the hungry and clothes to those in need; ⁸and if he grants loans without interest, stays away from sin, is honest and fair when judging others, ⁹and obeys my laws—that man is just," says the Lord, "and he shall surely live.

¹⁰"But if that man has a son who is a robber or murderer and who fulfills none of his responsibilities, ¹¹who refuses to obey the laws of God but

Family Devotions

☐ DEVOTION 231

TRUSTING GOD FOR HELP

Read Ezekiel 18:25-32

Trusting God for Help Memory Verse

God is our refuge and strength, a tested help in times of trouble.
Psalm 46:1

"The answer is no, Jason. That's final!" Mom was firm. As Jason flung himself out of the room, a swear word exploded from his lips. "Jason! Come back here this minute!" Mom ordered. "Did you say what I think you said?" Jason gritted his teeth and stared at the floor. Mom sighed deeply. "Son, what is the matter with you?" Jason did not answer, and tears filled Mom's eyes. "You will have to be punished for swearing. I'll talk to your father about it this evening."

"But, Mom, I didn't mean to," Jason pleaded. "It just slipped out. I'm sorry. Really I am. All the guys at school say those words, and they stick in my mind. I promise I'll never do it again. I'm sorry. Honest!"

Mom sighed and looked at him closely. "I believe you are," she decided. "Very well. We'll forget it this time."

Later that evening loud, angry words burst from Jason's room. "How many times have I told you to stay out of my stuff?" he roared.

As Mom started down the hall, she heard Tina cry, "But, Jason, I just wanted to borrow a pencil. I didn't mean to break your model. I'm sorry."

"That's what you said when you broke my watch. You're not really sorry! You're just sorry you got caught because you don't want to get in trouble. You cry and think I'll forget about it." Jason did not see his mother come into the room as he bent over to pick up the broken model, swearing softly.

"Jason!" At the sound of Mom's voice, Jason jumped and dropped the model. "Jason, look at me," Mom said. "Tina isn't the only one whose repentance is false. Didn't you tell me this afternoon you were sorry you swore?" Jason nodded slowly.

Mom continued, "True repentance is more than saying I'm sorry. It's being sorry enough for what you have done to stop doing it. Now let's go talk to your father."

How About You?
Do you ever say "I'm sorry" simply to keep out of trouble? False repentance might fool others for a while, but it never fools God. When your repentance is sincere, God promises to forgive you and to help you avoid making the same mistake again. He says he'll put "a new heart and a new spirit" in you! *B. W.*

• For the next devotional, turn to page 801. • For the next devotional on TRUSTING GOD FOR HELP, turn to page 1201. • For notes on TRUSTING GOD FOR HELP, see pages 240, 249, 464, 539, and 751.

worships idols on the mountains and commits adultery, [12]oppresses the poor and helpless, robs his debtors by refusing to let them redeem what they have given him in pledge, loves idols and worships them, [13]and loans out his money at interest—shall that man live? No! He shall surely die, and it is his own fault.

[14]"But if this sinful man has, in turn, a son who sees all his father's wickedness, so that he fears God and decides against that kind of life; [15]he doesn't go up on the mountains to feast before the idols and worship them and does not commit adultery; [16]he is fair to those who borrow from him and doesn't rob them, but feeds the hungry, clothes the needy, [17]helps the poor, does not loan money at interest, and obeys my laws—he shall not die because of his father's sins; he shall surely live. [18]But his father shall die for his own sins because he is cruel and robs and does wrong.

[19]"'What?' you ask. 'Doesn't the son pay for his father's sins?' No! For if the son does what is right and keeps my laws, he shall surely live. [20]The one who sins is the one who dies. The son shall not be punished for his father's sins, nor the father for his son's. The righteous person will be rewarded for his own goodness and the wicked person for his wickedness. [21]But if a wicked person turns away from all his sins and begins to obey my laws and do what is just and right, he shall surely live and not die. [22]All his past sins will be forgotten, and he shall live because of his goodness.

[23]"Do you think I like to see the wicked die?" asks the Lord. "Of course not! I only want him to turn from his wicked ways and live. [24]However, if a righteous person turns to sinning and acts like any other sinner, should he be allowed to live? No, of course not. All his previous goodness will be forgotten and he shall die for his sins.

[25]"Yet you say: 'The Lord isn't being fair!' Listen to me, O people of Israel. Am I the one who is unfair, or is it you? [26]When a good man turns away from being good, begins sinning, and dies in his sins, he dies for the evil he has done. [27]And if a wicked person turns away from his wickedness and obeys the law and does right, he shall save his soul, [28]for he has thought it over and decided to turn from his sins and live a good life. He shall surely live—he shall not die.

[29]"And yet the people of Israel keep saying: 'The Lord is unfair!' O people of Israel, it is you who are unfair, not I. [30]I will judge each of you, O Israel, and punish or reward each according to his own actions. Oh, turn from your sins while there is yet time. [31]Put them behind you and receive a new heart and a new spirit. For why will you die, O Israel? [32]I do not enjoy seeing you die," the Lord God says. "Turn, turn and live!

19 A Death Song

"Sing this death dirge for the leaders of Israel: [2]What a woman your mother was—like a lioness! Her children were like lion's cubs! [3]One of her cubs [King Jehoahaz] grew into a strong young lion and learned to catch prey and became a man-eater. [4]Then the nations called out their hunters; they trapped him in a pit and brought him in chains to Egypt.

[5]"When Israel, the mother lion, saw that all her hopes for him were gone, she took another of her cubs [King Jehoiachin] and taught him to be 'king of the beasts.' [6]He became a leader among the lions and learned to catch prey, and he too became a man-eater. [7]He demolished the palaces of the surrounding nations and ruined their cities; their farms were desolated, their crops destroyed; everyone in the land shook with terror when they heard him roar. [8]Then the armies of the nations surrounded him, coming from every side, and trapped him in a pit and captured him. [9]They prodded him into a cage and brought him before the king of Babylon. He was held in captivity so that his voice could never again be heard upon the mountains of Israel.

[10]"Your mother was like a vine beside an irrigation ditch, with lush, green foliage because of all the water. [11]Its strongest branch became a ruler's scepter, and it was very great, towering above the others and noticed from far away. [12]But the vine was uprooted in fury and thrown down to the ground. Its branches were broken and withered by a strong wind from the east; the fruit was destroyed by fire. [13]Now the vine is planted in the wilderness where the ground is hard and dry. [14]It is decaying from within; no strong branch remains. The fulfillment of this sad prophecy has already begun, and there is more ahead."

20 God Says "Remember!"

Late in July, six years after King Jeconiah was captured, some of the elders of Israel came to ask instructions from the Lord and sat before me awaiting his reply.

[2]Then the Lord gave me this message:

[3]"Son of dust, say to the elders of Israel, 'The Lord God says: How dare you come to ask my help? I swear that I will tell you nothing.' [4]Judge them, son of dust; condemn them; tell them of all the sins of this nation from the times of their fathers until now. [5,6]Tell them, 'The Lord God says: When I chose Israel and revealed myself to her in Egypt, I swore to her and her descendants that I would bring them out of Egypt to a land I had discovered and explored for them—a good land,

flowing as it were with milk and honey, the best of all lands anywhere.'

⁷"Then I said to them: 'Get rid of every idol; do not defile yourselves with the Egyptian gods, for I am the Lord your God.' ⁸But they rebelled against me and would not listen. They didn't get rid of their idols nor forsake the gods of Egypt. Then I thought, I will pour out my fury upon them and fulfill my anger against them while they are still in Egypt.

⁹,¹⁰"But I didn't do it, for I acted to protect the honor of my name, lest the Egyptians laugh at Israel's God who couldn't keep them back from harm. So I brought my people out of Egypt right before the Egyptians' eyes and led them into the wilderness. ¹¹There I gave them my laws so they could live by keeping them. If anyone keeps them, he will live. ¹²And I gave them the Sabbath—a day of rest every seventh day—as a symbol between them and me, to remind them that it is I, the Lord, who sanctifies them—that they are truly my people.

¹³"But Israel rebelled against me. There in the wilderness they refused my laws. They would not obey my rules even though obeying them means life. And they misused my Sabbaths. Then I thought, I will pour out my fury upon them and utterly consume them in the desert.

¹⁴"But again I refrained in order to protect the honor of my name, lest the nations who saw me bring them out of Egypt would say that it was because I couldn't care for them that I destroyed them. ¹⁵But I swore to them in the wilderness that I would not bring them into the land I had given them, a land full of milk and honey, the choicest spot on earth, ¹⁶because they laughed at my laws, ignored my wishes, and violated my Sabbaths—their hearts were with their idols! ¹⁷Nevertheless, I spared them. I didn't finish them off in the wilderness.

¹⁸"Then I spoke to their children and said: 'Don't follow your fathers' footsteps. Don't defile yourselves with their idols, ¹⁹for I am the Lord your God. Follow my laws; keep my ordinances; ²⁰hallow my Sabbaths; for they are a symbol of the contract between us to help you remember that I am the Lord your God.'

²¹"But their children, too, rebelled against me. They refused my laws—the laws that if a person keeps them, he will live. And they defiled my Sabbaths. So then I said: 'Now at last I will pour out my fury upon you in the wilderness.'

²²"Nevertheless, again I withdrew my judgment against them to protect my name among the nations who had seen my power in bringing them out of Egypt.

²³,²⁴But I took a solemn oath against them while they were in the wilderness that I would scatter them, dispersing them to the ends of the earth because they did not obey my laws but scorned them and violated my Sabbaths and longed for their fathers' idols. ²⁵I let them adopt customs and laws which were worthless. Through the keeping of them they could not attain life. ²⁶In the hope that they would draw back in horror and know that I alone am God, I let them pollute themselves with the very gifts I gave them. They burnt their firstborn children as offerings to their gods!

²⁷,²⁸"Son of dust, tell them that the Lord God says: 'Your fathers continued to blaspheme and betray me when I brought them into the land I promised them, for they offered sacrifices and incense on every high hill and under every tree! They roused my fury as they offered up their sacrifices to those "gods." They brought their perfumes and incense and poured out their drink offerings to them! ²⁹I said to them: "What is this place of sacrifice where you go?" And so it is still called 'The Place of Sacrifice'—that is how it got its name.

³⁰"The Lord God wants to know whether you are going to pollute yourselves just as your fathers did and keep on worshiping idols. ³¹For when you offer gifts to them and give your little sons to be burned to ashes as you do even today, shall I listen to you or help you, Israel? As I live," the Lord God says, "I will not give you any message, though you have come to me to ask.

³²"What you have in mind will not be done—to be like the nations all around you, serving gods of wood and stone. ³³I will rule you with an iron fist and in great anger and with power. ³⁴With might and fury I will bring you out from the lands where you are scattered, ³⁵,³⁶and will bring you into my desert judgment hall. I will judge you there and get rid of the rebels, just as I did in the wilderness after I brought you out of Egypt. ³⁷I will count you carefully and let only a small quota return. ³⁸And the others—the rebels and all those who sin against me—I will purge from among you. They shall not enter Israel, but I will bring them out of the countries where they are in exile. And when that happens, you will know I am the Lord.

³⁹"O Israel," the Lord God says: "If you insist on worshiping your idols, go right ahead, but then

---

PUTTING GOD FIRST 20:39 The people of Israel were worshiping idols and sacrificing to God at the same time! Often we think that some religion is better than none at all. While persisting in a life of sin, we may think, *Well, at least I go to church.* God will be pleased with this effort. But God wants first place in your life. No amount of religious ritual or personal sacrifice can make up for continuing sinful practices. What parts of your life have you not yet committed to God? **To begin the series of devotionals on PUTTING GOD FIRST, turn to page 115.**

don't bring your gifts to me as well! Such desecration of my holy name must stop!

⁴⁰"For at Jerusalem in my holy mountain," says the Lord, "all Israel shall worship me. There I will accept you and require you to bring me your offerings and the finest of your gifts. ⁴¹You will be to me as an offering of perfumed incense when I bring you back from exile, and the nations will see the great change in your hearts. ⁴²Then, when I have brought you home to the land I promised your fathers, you will know I am the Lord. ⁴³Then you will look back at all your sins and loathe yourselves because of the evil you have done. ⁴⁴And when I have honored my name by blessing you despite your wickedness, then, O Israel, you will know I am the Lord."

⁴⁵Then this message came to me from the Lord: ⁴⁶"Son of dust, look toward Jerusalem and speak out against it and the forest lands of the Negeb. ⁴⁷Prophesy to it and say: 'Hear the word of the Lord. I will set you on fire, O forest, and every tree will die, green and dry alike. The terrible flames will not be quenched, and they will scorch the world. ⁴⁸And all the world will see that I, the Lord, have set the fire. It shall not be put out.'"

⁴⁹Then I said, "O Lord God, they say of me, 'He only talks in riddles!'"

21 Ezekiel's Glittering Sword

Then this message came to me from the Lord:

²"Son of dust, face toward Jerusalem and prophesy against Israel and against my Temple! ³For the Lord says: 'I am against you, Israel. I will unsheath my sword and destroy your people, good and bad alike—⁴I will not spare even the righteous. I will make a clean sweep throughout the land from the Negeb to your northern borders. ⁵All the world shall know that it is I, the Lord. His sword is in his hand, and it will not return to its sheath again until its work is finished.'

⁶"Sigh and groan before the people, son of dust, in your bitter anguish; sigh with grief and broken heart. ⁷When they ask you why, tell them: 'Because of the fearsome news that God has given me. When it comes true, the boldest heart will melt with fear; all strength will disappear. Every spirit will faint; strong knees will tremble and become as weak as water.' And the Lord God says: 'Your doom is on the way; my judgments will be fulfilled!'"

⁸Then again this message came to me from God:

⁹⁻¹¹"Son of dust, tell them this: 'A sword is being sharpened and polished for terrible slaughter. Now will you laugh? For those far stronger than you have perished beneath its power. It is ready now to hand to the executioner.' ¹²Son of dust, with sobbing, beat upon your thigh, for that sword shall slay my people and all their leaders. All alike shall die. ¹³It will put them all to the test—and what chance do they have?" the Lord God asks.

¹⁴"Prophesy to them in this way: Clap your hands vigorously, then take a sword and brandish it twice, thrice, to symbolize the great massacre they face! ¹⁵Let their hearts melt with terror, for a sword glitters at every gate; it flashes like lightning; it is razor-edged for slaughter. ¹⁶O sword, slash to the right and slash to the left, wherever you will, wherever you want. ¹⁷And you have prophesied with clapping hands that I, the Lord, will smite Jerusalem and satisfy my fury."

¹⁸Then this message came to me. The Lord said: ¹⁹,²⁰"Son of dust, make a map and on it trace two routes for the king of Babylon to follow—one to Jerusalem and the other to Rabbah in Trans-Jordan. And put a signpost at the fork in the road from Babylon. ²¹For the king of Babylon stands at a fork, uncertain whether to attack Jerusalem or Rabbah. He will call his magicians to use divination; they will cast lots by shaking arrows from the quiver; they will sacrifice to idols and inspect the liver of their sacrifice. ²²They will decide to turn toward Jerusalem! With battering rams they will go against the gates, shouting for the kill; they will build siege towers and make a hill against the walls to reach the top. ²³Jerusalem won't understand this treachery; how could the diviners make this terrible mistake? For Babylon is Judah's ally and has sworn to defend Jerusalem! But (the king of Babylon) will think only of the times the people rebelled. He will attack and defeat them.

²⁴The Lord God says: "Again and again your guilt cries out against you, for your sins are open and unashamed. Wherever you go, whatever you do, all is filled with sin. And now the time of punishment has come.

²⁵"O King Zedekiah, evil prince of Israel, your final day of reckoning is here. ²⁶Take off your jeweled crown," the Lord God says. "The old order changes. Now the poor are exalted and the rich brought very low. ²⁷I will overturn, overturn, overturn the kingdom, so that even the new order that emerges will not succeed until the Man appears who has a right to it. And I will give it all to him.

²⁸"Son of dust, prophesy to the Ammonites too, for they mocked my people in their woe. Tell them this:

"'Against you also my glittering sword is drawn from its sheath; it is sharpened and polished and flashed like lightning. ²⁹Your magicians and false prophets have told you lies of safety and success—that your gods will save you from the king of Babylon. Thus they have caused your death along with all the other wicked, for when the day of final reckoning has come, you will be wounded unto death. ³⁰Shall I return my sword to its sheath before I deal with you? No, I will destroy you in your own country where you were born. ³¹I will pour out my fury upon you and blow upon the fire of my wrath until it becomes a roaring conflagration, and I will deliver you into the hands of cruel men skilled in destruction. ³²You are the fuel for the fire; your blood will be spilled in your own country, and you will be utterly wiped out, your memory lost in history. For I, the Lord, have spoken it.'"

22 God Lists the People's Sins

Now another message came from the Lord. He said:

²"Son of dust, indict Jerusalem as the City of Murder. Publicly denounce her terrible deeds. ³City of Murder, doomed and damned—City of Idols, filthy and foul—⁴you are guilty both of murder and idolatry. Now comes your day of doom. You have reached the limit of your years. I will make you a laughingstock and a reproach to all the nations of the world. ⁵Near and far they will mock you, a city of infamous rebels.

⁶"Every leader in Israel who lives within your walls is bent on murder. ⁷Fathers and mothers are contemptuously ignored; immigrants and visitors are forced to pay you for your 'protection'; orphans and widows are wronged and oppressed. ⁸The things of God are all despised; my Sabbaths are ignored. ⁹Prisoners are falsely accused and sent to their death. Every mountaintop is filled with idols; lewdness is everywhere. ¹⁰There are men who commit adultery with their fathers' wives and lie with menstruous women. ¹¹Adultery with a neighbor's wife, a daughter-in-law, a half sister—this is common. ¹²Hired murderers, loan racketeers, and extortioners are everywhere. You never even think of me and my commands," the Lord God says.

¹³"But now I snap my fingers and call a halt to your dishonest gain and bloodshed. ¹⁴How strong and courageous will you be then, in my day of reckoning? For I, the Lord, have spoken, and I will do all that I have said. ¹⁵I will scatter you throughout the world and burn out the wickedness within you. ¹⁶You will be dishonored among the nations, and you shall know I am the Lord."

¹⁷Then the Lord said this:

¹⁸⁻²⁰"Son of dust, the people of Israel are the worthless slag left when silver is smelted. They are the dross, compounded from the brass, the tin, the iron and the lead. Therefore the Lord God says: 'Because you are worthless dross, I will bring you to my crucible in Jerusalem, to smelt you with the heat of my wrath. ²¹I will blow the fire of my wrath upon you, ²²and you will melt like silver in fierce heat, and you will know that I, the Lord, have poured my wrath upon you.'"

²³Again the message of the Lord came to me, saying:

²⁴"Son of dust, say to the people of Israel: 'In the day of my indignation you shall be like an uncleared wilderness or a desert without rain.' ²⁵Your 'prophets' have plotted against you like lions stalking prey. They devour many lives; they seize treasures and extort wealth; they multiply the widows in the land. ²⁶Your priests have violated my laws and defiled my Temple and my holiness. To them the things of God are no more important than any daily task. They have not taught my people the difference between right and wrong, and they disregard my Sabbaths, so my holy name is greatly defiled among them. ²⁷Your leaders are like wolves, who tear apart their victims, and they destroy lives for profit. ²⁸Your 'prophets' describe false visions and speak false messages they claim are from God, when he hasn't spoken one word to them at all. Thus they repair the walls with whitewash! ²⁹Even the common people oppress and rob the poor and needy and cruelly extort from aliens.

³⁰"I looked in vain for anyone who would build again the wall of righteousness that guards the land, who could stand in the gap and defend you from my just attacks, but I found not one." ³¹And so the Lord God says: "I will pour out my anger upon you; I will consume you with the fire of my wrath. I have heaped upon you the full penalty for all your sins."

23 Two Sisters

The Lord's message came to me again, saying:

²,³"Son of dust, there were two sisters who as young girls became prostitutes in Egypt.

⁴,⁵"The older girl was named Oholah; her sister was Oholibah. (I am speaking of Samaria and Jerusalem!) I married them, and they bore me sons and daughters. But then Oholah turned to other gods instead of me and gave her love to the Assyrians, her neighbors, ⁶for they were all attractive young men, captains and commanders, in handsome blue, dashing about on their horses. ⁷And so she sinned with them—the choicest men of Assyria—worshiping their idols, defiling herself. ⁸For when she left Egypt, she did not leave her spirit of prostitution behind, but was still as lewd as in her youth when the Egyptians poured out their lusts upon her and robbed her of her virginity.

9"And so I delivered her into the evil clutches of the Assyrians whose gods she loved so much. 10They stripped her and killed her and took away her children as their slaves. Her name was known to every woman in the land as a sinner who had received what she deserved.

11"But when Oholibah [Jerusalem] saw what had happened to her sister she went right ahead in the same way and sinned even more than her sister. 12She fawned over her Assyrian neighbors, those handsome young men on fine steeds, those army officers in handsome uniforms—all of them desirable. 13I saw the way she was going, following right along behind her older sister.

14,15"She was in fact more debased than Samaria, for she fell in love with pictures she saw painted on a wall! They were pictures of Babylonian military officers, outfitted in striking red uniforms, with handsome belts, and flowing turbans on their heads. 16When she saw these paintings, she longed to give herself to the men pictured, so she sent messengers to Chaldea to invite them to come to her. 17And they came and committed adultery with her, defiling her in the bed of love, but afterward she hated them and broke off all relations with them.

18"And I despised her, just as I despised her sister, because she flaunted herself before them and gave herself to their lust. 19,20But that didn't bother her. She turned to even greater prostitution, sinning with the lustful men she remembered from her youth when she was a prostitute in Egypt. 21And thus you celebrated those former days when as a young girl you gave your virginity to those from Egypt.

22"And now the Lord God says that he will raise against you, O Oholibah [Jerusalem], those very nations from which you turned away, disgusted. 23 For the Babylonians will come, and all the Chaldeans from Pekod and Shoa and Koa; and all the Assyrians with them—handsome young men of high rank, riding their steeds. 24They will come against you from the north with chariots, wagons, and a great army fully prepared for attack. They will surround you on every side with armored men, and I will let them at you, to do with you as they wish. 25And I will send my jealousy against you and deal furiously with you. They will cut off your nose and ears; your survivors will be killed; your children will be taken away as slaves, and everything left will be burned. 26They will strip you of your beautiful clothes and jewels.

27"And so I will put a stop to your lewdness and prostitution brought from the land of Egypt; you will no more long for Egypt and her gods." 28For the Lord God says: "I will surely deliver you over to your enemies, to those you loathe. 29They will deal with you in hatred and rob you of all you own, leaving you naked and bare. And the shame of your prostitution shall be exposed to all the world.

30"You brought all this upon yourself by worshiping the gods of other nations, defiling yourself with all their idols. 31You have followed in your sister's footsteps, so I will punish you with the same terrors that destroyed her. 32Yes, the terrors that fell upon her will fall upon you—and the cup from which she drank was full and large. And all the world will mock you for your woe. 33You will reel like a drunkard beneath the awful blows of sorrow and distress, just as your sister Samaria did. 34In deep anguish you will drain that cup of terror to the very bottom and will lick the inside to get every drop. For I have spoken," says the Lord. 35"Because you have forgotten me and turned your backs on me, therefore you must bear the consequence of all your sin.

36"Son of dust, you must accuse Jerusalem and Samaria of all their awful deeds. 37For they have committed both adultery and murder; they have worshiped idols and murdered my children whom they bore to me, burning them as sacrifices on their altars. 38On the same day they defiled my Temple and ignored my Sabbaths, 39for when they had murdered their children in front of their idols, then even that same day they actually came into my Temple to worship! That is how much regard they have for me!

40"You even sent away to distant lands for priests to come with other gods for you to serve, and they have come and been welcomed! You bathed yourself, painted your eyelids, and put on your finest jewels for them. 41You sat together on a beautifully embroidered bed and put my incense and my oil upon a table spread before you. 42From your apartment came the sound of many men carousing—lewd men and drunkards from the wilderness, who put bracelets on your wrists and beautiful crowns upon your head. 43Will they commit adultery with these who have become old harlot hags? 44Yet that is what they did. They went in to them—to Samaria and Jerusalem, these shameless harlots—with all the zest of lustful men who visit prostitutes. 45But just persons everywhere will judge them for what they really are—adulteresses and murderers. They will mete out to them the sentences the law demands.

46The Lord God says: "Bring an army against them and hand them out to be crushed and despised. 47For their enemies will stone them and kill them with swords; they will butcher their sons and daughters and burn their homes. 48Thus will I make lewdness and idolatry to cease from the land. My judgment will be a lesson against idolatry for all to see. 49For you will be fully repaid for all your harlotry, your worshiping of idols. You will suffer the full penalty, and you will know that I alone am God."

24 A Cooking Pot

One day late in December of the ninth year (of King Jehoiachin's captivity), another message came to me from the Lord.

2"Son of dust," he said, "write down this date, for today the king of Babylon has attacked Jerusalem. 3And now give this parable to these rebels, Israel; tell them, 'The Lord God says: Put a pot of water on the fire to boil. 4Fill it with choicest mutton, the rump and shoulder and all the most tender cuts. 5Use only the best sheep from the flock, and heap fuel on the fire beneath the pot. Boil the meat well, until the flesh falls off the bones.'

6For the Lord God says: "Woe to Jerusalem, City of Murderers; you are a pot that is pitted with rust and with wickedness. So take out the meat chunk by chunk in whatever order it comes—for none is better than any other. 7For her wickedness is evident to all—she boldly murders, leaving blood upon the rocks in open view for all to see; she does not even try to cover it. 8And I have left it there, uncovered, to shout to me against her and arouse my wrath and vengeance.

9"Woe to Jerusalem, City of Murderers. I will pile on the fuel beneath her. 10Heap on the wood; let the fire roar and the pot boil. Cook the meat well, and then empty the pot and burn the bones. 11Now set it empty on the coals to scorch away the rust and corruption. 12But all for naught—it all remains despite the hottest fire. 13It is the rust and corruption of your filthy lewdness, of worshiping your idols. And now, because I wanted to cleanse you and you refused, remain filthy until my fury has accomplished all its terrors upon you! 14I, the Lord, have spoken it; it shall come to pass and I will do it."

15Again a message came to me from the Lord, saying:

16"Son of dust, I am going to take away your lovely wife. Suddenly, she will die. Yet you must show no sorrow. Do not weep; let there be no tears. 17You may sigh, but only quietly. Let there be no wailing at her grave; don't bare your head nor feet, and don't accept the food brought to you by consoling friends."

18I proclaimed this to the people in the morning, and in the evening my wife died. The next morning I did all the Lord had told me to.

19Then the people said: "What does all this mean? What are you trying to tell us?"

20,21And I answered, "The Lord told me to say to the people of Israel: 'I will destroy my lovely, beautiful Temple, the strength of your nation. And your sons and daughters in Judea will be slaughtered by the sword. 22And you will do as I have done; you may not mourn in public or console yourself by eating the food brought to you by sympathetic friends. 23Your head and feet shall not be bared; you shall not mourn or weep. But you will sorrow to one another for your sins and mourn privately for all the evil you have done. 24Ezekiel is an example to you,' the Lord God says. 'You will do as he has done. And when that time comes, then you will know I am the Lord.'"

25"Son of dust, on the day I finish taking from them in Jerusalem the joy of their hearts and their glory and joys—their wives and their sons and their daughters— 26on that day a refugee from Jerusalem will start on a journey to come to you in Babylon to tell you what has happened. 27And on the day of his arrival, your voice will suddenly return to you so that you can talk with him; and you will be a symbol for these people, and they shall know I am the Lord."

25 Thieves in the Desert

Then the Lord's message came to me again. He said:

2"Son of dust, look toward the land of Ammon and prophesy against its people. 3Tell them: 'Listen to what the Lord God says. Because you scoffed when my Temple was destroyed, and mocked Israel in her anguish, and laughed at Judah when she was marched away captive, 4therefore I will let the Bedouins from the desert to the east of you overrun your land. They will set up their encampments among you. They will harvest all your fruit and steal your dairy cattle. 5And I will turn the city of Rabbah into a pasture for camels and all the country of the Ammonites into a wasteland where flocks of sheep can graze. Then you will know I am the Lord.'

6For the Lord God says: "Because you clapped and stamped and cheered with glee at the destruction of my people, 7therefore I will lay my hand heavily upon you, delivering you to many nations for devastation. I will cut you off from being a nation any more. I will destroy you; then you shall know I am the Lord."

8And the Lord God says: "Because the Moabites have said that Judah is no better off than any other nation, 9,10therefore I will open up the eastern flank of Moab, wiping out her frontier cities, the glory of the nation—Beth-jeshimoth, Baal-meon and Kiriathaim. And Bedouin tribes from the desert to the east will pour in upon her, just as they will upon Ammon. And Moab will no longer be counted among the nations. 11Thus I will bring down my judgment upon the Moabites, and they shall know I am the Lord."

12And the Lord God says: "Because the people of Edom have sinned so greatly by avenging themselves upon the people of Judah, 13I will smash Edom with my fist and wipe out her people, her cattle, and her flocks. The sword will destroy everything from Teman to Dedan. 14By the hand of my people, Israel, this shall be done. They will carry out my furious vengeance."

15And the Lord God says: "Because the Philistines have acted against Judah out of revenge and long-standing hatred, 16I will shake my fist over the land of the Philistines, and I will wipe out the Cherithites and utterly destroy those along the seacoast. 17I will execute terrible vengeance upon them to rebuke them for what they have done. And when all this happens, then they shall know I am the Lord."

26 A City Will Be Ruined

Another message came to me from the Lord on the first day of the month, in the eleventh year (after King Jehoiachin was taken away to captivity).

2"Son of dust, Tyre has rejoiced over the fall of Jerusalem, saying, 'Ha! She who controlled the lucrative north-south trade routes along the coast and along the course of the Jordan River has been broken, and I have fallen heir! Because she has been laid waste, I shall become wealthy!'

3Therefore the Lord God says: "I stand against you, Tyre, and I will bring nations against you like ocean waves. 4They will destroy the walls of Tyre and tear down her towers. I will scrape away her soil and make her a bare rock! 5Her island shall become uninhabited, a place for fishermen to spread their nets, for I have spoken it," says the Lord God. "Tyre shall become the prey of many nations, 6and her mainland city shall perish by the sword. Then they shall know I am the Lord."

7For the Lord God says: "I will bring Nebuchadnezzar, king of Babylon—the king of kings from the north—against Tyre with a great army and cavalry and chariots. 8First he will destroy your suburbs; then he will attack your mainland city by building a siege wall and raising a roof of shields against it. 9He will set up battering rams against your walls and with sledgehammers demolish your forts. 10The hoofs of his cavalry will choke the city with dust, and your walls will shake as the horses gallop through your broken gates, pulling chariots behind them. 11Horsemen will occupy every street in the city; they will butcher your people, and your famous, huge pillars will topple.

12"They will plunder all your riches and merchandise and break down your walls. They will destroy your lovely homes and dump your stones and timber and even your dust into the sea. 13I will stop the music of your songs. No more will there be the sound of harps among you. 14I will make your island a bare rock, a place for fishermen to spread their nets. You will never be rebuilt, for I, the Lord, have spoken it." So says the Lord. 15"The whole country will shake with your fall; the wounded will scream as the slaughter goes on.

16"Then all the seaport rulers shall come down from their thrones and lay aside their robes and beautiful garments and sit on the ground shaking with fear at what they have seen. 17And they shall wail for you, singing this dirge: 'O mighty island city, with your naval power that terrorized the mainland, how you have vanished from the seas! 18How the islands tremble at your fall! They watch dismayed.'"

19For the Lord God says: "I will destroy Tyre to the ground. You will sink beneath the terrible waves of enemy attack. Great seas shall swallow you. 20I will send you to the pit of hell to lie there with those of long ago. Your city will lie in ruins, dead, like the bodies of those in the underworld who entered long ago the nether world of the dead. Never again will you be inhabited or be given beauty here in the land of those who live. 21I will bring you to a dreadful end; no search will be enough to find you," says the Lord.

27 A Great Seaport City

Then this message came to me from the Lord. He said:

2"Son of dust, sing this sad dirge for Tyre:

3"'O mighty seaport city, merchant center of the world, the Lord God speaks. You say, "I am the most beautiful city in all the world." 4You have extended your boundaries out into the sea; your architects have made you glorious. 5You are like a ship built of finest fir from Senir. They took a cedar from Lebanon to make a mast for you. 6They made your oars from oaks of Bashan. The walls of your cabin are of cypress from the southern coast of Cyprus. 7Your sails are made of Egypt's finest linens; you stand beneath awnings bright with purple and scarlet dyes from eastern Cyprus.

8"'Your sailors come from Sidon and Arvad; your helmsmen are skilled men from Zemer. 9Wise old craftsmen from Gebal do the calking. Ships come from every land with all their goods to barter for your trade.

10"'Your army includes men from far-off Paras, Lud, and Put. They serve you—it is a feather in your cap to have their shields hang upon your walls; it is the ultimate of honor. 11Men from Arvad and from Helech are the sentinels upon your walls; your towers are manned by men from Gamad. Their shields hang row on row upon the walls, perfecting your glory.

¹²"'From Tarshish come all kinds of riches to your markets—silver, iron, tin, and lead. ¹³Merchants from Javan, Tubal, and Meshech bring slaves and bronze dishes, ¹⁴while from Togarmah come chariot horses, steeds, and mules.

¹⁵"'Merchants come to you from Rhodes, and many coastlands are your captive markets, giving payment in ebony and ivory. ¹⁶Edom sends her traders to buy your many wares. They bring emeralds, purple dyes, embroidery, fine linen, and jewelry of coral and agate. ¹⁷Judah and the cities in what was once the kingdom of Israel send merchants with wheat from Minnith and Pannag, and with honey, oil, and balm. ¹⁸Damascus comes. She brings wines from Helbon and white Syrian wool to trade for all the rich variety of goods you make. ¹⁹Vedan and Javan bring Arabian yarn, wrought iron, cassia, and calamus, ²⁰while Dedan brings expensive saddlecloths for riding.

²¹"'The Arabians and Kedar's wealthy merchant princes bring you lambs and rams and goats. ²²The merchants of Sheba and Raamah come with all kinds of spices, jewels, and gold. ²³Haran, Canneh, Eden, Asshur, and Chilmad all send their wares. ²⁴They bring choice fabrics to trade—blue cloth, embroidery, and many-colored carpets bound with cords and made secure. ²⁵The ships of Tarshish are your ocean caravans; your island warehouse is filled to the brim!

²⁶"'But now your statesmen bring your ship of state into a hurricane! Your mighty vessel flounders in the heavy eastern gale, and you are wrecked in the heart of the seas! ²⁷Everything is lost. Your riches and wares, your sailors and pilots, your shipwrights, merchants, and soldiers; and all the people sink into the sea on the day of your vast ruin.

²⁸"'The surrounding cities quake at the sound as your pilots scream with fright. ²⁹All your sailors out at sea come to land and watch upon the mainland shore, ³⁰weeping bitterly and casting dust upon their heads and wallowing in ashes. ³¹They shave their heads in grief, put on sackcloth, and weep for you with bitterness of heart and deep mourning.

³²"'And this is the song of their sorrow; "Where in all the world was there ever such a wondrous city as Tyre, destroyed in the midst of the sea? ³³Your merchandise satisfied the desires of many nations. Kings at the ends of the earth rejoiced in the riches you sent them. ³⁴Now you lie broken beneath the sea; all your merchandise and all your crew have perished with you. ³⁵All who live along the coastlands watch, incredulous. Their kings are horribly afraid and look on with twisted faces.

³⁶The merchants of the nations shake their heads, for your fate is dreadful; you have forever perished."'"

28 A Proud King Will Fall

Here is another message given to me from the Lord:

²,³"Son of dust, say to the prince of Tyre, 'The Lord God says: You are so proud you think you are God, sitting on the throne of a god on your island home in the midst of the seas. But you are only a man and not a god, though you boast yourself to be like God. You are wiser than Daniel, for no secret is hidden from you. ⁴You have used your wisdom and understanding to get great wealth—gold and silver and many treasures. ⁵Yes, your wisdom has made you very rich and very proud."

⁶Therefore the Lord God says: "Because you claim that you are as wise as God, ⁷an enemy army, the terror of the nations, shall suddenly draw their swords against your marvelous wisdom and defile your splendor! ⁸They will bring you to the pit of hell, and you shall die as those pierced with many wounds, there on your island in the heart of the seas. ⁹Then will you boast as a god? At least to these invaders you will be no god, but merely man! ¹⁰ You will die like an outcast at the hands of foreigners. For I have spoken it," the Lord God says.

¹¹Then this further message came to me from the Lord:

¹²"Son of dust, weep for the king of Tyre. Tell him, 'The Lord God says: You were the perfection of wisdom and beauty. ¹³You were in Eden, the garden of God; your clothing was bejeweled with every precious stone—ruby, topaz, diamond, chrysolite, onyx, jasper, sapphire, carbuncle, and emerald—all in beautiful settings of finest gold. They were given to you on the day you were created. ¹⁴I appointed you to be the anointed Guardian Angel. You had access to the holy mountain of God. You walked among the stones of fire.

¹⁵"'You were perfect in all you did from the day you were created until that time when wrong was found in you. ¹⁶Your great wealth filled you with internal turmoil, and you sinned. Therefore, I cast you out of the mountain of God like a common sinner. I destroyed you, O Guardian Angel, from the midst of the stones of fire. ¹⁷Your heart was filled with pride because of all your beauty; you corrupted your wisdom for the sake of your splendor. Therefore, I have cast you down to the ground and exposed you helpless before the curious gaze of kings. ¹⁸You defiled your holiness with lust for gain; therefore, I brought forth fire from your own actions and let it burn you to ashes upon the earth in the sight of all those

watching you. ¹⁹All who know you are appalled at your fate; you are an example of horror; you are destroyed forever.'"

²⁰Then another message came to me from the Lord:

²¹"Son of dust, look toward the city of Sidon and prophesy against it. Say to it, ²²'The Lord God says: I am your enemy, O Sidon, and I will reveal my power over you. When I destroy you and show forth my holiness upon you, then all who see shall know I am the Lord. ²³I will send an epidemic of disease and an army to destroy; the wounded shall be slain in your streets by troops on every side. Then you will know I am the Lord. ²⁴No longer shall you and Israel's other neighbor nations prick and tear at Israel like thorns and briars, though they formerly despised her and treated her with great contempt.

²⁵"'The people of Israel will once more live in their own land, the land I gave their father Jacob. For I will gather them back again from distant lands where I have scattered them, and I will show the nations of the world my holiness among my people. ²⁶They will live safely in Israel and build their homes and plant their vineyards. When I punish all the bordering nations that treated them with such contempt, then they shall know I am the Lord their God.'"

29 A King like a Dragon

Late in December of the tenth year (of the imprisonment of King Jehoiachin), this message came to me from the Lord:

²"Son of dust, face toward Egypt and prophesy against Pharaoh her king and all her people. ³Tell them that the Lord God says: 'I am your enemy, Pharaoh, king of Egypt—mighty dragon lying in the middle of your rivers. For you have said, "The Nile is mine; I have made it for myself!" ⁴I will put hooks into your jaws and drag you out onto the land with fish sticking to your scales. ⁵And I will leave you and all the fish stranded in the desert to die, and you won't be buried, for I have given you as food to the wild animals and birds.

⁶"'Because of the way your might collapsed when Israel called on you for aid [instead of trusting me], all of you shall know I am the Lord. ⁷Israel leaned on you but, like a cracked staff, you snapped beneath her hand and wrenched her shoulder out of joint and made her stagger with the pain. ⁸Therefore the Lord God says: I will bring an army against you, O Egypt, and destroy both men and herds. ⁹The land of Egypt shall become a desolate wasteland, and the Egyptians will know that I, the Lord, have done it.

¹⁰"'Because you said: "The Nile is mine! I made it!" therefore I am against you and your river, and I will utterly destroy the land of Egypt, from Migdol to Syene, as far south as the border of Ethiopia. ¹¹For forty years not a soul will pass that way, neither men nor animals. It will be completely uninhabited. ¹²I will make Egypt desolate, surrounded by desolate nations, and her cities will lie as wastelands for forty years. I will exile the Egyptians to other lands.

¹³"'But the Lord God says that at the end of the forty years he will bring the Egyptians home again from the nations to which they will be banished. ¹⁴And I will restore the fortunes of Egypt and bring her people back to the land of Pathros in southern Egypt where they were born, but she will be an unimportant, minor kingdom. ¹⁵She will be the lowliest of all the nations; never again will she raise herself above the other nations; never again will Egypt be great enough for that.

¹⁶"'Israel will no longer expect any help from Egypt. Whenever she thinks of asking for it, then she will remember her sin in seeking it before. Then Israel will know that I alone am God.'"

¹⁷In the twenty-seventh year of King Jehoiachin's captivity, around the middle of March, this message came to me from the Lord:

¹⁸"Son of dust, the army of King Nebuchadnezzar of Babylon fought hard against Tyre. The soldiers' heads were bald (from carrying heavy basketfuls of earth); their shoulders were raw and blistered (from burdens of stones for the siege). And Nebuchadnezzar received no compensation and could not pay the army for all this work." ¹⁹Therefore, the Lord God says, "I will give the land of Egypt to Nebuchadnezzar, king of Babylon, and he will carry off her wealth, plundering everything she has, for his army. ²⁰Yes, I have given him the land of Egypt for his salary because he was working for me during those thirteen years at Tyre," says the Lord. ²¹"And the day will come when I will cause the ancient glory of Israel to revive, and then at last her words will be respected, and Egypt shall know I am the Lord."

30 A Day of Clouds and Gloom

Another message from the Lord!

²,³"Son of dust, prophesy and say: The Lord God says, 'Weep, for the terrible day is almost here; the day of the Lord; a day of clouds and gloom; a day of despair for the nations! ⁴A sword shall fall on Egypt; the slain shall cover the ground. Her wealth is taken away, her foundations destroyed. The land of Cush has been ravished. ⁵For Cush, Put, Lud, Arabia, and Libya, and all the countries leagued with them shall perish in that war.'

⁶For the Lord says: "All Egypt's allies shall fall, and the pride of her power shall end. From Migdol to Syene they shall perish by the sword. ⁷She

shall be desolate, surrounded by desolate nations, and her cities shall be in ruins, surrounded by other ruined cities. ⁸And they will know I am the Lord when I have set Egypt on fire and destroyed her allies. ⁹At that time I will send swift messengers to bring panic to the Ethiopians; great terror shall befall them at that time of Egypt's doom. This will all come true.

¹⁰For the Lord God says: "Nebuchadnezzar, king of Babylon, will destroy the multitudes of Egypt. ¹¹He and his armies—the terror of the nations—are sent to demolish the land. They shall war against Egypt and cover the ground with the slain. ¹²I will dry up the Nile and sell the whole land to wicked men. I will destroy Egypt and everything in it, using foreigners to do it. I, the Lord, have spoken it.

¹³"And I will smash the idols of Egypt and the images at Memphis, and there will be no king in Egypt; anarchy shall reign!

¹⁴"The cities of Pathros [along the upper Nile], Zoan, and Thebes shall lie in ruins by my hand. ¹⁵And I will pour out my fury upon Pelusium, the strongest fortress of Egypt, and I will stamp out the people of Thebes. ¹⁶Yes, I will set fire to Egypt; Pelusium will be racked with pain. Thebes will be torn apart; Memphis will be in daily terror. ¹⁷The young men of Heliopolis and Bubastis shall die by the sword, and the women will be taken away as slaves. ¹⁸When I come to break the power of Egypt, it will be a dark day for Tahpanhes too; a dark cloud will cover her, and her daughters will be taken away as captives. ¹⁹And so I will greatly punish Egypt and they shall know I am the Lord."

²⁰A year later, around the middle of March of the eleventh year of King Jehoiachin's captivity, this message came to me:

²¹"Son of dust, I have broken the arm of Pharaoh, king of Egypt, and it has not been set nor put into a cast to make it strong enough to hold a sword again. ²²For the Lord God says, I am against Pharaoh, king of Egypt, and I will break both his arms—the strong one and the one that was broken before, and I will make his sword clatter to the ground. ²³And I will banish the Egyptians to many lands. ²⁴And I will strengthen the arms of the king of Babylon and place my sword in his hand. But I will break the arms of Pharaoh, king of Egypt, and he shall groan before the king of Babylon as one who has been wounded unto death. ²⁵I will strengthen the hands of the king of Babylon, while the arms of Pharaoh fall useless to his sides. Yes, when I place my sword into the hand of the king of Babylon, and he swings it over the land of Egypt, Egypt shall know I am the Lord. ²⁶I will scatter the Egyptians among the nations; then they shall know I am the Lord."

31 A Magnificent Tree Cut Down

In mid-May of the eleventh year of King Jehoiachin's captivity, this message came to me from the Lord:

²,³"Son of dust, tell Pharaoh, king of Egypt, and all his people: 'You are as Assyria was—a great and mighty nation—like a cedar of Lebanon, full of thick branches and forest shade, with its head high up among the clouds. ⁴Its roots went deep into the moist earth. It grew luxuriantly and gave streamlets of water to all the trees around. ⁵It towered above all the other trees. It prospered and grew long thick branches because of all the water at its roots. ⁶The birds nested in its branches, and in its shade the flocks and herds gave birth to young. All the great nations of the world lived beneath its shadow. ⁷It was strong and beautiful, for its roots went deep to water. ⁸This tree was taller than any other in the garden of God; no cypress had branches equal to it; none had boughs to compare; none equaled it in beauty. ⁹Because of the magnificence that I gave it, it was the envy of all the other trees of Eden.'

¹⁰"But Egypt has become proud and arrogant", the Lord God says. "Therefore because she has set herself so high above the others, reaching to the clouds, ¹¹I will deliver her into the hands of a mighty nation, to destroy her as her wickedness deserves. I, myself, will cut her down. ¹²A foreign army (from Babylon)—the terror of the nations—will invade her land and cut her down and leave her fallen on the ground. Her branches will be scattered across the mountains and valleys and rivers of the land. All those who live beneath her shade will go away and leave her lying there. ¹³The birds will pluck off her twigs, and the wild animals will lie among her branches; ¹⁴let no other nation exult with pride for its own prosperity, though it be higher than the clouds, for all are doomed, and they will land in hell along with all the proud men of the world."

¹⁵The Lord God says: "When she fell, I made the oceans mourn for her and restrained their tides. I clothed Lebanon in black and caused the trees of Lebanon to weep. ¹⁶I made the nations shake with fear at the sound of her fall, for I threw her down to hell with all the others like her. And all the other proud trees of Eden, the choicest and the best of Lebanon, the ones whose roots went deep into the water, are comforted to find her there with them in hell. ¹⁷Her allies, too, are all destroyed and perish with her. They went down with her to the nether world—those nations that had lived beneath her shade.

¹⁸"O Egypt, you are great and glorious among the trees of Eden—the nations of the world. And you will be brought down to the pit of hell with

all these other nations. You will be among the nations you despise, killed by the sword. This is the fate of Pharaoh and all his teeming masses," says the Lord.

32 Lion or Crocodile?

In mid-February of the twelfth year of King Jehoiachin's captivity, this message came to me from the Lord:

2"Son of dust, mourn for Pharaoh, king of Egypt and say to him: 'You think of yourself as a strong young lion among the nations, but you are merely a crocodile along the banks of the Nile, making bubbles and muddying the stream.'"

3The Lord God says: "I will send a great army to catch you with my net. I will haul you out 4and leave you stranded on the land to die. And all the birds of the heavens will light upon you, and the wild animals of the whole earth will devour you until they are glutted and full. 5And I will cover the hills with your flesh and fill the valleys with your bones. 6And I will drench the earth with your gushing blood, filling the ravines to the tops of the mountains. 7I will blot you out, and I will veil the heavens and darken the stars. I will cover the sun with a cloud, and the moon shall not give you her light. 8Yes, darkness will be everywhere across your land—even the bright stars will be dark above you.

9"And when I destroy you, grief will be in many hearts among the distant nations you have never seen. 10Yes, terror shall strike in many lands, and their kings shall be terribly afraid because of all I do to you. They shall shudder with terror when I brandish my sword before them. They shall greatly tremble for their lives on the day of your fall.

11For the Lord God says: "The sword of the king of Babylon shall come upon you. 12I will destroy you with Babylon's mighty army—the terror of the nations. It will smash the pride of Egypt and all her people; all will perish. 13I will destroy all your flocks and herds that graze beside the streams, and neither man nor animal will disturb those waters any more. 14Therefore, the waters of Egypt will be as clear and flow as smoothly as olive oil," the Lord God says. 15"And when I destroy Egypt and wipe out everything she has, then she shall know that I, the Lord, have done it. 16Yes, cry for the sorrows of Egypt. Let all the nations weep for her and for her people," says the Lord.

17Two weeks later, another message came to me from the Lord. He said:

18"Son of dust, weep for the people of Egypt and for the other mighty nations. Send them down to the nether world among the denizens of death. 19What nation is as beautiful as you, O Egypt? Yet your doom is the pit; you will be laid beside the people you despise. 20The Egyptians will die with the multitudes slain by the sword, for the sword is drawn against the land of Egypt. She will be drawn down to judgment. 21The mighty warriors in the nether world will welcome her as she arrives with all her friends, to lie there beside the nations she despised, all victims of the sword.

22"The princes of Assyria lie there surrounded by the graves of all her people, those the sword has slain. 23Their graves are in the depths of hell, surrounded by their allies. All these mighty men who once struck terror into the hearts of everyone are now dead at the hands of their foes.

24"Great kings of Elam lie there with their people. They scourged the nations while they lived, and now they lie undone in hell; their fate is the same as that of ordinary men. 25They have a resting place among the slain, surrounded by the graves of all their people. Yes, they terrorized the nations while they lived, but now they lie in shame in the pit, slain by the sword.

26"The princes of Meshech and Tubal are there, surrounded by the graves of all their armies—all of them idolaters—who once struck terror to the hearts of all; now they lie dead. 27They are buried in a common grave and not as the fallen lords who are buried in great honor with their weapons beside them, with their shields covering them and their swords beneath their heads. They were a terror to all while they lived. 28Now you will lie crushed and broken among the idolaters, among those who are slain by the sword.

29"Edom is there with her kings and her princes; mighty as they were, they too lie among the others whom the sword has slain, with the idolaters who have gone down to the pit. 30All the princes of the north are there and the Sidonians, all slain. Once a terror, now they lie in shame; they lie in ignominy with all the other slain who go down to the pit.

31"When Pharaoh arrives, he will be comforted to find that he is not alone in having all his army slain," says the Lord God. 32"For I have caused my terror to fall upon all the living. And Pharaoh and his army shall lie among the idolaters who are slain by the sword."

33 God Will Be the Judge

Once again a message came to me from the Lord. He said:

2"Son of dust, tell your people: 'When I bring an army against a country, and the people of that land choose a watchman, 3and when he sees the army coming and blows the alarm to warn them, 4then anyone who hears the alarm but refuses to

FAMILY DEVOTIONS

☐ DEVOTION 232
RESPECTING GOD'S WARNINGS

Read Ezekiel 33:1-5

"I still don't see why I have to go!" Shanna slammed the car door. "Why can't I take care of Shawn at home? Why do I have to baby-sit in a waiting room?"

Mom shook her head. "I've explained that we're going to Grandma's house right after we visit Aunt Ruth in the hospital. It would take too long to come back home for you."

Shanna snorted and then went to her room and pouted. At the hospital, she rummaged through the magazines on a table and then picked up one she knew her parents would never allow her to read at home.

"Read your story out loud to me," Shawn begged.

Shanna grinned slyly. "I don't think so." She handed him another magazine. "Here, you look at the pictures." She was so engrossed in her reading that she jumped when a voice at her shoulder said, "Time to go, Shanna."

"Huh? Time to go?" Shanna asked quickly. "How is she?"

"Well, even though she has cancer," Dad replied, "she'll probably be fine. Because she went to the doctor at the first warning symptom, they found it in the early stages."

Shanna let out a big sigh. "Oh, that's good."

"It's important to heed early warnings," Mom said as they entered the empty elevator. "I see some danger signals in your life, Shanna." Shanna hung her head, and Mom continued, "Your attitude for one thing, and your reading material for another, tell me that you need a spiritual checkup. Sin is like a dreadful cancer."

As Shanna wiped a tear from her cheek, Dad spoke up. "Heeding a physical warning symptom may have saved Aunt Ruth's life. Heeding spiritual warnings could save you lots of trouble."

Respecting God's Warnings
Memory Verse

If my people will humble themselves and pray, and search for me, and turn from their wicked ways, I will hear them from heaven and forgive their sins and heal their land.
2 Chronicles 7:14

How About You?
Have you been warned about your attitude or actions lately? Did you resent it? It could be a blessing in disguise. An early warning could save you from trouble later. Work on the problem area in your life today. *B. W.*

• For the next devotional, turn to page 803. • For the next devotional on RESPECTING GOD'S WARNINGS, turn to page 867. • For notes on RESPECTING GOD'S WARNINGS, see pages 219, 874, and 1126.

heed it—well, if he dies, the fault is his own. ⁵For he heard the warning and wouldn't listen; the fault is his. If he had heeded the warning, he would have saved his life. ⁶But if the watchman sees the enemy coming and doesn't sound the alarm and warn the people, he is responsible for their deaths. They will die in their sins, but I will charge the watchman with their deaths.'

⁷"So with you, son of dust. I have appointed you as a watchman for the people of Israel; therefore, listen to what I say and warn them for me. ⁸When I say to the wicked, 'O wicked man, you will die!' and you don't tell him what I say, so that he does not repent—that wicked person will die in his sins, but I will hold you responsible for his death. ⁹But if you warn him to repent and he doesn't, he will die in his sin, and you will not be responsible.

¹⁰"O people of Israel, you are saying: 'Our sins are heavy upon us; we pine away with guilt. How can we live?' ¹¹Tell them: 'As I live, says the Lord God, I have no pleasure in the death of the wicked; *I desire that the wicked turn from his evil ways and live.* Turn, turn from your wickedness, for why will you die, O Israel? ¹²For the good works of a righteous man will not save him if he turns to sin; and the sins of an evil man will not destroy him if he repents and turns from his sins.'

¹³"I have said the good man will live. But if he sins, expecting his past goodness to save him, then none of his good deeds will be remembered. I will destroy him for his sins. ¹⁴And when I tell the wicked he will die, and then he turns from his sins and does what is fair and right— ¹⁵if he gives back the borrower's pledge, returns what he has stolen, and walks along the paths of right, not doing evil— he shall surely live. He shall not die. ¹⁶None of his past sins shall be brought up against him, for he has turned to the good and shall surely live.

¹⁷"And yet your people are saying the Lord isn't fair. The trouble is *they* aren't fair. ¹⁸For again I say, when the good man turns to evil, he shall die. ¹⁹But if the wicked turns from his wickedness and does what's fair and just, he shall live. ²⁰Yet you are saying the Lord isn't fair. But I will judge each of you in accordance with his deeds."

²¹In the eleventh year of our exile, late in December, one of those who escaped from Jerusalem arrived to tell me, "The city has fallen!" ²²Now the hand of the Lord had been upon me the previous evening, and he had healed me so that I could speak again by the time the man arrived.

²³Then this message came to me:

²⁴"Son of dust, the scattered remnants of Judah living among the ruined cities keep saying, 'Abraham was only one man and yet he got possession of the whole country! We are many, so we should certainly be able to get it back!' ²⁵But the Lord God says: 'You are powerless, for you do evil! You eat meat with the blood, you worship idols, and murder. Do you suppose I'll let you have the land? ²⁶Murderers! Idolators! Adulterers! Should you possess the land?'

²⁷"Tell them, 'The Lord God says: As I live, surely those living in the ruins shall die by the sword. Those living in the open fields shall be eaten by wild animals, and those in the forts and caves shall die of disease. ²⁸I will desolate the land and her pride, and her power shall come to an end. And the mountain villages of Israel shall be so ruined that no one will even travel through them. ²⁹When I have ruined the land because of their sins, then they shall know I am the Lord.'

³⁰"Son of dust, your people are whispering behind your back. They talk about you in their houses and whisper about you at the doors, saying, 'Come on, let's have some fun! Let's go hear him tell us what the Lord is saying!' ³¹So they come as though they are sincere and sit before you listening. But they have no intention of doing what I tell them to; they talk very sweetly about loving the Lord, but with their hearts they are loving their money. ³²You are very entertaining to them, like someone who sings lovely songs with a beautiful voice or plays well on an instrument. They hear what you say but don't pay any attention to it! ³³But when all these terrible things happen to them—as they will—then they will know a prophet has been among them."

34 God's Flock

Then this message came to me from the Lord:

²"Son of dust, prophesy against the shepherds, the leaders of Israel. Say to them, 'The Lord God says to you: Woe to the shepherds who feed themselves instead of their flocks. Shouldn't shepherds feed the sheep? ³You eat the best food and wear the finest clothes, but you let your flocks starve. ⁴You haven't taken care of the weak, nor tended the sick, nor bound up the broken bones, nor gone looking for those who have wandered away and are lost. Instead, you have ruled them with force and cruelty. ⁵So they were scattered, without a shepherd. They have become a prey to every animal that comes along. ⁶My sheep wandered through the mountains and hills and over the face of the earth, and there was no one to search for them or care about them.

⁷"'Therefore, O shepherds, hear the word of the Lord: ⁸As I live, says the Lord God, you abandoned my flock, leaving them to be attacked and destroyed, and you were no real shepherds at all, for you didn't search for them. You fed yourselves and let them starve; ⁹,¹⁰therefore, I am against the shepherds, and I will hold them responsible for

Family Devotions

☐ DEVOTION 233
BECOMING MORE LIKE JESUS

Read Ezekiel 34:23-31

One day, after Todd had helped his uncle pick apples for a couple of hours, he was resting beneath one of the trees when Uncle Mike came and sat next to him. "Ahhh!" exclaimed Uncle Mike, stretching. "A few minutes of rest sure sounds like a good idea. Here, how about having an apple?"

"No thanks, Uncle Mike," Todd replied. "I've been eating so many apples today, I can't look at another one. I've just been sitting here thinking. Why does a tree grow leaves as well as apples? You can't eat the leaves, and if there weren't leaves, there'd be more room for apples."

"Oh, but Todd, without the leaves there would be no apples," Uncle Mike stated.

"Really? I didn't know that! Are you sure?" Todd wanted to know.

"Oh, yes. Very sure," came his uncle's reply. "You see, Todd, the leaves absorb the sunshine and the rain, which then flow through the leaves, into the branch, and out into the fruit."

"How about that!" Todd exclaimed. "I probably heard that in school, but I'd forgotten it."

"Here's something else that's important," Todd's uncle continued. "Just as leaves soak up the sun, spelled s-u-n, in order to bear fruit, we need the Son, S-o-n, if we are to produce any fruit in our lives."

"Now you lost me, Uncle Mike. What do you mean?"

"Many people try their best to live good lives and do good things," explained Uncle Mike, "but without Jesus, the Son of God, their fruit—or good living—is worthless. Jesus told his disciples that without him they could do nothing. We need Jesus Christ living in our hearts and lives. That's why it's important to accept him as Savior while we're young and then learn all we can about him as we grow up. He can help us live the way we ought to."

Becoming More Like Jesus Memory Verse

Let everything you do reflect your love of the truth and the fact that you are in dead earnest about it.
Titus 2:7

How About You?

Do you think you can get along without the Son of God? Do you try to produce fruit, or good deeds, in your own strength? You can do nothing good by yourself. You need God's Son, Jesus. C. V. M.

• For the next devotional, turn to page 805. • For the next devotional on BECOMING MORE LIKE JESUS, turn to page 849. • For notes on BECOMING MORE LIKE JESUS, see pages 234, 983, 1105, and 1164.

what has happened to my flock. I will take away their right to feed the flock—and take away their right to eat. I will save my flock from being taken for their food.'"

[11]For the Lord God says: "I will search and find my sheep. [12]I will be like a shepherd looking for his flock. I will find my sheep and rescue them from all the places they were scattered in that dark and cloudy day. [13]And I will bring them back from among the people and nations where they were, back home to their own land of Israel, and I will feed them upon the mountains of Israel and by the rivers where the land is fertile and good. [14]Yes, I will give them good pasture on the high hills of Israel. There they will lie down in peace and feed in luscious mountain pastures. [15,16]I myself will be the Shepherd of my sheep and cause them to lie down in peace," the Lord God says. "I will seek my lost ones, those who strayed away, and bring them safely home again. I will put splints and bandages upon their broken limbs and heal the sick. And I will destroy the powerful, fat shepherds; I will feed them, yes—feed them punishment!

[17]"And as for you, O my flock—my people," the Lord God says, "I will judge you and separate good from bad, sheep from goats.

[18]"Is it a small thing to you, O evil shepherds, that you not only keep the best of the pastures for yourselves, but trample down the rest? That you take the best water for yourselves and muddy the rest with your feet? [19]All that's left for my flock is what you've trampled down; all they have to drink is water that you've fouled."

[20]Therefore the Lord God says: "I will surely judge between these fat shepherds and their scrawny sheep. [21]For these shepherds push and butt and crowd my sick and hungry flock until they're scattered far away. [22]So I myself will save my flock; no more will they be picked on and destroyed. And I will notice which is plump and which is thin, and why!

[23]"And I will set one Shepherd over all my people, even my Servant David. He shall feed them and be a Shepherd to them.

[24]"And I, the Lord, will be their God, and my Servant David shall be a Prince among my people. I, the Lord, have spoken it.

[25]"I will make a peace pact with them and drive away the dangerous animals from the land, so that my people can safely camp in the wildest places and sleep safely in the woods. [26]I will make my people and their homes around my hill a blessing. And there shall be showers, showers of blessing, for I will not shut off the rains but send them in their seasons. [27]Their fruit trees and fields will yield bumper crops, and everyone will live in safety. When I have broken off their chains of slavery and delivered them from those who profiteered at their expense, they shall know I am the Lord. [28]No more will other nations conquer them nor wild animals attack. They shall live in safety and no one shall make them afraid.

[29]"And I will raise up a notable Vine [the Messiah], in Israel so that my people will never again go hungry nor be shamed by heathen conquest. [30]In this way they will know that I, the Lord their God, am with them, and that they, the people of Israel, are my people," says the Lord God. [31]"You are my flock, the sheep of my pasture. You are my men and I am your God, so says the Lord."

35 Edom Will Be Ruined

Again a message came from the Lord. He said:

[2]"Son of dust, face toward Mount Seir and prophesy against the people saying, [3]'The Lord God says: I am against you, and I will smash you with my fist and utterly destroy you. [4,5]Because you hate my people Israel, I will demolish your cities and make you desolate, and then you shall know I am the Lord. You butchered my people when they were helpless, when I had punished them for all their sins. [6]As I live, the Lord God says, since you enjoy blood so much, I will give you a blood bath—your turn has come! [7]I will utterly wipe out the people of Mount Seir, killing off all those who try to escape and all those who return. [8]I will fill your mountains with the dead—your hills, your valleys, and your rivers will be filled with those the sword has killed. [9]Never again will you revive. You will be abandoned forever; your cities will never be rebuilt. Then you shall know I am the Lord.

[10]"'For you said, "Both Israel and Judah shall be mine. We will take possession of them. What do we care that God is there!" [11]Therefore as I live, the Lord God says, I will pay back your angry deeds with mine—I will punish you for all your acts of envy and of hate. And I will honor my name in Israel by what I do to you. [12]And you shall know that I have heard each evil word you spoke against the Lord, saying, "His people are helpless; they are food for us to eat!" [13]Saying that, you boasted great words against the Lord. And I have heard them all!

[14]"'The whole world will rejoice when I make you desolate. [15]You rejoiced at Israel's fearful fate. Now I will rejoice at yours! You will be wiped out, O people of Mount Seir and all who live in Edom! And then you will know I am the Lord!'

36 A Promise of Good Times

"Son of dust, prophesy to Israel's mountains. Tell them: 'Listen to this message from the Lord.

Family Devotions

☐ DEVOTION 234
AVOIDING SIN

Read Ezekiel 36:25-27

It was the day before rubbish pickup, and Dad was helping Jimmy with his chores. "I hate this job," said Jimmy as he put the clean cans in one container and the clean plastic bottles in another.

"It would be easier if you wouldn't let things pile up for a whole week," replied Dad.

"I liked it better when we just threw everything into one big plastic bag," grumbled Jimmy.

"Well, if we don't recycle what we can, soon there won't be any more room in the landfills," Dad told him.

Jimmy nodded. "I know," he said. "Our school bus goes past a landfill every day. There's a big mountain of rubbish. The kids on the bus call it Mount Trashmore!"

Dad pointed to a brown paper bag. "What's that stuff over there?"

"Oh, . . . well, those are things I wasn't sure how to sort," Jimmy mumbled, "but I'll figure it out."

"Let's see," said Dad. *"Hmmmm.* Records, some tapes, and magazines. Whoa! These magazines really are trash! Have you been reading these?"

"Some of the guys gave them to me," replied Jimmy. He was embarrassed.

"Do you enjoy these things?" asked Dad.

"At first I thought it was pretty neat and grown-up to read them," admitted Jimmy, "but then I didn't like what I kept thinking about. I'm throwing the stuff out, and I'm not taking any more."

"I'm glad," said Dad. "Things such as this could cause your mind and heart to become so full of trash it would crowd out God."

Avoiding Sin Memory Verse

How can a young man stay pure? By reading your Word and following its rules.
Psalm 119:9

How About You?

Have you thrown out all the trash in your life? Make sure your books, magazines, tapes, and TV shows are not the wrong kind. Ask God to tell you what to get rid of. He'll guide you as you pray and read the Bible. Don't build a Mount Trashmore in your life. H. A. D.

• For the next devotional, turn to page 819. • For the next devotional on AVOIDING SIN, turn to page 819. • For notes on AVOIDING SIN, see pages 220, 332, 392, and 657.

2"'Your enemies have sneered at you and claimed your ancient heights as theirs; ³they have destroyed you on every side and sent you away as slaves to many lands. You are mocked and slandered. ⁴Therefore, O mountains of Israel, hear the word of the Lord God. He says to the hills and mountains, dales and valleys, and to the ruined farms and the long-deserted cities, destroyed and mocked by heathen nations all around: ⁵My anger is afire against these nations, especially Edom, for grabbing my land with relish, in utter contempt for me, to take it for themselves.'

⁶"Therefore prophesy and say to the hills and mountains, dales and valleys of Israel: 'The Lord God says, I am full of fury because you suffered shame before the surrounding nations. ⁷Therefore, I have sworn with hand held high that those nations are going to have their turn of being covered with shame,⁸but for Israel good times will return. There will be heavy crops of fruit to prepare for my people's return—and they will be coming home again soon! ⁹See, I am for you, and I will come and help you as you prepare the ground and sow your crops. ¹⁰I will greatly increase your population throughout all Israel, and the ruined cities will be rebuilt and filled with people. ¹¹Not only the people, but your flocks and herds will also greatly multiply. O mountains of Israel, again you will be filled with homes. I will do even more for you than I did before. Then you shall know I am the Lord. ¹²My people will walk upon you once again, and you will belong to them again; and you will no longer be a place for burning their children on idol altars.'"

¹³The Lord God says: "Now the other nations taunt you, saying, 'Israel is a land that devours her people!' ¹⁴But they will not say this any more. Your birth rate will rise, and your infant mortality rate will drop off sharply," says the Lord. ¹⁵"No longer will those heathen nations sneer, for you will no longer be a nation of sinners," the Lord God says.

¹⁶Then this further word came to me from the Lord:

¹⁷"Son of dust, when the people of Israel were living in their own country, they defiled it by their evil deeds; to me their worship was as foul as filthy rags. ¹⁸They polluted the land with murder and with the worshiping of idols, so I poured out my fury upon them. ¹⁹And I exiled them to many lands; that is how I punished them for the evil way they lived. ²⁰But when they were scattered out among the nations, then they were a blight upon my holy name because the nations said, 'These are the people of God and he couldn't protect them from harm!' ²¹I am concerned about my reputation that was ruined by my people throughout the world.

²²"Therefore say to the people of Israel, 'The Lord God says: I am bringing you back again, but not because you deserve it; I am doing it to protect my holy name, which you tarnished among the nations. ²³I will honor my great name, that you defiled, and the people of the world shall know I am the Lord. I will be honored before their eyes by delivering you from exile among them. ²⁴For I will bring you back home again to the land of Israel.

²⁵"'Then it will be as though I had sprinkled clean water on you, for you will be clean—your filthiness will be washed away, your idol worship gone. ²⁶And I will give you a new heart—I will give you new and right desires—and put a new spirit within you. I will take out your stony hearts of sin and give you new hearts of love. ²⁷And I will put my Spirit within you so that you will obey my laws and do whatever I command.

²⁸"'And you shall live in Israel, the land which I gave your fathers long ago. And you shall be my people, and I will be your God. ²⁹I will cleanse away your sins. I will abolish crop failures and famine. ³⁰I will give you huge harvests from your fruit trees and fields, and never again will the surrounding nations be able to scoff at your land for its famines. ³¹Then you will remember your past sins and loathe yourselves for all the evils you did. ³²But always remember this: It is not for your own sakes that I will do this, but for mine. O my people Israel, be utterly ashamed of all that you have done!'

³³The Lord God says: "When I cleanse you from your sins, I will bring you home again to Israel, and rebuild the ruins. ³⁴Acreage will be cultivated again that through the years of exile lay empty as a barren wilderness; all who passed by were shocked to see the extent of ruin in your land. ³⁵But when I bring you back, they will say, 'This God-forsaken land has become like Eden's garden! The ruined cities are rebuilt and walled and filled with people!' ³⁶Then the nations all around—all those still left—will know that I, the Lord, rebuilt the ruins and planted lush crops in the wilderness. For I, the Lord, have promised it, and I will do it."

³⁷,³⁸The Lord God says: "I am ready to hear Israel's prayers for these blessings and to grant them their requests. Let them but ask, and I will multiply them like the flocks that fill Jerusalem's streets at time of sacrifice. The ruined cities will be crowded once more, and everyone will know I am the Lord."

37 Dried Bones

The power of the Lord was upon me and I was carried away by the Spirit of the Lord to a valley full of old, dry bones that were scattered everywhere across the ground. He led me around among them, ³and then he said to me:

"Son of dust, can these bones become people again?"

I replied, "Lord, you alone know the answer to that."

⁴Then he told me to speak to the bones and say: "O dry bones, listen to the words of God, ⁵for the Lord God says, 'See! I am going to make you live and breathe again! ⁶I will replace the flesh and muscles on you and cover you with skin. I will put breath into you, and you shall live and know I am the Lord.'"

⁷So I spoke these words from God, just as he told me to; and suddenly there was a rattling noise from all across the valley, and the bones of each body came together and attached to each other as they used to be. ⁸Then, as I watched, the muscles and flesh formed over the bones, and skin covered them, but the bodies had no breath. ⁹Then he told me to call to the wind and say: "The Lord God says: Come from the four winds, O Spirit, and breathe upon these slain bodies, that they may live again." ¹⁰So I spoke to the winds as he commanded me, and the bodies began breathing; they lived and stood up—a very great army.

¹¹Then he told me what the vision meant: "These bones," he said, "represent all the people of Israel. They say: 'We have become a heap of dried-out bones—all hope is gone.' ¹²But tell them, 'The Lord God says: My people, I will open your graves of exile and cause you to rise again and return to the land of Israel. ¹³And, then at last, O my people, you will know I am the Lord. ¹⁴I will put my Spirit into you, and you shall live and return home again to your own land. Then you will know that I, the Lord, have done just what I promised you.'"

¹⁵Again a message from the Lord came to me, saying:

¹⁶"Take a stick and carve on it these words: 'This stick represents Judah and her allied tribes.' Then take another stick and carve these words on it: 'This stick represents all the other tribes of Israel.' ¹⁷Now hold them together in your hand as one stick. ¹⁸⁻²⁰Tell these people (holding the sticks so they can see what you are doing), the Lord God says: 'I will take the tribes of Israel and join them to Judah and make them one stick in my hand.'

²¹For the Lord God says. "I am gathering the people of Israel from among the nations and bringing them home from around the world to their own land, ²²to unify them into one nation. One king shall be king of them all; no longer shall they be divided into two nations. ²³They shall stop polluting themselves with idols and their other sins, for I will save them from all this foulness. Then they shall truly be my people and I their God.

²⁴"And David, my Servant—the Messiah—shall be their King, their only Shepherd; and they shall obey my laws and all my wishes. ²⁵They shall live in the land of Israel where their fathers lived, the land I gave my servant Jacob. They and their children after them shall live there, and their grandchildren, for all generations. And my Servant David, their Messiah, shall be their Prince forever. ²⁶And I will make a covenant of peace with them, an everlasting pact. I will bless them and multiply them and put my Temple among them forever. ²⁷And I will make my home among them. Yes, I will be their God, and they shall be my people. ²⁸And when my Temple remains among them forever, then the nations will know that I, the Lord, have chosen Israel as my very own."

38 Ezekiel's Message to Gog

Here is another message to me from the Lord:

²,³"Son of dust, face northward toward the land of Magog and prophesy against Gog king of Meshech and Tubal. Tell him that the Lord God says: 'I am against you, Gog. ⁴I will put hooks into your jaws and pull you to your doom. I will mobilize your troops and armored cavalry and make you a mighty host, all fully armed. ⁵Peras, Cush, Put shall join you too with all their weaponry, ⁶and so shall Gomer and all his hordes and the armies of Togarmah from the distant north, as well as many others. ⁷Be prepared! Stay mobilized. You are their leader, Gog!

⁸"'A long time from now you will be called to action. In distant years you will swoop down onto the land of Israel that will be lying in peace after the return of its people from many lands. ⁹You and all your allies—a vast and awesome army—will roll down upon them like a storm and cover the land like a cloud. ¹⁰For at that time an evil thought will have come to your mind. ¹¹You will have said, "Israel is an unprotected land of unwalled villages! I will march against her and destroy these people living in such confidence! ¹²I will go to those once-desolate cities that are now filled with people again—those who have returned from all the nations—and I will capture vast amounts of loot and many slaves. For the people are rich with cattle now, and the whole earth revolves around them!"

¹³"But Sheba and Dedan and the merchant princes of Tarshish with whom she trades will ask, 'Who are you to rob them of silver and gold and drive away their cattle and seize their goods and make them poor?'"

¹⁴The Lord God says to Gog: "When my people are living in peace in their land, then you will rouse yourself. ¹⁵,¹⁶You will come from all over

the north with your vast host of cavalry and cover the land like a cloud. This will happen in the distant future—in the latter years of history. I will bring you against my land, and my holiness will be vindicated in your terrible destruction before their eyes, so that all the nations will know that I am God."

[17]The Lord God says: "You are the one I spoke of long ago through the prophets of Israel, saying that after many years had passed, I would bring you against my people. [18]But when you come to destroy the land of Israel, my fury will rise! [19]For in my jealousy and blazing wrath, I promise a mighty shaking in the land of Israel on that day. [20]All living things shall quake in terror at my presence; mountains shall be thrown down; cliffs shall tumble; walls shall crumble to the earth. [21]I will summon every kind of terror against you," says the Lord God, "and you will fight against yourselves in mortal combat! [22]I will fight you with sword, disease, torrential floods, great hailstones, fire, and brimstone! [23]Thus will I show my greatness and bring honor upon my name, and all the nations of the world will hear what I have done and know that I am God!

39 God's Holiness

"Son of dust, prophesy this also against Gog. Tell him:

"'I stand against you, Gog, leader of Meshech and Tubal. [2]I will turn you and drive you toward the mountains of Israel, bringing you from the distant north. And I will destroy 85 percent of your army in the mountains. [3]I will knock your weapons from your hands and leave you helpless. [4]You and all your vast armies will die upon the mountains. I will give you to the vultures and wild animals to devour you. [5]You will never reach the cities—you will fall upon the open fields; for I have spoken, the Lord God says. [6]And I will rain down fire on Magog and on all your allies who live safely on the coasts, and they shall know I am the Lord.

[7]"'Thus I will make known my holy name among my people Israel; I will not let it be mocked at anymore. And the nations, too, shall know I am the Lord, the Holy One of Israel. [8]That day of judgment will come; everything will happen just as I have declared it.

[9]"'The people of the cities of Israel will go out and pick up your shields and bucklers, bows and arrows, javelins and spears, to use for fuel—enough to last them seven years. [10]For seven years they will need nothing else for their fires. They won't cut wood from the fields or forests, for these weapons will give them all they need. They will use the possessions of those who abused them.

[11]"'And I will make a vast graveyard for Gog and his armies in the Valley of the Travelers, east of the Dead Sea. It will block the path of the travelers. There Gog and all his armies will be buried. And they will change the name of the place to 'The Valley of Gog's Army.' [12]It will take seven months for the people of Israel to bury the bodies. [13]Everyone in Israel will help, for it will be a glorious victory for Israel on that day when I demonstrate my glory, says the Lord. [14]At the end of the seven months, they will appoint men to search the land systematically for any skeletons left and bury them, so that the land will be cleansed. [15,16]Whenever anyone sees some bones, he will put up a marker beside them so that the buriers will see them and take them to the Valley of Gog's Army to bury them. A city named "Multitude" is there! And so the land will finally be cleansed.'

[17]"And now, son of dust, call all the birds and animals and say to them: 'Gather together for a mighty sacrificial feast. Come from far and near to the mountains of Israel. Come, eat the flesh and drink the blood! [18]Eat the flesh of mighty men and drink the blood of princes—they are the rams, the lambs, the goats, and the fat young bulls of Bashan for my feast! [19]Gorge yourselves with flesh until you are glutted, drink blood until you are drunk; this is the sacrificial feast I have prepared for you. [20]Feast at my banquet table—feast on horses, riders, and valiant warriors, says the Lord God.'

[21]"Thus I will demonstrate my glory among the nations; all shall see the punishment of Gog and know that I have done it. [22]And from that time onward the people of Israel will know I am the Lord their God. [23]And the nations will know why Israel was sent away to exile—it was punishment for sin, for they acted in treachery against their God. Therefore, I turned my face away from them and let their enemies destroy them. [24]I turned my face away and punished them in proportion to the vileness of their sins.

[25]"But now," the Lord God says, "I will end the captivity of my people and have mercy upon them and restore their fortunes, for I am concerned about my reputation! [26]Their time of treachery and shame will all be in the past; they will be home again, in peace and safety in their own land, with no one bothering them or making them afraid. [27]I will bring them home from the lands of their enemies—and my glory shall be evident to all the nations when I do it. Through them I will vindicate my holiness before the nations. [28]Then my people will know I am the Lord their God—responsible for sending them away to exile, and responsible for bringing them home. I will leave none of them remaining among the

nations. ²⁹And I will never hide my face from them again, for I will pour out my Spirit upon them," says the Lord God.

40 The New Temple

Early in April of the twenty-fifth year of our exile—the fourteenth year after Jerusalem was captured—the hand of the Lord was upon me, ²and in a vision he took me to the land of Israel and set me down on a high mountain where I saw what appeared to be a city opposite me. ³Going nearer, I saw a man whose face shone like bronze, standing beside the Temple gate, holding in his hand a measuring tape and a measuring stick.

⁴He said to me: "Son of dust, watch and listen and take to heart everything I show you, for you have been brought here so I can show you many things; and then you are to return to the people of Israel to tell them all you have seen." ⁵ The man began to measure the wall around the outside of the Temple area with his measuring stick, which was 10½ feet long. He told me, "This wall is 10½ feet high and 10½ feet wide." ⁶Then he took me over to the passageway that goes through the eastern wall. We climbed the seven steps into the entrance, and he measured the entry hall of the passage; it was 10½ feet wide.

⁷⁻¹²Walking on through the passageway I saw that there were three guardrooms on each side; each of these rooms was 10½ feet square, with a distance of 8¾ feet along the wall between them. In front of these rooms was a low barrier 18 inches high and 18 inches wide. Beyond the guardrooms was a 10½-foot doorway opening into a 14-foot hall with 3½-foot columns. Beyond this hall, at the inner end of the passageway, was a vestibule 22¾ feet wide and 17½ feet long.

¹³Then he measured the entire outside width of the passageway, measuring across the roof from the outside doors of the guardrooms; this distance was 43¾ feet. ¹⁴Then he estimated the pillars on each side of the porch to be about 100 feet high. ¹⁵The full length of the entrance passage was 87½ feet from one end to the other. ¹⁶There were windows that narrowed inward through the walls along both sides of the passageway and along the guardroom walls. The windows were also in the exit and in the entrance halls. The pillars were decorated with palm tree decorations.

¹⁷And so we passed through the passageway to the court inside. A stone pavement ran around the inside of the walls, and thirty rooms were built against the walls, opening onto this pavement. ¹⁸This was called "the lower pavement." It extended out from the walls into the court the same distance as the passageway did.

¹⁹Then he measured across to the wall on the other side of this court (which was called "the outer court" of the Temple) and found that the distance was 175 feet. ²⁰As I followed, he left the eastern passageway and went over to the passage through the northern wall and measured it. ²¹Here, too, there were three guardrooms on each side, and all the measurements were the same as for the east passageway—87½ feet long and 43¾ feet from side to side across the top of the guardrooms. ²²There were windows, an entry hall, and the palm tree decorations just the same as on the east side. And there were seven steps leading up to the doorway to the entry hall inside.

²³Here at the north entry, just as at the east, if one walked through the passageway into the court and straight across it, he came to an inner wall and a passageway through it to an inner court. The distance between the two passageways was 175 feet. ²⁴Then he took me around to the south gate and measured the various sections of its passageway and found they were just the same as in the others. ²⁵It had windows along the walls as the others did, and an entry hall. And like the others, it was 87½ feet long and 43¾ feet wide. ²⁶It, too, had a stairway of seven steps leading up to it, and there were palm tree decorations along the walls. ²⁷And here again, if one walked through the passageway into the court and straight across it, he came to the inner wall and a passageway through it to the inner court. And the distance between the passageways was 175 feet.

²⁸Then he took me over to the inner wall and its south passageway. He measured this passageway and found that it had the same measurements as the passageways of the outer wall. ²⁹,³⁰ Its guardrooms, pillars, and entrance and exit hall were identical to all the others, and so were the windows along its walls and entry. And, like the others, it was 87½ feet long by 43¾ feet wide. ³¹The only difference was that it had eight steps leading up to it instead of seven. It had palm tree decorations on the pillars, just as the others.

³²Then he took me along the court to the eastern entrance of the inner wall, and measured it. It, too, had the same measurements as the others. ³³Its guardrooms, pillars, and entrance hall were the same size as those of the other passageways, and there were windows along the walls and in the entry hall; and it was 87½ feet long by 43¾ feet wide. ³⁴Its entry hall faced the outer court, and there were palm tree decorations on its columns, but there were eight steps instead of seven going up to the entrance.

³⁵Then he took me around to the north gate of the inner wall, and the measurements there were

just like the others: ³⁶The guardrooms, pillars, and entry hall of this passageway were the same as the others, with a length of 87½ feet and a width of 43¾ feet. ³⁷Its entry hall faced toward the outer court; it had palm tree decorations on the walls of each side of the passageway, and there were eight steps leading up to the entrance.

³⁸But a door led from its entry hall into a side room where the flesh of the sacrifices was washed before being taken to the altar; ³⁹on each side of the entry hall of the passageway there were two tables where the animals for sacrifice were slaughtered for the burnt offerings, sin offerings, and guilt offerings to be presented in the Temple. ⁴⁰Outside the entry hall, on each side of the stairs going up to the north entrance, there were two more tables. ⁴¹So, in all there were eight tables, four inside and four outside, where the sacrifices were cut up and prepared. ⁴²There were also four stone tables where the butchering knives and other implements were laid. These tables were about 2⅝ feet square and 1¾ feet high. ⁴³There were hooks, 3 or 4 inches long, fastened along the walls of the entry hall, and on the tables the flesh of the offering was to be laid.

⁴⁴In the inner court there were two one-room buildings, one beside the northern entrance, facing south, and one beside the southern entrance, facing north.

⁴⁵And he said to me: "The building beside the inner northern gate is for the priests who supervise the maintenance. ⁴⁶The building beside the inner southern entrance is for the priests in charge of the altar—the descendants of Zadok—for they alone of all the Levites may come near to the Lord to minister to him."

⁴⁷Then he measured the inner court [in front of the Temple] and found it to be 175 feet square, and there was an altar in the court, standing in front of the Temple. ⁴⁸,⁴⁹Then he brought me to the entrance hall of the Temple. Ten steps led up to it from the inner court. Its walls extended up on either side to form two pillars, each of them 8¾ feet thick. The entrance was 24½ feet wide with 5¼-foot walls. Thus the entry hall was 35 feet wide and 19¼ feet long.

41 The Holy of Holies

Afterward he brought me into the nave, the large main room of the Temple, and measured the pillars that formed its doorway. They were 10½ feet square. ²The entrance hall was 17½ feet wide and 8¾ feet deep. The nave itself was 70 feet long by 35 feet.

³Then he went into the inner room at the end of the nave and measured the columns at the entrance and found them to be 3½ feet thick; its doorway was 10½ feet wide, with a hallway 12¼ feet deep behind it. ⁴The inner room was 35 feet square. "This," he told me, "is the Most Holy Place."

⁵Then he measured the wall of the Temple and found that it was 10½ feet thick, with a row of rooms along the outside. Each room was 7 feet wide. ⁶These rooms were in three tiers, one above the other, with thirty rooms in each tier. The whole structure was supported by girders and not attached to the Temple wall for support. ⁷Each tier was wider than the one below it, corresponding to the narrowing of the Temple wall as it rose higher. A stairway at the side of the Temple led up from floor to floor.

⁸I noticed that the Temple was built on a terrace and that the bottom row of rooms extended out 10½ feet onto the terrace. ⁹The outer wall of these rooms was 8¾ feet thick, leaving a free space of 8¾ feet out to the edge of the terrace, the same on both sides.

¹⁰Thirty-five feet away from the terrace, on both sides of the Temple, was another row of rooms down in the inner court. ¹¹Two doors opened from the tiers of rooms to the terrace yard, which was 8¾ feet wide; one door faced north and the other south.

¹²A large building stood on the west, facing the Temple yard, measuring 122½ feet wide by 157½ feet long. Its walls were 8¾ feet thick. ¹³Then he measured the Temple and its immediately surrounding yards. The area was 175 feet square. ¹⁴The inner court at the east of the Temple was also 175 feet wide, ¹⁵,¹⁶and so was the building west of the Temple, including its two walls.

The nave of the Temple and the Holy of Holies and the entry hall were paneled, and all three had recessed windows. The inner walls of the Temple were paneled with wood above and below the windows. ¹⁷,¹⁸The space above the door leading into the Holy of Holies was also paneled. The walls were decorated with carvings of Guardian Angels, each with two faces, and of palm trees alternating with the Guardian Angels. ¹⁹,²⁰One face—that of a man—looked toward the palm tree on one side, and the other face—that of a young lion—looked toward the palm tree on the other side. And so it was, all around the inner wall of the Temple.

²¹There were square doorposts at the doors of the nave, and in front of the Holy of Holies was what appeared to be an altar, but it was made of wood. ²² This altar was 3½ feet square and 5¼ feet high; its corners, base, and sides were all of wood. "This," he told me, "is the Table of the Lord."

²³Both the nave and the Holy of Holies had double doors, ²⁴each with two swinging sections. ²⁵The doors leading into the nave were decorated

with cherubim and palm trees, just as on the walls. And there was a wooden canopy over the entry hall. ²⁶There were recessed windows and carved palm trees on both sides of the entry hall, the hallways beside the Temple, and on the canopy over the entrance.

42 The Priests' Rooms

Then he led me out of the Temple, back into the inner court to the rooms north of the Temple yard, and to another building. ²This group of structures was 175 feet long by 87½ feet wide. ³The rows of rooms behind this building were the inner wall of the court. The rooms were in three tiers, overlooking the outer court on one side, and having a 35-foot strip of inner court on the other. ⁴A 17½-foot walk ran between the building and the tiers of rooms, extending the entire length, with the doors of the building facing north. ⁵The upper two tiers of rooms were not as wide as the lower one, because the upper tiers had wider walkways beside them. ⁶And since the building was not built with girders as those in the outer court were, the upper stories were set back from the ground floor.

⁷,⁸The north tiers, next to the outer court, were 87½ feet long—only half as long as the inner wing that faced the Temple court, which was 175 feet long. But a wall extended from the end of the shorter wing, parallel to the longer wing. ⁹,¹⁰And there was an entrance from the outer court to these rooms from the east. On the opposite side of the Temple a similar building composed of two units of tiers was on the south side of the inner court, between the Temple and the outer court, arranged the same as the other. ¹¹There was a walk between the two wings of the building, the same as in the other building across the court—the same length and width and the same exits and doors—they were identical units. ¹²And there was a door from the outer court at the east.

¹³Then he told me: "These north and south tiers of rooms facing the Temple yard are holy; there the priests who offer up the sacrifices to the Lord shall eat of the most holy offerings and store them—the cereal offerings, sin offerings, and guilt offerings, for these rooms are holy. ¹⁴When the priests leave the Holy Place—the nave of the Temple—they must change their clothes before going out to the outer court. The special robes in which they have been ministering must first be removed, for these robes are holy. They must put on other clothes before entering the parts of the building open to the public."

¹⁵When he had finished making these measurements, he led me out through the east passageway to measure the entire Temple area. ¹⁶⁻²⁰He found that it was in the form of a square, 875 feet long on each side, with a wall all around it to separate the restricted area from the public places.

43 Ezekiel Records Some Rules

Afterward he brought me out again to the passageway through the outer wall leading to the east. ²And suddenly the glory of the God of Israel appeared from the east. The sound of his coming was like the roar of rushing waters, and the whole landscape lighted up with his glory. ³It was just as I had seen it in the other visions, first by the Chebar Canal, and then later at Jerusalem when he came to destroy the city. And I fell down before him with my face in the dust. ⁴And the glory of the Lord came into the Temple through the eastern passageway.

⁵Then the Spirit took me up and brought me into the inner court; and the glory of the Lord filled the Temple. ⁶And I heard the Lord speaking to me from within the Temple (the man who had been measuring was still standing beside me).

⁷And the Lord said to me:

"Son of dust, this is the place of my throne and my footstool, where I shall remain, living among the people of Israel forever. They and their kings will not defile my holy name any longer through the adulterous worship of other gods or by worshiping the totem poles erected by their kings. ⁸They built their idol temples beside mine, with only a wall between, and worshiped their idols. Because they sullied my holy name by such wickedness, I consumed them in my anger. ⁹Now let them put away their idols and the totem poles erected by their kings, and I will live among them forever.

¹⁰"Son of dust, describe the Temple I have shown you to the people of Israel. Tell them its appearance and its plan so they will be ashamed of all their sins. ¹¹And if they are truly ashamed of what they have done, then explain to them the details of its construction—its doors and entrances—and everything about it. Write out all the directions and the rules for them to keep. ¹²And this is the basic law of the Temple: *Holiness!* The entire top of the hill where the Temple is built is *holy.* Yes, this is the primary law concerning it.

¹³"And these are the measurements of the altar: The base is 21 inches high, with a 9 inch rim around its edge, and it extends 21 inches beyond the altar on all sides. ¹⁴The first stage of the altar is a stone platform 3½ feet high. This platform is 21 inches narrower than the base block on all sides. Rising from this is a narrower platform, 21 inches narrower on all sides, and 7 feet high. ¹⁵From it a

still narrower platform rises 7 feet, and this is the top of the altar, with four horns projecting 21 inches up from the corners. ^{16}This top platform of the altar is 21 feet square. ^{17}The platform beneath it is $24\frac{1}{2}$ feet square with a $10\frac{1}{2}$-inch curb around the edges. The entire platform extends out from the top 21 inches on all sides. On the east side are steps to climb the altar."

^{18}And he said to me:

"Son of dust, the Lord God says: These are the measurements of the altar to be made in the future, when it is erected for the burning of offerings and the sprinkling of blood upon it. ^{19}At that time the Zadok family of the Levite tribe, who are my ministers, are to be given a bullock for a sin offering. ^{20}You shall take some of its blood and smear it on the four horns of the altar and on the four corners of the top platform and in the curb around it. This will cleanse and make atonement for the altar. ^{21}Then take the bullock for the sin offering and burn it at the appointed place outside the Temple area.

^{22}"The second day, sacrifice a young male goat without any defects—without sickness, deformities, cuts or scars—for a sin offering. Thus the altar shall be cleansed, as it was by the bullock. ^{23}When you have finished this cleansing ceremony, offer another perfect bullock and a perfect ram from the flock. ^{24}Present them before the Lord, and the priests shall sprinkle salt upon them as a burnt offering.

^{25}"Every day for seven days a male goat, a bullock and a ram from the flock shall be sacrificed as a sin offering. None are to have any defects or unhealthiness of any kind. ^{26}Do this each day for seven days to cleanse and make atonement for the altar, thus consecrating it. ^{27}On the eighth day, and on each day afterward, the priests will sacrifice on the altar the burnt offerings and thank offerings of the people, and I will accept you, says the Lord God."

44 What the Priests Should Do

Then the Lord brought me back to the outer wall's eastern passageway, but it was closed. ^{2}And he said to me:

"This gate shall remain closed; it shall never be opened. No man shall pass through it; for the Lord, the God of Israel, entered here, and so it shall remain shut. ^{3}Only the prince—because he is the prince—may sit inside the passageway to feast there before the Lord. But he shall go and come only through the entry hall of the passage."

^{4}Then he brought me through the north passageway to the front of the Temple. I looked and saw that the glory of the Lord filled the Temple of the Lord, and I fell to the ground with my face in the dust.

^{5}And the Lord said to me:

"Son of dust, notice carefully; use your eyes and ears. Listen to all I tell you about the laws and rules of the Temple of the Lord. Note carefully who may be admitted to the Temple and who is to be excluded from it. ^{6}And say to these rebels, the people of Israel, 'The Lord God says: O Israel, you have sinned greatly ^{7}by letting the uncircumcised into my sanctuary—those who have no heart for God—when you offer me my food, the fat and the blood. Thus you have broken my covenant in addition to all your other sins. ^{8}You have not kept the laws I gave you concerning these holy affairs, for you have hired foreigners to take charge of my sanctuary.'"

^{9}The Lord God says: "No foreigner of all the many among you shall enter my sanctuary if he has not been circumcised and does not love the Lord. ^{10}And the men of the tribe of Levi who abandoned me when Israel strayed away from God to idols must be punished for their unfaithfulness. ^{11}They may be Temple guards and gatemen; they may slay the animals brought for burnt offerings and be present to help the people. ^{12}But because they encouraged the people to worship other gods, causing Israel to fall into deep sin, I have raised my hand and taken oath," says the Lord God, "that they must be punished. ^{13}They shall not come near me to minister as priests; they may not touch any of my holy things, for they must bear their shame for all the sins they have committed. ^{14}They are the Temple caretakers, to do maintenance work and to assist the people in a general way.

^{15}"However, the sons of Zadok, of the tribe of Levi, continued as my priests in the Temple when Israel abandoned me for idols. These men shall be my ministers; they shall stand before me to offer the fat and blood of the sacrifices," says the Lord God. ^{16}"They shall enter my sanctuary and come to my Table to minister to me; they shall fulfill my requirements.

^{17}"They must wear only linen clothing when they enter the passageway to the inner court, for they must wear no wool while on duty in the inner court or in the Temple. ^{18}They must wear linen turbans and linen trousers; they must not wear anything that would cause them to perspire. ^{19}When they return to the outer court, they must take off the clothes they wear while ministering to me, leaving them in the sacred chambers, and put on other clothes lest they harm the people by touching them with this clothing.

^{20}"They must not let their hair grow too long nor shave it off. Regular, moderate haircuts are all they are allowed. ²¹No priest may drink wine before coming to the inner court. ²²He may marry only a Jewish maiden, or the widow of a priest; he may not marry a divorced woman.

²³"He shall teach my people the difference between what is holy and what is secular, what is right and what is wrong.

²⁴"They will serve as judges to resolve any disagreements among my people. Their decisions must be based upon my laws. And the priests themselves shall obey my rules and regulations at all the sacred festivals, and they shall see to it that the Sabbath is kept a sacred day.

²⁵"A priest must not defile himself by being in the presence of a dead person, unless it is his father, mother, child, brother, or unmarried sister. In such cases it is all right. ²⁶But afterward he must wait seven days before he is cleansed and able to perform his Temple duties again. ²⁷The first day he returns to work and enters the inner court and the sanctuary, he must offer a sin offering for himself," the Lord God says.

²⁸"As to property, they shall not own any, for I am their heritage! That is enough!

²⁹"Their food shall be the gifts and sacrifices brought to the Temple by the people—the cereal offerings, the sin offerings, and the guilt offerings. Whatever anyone gives to the Lord shall be the priests'. ³⁰The first of the first-ripe fruits and all the gifts for the Lord shall go to the priests. The first samples of each harvest of grain shall be donated to the priests too, so that the Lord will bless your homes. ³¹Priests may never eat meat from any bird or animal that dies a natural death or that dies after being attacked by other animals.

45 Some Land for the Lord

"When you divide the land among the tribes of Israel, you shall first give a section of it to the Lord as his holy portion. This piece shall be 8⅓ miles long and 6⅔ miles wide. It shall all be holy ground.

²"A section of this land, 875 feet square, shall be designated for the Temple. An additional 87½-foot strip all around is to be left empty. ³The Temple shall be built within the area which is 8⅓ miles long and 3⅓ miles wide. ⁴All this section shall be holy land; it will be used by the priests, who minister in the sanctuary, for their homes and for my Temple.

⁵"The strip next to it, 8⅓ miles long and 3⅓ miles wide, shall be the residence area for the Levites who work at the Temple. ⁶Adjacent to the holy lands will be a section 8⅓ miles by 1⅔ miles for a city open to everyone in Israel.

⁷"Two special sections of land shall be set apart for the prince—one on each side of the holy lands and city; it is contiguous with them in length, and its eastern and western boundaries are the same as those of the tribal sections. ⁸This shall be his allotment. My princes shall no longer oppress and rob my people but shall assign all the remainder of the land to the people, giving a portion to each tribe."

⁹For the Sovereign Lord says to the rulers: "Quit robbing and cheating my people out of their land and expelling them from their homes. Always be fair and honest. ¹⁰You must use honest scales, honest bushels, honest gallons. ¹¹A homer [about five bushels] shall be your standard unit of measurement for both liquid and dry measure. Smaller units shall be the ephah [about one half bushel] for dry measure, and the bath [about seventeen quarts] for liquid. ¹²The unit of weight shall be the silver shekel [about half an ounce]; it must always be exchanged for twenty gerahs, no less; five shekels shall be valued at five shekels, no less; and ten shekels at ten shekels! Fifty shekels shall always equal one mina.

¹³"This is the tax you must give to the prince: a bushel of wheat or barley for every sixty you reap; ¹⁴and one percent of your olive oil; ¹⁵from each 200 sheep in all your flocks in Israel, give him one sheep. These are the meal offerings, burnt offerings and thank offerings to make atonement for those who bring them," says the Lord God. ¹⁶"All the people of Israel shall bring their offerings to the prince.

¹⁷"The prince shall be required to furnish the people with sacrifices for public worship—sin offerings, burnt offerings, meal offerings, drink offerings, and thank offerings—to make reconciliation for the people of Israel. This shall be done at the time of the religious feasts, the new moon ceremonies, the Sabbaths, and all other similar occasions.

¹⁸The Lord God says: "On each New Year's Day sacrifice a young bull with no blemishes, to purify the Temple. ¹⁹The priest shall take some of the blood of this sin offering and put it on the door posts of the Temple, upon the four corners of the base of the altar, and upon the walls at the entry of the inner court. ²⁰Do this also on the seventh day of that month for anyone who has sinned

---

HONESTY 45:9-11 Greed and extortion were two of the major social sins of the nation during this time (see Amos 5:7-13). In the new economy there would be plenty of land for the "princes" (45:7-8) and no longer any basis for greed. Therefore, the princes and the people are commanded to be fair and honest, especially when they do business. Consider the ways you measure goods, money, or services. If you are paid for an hour of work, be sure you work for a full hour. If you sell a bushel of apples, make sure it is a full bushel. God is completely trustworthy, and his followers should be too. **To begin the series of devotionals on HONESTY, turn to page 33.**

through error or ignorance, and so the Temple will be cleansed.

[21] "On the fourteenth day of the same month, you shall celebrate the Passover. It will be a seven-day feast. Only bread without yeast shall be eaten during those days. [22] On the day of Passover the prince shall provide a young bull for a sin offering for himself and all the people of Israel. [23] On each of the seven days of the feast he shall prepare a burnt offering to the Lord. This daily offering will consist of seven young bulls and seven rams without blemish. A male goat shall also be given each day for a sin offering. [24] And the prince shall provide one half bushel of grain with each bullock and ram for a meal offering, and three quarts of olive oil.

[25] "Early in October during each of the seven days of the annual festival of shelters, he shall provide these same sacrifices for the sin offering, burnt offering, meal offering, and oil offering.

46 Special Offerings

The Lord God says, "The inner wall's eastern entrance shall be closed during the six work days but open on the Sabbath and on the days of the new moon celebrations. [2] The prince shall enter the outside entry hall of the passageway and proceed to the inner wall at the other end while the priest offers his burnt offering and peace offering. He shall worship inside the passageway and then return back to the entrance, which shall not be closed until evening. [3] The people shall worship the Lord in front of this passageway on the Sabbaths and on the days of the new moon celebrations.

[4] "The burnt offering that the prince sacrifices to the Lord on the Sabbath days shall be six lambs and a ram, all unblemished. [5] He shall present a meal offering of one half bushel of flour to go with the ram and whatever amount he is willing for to go with each lamb. And he shall bring three quarts of olive oil for each half bushel of flour. [6] At the new moon celebration, he shall bring one young bull in perfect condition, six lambs, and one ram, all without any blemish. [7] With the young bull, he must bring one half bushel of flour for a meal offering. With the ram he must bring one half bushel of flour. With the lamb he is to bring whatever he is willing to give. With each half bushel of grain he is to bring three quarts of olive oil.

[8] "The prince shall go in at the entry hall of the passageway and out the same way; [9] but when the people come in through the north passageway to sacrifice during the religious feasts, they must go out through the south passageway. Those coming in from the south must go out by the north. They must never go out the same way they come in, but must always use the opposite passageway. [10] The prince shall enter and leave with the common people on these occasions.

[11] "To summarize: At the special feasts and sacred festivals the meal offering shall be one half bushel with the young bull; one half bushel with the ram; as much as the prince is willing to give with each lamb; and three quarts of oil with each half bushel of grain. [12] Whenever the prince offers an extra burnt offering or peace offering to be sacrificed to the Lord, the inner eastern gate shall be opened up for him to enter, and he shall offer his sacrifices just as on the Sabbaths. Then he shall turn around and go out, and the passage shall be shut behind him.

[13] "Each morning a yearling lamb must be sacrificed as a burnt offering to the Lord. [14,15] And there must be a meal offering each morning—five pounds of flour with one quart of oil with which to mix it. This is a permanent ordinance—the lamb, the grain offering, and the olive oil shall be provided every morning for the daily sacrifice.

[16] The Sovereign Lord says: "If the prince gives a gift of land to one of his sons, it will belong to him forever. [17] But if he gives a gift of land to one of his servants, the servant may keep it only until the Year of Release (every seventh year) when he is set free; then the land returns to the prince. Only gifts to his sons are permanent. [18] And the prince may never take anyone's property by force. If he gives property to his sons, it must be from his own land, for I don't want my people losing their property and having to move away."

[19,20] After that, using the door through the wall at the side of the main passageway, he led me through the entrance to the block of sacred chambers that faced north. There, at the extreme west end of these rooms, I saw a place where, my guide told me, the priests boil the meat of the trespass offering and sin offering and bake the flour of the flour offerings into bread. They do it here to avoid the necessity of carrying the sacrifices through the outer court, in case they harm the people.

[21,22] Then he brought me out to the outer court again and led me to each of the four corners of the court. I saw that in each corner there was a room 70 feet long by 52½ feet wide, enclosed by walls. [23] Around the inside of these walls there ran a line of brick boiling vats with ovens underneath. [24] He said these rooms were where the Temple assistants—the Levites—boil the sacrifices the people offer.

47 The River of Healing

Then he brought me back to the door of the Temple. I saw a stream flowing eastward from beneath the Temple and passing to the right of the altar, that is, on its south side. [2] Then he brought me outside the wall through the north passageway and around to the eastern entrance, where I saw the stream flowing along on the south side [of the eastern passageway]. ³ Measuring as he went, he took me 1,500 feet east along the stream and told me to go across. At that point the water was up to my ankles. ⁴ He measured off another 1,500 feet and told me to cross again. This time the water was up to my knees. ⁵ Fifteen hundred feet after that it was up to my waist. Another 1,500 feet and it had become a river so deep I wouldn't be able to get across unless I were to swim. It was too deep to cross on foot.

⁶He told me to keep in mind what I had seen, then led me back along the bank. ⁷And now, to my surprise, many trees were growing on both sides of the river!

⁸He told me: "This river flows east through the desert and the Jordan Valley to the Dead Sea, where it will heal the salty waters and make them fresh and pure. ⁹Everything touching the water of this river shall live. Fish will abound in the Dead Sea, for its waters will be healed. Wherever this water flows, everything will live. ¹⁰Fishermen will stand along the shores of the Dead Sea, fishing all the way from Engedi to Eneglaim. The shores will be filled with nets drying in the sun. Fish of every kind will fill the Dead Sea just as they do the Mediterranean! ¹¹But the marshes and swamps will not be healed; they will still be salty. ¹²All kinds of fruit trees will grow along the riverbanks. The leaves will never turn brown and fall, and there will always be fruit. There will be a new crop every month—without fail! For they are watered by the river flowing from the Temple. The fruit will be for food and the leaves for medicine."

¹³The Lord God says: "Here are the instructions for dividing the land to the twelve tribes of Israel: The tribe of Joseph (Ephraim and Manasseh) shall be given two sections. ¹⁴Otherwise, each tribe will have an equal share. I promised with hand raised in oath of truth to give the land to your fathers, and you shall inherit it now.

¹⁵"The northern boundary will run from the Mediterranean toward Hethlon, then on through Labweh to Zedad; ¹⁶then to Berothah and Sibraim, which are on the border between Damascus and Hamath, and finally to Hazer-hatticon, on the border of Hauran. ¹⁷So the northern border will be from the Mediterranean to Hazar-enan, on the border with Hamath to the north and Damascus to the south.

¹⁸"The eastern border will run south from Hazar-enan to Mount Hauran, where it will bend westward to the Jordan at the southern tip of the Sea of Galilee, and down along the Jordan River separating Israel from Gilead, past the Dead Sea to Tamar.

¹⁹"The southern border will go west from Tamar to the springs at Meribath-kadesh and then follow the course of the Brook of Egypt (Wadi el-Arish) to the Mediterranean.

²⁰"On the west side, the Mediterranean itself will be your boundary, from the southern boundary to the point where the northern boundary begins.

²¹"Divide the land within these boundaries among the tribes of Israel. ²²Distribute the land as an inheritance for yourselves and for the foreigners who live among you with their families. All children born in the land—whether or not their parents are foreigners—are to be considered citizens and have the same rights your own children have. ²³All these immigrants are to be given land according to the tribe where they now live.

48 The Land Is Divided

"Here is the list of the tribes and the territory each is to get. For Dan: From the northwest boundary at the Mediterranean, across to Hethlon, then to Labweh, and then on to Hazarenan on the border between Damascus to the south and Hamath to the north. Those are the eastern and western limits of the land. ²Asher's territory lies south of Dan's and has the same east and west boundaries. ³Naphtali's land lies south of Asher's, with the same boundary lines on the east and the west. ⁴Then comes Manasseh, south of Naphtali, with the same eastern and western boundary lines. ⁵⁻⁷Next, to the south, is Ephraim, and then Reuben and then Judah, all with the same boundaries on the east and the west.

⁸"South of Judah is the land set aside for the Temple. It has the same eastern and western boundaries as the tribal units, with the Temple in the center. ⁹This Temple area will be 8⅓ miles long and 6⅔ miles wide.

¹⁰"A strip of land measuring 8⅓ miles long by 3⅓ miles wide, north to south, surrounds the Temple. ¹¹It is for the priests, that is, the sons of Zadok who obeyed me and didn't go into sin when the people of Israel and the rest of their tribe of Levi did. ¹²It is their special portion when the land is distributed, the most sacred land of all.

KNOWING GOD 48:35 The book of Ezekiel begins by describing the holiness of God, which Israel had despised and ignored. As a result, God's presence departed from the Temple, the city, and the people. The book ends with a detailed vision of the new Temple, the new city, and the new people—all demonstrating God's holiness. The pressures of everyday life can persuade us to focus on the here and now and thus forget God. That is why worship is so important; it takes our eyes off our current worries, gives us a glimpse of God's holiness, and allows us to look toward his future Kingdom. God's presence makes everything glorious, and worship brings us into his presence. **To begin the series of devotionals on KNOWING GOD, turn to page 197.**

Next to it lies the area where the other Levites will live. ¹³It will be of the same size and shape as the first. Together they measure 8⅓ miles by 6⅔ miles. ¹⁴None of this special land shall ever be sold or traded or used by others, for it belongs to the Lord; it is holy.

¹⁵"The strip of land 8⅓ miles long by 1⅔ miles wide, south of the Temple section, is for public use—homes, pasture, and parks, with a city in the center. ¹⁶The city itself is to be 1½ miles square. ¹⁷Open land for pastures shall surround the city for approximately a tenth of a mile. ¹⁸Outside the city, stretching east and west for three miles alongside the holy grounds, is garden area belonging to the city, for public use. ¹⁹It is open to anyone working in the city, no matter where he comes from in Israel.

²⁰"The entire area—including sacred lands and city lands—is 8⅓ miles square.

²¹,²²"The land on both sides of this area, extending clear out to the eastern and western boundaries of Israel, shall belong to the prince. This land, lying between the sections alloted to Judah and Benjamin, is 8⅓ miles square on each side of the sacred and city lands.

²³"The sections given to the remaining tribes are as follows: Benjamin's section extends across the entire country of Israel, from its eastern border clear across to the western border. ²⁴South of Benjamin's area lies that of Simeon, also extending out to these same eastern and western borders. ²⁵Next is Issachar, with the same boundaries. ²⁶Then comes Zebulun, also extending all the way across. ²⁷,²⁸Then Gad, with the same borders on east and west, while its south border runs from Tamar to the Spring at Meribath-kadesh, and then follows the Brook of Egypt (Wadi el-Arish) to the Mediterranean. ²⁹These are the allotments to be made to each tribe," says the Lord God.

³⁰,³¹"Each city gate will be named in honor of one of the tribes of Israel. On the north side, with its 1½-mile wall, there will be three gates, one named for Reuben, one for Judah, and one for Levi. ³²On the east side, with its 1½-mile wall, the gates will be named for Joseph, Benjamin, and Dan. ³³The south wall, also the same length, will have the gates of Simeon, Issachar, and Zebulun; ³⁴on the 1½ miles of the west side, they will be named for Gad, Asher, and Naphtali.

³⁵"The entire circumference of the city is six miles. And the name of the city will be 'The City of God.'"

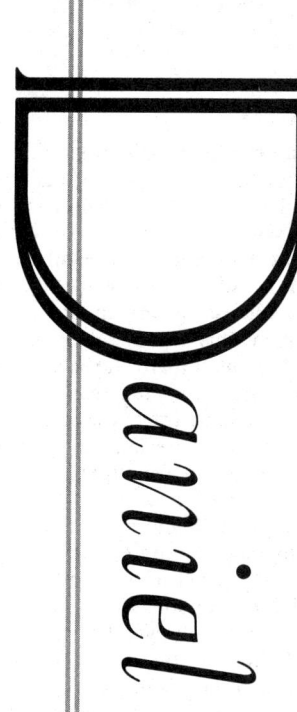

Daniel

PROBABLY EVERY day we see people who don't believe in God—at stores, at the community center, on TV, in school, and in our neighborhood. How can we keep our devotion to God strong when we're influenced by people who don't trust him?

Daniel was in the same situation. When he was a teenager, he was taken captive by the Babylonians with the rest of the people of Judah. The Babylonian king wanted some Judean men to serve in his court. So Daniel was chosen and trained in all the ways of the Babylonians.

Even though they were surrounded by people who didn't believe in God, Daniel and his friends stayed faithful to him. Sometimes it took courage—like when they were thrown into a flaming furnace or into a lions' den! But God used the faith of Daniel and his friends to teach the kings that he is real.

Through Daniel, God also gave messages about his future plans, though he gave them in symbols that are hard to understand.

As you read this book, look for the ways Daniel kept his faith even when it was hard.

1

Daniel Won't Eat the King's Food

Three years after King Jehoiakim began to rule in Judah, Babylon's King Nebuchadnezzar attacked Jerusalem with his armies, and the Lord gave him victory over Jehoiakim. When he returned to Babylon, he took along some of the sacred cups from the Temple of God and placed them in the treasury of his god in the land of Shinar.

³,⁴Then he ordered Ashpenaz, who was in charge of his palace personnel, to select some of the Jewish youths brought back as captives—young men of the royal family and nobility of Judah—and to teach them the Chaldean language and literature. "Pick strong, healthy, good-looking lads," he said; "those who have read widely in many fields, are well informed, alert and sensible, and have enough poise to look good around the palace."

⁵The king assigned them the best of food and wine from his own kitchen during their three-year training period, planning to make them his counselors when they graduated.

⁶Daniel, Hananiah, Mishael, and Azariah were four of the young men chosen, all from the tribe of Judah. ⁷However, their superintendent gave them Babylonian names, as follows:

Daniel was called Belteshazzar;
Hananiah was called Shadrach;
Mishael was called Meshach;
Azariah was called Abednego.

⁸But Daniel made up his mind not to eat the food and wine given to them by the king. He asked the superintendent for permission to eat other things instead. ⁹Now as it happened, God had given the superintendent a special appreciation for Daniel and sympathy for his predicament. ¹⁰But he was alarmed by Daniel's suggestion.

"I'm afraid you will become pale and thin compared with the other youths your age," he said, "and then the king will behead me for neglecting my responsibilities."

¹¹Daniel talked it over with the steward who was appointed by the superintendent to look after Daniel, Hananiah, Mishael, and Azariah, ¹²and suggested a ten-day diet of only vegetables and water; ¹³then, at the end of this trial period the steward could see how they looked in comparison with the other fellows who ate the king's rich food and decide whether or not to let them continue their diet.

¹⁴The steward finally agreed to the test. ¹⁵Well, at the end of the ten days, Daniel and his three friends looked healthier and better nourished than the youths who had been eating the food supplied by the king! ¹⁶So after that the steward fed them only vegetables and water, without the rich foods and wines!

¹⁷God gave these four youths great ability to learn, and they soon mastered all the literature and science of the time; and God gave to Daniel special ability in understanding the meanings of dreams and visions.

¹⁸,¹⁹When the three-year training period was completed, the superintendent brought all the young men to the king for oral exams, as he had been ordered to do. King Nebuchadnezzar had long talks with each of them, and none of them impressed him as much as Daniel, Hananiah, Mishael, and Azariah. So they were put on his regular staff of advisors. ²⁰And in all matters requiring information and balanced judgment, the king found these young men's advice ten times better than that of all the skilled magicians and wise astrologers in his realm.

²¹Daniel held this appointment as the king's counselor until the first year of the reign of King Cyrus.

2 Daniel Describes the King's Dream

One night in the second year of his reign, Nebuchadnezzar had a terrifying nightmare and awoke trembling with fear. And to make matters worse, he couldn't remember his dream! He immediately called in all his magicians, incantationists, sorcerers, and astrologers, and demanded that they tell him what his dream had been.

"I've had a terrible nightmare," he said as they stood before him, "and I can't remember what it was. Tell me, for I fear some tragedy awaits me."

⁴Then the astrologers (speaking in Aramaic) said to the king, "Sir, tell us the dream and then we can tell you what it means."

⁵But the king replied, "I tell you the dream is gone—I can't remember it. And if you won't tell me what it was and what it means, I'll have you torn limb from limb and your houses made into heaps of rubble! ⁶But I will give you many wonderful gifts and honors if you tell me what the dream was and what it means. So, begin!"

⁷They said again, "How can we tell you what the dream means unless you tell us what it was?"

⁸,⁹The king retorted, "I can see your trick! You're trying to stall for time until the calamity befalls me that the dream foretells. But if you don't tell me the dream, you certainly can't expect me to believe your interpretation!"

¹⁰The astrologers replied to the king, "There isn't a man alive who can tell others what they have dreamed! And there isn't a king in all the world who would ask such a thing! ¹¹This is an impossible thing the king requires. No one except the gods can tell you your dream, and they are not here to help."

¹²Upon hearing this, the king was furious and sent out orders to execute all the wise men of Babylon. ¹³And Daniel and his companions were rounded up with the others to be killed.

¹⁴But when Arioch, the chief executioner, came to kill them, Daniel handled the situation with great wisdom by asking, ¹⁵"Why is the king so angry? What is the matter?"

Then Arioch told him all that had happened.

¹⁶So Daniel went in to see the king. "Give me a little time," he said, "and I will tell you the dream and what it means."

¹⁷Then he went home and told Hananiah, Mishael, and Azariah, his companions. ¹⁸They asked the God of heaven to show them his mercy by telling them the secret, so they would not die with the others. ¹⁹And that night in a vision God told Daniel what the king had dreamed.

Then Daniel praised the God of heaven, ²⁰saying, "Blessed be the name of God forever and ever, for he alone has all wisdom and all power. ²¹World events are under his control. He removes

FAMILY DEVOTIONS

☐ DEVOTION 235
AVOIDING SIN

Read Daniel 1:8-16

"Our class is having a play," Tony told his parents one evening. "There's a scene with the devil in it, and Miss Clark gave me that part, but I really don't want to do it."

"Did you tell her?" Mom asked as she placed some food on Carrie's plate.

"No, I was going to, but—"

Tony's explanation was interrupted by Carrie. "I don't want that! I'm not going to eat it!"

"Then you will not get any dessert," said Mom sternly as she put some on Beth's plate, too.

"I was going to tell Miss Clark," Tony continued, "but Christi was talking to her. Christi was supposed to be a witch in the play, and she was telling Miss Clark she wouldn't do it. I was afraid—"

This time Tony was interrupted by Beth. "Mom, could I eat extra vegetables instead of this casserole, please?" Mom hesitated. "I suppose so."

"But what can I do about the play?" asked Tony.

He sighed as Carrie took over the conversation. "Why do I have to eat casserole if Beth doesn't?"

"Because your attitude is bad," Dad said sternly. "Beth asked politely if she could have a substitute. You declared rebelliously that you were not going to eat yours."

Mom turned to Tony. "Maybe that's your answer," she said. "Did Christi ask Miss Clark to excuse her from the play, or did she just say she wasn't going to do it?"

"She just said she wouldn't do it," replied Tony. "She was pretty rude about it. I guess that might be why Miss Clark got mad."

"Whether or not our requests are granted often depends on *how* we ask more than on *what* we ask," Dad said, as much to Carrie as to Tony.

The next day Tony came in from school grinning. "Guess what? Miss Clark excused me from the play. A right attitude does make a difference."

Avoiding Sin Memory Verse

Dear brothers, you are only visitors here. Since your real home is in heaven, I beg you to keep away from the evil pleasures of this world; they are not for you, for they fight against your very souls.
1 Peter 2:11

How About You?

When you are asked to do something you feel is wrong, don't be afraid to say no, but say it in the right way. Daniel made up his mind ahead of time that he would not do wrong. You need to do that, too, but don't be rebellious or super-holy about it. Be respectful but firm, as Daniel was. *B. W.*

• For the next devotional, turn to page 823. • For the next devotional on AVOIDING SIN, turn to page 973. • For notes on AVOIDING SIN, see pages 220, 332, 392, and 657.

kings and sets others on their thrones. He gives wise men their wisdom and scholars their intelligence. ²²He reveals profound mysteries beyond man's understanding. He knows all hidden things, for he is light, and darkness is no obstacle to him. ²³I thank and praise you, O God of my fathers, for you have given me wisdom and glowing health, and now even this vision of the king's dream and the understanding of what it means."

²⁴Then Daniel went in to see Arioch, who had been ordered to execute the wise men of Babylon, and said, "Don't kill them. Take me to the king, and I will tell him what he wants to know."

²⁵Then Arioch hurried Daniel in to the king and said, "I've found one of the Jewish captives who will tell you your dream!"

²⁶The king said to Daniel, "Is this true? Can you tell me what my dream was and what it means?"

²⁷Daniel replied, "No wise man, astrologer, magician, or wizard can tell the king such things, ²⁸but there is a God in heaven who reveals secrets, and he has told you in your dream what will happen in the future. This was your dream:

²⁹"You dreamed of coming events. He who reveals secrets was speaking to you. ³⁰(But remember, it's not because I am wiser than any living person that I know this secret of your dream, for God showed it to me for your benefit.)

³¹"O king, you saw a huge and powerful statue of a man, shining brilliantly, frightening and terrible. ³²The head of the statue was made of purest gold, its chest and arms were of silver, its belly and thighs of brass, ³³its legs of iron, its feet part iron and part clay. ³⁴But as you watched, a Rock was cut from the mountainside by supernatural means. It came hurtling toward the statue and crushed the feet of iron and clay, smashing them to bits. ³⁵Then the whole statue collapsed into a heap of iron, clay, brass, silver, and gold; its pieces were crushed as small as chaff, and the wind blew them all away. But the Rock that knocked the statue down became a great mountain that covered the whole earth.

³⁶"That was the dream; now for its meaning:

³⁷"Your Majesty, you are a king over many kings, for the God of heaven has given you your kingdom, power, strength, and glory. ³⁸You rule the farthest provinces, and even animals and birds are under your control, as God decreed. You are that head of gold.

³⁹"But after your kingdom has come to an end, another world power will arise to take your place. This empire will be inferior to yours. And after that kingdom has fallen, yet a third great power —represented by the bronze belly of the statue— will rise to rule the world. ⁴⁰Following it, the fourth kingdom will be strong as iron—smashing, bruising, and conquering. ⁴¹,⁴²The feet and toes you saw—part iron and part clay—show that later on, this kingdom will be divided. Some parts of it will be as strong as iron, and some as weak as clay. ⁴³This mixture of iron with clay also shows that these kingdoms will try to strengthen themselves by forming alliances with each other through intermarriage of their rulers; but this will not succeed, for iron and clay don't mix.

⁴⁴"During the reigns of those kings, the God of heaven will set up a kingdom that will never be destroyed; no one will ever conquer it. It will shatter all these kingdoms into nothingness, but it shall stand forever, indestructible. ⁴⁵That is the meaning of the Rock cut from the mountain without human hands—the Rock that crushed to powder all the iron and brass, the clay, the silver, and the gold.

"Thus the great God has shown what will happen in the future, and this interpretation of your dream is as sure and certain as my description of it."

⁴⁶Then Nebuchadnezzar fell to the ground before Daniel and worshiped him and commanded his people to offer sacrifices and burn sweet incense before him.

⁴⁷"Truly, O Daniel," the king said, "your God is the God of gods, Ruler of kings, the Revealer of mysteries, because he has told you this secret."

⁴⁸Then the king made Daniel very great; he gave him many valuable gifts and appointed him to be ruler over the whole province of Babylon, as well as chief over all his wise men.

⁴⁹Then, at Daniel's request, the king appointed Shadrach, Meshach, and Abednego as Daniel's assistants, to be in charge of all the affairs of the province of Babylon; Daniel served as chief magistrate in the king's court.

3 The Fiery Furnace

King Nebuchadnezzar made a gold statue ninety feet high and nine feet wide and set it up on the Plain of Dura, in the province of Babylon; ²then he sent messages to all the princes, governors, captains, judges, treasurers, counselors, sheriffs, and rulers of all the provinces of his empire, to come to the dedication of his statue. ³When they had all arrived and were standing before the monument, ⁴a herald shouted out, "O people of all nations and languages, this is the king's command:

⁵"When the band strikes up, you are to fall flat on the ground to worship King Nebuchadnezzar's gold statue; ⁶anyone who refuses to obey will immediately be thrown into a flaming furnace."

⁷So when the band began to play, everyone— whatever his nation, language, or religion —fell to the ground and worshiped the statue.

⁸But some officials went to the king and accused some of the Jews of refusing to worship!

⁹"Your Majesty," they said to him, ¹⁰"you made a law that everyone must fall down and worship the

gold statue when the band begins to play, ¹¹and that anyone who refuses will be thrown into a flaming furnace. ¹²But there are some Jews out there—Shadrach, Meshach, and Abednego, whom you have put in charge of Babylonian affairs—who have defied you, refusing to serve your gods or to worship the gold statue you set up."

¹³Then Nebuchadnezzar, in a terrible rage, ordered Shadrach, Meshach, and Abednego to be brought in before him.

¹⁴"Is it true, O Shadrach, Meshach, and Abednego," he demanded, "that you are refusing to serve my gods or to worship the gold statue I set up? ¹⁵I'll give you one more chance. When the music plays, if you fall down and worship the statue, all will be well. But if you refuse, you will be thrown into a flaming furnace within the hour. And what god can deliver you out of my hands then?"

¹⁶Shadrach, Meshach, and Abednego replied, "O Nebuchadnezzar, we are not worried about what will happen to us. ¹⁷If we are thrown into the flaming furnace, our God is able to deliver us; and he will deliver us out of your hand, Your Majesty. ¹⁸But if he doesn't, please understand, sir, that even then we will never under any circumstance serve your gods or worship the gold statue you have erected."

¹⁹Then Nebuchadnezzar was filled with fury and his face became dark with anger at Shadrach, Meshach, and Abednego. He commanded that the furnace be heated up seven times hotter than usual, ²⁰and called for some of the strongest men of his army to bind Shadrach, Meshach, and Abednego, and throw them into the fire. ²¹So they bound them tight with ropes and threw them into the furnace, fully clothed. ²²And because the king, in his anger, had demanded such a hot fire in the furnace, the flames leaped out and killed the soldiers as they threw them in! ²³So Shadrach, Meshach, and Abednego fell down bound into the roaring flames.

²⁴But suddenly, as he was watching, Nebuchadnezzar jumped up in amazement and exclaimed to his advisors, "Didn't we throw three men into the furnace?"

"Yes," they said, "we did indeed, Your Majesty."

²⁵"Well, look!" Nebuchadnezzar shouted. "I see *four* men, unbound, walking around in the fire, and they aren't even hurt by the flames! And the fourth looks like a god!"

²⁶Then Nebuchadnezzar came as close as he could to the open door of the flaming furnace and yelled: "Shadrach, Meshach, and Abednego, servants of the Most High God! Come out! Come here!" So they stepped out of the fire.

²⁷Then the princes, governors, captains, and counselors crowded around them and saw that the fire hadn't touched them—not a hair of their heads was singed; their coats were unscorched, and they didn't even smell of smoke!

²⁸Then Nebuchadnezzar said, "Blessed be the God of Shadrach, Meshach, and Abednego, for he sent his angel to deliver his trusting servants when they defied the king's commandment and were willing to die rather than serve or worship any god except their own. ²⁹Therefore, I make this decree, that any person of any nation, language, or religion who speaks a word against the God of Shadrach, Meshach, and Abednego shall be torn limb from limb and his house knocked into a heap of rubble. For no other God can do what this one does."

³⁰Then the king gave promotions to Shadrach, Meshach, and Abednego, so that they prospered greatly there in the province of Babylon.

4 The King Dreams about a Tree

This is the proclamation of Nebuchadnezzar the king, which he sent to people of every language in every nation of the world:

Greetings:

²I want you all to know about the strange thing that the Most High God did to me. ³It was incredible—a mighty miracle! And now I know for sure that his kingdom is everlasting; he reigns forever and ever.

⁴I, Nebuchadnezzar, was living in peace and prosperity, ⁵when one night I had a dream that greatly frightened me. ⁶I called in all the wise men of Babylon to tell me the meaning of my dream, ⁷but when they came—the magicians, astrologers, fortune-tellers, and wizards—and I told them the dream, they couldn't interpret it. ⁸At last Daniel came in—the man I named Belteshazzar after my god—the man in whom is the spirit of the holy gods, and I told him the dream.

⁹"O Belteshazzar, master magician," I said, "I know that the spirit of the holy gods is in you and no mystery is too great for you to solve. Tell me what my dream means:

¹⁰,¹¹"I saw a very tall tree out in a field, growing higher and higher into the sky until it could be seen by everyone in all the world. ¹²Its leaves were fresh and green, and its branches were weighted down with fruit, enough for everyone to eat. Wild animals rested beneath its shade and birds sheltered in its branches, and all the world was fed from it. ¹³Then as I lay there dreaming, I saw one of God's angels coming down from heaven.

¹⁴"He shouted, 'Cut down the tree; lop off its branches; shake off its leaves, and scatter its fruit. Get the animals out from under it and the birds from its branches, ¹⁵but leave its stump and roots in the ground, banded with a chain of iron and brass, surrounded by the tender grass. Let the dew of heaven drench him and let him eat grass with the wild animals! ¹⁶For seven years let him have the mind of an animal instead of a man. ¹⁷For this has

been decreed by the Watchers, demanded by the Holy Ones. The purpose of this decree is that all the world may understand that the Most High dominates the kingdoms of the world and gives them to anyone he wants to, even the lowliest of men!'

18"O Belteshazzar, that was my dream; now tell me what it means. For no one else can help me; all the wisest men of my kingdom have failed me. But you can tell me, for the spirit of the holy gods is in you."

19Then Daniel sat there stunned and silent for an hour, aghast at the meaning of the dream. Finally the king said to him: "Belteshazzar, don't be afraid to tell me what it means."

Daniel replied: "Oh, that the events foreshadowed in this dream would happen to your enemies, my lord, and not to you! 20For the tree you saw growing so tall, reaching high into the heavens for all the world to see, 21with its fresh green leaves, loaded with fruit for all to eat, the wild animals living in its shade, with its branches full of birds— 22that tree, Your Majesty, is you. For you have grown strong and great; your greatness reaches up to heaven, and your rule to the ends of the earth.

23"Then you saw God's angel coming down from heaven and saying, 'Cut down the tree and destroy it, but leave the stump and the roots in the earth surrounded by tender grass, banded with a chain of iron and brass. Let him be wet with the dew of heaven. For seven years let him eat grass with the animals of the field.'

24"Your Majesty, the Most High God has decreed—and it will surely happen—25that your people will chase you from your palace, and you will live in the fields like an animal, eating grass like a cow, your back wet with dew from heaven. For seven years this will be your life, until you learn that the Most High God dominates the kingdoms of men and gives power to anyone he chooses. 26But the stump and the roots were left in the ground! This means that you will get your kingdom back again when you have learned that heaven rules.

27"O King Nebuchadnezzar, listen to me—stop sinning; do what you know is right; be merciful to the poor. Perhaps even yet God will spare you."

28But all these things happened to Nebuchadnezzar. 29Twelve months after this dream, he was strolling on the roof of the royal palace in Babylon, 30and saying, "I, by my own mighty power, have built this beautiful city as my royal residence and as the capital of my empire."

31While he was still speaking these words, a voice called down from heaven, "O King Nebuchadnezzar, this message is for you: You are no longer ruler of this kingdom. 32You will be forced out of the palace to live with the animals in the fields and to eat grass like the cows for seven years, until you finally realize that God parcels out the kingdoms of men and gives them to anyone he chooses."

33That very same hour this prophecy was fulfilled. Nebuchadnezzar was chased from his palace and ate grass like the cows, and his body was wet with dew; his hair grew as long as eagles' feathers, and his nails were like birds' claws.

34"At the end of seven years I, Nebuchadnezzar, looked up to heaven, and my sanity returned, and I praised and worshiped the Most High God and honored him who lives forever, whose rule is everlasting, his kingdom evermore. 35All the people of the earth are nothing when compared to him; he does whatever he thinks best among the angels of heaven, as well as here on earth. No one can stop him or challenge him, saying, 'What do you mean by doing these things?' 36When my mind returned to me, so did my honor and glory and kingdom. My counselors and officers came back to me, and I was reestablished as head of my kingdom, with even greater honor than before.

37"Now, I, Nebuchadnezzar, praise and glorify and honor the King of Heaven, the Judge of all, whose every act is right and good; for he is able to take those who walk proudly and push them into the dust!"

5 Strange Writing on the Wall

Belshazzar the king invited a thousand of his officers to a great feast where the wine flowed freely. 2-4While Belshazzar was drinking, he was reminded of the gold and silver cups taken long before from the Temple in Jerusalem during Nebuchadnezzar's reign and brought to Babylon. Belshazzar ordered that these sacred cups be brought in to the feast, and when they arrived, he and his princes, wives, and concubines drank toasts from them to their idols made of gold and silver, brass and iron, wood and stone.

5Suddenly, as they were drinking from these cups, they saw the fingers of a man's hand writing on the plaster of the wall opposite the lampstand. The king himself saw the fingers as they wrote. 6His face blanched with fear, and such terror gripped him that his knees knocked together and his legs gave way beneath him.

FORGIVING OTHERS 4:19 When Daniel understood Nebuchadnezzar's dream, he was stunned. How could he be so deeply grieved at the fate of Nebuchadnezzar—the king who was responsible for the destruction of his home and nation? Daniel had forgiven him, so God was able to use Daniel. Very often when we have been wronged by someone, we find it difficult to forget the past. We may even be glad if that person suffers. Forgiving people means putting the past behind us. Can you love someone who has hurt you? Ask God to help you forgive, forget, and love. God may use you in an extraordinary way in that person's life! **To begin the series of devotionals on FORGIVING OTHERS, turn to page 39.**

FAMILY DEVOTIONS

☐ **DEVOTION 236**
HUMILITY

Read Daniel 4:28-33

"Look at that neat tree house!"

Sitting on the carpeted floor of his new hideout, Mark heard the voices float up from the street.

"Yeah. That's Mark Patterson's. His dad is a carpenter, so Mark had all the tools and materials he needed. He claims he built it all by himself, but I don't believe him." Mark recognized Delbert's voice. "I could do twice as good with half as much," Delbert bragged.

Mark shook his fist at the backs of the two boys disappearing down the street. "Ha! You couldn't do half as good with twice as much, you mean!"

When his grandparents came the following week, Mark proudly showed Grandpa Patterson his work.

"You did a good job," approved Grandpa. "It's nice to have a carpenter dad to supply knowledge, materials, and tools, isn't it?"

Mark frowned. Delbert had said the same thing. "But I built it!" Mark insisted. "I built it all by myself!"

"There are very few things we can do entirely alone without assistance from anyone else," answered Grandpa.

"You drive a truck by yourself," Mark argued.

"I do and I don't," Grandpa replied. "The company I work for supplies the job and the truck. God gives me the strength and knowledge to drive it. The government builds the highways I drive on. So you see, I'm dependent upon a lot of people for my job. I could never do it all by myself."

Mark grinned. "All right, Grandpa, you win. Dad taught me how to build things. He loaned me his tools, God gave me the strength, and together we built this tree house."

Humility Memory Verse

For everyone who tries to honor himself shall be humbled; and he who humbles himself shall be honored.
Luke 14:11

How About You?

Do you sometimes get proud of your work and forget to be thankful to those who help you? King Nebuchadnezzar bragged about his work and refused to give glory to God. Because he wanted all the credit for himself, God had to deal harshly with him. Don't make the same mistake he did. Take time right now to give thanks to God for helping you. And today be sure to thank some person who has helped you, too. B. W.

• For the next devotional, turn to page 825. • For the next devotional on *HUMILITY*, turn to page 875. • For notes on *HUMILITY*, see pages 57, 390, 428, 854, and 1228.

⁷"Bring the magicians and astrologers!" he screamed. "Bring the Chaldeans! Whoever reads that writing on the wall and tells me what it means will be dressed in purple robes of royal honor, with a gold chain around his neck, and he will become the third ruler in the kingdom!"

⁸But when they came, none of them could understand the writing or tell him what it meant.

⁹The king grew more and more hysterical; his face reflected the terror he felt, and his officers too were shaken. ¹⁰But when the queen-mother heard what was happening, she rushed to the banquet hall and said to Belshazzar, "Calm yourself, Your Majesty, don't be so pale and frightened over this. ¹¹For there is a man in your kingdom who has within him the spirit of the holy gods. In the days of your father this man was found to be as full of wisdom and understanding as though he were himself a god. And in the reign of King Nebuchadnezzar, he was made chief of all the magicians, astrologers, Chaldeans, and soothsayers of Babylon. ¹²Call for this man, Daniel—or Belteshazzar, as the king called him—for his mind is filled with divine knowledge and understanding. He can interpret dreams, explain riddles, and solve knotty problems. He will tell you what the writing means."

¹³So Daniel was rushed in to see the king. The king asked him, "Are you the Daniel brought from Israel as a captive by King Nebuchadnezzar? ¹⁴I have heard that you have the spirit of the gods within you and that you are filled with enlightenment and wisdom. ¹⁵My wise men and astrologers have tried to read that writing on the wall and tell me what it means, but they can't. ¹⁶I am told you can solve all kinds of mysteries. If you can tell me the meaning of those words, I will clothe you in purple robes, with a gold chain around your neck, and make you the third ruler in the kingdom."

¹⁷Daniel answered, "Keep your gifts or give them to someone else, but I will tell you what the writing means. ¹⁸Your Majesty, the Most High God gave Nebuchadnezzar, who long ago preceded you, a kingdom and majesty and glory and honor. ¹⁹He gave him such majesty that all the nations of the world trembled before him in fear. He killed any who offended him and spared any he liked. At his whim they rose or fell. ²⁰But when his heart and mind were hardened in pride, God removed him from his royal throne and took away his glory. ²¹He was chased out of his palace into the fields. His thoughts and feelings became those of an animal, and he lived among the wild donkeys; he ate grass like the cows, and his body was wet with the dew of heaven, until at last he knew that the Most High overrules the kingdoms of men and appoints anyone he desires to reign over them.

²²"And you, his successor, O Belshazzar—you knew all this, yet you have not been humble. ²³For you have defied the Lord of Heaven and brought here these cups from his Temple; and you and your officers and wives and concubines have been drinking wine from them while praising gods of silver, gold, brass, iron, wood, and stone—gods that neither see nor hear nor know anything at all. But you have not praised the God who gives you the breath of life and controls your destiny! ²⁴,²⁵And so God sent those fingers to write this message: 'Mene,' 'Mene,' 'Tekel,' 'Parsin.'

²⁶"This is what it means:

"*Mene* means 'numbered'—God has numbered the days of your reign, and they are ended.

²⁷"*Tekel* means 'weighed'—you have been weighed in God's balances and have failed the test.

²⁸"*Parsin* means 'divided'—your kingdom will be divided and given to the Medes and Persians."

²⁹Then at Belshazzar's command, Daniel was robed in purple, a gold chain was hung around his neck, and he was proclaimed third ruler in the kingdom.

³⁰That very night Belshazzar, the Chaldean king, was killed, ³¹and Darius the Mede entered the city and began reigning at the age of sixty-two.

6 Daniel in the Lions' Den

Darius divided the kingdom into 120 provinces, each under a governor. ²The governors were accountable to three presidents (Daniel was one of them) so the king could administer the kingdom efficiently.

³Daniel soon proved himself more capable than all the other presidents and governors, for he had great ability, and the king began to think of placing him over the entire empire as his administrative officer.

⁴This made the other presidents and governors very jealous, and they began searching for some fault in the way Daniel was handling his affairs so that they could complain to the king about him. But they couldn't find anything to criticize! He was faithful and honest and made no mistakes. ⁵So they concluded, "Our only chance is his religion!"

⁶They decided to go to the king and say, "King Darius, live forever! ⁷We presidents, governors, counselors, and deputies have unanimously decided that you should make a law, irrevocable under any circumstance, that for the next thirty days anyone who asks a favor of God or man—except from you, Your Majesty—shall be thrown to the lions. ⁸Your Majesty, we request your signature on this law; sign it so that it cannot be canceled or changed; it will be a 'law of the Medes and Persians' that cannot be revoked."

⁹So King Darius signed the law.

¹⁰But though Daniel knew about it, he went home and knelt down as usual in his upstairs

Family Devotions

☐ *Devotion 237*
Knowing God

Read Daniel 6:1-10

Knowing God
Memory Verse

Oh, that we might know the Lord! Let us press on to know him, and he will respond to us as surely as the coming of dawn or the rain of early spring.
Hosea 6:3

Josh struggled into his pajamas, raced to Elizabeth's bedroom, skidded on the shag rug next to the bed, and dropped to his knees next to his little sister. Elizabeth rolled her eyes and giggled. Josh was always late for bedtime prayers!

Elizabeth squeezed her eyes tightly shut and folded her hands on the bed. Josh also folded his hands and tried to keep his eyes shut. It was Mom's custom to pray with the children before she tucked them in each night. "Dear Lord," she prayed, "please keep my children safe tonight. Help us appreciate things we have and not worry over what we don't have. Thank you, Lord, for our health, our happiness, and our home. Help us to be kind to others." Twice Mom had to pause and wait patiently as Josh picked something off the floor and got back into position. When she finished, she shot Josh a warning glance as he once again dropped whatever he had. Then he prayed briefly, and Elizabeth did, too.

"Thank you for hearing our prayers and being with us always," Mom added in closing. "In Jesus' name. Amen."

Elizabeth hopped into bed as Josh fumbled around with something. "Josh, what do you have there?" asked Mom.

Josh held out a small metal key. "Just this key to my bike lock," he said. "I forgot to put it away after I locked my bike up tonight."

Mom smiled as she took the key. "This is very important, isn't it?" she asked. "You use it to unlock your bike every morning and lock it up every night. And you know, prayer is a key, too. It opens us up to the Lord in the morning and reminds us that we are locked under his protection at night. We must also remember that when we pray, we're in the presence of our great God. That's one reason why it's important to pay attention. We all have a key if we just choose to use it."

"Where's my key?" asked Elizabeth, not understanding.

Mom smiled. "Your key is your prayer to God. It's invisible, but it's very real."

How About You?
Do you use your key to talk to God? Prayer is a wonderful privilege. Make it your habit to open and close each day with sincere prayer. *V. R.*

• For the next devotional, turn to page 827. • For the next devotional on *Knowing God,* turn to page 935.
• For notes on *Knowing God,* see pages 129, 610, 815, and 1208.

bedroom, with its windows open toward Jerusalem, and prayed three times a day, just as he always had, giving thanks to his God.

¹¹Then the men thronged to Daniel's house and found him praying there, asking favors of his God. ¹²They rushed back to the king and reminded him about his law. "Haven't you signed a decree," they demanded, "that permits no petitions to any God or man—except you—for thirty days? And anyone disobeying will be thrown to the lions?"

"Yes," the king replied, "it is 'a law of the Medes and Persians,' that cannot be altered or revoked."

¹³Then they told the king, "That fellow Daniel, one of the Jewish captives, is paying no attention to you or your law. He is asking favors of his God three times a day."

¹⁴Hearing this, the king was very angry with himself for signing the law and determined to save Daniel. He spent the rest of the day trying to think of some way to get Daniel out of this predicament.

¹⁵In the evening the men came again to the king and said, "Your Majesty, there is nothing you can do. You signed the law, and it cannot be changed."

¹⁶So at last the king gave the order for Daniel's arrest, and he was taken to the den of lions. The king said to him, "May your God, whom you worship continually, deliver you." And then they threw him in. ¹⁷A stone was brought and placed over the mouth of the den; and the king sealed it with his own signet ring and with that of his government, so that no one could rescue Daniel from the lions.

¹⁸Then the king returned to his palace and went to bed without dinner. He refused his usual entertainment and didn't sleep all night. ¹⁹Very early the next morning he hurried out to the lions' den ²⁰and called out in anguish, "O Daniel, servant of the Living God, was your God, whom you worship continually, able to deliver you from the lions?"

²¹Then he heard a voice! "Your Majesty, live forever!" It was Daniel! ²²"My God has sent his angel," he said, "to shut the lions' mouths so that they can't touch me, for I am innocent before God; nor, sir, have I wronged you."

²³The king was beside himself with joy and ordered Daniel lifted from the den. And not a scratch was found on him because he believed in his God.

²⁴Then the king issued a command to bring the men who had accused Daniel and throw them into the den along with their children and wives, and the lions leaped upon them and tore them apart before they even hit the bottom of the den.

²⁵,²⁶Afterward King Darius wrote this message addressed to everyone in his empire:

"Greetings! I decree that everyone shall tremble and fear before the God of Daniel in every part of my kingdom. For his God is the living, unchanging God whose kingdom shall never be destroyed and whose power shall never end. ²⁷He delivers his people, preserving them from harm; he does great miracles in heaven and earth; it is he who delivered Daniel from the power of the lions."

²⁸So Daniel prospered in the reign of Darius and in the reign of Cyrus the Persian.

7 Daniel Dreams about Four Beasts

One night during the first year of Belshazzar's reign over the Babylonian Empire, Daniel had a dream and he wrote it down. This is his description of what he saw:

²In my dream I saw a great storm on a mighty ocean, with strong winds blowing from every direction. ³Then four huge animals came up out of the water, each different from the other. ⁴The first was like a lion, but it had eagle's wings! And as I watched, its wings were pulled off so that it could no longer fly, and it was left standing on the ground, on two feet, like a man; and a man's mind was given to it. ⁵The second animal looked like a bear with its paw raised, ready to strike. It held three ribs between its teeth, and I heard a voice saying to it, "Get up! Devour many people!" ⁶The third of these strange animals looked like a leopard, but on its back it had wings like those of birds, and it had four heads! And great power was given to it over all mankind.

⁷Then, as I watched in my dream, a fourth animal rose up out of the ocean, too dreadful to describe and incredibly strong. It devoured some of its victims by tearing them apart with its huge iron teeth, and others it crushed beneath its feet. It was far more brutal and vicious than any of the other animals, and it had ten horns.

⁸As I was looking at the horns, suddenly another small horn appeared among them, and three of the first ones were yanked out, roots and all, to give it room; this little horn had a man's eyes and a bragging mouth.

⁹I watched as thrones were put in place and the Ancient of Days—the Almighty God—sat down to judge. His clothing was as white as snow, his hair like whitest wool. He sat upon a fiery throne brought in on flaming wheels, and ¹⁰a river of fire flowed from before him. Millions of angels ministered to him, and hundreds of millions of people stood before him, waiting to be judged. Then the court began its session, and the books were opened.

¹¹As I watched, the brutal fourth animal was killed and its body handed over to be burned

Family Devotions

☐ *Devotion 238*
Praying at All Times

Read Daniel 6:11-28

"Ay-vee-air-ee," read Paul, looking at the name above the door of one of the buildings at the zoo. "What does that mean?" He was visiting the zoo with his uncle Mike.

"That's a building with all kinds of birds," his uncle answered. "Let's go see it." As they opened the door they heard a lot of chirping and squawking. Walking through the building, they saw many different kinds of birds. "Look over there," Uncle Mike said, pointing to a flamingo standing on one leg with his head on his back. "That one's asleep."

"What a funny way to sleep," said Paul. "How can that skinny leg hold that big bird?"

"God made it that way," answered Uncle Mike. "Isn't it amazing?" Paul nodded in agreement.

After leaving the aviary, Uncle Mike bought them each a snack, and they sat on a bench to eat. As they munched on their chips, Paul was very quiet. "Thinking about your parents again?" asked Uncle Mike finally.

"Yeah," Paul answered. "I just know they're going to get a divorce."

"Now you don't know for sure, Paul," Uncle Mike said comfortingly. "They had you come stay with me this weekend so that they could go to that marriage seminar. I believe they'll try to work things out."

"Yeah, I know," Paul said. "I just wish I could do something to help."

"You can pray," his uncle answered.

"Oh, I do that," said Paul. "All the time! But that's such a little thing."

"That's what you said about that flamingo's leg," Uncle Mike reminded him, "but that little leg held that bird up, didn't it? And your 'little' prayers can do great things, too. God made it that way."

Praying at All Times Memory Verse

Don't worry about anything; instead, pray about everything; tell God your needs, and don't forget to thank him for his answers.
Philippians 4:6

How About You?
Do you have problems you can do nothing about? Nothing, that is, except pray? You need to remember that God made prayer very powerful. It's the best thing you can do for your problems. Daniel knew how important prayer is—he even prayed when he knew he could get arrested and thrown into the lions' den! S. N.

- For the next devotional, turn to page 837.   • For the next devotional on *Praying at All Times,* turn to page 977.
- For notes on *Praying at All Times,* see pages 363, 442, 945, 1040, and 1051.

because of its arrogance against Almighty God and the boasting of its little horn. ¹²As for the other three animals, their kingdoms were taken from them, but they were allowed to live a short time longer.

¹³Next I saw the arrival of a Man—or so he seemed to be—brought there on clouds from heaven; he approached the Ancient of Days and was presented to him. ¹⁴He was given the ruling power and glory over all the nations of the world, so that all people of every language must obey him. His power is eternal—it will never end; his government shall never fall.

¹⁵I was confused and disturbed by all I had seen [Daniel wrote in his report], ¹⁶so I approached one of those standing beside the throne and asked him the meaning of all these things, and he explained them to me.

¹⁷"These four huge animals," he said, "represent four kings who will someday rule the earth. ¹⁸But in the end the people of the Most High God shall rule the governments of the world forever and forever."

¹⁹Then I asked about the fourth animal, the one so brutal and shocking, with its iron teeth and brass claws that tore men apart and stamped others to death with its feet. ²⁰I asked, too, about the ten horns and the little horn that came up afterward and destroyed three of the others—the horn with the eyes and the loud, bragging mouth, the one that was stronger than the others. ²¹For I had seen this horn warring against God's people and winning, ²²until the Ancient of Days came and opened his court and vindicated his people, giving them worldwide powers of government.

²³"This fourth animal," he told me, "is the fourth world power that will rule the earth. It will be more brutal than any of the others; it will devour the whole world, destroying everything before it. ²⁴His ten horns are ten kings that will rise out of his empire; then another king will arise, more brutal than the other ten, and will destroy three of them. ²⁵He will defy the Most High God and wear down the saints with persecution, and he will try to change all laws, morals, and customs. God's people will be helpless in his hands for three and a half years.

²⁶"But then the Ancient of Days will come and open his court of justice and take all power from this vicious king, to consume and destroy it until the end. ²⁷Then all nations under heaven and their power shall be given to the people of God; they shall rule all things forever, and all rulers shall serve and obey them."

²⁸That was the end of the dream. When I awoke, I was greatly disturbed, and my face was pale with fright, but I told no one what I had seen.

8 A Ram and a Goat

In the third year of the reign of King Belshazzar, I had another dream similar to the first.

²This time I was at Susa, the capital in the province of Elam, standing beside the Ulai River. ³As I was looking around, I saw a ram with two long horns standing on the riverbank; and as I watched, one of these horns began to grow, so that it was longer than the other. ⁴The ram butted everything out of its way, and no one could stand against it or help its victims. It did as it pleased and became very great.

⁵While I was wondering what this could mean, suddenly a buck goat appeared from the west so swiftly that it didn't even touch the ground. This goat, which had one very large horn between its eyes, ⁶rushed furiously at the two-horned ram. ⁷And the closer he came, the angrier he was. He charged into the ram and broke off both his horns. Now the ram was helpless, and the buck goat knocked him down and trampled him, for there was no one to rescue him.

⁸The victor became both proud and powerful, but suddenly, at the height of his power, his horn was broken, and in its place grew four good-sized horns pointing in four directions. ⁹One of these, growing slowly at first, soon became very strong and attacked the south and east, and warred against the land of Israel. ¹⁰He fought against the people of God and defeated some of their leaders. ¹¹He even challenged the Commander of the army of heaven by canceling the daily sacrifices offered to him and by defiling his Temple. ¹²But the army of heaven was restrained from destroying him for this transgression. As a result, truth and righteousness perished, and evil triumphed and prospered.

¹³Then I heard two of the holy angels talking to each other. One of them said, "How long will it be until the daily sacrifice is restored again? How long until the destruction of the Temple is avenged and God's people triumph?"

¹⁴The other replied, "Twenty-three hundred days must first go by."

¹⁵As I was trying to understand the meaning of this vision, suddenly a man was standing in front of me—or at least he looked like a man— ¹⁶and I heard a man's voice calling from across the river, "Gabriel, tell Daniel the meaning of his dream."

¹⁷So Gabriel started toward me. But as he approached, I was too frightened to stand and fell down with my face to the ground. "Son of man," he said, "you must understand that the events you have seen in your vision will not take place until the end times come."

¹⁸Then I fainted, lying face downward on the ground. But he roused me with a touch and

helped me to my feet. ¹⁹"I am here," he said, "to tell you what is going to happen in the last days of the coming time of terror—for what you have seen pertains to that final event in history.

²⁰"The two horns of the ram you saw are the kings of Media and Persia; ²¹the shaggy-haired goat is the nation of Greece, and its long horn represents the first great king of that country. ²²When you saw the horn break off and four smaller horns replace it, this meant that the Grecian Empire will break into four sections with four kings, none of them as great as the first.

²³"Toward the end of their kingdoms, when they have become morally rotten, an angry king shall rise to power with great shrewdness and intelligence. ²⁴His power shall be mighty, but it will be satanic strength and not his own. Prospering wherever he turns, he will destroy all who oppose him, though their armies be mighty, and he will devastate God's people.

²⁵"He will be a master of deception, defeating many by catching them off guard as they bask in false security. Without warning he will destroy them. So great will he fancy himself to be that he will even take on the Prince of Princes in battle; but in so doing he will seal his own doom, for he shall be broken by the hand of God, though no human means could overpower him.

²⁶"And then in your vision you heard about the twenty-three hundred days to pass before the rights of worship are restored. This number is literal, and means just that. But none of these things will happen for a long time, so don't tell anyone about them yet."

²⁷Then I grew faint and was sick for several days. Afterward I was up and around again and performed my duties for the king, but I was greatly distressed by the dream and did not understand it.

9 Daniel Prays for His People

It was now the first year of the reign of King Darius, the son of Ahasuerus. (Darius was a Mede but became king of the Chaldeans.) ²In that first year of his reign, I, Daniel, learned from the book of Jeremiah the prophet, that Jerusalem must lie desolate for seventy years. ³So I earnestly pleaded with the Lord God [to end our captivity and send us back to our own land].

As I prayed, I fasted and wore rough sackcloth, and I sprinkled myself with ashes ⁴and confessed my sins and those of my people.

"O Lord," I prayed, "you are a great and awesome God; you always fulfill your promises of mercy to those who love you and keep your laws. ⁵But we have sinned so much; we have rebelled against you and scorned your commands. ⁶We have refused to listen to your servants the prophets, whom you sent again and again down through the years, with your messages to our kings and princes and to all the people.

⁷"O Lord, you are righteous; but as for us, we are always shamefaced with sin, just as you see us now; yes, all of us—the men of Judah, the people of Jerusalem, and all Israel, scattered near and far wherever you have driven us because of our disloyalty to you. ⁸O Lord, we and our kings and princes and fathers are weighted down with shame because of all our sins.

⁹"But the Lord our God is merciful and pardons even those who have rebelled against him.

¹⁰"O Lord our God, we have disobeyed you; we have flouted all the laws you gave us through your servants, the prophets. ¹¹All Israel has disobeyed; we have turned away from you and haven't listened to your voice. And so the awesome curse of God has crushed us—the curse written in the law of Moses your servant. ¹²And you have done exactly as you warned us you would do, for never in all history has there been a disaster like what happened at Jerusalem to us and our rulers. ¹³Every curse against us written in the law of Moses has come true; all the evils he predicted—all have come. But even so we still refuse to satisfy the Lord our God by turning from our sins and doing right.

¹⁴"And so the Lord deliberately crushed us with the calamity he prepared; he is fair in everything he does, but we would not obey. ¹⁵O Lord our God, you brought lasting honor to your name by removing your people from Egypt in a great display of power. Lord, do it again! Though we have sinned so much and are full of wickedness, ¹⁶yet because of all your faithful mercies, Lord, please turn away your furious anger from Jerusalem, your own city, your holy mountain. For the heathen mock at you because your city lies in ruins for our sins.

¹⁷"O our God, hear your servant's prayer! Listen as I plead! Let your face shine again with peace and joy upon your desolate sanctuary—for your own glory, Lord.

¹⁸"O my God, bend down your ear and listen to my plea. Open your eyes and see our wretchedness, how your city lies in ruins—for everyone knows that it is yours. We don't ask because we merit help, but because you are so merciful despite our grievous sins.

¹⁹"O Lord, hear; O Lord, forgive. O Lord, listen to me and act! Don't delay—for your own sake, O my God, because your people and your city bear your name."

²⁰Even while I was praying and confessing my sin and the sins of my people, desperately pleading with the Lord my God for Jerusalem, his holy

mountain, [21]Gabriel, whom I had seen in the earlier vision, flew swiftly to me at the time of the evening sacrifice [22]and said to me, "Daniel, I am here to help you understand God's plans. [23]The moment you began praying a command was given. I am here to tell you what it was, for God loves you very much. Listen and try to understand the meaning of the vision that you saw!

[24]"The Lord has commanded 490 years of further punishment upon Jerusalem and your people. Then at last they will learn to stay away from sin, and their guilt will be cleansed; then the kingdom of everlasting righteousness will begin, and the Most Holy Place (in the Temple) will be rededicated, as the prophets have declared. [25]Now listen! It will be 49 years plus 434 years from the time the command is given to rebuild Jerusalem until the Anointed One comes! Jerusalem's streets and walls will be rebuilt despite the perilous times.

[26]"After this period of 434 years, the Anointed One will be killed, his kingdom still unrealized . . . and a king will arise whose armies will destroy the city and the Temple. They will be overwhelmed as with a flood, and war and its miseries are decreed from that time to the very end. [27]This king will make a seven-year treaty with the people, but after half that time, he will break his pledge and stop the Jews from all their sacrifices and their offerings; then, as a climax to all his terrible deeds, the Enemy shall utterly defile the sanctuary of God. But in God's time and plan, his judgment will be poured out upon this Evil One."

10 A Heavenly Messenger

In the third year of the reign of Cyrus, king of Persia, Daniel (also called Belteshazzar) had another vision. It concerned events certain to happen in the future: times of great tribulation—wars and sorrows, and this time he understood what the vision meant.

[2]When this vision came to me [Daniel said later], I had been in mourning for three full weeks. [3]All that time I tasted neither wine nor meat, and, of course, I went without desserts. I neither washed nor shaved nor combed my hair.

[4]Then one day early in April, as I was standing beside the great Tigris River, [5,6]I looked up, and suddenly there before me stood a person robed in linen garments, with a belt of purest gold around his waist and glowing, lustrous skin! From his face came blinding flashes like lightning, and his eyes were pools of fire; his arms and feet shone like polished brass, and his voice was like the roaring of a vast multitude of people.

[7]I, Daniel, alone saw this great vision; the men with me saw nothing, but they were suddenly filled with unreasoning terror and ran to hide, [8]so I was left alone. When I saw this frightening vision, my strength left me, and I grew pale and weak with fright.

[9]Then he spoke to me, and I fell to the ground face downward in a deep faint. [10]But a hand touched me and lifted me, still trembling, to my hands and knees. [11]And I heard his voice—"O Daniel, greatly beloved of God," he said, "stand up and listen carefully to what I have to say to you, for God has sent me to you." So I stood up, still trembling with fear.

[12]Then he said, "Don't be frightened, Daniel, for your request has been heard in heaven and was answered the very first day you began to fast before the Lord and pray for understanding; that very day I was sent here to meet you. [13]But for twenty-one days the mighty Evil Spirit who overrules the kingdom of Persia blocked my way. Then Michael, one of the top officers of the heavenly army, came to help me, so that I was able to break through these spirit rulers of Persia. [14]Now I am here to tell you what will happen to your people, the Jews, at the end times—for the fulfillment of this prophecy is many years away."

[15]All this time I was looking down, unable to speak a word. [16]Then someone—he looked like a man—touched my lips and I could talk again, and I said to the messenger from heaven, "Sir, I am terrified by your appearance and have no strength. [17]How can such a person as I even talk to you? For my strength is gone, and I can hardly breathe."

[18]Then the one who seemed to be a man touched me again, and I felt my strength returning. [19]"God loves you very much," he said; "don't be afraid! Calm yourself; be strong—yes, strong!"

Suddenly, as he spoke these words, I felt stronger and said to him, "Now you can go ahead and speak, sir, for you have strengthened me."

[20,21]He replied, "Do you know why I have come? I am here to tell you what is written in the 'Book of the Future.' Then, when I leave, I will go again to fight my way back, past the prince of Persia; and after him, the prince of Greece. Only Michael, the angel who guards your people Israel, will be there to help me.

11 The Messenger Predicts the Future

"I was the one sent to strengthen and help Darius the Mede in the first year of his reign. [2]But now I will show you what the future holds. Three more Persian kings will reign, to be succeeded by a fourth, far richer than the others. Using his wealth for political advantage, he will plan total war against Greece.

[3]"Then a mighty king will rise in Greece, a king

who will rule a vast kingdom and accomplish everything he sets out to do. ⁴But at the zenith of his power, his kingdom will break apart and be divided into four weaker nations, not even ruled by his sons. For his empire will be torn apart and given to others. ⁵One of them, the king of Egypt, will increase in power, but this king's own officials will rebel against him and take away his kingdom and make it still more powerful.

⁶"Several years later an alliance will be formed between the king of Syria and the king of Egypt. The daughter of the king of Egypt will be given in marriage to the king of Syria as a gesture of peace, but she will lose her influence over him, and not only will her hopes be blighted, but those of her father, the king of Egypt, and of her ambassador and child. ⁷But when her brother takes over as king of Egypt, he will raise an army against the king of Syria and march against him and defeat him. ⁸When he returns again to Egypt, he will carry back their idols with him, along with priceless gold and silver dishes; and for many years afterward he will leave the Syrian king alone.

⁹"Meanwhile, the king of Syria will invade Egypt briefly but will soon return again to his own land. ¹⁰,¹¹However, the sons of this Syrian king will assemble a mighty army that will overflow across Israel into Egypt, to a fortress there. Then the king of Egypt, in great anger, will rally against the vast forces of Syria and defeat them. ¹²Filled with pride after this great victory, he will have many thousands of his enemies killed, but his success will be short-lived.

¹³"A few years later the Syrian king will return with a fully-equipped army far greater than the one he lost, ¹⁴and other nations will join him in a crusade against Egypt. Insurgents among your own people, the Jews, will join them, thus fulfilling prophecy, but they will not succeed. ¹⁵Then the Syrian king and his allies will come and lay siege to a fortified city of Egypt and capture it, and the proud armies of Egypt will go down to defeat.

¹⁶"The Syrian king will march onward unopposed; none will be able to stop him. And he will also enter 'The Glorious Land' of Israel and pillage it. ¹⁷This will be his plot for conquering all Egypt: he, too, will form an alliance with the Egyptian king, giving him a daughter in marriage, so that she can work for him from within. But the plan will fail.

¹⁸"After this he will turn his attention to the coastal cities and conquer many. But a general will stop him and cause him to retreat in shame. ¹⁹He will turn homeward again but will have trouble on the way and disappear.

²⁰"His successor will be remembered as the king who sent a tax collector into Israel, but after a very brief reign, he will die mysteriously, though neither in battle nor in riot.

²¹"Next to come to power will be an evil man not directly in line for royal succession. But during a crisis he will take over the kingdom by flattery and intrigue. ²²Then all opposition will be swept away before him, including a leader of the priests. ²³His promises will be worthless. From the first his method will be deceit; with a mere handful of followers, he will become strong. ²⁴He will enter the richest areas of the land without warning and do something never done before: he will take the property and wealth of the rich and scatter it out among the people. With great success he will besiege and capture powerful strongholds throughout his dominions, but this will last for only a short while. ²⁵Then he will stir up his courage and raise a great army against Egypt; and Egypt, too, will raise a mighty army, but to no avail, for plots against him will succeed.

²⁶"Those of his own household will bring his downfall; his army will desert, and many be killed.

²⁷"Both these kings will be plotting against each other at the conference table, attempting to deceive each other. But it will make no difference, for neither can succeed until God's appointed time has come.

²⁸"The Syrian king will then return home with great riches, first marching through Israel and destroying it. ²⁹Then at the predestined time he will once again turn his armies southward, as he had threatened, but now it will be a very different story from those first two occasions. ³⁰,³¹For Roman warships will scare him off, and he will withdraw and return home. Angered by having to retreat, the Syrian king will again pillage Jerusalem and pollute the sanctuary, putting a stop to the daily sacrifices, and worshiping idols inside the Temple. He will leave godless Jews in power when he leaves—men who have abandoned their fathers' faith. ³²He will flatter those who hate the things of God and win them over to his side. But the people who know their God shall be strong and do great things.

³³"Those with spiritual understanding will have a wide ministry of teaching in those days. But they will be in constant danger, many of them dying by fire and sword, or being jailed and robbed. ³⁴Eventually these pressures will subside, and some ungodly

---

LEAVING THE FUTURE IN GOD'S HANDS 12:13 The promise of resurrection is reaffirmed to Daniel. He would one day see the fulfillment of his words, but he was not to spend the rest of his life wondering what his visions might mean. Instead, he was to rest in the comfort of God's sovereignty and look forward to the time when he would share eternal life with God. God does not reveal all things to us in this life. We must be content with the partial picture until it is his good time for us to see more. He will tell us all we need to know. **To begin the series of devotionals on LEAVING THE FUTURE IN GOD'S HANDS, turn to page 75.**

men will come, pretending to offer a helping hand, only to take advantage of them.

⁳⁵"And some who are most gifted in the things of God will stumble in those days and fall, but this will only refine and cleanse them and make them pure until the final end of all their trials, at God's appointed time.

³⁶"The king will do exactly as he pleases, claiming to be greater than every god there is, even blaspheming the God of gods, and prospering—until his time is up. For God's plans are unshakable. ³⁷He will have no regard for the gods of his fathers, nor for the god beloved of women, nor any other god, for he will boast that he is greater than them all. ³⁸Instead of these, he will worship the Fortress god—a god his fathers never knew—and lavish on him costly gifts! ³⁹Claiming this god's help, he will have great success against the strongest fortresses. He will honor those who submit to him, appointing them to positions of authority and dividing the land to them as their reward.

⁴⁰"Then at the time of the end, the king of the south will attack him again, and the northern king will react with the strength and fury of a whirlwind; his vast army and navy will rush out to bury him with their might. ⁴¹He will invade various lands on the way, including Israel, the Pleasant Land, and overthrow the governments of many nations. Moab, Edom, and most of Ammon will escape, ⁴²but Egypt and many other lands will be occupied. ⁴³ He will capture all the treasures of Egypt, and the Libyans and Ethiopians shall be his servants.

⁴⁴"But then news from the east and north will alarm him, and he will return in great anger to destroy as he goes. ⁴⁵He will halt between Jerusalem and the sea and there pitch his royal tents, but while he is there his time will suddenly run out, and there will be no one to help him.

12 A Message about the End of Time

"At that time Michael, the mighty angelic prince who stands guard over your nation, will stand up [and fight for you in heaven against satanic forces], and there will be a time of anguish for the Jews greater than any previous suffering in Jewish history. And yet every one of your people whose names are written in the Book will endure it.

²"And many of those whose bodies lie dead and buried will rise up, some to everlasting life and some to shame and everlasting contempt.

³"And those who are wise—the people of God—shall shine as brightly as the sun's brilliance, and those who turn many to righteousness will glitter like stars forever.

⁴"But Daniel, keep this prophecy a secret; seal it up so that it will not be understood until the end times, when travel and education shall be vastly increased!"

⁵Then I, Daniel, looked and saw two men on each bank of a river. ⁶And one of them asked the man in linen robes who was standing now above the river, "How long will it be until all these terrors end?"

⁷He replied, with both hands lifted to heaven, taking oath by him who lives forever and ever, that they will not end until three and a half years after the power of God's people has been crushed.

⁸I heard what he said, but I didn't understand what he meant. So I said, "Sir, how will all this finally end?"

⁹But he said, "Go now, Daniel, for what I have said is not to be understood until the time of the end. ¹⁰Many shall be purified by great trials and persecutions. But the wicked shall continue in their wickedness, and none of them will understand. Only those who are willing to learn will know what it means.

¹¹"From the time the daily sacrifice is taken away and the Horrible Thing is set up to be worshiped, there will be 1,290 days. ¹²And blessed are those who wait and remain until the 1335th day!

¹³"But go on now to the end of your life and your rest; for you will rise again and have your full share of those last days."

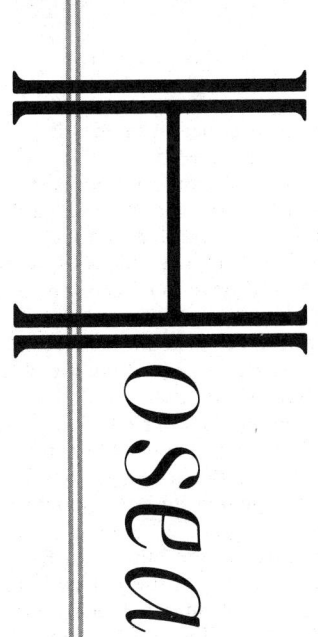

Hosea

DO YOU learn things faster when you see them acted out?

When God called Hosea to be a prophet, he called him to be an actor, too. In the prophets we've read so far, we've seen God speak through dreams, visions, symbols, objects, poems, and stories. But God wanted Hosea to be a living example of what God was trying to tell his people.

Hosea was a prophet during the reigns of Jereboam, Uzziah, Jotham, Ahaz, and Hezekiah. God asked Hosea to do something very hard—to marry a woman who would be unfaithful to him. And after she left him for other men, he was to forgive her, bring her home again, and keep loving her.

God and his people had a *covenant,* which is like being married. The people worshiped other gods, which is like a wife going out with other men. But God took his people back when they repented. That's what God wanted the people to think about when they saw Hosea accept and love his wife. God wanted his people to be faithful to him.

Hosea's Wife and Children

These are the messages from the Lord to Hosea, son of Beeri, during the reigns of these four kings of Judah:

Uzziah, Jotham, Ahaz, and Hezekiah; and one of the kings of Israel, Jeroboam, son of Joash.

²Here is the first message:

The Lord said to Hosea, "Go and marry a girl who is a prostitute, so that some of her children will be born to you from other men. This will illustrate the way my people have been untrue to me, committing open adultery against me by worshiping other gods."

³So Hosea married Gomer, daughter of Diblaim, and she conceived and bore him a son.

⁴,⁵And the Lord said, "Name the child Jezreel, for in the Valley of Jezreel I am about to punish King Jehu's dynasty to avenge the murders he committed; in fact, I will put an end to Israel as an independent kingdom, breaking the power of the nation in the Valley of Jezreel."

⁶Soon Gomer had another child—this one a

daughter. And God said to Hosea, "Name her Lo-ruhamah (meaning 'No more mercy') for I will have no more mercy upon Israel, to forgive her again. ⁷But I *will* have mercy on the tribe of Judah. I will personally free her from her enemies without any help from her armies or her weapons."

⁸After Gomer had weaned Lo-ruhamah, she again conceived and this time gave birth to a son. ⁹And God said, "Call him Lo-ammi (meaning 'Not mine'), for Israel is not mine and I am not her God.

¹⁰"Yet the time will come when Israel shall prosper and become a great nation; in that day her people will be too numerous to count—like sand along a seashore! Then, instead of saying to them, 'You are not my people,' I will tell them, 'You are my sons, children of the Living God.' ¹¹Then the people of Judah and Israel will unite and have one leader; they will return from exile together; what a day that will be—the day when God will sow his people in the fertile soil of their own land again.

2 Punishment and Forgiveness

"O Jezreel, rename your brother and sister. Call your brother Ammi (which means "Now you are mine"); name your sister Ruhamah ("Pitied"), for now God will have mercy upon her!

²"Plead with your mother, for she has become another man's wife—I am no longer her husband. Beg her to stop her harlotry, to quit giving herself to others. ³If she doesn't, I will strip her as naked as the day she was born and cause her to waste away and die of thirst as in a land riddled with famine and drought. ⁴And I will not give special favors to her children as I would to my own, for they are not my children; they belong to other men.

⁵"For their mother has committed adultery. She did a shameful thing when she said, 'I'll run after other men and sell myself to them for food and drinks and clothes.'

⁶"But I will fence her in with briars and thornbushes; I'll block the road before her to make her lose her way, so that ⁷when she runs after her lovers she will not catch up with them. She will search for them but not find them. Then she will think, 'I might as well return to my husband, for I was better off with him than I am now.'

⁸"She doesn't realize that all she has, has come from me. It was I who gave her all the gold and silver she used in worshiping Baal, her god!

⁹"But now I will take back the wine and ripened corn I constantly supplied, and the clothes I gave her to cover her nakedness—I will no longer give her rich harvests of grain in its season or wine at the time of the grape harvest. ¹⁰Now I will expose her nakedness in public for all her lovers to see, and no one will be able to rescue her from my hand.

¹¹"I will put an end to all her joys, her parties, holidays, and feasts. ¹²I will destroy her vineyards and her orchards—gifts she claims her lovers gave her—and let them grow into a jungle; wild animals will eat their fruit.

¹³"For all the incense she burned to Baal her idol and for the times when she put on her earrings and jewels and went out looking for her lovers and deserted me—for all these things I will punish her," says the Lord.

¹⁴"But I will court her again and bring her into the wilderness, and I will speak to her tenderly there. ¹⁵There I will give back her vineyards to her and transform her Valley of Troubles into a Door of Hope. She will respond to me there, singing with joy as in days long ago in her youth after I had freed her from captivity in Egypt.

¹⁶"In that coming day," says the Lord, "she will call me 'My Husband' instead of 'My Master.' ¹⁷O Israel, I will cause you to forget your idols, and their names will not be spoken anymore.

¹⁸"At that time I will make a treaty between you and the wild animals, birds, and snakes, not to fear each other any more; and I will destroy all weapons, and all wars will end.

"Then you will lie down in peace and safety, unafraid; ¹⁹and I will bind you to me forever with chains of righteousness and justice and love and mercy. ²⁰I will betroth you to me in faithfulness and love, and you will really know me then as you never have before.

²¹,²²"In that day," says the Lord, "I will answer the pleading of the sky for clouds, to pour down water on the earth in answer to its cry for rain. Then the earth can answer the parched cry of the grain, the grapes, and the olive trees for moisture and for dew—and the whole grand chorus shall sing together that "God sows!" He has given all!

²³"At that time I will sow a crop of Israelites and raise them for myself! I will pity those who are 'not pitied,' and I will say to those who are 'not my people,' 'Now you are my people'; and they will reply, 'You are our God!'"

GIVING THANKS 2:12 The people of Israel were so immersed in idolatry that they actually believed heathen gods gave them their orchards and vineyards. They had forgotten that the entire land was a gift from God (Deuteronomy 32:49). Today many people give credit to everything but God for their prosperity—luck, hard work, quick thinking, the right contacts. When you succeed, who gets the credit? **To begin the series of devotionals on GIVING THANKS, turn to page 169.**

3 Hosea Brings Gomer Back Home

Then the Lord said to me, "Go, and get your wife again and bring her back to you and love her, even though she loves adultery. For the Lord still loves Israel though she has turned to other gods and offered them choice gifts."

²So I bought her [back from her slavery] for a couple of dollars and eight bushels of barley, ³and I said to her, "You must live alone for many days; do not go out with other men nor be a prostitute, and I will wait for you."

⁴This illustrates the fact that Israel will be a long time without a king or prince, and without an altar, temple, priests, or even idols!

⁵Afterward they will return to the Lord their God and to the Messiah, their King, and they shall come trembling, submissive to the Lord and to his blessings in the end times.

4 God's Case against Israel

Hear the word of the Lord, O people of Israel. The Lord has filed a lawsuit against you listing the following charges: "There is no faithfulness, no kindness, no knowledge of God in your land. ²You swear and lie and kill and steal and commit adultery. There is violence everywhere, with one murder after another.

³"That is why your land is not producing; it is filled with sadness, and all living things grow sick and die; the animals, the birds, and even the fish begin to disappear.

⁴"Don't point your finger at someone else and try to pass the blame to him! Look, priest, I am pointing my finger at *you*. ⁵As a sentence for your crimes, you priests will stumble in broad daylight as well as in the night, and so will your false 'prophets' too; and I will destroy your mother, Israel. ⁶My people are destroyed because they don't know me, and it is all your fault, you priests, for you yourselves refuse to know me; therefore, I refuse to recognize you as my priests. Since you have forgotten my laws, I will 'forget' to bless your children. ⁷The more my people multiplied, the more they sinned against me. They exchanged the glory of God for the disgrace of idols.

⁸"The priests rejoice in the sins of the people; they lap it up and lick their lips for more! ⁹And thus it is: 'Like priests, like people'—because the priests are wicked, the people are too. Therefore, I will punish both priests and people for all their wicked deeds. ¹⁰They will eat and still be hungry. Though they do a big business as prostitutes, they shall have no children, for they have deserted me and turned to other gods.

¹¹"Wine, women, and song have robbed my people of their brains. ¹²For they are asking a piece of wood to tell them what to do. 'Divine Truth' comes to them through tea leaves! Longing after idols has made them foolish. For they have played the harlot, serving other gods, deserting me. ¹³They sacrifice to idols on the tops of mountains; they go up into the hills to burn incense in the pleasant shade of oaks and poplars and sumac trees.

"There your daughters turn to prostitution and your brides commit adultery. ¹⁴But why should I punish them? For you men are doing the same thing, sinning with harlots and temple prostitutes. Fools! Your doom is sealed, for you refuse to understand.

¹⁵"But though Israel is a prostitute, may Judah stay far from such a life. O Judah, do not join with those who insincerely worship me at Gilgal and at Bethel. Their worship is mere pretense. ¹⁶Don't be like Israel, stubborn as a heifer, resisting the Lord's attempts to lead her in green pastures. ¹⁷Stay away from her, for she is wedded to idolatry.

¹⁸"The men of Israel finish up their drinking bouts, and off they go to find some whores. Their love for shame is greater than for honor.

¹⁹"Therefore, a mighty wind shall sweep them away; they shall die in shame because they sacrifice to idols.

5 The Verdict Is In: Guilty

"Listen to this, you priests and all of Israel's leaders; listen, all you men of the royal family: You are doomed! For you have deluded the people with idols at Mizpah and Tabor ²and dug a deep pit to trap them at Acacia. But never forget—I will settle up with all of you for what you've done.

³I have seen your evil deeds: Israel, you have left me as a prostitute leaves her husband; you are utterly defiled. ⁴Your deeds won't let you come to God again, for the spirit of adultery is deep within you, and you cannot know the Lord.

⁵"The very arrogance of Israel testifies against her in my court. She will stumble under her load of guilt, and Judah, too, shall fall. ⁶Then at last, they will come with their flocks and herds to sacrifice to God, but it will be too late—they will not find him. He has withdrawn from them and they are left alone.

⁷"For they have betrayed the honor of the Lord, bearing children that aren't his. Suddenly they and all their wealth will disappear. ⁸Sound the alarm! Warn with trumpet blasts in Gibeah and Ramah, and on over to Beth-aven; tremble, land of Benjamin! ⁹Hear this announcement, Israel: When your day of punishment comes, you will become a heap of rubble.

10"The leaders of Judah have become the lowest sort of thieves. Therefore, I will pour my anger down upon them like a waterfall, 11and Ephraim will be crushed and broken by my sentence because she is determined to follow idols. 12I will destroy her as a moth does wool; I will sap away the strength of Judah like dry rot.

13"When Ephraim and Judah see how sick they are, Ephraim will turn to Assyria, to the great king there, but he can neither help nor cure.

14"I will tear Ephraim and Judah as a lion rips apart its prey; I will carry them off and chase all rescuers away.

15"I will abandon them and return to my home until they admit their guilt and look to me for help again, for as soon as trouble comes, they will search for me and say:

6 God Wants Israel's Love

"'Come, let us return to the Lord; it is he who has torn us—he will heal us. He has wounded—he will bind us up. 2In just a couple of days, or three at the most, he will set us on our feet again to live in his kindness! 3Oh, that we might know the Lord! Let us press on to know him, and he will respond to us as surely as the coming of dawn or the rain of early spring.'

4"O Ephraim and Judah, what shall I do with you? For your love vanishes like morning clouds, and disappears like dew. 5I sent my prophets to warn you of your doom; I have slain you with the words of my mouth, threatening you with death. Suddenly, without warning, my judgment will strike you as surely as day follows night.

6"I don't want your sacrifices—I want your love; I don't want your offerings—I want you to know me.

7"But like Adam, you broke my covenant; you refused my love. 8Gilead is a city of sinners, tracked with footprints of blood. 9Her citizens are gangs of robbers, lying in ambush for their victims; packs of priests murder along the road to Shechem and practice every kind of sin. 10Yes, I have seen a horrible thing in Israel—Ephraim chasing other gods, Israel utterly defiled.

11O Judah, for you also there is a plentiful harvest of punishment waiting—and I wanted so much to bless you!

7 Israel: Always Missing the Target

"I wanted to forgive Israel, but her sins were far too great—no one can even live in Samaria without being a liar, thief, and bandit!

2"Her people never seem to recognize that I am watching them. Their sinful deeds give them away on every side; I see them all. 3The king is glad about their wickedness; the princes laugh about their lies. 4They are all adulterers; as a baker's oven is constantly aflame—except after he kneads the dough and waits for it to rise again—so are these people constantly aflame with lust.

5"On the king's birthday, the princes get him drunk; he makes a fool of himself and drinks with those who mock him. 6Their hearts blaze like a furnace with intrigue. Their plot smolders through the night, and in the morning it flames forth like raging fire.

7"They kill their kings one after another, and none cries out to me for help.

8"My people mingle with the heathen, picking up their evil ways; thus they become as good-for-nothing as a half-baked cake!

9"Worshiping foreign gods has sapped their strength, but they don't know it. Ephraim's hair is turning gray, and he doesn't even realize how weak and old he is. 10His pride in other gods has openly condemned him; yet he doesn't return to his God, nor even try to find him.

11"Ephraim is a silly, witless dove, calling to Egypt, flying to Assyria. 12But as she flies, I throw my net over her and bring her down like a bird from the sky; I will punish her for all her evil ways.

13"Woe to my people for deserting me; let them perish, for they have sinned against me. I wanted to redeem them but their hard hearts would not accept the truth. 14They lie there sleepless with anxiety but won't ask my help. Instead, they worship heathen gods, asking them for crops and for prosperity.

15"I have helped them and made them strong, yet now they turn against me.

16"They look everywhere except to heaven, to the Most High God. They are like a crooked bow that always misses targets; their leaders will perish by the sword of the enemy for their insolence to me. And all Egypt will laugh at them.

8 A Prediction of Captivity

"Sound the alarm! They are coming! Like a vulture, the enemy descends upon the people of God because they have bro-

---

CONFESSING SIN 6:1-3 This is presumption, not true repentance. The people did not understand the seriousness of their sins. They did not turn from idols, pledge to change, or regret their sins. They thought God's wrath would only last a few days, when really their nation was about to be taken into exile. Israel was interested in God only for the material benefits he provided; they did not value the eternal benefits that come from worshiping him. Before judging them, however, consider your attitude. What do you hope to gain from your religion? Do you "repent" easily, without seriously considering what changes need to take place in your life? **To begin the series of devotionals on CONFESSING SIN, turn to page 41.**

Family Devotions

☐ **Devotion 239**

Showing Compassion

Read Hosea 6:1-3

"Look at the assignment Miss Linda gave us in Sunday school today," said Nancy, handing a paper to her mother.

Before Mom could read the paper, three-year-old Missi came bursting into the room. "Ohhhh! Mommy! Look at my finger. It's bleeding. That flower hurt me!"

A drop of blood almost hid the thorn in Missi's finger. Gently, Mom pulled out the thorn, wiped off the blood, and kissed the finger. Smiling, Missi went back outside.

Mom turned back to the paper Nancy had handed her. "Find a need and fill it; find a hurt and heal it," she read. She smiled at Nancy, "That's a good assignment."

"Sure," groaned Nancy, "except I'm not a doctor. How can I heal someone?"

"Didn't Miss Linda explain that there are different kinds of hurts?" Mom asked.

Nancy nodded. "Yes, she said that besides physical hurts, there are what she called mental and spiritual hurts. But what can I do about those things? I'm just a kid." She sighed. "I know that Karen's folks are getting a divorce. And I know that John's big brother is in jail for selling drugs. And Mandy's dad is out of work, so she never has money for extra projects at school. But I can't heal their hurts."

"When Missi came crying to me a while ago, I didn't really *heal* her finger. I just gave her a lot of love, and she forgot the pain," Mom said. "That's what you can do, too. You may not be able to solve anyone else's problems, but with God's help, you can encourage them and make their day brighter. And you can point them to Jesus, the one who really can heal their hurts. Pray about it, and the Lord will show you what you can do."

Nancy smiled. "OK. Maybe it isn't such a hard assignment after all."

Showing Compassion Memory Verse

What a wonderful God we have—he is the Father of our Lord Jesus Christ, the source of every mercy, and the one who so wonderfully comforts and strengthens us in our hardships and trials.
2 Corinthians 1:3

How About You?

Do you know someone who is hurting? God wants to heal that person's hurt, and he may want to use you to help. Smile at that person. Talk to him. Pray for her. Share something from God's Word. Try to heal at least one hurt this week. B. W.

• For the next devotional, turn to page 849. • For the next devotional on *Showing Compassion*, turn to page 883.
• For notes on *Showing Compassion*, see pages 206, 506, 515, 710, and 934.

ken my treaty and revolted against my laws.

²"Now Israel pleads with me and says, 'Help us, for you are our God!' ³But it is too late! Israel has thrown away her chance with contempt, and now her enemies will chase her. ⁴She has appointed kings and princes, but not with my consent. They have cut themselves off from my help by worshiping the idols that they made from their silver and gold.

⁵"O Samaria, I reject this calf—this idol you have made. My fury burns against you. How long will it be before one honest man is found among you? ⁶When will you admit this calf you worship was made by human hands! It is not God! Therefore, it must be smashed to bits.

⁷"They have sown the wind, and they will reap the whirlwind. Their cornstalks stand there barren, withered, sickly, with no grain; if it has any, foreigners will eat it.

⁸"Israel is destroyed; she lies among the nations as a broken pot. ⁹She is a lonely, wandering wild ass. The only friends she has are those she hires; Assyria is one of them.

¹⁰"But though she hires 'friends' from many lands, I will send her off to exile. Then for a while at least she will be free of the burden of her wonderful king! ¹¹Ephraim has built many altars, but they are not to worship me! They are altars of sin! ¹²Even if I gave her ten thousand laws, she'd say they weren't for her—that they applied to someone far away. ¹³Her people love the ritual of their sacrifice, but to me it is meaningless! I will call for an accounting of their sins and punish them; they shall return to Egypt.

¹⁴"Israel has built great palaces; Judah has constructed great defenses for her cities, but they have forgotten their Maker. Therefore, I will send down fire upon those palaces and burn those fortresses."

9 Wandering without God

O Israel, rejoice no more as others do, for you have deserted your God and sacrificed to other gods on every threshing floor.

²Therefore your harvests will be small; your grapes will blight upon the vine.

³You may no longer stay here in this land of God; you will be carried off to Egypt and Assyria and live there on scraps of food. ⁴There, far from home, you are not allowed to pour out wine for sacrifice to God. For no sacrifice that is offered there can please him; it is polluted, just as food of mourners is; all who eat such sacrifices are defiled. They may eat this food to feed themselves, but may not offer it to God. ⁵What then will you do on holy days, on days of feasting to the Lord, ⁶when you are carried off to Assyria as slaves? Who will inherit your possessions left behind? Egypt will! She will gather your dead; Memphis will bury them. And thorns and thistles will grow up among the ruins.

⁷The time of Israel's punishment has come; the day of recompense is almost here, and soon Israel will know it all too well. "The prophets are crazy"; "The inspired men are mad." Yes, so they mock, for the nation is weighted with sin and shows only hatred for those who love God.

⁸"I appointed the prophets to guard my people, but the people have blocked them at every turn and publicly declared their hatred, even in the Temple of the Lord. ⁹The things my people do are as depraved as what they did in Gibeah long ago. The Lord does not forget. He will surely punish them.

¹⁰"O Israel, how well I remember those first delightful days when I led you through the wilderness! How refreshing was your love! How satisfying, like the early figs of summer in their first season! But then you deserted me for Baal-peor, to give yourselves to other gods, and soon you were as foul as they. ¹¹The glory of Israel flies away like a bird, for your children will die at birth, or perish in the womb, or never even be conceived. ¹²And if your children grow, I will take them from you; all are doomed. Yes, it will be a sad day when I turn away and leave you alone."

¹³In my vision I have seen the sons of Israel doomed. The fathers are forced to lead their sons to slaughter. ¹⁴O Lord, what shall I ask for your people? I will ask for wombs that don't give birth, for breasts that cannot nourish.

¹⁵"All their wickedness began at Gilgal; there I began to hate them. I will drive them from my land because of their idolatry. I will love them no more, for all their leaders are rebels. ¹⁶Ephraim is doomed. The roots of Israel are dried up; she shall bear no more fruit. And if she gives birth, I will slay even her beloved child."

¹⁷My God will destroy the people of Israel because they will not listen or obey. They will be wandering Jews, homeless among the nations.

10 A Vine Full of Sin

"How prosperous Israel is—a luxuriant vine all filled with fruit! But the more wealth I give her, the more she pours it on the altars of her heathen gods; the

---

KEEPING YOUR PROMISES 10:4 God was angry with the people of Israel for their insincere promises to him, and in response he said that punishment would come. People break their promises, but God always keeps his. Are you remaining true to your promises, both to other people and to God? If not, ask God for forgiveness and help to get back on track. Then be careful about the promises you make. Never make a promise unless you are sure you can keep it. **To begin the series of devotionals on KEEPING YOUR PROMISES, turn to page 181.**

richer the harvests I give her, the more beautiful the statues and idols she erects. ²The hearts of her people are false toward God. They are guilty and must be punished. God will break down their heathen altars and smash their idols."

³Then they will say, "We deserted the Lord and he took away our king. But what's the difference? We don't need one anyway!"

⁴They make promises they don't intend to keep. Therefore punishment will spring up among them like poisonous weeds in the furrows of the field. ⁵The people of Samaria tremble lest their calf-god idols at Beth-aven should be hurt; the priests and people, too, mourn over the departed honor of their shattered gods. ⁶This idol—this calf-god thing—will be carted with them when they go as slaves to Assyria, a present to the great king there. Ephraim will be laughed at for trusting in this idol; Israel will be put to shame. ⁷As for Samaria, her king shall disappear like a chip of wood upon an ocean wave. ⁸And the idol altars of Aven at Bethel where Israel sinned will crumble. Thorns and thistles will grow up to surround them. And the people will cry to the mountains and hills to fall upon them and crush them.

⁹"O Israel, ever since that awful night in Gibeah, there has been only sin, sin, sin! You have made no progress whatever. Was it not right that the men of Gibeah were wiped out? ¹⁰I will come against you for your disobedience; I will gather the armies of the nations against you to punish you for your heaped-up sins.

¹¹"Ephraim is accustomed to treading out the grain—an easy job she loves. I have never put her under a heavy yoke before; I have spared her tender neck. But now I will harness her to the plow and harrow. Her days of ease are gone.

¹²"Plant the good seeds of righteousness, and you will reap a crop of my love; plow the hard ground of your hearts, for now is the time to seek the Lord, that he may come and shower salvation upon you.

¹³"But you have cultivated wickedness and raised a thriving crop of sins. You have earned the full reward of trusting in a lie—believing that military might and great armies can make a nation safe!

¹⁴"Therefore, the terrors of war shall rise among your people, and all your forts will fall, just as at Beth-arbel, which Shalman destroyed; even mothers and children were dashed to death there. ¹⁵That will be your fate, too, you people of Israel, because of your great wickedness. In one morning the king of Israel shall be destroyed.

11 God Still Loves Israel

"When Israel was a child I loved him as a son and brought him out of Egypt. ²But the more I called to him, the more he rebelled, sacrificing to Baal and burning incense to idols. ³I trained him from infancy, I taught him to walk, I held him in my arms. But he doesn't know or even care that it was I who raised him.

⁴"As a man would lead his favorite ox, so I led Israel with my ropes of love. I loosened his muzzle so he could eat. I myself have stooped and fed him. ⁵ But my people shall return to Egypt and Assyria because they won't return to me.

⁶"War will swirl through their cities; their enemies will crash through their gates and trap them in their own fortresses. ⁷For my people are determined to desert me. And so I have sentenced them to slavery, and no one shall set them free.

⁸"Oh, how can I give you up, my Ephraim? How can I let you go? How can I forsake you like Admah and Zeboiim? My heart cries out within me; how I long to help you! ⁹No, I will not punish you as much as my fierce anger tells me to. This is the last time I will destroy Ephraim. For I am God and not man; I am the Holy One living among you, and I did not come to destroy.

¹⁰"For the people shall walk after the Lord. I shall roar as a lion [at their enemies] and my people shall return trembling from the west. ¹¹Like a flock of birds, they will come from Egypt—like doves flying from Assyria. And I will bring them home again; it is a promise from the Lord."

¹²Israel surrounds me with lies and deceit, but Judah still trusts in God and is faithful to the Holy One.

12 God Wants His People Back

Israel is chasing the wind, yes, shepherding a whirlwind—a dangerous game! For she has given gifts to Egypt and Assyria to get their help, and in return she gets their worthless promises.

²But the Lord is bringing a lawsuit against Judah. Jacob will be justly punished for his ways. ³When he was born, he struggled with his brother; when he became a man, he even fought

---

RECEIVING CHRIST AS SAVIOR 14:1-2 The people could return to God by asking him to take away their sins. The same is true for us: we can pray Hosea's prayer and know our sins are forgiven because Christ died for them on the cross (John 3:16).

Forgiveness begins when we see the destructiveness of sin and the futility of life without God. Then we must admit we cannot save ourselves; our only hope is in God's mercy. When we request forgiveness, we must recognize that we do not deserve it and therefore cannot demand it. Our appeal must be for God's love and mercy, not for his justice. Although we cannot demand forgiveness, we can be confident we have received it, because God is gracious and loving and wants to restore us to himself, just as he wanted to restore Israel. **To begin the series of devotionals on RECEIVING CHRIST AS SAVIOR, turn to page 235.**

with God. ⁴Yes, he wrestled with the Angel and prevailed. He wept and pleaded for a blessing from him. He met God there at Bethel face to face. God spoke to him— ⁵the Lord, the God of heaven's armies—Jehovah is his name.

⁶Oh, come back to God. Live by the principles of love and justice, and always be expecting much from him, your God.

⁷But no, my people are like crafty merchants selling from dishonest scales—they love to cheat. ⁸Ephraim boasts, "I am so rich! I have gotten it all by myself !" But riches can't make up for sin.

⁹I am the same Lord, the same God, who delivered you from slavery in Egypt, and I am the one who will consign you to living in tents again, as you do each year at the Tabernacle Feast. ¹⁰I sent my prophets to warn you with many a vision and many a parable and dream."

¹¹But the sins of Gilgal flourish just the same. Row on row of altars—like furrows in a field—are used for sacrifices to your idols. And Gilead, too, is full of fools who worship idols. ¹²Jacob fled to Syria and earned a wife by tending sheep. ¹³Then the Lord led his people out of Egypt by a prophet, who guided and protected them. ¹⁴But Ephraim has bitterly provoked the Lord. The Lord will sentence him to death as payment for his sins.

13 God Is Angry

It used to be when Israel spoke, the nations shook with fear, for he was a mighty prince; but he worshiped Baal and sealed his doom.

²And now the people disobey more and more. They melt their silver to mold into idols, formed with skill by the hands of men. "Sacrifice to these!" they say—men kissing calves! ³They shall disappear like morning mist, like dew that quickly dries away, like chaff blown by the wind, like a cloud of smoke.

⁴"I alone am God, your Lord, and have been ever since I brought you out from Egypt. You have no God but me, for there is no other Savior. ⁵I took care of you in the wilderness, in that dry and thirsty land. ⁶But when you had eaten and were satisfied, then you became proud and forgot me. ⁷So I will come upon you like a lion, or a leopard lurking along the road. ⁸I will rip you to pieces like a bear whose cubs have been taken away, and like a lion I will devour you.

⁹"O Israel, if I destroy you, who can save you? ¹⁰Where is your king? Why don't you call on him for help? Where are all the leaders of the land? You asked for them, now let them save you! ¹¹I gave you kings in my anger, and I took them away in my wrath. ¹²Ephraim's sins are harvested and stored away for punishment.

¹³"New birth is offered him, but he is like a child resisting in the womb—how stubborn! how foolish! ¹⁴Shall I ransom him from hell? Shall I redeem him from Death? O Death, bring forth your terrors for his tasting! O Grave, demonstrate your plagues! For I will not relent!

¹⁵"He was called the most fruitful of all his brothers, but the east wind—a wind of the Lord from the desert—will blow hard upon him and dry up his land. All his flowing springs and green oases will dry away, and he will die of thirst. ¹⁶Samaria must bear her guilt, for she rebelled against her God. Her people will be killed by the invading army, her babies dashed to death against the ground, her pregnant women ripped open with a sword."

14 God Offers Forgiveness

O Israel, return to the Lord, your God, for you have been crushed by your sins. ²Bring your petition. Come to the Lord and say, "O Lord, take away our sins; be gracious to us and receive us, and we will offer you the sacrifice of praise. ³Assyria cannot save us, nor can our strength in battle; never again will we call the idols we have made 'our gods'; for in you alone, O Lord, the fatherless find mercy."

⁴"Then I will cure you of idolatry and faithlessness, and my love will know no bounds, for my anger will be forever gone! ⁵I will refresh Israel like the dew from heaven; she will blossom as the lily and root deeply in the soil like cedars in Lebanon. ⁶Her branches will spread out as beautiful as olive trees, fragrant as the forests of Lebanon. ⁷Her people will return from exile far away and rest beneath my shadow. They will be a watered garden and blossom like grapes; they will be as fragrant as the wines of Lebanon.

⁸"O Ephraim! Stay away from idols! I am living and strong! I look after you and care for you. I am like an evergreen tree, yielding my fruit to you throughout the year. My mercies never fail."

⁹Whoever is wise, let him understand these things. Whoever is intelligent, let him listen. For the paths of the Lord are true and right, and good men walk along them. But sinners trying them will fail.

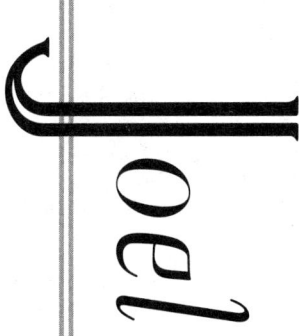

WHAT ARE some of the best promises that have been made to you? The book of Joel has some great promises of God that we can still see happen.

God's people were relying on false gods to protect them. God wanted his people to come back to him. To show the people that other gods are powerless, God brought a plague of locusts to destroy all the crops in their country.

God sent Joel to tell the people what was going to happen. God gave some great promises to them, and they also apply to us. God promised that when we're sorry for our sins, he will forgive us. He promised to take care of us when we trust him. He promised that everyone who calls on him will be saved. And he promised to give his Holy Spirit to all who believe in him. In the Old Testament, God's Spirit didn't live in people's hearts. This promise was first fulfilled in Acts 2, in the early church. And all these promises are still true for us.

As you read Joel, think of all the great promises God has made to you.

A Plague of Locusts

This message came from the Lord to Joel, son of Pethuel.

²Listen, you aged men of Israel! Everyone, listen! In all your lifetime, yes, in all your history, have you ever heard of such a thing as I am going to tell you? ³In years to come, tell your children about it; pass the awful story down from generation to generation. ⁴After the cutter-locusts finish eating your crops, the swarmer-locusts will take what's left! After them will come the hopper-locusts! And then the stripper-locusts too!

⁵Wake up and weep, you drunkards, for all the grapes are ruined, and all your wine is gone! ⁶A vast army of locusts covers the land. It is a terrible army too numerous to count, with teeth as sharp as those of lions! ⁷They have ruined my vines and stripped the bark from the fig trees, leaving trunks and branches white and bare.

⁸Weep with sorrow, as a virgin weeps whose

fiancé is dead. ⁹Gone are the offerings of grain and wine to bring to the Temple of the Lord; the priests are starving. Hear the crying of these ministers of God. ¹⁰The fields are bare of crops. Sorrow and sadness are everywhere. The grain, the grapes, the olive oil are gone.

¹¹Well may you farmers stand so shocked and stricken; well may you vinedressers weep. Weep for the wheat and the barley, too, for they are gone. ¹²The grapevines are dead; the fig trees are dying; the pomegranates wither; the apples shrivel on the trees; all joy has withered with them.

¹³O priests, robe yourselves in sackcloth. O ministers of my God, lie all night before the altar, weeping. For there are no more offerings of grain and wine for you. ¹⁴Announce a fast; call a solemn meeting. Gather the elders and all the people into the Temple of the Lord your God, and weep before him there.

¹⁵Alas, this terrible day of punishment is on the way. Destruction from the Almighty is almost here! ¹⁶Our food will disappear before our eyes; all joy and gladness will be ended in the Temple of our God. ¹⁷The seed rots in the ground; the barns and granaries are empty; the grain has dried up in the fields. ¹⁸The cattle groan with hunger; the herds stand perplexed, for there is no pasture for them; the sheep bleat in misery.

¹⁹Lord, help us! For the heat has withered the pastures and burned up all the trees. ²⁰Even the wild animals cry to you for help, for there is no water for them. The creeks are dry, and the pastures are scorched.

2 Judgment Will Come

Sound the alarm in Jerusalem! Let the blast of the warning trumpet be heard upon my holy mountain! Let everyone tremble in fear, for the day of the Lord's judgment approaches.

²It is a day of darkness and gloom, of black clouds and thick darkness. What a mighty army! It covers the mountains like night! How great, how powerful these "people" are! The likes of them have not been seen before, and never will again throughout the generations of the world! ³Fire goes before them and follows them on every side! Ahead of them the land lies fair as Eden's Garden in all its beauty, but they destroy it to the ground; not one thing escapes. ⁴They look like tiny horses, and they run as fast. ⁵Look at them leaping along the tops of the mountain! Listen to the noise they make, like the rumbling of chariots, or the roar of fire sweeping across a field, and like a mighty army moving into battle.

⁶Fear grips the waiting people; their faces grow pale with fright. ⁷These "soldiers" charge like infantry; they scale the walls like picked and trained commandos. Straight forward they march, never breaking ranks. ⁸They never crowd each other. Each is right in place. No weapon can stop them. ⁹They swarm upon the city; they run upon the walls; they climb up into the houses, coming like thieves through the windows. ¹⁰The earth quakes before them and the heavens tremble. The sun and moon are obscured and the stars are hid.

¹¹The Lord leads them with a shout. This is his mighty army, and they follow his orders. The day of the judgment of the Lord is an awesome, terrible thing. Who can endure it?

¹²That is why the Lord says, "Turn to me now, while there is time. Give me all your hearts. Come with fasting, weeping, mourning. ¹³Let your remorse tear at your hearts and not your garments." Return to the Lord your God, for he is gracious and merciful. He is not easily angered; he is full of kindness and anxious not to punish you.

¹⁴Who knows? Perhaps even yet he will decide to let you alone and give you a blessing instead of his terrible curse. Perhaps he will give you so much that you can offer your grain and wine to the Lord as before!

¹⁵Sound the trumpet in Zion! Call a fast and gather all the people together for a solemn meeting. ¹⁶Bring everyone—the elders, the children, and even the babies. Call the bridegroom from his quarters and the bride from her privacy.

¹⁷The priests, the ministers of God, will stand between the people and the altar, weeping; and they will pray, "Spare your people, O our God; don't let the heathen rule them, for they belong to you. Don't let them be disgraced by the taunts of the heathen who say, 'Where is this God of theirs? How weak and helpless he must be!'"

¹⁸Then the Lord will pity his people and be indignant for the honor of his land! ¹⁹He will reply, "See, I am sending you much corn and wine and oil, to fully satisfy your need. No longer will I make you a laughingstock among the nations. ²⁰I will remove these armies from the north and send them far away; I will turn them back into the parched wastelands where they will die; half shall be driven into the Dead Sea and the rest into the Mediterranean, and then their rotting stench will rise

---

RECEIVING CHRIST AS SAVIOR 2:12-13 God told the people to turn to him while there was still time. Time was running out and destruction would soon be upon them. Time is also running out for us. Because we don't know when our lives will end, we should turn to the Lord now, while we can. Don't let anything hold you back from turning to God and accepting his free gift of salvation through Jesus. **To begin the series of devotionals on RECEIVING CHRIST AS SAVIOR, turn to page 235.**

upon the land. The Lord has done a mighty miracle for you."

²¹Fear not, my people; be glad now and rejoice, for he has done amazing things for you. ²²Let the flocks and herds forget their hunger; the pastures will turn green again. The trees will bear their fruit; the fig trees and grape vines will flourish once more. ²³Rejoice, O people of Jerusalem, rejoice in the Lord your God! For the rains he sends are tokens of forgiveness. Once more the autumn rains will come, as well as those of spring. ²⁴The threshing floors will pile high again with wheat, and the presses overflow with olive oil and wine.

²⁵"And I will give you back the crops the locusts ate!—my great destroying army that I sent against you. ²⁶Once again you will have all the food you want.

"Praise the Lord, who does these miracles for you. Never again will my people experience disaster such as this. ²⁷And you will know that I am here among my people Israel, and that I alone am the Lord your God. And my people shall never again be dealt a blow like this.

²⁸"After I have poured out my rains again, I will pour out my Spirit upon all of you! Your sons and daughters will prophesy; your old men will dream dreams, and your young men see visions. ²⁹And I will pour out my Spirit even on your slaves, men and women alike, ³⁰and put strange symbols in the earth and sky—blood and fire and pillars of smoke.

³¹"The sun will be turned into darkness and the moon to blood before the great and terrible Day of the Lord shall come.

³²"Everyone who calls upon the name of the Lord will be saved; even in Jerusalem some will escape, just as the Lord has promised, for he has chosen some to survive.

3 Bad News for Israel's Enemies

"At that time, when I restore the prosperity of Judah and Jerusalem," says the Lord, ²"I will gather the armies of the world into the 'Valley Where Jehovah Judges' and punish them there for harming my people, for scattering my inheritance among the nations and dividing up my land.

³"They divided up my people as their slaves; they traded a young lad for a prostitute, and a little girl for wine enough to get drunk. ⁴Tyre and Sidon, don't you try to interfere! Are you trying to take revenge on me, you cities of Philistia? Beware, for I will strike back swiftly and return the harm to your own heads.

⁵"You have taken my silver and gold and all my precious treasures and carried them off to your heathen temples. ⁶You have sold the people of Judah and Jerusalem to the Greeks, who took them far from their own land. ⁷But I will bring them back again from all these places you have sold them to, and I will pay you back for all that you have done. ⁸I will sell your sons and daughters to the people of Judah, and they will sell them to the Sabeans far away. This is a promise from the Lord."

⁹Announce this far and wide: Get ready for war! Conscript your best soldiers; collect all your armies. ¹⁰Melt your plowshares into swords, and beat your pruning hooks into spears. Let the weak be strong. ¹¹Gather together and come, all nations everywhere. And now, O Lord, bring down your warriors!

¹²"Collect the nations; bring them to the Valley of Jehoshaphat, for there I will sit to pronounce judgment on them all. ¹³Now let the sickle do its work; the harvest is ripe and waiting. Tread the winepress, for it is full to overflowing with the wickedness of these men."

¹⁴Multitudes, multitudes waiting in the valley for the verdict of their doom! For the Day of the Lord is near, in the Valley of Judgment. ¹⁵The sun and moon will be darkened and the stars withdraw their light. ¹⁶The Lord shouts from his Temple in Jerusalem, and the earth and sky begin to shake. But to his people Israel, the Lord will be very gentle. He is their Refuge and Strength.

¹⁷"Then you shall know at last that I am the Lord your God in Zion, my holy mountain. Jerusalem shall be mine forever; the time will come when no foreign armies will pass through her any more.

¹⁸"Sweet wine will drip from the mountains, and the hills shall flow with milk. Water will fill the dry stream beds of Judah, and a fountain will burst forth from the Temple of the Lord to water Acacia Valley. ¹⁹Egypt will be destroyed, and Edom, too, because of their violence against the Jews, for they killed innocent people in those nations.

²⁰"But Israel will prosper forever, and Jerusalem will thrive as generations pass. ²¹For I will avenge the blood of my people; I will not clear their oppressors of guilt. For my home is in Jerusalem with my people."

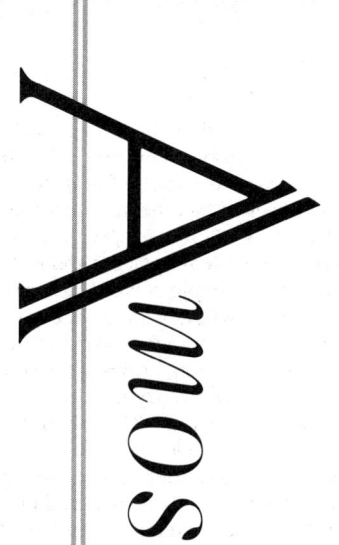

IN THE Bible, God gives us lots of instructions for living. He tells us what's important for us to do and what he cares about. One theme that is repeated in the Bible is being kind to the poor. God sent Amos to tell the Israelites that this is very important.

During the reigns of Uzziah and Jereboam II, the Israelites were doing well. They were powerful; their crops were growing well; many people were rich. It would have been easy for the Israelites to help the poor people who lived among them. But the rich people were stuck-up and selfish.

God had told them to help the people who were poor, but they didn't want to share. Instead, they went to the Temple and gave gifts to God. God didn't want their gifts, because he knew the people were just pretending to love him. He told them that if they *really* loved him, they would help the poor people and try to do good things.

Amos used symbols to show the Israelites what they were like. They looked great at a glance, but underneath they were rotten.

God Punishes Israel's Neighbors

Amos was a herdsman living in the village of Tekoa. [All day long he sat on the hillsides watching the sheep, keeping them from straying.]

²One day, in a vision, God told him some of the things that were going to happen to his nation, Israel. This vision came to him at the time Uzziah was king of Judah and while Jeroboam (son of Joash) was king of Israel—two years before the earthquake.

This is his report of what he saw and heard: The Lord roared—like a ferocious lion from his lair—from his Temple on Mount Zion. And suddenly the lush pastures of Mount Carmel withered and dried, and all the shepherds mourned.

³The Lord says, "The people of Damascus have sinned again and again, and I will not forget it. I will not leave her unpunished any more. For they have threshed my people in Gilead as grain is threshed with iron rods. ⁴So I will set fire to King Hazael's palace, destroying the strong fortress of Ben-hadad. ⁵I will snap the bars that locked the

gates of Damascus and kill her people as far away as the plain of Aven, and the people of Syria shall return to Kir as slaves." The Lord has spoken.

⁶The Lord says, "Gaza has sinned again and again, and I will not forget it. I will not leave her unpunished any more. For she sent my people into exile, selling them as slaves in Edom. ⁷So I will set fire to the walls of Gaza, and all her forts shall be destroyed. ⁸I will kill the people of Ashdod and destroy Ekron and the king of Ashkelon; all Philistines left will perish." The Lord has spoken.

⁹The Lord says, "The people of Tyre have sinned again and again, and I will not forget it. I will not leave them unpunished any more. For they broke their treaty with their brother, Israel; they attacked and conquered him, and led him into slavery to Edom. ¹⁰So I will set fire to the walls of Tyre, and it will burn down all his forts and palaces."

¹¹The Lord says, "Edom has sinned again and again, and I will not forget it. I will not leave him unpunished any more. For he chased his brother, Israel, with the sword; he was pitiless in unrelenting anger. ¹²So I will set fire to Teman, and it will burn down all the forts of Bozrah."

¹³The Lord says, "The people of Ammon have sinned again and again, and I will not forget it. I will not leave them unpunished any more. For in their wars in Gilead to enlarge their borders they committed cruel crimes, ripping open pregnant women with their swords.

¹⁴"So I will set fire to the walls of Rabbah, and it will burn down their forts and palaces; there will be wild shouts of battle like a whirlwind in a mighty storm. ¹⁵And their king and his princes will go into exile together." The Lord has spoken.

2 God Punishes Israel, Too

The Lord says, "The people of Moab have sinned again and again, and I will not forget it. I will not leave them unpunished any more. For they desecrated the tombs of the kings of Edom, with no respect for the dead. ²Now in return I will send fire upon Moab, and it will destroy all the palaces in Kerioth. Moab shall go down in tumult as the warriors shout and trumpets blare. ³And I will destroy their king and slay all the leaders under him." The Lord has spoken.

⁴The Lord says, "The people of Judah have sinned again and again, and I will not forget it. I will not leave them unpunished any more. For they have rejected the laws of God, refusing to obey him. They have hardened their hearts and sinned as their fathers did. ⁵So I will destroy Judah with fire and burn down all Jerusalem's palaces and forts."

⁶The Lord says, "The people of Israel have sinned again and again, and I will not forget it. I will not leave them unpunished any more. For they have perverted justice by accepting bribes and sold into slavery the poor who can't repay their debts; they trade them for a pair of shoes. ⁷They trample the poor in the dust and kick aside the meek.

"And a man and his father defile the same temple-girl, corrupting my holy name. ⁸At their religious feasts they lounge in clothing stolen from their debtors, and in my own Temple they offer sacrifices of wine they purchased with stolen money.

⁹"Yet think of all I did for them! I cleared the land of the Amorites before them—the Amorites, as tall as cedar trees, and strong as oaks! But I lopped off their fruit and cut their roots. ¹⁰And I brought you out from Egypt and led you through the desert forty years, to possess the land of the Amorites. ¹¹And I chose your sons to be Nazirites and prophets—can you deny this, Israel?" asks the Lord. ¹²"But you caused the Nazirites to sin by urging them to drink your wine, and you silenced my prophets, telling them, 'Shut up!'

¹³"Therefore, I will make you groan as a wagon groans that is loaded with sheaves. ¹⁴Your swiftest warriors will stumble in flight. The strong will all be weak, and the great ones can no longer save themselves. ¹⁵The archer's aim will fail, the swiftest runners won't be fast enough to flee, and even the best of horsemen can't outrun the danger then. ¹⁶The most courageous of your mighty men will drop their weapons and run for their lives that day." The Lord God has spoken.

3 They Cannot Walk with God

Listen! This is your doom! It is spoken by the Lord against both Israel and Judah—against the entire family I brought from Egypt:

²"Of all the peoples of the earth, I have chosen you alone. That is why I must punish you the more for all your sins. ³For how can we walk together with your sins between us?

⁴"Would I be roaring as a lion unless I had a reason? The fact is, I am getting ready to destroy you. Even a young lion, when it growls, shows it is ready for its food. ⁵A trap doesn't snap shut unless it is stepped on; your punishment is well deserved. ⁶The

---

FAITH IN ACTION 2:6-7 Amos spoke to the upper class. There was no middle class in the country—only the very rich and the very poor. The rich kept religious rituals. They gave extra tithes, went to places of worship, and offered sacrifices. But they were greedy and unjust, and they took advantage of the helpless. Be sure that you do not neglect the needs of the poor while you faithfully attend church and fulfill religious rituals. God expects us to live out our faith, and this means responding to those in need. **To begin the series of devotionals on FAITH IN ACTION, turn to page 141.**

alarm has sounded—listen and fear! For I, the Lord, am sending disaster into your land.

⁷"But always, first of all, I warn you through my prophets. This I now have done."

⁸The Lion has roared—tremble in fear. The Lord God has sounded your doom—I dare not refuse to proclaim it.

⁹"Call together the Assyrian and Egyptian leaders, saying, 'Take your seats now on the mountains of Samaria to witness the scandalous spectacle of all Israel's crimes.' ¹⁰My people have forgotten what it means to do right," says the Lord. "Their beautiful homes are full of the loot from their thefts and banditry. ¹¹Therefore," the Lord God says, "an enemy is coming! He is surrounding them and will shatter their forts and plunder those beautiful homes."

¹²The Lord says, "A shepherd tried to rescue his sheep from a lion, but it was too late; he snatched from the lion's mouth two legs and a piece of ear. So it will be when the Israelites in Samaria are finally rescued—all they will have left is half a chair and a tattered pillow.

¹³"Listen to this announcement and publish it throughout all Israel," says the Lord, the Lord Almighty: ¹⁴"On the same day that I punish Israel for her sins I will also destroy the idol altars at Bethel. The horns of the altar will be cut off and fall to the ground.

¹⁵"And I will destroy the beautiful homes of the wealthy—their winter mansions and their summer houses too—and demolish their ivory palaces."

4 The People Continue to Sin

Listen to me, you "fat cows" of Bashan living in Samaria—you women who encourage your husbands to rob the poor and crush the needy—you who never have enough to drink! ²The Lord God has sworn by his holiness that the time will come when he will put hooks in your noses and lead you away like the cattle you are; they will drag the last of you away with fishhooks! ³You will be hauled from your beautiful homes and tossed out through the nearest breach in the wall. The Lord has said it.

⁴Go ahead and sacrifice to idols at Bethel and Gilgal. Keep disobeying—your sins are mounting up. Sacrifice each morning and bring your tithes twice a week! ⁵Go through all your proper forms and give extra offerings. How you pride yourselves and crow about it everywhere!

⁶"I sent you hunger," says the Lord, "but it did no good; you still would not return to me. ⁷I ruined your crops by holding back the rain three months before the harvest. I sent rain on one city but not another. While rain fell on one field, another was dry and withered. ⁸People from two or three cities would make their weary journey for a drink of water to a city that had rain, but there wasn't ever enough. Yet you wouldn't return to me," says the Lord.

⁹"I sent blight and mildew on your farms and your vineyards; the locusts ate your figs and olive trees. And still you wouldn't return to me," says the Lord. ¹⁰"I sent you plagues like those of Egypt long ago. I killed your lads in war and drove away your horses. The stench of death was terrible to smell. And yet you refused to come. ¹¹I destroyed some of your cities, as I did Sodom and Gomorrah; those left are like half-burned firebrands snatched away from fire. And still you won't return to me," says the Lord.

¹²"Therefore, I will bring upon you all these further evils I have spoken of. Prepare to meet your God in judgment, Israel. ¹³For you are dealing with the One who formed the mountains, made the winds, and knows your every thought; he turns the morning to darkness and crushes down the mountains underneath his feet: Jehovah, the Lord, the Lord Almighty, is his name."

5 A Sad Song of Grief

Sadly I sing this song of grief for you, O Israel:

²"Beautiful Israel lies broken and crushed upon the ground and cannot rise. No one will help her. She is left alone to die." ³For the Lord God says, "The city that sends a thousand men to battle, a hundred will return. The city that sends a hundred, only ten will come back alive."

⁴The Lord says to the people of Israel, "Seek me—and live. ⁵Don't seek the idols of Bethel, Gilgal, or Beersheba; for the people of Gilgal will be carried off to exile, and those of Bethel shall surely come to grief."

⁶Seek the Lord and live, or else he will sweep like fire through Israel and consume her, and none of the idols in Bethel can put it out.

⁷O evil men, you make "justice" a bitter pill for the poor and oppressed. "Righteousness" and "fair play" are meaningless fictions to you!

⁸Seek him who created the Seven Stars and the constellation Orion, who turns darkness into morning and day into night, who calls forth the water from the ocean and pours it out as rain upon the land. The Lord, Jehovah, is his name. ⁹With blinding speed and violence he brings destruction on the strong, breaking all defenses.

¹⁰How you hate honest judges! How you despise people who tell the truth! ¹¹You trample the poor and steal their smallest crumb by all your taxes, fines, and usury; therefore, you will never live in the beautiful stone houses you are

building, nor drink the wine from the lush vineyards you are planting.

¹²For many and great are your sins. I know them all so well. You are the enemies of everything good; you take bribes; you refuse justice to the poor. ¹³Therefore, those who are wise will not try to interfere with the Lord in the dread day of your punishment.

¹⁴Be good, flee evil—and live! Then the Lord, the Lord Almighty, will truly be your Helper, as you have claimed he is. ¹⁵Hate evil and love the good; remodel your courts into true halls of justice. Perhaps even yet the Lord God of Hosts will have mercy on his people who remain.

¹⁶Therefore the Lord God says this: "There will be crying in all the streets and every road. Call for the farmers to weep with you too; call for professional mourners to wail and lament. ¹⁷There will be sorrow and crying in every vineyard, for I will pass through and destroy. ¹⁸You say, 'If only the Day of the Lord were here, for then God would deliver us from all our foes.' But you have no idea what you ask. For that day will *not* be light and prosperity, but darkness and doom! How terrible the darkness will be for you; not a ray of joy or hope will shine. ¹⁹In that day you will be as a man who is chased by a lion and is met by a bear, or a man in a dark room who leans against a wall and puts his hand on a snake. ²⁰Yes, that will be a dark and hopeless day for you.

²¹"I hate your show and pretense—your hypocrisy of 'honoring' me with your religious feasts and solemn assemblies. ²²I will not accept your burnt offerings and thank offerings. I will not look at your offerings of peace. ²³Away with your hymns of praise—they are mere noise to my ears. I will not listen to your music, no matter how lovely it is.

²⁴"I want to see a mighty flood of justice—a torrent of doing good.

²⁵⁻²⁷"You sacrificed to me for forty years while you were in the desert, Israel—but always your real interest has been in your heathen gods—in Sakkuth your king, and in Kaiwan, your god of the stars, and in all the images of them you made. So I will send them into captivity with you far to the east of Damascus," says the Lord, the Lord Almighty.

6 God Hates Israel's Pride

Woe to those lounging in luxury at Jerusalem and Samaria, so famous and popular among the people of Israel. ²Go over to Calneh and see what happened there; then go to great Hamath and down to Gath in the Philistines' land. Once they were better and greater than you, but look at them now. ³You push away all thought of punishment awaiting you, but by your deeds you bring the Day of Judgment near.

⁴You lie on ivory beds surrounded with luxury, eating the meat of the tenderest lambs and the choicest calves. ⁵You sing idle songs to the sound of the harp and fancy yourselves to be as great musicians as King David was.

⁶You drink wine by the bucketful and perfume yourselves with sweet ointments, caring nothing at all that your brothers need your help. ⁷Therefore you will be the first to be taken as slaves; suddenly your revelry will end.

⁸Jehovah the Almighty Lord has sworn by his own name, "I despise the pride and false glory of Israel and hate their beautiful homes. I will turn over this city and everything in it to her enemies."

⁹If there are as few as ten of them left and only one house, they too will perish. ¹⁰A man's uncle will be the only one left to bury him, and when he goes in to carry his body from the house, he will ask the only one still alive inside, "Are any others left?" And the answer will be, "No," and he will add, "Shhh . . . don't mention the name of the Lord—he might hear you."

¹¹For the Lord commanded this: That homes both great and small should be smashed to pieces. ¹²Can horses run on rocks? Can oxen plow the sea? Stupid even to ask—but no more stupid than what you do when you make a mockery of justice and corrupt and sour all that should be good and right. ¹³ And just as stupid is your rejoicing in how great you are when you are less than nothing—and priding yourselves on your own tiny power!

¹⁴"O Israel, I will bring against you a nation that will bitterly oppress you from your northern boundary to your southern tip, all the way from Hamath to the brook of Arabah," says the Lord, the Lord Almighty.

7 Locusts, Fire, and a Plumbline

This is what the Lord God showed me in a vision: He was preparing a vast swarm of locusts to destroy all the main crop that sprang up after the first mowing, which went as taxes to the king. ²They ate everything in sight. Then I said, "O Lord God, please forgive your people! Don't send them this plague! If you turn against Israel, what hope is there? For Israel is so small!"

³So the Lord relented and did not fulfill the vision. "I won't do it," he told me.

⁴Then the Lord God showed me a great fire he had prepared to punish them; it had burned up the waters and was devouring the entire land.

⁵Then I said, "O Lord God, please don't do it. If you turn against them, what hope is there? For Israel is so small!"

Family Devotions

☐ DEVOTION 240
BECOMING MORE LIKE JESUS

Read Amos 7:7-8

Andrea could hardly wait till Grandpa finished building the playhouse he was making for her. She watched as he raised his arm to the top of the wall he was erecting. In his hand he held a long cord with a weight attached at the bottom. "I know what that is," said Andrea proudly.

Grandpa was surprised. "You do?"

Andrea nodded. "It's a plumbline," she said. "The weight at the end makes the string hang straight down. When you hold it along the wall, you can tell if the wall is straight or not."

"Well, I'm impressed!" exclaimed Grandpa. "Where did a little girl like you learn about plumblines?"

"In Sunday school," replied Andrea.

Grandpa was even more surprised. "In Sunday school?"

"Yep." Andrea nodded. "My teacher talked about the prophet Amos. She read from the Bible about how God showed him a plumbline and told him he would check the people to see whether or not they were living as they should. He was going to punish them if they didn't measure up to what they should be."

"Very good!" approved Grandpa. He wound up the cord. "Did you talk about the plumbline God uses to measure his children today?"

"My teacher said God tells us in the Bible that he expects us to live godly lives—to be like him," replied Andrea. "That's hard."

"Yes, it is," agreed Grandpa. "His standard for us is to be holy, just as he is holy. We can't do it without his help. I'm very thankful that he's willing to forgive us when we ask him and to give us the help we need."

> *Becoming More Like Jesus*
> *Memory Verse*
>
> No, he has told you what he wants, and this is all it is: *to be fair, just, merciful, and to walk humbly with your God.*
> Micah 6:8

How About You?

Are you aware of God's standard for Christians? Maybe you think you're better than your neighbors or than other kids in your class. Perhaps you think you behave better than other Christians you know. But God isn't comparing you to any of them. He isn't comparing you to your parents, teachers, or pastor. His standard is himself; he wants you to be like Jesus. Ask him to help you measure up and be the person he wants you to be. H. M.

• For the next devotional, turn to page 857. • For the next devotional on BECOMING MORE LIKE JESUS, turn to page 1019. • For notes on BECOMING MORE LIKE JESUS, see pages 234, 983, 1105, and 1164.

⁶Then the Lord turned from this plan too, and said, "I won't do that either."

⁷Then he showed me this: The Lord was standing beside a wall built with a plumbline, checking it with a plumbline to see if it was straight. ⁸And the Lord said to me, "Amos, what do you see?"

I answered, "A plumbline."

And he replied, "I will test my people with a plumbline. I will no longer turn away from punishing. ⁹The idol altars and temples of Israel will be destroyed, and I will destroy the dynasty of King Jeroboam by the sword."

¹⁰But when Amaziah, the priest of Bethel, heard what Amos was saying, he rushed a message to Jeroboam, the king: "Amos is a traitor to our nation and is plotting your death. This is intolerable. It will lead to rebellion all across the land. ¹¹He says you will be killed and Israel will be sent far away into exile and slavery."

¹²Then Amaziah sent orders to Amos, "Get out of here, you prophet, you! Flee to the land of Judah and do your prophesying there! ¹³Don't bother us here with your visions, not here in the capital where the king's chapel is!"

¹⁴But Amos replied, "I am not really one of the prophets. I do not come from a family of prophets. I am just a herdsman and fruit picker. ¹⁵But the Lord took me from caring for the flocks and told me, 'Go and prophesy to my people Israel.'

¹⁶"Now, therefore, listen to this message to you from the Lord. You say, 'Don't prophesy against Israel.' ¹⁷The Lord's reply is this: 'Because of your interference, your wife will become a prostitute in this city, your sons and daughters will be killed, and your land divided up. You yourself will die in a heathen land, and the people of Israel will certainly become slaves in exile, far from their land.'"

8 Amos Sees a Basket of Fruit

Then the Lord God showed me, in a vision, a basket full of ripe fruit.

²"What do you see, Amos?" he asked.

I replied, "A basket full of ripe fruit."

Then the Lord said, "This fruit represents my people Israel—ripe for punishment. I will not defer their punishment again. ³The riotous sound of singing in the Temple will turn to weeping then. Dead bodies will be scattered everywhere. They will be carried out of the city in silence." The Lord has spoken.

⁴Listen, you merchants who rob the poor, trampling on the needy; ⁵you who long for the Sabbath to end and the religious holidays to be over so you can get out and start cheating again—using your weighted scales and under-sized measures; ⁶you who make slaves of the poor, buying them for their debt of a piece of silver or a pair of shoes, or selling them your moldy wheat:

⁷The Lord, the Pride of Israel, has sworn: "I won't forget your deeds! ⁸The land will tremble as it awaits its doom, and everyone will mourn. It will rise up like the river Nile at floodtime, toss about, and sink again. ⁹At that time I will make the sun go down at noon and darken the earth in the daytime. ¹⁰And I will turn your parties into times of mourning, and your songs of joy will be turned to cries of despair. You will wear funeral clothes and shave your heads as signs of sorrow, as if your only son had died; bitter, bitter will be that day.

¹¹"The time is surely coming," says the Lord God, "when I will send a famine on the land—not a famine of bread or water, but of hearing the words of the Lord. ¹²Men will wander everywhere from sea to sea, seeking the word of the Lord, searching, running here and going there, but will not find it. ¹³Beautiful girls and fine young men alike will grow faint and weary, thirsting for the word of God. ¹⁴And those who worship the idols of Samaria, Dan, and Beersheba shall fall and never rise again."

9 Israel Will Be Destroyed

I saw the Lord standing beside the altar, saying, "Smash the tops of the pillars and shake the Temple until the pillars crumble and the roof crashes down upon the people below. Though they run, they will not escape; they all will be killed.

²"Though they dig down to Sheol, I will reach down and pull them up; though they climb into the heavens, I will bring them down. ³Though they hide among the rocks at the top of Carmel, I will search them out and capture them. Though they hide at the bottom of the ocean, I will send the sea-serpent after them to bite and destroy them. ⁴Though they volunteer for exile, I will command the sword to kill them there. I will see to it that they receive evil and not good."

⁵The Lord Almighty touches the land and it melts, and all its people mourn. It rises like the river Nile in Egypt and then sinks again. ⁶The upper stories of his home are in the heavens, the first floor on the earth. He calls for the vapor to rise from the ocean and pours it down as rain upon the ground. Jehovah, the Lord, is his name.

⁷"O people of Israel, are you any more to me than the Ethiopians are? Have not I, who brought you out of Egypt, done as much for other people too? I brought the Philistines from Caphtor and the Syrians out of Kir.

⁸"The eyes of the Lord God are watching Israel, that sinful nation, and I will root her up and scatter her across the world. *Yet I have promised that this*

rooting out will not be permanent. ⁹For I have commanded that Israel be sifted by the other nations as grain is sifted in a sieve, yet not one true kernel will be lost. ¹⁰But all these sinners who say, 'God will not touch us,' will die by the sword.

¹¹"Then, at that time I will rebuild the City of David, which is now lying in ruins, and return it to its former glory, ¹²and Israel will possess what is left of Edom and of all the nations that belong to me." For so the Lord, who plans it all, has said.

¹³"The time will come when there will be such abundance of crops that the harvesttime will scarcely end before the farmer starts again to sow another crop, and the terraces of grapes upon the hills of Israel will drip sweet wine! ¹⁴I will restore the fortunes of my people Israel, and they will rebuild their ruined cities and live in them again; they will plant vineyards and gardens; they will eat their crops and drink their wine. ¹⁵I will firmly plant them there upon the land that I have given them; they shall not be pulled up again," says the Lord your God.

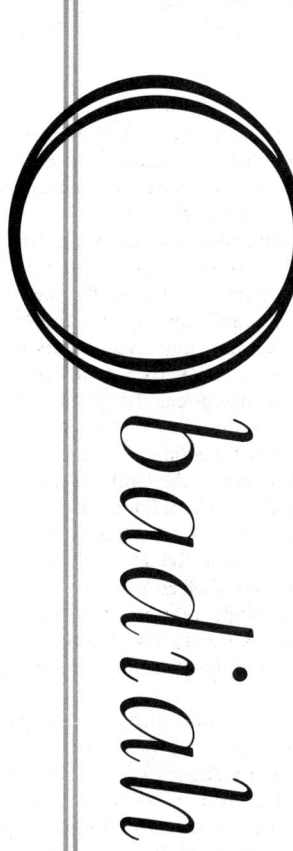

Obadiah

HOLDING a grudge doesn't do anything to solve problems. It doesn't make anyone feel better—especially the person who won't let go of the bad memory. Some people can hold a grudge for a long time. The nation of Edom held a grudge against Israel for centuries.

Think back to Jacob and Esau, who were twin sons of Isaac. Esau was the oldest son. In their culture that meant lots of benefits and privileges. But Esau wasn't careful about his position. Jacob played a trick on Esau and took his firstborn blessings.

Jacob's descendants became the nation of Israel. Esau's descendants became the nation of Edom. The Edomites always held a grudge against Israel and were mean to them. God sent Obadiah to tell Edom that because of their pride and the wrong things they did against Jacob's descendants, they would be punished. They would be treated by other countries the same way they treated Israel.

Grudges don't help anything. And God doesn't like them, either. As you read Obadiah, think of better ways to respond to a conflict than by holding a grudge.

Edom Will Be Destroyed

In a vision the Lord God showed Obadiah the future of the land of Edom.

"A report has come from the Lord," he said, "that God has sent an ambassador to the nations with this message: 'Attention! You are to send your armies against Edom and destroy her!'"

²"I will cut you down to size among the nations, Edom, making you small and despised.

³"You are proud because you live in those high, inaccessible cliffs. 'Who can ever reach us way up here!' you boast. Don't fool yourselves! ⁴Though you soar as high as eagles, and build your nest among the stars, I will bring you plummeting down," says the Lord.

⁵"Far better it would be for you if thieves had come at night to plunder you—for they would not take everything! Or if your vineyards were robbed of all their fruit—for at least the gleanings would be left! ⁶Every nook and cranny will be searched and robbed, and every treasure found and taken.

⁷"All your allies will turn against you and help to push you out of your land. They will promise peace while plotting your destruction. Your trusted friends will set traps for you, and all your counterstrategy will fail. ⁸In that day not one wise man will be left in all of Edom!" says the Lord. "For I will fill the wise men of Edom with stupidity. ⁹The mightiest soldiers of Teman will be confused, and helpless to prevent the slaughter.

¹⁰"And why? Because of what you did to your brother Israel. Now your sins will be exposed for all to see; ashamed and defenseless, you will be cut off forever. ¹¹For you deserted Israel in his time of need. You stood aloof, refusing to lift a finger to help him when invaders carried off his wealth and divided Jerusalem among them by lot; you were as one of his enemies.

¹²"You should not have done it. You should not have gloated when they took him far away to foreign lands; you should not have rejoiced in the day of his misfortune; you should not have mocked in his time of need. ¹³You yourselves went into the land of Israel in the day of his calamity and looted him. You made yourselves rich at his expense. ¹⁴You stood at the crossroads and killed those trying to escape; you captured the survivors and returned them to their enemies in that terrible time of his distress.

¹⁵The Lord's vengeance will soon fall upon all Gentile nations. As you have done to Israel, so will it be done to you. Your acts will boomerang upon your heads. ¹⁶You drank my cup of punishment upon my holy mountain, and the nations round about will drink it too; yes, they will drink and stagger back and disappear from history, no longer nations any more.

¹⁷"But Jerusalem will become a refuge, a way of escape. Israel will reoccupy the land. ¹⁸Israel will be a fire that sets the dry fields of Edom aflame. There will be no survivors," for the Lord has spoken.

¹⁹Then my people who live in the Negeb shall occupy the hill country of Edom; those living in Judean lowlands shall possess the Philistine plains and repossess the fields of Ephraim and Samaria. And the people of Benjamin shall possess Gilead.

²⁰The Israeli exiles shall return and occupy the Phoenician coastal strip as far north as Zarephath. Those exiled in Asia Minor shall return to their homeland and conquer the Negeb's outlying villages. ²¹For deliverers will come to Jerusalem and rule all Edom. And the Lord shall be King!

HUMILITY 1:4 The Edomites were proud of their city carved right into the rock. Today it is considered one of the marvels of the ancient world, but only as a tourist attraction. The Bible warns that pride is the surest route to self-destruction (Proverbs 16:18). Just as Petra and Edom fell, so will proud people fall. A humble person is more secure than a proud person, because humility gives one a more accurate perspective of oneself and the world. **To begin the series of devotionals on HUMILITY, turn to page 449.**

Jonah

GOD CARES about other people more than we do. And it's a good thing! We can be selfish, but God shows us how to love others. This is what the book of Jonah is about.

Jonah was an Israelite, and the Israelites were enemies of a city called Nineveh. But God loved the Ninevites and wanted them to know him and worship him. So he told Jonah to go to Nineveh and tell the people to stop doing wrong and worshiping false gods. If they didn't, God would destroy their city.

Jonah thought that destroying Nineveh was a pretty good idea, so he didn't want to help them by telling them God's message. God had to convince Jonah with an adventure. Finally Jonah went to Nineveh and obeyed God. Sure enough, the Ninevites were sorry and turned to God, and God didn't have to destroy them.

Jonah was upset. He didn't want God to love the Ninevites!

God is loving and forgiving to *all* people so that they can stop doing wrong and start trusting him. As you read, look for the differences between God and Jonah.

A Big Fish Swallows Jonah

The Lord sent this message to Jonah, the son of Amittai:

²"Go to the great city of Nineveh, and give them this announcement from the Lord: 'I am going to destroy you, for your wickedness rises before me; it smells to highest heaven.'"

³But Jonah was afraid to go and ran away from the Lord. He went down to the seacoast, to the port of Joppa, where he found a ship leaving for Tarshish. He bought a ticket, went on board, and climbed down into the dark hold of the ship to hide there from the Lord.

⁴But as the ship was sailing along, suddenly the Lord flung a terrific wind over the sea, causing a great storm that threatened to send them to the bottom. ⁵Fearing for their lives, the desperate sailors shouted to their gods for help and threw the cargo overboard to lighten the ship. And all this time Jonah was sound asleep down in the hold.

⁶So the captain went down after him. "What do

you mean," he roared, "sleeping at a time like this? Get up and cry to your god, and see if he will have mercy on us and save us!"

⁷Then the crew decided to draw straws to see which of them had offended the gods and caused this terrible storm; and Jonah drew the short one.

⁸"What have you done," they asked, "to bring this awful storm upon us? Who are you? What is your work? What country are you from? What is your nationality?"

⁹,¹⁰And he said, "I am a Jew; I worship Jehovah, the God of heaven, who made the earth and sea." Then he told them he was running away from the Lord.

The men were terribly frightened when they heard this. "Oh, why did you do it?" they shouted. ¹¹"What should we do to you to stop the storm?" For it was getting worse and worse.

¹²"Throw me out into the sea," he said, "and it will become calm again. For I know this terrible storm has come because of me."

¹³They tried harder to row the boat ashore, but couldn't make it. The storm was too fierce to fight against. ¹⁴Then they shouted out a prayer to Jehovah, Jonah's God. "O Jehovah," they pleaded, "don't make us die for this man's sin, and don't hold us responsible for his death, for it is not our fault—you have sent this storm upon him for your own good reasons."

¹⁵Then they picked up Jonah and threw him overboard into the raging sea—and the storm stopped!

¹⁶The men stood there in awe before Jehovah, and they sacrificed to him and vowed to serve him.

¹⁷Now the Lord had arranged for a great fish to swallow Jonah. And Jonah was inside the fish three days and three nights.

2 Then Jonah prayed to the Lord his God from inside the fish:

²"In my great trouble I cried to the Lord and he answered me; from the depths of death I called, and Lord, you heard me! ³You threw me into the ocean depths; I sank down into the floods of waters and was covered by your wild and stormy waves. ⁴Then I said, 'O Lord, you have rejected me and cast me away. How shall I ever again see your holy Temple?'

⁵"I sank beneath the waves, and death was very near. The waters closed above me; the seaweed wrapped itself around my head. ⁶I went down to the bottoms of the mountains that rise from off the ocean floor. I was locked out of life and imprisoned in the land of death. But, O Lord my God, you have snatched me from the yawning jaws of death!

⁷"When I had lost all hope, I turned my thoughts once more to the Lord. And my earnest prayer went to you in your holy Temple. ⁸(Those who worship false gods have turned their backs on all the mercies waiting for them from the Lord!)

⁹"I will never worship anyone but you! For how can I thank you enough for all you have done? I will surely fulfill my promises. For my deliverance comes from the Lord alone."

¹⁰And the Lord ordered the fish to spit up Jonah on the beach, and it did.

Jonah Preaches at Nineveh

3 Then the Lord spoke to Jonah again: "Go to that great city, Nineveh," he said, "and warn them of their doom, as I told you to before!"

³So Jonah obeyed and went to Nineveh. Now Nineveh was a very large city with many villages around it—so large that it would take three days to walk through it.

⁴,⁵But the very first day when Jonah entered the city and began to preach, the people repented. Jonah shouted to the crowds that gathered around him, "Forty days from now Nineveh will be destroyed!" And they believed him and declared a fast; from the king on down, everyone put on sackcloth—the rough, coarse garments worn at times of mourning.

⁶For when the king of Nineveh heard what Jonah was saying, he stepped down from his throne, laid aside his royal robes, put on sackcloth, and sat in ashes. ⁷And the king and his nobles sent this message throughout the city: "Let no one, not even the animals, eat anything at all, nor even drink any water. ⁸Everyone must wear sackcloth and cry mightily to God, and let everyone turn from his evil ways, from his violence and robbing. ⁹Who can tell? Perhaps even yet God will decide to let us live and will hold back his fierce anger from destroying us."

¹⁰And when God saw that they had put a stop to their evil ways, he abandoned his plan to destroy them and didn't carry it through.

4 This change of plans made Jonah very angry. ²He complained to the Lord about it: "This is exactly what I thought you'd do, Lord, when I was there in my own country and you first told me to come here. That's why I ran away to Tarshish. For I knew you were a gracious God, merciful, slow to

---

SERVING GOD BOLDLY 1:3 Jonah was afraid. He knew God had a specific job for him, but he didn't want to do it. When God gives us directions through his Word, sometimes we run in fear, claiming that God is asking too much. Fear made Jonah run. But running got him into worse trouble. In the end, he knew it was best to do what God had asked in the first place. But by then he had paid a costly price for running. It is far better to obey from the start. **To begin the series of devotionals on SERVING GOD BOLDLY, turn to page 17.**

Family Devotions

☐ **DEVOTION 241**
OVERCOMING ANGER

Read Jonah 4

*B*ang! went Marvin's ankle against the dining room chair. *Crash!* went the chair as Marvin kicked it over with his bare foot. And "Ouch!" said Marvin as he sat down to rub his sore ankle and aching toes.

"That dumb chair!" Marvin shouted. "It always gets in the way." He continued to complain as he rubbed his bruises.

Just then Dad walked in. He quietly set the chair up, then asked, "Who are you mad at, Son?"

"At the chair," replied Marvin. "It hurt my foot!"

"I'm sorry you got hurt," Dad said. "But surely you're not really angry with the chair, are you?"

Marvin pouted. "No, I guess not," he admitted. "But what's the big deal? Who cares if I yell at the chair? It can't hear me."

"No, the chair can't, but God can," Dad replied. "Do you think he's pleased when you shout and kick the furniture whenever things don't go your way?" Marvin hung his head. This was the first time Dad had spoken to him about his problem with anger. "You're responsible for your actions and for the words that come out of your mouth," continued Dad. "Displaying your temper won't make your anger go away. It only makes you, and everyone around you, more tense and unhappy."

"Well, what should I do?" grumbled Marvin.

"Deal with your anger God's way," Dad replied. "Pray immediately that God will help you get rid of it. Do what you can to solve the problem—like walking more slowly through the dining room, for example. Also, confess any feelings of self-pity or pride that may be causing your anger."

"I'll try, Dad," sighed Marvin. He turned toward the chair and smiled. "Sorry, chair. I'll think twice before I yell at you again. Even if you can't hear me, God can!"

Overcoming Anger Memory Verses

Dear brothers, don't ever forget that it is best to listen much, speak little, and not become angry; for anger doesn't make us good, as God demands that we must be.
James 1:19-20

How About You?

Do you get angry when things don't turn out your way, as Jonah did when God changed his mind about destroying Nineveh? Do you control your feelings of anger, or do you let them control you? People who lose their temper displease God and irritate those around them. Anger can easily lead to other kinds of sin as well. Don't lose your temper! S. K.

• For the next devotional, turn to page 861.   • For the next devotional on OVERCOMING ANGER, turn to page 903.
• For notes on OVERCOMING ANGER, see pages 176, 511, 936, and 1003.

get angry, and full of kindness; I knew how easily you could cancel your plans for destroying these people.

³"Please kill me, Lord; I'd rather be dead than alive [when nothing that I told them happens]."

⁴Then the Lord said, "Is it right to be *angry* about *this?*"

⁵So Jonah went out and sat sulking on the east side of the city, and he made a leafy shelter to shade him as he waited there to see if anything would happen to the city. ⁶And when the leaves of the shelter withered in the heat, the Lord arranged for a vine to grow up quickly and spread its broad leaves over Jonah's head to shade him. This made him comfortable and very grateful.

⁷But God also prepared a worm! The next morning the worm ate through the stem of the plant, so that it withered away and died.

⁸Then when the sun was hot, God ordered a scorching east wind to blow on Jonah, and the sun beat down upon his head until he grew faint and wished to die. For he said, "Death is better than this!"

⁹And God said to Jonah, "Is it right for you to be angry because the plant died?"

"Yes," Jonah said, "it is; it is right for me to be angry enough to die!"

¹⁰Then the Lord said, "You feel sorry for yourself when your shelter is destroyed, though you did no work to put it there, and it is, at best, short-lived. ¹¹And why shouldn't I feel sorry for a great city like Nineveh with its 120,000 people in utter spiritual darkness and all its cattle?"

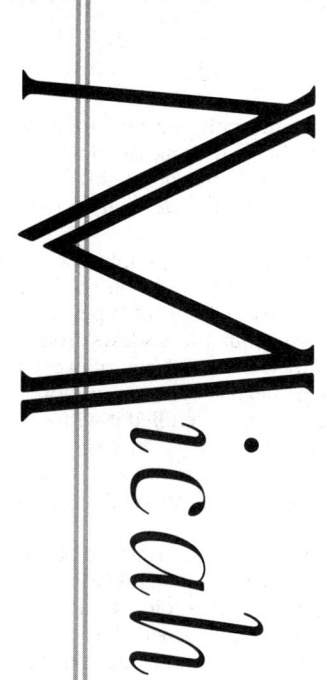

Micah

HOW DO you describe God? If you had to write down what he is like and what he does, what words would you use?

Micah used poetic words to describe God. Sometimes he drew pictures with his words. Sometimes he got caught up in how awesome God's actions are and just spilled over with words of praise. He reminded the people that God is a good and fair judge, that he is all-powerful, and that he is forgiving and accepting.

Micah gave God's messages during the same time as Isaiah, Hosea, and Amos. Like Amos, he told the selfish rich people they needed to start being kind and generous to the poor, or the nation would be punished. Micah reminded the people that they should do this because of who God is. Micah also gave them the special message that one day their Messiah would be born in Bethlehem.

As you read Micah, look for descriptions of God's character—who he is and what he does. Think of how *you* would describe God.

Dark Days for Israel and Judah

These are messages from the Lord to Micah, who lived in the town of Moresheth during the reigns of King Jotham, King Ahaz, and King Hezekiah, all kings of Judah. The messages were addressed to both Samaria and Judah and came to Micah in the form of visions.

²Attention! Let all the peoples of the world listen. For the Lord in his holy Temple has made accusations against you!

³Look! He is coming! He leaves his throne in heaven and comes to earth, walking on the mountaintops. ⁴They melt beneath his feet and flow into the valleys like wax in fire, like water pouring down a hill.

⁵And why is this happening? Because of the sins of Israel and Judah. What sins? The idolatry and oppression centering in the capital cities, Samaria and Jerusalem!

⁶Therefore, the entire city of Samaria will crumble into a heap of rubble and become an open field, her streets plowed up for planting grapes!

The Lord will tear down her wall and her forts, exposing their foundations, and pour their stones into the valleys below. ⁷All her carved images will be smashed to pieces; her ornate idol temples, built with the gifts of worshipers, will all be burned.

⁸I will wail and lament, howling as a jackal, mournful as an ostrich crying across the desert sands at night. I will walk naked and barefoot in sorrow and shame; ⁹for my people's wound is far too deep to heal. The Lord stands ready at Jerusalem's gates to punish her. ¹⁰Woe to the city of Gath. Weep, men of Bakah. In Beth-le-aphrah roll in the dust in your anguish and shame. ¹¹There go the people of Shaphir, led away as slaves—stripped, naked and ashamed. The people of Zaanan dare not show themselves outside their walls. The foundations of Beth-ezel are swept away—the very ground on which it stood. ¹²The people of Maroth vainly hope for better days, but only bitterness awaits them as the Lord stands poised against Jerusalem.

¹³Quick! Use your swiftest chariots and flee, O people of Lachish, for you were the first of the cities of Judah to follow Israel in her sin of idol worship. Then all the cities of the south began to follow your example.

¹⁴Write off Moresheth of Gath; there is no hope of saving her. The town of Achzib has deceived the kings of Israel, for she promised help she cannot give. ¹⁵You people of Mareshah will be a prize to your enemies. They will penetrate to Adullum, the "Pride of Israel."

¹⁶Weep, weep for your little ones. For they are snatched away, and you will never see them again. They have gone as slaves to distant lands. Shave your heads in sorrow.

2 God Punishes Injustice

Woe to you who lie awake at night, plotting wickedness; you rise at dawn to carry out your schemes; because you can, you do. ²You want a certain piece of land or someone else's house (though it is all he has); you take it by fraud and threats and violence.

³But the Lord God says, "I will reward your evil with evil; nothing can stop me; never again will you be proud and haughty after I am through with you. ⁴Then your enemies will taunt you and mock your dirge of despair: 'We are finished, ruined. God has confiscated our land and sent us far away; he has given what is ours to others.' ⁵Others will set your boundaries then. "The People of the Lord" will live where they are sent.

⁶"Don't say such things," the people say. "Don't harp on things like that. It's disgraceful, that sort of talk. Such evils surely will not come our way."

⁷Is that the right reply for you to make, O House of Jacob? Do you think the Spirit of the Lord likes to talk to you so roughly? No! His threats are for your good, to get you on the path again.

⁸Yet to this very hour my people rise against me. For you steal the shirts right off the backs of those who trusted you, who walk in peace.

⁹You have driven out the widows from their homes and stripped their children of every God-given right. ¹⁰Up! Begone! This is no more your land and home, for you have filled it with sin, and it will vomit you out.

¹¹"I'll preach to you the joys of wine and drink"—that is the kind of drunken, lying prophet that you like!

¹²"The time will come, O Israel, when I will gather you—all that are left—and bring you together again like sheep in a fold, like a flock in a pasture—a noisy, happy crowd. ¹³The Messiah will lead you out of exile and bring you through the gates of your cities of captivity, back to your own land. Your King will go before you—the Lord leads on.

3 God Punishes the Leaders

Listen, you leaders of Israel—you are supposed to know right from wrong, ²yet you are the very ones who hate good and love evil; you skin my people and strip them to the bone.

³You devour them, flog them, break their bones, and chop them up like meat for the cooking pot—⁴and then you plead with the Lord for his help in times of trouble! Do you really expect him to listen? He will look the other way! ⁵You false prophets! You who lead his people astray! You who cry "Peace" to those who give you food and threaten those who will not pay!

This is God's message to you: ⁶"The night will close about you and cut off all your visions; darkness will cover you with never a word from God. The sun will go down upon you, and your day will end. ⁷Then at last you will cover your faces in shame and admit that your messages were not from God."

⁸But as for me, I am filled with power, with the Spirit of the Lord, fearlessly announcing God's punishment on Israel for her sins.

⁹Listen to me, you leaders of Israel who hate justice and love unfairness ¹⁰ and fill Jerusalem with murder and sin of every kind— ¹¹you leaders who take bribes; you priests and prophets who won't preach and prophesy until you're paid. (And yet you fawn upon the Lord and say, "All is well—the Lord is here among us. No harm can come to us.") ¹²It is because of you that Jerusalem will be plowed like a field and become a

Family Devotions

☐ *Devotion 242*

Leaving the Future in God's Hands

Read Micah 5:10-15

"Did either of you children make those expensive phone calls to this nine hundred number?" Mom asked Liz and Garth. She and Dad were discussing the phone bill.

"We did call a number advertised on TV," admitted Liz.

"You called ten times in one month!" exclaimed Mom.

"It was a 'Dial-a-Fortune' thing, and when some things came true, we figured there must be something to it," explained Liz, "so we called back to find out more."

"It's no big deal," added Garth.

Dad frowned. "It's a very big deal," he said, "not just because you made these calls without permission, but also because fortune-telling is wrong, according to the Bible."

"But why was some of the stuff they said true?" Liz wanted to know.

"Well, sometimes they give general or vague statements that may be true by chance," Mom explained.

"And other times the information given is lies devised by the evil forces in the world," Dad added. "Sometimes they too may appear to be correct, but they are really a scheme to trap people into believing false messages."

"Stick to the Bible," advised Mom. "All of its messages are true."

"Yes," said Dad. He took the phone bill. "As for this, money will be taken from your allowance each week until these calls are paid for. Did the fortune-teller mention that?" Sadly Garth and Liz shook their heads.

Leaving the Future in God's Hands Memory Verse

For I know the plans I have for you, says the Lord. They are plans for good and not for evil, to give you a future and a hope.
Jeremiah 29:11

How About You?

Have you ever been curious about fortune-telling? Don't look to people, the stars, or crystal balls for help. Depend on God's truth for the real answers. There are many things he doesn't choose to let you know right now. Trust him for the future day by day. *N. E. K.*

• For the next devotional, turn to page 867. • To start the next topic, turn to page 313. • For notes on *Leaving the Future in God's Hands*, see pages 405, 452, 831, and 1061.

heap of rubble; the mountaintop where the Temple stands will be overgrown with brush.

4 Someday the Lord Will Be King

But in the last days Mount Zion will be the most renowned of all the mountains of the world, praised by all nations; people from all over the world will make pilgrimages there.

²"Come," they will say to one another, "let us visit the mountain of the Lord, and see the Temple of the God of Israel; he will tell us what to do, and we will do it." For in those days the whole world will be ruled by the Lord from Jerusalem! He will issue his laws and announce his decrees from there.

³He will arbitrate among the nations and dictate to strong nations far away. They will beat their swords into plowshares and their spears into pruning-hooks; nations shall no longer fight each other, for all war will end. There will be universal peace, and all the military academies and training camps will be closed down.

⁴Everyone will live quietly in his own home in peace and prosperity, for there will be nothing to fear. The Lord himself has promised this. ⁵(Therefore we will follow the Lord our God forever and ever, even though all the nations around us worship idols!)

⁶In that coming day, the Lord says that he will bring back his punished people—sick and lame and dispossessed— ⁷and make them strong again in their own land, a mighty nation, and the Lord himself shall be their King from Mount Zion forever. ⁸O Jerusalem—the Watchtower of God's people—your royal might and power will come back to you again, just as before.

⁹But for now, now you scream in terror. Where is your king to lead you? He is dead! Where are your wise men? All are gone! Pain has gripped you like a woman in labor. ¹⁰Writhe and groan in your terrible pain, O people of Zion, for you must leave this city and live in the fields; you will be sent far away into exile in Babylon. But there I will rescue you and free you from the grip of your enemies.

¹¹True, many nations have gathered together against you, calling for your blood, eager to destroy you. ¹²But they do not know the thoughts of the Lord nor understand his plan, for the time will come when the Lord will gather together the enemies of his people like sheaves upon the threshing floor, helpless before Israel.

¹³Rise, thresh, O daughter of Zion; I will give you horns of iron and hoofs of brass; you will trample to pieces many people, and you will give their wealth as offerings to the Lord, the Lord of all the earth.

5 A Ruler Will Come from Bethlehem

Mobilize! The enemy lays siege to Jerusalem! With a rod they shall strike the Judge of Israel on the face.

²"O Bethlehem Ephrathah, you are but a small Judean village, yet you will be the birthplace of my King who is alive from everlasting ages past!" ³God will abandon his people to their enemies until she who is to give birth has her son; then at last his fellow countrymen—the exile remnants of Israel—will rejoin their brethren in their own land.

⁴And he shall stand and feed his flock in the strength of the Lord, in the majesty of the name of the Lord his God, and his people shall remain there undisturbed, for he will be greatly honored all around the world. ⁵He will be our Peace. And when the Assyrian invades our land and marches across our hills, he will appoint seven shepherds to watch over us, eight princes to lead us. ⁶They will rule Assyria with drawn swords and enter the gates of the land of Nimrod. He will deliver us from the Assyrians when they invade our land.

⁷Then the nation of Israel will refresh the world like a gentle dew or the welcome showers of rain, ⁸and Israel will be as strong as a lion. The nations will be like helpless sheep before her! ⁹She will stand up to her foes; all her enemies will be wiped out.

¹⁰"At that same time," says the Lord, "I will destroy all the weapons you depend on, ¹¹tear down your walls, and demolish the defenses of your cities. ¹²I will put an end to all witchcraft—there will be no more fortune-tellers to consult— ¹³and destroy all your idols. Never again will you worship what you have made, ¹⁴for I will abolish the heathen shrines from among you, and destroy the cities where your idol temples stand.

¹⁵"I will pour out my vengeance upon the nations who refuse to obey me."

6 God's Case against His People

Listen to what the Lord is saying to his people:

"Stand up and state your case against me. Let the mountains and hills be called to witness your complaint.

²"And now, O mountains, listen to the Lord's complaint! For he has a case against his people Israel! He will prosecute them to the full. ³O my people, what have I done that makes you turn away from me? Tell me why your patience is exhausted! Answer me! ⁴For I brought you out of Egypt and cut your chains of slavery. I gave you Moses, Aaron, and Miriam to help you.

⁵"Don't you remember, O my people, how Balak, king of Moab, tried to destroy you through the

curse of Balaam, son of Beor, but I made him bless you instead? That is the kindness I showed you again and again. Have you no memory at all of what happened at Acacia and Gilgal and how I blessed you there?"

6"How can we make up to you for what we've done?" you ask. "Shall we bow before the Lord with offerings of yearling calves?"

Oh no! 7For if you offered him thousands of rams and ten thousands of rivers of olive oil—would that please him? Would he be satisfied? If you sacrificed your oldest child, would that make him glad? Then would he forgive your sins? Of course not!

8No, he has told you what he wants, and this is all it is: *to be fair, just, merciful, and to walk humbly with your God.*

9The Lord's voice calls out to all Jerusalem—listen to the Lord if you are wise! "The armies of destruction are coming; the Lord is sending them. 10For your sins are very great—is there to be no end of getting rich by cheating? The homes of the wicked are full of ungodly treasures and lying scales. 11Shall I say 'Good!' to all your merchants with their bags of false, deceitful weights? How could God be just while saying that? 12Your rich men are wealthy through extortion and violence; your citizens are so used to lying that their tongues can't tell the truth!

13"Therefore I will wound you! I will make your hearts miserable for all your sins. 14You will eat but never have enough; hunger pangs and emptiness will still remain. And though you try and try to save your money, it will come to nothing at the end, and what little you succeed in storing up I'll give to those who conquer you! 15You will plant crops but not harvest them; you will press out the oil from the olives and not get enough to anoint yourself! You will trample the grapes but get no juice to make your wine.

16"The only commands you keep are those of Omri; the only example you follow is that of Ahab! Therefore, I will make an awesome example of you—I will destroy you. I will make you the laughingstock of the world; all who see you will snicker and sneer!"

7 Hard Times for Everyone

Woe is me! It is as hard to find an honest man as grapes and figs when harvest days are over. Not a cluster to eat, not a single early fig, however much I long for it! The good men have disappeared from the earth; not one fair-minded man is left. They are all murderers, turning against even their own brothers.

3They go at their evil deeds with both hands, and how skilled they are in using them! The governor and judge alike demand bribes. The rich man pays them off and tells them whom to ruin. Justice is twisted between them. 4Even the best of them are prickly as briars; the straightest is more crooked than a hedge of thorns. But your judgment day is coming swiftly now; your time of punishment is almost here; confusion, destruction, and terror will be yours.

5Don't trust anyone, not your best friend—not even your wife! 6For the son despises his father; the daughter defies her mother; the bride curses her mother-in-law. Yes, a man's enemies will be found in his own home.

7As for me, I look to the Lord for his help; I wait for God to save me; he will hear me. 8Do not rejoice against me, O my enemy, for though I fall, I will rise again! When I sit in darkness, the Lord himself will be my Light. 9I will be patient while the Lord punishes me, for I have sinned against him; then he will defend me from my enemies and punish them for all the evil they have done to me. God will bring me out of my darkness into the light, and I will see his goodness. 10Then my enemy will see that God is for me and be ashamed for taunting, "Where is that God of yours?" Now with my own eyes I see them trampled down like mud in the street.

11Your cities, people of God, will be rebuilt, much larger and more prosperous than before. 12Citizens of many lands will come and honor you—from Assyria to Egypt, and from Egypt to the Euphrates, from sea to sea and from distant hills and mountains.

13But first comes terrible destruction to Israel for the great wickedness of her people. 14O Lord, come and rule your people; lead your flock; make them live in peace and prosperity; let them enjoy the fertile pastures of Bashan and Gilead as they did long ago.

15"Yes," replies the Lord, "I will do mighty miracles for you, like those when I brought you out of slavery in Egypt. 16All the world will stand amazed at what I will do for you and be embarrassed at their puny might. They will stand in silent awe, deaf to all around them." 17They will see what snakes they are, lowly as worms crawling from their holes. They will come trembling out from their fortresses to meet the Lord our God. They will fear him; they will stand in awe.

HONESTY 7:1-4 Micah could not find an honest person anywhere in the land. Even today, real honesty is difficult to find. Society rationalizes sin, and even Christians sometimes compromise Christian principles in order to do what they want. It is easy to convince ourselves that we deserve a few breaks, especially when "everyone else is doing it." But the standards for honesty come from God, not society. We are honest because God is truth, and we are to be like him. **To begin the series of devotionals on HONESTY, turn to page 33.**

¹⁸Where is another God like you, who pardons the sins of the survivors among his people? You cannot stay angry with your people, for you love to be merciful. ¹⁹Once again you will have compassion on us. You will tread our sins beneath your feet; you will throw them into the depths of the ocean! ²⁰You will bless us as you promised Jacob long ago. You will set your love upon us, as you promised our father Abraham!

Nahum

SOME PEOPLE have to be punished to learn a lesson. Others can learn from watching someone else. Which type of person are you?

God sent Nahum to tell the people of Judah that their neighboring enemy—Assyria—was about to be destroyed. Assyria had attacked Judah again and again. The capital of Assyria was Nineveh. Though the Ninevites had turned to God when Jonah warned them, they later turned back to false gods and were persecuting the people of Judah.

The people of Judah were probably happy to hear that God was going to destroy their worst enemy. But God meant this as a warning to Judah, too. The people of Judah were falling away from God. What God was going to do to Nineveh he could do to Judah as well.

We can learn a lesson from Nineveh: God punishes wrongdoing. God is concerned about fairness and justice. He cares for those who trust him, but he punishes those who turn away from him. As you read Nahum, look for the lesson you can learn from Nineveh. Look for ways to grow closer to God and turn away from wrongdoing.

God Is Patient and Powerful

This is the vision God gave to Nahum, who lived in Elkosh, concerning the impending doom of Nineveh:

²God is jealous over those he loves; that is why he takes vengeance on those who hurt them. He furiously destroys their enemies. ³He is slow in getting angry, but when aroused, his power is incredible, and he does not easily forgive. He shows his power in the terrors of the cyclone and the raging storms; clouds are billowing dust beneath his feet! ⁴At his command the oceans and rivers become dry sand; the lush pastures of Bashan and Carmel fade away; the green forests of Lebanon wilt. ⁵In his presence mountains quake and hills melt; the earth crumbles, and its people are destroyed.

⁶Who can stand before an angry God? His fury is like fire; the mountains tumble down before his anger.

⁷The Lord is good. When trouble comes, he is the place to go! And he knows everyone who

trusts in him! ⁸But he sweeps away his enemies with an overwhelming flood; he pursues them all night long.

⁹What are you thinking of, Nineveh, to defy the Lord? He will stop you with one blow; he won't need to strike again. ¹⁰He tosses his enemies into the fire like a tangled mass of thorns. They burst into flames like straw. ¹¹Who is this king of yours who dares to plot against the Lord? ¹²But the Lord is not afraid of him! "Though he build his army millions strong," the Lord declares, "it will vanish.

"O my people, I have punished you enough! ¹³Now I will break your chains and release you from the yoke of slavery to this Assyrian king." ¹⁴And to the king he says, "I have ordered an end to your dynasty; your sons will never sit upon your throne. And I will destroy your gods and temples, and I will bury you! For how you stink with sin!"

¹⁵See, the messengers come running down the mountains with glad news: "The invaders have been wiped out and we are safe!" O Judah, proclaim a day of thanksgiving and worship only the Lord, as you have vowed. For this enemy from Nineveh will never come again. He is cut off forever; he will never be seen again.

2 Nineveh Will Fall

Nineveh, you are finished! You are already surrounded by enemy armies! Sound the alarm! Man the ramparts! Muster your defenses, full force, and keep a sharp watch for the enemy attack to begin! ²For the land of the people of God lies empty and broken after your attacks, but the Lord will restore their honor and power again!

³Shields flash red in the sunlight! The attack begins! See their scarlet uniforms! See their glittering chariots moving forward side by side, pulled by prancing steeds! ⁴Your own chariots race recklessly along the streets and through the squares, darting like lightning, gleaming like torches. ⁵The king shouts for his officers; they stumble in their haste, rushing to the walls to set up their defenses. ⁶But too late! The river gates are open! The enemy has entered! The palace is in panic!

⁷The queen of Nineveh is brought out naked to the streets and led away, a slave, with all her maidens weeping after her; listen to them mourn like doves and beat their breasts! ⁸Nineveh is like a leaking water tank! Her soldiers slip away, deserting her; she cannot hold them back. "Stop, stop," she shouts, but they keep on running.

⁹Loot the silver! Loot the gold! There seems to be no end of treasures. Her vast, uncounted wealth is stripped away. ¹⁰Soon the city is an empty shambles; hearts melt in horror; knees quake; her people stand aghast, pale-faced and trembling.

¹¹Where now is that great Nineveh, lion of the nations, full of fight and boldness, where even the old and feeble, as well as the young and tender, lived unafraid?

¹²O Nineveh, once mighty lion! You crushed your enemies to feed your children and your wives and filled your city and your homes with captured goods and slaves.

¹³But now the Lord Almighty has turned against you. He destroys your weapons. Your chariots stand there, silent and unused. Your finest youth lie dead. Never again will you bring back slaves from conquered nations; never again will you rule the earth.

3 Destruction

Woe to Nineveh, City of Blood, full of lies, crammed with plunder. ²Listen! Hear the crack of the whips as the chariots rush forward against her, wheels rumbling, horses' hoofs pounding, and chariots clattering as they bump wildly through the streets! ³See the flashing swords and glittering spears in the upraised arms of the cavalry! The dead are lying in the streets—bodies, heaps of bodies, everywhere. Men stumble over them, scramble to their feet, and fall again.

⁴All this because Nineveh sold herself to the enemies of God. The beautiful and faithless city, mistress of deadly charms, enticed the nations with her beauty, then taught them all to worship her false gods, bewitching people everywhere.

⁵"No wonder I stand against you," says the Lord Almighty; "and now all the earth will see your nakedness and shame. ⁶I will cover you with filth and show the world how really vile you are." ⁷All who see you will shrink back in horror: "Nineveh lies in utter ruin." Yet no one anywhere regrets your fate!

⁸Are you any better than Thebes, straddling the Nile, protected on all sides by the river? ⁹Ethiopia and the whole land of Egypt were her mighty allies, and she could call on them for infinite assistance, as well as Put and Libya. ¹⁰Yet Thebes fell and her people were led off as slaves; her babies were dashed to death against the stones of the streets. Soldiers drew straws to see who would get her officers as servants. All her leaders were bound in chains.

¹¹Nineveh, too, will stagger like a drunkard and hide herself in fear. ¹²All your forts will fall. They will be devoured like first-ripe figs that fall into the mouths of those who shake the trees. ¹³Your troops will be weak and helpless as women. The gates of your land will be opened wide to the enemy and set on fire and burned. ¹⁴Get ready for the siege!

FAMILY DEVOTIONS

☐ DEVOTION 243
RESPECTING GOD'S WARNINGS

Read Nahum 1:1-3, 7-12

Michelle came home from school by herself. "Where's your brother?" asked Mom as Michelle came in the door.

Michelle hesitated. "Uh . . . well . . . he went to the drugstore with some friends," she said slowly.

"What friends?" asked Mom suspiciously. "I hope it's not the same group that was caught shoplifting." Michelle didn't answer. "Is it that group?" demanded Mom, and finally Michelle admitted that it was.

When Roger came home about an hour later, Dad was already home. "Where have you been?" asked Dad.

"Oh, I was just in town at the drugstore," Roger replied.

"Who were you with?" Dad asked him.

"Uh . . . nobody," answered Roger sheepishly.

"That's funny," Dad said. "Michelle tried to get out of telling, but when Mom insisted, she admitted that you went with some other kids. The same ones, in fact, who were caught shoplifting last week."

Roger stared at the floor. "All right," he finally said with a sigh, "but nobody shoplifted anything today. Besides, I'll never go with them again. I promise. I really mean it!"

Dad reached for his Bible. "I think we need to read about Nineveh from the book of Nahum."

As Dad began reading, Roger squirmed in his chair. "That's talking about God's destruction of Nineveh," said Dad when he had finished. "Earlier, in the book of Jonah, God showed mercy to Nineveh. But the people sinned again, and God had enough of their sin." Dad looked at Roger and shook his head. "I'm afraid I can't be merciful with you this time, Son. You didn't learn your lesson when I was merciful, so now you must be disciplined."

Respecting God's Warnings
Memory Verse

If my people will humble themselves and pray, and search for me, and turn from their wicked ways, I will hear them from heaven and forgive their sins and heal their land.

2 Chronicles 7:14

How About You?
Do you know that God hates sin? As this passage says, he is slow in getting angry, but we must never take this to mean he overlooks sin. He is a God of holiness as well as of mercy. When people will not turn from their sin, he must punish. *S. N.*

• For the next devotional, turn to page 871. • For the next devotional on *RESPECTING GOD'S WARNINGS*, turn to page 1171. • For notes on *RESPECTING GOD'S WARNINGS*, see pages 219, 874, and 1126.

Store up water! Strengthen the forts! Prepare many bricks for repairing your walls! Go into the pits to trample the clay, and pack it in the molds!

¹⁵But in the middle of your preparations, the fire will devour you; the sword will cut you down; the enemy will consume you like young locusts that eat up everything before them. There is no escape, though you multiply like grasshoppers. ¹⁶Merchants, numerous as stars, filled your city with vast wealth, but your enemies swarm like locusts and carry it away. ¹⁷Your princes and officials crowd together like grasshoppers in the hedges in the cold, but all of them will flee away and disappear, like locusts when the sun comes up and warms the earth.

¹⁸O Assyrian king, your princes lie dead in the dust; your people are scattered across the mountains; there is no shepherd now to gather them. ¹⁹There is no healing for your wound—it is far too deep to cure. All who hear your fate will clap their hands for joy, for where can one be found who has not suffered from your cruelty?

Habakkuk

IT'S FRUSTRATING to look around our world and see people getting away with awful things. This is how Habakkuk felt when he looked at Judah. The people were disobeying God and getting away with it.

God told Habakkuk that he planned to punish the Judeans by sending the Babylonian (Chaldean) army. The Babylonians were far more disobedient than the Judeans. How could God use a totally bad nation to punish his chosen people? Habakkuk was still confused.

So then God gave Habakkuk a glimpse of his overall plan—a plan that *we* have a part in. Habakkuk wrote that someday the whole world—not just God's chosen people—would know about God. Because God now sends his Word to all people, *we* can know him, too. Habakkuk wrote that people should trust in God—and live by faith. This is repeated in the New Testament, and we trust and have faith in Jesus.

After Habakkuk saw God's plan, he decided that no matter how terrible things got in Judah, he would praise and trust God. We can choose to do the same thing. As you read Habakkuk, look for reasons to praise God even when things are bad.

1

Habakkuk Has Questions for God
This is the message that came to the prophet Habakkuk in a vision from God:

²O Lord, how long must I call for help before you will listen? I shout to you in vain; there is no answer. "Help! Murder!" I cry, but no one comes to save. ³Must I forever see this sin and sadness all around me?

Wherever I look I see oppression and bribery and men who love to argue and to fight. ⁴The law is not enforced, and there is no justice given in the courts, for the wicked far outnumber the righteous, and bribes and trickery prevail.

⁵The Lord replied: "Look, and be amazed! You will be astounded at what I am about to do! For I am going to do something in your own lifetime that you will have to see to believe. ⁶I am raising a new force on the world scene, the Chaldeans, a cruel and violent nation who will march across the world and conquer it. ⁷They are notorious for their cruelty. They do as they like, and no one can interfere. ⁸Their horses are swifter than leopards. They

are a fierce people, more fierce than wolves at dusk. Their cavalry move proudly forward from a distant land; like eagles they come swooping down to pounce upon their prey. ⁹All opposition melts away before the terror of their presence. They collect captives like sand.

¹⁰"They scoff at kings and princes and scorn their forts. They simply heap up dirt against their walls and capture them! ¹¹They sweep past like wind and are gone, but their guilt is deep, for they claim their power is from their gods."

¹²O Lord my God, my Holy One, you who are eternal—is your plan in all of this to wipe us out? Surely not! O God our Rock, you have decreed the rise of these Chaldeans to chasten and correct us for our awful sins. ¹³We are wicked, but they far more! Will you, who cannot allow sin in any form, stand idly by while they swallow us up? Should you be silent while the wicked destroy those who are better than they?

¹⁴Are we but fish, to be caught and killed? Are we but creeping things that have no leader to defend them from their foes? ¹⁵Must we be strung up on their hooks and dragged out in their nets, while they rejoice? ¹⁶Then they will worship their nets and burn incense before them! "These are the gods who make us rich," they'll say.

¹⁷Will you let them get away with this forever? Will they succeed forever in their heartless wars?

2 God Explains His Ways

I will climb my watchtower now and wait to see what answer God will give to my complaint.

²And the Lord said to me, "Write my answer on a billboard, large and clear, so that anyone can read it at a glance and rush to tell the others. ³But these things I plan won't happen right away. Slowly, steadily, surely, the time approaches when the vision will be fulfilled. If it seems slow, do not despair, for these things will surely come to pass. Just be patient! They will not be overdue a single day!

⁴"Note this: Wicked men trust themselves alone [as these Chaldeans do], and fail; but the righteous man trusts in me and lives! ⁵What's more, these arrogant Chaldeans are betrayed by all their wine, for it is treacherous. In their greed they have collected many nations, but like death and hell, they are never satisfied. ⁶The time is coming when all their captives will taunt them, saying: 'You robbers! At last justice has caught up with you! Now you will get your just deserts for your oppression and extortion!'

⁷"Suddenly your debtors will rise up in anger and turn on you and take all you have, while you stand trembling and helpless. ⁸You have ruined many nations; now they will ruin you. You murderers! You have filled the countryside with lawlessness and all the cities too.

⁹"Woe to you for getting rich by evil means, attempting to live beyond the reach of danger. ¹⁰By the murders you commit, you have shamed your name and forfeited your lives. ¹¹The very stones in the walls of your homes cry out against you, and the beams in the ceilings echo what they say.

¹²"Woe to you who build cities with money gained from murdering and robbery! ¹³Has not the Lord decreed that godless nations' gains will turn to ashes in their hands? They work so hard, but all in vain!

¹⁴("The time will come when all the earth is filled, as the waters fill the sea, with an awareness of the glory of the Lord.)

¹⁵"Woe to you for making your neighboring lands reel and stagger like drunkards beneath your blows, and then gloating over their nakedness and shame. ¹⁶Soon your own glory will be replaced by shame. Drink down God's judgment on yourselves. Stagger and fall! ¹⁷You cut down the forests of Lebanon—now you will be cut down! You terrified the wild animals you caught in your traps—now terror will strike you because of all your murdering and violence in cities everywhere.

¹⁸"What profit was there in worshiping all your man-made idols? What a foolish lie that they could help! What fools you were to trust what you yourselves had made. ¹⁹Woe to those who command their lifeless wooden idols to arise and save them, who call out to the speechless stone to tell them what to do. Can images speak for God? They are overlaid with gold and silver, but there is no breath at all inside!

²⁰"But the Lord is in his holy Temple; let all the earth be silent before him."

3 Habakkuk's Prayer

This is the prayer of triumph that Habakkuk sang before the Lord:

²O Lord, now I have heard your report, and I worship you in awe for the fearful things you are going to do. In this time of our deep need, begin again to help us, as you did in years gone by. Show us your power to save us. In your wrath, remember mercy.

³I see God moving across the deserts from Mount Sinai. His brilliant splendor fills the earth

---

TRUSTING GOD'S PLAN   2:4   Another translation of this passage is "the righteous shall live by his faith." This verse has inspired countless Christians. Paul refers to it in Romans 1:17 and quotes it in Galatians 3:11. The writer of Hebrews quotes it in 10:38, just before the famous chapter on faith. And it is helpful to all Christians who must live through difficult times without seeing the outcome. Christians must trust that God is directing all things according to his purposes. **To begin the series of devotionals on TRUSTING GOD'S PLAN, turn to page 9.**

Family Devotions

☐ DEVOTION 244
RECEIVING CHRIST AS SAVIOR

Read Habakkuk 3:18

Receiving Christ as Savior
Memory Verse

For God loved the world so much that he gave his only Son so that anyone who believes in him shall not perish but have eternal life.
John 3:16

One day the biggest, fanciest car Billy had ever seen pulled in at his dad's repair shop. Out climbed a man and a boy. "Hi, Kevin," Billy greeted the boy. "That your car?"

Kevin nodded. "Yep, it's ours," he said.

"It looks neat!" exclaimed Billy. "Is it fun to ride in?"

Kevin shrugged. "It's OK," he said. While their fathers talked about the work needed on the car, Billy tried to get Kevin to show him some of its special features, but Kevin didn't seem much interested.

"Is Kevin a friend of yours?" asked Dad after they had left. "I haven't seen him around before."

"He's new at school," replied Billy, "and he's kind of different. I mean . . . he's smart and rich—his family seems to have a lot of money—but he never seems very happy about anything."

"Hmmmm." Dad stood up with a spark plug in his hand. "All that fancy equipment on this car," he said, "but Mr. Peters said it didn't have much spark—and no wonder. The spark plugs are bad." He shook his head. "Apparently Kevin has a lot going for him, but maybe he doesn't have any spark, either," he added.

Billy looked at his father suspiciously. "Huh?"

"God is the spark Kevin needs to be happy," Dad explained.

How About You?
Have you learned that being smart, good-looking, or having lots of money does not bring happiness? Do you have spark in your life—do you know Jesus as Savior? Talk to your mom or dad about how you can receive Jesus as your Savior. *D. K.*

"Ohhh . . . !" Billy began to see what Dad was getting at. "Now that you mention it, I don't think his family goes to church anywhere," said Billy thoughtfully. "I think I'll invite him to Sunday school."

"That's a great idea," approved Dad. "Perhaps at church—or perhaps through your witness—Kevin will see that he needs Jesus as his Savior. Then there will be some spark in his life, too."

• For the next devotional, turn to page 875. • For the next devotional on RECEIVING CHRIST AS SAVIOR, turn to page 989. • For notes on RECEIVING CHRIST AS SAVIOR, see pages 839, 842, 1146, 1234, and 1240.

and sky; his glory fills the heavens, and the earth is full of his praise! What a wonderful God he is! ⁴From his hands flash rays of brilliant light. He rejoices in his awesome power. ⁵Pestilence marches before him; plague follows close behind. ⁶He stops; he stands still for a moment, gazing at the earth. Then he shakes the nations, scattering the everlasting mountains and leveling the hills. His power is just the same as always! ⁷I see the people of Cushan and of Midian in mortal fear.

⁸,⁹ Was it in anger, Lord, you smote the rivers and parted the sea? Were you displeased with them? No, you were sending your chariots of salvation! All saw your power! Then springs burst forth upon the earth at your command! ¹⁰The mountains watched and trembled. Onward swept the raging water. The mighty deep cried out, announcing its surrender to the Lord. ¹¹ The lofty sun and moon began to fade, obscured by brilliance from your arrows and the flashing of your glittering spear.

¹²You marched across the land in awesome anger and trampled down the nations in your wrath. ¹³You went out to save your chosen people. You crushed the head of the wicked and laid bare his bones from head to toe. ¹⁴You destroyed with their own weapons those who came out like a whirlwind, thinking Israel would be an easy prey.

¹⁵Your horsemen marched across the sea; the mighty waters piled high. ¹⁶ I tremble when I hear all this; my lips quiver with fear. My legs give way beneath me, and I shake in terror. I will quietly wait for the day of trouble to come upon the people who invade us.

¹⁷Even though the fig trees are all destroyed, and there is neither blossom left nor fruit; though the olive crops all fail, and the fields lie barren; even if the flocks die in the fields and the cattle barns are empty, ¹⁸yet I will rejoice in the Lord; I will be happy in the God of my salvation. ¹⁹The Lord God is my strength; he will give me the speed of a deer and bring me safely over the mountains.

(A note to the choir director: When singing this ode, the choir is to be accompanied by stringed instruments.)

Zephaniah

SOME PEOPLE are so proud of their abilities or positions that they think the wrong things they do aren't worth punishing. They might feel that way because they star in a play or on a team, or because their family is important in town.

In Zephaniah's day, the people of Judah had a lot of pride. After all, they were God's chosen people! They were proud of that and thought they could do anything they wanted because of it.

God sent Zephaniah to tell them they were wrong. Because God loved his chosen people, he wanted them to be the best they could be. He was going to punish those who did wrong and get rid of people who were against God. But he would save the people who loved and obeyed him. *These* would be his chosen people.

Zephaniah took this message to King Josiah. This good king listened to Zephaniah and led the people to stop sinning and start worshiping God again.

As you read Zephaniah, think about sins you might be hiding behind pride.

A Grim Prediction for Judah

Subject: a message from the Lord.

To: Zephaniah (son of Cushi, grandson of Gedaliah, great-grandson of Amariah, and great-great-grandson of Hezekiah). *When:* During the reign of Josiah (son of Amon) king of Judah.

²"I will sweep away everything in all your land," says the Lord. "I will destroy it to the ground. ³I will sweep away both men and animals alike. Mankind and all the idols that he worships—all will vanish. Even the birds of the air and the fish in the sea will perish. ⁴I will crush Judah and Jerusalem with my fist and destroy every remnant of those who worship Baal; I will put an end to their idolatrous priests, so that even the memory of them will disappear. ⁵They go up on their roofs and bow to the sun, moon, and stars. They 'follow the Lord,' but worship Molech too! I will destroy them. ⁶And I will destroy those who formerly worshiped the Lord, but now no longer do, and those who never loved him and never wanted to."

⁷Stand in silence in the presence of the Lord. For the awesome Day of his Judgment has come; he has prepared a great slaughter of his people and has chosen their executioners. ⁸"On that Day of Judgment I will punish the leaders and princes of Judah and all others wearing heathen clothing. ⁹Yes, I will punish those who follow heathen customs and who rob and kill to fill their masters' homes with evil gain of violence and fraud. ¹⁰A cry of alarm will begin at the farthest gate of Jerusalem, coming closer and closer until the noise of the advancing army reaches the very top of the hill where the city is built.

¹¹"Wail in sorrow, you people of Jerusalem. All your greedy businessmen, all your loan sharks—all will die.

¹²"I will search with lanterns in Jerusalem's darkest corners to find and punish those who sit contented in their sins, indifferent to God, thinking he will let them alone. ¹³They are the very ones whose property will be plundered by the enemy, whose homes will be ransacked; they will never have a chance to live in the new homes they have built. They will never drink wine from the vineyards they have planted.

¹⁴"That terrible day is near. Swiftly it comes—a day when strong men will weep bitterly. ¹⁵It is a day of the wrath of God poured out; it is a day of terrible distress and anguish, a day of ruin and desolation, a day of darkness and gloom, of clouds, blackness, ¹⁶trumpet calls, and battle cries; down go the walled cities and strongest battlements!

¹⁷"I will make you as helpless as a blind man searching for a path because you have sinned against the Lord; therefore, your blood will be poured out into the dust and your bodies will lie there rotting on the ground."

¹⁸Your silver and gold will be of no use to you in that day of the Lord's wrath. You cannot ransom yourselves with it. For the whole land will be devoured by the fire of his jealousy. He will make a speedy riddance of all the people of Judah.

2 Change and God May Save You

Gather together and pray, you shameless nation, ²while there still is time—before judgment begins and your opportunity is blown away like chaff; before the fierce anger of the Lord falls and the terrible day of his wrath begins. ³Beg him to save you, all who are humble—all who have tried to obey.

Walk humbly and do what is right; perhaps even yet the Lord will protect you from his wrath in that day of doom.

⁴Gaza, Ashkelon, Ashdod, Ekron—these Philistine cities, too, will be rooted out and left in desolation. ⁵And woe to you Philistines living on the coast and in the land of Canaan, for the judgment is against you too. The Lord will destroy you until not one of you is left. ⁶The coastland will become a pasture, a place of shepherd camps and folds for sheep.

⁷There the little remnant of the tribe of Judah will be pastured. They will lie down to rest in the abandoned houses in Ashkelon. For the Lord God will visit his people in kindness and restore their prosperity again.

⁸"I have heard the taunts of the people of Moab and Ammon, mocking my people and invading their land. ⁹Therefore as I live," says the Lord Almighty, God of Israel, "Moab and Ammon will be destroyed like Sodom and Gomorrah and become a place of stinging nettles, salt pits, and eternal desolation; those of my people who are left will plunder and possess them."

¹⁰They will receive the wages of their pride, for they have scoffed at the people of the Lord Almighty. ¹¹The Lord will do terrible things to them. He will starve out all those gods of foreign powers, and everyone shall worship him, each in his own land throughout the world.

¹²You Ethiopians, too, will be slain by his sword, ¹³and so will the lands of the north; he will destroy Assyria and make its great capital Nineveh a desolate wasteland like a wilderness. ¹⁴That once proud city will become a pastureland for sheep. All sorts of wild animals will have their homes in her. Hedgehogs will burrow there; the vultures and the owls will live among the ruins of her palaces, hooting from the gaping windows; the ravens will croak from her doors. All her cedar paneling will lie open to the wind and weather.

¹⁵This is the fate of that vast, prosperous city that lived in such security, that said to herself, "In all the world there is no city as great as I." But now—see how she has become a place of utter ruins, a place for animals to live! Everyone passing that way will mock or shake his head in disbelief.

RESPECTING GOD'S WARNINGS 3:2 Do you know people who refuse to listen when someone disagrees with their opinions? Those who are proud often refuse to listen to anything that contradicts their inflated self-esteem, and God's people had become so proud that they would not hear or accept God's correction. Do you find it difficult to listen to the spiritual counsel of others or God's words from the Bible? You will be more willing to listen when you consider how weak and sinful you really are. **To begin the series of devotionals on *RESPECTING GOD'S WARNINGS*, turn to page 21.**

Family Devotions

☐ DEVOTION 245
HUMILITY

Read Zephaniah 2:3

Adam watched his father cut branch after branch off the fruit trees in the backyard. "Won't that ruin the trees?" he asked after a time.

Dad stepped away from his work. "Just the opposite," he replied. "If I do this now, these trees will grow into straight, strong, and productive trees."

"That doesn't make sense to me," Adam retorted.

Dad grinned. "Neither do the spankings I give you from time to time, but they're necessary."

Adam scratched his head in wonderment. "What do the spankings have to do with pruning trees?" he asked.

"Well, you may not agree," Dad answered, "but they make you a better person—just as pruning results in better trees. When you take something that doesn't belong to you, as you did this morning, a spanking is important."

Adam remembered what happened that morning. He had taken a baseball that belonged to the boy next door. As a result, he had been punished.

"It's like I told you," Dad continued. "If I let you get away with stealing little things now, you may grow up and try to steal bigger things. The punishment you'd get then would be a whole lot worse than what I give you."

Deep down, Adam knew his father was right. It seemed strange to think that he was "lucky" to be punished now, but he supposed it was true. His thoughts were interrupted as his father spoke again. "I punish you because I love you, Son. That's why I want to correct you while you're young. You're something like the trees I'm pruning. If you let the bad things in your life be cut away, you will grow to be a better person."

Humility Memory Verse

For everyone who tries to honor himself shall be humbled; and he who humbles himself shall be honored.
Luke 14:11

How About You?
Do you get angry when you are corrected? Try to realize that it is helpful. It is done because someone loves you and wants you to be the very best person you can possibly be. R.J.

• For the next devotional, turn to page 883.   • For the next devotional on HUMILITY, turn to page 961.
• For notes on HUMILITY, see pages 57, 390, 428, 854, and 1228.

3 Judgment for Jerusalem

Woe to filthy, sinful Jerusalem, city of violence and crime. ²In her pride she won't listen even to the voice of God. No one can tell her anything; she refuses all correction. She does not trust the Lord nor seek for God.

³Her leaders are like roaring lions hunting for their victims—out for everything that they can get. Her judges are like ravenous wolves at evening time, who by dawn have left no trace of their prey.

⁴Her "prophets" are liars seeking their own gain; her priests defile the Temple by their disobedience to God's laws.

⁵But the Lord is there within the city, and he does no wrong. Day by day his justice is more evident, but no one heeds—the wicked know no shame.

⁶"I have cut off many nations, laying them waste to their farthest borders; I have left their streets in silent ruin and their cities deserted without a single survivor to remember what happened. ⁷I thought, 'Surely they will listen to me now—surely they will heed my warnings, so that I'll not need to strike again.' But no; however much I punish them, they continue all their evil ways from dawn to dusk and dusk to dawn." ⁸But the Lord says, "Be patient; the time is coming soon when I will stand up and accuse these evil nations. For it is my decision to gather together the kingdoms of the earth and pour out my fiercest anger and wrath upon them. All the earth shall be devoured with the fire of my jealousy.

⁹"At that time I will change the speech of my returning people to pure Hebrew so that all can worship the Lord together. ¹⁰My scattered people who live in the Sudan, beyond the rivers of Ethiopia, will come with their offerings, asking me to be their God again. ¹¹And then you will no longer need to be ashamed of yourselves, for you will no longer be rebels against me. I will remove all your proud and arrogant people from among you; there will be no pride or haughtiness on my holy mountain. ¹²Those who are left will be the poor and the humble, and they will trust in the name of the Lord. ¹³They will not be sinners, full of lies and deceit. They will live quietly, in peace, and lie down in safety, and no one will make them afraid."

¹⁴Sing, O daughter of Zion; shout, O Israel; be glad and rejoice with all your heart, O daughter of Jerusalem. ¹⁵For the Lord will remove his hand of judgment and disperse the armies of your enemy. And the Lord himself, the King of Israel, will live among you! At last your troubles will be over—you need fear no more.

¹⁶On that day the announcement to Jerusalem will be, "Cheer up, don't be afraid. ¹⁷,¹⁸For the Lord your God has arrived to live among you. He is a mighty Savior. He will give you victory. He will rejoice over you with great gladness; he will love you and not accuse you." Is that a joyous choir I hear? No, it is the Lord himself exulting over you in happy song.

"I have gathered your wounded and taken away your reproach. ¹⁹And I will deal severely with all who have oppressed you. I will save the weak and helpless ones, and bring together those who were chased away. I will give glory to my former exiles, mocked and shamed.

²⁰"At that time, I will gather you together and bring you home again, and give you a good name, a name of distinction among all the peoples of the earth, and they will praise you when I restore your fortunes before your very eyes," says the Lord.

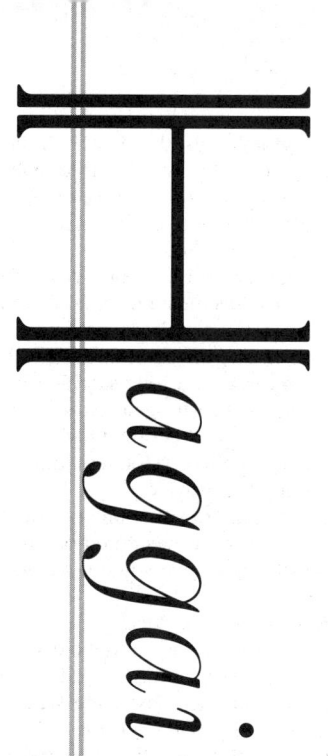

Haggai

HOW DO you decide what's the most important thing for you to do? Does it depend on how much money you have, how much time you have, or what your parents want you to do? How about if you know God wants you to do something?

Haggai was a prophet during the time when God's people came back to Jerusalem after their seventy years of captivity. When they came back, they knew they were to rebuild the Temple first. Worshiping God was the most important thing for them to do—their top priority. They started out rebuilding with enthusiasm, but after sixteen years, they still hadn't finished! God sent Haggai to talk to the people about this.

The people said they didn't have enough money . . . there was a drought . . . they had to take care of their own houses, so there wasn't time to build. Haggai told them the problem was their priorities. God promised to give the people all they needed if they would start working on the Temple again!

When you know God wants you to do something, what keeps you from it? As you read Haggai, think about how you set your priorities.

1

Let's Rebuild the Temple

Subject: a message from the Lord.

To: Haggai the prophet, who delivered it to Zerubbabel (son of Shealtiel), governor of Judah; and to Joshua (son of Josedech), the High Priest—for it was addressed to them.

When: In late August of the second year of the reign of King Darius I.

[2] "Why is everyone saying it is not the right time for rebuilding my Temple?" asks the Lord.

[3,4] His reply to them is this: "Is it then the right time for you to live in luxurious homes, when the Temple lies in ruins? [5] Look at the result: [6] You plant much but harvest little. You have scarcely enough to eat or drink and not enough clothes to keep you warm. Your income disappears, as though you were putting it into pockets filled with holes!

[7] "Think it over," says the Lord Almighty. "Consider how you have acted and what has happened

as a result! ⁸Then go up into the mountains, bring down timber, and rebuild my Temple, and I will be pleased with it and appear there in my glory," says the Lord.

⁹"You hope for much but get so little. And when you bring it home, I blow it away—it doesn't last at all. Why? Because my Temple lies in ruins, and you don't care. Your only concern is your own fine homes. ¹⁰That is why I am holding back the rains from heaven and giving you such scant crops. ¹¹In fact, I have called for a drought upon the land, yes, and in the highlands too—a drought to wither the grain and grapes and olives and all your other crops, a drought to starve both you and all your cattle and ruin everything you have worked so hard to get."

¹²Then Zerubbabel (son of Shealtiel), the governor of Judah, and Joshua (son of Josedech), the High Priest, and the few people remaining in the land obeyed Haggai's message from the Lord their God; they began to worship him in earnest.

¹³Then the Lord told them (again sending the message through Haggai, his messenger), "I am with you; I will bless you." ¹⁴,¹⁵And the Lord gave them a desire to rebuild his Temple; so they all gathered in early September of the second year of King Darius' reign and volunteered their help.

2 God Promises to Bless His People

In early October of the same year, the Lord sent them this message through Haggai:

²"Ask this question of the governor and High Priest and everyone left in the land:

³"Who among you can remember the Temple as it was before? How glorious it was! In comparison, it is nothing now, is it? ⁴But take courage, O Zerubbabel and Joshua and all the people; take courage and work, for I am with you, says the Lord Almighty. ⁵For I promised when you left Egypt that my Spirit would remain among you; so don't be afraid.'"

⁶"For the Lord Almighty says, 'In just a little while I will begin to shake the heavens and earth—and the oceans, too, and the dry land. ⁷I will shake all nations, and the Desire of All Nations shall come to this Temple, and I will fill this place with my glory,' says the Lord Almighty. ⁸,⁹'The future splendor of this Temple will be greater than the splendor of the first one! For I have plenty of silver and gold to do it! And here I will give peace,'" says the Lord.

¹⁰In early December, in the second year of the reign of King Darius, this message came from the Lord through Haggai the prophet:

¹¹"Ask the priests this question about the law: ¹²'If one of you is carrying a holy sacrifice in his robes and happens to brush against some bread or wine or meat, will it too become holy?'"

"No," the priests replied. "Holiness does not pass to other things that way."

¹³Then Haggai asked, "But if someone touches a dead person, and so becomes ceremonially impure, and then brushes against something, does it become contaminated?"

And the priests answered, "Yes."

¹⁴Haggai then made his meaning clear. "You people," he said (speaking for the Lord), "'were contaminating your sacrifices by living with selfish attitudes and evil hearts—and not only your sacrifices, but everything else that you did as a "service" to me. ¹⁵And so everything you did went wrong. But all is different now because you have begun to build the Temple. ¹⁶,¹⁷Before, when you expected a twenty-bushel crop, there were only ten. When you came to draw fifty gallons from the olive press, there were only twenty. I rewarded all your labor with rust and mildew and hail. Yet, even so, you refused to return to me,'" says the Lord.

¹⁸,¹⁹"'But now note this: From today, this 24th day of the month, as the foundation of the Lord's Temple is finished, and from this day onward, I will bless you. Notice, I am giving you this promise now before you have even begun to rebuild the Temple structure, and before you have harvested your grain, and before the grapes, the figs, the pomegranates, and olives have produced their next crops: *From this day I will bless you.*'"

²⁰Another message came to Haggai from the Lord that same day:

²¹"Tell Zerubbabel, the governor of Judah, 'I am about to shake the heavens and the earth, ²²to overthrow thrones, destroy the strength of the kingdoms of the nations. I will overthrow their armed might, and brothers and companions will kill each other. ²³But when that happens, I will take you, O Zerubbabel my servant, and honor you like a signet ring upon my finger; for I have specially chosen you,'" says the Lord Almighty.

KNOWING YOU'RE SPECIAL TO GOD 2:23 God closes his message to Zerubbabel with this tremendous affirmation: "I have specially chosen you." Such a proclamation is ours as well—each of us has been chosen by God (Ephesians 1:4). This truth should make us see our value in God's eyes and motivate us to work for him. When you feel down, remind yourself, "God has chosen me!" **To begin the series of devotionals on** *KNOWING YOU'RE SPECIAL TO GOD,* **turn to page 307.**

Zechariah

IT'S HARD to go on without hope for the future. A lot of what we do today depends on our hope for what will happen in the future.

God sent Zechariah to give short-term warnings and long-term hope to the people who had returned to Jerusalem. God wanted to motivate his people to do good by letting them know of the great future they had coming.

God spoke to Zechariah through visions and symbols. His messages were about horse riders, animal horns, a yardstick, the High Priest's clothes, lampstands, olive trees, a flying scroll, a woman in a basket, and chariots. These may sound strange, but they were symbols that had special importance for the people living then.

Zechariah also said things about the Messiah. Even though this was many years before Jesus was born, Zechariah said that the Messiah would ride into Jerusalem on a donkey, which is what Jesus did the week before he was crucified. Zechariah mentions thirty pieces of silver, which Judas used to betray Jesus. Zechariah also talks about the very end of time, when the Lord will rule the whole earth.

1

Return to the Lord

Subject: messages from the Lord. These messages from the Lord were given to Zechariah (son of Berechiah and grandson of Iddo the prophet) in early November of the second year of the reign of King Darius.

²The Lord Almighty was very angry with your fathers. ³But he will turn again and favor you if only you return to him. ⁴Don't be like your fathers were! The earlier prophets pled in vain with them to turn from all their evil ways.

"Come, return to me," the Lord God said. But no, they wouldn't listen; they paid no attention at all.

⁵,⁶Your fathers and their prophets are now long dead, but remember the lesson they learned, that *God's Word endures!* It caught up with them and punished them. Then at last they repented.

"We have gotten what we deserved from God,"

they said. "He has done just what he warned us he would."

⁷The following February, still in the second year of the reign of King Darius, another message from the Lord came to Zechariah (son of Berechiah and grandson of Iddo the prophet), in a vision in the night: ⁸I saw a Man sitting on a red horse that was standing among the myrtle trees beside a river. Behind him were other horses, red and bay and white, each with its rider.

⁹An angel stood beside me, and I asked him, "Sir, what are all those horses for?"

"I'll tell you," he replied.

¹⁰Then the rider on the red horse—he was the Angel of the Lord—answered me, "The Lord has sent them to patrol the earth for him."

¹¹Then the other riders reported to the Angel of the Lord, "We have patrolled the whole earth, and everywhere there is prosperity and peace."

¹²Upon hearing this, the Angel of the Lord prayed this prayer: "O Lord Almighty, for seventy years your anger has raged against Jerusalem and the cities of Judah. How long will it be until you again show mercy to them?"

¹³And the Lord answered the angel who stood beside me, speaking words of comfort and assurance.

¹⁴Then the angel said, "Shout out this message from the Lord Almighty: 'Don't you think I care about what has happened to Judah and Jerusalem? I am as jealous as a husband for his captive wife. ¹⁵I am very angry with the heathen nations sitting around at ease, for I was only a little displeased with my people, but the nations afflicted them far beyond my intentions.' ¹⁶Therefore the Lord declares: 'I have returned to Jerusalem filled with mercy; my Temple will be rebuilt,' says the Lord Almighty, 'and so will all Jerusalem.' ¹⁷Say it again: 'The Lord Almighty declares that the cities of Israel will again overflow with prosperity, and the Lord will again comfort Jerusalem and bless her and live in her.' "

¹⁸Then I looked and saw four animal horns!

¹⁹"What are these?" I asked the angel.

He replied, "They represent the four world powers that have scattered Judah, Israel, and Jerusalem."

²⁰Then the Lord showed me four blacksmiths.

²¹"What have these men come to do?" I asked.

The angel replied, "They have come to take hold of the four horns that scattered Judah so terribly, and to pound them on the anvil and throw them away."

2 A Man with a Yardstick

When I looked around me again, I saw a man carrying a yardstick in his hand.

²"Where are you going?" I asked.

"To measure Jerusalem," he said. "I want to see whether it is big enough for all the people!"

³Then the angel who was talking to me went over to meet another angel coming toward him.

⁴"Go tell this young man," said the other angel, "that Jerusalem will some day be so full of people that she won't have room enough for all! Many will live outside the city walls, with all their many cattle—and yet they will be safe. ⁵For the Lord himself will be a wall of fire protecting them and all Jerusalem; he will be the glory of the city.

⁶,⁷"Come, flee from the land of the north, from Babylon," says the Lord to all his exiles there; "I scattered you to the winds, but I will bring you back again. Escape, escape to Zion now!" says the Lord.

⁸"The Lord of Glory has sent me against the nations that oppressed you, for he who harms you sticks his finger in Jehovah's eye!

⁹"I will smash them with my fist and their slaves will be their rulers! *Then you will know it was the Lord Almighty who sent me.* ¹⁰Sing, Jerusalem, and rejoice! For I have come to live among you," says the Lord. ¹¹,¹²"At that time many nations will be converted to the Lord, and they too shall be my people; I will live among them all. *Then you will know it was the Lord Almighty who sent me to you.* And Judah shall be the Lord's inheritance in the Holy Land, for God shall once more choose to bless Jerusalem.

¹³"Be silent, all mankind, before the Lord, for he has come to earth from heaven, from his holy home."

3 Zechariah Sees the High Priest

Then the Angel showed me (in my vision) Joshua the High Priest standing before the Angel of the Lord; and Satan was there too, at the Angel's right hand, accusing Joshua of many things.

²And the Lord said to Satan, "I reject your accusations, Satan; yes, I, the Lord, for I have decided to be merciful to Jerusalem—I rebuke you. I have decreed mercy to Joshua and his nation; they are like a burning stick pulled out of the fire."

³Joshua's clothing was filthy as he stood before the Angel of the Lord.

⁴Then the Angel said to the others standing there, "Remove his filthy clothing." And turning to Joshua he said, "See, I have taken away your sins, and now I am giving you these fine new clothes."

SHOWING KINDNESS 2:8 Believers are precious to God (Psalm 116:15); they are his very own children (Psalm 103:13). Treating any believer unkindly is the same as treating God that way. As Jesus told his disciples, when we help others we are helping him; when we neglect them we are neglecting him (Matthew 25:34-46). Be careful, therefore, how you treat fellow believers—that is the way you are treating God. **To begin the series of devotionals on SHOWING KINDNESS, turn to page 81.**

5,6Then I said, "Please, could he also have a clean turban on his head?" So they gave him one.

Then the Angel of the Lord spoke very solemnly to Joshua and said, 7"The Lord Almighty declares: 'If you will follow the paths I set for you and do all I tell you to, then I will put you in charge of my Temple, to keep it holy; and I will let you walk in and out of my presence with these angels. 8Listen to me, O Joshua the High Priest, and all you other priests, you are illustrations of the good things to come. Don't you see?—Joshua represents my servant the Branch whom I will send. 9He will be the Foundation Stone of the Temple that Joshua is standing beside, and I will engrave this inscription on it seven times: *I will remove the sins of this land in a single day.* 10And after that,' the Lord Almighty declares, 'you will all live in peace and prosperity, and each of you will own a home of your own where you can invite your neighbors.'"

4 The Golden Lampstand

Then the angel who had been talking with me woke me, as though I had been asleep.

2"What do you see now?" he asked.

I answered, "I see a gold lampstand holding seven lamps, and at the top there is a reservoir for the olive oil that feeds the lamps, flowing into them through seven tubes. 3And I see two olive trees carved upon the lampstand, one on each side of the reservoir. 4What is it, sir?" I asked. "What does this mean?"

5"Don't you really know?" the angel asked.

"No, sir," I said, "I don't."

6Then he said, "This is God's message to Zerubbabel: 'Not by might, nor by power, but by my Spirit, says the Lord Almighty—you will succeed because of my Spirit, though you are few and weak.' 7Therefore no mountain, however high, can stand before Zerubbabel! For it will flatten out before him! And Zerubbabel will finish building this Temple with mighty shouts of thanksgiving for God's mercy, declaring that all was done by grace alone."

8Another message that I received from the Lord said:

9"Zerubbabel laid the foundation of this Temple, and he will complete it. (Then you will know these messages are from God, the Lord Almighty.) 10Do not despise this small beginning, for the eyes of the Lord rejoice to see the work begin, to see the plumbline in the hand of Zerubbabel. For these seven lamps represent the eyes of the Lord that see everywhere around the world."

11Then I asked him about the two olive trees on each side of the lampstand, 12and about the two olive branches that emptied oil into gold bowls through two gold tubes.

13"Don't you know?" he asked.

"No, sir," I said.

14Then he told me, "They represent the two anointed ones who assist the Lord of all the earth."

5 Zechariah Sees a Flying Scroll

I looked up again and saw a scroll flying through the air.

2"What do you see?" he asked.

"A flying scroll!" I replied. "It appears to be about thirty feet long and fifteen feet wide!"

3"This scroll," he told me, "represents the words of God's curse going out over the entire land. It says that all who steal and lie have been judged and sentenced to death."

4"I am sending this curse into the home of every thief and everyone who swears falsely by my name," says the Lord Almighty. "And my curse shall remain upon his home and completely destroy it."

5Then the angel left me for awhile, but he returned and said, "Look up! Something is traveling through the sky!"

6"What is it?" I asked.

He replied, "It is a bushel basket filled with the sin prevailing everywhere throughout the land."

7Suddenly the heavy lead cover on the basket was lifted off, and I could see a woman sitting inside the basket!

8He said, "She represents wickedness," and he pushed her back into the basket and clamped down the heavy lid again.

9Then I saw two women flying toward us, with wings like those of a stork. And they took the bushel basket and flew off with it, high in the sky.

10"Where are they taking her?" I asked the angel.

11He replied, "To Babylon where they will build a temple for the basket, to worship it!"

6 Zechariah Sees Four Chariots

Then I looked up again and saw four chariots coming from between what looked like two mountains made of brass. 2The first chariot was pulled by red horses, the second by black ones,

---

CONFESSING SIN 3:2-4 Zechariah's vision graphically portrays how we obtain God's mercy. We do nothing ourselves. It is at God's initiative that our filthy garments (sins) are removed, and God provides us with new, clean clothes (the righteousness of Christ—Revelation 19:8). All we need to do is repent and ask God to forgive us. When Satan tries to make you feel dirty and unworthy, remember that the clean clothes of Christ's righteousness make you worthy to draw near to God.
To begin the series of devotionals on CONFESSING SIN, turn to page 41.

³the third by white horses and the fourth by dappled-grays.

⁴"And what are these, sir?" I asked the angel.

⁵He replied, "These are the four heavenly spirits who stand before the Lord of all the earth; they are going out to do his work. ⁶The chariot pulled by the black horses will go north, and the one pulled by white horses will follow it there, while the dappled-grays will go south."

⁷The red horses were impatient to be off, to patrol back and forth across the earth, so the Lord said, "Go. Begin your patrol." So they left at once.

⁸Then the Lord summoned me and said, "Those who went north have executed my judgment and quieted my anger there."

⁹In another message the Lord said:

¹⁰,¹¹"Heldai, Tobijah, and Jedaiah will bring gifts of silver and gold from the Jews exiled in Babylon. The same day they arrive, meet them at the home of Josiah (son of Zephaniah), where they will stay. Accept their gifts and make from them a crown from the silver and gold. Then put the crown on the head of Joshua (son of Josedech) the High Priest. ¹²Tell him that the Lord Almighty says, 'You represent the Man who will come, whose name is "The Branch"—he will grow up from himself—and will build the Temple of the Lord. ¹³To him belongs the royal title. He will rule both as King and as Priest, with perfect harmony between the two!'

¹⁴"Then put the crown in the Temple of the Lord, to honor those who gave it—Heldai, Tobijah, Jedaiah, and also Josiah. ¹⁵These three who have come from so far away represent many others who will some day come from distant lands to rebuild the Temple of the Lord. And when this happens, you will know my messages have been from God, the Lord Almighty. But none of this will happen unless you carefully obey the commandments of the Lord your God."

7 Be Just and Kind

Another message came to me from the Lord in late November of the fourth year of the reign of King Darius.

²The Jews of the city of Bethel had sent a group of men headed by Sharezer, the chief administrative officer of the king, and Regem-melech, to the Lord's Temple at Jerusalem, to seek his blessing ³and to speak with the priests and prophets about whether they must continue their traditional custom of fasting and mourning during the month of August each year, as they had been doing so long.

⁴This was the Lord's reply:

⁵"When you return to Bethel, say to all your people and your priests, 'During those seventy years of exile when you fasted and mourned in August and October, were you really in earnest about leaving your sins behind and coming back to me? No, not at all! ⁶And even now in your holy feasts to God, you don't think of me, but only of the food and fellowship and fun. ⁷Long years ago, when Jerusalem was prosperous and her southern suburbs out along the plain were filled with people, the prophets warned them that this attitude would surely lead to ruin, as it has.'"

⁸,⁹Then this message from the Lord came to Zechariah. "Tell them to be honest and fair—and not to take bribes—and to be merciful and kind to everyone. ¹⁰Tell them to stop oppressing widows and orphans, foreigners and poor people, and to stop plotting evil against each other. ¹¹Your fathers would not listen to this message. They turned stubbornly away and put their fingers in their ears to keep from hearing me. ¹²They hardened their hearts like flint, afraid to hear the words that God, the Lord Almighty, commanded them—the laws he had revealed to them by his Spirit through the early prophets. That is why such great wrath came down on them from God. ¹³I called, but they refused to listen, so when they cried to me, I turned away. ¹⁴I scattered them as with a whirlwind among the far-off nations. Their land became desolate; no one even traveled through it; the Pleasant Land lay bare and blighted."

8 Judah Will Be Blessed

Again the Lord's message came to me:

²The Lord Almighty says, "I am greatly concerned—yes, furiously angry—because of all that Jerusalem's enemies have done to her. ³Now I am going to return to my land, and I, myself, will live within Jerusalem. Then Jerusalem shall be called 'The Faithful City,' and 'The Holy Mountain,' and 'The Mountain of the Lord Almighty.'"

⁴The Lord Almighty declares that Jerusalem will have peace and prosperity so long that there will once again be aged men and women hobbling through her streets on canes, ⁵and the streets will be filled with boys and girls at play.

⁶The Lord says, "This seems unbelievable to you—a remnant, small, discouraged as you are—but it is no great thing for me. ⁷You can be sure that I will rescue my people from east and west, wherever they are scattered. ⁸I will bring them home again to live safely in Jerusalem, and they will be my people, and I will be their God, just and true and yet forgiving them their sins!"

⁹The Lord Almighty says, "Get on with the job and finish it! You have been listening long enough! For since you began laying the foundation of the Temple, the prophets have been telling

FAMILY DEVOTIONS

☐ DEVOTION 246
SHOWING COMPASSION

Read Zechariah 7:8-10

Christy was sorry when she heard that Nicole's mother had been in a car accident and was in critical condition in the hospital. Many of the children stared curiously at Nicole but stayed away from her because they didn't know what to say. And most of those who did talk to her felt very awkward about it. Christy didn't know Nicole very well, but she could truly understand how Nicole felt because her own dad had been in a serious accident the year before. There were still some things he couldn't do because of the accident.

At lunchtime Christy sat next to Nicole. "I know how hard it is," she said softly. "My father was in a car wreck last year."

"Oh," sighed Nicole, "then you understand how I feel!"

"Yes, I do," Christy assured her. "Would you like me to pray for your mother right now?"

"Oh, would you?" Nicole's face showed her first smile of the day.

When Christy got home from school that afternoon, she told her dad about Nicole's mother. "I told her that knowing the Lord helped me. She listened to what I had to say, Dad, because she knew I understood how she felt."

Dad smiled and nodded. "It often happens like that, Christy," he said. "In fact, the Bible tells us that because God comforts us during the bad times, we can, in turn, comfort others who are going through bad times. One way we can do this is by telling them about the Lord."

Showing Compassion Memory Verse

What a wonderful God we have—he is the Father of our Lord Jesus Christ, the source of every mercy, and the one who so wonderfully comforts and strengthens us in our hardships and trials.
2 Corinthians 1:3

How About You?

The Lord tells us that he will comfort us during any situation, and that we, in turn, can comfort others with his love. Even if nothing really bad has happened to you, you can still pray for those who are going through a tough situation. You can still tell them about God's love. In this way, you can "be merciful and kind to everyone." *L. M. W.*

• For the next devotional, turn to page 885.   • For the next devotional on *SHOWING COMPASSION,* turn to page 1017.
• For notes on *SHOWING COMPASSION,* see pages 206, 506, 515, 710, and 934.

you about the blessings that await you when it's finished. ¹⁰Before the work began there were no jobs, no wages, no security; if you left the city, there was no assurance you would ever return, for crime was rampant.

¹¹"But it is all so different now!" says the Lord Almighty. ¹²"For I am sowing peace and prosperity among you. Your crops will prosper; the grapevines will be weighted down with fruit; the ground will be fertile, with plenty of rain; all these blessings will be given to the people left in the land. ¹³'May you be as poor as Judah,' the heathen used to say to those they cursed! But no longer! For now *Judah* is a word of blessing, not a curse. 'May you be as prosperous and happy as Judah is,' they'll say. So don't be afraid or discouraged! Get on with rebuilding the Temple! ¹⁴,¹⁵If you do, I will certainly bless you. And don't think that I might change my mind. I did what I said I would when your fathers angered me and I promised to punish them, and I won't change this decision of mine to bless you. ¹⁶Here is your part: Tell the truth. Be fair. Live at peace with everyone. ¹⁷Don't plot harm to others; don't swear that something is true when it isn't! How I hate all that sort of thing!" says the Lord.

¹⁸Here is another message that came to me from the Lord Almighty:

¹⁹"The traditional fasts and times of mourning you have kept in July, August, October, and January are ended. They will be changed to joyous festivals if you love truth and peace! ²⁰,²¹People from around the world will come on pilgrimages and pour into Jerusalem from many foreign cities to attend these celebrations. People will write their friends in other cities and say, 'Let's go to Jerusalem to ask the Lord to bless us and be merciful to us. I'm going! Please come with me. Let's go *now!*' ²²Yes, many people, even strong nations, will come to the Lord Almighty in Jerusalem to ask for his blessing and help. ²³In those days ten men from ten different nations will clutch at the coat sleeves of one Jew and say, 'Please be my friend, for I know that God is with you.'"

9 Israel's Enemies Will Be Punished

This is the message concerning God's curse on the lands of Hadrach and Damascus, for the Lord is closely watching all mankind, as well as Israel.

²"Doomed is Hamath, near Damascus, and Tyre and Zidon too, shrewd though they be. ³Though Tyre has armed herself to the hilt and become so rich that silver is like dirt to her, and fine gold like dust in the streets, ⁴yet the Lord will dispossess her and hurl her fortifications into the sea; and she shall be set on fire and burned to the ground.

⁵"Ashkelon will see it happen and be filled with fear; Gaza will huddle in desperation, and Ekron will shake with terror, for their hopes that Tyre would stop the enemies' advance will all be dashed. Gaza will be conquered, her king killed, and Ashkelon will be completely destroyed.

⁶"Foreigners will take over the city of Ashdod, the rich city of the Philistines. ⁷I will yank her idolatry out of her mouth and pull from her teeth her sacrifices that she eats with blood. Everyone left will worship God and be adopted into Israel as a new clan: the Philistines of Ekron will intermarry with the Jews, just as the Jebusites did so long ago. ⁸And I will surround my Temple like a guard to keep invading armies from entering Israel. I am closely watching their movements, and I will keep them away; no foreign oppressors will again overrun my people's land.

⁹"Rejoice greatly, O my people! Shout with joy! For look—your King is coming! He is the Righteous One, the Victor! Yet he is lowly, riding on a donkey's colt! ¹⁰I will disarm all peoples of the earth, including my people in Israel, and he shall bring peace among the nations. His realm shall stretch from sea to sea, from the river to the ends of the earth.

¹¹"I have delivered you from death in a waterless pit because of the covenant I made with you, sealed with blood. ¹²Come to the place of safety, all you prisoners, for there is yet hope! I promise right now, I will repay you two mercies for each of your woes! ¹³Judah, you are my bow! Ephraim, you are my arrow! Both of you will be my sword, like the sword of a mighty soldier brandished against the sons of Greece."

¹⁴The Lord shall lead his people as they fight! His arrows shall fly like lightning; the Lord God shall sound the trumpet call and go out against his enemies like a whirlwind off the desert from the south. ¹⁵He will defend his people, and they will subdue their enemies, treading them beneath their feet. They will taste victory and shout with triumph. They will slaughter their foes, leaving horrible carnage everywhere. ¹⁶,¹⁷The Lord their God will save his people in that day, as a Shepherd caring for his sheep. They shall shine in his land as glittering jewels in a crown. How wonderful and beautiful all shall be! The abundance of grain and grapes will make the young men and girls flourish; they will be radiant with health and happiness.

10 Promises for Israel and Judah

Ask the Lord for rain in the springtime, and he will answer with lightning and showers. Every

Family Devotions

☐ *Devotion 247*
Making the Best Choices

Read Zechariah 8:9-23

Making the Best Choices Memory Verse

He will always give you all you need from day to day if you will make the Kingdom of God your primary concern. Luke 12:31

At the first meeting of his church youth group, Jimmy was given a quiet-time diary. At first he was very faithful in reading his Bible and writing responses to the questions. One day, however, Jimmy's father bought a video game for the family. Jimmy loved it. He never seemed to grow weary of rescuing princesses or shooting down enemy planes. He often had to be told to turn the game off and do his homework or finish his chores.

One day as Jimmy's father was walking past his son's room, he noticed the quiet-time diary on the dresser. He stopped. "Mind if I look at this, Son?" he asked.

Jimmy shrugged. "Go ahead," he said on his way out.

As Dad thumbed through the book, he noticed that no questions had been answered since the day he had brought the video game home. Still holding the diary, Dad went to the family room where Jimmy was on the verge of rescuing the princess. Receiving no reply when he spoke to Jimmy, Dad went over and switched off the monitor.

Jimmy was shocked. "Dad, I—"

"Son, I'm sorry I ever bought that game," said Dad as Jimmy began to object. "I can see it has had a bad effect on you. We're going to put it away for a while."

"Aw, Dad," protested Jimmy, "there's nothing wrong with this. What's it hurting?"

Dad looked very solemn. "There's nothing wrong with the game," he agreed. "The problem is with you. You're obsessed with it, and that's wrong." Jimmy was about to argue when he noticed the quiet-time diary in his father's hand. "A little recreation is good," continued Dad, "but something good can become bad when it takes the place of what is best."

How About You?
Does God have first place in your time schedule? In today's Scripture reading, God had to remind the Temple workers to get on with the job he had given them. We need to be sure to give top priority to God's work, too, starting with spending time in his Word to learn more about him and what he wants. D. C. C.

• For the next devotional, turn to page 891. • For the next devotional on *Making the Best Choices,* turn to page 941. • For notes on *Making the Best Choices,* see pages 358, 652, and 944.

field will become a lush pasture. ²How foolish to ask the idols for anything like that! Fortune-tellers' predictions are all a bunch of silly lies; what comfort is there in promises that don't come true? Judah and Israel have been led astray and wander like lost sheep; everyone attacks them, for they have no shepherd to protect them.

³"My anger burns against your 'shepherds'—your leaders—and I will punish them—these goats. For the Lord Almighty has arrived to help his flock of Judah. I will make them strong and glorious like a proud steed in battle. ⁴From them will come the Cornerstone, the Peg on which all hope hangs, the Bow that wins the battle, the Ruler over all the earth. ⁵They will be mighty warriors for God, grinding their enemies' faces into the dust beneath their feet. The Lord is with them as they fight; their enemy is doomed.

⁶"I will strengthen Judah, yes, and Israel too; I will reestablish them because I love them. It will be as though I had never cast them all away, for I, the Lord their God, will hear their cries. ⁷They shall be like mighty warriors. They shall be happy as with wine. Their children, too, shall see the mercies of the Lord and be glad. Their hearts shall rejoice in the Lord. ⁸When I whistle to them, they'll come running, for I have bought them back again. From the few that are left, their population will grow again to former size. ⁹ Though I have scattered them like seeds among the nations, still they will remember me and return again to God; with all their children, they will come home again to Israel. ¹⁰I will bring them back from Egypt and Assyria and resettle them in Israel—in Gilead and Lebanon; there will scarcely be room for all of them! ¹¹They shall pass safely through the sea of distress, for the waves will be held back. The Nile will become dry—the rule of Assyria and Egypt over my people will end."

¹²The Lord says, "I will make my people strong with power from me! They will go wherever they wish, and wherever they go they will be under my personal care."

11 The Two Shepherds

Open your doors, O Lebanon, to judgment. You will be destroyed as though by fire raging through your forests. ²Weep, O cypress trees, for all the ruined cedars; the tallest and most beautiful of them are fallen. Cry in fear, you oaks of Bashan, as you watch the thickest forests felled. ³Listen to the wailing of Israel's leaders—all these evil shepherds—for their wealth is gone. Hear the young lions roaring—the princes are weeping, for their glorious Jordan valley lies in ruins.

⁴Then said the Lord my God to me, "Go and take a job as shepherd of a flock being fattened for the butcher. ⁵This will illustrate the way my people have been bought and slain by wicked leaders, who go unpunished. 'Thank God, now I am rich!' say those who have betrayed them—their own shepherds have sold them without mercy. ⁶And I won't spare them either," says the Lord, "for I will let them fall into the clutches of their own wicked leaders, and they will slay them. They shall turn the land into a wilderness, and I will not protect it from them."

⁷So I took two shepherd's staffs, naming one Grace and the other Union, and I fed the flock as I had been told to do. ⁸And I got rid of their three evil shepherds in a single month. But I became impatient with these sheep—this nation—and they hated me too.

⁹So I told them, "I won't be your shepherd any longer. If you die, you die; if you are killed, I don't care. Go ahead and destroy yourselves!"

¹⁰And I took my staff called Grace and snapped it in two, showing that I had broken my contract to lead and protect them. ¹¹That was the end of the agreement. Then those who bought and sold sheep, who were watching, realized that God was telling them something through what I did.

¹²And I said to their leaders, "If you like, give me my pay, whatever I am worth; but only if you want to."

So they counted out thirty little silver coins as my wages.

¹³And the Lord told me, "Use it to buy a field from the pottery makers—this magnificent sum they value you at!"

So I took the thirty coins and threw them into the Temple for the pottery makers. ¹⁴Then I broke my other staff, "Union," to show that the bond of unity between Judah and Israel was broken.

¹⁵Then the Lord told me to go again and get a job as a shepherd; this time I was to act the part of a worthless, wicked shepherd.

¹⁶And he said to me, "This illustrates how I will give this nation a shepherd who will not care for the dying ones, nor look after the young, nor heal the broken bones, nor feed the healthy ones, nor carry the lame that cannot walk; instead, he will eat the fat ones, even tearing off their feet. ¹⁷Woe to this worthless shepherd who doesn't care for the flock. God's sword will cut his arm and pierce through his right eye; his arm will become useless and his right eye blinded."

12 God Defends His People

This is the fate of Israel, as pronounced by the Lord, who stretched out the heavens, laid the foundation of the earth, and formed the spirit of man within him:

²"I will make Jerusalem and Judah like a cup of

poison to all the nearby nations that send their armies to surround Jerusalem. ³Jerusalem will be a heavy stone burdening the world. And though all the nations of the earth unite in an attempt to move her, they will all be crushed.

⁴"In that day," says the Lord, "I will bewilder the armies drawn up against her, and make fools of them, for I will watch over the people of Judah, but blind all her enemies.

⁵"And the clans of Judah shall say to themselves, 'The people of Jerusalem have found strength in the Lord Almighty, their God.'

⁶"In that day I will make the clans of Judah like a little fire that sets the forest aflame—like a burning match among the sheaves; they will burn up all the neighboring nations right and left, while Jerusalem stands unmoved. ⁷The Lord will give victory to the rest of Judah first, before Jerusalem, so that the people of Jerusalem and the royal line of David won't be filled with pride at their success.

⁸"The Lord will defend the people of Jerusalem; the weakest among them will be as mighty as King David! And the royal line will be as God, like the Angel of the Lord who goes before them! ⁹For my plan is to destroy all the nations that come against Jerusalem.

¹⁰"Then I will pour out the spirit of grace and prayer on all the people of Jerusalem. They will look on him they pierced, and mourn for him as for an only son, and grieve bitterly for him as for an oldest child who died. ¹¹The sorrow and mourning in Jerusalem at that time will be even greater than the grievous mourning for the godly King Josiah, who was killed in the valley of Megiddo.

¹²⁻¹⁴"All of Israel will weep in profound sorrow. The whole nation will be bowed down with universal grief—king, prophet, priest, and people. Each family will go into private mourning, husbands and wives apart, to face their sorrow alone.

13 God's Fountain of Forgiveness

"At that time a Fountain will be opened to the people of Israel and Jerusalem, a Fountain to cleanse them from all their sins and defilement."

²And the Lord Almighty declares, "In that day I will get rid of every vestige of idol worship throughout the land, so that even the names of the idols will be forgotten. All false prophets and fortune-tellers will be wiped out, ³and if anyone begins false prophecy again, his own father and mother will slay him! 'You must die,' they will tell him, 'for you are prophesying lies in the name of the Lord.'

⁴"No one will be boasting then of his prophetic gift! No one will wear prophet's clothes to try to fool the people then.

⁵"'No,' he will say. 'I am not a prophet; I am a farmer. The soil has been my livelihood from my earliest youth.'

⁶"And if someone asks, 'Then what are these scars on your chest and your back?' he will say, 'I got into a brawl at the home of a friend!'

⁷"Awake, O sword, against my Shepherd, the man who is my associate and equal," says the Lord Almighty. "Strike down the Shepherd and the sheep will scatter, but I will come back and comfort and care for the lambs. ⁸Two-thirds of all the nation of Israel will be cut off and die, but a third will be left in the land. ⁹I will bring the third that remain through the fire and make them pure, as gold and silver are refined and purified by fire. They will call upon my name and I will hear them; I will say, 'These are my people,' and they will say, 'The Lord is our God.'"

14 God's Rule over All the Earth

Watch, for the day of the Lord is coming soon! On that day the Lord will gather together the nations to fight Jerusalem; the city will be taken, the houses rifled, the loot divided, the women raped; half the population will be taken away as slaves, and half will be left in what remains of the city.

³Then the Lord will go out fully armed for war, to fight against those nations. ⁴That day his feet will stand upon the Mount of Olives, to the east of Jerusalem, and the Mount of Olives will split apart, making a very wide valley running from east to west, for half the mountain will move toward the north and half toward the south. ⁵You will escape through that valley, for it will reach across to the city gate. Yes, you will escape as your people did long centuries ago from the earthquake in the days of Uzziah, king of Judah, and the Lord my God shall come, and all his saints and angels with him.

⁶The sun and moon and stars will no longer shine, ⁷yet there will be continuous day! Only the Lord knows how! There will be no normal day and night—at evening time it will still be light. ⁸Life-giving waters will flow out from Jerusalem, half toward the Dead Sea and half toward the Mediterranean, flowing continuously both in winter and in summer.

⁹And the Lord shall be King over all the earth. In that day there shall be one Lord—his name alone will be worshiped. ¹⁰All the land from Geba (the northern border of Judah) to Rimmon (the southern border) will become one vast plain, but Jerusalem will be on an elevated site, covering the area all the way from the Gate of Benjamin over to the site

of the old gate, then to the Corner Gate, and from the Tower of Hananel to the king's wine presses. ¹¹And Jerusalem shall be inhabited, safe at last, never again to be cursed and destroyed.

¹²And the Lord will send a plague on all the people who fought Jerusalem. They will become like walking corpses, their flesh rotting away; their eyes will shrivel in their sockets, and their tongues will decay in their mouths.

¹³They will be seized with terror, panic-stricken from the Lord, and will fight against each other in hand-to-hand combat. ¹⁴All Judah will be fighting at Jerusalem. The wealth of all the neighboring nations will be confiscated—great quantities of gold and silver and fine clothing. ¹⁵(This same plague will strike the horses, mules, camels, donkeys, and all the other animals in the enemy camp.)

¹⁶In the end, those who survive the plague will go up to Jerusalem each year to worship the King, the Lord Almighty, to celebrate a time of thanksgiving. ¹⁷And any nation anywhere in all the world that refuses to come to Jerusalem to worship the King, the Lord Almighty, will have no rain. ¹⁸But if Egypt refuses to come, God will punish her with some other plague. ¹⁹And so Egypt and the other nations will all be punished if they refuse to come.

²⁰In that day the bells on the horses will have written on them, "These Are Holy Property"; and the trash cans in the Temple of the Lord will be as sacred as the bowls beside the altar. ²¹In fact, every container in Jerusalem and Judah shall be sacred to the Lord Almighty; all who come to worship may use any of them free of charge to boil their sacrifices in; there will be no more grasping traders in the Temple of the Lord Almighty!

DO YOU know people who do things halfway? When it's time to clean their room, for example, they shove everything under the bed instead of putting things away. Then they claim they've honestly cleaned their room.

God's people were acting like this. The people said they were offering sacrifices properly. But the animals for the sacrifices were damaged, and that wasn't right.

The people said they were bringing their tithes and offerings. But they brought what little money they had left over instead of giving to God *first,* and that wasn't right.

God said the people weren't sorry for their sins. The people pointed out that they cried over their sins. But they kept sinning anyway, and that wasn't right.

The people were obeying God with only half their heart and half their effort. It proved that deep down they didn't love God. God wanted their hearts.

Are there ways that you're only loving God halfway? Search your heart for the answer as you read Malachi.

1

God Loves His People

Here is the Lord's message to Israel, given through the prophet Malachi:

2,3"I have loved you very deeply," says the Lord. But you retort, "Really? When was this?"

And the Lord replies, "I showed my love for you by loving your father, Jacob. I didn't need to. I even rejected his very own brother, Esau, and destroyed Esau's mountains and inheritance, to give it to the jackals of the desert. 4And if his descendants should say, 'We will rebuild the ruins,' then the Lord Almighty will say, 'Try to if you like, but I will destroy it again,' for their country is named 'The Land of Wickedness,' and their people are called 'Those Whom God Does Not Forgive.'"

5O Israel, lift your eyes to see what God is doing all around the world; then you will say, "Truly, the Lord's great power goes far beyond our borders!"

6"A son honors his father, a servant honors his master. I am your Father and Master, yet you don't honor me, O priests, but you despise my name."

"Who? Us?" you say. "When did we ever despise your name?"

⁷"When you offer polluted sacrifices on my altar."

"Polluted sacrifices? When have we ever done a thing like that?"

"Every time you say, 'Don't bother bringing anything very valuable to offer to God!' ⁸You tell the people, 'Lame animals are all right to offer on the altar of the Lord—yes, even the sick and the blind ones.' And you claim this isn't evil? Try it on your governor sometime—give him gifts like that—and see how pleased he is!

⁹"'God have mercy on us,' you recite; 'God be gracious to us!' But when you bring that kind of gift, why should he show you any favor at all?

¹⁰"Oh, to find one priest among you who would shut the doors and refuse this kind of sacrifice! I have no pleasure in you," says the Lord Almighty, "and I will not accept your offerings.

¹¹"But my name will be honored by the Gentiles from morning till night. All around the world they will offer sweet incense and pure offerings in honor of my name. For my name shall be great among the nations," says the Lord Almighty. ¹²"But you dishonor it, saying that my altar is not important and encouraging people to bring cheap, sick animals to offer to me on it.

¹³"You say, 'Oh, it's too difficult to serve the Lord and do what he asks.' And you turn up your noses at the rules he has given you to obey. Think of it! Stolen animals, lame and sick—as offerings to God! Should I accept such offerings as these?" asks the Lord. ¹⁴"Cursed is that man who promises a fine ram from his flock and substitutes a sick one to sacrifice to God. For I am a Great King," says the Lord Almighty, "and my name is to be mightily revered among the Gentiles."

2 God Warns His Priests

Listen, you priests, to this warning from the Lord Almighty:

"If you don't change your ways and give glory to my name, then I will send terrible punishment upon you, and instead of giving you blessings as I would like to, I will turn on you with curses. Indeed, I have cursed you already because you haven't taken seriously the things that are most important to me.

³"Take note that I will rebuke your children; I will spread on your faces the manure of these animals you offer me and throw you out like dung. ⁴Then at last you will know it was I who sent you this warning to return to the laws I gave your father Levi," says the Lord Almighty. ⁵"The purpose of these laws was to give him life and peace, to be a means of showing his respect and awe for me by keeping them. ⁶He passed on to the people all the truth he got from me. He did not lie or cheat; he walked with me, living a good and righteous life, and turned many from their lives of sin.

⁷"Priests' lips should flow with the knowledge of God so the people will learn God's laws. The priests are the messengers of the Lord Almighty, and men should come to them for guidance. ⁸But not to you! For you have left God's paths. Your 'guidance' has caused many to stumble in sin. You have distorted the covenant of Levi and made it into a grotesque parody," says the Lord Almighty. ⁹"Therefore, I have made you contemptible in the eyes of all the people; for you have not obeyed me, but you let your favorites break the law without rebuke."

¹⁰We are children of the same father, Abraham, all created by the same God. And yet we are faithless to each other, violating the covenant of our fathers! ¹¹In Judah, in Israel, and in Jerusalem, there is treachery, for the men of Judah have defiled God's holy and beloved Temple by marrying heathen women who worship idols. ¹²May the Lord cut off from his covenant every last man, whether priest or layman, who has done this thing!

¹³Yet you cover the altar with your tears because the Lord doesn't pay attention to your offerings anymore, and you receive no blessing from him. ¹⁴"Why has God abandoned us?" you cry. I'll tell you why; it is because the Lord has seen your treachery in divorcing your wives who have been faithful to you through the years, the companions you promised to care for and keep. ¹⁵You were united to your wife by the Lord. In God's wise plan, when you married, the two of you became one person in his sight. And what does he want? Godly children from your union. Therefore, guard your passions! Keep faith with the wife of your youth.

¹⁶For the Lord, the God of Israel, says he hates divorce and cruel men. Therefore, control your passions—let there be no divorcing of your wives.

¹⁷You have wearied the Lord with your words.

"Wearied him?" you ask in fake surprise. "How have we wearied him?"

By saying that evil is good, that it pleases the Lord! Or by saying that God won't punish us—he doesn't care.

SERVING GOD WILLINGLY 1:6-8 God accused Israel of dishonoring him by offering imperfect sacrifices. Our lives should be living sacrifices to God (Romans 12:1). If we give God only our leftover time, money, and energy, we repeat the same sin as these worshipers who didn't want to bring anything valuable to God. What we give God reflects our true attitude toward him. **To begin the series of devotionals on SERVING GOD WILLINGLY, turn to page 291.**

Family Devotions

☐ DEVOTION 248
GIVING TO GOD

Read Malachi 3:8-12

*Giving to God
Memory Verse*

Bring all the tithes into the storehouse so that there will be food enough in my Temple; if you do, I will open up the windows of heaven for you and pour out a blessing so great you won't have room enough to take it in! Try it! Let me prove it to you!
Malachi 3:10

As church began, Janice was thinking about how she had finally earned enough for a whole week at Bible camp, plus a few dollars for crafts and treats. Her thoughts were interrupted by a nudge on her elbow. The offering was being taken, and it made her feel a little guilty. For weeks she had been putting every cent she earned into the bank. She hadn't put anything into the offering. *After all,* she reasoned, *it's for camp where I'll be learning more about the Lord, so in a way, it's for him.*

After church, Janice went to her Sunday school teacher's home for a picnic lunch. As they ate, Janice told Mrs. Harper about her decision not to tithe while she was saving for camp.

"It doesn't seem like it's wrong since the money is all going for something good, but I do have a funny feeling about not giving," Janice admitted. "The problem is, I won't have enough for camp if I give 10 percent of the money. Maybe I could just give a dollar."

"Watch this," Mrs. Harper said, throwing a ball far across the lawn. Pixie, her little dog, appeared as if by magic, burrowed under the bushes to find the ball, and ran back to drop it into Mrs. Harper's hand. Each time Mrs. Harper threw the ball, Pixie got it and brought it back.

"This game wasn't much fun for either Pixie or me at first," said Mrs. Harper. "She didn't know me very well or trust me very much. When I threw the ball, she would grab it and hold it. Then she learned to bring it back, but she wouldn't let go. She was afraid the game would be over. Now she knows that if there is to be a game of catch, she has to give up the ball."

Mrs. Harper turned to Janice. "God has commanded us to give back to him a part of everything he gives us. Trust him, Janice. God says the more we give, the more he will bless us. If we hold on, we only cheat ourselves."

How About You?
Have you been giving God part of all the money that comes to you? God doesn't use only large offerings. He also uses the pennies, nickels, and dimes of boys and girls. Giving to God is exciting and rewarding. See how much you can give, not how much you can keep. *C. R.*

• For the next devotional, turn to page 897. • For the next devotional on GIVING TO GOD, turn to page 1047.
• For notes on GIVING TO GOD, see pages 182, 433, and 1128.

3 The Coming of the Messiah

"Listen: I will send my messenger before me to prepare the way. And then the One you are looking for will come suddenly to his Temple—the Messenger of God's promises, to bring you great joy. Yes, he is surely coming," says the Lord Almighty. ²"But who can live when he appears? Who can endure his coming? For he is like a blazing fire refining precious metal, and he can bleach the dirtiest garments! ³Like a refiner of silver he will sit and closely watch as the dross is burned away. He will purify the Levites, the ministers of God, refining them like gold or silver, so that they will do their work for God with pure hearts. ⁴Then once more the Lord will enjoy the offerings brought to him by the people of Judah and Jerusalem, as he did before. ⁵At that time my punishments will be quick and certain; I will move swiftly against wicked men who trick the innocent, against adulterers and liars, against all those who cheat their hired hands, who oppress widows and orphans, or defraud strangers, and do not fear me," says the Lord Almighty.

⁶"For I am the Lord—I do not change. That is why you are not already utterly destroyed [for my mercy endures forever].

⁷"Though you have scorned my laws from earliest time, yet you may still return to me," says the Lord Almighty. "Come and I will forgive you.

"But you say, 'We have never even gone away!'

⁸"Will a man rob God? Surely not! And yet you have robbed me.

"'What do you mean? When did we ever rob you?'

"You have robbed me of the tithes and offerings due to me. ⁹And so the awesome curse of God is cursing you, for your whole nation has been robbing me. ¹⁰Bring all the tithes into the storehouse so that there will be food enough in my Temple; if you do, I will open up the windows of heaven for you and pour out a blessing so great you won't have room enough to take it in!

"Try it! Let me prove it to you! ¹¹Your crops will be large, for I will guard them from insects and plagues. Your grapes won't shrivel away before they ripen," says the Lord Almighty. ¹²"And all nations will call you blessed, for you will be a land sparkling with happiness. These are the promises of the Lord Almighty.

¹³"Your attitude toward me has been proud and arrogant," says the Lord.

"But you say, 'What do you mean? What have we said that we shouldn't?'

¹⁴,¹⁵"Listen; you have said, 'It is foolish to worship God and obey him. What good does it do to obey his laws, and to sorrow and mourn for our sins? From now on, as far as we're concerned, "Blessed are the arrogant." For those who do evil shall prosper, and those who dare God to punish them shall get off scot-free.'"

¹⁶Then those who feared and loved the Lord spoke often of him to each other. And he had a Book of Remembrance drawn up in which he recorded the names of those who feared him and loved to think about him.

¹⁷"They shall be mine," says the Lord Almighty, "in that day when I make up my jewels. And I will spare them as a man spares an obedient and dutiful son. ¹⁸Then you will see the difference between God's treatment of good men and bad, between those who serve him and those who don't.

4 The Great Judgment Day

"Watch now," the Lord Almighty declares, "the day of judgment is coming, burning like a furnace. The proud and wicked will be burned up like straw; like a tree, they will be consumed—roots and all.

²"But for you who fear my name, the Sun of Righteousness will rise with healing in his wings. And you will go free, leaping with joy like calves let out to pasture. ³Then you will tread upon the wicked as ashes underfoot," says the Lord Almighty. ⁴"Remember to obey the laws I gave all Israel through Moses my servant on Mount Horeb.

⁵"See, I will send you another prophet like Elijah before the coming of the great and dreadful judgment day of God. ⁶His preaching will bring fathers and children together again, to be of one mind and heart, for they will know that if they do not repent, I will come and utterly destroy their land."

New Testament

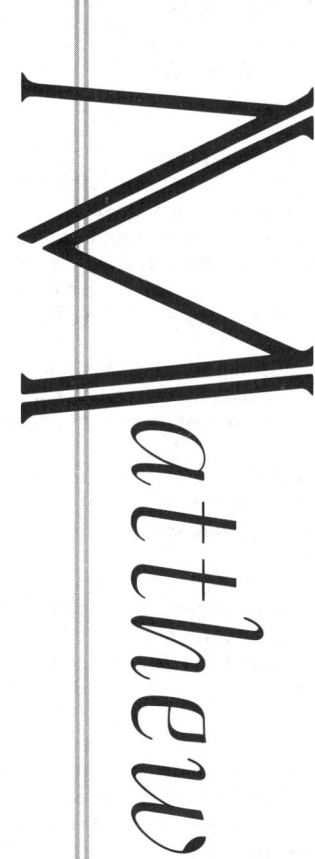

DO YOU ever feel as if God has stopped speaking to you? How do you find out what God wants of you?

This is what the Jewish people thought was their problem. It had been four hundred years since God had spoken to them through the prophet Malachi. They had God's Word written down, but they didn't want to obey it. And they wondered why God had stopped speaking to them!

God's people and their Promised Land were now part of the Roman Empire. The Jews remembered God's promise to send a Messiah. They hoped for a warrior-king to deliver them from the Romans.

When Jesus came, many of the Jews did not believe he was the Messiah, even though he fulfilled the prophecies God had given. They did not want to believe or obey what Jesus told them.

Sometimes God stops speaking when he's already told us what to do and he's waiting for us to obey. As you read Matthew, look for God speaking to you.

1 Jesus' Family Tree
These are the ancestors of Jesus Christ, a descendant of King David and of Abraham:

²Abraham was the father of Isaac; Isaac was the father of Jacob; Jacob was the father of Judah and his brothers.

³Judah was the father of Perez and Zerah (Tamar was their mother); Perez was the father of Hezron; Hezron was the father of Aram;

⁴Aram was the father of Amminadab; Amminadab was the father of Nahshon; Nahshon was the father of Salmon;

⁵Salmon was the father of Boaz (Rahab was his mother); Boaz was the father of Obed (Ruth was his mother); Obed was the father of Jesse;

⁶Jesse was the father of King David. David was the father of Solomon (his mother was the widow of Uriah);

⁷Solomon was the father of Rehoboam; Rehoboam was the father of Abijah; Abijah was the father of Asa;

⁸Asa was the father of Jehoshaphat; Jehoshaphat was the father of Jehoram; Jehoram was the father of Uzziah;

⁹Uzziah was the father of Jotham; Jotham was the father of Ahaz; Ahaz was the father of Hezekiah;

¹⁰Hezekiah was the father of Manasseh; Manasseh was the father of Amos; Amos was the father of Josiah;

¹¹Josiah was the father of Jechoniah and his brothers (born at the time of the exile to Babylon).

¹²After the exile: Jechoniah was the father of Shealtiel; Shealtiel was the father of Zerubbabel;

¹³Zerubbabel was the father of Abiud; Abiud was the father of Eliakim; Eliakim was the father of Azor;

¹⁴Azor was the father of Zadok; Zadok was the father of Achim; Achim was the father of Eliud;

¹⁵Eliud was the father of Eleazar; Eleazar was the father of Matthan; Matthan was the father of Jacob;

¹⁶Jacob was the father of Joseph (who was the husband of Mary, the mother of Jesus Christ the Messiah).

¹⁷These are fourteen of the generations from Abraham to King David; and fourteen from King David's time to the exile; and fourteen from the exile to Christ.

¹⁸These are the facts concerning the birth of Jesus Christ: His mother, Mary, was engaged to be married to Joseph. But while she was still a virgin she became pregnant by the Holy Spirit. ¹⁹Then Joseph, her fiancé, being a man of stern principle, decided to break the engagement but to do it quietly, as he didn't want to publicly disgrace her.

²⁰As he lay awake considering this, he fell into a dream, and saw an angel standing beside him. "Joseph, son of David," the angel said, "don't hesitate to take Mary as your wife! For the child within her has been conceived by the Holy Spirit. ²¹And she will have a Son, and you shall name him Jesus (meaning 'Savior'), for he will save his people from their sins. ²²This will fulfill God's message through his prophets—

²³*'Listen! The virgin shall conceive a child!*
She shall give birth to a Son, and he shall
be called "Emmanuel" (meaning "God is
with us").'

²⁴When Joseph awoke, he did as the angel commanded and brought Mary home to be his wife, ²⁵but she remained a virgin until her Son was born; and Joseph named him "Jesus."

2 Wise Men Visit Baby Jesus

Jesus was born in the town of Bethlehem, in Judea, during the reign of King Herod.

At about that time some astrologers from eastern lands arrived in Jerusalem, asking, ²"Where is the newborn King of the Jews? for we have seen his star in far-off eastern lands and have come to worship him."

³King Herod was deeply disturbed by their question, and all Jerusalem was filled with rumors. ⁴He called a meeting of the Jewish religious leaders.

"Did the prophets tell us where the Messiah would be born?" he asked.

⁵"Yes, in Bethlehem," they said, "for this is what the prophet Micah wrote:

⁶'O little town of Bethlehem, you are not just
    an unimportant Judean village, for a Governor shall rise from you to rule my
    people Israel.'"

⁷Then Herod sent a private message to the astrologers, asking them to come to see him; at this meeting he found out from them the exact time when they first saw the star. Then he told them, ⁸"Go to Bethlehem and search for the child. And when you find him, come back and tell me so that I can go and worship him too!"

⁹After this interview the astrologers started out again. And look! The star appeared to them again, standing over Bethlehem. ¹⁰Their joy knew no bounds!

¹¹Entering the house where the baby and Mary, his mother, were, they threw themselves down before him, worshiping. Then they opened their presents and gave him gold, frankincense, and myrrh. ¹²But when they returned to their own land, they didn't go through Jerusalem to report to Herod, for God had warned them in a dream to go home another way.

¹³After they were gone, an angel of the Lord appeared to Joseph in a dream. "Get up and flee to Egypt with the baby and his mother," the angel said, "and stay there until I tell you to return, for King Herod is going to try to kill the child." ¹⁴That same night he left for Egypt with Mary and the baby, ¹⁵and stayed there until King Herod's death. This fulfilled the prophet's prediction,

"I have called my Son from Egypt."

¹⁶Herod was furious when he learned that the astrologers had disobeyed him. Sending soldiers to Bethlehem, he ordered them to kill every baby boy two years old and under, both in the town and on the nearby farms, for the astrologers had

FAMILY DEVOTIONS

☐ DEVOTION 249
SHARING YOUR FAITH

Read Matthew 4:18-22

Though the days were getting chilly, Johnny sat on the front steps singing a song. Johnny liked to sing, and he sang a chorus he had often sung in Sunday school. "I will make you fishers of men . . . if you follow me." Just as he finished the song, his mother came outside with a cup of hot chocolate.

"Here, Johnny," she said, "I thought you might like this to warm you up. What was the song I heard you singing just now?"

"Thanks, Mom! I was singing 'Fishers of Men.' Want to hear it?"

"Sure," said Mom. After Johnny had sung it again, she asked, "Do you know what that means?"

"Sure," Johnny answered, but he looked a bit startled. After Mom went back inside, he sipped the steaming hot chocolate and thought about Mom's question. Long ago his Sunday school teacher had explained that instead of fishing for fish, Jesus wants Christians to go fishing for people—to help others come to know him.

Suddenly Johnny jumped off the step and ran to Danny's house. "Hi, Danny," he said. "Want to go to Bible club on Thursday with me?"

"Bible club? What do you do there?" Danny asked.

"Oh, it's neat," answered Johnny. "We play games, sing songs, and learn things from the Bible. How about going with me?" Johnny was pleased when Danny agreed to go. "Great!" he said. "Hey, let's go and ask Jim if he wants to go, too!" They did, and Jim agreed to join them.

As Johnny was getting ready for bed that night, he told his mother about his "fishing trip" that afternoon. "Well, Johnny, I see you really did learn the meaning of that song," she smiled. "I hope you'll be a fisherman for Jesus as long as you live."

Sharing Your Faith Memory Verse

And let us not get tired of doing what is right, for after a while we will reap a harvest of blessing if we don't get discouraged and give up.
Galatians 6:9

How About You?

Are you trying to win your friends to Jesus? If you're a Christian, you should be doing this by your actions and your words. Lots of kids get excited about fishing for fish. Get excited about fishing for people, too! C. V. M.

• For the next devotional, turn to page 899.   • For the next devotional on *SHARING YOUR FAITH*, turn to page 927.
• For notes on *SHARING YOUR FAITH*, see pages 462, 776, 1015, and 1074.

told him the star first appeared to them two years before. ¹⁷This brutal action of Herod's fulfilled the prophecy of Jeremiah,

¹⁸"Screams of anguish come from Ramah,
Weeping unrestrained;
Rachel weeping for her children,
Uncomforted—
For they are dead."

¹⁹When Herod died, an angel of the Lord appeared in a dream to Joseph in Egypt and told him, ²⁰"Get up and take the baby and his mother back to Israel, for those who were trying to kill the child are dead."

²¹So he returned immediately to Israel with Jesus and his mother. ²²But on the way he was frightened to learn that the new king was Herod's son, Archelaus. Then, in another dream, he was warned not to go to Judea, so they went to Galilee instead ²³and lived in Nazareth. This fulfilled the prediction of the prophets concerning the Messiah,

"He shall be called a Nazarene."

3 John the Baptist Preaches

While they were living in Nazareth, John the Baptist began preaching out in the Judean wilderness. His constant theme was, ²"Turn from your sins ... turn to God ... for the Kingdom of Heaven is coming soon." ³Isaiah the prophet had told about John's ministry centuries before! He had written,

"I hear a shout from the wilderness, 'Prepare a
road for the Lord—straighten out the
path where he will walk.'"

⁴John's clothing was woven from camel's hair and he wore a leather belt; his food was locusts and wild honey. ⁵People from Jerusalem and from all over the Jordan Valley, and, in fact, from every section of Judea went out to the wilderness to hear him preach, ⁶and when they confessed their sins, he baptized them in the Jordan River.

⁷But when he saw many Pharisees and Sadducees coming to be baptized, he denounced them.

"You sons of snakes!" he warned. "Who said that you could escape the coming wrath of God? ⁸Before being baptized, prove that you have turned from sin by doing worthy deeds. ⁹Don't try to get by as you are, thinking, 'We are safe for we are Jews—descendants of Abraham.' That proves nothing. God can change these stones here into Jews!

¹⁰"And even now the axe of God's judgment is poised to chop down every unproductive tree. They will be chopped and burned.

¹¹"With water I baptize those who repent of their sins; but someone else is coming, far greater than I am, so great that I am not worthy to carry his shoes! He shall baptize you with the Holy Spirit and with fire. ¹²He will separate the chaff from the grain, burning the chaff with never-ending fire and storing away the grain."

¹³Then Jesus went from Galilee to the Jordan River to be baptized there by John. ¹⁴John didn't want to do it.

"This isn't proper," he said. "I am the one who needs to be baptized by you."

¹⁵But Jesus said, "Please do it, for I must do all that is right." So then John baptized him.

¹⁶After his baptism, as soon as Jesus came up out of the water, the heavens were opened to him and he saw the Spirit of God coming down in the form of a dove. ¹⁷And a voice from heaven said, "This is my beloved Son, and I am wonderfully pleased with him."

4 Jesus Is Tempted

Then Jesus was led out into the wilderness by the Holy Spirit, to be tempted there by Satan. ²For forty days and forty nights he ate nothing and became very hungry. ³Then Satan tempted him to get food by changing stones into loaves of bread.

"It will prove you are the Son of God," he said.

⁴But Jesus told him, "No! For the Scriptures tell us that bread won't feed men's souls: obedience to every word of God is what we need."

⁵Then Satan took him to Jerusalem to the roof of the Temple. ⁶"Jump off," he said, "and prove you are the Son of God; for the Scriptures declare, 'God will send his angels to keep you from harm,' ... they will prevent you from smashing on the rocks below."

⁷Jesus retorted, "It also says not to put the Lord your God to a foolish test!"

⁸Next Satan took him to the peak of a very high mountain and showed him the nations of the world and all their glory. ⁹"I'll give it all to you," he said, "if you will only kneel and worship me."

¹⁰"Get out of here, Satan," Jesus told him. "The Scriptures say, 'Worship only the Lord God. Obey only him.'"

¹¹Then Satan went away, and angels came and cared for Jesus.

¹²,¹³When Jesus heard that John had been arrested, he left Judea and returned home to Nazareth in Galilee; but soon he moved to Capernaum, beside the Lake of Galilee, close to Zebulun and Naphtali. ¹⁴This fulfilled Isaiah's prophecy:

Family Devotions

☐ **Devotion 250**
Showing Kindness

Read Matthew 5:7

"Look! Here comes that retard on her three-wheeled bike," said Jason. "Let's act like we're going to run into her and see what she does."

Jason and Terry steered their bikes toward the girl. Fear spread across her face as they came closer. "Stop!" she shouted.

"Retard! Retard! You're just a retard," chanted Jason, and Terry joined in. Laughing loudly, they steered away before actually running into the frightened girl.

Just then Mrs. Brown, Jason's Sunday school teacher, came out of her house. Feeling guilty, Jason turned his head away, and before he realized what was happening, he had run into Terry. Down they went, a tangle of boys and bikes! Jason felt a sharp pain where his arm was badly skinned, and Terry was limping when he got up. Mrs. Brown invited them into her house to get cleaned up.

"Do you like to get hurt?" Mrs. Brown asked as she got out the bandages. The boys shook their heads. "How would you have felt," she continued, "if I had come out and pushed you over and then laughed when you got hurt?"

"That would have been mean," Jason answered.

Mrs. Brown nodded. "Yet that's something like what you did to that little girl."

"We didn't touch her," protested Terry. "We just teased her a little. We didn't hurt her."

"You didn't hurt her on the outside," corrected Mrs. Brown, "but you hurt her on the inside. It hurts her to be made fun of because she's retarded." In his heart Jason truly felt sorry. "Jesus taught us to treat others kindly," continued Mrs. Brown. "He treated everyone with love, and he wants us to do that, too."

As the boys got ready to leave, both of them looked ashamed. "We're sorry," they said.

Jason got on his bike, but he turned back. "We'll remember that it hurts to be hurt," he called to Mrs. Brown, "and we won't make fun of that girl again."

Showing Kindness Memory Verse

That's why whenever we can we should always be kind to everyone, and especially to our Christian brothers.
Galatians 6:10

How About You?
Do you sometimes tease others who are different? Teasing can be very painful. Jesus taught us to be kind to everyone, and he lived that way. Be a friend, not a tease or a bully. *C. Y.*

• For the next devotional, turn to page 901.   • To start the next topic, turn to page 139.   • For notes on *Showing Kindness*, see pages 664, 880, 1038, and 1244.

15,16 "The land of Zebulun and the land of Naphtali, beside the Lake, and the countryside beyond the Jordan River, and Upper Galilee where so many foreigners live—there the people who sat in darkness have seen a great Light; they sat in the land of death, and the Light broke through upon them."

17 From then on, Jesus began to preach, "Turn from sin and turn to God, for the Kingdom of Heaven is near."

18 One day as he was walking along the beach beside the Lake of Galilee, he saw two brothers—Simon, also called Peter, and Andrew—out in a boat fishing with a net, for they were commercial fishermen.

19 Jesus called out, "Come along with me and I will show you how to fish for the souls of men!" 20 And they left their nets at once and went with him.

21 A little farther up the beach he saw two other brothers, James and John, sitting in a boat with their father, Zebedee, mending their nets; and he called to them to come too. 22 At once they stopped their work and, leaving their father behind, went with him.

23 Jesus traveled all through Galilee teaching in the Jewish synagogues, everywhere preaching the Good News about the Kingdom of Heaven. And he healed every kind of sickness and disease. 24 The report of his miracles spread far beyond the borders of Galilee so that sick folk were soon coming to be healed from as far away as Syria. And whatever their illness and pain, or if they were possessed by demons, or were insane, or paralyzed—he healed them all. 25 Enormous crowds followed him wherever he went—people from Galilee, and the Ten Cities, and Jerusalem, and from all over Judea, and even from across the Jordan River.

5 The Sermon on the Mount

One day as the crowds were gathering, he went up the hillside with his disciples and sat down and taught them there.

3 "Humble men are very fortunate!" he told them, "for the Kingdom of Heaven is given to them. 4 Those who mourn are fortunate! for they shall be comforted. 5 The meek and lowly are fortunate! for the whole wide world belongs to them.

6 "Happy are those who long to be just and good, for they shall be completely satisfied. 7 Happy are the kind and merciful, for they shall be shown mercy. 8 Happy are those whose hearts are pure, for they shall see God. 9 Happy are those who strive for peace—they shall be called the sons of God. 10 Happy are those who are persecuted because they are good, for the Kingdom of Heaven is theirs.

11 "When you are reviled and persecuted and lied about because you are my followers—wonderful! 12 Be *happy* about it! Be *very glad!* for a *tremendous reward* awaits you up in heaven. And remember, the ancient prophets were persecuted too.

13 "You are the world's seasoning, to make it tolerable. If you lose your flavor, what will happen to the world? And you yourselves will be thrown out and trampled underfoot as worthless. 14 You are the world's light—a city on a hill, glowing in the night for all to see. 15,16 Don't hide your light! Let it shine for all; let your good deeds glow for all to see, so that they will praise your heavenly Father.

17 "Don't misunderstand why I have come—it isn't to cancel the laws of Moses and the warnings of the prophets. No, I came to fulfill them and to make them all come true. 18 With all the earnestness I have I say: Every law in the Book will continue until its purpose is achieved. 19 And so if anyone breaks the least commandment and teaches others to, he shall be the least in the Kingdom of Heaven. But those who teach God's laws *and obey them* shall be great in the Kingdom of Heaven.

20 "But I warn you—unless your goodness is greater than that of the Pharisees and other Jewish leaders, you can't get into the Kingdom of Heaven at all!

21 "Under the laws of Moses the rule was, 'If you murder, you must die.' 22 But I have added to that rule and tell you that if you are only *angry,* even in your own home, you are in danger of judgment! If you call your friend an idiot, you are in danger of being brought before the court. And if you curse him, you are in danger of the fires of hell.

23 "So if you are standing before the altar in the Temple, offering a sacrifice to God, and suddenly remember that a friend has something against you, 24 leave your sacrifice there beside the altar and go and apologize and be reconciled to him, and then come and offer your sacrifice to God. 25 Come to terms quickly with your enemy before it is too late and he drags you into court and you are thrown into a debtor's cell, 26 for you will stay there until you have paid the last penny.

27 "The laws of Moses said, 'You shall not commit adultery.' 28 But I say: Anyone who even looks at a woman with lust in his eye has already committed adultery with her in his heart. 29 So if your

Family Devotions

☐ DEVOTION 251
SERVING GOD BOLDLY

Read Matthew 5:14-16

Serving God Boldly
Memory Verse

Yes, be bold and strong!
Banish fear and doubt!
For remember, the Lord
your God is with you
wherever you go.
Joshua 1:9

"Here's Mom now," Julie told her little brother, as the old, blue car pulled up in front of the church. Julie opened the door and plopped Benjie into his car seat. She fastened the seat belt, then got in and fastened her own.

"How was vacation Bible school?" Mother asked.

"Great," answered Julie, "except that Mrs. Wilson asked me to play the piano for the primary department's song time the rest of the week."

Mom frowned. "That's bad?" she asked.

Julie nodded. "I'm not going to do it," she said. "I just can't. I'd be so nervous with all those little kids looking at me." Her stomach felt fluttery just thinking about it.

Her mother sighed. "I wish you'd try it," she said quietly.

Three-year-old Benjie decided he had been quiet long enough. "Sissy," he said, tugging at Julie's sleeve, "listen to my song!" Holding one chubby finger straight up before him, he began to sing. "This little light of mine—I'm gonna let it shine. . . ."

When he had finished, Julie gave him a big hug. "Good job," she said. "When I was little like you, that was one of my favorite songs. Shall we sing it together?"

"Maybe you shouldn't sing it if you don't mean it anymore," suggested Mom.

"What?" Julie turned to her mother with a puzzled frown.

"Aren't you hiding your light under a bushel, dear?" Mom asked. "I'm thinking of your refusal to play the piano."

"Oh, Mom!" grumbled Julie, as Benjie began to sing again, but she didn't join in. Not until the very last line, that is. When the song ended, she grinned at her mother.

How About You?
Are you ever afraid to use the talents God gave you? Do your knees shake, and does your throat get dry when you get up in front of others? Are you afraid you'll mess up? God gave you certain talents. Ask him for the courage to use them to help other people. P. M.

"I guess if God gave me the talent to play, he can give me the courage to do it in front of those kids," she said. "I'll try it. My turn to sing a verse, Benjie." Mother smiled as Julie sang the verse she made up to the old familiar tune, "I'm gonna play for Jesus. Let my light now shine . . ."

• For the next devotional, turn to page 903.   • For the next devotional on *SERVING GOD BOLDLY,* turn to page 913.
• For notes on *SERVING GOD BOLDLY,* see pages 327, 404, 501, 720, and 856.

eye—even if it is your best eye! —causes you to lust, gouge it out and throw it away. Better for part of you to be destroyed than for all of you to be cast into hell. ³⁰And if your hand—even your right hand—causes you to sin, cut it off and throw it away. Better that than find yourself in hell.

³¹"The law of Moses says, 'If anyone wants to be rid of his wife, he can divorce her merely by giving her a letter of dismissal.' ³²But I say that a man who divorces his wife, except for fornication, causes her to commit adultery if she marries again. And he who marries her commits adultery.

³³"Again, the law of Moses says, 'You shall not break your vows to God but must fulfill them all.' ³⁴But I say: Don't make any vows! And even to say 'By heavens!' is a sacred vow to God, for the heavens are God's throne. ³⁵And if you say 'By the earth!' it is a sacred vow, for the earth is his footstool. And don't swear 'By Jerusalem!' for Jerusalem is the capital of the great King. ³⁶Don't even swear 'By my head!' for you can't turn one hair white or black. ³⁷Say just a simple 'Yes, I will' or 'No, I won't.' Your word is enough. To strengthen your promise with a vow shows that something is wrong.

³⁸"The law of Moses says, 'If a man gouges out another's eye, he must pay with his own eye. If a tooth gets knocked out, knock out the tooth of the one who did it.' ³⁹But I say: Don't resist violence! If you are slapped on one cheek, turn the other too. ⁴⁰If you are ordered to court, and your shirt is taken from you, give your coat too. ⁴¹If the military demand that you carry their gear for a mile, carry it two. ⁴²Give to those who ask, and don't turn away from those who want to borrow.

⁴³"There is a saying, 'Love your *friends* and hate your enemies.' ⁴⁴But I say: Love your *enemies!* Pray for those who *persecute* you! ⁴⁵In that way you will be acting as true sons of your Father in heaven. For he gives his sunlight to both the evil and the good, and sends rain on the just and on the unjust too. ⁴⁶If you love only those who love you, what good is that? Even scoundrels do that much. ⁴⁷If you are friendly only to your friends, how are you different from anyone else? Even the heathen do that. ⁴⁸But you are to be perfect, even as your Father in heaven is perfect.

6 Help Others without Bragging

"Take care! Don't do your good deeds publicly, to be admired, for then you will lose the reward from your Father in heaven. ²When you give a gift to a beggar, don't shout about it as the hypocrites do—blowing trumpets in the synagogues and streets to call attention to their acts of charity! I tell you in all earnestness, they have received all the reward they will ever get. ³But when you do a kindness to someone, do it secretly—don't tell your left hand what your right hand is doing. ⁴And your Father, who knows all secrets, will reward you.

⁵"And now about prayer. When you pray, don't be like the hypocrites who pretend piety by praying publicly on street corners and in the synagogues where everyone can see them. Truly, that is all the reward they will ever get. ⁶But when you pray, go away by yourself, all alone, and shut the door behind you and pray to your Father secretly, and your Father, who knows your secrets, will reward you.

⁷,⁸"Don't recite the same prayer over and over as the heathen do, who think prayers are answered only by repeating them again and again. Remember, your Father knows exactly what you need even before you ask him!

⁹"Pray along these lines: 'Our Father in heaven, we honor your holy name. ¹⁰We ask that your kingdom will come now. May your will be done here on earth, just as it is in heaven. ¹¹Give us our food again today, as usual, ¹²and forgive us our sins, just as we have forgiven those who have sinned against us. ¹³Don't bring us into temptation, but deliver us from the Evil One. Amen.' ¹⁴,¹⁵Your heavenly Father will forgive you if you forgive those who sin against you; but if *you* refuse to forgive *them, he* will not forgive *you.*

¹⁶"And now about fasting. When you fast, declining your food for a spiritual purpose, don't do it publicly, as the hypocrites do, who try to look wan and disheveled so people will feel sorry for them. Truly, that is the only reward they will ever get. ¹⁷But when you fast, put on festive clothing, ¹⁸so that no one will suspect you are hungry, except your Father who knows every secret. And he will reward you.

¹⁹"Don't store up treasures here on earth where they can erode away or may be stolen. ²⁰Store them in heaven where they will never lose their value and are safe from thieves. ²¹If your profits are in heaven, your heart will be there too.

²²"If your eye is pure, there will be sunshine in your soul. ²³But if your eye is clouded with evil thoughts and desires, you are in deep spiritual darkness. And oh, how deep that darkness can be!

²⁴"You cannot serve two masters:

CONTENTMENT 6:24 Jesus contrasted heavenly values with earthly values when he explained that our first loyalty should be to those things that do not fade, cannot be stolen or used up, and never wear out. We should not be so tied to our possessions that *they* possess *us.* We may have to do some cutting back if our possessions are becoming too important to us. Jesus is calling for a decision that allows us to live contentedly with whatever we have because we have chosen what is eternal and lasting as our first priority. **To begin the series of devotionals on CONTENTMENT, turn to page 89.**

Family Devotions

☐ DEVOTION 252
OVERCOMING ANGER

Read Matthew 5:21-22

*Overcoming Anger
Memory Verse*

Dear brothers, don't ever forget that it is best to listen much, speak little, and not become angry; for anger doesn't make us good, as God demands that we must be.
James 1:19-20

Judy woke up in a terrible mood. She had an oral book report to do at school today, and she wasn't well prepared. Besides, it was pouring rain! Her hair would get all kinky and frizzy!

Judy and her brother, Jerry, both reached the bathroom door at the same time. "Ouch!" cried Jerry as Judy grabbed his arm. "Mom, Judy pushed me against the wall!"

When Judy emerged from the bathroom, Mom was waiting. "I'm ready to hear an explanation from you, young lady. What did Jerry do to deserve this?" She showed Judy the long scrape on the little boy's arm.

"He got in my way, that's what!" exclaimed Judy. "My bus comes twenty minutes earlier than his. I've tried to tell the idiot that I should always be in the bathroom first, but he won't listen to me!"

"Judy, I'm ashamed of the way you're acting," scolded Mom. "Jerry hasn't done anything to you this morning. Now apologize, and get downstairs for breakfast!"

"I'm sorry," Judy spat. Then, as she headed for the kitchen, she whispered, "But I hate you, you big baby."

After breakfast the family had devotions. At Mom's request, Dad read Matthew 5:21-22 and 1 John 3:15. "Jesus is teaching the Ten Commandments," Dad said. "Here he explains that being angry with no cause, or hating someone, or calling someone an idiot is just as wrong in God's eyes as murder."

Judy looked shocked as she glanced at Jerry. She definitely didn't want to be a murderer! "I'm sorry," she whispered. "I didn't mean it. You can even have the bathroom first after this."

How About You?
Do you ever get angry at people for no good reason? Do you call them names? Christ said anyone guilty of these things is like someone who has broken the sixth commandment. The words I hate you **are words you should never use.** P. R.

- For the next devotional, turn to page 905.
- For the next devotional on OVERCOMING ANGER, turn to page 1123.
- For notes on OVERCOMING ANGER, see pages 176, 511, 936, and 1003.

God and money. For you will hate one and love the other, or else the other way around.

²⁵"So my counsel is: Don't worry about *things*—food, drink, and clothes. For you already have life and a body—and they are far more important than what to eat and wear. ²⁶Look at the birds! They don't worry about what to eat—they don't need to sow or reap or store up food—for your heavenly Father feeds them. And you are far more valuable to him than they are. ²⁷Will all your worries add a single moment to your life?

²⁸"And why worry about your clothes? Look at the field lilies! They don't worry about theirs. ²⁹Yet King Solomon in all his glory was not clothed as beautifully as they. ³⁰And if God cares so wonderfully for flowers that are here today and gone tomorrow, won't he more surely care for you, O men of little faith?

³¹,³²"So don't worry at all about having enough food and clothing. Why be like the heathen? For they take pride in all these things and are deeply concerned about them. But your heavenly Father already knows perfectly well that you need them, ³³and he will give them to you if you give him first place in your life and live as he wants you to.

³⁴"So don't be anxious about tomorrow. God will take care of your tomorrow too. Live one day at a time.

7 Don't Criticize Others

"Don't criticize, and then you won't be criticized. ²For others will treat you as you treat them. ³And why worry about a speck in the eye of a brother when you have a board in your own? ⁴Should you say, 'Friend, let me help you get that speck out of your eye,' when you can't even see because of the board in your own? ⁵Hypocrite! First get rid of the board. Then you can see to help your brother.

⁶"Don't give holy things to depraved men. Don't give pearls to swine! They will trample the pearls and turn and attack you.

⁷"Ask, and you will be given what you ask for. Seek, and you will find. Knock, and the door will be opened. ⁸For everyone who asks, receives. Anyone who seeks, finds. If only you will knock, the door will open. ⁹If a child asks his father for a loaf of bread, will he be given a stone instead? ¹⁰If he asks for fish, will he be given a poisonous snake? Of course not! ¹¹And if you hardhearted, sinful men know how to give good gifts to your children, won't your Father in heaven even more certainly give good gifts to those who ask him for them?

¹²"Do for others what you want them to do for you. This is the teaching of the laws of Moses in a nutshell.

¹³"Heaven can be entered only through the narrow gate! The highway to hell is broad, and its gate is wide enough for all the multitudes who choose its easy way. ¹⁴But the Gateway to Life is small, and the road is narrow, and only a few ever find it.

¹⁵"Beware of false teachers who come disguised as harmless sheep, but are wolves and will tear you apart. ¹⁶You can detect them by the way they act, just as you can identify a tree by its fruit. You need never confuse grapevines with thorn bushes or figs with thistles. ¹⁷Different kinds of fruit trees can quickly be identified by examining their fruit. ¹⁸A variety that produces delicious fruit never produces an inedible kind. And a tree producing an inedible kind can't produce what is good. ¹⁹So the trees having the inedible fruit are chopped down and thrown on the fire. ²⁰Yes, the way to identify a tree or a person is by the kind of fruit produced.

²¹"Not all who sound religious are really godly people. They may refer to me as 'Lord,' but still won't get to heaven. For the decisive question is whether they obey my Father in heaven. ²²At the Judgment many will tell me, 'Lord, Lord, we told others about you and used your name to cast out demons and to do many other great miracles.' ²³But I will reply, 'You have never been mine. Go away, for your deeds are evil.'

²⁴"All who listen to my instructions and follow them are wise, like a man who builds his house on solid rock. ²⁵Though the rain comes in torrents, and the floods rise and the storm winds beat against his house, it won't collapse, for it is built on rock.

²⁶"But those who hear my instructions and ignore them are foolish, like a man who builds his house on sand. ²⁷For when the rains and floods come, and storm winds beat against his house, it will fall with a mighty crash." ²⁸The crowds were amazed at Jesus' sermons, ²⁹for he taught as one who had great authority, and not as their Jewish leaders.

8 Two Men Believe and Are Healed

Large crowds followed Jesus as he came down the hillside.

²*Look! A leper is approaching. He kneels before him, worshiping.* "Sir," *the leper pleads,* "if you want to, you can heal me."

³*Jesus touches the man.* "I want to," *he says.* "Be healed." *And instantly the leprosy disappears.*

⁴*Then Jesus says to him,* "Don't stop to talk to anyone; go right over to the priest to be examined; and take with you the offering required by

Family Devotions

□ DEVOTION 253
LOVING OTHERS

Read Matthew 9:18-26

Eric savagely kicked a stone, sending it flying along the sidewalk. He heard someone coming up behind him and turned. It was Doug, one of the few people in his class at school who didn't make fun of Eric's bald head. "What's wrong?" Doug asked when he saw how upset Eric looked.

"Oh, not much," mumbled Eric. "It's just that the kids have been making fun of me again."

"Does having leukemia make your hair fall out?" Doug asked cautiously.

Eric shook his head. "That's caused by the treatments I have to take," he explained. He bit his lip, struggling not to show how much the teasing hurt. "Thanks for not teasing me, Doug," he added.

"Oh, that's all right," Doug replied, smiling. "Want to come over and play with my race-car set? You can call your mom from my house."

After getting permission from his mother, Eric followed Doug to the basement. As his little car sped around the track, Doug asked, "Does it hurt to have leukemia?"

"Some of the tests hurt, and the treatment makes me feel sick to my stomach. But for me, the worst part is that my hair falls out," said Eric, stopping his car. "I look so strange, and the teasing just makes it worse. If it weren't for you not joining them, I think I'd give up. How come you don't tease like the others?"

"Because Jesus wouldn't want me to," Doug said.

"Wish the other kids knew more about Jesus then," said Eric. "I don't know much about him, either."

Doug smiled. "Let's go upstairs and have some cookies and milk, and I'll tell you more about him," he said.

Loving Others Memory Verse

Little children, let us stop just *saying* we love people; let us *really* love them, and *show it* by our *actions.*
1 John 3:18

How About You?

Jesus treated everyone with love and compassion—even people with serious illnesses. It didn't matter to him if the person looked or acted strange. If you know someone who is teased because he or she looks different, you can make life easier for that person by refusing to join in the teasing. C. Y.

- For the next devotional, turn to page 913.   • For the next devotional on LOVING OTHERS, turn to page 953.
- For notes on LOVING OTHERS, see pages 658, 951, 967, and 1242.

Moses' law for lepers who are healed—a public testimony of your cure."

⁵,⁶When Jesus arrived in Capernaum, a Roman army captain came and pled with him to come to his home and heal his servant boy who was in bed paralyzed and racked with pain.

⁷"Yes," Jesus said, "I will come and heal him."

⁸,⁹Then the officer said, "Sir, I am not worthy to have you in my home; [and it isn't necessary for you to come]. If you will only stand here and say, 'Be healed,' my servant will get well! I know, because I am under the authority of my superior officers and I have authority over my soldiers, and I say to one, 'Go,' and he goes, and to another, 'Come,' and he comes, and to my slave boy, 'Do this or that,' and he does it. And I know you have authority to tell his sickness to go—and it will go!"

¹⁰Jesus stood there amazed! Turning to the crowd he said, "I haven't seen faith like this in all the land of Israel! ¹¹And I tell you this, that many Gentiles [like this Roman officer], shall come from all over the world and sit down in the Kingdom of Heaven with Abraham, Isaac, and Jacob. ¹²And many an Israelite—those for whom the Kingdom was prepared—shall be cast into outer darkness, into the place of weeping and torment."

¹³Then Jesus said to the Roman officer, "Go on home. What you have believed has happened!" And the boy was healed that same hour!

¹⁴When Jesus arrived at Peter's house, Peter's mother-in-law was in bed with a high fever. ¹⁵But when Jesus touched her hand, the fever left her; and she got up and prepared a meal for them!

¹⁶That evening several demon-possessed people were brought to Jesus; and when he spoke a single word, all the demons fled; and all the sick were healed. ¹⁷This fulfilled the prophecy of Isaiah, "He took our sicknesses and bore our diseases."

¹⁸When Jesus noticed how large the crowd was growing, he instructed his disciples to get ready to cross to the other side of the lake.

¹⁹Just then one of the Jewish religious teachers said to him, "Teacher, I will follow you no matter where you go!"

²⁰But Jesus said, "Foxes have dens and birds have nests, but I, the Messiah, have no home of my own—no place to lay my head."

²¹Another of his disciples said, "Sir, when my father is dead, then I will follow you."

²²But Jesus told him, "Follow me *now!* Let those who are spiritually dead care for their own dead."

²³Then he got into a boat and started across the lake with his disciples. ²⁴Suddenly a terrible storm came up, with waves higher than the boat. But Jesus was asleep.

²⁵The disciples went to him and wakened him, shouting, "Lord, save us! We're sinking!"

²⁶But Jesus answered, "O you men of little faith! Why are you so frightened?" Then he stood up and rebuked the wind and waves, and the storm subsided and all was calm. ²⁷The disciples just sat there, awed! "Who is this," they asked themselves, "that even the winds and the sea obey him?"

²⁸When they arrived on the other side of the lake, in the country of the Gadarenes, two men with demons in them met him. They lived in a cemetery and were so dangerous that no one could go through that area.

²⁹They began screaming at him, "What do you want with us, O Son of God? You have no right to torment us yet."

³⁰A herd of pigs was feeding in the distance, ³¹so the demons begged, "If you cast us out, send us into that herd of pigs."

³²"All right," Jesus told them. "Begone."

And they came out of the men and entered the pigs, and the whole herd rushed over a cliff and drowned in the water below. ³³The herdsmen fled to the nearest city with the story of what had happened, ³⁴and the entire population came rushing out to see Jesus and begged him to go away and leave them alone.

9 Jesus Heals a Paralyzed Man

So Jesus climbed into a boat and went across the lake to Capernaum, his hometown.

²Soon some men brought him a paralyzed boy on a mat. When Jesus saw their faith, he said to the sick boy, "Cheer up, son! For I have forgiven your sins!"

³"Blasphemy! This man is saying he is God!" exclaimed some of the religious leaders to themselves.

⁴Jesus knew what they were thinking and asked them, "Why are you thinking such evil thoughts? ⁵,⁶I, the Messiah, have the authority on earth to forgive sins. But talk is cheap—anybody could say that. So I'll prove it to you by healing this man." Then, turning to the paralyzed man, he commanded, "Pick up your stretcher and go on home, for you are healed."

⁷And the boy jumped up and left!

⁸A chill of fear swept through the crowd as they saw this happen right before their eyes. How they praised God for giving such authority to a man!

⁹As Jesus was going on down the road, he saw a tax collector, Matthew, sitting at a tax collection booth. "Come and be my disciple," Jesus said to him, and Matthew jumped up and went along with him.

¹⁰Later, as Jesus and his disciples were eating

dinner [at Matthew's house], there were many notorious swindlers there as guests!

¹¹The Pharisees were indignant. "Why does your teacher associate with men like that?"

¹²"Because people who are well don't need a doctor! It's the sick people who do!" was Jesus' reply. ¹³Then he added, "Now go away and learn the meaning of this verse of Scripture,

'It isn't your sacrifices and your gifts I want—
I want you to be merciful.'

For I have come to urge sinners, not the self-righteous, back to God."

¹⁴One day the disciples of John the Baptist came to Jesus and asked him, "Why don't your disciples fast as we do and as the Pharisees do?"

¹⁵"Should the bridegroom's friends mourn and go without food while he is with them?" Jesus asked. "But the time is coming when I will be taken from them. Time enough then for them to refuse to eat.

¹⁶"And who would patch an old garment with unshrunk cloth? For the patch would tear away and make the hole worse. ¹⁷And who would use old wineskins to store new wine? For the old skins would burst with the pressure, and the wine would be spilled and skins ruined. Only new wineskins are used to store new wine. That way both are preserved."

¹⁸As he was saying this, the rabbi of the local synagogue came and worshiped him. "My little daughter has just died," he said, "but you can bring her back to life again if you will only come and touch her."

¹⁹As Jesus and the disciples were going to the rabbi's home, ²⁰a woman who had been sick for twelve years with internal bleeding came up behind him and touched a tassel of his robe, ²¹for she thought, "If I only touch him, I will be healed."

²²Jesus turned around and spoke to her. "Daughter," he said, "all is well! Your faith has healed you." And the woman was well from that moment.

²³When Jesus arrived at the rabbi's home and saw the noisy crowds and heard the funeral music, ²⁴he said, "Get them out, for the little girl isn't dead; she is only sleeping!" Then how they all scoffed and sneered at him!

²⁵When the crowd was finally outside, Jesus went in where the little girl was lying and took her by the hand, and she jumped up and was all right again! ²⁶The report of this wonderful miracle swept the entire countryside.

²⁷As Jesus was leaving her home, two blind men followed along behind, shouting, "O Son of King David, have mercy on us."

²⁸They went right into the house where he was staying, and Jesus asked them, "Do you believe I can make you see?"

"Yes, Lord," they told him, "we do."

²⁹Then he touched their eyes and said, "Because of your faith it will happen."

³⁰And suddenly they could see! Jesus sternly warned them not to tell anyone about it, ³¹but instead they spread his fame all over the town.

³²Leaving that place, Jesus met a man who couldn't speak because a demon was inside him. ³³So Jesus cast out the demon, and instantly the man could talk. How the crowds marveled! "Never in all our lives have we seen anything like this," they exclaimed.

³⁴But the Pharisees said, "The reason he can cast out demons is that he is demon-possessed himself—possessed by Satan, the demon king!"

³⁵Jesus traveled around through all the cities and villages of that area, teaching in the Jewish synagogues and announcing the Good News about the Kingdom. And wherever he went he healed people of every sort of illness. ³⁶And what pity he felt for the crowds that came, because their problems were so great and they didn't know what to do or where to go for help. They were like sheep without a shepherd.

³⁷"The harvest is so great, and the workers are so few," he told his disciples. ³⁸"So pray to the one in charge of the harvesting, and ask him to recruit more workers for his harvest fields."

10 Jesus Sends Out the Disciples

Jesus called his twelve disciples to him and gave them authority to cast out evil spirits and to heal every kind of sickness and disease.

²⁻⁴Here are the names of his twelve disciples: Simon (also called Peter), Andrew (Peter's brother), James (Zebedee's son), John (James' brother), Philip, Bartholomew, Thomas, Matthew (the tax collector), James (Alphaeus' son), Thaddaeus, Simon (a member of "The Zealots," a subversive political party), Judas Iscariot (the one who betrayed him).

⁵Jesus sent them out with these instructions: "Don't go to the Gentiles or the Samaritans, ⁶but only to the people of Israel—God's lost sheep. ⁷Go and announce to them that the Kingdom of Heaven is near. ⁸Heal the sick, raise the dead, cure the lepers, and cast out demons. Give as freely as you have received!

⁹"Don't take any money with you; ¹⁰don't even carry a duffle bag with extra clothes and shoes, or even a walking stick; for those you help should feed and care for you. ¹¹Whenever you enter a city or village, search for a godly man and stay in his home until you leave for the next town.

¹²When you ask permission to stay, be friendly, ¹³and if it turns out to be a godly home, give it your blessing; if not, keep the blessing. ¹⁴Any city or home that doesn't welcome you—shake off the dust of that place from your feet as you leave. ¹⁵Truly, the wicked cities of Sodom and Gomorrah will be better off at Judgment Day than they.

¹⁶"I am sending you out as sheep among wolves. Be as wary as serpents and harmless as doves. ¹⁷But beware! For you will be arrested and tried, and whipped in the synagogues. ¹⁸Yes, and you must stand trial before governors and kings for my sake. This will give you the opportunity to tell them about me, yes, to witness to the world.

¹⁹"When you are arrested, don't worry about what to say at your trial, for you will be given the right words at the right time. ²⁰For it won't be you doing the talking—it will be the Spirit of your heavenly Father speaking through you!

²¹"Brother shall betray brother to death, and fathers shall betray their own children. And children shall rise against their parents and cause their deaths. ²²Everyone shall hate you because you belong to me. But all of you who endure to the end shall be saved.

²³"When you are persecuted in one city, flee to the next! I will return before you have reached them all!

²⁴"A student is not greater than his teacher. A servant is not above his master. ²⁵The student shares his teacher's fate. The servant shares his master's! And since I, the master of the household, have been called 'Satan,' how much more will you! ²⁶But don't be afraid of those who threaten you. For the time is coming when the truth will be revealed: their secret plots will become public information.

²⁷"What I tell you now in the gloom, shout abroad when daybreak comes. What I whisper in your ears, proclaim from the housetops!

²⁸"Don't be afraid of those who can kill only your bodies—but can't touch your souls! Fear only God who can destroy both soul and body in hell. ²⁹Not one sparrow (What do they cost? Two for a penny?) can fall to the ground without your Father knowing it. ³⁰And the very hairs of your head are all numbered. ³¹So don't worry! You are more valuable to him than many sparrows.

³²"If anyone publicly acknowledges me as his friend, I will openly acknowledge him as my friend before my Father in heaven. ³³But if anyone publicly denies me, I will openly deny him before my Father in heaven.

³⁴"Don't imagine that I came to bring peace to the earth! No, rather, a sword. ³⁵I have come to set a man against his father, and a daughter against her mother, and a daughter-in-law against her mother-in-law— ³⁶a man's worst enemies will be right in his own home! ³⁷If you love your father and mother more than you love me, you are not worthy of being mine; or if you love your son or daughter more than me, you are not worthy of being mine. ³⁸If you refuse to take up your cross and follow me, you are not worthy of being mine.

³⁹"If you cling to your life, you will lose it; but if you give it up for me, you will save it.

⁴⁰"Those who welcome you are welcoming me. And when they welcome me they are welcoming God who sent me. ⁴¹If you welcome a prophet because he is a man of God, you will be given the same reward a prophet gets. And if you welcome good and godly men because of their godliness, you will be given a reward like theirs.

⁴²"And if, as my representatives, you give even a cup of cold water to a little child, you will surely be rewarded."

John's Questions about Jesus

11 When Jesus had finished giving these instructions to his twelve disciples, he went off preaching in the cities where they were scheduled to go.

²John the Baptist, who was now in prison, heard about all the miracles the Messiah was doing, so he sent his disciples to ask Jesus, ³"Are you really the one we are waiting for, or shall we keep on looking?"

⁴Jesus told them, "Go back to John and tell him about the miracles you've seen me do— ⁵the blind people I've healed, and the lame people now walking without help, and the cured lepers, and the deaf who hear, and the dead raised to life; and tell him about my preaching the Good News to the poor. ⁶Then give him this message, 'Blessed are those who don't doubt me.'"

⁷When John's disciples had gone, Jesus began talking about him to the crowds. "When you went out into the barren wilderness to see John, what did you expect him to be like? Grass

---

KNOWING YOU'RE SPECIAL TO GOD 10:29-31 Jesus said that God cares for the sparrows' every need, and we are far more valuable to God than these little birds, so valuable that God sent his only Son to die for us (John 3:16). You are of great worth to God. You are never lost in his inventory. Because God places such value on us, we need never fear personal threats or difficult trials. These can't dislodge God's love and Spirit from within us.

But don't think that because you are valuable to God he will take away all your troubles (see 10:16). The real test of value is how well something holds up under the wear, tear, and abuse of everyday life. Those who stand up for Christ in spite of their troubles truly have lasting value and will receive great rewards (see 5:11-12). **To begin the series of devotionals on KNOWING YOU'RE SPECIAL TO GOD, turn to page 307.**

blowing in the wind? ⁸Or were you expecting to see a man dressed as a prince in a palace? ⁹Or a prophet of God? Yes, and he is more than just a prophet. ¹⁰For John is the man mentioned in the Scriptures—a messenger to precede me, to announce my coming, and prepare people to receive me.

¹¹"Truly, of all men ever born, none shines more brightly than John the Baptist. And yet, even the lesser lights in the Kingdom of Heaven will be greater than he is! ¹²And from the time John the Baptist began preaching and baptizing until now, ardent multitudes have been crowding toward the Kingdom of Heaven, ¹³for all the laws and prophets looked forward [to the Messiah]. Then John appeared, ¹⁴and if you are willing to understand what I mean, he is Elijah, the one the prophets said would come [at the time the Kingdom begins]. ¹⁵If ever you were willing to listen, listen now!

¹⁶"What shall I say about this nation? These people are like children playing, who say to their little friends, ¹⁷'We played wedding and you weren't happy, so we played funeral but you weren't sad.' ¹⁸For John the Baptist doesn't even drink wine and often goes without food, and you say, 'He's crazy.' ¹⁹And I, the Messiah, feast and drink, and you complain that I am 'a glutton and a drinking man, and hang around with the worst sort of sinners!' But brilliant men like you can justify your every inconsistency!"

²⁰Then he began to pour out his denunciations against the cities where he had done most of his miracles, because they hadn't turned to God.

²¹"Woe to you, Chorazin, and woe to you, Bethsaida! For if the miracles I did in your streets had been done in wicked Tyre and Sidon their people would have repented long ago in shame and humility. ²²Truly, Tyre and Sidon will be better off on the Judgment Day than you! ²³And Capernaum, though highly honored, shall go down to hell! For if the marvelous miracles I did in you had been done in Sodom, it would still be here today. ²⁴Truly, Sodom will be better off at the Judgment Day than you."

²⁵And Jesus prayed this prayer: "O Father, Lord of heaven and earth, thank you for hiding the truth from those who think themselves so wise, and for revealing it to little children. ²⁶Yes, Father, for it pleased you to do it this way! . . .

²⁷"Everything has been entrusted to me by my Father. Only the Father knows the Son, and the Father is known only by the Son and by those to whom the Son reveals him. ²⁸Come to me and I will give you rest—all of you who work so hard beneath a heavy yoke. ²⁹,³⁰Wear my yoke—for it fits perfectly—and let me teach you; for I am gentle and humble, and you shall find rest for your souls; for I give you only light burdens."

12 Jesus Talks about the Sabbath

About that time, Jesus was walking one day through some grainfields with his disciples. It was on the Sabbath, the Jewish day of worship, and his disciples were hungry; so they began breaking off heads of wheat and eating the grain.

²But some Pharisees saw them do it and protested, "Your disciples are breaking the law. They are harvesting on the Sabbath."

³But Jesus said to them, "Haven't you ever read what King David did when he and his friends were hungry? ⁴He went into the Temple and they ate the special bread permitted to the priests alone. That was breaking the law too. ⁵And haven't you ever read in the law of Moses how the priests on duty in the Temple may work on the Sabbath? ⁶And truly, one is here who is greater than the Temple! ⁷But if you had known the meaning of this Scripture verse, 'I want you to be merciful more than I want your offerings,' you would not have condemned those who aren't guilty! ⁸For I, the Messiah, am master even of the Sabbath."

⁹Then he went over to the synagogue ¹⁰and noticed there a man with a deformed hand. The Pharisees asked Jesus, "Is it legal to work by healing on the Sabbath day?" (They were, of course, hoping he would say yes, so they could arrest him!) ¹¹This was his answer: "If you had just one sheep, and it fell into a well on the Sabbath, would you work to rescue it that day? Of course you would. ¹²And how much more valuable is a person than a sheep! Yes, it is right to do good on the Sabbath." ¹³Then he said to the man, "Stretch out your arm." And as he did, his hand became normal, just like the other one!

¹⁴Then the Pharisees called a meeting to plot Jesus' arrest and death.

¹⁵But he knew what they were planning and left the synagogue, with many following him. He healed all the sick among them, ¹⁶but he cautioned them against spreading the news about his miracles. ¹⁷This fulfilled the prophecy of Isaiah concerning him:

¹⁸"Look at my Servant.
See my Chosen One.
He is my Beloved, in whom my soul delights.
I will put my Spirit upon him,
And he will judge the nations.
¹⁹He does not fight nor shout;
He does not raise his voice!
²⁰He does not crush the weak,
Or quench the smallest hope;
He will end all conflict with his final victory,

²¹And his name shall be the hope
Of all the world."

²²Then a demon-possessed man—he was both blind and unable to talk—was brought to Jesus, and Jesus healed him so that he could both speak and see. ²³The crowd was amazed. "Maybe Jesus is the Messiah!" they exclaimed.

²⁴But when the Pharisees heard about the miracle they said, "He can cast out demons because he is Satan, king of devils."

²⁵Jesus knew their thoughts and replied, "A divided kingdom ends in ruin. A city or home divided against itself cannot stand. ²⁶And if Satan is casting out Satan, he is fighting himself and destroying his own kingdom. ²⁷And if, as you claim, I am casting out demons by invoking the powers of Satan, then what power do your own people use when they cast them out? Let them answer your accusation! ²⁸But if I am casting out demons by the Spirit of God, then the Kingdom of God has arrived among you. ²⁹One cannot rob Satan's kingdom without first binding Satan. Only then can his demons be cast out! ³⁰Anyone who isn't helping me is harming me.

³¹,³²"Even blasphemy against me or any other sin can be forgiven—all except one: speaking against the Holy Spirit shall never be forgiven, either in this world or in the world to come.

³³"A tree is identified by its fruit. A tree from a select variety produces good fruit; poor varieties don't. ³⁴You brood of snakes! How could evil men like you speak what is good and right? For a man's heart determines his speech. ³⁵A good man's speech reveals the rich treasures within him. An evil-hearted man is filled with venom, and his speech reveals it. ³⁶And I tell you this, that you must give account on Judgment Day for every idle word you speak. ³⁷Your words now reflect your fate then: either you will be justified by them or you will be condemned."

³⁸One day some of the Jewish leaders, including some Pharisees, came to Jesus asking him to show them a miracle.

³⁹,⁴⁰But Jesus replied, "Only an evil, faithless nation would ask for further proof; and none will be given except what happened to Jonah the prophet! For as Jonah was in the great fish for three days and three nights, so I, the Messiah, shall be in the heart of the earth three days and three nights. ⁴¹The men of Nineveh shall arise against this nation at the judgment and condemn you. For when Jonah preached to them, they repented and turned to God from all their evil ways. And now a greater than Jonah is here—and you refuse to believe him. ⁴²The Queen of Sheba shall rise against this nation in the judgment and condemn it; for she came from a distant land to hear the wisdom of Solomon; and now a greater than Solomon is here—and you refuse to believe him.

⁴³⁻⁴⁵"This evil nation is like a man possessed by a demon. For if the demon leaves, it goes into the deserts for a while, seeking rest but finding none. Then it says, 'I will return to the man I came from.' So it returns and finds the man's heart clean but empty! Then the demon finds seven other spirits more evil than itself, and all enter the man and live in him. And so he is worse off than before."

⁴⁶,⁴⁷As Jesus was speaking in a crowded house his mother and brothers were outside, wanting to talk with him. When someone told him they were there, ⁴⁸he remarked, "Who is my mother? Who are my brothers?" ⁴⁹He pointed to his disciples. "Look!" he said, "these are my mother and brothers." ⁵⁰Then he added, "Anyone who obeys my Father in heaven is my brother, sister, and mother!"

13 A Story about a Farmer

Later that same day, Jesus left the house and went down to the shore, ²,³where an immense crowd soon gathered. He got into a boat and taught from it while the people listened on the beach. He used many illustrations such as this one in his sermon:

"A farmer was sowing grain in his fields. ⁴As he scattered the seed across the ground, some fell beside a path, and the birds came and ate it. ⁵And some fell on rocky soil where there was little depth of earth; the plants sprang up quickly enough in the shallow soil, ⁶but the hot sun soon scorched them and they withered and died, for they had so little root. ⁷Other seeds fell among thorns, and the thorns choked out the tender blades. ⁸But some fell on good soil and produced a crop that was thirty, sixty, and even a hundred times as much as he had planted. ⁹If you have ears, listen!"

¹⁰His disciples came and asked him, "Why do you always use these hard-to-understand illustrations?"

¹¹Then he explained to them that only they were permitted to understand about the Kingdom of Heaven, and others were not.

¹²,¹³"For to him who has will more be given," he told them, "and he will have great plenty; but from him who has not, even the little he has will be taken away. That is why I use these illustrations, so people will hear and see but not understand.

¹⁴"This fulfills the prophecy of Isaiah:

> 'They hear, but don't understand; they look, but don't see! ¹⁵For their hearts are fat and heavy, and their ears are dull, and they have closed their eyes in sleep, ¹⁶so they won't see and hear and understand and turn to God again, and let me heal them.'

But blessed are your eyes, for they see; and your ears, for they hear. [17]Many a prophet and godly man has longed to see what you have seen and hear what you have heard, but couldn't.

[18]"Now here is the explanation of the story I told about the farmer planting grain: [19]The hard path where some of the seeds fell represents the heart of a person who hears the Good News about the Kingdom and doesn't understand it; then Satan comes and snatches away the seeds from his heart. [20]The shallow, rocky soil represents the heart of a man who hears the message and receives it with real joy, [21]but he doesn't have much depth in his life, and the seeds don't root very deeply, and after a while when trouble comes, or persecution begins because of his beliefs, his enthusiasm fades, and he drops out. [22]The ground covered with thistles represents a man who hears the message, but the cares of this life and his longing for money choke out God's Word, and he does less and less for God. [23]The good ground represents the heart of a man who listens to the message and understands it and goes out and brings thirty, sixty, or even a hundred others into the Kingdom."

[24]Here is another illustration Jesus used: "The Kingdom of Heaven is like a farmer sowing good seed in his field; [25]but one night as he slept, his enemy came and sowed thistles among the wheat. [26]When the crop began to grow, the thistles grew too.

[27]"The farmer's men came and told him, 'Sir, the field where you planted that choice seed is full of thistles!'

[28]"'An enemy has done it,' he exclaimed.

"'Shall we pull out the thistles?' they asked.

[29]"'No,' he replied. 'You'll hurt the wheat if you do. [30]Let both grow together until the harvest, and I will tell the reapers to sort out the thistles and burn them, and put the wheat in the barn.'"

[31,32]Here is another of his illustrations: "The Kingdom of Heaven is like a tiny mustard seed planted in a field. It is the smallest of all seeds but becomes the largest of plants, and grows into a tree where birds can come and find shelter."

[33]He also used this example:

"The Kingdom of Heaven can be compared to a woman making bread. She takes a measure of flour and mixes in the yeast until it permeates every part of the dough."

[34,35]Jesus constantly used these illustrations when speaking to the crowds. In fact, because the prophets said that he would use so many, he never spoke to them without at least one illustration. For it had been prophesied, "I will talk in parables; I will explain mysteries hidden since the beginning of time."

[36]Then, leaving the crowds outside, he went into the house. His disciples asked him to explain to them the illustration of the thistles and the wheat.

[37]"All right," he said, "I am the farmer who sows the choice seed. [38]The field is the world, and the seed represents the people of the Kingdom; the thistles are the people belonging to Satan. [39]The enemy who sowed the thistles among the wheat is the devil; the harvest is the end of the world, and the reapers are the angels.

[40]"Just as in this story the thistles are separated and burned, so shall it be at the end of the world: [41]I will send my angels, and they will separate out of the Kingdom every temptation and all who are evil, [42]and throw them into the furnace and burn them. There shall be weeping and gnashing of teeth. [43]Then the godly shall shine as the sun in their Father's Kingdom. Let those with ears, listen!

[44]"The Kingdom of Heaven is like a treasure a man discovered in a field. In his excitement, he sold everything he owned to get enough money to buy the field—and get the treasure, too!

[45]"Again, the Kingdom of Heaven is like a pearl merchant on the lookout for choice pearls. [46]He discovered a real bargain—a pearl of great value—and sold everything he owned to purchase it!

[47,48]"Again, the Kingdom of Heaven can be illustrated by a fisherman—he casts a net into the water and gathers in fish of every kind, valuable and worthless. When the net is full, he drags it up onto the beach and sits down and sorts out the edible ones into crates and throws the others away. [49]That is the way it will be at the end of the world—the angels will come and separate the wicked people from the godly, [50]casting the wicked into the fire; there shall be weeping and gnashing of teeth. [51]Do you understand?"

"Yes," they said, "we do."

[52]Then he added, "Those experts in Jewish law who are now my disciples have double treasures—from the Old Testament as well as from the New!"

[53,54]When Jesus had finished giving these illustrations, he returned to his hometown, Nazareth in Galilee, and taught there in the synagogue and astonished everyone with his wisdom and his miracles.

[55]"How is this possible?" the people exclaimed. "He's just a carpenter's son, and we know Mary his mother and his brothers—James, Joseph, Simon, and Judas. [56]And his sisters—they all live here. How can he be so great?" [57]And they became angry with him!

Then Jesus told them, "A prophet is honored everywhere except in his own country, and among his own people!" [58]And so he did only a few great miracles there, because of their unbelief.

14

Herod Kills John the Baptist

When King Herod heard about Jesus, ²he said to his men, "This must be John the Baptist, come back to life again. That is why he can do these miracles." ³For Herod had arrested John and chained him in prison at the demand of his wife Herodias, his brother Philip's ex-wife, ⁴because John had told him it was wrong for him to marry her. ⁵He would have killed John but was afraid of a riot, for all the people believed John was a prophet.

⁶But at a birthday party for Herod, Herodias' daughter performed a dance that greatly pleased him, ⁷so he vowed to give her anything she wanted. ⁸Consequently, at her mother's urging, the girl asked for John the Baptist's head on a tray.

⁹The king was grieved, but because of his oath, and because he didn't want to back down in front of his guests, he issued the necessary orders.

¹⁰So John was beheaded in the prison, ¹¹and his head was brought on a tray and given to the girl, who took it to her mother.

¹²Then John's disciples came for his body and buried it, and came to tell Jesus what had happened.

¹³As soon as Jesus heard the news, he went off by himself in a boat to a remote area to be alone. But the crowds saw where he was headed and followed by land from many villages.

¹⁴So when Jesus came out of the wilderness, a vast crowd was waiting for him, and he pitied them and healed their sick.

¹⁵That evening the disciples came to him and said, "It is already past time for supper, and there is nothing to eat here in the desert; send the crowds away so they can go to the villages and buy some food."

¹⁶But Jesus replied, "That isn't necessary—you feed them!"

¹⁷"What!" they exclaimed. "We have exactly five small loaves of bread and two fish!"

¹⁸"Bring them here," he said.

¹⁹Then he told the people to sit down on the grass; and he took the five loaves and two fish, looked up into the sky, and asked God's blessing on the meal, then broke the loaves apart and gave them to the disciples to place before the people.

²⁰And everyone ate until full! And when the scraps were picked up afterwards, there were twelve basketfuls left over! ²¹(About five thousand men were in the crowd that day, besides all the women and children.)

²²Immediately after this, Jesus told his disciples to get into their boat and cross to the other side of the lake while he stayed to get the people started home.

²³,²⁴Then afterwards he went up into the hills to pray. Night fell, and out on the lake the disciples were in trouble. For the wind had risen and they were fighting heavy seas.

²⁵About four o'clock in the morning Jesus came to them, walking on the water! ²⁶They screamed in terror, for they thought he was a ghost.

²⁷But Jesus immediately spoke to them, reassuring them. "Don't be afraid!" he said.

²⁸Then Peter called to him: "Sir, if it is really you, tell me to come over to you, walking on the water."

²⁹"All right," the Lord said, "come along!"

So Peter went over the side of the boat and walked on the water toward Jesus. ³⁰But when he looked around at the high waves, he was terrified and began to sink. "Save me, Lord!" he shouted.

³¹Instantly Jesus reached out his hand and rescued him. "O man of little faith," Jesus said. "Why did you doubt me?" ³²And when they had climbed back into the boat, the wind stopped.

³³The others sat there, awestruck. "You really are the Son of God!" they exclaimed.

³⁴They landed at Gennesaret. ³⁵The news of their arrival spread quickly throughout the city, and soon people were rushing around, telling everyone to bring in their sick to be healed. ³⁶The sick begged him to let them touch even the tassel of his robe, and all who did were healed.

15

The Rules That Count

Some Pharisees and other Jewish leaders now arrived from Jerusalem to interview Jesus.

²"Why do your disciples disobey the ancient Jewish traditions?" they demanded. "For they ignore our ritual of ceremonial handwashing before they eat." ³He replied, "And why do your traditions violate the direct commandments of God? ⁴For instance, God's law is 'Honor your father and mother; anyone who reviles his parents must die.' ⁵,⁶But you say, 'Even if your parents are in need, you may give their support money to the church instead.' And so, by your man-made rule, you nullify the direct command of God to honor and care for your parents. ⁷You hypocrites! Well did Isaiah prophesy of you, ⁸'These people say they honor

---

OVERCOMING FEAR 14:28 Peter was not testing Jesus, something we are told not to do (4:7). Instead he was the only one in the boat to react in faith. His impulsive request led him to experience a rather unusual demonstration of God's power. Peter started to sink because he took his eyes off Jesus and focused on the high waves around him. Then his faith wavered when he realized what he was doing. We may not walk on water, but we do walk through tough situations. If we focus on the waves of difficult circumstances around us without looking to Christ for help, we too may despair and sink. To maintain your faith in the midst of difficult situations, keep your eyes on Christ's power rather than on your inadequacies. **To begin the series of devotionals on OVERCOMING FEAR, turn to page 13.**

Family Devotions

☐ DEVOTION 254
SERVING GOD BOLDLY

Read Matthew 14:23-33

I'd like to do that, thought Melissa when Miss Baker asked for a volunteer to memorize Psalm 100 and recite it at the Thanksgiving program. *But if I made a mistake in front of all those people, I'd just die.* Some of the other girls in Melissa's Sunday school class expressed the same fear, and no one volunteered.

A little later Miss Baker told the Bible story of Peter walking on the water. She was such a good storyteller that Melissa could almost feel the water beneath her feet. The entire class seemed to relax when Peter and Jesus were finally in the boat with the other disciples, and the sea was calm. "Who in this story made the biggest mistake?" asked Miss Baker.

"Peter," was Dawn's quick reply.

"Why do you think it was Peter?" Miss Baker asked.

"I think it was because he was afraid," suggested Lucy.

"And he didn't trust Jesus," added Melissa.

Miss Baker shook her head. "Actually, Peter was the only one who *did* trust Jesus. He got out of the boat while the others sat and watched. The ones who made the biggest mistake were the eleven disciples who didn't have faith to do it. We're a lot like them. One of the worst mistakes we make is to allow fear to keep us from trying."

At the Thanksgiving program two weeks later, Melissa trembled as she stood before the audience. Then she remembered Peter. *Lord Jesus, help me,* she prayed silently as she began to recite. Twice she forgot a word, and Miss Baker had to prompt her. But when she finished, Miss Baker gave her a big smile. Suddenly it was not so important that she had made a couple of mistakes. The important thing was that she had not let fear keep her from trying.

Serving God Boldly Memory Verse

Yes, be bold and strong!
Banish fear and doubt!
For remember, the Lord
your God is with you
wherever you go.
Joshua 1:9

How About You?

Is there something you want to do for the Lord Jesus, but you're afraid to try? Remember Peter. He tried, and when he began to sink, Jesus was there to lift him up. Trying and failing isn't a mistake, but it's a big mistake to fail to try. B. W.

• For the next devotional, turn to page 917.   • For the next devotional on SERVING GOD BOLDLY, turn to page 947.
• For notes on SERVING GOD BOLDLY, see pages 327, 404, 501, 720, and 856.

me, but their hearts are far away. ⁹Their worship is worthless, for they teach their man-made laws instead of those from God.'"

¹⁰Then Jesus called to the crowds and said, "Listen to what I say and try to understand: ¹¹You aren't made unholy by eating nonkosher food! It is what you *say* and *think* that makes you unclean."

¹²Then the disciples came and told him, "You offended the Pharisees by that remark."

¹³,¹⁴Jesus replied, "Every plant not planted by my Father shall be rooted up, so ignore them. They are blind guides leading the blind, and both will fall into a ditch."

¹⁵Then Peter asked Jesus to explain what he meant when he said that people are not defiled by nonkosher food.

¹⁶"Don't you understand?" Jesus asked him. ¹⁷"Don't you see that anything you eat passes through the digestive tract and out again? ¹⁸But evil words come from an evil heart and defile the man who says them. ¹⁹For from the heart come evil thoughts, murder, adultery, fornication, theft, lying, and slander. ²⁰These are what defile; but there is no spiritual defilement from eating without first going through the ritual of ceremonial handwashing!"

²¹Jesus then left that part of the country and walked the fifty miles to Tyre and Sidon.

²²A woman from Canaan who was living there came to him, pleading, "Have mercy on me, O Lord, King David's Son! For my daughter has a demon within her, and it torments her constantly."

²³But Jesus gave her no reply—not even a word. Then his disciples urged him to send her away. "Tell her to get going," they said, "for she is bothering us with all her begging."

²⁴Then he said to the woman, "I was sent to help the Jews—the lost sheep of Israel—not the Gentiles."

²⁵But she came and worshiped him and pled again, "Sir, help me!"

²⁶"It doesn't seem right to take bread from the children and throw it to the dogs," he said.

²⁷"Yes, it is!" she replied, "for even the puppies beneath the table are permitted to eat the crumbs that fall."

²⁸"Woman," Jesus told her, "your faith is large, and your request is granted." And her daughter was healed right then.

²⁹Jesus now returned to the Sea of Galilee and climbed a hill and sat there. ³⁰And a vast crowd brought him their lame, blind, maimed, and those who couldn't speak, and many others, and laid them before Jesus, and he healed them all. ³¹What a spectacle it was! Those who hadn't been able to say a word before were talking excitedly, and those with missing arms and legs had new ones; the crippled were walking and jumping around, and those who had been blind were gazing about them! The crowds just marveled, and praised the God of Israel.

³²Then Jesus called his disciples to him and said, "I pity these people—they've been here with me for three days now and have nothing left to eat; I don't want to send them away hungry or they will faint along the road."

³³The disciples replied, "And where would we get enough here in the desert for all this mob to eat?"

³⁴Jesus asked them, "How much food do you have?" And they replied, "Seven loaves of bread and a few small fish!"

³⁵Then Jesus told all of the people to sit down on the ground, ³⁶and he took the seven loaves and the fish, and gave thanks to God for them, and divided them into pieces, and gave them to the disciples who presented them to the crowd. ³⁷,³⁸And everyone ate until full—four thousand men besides the women and children! And afterwards, when the scraps were picked up, there were seven basketfuls left over!

³⁹Then Jesus sent the people home and got into the boat and crossed to Magadan.

16 The Leaders Want a Miracle

One day the Pharisees and Sadducees came to test Jesus' claim of being the Messiah by asking him to show them some great demonstrations in the skies.

²,³He replied, "You are good at reading the weather signs of the skies—red sky tonight means fair weather tomorrow; red sky in the morning means foul weather all day—but you can't read the obvious signs of the times! ⁴This evil, unbelieving nation is asking for some strange sign in the heavens, but no further proof will be given except the miracle that happened to Jonah." Then Jesus walked out on them.

⁵Arriving across the lake, the disciples discovered they had forgotten to bring any food.

⁶"Watch out!" Jesus warned them; "beware of the yeast of the Pharisees and Sadducees."

⁷They thought he was saying this because they had forgotten to bring bread.

⁸Jesus knew what they were thinking and told them, "O men of little faith! Why are you so worried about having no food? ⁹Won't you ever understand? Don't you remember at all the five thousand I fed with five loaves, and the basketfuls left over? ¹⁰Don't you remember the four thousand I fed, and all that was left? ¹¹How could you even think I was talking about food? But again I

say, 'Beware of the yeast of the Pharisees and Sadducees.'"

¹²Then at last they understood that by *yeast* he meant the *wrong teaching* of the Pharisees and Sadducees.

¹³When Jesus came to Caesarea Philippi, he asked his disciples, "Who are the people saying I am?"

¹⁴"Well," they replied, "some say John the Baptist; some, Elijah; some, Jeremiah or one of the other prophets."

¹⁵Then he asked them, "Who do *you* think I am?"

¹⁶Simon Peter answered, "The Christ, the Messiah, the Son of the living God."

¹⁷"God has blessed you, Simon, son of Jonah," Jesus said, "for my Father in heaven has personally revealed this to you—this is not from any human source. ¹⁸You are Peter, a stone; and upon this rock I will build my church; and all the powers of hell shall not prevail against it. ¹⁹And I will give you the keys of the Kingdom of Heaven; whatever doors you lock on earth shall be locked in heaven; and whatever doors you open on earth shall be open in heaven!"

²⁰Then he warned the disciples against telling others that he was the Messiah.

²¹From then on Jesus began to speak plainly to his disciples about going to Jerusalem, and what would happen to him there—that he would suffer at the hands of the Jewish leaders, that he would be killed, and that three days later he would be raised to life again.

²²But Peter took him aside to remonstrate with him. "Heaven forbid, sir," he said. "This is not going to happen to you!"

²³Jesus turned on Peter and said, "Get away from me, you Satan! You are a dangerous trap to me. You are thinking merely from a human point of view, and not from God's."

²⁴Then Jesus said to the disciples, "If anyone wants to be a follower of mine, let him deny himself and take up his cross and follow me. ²⁵For anyone who keeps his life for himself shall lose it; and anyone who loses his life for me shall find it again. ²⁶What profit is there if you gain the whole world—and lose eternal life? What can be compared with the value of eternal life? ²⁷For I, the Son of Mankind, shall come with my angels in the glory of my Father and judge each person according to his deeds. ²⁸And some of you standing right here now will certainly live to see me coming in my Kingdom."

17 Jesus Shines like the Sun

Six days later Jesus took Peter, James, and his brother John to the top of a high and lonely hill, ²and as they watched, his appearance changed so that his face shone like the sun and his clothing became dazzling white.

³Suddenly Moses and Elijah appeared and were talking with him. ⁴Peter blurted out, "Sir, it's wonderful that we can be here! If you want me to, I'll make three shelters, one for you and one for Moses and one for Elijah."

⁵But even as he said it, a bright cloud came over them, and a voice from the cloud said, *"This* is my beloved Son, and I am wonderfully pleased with him. Obey him."

⁶At this the disciples fell face downward to the ground, terribly frightened. ⁷Jesus came over and touched them. "Get up," he said, "don't be afraid."

⁸And when they looked, only Jesus was with them.

⁹As they were going down the mountain, Jesus commanded them not to tell anyone what they had seen until after he had risen from the dead.

¹⁰His disciples asked, "Why do the Jewish leaders insist Elijah must return before the Messiah comes?"

¹¹Jesus replied, "They are right. Elijah must come and set everything in order. ¹²And, in fact, he has already come, but he wasn't recognized, and was badly mistreated by many. And I, the Messiah, shall also suffer at their hands."

¹³Then the disciples realized he was speaking of John the Baptist.

¹⁴When they arrived at the bottom of the hill, a huge crowd was waiting for them. A man came and knelt before Jesus and said, ¹⁵"Sir, have mercy on my son, for he is mentally deranged and in great trouble, for he often falls into the fire or into the water; ¹⁶so I brought him to your disciples, but they couldn't cure him."

¹⁷Jesus replied, "Oh, you stubborn, faithless people! How long shall I bear with you? Bring him here to me." ¹⁸Then Jesus rebuked the demon in the boy and it left him, and from that moment the boy was well.

¹⁹Afterwards the disciples asked Jesus privately, "Why couldn't we cast that demon out?"

²⁰"Because of your little faith," Jesus told them. "For if you had faith even as small as a tiny mustard seed you could say to this mountain, 'Move!' and it would go far away. Nothing would be impossible. ²¹But this kind of demon won't leave unless you have prayed and gone without food."

²²,²³One day while they were still in Galilee, Jesus told them, "I am going to be betrayed into the power of those who will kill me, and on the third day afterwards I will be brought back to life again." And the disciples' hearts were filled with sorrow and dread.

²⁴On their arrival in Capernaum, the Temple tax

collectors came to Peter and asked him, "Doesn't your master pay taxes?"

25 "Of course he does," Peter replied.

Then he went into the house to talk to Jesus about it, but before he had a chance to speak, Jesus asked him, "What do you think, Peter? Do kings levy assessments against their own people or against conquered foreigners?"

26,27 "Against the foreigners," Peter replied.

"Well, then," Jesus said, "the citizens are free! However, we don't want to offend them, so go down to the shore and throw in a line, and open the mouth of the first fish you catch. You will find a coin to cover the taxes for both of us; take it and pay them."

18 Who Is the Greatest?

About that time the disciples came to Jesus to ask which of them would be greatest in the Kingdom of Heaven!

2 Jesus called a small child over to him and set the little fellow down among them, 3 and said, "Unless you turn to God from your sins and become as little children, you will never get into the Kingdom of Heaven. 4 Therefore anyone who humbles himself as this little child is the greatest in the Kingdom of Heaven. 5 And any of you who welcomes a little child like this because you are mine is welcoming me and caring for me. 6 But if any of you causes one of these little ones who trusts in me to lose his faith, it would be better for you to have a rock tied to your neck and be thrown into the sea.

7 "Woe upon the world for all its evils. Temptation to do wrong is inevitable, but woe to the man who does the tempting. 8 So if your hand or foot causes you to sin, cut it off and throw it away. Better to enter heaven crippled than to be in hell with both of your hands and feet. 9 And if your eye causes you to sin, gouge it out and throw it away. Better to enter heaven with one eye than to be in hell with two.

10 "Beware that you don't look down upon a single one of these little children. For I tell you that in heaven their angels have constant access to my Father. 11 And I, the Messiah, came to save the lost.

12 "If a man has a hundred sheep, and one wanders away and is lost, what will he do? Won't he leave the ninety-nine others and go out into the hills to search for the lost one? 13 And if he finds it, he will rejoice over it more than over the ninety-nine others safe at home! 14 Just so, it is not my Father's will that even one of these little ones should perish.

15 "If a brother sins against you, go to him privately and confront him with his fault. If he listens and confesses it, you have won back a brother. 16 But if not, then take one or two others with you and go back to him again, proving everything you say by these witnesses. 17 If he still refuses to listen, then take your case to the church, and if the church's verdict favors you, but he won't accept it, then the church should excommunicate him. 18 And I tell you this—whatever you bind on earth is bound in heaven, and whatever you free on earth will be freed in heaven.

19 "I also tell you this—if two of you agree down here on earth concerning anything you ask for, my Father in heaven will do it for you. 20 For where two or three gather together because they are mine, I will be right there among them."

21 Then Peter came to him and asked, "Sir, how often should I forgive a brother who sins against me? Seven times?"

22 "No!" Jesus replied, "seventy times seven!

23 "The Kingdom of Heaven can be compared to a king who decided to bring his accounts up to date. 24 In the process, one of his debtors was brought in who owed him $10 million! 25 He couldn't pay, so the king ordered him sold for the debt, also his wife and children and everything he had.

26 "But the man fell down before the king, his face in the dust, and said, 'Oh, sir, be patient with me and I will pay it all.'

27 "Then the king was filled with pity for him and released him and forgave his debt.

28 "But when the man left the king, he went to a man who owed him $2,000 and grabbed him by the throat and demanded instant payment.

29 "The man fell down before him and begged him to give him a little time. 'Be patient and I will pay it,' he pled.

30 "But his creditor wouldn't wait. He had the man arrested and jailed until the debt would be paid in full.

31 "Then the man's friends went to the king and told him what had happened. 32 And the king called before him the man he had forgiven and said, 'You evil-hearted wretch! Here I forgave you all that tremendous debt, just because you asked me to— 33 shouldn't you have mercy on others, just as I had mercy on you?'

34 "Then the angry king sent the man to the torture chamber until he had paid every last penny due. 35 So shall my heavenly Father do to you if you refuse to truly forgive your brothers."

19 Marriage and Divorce

After Jesus had finished this address, he left Galilee and circled back to Judea from across the Jordan River. 2 Vast crowds followed him, and he healed their sick. 3 Some Pharisees came to interview him and tried to trap him into saying something that would ruin him.

"Do you permit divorce?" they asked.

4 "Don't you read the Scriptures?" he replied. "In

Family Devotions

☐ **Devotion 255**
Forgiving Others

Read Matthew 18:21-22

At the first ring of the telephone, Kevin rushed to answer. He figured it would be Grandma calling to wish him a happy birthday. "Kevin?" said a man's voice. Kevin wondered who it could be. "This is your father," the man continued. Kevin fingered the cord of the telephone, uncertain how to respond. "I called to wish you a happy birthday," his father added when Kevin didn't answer.

"You said you didn't want any more to do with me," said Kevin finally, "so I don't want to talk to you." With that, he hung up the phone.

Kevin went to tell his mother about the call. He thought she would be pleased with the way he had handled it. After all, during the time of the divorce nearly two years before, she had often had harsh words for his father. So he was surprised when she said, "Kevin, we need to talk about this." Then Mom did something very strange. She called Kevin's dog, Splash, to join them. Kevin laughed when Splash ran in, jumped up on his lap, and tried to lick his face. "See how much Splash loves you," said Mom.

"I love him, too." Kevin gave Splash an affectionate pat on the head.

"I know you do," said Mom, "but do you remember what you said when you got mad at him last week?"

Kevin thought for a moment. Then he nodded. "I said, 'Bad dog. I don't want you any more,' didn't I, old fellow?" He hugged his pet. "I'm sorry, Splash. I didn't mean it."

"Your father may feel the way you do," Mom said gently. "Two years ago, we all said many things out of anger. Now we need to learn to forgive one another just as God forgives us."

Kevin thought about what Mom was saying. "Mom, do you know Dad's phone number?" he asked at last.

"Yes. I'll get it for you," said Mom as her arm circled Kevin's shoulder.

Forgiving Others
Memory Verse

Be gentle and ready to forgive; never hold grudges. Remember, the Lord forgave you, so you must forgive others.
Colossians 3:13

How About You?

Do you have trouble forgiving someone? Most people do, but it's one of the commands of our Lord. Would it help to remember how often you have been forgiven? By your parents? By your friends? By an enemy? Most of all, it's important to remember that God forgives. E. M. B.

- For the next devotional, turn to page 919.   • For the next devotional on *Forgiving Others*, turn to page 1147.
- For notes on *Forgiving Others*, see pages 273, 356, 586, and 822.

them it is written that at the beginning God created man and woman, 5,6and that a man should leave his father and mother, and be forever united to his wife. The two shall become one—no longer two, but one! And no man may divorce what God has joined together."

7"Then, why," they asked, "did Moses say a man may divorce his wife by merely writing her a letter of dismissal?"

8Jesus replied, "Moses did that in recognition of your hard and evil hearts, but it was not what God had originally intended. 9And I tell you this, that anyone who divorces his wife, except for fornication, and marries another, commits adultery."

10Jesus' disciples then said to him, "If that is how it is, it is better not to marry!"

11"Not everyone can accept this statement," Jesus said. "Only those whom God helps. 12Some are born without the ability to marry, and some are disabled by men, and some refuse to marry for the sake of the Kingdom of Heaven. Let anyone who can, accept my statement."

13Little children were brought for Jesus to lay his hands on them and pray. But the disciples scolded those who brought them. "Don't bother him," they said.

14But Jesus said, "Let the little children come to me, and don't prevent them. For of such is the Kingdom of Heaven." 15And he put his hands on their heads and blessed them before he left.

16Someone came to Jesus with this question: "Good master, what must I do to have eternal life?"

17"When you call me good you are calling me God," Jesus replied, "for God alone is truly good. But to answer your question, you can get to heaven if you keep the commandments."

18"Which ones?" the man asked.

And Jesus replied, "Don't kill, don't commit adultery, don't steal, don't lie, 19honor your father and mother, and love your neighbor as yourself!"

20"I've always obeyed every one of them," the youth replied. "What else must I do?"

21Jesus told him, "If you want to be perfect, go and sell everything you have and give the money to the poor, and you will have treasure in heaven; and come, follow me." 22But when the young man heard this, he went away sadly, for he was very rich.

23Then Jesus said to his disciples, "It is almost impossible for a rich man to get into the Kingdom of Heaven. 24I say it again—it is easier for a camel to go through the eye of a needle than for a rich man to enter the Kingdom of God!"

25This remark confounded the disciples. "Then who in the world can be saved?" they asked.

26Jesus looked at them intently and said, "Humanly speaking, no one. But with God, everything is possible."

27Then Peter said to him, "We left everything to follow you. What will we get out of it?"

28And Jesus replied, "When I, the Messiah, shall sit upon my glorious throne in the Kingdom, you my disciples shall certainly sit on twelve thrones judging the twelve tribes of Israel. 29And anyone who gives up his home, brothers, sisters, father, mother, wife, children, or property, to follow me, shall receive a hundred times as much in return, and shall have eternal life. 30But many who are first now will be last then; and some who are last now will be first then."

20 A Story about a Vineyard

Here is another illustration of the Kingdom of Heaven. "The owner of an estate went out early one morning to hire workers for his harvest field. 2He agreed to pay them $20 a day and sent them out to work.

3"A couple of hours later he was passing a hiring hall and saw some men standing around waiting for jobs, 4so he sent them also into his fields, telling them he would pay them whatever was right at the end of the day. 5At noon and again around three o'clock in the afternoon he did the same thing.

6"At five o'clock that evening he was in town again and saw some more men standing around and asked them, 'Why haven't you been working today?'

7"'Because no one hired us,' they replied.

"'Then go on out and join the others in my fields,' he told them.

8"That evening he told the paymaster to call the men in and pay them, beginning with the last men first. 9When the men hired at five o'clock were paid, each received $20. 10So when the men hired earlier came to get theirs, they assumed they would receive much more. But they, too, were paid $20.

11,12"They protested, 'Those fellows worked only one hour, and yet you've paid them just as much as those of us who worked all day in the scorching heat.'

13"'Friend,' he answered one of them, 'I did you no wrong! Didn't you agree to work all day for $20? 14Take it and go. It is my desire to pay all the same; 15is it against the law to give away my money if I want to? Should you be angry because I am kind?' 16And so it is that the last shall be first, and the first, last."

17As Jesus was on the way to Jerusalem, he took the twelve disciples aside 18and talked to them about what would happen to him when they arrived.

"I will be betrayed to the chief priests and other Jewish leaders, and they will condemn me to die. 19And they will hand me over to the Roman government, and I will be mocked and crucified, and the third day I will rise to life again."

Family Devotions

☐ DEVOTION 256
FAITH IN ACTION

Read Matthew 21:28-32

"You'd hardly know Jay Snider lately!" Mark reported enthusiastically at the family dinner table. "He quit going to all those drinking parties on weekends, and he even carries a Bible with him to church now."

"Well, Laura Perry is just the opposite," said Mark's sister, Lisa. "She's always gone to church, and she talks like a Christian in Sunday school and youth group. But now she's started going to those same parties that Jay quit. You should hear the stories she's been telling about how much she can drink and everything. So now Jay, the drinker, goes to church and Laura, the churchgoer, goes out drinking. Seems odd, doesn't it?"

"Well," said Mother thoughtfully, "do you remember when I asked you to empty the dishwasher the other night, Lisa? You said you would, but then a friend called and you took off without getting it done. I was frustrated with you, and I asked Mark to do your job. Mark told me he couldn't because he had some important homework to do."

"That's true," put in Mark defensively, "but then I realized it was just an excuse, and so I did it anyway."

"So . . . who emptied the dishwasher? The person who said yes or the one who said no?" asked Mother.

"I guess it was the one who said no," said Laura.

"That's right," said Mother. "And that's the kind of thing I see happening with your friends."

Dad nodded. "Laura has always gone to church, and she seemed to have said yes to God. But now her actions seem to show that she never really said yes in her heart. We need to pray that Laura will say a true yes to God and show it by her life. On the other hand, Jay said no to God for several years, but once he said yes, he meant it. We know that by his actions."

"We all need to be sure our lives show that we're saying yes to God by the things that we do," added Mother.

Faith in Action
Memory Verse

In response to all he has done for us, let us outdo each other in being helpful and kind to each other and in doing good.
Hebrews 10:24

How About You?
Have you said yes to Jesus in words? That's good, but what are your actions saying? Do they show that your yes was genuine? Does your language reflect it? Remember, actions often speak louder than words. Make sure your actions are a testimony for Jesus. L. W.

• For the next devotional, turn to page 925. • For the next devotional on *FAITH IN ACTION*, turn to page 1217.
• For notes on *FAITH IN ACTION*, see pages 583, 846, 1068, and 1232.

²⁰Then the mother of James and John, the sons of Zebedee, brought them to Jesus and respectfully asked a favor.

²¹"What is your request?" he asked. She replied, "In your Kingdom, will you let my two sons sit on two thrones next to yours?"

²²But Jesus told her, "You don't know what you are asking!" Then he turned to James and John and asked them, "Are you able to drink from the terrible cup I am about to drink from?"

"Yes," they replied, "we are able!"

²³"You shall indeed drink from it," he told them. "But I have no right to say who will sit on the thrones next to mine. Those places are reserved for the persons my Father selects."

²⁴The other ten disciples were indignant when they heard what James and John had asked for.

²⁵But Jesus called them together and said, "Among the heathen, kings are tyrants and each minor official lords it over those beneath him. ²⁶But among you it is quite different. Anyone wanting to be a leader among you must be your servant. ²⁷And if you want to be right at the top, you must serve like a slave. ²⁸Your attitude must be like my own, for I, the Messiah, did not come to be served, but to serve, and to give my life as a ransom for many."

²⁹As Jesus and the disciples left the city of Jericho, a vast crowd surged along behind.

³⁰Two blind men were sitting beside the road, and when they heard that Jesus was coming that way, they began shouting, "Sir, King David's Son, have mercy on us!"

³¹The crowd told them to be quiet, but they only yelled the louder.

³²,³³When Jesus came to the place where they were, he stopped in the road and called, "What do you want me to do for you?"

"Sir," they said, "we want to see!"

³⁴Jesus was moved with pity for them and touched their eyes. And instantly they could see, and followed him.

21 Jesus Rides into Jerusalem

As Jesus and the disciples approached Jerusalem, and were near the town of Bethphage on the Mount of Olives, Jesus sent two of them into the village ahead.

²"Just as you enter," he said, "you will see a donkey tied there, with its colt beside it. Untie them and bring them here. ³If anyone asks you what you are doing, just say, 'The Master needs them,' and there will be no trouble."

⁴This was done to fulfill the ancient prophecy, ⁵"Tell Jerusalem her King is coming to her, riding humbly on a donkey's colt!"

⁶The two disciples did as Jesus said, ⁷and brought the animals to him and threw their garments over the colt for him to ride on. ⁸And some in the crowd threw down their coats along the road ahead of him, and others cut branches from the trees and spread them out before him.

⁹Then the crowds surged on ahead and pressed along behind, shouting, "God bless King David's Son!" . . . "God's Man is here!". . . Bless him, Lord!" . . . "Praise God in highest heaven!"

¹⁰The entire city of Jerusalem was stirred as he entered. "Who is this?" they asked.

¹¹And the crowds replied, "It's Jesus, the prophet from Nazareth up in Galilee."

¹²Jesus went into the Temple, drove out the merchants, and knocked over the moneychangers' tables and the stalls of those selling doves.

¹³"The Scriptures say my Temple is a place of prayer," he declared, "but you have turned it into a den of thieves."

¹⁴And now the blind and crippled came to him, and he healed them there in the Temple. ¹⁵But when the chief priests and other Jewish leaders saw these wonderful miracles and heard even the little children in the Temple shouting, "God bless the Son of David," they were disturbed and indignant and asked him, "Do you hear what these children are saying?"

¹⁶"Yes," Jesus replied. "Didn't you ever read the Scriptures? For they say, 'Even little babies shall praise him!'"

¹⁷Then he returned to Bethany, where he stayed overnight.

¹⁸In the morning, as he was returning to Jerusalem, he was hungry ¹⁹and noticed a fig tree beside the road. He went over to see if there were any figs, but there were only leaves. Then he said to it, "Never bear fruit again!" And soon the fig tree withered up.

²⁰The disciples were utterly amazed and asked, "How did the fig tree wither so quickly?"

²¹Then Jesus told them, "Truly, if you have faith and don't doubt, you can do things like this and much more. You can even say to this Mount of Olives, 'Move over into the ocean,' and it will. ²²You can get anything—*anything* you ask for in prayer—if you believe."

²³When he had returned to the Temple and was teaching, the chief priests and other Jewish leaders came up to him and de-

---

SERVING GOD WILLINGLY 20:27 Jesus described leadership from a new perspective. Instead of using people, we are to *serve* them. Jesus' purpose in life was to serve others and to give his life away. A real leader has a servant's heart. He appreciates others' worth and realizes he's not above any job. If you see something that needs to be done, don't wait to be asked. Take the initiative and do it like a faithful servant. **To begin the series of devotionals on SERVING GOD WILLINGLY, turn to page 291.**

manded to know by whose authority he had thrown out the merchants the day before.

24"I'll tell you if you answer one question first," Jesus replied. 25"Was John the Baptist sent from God or not?"

They talked it over among themselves. "If we say, 'From God,'" they said, "then he will ask why we didn't believe what John said. 26And if we deny that God sent him, we'll be mobbed, for the crowd all think he was a prophet." 27So they finally replied, "We don't know!"

And Jesus said, "Then I won't answer your question either.

28"But what do you think about this? A man with two sons told the older boy, 'Son, go out and work on the farm today.' 29'I won't,' he answered, but later he changed his mind and went. 30Then the father told the youngest, 'You go!' and he said, 'Yes, sir, I will.' But he didn't. 31Which of the two was obeying his father?"

They replied, "The first, of course."

Then Jesus explained his meaning: "Surely evil men and prostitutes will get into the Kingdom before you do. 32For John the Baptist told you to repent and turn to God, and you wouldn't, while very evil men and prostitutes did. And even when you saw this happening, you refused to repent, and so you couldn't believe.

33"Now listen to this story: A certain landowner planted a vineyard with a hedge around it, and built a platform for the watchman, then leased the vineyard to some farmers on a sharecrop basis, and went away to live in another country.

34"At the time of the grape harvest he sent his agents to the farmers to collect his share. 35But the farmers attacked his men, beat one, killed one, and stoned another.

36"Then he sent a larger group of his men to collect for him, but the results were the same. 37Finally the owner sent his son, thinking they would surely respect him.

38"But when these farmers saw the son coming they said among themselves, 'Here comes the heir to this estate; come on, let's kill him and get it for ourselves!' 39So they dragged him out of the vineyard and killed him.

40"When the owner returns, what do you think he will do to those farmers?"

41The Jewish leaders replied, "He will put the wicked men to a horrible death and lease the vineyard to others who will pay him promptly."

42Then Jesus asked them, "Didn't you ever read in the Scriptures: 'The stone rejected by the builders has been made the honored cornerstone; how remarkable! what an amazing thing the Lord has done'?

43"What I mean is that the Kingdom of God shall be taken away from you, and given to a nation that will give God his share of the crop. 44All who stumble on this rock of truth shall be broken, but those it falls on will be scattered as dust."

45When the chief priests and other Jewish leaders realized that Jesus was talking about them—that they were the farmers in his story—46they wanted to get rid of him but were afraid to try because of the crowds, for they accepted Jesus as a prophet.

22 A Story about a Wedding

Jesus told several other stories to show what the Kingdom of Heaven is like.

"For instance," he said, "it can be illustrated by the story of a king who prepared a great wedding dinner for his son. 3Many guests were invited, and when the banquet was ready he sent messengers to notify everyone that it was time to come. But all refused! 4So he sent other servants to tell them, 'Everything is ready and the roast is in the oven. Hurry!'

5"But the guests he had invited merely laughed and went on about their business, one to his farm, another to his store; 6others beat up his messengers and treated them shamefully, even killing some of them.

7"Then the angry king sent out his army and destroyed the murderers and burned their city. 8And he said to his servants, 'The wedding feast is ready, and the guests I invited aren't worthy of the honor. 9Now go out to the street corners and invite everyone you see.'

10"So the servants did, and brought in all they could find, good and bad alike; and the banquet hall was filled with guests. 11But when the king came in to meet the guests, he noticed a man who wasn't wearing the wedding robe [provided for him].

12"'Friend,' he asked, 'how does it happen that you are here without a wedding robe?' And the man had no reply.

13"Then the king said to his aides, 'Bind him hand and foot and throw him out into the outer darkness where there is weeping and gnashing of teeth.' 14For many are called, but few are chosen."

15Then the Pharisees met together to try to think of some way to trap Jesus into saying something for which they could arrest him. 16They decided to send some of their men along with the Herodians to ask him this question: "Sir, we know you are very honest and teach the truth regardless of the consequences, without fear or favor. 17Now tell us, is it right to pay taxes to the Roman government or not?"

18But Jesus saw what they were after. "You hypocrites!" he exclaimed. "Who are you trying to fool with your trick questions? ¹⁹Here, show me a coin." And they handed him a penny.

²⁰"Whose picture is stamped on it?" he asked them. "And whose name is this beneath the picture?"

²¹"Caesar's," they replied.

"Well, then," he said, "give it to Caesar if it is his, and give God everything that belongs to God."

²²His reply surprised and baffled them, and they went away.

²³But that same day some of the Sadducees, who say there is no resurrection after death, came to him and asked, ²⁴"Sir, Moses said that if a man died without children, his brother should marry the widow and their children would get all the dead man's property. ²⁵Well, we had among us a family of seven brothers. The first of these men married and then died, without children, so his widow became the second brother's wife. ²⁶This brother also died without children, and the wife was passed to the next brother, and so on until she had been the wife of each of them. ²⁷And then she also died. ²⁸So whose wife will she be in the resurrection? For she was the wife of all seven of them!"

²⁹But Jesus said, "Your error is caused by your ignorance of the Scriptures and of God's power! ³⁰For in the resurrection there is no marriage; everyone is as the angels in heaven. ³¹But now, as to whether there is a resurrection of the dead—don't you ever read the Scriptures? Don't you realize that God was speaking directly to you when he said, ³²'I *am* the God of Abraham, Isaac, and Jacob'? So God is not the God of the dead, but of the *living*."

³³The crowds were profoundly impressed by his answers—³⁴,³⁵but not the Pharisees! When they heard that he had routed the Sadducees with his reply, they thought up a fresh question of their own to ask him. One of them, a lawyer, spoke up: ³⁶"Sir, which is the most important command in the laws of Moses?"

³⁷Jesus replied, "'Love the Lord your God with all your heart, soul, and mind.' ³⁸,³⁹This is the first and greatest commandment. The second most important is similar: 'Love your neighbor as much as you love yourself.' ⁴⁰All the other commandments and all the demands of the prophets stem from these two laws and are fulfilled if you obey them. Keep only these and you will find that you are obeying all the others."

⁴¹Then, surrounded by the Pharisees, he asked them a question: ⁴²"What about the Messiah? Whose son is he?"

"The son of David," they replied.

⁴³"Then why does David, speaking under the inspiration of the Holy Spirit, call him 'Lord'?" Jesus asked. "For David said,

⁴⁴'God said to my Lord, Sit at my right hand until I put your enemies beneath your feet.'

⁴⁵Since David called him 'Lord,' how can he be merely his son?"

⁴⁶They had no answer. And after that no one dared ask him any more questions.

23 Jesus Warns the People

Then Jesus said to the crowds, and to his disciples, ²"You would think these Jewish leaders and these Pharisees were Moses, the way they keep making up so many laws! ³And of course you should obey their every whim! It may be all right to do what they say, but above anything else, *don't follow their example.* For they don't do what they tell you to do. ⁴They load you with impossible demands that they themselves don't even try to keep.

⁵"Everything they do is done for show. They act holy by wearing on their arms little prayer boxes with Scripture verses inside, and by lengthening the memorial fringes of their robes. ⁶And how they love to sit at the head table at banquets and in the reserved pews in the synagogue! ⁷How they enjoy the deference paid them on the streets and to be called 'Rabbi' and 'Master'! ⁸Don't ever let anyone call you that. For only God is your Rabbi and all of you are on the same level, as brothers. ⁹And don't address anyone here on earth as 'Father,' for only God in heaven should be addressed like that. ¹⁰And don't be called 'Master,' for only one is your master, even the Messiah.

¹¹"The more lowly your service to others, the greater you are. To be the greatest, be a servant. ¹²But those who think themselves great shall be disappointed and humbled; and those who humble themselves shall be exalted.

¹³,¹⁴"Woe to you, Pharisees, and you other religious leaders. Hypocrites! For you won't let others enter the Kingdom of Heaven and won't go in yourselves. And you pretend to be holy, with all your long, public prayers in the streets, while you are evicting widows from their homes. Hypocrites! ¹⁵Yes, woe upon you hypocrites. For you go to all lengths to make one convert, and then turn him into twice the son of hell you are yourselves. ¹⁶Blind guides! Woe upon you! For your

---

SERVING GOD WILLINGLY 23:11-12 Jesus challenged society's norms. To him, greatness comes from serving—giving of yourself to help God and others. Service keeps us aware of others' needs, and it stops us from focusing only on ourselves. Jesus came as a servant. What kind of greatness do you seek? **To begin the series of devotionals on SERVING GOD WILLINGLY, turn to page 291.**

rule is that to swear 'By God's Temple' means nothing—you can break that oath, but to swear 'By the gold in the Temple' is binding! [17]Blind fools! Which is greater, the gold, or the Temple that sanctifies the gold? [18]And you say that to take an oath 'By the altar' can be broken, but to swear 'By the gifts on the altar' is binding! [19]Blind! For which is greater, the gift on the altar, or the altar itself that sanctifies the gift? [20]When you swear 'By the altar' you are swearing by it and everything on it, [21]and when you swear 'By the Temple' you are swearing by it and by God who lives in it. [22]And when you swear 'By heavens' you are swearing by the Throne of God and by God himself.

[23]"Yes, woe upon you, Pharisees, and you other religious leaders—hypocrites! For you tithe down to the last mint leaf in your garden, but ignore the important things—justice and mercy and faith. Yes, you should tithe, but you shouldn't leave the more important things undone. [24]Blind guides! You strain out a gnat and swallow a camel.

[25]"Woe to you, Pharisees, and you religious leaders—hypocrites! You are so careful to polish the outside of the cup, but the inside is foul with extortion and greed. [26]Blind Pharisees! First cleanse the inside of the cup, and then the whole cup will be clean.

[27]"Woe to you, Pharisees, and you religious leaders! You are like beautiful mausoleums—full of dead men's bones, and of foulness and corruption. [28]You try to look like saintly men, but underneath those pious robes of yours are hearts besmirched with every sort of hypocrisy and sin.

[29,30]"Yes, woe to you, Pharisees, and you religious leaders—hypocrites! For you build monuments to the prophets killed by your fathers and lay flowers on the graves of the godly men they destroyed, and say, 'We certainly would never have acted as our fathers did.'

[31]"In saying that, you are accusing yourselves of being the sons of wicked men. [32]And you are following in their steps, filling up the full measure of their evil. [33]Snakes! Sons of vipers! How shall you escape the judgment of hell?

[34]"I will send you prophets, and wise men, and inspired writers, and you will kill some by crucifixion, and rip open the backs of others with whips in your synagogues, and hound them from city to city, [35]so that you will become guilty of all the blood of murdered godly men from righteous Abel to Zechariah (son of Barachiah), slain by you in the Temple between the altar and the sanctuary. [36]Yes, all the accumulated judgment of the centuries shall break upon the heads of this very generation.

[37]"O Jerusalem, Jerusalem, the city that kills the prophets and stones all those God sends to her! How often I have wanted to gather your children together as a hen gathers her chicks beneath her wings, but you wouldn't let me. [38]And now your house is left to you, desolate. [39]For I tell you this, you will never see me again until you are ready to welcome the one sent to you from God."

24 Jesus Tells about the Future

As Jesus was leaving the Temple grounds, his disciples came along and wanted to take him on a tour of the various Temple buildings.

[2]But he told them, "All these buildings will be knocked down, with not one stone left on top of another!"

[3]"When will this happen?" the disciples asked him later, as he sat on the slopes of the Mount of Olives. "What events will signal your return and the end of the world?"

[4]Jesus told them, "Don't let anyone fool you. [5]For many will come claiming to be the Messiah and will lead many astray. [6]When you hear of wars beginning, this does not signal my return; these must come, but the end is not yet. [7]The nations and kingdoms of the earth will rise against each other, and there will be famines and earthquakes in many places. [8]But all this will be only the beginning of the horrors to come.

[9]"Then you will be tortured and killed and hated all over the world because you are mine, [10]and many of you shall fall back into sin and betray and hate each other. [11]And many false prophets will appear and lead many astray. [12]Sin will be rampant everywhere and will cool the love of many. [13]But those enduring to the end shall be saved.

[14]"And the Good News about the Kingdom will be preached throughout the whole world, so that all nations will hear it, and then, finally, the end will come.

[15]"So, when you see the horrible thing (told about by Daniel the prophet) standing in a holy place (Note to the reader: You know what is meant!), [16]then those in Judea must flee into the Judean hills. [17]Those on their porches must not even go inside to pack before they flee. [18]Those in the fields should not return to their homes for their clothes.

[19]"And woe to pregnant women and to those with babies in those days. [20]And pray that your flight will not be in winter, or on the Sabbath. [21]For there will be persecution such as the world has never before seen in all its history and will never see again.

[22]"In fact, unless those days are shortened, all mankind will perish. But they will be shortened for the sake of God's chosen people.

23"Then if anyone tells you, 'The Messiah has arrived at such and such a place, or has appeared here or there,' don't believe it. 24For false Christs shall arise, and false prophets, and will do wonderful miracles so that if it were possible, even God's chosen ones would be deceived. 25See, I have warned you.

26"So if someone tells you the Messiah has returned and is out in the desert, don't bother to go and look. Or, that he is hiding at a certain place, don't believe it! 27For as the lightning flashes across the sky from east to west, so shall my coming be, when I, the Messiah, return. 28And wherever the carcass is, there the vultures will gather.

29"Immediately after the persecution of those days the sun will be darkened, and the moon will not give light, and the stars will seem to fall from the heavens, and the powers overshadowing the earth will be convulsed.

30"And then at last the signal of my coming will appear in the heavens, and there will be deep mourning all around the earth. And the nations of the world will see me arrive in the clouds of heaven, with power and great glory. 31And I shall send forth my angels with the sound of a mighty trumpet blast, and they shall gather my chosen ones from the farthest ends of the earth and heaven.

32"Now learn a lesson from the fig tree. When her branch is tender and the leaves begin to sprout, you know that summer is almost here. 33Just so, when you see all these things beginning to happen, you can know that my return is near, even at the doors. 34Then at last this age will come to its close.

35"Heaven and earth will disappear, but my words remain forever.36But no one knows the date and hour when the end will be—not even the angels. No, nor even God's Son. Only the Father knows.

37,38"The world will be at ease—banquets and parties and weddings—just as it was in Noah's time before the sudden coming of the flood; 39people wouldn't believe what was going to happen until the flood actually arrived and took them all away. So shall my coming be.

40"Two men will be working together in the fields, and one will be taken, the other left. 41Two women will be going about their household tasks; one will be taken, the other left.

42"So be prepared, for you don't know what day your Lord is coming.

43"Just as a man can prevent trouble from thieves by keeping watch for them, 44so you can avoid trouble by always being ready for my unannounced return.

45"Are you a wise and faithful servant of the Lord? Have I given you the task of managing my household, to feed my children day by day? 46Blessings on you if I return and find you faithfully doing your work. 47I will put such faithful ones in charge of everything I own!

48"But if you are evil and say to yourself, 'My Lord won't be coming for a while,' 49and begin oppressing your fellow servants, partying and getting drunk, 50your Lord will arrive unannounced and unexpected, 51and severely whip you and send you off to the judgment of the hypocrites; there will be weeping and gnashing of teeth.

25 A Story about Ten Bridesmaids

"The Kingdom of Heaven can be illustrated by the story of ten bridesmaids who took their lamps and went to meet the bridegroom. 2-4But only five of them were wise enough to fill their lamps with oil, while the other five were foolish and forgot.

5,6"So, when the bridegroom was delayed, they lay down to rest until midnight, when they were roused by the shout, 'The bridegroom is coming! Come out and welcome him!'

7,8"All the girls jumped up and trimmed their lamps. Then the five who hadn't any oil begged the others to share with them, for their lamps were going out.

9"But the others replied, 'We haven't enough. Go instead to the shops and buy some for yourselves.'

10"But while they were gone, the bridegroom came, and those who were ready went in with him to the marriage feast, and the door was locked.

11"Later, when the other five returned, they stood outside, calling, 'Sir, open the door for us!'

12"But he called back, 'Go away! It is too late!'

13"So stay awake and be prepared, for you do not know the date or moment of my return.

14"Again, the Kingdom of Heaven can be illustrated by the story of a man going into another country, who called together his servants and loaned them money to invest for him while he was gone.

15"He gave $5,000 to one, $2,000 to another, and $1,000 to the last—dividing it in proportion to their abilities—and then left on his trip. 16The man who received the $5,000 began immediately to buy and sell with it and soon earned another $5,000. 17The man with $2,000 went right to work, too, and earned another $2,000.

18"But the man who received the $1,000 dug a hole in the ground and hid the money for safekeeping.

19"After a long time their master returned from his trip and called them to him to account for his money. 20The man to whom he had entrusted the $5,000 brought him $10,000.

21"His master praised him for good work. 'You

Family Devotions

☐ DEVOTION 257
KEEPING YOUR PROMISES

Read Matthew 25:14-23

Jimmy was confused. "Mom," he said, "I've been trying to learn the fruit of the Spirit, and the seventh one is faithfulness. I don't understand how that can be one of them since it takes faith to become a Christian in the first place."

Mom smiled. "That's true," she agreed, "but the Bible also tells us to have faith after we're Christians. For example, when we pray, we are to have faith that God will answer. But I think there's something else here, too. Do you understand the word *faithfulness*?"

Jimmy nodded. "Dad always says that Tippy is a faithful old dog. I guess that means she's always here when I need her," he said.

Mom laughed. "Yes, we got Tippy to be a companion to you, and she faithfully does her job, doesn't she? In much the same way, we should be faithful in what we do."

The next day Jimmy had a job to do. Mrs. King lived three doors down the street, and she was old and sick. At the beginning of the summer she had hired Jimmy to take care of mowing her grass for the whole summer. They had made a bargain that Jimmy would mow the lawn every Friday morning, and she would pay him ten dollars each time. Just as Jimmy was putting gas in the mower, some of his friends approached.

"Hey, Jim! A bunch of us are going to play baseball. C'mon," they urged. "We need a good third baseman."

Now there was nothing Jimmy would rather do than play baseball, so he put the gas can away and reached for his mitt. But just then old Tippy came running around the corner of the garage. Stopping, Jimmy thought about his conversation with Mom yesterday. *The fruit of the Spirit is faithfulness,* he remembered. Reaching down, he patted Tippy on the head and called to his friends, "You guys go on! I have a job to do right now."

Keeping Your Promises Memory Verse

God delights in those who keep their promises and abhors those who don't.
Proverbs 12:22

How About You?

When someone gives you a job to do, do you do it faithfully, no matter how large or small it is? Perhaps the job God has given you right now is to help Mom, mow the lawn, or be a good student. Are you faithful in whatever it is that he has given you to do? When you stand before him someday, will you hear the words, "Good work. You are a good and faithful servant"? R. P.

• For the next devotional, turn to page 927.   • For the next devotional on KEEPING YOUR PROMISES, turn to page 985.
• For notes on KEEPING YOUR PROMISES, see pages 183, 284, and 838.

have been faithful in handling this small amount,' he told him, 'so now I will give you many more responsibilities. Begin the joyous tasks I have assigned to you.'

22"Next came the man who had received the $2,000, with the report, 'Sir, you gave me $2,000 to use, and I have doubled it.'

23"'Good work,' his master said. 'You are a good and faithful servant. You have been faithful over this small amount, so now I will give you much more.'

24,25"Then the man with the $1,000 came and said, 'Sir, I knew you were a hard man, and I was afraid you would rob me of what I earned, so I hid your money in the earth and here it is!'

26"But his master replied, 'Wicked man! Lazy slave! Since you knew I would demand your profit, 27you should at least have put my money into the bank so I could have some interest. 28Take the money from this man and give it to the man with the $10,000. 29For the man who uses well what he is given shall be given more, and he shall have abundance. But from the man who is unfaithful, even what little responsibility he has shall be taken from him. 30And throw the useless servant out into outer darkness: there shall be weeping and gnashing of teeth.'

31"But when I, the Messiah, shall come in my glory, and all the angels with me, then I shall sit upon my throne of glory. 32And all the nations shall be gathered before me. And I will separate the people as a shepherd separates the sheep from the goats, 33and place the sheep at my right hand, and the goats at my left.

34"Then I, the King, shall say to those at my right, 'Come, blessed of my Father, into the Kingdom prepared for you from the founding of the world. 35For I was hungry and you fed me; I was thirsty and you gave me water; I was a stranger and you invited me into your homes; 36naked and you clothed me; sick and in prison, and you visited me.'

37"Then these righteous ones will reply, 'Sir, when did we ever see you hungry and feed you? Or thirsty and give you anything to drink? 38Or a stranger, and help you? Or naked, and clothe you? 39When did we ever see you sick or in prison, and visit you?'

40"And I, the King, will tell them, 'When you did it to these my brothers you were doing it to me!' 41Then I will turn to those on my left and say, 'Away with you, you cursed ones, into the eternal fire prepared for the devil and his demons. 42For I was hungry and you wouldn't feed me; thirsty, and you wouldn't give me anything to drink; 43a stranger, and you refused me hospitality; naked, and you wouldn't clothe me; sick, and in prison, and you didn't visit me.'

44"Then they will reply, 'Lord, when did we ever see you hungry or thirsty or a stranger or naked or sick or in prison, and not help you?'

45"And I will answer, 'When you refused to help the least of these my brothers, you were refusing help to me.'

46"And they shall go away into eternal punishment; but the righteous into everlasting life."

26 A Story about Talents

When Jesus had finished this talk with his disciples, he told them,

2"As you know, the Passover celebration begins in two days, and I shall be betrayed and crucified."

3At that very moment the chief priests and other Jewish officials were meeting at the residence of Caiaphas the High Priest, 4to discuss ways of capturing Jesus quietly and killing him. 5"But not during the Passover celebration," they agreed, "for there would be a riot."

6Jesus now proceeded to Bethany, to the home of Simon the leper. 7While he was eating, a woman came in with a bottle of very expensive perfume and poured it over his head.

8,9The disciples were indignant. "What a waste of good money," they said. "Why, she could have sold it for a fortune and given it to the poor."

10Jesus knew what they were thinking and said, "Why are you criticizing her? For she has done a good thing to me. 11You will always have the poor among you, but you won't always have me. 12She has poured this perfume on me to prepare my body for burial. 13And she will always be remembered for this deed. The story of what she has done will be told throughout the whole world, wherever the Good News is preached."

14Then Judas Iscariot, one of the twelve apostles, went to the chief priests 15and asked, "How much will you pay me to get Jesus into your hands?" And they gave him thirty silver coins. 16From that time on, Judas watched for an opportunity to betray Jesus to them.

17On the first day of the Passover ceremonies, when bread made with yeast was purged from every Jewish home, the disciples came to Jesus and asked, "Where shall we plan to eat the Passover?"

18He replied, "Go into the city and see Mr. So-and-So, and tell him, 'Our Master says, my time has come, and I will eat the Passover meal with my disciples at your house.'" 19So the disciples did as he told them and prepared the supper there.

20,21That evening as he sat eating with the Twelve, he said, "One of you will betray me."

22Sorrow chilled their hearts, and each one asked, "Am I the one?"

23He replied, "It is the one I served first. 24For I must die just as was prophesied, but woe to the

Family Devotions

☐ **Devotion 258**
Sharing Your Faith

Read Matthew 26:69-75

"Hey, Matt!" called Billy from the other side of the playground. "Where were you last night? I called your house at least six times, but you weren't home. I wanted to know if you could go to the video arcade."

"Oh, well, we were . . . uh . . . out," Matt stammered. He didn't want to tell Billy he had been at church. They were having a missionary conference, and Matt enjoyed the speakers. But Billy wouldn't understand! He'd only laugh.

"How about tonight?" Billy asked. "They've got a new game. I tried it a couple of times, and it's a blast!"

"Well, we're going to be busy again tonight," Matt said. The conference lasted all week, and Matt's family was going to attend each night.

"Tomorrow night?"

"No, I can't."

"What does your family do every night?" asked Billy. "No one goes out that much!"

Again Matt hesitated. Then it hit him: Here he was, going to a missionary conference and praying for the missionaries to reach more people for the Lord, yet he didn't even have the courage to admit to one of his closest friends that he was going to church! Something was wrong, but Matt knew he could correct it!

"Billy," he began, "we're having a missionary conference at church, and our whole family is going. In fact, maybe you'd like to come, too?"

Sharing Your Faith Memory Verse

And I assure you of this: I, the Messiah, will publicly honor you in the presence of God's angels if you publicly acknowledge me here on earth as your Friend.
Luke 12:8

How About You?

Are you ashamed to tell your friends you go to church? Are you ashamed to tell them about Christ? Do you deny that you love him by your actions if not by your words? Should you, like Peter, be "crying bitterly" because you've denied the Lord Jesus Christ? Don't feel embarrassed to talk about him. Look for opportunities to tell your friends about your relationship with the Lord. L. M. W.

• For the next devotional, turn to page 931.   • For the next devotional on *Sharing Your Faith,* turn to page 957.
• For notes on *Sharing Your Faith,* see pages 462, 776, 1015, and 1074.

man by whom I am betrayed. Far better for that one if he had never been born."

²⁵Judas, too, had asked him, "Rabbi, am I the one?" And Jesus had told him, "Yes."

²⁶As they were eating, Jesus took a small loaf of bread and blessed it and broke it apart and gave it to the disciples and said, "Take it and eat it, for this is my body."

²⁷And he took a cup of wine and gave thanks for it and gave it to them and said, "Each one drink from it, ²⁸for this is my blood, sealing the New Covenant. It is poured out to forgive the sins of multitudes. ²⁹Mark my words—I will not drink this wine again until the day I drink it new with you in my Father's Kingdom."

³⁰And when they had sung a hymn, they went out to the Mount of Olives.

³¹Then Jesus said to them, "Tonight you will all desert me. For it is written in the Scriptures that God will smite the Shepherd, and the sheep of the flock will be scattered. ³²But after I have been brought back to life again, I will go to Galilee and meet you there."

³³Peter declared, "If everyone else deserts you, I won't."

³⁴Jesus told him, "The truth is that this very night, before the cock crows at dawn, you will deny me three times!"

³⁵"I would die first!" Peter insisted. And all the other disciples said the same thing.

³⁶Then Jesus brought them to a garden grove, Gethsemane, and told them to sit down and wait while he went on ahead to pray. ³⁷He took Peter with him and Zebedee's two sons James and John, and began to be filled with anguish and despair.

³⁸Then he told them, "My soul is crushed with horror and sadness to the point of death . . . stay here . . . stay awake with me."

³⁹He went forward a little, and fell face downward on the ground, and prayed, "My Father! If it is possible, let this cup be taken away from me. But I want your will, not mine."

⁴⁰Then he returned to the three disciples and found them asleep. "Peter," he called, "couldn't you even stay awake with me one hour? ⁴¹Keep alert and pray. Otherwise temptation will overpower you. For the spirit indeed is willing, but how weak the body is!"

⁴²Again he left them and prayed, "My Father! If this cup cannot go away until I drink it all, your will be done."

⁴³He returned to them again and found them sleeping, for their eyes were heavy, ⁴⁴so he went back to prayer the third time, saying the same things again.

⁴⁵Then he came to the disciples and said, "Sleep on now and take your rest . . . but no! The time has come! I am betrayed into the hands of evil men! ⁴⁶Up! Let's be going! Look! Here comes the man who is betraying me!"

⁴⁷At that very moment while he was still speaking, Judas, one of the Twelve, arrived with a great crowd armed with swords and clubs, sent by the Jewish leaders. ⁴⁸Judas had told them to arrest the man he greeted, for that would be the one they were after. ⁴⁹So now Judas came straight to Jesus and said, "Hello, Master!" and embraced him in friendly fashion.

⁵⁰Jesus said, "My friend, go ahead and do what you have come for." Then the others grabbed him.

⁵¹One of the men with Jesus pulled out a sword and slashed off the ear of the High Priest's servant.

⁵²"Put away your sword," Jesus told him. "Those using swords will get killed. ⁵³Don't you realize that I could ask my Father for thousands of angels to protect us, and he would send them instantly? ⁵⁴But if I did, how would the Scriptures be fulfilled that describe what is happening now?" ⁵⁵Then Jesus spoke to the crowd. "Am I some dangerous criminal," he asked, "that you had to arm yourselves with swords and clubs before you could arrest me? I was with you teaching daily in the Temple and you didn't stop me then. ⁵⁶But this is all happening to fulfill the words of the prophets as recorded in the Scriptures."

At that point, all the disciples deserted him and fled.

⁵⁷Then the mob led him to the home of Caiaphas, the High Priest, where all the Jewish leaders were gathering. ⁵⁸Meanwhile, Peter was following far to the rear, and came to the courtyard of the High Priest's house and went in and sat with the soldiers, and waited to see what was going to be done to Jesus.

⁵⁹The chief priests and, in fact, the entire Jewish Supreme Court assembled there and looked for witnesses who would lie about Jesus, in order to build a case against him that would result in a death sentence. ⁶⁰,⁶¹But even though they found many who agreed to be false witnesses, these always contradicted each other.

Finally two men were found who declared, "This man said, 'I am able to destroy the Temple of God and rebuild it in three days.'"

⁶²Then the High Priest stood up and said to Jesus, "Well, what about it? Did you say that, or didn't you?" ⁶³But Jesus remained silent.

Then the High Priest said to him, "I demand in the name of the living God that you tell us whether you claim to be the Messiah, the Son of God."

⁶⁴"Yes," Jesus said, "I am. And in the future you will see me, the Messiah, sitting at the right hand of God and returning on the clouds of heaven."

⁶⁵,⁶⁶Then the High Priest tore at his own clothing, shouting, "Blasphemy! What need have we for

other witnesses? You have all heard him say it! What is your verdict?"

They shouted, "Death!—Death!—Death!"

⁶⁷Then they spat in his face and struck him and some slapped him, ⁶⁸saying, "Prophesy to us, you Messiah! Who struck you that time?"

⁶⁹Meanwhile, as Peter was sitting in the courtyard, a girl came over and said to him, "You were with Jesus, for both of you are from Galilee."

⁷⁰But Peter denied it loudly. "I don't even know what you are talking about," he angrily declared.

⁷¹Later, out by the gate, another girl noticed him and said to those standing around, "This man was with Jesus—from Nazareth."

⁷²Again Peter denied it, this time with an oath. "I don't even know the man," he said.

⁷³But after a while the men who had been standing there came over to him and said, "We know you are one of his disciples, for we can tell by your Galilean accent."

⁷⁴Peter began to curse and swear. "I don't even know the man," he said.

And immediately the cock crowed. ⁷⁵Then Peter remembered what Jesus had said, "Before the cock crows, you will deny me three times." And he went away, crying bitterly.

27 Judas Hangs Himself

When it was morning, the chief priests and Jewish leaders met again to discuss how to induce the Roman government to sentence Jesus to death. ²Then they sent him in chains to Pilate, the Roman governor.

³About that time Judas, who betrayed him, when he saw that Jesus had been condemned to die, changed his mind and deeply regretted what he had done, and brought back the money to the chief priests and other Jewish leaders

⁴"I have sinned," he declared, "for I have betrayed an innocent man."

"That's your problem," they retorted.

⁵Then he threw the money onto the floor of the Temple and went out and hanged himself. ⁶The chief priests picked the money up. "We can't put it in the collection," they said, "since it's against our laws to accept money paid for murder."

⁷They talked it over and finally decided to buy a certain field where the clay was used by potters, and to make it into a cemetery for foreigners who died in Jerusalem. ⁸That is why the cemetery is still called "The Field of Blood."

⁹This fulfilled the prophecy of Jeremiah which says,

"They took the thirty pieces of silver—the price at which he was valued by the people of Israel—¹⁰and purchased a field from the potters as the Lord directed me."

¹¹Now Jesus was standing before Pilate, the Roman governor. "Are you the Jews' Messiah?" the governor asked him.

"Yes," Jesus replied.

¹²But when the chief priests and other Jewish leaders made their many accusations against him, Jesus remained silent.

¹³"Don't you hear what they are saying?" Pilate demanded.

¹⁴But Jesus said nothing, much to the governor's surprise.

¹⁵Now the governor's custom was to release one Jewish prisoner each year during the Passover celebration—anyone they wanted. ¹⁶This year there was a particularly notorious criminal in jail named Barabbas, ¹⁷and as the crowds gathered before Pilate's house that morning he asked them, "Which shall I release to you—Barabbas, or Jesus your Messiah?" ¹⁸For he knew very well that the Jewish leaders had arrested Jesus out of envy because of his popularity with the people.

¹⁹Just then, as he was presiding over the court, Pilate's wife sent him this message: "Leave that good man alone; for I had a terrible nightmare concerning him last night."

²⁰Meanwhile the chief priests and Jewish officials persuaded the crowds to ask for Barabbas' release, and for Jesus' death. ²¹So when the governor asked again, "Which of these two shall I release to you?" the crowd shouted back their reply: "Barabbas!"

²²"Then what shall I do with Jesus, your Messiah?" Pilate asked.

And they shouted, "Crucify him!"

²³"Why?" Pilate demanded. "What has he done wrong?" But they kept shouting, "Crucify! Crucify!"

²⁴When Pilate saw that he wasn't getting anywhere and that a riot was developing, he sent for a bowl of water and washed his hands before the crowd, saying, "I am innocent of the blood of this good man. The responsibility is yours!"

²⁵And the mob yelled back, "His blood be on us and on our children!"

²⁶Then Pilate released Barabbas to them. And after he had whipped Jesus, he gave him to the Roman soldiers to take away and crucify.

²⁷But first they took him into the armory and called out the entire contingent. ²⁸They stripped him and put a scarlet robe on him, ²⁹and made a crown from long thorns and put it on his head, and placed a stick in his right hand as a scepter and knelt before him in mockery. "Hail, King of the Jews," they yelled. ³⁰And they spat on him and grabbed the stick and beat him on the head with it.

³¹After the mockery, they took off the robe and put his own garment on him again, and took him out to crucify him.

³²As they were on the way to the execution grounds they came across a man from Cyrene, in Africa—Simon was his name—and forced him to carry Jesus' cross. ³³Then they went out to an area known as Golgotha, that is, "Skull Hill," ³⁴where the soldiers gave him drugged wine to drink; but when he had tasted it, he refused.

³⁵After the crucifixion, the soldiers threw dice to divide up his clothes among themselves. ³⁶Then they sat around and watched him as he hung there. ³⁷And they put a sign above his head, "This is Jesus, the King of the Jews."

³⁸Two robbers were also crucified there that morning, one on either side of him. ³⁹And the people passing by hurled abuse, shaking their heads at him and saying, ⁴⁰"So! You can destroy the Temple and build it again in three days, can you? Well, then, come on down from the cross if you are the Son of God!"

⁴¹⁻⁴³And the chief priests and Jewish leaders also mocked him. "He saved others," they scoffed, "but he can't save himself! So you are the King of Israel, are you? Come down from the cross and we'll believe you! He trusted God—let God show his approval by delivering him! Didn't he say, 'I am God's Son'?"

⁴⁴And the robbers also threw the same in his teeth.

⁴⁵That afternoon, the whole earth was covered with darkness for three hours, from noon until three o'clock.

⁴⁶About three o'clock, Jesus shouted, "Eli, Eli, lama sabachthani?" which means, "My God, my God, why have you forsaken me?"

⁴⁷Some of the bystanders misunderstood and thought he was calling for Elijah. ⁴⁸One of them ran and filled a sponge with sour wine and put it on a stick and held it up to him to drink. ⁴⁹But the rest said, "Leave him alone. Let's see whether Elijah will come and save him."

⁵⁰Then Jesus shouted out again, dismissed his spirit, and died.

⁵¹And look! The curtain secluding the Holiest Place in the Temple was split apart from top to bottom; and the earth shook, and rocks broke, ⁵²and tombs opened, and many godly men and women who had died came back to life again. ⁵³After Jesus' resurrection, they left the cemetery and went into Jerusalem, and appeared to many people there.

⁵⁴The soldiers at the crucifixion and their sergeant were terribly frightened by the earthquake and all that happened. They exclaimed, "Surely this was God's Son."

⁵⁵And many women who had come down from Galilee with Jesus to care for him were watching from a distance. ⁵⁶Among them were Mary Magdalene and Mary the mother of James and Joseph, and the mother of James and John (the sons of Zebedee).

⁵⁷When evening came, a rich man from Arimathea named Joseph, one of Jesus' followers, ⁵⁸went to Pilate and asked for Jesus' body. And Pilate issued an order to release it to him. ⁵⁹Joseph took the body and wrapped it in a clean linen cloth, ⁶⁰and placed it in his own new rock-hewn tomb, and rolled a great stone across the entrance as he left. ⁶¹Both Mary Magdalene and the other Mary were sitting nearby watching.

⁶²The next day—at the close of the first day of the Passover ceremonies—the chief priests and Pharisees went to Pilate, ⁶³and told him, "Sir, that liar once said, 'After three days I will come back to life again.' ⁶⁴So we request an order from you sealing the tomb until the third day, to prevent his disciples from coming and stealing his body and then telling everyone he came back to life! If that happens, we'll be worse off than we were at first."

⁶⁵"Use your own Temple police," Pilate told them. "They can guard it safely enough."

⁶⁶So they sealed the stone and posted guards to protect it from intrusion.

28 Jesus Comes Back to Life!

Early on Sunday morning, as the new day was dawning, Mary Magdalene and the other Mary went out to the tomb.

²Suddenly there was a great earthquake; for an angel of the Lord came down from heaven and rolled aside the stone and sat on it. ³His face shone like lightning and his clothing was a brilliant white. ⁴The guards shook with fear when they saw him, and fell into a dead faint.

⁵Then the angel spoke to the women. "Don't be frightened!" he said. "I know you are looking for Jesus, who was crucified, ⁶but he isn't here! For he has come back to life again, just as he said he would. Come in and see where his body was lying. . . . ⁷And now, go quickly and tell his disciples that he has risen from the dead, and that he is going to Galilee to meet them there. That is my message to them."

⁸The women ran from the tomb, badly frightened, but also filled with joy, and rushed to find the disciples to give them the angel's message. ⁹And as they were running, suddenly Jesus was there in front of them!

"Good morning!" he said. And they fell to the ground before him, holding his feet and worshiping him.

¹⁰Then Jesus said to them, "Don't be fright-

Family Devotions

☐ **Devotion 259**
Obedience

Read Matthew 28:19-20

Obedience
Memory Verse

Oh, that they would always have such a heart for me, wanting to obey my commandments. Then all would go well with them in the future, and with their children throughout all generations!
Deuteronomy 5:29

Marty's uncle Rick was visiting them while he was on furlough from the army, and Marty had lots of questions to ask. He had never talked to any soldiers, and he wasn't even sure what they did in the army.

"Do you have a job?" Marty asked bluntly.

"I sure do," Uncle Rick replied. "I work on jeeps, just like I did before I entered the service."

"Do you have a boss?" Marty pressed.

"Yes," Uncle Rick replied again, "my commanding officer is my boss."

"What do you do for him?" Marty persisted.

"Well, I follow every order he gives me."

And so the question-and-answer session continued. Marty really enjoyed it, and he hoped his uncle didn't mind. One Sunday evening, Uncle Rick was asked to give his testimony at church. He wore his uniform, and Marty listened proudly as Uncle Rick spoke. He started by telling the people about some of Marty's questions.

"When Marty asked me what I did for my commanding officer, it reminded me of my spiritual commanding officer, Jesus Christ. I wonder if I'm as careful about obeying his orders as I am about obeying the orders given to me in the army," Uncle Rick said. "God has commanded us to 'go and make disciples in all the nations.' He has also commanded us to love each other as much as he loved us."

Marty's thoughts became very serious as he listened to his uncle talk about other commands given by God. Silently Marty prayed, asking God to help him to be obedient to the commands in the Bible. He was going to follow all the orders from his commanding officer, the Lord Jesus.

How About You?
If you're a Christian, God expects you to obey the commands in the Bible. Each time you come across a command in Scripture, ask yourself, "Am I obeying this command?" Good soldiers don't question their orders—they just obey them. R.J.

ened! Go tell my brothers to leave at once for Galilee, to meet me there."

¹¹As the women were on the way into the city, some of the Temple police who had been guarding the tomb went to the chief priests and told them what had happened. ¹²,¹³A meeting of all the Jewish leaders was called, and it was decided to bribe the police to say they had all been asleep when Jesus' disciples came during the night and stole his body.

¹⁴"If the governor hears about it," the Council promised, "we'll stand up for you and everything will be all right."

¹⁵So the police accepted the bribe and said what they were told to. Their story spread widely among the Jews and is still believed by them to this very day.

¹⁶Then the eleven disciples left for Galilee, going to the mountain where Jesus had said they would find him. ¹⁷There they met him and worshiped him—but some of them weren't sure it really was Jesus!

¹⁸He told his disciples, "I have been given all authority in heaven and earth. ¹⁹Therefore go and make disciples in all the nations, baptizing them into the name of the Father and of the Son and of the Holy Spirit, ²⁰and then teach these new disciples to obey all the commands I have given you; and be sure of this—that I am with you always, even to the end of the world."

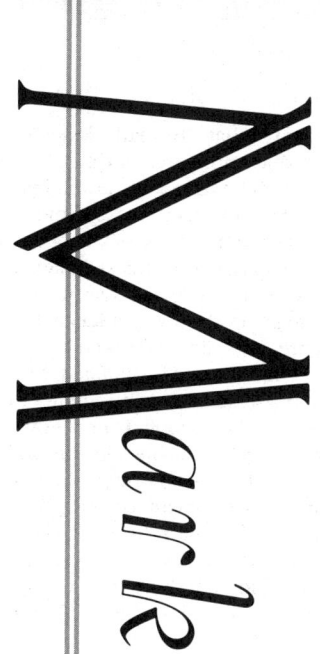

Mark

WHAT DO you like best about Jesus? If you had to write about him, what would you say?

Each Gospel writer picked different things to say about Jesus. Mark really liked Jesus' miracles and the ways he helped people, and most of his book focuses on these things. Mark wanted people to learn about Jesus' love in action.

Mark gives us a clear picture of Jesus as a servant. Because Jesus was the Messiah, he could do anything he wanted. But he chose to *serve* by getting involved in people's lives. He didn't stand on a stage and preach at them from a distance. Instead, he sat down in the middle of a crowd, where people could touch him and get to know him.

What would you write about Jesus? As you read this book, look for things you like best about him.

Preparing the Way for Jesus

Here begins the wonderful story of Jesus the Messiah, the Son of God.

²In the book written by the prophet Isaiah, God announced that he would send his Son to earth, and that a special messenger would arrive first to prepare the world for his coming.

³"This messenger will live out in the barren wilderness," Isaiah said, "and will proclaim that everyone must straighten out his life to be ready for the Lord's arrival."

⁴This messenger was John the Baptist. He lived in the wilderness and taught that all should be baptized as a public announcement of their decision to turn their backs on sin, so that God could forgive them. ⁵People from Jerusalem and from all over Judea traveled out into the Judean wastelands to see and hear John, and when they confessed their sins he baptized them in the Jordan River. ⁶His clothes were woven from camel's hair and he wore a leather belt; locusts and wild honey were his food. ⁷Here is a sample of his preaching:

"Someone is coming soon who is far greater than I am, so much greater that I am not even worthy to be his slave. ⁸I baptize you with water but he will baptize you with God's Holy Spirit!"

⁹Then one day Jesus came from Nazareth in Galilee, and was baptized by John there in the Jordan River. ¹⁰The moment Jesus came up out of the water, he saw the heavens open and the Holy Spirit in the form of a dove descending on him, ¹¹and a voice from heaven said, "You are my beloved Son; you are my Delight."

¹²,¹³Immediately the Holy Spirit urged Jesus into the desert. There, for forty days, alone except for desert animals, he was subjected to Satan's temptations to sin. And afterwards the angels came and cared for him.

¹⁴Later on, after John was arrested by King Herod, Jesus went to Galilee to preach God's Good News.

¹⁵"At last the time has come!" he announced. "God's Kingdom is near! Turn from your sins and act on this glorious news!"

¹⁶One day as Jesus was walking along the shores of the Sea of Galilee, he saw Simon and his brother Andrew fishing with nets, for they were commercial fishermen.

¹⁷Jesus called out to them, "Come, follow me! And I will make you fishermen for the souls of men!" ¹⁸At once they left their nets and went along with him.

¹⁹A little farther up the beach, he saw Zebedee's sons, James and John, in a boat mending their nets. ²⁰He called them too, and immediately they left their father Zebedee in the boat with the hired men and went with him.

²¹Jesus and his companions now arrived at the town of Capernaum and on Saturday morning went into the Jewish place of worship—the synagogue—where he preached. ²²The congregation was surprised at his sermon because he spoke as an authority and didn't try to prove his points by quoting others—quite unlike what they were used to hearing!

²³A man possessed by a demon was present and began shouting, ²⁴"Why are you bothering us, Jesus of Nazareth—have you come to destroy us demons? I know who you are—the holy Son of God!"

²⁵Jesus curtly commanded the demon to say no more and to come out of the man. ²⁶At that the evil spirit screamed and convulsed the man violently and left him. ²⁷Amazement gripped the audience and they began discussing what had happened.

"What sort of new religion is this?" they asked excitedly. "Why, even evil spirits obey his orders!"

²⁸The news of what he had done spread quickly through that entire area of Galilee.

²⁹,³⁰Then, leaving the synagogue, he and his disciples went over to Simon and Andrew's home, where they found Simon's mother-in-law sick in bed with a high fever. They told Jesus about her right away. ³¹He went to her bedside, and as he took her by the hand and helped her to sit up, the fever suddenly left, and she got up and prepared dinner for them!

³²,³³By sunset the courtyard was filled with the sick and demon-possessed, brought to him for healing; and a huge crowd of people from all over the city of Capernaum gathered outside the door to watch. ³⁴So Jesus healed great numbers of sick folk that evening and ordered many demons to come out of their victims. (But he refused to allow the demons to speak, because they knew who he was.)

³⁵The next morning he was up long before daybreak and went out alone into the wilderness to pray.

³⁶,³⁷Later, Simon and the others went out to find him, and told him, "Everyone is asking for you."

³⁸But he replied, "We must go on to other towns as well, and give my message to them too, for that is why I came."

³⁹So he traveled throughout the province of Galilee, preaching in the synagogues and releasing many from the power of demons.

⁴⁰Once a leper came and knelt in front of him and begged to be healed. "If you want to, you can make me well again," he pled.

⁴¹And Jesus, moved with pity, touched him and said, "I want to! Be healed!" ⁴²Immediately the leprosy was gone—the man was healed!

⁴³,⁴⁴Jesus then told him sternly, "Go and be examined immediately by the Jewish priest. Don't stop to speak to anyone along the way. Take along the offering prescribed by Moses for a leper who is healed, so that everyone will have proof that you are well again."

⁴⁵But as the man went on his way he began to shout the good news that he was healed; as a result, such throngs soon surrounded Jesus that he couldn't publicly enter a city anywhere, but had to stay out in the barren wastelands. And people from everywhere came to him there.

2 A Hole in the Roof

Several days later he returned to Capernaum, and the news of his arrival spread quickly through the city. ²Soon the house where he was staying was so packed with visitors that there wasn't room for a single person more, not even outside the door. And he preached the Word to them. ³Four men ar-

---

SHOWING COMPASSION 2:3 The paralyzed man's need moved his friends to action, and they brought him to Jesus. When you recognize someone's need, do you act? Many people have physical and spiritual needs you can meet, either by yourself or with others who are also concerned. Human need moved these four men; let it also move you to compassionate action. **To begin the series of devotionals on SHOWING COMPASSION, turn to page 569.**

Family Devotions

☐ DEVOTION 260
KNOWING GOD

Read Mark 1:35

Brian loved seeing the animals, climbing on the haystacks, swinging on the rope in the barn, and fishing and wading in the creek when his family went to visit his grandparents' farm. "This sure is a neat place!" he exclaimed as he washed up for supper one evening.

Mom smiled. "You seem to be enjoying yourself in spite of no playgrounds or ice-cream stores out here, or even a TV."

"Yeah, it's kind of nice to have it quiet—a guy has a chance to think out here."

After a hearty supper, Dad looked over at Brian. "Your grandpa and I have a surprise for you, Son. We thought you might enjoy camping out in the woods with us tonight."

Three hours later, they sat contentedly by the smoldering campfire. "Time for devotions," Grandpa announced as he pulled out his Bible.

As Brian reached in his duffle bag for his own Bible, he glanced upward. "Wow! Look at all those stars!" he cried. "We sure can't see this many at our house. They must be a lot closer here."

Dad and Grandpa laughed. "No, the stars aren't any closer," Dad replied, "but we're out in the country now, away from all the city lights, which tend to blot out the smaller lights of the stars."

"I think there's a spiritual lesson here," Grandpa said thoughtfully as he leafed through his Bible. "Just as the glaring lights of the city blot out the stars, so the busyness of everyday activities can make it hard to see how God is working in our lives. That's why it's good to draw apart to a quiet place—a place where you can be alone and concentrate on God's Word and your relationship to him."

"I'll try to remember that," Brian said. He listened very carefully as Grandpa read from the Bible.

Knowing God Memory Verse

Oh, that we might know the Lord! Let us press on to know him, and he will respond to us as surely as the coming of dawn or the rain of early spring.
Hosea 6:3

How About You?
Is your time so filled with school activities and recreation that you hardly ever think about God or the Bible? Be careful! If you don't set aside quiet times to be alone with God, you'll miss many of the wonderful blessings the Lord has planned for you. *S. K.*

- For the next devotional, turn to page 939. • For the next devotional on KNOWING GOD, turn to page 1059.
- For notes on KNOWING GOD, see pages 129, 610, 815, and 1208.

rived carrying a paralyzed man on a stretcher. ⁴They couldn't get to Jesus through the crowd, so they dug through the clay roof above his head and lowered the sick man on his stretcher, right down in front of Jesus.

⁵When Jesus saw how strongly they believed that he would help, Jesus said to the sick man, "Son, your sins are forgiven!"

⁶But some of the Jewish religious leaders said to themselves as they sat there, ⁷"What? This is blasphemy! Does he think he is God? For only God can forgive sins."

⁸Jesus could read their minds and said to them at once, "Why does this bother you? ⁹⁻¹¹I, the Messiah, have the authority on earth to forgive sins. But talk is cheap—anybody could say that. So I'll prove it to you by healing this man." Then, turning to the paralyzed man, he commanded, "Pick up your stretcher and go on home, for you are healed!"

¹²The man jumped up, took the stretcher, and pushed his way through the stunned onlookers! Then how they praised God. "We've never seen anything like this before!" they all exclaimed.

¹³Then Jesus went out to the seashore again and preached to the crowds that gathered around him. ¹⁴As he was walking up the beach he saw Levi, the son of Alphaeus, sitting at his tax collection booth. "Come with me," Jesus told him. "Come be my disciple."

And Levi jumped to his feet and went along.

¹⁵That night Levi invited his fellow tax collectors and many other notorious sinners to be his dinner guests so that they could meet Jesus and his disciples. (There were many men of this type among the crowds that followed him.) ¹⁶But when some of the Jewish religious leaders saw him eating with these men of ill repute, they said to his disciples, "How can he stand it, to eat with such scum?"

¹⁷When Jesus heard what they were saying, he told them, "Sick people need the doctor, not healthy ones! I haven't come to tell good people to repent, but the bad ones."

¹⁸John's disciples and the Jewish leaders sometimes fasted, that is, went without food as part of their religion. One day some people came to Jesus and asked why his disciples didn't do this too.

¹⁹Jesus replied, "Do friends of the bridegroom refuse to eat at the wedding feast? Should they be sad while he is with them? ²⁰But some day he will be taken away from them, and then they will mourn. ²¹[Besides, going without food is part of the old way of doing things.] It is like patching an old garment with unshrunk cloth! What happens? The patch pulls away and leaves the hole worse than before. ²²You know better than to put new wine into old wineskins. They would burst. The wine would be spilled out and the wineskins ruined. New wine needs fresh wineskins."

²³Another time, on a Sabbath day as Jesus and his disciples were walking through the fields, the disciples were breaking off heads of wheat and eating the grain.

²⁴Some of the Jewish religious leaders said to Jesus, "They shouldn't be doing that! It's against our laws to work by harvesting grain on the Sabbath."

²⁵,²⁶But Jesus replied, "Didn't you ever hear about the time King David and his companions were hungry, and he went into the house of God—Abiathar was High Priest then—and they ate the special bread only priests were allowed to eat? That was against the law too. ²⁷But the Sabbath was made to benefit man, and not man to benefit the Sabbath. ²⁸And I, the Messiah, have authority even to decide what men can do on Sabbath days!"

3 Jesus Heals a Crippled Hand

While in Capernaum Jesus went over to the synagogue again, and noticed a man there with a deformed hand.

²Since it was the Sabbath, Jesus' enemies watched him closely. Would he heal the man's hand? If he did, they planned to arrest him!

³Jesus asked the man to come and stand in front of the congregation. ⁴Then turning to his enemies he asked, "Is it all right to do kind deeds on Sabbath days? Or is this a day for doing harm? Is it a day to save lives or to destroy them?" But they wouldn't answer him. ⁵Looking around at them angrily, for he was deeply disturbed by their indifference to human need, he said to the man, "Reach out your hand." He did, and instantly his hand was healed!

⁶At once the Pharisees went away and met with the Herodians to discuss plans for killing Jesus.

⁷,⁸Meanwhile, Jesus and his disciples withdrew to the beach, followed by a huge crowd from all over Galilee, Judea, Jerusalem, Idumea, from beyond the Jordan River, and even from as far away as Tyre and Sidon. For the news about his miracles had spread far and wide and vast numbers came to see him for themselves.

OVERCOMING ANGER 3:5 Jesus was angry about the Pharisees' uncaring attitude. Anger itself is not wrong, but we need to consider what makes us angry and what we do with our anger. Too often we express our anger in selfish and harmful ways. By contrast, Jesus expressed his anger by correcting a problem—healing the man's hand. Use your anger to find constructive solutions rather than to add to the problem by tearing people down. **To begin the series of devotionals on** OVERCOMING ANGER, **turn to pag 133.**

⁹He instructed his disciples to bring around a boat and to have it standing ready to rescue him in case he was crowded off the beach. ¹⁰For there had been many healings that day and as a result great numbers of sick people were crowding around him, trying to touch him.

¹¹And whenever those possessed by demons caught sight of him they would fall down before him shrieking, "You are the Son of God!" ¹²But he strictly warned them not to make him known.

¹³Afterwards he went up into the hills and summoned certain ones he chose, inviting them to come and join him there; and they did. ¹⁴,¹⁵Then he selected twelve of them to be his regular companions and to go out to preach and to cast out demons. ¹⁶⁻¹⁹These are the names of the twelve he chose: Simon (he renamed him "Peter"), James and John (the sons of Zebedee, but Jesus called them "Sons of Thunder"), Andrew, Philip, Bartholomew, Matthew, Thomas, James (the son of Alphaeus), Thaddaeus, Simon (a member of a political party advocating violent overthrow of the Roman government), Judas Iscariot (who later betrayed him).

²⁰When he returned to the house where he was staying, the crowds began to gather again, and soon it was so full of visitors that he couldn't even find time to eat. ²¹When his friends heard what was happening they came to try to take him home with them.

"He's out of his mind," they said.

²²But the Jewish teachers of religion who had arrived from Jerusalem said, "His trouble is that he's possessed by Satan, king of demons. That's why demons obey him."

²³Jesus summoned these men and asked them (using proverbs they all understood), "How can Satan cast out Satan? ²⁴A kingdom divided against itself will collapse. ²⁵A home filled with strife and division destroys itself. ²⁶And if Satan is fighting against himself, how can he accomplish anything? He would never survive. ²⁷[Satan must be bound before his demons are cast out], just as a strong man must be tied up before his house can be ransacked and his property robbed.

²⁸"I solemnly declare that any sin of man can be forgiven, even blasphemy against me; ²⁹but blasphemy against the Holy Spirit can never be forgiven. It is an eternal sin."

³⁰He told them this because they were saying he did his miracles by Satan's power [instead of acknowledging it was by the Holy Spirit's power].

³¹,³²Now his mother and brothers arrived at the crowded house where he was teaching, and they sent word for him to come out and talk with them. "Your mother and brothers are outside and want to see you," he was told.

³³He replied, "Who is my mother? Who are my brothers?" ³⁴Looking at those around him he said, "These are my mother and brothers! ³⁵Anyone who does God's will is my brother, and my sister, and my mother."

4 A Story about Four Kinds of Soil

Once again an immense crowd gathered around him on the beach as he was teaching, so he got into a boat and sat down and talked from there. ²His usual method of teaching was to tell the people stories. One of them went like this:

³"Listen! A farmer decided to sow some grain. As he scattered it across his field, ⁴some of it fell on a path, and the birds came and picked it off the hard ground and ate it. ⁵,⁶Some fell on thin soil with underlying rock. It grew up quickly enough, but soon wilted beneath the hot sun and died because the roots had no nourishment in the shallow soil. ⁷Other seeds fell among thorns that shot up and crowded the young plants so that they produced no grain. ⁸But some of the seeds fell into good soil and yielded thirty times as much as he had planted—some of it even sixty or a hundred times as much! ⁹If you have ears, listen!"

¹⁰Afterwards, when he was alone with the twelve and with his other disciples, they asked him, "What does your story mean?"

¹¹,¹²He replied, "You are permitted to know some truths about the Kingdom of God that are hidden to those outside the Kingdom:

'Though they see and hear, they will not understand or turn to God, or be forgiven for their sins.'

¹³But if you can't understand *this* simple illustration, what will you do about all the others I am going to tell?

¹⁴"The farmer I talked about is anyone who brings God's message to others, trying to plant good seed within their lives. ¹⁵The hard pathway, where some of the seed fell, represents the hard hearts of some of those who hear God's message; Satan comes at once to try to make them forget it. ¹⁶The rocky soil represents the hearts of those who hear the message with joy, ¹⁷but, like young plants in such soil, their roots don't go very deep, and though at first they get along fine, as soon as persecution begins, they wilt.

¹⁸"The thorny ground represents the hearts of people who listen to the Good News and receive it, ¹⁹but all too quickly the attractions of this world and the delights of wealth, and the search

for success and lure of nice things come in and crowd out God's message from their hearts, so that no crop is produced.

20"But the good soil represents the hearts of those who truly accept God's message and produce a plentiful harvest for God—thirty, sixty, or even a hundred times as much as was planted in their hearts." 21Then he asked them, "When someone lights a lamp, does he put a box over it to shut out the light? Of course not! The light couldn't be seen or used. A lamp is placed on a stand to shine and be useful.

22"All that is now hidden will someday come to light. 23If you have ears, listen! 24And be sure to put into practice what you hear. The more you do this, the more you will understand what I tell you. 25To him who has shall be given; from him who has not shall be taken away even what he has.

26"Here is another story illustrating what the Kingdom of God is like:

"A farmer sowed his field 27and went away, and as the days went by, the seeds grew and grew without his help. 28For the soil made the seeds grow. First a leaf-blade pushed through, and later the wheat-heads formed and finally the grain ripened, 29and then the farmer came at once with his sickle and harvested it."

30Jesus asked, "How can I describe the Kingdom of God? What story shall I use to illustrate it? 31,32It is like a tiny mustard seed! Though this is one of the smallest of seeds, yet it grows to become one of the largest of plants, with long branches where birds can build their nests and be sheltered."

33He used many such illustrations to teach the people as much as they were ready to understand. 34In fact, he taught only by illustrations in his public teaching, but afterwards, when he was alone with his disciples, he would explain his meaning to them.

35As evening fell, Jesus said to his disciples, "Let's cross to the other side of the lake." 36So they took him just as he was and started out, leaving the crowds behind (though other boats followed). 37But soon a terrible storm arose. High waves began to break into the boat until it was nearly full of water and about to sink. 38Jesus was asleep at the back of the boat with his head on a cushion. Frantically they wakened him, shouting, "Teacher, don't you even care that we are all about to drown?"

39Then he rebuked the wind and said to the sea, "Quiet down!" And the wind fell, and there was a great calm!

40And he asked them, "Why were you so fearful? Don't you even yet have confidence in me?"

41And they were filled with awe and said among themselves, "Who is this man, that even the winds and seas obey him?"

5 Jesus Heals a Man with Demons

When they arrived at the other side of the lake, a demon-possessed man ran out from a graveyard, just as Jesus was climbing from the boat.

3,4This man lived among the gravestones and had such strength that whenever he was put into handcuffs and shackles—as he often was—he snapped the handcuffs from his wrists and smashed the shackles and walked away. No one was strong enough to control him. 5All day long and through the night he would wander among the tombs and in the wild hills, screaming and cutting himself with sharp pieces of stone.

6When Jesus was still far out on the water, the man had seen him and had run to meet him, and fell down before him.

7,8Then Jesus spoke to the demon within the man and said, "Come out, you evil spirit."

It gave a terrible scream, shrieking, "What are you going to do to me, Jesus, Son of the Most High God? For God's sake, don't torture me!"

9"What is your name?" Jesus asked, and the demon replied, "Legion, for there are many of us here within this man."

10Then the demons begged him again and again not to send them to some distant land.

11Now as it happened there was a huge herd of hogs rooting around on the hill above the lake. 12"Send us into those hogs," the demons begged.

13And Jesus gave them permission. Then the evil spirits came out of the man and entered the hogs, and the entire herd plunged down the steep hillside into the lake and drowned.

14The herdsmen fled to the nearby towns and countryside, spreading the news as they ran. Everyone rushed out to see for themselves. 15And a large crowd soon gathered where Jesus was; but as they saw the man sitting there, fully clothed and perfectly sane, they were frightened. 16Those who saw what happened were telling everyone about it, 17and the crowd began pleading with Jesus to go away and leave them alone! 18So he got back into the boat. The man who had been possessed by the demons begged Jesus to let him go along. 19But Jesus said no.

"Go home to your friends," he told him, "and tell them what wonderful things God has done for you; and how merciful he has been."

20So the man started off to visit the Ten Towns of that region and began to tell everyone about the great things Jesus had done for him; and they were awestruck by his story.

21When Jesus had gone across by boat to the other side of the lake, a vast crowd gathered around him on the shore.

22The leader of the local synagogue, whose

Family Devotions

☐ *Devotion 261*
Overcoming Fear

Read Mark 4:36-41

Scott glanced nervously out the school window. He hoped there wasn't going to be another tornado alert today. They always made him afraid.

As Scott began the first problem, a bell rang. "Tornado drill," said Miss Greely. But there was something different today. Scott could hear a siren blowing, and as he listened, he knew it came from a nearby fire station. It was a signal that a tornado had been seen nearby!

Scott had never been so scared before! But as he sat, trembling, he remembered something Dad had said just the weekend before. They had gone swimming, and as Dad walked out into the deep water, Scott's little brother Brian hung on to Dad's shoulders. "Are you scared in the deep water, Brian?" Scott asked.

Brian had shook his head and said, "Nope, Dad's got me."

Dad had laughed as he replied, "Good boy! I'm in control here, and I'm glad you trust your father." Then he added, "I hope both you boys will remember that you can always trust your Father in heaven, too. He's in control of all the circumstances of your lives."

A few minutes later, Scott heard a roaring sound. It almost sounded like a train rushing by. He had heard that a tornado sounded that way. *I'm still scared,* Scott thought, *but not so awfully scared. God's my heavenly Father, and he's in control.*

After the all-clear whistle sounded, the children returned to their classrooms and were soon dismissed to go home. They learned that a tornado had indeed passed by, not far from their school. Much damage had been done, but no one had been hurt. With his family, Scott thanked God for watching over them.

Overcoming Fear Memory Verse

Fear not, for I am with you. Do not be dismayed. I am your God. I will strengthen you; I will help you; I will uphold you with my victorious right hand.
Isaiah 41:10

How About You?

Storms can be frightening, can't they? They are powerful and can cause a lot of damage. But God is even more powerful. Even the wind has to obey him! Remember that God is in control. *H. M.*

- For the next devotional, turn to page 941. • For the next devotional on *Overcoming Fear*, turn to page 993.
- For notes on *Overcoming Fear*, see pages 191, 482, 554, 592, and 912.

name was Jairus, came and fell down before him, ²³pleading with him to heal his little daughter.

"She is at the point of death," he said in desperation. "Please come and place your hands on her and make her live."

²⁴Jesus went with him, and the crowd thronged behind. ²⁵In the crowd was a woman who had been sick for twelve years with a hemorrhage. ²⁶She had suffered much from many doctors through the years and had become poor from paying them, and was no better but, in fact, was worse. ²⁷She had heard all about the wonderful miracles Jesus did, and that is why she came up behind him through the crowd and touched his clothes.

²⁸For she thought to herself, "If I can just touch his clothing, I will be healed." ²⁹And sure enough, as soon as she had touched him, the bleeding stopped and she knew she was well!

³⁰Jesus realized at once that healing power had gone out from him, so he turned around in the crowd and asked, "Who touched my clothes?"

³¹His disciples said to him, "All this crowd pressing around you, and you ask who touched you?"

³²But he kept on looking around to see who it was who had done it. ³³Then the frightened woman, trembling at the realization of what had happened to her, came and fell at his feet and told him what she had done. ³⁴And he said to her, "Daughter, your faith has made you well; go in peace, healed of your disease."

³⁵While he was still talking to her, messengers arrived from Jairus' home with the news that it was too late—his daughter was dead and there was no point in Jesus' coming now. ³⁶But Jesus ignored their comments and said to Jairus, "Don't be afraid. Just trust me."

³⁷Then Jesus halted the crowd and wouldn't let anyone go on with him to Jairus' home except Peter and James and John. ³⁸When they arrived, Jesus saw that all was in great confusion, with unrestrained weeping and wailing. ³⁹He went inside and spoke to the people.

"Why all this weeping and commotion?" he asked. "The child isn't dead; she is only asleep!"

⁴⁰They laughed at him in bitter derision, but he told them all to leave, and taking the little girl's father and mother and his three disciples, he went into the room where she was lying.

⁴¹,⁴²Taking her by the hand he said to her, "Get up, little girl!" (She was twelve years old.) And she jumped up and walked around! Her parents just couldn't get over it. ⁴³Jesus instructed them very earnestly not to tell what had happened and told them to give her something to eat.

6 Rejected in His Hometown

Soon afterwards he left that section of the country and returned with his disciples to Nazareth, his hometown. ²,³The next Sabbath he went to the synagogue to teach, and the people were astonished at his wisdom and his miracles because he was just a local man like themselves.

"He's no better than we are," they said. "He's just a carpenter, Mary's boy, and a brother of James and Joseph, Judas and Simon. And his sisters live right here among us." And they were offended!

⁴Then Jesus told them, "A prophet is honored everywhere except in his hometown and among his relatives and by his own family." ⁵And because of their unbelief he couldn't do any mighty miracles among them except to place his hands on a few sick people and heal them. ⁶And he could hardly accept the fact that they wouldn't believe in him.

Then he went out among the villages, teaching.

⁷And he called his twelve disciples together and sent them out two by two, with power to cast out demons. ⁸,⁹He told them to take nothing with them except their walking sticks—no food, no knapsack, no money, not even an extra pair of shoes or a change of clothes.

¹⁰"Stay at one home in each village—don't shift around from house to house while you are there," he said. ¹¹"And whenever a village won't accept you or listen to you, shake off the dust from your feet as you leave; it is a sign that you have abandoned it to its fate."

¹²So the disciples went out, telling everyone they met to turn from sin. ¹³And they cast out many demons and healed many sick people, anointing them with olive oil.

¹⁴King Herod soon heard about Jesus, for his miracles were talked about everywhere. The king thought Jesus was John the Baptist come back to life again. So the people were saying, "No wonder he can do such miracles." ¹⁵Others thought Jesus was Elijah the ancient prophet, now returned to life again; still others claimed he was a new prophet like the great ones of the past.

¹⁶"No," Herod said, "it is John, the man I beheaded. He has come back from the dead."

¹⁷,¹⁸For Herod had sent soldiers to arrest and imprison John

OPTIMISM 5:36 Jesus' words to Jairus in the midst of crisis speak to us as well: "Don't be afraid. Just trust me." In Jesus' mind, there was both hope and promise. The next time you feel confused, afraid, and without hope—as Jairus did—remember to see your problem from Jesus' point of view. He is the source of all hope and promise. **To begin the series of devotionals on OPTIMISM, turn to page 19.**

FAMILY DEVOTIONS

☐ DEVOTION 262
MAKING THE BEST CHOICES

Read Mark 6: 7-13, 30-31

The Taylors were on their way to a cottage they were renting near Sunshine Lake. "It's already dark out," observed Sue as she stared out the car window. "I can hardly wait to get there. It seems like years since we've been on a real vacation!"

"I know," sighed Mom. "We've been so busy getting your father's business started and redecorating the house. It's hard to find a time when we're all free to take a vacation. I'm glad we're getting a few days together before school starts."

When they arrived at the cottage, Sue and her brother, Jimmy, helped Dad unpack the car while Mom swept and dusted inside. "Phew! This place sure is musty," Jimmy commented.

"It'll be all right once we've opened it up," replied Mom. "It's pretty rustic, but at least it has electricity. I'll plug in the coffeepot and put some water on the stove for hot chocolate." As soon as she did so, however, all the lights went off. "Oh no! I must have blown a fuse," she moaned.

"I'll check," said Dad, getting the flashlight and going to find the fuse box. A few minutes later he called, "Looks to me like there are too many things on one small circuit. You'll have to turn off a few lights before you can make that coffee and use the stove." Mom hurried to do so, and soon the lights came back on.

Later, as they sat together near the fireplace, Mom said thoughtfully, "This incident reminds me of our family lately. We've been overloaded, too. We've all been so busy that we don't have much time to spend together anymore."

Dad nodded. "I think we should take some time during this vacation to evaluate our activities and see which ones we could cut out of our schedules," he said. Then he picked up his Bible. "Let's have family devotions right now. That's one activity we should always take time for."

Making the Best Choices
Memory Verse

He will always give you all you need from day to day if you will make the Kingdom of God your primary concern.
Luke 12:31

How About You?

Have you been too busy lately? Make a list of things you do, and put the really important ones first. Be sure to put daily devotions near the top, along with time spent with your family, proper rest, and meals. If there isn't time for everything else on your list, decide which things can be omitted. Don't get overloaded. S. K.

• For the next devotional, turn to page 947. • For the next devotional on MAKING THE BEST CHOICES, turn to page 1183. • For notes on MAKING THE BEST CHOICES, see pages 358, 652, and 944.

because he kept saying it was wrong for the king to marry Herodias, his brother Philip's wife. ¹⁹Herodias wanted John killed in revenge, but without Herod's approval she was powerless. ²⁰And Herod respected John, knowing that he was a good and holy man, and so he kept him under his protection. Herod was disturbed whenever he talked with John, but even so he liked to listen to him.

²¹Herodias' chance finally came. It was Herod's birthday and he gave a stag party for his palace aides, army officers, and the leading citizens of Galilee. ²²,²³Then Herodias' daughter came in and danced before them and greatly pleased them all.

"Ask me for anything you like," the king vowed, "even half of my kingdom, and I will give it to you!"

²⁴She went out and consulted her mother, who told her, "Ask for John the Baptist's head!"

²⁵So she hurried back to the king and told him, "I want the head of John the Baptist—right now—on a tray!"

²⁶Then the king was sorry, but he was embarrassed to break his oath in front of his guests. ²⁷So he sent one of his bodyguards to the prison to cut off John's head and bring it to him. The soldier killed John in the prison, ²⁸and brought back his head on a tray, and gave it to the girl and she took it to her mother.

²⁹When John's disciples heard what had happened, they came for his body and buried it in a tomb.

³⁰The apostles now returned to Jesus from their tour and told him all they had done and what they had said to the people they visited.

³¹Then Jesus suggested, "Let's get away from the crowds for a while and rest." For so many people were coming and going that they scarcely had time to eat. ³²So they left by boat for a quieter spot. ³³But many people saw them leaving and ran on ahead along the shore and met them as they landed. ³⁴So the usual vast crowd was there as he stepped from the boat; and he had pity on them because they were like sheep without a shepherd, and he taught them many things they needed to know.

³⁵,³⁶Late in the afternoon his disciples came to him and said, "Tell the people to go away to the nearby villages and farms and buy themselves some food, for there is nothing to eat here in this desolate spot, and it is getting late."

³⁷But Jesus said, *"You* feed them."

"With what?" they asked. "It would take a fortune to buy food for all this crowd!"

³⁸"How much food do we have?" he asked. "Go and find out."

They came back to report that there were five loaves of bread and two fish. ³⁹,⁴⁰Then Jesus told the crowd to sit down, and soon colorful groups of fifty or a hundred each were sitting on the green grass.

⁴¹He took the five loaves and two fish and looking up to heaven, gave thanks for the food. Breaking the loaves into pieces, he gave some of the bread and fish to each disciple to place before the people. ⁴²And the crowd ate until they could hold no more!

⁴³,⁴⁴There were about 5,000 men there for that meal, and afterwards twelve basketfuls of scraps were picked up off the grass!

⁴⁵Immediately after this Jesus instructed his disciples to get back into the boat and strike out across the lake to Bethsaida, where he would join them later. He himself would stay and tell the crowds good-bye and get them started home.

⁴⁶Afterwards he went up into the hills to pray. ⁴⁷During the night, as the disciples in their boat were out in the middle of the lake, and he was alone on land, ⁴⁸he saw that they were in serious trouble, rowing hard and struggling against the wind and waves.

About three o'clock in the morning he walked out to them on the water. He started past them, ⁴⁹but when they saw something walking along beside them they screamed in terror, thinking it was a ghost, ⁵⁰for they all saw him.

But he spoke to them at once. "It's all right," he said. "It is I! Don't be afraid." ⁵¹Then he climbed into the boat and the wind stopped!

They just sat there, unable to take it in! ⁵²For they still didn't realize who he was, even after the miracle the evening before! For they didn't want to believe!

⁵³When they arrived at Gennesaret on the other side of the lake, they moored the boat ⁵⁴and climbed out.

The people standing around there recognized him at once, ⁵⁵and ran throughout the whole area to spread the news of his arrival, and began carrying sick folks to him on mats and stretchers. ⁵⁶Wherever he went—in villages and cities, and out on the farms—they laid the sick in the market plazas and streets, and begged him to let them at least touch the fringes of his clothes; and as many as touched him were healed.

7 A Bunch of Hypocrites

One day some Jewish religious leaders arrived from Jerusalem to investigate him, ²and noticed that some of his disciples failed to follow the usual Jewish rituals before eating. ³(For the Jews, especially the Pharisees, will never eat until they have sprinkled their arms to the elbows, as required by their ancient traditions. ⁴So when they come home from the market they must always sprinkle themselves in this way before touching any food. This is but one of many examples of laws and regulations they have clung to for centuries, and still follow, such as their ceremony of cleansing for pots, pans and dishes.)

⁵So the religious leaders asked him, "Why don't your disciples follow our age-old customs? For they eat without first performing the washing ceremony."

⁶,⁷Jesus replied, "You bunch of hypocrites! Isaiah the prophet described you very well when he said, 'These people speak very prettily about the Lord but they have no love for him at all. Their worship is a farce, for they claim that God commands the people to obey their petty rules.' How right Isaiah was! ⁸For you ignore God's specific orders and substitute your own traditions. ⁹You are simply rejecting God's laws and trampling them under your feet for the sake of tradition.

¹⁰For instance, Moses gave you this law from God: 'Honor your father and mother.' And he said that anyone who speaks against his father or mother must die. ¹¹But you say it is perfectly all right for a man to disregard his needy parents, telling them, 'Sorry, I can't help you! For I have given to God what I could have given to you.' ¹²,¹³And so you break the law of God in order to protect your man-made tradition. And this is only one example. There are many, many others."

¹⁴Then Jesus called to the crowd to come and hear. "All of you listen," he said, "and try to understand. ¹⁵,¹⁶Your souls aren't harmed by what you eat, but by what you think and say!"

¹⁷Then he went into a house to get away from the crowds, and his disciples asked him what he meant by the statement he had just made.

¹⁸"Don't you understand either?" he asked. "Can't you see that what you eat won't harm your soul? ¹⁹For food doesn't come in contact with your heart, but only passes through the digestive system." (By saying this he showed that every kind of food is kosher.)

²⁰And then he added, "It is the thought-life that pollutes. ²¹For from within, out of men's hearts, come evil thoughts of lust, theft, murder, adultery, ²²wanting what belongs to others, wickedness, deceit, lewdness, envy, slander, pride, and all other folly. ²³All these vile things come from within; they are what pollute you and make you unfit for God."

²⁴Then he left Galilee and went to the region of Tyre and Sidon, and tried to keep it a secret that he was there, but couldn't. For as usual the news of his arrival spread fast.

²⁵Right away a woman came to him whose little girl was possessed by a demon. She had heard about Jesus and now she came and fell at his feet, ²⁶and pled with him to release her child from the demon's control. (But she was Syrophoenician—a "despised Gentile!")

²⁷Jesus told her, "First I should help my own family—the Jews. It isn't right to take the children's food and throw it to the dogs."

²⁸She replied, "That's true, sir, but even the puppies under the table are given some scraps from the children's plates."

²⁹"Good!" he said. "You have answered well—so well that I have healed your little girl. Go on home, for the demon has left her!"

³⁰And when she arrived home, her little girl was lying quietly in bed, and the demon was gone.

³¹From Tyre he went to Sidon, then back to the Sea of Galilee by way of the Ten Towns. ³²A deaf man with a speech impediment was brought to him, and everyone begged Jesus to lay his hands on the man and heal him.

³³Jesus led him away from the crowd and put his fingers into the man's ears, then spat and touched the man's tongue with the spittle. ³⁴Then, looking up to heaven, he sighed and commanded, "Open!" ³⁵Instantly the man could hear perfectly and speak plainly!

³⁶Jesus told the crowd not to spread the news, but the more he forbade them, the more they made it known, ³⁷for they were overcome with utter amazement. Again and again they said, "Everything he does is wonderful; he even corrects deafness and stammering!"

8 Another Mealtime Miracle

One day about this time as another great crowd gathered, the people ran out of food again. Jesus called his disciples to discuss the situation.

"I pity these people," he said, "for they have been here three days and have nothing left to eat. ³And if I send them home without feeding them, they will faint along the road! For some of them have come a long distance."

⁴"Are we supposed to find food for them here in the desert?" his disciples scoffed.

⁵"How many loaves of bread do you have?" he asked.

"Seven," they replied. ⁶So he told the crowd to sit down on the ground. Then he took the seven loaves, thanked God for them, broke them into pieces and passed them to his disciples; and the disciples placed them before the people. ⁷A few small fish were found, too, so Jesus also blessed these and told the disciples to serve them.

⁸,⁹And the whole crowd ate until they were full, and afterwards he sent them home. There were about 4,000 people in the crowd that day and when the scraps were picked up after the meal, there were seven very large basketfuls left over!

¹⁰Immediately after this he got into a boat with his disciples and came to the region of Dalmanutha.

¹¹When the local Jewish leaders learned of his arrival, they came to argue with him.

"Do a miracle for us," they said. "Make something happen in the sky. Then we will believe in you."

¹²He sighed deeply when he heard this and he said, "Certainly not. How many more miracles do you people need?"

¹³So he got back into the boat and left them, and crossed to the other side of the lake. ¹⁴But the disciples had forgotten to stock up on food before they left and had only one loaf of bread in the boat.

¹⁵As they were crossing, Jesus said to them very solemnly, "Beware of the yeast of King Herod and of the Pharisees."

¹⁶"What does he mean?" the disciples asked each other. They finally decided that he must be talking about their forgetting to bring bread.

¹⁷Jesus realized what they were discussing and said, "No, that isn't it at all! Can't you understand? Are your hearts too hard to take it in? ¹⁸'Your eyes are to see with—why don't you look? Why don't you open your ears and listen?' Don't you remember anything at all?

¹⁹"What about the 5,000 men I fed with five loaves of bread? How many basketfuls of scraps did you pick up afterwards?"

"Twelve," they said.

²⁰"And when I fed the 4,000 with seven loaves, how much was left?"

"Seven basketfuls," they said.

²¹"And yet you think I'm worried that we have no bread?"

²²When they arrived at Bethsaida, some people brought a blind man to him and begged him to touch and heal him. ²³Jesus took the blind man by the hand and led him out of the village, and spat upon his eyes, and laid his hands over them.

"Can you see anything now?" Jesus asked him.

²⁴The man looked around. "Yes!" he said, "I see men! But I can't see them very clearly; they look like tree trunks walking around!"

²⁵Then Jesus placed his hands over the man's eyes again and as the man stared intently, his sight was completely restored, and he saw everything clearly, drinking in the sights around him.

²⁶Jesus sent him home to his family. "Don't even go back to the village first," he said.

²⁷Jesus and his disciples now left Galilee and went out to the villages of Caesarea Philippi. As they were walking along he asked them, "Who do the people think I am? What are they saying about me?"

²⁸"Some of them think you are John the Baptist," the disciples replied, "and others say you are Elijah or some other ancient prophet come back to life again."

²⁹Then he asked, "Who do you think I am?" Peter replied, "You are the Messiah." ³⁰But Jesus warned them not to tell anyone!

³¹Then he began to tell them about the terrible things he would suffer, and that he would be rejected by the elders and the Chief Priests and the other Jewish leaders—and be killed, and that he would rise again three days afterwards. ³²He talked about it quite frankly with them, so Peter took him aside and chided him. "You shouldn't say things like that," he told Jesus.

³³Jesus turned and looked at his disciples and then said to Peter very sternly, "Satan, get behind me! You are looking at this only from a human point of view and not from God's."

³⁴Then he called his disciples and the crowds to come over and listen. "If any of you wants to be my follower," he told them, "you must put aside your own pleasures and shoulder your cross, and follow me closely. ³⁵If you insist on saving your life, you will lose it. Only those who throw away their lives for my sake and for the sake of the Good News will ever know what it means to really live.

³⁶"And how does a man benefit if he gains the whole world and loses his soul in the process? ³⁷For is anything worth more than his soul? ³⁸And anyone who is ashamed of me and my message in these days of unbelief and sin, I, the Messiah, will be ashamed of him when I return in the glory of my Father, with the holy angels."

9 The Transfiguration

Jesus went on to say to his disciples, "Some of you who are standing here right now will live to see the Kingdom of God arrive in great power!"

²Six days later Jesus took Peter, James and John to the top of a mountain. No one else was there.

Suddenly his face began to shine with glory, ³and his clothing became dazzling white, far more glorious than any earthly process could ever make it! ⁴Then Elijah and Moses appeared and began talking with Jesus!

MAKING THE BEST CHOICES 8:36-37 Many people spend their lives seeking pleasure. Jesus said, however, that the world of pleasure centered on possessions, position, or power is ultimately worthless. Whatever we have on earth is only temporary; it cannot be exchanged for our souls. If you work hard at getting what you want, you might eventually have a "pleasurable" life, but in the end you will find it hollow and empty. Are you willing to make the pursuit of God more important than the selfish pursuit of pleasure? Follow Jesus, and you will know what it means to really live in this life and to have life eternal as well. **To begin the series of devotionals on MAKING THE BEST CHOICES, turn to page 275.**

⁵"Teacher, this is wonderful!" Peter exclaimed. "We will make three shelters here, one for each of you...."

⁶He said this just to be talking, for he didn't know what else to say and they were all terribly frightened.

⁷But while he was still speaking these words, a cloud covered them, blotting out the sun, and a voice from the cloud said, *"This* is my beloved Son. Listen to *him."*

⁸Then suddenly they looked around and Moses and Elijah were gone, and only Jesus was with them.

⁹As they descended the mountainside he told them never to mention what they had seen until after he had risen from the dead. ¹⁰So they kept it to themselves, but often talked about it, and wondered what he meant by "rising from the dead."

¹¹Now they began asking him about something the Jewish religious leaders often spoke of, that Elijah must return [before the Messiah could come].

¹²,¹³Jesus agreed that Elijah must come first and prepare the way—and that he had, in fact, already come! And that he had been terribly mistreated, just as the prophets had predicted. Then Jesus asked them what the prophets could have been talking about when they predicted that the Messiah would suffer and be treated with utter contempt.

¹⁴At the bottom of the mountain they found a great crowd surrounding the other nine disciples, as some Jewish leaders argued with them. ¹⁵The crowd watched Jesus in awe as he came toward them, and then ran to greet him. ¹⁶"What's all the argument about?" he asked.

¹⁷One of the men in the crowd spoke up and said, "Teacher, I brought my son for you to heal—he can't talk because he is possessed by a demon. ¹⁸And whenever the demon is in control of him it dashes him to the ground and makes him foam at the mouth and grind his teeth and become rigid. So I begged your disciples to cast out the demon, but they couldn't do it."

¹⁹Jesus said [to his disciples], "Oh, what tiny faith you have; how much longer must I be with you until you believe? How much longer must I be patient with you? Bring the boy to me."

²⁰So they brought the boy, but when he saw Jesus the demon convulsed the child horribly, and he fell to the ground writhing and foaming at the mouth.

²¹"How long has he been this way?" Jesus asked the father.

And he replied, "Since he was very small, ²²and the demon often makes him fall into the fire or into water to kill him. Oh, have mercy on us and do something if you can."

²³"If I can?" Jesus asked. *"Anything* is possible if you have faith."

²⁴The father instantly replied, "I *do* have faith; oh, help me to have *more!"*

²⁵When Jesus saw the crowd was growing he rebuked the demon.

"O demon of deafness and dumbness," he said, "I command you to come out of this child and enter him no more!"

²⁶Then the demon screamed terribly and convulsed the boy again and left him; and the boy lay there limp and motionless, to all appearance dead. A murmur ran through the crowd—"He is dead." ²⁷But Jesus took him by the hand and helped him to his feet and he stood up and was all right! ²⁸Afterwards, when Jesus was alone in the house with his disciples, they asked him, "Why couldn't we cast that demon out?"

²⁹Jesus replied, "Cases like this require prayer."

³⁰,³¹Leaving that region they traveled through Galilee where he tried to avoid all publicity in order to spend more time with his disciples, teaching them. He would say to them, "I, the Messiah, am going to be betrayed and killed and three days later I will return to life again."

³²But they didn't understand and were afraid to ask him what he meant.

³³And so they arrived at Capernaum. When they were settled in the house where they were to stay he asked them, "What were you discussing out on the road?"

³⁴But they were ashamed to answer, for they had been arguing about which of them was the greatest!

³⁵He sat down and called them around him and said, "Anyone wanting to be the greatest must be the least—the servant of all!"

³⁶Then he placed a little child among them; and taking the child in his arms he said to them, ³⁷"Anyone who welcomes a little child like this in my name is welcoming me, and anyone who welcomes me is welcoming my Father who sent me!"

³⁸One of his disciples, John, told him one day, "Teacher, we saw a man using your name to cast out demons; but we told him not to, for he isn't one of our group."

³⁹"Don't forbid him!" Jesus said. "For no one doing miracles in my name will quickly turn against me. ⁴⁰Anyone who isn't against us is for us.

PRAYING AT ALL TIMES 9:23 These words of Jesus do not mean we can automatically obtain anything we want if we just think positively. Jesus meant that anything is *possible* with faith because nothing is too difficult for God. This is not a teaching on how to pray as much as a statement about God's power to overcome obstacles to his work. We cannot have everything we pray for as if by magic; but with faith, we can have everything we need to serve him. **To begin the series of devotionals on PRAYING AT ALL TIMES, turn to page 45.**

⁴¹If anyone so much as gives you a cup of water because you are Christ's—I say this solemnly—he won't lose his reward. ⁴²But if someone causes one of these little ones who believe in me to lose faith—it would be better for that man if a huge millstone were tied around his neck and he were thrown into the sea.

⁴³,⁴⁴ "If your hand does wrong, cut it off. Better live forever with one hand than be thrown into the unquenchable fires of hell with two! ⁴⁵,⁴⁶ If your foot carries you toward evil, cut it off! Better be lame and live forever than have two feet that carry you to hell.

⁴⁷"And if your eye is sinful, gouge it out. Better enter the Kingdom of God half blind than have two eyes and see the fires of hell, ⁴⁸where the worm never dies, and the fire never goes out— ⁴⁹where all are salted with fire.

⁵⁰"Good salt is worthless if it loses its saltiness; it can't season anything. So don't lose your flavor! Live in peace with each other."

10 Marriage and Divorce

Then he left Capernaum and went southward to the Judean borders and into the area east of the Jordan River. And as always there were the crowds; and as usual he taught them.

²Some Pharisees came and asked him, "Do you permit divorce?" Of course they were trying to trap him.

³"What did Moses say about divorce?" Jesus asked them.

⁴"He said it was all right," they replied. "He said that all a man has to do is write his wife a letter of dismissal."

⁵"And why did he say that?" Jesus asked. "I'll tell you why—it was a concession to your hardhearted wickedness. ⁶,⁷But it certainly isn't God's way. For from the very first he made man and woman to be joined together permanently in marriage; therefore a man is to leave his father and mother, ⁸and he and his wife are united so that they are no longer two, but one. ⁹And no man may separate what God has joined together."

¹⁰Later, when he was alone with his disciples in the house, they brought up the subject again.

¹¹He told them, "When a man divorces his wife to marry someone else, he commits adultery against her. ¹²And if a wife divorces her husband and remarries, she, too, commits adultery."

¹³Once when some mothers were bringing their children to Jesus to bless them, the disciples shooed them away, telling them not to bother him.

¹⁴But when Jesus saw what was happening he was very much displeased with his disciples and said to them, "Let the children come to me, for the Kingdom of God belongs to such as they. Don't send them away! ¹⁵I tell you as seriously as I know how that anyone who refuses to come to God as a little child will never be allowed into his Kingdom."

¹⁶Then he took the children into his arms and placed his hands on their heads and he blessed them.

¹⁷As he was starting out on a trip, a man came running to him and knelt down and asked, "Good Teacher, what must I do to get to heaven?"

¹⁸"Why do you call me good?" Jesus asked. "Only God is truly good! ¹⁹But as for your question—you know the commandments: don't kill, don't commit adultery, don't steal, don't lie, don't cheat, respect your father and mother."

²⁰"Teacher," the man replied, "I've never once broken a single one of those laws."

²¹Jesus felt genuine love for this man as he looked at him. "You lack only one thing," he told him; "go and sell all you have and give the money to the poor—and you shall have treasure in heaven—and come, follow me."

²²Then the man's face fell, and he went sadly away, for he was very rich.

²³Jesus watched him go, then turned around and said to his disciples, "It's almost impossible for the rich to get into the Kingdom of God!"

²⁴This amazed them. So Jesus said it again: "Dear children, how hard it is for those who trust in riches to enter the Kingdom of God. ²⁵It is easier for a camel to go through the eye of a needle than for a rich man to enter the Kingdom of God."

²⁶The disciples were incredulous! "Then who in the world can be saved, if not a rich man?" they asked.

²⁷Jesus looked at them intently, then said, "Without God, it is utterly impossible. But with God everything is possible."

²⁸Then Peter began to mention all that he and the other disciples had left behind. "We've given up everything to follow you," he said.

²⁹And Jesus replied, "Let me assure you that no one has ever given up anything—home, brothers, sisters, mother, father, children, or property—for love of me and to tell others the Good News, ³⁰who won't be given back, a hundred times over, homes, brothers, sisters, mothers, children, and land—with persecutions!

"All these will be his here on earth, and in the world to come he shall have eternal life. ³¹But many people who seem to be important now will be the least important then; and many who are considered least here shall be greatest there."

³²Now they were on the way to Jerusalem, and Jesus was walking along ahead; and as the disciples were following they were filled with terror and dread.

Family Devotions

☐ DEVOTION 263
SERVING GOD BOLDLY

Read Mark 11:1-11

"What can you do to serve Jesus, boys and girls?" asked Mr. Jim, the leader of children's church.

Good question, thought Mary Lou. She wanted to be used by God, but she didn't see any way the Lord could possibly use her. Some kids brought money to Sunday school, but she didn't have any money of her own to give. Some kids sang in the children's choir, but Mary Lou was sure she didn't have a good voice. Some kids always gave testimonies on Sunday nights, but she just knew she would stutter if she tried to do that.

Just then Mr. Jim asked, "Are you smarter than a donkey?" All the kids laughed. "Then," continued Mr. Jim, "you can serve Jesus." He went on to read Mark 11:1-11, and then he explained how a donkey colt was once a perfect picture of a servant. "First of all," said Mr. Jim, "he was where God wanted him to be. He was available."

Hmmm, thought Mary Lou. *Well, I want God to be able to use me. I guess I'm available.*

"Second," added Mr. Jim, "he was untied, as Jesus said he should be. This makes me think that maybe you're afraid to try to serve Jesus. Maybe you need to let him untie your fears." Now Mary Lou knew that this lesson was just for her. She had to admit that she was afraid to try to sing or witness for Jesus.

"Also, the colt was controlled," Mr. Jim continued. He explained how, even though this colt had never been ridden before, he didn't buck in fright when Jesus sat on him. He just let Jesus control him. "Have you truly let Jesus control you, or have you been stubborn?" asked Mr. Jim. Mary Lou began to feel uncomfortable. She knew she had been thinking only about how she felt and what she would like to do. She hadn't asked Jesus to control her life.

When Mr. Jim asked the children to bow their heads for prayer, Mary Lou asked God to take control of her life. She asked him to untie all her fear of failure. *Let me be a servant just like the little donkey,* she prayed.

Serving God Boldly Memory Verse

Yes, be bold and strong!
Banish fear and doubt!
For remember, the Lord
your God is with you
wherever you go.
Joshua 1:9

How About You?

Are you afraid to try to speak out for Jesus? Are you afraid that if you try to sing a song or play an instrument to serve him, you will make a mistake? Take a lesson from the donkey colt. Be available. Be untied. And be controlled. The Lord needs you! R. P.

- For the next devotional, turn to page 949.   • For the next devotional on SERVING GOD BOLDLY, turn to page 1169.
- For notes on SERVING GOD BOLDLY, see pages 327, 404, 501, 720, and 856.

Taking them aside, Jesus once more began describing all that was going to happen to him when they arrived at Jerusalem.

³³"When we get there," he told them, "I, the Messiah, will be arrested and taken before the chief priests and the Jewish leaders, who will sentence me to die and hand me over to the Romans to be killed. ³⁴They will mock me and spit on me and flog me with their whips and kill me; but after three days I will come back to life again."

³⁵Then James and John, the sons of Zebedee, came over and spoke to him in a low voice. "Master," they said, "we want you to do us a favor."

³⁶"What is it?" he asked.

³⁷"We want to sit on the thrones next to yours in your Kingdom," they said, "one at your right and the other at your left!"

³⁸But Jesus answered, "You don't know what you are asking! Are you able to drink from the bitter cup of sorrow I must drink from? Or to be baptized with the baptism of suffering I must be baptized with?"

³⁹"Oh, yes," they said, "we are!"

And Jesus said, "You shall indeed drink from my cup and be baptized with my baptism, ⁴⁰but I do not have the right to place you on thrones next to mine. Those appointments have already been made."

⁴¹When the other disciples discovered what James and John had asked, they were very indignant. ⁴²So Jesus called them to him and said, "As you know, the kings and great men of the earth lord it over the people; ⁴³but among you it is different. Whoever wants to be great among you must be your servant. ⁴⁴And whoever wants to be greatest of all must be the slave of all. ⁴⁵For even I, the Messiah, am not here to be served, but to help others, and to give my life as a ransom for many."

⁴⁶And so they reached Jericho. Later, as they left town, a great crowd was following. Now it happened that a blind beggar named Bartimaeus (the son of Timaeus) was sitting beside the road as Jesus was going by.

⁴⁷When Bartimaeus heard that Jesus from Nazareth was near, he began to shout out, "Jesus, Son of David, have mercy on me!"

⁴⁸"Shut up!" some of the people yelled at him. But he only shouted the louder, again and again, "O Son of David, have mercy on me!"

⁴⁹When Jesus heard him, he stopped there in the road and said, "Tell him to come here."

So they called the blind man. "You lucky fellow," they said, "come on, he's calling you!" ⁵⁰Bartimaeus yanked off his old coat and flung it aside, jumped up and came to Jesus.

⁵¹"What do you want me to do for you?" Jesus asked.

"O Teacher," the blind man said, "I want to see!"

⁵²And Jesus said to him, "All right, it's done. Your faith has healed you."

And instantly the blind man could see and followed Jesus down the road!

Crowds Welcome Jesus

As they neared Bethphage and Bethany on the outskirts of Jerusalem and came to the Mount of Olives, Jesus sent two of his disciples on ahead.

²"Go into that village over there," he told them, "and just as you enter you will see a colt tied up that has never been ridden. Untie him and bring him here. ³And if anyone asks you what you are doing, just say, 'Our Master needs him and will return him soon.'"

⁴,⁵Off went the two men and found the colt standing in the street, tied outside a house. As they were untying it, some who were standing there demanded, "What are you doing, untying that colt?"

⁶So they said what Jesus had told them to, and then the men agreed.

⁷So the colt was brought to Jesus, and the disciples threw their cloaks across its back for him to ride on. ⁸Then many in the crowd spread out their coats along the road before him, while others threw down leafy branches from the fields.

⁹He was in the center of the procession with crowds ahead and behind, and all of them shouting, "Hail to the King!" "Praise God for him who comes in the name of the Lord!" . . . ¹⁰"Praise God for the return of our father David's kingdom . . . " "Hail to the King of the universe!"

¹¹And so he entered Jerusalem and went into the Temple. He looked around carefully at everything and then left—for now it was late in the afternoon—and went out to Bethany with the twelve disciples.

¹²The next morning as they left Bethany, he felt hungry. ¹³A little way off he noticed a fig tree in full leaf, so he went over to see if he could find any figs on it. But no, there were only leaves, for it was too early in the season for fruit.

¹⁴Then Jesus said to the tree, "You shall never bear fruit again!" And the disciples heard him say it.

STANDING FOR RIGHTEOUSNESS **11:14-15** Jesus became angry, but he did not sin in his anger. There is a place for righteous indignation. Christians should be upset about sin and injustice and should take a stand against them. Unfortunately, believers are often passive about these important issues and get angry instead over personal insults and petty irritations. Make sure your anger is directed toward the right issues. **To begin the series of devotionals on STANDING FOR RIGHTEOUSNESS, turn to page 139.**

FAMILY DEVOTIONS

☐ *DEVOTION 264*
PATIENCE

Read Mark 11:22-25

"God sure has answered a lot of prayers for us lately, hasn't he?" Mark asked his big sister, Mary.

"He sure has," Mary agreed. "He healed Grandma, gave Daddy a job, and even sent us some new friends!"

"I guess God will give us anything we want. All we have to do is ask him," five-year-old Mark reasoned.

After Mother had tucked the children into bed that night, she returned to the living room, a frown on her face. "In their prayers tonight Mary asked God to send a piano, and Mark asked for a bike."

Dad grinned. "I guess they're taking their requests over our heads."

After a week of watching and waiting, Mark and Mary went to their mother. "I thought God always answered our prayers," Mary began.

"He does, Mary." Mother knew what was coming. "Did you ask for something you haven't received?"

Both children nodded. "We asked for a bicycle and a piano, but I guess God didn't hear us. Maybe we should pray louder," Mark said.

"I'm sure God heard you," replied Mother, "but I don't think you're hearing his answer. He's telling you the same thing Daddy and I told you when you asked us. He's telling you to wait."

Mary frowned. "But we don't want to wait."

"Your daddy and I know that you need to wait, and God agrees with us," Mother explained.

Mary patted Mark's shoulder. "Well, Mark, we tried. Now I guess we'll just have to wait."

Patience Memory Verse

Now as for you, dear brothers who are waiting for the Lord's return, be patient, like a farmer who waits until the autumn for his precious harvest to ripen.
James 5:7

How About You?

Are you asking God for something your parents have said you cannot have or will have to wait for? Perhaps what you want may not be good for you right now. When you pray, listen for God's answer. Sometimes he says yes. Sometimes he says no. And sometimes he tells you, "Wait." God always answers your prayers. Do you always hear his answer? B. W.

• For the next devotional, turn to page 953. • For the next devotional on *PATIENCE*, turn to page 1139. • For notes on *PATIENCE*, see pages 35, 242, 329, and 502.

[15]When they arrived back to Jerusalem he went to the Temple and began to drive out the merchants and their customers, and knocked over the tables of the moneychangers and the stalls of those selling doves, [16]and stopped everyone from bringing in loads of merchandise.

[17]He told them, "It is written in the Scriptures, 'My Temple is to be a place of prayer for all nations,' but you have turned it into a den of robbers."

[18]When the chief priests and other Jewish leaders heard what he had done, they began planning how best to get rid of him. Their problem was their fear of riots because the people were so enthusiastic about Jesus' teaching.

[19]That evening as usual they left the city.

[20]Next morning, as the disciples passed the fig tree he had cursed, they saw that it was withered from the roots! [21]Then Peter remembered what Jesus had said to the tree on the previous day and exclaimed, "Look, Teacher! The fig tree you cursed has withered!"

[22,23]In reply Jesus said to the disciples, "If you only have faith in God—this is the absolute truth—you can say to this Mount of Olives, 'Rise up and fall into the Mediterranean,' and your command will be obeyed. All that's required is that you really believe and have no doubt! [24]Listen to me! You can pray for *anything*, and *if you believe, you have it*; it's yours! [25]But when you are praying, first forgive anyone you are holding a grudge against, so that your Father in heaven will forgive you your sins too."

[26-28] By this time they had arrived in Jerusalem again, and as he was walking through the Temple area, the chief priests and other Jewish leaders came up to him demanding, "What's going on here? Who gave you the authority to drive out the merchants?"

[29]Jesus replied, "I'll tell you if you answer one question! [30]What about John the Baptist? Was he sent by God, or not? Answer me!"

[31]They talked it over among themselves. "If we reply that God sent him, then he will say, 'All right, why didn't you accept him?' [32]But if we say God didn't send him, then the people will start a riot." (For the people all believed strongly that John was a prophet.)

[33]So they said, "We can't answer. We don't know."

To which Jesus replied, "Then I won't answer your question either!"

12 A Story about a Farm

Here are some of the story-illustrations Jesus gave to the people at that time:

"A man planted a vineyard and built a wall around it and dug a pit for pressing out the grape juice, and built a watchman's tower. Then he leased the farm to tenant farmers and moved to another country. [2]At grape-picking time he sent one of his men to collect his share of the crop. [3]But the farmers beat up the man and sent him back empty-handed.

[4]"The owner then sent another of his men, who received the same treatment, only worse, for his head was seriously injured. [5]The next man he sent was killed; and later, others were either beaten or killed, until [6]there was only one left—his only son. He finally sent him, thinking they would surely give him their full respect.

[7]"But when the farmers saw him coming they said, 'He will own the farm when his father dies. Come on, let's kill him—and then the farm will be ours!' [8]So they caught him and murdered him and threw his body out of the vineyard.

[9]"What do you suppose the owner will do when he hears what happened? He will come and kill them all, and lease the vineyard to others. [10]Don't you remember reading this verse in the Scriptures? 'The Rock the builders threw away became the cornerstone, the most honored stone in the building! [11]This is the Lord's doing and it is an amazing thing to see.'"

[12]The Jewish leaders wanted to arrest him then and there for using this illustration, for they knew he was pointing at them—they were the wicked farmers in his story. But they were afraid to touch him for fear of a mob. So they left him and went away.

[13]But they sent other religious and political leaders to talk with him and try to trap him into saying something he could be arrested for.

[14]"Teacher," these spies said, "we know you tell the truth no matter what! You aren't influenced by the opinions and desires of men, but sincerely teach the ways of God. Now tell us, is it right to pay taxes to Rome, or not?"

[15]Jesus saw their trick and said, "Show me a coin and I'll tell you."

[16]When they handed it to him he asked, "Whose picture and title is this on the coin?" They replied, "The emperor's."

[17]"All right," he said, "if it is his, give it to him. But everything that belongs to God must be given to God!" And they scratched their heads in bafflement at his reply.

[18]Then the Sadducees stepped forward—a group of men who say there is no resurrection. Here was their question:

[19]"Teacher, Moses gave us a law that when a man dies without children, the man's brother should marry his widow and have children in his brother's name. [20-22]Well, there were seven brothers and the oldest married and died, and left no children. So the second brother married the

widow, but soon he died too and left no children. Then the next brother married her and died without children, and so on until all were dead, and still there were no children; and last of all, the woman died too.

²³"What we want to know is this: In the resurrection, whose wife will she be, for she had been the wife of each of them?"

²⁴Jesus replied, "Your trouble is that you don't know the Scriptures and don't know the power of God. ²⁵For when these seven brothers and the woman rise from the dead, they won't be married—they will be like the angels.

²⁶"But now as to whether there will be a resurrection—have you never read in the book of Exodus about Moses and the burning bush? God said to Moses, 'I *am* the God of Abraham, and I *am* the God of Isaac, and I *am* the God of Jacob.'

²⁷"God was telling Moses that these men, though dead for hundreds of years, were still very much alive, for he would not have said, 'I *am* the God' of those who don't exist! You have made a serious error."

²⁸One of the teachers of religion who was standing there listening to the discussion realized that Jesus had answered well. So he asked, "Of all the commandments, which is the most important?"

²⁹Jesus replied, "The one that says, 'Hear, O Israel! The Lord our God is the one and only God. ³⁰And you must love him with all your heart and soul and mind and strength.'

³¹"The second is: 'You must love others as much as yourself.' No other commandments are greater than these."

³²The teacher of religion replied, "Sir, you have spoken a true word in saying that there is only one God and no other. ³³And I know it is far more important to love him with all my heart and understanding and strength, and to love others as myself, than to offer all kinds of sacrifices on the altar of the Temple."

³⁴Realizing this man's understanding, Jesus said to him, "You are not far from the Kingdom of God." And after that, no one dared ask him any more questions.

³⁵Later, as Jesus was teaching the people in the Temple area, he asked them this question:

"Why do your religious teachers claim that the Messiah must be a descendant of King David? ³⁶For David himself said—and the Holy Spirit was speaking through him when he said it—'God said to my Lord, sit at my right hand until I make your enemies your footstool.' ³⁷Since David called him his Lord, how can he be his *son?*"

(This sort of reasoning delighted the crowd and they listened to him with great interest.)

³⁸Here are some of the other things he taught them at this time:

"Beware of the teachers of religion! For they love to wear the robes of the rich and scholarly, and to have everyone bow to them as they walk through the markets. ³⁹They love to sit in the best seats in the synagogues and at the places of honor at banquets—⁴⁰but they shamelessly cheat widows out of their homes and then, to cover up the kind of men they really are, they pretend to be pious by praying long prayers in public. Because of this, their punishment will be the greater."

⁴¹Then he went over to the collection boxes in the Temple and sat and watched as the crowds dropped in their money. Some who were rich put in large amounts. ⁴²Then a poor widow came and dropped in two pennies.

⁴³,⁴⁴He called his disciples to him and remarked, "That poor widow has given more than all those rich men put together! For they gave a little of their extra fat, while she gave up her last penny."

13 Jesus Tells about the Future

As he was leaving the Temple that day, one of his disciples said, "Teacher, what beautiful buildings these are! Look at the decorated stonework on the walls."

²Jesus replied, "Yes, look! For not one stone will be left upon another, except as ruins."

³,⁴And as he sat on the slopes of the Mount of Olives across the valley from Jerusalem, Peter, James, John, and Andrew got alone with him and asked him, "Just when is all this going to happen to the Temple? Will there be some warning ahead of time?"

⁵So Jesus launched into an extended reply. "Don't let anyone mislead you," he said, ⁶"for many will come declaring themselves to be your Messiah and will lead many astray. ⁷And wars will break out near and far, but this is not the signal of the end-time.

⁸"For nations and kingdoms will proclaim war against each other, and there will be earthquakes in many lands, and famines. These herald only the early stages of the anguish ahead. ⁹But when

---

LOVING OTHERS 12:29-31 God's laws can be reduced to two simple rules for life: love God and love others. These commands are from the Old Testament (Leviticus 19:18; Deuteronomy 6:5). When you love God completely and care for others as you care for yourself, then you have fulfilled the intent of the Ten Commandments and the other Old Testament laws. According to Jesus, these two rules summarize all God's laws. When you are uncertain about what to do, ask yourself which course of action best demonstrates love for God and love for others. **To begin the series of devotionals on LOVING OTHERS, turn to page 313.**

these things begin to happen, watch out! For you will be in great danger. You will be dragged before the courts, and beaten in the synagogues, and accused before governors and kings of being my followers. This is your opportunity to tell them the Good News. 10And the Good News must first be made known in every nation before the end-time finally comes. 11But when you are arrested and stand trial, don't worry about what to say in your defense. Just say what God tells you to. Then you will not be speaking, but the Holy Spirit will.

12"Brothers will betray each other to death, fathers will betray their own children, and children will betray their parents to be killed. 13And everyone will hate you because you are mine. But all who endure to the end without renouncing me shall be saved.

14"When you see the horrible thing standing in the Temple—reader, pay attention!—flee, if you can, to the Judean hills. 15,16Hurry! If you are on your rooftop porch, don't even go back into the house. If you are out in the fields, don't even return for your money or clothes.

17"Woe to pregnant women in those days, and to mothers nursing their children. 18And pray that your flight will not be in winter. 19For those will be days of such horror as have never been since the beginning of God's creation, nor will ever be again. 20And unless the Lord shortens that time of calamity, not a soul in all the earth will survive. But for the sake of his chosen ones he will limit those days.

21"And then if anyone tells you, 'This is the Messiah,' or, 'That one is,' don't pay any attention. 22For there will be many false Messiahs and false prophets who will do wonderful miracles that would deceive, if possible, even God's own children. 23Take care! I have warned you!

24"After the tribulation ends, then the sun will grow dim and the moon will not shine, 25and the stars will fall—the heavens will convulse.

26"Then all mankind will see me, the Messiah, coming in the clouds with great power and glory. 27And I will send out the angels to gather together my chosen ones from all over the world—from the farthest bounds of earth and heaven.

28"Now, here is a lesson from a fig tree. When its buds become tender and its leaves begin to sprout, you know that spring has come. 29And when you see these things happening that I've described, you can be sure that my return is very near, that I am right at the door.

30"Yes, these are the events that will signal the end of the age. 31Heaven and earth shall disappear, but my words stand sure forever.

32"However, no one, not even the angels in heaven, nor I myself, knows the day or hour when these things will happen; only the Father knows. 33And since you don't know when it will happen, stay alert. Be on the watch [for my return].

34"My coming can be compared with that of a man who went on a trip to another country. He laid out his employees' work for them to do while he was gone and told the gatekeeper to watch for his return.

35-37"Keep a sharp lookout! For you do not know when I will come, at evening, at midnight, early dawn or late daybreak. Don't let me find you sleeping. *Watch for my return!* This is my message to you and to everyone else."

14 A Plot to Kill Jesus

The Passover observance began two days later—an annual Jewish holiday when no bread made with yeast was eaten. The chief priests and other Jewish leaders were still looking for an opportunity to arrest Jesus secretly and put him to death.

2"But we can't do it during the Passover," they said, "or there will be a riot."

3Meanwhile Jesus was in Bethany, at the home of Simon the leper; during supper a woman came in with a beautiful flask of expensive perfume. Then, breaking the seal, she poured it over his head.

4,5Some of those at the table were indignant among themselves about this "waste," as they called it.

"Why, she could have sold that perfume for a fortune and given the money to the poor!" they snarled.

6But Jesus said, "Let her alone; why berate her for doing a good thing? 7You always have the poor among you, and they badly need your help, and you can aid them whenever you want to; but I won't be here much longer.

8"She has done what she could and has anointed my body ahead of time for burial. 9And I tell you this in solemn truth, that wherever the Good News is preached throughout the world, this woman's deed will be remembered and praised."

10Then Judas Iscariot, one of his disciples, went to the chief priests to arrange to betray Jesus to them.

11When the chief priests heard why he had come, they were excited and happy and promised him a reward. So he began looking for the right time and place to betray Jesus.

12On the first day of the Passover, the day the lambs were sacrificed, his disciples asked him where he wanted to go to eat the traditional Pass-

FAMILY DEVOTIONS

☐ *DEVOTION 265*
LOVING OTHERS

Read Mark 14:3-9

Loving Others
Memory Verse

Little children, let us stop just *saying* we love people; let us *really* love them, and *show it* by our *actions*.
1 John 3:18

John busily worked on a picture for his grandmother, who would be coming for a visit soon. He finished drawing a house, then worked on trees and other objects. John enjoyed art, and his teacher had told him he had a talent for it. "There!" he said, checking the finished picture to make sure he had done it as well as he could.

Nearby John's younger sister, Sara, worked on a picture of her own. "Mine's done, too," she said, holding it up.

"Looks like scribbling to me," John scoffed.

When Grandma arrived, John gave her his drawing. "My, but this is good work, John," Grandma exclaimed. When Sara shyly held out her picture, Grandma exclaimed over it, too. But she noticed John's scowl.

Later, when John and Grandma were alone, she asked him about it. "You seemed displeased when I praised Sara for her picture. Why?"

"It wasn't as good as mine," replied John. "It was just scribbling. Why would you like it?"

"I saw the love that went into it," Grandma explained. "I saw that Sara had worked just as hard to please me as you had. Maybe it wasn't done with a practiced hand, as yours was, but the love was there."

John still looked a little doubtful, but he nodded slowly. "I guess that means you'd love me just as much if I couldn't draw well," he said. Then he added with a smile, "And that's good."

"That's right," agreed Grandma. "Shall I tell you something else that's good? God sees the things we do for him out of love. We see some actions, or deeds, as being little or unimportant, but they're important to God because he notices the love put into them. Giving a helping hand, a friendly smile, or an encouraging word is just as important to God as any other job."

How About You?
Do you sometimes feel that what you have done for God may be more important than what someone else has done? Or perhaps you feel your actions are less important. God sees the love in your deeds, no matter what they are. All acts done in love are precious in God's sight. *C. Y.*

• For the next devotional, turn to page 957. • For the next devotional on LOVING OTHERS, turn to page 975.
• For notes on LOVING OTHERS, see pages 658, 951, 967, and 1242.

over supper. ¹³He sent two of them into Jerusalem to make the arrangements.

"As you are walking along," he told them, "you will see a man coming toward you carrying a pot of water. Follow him. ¹⁴At the house he enters, tell the man in charge, 'Our Master sent us to see the room you have ready for us, where we will eat the Passover supper this evening!' ¹⁵He will take you upstairs to a large room all set up. Prepare our supper there."

¹⁶So the two disciples went on ahead into the city and found everything as Jesus had said, and prepared the Passover.

¹⁷In the evening Jesus arrived with the other disciples, ¹⁸and as they were sitting around the table eating, Jesus said, "I solemnly declare that one of you will betray me, one of you who is here eating with me."

¹⁹A great sadness swept over them, and one by one they asked him, "Am I the one?"

²⁰He replied, "It is one of you twelve eating with me now. ²¹I must die, as the prophets declared long ago; but, oh, the misery ahead for the man by whom I am betrayed. Oh, that he had never been born!"

²²As they were eating, Jesus took bread and asked God's blessing on it and broke it in pieces and gave it to them and said, "Eat it—this is my body."

²³Then he took a cup of wine and gave thanks to God for it and gave it to them; and they all drank from it. ²⁴And he said to them, "This is my blood, poured out for many, sealing the new agreement between God and man. ²⁵I solemnly declare that I shall never again taste wine until the day I drink a different kind in the Kingdom of God."

²⁶Then they sang a hymn and went out to the Mount of Olives.

²⁷"All of you will desert me," Jesus told them, "for God has declared through the prophets, 'I will kill the Shepherd, and the sheep will scatter.' ²⁸But after I am raised to life again, I will go to Galilee and meet you there."

²⁹Peter said to him, "I will never desert you no matter what the others do!"

³⁰"Peter," Jesus said, "before the cock crows a second time tomorrow morning you will deny me three times."

³¹"No!" Peter exploded. "Not even if I have to die with you! I'll *never* deny you!" And all the others vowed the same.

³²And now they came to an olive grove called the Garden of Gethsemane, and he instructed his disciples, "Sit here, while I go and pray."

³³He took Peter, James, and John with him and began to be filled with horror and deepest distress. ³⁴And he said to them, "My soul is crushed by sorrow to the point of death; stay here and watch with me."

³⁵He went on a little further and fell to the ground and prayed that if it were possible the awful hour awaiting him might never come.

³⁶"Father, Father," he said, "everything is possible for you. Take away this cup from me. Yet I want your will, not mine."

³⁷Then he returned to the three disciples and found them asleep.

"Simon!" he said. "Asleep? Couldn't you watch with me even one hour? ³⁸Watch with me and pray lest the Tempter overpower you. For though the spirit is willing enough, the body is weak."

³⁹And he went away again and prayed, repeating his pleadings. ⁴⁰Again he returned to them and found them sleeping, for they were very tired. And they didn't know what to say.

⁴¹The third time when he returned to them he said, "Sleep on; get your rest! But no! The time for sleep has ended! Look! I am betrayed into the hands of wicked men. ⁴²Come! Get up! We must go! Look! My betrayer is here!"

⁴³And immediately, while he was still speaking, Judas (one of his disciples) arrived with a mob equipped with swords and clubs, sent out by the chief priests and other Jewish leaders.

⁴⁴Judas had told them, "You will know which one to arrest when I go over and greet him. Then you can take him easily." ⁴⁵So as soon as they arrived he walked up to Jesus. "Master!" he exclaimed, and embraced him with a great show of friendliness. ⁴⁶Then the mob arrested Jesus and held him fast. ⁴⁷But someone pulled a sword and slashed at the High Priest's servant, cutting off his ear.

⁴⁸Jesus asked them, "Am I some dangerous robber, that you come like this, armed to the teeth to capture me? ⁴⁹Why didn't you arrest me in the Temple? I was there teaching every day. But these things are happening to fulfill the prophecies about me."

⁵⁰Meanwhile, all his disciples had fled. ⁵¹,⁵²There was, however, a young man following along behind, clothed only in a linen nightshirt. When the mob tried to grab him, he escaped, though his clothes were torn off in the process, so that he ran away completely naked.

⁵³Jesus was led to the High Priest's home where all of the chief priests and other Jewish leaders soon gathered. ⁵⁴Peter followed far behind and then slipped inside the gates of the High Priest's residence and crouched beside a fire among the servants.

⁵⁵Inside, the chief priests and the whole Jewish Supreme Court were trying to find something against Jesus that would be sufficient to condemn

him to death. But their efforts were in vain. ⁵⁶Many false witnesses volunteered, but they contradicted each other.

⁵⁷Finally some men stood up to lie about him and said, ⁵⁸"We heard him say, 'I will destroy this Temple made with human hands and in three days I will build another, made without human hands!'" ⁵⁹But even then they didn't get their stories straight!

⁶⁰Then the High Priest stood up before the Court and asked Jesus, "Do you refuse to answer this charge? What do you have to say for yourself?"

⁶¹To this Jesus made no reply.

Then the High Priest asked him. "Are you the Messiah, the Son of God?"

⁶²Jesus said, "I am, and you will see me sitting at the right hand of God, and returning to earth in the clouds of heaven."

⁶³,⁶⁴Then the High Priest tore at his clothes and said, "What more do we need? Why wait for witnesses? You have heard his blasphemy. What is your verdict?" And the vote for the death sentence was unanimous.

⁶⁵Then some of them began to spit at him, and they blindfolded him and began to hammer his face with their fists.

"Who hit you that time, you prophet?" they jeered. And even the bailiffs were using their fists on him as they led him away.

⁶⁶,⁶⁷Meanwhile Peter was below in the courtyard. One of the maids who worked for the High Priest noticed Peter warming himself at the fire.

She looked at him closely and then announced, *"You* were with Jesus, the Nazarene."

⁶⁸Peter denied it. "I don't know what you're talking about!" he said, and walked over to the edge of the courtyard.

Just then, a rooster crowed.

⁶⁹The maid saw him standing there and began telling the others, "There he is! There's that disciple of Jesus!"

⁷⁰Peter denied it again.

A little later others standing around the fire began saying to Peter, "You are, too, one of them, for you are from Galilee!"

⁷¹He began to curse and swear. "I don't even know this fellow you are talking about," he said.

⁷²And immediately the rooster crowed the second time. Suddenly Jesus' words flashed through Peter's mind: "Before the cock crows twice, you will deny me three times." And he began to cry.

15 Pilate Questions Jesus

Early in the morning the chief priests, elders and teachers of religion—the entire Supreme Court—met to discuss their next steps. Their decision was to send Jesus under armed guard to Pilate, the Roman governor.

²Pilate asked him, "Are you the King of the Jews?"

"Yes," Jesus replied, "it is as you say."

³,⁴Then the chief priests accused him of many crimes, and Pilate asked him, "Why don't you say something? What about all these charges against you?"

⁵But Jesus said no more, much to Pilate's amazement.

⁶Now, it was Pilate's custom to release one Jewish prisoner each year at Passover time—any prisoner the people requested. ⁷One of the prisoners at that time was Barabbas, convicted along with others for murder during an insurrection.

⁸Now a mob began to crowd in toward Pilate, asking him to release a prisoner as usual.

⁹"How about giving you the 'King of Jews'?" Pilate asked. "Is he the one you want released?" ¹⁰(For he realized by now that this was a frameup, backed by the chief priests because they envied Jesus' popularity.)

¹¹But at this point the chief priests whipped up the mob to demand the release of Barabbas instead of Jesus.

¹²"But if I release Barabbas," Pilate asked them, "what shall I do with this man you call your king?"

¹³They shouted back, "Crucify him!"

¹⁴"But why?" Pilate demanded. "What has he done wrong?" They only roared the louder, "Crucify him!"

¹⁵Then Pilate, afraid of a riot and anxious to please the people, released Barabbas to them. And he ordered Jesus flogged with a leaded whip, and handed him over to be crucified.

¹⁶,¹⁷Then the Roman soldiers took him into the barracks of the palace, called out the entire palace guard, dressed him in a purple robe, and made a crown of long, sharp thorns and put it on his head. ¹⁸Then they saluted, yelling, "Yea! King of the Jews!" ¹⁹And they beat him on the head with a cane, and spat on him, and went down on their knees to "worship" him.

²⁰When they finally tired of their sport, they took off the purple robe and put his own clothes on him again, and led him away to be crucified.

²¹Simon of Cyrene, who was coming in from the country just then, was pressed into service to carry Jesus' cross. (Simon is the father of Alexander and Rufus.)

²²And they brought Jesus to a place called Golgotha. (Golgotha means skull.) ²³Wine drugged with bitter herbs was offered to him there, but he refused it. ²⁴And then they crucified him—and threw dice for his clothes.

25It was about nine o'clock in the morning when the crucifixion took place.

26A signboard was fastened to the cross above his head, announcing his crime. It read, "The King of the Jews."

27Two robbers were also crucified that morning, their crosses on either side of his. 28 And so the Scripture was fulfilled that said, "He was counted among evil men."

29,30The people jeered at him as they walked by, and wagged their heads in mockery.

"Ha! Look at you now!" they yelled at him. "Sure, you can destroy the Temple and rebuild it in three days! If you're so wonderful, save yourself and come down from the cross."

31The chief priests and religious leaders were also standing around joking about Jesus.

"He's quite clever at 'saving' others," they said, "but he can't save himself!"

32"Hey there, Messiah!" they yelled at him. "You 'King of Israel'! Come on down from the cross and we'll believe you!"

And even the two robbers dying with him, cursed him.

33About noon, darkness fell across the entire land, lasting until three o'clock that afternoon.

34Then Jesus called out with a loud voice, "Eli, Eli, lama sabachthani?" ("My God, my God, why have you deserted me?")

35Some of the people standing there thought he was calling for the prophet Elijah. 36So one man ran and got a sponge and filled it with sour wine and held it up to him on a stick.

"Let's see if Elijah will come and take him down!" he said.

37Then Jesus uttered another loud cry and dismissed his spirit.

38And the curtain in the Temple was split apart from top to bottom.

39When the Roman officer standing beside his cross saw how he dismissed his spirit, he exclaimed, "Truly, this was the Son of God!"

40Some women were there watching from a distance—Mary Magdalene, Mary (the mother of James the Younger and of Joses), Salome, and others. 41They and many other Galilean women who were his followers had ministered to him when he was up in Galilee, and had come with him to Jerusalem.

42,43This all happened the day before the Sabbath. Late that afternoon Joseph from Arimathea, an honored member of the Jewish Supreme Court (who personally was eagerly expecting the arrival of God's Kingdom), gathered his courage and went to Pilate and asked for Jesus' body.

44Pilate couldn't believe that Jesus was already dead so he called for the Roman officer in charge and asked him. 45The officer confirmed the fact, and Pilate told Joseph he could have the body.

46Joseph bought a long sheet of linen cloth and, taking Jesus' body down from the cross, wound it in the cloth and laid it in a rock-hewn tomb, and rolled a stone in front of the entrance.

47(Mary Magdalene and Mary the mother of Joses were watching as Jesus was laid away.)

16 Women Visit Jesus' Tomb

The next evening, when the Sabbath ended, Mary Magdalene and Salome and Mary the mother of James went out and purchased embalming spices.

Early the following morning, just at sunrise, they carried them out to the tomb. 3On the way they were discussing how they could ever roll aside the huge stone from the entrance.

4But when they arrived they looked up and saw that the stone—a *very* heavy one—was already moved away and the entrance was open! 5So they entered the tomb—and there on the right sat a young man clothed in white. The women were startled, 6but the angel said, "Don't be so surprised. Aren't you looking for Jesus, the Nazarene who was crucified? He isn't here! He has come back to life! Look, that's where his body was lying. 7Now go and give this message to his disciples including Peter:

"'Jesus is going ahead of you to Galilee. You will see him there, just as he told you before he died!'"

8The women fled from the tomb, trembling and bewildered, too frightened to talk.

9 It was early on Sunday morning when Jesus came back to life, and the first person who saw him was Mary Magdalene—the woman from whom he had cast out seven demons. 10,11She found the disciples wet-eyed with grief and exclaimed that she had seen Jesus, and he was alive! But they didn't believe her!

12Later that day he appeared to two who were walking from Jerusalem into the country, but they didn't recognize him at first because he had changed his appearance. 13When they finally realized who he was, they rushed back to Jerusalem to tell the others, but no one believed them.

14Still later he appeared to the eleven disciples as they were eating together. He rebuked them for their unbelief—their stubborn refusal to believe those who had seen him alive from the dead.

15And then he told them, "You are to go into all the world and preach the Good News to everyone, everywhere. 16Those who believe and are baptized will be saved. But those who refuse to believe will be condemned.

Family Devotions

☐ *Devotion 266*
Sharing Your Faith

Read Mark 16:15

Paul and his parents joined the long line of people standing side by side for the community "book pass." The line began inside the old library and extended all the way down the street and into the new library. "This is going to be fun," said Paul, waving to some of his friends.

After the mayor gave a speech, the book pass began. Someone inside the old library removed books from the shelves and handed them to the first person in line. Then, one by one, the people passed the books all the way down the line from the old library right into the new one.

"I'm getting tired of passing books," Paul said after a while. "My arms are getting sore." He stepped out of the line, leaving a gap where he had been standing between his parents. Mom stretched toward Dad as she passed the books. Dad reached out to get them. It was much more difficult without Paul in his place. Soon he stepped back in line. "I'll finish my part," he mumbled. "You're slowing things down with all that reaching."

That evening, Paul was studying his Sunday school lesson about witnessing. "It's hard to tell people about Jesus," he said. "I tried to talk to my friend Pete the other day, but I'm no good at it."

Dad looked up from his newspaper. "It can be hard," he agreed, "but it's our responsibility—and it *is* a command."

"I know," Paul said, "but since some people can do it better than others, why not just let them do it?"

"The gospel message needs to be passed on from one person to the next, just like those books we passed today," said Dad. "When you got tired and dropped out of the book line, the work was much more difficult for your mother and me. When someone fails to do his part, it puts more work on other people and slows down the spreading of the Word."

"That's right," agreed Mother. She ruffled Paul's hair. "I hope you'll decide to stay in line and do what you can to win your friends to Jesus."

Sharing Your Faith Memory Verse

And let us not get tired of doing what is right, for after a while we will reap a harvest of blessing if we don't get discouraged and give up.
Galatians 6:9

How About You?

Do you tell others about Jesus or do you think it's someone else's job? It is your responsibility to help spread the gospel message. Get in line and do your share. N. E. K.

- For the next devotional, turn to page 961. • For the next devotional on *Sharing Your Faith*, turn to page 979.
- For notes on *Sharing Your Faith*, see pages 462, 776, 1015, and 1074.

[17]"And those who believe shall use my authority to cast out demons, and they shall speak new languages. [18]They will be able even to handle snakes with safety, and if they drink anything poisonous, it won't hurt them; and they will be able to place their hands on the sick and heal them."

[19]When the Lord Jesus had finished talking with them, he was taken up into heaven and sat down at God's right hand.

[20]And the disciples went everywhere preaching, and the Lord was with them and confirmed what they said by the miracles that followed their messages.

SOMETIMES WE might wonder how we can know that the Gospels really tell the truth about Jesus. The Gospel of Luke can reassure us about the truth.

Luke was a doctor and a historian. He was a friend of Paul, Mark, and other people in the New Testament. Before he wrote his Gospel, Luke set out to find the truth about Jesus. He wanted to tell one of his friends the important facts about Jesus in an orderly way—like a newspaper article or a school book report. The details and quotes he included show that he talked to many people who knew Jesus well. Luke also explained some Jewish customs that would be hard for his Roman friend—and us—to understand.

Luke wanted his friend to understand who Jesus really was and why he came. And Luke himself believed the truth he wrote about.

You may know lots of stories about Jesus. As you read Luke, look for things you didn't know and truths about Jesus that are new to you.

An Angel Visits Zacharias

Dear friend who loves God:

1,2 Several biographies of Christ have already been written using as their source material the reports circulating among us from the early disciples and other eyewitnesses. 3However, it occurred to me that it would be well to recheck all these accounts from first to last and after thorough investigation to pass this summary on to you, 4to reassure you of the truth of all you were taught.

5My story begins with a Jewish priest, Zacharias, who lived when Herod was king of Judea. Zacharias was a member of the Abijah division of the Temple service corps. (His wife, Elizabeth, was, like himself, a member of the priest tribe of the Jews, a descendant of Aaron.) 6Zacharias and Elizabeth were godly folk, careful to obey all of God's laws in spirit as well as in letter. 7But they had no children, for Elizabeth was barren; and now they were both very old.

8,9One day as Zacharias was going about his

work in the Temple—for his division was on duty that week—the honor fell to him by lot to enter the inner sanctuary and burn incense before the Lord. ¹⁰Meanwhile, a great crowd stood outside in the Temple court, praying as they always did during that part of the service when the incense was being burned.

¹¹,¹²Zacharias was in the sanctuary when suddenly an angel appeared, standing to the right of the altar of incense! Zacharias was startled and terrified.

¹³But the angel said, "Don't be afraid, Zacharias! For I have come to tell you that God has heard your prayer, and your wife, Elizabeth, will bear you a son! And you are to name him John. ¹⁴You will both have great joy and gladness at his birth, and many will rejoice with you. ¹⁵For he will be one of the Lord's great men. He must never touch wine or hard liquor—and he will be filled with the Holy Spirit, even from before his birth! ¹⁶And he will persuade many a Jew to turn to the Lord his God. ¹⁷He will be a man of rugged spirit and power like Elijah, the prophet of old; and he will precede the coming of the Messiah, preparing the people for his arrival. He will soften adult hearts to become like little children's, and will change disobedient minds to the wisdom of faith."

¹⁸Zacharias said to the angel, "But this is impossible! I'm an old man now, and my wife is also well along in years."

¹⁹Then the angel said, "I am Gabriel! I stand in the very presence of God. It was he who sent me to you with this good news! ²⁰And now, because you haven't believed me, you are to be stricken silent, unable to speak until the child is born. For my words will certainly come true at the proper time."

²¹Meanwhile the crowds outside were waiting for Zacharias to appear and wondered why he was taking so long. ²²When he finally came out, he couldn't speak to them, and they realized from his gestures that he must have seen a vision in the Temple. ²³He stayed on at the Temple for the remaining days of his Temple duties and then returned home. ²⁴Soon afterwards Elizabeth his wife became pregnant and went into seclusion for five months.

²⁵"How kind the Lord is," she exclaimed, "to take away my disgrace of having no children!"

²⁶The following month God sent the angel Gabriel to Nazareth, a village in Galilee, ²⁷to a virgin, Mary, engaged to be married to a man named Joseph, a descendant of King David.

²⁸Gabriel appeared to her and said, "Congratulations, favored lady! The Lord is with you!"

²⁹Confused and disturbed, Mary tried to think what the angel could mean.

³⁰"Don't be frightened, Mary," the angel told her, "for God has decided to wonderfully bless you! ³¹Very soon now, you will become pregnant and have a baby boy, and you are to name him 'Jesus.' ³²He shall be very great and shall be called the Son of God. And the Lord God shall give him the throne of his ancestor David. ³³And he shall reign over Israel forever; his Kingdom shall never end!"

³⁴Mary asked the angel, "But how can I have a baby? I am a virgin."

³⁵The angel replied, "The Holy Spirit shall come upon you, and the power of God shall overshadow you; so the baby born to you will be utterly holy—the Son of God. ³⁶Furthermore, six months ago your Aunt Elizabeth—'the barren one,' they called her—became pregnant in her old age! ³⁷For every promise from God shall surely come true."

³⁸Mary said, "I am the Lord's servant, and I am willing to do whatever he wants. May everything you said come true." And then the angel disappeared.

³⁹,⁴⁰A few days later Mary hurried to the highlands of Judea to the town where Zacharias lived, to visit Elizabeth.

⁴¹At the sound of Mary's greeting, Elizabeth's child leaped within her and she was filled with the Holy Spirit.

⁴²She gave a glad cry and exclaimed to Mary, "You are favored by God above all other women, and your child is destined for God's mightiest praise. ⁴³What an honor this is, that the mother of my Lord should visit me! ⁴⁴When you came in and greeted me, the instant I heard your voice, my baby moved in me for joy! ⁴⁵You believed that God would do what he said; that is why he has given you this wonderful blessing."

⁴⁶Mary responded, "Oh, how I praise the Lord. ⁴⁷How I rejoice in God my Savior! ⁴⁸For he took notice of his lowly servant girl, and now generation after generation forever shall call me blest of God. ⁴⁹For he, the mighty Holy One, has done great things to me. ⁵⁰His mercy goes on from generation to generation, to all who reverence him.

⁵¹"How powerful is his mighty arm! How he scatters the proud and haughty ones! ⁵²He has torn princes from their thrones and exalted the lowly. ⁵³He has satisfied the hungry hearts and sent

---

KNOWING YOU'RE SPECIAL TO GOD 1:46-55 Mary was young, poor, female—all characteristics that, to the people of her day, would make her seem unusable by God for any major task. But God chose Mary for one of the most important acts of obedience he has ever demanded of anyone. You may feel that your situation in life makes you an unlikely candidate for God's service. Don't limit God's choices. He can use you if you trust him. **To begin the series of devotionals on KNOWING YOU'RE SPECIAL TO GOD, turn to page 307.**

FAMILY DEVOTIONS

☐ *DEVOTION 267*
HUMILITY

Read Luke 1:26-33, 46-49

Humility
Memory Verse

For everyone who tries to honor himself shall be humbled; and he who humbles himself shall be honored.
Luke 14:11

Shelly waited to hear the teacher call her name. She knew she was the perfect one to take the part of Mary, the mother of Jesus. No one could memorize the lines as well as she could. And her mother was the best seamstress in the church. She could have the best costume.

"Julie," said Mrs. Roberts, "I think you would be a good Mary."

Shelly gasped! Who was Julie but a poor, stammering girl who missed church half the time in order to help her sick mother. What kind of Mary would she be? "That's just fine with me," Shelly muttered to herself. "Who wants to be in a dumb old play anyway!" When Mrs. Roberts offered her another part, she made excuses and refused to be in the program at all.

Shelly sat in the front row the night of the program. She had come to laugh at Julie's mistakes. Mrs. Roberts would be embarrassed for making such a foolish choice! Shelly watched as Julie walked up front wearing a drab outfit that looked like it came from a feed sack. *What a peasant!* Shelly thought in disgust.

Hesitantly Julie began reciting from Luke. "For he . . . hath regarded . . . the low estate . . . of his handmaiden. . . ."

"Low estate," grumbled Shelly to herself. "That sure fits Julie." And then suddenly it struck her that Mrs. Roberts was right! Julie was a good Mary! Julie was humble and stood in awe before God like Mary did—a servant willing to obey and carry out his commands. Shelly had to admit that she would have exalted herself, but Julie sought to glorify Jesus.

While the program continued, Shelly bowed her head. Silently she asked God to forgive her proud spirit and make her his humble servant.

How About You?

Do you think you're better than some people because you feel you are more talented than they are? Do you think you should always be the one chosen to play special music, answer the questions, or lead in prayer because you do it best? Jesus wants obedient servants who are willing to stoop to help others so that he might be lifted up. *J. H.*

• For the next devotional, turn to page 973. • To start the next topic, turn to page 181. • For notes on *HUMILITY*, see pages 57, 390, 428, 854, and 1228.

the rich away with empty hands. ⁵⁴And how he has helped his servant Israel! He has not forgotten his promise to be merciful. ⁵⁵For he promised our fathers—Abraham and his children—to be merciful to them forever."

⁵⁶Mary stayed with Elizabeth about three months and then went back to her own home.

⁵⁷By now Elizabeth's waiting was over, for the time had come for the baby to be born—and it was a boy. ⁵⁸The word spread quickly to her neighbors and relatives of how kind the Lord had been to her, and everyone rejoiced.

⁵⁹When the baby was eight days old, all the relatives and friends came for the circumcision ceremony. They all assumed the baby's name would be Zacharias, after his father.

⁶⁰But Elizabeth said, "No! He must be named John!"

⁶¹"What?" they exclaimed. "There is no one in all your family by that name." ⁶²So they asked the baby's father, talking to him by gestures.

⁶³He motioned for a piece of paper and to everyone's surprise wrote, "His name is *John!*" ⁶⁴Instantly Zacharias could speak again, and he began praising God.

⁶⁵Wonder fell upon the whole neighborhood, and the news of what had happened spread through the Judean hills. ⁶⁶And everyone who heard about it thought long thoughts and asked, "I wonder what this child will turn out to be? For the hand of the Lord is surely upon him in some special way."

⁶⁷Then his father, Zacharias, was filled with the Holy Spirit and gave this prophecy:

⁶⁸"Praise the Lord, the God of Israel, for he has come to visit his people and has redeemed them. ⁶⁹He is sending us a Mighty Savior from the royal line of his servant David, ⁷⁰just as he promised through his holy prophets long ago—⁷¹someone to save us from our enemies, from all who hate us.

⁷²,⁷³"He has been merciful to our ancestors, yes, to Abraham himself, by remembering his sacred promise to him, ⁷⁴and by granting us the privilege of serving God fearlessly, freed from our enemies, ⁷⁵and by making us holy and acceptable, ready to stand in his presence forever.

⁷⁶"And you, my little son, shall be called the prophet of the glorious God, for you will prepare the way for the Messiah. ⁷⁷You will tell his people how to find salvation through forgiveness of their sins. ⁷⁸All this will be because the mercy of our God is very tender, and heaven's dawn is about to break upon us, ⁷⁹to give light to those who sit in darkness and death's shadow, and to guide us to the path of peace."

⁸⁰The little boy greatly loved God and when he grew up he lived out in the lonely wilderness until he began his public ministry to Israel.

2 Jesus Is Born

About this time Caesar Augustus, the Roman emperor, decreed that a census should be taken throughout the nation. ²(This census was taken when Quirinius was governor of Syria.)

³Everyone was required to return to his ancestral home for this registration. ⁴And because Joseph was a member of the royal line, he had to go to Bethlehem in Judea, King David's ancient home—journeying there from the Galilean village of Nazareth. ⁵He took with him Mary, his fiancée, who was obviously pregnant by this time.

⁶And while they were there, the time came for her baby to be born; ⁷and she gave birth to her first child, a son. She wrapped him in a blanket and laid him in a manger, because there was no room for them in the village inn.

⁸That night some shepherds were in the fields outside the village, guarding their flocks of sheep. ⁹Suddenly an angel appeared among them, and the landscape shone bright with the glory of the Lord. They were badly frightened, ¹⁰but the angel reassured them.

"Don't be afraid!" he said. "I bring you the most joyful news ever announced, and it is for everyone! ¹¹The Savior—yes, the Messiah, the Lord—has been born tonight in Bethlehem! ¹²How will you recognize him? You will find a baby wrapped in a blanket, lying in a manger!"

¹³Suddenly, the angel was joined by a vast host of others—the armies of heaven—praising God:

¹⁴"Glory to God in the highest heaven," they sang, "and peace on earth for all those pleasing him."

¹⁵When this great army of angels had returned again to heaven, the shepherds said to each other, "Come on! Let's go to Bethlehem! Let's see this wonderful thing that has happened, which the Lord has told us about."

¹⁶They ran to the village and found their way to Mary and Joseph. And there was the baby, lying in the manger. ¹⁷The shepherds told everyone what had happened and what the angel had said to them about this child. ¹⁸All who heard the shepherds' story expressed astonishment, ¹⁹but Mary quietly treasured these things in her heart and often thought about them.

²⁰Then the shepherds went back again to their fields and flocks, praising God for the visit of the angels, and because they had seen the child, just as the angel had told them.

²¹Eight days later, at the baby's circumcision ceremony, he was named Jesus, the name given him by the angel before he was even conceived.

²²When the time came for Mary's purification offering at the Temple, as required by the laws of Moses after the birth of a child, his parents took him to Jerusalem to present him to the Lord; ²³for in these laws God had said, "If a woman's first child is a boy, he shall be dedicated to the Lord."

²⁴At that time Jesus' parents also offered their sacrifice for purification—"either a pair of turtledoves or two young pigeons" was the legal requirement. ²⁵That day a man named Simeon, a Jerusalem resident, was in the Temple. He was a good man, very devout, filled with the Holy Spirit and constantly expecting the Messiah to come soon. ²⁶For the Holy Spirit had revealed to him that he would not die until he had seen him—God's anointed King. ²⁷The Holy Spirit had impelled him to go to the Temple that day; and so, when Mary and Joseph arrived to present the baby Jesus to the Lord in obedience to the law, ²⁸Simeon was there and took the child in his arms, praising God.

²⁹⁻³¹"Lord," he said, "now I can die content! For I have seen him as you promised me I would. I have seen the Savior you have given to the world. ³² He is the Light that will shine upon the nations, and he will be the glory of your people Israel!"

³³Joseph and Mary just stood there, marveling at what was being said about Jesus.

³⁴,³⁵Simeon blessed them but then said to Mary, "A sword shall pierce your soul, for this child shall be rejected by many in Israel, and this to their undoing. But he will be the greatest joy of many others. And the deepest thoughts of many hearts shall be revealed."

³⁶,³⁷Anna, a prophetess, was also there in the Temple that day. She was the daughter of Phanuel, of the Jewish tribe of Asher, and was very old, for she had been a widow for eighty-four years following seven years of marriage. She never left the Temple but stayed there night and day, worshiping God by praying and often fasting.

³⁸She came along just as Simeon was talking with Mary and Joseph, and she also began thanking God and telling everyone in Jerusalem who had been awaiting the coming of the Savior that the Messiah had finally arrived.

³⁹When Jesus' parents had fulfilled all the requirements of the Law of God they returned home to Nazareth in Galilee. ⁴⁰There the child became a strong, robust lad, and was known for wisdom beyond his years; and God poured out his blessings on him.

⁴¹,⁴²When Jesus was twelve years old he accompanied his parents to Jerusalem for the annual Passover Festival, which they attended each year. ⁴³After the celebration was over they started home to Nazareth, but Jesus stayed behind in Jerusalem. His parents didn't miss him the first day, ⁴⁴for they assumed he was with friends among the other travelers. But when he didn't show up that evening, they started to look for him among their relatives and friends; ⁴⁵and when they couldn't find him, they went back to Jerusalem to search for him there.

⁴⁶,⁴⁷Three days later they finally discovered him. He was in the Temple, sitting among the teachers of Law, discussing deep questions with them and amazing everyone with his understanding and answers.

⁴⁸His parents didn't know what to think. "Son!" his mother said to him. "Why have you done this to us? Your father and I have been frantic, searching for you everywhere."

⁴⁹"But why did you need to search?" he asked. "Didn't you realize that I would be here at the Temple, in my Father's House?" ⁵⁰But they didn't understand what he meant.

⁵¹Then he returned to Nazareth with them and was obedient to them; and his mother stored away all these things in her heart. ⁵²So Jesus grew both tall and wise, and was loved by God and man.

3 John the Baptist Preaches

In the fifteenth year of the reign of Emperor Tiberius Caesar, a message came from God to John (the son of Zacharias), as he was living out in the deserts. (Pilate was governor over Judea at that time; Herod, over Galilee; his brother Philip, over Iturea and Trachonitis; Lysanias, over Abilene; and Annas and Caiaphas were High Priests.) ³Then John went from place to place on both sides of the Jordan River, preaching that people should be baptized to show that they had turned to God and away from their sins, in order to be forgiven.

⁴In the words of Isaiah the prophet, John was "a voice shouting from the barren wilderness, 'Prepare a road for the Lord to travel on! Widen the pathway before him! ⁵Level the mountains! Fill up the valleys! Straighten the curves! Smooth out the ruts! ⁶And then all mankind shall see the Savior sent from God.'"

⁷Here is a sample of John's preaching to the crowds that came for baptism: "You brood of snakes! You are trying to escape hell without truly turning to God! That is why you want to be baptized! ⁸First go and prove by the way you live that you really have repented. And don't think you are safe because you are descendants of Abraham. That isn't enough. God can produce children of Abraham from these desert stones! ⁹The axe of his judgment is poised over you, ready to sever your roots and cut you down. Yes, every tree that

does not produce good fruit will be chopped down and thrown into the fire."

¹⁰The crowd replied, "What do you want us to do?"

¹¹"If you have two coats," he replied, "give one to the poor. If you have extra food, give it away to those who are hungry."

¹²Even tax collectors—notorious for their corruption—came to be baptized and asked, "How shall we prove to you that we have abandoned our sins?"

¹³"By your honesty," he replied. "Make sure you collect no more taxes than the Roman government requires you to."

¹⁴"And us," asked some soldiers, "what about us?"

John replied, "Don't extort money by threats and violence; don't accuse anyone of what you know he didn't do; and be content with your pay!"

¹⁵Everyone was expecting the Messiah to come soon, and eager to know whether or not John was he. This was the question of the hour and was being discussed everywhere.

¹⁶John answered the question by saying, "I baptize only with water; but someone is coming soon who has far higher authority than mine; in fact, I am not even worthy of being his slave. He will baptize you with fire—with the Holy Spirit. ¹⁷He will separate chaff from grain, and burn up the chaff with eternal fire and store away the grain." ¹⁸He used many such warnings as he announced the Good News to the people.

¹⁹,²⁰(But after John had publicly criticized Herod, governor of Galilee, for marrying Herodias, his brother's wife, and for many other wrongs he had done, Herod put John in prison, thus adding this sin to all his many others.)

²¹Then one day, after the crowds had been baptized, Jesus himself was baptized; and as he was praying, the heavens opened, ²²and the Holy Spirit in the form of a dove settled upon him, and a voice from heaven said, "You are my much loved Son, yes, my delight."

²³⁻³⁸Jesus was about thirty years old when he began his public ministry.

Jesus was known as the son of Joseph. Joseph's father was Heli; Heli's father was Matthat; Matthat's father was Levi; Levi's father was Melchi; Melchi's father was Jannai; Jannai's father was Joseph; Joseph's father was Mattathias; Mattathias' father was Amos; Amos' father was Nahum; Nahum's father was Esli; Esli's father was Naggai; Naggai's father was Maath; Maath's father was Mattathias; Mattathias' father was Semein; Semein's father was Josech; Josech's father was Joda; Joda's father was Joanan; Joanan's father was Rhesa; Rhesa's father was Zerubbabel; Zerubbabel's father was Shealtiel; Shealtiel's father was Neri; Neri's father was Melchi; Melchi's father was Addi; Addi's father was Cosam; Cosam's father was Elmadam; Elmadam's father was Er; Er's father was Joshua; Joshua's father was Eliezer; Eliezer's father was Jorim; Jorim's father was Matthat; Matthat's father was Levi; Levi's father was Simeon; Simeon's father was Judah; Judah's father was Joseph; Joseph's father was Jonam; Jonam's father was Eliakim; Eliakim's father was Melea; Melea's father was Menna; Menna's father was Mattatha; Mattatha's father was Nathan; Nathan's father was David; David's father was Jesse; Jesse's father was Obed; Obed's father was Boaz; Boaz' father was Salmon; Salmon's father was Nahshon; Nahshon's father was Amminadab; Amminadab's father was Admin; Admin's father was Arni; Arni's father was Hezron; Hezron's father was Perez; Perez' father was Judah; Judah's father was Jacob; Jacob's father was Isaac; Isaac's father was Abraham; Abraham's father was Terah; Terah's father was Nahor; Nahor's father was Serug; Serug's father was Reu; Reu's father was Peleg; Peleg's father was Eber; Eber's father was Shelah; Shelah's father was Cainan; Cainan's father was Arphaxad; Arphaxad's father was Shem; Shem's father was Noah; Noah's father was Lamech; Lamech's father was Methuselah; Methuselah's father was Enoch; Enoch's father was Jared; Jared's father was Mahalaleel; Mahalaleel's father was Cainan; Cainan's father was Enos; Enos' father was Seth; Seth's father was Adam; Adam's father was God.

4 Jesus Resists Temptation

Then Jesus, full of the Holy Spirit, left the Jordan River, being urged by the Spirit out into the barren wastelands of Judea, where Satan tempted him for forty days. He ate nothing all that time and was very hungry.

³Satan said, "If you are God's Son, tell this stone to become a loaf of bread."

⁴But Jesus replied, "It is written in the Scriptures, 'Other things in life are much more important than bread!'"

⁵Then Satan took him up and revealed to him all the kingdoms

RESISTING TEMPTATION 4:3 Sometimes what we are tempted to do isn't wrong in itself. Turning stones into bread wasn't necessarily bad. The sin was not in the act but in the reason for it. Satan was trying to get Jesus to take a shortcut, to solve his immediate problem at the expense of his long-range goals. Satan often works that way—persuading us to do things, even good things, for the wrong reason. The fact that something is not wrong in itself does not mean it is good for you at a given time. First ask, "Is the Holy Spirit leading me to do this? Or is Satan nudging me to do this in order to get me off the track?" **To begin the series of devotionals on RESISTING TEMPTATION, turn to page 7.**

of the world in a moment of time; ⁶,⁷and the devil told him, "I will give you all these splendid kingdoms and their glory—for they are mine to give to anyone I wish—if you will only get down on your knees and worship me."

⁸Jesus replied, "We must worship God, and him alone. So it is written in the Scriptures."

⁹⁻¹¹Then Satan took him to Jerusalem to a high roof of the Temple and said, "If you are the Son of God, jump off! For the Scriptures say that God will send his angels to guard you and to keep you from crashing to the pavement below!"

¹²Jesus replied, "The Scriptures also say, 'Do not put the Lord your God to a foolish test.'"

¹³When the devil had ended all the temptations, he left Jesus for a while and went away.

¹⁴Then Jesus returned to Galilee, full of the Holy Spirit's power. Soon he became well known throughout all that region ¹⁵for his sermons in the synagogues; everyone praised him.

¹⁶When he came to the village of Nazareth, his boyhood home, he went as usual to the synagogue on Saturday, and stood up to read the Scriptures. ¹⁷The book of Isaiah the prophet was handed to him, and he opened it to the place where it says:

¹⁸,¹⁹"The Spirit of the Lord is upon me; he has appointed me to preach Good News to the poor; he has sent me to heal the brokenhearted and to announce that captives shall be released and the blind shall see, that the downtrodden shall be freed from their oppressors, and that God is ready to give blessings to all who come to him."

²⁰He closed the book and handed it back to the attendant and sat down, while everyone in the synagogue gazed at him intently. ²¹Then he added, "These Scriptures came true today!"

²²All who were there spoke well of him and were amazed by the beautiful words that fell from his lips. "How can this be?" they asked. "Isn't this Joseph's son?"

²³Then he said, "Probably you will quote me that proverb, 'Physician, heal yourself'—meaning, 'Why don't you do miracles here in your hometown like those you did in Capernaum?' ²⁴But I solemnly declare to you that no prophet is accepted in his own hometown! ²⁵,²⁶For example, remember how Elijah the prophet used a miracle to help the widow of Zarephath—a foreigner from the land of Sidon. There were many Jewish widows needing help in those days of famine, for there had been no rain for three and a half years, and hunger stalked the land; yet Elijah was not sent to them. ²⁷Or think of the prophet Elisha, who healed Naaman, a Syrian, rather than the many Jewish lepers needing help."

²⁸These remarks stung them to fury; ²⁹and jumping up, they mobbed him and took him to the edge of the hill on which the city was built, to push him over the cliff. ³⁰But he walked away through the crowd and left them.

³¹Then he returned to Capernaum, a city in Galilee, and preached there in the synagogue every Saturday. ³²Here, too, the people were amazed at the things he said. For he spoke as one who knew the truth, instead of merely quoting the opinions of others as his authority.

³³Once as he was teaching in the synagogue, a man possessed by a demon began shouting at Jesus, ³⁴"Go away! We want nothing to do with you, Jesus from Nazareth. You have come to destroy us. I know who you are—the Holy Son of God."

³⁵Jesus cut him short. "Be silent!" he told the demon. "Come out!" The demon threw the man to the floor as the crowd watched, and then left him without hurting him further.

³⁶Amazed, the people asked, "What is in this man's words that even demons obey him?" ³⁷The story of what he had done spread like wildfire throughout the whole region.

³⁸After leaving the synagogue that day, he went to Simon's home where he found Simon's mother-in-law very sick with a high fever. "Please heal her," everyone begged.

³⁹Standing at her bedside he spoke to the fever, rebuking it, and immediately her temperature returned to normal, and she got up and prepared a meal for them!

⁴⁰As the sun went down that evening, all the villagers who had any sick people in their homes, no matter what their diseases were, brought them to Jesus; and the touch of his hands healed every one! ⁴¹Some were possessed by demons; and the demons came out at his command, shouting, "You are the Son of God." But because they knew he was the Christ, he stopped them and told them to be silent.

⁴²Early the next morning he went out into the desert. The crowds searched everywhere for him, and when they finally found him, they begged him not to leave them but to stay at Capernaum. ⁴³But he replied, "I must preach the Good News of the Kingdom of God in other places too, for that is why I was sent." ⁴⁴So he continued to travel around preaching in synagogues throughout Judea.

GOING TO CHURCH 4:16 Jesus went to the synagogue "as usual." Even though he was the perfect Son of God, and his local synagogue undoubtedly left much to be desired, Jesus attended services every week. His example makes our excuses for not attending church sound weak and self-serving. Make regular worship a part of your life. **To begin the series of devotionals on GOING TO CHURCH, turn to page 193.**

5 Fishing with Jesus

One day as he was preaching on the shore of Lake Gennesaret, great crowds pressed in on him to listen to the Word of God. ²He noticed two empty boats standing at the water's edge while the fishermen washed their nets. ³Stepping into one of the boats, Jesus asked Simon, its owner, to push out a little into the water, so that he could sit in the boat and speak to the crowds from there.

⁴When he had finished speaking, he said to Simon, "Now go out where it is deeper and let down your nets and you will catch a lot of fish!"

⁵"Sir," Simon replied, "we worked hard all last night and didn't catch a thing. But if you say so, we'll try again."

⁶And this time their nets were so full that they began to tear! ⁷A shout for help brought their partners in the other boat, and soon both boats were filled with fish and on the verge of sinking.

⁸When Simon Peter realized what had happened, he fell to his knees before Jesus and said, "Oh, sir, please leave us—I'm too much of a sinner for you to have around." ⁹For he was awestruck by the size of their catch, as were the others with him, ¹⁰and his partners too—James and John, the sons of Zebedee. Jesus replied, "Don't be afraid! From now on you'll be fishing for the souls of men!"

¹¹And as soon as they landed, they left everything and went with him.

¹²One day in a certain village he was visiting, there was a man with an advanced case of leprosy. When he saw Jesus he fell to the ground before him, face downward in the dust, begging to be healed.

"Sir," he said, "if you only will, you can clear me of every trace of my disease."

¹³Jesus reached out and touched the man and said, "Of course I will. Be healed." And the leprosy left him instantly! ¹⁴Then Jesus instructed him to go at once without telling anyone what had happened and be examined by the Jewish priest. "Offer the sacrifice Moses' law requires for lepers who are healed," he said. "This will prove to everyone that you are well." ¹⁵Now the report of his power spread even faster and vast crowds came to hear him preach and to be healed of their diseases. ¹⁶But he often withdrew to the wilderness for prayer.

¹⁷One day while he was teaching, some Jewish religious leaders and teachers of the Law were sitting nearby. (It seemed that these men showed up from every village in all Galilee and Judea, as well as from Jerusalem.) And the Lord's healing power was upon him.

¹⁸,¹⁹Then—look! Some men came carrying a paralyzed man on a sleeping mat. They tried to push through the crowd to Jesus but couldn't reach him. So they went up on the roof above him, took off some tiles and lowered the sick man down into the crowd, still on his sleeping mat, right in front of Jesus.

²⁰Seeing their faith, Jesus said to the man, "My friend, your sins are forgiven!"

²¹"Who does this fellow think he is?" the Pharisees and teachers of the Law exclaimed among themselves. "This is blasphemy! Who but God can forgive sins?"

²²Jesus knew what they were thinking, and he replied, "Why is it blasphemy? ²³,²⁴I, the Messiah, have the authority on earth to forgive sins. But talk is cheap—anybody could say that. So I'll prove it to you by healing this man." Then, turning to the paralyzed man, he commanded, "Pick up your stretcher and go on home, for you are healed!"

²⁵And immediately, as everyone watched, the man jumped to his feet, picked up his mat and went home praising God! ²⁶Everyone present was gripped with awe and fear. And they praised God, remarking over and over again, "We have seen strange things today."

²⁷Later on as Jesus left the town he saw a tax collector—with the usual reputation for cheating—sitting at a tax collection booth. The man's name was Levi. Jesus said to him, "Come and be one of my disciples!" ²⁸So Levi left everything, sprang up and went with him.

²⁹Soon Levi held a reception in his home with Jesus as the guest of honor. Many of Levi's fellow tax collectors and other guests were there.

³⁰But the Pharisees and teachers of the Law complained bitterly to Jesus' disciples about his eating with such notorious sinners.

³¹Jesus answered them, "It is the sick who need a doctor, not those in good health. ³²My purpose is to invite sinners to turn from their sins, not to spend my time with those who think themselves already good enough."

³³Their next complaint was that Jesus' disciples were feasting instead of fasting. "John the Baptist's disciples are constantly going without food and praying," they declared, "and so do the disciples of the Pharisees. Why are yours wining and dining?"

³⁴Jesus asked, "Do happy men fast? Do wedding guests go hungry while celebrating with the groom? ³⁵But the time will come when the bridegroom will be killed; then they won't want to eat."

³⁶Then Jesus used this illustration: "No one tears off a piece of a new garment to make a patch for an old one. Not only will the new garment be ruined, but the old garment will look worse with a new patch on it! ³⁷And no one puts new wine into old wineskins, for the new wine bursts the old skins, ruining the skins and spilling the wine. ³⁸New wine must be put into new wineskins. ³⁹But no one after drinking the old wine seems to want the fresh and the new. 'The old ways are best,' they say."

6 Picking Wheat on the Sabbath

One Sabbath as Jesus and his disciples were walking through some grainfields, they were breaking off the heads of wheat, rubbing off the husks in their hands and eating the grains.

[2] But some Pharisees said, "That's illegal! Your disciples are harvesting grain, and it's against the Jewish law to work on the Sabbath."

[3] Jesus replied, "Don't you read the Scriptures? Haven't you ever read what King David did when he and his men were hungry? [4] He went into the Temple and took the shewbread, the special bread that was placed before the Lord, and ate it—illegal as this was—and shared it with others." [5] And Jesus added, "I am master even of the Sabbath."

[6] On another Sabbath he was in the synagogue teaching, and a man was present whose right hand was deformed. [7] The teachers of the Law and the Pharisees watched closely to see whether he would heal the man that day, since it was the Sabbath. For they were eager to find some charge to bring against him.

[8] How well he knew their thoughts! But he said to the man with the deformed hand, "Come and stand here where everyone can see." So he did.

[9] Then Jesus said to the Pharisees and teachers of the Law, "I have a question for you. Is it right to do good on the Sabbath day, or to do harm? To save life, or to destroy it?"

[10] He looked around at them one by one and then said to the man, "Reach out your hand." And as he did, it became completely normal again. [11] At this, the enemies of Jesus were wild with rage and began to plot his murder.

[12] One day soon afterwards he went out into the mountains to pray, and prayed all night. [13] At daybreak he called together his followers and chose twelve of them to be the inner circle of his disciples. (They were appointed as his "apostles," or "missionaries.") [14][16] Here are their names:

Simon (he also called him Peter), Andrew (Simon's brother), James, John, Philip, Bartholomew, Matthew, Thomas, James (the son of Alphaeus), Simon (a member of the Zealots, a subversive political party), Judas (son of James), Judas Iscariot (who later betrayed him).

[17,18] When they came down the slopes of the mountain, they stood with Jesus on a large, level area, surrounded by many of his followers who, in turn, were surrounded by the crowds. For people from all over Judea and from Jerusalem and from as far north as the seacoasts of Tyre and Sidon had come to hear him or to be healed. And he cast out many demons. [19] Everyone was trying to touch him, for when they did, healing power went out from him and they were cured.

[20] Then he turned to his disciples and said, "What happiness there is for you who are poor, for the Kingdom of God is yours! [21] What happiness there is for you who are now hungry, for you are going to be satisfied! What happiness there is for you who weep, for the time will come when you shall laugh with joy! [22] What happiness it is when others hate you and exclude you and insult you and smear your name because you are mine! [23] When that happens, rejoice! Yes, leap for joy! For you will have a great reward awaiting you in heaven. And you will be in good company—the ancient prophets were treated that way too!

[24] "But, oh, the sorrows that await the rich. For they have their only happiness down here. [25] They are fat and prosperous now, but a time of awful hunger is before them. Their careless laughter now means sorrow then. [26] And what sadness is ahead for those praised by the crowds—for *false* prophets have *always* been praised.

[27] "Listen, all of you. Love your *enemies*. Do *good* to those who *hate* you. [28] Pray for the happiness of those who *curse* you; implore God's blessing on those who *hurt* you.

[29] "If someone slaps you on one cheek, let him slap the other too! If someone demands your coat, give him your shirt besides. [30] Give what you have to anyone who asks you for it; and when things are taken away from you, don't worry about getting them back. [31] Treat others as you want them to treat you.

[32] "Do you think you deserve credit for merely loving those who love you? Even the godless do that! [33] And if you do good only to those who do you good—is that so wonderful? Even sinners do that much! [34] And if you lend money only to those who can repay you, what good is that? Even the most wicked will lend to their own kind for full return!

[35] "Love your *enemies!* Do good to *them!* Lend to *them!* And don't be concerned about the fact that they won't repay. Then your reward from heaven will be very great, and you will truly be acting as sons of God: for he is kind to the *unthankful* and to those who are *very wicked*.

***Loving Others* 6:27** The Jews despised the Romans because they oppressed God's people, but Jesus told them to love these enemies. Such words turned many away from Christ. But Jesus wasn't talking about having affection for enemies; he was talking about an act of the will. You can't "fall into" this kind of love—it takes conscious effort. Loving our enemies means acting in their best interests. We can pray for them, and we can think of ways to help them. Jesus loved the whole world, even though the world was in rebellion against God. He asks us to follow his example by loving our enemies. **To begin the series of devotionals on *Loving Others*, turn to page 313.**

36 "Try to show as much compassion as your Father does.

37 "Never criticize or condemn—or it will all come back on you. Go easy on others; then they will do the same for you. 38 For if you give, you will get! Your gift will return to you in full and overflowing measure, pressed down, shaken together to make room for more, and running over. Whatever measure you use to give—large or small—will be used to measure what is given back to you."

39 Here are some of the story-illustrations Jesus used in his sermons: "What good is it for one blind man to lead another? He will fall into a ditch and pull the other down with him. 40 How can a student know more than his teacher? But if he works hard, he may learn as much.

41 "And why quibble about the speck in someone else's eye—his little fault—when a board is in your own? 42 How can you think of saying to him, 'Brother, let me help you get rid of that speck in your eye,' when you can't see past the board in yours? Hypocrite! First get rid of the board, and then perhaps you can see well enough to deal with his speck!

43 "A tree from good stock doesn't produce scrub fruit nor do trees from poor stock produce choice fruit. 44 A tree is identified by the kind of fruit it produces. Figs never grow on thorns, or grapes on bramble bushes. 45 A good man produces good deeds from a good heart. And an evil man produces evil deeds from his hidden wickedness. Whatever is in the heart overflows into speech.

46 "So why do you call me 'Lord' when you won't obey me? 47,48 But all those who come and listen and obey me are like a man who builds a house on a strong foundation laid upon the underlying rock. When the floodwaters rise and break against the house, it stands firm, for it is strongly built.

49 "But those who listen and don't obey are like a man who builds a house without a foundation. When the floods sweep down against that house, it crumbles into a heap of ruins."

7 A Man Is Healed Far Away

When Jesus had finished his sermon he went back into the city of Capernaum.

2 Just at that time the highly prized slave of a Roman army captain was sick and near death. 3 When the captain heard about Jesus, he sent some respected Jewish elders to ask him to come and heal his slave. 4 So they began pleading earnestly with Jesus to come with them and help the man. They told him what a wonderful person the captain was.

"If anyone deserves your help, it is he," they said, 5 "for he loves the Jews and even paid personally to build us a synagogue!"

6-8 Jesus went with them; but just before arriving at the house, the captain sent some friends to say, "Sir, don't inconvenience yourself by coming to my home, for I am not worthy of any such honor or even to come and meet you. Just speak a word from where you are, and my servant boy will be healed! I know, because I am under the authority of my superior officers, and I have authority over my men. I only need to say 'Go!' and they go; or 'Come!' and they come; and to my slave, 'Do this or that,' and he does it. So just say, 'Be healed!' and my servant will be well again!"

9 Jesus was amazed. Turning to the crowd he said, "Never among all the Jews in Israel have I met a man with faith like this."

10 And when the captain's friends returned to his house, they found the slave completely healed.

11 Not long afterwards Jesus went with his disciples to the village of Nain, with the usual great crowd at his heels. 12 A funeral procession was coming out as he approached the village gate. The boy who had died was the only son of his widowed mother, and many mourners from the village were with her.

13 When the Lord saw her, his heart overflowed with sympathy. "Don't cry!" he said. 14 Then he walked over to the coffin and touched it, and the bearers stopped. "Laddie," he said, "come back to life again."

15 Then the boy sat up and began to talk to those around him! And Jesus gave him back to his mother.

16 A great fear swept the crowd, and they exclaimed with praises to God, "A mighty prophet has risen among us," and, "We have seen the hand of God at work today."

17 The report of what he did that day raced from end to end of Judea and even out across the borders.

18 The disciples of John the Baptist soon heard of all that Jesus was doing. When they told John about it, 19 he sent two of his disciples to Jesus to ask him, "Are you really the Messiah? Or shall we keep on looking for him?"

20-22 The two disciples found Jesus while he was curing many sick people of their various diseases—healing the lame and the blind and casting out evil spirits. When they asked him John's question, this was his reply: "Go back to John and tell him all you have seen and heard here today: how those who were blind can see. The lame are walking without a limp. The lepers are completely healed. The deaf can hear again. The dead come back to life. And the poor are hearing the Good

News. ²³And tell him, 'Blessed is the one who does not lose his faith in me.'"

²⁴After they left, Jesus talked to the crowd about John. "Who is this man you went out into the Judean wilderness to see?" he asked. "Did you find him weak as grass, moved by every breath of wind? ²⁵Did you find him dressed in expensive clothes? No! Men who live in luxury are found in palaces, not out in the wilderness. ²⁶But did you find a prophet? Yes! And more than a prophet. ²⁷He is the one to whom the Scriptures refer when they say, 'Look! I am sending my messenger ahead of you, to prepare the way before you.' ²⁸In all humanity there is no one greater than John. And yet the least citizen of the Kingdom of God is greater than he."

²⁹And all who heard John preach—even the most wicked of them—agreed that God's requirements were right, and they were baptized by him. ³⁰All, that is, except the Pharisees and teachers of Moses' Law. They rejected God's plan for them and refused John's baptism.

³¹"What can I say about such men?" Jesus asked. "With what shall I compare them? ³²They are like a group of children who complain to their friends, 'You don't like it if we play "wedding" and you don't like it if we play "funeral"'! ³³For John the Baptist used to go without food and never took a drop of liquor all his life, and you said, 'He must be crazy!' ³⁴But I eat my food and drink my wine, and you say, 'What a glutton Jesus is! And he drinks! And has the lowest sort of friends!' ³⁵But I am sure you can always justify your inconsistencies."

³⁶One of the Pharisees asked Jesus to come to his home for lunch and Jesus accepted the invitation. As they sat down to eat, ³⁷a woman of the streets—a prostitute—heard he was there and brought an exquisite flask filled with expensive perfume. ³⁸Going in, she knelt behind him at his feet, weeping, with her tears falling down upon his feet; and she wiped them off with her hair and kissed them and poured the perfume on them.

³⁹When Jesus' host, a Pharisee, saw what was happening and who the woman was, he said to himself, "This proves that Jesus is no prophet, for if God had really sent him, he would know what kind of woman this one is!"

⁴⁰Then Jesus spoke up and answered his thoughts. "Simon," he said to the Pharisee, "I have something to say to you."

"All right, Teacher," Simon replied, "go ahead."

⁴¹Then Jesus told him this story: "A man loaned money to two people—$5,000 to one and $500 to the other. ⁴²But neither of them could pay him back, so he kindly forgave them both, letting them keep the money! Which do you suppose loved him most after that?"

⁴³"I suppose the one who had owed him the most," Simon answered.

"Correct," Jesus agreed.

⁴⁴Then he turned to the woman and said to Simon, "Look! See this woman kneeling here! When I entered your home, you didn't bother to offer me water to wash the dust from my feet, but she has washed them with her tears and wiped them with her hair. ⁴⁵You refused me the customary kiss of greeting, but she has kissed my feet again and again from the time I first came in. ⁴⁶You neglected the usual courtesy of olive oil to anoint my head, but she has covered my feet with rare perfume. ⁴⁷Therefore her sins—and they are many—are forgiven, for she loved me much; but one who is forgiven little, shows little love."

⁴⁸And he said to her, "Your sins are forgiven."

⁴⁹Then the men at the table said to themselves, "Who does this man think he is, going around forgiving sins?"

⁵⁰And Jesus said to the woman, "Your faith has saved you; go in peace."

8 Women Go with Jesus

Not long afterwards he began a tour of the cities and villages of Galilee to announce the coming of the Kingdom of God, and took his twelve disciples with him. ²Some women went along, from whom he had cast out demons or whom he had healed; among them were Mary Magdalene (Jesus had cast out seven demons from her), ³Joanna, Chuza's wife (Chuza was King Herod's business manager and was in charge of his palace and domestic affairs), Susanna, and many others who were contributing from their private means to the support of Jesus and his disciples.

⁴One day he gave this illustration to a large crowd that was gathering to hear him—while many others were still on the way, coming from other towns.

⁵"A farmer went out to his field to sow grain. As he scattered the seed on the ground, some of it fell on a footpath and was trampled on; and the birds came and ate it as it lay exposed. ⁶Other seed fell on shallow soil with rock beneath. This seed began to grow, but soon withered and died for lack of moisture. ⁷Other seed landed in thistle patches, and the young grain stalks were soon choked out. ⁸Still other fell on fertile soil; this seed grew and produced a crop one hundred times as large as he had planted." (As he was giving this illustration he said, "If anyone has listening ears, use them now!")

⁹His apostles asked him what the story meant.

¹⁰He replied, "God has granted you to know the meaning of these parables, for they tell a great

deal about the Kingdom of God. But these crowds hear the words and do not understand, just as the ancient prophets predicted.

¹¹"This is its meaning: The seed is God's message to men. ¹²The hard path where some seed fell represents the hard hearts of those who hear the words of God, but then the devil comes and steals the words away and prevents people from believing and being saved. ¹³The stony ground represents those who enjoy listening to sermons, but somehow the message never really gets through to them and doesn't take root and grow. They know the message is true, and sort of believe for awhile; but when the hot winds of persecution blow, they lose interest. ¹⁴The seed among the thorns represents those who listen and believe God's words but whose faith afterwards is choked out by worry and riches and the responsibilities and pleasures of life. And so they are never able to help anyone else to believe the Good News.

¹⁵"But the good soil represents honest, goodhearted people. They listen to God's words and cling to them and steadily spread them to others who also soon believe."

¹⁶[Another time he asked,] "Who ever heard of someone lighting a lamp and then covering it up to keep it from shining? No, lamps are mounted in the open where they can be seen. ¹⁷This illustrates the fact that someday everything [in men's hearts] shall be brought to light and made plain to all. ¹⁸So be careful how you listen; for whoever has, to him shall be given more; and whoever does not have, even what he thinks he has shall be taken away from him."

¹⁹Once when his mother and brothers came to see him, they couldn't get into the house where he was teaching because of the crowds. ²⁰When Jesus heard they were standing outside and wanted to see him, ²¹he remarked, "My mother and my brothers are all those who hear the message of God and obey it."

²²One day about that time, as he and his disciples were out in a boat, he suggested that they cross to the other side of the lake. ²³On the way across he lay down for a nap, and while he was sleeping the wind began to rise. A fierce storm developed that threatened to swamp them, and they were in real danger.

²⁴They rushed over and woke him up. "Master, Master, we are sinking!" they screamed.

So he spoke to the storm: "Quiet down," he said, and the wind and waves subsided and all was calm! ²⁵Then he asked them, "Where is your faith?"

And they were filled with awe and fear of him and said to one another, "Who is this man, that even the winds and waves obey him?"

²⁶So they arrived at the other side, in the Gerasene country across the lake from Galilee. ²⁷As he was climbing out of the boat a man from the city of Gadara came to meet him, a man who had been demon-possessed for a long time. Homeless and naked, he lived in a cemetery among the tombs. ²⁸As soon as he saw Jesus he shrieked and fell to the ground before him, screaming, "What do you want with me, Jesus, Son of God Most High? Please, I beg you, oh, don't torment me!"

²⁹For Jesus was already commanding the demon to leave him. This demon had often taken control of the man so that even when shackled with chains he simply broke them and rushed out into the desert, completely under the demon's power. ³⁰"What is your name?" Jesus asked the demon. "Legion," they replied—for the man was filled with thousands of them! ³¹They kept begging Jesus not to order them into the Bottomless Pit.

³²A herd of pigs was feeding on the mountainside nearby, and the demons pled with him to let them enter into the pigs. And Jesus said they could. ³³So they left the man and went into the pigs, and immediately the whole herd rushed down the mountainside and fell over a cliff into the lake below, where they drowned. ³⁴The herdsmen rushed away to the nearby city, spreading the news as they ran.

³⁵Soon a crowd came out to see for themselves what had happened and saw the man who had been demon-possessed sitting quietly at Jesus' feet, clothed and sane! And the whole crowd was badly frightened. ³⁶Then those who had seen it happen told how the demon-possessed man had been healed. ³⁷And everyone begged Jesus to go away and leave them alone (for a deep wave of fear had swept over them). So he returned to the boat and left, crossing back to the other side of the lake.

³⁸The man who had been demon-possessed begged to go too, but Jesus said no.

³⁹"Go back to your family," he told him, "and tell them what a wonderful thing God has done for you."

So he went all through the city telling everyone about Jesus' mighty miracle.

⁴⁰On the other side of the lake the crowds received him with open arms, for they had been waiting for him.

⁴¹And now a man named Jairus, a leader of a Jewish synagogue, came and fell down at Jesus' feet and begged him to come home with him, ⁴²for his only child was dying, a little girl twelve years old. Jesus went with him, pushing through the crowds.

⁴³,⁴⁴As they went a woman who wanted to be healed came up behind and touched him, for she

had been slowly bleeding for twelve years, and could find no cure (though she had spent everything she had on doctors). But the instant she touched the edge of his robe, the bleeding stopped.

⁴⁵"Who touched me?" Jesus asked.

Everyone denied it, and Peter said, "Master, so many are crowding against you...."

⁴⁶But Jesus told him, "No, it was someone who deliberately touched me, for I felt healing power go out from me."

⁴⁷When the woman realized that Jesus knew, she began to tremble and fell to her knees before him and told why she had touched him and that now she was well.

⁴⁸"Daughter," he said to her, "your faith has healed you. Go in peace."

⁴⁹While he was still speaking to her, a messenger arrived from the Jairus' home with the news that the little girl was dead. "She's gone," he told her father; "there's no use troubling the Teacher now."

⁵⁰But when Jesus heard what had happened, he said to the father, "Don't be afraid! Just trust me, and she'll be all right."

⁵¹When they arrived at the house, Jesus wouldn't let anyone into the room except Peter, James, John, and the little girl's father and mother. ⁵²The home was filled with mourning people, but he said, "Stop the weeping! She isn't dead; she is only asleep!" ⁵³This brought scoffing and laughter, for they all knew she was dead.

⁵⁴Then he took her by the hand and called, "Get up, little girl!" ⁵⁵And at that moment her life returned and she jumped up! "Give her something to eat!" he said. ⁵⁶Her parents were overcome with happiness, but Jesus insisted that they not tell anyone the details of what had happened.

9 An Assignment for the Disciples

One day Jesus called together his twelve apostles and gave them authority over all demons—power to cast them out—and to heal all diseases. ²Then he sent them away to tell everyone about the coming of the Kingdom of God and to heal the sick.

³"Don't even take along a walking stick," he instructed them, "nor a beggar's bag, nor food, nor money. Not even an extra coat. ⁴Be a guest in only one home at each village.

⁵"If the people of a town won't listen to you when you enter it, turn around and leave, demonstrating God's anger against it by shaking its dust from your feet as you go."

⁶So they began their circuit of the villages, preaching the Good News and healing the sick.

⁷When reports of Jesus' miracles reached Herod, the governor, he was worried and puzzled, for some were saying, "This is John the Baptist come back to life again"; ⁸and others, "It is Elijah or some other ancient prophet risen from the dead." These rumors were circulating all over the land.

⁹"I beheaded John," Herod said, "so who is this man about whom I hear such strange stories?" And he tried to see him.

¹⁰After the apostles returned to Jesus and reported what they had done, he slipped quietly away with them toward the city of Bethsaida. ¹¹But the crowds found out where he was going and followed. And he welcomed them, teaching them again about the Kingdom of God and curing those who were ill.

¹²Late in the afternoon all twelve of the disciples came and urged him to send the people away to the nearby villages and farms, to find food and lodging for the night. "For there is nothing to eat here in this deserted spot," they said.

¹³But Jesus replied, *"You* feed them!"

"Why, we have only five loaves of bread and two fish among the lot of us," they protested; "or are you expecting us to go and buy enough for this whole mob?" ¹⁴For there were about 5,000 men there!

"Just tell them to sit down on the ground in groups of about fifty each," Jesus replied. ¹⁵So they did.

¹⁶Jesus took the five loaves and two fish and looked up into the sky and gave thanks; then he broke off pieces for his disciples to set before the crowd. ¹⁷And everyone ate and ate; still, twelve basketfuls of scraps were picked up afterwards!

¹⁸One day as he was alone, praying, with his disciples nearby, he came over and asked them, "Who are the people saying I am?"

¹⁹"John the Baptist," they told him, "or perhaps Elijah or one of the other ancient prophets risen from the dead."

²⁰Then he asked them, "Who do you think I am?"

Peter replied, "The Messiah—the Christ of God!"

²¹He gave them strict orders not to speak of this to anyone. ²²"For I, the Messiah, must suffer much," he said, "and be rejected by the Jewish leaders—the elders, chief priests, and teachers of the Law—and be killed; and three days later I will come back to life again!"

²³Then he said to all, "Anyone who wants to follow me must put aside his own desires and conveniences and carry his cross with him every day and *keep close to me!* ²⁴Whoever loses his life for my sake will save it, but whoever insists on keeping his life will lose it; ²⁵and what profit is

there in gaining the whole world when it means forfeiting one's self?

²⁶"When I, the Messiah, come in my glory and in the glory of the Father and the holy angels, I will be ashamed then of all who are ashamed of me and of my words now. ²⁷But this is the simple truth—some of you who are standing here right now will not die until you have seen the Kingdom of God."

²⁸Eight days later he took Peter, James, and John with him into the hills to pray. ²⁹And as he was praying, his face began to shine, and his clothes became dazzling white and blazed with light. ³⁰Then two men appeared and began talking with him—Moses and Elijah! ³¹They were splendid in appearance, glorious to see; and they were speaking of his death at Jerusalem, to be carried out in accordance with God's plan.

³²Peter and the others had been very drowsy and had fallen asleep. Now they woke up and saw Jesus covered with brightness and glory, and the two men standing with him. ³³As Moses and Elijah were starting to leave, Peter, all confused and not even knowing what he was saying, blurted out, "Master, this is wonderful! We'll put up three shelters—one for you and one for Moses and one for Elijah!"

³⁴But even as he was saying this, a bright cloud formed above them; and terror gripped them as it covered them. ³⁵And a voice from the cloud said, *"This* is my Son, my Chosen One; listen to *him."*

³⁶Then, as the voice died away, Jesus was there alone with his disciples. They didn't tell anyone what they had seen until long afterwards.

³⁷The next day as they descended from the hill, a huge crowd met him, ³⁸and a man in the crowd called out to him, "Teacher, this boy here is my only son, ³⁹and a demon keeps seizing him, making him scream; and it throws him into convulsions so that he foams at the mouth; it is always hitting him and hardly ever leaves him alone. ⁴⁰I begged your disciples to cast the demon out, but they couldn't."

⁴¹"O you stubborn faithless people," Jesus said [to his disciples], "how long should I put up with you? Bring him here."

⁴²As the boy was coming the demon knocked him to the ground and threw him into a violent convulsion. But Jesus ordered the demon to come out, and healed the boy and handed him over to his father.

⁴³Awe gripped the people as they saw this display of the power of God.

Meanwhile, as they were exclaiming over all the wonderful things he was doing, Jesus said to his disciples, ⁴⁴"Listen to me and remember what I say. I, the Messiah, am going to be betrayed."

⁴⁵But the disciples didn't know what he meant, for their minds had been sealed and they were afraid to ask him.

⁴⁶Now came an argument among them as to which of them would be greatest [in the coming Kingdom]! ⁴⁷But Jesus knew their thoughts, so he stood a little child beside him ⁴⁸and said to them, "Anyone who takes care of a little child like this is caring for me! And whoever cares for me is caring for God who sent me. Your care for others is the measure of your greatness." ⁴⁹His disciple John came to him and said, "Master, we saw someone using your name to cast out demons. And we told him not to. After all, he isn't in our group."

⁵⁰But Jesus said, "You shouldn't have done that! For anyone who is not against you is for you."

⁵¹As the time drew near for his return to heaven, he moved steadily onward toward Jerusalem with an iron will.

⁵²One day he sent messengers ahead to reserve rooms for them in a Samaritan village. ⁵³But they were turned away! The people of the village refused to have anything to do with them because they were headed for Jerusalem.

⁵⁴When word came back of what had happened, James and John said to Jesus, "Master, shall we order fire down from heaven to burn them up?" ⁵⁵But Jesus turned and rebuked them, ⁵⁶and they went on to another village.

⁵⁷As they were walking along someone said to Jesus, "I will always follow you no matter where you go."

⁵⁸But Jesus replied, "Remember, I don't even own a place to lay my head. Foxes have dens to live in, and birds have nests, but I, the Messiah, have no earthly home at all."

⁵⁹Another time, when he invited a man to come with him and to be his disciple, the man agreed—but wanted to wait until his father's death.

⁶⁰Jesus replied, "Let those without eternal life concern themselves with things like that. Your duty is to come and preach the coming of the Kingdom of God to all the world."

⁶¹Another said, "Yes, Lord, I will come, but first let me ask permission of those at home."

⁶²But Jesus told him, "Anyone who lets himself be distracted from the work I plan for him is not fit for the Kingdom of God."

10 Jesus Sends Out 70 Messengers

The Lord now chose seventy other disciples and sent them on ahead in pairs to all the towns and villages he planned to visit later.

²These were his instructions to them: "Plead with the Lord of the harvest to send out more laborers to help you, for the harvest is so plentiful and the workers so few. ³Go now, and remember that I am sending you out as lambs among wolves.

FAMILY DEVOTIONS

☐ *DEVOTION 268*
AVOIDING SIN

Read Luke 9:57-62

Scott had been a Christian only a short time. His old friends kept after him to join them in things they all used to do before he was saved, but he knew from experience that they often got into trouble. It was a real struggle for him.

"Scott, I need some help getting my garden ready for spring planting," said Mr. Lockwood, Scott's Sunday school teacher. "Would you care to come over after school tomorrow and help me?"

"Sure," responded Scott. He really liked Mr. Lockwood.

The next day Mr. Lockwood started the garden tiller and showed Scott how it worked. "Start here, and don't take your eyes off that post down there," said Mr. Lockwood, pointing to the other end of the garden. "Make a straight row toward it. When you come back this way, you follow the furrow you've just made."

Scott began eagerly, hoping he would do a good job. Soon his confidence began to build as row after row of neatly turned earth appeared. He was almost finished when his teacher came out with a big glass of lemonade for him.

"Shut it off and take a break," shouted Mr. Lockwood.

Scott turned around to grin and nod his head, then turned back to shut off the machine. To his dismay, he saw that the tiller had made a big swerve to the right while he had been looking back. Mr. Lockwood saw what had happened, too.

"Come and have your lemonade," he said, "and then we'll see what can be done to straighten this last row."

As they sat under a tree and drank the lemonade, Scott mentioned the problems he was having with his old friends.

"Hmmm," murmured Mr. Lockwood thoughtfully as he gazed over the garden. "Looking back messes up a field, and looking back often messes up a life, too. Sometimes we have to break friendships to serve the Lord. Don't look back on your old life, Scott. Look to Jesus."

Avoiding Sin Memory Verse

How can a young man stay pure? By reading your Word and following its rules.
Psalm 119:9

How About You?

Do you have old friends who want you to join them in doing things that would displease the Lord? Do those old ways seem attractive? It may be necessary to replace old friendships and old habits with new ones. Ask the Lord to help you not to be distracted by looking back or by anything else. *R. P.*

• For the next devotional, turn to page 975.   • For the next devotional on *AVOIDING SIN*, turn to page 1081.
• For notes on *AVOIDING SIN*, see pages 220, 332, 392, and 657.

⁴"Don't take any money with you, or a beggar's bag, or even an extra pair of shoes. And don't waste time along the way.

⁵"Whenever you enter a home, give it your blessing. ⁶If it is worthy of the blessing, the blessing will stand; if not, the blessing will return to you.

⁷"When you enter a village, don't shift around from home to home, but stay in one place, eating and drinking without question whatever is set before you. And don't hesitate to accept hospitality, for the workman is worthy of his wages!

⁸,⁹"If a town welcomes you, follow these two rules:

(1) Eat whatever is set before you.
(2) Heal the sick; and as you heal them, say, 'The Kingdom of God is very near you now.'

¹⁰"But if a town refuses you, go out into its streets and say, ¹¹'We wipe the dust of your town from our feet as a public announcement of your doom. Never forget how close you were to the Kingdom of God!' ¹²Even wicked Sodom will be better off than such a city on the Judgment Day. ¹³What horrors await you, you cities of Chorazin and Bethsaida! For if the miracles I did for you had been done in the cities of Tyre and Sidon, their people would have sat in deep repentance long ago, clothed in sackcloth and throwing ashes on their heads to show their remorse. ¹⁴Yes, Tyre and Sidon will receive less punishment on the Judgment Day than you. ¹⁵And you people of Capernaum, what shall I say about you? Will you be exalted to heaven? No, you shall be brought down to hell."

¹⁶Then he said to the disciples, "Those who welcome you are welcoming me. And those who reject you are rejecting me. And those who reject me are rejecting God who sent me."

¹⁷When the seventy disciples returned, they joyfully reported to him, "Even the demons obey us when we use your name."

¹⁸"Yes," he told them, "I saw Satan falling from heaven as a flash of lightning! ¹⁹And I have given you authority over all the power of the Enemy, and to walk among serpents and scorpions and to crush them. Nothing shall injure you! ²⁰However, the important thing is not that demons obey you, but that your names are registered as citizens of heaven."

²¹Then he was filled with the joy of the Holy Spirit and said, "I praise you, O Father, Lord of heaven and earth, for hiding these things from the intellectuals and worldly wise and for revealing them to those who are as trusting as little children. Yes, thank you, Father, for that is the way you wanted it. ²²I am the Agent of my Father in everything; and no one really knows the Son except the Father, and no one really knows the Father except the Son and those to whom the Son chooses to reveal him."

²³Then, turning to the twelve disciples, he said quietly, "How privileged you are to see what you have seen. ²⁴Many a prophet and king of old has longed for these days, to see and hear what you have seen and heard!"

²⁵One day an expert on Moses' laws came to test Jesus' orthodoxy by asking him this question: "Teacher, what does a man need to do to live forever in heaven?"

²⁶Jesus replied, "What does Moses' law say about it?"

²⁷"It says," he replied, "that you must love the Lord your God with all your heart, and with all your soul, and with all your strength, and with all your mind. And you must love your neighbor just as much as you love yourself."

²⁸"Right!" Jesus told him. *"Do this and you shall live!"*

²⁹The man wanted to justify (his lack of love for some kinds of people), so he asked, "Which neighbors?"

³⁰Jesus replied with an illustration: "A Jew going on a trip from Jerusalem to Jericho was attacked by bandits. They stripped him of his clothes and money, and beat him up and left him lying half dead beside the road.

³¹"By chance a Jewish priest came along; and when he saw the man lying there, he crossed to the other side of the road and passed him by. ³²A Jewish Temple-assistant walked over and looked at him lying there, but then went on.

³³"But a despised Samaritan came along, and when he saw him, he felt deep pity. ³⁴Kneeling beside him the Samaritan soothed his wounds with medicine and bandaged them. Then he put the man on his donkey and walked along beside him till they came to an inn, where he nursed him through the night. ³⁵The next day he handed the innkeeper two twenty-dollar bills and told him to take care of the man. 'If his bill runs higher than that,' he said, 'I'll pay the difference the next time I am here.'

³⁶"Now which of these three would you say was a neighbor to the bandits' victim?"

³⁷The man replied, "The one who showed him some pity."

Then Jesus said, "Yes, now go and do the same."

³⁸As Jesus and the disciples continued on their way to Jerusalem they came to a village where a woman named Martha welcomed them into her home. ³⁹Her sister Mary sat on the floor, listening to Jesus as he talked.

⁴⁰But Martha was the jittery type and was worrying over the big dinner she was preparing.

Family Devotions

☐ DEVOTION 269
LOVING OTHERS

Read Luke 10:30-37

Loving Others Memory Verse

Little children, let us stop just *saying* we love people; let us *really* love them, and *show it* by our *actions*.
1 John 3:18

It was almost supper time, so Mollie and Joy Barton started walking home from their friend's house. As they passed an empty lot, they heard the sound of crying. And there, in the empty lot, was Ricky Taylor—"Icky Ricky," the children called him. Not only was he usually dirty and smelly and looked like he needed a bath, he was also the school bully. Yet there he was, crying like a baby! Nearby, a rather badly wrecked bike lay in a heap. The boy had a skinned knee and some blood on his nose. The girls looked at him and hurried on by, both secretly thinking that finally "Icky Ricky" had gotten what was coming to him.

When they arrived at home, the girls hurried to wash up for supper. Soon they heard their father coming home. When they returned to the kitchen, they were amazed to find Ricky Taylor being helped into the house by Dad.

"Look what happened to this poor young man!" Dad said, pulling up a chair for Ricky. Mom quickly began cleaning the knee and nose. The girls hung back near the wall as their dad got a phone number from Ricky and called his grandma. Soon Ricky and his wrecked bike were on their way home in Dad's car.

"Well! It surely was nice for Ricky that your dad came along," declared Mom. "Not everyone helps people out like your father does. He's really a good Samaritan."

"A good Samaritan?" asked Mollie guiltily.

"You mean like in the Bible?" added Joy. Both girls had heard the story many times, and they now felt ashamed.

"That's right." Mother nodded. "You know, God is pleased when we show his love to others—even to those who seem unlovely to us."

How About You?

Do you help other people whenever you can—even when they seem icky to you? God loves them, and he wants you to love them, too. He wants you to treat them as neighbors and to love them as you love yourself. That's loving quite a lot, isn't it? *C. G.*

She came to Jesus and said, "Sir, doesn't it seem unfair to you that my sister just sits here while I do all the work? Tell her to come and help me."

⁴¹But the Lord said to her, "Martha, dear friend, you are so upset over all these details! ⁴²There is really only one thing worth being concerned about. Mary has discovered it—and I won't take it away from her!"

Jesus Teaches about Prayer

Once when Jesus had been out praying, one of his disciples came to him as he finished and said, "Lord, teach us a prayer to recite just as John taught one to his disciples."

²And this is the prayer he taught them: "Father, may your name be honored for its holiness; send your Kingdom soon. ³Give us our food day by day. ⁴And forgive our sins—for we have forgiven those who sinned against us. And don't allow us to be tempted."

⁵,⁶Then, teaching them more about prayer, he used this illustration: "Suppose you went to a friend's house at midnight, wanting to borrow three loaves of bread. You would shout up to him, 'A friend of mine has just arrived for a visit and I've nothing to give him to eat.' ⁷He would call down from his bedroom, 'Please don't ask me to get up. The door is locked for the night and we are all in bed. I just can't help you this time.'

⁸"But I'll tell you this—though he won't do it as a friend, if you keep knocking long enough, he will get up and give you everything you want—just because of your persistence. ⁹And so it is with prayer—keep on asking and you will keep on getting; keep on looking and you will keep on finding; knock and the door will be opened. ¹⁰Everyone who asks, receives; all who seek, find; and the door is opened to everyone who knocks.

¹¹"You men who are fathers—if your boy asks for bread, do you give him a stone? If he asks for fish, do you give him a snake? ¹²If he asks for an egg, do you give him a scorpion? [Of course not!] ¹³And if even sinful persons like yourselves give children what they need, don't you realize that your heavenly Father will do at least as much, and give the Holy Spirit to those who ask for him?"

¹⁴Once, when Jesus cast out a demon from a man who couldn't speak, his voice returned to him. The crowd was excited and enthusiastic, ¹⁵but some said, "No wonder he can cast them out. He gets his power from Satan, the king of demons!" ¹⁶Others asked for something to happen in the sky to prove his claim of being the Messiah.

¹⁷He knew the thoughts of each of them, so he said, "Any kingdom filled with civil war is doomed; so is a home filled with argument and strife. ¹⁸Therefore, if what you say is true, that Satan is fighting against himself by empowering me to cast out his demons, how can his kingdom survive? ¹⁹And if I am empowered by Satan, what about your own followers? For they cast out demons! Do you think this proves they are possessed by Satan? Ask *them* if you are right! ²⁰But if I am casting out demons because of power from God, it proves that the Kingdom of God has arrived.

²¹"For when Satan, strong and fully armed, guards his palace, it is safe—²²until someone stronger and better-armed attacks and overcomes him and strips him of his weapons and carries off his belongings.

²³"Anyone who is not for me is against me; if he isn't helping me, he is hurting my cause.

²⁴"When a demon is cast out of a man, it goes to the deserts, searching there for rest; but finding none, it returns to the person it left, ²⁵and finds that its former home is all swept and clean. ²⁶Then it goes and gets seven other demons more evil than itself, and they all enter the man. And so the poor fellow is seven times worse off than he was before."

²⁷As he was speaking, a woman in the crowd called out, "God bless your mother—the womb from which you came, and the breasts that gave you suck!"

²⁸He replied, "Yes, but even more blessed are all who hear the Word of God and put it into practice."

²⁹,³⁰As the crowd pressed in upon him, he preached them this sermon: "These are evil times, with evil people. They keep asking for some strange happening in the skies [to prove I am the Messiah], but the only proof I will give them is a miracle like that of Jonah, whose experiences proved to the people of Nineveh that God had sent him. My similar experience will prove that God has sent me to these people.

³¹"And at the Judgment Day the Queen of Sheba shall arise and point her finger at this generation, condemning it, for she went on a long, hard journey to listen to the wisdom of Solomon; but one far greater than Solomon is here [and few pay any attention].

³²"The men of Nineveh, too, shall arise and condemn this nation, for they repented at the preaching of Jonah; and someone far greater than Jonah is here [but this nation won't listen].

³³"No one lights a lamp and hides it! Instead, he puts it on a lampstand to give light to all who enter the room. ³⁴Your eyes light up your inward being. A pure eye lets sunshine into your soul. A lustful eye shuts out the light and plunges you into darkness. ³⁵So watch out that the sunshine isn't blotted out. ³⁶If you are filled with light within, with no dark corners, then your face will

Family Devotions

☐ *Devotion 270*
Praying at All Times

Read Luke 11:5-8

Praying at All Times
Memory Verse

Don't worry about anything; instead, pray about everything; tell God your needs, and don't forget to thank him for his answers.
Philippians 4:6

It was Kyle's birthday, and right after supper he opened a large present from his parents. "Oh, boy! A chemistry set!" he exclaimed. "It's just what I wanted!"

His parents chuckled. "We know," Mother smiled. "How could we help but know with all the hints you've given?"

"Huh?" asked Kyle innocently. "Have I been hinting?"

"Ever since you saw that chemistry set at the store, you've been talking about how much you wanted one," Dad said.

"And when I went out to buy your present," Mother added, "I found a note in my purse that said, 'Don't forget the C. S.! Love, Guess Who.'"

Kyle laughed and turned red. "I guess I have been kind of a pest. I hope you're not mad at me."

"Of course not," replied his father. "You weren't rude about it, just persistent. Actually, we like it when you tell us what you really want."

"I can't wait to show Steve," said Kyle eagerly.

"That reminds me—you were going to pray for an opportunity to witness to Steve," said Dad. "How did that turn out?"

Kyle looked uncomfortable. "Oh, well, I did pray about it for a while, but nothing seemed to happen, so I kinda forgot about it."

"Speaking of prayer," said Mother, "you also said you were going to pray for money to go to the church youth camp this summer. Have you gotten it yet?"

Kyle shook his head. "I saved about ten dollars," he explained, "but I didn't get any more for a long time, so I quit praying about it."

Dad looked serious. "You've learned to be persistent when it comes to asking for birthday presents," he said. "It's a shame you haven't applied this principle to your praying. You see, it pleases God to give his children what they really want and need, but too often we say a halfhearted prayer about something and then forget all about it. Who knows how many wonderful answers to prayer we'd receive if only we kept on asking!"

How About You?
Is there a problem or a need in your life that you have prayed about? If so, that's fine, but don't forget to keep on praying. In his Word, God sets down several conditions for effective prayer. One of them is persistence. So keep on asking and believing. *S. K.*

• For the next devotional, turn to page 979. • To start the next topic, turn to page 115. • For notes on *Praying at All Times*, see pages 363, 442, 945, 1040, and 1051.

be radiant too, as though a floodlight is beamed upon you."

37,38 As he was speaking, one of the Pharisees asked him home for a meal. When Jesus arrived, he sat down to eat without first performing the ceremonial washing required by Jewish custom. This greatly surprised his host.

39 Then Jesus said to him, "You Pharisees wash the outside, but inside you are still dirty—full of greed and wickedness! 40 Fools! Didn't God make the inside as well as the outside? 41 Purity is best demonstrated by generosity.

42 "But woe to you Pharisees! For though you are careful to tithe even the smallest part of your income, you completely forget about justice and the love of God. You should tithe, yes, but you should not leave these other things undone.

43 "Woe to you Pharisees! For how you love the seats of honor in the synagogues and the respectful greetings from everyone as you walk through the markets! 44 Yes, awesome judgment is awaiting you. For you are like hidden graves in a field. Men go by you with no knowledge of the corruption they are passing."

45 "Sir," said an expert in religious law who was standing there, "you have insulted my profession, too, in what you just said."

46 "Yes," said Jesus, "the same horrors await you! For you crush men beneath impossible religious demands—demands that you yourselves would never think of trying to keep. 47 Woe to you! For you are exactly like your ancestors who killed the prophets long ago. 48 Murderers! You agree with your fathers that what they did was right—you would have done the same yourselves.

49 "This is what God says about you: 'I will send prophets and apostles to you, and you will kill some of them and chase away the others.'

50 "And you of this generation will be held responsible for the murder of God's servants from the founding of the world— 51 from the murder of Abel to the murder of Zechariah who perished between the altar and the sanctuary. Yes, it will surely be charged against you.

52 "Woe to you experts in religion! For you hide the truth from the people. You won't accept it for yourselves, and you prevent others from having a chance to believe it."

53,54 The Pharisees and legal experts were furious; and from that time on they plied him fiercely with a host of questions, trying to trap him into saying something for which they could have him arrested.

12 Jesus Warns against Hypocrisy

Meanwhile the crowds grew until thousands upon thousands were milling about and crushing each other. He turned now to his disciples and warned them, "More than anything else, beware of these Pharisees and the way they pretend to be good when they aren't. But such hypocrisy cannot be hidden forever. 2 It will become as evident as yeast in dough. 3 Whatever they have said in the dark shall be heard in the light, and what you have whispered in the inner rooms shall be broadcast from the housetops for all to hear!

4 "Dear friends, don't be afraid of these who want to murder you. They can only kill the body; they have no power over your souls. 5 But I'll tell you whom to fear—fear God who has the power to kill and then cast into hell.

6 "What is the price of five sparrows? A couple of pennies? Not much more than that. Yet God does not forget a single one of them. 7 And he knows the number of hairs on your head! Never fear, you are far more valuable to him than a whole flock of sparrows.

8 "And I assure you of this: I, the Messiah, will publicly honor you in the presence of God's angels if you publicly acknowledge me here on earth as your Friend. 9 But I will deny before the angels those who deny me here among men. 10 (Yet those who speak against me may be forgiven—while those who speak against the Holy Spirit shall never be forgiven.)

11 "And when you are brought to trial before these Jewish rulers and authorities in the synagogues, don't be concerned about what to say in your defense, 12 for the Holy Spirit will give you the right words even as you are standing there."

13 Then someone called from the crowd, "Sir, please tell my brother to divide my father's estate with me."

14 But Jesus replied, "Man, who made me a judge over you to decide such things as that? 15 Beware! Don't always be wishing for what you don't have. For real life and real living are not related to how rich we are."

16 Then he gave an illustration: "A rich man had a fertile farm that produced fine crops. 17 In fact, his barns were full to overflowing—he couldn't get everything in. He thought about his problem, 18 and finally exclaimed, 'I know—I'll tear down my barns and build bigger ones! Then I'll have room enough. 19 And I'll sit back and say to myself, "Friend, you have enough stored away for years to come. Now take it easy! Wine, women, and song for you!"'

20 "But God said to him, 'Fool! Tonight you die. Then who will get it all?'

21 "Yes, every man is a fool who gets rich on earth but not in heaven."

22 Then turning to his disciples he said, "Don't worry about whether you have enough food to eat or clothes to wear. 23 For life consists of far

Family Devotions

☐ DEVOTION 271
SHARING YOUR FAITH

Read Luke 12:8-12

Jenny and her family were spending spring break at Mountain View Bible Camp, and Jenny was having a wonderful time. "Can I please buy a camp T-shirt?" she begged one day. "Everyone else has one." Mom agreed, and Jenny promptly went to buy one. On the front was a picture of the chapel with the words "Proclaiming his Word to the World." On the back it said, "Mountain View Bible Camp." Jenny wore the shirt regularly, proud to be a part of the group.

Back home, Jenny stuffed the shirt into a drawer and forgot about it. Mom didn't forget, though. From time to time she suggested that Jenny wear it, but Jenny always refused. "I like it," she insisted, "but it just wouldn't look right here."

One Friday was declared T-shirt day at school. Again Jenny begged for a new shirt. "Not this time," Mom replied. "Wear your camp shirt. It's almost new."

"I can't wear that," protested Jenny. "It wouldn't look right. Everyone else will wear shirts with cute sayings on them, or they'll be from exciting places like Fun Haven."

"Wasn't camp exciting?" asked Mom. "You loved your shirt before."

Jenny bit her lip. "It was different at camp," she said.

"Yes, it was," Mom admitted. "It was comfortable to be identified as a Christian then, because others shared your faith."

Jenny bristled. "Are you saying I'm ashamed now to let others see I'm a Christian?"

"Are you?" asked Mom softly.

Jenny thought about it. "I guess maybe I have been," she confessed. "I'll wear my camp shirt to school after all. Maybe I can interest my friends in attending Bible camp in the summer.

"Good," Mom said. "Then you'll be proclaiming God's Word, just like your shirt says!"

Sharing Your Faith Memory Verse

And I assure you of this: I, the Messiah, will publicly honor you in the presence of God's angels if you publicly acknowledge me here on earth as your Friend.
Luke 12:8

How About You?
Do your friends and teachers know you're a Christian? Do you pray before you eat, witness when you can, and speak up for your faith in the classroom? Don't be ashamed of Jesus. Others need to know him, too. *J. H.*

• For the next devotional, turn to page 981. • For the next devotional on SHARING YOUR FAITH, turn to page 1011.
• For notes on SHARING YOUR FAITH, see pages 462, 776, 1015, and 1074.

more than food and clothes. ²⁴Look at the ravens—they don't plant or harvest or have barns to store away their food, and yet they get along all right—for God feeds them. And you are far more valuable to him than any birds!

²⁵"And besides, what's the use of worrying? What good does it do? Will it add a single day to your life? Of course not! ²⁶And if worry can't even do such little things as that, what's the use of worrying over bigger things?

²⁷"Look at the lilies! They don't toil and spin, and yet Solomon in all his glory was not robed as well as they are. ²⁸And if God provides clothing for the flowers that are here today and gone tomorrow, don't you suppose that he will provide clothing for you, you doubters? ²⁹And don't worry about food—what to eat and drink; don't worry at all that God will provide it for you. ³⁰All mankind scratches for its daily bread, but your heavenly Father knows your needs. ³¹He will always give you all you need from day to day if you will make the Kingdom of God your primary concern.

³²"So don't be afraid, little flock. For it gives your Father great happiness to give you the Kingdom. ³³Sell what you have and give to those in need. This will fatten your purses in heaven! And the purses of heaven have no rips or holes in them. Your treasures there will never disappear; no thief can steal them; no moth can destroy them. ³⁴Wherever your treasure is, there your heart and thoughts will also be.

³⁵"Be prepared—all dressed and ready— ³⁶for your Lord's return from the wedding feast. Then you will be ready to open the door and let him in the moment he arrives and knocks. ³⁷There will be great joy for those who are ready and waiting for his return. He himself will seat them and put on a waiter's uniform and serve them as they sit and eat! ³⁸He may come at nine o'clock at night— or even at midnight. But whenever he comes, there will be joy for his servants who are ready!

³⁹"Everyone would be ready for him if they knew the exact hour of his return—just as they would be ready for a thief if they knew when he was coming. ⁴⁰So be ready all the time. For I, the Messiah, will come when least expected."

⁴¹Peter asked, "Lord, are you talking just to us or to everyone?"

⁴²⁻⁴⁴And the Lord replied, "I'm talking to any faithful, sensible man whose master gives him the responsibility of feeding the other servants. If his master returns and finds that he has done a good job, there will be a reward—his master will put him in charge of all he owns.

⁴⁵"But if the man begins to think, 'My Lord won't be back for a long time,' and begins to whip the men and women he is supposed to protect, and to spend his time at drinking parties and in drunkenness— ⁴⁶well, his master will return without notice and remove him from his position of trust and assign him to the place of the unfaithful. ⁴⁷He will be severely punished, for though he knew his duty he refused to do it.

⁴⁸"But anyone who is not aware that he is doing wrong will be punished only lightly. Much is required from those to whom much is given, for their responsibility is greater.

⁴⁹"I have come to bring fire to the earth, and, oh, that my task were completed! ⁵⁰There is a terrible baptism ahead of me, and how I am pent up until it is accomplished!

⁵¹"Do you think I have come to give peace to the earth? *No!* Rather, strife and division! ⁵²From now on families will be split apart, three in favor of me, and two against—or perhaps the other way around. ⁵³A father will decide one way about me; his son, the other; mother and daughter will disagree; and the decision of an honored mother-in-law will be spurned by her daughter-in-law."

⁵⁴Then he turned to the crowd and said, "When you see clouds beginning to form in the west, you say, 'Here comes a shower.' And you are right.

⁵⁵"When the south wind blows you say, 'Today will be a scorcher.' And it is. ⁵⁶Hypocrites! You interpret the sky well enough, but you refuse to notice the warnings all around you about the crisis ahead. ⁵⁷Why do you refuse to see for yourselves what is right?

⁵⁸"If you meet your accuser on the way to court, try to settle the matter before it reaches the judge, lest he sentence you to jail; ⁵⁹for if that happens, you won't be free again until the last penny is paid in full."

13 Jesus Tells the People to Repent

About this time he was informed that Pilate had butchered some Jews from Galilee as they were sacrificing at the Temple in Jerusalem.

²"Do you think they were worse sinners than other men from Galilee?" he asked. "Is that why they suffered? ³Not at all! And don't you realize that you also will perish unless you leave your evil ways and turn to God?

⁴"And what about the eighteen men who died when the Tower of Siloam fell on them? Were they the worst sinners in Jerusalem? ⁵Not at all! And you, too, will perish unless you repent."

⁶Then he used this illustration: "A man planted a fig tree in his garden and came again and again to see if he could find any fruit on it, but he was always disappointed. ⁷Finally he told his gardener to cut it down. 'I've waited three years and there hasn't been a single fig!' he said. 'Why bother with it any longer? It's taking up space we can use for something else.'

Family Devotions

☐ DEVOTION 272
TRUSTING GOD'S PLAN

Read Luke 12:16-21

Jordan's parents were serving as missionaries in Africa, and he was learning many new things. One day his friend Paul helped him make a trap to catch a monkey. "It's easy," said Paul, handing Jordan a gourd. "First, make a hole in this gourd, just big enough for a monkey to put his hand through." He supervised while Jordan worked. "There," Paul said, "that's big enough. The gourd is hollow, so now we'll put some nuts and fruit in it. Then we'll fasten it to a branch of a tree at the edge of the village."

"I don't get it," said Jordan as the boys walked to the tree Paul had selected. "How will this work? I can see that a monkey might reach into the gourd to get the food out, but what will keep him from getting away with it?"

"When he has nuts in his fist, his hand won't go through the hole," explained Paul. "If he'd just let them go, he could get away. But he won't. He hangs on even though it means he gets caught." Paul helped Jordan attach the gourd to a tree. "There. By tomorrow morning, you'll probably have a monkey."

When he returned home, Jordan told his mother about the monkeys. Mom nodded. "They certainly are silly," she agreed. "But do you know I was just as foolish myself once? I wanted certain things," she explained. "A nice home, pretty clothes, a nice car, a grassy lawn. I wanted to hang on to them. I didn't want to give them up and come to the mission field. But the Lord showed me that by following his will, I wasn't really giving up anything important. I was just letting those things go for something better. I've never been as happy as I've been here in Africa, bringing the message of salvation to these people."

Trusting God's Plan Memory Verse

This plan of mine is not what you would work out, neither are my thoughts the same as yours! For just as the heavens are higher than the earth, so are my ways higher than yours, and my thoughts than yours.
Isaiah 55:8-9

How About You?

What things do you want very badly? What goals do you have for your life? Good grades? Money? Fun? Pretty clothes? A big car? Don't set your heart on the things of this world. Don't let them trap you into missing what God intends for you. It may be that he has those things in his plan for you, but you need to be willing to let them go. If they are not in his plan, you can be sure he has something even better. H. M.

• For the next devotional, turn to page 985. • For the next devotional on TRUSTING GOD'S PLAN, turn to page 1033.
• For notes on TRUSTING GOD'S PLAN, see pages 252, 296, 731, and 870.

⁸"'Give it one more chance,' the gardener answered. 'Leave it another year, and I'll give it special attention and plenty of fertilizer. ⁹If we get figs next year, fine; if not, I'll cut it down.'"

¹⁰One Sabbath as he was teaching in a synagogue, ¹¹he saw a seriously handicapped woman who had been bent double for eighteen years and was unable to straighten herself.

¹²Calling her over to him Jesus said, "Woman, you are healed of your sickness!" ¹³He touched her, and instantly she could stand straight. How she praised and thanked God!

¹⁴But the local Jewish leader in charge of the synagogue was very angry about it because Jesus had healed her on the Sabbath day. "There are six days of the week to work," he shouted to the crowd. "Those are the days to come for healing, not on the Sabbath!"

¹⁵But the Lord replied, "You hypocrite! You work on the Sabbath! Don't you untie your cattle from their stalls on the Sabbath and lead them out for water? ¹⁶And is it wrong for me, just because it is the Sabbath day, to free this Jewish woman from the bondage in which Satan has held her for eighteen years?"

¹⁷This shamed his enemies. And all the people rejoiced at the wonderful things he did.

¹⁸Now he began teaching them again about the Kingdom of God: "What is the Kingdom like?" he asked. "How can I illustrate it? ¹⁹It is like a tiny mustard seed planted in a garden; soon it grows into a tall bush and the birds live among its branches.

²⁰,²¹"It is like yeast kneaded into dough, which works unseen until it has risen high and light."

²²He went from city to city and village to village, teaching as he went, always pressing onward toward Jerusalem.

²³Someone asked him, "Will only a few be saved?"

And he replied, ²⁴,²⁵"The door to heaven is narrow. Work hard to get in, for the truth is that many will try to enter but when the head of the house has locked the door, it will be too late. Then if you stand outside knocking, and pleading, 'Lord, open the door for us,' he will reply, 'I do not know you.'

²⁶"But we ate with you, and you taught in our streets," you will say.

²⁷"And he will reply, 'I tell you, I don't know you. You can't come in here, guilty as you are. Go away.'

²⁸"And there will be great weeping and gnashing of teeth as you stand outside and see Abraham, Isaac, Jacob, and all the prophets within the Kingdom of God— ²⁹for people will come from all over the world to take their places there. ³⁰And note this: some who are despised now will be greatly honored then; and some who are highly thought of now will be least important then."

³¹A few minutes later some Pharisees said to him, "Get out of here if you want to live, for King Herod is after you!"

³²Jesus replied, "Go tell that fox that I will keep on casting out demons and doing miracles of healing today and tomorrow; and the third day I will reach my destination. ³³Yes, today, tomorrow, and the next day! For it wouldn't do for a prophet of God to be killed except in Jerusalem!

³⁴"O Jerusalem, Jerusalem! The city that murders the prophets. The city that stones those sent to help her. How often I have wanted to gather your children together even as a hen protects her brood under her wings, but you wouldn't let me. ³⁵And now—now your house is left desolate. And you will never again see me until you say, 'Welcome to him who comes in the name of the Lord.'"

14 Healing on the Sabbath

One Sabbath as he was in the home of a member of the Jewish Council, the Pharisees were watching him like hawks to see if he would heal a man who was present who was suffering from dropsy.

³Jesus said to the Pharisees and legal experts standing around, "Well, is it within the Law to heal a man on the Sabbath day, or not?"

⁴And when they refused to answer, Jesus took the sick man by the hand and healed him and sent him away.

⁵Then he turned to them: "Which of you doesn't work on the Sabbath?" he asked. "If your cow falls into a pit, don't you proceed at once to get it out?"

⁶Again they had no answer.

⁷When he noticed that all who came to the dinner were trying to sit near the head of the table, he gave them this advice: ⁸"If you are invited to a wedding feast, don't always head for the best seat. For if someone more respected than you shows up, ⁹the host will bring him over to where you are sitting and say, 'Let this man sit here instead.' And you, embarrassed, will have to

---

PUTTING GOD FIRST 13:30 There will be many surprises in God's Kingdom. Some who are despised now will be greatly honored then; some influential people here will be left outside the gates. Many people who are great in God's eyes are virtually ignored by this world. What matters to God is not one's earthly popularity, status, wealth, heritage, or power, but one's commitment to Christ. How do your values match what the Bible tells us to value? Make sure you put God in first place so you will join the people from all over the world who will take their places in the Kingdom of Heaven. **To begin the series of devotionals on PUTTING GOD FIRST, turn to page 115.**

take whatever seat is left at the foot of the table! ¹⁰"Do this instead—start at the foot; and when your host sees you he will come and say, 'Friend, we have a better place than this for you!' Thus you will be honored in front of all the other guests. ¹¹For everyone who tries to honor himself shall be humbled; and he who humbles himself shall be honored." ¹²Then he turned to his host. "When you put on a dinner," he said, "don't invite friends, brothers, relatives, and rich neighbors! For they will return the invitation. ¹³Instead, invite the poor, the crippled, the lame, and the blind. ¹⁴Then at the resurrection of the godly, God will reward you for inviting those who can't repay you."

¹⁵Hearing this, a man sitting at the table with Jesus exclaimed, "What a privilege it would be to get into the Kingdom of God!"

¹⁶Jesus replied with this illustration: "A man prepared a great feast and sent out many invitations. ¹⁷When all was ready, he sent his servant around to notify the guests that it was time for them to arrive. ¹⁸But they all began making excuses. One said he had just bought a field and wanted to inspect it, and asked to be excused. ¹⁹Another said he had just bought five pair of oxen and wanted to try them out. ²⁰Another had just been married and for that reason couldn't come.

²¹"The servant returned and reported to his master what they had said. His master was angry and told him to go quickly into the streets and alleys of the city and to invite the beggars, crippled, lame, and blind. ²²But even then, there was still room.

²³"'Well, then,' said his master, 'go out into the country lanes and out behind the hedges and urge anyone you find to come, so that the house will be full. ²⁴For none of those I invited first will get even the smallest taste of what I had prepared for them.'"

²⁵Great crowds were following him. He turned around and addressed them as follows: ²⁶"Anyone who wants to be my follower must love me far more than he does his own father, mother, wife, children, brothers, or sisters—yes, more than his own life—otherwise he cannot be my disciple. ²⁷And no one can be my disciple who does not carry his own cross and follow me.

²⁸"But don't begin until you count the cost. For who would begin construction of a building without first getting estimates and then checking to see if he has enough money to pay the bills? ²⁹Otherwise he might complete only the foundation before running out of funds. And then how everyone would laugh! ³⁰"'See that fellow there?' they would mock. 'He started that building and ran out of money before it was finished!'

³¹"Or what king would ever dream of going to war without first sitting down with his counselors and discussing whether his army of 10,000 is strong enough to defeat the 20,000 men who are marching against him?

³²"If the decision is negative, then while the enemy troops are still far away, he will send a truce team to discuss terms of peace. ³³So no one can become my disciple unless he first sits down and counts his blessings—and then renounces them all for me.

³⁴"What good is salt that has lost its saltiness? ³⁵Flavorless salt is fit for nothing—not even for fertilizer. It is worthless and must be thrown out. Listen well if you would understand my meaning."

15 A Story about a Lost Sheep

Dishonest tax collectors and other notorious sinners often came to listen to Jesus' sermons; ²but this caused complaints from the Jewish religious leaders and the experts on Jewish law because he was associating with such despicable people—even eating with them!

³,⁴So Jesus used this illustration: "If you had a hundred sheep and one of them strayed away and was lost in the wilderness, wouldn't you leave the ninety-nine others to go and search for the lost one until you found it? ⁵And then you would joyfully carry it home on your shoulders. ⁶When you arrived you would call together your friends and neighbors to rejoice with you because your lost sheep was found.

⁷"Well, in the same way heaven will be happier over one lost sinner who returns to God than over ninety-nine others who haven't strayed away!

⁸"Or take another illustration: A woman has ten valuable silver coins and loses one. Won't she light a lamp and look in every corner of the house and sweep every nook and cranny until she finds it? ⁹And then won't she call in her friends and neighbors to rejoice with her? ¹⁰In the same way there is joy in the presence of the angels of God when one sinner repents."

¹¹To further illustrate the point, he told them

BECOMING MORE LIKE JESUS **14:34** Salt can lose its flavor. When it gets wet and then dries, nothing is left but a tasteless residue. Many Christians blend into the world instead of standing out and representing Christ, but Jesus says if Christians lose their distinctive saltiness, they become worthless. Just as salt flavors and preserves food, we are to preserve the good in the world, help keep it from spoiling, and bring new flavor to life. Being "salty" is not easy, but if a Christian fails in this function, he fails to represent Christ in the world. How salty are you? **To begin the series of devotionals on *Becoming More Like Jesus*, turn to page 131.**

this story: "A man had two sons. ¹²When the younger told his father, 'I want my share of your estate now, instead of waiting until you die!' his father agreed to divide his wealth between his sons.

¹³"A few days later this younger son packed all his belongings and took a trip to a distant land, and there wasted all his money on parties and prostitutes. ¹⁴About the time his money was gone a great famine swept over the land, and he began to starve. ¹⁵He persuaded a local farmer to hire him to feed his pigs. ¹⁶The boy became so hungry that even the pods he was feeding the swine looked good to him. And no one gave him anything.

¹⁷"When he finally came to his senses, he said to himself, 'At home even the hired men have food enough and to spare, and here I am, dying of hunger! ¹⁸I will go home to my father and say, "Father, I have sinned against both heaven and you, ¹⁹and am no longer worthy of being called your son. Please take me on as a hired man."'

²⁰"So he returned home to his father. And while he was still a long distance away, his father saw him coming, and was filled with loving pity and ran and embraced him and kissed him.

²¹"His son said to him, 'Father, I have sinned against heaven and you, and am not worthy of being called your son—'

²²"But his father said to the slaves, 'Quick! Bring the finest robe in the house and put it on him. And a jeweled ring for his finger; and shoes! ²³And kill the calf we have in the fattening pen. We must celebrate with a feast, ²⁴for this son of mine was dead and has returned to life. He was lost and is found.' So the party began.

²⁵"Meanwhile, the older son was in the fields working; when he returned home, he heard dance music coming from the house, ²⁶and he asked one of the servants what was going on.

²⁷"'Your brother is back,' he was told, 'and your father has killed the calf we were fattening and has prepared a great feast to celebrate his coming home again unharmed.'

²⁸"The older brother was angry and wouldn't go in. His father came out and begged him, ²⁹but he replied, 'All these years I've worked hard for you and never once refused to do a single thing you told me to; and in all that time you never gave me even one young goat for a feast with my friends. ³⁰Yet when this son of yours comes back after spending your money on prostitutes, you celebrate by killing the finest calf we have on the place.'

³¹"'Look, dear son,' his father said to him, 'you and I are very close, and everything I have is yours. ³²But it is right to celebrate. For he is your brother; and he was dead and has come back to life! He was lost and is found!'"

16 A Shrewd Accountant

Jesus now told this story to his disciples: "A rich man hired an accountant to handle his affairs, but soon a rumor went around that the accountant was thoroughly dishonest.

²"So his employer called him in and said, 'What's this I hear about your stealing from me? Get your report in order, for you are to be dismissed.'

³"The accountant thought to himself, 'Now what? I'm through here, and I haven't the strength to go out and dig ditches, and I'm too proud to beg. ⁴I know just the thing! And then I'll have plenty of friends to take care of me when I leave!'

⁵,⁶"So he invited each one who owed money to his employer to come and discuss the situation. He asked the first one, 'How much do you owe him?' 'My debt is 850 gallons of olive oil,' the man replied. 'Yes, here is the contract you signed,' the accountant told him. 'Tear it up and write another one for half that much!'

⁷"'And how much do you owe him?' he asked the next man. 'A thousand bushels of wheat,' was the reply. 'Here,' the accountant said, 'take your note and replace it with one for only 800 bushels!'

⁸"The rich man had to admire the rascal for being so shrewd. And it is true that the citizens of this world are more clever [in dishonesty!] than the godly are. ⁹But shall I tell *you* to act that way, to buy friendship through cheating? Will this ensure your entry into an everlasting home in heaven? ¹⁰No! For unless you are honest in small matters, you won't be in large ones. If you cheat even a little, you won't be honest with greater responsibilities. ¹¹And if you are untrustworthy about worldly wealth, who will trust you with the true riches of heaven? ¹²And if you are not faithful with other people's money, why should you be entrusted with money of your own?

¹³"For neither you nor anyone else can serve two masters. You will hate one and show loyalty to the other, or else the other way around—you will be enthusiastic about one and despise the other. You cannot serve both God and money."

¹⁴The Pharisees, who dearly loved their money, naturally scoffed at all this.

¹⁵Then he said to them, "You wear a noble, pious expression in public, but God knows your evil hearts. Your pretense brings you honor from the people, but it is an abomination in the sight of God. ¹⁶Until John the Baptist began to preach, the laws of Moses and the messages of the prophets

FAMILY DEVOTIONS

☐ DEVOTION 273
KEEPING YOUR PROMISES

Read Luke 16:10-12

Keeping Your Promises Memory Verse

God delights in those who keep their promises and abhors those who don't.
Proverbs 12:22

Rex was angry! His little sister, Lisa, was on the front porch playing with her new puppy, but he was sulking in the living room. If Lisa could have a puppy, he didn't see why he couldn't have a kitten! "Rex," said Dad when he saw his son's unhappy face, "you don't have any excuse for acting this way. You had the same chance to have a kitten that Lisa had for a puppy. If you had taken good care of your goldfish, we'd have allowed you to get a kitten. Instead of caring for the fish, you failed to clean its bowl and feed it. Lisa had to take over its care."

"But I don't like goldfish!" wailed Rex.

"You didn't have to like the fish," said Dad, "but you did have to take good care of it if you wanted a kitten. If we can't trust you to take care of something small, how can we expect you to take care of something bigger and more complicated—like a cat?" Dad paused, then added, "You know, this is often how God works as well."

"What do you mean?" asked Rex. "Are you saying I shouldn't ask him for a kitten?"

"No, but I'm saying that God generally first trusts his children with small tasks," replied Dad. "I've known people who had dreams of doing great things for God, but they lacked the discipline to follow through on small things—like reading the Bible and praying, helping a neighbor, or doing a good job where they were. We need to do well in small things before God is likely to trust us with a bigger task—such as going out and saving the world."

Rex thought about his father's words. "Dad?" he said after a few moments.

"Yes, Son?"

"Could I have my goldfish back?" asked Rex.

"Hmmmm," said Dad with a smile, "I suppose we could give it another try."

How About You?
Do you do your best in small things? Do you do a good job with your chores? With your schoolwork? Be faithful in whatever God gives you to do now. Then you can be trusted with even greater things. *L. W.*

• For the next devotional, turn to page 987. • To start the next topic, turn to page 197. • For notes on KEEPING YOUR PROMISES, see pages 183, 284, and 838.

were your guides. But John introduced the Good News that the Kingdom of God would come soon. And now eager multitudes are pressing in. ¹⁷But that doesn't mean that the Law has lost its force in even the smallest point. It is as strong and unshakable as heaven and earth.

¹⁸"So anyone who divorces his wife and marries someone else commits adultery, and anyone who marries a divorced woman commits adultery."

¹⁹"There was a certain rich man," Jesus said, "who was splendidly clothed and lived each day in mirth and luxury. ²⁰One day Lazarus, a diseased beggar, was laid at his door. ²¹As he lay there longing for scraps from the rich man's table, the dogs would come and lick his open sores. ²²Finally the beggar died and was carried by the angels to be with Abraham in the place of the righteous dead. The rich man also died and was buried, ²³and his soul went into hell. There, in torment, he saw Lazarus in the far distance with Abraham.

²⁴"'Father Abraham,' he shouted, 'have some pity! Send Lazarus over here if only to dip the tip of his finger in water and cool my tongue, for I am in anguish in these flames.'

²⁵"But Abraham said to him, 'Son, remember that during your lifetime you had everything you wanted, and Lazarus had nothing. So now he is here being comforted and you are in anguish. ²⁶And besides, there is a great chasm separating us, and anyone wanting to come to you from here is stopped at its edge; and no one over there can cross to us.'

²⁷"Then the rich man said, 'O Father Abraham, then please send him to my father's home— ²⁸for I have five brothers—to warn them about this place of torment lest they come here when they die.'

²⁹"But Abraham said, 'The Scriptures have warned them again and again. Your brothers can read them any time they want to.'

³⁰"The rich man replied, 'No, Father Abraham, they won't bother to read them. But if someone is sent to them from the dead, then they will turn from their sins.'

³¹"But Abraham said, 'If they won't listen to Moses and the prophets, they won't listen even though someone rises from the dead.'"

17 A Story about a Servant

"There will always be temptations to sin," Jesus said one day to his disciples, "but woe to the man who does the tempting. ²,³If he were thrown into the sea with a huge rock tied to his neck, he would be far better off than facing the punishment in store for those who harm these little children's souls. I am warning you!

"Rebuke your brother if he sins, and forgive him if he is sorry. ⁴Even if he wrongs you seven times a day and each time turns again and asks forgiveness, forgive him."

⁵One day the apostles said to the Lord, "We need more faith; tell us how to get it."

⁶"If your faith were only the size of a mustard seed," Jesus answered, "it would be large enough to uproot that mulberry tree over there and send it hurtling into the sea! Your command would bring immediate results! ⁷⁻⁹When a servant comes in from plowing or taking care of sheep, he doesn't just sit down and eat, but first prepares his master's meal and serves him his supper before he eats his own. And he is not even thanked, for he is merely doing what he is supposed to do. ¹⁰Just so, if you merely obey me, you should not consider yourselves worthy of praise. For you have simply done your duty!"

¹¹As they continued onward toward Jerusalem, they reached the border between Galilee and Samaria, ¹²and as they entered a village there, ten lepers stood at a distance, ¹³crying out, "Jesus, sir, have mercy on us!"

¹⁴He looked at them and said, "Go to the Jewish priest and show him that you are healed!" And as they were going, their leprosy disappeared.

¹⁵One of them came back to Jesus, shouting, "Glory to God, I'm healed!" ¹⁶He fell flat on the ground in front of Jesus, face downward in the dust, thanking him for what he had done. This man was a despised Samaritan.

¹⁷Jesus asked, "Didn't I heal ten men? Where are the nine? ¹⁸Does only this foreigner return to give glory to God?"

¹⁹And Jesus said to the man, "Stand up and go; your faith has made you well."

²⁰One day the Pharisees asked Jesus, "When will the Kingdom of God begin?" Jesus replied, "The Kingdom of God isn't ushered in with visible signs. ²¹You won't be able to say, 'It has begun here in this place or there in that part of the country.' For the Kingdom of God is within you."

²²Later he talked again about this with his disciples. "The time is coming when you will long for me to be with you even for a single day, but I won't be here," he said. ²³"Reports will reach you that I have returned and that I am in this place or that; don't believe it or go out to look for me. ²⁴For when I return, you will know it beyond all doubt. It will be as evident as the lightning that flashes across the skies. ²⁵But first I must suffer terribly and be rejected by this whole nation.

²⁶"[When I return] the world will be [as indifferent to the things of God] as the people were in Noah's day. ²⁷They ate and drank and married—

Family Devotions

☐ *Devotion 274*
Giving Thanks

Read Luke 17:11-19

"This has been one of the best birthdays I've ever had," said Jerry as he looked at his gifts. There was a video game, a magazine subscription, a sweater, a twenty-dollar check, a new jacket, and a bike.

"Here's one more gift for you." Mom smiled as she handed him a small box.

"Another one?" Jerry was surprised. "I thought I had opened them all." Quickly he ripped the paper off. "What is this? A box of stationery for a boy?"

"A box of thank-you notes, complete with stamps," said Mom. "Before you do another thing, sit down here and write thank-you notes to everyone who gave you a gift."

"Oh, Mom, I'll do it later," argued Jerry. "I don't have time right now. I want to ride my bike and play my computer game."

"Everyone who bought you a gift spent time and money on you—time and money they could well have used somewhere else. Certainly you have time to sit down and write a short note of thanks to each one."

Jerry grumbled a bit, but he obeyed. Thirty minutes later the notes were written, and Jerry spent the rest of the evening enjoying his gifts.

At bedtime Dad remarked, "Every day the Lord gives us gifts, too, but so often we're in such a hurry to enjoy them that we neglect to tell him thanks."

"Know what I'm going to start doing?" asked Jerry. "I'm going to start with thank-you prayers before I ask the Lord for anything. And I'm going to start right now!"

Giving Thanks
Memory Verse

Is anyone among you suffering? He should keep on praying about it. And those who have reason to be thankful should continually be singing praises to the Lord.
James 5:13

How About You?
Have you been putting off writing a thank-you note to someone? And what about the Lord? Do you owe him a thank-you prayer? Take time to offer your thanks now. You'll be glad you did. *L. M. W.*

• For the next devotional, turn to page 989. • To start the next topic, turn to page 105. • For notes on *Giving Thanks*, see pages 582, 608, and 834.

everything just as usual right up to the day when Noah went into the ark and the flood came and destroyed them all.

28"And the world will be as it was in the days of Lot: people went about their daily business—eating and drinking, buying and selling, farming and building— 29until the morning Lot left Sodom. Then fire and brimstone rained down from heaven and destroyed them all. 30Yes, it will be 'business as usual' right up to the hour of my return.

31"Those away from home that day must not return to pack; those in the fields must not return to town— 32remember what happened to Lot's wife! 33Whoever clings to his life shall lose it, and whoever loses his life shall save it. 34That night two men will be asleep in the same room, and one will be taken away, the other left. 35,36Two women will be working together at household tasks; one will be taken, the other left; and so it will be with men working side by side in the fields."

37"Lord, where will they be taken?" the disciples asked.

Jesus replied, "Where the body is, the vultures gather!"

18 A Story about a Persistent Widow

One day Jesus told his disciples a story to illustrate their need for constant prayer and to show them that they must keep praying until the answer comes.

2"There was a city judge," he said, "a very godless man who had great contempt for everyone. 3A widow of that city came to him frequently to appeal for justice against a man who had harmed her. 4,5The judge ignored her for a while, but eventually she got on his nerves.

"'I fear neither God nor man,' he said to himself, 'but this woman bothers me. I'm going to see that she gets justice, for she is wearing me out with her constant coming!'"

6Then the Lord said, "If even an evil judge can be worn down like that, 7don't you think that God will surely give justice to his people who plead with him day and night? 8Yes! He will answer them quickly! But the question is: When I, the Messiah, return, how many will I find who have faith [and are praying]?"

9Then he told this story to some who boasted of their virtue and scorned everyone else:

10"Two men went to the Temple to pray. One was a proud, self-righteous Pharisee, and the other a cheating tax collector. 11The proud Pharisee 'prayed' this prayer: 'Thank God, I am not a sinner like everyone else, especially like that tax collector over there! For I never cheat, I don't commit adultery, 12I go without food twice a week, and I give to God a tenth of everything I earn.'

13"But the corrupt tax collector stood at a distance and dared not even lift his eyes to heaven as he prayed, but beat upon his chest in sorrow, exclaiming, 'God, be merciful to me, a sinner.' 14I tell you, this sinner, not the Pharisee, returned home forgiven! For the proud shall be humbled, but the humble shall be honored."

15One day some mothers brought their babies to him to touch and bless. But the disciples told them to go away.

16,17Then Jesus called the children over to him and said to the disciples, "Let the little children come to me! Never send them away! For the Kingdom of God belongs to men who have hearts as trusting as these little children's. And anyone who doesn't have their kind of faith will never get within the Kingdom's gates."

18Once a Jewish religious leader asked him this question: "Good sir, what shall I do to get to heaven?"

19"Do you realize what you are saying when you call me 'good'?" Jesus asked him. "Only God is truly good, and no one else.

20"But as to your question, you know what the Ten Commandments say—don't commit adultery, don't murder, don't steal, don't lie, honor your parents, and so on." 21The man replied, "I've obeyed every one of these laws since I was a small child."

22"There is still one thing you lack," Jesus said. "Sell all you have and give the money to the poor—it will become treasure for you in heaven—and come, follow me."

23But when the man heard this he went sadly away, for he was very rich.

24Jesus watched him go and then said to his disciples, "How hard it is for the rich to enter the Kingdom of God! 25It is easier for a camel to go through the eye of a needle than for a rich man to enter the Kingdom of God."

26Those who heard him say this exclaimed, "If it is that hard, how can *anyone* be saved?"

27He replied, "God can do what men can't!"

28And Peter said, "We have left our homes and followed you."

29"Yes," Jesus replied, "and everyone who has done as you have, leaving home, wife, brothers, parents, or children for the sake of the Kingdom of God, 30will be repaid many times over now, as well as receiving eternal life in the world to come."

31Gathering the Twelve around him he told them, "As you know, we are going to Jerusalem. And when we get there, all the predictions of the ancient prophets concerning me will come true.

FAMILY DEVOTIONS

☐ DEVOTION 275
RECEIVING CHRIST AS SAVIOR

Read Luke 18:10-14

"Oh, well! Nobody's perfect!" laughed Jody as she missed the basket, and the other girls laughed with her. "Nobody's perfect" was one of Jody's favorite phrases, and the girls almost knew ahead of time when they would hear it again.

Later that day, Jody went with her friend Robin to an after-school Bible class. She enjoyed it, but she did not agree with what Mrs. Gates, the Bible teacher, said. "No matter how good you are," said Mrs. Gates, "you're not good enough for heaven. You're a sinner, but Jesus took the punishment for your sins. The only way you can get into heaven is to believe that and accept Jesus as your Savior."

Jody discussed it with Robin as the girls walked home. "She makes it sound like everybody's such a terrible sinner. I'm not all that bad!"

"You may be a pretty decent kid," replied Robin, "but you've done some things that are wrong. I remember the time you and I sneaked . . ."

Jody laughed. "But even that wasn't *so* awful bad. And what about people like my uncle Joe? He's always helping others. He gives lots of money to places like the city mission—even the church. And last year when his neighbor's house was on fire, he rushed in himself to get the baby out." Suddenly she stopped. "Oh, I'm so busy talking, I'm not paying attention! We just passed my street, and I forgot to turn. How dumb can you be! Oh, well! Nobody's perfect!"

"You said it," laughed Robin. "I didn't. But you know what? God said it, too. He said we've all sinned, even the best of us, and no sin can enter heaven. No matter how much good you or your uncle do, you still have to get rid of your sin. Only Jesus can take it away. Think about that."

Jody did think about it as she turned and slowly headed back toward her own street.

Receiving Christ as Savior
Memory Verse

If you tell others with your own mouth that Jesus Christ is your Lord and believe in your own heart that God has raised him from the dead, you will be saved.
Romans 10:9

How About You?
Are you fit for heaven? No lying, disobedience, cheating, gossip—nor any other sin—is allowed to enter heaven. Today's Scripture tells of two men. One had done good things. The other admitted his sin and his need. Jesus says the one who asked for God's mercy is the one who was saved. Which of these men are you like? Confess your sin, and ask Jesus to forgive you and save you. H. M.

• For the next devotional, turn to page 993. • For the next devotional on RECEIVING CHRIST AS SAVIOR, turn to page 1007. • For notes on RECEIVING CHRIST AS SAVIOR, see pages 839, 842, 1146, 1234, and 1240.

³²I will be handed over to the Gentiles to be mocked and treated shamefully and spat upon, ³³and lashed and killed. And the third day I will rise again."

³⁴But they didn't understand a thing he said. He seemed to be talking in riddles.

³⁵As they approached Jericho, a blind man was sitting beside the road, begging from travelers. ³⁶When he heard the noise of a crowd going past, he asked what was happening. ³⁷He was told that Jesus from Nazareth was going by, ³⁸so he began shouting, "Jesus, Son of David, have mercy on me!"

³⁹The crowds ahead of Jesus tried to hush the man, but he only yelled the louder, "Son of David, have mercy on me!"

⁴⁰When Jesus arrived at the spot, he stopped. "Bring the blind man over here," he said. ⁴¹Then Jesus asked the man, "What do you want?"

"Lord," he pleaded, "I want to see!"

⁴²And Jesus said, "All right, begin seeing! Your faith has healed you."

⁴³And instantly the man could see and followed Jesus, praising God. And all who saw it happen praised God too.

19 Jesus Gives Zacchaeus a New Life

As Jesus was passing through Jericho, a man named Zacchaeus, one of the most influential Jews in the Roman tax-collecting business (and, of course, a very rich man), ³tried to get a look at Jesus, but he was too short to see over the crowds. ⁴So he ran ahead and climbed into a sycamore tree beside the road, to watch from there.

⁵When Jesus came by, he looked up at Zacchaeus and called him by name! "Zacchaeus!" he said. "Quick! Come down! For I am going to be a guest in your home today!"

⁶Zacchaeus hurriedly climbed down and took Jesus to his house in great excitement and joy.

⁷But the crowds were displeased. "He has gone to be the guest of a notorious sinner," they grumbled.

⁸Meanwhile, Zacchaeus stood before the Lord and said, "Sir, from now on I will give half my wealth to the poor, and if I find I have overcharged anyone on his taxes, I will penalize myself by giving him back four times as much!"

⁹,¹⁰Jesus told him, "This shows that salvation has come to this home today. This man was one of the lost sons of Abraham, and I, the Messiah, have come to search for and to save such souls as his."

¹¹And because Jesus was nearing Jerusalem, he told a story to correct the impression that the Kingdom of God would begin right away.

¹²"A nobleman living in a certain province was called away to the distant capital of the empire to be crowned king of his province. ¹³Before he left he called together ten assistants and gave them each $2,000 to invest while he was gone. ¹⁴But some of his people hated him and sent him their declaration of independence, stating that they had rebelled and would not acknowledge him as their king.

¹⁵"Upon his return he called in the men to whom he had given the money, to find out what they had done with it, and what their profits were.

¹⁶"The first man reported a tremendous gain—ten times as much as the original amount!

¹⁷"'Fine!' the king exclaimed. 'You are a good man. You have been faithful with the little I entrusted to you, and as your reward, you shall be governor of ten cities.'

¹⁸"The next man also reported a splendid gain—five times the original amount.

¹⁹"'All right!' his master said. 'You can be governor over five cities.'

²⁰"But the third man brought back only the money he had started with. 'I've kept it safe,' he said, ²¹'because I was afraid [you would demand my profits], for you are a hard man to deal with, taking what isn't yours and even confiscating the crops that others plant.' ²²'You vile and wicked slave,' the king roared. 'Hard, am I? That's exactly how I'll be toward you! If you knew so much about me and how tough I am, ²³then why didn't you deposit the money in the bank so that I could at least get some interest on it?'

²⁴"Then turning to the others standing by he ordered, 'Take the money away from him and give it to the man who earned the most.'

²⁵"'But, sir,' they said, 'he has enough already!'

²⁶"'Yes,' the king replied, 'but it is always true that those who have, get more, and those who have little, soon lose even that. ²⁷And now about these enemies of mine who revolted—bring them in and execute them before me.'"

²⁸After telling this story, Jesus went on toward Jerusalem, walking along ahead of his disciples. ²⁹As they came to the towns of Bethphage and Bethany, on the Mount of Olives, he sent two disciples ahead, ³⁰with instructions to go to the next village, and as they entered they were to look for a donkey tied beside the road. It would be a colt, not yet broken for riding.

"Untie him," Jesus said, "and bring him here. ³¹And if anyone asks you what you are doing, just say, 'The Lord needs him.'"

³²They found the colt as Jesus said, ³³and sure enough, as they were untying it, the owners demanded an explanation.

"What are you doing?" they asked. "Why are you untying our colt?"

³⁴And the disciples simply replied, "The Lord

needs him!" ³⁵So they brought the colt to Jesus and threw some of their clothing across its back for Jesus to sit on.

³⁶,³⁷Then the crowds spread out their robes along the road ahead of him, and as they reached the place where the road started down from the Mount of Olives, the whole procession began to shout and sing as they walked along, praising God for all the wonderful miracles Jesus had done.

³⁸"God has given us a King!" they exulted. "Long live the King! Let all heaven rejoice! Glory to God in the highest heavens!"

³⁹But some of the Pharisees among the crowd said, "Sir, rebuke your followers for saying things like that!"

⁴⁰He replied, "If they keep quiet, the stones along the road will burst into cheers!"

⁴¹But as they came closer to Jerusalem and he saw the city ahead, he began to cry. ⁴²"Eternal peace was within your reach and you turned it down," he wept, "and now it is too late. ⁴³Your enemies will pile up earth against your walls and encircle you and close in on you, ⁴⁴and crush you to the ground, and your children within you; your enemies will not leave one stone upon another—for you have rejected the opportunity God offered you."

⁴⁵Then he entered the Temple and began to drive out the merchants from their stalls, ⁴⁶saying to them, "The Scriptures declare, 'My Temple is a place of prayer; but you have turned it into a den of thieves.'"

⁴⁷After that he taught daily in the Temple, but the chief priests and other religious leaders and the business community were trying to find some way to get rid of him. ⁴⁸But they could think of nothing, for he was a hero to the people—they hung on every word he said.

20 Leaders Challenge Jesus' Authority

On one of those days when he was teaching and preaching the Good News in the Temple, he was confronted by the chief priests and other religious leaders and councilmen. ²They demanded to know by what authority he had driven out the merchants from the Temple.

³"I'll ask you a question before I answer," he replied ⁴"Was John sent by God, or was he merely acting under his own authority?"

⁵They talked it over among themselves. "If we say his message was from heaven, then we are trapped because he will ask, 'Then why didn't you believe him?' ⁶But if we say John was not sent from God, the people will mob us, for they are convinced that he was a prophet." ⁷Finally they replied, "We don't know!"

⁸And Jesus responded, "Then I won't answer your question either."

⁹Now he turned to the people again and told them this story: "A man planted a vineyard and rented it out to some farmers, and went away to a distant land to live for several years. ¹⁰When harvest time came, he sent one of his men to the farm to collect his share of the crops. But the tenants beat him up and sent him back empty-handed. ¹¹Then he sent another, but the same thing happened; he was beaten up and insulted and sent away without collecting. ¹²A third man was sent and the same thing happened. He, too, was wounded and chased away.

¹³"'What shall I do?' the owner asked himself. 'I know! I'll send my cherished son. Surely they will show respect for him.'

¹⁴"But when the tenants saw his son, they said, 'This is our chance! This fellow will inherit all the land when his father dies. Come on. Let's kill him, and then it will be ours.' ¹⁵So they dragged him out of the vineyard and killed him.

"What do you think the owner will do? ¹⁶I'll tell you—he will come and kill them and rent the vineyard to others."

"But they would never do a thing like that," his listeners protested.

¹⁷Jesus looked at them and said, "Then what does the Scripture mean where it says, 'The Stone rejected by the builders was made the cornerstone'?" ¹⁸And he added, "Whoever stumbles over that Stone shall be broken; and those on whom it falls will be crushed to dust."

¹⁹When the chief priests and religious leaders heard about this story he had told, they wanted him arrested immediately, for they realized that he was talking about them. They were the wicked tenants in his illustration. But they were afraid that if they themselves arrested him, there would be a riot. So they tried to get him to say something that could be reported to the Roman governor as reason for arrest by him.

²⁰Watching their opportunity, they sent secret agents pretending to be honest men. ²¹They said to Jesus, "Sir, we know what an honest teacher you are. You always tell the truth and don't budge an inch in the face of what others think, but teach the ways of God. ²²Now tell us—is it right to pay taxes to the Roman government or not?"

²³He saw through their trickery and said, ²⁴"Show me a coin. Whose portrait is this on it? And whose name?"

They replied, "Caesar's—the Roman emperor's."

²⁵He said, "Then give the emperor all that is his—and give to God all that is his!"

²⁶Thus their attempt to outwit him before the people failed; and marveling at his answer, they were silent.

²⁷Then some Sadducees—men who believed

that death is the end of existence, that there is no resurrection—²⁸came to Jesus with this:

"The laws of Moses state that if a man dies without children, the man's brother shall marry the widow, and their children will legally belong to the dead man, to carry on his name. ²⁹We know of a family of seven brothers. The oldest married and then died without any children. ³⁰His brother married the widow and he, too, died. Still no children. ³¹And so it went, one after the other, until each of the seven had married her and died, leaving no children. ³²Finally the woman died also. ³³Now here is our question: Whose wife will she be in the resurrection? For all of them were married to her!"

³⁴,³⁵Jesus replied, "Marriage is for people here on earth, but when those who are counted worthy of being raised from the dead get to heaven, they do not marry. ³⁶And they never die again; in these respects they are like angels, and are sons of God, for they are raised up in new life from the dead.

³⁷,³⁸"But as to your real question—whether or not there is a resurrection—why, even the writings of Moses himself prove this. For when he describes how God appeared to him in the burning bush, he speaks of God as 'the God of Abraham, the God of Isaac, and the God of Jacob.' To say that the Lord *is* some person's God means that person is *alive*, not dead! So from God's point of view, all men are living."

³⁹"Well said, sir!" remarked some of the experts in the Jewish law who were standing there. ⁴⁰And that ended their questions, for they dared ask no more!

⁴¹Then he presented *them* with a question. "Why is it," he asked, "that Christ, the Messiah, is said to be a descendant of King David? ⁴²,⁴³For David himself wrote in the book of Psalms: 'God said to my Lord, the Messiah, "Sit at my right hand until I place your enemies beneath your feet."' ⁴⁴How can the Messiah be both David's son and David's God at the same time?"

⁴⁵Then, with the crowds listening, he turned to his disciples and said, ⁴⁶"Beware of these experts in religion, for they love to parade in dignified robes and to be bowed to by the people as they walk along the street. And how they love the seats of honor in the synagogues and at religious festivals! ⁴⁷But even while they are praying long prayers with great outward piety, they are planning schemes to cheat widows out of their property. Therefore God's heaviest sentence awaits these men."

21 The Widow's Small Coins

As he stood in the Temple, he was watching the rich tossing their gifts into the collection box. ²Then a poor widow came by and dropped in two small copper coins.

³"Really," he remarked, "this poor widow has given more than all the rest of them combined. ⁴For they have given a little of what they didn't need, but she, poor as she is, has given everything she has."

⁵Some of his disciples began talking about the beautiful stonework of the Temple and the memorial decorations on the walls.

⁶But Jesus said, "The time is coming when all these things you are admiring will be knocked down, and not one stone will be left on top of another; all will become one vast heap of rubble."

⁷"Master!" they exclaimed. "When? And will there be any warning ahead of time?"

⁸He replied, "Don't let anyone mislead you. For many will come announcing themselves as the Messiah, and saying, 'The time has come.' But don't believe them! ⁹And when you hear of wars and insurrections beginning, don't panic. True, wars must come, but the end won't follow immediately—¹⁰for nation shall rise against nation and kingdom against kingdom, ¹¹and there will be great earthquakes, and famines in many lands, and epidemics, and terrifying things happening in the heavens.

¹²"But before all this occurs, there will be a time of special persecution, and you will be dragged into synagogues and prisons and before kings and governors for my name's sake. ¹³But as a result, the Messiah will be widely known and honored. ¹⁴Therefore, don't be concerned about how to answer the charges against you, ¹⁵for I will give you the right words and such logic that none of your opponents will be able to reply! ¹⁶Even those closest to you—your parents, brothers, relatives, and friends will betray you and have you arrested; and some of you will be killed. ¹⁷And everyone will hate you because you are mine and are called by my name. ¹⁸But not a hair of your head will perish! ¹⁹For if you stand firm, you will win your souls.

²⁰"But when you see Jerusalem surrounded by armies, then you will know that the time of its destruction has arrived. ²¹Then let the people of Judea flee to the hills. Let those in Jerusalem try to escape, and those outside the city must not attempt to return. ²²For those will be days of God's judgment, and the words of the ancient Scriptures written by the prophets will be abundantly fulfilled. ²³Woe to expectant mothers in those days, and those with tiny babies. For there will be great distress upon this nation and wrath upon this people. ²⁴They will be brutally killed by enemy weapons, or sent away as exiles and captives to all the nations of the world; and Jerusalem shall be conquered and trampled down by the Gentiles until the period of Gentile triumph ends in God's good time.

²⁵"Then there will be strange events in the

FAMILY DEVOTIONS

☐ *DEVOTION 276*
OVERCOMING FEAR

Read Luke 21:9-19

As soon as Matt walked in the door, his mother knew something was wrong. He was quiet and troubled, not his usual happy self.

"How was school, Matt?" Mom asked.

Matt shrugged. "It was OK."

"You don't seem very happy," observed Mom.

Matt hesitated. "We had a discussion in social studies class. One of the kids started talking about nuclear war and how the whole world was going to end. Mr. Morgan, our teacher, agreed with him."

"What do you think, Matt?" asked Mom.

Matt gave his mother a little smile. "I think it's sort of scary." Matt paused. "Aren't you afraid, Mom?"

"Matt, this world is a messed-up place," answered Mom, "but when people tell frightening stories about nuclear war, I take time to thank the Lord that my future is in *his* hands. As Christians, we know that the Lord loves and cares for us. He is still in control. Only what he allows will happen, and we can trust him to allow only what is best for us."

"But our teacher says that if everyone would stop making nuclear weapons, the world would be peaceful and no one would fight," offered Matt.

"That sounds good, Matt," answered Mom, "but it's not what the Bible says. Nations want to be powerful and will do anything to gain that power. It's unrealistic to think that all nations will suddenly decide to stop fighting. There will always be war. Again, we must remember to put our trust in the Lord."

Matt thought about it for a moment. Then he grinned at his mother. "It's good to be a Christian, Mom—and to trust the Lord to know what's best for me!"

Overcoming Fear
Memory Verse

Fear not, for I am with you. Do not be dismayed. I am your God. I will strengthen you; I will help you; I will uphold you with my victorious right hand.
Isaiah 41:10

How About You?
Are you frightened when you think about war? As a Christian, you don't have to be afraid. The Lord says that your future is in his hands. Whatever that future holds, he will be with you and help you through it. And isn't it nice to look forward to a wonderful future life in heaven? L. M. W.

• For the next devotional, turn to page 995.   • For the next devotional on *OVERCOMING FEAR*, turn to page 1113.
• For notes on *OVERCOMING FEAR*, see pages 191, 482, 554, 592, and 912.

skies—warnings, evil omens and portents in the sun, moon and stars; and down here on earth the nations will be in turmoil, perplexed by the roaring seas and strange tides. ²⁶The courage of many people will falter because of the fearful fate they see coming upon the earth, for the stability of the very heavens will be broken up. ²⁷Then the peoples of the earth shall see me, the Messiah, coming in a cloud with power and great glory. ²⁸So when all these things begin to happen, stand straight and look up! For your salvation is near."

²⁹Then he gave them this illustration: "Notice the fig tree, or any other tree. ³⁰When the leaves come out, you know without being told that summer is near. ³¹In the same way, when you see the events taking place that I've described you can be just as sure that the Kingdom of God is near.

³²"I solemnly declare to you that when these things happen, the end of this age has come. ³³And though all heaven and earth shall pass away, yet my words remain forever true.

³⁴,³⁵"Watch out! Don't let my sudden coming catch you unawares; don't let me find you living in careless ease, carousing and drinking, and occupied with the problems of this life, like all the rest of the world. ³⁶Keep a constant watch. And pray that if possible you may arrive in my presence without having to experience these horrors."

³⁷,³⁸Every day Jesus went to the Temple to teach, and the crowds began gathering early in the morning to hear him. And each evening he returned to spend the night on the Mount of Olives.

22 A Plan to Kill Jesus

And now the Passover celebration was drawing near—the Jewish festival when only bread made without yeast was used. ²The chief priests and other religious leaders were actively plotting Jesus' murder, trying to find a way to kill him without starting a riot—a possibility they greatly feared.

³Then Satan entered into Judas Iscariot, who was one of the twelve disciples, ⁴and he went over to the chief priests and captains of the Temple guards to discuss the best way to betray Jesus to them. ⁵They were, of course, delighted to know that he was ready to help them and promised him a reward. ⁶So he began to look for an opportunity for them to arrest Jesus quietly when the crowds weren't around.

⁷Now the day of the Passover celebration arrived, when the Passover lamb was killed and eaten with the unleavened bread. ⁸Jesus sent Peter and John ahead to find a place to prepare their Passover meal.

⁹"Where do you want us to go?" they asked.

¹⁰And he replied, "As soon as you enter Jerusalem, you will see a man walking along carrying a pitcher of water. Follow him into the house he enters, ¹¹and say to the man who lives there, 'Our Teacher says for you to show us the guest room where he can eat the Passover meal with his disciples.' ¹²He will take you upstairs to a large room all ready for us. That is the place. Go ahead and prepare the meal there."

¹³They went off to the city and found everything just as Jesus had said, and prepared the Passover supper.

¹⁴Then Jesus and the others arrived, and at the proper time all sat down together at the table; ¹⁵and he said, "I have looked forward to this hour with deep longing, anxious to eat this Passover meal with you before my suffering begins. ¹⁶For I tell you now that I won't eat it again until what it represents has occurred in the Kingdom of God."

¹⁷Then he took a glass of wine, and when he had given thanks for it, he said, "Take this and share it among yourselves. ¹⁸For I will not drink wine again until the Kingdom of God has come."

¹⁹Then he took a loaf of bread; and when he had thanked God for it, he broke it apart and gave it to them, saying, "This is my body, given for you. Eat it in remembrance of me."

²⁰After supper he gave them another glass of wine, saying, "This wine is the token of God's new agreement to save you—an agreement sealed with the blood I shall pour out to purchase back your souls. ²¹But here at this table, sitting among us as a friend, is the man who will betray me. ²²I must die. It is part of God's plan. But, oh, the horror awaiting that man who betrays me."

²³Then the disciples wondered among themselves which of them would ever do such a thing.

²⁴And they began to argue among themselves as to who would have the highest rank [in the coming Kingdom].

²⁵Jesus told them, "In this world the kings and great men order their slaves around, and the slaves have no choice but to like it! ²⁶But among you, the one who serves you best will be your leader. ²⁷Out in the world the master sits at the table and is served by his servants. But not here! For I am your servant. ²⁸Nevertheless, because you have stood true to me in these terrible days, ²⁹and because my Father has granted me a Kingdom, I, here and now, grant you the right ³⁰to eat and drink at my table in that Kingdom; and you will sit on thrones judging the twelve tribes of Israel.

³¹"Simon, Simon, Satan has asked to have you, to sift you like wheat, ³²but I have pleaded in prayer for you that your faith should not completely fail. So when you have repented and

FAMILY DEVOTIONS

☐ DEVOTION 277
ENCOURAGING OTHERS

Read Luke 22:25-32

Encouraging Others
Memory Verse

So encourage each other to build each other up, just as you are already doing.
1 Thessalonians 5:11

"Good morning, Hendrick," William greeted his lamb as he entered the fenced enclosure. "You're going to win that blue ribbon at the fair in a couple of months." He groomed Hendrick until Mom called him for lunch.

"Hendrick is going to win that blue ribbon, Mom. I just know he is," William said.

Mom smiled. "He just might," she agreed. "By the way, have you called Kevin to see if he'll be going to church with us tomorrow?"

"No," William shook his head. "But it doesn't matter, because he got saved last week." William walked over to the door. "I'm going to see what Hendrick's up to."

When William reached the enclosure, he discovered that he had left the gate open, and the lamb was gone. Quickly he ran to the house, calling for his mother. She helped William search for his lamb, and before long they found him in a field—right in the middle of nettles and spiny flowers which caught and stuck in his coat.

"Oh, Hendrick, you naughty lamb," William moaned. "I had you all cleaned and brushed. Now look at you!"

Mom stood and eyed the lamb. "We wouldn't want this to happen to your friend Kevin, would we?" she said.

"Kevin?" William was puzzled. "What do you mean?"

"Hendrick needs guidance and restrictions even after he has been brushed and fed. Left to himself, he gets all messed up again," explained Mom. "And Kevin—even now that he's saved—needs guidance, too. He needs to be around people of God, who can guide him in the way he should go. God wants you to be not only your lamb's keeper, but also your brother's keeper."

William nodded slowly. "I get it," he said. "I'll ride over to Kevin's and ask him to go to church with us—as soon as I get this lamb locked up."

How About You?
Do you think a newly saved person should take care of himself? All Christians need help and guidance, especially those who are new converts. You can help them. Jesus' advice to Peter is good advice for you, too. D. A. L.

• For the next devotional, turn to page 1005. • For the next devotional on ENCOURAGING OTHERS, turn to page 1091.
• For notes on ENCOURAGING OTHERS, see pages 108, 157, 474, 1156, and 1170.

turned to me again, strengthen and build up the faith of your brothers."

³³Simon said, "Lord, I am ready to go to jail with you, and even to die with you."

³⁴But Jesus said, "Peter, let me tell you something. Between now and tomorrow morning when the rooster crows, you will deny me three times, declaring that you don't even know me."

³⁵Then Jesus asked them, "When I sent you out to preach the Good News and you were without money, duffle bag, or extra clothing, how did you get along?"

"Fine," they replied.

³⁶"But now," he said, "take a duffle bag if you have one and your money. And if you don't have a sword, better sell your clothes and buy one! ³⁷For the time has come for this prophecy about me to come true: 'He will be condemned as a criminal!' Yes, everything written about me by the prophets will come true."

³⁸"Master," they replied, "we have two swords among us."

"Enough!" he said.

³⁹Then, accompanied by the disciples, he left the upstairs room and went as usual to the Mount of Olives. ⁴⁰There he told them, "Pray God that you will not be overcome by temptation."

⁴¹,⁴²He walked away, perhaps a stone's throw, and knelt down and prayed this prayer: "Father, if you are willing, please take away this cup of horror from me. But I want your will, not mine." ⁴³Then an angel from heaven appeared and strengthened him, ⁴⁴for he was in such agony of spirit that he broke into a sweat of blood, with great drops falling to the ground as he prayed more and more earnestly. ⁴⁵At last he stood up again and returned to the disciples—only to find them asleep, exhausted from grief.

⁴⁶"Asleep!" he said. "Get up! Pray God that you will not fall when you are tempted."

⁴⁷But even as he said this, a mob approached, led by Judas, one of his twelve disciples. Judas walked over to Jesus and kissed him on the cheek in friendly greeting.

⁴⁸But Jesus said, "Judas, how can you do this—betray the Messiah with a kiss?"

⁴⁹When the other disciples saw what was about to happen, they exclaimed, "Master, shall we fight? We brought along the swords!" ⁵⁰And one of them slashed at the High Priest's servant and cut off his right ear.

⁵¹But Jesus said, "Don't resist any more." And he touched the place where the man's ear had been and restored it. ⁵²Then Jesus addressed the chief priests and captains of the Temple guards and the religious leaders who headed the mob. "Am I a robber," he asked, "that you have come armed with swords and clubs to get me? ⁵³Why didn't you arrest me in the Temple? I was there every day. But this is your moment—the time when Satan's power reigns supreme."

⁵⁴So they seized him and led him to the High Priest's residence, and Peter followed at a distance. ⁵⁵The soldiers lit a fire in the courtyard and sat around it for warmth, and Peter joined them there.

⁵⁶A servant girl noticed him in the firelight and began staring at him. Finally she spoke: "This man was with Jesus!"

⁵⁷Peter denied it. "Woman," he said, "I don't even know the man!"

⁵⁸After a while someone else looked at him and said, "You must be one of them!"

"No sir, I am not!" Peter replied.

⁵⁹About an hour later someone else flatly stated, "I know this fellow is one of Jesus' disciples, for both are from Galilee."

⁶⁰But Peter said, "Man, I don't know what you are talking about." And as he said the words, a rooster crowed.

⁶¹At that moment Jesus turned and looked at Peter. Then Peter remembered what he had said—"Before the rooster crows tomorrow morning, you will deny me three times." ⁶²And Peter walked out of the courtyard, crying bitterly.

⁶³,⁶⁴Now the guards in charge of Jesus began mocking him. They blindfolded him and hit him with their fists and asked, "Who hit you that time, prophet?" ⁶⁵And they threw all sorts of other insults at him.

⁶⁶Early the next morning at daybreak the Jewish Supreme Court assembled, including the chief priests and all the top religious authorities of the nation. Jesus was led before this Council ⁶⁷,⁶⁸and instructed to state whether or not he claimed to be the Messiah.

But he replied, "If I tell you, you won't believe me or let me present my case. ⁶⁹But the time is soon coming when I, the Messiah, shall be enthroned beside Almighty God."

⁷⁰They all shouted, "Then you claim you are the Son of God?"

And he replied, "Yes, I am."

⁷¹"What need do we have for other witnesses?" they shouted. "For we ourselves have heard him say it."

23 Jesus Stands before Pilate

Then the entire Council took Jesus over to Pilate, the governor. ²They began at once accusing him: "This fellow has been leading our people to ruin by telling them not to pay their taxes to the Roman government and by claiming he is our Messiah—a King."

³So Pilate asked him, "Are you their Messiah—their King?"

"Yes," Jesus replied, "it is as you say."

⁴Then Pilate turned to the chief priests and to the mob and said, "So? That isn't a crime!"

⁵Then they became desperate. "But he is causing riots against the government everywhere he goes, all over Judea, from Galilee to Jerusalem!"

⁶"Is he then a Galilean?" Pilate asked.

⁷When they told him yes, Pilate said to take him to King Herod, for Galilee was under Herod's jurisdiction; and Herod happened to be in Jerusalem at the time. ⁸Herod was delighted at the opportunity to see Jesus, for he had heard a lot about him and had been hoping to see him perform a miracle.

⁹He asked Jesus question after question, but there was no reply. ¹⁰Meanwhile, the chief priests and the other religious leaders stood there shouting their accusations.

¹¹Now Herod and his soldiers began mocking and ridiculing Jesus; and putting a kingly robe on him, they sent him back to Pilate. ¹²That day Herod and Pilate—enemies before—became fast friends.

¹³Then Pilate called together the chief priests and other Jewish leaders, along with the people, ¹⁴and announced his verdict:

"You brought this man to me, accusing him of leading a revolt against the Roman government. I have examined him thoroughly on this point and find him innocent. ¹⁵Herod came to the same conclusion and sent him back to us—nothing this man has done calls for the death penalty. ¹⁶I will therefore have him scourged with leaded thongs and release him."

¹⁷,¹⁸But now a mighty roar rose from the crowd as with one voice they shouted. "Kill him, and release Barabbas to us!" ¹⁹(Barabbas was in prison for starting an insurrection in Jerusalem against the government, and for murder.) ²⁰Pilate argued with them, for he wanted to release Jesus. ²¹But they shouted, "Crucify him! Crucify him!"

²²Once more, for the third time, he demanded, "Why? What crime has he committed? I have found no reason to sentence him to death. I will therefore scourge him and let him go." ²³But they shouted louder and louder for Jesus' death, and their voices prevailed.

²⁴So Pilate sentenced Jesus to die as they demanded. ²⁵And he released Barabbas, the man in prison for insurrection and murder, at their request. But he delivered Jesus over to them to do with as they would.

²⁶As the crowd led Jesus away to his death, Simon of Cyrene, who was just coming into Jerusalem from the country, was forced to follow, carrying Jesus' cross. ²⁷Great crowds trailed along behind, and many grief-stricken women.

²⁸But Jesus turned and said to them, "Daughters of Jerusalem, don't weep for me, but for yourselves and for your children. ²⁹For the days are coming when the women who have no children will be counted fortunate indeed. ³⁰Mankind will beg the mountains to fall on them and crush them, and the hills to bury them. ³¹For if such things as this are done to me, the Living Tree, what will they do to you?"

³²,³³Two others, criminals, were led out to be executed with him at a place called "The Skull." There all three were crucified—Jesus on the center cross, and the two criminals on either side.

³⁴"Father, forgive these people," Jesus said, "for they don't know what they are doing."

And the soldiers gambled for his clothing, throwing dice for each piece. ³⁵The crowd watched. And the Jewish leaders laughed and scoffed. "He was so good at helping others," they said, "let's see him save himself if he is really God's Chosen One, the Messiah."

³⁶The soldiers mocked him, too, by offering him a drink—of sour wine. ³⁷And they called to him, "If you are the King of the Jews, save yourself!"

³⁸A signboard was nailed to the cross above him with these words: "This is the King of the Jews."

³⁹One of the criminals hanging beside him scoffed, "So you're the Messiah, are you? Prove it by saving yourself—and us, too, while you're at it!"

⁴⁰,⁴¹But the other criminal protested. "Don't you even fear God when you are dying? We deserve to die for our evil deeds, but this man hasn't done one thing wrong." ⁴²Then he said, "Jesus, remember me when you come into your Kingdom."

⁴³And Jesus replied, "Today you will be with me in Paradise. This is a solemn promise."

⁴⁴By now it was noon, and darkness fell across the whole land for three hours, until three o'clock. ⁴⁵The light from the sun was gone—and suddenly the thick veil hanging in the Temple split apart.

⁴⁶Then Jesus shouted, "Father, I commit my spirit to you," and with those words he died.

⁴⁷When the captain of the Roman military unit handling the executions saw what had happened, he was stricken with awe before God and said, "Surely this man was innocent."

⁴⁸And when the crowd that came to see the crucifixion saw that Jesus was dead they went home in deep sorrow. ⁴⁹Meanwhile, Jesus' friends, including the women who had followed him down from Galilee, stood in the distance watching.

⁵⁰⁻⁵²Then a man named Joseph, a member of the Jewish Supreme Court, from the city of Arimathea in Judea, went to Pilate and asked for the body of Jesus. He was a godly man who had been expecting the Messiah's coming and had not agreed with the decision and actions of the other Jewish leaders. ⁵³So he took down Jesus' body and wrapped it in a long linen cloth and laid it in a new, unused tomb hewn into the rock [at the side of a hill]. ⁵⁴This was done late on Friday afternoon, the day of preparation for the Sabbath.

⁵⁵As the body was taken away, the women from Galilee followed and saw it carried into the tomb. ⁵⁶Then they went home and prepared spices and ointments to embalm him; but by the time they were finished it was the Sabbath, so they rested all that day as required by the Jewish law.

24 Jesus Is Alive!

But very early on Sunday morning they took the ointments to the tomb—²and found that the huge stone covering the entrance had been rolled aside. ³So they went in—but the Lord Jesus' body was gone.

⁴They stood there puzzled, trying to think what could have happened to it. Suddenly two men appeared before them, clothed in shining robes so bright their eyes were dazzled. ⁵The women were terrified and bowed low before them.

Then the men asked, "Why are you looking in a tomb for someone who is alive? ⁶,⁷He isn't here! He has come back to life again! Don't you remember what he told you back in Galilee—that the Messiah must be betrayed into the power of evil men and be crucified and that he would rise again the third day?"

⁸Then they remembered ⁹and rushed back to Jerusalem to tell his eleven disciples—and everyone else—what had happened. ¹⁰(The women who went to the tomb were Mary Magdalene and Joanna and Mary the mother of James, and several others.) ¹¹But the story sounded like a fairy tale to the men—they didn't believe it.

¹²However, Peter ran to the tomb to look. Stooping, he peered in and saw the empty linen wrappings; and then he went back home again, wondering what had happened.

¹³That same day, Sunday, two of Jesus' followers were walking to the village of Emmaus, seven miles out of Jerusalem. ¹⁴As they walked along they were talking of Jesus' death, ¹⁵when suddenly Jesus himself came along and joined them and began walking beside them. ¹⁶But they didn't recognize him, for God kept them from it.

¹⁷"You seem to be in a deep discussion about something," he said. "What are you so concerned about?" They stopped short, sadness written across their faces. ¹⁸And one of them, Cleopas, replied, "You must be the only person in Jerusalem who hasn't heard about the terrible things that happened there last week."

¹⁹"What things?" Jesus asked.

"The things that happened to Jesus, the Man from Nazareth," they said. "He was a Prophet who did incredible miracles and was a mighty Teacher, highly regarded by both God and man. ²⁰But the chief priests and our religious leaders arrested him and handed him over to the Roman government to be condemned to death, and they crucified him. ²¹We had thought he was the glorious Messiah and that he had come to rescue Israel.

"And now, besides all this—which happened three days ago— ²²,²³some women from our group of his followers were at his tomb early this morning and came back with an amazing report that his body was missing, and that they had seen some angels there who told them Jesus is alive! ²⁴Some of our men ran out to see, and sure enough, Jesus' body was gone, just as the women had said."

²⁵Then Jesus said to them, "You are such foolish, foolish people! You find it so hard to believe all that the prophets wrote in the Scriptures! ²⁶Wasn't it clearly predicted by the prophets that the Messiah would have to suffer all these things before entering his time of glory?"

²⁷Then Jesus quoted them passage after passage from the writings of the prophets, beginning with the book of Genesis and going right on through the Scriptures, explaining what the passages meant and what they said about himself.

²⁸By this time they were nearing Emmaus and the end of their journey. Jesus would have gone on, ²⁹but they begged him to stay the night with them, as it was getting late. So he went home with them. ³⁰As they sat down to eat, he asked God's blessing on the food and then took a small loaf of bread and broke it and was passing it over to them, ³¹when suddenly—it was as though their eyes were opened—they recognized him! And at that moment he disappeared!

³²They began telling each other how their hearts had felt strangely warm as he talked with them and explained the Scriptures during the walk down the road. ³³,³⁴Within the hour they were on their way back to Jerusalem, where the eleven disciples and the other followers of Jesus greeted them with these words, "The Lord has really risen! He appeared to Peter!"

³⁵Then the two from Emmaus told their story of how Jesus had appeared to them as they were walking along the road and how they had recognized him as he was breaking the bread.

³⁶And just as they were telling about it, Jesus himself was suddenly standing there among them,

and greeted them. ³⁷But the whole group was terribly frightened, thinking they were seeing a ghost!

³⁸"Why are you frightened?" he asked. "Why do you doubt that it is really I? ³⁹Look at my hands! Look at my feet! You can see that it is I, myself! Touch me and make sure that I am not a ghost! For ghosts don't have bodies, as you see that I do!" ⁴⁰As he spoke, he held out his hands for them to see [the marks of the nails], and showed them [the wounds in] his feet.

⁴¹Still they stood there undecided, filled with joy and doubt.

Then he asked them, "Do you have anything here to eat?"

⁴²They gave him a piece of broiled fish, ⁴³and he ate it as they watched!

⁴⁴Then he said, "When I was with you before, don't you remember my telling you that everything written about me by Moses and the prophets and in the Psalms must all come true?" ⁴⁵Then he opened their minds to understand at last these many Scriptures! ⁴⁶And he said, "Yes, it was written long ago that the Messiah must suffer and die and rise again from the dead on the third day; ⁴⁷and that this message of salvation should be taken from Jerusalem to all the nations: *There is forgiveness of sins for all who turn to me.* ⁴⁸You have seen these prophecies come true.

⁴⁹"And now I will send the Holy Spirit upon you, just as my Father promised. Don't begin telling others yet—stay here in the city until the Holy Spirit comes and fills you with power from heaven."

⁵⁰Then Jesus led them out along the road to Bethany, and lifting his hands to heaven, he blessed them, ⁵¹and then began rising into the sky, and went on to heaven. ⁵²And they worshiped him, and returned to Jerusalem filled with mighty joy, ⁵³and were continually in the Temple, praising God.

John

WHAT ARE your reasons for believing in Jesus? What is your relationship with him like?

John wrote his Gospel to give reasons for believing in Jesus. John was one of the twelve disciples and one of Jesus' closest friends when Jesus lived on earth. John assumed his readers already knew the facts about Jesus. So instead of telling too many details of what Jesus did, John told *who Jesus was.* John wrote down what Jesus said about himself and why he came.

Jesus used many different names for himself to help people understand and believe in him. John wrote them all down. Jesus said he was the Bread of Life, the Light of the World, the Good Shepherd, the Gate for the sheep, the Way, the Truth, the Life, and the Vine.

Who is Jesus to you? As you read John, look for reasons to believe in Jesus.

God Becomes a Human

Before anything else existed, there was Christ, with God. He has always been alive and is himself God. ³He created everything there is—nothing exists that he didn't make. ⁴Eternal life is in him, and this life gives light to all mankind. ⁵His life is the light that shines through the darkness—and the darkness can never extinguish it.

⁶,⁷God sent John the Baptist as a witness to the fact that Jesus Christ is the true Light. ⁸John himself was not the Light; he was only a witness to identify it.

⁹Later on, the one who is the true Light arrived to shine on everyone coming into the world.

¹⁰But although he made the world, the world didn't recognize him when he came. ¹¹,¹²Even in his own land and among his own people, the Jews, he was not accepted. Only a few would welcome and receive him. But to all who received him, he gave the right to become children of God. All they

needed to do was to trust him to save them. ¹³All those who believe this are reborn!—not a physical rebirth resulting from human passion or plan—but from the will of God.

¹⁴And Christ became a human being and lived here on earth among us and was full of loving forgiveness and truth. And some of us have seen his glory—the glory of the only Son of the heavenly Father!

¹⁵John pointed him out to the people, telling the crowds, "This is the one I was talking about when I said, 'Someone is coming who is greater by far than I am—for he existed long before I did!'" ¹⁶We have all benefited from the rich blessings he brought to us—blessing upon blessing heaped upon us! ¹⁷For Moses gave us only the Law with its rigid demands and merciless justice, while Jesus Christ brought us loving forgiveness as well. ¹⁸No one has ever actually seen God, but, of course, his only Son has, for he is the companion of the Father and has told us all about him.

¹⁹The Jewish leaders sent priests and assistant priests from Jerusalem to ask John whether he claimed to be the Messiah.

²⁰He denied it flatly. "I am not the Christ," he said.

²¹"Well then, who are you?" they asked. "Are you Elijah?"

"No," he replied.

"Are you the Prophet?"

"No."

²²"Then who are you? Tell us, so we can give an answer to those who sent us. What do you have to say for yourself?"

²³He replied, "I am a voice from the barren wilderness, shouting as Isaiah prophesied, 'Get ready for the coming of the Lord!'"

²⁴,²⁵Then those who were sent by the Pharisees asked him, "If you aren't the Messiah or Elijah or the Prophet, what right do you have to baptize?"

²⁶John told them, "I merely baptize with water, but right here in the crowd is someone you have never met, ²⁷who will soon begin his ministry among you, and I am not even fit to be his slave."

²⁸This incident took place at Bethany, a village on the other side of the Jordan River where John was baptizing.

²⁹The next day John saw Jesus coming toward him and said, "Look! There is the Lamb of God who takes away the world's sin! ³⁰He is the one I was talking about when I said, 'Soon a man far greater than I am is coming, who existed long before me!' ³¹I didn't know he was the one, but I am here baptizing with water in order to point him out to the nation of Israel."

³²Then John told about seeing the Holy Spirit in the form of a dove descending from heaven and resting upon Jesus.

³³"I didn't know he was the one," John said again, "but at the time God sent me to baptize he told me, 'When you see the Holy Spirit descending and resting upon someone—he is the one you are looking for. He is the one who baptizes with the Holy Spirit.' ³⁴I saw it happen to this man, and I therefore testify that he is the Son of God."

³⁵The following day as John was standing with two of his disciples, ³⁶Jesus walked by. John looked at him intently and then declared, "See! There is the Lamb of God!"

³⁷Then John's two disciples turned and followed Jesus.

³⁸Jesus looked around and saw them following. "What do you want?" he asked them.

"Sir," they replied, "where do you live?"

³⁹"Come and see," he said. So they went with him to the place where he was staying and were with him from about four o'clock that afternoon until the evening. ⁴⁰(One of these men was Andrew, Simon Peter's brother.)

⁴¹Andrew then went to find his brother Peter and told him, "We have found the Messiah!" ⁴²And he brought Peter to meet Jesus.

Jesus looked intently at Peter for a moment and then said, "You are Simon, John's son—but you shall be called Peter, the rock!"

⁴³The next day Jesus decided to go to Galilee. He found Philip and told him, "Come with me." ⁴⁴(Philip was from Bethsaida, Andrew and Peter's hometown.)

⁴⁵Philip now went off to look for Nathanael and told him, "We have found the Messiah!—the very person Moses and the prophets told about! His name is Jesus, the son of Joseph from Nazareth!"

⁴⁶"Nazareth!" exclaimed Nathanael. "Can anything good come from there?"

"Just come and see for yourself," Philip declared.

⁴⁷As they approached, Jesus said, "Here comes an honest man—a true son of Israel."

⁴⁸"How do you know what I am like?" Nathanael demanded.

And Jesus replied, "I could see you under the fig tree before Philip found you."

⁴⁹Nathanael replied, "Sir, you are the Son of God—the King of Israel!"

⁵⁰Jesus asked him, "Do you be-

GOING TO CHURCH 2:14-16 God's Temple was being misused by people who had turned it into a marketplace. They had forgotten, or didn't care, that God's house is a place of worship, not a place for making a profit. Our attitude toward the church is wrong if we see it as a place for personal contacts or business advantage, or even as just a place to see our friends. Make sure you attend church to worship God. **To begin the series of devotionals on** GOING TO CHURCH, **turn to page 193.**

lieve all this just because I told you I had seen you under the fig tree? You will see greater proofs than this. ⁵¹You will even see heaven open and the angels of God coming back and forth to me, the Messiah."

2 Jesus Turns Water into Wine

Two days later Jesus' mother was a guest at a wedding in the village of Cana in Galilee, ²and Jesus and his disciples were invited too. ³The wine supply ran out during the festivities, and Jesus' mother came to him with the problem.

⁴"I can't help you now," he said. "It isn't yet my time for miracles."

⁵But his mother told the servants, "Do whatever he tells you to."

⁶Six stone waterpots were standing there; they were used for Jewish ceremonial purposes and held perhaps twenty to thirty gallons each. ⁷,⁸Then Jesus told the servants to fill them to the brim with water. When this was done he said, "Dip some out and take it to the master of ceremonies."

⁹When the master of ceremonies tasted the water that was now wine, not knowing where it had come from (though, of course, the servants did), he called the bridegroom over.

¹⁰"This is wonderful stuff!" he said. "You're different from most. Usually a host uses the best wine first, and afterwards, when everyone is full and doesn't care, then he brings out the less expensive brands. But you have kept the best for the last!"

¹¹This miracle at Cana in Galilee was Jesus' first public demonstration of his heaven-sent power. And his disciples believed that he really was the Messiah.

¹²After the wedding he left for Capernaum for a few days with his mother, brothers, and disciples.

¹³Then it was time for the annual Jewish Passover celebration, and Jesus went to Jerusalem.

¹⁴In the Temple area he saw merchants selling cattle, sheep, and doves for sacrifices, and moneychangers behind their counters. ¹⁵Jesus made a whip from some ropes and chased them all out, and drove out the sheep and oxen, scattering the moneychangers' coins over the floor and turning over their tables! ¹⁶Then, going over to the men selling doves, he told them, "Get these things out of here. Don't turn my Father's House into a market!"

¹⁷Then his disciples remembered this prophecy from the Scriptures: "Concern for God's House will be my undoing."

¹⁸"What right have you to order them out?" the Jewish leaders demanded. "If you have this authority from God, show us a miracle to prove it."

¹⁹"All right," Jesus replied, "this is the miracle I will do for you: Destroy this sanctuary and in three days I will raise it up!"

²⁰"What!" they exclaimed. "It took forty-six years to build this Temple, and you can do it in three days?" ²¹But by "this sanctuary" he meant his body. ²²After he came back to life again, the disciples remembered his saying this and realized that what he had quoted from the Scriptures really did refer to him, and had all come true!

²³Because of the miracles he did in Jerusalem at the Passover celebration, many people were convinced that he was indeed the Messiah. ²⁴,²⁵But Jesus didn't trust them, for he knew mankind to the core. No one needed to tell him how changeable human nature is!

3 Jesus Talks with Nicodemus

After dark one night a Jewish religious leader named Nicodemus, a member of the sect of the Pharisees, came for an interview with Jesus. "Sir," he said, "we all know that God has sent you to teach us. Your miracles are proof enough of this."

³Jesus replied, "With all the earnestness I possess I tell you this: Unless you are born again, you can never get into the Kingdom of God."

⁴"Born again!" exclaimed Nicodemus. "What do you mean? How can an old man go back into his mother's womb and be born again?"

⁵Jesus replied, "What I am telling you so earnestly is this: Unless one is born of water and the Spirit, he cannot enter the Kingdom of God. ⁶Men can only reproduce human life, but the Holy Spirit gives new life from heaven; ⁷so don't be surprised at my statement that you must be born again! ⁸Just as you can hear the wind but can't tell where it comes from or where it will go next, so it is with the Spirit. We do not know on whom he will next bestow this life from heaven."

⁹"What do you mean?" Nicodemus asked.

¹⁰,¹¹Jesus replied, "You, a respected Jewish teacher, and yet you don't understand these things? I am telling you what I know and have seen—and yet you won't believe me. ¹²But if you don't even believe me when I tell you about such things as these that happen here among men, how can you possibly believe if I tell you what is

---

OVERCOMING ANGER **2:15-16** Jesus was obviously angry at the merchants who exploited those who had come to God's house to worship. There is a difference between uncontrolled rage and righteous indignation—yet both are called anger. We must be very careful how we use the powerful emotion of anger. It is right to be angry about injustice and sin; it is wrong to be angry over trivial personal offenses. **To begin the series of devotionals on *OVERCOMING ANGER*, turn to page 133.**

going on in heaven? ¹³For only I, the Messiah, have come to earth and will return to heaven again. ¹⁴And as Moses in the wilderness lifted up the bronze image of a serpent on a pole, even so I must be lifted up upon a pole, ¹⁵so that anyone who believes in me will have eternal life. ¹⁶For God loved the world so much that he gave his only Son so that anyone who believes in him shall not perish but have eternal life. ¹⁷God did not send his Son into the world to condemn it, but to save it.

¹⁸"There is no eternal doom awaiting those who trust him to save them. But those who don't trust him have already been tried and condemned for not believing in the only Son of God. ¹⁹Their sentence is based on this fact: that the Light from heaven came into the world, but they loved the darkness more than the Light, for their deeds were evil. ²⁰They hated the heavenly Light because they wanted to sin in the darkness. They stayed away from that Light for fear their sins would be exposed and they would be punished. ²¹But those doing right come gladly to the Light to let everyone see that they are doing what God wants them to."

²²Afterwards Jesus and his disciples left Jerusalem and stayed for a while in Judea and baptized there.

²³,²⁴At this time John the Baptist was not yet in prison. He was baptizing at Aenon, near Salim, because there was plenty of water there. ²⁵One day someone began an argument with John's disciples, telling them that Jesus' baptism was best. ²⁶So they came to John and said, "Master, the man you met on the other side of the Jordan River—the one you said was the Messiah—he is baptizing too, and everybody is going over there instead of coming here to us."

²⁷John replied, "God in heaven appoints each man's work. ²⁸My work is to prepare the way for that man so that everyone will go to him. You yourselves know how plainly I told you that I am not the Messiah. I am here to prepare the way for him—that is all. ²⁹The crowds will naturally go to the main attraction—the bride will go where the bridegroom is! A bridegroom's friends rejoice with him. I am the Bridegroom's friend, and I am filled with joy at his success. ³⁰He must become greater and greater, and I must become less and less.

³¹"He has come from heaven and is greater than anyone else. I am of the earth, and my understanding is limited to the things of earth. ³²He tells what he has seen and heard, but how few believe what he tells them! ³³,³⁴Those who believe him discover that God is a fountain of truth. For this one—sent by God—speaks God's words, for God's Spirit is upon him without measure or limit.

³⁵The Father loves this man because he is his Son, and God has given him everything there is. ³⁶And all who trust him—God's Son—to save them have eternal life; those who don't believe and obey him shall never see heaven, but the wrath of God remains upon them."

4 Jesus and the Woman at a Well

When the Lord knew that the Pharisees had heard about the greater crowds coming to him than to John to be baptized and to become his disciples—(though Jesus himself didn't baptize them, but his disciples did)— ³he left Judea and returned to the province of Galilee.

⁴He had to go through Samaria on the way, ⁵,⁶and around noon as he approached the village of Sychar, he came to Jacob's Well, located on the parcel of ground Jacob gave to his son Joseph. Jesus was tired from the long walk in the hot sun and sat wearily beside the well.

⁷Soon a Samaritan woman came to draw water, and Jesus asked her for a drink. ⁸He was alone at the time as his disciples had gone into the village to buy some food. ⁹The woman was surprised that a Jew would ask a "despised Samaritan" for anything—usually they wouldn't even speak to them!—and she remarked about this to Jesus.

¹⁰He replied, "If you only knew what a wonderful gift God has for you, and who I am, you would ask me for some *living* water!"

¹¹"But you don't have a rope or a bucket," she said, "and this is a very deep well! Where would you get this living water? ¹²And besides, are you greater than our ancestor Jacob? How can you offer better water than this which he and his sons and cattle enjoyed?"

¹³Jesus replied that people soon became thirsty again after drinking this water. ¹⁴"But the water I give them," he said, "becomes a perpetual spring within them, watering them forever with eternal life."

¹⁵"Please, sir," the woman said, "give me some of that water! Then I'll never be thirsty again and won't have to make this long trip out here every day."

¹⁶"Go and get your husband," Jesus told her.

¹⁷,¹⁸"But I'm not married," the woman replied.

"All too true!" Jesus said. "For you have had five husbands, and you aren't even married to the man you're living with now."

¹⁹"Sir," the woman said, "you must be a prophet. ²⁰But say, tell me, why is it that you Jews insist that Jerusalem is the only place of worship, while we Samaritans claim it is here [at Mount Gerizim], where our ancestors worshiped?"

²¹⁻²⁴Jesus replied, "The time is coming, ma'am, when we will no longer be concerned about

FAMILY DEVOTIONS

☐ **DEVOTION 278**
CULTIVATING GODLY ATTITUDES

Read John 3:1-8

"Look at the wind!" exclaimed Sue as she stood at the window. "The trees are swaying back and forth, and some of the branches are breaking off."

"Wow! It's really blowing!" agreed Todd as he came into the room. "I've never seen such a big wind!"

Dad joined them at the window. "You can't really see wind," he reminded them. "You only see what it does."

"Like making that garbage can roll down the street," remarked Sue.

The three of them watched in silence for a few minutes, then Dad said, "Jesus compared the blowing of the wind to becoming a Christian. We can't see the wind, and we can't see Jesus coming into somebody's life, because it's his Spirit that comes in."

"And spirits are invisible," said Todd. He looked at his sister. "That's why Sue still looks the same. She has a turned-up nose and freckles just like before she invited Jesus into her heart last summer." He loved to tease Sue about her freckles.

Dad smiled. "We see what the wind does, though," he said, "and we also see what Jesus does. When he comes into a person's life, he changes that person. A Christian wants to please the Lord and be obedient. He tries not to do the things that displease God."

Sue nodded. "I still do bad things sometimes, but I try not to," she said. "When I do, I feel awful, and I ask Jesus to forgive me. Before I was saved, I didn't care much."

"And I've noticed that you don't get as mad when I tease you," admitted Todd.

Sue slipped her hand into her father's and looked up at him. "I'm glad the wind doesn't always blow this hard," she said. "But I'm glad Jesus is always in my heart."

Cultivating Godly Attitudes
Memory Verse

Your attitude should be the kind that was shown us by Jesus Christ.
Philippians 2:5

How About You?
Does your life show that you are a Christian? Has there been any change since you invited Jesus to come in? Make sure you're really born again. Then ask God to help you live in such a way that those around you will see what he is doing for you. M. N.

• For the next devotional, turn to page 1007. • For the next devotional on CULTIVATING GODLY ATTITUDES, turn to page 1097. • For notes on CULTIVATING GODLY ATTITUDES, see pages 337, 383, 472, 622, and 1216.

whether to worship the Father here or in Jerusalem. For it's not *where* we worship that counts, but *how* we worship—is our worship spiritual and real? Do we have the Holy Spirit's help? For God is Spirit, and we must have his help to worship as we should. The Father wants this kind of worship from us. But you Samaritans know so little about him, worshiping blindly, while we Jews know all about him, for salvation comes to the world through the Jews."

25The woman said, "Well, at least I know that the Messiah will come—the one they call Christ—and when he does, he will explain everything to us."

26Then Jesus told her, "I am the Messiah!"

27Just then his disciples arrived. They were surprised to find him talking to a woman, but none of them asked him why, or what they had been discussing.

28,29Then the woman left her waterpot beside the well and went back to the village and told everyone, "Come and meet a man who told me everything I ever did! Can this be the Messiah?" 30So the people came streaming from the village to see him.

31Meanwhile, the disciples were urging Jesus to eat. 32"No," he said, "I have some food you don't know about."

33"Who brought it to him?" the disciples asked each other.

34Then Jesus explained: "My nourishment comes from doing the will of God who sent me, and from finishing his work. 35Do you think the work of harvesting will not begin until the summer ends four months from now? Look around you! Vast fields of human souls are ripening all around us, and are ready now for reaping. 36The reapers will be paid good wages and will be gathering eternal souls into the granaries of heaven! What joys await the sower and the reaper, both together! 37For it is true that one sows and someone else reaps. 38I sent you to reap where you didn't sow; others did the work, and you received the harvest."

39Many from the Samaritan village believed he was the Messiah because of the woman's report: "He told me everything I ever did!" 40,41When they came out to see him at the well, they begged him to stay at their village; and he did, for two days, long enough for many of them to believe in him after hearing him. 42Then they said to the woman, "Now we believe because we have heard him ourselves, not just because of what you told us. He is indeed the Savior of the world."

43,44At the end of the two days' stay he went on into Galilee. Jesus used to say, "A prophet is honored everywhere except in his own country!" 45But the Galileans welcomed him with open arms, for they had been in Jerusalem at the Passover celebration and had seen some of his miracles.

46,47In the course of his journey through Galilee he arrived at the town of Cana, where he had turned the water into wine. While he was there, a man in the city of Capernaum, a government official, whose son was very sick, heard that Jesus had come from Judea and was traveling in Galilee. This man went over to Cana, found Jesus, and begged him to come to Capernaum with him and heal his son, who was now at death's door.

48Jesus asked, "Won't any of you believe in me unless I do more and more miracles?"

49The official pled, "Sir, please come now before my child dies."

50Then Jesus told him, "Go back home. Your son is healed!" And the man believed Jesus and started home. 51While he was on his way, some of his servants met him with the news that all was well—his son had recovered. 52He asked them when the lad had begun to feel better, and they replied, "Yesterday afternoon at about one o'clock his fever suddenly disappeared!" 53Then the father realized it was the same moment that Jesus had told him, "Your son is healed." And the officer and his entire household believed that Jesus was the Messiah.

54This was Jesus' second miracle in Galilee after coming from Judea.

5 Jesus Heals a Sick Man

Afterwards Jesus returned to Jerusalem for one of the Jewish religious holidays. 2Inside the city, near the Sheep Gate, was Bethesda Pool, with five covered platforms or porches surrounding it. 3Crowds of sick folks—lame, blind, or with paralyzed limbs—lay on the platforms (waiting for a certain movement of the water, 4for an angel of the Lord came from time to time and disturbed the water, and the first person to step down into it afterwards was healed).

5One of the men lying there had been sick for thirty-eight years. 6When Jesus saw him and knew how long he had been ill, he asked him, "Would you like to get well?"

7"I can't," the sick man said, "for I have no one to help me into the pool at the movement of the water. While I am trying to get there, someone else always gets in ahead of me."

8Jesus told him, "Stand up, roll up your sleeping mat and go on home!"

9Instantly, the man was healed! He rolled up the mat and began walking!

But it was on the Sabbath when this miracle was done. 10So the Jewish leaders objected. They said to the man who was cured, "You can't work

FAMILY DEVOTIONS

☐ *DEVOTION 279*
RECEIVING CHRIST AS SAVIOR

Read John 3:16-21

Receiving Christ as Savior
Memory Verse

For God loved the world so much that he gave his only Son so that anyone who believes in him shall not perish but have eternal life.
John 3:16

One of the places the Carr family visited on their vacation was Jewel Cave. Ryan was excited about being in a cave. He listened carefully as Peter, their tour guide, led them down the narrow paths and told about the cave. Ryan was fascinated by the different rock formations and was interested in hearing about the people who first explored the cave.

"Now," Peter said, as they stopped in a small opening, "I'm going to turn off the lights so you can see what it means to be truly in the dark." Peter was certainly right about its being dark. Ryan couldn't see a thing! He could not even see his fingers, though he put them right in front of his face. It was darker than night. At night Ryan could at least see shadows.

Peter made a joke about leaving the people in the darkness while he went on a coffee break. Everyone laughed, but it made Ryan think. He knew the Bible described people who didn't know Jesus as Savior as being lost in darkness. Now that he was in the dark, he realized that it was a scary place to be.

Of course, Peter was just joking about leaving the tour group in the dark cave, but Ryan knew the Lord wasn't joking when he talked about the darkness of sin. He remembered, too, that Jesus spoke of being the Light of the World, and he was thankful he knew Jesus as Savior.

How About You?
Are you still in darkness—the darkness of sin? Jesus is called the Light of the World, and he is willing to take away the darkness from those who trust in him. Won't you ask him to do that today? L. M. W.

• For the next devotional, turn to page 1009.   • For the next devotional on *RECEIVING CHRIST AS SAVIOR*, turn to page 1021.   • For notes on *RECEIVING CHRIST AS SAVIOR*, see pages 839, 842, 1146, 1234, and 1240.

on the Sabbath! It's illegal to carry that sleeping mat!"

11"The man who healed me told me to," was his reply.

12"Who said such a thing as that?" they demanded.

13The man didn't know, and Jesus had disappeared into the crowd. 14But afterwards Jesus found him in the Temple and told him, "Now you are well; don't sin as you did before, or something even worse may happen to you."

15Then the man went to find the Jewish leaders and told them it was Jesus who had healed him.

16So they began harassing Jesus as a Sabbath breaker.

17But Jesus replied, "My Father constantly does good, and I'm following his example."

18Then the Jewish leaders were all the more eager to kill him because in addition to disobeying their Sabbath laws, he had spoken of God as his Father, thereby making himself equal with God.

19Jesus replied, "The Son can do nothing by himself. He does only what he sees the Father doing, and in the same way. 20For the Father loves the Son, and tells him everything he is doing; and the Son will do far more awesome miracles than this man's healing. 21He will even raise from the dead anyone he wants to, just as the Father does. 22And the Father leaves all judgment of sin to his Son, 23so that everyone will honor the Son, just as they honor the Father. But if you refuse to honor God's Son, whom he sent to you, then you are certainly not honoring the Father.

24"I say emphatically that anyone who listens to my message and believes in God who sent me has eternal life, and will never be damned for his sins, but has already passed out of death into life.

25"And I solemnly declare that the time is coming, in fact, it is here, when the dead shall hear my voice—the voice of the Son of God—and those who listen shall live. 26The Father has life in himself, and has granted his Son to have life in himself, 27and to judge the sins of all mankind because he is the Son of Man. 28Don't be so surprised! Indeed the time is coming when all the dead in their graves shall hear the voice of God's Son, 29and shall rise again—those who have done good, to eternal life; and those who have continued in evil, to judgment.

30"But I pass no judgment without consulting the Father. I judge as I am told. And my judgment is absolutely fair and just, for it is according to the will of God who sent me and is not merely my own.

31"When I make claims about myself they aren't believed, 32,33but someone else, yes, John the Baptist, is making these claims for me too. You have gone out to listen to his preaching, and I can assure you that all he says about me is true! 34But the truest witness I have is not from a man, though I have reminded you about John's witness so that you will believe in me and be saved. 35John shone brightly for a while, and you benefited and rejoiced, 36but I have a greater witness than John. I refer to the miracles I do; these have been assigned me by the Father, and they prove that the Father has sent me. 37And the Father himself has also testified about me, though not appearing to you personally, or speaking to you directly. 38But you are not listening to him, for you refuse to believe me—the one sent to you with God's message.

39"You search the Scriptures, for you believe they give you eternal life. And the Scriptures point to me! 40Yet you won't come to me so that I can give you this life eternal!

41,42"Your approval or disapproval means nothing to me, for as I know so well, you don't have God's love within you. 43I know, because I have come to you representing my Father and you refuse to welcome me, though you readily enough receive those who aren't sent from him, but represent only themselves! 44No wonder you can't believe! For you gladly honor each other, but you don't care about the honor that comes from the only God!

45"Yet it is not I who will accuse you of this to the Father—Moses will! Moses, on whose laws you set your hopes of heaven. 46For you have refused to believe Moses. He wrote about me, but you refuse to believe him, so you refuse to believe in me. 47And since you don't believe what he wrote, no wonder you don't believe me either."

6 Jesus Feeds 5,000 People

After this, Jesus crossed over the Sea of Galilee, also known as the Sea of Tiberias. 2-5And a huge crowd, many of them pilgrims on their way to Jerusalem for the annual Passover celebration, were following him wherever he went, to watch him heal the sick. So when Jesus went up into the hills and sat down with his disciples around him, he soon saw a great multitude of people climbing the hill, looking for him.

Turning to Philip he asked, "Philip, where can we buy bread to feed all these people?" 6(He was testing Philip, for he already knew what he was going to do.)

7Philip replied, "It would take a fortune to begin to do it!"

8,9Then Andrew, Simon Peter's brother, spoke up. "There's a youngster here with five barley loaves and a couple of fish! But what good is that with all this mob?"

FAMILY DEVOTIONS

☐ *DEVOTION 280*
KNOWING YOU'RE SPECIAL TO GOD

Read John 6:1-13

The chatter of the grown-ups surrounded Marcie as she pushed her food around on her plate. Pastor James had come for dinner, and they were discussing their church's campaign to reach every family in their small town with the gospel message. A men's breakfast was being planned, and Dad was going to be master of ceremonies. Mom was going to sing at a women's luncheon. Dan, Marcie's big brother, was going to make posters to advertise a citywide youth rally. Marcie sighed. *I wish I were big enough to help,* she thought.

Just then, Pastor James turned to Marcie. "Will you invite your friends to our special meetings?" he asked.

Marcie shrugged and nodded. "I suppose," she murmured, "but I wish I could do something important." Discouraged, she excused herself and left the table.

Later that night Mom tucked Marcie into bed. "Don't forget to fix the night-light for me," said Marcie.

"Right," said Mom, snapping off Marcie's bedside light and going out into the hall. "I'm plugging it in right now." Suddenly, a bright light filled the hall, spilling over into Marcie's room.

Marcie jumped out of bed and ran to the door. Instead of the usual little night-light, she saw a bright lamp plugged into the outlet. "Mom, that light's too bright."

Mom turned back. "Why, you're right," she agreed. She turned off the lamp and plugged in the usual night-light. "You see," she said, "little lights are needed, just as big ones are. And little jobs need to be done, just as big ones do. Little people, as well as big ones, need to be invited to come to Jesus."

Marcie was thoughtful. "I'll invite all my friends," she decided. "I'll invite my whole class. I'll be a night-light."

Knowing You're Special to God Memory Verse

But now the Lord who created you, O Israel, says, Don't be afraid, for I have ransomed you; I have called you by name; you are mine.
Isaiah 43:1

How About You?

Are you too small to preach? To organize meetings? To prepare a dinner? That's all right. Perhaps you—not your father—can be a friend to the lonesome child down the block. You—not your mother—can invite your teacher and classmates to come to church. Whatever God asks you to do, do it for his glory, just like the child who offered his lunch to Jesus. H. M.

• For the next devotional, turn to page 1011.   • For the next devotional on KNOWING YOU'RE SPECIAL TO GOD, turn to page 1027.   • For notes on KNOWING YOU'RE SPECIAL TO GOD, see pages 260, 878, 908, and 960.

¹⁰"Tell everyone to sit down," Jesus ordered. And all of them—the approximate count of the men only was five thousand—sat down on the grassy slopes. ¹¹Then Jesus took the loaves and gave thanks to God and passed them out to the people. Afterwards he did the same with the fish. And everyone ate until full!

¹²"Now gather the scraps," Jesus told his disciples, "so that nothing is wasted." ¹³And twelve baskets were filled with the leftovers!

¹⁴When the people realized what a great miracle had happened, they exclaimed, "Surely, he is the Prophet we have been expecting!"

¹⁵Jesus saw that they were ready to take him by force and make him their king, so he went higher into the mountains alone.

¹⁶That evening his disciples went down to the shore to wait for him. ¹⁷But as darkness fell and Jesus still hadn't come back, they got into the boat and headed out across the lake toward Capernaum. ¹⁸,¹⁹But soon a gale swept down upon them as they rowed, and the sea grew very rough. They were three or four miles out when suddenly they saw Jesus walking toward the boat! They were terrified, ²⁰but he called out to them and told them not to be afraid. ²¹Then they were willing to let him in, and immediately the boat was where they were going!

²²,²³The next morning, back across the lake, crowds began gathering on the shore [waiting to see Jesus]. For they knew that he and his disciples had come over together and that the disciples had gone off in their boat, leaving him behind. Several small boats from Tiberias were nearby, ²⁴so when the people saw that Jesus wasn't there, nor his disciples, they got into the boats and went across to Capernaum to look for him.

²⁵When they arrived and found him, they said, "Sir, how did you get here?" ²⁶Jesus replied, "The truth of the matter is that you want to be with me because I fed you, not because you believe in me. ²⁷But you shouldn't be so concerned about perishable things like food. No, spend your energy seeking the eternal life that I, the Messiah, can give you. For God the Father has sent me for this very purpose."

²⁸They replied, "What should we do to satisfy God?"

²⁹Jesus told them, "This is the will of God, that you believe in the one he has sent."

³⁰,³¹They replied, "You must show us more miracles if you want us to believe you are the Messiah. Give us free bread every day, like our fathers had while they journeyed through the wilderness! As the Scriptures say, 'Moses gave them bread from heaven.'"

³²Jesus said, "Moses didn't give it to them. My Father did. And now he offers you true Bread from heaven. ³³The true Bread is a Person—the one sent by God from heaven, and he gives life to the world."

³⁴"Sir," they said, "give us that bread every day of our lives!"

³⁵Jesus replied, "I am the Bread of Life. No one coming to me will ever be hungry again. Those believing in me will never thirst. ³⁶But the trouble is, as I have told you before, you haven't believed even though you have seen me. ³⁷But some will come to me—those the Father has given me—and I will never, never reject them. ³⁸For I have come here from heaven to do the will of God who sent me, not to have my own way. ³⁹And this is the will of God, that I should not lose even one of all those he has given me, but that I should raise them to eternal life at the Last Day. ⁴⁰For it is my Father's will that everyone who sees his Son and believes on him should have eternal life—that I should raise him at the Last Day."

⁴¹Then the Jews began to murmur against him because he claimed to be the Bread from heaven.

⁴²"What?" they exclaimed. "Why, he is merely Jesus the son of Joseph, whose father and mother we know. What is this he is saying, that he came down from heaven?"

⁴³But Jesus replied, "Don't murmur among yourselves about my saying that. ⁴⁴For no one can come to me unless the Father who sent me draws him to me, and at the Last Day I will cause all such to rise again from the dead. ⁴⁵As it is written in the Scriptures, 'They shall all be taught of God.' Those the Father speaks to, who learn the truth from him, will be attracted to me. ⁴⁶(Not that anyone actually sees the Father, for only I have seen him.)

⁴⁷"How earnestly I tell you this—anyone who believes in me already has eternal life! ⁴⁸⁻⁵¹Yes, I am the Bread of Life! When your fathers in the wilderness ate bread from the skies, they all died. But the Bread from heaven gives eternal life to everyone who eats it. I am that Living Bread that came down out of heaven. Anyone eating this Bread shall live forever; this Bread is my flesh given to redeem humanity."

⁵²Then the Jews began arguing with each other about what he meant. "How can this man give us his flesh to eat?" they asked.

⁵³So Jesus said it again, "With all the earnestness I possess I tell you this: Unless you eat the flesh of the Messiah and drink his blood, you cannot have eternal life within you. ⁵⁴But anyone who does eat my flesh and drink my blood has eternal life, and I will raise him at the Last Day. ⁵⁵For my flesh is the true food, and my blood is the true drink. ⁵⁶Everyone who eats my flesh and drinks my blood is in me, and I in him. ⁵⁷I live by the power of the living Father who sent me, and

FAMILY DEVOTIONS

☐ *DEVOTION 281*
SHARING YOUR FAITH

Read John 7:1-5

The Sunday school lesson had been about sharing Christ with others. During class, the children had talked about different ways they could witness to their friends. Mike, however, hadn't participated in the discussion. When class was over, he waited until the others had left so that he could talk to Mrs. Winfield privately. "What is it, Mike?" she asked gently. "You were very quiet today."

"It's my family," Mike told her. "I'm the only one who believes in Christ. I come to church with my neighbors. My parents are the ones I really want most to witness to. But my dad is always telling me that church is crazy, and my mother laughs when I try to tell her about the Bible. The other kids in the class all come from Christian homes. They don't know how good they have it!"

"It is hard to be the only Christian in the family," agreed Mrs. Winfield. "I know, because I started attending church with a friend, too, and then I accepted the Lord. I prayed for my parents daily, yet they seemed to grow angry about what I was learning."

"What did you do?" Mike asked.

"What I did was talk to *my* Sunday school teacher, and she reminded me that the Lord understood my situation and the problems I was having in a non-Christian home. Then she showed me a verse I hadn't seen before." Mrs. Winfield opened her Bible. "Did you know, Mike, that the Lord's own brothers didn't believe in him? Look at John 7:1-5."

"I never knew that before," Mike said thoughtfully. "The Lord does understand my problem, doesn't he?"

"He sure does, Mike," agreed the teacher. "Remember that truth as you pray for your parents, and live each day so that they can see Christ in you."

Sharing Your Faith Memory Verse

And let us not get tired of doing what is right, for after a while we will reap a harvest of blessing if we don't get discouraged and give up.
Galatians 6:9

How About You?

Are you the only Christian in your family? Do your parents or brothers and sisters think it's silly to believe the Bible? The Lord does understand. He knows you are in a tough situation. There was a time when his own brothers did not believe in him. Talk to the Lord about your feelings. He will help you. L. M. W.

• For the next devotional, turn to page 1017. • For the next devotional on *SHARING YOUR FAITH*, turn to page 1037.
• For notes on *SHARING YOUR FAITH*, see pages 462, 776, 1015, and 1074.

in the same way those who partake of me shall live because of me! ⁵⁸I am the true Bread from heaven; and anyone who eats this Bread shall live forever, and not die as your fathers did—though they ate bread from heaven." ⁵⁹(He preached this sermon in the synagogue in Capernaum.)

⁶⁰Even his disciples said, "This is very hard to understand. Who can tell what he means?"

⁶¹Jesus knew within himself that his disciples were complaining and said to them, "Does *this* offend you? ⁶²Then what will you think if you see me, the Messiah, return to heaven again? ⁶³Only the Holy Spirit gives eternal life. Those born only once, with physical birth, will never receive this gift. But now I have told you how to get this true spiritual life. ⁶⁴But some of you don't believe me." (For Jesus knew from the beginning who didn't believe and knew the one who would betray him.)

⁶⁵And he remarked, "That is what I meant when I said that no one can come to me unless the Father attracts him to me."

⁶⁶At this point many of his disciples turned away and deserted him.

⁶⁷Then Jesus turned to the Twelve and asked, "Are you going too?"

⁶⁸Simon Peter replied, "Master, to whom shall we go? You alone have the words that give eternal life, ⁶⁹and we believe them and know you are the holy Son of God."

⁷⁰Then Jesus said, "I chose the twelve of you, and one is a devil." ⁷¹He was speaking of Judas, son of Simon Iscariot, one of the Twelve, who would betray him.

7

Jesus' Brothers Make Fun of Him

After this, Jesus went to Galilee, going from village to village, for he wanted to stay out of Judea where the Jewish leaders were plotting his death. ²But soon it was time for the Tabernacle Ceremonies, one of the annual Jewish holidays, ³and Jesus' brothers urged him to go to Judea for the celebration.

"Go where more people can see your miracles!" they scoffed. ⁴"You can't be famous when you hide like this! If you're so great, prove it to the world!" ⁵For even his brothers didn't believe in him.

⁶Jesus replied, "It is not the right time for me to go now. But you can go anytime and it will make no difference, ⁷for the world can't hate you; but it does hate me, because I accuse it of sin and evil. ⁸You go on, and I'll come later when it is the right time." ⁹So he remained in Galilee.

¹⁰But after his brothers had left for the celebration, then he went too, though secretly, staying out of the public eye. ¹¹The Jewish leaders tried to find him at the celebration and kept asking if anyone had seen him. ¹²There was a lot of discussion about him among the crowds. Some said, "He's a wonderful man," while others said, "No, he's duping the public." ¹³But no one had the courage to speak out for him in public for fear of reprisals from the Jewish leaders.

¹⁴Then, midway through the festival, Jesus went up to the Temple and preached openly. ¹⁵The Jewish leaders were surprised when they heard him. "How can he know so much when he's never been to our schools?" they asked.

¹⁶So Jesus told them, "I'm not teaching you my own thoughts, but those of God who sent me. ¹⁷If any of you really determines to do God's will, then you will certainly know whether my teaching is from God or is merely my own. ¹⁸Anyone presenting his own ideas is looking for praise for himself, but anyone seeking to honor the one who sent him is a good and true person. ¹⁹None of *you* obeys the laws of Moses! So why pick on *me* for breaking them? Why kill *me* for this?"

²⁰The crowd replied, "You're out of your mind! Who's trying to kill you?"

²¹⁻²³Jesus replied, "I worked on the Sabbath by healing a man, and you were surprised. But you work on the Sabbath, too, whenever you obey Moses' law of circumcision (actually, however, this tradition of circumcision is older than the Mosaic law); for if the correct time for circumcising your children falls on the Sabbath, you go ahead and do it, as you should. So why should I be condemned for making a man completely well on the Sabbath? ²⁴Think this through and you will see that I am right."

²⁵Some of the people who lived there in Jerusalem said among themselves, "Isn't this the man they are trying to kill? ²⁶But here he is preaching in public, and they say nothing to him. Can it be that our leaders have learned, after all, that he really is the Messiah? ²⁷But how could he be? For we know where this man was born; when Christ comes, he will just appear and no one will know where he comes from."

²⁸So Jesus, in a sermon in the Temple, called out, "Yes, you know me and where I was born and raised, but I am the representative of one you don't know, and he is Truth. ²⁹I know him because I was with him, and he sent me to you."

³⁰Then the Jewish leaders sought to arrest him; but no hand was laid on him, for God's time had not yet come.

³¹Many among the crowds at the Temple believed on him. "After all," they said, "what miracles do you expect the Messiah to do that this man hasn't done?"

³²When the Pharisees heard that the crowds were in this mood, they and the chief priests sent officers to arrest Jesus. ³³But Jesus told them,

"[Not yet!] I am to be here a little longer. Then I shall return to the one who sent me. ³⁴You will search for me but not find me. And you won't be able to come where I am!"

³⁵The Jewish leaders were puzzled by this statement. "Where is he planning to go?" they asked. "Maybe he is thinking of leaving the country and going as a missionary among the Jews in other lands, or maybe even to the Gentiles! ³⁶What does he mean about our looking for him and not being able to find him, and, 'You won't be able to come where I am'?"

³⁷On the last day, the climax of the holidays, Jesus shouted to the crowds, "If anyone is thirsty, let him come to me and drink. ³⁸For the Scriptures declare that rivers of living water shall flow from the inmost being of anyone who believes in me." ³⁹(He was speaking of the Holy Spirit, who would be given to everyone believing in him; but the Spirit had not yet been given, because Jesus had not yet returned to his glory in heaven.)

⁴⁰When the crowds heard him say this, some of them declared, "This man surely is the prophet who will come just before the Messiah." ⁴¹,⁴²Others said, "He *is* the Messiah." Still others, "But he *can't* be! Will the Messiah come from *Galilee?* For the Scriptures clearly state that the Messiah will be born of the royal line of David, in *Bethlehem,* the village where David was born." ⁴³So the crowd was divided about him. ⁴⁴And some wanted him arrested, but no one touched him.

⁴⁵The Temple police who had been sent to arrest him returned to the chief priests and Pharisees. "Why didn't you bring him in?" they demanded.

⁴⁶"He says such wonderful things!" they mumbled. "We've never heard anything like it."

⁴⁷"So you also have been led astray?" the Pharisees mocked. ⁴⁸"Is there a single one of us Jewish rulers or Pharisees who believes he is the Messiah? ⁴⁹These stupid crowds do, yes; but what do they know about it? A curse upon them anyway!"

⁵⁰Then Nicodemus spoke up. (Remember him? He was the Jewish leader who came secretly to interview Jesus.) ⁵¹"Is it legal to convict a man before he is even tried?" he asked.

⁵²They replied, "Are you a wretched Galilean too? Search the Scriptures and see for yourself—no prophets will come from Galilee!"

⁵³ Then the meeting broke up and everybody went home.

8 Jesus Forgives a Guilty Woman

Jesus returned to the Mount of Olives, ²but early the next morning he was back again at the Temple. A crowd soon gathered, and he sat down and talked to them. ³As he was speaking, the Jewish leaders and Pharisees brought a woman caught in adultery and placed her out in front of the staring crowd.

⁴"Teacher," they said to Jesus, "this woman was caught in the very act of adultery. ⁵Moses' law says to kill her. What about it?"

⁶They were trying to trap him into saying something they could use against him, but Jesus stooped down and wrote in the dust with his finger. ⁷They kept demanding an answer, so he stood up again and said, "All right, hurl the stones at her until she dies. But only he who never sinned may throw the first!"

⁸Then he stooped down again and wrote some more in the dust. ⁹And the Jewish leaders slipped away one by one, beginning with the eldest, until only Jesus was left in front of the crowd with the woman.

¹⁰Then Jesus stood up again and said to her, "Where are your accusers? Didn't even one of them condemn you?"

¹¹"No, sir," she said.

And Jesus said, "Neither do I. Go and sin no more."

¹²Later, in one of his talks, Jesus said to the people, "I am the Light of the world. So if you follow me, you won't be stumbling through the darkness, for living light will flood your path."

¹³The Pharisees replied, "You are boasting—and lying!"

¹⁴Jesus told them, "These claims are true even though I make them concerning myself. For I know where I came from and where I am going, but you don't know this about me. ¹⁵You pass judgment on me without knowing the facts. I am not judging you now; ¹⁶but if I were, it would be an absolutely correct judgment in every respect, for I have with me the Father who sent me. ¹⁷Your laws say that if two men agree on something that has happened, their witness is accepted as fact. ¹⁸Well, I am one witness, and my Father who sent me is the other."

¹⁹"Where is your father?" they asked.

Jesus answered, "You don't know who I am, so you don't know who my Father is. If you knew me, then you would know him too."

²⁰Jesus made these statements while in the section of the Temple known as the Treasury. But he was not arrested, for his time had not yet run out.

²¹Later he said to them again, "I am going away; and you will search for me, and die in your sins. And you cannot come where I am going."

²²The Jews asked, "Is he planning suicide? What does he mean, 'You cannot come where I am going'?"

²³Then he said to them, "You are from below; I am from above. You are of this world; I am not.

24That is why I said that you will die in your sins; for unless you believe that I am the Messiah, the Son of God, you will die in your sins."

25"Tell us who you are," they demanded.

He replied, "I am the one I have always claimed to be. 26I could condemn you for much and teach you much, but I won't, for I say only what I am told to by the one who sent me; and he is Truth." 27But they still didn't understand that he was talking to them about God.

28So Jesus said, "When you have killed the Messiah, then you will realize that I am he and that I have not been telling you my own ideas, but have spoken what the Father taught me. 29And he who sent me is with me—he has not deserted me—for I always do those things that are pleasing to him."

30,31Then many of the Jewish leaders who heard him say these things began believing him to be the Messiah.

Jesus said to them, "You are truly my disciples if you live as I tell you to, 32and you will know the truth, and the truth will set you free."

33"But we are descendants of Abraham," they said, "and have never been slaves to any man on earth! What do you mean, 'set free'?"

34Jesus replied, "You are slaves of sin, every one of you. 35And slaves don't have rights, but the Son has every right there is! 36So if the Son sets you free, you will indeed be free—37(Yes, I realize that you are descendants of Abraham!) And yet some of you are trying to kill me because my message does not find a home within your hearts. 38I am telling you what I saw when I was with my Father. But you are following the advice of *your* father."

39"Our father is Abraham," they declared.

"No!" Jesus replied, "for if he were, you would follow his good example. 40But instead you are trying to kill me—and all because I told you the truth I heard from God. Abraham wouldn't do a thing like that! 41No, you are obeying your *real* father when you act that way."

They replied, "We were not born out of wedlock—our true Father is God himself."

42Jesus told them, "If that were so, then you would love me, for I have come to you from God. I am not here on my own, but he sent me. 43Why can't you understand what I am saying? It is because you are prevented from doing so! 44For you are the children of your father the devil and you love to do the evil things he does. He was a murderer from the beginning and a hater of truth—there is not an iota of truth in him. When he lies, it is perfectly normal; for he is the father of liars. 45And so when I tell the truth, you just naturally don't believe it!

46"Which of you can truthfully accuse me of one single sin? [No one!] And since I am telling you the truth, why don't you believe me? 47Anyone whose Father is God listens gladly to the words of God. Since you don't, it proves you aren't his children."

48"You Samaritan! Foreigner! Devil!" the Jewish leaders snarled. "Didn't we say all along you were possessed by a demon?"

49"No," Jesus said, "I have no demon in me. For I honor my Father—and you dishonor me. 50And though I have no wish to make myself great, God wants this for me and judges [those who reject me]. 51With all the earnestness I have I tell you this—no one who obeys me shall ever die!"

52The leaders of the Jews said, "Now we know you are possessed by a demon. Even Abraham and the mightiest prophets died, and yet you say that obeying you will keep a man from dying! 53So you are greater than our father Abraham, who died? And greater than the prophets, who died? Who do you think you are?" 54Then Jesus told them this: "If I am merely boasting about myself, it doesn't count. But it is my Father—and you claim him as your God—who is saying these glorious things about me. 55But you do not even know him. I do. If I said otherwise, I would be as great a liar as you! But it is true—I know him and fully obey him. 56Your father Abraham rejoiced to see my day. He knew I was coming and was glad."

57*The Jewish leaders:* "You aren't even fifty years old—sure, you've seen Abraham!"

58*Jesus:* "The absolute truth is that I was in existence before Abraham was ever born!"

59At that point the Jewish leaders picked up stones to kill him. But Jesus was hidden from them, and walked past them and left the Temple.

9 Jesus Heals a Blind Man

As he was walking along, he saw a man blind from birth.

2"Master," his disciples asked him, "why was this man born blind? Was it a result of his own sins or those of his parents?"

3"Neither," Jesus answered. "But to demonstrate the power of God. 4All of us must quickly carry out the tasks assigned us by the one who sent me, for there is little time left before the night falls and all work comes to an end. 5But while I am still here in the world, I give it my light."

6Then he spat on the ground and made mud from the spittle and smoothed the mud over the blind man's eyes, 7and told him, "Go and wash in the Pool of Siloam" (the word *Siloam* means "Sent"). So the man went where he was sent and washed and came back seeing!

8His neighbors and others who knew him as a blind beggar asked each other, "Is this the same fellow—that beggar?"

9Some said yes, and some said no. "It can't be

the same man," they thought, "but he surely looks like him!"

And the beggar said, "I *am* the same man!"

¹⁰Then they asked him how in the world he could see. What had happened?

¹¹And he told them, "A man they call Jesus made mud and smoothed it over my eyes and told me to go to the Pool of Siloam and wash off the mud. I did, and I can see!"

¹²"Where is he now?" they asked.

"I don't know," he replied.

¹³Then they took the man to the Pharisees. ¹⁴Now as it happened, this all occurred on a Sabbath. ¹⁵Then the Pharisees asked him all about it. So he told them how Jesus had smoothed the mud over his eyes, and when it was washed away, he could see!

¹⁶Some of them said, "Then this fellow Jesus is not from God because he is working on the Sabbath."

Others said, "But how could an ordinary sinner do such miracles?" So there was a deep division of opinion among them.

¹⁷Then the Pharisees turned on the man who had been blind and demanded, "This man who opened your eyes—who do you say he is?"

"I think he must be a prophet sent from God," the man replied.

¹⁸The Jewish leaders wouldn't believe he had been blind, until they called in his parents ¹⁹and asked them, "Is this your son? Was he born blind? If so, how can he see?"

²⁰His parents replied, "We know this is our son and that he was born blind, ²¹but we don't know what happened to make him see, or who did it. He is old enough to speak for himself. Ask him."

²²,²³They said this in fear of the Jewish leaders who had announced that anyone saying Jesus was the Messiah would be excommunicated.

²⁴So for the second time they called in the man who had been blind and told him, "Give the glory to God, not to Jesus, for we know Jesus is an evil person."

²⁵"I don't know whether he is good or bad," the man replied, "but I know this: *I was blind, and now I see!*"

²⁶"But what did he do?" they asked. "How did he heal you?"

²⁷"Look!" the man exclaimed. "I told you once; didn't you listen? Why do you want to hear it again? Do you want to become his disciples too?"

²⁸Then they cursed him and said, "You are his disciple, but we are disciples of Moses. ²⁹We know God has spoken to Moses, but as for this fellow, we don't know anything about him."

³⁰"Why, that's very strange!" the man replied. "He can heal blind men, and yet you don't know anything about him! ³¹Well, God doesn't listen to evil men, but he has open ears to those who worship him and do his will. ³²Since the world began there has never been anyone who could open the eyes of someone born blind. ³³If this man were not from God, he couldn't do it."

³⁴"You illegitimate bastard, you!" they shouted. "Are you trying to teach *us*?" And they threw him out.

³⁵When Jesus heard what had happened, he found the man and said, "Do you believe in the Messiah?"

³⁶The man answered, "Who is he, sir, for I want to."

³⁷"You have seen him," Jesus said, "and he is speaking to you!"

³⁸"Yes, Lord," the man said, "I believe!" And he worshiped Jesus.

³⁹Then Jesus told him, "I have come into the world to give sight to those who are spiritually blind and to show those who think they see that they are blind."

⁴⁰The Pharisees who were standing there asked, "Are you saying we are blind?"

⁴¹"If you were blind, you wouldn't be guilty," Jesus replied. "But your guilt remains because you claim to know what you are doing.

10 Jesus: The Good Shepherd

"Anyone refusing to walk through the gate into a sheepfold, who sneaks over the wall, must surely be a thief! ²For a shepherd comes through the gate. ³The gatekeeper opens the gate for him, and the sheep hear his voice and come to him; and he calls his own sheep by name and leads them out. ⁴He walks ahead of them; and they follow him, for they recognize his voice. ⁵They won't follow a stranger but will run from him, for they don't recognize his voice."

⁶Those who heard Jesus use this illustration didn't understand what he meant, ⁷so he explained it to them.

"I am the Gate for the sheep," he said. ⁸"All others who came before me were thieves and robbers. But the true sheep did not listen to them. ⁹Yes, I am the Gate. Those who come in by way of the Gate will be saved and will go in and out and find green pastures. ¹⁰The thief's purpose is to

---

SHARING YOUR FAITH 9:25 By now the man who had been blind had heard the same questions over and over. He did not know how he was healed, but he knew that his life had been miraculously changed, and he was not afraid to tell the truth. You don't need to know all the answers in order to share Christ with others. It is important to tell them what Christ has done for you and how he has changed your life. Then trust that God will use your words to help others believe in him, too. **To begin the series of devotionals on SHARING YOUR FAITH, turn to page 427.**

steal, kill and destroy. My purpose is to give life in all its fullness.

¹¹"I am the Good Shepherd. The Good Shepherd lays down his life for the sheep. ¹²A hired man will run when he sees a wolf coming and will leave the sheep, for they aren't his and he isn't their shepherd. And so the wolf leaps on them and scatters the flock. ¹³The hired man runs because he is hired and has no real concern for the sheep.

¹⁴"I am the Good Shepherd and know my own sheep, and they know me, ¹⁵just as my Father knows me and I know the Father; and I lay down my life for the sheep. ¹⁶I have other sheep, too, in another fold. I must bring them also, and they will heed my voice; and there will be one flock with one Shepherd.

¹⁷"The Father loves me because I lay down my life that I may have it back again. ¹⁸No one can kill me without my consent—I lay down my life voluntarily. For I have the right and power to lay it down when I want to and also the right and power to take it again. For the Father has given me this right."

¹⁹When he said these things, the Jewish leaders were again divided in their opinions about him. ²⁰Some of them said, "He has a demon or else is crazy. Why listen to a man like that?"

²¹Others said, "This doesn't sound to us like a man possessed by a demon! Can a demon open the eyes of blind men?"

²²,²³It was winter, and Jesus was in Jerusalem at the time of the Dedication Celebration. He was at the Temple, walking through the section known as Solomon's Hall. ²⁴The Jewish leaders surrounded him and asked, "How long are you going to keep us in suspense? If you are the Messiah, tell us plainly."

²⁵"I have already told you, and you don't believe me," Jesus replied. "The proof is in the miracles I do in the name of my Father. ²⁶But you don't believe me because you are not part of my flock. ²⁷My sheep recognize my voice, and I know them, and they follow me. ²⁸I give them eternal life and they shall never perish. No one shall snatch them away from me, ²⁹for my Father has given them to me, and he is more powerful than anyone else, so no one can kidnap them from me. ³⁰I and the Father are one."

³¹Then again the Jewish leaders picked up stones to kill him.

³²Jesus said, "At God's direction I have done many a miracle to help the people. For which one are you killing me?"

³³They replied, "Not for any good work, but for blasphemy; you, a mere man, have declared yourself to be God."

³⁴⁻³⁶"In your own Law it says that men are gods!" he replied. "So if the Scripture, which cannot be untrue, speaks of those as gods to whom the message of God came, do you call it blasphemy when the one sanctified and sent into the world by the Father says, 'I am the Son of God'? ³⁷Don't believe me unless I do miracles of God. ³⁸But if I do, believe them even if you don't believe me. Then you will become convinced that the Father is in me, and I in the Father."

³⁹Once again they started to arrest him. But he walked away and left them, ⁴⁰and went beyond the Jordan River to stay near the place where John was first baptizing. ⁴¹And many followed him.

"John didn't do miracles," they remarked to one another, "but all his predictions concerning this man have come true." ⁴²And many came to the decision that he was the Messiah.

Jesus Brings Lazarus to Life

Do you remember Mary, who poured the costly perfume on Jesus' feet and wiped them with her hair? Well, her brother Lazarus, who lived in Bethany with Mary and her sister Martha, was sick. ³So the two sisters sent a message to Jesus telling him, "Sir, your good friend is very, very sick."

⁴But when Jesus heard about it he said, "The purpose of his illness is not death, but for the glory of God. I, the Son of God, will receive glory from this situation."

⁵Although Jesus was very fond of Martha, Mary, and Lazarus, ⁶he stayed where he was for the next two days and made no move to go to them. ⁷Finally, after the two days, he said to his disciples, "Let's go to Judea."

⁸But his disciples objected. "Master," they said, "only a few days ago the Jewish leaders in Judea were trying to kill you. Are you going there again?"

⁹Jesus replied, "There are twelve hours of daylight every day, and during every hour of it a man can walk safely and not stumble. ¹⁰Only at night is there danger of a wrong step, because of the dark." ¹¹Then he said, "Our friend Lazarus has gone to sleep, but now I will go and waken him!"

¹²,¹³The disciples, thinking Jesus meant Lazarus was having a good night's rest, said, "That means he is getting better!" But Jesus meant Lazarus had died.

¹⁴Then he told them plainly, "Lazarus is dead. ¹⁵And for your sake, I am glad I wasn't there, for this will give you another opportunity to believe in me. Come, let's go to him."

¹⁶Thomas, nicknamed "The Twin," said to his fellow disciples, "Let's go too—and die with him."

¹⁷When they arrived at Bethany, they were told

FAMILY DEVOTIONS

☐ DEVOTION 282
SHOWING COMPASSION

Read John 11:32-36

As Kurt turned his bike into the driveway, he skidded on some gravel and fell, scraping his elbow. "It doesn't hurt," he said as Mom bandaged it. Actually, his arm hurt quite a bit, but Kurt would never admit it. He thought he should be brave and not show his feelings.

"Come on, " Mom said. "Let's see if the TV news has anything about the fire this afternoon." As they watched, they saw a film clip of Kurt's father, a fireman, climbing a tall ladder to help a woman escape from the burning house.

"Boy, did you see that?" asked Kurt. "Dad sure is brave."

Kurt was excited when his father arrived home, dirty and smelling like smoke. "Hey, Dad, we saw you on TV!" Kurt began, but his father didn't smile. Instead, he slumped down in a chair, put his face in his hands, and started to cry. Kurt was horrified!

"What's wrong, honey?" asked Kurt's mother.

Dad wiped his eyes. "I'm all right. But the man we rescued from the burning house died in the hospital. His wife is terribly upset and frightened. I just feel so sorry for her!"

Kurt grew quiet and went to his room. A short time later, his father came in to see him. "Are you all right, Son?" Dad asked.

Kurt looked away. "Well," he mumbled, "I thought that men never—at least, a fireman wouldn't—well, I never thought *you* would."

Dad smiled kindly. "You mean you thought men never cried, right?" Kurt nodded, and his father continued. "I know that I don't usually seem very emotional, but I wouldn't make a very good fireman if I didn't care about people—or a good Christian, either. Jesus cried when his friend Lazarus died, remember? You don't think he was a sissy, do you?"

"No," Kurt replied slowly. "He was brave enough to go to the cross and die for us. I guess I've got a lot to learn about being a real man, haven't I?"

Showing Compassion Memory Verse

What a wonderful God we have—he is the Father of our Lord Jesus Christ, the source of every mercy, and the one who so wonderfully comforts and strengthens us in our hardships and trials.
2 Corinthians 1:3

How About You?

Do you think that men should be tough—that they should hide their feelings to prove how brave they are? Jesus didn't hide his feelings, and he was no weakling either. He accomplished the difficult through the power of God. You can do the same, whether you're a young man or a young woman. S. K.

• For the next devotional, turn to page 1019. • For the next devotional on SHOWING COMPASSION, turn to page 1121. • For notes on SHOWING COMPASSION, see pages 206, 506, 515, 710, and 934.

that Lazarus had already been in his tomb for four days. ¹⁸Bethany was only a couple of miles down the road from Jerusalem, ¹⁹and many of the Jewish leaders had come to pay their respects and to console Martha and Mary on their loss. ²⁰When Martha got word that Jesus was coming, she went to meet him. But Mary stayed at home.

²¹Martha said to Jesus, "Sir, if you had been here, my brother wouldn't have died. ²²And even now it's not too late, for I know that God will bring my brother back to life again, if you will only ask him to."

²³Jesus told her, "Your brother will come back to life again."

²⁴"Yes," Martha said, "when everyone else does, on Resurrection Day."

²⁵Jesus told her, "I am the one who raises the dead and gives them life again. Anyone who believes in me, even though he dies like anyone else, shall live again. ²⁶He is given eternal life for believing in me and shall never perish. Do you believe this, Martha?"

²⁷"Yes, Master," she told him. "I believe you are the Messiah, the Son of God, the one we have so long awaited."

²⁸Then she left him and returned to Mary and, calling her aside from the mourners, told her, "He is here and wants to see you." ²⁹So Mary went to him at once.

³⁰Now Jesus had stayed outside the village, at the place where Martha met him. ³¹When the Jewish leaders who were at the house trying to console Mary saw her leave so hastily, they assumed she was going to Lazarus' tomb to weep; so they followed her.

³²When Mary arrived where Jesus was, she fell down at his feet, saying, "Sir, if you had been here, my brother would still be alive."

³³When Jesus saw her weeping and the Jewish leaders wailing with her, he was moved with indignation and deeply troubled. ³⁴"Where is he buried?" he asked them.

They told him, "Come and see." ³⁵Tears came to Jesus' eyes.

³⁶"They were close friends," the Jewish leaders said. "See how much he loved him."

³⁷,³⁸But some said, "This fellow healed a blind man—why couldn't he keep Lazarus from dying?"

And again Jesus was moved with deep anger. Then they came to the tomb. It was a cave with a heavy stone rolled across its door.

³⁹"Roll the stone aside," Jesus told them.

But Martha, the dead man's sister, said, "By now the smell will be terrible, for he has been dead four days."

⁴⁰"But didn't I tell you that you will see a wonderful miracle from God if you believe?" Jesus asked her.

⁴¹So they rolled the stone aside. Then Jesus looked up to heaven and said, "Father, thank you for hearing me. ⁴²(You always hear me, of course, but I said it because of all these people standing here, so that they will believe you sent me.)" ⁴³Then he shouted, "Lazarus, come out!"

⁴⁴And Lazarus came—bound up in the gravecloth, his face muffled in a head swath. Jesus told them, "Unwrap him and let him go!"

⁴⁵And so at last many of the Jewish leaders who were with Mary and saw it happen, finally believed on him. ⁴⁶But some went away to the Pharisees and reported it to them.

⁴⁷Then the chief priests and Pharisees convened a council to discuss the situation.

"What are we going to do?" they asked each other. "For this man certainly does miracles. ⁴⁸If we let him alone the whole nation will follow him—and then the Roman army will come and kill us and take over the Jewish government."

⁴⁹And one of them, Caiaphas, who was High Priest that year, said, "You stupid idiots— ⁵⁰let this one man die for the people—why should the whole nation perish?"

⁵¹This prophecy that Jesus should die for the entire nation came from Caiaphas in his position as High Priest—he didn't think of it by himself, but was inspired to say it. ⁵²It was a prediction that Jesus' death would not be for Israel only, but for all the children of God scattered around the world. ⁵³So from that time on the Jewish leaders began plotting Jesus' death.

⁵⁴Jesus now stopped his public ministry and left Jerusalem; he went to the edge of the desert, to the village of Ephraim, and stayed there with his disciples.

⁵⁵The Passover, a Jewish holy day, was near, and many country people arrived in Jerusalem several days early so that they could go through the cleansing ceremony before the Passover began. ⁵⁶They wanted to see Jesus, and as they gossiped in the Temple, they asked each other, "What do you think? Will he come for the Passover?" ⁵⁷Meanwhile the chief priests and Pharisees had publicly announced that anyone seeing Jesus must report him immediately so that they could arrest him.

12 Mary Anoints Jesus' Feet

Six days before the Passover ceremonies began, Jesus arrived in Bethany where Lazarus was—the man he had brought back to life. ²A banquet was prepared in Jesus' honor. Martha served, and Lazarus sat at the table with him. ³Then Mary took a jar of costly perfume made

Family Devotions

☐ DEVOTION 283
BECOMING MORE LIKE JESUS

Read John 13:34-35

"Back so soon?" asked Mom as Peggy came in with a grocery sack. "Did you find the tomato sauce all right?"

"Sure did. And look what else I bought," said Peggy, taking several cans from the bag. "These were really cheap because the labels are gone. I saved lots of money for you."

"But we don't know what they are!" Mom said with a frown. Then she laughed. "Very well," she said, "choose one for dinner tonight. Whatever it turns out to be, you'll have to eat some, OK? You bought it—you eat it!"

Peggy agreed. She looked over the array of unlabeled cans, finally setting one aside for dinner. "I think it's corn," she guessed.

At the dinner table that evening, Peggy's brother Todd wrinkled his nose as Mom brought in the food. "What's that strange smell?" he asked.

Mom set a bowl on the table. "It's sauerkraut. Peggy chose it for us tonight," she said. "I hope you like it. You go first, Peggy. Not too small a serving!"

Dad laughed when he heard the story of the unlabeled cans, and he took a large serving of the sauerkraut. "Well, I'm glad you bought this," he said. "I haven't had it for years. I like it! It's good."

But Peggy and Todd didn't agree. "I wonder what else I bought," said Peggy in a worried tone. "I see now why they sold that stuff so cheap. Labels are important."

For family devotions that night, Dad handed each of the children a Bible. "As we've learned, labels are important," he said, "and as Christians, we have a label, too. It's found in John 13:34-35."

Peggy and Todd scrambled to see who could find it first. "Oh! I've got it!" exclaimed Peggy. "It's love."

"Right," nodded Dad. "People should be able to see by our label of love that we are Christians. Let's make sure others can see our label."

Becoming More Like Jesus Memory Verse

No, he has told you what he wants, and this is all it is: *to be fair, just, merciful, and to walk humbly with your God.*
Micah 6:8

How About You?

Can others tell by your label that you're a Christian? Do they see love in your works? In your actions? They should not only see you display love toward the unsaved, but especially toward other Christians. Check your actions today. Make sure the label of love is there for everyone to see. *H. M.*

• For the next devotional, turn to page 1021. • For the next devotional on BECOMING MORE LIKE JESUS, turn to page 1079. • For notes on BECOMING MORE LIKE JESUS, see pages 234, 983, 1105, and 1164.

from essence of nard, and anointed Jesus' feet with it and wiped them with her hair. And the house was filled with fragrance.

⁴But Judas Iscariot, one of his disciples—the one who would betray him—said, ⁵"That perfume was worth a fortune. It should have been sold and the money given to the poor." ⁶Not that he cared for the poor, but he was in charge of the disciples' funds and often dipped into them for his own use!

⁷Jesus replied, "Let her alone. She did it in preparation for my burial. ⁸You can always help the poor, but I won't be with you very long."

⁹When the ordinary people of Jerusalem heard of his arrival, they flocked to see him and also to see Lazarus—the man who had come back to life again. ¹⁰Then the chief priests decided to kill Lazarus too, ¹¹for it was because of him that many of the Jewish leaders had deserted and believed in Jesus as their Messiah.

¹²The next day, the news that Jesus was on the way to Jerusalem swept through the city, and a huge crowd of Passover visitors ¹³took palm branches and went down the road to meet him, shouting, "The Savior! God bless the King of Israel! Hail to God's Ambassador!"

¹⁴Jesus rode along on a young donkey, fulfilling the prophecy that said: ¹⁵"Don't be afraid of your King, people of Israel, for he will come to you meekly, sitting on a donkey's colt!"

¹⁶(His disciples didn't realize at the time that this was a fulfillment of prophecy; but after Jesus returned to his glory in heaven, then they noticed how many prophecies of Scripture had come true before their eyes.)

¹⁷And those in the crowd who had seen Jesus call Lazarus back to life were telling all about it. ¹⁸That was the main reason why so many went out to meet him—because they had heard about this mighty miracle.

¹⁹Then the Pharisees said to each other, "We've lost. Look—the whole world has gone after him!"

²⁰Some Greeks who had come to Jerusalem to attend the Passover ²¹paid a visit to Philip, who was from Bethsaida, and said, "Sir, we want to meet Jesus." ²²Philip told Andrew about it, and they went together to ask Jesus.

²³,²⁴Jesus replied that the time had come for him to return to his glory in heaven, and that "I must fall and die like a kernel of wheat that falls into the furrows of the earth. Unless I die I will be alone—a single seed. But my death will produce many new wheat kernels—a plentiful harvest of new lives. ²⁵If you love your life down here—you will lose it. If you despise your life down here—you will exchange it for eternal glory.

²⁶"If these Greeks want to be my disciples, tell them to come and follow me, for my servants must be where I am. And if they follow me, the Father will honor them. ²⁷Now my soul is deeply troubled. Shall I pray, 'Father, save me from what lies ahead'? But that is the very reason why I came! ²⁸Father, bring glory and honor to your name."

Then a voice spoke from heaven saying, "I have already done this, and I will do it again." ²⁹When the crowd heard the voice, some of them thought it was thunder, while others declared an angel had spoken to him.

³⁰Then Jesus told them, "The voice was for your benefit, not mine. ³¹The time of judgment for the world has come—and the time when Satan, the prince of this world, shall be cast out. ³²And when I am lifted up [on the cross], I will draw everyone to me." ³³He said this to indicate how he was going to die.

³⁴"Die?" asked the crowd. "We understood that the Messiah would live forever and never die. Why are you saying he will die? What Messiah are you talking about?"

³⁵Jesus replied, "My light will shine out for you just a little while longer. Walk in it while you can, and go where you want to go before the darkness falls, for then it will be too late for you to find your way. ³⁶Make use of the Light while there is still time; then you will become light bearers."

After saying these things, Jesus went away and was hidden from them.

³⁷But despite all the miracles he had done, most of the people would not believe he was the Messiah. ³⁸This is exactly what Isaiah the prophet had predicted: "Lord, who will believe us? Who will accept God's mighty miracles as proof?" ³⁹But they couldn't believe, for as Isaiah also said: ⁴⁰"God has blinded their eyes and hardened their hearts so that they can neither see nor understand nor turn to me to heal them." ⁴¹Isaiah was referring to Jesus when he made this prediction, for he had seen a vision of the Messiah's glory.

⁴²However, even many of the Jewish leaders believed him to be the Messiah but wouldn't admit it to anyone because of their fear that the Pharisees would excommunicate them from the synagogue; ⁴³for they loved the praise of men more than the praise of God.

⁴⁴Jesus shouted to the crowds, "If you trust me, you are really trusting God. ⁴⁵For when you see me, you are seeing the one who sent me. ⁴⁶I have come as a Light to shine in this dark world, so that all who put their trust in me will no longer wander in the darkness. ⁴⁷If anyone hears me and doesn't obey me, I am not his judge—for I have come to save the world and not to judge it. ⁴⁸But all who reject me and my message will be judged at the Day of Judgment by the truths I have spoken. ⁴⁹For these are not my own ideas, but I have

FAMILY DEVOTIONS

☐ *DEVOTION 284*
RECEIVING CHRIST AS SAVIOR

Read John 14:1-6

Receiving Christ as Savior
Memory Verse

If you tell others with your own mouth that Jesus Christ is your Lord and believe in your own heart that God has raised him from the dead, you will be saved.
Romans 10:9

Passenger trains had not stopped at Centerville for years, but for the city's anniversary celebration there was going to be a train with free rides for everyone. John had urged his dad to go with him, and together they climbed aboard. But it seemed as though the train would never start. "Shouldn't we be going pretty soon?" John asked.

"Maybe they're waiting for more people," suggested Dad. The car was not very full.

At that moment a man dressed as a conductor stepped into the car. "Guess you folks didn't read the sign," he said. "This car's not going anywhere."

John looked at the few people on the train and then at the conductor. "How come?" he asked, looking bewildered.

"'Cause this car's not hooked up to the engine," the man laughed. "It's on the second track. The train with the cars we're using will be back soon."

John and his father and the others got off the train to wait. "We had good intentions of taking that ride," Dad said, putting his hand on John's shoulder, "but good intentions didn't get us there."

"That sounds like a good sermon topic," John said, looking down the track to see if there was a train coming.

Dad agreed. "You're right. Some people think they're headed for heaven just because they attend church. But being in a church doesn't necessarily mean you're in Christ."

"Guess you have to be hooked up to the engine," John added.

When the train returned, John and his father were careful to board one of the cars right behind the engine. "I know we're going somewhere," John said as they sat waiting for the train to start. "This time I checked to see if the car is hooked up!"

How About You?
Some people do not check to see what the Bible says about the way to heaven. They think that whatever their church teaches must be right. God's Word says there is only one way to heaven, and Jesus is that way. If you haven't come to Christ and confessed your sin and asked him to be your Savior, you're just not on the right track. Have you accepted him as the Way? You must if you expect to go to heaven. *R.J.*

• For the next devotional, turn to page 1023. • For the next devotional on *RECEIVING CHRIST AS SAVIOR*, turn to page 1025. • For notes on *RECEIVING CHRIST AS SAVIOR*, see pages 839, 842, 1146, 1234, and 1240.

told you what the Father said to tell you. ⁵⁰And I know his instructions lead to eternal life; so whatever he tells me to say, I say!"

13. Jesus Washes His Disciples' Feet

Jesus knew on the evening of Passover Day that it would be his last night on earth before returning to his Father. During supper the devil had already suggested to Judas Iscariot, Simon's son, that this was the night to carry out his plan to betray Jesus. Jesus knew that the Father had given him everything and that he had come from God and would return to God. And how he loved his disciples! ⁴So he got up from the supper table, took off his robe, wrapped a towel around his loins, ⁵poured water into a basin, and began to wash the disciples' feet and to wipe them with the towel he had around him.

⁶When he came to Simon Peter, Peter said to him, "Master, you shouldn't be washing our feet like this!"

⁷Jesus replied, "You don't understand now why I am doing it; some day you will."

⁸"No," Peter protested, "you shall never wash my feet!"

"But if I don't, you can't be my partner," Jesus replied.

⁹Simon Peter exclaimed, "Then wash my hands and head as well—not just my feet!"

¹⁰Jesus replied, "One who has bathed all over needs only to have his feet washed to be entirely clean. Now you are clean—but that isn't true of everyone here." ¹¹For Jesus knew who would betray him. That is what he meant when he said, "Not all of you are clean."

¹²After washing their feet he put on his robe again and sat down and asked, "Do you understand what I was doing? ¹³You call me 'Master' and 'Lord,' and you do well to say it, for it is true. ¹⁴And since I, the Lord and Teacher, have washed your feet, you ought to wash each other's feet. ¹⁵I have given you an example to follow: do as I have done to you. ¹⁶How true it is that a servant is not greater than his master. Nor is the messenger more important than the one who sends him. ¹⁷You know these things—now do them! That is the path of blessing.

¹⁸"I am not saying these things to all of you; I know so well each one of you I chose. The Scripture declares, 'One who eats supper with me will betray me,' and this will soon come true. ¹⁹I tell you this now so that when it happens, you will believe on me.

²⁰"Truly, anyone welcoming my messenger is welcoming me. And to welcome me is to welcome the Father who sent me."

²¹Now Jesus was in great anguish of spirit and exclaimed, "Yes, it is true—one of you will betray me." ²²The disciples looked at each other, wondering whom he could mean. ²³Since I was sitting next to Jesus at the table, being his closest friend, ²⁴Simon Peter motioned to me to ask him who it was who would do this terrible deed.

²⁵So I turned and asked him, "Lord, who is it?"

²⁶He told me, "It is the one I honor by giving the bread dipped in the sauce."

And when he had dipped it, he gave it to Judas, son of Simon Iscariot.

²⁷As soon as Judas had eaten it, Satan entered into him. Then Jesus told him, "Hurry—do it now."

²⁸None of the others at the table knew what Jesus meant. ²⁹Some thought that since Judas was their treasurer, Jesus was telling him to go and pay for the food or to give some money to the poor. ³⁰Judas left at once, going out into the night.

³¹As soon as Judas left the room, Jesus said, "My time has come; the glory of God will soon surround me—and God shall receive great praise because of all that happens to me. ³²And God shall give me his own glory, and this so very soon. ³³Dear, dear children, how brief are these moments before I must go away and leave you! Then, though you search for me, you cannot come to me—just as I told the Jewish leaders.

³⁴"And so I am giving a new commandment to you now—love each other just as much as I love you. ³⁵Your strong love for each other will prove to the world that you are my disciples."

³⁶Simon Peter said, "Master, where are you going?"

And Jesus replied, "You can't go with me now; but you will follow me later."

³⁷"But why can't I come now?" he asked, "for I am ready to die for you."

³⁸Jesus answered, "Die for me? No—three times before the cock crows tomorrow morning, you will deny that you even know me!

14. Jesus: The Way, Truth, and Life

"Let not your heart be troubled. You are trusting God, now trust in me. ²,³There are many homes up there where my Father lives, and I am going to prepare them for your coming. When everything is ready, then I will come and get you, so that you can always be with me where I am. If this weren't so, I would tell you plainly. ⁴And you know where I am going and how to get there."

⁵"No, we don't," Thomas said. "We haven't any idea where you are going, so how can we know the way?"

⁶Jesus told him, "I am the Way—yes, and the Truth and the Life. No one can get to the Father except by means of me. ⁷If you had known who I

Family Devotions

☐ DEVOTION 285
OBEDIENCE

Read John 14:15-21

One Saturday morning Nancy reminded her brother, Dan, that they were planning to go and buy their mother a present because the next day was Mom's Day. "Can't," Dan said crossly. "Mom says I can't leave the house."

"Why not?" Nancy asked. "What did you do?"

"Just what she told me," Dan grumbled. "I cleaned my closet. When I got done, I asked, 'Now does it suit you?' She said my closet did but not my attitude. So I have to stay home today."

"Oh, Dan," moaned Nancy, "this spoils everything. Look—I'll go ask her if you can go to the store with me."

Nancy went into the house, but when Mom said no, Nancy argued with her mother and spoke disrespectfully to her. As a result, she got grounded, too.

After dinner the next day, Nancy told her mother that they'd wanted to get her a present. "But you wouldn't let us go to the store," she complained.

"I didn't want a gift from you children," said Mom.

"You didn't?" asked Dan. "Why not?"

"Well, there's a better way than that to show love for someone. Do you remember what we read from the Bible last night?"

"I do," said Nancy slowly. "'If you love me, obey me.' I guess we didn't act like we loved you yesterday. I'm sorry, Mom—honest I am! I'm going to prove it by acting like I love you. You'll see!"

"Me, too," added Dan. "Will you forgive me?"

"Of course I will," answered Mom.

Obedience Memory Verse

Oh, that they would always have such a heart for me, wanting to obey my commandments. Then all would go well with them in the future, and with their children throughout all generations!
Deuteronomy 5:29

How About You?

Can your parents tell by your actions that you love them? Have you told them lately—not by words, but by quick and cheerful obedience—that they are precious to you? Right now ask God to help you obey. A. G. L.

• For the next devotional, turn to page 1025. • For the next devotional on OBEDIENCE, turn to page 1253.
• For notes on OBEDIENCE, see pages 319, 425, 500, 510, and 757.

am, then you would have known who my Father is. From now on you know him—and have seen him!"

⁸Philip said, "Sir, show us the Father and we will be satisfied."

⁹Jesus replied, "Don't you even yet know who I am, Philip, even after all this time I have been with you? Anyone who has seen me has seen the Father! So why are you asking to see him? ¹⁰Don't you believe that I am in the Father and the Father is in me? The words I say are not my own but are from my Father who lives in me. And he does his work through me. ¹¹Just believe it—that I am in the Father and the Father is in me. Or else believe it because of the mighty miracles you have seen me do.

¹²,¹³"In solemn truth I tell you, anyone believing in me shall do the same miracles I have done, and even greater ones, because I am going to be with the Father. You can ask him for *anything*, using my name, and I will do it, for this will bring praise to the Father because of what I, the Son, will do for you. ¹⁴Yes, ask *anything*, using my name, and I will do it!

¹⁵,¹⁶"If you love me, obey me; and I will ask the Father and he will give you another Comforter, and he will never leave you. ¹⁷He is the Holy Spirit, the Spirit who leads into all truth. The world at large cannot receive him, for it isn't looking for him and doesn't recognize him. But you do, for he lives with you now and some day shall be in you. ¹⁸No, I will not abandon you or leave you as orphans in the storm—I will come to you. ¹⁹In just a little while I will be gone from the world, but I will still be present with you. For I will live again—and you will too. ²⁰When I come back to life again, you will know that I am in my Father, and you in me, and I in you. ²¹The one who obeys me is the one who loves me; and because he loves me, my Father will love him; and I will too, and I will reveal myself to him."

²²Judas (not Judas Iscariot, but his other disciple with that name) said to him, "Sir, why are you going to reveal yourself only to us disciples and not to the world at large?"

²³Jesus replied, "Because I will only reveal myself to those who love me and obey me. The Father will love them too, and we will come to them and live with them. ²⁴Anyone who doesn't obey me doesn't love me. And remember, I am not making up this answer to your question! It is the answer given by the Father who sent me.

²⁵"I am telling you these things now while I am still with you. ²⁶But when the Father sends the Comforter instead of me—and by the Comforter I mean the Holy Spirit—he will teach you much, as well as remind you of everything I myself have told you.

²⁷"I am leaving you with a gift—peace of mind and heart! And the peace I give isn't fragile like the peace the world gives. So don't be troubled or afraid. ²⁸Remember what I told you—I am going away, but I will come back to you again. If you really love me, you will be very happy for me, for now I can go to the Father, who is greater than I am. ²⁹I have told you these things before they happen so that when they do, you will believe [in me].

³⁰"I don't have much more time to talk to you, for the evil prince of this world approaches. He has no power over me, ³¹but I will freely do what the Father requires of me so that the world will know that I love the Father. Come, let's be going.

15 The Vine and the Branches

"I am the true Vine, and my Father is the Gardener. ²He lops off every branch that doesn't produce. And he prunes those branches that bear fruit for even larger crops. ³He has already tended you by pruning you back for greater strength and usefulness by means of the commands I gave you. ⁴Take care to live in me, and let me live in you. For a branch can't produce fruit when severed from the vine. Nor can you be fruitful apart from me.

⁵"Yes, I am the Vine; you are the branches. Whoever lives in me and I in him shall produce a large crop of fruit. For apart from me you can't do a thing. ⁶If anyone separates from me, he is thrown away like a useless branch, withers, and is gathered into a pile with all the others and burned. ⁷But if you stay in me and obey my commands, you may ask any request you like, and it will be granted! ⁸My true disciples produce bountiful harvests. This brings great glory to my Father.

⁹"I have loved you even as the Father has loved me. Live within my love. ¹⁰When you obey me you are living in my love, just as I obey my Father and live in his love. ¹¹I have told you this so that you will be filled with my joy. Yes, your cup of joy will overflow! ¹²I demand that you love each other as much as I love you. ¹³And here is how to measure it—the greatest love is shown when a person lays down his life for his friends; ¹⁴and you are my friends if you obey me. ¹⁵I no longer call you slaves, for a master doesn't confide in his slaves; now you are my friends, proved by the fact that I have told you everything the Father told me.

¹⁶"You didn't choose me! I chose you! I appointed you to go and produce lovely fruit always, so

---

TRUE JOY   15:11   When things are going well, we feel elated. When hardships come, we sink into depression. But true joy transcends the rolling waves of circumstance. Joy comes from a consistent relationship with Jesus Christ. He will help us walk through adversity without sinking into devastating lows and manage prosperity without moving into deceptive highs. The joy of living with Jesus Christ daily will keep us levelheaded, no matter how high or low our circumstances.
To begin the series of devotionals on TRUE JOY, turn to page 83.

Family Devotions

☐ DEVOTION 286
RECEIVING CHRIST AS SAVIOR

Read John 15:1-8

Randy bounced alongside of Grandpa in the pickup truck. They were on their way to the vineyard, where Grandpa was going to do some pruning.

"How do you know which branches to cut off?" Randy asked when they got there.

"The ones that are attached to the main vine are the branches that I leave," answered Grandpa. "They're the strongest and will grow nice, fat grapes. The branches that only grow from other branches, not right from the main vine, won't grow good grapes, so I cut those off." Grandpa showed Randy how he followed a branch to its beginning to see whether or not it was attached to the main vine. "Whenever I prune the grapevines, I'm reminded of what Jesus said about them," said Grandpa.

"Jesus talked about grapevines?" Randy asked.

"Sure," answered Grandpa, nodding. "Jesus compared himself to the main vine of a grapevine, and he said people are like the branches. Some are the true branches attached to the vine and will be fruitful, and others are just secondary branches to be cut off."

"Which people are the true branches?" asked Randy.

"Those who trust in Jesus as the way to heaven," replied Grandpa. "The other branches are those who try to get there on their own."

"I've asked Jesus to forgive my sins, and I love him. So I'm a true branch, right?" Randy asked.

"Right you are," said Grandpa while he cut another branch.

Receiving Christ as Savior
Memory Verse

For God loved the world so much that he gave his only Son so that anyone who believes in him shall not perish but have eternal life.
John 3:16

How About You?

Are you attached to Jesus, the Vine? Or are you attached to your church membership, your baptism, or your good works? There is only one way to get to heaven, and that is to trust Jesus to forgive your sins. If you do that, you'll be like a fruitful branch attached to the vine. If you've never asked Jesus to be your Savior, do it now. Don't be cast away like an unfruitful branch. *C. Y.*

• For the next devotional, turn to page 1027. • For the next devotional on RECEIVING CHRIST AS SAVIOR, turn to page 1053. • For notes on RECEIVING CHRIST AS SAVIOR, see pages 839, 842, 1146, 1234, and 1240.

that no matter what you ask for from the Father, using my name, he will give it to you. ¹⁷I demand that you love each other, ¹⁸for you get enough hate from the world! But then, it hated me before it hated you. ¹⁹The world would love you if you belonged to it; but you don't—for I chose you to come out of the world, and so it hates you. ²⁰Do you remember what I told you? 'A slave isn't greater than his master!' So since they persecuted me, naturally they will persecute you. And if they had listened to me, they would listen to you! ²¹The people of the world will persecute you because you belong to me, for they don't know God who sent me.

²²"They would not be guilty if I had not come and spoken to them. But now they have no excuse for their sin. ²³Anyone hating me is also hating my Father. ²⁴If I hadn't done such mighty miracles among them they would not be counted guilty. But as it is, they saw these miracles and yet they hated both of us—me and my Father. ²⁵This has fulfilled what the prophets said concerning the Messiah, 'They hated me without reason.'

²⁶"But I will send you the Comforter—the Holy Spirit, the source of all truth. He will come to you from the Father and will tell you all about me. ²⁷And you also must tell everyone about me because you have been with me from the beginning.

16 The Holy Spirit

"I have told you these things so that you won't be staggered [by all that lies ahead.] ²For you will be excommunicated from the synagogues, and indeed the time is coming when those who kill you will think they are doing God a service. ³This is because they have never known the Father or me. ⁴Yes, I'm telling you these things now so that when they happen you will remember I warned you. I didn't tell you earlier because I was going to be with you for a while longer.

⁵"But now I am going away to the one who sent me; and none of you seems interested in the purpose of my going; none wonders why. ⁶Instead you are only filled with sorrow. ⁷But the fact of the matter is that it is best for you that I go away, for if I don't, the Comforter won't come. If I do, he will—for I will send him to you.

⁸"And when he has come he will convince the world of its sin, and of the availability of God's goodness, and of deliverance from judgment. ⁹The world's sin is unbelief in me; ¹⁰there is righteousness available because I go to the Father and you shall see me no more; ¹¹there is deliverance from judgment because the prince of this world has already been judged.

¹²"Oh, there is so much more I want to tell you, but you can't understand it now. ¹³When the Holy Spirit, who is truth, comes, he shall guide you into all truth, for he will not be presenting his own ideas, but will be passing on to you what he has heard. He will tell you about the future. ¹⁴He shall praise me and bring me great honor by showing you my glory. ¹⁵All the Father's glory is mine; this is what I mean when I say that he will show you my glory.

¹⁶"In just a little while I will be gone, and you will see me no more; but just a little while after that, and you will see me again!"

¹⁷,¹⁸"Whatever is he saying?" some of his disciples asked. "What is this about 'going to the Father'? We don't know what he means."

¹⁹Jesus realized they wanted to ask him so he said, "Are you asking yourselves what I mean? ²⁰The world will greatly rejoice over what is going to happen to me, and you will weep. But your weeping shall suddenly be turned to wonderful joy [when you see me again]. ²¹It will be the same joy as that of a woman in labor when her child is born—her anguish gives place to rapturous joy and the pain is forgotten. ²²You have sorrow now, but I will see you again and then you will rejoice; and no one can rob you of that joy. ²³At that time you won't need to ask me for anything, for you can go directly to the Father and ask him, and he will give you what you ask for because you use my name. ²⁴You haven't tried this before, [but begin now]. Ask, using my name, and you will receive, and your cup of joy will overflow.

²⁵"I have spoken of these matters very guardedly, but the time will come when this will not be necessary and I will tell you plainly all about the Father. ²⁶Then you will present your petitions over my signature! And I won't need to ask the Father to grant you these requests, ²⁷for the Father himself loves you dearly because you love me and believe that I came from the Father. ²⁸Yes, I came from the Father into the world and will leave the world and return to the Father."

²⁹"At last you are speaking plainly," his disciples said, "and not in riddles. ³⁰Now we understand that you know everything and don't need anyone to tell you anything. From this we believe that you came from God."

³¹"Do you finally believe this?" Jesus asked. ³²"But the time is coming—in fact, it is here—when you will be scattered, each one returning to his own home, leaving me alone. Yet I will not be alone, for the Father is with me. ³³I have told you all this so that you will have peace of heart and mind. Here on earth you will have many trials and sorrows; but cheer up, for I have overcome the world."

17 Jesus Prays for Himself

When Jesus had finished saying all these things he looked up to heaven and said, "Father, the time has come. Reveal the glory of your Son

Family Devotions

☐ DEVOTION 287
KNOWING YOU'RE SPECIAL TO GOD

Read John 15:16

Jerry shifted nervously from one foot to the other, wiping his sweating palms on his jeans. How he wished his gym teacher would just assign teams for the various games they played, but once again they were choosing sides. Jerry was smaller and slower than the other boys in gym, and he was usually left till last. It just wasn't fair! Why did God make him so small? He was close to tears, and his heart pounded. Already there were only six boys left to be chosen.

"Tim," called Brent, the biggest boy in class, one of the team leaders.

"Justin," barked Clint, the other leader.

"Phil."

"David."

Jerry licked his dry lips nervously as Brent and Clint looked at each other and grimaced. "Byron," Brent called, motioning to the boy beside Jerry.

"All right, Jerry, come on," Clint called grudgingly.

Fighting tears, Jerry loped over to the team. Though he tried his very best, he didn't do very well in the game and got withering looks from the other team members.

After school, his tears mingled with his peanut butter sandwich as he told his mother about his problems. She spoke tenderly. "I know it hurts very much not to be chosen until last," she said. "Maybe it will help a little if you remember that you have been chosen for a team that's more important than all the others, and whose team captain is over all those other team captains."

Jerry wiped his eyes. "I have?" he asked hopefully. "What team is that?"

"God's team—and size doesn't count, either!" said Mom triumphantly. "God says in the Bible that he has chosen each of us!" She gave Jerry a bright smile. "And you're made just to order for the part you'll play on his team!"

Knowing You're Special to God Memory Verse

But now the Lord who created you, O Israel, says, Don't be afraid, for I have ransomed you; I have called you by name; you are mine.
Isaiah 43:1

How About You?

Do you sometimes wish God had made you differently because you don't fit in a sport or musical activity? God does not make mistakes. He has a very wonderful plan for each life. If you have accepted Jesus as your personal Savior, you have been chosen for God's team. Follow him daily, and you'll find the purpose for which you were made in your own special way. D. E.

• For the next devotional, turn to page 1029. • For the next devotional on KNOWING YOU'RE SPECIAL TO GOD, turn to page 1109. • For notes on KNOWING YOU'RE SPECIAL TO GOD, see pages 260, 878, 908, and 960.

so that he can give the glory back to you. ²For you have given him authority over every man and woman in all the earth. He gives eternal life to each one you have given him. ³And this is the way to have eternal life—by knowing you, the only true God, and Jesus Christ, the one you sent to earth! ⁴I brought glory to you here on earth by doing everything you told me to. ⁵And now, Father, reveal my glory as I stand in your presence, the glory we shared before the world began.

⁶"I have told these men all about you. They were in the world, but then you gave them to me. Actually, they were always yours, and you gave them to me; and they have obeyed you. ⁷Now they know that everything I have is a gift from you, ⁸for I have passed on to them the commands you gave me; and they accepted them and know of a certainty that I came down to earth from you, and they believe you sent me.

⁹"My plea is not for the world but for those you have given me because they belong to you. ¹⁰And all of them, since they are mine, belong to you; and you have given them back to me with everything else of yours, and so *they are my glory!* ¹¹Now I am leaving the world, and leaving them behind, and coming to you. Holy Father, keep them in your own care—all those you have given me—so that they will be united just as we are, with none missing. ¹²During my time here I have kept safe within your family all of these you gave me. I guarded them so that not one perished, except the son of hell, as the Scriptures foretold.

¹³"And now I am coming to you. I have told them many things while I was with them so that they would be filled with my joy. ¹⁴I have given them your commands. And the world hates them because they don't fit in with it, just as I don't. ¹⁵I'm not asking you to take them out of the world, but to keep them safe from Satan's power. ¹⁶They are not part of this world any more than I am. ¹⁷Make them pure and holy through teaching them your words of truth. ¹⁸As you sent me into the world, I am sending them into the world, ¹⁹and I consecrate myself to meet their need for growth in truth and holiness.

²⁰"I am not praying for these alone but also for the future believers who will come to me because of the testimony of these. ²¹My prayer for all of them is that they will be of one heart and mind, just as you and I are, Father—that just as you are in me and I am in you, so they will be in us, and the world will believe you sent me.

²²"I have given them the glory you gave me— the glorious unity of being one, as we are—²³I in them and you in me, all being perfected into one—so that the world will know you sent me and will understand that you love them as much as you love me. ²⁴Father, I want them with me— these you've given me—so that they can see my glory. You gave me the glory because you loved me before the world began!

²⁵"O righteous Father, the world doesn't know you, but I do; and these disciples know you sent me. ²⁶And I have revealed you to them and will keep on revealing you so that the mighty love you have for me may be in them, and I in them."

18 Jesus Is Arrested

After saying these things Jesus crossed the Kidron ravine with his disciples and entered a grove of olive trees. ²Judas, the betrayer, knew this place, for Jesus had gone there many times with his disciples.

³The chief priests and Pharisees had given Judas a squad of soldiers and police to accompany him. Now with blazing torches, lanterns, and weapons they arrived at the olive grove.

⁴,⁵Jesus fully realized all that was going to happen to him. Stepping forward to meet them he asked, "Whom are you looking for?"

"Jesus of Nazareth," they replied.

"I am he," Jesus said. ⁶And as he said it, they all fell backwards to the ground!

⁷Once more he asked them, "Whom are you searching for?"

And again they replied, "Jesus of Nazareth."

⁸"I told you I am he," Jesus said; "and since I am the one you are after, let these others go." ⁹He did this to carry out the prophecy he had just made, "I have not lost a single one of those you gave me. . . ."

¹⁰Then Simon Peter drew a sword and slashed off the right ear of Malchus, the High Priest's servant.

¹¹But Jesus said to Peter, "Put your sword away. Shall I not drink from the cup the Father has given me?"

¹²So the Jewish police, with the soldiers and their lieutenant, arrested Jesus and tied him. ¹³First they took him to Annas, the father-in-law of Caiaphas, the High Priest that year. ¹⁴Caiaphas was the one who told the other Jewish leaders, "Better that one should die for all."

¹⁵Simon Peter followed along behind, as did another of the disciples who was acquainted with the High Priest. So that other disciple was permitted into the courtyard along with Jesus, ¹⁶while Peter stood outside the gate. Then the other disciple spoke to the girl watching at the gate, and she let Peter in. ¹⁷The girl asked Peter, "Aren't you one of Jesus' disciples?"

"No," he said, "I am not!"

¹⁸The police and the household servants were

Family Devotions

☐ **Devotion 288**
Accepting Others

Read John 17:20-23

"Dad, we do things differently at our church than they do at Bob's church," Kenny said one day. "We had an argument about it. He said his church is right, and I said my church is right. Whose way is really right?"

Before Dad could attempt an answer, Kenny's little sister and brother came into the kitchen, carrying a keyboard. They set it on the table. "We want to play a song Daddy taught us," announced Cathy, and they proceeded to do so. At first, they carefully pressed the keys, and Kenny thought he recognized "Twinkle, Twinkle, Little Star." But then it became obvious that they were playing two different songs.

"That sounds awful," declared Kenny. "I think you need a new teacher."

"Wait a minute!" protested Dad. "The teacher's not the problem. They're not following my instructions."

When the children were gone, Dad grinned at Kenny. "That sure wasn't the way I intended their music to turn out," he said. "But, what just happened reminds me of what happens to Christians. Can't you almost hear God saying, 'That wasn't what I intended,' as he watches us? Jesus intended for his followers to all play the same song. He wanted all Christians to be unified—to be one."

"But which song should we be playing? Whose way is right—Bob's church or our church?" Kenny asked again.

"God's way is right," Dad answered. "I don't know what church Bob attends. But we believe the church we go to teaches what God says in his Word. That's why we go there."

"So that's what I should tell Bob the next time we argue about our differences?" Kenny persisted.

"Why argue? Why not agree to read your Bible and do your best to do what it says?" suggested Dad. "That's what Jesus would want you to do."

Accepting Others Memory Verse

How wonderful it is, how pleasant, when brothers live in harmony!
Psalm 133:1

How About You?

Do you argue with someone from another church? You should attend a church that you believe agrees with what God says in his Word, and then quit arguing. By reading the Bible and putting its teaching into practice, and by encouraging others to do the same, we can have the unity Jesus wants for us. K. R. A.

- For the next devotional, turn to page 1031. • For the next devotional on Accepting Others, turn to page 1049.
- For notes on Accepting Others, see pages 270, 1140, 1196, and 1254.

standing around a fire they had made, for it was cold. And Peter stood there with them, warming himself.

[19] Inside, the High Priest began asking Jesus about his followers and what he had been teaching them.

[20] Jesus replied, "What I teach is widely known, for I have preached regularly in the synagogue and Temple; I have been heard by all the Jewish leaders and teach nothing in private that I have not said in public. [21] Why are you asking me this question? Ask those who heard me. You have some of them here. They know what I said."

[22] One of the soldiers standing there struck Jesus with his fist. "Is that the way to answer the High Priest?" he demanded.

[23] "If I lied, prove it," Jesus replied. "Should you hit a man for telling the truth?"

[24] Then Annas sent Jesus, bound, to Caiaphas the High Priest.

[25] Meanwhile, as Simon Peter was standing by the fire, he was asked again, "Aren't you one of his disciples?"

"Of course not," he replied.

[26] But one of the household slaves of the High Priest—a relative of the man whose ear Peter had cut off—asked, "Didn't I see you out there in the olive grove with Jesus?"

[27] Again Peter denied it. And immediately a rooster crowed.

[28] Jesus' trial before Caiaphas ended in the early hours of the morning. Next he was taken to the palace of the Roman governor. His accusers wouldn't go in themselves for that would "defile" them, they said, and they wouldn't be allowed to eat the Passover lamb. [29] So Pilate, the governor, went out to them and asked, "What is your charge against this man? What are you accusing him of doing?"

[30] "We wouldn't have arrested him if he weren't a criminal!" they retorted.

[31] "Then take him away and judge him yourselves by your own laws," Pilate told them.

"But we want him crucified," they demanded, "and your approval is required." [32] This fulfilled Jesus' prediction concerning the method of his execution.

[33] Then Pilate went back into the palace and called for Jesus to be brought to him. "Are you the King of the Jews?" he asked him.

[34] "'King' as *you* use the word or as the *Jews* use it?" Jesus asked.

[35] "Am I a Jew?" Pilate retorted. "Your own people and their chief priests brought you here. Why? What have you done?"

[36] Then Jesus answered, "I am not an earthly king. If I were, my followers would have fought when I was arrested by the Jewish leaders. But my Kingdom is not of the world."

[37] Pilate replied, "But you are a king then?"

"Yes," Jesus said. "I was born for that purpose. And I came to bring truth to the world. All who love the truth are my followers."

[38] "What is truth?" Pilate exclaimed. Then he went out again to the people and told them, "He is not guilty of any crime. [39] But you have a custom of asking me to release someone from prison each year at Passover. So if you want me to, I'll release the 'King of the Jews.'"

[40] But they screamed back. "No! Not this man, but Barabbas!" Barabbas was a robber.

19 Pilate Judges Jesus

Then Pilate laid open Jesus' back with a leaded whip, [2] and the soldiers made a crown of thorns and placed it on his head and robed him in royal purple. [3] "Hail, 'King of the Jews!'" they mocked, and struck him with their fists.

[4] Pilate went outside again and said to the Jews, "I am going to bring him out to you now, but understand clearly that I find him *not guilty*."

[5] Then Jesus came out wearing the crown of thorns and the purple robe. And Pilate said, "Behold the man!"

[6] At sight of him the chief priests and Jewish officials began yelling, "Crucify! Crucify!"

"*You* crucify him," Pilate said. "I find him *not guilty*."

[7] They replied, "By our laws he ought to die because he called himself the Son of God."

[8] When Pilate heard this, he was more frightened than ever. [9] He took Jesus back into the palace again and asked him, "Where are you from?" but Jesus gave no answer.

[10] "You won't talk to me?" Pilate demanded. "Don't you realize that I have the power to release you or to crucify you?"

[11] Then Jesus said, "You would have no power at all over me unless it were given to you from above. So those who brought me to you have the greater sin."

[12] Then Pilate tried to release him, but the Jewish leaders told him, "If you release this man, you are no friend of Caesar's. Anyone who declares himself a king is a rebel against Caesar."

[13] At these words Pilate brought Jesus out to them again and sat down at the judgment bench on the stone-paved platform. [14] It was now about noon of the day before Passover.

And Pilate said to the Jews, "Here is your king!"

[15] "Away with him," they yelled. "Away with him—crucify him!"

"What? Crucify your king?" Pilate asked.

"We have no king but Caesar," the chief priests shouted back.

Family Devotions

☐ *Devotion 289*
Trusting God for Guidance

Read John 20:24-29

Trusting God for Guidance Memory Verse

I will instruct you (says the Lord) and guide you along the best pathway for your life; I will advise you and watch your progress.
Psalm 32:8

I wish this feeling would never end, Julie thought as she sat near the campfire with her youth group friends. At this moment, as she and her Christian friends sang God's praises, she felt closer to him than ever before. But the feeling would end. She'd been to retreats before, and she knew that on Monday morning she wouldn't feel nearly as close to God. *If I don't feel close to God on Monday, maybe this feeling of God's presence is just in my head. Maybe he isn't real at all.* Julie tried to forget these ideas, but she couldn't.

When Julie arrived home the next day, Mom was busy with dinner preparations. "My cousin Pauline is coming for dinner," Mom explained as she scurried about.

"I didn't know you had a cousin named Pauline," said Julie as she began to help.

Julie found Pauline delightful. She entertained them all during dinner with funny stories about Mom's childhood. "I'm glad I got to know you," Julie told her. "And just think, a few hours ago I didn't know you existed."

"Shame on your mom for not mentioning me," Pauline said with a wink. "But I've been here all along."

The words stuck with Julie. Cousin Pauline's existence wasn't dependent on Julie knowing about her or "feeling her presence." It was the same with God. *I've been a doubting Thomas,* Julie told herself. Thomas doubted Jesus was really alive until he saw him. Julie had doubted God was real because she didn't always feel his presence.

"Tell us about the retreat," suggested Mom.

"It was great," Julie said. "Really great."

How About You?

Have you ever felt God to be especially close, only to be doubtful of his presence when you no longer felt that way? It's nice to feel God's presence, but it's important to know he is there whether you have the "feeling" or not. Don't rely on feelings. Rely on God's Word. He promises to guide you all the time. K. R. A.

• For the next devotional, turn to page 1033. • To start the next topic, turn to page 29. • For notes on *Trusting God for Guidance*, see pages 522, 553, 614, 676, and 1056.

¹⁶Then Pilate gave Jesus to them to be crucified.

¹⁷So they had him at last, and he was taken out of the city, carrying his cross to the place known as "The Skull," in Hebrew, "Golgotha." ¹⁸There they crucified him and two others with him, one on either side, with Jesus between them. ¹⁹And Pilate posted a sign over him reading, "Jesus of Nazareth, the King of the Jews." ²⁰The place where Jesus was crucified was near the city; and the signboard was written in Hebrew, Latin, and Greek, so that many people read it.

²¹Then the chief priests said to Pilate, "Change it from 'The King of the Jews' to '*He said,* I am King of the Jews.'"

²²Pilate replied, "What I have written, I have written. It stays exactly as it is."

²³,²⁴When the soldiers had crucified Jesus, they put his garments into four piles, one for each of them. But they said, "Let's not tear up his robe," for it was seamless. "Let's throw dice to see who gets it." This fulfilled the Scripture that says,

> "They divided my clothes among them and
> cast lots for my robe."

²⁵So that is what they did.

Standing near the cross were Jesus' mother, Mary, his aunt, the wife of Cleopas, and Mary Magdalene. ²⁶When Jesus saw his mother standing there beside me, his close friend, he said to her, "He is your son."

²⁷And to me he said, "She is your mother!" And from then on I took her into my home.

²⁸Jesus knew that everything was now finished, and to fulfill the Scriptures said, "I'm thirsty." ²⁹A jar of sour wine was sitting there, so a sponge was soaked in it and put on a hyssop branch and held up to his lips.

³⁰When Jesus had tasted it, he said, "It is finished," and bowed his head and dismissed his spirit.

³¹The Jewish leaders didn't want the victims hanging there the next day, which was the Sabbath (and a very special Sabbath at that, for it was the Passover), so they asked Pilate to order the legs of the men broken to hasten death; then their bodies could be taken down. ³²So the soldiers came and broke the legs of the two men crucified with Jesus; ³³but when they came to him, they saw that he was dead already, so they didn't break his. ³⁴However, one of the soldiers pierced his side with a spear, and blood and water flowed out. ³⁵I saw all this myself and have given an accurate report so that you also can believe. ³⁶,³⁷The soldiers did this in fulfillment of the Scripture that says, "Not one of his bones shall be broken," and, "They shall look on him whom they pierced."

³⁸Afterwards Joseph of Arimathea, who had been a secret disciple of Jesus for fear of the Jewish leaders, boldly asked Pilate for permission to take Jesus' body down; and Pilate told him to go ahead. So he came and took it away. ³⁹Nicodemus, the man who had come to Jesus at night, came too, bringing a hundred pounds of embalming ointment made from myrrh and aloes. ⁴⁰Together they wrapped Jesus' body in a long linen cloth saturated with the spices, as is the Jewish custom of burial. ⁴¹The place of crucifixion was near a grove of trees, where there was a new tomb, never used before. ⁴²And so, because of the need for haste before the Sabbath, and because the tomb was close at hand, they laid him there.

20 Peter and John at Jesus' Tomb

Early Sunday morning, while it was still dark, Mary Magdalene came to the tomb and found that the stone was rolled aside from the entrance.

²She ran and found Simon Peter and me and said, "They have taken the Lord's body out of the tomb, and I don't know where they have put him!"

³,⁴We ran to the tomb to see; I outran Peter and got there first, ⁵and stooped and looked in and saw the linen cloth lying there, but I didn't go in. ⁶Then Simon Peter arrived and went on inside. He also noticed the cloth lying there, ⁷while the swath that had covered Jesus' head was rolled up in a bundle and was lying at the side. ⁸Then I went in too, and saw, and believed [that he had risen]—⁹for until then we hadn't realized that the Scriptures said he would come to life again!

¹⁰We went on home, ¹¹and by that time Mary had returned to the tomb and was standing outside crying. And as she wept, she stooped and looked in ¹²and saw two white-robed angels sitting at the head and foot of the place where the body of Jesus had been lying.

¹³"Why are you crying?" the angels asked her.

"Because they have taken away my Lord," she replied, "and I don't know where they have put him."

¹⁴She glanced over her shoulder and saw someone standing behind her. It was Jesus, but she didn't recognize him!

¹⁵"Why are you crying?" he asked her. "Whom are you looking for?"

She thought he was the gardener. "Sir," she said, "if you have taken him away, tell me where you have put him, and I will go and get him."

¹⁶"Mary!" Jesus said. She turned toward him.

"Master!" she exclaimed.

¹⁷"Don't touch me," he cautioned, "for I haven't yet ascended to the Father. But go find my brothers

Family Devotions

☐ DEVOTION 290
TRUSTING GOD'S PLAN

Read John 21:17-22

"It's not fair!" Troy whined. "It's just not fair! I go to children's choir practice every Saturday morning. I've never missed once. And I've been practicing the solo part for weeks, but now Mr. Widmark says that Joel gets to do the solo when we sing next Sunday." The nine-year-old boy was fighting tears as he rode home in the car with Mom.

"Now wait a minute, Troy," said Mom. "Did Mr. Widmark ever say that you were going to sing the solo?"

"Well, no," admitted Troy, "but I'm the most faithful boy in the choir! I just took it for granted that I'd get to sing it. I've got the best voice in—"

"Stop it, Troy," Mom reprimanded. "You do have a nice voice, but evidently Joel does, too. Maybe Mr. Widmark is hoping that Joel's parents will come to church if he has the solo. Or maybe Joel has the better voice. Whatever the reason, it shouldn't matter to you who sings the solo part."

"But Mom, doesn't being faithful for all these weeks of practice count for anything?" asked Troy. "Joel has only been coming for a few weeks."

Mom sighed. "I can understand how you feel," she said gently, "but I think you need to remember the reason for being in the choir. You remind me a little of the apostle Peter at the end of the book of John. Peter had just been told by Jesus how he would die, and Peter immediately wondered how John would have to die. Jesus said, 'What is that to you? *You* follow me!'"

Now Troy was quiet for a long time. Finally he said, "So Jesus just wants me to follow him and not worry about what Joel does. I hope Joel does a good job."

Trusting God's Plan Memory Verses

This plan of mine is not what you would work out, neither are my thoughts the same as yours! For just as the heavens are higher than the earth, so are my ways higher than yours, and my thoughts than yours.
Isaiah 55:8-9

How About You?

Have you ever been upset because, as you tried to serve the Lord, it seemed someone else got more glory than you or had an easier time of it? Peter had the same problem. He wondered if John was going to get to live a normal life, when he, Peter, was going to have to die for Jesus. You should not worry about what other people get to do. Your job is to follow Jesus, in whatever plan he has for you. R. P.

• For the next devotional, turn to page 1037. • For notes on TRUSTING GOD'S PLAN, see pages 252, 296, 731, and 870.

and tell them that I ascend to my Father and your Father, my God and your God."

[18]Mary Magdalene found the disciples and told them, "I have seen the Lord!" Then she gave them his message.

[19]That evening the disciples were meeting behind locked doors, in fear of the Jewish leaders, when suddenly Jesus was standing there among them! After greeting them, [20]he showed them his hands and side. And how wonderful was their joy as they saw their Lord!

[21]He spoke to them again and said, "As the Father has sent me, even so I am sending you." [22]Then he breathed on them and told them, "Receive the Holy Spirit. [23]If you forgive anyone's sins, they are forgiven. If you refuse to forgive them, they are unforgiven."

[24]One of the disciples, Thomas, "The Twin," was not there at the time with the others. [25]When they kept telling him, "We have seen the Lord," he replied, "I won't believe it unless I see the nail wounds in his hands—and put my fingers into them—and place my hand into his side."

[26]Eight days later the disciples were together again, and this time Thomas was with them. The doors were locked; but suddenly, as before, Jesus was standing among them and greeting them.

[27]Then he said to Thomas, "Put your finger into my hands. Put your hand into my side. Don't be faithless any longer. Believe!"

[28]"My Lord and my God!" Thomas said.

[29]Then Jesus told him, "You believe because you have seen me. But blessed are those who haven't seen me and believe anyway."

[30,31]Jesus' disciples saw him do many other miracles besides the ones told about in this book, but these are recorded so that you will believe that he is the Messiah, the Son of God, and that believing in him you will have life.

21 Jesus Helps Catch Fish

Later Jesus appeared again to the disciples beside the Lake of Galilee. This is how it happened:

[2]A group of us were there—Simon Peter, Thomas, "The Twin," Nathanael from Cana in Galilee, my brother James and I and two other disciples.

[3]Simon Peter said, "I'm going fishing."

"We'll come too," we all said. We did, but caught nothing all night. [4]At dawn we saw a man standing on the beach but couldn't see who he was.

[5]He called, "Any fish, boys?"

"No," we replied.

[6]Then he said, "Throw out your net on the right-hand side of the boat, and you'll get plenty of them!" So we did, and couldn't draw in the net because of the weight of the fish, there were so many!

[7]Then I said to Peter, "It is the Lord!" At that, Simon Peter put on his tunic (for he was stripped to the waist) and jumped into the water [and swam ashore]. [8]The rest of us stayed in the boat and pulled the loaded net to the beach, about 300 feet away. [9]When we got there, we saw that a fire was kindled and fish were frying over it, and there was bread.

[10]"Bring some of the fish you've just caught," Jesus said. [11]So Simon Peter went out and dragged the net ashore. By his count there were 153 large fish; and yet the net hadn't torn.

[12]"Now come and have some breakfast!" Jesus said; and none of us dared ask him if he really was the Lord, for we were quite sure of it. [13]Then Jesus went around serving us the bread and fish.

[14]This was the third time Jesus had appeared to us since his return from the dead.

[15]After breakfast Jesus said to Simon Peter, "Simon, son of John, do you love me more than these others?"

"Yes," Peter replied, "you know I am your friend."

"Then feed my lambs," Jesus told him.

[16]Jesus repeated the question: "Simon, son of John, do you *really* love me?"

"Yes, Lord," Peter said, "you know I am your friend."

"Then take care of my sheep," Jesus said.

[17]Once more he asked him, "Simon, son of John, are you even my friend?"

Peter was grieved at the way Jesus asked the question this third time. "Lord, you know my heart; you know I am," he said.

Jesus said, "Then feed my little sheep. [18]When you were young, you were able to do as you liked and go wherever you wanted to; but when you are old, you will stretch out your hands and others will direct you and take you where you don't want to go." [19]Jesus said this to let him know what kind of death he would die to glorify God. Then Jesus told him, "Follow me."

[20]Peter turned around and saw the disciple Jesus loved following, the one who had leaned around at supper that time to ask Jesus, "Master, which of us will betray you?" [21]Peter asked Jesus, "What about him, Lord? What sort of death will he die?"

[22]Jesus replied, "If I want him to live until I return, what is that to you? *You* follow me."

[23]So the rumor spread among the brotherhood that that disciple wouldn't die! But that isn't what Jesus said at all! He only said, "If I want him to live until I come, what is that to you?"

[24]*I am that disciple!* I saw these events and have recorded them here. And we all know that my account of these things is accurate.

[25]And I suppose that if all the other events in Jesus' life were written, the whole world could hardly contain the books!

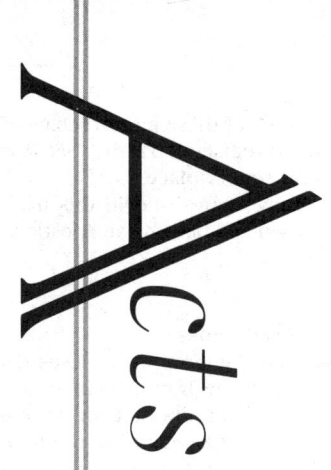

Acts

WHO HELPS you understand the Bible and grow in your relationship with Jesus? Think about how your life would be different if these people didn't teach and help you.

The book of Acts tells about the Christian teachers. It tells about the first Christian churches and congregations, the first pastors and elders, the first deacons and missions committees. These people focused their time, money, and energy on worshiping God, helping people in need, and telling others what Jesus had done for them.

The early Christians were excited to tell others about Jesus. Some people, like Paul and Barnabas, traveled far away to bring the gospel. Those who stayed home, like Peter and James, told people nearby.

We have the chance to tell others about Jesus, too. As you read Acts, think of the people who teach you about Jesus. And think of people *you* can tell about him.

Jesus Goes Up to Heaven

Dear friend who loves God:

In my first letter I told you about Jesus' life and teachings and how he returned to heaven after giving his chosen apostles further instructions from the Holy Spirit. ³During the forty days after his crucifixion he appeared to the apostles from time to time, actually alive, and proved to them in many ways that it was really he himself they were seeing. And on these occasions he talked to them about the Kingdom of God.

⁴In one of these meetings he told them not to leave Jerusalem until the Holy Spirit came upon them in fulfillment of the Father's promise, a matter he had previously discussed with them.

⁵"John baptized you with water," he reminded them, "but you shall be baptized with the Holy Spirit in just a few days."

⁶And another time when he appeared to them, they asked him, "Lord, are you going to free Israel [from Rome] now and restore us as an independent nation?"

⁷"The Father sets those dates," he replied, "and they are not for you to know. ⁸But when the Holy Spirit has come upon you, you will receive power to testify about me with great effect, to the people in Jerusalem, throughout Judea, in Samaria, and to the ends of the earth, about my death and resurrection."

⁹It was not long afterwards that he rose into the sky and disappeared into a cloud, leaving them staring after him. ¹⁰As they were straining their eyes for another glimpse, suddenly two white-robed men were standing there among them, ¹¹and said, "Men of Galilee, why are you standing here staring at the sky? Jesus has gone away to heaven, and some day, just as he went, he will return!"

¹²They were at the Mount of Olives when this happened, so now they walked the half mile back to Jerusalem ¹³and held a prayer meeting in an upstairs room of the house where they were staying.

¹⁴Here is the list of those who were present at the meeting: Peter, John, James, Andrew, Philip, Thomas, Bartholomew, Matthew, James (son of Alphaeus), Simon (also called "The Zealot"), Judas (son of James), and the brothers of Jesus. Several women, including Jesus' mother, were also there.

¹⁵This prayer meeting went on for several days. During this time, on a day when about 120 people were present, Peter stood up and addressed them as follows:

¹⁶"Brothers, it was necessary for the Scriptures to come true concerning Judas, who betrayed Jesus by guiding the mob to him, for this was predicted long ago by the Holy Spirit, speaking through King David. ¹⁷Judas was one of us, chosen to be an apostle just as we were. ¹⁸He bought a field with the money he received for his treachery and falling headlong there, he burst open, spilling out his bowels. ¹⁹The news of his death spread rapidly among all the people of Jerusalem, and they named the place 'The Field of Blood.' ²⁰King David's prediction of this appears in the Book of Psalms, where he says, 'Let his home become desolate with no one living in it.' And again, 'Let his work be given to someone else to do.'

²¹,²²"So now we must choose someone else to take Judas' place and to join us as witnesses of Jesus' resurrection. Let us select someone who has been with us constantly from our first association with the Lord—from the time he was baptized by John until the day he was taken from us into heaven."

²³The assembly nominated two men: Joseph Justus (also called Barsabbas) and Matthias. ²⁴,²⁵Then they all prayed for the right man to be chosen. "O Lord," they said, "you know every heart; show us which of these men you have chosen as an apostle to replace Judas the traitor, who has gone on to his proper place."

²⁶Then they drew straws, and in this manner Matthias was chosen and became an apostle with the other eleven.

2 The Holy Spirit Comes

Seven weeks had gone by since Jesus' death and resurrection, and the Day of Pentecost had now arrived. As the believers met together that day, ²suddenly there was a sound like the roaring of a mighty windstorm in the skies above them and it filled the house where they were meeting. ³Then, what looked like flames or tongues of fire appeared and settled on their heads. ⁴And everyone present was filled with the Holy Spirit and began speaking in languages they didn't know, for the Holy Spirit gave them this ability.

⁵Many godly Jews were in Jerusalem that day for the religious celebrations, having arrived from many nations. ⁶And when they heard the roaring in the sky above the house, crowds came running to see what it was all about, and were stunned to hear their own languages being spoken by the disciples.

⁷"How can this be?" they exclaimed. "For these men are all from Galilee, ⁸and yet we hear them speaking all the native languages of the lands where we were born! ⁹Here we are—Parthians, Medes, Elamites, men from Mesopotamia, Judea, Cappadocia, Pontus, Asia Minor, ¹⁰Phrygia, Pamphylia, Egypt, the Cyrene language areas of Libya, visitors from Rome—both Jews and Jewish converts—¹¹Cretans, and Arabians. And we all hear these men telling in our own languages about the mighty miracles of God!"

¹²They stood there amazed and perplexed. "What can this mean?" they asked each other.

¹³But others in the crowd were mocking. "They're drunk, that's all!" they said.

¹⁴Then Peter stepped forward with the eleven apostles and shouted to the crowd, "Listen, all of you, visitors and residents of Jerusalem alike! ¹⁵Some of you are saying these men are drunk! It isn't true! It's much too early for that! People don't get drunk by 9:00 A.M.! ¹⁶No! What you see this morning was predicted centuries ago by the prophet Joel—¹⁷'In the last days,' God said, 'I will pour out my Holy Spirit upon all mankind, and your sons and daughters shall prophesy, and your young men shall see visions, and your old men dream dreams. ¹⁸Yes, the Holy Spirit shall come upon all my servants, men and women alike, and they shall prophesy. ¹⁹And I will cause strange demonstrations in the heavens and on the earth—blood and fire and clouds of smoke; ²⁰the

FAMILY DEVOTIONS

☐ *DEVOTION 291*
SHARING YOUR FAITH

Read Acts 2:41-47

Sharing Your Faith Memory Verse

And I assure you of this: I, the Messiah, will publicly honor you in the presence of God's angels if you publicly acknowledge me here on earth as your Friend.
Luke 12:8

Phil Evans wasn't really listening to the Scripture his father was reading. He had something else on his mind—Jim Kardon. Phil had invited Jim to church and Sunday school three different times, but Jim wanted no part of it. Phil was ready to give up. After they finished their devotional time, he spoke of his feelings. "I'm never going to invite Jim to church again," he said bluntly.

"Why not?" Dad wanted to know.

"Because he always turns me down," Phil said emphatically.

Phil's father was quiet for a time. "Did you notice what tonight's Scripture lesson was about?" he asked finally. Phil admitted that his thoughts were elsewhere, so Dad added, "It was about the growth of the early church. The early Christians were steadfast, and God added souls to the church. We need to be steadfast, too. By the way, how long has it been since you accepted Jesus as your Savior?"

Phil looked up at his father in surprise. "About a year," he replied. "Why?"

"And how long before you made your decision did you hear the gospel from church and Sunday school—and from your mother and me?" asked Dad.

Phil shrugged. "Seems like I heard it over and over all my life." He stopped suddenly. He was beginning to see what his father was trying to tell him. If Dad and Mom or his pastor and Sunday school teachers had only talked with him three times about the Lord and then quit, maybe he wouldn't be a Christian now. Suddenly he knew what it meant to be steadfast. It meant to keep on even when things got hard or people didn't respond right away.

"I guess I'm giving up too quickly," he said finally. "I'll ask Jim again this week."

How About You?
Do you know someone who needs Jesus as Savior? Have you talked with him about it? How many times? How often? Learn to be steadfast in witnessing and praying for your friends, then leave the results to the Lord. *R.J.*

• For the next devotional, turn to page 1041.   • For the next devotional on *SHARING YOUR FAITH,* turn to page 1041.
• For notes on *SHARING YOUR FAITH,* see pages 462, 776, 1015, and 1074.

sun shall turn black and the moon blood-red before that awesome Day of the Lord arrives. ²¹But anyone who asks for mercy from the Lord shall have it and shall be saved.'

²²"O men of Israel, listen! God publicly endorsed Jesus of Nazareth by doing tremendous miracles through him, as you well know. ²³But God, following his prearranged plan, let you use the Roman government to nail him to the cross and murder him. ²⁴Then God released him from the horrors of death and brought him back to life again, for death could not keep this man within its grip.

²⁵"King David quoted Jesus as saying:

'I know the Lord is always with me. He is helping me. God's mighty power supports me.
²⁶'No wonder my heart is filled with joy and my tongue shouts his praises! For I know all will be well with me in death—
²⁷'You will not leave my soul in hell or let the body of your Holy Son decay.
²⁸'You will give me back my life and give me wonderful joy in your presence.'

²⁹"Dear brothers, think! David wasn't referring to himself when he spoke these words I have quoted, for he died and was buried, and his tomb is still here among us. ³⁰But he was a prophet, and knew God had promised with an unbreakable oath that one of David's own descendants would [be the Messiah and] sit on David's throne. ³¹David was looking far into the future and predicting the Messiah's resurrection, and saying that the Messiah's soul would not be left in hell and his body would not decay. ³²He was speaking of Jesus, and we all are witnesses that Jesus rose from the dead.

³³"And now he sits on the throne of highest honor in heaven, next to God. And just as promised, the Father gave him the authority to send the Holy Spirit—with the results you are seeing and hearing today.

³⁴"[No, David was not speaking of himself in these words of his I have quoted], for he never ascended into the skies. Moreover, he further stated, 'God spoke to my Lord, the Messiah, and said to him, Sit here in honor beside me ³⁵until I bring your enemies into complete subjection.'

³⁶"Therefore I clearly state to everyone in Israel that God has made this Jesus you crucified to be the Lord, the Messiah!"

³⁷These words of Peter's moved them deeply, and they said to him and to the other apostles, "Brothers, what should we do?"

³⁸And Peter replied, "Each one of you must turn from sin, return to God, and be baptized in the name of Jesus Christ for the forgiveness of your sins; then you also shall receive this gift, the Holy Spirit. ³⁹For Christ promised him to each one of you who has been called by the Lord our God, and to your children and even to those in distant lands!"

⁴⁰Then Peter preached a long sermon, telling about Jesus and strongly urging all his listeners to save themselves from the evils of their nation. ⁴¹And those who believed Peter were baptized—about three thousand in all! ⁴²They joined with the other believers in regular attendance at the apostles' teaching sessions and at the Communion services and prayer meetings.

⁴³A deep sense of awe was on them all, and the apostles did many miracles.

⁴⁴And all the believers met together constantly and shared everything with each other, ⁴⁵selling their possessions and dividing with those in need. ⁴⁶They worshiped together regularly at the Temple each day, met in small groups in homes for Communion, and shared their meals with great joy and thankfulness, ⁴⁷praising God. The whole city was favorable to them, and each day God added to them all who were being saved.

3 Peter and John Heal a Man

Peter and John went to the Temple one afternoon to take part in the three o'clock daily prayer meeting. ²As they approached the Temple, they saw a man lame from birth carried along the street and laid beside the Temple gate—the one called The Beautiful Gate—as was his custom every day. ³As Peter and John were passing by, he asked them for some money.

⁴They looked at him intently, and then Peter said, "Look here!"

⁵The lame man looked at them eagerly, expecting a gift.

⁶But Peter said, "We don't have any money for you! But I'll give you something else! I command you in the name of Jesus Christ of Nazareth, *walk!* "

⁷,⁸Then Peter took the lame man by the hand and pulled him to his feet. And as he did, the man's feet and ankle-bones were healed and strengthened so that he came up with a leap, stood there a moment

---

SHOWING KINDNESS 2:44 Recognizing the other believers as brothers and sisters in the family of God, the Christians in Jerusalem shared all they had so that all could benefit from God's blessings. It is tempting—especially if we have material wealth—to cut ourselves off from one another, each taking care of his own, each providing for and enjoying his own little piece of the world. But as part of God's spiritual family, we have a responsibility to help one another in every way possible. God's family works best when its members work together.
To begin the series of devotionals on SHOWING KINDNESS, turn to page 81.

and began walking! Then, walking, leaping, and praising God, he went into the Temple with them.

⁹When the people inside saw him walking and heard him praising God, ¹⁰and realized he was the lame beggar they had seen so often at The Beautiful Gate, they were inexpressibly surprised! ¹¹They all rushed out to Solomon's Hall, where he was holding tightly to Peter and John! Everyone stood there awed by the wonderful thing that had happened.

¹²Peter saw his opportunity and addressed the crowd. "Men of Israel," he said, "what is so surprising about this? And why look at us as though we by our own power and godliness had made this man walk? ¹³For it is the God of Abraham, Isaac, Jacob and of all our ancestors who has brought glory to his servant Jesus by doing this. I refer to the Jesus whom you rejected before Pilate, despite Pilate's determination to release him. ¹⁴You didn't want him freed—this holy, righteous one. Instead you demanded the release of a murderer. ¹⁵And you killed the Author of Life; but God brought him back to life again. And John and I are witnesses of this fact, for after you killed him we saw him alive!

¹⁶"Jesus' name has healed this man—and you know how lame he was before. Faith in Jesus' name—faith given us from God—has caused this perfect healing.

¹⁷"Dear brothers, I realize that what you did to Jesus was done in ignorance; and the same can be said of your leaders. ¹⁸But God was fulfilling the prophecies that the Messiah must suffer all these things. ¹⁹Now change your mind and attitude to God and turn to him so he can cleanse away your sins and send you wonderful times of refreshment from the presence of the Lord ²⁰and send Jesus your Messiah back to you again. ²¹,²²For he must remain in heaven until the final recovery of all things from sin, as prophesied from ancient times. Moses, for instance, said long ago, 'The Lord God will raise up a Prophet among you, who will resemble me! Listen carefully to everything he tells you. ²³Anyone who will not listen to him shall be utterly destroyed.'

²⁴"Samuel and every prophet since have all spoken about what is going on today. ²⁵You are the children of those prophets; and you are included in God's promise to your ancestors to bless the entire world through the Jewish race—that is the promise God gave to Abraham. ²⁶And as soon as God had brought his servant to life again, he sent him first of all to you men of Israel, to bless you by turning you back from your sins."

4 Peter and John's Courage

While they were talking to the people, the chief priests, the captain of the Temple police, and some of the Sadducees came over to them, ²very disturbed that Peter and John were claiming that Jesus had risen from the dead. ³They arrested them and since it was already evening, jailed them overnight. ⁴But many of the people who heard their message believed it, so that the number of believers now reached a new high of about five thousand men!

⁵The next day it happened that the Council of all the Jewish leaders was in session in Jerusalem— ⁶Annas the High Priest was there, and Caiaphas, John, Alexander, and others of the High Priest's relatives. ⁷So the two disciples were brought in before them.

"By what power, or by whose authority have you done this?" the Council demanded.

⁸Then Peter, filled with the Holy Spirit, said to them, "Honorable leaders and elders of our nation, ⁹if you mean the good deed done to the cripple, and how he was healed, ¹⁰let me clearly state to you and to all the people of Israel that it was done in the name and power of Jesus from Nazareth, the Messiah, the man you crucified—but God raised back to life again. It is by his authority that this man stands here healed! ¹¹For Jesus the Messiah is (the one referred to in the Scriptures when they speak of) a 'stone discarded by the builders which became the capstone of the arch.' ¹²There is salvation in no one else! Under all heaven there is no other name for men to call upon to save them."

¹³When the Council saw the boldness of Peter and John and could see that they were obviously uneducated non-professionals, they were amazed and realized what being with Jesus had done for them! ¹⁴And the Council could hardly discredit the healing when the man they had healed was standing right there beside them! ¹⁵So they sent them out of the Council chamber and conferred among themselves.

¹⁶"What shall we do with these men?" they asked each other. "We can't deny that they have done a tremendous miracle, and everybody in Jerusalem knows about it. ¹⁷But perhaps we can stop them from spreading their propaganda. We'll tell them that if they do it again we'll really throw the book at them." ¹⁸So they called them back in, and told them never again to speak about Jesus.

¹⁹But Peter and John replied, "You decide whether God wants us to obey you instead of him! ²⁰We cannot stop telling about the wonderful things we saw Jesus do and heard him say."

²¹The Council then threatened them further and finally let them go because they didn't know how to punish them without starting a riot. For everyone was praising God for this wonderful miracle— ²²the healing of a man who had been lame for forty years.

²³As soon as they were freed, Peter and John

found the other disciples and told them what the Council had said.

²⁴Then all the believers united in this prayer:

"O Lord, Creator of heaven and earth and of the sea and everything in them— ²⁵,²⁶you spoke long ago by the Holy Spirit through our ancestor King David, your servant, saying, 'Why do the heathen rage against the Lord, and the foolish nations plan their little plots against Almighty God? The kings of the earth unite to fight against him and against the anointed Son of God!'

²⁷"That is what is happening here in this city today! For Herod the king, and Pontius Pilate the governor, and all the Romans—as well as the people of Israel—are united against Jesus, your anointed Son, your holy servant. ²⁸They won't stop at anything that you in your wise power will let them do. ²⁹And now, O Lord, hear their threats, and grant to your servants great boldness in their preaching, ³⁰and send your healing power, and may miracles and wonders be done by the name of your holy servant Jesus."

³¹After this prayer, the building where they were meeting shook, and they were all filled with the Holy Spirit and boldly preached God's message.

³²All the believers were of one heart and mind, and no one felt that what he owned was his own; everyone was sharing. ³³And the apostles preached powerful sermons about the resurrection of the Lord Jesus, and there was warm fellowship among all the believers, ³⁴,³⁵and no poverty—for all who owned land or houses sold them and brought the money to the apostles to give to others in need.

³⁶For instance, there was Joseph (the one the apostles nicknamed "Barnabas, the encourager." He was of the tribe of Levi, from the island of Cyprus). ³⁷He was one of those who sold a field he owned and brought the money to the apostles for distribution to those in need.

5 Ananias and Sapphira Lie to God

But there was a man named Ananias (with his wife Sapphira) who sold some property ²and brought only part of the money, claiming it was the full price. (His wife had agreed to this deception.)

³But Peter said, "Ananias, Satan has filled your heart. When you claimed this was the full price, you were lying to the Holy Spirit. ⁴The property was yours to sell or not, as you wished. And after selling it, it was yours to decide how much to give. How could you do a thing like this? You weren't lying to us, but to God."

⁵As soon as Ananias heard these words, he fell to the floor, dead! Everyone was terrified, ⁶and the younger men covered him with a sheet and took him out and buried him.

⁷About three hours later his wife came in, not knowing what had happened. ⁸Peter asked her, "Did you people sell your land for such and such a price?"

"Yes," she replied, "we did."

⁹And Peter said, "How could you and your husband even think of doing a thing like this—conspiring together to test the Spirit of God's ability to know what is going on? Just outside that door are the young men who buried your husband, and they will carry you out too."

¹⁰Instantly she fell to the floor, dead, and the young men came in and, seeing that she was dead, carried her out and buried her beside her husband. ¹¹Terror gripped the entire church and all others who heard what had happened.

¹²Meanwhile, the apostles were meeting regularly at the Temple in the area known as Solomon's Hall, and they did many remarkable miracles among the people. ¹³The other believers didn't dare join them, though, but all had the highest regard for them. ¹⁴And more and more believers were added to the Lord, crowds both of men and women. ¹⁵Sick people were brought out into the streets on beds and mats so that at least Peter's shadow would fall across some of them as he went by! ¹⁶And crowds came in from the Jerusalem suburbs, bringing their sick folk and those possessed by demons; and every one of them was healed.

¹⁷The High Priest and his relatives and friends among the Sadducees reacted with violent jealousy ¹⁸and arrested the apostles, and put them in the public jail.

¹⁹But an angel of the Lord came at night, opened the gates of the jail and brought them out. Then he told them, ²⁰"Go over to the Temple and preach about this Life!"

²¹They arrived at the Temple about daybreak and immediately began preaching! Later that morning the High Priest and his courtiers arrived at the Temple, and, convening the Jewish Council and the entire Senate, they sent for the apostles to be brought for trial. ²²But when the police arrived at the jail, the men weren't there, so they returned to the Council and reported, ²³"The jail doors were locked, and the

---

PRAYING AT ALL TIMES 4:24-30 Notice how the believers prayed. First they praised God; then they told God their specific problem and asked for his help. They did not ask God to remove the problem, but to help them deal with it. This is a model for us to follow when we pray. We may ask God to remove our problems, and he may choose to do so, but we must recognize that often he will leave the problem in place and give us the grace to deal with it. **To begin the series of devotionals on PRAYING AT ALL TIMES, turn to page 45.**

FAMILY DEVOTIONS

☐ DEVOTION 292
SHARING YOUR FAITH

Read Acts 4:13-20; 5:12-32

The police car drew quickly to the curb where Todd was standing with some other children. "Do you kids know Jason Connor?" the officer asked.

"No, sir," answered one of the children.

"I've got to find him in a hurry," the policeman said.

When Todd later told his friend Kurt what had happened, Kurt frowned. "I think you should have told him where Jason was," said Kurt. "You know he's probably playing ball at the park."

"I know, but what if he's in trouble? I was afraid we might get in trouble too, if the policeman knew we were his friends," explained Todd.

"Well, some friend you are!" scolded Kurt. "Seems like you should stand by him, not act like you don't know him."

Later both boys were sorry to learn why the police were looking for Jason. His parents had been badly injured in a car accident and were hospitalized.

As Kurt and Todd stood in a checkout lane at the supermarket the next day, two men behind them began talking. "I hear your neighbors, the Connors, were in a really bad accident," said one.

"They sure were," replied the other. "They both were really battered. Be out of work at least a month. That will give them plenty of time to wonder where their God was when they got hit. They've been on my back for years about trusting in their God." He glanced at Kurt, who was staring at him. "Don't let anybody fool you about a loving, caring God, kid. There isn't any."

Kurt looked away and said nothing, but Todd looked up and smiled at the man. "Sir, I know the Connors," he said. "And God *is* their friend, and mine, too. He was with them when they got hurt, and he'll take good care of them. Right, Kurt?"

"Right, Todd," Kurt agreed nervously. With shame he thought of how he had scolded Todd for not admitting he knew Jason. Now by his silence, Kurt had almost denied his very best friend, the Lord Jesus.

Sharing Your Faith Memory Verse

And let us not get tired of doing what is right, for after a while we will reap a harvest of blessing if we don't get discouraged and give up.
Galatians 6:9

How About You?

Do you speak up for the Lord when you have a chance? Or, by your silence, do you deny that you even know him? Ask God to give you the courage to speak up for him. *A. G. L.*

• For the next devotional, turn to page 1043. • For the next devotional on *SHARING YOUR FAITH*, turn to page 1071.
• For notes on *SHARING YOUR FAITH*, see pages 462, 776, 1015, and 1074.

guards were standing outside, but when we opened the gates, no one was there!"

²⁴When the police captain and the chief priests heard this, they were frantic, wondering what would happen next and where all this would end! ²⁵Then someone arrived with the news that the men they had jailed were out in the Temple, preaching to the people!

²⁶,²⁷The police captain went with his officers and arrested them (without violence, for they were afraid the people would kill them if they roughed up the disciples) and brought them in before the Council.

²⁸"Didn't we tell you never again to preach about this Jesus?" the High Priest demanded. "And instead you have filled all Jerusalem with your teaching and intend to bring the blame for this man's death on us!"

²⁹But Peter and the apostles replied, "We must obey God rather than men. ³⁰The God of our ancestors brought Jesus back to life again after you had killed him by hanging him on a cross. ³¹Then, with mighty power, God exalted him to be a Prince and Savior, so that the people of Israel would have an opportunity for repentance, and for their sins to be forgiven. ³²And we are witnesses of these things and so is the Holy Spirit, who is given by God to all who obey him."

³³At this, the Council was furious and decided to kill them. ³⁴But one of their members, a Pharisee named Gamaliel (an expert on religious law and very popular with the people), stood up and requested that the apostles be sent outside the Council chamber while he talked.

³⁵Then he addressed his colleagues as follows:

"Men of Israel, take care what you are planning to do to these men! ³⁶Some time ago there was that fellow Theudas, who pretended to be someone great. About four hundred others joined him, but he was killed, and his followers were harmlessly dispersed.

³⁷"After him, at the time of the taxation, there was Judas of Galilee. He drew away some people as disciples, but he also died, and his followers scattered.

³⁸"And so my advice is, leave these men alone. If what they teach and do is merely on their own, it will soon be overthrown. ³⁹But if it is of God, you will not be able to stop them, lest you find yourselves fighting even against God."

⁴⁰The Council accepted his advice, called in the apostles, had them beaten, and then told them never again to speak in the name of Jesus, and finally let them go. ⁴¹They left the Council chamber rejoicing that God had counted them worthy to suffer dishonor for his name. ⁴²And every day, in the Temple and in their home Bible classes, they continued to teach and preach that Jesus is the Messiah.

6 Seven Men with Special Work

But with the believers multiplying rapidly, there were rumblings of discontent. Those who spoke only Greek complained that their widows were being discriminated against, that they were not being given as much food in the daily distribution as the widows who spoke Hebrew. ²So the Twelve called a meeting of all the believers.

"We should spend our time preaching, not administering a feeding program," they said. ³"Now look around among yourselves, dear brothers, and select seven men, wise and full of the Holy Spirit, who are well thought of by everyone; and we will put them in charge of this business. ⁴Then we can spend our time in prayer, preaching, and teaching."

⁵This sounded reasonable to the whole assembly, and they elected the following: Stephen (a man unusually full of faith and the Holy Spirit), Philip, Prochorus, Nicanor, Timon, Parmenas, Nicolaus of Antioch (a Gentile convert to the Jewish faith, who had become a Christian).

⁶These seven were presented to the apostles, who prayed for them and laid their hands on them in blessing.

⁷God's message was preached in ever-widening circles, and the number of disciples increased vastly in Jerusalem; and many of the Jewish priests were converted too.

⁸Stephen, the man so full of faith and the Holy Spirit's power, did spectacular miracles among the people.

⁹But one day some of the men from the Jewish cult of "The Freedmen" started an argument with him, and they were soon joined by Jews from Cyrene, Alexandria in Egypt, and the Turkish provinces of Cilicia, and Asia Minor. ¹⁰But none of them was able to stand against Stephen's wisdom and spirit.

¹¹So they brought in some men to lie about him, claiming they had heard Stephen curse Moses, and even God.

¹²This accusation roused the crowds to fury against Stephen, and the Jewish leaders arrested him and brought him before the Council. ¹³The lying witnesses testified again that Stephen was constantly speaking against the Temple and against the laws of Moses.

¹⁴They declared, "We have heard him say that this fellow Jesus of Nazareth will destroy the Temple and throw out all of Moses' laws." ¹⁵At this point everyone in the Council chamber saw Stephen's face become as radiant as an angel's!

Family Devotions

☐ *Devotion 293*
Standing for Righteousness

Read Acts 5:1-11

"I'll get it!" David jumped up as the teakettle started to whistle. He had been waiting for the water to boil so he could fix himself a cup of hot chocolate.

"Careful!" called Mom. "That handle gets very, very hot. Better use a pot holder."

But David wasn't paying attention. He put a scoop of hot chocolate mix into a cup and then reached out to pick up the teakettle. "Ouch!" He dropped the kettle almost as soon as he touched it. "Oh, that hurts!" He ran cold water over his hand as Mom came to help.

"I tried to warn you, because I've gotten burned on that teakettle, too," said Mom as she checked his hand. "Too bad you couldn't learn from my experience."

At school the next day, David's teacher called him up to her desk and showed him a baseball mitt. "You said you lost your mitt," said Miss Wiley, "and this one was found out on the playground. Is it yours?"

The mitt Miss Wiley held out was just like David's, only his was more worn. *Should I say it's mine, anyway?* he wondered. He felt guilty even thinking about it. Just the night before, he'd read about the lies Ananias and Sapphira had told. Still, well, he was sure God wouldn't strike him dead for telling a little lie. As David took the mitt, he felt a bit of pain in his burned palm. *I didn't learn from Mom's experience, but I am going to learn from Ananias and Sapphira's,* he thought. He handed the mitt back to Miss Wiley. "It's like mine," he said, "but mine isn't this new."

As David walked back to his seat, he felt happy inside. He didn't have a mitt, but he had a clear conscience, and that was even better.

Standing for Righteousness Memory Verse

For the eyes of the Lord search back and forth across the whole earth, looking for people whose hearts are perfect toward him, so that he can show his great power in helping them.
2 Chronicles 16:9

How About You?
Do you learn from the examples and experiences of others? Do you learn from things written in God's Word? The Bible gives many examples from which you should learn. Read about these in the Bible. Pay attention to what happened to them and profit from their experiences, then take a stand for righteousness. *H. M.*

• For the next devotional, turn to page 1047. • For the next devotional on *Standing for Righteousness*, turn to page 1149. • For notes on *Standing for Righteousness*, see pages 62, 298, 371, 678, and 948.

7

Stephen Is Executed

Then the High Priest asked him, "Are these accusations true?"

²This was Stephen's lengthy reply: "The glorious God appeared to our ancestor Abraham in Iraq before he moved to Syria, ³and told him to leave his native land, to say good-bye to his relatives and to start out for a country that God would direct him to. ⁴So he left the land of the Chaldeans and lived in Haran, in Syria, until his father died. Then God brought him here to the land of Israel, ⁵but gave him no property of his own, not one little tract of land.

"However, God promised that eventually the whole country would belong to him and his descendants—though as yet he had no children! ⁶But God also told him that these descendants of his would leave the land and live in a foreign country and there become slaves for 400 years. ⁷'But I will punish the nation that enslaves them,' God told him, 'and afterwards my people will return to this land of Israel and worship me here.'

⁸"God also gave Abraham the ceremony of circumcision at that time, as evidence of the covenant between God and the people of Abraham. And so Isaac, Abraham's son, was circumcised when he was eight days old. Isaac became the father of Jacob, and Jacob was the father of the twelve patriarchs of the Jewish nation. ⁹These men were very jealous of Joseph and sold him to be a slave in Egypt. But God was with him, ¹⁰and delivered him out of all of his anguish, and gave him favor before Pharaoh, king of Egypt. God also gave Joseph unusual wisdom so that Pharaoh appointed him governor over all Egypt, as well as putting him in charge of all the affairs of the palace.

¹¹"But a famine developed in Egypt and Canaan, and there was great misery for our ancestors. When their food was gone, ¹²Jacob heard that there was still grain in Egypt, so he sent his sons to buy some. ¹³The second time they went, Joseph revealed his identity to his brothers, and they were introduced to Pharaoh. ¹⁴Then Joseph sent for his father Jacob and all his brothers' families to come to Egypt, seventy-five persons in all. ¹⁵So Jacob came to Egypt, where he died, and all his sons. ¹⁶All of them were taken to Shechem and buried in the tomb Abraham bought from the sons of Hamor, Shechem's father.

¹⁷,¹⁸"As the time drew near when God would fulfill his promise to Abraham to free his descendants from slavery, the Jewish people greatly multiplied in Egypt; but then a king was crowned who had no respect for Joseph's memory. ¹⁹This king plotted against our race, forcing parents to abandon their children in the fields.

²⁰"About that time Moses was born—a child of divine beauty. His parents hid him at home for three months, ²¹and when at last they could no longer keep him hidden and had to abandon him, Pharaoh's daughter found him and adopted him as her own son, ²²and taught him all the wisdom of the Egyptians, and he became a mighty prince and orator.

²³"One day as he was nearing his fortieth birthday, it came into his mind to visit his brothers, the people of Israel. ²⁴During this visit he saw an Egyptian mistreating a man of Israel. So Moses killed the Egyptian. ²⁵Moses supposed his brothers would realize that God had sent him to help them, but they didn't.

²⁶"The next day he visited them again and saw two men of Israel fighting. He tried to be a peacemaker. 'Gentlemen,' he said, 'you are brothers and shouldn't be fighting like this! It is wrong!'

²⁷"But the man in the wrong told Moses to mind his own business. 'Who made *you* a ruler and judge over us?' he asked. ²⁸'Are you going to kill me as you killed that Egyptian yesterday?'

²⁹"At this, Moses fled the country and lived in the land of Midian, where his two sons were born.

³⁰"Forty years later, in the desert near Mount Sinai, an Angel appeared to him in a flame of fire in a bush. ³¹Moses saw it and wondered what it was, and as he ran to see, the voice of the Lord called out to him, ³²'I am the God of your ancestors—of Abraham, Isaac and Jacob.' Moses shook with terror and dared not look.

³³"And the Lord said to him, 'Take off your shoes, for you are standing on holy ground. ³⁴I have seen the anguish of my people in Egypt and have heard their cries. I have come down to deliver them. Come, I will send you to Egypt.' ³⁵And so God sent back the same man his people had previously rejected by demanding, 'Who made *you* a ruler and judge over us?' Moses was sent to be their ruler and savior. ³⁶And by means of many remarkable miracles he led them out of Egypt and through the Red Sea, and back and forth through the wilderness for forty years.

³⁷"Moses himself told the people of Israel, 'God will raise up a Prophet much like me from among your brothers.' ³⁸How true this proved to be, for in the wilderness, Moses was the go-between—the mediator between the people of Israel and the Angel who gave them the Law of God—the Living Word—on Mount Sinai.

³⁹"But our fathers rejected Moses and wanted to return to Egypt. ⁴⁰They told Aaron, 'Make idols for us, so that we will have gods to lead us back; for we don't know what has become of this Moses, who brought us out of Egypt.' ⁴¹So they made

a calf idol and sacrificed to it, and rejoiced in this thing they had made.

⁴²"Then God turned away from them and gave them up, and let them serve the sun, moon, and stars as their gods! In the book of Amos' prophecies the Lord God asks, 'Was it to me you were sacrificing during those forty years in the desert, Israel? ⁴³No, your real interest was in your heathen gods—Sakkuth, and the star god Kaiway, and in all the images you made. So I will send you into captivity far away beyond Babylon.'

⁴⁴"Our ancestors carried along with them a portable Temple, or Tabernacle, through the wilderness. In it they kept the stone tablets with the Ten Commandments written on them. This building was constructed in exact accordance with the plan shown to Moses by the Angel. ⁴⁵Years later, when Joshua led the battles against the Gentile nations, this Tabernacle was taken with them into their new territory, and used until the time of King David.

⁴⁶"God blessed David greatly, and David asked for the privilege of building a permanent Temple for the God of Jacob. ⁴⁷But it was Solomon who actually built it. ⁴⁸,⁴⁹However, God doesn't live in temples made by human hands. 'The heaven is my throne,' says the Lord through his prophets, 'and earth is my footstool. What kind of home could you build?' asks the Lord. 'Would I stay in it? ⁵⁰Didn't I make both heaven and earth?'

⁵¹"You stiff-necked heathen! Must you forever resist the Holy Spirit? But your fathers did, and so do you! ⁵²Name one prophet your ancestors didn't persecute! They even killed the ones who predicted the coming of the Righteous One—the Messiah whom you betrayed and murdered. ⁵³Yes, and you deliberately destroyed God's laws, though you received them from the hands of angels."

⁵⁴The Jewish leaders were stung to fury by Stephen's accusation and ground their teeth in rage. ⁵⁵But Stephen, full of the Holy Spirit, gazed steadily upward into heaven and saw the glory of God and Jesus standing at God's right hand. ⁵⁶And he told them, "Look, I see the heavens opened and Jesus the Messiah standing beside God, at his right hand!"

⁵⁷Then they mobbed him, putting their hands over their ears, and drowning out his voice with their shouts, ⁵⁸and dragged him out of the city to stone him. The official witnesses—the executioners—took off their coats and laid them at the feet of a young man named Paul.

⁵⁹And as the murderous stones came hurtling at him, Stephen prayed, "Lord Jesus, receive my spirit." ⁶⁰And he fell to his knees, shouting, "Lord, don't charge them with this sin!" and with that, he died.

8 Philip and an Ethiopian

Paul was in complete agreement with the killing of Stephen.

And a great wave of persecution of the believers began that day, sweeping over the church in Jerusalem, and everyone except the apostles fled into Judea and Samaria. ²(But some godly Jews came and with great sorrow buried Stephen.) ³Paul was like a wild man, going everywhere to devastate the believers, even entering private homes and dragging out men and women alike and jailing them.

⁴But the believers who had fled Jerusalem went everywhere preaching the Good News about Jesus! ⁵Philip, for instance, went to the city of Samaria and told the people there about Christ. ⁶Crowds listened intently to what he had to say because of the miracles he did. ⁷Many evil spirits were cast out, screaming as they left their victims, and many who were paralyzed or lame were healed, ⁸so there was much joy in that city!

⁹⁻¹¹A man named Simon had formerly been a sorcerer there for many years; he was a very influential, proud man because of the amazing things he could do—in fact, the Samaritan people often spoke of him as the Messiah. ¹²But now they believed Philip's message that Jesus was the Messiah, and his words concerning the Kingdom of God; and many men and women were baptized. ¹³Then Simon himself believed and was baptized and began following Philip wherever he went, and was amazed by the miracles he did.

¹⁴When the apostles back in Jerusalem heard that the people of Samaria had accepted God's message, they sent down Peter and John. ¹⁵As soon as they arrived, they began praying for these new Christians to receive the Holy Spirit, ¹⁶for as yet he had not come upon any of them. For they had only been baptized in the name of the Lord Jesus. ¹⁷Then Peter and John laid their hands upon these believers, and they received the Holy Spirit.

¹⁸When Simon saw this—that the Holy Spirit was given when the apostles placed their hands upon people's heads—he offered money to buy this power.

¹⁹"Let me have this power too," he exclaimed, "so that when I lay my hands on people, they will receive the Holy Spirit!"

²⁰But Peter replied, "Your money perish with you for thinking God's gift can be bought! ²¹You can have no part in this, for your heart is not right before God. ²²Turn from this great wickedness and pray. Perhaps God will yet forgive your evil thoughts— ²³for I can see that there is jealousy and sin in your heart."

²⁴"Pray for me," Simon exclaimed, "that these terrible things won't happen to me."

²⁵After testifying and preaching in Samaria, Peter and John returned to Jerusalem, stopping at several Samaritan villages along the way to preach the Good News to them too.

²⁶But as for Philip, an angel of the Lord said to him, "Go over to the road that runs from Jerusalem through the Gaza Desert, arriving around noon." ²⁷So he did, and who should be coming down the road but the Treasurer of Ethiopia, a eunuch of great authority under Candace the queen. He had gone to Jerusalem to worship ²⁸and was now returning in his chariot, reading aloud from the book of the prophet Isaiah.

²⁹The Holy Spirit said to Philip, "Go over and walk along beside the chariot."

³⁰Philip ran over and heard what he was reading and asked, "Do you understand it?"

³¹"Of course not!" the man replied. "How can I when there is no one to instruct me?" And he begged Philip to come up into the chariot and sit with him.

³²The passage of Scripture he had been reading from was this:

> "He was led as a sheep to the slaughter, and as a lamb is silent before the shearers, so he opened not his mouth; ³³in his humiliation, justice was denied him; and who can express the wickedness of the people of his generation? For his life is taken from the earth."

³⁴The eunuch asked Philip, "Was Isaiah talking about himself or someone else?"

³⁵So Philip began with this same Scripture and then used many others to tell him about Jesus.

³⁶As they rode along, they came to a small body of water, and the eunuch said, "Look! Water! Why can't I be baptized?"

³⁷"You can," Philip answered, "if you believe with all your heart."

And the eunuch replied, "I believe that Jesus Christ is the Son of God."

³⁸He stopped the chariot, and they went down into the water and Philip baptized him. ³⁹And when they came up out of the water, the Spirit of the Lord caught away Philip, and the eunuch never saw him again, but went on his way rejoicing. ⁴⁰Meanwhile, Philip found himself at Azotus! He preached the Good News there and in every city along the way, as he traveled to Caesarea.

 Paul Meets Jesus

But Paul, threatening with every breath and to destroy every Christian, went to the High Priest in Jerusalem. ²He requested a letter addressed to synagogues in Damascus, requiring their cooperation in the persecution of any believers he found there, both men and women, so that he could bring them in chains to Jerusalem.

³As he was nearing Damascus on this mission, suddenly a brilliant light from heaven spotted down upon him! ⁴He fell to the ground and heard a voice saying to him, "Paul! Paul! Why are you persecuting me?"

⁵"Who is speaking, sir?" Paul asked.

And the voice replied, "I am Jesus, the one you are persecuting! ⁶Now get up and go into the city and await my further instructions."

⁷The men with Paul stood speechless with surprise, for they heard the sound of someone's voice but saw no one! ⁸,⁹As Paul picked himself up off the ground, he found that he was blind. He had to be led into Damascus and was there three days, blind, going without food and water all that time.

¹⁰Now there was in Damascus a believer named Ananias. The Lord spoke to him in a vision, calling, "Ananias!"

"Yes, Lord!" he replied.

¹¹And the Lord said, "Go over to Straight Street and find the house of a man named Judas and ask there for Paul of Tarsus. He is praying to me right now, for ¹²I have shown him a vision of a man named Ananias coming in and laying his hands on him so that he can see again!"

¹³"But Lord," exclaimed Ananias, "I have heard about the terrible things this man has done to the believers in Jerusalem! ¹⁴And we hear that he has arrest warrants with him from the chief priests, authorizing him to arrest every believer in Damascus!"

¹⁵But the Lord said, "Go and do what I say. For Paul is my chosen instrument to take my message to the nations and before kings, as well as to the people of Israel. ¹⁶And I will show him how much he must suffer for me."

¹⁷So Ananias went over and found Paul and laid his hands on him and said, "Brother Paul, the Lord Jesus, who appeared to you on the road, has sent me so that you may be filled with the Holy Spirit and get your sight back."

¹⁸Instantly (it was as though scales fell from his eyes) Paul could see and was immediately baptized. ¹⁹Then he ate and was strengthened.

He stayed with the believers in Damascus for a few days ²⁰and went at once to the synagogue to tell everyone there the Good News about Jesus—that he is indeed the Son of God!

²¹All who heard him were amazed. "Isn't this the same man who persecuted Jesus' followers so bitterly in Jerusalem?" they asked. "And we under-

FAMILY DEVOTIONS

☐ *DEVOTION 294*
GIVING TO GOD

Read Acts 9:36-43

"What are you making, Mom?" Jody asked as she looked up from her book.

"I'm making a baby sweater for one of the ladies at church," answered Mom. "Mrs. Pauley is having a baby next month."

"How come you do so many things like that for other people?" Jody asked.

"I enjoy making things, and I enjoy giving them away." Mom smiled. "When you make something special at school you enjoy bringing it home to me, don't you?"

Jody nodded. "Sure, but that seems different," she said. "I mean, you're my mom! But you do a lot of things for people you hardly know."

"Not as much as Dorcas did," Mom answered.

"Dorcas?" Jody asked. "Who's she?"

"The book of Acts tells about a lady named Dorcas," explained Mom. "She was probably one of the first women inspired by Christ to be active in works of love. She knew how to sew, and she devoted time to making clothes for widows and poor people."

"Oh, I remember hearing about her in Sunday school," Jody said thoughtfully.

Mom smiled. "When Dorcas died, everyone was very sad. Do you remember what happened then?"

Jody thought for a moment, then her face brightened. "Was she raised from the dead?"

"That's right," said Mom. "The apostle Peter was in town at the time, and when he was told about it, he prayed, and God used him to raise her to life."

"When I get older I'm going to do things for other people, too—like Dorcas and you," Jody decided.

"You don't have to wait that long," said Mom. "Let's think of something you can do for someone else right now."

Giving to God Memory Verse

Bring all the tithes into the storehouse so that there will be food enough in my Temple; if you do, I will open up the windows of heaven for you and pour out a blessing so great you won't have room enough to take it in! Try it! Let me prove it to you!
Malachi 3:10

H o w   A b o u t   Y o u ?

What can you do for someone? Could you draw a picture, or make a small gift, and give it to your grandparents? Help them by dusting or cleaning? Help your mother make cookies for someone who is ill? Make a card for a shut-in? Mow the lawn for an elderly neighbor? When you give to others, you please the Lord, too. *V. L. C.*

• For the next devotional, turn to page 1049.   • For the next devotional on *GIVING TO GOD,* turn to page 1127.
• For notes on *GIVING TO GOD,* see pages 182, 433, and 1128.

stand that he came here to arrest them all and take them in chains to the chief priests."

²²Paul became more and more fervent in his preaching, and the Damascus Jews couldn't withstand his proofs that Jesus was indeed the Christ.

²³After a while the Jewish leaders determined to kill him. ²⁴But Paul was told about their plans, that they were watching the gates of the city day and night prepared to murder him. ²⁵So during the night some of his converts let him down in a basket through an opening in the city wall!

²⁶Upon arrival in Jerusalem he tried to meet with the believers, but they were all afraid of him. They thought he was faking! ²⁷Then Barnabas brought him to the apostles and told them how Paul had seen the Lord on the way to Damascus, what the Lord had said to him, and all about his powerful preaching in the name of Jesus. ²⁸Then they accepted him, and after that he was constantly with the believers ²⁹and preached boldly in the name of the Lord. But then some Greek-speaking Jews with whom he had argued plotted to murder him. ³⁰However, when the other believers heard about his danger, they took him to Caesarea and then sent him to his home in Tarsus.

³¹Meanwhile, the church had peace throughout Judea, Galilee and Samaria, and grew in strength and numbers. The believers learned how to walk in the fear of the Lord and in the comfort of the Holy Spirit.

³²Peter traveled from place to place to visit them, and in his travels came to the believers in the town of Lydda. ³³There he met a man named Aeneas, paralyzed and bedridden for eight years.

³⁴Peter said to him, "Aeneas! Jesus Christ has healed you! Get up and make your bed." And he was healed instantly. ³⁵Then the whole population of Lydda and Sharon turned to the Lord when they saw Aeneas walking around.

³⁶In the city of Joppa there was a woman named Dorcas ("Gazelle"), a believer who was always doing kind things for others, especially for the poor. ³⁷About this time she became ill and died. Her friends prepared her for burial and laid her in an upstairs room. ³⁸But when they learned that Peter was nearby at Lydda, they sent two men to beg him to return with them to Joppa. ³⁹This he did; as soon as he arrived, they took him upstairs where Dorcas lay. The room was filled with weeping widows who were showing one another the coats and other garments Dorcas had made for them. ⁴⁰But Peter asked them all to leave the room; then he knelt and prayed. Turning to the body he said, "Get up, Dorcas," and she opened her eyes! And when she saw Peter, she sat up! ⁴¹He gave her his hand and helped her up and called in the believers and widows, presenting to them.

⁴²The news raced through the town, and many believed in the Lord. ⁴³And Peter stayed a long time in Joppa, living with Simon, the tanner.

10 A Roman Captain Calls for Peter

In Caesarea there lived a Roman army officer, Cornelius, a captain of an Italian regiment. ²He was a godly man, deeply reverent, as was his entire household. He gave generously to charity and was a man of prayer. ³While wide awake one afternoon he had a vision—it was about three o'clock—and in this vision he saw an angel of God coming toward him.

"Cornelius!" the angel said.

⁴Cornelius stared at him in terror. "What do you want, sir?" he asked the angel.

And the angel replied, "Your prayers and charities have not gone unnoticed by God! ⁵,⁶Now send some men to Joppa to find a man named Simon Peter, who is staying with Simon, the tanner, down by the shore, and ask him to come and visit you."

⁷As soon as the angel was gone, Cornelius called two of his household servants and a godly soldier, one of his personal bodyguard, ⁸and told them what had happened and sent them off to Joppa.

⁹,¹⁰The next day as they were nearing the city, Peter went up on the flat roof of his house to pray. It was noon and he was hungry, but while lunch was being prepared, he fell into a trance. ¹¹He saw the sky open and a great canvas sheet, suspended by its four corners, settle to the ground. ¹²In the sheet were all sorts of animals, snakes, and birds [forbidden to the Jews for food].

¹³Then a voice said to him, "Go kill and eat any of them you wish."

¹⁴"Never, Lord," Peter declared, "I have never in all my life eaten such creatures, for they are forbidden by our Jewish laws."

¹⁵The voice spoke again, "Don't contradict God! If he says something is kosher, then it is."

¹⁶The same vision was repeated three times. Then the sheet was pulled up again to heaven.

¹⁷Peter was very perplexed. What could the vision mean? What was he supposed to do?

Just then the men sent by Cornelius had found the house and were standing outside at the gate, ¹⁸inquiring whether this was the place where Simon Peter lived!

¹⁹Meanwhile, as Peter was puzzling over the vision, the Holy Spirit said to him, "Three men have come to see you. ²⁰Go down and meet them and go with them. All is well, I have sent them."

²¹So Peter went down. "I'm the man you're looking for," he said. "Now what is it you want?"

²²Then they told him about Cornelius the Ro-

Family Devotions

☐ **Devotion 295**
Accepting Others

Read Acts 10:25-28

Accepting Others Memory Verse

How wonderful it is, how pleasant, when brothers live in harmony!
Psalm 133:1

Jessica and her friend Jimmy shouted with glee as they stood back to admire the snowman they were making. As they began to fashion some arms, a classmate, Aiko, came along. She grinned and stopped to help. "Go away," said Jessica with a scowl. "This is our snowman." Aiko's grin faded, and she slowly left. "She'd have wanted to give him slanting eyes," Jessica said loudly enough for Aiko to hear. At the window Jessica's mother frowned.

A little later Jason, another classmate, stopped to help, and he, too, was soon sent on his way. "You'd probably want to cover his face with mud and make him all black," Jessica laughed.

"Oh, who wants to help you anyway, Whitey?" Jason retorted.

Jessica angrily stomped her foot. "You stop calling us names!" she shouted. Still watching, Mom decided to call Jessica in.

"Oh, Mom! Did you see our snowman?" Jessica asked as she came in the door. "We call him Mr. Snowflake!"

Mom smiled. "Really?" she asked. "What have you learned about snowflakes in school?"

"Well, my teacher said each one is a perfect crystal, and no two are ever alike. But they're all beautiful!"

Mom nodded. "Kind of like people," she said. "They have different kinds of hair and eyes and skin. But they're all made by the great artist—God—and in his sight, each one is beautiful. So, unless we're going to disagree with God, we should consider them beautiful, too."

Jessica was quiet for a time. "Mom," she said finally, "may I have some kids over after school tomorrow? I need to apologize to Aiko and Jason, and I'd like to ask them to come help me build another snowman."

How About You?
Do you think you're better than people who look different from you, are poorer, or don't seem as smart? God made everyone according to his own special plan. Be careful not to say he made anyone poorly. *H. M.*

• For the next devotional, turn to page 1053.   • To start the next topic, turn to page 195.   • For notes on Accepting Others, see pages 270, 1140, 1196, and 1254.

man officer, a good and godly man, well thought of by the Jews, and how an angel had instructed him to send for Peter to come and tell him what God wanted him to do.

²³So Peter invited them in and lodged them overnight.

The next day he went with them, accompanied by some other believers from Joppa.

²⁴They arrived in Caesarea the following day, and Cornelius was waiting for him and had called together his relatives and close friends to meet Peter. ²⁵As Peter entered his home, Cornelius fell to the floor before him in worship.

²⁶But Peter said, "Stand up! I'm not a god!"

²⁷So he got up, and they talked together for a while and then went in where the others were assembled.

²⁸Peter told them, "You know it is against the Jewish laws for me to come into a Gentile home like this. But God has shown me in a vision that I should never think of anyone as inferior. ²⁹So I came as soon as I was sent for. Now tell me what you want."

³⁰Cornelius replied, "Four days ago I was praying as usual at this time of the afternoon, when suddenly a man was standing before me clothed in a radiant robe! ³¹He told me, 'Cornelius, your prayers are heard and your charities have been noticed by God! ³²Now send some men to Joppa and summon Simon Peter, who is staying in the home of Simon, a tanner, down by the shore.' ³³So I sent for you at once, and you have done well to come so soon. Now here we are, waiting before the Lord, anxious to hear what he has told you to tell us!"

³⁴Then Peter replied, "I see very clearly that the Jews are not God's only favorites! ³⁵In every nation he has those who worship him and do good deeds and are acceptable to him. ^{36,37}I'm sure you have heard about the Good News for the people of Israel—that there is peace with God through Jesus, the Messiah, who is Lord of all creation. This message has spread all through Judea, beginning with John the Baptist in Galilee. ³⁸And you no doubt know that Jesus of Nazareth was anointed by God with the Holy Spirit and with power, and he went around doing good and healing all who were possessed by demons, for God was with him.

³⁹"And we apostles are witnesses of all he did throughout Israel and in Jerusalem, where he was murdered on a cross. ^{40,41}But God brought him back to life again three days later and showed him to certain witnesses God had selected beforehand—not to the general public, but to us who ate and drank with him after he rose from the dead. ⁴²And he sent us to preach the Good News everywhere and to testify that Jesus is ordained of God to be the Judge of all—living and dead. ⁴³And all the prophets have written about him, saying that everyone who believes in him will have their sins forgiven through his name."

⁴⁴Even as Peter was saying these things, the Holy Spirit fell upon all those listening! ⁴⁵The Jews who came with Peter were amazed that the gift of the Holy Spirit would be given to Gentiles too! ^{46,47}But there could be no doubt about it, for they heard them speaking in tongues and praising God.

Peter asked, "Can anyone object to my baptizing them, now that they have received the Holy Spirit just as we did?" ⁴⁸So he did, baptizing them in the name of Jesus, the Messiah. Afterwards Cornelius begged him to stay with them for several days.

Why Peter Preaches to Gentiles

Soon the news reached the apostles and other brothers in Judea that Gentiles also were being converted! ²But when Peter arrived back in Jerusalem, the Jewish believers argued with him.

³"You fellowshiped with Gentiles and even ate with them," they accused.

⁴Then Peter told them the whole story. ⁵"One day in Joppa," he said, "while I was praying, I saw a vision—a huge sheet, let down by its four corners from the sky. ⁶Inside the sheet were all sorts of animals, reptiles, and birds [which we are not to eat]. ⁷And I heard a voice say, 'Kill and eat whatever you wish.'

⁸"'Never, Lord,' I replied. 'For I have never yet eaten anything forbidden by our Jewish laws!'

⁹"But the voice came again, 'Don't say it isn't right when God declares it is!'

¹⁰"This happened *three times* before the sheet and all it contained disappeared into heaven. ¹¹Just then three men who had come to take me with them to Caesarea arrived at the house where I was staying! ¹²The Holy Spirit told me to go with them and not to worry about their being Gentiles! These six brothers here accompanied me, and we soon arrived at the home of the man who had sent the messengers. ¹³He told us how an angel had appeared to him and told him to send messengers to Joppa to find Simon Peter! ¹⁴'He will tell you how you and all your household can be saved!' the angel had told him.

¹⁵"Well, I began telling them the Good News, but just as I was getting started with my sermon, the Holy Spirit fell on them, just as he fell on us at the beginning! ¹⁶Then I thought of the Lord's words when he said, 'Yes, John baptized with water, but you shall be baptized with the Holy Spirit.' ¹⁷And since it was *God* who gave these Gentiles

the same gift he gave us when we believed on the Lord Jesus Christ, who was I to argue?"

[18] When the others heard this, all their objections were answered and they began praising God! "Yes," they said, "God has given to the Gentiles, too, the privilege of turning to him and receiving eternal life!"

[19] Meanwhile, the believers who fled from Jerusalem during the persecution after Stephen's death traveled as far as Phoenicia, Cyprus, and Antioch, scattering the Good News, but only to Jews. [20] However, some of the believers who went to Antioch from Cyprus and Cyrene also gave their message about the Lord Jesus to some Greeks. [21] And the Lord honored this effort so that large numbers of these Gentiles became believers.

[22] When the church at Jerusalem heard what had happened, they sent Barnabas to Antioch to help the new converts. [23] When he arrived and saw the wonderful things God was doing, he was filled with excitement and joy, and encouraged the believers to stay close to the Lord, whatever the cost. [24] Barnabas was a kindly person, full of the Holy Spirit and strong in faith. As a result, large numbers of people were added to the Lord.

[25] Then Barnabas went on to Tarsus to hunt for Paul. [26] When he found him, he brought him back to Antioch; and both of them stayed there for a full year teaching the many new converts. (It was there at Antioch that the believers were first called "Christians.")

[27] During this time some prophets came down from Jerusalem to Antioch, [28] and one of them, named Agabus, stood up in one of the meetings to predict by the Spirit that a great famine was coming upon the land of Israel. (This was fulfilled during the reign of Claudius.) [29] So the believers decided to send relief to the Christians in Judea, each giving as much as he could. [30] This they did, consigning their gifts to Barnabas and Paul to take to the elders of the church in Jerusalem.

12 An Angel Lets Peter Out of Prison

About that time King Herod moved against some of the believers [2] and killed the apostle James (John's brother). [3] When Herod saw how much this pleased the Jewish leaders, he arrested Peter during the Passover celebration [4] and imprisoned him, placing him under the guard of sixteen soldiers. Herod's intention was to deliver Peter to the Jews for execution after the Passover. [5] But earnest prayer was going up to God from the church for his safety all the time he was in prison.

[6] The night before he was to be executed, he was asleep, double-chained between two soldiers with others standing guard before the prison gate, [7] when suddenly there was a light in the cell and an angel of the Lord stood beside Peter! The angel slapped him on the side to awaken him and said, "Quick! Get up!" And the chains fell off his wrists! [8] Then the angel told him, "Get dressed and put on your shoes." And he did. "Now put on your coat and follow me!" the angel ordered.

[9] So Peter left the cell, following the angel. But all the time he thought it was a dream or vision and didn't believe it was really happening. [10] They passed the first and second cell blocks and came to the iron gate to the street, and this opened to them of its own accord! So they passed through and walked along together for a block, and then the angel left him.

[11] Peter finally realized what had happened! "It's really true!" he said to himself. "The Lord has sent his angel and saved me from Herod and from what the Jews were hoping to do to me!"

[12] After a little thought he went to the home of Mary, mother of John Mark, where many were gathered for a prayer meeting.

[13] He knocked at the door in the gate, and a girl named Rhoda came to open it. [14] When she recognized Peter's voice, she was so overjoyed that she ran back inside to tell everyone that Peter was standing outside in the street. [15] They didn't believe her. "You're out of your mind," they said. When she insisted they decided, "It must be his angel. [They must have killed him.]"

[16] Meanwhile Peter continued knocking. When they finally went out and opened the door, their surprise knew no bounds. [17] He motioned for them to quiet down and told them what had happened and how the Lord had brought him out of jail. "Tell James and the others what happened," he said—and left for safer quarters.

[18] At dawn, the jail was in great commotion. What had happened to Peter? [19] When Herod sent for him and found that he wasn't there, he had the sixteen guards arrested, court-martialed and sentenced to death. Afterwards he left to live in Caesarea for a while.

[20] While he was in Caesarea, a delegation from Tyre and Sidon arrived to see him. He was highly displeased with the people of those two cities, but the delegates made friends with Blastus, the royal secretary, and asked for peace, for their cities were economically dependent upon trade

---

PRAYING AT ALL TIMES 12:5 In the midst of the plots, execution, and arrest, Luke injects the very important word *but*. Herod's plan was to execute Peter, *but* the believers were praying for Peter's safety. The earnest prayer of the church significantly affected the outcome of these events. We know from the testimony of the Bible that prayer changes attitudes and events. So pray often, and pray with confidence. **To begin the series of devotionals on PRAYING AT ALL TIMES, turn to page 45.**

with Herod's country. ²¹An appointment with Herod was granted, and when the day arrived he put on his royal robes, sat on his throne, and made a speech to them. ²²At its conclusion the people gave him a great ovation, shouting, "It is the voice of a god and not of a man!"

²³Instantly, an angel of the Lord struck Herod with a sickness so that he was filled with maggots and died—because he accepted the people's worship instead of giving the glory to God.

²⁴God's Good News was spreading rapidly and there were many new believers.

²⁵Barnabas and Paul now visited Jerusalem and as soon as they had finished their business, returned to Antioch, taking John Mark with them.

13 Paul's First Missionary Journey

Among the prophets and teachers of the church at Antioch were Barnabas and Symeon (also called "The Black Man"), Lucius (from Cyrene), Manaen (the foster-brother of King Herod), and Paul. ²One day as these men were worshiping and fasting the Holy Spirit said, "Dedicate Barnabas and Paul for a special job I have for them." ³So after more fasting and prayer, the men laid their hands on them—and sent them on their way.

⁴Directed by the Holy Spirit they went to Seleucia and then sailed for Cyprus. ⁵There, in the town of Salamis, they went to the Jewish synagogue and preached. (John Mark went with them as their assistant.)

⁶,⁷Afterwards they preached from town to town across the entire island until finally they reached Paphos where they met a Jewish sorcerer, a fake prophet named Bar-Jesus. He had attached himself to the governor, Sergius Paulus, a man of considerable insight and understanding. The governor invited Barnabas and Paul to visit him, for he wanted to hear their message from God. ⁸But the sorcerer, Elymas (his name in Greek), interfered and urged the governor to pay no attention to what Paul and Barnabas said, trying to keep him from trusting the Lord.

⁹Then Paul, filled with the Holy Spirit, glared angrily at the sorcerer and said, ¹⁰"You son of the devil, full of every sort of trickery and villainy, enemy of all that is good, will you never end your opposition to the Lord? ¹¹And now God has laid his hand of punishment upon you, and you will be stricken awhile with blindness."

Instantly mist and darkness fell upon him, and he began wandering around begging for someone to take his hand and lead him. ¹²When the governor saw what happened, he believed and was astonished at the power of God's message.

¹³Now Paul and those with him left Paphos by ship for Turkey, landing at the port town of Perga. There John deserted them and returned to Jerusalem. ¹⁴But Barnabas and Paul went on to Antioch, a city in the province of Pisidia.

On the Sabbath they went into the synagogue for the services. ¹⁵After the usual readings from the Books of Moses and from the Prophets, those in charge of the service sent them this message: "Brothers, if you have any word of instruction for us come and give it!"

¹⁶So Paul stood, waved a greeting to them and began. "Men of Israel," he said, "and all others here who reverence God, [let me begin my remarks with a bit of history].

¹⁷"The God of this nation Israel chose our ancestors and honored them in Egypt by gloriously leading them out of their slavery. ¹⁸And he nursed them through forty years of wandering around in the wilderness. ¹⁹,²⁰Then he destroyed seven nations in Canaan and gave Israel their land as an inheritance. Judges ruled for about four hundred and fifty years and were followed by Samuel the prophet.

²¹"Then the people begged for a king, and God gave them Saul (son of Kish), a man of the tribe of Benjamin, who reigned for forty years. ²²But God removed him and replaced him with David as king, a man about whom God said, 'David (son of Jesse) is a man after my own heart, for he will obey me.' ²³And it is one of King David's descendants, Jesus, who is God's promised Savior of Israel!

²⁴"But before he came, John the Baptist preached the need for everyone in Israel to turn from sin to God. ²⁵As John was finishing his work he asked, 'Do you think I am the Messiah? No! But he is coming soon—and in comparison with him, I am utterly worthless.'

²⁶"Brothers—you sons of Abraham, and also all of you Gentiles here who reverence God—this salvation is for all of us! ²⁷The Jews in Jerusalem and their leaders fulfilled prophecy by killing Jesus; for they didn't recognize him or realize that he is the one the prophets had written about, though they heard the prophets' words read every Sabbath. ²⁸They found no just cause to execute him, but asked Pilate to have him killed anyway. ²⁹When they had fulfilled all the prophecies concerning his death, he was taken from the cross and placed in a tomb.

³⁰"But God brought him back to life again! ³¹And he was seen many times during the next few days by the men who had accompanied him to Jerusalem from Galilee—these men have constantly testified to this in public witness.

³²,³³"And now Barnabas and I are here to bring you this Good News—that God's promise to our ancestors has come true in our own time, in that God brought Jesus back to life again. This is what the second Psalm is talking about when it says concerning Jesus, 'Today I have honored you as my Son.'

Family Devotions

☐ DEVOTION 296
RECEIVING CHRIST AS SAVIOR

Read Acts 13:26-39

"Oh, no!" groaned Dana as she and her mother stood looking at the dent in their car. "What happened?"

"Apparently someone backed into the car while we were shopping," replied Mom. "Whoever it was didn't leave a note admitting his fault." She sighed. "Well, there's nothing to be done, I guess, but I suppose we should make a police report."

After the report was made, Dana and Mom hurried home to tell Dad about the accident. "Well," he said as he looked at the car, "this isn't major damage, but the body work will be an expensive repair job. I'll call our insurance agent—I think this will be covered."

"The person who did it ought to pay the bill," declared Dana. "It was his fault."

"Yes, but we can't get him to pay the bill when we don't know who he is," replied Mom, "so if the insurance doesn't cover it, we'll just have to take care of it ourselves."

"Well, you certainly shouldn't have to pay to get the car fixed," Dana insisted. "That isn't fair!"

"No," said Mom, "but there's not a whole lot we can do about it."

"I know one thing we can do," said Dad. "We can all be thankful it's just a car that's damaged. Nobody got hurt."

Mom nodded. "I'm also thankful that the damage is so minor that the car can still be driven," she added.

"I'm thinking of something else, too," said Dad. "We can use this as a reminder to be thankful that Jesus paid the price for sin even when he knew who was at fault—us. I must admit that I'm not happy about paying for repairs that are someone else's fault, but Jesus willingly paid the price when the fault was ours. Let's never forget to thank him for that."

Receiving Christ as Savior Memory Verse

If you tell others with your own mouth that Jesus Christ is your Lord and believe in your own heart that God has raised him from the dead, you will be saved.
Romans 10:9

How About You?

Does paying the price for something that was someone else's fault make you feel angry? That's natural. But just think! Jesus died willingly to pay the price for your sin. His love for you is that great! If you haven't already accepted what he did for you, do so today. N. E. K.

• For the next devotional, turn to page 1057. • For the next devotional on RECEIVING CHRIST AS SAVIOR, turn to page 1255. • For notes on RECEIVING CHRIST AS SAVIOR, see pages 839, 842, 1146, 1234, and 1240.

34"For God had promised to bring him back to life again, no more to die. This is stated in the Scripture that says, 'I will do for you the wonderful thing I promised David.' 35In another Psalm he explained more fully, saying, 'God will not let his Holy One decay.' 36This was not a reference to David, for after David had served his generation according to the will of God, he died and was buried, and his body decayed. 37[No, it was a reference to another]—someone God brought back to life, whose body was not touched at all by the ravages of death.

38"Brothers! Listen! In this man Jesus there is forgiveness for your sins! 39Everyone who trusts in him is freed from all guilt and declared righteous—something the Jewish law could never do. 40Oh, be careful! Don't let the prophets' words apply to you. For they said, 41'Look and perish, you despisers [of the truth], for I am doing something in your day—something that you won't believe when you hear it announced.'"

42As the people left the synagogue that day, they asked Paul to return and speak to them again the next week. 43And many Jews and godly Gentiles who worshiped at the synagogue followed Paul and Barnabas down the street as the two men urged them to accept the mercies God was offering. 44The following week almost the entire city turned out to hear them preach the Word of God.

45But when the Jewish leaders saw the crowds, they were jealous, and cursed and argued against whatever Paul said.

46Then Paul and Barnabas spoke out boldly and declared, "It was necessary that this Good News from God should be given first to you Jews. But since you have rejected it and shown yourselves unworthy of eternal life—well, we will offer it to Gentiles. 47For this is as the Lord commanded when he said, 'I have made you a light to the Gentiles, to lead them from the farthest corners of the earth to my salvation.'"

48When the Gentiles heard this, they were very glad and rejoiced in Paul's message; and as many as wanted eternal life, believed. 49So God's message spread all through that region. 50Then the Jewish leaders stirred up both the godly women and the civic leaders of the city and incited a mob against Paul and Barnabas, and ran them out of town. 51But they shook off the dust of their feet against the town and went on to the city of Iconium. 52And their converts were filled with joy and with the Holy Spirit.

14 Paul and Barnabas Seen As Gods

At Iconium, Paul and Barnabas went together to the synagogue and preached with such power that many—both Jews and Gentiles—believed.

2But the Jews who spurned God's message stirred up distrust among the Gentiles against Paul and Barnabas, saying all sorts of evil things about them. 3Nevertheless, they stayed there a long time, preaching boldly, and the Lord proved their message was from him by giving them power to do great miracles. 4But the people of the city were divided in their opinion about them. Some agreed with the Jewish leaders, and some backed the apostles.

5,6When Paul and Barnabas learned of a plot to incite a mob of Gentiles, Jews, and Jewish leaders to attack and stone them, they fled for their lives, going to the cities of Lycaonia, Lystra, Derbe, and the surrounding area, 7and preaching the Good News there.

8While they were at Lystra, they came upon a man with crippled feet who had been that way from birth, so he had never walked. 9He was listening as Paul preached, and Paul noticed him and realized he had faith to be healed. 10So Paul called to him, "Stand up!" and the man leaped to his feet and started walking!

11When the listening crowd saw what Paul had done, they shouted (in their local dialect, of course), "These men are gods in human bodies!" 12They decided that Barnabas was the Greek god Jupiter, and that Paul, because he was the chief speaker, was Mercury! 13The local priest of the Temple of Jupiter, located on the outskirts of the city, brought them cartloads of flowers and prepared to sacrifice oxen to them at the city gates before the crowds.

14But when Barnabas and Paul saw what was happening, they ripped at their clothing in dismay and ran out among the people, shouting, 15"Men! What are you doing? We are merely human beings like yourselves! We have come to bring you the Good News that you are invited to turn from the worship of these foolish things and to pray instead to the living God, who made heaven and earth and sea and everything in them. 16In bygone days he permitted the nations to go their own ways, 17but he never left himself without a witness; there were always his reminders—the kind things he did such as sending you rain and good crops and giving you food and gladness."

18But even so, Paul and Barnabas could scarcely restrain the people from sacrificing to them!

19Yet only a few days later, some Jews arrived from Antioch and Iconium and turned the crowds into a murderous mob that stoned Paul and dragged him out of the city, apparently dead. 20But as the believers stood around him, he got up and went back into the city!

The next day he left with Barnabas for Derbe. 21After preaching the Good News there and making many disciples, they returned again to Lystra, Iconium and Antioch, ²²where they helped the believers to grow in love for God and each other. They encouraged them to continue in the faith in spite of all the persecution, reminding them that they must enter into the Kingdom of God through many tribulations. ²³Paul and Barnabas also appointed elders in every church and prayed for them with fasting, turning them over to the care of the Lord in whom they trusted.

²⁴Then they traveled back through Pisidia to Pamphylia, ²⁵preached again in Perga, and went on to Attalia.

²⁶Finally they returned by ship to Antioch, where their journey had begun and where they had been committed to God for the work now completed.

²⁷Upon arrival they called together the believers and reported on their trip, telling how God had opened the door of faith to the Gentiles too. ²⁸And they stayed there with the believers at Antioch for a long while.

15 A Church Conflict

While Paul and Barnabas were at Antioch, some men from Judea arrived and began to teach the believers that unless they adhered to the ancient Jewish custom of circumcision, they could not be saved. ²Paul and Barnabas argued and discussed this with them at length, and finally the believers sent them to Jerusalem, accompanied by some local men, to talk to the apostles and elders there about this question. ³After the entire congregation had escorted them out of the city, the delegates went on to Jerusalem, stopping along the way in the cities of Phoenicia and Samaria to visit the believers, telling them—much to everyone's joy—that the Gentiles, too, were being converted.

⁴Arriving in Jerusalem, they met with the church leaders—all the apostles and elders were present—and Paul and Barnabas reported on what God had been doing through their ministry. ⁵But then some of the men who had been Pharisees before their conversion stood to their feet and declared that all Gentile converts must be circumcised and required to follow all the Jewish customs and ceremonies.

⁶So the apostles and church elders set a further meeting to decide this question.

⁷At the meeting, after long discussion, Peter stood and addressed them as follows: "Brothers, you all know that God chose me from among you long ago to preach the Good News to the Gentiles so that they also could believe. ⁸God, who knows men's hearts, confirmed the fact that he accepts Gentiles by giving them the Holy Spirit, just as he gave him to us. ⁹He made no distinction between them and us, for he cleansed their lives through faith, just as he did ours. ¹⁰And now are you going to correct God by burdening the Gentiles with a yoke that neither we nor our fathers were able to bear? ¹¹Don't you believe that all are saved the same way, by the free gift of the Lord Jesus?"

¹²There was no further discussion, and everyone now listened as Barnabas and Paul told about the miracles God had done through them among the Gentiles.

¹³When they had finished, James took the floor. "Brothers," he said, "listen to me. ¹⁴Peter has told you about the time God first visited the Gentiles to take from them a people to bring honor to his name. ¹⁵And this fact of Gentile conversion agrees with what the prophets predicted. For instance, listen to this passage from the prophet Amos:

> ¹⁶'Afterwards' [says the Lord], 'I will return and renew the broken contract with David,
> ¹⁷so that Gentiles, too, will find the Lord—
> all those marked with my name.'

¹⁸That is what the Lord says, who reveals his plans made from the beginning.

¹⁹"And so my judgment is that we should not insist that the Gentiles who turn to God must obey our Jewish laws, ²⁰except that we should write to them to refrain from eating meat sacrificed to idols, from all fornication, and also from eating unbled meat of strangled animals. ²¹For these things have been preached against in Jewish synagogues in every city on every Sabbath for many generations."

²²Then the apostles and elders and the whole congregation voted to send delegates to Antioch with Paul and Barnabas, to report on this decision. The men chosen were two of the church leaders—Judas (also called Barsabbas) and Silas.

²³This is the letter they took along with them:

"*From:* The apostles, elders and brothers at Jerusalem.

"*To:* The Gentile brothers in Antioch, Syria and Cilicia. Greetings!

²⁴"We understand that some believers from here have upset you and questioned your salvation, but they had no such instructions from us. ²⁵So it seemed wise to us, having unanimously agreed on our decision, to send to you these two official representatives, along with our beloved Barnabas and Paul. ²⁶These men—Judas and Silas, who have risked their lives for the sake of our Lord Jesus Christ—will confirm orally what we have decided concerning your question.

²⁷⁻²⁹"For it seemed good to the Holy Spirit and to us to lay no greater burden of Jewish laws on

you than to abstain from eating food offered to idols and from unbled meat of strangled animals, and, of course, from fornication. If you do this, it is enough. Farewell."

[30] The four messengers went at once to Antioch, where they called a general meeting of the Christians and gave them the letter. [31] And there was great joy throughout the church that day as they read it.

[32] Then Judas and Silas, both being gifted speakers, preached long sermons to the believers, strengthening their faith. [33] They stayed several days, and then Judas and Silas returned to Jerusalem taking greetings and appreciation to those who had sent them. [34,35] Paul and Barnabas stayed on at Antioch to assist several others who were preaching and teaching there.

[36] Several days later Paul suggested to Barnabas that they return again to Turkey and visit each city where they had preached before, to see how the new converts were getting along. [37] Barnabas agreed and wanted to take along John Mark. [38] But Paul didn't like that idea at all, since John had deserted them in Pamphylia. [39] Their disagreement over this was so sharp that they separated. Barnabas took Mark with him and sailed for Cyprus, [40,41] while Paul chose Silas and, with the blessing of the believers, left for Syria and Cilicia to encourage the churches there.

16 Timothy Is Paul's Helper

Paul and Silas went first to Derbe and then on to Lystra where they met Timothy, a believer whose mother was a Christian Jewess, but his father a Greek. [2] Timothy was well thought of by the brothers in Lystra and Iconium, [3] so Paul asked him to join them on their journey. In deference to the Jews of the area, he circumcised Timothy before they left, for everyone knew that his father was a Greek [and hadn't permitted this before]. [4] Then they went from city to city, making known the decision concerning the Gentiles, as decided by the apostles and elders in Jerusalem. [5] So the church grew daily in faith and numbers.

[6] Next they traveled through Phrygia and Galatia because the Holy Spirit had told them not to go into the Turkish province of Asia Minor at that time. [7] Then going along the borders of Mysia they headed north for the province of Bithynia, but again the Spirit of Jesus said no. [8] So instead they went on through Mysia province to the city of Troas.

[9] That night Paul had a vision. In his dream he saw a man over in Macedonia, Greece, pleading with him, "Come over here and help us." [10] Well, that settled it. We would go to Macedonia, for we could only conclude that God was sending us to preach the Good News there.

[11] We went aboard a boat at Troas, and sailed straight across to Samothrace, and the next day on to Neapolis, [12] and finally reached Philippi, a Roman colony just inside the Macedonian border, and stayed there several days.

[13] On the Sabbath we went a little way outside the city to a riverbank where we understood some people met for prayer; and we taught the Scriptures to some women who came. [14] One of them was Lydia, a saleswoman from Thyatira, a merchant of purple cloth. She was already a worshiper of God and as she listened to us, the Lord opened her heart and she accepted all that Paul was saying. [15] She was baptized along with all her household and asked us to be her guests. "If you agree that I am faithful to the Lord," she said, "come and stay at my home." And she urged us until we did.

[16] One day as we were going down to the place of prayer beside the river, we met a demon-possessed slave girl, who was a fortune-teller and earned much money for her masters. [17] She followed along behind us shouting, "These men are servants of God, and they have come to tell you how to have your sins forgiven."

[18] This went on day after day until Paul, in great distress, turned and spoke to the demon within her. "I command you in the name of Jesus Christ to come out of her," he said. And instantly it left her.

[19] Her masters' hopes of wealth were now shattered; they grabbed Paul and Silas and dragged them before the judges at the marketplace.

[20,21] "These Jews are corrupting our city," they shouted. "They are teaching the people to do things that are against the Roman laws."

[22] A mob was quickly formed against Paul and Silas, and the judges ordered them stripped and beaten with wooden whips. [23] Again and again the rods slashed down across their bared backs; and afterwards they were thrown into prison. The jailer was threatened with death if they escaped, [24] so he took no chances, but put them into the inner dungeon and clamped their feet into the stocks.

[25] Around midnight, as Paul and

TRUSTING GOD FOR GUIDANCE 16:6 We don't know how the Holy Spirit told Paul that he and his men were not to go into Asia. It may have been through a prophet, a vision, an inner conviction, or some other circumstance. To know God's will does not mean we must hear his voice. He leads in different ways. When seeking God's will (1) make sure your plan is in harmony with God's Word; (2) ask mature Christians for their advice; (3) check your own motives—are you seeking to do what you want or what you think God wants? (4) pray for God to open and close the doors of circumstances. **To begin the series of devotionals on** *TRUSTING GOD FOR GUIDANCE,* **turn to page 27.**

FAMILY DEVOTIONS

☐ DEVOTION 297
OPTIMISM

Read Acts 16:22-32

"I didn't make the basketball team, Mom." Joe slumped down in a chair as he came in from school one day. "I'm not bragging or anything, but I do play basketball well."

"Yes, you do, Son," agreed Mom, "but there were only two openings on the team, and the coach had to choose, didn't he? Who did make it?"

"Kevin, which we all expected. Kevin is good! Then they chose Randy for the other opening. In the tryouts, I made more baskets than he did, and I dribbled the ball longer. But his dad is a teacher at school, and I think that's why he made it," Joe concluded bitterly.

Mom was quiet for a few minutes. She knew there had been other times when Randy was chosen for something because his dad was a teacher. She sighed. "I suppose that may be possible. If you really believe that, perhaps you should ask the coach about it," she suggested, "but do be careful not to make accusations you can't prove. And, Joe, you must learn that life isn't always fair. Another thing you must learn is to maintain a Christlike attitude no matter what happens."

"Aw, Mom," Joe whined.

"Think of Paul and Silas. It wasn't fair that they were thrown in jail for preaching about the Lord," continued Mom, "and yet they sang! They weren't going to let the unfair actions of others get them down. I know this experience is hard for you, but you can learn something from it. Accept it as a challenge. Ask the Lord to help you handle the situation. You will come out of it a stronger and more mature Christian."

Joe sighed. He knew his mom was right. It wasn't going to help to be upset. He would ask the Lord to help him turn a bad experience into a growing experience.

Optimism Memory Verse

Fix your thoughts on what is true and good and right. Think about things that are pure and lovely, and dwell on the fine, good things in others. Think about all you can praise God for and be glad about.
Philippians 4:8

How About You?

Are you ever treated unfairly? It happens to everyone. The next time you're faced with an unfair situation that you can't change, remember Paul and Silas. Instead of complaining, they sang! God used them through that experience, and he can also use you. Maintain a good attitude. Grow through what has happened. L. M. W.

• For the next devotional, turn to page 1059.   • To start the next topic, turn to page 133.   • For notes on OPTIMISM, see pages 143, 536, 677, and 940.

Silas were praying and singing hymns to the Lord—and the other prisoners were listening—²⁶suddenly there was a great earthquake; the prison was shaken to its foundations, all the doors flew open—and the chains of every prisoner fell off! ²⁷The jailer wakened to see the prison doors wide open, and assuming the prisoners had escaped, he drew his sword to kill himself.

²⁸But Paul yelled to him, "Don't do it! We are all here!"

²⁹Trembling with fear, the jailer called for lights and ran to the dungeon and fell down before Paul and Silas. ³⁰He brought them out and begged them, "Sirs, what must I do to be saved?"

³¹They replied, "Believe on the Lord Jesus and you will be saved, and your entire household."

³²Then they told him and all his household the Good News from the Lord. ³³That same hour he washed their stripes, and he and all his family were baptized. ³⁴Then he brought them up into his house and set a meal before them. How he and his household rejoiced because all were now believers! ³⁵The next morning the judges sent police officers over to tell the jailer, "Let those men go!" ³⁶So the jailer told Paul they were free to leave.

³⁷But Paul replied, "Oh no they don't! They have publicly beaten us without trial and jailed us—and we are Roman citizens! So now they want us to leave secretly? Never! Let them come themselves and release us!"

³⁸The police officers reported to the judges, who feared for their lives when they heard Paul and Silas were Roman citizens. ³⁹So they came to the jail and begged them to go, and brought them out and pled with them to leave the city. ⁴⁰Paul and Silas then returned to the home of Lydia, where they met with the believers and preached to them once more before leaving town.

17 Paul Visits Two Towns

Now they traveled through the cities of Amphipolis and Apollonia and came to Thessalonica, where there was a Jewish synagogue. ²As was Paul's custom, he went there to preach, and for three Sabbaths in a row he opened the Scriptures to the people, ³explaining the prophecies about the sufferings of the Messiah and his coming back to life, and proving that Jesus is the Messiah. ⁴Some who listened were persuaded and became converts—including a large number of godly Greek men and also many important women of the city.

⁵But the Jewish leaders were jealous and incited some worthless fellows from the streets to form a mob and start a riot. They attacked the home of Jason, planning to take Paul and Silas to the City Council for punishment.

⁶Not finding them there, they dragged out Jason and some of the other believers, and took them before the Council instead. "Paul and Silas have turned the rest of the world upside down, and now they are here disturbing our city," they shouted, ⁷"and Jason has let them into his home. They are all guilty of treason, for they claim another king, Jesus, instead of Caesar."

⁸,⁹The people of the city, as well as the judges, were concerned at these reports and let them go only after they had posted bail.

¹⁰That night the Christians hurried Paul and Silas to Beroea, and, as usual, they went to the synagogue to preach. ¹¹But the people of Beroea were more open-minded than those in Thessalonica, and gladly listened to the message. They searched the Scriptures day by day to check up on Paul and Silas' statements to see if they were really so. ¹²As a result, many of them believed, including several prominent Greek women and many men also.

¹³But when the Jews in Thessalonica learned that Paul was preaching in Beroea, they went over and stirred up trouble. ¹⁴The believers acted at once, sending Paul on to the coast, while Silas and Timothy remained behind. ¹⁵Those accompanying Paul went on with him to Athens and then returned to Beroea with a message for Silas and Timothy to hurry and join him.

¹⁶While Paul was waiting for them in Athens, he was deeply troubled by all the idols he saw everywhere throughout the city. ¹⁷He went to the synagogue for discussions with the Jews and the devout Gentiles, and spoke daily in the public square to all who happened to be there.

¹⁸He also had an encounter with some of the Epicurean and Stoic philosophers. Their reaction, when he told them about Jesus and his resurrection, was, "He's a dreamer," or, "He's pushing some foreign religion."

¹⁹But they invited him to the forum at Mars Hill. "Come and tell us more about this new religion," they said, ²⁰"for you are saying some rather startling things and we want to hear more." ²¹(I should explain that all the Athenians as well as the foreigners in Athens seemed to spend all their time discussing the latest new ideas!)

²²So Paul, standing before them at the Mars Hill forum, addressed them as follows:

"Men of Athens, I notice that you are very religious, ²³for as I was out walking I saw your many altars, and one of them had this inscription on it—'To the Unknown God.' You have been worshiping him without knowing who he is, and now I wish to tell you about him.

²⁴"He made the world and everything in it, and

Family Devotions

☐ **DEVOTION 298**
KNOWING GOD

Read Acts 17:10-12

"If God loved us, he wouldn't let us have all this trouble," Keith argued with his big brother, Mark. "What good does it do to pray? I asked God to heal Grandma Davis, and she died. I asked him to give Dad a job, but he hasn't. And don't start preaching at me either, just 'cause you're going to seminary now."

Mark shrugged and sighed, "Very well. Have it your way. Nothing I say seems to help. But your attitude sure is making it hard on Dad. Isn't it bad enough that he's lost his job without your acting like a spoiled brat? So what if you won't get a new bike for your birthday? You'll live."

"That's easy for you to say!" Keith ran out of the house, slamming the door behind him.

Later, Keith went downstairs where Dad and Mom were using Mark's new weight-lifting equipment. After watching a while he grinned. "What's the matter, Dad? You getting soft in your old age?" he teased as his father strained to lift the weights.

Dad laughed, "Been sitting at a desk too long, I guess. I didn't realize I was so out of shape."

"You need to spend some time working out every day, Dad." Keith grinned as he took a turn at the weights. "I'm not nearly as big as you, and I can lift these."

"You're not nearly as old as I am, either." Dad playfully took a jab at Keith.

"It's not your age nor size," Keith replied. "It's keeping fit."

Mark put his arm around his young brother's shoulders and drew him aside. "And that's also why it's important to keep in touch with God every day," Mark quietly told his brother. "So your spiritual muscles won't become flabby. If you were in good spiritual shape, Keith, your attitude about our problems would be a lot different," Mark said pointedly. "You would trust God instead of pouting. You would wait for a bike without complaining."

Knowing God Memory Verse

Oh, that we might know the Lord! Let us press on to know him, and he will respond to us as surely as the coming of dawn or the rain of early spring.
Hosea 6:3

How About You?

Are you out of shape spiritually? Have you been skipping daily prayer and Bible reading? If so, your attitude probably shows it. Don't allow your spiritual muscles of faith to become flabby. Determine now to work out spiritually every day. B. W.

• For the next devotional, turn to page 1067.   • For the next devotional on KNOWING GOD, turn to page 1181.
• For notes on KNOWING GOD, see pages 129, 610, 815, and 1208.

since he is Lord of heaven and earth, he doesn't live in man-made temples; ²⁵and human hands can't minister to his needs—for he has no needs! He himself gives life and breath to everything, and satisfies every need there is. ²⁶He created all the people of the world from one man, Adam, and scattered the nations across the face of the earth. He decided beforehand which should rise and fall, and when. He determined their boundaries.

²⁷"His purpose in all of this is that they should seek after God, and perhaps feel their way toward him and find him—though he is not far from any one of us. ²⁸For in him we live and move and are! As one of your own poets says it, 'We are the sons of God.' ²⁹If this is true, we shouldn't think of God as an idol made by men from gold or silver or chipped from stone. ³⁰God tolerated man's past ignorance about these things, but now he commands everyone to put away idols and worship only him. ³¹For he has set a day for justly judging the world by the man he has appointed, and has pointed him out by bringing him back to life again."

³²When they heard Paul speak of the resurrection of a person who had been dead, some laughed, but others said, "We want to hear more about this later." ³³That ended Paul's discussion with them, ³⁴but a few joined him and became believers. Among them was Dionysius, a member of the City Council, and a woman named Damaris, and others.

18 Paul with Priscilla and Aquila

Then Paul left Athens and went to Corinth. ²,³There he became acquainted with a Jew named Aquila, born in Pontus, who had recently arrived from Italy with his wife, Priscilla. They had been expelled from Italy as a result of Claudius Caesar's order to deport all Jews from Rome. Paul lived and worked with them, for they were tentmakers just as he was.

⁴Each Sabbath found Paul at the synagogue, trying to convince the Jews and Greeks alike. ⁵And after the arrival of Silas and Timothy from Macedonia, Paul spent his full time preaching and testifying to the Jews that Jesus is the Messiah. ⁶But when the Jews opposed him and blasphemed, hurling abuse at Jesus, Paul shook off the dust from his robe and said, "Your blood be upon your own heads—I am innocent—from now on I will preach to the Gentiles."

⁷After that he stayed with Titus Justus, a Gentile who worshiped God and lived next door to the synagogue. ⁸However, Crispus, the leader of the synagogue, and all his household believed in the Lord and were baptized—as were many others in Corinth.

⁹One night the Lord spoke to Paul in a vision and told him, "Don't be afraid! Speak out! Don't quit! ¹⁰For I am with you and no one can harm you. Many people here in this city belong to me." ¹¹So Paul stayed there the next year and a half, teaching the truths of God.

¹²But when Gallio became governor of Achaia, the Jews rose in concerted action against Paul and brought him before the governor for judgment. ¹³They accused Paul of "persuading men to worship God in ways that are contrary to Roman law." ¹⁴But just as Paul started to make his defense, Gallio turned to his accusers and said, "Listen, you Jews, if this were a case involving some crime, I would be obliged to listen to you, ¹⁵but since it is merely a bunch of questions of semantics and personalities and your silly Jewish laws, you take care of it. I'm not interested and I'm not touching it." ¹⁶And he drove them out of the courtroom.

¹⁷Then the mob grabbed Sosthenes, the new leader of the synagogue, and beat him outside the courtroom. But Gallio couldn't have cared less.

¹⁸Paul stayed in the city several days after that and then said good-bye to the Christians and sailed for the coast of Syria, taking Priscilla and Aquila with him. At Cenchreae Paul had his head shaved according to Jewish custom, for he had taken a vow. ¹⁹Arriving at the port of Ephesus, he left us aboard ship while he went over to the synagogue for a discussion with the Jews. ²⁰They asked him to stay for a few days, but he felt that he had no time to lose.

²¹"I must by all means be at Jerusalem for the holiday," he said. But he promised to return to Ephesus later if God permitted; and so he set sail again.

²²The next stop was at the port of Caesarea from where he visited the church [at Jerusalem] and then sailed on to Antioch. ²³After spending some time there, he left for Turkey again, going through Galatia and Phrygia visiting all the believers, encouraging them and helping them grow in the Lord.

²⁴As it happened, a Jew named Apollos, a wonderful Bible teacher and preacher, had just arrived in Ephesus from Alexandria in Egypt. ²⁵,²⁶While he was in Egypt, someone had told him about John the Baptist and what John had said about Jesus, but that is all he knew. He had never heard the rest of the story! So he was preaching boldly and enthusiastically in the synagogue, "The Messiah is coming! Get ready to receive him!" Priscilla and Aquila were there and heard him—and it was a powerful sermon. Afterwards they met with him and explained what had happened to Jesus since the time of John, and all that it meant!

²⁷Apollos had been thinking about going to Greece, and the believers encouraged him in this.

They wrote to their fellow-believers there, telling them to welcome him. And upon his arrival in Greece, he was greatly used of God to strengthen the church, [28]for he powerfully refuted all the Jewish arguments in public debate, showing by the Scriptures that Jesus is indeed the Messiah.

19 God Sends the Holy Spirit

While Apollos was in Corinth, Paul traveled through Turkey and arrived in Ephesus, where he found several disciples. [2]"Did you receive the Holy Spirit when you believed?" he asked them.

"No," they replied, "we don't know what you mean. What is the Holy Spirit?"

[3]"Then what beliefs did you acknowledge at your baptism?" he asked.

And they replied, "What John the Baptist taught."

[4]Then Paul pointed out to them that John's baptism was to demonstrate a desire to turn from sin to God and that those receiving his baptism must then go on to believe in Jesus, the one John said would come later.

[5]As soon as they heard this, they were baptized in the name of the Lord Jesus. [6]Then, when Paul laid his hands upon their heads, the Holy Spirit came on them, and they spoke in other languages and prophesied. [7]The men involved were about twelve in number.

[8]Then Paul went to the synagogue and preached boldly each Sabbath day for three months, telling what he believed and why, and persuading many to believe in Jesus. [9]But some rejected his message and publicly spoke against Christ, so he left, refusing to preach to them again. Pulling out the believers, he began a separate meeting at the lecture hall of Tyrannus and preached there daily. [10]This went on for the next two years, so that everyone in the Turkish province of Asia Minor—both Jews and Greeks—heard the Lord's message.

[11]And God gave Paul the power to do unusual miracles, [12]so that even when his handkerchiefs or parts of his clothing were placed upon sick people, they were healed, and any demons within them came out.

[13]A team of itinerant Jews who were traveling from town to town casting out demons planned to experiment by using the name of the Lord Jesus. The incantation they decided on was this: "I adjure you by Jesus, whom Paul preaches, to come out!" [14]Seven sons of Sceva, a Jewish priest, were doing this. [15]But when they tried it on a man possessed by a demon, the demon replied, "I know Jesus and I know Paul, but who are you?" [16]And he leaped on two of them and beat them up, so that they fled out of his house naked and badly injured.

[17]The story of what happened spread quickly all through Ephesus, to Jews and Greeks alike; and a solemn fear descended on the city, and the name of the Lord Jesus was greatly honored. [18,19]Many of the believers who had been practicing black magic confessed their deeds and brought their incantation books and charms and burned them at a public bonfire. (Someone estimated the value of the books at $10,000.) [20]This indicates how deeply the whole area was stirred by God's message.

[21]Afterwards Paul felt impelled by the Holy Spirit to go across to Greece before returning to Jerusalem. "And after that," he said, "I must go on to Rome!" [22]He sent his two assistants, Timothy and Erastus, on ahead to Greece while he stayed awhile longer in Asia Minor.

[23]But about that time, a big blowup developed in Ephesus concerning the Christians. [24]It began with Demetrius, a silversmith who employed many craftsmen to manufacture silver shrines of the Greek goddess Diana. [25]He called a meeting of his men, together with others employed in related trades, and addressed them as follows:

"Gentlemen, this business is our income. [26]As you know so well from what you've seen and heard, this man Paul has persuaded many, many people that handmade gods aren't gods at all. As a result, our sales volume is going down! And this trend is evident not only here in Ephesus, but throughout the entire province! [27]Of course, I am not only talking about the business aspects of this situation and our loss of income, but also of the possibility that the temple of the great goddess Diana will lose its influence, and that Diana—this magnificent goddess worshiped not only throughout this part of Turkey but all around the world—will be forgotten!"

[28]At this their anger boiled and they began shouting, "Great is Diana of the Ephesians!"

[29]A crowd began to gather, and soon the city

LEAVING THE FUTURE IN GOD'S HANDS 19:18-19 Ephesus was a center for black magic and other occult practices. The people cooked up magical formulas to give them wealth, happiness, and success in marriage. Superstition and sorcery were commonplace. God clearly forbids such practices (Deuteronomy 18:9-13). You cannot be a believer and hold on to the occult, black magic, or sorcery. Once you begin to dabble in these areas, it is extremely easy to become obsessed by them because Satan is very powerful. But God's power is even greater (1 John 4:4; Revelation 20:10). If you are mixed up in the occult, learn a lesson from the Ephesians and get rid of anything that could keep you trapped in such practices. **To begin the series of devotionals on LEAVING THE FUTURE IN GOD'S HANDS, turn to page 75.**

was filled with confusion. Everyone rushed to the amphitheater, dragging along Gaius and Aristarchus, Paul's traveling companions, for trial. ³⁰Paul wanted to go in, but the disciples wouldn't let him. ³¹Some of the Roman officers of the province, friends of Paul, also sent a message to him, begging him not to risk his life by entering.

³²Inside the people were all shouting, some one thing and some another—everything was in confusion. In fact, most of them didn't even know why they were there.

³³Alexander was spotted among the crowd by some of the Jews and dragged forward. He motioned for silence and tried to speak. ³⁴But when the crowd realized he was a Jew, they started shouting again and kept it up for two hours: "Great is Diana of the Ephesians! Great is Diana of the Ephesians!"

³⁵At last the mayor was able to quiet them down enough to speak. "Men of Ephesus," he said, "everyone knows that Ephesus is the center of the religion of the great Diana, whose image fell down to us from heaven. ³⁶Since this is an indisputable fact, you shouldn't be disturbed no matter what is said, and should do nothing rash. ³⁷Yet you have brought these men here who have stolen nothing from her temple and have not defamed her. ³⁸If Demetrius and the craftsmen have a case against them, the courts are currently in session and the judges can take the case at once. Let them go through legal channels. ³⁹And if there are complaints about other matters, they can be settled at the regular City Council meetings; ⁴⁰for we are in danger of being called to account by the Roman government for today's riot, since there is no cause for it. And if Rome demands an explanation, I won't know what to say."

⁴¹Then he dismissed them, and they dispersed.

20 On to Greece and Macedonia

When it was all over, Paul sent for the disciples, preached a farewell message to them, said good-bye and left for Greece, ²preaching to the believers along the way in all the cities he passed through. ³He was in Greece three months and was preparing to sail for Syria when he discovered a plot by the Jews against his life, so he decided to go north to Macedonia first.

⁴Several men were traveling with him, going as far as Turkey; they were Sopater of Beroea, the son of Pyrrhus; Aristarchus and Secundus, from Thessalonica; Gaius, from Derbe; and Timothy; and Tychicus and Trophimus, who were returning to their homes in Turkey, ⁵and had gone on ahead and were waiting for us at Troas. ⁶As soon as the Passover ceremonies ended, we boarded ship at Philippi in northern Greece and five days later arrived in Troas, Turkey, where we stayed a week.

⁷On Sunday we gathered for a Communion service, with Paul preaching. And since he was leaving the next day, he talked until midnight! ⁸The upstairs room where we met was lighted with many flickering lamps; ⁹and as Paul spoke on and on, a young man named Eutychus, sitting on the windowsill, went fast asleep and fell three stories to his death below. ¹⁰⁻¹²Paul went down and took him into his arms. "Don't worry," he said, "he's all right!" And he was! What a wave of awesome joy swept through the crowd! They all went back upstairs and ate the Lord's Supper together; then Paul preached another long sermon—so it was dawn when he finally left them!

¹³Paul was going by land to Assos, and we went on ahead by ship. ¹⁴He joined us there and we sailed together to Mitylene; ¹⁵the next day we passed Chios; the next, we touched at Samos; and a day later we arrived at Miletus.

¹⁶Paul had decided against stopping at Ephesus this time, as he was hurrying to get to Jerusalem, if possible, for the celebration of Pentecost.

¹⁷But when we landed at Miletus, he sent a message to the elders of the church at Ephesus asking them to come down to the boat to meet him.

¹⁸When they arrived he told them, "You men know that from the day I set foot in Turkey until now ¹⁹I have done the Lord's work humbly—yes, and with tears—and have faced grave danger from the plots of the Jews against my life. ²⁰Yet I never shrank from telling you the truth, either publicly or in your homes. ²¹I have had one message for Jews and Gentiles alike—the necessity of turning from sin to God through faith in our Lord Jesus Christ.

²²"And now I am going to Jerusalem, drawn there irresistibly by the Holy Spirit, not knowing what awaits me, ²³except that the Holy Spirit has told me in city after city that jail and suffering lie ahead. ²⁴But life is worth nothing unless I use it for doing the work assigned me by the Lord Jesus—the work of telling others the Good News about God's mighty kindness and love.

²⁵"And now I know that none of you among whom I went about teaching the Kingdom will ever see me again. ²⁶Let me say plainly that no man's blood can be laid at my door, ²⁷for I didn't shrink from declaring all God's message to you.

²⁸"And now beware! Be sure that you feed and shepherd God's flock—his church, purchased with his blood—for the Holy Spirit is holding you responsible as overseers. ²⁹I know full well that after I leave you, false teachers, like vicious wolves, will appear among you, not sparing the flock. ³⁰Some of you yourselves will distort the

truth in order to draw a following. ³¹Watch out! Remember the three years I was with you—my constant watchcare over you night and day and my many tears for you.

³²"And now I entrust you to God and his care and to his wonderful words that are able to build your faith and give you all the inheritance of those who are set apart for himself.

³³"I have never been hungry for money or fine clothing— ³⁴you know that these hands of mine worked to pay my own way and even to supply the needs of those who were with me. ³⁵And I was a constant example to you in helping the poor; for I remembered the words of the Lord Jesus, 'It is more blessed to give than to receive.'"

³⁶When he had finished speaking, he knelt and prayed with them, ³⁷and they wept aloud as they embraced him in farewell, ³⁸sorrowing most of all because he said that he would never see them again. Then they accompanied him down to the ship.

21 Paul Journeys to Jerusalem

After parting from the Ephesian elders, we sailed straight to Cos. The next day we reached Rhodes and then went to Patara. ²There we boarded a ship sailing for the Syrian province of Phoenicia. ³We sighted the island of Cyprus, passed it on our left, and landed at the harbor of Tyre, in Syria, where the ship unloaded. ⁴We went ashore, found the local believers, and stayed with them a week. These disciples warned Paul—the Holy Spirit prophesying through them—not to go on to Jerusalem. ⁵At the end of the week when we returned to the ship, the entire congregation including wives and children walked down to the beach with us where we prayed and said our farewells. ⁶Then we went aboard, and they returned home.

⁷The next stop after leaving Tyre was Ptolemais, where we greeted the believers but stayed only one day. ⁸Then we went on to Caesarea and stayed at the home of Philip the Evangelist, one of the first seven deacons. ⁹He had four unmarried daughters who had the gift of prophecy.

¹⁰During our stay of several days, a man named Agabus, who also had the gift of prophecy, arrived from Judea ¹¹and visited us. He took Paul's belt, bound his own feet and hands with it, and said, "The Holy Spirit declares, 'So shall the owner of this belt be bound by the Jews in Jerusalem and turned over to the Romans.'" ¹²Hearing this, all of us—the local believers and his traveling companions—begged Paul not to go on to Jerusalem.

¹³But he said, "Why all this weeping? You are breaking my heart! For I am ready not only to be jailed at Jerusalem but also to die for the sake of the Lord Jesus." ¹⁴When it was clear that he wouldn't be dissuaded, we gave up and said, "The will of the Lord be done."

¹⁵So shortly afterwards we packed our things and left for Jerusalem. ¹⁶Some disciples from Caesarea accompanied us, and on arrival we were guests at the home of Mnason, originally from Cyprus, one of the early believers; ¹⁷and all the believers at Jerusalem welcomed us cordially.

¹⁸The second day Paul took us with him to meet with James and the elders of the Jerusalem church. ¹⁹After greetings were exchanged, Paul recounted the many things God had accomplished among the Gentiles through his work.

²⁰They praised God but then said, "You know, dear brother, how many thousands of Jews have also believed, and they are all very insistent that Jewish believers must continue to follow the Jewish traditions and customs. ²¹Our Jewish Christians here at Jerusalem have been told that you are against the laws of Moses, against our Jewish customs, and that you forbid the circumcision of their children. ²²Now what can be done? For they will certainly hear that you have come.

²³"We suggest this: We have four men here who are preparing to shave their heads and take some vows. ²⁴Go with them to the Temple and have your head shaved too—and pay for theirs to be shaved.

"Then everyone will know that you approve of this custom for the Hebrew Christians and that you yourself obey the Jewish laws and are in line with our thinking in these matters.

²⁵"As for the Gentile Christians, we aren't asking them to follow these Jewish customs at all—except for the ones we wrote to them about: not to eat food offered to idols, not to eat unbled meat from strangled animals, and not to commit fornication."

²⁶,²⁷So Paul agreed to their request and the next day went with the men to the Temple for the ceremony, thus publicizing his vow to offer a sacrifice seven days later with the others.

The seven days were almost ended when some Jews from Turkey saw him in the Temple and roused a mob against him. They grabbed him, ²⁸yelling, "Men of Israel! Help! Help! This is the man who preaches against our people and tells everybody to disobey the Jewish laws. He even

---

CONTENTMENT 20:33 Paul was satisfied with whatever he had, wherever he was, as long as he could do God's work. Examine your attitudes toward wealth and comfort. If you focus more on what you don't have than on what you do have, it's time to reexamine your priorities and put God's work back in first place. Then you'll be able to be content with what God has given you. **To begin the series of devotionals on CONTENTMENT, turn to page 89.**

talks against the Temple and defiles it by bringing Gentiles in!" ²⁹(For down in the city earlier that day, they had seen him with Trophimus, a Gentile from Ephesus in Turkey, and assumed that Paul had taken him into the Temple.)

³⁰The whole population of the city was electrified by these accusations and a great riot followed. Paul was dragged out of the Temple, and immediately the gates were closed behind him. ³¹As they were killing him, word reached the commander of the Roman garrison that all Jerusalem was in an uproar. ³²He quickly ordered out his soldiers and officers and ran down among the crowd. When the mob saw the troops coming, they quit beating Paul. ³³The commander arrested him and ordered him bound with double chains. Then he asked the crowd who he was and what he had done. ³⁴Some shouted one thing and some another. When he couldn't find out anything in all the uproar and confusion, he ordered Paul to be taken to the armory. ³⁵As they reached the stairs, the mob grew so violent that the soldiers lifted Paul to their shoulders to protect him, ³⁶and the crowd surged behind shouting, "Away with him, away with him!"

³⁷,³⁸As Paul was about to be taken inside, he said to the commander, "May I have a word with you?"

"Do you know Greek?" the commander asked, surprised. "Aren't you that Egyptian who led a rebellion a few years ago and took 4,000 members of the Assassins with him into the desert?"

³⁹"No," Paul replied, "I am a Jew from Tarsus in Cilicia which is no small town. I request permission to talk to these people."

⁴⁰The commander agreed, so Paul stood on the stairs and motioned to the people to be quiet; soon a deep silence enveloped the crowd, and he addressed them in Hebrew as follows:

22 Paul Is Arrested

"Brothers and fathers, listen to me as I offer my defense." ²(When they heard him speaking in Hebrew, the silence was even greater.) ³"I am a Jew," he said, "born in Tarsus, a city in Cilicia, but educated here in Jerusalem under Gamaliel, at whose feet I learned to follow our Jewish laws and customs very carefully. I became very anxious to honor God in everything I did, just as you have tried to do today. ⁴And I persecuted the Christians, hounding them to death, binding and delivering both men and women to prison. ⁵The High Priest or any member of the Council can testify that this is so. For I asked them for letters to the Jewish leaders in Damascus, with instructions to let me bring any Christians I found to Jerusalem in chains to be punished.

⁶"As I was on the road, nearing Damascus, suddenly about noon a very bright light from heaven shone around me. ⁷And I fell to the ground and heard a voice saying to me, 'Paul, Paul, why are you persecuting me?'

⁸"Who is it speaking to me, sir?' I asked. And he replied, 'I am Jesus of Nazareth, the one you are persecuting.' ⁹The men with me saw the light but didn't understand what was said.

¹⁰"And I said, 'What shall I do, Lord?'

"And the Lord told me, 'Get up and go into Damascus, and there you will be told what awaits you in the years ahead.'

¹¹"I was blinded by the intense light and had to be led into Damascus by my companions. ¹²There a man named Ananias, as godly a man as you could find for obeying the law and well thought of by all the Jews of Damascus, ¹³came to me, and standing beside me said, 'Brother Paul, receive your sight!' And that very hour I could see him!

¹⁴"Then he told me, 'The God of our fathers has chosen you to know his will and to see the Messiah and hear him speak. ¹⁵You are to take his message everywhere, telling what you have seen and heard. ¹⁶And now, why delay? Go and be baptized and be cleansed from your sins, calling on the name of the Lord.'

¹⁷,¹⁸"One day after my return to Jerusalem, while I was praying in the Temple, I fell into a trance and saw a vision of God saying to me, 'Hurry! Leave Jerusalem, for the people here won't believe you when you give them my message.'

¹⁹"But Lord,' I argued, 'they certainly know that I imprisoned and beat those in every synagogue who believed on you. ²⁰And when your witness Stephen was killed, I was standing there agreeing—keeping the coats they laid aside as they stoned him.'

²¹"But God said to me, 'Leave Jerusalem, for I will send you far away to the *Gentiles!*'"

²²The crowd listened until Paul came to that word, then with one voice they shouted, "Away with such a fellow! Kill him! He isn't fit to live!" ²³They yelled and threw their coats in the air and tossed up handfuls of dust.

²⁴So the commander brought him inside and ordered him lashed with whips to make him confess his crime. He wanted to find out why the crowd had become so furious!

²⁵As they tied Paul down to lash him, Paul said to an officer standing there, "Is it legal for you to whip a Roman citizen who hasn't even been tried?"

²⁶The officer went to the commander and asked, "What are you doing? This man is a Roman citizen!"

²⁷So the commander went over and asked Paul, "Tell me, are you a Roman citizen?"

"Yes, I certainly am."

²⁸"I am too," the commander muttered, "and it cost me plenty!"

"But I am a citizen by birth!"

²⁹The soldiers standing ready to lash him, quickly disappeared when they heard Paul was a Roman citizen, and the commander was frightened because he had ordered him bound and whipped.

³⁰The next day the commander freed him from his chains and ordered the chief priests into session with the Jewish Council. He had Paul brought in before them to try to find out what the trouble was all about.

23

Gazing intently at the Council, Paul began:

"Brothers, I have always lived before God in all good conscience!"

²Instantly Ananias the High Priest commanded those close to Paul to slap him on the mouth.

³Paul said to him, "God shall slap you, you whitewashed pigpen. What kind of judge are you to break the law yourself by ordering me struck like that?"

⁴Those standing near Paul said to him, "Is that the way to talk to God's High Priest?"

⁵"I didn't realize he was the High Priest, brothers," Paul replied, "for the Scriptures say, 'Never speak evil of any of your rulers.'"

⁶Then Paul thought of something! Part of the Council were Sadducees, and part were Pharisees! So he shouted, "Brothers, I am a Pharisee, as were all my ancestors! And I am being tried here today because I believe in the resurrection of the dead!"

⁷This divided the Council right down the middle—the Pharisees against the Sadducees—⁸for the Sadducees say there is no resurrection or angels or even eternal spirit within us, but the Pharisees believe in all of these.

⁹So a great clamor arose. Some of the Jewish leaders jumped up to argue that Paul was all right. "We see nothing wrong with him," they shouted. "Perhaps a spirit or angel spoke to him [there on the Damascus road]."

¹⁰The shouting grew louder and louder, and the men were tugging at Paul from both sides, pulling him this way and that. Finally the commander, fearing they would tear him apart, ordered his soldiers to take him away from them by force and bring him back to the armory.

¹¹That night the Lord stood beside Paul and said, "Don't worry, Paul; just as you have told the people about me here in Jerusalem, so you must also in Rome."

¹²,¹³The next morning some forty or more of the Jews got together and bound themselves by a curse neither to eat nor drink until they had killed Paul! ¹⁴Then they went to the chief priests and elders and told them what they had done. ¹⁵"Ask the commander to bring Paul back to the Council again," they requested. "Pretend you want to ask a few more questions. We will kill him on the way."

¹⁶But Paul's nephew got wind of their plan and came to the armory and told Paul.

¹⁷Paul called one of the officers and said, "Take this boy to the commander. He has something important to tell him."

¹⁸So the officer did, explaining, "Paul, the prisoner, called me over and asked me to bring this young man to you to tell you something."

¹⁹The commander took the boy by the hand, and leading him aside asked, "What is it you want to tell me, lad?"

²⁰"Tomorrow," he told him, "the Jews are going to ask you to bring Paul before the Council again, pretending they want to get some more information. ²¹But don't do it! There are more than forty men hiding along the road ready to jump him and kill him. They have bound themselves under a curse to neither eat nor drink till he is dead. They are out there now, expecting you to agree to their request."

²²"Don't let a soul know you told me this," the commander warned the boy as he left. ²³,²⁴Then the commander called two of his officers and ordered, "Get 200 soldiers ready to leave for Caesarea at nine o'clock tonight! Take 200 spearmen and 70 mounted cavalry. Give Paul a horse to ride and get him safely to Governor Felix."

²⁵Then he wrote this letter to the governor:

²⁶"*From:* Claudius Lysias

"*To:* His Excellency, Governor Felix.

"Greetings!

²⁷"This man was seized by the Jews, and they were killing him when I sent the soldiers to rescue him, for I learned that he was a Roman citizen. ²⁸Then I took him to their Council to try to find out what he had done. ²⁹I soon discovered it was something about their Jewish beliefs, certainly nothing worthy of imprisonment or death. ³⁰But when I was informed of a plot to kill him, I decided to send him on to you and will tell his accusers to bring their charges before you."

³¹So that night, as ordered, the soldiers took Paul to Antipatris. ³²They returned to the armory the next morning, leaving him with the cavalry to take him on to Caesarea.

³³When they arrived in Caesarea, they pre-

sented Paul and the letter to the governor. ³⁴He read it and then asked Paul where he was from.

"Cilicia," Paul answered.

³⁵"I will hear your case fully when your accusers arrive," the governor told him, and ordered him kept in the prison at King Herod's palace.

24 Paul before Felix

Five days later Ananias the High Priest arrived with some of the Jewish leaders and the lawyer Tertullus, to make their accusations against Paul. ²When Tertullus was called forward, he laid charges against Paul in the following address to the governor:

"Your Excellency, you have given quietness and peace to us Jews and have greatly reduced the discrimination against us. ³And for this we are very, very grateful to you. ⁴But lest I bore you, kindly give me your attention for only a moment as I briefly outline our case against this man. ⁵For we have found him to be a troublemaker, a man who is constantly inciting the Jews throughout the entire world to riots and rebellions against the Roman government. He is a ringleader of the sect known as the Nazarenes. ⁶Moreover, he was trying to defile the Temple when we arrested him.

"We would have given him what he justly deserves, ⁷but Lysias, the commander of the garrison, came and took him violently away from us, ⁸demanding that he be tried by Roman law. You can find out the truth of our accusations by examining him yourself."

⁹Then all the other Jews chimed in, declaring that everything Tertullus said was true.

¹⁰Now it was Paul's turn. The governor motioned for him to rise and speak.

Paul began: "I know, sir, that you have been a judge of Jewish affairs for many years, and this gives me confidence as I make my defense. ¹¹You can quickly discover that it was no more than twelve days ago that I arrived in Jerusalem to worship at the Temple, ¹²and you will discover that I have never incited a riot in any synagogue or on the streets of any city; ¹³and these men certainly cannot prove the things they accuse me of doing.

¹⁴"But one thing I do confess, that I believe in the way of salvation, which they refer to as a sect; I follow that system of serving the God of our ancestors; I firmly believe in the Jewish law and everything written in the books of prophecy; ¹⁵and I believe, just as these men do, that there will be a resurrection of both the righteous and ungodly. ¹⁶Because of this, I try with all my strength to always maintain a clear conscience before God and man.

¹⁷"After several years away, I returned to Jerusalem with money to aid the Jews and to offer a sacrifice to God. ¹⁸My accusers saw me in the Temple as I was presenting my thank offering. I had shaved my head as their laws required, and there was no crowd around me, and no rioting! But some Jews from Turkey were there ¹⁹(who ought to be here if they have anything against me)— ²⁰but look! Ask these men right here what wrongdoing their Council found in me, ²¹except that I said one thing I shouldn't when I shouted out, 'I am here before the Council to defend myself for believing that the dead will rise again!'"

²²Felix, who knew Christians didn't go around starting riots, told the Jews to wait for the arrival of Lysias, the garrison commander, and then he would decide the case. ²³He ordered Paul to prison but instructed the guards to treat him gently and not to forbid any of his friends from visiting him or bringing him gifts to make his stay more comfortable.

²⁴A few days later Felix came with Drusilla, his legal wife, a Jewess. Sending for Paul, they listened as he told them about faith in Christ Jesus. ²⁵And as he reasoned with them about righteousness and self-control and the judgment to come, Felix was terrified.

"Go away for now," he replied, "and when I have a more convenient time, I'll call for you again."

²⁶He also hoped that Paul would bribe him, so he sent for him from time to time and talked with him. ²⁷Two years went by in this way; then Felix was succeeded by Porcius Festus. And because Felix wanted to gain favor with the Jews, he left Paul in chains.

25 Paul before Festus

Three days after Festus arrived in Caesarea to take over his new responsibilities, he left for Jerusalem, ²where the chief priests and other Jewish leaders got hold of him and gave him their story about Paul. ³They begged him to bring Paul to Jerusalem at once. (Their plan was to waylay and kill him.) ⁴But Festus replied that since Paul was at Caesarea and he himself was returning there soon, ⁵those with authority in this affair should return with him for the trial.

⁶Eight or ten days later he returned to Caesarea and the following day opened Paul's trial.

⁷On Paul's arrival in court the Jews from Jerusalem gathered around, hurling many serious accusations which they couldn't prove. ⁸Paul denied the charges: "I am not guilty," he said. "I have not opposed the Jewish laws or desecrated

FAMILY DEVOTIONS

☐ DEVOTION 299
HONESTY

Read Acts 24:16

"Dad, what's a falsehood?" asked Katie as she plunked herself in a chair beside her father.

"A falsehood?" Dad asked in surprise. "Well, a falsehood is a lie or untruth."

"That's what I thought," said Katie, "but it's a funny word. Why would a lie be called a falsehood?"

"Hmmm," pondered Dad. "Well, one explanation I've heard is that it comes from something done hundreds of years ago. It was during a time when people wore hoods instead of hats, and they wore cloaks instead of coats."

"Like Little Red Riding Hood?" asked Katie.

"Sort of," answered Dad. "A person like a doctor or lawyer—or whatever profession—wore a certain type and color of hood."

"Then if you saw someone with a certain kind of hood, you would know what he was?" asked Katie.

"Yes, and that's where the falsehood comes in," Dad answered. "Some dishonest people would go to a town where they weren't known, wear a hood they hadn't earned, and set up a practice. They were living a lie. They were wearing a false hood."

Katie nodded. "I can see how the word came to mean a lie," she said. "I think it's a good word to use to describe people who pretend to be something they're not today, too. Some kids cheat and swear at school, but pretend to be Christians on Sunday. It's like they're hiding under a false hood."

"That's right!" answered Dad. "On more than one occasion Jesus condemned the scribes and Pharisees for making long prayers—pretending to be worshiping God when they were really just putting on a show to impress people. Be careful always to be honest before God and others."

"I will," Katie promised.

Honesty Memory Verse

Stop lying to each other; tell the truth, for we are parts of each other and when we lie to each other we are hurting ourselves.
Ephesians 4:25

How About You?
Are you pretending to be something you aren't? If you feel the need to pretend, ask yourself why. If you're honest and obedient as God wants you to be, you will not feel the need to hide under a "false hood." *A. G. L.*

• For the next devotional, turn to page 1071. • To start the next topic, turn to page 449. • For notes on *HONESTY*, see pages 304, 813, and 863.

the Temple or rebelled against the Roman government."

⁹Then Festus, anxious to please the Jews, asked him, "Are you willing to go to Jerusalem and stand trial before me?"

¹⁰,¹¹But Paul replied, "No! I demand my privilege of a hearing before the emperor himself. You know very well I am not guilty. If I have done something worthy of death, I don't refuse to die! But if I am innocent, neither you nor anyone else has a right to turn me over to these men to kill me. *I appeal to Caesar.*"

¹²Festus conferred with his advisors and then replied, "Very well! You have appealed to Caesar, and to Caesar you shall go!"

¹³A few days later King Agrippa arrived with Bernice for a visit with Festus. ¹⁴During their stay of several days Festus discussed Paul's case with the king. "There is a prisoner here," he told him, "whose case was left for me by Felix. ¹⁵When I was in Jerusalem, the chief priests and other Jewish leaders gave me their side of the story and asked me to have him killed. ¹⁶Of course I quickly pointed out to them that Roman law does not convict a man before he is tried. He is given an opportunity to defend himself face to face with his accusers.

¹⁷"When they came here for the trial, I called the case the very next day and ordered Paul brought in. ¹⁸But the accusations made against him weren't at all what I supposed they would be. ¹⁹It was something about their religion and about someone called Jesus who died, but Paul insists is alive! ²⁰I was perplexed as to how to decide a case of this kind and asked him whether he would be willing to stand trial on these charges in Jerusalem. ²¹But Paul appealed to Caesar! So I ordered him back to jail until I could arrange to get him to the emperor."

²²"I'd like to hear the man myself," Agrippa said.

And Festus replied, "You shall—tomorrow!"

²³So the next day, after the king and Bernice had arrived at the courtroom with great pomp, accompanied by military officers and prominent men of the city, Festus ordered Paul brought in.

²⁴Then Festus addressed the audience: "King Agrippa and all present," he said, "this is the man whose death is demanded both by the local Jews and by those in Jerusalem! ²⁵But in my opinion he has done nothing worthy of death. However, he appealed his case to Caesar, and I have no alternative but to send him. ²⁶But what shall I write the emperor? For there is no real charge against him! So I have brought him before you all, and especially you, King Agrippa, to examine him and then tell me what to write. ²⁷For it doesn't seem reasonable to send a prisoner to the emperor without any charges against him!"

26 Agrippa Wants to Hear Paul

Then Agrippa said to Paul, "Go ahead. Tell us your story."

So Paul, with many gestures, presented his defense:

²"I am fortunate, King Agrippa," he began, "to be able to present my answer before you, ³for I know you are an expert on Jewish laws and customs. Now please listen patiently!

⁴"As the Jews are well aware, I was given a thorough Jewish training from my earliest childhood in Tarsus and later at Jerusalem, and I lived accordingly. ⁵If they would admit it, they know that I have always been the strictest of Pharisees when it comes to obedience to Jewish laws and customs. ⁶But the real reason behind their accusations is something else—it is because I am looking forward to the fulfillment of God's promise made to our ancestors. ⁷The twelve tribes of Israel strive night and day to attain this same hope I have! Yet, O King, for me it is a crime, they say! ⁸But is it a crime to believe in the resurrection of the dead? Does it seem incredible to you that God can bring men back to life again?

⁹"I used to believe that I ought to do many horrible things to the followers of Jesus of Nazareth. ¹⁰I imprisoned many of the saints in Jerusalem, as authorized by the High Priests; and when they were condemned to death, I cast my vote against them. ¹¹I used torture to try to make Christians everywhere curse Christ. I was so violently opposed to them that I even hounded them in distant cities in foreign lands.

¹²"I was on such a mission to Damascus, armed with the authority and commission of the chief priests, ¹³when one day about noon, sir, a light from heaven brighter than the sun shone down on me and my companions. ¹⁴We all fell down, and I heard a voice speaking to me in Hebrew, 'Paul, Paul, why are you persecuting me? You are only hurting yourself.'

¹⁵"'Who are you, sir?' I asked.

"And the Lord replied, 'I am Jesus, the one you are persecuting. ¹⁶Now stand up! For I have appeared to you to appoint you as my servant and my witness. You are to tell the world about this

---

FAITH IN ACTION 25:11 Paul knew he was blameless of the charges against him and could appeal to Caesar's judgment. He knew his rights as a Roman citizen and as an innocent person. Paul had met his responsibilities as a Roman, and so he had the opportunity to claim Rome's protection. The good reputation and clear conscience that result from our walk with God can help us remain not only guilt-free before God, but blame-free before the world as well. **To begin the series of devotionals on FAITH IN ACTION, turn to page 141.**

experience and about the many other occasions when I shall appear to you. [17]And I will protect you from both your own people and the Gentiles. Yes, I am going to send you to the Gentiles [18]to open their eyes to their true condition so that they may repent and live in the light of God instead of in Satan's darkness, so that they may receive forgiveness for their sins and God's inheritance along with all people everywhere whose sins are cleansed away, who are set apart by faith in me.'

[19]"And so, O King Agrippa, I was not disobedient to that vision from heaven! [20]I preached first to those in Damascus, then in Jerusalem and through Judea, and also to the Gentiles that all must forsake their sins and turn to God—and prove their repentance by doing good deeds. [21]The Jews arrested me in the Temple for preaching this and tried to kill me, [22]but God protected me so that I am still alive today to tell these facts to everyone, both great and small. I teach nothing except what the Prophets and Moses said— [23]that the Messiah would suffer and be the First to rise from the dead, to bring light to Jews and Gentiles alike."

[24]Suddenly Festus shouted, "Paul, you are insane. Your long studying has broken your mind!"

[25]But Paul replied, "I am not insane, Most Excellent Festus. I speak words of sober truth. [26]And King Agrippa knows about these things. I speak frankly for I am sure these events are all familiar to him, for they were not done in a corner! [27]King Agrippa, do you believe the Prophets? But I know you do—"

[28]Agrippa interrupted him. "With trivial proofs like these, you expect me to become a Christian?"

[29]And Paul replied, "Would to God that whether my arguments are trivial or strong, both you and everyone here in this audience might become the same as I am, except for these chains."

[30]Then the king, the governor, Bernice, and all the others stood and left. [31]As they talked it over afterwards they agreed, "This man hasn't done anything worthy of death or imprisonment."

[32]And Agrippa said to Festus, "He could be set free if he hadn't appealed to Caesar!"

27 Paul's Ship Is Wrecked

Arrangements were finally made to start us on our way to Rome by ship; so Paul and several other prisoners were placed in the custody of an officer named Julius, a member of the imperial guard. [2]We left on a boat that was scheduled to make several stops along the Turkish coast. I should add that Aristarchus, a Greek from Thessalonica, was with us.

[3]The next day when we docked at Sidon, Julius was very kind to Paul and let him go ashore to visit with friends and receive their hospitality. [4]Putting to sea from there, we encountered headwinds that made it difficult to keep the ship on course, so we sailed north of Cyprus between the island and the mainland [5]and passed along the coast of the provinces of Cilicia and Pamphylia, landing at Myra, in the province of Lycia. [6]There our officer found an Egyptian ship from Alexandria, bound for Italy, and put us aboard.

[7,8]We had several days of rough sailing, and finally neared Cnidus; but the winds had become too strong, so we ran across to Crete, passing the port of Salome. Beating into the wind with great difficulty and moving slowly along the southern coast, we arrived at Fair Havens, near the city of Lasea. [9]There we stayed for several days. The weather was becoming dangerous for long voyages by then because it was late in the year, and Paul spoke to the ship's officers about it.

[10]"Sirs," he said, "I believe there is trouble ahead if we go on—perhaps shipwreck, loss of cargo, injuries, and death." [11]But the officers in charge of the prisoners listened more to the ship's captain and the owner than to Paul. [12]And since Fair Havens was an exposed harbor—a poor place to spend the winter—most of the crew advised trying to go further up the coast to Phoenix in order to winter there; Phoenix was a good harbor with only a northwest and southwest exposure.

[13]Just then a light wind began blowing from the south, and it looked like a perfect day for the trip; so they pulled up anchor and sailed along close to shore.

[14,15]But shortly afterwards the weather changed abruptly, and a heavy wind of typhoon strength (a "northeaster," they called it) caught the ship and blew it out to sea. They tried at first to face back to shore but couldn't, so they gave up and let the ship run before the gale.

[16]We finally sailed behind a small island named Clauda, where with great difficulty we hoisted aboard the lifeboat that was being towed behind us, [17]and then banded the ship with ropes to strengthen the hull. The sailors were afraid of being driven across to the quicksands of the African coast, so they lowered the topsails and were thus driven before the wind.

[18]The next day as the seas grew higher, the crew began throwing the cargo overboard. [19]The following day they threw out the tackle and anything else they could lay their hands on. [20]The terrible storm raged unabated many days, until at last all hope was gone.

[21]No one had eaten for a long time, but finally Paul called the crew together and said, "Men, you should have listened to me in the first place and not left Fair Havens—you would have avoided all this injury and loss! [22]But cheer up! Not one of us will lose our lives, even though the ship will go down.

[23]"For last night an angel of the God to whom I

belong and whom I serve stood beside me ²⁴and said, 'Don't be afraid, Paul—for you will surely stand trial before Caesar! What's more, God has granted your request and will save the lives of all those sailing with you.' ²⁵So take courage! For I believe God! It will be just as he said! ²⁶But we will be shipwrecked on an island."

²⁷About midnight on the fourteenth night of the storm, as we were being driven to and fro on the Adriatic Sea, the sailors suspected land was near. ²⁸They sounded and found 120 feet of water below them. A little later they sounded again and found only 90 feet. ²⁹At this rate they knew they would soon be driven ashore; and fearing rocks along the coast, they threw out four anchors from the stern and prayed for daylight.

³⁰Some of the sailors planned to abandon the ship and lowered the emergency boat as though they were going to put out anchors from the prow. ³¹But Paul said to the soldiers and commanding officer, "You will all die unless everyone stays aboard." ³²So the soldiers cut the ropes and let the boat fall off.

³³As the darkness gave way to the early morning light, Paul begged everyone to eat. "You haven't touched food for two weeks," he said. ³⁴"Please eat something now for your own good! For not a hair of your heads shall perish!"

³⁵Then he took some hardtack and gave thanks to God before them all, and broke off a piece and ate it. ³⁶Suddenly everyone felt better and began eating, ³⁷all 276 of us—for that is the number we had aboard. ³⁸After eating, the crew lightened the ship further by throwing all the wheat overboard.

³⁹When it was day, they didn't recognize the coastline, but noticed a bay with a beach and wondered whether they could get between the rocks and be driven up onto the beach. ⁴⁰They finally decided to try. Cutting off the anchors and leaving them in the sea, they lowered the rudders, raised the foresail, and headed ashore. ⁴¹But the ship hit a sandbar and ran aground. The bow of the ship stuck fast, while the stern was exposed to the violence of the waves and began to break apart.

⁴²The soldiers advised their commanding officer to let them kill the prisoners lest any of them swim ashore and escape. ⁴³But Julius wanted to spare Paul, so he told them no. Then he ordered all who could swim to jump overboard and make for land, ⁴⁴and the rest to try for it on planks and debris from the broken ship. So everyone escaped safely ashore!

28 Paul Is Shipwrecked on Malta

We soon learned that we were on the island of Malta. The people of the island were very kind to us, building a bonfire on the beach to welcome and warm us in the rain and cold. ³As Paul gathered an armful of sticks to lay on the fire, a poisonous snake, driven out by the heat, fastened itself onto his hand! ⁴The people of the island saw it hanging there and said to each other, "A murderer, no doubt! Though he escaped the sea, justice will not permit him to live!"

⁵But Paul shook off the snake into the fire and was unharmed. ⁶The people waited for him to begin swelling or suddenly fall dead; but when they had waited a long time and no harm came to him, they changed their minds and decided he was a god.

⁷Near the shore where we landed was an estate belonging to Publius, the governor of the island. He welcomed us courteously and fed us for three days. ⁸As it happened, Publius' father was ill with fever and dysentery. Paul went in and prayed for him, and laying his hands on him, healed him! ⁹Then all the other sick people in the island came and were cured. ¹⁰As a result we were showered with gifts, and when the time came to sail, people put on board all sorts of things we would need for the trip.

¹¹It was three months after the shipwreck before we set sail again, and this time it was in *The Twin Brothers* of Alexandria, a ship that had wintered at the island. ¹²Our first stop was Syracuse, where we stayed three days. ¹³From there we circled around to Rhegium; a day later a south wind began blowing, so the following day we arrived at Puteoli, ¹⁴where we found some believers! They begged us to stay with them seven days. Then we went on to Rome.

¹⁵The brothers in Rome had heard we were coming and came to meet us at the Forum on the Appian Way. Others joined us at The Three Taverns. When Paul saw them, he thanked God and took courage.

¹⁶When we arrived in Rome, Paul was permitted to live wherever he wanted to, though guarded by a soldier.

¹⁷Three days after his arrival, he called together the local Jewish leaders and spoke to them as follows:

"Brothers, I was arrested by the Jews in Jerusalem and handed over to the Roman government for prosecution, even though I had harmed no one nor violated the customs of our ancestors. ¹⁸The Romans gave me a trial and wanted to release me, for they found no cause for the death sentence demanded by the Jewish leaders. ¹⁹But when the Jews protested the decision, I felt it necessary, with no malice against them, to appeal to Caesar. ²⁰I asked you to come here today so we could get acquainted and I could tell you that it is because I believe the Messiah has come that I am bound with this chain."

²¹They replied, "We have heard nothing against

Family Devotions

☐ DEVOTION 300
SHARING YOUR FAITH

Read Acts 28:16-31

"Hi, Gordy." Ken nervously greeted his longtime friend. He always felt guilty when he saw Gordy lately. That was because Ken had accepted Jesus as Savior, but he'd never told Gordy. He knew he should. In fact, he wanted to—it was just that he was afraid Gordy would laugh.

"What did you get for your birthday yesterday?" Gordy asked now. "Anything good?"

"You bet," replied Ken. He lifted his left hand and displayed a new baseball mitt. "How about this? No balls are going to get away from me now!"

"Neat," approved Gordy. "I could really use that."

"My grandparents gave it to me," said Ken, "and this shirt is from my brother. My folks gave me a skateboard."

"Wow!" Gordy let out a long whistle. "I could use all those things."

"Well, you can't have 'em," laughed Ken. Suddenly he thought about the gift of eternal life he had received a month ago. He'd told Gordy about all his other gifts. He knew he should tell him about that one, too. That was a gift Gordy could have. He took a deep breath. "A month ago I got . . ." He took another deep breath. "A month ago I got . . ." He stopped, afraid to finish. "I got a gift from God. I got my sins forgiven."

"Huh?" Gordy looked startled. "What on earth are you talking about?"

"I'm a Christian now, and if you want to, you can have that gift, too." Ken finished in a hurry. "I gotta go. Bye." He hurried down the street as Gordy stared after him. Ken felt a little funny because he was sure he hadn't done that very well. At the same time, he felt lighthearted because he knew that at least it was a start. *I'm going to invite Gordy to Sunday school this week,* he decided. *I'll ask him tomorrow. I'll pray that he'll be saved soon, too!*

Sharing Your Faith Memory Verse

And let us not get tired of doing what is right, for after a while we will reap a harvest of blessing if we don't get discouraged and give up.
Galatians 6:9

How About You?

Do you talk with your friends about anything and everything except the Lord? Paul couldn't stop talking about everything God had done for him! Don't be afraid to tell your friends about the wonderful gift God has given you. They may want it, too. H. M.

- For the next devotional, turn to page 1075. • For the next devotional on SHARING YOUR FAITH, turn to page 1099.
- For notes on SHARING YOUR FAITH, see pages 462, 776, 1015, and 1074.

you! We have had no letters from Judea or reports from those arriving from Jerusalem. ²²But we want to hear what you believe, for the only thing we know about these Christians is that they are denounced everywhere!"

²³So a time was set, and on that day large numbers came to his house. He told them about the Kingdom of God and taught them about Jesus from the Scriptures—from the five books of Moses and the books of prophecy. He began lecturing in the morning and went on into the evening!

²⁴Some believed and some didn't. ²⁵But after they had argued back and forth among themselves, they left with this final word from Paul ringing in their ears: "The Holy Spirit was right when he said through Isaiah the prophet,

²⁶"'Say to the Jews, "You will hear and see but not understand, ²⁷for your hearts are too fat and your ears don't listen and you have closed your eyes against understanding, for you don't want to see and hear and understand and turn to me to heal you.'"

²⁸,²⁹So I want you to realize that this salvation from God is available to the Gentiles too, and they will accept it."

³⁰Paul lived for the next two years in his rented house and welcomed all who visited him, ³¹telling them with all boldness about the Kingdom of God and about the Lord Jesus Christ; and no one tried to stop him.

Romans

WHAT QUESTIONS do you have about what you believe? In Romans, Paul tackles some big questions about our faith.

Paul wrote this letter to the Christians living in Rome. Paul had never met them, but he wanted to visit them. Rome was the capital city of the Roman Empire. Most Romans believed in many gods, but some believed in Jesus. Those Christians had a lot of questions about salvation and growing in Jesus.

These are some of the hard questions Paul answered: Does *everyone* deserve God's punishment? Does doing good things make up for sin? What is the proof that we are really Christians? How do we learn to stop doing wrong things? Can we do anything so bad that God will stop loving us? How are we supposed to treat other Christians? How are we supposed to treat non-Christians?

As you read Romans, look for answers to these questions and to other questions you might have. Ask God to help you understand his answers.

Paul Writes with Good News

Dear friends in Rome: [1]This letter is from Paul, Jesus Christ's slave, chosen to be a missionary, and sent out to preach God's Good News. [2]This Good News was promised long ago by God's prophets in the Old Testament. [3]It is the Good News about his Son, Jesus Christ our Lord, who came as a human baby, born into King David's royal family line; [4]and by being raised from the dead he was proved to be the mighty Son of God, with the holy nature of God himself.

[5]And now, through Christ, all the kindness of God has been poured out upon us undeserving sinners; and now he is sending us out around the world to tell all people everywhere the great things God has done for them, so that they, too, will believe and obey him.

[6,7]And you, dear friends in Rome, are among those he dearly loves; you, too, are invited by Jesus Christ to be God's very own—yes, his holy people. May all God's mercies and peace be yours from God our Father and from Jesus Christ our Lord.

⁸Let me say first of all that wherever I go I hear you being talked about! For your faith in God is becoming known around the world. How I thank God through Jesus Christ for this good report, and for each one of you. ⁹God knows how often I pray for you. Day and night I bring you and your needs in prayer to the one I serve with all my might, telling others the Good News about his Son.

¹⁰And one of the things I keep on praying for is the opportunity, God willing, to come at last to see you and, if possible, that I will have a safe trip. ¹¹,¹²For I long to visit you so that I can impart to you the faith that will help your church grow strong in the Lord. Then, too, I need your help, for I want not only to share my faith with you but to be encouraged by yours: Each of us will be a blessing to the other.

¹³I want you to know, dear brothers, that I planned to come many times before (but was prevented) so that I could work among you and see good results, just as I have among the other Gentile churches. ¹⁴For I owe a great debt to you and to everyone else, both to civilized people and uncivilized alike; yes, to the educated and uneducated alike. ¹⁵So, to the fullest extent of my ability, I am ready to come also to you in Rome to preach God's Good News.

¹⁶For I am not ashamed of this Good News about Christ. It is God's powerful method of bringing all who believe it to heaven. This message was preached first to the Jews alone, but now everyone is invited to come to God in this same way. ¹⁷This Good News tells us that God makes us ready for heaven—makes us right in God's sight—when we put our faith and trust in Christ to save us. This is accomplished from start to finish by faith. As the Scripture says it, "The man who finds life will find it through trusting God."

¹⁸But God shows his anger from heaven against all sinful, evil men who push away the truth from them. ¹⁹For the truth about God is known to them instinctively; God has put this knowledge in their hearts. ²⁰Since earliest times men have seen the earth and sky and all God made, and have known of his existence and great eternal power. So they will have no excuse [when they stand before God at Judgment Day].

²¹Yes, they knew about him all right, but they wouldn't admit it or worship him or even thank him for all his daily care. And after awhile they began to think up silly ideas of what God was like and what he wanted them to do. The result was that their foolish minds became dark and confused. ²²Claiming themselves to be wise without God, they became utter fools instead. ²³And then, instead of worshiping the glorious, ever-living God, they took wood and stone and made idols for themselves, carving them to look like mere birds and animals and snakes and puny men.

²⁴So God let them go ahead into every sort of sex sin, and do whatever they wanted to—yes, vile and sinful things with each other's bodies. ²⁵Instead of believing what they knew was the truth about God, they deliberately chose to believe lies. So they prayed to the things God made, but wouldn't obey the blessed God who made these things.

²⁶That is why God let go of them and let them do all these evil things, so that even their women turned against God's natural plan for them and indulged in sex sin with each other. ²⁷And the men, instead of having normal sex relationships with women, burned with lust for each other, men doing shameful things with other men and, as a result, getting paid within their own souls with the penalty they so richly deserved.

²⁸So it was that when they gave God up and would not even acknowledge him, God gave them up to doing everything their evil minds could think of. ²⁹Their lives became full of every kind of wickedness and sin, of greed and hate, envy, murder, fighting, lying, bitterness, and gossip.

³⁰They were backbiters, haters of God, insolent, proud, braggarts, always thinking of new ways of sinning and continually being disobedient to their parents. ³¹They tried to misunderstand, broke their promises, and were heartless—without pity. ³²They were fully aware of God's death penalty for these crimes, yet they went right ahead and did them anyway and encouraged others to do them, too.

2 God Will Judge Us All

"Well," you may be saying, "what terrible people you have been talking about!" But wait a minute! You are just as bad. When you say they are wicked and should be punished, you are talking about yourselves, for you do these very same things. ²And we know that God, in justice, will punish anyone who does such things as these. ³Do you think that God will judge and condemn others for doing them and overlook you when you do them, too? ⁴Don't you realize how pa-

---

SHARING YOUR FAITH 1:5 There is a privilege and a responsibility for Christians. God graciously forgives the sins of those who, by faith, believe in him as Lord. When we believe, we receive his forgiveness. In doing this, however, we are committing ourselves to live a new life. Paul points out that this new life, a gift from God, also involves a call from God—a God-given responsibility—to witness to the world as a missionary. God may or may not call you to be an overseas missionary, but he does call you (and all believers) to be a witness and an example of the changed life Jesus Christ has worked in you. **To begin the series of devotionals on SHARING YOUR FAITH, turn to page 427.**

Family Devotions

☐ **Devotion 301**
Confessing Sin

Read Romans 2:18-23

As Janie turned over a rock in the backyard, she drew back. "Yuck, Mom! Look at all these icky bugs hiding under this rock! They don't seem to like the sun. I think they're looking for a dark place to hide."

"They're a little like us then, aren't they?" Mom said thoughtfully.

Janie glanced at her mother in surprise. "Huh?"

"Well, just as these bugs are scrambling for hiding places, we sometimes scramble to find hiding places for the sin in our hearts," explained Mom. "We try to keep it in the dark, but God sees it."

"My Sunday school teacher was talking about sin last week. She says there are two kinds, sins of *commission* and sins of *omission*."

"And do you know what that means?" said Mom, smiling.

"The sins of commission are the bad things we think or do," answered Janie. "Sins of omission are when we don't do things we should do, like not calling a friend when we know she's sad, or not telling someone about Jesus when we get the chance."

"Good for you!" said Mom. "You remembered that lesson very well. It's even more important to remember that God sees every sin."

Janie nodded as she watched the last of the insects disappear. "I'll think of these as 'sin bugs' from now on." She shuddered. "They'll be a reminder that I don't want sin in my heart."

Confessing Sin Memory Verse

But if we confess our sins to him, he can be depended on to forgive us and to cleanse us from every wrong. [And it is perfectly proper for God to do this for us because Christ died to wash away our sins.]
1 John 1:9

How About You?

Are sins of commission *and* sins of omission *new terms to you? It's sometimes easy to recognize the things we do wrong, but it's harder to realize that "not doing" something may be a sin, too. Check your life. Is there something you should do for a friend? Are there things you should do around your home, even though no one has told you to do them? Confess them to God. Then get busy and do the things he wants you to do.* V. L. C.

• For the next devotional, turn to page 1079.   • For the next devotional on *Confessing Sin*, turn to page 1179.
• For notes on *Confessing Sin*, see pages 429, 479, 836, 881, and 1220.

tient he is being with you? Or don't you care? Can't you see that he has been waiting all this time without punishing you, to give you time to turn from your sin? His kindness is meant to lead you to repentance.

⁵But no, you won't listen; and so you are saving up terrible punishment for yourselves because of your stubbornness in refusing to turn from your sin; for there is going to come a day of wrath when God will be the just Judge of all the world. ⁶He will give each one whatever his deeds deserve. ⁷He will give eternal life to those who patiently do the will of God, seeking for the unseen glory and honor and eternal life that he offers. ⁸But he will terribly punish those who fight against the truth of God and walk in evil ways— God's anger will be poured out upon them. ⁹There will be sorrow and suffering for Jews and Gentiles alike who keep on sinning. ¹⁰But there will be glory and honor and peace from God for all who obey him, whether they are Jews or Gentiles. ¹¹For God treats everyone the same.

¹²⁻¹⁵He will punish sin wherever it is found. He will punish the heathen when they sin, even though they never had God's written laws, for down in their hearts they know right from wrong. God's laws are written within them; their own conscience accuses them, or sometimes excuses them. And God will punish the Jews for sinning because they have his written laws but don't obey them. They know what is right but don't do it. After all, salvation is not given to those who know what to do, unless they do it. ¹⁶The day will surely come when at God's command Jesus Christ will judge the secret lives of everyone, their inmost thoughts and motives; this is all part of God's great plan, which I proclaim.

¹⁷You Jews think all is well between yourselves and God because he gave his laws to you; you brag that you are his special friends. ¹⁸Yes, you know what he wants; you know right from wrong and favor the right because you have been taught his laws from earliest youth. ¹⁹You are so sure of the way to God that you could point it out to a blind man. You think of yourselves as beacon lights, directing men who are lost in darkness to God. ²⁰You think that you can guide the simple and teach even children the affairs of God, for you really know his laws, which are full of all knowledge and truth.

²¹Yes, you teach others—then why don't you teach yourselves? You tell others not to steal—do *you* steal? ²²You say it is wrong to commit adultery—do *you* do it? You say "Don't pray to idols" and then make money your god instead.

²³You are so proud of knowing God's laws, *but you dishonor him by breaking them*. ²⁴No wonder the Scriptures say that the world speaks evil of God because of you.

²⁵Being a Jew is worth something if you obey God's laws; but if you don't, then you are no better off than the heathen. ²⁶And if the heathen obey God's laws, won't God give them all the rights and honors he planned to give the Jews? ²⁷In fact, those heathen will be much better off than you Jews who know so much about God and have his promises but don't obey his laws.

²⁸For you are not real Jews just because you were born of Jewish parents or because you have gone through the Jewish initiation ceremony of circumcision. ²⁹No, a real Jew is anyone whose heart is right with God. For God is not looking for those who cut their bodies in actual body circumcision, but he is looking for those with changed hearts and minds. Whoever has that kind of change in his life will get his praise from God, even if not from you.

3 God Remains Faithful

Then what's the use of being a Jew? Are there any special benefits for them from God? Is there any value in the Jewish circumcision ceremony? ²Yes, being a Jew has many advantages.

First of all, God trusted them with his laws [so that they could know and do his will]. ³True, some of them were unfaithful, but just because they broke their promises to God, does that mean God will break his promises? ⁴Of course not! Though everyone else in the world is a liar, God is not. Do you remember what the book of Psalms says about this? That God's words will always prove true and right, no matter who questions them.

⁵"But," some say, "our breaking faith with God is good, our sins serve a good purpose, for people will notice how good God is when they see how bad we are. Is it fair, then, for him to punish us when our sins are helping him?" (That is the way some people talk.) ⁶God forbid! Then what kind of God would he be, to overlook sin? How could he ever condemn anyone? ⁷For he could not judge and condemn me as a sinner if my dishonesty brought him glory by pointing up his honesty in contrast to my lies. ⁸If you follow through with that idea you come to this: the worse we are, the better God likes it! But the damnation of those who say such things is just. Yet some claim that this is what I preach!

⁹Well, then, are we Jews *better* than others? No, not at all, for we have already shown that all men alike are sinners, whether Jews or Gentiles. ¹⁰As the Scriptures say,

"No one is good—no one in all the world is innocent."

¹¹No one has ever really followed God's paths or even truly wanted to.

¹²Every one has turned away; all have gone wrong. No one anywhere has kept on doing what is right; not one.

¹³Their talk is foul and filthy like the stench from an open grave. Their tongues are loaded with lies. Everything they say has in it the sting and poison of deadly snakes.

¹⁴Their mouths are full of cursing and bitterness.

¹⁵They are quick to kill, hating anyone who disagrees with them.

¹⁶Wherever they go they leave misery and trouble behind them, ¹⁷and they have never known what it is to feel secure or enjoy God's blessing.

¹⁸They care nothing about God nor what he thinks of them.

¹⁹So the judgment of God lies very heavily upon the Jews, for they are responsible to keep God's laws instead of doing all these evil things; not one of them has any excuse; in fact, all the world stands hushed and guilty before Almighty God.

²⁰Now do you see it? No one can ever be made right in God's sight by doing what the law commands. For the more we know of God's laws, the clearer it becomes that we aren't obeying them; his laws serve only to make us see that we are sinners.

²¹,²²But now God has shown us a different way to heaven—not by "being good enough" and trying to keep his laws, but by a new way (though not new, really, for the Scriptures told about it long ago). Now God says he will accept and acquit us—declare us "not guilty"—if we trust Jesus Christ to take away our sins. And we all can be saved in this same way, by coming to Christ, no matter who we are or what we have been like. ²³Yes, all have sinned; all fall short of God's glorious ideal; ²⁴yet now God declares us "not guilty" of offending him if we trust in Jesus Christ, who in his kindness freely takes away our sins.

²⁵For God sent Christ Jesus to take the punishment for our sins and to end all God's anger against us. He used Christ's blood and our faith as the means of saving us from his wrath. In this way he was being entirely fair, even though he did not punish those who sinned in former times. For he was looking forward to the time when Christ would come and take away those sins. ²⁶And now in these days also he can receive sinners in this same way because Jesus took away their sins.

But isn't this unfair for God to let criminals go free, and say that they are innocent? No, for he does it on the basis of their trust in Jesus who took away their sins.

²⁷Then what can we boast about doing for our salvation? Nothing at all. Why? Because acquittal is not based on our good deeds; based on what Christ has done and our faith in him. ²⁸So it is that we are saved by faith in Christ and not by the good things we do.

²⁹And does God save only the Jews in this way? No, the Gentiles, too, may come to him in this same manner. ³⁰God treats us all the same; all, whether Jews or Gentiles, are acquitted if they have faith. ³¹Well then, if we are saved by faith, does this mean that we no longer need obey God's laws? Just the opposite! In fact, only when we trust Jesus can we truly obey him.

4 Abraham Believed God

Abraham was, humanly speaking, the founder of our Jewish nation. What were his experiences concerning this question of being saved by faith? Was it because of his good deeds that God accepted him? If so, then he would have something to boast about. But from God's point of view Abraham had no basis at all for pride. ³For the Scriptures tell us Abraham *believed God,* and that is why God canceled his sins and declared him "not guilty."

⁴,⁵But didn't he earn his right to heaven by all the good things he did? No, for being saved is a gift; if a person could earn it by being good, then it wouldn't be free—but it is! It is *given* to those who do *not* work for it. For God declares sinners to be good in his sight if they have faith in Christ to save them from God's wrath.

⁶King David spoke of this, describing the happiness of an undeserving sinner who is declared "not guilty" by God. ⁷"Blessed and to be envied," he said, "are those whose sins are forgiven and put out of sight. ⁸Yes, what joy there is for anyone whose sins are no longer counted against him by the Lord."

⁹Now then, the question: Is this blessing given only to those who have faith in Christ but also keep the Jewish laws, or is the blessing also given to those who do not keep the Jewish rules but only trust in Christ? Well, what about Abraham? We say that he received these blessings through his faith. Was it by faith alone, or because he also kept the Jewish rules?

¹⁰For the answer to that question, answer this one: *When* did God give this blessing to Abraham? It was *before he became a Jew*—before he went through the Jewish initiation ceremony of circumcision.

¹¹It wasn't until later on, *after* God had promised to bless him *because of his faith,* that he was circumcised. The circumcision ceremony was a sign that Abraham already had faith and that God

im and declared him just
before the ceremony took
e spiritual father of those
ved without obeying Jew-
at those who do not keep
d by God through faith.
he spiritual father of those
Jews who have been circumcised. They can see from his example that it is not this ceremony that saves them, for Abraham found favor with God by faith alone *before he was circumcised.*

¹³It is clear, then, that God's promise to give the whole earth to Abraham and his descendants was not because Abraham obeyed God's laws but because he trusted God to keep his promise. ¹⁴So if you still claim that God's blessings go to those who are "good enough," then you are saying that God's promises to those who have faith are meaningless, and faith is foolish. ¹⁵But the fact of the matter is this: when we try to gain God's blessing and salvation by keeping his laws we always end up under his anger, for we always fail to keep them. The only way we can keep from breaking laws is not to have any to break!

¹⁶So God's blessings are given to us by faith, as a free gift; we are certain to get them whether or not we follow Jewish customs if we have faith like Abraham's, for Abraham is the father of us all when it comes to these matters of faith. ¹⁷That is what the Scriptures mean when they say that God made Abraham the father of many nations. God will accept all people in every nation who trust God as Abraham did. And this promise is from God himself, who makes the dead live again and speaks of future events with as much certainty as though they were already past.

¹⁸So, when God told Abraham that he would give him a son who would have many descendants and become a great nation, Abraham believed God even though such a promise just couldn't come to pass! ¹⁹And because his faith was strong, he didn't worry about the fact that he was too old to be a father at the age of one hundred, and that Sarah his wife, at ninety, was also much too old to have a baby.

²⁰But Abraham never doubted. He believed God, for his faith and trust grew ever stronger, and he praised God for this blessing even before it happened. ²¹He was completely sure that God was well able to do anything he promised. ²²And because of Abraham's faith God forgave his sins and declared him "not guilty."

²³Now this wonderful statement—that he was accepted and approved through his faith—wasn't just for Abraham's benefit. ²⁴It was for us, too, assuring us that God will accept us in the same way he accepted Abraham—when we believe the promises of God who brought back Jesus our Lord from the dead. ²⁵He died for our sins and rose again to make us right with God, filling us with God's goodness.

5 Finding Peace and Joy

So now, since we have been made right in God's sight by faith in his promises, we can have real peace with him because of what Jesus Christ our Lord has done for us. ²For because of our faith, he has brought us into this place of highest privilege where we now stand, and we confidently and joyfully look forward to actually becoming all that God has had in mind for us to be.

³We can rejoice, too, when we run into problems and trials, for we know that they are good for us—they help us learn to be patient. ⁴And patience develops strength of character in us and helps us trust God more each time we use it until finally our hope and faith are strong and steady. ⁵Then, when that happens, we are able to hold our heads high no matter what happens and know that all is well, for we know how dearly God loves us, and we feel this warm love everywhere within us because God has given us the Holy Spirit to fill our hearts with his love.

⁶When we were utterly helpless, with no way of escape, Christ came at just the right time and died for us sinners who had no use for him. ⁷Even if we were good, we really wouldn't expect anyone to die for us, though, of course, that might be barely possible. ⁸But God showed his great love for us by sending Christ to die for us while we were still sinners. ⁹And since by his blood he did all this for us as sinners, how much more will he do for us now that he has declared us not guilty? Now he will save us from all of God's wrath to come. ¹⁰And since, when we were his enemies, we were brought back to God by the death of his Son, what blessings he must have for us now that we are his friends and he is living within us!

¹¹Now we rejoice in our wonderful new relationship with God—all because of what our Lord Jesus Christ has done in dying for our sins—making us friends of God.

¹²When Adam sinned, sin entered the entire human race. His sin spread death throughout all the world, so everything began to grow old and die, for all sinned. ¹³[We know that it was Adam's sin that caused this] because although, of course, people were sinning from the time of Adam until Moses, God did not in those days judge them guilty of death for breaking his laws—because he had not yet given his laws to them nor told them what he wanted them to do. ¹⁴So when their bodies died it was not for their own sins since they themselves had never disobeyed God's special law against eating the forbidden fruit, as Adam had.

Family Devotions

☐ *Devotion 302*
Becoming More Like Jesus

Read Romans 5:1-5

Becoming More Like Jesus Memory Verse

No, he has told you what he wants, and this is all it is: *to be fair, just, merciful, and to walk humbly with your God.* Micah 6:8

"I feel terrible," Tim complained. "I can hardly breathe, and my throat is so sore."

"I know," sympathized Mom. "Here's some juice for you. Just stay on the couch. In a few days your cold will be better."

A short time later Tim called his mother. "I still feel terrible," he said in a whining voice.

Mom brought a wet cloth for Tim's forehead, fixed his pillow, and tucked his cover around him. "Now you just rest," she said.

But Tim didn't feel like resting. He kept on moaning, sighing, and whining until finally Mom said, "Tim, I've done all I can for you. I know you're uncomfortable and that it's not fun to be sick. But you must learn not to complain. The Bible tells us to be patient when we have problems and trials—circumstances that make you miserable or unhappy."

"But I hate being sick. How can I be patient about that?" Tim argued.

"Complaining won't help you or anyone else. In fact, it will make you and those around you feel worse. If you learn to be cheerful and uncomplaining even when you're not feeling well, you bring glory to God," explained Mom. "Follow Jesus' example. He didn't complain when he suffered."

"Well, I never knew the Bible said anything about how to act when I have a cold," said Tim. "OK, from now on I'll try to be more patient, but it's going to be hard."

"Asking the Lord for help will make it easier," Mom said.

How About You?
When you're sick do you complain about your aches and pains all the time? You need to let your parents know if you're not feeling well, but once you're getting treatment, there's no need to keep on complaining. Instead, think happy thoughts, and thank God for all the blessings you do have. *C. Y.*

• For the next devotional, turn to page 1081. • For the next devotional on *Becoming More Like Jesus*, turn to page 1193. • For notes on *Becoming More Like Jesus*, see pages 234, 983, 1105, and 1164.

What a contrast between Adam and Christ who was yet to come! ¹⁵And what a difference between man's sin and God's forgiveness!

For this one man, Adam, brought death to many through his *sin*. But this one man, Jesus Christ, brought forgiveness to many through God's *mercy*. ¹⁶Adam's *one* sin brought the penalty of death to many, while Christ freely takes away *many* sins and gives glorious life instead. ¹⁷The sin of this one man, Adam, caused *death to be king over all*, but all who will take God's gift of forgiveness and acquittal are *kings of life* because of this one man, Jesus Christ. ¹⁸Yes, Adam's *sin* brought *punishment* to all, but Christ's *righteousness* makes men *right with God*, so that they can live. ¹⁹Adam caused many to be sinners because he *disobeyed* God, and Christ caused many to be made acceptable to God because he *obeyed*.

²⁰The Ten Commandments were given so that all could see the extent of their failure to obey God's laws. But the more we see our sinfulness, the more we see God's abounding grace forgiving us. ²¹Before, sin ruled over all men and brought them to death, but now God's kindness rules instead, giving us right standing with God and resulting in eternal life through Jesus Christ our Lord.

6 Christ Broke Sin's Power

Well then, shall we keep on sinning so that God can keep on showing us more and more kindness and forgiveness?

²,³Of course not! Should we keep on sinning when we don't have to? For sin's power over us was broken when we became Christians and were baptized to become a part of Jesus Christ; through his death the power of your sinful nature was shattered. ⁴Your old sin-loving nature was buried with him by baptism when he died; and when God the Father, with glorious power, brought him back to life again, you were given his wonderful new life to enjoy.

⁵For you have become a part of him, and so you died with him, so to speak, when he died; and now you share his new life and shall rise as he did. ⁶Your old evil desires were nailed to the cross with him; that part of you that loves to sin was crushed and fatally wounded, so that your sin-loving body is no longer under sin's control, no longer needs to be a slave to sin; ⁷for when you are deadened to sin you are freed from all its allure and its power over you. ⁸And since your old sin-loving nature "died" with Christ, we know that you will share his new life. ⁹Christ rose from the dead and will never die again. Death no longer has any power over him. ¹⁰He died once for all to end sin's power, but now he lives forever in unbroken fellowship with God. ¹¹So look upon your old sin nature as dead and unresponsive to sin, and instead be alive to God, alert to him, through Jesus Christ our Lord.

¹²Do not let sin control your puny body any longer; do not give in to its sinful desires. ¹³Do not let any part of your bodies become tools of wickedness, to be used for sinning; but give yourselves completely to God—every part of you—for you are back from death and you want to be tools in the hands of God, to be used for his good purposes. ¹⁴Sin need never again be your master, for now you are no longer tied to the law where sin enslaves you, but you are free under God's favor and mercy.

¹⁵Does this mean that now we can go ahead and sin and not worry about it? (For our salvation does not depend on keeping the law but on receiving God's grace!) Of course not!

¹⁶Don't you realize that you can choose your own master? You can choose sin (with death) or else obedience (with acquittal). The one to whom you offer yourself—he will take you and be your master, and you will be his slave. ¹⁷Thank God that though you once chose to be slaves of sin, now you have obeyed with all your heart the teaching to which God has committed you. ¹⁸And now you are free from your old master, sin; and you have become slaves to your new master, righteousness.

¹⁹I speak this way, using the illustration of slaves and masters, because it is easy to understand: just as you used to be slaves to all kinds of sin, so now you must let yourselves be slaves to all that is right and holy.

²⁰In those days when you were slaves of sin you didn't bother much with goodness. ²¹And what was the result? Evidently not good, since you are ashamed now even to think about those things you used to do, for all of them end in eternal doom. ²²But now you are free from the power of sin and are slaves of God, and his benefits to you include holiness and everlasting life. ²³For the wages of sin is death, but the free gift of God is eternal life through Jesus Christ our Lord.

7 You Can Serve God

Don't you understand yet, dear Jewish brothers in Christ, that when a person dies the law no longer holds him in its power?

²Let me illustrate: when a woman marries, the law binds her to her husband as long as he is alive. But if he dies, she is no longer bound to him; the laws of marriage no longer apply to her. ³Then she can marry someone else if she wants to. That

FAMILY DEVOTIONS

☐ DEVOTION 303
AVOIDING SIN

Read Romans 6:20-23

"Mom, the itchy spots are back on my skin," Allen said, holding out his arms. "I have bumps on my legs, too."

"Oh, Allen," said Mom, "your allergies are acting up again. I haven't changed the laundry detergent or any of our soaps. I can't imagine what has caused an allergic reaction this time, can you?"

Allen scratched his arms as he thought. "When I was over at Bob's this morning, his Mom had some stuff out to send to the mission," he said. "Bob and I dressed up in some of his dad's old camouflage clothes. I suppose they were washed in something that caused my reaction."

"I expect that's it," said Mom. "Go take a shower, and then we'll go and get your prescription refilled."

As Allen and his mother drove home after picking up the medicine, Allen sighed. "It's hard to remember that I need to be careful what touches my skin," he said. "We were having so much fun that I didn't even think about it." He rubbed his arms. "My allergies remind me, though," he added. "It's too bad they don't remind me ahead of time!"

"Isn't that the truth!" agreed Mom. She smiled at her son. "You know," she added thoughtfully, "dressing in those clothes was innocent fun, and it seems too bad you have to avoid things like that. But you do, or you get this negative reaction. There are other things that we need to be very careful to avoid, too, even though they seem like innocent fun. We need to think ahead to the consequences before getting involved in those things."

"Like what?" asked Allen.

"Well, like watching bad TV shows, or reading dirty books, or going places where we'll be tempted to do wrong," said Mom. "Those kinds of things, like any sinful activity, will stir up a negative reaction in our lives. We need to ask the Lord to remind us to avoid things that will harm us."

Avoiding Sin Memory Verse

Dear brothers, you are only visitors here. Since your real home is in heaven, I beg you to keep away from the evil pleasures of this world; they are not for you, for they fight against your very souls.
1 Peter 2:11

How About You?
Are you allergic to anything—foods, bees, medicine, weeds, soap? If so, you know it's best for you to avoid those things. Sin can cause a very bad reaction in your life as well. Now that you are free from the power of sin, avoid sinful activity, and you will avoid its consequences. N. E. K.

- For the next devotional, turn to page 1083. • For the next devotional on AVOIDING SIN, turn to page 1087.
- For notes on AVOIDING SIN, see pages 220, 332, 392, and 657.

would be wrong while he was alive, but it is perfectly all right after he dies.

⁴Your "husband," your master, used to be the Jewish law; but you "died," as it were, with Christ on the cross; and since you are "dead," you are no longer "married to the law," and it has no more control over you. Then you came back to life again when Christ did and are a new person. And now you are "married," so to speak, to the one who rose from the dead, so that you can produce good fruit, that is, good deeds for God. ⁵When your old nature was still active, sinful desires were at work within you, making you want to do whatever God said not to and producing sinful deeds, the rotting fruit of death. ⁶But now you need no longer worry about the Jewish laws and customs because you "died" while in their captivity, and now you can really serve God; not in the old way, mechanically obeying a set of rules, but in the new way, [with all of your hearts and minds].

⁷Well then, am I suggesting that these laws of God are evil? Of course not! No, the law is not sinful, but it was the law that showed me my sin. I would never have known the sin in my heart—the evil desires that are hidden there—if the law had not said, "You must not have evil desires in your heart." ⁸But sin used this law against evil desires by reminding me that such desires are wrong, and arousing all kinds of forbidden desires within me! Only if there were no laws to break would there be no sinning.

⁹That is why I felt fine so long as I did not understand what the law really demanded. But when I learned the truth, I realized that I had broken the law and was a sinner, doomed to die. ¹⁰So as far as I was concerned, the good law which was supposed to show me the way of life resulted instead in my being given the death penalty. ¹¹Sin fooled me by taking the good laws of God and using them to make me guilty of death. ¹²But still, you see, the law itself was wholly right and good.

¹³But how can that be? Didn't the law cause my doom? How then can it be good? No, it was sin, devilish stuff that it is, that used what was good to bring about my condemnation. So you can see how cunning and deadly and damnable it is. For it uses God's good laws for its own evil purposes.

¹⁴The law is good, then, and the trouble is not there but with *me* because I am sold into slavery with Sin as my owner.

¹⁵I don't understand myself at all, for I really want to do what is right, but I can't. I do what I don't want to—what I hate. ¹⁶I know perfectly well that what I am doing is wrong, and my bad conscience proves that I agree with these laws I am breaking. ¹⁷But I can't help myself because I'm no longer doing it. It is sin inside me that is stronger than I am that makes me do these evil things.

¹⁸I know I am rotten through and through so far as my old sinful nature is concerned. No matter which way I turn I can't make myself do right. I want to but I can't. ¹⁹When I want to do good, I don't; and when I try not to do wrong, I do it anyway. ²⁰Now if I am doing what I don't want to, it is plain where the trouble is: sin still has me in its evil grasp.

²¹It seems to be a fact of life that when I want to do what is right, I inevitably do what is wrong. ²²I love to do God's will so far as my new nature is concerned; ²³⁻²⁵but there is something else deep within me, in my lower nature, that is at war with my mind and wins the fight and makes me a slave to the sin that is still within me. In my mind I want to be God's willing servant, but instead I find myself still enslaved to sin.

So you see how it is: my new life tells me to do right, but the old nature that is still inside me loves to sin. Oh, what a terrible predicament I'm in! Who will free me from my slavery to this deadly lower nature? Thank God! It has been done by Jesus Christ our Lord. He has set me free.

8 The Holy Spirit Frees Us from Sin

So there is now no condemnation awaiting those who belong to Christ Jesus. ²For the power of the life-giving Spirit—and this power is mine through Christ Jesus—has freed me from the vicious circle of sin and death. ³We aren't saved from sin's grasp by knowing the commandments of God because we can't and don't keep them, but God put into effect a different plan to save us. He sent his own Son in a human body like ours—except that ours are sinful—and destroyed sin's control over us by giving himself as a sacrifice for our sins. ⁴So now we can obey God's laws if we follow after the Holy Spirit and no longer obey the old evil nature within us.

⁵Those who let themselves be controlled by their lower natures live only to please themselves, but those who follow after the Holy Spirit find themselves doing those things that please God. ⁶Following after the Holy Spirit leads to life and peace, but following after the old nature leads to death ⁷because the old sinful nature within us is against God. It never did obey God's laws and it never will. ⁸That's why those who are still under the control of their old sinful selves, bent on following their old evil desires, can never please God.

⁹But you are not like that. You are controlled by your new nature if you have the Spirit of God living in you. (And remember that if anyone

FAMILY DEVOTIONS

☐ *DEVOTION 304*
DEALING WITH CHANGE

Read Romans 8:26-31

Jon propped his chin in his hand as he watched his grandmother mix shortening and sugar. "I'm making your favorite cake, Jon—chocolate." As Jon smiled faintly, Grandma added, "Why so quiet? Is anything wrong?"

Jon snorted. "Everything's wrong! Dad's getting transferred, so I have to leave all my friends. Mom says I have to give up my dog, too. And the doctor says I have to wear a brace on my leg. How can I ever make new friends wearing a metal monster? If God loved me, he wouldn't let all this happen to me." Jon slammed his fist on the table. "It's not fair!"

"Here, have a taste." Grandma handed him the cocoa.

"Yuck!" Jon drew back.

"Then how about this?" Grandma dipped a spoon into the shortening and sugar mixture.

Jon frowned. "No way am I going to taste that!"

Grandma raised her eyebrows. "Then how about some flour, or baking soda, or this egg?"

Jon grinned. "Awww, Grandma, you're teasing me."

Grandma smiled. "You know, the Bible says all that happens is working for good in the life of a Christian. It doesn't say all things *are* good. Cocoa or a raw egg isn't good alone, but when I mix all the ingredients together—"

"Yummmm, yummmm, good!" Jon sang.

"So in life," Grandma continued as she mixed flour into the batter, "when God gets through mixing a Christian's experiences together—the bitter, the sweet, the happy, the sad—life comes out good. Moving and wearing a brace are bitter experiences for you now, but trust God, Jon. He'll add some sugar and some flavoring, and in the end it will be good. Even better than my cake," Grandma laughed.

"Maybe so," John agreed. Then he grinned. "Grandma, may I lick the beater?"

Dealing with Change
Memory Verse

We know that all that happens to us is working for our good if we love God and are fitting into his plans.
Romans 8:28

How About You?
Have you had to swallow some bitter experiences lately? Some changes you don't understand? Be patient. All the ingredients are not in yet, but God is making something special out of you. *B. W.*

• For the next devotional, turn to page 1087. • To start the next topic, turn to page 705. • For notes on *DEALING WITH CHANGE*, see pages 56, 156, 288, 1186, and 1198.

doesn't have the Spirit of Christ living in him, he is not a Christian at all.) [10]Yet, even though Christ lives within you, your body will die because of sin; but your spirit will live, for Christ has pardoned it. [11]And if the Spirit of God, who raised up Jesus from the dead, lives in you, he will make your dying bodies live again after you die, by means of this same Holy Spirit living within you.

[12]So, dear brothers, you have no obligations whatever to your old sinful nature to do what it begs you to do. [13]For if you keep on following it you are lost and will perish, but if through the power of the Holy Spirit you crush it and its evil deeds, you shall live. [14]For all who are led by the Spirit of God are sons of God.

[15]And so we should not be like cringing, fearful slaves, but we should behave like God's very own children, adopted into the bosom of his family, and calling to him, "Father, Father." [16]For his Holy Spirit speaks to us deep in our hearts and tells us that we really are God's children. [17]And since we are his children, we will share his treasures—for all God gives to his Son Jesus is now ours too. But if we are to share his glory, we must also share his suffering.

[18]Yet what we suffer now is nothing compared to the glory he will give us later. [19]For all creation is waiting patiently and hopefully for that future day when God will resurrect his children. [20,21]For on that day thorns and thistles, sin, death, and decay—the things that overcame the world against its will at God's command—will all disappear, and the world around us will share in the glorious freedom from sin which God's children enjoy.

[22]For we know that even the things of nature, like animals and plants, suffer in sickness and death as they await this great event. [23]And even we Christians, although we have the Holy Spirit within us as a foretaste of future glory, also groan to be released from pain and suffering. We, too, wait anxiously for that day when God will give us our full rights as his children, including the new bodies he has promised us—bodies that will never be sick again and will never die.

[24]We are saved by trusting. And trusting means looking forward to getting something we don't yet have—for a man who already has something doesn't need to hope and trust that he will get it. [25]But if we must keep trusting God for something that hasn't happened yet, it teaches us to wait patiently and confidently.

[26]And in the same way—by our faith—the Holy Spirit helps us with our daily problems and in our praying. For we don't even know what we should pray for nor how to pray as we should, but the Holy Spirit prays for us with such feeling that it cannot be expressed in words. [27]And the Father who knows all hearts knows, of course, what the Spirit is saying as he pleads for us in harmony with God's own will. [28]And we know that all that happens to us is working for our good if we love God and are fitting into his plans.

[29]For from the very beginning God decided that those who came to him—and all along he knew who would—should become like his Son, so that his Son would be the First, with many brothers. [30]And having chosen us, he called us to come to him; and when we came, he declared us "not guilty," filled us with Christ's goodness, gave us right standing with himself, and promised us his glory.

[31]What can we ever say to such wonderful things as these? If God is on our side, who can ever be against us? [32]Since he did not spare even his own Son for us but gave him up for us all, won't he also surely give us everything else?

[33]Who dares accuse us whom God has chosen for his own? Will God? No! He is the one who has forgiven us and given us right standing with himself.

[34]Who then will condemn us? Will Christ? *No!* For he is the one who died for us and came back to life again for us and is sitting at the place of highest honor next to God, pleading for us there in heaven.

[35]Who then can ever keep Christ's love from us? When we have trouble or calamity, when we are hunted down or destroyed, is it because he doesn't love us anymore? And if we are hungry or penniless or in danger or threatened with death, has God deserted us?

[36]No, for the Scriptures tell us that for his sake we must be ready to face death at every moment of the day—we are like sheep awaiting slaughter; [37]but despite all this, overwhelming victory is ours through Christ who loved us enough to die for us. [38]For I am convinced that nothing can ever separate us from his love. Death can't, and life can't. The angels won't, and all the powers of hell itself cannot keep God's love away. Our fears for today, our worries about tomorrow, [39]or where we are—high above the sky, or in the deepest ocean—nothing will ever be able to separate us from the love of God demonstrated by our Lord Jesus Christ when he died for us.

9 God Is Sovereign

O Israel, my people! O my Jewish brothers! How I long for you to come to Christ. My heart is heavy within me, and I grieve bitterly day and night because of you. Christ knows and the Holy Spirit knows that it is no mere pretense when I say that I would be willing to be forever damned if that would save you. [4]God has given you so much, but still you will not listen to him. He took you as his own special, chosen people and led you along with a bright cloud of glory and told you how very much he wanted to bless you. He gave you his rules for daily life so you would know what he wanted you to do. He let you worship him and gave you mighty promises. 5Great men of God were your fathers, and Christ himself was one of you, a Jew so far as his human nature is concerned, he who now rules over all things. Praise God forever!

6Well then, has God failed to fulfill his promises to the Jews? No! [For these promises are only to those who are truly Jews.] And not everyone born into a Jewish family is truly a Jew! 7Just the fact that they come from Abraham doesn't make them truly Abraham's children. For the Scriptures say that the promises apply only to Abraham's son Isaac and Isaac's descendants, though Abraham had other children too. 8This means that not all of Abraham's children are children of God, but only those who believe the promise of salvation which he made to Abraham.

9For God had promised, "Next year I will give you and Sarah a son." 10-13And years later, when this son Isaac was grown up and married and Rebecca his wife was about to bear him twin children, God told her that Esau, the child born first, would be a servant to Jacob, his twin brother. In the words of the Scripture, "I chose to bless Jacob but not Esau." And God said this before the children were even born, before they had done anything either good or bad. This proves that God was doing what he had decided from the beginning; it was not because of what the children did but because of what God wanted and chose.

14Was God being unfair? Of course not. 15For God had said to Moses, "If I want to be kind to someone, I will. And I will take pity on anyone I want to." 16And so God's blessings are not given just because someone decides to have them or works hard to get them. They are given because God takes pity on those he wants to.

17Pharaoh, king of Egypt, was an example of this fact. For God told him he had given him the kingdom of Egypt for the very purpose of displaying the awesome power of God against him, so that all the world would hear about God's glorious name. 18So you see, God is kind to some just because he wants to be, and he makes some refuse to listen.

19Well then, why does God blame them for not listening? Haven't they done what he made them do?

20No, don't say that. Who are you to criticize God? Should the thing made say to the one who made it, "Why have you made me like this?" 21When a man makes a jar out of clay, doesn't he have a right to use the same lump of clay to make one jar beautiful, to be used for holding flowers, and another to throw garbage into? 22Does not God have a perfect right to show his fury and power against those who are fit only for destruction, those he has been patient with for all this time? 23,24And he has a right to take others such as ourselves, who have been made for pouring the riches of his glory into, whether we are Jews or Gentiles, and to be kind to us so that everyone can see how very great his glory is.

25Remember what the prophecy of Hosea says? There God says that he will find other children for himself (who are not from his Jewish family) and will love them, though no one had ever loved them before. 26And the heathen, of whom it once was said, "You are not my people," shall be called "sons of the Living God."

27Isaiah the prophet cried out concerning the Jews that though there would be millions of them, only a small number would ever be saved. 28"For the Lord will execute his sentence upon the earth, quickly ending his dealings, justly cutting them short."

29And Isaiah says in another place that except for God's mercy all the Jews would be destroyed—all of them—just as everyone in the cities of Sodom and Gomorrah perished.

30Well then, what shall we say about these things? Just this, that God has given the Gentiles the opportunity to be acquitted by faith, even though they had not been really seeking God. 31But the Jews, who tried so hard to get right with God by keeping his laws, never succeeded. 32Why not? Because they were trying to be saved by keeping the law and being good instead of by depending on faith. They have stumbled over the great stumbling stone. 33God warned them of this in the Scriptures when he said, "I have put a Rock in the path of the Jews, and many will stumble over him (Jesus). Those who believe in him will never be disappointed."

10 Some Don't Understand

Dear brothers, the longing of my heart and my prayer is that the Jewish people might be saved. 2I know what enthusiasm they have for the honor of God, but it is misdirected zeal. 3For they don't understand that Christ has died to make them right with God. Instead they are trying to make themselves good enough to gain God's favor by keeping the Jewish laws and customs, but that is not God's way of salvation. 4They don't understand that Christ gives to those who trust in him everything they are trying to get by keeping his laws. He ends all of that.

5For Moses wrote that if a person could be perfectly good and hold out against temptation all his life and never sin once, only then could he be pardoned and saved. ⁶But the salvation that comes through faith says, "You don't need to search the heavens to find Christ and bring him down to help you," and, ⁷"You don't need to go among the dead to bring Christ back to life again."

⁸For salvation that comes from trusting Christ—which is what we preach—is already within easy reach of each of us; in fact, it is as near as our own hearts and mouths. ⁹For if you tell others with your own mouth that Jesus Christ is your Lord and believe in your own heart that God has raised him from the dead, you will be saved. ¹⁰For it is by believing in his heart that a man becomes right with God; and with his mouth he tells others of his faith, confirming his salvation.

¹¹For the Scriptures tell us that no one who believes in Christ will ever be disappointed. ¹²Jew and Gentile are the same in this respect: they all have the same Lord who generously gives his riches to all those who ask him for them. ¹³Anyone who calls upon the name of the Lord will be saved.

¹⁴But how shall they ask him to save them unless they believe in him? And how can they believe in him if they have never heard about him? And how can they hear about him unless someone tells them? ¹⁵And how will anyone go and tell them unless someone sends him? That is what the Scriptures are talking about when they say, "How beautiful are the feet of those who preach the Gospel of peace with God and bring glad tidings of good things." In other words, how welcome are those who come preaching God's Good News!

¹⁶But not everyone who hears the Good News has welcomed it, for Isaiah the prophet said, "Lord, who has believed me when I told them?" ¹⁷Yet faith comes from listening to this Good News—the Good News about Christ.

¹⁸But what about the Jews? Have they heard God's Word? Yes, for it has gone wherever they are; the Good News has been told to the ends of the earth. ¹⁹And did they understand [that God would give his salvation to others if they refused to take it]? Yes, for even back in the time of Moses, God had said that he would make his people jealous and try to wake them up by giving his salvation to the foolish heathen nations. ²⁰And later on Isaiah said boldly that God would be found by people who weren't even looking for him. ²¹In the meantime, he keeps on reaching out his hands to the Jews, but they keep arguing and refusing to come.

God's Kindness for Israel

I ask then, has God rejected and deserted his people the Jews? Oh no, not at all. Remember that I myself am a Jew, a descendant of Abraham and a member of Benjamin's family.

²,³No, God has not discarded his own people whom he chose from the very beginning. Do you remember what the Scriptures say about this? Elijah the prophet was complaining to God about the Jews, telling God how they had killed the prophets and torn down God's altars; Elijah claimed that he was the only one left in all the land who still loved God, and now they were trying to kill him too.

⁴And do you remember how God replied? God said, "No, you are not the only one left. I have seven thousand others besides you who still love me and have not bowed down to idols!"

⁵It is the same today. Not all the Jews have turned away from God; there are a few being saved as a result of God's kindness in choosing them. ⁶And if it is by God's kindness, then it is not by their being good enough. For in that case the free gift would no longer be free—it isn't free when it is earned.

⁷So this is the situation: Most of the Jews have not found the favor of God they are looking for. A few have—the ones God has picked out—but the eyes of the others have been blinded. ⁸This is what our Scriptures refer to when they say that God has put them to sleep, shutting their eyes and ears so that they do not understand what we are talking about when we tell them of Christ. And so it is to this very day.

⁹King David spoke of this same thing when he said, "Let their good food and other blessings trap them into thinking all is well between themselves and God. Let these good things boomerang on them and fall back upon their heads to justly crush them. ¹⁰Let their eyes be dim," he said, "so that they cannot see, and let them walk bent-backed forever with a heavy load."

¹¹Does this mean that God has rejected his Jewish people forever? Of course not! His purpose was to make his salvation available to the Gentiles, and then the Jews would be jealous and begin to want God's salvation for themselves. ¹²Now if the whole world became rich as a result of God's offer of salvation, when the Jews stumbled over it and turned it down, think how much greater a blessing the world will share in later on when the Jews, too, come to Christ.

¹³As you know, God has appointed me as a special messenger to you Gentiles. I lay great stress on this and remind the Jews about it as often as I can, ¹⁴so that if possible I can make them want what you Gentiles have and in that way save some of them. ¹⁵And how wonderful it will be when they become Christians! When God turned away from them it meant that he turned to the rest of the world to offer his salvation; and

Family Devotions

☐ **Devotion 305**
Avoiding Sin

Read Romans 12:1-2

Stephanie clapped a hand over her mouth. As Mom took out the coffeepot, she looked at her daughter. "See that you don't use that word again," she said sternly.

"I'm sorry, Mom," apologized Stephanie. "I didn't mean to say it, but I hear it so often at school." She watched as Mom put a white paper into the coffeepot. "What's that thing for?"

"This is a filter," said Mom. "It lets the water through but keeps the coffee grounds from going into the coffee. I realize that you can't always help hearing bad words, but you need to learn to filter all the things you hear and see and think. When we see someone do something wrong, we don't have to do it, too. Allow only the good things to settle down and stay with you. You'll need God's help, but you can do it."

"OK, Mom," agreed Stephanie. "I'll try." She showed her mother a listing in the TV section of the paper. "Can I watch this program tonight?"

Mom read the description and shook her head. "I'm quite sure this isn't the type of program you should see," she said. "I'm sure the language and morals will be very ungodly."

"Oh, it'll be all right if I watch it, Mom," teased Stephanie. "I'll filter out all the bad stuff."

Mom shook her head. "Would it be OK to put garbage in the coffeepot and expect the filter to make it fit to drink?"

"Yuck!" exclaimed Stephanie.

"The filter helps keep the coffee clean, but we need to be responsible and avoid putting things in the coffeepot that don't belong there in the first place. Your mind is the same way. We shouldn't dump 'garbage' in our minds on purpose. But when we can't help what we see and hear, that's when we should use our filters."

Avoiding Sin
Memory Verse

How can a young man stay pure? By reading your Word and following its rules.
Psalm 119:9

H o w   A b o u t   Y o u ?
Do you find yourself automatically copying "the behavior and customs of this world"? The best policy is to avoid being where you will hear or see bad things. If that's impossible, ask the Lord to help you filter out the bad influences and to keep only the thoughts and ideas that are good and pleasing to him. Then deliberately think about other things—wholesome things. *H. M.*

• For the next devotional, turn to page 1091. • For the next devotional on *Avoiding Sin,* turn to page 1187.
• For notes on *Avoiding Sin,* see pages 220, 332, 392, and 657.

now it is even more wonderful when the Jews come to Christ. It will be like dead people coming back to life. ¹⁶And since Abraham and the prophets are God's people, their children will be too. For if the roots of the tree are holy, the branches will be too.

¹⁷But some of these branches from Abraham's tree, some of the Jews, have been broken off. And you Gentiles who were branches from, we might say, a wild olive tree, were grafted in. So now you, too, receive the blessing God has promised Abraham and his children, sharing in God's rich nourishment of his own special olive tree.

¹⁸But you must be careful not to brag about being put in to replace the branches that were broken off. Remember that you are important only because you are now a part of God's tree; you are just a branch, not a root.

¹⁹"Well," you may be saying, "those branches were broken off to make room for me, so I must be pretty good."

²⁰Watch out! Remember that those branches, the Jews, were broken off because they didn't believe God, and you are there only because you do. Do not be proud; be humble and grateful—and careful. ²¹For if God did not spare the branches he put there in the first place, he won't spare you either.

²²Notice how God is both kind and severe. He is very hard on those who disobey, but very good to you if you continue to love and trust him. But if you don't, you too will be cut off. ²³On the other hand, if the Jews leave their unbelief behind them and come back to God, God will graft them back into the tree again. He has the power to do it.

²⁴For if God was willing to take you who were so far away from him—being part of a wild olive tree—and graft you into his own good tree—a very unusual thing to do—don't you see that he will be far more ready to put the Jews back again, who were there in the first place?

²⁵I want you to know about this truth from God, dear brothers, so that you will not feel proud and start bragging. Yes, it is true that some of the Jews have set themselves against the Gospel now, but this will last only until all of you Gentiles have come to Christ—those of you who will. ²⁶And then all Israel will be saved.

Do you remember what the prophets said about this? "There shall come out of Zion a Deliverer, and he shall turn the Jews from all ungodliness. ²⁷At that time I will take away their sins, just as I promised."

²⁸Now many of the Jews are enemies of the Gospel. They hate it. But this has been a benefit to you, for it has resulted in God's giving his gifts to you Gentiles. Yet the Jews are still beloved of God because of his promises to Abraham, Isaac, and Jacob. ²⁹For God's gifts and his call can never be withdrawn; he will never go back on his promises. ³⁰Once you were rebels against God, but when the Jews refused his gifts God was merciful to you instead. ³¹And now the Jews are the rebels, but some day they, too, will share in God's mercy upon you. ³²For God has given them all up to sin so that he could have mercy upon all alike.

³³Oh, what a wonderful God we have! How great are his wisdom and knowledge and riches! How impossible it is for us to understand his decisions and his methods! ³⁴For who among us can know the mind of the Lord? Who knows enough to be his counselor and guide? ³⁵And who could ever offer to the Lord enough to induce him to act? ³⁶For everything comes from God alone. Everything lives by his power, and everything is for his glory. To him be glory evermore.

12 Give Your Life to God

And so, dear brothers, I plead with you to give your bodies to God. Let them be a living sacrifice, holy—the kind he can accept. When you think of what he has done for you, is this too much to ask? ²Don't copy the behavior and customs of this world, but be a new and different person with a fresh newness in all you do and think. Then you will learn from your own experience how his ways will really satisfy you.

³As God's messenger I give each of you God's warning: Be honest in your estimate of yourselves, measuring your value by how much faith God has given you. ⁴,⁵Just as there are many parts to our bodies, so it is with Christ's body. We are all parts of it, and it takes every one of us to make it complete, for we each have different work to do. So we belong to each other, and each needs all the others.

⁶God has given each of us the ability to do certain things well. So if God has given you the ability to prophesy, then prophesy whenever you can—as often as your faith is strong enough to receive a

---

RESPECTING OTHERS 12:10 We can honor others in one of two ways. One involves ulterior motives. We honor our bosses so they will reward us, our employees so they will work harder, the wealthy so they will contribute to our cause, the powerful so they will use their power for us and not against us. The other way—God's way—involves love. As Christians, we honor people because they have been created in God's image. We should especially honor fellow Christians, because they are our brothers and sisters in Christ. Does God's way of honoring others sound too difficult for your competitive nature? Why not try to outdo one another in showing honor? Put others first! **To begin the series of devotionals on RESPECTING OTHERS, turn to page 5.**

message from God. ⁷If your gift is that of serving others, serve them well. If you are a teacher, do a good job of teaching. ⁸If you are a preacher, see to it that your sermons are strong and helpful. If God has given you money, be generous in helping others with it. If God has given you administrative ability and put you in charge of the work of others, take the responsibility seriously. Those who offer comfort to the sorrowing should do so with Christian cheer.

⁹Don't just pretend that you love others: really love them. Hate what is wrong. Stand on the side of the good. ¹⁰Love each other with brotherly affection and take delight in honoring each other. ¹¹Never be lazy in your work, but serve the Lord enthusiastically.

¹²Be glad for all God is planning for you. Be patient in trouble, and prayerful always. ¹³When God's children are in need, you be the one to help them out. And get into the habit of inviting guests home for dinner or, if they need lodging, for the night.

¹⁴If someone mistreats you because you are a Christian, don't curse him; pray that God will bless him. ¹⁵When others are happy, be happy with them. If they are sad, share their sorrow. ¹⁶Work happily together. Don't try to act big. Don't try to get into the good graces of important people, but enjoy the company of ordinary folks. And don't think you know it all!

¹⁷Never pay back evil for evil. Do things in such a way that everyone can see you are honest clear through. ¹⁸Don't quarrel with anyone. Be at peace with everyone, just as much as possible.

¹⁹Dear friends, never avenge yourselves. Leave that to God, for he has said that he will repay those who deserve it. [Don't take the law into your own hands.] ²⁰Instead, feed your enemy if he is hungry. If he is thirsty give him something to drink and you will be "heaping coals of fire on his head." In other words, he will feel ashamed of himself for what he has done to you. ²¹Don't let evil get the upper hand, but conquer evil by doing good.

13 Obey the Government

Obey the government, for God is the one who has put it there. There is no government anywhere that God has not placed in power. ²So those who refuse to obey the laws of the land are refusing to obey God, and punishment will follow. ³For the policeman does not frighten people who are doing right; but those doing evil will always fear him. So if you don't want to be afraid, keep the laws and you will get along well. ⁴The policeman is sent by God to help you. But if you are doing something wrong, of course you should be afraid, for he will have you punished. He is sent by God for that very purpose. ⁵Obey the laws, then, for two reasons: first, to keep from being punished, and second, just because you know you should.

⁶Pay your taxes too, for these same two reasons. For government workers need to be paid so that they can keep on doing God's work, serving you. ⁷Pay everyone whatever he ought to have: pay your taxes and import duties gladly, obey those over you, and give honor and respect to all those to whom it is due.

⁸Pay all your debts except the debt of love for others—never finish paying that! For if you love them, you will be obeying all of God's laws, fulfilling all his requirements. ⁹If you love your neighbor as much as you love yourself you will not want to harm or cheat him, or kill him or steal from him. And you won't sin with his wife or want what is his, or do anything else the Ten Commandments say is wrong. All ten are wrapped up in this one, to love your neighbor as you love yourself. ¹⁰Love does no wrong to anyone. That's why it fully satisfies all of God's requirements. It is the only law you need.

¹¹Another reason for right living is this: you know how late it is; time is running out. Wake up, for the coming of the Lord is nearer now than when we first believed. ¹²,¹³The night is far gone, the day of his return will soon be here. So quit the evil deeds of darkness and put on the armor of right living, as we who live in the daylight should! Be decent and true in everything you do so that all can approve your behavior. Don't spend your time in wild parties and getting drunk or in adultery and lust or fighting or jealousy. ¹⁴But ask the Lord Jesus Christ to help you live as you should, and don't make plans to enjoy evil.

14 Don't Criticize Other Christians

Give a warm welcome to any brother who wants to join you, even though his faith is weak. Don't criticize him for having different ideas from yours about what is right and wrong. ²For instance, don't argue with him about whether or not to eat meat that has been offered to idols. You may believe there is no harm in this, but the faith of others is weaker; they think it is wrong and will go without any meat at all and eat vegetables rather than eat that kind of meat. ³Those who think it is all right to eat such meat must not look down on those who won't. And if you are one of those who won't, don't find fault with those who do. For God has accepted them to be his children. ⁴They are God's servants, not yours. They are responsible to him, not to you. Let him tell them whether they are right or wrong. And God is able to make them do as they should.

⁵Some think that Christians should observe the Jewish holidays as special days to worship God, but others say it is wrong and foolish to go to all that trouble, for every day alike belongs to God. On questions of this kind everyone must decide for himself. ⁶If you have special days for worshiping the Lord, you are trying to honor him; you are doing a good thing. So is the person who eats meat that has been offered to idols; he is thankful to the Lord for it; he is doing right. And the person who won't touch such meat, he, too, is anxious to please the Lord, and is thankful. ⁷We are not our own bosses to live or die as we ourselves might choose. ⁸Living or dying we follow the Lord. Either way we are his. ⁹Christ died and rose again for this very purpose, so that he can be our Lord both while we live and when we die.

¹⁰You have no right to criticize your brother or look down on him. Remember, each of us will stand personally before the Judgment Seat of God. ¹¹For it is written, "As I live," says the Lord, "every knee shall bow to me and every tongue confess to God." ¹²Yes, each of us will give an account of himself to God.

¹³So don't criticize each other anymore. Try instead to live in such a way that you will never make your brother stumble by letting him see you doing something he thinks is wrong.

¹⁴As for myself, I am perfectly sure on the authority of the Lord Jesus that there is nothing really wrong with eating meat that has been offered to idols. But if someone believes it is wrong, then he shouldn't do it because for him it is wrong. ¹⁵And if your brother is bothered by what you eat, you are not acting in love if you go ahead and eat it. Don't let your eating ruin someone for whom Christ died. ¹⁶Don't do anything that will cause criticism against yourself even though you know that what you do is right.

¹⁷For, after all, the important thing for us as Christians is not what we eat or drink but stirring up goodness and peace and joy from the Holy Spirit. ¹⁸If you let Christ be Lord in these affairs, God will be glad; and so will others. ¹⁹In this way aim for harmony in the church, and try to build each other up.

²⁰Don't undo the work of God for a chunk of meat. Remember, there is nothing wrong with the meat, but it is wrong to eat it if it makes another stumble. ²¹The right thing to do is to quit eating meat or drinking wine or doing anything else that offends your brother or makes him sin. ²²You may know that there is nothing wrong with what you do, even from God's point of view, but keep it to yourself; don't flaunt your faith in front of others who might be hurt by it. In this situation, happy is the man who does not sin by doing what he knows is right. ²³But anyone who believes that something he wants to do is wrong shouldn't do it. He sins if he does, for he thinks it is wrong, and so for him it *is* wrong. Anything that is done apart from what he feels is right is sin.

15 Think of Others First

Even if we believe that it makes no difference to the Lord whether we do these things, still we cannot just go ahead and do them to please ourselves; for we must bear the "burden" of being considerate of the doubts and fears of others—of those who feel these things are wrong. Let's please the other fellow, not ourselves, and do what is for his good and thus build him up in the Lord. ³Christ didn't please himself. As the Psalmist said, "He came for the very purpose of suffering under the insults of those who were against the Lord." ⁴These things that were written in the Scriptures so long ago are to teach us patience and to encourage us so that we will look forward expectantly to the time when God will conquer sin and death.

⁵May God who gives patience, steadiness, and encouragement help you to live in complete harmony with each other—each with the attitude of Christ toward the other. ⁶And then all of us can praise the Lord together with one voice, giving glory to God, the Father of our Lord Jesus Christ.

⁷So warmly welcome each other into the church, just as Christ has warmly welcomed you; then God will be glorified. ⁸Remember that Jesus Christ came to show that God is true to his promises and to help the Jews. ⁹And remember that he came also that the Gentiles might be saved and give glory to God for his mercies to them. That is what the psalmist meant when he wrote: "I will praise you among the Gentiles and sing to your name."

¹⁰And in another place, "Be glad, O you Gentiles, along with his people the Jews."

¹¹And yet again, "Praise the Lord, O you Gentiles; let everyone praise him."

¹²And the prophet Isaiah said, "There shall be an Heir in the house of Jesse, and he will be King over the Gentiles; they will pin their hopes on him alone."

¹³So I pray for you Gentiles that God who gives you hope will keep you happy and full of peace as you believe in him. I pray that God will help you overflow with hope in him through the Holy Spirit's power within you.

¹⁴I know that you are wise and good, my brothers, and that you know these things so well that you are able to teach others all about them. ¹⁵,¹⁶But even so I have been bold enough to emphasize some of these points, knowing that all you need is this reminder from me; for I am, by

FAMILY DEVOTIONS

☐ DEVOTION 306
ENCOURAGING OTHERS

Read Romans 14:1-4

Encouraging Others Memory Verse

So encourage each other to build each other up, just as you are already doing.
1 Thessalonians 5:11

Jimmy slouched in a kitchen chair. "Hey, Mom," he sighed, "remember I told you that my friend, Pete, accepted Christ last month?"

"Of course I remember," said Mom. "You were really happy and excited about it. But what's wrong now?"

"Well, I saw Pete smoking in the school parking lot today," Jimmy said. "I figured he would quit smoking now that he's a Christian." Jimmy shook his head sadly. "I even heard him use a swear word. Some Christian he turned out to be!"

Mom looked thoughtful. "That's too bad, Jimmy," she began. Just then, they heard a faint cry coming from down the hall. "Your sister's awake," said Mom. "Would you go tell her she can get up from her nap?"

Jimmy stared at Mom. "But Jennifer's only six months old," he said. "You know she can't walk out here by herself."

"Why not?" asked Mom. "After all, I've been carrying her around for a long time. I think it's about time she started walking."

"But—but, Mom!" argued Jimmy. "You know that babies can't walk until they're about a year old. Give her a chance to grow up!"

"The same chance you're giving Pete, you mean?" asked Mother. Jimmy looked confused, so after she had gone to get Jennifer, Mom explained. "Babies can't do everything as soon as they're born. They have to grow up gradually. It's the same way with Christians. Some people, after they accept Christ as their Savior, seem to grow very quickly. Others take more time. As they go to church, read the Bible and pray, and fellowship with other Christians, God will help them to grow. But we have to be patient. It takes time!"

"I see," said Jimmy. "I'll try being more of a friend to Pete, and not expect too much of him all at once. And I'll pray that God will help him grow—and me, too!"

How About You?
You may be tempted to criticize when you see a new Christian falling into sin, or doing things you think Christians shouldn't do. But he or she needs help, not criticism. Perhaps you can share some Bible verses that deal with the problem. Then, pray for that person and wait for God to help him or her grow. Making Christians feel discouraged is the devil's work. Your job is to build them up! S. K.

• For the next devotional, turn to page 1093.   • For the next devotional on ENCOURAGING OTHERS, turn to page 1093.
• For notes on ENCOURAGING OTHERS, see pages 108, 157, 474, 1156, and 1170.

God's grace, a special messenger from Jesus Christ to you Gentiles, bringing you the Gospel and offering you up as a fragrant sacrifice to God; for you have been made pure and pleasing to him by the Holy Spirit. [17]So it is right for me to be a little proud of all Christ Jesus has done through me. [18]I dare not judge how effectively he has used others, but I know this: he has used me to win the Gentiles to God. [19]I have won them by my message and by the good way I have lived before them and by the miracles done through me as signs from God—all by the Holy Spirit's power. In this way I have preached the full Gospel of Christ all the way from Jerusalem clear over into Illyricum.

[20]But all the while my ambition has been to go still farther, preaching where the name of Christ has never yet been heard, rather than where a church has already been started by someone else. [21]I have been following the plan spoken of in the Scriptures where Isaiah says that those who have never heard the name of Christ before will see and understand. [22]In fact, that is the very reason I have been so long in coming to visit you.

[23]But now at last I am through with my work here, and I am ready to come after all these long years of waiting. [24]For I am planning to take a trip to Spain, and when I do, I will stop off there in Rome; and after we have had a good time together for a little while, you can send me on my way again.

[25]But before I come, I must go down to Jerusalem to take a gift to the Jewish Christians there. [26]For you see, the Christians in Macedonia and Achaia have taken up an offering for those in Jerusalem who are going through such hard times. [27]They were very glad to do this, for they feel that they owe a real debt to the Jerusalem Christians. Why? Because the news about Christ came to these Gentiles from the church in Jerusalem. And since they received this wonderful spiritual gift of the Gospel from there, they feel that the least they can do in return is to give some material aid. [28]As soon as I have delivered this money and completed this good deed of theirs, I will come to see you on my way to Spain. [29]And I am sure that when I come the Lord will give me a great blessing for you.

[30]Will you be my prayer partners? For the Lord Jesus Christ's sake and because of your love for me—given to you by the Holy Spirit—pray much with me for my work. [31]Pray that I will be protected in Jerusalem from those who are not Christians. Pray also that the Christians there will be willing to accept the money I am bringing them. [32]Then I will be able to come to you with a happy heart by the will of God, and we can refresh each other.

[33]And now may our God, who gives peace, be with you all. Amen.

16 Paul Greets His Friends

Phoebe, a dear Christian woman from the town of Cenchreae, will be coming to see you soon. She has worked hard in the church there. Receive her as your sister in the Lord, giving her a warm Christian welcome. Help her in every way you can, for she has helped many in their needs, including me. [3]Tell Priscilla and Aquila hello. They have been my fellow workers in the affairs of Christ Jesus. [4]In fact, they risked their lives for me, and I am not the only one who is thankful to them; so are all the Gentile churches.

[5]Please give my greetings to all those who meet to worship in their home. Greet my good friend Epaenetus. He was the very first person to become a Christian in Asia. [6]Remember me to Mary, too, who has worked so hard to help us. [7]Then there are Andronicus and Junias, my relatives who were in prison with me. They are respected by the apostles and became Christians before I did. Please give them my greetings. [8]Say hello to Ampliatus, whom I love as one of God's own children, [9]and Urbanus, our fellow worker, and beloved Stachys.

[10]Then there is Apelles, a good man whom the Lord approves; greet him for me. And give my best regards to those working at the house of Aristobulus. [11]Remember me to Herodion my relative. Remember me to the Christian slaves over at Narcissus House. [12]Say hello to Tryphaena and Tryphosa, the Lord's workers, and to dear Persis, who has worked so hard for the Lord. [13]Greet Rufus for me, whom the Lord picked out to be his very own; and also his dear mother who has been such a mother to me. [14]And please give my greetings to Asyncritus, Phlegon, Hermes, Patrobas, Hermas, and the other brothers who are with them. [15]Give my love to Philologus, Julia, Nereus and his sister, and to Olympas, and all the Christians who are with them. [16]Shake hands warmly with each other. All the churches here send you their greetings.

[17]And now there is one more thing to say before I end this letter. Stay away from those who cause divisions and are upsetting people's faith, teaching things about Christ that are contrary to what you have been taught. [18]Such teachers are not working for our Lord Jesus but only want gain for themselves. They are good speakers, and simple-minded people are often fooled by them. [19]But everyone knows that you stand loyal and true. This makes me very happy. I want you always to remain very clear about what is right and to stay innocent of any wrong. [20]The God of

Family Devotions

☐ DEVOTION 307
ENCOURAGING OTHERS

Read Romans 16:3-10

Encouraging Others
Memory Verse

So encourage each other to build each other up, just as you are already doing.
1 Thessalonians 5:11

Every morning Michael read a chapter of the Bible and prayed. One morning he read Romans 16. *This is kind of a different chapter,* he thought. *It's mostly a list of the people Paul appreciated.* He studied it for a moment. *Maybe this chapter is in the Bible to show us how important it is to let others know how much we appreciate them.*

So at breakfast Michael said to his mother, "Thanks for cooking these eggs for me, Mom." Then when his brother Steve came into the kitchen, Michael said, "Steve, I appreciate you for letting me use your markers for my report." Mom and Steve both looked surprised, but they gave Michael such big smiles that he decided to keep on telling people how much he appreciated them.

At school, Michael said to his friend Keith, "Thanks for sticking up for me when those guys teased me yesterday. I appreciate that."

After class he told his teacher, "I appreciate the neat way you've been telling us about the Civil War. It makes studying so much more interesting."

On the way home from school, Michael walked by his church. Pastor Grey was standing in the parking lot, talking to the organist. "Pastor," Michael called, "I want you to know I appreciate your messages. And Mrs. Johnson, I appreciate you for playing the organ each week." Michael received two more big smiles.

That night as Michael was getting ready for bed, he thought once again about appreciation. People needed to be appreciated. He could tell that by the big smiles he had been getting all day. He was glad he had learned a lesson from the apostle Paul.

How About You?
You probably do appreciate all the people who do things for you, but do you let them know it? Make a list of five people whom you appreciate, and then tell them. You'll feel good because you will be helping others feel good. And don't forget to include Jesus on your list. He deserves the most appreciation.
L. M. W.

• For the next devotional, turn to page 1097. • For the next devotional on ENCOURAGING OTHERS, turn to page 1103.
• For notes on ENCOURAGING OTHERS, see pages 108, 157, 474, 1156, and 1170.

peace will soon crush Satan under your feet. The blessings from our Lord Jesus Christ be upon you.

²¹Timothy my fellow worker, and Lucius and Jason and Sosipater, my relatives, send you their good wishes. ²²I, Tertius, the one who is writing this letter for Paul, send my greetings too, as a Christian brother. ²³Gaius says to say hello to you for him. I am his guest, and the church meets here in his home. Erastus, the city treasurer, sends you his greetings and so does Quartus, a Christian brother. ²⁴Good-bye. May the grace of our Lord Jesus Christ be with you all.

²⁵⁻²⁷I commit you to God, who is able to make you strong and steady in the Lord, just as the Gospel says, and just as I have told you. This is God's plan of salvation for you Gentiles, kept secret from the beginning of time. But now as the prophets foretold and as God commands, this message is being preached everywhere, so that people all around the world will have faith in Christ and obey him. To God, who alone is wise, be the glory forever through Jesus Christ our Lord. Amen.

Sincerely, Paul

1 Corinthians

DO YOU ever wonder if what you're doing is right or wrong? The book of Romans told us about what to believe. Now 1 Corinthians tells us how to *act* because of what we believe.

Corinth was an important city when Paul wrote this letter. People of all nationalities lived there or traveled there to buy and sell things. Corinth was known for being a bad place. People who lived there committed every sin you can imagine.

Paul had started the church in Corinth on one of his missionary journeys. Now he heard that some people in the church had started doing the bad things that other people in the city did, and the church had sent him a letter with some questions. Paul wrote back to answer their questions and to help them correct the bad habits the Christians had gotten into.

Christians today still need to learn what Paul taught the Corinthians. As you read, look for ways you can make your actions show what you believe.

Paul: Chosen to Be a Missionary

From: Paul, chosen by God to be Jesus Christ's missionary, and from brother Sosthenes.

²*To:* The Christians in Corinth, invited by God to be his people and made acceptable to him by Christ Jesus. *And to:* All Christians everywhere—whoever calls upon the name of Jesus Christ, our Lord and theirs.

³May God our Father and the Lord Jesus Christ give you all of his blessings, and great peace of heart and mind.

⁴I can never stop thanking God for all the wonderful gifts he has given you, now that you are Christ's: ⁵he has enriched your whole life. He has helped you speak out for him and has given you a full understanding of the truth; ⁶what I told you Christ could do for you has happened! ⁷Now you have every grace and blessing; every spiritual gift and power for doing his will are yours during this time of waiting for the return of our Lord Jesus Christ. ⁸And he guarantees right up to the end that you will be counted free from all sin and

guilt on that day when he returns. ⁹God will surely do this for you, for he always does just what he says, and he is the one who invited you into this wonderful friendship with his Son, even Christ our Lord.

¹⁰But, dear brothers, I beg you in the name of the Lord Jesus Christ to stop arguing among yourselves. Let there be real harmony so that there won't be splits in the church. I plead with you to be of one mind, united in thought and purpose. ¹¹For some of those who live at Chloe's house have told me of your arguments and quarrels, dear brothers. ¹²Some of you are saying, "I am a follower of Paul"; and others say that they are for Apollos or for Peter; and some that they alone are the true followers of Christ. ¹³And so, in effect, you have broken Christ into many pieces.

But did I, Paul, die for your sins? Were any of you baptized in my name? ¹⁴I am so thankful now that I didn't baptize any of you except Crispus and Gaius. ¹⁵For now no one can think that I have been trying to start something new, beginning a "Church of Paul." ¹⁶Oh, yes, and I baptized the family of Stephanas. I don't remember ever baptizing anyone else. ¹⁷For Christ didn't send me to baptize, but to preach the Gospel; and even my preaching sounds poor, for I do not fill my sermons with profound words and high sounding ideas, for fear of diluting the mighty power there is in the simple message of the cross of Christ.

¹⁸I know very well how foolish it sounds to those who are lost, when they hear that Jesus died to save them. But we who are saved recognize this message as the very power of God. ¹⁹For God says, "I will destroy all human plans of salvation no matter how wise they seem to be, and ignore the best ideas of men, even the most brilliant of them."

²⁰So what about these wise men, these scholars, these brilliant debaters of this world's great affairs? God has made them all look foolish and shown their wisdom to be useless nonsense. ²¹For God in his wisdom saw to it that the world would never find God through human brilliance, and then he stepped in and saved all those who believed his message, which the world calls foolish and silly. ²²It seems foolish to the Jews because they want a sign from heaven as proof that what is preached is true; and it is foolish to the Gentiles because they believe only what agrees with their philosophy and seems wise to them. ²³So when we preach about Christ dying to save them, the Jews are offended and the Gentiles say it's all nonsense. ²⁴But God has opened the eyes of those called to salvation, both Jews and Gentiles, to see that Christ is the mighty power of God to save them; Christ himself is the center of God's wise plan for their salvation. ²⁵This so-called "foolish" plan of God is far wiser than the wisest plan of the wisest man, and God in his weakness—Christ dying on the cross—is far stronger than any man.

²⁶Notice among yourselves, dear brothers, that few of you who follow Christ have big names or power or wealth. ²⁷Instead, God has deliberately chosen to use ideas the world considers foolish and of little worth in order to shame those people considered by the world as wise and great. ²⁸He has chosen a plan despised by the world, counted as nothing at all, and used it to bring down to nothing those the world considers great, ²⁹so that no one anywhere can ever brag in the presence of God.

³⁰For it is from God alone that you have your life through Christ Jesus. He showed us God's plan of salvation; he was the one who made us acceptable to God; he made us pure and holy and gave himself to purchase our salvation. ³¹As it says in the Scriptures, "If anyone is going to boast, let him boast only of what the Lord has done."

2 The Holy Spirit Gives Us Wisdom

Dear brothers, even when I first came to you I didn't use lofty words and brilliant ideas to tell you God's message. ²For I decided that I would speak only of Jesus Christ and his death on the cross. ³I came to you in weakness—timid and trembling. ⁴And my preaching was very plain, not with a lot of oratory and human wisdom, but the Holy Spirit's power was in my words, proving to those who heard them that the message was from God. ⁵I did this because I wanted your faith to stand firmly upon God, not on man's great ideas.

⁶Yet when I am among mature Christians I do speak with words of great wisdom, but not the kind that comes from here on earth, and not the kind that appeals to the great men of this world, who are doomed to fall. ⁷Our words are wise because they are from God, telling of God's wise plan to bring us into the glories of heaven. This plan was hidden in former times, though it was made for our benefit before the world began. ⁸But the great men of the world have not understood it; if they had, they never would have crucified the Lord of Glory.

⁹That is what is meant by the Scriptures which say that no mere man has ever seen, heard, or even imagined what wonderful things God has ready for those who love the Lord. ¹⁰But we know about these things because God has sent his Spirit to tell us, and his Spirit searches out and shows us all of God's deepest secrets. ¹¹No one can really know what anyone else is thinking or what he is really like except that person himself. And no one can know God's thoughts except God's own Spirit. ¹²And God has actually given us his Spirit (not the world's spirit) to tell us about the wonderful free gifts of

FAMILY DEVOTIONS

☐ DEVOTION 308
CULTIVATING GODLY ATTITUDES

Read 1 Corinthians 3:10-15

Cultivating Godly Attitudes
Memory Verse

Whatever you do or say, let it be as a representative of the Lord Jesus, and come with him into the presence of God the Father to give him your thanks.
Colossians 3:17

"But even though he huffed and he puffed, the mean old wolf couldn't blow down the house of the third little pig. It was made of bricks." Little Joanie looked proudly around the table.

"Big deal," scoffed her brother, Matt. "You've known that story ever since you were a baby."

"Yes, but now she can read it all by herself," said Dad, smiling at his little daughter. "Good for you, Little Pig."

"Daddy!" protested Joanie. "I'm not a pig."

"No, you're not," agreed Dad. "I called you that because the little pigs were builders, and you are, too."

"Me?" asked Joanie. "I'm not building a house."

Dad smiled. "No," he said, "but you're building your life. We all are. We add a little to it every day by the things we do or say and the places we go. Sometimes we add straw or sticks. Sometimes we add something even better than brick—the Bible talks about using gold and silver and jewels to build with. They're the only things that will last."

"What do you think are some of the things we do that are like straw or sticks?" asked Mom.

"Cheating and lying and disobeying are all bad things," said Matt promptly. "They're straw and sticks."

"Yes," agreed Dad, "and so are the good works that we do with the wrong attitude."

"Like helping, but being mad about it?" asked Joanie.

Dad nodded. "Now, what are some things that will last?"

"Inviting a friend to Sunday school," suggested Matt.

"Running errands for Grandma," said Joanie.

"Good," said Dad, nodding his approval. "As we build our life houses, let's be careful to use materials that last."

How About You?
What are you using to build your life house? Will you use sticks, hay, or straw today? Or will you build with materials that will last for all eternity—with actions and attitudes that please God? *H. M.*

grace and blessing that God has given us. ¹³In telling you about these gifts we have even used the very words given to us by the Holy Spirit, not words that we as men might choose. So we use the Holy Spirit's words to explain the Holy Spirit's facts. ¹⁴But the man who isn't a Christian can't understand and can't accept these thoughts from God, which the Holy Spirit teaches us. They sound foolish to him because only those who have the Holy Spirit within them can understand what the Holy Spirit means. Others just can't take it in. ¹⁵But the spiritual man has insight into everything, and that bothers and baffles the man of the world, who can't understand him at all. ¹⁶How could he? For certainly he has never been one to know the Lord's thoughts, or to discuss them with him, or to move the hands of God by prayer. But, strange as it seems, we Christians actually do have within us a portion of the very thoughts and mind of Christ.

3 Dear brothers, I have been talking to you as though you were still just babies in the Christian life who are not following the Lord but your own desires; I cannot talk to you as I would to healthy Christians who are filled with the Spirit. ²I have had to feed you with milk and not with solid food because you couldn't digest anything stronger. And even now you still have to be fed on milk. ³For you are still only baby Christians, controlled by your own desires, not God's. When you are jealous of one another and divide up into quarreling groups, doesn't that prove you are still babies, wanting your own way? In fact, you are acting like people who don't belong to the Lord at all. ⁴There you are, quarreling about whether I am greater than Apollos, and dividing the church. Doesn't this show how little you have grown in the Lord?

⁵Who am I, and who is Apollos, that we should be the cause of a quarrel? Why, we're just God's servants, each of us with certain special abilities, and with our help you believed. ⁶My work was to plant the seed in your hearts, and Apollos' work was to water it, but it was God, not we, who made the garden grow in your hearts. ⁷The person who does the planting or watering isn't very important, but God is important because he is the one who makes things grow. ⁸Apollos and I are working as a team, with the same aim, though each of us will be rewarded for his own hard work. ⁹We are only God's coworkers. You are *God's* garden, not ours; you are *God's* building, not ours.

¹⁰God, in his kindness, has taught me how to be an expert builder. I have laid the foundation and Apollos has built on it. But he who builds on the foundation must be very careful. ¹¹And no one can ever lay any other real foundation than that one we already have—Jesus Christ. ¹²But there are various kinds of materials that can be used to build on that foundation. Some use gold and silver and jewels; and some build with sticks and hay or even straw! ¹³There is going to come a time of testing at Christ's Judgment Day to see what kind of material each builder has used. Everyone's work will be put through the fire so that all can see whether or not it keeps its value, and what was really accomplished. ¹⁴Then every workman who has built on the foundation with the right materials, and whose work still stands, will get his pay. ¹⁵But if the house he has built burns up, he will have a great loss. He himself will be saved, but like a man escaping through a wall of flames.

¹⁶Don't you realize that all of you together are the house of God, and that the Spirit of God lives among you in his house? ¹⁷If anyone defiles and spoils God's home, God will destroy him. For God's home is holy and clean, and you are that home.

¹⁸Stop fooling yourselves. If you count yourself above average in intelligence, as judged by this world's standards, you had better put this all aside and be a fool rather than let it hold you back from the true wisdom from above. ¹⁹For the wisdom of this world is foolishness to God. As it says in the book of Job, God uses man's own brilliance to trap him; he stumbles over his own "wisdom" and falls. ²⁰And again, in the book of Psalms, we are told that the Lord knows full well how the human mind reasons and how foolish and futile it is.

²¹So don't be proud of following the wise men of this world. For God has already given you everything you need. ²²He has given you Paul and Apollos and Peter as your helpers. He has given you the whole world to use, and life and even death are your servants. He has given you all of the present and all of the future. All are yours, ²³and you belong to Christ, and Christ is God's.

4 Cliques in the Church

So Apollos and I should be looked upon as Christ's servants who distribute God's blessings by explaining God's secrets. ²Now the most important thing about a servant is that he does just what his master tells him to. ³What about me? Have I been a good servant? Well, I don't worry over what you think about this or what anyone else thinks. I don't even trust my own judgment on this point. ⁴My conscience is clear, but even that isn't final proof. It is the Lord himself who must examine me and decide.

⁵So be careful not to jump to conclusions before the Lord returns as to whether someone is a good servant or not. When the Lord comes, he will turn on the light so that everyone can see exactly what each one of us is really like, deep down in our hearts. Then everyone will know

FAMILY DEVOTIONS

☐ DEVOTION 309
SHARING YOUR FAITH

Read 1 Corinthians 4:1-5

"Dad, are you in here?" Joel's voice sailed over the top of the roses, carnations, and daffodils in the greenhouse.

"Back here with the orchids, Joel," Dad responded. Joel plodded to the back of the greenhouse, where his father was patting down the soil in a flower pot. "Well, how was your first day at Mr. Callaway's store?" asked Dad.

"Just terrible," grumbled Joel. "I stocked; I swept; I painted. Still all Mr. Callaway said was, 'You can stack those cans better. You missed some dirt. You didn't put enough paint on your brush.' It made me so mad."

"Hmmm," murmured Dad. "Well, I know he can be gruff, but I hope you were polite anyway. You can be a testimony for the Lord by your attitude as well as your words." He paused, and Joel just looked glum. "You can be like the *Rhizanthella gardneri*," added Dad.

"The what?" gasped Joel.

Dad chuckled. *"Rhizanthella gardneri* is the scientific name for an all-white orchid from Australia. The orchid spends its entire life underground, except when it pokes its pod above the ground to disperse its seeds." He took the flower pot he had been working with and motioned for Joel to follow him into a dark room. Digging carefully, Joel's father revealed a small white flower under the soil.

"Neat!" Joel exclaimed. "But how does my working for Mr. Callaway compare to that flower?"

"You can be like the white orchid by poking your head above Mr. Callaway's gruffness and spreading Christian seeds of kindness, patience, and love," explained Dad. "You can serve the Lord by serving Mr. Callaway. In time, he's almost sure to notice. Even more important, God sees. He's the one who really matters."

Sharing Your Faith Memory Verse

And I assure you of this: I, the Messiah, will publicly honor you in the presence of God's angels if you publicly acknowledge me here on earth as your Friend.
Luke 12:8

How About You?
Do you remain kind, loving, and thoughtful even when it seems you're not appreciated? Your actions and attitudes are an important part of your testimony for the Lord. Don't look for the praise of man. Instead, look for God's future praise of, "You are a good and faithful servant." D. A. L.

• For the next devotional, turn to page 1101. • To start the next topic, turn to page 569. • For notes on SHARING YOUR FAITH, see pages 462, 776, 1015, and 1074.

why we have been doing the Lord's work. At that time God will give to each one whatever praise is coming to him.

⁶I have used Apollos and myself as examples to illustrate what I have been saying: that you must not have favorites. You must not be proud of one of God's teachers more than another. ⁷What are you so puffed up about? What do you have that God hasn't given you? And if all you have is from God, why act as though you are so great, and as though you have accomplished something on your own?

⁸You seem to think you already have all the spiritual food you need. You are full and spiritually contented, rich kings on your thrones, leaving us far behind! I wish you really were already on your thrones, for when that time comes you can be sure that we will be there, too, reigning with you. ⁹Sometimes I think God has put us apostles at the very end of the line, like prisoners soon to be killed, put on display at the end of a victor's parade, to be stared at by men and angels alike.

¹⁰Religion has made us foolish, you say, but of course you are all such wise and sensible Christians! We are weak, but not you! You are well thought of, while we are laughed at. ¹¹To this very hour we have gone hungry and thirsty, without even enough clothes to keep us warm. We have been kicked around without homes of our own. ¹²We have worked wearily with our hands to earn our living. We have blessed those who cursed us. We have been patient with those who injured us. ¹³We have replied quietly when evil things have been said about us. Yet right up to the present moment we are like dirt underfoot, like garbage.

¹⁴I am not writing about these things to make you ashamed, but to warn and counsel you as beloved children. ¹⁵For although you may have ten thousand others to teach you about Christ, remember that you have only me as your father. For I was the one who brought you to Christ when I preached the Gospel to you. ¹⁶So I beg you to follow my example and do as I do.

¹⁷That is the very reason why I am sending Timothy—to help you do this. For he is one of those I won to Christ, a beloved and trustworthy child in the Lord. He will remind you of what I teach in all the churches wherever I go.

¹⁸I know that some of you will have become proud, thinking that I am afraid to come to deal with you. ¹⁹But I will come, and soon, if the Lord will let me, and then I'll find out whether these proud men are just big talkers or whether they really have God's power. ²⁰The Kingdom of God is not just talking; it is living by God's power. ²¹Which do you choose? Shall I come with punishment and scolding, or shall I come with quiet love and gentleness?

5 Sin in the Church

Everyone is talking about the terrible thing that has happened there among you, something so evil that even the heathen don't do it: you have a man in your church who is living in sin with his father's wife. ²And are you still so conceited, so "spiritual"? Why aren't you mourning in sorrow and shame and seeing to it that this man is removed from your membership?

³,⁴Although I am not there with you, I have been thinking a lot about this, and in the name of the Lord Jesus Christ I have already decided what to do, just as though I were there. You are to call a meeting of the church—and the power of the Lord Jesus will be with you as you meet, and I will be there in spirit—⁵and cast out this man from the fellowship of the church and into Satan's hands, to punish him, in the hope that his soul will be saved when our Lord Jesus Christ returns.

⁶What a terrible thing it is that you are boasting about your purity and yet you let this sort of thing go on. Don't you realize that if even one person is allowed to go on sinning, soon all will be affected? ⁷Remove this evil cancer—this wicked person—from among you, so that you can stay pure. Christ, God's Lamb, has been slain for us. ⁸So let us feast upon him and grow strong in the Christian life, leaving entirely behind us the cancerous old life with all its hatreds and wickedness. Let us feast instead upon the pure bread of honor and sincerity and truth.

⁹When I wrote to you before I said not to mix with evil people. ¹⁰But when I said that I wasn't talking about unbelievers who live in sexual sin or are greedy cheats and thieves and idol worshipers. For you can't live in this world without being with people like that. ¹¹What I meant was that you are not to keep company with anyone who claims to be a brother Christian but indulges in sexual sins, or is greedy, or is a swindler, or worships idols, or is a drunkard, or abusive. Don't even eat lunch with such a person.

¹²It isn't our job to judge outsiders. But it certainly is our job to judge and deal strongly with those who are members of the church and who are sinning in these ways. ¹³God alone is the Judge of those on the outside. But you yourselves must deal with this man and put him out of your church.

6 Lawsuits

How is it that when you have something against another Christian, you "go to law" and ask a heathen court to decide the matter instead of taking it to other Christians to decide which of you is right? ²Don't you know that someday we Christians are going to judge and govern the

Family Devotions

☐ DEVOTION 310
CULTIVATING GODLY ATTITUDES

Read 1 Corinthians 6:19-20

Cultivating Godly Attitudes Memory Verse

Your attitude should be the kind that was shown us by Jesus Christ.
Philippians 2:5

"Are you going to wear *that* to school?" Mother's familiar question made Tammy sigh as she came into the kitchen. She said nothing, but sat down and poured herself some cereal, hoping the question would go away. "I want you to change," added Mom.

If Mom had her way, Tammy thought, *I'd be dressed like an old lady!* Aloud, she said, "I could wear the T-shirt Brenda gave me—the one that says—"

"No," her mother interrupted, "that's even worse."

"I thought what's on the inside of a person was what counted," muttered Tammy as she went to change. When she returned, she looked around the kitchen. "I'm going to Darcy's birthday party right after school, remember?" she said. "Did someone move the present I wrapped? I left it right here by the sink when I went to bed last night."

"What did it look like?" asked Mom.

"It's a little pearl necklace," replied Tammy. "I put it in a box, and then, for a joke, I wrapped it in newspaper and tied it with a string. Then I put it in one of these little plastic bags you use for—"

"For garbage!" gasped Mom. "I thought it *was* garbage, and I put it out with the rest of the trash."

Tammy ran out to the curb and began lifting the lid on first one garbage can, then another. In the distance, she could hear the whine of the approaching garbage truck. At last she found the bag and ran back into the house.

As she went to change her clothes, Tammy realized that by wrapping her gift as garbage, she had made it look like what was inside was not very valuable. *Maybe my wrappings give a false message, too,* she thought, looking at herself in the mirror. *God can see inside of me, but nobody else can. I should dress like there's something worthwhile inside.*

How About You?

What does your appearance say? Would Jesus approve of the clothes you wear? Your appearance gives people an impression of you—be sure it's an impression you want them to have. You should give glory to God by the clothes you choose. And don't forget that the perfect accessory for every outfit is a smile. *C. R.*

• For the next devotional, turn to page 1103. • For the next devotional on *CULTIVATING GODLY ATTITUDES,* turn to page 1141. • For notes on *CULTIVATING GODLY ATTITUDES,* see pages 337, 383, 472, 622, and 1216.

world? So why can't you decide even these little things among yourselves? ³Don't you realize that we Christians will judge and reward the very angels in heaven? So you should be able to decide your problems down here on earth easily enough. ⁴Why then go to outside judges who are not even Christians? ⁵I am trying to make you ashamed. Isn't there anyone in all the church who is wise enough to decide these arguments? ⁶But, instead, one Christian sues another and accuses his Christian brother in front of unbelievers.

⁷To have such lawsuits at all is a real defeat for you as Christians. Why not just accept mistreatment and leave it at that? It would be far more honoring to the Lord to let yourselves be cheated. ⁸But, instead, you yourselves are the ones who do wrong, cheating others, even your own brothers.

⁹,¹⁰Don't you know that those doing such things have no share in the Kingdom of God? Don't fool yourselves. Those who live immoral lives, who are idol worshipers, adulterers or homosexuals—will have no share in his Kingdom. Neither will thieves or greedy people, drunkards, slanderers, or robbers. ¹¹There was a time when some of you were just like that but now your sins are washed away, and you are set apart for God; and he has accepted you because of what the Lord Jesus Christ and the Spirit of our God have done for you.

¹²I can do anything I want to if Christ has not said no, but some of these things aren't good for me. Even if I am allowed to do them, I'll refuse to if I think they might get such a grip on me that I can't easily stop when I want to. ¹³For instance, take the matter of eating. God has given us an appetite for food and stomachs to digest it. But that doesn't mean we should eat more than we need. Don't think of eating as important because someday God will do away with both stomachs and food.

But sexual sin is never right: our bodies were not made for that but for the Lord, and the Lord wants to fill our bodies with himself. ¹⁴And God is going to raise our bodies from the dead by his power just as he raised up the Lord Jesus Christ. ¹⁵Don't you realize that your bodies are actually parts and members of Christ? So should I take part of Christ and join him to a prostitute? Never! ¹⁶And don't you know that if a man joins himself to a prostitute she becomes a part of him and he becomes a part of her? For God tells us in the Scripture that in his sight the two become one person. ¹⁷But if you give yourself to the Lord, you and Christ are joined together as one person.

¹⁸That is why I say to run from sex sin. No other sin affects the body as this one does. When you sin this sin it is against your own body. ¹⁹Haven't you yet learned that your body is the home of the Holy Spirit God gave you, and that he lives within you? Your own body does not belong to you. ²⁰For God has bought you with a great price. So use every part of your body to give glory back to God because he owns it.

7 Questions about Marriage

Now about those questions you asked in your last letter: my answer is that if you do not marry, it is good. ²But usually it is best to be married, each man having his own wife, and each woman having her own husband, because otherwise you might fall back into sin.

³The man should give his wife all that is her right as a married woman, and the wife should do the same for her husband: ⁴for a girl who marries no longer has full right to her own body, for her husband then has his rights to it, too; and in the same way the husband no longer has full right to his own body, for it belongs also to his wife. ⁵So do not refuse these rights to each other. The only exception to this rule would be the agreement of both husband and wife to refrain from the rights of marriage for a limited time, so that they can give themselves more completely to prayer. Afterwards, they should come together again so that Satan won't be able to tempt them because of their lack of self-control.

⁶I'm not saying you *must* marry, but you certainly *may* if you wish. ⁷I wish everyone could get along without marrying, just as I do. But we are not all the same. God gives some the gift of a husband or wife, and others he gives the gift of being able to stay happily unmarried. ⁸So I say to those who aren't married and to widows—better to stay unmarried if you can, just as I am. ⁹But if you can't control yourselves, go ahead and marry. It is better to marry than to burn with lust.

¹⁰Now, for those who are married I have a command, not just a suggestion. And it is not a command from me, for this is what the Lord himself has said: A wife must not leave her husband. ¹¹But if she is separated from him, let her remain single or else go back to him. And the husband must not divorce his wife.

¹²Here I want to add some suggestions of my own. These are not direct commands from the Lord, but they seem right to me: If a Christian has a wife who is not a Christian, but she wants to stay with him anyway, he must not leave her or divorce her. ¹³And if a Christian woman has a husband who isn't a Christian, and he wants her to stay with him, she must not leave him. ¹⁴For perhaps the husband who isn't a Christian may become a Christian with the help of his Christian wife. And the wife who isn't a Christian may become a Christian with the help of her Christian

Family Devotions

☐ DEVOTION 311
ENCOURAGING OTHERS

Read 1 Corinthians 8:8-13

Encouraging Others
Memory Verse

So encourage each other to build each other up, just as you are already doing.
1 Thessalonians 5:11

Darrell burst into the room. "Mom, guess what happened at Bible club!" he exclaimed. "Troy accepted Jesus as his Savior!"

"How wonderful!" Mother responded. "I'm happy Troy's a Christian, but I'm afraid he won't get much encouragement at home. His dad is an alcoholic and doesn't have much use for God or the church."

"I'll help Troy," Darrell said eagerly.

But a few weeks later, Darrell wasn't so sure about that. "I asked Troy to go with me to Don's house to play pool," he grumbled, "but you know what he said?" He said, 'Darrell, I thought you were a Christian!' Then he walked away! I've been a Christian longer than he has. Who does he think he is? What's wrong with playing pool?"

Mother was thoughtful. "Maybe Troy's father plays a lot of pool in the bars, so Troy associates playing pool with drinking, wasting money, and being away from home too much. He probably doesn't understand that a quiet game of pool in somebody's basement can be OK. Darrell, I think you may need to stay away from playing pool, so you don't cause Troy to sin."

"I don't see why I shouldn't play," objected Darrell. "I can't help it if he doesn't like it."

Mother thought for a moment. "Troy's a baby Christian. Seeing you do something he considers wrong might hurt him spiritually. If he thinks he shouldn't play pool, it would be wrong for him to join you. As he grows in his Christian life, he'll learn how to handle his actions. But right now, pool playing is a problem for him."

Darrell nodded thoughtfully. "I don't want to do anything that would make Troy stumble in his faith. Maybe next time I'll just invite him over here to work on my model airplanes."

How About You?

Are there things you think are OK to do, but which bother other people? Remember, a Christian doesn't live for himself. His actions influence others. Do your activities draw people to Christ or turn them away? Be careful not to cause someone else to do something he feels is wrong, even if it means you have to give up something you enjoy. J. H.

- For the next devotional, turn to page 1107. • For the next devotional on ENCOURAGING OTHERS, turn to page 1221.
- For notes on ENCOURAGING OTHERS, see pages 108, 157, 474, 1156, and 1170.

husband. Otherwise, if the family separates, the children might never come to know the Lord; whereas a united family may, in God's plan, result in the children's salvation.

¹⁵But if the husband or wife who isn't a Christian is eager to leave, it is permitted. In such cases the Christian husband or wife should not insist that the other stay, for God wants his children to live in peace and harmony. ¹⁶For, after all, there is no assurance to you wives that your husbands will be converted if they stay; and the same may be said to you husbands concerning your wives.

¹⁷But be sure in deciding these matters that you are living as God intended, marrying or not marrying in accordance with God's direction and help, and accepting whatever situation God has put you into. This is my rule for all the churches.

¹⁸For instance, a man who already has gone through the Jewish ceremony of circumcision before he became a Christian shouldn't worry about it; and if he hasn't been circumcised, he shouldn't do it now. ¹⁹For it doesn't make any difference at all whether a Christian has gone through this ceremony or not. But it makes a lot of difference whether he is pleasing God and keeping God's commandments. That is the important thing.

²⁰Usually a person should keep on with the work he was doing when God called him. ²¹Are you a slave? Don't let that worry you—but of course, if you get a chance to be free, take it. ²²If the Lord calls you, and you are a slave, remember that Christ has set you free from the awful power of sin; and if he has called you and you are free, remember that you are now a slave of Christ. ²³You have been bought and paid for by Christ, so you belong to him—be free now from all these earthly prides and fears. ²⁴So, dear brothers, whatever situation a person is in when he becomes a Christian, let him stay there, for now the Lord is there to help him.

²⁵Now I will try to answer your other question. What about girls who are not yet married? Should they be permitted to do so? In answer to this question, I have no special command for them from the Lord. But the Lord in his kindness has given me wisdom that can be trusted, and I will be glad to tell you what I think.

²⁶Here is the problem: We Christians are facing great dangers to our lives at present. In times like these I think it is best for a person to remain unmarried. ²⁷Of course, if you already are married, don't separate because of this. But if you aren't, don't rush into it at this time. ²⁸But if you men decide to go ahead anyway and get married now, it is all right; and if a girl gets married in times like these, it is no sin. However, marriage will bring extra problems that I wish you didn't have to face right now.

²⁹The important thing to remember is that our remaining time is very short, [and so are our opportunities for doing the Lord's work]. For that reason those who have wives should stay as free as possible for the Lord; ³⁰happiness or sadness or wealth should not keep anyone from doing God's work. ³¹Those in frequent contact with the exciting things the world offers should make good use of their opportunities without stopping to enjoy them; for the world in its present form will soon be gone.

³²In all you do, I want you to be free from worry. An unmarried man can spend his time doing the Lord's work and thinking how to please him. ³³But a married man can't do that so well; he has to think about his earthly responsibilities and how to please his wife. ³⁴His interests are divided. It is the same with a girl who marries. She faces the same problem. A girl who is not married is anxious to please the Lord in all she is and does. But a married woman must consider other things such as housekeeping and the likes and dislikes of her husband.

³⁵I am saying this to help you, not to try to keep you from marrying. I want you to do whatever will help you serve the Lord best, with as few other things as possible to distract your attention from him.

³⁶But if anyone feels he ought to marry because he has trouble controlling his passions, it is all right; it is not a sin; let him marry. ³⁷But if a man has the willpower not to marry and decides that he doesn't need to and won't, he has made a wise decision. ³⁸So the person who marries does well, and the person who doesn't marry does even better.

³⁹The wife is part of her husband as long as he lives; if her husband dies, then she may marry again, but only if she marries a Christian. ⁴⁰But in my opinion she will be happier if she doesn't marry again; and I think I am giving you counsel from God's Spirit when I say this.

8 Food Offered to Idols

Next is your question about eating food that has been sacrificed to idols. On this question everyone feels that only his answer is the right one! But although being a "know-it-all" makes us feel important, what is really needed to build the church is love. ²If anyone thinks he knows all the answers, he is just showing his ignorance. ³But the person who truly loves God is the one who is open to God's knowledge.

⁴So now, what about it? Should we eat meat that has been sacrificed to idols? Well, we all know that an idol is not really a god, and that there is only one God, and no other. ⁵According to

some people, there are a great many gods, both in heaven and on earth. ⁶But we know that there is only one God, the Father, who created all things and made us to be his own; and one Lord Jesus Christ, who made everything and gives us life.

⁷However, some Christians don't realize this. All their lives they have been used to thinking of idols as alive, and have believed that food offered to the idols is really being offered to actual gods. So when they eat such food it bothers them and hurts their tender consciences. ⁸Just remember that God doesn't care whether we eat it or not. We are no worse off if we don't eat it, and no better off if we do. ⁹But be careful not to use your freedom to eat it, lest you cause some Christian brother to sin whose conscience is weaker than yours.

¹⁰You see, this is what may happen: Someone who thinks it is wrong to eat this food will see you eating at a temple restaurant, for you know there is no harm in it. Then he will become bold enough to do it too, although all the time he still feels it is wrong. ¹¹So because you "know it is all right to do it," you will be responsible for causing great spiritual damage to a brother with a tender conscience for whom Christ died. ¹²And it is a sin against Christ to sin against your brother by encouraging him to do something he thinks is wrong. ¹³So if eating meat offered to idols is going to make my brother sin, I'll not eat any of it as long as I live because I don't want to do this to him.

9 The Right of an Apostle

I am an apostle, God's messenger, responsible to no mere man. I am one who has actually seen Jesus our Lord with my own eyes. And your changed lives are the result of my hard work for him. ²If in the opinion of others, I am not an apostle, I certainly am to you, for you have been won to Christ through me. ³This is my answer to those who question my rights.

⁴Or don't I have any rights at all? Can't I claim the same privilege the other apostles have of being a guest in your homes? ⁵If I had a wife, and if she were a believer, couldn't I bring her along on these trips just as the other disciples do, and as the Lord's brothers do, and as Peter does? ⁶And must Barnabas and I alone keep working for our living while you supply these others? ⁷What soldier in the army has to pay his own expenses? And have you ever heard of a farmer who harvests his crop and doesn't have the right to eat some of it? What shepherd takes care of a flock of sheep and goats and isn't allowed to drink some of the milk? ⁸And I'm not merely quoting the opinions of men as to what is right. I'm telling you what God's law says. ⁹For in the law God gave to Moses he said that you must not put a muzzle on an ox to keep it from eating when it is treading out the wheat. Do you suppose God was thinking only about oxen when he said this? ¹⁰Wasn't he also thinking about us? Of course he was. He said this to show us that Christian workers should be paid by those they help. Those who do the plowing and threshing should expect some share of the harvest.

¹¹We have planted good spiritual seed in your souls. Is it too much to ask, in return, for mere food and clothing? ¹²You give them to others who preach to you, and you should. But shouldn't we have an even greater right to them? Yet we have *never* used this right but supply our own needs without your help. We have never demanded payment of any kind for fear that, if we did, you might be less interested in our message to you from Christ.

¹³Don't you realize that God told those working in his temple to take for their own needs some of the food brought there as gifts to him? And those who work at the altar of God get a share of the food that is brought by those offering it to the Lord. ¹⁴In the same way the Lord has given orders that those who preach the Gospel should be supported by those who accept it.

¹⁵Yet I have never asked you for one penny. And I am not writing this to hint that I would like to start now. In fact, I would rather die of hunger than lose the satisfaction I get from preaching to you without charge. ¹⁶For just preaching the Gospel isn't any special credit to me—I couldn't keep from preaching it if I wanted to. I would be utterly miserable. Woe unto me if I don't.

¹⁷If I were volunteering my services of my own free will, then the Lord would give me a special reward; but that is not the situation, for God has picked me out and given me this sacred trust, and I have no choice. ¹⁸Under this circumstance, what is my pay? It is the special joy I get from preaching the Good News without expense to anyone, never demanding my rights.

¹⁹And this has a real advantage: I am not bound to obey anyone just because he pays my salary; yet I have freely and happily become a servant of any and all so that I can win them to Christ.

BECOMING MORE LIKE JESUS 9:24-27 Winning a race requires purpose and discipline. Paul used this illustration to explain that the Christian life takes hard work, self-denial, and grueling preparation. As Christians, we are running toward our heavenly reward. Prayer, Bible study, and worship equip us to run with strength and endurance. Don't merely observe from the grandstand; don't just turn out to jog a couple of laps each morning. Train diligently, because the Christian life truly is important. **To begin the series of devotionals on BECOMING MORE LIKE JESUS, turn to page 131.**

20When I am with the Jews I seem as one of them so that they will listen to the Gospel and I can win them to Christ. When I am with Gentiles who follow Jewish customs and ceremonies I don't argue, even though I don't agree, because I want to help them. 21When with the heathen I agree with them as much as I can, except of course that I must always do what is right as a Christian. And so, by agreeing, I can win their confidence and help them too.

22When I am with those whose consciences bother them easily, I don't act as though I know it all and don't say they are foolish; the result is that they are willing to let me help them. Yes, whatever a person is like, I try to find common ground with him so that he will let me tell him about Christ and let Christ save him. 23I do this to get the Gospel to them and also for the blessing I myself receive when I see them come to Christ.

24In a race everyone runs, but only one person gets first prize. So run your race to win. 25To win the contest you must deny yourselves many things that would keep you from doing your best. An athlete goes to all this trouble just to win a blue ribbon or a silver cup, but we do it for a heavenly reward that never disappears. 26So I run straight to the goal with purpose in every step. I fight to win. I'm not just shadow-boxing or playing around. 27Like an athlete I punish my body, treating it roughly, training it to do what it should, not what it wants to. Otherwise I fear that after enlisting others for the race, I myself might be declared unfit and ordered to stand aside.

10 Lessons about Idol Worship

For we must never forget, dear brothers, what happened to our people in the wilderness long ago. God guided them by sending a cloud that moved along ahead of them; and he brought them all safely through the waters of the Red Sea. 2This might be called their "baptism"—baptized both in sea and cloud!—as followers of Moses—their commitment to him as their leader. 3,4And by a miracle God sent them food to eat and water to drink there in the desert; they drank the water that Christ gave them. He was there with them as a mighty Rock of spiritual refreshment. 5Yet after all this most of them did not obey God, and he destroyed them in the wilderness.

6From this lesson we are warned that we must not desire evil things as they did, 7nor worship idols as they did. (The Scriptures tell us, "The people sat down to eat and drink and then got up to dance" in worship of the golden calf.)

8Another lesson for us is what happened when some of them sinned with other men's wives, and 23,000 fell dead in one day. 9And don't try the Lord's patience—they did and died from snake bites. 10And don't murmur against God and his dealings with you as some of them did, for that is why God sent his Angel to destroy them.

11All these things happened to them as examples—as object lessons to us—to warn us against doing the same things; they were written down so that we could read about them and learn from them in these last days as the world nears its end.

12So be careful. If you are thinking, "Oh, I would never behave like that"—let this be a warning to you. For you too may fall into sin. 13But remember this—the wrong desires that come into your life aren't anything new and different. Many others have faced exactly the same problems before you. And no temptation is irresistible. You can trust God to keep the temptation from becoming so strong that you can't stand up against it, for he has promised this and will do what he says. He will show you how to escape temptation's power so that you can bear up patiently against it.

14So, dear friends, carefully avoid idol worship of every kind.

15You are intelligent people. Look now and see for yourselves whether what I am about to say is true. 16When we ask the Lord's blessing upon our drinking from the cup of wine at the Lord's Table, this means, doesn't it, that all who drink it are sharing together the blessing of Christ's blood? And when we break off pieces of the bread from the loaf to eat there together, this shows that we are sharing together in the benefits of his body. 17No matter how many of us there are, we all eat from the same loaf, showing that we are all parts of the one body of Christ. 18And the Jewish people, all who eat the sacrifices, are united by that act.

19What am I trying to say? Am I saying that the idols to whom the heathen bring sacrifices are really alive and are real gods, and that these sacrifices are of some value? No, not at all. 20What I am saying is that those who offer food to these idols are united together in sacrificing to demons, certainly not to God. And I don't want any of you to be partners with demons when you eat the same food, along with the heathen, that has been offered to these idols. 21You cannot drink from the cup at the Lord's Table and at Satan's table, too. You cannot eat bread both at the Lord's Table and at Satan's table.

22What? Are you tempting the Lord to be angry with you? Are you stronger than he is?

23You are certainly free to eat food offered to idols if you want to; it's not against God's laws to eat such meat, but that doesn't mean that you should go ahead and do it. It may be perfectly legal, but it may not be best and helpful. 24Don't

Family Devotions

☐ DEVOTION 312
RESISTING TEMPTATION

Read 1 Corinthians 10:12-13

Will it be so awful if I cheat a little just once? Jon thought as he walked home from school. *I don't know why Mrs. Gray has that stupid rule anyway.* The rule was that those who got 100 percent on a trial spelling test in the middle of the week could go out early for recess on Friday, while the rest of the class repeated the test. Jon and his friends seldom got out early, but this week they figured out a way to sneak a peek at the answers so they'd all get extra time to play.

Jon had agreed to the plan, and almost immediately his conscience started to bother him. He was a Christian and knew it was wrong to cheat. But now the others were counting on him. He didn't know what to do.

As Mom was fixing dinner that evening, the lights suddenly went out. "Oh, no!" she exclaimed. "I blew a fuse."

Jon went to the basement with his father and watched him replace the burned-out fuse. "How do those things work?" Jon asked.

"Well, it's a little complicated," said Dad. "You see, there are wires running through the walls to various switches and electrical outlets. If too many things are turned on at once, it requires so much electricity that the wires could get very hot and even cause a fire. But the fuse will burn out and stop the flow of electricity when there is too much being used. The fuse won't let more electricity go through the wires than is safe."

Jon and Dad started back up the stairs. "The fuse reminds me of what God does for us," Dad added. "He'll never let such a great temptation come our way that we can't handle it. He stops it before it can get that bad."

As Jon went to his room, he thought about the things Dad had said. He knew he didn't have to cheat. God would help him to be honest. He'd tell his friends tomorrow.

Resisting Temptation Memory Verse

For since he himself has now been through suffering and temptation, he knows what it is like when we suffer and are tempted, and he is wonderfully able to help us.
Hebrews 2:18

How About You?

Do you sometimes feel that you can't help doing something wrong? That the temptation is just too great? You're wrong. No matter what the temptation, you can be sure that God will help you overcome it if you are willing to let him do so. H. M.

• For the next devotional, turn to page 1109. • To start the next topic, turn to page 225. • For notes on *RESISTING TEMPTATION*, see pages 268, 448, 964, and 1258.

think only of yourself. Try to think of the other fellow, too, and what is best for him.

²⁵Here's what you should do. Take any meat you want that is sold at the market. Don't ask whether or not it was offered to idols, lest the answer hurt your conscience. ²⁶For the earth and every good thing in it belongs to the Lord and is yours to enjoy.

²⁷If someone who isn't a Christian asks you out to dinner, go ahead; accept the invitation if you want to. Eat whatever is on the table and don't ask any questions about it. Then you won't know whether or not it has been used as a sacrifice to idols, and you won't risk having a bad conscience over eating it. ²⁸But if someone warns you that this meat has been offered to idols, then don't eat it for the sake of the man who told you, and of his conscience. ²⁹In this case *his* feeling about it is the important thing, not yours.

But why, you may ask, must I be guided and limited by what someone else thinks? ³⁰If I can thank God for the food and enjoy it, why let someone spoil everything just because he thinks I am wrong? ³¹Well, I'll tell you why. It is because you must do everything for the glory of God, even your eating and drinking. ³²So don't be a stumbling block to anyone, whether they are Jews or Gentiles or Christians. ³³That is the plan I follow, too. I try to please everyone in everything I do, not doing what I like or what is best for me but what is best for them, so that they may be saved.

11 Honor and Respect in Worship

And you should follow my example, just as I follow Christ's.

²I am so glad, dear brothers, that you have been remembering and doing everything I taught you. ³But there is one matter I want to remind you about: that a wife is responsible to her husband, her husband is responsible to Christ, and Christ is responsible to God. ⁴That is why, if a man refuses to remove his hat while praying or preaching, he dishonors Christ. ⁵And that is why a woman who publicly prays or prophesies without a covering on her head dishonors her husband [for her covering is a sign of her subjection to him]. ⁶Yes, if she refuses to wear a head covering, then she should cut off all her hair. And if it is shameful for a woman to have her head shaved, then she should wear a covering. ⁷But a man should not wear anything on his head [when worshiping, for his hat is a sign of subjection to men].

God's glory is man made in his image, and man's glory is the woman. ⁸The first man didn't come from woman, but the first woman came out of man. ⁹And Adam, the first man, was not made for Eve's benefit, but Eve was made for Adam. ¹⁰So a woman should wear a covering on her head as a sign that she is under man's authority, a fact for all the angels to notice and rejoice in.

¹¹But remember that in God's plan men and women need each other. ¹²For although the first woman came out of man, all men have been born from women ever since, and both men and women come from God their Creator.

¹³What do you yourselves really think about this? Is it right for a woman to pray in public without covering her head? ¹⁴,¹⁵Doesn't even instinct itself teach us that women's heads should be covered? For women are proud of their long hair, while a man with long hair tends to be ashamed. ¹⁶But if anyone wants to argue about this, all I can say is that we never teach anything else than this—that a woman should wear a covering when prophesying or praying publicly in the church, and all the churches feel the same way about it.

¹⁷Next on my list of items to write you about is something else I cannot agree with. For it sounds as if more harm than good is done when you meet together for your communion services. ¹⁸Everyone keeps telling me about the arguing that goes on in these meetings, and the divisions developing among you, and I can just about believe it. ¹⁹But I suppose you feel this is necessary so that you who are always right will become known and recognized!

²⁰When you come together to eat, it isn't the Lord's Supper you are eating, ²¹but your own. For I am told that everyone hastily gobbles all the food he can without waiting to share with the others, so that one doesn't get enough and goes hungry while another has too much to drink and gets drunk. ²²What? Is this really true? Can't you do your eating and drinking at home to avoid disgracing the church and shaming those who are poor and can bring no food? What am I supposed to say about these things? Do you want me to praise you? Well, I certainly do not!

²³For this is what the Lord himself has said about his Table, and I have passed it on to you before: That on the night when Judas betrayed him, the Lord Jesus took bread, ²⁴and when he had given thanks to God for it, he broke it and gave it to his disciples and said, "Take this and eat it. This is my body, which is given for you. Do this to remember me." ²⁵In the same way, he took the cup of wine after supper, saying, "This cup is the new agreement between God and you that has been established and set in motion by my blood. Do this in remembrance of me whenever you drink it." ²⁶For every time you eat this bread and drink this cup you are retelling the message of the Lord's death, that he has died for you. Do this until he comes again.

Family Devotions

☐ DEVOTION 313
KNOWING YOU'RE SPECIAL TO GOD

Read 1 Corinthians 12:20-27

Jana sighed as she sat down at the table one morning. "I wish I could do something important for the special services at church," she said. "Carl and Jack are going to play a trumpet duet, and Melanie and Sherri and Tara are singing a trio. Holly's playing the piano one evening, and Bonnie was asked to read her poem on prayer. Everybody's doing something but me."

"I thought you were helping in the nursery," said Mom.

"Oh, I always do that," said Jana, "but I'd like to do something really important for once."

Jana's older sister, Traci, limped into the room. "How's the toe you hurt yesterday?" asked Mom.

"Much better," reported Traci, pushing a strand of hair from her face. "Before long, I'll be able to walk normally." She stuck out her foot. "I never realized before how important a little toe is! I recommend that everyone pay more attention to their little toes."

Mom smiled. "Did you look at your little toes this morning, Jana?" she asked.

"Probably not," laughed Jana.

"Did you comb your hair?" asked Mom. "Did you look at your face?"

"Sure," said Jana. "What are you getting at, Mom?"

"Well," said Mom, "I'm just trying to point out that although we normally pay more attention to some parts of our bodies, like our hair and our face, every part is important. Even our little toes. Every member of the body of Christ—that is, every believer—is important, too. We tend to pay more attention to those who play or sing or speak. But those who work in the nursery or sweep the church or pray as they sit quietly in their seats are just as important. We often notice them only when they get hurt and don't perform their jobs, but God notices them all the time. They're very important."

Knowing You're Special to God Memory Verse

But now the Lord who created you, O Israel, says, Don't be afraid, for I have ransomed you; I have called you by name; you are mine.
Isaiah 43:1

How About You?
Do you feel unimportant? Some jobs seem more glamorous to us than others, but God won't reward you according to how glamorous your task is. He'll reward you according to how faithfully you perform the task he has given you to do. It's important in his sight, and so are you! *H. M.*

• For the next devotional, turn to page 1111. • To start the next topic, turn to page 75. • For notes on KNOWING YOU'RE SPECIAL TO GOD, see pages 260, 878, 908, and 960.

27So if anyone eats this bread and drinks from this cup of the Lord in an unworthy manner, he is guilty of sin against the body and the blood of the Lord. 28That is why a man should examine himself carefully before eating the bread and drinking from the cup. 29For if he eats the bread and drinks from the cup unworthily, not thinking about the body of Christ and what it means, he is eating and drinking God's judgment upon himself; for he is trifling with the death of Christ. 30That is why many of you are weak and sick, and some have even died.

31But if you carefully examine yourselves before eating you will not need to be judged and punished. 32Yet, when we are judged and punished by the Lord, it is so that we will not be condemned with the rest of the world. 33So, dear brothers, when you gather for the Lord's Supper—the communion service—wait for each other; 34if anyone is really hungry he should eat at home so that he won't bring punishment upon himself when you meet together.

I'll talk to you about the other matters after I arrive.

12 Everyone Has Special Abilities

And now, brothers, I want to write about the special abilities the Holy Spirit gives to each of you, for I don't want any misunderstanding about them. 2You will remember that before you became Christians you went around from one idol to another, not one of which could speak a single word. 3But now you are meeting people who claim to speak messages from the Spirit of God. How can you know whether they are really inspired by God or whether they are fakes? Here is the test: no one speaking by the power of the Spirit of God can curse Jesus, and no one can say, "Jesus is Lord," and really mean it, unless the Holy Spirit is helping him.

4Now God gives us many kinds of special abilities, but it is the same Holy Spirit who is the source of them all. 5There are different kinds of service to God, but it is the same Lord we are serving. 6There are many ways in which God works in our lives, but it is the same God who does the work in and through all of us who are his. 7The Holy Spirit displays God's power through each of us as a means of helping the entire church.

8To one person the Spirit gives the ability to give wise advice; someone else may be especially good at studying and teaching, and this is his gift from the same Spirit. 9He gives special faith to another, and to someone else the power to heal the sick. 10He gives power for doing miracles to some, and to others power to prophesy and preach. He gives someone else the power to know whether evil spirits are speaking through those who claim to be giving God's messages—or whether it is really the Spirit of God who is speaking. Still another person is able to speak in languages he never learned; and others, who do not know the language either, are given power to understand what he is saying. 11It is the same and only Holy Spirit who gives all these gifts and powers, deciding which each one of us should have.

12Our bodies have many parts, but the many parts make up only one body when they are all put together. So it is with the "body" of Christ. 13Each of us is a part of the one body of Christ. Some of us are Jews, some are Gentiles, some are slaves, and some are free. But the Holy Spirit has fitted us all together into one body. We have been baptized into Christ's body by the one Spirit, and have all been given that same Holy Spirit.

14Yes, the body has many parts, not just one part. 15If the foot says, "I am not a part of the body because I am not a hand," that does not make it any less a part of the body. 16And what would you think if you heard an ear say, "I am not part of the body because I am only an ear and not an eye"? Would that make it any less a part of the body? 17Suppose the whole body were an eye—then how would you hear? Or if your whole body were just one big ear, how could you smell anything?

18But that isn't the way God has made us. He has made many parts for our bodies and has put each part just where he wants it. 19What a strange thing a body would be if it had only one part! 20So he has made many parts, but still there is only one body.

21The eye can never say to the hand, "I don't need you." The head can't say to the feet, "I don't need you."

22And some of the parts that seem weakest and least important are really the most necessary. 23Yes, we are especially glad to have some parts that seem rather odd! And we carefully protect from the eyes of others those parts that should not be seen, 24while of course the parts that may be seen do not require this special care. So God has put the body together in such a way that extra honor and care are given to those parts that might otherwise seem less important. 25This makes for happiness among the parts, so that the parts have the same care for each other that they do for themselves. 26If one part suffers, all parts suffer with it, and if one part is honored, all the parts are glad.

27Now here is what I am trying to say: All of you together are the one body of Christ, and each one of you is a separate and necessary part of it.

FAMILY DEVOTIONS

☐ *DEVOTION 314*
LOVING OTHERS

Read 1 Corinthians 13:4-10

Tina sighed happily as she walked into the living room. "I'm in love!" she announced. "Gregg's such a wonderful guy! He's always so nice to me!"

Mother frowned slightly. "I'm glad you and Gregg are friends, but remember, *love* is a pretty strong word."

Tina's brother, Joel, laughed. "Tina thinks that just because she's fifteen, she knows everything about love." He reached down to pat his dog. "Now, me and Ralph here—that's love! He does whatever I tell him, he's always ready to play, and he doesn't talk my ear off like some drippy girl would. That's what I call true love."

Shortly afterwards, Tina had a phone call that left her looking upset. "That rotten Gregg!" she said. "He took another girl to the basketball game last night and never even asked me! I'll never speak to him again!"

"Ha, ha!" laughed Joel. "All that true love gone right down the drain!" Joel was laughing so hard that he didn't see Ralph sitting on the floor beside him. He stepped right on the dog's tail, and Ralph nipped him on the leg!

"Ouch! You bad dog!" scolded Joel. "Get out of here!"

Hearing the commotion, Mother hurried in. "What's going on here?"

"Well, I decided I don't love Gregg anymore!" said Tina. "I can't believe how inconsiderate he is."

"Oh, and I got mad at Ralph when he nipped me," explained Joel, rubbing his leg.

"Well, kids, just a few minutes ago you were both sure you knew what true love was. I'm afraid you still have a few things to learn. Real love doesn't change just because someone makes you mad. It's a choice you make, not just a nice feeling."

Loving Others Memory Verse

Little children, let us stop just *saying* we love people; let us *really* love them, and *show it* by our *actions*.
1 John 3:18

How About You?

Do you ever wonder what true love is? Some people think that love is a feeling, an emotional high, something that just happens. But the Bible teaches that loving is something you decide to do. God commands you to love others. And he'll help you to do it! S. K.

• For the next devotional, turn to page 1113. • To start the next topic, turn to page 275. • For notes on *LOVING OTHERS*, see pages 658, 951, 967, and 1242.

²⁸Here is a list of some of the parts he has placed in his Church, which is his body:

Apostles,
Prophets—those who preach God's Word,
Teachers,
Those who do miracles,
Those who have the gift of healing;
Those who can help others,
Those who can get others to work together,
Those who speak in languages they have
    never learned.

²⁹Is everyone an apostle? Of course not. Is everyone a preacher? No. Are all teachers? Does everyone have the power to do miracles? ³⁰Can everyone heal the sick? Of course not. Does God give all of us the ability to speak in languages we've never learned? Can just anyone understand and translate what those are saying who have that gift of foreign speech? ³¹No, but try your best to have the more important of these gifts.

First, however, let me tell you about something else that is better than any of them!

13 What Is Love?

If I had the gift of being able to speak in other languages without learning them and could speak in every language there is in all of heaven and earth, but didn't love others, I would only be making noise. ²If I had the gift of prophecy and knew all about what is going to happen in the future, knew everything about *everything*, but didn't love others, what good would it do? Even if I had the gift of faith so that I could speak to a mountain and make it move, I would still be worth nothing at all without love. ³If I gave everything I have to poor people, and if I were burned alive for preaching the Gospel but didn't love others, it would be of no value whatever.

⁴Love is very patient and kind, never jealous or envious, never boastful or proud, ⁵never haughty or selfish or rude. Love does not demand its own way. It is not irritable or touchy. It does not hold grudges and will hardly even notice when others do it wrong. ⁶It is never glad about injustice, but rejoices whenever truth wins out. ⁷If you love someone, you will be loyal to him no matter what the cost. You will always believe in him, always expect the best of him, and always stand your ground in defending him.

⁸All the special gifts and powers from God will someday come to an end, but love goes on forever. Someday prophecy and speaking in unknown languages and special knowledge—these gifts will disappear. ⁹Now we know so little, even with our special gifts, and the preaching of those most gifted is still so poor. ¹⁰But when we have been made perfect and complete, then the need for these inadequate special gifts will come to an end, and they will disappear.

¹¹It's like this: when I was a child I spoke and thought and reasoned as a child does. But when I became a man my thoughts grew far beyond those of my childhood, and now I have put away the childish things. ¹²In the same way, we can see and understand only a little about God now, as if we were peering at his reflection in a poor mirror; but someday we are going to see him in his completeness, face to face. Now all that I know is hazy and blurred, but then I will see everything clearly, just as clearly as God sees into my heart right now.

¹³There are three things that remain—faith, hope, and love—and the greatest of these is love.

14 Prophecy and Tongues

Let love be your greatest aim; nevertheless, ask also for the special abilities the Holy Spirit gives, and especially the gift of prophecy, being able to preach the messages of God.

²But if your gift is that of being able to "speak in tongues," that is, to speak in languages you haven't learned, you will be talking to God but not to others, since they won't be able to understand you. You will be speaking by the power of the Spirit, but it will all be a secret. ³But one who prophesies, preaching the messages of God, is helping others grow in the Lord, encouraging and comforting them. ⁴So a person "speaking in tongues" helps himself grow spiritually, but one who prophesies, preaching messages from God, helps the entire church grow in holiness and happiness.

⁵I wish you all had the gift of "speaking in tongues," but even more I wish you were all able to prophesy, preaching God's messages, for that is a greater and more useful power than to speak in unknown languages—unless, of course, you can tell everyone afterwards what you were saying, so that they can get some good out of it too.

⁶Dear friends, even if I myself should come to you talking in some language you don't understand, how would that help you? But if I speak plainly what God has revealed to me, and tell you the things I know, and what is going to happen, and the great truths of God's Word—that is what you need; that is what will help you. ⁷Even musical instruments—the flute, for instance, or the harp—are examples of the need for speaking in plain, simple English rather than in unknown languages. For no one will recognize the tune the flute is playing unless each note is sounded clearly. ⁸And if the army bugler doesn't play the

FAMILY DEVOTIONS

☐ *DEVOTION 315*
OVERCOMING FEAR

Read 1 Corinthians 15:51-57

Overcoming Fear
Memory Verse

Fear not, for I am with you. Do not be dismayed. I am your God. I will strengthen you; I will help you; I will uphold you with my victorious right hand.
Isaiah 41:10

"Do you really think this thing is ever going to turn into something beautiful, Grandma?" asked Nathan, bringing a jar to the sofa where his grandmother was resting. He had caught a caterpillar, and it had spun itself into a cocoon. Nathan liked to share things with Grandma. She was always interested even though she was sick.

Grandma smiled as she looked at the dried-up, greenish thing in the jar Nathan held. "Oh, yes. Just wait," she answered. "Sit down a minute, Nathan, and let's talk." She patted the seat beside her. "Nathan, someday soon I'm going to be like the caterpillar inside that cocoon," Grandma continued. "The doctor says I won't be here much longer—I will die soon." A big lump came into Nathan's throat, and tears sprang to his eyes. Grandma patted his hand. "I don't want you to feel too bad when that happens, Nathan, because I'll be going to heaven. My old body will be buried in the ground, but the real me will be with Jesus, because I have received him as my Savior. And someday God is going to give me a wonderful new body that won't get sick anymore. You keep watching the cocoon, and when you see the beautiful creature that comes out of it, think about the beautiful new body your grandma is going to get."

One night while Nathan was asleep, Grandma died. When Nathan saw her lying so still in her casket, he knew it was only her body. Grandma was with Jesus. Thinking about that helped, but he still felt sad.

The morning after Grandma's funeral, Nathan noticed something that made him very excited. "Mom! Dad!" he called. "Look at my butterfly!" Sure enough, a beautiful butterfly had emerged from the cocoon.

They admired the lovely creature together, and finally Nathan decided to let it go free. As he watched the butterfly stretch its wings and fly away, he remembered what his grandma had told him about the beautiful new body God was going to give her.

How About You?
Do you realize that you don't need to fear death when you have trusted Jesus to be your Savior? Just as the caterpillar turned into a beautiful butterfly, so you will receive a new body that will live forever. Thank God for this wonderful hope. *M. N.*

• For the next devotional, turn to page 1121. • To start the next topic, turn to page 549. • For notes on OVERCOMING FEAR, see pages 191, 482, 554, 592, and 912.

right notes, how will the soldiers know that they are being called to battle? ⁹In the same way, if you talk to a person in some language he doesn't understand, how will he know what you mean? You might as well be talking to an empty room.

¹⁰I suppose that there are hundreds of different languages in the world, and all are excellent for those who understand them, ¹¹but to me they mean nothing. A person talking to me in one of these languages will be a stranger to me and I will be a stranger to him. ¹²Since you are so anxious to have special gifts from the Holy Spirit, ask him for the very best, for those that will be of real help to the whole church.

¹³If someone is given the gift of speaking in unknown tongues, he should pray also for the gift of knowing what he has said, so that he can tell people afterwards plainly. ¹⁴For if I pray in a language I don't understand, my spirit is praying, but I don't know what I am saying.

¹⁵Well, then, what shall I do? I will do both. I will pray in unknown tongues and also in ordinary language that everyone understands. I will sing in unknown tongues and also in ordinary language so that I can understand the praise I am giving; ¹⁶for if you praise and thank God with the spirit alone, speaking in another language, how can those who don't understand you be praising God along with you? How can they join you in giving thanks when they don't know what you are saying? ¹⁷You will be giving thanks very nicely, no doubt, but the other people present won't be helped.

¹⁸I thank God that I "speak in tongues" privately more than any of the rest of you. ¹⁹But in public worship I would much rather speak five words that people can understand and be helped by than ten thousand words while "speaking in tongues" in an unknown language.

²⁰Dear brothers, don't be childish in your understanding of these things. Be innocent babies when it comes to planning evil, but be men of intelligence in understanding matters of this kind. ²¹We are told in the ancient Scriptures that God would send men from other lands to speak in foreign languages to his people, but even then they would not listen. ²²So you see that being able to "speak in tongues" is not a sign to God's children concerning his power, but is a sign to the unsaved. However, prophecy (preaching the deep truths of God) is what the Christians need, and unbelievers aren't yet ready for it. ²³Even so, if an unsaved person, or someone who doesn't have these gifts, comes to church and hears you all talking in other languages, he is likely to think you are crazy. ²⁴But if you prophesy, preaching God's Word, [even though such preaching is mostly for believers] and an unsaved person or a new Christian comes in who does not understand about these things, all these sermons will convince him of the fact that he is a sinner, and his conscience will be pricked by everything he hears. ²⁵As he listens, his secret thoughts will be laid bare, and he will fall down on his knees and worship God, declaring that God is really there among you.

²⁶Well, my brothers, let's add up what I am saying. When you meet together some will sing, another will teach, or tell some special information God has given him, or speak in an unknown language, or tell what someone else is saying who is speaking in the unknown language, but everything that is done must be useful to all, and build them up in the Lord. ²⁷No more than two or three should speak in an unknown language, and they must speak one at a time, and someone must be ready to interpret what they are saying. ²⁸But if no one is present who can interpret, they must not speak out loud. They must talk silently to themselves and to God in the unknown language but not publicly.

²⁹,³⁰Two or three may prophesy, one at a time, if they have the gift, while all the others listen. But if, while someone is prophesying, someone else receives a message or idea from the Lord, the one who is speaking should stop. ³¹In this way all who have the gift of prophecy can speak, one after the other, and everyone will learn and be encouraged and helped. ³²Remember that a person who has a message from God has the power to stop himself or wait his turn. ³³God is not one who likes things to be disorderly and upset. He likes harmony, and he finds it in all the other churches.

³⁴Women should be silent during the church meetings. They are not to take part in the discussion, for they are subordinate to men as the Scriptures also declare. ³⁵If they have any questions to ask, let them ask their husbands at home, for it is improper for women to express their opinions in church meetings.

³⁶You disagree? And do you think that the knowledge of God's will begins and ends with you Corinthians? Well, you are mistaken! ³⁷You who claim to have the gift of prophecy or any other special ability from the Holy Spirit should be the first to realize that what I am saying is a commandment from the Lord himself. ³⁸But if anyone still disagrees—well, we will leave him in his ignorance.

³⁹So, my fellow believers, long to be prophets so that you can preach God's message plainly; and never say it is wrong to "speak in tongues"; ⁴⁰however, be sure that everything is done properly in a good and orderly way.

15 Christ Rose from the Dead

Now let me remind you, brothers, of what the Gospel really is, for it has not changed—it is the same Good News I preached to you before. You welcomed it then and still do now, for your faith is squarely built upon this wonderful message; ²and it is this Good News that saves you if you still firmly believe it, unless of course you never really believed it in the first place.

³I passed on to you right from the first what had been told to me, that Christ died for our sins just as the Scriptures said he would, ⁴and that he was buried, and that three days afterwards he arose from the grave just as the prophets foretold. ⁵He was seen by Peter and later by the rest of "the Twelve." ⁶After that he was seen by more than five hundred Christian brothers at one time, most of whom are still alive, though some have died by now. ⁷Then James saw him, and later all the apostles. ⁸Last of all I saw him too, long after the others, as though I had been born almost too late for this. ⁹For I am the least worthy of all the apostles, and I shouldn't even be called an apostle at all after the way I treated the church of God.

¹⁰But whatever I am now it is all because God poured out such kindness and grace upon me—and not without results: for I have worked harder than all the other apostles, yet actually I wasn't doing it, but God working in me, to bless me. ¹¹It makes no difference who worked the hardest, I or they; the important thing is that we preached the Gospel to you and you believed it.

¹²But tell me this! Since you believe what we preach, that *Christ* rose from the dead, why are some of you saying that dead people will never come back to life again? ¹³For if there is no resurrection of the dead, then Christ must still be dead. ¹⁴And if he is still dead, then all our preaching is useless and your trust in God is empty, worthless, hopeless; ¹⁵and we apostles are all liars because we have said that God raised Christ from the grave, and of course that isn't true if the dead do not come back to life again. ¹⁶If they don't, then Christ is still dead, ¹⁷and you are very foolish to keep on trusting God to save you, and you are still under condemnation for your sins; ¹⁸in that case, all Christians who have died are lost! ¹⁹And if being a Christian is of value to us only now in this life, we are the most miserable of creatures.

²⁰But the fact is that Christ did actually rise from the dead and has become the first of millions who will come back to life again someday.

²¹Death came into the world because of what one man (Adam) did, and it is because of what this other man (Christ) has done that now there is the resurrection from the dead. ²²Everyone dies because all of us are related to Adam, being members of his sinful race, and wherever there is sin, death results. But all who are related to Christ will rise again. ²³Each, however, in his own turn: Christ rose first; then when Christ comes back, all his people will become alive again.

²⁴After that the end will come when he will turn the Kingdom over to God the Father, having put down all enemies of every kind. ²⁵For Christ will be King until he has defeated all his enemies, ²⁶including the last enemy—death. This too must be defeated and ended. ²⁷For the rule and authority over all things has been given to Christ by his Father; except, of course, Christ does not rule over the Father himself, who gave him this power to rule. ²⁸When Christ has finally won the battle against all his enemies, then he, the Son of God, will put himself also under his Father's orders, so that God who has given him the victory over everything else will be utterly supreme.

²⁹If the dead will not come back to life again, then what point is there in people being baptized for those who are gone? Why do it unless you believe that the dead will someday rise again?

³⁰And why should we ourselves be continually risking our lives, facing death hour by hour? ³¹For it is a fact that I face death daily; that is as true as my pride in your growth in the Lord. ³²And what value was there in fighting wild beasts—those men of Ephesus—if it was only for what I gain in this life down here? If we will never live again after we die, then we might as well go and have ourselves a good time: let us eat, drink, and be merry. What's the difference? For tomorrow we die, and that ends everything!

³³Don't be fooled by those who say such things. If you listen to them you will start acting like them. ³⁴Get some sense and quit your sinning. For to your shame I say it; some of you are not even Christians at all and have never really known God.

³⁵But someone may ask, "How will the dead be brought back to life again? What kind of bodies will they have?" ³⁶What a foolish question! You will find the answer in your own garden! When you put a seed into the ground it doesn't grow into a plant unless it "dies" first. ³⁷And when the green shoot comes up out of the seed, it is very different from the seed you first planted. For all you put into the ground is a dry little seed of wheat or whatever it is you are planting, ³⁸then God gives it a beautiful new body—just the kind he wants it to have; a different kind of plant grows from each kind of seed. ³⁹And just as there are different kinds of seeds and plants, so also there are different kinds of flesh. Humans, animals, fish, and birds are all different.

⁴⁰The angels in heaven have bodies far different from ours, and the beauty and the glory of their bodies is different from the beauty and the

glory of ours. ⁴¹The sun has one kind of glory while the moon and stars have another kind. And the stars differ from each other in their beauty and brightness.

⁴²In the same way, our earthly bodies which die and decay are different from the bodies we shall have when we come back to life again, for they will never die. ⁴³The bodies we have now embarrass us, for they become sick and die; but they will be full of glory when we come back to life again. Yes, they are weak, dying bodies now, but when we live again they will be full of strength. ⁴⁴They are just human bodies at death, but when they come back to life they will be superhuman bodies. For just as there are natural, human bodies, there are also supernatural, spiritual bodies.

⁴⁵The Scriptures tell us that the first man, Adam, was given a natural, human body but Christ is more than that, for he was life-giving Spirit.

⁴⁶First, then, we have these human bodies, and later on God gives us spiritual, heavenly bodies. ⁴⁷Adam was made from the dust of the earth, but Christ came from heaven above. ⁴⁸Every human being has a body just like Adam's, made of dust, but all who become Christ's will have the same kind of body as his—a body from heaven. ⁴⁹Just as each of us now has a body like Adam's, so we shall some day have a body like Christ's.

⁵⁰I tell you this, my brothers: an earthly body made of flesh and blood cannot get into God's Kingdom. These perishable bodies of ours are not the right kind to live forever.

⁵¹But I am telling you this strange and wonderful secret: we shall not all die, but we shall all be given new bodies! ⁵²It will all happen in a moment, in the twinkling of an eye, when the last trumpet is blown. For there will be a trumpet blast from the sky, and all the Christians who have died will suddenly become alive, with new bodies that will never, never die; and then we who are still alive shall suddenly have new bodies too. ⁵³For our earthly bodies, the ones we have now that can die, must be transformed into heavenly bodies that cannot perish but will live forever.

⁵⁴When this happens, then at last this Scripture will come true—"Death is swallowed up in victory." ⁵⁵,⁵⁶O death, where then your victory? Where then your sting? For sin—the sting that causes death—will all be gone; and the law, which reveals our sins, will no longer be our judge. ⁵⁷How we thank God for all of this! It is he who makes us victorious through Jesus Christ our Lord!

⁵⁸So, my dear brothers, since future victory is sure, be strong and steady, always abounding in the Lord's work, for you know that nothing you do for the Lord is ever wasted as it would be if there were no resurrection.

16 Giving an Offering

Now here are the directions about the money you are collecting to send to the Christians in Jerusalem; (and, by the way, these are the same directions I gave to the churches in Galatia). ²On every Lord's Day each of you should put aside something from what you have earned during the week, and use it for this offering. The amount depends on how much the Lord has helped you earn. Don't wait until I get there and then try to collect it all at once. ³When I come I will send your loving gift with a letter to Jerusalem, to be taken there by trustworthy messengers you yourselves will choose. ⁴And if it seems wise for me to go along too, then we can travel together.

⁵I am coming to visit you after I have been to Macedonia first, but I will be staying there only for a little while. ⁶It could be that I will stay longer with you, perhaps all winter, and then you can send me on to my next destination. ⁷This time I don't want to make just a passing visit and then go right on; I want to come and stay awhile, if the Lord will let me. ⁸I will be staying here at Ephesus until the holiday of Pentecost, ⁹for there is a wide open door for me to preach and teach here. So much is happening, but there are many enemies.

¹⁰If Timothy comes make him feel at home, for he is doing the Lord's work just as I am. ¹¹Don't let anyone despise or ignore him [because he is young], but send him back to me happy with his time among you; I am looking forward to seeing him soon, along with the others who are returning.

¹²I begged Apollos to visit you along with the others, but he thought that it was not at all God's will for him to go now; he will be seeing you later on when he has the opportunity.

¹³Keep your eyes open for spiritual danger; stand true to the Lord; act like men; be strong; ¹⁴and whatever you do, do it with kindness and love.

¹⁵Do you remember Stephanas and his family? They were the first to become Christians in Greece, and they are spending their lives helping and serving Christians everywhere. ¹⁶Please follow their instructions and do everything you can to help them as well as all others like them who work hard at your side with such real devotion. ¹⁷I am so glad that Stephanas, Fortunatus, and Achaicus have arrived here for a visit. They have been making up for the help you aren't here to give me. ¹⁸They have cheered me greatly and have been a wonderful encouragement to me, as I am sure they were to you, too. I hope you properly appreciate the work of such men as these.

¹⁹The churches here in Asia send you their loving greetings. Aquila and Priscilla send you their

love, and so do all the others who meet in their home for their church service. [20]All the friends here have asked me to say hello to you for them. And give each other a loving handshake when you meet.

[21]I will write these final words of this letter with my own hand: [22]if anyone does not love the Lord, that person is cursed. Lord Jesus, come! [23]May the love and favor of the Lord Jesus Christ rest upon you. [24]My love to all of you, for we all belong to Christ Jesus.

Sincerely, Paul

2 Corinthians

WHEN YOU'RE going through a hard time, doesn't it feel good to have someone really understand what you're going through? When Paul wrote his letters, he could write with understanding because he had been through lots of hard times.

After he sent his first letter to the Corinthians, Paul probably visited them and then wrote a strong letter so they would start obeying God. The Corinthians felt hurt and angry about Paul's harsh words to them. They kept on questioning Paul's authority.

The letter we call 2 Corinthians is probably the third letter Paul wrote to the Christians at Corinth. He wanted to clear up their hurt feelings and let them know how much he cared for them. The Corinthians were going through hard times, so Paul comforted them with reminders of what faith is about and examples from his own life.

As you read 2 Corinthians, look for the ways Paul learned compassion through hard times. Think about how you can be more understanding to others in hard times.

Paul: A Messenger of God

Dear friends: This letter is from me, Paul, appointed by God to be Jesus Christ's messenger; and from our dear brother Timothy. We are writing to all of you Christians there in Corinth and throughout Greece. 2May God our Father and the Lord Jesus Christ mightily bless each one of you and give you peace.

3,4What a wonderful God we have—he is the Father of our Lord Jesus Christ, the source of every mercy, and the one who so wonderfully comforts and strengthens us in our hardships and trials. And why does he do this? So that when others are troubled, needing our sympathy and encouragement, we can pass on to them this same help and comfort God has given us. 5You can be sure that the more we undergo sufferings for Christ, the more he will shower us with his comfort and encouragement. 6,7We are in deep trouble for bringing you God's comfort and salvation. But in our trouble God has comforted us—and this, too, to help you: to show you from our personal experience how God will tenderly comfort you when you undergo these same sufferings. He will give you the strength to endure.

⁸I think you ought to know, dear brothers, about the hard time we went through in Asia. We were really crushed and overwhelmed, and feared we would never live through it. ⁹We felt we were doomed to die and saw how powerless we were to help ourselves; but that was good, for then we put everything into the hands of God, who alone could save us, for he can even raise the dead. ¹⁰And he did help us and saved us from a terrible death; yes, and we expect him to do it again and again. ¹¹But you must help us too by praying for us. For much thanks and praise will go to God from you who see his wonderful answers to your prayers for our safety!

¹²We are so glad that we can say with utter honesty that in all our dealings we have been pure and sincere, quietly depending upon the Lord for his help and not on our own skills. And that is even more true, if possible, about the way we have acted toward you. ¹³,¹⁴My letters have been straightforward and sincere; nothing is written between the lines! And even though you don't know me very well (I hope someday you will), I want you to try to accept me and be proud of me as you already are to some extent; just as I shall be of you on that day when our Lord Jesus comes back again.

¹⁵,¹⁶It was because I was so sure of your understanding and trust that I planned to stop and see you on my way to Macedonia, as well as afterwards when I returned, so that I could be a double blessing to you and so that you could send me on my way to Judea.

¹⁷Then why, you may be asking, did I change my plan? Hadn't I really made up my mind yet? Or am I like a man of the world who says yes when he really means no? ¹⁸Never! As surely as God is true, I am not that sort of person. My yes means yes.

¹⁹Timothy and Silvanus and I have been telling you about Jesus Christ the Son of God. He isn't one to say yes when he means no. He always does exactly what he says. ²⁰He carries out and fulfills all of God's promises, no matter how many of them there are; and we have told everyone how faithful he is, giving glory to his name. ²¹It is this God who has made you and me into faithful Christians and commissioned us apostles to preach the Good News. ²²He has put his brand upon us—his mark of ownership—and given us his Holy Spirit in our hearts as guarantee that we belong to him and as the first installment of all that he is going to give us.

²³I call upon this God to witness against me if I am not telling the absolute truth: the reason I haven't come to visit you yet is that I don't want to sadden you with a severe rebuke. ²⁴When I come, although I can't do much to help your faith, for it is strong already, I want to be able to do something about your joy: I want to make you happy, not sad.

2 Forgiveness and Acceptance

"No," I said to myself, "I won't do it. I'll not make them unhappy with another painful visit." ²For if I make you sad, who is going to make me happy? You are the ones to do it, and how can you if I cause you pain? ³That is why I wrote as I did in my last letter, so that you will get things straightened out before I come. Then, when I do come, I will not be made sad by the very ones who ought to give me greatest joy. I felt sure that your happiness was so bound up in mine that you would not be happy either unless I came with joy.

⁴Oh, how I hated to write that letter! It almost broke my heart, and I tell you honestly that I cried over it. I didn't want to hurt you, but I had to show you how very much I loved you and cared about what was happening to you.

⁵,⁶Remember that the man I wrote about, who caused all the trouble, has not caused sorrow to me as much as to all the rest of you—though I certainly have my share in it too. I don't want to be harder on him than I should. He has been punished enough by your united disapproval. ⁷Now it is time to forgive him and comfort him. Otherwise he may become so bitter and discouraged that he won't be able to recover. ⁸Please show him now that you still do love him very much.

⁹I wrote to you as I did so that I could find out how far you would go in obeying me. ¹⁰When you forgive anyone, I do too. And whatever I have forgiven (to the extent that this affected me too) has been by Christ's authority, and for your good. ¹¹A further reason for forgiveness is to keep from being outsmarted by Satan, for we know what he is trying to do.

¹²Well, when I got as far as the city of Troas, the Lord gave me tremendous opportunities to preach the Gospel. ¹³But Titus, my dear brother, wasn't there to meet me and I couldn't rest, wondering where he was and what had happened to him. So I said good-bye and went right on to Macedonia to try to find him.

¹⁴But thanks be to God! For through what Christ has done, he has triumphed over us so that now wherever we go he uses us to tell others about the Lord and to spread the Gospel like a sweet perfume. ¹⁵As far as God is concerned there is a sweet, wholesome fragrance in our lives. It is the fragrance of Christ within us, an aroma to both the saved and the unsaved all around us. ¹⁶To those who are not being saved, we seem a

Family Devotions

☐ *Devotion 316*
Showing Compassion

Read 2 Corinthians 1:3-7

Jenny and Jane. Strangers thought they were twins, but their friends knew them as best buddies. They were inseparable. But one day that all changed.

"Jenny, aren't you going to stay for the pep assembly?" Jane asked.

"No, I don't feel too well," Jenny said. "I called my mom to come and get me."

"See you tomorrow then," said Jane.

But Jenny didn't come to school the next day. Jane stopped to see her at home, but she was resting. Before long, she was in the hospital.

At first, Jane went there to see Jenny. She brought their favorite flower, a pink rose. Jane could tell Jenny liked the rose by the smile in her eyes, but Jenny didn't say much. She was hooked up to several tubes, and nurses kept checking her.

Jane felt uncomfortable visiting Jane. The longer Jenny stayed in the hospital, the less Jane visited her. Finally Jane stopped going altogether.

"Jane, who's your best friend?" asked Mom one day.

Jane looked puzzled. "Jenny, of course!"

"I thought best friends like to be together," Mom answered, "and you haven't seen Jenny in days."

Jane burst into tears. "Mom, I can't go there. Jenny can barely talk. And she looks so different. I'm sure she's going to die. What can I say?"

"You don't need to say anything," answered Mom. "Just be there. Jenny really needs a friend now. She misses you so much, Jane. Her mom told me that. She thinks you don't care about her anymore."

"But I do, Mom!" exclaimed Jane. "I care so much it hurts!"

"Then go be with her," encouraged Mom. "Show her you still care. Let her know you're praying for her."

Jane got her coat. How could a real friend stay away?

Showing Compassion Memory Verse

What a wonderful God we have—he is the Father of our Lord Jesus Christ, the source of every mercy, and the one who so wonderfully comforts and strengthens us in our hardships and trials.

2 Corinthians 1:3

How About You?

Do you know someone who is ill? Be a comfort. Visit if possible. Read a few comforting Bible verses. Send a card, a note, flowers, or something else your friend or relative would like. Let him or her know how much you care. *J. H.*

• For the next devotional, turn to page 1123. • To start the next topic, turn to page 81. • For notes on *Showing Compassion*, see pages 206, 506, 515, 710, and 934.

fearful smell of death and doom, while to those who know Christ we are a life-giving perfume. But who is adequate for such a task as this? ¹⁷Only those who, like ourselves, are men of integrity, sent by God, speaking with Christ's power, with God's eye upon us. We are not like those hucksters—and there are many of them—whose idea in getting out the Gospel is to make a good living out of it.

3 Our Success Comes from God

Are we beginning to be like those false teachers of yours who must tell you all about themselves and bring long letters of recommendation with them? I think you hardly need someone's letter to tell you about us, do you? And we don't need a recommendation from you, either! ²The only letter I need is you yourselves! By looking at the good change in your hearts, everyone can see that we have done a good work among you. ³They can see that you are a letter from Christ, written by us. It is not a letter written with pen and ink, but by the Spirit of the living God; not one carved on stone, but in human hearts.

⁴We dare to say these good things about ourselves only because of our great trust in God through Christ, that he will help us to be true to what we say, ⁵and not because we think we can do anything of lasting value by ourselves. Our only power and success comes from God. ⁶He is the one who has helped us tell others about his new agreement to save them. We do not tell them that they must obey every law of God or die; but we tell them there is life for them from the Holy Spirit. The old way, trying to be saved by keeping the Ten Commandments, ends in death; in the new way, the Holy Spirit gives them life.

⁷Yet that old system of law that led to death began with such glory that people could not bear to look at Moses' face. For as he gave them God's law to obey, his face shone out with the very glory of God—though the brightness was already fading away. ⁸Shall we not expect far greater glory in these days when the Holy Spirit is giving life? ⁹If the plan that leads to doom was glorious, much more glorious is the plan that makes men right with God. ¹⁰In fact, that first glory as it shone from Moses' face is worth nothing at all in comparison with the overwhelming glory of the new agreement. ¹¹So if the old system that faded into nothing was full of heavenly glory, the glory of God's new plan for our salvation is certainly far greater, for it is eternal.

¹²Since we know that this new glory will never go away, we can preach with great boldness, ¹³and not as Moses did, who put a veil over his face so that the Israelis could not see the glory fade away.

¹⁴Not only Moses' face was veiled, but his people's minds and understanding were veiled and blinded too. Even now when the Scripture is read it seems as though Jewish hearts and minds are covered by a thick veil, because they cannot see and understand the real meaning of the Scriptures. For this veil of misunderstanding can be removed only by believing in Christ. ¹⁵Yes, even today when they read Moses' writings their hearts are blind and they think that obeying the Ten Commandments is the way to be saved.

¹⁶But whenever anyone turns to the Lord from his sins, then the veil is taken away. ¹⁷The Lord is the Spirit who gives them life, and where he is there is freedom [from trying to be saved by keeping the laws of God]. ¹⁸But we Christians have no veil over our faces; we can be mirrors that brightly reflect the glory of the Lord. And as the Spirit of the Lord works within us, we become more and more like him.

4 Satan Blinds, but God Gives Light

It is God himself, in his mercy, who has given us this wonderful work [of telling his Good News to others], and so we never give up. ²We do not try to trick people into believing—we are not interested in fooling anyone. We never try to get anyone to believe that the Bible teaches what it doesn't. All such shameful methods we forego. We stand in the presence of God as we speak and so we tell the truth, as all who know us will agree.

³If the Good News we preach is hidden to anyone, it is hidden from the one who is on the road to eternal death. ⁴Satan, who is the god of this evil world, has made him blind, unable to see the glorious light of the Gospel that is shining upon him or to understand the amazing message we preach about the glory of Christ, who is God. ⁵We don't go around preaching about ourselves but about Christ Jesus as Lord. All we say of ourselves is that we are your slaves because of what Jesus has done for us. ⁶For God, who said, "Let there be light in the darkness," has made us understand that it is the brightness of his glory that is seen in the face of Jesus Christ.

⁷But this precious treasure—this light and power that now shine within us—is held in a perishable container, that is, in our weak bodies. Everyone can see that the glorious power within must be from God and is not our own.

⁸We are pressed on every side by troubles, but not crushed and broken. We are perplexed because we don't know why things happen as they do, but we don't give up and quit. ⁹We are hunted down, but God never abandons us. We get knocked down, but we get up again and keep going. ¹⁰These bodies of ours are constantly facing death just as Jesus did;

FAMILY DEVOTIONS

☐ *DEVOTION 317*
OVERCOMING ANGER

Read 2 Corinthians 2:5-11

Overcoming Anger Memory Verses

Dear brothers, don't ever forget that it is best to listen much, speak little, and not become angry; for anger doesn't make us good, as God demands that we must be.
James 1:19-20

Stephie had a sick feeling in the pit of her stomach as she opened her eyes one morning. She felt the anger rise within her, as it did so often lately. Her former best friend, Susan, had been spreading rumors about her ever since Stephie had won the science fair competition. She reluctantly sat up in bed. "I hate her," she breathed quietly. "Why can't she just leave me alone?"

Stephie got out of bed and went into the kitchen where her mother was peeling vegetables for stew.

"Good morning," her mother said, smiling. "How did you sleep?"

"Oh, fair, I guess," Stephie muttered with a shrug. Then her eyes filled with tears. "I'm so sick of the things Susan is telling people about me!" she blurted out angrily. "She used to be my best friend!"

Her mother thought for a moment. "Well, it's easy to feel bitter when someone tries to hurt you like that," she agreed, "but the Lord doesn't want us to be bitter. Bitterness is not easy to overcome, though, so you need to deal with it one day at a time." She picked up an onion for the stew. "Dealing with bitterness is something like peeling an onion," she added. "You peel off one layer at a time. With each layer comes tears, but eventually there will be no more onion."

"So, you can't really get over it right away?" Stephie asked.

"Well, you can't pray just once about something like bitterness," Mom replied. "It takes daily prayer. It can take weeks, months, and sometimes years, but you will see victory. You must deal with it one day at a time."

"Will you pray with me, Mom? I want God to start peeling away this onion for me!"

Mom gave Stephie a hug as they sat down to pray together.

How About You?
Are you angry about things that are happening to you that you cannot change? Does that anger keep growing and growing inside of you? That's called bitterness. You need to ask God daily to help you overcome bitterness. It will take time, but as you learn to trust him, you will have victory. *S. N.*

• For the next devotional, turn to page 1125. • For the next devotional on *OVERCOMING ANGER*, turn to page 1133.
• For notes on *OVERCOMING ANGER*, see pages 176, 511, 936, and 1003.

so it is clear to all that it is only the living Christ within [who keeps us safe].

¹¹Yes, we live under constant danger to our lives because we serve the Lord, but this gives us constant opportunities to show forth the power of Jesus Christ within our dying bodies. ¹²Because of our preaching we face death, but it has resulted in eternal life for you.

¹³We boldly say what we believe [trusting God to care for us], just as the psalm writer did when he said, "I believe and therefore I speak." ¹⁴We know that the same God who brought the Lord Jesus back from death will also bring us back to life again with Jesus and present us to him along with you. ¹⁵These sufferings of ours are for your benefit. And the more of you who are won to Christ, the more there are to thank him for his great kindness, and the more the Lord is glorified.

¹⁶That is why we never give up. Though our bodies are dying, our inner strength in the Lord is growing every day. ¹⁷These troubles and sufferings of ours are, after all, quite small and won't last very long. Yet this short time of distress will result in God's richest blessing upon us forever and ever! ¹⁸So we do not look at what we can see right now, the troubles all around us, but we look forward to the joys in heaven which we have not yet seen. The troubles will soon be over, but the joys to come will last forever.

5 We Will Have New Bodies

For we know that when this tent we live in now is taken down—when we die and leave these bodies—we will have wonderful new bodies in heaven, homes that will be ours forevermore, made for us by God himself and not by human hands. ²How weary we grow of our present bodies. That is why we look forward eagerly to the day when we shall have heavenly bodies that we shall put on like new clothes. ³For we shall not be merely spirits without bodies. ⁴These earthly bodies make us groan and sigh, but we wouldn't like to think of dying and having no bodies at all. We want to slip into our new bodies so that these dying bodies will, as it were, be swallowed up by everlasting life. ⁵This is what God has prepared for us, and as a guarantee he has given us his Holy Spirit.

⁶Now we look forward with confidence to our heavenly bodies, realizing that every moment we spend in these earthly bodies is time spent away from our eternal home in heaven with Jesus. ⁷We know these things are true by believing, not by seeing. ⁸And we are not afraid but are quite content to die, for then we will be at home with the Lord. ⁹So our aim is to please him always in everything we do, whether we are here in this body or away from this body and with him in heaven. ¹⁰For we must all stand before Christ to be judged and have our lives laid bare—before him. Each of us will receive whatever he deserves for the good or bad things he has done in his earthly body.

¹¹It is because of this solemn fear of the Lord, which is ever present in our minds, that we work so hard to win others. God knows our hearts, that they are pure in this matter, and I hope that, deep within, you really know it too.

¹²Are we trying to pat ourselves on the back again? No, I am giving you some good ammunition! You can use this on those preachers of yours who brag about how well they look and preach but don't have true and honest hearts. You can boast about us that we, at least, are well intentioned and honest.

¹³,¹⁴Are we insane [to say such things about ourselves]? If so, it is to bring glory to God. And if we are in our right minds, it is for your benefit. Whatever we do, it is certainly not for our own profit but because Christ's love controls us now. Since we believe that Christ died for all of us, we should also believe that we have died to the old life we used to live. ¹⁵He died for all so that all who live—having received eternal life from him—might live no longer for themselves, to please themselves, but to spend their lives pleasing Christ who died and rose again for them. ¹⁶So stop evaluating Christians by what the world thinks about them or by what they seem to be like on the outside. Once I mistakenly thought of Christ that way, merely as a human being like myself. How differently I feel now! ¹⁷When someone becomes a Christian, he becomes a brand new person inside. He is not the same anymore. A new life has begun!

¹⁸All these new things are from God who brought us back to himself through what Christ Jesus did. And God has given us the privilege of urging everyone to come into his favor and be reconciled to him. ¹⁹For God was in Christ, restoring the world to himself, no longer counting men's sins against them but blotting them out. This is the wonderful message he has given us to tell others. ²⁰We are Christ's ambassadors. God is using us to speak to you: we beg you, as though Christ himself were here pleading with you, receive the love he offers you—be reconciled to God. ²¹For God took the sinless Christ and poured into him our sins. Then, in exchange, he poured God's goodness into us!

6 When Life Is Hard, Lean on God

As God's partners, we beg you not to toss aside this marvelous message of God's great kindness. ²For God says, "Your cry came to me at a

Family Devotions

☐ *Devotion 318*
Going to Church

Read 2 Corinthians 4:7-10, 16

As Pastor Page began his sermon, Debbie yawned. She began scribbling a note on her bulletin, but she noticed Mother frowning at her. So she stuffed it into her purse and read her Sunday school paper instead.

The next night, Debbie excitedly went with her mother to an exercise class they'd signed up for at the YMCA. She was impressed with all the exercise equipment, and she had a great time trying it out during the class.

"That sure was neat, Mom," Debbie said happily as they drove home. "I like the rowing machine, and it was fun lifting weights. Maybe we can try out the pool next time."

Mother yawned. "It sure made me tired," she said.

"I'm tired, too," agreed Debbie, "but it was fun. My muscles are a little sore, but I feel good. I know that working out makes me stronger."

Mother smiled. "I know what you mean," she said with a nod. "That's how I felt after my workout yesterday, too."

"Yesterday?" Debbie frowned. "You didn't exercise yesterday, Mom. We just went to church."

"Ah, but I got a spiritual workout yesterday," said Mother, "and I needed that. You missed it, though. You see, you can't just sit in church on Sundays and expect to grow spiritually. If you ever expect to become strong in the Lord, you need to exercise your faith, like you do your body."

Going to Church Memory Verse

Let us not neglect our church meetings, as some people do, but encourage and warn each other, especially now that the day of his coming back again is drawing near.
Hebrews 10:25

How About You?

Do you feel that church is a waste of time—that you don't get anything out of it? Just as you may exercise physically to strengthen your body, you need to pay attention in church to help your inner strength in the Lord to grow. Church is a place where true believers in Christ meet to worship and serve God and to learn how to live for him. Don't let church become a bore. Get involved. S. K.

• For the next devotional, turn to page 1127. • For the next devotional on *Going to Church*, turn to page 1189.
• For notes on *Going to Church*, see pages 770, 965, and 1002.

favorable time, when the doors of welcome were wide open. I helped you on a day when salvation was being offered." Right now God is ready to welcome you. Today he is ready to save you.

³We try to live in such a way that no one will ever be offended or kept back from finding the Lord by the way we act, so that no one can find fault with us and blame it on the Lord. ⁴In fact, in everything we do we try to show that we are true ministers of God.

We patiently endure suffering and hardship and trouble of every kind. ⁵We have been beaten, put in jail, faced angry mobs, worked to exhaustion, stayed awake through sleepless nights of watching, and gone without food. ⁶We have proved ourselves to be what we claim by our wholesome lives and by our understanding of the Gospel and by our patience. We have been kind and truly loving and filled with the Holy Spirit. ⁷We have been truthful, with God's power helping us in all we do. All of the godly man's arsenal—weapons of defense, and weapons of attack—have been ours.

⁸We stand true to the Lord whether others honor us or despise us, whether they criticize us or commend us. We are honest, but they call us liars.

⁹The world ignores us, but we are known to God; we live close to death, but here we are, still very much alive. We have been injured but kept from death. ¹⁰Our hearts ache, but at the same time we have the joy of the Lord. We are poor, but we give rich spiritual gifts to others. We own nothing, and yet we enjoy everything.

¹¹Oh, my dear Corinthian friends! I have told you all my feelings; I love you with all my heart. ¹²Any coldness still between us is not because of any lack of love on my part but because your love is too small and does not reach out to me and draw me in. ¹³I am talking to you now as if you truly were my very own children. Open your hearts to us! Return our love!

¹⁴Don't be teamed with those who do not love the Lord, for what do the people of God have in common with the people of sin? How can light live with darkness? ¹⁵And what harmony can there be between Christ and the devil? How can a Christian be a partner with one who doesn't believe? ¹⁶And what union can there be between God's temple and idols? For you are God's temple, the home of the living God, and God has said of you, "I will live in them and walk among them, and I will be their God and they shall be my people." ¹⁷That is why the Lord has said, "Leave them; separate yourselves from them; don't touch their filthy things, and I will welcome you ¹⁸and be a Father to you, and you will be my sons and daughters."

7 Paul Is Proud of the Christians

Having such great promises as these, dear friends, let us turn away from everything wrong, whether of body or spirit, and purify ourselves, living in the wholesome fear of God, giving ourselves to him alone. ²Please open your hearts to us again, for not one of you has suffered any wrong from us. Not one of you was led astray. We have cheated no one nor taken advantage of anyone. ³I'm not saying this to scold or blame you, for, as I have said before, you are in my heart forever, and I live and die with you. ⁴I have the highest confidence in you, and my pride in you is great. You have greatly encouraged me; you have made me so happy in spite of all my suffering.

⁵When we arrived in Macedonia there was no rest for us; outside, trouble was on every hand and all around us; within us, our hearts were full of dread and fear. ⁶Then God who cheers those who are discouraged refreshed us by the arrival of Titus. ⁷Not only was his presence a joy, but also the news that he brought of the wonderful time he had with you. When he told me how much you were looking forward to my visit, and how sorry you were about what had happened, and about your loyalty and warm love for me, well, I overflowed with joy!

⁸I am no longer sorry that I sent that letter to you, though I was very sorry for a time, realizing how painful it would be to you. But it hurt you only for a little while. ⁹Now I am glad I sent it, not because it hurt you but because the pain turned you to God. It was a good kind of sorrow you felt, the kind of sorrow God wants his people to have, so that I need not come to you with harshness. ¹⁰For God sometimes uses sorrow in our lives to help us turn away from sin and seek eternal life. We should never regret his sending it. But the sorrow of the man who is not a Christian is not the sorrow of true repentance and does not prevent eternal death.

¹¹Just see how much good this grief from the Lord did for you! You no longer shrugged your shoulders but became earnest and sincere and very anxious to get rid of the sin that I wrote you about. You became frightened

---

RESPECTING GOD'S WARNINGS 7:11 It is difficult to be confronted with our sin, and even more difficult to get rid of sin. Paul praised the Corinthians for clearing up an especially troublesome situation. Do you tend to be defensive when confronted? Don't let pride keep you from admitting your sins. Accept correction as a tool for your growth, and do all you can to correct problems that are pointed out to you. **To begin the series of devotionals on RESPECTING GOD'S WARNINGS, turn to page 21.**

Family Devotions

☐ DEVOTION 319
GIVING TO GOD

Read 2 Corinthians 8:2-15

"I hope you made a lot of those," Steve said when he saw the fresh cinnamon rolls on the kitchen table.

"I did," Mom replied. "I even baked a dozen for the Carlsons."

"The Carlsons?" Steve questioned. "What for?"

"Because they don't have money for such things," she answered, "and I thought they might enjoy some."

"Can't you give them bread or potatoes or something?" grumbled Steve. As soon as he spoke, he knew he had said the wrong thing. He was being selfish, and both he and his mother knew it. He blushed with embarrassment.

"The Bible tells us to share each other's troubles," Mom replied, referring to a Scripture verse that Steve had memorized. He did not answer immediately. He didn't really mind helping a family like the Carlsons, but did his mother have to give away something that he liked as much as her homemade cinnamon rolls?

Mom broke into his thoughts just as though she knew what he was thinking. "You know," she said, "when God the Father saw the need of people, he gave his very best." She paused significantly. "Is it too much for us to give a needy family something that we like?"

Steve had no answer for his mother's question. He was a Christian, and he knew that selfishness was not to be part of the Christian life. "You're right," he said finally. "But then, you usually are."

There was a smile on his face as he picked up the plate of cinnamon rolls and made his way to the Carlsons' house. With every step, he took a deep breath, so as to inhale the good aroma of the rolls. The Carlsons would enjoy them—he was sure of that!

Giving to God Memory Verse

Bring all the tithes into the storehouse so that there will be food enough in my Temple; if you do, I will open up the windows of heaven for you and pour out a blessing so great you won't have room enough to take it in! Try it! Let me prove it to you!
Malachi 3:10

How About You?
Are you willing to help someone in need even if it means giving something that is very special to you? God was! By sharing with others—sharing your time, your money, your things, your prayers—you can prove that your love is real. R.J.

• For the next devotional, turn to page 1129.   • For the next devotional on GIVING TO GOD, turn to page 1129.
• For notes on GIVING TO GOD, see pages 182, 433, and 1128.

about what had happened and longed for me to come and help. You went right to work on the problem and cleared it up [punishing the man who sinned]. You have done everything you could to make it right.

12 I wrote as I did so the Lord could show how much you really do care for us. That was my purpose even more than to help the man who sinned or his father to whom he did the wrong.

13 In addition to the encouragement you gave us by your love, we were made happier still by Titus' joy when you gave him such a fine welcome and set his mind at ease. 14 I told him how it would be—told him before he left me of my pride in you—and you didn't disappoint me. I have always told you the truth and now my boasting to Titus has also proved true! 15 He loves you more than ever when he remembers the way you listened to him so willingly and received him so anxiously and with such deep concern. 16 How happy this makes me, now that I am sure all is well between us again. Once again I can have perfect confidence in you.

8 Generous Giving Pleases God

Now I want to tell you what God in his grace has done for the churches in Macedonia.

2 Though they have been going through much trouble and hard times, they have mixed their wonderful joy with their deep poverty, and the result has been an overflow of giving to others. 3 They gave not only what they could afford but far more; and I can testify that they did it because they wanted to and not because of nagging on my part. 4 They begged us to take the money so they could share in the joy of helping the Christians in Jerusalem. 5 Best of all, they went beyond our highest hopes, for their first action was to dedicate themselves to the Lord and to us, for whatever directions God might give to them through us. 6 They were so enthusiastic about it that we have urged Titus, who encouraged your giving in the first place, to visit you and encourage you to complete your share in this ministry of giving. 7 You people there are leaders in so many ways—you have so much faith, so many good preachers, so much learning, so much enthusiasm, so much love for us. Now I want you to be leaders also in the spirit of cheerful giving.

8 I am not giving you an order; I am not saying you must do it, but others are eager for it. This is one way to prove that your love is real, that it goes beyond mere words.

9 You know how full of love and kindness our Lord Jesus was: though he was so very rich, yet to help you he became so very poor, so that by being poor he could make you rich.

10 I want to suggest that you finish what you started to do a year ago, for you were not only the first to propose this idea, but the first to begin doing something about it. 11 Having started the ball rolling so enthusiastically, you should carry this project through to completion just as gladly, giving whatever you can out of whatever you have. Let your enthusiastic idea at the start be equalled by your realistic action now. 12 If you are really eager to give, then it isn't important how much you have to give. God wants you to give what you have, not what you haven't.

13 Of course, I don't mean that those who receive your gifts should have an easy time of it at your expense, 14 but you should divide with them. Right now you have plenty and can help them; then at some other time they can share with you when you need it. In this way, each will have as much as he needs. 15 Do you remember what the Scriptures say about this? "He that gathered much had nothing left over, and he that gathered little had enough." So you also should share with those in need.

16 I am thankful to God that he has given Titus the same real concern for you that I have. 17 He is glad to follow my suggestion that he visit you again—but I think he would have come anyway, for he is very eager to see you! 18 I am sending another well-known brother with him, who is highly praised as a preacher of the Good News in all the churches. 19 In fact, this man was elected by the churches to travel with me to take the gift to Jerusalem. This will glorify the Lord and show our eagerness to help each other. 20 By traveling together we will guard against any suspicion, for we are anxious that no one should find fault with the way we are handling this large gift. 21 God knows we are honest, but I want everyone else to know it too. That is why we have made this arrangement.

22 And I am sending you still another brother, whom we know from experience to be an earnest Christian. He is especially interested as he looks forward to this trip because I have told him all about your eagerness to help.

23 If anyone asks who Titus is,

GIVING TO GOD **8:10-15** The Corinthian Christians had money, and Paul challenged them to share with the Jerusalem Christians just as the Macedonian churches had done. Four principles of giving emerge here: (1) your willingness to give cheerfully is more important than the amount you give; (2) you should strive to fulfill your financial commitments; (3) if you give to others in need, they will in turn help you when you are in need; (4) nevertheless, you should give as a response to Christ, not for anything you can get out of it. How you give reflects your devotion to Christ. These principles apply regardless of your financial condition. **To begin the series of devotionals on GIVING TO GOD, turn to page 105.**

FAMILY DEVOTIONS

☐ DEVOTION 320
GIVING TO GOD

Read 2 Corinthians 9:6-8

"What are you going to do with that?" Tiffany asked when she saw her sister slip some money into her Bible.

"It's for our special missionary project," Tara told her. "It's half of my birthday money plus what I got from our baby-sitting job. How much are you giving?"

Tiffany got up to leave the room. "That's none of your business," she mumbled. She certainly didn't want to admit that she was giving only fifty cents.

As they returned home from church that morning, Mom pointed to the flowers along the front walk. "Look at my pansies," she said. "Aren't they pretty?"

"How can they have so many flowers already?" asked Tiffany. "You just picked all the pansies two days ago."

"Pansies need to be picked often," said Mom. "The more they give, the more they have to give. It makes me think of our gifts to the Lord. When we give generously and cheerfully to him, he gives back to us. It seems like the more we give, the more we have from which to give."

Tiffany stooped to pick a pansy as she thought about that. "You mean if we give lots of money, God will send more money to us?" she asked.

Mom smiled. "Well, I can't promise you that," she said, "although it often does seem to work out that way. Sometimes, though, the extra blessings God gives back to us may be in some other form. Maybe he'll keep our clothes from wearing out too fast, or perhaps he'll give a special sense of joy and peace and well-being."

Tiffany thought about her sister, who was always generous and happy. Then she thought about the discontentment she often felt herself. *I want to start giving like the pansies, too,* she decided at last.

Giving to God
Memory Verse

Bring all the tithes into the storehouse so that there will be food enough in my Temple; if you do, I will open up the windows of heaven for you and pour out a blessing so great you won't have room enough to take it in! Try it! Let me prove it to you!
Malachi 3:10

How About You?
Do you give cheerfully to the Lord, or do you grumble and complain about giving money? The Lord loves a cheerful giver. He's promised to give you more than you give him. It may not be money, but it will be whatever blessing you need most. *M. R. P.*

• For the next devotional, turn to page 1133.   • To start the next topic, turn to page 193.   • For notes on *GIVING TO GOD,* see pages 182, 433, and 1128.

say that he is my partner, my helper in helping you, and you can also say that the other two brothers represent the assemblies here and are splendid examples of those who belong to the Lord.

²⁴Please show your love for me to these men and do for them all that I have publicly boasted you would.

9 God Likes People Who Give Happily

I realize that I really don't even need to mention this to you, about helping God's people. ²For I know how eager you are to do it, and I have boasted to the friends in Macedonia that you were ready to send an offering a year ago. In fact, it was this enthusiasm of yours that stirred up many of them to begin helping. ³But I am sending these men just to be sure that you really are ready, as I told them you would be, with your money all collected; I don't want it to turn out that this time I was wrong in my boasting about you. ⁴I would be very much ashamed—and so would you—if some of these Macedonian people come with me, only to find that you still aren't ready after all I have told them!

⁵So I have asked these other brothers to arrive ahead of me to see that the gift you promised is on hand and waiting. I want it to be a real gift and not look as if it were being given under pressure.

⁶But remember this—if you give little, you will get little. A farmer who plants just a few seeds will get only a small crop, but if he plants much, he will reap much. ⁷Everyone must make up his own mind as to how much he should give. Don't force anyone to give more than he really wants to, for cheerful givers are the ones God prizes. ⁸God is able to make it up to you by giving you everything you need and more so that there will not only be enough for your own needs but plenty left over to give joyfully to others. ⁹It is as the Scriptures say: "The godly man gives generously to the poor. His good deeds will be an honor to him forever."

¹⁰For God, who gives seed to the farmer to plant, and later on good crops to harvest and eat, will give you more and more seed to plant and will make it grow so that you can give away more and more fruit from your harvest.

¹¹Yes, God will give you much so that you can give away much, and when we take your gifts to those who need them they will break out into thanksgiving and praise to God for your help. ¹²So two good things happen as a result of your gifts—those in need are helped, and they overflow with thanks to God. ¹³Those you help will be glad not only because of your generous gifts to themselves and to others, but they will praise God for this proof that your deeds are as good as your doctrine. ¹⁴And they will pray for you with deep fervor and feeling because of the wonderful grace of God shown through you.

¹⁵Thank God for his Son—his Gift too wonderful for words.

10 Paul's Authority

I plead with you—yes, I, Paul—and I plead gently, as Christ himself would do. Yet some of you are saying, "Paul's letters are bold enough when he is far away, but when he gets here he will be afraid to raise his voice!"

²I hope I won't need to show you when I come how harsh and rough I can be. I don't want to carry out my present plans against some of you who seem to think my deeds and words are merely those of an ordinary man. ³It is true that I am an ordinary, weak human being, but I don't use human plans and methods to win my battles. ⁴I use God's mighty weapons, not those made by men, to knock down the devil's strongholds. ⁵These weapons can break down every proud argument against God and every wall that can be built to keep men from finding him. With these weapons I can capture rebels and bring them back to God and change them into men whose hearts' desire is obedience to Christ. ⁶I will use these weapons against every rebel who remains after I have first used them on you yourselves and you surrender to Christ.

⁷The trouble with you is that you look at me and I seem weak and powerless, but you don't look beneath the surface. Yet if anyone can claim the power and authority of Christ, I certainly can. ⁸I may seem to be boasting more than I should about my authority over you—authority to help you, not to hurt you—but I shall make good every claim. ⁹I say this so that you will not think I am just blustering when I scold you in my letters.

¹⁰"Don't bother about his letters," some say. "He sounds big, but it's all noise. When he gets here you will see that there is nothing great about him, and you have never heard a worse preacher!" ¹¹This time my personal presence is going to be just as rough on you as my letters are!

¹²Oh, don't worry, I wouldn't dare say that I am as wonderful as these other men who tell you how good they are! Their trouble is that they are only comparing themselves with each other and measuring themselves against their own little ideas. What stupidity!

¹³But we will not boast of authority we do not have. Our goal is to measure up to God's plan for us, and this plan includes our working there with you. ¹⁴We are not going too far when we claim authority over you, for we were the first to come

to you with the Good News concerning Christ. ¹⁵It is not as though we were trying to claim credit for the work someone else has done among you. Instead, we hope that your faith will grow and that, still within the limits set for us, our work among you will be greatly enlarged.

¹⁶After that, we will be able to preach the Good News to other cities that are far beyond you, where no one else is working; then there will be no question about being in someone else's field. ¹⁷As the Scriptures say, "If anyone is going to boast, let him boast about what the Lord has done and not about himself." ¹⁸When someone boasts about himself and how well he has done, it doesn't count for much. But when the Lord commends him, that's different!

Smooth Talkers and Phony Teachers

I hope you will be patient with me as I keep on talking like a fool. Do bear with me and let me say what is on my heart. ²I am anxious for you with the deep concern of God himself—anxious that your love should be for Christ alone, just as a pure maiden saves her love for one man only, for the one who will be her husband. ³But I am frightened, fearing that in some way you will be led away from your pure and simple devotion to our Lord, just as Eve was deceived by Satan in the Garden of Eden. ⁴You seem so gullible: you believe whatever anyone tells you even if he is preaching about another Jesus than the one we preach, or a different spirit than the Holy Spirit you received, or shows you a different way to be saved. You swallow it all.

⁵Yet I don't feel that these marvelous "messengers from God," as they call themselves, are any better than I am. ⁶If I am a poor speaker, at least I know what I am talking about, as I think you realize by now, for we have proved it again and again.

⁷Did I do wrong and cheapen myself and make you look down on me because I preached God's Good News to you without charging you anything? ⁸,⁹Instead I "robbed" other churches by taking what they sent me and using it up while I was with you so that I could serve you without cost. And when that was gone and I was getting hungry, I still didn't ask you for anything, for the Christians from Macedonia brought me another gift. I have never yet asked you for one cent, and I never will. ¹⁰I promise this with every ounce of truth I possess—that I will tell everyone in Greece about it! ¹¹Why? Because I don't love you? God knows I do. ¹²But I will do it to cut out the ground from under the feet of those who boast that they are doing God's work in just the same way we are.

¹³God never sent those men at all; they are "phonies" who have fooled you into thinking they are Christ's apostles. ¹⁴Yet I am not surprised! Satan can change himself into an angel of light, ¹⁵so it is no wonder his servants can do it too, and seem like godly ministers. In the end they will get every bit of punishment their wicked deeds deserve.

¹⁶Again I plead, don't think that I have lost my wits to talk like this; but even if you do, listen to me anyway—a witless man, a fool—while I also boast a little as they do. ¹⁷Such bragging isn't something the Lord commanded me to do, for I am acting like a brainless fool. ¹⁸Yet those other men keep telling you how wonderful they are, so here I go: ¹⁹,²⁰(You think you are so wise—yet you listen gladly to those fools; you don't mind at all when they make you their slaves and take everything you have, and take advantage of you, and put on airs, and slap you in the face. ²¹I'm ashamed to say that I'm not strong and daring like that!

But whatever they can boast about—I'm talking like a fool again—I can boast about it, too.)

²²They brag that they are Hebrews, do they? Well, so am I. And they say that they are Israelites, God's chosen people? So am I. And they are descendants of Abraham? Well, I am too.

²³They say they serve Christ? But I have served him far more! (Have I gone mad to boast like this?) I have worked harder, been put in jail more often, been whipped times without number, and faced death again and again and again. ²⁴Five different times the Jews gave me their terrible thirty-nine lashes. ²⁵Three times I was beaten with rods. Once I was stoned. Three times I was shipwrecked. Once I was in the open sea all night and the whole next day. ²⁶I have traveled many weary miles and have been often in great danger from flooded rivers and from robbers and from my own people, the Jews, as well as from the hands of the Gentiles. I have faced grave dangers from mobs in the cities and from death in the deserts and in the stormy seas and from men who claim to be brothers in Christ but are not. ²⁷I have lived with weariness and pain and sleepless nights. Often I have been hungry and thirsty and have gone without food; often I have shivered with cold, without enough clothing to keep me warm.

²⁸Then, besides all this, I have the constant worry of how the churches are getting along: ²⁹Who makes a mistake and I do not feel his sadness? Who falls without my longing to help him? Who is spiritually hurt without my fury rising against the one who hurt him?

³⁰But if I must brag, I would rather brag about the things that show how weak I am. ³¹God, the Father of our Lord Jesus Christ, who is to be

praised forever and ever, knows I tell the truth. ³²For instance, in Damascus the governor under King Aretas kept guards at the city gates to catch me; ³³but I was let down by rope and basket from a hole in the city wall, and so I got away! [What popularity!]

12 Paul's Physical Problems

This boasting is all so foolish, but let me go on. Let me tell about the visions I've had, and revelations from the Lord.

²,³Fourteen years ago I was taken up to heaven for a visit. Don't ask me whether my body was there or just my spirit, for I don't know; only God can answer that. But anyway, there I was in paradise, ⁴and heard things so astounding that they are beyond a man's power to describe or put in words (and anyway I am not allowed to tell them to others). ⁵That experience is something worth bragging about, but I am not going to do it. I am going to boast only about how weak I am and how great God is to use such weakness for his glory. ⁶I have plenty to boast about and would be no fool in doing it, but I don't want anyone to think more highly of me than he should from what he can actually see in my life and my message.

⁷I will say this: because these experiences I had were so tremendous, God was afraid I might be puffed up by them; so I was given a physical condition which has been a thorn in my flesh, a messenger from Satan to hurt and bother me and prick my pride. ⁸Three different times I begged God to make me well again.

⁹Each time he said, "No. But I am with you; that is all you need. My power shows up best in weak people." Now I am glad to boast about how weak I am; I am glad to be a living demonstration of Christ's power, instead of showing off my own power and abilities. ¹⁰Since I know it is all for Christ's good, I am quite happy about "the thorn," and about insults and hardships, persecutions and difficulties; for when I am weak, then I am strong—the less I have, the more I depend on him.

¹¹You have made me act like a fool—boasting like this—for you people ought to be writing about me and not making me write about myself. There isn't a single thing these other marvelous fellows have that I don't have too, even though I am really worth nothing at all. ¹²When I was there I certainly gave you every proof that I was truly an apostle, sent to you by God himself, for I patiently did many wonders and signs and mighty works among you. ¹³The only thing I didn't do for you, which I do everywhere else in all other churches, was to become a burden to you—I didn't ask you to give me food to eat and a place to stay. Please forgive me for this wrong!

¹⁴Now I am coming to you again, the third time; and it is still not going to cost you anything, for I don't want your money. I want *you!* And anyway, you are my children, and little children don't pay for their father's and mother's food—it's the other way around; parents supply food for their children. ¹⁵I am glad to give you myself and all I have for your spiritual good, even though it seems that the more I love you, the less you love me.

¹⁶Some of you are saying, "It's true that his visits didn't seem to cost us anything, but he is a sneaky fellow, that Paul, and he fooled us. As sure as anything he must have made money from us some way."

¹⁷But how? Did any of the men I sent to you take advantage of you? ¹⁸When I urged Titus to visit you and sent our other brother with him, did they make any profit? No, of course not. For we have the same Holy Spirit and walk in each other's steps, doing things the same way.

¹⁹I suppose you think I am saying all this to get back into your good graces. That isn't it at all. I tell you, with God listening as I say it, that I have said this to help *you*, dear friends—to build you up spiritually—and not to help myself. ²⁰For I am afraid that when I come to visit you I won't like what I find, and then you won't like the way I will have to act. I am afraid that I will find you quarreling, and envying each other, and being angry with each other, and acting big, and saying wicked things about each other, and whispering behind each other's backs, filled with conceit and disunity. ²¹Yes, I am afraid that when I come God will humble me before you and I will be sad and mourn because many of you have sinned before and don't even care about the wicked, impure things you have done: your lust and immorality, and the taking of other men's wives.

13 Check Up on Yourselves

This is the third time I am coming to visit you. The Scriptures tell us that if two or three have seen a wrong, it must be punished. [Well, this is my third warning as I come now for this visit.] ²I have already warned those who had been sinning when I was there last; now I warn them again and all others, just as I did then, that this time I come ready to punish severely and I will not spare them.

³I will give you all the proof you want that Christ speaks through me. Christ is not weak in his dealings with you but is a mighty power within you. ⁴His weak, human body died on the cross, but now he lives by the mighty power of God. We, too, are weak in our bodies, as he was, but now we live and are strong, as he is, and have all of God's power to use in dealing with you.

FAMILY DEVOTIONS

☐ *DEVOTION 321*
OVERCOMING ANGER

Read 2 Corinthians 12:20

Overcoming Anger
Memory Verses

Dear brothers, don't ever forget that it is best to listen much, speak little, and not become angry; for anger doesn't make us good, as God demands that we must be.
James 1:19-20

Mom sighed deeply as she heard raised voices coming from the patio. Soon Brad came bursting into the house. "Mom, Tyler's being mean again! I wish he wouldn't even come over if he's going to act like that."

"I know you boys haven't gotten along very well lately," said Mom, "but why can't you be the one to stop all the quarreling that goes on between you?"

"Why me? Tyler's the one who always starts it," Brad defended himself.

"It takes *two* to quarrel," Mom pointed out. "If you refuse to fight, and if you ignore his teasing, there won't be any quarrel."

"If I don't stand up for my rights, he'll think I'm a sissy," protested Brad.

"Do you know what God thinks about all this?" asked Mom. "He says it's an honor for a man to stay out of a fight. Read it yourself in Proverbs—chapter 20, verse 3. Anybody can quarrel, you know, but it takes a wise person to stop a quarrel. The same verse says that only fools insist on quarreling."

"Tell that to Tyler!" demanded Brad.

"I'm not Tyler's mother, I'm yours—so I'm telling you," said Mom. "Do you choose to be an honorable man or a foolish one?"

Brad took a deep breath. "All right, I'll try."

Several times in the next few days, Tyler tried to pick a quarrel. He rode Brad's bike without permission, he tossed pebbles at him, and he called him a sissy, but Brad ignored him. Whenever Tyler teased him, Brad just walked away. Finally Tyler could stand it no longer. "What's the matter with you?" he asked.

Brad grinned. "Read Proverbs 20, verse 3," he advised. "If you follow its advice, it'll make a man—an honorable man—out of you." Brad walked away, laughing.

How About You?
Do you often quarrel with your brothers and sisters or with friends? Remember what God says about someone who insists on quarreling. Even if it's really the other person's fault, avoid arguing and fighting. It takes two to quarrel, so don't be one of the two. *B. W.*

• For the next devotional, turn to page 1137. • To start the next topic, turn to page 13. • For notes on *OVERCOMING ANGER*, see pages 176, 511, 936, and 1003.

⁵Check up on yourselves. Are you really Christians? Do you pass the test? Do you feel Christ's presence and power more and more within you? Or are you just pretending to be Christians when actually you aren't at all? ⁶I hope you can agree that I have stood that test and truly belong to the Lord.

⁷I pray that you will live good lives, not because that will be a feather in our caps, proving that what we teach is right; no, for we want you to do right even if we ourselves are despised. ⁸Our responsibility is to encourage the right at all times, not to hope for evil. ⁹We are glad to be weak and despised if you are really strong. Our greatest wish and prayer is that you will become mature Christians.

¹⁰I am writing this to you now in the hope that I won't need to scold and punish when I come; for I want to use the Lord's authority that he has given me, not to punish you but to make you strong.

¹¹I close my letter with these last words: Be happy. Grow in Christ. Pay attention to what I have said. Live in harmony and peace. And may the God of love and peace be with you.

¹²Greet each other warmly in the Lord. ¹³All the Christians here send you their best regards. ¹⁴May the grace of our Lord Jesus Christ be with you all. May God's love and the Holy Spirit's friendship be yours.

Paul

Galatians

WHY DO you obey God's rules? Is it because God's Spirit is helping you become like Jesus? Or is it because you think God will love you more if you do good things?

When Paul traveled in the area called Galatia, many people accepted Christ. Some of them had been faithful Jews. After Paul left, these Jewish Christians started teaching that people had to obey all the Old Testament laws or else they weren't really saved.

When Paul heard about this, he was alarmed. He wrote this letter to remind the people that they couldn't "earn" salvation by doing good things or by obeying a lot of rules. He told the people they must be crazy because they'd forgotten that they were saved by believing in Christ and fully trusting him— not by obeying religious rules and laws!

As you read Galatians, look for what *really* makes us right with God.

Paul: Christ's Missionary

From: Paul the missionary and all the other Christians here.

To: The churches of Galatia.

I was not called to be a missionary by any group or agency. My call is from Jesus Christ himself and from God the Father who raised him from the dead. ³May peace and blessing be yours from God the Father and from the Lord Jesus Christ. ⁴He died for our sins just as God our Father planned, and rescued us from this evil world in which we live. ⁵All glory to God through all the ages of eternity. Amen.

⁶I am amazed that you are turning away so soon from God who, in his love and mercy, invited you to share the eternal life he gives through Christ; you are already following a different "way to heaven," which really doesn't go to heaven at all. ⁷For there is no other way than the one we showed you; you are being fooled by those who twist and change the truth concerning Christ.

⁸Let God's curses fall on anyone, including my-

self, who preaches any other way to be saved than the one we told you about; yes, if an angel comes from heaven and preaches any other message, let him be forever cursed. ⁹I will say it again: if anyone preaches any other gospel than the one you welcomed, let God's curse fall upon him.

¹⁰You can see that I am not trying to please you by sweet talk and flattery; no, I am trying to please God. If I were still trying to please men I could not be Christ's servant.

¹¹Dear friends, I solemnly swear that the way to heaven that I preach is not based on some mere human whim or dream. ¹²For my message comes from no less a person than Jesus Christ himself, who told me what to say. No one else has taught me.

¹³You know what I was like when I followed the Jewish religion—how I went after the Christians mercilessly, hunting them down and doing my best to get rid of them all. ¹⁴I was one of the most religious Jews of my own age in the whole country and tried as hard as I possibly could to follow all the old, traditional rules of my religion.

¹⁵But then something happened! For even before I was born, God had chosen me to be his and called me—what kindness and grace—¹⁶to reveal his Son within me so that I could go to the Gentiles and show them the Good News about Jesus.

When all this happened to me I didn't go at once and talk it over with anyone else; ¹⁷I didn't go up to Jerusalem to consult with those who were apostles before I was. No, I went away into the deserts of Arabia and then came back to the city of Damascus. ¹⁸It was not until three years later that I finally went to Jerusalem for a visit with Peter and stayed there with him for fifteen days. ¹⁹And the only other apostle I met at that time was James, our Lord's brother. ²⁰(Listen to what I am saying, for I am telling you this in the very presence of God. This is exactly what happened—I am not lying to you.) ²¹Then after this visit I went to Syria and Cilicia. ²²And still the Christians in Judea didn't even know what I looked like. ²³All they knew was what people were saying, that "our former enemy is now preaching the very faith he tried to wreck." ²⁴And they gave glory to God because of me.

2 Church Leaders Accepted Paul

Then fourteen years later I went back to Jerusalem again, this time with Barnabas; and Titus came along too. ²I went there with definite orders from God to confer with the brothers there about the message I was preaching to the Gentiles. I talked privately to the leaders of the church so that they would all understand just what I had been teaching and, I hoped, agree that it was right. ³And they did agree; they did not even demand that Titus, my companion, should be circumcised, though he was a Gentile.

⁴Even that question wouldn't have come up except for some so-called "Christians" there—false ones, really—who came to spy on us and see what freedom we enjoyed in Christ Jesus, as to whether we obeyed the Jewish laws or not. They tried to get us all tied up in their rules, like slaves in chains. ⁵But we did not listen to them for a single moment, for we did not want to confuse you into thinking that salvation can be earned by being circumcised and by obeying Jewish laws.

⁶And the great leaders of the church who were there had nothing to add to what I was preaching. (By the way, their being great leaders made no difference to me, for all are the same to God.) ⁷⁻⁹In fact, when Peter, James, and John, who were known as the pillars of the church, saw how greatly God had used me in winning the Gentiles, just as Peter had been blessed so greatly in his preaching to the Jews—for the same God gave us each our special gifts—they shook hands with Barnabas and me and encouraged us to keep right on with our preaching to the Gentiles while they continued their work with the Jews. ¹⁰The only thing they did suggest was that we must always remember to help the poor, and I, too, was eager for that.

¹¹But when Peter came to Antioch I had to oppose him publicly, speaking strongly against what he was doing, for it was very wrong. ¹²For when he first arrived, he ate with the Gentile Christians [who don't bother with circumcision and the many other Jewish laws]. But afterwards, when some Jewish friends of James came, he wouldn't eat with the Gentiles anymore because he was afraid of what these Jewish legalists, who insisted that circumcision was necessary for salvation, would say; ¹³and then all the other Jewish Christians and even Barnabas became hypocrites too, following Peter's example, though they certainly knew better. ¹⁴When I saw what was happening and that they weren't being honest about what they really believed and weren't following the truth of the Gospel, I said to Peter in front of all the others, "Though you are a Jew by birth, you have long since discarded the Jewish laws; so why, all of a sudden, are you trying to make these Gentiles obey them? ¹⁵You and I are Jews by birth, not mere Gentile sinners, ¹⁶and yet we Jewish Christians know very well that we cannot become right with God by obeying our Jewish laws but only by faith in Jesus Christ to take away our sins. And so we, too, have trusted Jesus Christ, that we might be accepted by God because of faith—and not because we have obeyed the Jewish laws. For no one will ever be saved by obeying them."

FAMILY DEVOTIONS

☐ *DEVOTION 322*
RESPECTING OTHERS

Read Galatians 3:26-29

"Go, Jon! Go!" yelled Greg, as he jumped up and down. "Make that touchdown! All right!" He cheered wildly as his teammate scored the first touchdown of the game.

At the dinner table that evening Greg gave his family a blow-by-blow account of the afternoon's game. Over and over they heard the name *Jon* as Greg described the various plays. Finally Greg's sister, Fran, looked at her brother in disgust. "I am sick of hearing about all the wonderful plays Jon made," she declared. "I was under the impression that you didn't even like him, and frankly, I agreed with you. But now all you can do is sing his praises."

"Well, he may not be my favorite person in all the world," admitted Greg. "He's not my best friend or anything, but he's on our team. We're fighting for the same cause. We're both Coreyville Cougars, the 'best in the west!' You should have seen him run this afternoon. Peter passed him the ball, and he was off down the field like a streak. The other team didn't—"

"Oh, help me," moaned Fran. "Here we go again."

Mother laughed. "I'm glad you enjoyed your game so much, Son," she said. "It's nice you were able to win, and it's also nice that you've found something to admire in Jon. We should always look for positive things in others."

"I think Greg has given us a good example of how we should view other Christians," observed Dad. "We don't have to like everything about them, and they don't have to like everything about us, and they don't all have to be our best friends. But we should remember that we're on the same team. We're fighting for the same cause—that of winning others to Jesus and bringing glory to God. We should love them, and I believe we can even find something to admire in each of them. We should regard them as teammates."

Respecting Others Memory Verse

Don't be selfish; don't live to make a good impression on others. Be humble, thinking of others as better than yourself.
Philippians 2:3

How About You?

Is there a fellow Christian whom you dislike? Look for some good quality in him, and then concentrate on that rather than on the things that annoy you. Remember, you both belong to Christ, and that should bind you together. You are teammates. As such, work together to glorify the Lord. H. M.

• For the next devotional, turn to page 1139.   • For the next devotional on RESPECTING OTHERS, turn to page 1151.
• For notes on RESPECTING OTHERS, see pages 322, 382, 1088, and 1218.

17But what if we trust Christ to save us and then find that we are wrong and that we cannot be saved without being circumcised and obeying all the other Jewish laws? Wouldn't we need to say that faith in Christ had ruined us? God forbid that anyone should dare to think such things about our Lord. 18Rather, we are sinners if we start rebuilding the old systems I have been destroying of trying to be saved by keeping Jewish laws, 19for it was through reading the Scripture that I came to realize that I could never find God's favor by trying—and failing—to obey the laws. I came to realize that acceptance with God comes by believing in Christ.

20I have been crucified with Christ: and I myself no longer live, but Christ lives in me. And the real life I now have within this body is a result of my trusting in the Son of God, who loved me and gave himself for me. 21I am not one of those who treats Christ's death as meaningless. For if we could be saved by keeping Jewish laws, then there was no need for Christ to die.

3 Jewish Law and Faith in Christ

Oh, foolish Galatians! What magician has hypnotized you and cast an evil spell upon you? For you used to see the meaning of Jesus Christ's death as clearly as though I had waved a placard before you with a picture on it of Christ dying on the cross. 2Let me ask you this one question: Did you receive the Holy Spirit by trying to keep the Jewish laws? Of course not, for the Holy Spirit came upon you only after you heard about Christ and trusted him to save you. 3Then have you gone completely crazy? For if trying to obey the Jewish laws never gave you spiritual life in the first place, why do you think that trying to obey them now will make you stronger Christians? 4You have suffered so much for the Gospel. Now are you going to just throw it all overboard? I can hardly believe it!

5I ask you again, does God give you the power of the Holy Spirit and work miracles among you as a result of your trying to obey the Jewish laws? No, of course not. It is when you believe in Christ and fully trust him.

6Abraham had the same experience—God declared him fit for heaven only because he believed God's promises. 7You can see from this that the real children of Abraham are all the men of faith who truly trust in God.

8,9What's more, the Scriptures looked forward to this time when God would save the Gentiles also, through their faith. God told Abraham about this long ago when he said, "I will bless those in every nation who trust in me as you do." And so it is: all who trust in Christ share the same blessing Abraham received.

10Yes, and those who depend on the Jewish laws to save them are under God's curse, for the Scriptures point out very clearly, "Cursed is everyone who at any time breaks a single one of these laws that are written in God's Book of the Law." 11Consequently, it is clear that no one can ever win God's favor by trying to keep the Jewish laws because God has said that the only way we can be right in his sight is by faith. As the prophet Habakkuk says it, "The man who finds life will find it through trusting God." 12How different from this way of faith is the way of law, which says that a man is saved by obeying every law of God, without one slip. 13But Christ has bought us out from under the doom of that impossible system by taking the curse for our wrongdoing upon himself. For it is written in the Scripture, "Anyone who is hanged on a tree is cursed" [as Jesus was hung upon a wooden cross].

14Now God can bless the Gentiles, too, with this same blessing he promised to Abraham; and all of us as Christians can have the promised Holy Spirit through this faith.

15Dear brothers, even in everyday life a promise made by one man to another, if it is written down and signed, cannot be changed. He cannot decide afterward to do something else instead.

16Now, God gave some promises to Abraham and his Child. And notice that it doesn't say the promises were to his *children,* as it would if all his sons—all the Jews—were being spoken of, but to his *Child*—and that, of course, means Christ. 17Here's what I am trying to say: God's promise to save through faith—and God wrote this promise down and signed it—could not be canceled or changed four hundred and thirty years later when God gave the Ten Commandments. 18If *obeying those laws* could save us, then it is obvious that this would be a different way of gaining God's favor than Abraham's way, for he simply accepted God's promise.

19Well then, why were the laws given? They were added after the promise was given, to show men how guilty they are of breaking God's laws. But this system of law was to last only until the coming of Christ, the Child to whom God's promise was made. (And there is this further difference. God gave his laws to angels to give to Moses, who then gave them to the people; 20but when God gave his promise to Abraham, he did it by himself alone, without angels or Moses as go-betweens.)

21,22Well then, are God's laws and God's promises against each other? Of course not! If we could be saved by his laws, then God would not have had to give us a different way to get out of the grip of sin—for the Scriptures insist we are all

Family Devotions

☐ DEVOTION 323
PATIENCE

Read Galatians 5:22–6:1

Patience
Memory Verse

Now as for you, dear brothers who are waiting for the Lord's return, be patient, like a farmer who waits until the autumn for his precious harvest to ripen.
James 5:7

"It seems to me that if Mary Jane really meant it when she said she accepted Jesus, she'd be a little nicer to the kids at school," Barbara told her mother as they finished the dishes. "We've been studying the fruit of the Spirit in Sunday school, but she acts like she never heard of them." As Barbara hung up the dishcloth, her yellow kitten jumped up on the counter. "Buddy! Get down from there!" screeched Barbara. Buddy jumped down and walked calmly across the room as if nothing had happened. "Oh!" sputtered Barbara. "That cat makes me mad! Now I've got to wash the counter again!"

"Now, now," sympathized Barbara's mother. "No need to get so upset. Just keep after Buddy, and he'll eventually learn that he's not allowed up there."

Barbara quickly wiped the counter, then tromped outside and plopped down on the steps. "Sometimes I wish I didn't even have a cat," she pouted. "He can be such a pain!"

"Honey," said Mom, sitting down next to her daughter, "you know you wouldn't give Buddy up. But you have to remember that he's still a baby. You need to train him and teach him the rules."

Purring loudly, Buddy rubbed up against Barbara, and she softened a little. "Like you did for me?" she asked.

"Yes," agreed Mom, "and like older Christians do for new Christians. Those who are babies in Christ can't be expected to immediately know the whole Bible or to do everything right. We must have lots of patience and teach them. Then they'll learn to be strong Christians!"

Barbara reached down and picked up Buddy. "I guess I can't expect you to know the rules completely yet," she murmured to him, "and I guess I shouldn't expect quite so much of Mary Jane, either. I'll try to be more patient."

How About You?
Do you expect too much from those who are new Christians? Remember that one fruit of the Spirit is patience. As you pray for new Christians, also be patient with them. As you develop patience, you will be growing in the Lord along with them. *V. R.*

• For the next devotional, turn to page 1141. • For the next devotional on *PATIENCE*, turn to page 1175.
• For notes on *PATIENCE*, see pages 35, 242, 329, and 502.

its prisoners. The only way out is through faith in Jesus Christ; the way of escape is open to all who believe him.

23Until Christ came we were guarded by the law, kept in protective custody, so to speak, until we could believe in the coming Savior.

24Let me put it another way. The Jewish laws were our teacher and guide until Christ came to give us right standing with God through our faith. 25But now that Christ has come, we don't need those laws any longer to guard us and lead us to him. 26For now we are all children of God through faith in Jesus Christ, 27and we who have been baptized into union with Christ are enveloped by him. 28We are no longer Jews or Greeks or slaves or free men or even merely men or women, but we are all the same—we are Christians; we are one in Christ Jesus. 29And now that we are Christ's we are the true descendants of Abraham, and all of God's promises to him belong to us.

4 Paul's Concern for the Galatians

But remember this, that if a father dies and leaves great wealth for his little son, that child is not much better off than a slave until he grows up, even though he actually owns everything his father had. 2He has to do what his guardians and managers tell him to until he reaches whatever age his father set.

3And that is the way it was with us before Christ came. We were slaves to Jewish laws and rituals, for we thought they could save us. 4But when the right time came, the time God decided on, he sent his Son, born of a woman, born as a Jew, 5to buy freedom for us who were slaves to the law so that he could adopt us as his very own sons. 6And because we are his sons, God has sent the Spirit of his Son into our hearts, so now we can rightly speak of God as our dear Father. 7 Now we are no longer slaves but God's own sons. And since we are his sons, everything he has belongs to us, for that is the way God planned.

8Before you Gentiles knew God you were slaves to so-called gods that did not even exist. 9And now that you have found God (or I should say, now that God has found you), how can it be that you want to go back again and become slaves once more to another poor, weak, useless religion of trying to get to heaven by obeying God's laws?

10You are trying to find favor with God by what you do or don't do on certain days or months or seasons or years. 11I fear for you. I am afraid that all my hard work for you was worth nothing.

12Dear brothers, please feel as I do about these things, for I am as free from these chains as you used to be. You did not despise me then when I first preached to you, 13even though I was sick when I first brought you the Good News of Christ. 14But even though my sickness was revolting to you, you didn't reject me and turn me away. No, you took me in and cared for me as though I were an angel from God or even Jesus Christ himself.

15Where is that happy spirit that we felt together then? For in those days I know you would gladly have taken out your own eyes and given them to replace mine if that would have helped me.

16And now have I become your enemy because I tell you the truth?

17Those false teachers who are so anxious to win your favor are not doing it for your good. What they are trying to do is to shut you off from me so that you will pay more attention to them. 18It is a fine thing when people are nice to you with good motives and sincere hearts, especially if they aren't doing it just when I am with you! 19Oh, my children, how you are hurting me! I am once again suffering for you the pains of a mother waiting for her child to be born—longing for the time when you will finally be filled with Christ. 20How I wish I could be there with you right now and not have to reason with you like this, for at this distance I frankly don't know what to do.

21Listen to me, you friends who think you have to obey the Jewish laws to be saved: Why don't you find out what those laws really mean? 22For it is written that Abraham had two sons, one from his slave-wife and one from his freeborn wife. 23There was nothing unusual about the birth of the slave-wife's baby. But the baby of the freeborn wife was born only after God had especially promised he would come.

24,25Now this true story is an illustration of God's two ways of helping people. One way was by giving them his laws to obey. He did this on Mount Sinai, when he gave the Ten Commandments to Moses. Mount Sinai, by the way, is called "Mount Hagar" by the Arabs—and in my illustration, Abraham's slave-wife Hagar represents Jerusalem, the mother-city of the Jews, the center of that system of trying to please God by trying to obey the Commandments; and the Jews, who try to follow that system, are her slave children. 26But our mother-city is the heavenly Jerusalem, and she is not a slave to Jewish laws.

27That is what Isaiah meant when he prophesied, "Now you

ACCEPTING OTHERS 3:28 It's natural to feel uncomfortable around those who are different from us and to prefer to be with those who resemble us. But when we allow our differences to separate us from our fellow believers, we are disobeying clear biblical teaching. Make a point of seeking out and appreciating people who are not just like you and your friends. You may find that you and they have a lot in common. **To begin the series of devotionals on ACCEPTING OTHERS, turn to page 207.**

Family Devotions

☐ DEVOTION 324
CULTIVATING GODLY ATTITUDES

Read Galatians 6:4

One Saturday morning, Molly was moping around the house. Mother noticed and said, "Why is my favorite nine-year-old so sad today?"

"Oh, Mom," Molly whimpered, "I'm no good at anything! I can't sing like Cheryl, and I can't play the piano half as good as she does!"

"No good, huh?" her mother replied. "Well, I know one thing you're very good at, and that's helping me to get lunch on the table." Molly smiled and seemed to forget her blue mood while they ate.

After lunch, much to the surprise of Molly and her mother, Dad sat down on the piano bench. He began to bang on the piano keys as he playfully sang in an off-key voice. Soon Molly and Mother were laughing hard. Molly put her hands over her ears as she shouted, "Daddy, please! Give our ears a break!"

As Dad stopped playing, Mother said, "Remember, Molly, you said you couldn't play the piano very well. But it all depends on what you compare yourself to. Compared to Daddy, you play the piano very well."

Molly still wasn't convinced. "That doesn't matter. I'm not good at sports like Daddy is, and I can't sing high notes like Cheryl does either!"

"Oh, Molly," Mother chuckled, "don't compare yourself with others so much! You're much better at sports than I ever was! And Mrs. Pierce told me just last week that you are one of the best altos in the junior choir."

"Molly, I know a verse from the Bible that you need to learn," said Dad. As Molly looked at Galatians 6:4, Dad pointed out that God wants his children to develop their own talents and not waste their time comparing themselves with their friends. Molly promised to learn the verse, and Mother and Dad promised to pray for her.

Cultivating Godly Attitudes
Memory Verse

Whatever you do or say, let it be as a representative of the Lord Jesus, and come with him into the presence of God the Father to give him your thanks.
Colossians 3:17

How About You?
Do you want to be like someone you know, and are you constantly comparing yourself with that person? God wants you to just be you! He expects you to be a good steward with the gifts he has given you. Use them to cheerfully serve others—and him! R. P.

• For the next devotional, turn to page 1147. • For the next devotional on CULTIVATING GODLY ATTITUDES, turn to page 1163. • For notes on CULTIVATING GODLY ATTITUDES, see pages 337, 383, 472, 622, and 1216.

can rejoice, O childless woman; you can shout with joy though you never before had a child. For I am going to give you many children—more children than the slave-wife has."

28You and I, dear brothers, are the children that God promised, just as Isaac was. 29And so we who are born of the Holy Spirit are persecuted now by those who want us to keep the Jewish laws, just as Isaac, the child of promise, was persecuted by Ishmael, the slave-wife's son.

30But the Scriptures say that God told Abraham to send away the slave-wife and her son, for the slave-wife's son could not inherit Abraham's home and lands along with the free woman's son. 31Dear brothers, we are not slave children, obligated to the Jewish laws, but children of the free woman, acceptable to God because of our faith.

5 Freedom: Christ's Special Gift

So Christ has made us free. Now make sure that you stay free, and don't get all tied up again in the chains of slavery to Jewish laws and ceremonies. 2Listen to me, for this is serious: *if you are counting on circumcision and keeping the Jewish laws to make you right with God, then Christ cannot save you.* 3I'll say it again. Anyone trying to find favor with God by being circumcised must always obey every other Jewish law or perish. 4Christ is useless to you if you are counting on clearing your debt to God by keeping those laws; you are lost from God's grace.

5But we by the help of the Holy Spirit are counting on Christ's death to clear away our sins and make us right with God. 6And we to whom Christ has given eternal life don't need to worry about whether we have been circumcised or not, or whether we are obeying the Jewish ceremonies or not; for all we need is faith working through love.

7You were getting along so well. Who has interfered with you to hold you back from following the truth? 8It certainly isn't God who has done it, for he is the one who has called you to freedom in Christ. 9But it takes only one wrong person among you to infect all the others.

10I am trusting the Lord to bring you back to believing as I do about these things. God will deal with that person, whoever he is, who has been troubling and confusing you.

11Some people even say that I myself am preaching that circumcision and Jewish laws are necessary to the plan of salvation. Well, if I preached that, I would be persecuted no more—for that message doesn't offend anyone. The fact that I am still being persecuted proves that I am still preaching salvation through faith in the cross of Christ alone.

12I only wish these teachers who want you to cut yourselves by being circumcised would cut themselves off from you and leave you alone!

13For, dear brothers, you have been given freedom: not freedom to do wrong, but freedom to love and serve each other. 14For the whole Law can be summed up in this one command: "Love others as you love yourself." 15But if instead of showing love among yourselves you are always critical and catty, watch out! Beware of ruining each other.

16I advise you to obey only the Holy Spirit's instructions. He will tell you where to go and what to do, and then you won't always be doing the wrong things your evil nature wants you to. 17For we naturally love to do evil things that are just the opposite from the things that the Holy Spirit tells us to do; and the good things we want to do when the Spirit has his way with us are just the opposite of our natural desires. These two forces within us are constantly fighting each other to win control over us, and our wishes are never free from their pressures. 18When you are guided by the Holy Spirit, you need no longer force yourself to obey Jewish laws.

19But when you follow your own wrong inclinations, your lives will produce these evil results: impure thoughts, eagerness for lustful pleasure, 20idolatry, spiritism (that is, encouraging the activity of demons), hatred and fighting, jealousy and anger, constant effort to get the best for yourself, complaints and criticisms, the feeling that everyone else is wrong except those in your own little group—and there will be wrong doctrine, 21envy, murder, drunkenness, wild parties, and all that sort of thing. Let me tell you again, as I have before, that anyone living that sort of life will not inherit the Kingdom of God.

22But when the Holy Spirit controls our lives he will produce this kind of fruit in us: love, joy, peace, patience, kindness, goodness, faithfulness, 23gentleness and self-control; and here there is no conflict with Jewish laws.

24Those who belong to Christ have nailed their natural evil desires to his cross and crucified them there.

25If we are living now by the Holy Spirit's power, let us follow the Holy Spirit's leading in every part of our lives. 26Then we won't need to look for honors and popularity, which lead to jealousy and hard feelings.

6 We Reap What We Sow

Dear brothers, if a Christian is overcome by some sin, you who are godly should gently and humbly help him back onto the right path, remembering that next time it might be one of you who is in the wrong. ²Share each other's troubles and problems, and so obey our Lord's command. ³If anyone thinks he is too great to stoop to this, he is fooling himself. He is really a nobody.

⁴Let everyone be sure that he is doing his very best, for then he will have the personal satisfaction of work well done and won't need to compare himself with someone else. ⁵Each of us must bear some faults and burdens of his own. For none of us is perfect!

⁶Those who are taught the Word of God should help their teachers by paying them.

⁷Don't be misled; remember that you can't ignore God and get away with it: a man will always reap just the kind of crop he sows! ⁸If he sows to please his own wrong desires, he will be planting seeds of evil and he will surely reap a harvest of spiritual decay and death; but if he plants the good things of the Spirit, he will reap the everlasting life that the Holy Spirit gives him. ⁹And let us not get tired of doing what is right, for after a while we will reap a harvest of blessing if we don't get discouraged and give up. ¹⁰That's why whenever we can we should always be kind to everyone, and especially to our Christian brothers.

¹¹I will write these closing words in my own handwriting. See how large I have to make the letters! ¹²Those teachers of yours who are trying to convince you to be circumcised are doing it for just one reason: so that they can be popular and avoid the persecution they would get if they admitted that the cross of Christ alone can save. ¹³And even those teachers who submit to circumcision don't try to keep the other Jewish laws; but they want you to be circumcised in order that they can boast that you are their disciples.

¹⁴As for me, God forbid that I should boast about anything except the cross of our Lord Jesus Christ. Because of that cross, my interest in all the attractive things of the world was killed long ago, and the world's interest in me is also long dead. ¹⁵It doesn't make any difference now whether we have been circumcised or not; what counts is whether we really have been changed into new and different people.

¹⁶May God's mercy and peace be upon all of you who live by this principle and upon those everywhere who are really God's own.

¹⁷From now on please don't argue with me about these things, for I carry on my body the scars of the whippings and wounds from Jesus' enemies that mark me as his slave.

¹⁸Dear brothers, may the grace of our Lord Jesus Christ be with you all.

Sincerely, Paul

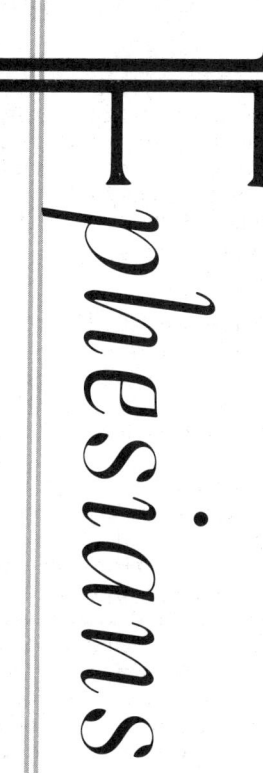

Ephesians

WHAT DO you ask God for when you pray for other people? Sometimes it's hard to think of things to pray besides "be with them" and "help them." In Ephesians, Paul shows us how to pray.

Paul wanted the people in the church to care about each other. He wanted them to learn how to live in a way that would please God. He was concerned about family relationships. He probably prayed about all these things.

Paul knew how important our prayers are. He knew that the spiritual world is real, even though we can't see it. Through prayer we win battles against enemy spiritual forces. Paul wrote about the "armor" God gives us to fight those battles.

As you read Ephesians, think about how important prayer is. And look for things you can pray about for your friends and family.

Paul: A Loyal Follower of Christ

Dear Christian friends at Ephesus, ever loyal to the Lord: This is Paul writing to you, chosen by God to be Jesus Christ's messenger. ²May his blessings and peace be yours, sent to you from God our Father and Jesus Christ our Lord.

³How we praise God, the Father of our Lord Jesus Christ, who has blessed us with every blessing in heaven because we belong to Christ.

⁴Long ago, even before he made the world, God chose us to be his very own through what Christ would do for us; he decided then to make us holy in his eyes, without a single fault—we who stand before him covered with his love. ⁵His unchanging plan has always been to adopt us into his own family by sending Jesus Christ to die for us. And he did this because he wanted to!

⁶Now all praise to God for his wonderful kindness to us and his favor that he has poured out upon us because we belong to his dearly loved Son. ⁷So overflowing is his kindness toward us that he took away all our sins through the blood

of his Son, by whom we are saved; [8]and he has showered down upon us the richness of his grace—for how well he understands us and knows what is best for us at all times.

[9]God has told us his secret reason for sending Christ, a plan he decided on in mercy long ago; [10]and this was his purpose: that when the time is ripe he will gather us all together from wherever we are—in heaven or on earth—to be with him in Christ forever. [11]Moreover, because of what Christ has done, we have become gifts to God that he delights in, for as part of God's sovereign plan we were chosen from the beginning to be his, and all things happen just as he decided long ago. [12]God's purpose in this was that we should praise God and give glory to him for doing these mighty things for us, who were the first to trust in Christ.

[13]And because of what Christ did, all you others too, who heard the Good News about how to be saved, and trusted Christ, were marked as belonging to Christ by the Holy Spirit, who long ago had been promised to all of us Christians. [14]His presence within us is God's guarantee that he really will give us all that he promised; and the Spirit's seal upon us means that God has already purchased us and that he guarantees to bring us to himself. This is just one more reason for us to praise our glorious God.

[15]That is why, ever since I heard of your strong faith in the Lord Jesus and of the love you have for Christians everywhere, [16,17]I have never stopped thanking God for you. I pray for you constantly, asking God, the glorious Father of our Lord Jesus Christ, to give you wisdom to see clearly and really understand who Christ is and all that he has done for you. [18]I pray that your hearts will be flooded with light so that you can see something of the future he has called you to share. I want you to realize that God has been made rich because we who are Christ's have been given to him! [19]I pray that you will begin to understand how incredibly great his power is to help those who believe him. It is that same mighty power [20]that raised Christ from the dead and seated him in the place of honor at God's right hand in heaven, [21]far, far above any other king or ruler or dictator or leader. Yes, his honor is far more glorious than that of anyone else either in this world or in the world to come. [22]And God has put all things under his feet and made him the supreme Head of the Church—[23]which is his body, filled with himself, the Author and Giver of everything everywhere.

2 Our Life Before and After Christ

Once you were under God's curse, doomed forever for your sins. [2]You went along with the crowd and were just like all the others, full of sin, obeying Satan, the mighty prince of the power of the air, who is at work right now in the hearts of those who are against the Lord. [3]All of us used to be just as they are, our lives expressing the evil within us, doing every wicked thing that our passions or our evil thoughts might lead us into. We started out bad, being born with evil natures, and were under God's anger just like everyone else.

[4]But God is so rich in mercy; he loved us so much [5]that even though we were spiritually dead and doomed by our sins, he gave us back our lives again when he raised Christ from the dead—only by his undeserved favor have we ever been saved—[6]and lifted us up from the grave into glory along with Christ, where we sit with him in the heavenly realms—all because of what Christ Jesus did. [7]And now God can always point to us as examples of how very, very rich his kindness is, as shown in all he has done for us through Jesus Christ.

[8]Because of his kindness, you have been saved through trusting Christ. And even trusting is not of yourselves; it too is a gift from God. [9]Salvation is not a reward for the good we have done, so none of us can take any credit for it. [10]It is God himself who has made us what we are and given us new lives from Christ Jesus; and long ages ago he planned that we should spend these lives in helping others.

[11]Never forget that once you were heathen and that you were called godless and "unclean" by the Jews. (But their hearts, too, were still unclean, even though they were going through the ceremonies and rituals of the godly, for they circumcised themselves as a sign of godliness.) [12]Remember that in those days you were living utterly apart from Christ; you were enemies of God's children, and he had promised you no help. You were lost, without God, without hope.

[13]But now you belong to Christ Jesus, and though you once were far away from God, now you have been brought very near to him because of what Jesus Christ has done for you with his blood.

RECEIVING CHRIST AS SAVIOR **2:3** The fact that all people, without exception, commit sin proves that they share in the sinful nature. Does this mean there are no good people who are not Christians? Of course not—many people do good to others. On a relative scale, many are moral, kind, keep the laws, and so on. Comparing these people to criminals, we would say they are very good indeed. But on God's absolute scale, *no one* is good. Only by accepting the forgiveness made possible by Jesus' death on the cross can we be made acceptable in God's sight. **To begin the series of devotionals on RECEIVING CHRIST AS SAVIOR, turn to page 235.**

FAMILY DEVOTIONS

☐ DEVOTION 325
FORGIVING OTHERS

Read Ephesians 4:17-32

Heidi darted out of Stacy's house, slamming the door behind her. "Some friend Stacy is!" she fumed, as she walked home. "I'm never going to play with her again!"

As she stomped up the steps to her house, Heidi stumbled and fell. She wasn't hurt, but when she picked herself up, she saw that she had torn her skirt. Tears filled her eyes, and she ran into the house to find her mother. "Oh, Mom," she cried, "this is the very worst day of my life! I fell on the steps and tore my best skirt. Just look at it!"

Mom examined the skirt carefully. "This isn't a bad tear," she said. "I'll mend it right now, before it gets worse, and you'll never know it was torn." Heidi changed clothes, and her mother got busy with needle and thread.

As Mom worked, Heidi told her about the quarrel with Stacy. "You should have heard what she called me," whined Heidi.

"And what did you call her?" Mom asked.

"Uh—well, I don't exactly remember what I said," stammered Heidi. "I was pretty mad."

Soon the ripped skirt was mended. "It's just as good as new," Mom told Heidi, holding up the skirt. "I'm glad you showed it to me right away, though. If it had ripped further, it would have been a lot harder to fix."

"Thanks, Mom," said Heidi, managing a smile. "I'm glad you could mend it. This is my favorite skirt."

"And what about your friendship with Stacy, your favorite friend?" Mom asked. "Shouldn't that be mended, too?" Heidi looked down at the floor. "Isn't that a great deal more important than fixing your ripped skirt?" persisted Mom. "Why don't you go and mend that ripped friendship before it gets worse?" Slowly Heidi nodded.

Forgiving Others Memory Verse

Be gentle and ready to forgive; never hold grudges. Remember, the Lord forgave you, so you must forgive others.
Colossians 3:13

How About You?

Have you had a quarrel with a friend or relative? Even if your feelings were hurt, isn't your relationship with that person important enough for you to forgive and just forget about the hurt? Perhaps that will be easier to do if you'll remember how much God has forgiven you. Besides, you probably need to ask for forgiveness yourself, since it takes two to quarrel. Mend the torn relationship quickly—while you can still do it. M. R. P.

• For the next devotional, turn to page 1149.   • For the next devotional on FORGIVING OTHERS, turn to page 1165.
• For notes on FORGIVING OTHERS, see pages 273, 356, 586, and 822.

¹⁴For Christ himself is our way of peace. He has made peace between us Jews and you Gentiles by making us all one family, breaking down the wall of contempt that used to separate us. ¹⁵By his death he ended the angry resentment between us, caused by the Jewish laws that favored the Jews and excluded the Gentiles, for he died to annul that whole system of Jewish laws. Then he took the two groups that had been opposed to each other and made them parts of himself; thus he fused us together to become one new person, and at last there was peace. ¹⁶As parts of the same body, our anger against each other has disappeared, for both of us have been reconciled to God. And so the feud ended at last at the cross. ¹⁷And he has brought this Good News of peace to you Gentiles who were very far away from him, and to us Jews who were near. ¹⁸Now all of us, whether Jews or Gentiles, may come to God the Father with the Holy Spirit's help because of what Christ has done for us.

¹⁹Now you are no longer strangers to God and foreigners to heaven, but you are members of God's very own family, citizens of God's country, and you belong in God's household with every other Christian.

²⁰What a foundation you stand on now: the apostles and the prophets; and the cornerstone of the building is Jesus Christ himself! ²¹We who believe are carefully joined together with Christ as parts of a beautiful, constantly growing temple for God. ²²And you also are joined with him and with each other by the Spirit and are part of this dwelling place of God.

3 Salvation Is for Everyone

I, Paul, the servant of Christ, am here in jail because of you—for preaching that you Gentiles are a part of God's house. ²,³No doubt you already know that God has given me this special work of showing God's favor to you Gentiles, as I briefly mentioned before in one of my letters. God himself showed me this secret plan of his, that the Gentiles, too, are included in his kindness. ⁴I say this to explain to you how I know about these things. ⁵In olden times God did not share this plan with his people, but now he has revealed it by the Holy Spirit to his apostles and prophets.

⁶And this is the secret: that the Gentiles will have their full share with the Jews in all the riches inherited by God's sons; both are invited to belong to his Church, and all of God's promises of mighty blessings through Christ apply to them both when they accept the Good News about Christ and what he has done for them. ⁷God has given me the wonderful privilege of telling everyone about this plan of his; and he has given me his power and special ability to do it well.

⁸Just think! Though I did nothing to deserve it, and though I am the most useless Christian there is, yet I was the one chosen for this special joy of telling the Gentiles the Glad News of the endless treasures available to them in Christ; ⁹and to explain to everyone that God is the Savior of the Gentiles too, just as he who made all things had secretly planned from the very beginning.

¹⁰And his reason? To show to all the rulers in heaven how perfectly wise he is when all of his family—Jews and Gentiles alike—are seen to be joined together in his Church ¹¹in just the way he had always planned it through Jesus Christ our Lord.

¹²Now we can come fearlessly right into God's presence, assured of his glad welcome when we come with Christ and trust in him.

¹³So please don't lose heart at what they are doing to me here. It is for you I am suffering, and you should feel honored and encouraged.

¹⁴,¹⁵When I think of the wisdom and scope of his plan, I fall down on my knees and pray to the Father of all the great family of God—some of them already in heaven and some down here on earth—¹⁶that out of his glorious, unlimited resources he will give you the mighty inner strengthening of his Holy Spirit. ¹⁷And I pray that Christ will be more and more at home in your hearts, living within you as you trust in him. May your roots go down deep into the soil of God's marvelous love; ¹⁸,¹⁹and may you be able to feel and understand, as all God's children should, how long, how wide, how deep, and how high his love really is; and to experience this love for yourselves, though it is so great that you will never see the end of it or fully know or understand it. And so at last you will be filled up with God himself.

²⁰Now glory be to God, who by his mighty power at work within us is able to do far more than we would ever dare to ask or even dream of—infinitely beyond our highest prayers, desires, thoughts, or hopes. ²¹May he be given glory forever and ever through endless ages because of his master plan of salvation for the Church through Jesus Christ.

4 Special Abilities

I beg you—I, a prisoner here in jail for serving the Lord—to live and act in a way worthy of those who have been chosen for such wonderful blessings as these. ²Be humble and gentle. Be patient with each other, making allowance for each other's faults because of your love. ³Try always to be led along together by the Holy Spirit and so be at peace with one another.

FAMILY DEVOTIONS

☐ *DEVOTION 326*
STANDING FOR RIGHTEOUSNESS

Read Ephesians 5:14-21

Standing for Righteousness Memory Verse

For the eyes of the Lord search back and forth across the whole earth, looking for people whose hearts are perfect toward him, so that he can show his great power in helping them.
2 Chronicles 16:9

Aaron was excited as he and his father took their places on the tree stand. It was the first time Dad had taken him bow hunting. As Aaron squinted into the low sun, he noticed rows of standing corn in the field nearby. Glancing around, his gaze froze on something large and black. Black? Deer are tan, so what was this thing? Aaron shivered with something close to fear. He nudged his father, and whispered, "Dad, there's something out there, and it's coming this way!"

Just then the animal stood on its hind legs, revealing itself to be a large black bear. It raised its head and sniffed the air. Aaron and Dad stood still in shocked amazement. This was a rare sight in that area. Still sniffing, the bear cautiously moved to the edge of the woods. Checking for danger, it sat on its haunches where field and woods met, gazing longingly at the corn. After several minutes, the bear ventured cautiously toward the field. Soon, however, it returned to the woods.

Driving home later, Dad and Aaron talked about the bear's interesting behavior. "Did you see how much it wanted to get that corn?" asked Aaron.

"Yes, but apparently it sensed danger, and it was too smart to take a chance by staying out in the open," replied Dad. "We could take a lesson from that bear." Then he quoted Ephesians 5:15.

"What does that mean, Dad?" asked Aaron.

"Well, it means that, as Christians, we are to be very careful how we live and where we go—looking all around and being alert to every temptation—so we don't get trapped by some sin or trick of the devil," explained Dad.

When they got home, Mother asked about their hunting trip. "Don't make up some big story about hundreds of deer," she joked. "Just tell me the bare facts."

Dad grinned and winked at Aaron. "That's what we'll tell you," he replied. "Just the 'bear' facts."

How About You?
Are you foolish about the way you live, or are you careful in all that you do? Do you stay away from places where you might be tempted to do wrong? Do you avoid people who encourage you to sin? Be careful to live as God wants you to live. Be wise. *L. A. T.*

• For the next devotional, turn to page 1151. • To start the next topic, turn to page 83. • For notes on *STANDING FOR RIGHTEOUSNESS*, see pages 62, 298, 371, 678, and 948.

[4] We are all parts of one body, we have the same Spirit, and we have all been called to the same glorious future. [5] For us there is only one Lord, one faith, one baptism, [6] and we all have the same God and Father who is over us all and in us all, and living through every part of us. [7] However, Christ has given each of us special abilities—whatever he wants us to have out of his rich storehouse of gifts.

[8] The psalmist tells about this, for he says that when Christ returned triumphantly to heaven after his resurrection and victory over Satan, he gave generous gifts to men. [9] Notice that it says he returned to heaven. This means that he had first come down from the heights of heaven, far down to the lowest parts of the earth. [10] The same one who came down is the one who went back up, that he might fill all things everywhere with himself, from the very lowest to the very highest.

[11] Some of us have been given special ability as apostles; to others he has given the gift of being able to preach well; some have special ability in winning people to Christ, helping them to trust him as their Savior; still others have a gift for caring for God's people as a shepherd does his sheep, leading and teaching them in the ways of God.

[12] Why is it that he gives us these special abilities to do certain things best? It is that God's people will be equipped to do better work for him, building up the Church, the body of Christ, to a position of strength and maturity; [13] until finally we all believe alike about our salvation and about our Savior, God's Son, and all become full-grown in the Lord—yes, to the point of being filled full with Christ.

[14] Then we will no longer be like children, forever changing our minds about what we believe because someone has told us something different or has cleverly lied to us and made the lie sound like the truth. [15,16] Instead, we will lovingly follow the truth at all times—speaking truly, dealing truly, living truly—and so become more and more in every way like Christ who is the Head of his body, the Church. Under his direction, the whole body is fitted together perfectly, and each part in its own special way helps the other parts, so that the whole body is healthy and growing and full of love.

[17,18] Let me say this, then, speaking for the Lord: Live no longer as the unsaved do, for they are blinded and confused. Their closed hearts are full of darkness; they are far away from the life of God because they have shut their minds against him, and they cannot understand his ways. [19] They don't care anymore about right and wrong and have given themselves over to impure ways. They stop at nothing, being driven by their evil minds and reckless lusts.

[20] But that isn't the way Christ taught you! [21] If you have really heard his voice and learned from him the truths concerning himself, [22] then throw off your old evil nature—the old you that was a partner in your evil ways—rotten through and through, full of lust and sham.

[23] Now your attitudes and thoughts must all be constantly changing for the better. [24] Yes, you must be a new and different person, holy and good. Clothe yourself with this new nature.

[25] Stop lying to each other; tell the truth, for we are parts of each other and when we lie to each other we are hurting ourselves. [26] If you are angry, don't sin by nursing your grudge. Don't let the sun go down with you still angry—get over it quickly; [27] for when you are angry, you give a mighty foothold to the devil.

[28] If anyone is stealing he must stop it and begin using those hands of his for honest work so he can give to others in need. [29] Don't use bad language. Say only what is good and helpful to those you are talking to, and what will give them a blessing.

[30] Don't cause the Holy Spirit sorrow by the way you live. Remember, he is the one who marks you to be present on that day when salvation from sin will be complete.

[31] Stop being mean, bad-tempered, and angry. Quarreling, harsh words, and dislike of others should have no place in your lives. [32] Instead, be kind to each other, tenderhearted, forgiving one another, just as God has forgiven you because you belong to Christ.

5 Learn What Pleases God

Follow God's example in everything you do just as a much loved child imitates his father. [2] Be full of love for others, following the example of Christ who loved you and gave himself to God as a sacrifice to take away your sins. And God was pleased, for Christ's love for you was like sweet perfume to him.

[3] Let there be no sex sin, impurity or greed among you. Let no one be able to accuse you of any such things. [4] Dirty stories, foul talk, and coarse jokes—these are not for you. Instead, remind each other of God's goodness, and be thankful.

[5] You can be sure of this: The Kingdom of Christ and of God will never belong to anyone who is impure or greedy, for a greedy person is really an idol worshiper—he loves and worships the good things of this life more than God. [6] Don't be fooled by those who try to excuse these sins, for the terrible wrath of God is upon all those who do

Family Devotions

☐ **Devotion 327**
Respecting Others

Read Ephesians 6:1-4

Mary scuffed her shoe in the dirt beneath the swing as a classmate, Joan, sat down beside her. "Hi, Mary. Would you like to jump rope with me?" asked Joan.

Mary scowled. "No, thanks," she said gruffly.

"Is something wrong?" asked Joan.

"I just don't like it here," replied Mary. "All my friends are at my old school across town." She pushed off with her foot and began to swing.

Joan watched the back-and-forth rhythm of Mary's swing for a few moments and then joined her. "Why don't you still go there?" asked Joan.

"We moved because our family was getting too big for our house," replied Mary, "and now we're in this district. I want to live with my grandma and stay in my old school, but my parents say they want me with them."

"Oh. That reminds me of something I learned in Sunday school last week. Do you go to church and Sunday school?"

Mary nodded as she let her swing come to a stop. "What did you learn?"

"It was one of the Ten Commandments. It says, 'Honor your father and mother,'" Joan answered, letting her swing stop.

Mary had recently learned the Ten Commandments in Sunday school, too. "But I obey them," said Mary. "I'm here, aren't I?"

Joan fingered her braid. "Well, my teacher said *honor* means to respect your parents," she said.

Mary scowled as she drew a pattern in the dust with her shoe. She felt guilty—she knew her attitude was wrong. Finally she looked up. "I guess I could always make some new friends," she said. "Do you still want to jump rope?"

Respecting Others
Memory Verse

You must love the Lord your God with all your heart, and with all your soul, and with all your strength, and with all your mind. And you must love your neighbor just as much as you love yourself.
Luke 10:27

How About You?

Do you honor your parents as well as obey them? Or do you obey them just so you won't get in trouble? Do you grumble and complain when they tell you to do something? God gave you parents to guide you and care for you. Thank God for them. And thank them for caring for you. V. M.

• For the next devotional, turn to page 1157. • To start the next topic, turn to page 17. • For notes on *Respecting Others*, see pages 322, 382, 1088, and 1218.

them. ⁷Don't even associate with such people. ⁸For though once your heart was full of darkness, now it is full of light from the Lord, and your behavior should show it! ⁹Because of this light within you, you should do only what is good and right and true.

¹⁰Learn as you go along what pleases the Lord. ¹¹Take no part in the worthless pleasures of evil and darkness, but instead, rebuke and expose them. ¹²It would be shameful even to mention here those pleasures of darkness that the ungodly do. ¹³But when you expose them, the light shines in upon their sin and shows it up, and when they see how wrong they really are, some of them may even become children of light! ¹⁴That is why God says in the Scriptures, "Awake, O sleeper, and rise up from the dead; and Christ shall give you light."

¹⁵,¹⁶So be careful how you act; these are difficult days. Don't be fools; be wise: make the most of every opportunity you have for doing good. ¹⁷Don't act thoughtlessly, but try to find out and do whatever the Lord wants you to. ¹⁸Don't drink too much wine, for many evils lie along that path; be filled instead with the Holy Spirit and controlled by him.

¹⁹Talk with each other much about the Lord, quoting psalms and hymns and singing sacred songs, making music in your hearts to the Lord. ²⁰Always give thanks for everything to our God and Father in the name of our Lord Jesus Christ.

²¹Honor Christ by submitting to each other. ²²You wives must submit to your husbands' leadership in the same way you submit to the Lord. ²³For a husband is in charge of his wife in the same way Christ is in charge of his body the Church. (He gave his very life to take care of it and be its Savior!) ²⁴So you wives must willingly obey your husbands in everything, just as the Church obeys Christ.

²⁵And you husbands, show the same kind of love to your wives as Christ showed to the Church when he died for her, ²⁶to make her holy and clean, washed by baptism and God's Word; ²⁷so that he could give her to himself as a glorious Church without a single spot or wrinkle or any other blemish, being holy and without a single fault. ²⁸That is how husbands should treat their wives, loving them as parts of themselves. For since a man and his wife are now one, a man is really doing himself a favor and loving himself when he loves his wife! ²⁹,³⁰No one hates his own body but lovingly cares for it, just as Christ cares for his body the Church, of which we are parts.

³¹(That the husband and wife are one body is proved by the Scripture, which says, "A man must leave his father and mother when he marries so that he can be perfectly joined to his wife, and the two shall be one.") ³²I know this is hard to understand, but it is an illustration of the way we are parts of the body of Christ.

³³So again I say, a man must love his wife as a part of himself; and the wife must see to it that she deeply respects her husband—obeying, praising, and honoring him.

6 Family Advice

Children, obey your parents; this is the right thing to do because God has placed them in authority over you. ²Honor your father and mother. This is the first of God's Ten Commandments that ends with a promise. ³And this is the promise: that if you honor your father and mother, yours will be a long life, full of blessing.

⁴And now a word to you parents. Don't keep on scolding and nagging your children, making them angry and resentful. Rather, bring them up with the loving discipline the Lord himself approves, with suggestions and godly advice.

⁵Slaves, obey your masters; be eager to give them your very best. Serve them as you would Christ. ⁶,⁷Don't work hard only when your master is watching and then shirk when he isn't looking; work hard and with gladness all the time, as though working for Christ, doing the will of God with all your hearts. ⁸Remember, the Lord will pay you for each good thing you do, whether you are slave or free.

⁹And you slave owners must treat your slaves right, just as I have told them to treat you. Don't keep threatening them; remember, you yourselves are slaves to Christ; you have the same Master they do, and he has no favorites.

¹⁰Last of all I want to remind you that your strength must come from the Lord's mighty power within you. ¹¹Put on all of God's armor so that you will be able to stand safe against all strategies and tricks of Satan. ¹²For we are not fighting against people made of flesh and blood, but against persons without bodies—the evil rulers of the unseen world, those mighty satanic beings and great evil princes of darkness who rule this world; and against huge numbers of wicked spirits in the spirit world.

¹³So use every piece of God's armor to resist the enemy whenever he attacks, and when it is all over, you will still be standing up.

¹⁴But to do this, you will need the strong belt of truth and the breastplate of God's approval. ¹⁵Wear shoes that are able to speed you on as you preach the Good News of peace with God. ¹⁶In every battle you will need faith as your shield to stop the fiery arrows aimed at you by Satan. ¹⁷And you will need the helmet of salvation and the sword of the Spirit—which is the Word of God.

¹⁸Pray all the time. Ask God for anything in line

with the Holy Spirit's wishes. Plead with him, reminding him of your needs, and keep praying earnestly for all Christians everywhere. [19]Pray for me, too, and ask God to give me the right words as I boldly tell others about the Lord and as I explain to them that his salvation is for the Gentiles too. [20]I am in chains now for preaching this message from God. But pray that I will keep on speaking out boldly for him even here in prison, as I should.

[21]Tychicus, who is a much-loved brother and faithful helper in the Lord's work, will tell you all about how I am getting along. [22]I am sending him to you for just this purpose: to let you know how we are and be encouraged by his report.

[23]May God give peace to you, my Christian brothers, and love, with faith from God the Father and the Lord Jesus Christ. [24]May God's grace and blessing be upon all who sincerely love our Lord Jesus Christ.

Sincerely, Paul

Philippians

WHAT WOULD you give up in order to have a relationship with Jesus? Would you give up your family? Your reputation or popularity? Your money or job? Your health?

The apostle Paul gave up all these things to have Jesus in his life. He came from a family that all the Jews looked up to. He was educated and had influence in the synagogues.

When Paul gave his life to Jesus, he gave up teaching Jewish law, lost his influence, and realized that his family background wasn't important. When he started teaching about Jesus, he was beaten up and persecuted.

Paul wrote in Philippians that nothing could compare to his relationship with Jesus. *Nothing* in his life was as important as that was. His life's goal was to know Jesus better and to be like him. Paul put everything he had into reaching that goal.

How can you make your life's goal more like Paul's? As you read Philippians, look for ways to make knowing and serving Jesus your goal.

Paul's Prayer: Keep Growing

From: Paul and Timothy, slaves of Jesus Christ.

To: The pastors and deacons and all the Christians in the city of Philippi.

²May God bless you all. Yes, I pray that God our Father and the Lord Jesus Christ will give each of you his fullest blessings and his peace in your hearts and your lives.

³All my prayers for you are full of praise to God! ⁴When I pray for you, my heart is full of joy ⁵because of all your wonderful help in making known the Good News about Christ from the time you first heard it until now. ⁶And I am sure that God who began the good work within you will keep right on helping you grow in his grace until his task within you is finally finished on that day when Jesus Christ returns.

⁷How natural it is that I should feel as I do about you, for you have a very special place in my heart. We have shared together the blessings of God, both when I was in prison and when I was out, defending the truth and telling others

about Christ. ⁸Only God knows how deep is my love and longing for you—with the tenderness of Jesus Christ. ⁹My prayer for you is that you will overflow more and more with love for others, and at the same time keep on growing in spiritual knowledge and insight, ¹⁰for I want you always to see clearly the difference between right and wrong, and to be inwardly clean, no one being able to criticize you from now until our Lord returns. ¹¹May you always be doing those good, kind things that show you are a child of God, for this will bring much praise and glory to the Lord.

¹²And I want you to know this, dear brothers: Everything that has happened to me here has been a great boost in getting out the Good News concerning Christ. ¹³For everyone around here, including all the soldiers over at the barracks, knows that I am in chains simply because I am a Christian. ¹⁴And because of my imprisonment, many of the Christians here seem to have lost their fear of chains! Somehow my patience has encouraged them, and they have become more and more bold in telling others about Christ.

¹⁵Some, of course, are preaching the Good News because they are jealous of the way God has used me. They want reputations as fearless preachers! But others have purer motives, ¹⁶,¹⁷preaching because they love me, for they know that the Lord has brought me here to use me to defend the Truth. And some preach to make me jealous, thinking that their success will add to my sorrows here in jail! ¹⁸But whatever their motive for doing it, the fact remains that the Good News about Christ is being preached, and I am glad.

¹⁹I am going to keep on being glad, for I know that as you pray for me, and as the Holy Spirit helps me, this is all going to turn out for my good. ²⁰For I live in eager expectation and hope that I will never do anything that will cause me to be ashamed of myself but that I will always be ready to speak out boldly for Christ while I am going through all these trials here, just as I have in the past; and that I will always be an honor to Christ, whether I live or whether I must die. ²¹For to me, living means opportunities for Christ, and dying—well, that's better yet! ²²But if living will give me more opportunities to win people to Christ, then I really don't know which is better, to live or die! ²³Sometimes I want to live, and at other times I don't, for I long to go and be with Christ. How much happier for *me* than being here! ²⁴But the fact is that I can be of more help to *you* by staying!

²⁵Yes, I am still needed down here, and so I feel certain I will be staying on earth a little longer, to help you grow and become happy in your faith; ²⁶my staying will make you glad and give you reason to glorify Christ Jesus for keeping me safe when I return to visit you again.

²⁷But whatever happens to me, remember always to live as Christians should, so that whether I ever see you again or not, I will keep on hearing good reports that you are standing side by side with one strong purpose—to tell the Good News ²⁸fearlessly, no matter what your enemies may do. They will see this as a sign of their downfall, but for you it will be a clear sign from God that he is with you, and that he has given you eternal life with him. ²⁹For to you has been given the privilege not only of trusting him but also of suffering for him. ³⁰We are in this fight together. You have seen me suffer for him in the past; and I am still in the midst of a great and terrible struggle now, as you know so well.

2 A Christlike Attitude

Is there any such thing as Christians cheering each other up? Do you love me enough to want to help me? Does it mean anything to you that we are brothers in the Lord, sharing the same Spirit? Are your hearts tender and sympathetic at all? ²Then make me truly happy by loving each other and agreeing wholeheartedly with each other, working together with one heart and mind and purpose.

³Don't be selfish; don't live to make a good impression on others. Be humble, thinking of others as better than yourself. ⁴Don't just think about your own affairs, but be interested in others, too, and in what they are doing.

⁵Your attitude should be the kind that was shown us by Jesus Christ, ⁶who, though he was God, did not demand and cling to his rights as God, ⁷but laid aside his mighty power and glory, taking the disguise of a slave and becoming like men. ⁸And he humbled himself even further, going so far as actually to die a criminal's death on a cross.

⁹Yet it was because of this that God raised him up to the heights of heaven and gave him a name which is above every other name, ¹⁰that at the name of Jesus every knee shall bow in

---

ENCOURAGING OTHERS **1:3-11** Paul consistently prayed for his friends at Philippi. Although they were separated from each other, Paul said the Philippians had a very special place in his heart because of all they had shared together. We too should pray consistently for others, especially for those with whom we share in God's blessings—our brothers and sisters in Christ. In this way we can be an encouragement to them. **To begin the series of devotionals on ENCOURAGING OTHERS, turn to page 705.**

Family Devotions

☐ *Devotion 329*
True Joy

Read Philippians 2:14-18

True Joy
Memory Verse

Always be full of joy in the Lord; I say it again, rejoice!
Philippians 4:4

"Peter, don't stop practicing your trumpet yet! You've only been playing for about ten minutes," Mrs. Nelson called from the kitchen.

"But Mom, I've played each of the songs."

"Then play them each again and again, young man. You promised you would practice thirty minutes every day, without arguing, if we let you join the band," his mother replied.

"But I never get any better at it," Peter grumbled as he picked up the trumpet.

"Peter," said Mom, "some things take lots and lots of practice to be able to do them well. Nothing worthwhile in life comes simply."

After dinner that night, the Nelson family read from the letter to the Philippians during family devotions. Then Dad said, "Did either of you children notice a theme to the verses we read?"

Nine-year-old Sara knew. "The same words are used over again and again—*joy* and *rejoice!*"

"Right!" Dad agreed. Then addressing Peter, he asked, "Son, why do you suppose Paul repeated those words—*joy* and *rejoice*—so much?"

"I don't know," Peter answered.

"Maybe joy is a bit like trumpet playing, Peter," Mom suggested. "Maybe it takes practice. We have to practice being joyful over and over, even though we may not feel like being joyful. Some day in the future, rejoicing will get easier for us, just like your trumpet playing will get easier for you. Let's all start practicing joy in this house, OK?"

As Dad closed their discussion with prayer, Peter determined in his heart to practice his trumpet *and* his joy every day!

How About You?
Are you often gloomy with your family? When things go wrong do you pout and grumble? If you do, you need to practice finding something to rejoice about. R. P.

• For the next devotional, turn to page 1159. • To start the next topic, turn to page 27. • For notes on *True Joy*, see pages 532, 1024, and 1160.

heaven and on earth and under the earth, ¹¹and every tongue shall confess that Jesus Christ is Lord, to the glory of God the Father.

¹²Dearest friends, when I was there with you, you were always so careful to follow my instructions. And now that I am away you must be even more careful to do the good things that result from being saved, obeying God with deep reverence, shrinking back from all that might displease him. ¹³For God is at work within you, helping you want to obey him, and then helping you do what he wants.

¹⁴In everything you do, stay away from complaining and arguing ¹⁵so that no one can speak a word of blame against you. You are to live clean, innocent lives as children of God in a dark world full of people who are crooked and stubborn. Shine out among them like beacon lights, ¹⁶holding out to them the Word of Life.

Then when Christ returns, how glad I will be that my work among you was so worthwhile. ¹⁷And if my lifeblood is, so to speak, to be poured out over your faith, which I am offering up to God as a sacrifice—that is, if I am to die for you—even then I will be glad and will share my joy with each of you. ¹⁸For you should be happy about this, too, and rejoice with me for having this privilege of dying for you.

¹⁹If the Lord is willing, I will send Timothy to see you soon. Then when he comes back, he can cheer me up by telling me all about you and how you are getting along. ²⁰There is no one like Timothy for having a real interest in you; ²¹everyone else seems to be worrying about his own plans and not those of Jesus Christ. ²²But you know Timothy. He has been just like a son to me in helping me preach the Good News. ²³I hope to send him to you just as soon as I find out what is going to happen to me here. ²⁴And I am trusting the Lord that soon I myself may come to see you.

²⁵Meanwhile, I thought I ought to send Epaphroditus back to you. You sent him to help me in my need; well, he and I have been real brothers, working and battling side by side. ²⁶Now I am sending him home again, for he has been homesick for all of you and upset because you heard that he was ill. ²⁷And he surely was; in fact, he almost died. But God had mercy on him and on me, too, not allowing me to have this sorrow on top of everything else.

²⁸So I am all the more anxious to get him back to you again, for I know how thankful you will be to see him, and that will make me happy and lighten all my cares. ²⁹Welcome him in the Lord with great joy, and show your appreciation, ³⁰for he risked his life for the work of Christ and was at the point of death while trying to do for me the things you couldn't do because you were far away.

3

Know Him

Whatever happens, dear friends, be glad in the Lord. I never get tired of telling you this, and it is good for you to hear it again and again.

²Watch out for those wicked men—dangerous dogs, I call them—who say you must be circumcised to be saved. ³For it isn't the *cutting of our bodies* that makes us children of God; it is *worshiping him with our spirits.* That is the only true "circumcision." We Christians glory in what Christ Jesus has done for us and realize that we are helpless to save ourselves.

⁴Yet if anyone ever had reason to hope that he could save himself, it would be I. If others could be saved by what they are, certainly I could! ⁵For I went through the Jewish initiation ceremony when I was eight days old, having been born into a pure-blooded Jewish home that was a branch of the old original Benjamin family. So I was a real Jew if there ever was one! What's more, I was a member of the Pharisees who demand the strictest obedience to every Jewish law and custom. ⁶And sincere? Yes, so much so that I greatly persecuted the Church; and I tried to obey every Jewish rule and regulation right down to the very last point.

⁷But all these things that I once thought very worthwhile—now I've thrown them all away so that I can put my trust and hope in Christ alone. ⁸Yes, everything else is worthless when compared with the priceless gain of knowing Christ Jesus my Lord. I have put aside all else, counting it worth less than nothing, in order that I can have Christ, ⁹and become one with him, no longer counting on being saved by being good enough or by obeying God's laws, but by trusting Christ to save me; for God's way of making us right with himself depends on faith—counting on Christ alone. ¹⁰Now I have given up everything else—I have found it to be the only way to really know Christ and to experience the mighty power that brought him back to life again, and to find out what it means to suffer and to die with him. ¹¹So whatever it takes, I will be one who lives in the fresh newness of life of those who are alive from the dead.

¹²I don't mean to say I am perfect. I haven't learned all I should even yet, but I keep working toward that day when I will finally be all that Christ saved me for and wants me to be.

¹³No, dear brothers, I am still not all I should be, but I am bringing all my energies to bear on this one thing: Forgetting the past and looking forward to what lies ahead, ¹⁴I strain to reach the

Family Devotions

☐ *Devotion 330*
CONTENTMENT

Read Philippians 4:6-13

Contentment Memory Verse

I know how to live on almost nothing or with everything. I have learned the secret of contentment in every situation, whether it be a full stomach or hunger, plenty or want. *Philippians 4:12*

"I wish my dad had time to spend with us like yours does," Sonya complained. "He's always so busy!"

Bethany looked at the beautiful furnishings in Sonya's home. "Well, you sure have lots of nice things," she sighed. "At our house we have lots of time, but no money."

After listening to the girls complain for several minutes, Sonya's mother persuaded them to join her in making some visits for the church welcoming committee. At the first stop, a young mother invited them in. "You'll have to excuse this house," she sighed. "The children are about to drive me crazy. I'll be glad when they're all in school. Then maybe I'll have some peace and quiet." Motioning them to sit down, she continued, "It's so lonesome here. Everyone is so unfriendly." For thirty minutes Mrs. Marshall continued her tirade.

When they finally left, Bethany whistled. "Wow! I wonder if she's happy about anything."

Reluctantly, the girls followed Mother up the steps of another house. A smiling lady answered the door. "We're so happy here," Mrs. Perry bubbled to her guests. "We're thankful we found a loving church family so quickly."

On the way home, Mother spoke quietly. "There are two tents in which we can live. One is contentment, and the other is discontentment. Mrs. Marshall and Mrs. Perry moved to town about the same time. Their husbands work for the same company. They live in the same neighborhood and attend the same church. Mrs. Marshall has chosen to live in discontentment, but Mrs. Perry lives in contentment." Mother smiled, then continued, "It's not how much time or money you have that determines how happy you are. It's whether you choose to live in contentment or discontentment."

Remembering their earlier conversation, Sonya grinned at her friend. "Well, Beth, it looks like we need to move," she whispered. "We've been camping in the wrong tent!"

How About You?
Where do you live? Do you find yourself complaining about what you don't have instead of counting your blessings? If so, now is the time to move out of that state of discontentment. Determine to be content in every situation. *B. W.*

• For the next devotional, turn to page 1163. • For the next devotional on *Contentment*, turn to page 1211. • For notes on *Contentment*, see pages 542, 547, 902, and 1063.

end of the race and receive the prize for which God is calling us up to heaven because of what Christ Jesus did for us.

15 I hope all of you who are mature Christians will see eye-to-eye with me on these things, and if you disagree on some point, I believe that God will make it plain to you— 16 if you fully obey the truth you have.

17 Dear brothers, pattern your lives after mine, and notice who else lives up to my example. 18 For I have told you often before, and I say it again now with tears in my eyes, there are many who walk along the Christian road who are really enemies of the cross of Christ. 19 Their future is eternal loss, for their god is their appetite: they are proud of what they should be ashamed of; and all they think about is this life here on earth. 20 But our homeland is in heaven, where our Savior, the Lord Jesus Christ, is; and we are looking forward to his return from there. 21 When he comes back, he will take these dying bodies of ours and change them into glorious bodies like his own, using the same mighty power that he will use to conquer all else everywhere.

4 Think about the Good

Dear brother Christians, I love you and long to see you, for you are my joy and my reward for my work. My beloved friends, stay true to the Lord.

2 And now I want to plead with those two dear women, Euodias and Syntyche. Please, please, with the Lord's help, quarrel no more—be friends again. 3 And I ask you, my true teammate, to help these women, for they worked side by side with me in telling the Good News to others; and they worked with Clement, too, and the rest of my fellow workers whose names are written in the Book of Life.

4 Always be full of joy in the Lord; I say it again, rejoice! 5 Let everyone see that you are unselfish and considerate in all you do. Remember that the Lord is coming soon. 6 Don't worry about anything; instead, pray about everything; tell God your needs, and don't forget to thank him for his answers. 7 If you do this, you will experience God's peace, which is far more wonderful than the human mind can understand. His peace will keep your thoughts and your hearts quiet and at rest as you trust in Christ Jesus.

8 And now, brothers, as I close this letter, let me say this one more thing: Fix your thoughts on what is true and good and right. Think about things that are pure and lovely, and dwell on the fine, good things in others. Think about all you can praise God for and be glad about. 9 Keep putting into practice all you learned from me and saw me doing, and the God of peace will be with you.

10 How grateful I am and how I praise the Lord that you are helping me again. I know you have always been anxious to send what you could, but for a while you didn't have the chance. 11 Not that I was ever in need, for I have learned how to get along happily whether I have much or little. 12 I know how to live on almost nothing or with everything. I have learned the secret of contentment in every situation, whether it be a full stomach or hunger, plenty or want; 13 for I can do everything God asks me to with the help of Christ who gives me the strength and power. 14 But even so, you have done right in helping me in my present difficulty.

15 As you well know, when I first brought the Gospel to you and then went on my way, leaving Macedonia, only you Philippians became my partners in giving and receiving. No other church did this. 16 Even when I was over in Thessalonica you sent help twice. 17 But though I appreciate your gifts, what makes me happiest is the well-earned reward you will have because of your kindness.

18 At the moment I have all I need—more than I need! I am generously supplied with the gifts you sent me when Epaphroditus came. They are a sweet-smelling sacrifice that pleases God well. 19 And it is he who will supply all your needs from his riches in glory because of what Christ Jesus has done for us. 20 Now unto God our Father be glory forever and ever. Amen.

Sincerely, Paul

P.S. 21 Say hello for me to all the Christians there; the brothers with me send their greetings, too. 22 And all the other Christians here want to be remembered to you, especially those who work in Caesar's palace. 23 The blessings of our Lord Jesus Christ be upon your spirits

---

TRUE JOY **4:4** It seems strange that a man in prison would be telling a church to rejoice. But Paul's attitude teaches us an important lesson: our inner attitude does not have to reflect our outward circumstances. Paul was full of joy because he knew that no matter what happened to him, Jesus Christ was with him. It's easy to get discouraged about unpleasant circumstances or to take unimportant events too seriously. If you haven't been joyful lately, you may not be looking at life from the right perspective. **To begin the series of devotionals on** *TRUE JOY,* **turn to page 83.**

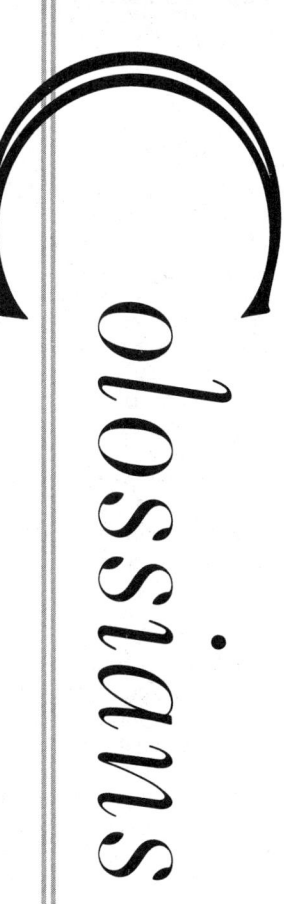

Colossians

WHAT IS life as a Christian supposed to be like? The Bible tells us that when we accept Christ, he lives in us. In Colossians, Paul wrote about what we have when we have Jesus in our lives.

Paul said that before we knew Jesus, we were far away from God. But Jesus brought us close to God. We have been made new in Christ, and all our sins are forgiven. We have been set free from following the world's ideas of how to be saved—by doing good and trying to obey a lot of rules.

Life in Christ is great. Look in Colossians for what you can expect from a relationship with Jesus.

Paul: Chosen by God

From: Paul, chosen by God to be Jesus Christ's messenger, and from Brother Timothy.

²*To:* The faithful Christian brothers—God's people—in the city of Colosse.

May God our Father shower you with blessings and fill you with his great peace.

³Whenever we pray for you, we always begin by giving thanks to God the Father of our Lord Jesus Christ, ⁴for we have heard how much you trust the Lord, and how much you love his people. ⁵And you are looking forward to the joys of heaven, and have been ever since the Gospel first was preached to you. ⁶The same Good News that came to you is going out all over the world and changing lives everywhere, just as it changed yours that very first day you heard it and understood about God's great kindness to sinners.

⁷Epaphras, our much-loved fellow worker, was the one who brought you this Good News. He is Jesus Christ's faithful slave, here to help us in your place. ⁸And he is the one who has told us about

the great love for others that the Holy Spirit has given you.

⁹So ever since we first heard about you we have kept on praying and asking God to help you understand what he wants you to do; asking him to make you wise about spiritual things; ¹⁰and asking that the way you live will always please the Lord and honor him, so that you will always be doing good, kind things for others, while all the time you are learning to know God better and better.

¹¹We are praying, too, that you will be filled with his mighty, glorious strength so that you can keep going no matter what happens—always full of the joy of the Lord, ¹²and always thankful to the Father who has made us fit to share all the wonderful things that belong to those who live in the Kingdom of light. ¹³For he has rescued us out of the darkness and gloom of Satan's kingdom and brought us into the Kingdom of his dear Son, ¹⁴who bought our freedom with his blood and forgave us all our sins.

¹⁵Christ is the exact likeness of the unseen God. He existed before God made anything at all, and, in fact, ¹⁶Christ himself is the Creator who made everything in heaven and earth, the things we can see and the things we can't; the spirit world with its kings and kingdoms, its rulers and authorities; all were made by Christ for his own use and glory. ¹⁷He was before all else began and it is his power that holds everything together. ¹⁸He is the Head of the body made up of his people—that is, his Church—which he began; and he is the Leader of all those who arise from the dead, so that he is first in everything; ¹⁹for God wanted all of himself to be in his Son.

²⁰It was through what his Son did that God cleared a path for everything to come to him—all things in heaven and on earth—for Christ's death on the cross has made peace with God for all by his blood. ²¹This includes you who were once so far away from God. You were his enemies and hated him and were separated from him by your evil thoughts and actions, yet now he has brought you back as his friends. ²²He has done this through the death on the cross of his own human body, and now as a result Christ has brought you into the very presence of God, and you are standing there before him with nothing left against you—nothing left that he could even chide you for; ²³the only condition is that you fully believe the Truth, standing in it steadfast and firm, strong in the Lord, convinced of the Good News that Jesus died for you, and never shifting from trusting him to save you. This is the wonderful news that came to each of you and is now spreading all over the world. And I, Paul, have the joy of telling it to others.

²⁴But part of my work is to suffer for you; and I am glad, for I am helping to finish up the remainder of Christ's sufferings for his body, the Church.

²⁵God has sent me to help his Church and to tell his secret plan to you Gentiles. ²⁶,²⁷He has kept this secret for centuries and generations past, but now at last it has pleased him to tell it to those who love him and live for him, and the riches and glory of his plan are for you Gentiles, too. And this is the secret: *Christ in your hearts is your only hope of glory.*

²⁸So everywhere we go we talk about Christ to all who will listen, warning them and teaching them as well as we know how. We want to be able to present each one to God, perfect because of what Christ has done for each of them. ²⁹This is my work, and I can do it only because Christ's mighty energy is at work within me.

2 A New Life in Christ

I wish you could know how much I have struggled in prayer for you and for the church at Laodicea, and for my many other friends who have never known me personally. ²This is what I have asked of God for you: that you will be encouraged and knit together by strong ties of love, and that you will have the rich experience of knowing Christ with real certainty and clear understanding. *For God's secret plan, now at last made known, is Christ himself.* ³In him lie hidden all the mighty, untapped treasures of wisdom and knowledge.

⁴I am saying this because I am afraid that someone may fool you with smooth talk. ⁵For though I am far away from you my heart is with you, happy because you are getting along so well, happy because of your strong faith in Christ. ⁶And now just as you trusted Christ to save you, trust him, too, for each day's problems; live in vital union with him. ⁷Let your roots grow down into him and draw up nourishment from him. See that you go on growing in the Lord, and become strong and vigorous in the truth you were taught. Let your lives overflow with joy and thanksgiving for all he has done.

⁸Don't let others spoil your faith and joy with their philosophies, their wrong and shallow answers built on men's thoughts and ideas, instead of on what Christ has said. ⁹For in Christ there is all of God in a human body; ¹⁰*so you have everything when you have Christ,* and you are filled with God through your union with Christ. He is the highest Ruler, with authority over every other power.

¹¹When you came to Christ, he set you free from your evil desires, not by a bodily operation of circumcision but by a spiritual operation, the baptism of your souls. ¹²For in baptism you see how your old, evil nature died with him and was buried with him; and then you came up out of

FAMILY DEVOTIONS

☐ **DEVOTION 331**
CULTIVATING GODLY ATTITUDES

Read Colossians 3 : 8 - 15

Cultivating Godly Attitudes
Memory Verse

Your attitude should be the kind that was shown us by Jesus Christ.
Philippians 2:5

"You should see all the stuff Mom and I got on sale today," Bonnie told her father one evening. "Cheap, too."

Mom sighed. "Yes," she agreed, "but it was such a hassle getting through the crowds at the mall and pawing through piles of merchandise. I wondered at times if it was really worth it. But as Bonnie says, it was cheap. It makes you wonder how the stores can afford to sell things at those prices."

"They know what they're doing," Dad assured her. "They're clearing out things that are no longer profitable and making room to restock their shelves with new things from which they *can* make a good profit. We could take a lesson from them."

"Like what?" asked Bonnie curiously.

"There are things on the shelves of our lives that we should clear out from time to time," explained Dad as he reached for his Bible. "Let's read about them for devotions tonight." He read aloud from Colossians 3.

"That makes me feel guilty for getting angry at some pushy women in the store today," confessed Mom. "I need to get rid of anger from the shelves of my life."

"Well, how much do you suppose we can sell our bad qualities for?" asked Bonnie with a mischievous grin.

Dad smiled. "I trust there would be no buyers for them. Forget selling them and just trash them," he advised. "And let's not forget to restock our shelves with this list of traits that are pleasing to God."

How About You?
What traits are found on the shelves of your life? Do you need to get rid of lying, filthy language, or a desire to get even with someone? Do you need to add kindness, a forgiving spirit, or humility? Ask God right now to help you do that. H. M.

• For the next devotional, turn to page 1165.   • For the next devotional on *CULTIVATING GODLY ATTITUDES*, turn to page 1251.   • For notes on *CULTIVATING GODLY ATTITUDES*, see pages 337, 383, 472, 622, and 1216.

death with him into a new life because you trusted the Word of the mighty God who raised Christ from the dead.

[13] You were dead in sins, and your sinful desires were not yet cut away. Then he gave you a share in the very life of Christ, for he forgave all your sins, [14] and blotted out the charges proved against you, the list of his commandments which you had not obeyed. He took this list of sins and destroyed it by nailing it to Christ's cross. [15] In this way God took away Satan's power to accuse you of sin, and God openly displayed to the whole world Christ's triumph at the cross where your sins were all taken away.

[16] So don't let anyone criticize you for what you eat or drink, or for not celebrating Jewish holidays and feasts or new moon ceremonies or Sabbaths. [17] For these were only temporary rules that ended when Christ came. They were only shadows of the real thing—of Christ himself. [18] Don't let anyone declare you lost when you refuse to worship angels, as they say you must. They have seen a vision, they say, and know you should. These proud men (though they claim to be so humble) have a very clever imagination. [19] But they are not connected to Christ, the Head to which all of us who are his body are joined; for we are joined together by his strong sinews, and we grow only as we get our nourishment and strength from God.

[20] Since you died, as it were, with Christ and this has set you free from following the world's ideas of how to be saved—by doing good and obeying various rules—why do you keep right on following them anyway, still bound by such rules as [21] not eating, tasting, or even touching certain foods? [22] Such rules are mere human teachings, for food was made to be eaten and used up. [23] These rules may seem good, for rules of this kind require strong devotion and are humiliating and hard on the body, but they have no effect when it comes to conquering a person's evil thoughts and desires. They only make him proud.

3 Some Rules to Obey

Since you became alive again, so to speak, when Christ arose from the dead, now set your sights on the rich treasures and joys of heaven where he sits beside God in the place of honor and power. [2] Let heaven fill your thoughts; don't spend your time worrying about things down here. [3] You should have as little desire for this world as a dead person does. Your real life is in heaven with Christ and God. [4] And when Christ who is our real life comes back again, you will shine with him and share in all his glories.

[5] Away then with sinful, earthly things; deaden the evil desires lurking within you; have nothing to do with sexual sin, impurity, lust, and shameful desires; don't worship the good things of life, for that is idolatry. [6] God's terrible anger is upon those who do such things. [7] You used to do them when your life was still part of this world; [8] but now is the time to cast off and throw away all these rotten garments of anger, hatred, cursing, and dirty language.

[9] Don't tell lies to each other; it was your old life with all its wickedness that did that sort of thing; now it is dead and gone. [10] You are living a brand new kind of life that is continually learning more and more of what is right, and trying constantly to be more and more like Christ who created this new life within you. [11] In this new life one's nationality or race or education or social position is unimportant; such things mean nothing. Whether a person has Christ is what matters, and he is equally available to all.

[12] Since you have been chosen by God who has given you this new kind of life, and because of his deep love and concern for you, you should practice tenderhearted mercy and kindness to others. Don't worry about making a good impression on them, but be ready to suffer quietly and patiently. [13] Be gentle and ready to forgive; never hold grudges. Remember, the Lord forgave you, so you must forgive others.

[14] Most of all, let love guide your life, for then the whole church will stay together in perfect harmony. [15] Let the peace of heart that comes from Christ be always present in your hearts and lives, for this is your responsibility and privilege as members of his body. And always be thankful.

[16] Remember what Christ taught, and let his words enrich your lives and make you wise; teach them to each other and sing them out in psalms and hymns and spiritual songs, singing to the Lord with thankful hearts. [17] And whatever you do or say, let it be as a representative of the Lord Jesus, and come with him into the presence of God the Father to give him your thanks.

[18] You wives, submit yourselves to your husbands, for that is what the Lord has planned for you. [19] And you husbands must be loving and kind to your wives and not bitter against them nor harsh.

BECOMING MORE LIKE JESUS 2:20-23 People should be able to see a difference between the way Christians and non-Christians live. Still, we should not expect instant maturity in Christ. The Christian life is a process. Although we have a new nature, we don't automatically have all good thoughts and attitudes when we become a new person in Christ. But if we keep listening to God, we will be changing all the time. As you look over the last year, what changes for the better have you seen in your thoughts and attitudes? Change may be slow, but your life will change significantly if you trust God to change you. **To begin the series of devotionals on BECOMING MORE LIKE JESUS, turn to page 131.**

FAMILY DEVOTIONS

☐ *DEVOTION 332*
FORGIVING OTHERS

Read Colossians 3 : 12 -15

Kim and Judy were visiting Uncle Dale in the hospital. As they were playing a board game the girls had brought along, a man entered the room. "Hi, Joe!" said Uncle Dale cheerfully.

"Hello," the visitor replied.

"Kim, Judy, meet Joe Turner." Uncle Dale introduced his nieces. "Joe comes to see me every day, and we have a Bible study," he explained to the girls.

"Don't let me interrupt you," said Joe. "I have some errands to run. I'll come back in a little while."

"That will be fine." Uncle Dale smiled and added, "Don't forget."

"No chance," replied Joe as he left.

The girls were silent for a while. "Joe is the man who caused your accident, isn't he?" Kim said at last. "Why are you friends with him? It's his fault you can't walk!"

"I was angry right after the accident," Uncle Dale admitted. "Then one day I read Colossians 3:13. Judy, will you find that in my Bible?"

Judy quickly found the verse in Uncle Dale's Bible and began reading. "Be gentle and ready to forgive; never hold grudges. Remember, the Lord forgave you, so you must forgive others."

"Shortly after I finished my devotions that day," continued Uncle Dale, "Joe came into my room. I sure had a quarrel against him! But he asked me to forgive him." Uncle Dale cleared his throat. "God used the accident to bring Joe and me both closer to him," he added quietly.

Kim had tears in her eyes. "I just don't think I can forgive Joe," she said. "Is there something the matter with me, Uncle Dale?"

"Nothing God can't cure," Uncle Dale assured her. "It's just that you love me, so you don't like to see me hurt. That's natural. But listen—why don't you girls stay for our Bible study today? Then you can get to know Joe better. It's easier to forgive someone when he's your friend."

Forgiving Others Memory Verse

Be gentle and ready to forgive; never hold grudges. Remember, the Lord forgave you, so you must forgive others.

Colossians 3:13

How About You?

Has someone hurt you so badly that you can't forgive him? Be nice to him even when he isn't nice to you. Get to know him better— you may even become friends. Above all, remember how much God has forgiven you; follow his example. *A. L.*

²⁰You children must always obey your fathers and mothers, for that pleases the Lord. ²¹Fathers, don't scold your children so much that they become discouraged and quit trying.

²²You slaves must always obey your earthly masters, not only trying to please them when they are watching you but all the time; obey them willingly because of your love for the Lord and because you want to please him. ²³Work hard and cheerfully at all you do, just as though you were working for the Lord and not merely for your masters, ²⁴remembering that it is the Lord Christ who is going to pay you, giving you your full portion of all he owns. He is the one you are really working for. ²⁵And if you don't do your best for him, he will pay you in a way that you won't like—for he has no special favorites who can get away with shirking.

4 Paul Says Good-bye

You slave owners must be just and fair to all your slaves. Always remember that you, too, have a Master in heaven who is closely watching you.

²Don't be weary in prayer; keep at it; watch for God's answers, and remember to be thankful when they come. ³Don't forget to pray for us too, that God will give us many chances to preach the Good News of Christ for which I am here in jail. ⁴Pray that I will be bold enough to tell it freely and fully and make it plain, as, of course, I should.

⁵Make the most of your chances to tell others the Good News. Be wise in all your contacts with them. ⁶Let your conversation be gracious as well as sensible, for then you will have the right answer for everyone.

⁷Tychicus, our much-loved brother, will tell you how I am getting along. He is a hard worker and serves the Lord with me. ⁸I have sent him on this special trip just to see how you are and to comfort and encourage you. ⁹I am also sending Onesimus, a faithful and much-loved brother, one of your own people. He and Tychicus will give you all the latest news.

¹⁰Aristarchus, who is with me here as a prisoner, sends you his love, and so does Mark, a relative of Barnabas. And as I said before, give Mark a hearty welcome if he comes your way. ¹¹Jesus Justus also sends his love. These are the only Jewish Christians working with me here, and what a comfort they have been!

¹²Epaphras, from your city, a servant of Christ Jesus, sends you his love. He is always earnestly praying for you, asking God to make you strong and perfect and to help you know his will in everything you do. ¹³I can assure you that he has worked hard for you with his prayers, and also for the Christians in Laodicea and Hierapolis.

¹⁴Dear Doctor Luke sends his love, and so does Demas.

¹⁵Please give my greeting to the Christian friends at Laodicea, and to Nymphas, and to those who meet in his home. ¹⁶By the way, after you have read this letter, will you pass it on to the church at Laodicea? And read the letter I wrote to them. ¹⁷And say to Archippus, "Be sure that you do all the Lord has told you to."

¹⁸Here is my own greeting in my own handwriting: Remember me here in jail. May God's blessings surround you.

Sincerely, Paul

1 Thessalonians

ARE THERE people in your life who set good examples for you to follow? What kind of example are *you* for your friends or your brothers and sisters? When Paul wrote his first letter to the Thessalonians, he told them they were an example to other Christians in the area.

Paul had started the church in Thessalonica when he was on his second missionary trip. The new believers had trouble right away with people in the city. The church had sent Paul away for his own safety, but he was concerned about them.

Paul sent Timothy to get news. Timothy brought back a great report. The Thessalonians were living to please God, caring for others, and sharing their faith. Because of this, Paul wrote to them and said that the church in Thessalonica would be a great example for other churches in the area to follow.

In addition to encouraging the people of Thessalonica, Paul gave them advice about their weaknesses and answered their questions about Jesus' return.

As you read 1 Thessalonians, look for ways you can *follow* the example of the Thessalonian Christians and *be* an example to others.

Chosen by God

From: Paul, Silas, and Timothy.

To: The church at Thessalonica—to you who belong to God the Father and the Lord Jesus Christ: May blessing and peace of heart be your rich gifts from God our Father and from Jesus Christ our Lord.

[2] We always thank God for you and pray for you constantly. [3] We never forget your loving deeds as we talk to our God and Father about you, and your strong faith and steady looking forward to the return of our Lord Jesus Christ.

[4] We know that God has chosen you, dear brothers, much beloved of God. [5] For when we brought you the Good News, it was not just meaningless chatter to you; no, you listened with great interest. What we told you produced a powerful effect upon you, for the Holy Spirit gave you great and full assurance that what we said was true. And you know how our very lives were further proof to you of the truth of our message. [6] So you became our followers and the Lord's; for you received our message with joy from the Holy

Spirit in spite of the trials and sorrows it brought you.

⁷Then you yourselves became an example to all the other Christians in Greece. ⁸And now the Word of the Lord has spread out from you to others everywhere, far beyond your boundaries, for wherever we go we find people telling us about your remarkable faith in God. We don't need to tell *them* about it, ⁹for *they* keep telling *us* about the wonderful welcome you gave us, and how you turned away from your idols to God so that now the living and true God only is your Master. ¹⁰And they speak of how you are looking forward to the return of God's Son from heaven—Jesus, whom God brought back to life—and he is our only Savior from God's terrible anger against sin.

2 Paul's Friends

You yourselves know, dear brothers, how worthwhile that visit was. ²You know how badly we had been treated at Philippi just before we came to you and how much we suffered there. Yet God gave us the courage to boldly repeat the same message to you, even though we were surrounded by enemies. ³So you can see that we were not preaching with any false motives or evil purposes in mind; we were perfectly straightforward and sincere.

⁴For we speak as messengers from God, trusted by him to tell the truth; we change his message not one bit to suit the taste of those who hear it; for we serve God alone, who examines our hearts' deepest thoughts. ⁵Never once did we try to win you with flattery, as you very well know, and God knows we were not just pretending to be your friends so that you would give us money! ⁶As for praise, we have never asked for it from you or anyone else, although as apostles of Christ we certainly had a right to some honor from you. ⁷But we were as gentle among you as a mother feeding and caring for her own children. ⁸We loved you dearly—so dearly that we gave you not only God's message, but our own lives too.

⁹Don't you remember, dear brothers, how hard we worked among you? Night and day we toiled and sweated to earn enough to live on so that our expenses would not be a burden to anyone there, as we preached God's Good News among you. ¹⁰You yourselves are our witnesses—as is God—that we have been pure and honest and faultless toward every one of you. ¹¹We talked to you as a father to his own children—don't you remember?—pleading with you, encouraging you and even demanding ¹²that your daily lives should not embarrass God but bring joy to him who invited you into his Kingdom to share his glory.

¹³And we will never stop thanking God for this: that when we preached to you, you didn't think of the words we spoke as being just our own, but you accepted what we said as the very Word of God—which, of course, it was—and it changed your lives when you believed it.

¹⁴And then, dear brothers, you suffered what the churches in Judea did, persecution from your own countrymen, just as they suffered from their own people, the Jews. ¹⁵After they had killed their own prophets, they even executed the Lord Jesus; and now they have brutally persecuted us and driven us out. They are against both God and man, ¹⁶trying to keep us from preaching to the Gentiles for fear some might be saved; and so their sins continue to grow. But the anger of God has caught up with them at last.

¹⁷Dear brothers, after we left you and had been away from you but a very little while (though our hearts never left you), we tried hard to come back to see you once more. ¹⁸We wanted very much to come, and I, Paul, tried again and again, but Satan stopped us. ¹⁹For what is it we live for, that gives us hope and joy and is our proud reward and crown? It is you! Yes, you will bring us much joy as we stand together before our Lord Jesus Christ when he comes back again. ²⁰For you are our trophy and joy.

3 A Job Well Done

Finally, when I could stand it no longer, I decided to stay alone in Athens ²,³and send Timothy, our brother and fellow worker, God's minister, to visit you to strengthen your faith and encourage you and to keep you from becoming fainthearted in all the troubles you were going through. (But of course you know that such troubles are a part of God's plan for us Christians. ⁴Even while we were still with you we warned you ahead of time that suffering would soon come—and it did.)

⁵As I was saying, when I could bear the suspense no longer, I sent Timothy to find out whether your faith was still strong. I was afraid that perhaps Satan had gotten the best of you and that all our work had been useless. ⁶And now Timothy has just returned and brings the welcome news that your faith and love are as strong as ever and that you remember our visit with joy and want to see us just as much as we want to see you. ⁷So we are greatly comforted, dear brothers, in all of our own crushing troubles and suffering here, now that we know you are standing true to the Lord. ⁸We can bear anything as long as we know that you remain strong in him.

⁹How can we thank God enough for you and for the joy and delight you have given us in our

Family Devotions

☐ DEVOTION 333
SERVING GOD BOLDLY

Read 1 Thessalonians 2:2-8

Matt and his father were on a fishing trip when Matt made a discovery—an eagle's nest way up near the top of a tall tree. In the sky, they saw a large bird soaring high over the river. Matt let out a long breath. "Wow!" he exclaimed. "I wish I could fly like that!" Eagles were his favorite bird, but he had never seen a real one before, except in a zoo.

"Well, that eagle didn't always have such great flying skills," Dad told him. "Baby eagles are afraid of flying. In fact, it takes a great deal of their mother's prodding to get them out of their soft, warm nest."

"I know. I read about that," said Matt. "My book said the mother eagle pushes them right out over the side of the nest. That must be scary for them." Matt looked again at the nest.

Dad nodded. "They probably think they'll fall to the ground," he said. "But after the mother eagle lets the little eaglet flutter and fall for a time, she soars underneath it and lets it land on her wings. Then she takes it back safely to the nest. Over and over she helps each eaglet practice flying until they are all brave enough and strong enough to fly on their own."

A few days later, Matt was asked to do something he had never done before—to give his testimony at his youth group meeting. He agreed to do it, but he felt so scared! "If only they hadn't asked me!" he groaned on the afternoon of the meeting.

His father overheard him. "Of course it's scary, Matt," he said, "but you haven't forgotten how little eagles learn to fly, have you?"

"What does that have to do with giving a testimony?" Matt wanted to know.

"God is somewhat like the mother eagle," explained Dad. "Sometimes he has to prod you to try new things—things that make you feel helpless or afraid. But he'll be there to teach you and catch you!"

Serving God Boldly Memory Verse

Yes, be bold and strong!
Banish fear and doubt!
For remember, the Lord
your God is with you
wherever you go.
Joshua 1:9

How About You?

Do you hang back when there are challenges to face? God will not forsake you as you try out your wings. Even when you feel as if you are falling—or failing—you will discover that "the eternal God is your Refuge, and underneath are the everlasting arms." As a Christian, you can fly! T. V.

• For the next devotional, turn to page 1171. • To start the next topic, turn to page 291. • For notes on SERVING GOD BOLDLY, see pages 327, 404, 501, 720, and 856.

praying for you? ¹⁰For night and day we pray on and on for you, asking God to let us see you again, to fill up any little cracks there may yet be in your faith.

¹¹May God our Father himself and our Lord Jesus send us back to you again. ¹²And may the Lord make your love to grow and overflow to each other and to everyone else, just as our love does toward you. ¹³This will result in your hearts being made strong, sinless, and holy by God our Father so that you may stand before him guiltless on that day when our Lord Jesus Christ returns with all those who belong to him.

4 How Can I Please God?

Let me add this, dear brothers: You already know how to please God in your daily living, for you know the commands we gave you from the Lord Jesus himself. Now we beg you—yes, we demand of you in the name of the Lord Jesus—that you live more and more closely to that ideal. ³,⁴For God wants you to be holy and pure and to keep clear of all sexual sin so that each of you will marry in holiness and honor— ⁵not in lustful passion as the heathen do, in their ignorance of God and his ways.

⁶And this also is God's will: that you never cheat in this matter by taking another man's wife because the Lord will punish you terribly for this, as we have solemnly told you before. ⁷For God has not called us to be dirty-minded and full of lust but to be holy and clean. ⁸If anyone refuses to live by these rules, he is not disobeying the rules of men but of God who gives his *Holy* Spirit to you.

⁹But concerning the pure brotherly love that there should be among God's people, I don't need to say very much, I'm sure! For God himself is teaching you to love one another. ¹⁰Indeed, your love is already strong toward all the Christian brothers throughout your whole nation. Even so, dear friends, we beg you to love them more and more. ¹¹This should be your ambition: to live a quiet life, minding your own business and doing your own work, just as we told you before. ¹²As a result, people who are not Christians will trust and respect you, and you will not need to depend on others for enough money to pay your bills.

¹³And now, dear brothers, I want you to know what happens to a Christian when he dies so that when it happens, you will not be full of sorrow, as those are who have no hope. ¹⁴For since we believe that Jesus died and then came back to life again, we can also believe that when Jesus returns, God will bring back with him all the Christians who have died.

¹⁵I can tell you this directly from the Lord: that we who are still living when the Lord returns will not rise to meet him ahead of those who are in their graves. ¹⁶For the Lord himself will come down from heaven with a mighty shout and with the soul-stirring cry of the archangel and the great trumpet-call of God. And the believers who are dead will be the first to rise to meet the Lord. ¹⁷Then we who are still alive and remain on the earth will be caught up with them in the clouds to meet the Lord in the air and remain with him forever. ¹⁸So comfort and encourage each other with this news.

5 Are You Ready for Christ's Return?

When is all this going to happen? I really don't need to say anything about that, dear brothers, ²for you know perfectly well that no one knows. That day of the Lord will come unexpectedly, like a thief in the night. ³When people are saying, "All is well; everything is quiet and peaceful"—then, all of a sudden, disaster will fall upon them as suddenly as a woman's birth pains begin when her child is born. And these people will not be able to get away anywhere—there will be no place to hide.

⁴But, dear brothers, you are not in the dark about these things, and you won't be surprised as by a thief when that day of the Lord comes. ⁵For you are all children of the light and of the day, and do not belong to darkness and night. ⁶So be on your guard, not asleep like the others. Watch for his return and stay sober. ⁷Night is the time for sleep and the time when people get drunk. ⁸But let us who live in the light keep sober, protected by the armor of faith and love, and wearing as our helmet the happy hope of salvation.

⁹For God has not chosen to pour out his anger upon us but to save us through our Lord Jesus Christ; ¹⁰he died for us so that we can live with him forever, whether we are dead or alive at the time of his return. ¹¹So encourage each other to build each other up, just as you are already doing.

¹²Dear brothers, honor the officers of your church who work hard among you and warn you against all that is wrong. ¹³Think highly of them and give them your wholehearted love because

---

ENCOURAGING OTHERS 5:9-11 As you near the end of a foot race, your legs ache, your throat burns, and your whole body cries out for you to stop. This is when supporters are most valuable. Their encouragement helps you push through the pain to the finish. In the same way, Christians are to encourage one another. A word of encouragement offered at the right moment can make the difference between finishing well and collapsing along the way. Look around you. Be sensitive to others' need for encouragement, and offer it in words or actions whenever you can. **To begin the series of devotionals on ENCOURAGING OTHERS, turn to page 705.**

Family Devotions

☐ DEVOTION 334
RESPECTING GOD'S WARNINGS

Read 1 Thessalonians 5:1-11

Respecting God's Warnings
Memory Verse

If my people will humble themselves and pray, and search for me, and turn from their wicked ways, I will hear them from heaven and forgive their sins and heal their land.
2 Chronicles 7:14

Dark, threatening clouds rolled overhead as the Martin family drove home from church. "Jesus is coming in the clouds," five-year-old Mark said as he intently watched the sky. "Do you think he's coming today?"

"He could," Mother replied.

"I've heard that all my life," fifteen-year-old Merri sneered. "I think preachers just say that to scare people into living right."

Suddenly they heard the thin, piercing wail of the tornado siren. The wind began to blow fiercely, and large drops of rain pelted the car.

"Maybe Jesus is coming," Mark said excitedly.

"Don't say that!" Merri cried. "Hurry, Dad!"

"Calm down, Merri," Dad repeated as he turned the car into the driveway. Hail began to salt the ground as the Martins ran for the storm cellar in their backyard. Next door, Mr. Carson stood on his porch, watching the clouds.

"Better come to the cellar with us, Mr. Carson!" Mother called as they ran past him.

Mr. Carson laughed. "No thanks!" he said. "They blow that tornado siren every time a little cloud comes up. No need to hide in a dark hole in the ground!" As the cellar door closed behind the Martin family, a loud roar filled the air.

About half an hour later Dad left the cellar to see what had happened. When he returned, his face was grim. "It was a tornado. It took only part of the roof off our house, but Mr. Carson's house was demolished."

"What about Mr. Carson?" Merri asked.

"He's on his way to the hospital," answered Dad sadly.

"I guess he thought the sirens were just to scare people—like I was saying about the preachers," Merri said softly. "I'm glad we took the warning seriously—and I guess I need to take it seriously that Jesus is coming back, too."

How About You?
Everywhere there are signs that warn us that Jesus is coming soon. It will be a wonderful day for those who are ready, but a day of destruction for those who are not. Don't be foolish and ignore the warnings. *B. W.*

• For the next devotional, turn to page 1175. • For the next devotional on *RESPECTING GOD'S WARNINGS*, turn to page 1263. • For notes on *RESPECTING GOD'S WARNINGS*, see pages 219, 874, and 1126.

they are straining to help you. And remember, no quarreling among yourselves.

¹⁴Dear brothers, warn those who are lazy, comfort those who are frightened, take tender care of those who are weak, and be patient with everyone. ¹⁵See that no one pays back evil for evil, but always try to do good to each other and to everyone else. ¹⁶Always be joyful. ¹⁷Always keep on praying. ¹⁸No matter what happens, always be thankful, for this is God's will for you who belong to Christ Jesus.

¹⁹Do not smother the Holy Spirit. ²⁰Do not scoff at those who prophesy, ²¹ but test everything that is said to be sure it is true, and if it is, then accept it. ²²Keep away from every kind of evil. ²³May the God of peace himself make you entirely pure and devoted to God; and may your spirit and soul and body be kept strong and blameless until that day when our Lord Jesus Christ comes back again. ²⁴God, who called you to become his child, will do all this for you, just as he promised. ²⁵Dear brothers, pray for us. ²⁶Shake hands for me with all the brothers there. ²⁷I command you in the name of the Lord to read this letter to all the Christians. ²⁸And may rich blessings from our Lord Jesus Christ be with you, every one.

Sincerely, Paul

2 Thessalonians

HOW MUCH are you willing to put up with to stick to your faith? People were making trouble for the Thessalonian Christians because of the way they lived. Paul praised the Thessalonian Christians for standing firm in their faith even though they were having hard times.

Paul wrote this letter to encourage them to keep loving God and others and not to get sidetracked. Paul reminded them that people who do wrong—whether inside or outside the church—will be punished. So Christians don't need to envy people who seem to get away with wrongdoing. Paul told the Thessalonians *why* they should be faithful to God—because God would always be faithful to them.

Paul also told them to keep busy working for God. Some people were getting lazy and didn't work because they thought Jesus was coming back any day.

When you have a hard time standing firm in your faith, think of the Thessalonians. If you're being treated unfairly because of your faith or you're tempted to do wrong, remember that God is faithful to you. Look for ways to stand firm as you read 2 Thessalonians.

1

Patience in Suffering

From: Paul, Silas, and Timothy.

To: The church of Thessalonica—kept safe in God our Father and in the Lord Jesus Christ.

²May God the Father and the Lord Jesus Christ give you rich blessings and peace-filled hearts and minds.

³Dear brothers, giving thanks to God for you is not only the right thing to do, but it is our duty to God because of the really wonderful way your faith has grown and because of your growing love for each other. ⁴We are happy to tell other churches about your patience and complete faith in God, in spite of all the crushing troubles and hardships you are going through.

⁵This is only one example of the fair, just way God does things, for he is using your sufferings to make you ready for his Kingdom, ⁶while at the same time he is preparing judgment and punishment for those who are hurting you.

⁷And so I would say to you who are suffering, God will give you rest along with us when the

Lord Jesus appears suddenly from heaven in flaming fire with his mighty angels, ⁸bringing judgment on those who do not wish to know God and who refuse to accept his plan to save them through our Lord Jesus Christ. ⁹They will be punished in everlasting hell, forever separated from the Lord, never to see the glory of his power ¹⁰when he comes to receive praise and admiration because of all he has done for his people, his saints. And you will be among those praising him because you have believed what we told you about him.

¹¹And so we keep on praying for you, that our God will make you the kind of children he wants to have—will make you as good as you wish you could be!—rewarding your faith with his power. ¹²Then everyone will be praising the name of the Lord Jesus Christ because of the results they see in you; and your greatest glory will be that you belong to him. The tender mercy of our God and of the Lord Jesus Christ has made all this possible for you.

2 The Antichrist

And now, what about the coming again of our Lord Jesus Christ and our being gathered together to meet him? Please don't be upset and excited, dear brothers, by the rumor that this day of the Lord has already begun. If you hear of people having visions and special messages from God about this, or letters that are supposed to have come from me, don't believe them. ³Don't be carried away and deceived regardless of what they say.

For that day will not come until two things happen: first, there will be a time of great rebellion against God, and then the man of rebellion will come—the son of hell. ⁴He will defy every god there is and tear down every other object of adoration and worship. He will go in and sit as God in the temple of God, claiming that he himself is God. ⁵Don't you remember that I told you this when I was with you? ⁶And you know what is keeping him from being here already; for he can come only when his time is ready.

⁷As for the work this man of rebellion and hell will do when he comes, it is already going on, but he himself will not come until the one who is holding him back steps out of the way. ⁸Then this wicked one will appear, whom the Lord Jesus will burn up with the breath of his mouth and destroy by his presence when he returns. ⁹This man of sin will come as Satan's tool, full of satanic power, and will trick everyone with strange demonstrations, and will do great miracles. ¹⁰He will completely fool those who are on their way to hell because they have said no to the Truth; they have refused to believe it and love it and let it save them, ¹¹so God will allow them to believe lies with all their hearts, ¹²and all of them will be justly judged for believing falsehood, refusing the Truth, and enjoying their sins.

¹³But we must forever give thanks to God for you, our brothers loved by the Lord, because God chose from the very first to give you salvation, cleansing you by the work of the Holy Spirit and by your trusting in the Truth. ¹⁴Through us he told you the Good News. Through us he called you to share in the glory of our Lord Jesus Christ.

¹⁵With all these things in mind, dear brothers, stand firm and keep a strong grip on the truth that we taught you in our letters and during the time we were with you.

¹⁶May our Lord Jesus Christ himself and God our Father, who has loved us and given us everlasting comfort and hope, which we don't deserve, ¹⁷comfort your hearts with all comfort, and help you in every good thing you say and do.

3 God Makes Us Strong

Finally, dear brothers, as I come to the end of this letter, I ask you to pray for us. Pray first that the Lord's message will spread rapidly and triumph wherever it goes, winning converts everywhere as it did when it came to you. ²Pray, too, that we will be saved out of the clutches of evil men, for not everyone loves the Lord. ³But the Lord is faithful; he will make you strong and guard you from satanic attacks of every kind. ⁴And we trust the Lord that you are putting into practice the things we taught you, and that you always will. ⁵May the Lord bring you into an ever deeper understanding of the love of God and of the patience that comes from Christ.

⁶Now here is a command, dear brothers, given in the name of our Lord Jesus Christ by his authority: Stay away from any Christian who spends his days in laziness and does not follow the ideal of hard work we set up for you. ⁷For you well know that you ought to follow our example: you never saw us loafing; ⁸we never accepted food from anyone without buying it; we worked hard day and night

---

PERSEVERANCE 1:5 As we live for Christ, we will experience troubles and hardships. Some say troubles are a result of sin or lack of faith. But Paul teaches that they may be a part of God's plan for believers. Our problems help us look upward and forward, not inward (Mark 13:35-36); they help build strong character (Romans 5:3-4); and they help us be sensitive to others who also must struggle (2 Corinthians 1:3-5). In addition, problems are unavoidable because we are trying to be godly people in an ungodly world. Your troubles may well be a sign of effective Christian living. **To begin the series of devotionals on PERSEVERANCE, turn to page 37.**

Family Devotions

☐ **DEVOTION 335**
PATIENCE

Read 2 Thessalonians 3:5

Patience
Memory Verse

Now as for you, dear brothers who are waiting for the Lord's return, be patient, like a farmer who waits until the autumn for his precious harvest to ripen.
James 5:7

Tears trickled down Katrina's cheeks as she repeated her argument. "It wouldn't be a real date—just Jeff and Shana and Mark and me. I told you Jeff's folks would be there."

Mom sighed deeply. "Katrina, I'm sorry. But twelve is too young."

"I'm too young for everything!" Katrina wailed.

Mom put her arm around Katrina's stiff shoulders. "Not too young to make fudge for your entry in the pecan show. You'll find the pecans on the table. If you need help, I'll be in the backyard."

As Katrina cooked, she sniffed, sighed, and slammed pans. The fudge was in the refrigerator and Katrina was cleaning up the kitchen when Mom came in carrying another pail of pecans. "Remember when we planted our pecan tree, Katie?" she asked. "You were just a little girl. It took a long time, but it's finally producing!"

Katrina ignored her mother and opened the refrigerator to check on the fudge. "It isn't getting hard!" she whined.

Mom looked over her shoulder. "I'm afraid you got in too big a hurry, honey, and didn't cook it long enough."

Later, as Mom helped Katrina pick pecans out of the shells for a second batch of fudge, Mom said softly, "A lot of things in life take time—things like fudge and pecan trees and growing up. When we rush them, we often ruin them. Be patient, honey."

Katrina hated to admit it, but she knew her mother was right. She gave Mom a tearful smile. "This time I'm going to let you help me decide when the fudge is ready," she said. "You've had more experience with it. And with growing up, too."

How About You?

Are you fretting and stewing, wanting to do something your parents say you're not old enough to do? Ask the Lord to help you be patient. Whatever you're waiting for will be more enjoyable and valuable because of the wait. Meanwhile, use the experiences God is giving you right now to develop Christian virtues (including patience). Trust him to give you opportunities. B. W.

• For the next devotional, turn to page 1179. • For the next devotional on *PATIENCE*, turn to page 1207. • For notes on *PATIENCE*, see pages 35, 242, 329, and 502.

for the money we needed to live on, in order that we would not be a burden to any of you. ⁹It wasn't that we didn't have the right to ask you to feed us, but we wanted to show you firsthand how you should work for your living. ¹⁰Even while we were still there with you, we gave you this rule: "He who does not work shall not eat."

¹¹Yet we hear that some of you are living in laziness, refusing to work, and wasting your time in gossiping. ¹²In the name of the Lord Jesus Christ we appeal to such people—we command them—to quiet down, get to work, and earn their own living. ¹³And to the rest of you I say, dear brothers, never be tired of doing right.

¹⁴If anyone refuses to obey what we say in this letter, notice who he is and stay away from him, that he may be ashamed of himself. ¹⁵Don't think of him as an enemy, but speak to him as you would to a brother who needs to be warned.

¹⁶May the Lord of peace himself give you his peace no matter what happens. The Lord be with you all.

¹⁷Now here is my greeting, which I am writing with my own hand, as I do at the end of all my letters, for proof that it really is from me. This is in my own handwriting. ¹⁸May the blessing of our Lord Jesus Christ be upon you all.

Sincerely, Paul

1 Timothy

WHAT'S IMPORTANT in running a church? What were the roles of pastors and congregations in New Testament times? We have some clues in Paul's first letter to Timothy.

Timothy had been Paul's friend and fellow worker for many years. They traveled together on some missionary trips. Paul trained Timothy and appointed him to be a pastor and teacher at some of the churches they started. This letter gives Timothy instructions on what to teach the Ephesian Christians when Paul couldn't be there.

Some people were teaching false things about Jesus. Timothy's job was to teach the truth so that Christians wouldn't believe wrong things. Paul also gave him some advice on prayer and worship.

A large part of this letter explains what church leaders should be like. It's important that they live in a way that honors God. But Paul also talks about how people in the congregation should act.

Paul's teaching on church life is still true for us today. As you read 1 Timothy, look for something in Paul's advice that you can put into practice.

Paul's Son in the Lord

From: Paul, a missionary of Jesus Christ, sent out by the direct command of God our Savior and by Jesus Christ our Lord—our only hope.

²*To:* Timothy.

Timothy, you are like a son to me in the things of the Lord. May God our Father and Jesus Christ our Lord show you his kindness and mercy and give you great peace of heart and mind.

³,⁴As I said when I left for Macedonia, please stay there in Ephesus and try to stop the men who are teaching such wrong doctrine. Put an end to their myths and fables, and their idea of being saved by finding favor with an endless chain of angels leading up to God—wild ideas that stir up questions and arguments instead of helping people accept God's plan of faith. ⁵What I am eager for is that all the Christians there will be filled with love that comes from pure hearts, and that their minds will be clean and their faith strong.

⁶But these teachers have missed this whole

idea and spend their time arguing and talking foolishness. ⁷They want to become famous as teachers of the laws of Moses when they haven't the slightest idea what those laws really show us. ⁸Those laws are good when used as God intended. ⁹But they were not made for us, whom God has saved; they are for sinners who hate God, have rebellious hearts, curse and swear, attack their fathers and mothers, and murder. ¹⁰,¹¹Yes, these laws are made to identify as sinners all who are immoral and impure: homosexuals, kidnappers, liars, and all others who do things that contradict the glorious Good News of our blessed God, whose messenger I am.

¹²How thankful I am to Christ Jesus our Lord for choosing me as one of his messengers, and giving me the strength to be faithful to him, ¹³even though I used to scoff at the name of Christ. I hunted down his people, harming them in every way I could. But God had mercy on me because I didn't know what I was doing, for I didn't know Christ at that time. ¹⁴Oh, how kind our Lord was, for he showed me how to trust him and become full of the love of Christ Jesus.

¹⁵How true it is, and how I long that everyone should know it, that Christ Jesus came into the world to save sinners—and I was the greatest of them all. ¹⁶But God had mercy on me so that Christ Jesus could use me as an example to show everyone how patient he is with even the worst sinners, so that others will realize that they, too, can have everlasting life. ¹⁷Glory and honor to God forever and ever. He is the King of the ages, the unseen one who never dies; he alone is God, and full of wisdom. Amen.

¹⁸Now, Timothy, my son, here is my command to you: Fight well in the Lord's battles, just as the Lord told us through his prophets that you would. ¹⁹Cling tightly to your faith in Christ and always keep your conscience clear, doing what you know is right. For some people have disobeyed their consciences and have deliberately done what they knew was wrong. It isn't surprising that soon they lost their faith in Christ after defying God like that. ²⁰Hymenaeus and Alexander are two examples of this. I had to give them over to Satan to punish them until they could learn not to bring shame to the name of Christ.

2 Guidelines for Worship

Here are my directions: Pray much for others; plead for God's mercy upon them; give thanks for all he is going to do for them.

²Pray in this way for kings and all others who are in authority over us, or are in places of high responsibility, so that we can live in peace and quietness, spending our time in godly living and thinking much about the Lord. ³This is good and pleases God our Savior, ⁴for he longs for all to be saved and to understand this truth: ⁵*That God is on one side and all the people on the other side, and Christ Jesus, himself man, is between them to bring them together,* ⁶*by giving his life for all mankind.*

This is the message that at the proper time God gave to the world. ⁷And I have been chosen—this is the absolute truth—as God's minister and missionary to teach this truth to the Gentiles and to show them God's plan of salvation through faith.

⁸So I want men everywhere to pray with holy hands lifted up to God, free from sin and anger and resentment. ⁹,¹⁰And the women should be the same way, quiet and sensible in manner and clothing. Christian women should be noticed for being kind and good, not for the way they fix their hair or because of their jewels or fancy clothes. ¹¹Women should listen and learn quietly and humbly.

¹²I never let women teach men or lord it over them. Let them be silent in your church meetings. ¹³Why? Because God made Adam first, and afterwards he made Eve. ¹⁴And it was not Adam who was fooled by Satan, but Eve, and sin was the result. ¹⁵So God sent pain and suffering to women when their children are born, but he will save their souls if they trust in him, living quiet, good, and loving lives.

3 Guidelines for Church Leaders

It is a true saying that if a man wants to be a pastor he has a good ambition. ²For a pastor must be a good man whose life cannot be spoken against. He must have only one wife, and he must be hard working and thoughtful, orderly, and full of good deeds. He must enjoy having guests in his home and must be a good Bible teacher. ³He must not be a drinker or quarrelsome, but he must be gentle and kind and not be one who loves money. ⁴He must have a well-behaved family, with children who obey quickly and quietly. ⁵For if a man can't make his own little family behave, how can he help the whole church?

⁶The pastor must not be a new Christian because he might be proud of being chosen so soon, and pride comes before a fall. (Satan's downfall is an example.) ⁷Also, he must be well spoken of by people outside the church—those who aren't Christians—so that Satan can't trap him with many accusations and leave him without freedom to lead his flock.

⁸The deacons must be the same sort of good, steady men as the pastors. They must not be heavy drinkers and must not be greedy for money. ⁹They must be earnest, wholehearted followers of

FAMILY DEVOTIONS

☐ **DEVOTION 336**
CONFESSING SIN

Read 1 Timothy 1 : 12 - 17

Gary felt a little guilty as he jumped into bed. Earlier at his friend's house he had watched a TV program that he was not allowed to see at home. Now he had decided not to take time to read his Bible or pray. He knew he should, but he really didn't want to. Somehow Bible reading and praying didn't appeal to him tonight, so he went to sleep instead.

After school the next day, Gary idly bounced his ball against the wall of the family room. He knew it was against the rules to play with his ball in the house, but he didn't see why. He tossed the ball again and was horrified at the loud crash that followed. His father's glass-bottled model ship lay shattered on the floor! "Oh, no!" Gary cried. He quickly swept up the pieces and threw them out.

At the supper table Gary tried to avoid his father's gaze. "How about a game of chess tonight?" Dad asked. "Maybe I can beat you this time."

"No, I'd rather not play," said Gary.

After Dad suggested a couple of other activities, Gary couldn't keep quiet any longer. "You won't want to play with me when you know what I did," he said. Then he told what had happened.

"I'm disappointed that you disobeyed me," Dad said, "but I'm glad you told me. I want you to always feel free to come to me, no matter what you've done. I may have to punish you, but I'll never turn you away."

"Thanks, Dad," Gary said through his tears.

"Our heavenly Father has set an example for us," Dad replied. "When we confess our sin, he won't turn us away. He wants our fellowship."

As Gary thought about that, he knew he had some things he needed to confess to God. His guilt had caused him to avoid Dad's company, and it had caused him to avoid God's fellowship, too. He wanted to make things right. He had a great dad and an even greater God!

Confessing Sin
Memory Verse

Create in me a new, clean heart, O God, filled with clean thoughts and right desires.
Psalm 51:10

H o w   A b o u t   Y o u ?
When you have done something wrong, do you sometimes avoid God's Word and prayer? Are you ever afraid to come to God because you've sinned? He wants you to come to him. Confess your sin. He'll forgive you and restore your fellowship with him. *J. H.*

• For the next devotional, turn to page 1181.   • To start the next topic, turn to page 89.   • For notes on CONFESSING SIN, see pages 429, 479, 836, 881, and 1220.

Christ, who is the hidden Source of their faith. ¹⁰Before they are asked to be deacons, they should be given other jobs in the church as a test of their character and ability, and if they do well, then they may be chosen as deacons.

¹¹Their wives must be thoughtful, not heavy drinkers, not gossipers, but faithful in everything they do. ¹²Deacons should have only one wife, and they should have happy, obedient families. ¹³Those who do well as deacons will be well rewarded both by respect from others and also by developing their own confidence and bold trust in the Lord.

¹⁴I am writing these things to you now, even though I hope to be with you soon, ¹⁵so that if I don't come for awhile, you will know what kind of men you should choose as officers for the church of the living God, which contains and holds high the truth of God.

¹⁶It is quite true that the way to live a godly life is not an easy matter. But the answer lies in Christ, who came to earth as a man, was proved spotless and pure in his Spirit, was served by angels, was preached among the nations, was accepted by men everywhere, and was received up again to his glory in heaven.

4 Ignore False Teachers: They Lie

But the Holy Spirit tells us clearly that in the last times some in the church will turn away from Christ and become eager followers of teachers with devil-inspired ideas. ²These teachers will tell lies with straight faces and do it so often that their consciences won't even bother them.

³They will say it is wrong to be married and wrong to eat meat, even though God gave these things to well-taught Christians to enjoy and be thankful for. ⁴For everything God made is good, and we may eat it gladly if we are thankful for it, ⁵and if we ask God to bless it, for it is made good by the Word of God and prayer.

⁶If you explain this to the others you will be doing your duty as a worthy pastor who is fed by faith and by the true teaching you have followed.

⁷Don't waste time arguing over foolish ideas and silly myths and legends. Spend your time and energy in the exercise of keeping spiritually fit. ⁸Bodily exercise is all right, but spiritual exercise is much more important and is a tonic for all you do. So exercise yourself spiritually, and practice being a better Christian because that will help you not only now in this life, but in the next life too. ⁹,¹⁰This is the truth and everyone should accept it. We work hard and suffer much in order that people will believe it, for our hope is in the living God who died for all, and particularly for those who have accepted his salvation.

¹¹Teach these things and make sure everyone learns them well. ¹²Don't let anyone think little of you because you are young. Be their ideal; let them follow the way you teach and live; be a pattern for them in your love, your faith, and your clean thoughts. ¹³Until I get there, read and explain the Scriptures to the church; preach God's Word.

¹⁴Be sure to use the abilities God has given you through his prophets when the elders of the church laid their hands upon your head. ¹⁵Put these abilities to work; throw yourself into your tasks so that everyone may notice your improvement and progress. ¹⁶Keep a close watch on all you do and think. Stay true to what is right and God will bless you and use you to help others.

5 Your Part

Never speak sharply to an older man, but plead with him respectfully just as though he were your own father. Talk to the younger men as you would to much-loved brothers. ²Treat the older women as mothers, and the girls as your sisters, thinking only pure thoughts about them.

³The church should take loving care of women whose husbands have died if they don't have anyone else to help them. ⁴But if they have children or grandchildren, these are the ones who should take the responsibility, for kindness should begin at home, supporting needy parents. This is something that pleases God very much.

⁵The church should care for widows who are poor and alone in the world if they are looking to God for his help and spending much time in prayer; ⁶but not if they are spending their time running around gossiping, seeking only pleasure and thus ruining their souls. ⁷This should be your church rule so that the Christians will know and do what is right.

⁸But anyone who won't care for his own relatives when they need help, especially those living in his own family, has no right to say he is a Christian. Such a person is worse than the heathen.

⁹A widow who wants to become one of the special church workers should be at least sixty years old and have been married only once. ¹⁰She must be well thought of by everyone because of the good she has done. Has she brought up her children well? Has she been kind to strangers as well as to other Christians? Has she helped those who are sick and hurt? Is she always ready to show kindness?

¹¹The younger widows should not become members of this special group because after awhile they are likely to disregard their vow to Christ and marry again. ¹²And so they will stand condemned because they broke their first promise. ¹³Besides, they are likely to be lazy and spend

Family Devotions

☐ *Devotion 337*
Knowing God

Read 1 Timothy 4:7-10

Don had never been so glad to see the end of a week. Band camp had been hard work! There had been fun times like the huge pillow fight the other night, but for the most part, this week of camp had been too much work. What a way to spend Christmas vacation!

On Monday, Don had played his trumpet so long and so hard that he'd split his lip, and the nurse had given him ointment to soothe it. He had to admit, though, that after all the hours of practice this week, his lips were stronger.

It wasn't just his lips that had been put to the test. Every morning the band had gotten up and done exercises at six o'clock. They had also marched two hours each day. After the first day, Don's legs had been so sore he felt like he never wanted to walk again! But his legs felt really strong and tough now that the week was over.

The very first day back at school, Don turned his ankle in gym and had to stay off it for several days. He was almost glad. At least he didn't have to march with the band! They were preparing for a long parade, and Mr. Artz, the band director, was really making them work hard.

Then just as Don was getting ready to rejoin the band, he got the flu. Now he began to get worried. He *did* want to march in that parade. He hoped nothing else would happen to him!

And nothing did. On the day of the parade he was feeling fine. Off Don marched with the band. He couldn't believe how tired it made him!

At church the next day, Pastor Stewart talked about being spiritually strong. "Our spiritual lives are like our physical lives," concluded the pastor. "We don't have to do anything to get *out* of shape, but we must exercise daily to stay *in* shape."

Don knew exactly what the pastor meant, and he knew that he had allowed himself to get out of shape spiritually, too. He asked the Lord to help him get his spiritual body back in shape and keep it that way.

Knowing God
Memory Verse

Oh, that we might know the Lord! Let us press on to know him, and he will respond to us as surely as the coming of dawn or the rain of early spring.
Hosea 6:3

How About You?
Is your spirit out of shape from lack of exercise? Doing nothing will get you out of shape very quickly, so discipline yourself to read the Bible, pray, and live for Jesus every day. *R. P.*

• For the next devotional, turn to page 1183. • To start the next topic, turn to page 307. • For notes on *Knowing God*, see pages 129, 610, 815, and 1208.

their time gossiping around from house to house, getting into other people's business. ¹⁴So I think it is better for these younger widows to marry again and have children and take care of their own homes; then no one will be able to say anything against them. ¹⁵For I am afraid that some of them have already turned away from the church and been led astray by Satan.

¹⁶Let me remind you again that a widow's relatives must take care of her and not leave this to the church to do. Then the church can spend its money for the care of widows who are all alone and have nowhere else to turn.

¹⁷Pastors who do their work well should be paid well and should be highly appreciated, especially those who work hard at both preaching and teaching. ¹⁸For the Scriptures say, "Never tie up the mouth of an ox when it is treading out the grain—let him eat as he goes along!" And in another place, "Those who work deserve their pay!"

¹⁹Don't listen to complaints against the pastor unless there are two or three witnesses to accuse him. ²⁰If he has really sinned, then he should be rebuked in front of the whole church so that no one else will follow his example.

²¹I solemnly command you in the presence of God and the Lord Jesus Christ and of the holy angels to do this whether the pastor is a special friend of yours or not. All must be treated exactly the same. ²²Never be in a hurry about choosing a pastor; you may overlook his sins, and it will look as if you approve of them. Be sure that you yourself stay away from all sin. ²³(By the way, this doesn't mean you should completely give up drinking wine. You ought to take a little sometimes as medicine for your stomach because you are sick so often.)

²⁴Remember that some men, even pastors, lead sinful lives, and everyone knows it. In such situations you can do something about it. But in other cases only the judgment day will reveal the terrible truth. ²⁵In the same way, everyone knows how much good some pastors do, but sometimes their good deeds aren't known until long afterward.

6 Money Isn't Everything

Christian slaves should work hard for their owners and respect them; never let it be said that Christ's people are poor workers. Don't let the name of God or his teaching be laughed at because of this.

²If their owner is a Christian, that is no excuse for slowing down; rather they should work all the harder because a brother in the faith is being helped by their efforts.

Teach these truths, Timothy, and encourage all to obey them.

³Some may deny these things, but they are the sound, wholesome teachings of the Lord Jesus Christ and are the foundation for a godly life. ⁴Anyone who says anything different is both proud and stupid. He is quibbling over the meaning of Christ's words and stirring up arguments ending in jealousy and anger, which only lead to name-calling, accusations, and evil suspicions. ⁵These arguers—their minds warped by sin—don't know how to tell the truth; to them the Good News is just a means of making money. Keep away from them.

⁶Do you want to be truly rich? You already are if you are happy and good. ⁷After all, we didn't bring any money with us when we came into the world, and we can't carry away a single penny when we die. ⁸So we should be well satisfied without money if we have enough food and clothing. ⁹But people who long to be rich soon begin to do all kinds of wrong things to get money, things that hurt them and make them evil-minded and finally send them to hell itself. ¹⁰For the love of money is the first step toward all kinds of sin. Some people have even turned away from God because of their love for it, and as a result have pierced themselves with many sorrows.

¹¹O Timothy, you are God's man. Run from all these evil things, and work instead at what is right and good, learning to trust him and love others and to be patient and gentle. ¹²Fight on for God. Hold tightly to the eternal life that God has given you and that you have confessed with such a ringing confession before many witnesses.

¹³I command you before God, who gives life to all, and before Christ Jesus, who gave a fearless testimony before Pontius Pilate, ¹⁴that you fulfill all he has told you to do so that no one can find fault with you from now until our Lord Jesus Christ returns. ¹⁵For in due season Christ will be revealed from heaven by the blessed and only Almighty God, the King of kings and Lord of lords, ¹⁶who alone can never die, who lives in light so terrible that no human being can approach him. No mere man has ever seen him nor ever will. Unto him be honor and everlasting power and dominion forever and ever. Amen.

RESPECTING AUTHORITY 5:17-18 Faithful, diligent church leaders should be supported and appreciated. Too often they are targets for criticism because the congregation has unrealistic expectations. How do you treat your church leaders? Do you enjoy finding fault, or do you show your appreciation? Do they receive enough financial support to allow them to live without worry and provide for the needs of their families? Jesus and Paul emphasized the importance of supporting ministers who lead and teach us (see Galatians 6:6). **To begin the series of devotionals on RESPECTING AUTHORITY, turn to page 225.**

Family Devotions

☐ DEVOTION 338
MAKING THE BEST CHOICES

Read 1 Timothy 6:9-18

Jason whistled as he rang the doorbell of the big house on the hill.

"Hey! What do you want?" The door was jerked open, and Mr. Atkins stood there frowning.

"I'm Jason Parker, your new paperboy," Jason replied. "I'd like to collect for the paper, please. It's—"

"I know how much it is! It's *too* much!" the old man snapped. "And I suppose you expect a tip for putting it on the porch. Well, you aren't going to get it."

Jason stood quietly as Mr. Atkins counted out the exact amount. "Thank you, sir," Jason said. The old man just slammed the door.

Jason wasn't whistling when he knocked on the door of the little house where Miss Patterson lived. "Yes? Oh, it's the new paperboy." A sweet voice came from a wrinkled face. "Just a minute. I'll get your money." Soon she was back with the money and a plastic bag. "I do so appreciate having the paper put on my porch. I'd like to give you a tip, but I don't have any extra money this month. However, I do have some homemade cookies."

Later Jason told his mother about Mr. Atkins and Miss Patterson.

"Mr. Atkins is so stingy!" Jason snorted. "And he's the richest man in town!"

"He's also one of the poorest men in town," replied Mother. "He was determined to make lots of money, and he did. But in the process, he turned his back on God and on his friends. Now Miss Patterson may not have much money, but she's what the Bible would call 'rich in good works.' She's also rich in friends. She's a good example of the way Christians ought to love and care for others."

"So Mr. Atkins is a poor rich man, and Miss Patterson is a rich poor lady," Jason reasoned.

Making the Best Choices
Memory Verse

He will always give you all you need from day to day if you will make the Kingdom of God your primary concern.
Luke 12:31

How About You?

Do you want to be rich? There's nothing wrong with having money if God has provided it, but a strong desire for lots of money is dangerous. Don't make the mistake of thinking money brings happiness. There is a better kind of riches. Invest your time and efforts in making friends, in helping others, and in serving the Lord. B. W.

• For the next devotional, turn to page 1187. • To start the next topic, turn to page 25. • For notes on MAKING THE BEST CHOICES, see pages 358, 652, and 944.

¹⁷Tell those who are rich not to be proud and not to trust in their money, which will soon be gone, but their pride and trust should be in the living God who always richly gives us all we need for our enjoyment. ¹⁸Tell them to use their money to do good. They should be rich in good works and should give happily to those in need, always being ready to share with others whatever God has given them. ¹⁹By doing this they will be storing up real treasure for themselves in heaven—it is the only safe investment for eternity! And they will be living a fruitful Christian life down here as well.

²⁰Oh, Timothy, don't fail to do these things that God entrusted to you. Keep out of foolish arguments with those who boast of their "knowledge" and thus prove their lack of it. ²¹Some of these people have missed the most important thing in life—they don't know God. May God's mercy be upon you.

Sincerely, Paul

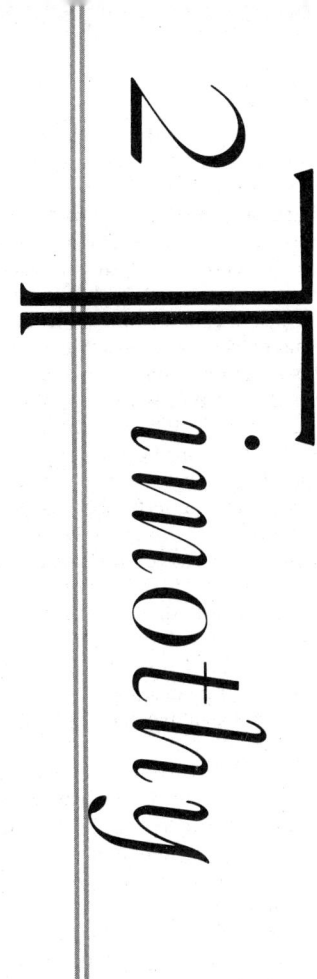

2 Timothy

DO YOU ever feel like you're not important enough to do anything valuable for God? Timothy is an example of how God can use someone to do great things even though he has weaknesses.

Timothy's father was Greek and his mother was Jewish, which meant that he probably wasn't accepted by either group. He was young, and in his culture older people were more respected than young people. He was often sick and had stomach problems. He was not very brave and may have even been shy—several times Paul told him not to be afraid of people and to be bold. Could someone like this be useful to God?

Timothy was a good leader who ended up being a great help to Paul and to Christians in several cities. God used Timothy despite his weaknesses. In this letter, Paul encouraged Timothy to confidently teach the truth to the churches he pastored.

A Letter to Encourage Timothy

From: Paul, Jesus Christ's missionary, sent out by God to tell men and women everywhere about the eternal life he has promised them through faith in Jesus Christ.

²*To:* Timothy, my dear son. May God the Father and Christ Jesus our Lord shower you with his kindness, mercy, and peace.

³How I thank God for you, Timothy. I pray for you every day, and many times during the long nights I beg my God to bless you richly. He is my fathers' God and mine, and my only purpose in life is to please him.

⁴How I long to see you again. How happy I would be, for I remember your tears as we left each other.

⁵I know how much you trust the Lord, just as your mother Eunice and your grandmother Lois do; and I feel sure you are still trusting him as much as ever.

⁶This being so, I want to remind you to stir into flame the strength and boldness that is in you,

that entered into you when I laid my hands upon your head and blessed you. ⁷For the Holy Spirit, God's gift, does not want you to be afraid of people, but to be wise and strong, and to love them and enjoy being with them.

⁸If you will stir up this inner power, you will never be afraid to tell others about our Lord or to let them know that I am your friend even though I am here in jail for Christ's sake. You will be ready to suffer with me for the Lord, for he will give you strength in suffering.

⁹It is he who saved us and chose us for his holy work not because we deserved it but because that was his plan long before the world began—to show his love and kindness to us through Christ. ¹⁰And now he has made all of this plain to us by the coming of our Savior Jesus Christ, who broke the power of death and showed us the way of everlasting life through trusting him. ¹¹And God has chosen me to be his missionary, to preach to the Gentiles and teach them.

¹²That is why I am suffering here in jail, and I am certainly not ashamed of it, for I know the one in whom I trust, and I am sure that he is able to safely guard all that I have given him until the day of his return.

¹³Hold tightly to the pattern of truth I taught you, especially concerning the faith and love Christ Jesus offers you. ¹⁴Guard well the splendid, God-given ability you received as a gift from the Holy Spirit who lives within you.

¹⁵As you know, all the Christians who came here from Asia have deserted me; even Phygellus and Hermogenes are gone. ¹⁶May the Lord bless Onesiphorus and all his family because he visited me and encouraged me often. His visits revived me like a breath of fresh air, and he was never ashamed of my being in jail. ¹⁷In fact, when he came to Rome, he searched everywhere trying to find me, and finally did. ¹⁸May the Lord give him a special blessing at the day of Christ's return. And you know better than I can tell you how much he helped me at Ephesus.

2 Be a Good Soldier

O Timothy, my son, be strong with the strength Christ Jesus gives you. ²For you must teach others those things you and many others have heard me speak about. Teach these great truths to trustworthy men who will, in turn, pass them on to others.

³Take your share of suffering as a good soldier of Jesus Christ, just as I do; ⁴and as Christ's soldier, do not let yourself become tied up in worldly affairs, for then you cannot satisfy the one who has enlisted you in his army. ⁵Follow the Lord's rules for doing his work, just as an athlete either follows the rules or is disqualified and wins no prize. ⁶Work hard like a farmer who gets paid well if he raises a large crop. ⁷Think over these three illustrations, and may the Lord help you to understand how they apply to you.

⁸Don't ever forget the wonderful fact that Jesus Christ was a man, born into King David's family; and that he was God, as shown by the fact that he rose again from the dead. ⁹It is because I have preached these great truths that I am in trouble here and have been put in jail like a criminal. But the Word of God is not chained, even though I am. ¹⁰I am more than willing to suffer if that will bring salvation and eternal glory in Christ Jesus to those God has chosen.

¹¹I am comforted by this truth, that when we suffer and die for Christ it only means that we will begin living with him in heaven. ¹²And if we think that our present service for him is hard, just remember that some day we are going to sit with him and rule with him. But if we give up when we suffer, and turn against Christ, then he must turn against us. ¹³Even when we are too weak to have any faith left, he remains faithful to us and will help us, for he cannot disown us who are part of himself, and he will always carry out his promises to us.

¹⁴Remind your people of these great facts, and command them in the name of the Lord not to argue over unimportant things. Such arguments are confusing and useless and even harmful. ¹⁵Work hard so God can say to you, "Well done." Be a good workman, one who does not need to be ashamed when God examines your work. Know what his Word says and means. ¹⁶Steer clear of foolish discussions that lead people into the sin of anger with each other. ¹⁷Things will be said that will burn and hurt for a long time to come. Hymenaeus and Philetus, in their love of argument, are men like that. ¹⁸They have left the path of truth, preaching the lie that the resurrection of the dead has already occurred; and they have weakened the faith of some who believe them.

¹⁹But God's truth stands firm like a great rock, and nothing can shake it. It is a foundation stone with these words written on it:

DEALING WITH CHANGE 1:13-14 Timothy was in a time of transition. He had been Paul's bright young helper; soon he would be on his own as leader of a church in a difficult environment. Although his responsibilities were changing, Timothy was not without help. He had everything he needed to face the future, if he would hold on tightly to the Lord's resources. When you are facing difficult transitions, it is good to follow Paul's advice to Timothy and look back at your experience. Who is the foundation of your faith? How can you build on that foundation? What gifts has the Holy Spirit given you? Use the gifts you have already been given. **To begin the series of devotionals on DEALING WITH CHANGE, turn to page 15.**

Family Devotions

☐ **DEVOTION 339**
AVOIDING SIN

Read 2 Timothy 2:19-22

"I'll be glad to set the table," offered Grandmother, coming into the kitchen as Mom was preparing supper. Though nearly blind, she liked to help whenever she could.

"That will be a big help," said Mom. "Use the dishes that are in the dishwasher."

When supper was ready, Mom called everyone to the table. Jill was the first to notice that something was wrong. "Yuck!" she exclaimed. "These dishes are dirty. Why are they on the table?"

Mom looked at her plate. "Oh!" she gasped. "I must have forgotten to run the dishwasher last night!"

"And I couldn't see that they were dirty," said Grandma. After a good laugh, everyone helped remove the dishes and replace them with clean ones.

After reading Scripture for family devotions later, Dad closed his Bible thoughtfully. "In the verses we just read, we are compared to dishes," he said. "I'm sure we all saw tonight how unpleasant it would be to eat off of dirty plates, right? We want clean dishes for our food. In the same way, we need to keep ourselves 'clean' so God can use us."

"Well, when I'm dirty, Mom tells me cleanliness is next to godliness," said Dana.

Jill nodded. "Is that in the Bible?" she asked.

Dad laughed. "No, though we should keep our bodies clean, of course," he said. "But God is more concerned that we live clean, pure lives. That's what the apostle Paul is talking about here. He tells Timothy to do that by running away from anything that might make him want to do wrong. It's a good thing to keep in mind when you're tempted to do such things as smoke, drink, use drugs, or commit immoral, impure actions with your body. When you're faced with those temptations, remember the dirty dishes. I'm sure you don't want to be like them."

Dana and Jill vigorously nodded their heads.

Avoiding Sin Memory Verse

Dear brothers, you are only visitors here. Since your real home is in heaven, I beg you to keep away from the evil pleasures of this world; they are not for you, for they fight against your very souls.
1 Peter 2:11

How About You?
Are you keeping yourself clean and pure for God? Follow Paul's advice to Timothy, and then you'll be someone God can use. M. R. P.

- For the next devotional, turn to page 1189. • For the next devotional on *AVOIDING SIN*, turn to page 1225.
- For notes on *AVOIDING SIN*, see pages 220, 332, 392, and 657.

"The Lord knows those who are really his," and "A person who calls himself a Christian should not be doing things that are wrong."

²⁰In a wealthy home there are dishes made of gold and silver as well as some made from wood and clay. The expensive dishes are used for guests, and the cheap ones are used in the kitchen or to put garbage in. ²¹If you stay away from sin you will be like one of these dishes made of purest gold—the very best in the house—so that Christ himself can use you for his highest purposes.

²²Run from anything that gives you the evil thoughts that young men often have, but stay close to anything that makes you want to do right. Have faith and love, and enjoy the companionship of those who love the Lord and have pure hearts.

²³Again I say, don't get involved in foolish arguments, which only upset people and make them angry. ²⁴God's people must not be quarrelsome; they must be gentle, patient teachers of those who are wrong. ²⁵Be humble when you are trying to teach those who are mixed up concerning the truth. For if you talk meekly and courteously to them, they are more likely, with God's help, to turn away from their wrong ideas and believe what is true. ²⁶Then they will come to their senses and escape from Satan's trap of slavery to sin, which he uses to catch them whenever he likes, and then they can begin doing the will of God.

3 Being a Christian Can Be Tough

You may as well know this too, Timothy, that in the last days it is going to be very difficult to be a Christian. ²For people will love only themselves and their money; they will be proud and boastful, sneering at God, disobedient to their parents, ungrateful to them, and thoroughly bad. ³They will be hardheaded and never give in to others; they will be constant liars and troublemakers and will think nothing of immorality. They will be rough and cruel, and sneer at those who try to be good. ⁴They will betray their friends; they will be hotheaded, puffed up with pride, and prefer good times to worshiping God. ⁵They will go to church, yes, but they won't really believe anything they hear. Don't be taken in by people like that.

⁶They are the kind who craftily sneak into other people's homes and make friendships with silly, sin-burdened women and teach them their new doctrines. ⁷Women of that kind are forever following new teachers, but they never understand the truth. ⁸And these teachers fight truth just as Jannes and Jambres fought against Moses. They have dirty minds, warped and twisted, and have turned against the Christian faith.

⁹But they won't get away with all this forever. Someday their deceit will be well known to everyone, as was the sin of Jannes and Jambres.

¹⁰But you know from watching me that I am not that kind of person. You know what I believe and the way I live and what I want. You know my faith in Christ and how I have suffered. You know my love for you, and my patience. ¹¹You know how many troubles I have had as a result of my preaching the Good News. You know about all that was done to me while I was visiting in Antioch, Iconium, and Lystra, but the Lord delivered me. ¹²Yes, and those who decide to please Christ Jesus by living godly lives will suffer at the hands of those who hate him. ¹³In fact, evil men and false teachers will become worse and worse, deceiving many, they themselves having been deceived by Satan.

¹⁴But you must keep on believing the things you have been taught. You know they are true, for you know that you can trust those of us who have taught you. ¹⁵You know how, when you were a small child, you were taught the holy Scriptures; and it is these that make you wise to accept God's salvation by trusting in Christ Jesus. ¹⁶The whole Bible was given to us by inspiration from God and is useful to teach us what is true and to make us realize what is wrong in our lives; it straightens us out and helps us do what is right. ¹⁷It is God's way of making us well prepared at every point, fully equipped to do good to everyone.

4 Share Your Faith

And so I solemnly urge you before God and before Christ Jesus—who will someday judge the living and the dead when he appears to set up his Kingdom— ²to preach the Word of God urgently at all times, whenever you get the chance, in season and out, when it is convenient and when it is not. Correct and rebuke your people when they need it, encourage them to do right, and all the time be feeding them patiently with God's Word.

³For there is going to come a time when people won't listen to the truth but will go around

---

RESPECTING GOD'S WORD **3:16** The whole Bible is God's inspired Word. Because it is inspired and trustworthy, we should *read it* and *apply it* to our lives. The Bible is our standard for testing everything else that claims to be true. It is our safeguard against false teaching and our source of guidance for how we should live. It is our only source of knowledge about how we can be saved. God wants to show you what is true and equip you to live for him. How much time do you spend in God's Word? Read it regularly to discover God's truth and become confident in your life and faith. Develop a plan for reading the whole Bible, not just the same familiar passages. **To begin the series of devotionals on RESPECTING GOD'S WORD, turn to page 11.**

Family Devotions

☐ DEVOTION 340
GOING TO CHURCH

Read 2 Timothy 2:15; 3:14-17

"Well, Greg, what's on your schedule for tomorrow?" asked Dad, as he sat down in an easy chair.

Greg snapped off the TV and picked up the paper. "Oh," he said, "tomorrow afternoon we have a youth group party." He quickly read through the comic page while his dad took off his shoes. Then, handing Dad the newspaper, Greg added, "They're having a Bible quiz at the beginning of the party. Maybe I'll go late."

"Oh?" asked Dad. "You used to enjoy quizzes. Why don't you like them now?"

Greg leafed through a sports magazine. "Because Joel always wins, that's why. They're no fun anymore."

"Do you know what chapters the quiz will cover?"

"Yes," replied Greg, "but it doesn't matter what chapters they are. Joel will know everything in them. That guy really knows his Bible. The other day in science class, Joel and our teacher got into quite a discussion about creation, and Joel did really good. He quoted verses from the Bible and talked about why he believed it was true. He really knew what he was talking about."

"Good for Joel!" cheered Dad.

"I've heard him do the same kind of thing in history class. I wish I knew the Bible like that." Greg sighed and began reading an article.

Dad watched Greg for a moment, then he asked, "How do you suppose Joel learned so much?" Greg shrugged. "Well," said Dad, "I don't think it came from reading magazines or newspapers or watching TV. If you want to know the Bible, you have to study the Bible."

Greg looked at Dad thoughtfully. He looked down at his magazine. Then, putting it down, he got to his feet. "Excuse me, please." He grinned at his dad. "I have to go study a couple of chapters in my Bible. Joel's gonna get some competition tomorrow!"

Going to Church Memory Verse

Let us not neglect our church meetings, as some people do, but encourage and warn each other, especially now that the day of his coming back again is drawing near.
Hebrews 10:25

How About You?

Do you wish you had as much Bible knowledge as your pastor, your Sunday school teacher, or even a friend? It's available to you, too, but it won't come automatically. One of the benefits of going to church and Sunday school is the chance to learn more about the Bible. Listen carefully when God's Word is taught there. Also, study it for yourself. *H. M.*

- For the next devotional, turn to page 1193. • For the next devotional on GOING TO CHURCH, turn to page 1205.
- For notes on GOING TO CHURCH, see pages 770, 965, and 1002.

looking for teachers who will tell them just what they want to hear. ⁴They won't listen to what the Bible says but will blithely follow their own misguided ideas.

⁵Stand steady, and don't be afraid of suffering for the Lord. Bring others to Christ. Leave nothing undone that you ought to do.

⁶I say this because I won't be around to help you very much longer. My time has almost run out. Very soon now I will be on my way to heaven. ⁷I have fought long and hard for my Lord, and through it all I have kept true to him. And now the time has come for me to stop fighting and rest. ⁸In heaven a crown is waiting for me, which the Lord, the righteous Judge, will give me on that great day of his return. And not just to me but to all those whose lives show that they are eagerly looking forward to his coming back again.

⁹Please come as soon as you can, ¹⁰for Demas has left me. He loved the good things of this life and went to Thessalonica. Crescens has gone to Galatia, Titus to Dalmatia. ¹¹Only Luke is with me. Bring Mark with you when you come, for I need him. ¹²(Tychicus is gone too, as I sent him to Ephesus.) ¹³When you come, be sure to bring the coat I left at Troas with Brother Carpus, and also the books, but especially the parchments.

¹⁴Alexander the coppersmith has done me much harm. The Lord will punish him, ¹⁵but be careful of him, for he fought against everything we said.

¹⁶The first time I was brought before the judge, no one was here to help me. Everyone had run away. I hope that they will not be blamed for it. ¹⁷But the Lord stood with me and gave me the opportunity to boldly preach a whole sermon for all the world to hear. And he saved me from being thrown to the lions. ¹⁸Yes, and the Lord will always deliver me from all evil and will bring me into his heavenly Kingdom. To God be the glory forever and ever. Amen.

¹⁹Please say hello for me to Priscilla and Aquila and those living at the home of Onesiphorus. ²⁰Erastus stayed at Corinth, and I left Trophimus sick at Miletus.

²¹Do try to be here before winter. Eubulus sends you greetings, and so do Pudens, Linus, Claudia, and all the others. ²²May the Lord Jesus Christ be with your spirit.

Farewell, Paul

Titus

SOMETIMES OUR bad habits seem so much a part of us that we think we'll never get rid of them. This was a problem for Christians on the island of Crete.

The Cretans had a culture all their own. They were well known for lying, laziness, and violence. When Cretans became Christians, they brought their bad habits into the church. Paul wrote this letter to Titus, who was working with the churches in Crete, to remind him of what the Christians needed to learn and do. If they really believed in Jesus, their lives would show it.

But bad habits can't be changed just by trying hard. Paul also wrote about the work of the Holy Spirit. After we accept Jesus into our hearts, his Spirit washes us clean and makes us new. The Spirit helps us change our actions to be what God wants us to be.

Do you struggle with bad habits? Look for the help of God's Spirit as you read Titus.

Paul Is Sent to Bring Faith

From: Paul, the slave of God and the messenger of Jesus Christ.

I have been sent to bring faith to those God has chosen and to teach them to know God's truth—the kind of truth that changes lives—so that they can have eternal life, which God promised them before the world began—and he cannot lie. ³And now in his own good time he has revealed this Good News and permits me to tell it to everyone. By command of God our Savior, I have been trusted to do this work for him.

⁴*To:* Titus, who is truly my son in the affairs of the Lord.

May God the Father and Christ Jesus our Savior give you his blessings and his peace.

⁵I left you there on the island of Crete so that you could do whatever was needed to help strengthen each of its churches, and I asked you to appoint pastors in every city who would follow

the instructions I gave you. ⁶The men you choose must be well thought of for their good lives; they must have only one wife and their children must love the Lord and not have a reputation for being wild or disobedient to their parents.

⁷These pastors must be men of blameless lives because they are God's ministers. They must not be proud or impatient; they must not be drunkards or fighters or greedy for money. ⁸They must enjoy having guests in their homes and must love all that is good. They must be sensible men, and fair. They must be clean minded and level headed. ⁹Their belief in the truth that they have been taught must be strong and steadfast so that they will be able to teach it to others and show those who disagree with them where they are wrong.

¹⁰For there are many who refuse to obey; this is especially true among those who say that all Christians must obey the Jewish laws. But this is foolish talk; it blinds people to the truth, ¹¹and it must be stopped. Already whole families have been turned away from the grace of God. Such teachers are only after your money. ¹²One of their own men, a prophet from Crete, has said about them, "These men of Crete are all liars; they are like lazy animals, living only to satisfy their stomachs." ¹³And this is true. So speak to the Christians there as sternly as necessary to make them strong in the faith ¹⁴and to stop them from listening to Jewish folk tales and the demands of men who have turned their backs on the truth.

¹⁵A person who is pure of heart sees goodness and purity in everything; but a person whose own heart is evil and untrusting finds evil in everything, for his dirty mind and rebellious heart color all he sees and hears. ¹⁶Such persons claim they know God, but from seeing the way they act, one knows they don't. They are rotten and disobedient, worthless so far as doing anything good is concerned.

2 Special Guidelines

But as for you, speak up for the right living that goes along with true Christianity. ²Teach the older men to be serious and unruffled; they must be sensible, knowing and believing the truth and doing everything with love and patience.

³Teach the older women to be quiet and respectful in everything they do. They must not go around speaking evil of others and must not be heavy drinkers, but they should be teachers of goodness. ⁴These older women must train the younger women to live quietly, to love their husbands and their children, ⁵and to be sensible and clean minded, spending their time in their own homes, being kind and obedient to their husbands so that the Christian faith can't be spoken against by those who know them.

⁶In the same way, urge the young men to behave carefully, taking life seriously. ⁷And here you yourself must be an example to them of good deeds of every kind. Let everything you do reflect your love of the truth and the fact that you are in dead earnest about it. ⁸Your conversation should be so sensible and logical that anyone who wants to argue will be ashamed of himself because there won't be anything to criticize in anything you say!

⁹Urge slaves to obey their masters and to try their best to satisfy them. They must not talk back, ¹⁰nor steal, but must show themselves to be entirely trustworthy. In this way they will make people want to believe in our Savior and God.

¹¹For the free gift of eternal salvation is now being offered to everyone; ¹²and along with this gift comes the realization that God wants us to turn from godless living and sinful pleasures and to live good, God-fearing lives day after day, ¹³looking forward to that wonderful time we've been expecting, when his glory shall be seen—the glory of our great God and Savior Jesus Christ. ¹⁴He died under God's judgment against our sins so that he could rescue us from constant falling into sin and make us his very own people, with cleansed hearts and real enthusiasm for doing kind things for others. ¹⁵You must teach these things and encourage your people to do them, correcting them when necessary as one who has every right to do so. Don't let anyone think that what you say is not important.

3 Obey the Government

Remind your people to obey the government and its officers, and always to be obedient and ready for any honest work. ²They must not speak evil of anyone, nor quarrel, but be gentle and truly courteous to all.

³Once we, too, were foolish and disobedient; we were misled by others and became slaves to many evil pleasures and wicked desires. Our lives were full of resentment and envy. We hated others and they hated us.

⁴But when the time came for the kindness and love of God our Savior to appear, ⁵then he saved us—not because we were good enough to be saved but because of his kindness and pity—by washing away our sins and giving us the new joy of the indwelling Holy Spirit, ⁶whom he poured out upon us with wonderful fullness—and all because of what Jesus Christ our Savior did ⁷so that he could declare us good in God's eyes—all because of his great kindness; and now we can share in the wealth of the eternal life he gives us, and we are eagerly looking forward to receiving it.

Family Devotions

☐ *Devotion 341*
Becoming More Like Jesus

Read Titus 2:6-8

Becoming More Like Jesus Memory Verse

Let everything you do reflect your love of the truth and the fact that you are in dead earnest about it. *Titus 2:7*

Joey ran from the store with tears running down his cheeks, his feet barely touching the pavement. He felt like his heart was about to explode. When he reached home, he collapsed on the sofa. Mom gathered the little boy into her arms. "Whatever is the matter?" she asked.

"Hank . . . at the s-s-store said . . . said . . ." Joey trembled. "He said . . ." His eyes widened as he remembered. "But I didn't! I didn't!" he choked.

Mom held him tightly and asked calmly, "You didn't what, Joey?"

Joey took a deep breath. "I didn't steal candy from the store yesterday after school—or any time! Hank, the new clerk, said I did. He said if I'd give him five dollars, he wouldn't tell anyone. You do believe me, don't you!"

Mom's mouth tightened. "Certainly, I believe you." She stood up. "I'm going to the store."

When she returned later, Joey asked, "What happened?"

Mom smiled grimly. "When I talked to Hank, he smirked and asked how I knew you hadn't stolen the candy. I told him, 'Because I know my son.' Then Mr. Johnson, your teacher, came in. When he heard what had happened, he said, 'Joey didn't take that candy. He was with me after school. But even if he hadn't been, I'd never believe you, Hank, because Joey is one of the most honest boys I know.'"

Joey's mouth fell open. "I was so scared, I forgot about going with Mr. Johnson to the library."

Mom squeezed Joey's shoulders. "Hank was mighty embarrassed. He's been getting money from little kids by threatening them. But he picked the wrong one this time."

Joey hugged his mother. "Thanks, Mom, for believing me," he said.

Mom ruffled Joey's hair. "Thanks, Son, for being trustworthy."

How About You?
If something like this happened to you, could your parents believe you? Are you trustworthy (worthy of their trust)? It's important to build a good reputation—for your own sake, for your parent's sake, and also for the Lord's sake. Your reputation reflects on him. *B. W.*

• For the next devotional, turn to page 1201. • For the next devotional on *Becoming More Like Jesus*, turn to page 1219. • For notes on *Becoming More Like Jesus*, see pages 234, 983, 1105, and 1164.

⁸These things I have told you are all true. Insist on them so that Christians will be careful to do good deeds all the time, for this is not only right, but it brings results.

⁹Don't get involved in arguing over unanswerable questions and controversial theological ideas; keep out of arguments and quarrels about obedience to Jewish laws, for this kind of thing isn't worthwhile; it only does harm. ¹⁰If anyone is causing divisions among you, he should be given a first and second warning. After that have nothing more to do with him, ¹¹for such a person has a wrong sense of values. He is sinning, and he knows it.

¹²I am planning to send either Artemas or Tychicus to you. As soon as one of them arrives, please try to meet me at Nicopolis as quickly as you can, for I have decided to stay there for the winter. ¹³Do everything you can to help Zenas the lawyer and Apollos with their trip; see that they are given everything they need. ¹⁴For our people must learn to help all who need their assistance, that their lives will be fruitful.

¹⁵Everybody here sends greetings. Please say hello to all of the Christian friends there. May God's blessings be with you all.

Sincerely, Paul

Philemon

WHEN SOMEONE does something that really hurts us, it can be hard to forgive. Paul knew this when he wrote to Philemon.

Philemon was a wealthy man who lived in Colosse. He owned a large home and also kept slaves. One of his slaves stole some money and ran away, and Philemon was probably angry about it.

One day Philemon got a letter from his friend Paul. Philemon was probably surprised to hear that Paul had met his runaway slave, Onesimus. Paul and Onesimus were both in prison, and Onesimus had become a Christian. Onesimus was about to be released, and Paul urged him to return to Philemon. Paul wanted Philemon to forgive Onesimus and accept him back into the household. Paul said that he would be coming to visit soon to make sure everything worked out.

The Bible doesn't tell us Philemon's response to this letter, but Paul's message is clear. When we've wronged someone, we are to return and ask forgiveness. When other people wrong us, we are to forgive them. As you read Philemon, think about the need for forgiveness in your life.

Onesimus Comes Home

From: Paul, in jail for preaching the Good News about Jesus Christ, and from Brother Timothy.

To: Philemon, our much-loved fellow worker, and to the church that meets in your home, and to Apphia our sister, and to Archippus who, like myself, is a soldier of the cross.

³May God our Father and the Lord Jesus Christ give you his blessings and his peace.

⁴I always thank God when I am praying for you, dear Philemon, ⁵because I keep hearing of your love and trust in the Lord Jesus and in his people. ⁶And I pray that as you share your faith with others it will grip their lives too, as they see the wealth of good things in you that come from Christ Jesus. ⁷I myself have gained much joy and comfort from your love, my brother, because your kindness has so often refreshed the hearts of God's people.

⁸,⁹Now I want to ask a favor of you. I could demand it of you in the name of Christ because it

is the right thing for you to do, but I love you and prefer just to ask you—I, Paul, an old man now, here in jail for the sake of Jesus Christ. ¹⁰My plea is that you show kindness to my child Onesimus, whom I won to the Lord while here in my chains. ¹¹Onesimus (whose name means "Useful") hasn't been of much use to you in the past, but now he is going to be of real use to both of us. ¹²I am sending him back to you, and with him comes my own heart.

¹³I really wanted to keep him here with me while I am in these chains for preaching the Good News, and you would have been helping me through him, ¹⁴but I didn't want to do it without your consent. I didn't want you to be kind because you had to but because you wanted to. ¹⁵Perhaps you could think of it this way: that he ran away from you for a little while so that now he can be yours forever, ¹⁶no longer only a slave, but something much better—a beloved brother, especially to me. Now he will mean much more to you too, because he is not only a servant but also your brother in Christ.

¹⁷If I am really your friend, give him the same welcome you would give to me if I were the one who was coming. ¹⁸If he has harmed you in any way or stolen anything from you, charge me for it. ¹⁹I will pay it back (I, Paul, personally guarantee this by writing it here with my own hand) but I won't mention how much you owe me! The fact is, you even owe me your very soul! ²⁰Yes, dear brother, give me joy with this loving act and my weary heart will praise the Lord.

²¹I've written you this letter because I am positive that you will do what I ask and even more!

²²Please keep a guest room ready for me, for I am hoping that God will answer your prayers and let me come to you soon.

²³Epaphras my fellow prisoner, who is also here for preaching Christ Jesus, sends you his greetings. ²⁴So do Mark, Aristarchus, Demas, and Luke, my fellow workers.

²⁵The blessings of our Lord Jesus Christ be upon your spirit.

Paul

ACCEPTING OTHERS 1:13-16 What a difference Onesimus's status as a Christian made in his relationship to Philemon. He was no longer merely a slave, he was also a brother. Now both Onesimus and Philemon were members of God's family—equals in Christ. A Christian's status as a member of God's family transcends all other distinctions among believers. Do you look down on any fellow Christians? Remember, they are your brothers and sisters, your equals before Christ (Galatians 3:28). How you treat your brothers and sisters in Christ's family reflects your true Christian commitment. **To begin the series of devotionals on ACCEPTING OTHERS, turn to page 207.**

SOME PEOPLE think of Christianity as a set of rules instead of as a relationship with Jesus.

Hebrews is a letter that was written to Jewish Christians who were putting too much emphasis on obeying religious rules and laws. The writer of Hebrews told these Christians that knowing Jesus is the most important thing. Jesus is God. He fulfilled the Old Testament prophecies and promises. We don't need to offer sacrifices again and again because Jesus was the perfect, onetime sacrifice to pay for our sins. Jesus opened the way for each person to come directly to God. In the Tabernacle and Temple system, only a few special people—the priests—could enter God's house.

The Jewish Christians needed to be reminded that their *faith* was what counted, not how many rules they followed. Even in the Old Testament, it was faith that God really wanted from his people.

Jesus Christ Is God's Son

Long ago God spoke in many different ways to our fathers through the prophets [in visions, dreams, and even face to face], telling them little by little about his plans.

²But now in these days he has spoken to us through his Son to whom he has given everything and through whom he made the world and everything there is.

³God's Son shines out with God's glory, and all that God's Son is and does marks him as God. He regulates the universe by the mighty power of his command. He is the one who died to cleanse us and clear our record of all sin, and then sat down in highest honor beside the great God of heaven.

⁴Thus he became far greater than the angels, as proved by the fact that his name "Son of God," which was passed on to him from his Father, is far greater than the names and titles of the angels. ⁵,⁶For God never said to any angel, "You are my Son, and today I have given you the honor that goes with that name." But God said it about Jesus.

Another time he said, "I am his Father and he is my Son." And still another time—when his firstborn Son came to earth—God said, "Let all the angels of God worship him."

⁷God speaks of his angels as messengers swift as the wind and as servants made of flaming fire; ⁸but of his Son he says, "Your Kingdom, O God, will last forever and ever; its commands are always just and right. ⁹You love right and hate wrong; so God, even your God, has poured out more gladness upon you than on anyone else."

¹⁰God also called him "Lord" when he said, "Lord, in the beginning you made the earth, and the heavens are the work of your hands. ¹¹They will disappear into nothingness, but you will remain forever. They will become worn out like old clothes, ¹²and some day you will fold them up and replace them. But you yourself will never change, and your years will never end."

¹³And did God ever say to an angel, as he does to his Son, "Sit here beside me in honor until I crush all your enemies beneath your feet"?

¹⁴No, for the angels are only spirit-messengers sent out to help and care for those who are to receive his salvation.

2 Listen Carefully and Obey God

So we must listen very carefully to the truths we have heard, or we may drift away from them. ²For since the messages from angels have always proved true and people have always been punished for disobeying them, ³what makes us think that we can escape if we are indifferent to this great salvation announced by the Lord Jesus himself and passed on to us by those who heard him speak?

⁴God always has shown us that these messages are true by signs and wonders and various miracles and by giving certain special abilities from the Holy Spirit to those who believe; yes, God has assigned such gifts to each of us.

⁵And the future world we are talking about will not be controlled by angels. ⁶No, for in the book of Psalms David says to God, "What is mere man that you are so concerned about him? And who is this Son of Man you honor so highly? ⁷For though you made him lower than the angels for a little while, now you have crowned him with glory and honor. ⁸And you have put him in complete charge of everything there is. Nothing is left out."

We have not yet seen all of this take place, ⁹but we do see Jesus—who for awhile was a little lower than the angels—crowned now by God with glory and honor because he suffered death for us. Yes, because of God's great kindness, Jesus tasted death for everyone in all the world.

¹⁰And it was right and proper that God, who made everything for his own glory, should allow Jesus to suffer, for in doing this he was bringing vast multitudes of God's people to heaven; for his suffering made Jesus a perfect Leader, one fit to bring them into their salvation.

¹¹We who have been made holy by Jesus, now have the same Father he has. That is why Jesus is not ashamed to call us his brothers. ¹²For he says in the book of Psalms, "I will talk to my brothers about God my Father, and together we will sing his praises." ¹³At another time he said, "I will put my trust in God along with my brothers." And at still another time, "See, here am I and the children God gave me."

¹⁴Since we, God's children, are human beings—made of flesh and blood—he became flesh and blood too by being born in human form; for only as a human being could he die and in dying break the power of the devil who had the power of death. ¹⁵Only in that way could he deliver those who through fear of death have been living all their lives as slaves to constant dread.

¹⁶We all know he did not come as an angel but as a human being—yes, a Jew. ¹⁷And it was necessary for Jesus to be like us, his brothers, so that he could be our merciful and faithful High Priest before God, a Priest who would be both merciful to us and faithful to God in dealing with the sins of the people. ¹⁸For since he himself has now been through suffering and temptation, he knows what it is like when we suffer and are tempted, and he is wonderfully able to help us.

3 Jesus: Greater Than Moses

Therefore, dear brothers whom God has set apart for himself—you who are chosen for heaven—I want you to think now about this Jesus who is God's Messenger and the High Priest of our faith.

²For Jesus was faithful to God who appointed him High Priest, just as Moses also faithfully served in God's house. ³But Jesus has far more glory than Moses, just as a man who builds a fine house gets more praise than his house does. ⁴And many people can build houses, but only God made everything.

⁵Well, Moses did a fine job working in God's house, but he was only a servant; and his work

---

DEALING WITH CHANGE 2:9 God has put Jesus in charge of everything and Jesus has revealed himself to us. We do not yet see Jesus reigning on earth, but we can picture him in his heavenly glory. When confused by tomorrow and anxious about the future, strive to keep a clear view of Jesus Christ—who he is, what he has done, and what he is doing for us right now. This will give stability to your life day by day. **To begin the series of devotionals on DEALING WITH CHANGE, turn to page 15.**

was mostly to illustrate and suggest those things that would happen later on. ⁶But Christ, God's faithful Son, is in complete charge of God's house. And we Christians are God's house—he lives in us!—if we keep up our courage firm to the end, and our joy and our trust in the Lord.

⁷,⁸And since Christ is so much superior, the Holy Spirit warns us to listen to him, to be careful to hear his voice today and not let our hearts become set against him, as the people of Israel did. They steeled themselves against his love and complained against him in the desert while he was testing them. ⁹But God was patient with them forty years, though they tried his patience sorely; he kept right on doing his mighty miracles for them to see. ¹⁰"But," God says, "I was very angry with them, for their hearts were always looking somewhere else instead of up to me, and they never found the paths I wanted them to follow."

¹¹Then God, full of this anger against them, bound himself with an oath that he would never let them come to his place of rest.

¹²Beware then of your own hearts, dear brothers, lest you find that they, too, are evil and unbelieving and are leading you away from the living God. ¹³Speak to each other about these things every day while there is still time so that none of you will become hardened against God, being blinded by the glamor of sin. ¹⁴For if we are faithful to the end, trusting God just as we did when we first became Christians, we will share in all that belongs to Christ.

¹⁵But *now* is the time. Never forget the warning, "*Today* if you hear God's voice speaking to you, do not harden your hearts against him, as the people of Israel did when they rebelled against him in the desert."

¹⁶And who were those people I speak of, who heard God's voice speaking to them but then rebelled against him? They were the ones who came out of Egypt with Moses their leader. ¹⁷And who was it who made God angry for all those forty years? These same people who sinned and as a result died in the wilderness. ¹⁸And to whom was God speaking when he swore with an oath that they could never go into the land he had promised his people? He was speaking to all those who disobeyed him. ¹⁹And why couldn't they go in? Because they didn't trust him.

4 God's Promise of Rest

Although God's promise still stands—his promise that all may enter his place of rest—we ought to tremble with fear because some of you may be on the verge of failing to get there after all. ²For this wonderful news—the message that God wants to save us—has been given to us just as it was to those who lived in the time of Moses. But it didn't do them any good because they didn't believe it. They didn't mix it with faith. ³For only we who believe God can enter into his place of rest. He has said, "I have sworn in my anger that those who don't believe me will never get in," even though he has been ready and waiting for them since the world began.

⁴We know he is ready and waiting because it is written that God rested on the seventh day of creation, having finished all that he had planned to make.

⁵Even so they didn't get in, for God finally said, "They shall never enter my rest." ⁶Yet the promise remains and some get in—but not those who had the first chance, for they disobeyed God and failed to enter.

⁷But he has set another time for coming in, and that time is now. He announced this through King David long years after man's first failure to enter, saying in the words already quoted, "Today when you hear him calling, do not harden your hearts against him."

⁸This new place of rest he is talking about does not mean the land of Israel that Joshua led them into. If that were what God meant, he would not have spoken long afterwards about "today" being the time to get in. ⁹So there is a full complete rest *still waiting* for the people of God. ¹⁰Christ has already entered there. He is resting from his work, just as God did after the creation. ¹¹Let us do our best to go into that place of rest, too, being careful not to disobey God as the children of Israel did, thus failing to get in.

¹²For whatever God says to us is full of living power: it is sharper than the sharpest dagger, cutting swift and deep into our innermost thoughts and desires with all their parts, exposing us for what we really are. ¹³He knows about everyone, everywhere. Everything about us is bare and wide open to the all-seeing eyes of our living God; nothing can be hidden from him to whom we must explain all that we have done.

¹⁴But Jesus the Son of God is our great High Priest who has gone to heaven itself to help us; therefore let us never stop trusting him. ¹⁵This High Priest of ours understands our weaknesses since he had the same temptations we do, though he never once gave way to them and sinned. ¹⁶So let us come boldly to the very throne of God and stay there to receive his mercy and to find grace to help us in our times of need.

5 Jesus Christ Is Our High Priest

The Jewish high priest is merely a man like anyone else, but he is chosen to speak for all other men in their dealings with God. He presents their gifts to God and offers to him the blood of animals that are sacrificed to cover the sins of the people and his own sins too. And because he is a man, he can deal gently with other men, though they are foolish and ignorant, for he, too, is surrounded with the same temptations and understands their problems very well.

⁴Another thing to remember is that no one can be a high priest just because he wants to be. He has to be called by God for this work in the same way God chose Aaron.

⁵That is why Christ did not elect himself to the honor of being High Priest; no, he was chosen by God. God said to him, "My Son, today I have honored you." ⁶And another time God said to him, "You have been chosen to be a priest forever, with the same rank as Melchizedek."

⁷Yet while Christ was here on earth he pleaded with God, praying with tears and agony of soul to the only one who would save him from [premature] death. And God heard his prayers because of his strong desire to obey God at all times.

⁸And even though Jesus was God's Son, he had to learn from experience what it was like to obey when obeying meant suffering. ⁹It was after he had proved himself perfect in this experience that Jesus became the Giver of eternal salvation to all those who obey him. ¹⁰For remember that God has chosen him to be a High Priest with the same rank as Melchizedek.

¹¹There is much more I would like to say along these lines, but you don't seem to listen, so it's hard to make you understand.

¹²,¹³You have been Christians a long time now, and you ought to be teaching others, but instead you have dropped back to the place where you need someone to teach you all over again the very first principles in God's Word. You are like babies who can drink only milk, not old enough for solid food. And when a person is still living on milk it shows he isn't very far along in the Christian life, and doesn't know much about the difference between right and wrong. He is still a baby Christian! ¹⁴You will never be able to eat solid spiritual food and understand the deeper things of God's Word until you become better Christians and learn right from wrong by practicing doing right.

6 Count on God's Promises

Let us stop going over the same old ground again and again, always teaching those first lessons about Christ. Let us go on instead to other things and become mature in our understanding, as strong Christians ought to be. Surely we don't need to speak further about the foolishness of trying to be saved by being good, or about the necessity of faith in God; ²you don't need further instruction about baptism and spiritual gifts and the resurrection of the dead and eternal judgment.

³The Lord willing, we will go on now to other things.

⁴There is no use trying to bring you back to the Lord again if you have once understood the Good News and tasted for yourself the good things of heaven and shared in the Holy Spirit, ⁵and know how good the Word of God is, and felt the mighty powers of the world to come, ⁶and then have turned against God. You cannot bring yourself to repent again if you have nailed the Son of God to the cross again by rejecting him, holding him up to mocking and to public shame.

⁷When a farmer's land has had many showers upon it and good crops come up, that land has experienced God's blessing upon it. ⁸But if it keeps on having crops of thistles and thorns, the land is considered no good and is ready for condemnation and burning off.

⁹Dear friends, even though I am talking like this I really don't believe that what I am saying applies to you. I am confident you are producing the good fruit that comes along with your salvation. ¹⁰For God is not unfair. How can he forget your hard work for him, or forget the way you used to show your love for him—and still do—by helping his children? ¹¹And we are anxious that you keep right on loving others as long as life lasts, so that you will get your full reward.

¹²Then, knowing what lies ahead for you, you won't become bored with being a Christian nor become spiritually dull and indifferent, but you will be anxious to follow the example of those who receive all that God has promised them because of their strong faith and patience.

¹³For instance, there was God's promise to Abraham: God took an oath in his own name, since there was no one greater to swear by, ¹⁴that he would bless Abraham again and again, and give him a son and make him the father of a great nation of people. ¹⁵Then Abraham waited patiently until finally God gave him a son, Isaac, just as he had promised.

¹⁶When a man takes an oath, he is calling upon someone greater than himself to force him to do what he has promised or to punish him if he later refuses to do it; the oath ends all argument about it. ¹⁷God also bound himself with an oath, so that those he promised to help would be perfectly sure and never need to wonder whether he might change his plans.

¹⁸He has given us both his promise and his oath, two things we can completely count on, for it is impossible for God to tell a lie. Now all those

FAMILY DEVOTIONS

☐ *Devotion 342*
Trusting God for Help

Read Hebrews 4:12-16

Trusting God for Help
Memory Verse

God is our refuge and strength, a tested help in times of trouble.
Psalm 46:1

Gene and his father were taking advantage of a lovely fall afternoon for one last fishing trip before winter, and they were having a serious discussion. "I know we're supposed to love everyone," said Gene as he stared at the river, "but to tell you the truth, I don't think I'll ever love Bruce. He's such a bully, and he makes me so mad. How can I love someone who acts the way he does?"

Dad was thoughtful as he reeled in his line. "Say, Gene," he said, taking out his pocket knife, "what do you think will happen if I toss this knife in the water?"

Gene took the knife from Dad's hand and examined it before handing it back. "It will sink like a rock, of course."

"I disagree," said Dad. "I think it will stay right at the top—I'll show you. Just watch."

"Don't throw it in the water," protested Gene. "You'll lose it. Give it to me if you don't want it anymore. It won't do anybody any good on the bottom of the river."

But Dad had turned to his tackle box. Taking out the biggest cork bobber he could find, he tied it to his fishing line. Just above it, he attached the knife. Gene watched as Dad threw the whole assembly into the river. It sank beneath the water, then began to float.

"Oh, no fair," protested Gene. "The cork is floating and the knife is just riding along."

"Well, I didn't say it would float by itself," replied Dad, reeling it in. "It would be impossible for it to do that. But with the help of the cork, it's carried along at the top of the water. It reminds me that with God, nothing is impossible. God gives many commands I can't carry out by myself, but when I trust him to help me, he just holds me up and carries me along—even when it's against my natural instincts."

"I get the point, Dad," said Gene, with a grin. "I'll ask God to help me love Bruce. I really will."

How About You?
Is it unnatural for you to witness for Jesus? To quit complaining? To be cheerful? To be unselfish? God gives many commands that go against your natural inclinations. By yourself, you can't obey them—but with his help, you can. *H. M.*

• For the next devotional, turn to page 1203. • To start the next topic, turn to page 9. • For notes on *Trusting God for Help*, see pages 240, 249, 464, 539, and 751.

who flee to him to save them can take new courage when they hear such assurances from God; now they can know without doubt that he will give them the salvation he has promised them.

[19]This certain hope of being saved is a strong and trustworthy anchor for our souls, connecting us with God himself behind the sacred curtains of heaven, [20]where Christ has gone ahead to plead for us from his position as our High Priest, with the honor and rank of Melchizedek.

7 Melchizedek: Justice and Peace

This Melchizedek was king of the city of Salem and also a priest of the Most High God. When Abraham was returning home after winning a great battle against many kings, Melchizedek met him and blessed him; [2]then Abraham took a tenth of all he had won in the battle and gave it to Melchizedek.

Melchizedek's name means "Justice," so he is the King of Justice; and he is also the King of Peace because of the name of his city, Salem, which means "Peace." [3]Melchizedek had no father or mother and there is no record of any of his ancestors. He was never born and he never died but his life is like that of the Son of God—a priest forever.

[4]See then how great this Melchizedek is:

*(a)*Even Abraham, the first and most honored of all God's chosen people, gave Melchizedek a tenth of the spoils he took from the kings he had been fighting. [5]One could understand why Abraham would do this if Melchizedek had been a Jewish priest, for later on God's people were required by law to give gifts to help their priests because the priests were their relatives. [6]But Melchizedek was not a relative, and yet Abraham paid him.

*(b)*Melchizedek placed a blessing upon mighty Abraham, [7]and as everyone knows, a person who has the power to bless is always greater than the person he blesses.

[8]*(c)*The Jewish priests, though mortal, received tithes; but we are told that Melchizedek lives on.

[9]*(d)*One might even say that Levi himself (the ancestor of all Jewish priests, of all who receive tithes), paid tithes to Melchizedek through Abraham. [10]For although Levi wasn't born yet, the seed from which he came was in Abraham when Abraham paid the tithes to Melchizedek.

[11]*(e)*If the Jewish priests and their laws had been able to save us, why then did God need to send Christ as a priest with the rank of Melchizedek, instead of sending someone with the rank of Aaron—the same rank all other priests had?

[12-14]And when God sends a new kind of priest, his law must be changed to permit it. As we all know, Christ did not belong to the priest-tribe of Levi, but came from the tribe of Judah, which had not been chosen for priesthood; Moses had never given them that work.

[15]So we can plainly see that God's method changed, for Christ, the new High Priest who came with the rank of Melchizedek, [16]did not become a priest by meeting the old requirement of belonging to the tribe of Levi, but on the basis of power flowing from a life that cannot end. [17]And the psalmist points this out when he says of Christ, "You are a priest forever with the rank of Melchizedek."

[18]Yes, the old system of priesthood based on family lines was canceled because it didn't work. It was weak and useless for saving people. [19]It never made anyone really right with God. But now we have a far better hope, for Christ makes us acceptable to God, and now we may draw near to him.

[20]God took an oath that Christ would always be a Priest, [21]although he never said that of other priests. Only to Christ he said, "The Lord has sworn and will never change his mind: You are a Priest forever, with the rank of Melchizedek." [22]Because of God's oath, Christ can guarantee forever the success of this new and better arrangement.

[23]Under the old arrangement there had to be many priests so that when the older ones died off, the system could still be carried on by others who took their places.

[24]But Jesus lives forever and continues to be a Priest so that no one else is needed. [25]He is able to save completely all who come to God through him. Since he will live forever, he will always be there to remind God that he has paid for their sins with his blood.

[26]He is, therefore, exactly the kind of High Priest we need; for he is holy and blameless, unstained by sin, undefiled by sinners, and to him has been given the place of honor in heaven. [27]He never needs the daily blood of animal sacrifices, as other priests did, to cover over first their own sins and then the sins of the people; for he finished all sacrifices, once and for all, when he sacrificed himself on the cross. [28]Under the old system, even the high priests were weak and sinful men who could not keep from doing wrong, but later God appointed by his oath his Son who is perfect forever.

8 Our New High Priest

What we are saying is this: Christ, whose priesthood we have just described, is our High Priest and is in heaven at the place of greatest honor next to God himself. [2]He ministers in the

FAMILY DEVOTIONS

☐ **DEVOTION 343**
SERVING GOD WILLINGLY

Read Hebrews 6:10-12

Matt sat idly on the porch swing. When Jerry came riding by on his bicycle at top speed, Matt almost didn't see him. "Hey, Jerry," he called to his friend's back, "where's the fire?"

Jerry slammed on his brakes. "No fire," he responded. "I've just got a lot to do today."

"Boy, I don't," Matt grumbled. "I'm so bored. There's nothing to do around here."

"Nothing to do?" echoed Jerry. "I'm really busy. I'm on my way to mow Gramp Norton's lawn. Want to help me?"

"Sure," Matt answered. "How much will we get paid?"

"Nothing." Jerry grinned. "I'm doing it for the Lord and for fun."

"For the Lord and for fun?" Matt slapped his forehead. "You're mowing a lawn for fun? Does Gramps have a riding mower or something?"

Jerry shook his head. "No. I'm doing it because it's fun to do things for other people. And, besides, Jesus said when I do something for others, I'm doing it for him. I've decided to spend this summer working for Jesus."

Matt raised his eyebrows and moaned. But because he didn't have anything else to do, he went with Jerry. He also went with him the next day—and the next day, too—as Jerry "worked for the Lord."

"Say, this is fun," Matt told Jerry as they cleaned his dad's garage without having been asked to do so.

"My mom says we get bored because we think about ourselves too much," Jerry told Matt. "She says it's less likely to happen when we're busy helping others."

"Well, I sure haven't been bored the last few days," Matt said grinning. "Maybe this summer won't be so dull after all."

Serving God Willingly Memory Verse

Anyone who takes care of a little child like this is caring for me! And whoever cares for me is caring for God who sent me. Your care for others is the measure of your greatness.
Luke 9:48

How About You?

Is "I'm bored" your theme song? Could that be because you're thinking too much about yourself? There are many things you can do to keep busy and help others. Ask the Lord to show you some way you can help another person each day. Then do it. When you do something for someone else, you are doing it for Jesus, too. B. W.

temple in heaven, the true place of worship built by the Lord and not by human hands.

³And since every high priest is appointed to offer gifts and sacrifices, Christ must make an offering too. ⁴The sacrifice he offers is far better than those offered by the earthly priests. (But even so, if he were here on earth he wouldn't even be permitted to be a priest because down here the priests still follow the old Jewish system of sacrifices.) ⁵Their work is connected with a mere earthly model of the real tabernacle in heaven; for when Moses was getting ready to build the tabernacle, God warned him to follow exactly the pattern of the heavenly tabernacle as shown to him on Mount Sinai. ⁶But Christ, as a Minister in heaven, has been rewarded with a far more important work than those who serve under the old laws because the new agreement that he passes on to us from God contains far more wonderful promises.

⁷The old agreement didn't even work. If it had, there would have been no need for another to replace it. ⁸But God himself found fault with the old one, for he said, "The day will come when I will make a new agreement with the people of Israel and the people of Judah. ⁹This new agreement will not be like the old one I gave to their fathers on the day when I took them by the hand to lead them out of the land of Egypt; they did not keep their part in that agreement, so I had to cancel it. ¹⁰But this is the new agreement I will make with the people of Israel, says the Lord: I will write my laws in their minds so that they will know what I want them to do without my even telling them, and these laws will be in their hearts so that they will want to obey them, and I will be their God and they shall be my people. ¹¹And no one then will need to speak to his friend or neighbor or brother, saying, 'You, too, should know the Lord,' because everyone, great and small, will know me already. ¹²And I will be merciful to them in their wrongdoings, and I will remember their sins no more."

¹³God speaks of these new promises, of this new agreement, as taking the place of the old one; for the old one is out of date now and has been put aside forever.

9 Old Rules about Worship

Now in that first agreement between God and his people there were rules for worship and there was a sacred tent down here on earth. Inside this place of worship there were two rooms. The first one contained the golden candlestick and a table with special loaves of holy bread upon it; this part was called the Holy Place. ³Then there was a curtain, and behind the curtain was a room called the Holy of Holies. ⁴In that room there were a golden incense-altar and the golden chest, called the ark of the covenant, completely covered on all sides with pure gold. Inside the ark were the tablets of stone with the Ten Commandments written on them, and a golden jar with some manna in it, and Aaron's wooden cane that budded. ⁵Above the golden chest were statues of angels called the cherubim—the guardians of God's glory—with their wings stretched out over the ark's golden cover, called the mercy seat. But enough of such details.

⁶Well, when all was ready, the priests went in and out of the first room whenever they wanted to, doing their work. ⁷But only the high priest went into the inner room, and then only once a year, all alone, and always with blood that he sprinkled on the mercy seat as an offering to God to cover his own mistakes and sins and the mistakes and sins of all the people.

⁸And the Holy Spirit uses all this to point out to us that under the old system the common people could not go into the Holy of Holies as long as the outer room and the entire system it represents were still in use.

⁹This has an important lesson for us today. For under the old system, gifts and sacrifices were offered, but these failed to cleanse the hearts of the people who brought them. ¹⁰For the old system dealt only with certain rituals—what foods to eat and drink, rules for washing themselves, and rules about this and that. The people had to keep these rules to tide them over until Christ came with God's new and better way.

¹¹He came as High Priest of this better system that we now have. He went into that greater, perfect tabernacle in heaven, not made by men nor part of this world, ¹²and once for all took blood into that inner room, the Holy of Holies, and sprinkled it on the mercy seat; but it was not the blood of goats and calves. No, he took his own blood, and with it he, by himself, made sure of our eternal salvation.

¹³And if under the old system the blood of bulls and goats and the ashes of young cows could cleanse men's bodies from sin, ¹⁴just think how much more surely the blood of Christ will transform our lives and hearts. His sacrifice frees us from the worry of having to obey the old rules and makes us want to serve the living God. For by the help of the eternal Holy Spirit, Christ willingly gave himself to God to die for our sins—he being perfect, without a single sin or fault. ¹⁵Christ came with this new agreement so that all who are invited may come and have forever all the wonders God has promised them. For Christ died to rescue them from the penalty of the sins they had committed while still under that old system.

FAMILY DEVOTIONS

☐ *DEVOTION 344*
GOING TO CHURCH

Read Hebrews 10 : 19 - 25

"Mom, can I go skiing with Jan and her family next Sunday?" asked Amy. She hurried on as she saw her mother begin to shake her head. "Jan and her family go skiing almost every weekend, but they worship God just as well as we do. Jan told me they feel God's presence in nature—in the snow and the hills and everything."

"That sounds good," Mom said, "but I wonder how much you'd even think about God if you were skiing instead of attending church. What Jan's family does is up to them, but you're our responsibility, and Dad and I don't think it's right to skip church in favor of skiing."

Amy knew it was useless to argue.

That evening Dad added a log to the fire in the fireplace and stirred it with a poker. Suddenly, with a loud crack, a small ember flew out onto the hearth. Amy jumped and then laughed as she watched it glow for a few minutes before slowly fading and turning black.

"Did that scare you?" asked Dad.

"For a minute," said Amy, grinning. "It sure didn't burn long when it got separated from the rest of the logs, did it?"

"No, it didn't," answered Mom thoughtfully. "You know, that ember that fell from the fireplace is a good illustration of what can happen to God's children when they no longer meet with God's people. That ember was giving light and warmth with the others, but all by itself, it soon grew cold. And God's people, united in fellowship, worship, and prayer, are like the glowing coals. They give and receive strength for everyday living. But, all alone, they often grow cold, too."

---

*Going to Church
Memory Verse*

Let us not neglect our church meetings, as some people do, but encourage and warn each other, especially now that the day of his coming back again is drawing near.
Hebrews 10:25

H o w   A b o u t   Y o u ?
Do you worship regularly with God's people? He says you should do that. He knows you need the encouragement and warmth of their fellowship. Together you can do great things for him. *H. M.*

• For the next devotional, turn to page 1207.   • To start the next topic, turn to page 33.   • For notes on *GOING TO CHURCH*, see pages 770, 965, and 1002.

[16]Now, if someone dies and leaves a will—a list of things to be given away to certain people when he dies—no one gets anything until it is proved that the person who wrote the will is dead. [17]The will goes into effect only after the death of the person who wrote it. While he is still alive no one can use it to get any of those things he has promised them.

[18]That is why blood was sprinkled [as proof of Christ's death] before even the first agreement could go into effect. [19]For after Moses had given the people all of God's laws, he took the blood of calves and goats, along with water, and sprinkled the blood over the book of God's laws and over all the people, using branches of hyssop bushes and scarlet wool to sprinkle with. [20]Then he said, "This is the blood that marks the beginning of the agreement between you and God, the agreement God commanded me to make with you." [21]And in the same way he sprinkled blood on the sacred tent and on whatever instruments were used for worship. [22]In fact we can say that under the old agreement almost everything was cleansed by sprinkling it with blood, and without the shedding of blood there is no forgiveness of sins.

[23]That is why the sacred tent down here on earth and everything in it—all copied from things in heaven—all had to be made pure by Moses in this way, by being sprinkled with the blood of animals. But the real things in heaven, of which these down here are copies, were made pure with far more precious offerings.

[24]For Christ has entered into heaven itself to appear now before God as our Friend. It was not in the earthly place of worship that he did this, for that was merely a copy of the real temple in heaven. [25]Nor has he offered himself again and again, as the high priest down here on earth offers animal blood in the Holy of Holies each year. [26]If that had been necessary, then he would have had to die again and again, ever since the world began. But no! He came once for all, at the end of the age, to put away the power of sin forever by dying for us.

[27]And just as it is destined that men die only once, and after that comes judgment, [28]so also Christ died only once as an offering for the sins of many people; and he will come again, but not to deal again with our sins.

This time he will come bringing salvation to all those who are eagerly and patiently waiting for him.

10 Forgiveness: Once and for All

The old system of Jewish laws gave only a dim foretaste of the good things Christ would do for us. The sacrifices under the old system were repeated again and again, year after year, but even so they could never save those who lived under their rules. [2]If they could have, one offering would have been enough; the worshipers would have been cleansed once for all and their feeling of guilt would be gone.

[3]But just the opposite happened: those yearly sacrifices reminded them of their disobedience and guilt instead of relieving their minds. [4]For it is not possible for the blood of bulls and goats really to take away sins.

[5]That is why Christ said as he came into the world, "O God, the blood of bulls and goats cannot satisfy you, so you have made ready this body of mine for me to lay as a sacrifice upon your altar. [6]You were not satisfied with the animal sacrifices, slain and burnt before you as offerings for sin. [7]Then I said, 'See, I have come to do your will, to lay down my life, just as the Scriptures said that I would.'"

[8]After Christ said this about not being satisfied with the various sacrifices and offerings required under the old system, [9]he then added, "Here I am. I have come to give my life."

He cancels the first system in favor of a far better one. [10]Under this new plan we have been forgiven and made clean by Christ's dying for us once and for all.

[11]Under the old agreement the priests stood before the altar day after day offering sacrifices that could never take away our sins. [12]But Christ gave himself to God for our sins as one sacrifice for all time and then sat down in the place of highest honor at God's right hand, [13]waiting for his enemies to be laid under his feet. [14]For by that one offering he made forever perfect in the sight of God all those whom he is making holy.

[15]And the Holy Spirit testifies that this is so, for he has said, [16]"This is the agreement I will make with the people of Israel, though they broke their first agreement: I will write my laws into their minds so that they will always know my will, and I will put my laws in their hearts so that they will want to obey them." [17]And then he adds, "I will never again remember their sins and lawless deeds."

[18]Now, when sins have once been forever forgiven and forgotten, there is no need to offer more sacrifices to get rid of them.

[19]And so, dear brothers, now we may walk right into the very Holy of Holies, where God is, because of the blood of Jesus. [20]This is the fresh, new, life-giving way that Christ has opened up for us by tearing the curtain—his human body—to let us into the holy presence of God.

[21]And since this great High Priest of ours rules over God's household, [22]let us go right in to God himself, with true hearts fully trusting him to

Family Devotions

☐ *Devotion 345*
Patience

Read Hebrews 10 : 32 - 38

As Dad read from the Bible about people being laughed at for their faith in Christ, Tina was thinking about a girl at school. Judy, who was a whole head taller than Tina, constantly made fun of her because she was a Christian.

The next day at school Judy shouted, "Everyone be real good! Here comes the perfect Christian. Hail to Tina! Should we bow down?" Tina wondered if it was because Judy was so big and the other kids were afraid of her that they laughed with her, or did they feel that way, too?

At lunch Judy tripped Tina as she was carrying her tray to the table, and Tina got peas and carrots all over her blouse. She wanted so badly to do something back to Judy, but she remembered that she was supposed to be willing to suffer for the Lord.

After school Tina was surprised when a new girl named Chris came to walk with her. "Tina, why do you just take all this trouble from Judy? Why don't you do something to get even? I know I would! At least talk to the teacher or the principal or something!" Chris urged.

"Well," Tina replied, "I'm a Christian, and the Bible tells me I should be willing to suffer for Jesus' sake. I'm trying to do what God wants me to do."

Chris looked thoughtful. "I don't understand what you mean, but I sure would like to find out more about God if he gives you that kind of patience. I have such a terrible temper!" she confessed.

"Daddy!" Tina shouted as she came in from school. "I may not ever lead Judy to Christ by being patient, but it might help me win Chris for the Lord!"

Patience
Memory Verse

Now as for you, dear brothers who are waiting for the Lord's return, be patient, like a farmer who waits until the autumn for his precious harvest to ripen.
James 5:7

How About You?
Do you feel like you have suffered for a long time at the hands of another person? Maybe the Lord is trying to teach you to trust him in everything, so that you can be an effective witness for him. *R. P.*

• For the next devotional, turn to page 1209. • To start the next topic, turn to page 37. • For notes on *Patience*, see pages 35, 242, 329, and 502.

receive us because we have been sprinkled with Christ's blood to make us clean and because our bodies have been washed with pure water.

23Now we can look forward to the salvation God has promised us. There is no longer any room for doubt, and we can tell others that salvation is ours, for there is no question that he will do what he says.

24In response to all he has done for us, let us outdo each other in being helpful and kind to each other and in doing good.

25Let us not neglect our church meetings, as some people do, but encourage and warn each other, especially now that the day of his coming back again is drawing near.

26If anyone sins deliberately by rejecting the Savior after knowing the truth of forgiveness, this sin is not covered by Christ's death; there is no way to get rid of it. 27There will be nothing to look forward to but the terrible punishment of God's awful anger, which will consume all his enemies. 28A man who refused to obey the laws given by Moses was killed without mercy if there were two or three witnesses to his sin. 29Think how much more terrible the punishment will be for those who have trampled underfoot the Son of God and treated his cleansing blood as though it were common and unhallowed, and insulted and outraged the Holy Spirit who brings God's mercy to his people.

30For we know him who said, "Justice belongs to me; I will repay them"; who also said, "The Lord himself will handle these cases." 31It is a fearful thing to fall into the hands of the living God.

32Don't ever forget those wonderful days when you first learned about Christ. Remember how you kept right on with the Lord even though it meant terrible suffering. 33Sometimes you were laughed at and beaten, and sometimes you watched and sympathized with others suffering the same things. 34You suffered with those thrown into jail, and you were actually joyful when all you owned was taken from you, knowing that better things were awaiting you in heaven, things that would be yours forever.

35Do not let this happy trust in the Lord die away, no matter what happens. Remember your reward! 36You need to keep on patiently doing God's will if you want him to do for you all that he has promised. 37His coming will not be delayed much longer. 38And those whose faith has made them good in God's sight must live by faith, trusting him in everything. Otherwise, if they shrink back, God will have no pleasure in them.

39But we have never turned our backs on God and sealed our fate. No, our faith in him assures our souls' salvation.

Great Heroes of the Faith

What is faith? It is the confident assurance that something we want is going to happen. It is the certainty that what we hope for is waiting for us, even though we cannot see it up ahead. 2Men of God in days of old were famous for their faith.

3By faith—by believing God—we know that the world and the stars—in fact, all things—were made at God's command; and that they were all made from things that can't be seen.

4It was by faith that Abel obeyed God and brought an offering that pleased God more than Cain's offering did. God accepted Abel and proved it by accepting his gift; and though Abel is long dead, we can still learn lessons from him about trusting God.

5Enoch trusted God too, and that is why God took him away to heaven without dying; suddenly he was gone because God took him. Before this happened God had said how pleased he was with Enoch. 6You can never please God without faith, without depending on him. Anyone who wants to come to God must believe that there is a God and that he rewards those who sincerely look for him.

7Noah was another who trusted God. When he heard God's warning about the future, Noah believed him even though there was then no sign of a flood, and wasting no time, he built the ark and saved his family. Noah's belief in God was in direct contrast to the sin and disbelief of the rest of the world—which refused to obey—and because of his faith he became one of those whom God has accepted.

8Abraham trusted God, and when God told him to leave home and go far away to another land that he promised to give him, Abraham obeyed. Away he went, not even knowing where he was going. 9And even when he reached God's promised land, he lived in tents like a mere visitor as did Isaac and Jacob, to whom God gave the same promise. 10Abraham did this because he was confidently waiting for God to bring him to that strong heavenly city whose designer and builder is God.

KNOWING GOD **11:1** How do you feel when you know your birthday is coming soon? Are you excited and anxious? You know you will certainly receive gifts and other special treats. But some things will be a surprise. Birthdays combine assurance and anticipation, and so does faith! Faith is the conviction based on past experience that God's new and fresh surprises will surely be ours. Two words describe our faith: *confidence* and *certainty*. We believe that God will fulfill his promises even though we don't see those promises materializing *now*—this is true faith (see John 20:24-31). **To begin the series of devotionals on KNOWING GOD, turn to page 197.**

Family Devotions

□ *Devotion 346*
Perseverance

Read Hebrews 12 : 1-3

*Perseverance
Memory Verse*

Be strong and courageous and get to work. Don't be frightened by the size of the task, for the Lord my God is with you; he will not forsake you. He will see to it that everything is finished correctly.
1 Chronicles 28:20

Aaron and his mother sadly arrived home from his grandfather's funeral. "I'm sure going to miss Grandpa," said Aaron, tears filling his eyes. "He was the best grandfather a guy could have!"

"Yes," agreed Mom as Aaron picked up a picture of his grandfather and gazed at it. "Grandpa set a good example for you as a Christian. He witnessed for Christ everywhere he went, and he always gave his time and his money to help others, too."

Aaron nodded. "I don't know of anyone who can take Grandpa's place," he said with a sigh.

His mother smiled. "You can," she said. Aaron looked up, startled. "You see, the Bible says that living the Christian life is like running a race. In a way, it's like a relay race," Mom explained. "Remember your big race last month?"

"I sure do!" Aaron exclaimed, his face lighting up as he remembered the exciting race. His team, the Eagles, had been determined to take the trophy away from the Panthers, who had been unbeaten for four years.

When it was Aaron's turn to run, the race between the two teams was almost dead even. Sprinting along the track at full speed and pushing himself to his limit, Aaron had streaked ahead of his opponent. They were a full yard apart by the end of his run. The Panthers never made up the difference, and the Eagles had won the race.

"The Christians who've died and gone to heaven ran in their appointed place and time—some running well, and some not so well," Mom continued.

"Grandpa sure ran well," said Aaron. "I think he was one of the best runners. And now I'm next in the relay?"

"Yes," replied Mom. "Grandpa has run his race. Now he's passed the torch on to you. With God's help, take the torch and run the very best you can."

How About You?
Do you know that you, too, are a runner in life's race? Many heroes of the faith have run ahead of you. But now they're gone, and the torch is passed on to you. What kind of race are you running? M. R. P.

• For the next devotional, turn to page 1211. • To start the next topic, turn to page 45. • For notes on *Perseverance*, see pages 326, 461, 503, 760, and 1174.

¹¹Sarah, too, had faith, and because of this she was able to become a mother in spite of her old age, for she realized that God, who gave her his promise, would certainly do what he said. ¹²And so a whole nation came from Abraham, who was too old to have even one child—a nation with so many millions of people that, like the stars of the sky and the sand on the ocean shores, there is no way to count them.

¹³These men of faith I have mentioned died without ever receiving all that God had promised them; but they saw it all awaiting them on ahead and were glad, for they agreed that this earth was not their real home but that they were just strangers visiting down here. ¹⁴And quite obviously when they talked like that, they were looking forward to their real home in heaven.

¹⁵If they had wanted to, they could have gone back to the good things of this world. ¹⁶But they didn't want to. They were living for heaven. And now God is not ashamed to be called their God, for he has made a heavenly city for them.

¹⁷While God was testing him, Abraham still trusted in God and his promises, and so he offered up his son Isaac and was ready to slay him on the altar of sacrifice; ¹⁸yes, to slay even Isaac, through whom God had promised to give Abraham a whole nation of descendants!

¹⁹He believed that if Isaac died God would bring him back to life again; and that is just about what happened, for as far as Abraham was concerned, Isaac was doomed to death, but he came back again alive! ²⁰It was by faith that Isaac knew God would give future blessings to his two sons, Jacob and Esau.

²¹By faith Jacob, when he was old and dying, blessed each of Joseph's two sons as he stood and prayed, leaning on the top of his cane.

²²And it was by faith that Joseph, as he neared the end of his life, confidently spoke of God bringing the people of Israel out of Egypt; and he was so sure of it that he made them promise to carry his bones with them when they left!

²³Moses' parents had faith too. When they saw that God had given them an unusual child, they trusted that God would save him from the death the king commanded, and they hid him for three months and were not afraid.

²⁴,²⁵It was by faith that Moses, when he grew up, refused to be treated as the grandson of the king, but chose to share ill-treatment with God's people instead of enjoying the fleeting pleasures of sin. ²⁶He thought that it was better to suffer for the promised Christ than to own all the treasures of Egypt, for he was looking forward to the great reward that God would give him. ²⁷And it was because he trusted God that he left the land of Egypt and wasn't afraid of the king's anger. Moses kept right on going; it seemed as though he could see God right there with him. ²⁸And it was because he believed God would save his people that he commanded them to kill a lamb as God had told them to and sprinkle the blood on the doorposts of their homes so that God's terrible Angel of Death could not touch the oldest child in those homes as he did among the Egyptians.

²⁹The people of Israel trusted God and went right through the Red Sea as though they were on dry ground. But when the Egyptians chasing them tried it, they all were drowned.

³⁰It was faith that brought the walls of Jericho tumbling down after the people of Israel had walked around them seven days as God had commanded them. ³¹By faith—because she believed in God and his power—Rahab the harlot did not die with all the others in her city when they refused to obey God, for she gave a friendly welcome to the spies.

³²Well, how much more do I need to say? It would take too long to recount the stories of the faith of Gideon and Barak and Samson and Jephthah and David and Samuel and all the other prophets. ³³These people all trusted God and as a result won battles, overthrew kingdoms, ruled their people well, and received what God had promised them; they were kept from harm in a den of lions ³⁴and in a fiery furnace. Some, through their faith, escaped death by the sword. Some were made strong again after they had been weak or sick. Others were given great power in battle; they made whole armies turn and run away. ³⁵And some women, through faith, received their loved ones back again from death. But others trusted God and were beaten to death, preferring to die rather than turn from God and be free—trusting that they would rise to a better life afterwards.

³⁶Some were laughed at and their backs cut open with whips, and others were chained in dungeons. ³⁷,³⁸Some died by stoning and some by being sawed in two; others were promised freedom if they would renounce their faith, then were killed with the sword. Some went about in skins of sheep and goats, wandering over deserts and mountains, hiding in dens and caves. They were hungry and sick and ill-treated—too good for this world. ³⁹And these men of faith, though they trusted God and won his approval, none of them received all that God had promised them; ⁴⁰for God wanted them to wait and share the even better rewards that were prepared for us.

12 Let God Train You

Since we have such a huge crowd of men of faith watching us from the grandstands, let us strip off anything that slows us down or holds us

Family Devotions

☐ DEVOTION 347
CONTENTMENT

Read Hebrews 13:5

"There's a For Sale sign at the house on the corner," called Margie as she burst through the door. "Can we look at it again, Mom? It's so neat!"

"It is lovely," agreed Mom, "but it was too expensive when we looked at it before, and I'm afraid it still is. God has provided well for us, however. I love this house, too."

"But that one is so much bigger!" said Margie.

Mom smiled. "I think the only way we could pay for that house would be to live on canned spaghetti and powdered milk for twenty or thirty years," she said. "How does that sound to you?"

Margie laughed. "Not so good." She sighed. "I wish we were richer. Couldn't you get a job maybe?"

"Margie," said her mother, "do you remember what happened when we tried to make a super-duper buffet lunch last week?"

"Yeah," Margie laughed. "We had the oven going, and every appliance we own was plugged in. And we blew one fuse after another, so we couldn't get anything done!"

"Yes," said Mom. "We ended up with a lot of half-cooked food because we tried to do too much. Can you see how we might learn something from that experience?"

"Sure," Margie giggled. "We learned that you need to get circuit breakers!"

Mom smiled. "I had in mind a more spiritual lesson."

"Well," said Margie thoughtfully, "do you mean that we could overload ourselves, like we overloaded the wiring?"

Mom nodded. "More possessions, along with more debt, might make us lose track of what really matters," she said. "Let's just thank the Lord for leading us to a safe and comfortable home we can afford."

Contentment Memory Verse

I know how to live on almost nothing or with everything. I have learned the secret of contentment in every situation, whether it be a full stomach or hunger, plenty or want.
Philippians 4:12

How About You?

Do you sometimes wish your parents were richer? Surprisingly, many rich people worry so much about their possessions that they can't enjoy them. Money provides physical comforts, but it cannot satisfy the hunger and thirst of the spirit. It's much better to be "rich toward God" than to be rich in the things of this world. Don't overburden yourself seeking riches that don't satisfy. L. B. M.

• For the next devotional, turn to page 1217.   • For the next devotional on CONTENTMENT, turn to page 1261.   • For notes on CONTENTMENT, see pages 542, 547, 902, and 1063.

back, and especially those sins that wrap themselves so tightly around our feet and trip us up; and let us run with patience the particular race that God has set before us.

²Keep your eyes on Jesus, our leader and instructor. He was willing to die a shameful death on the cross because of the joy he knew would be his afterwards; and now he sits in the place of honor by the throne of God.

³If you want to keep from becoming fainthearted and weary, think about his patience as sinful men did such terrible things to him. ⁴After all, you have never yet struggled against sin and temptation until you sweat great drops of blood.

⁵And have you quite forgotten the encouraging words God spoke to you, his child? He said, "My son, don't be angry when the Lord punishes you. Don't be discouraged when he has to show you where you are wrong. ⁶For when he punishes you, it proves that he loves you. When he whips you, it proves you are really his child."

⁷Let God train you, for he is doing what any loving father does for his children. Whoever heard of a son who was never corrected? ⁸If God doesn't punish you when you need it, as other fathers punish their sons, then it means that you aren't really God's son at all—that you don't really belong in his family. ⁹Since we respect our fathers here on earth, though they punish us, should we not all the more cheerfully submit to God's training so that we can begin really to live?

¹⁰Our earthly fathers trained us for a few brief years, doing the best for us that they knew how, but God's correction is always right and for our best good, that we may share his holiness. ¹¹Being punished isn't enjoyable while it is happening—it hurts! But afterwards we can see the result, a quiet growth in grace and character.

¹²So take a new grip with your tired hands, stand firm on your shaky legs, ¹³and mark out a straight, smooth path for your feet so that those who follow you, though weak and lame, will not fall and hurt themselves but become strong.

¹⁴Try to stay out of all quarrels, and seek to live a clean and holy life, for one who is not holy will not see the Lord. ¹⁵Look after each other so that not one of you will fail to find God's best blessings. Watch out that no bitterness takes root among you, for as it springs up it causes deep trouble, hurting many in their spiritual lives. ¹⁶Watch out that no one becomes involved in sexual sin or becomes careless about God as Esau did: he traded his rights as the oldest son for a single meal. ¹⁷And afterwards, when he wanted those rights back again, it was too late, even though he wept bitter tears of repentance. So remember, and be careful.

¹⁸You have not had to stand face to face with terror, flaming fire, gloom, darkness, and a terrible storm as the Israelites did at Mount Sinai when God gave them his laws. ¹⁹For there was an awesome trumpet blast and a voice with a message so terrible that the people begged God to stop speaking. ²⁰They staggered back under God's command that if even an animal touched the mountain it must die. ²¹Moses himself was so frightened at the sight that he shook with terrible fear.

²²But you have come right up into Mount Zion, to the city of the living God, the heavenly Jerusalem, and to the gathering of countless happy angels; ²³and to the church, composed of all those registered in heaven; and to God who is Judge of all; and to the spirits of the redeemed in heaven, already made perfect; ²⁴and to Jesus himself, who has brought us his wonderful new agreement; and to the sprinkled blood, which graciously forgives instead of crying out for vengeance as the blood of Abel did.

²⁵So see to it that you obey him who is speaking to you. For if the people of Israel did not escape when they refused to listen to Moses, the earthly messenger, how terrible our danger if we refuse to listen to God who speaks to us from heaven! ²⁶When he spoke from Mount Sinai his voice shook the earth, but, "Next time," he says, "I will not only shake the earth but the heavens too." ²⁷By this he means that he will sift out everything without solid foundations so that only unshakable things will be left.

²⁸Since we have a Kingdom nothing can destroy, let us please God by serving him with thankful hearts and with holy fear and awe. ²⁹For our God is a consuming fire.

13 Live Good and Obedient Lives

Continue to love each other with true brotherly love. ²Don't forget to be kind to strangers, for some who have done this have entertained angels without realizing it! ³Don't forget about those in jail. Suffer with them as though you were there yourself. Share the sorrow of those being mistreated, for you know what they are going through.

⁴Honor your marriage and its vows, and be pure; for God will surely punish all those who are immoral or commit adultery.

⁵Stay away from the love of money; be satisfied with what you have. For God has said, "I will never, *never* fail you nor forsake you." ⁶That is why we can say without any doubt or fear, "The Lord is my Helper, and I am not afraid of anything that mere man can do to me."

⁷Remember your leaders who have taught you the Word of God. Think of all the good that has

come from their lives, and try to trust the Lord as they do.

⁸Jesus Christ is the same yesterday, today, and forever. ⁹So do not be attracted by strange, new ideas. Your spiritual strength comes as a gift from God, not from ceremonial rules about eating certain foods—a method which, by the way, hasn't helped those who have tried it!

¹⁰We have an altar—the cross where Christ was sacrificed—where those who continue to seek salvation by obeying Jewish laws can never be helped. ¹¹Under the system of Jewish laws, the high priest brought the blood of the slain animals into the sanctuary as a sacrifice for sin, and then the bodies of the animals were burned outside the city. ¹²That is why Jesus suffered and died outside the city, where his blood washed our sins away.

¹³So let us go out to him beyond the city walls [that is, outside the interests of this world, being willing to be despised] to suffer with him there, bearing his shame. ¹⁴For this world is not our home; we are looking forward to our everlasting home in heaven.

¹⁵With Jesus' help we will continually offer our sacrifice of praise to God by telling others of the glory of his name. ¹⁶Don't forget to do good and to share what you have with those in need, for such sacrifices are very pleasing to him. ¹⁷Obey your spiritual leaders and be willing to do what they say. For their work is to watch over your souls, and God will judge them on how well they do this. Give them reason to report joyfully about you to the Lord and not with sorrow, for then you will suffer for it too.

¹⁸Pray for us, for our conscience is clear and we want to keep it that way. ¹⁹I especially need your prayers right now so that I can come back to you sooner.

²⁰,²¹And now may the God of peace, who brought again from the dead our Lord Jesus, equip you with all you need for doing his will. May he who became the great Shepherd of the sheep by an everlasting agreement between God and you, signed with his blood, produce in you through the power of Christ all that is pleasing to him. To him be glory forever and ever. Amen.

²²Brethren, please listen patiently to what I have said in this letter, for it is a short one. ²³I want you to know that Brother Timothy is now out of jail; if he comes here soon, I will come with him to see you. ²⁴,²⁵Give my greetings to all your leaders and to the other believers there. The Christians from Italy who are here with me send you their love. God's grace be with you all. Goodbye.

James

HAVE YOU ever been asked to prove something? Have you ever wanted someone else to prove his or her sincerity or loyalty or knowledge? James wrote this letter to demand proof—proof that people who *say* they're Christians really *are*.

The people who received this letter were used to following many laws before they became Christians. Now they had freedom in Christ and thought they could do whatever they wanted. Since they knew they didn't earn salvation by doing good works, they thought they didn't have to do good things anymore.

James wrote that Christians can prove themselves by obeying God's laws of love. The proof includes trusting God during hard times, not giving special treatment to rich people, watching what they say, growing in God's wisdom, and helping the poor. When Christians act with this kind of love, they prove they are Christians.

Do your actions prove you're a Christian? As you read James, look for ways to make your actions line up with your faith.

James: A Servant of God

From: James, a servant of God and of the Lord Jesus Christ.

To: Jewish Christians scattered everywhere. Greetings!

2Dear brothers, is your life full of difficulties and temptations? Then be happy, 3for when the way is rough, your patience has a chance to grow. 4So let it grow, and don't try to squirm out of your problems. For when your patience is finally in full bloom, then you will be ready for anything, strong in character, full and complete.

5If you want to know what God wants you to do, ask him, and he will gladly tell you, for he is always ready to give a bountiful supply of wisdom to all who ask him; he will not resent it. 6But when you ask him, be sure that you really expect him to tell you, for a doubtful mind will be as unsettled as a wave of the sea that is driven and tossed by the wind; 7,8and every decision you then make will be uncertain, as you turn first this way and then that. If you don't ask with faith, don't expect the Lord to give you any solid answer.

⁹A Christian who doesn't amount to much in this world should be glad, for he is great in the Lord's sight. ¹⁰,¹¹But a rich man should be glad that his riches mean nothing to the Lord, for he will soon be gone, like a flower that has lost its beauty and fades away, withered—killed by the scorching summer sun. So it is with rich men. They will soon die and leave behind all their busy activities.

¹²Happy is the man who doesn't give in and do wrong when he is tempted, for afterwards he will get as his reward the crown of life that God has promised those who love him. ¹³And remember, when someone wants to do wrong it is never God who is tempting him, for God never wants to do wrong and never tempts anyone else to do it. ¹⁴Temptation is the pull of man's own evil thoughts and wishes. ¹⁵These evil thoughts lead to evil actions and afterwards to the death penalty from God. ¹⁶So don't be misled, dear brothers.

¹⁷But whatever is good and perfect comes to us from God, the Creator of all light, and he shines forever without change or shadow. ¹⁸And it was a happy day for him when he gave us our new lives through the truth of his Word, and we became, as it were, the first children in his new family.

¹⁹Dear brothers, don't ever forget that it is best to listen much, speak little, and not become angry; ²⁰for anger doesn't make us good, as God demands that we must be.

²¹So get rid of all that is wrong in your life, both inside and outside, and humbly be glad for the wonderful message we have received, for it is able to save our souls as it takes hold of our hearts.

²²And remember, it is a message to obey, not just to listen to. So don't fool yourselves. ²³For if a person just listens and doesn't obey, he is like a man looking at his face in a mirror; ²⁴as soon as he walks away, he can't see himself anymore or remember what he looks like. ²⁵But if anyone keeps looking steadily into God's law for free men, he will not only remember it but he will do what it says, and God will greatly bless him in everything he does.

²⁶Anyone who says he is a Christian but doesn't control his sharp tongue is just fooling himself, and his religion isn't worth much. ²⁷The Christian who is pure and without fault, from God the Father's point of view, is the one who takes care of orphans and widows, and who remains true to the Lord—not soiled and dirtied by his contacts with the world.

2 No Special Treatment

Dear brothers, how can you claim that you belong to the Lord Jesus Christ, the Lord of glory, if you show favoritism to rich people and look down on poor people?

²If a man comes into your church dressed in expensive clothes and with valuable gold rings on his fingers, and at the same moment another man comes in who is poor and dressed in threadbare clothes, ³and you make a lot of fuss over the rich man and give him the best seat in the house and say to the poor man, "You can stand over there if you like or else sit on the floor"—well, ⁴judging a man by his wealth shows that you are guided by wrong motives.

⁵Listen to me, dear brothers: God has chosen poor people to be rich in faith, and the Kingdom of Heaven is theirs, for that is the gift God has promised to all those who love him. ⁶And yet, of the two strangers, you have despised the poor man. Don't you realize that it is usually the rich men who pick on you and drag you into court? ⁷And all too often they are the ones who laugh at Jesus Christ, whose noble name you bear.

⁸Yes indeed, it is good when you truly obey our Lord's command, "You must love and help your neighbors just as much as you love and take care of yourself." ⁹But you are breaking this law of our Lord's when you favor the rich and fawn over them; it is sin.

¹⁰And the person who keeps every law of God but makes one little slip is just as guilty as the person who has broken every law there is. ¹¹For the God who said you must not marry a woman who already has a husband also said you must not murder, so even though you have not broken the marriage laws by committing adultery, but have murdered someone, you have entirely broken God's laws and stand utterly guilty before him.

¹²You will be judged on whether or not you are doing what Christ wants you to. So watch what you do and what you think; ¹³for there will be no mercy to those who have shown no mercy. But if you have been merciful, then God's mercy toward you will win out over his judgment against you.

CULTIVATING GODLY ATTITUDES 1:5 When James speaks of wisdom, he means practical discernment. God is willing to give us this wisdom, but we will be unable to receive it if we are self-centered instead of God-centered. To learn God's will, we need to ask him to reveal it to us, and then we must be willing to do what he tells us to do. Wisdom begins with respect for God, leads to right living, and results in increased ability to tell right from wrong. **To begin the series of devotionals on CULTIVATING GODLY ATTITUDES, turn to page 121.**

FAMILY DEVOTIONS

☐ DEVOTION 348
FAITH IN ACTION

Read James 2 : 14 - 20

School began in the usual boring way for Roger—first math, then reading. *We need some action around here,* Roger thought. He peeked into his desk to check on the little mouse he had in a small box there.

A few minutes later, his teacher, Mrs. Madden, had to go to the office. She appointed Jennifer to be class monitor in her absence. Roger decided this was his chance. Quietly he took the mouse from his desk and released it. It scampered across the floor. "There's a mouse!" The girls screamed, and several of them ran to the back of the room.

"Take your seats," Jennifer instructed. "It won't hurt you." The mouse dashed across the floor, running right over Jennifer's foot. "Ahhhh!" she shrieked. She climbed onto her chair, and some of the other girls did the same.

"Quiet," Jennifer ordered. "Everyone sit down. There's nothing to worry about." But she continued to stand on her chair.

Just then Mrs. Madden returned and restored order to the classrooom.

After school, Roger told his mother about Jennifer and the mouse. He told her everything except how the mouse got there. "It was pretty funny," he said. "Jennifer told the class to sit down because there was nothing to worry about, but she stayed standing on her chair!"

"That's a good example of what we discussed in my ladies' Bible study this morning," said Mom. "Just as Jennifer's actions didn't match her words, Christians' actions don't always match what they profess to believe. If we claim to love Jesus, yet do things in disobedience to him, we're not putting our faith into action."

Roger felt guilty. He knew that disrupting the class was not Christlike. When he reached his room, he asked God to forgive him for not living according to his faith.

Faith in Action Memory Verse

In response to all he has done for us, let us outdo each other in being helpful and kind to each other and in doing good.
Hebrews 10:24

How About You?
Do you say you believe in Jesus but carelessly lie, cheat, or treat others unkindly? Or do you act out your faith by living a godly life? Ask God to help you act according to your faith. *N. E. K.*

• For the next devotional, turn to page 1219. • For the next devotional on *FAITH IN ACTION*, turn to page 1229.
• For notes on *FAITH IN ACTION*, see pages 583, 846, 1068, and 1232.

¹⁴Dear brothers, what's the use of saying that you have faith and are Christians if you aren't proving it by helping others? Will *that* kind of faith save anyone? ¹⁵If you have a friend who is in need of food and clothing, ¹⁶and you say to him, "Well, good-bye and God bless you; stay warm and eat hearty," and then don't give him clothes or food, what good does that do?

¹⁷So you see, it isn't enough just to have faith. You must also do good to prove that you have it. Faith that doesn't show itself by good works is no faith at all—it is dead and useless.

¹⁸But someone may well argue, "You say the way to God is by faith alone, plus nothing; well, I say that good works are important too, for without good works you can't prove whether you have faith or not; but anyone can see that I have faith by the way I act."

¹⁹Are there still some among you who hold that "only believing" is enough? Believing in one God? Well, remember that the demons believe this too—so strongly that they tremble in terror! ²⁰Fool! When will you ever learn that "believing" is useless without *doing* what God wants you to? Faith that does not result in good deeds is not real faith.

²¹Don't you remember that even our father Abraham was declared good because of what he *did* when he was willing to obey God, even if it meant offering his son Isaac to die on the altar? ²²You see, he was trusting God so much that he was willing to do whatever God told him to; his faith was made complete by what he did—by his actions, his good deeds. ²³And so it happened just as the Scriptures say, that Abraham trusted God, and the Lord declared him good in God's sight, and he was even called "the friend of God." ²⁴So you see, a man is saved by what he does, as well as by what he believes.

²⁵Rahab, the prostitute, is another example of this. She was saved because of what she did when she hid those messengers and sent them safely away by a different road. ²⁶Just as the body is dead when there is no spirit in it, so faith is dead if it is not the kind that results in good deeds.

3 Control What You Say

Dear brothers, don't be too eager to tell others their faults, for we all make many mistakes; and when we teachers of religion, who should know better, do wrong, our punishment will be greater than it would be for others.

If anyone can control his tongue, it proves that he has perfect control over himself in every other way. ³We can make a large horse turn around and go wherever we want by means of a small bit in his mouth. ⁴And a tiny rudder makes a huge ship turn wherever the pilot wants it to go, even though the winds are strong.

⁵So also the tongue is a small thing, but what enormous damage it can do. A great forest can be set on fire by one tiny spark. ⁶And the tongue is a flame of fire. It is full of wickedness, and poisons every part of the body. And the tongue is set on fire by hell itself and can turn our whole lives into a blazing flame of destruction and disaster.

⁷Men have trained, or can train, every kind of animal or bird that lives and every kind of reptile and fish, ⁸but no human being can tame the tongue. It is always ready to pour out its deadly poison. ⁹Sometimes it praises our heavenly Father, and sometimes it breaks out into curses against men who are made like God. ¹⁰And so blessing and cursing come pouring out of the same mouth. Dear brothers, surely this is not right! ¹¹Does a spring of water bubble out first with fresh water and then with bitter water? ¹²Can you pick olives from a fig tree, or figs from a grape vine? No, and you can't draw fresh water from a salty pool.

¹³If you are wise, live a life of steady goodness so that only good deeds will pour forth. And if you don't brag about them, then you will be truly wise! ¹⁴And by all means don't brag about being wise and good if you are bitter and jealous and selfish; that is the worst sort of lie. ¹⁵For jealousy and selfishness are not God's kind of wisdom. Such things are earthly, unspiritual, inspired by the devil. ¹⁶For wherever there is jealousy or selfish ambition, there will be disorder and every other kind of evil.

¹⁷But the wisdom that comes from heaven is first of all pure and full of quiet gentleness. Then it is peace-loving and courteous. It allows discussion and is willing to yield to others; it is full of mercy and good deeds. It is wholehearted and straightforward and sincere. ¹⁸And those who are peacemakers will plant seeds of peace and reap a harvest of goodness.

RESPECTING OTHERS 2:2-4 Why is it wrong to judge a person by his or her economic status? Wealth may indicate intelligence, wise decisions, and hard work. On the other hand, it may mean only that a person had the good fortune of being born into a wealthy family. Or it can even be the sign of greed, dishonesty, and selfishness. By honoring someone just because he or she dresses well, we are making appearance more important than character. Sometimes we do this because (1) poverty makes us uncomfortable; we don't want to face our responsibilities to those who have less than we do; (2) we want to be wealthy too, and we hope to use the rich person as a means to that end; (3) we want the rich person to join our church and help support it financially. All these motives are selfish; they view neither the rich nor the poor person as a human being in need of fellowship. If we say that Christ is our Lord, then we must live as he requires, showing no favoritism and loving all people regardless of whether they are rich or poor. **To begin the series of devotionals on RESPECTING OTHERS, turn to page 5.**

Family Devotions

☐ DEVOTION 349
BECOMING MORE LIKE JESUS

Read James 3:5-10

Gina and her mother stopped at the center square in the mall and watched a ventriloquist perform. "That was fun!" Gina said later. "I know that man was really doing the talking for the dummy, but I couldn't even see his lips move. It seemed like the dummy was actually talking."

That evening, Gina had a big argument with her brother, Lyle. "You pig!" Gina shouted at him.

"Gina," Mom said, "watch your tongue! You know how I feel about that kind of name calling."

A little later, Gina and Lyle were fighting again. "You're an ugly rat!" grumbled Gina.

"Gina!" Mom called sternly. "Come here right now and sit on this chair for a while." Embarrassed, Gina did as she was told. "Where are those words coming from?" asked Mom after a little while. "Do you forget that you're a Christian?"

Gina sighed. "I just say them without thinking," she said. "But why doesn't God stop me? I don't understand why he lets bad words come out of my mouth."

"Well," said Mom, "God isn't a big ventriloquist in the sky, you know."

"You mean like the man at the mall?" Gina asked.

Mom nodded. "The man at the mall worked that dummy like a puppet and spoke for it. But God gives us the responsibility to move our own mouths and to choose the words we speak."

"We're not dummies, are we?" murmured Gina.

"If you were, you wouldn't be a free child of God serving him out of a willing, obedient heart," replied Mom. "But instead of spouting out whatever you want, you can choose to say words that are pleasing to God. Ask him to help you do that."

Becoming More Like Jesus Memory Verse

Let everything you do reflect your love of the truth and the fact that you are in dead earnest about it.
Titus 2:7

How About You?

Are you careful to say only things that are pleasing to God? When you say unkind words, you're making a poor choice. Ask God to help you speak for him. N. E. K.

• For the next devotional, turn to page 1221. • For the next devotional on BECOMING MORE LIKE JESUS, turn to page 1233. • For notes on BECOMING MORE LIKE JESUS, see pages 234, 983, 1105, and 1164.

4 How Can You Get Close to God?

What is causing the quarrels and fights among you? Isn't it because there is a whole army of evil desires within you? ²You want what you don't have, so you kill to get it. You long for what others have, and can't afford it, so you start a fight to take it away from them. And yet the reason you don't have what you want is that you don't ask God for it. ³And even when you do ask you don't get it because your whole aim is wrong—you want only what will give *you* pleasure.

⁴You are like an unfaithful wife who loves her husband's enemies. Don't you realize that making friends with God's enemies—the evil pleasures of this world—makes you an enemy of God? I say it again, that if your aim is to enjoy the evil pleasure of the unsaved world, you cannot also be a friend of God. ⁵Or what do you think the Scripture means when it says that the Holy Spirit, whom God has placed within us, watches over us with tender jealousy? ⁶But he gives us more and more strength to stand against all such evil longings. As the Scripture says, God gives strength to the humble but sets himself against the proud and haughty.

⁷So give yourselves humbly to God. Resist the devil and he will flee from you. ⁸And when you draw close to God, God will draw close to you. Wash your hands, you sinners, and let your hearts be filled with God alone to make them pure and true to him. ⁹Let there be tears for the wrong things you have done. Let there be sorrow and sincere grief. Let there be sadness instead of laughter, and gloom instead of joy. ¹⁰Then when you realize your worthlessness before the Lord, he will lift you up, encourage and help you.

¹¹Don't criticize and speak evil about each other, dear brothers. If you do, you will be fighting against God's law of loving one another, declaring it is wrong. But your job is not to decide whether this law is right or wrong, but to obey it. ¹²Only he who made the law can rightly judge among us. He alone decides to save us or destroy. So what right do you have to judge or criticize others?

¹³Look here, you people who say, "Today or tomorrow we are going to such and such a town, stay there a year, and open up a profitable business." ¹⁴How do you know what is going to happen tomorrow? For the length of your lives is as uncertain as the morning fog—now you see it; soon it is gone. ¹⁵What you ought to say is, "If the Lord wants us to, we shall live and do this or that." ¹⁶Otherwise you will be bragging about your own plans, and such self-confidence never pleases God.

¹⁷Remember, too, that knowing what is right to do and then not doing it is sin.

5 A Warning to the Rich

Look here, you rich men, now is the time to cry and groan with anguished grief because of all the terrible troubles ahead of you. ²Your wealth is even now rotting away, and your fine clothes are becoming mere moth-eaten rags. ³The value of your gold and silver is dropping fast, yet it will stand as evidence against you and eat your flesh like fire. That is what you have stored up for yourselves to receive on that coming day of judgment. ⁴For listen! Hear the cries of the field workers whom you have cheated of their pay. Their cries have reached the ears of the Lord of Hosts.

⁵You have spent your years here on earth having fun, satisfying your every whim, and now your fat hearts are ready for the slaughter. ⁶You have condemned and killed good men who had no power to defend themselves against you.

⁷Now as for you, dear brothers who are waiting for the Lord's return, be patient, like a farmer who waits until the autumn for his precious harvest to ripen. ⁸Yes, be patient. And take courage, for the coming of the Lord is near.

⁹Don't grumble about each other, brothers. Are you yourselves above criticism? For see! The great Judge is coming. He is almost here. [Let him do whatever criticizing must be done.]

¹⁰For examples of patience in suffering, look at the Lord's prophets. ¹¹We know how happy they are now because they stayed true to him then, even though they suffered greatly for it. Job is an example of a man who continued to trust the Lord in sorrow; from his experiences we can see how the Lord's plan finally ended in good, for he is full of tenderness and mercy.

¹²But most of all, dear brothers, do not swear either by heaven or earth or anything else; just say a simple yes or no so that you will not sin and be condemned for it.

¹³Is anyone among you suffering? He should keep on praying about it. And those who have reason to be thankful should continually be singing praises to the Lord.

¹⁴Is anyone sick? He should call for the elders of the church and they should pray over him and pour a little oil upon him, calling on the Lord to heal him. ¹⁵And their prayer, if offered in faith, will heal him, for the Lord will make him well; and

---

CONFESSING SIN 5:9 When things go wrong, we tend to blame others for our miseries. Blaming others is easier than taking our share of the responsibility, but it is both destructive and sinful. Before you judge others for their shortcomings, remember that Christ the Judge will come to evaluate each of us (Matthew 7:1-5). He will not let us get away with shifting the blame to others. **To begin the series of devotionals on CONFESSING SIN, turn to page 41.**

Family Devotions

☐ **Devotion 350**
Encouraging Others

Read James 3:8-10, 13-18

Encouraging Others Memory Verse

So encourage each other to build each other up, just as you are already doing.
1 Thessalonians 5:11

"Am I doing this right, Grandma?"

Grandmother examined the strip of crocheted lace Sarah handed her. "Looks good to me," she said.

"This is going to be a pretty collar," Sarah said proudly. "What do I do next?"

"Make the next row exactly like this one," Grandmother replied. "By next week when I go to stay with your aunt Denise, you should be able to follow the pattern by yourself."

"We wish you could stay with us all the time, don't we, Mittens?" Sarah brushed her bare toes over the fur of the cat at her feet. "Aunt Denise and Darci are so stuck-up. They may have more money, but they're not any better than we are! In fact, Darci is nothing but a spoiled brat. She tells lies to get what she wants, and she—"

"That's enough, Sarah Jane!" Grandmother said sternly. "Remember, Darci is my granddaughter, and I love her as much as I love you."

"Dinner is ready!" Mom's call from the kitchen interrupted their conversation.

After dinner, Sarah and Grandmother returned to the family room. "I'm going to work on my—oh no! Look, Grandma!" Sarah pointed at the cat, who was playing with a mass of tangled thread. "Mittens unraveled all my hard work! I'll have to start all over."

Grandmother smiled sympathetically. "It takes time and careful thought to crochet a lace collar, but anyone—even a cat—can unravel one. It's like that with everything. It always takes more effort to build up than to tear down. It's easy to find fault with people and run them down, but it seems hard to find their good points and build them up. God commands us to do just that. He tells us to build each other up."

Sarah sighed as she started winding the thread around the spool. "You mean my remarks about Darci, I know. I guess I was just being catty, Grandma. I'm sorry."

How About You?
Do you say catty things about others? Do you run them down? This would be a good day to stop tearing others down and start building them up as God wants you to do. *B. W.*

• For the next devotional, turn to page 1225. • For the next devotional on *Encouraging Others*, turn to page 1239.
• For notes on *Encouraging Others*, see pages 108, 157, 474, 1156, and 1170.

if his sickness was caused by some sin, the Lord will forgive him.

¹⁶Admit your faults to one another and pray for each other so that you may be healed. The earnest prayer of a righteous man has great power and wonderful results. ¹⁷Elijah was as completely human as we are, and yet when he prayed earnestly that no rain would fall, none fell for the next three and a half years! ¹⁸Then he prayed again, this time that it *would* rain, and down it poured, and the grass turned green and the gardens began to grow again.

¹⁹Dear brothers, if anyone has slipped away from God and no longer trusts the Lord and someone helps him understand the Truth again, ²⁰that person who brings him back to God will have saved a wandering soul from death, bringing about the forgiveness of his many sins.

Sincerely, James

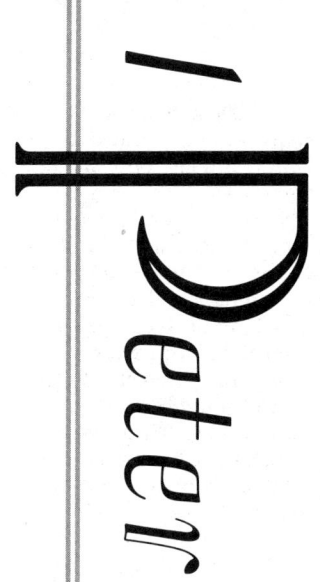

1 Peter

THERE ARE many ways to grow. We grow physically as we get older. We grow intellectually as we learn more in school. We grow socially as we deepen friendships and learn to handle new situations. There's another way we can grow, too: spiritually.

Peter wrote that growing spiritually takes concentration, just as studying or being a good friend takes effort. Being holy and humble is the way to grow spiritually. In this letter, Peter tells many ways to be holy and humble.

Peter was one of Jesus' disciples and an important leader in the early church. Peter was writing to warn Christians about persecution headed their way. They would need to be strong in their faith to come through it.

Peter wanted the Christians to grow as much as they could before the persecution got bad. We can make the same effort to grow spiritually. As you read 1 Peter, look for ways you can help your spirit grow.

God's Missionary

From: Peter, Jesus Christ's missionary.

To: The Jewish Christians driven out of Jerusalem and scattered throughout Pontus, Galatia, Cappadocia, Asia Minor, and Bithynia.

²Dear friends, God the Father chose you long ago and knew you would become his children. And the Holy Spirit has been at work in your hearts, cleansing you with the blood of Jesus Christ and making you to please him. May God bless you richly and grant you increasing freedom from all anxiety and fear.

³All honor to God, the God and Father of our Lord Jesus Christ; for it is his boundless mercy that has given us the privilege of being born again so that we are now members of God's own family. Now we live in the hope of eternal life because Christ rose again from the dead. ⁴And God has reserved for his children the priceless gift of eternal life; it is kept in heaven for you, pure and

undefiled, beyond the reach of change and decay. ⁵And God, in his mighty power, will make sure that you get there safely to receive it because you are trusting him. It will be yours in that coming last day for all to see. ⁶So be truly glad! There is wonderful joy ahead, even though the going is rough for a while down here.

⁷These trials are only to test your faith, to see whether or not it is strong and pure. It is being tested as fire tests gold and purifies it—and your faith is far more precious to God than mere gold; so if your faith remains strong after being tried in the test tube of fiery trials, it will bring you much praise and glory and honor on the day of his return.

⁸You love him even though you have never seen him; though not seeing him, you trust him; and even now you are happy with the inexpressible joy that comes from heaven itself. ⁹And your further reward for trusting him will be the salvation of your souls.

¹⁰This salvation was something the prophets did not fully understand. Though they wrote about it, they had many questions as to what it all could mean. ¹¹They wondered what the Spirit of Christ within them was talking about, for he told them to write down the events which, since then, have happened to Christ: his suffering, and his great glory afterwards. And they wondered when and to whom all this would happen.

¹²They were finally told that these things would not occur during their lifetime, but long years later, during yours. And now at last this Good News has been plainly announced to all of us. It was preached to us in the power of the same heaven-sent Holy Spirit who spoke to them; and it is all so strange and wonderful that even the angels in heaven would give a great deal to know more about it.

¹³So now you can look forward soberly and intelligently to more of God's kindness to you when Jesus Christ returns.

¹⁴Obey God because you are his children; don't slip back into your old ways—doing evil because you knew no better. ¹⁵But be holy now in everything you do, just as the Lord is holy, who invited you to be his child. ¹⁶He himself has said, "You must be holy, for I am holy."

¹⁷And remember that your heavenly Father to whom you pray has no favorites when he judges. He will judge you with perfect justice for everything you do; so act in reverent fear of him from now on until you get to heaven. ¹⁸God paid a ransom to save you from the impossible road to heaven which your fathers tried to take, and the ransom he paid was not mere gold or silver as you very well know. ¹⁹But he paid for you with the precious lifeblood of Christ, the sinless, spotless Lamb of God. ²⁰God chose him for this purpose long before the world began, but only recently was he brought into public view, in these last days, as a blessing to you.

²¹Because of this, your trust can be in God who raised Christ from the dead and gave him great glory. Now your faith and hope can rest in him alone. ²²Now you can have real love for everyone because your souls have been cleansed from selfishness and hatred when you trusted Christ to save you; so see to it that you really do love each other warmly, with all your hearts.

²³For you have a new life. It was not passed on to you from your parents, for the life they gave you will fade away. This new one will last forever, for it comes from Christ, God's ever-living Message to men. ²⁴Yes, our natural lives will fade as grass does when it becomes all brown and dry. All our greatness is like a flower that droops and falls; ²⁵but the Word of the Lord will last forever. And his message is the Good News that was preached to you.

2 A Living Stone for God's House

So get rid of your feelings of hatred. Don't just pretend to be good! Be done with dishonesty and jealousy and talking about others behind their backs. ²,³ Now that you realize how kind the Lord has been to you, put away all evil, deception, envy, and fraud. Long to grow up into the fullness of your salvation; cry for this as a baby cries for his milk.

⁴Come to Christ, who is the living Foundation of Rock upon which God builds; though men have spurned him, he is very precious to God who has chosen him above all others.

⁵And now you have become living buildingstones for God's use in building his house. What's more, you are his holy priests; so come to him—[you who are acceptable to him because of Jesus Christ]—and offer to God those things that please him. ⁶As the Scriptures express it, "See, I am sending Christ to be the carefully chosen, precious Cornerstone of my church, and I will never disappoint those who trust in him."

⁷Yes, he is very precious to you who believe; and to those who reject him, well—"The same Stone that was rejected by the builders has become the Cornerstone, the most honored and important part of the building." ⁸And the Scriptures also say, "He is the Stone that some will stumble over, and the Rock that will make them fall." They will stumble because they will not listen to God's Word nor obey it, and so this punishment must follow—that they will fall.

⁹But you are not like that, for you have been chosen by God himself—you are priests of the

Family Devotions

☐ DEVOTION 351
AVOIDING SIN

Read 1 Peter 1 : 22 – 2 : 3

Avoiding Sin Memory Verse

How can a young man stay pure? By reading your Word and following its rules.
Psalm 119:9

"Somebody must have decided we shouldn't eat junk food," grumbled Leslie when she came home from school one day. "They're taking the candy and pop machines out of the cafeteria. Now what are we supposed to do if we want something to eat between classes?"

"Won't they put something in their place?" Mom asked.

"Well, yeah," admitted Leslie. "Apples, raisins, milk, and juice."

"Good," approved Mom. "Those are better foods to eat. After all, food affects your health." Mom watched as Leslie picked up the remote control and switched through the channels on the TV, then she added, "Did you know that this applies to the mind as well as the body?"

"And you classify TV as junk food." Leslie flipped the TV back off and stared at the blank screen.

"Suppose we didn't have television," suggested Mom. "Then what would you do instead of plopping yourself down in front of the TV each night?"

Leslie thought about it. "I don't know. Call a friend. Read a book. Maybe even do homework!" She laughed.

"I think that would be considered good food, like apples, raisins, and juices," said Mom. "Now, let's see. You need some meat in your diet, too. What do you think that might be?"

"Bible reading," answered Leslie promptly. "And maybe attending church and Sunday school."

"Good," agreed Mom. "Let's both work on improving our diets. You can start by having some milk and crackers while you memorize your verse for Sunday school."

How About You?

How is your diet? Are there some mental and spiritual junk foods you need to get rid of— things like books or TV programs that use bad language or have ungodly characters and dirty jokes? Are there healthy foods you need to add—like daily devotions and faithful attendance at church? Follow a spiritual diet that is pleasing to the Lord. V. L. C.

• For the next devotional, turn to page 1227. • For the next devotional on *AVOIDING SIN*, turn to page 1227. • For notes on *AVOIDING SIN*, see pages 220, 332, 392, and 657.

King, you are holy and pure, you are God's very own—all this so that you may show to others how God called you out of the darkness into his wonderful light. [10]Once you were less than nothing; now you are God's own. Once you knew very little of God's kindness; now your very lives have been changed by it.

[11]Dear brothers, you are only visitors here. Since your real home is in heaven, I beg you to keep away from the evil pleasures of this world; they are not for you, for they fight against your very souls.

[12]Be careful how you behave among your unsaved neighbors; for then, even if they are suspicious of you and talk against you, they will end up praising God for your good works when Christ returns.

[13]For the Lord's sake, obey every law of your government: those of the king as head of the state, [14]and those of the king's officers, for he has sent them to punish all who do wrong, and to honor those who do right.

[15]It is God's will that your good lives should silence those who foolishly condemn the Gospel without knowing what it can do for them, having never experienced its power. [16]You are free from the law, but that doesn't mean you are free to do wrong. Live as those who are free to do only God's will at all times.

[17]Show respect for everyone. Love Christians everywhere. Fear God and honor the government.

[18]Servants, you must respect your masters and do whatever they tell you—not only if they are kind and reasonable, but even if they are tough and cruel. [19]Praise the Lord if you are punished for doing right! [20]Of course, you get no credit for being patient if you are beaten for doing wrong; but if you do right and suffer for it, and are patient beneath the blows, God is well pleased.

[21]This suffering is all part of the work God has given you. Christ, who suffered for you, is your example. Follow in his steps: [22]He never sinned, never told a lie, [23]never answered back when insulted; when he suffered he did not threaten to get even; he left his case in the hands of God who always judges fairly. [24]He personally carried the load of our sins in his own body when he died on the cross so that we can be finished with sin and live a good life from now on. For his wounds have healed ours! [25]Like sheep you wandered away from God, but now you have returned to your Shepherd, the Guardian of your souls who keeps you safe from all attacks.

3 Advice for Husbands and Wives

Wives, fit in with your husbands' plans; for then if they refuse to listen when you talk to them about the Lord, they will be won by your respectful, pure behavior. Your godly lives will speak to them better than any words.

[3]Don't be concerned about the outward beauty that depends on jewelry, or beautiful clothes, or hair arrangement. [4]Be beautiful inside, in your hearts, with the lasting charm of a gentle and quiet spirit that is so precious to God. [5]That kind of deep beauty was seen in the saintly women of old, who trusted God and fitted in with their husbands' plans.

[6]Sarah, for instance, obeyed her husband Abraham, honoring him as head of the house. And if you do the same, you will be following in her steps like good daughters and doing what is right; then you will not need to fear [offending your husbands].

[7]You husbands must be careful of your wives, being thoughtful of their needs and honoring them as the weaker sex. Remember that you and your wife are partners in receiving God's blessings, and if you don't treat her as you should, your prayers will not get ready answers.

[8]And now this word to all of you: You should be like one big happy family, full of sympathy toward each other, loving one another with tender hearts and humble minds. [9]Don't repay evil for evil. Don't snap back at those who say unkind things about you. Instead, pray for God's help for them, for we are to be kind to others, and God will bless us for it.

[10]If you want a happy, good life, keep control of your tongue, and guard your lips from telling lies. [11]Turn away from evil and do good. Try to live in peace even if you must run after it to catch and hold it! [12]For the Lord is watching his children, listening to their prayers; but the Lord's face is hard against those who do evil.

[13]Usually no one will hurt you for wanting to do good. [14]But even if they should, you are to be envied, for God will reward you for it. [15]Quietly trust yourself to Christ your Lord, and if anybody asks why you believe as you do, be ready to tell him, and do it in a gentle and respectful way.

[16]Do what is right; then if men speak against you, calling you evil names, they will become ashamed of themselves for falsely accusing you when you have only done what is good. [17]Remember, if God wants you to suffer, it is better to suffer for doing good than for doing wrong!

[18]Christ also suffered. He died once for the sins of all us guilty sinners although he himself was innocent of any sin at any time, that he might bring us safely home to God. But though his body died, his spirit lived on, [19]and it was in the spirit that he visited the spirits in prison and preached to them—[20]spirits of those who, long before in the days of Noah, had refused to listen to God,

Family Devotions

☐ **Devotion 352**
Avoiding Sin

Read 1 Peter 2 : 11-16

Avoiding Sin
Memory Verse

Dear brothers, you are only visitors here. Since your real home is in heaven, I beg you to keep away from the evil pleasures of this world; they are not for you, for they fight against your very souls.
1 Peter 2:11

"Aliens!"

"There go the aliens!"

Ginny and her friend Alicia cringed as the taunting cries followed them. They had once again refused to join the activities of a certain group of classmates. They had so often separated themselves from the bad behavior of other kids that they had been dubbed "aliens" by the other children. Ginny sighed. "My mother keeps reminding me not to give in to the temptation to be like those kids," she remarked, "but I don't think she knows what it's like for kids in school these days."

"Yeah," agreed Alicia. "My mom keeps saying I should 'just say no' to drugs, but sometimes I feel like giving in to some of the other stuff—like looking at the magazines the kids are passing around. Then maybe they wouldn't call us names all the time."

At home that evening, Ginny told her mother about what happened. "They call Alicia and me *aliens* because we don't do the things they do," she complained.

Mom nodded. "I can understand how you feel," she said. "But I guess it's not so strange they call you that. You really are aliens, you know."

"Mom," said Ginny, "we are not!"

Mom smiled. "Yes," she insisted, "you are. You girls have both accepted Jesus as Savior, so now your citizenship is really in heaven. The Bible says we're just visitors here in this world. You're different because you live for Christ."

"Then I guess it's not so bad to be called *aliens* after all, is it?" said Ginny with a sigh. "I'll have to tell Alicia."

H o w   A b o u t   Y o u ?
Do other boys and girls pressure you to join them in some ungodly ways? Do they tease you when you refuse? Perhaps you don't find it hard to say no to such things as smoking, drinking, or doing drugs, but you're tempted to laugh at dirty jokes, show disrespect to a teacher, or do some other thing you know is wrong. Don't do it. If you belong to Jesus, you don't belong to this world. Act the way a citizen of heaven should act. *N. E. K.*

• For the next devotional, turn to page 1229.   • To start the next topic, turn to page 131.   • For notes on *Avoiding Sin,* see pages 220, 332, 392, and 657.

though he waited patiently for them while Noah was building the ark. Yet only eight persons were saved from drowning in that terrible flood. ²¹(That, by the way, is what baptism pictures for us: In baptism we show that we have been saved from death and doom by the resurrection of Christ; not because our bodies are washed clean by the water but because in being baptized we are turning to God and asking him to cleanse our *hearts* from sin.) ²²And now Christ is in heaven, sitting in the place of honor next to God the Father, with all the angels and powers of heaven bowing before him and obeying him.

4 Continue to Love One Another

Since Christ suffered and underwent pain, you must have the same attitude he did; you must be ready to suffer, too. For remember, when your body suffers, sin loses its power, ²and you won't be spending the rest of your life chasing after evil desires but will be anxious to do the will of God. ³You have had enough in the past of the evil things the godless enjoy—sex sin, lust, getting drunk, wild parties, drinking bouts, and the worship of idols, and other terrible sins.

⁴Of course, your former friends will be very surprised when you don't eagerly join them anymore in the wicked things they do, and they will laugh at you in contempt and scorn. ⁵But just remember that they must face the Judge of all, living and dead; they will be punished for the way they have lived. ⁶That is why the Good News was preached even to those who were dead—killed by the flood—so that although their bodies were punished with death, they could still live in their spirits as God lives.

⁷The end of the world is coming soon. Therefore be earnest, thoughtful men of prayer. ⁸Most important of all, continue to show deep love for each other, for love makes up for many of your faults. ⁹Cheerfully share your home with those who need a meal or a place to stay for the night.

¹⁰God has given each of you some special abilities; be sure to use them to help each other, passing on to others God's many kinds of blessings. ¹¹Are you called to preach? Then preach as though God himself were speaking through you. Are you called to help others? Do it with all the strength and energy that God supplies so that God will be glorified through Jesus Christ—to him be glory and power forever and ever. Amen.

¹²Dear friends, don't be bewildered or surprised when you go through the fiery trials ahead, for this is no strange, unusual thing that is going to happen to you. ¹³Instead, be really glad—because these trials will make you partners with Christ in his suffering, and afterwards you will have the wonderful joy of sharing his glory in that coming day when it will be displayed.

¹⁴Be happy if you are cursed and insulted for being a Christian, for when that happens the Spirit of God will come upon you with great glory. ¹⁵Don't let me hear of your suffering for murdering or stealing or making trouble or being a busybody and prying into other people's affairs. ¹⁶But it is no shame to suffer for being a Christian. Praise God for the privilege of being in Christ's family and being called by his wonderful name! ¹⁷For the time has come for judgment, and it must begin first among God's own children. And if even we who are Christians must be judged, what terrible fate awaits those who have never believed in the Lord? ¹⁸If the righteous are barely saved, what chance will the godless have?

¹⁹So if you are suffering according to God's will, keep on doing what is right and trust yourself to the God who made you, for he will never fail you.

5 Advice for Teachers and Students

And now, a word to you elders of the church. I, too, am an elder; with my own eyes I saw Christ dying on the cross; and I, too, will share his glory and his honor when he returns. Fellow elders, this is my plea to you: ²Feed the flock of God; care for it willingly, not grudgingly; not for what you will get out of it but because you are eager to serve the Lord. ³Don't be tyrants, but lead them by your good example, ⁴and when the Head Shepherd comes, your reward will be a never-ending share in his glory and honor.

⁵You younger men, follow the leadership of those who are older. And all of you serve each other with humble spirits, for God gives special blessings to those who are humble, but sets himself against those who are proud. ⁶If you will humble yourselves under the mighty hand of God, in his good time he will lift you up.

⁷Let him have all your worries and cares, for he is always thinking about you and watching everything that concerns you.

⁸Be careful—watch out for attacks from Satan, your great enemy. He prowls around like a hungry, roaring lion, looking for some victim to tear apart. ⁹Stand firm when he attacks.

HUMILITY 5:6 We often worry about our position and status, hoping we'll get proper recognition for what we do. But Peter advises us to remember that God's recognition counts more than human praise. God is able and willing to bless us according to his own timing. Obey God regardless of present circumstances, and in his good time—either in this life or in the next—he will lift you up. **To begin the series of devotionals on HUMILITY, turn to page 449.**

FAMILY DEVOTIONS

☐ DEVOTION 353
FAITH IN ACTION

Read 1 Peter 2 : 12

Faith in Action Memory Verse

In response to all he has done for us, let us outdo each other in being helpful and kind to each other and in doing good.
Hebrews 10:24

"It's not my turn anyway. Make Cindi do it!" Brad yelled over his shoulder as he slammed the door behind him.

"Hi, Brad. You mad about something?" a voice called.

Brad looked up to see Nathan, his new neighbor, leaning against the gate, grinning. "I sure am!" exclaimed Brad. "You would be, too, if your mother was always on your back."

"Oh, she is," Nathan replied, "but I just let it go in one ear and out the other. Hey, why does your T-shirt say 'I am a King's Kid'? Your dad's a plumber."

"That's talking about God," Brad said impatiently. "I'm a child of God."

Nathan shrugged. "Well, if you say so."

Brad picked up his bat and glove. "I'm going to the park to play ball with the gang. You want to go?"

All the way to the park Nathan bragged about what a good pitcher he was. When the boys chose teams, Brad chose Nathan.

After Nathan had walked the first three batters, Brad began to have doubts about Nathan's pitching ability. By the end of the second inning, Brad's team was behind six to one, and Brad was angry. He told Nathan what he thought about his pitching and replaced him with Clint.

That evening, he told his parents about Nathan. "He's just a bunch of talk. He couldn't hit the side of the barn, and he wouldn't know a good pitcher if he saw one."

Mom raised her eyebrows. "I heard you talking to Nathan this afternoon, Brad."

Brad shrugged. "So?"

"So, Nathan claimed to be a pitcher, but you think he's a poor one. You claim to be a Christian, but I wonder what kind of Christian Nathan thinks you are—especially after your little exhibition this afternoon. You said Nathan wouldn't recognize a good pitcher if he saw one. I wonder if he would recognize a good Christian."

How About You?
Do your works match your words? While you claim to be a Christian, do your actions deny it? Being a Christian is more than wearing a T-shirt. *B. W.*

Trust the Lord; and remember that other Christians all around the world are going through these sufferings too.

¹⁰After you have suffered a little while, our God, who is full of kindness through Christ, will give you his eternal glory. He personally will come and pick you up, and set you firmly in place, and make you stronger than ever. ¹¹To him be all power over all things, forever and ever. Amen.

¹²I am sending this note to you through the courtesy of Silvanus who is, in my opinion, a very faithful brother. I hope I have encouraged you by this letter, for I have given you a true statement of the way God blesses. What I have told you here should help you to stand firmly in his love.

¹³The church here in Rome—she is your sister in the Lord—sends you her greetings; so does my son Mark. ¹⁴Give each other the handshake of Christian love. Peace be to all of you who are in Christ.

2 Peter

SOMETIMES IT'S helpful to refresh your memory on something important. How often do you need reminders about what you're supposed to do?

Peter's second letter was written as a reminder. The Christians who received this letter had heard all of these teachings before. But some of those Christians didn't listen very well, and they had stopped doing what pleased God.

Peter wrote to remind Christians that they needed to keep learning to know God better. Peter said he would remind them of this over and over. It's important to study God's Word again and again to refresh our memory about who Jesus is and how we can please him. It's also important not to just listen to God's Word, but to do what it says.

As you read 2 Peter, refresh your memory with truths about Jesus.

Steps to Spiritual Growth

From: Simon Peter, a servant and missionary of Jesus Christ.

To: All of you who have our kind of faith. The faith I speak of is the kind that Jesus Christ our God and Savior gives to us. How precious it is, and how just and good he is to give this same faith to each of us.

²Do you want more and more of God's kindness and peace? Then learn to know him better and better. ³For as you know him better, he will give you, through his great power, everything you need for living a truly good life: he even shares his own glory and his own goodness with us! ⁴And by that same mighty power he has given us all the other rich and wonderful blessings he promised; for instance, the promise to save us from the lust and rottenness all around us, and to give us his own character.

⁵But to obtain these gifts, you need more than faith; you must also work hard to be good, and even that is not enough. For then you must learn

to know God better and discover what he wants you to do. ⁶Next, learn to put aside your own desires so that you will become patient and godly, gladly letting God have his way with you. ⁷This will make possible the next step, which is for you to enjoy other people and to like them, and finally you will grow to love them deeply. ⁸The more you go on in this way, the more you will grow strong spiritually and become fruitful and useful to our Lord Jesus Christ. ⁹But anyone who fails to go after these additions to faith is blind indeed, or at least very shortsighted and has forgotten that God delivered him from the old life of sin so that now he can live a strong, good life for the Lord.

¹⁰So, dear brothers, work hard to prove that you really are among those God has called and chosen, and then you will never stumble or fall away. ¹¹And God will open wide the gates of heaven for you to enter into the eternal kingdom of our Lord and Savior Jesus Christ.

¹²I plan to keep on reminding you of these things even though you already know them and are really getting along quite well! ¹³,¹⁴But the Lord Jesus Christ has showed me that my days here on earth are numbered, and I am soon to die. As long as I am still here I intend to keep sending these reminders to you, ¹⁵hoping to impress them so clearly upon you that you will remember them long after I have gone.

¹⁶For we have not been telling you fairy tales when we explained to you the power of our Lord Jesus Christ and his coming again. My own eyes have seen his splendor and his glory: ¹⁷,¹⁸I was there on the holy mountain when he shone out with honor given him by God his Father; I heard that glorious, majestic voice calling down from heaven, saying, "This is my much-loved Son; I am well pleased with him."

¹⁹So we have seen and proved that what the prophets said came true. You will do well to pay close attention to everything they have written, for, like lights shining into dark corners, their words help us to understand many things that otherwise would be dark and difficult. But when you consider the wonderful truth of the prophets' words, then the light will dawn in your souls and Christ the Morning Star will shine in your hearts. ²⁰,²¹For no prophecy recorded in Scripture was ever thought up by the prophet himself. It was the Holy Spirit within these godly men who gave them true messages from God.

2 Beware of False Teachers

But there were false prophets, too, in those days, just as there will be false teachers among you. They will cleverly tell their lies about God, turning against even their Master who bought them; but theirs will be a swift and terrible end. ²Many will follow their evil teaching that there is nothing wrong with sexual sin. And because of them Christ and his way will be scoffed at.

³These teachers in their greed will tell you anything to get hold of your money. But God condemned them long ago and their destruction is on the way. ⁴For God did not spare even the angels who sinned, but threw them into hell, chained in gloomy caves and darkness until the judgment day. ⁵And he did not spare any of the people who lived in ancient times before the flood except Noah, the one man who spoke up for God, and his family of seven. At that time God completely destroyed the whole world of ungodly men with the vast flood. ⁶Later, he turned the cities of Sodom and Gomorrah into heaps of ashes and blotted them off the face of the earth, making them an example for all the ungodly in the future to look back upon and fear.

⁷,⁸But at the same time the Lord rescued Lot out of Sodom because he was a good man, sick of the terrible wickedness he saw everywhere around him day after day. ⁹So also the Lord can rescue you and me from the temptations that surround us, and continue to punish the ungodly until the day of final judgment comes. ¹⁰He is especially hard on those who follow their own evil, lustful thoughts, and those who are proud and willful, daring even to scoff at the Glorious Ones without so much as trembling, ¹¹although the angels in heaven who stand in the very presence of the Lord, and are far greater in power and strength than these false teachers, never speak out disrespectfully against these evil Mighty Ones.

¹²But false teachers are fools—no better than animals. They do whatever they feel like; born only to be caught and killed, they laugh at the terrifying powers of the underworld which they know so little about; and they will be destroyed along with all the demons and powers of hell.

¹³That is the pay these teachers will have for their sin. For they live in evil pleasures day after day. They are a disgrace and a stain among you, deceiving you by living in foul sin on the side while they join your love feasts as though they were honest men. ¹⁴No woman can escape their sinful stare, and of adultery

---

FAITH IN ACTION 1:6 False teachers were saying that learning to put aside your own desires was not needed because works do not help the believer anyway (2:19). It is true that works cannot save us, but it is absolutely false to think they are unimportant. We are saved so that we can grow to resemble Christ and so that we can serve others. God wants us to model his character, and the way we do that is by our actions. **To begin the series of devotionals on FAITH IN ACTION, turn to page 141.**

FAMILY DEVOTIONS

☐ *DEVOTION 354*
BECOMING MORE LIKE JESUS

Read 2 Peter 1:5-9

Lori was jealous of her brother Lance. *He gets along with Mom and Dad so much better than I do,* she thought. *Even Todd likes him better than he likes me.*

"Play with me," begged three-year-old Todd, pulling at her arm and interrupting her thoughts.

"No," answered Lori, "play by yourself."

Mom came in from the yard. "Lori," she said, "come help me weed the flower beds."

"Do I have to?" whined Lori, following her mother unwillingly. "Why doesn't Lance ever have to weed?"

"He has other chores," replied Mom. "You start here." Mom guided her to the end of a row.

Lori pouted as she slowly pulled weeds. Suddenly she shrieked. "Oh, that awful mosquito. He bit me!"

"Too bad you couldn't whack him before he got a chance to bite you," said Mom.

Just then Lori noticed a ladybug on one of the plants. "Look, Mom," she said. "A ladybug. Shall I whack it?"

"No," said Mom. "Mosquitoes are pests, but ladybugs are our friends. I read somewhere that ladybugs eat the harmful insects that destroy crops. Thank God for ladybugs."

Just then Lance called from the patio. "I finished cleaning the garage, Mom," he said. "Todd wants me to take him to the playground. Is that OK?"

"Wonderful!" said Mom. "Thank you, Lance."

Lori thought hard. *Maybe if I'm more helpful, I'll be appreciated, too—like Lance and the ladybugs. Maybe people would even thank God for me!*

Becoming More Like Jesus Memory Verse

No, he has told you what he wants, and this is all it is: *to be fair, just, merciful, and to walk humbly with your God.*
Micah 6:8

How About You?
Are you like a mosquito or like a ladybug? Are you pesky or helpful? Do others like to have you around? With God's help, become a more useful person. Others will appreciate it, God will be pleased, and you'll be happier, too. *M. N.*

• For the next devotional, turn to page 1237. • For the next devotional on BECOMING MORE LIKE JESUS, turn to page 1237. • For notes on BECOMING MORE LIKE JESUS, see pages 234, 983, 1105, and 1164.

they never have enough. They make a game of luring unstable women. They train themselves to be greedy; and are doomed and cursed. [15]They have gone off the road and become lost like Balaam, the son of Beor, who fell in love with the money he could make by doing wrong; [16]but Balaam was stopped from his mad course when his donkey spoke to him with a human voice, scolding and rebuking him.

[17]These men are as useless as dried-up springs of water, promising much and delivering nothing; they are as unstable as clouds driven by the storm winds. They are doomed to the eternal pits of darkness. [18]They proudly boast about their sins and conquests, and, using lust as their bait, they lure back into sin those who have just escaped from such wicked living.

[19]"You aren't saved by being good," they say, "so you might as well be bad. Do what you like; be free."

But these very teachers who offer this "freedom" from law are themselves slaves to sin and destruction. For a man is a slave to whatever controls him. [20]And when a person has escaped from the wicked ways of the world by learning about our Lord and Savior Jesus Christ, and then gets tangled up with sin and becomes its slave again, he is worse off than he was before. [21]It would be better if he had never known about Christ at all than to learn of him and then afterwards turn his back on the holy commandments that were given to him. [22]There is an old saying that "A dog comes back to what he has vomited, and a pig is washed only to come back and wallow in the mud again." That is the way it is with those who turn again to their sin.

3 Hope for Growing Christians

This is my second letter to you, dear brothers, and in both of them I have tried to remind you—if you will let me—about facts you already know: facts you learned from the holy prophets and from us apostles who brought you the words of our Lord and Savior.

[3]First, I want to remind you that in the last days there will come scoffers who will do every wrong they can think of and laugh at the truth. [4]This will be their line of argument: "So Jesus promised to come back, did he? Then where is he? He'll never come! Why, as far back as anyone can remember, everything has remained exactly as it was since the first day of creation."

[5,6]They deliberately forget this fact: that God did destroy the world with a mighty flood long after he had made the heavens by the word of his command and had used the waters to form the earth and surround it. [7]And God has commanded that the earth and the heavens be stored away for a great bonfire at the judgment day, when all ungodly men will perish.

[8]But don't forget this, dear friends, that a day or a thousand years from now is like tomorrow to the Lord. [9]He isn't really being slow about his promised return, even though it sometimes seems that way. But he is waiting, for the good reason that he is not willing that any should perish, and he is giving more time for sinners to repent. [10]The day of the Lord is surely coming, as unexpectedly as a thief, and then the heavens will pass away with a terrible noise, and the heavenly bodies will disappear in fire, and the earth and everything on it will be burned up.

[11]And so since everything around us is going to melt away, what holy, godly lives we should be living! [12]You should look forward to that day and hurry it along—the day when God will set the heavens on fire, and the heavenly bodies will melt and disappear in flames. [13]But we are looking forward to God's promise of new heavens and a new earth afterwards, where there will be only goodness.

[14]Dear friends, while you are waiting for these things to happen and for him to come, try hard to live without sinning; and be at peace with everyone so that he will be pleased with you when he returns.

[15,16]And remember why he is waiting. He is giving us time to get his message of salvation out to others. Our wise and beloved brother Paul has talked about these same things in many of his letters. Some of his comments are not easy to understand, and there are people who are deliberately stupid, and always demand some unusual interpretation—they have twisted his letters around to mean something quite different from what he meant, just as they do the other parts of the Scripture—and the result is disaster for them.

[17]I am warning you ahead of time, dear brothers, so that you can watch out and not be carried away by the mistakes of these wicked men, lest you yourselves become mixed up too. [18]But grow in spiritual strength and become better acquainted with our Lord and Savior Jesus Christ. To him be all glory and splendid honor, both now and forevermore. Good-bye.

Peter

RECEIVING CHRIST AS SAVIOR 2:19 Many believe freedom means doing anything you want. But no one is ever completely free in that sense. If we refuse to follow God, we will follow our own sinful desires and become enslaved to what our bodies want. If we submit our lives to Christ and receive him as Savior, he will free us from slavery to sin. **To begin the series of devotionals on RECEIVING CHRIST AS SAVIOR, turn to page 235.**

1 John

WHAT'S THE hardest command you've had to obey? Are you ever "commanded" to do something fun? In 1 John we get a command to do something great! We are commanded to show love.

John wanted Christians to show the love of Jesus to everyone. In fact, John said that people who love Jesus *will* love others. If they don't, it shows that they don't really love Jesus after all. The command to be loving came right from Jesus, and Jesus lived out his own command. Some of the ways Jesus showed love are named in this letter.

The John who wrote this letter is the same person who wrote the Gospel of John, the letters called 2 John and 3 John, and the book of Revelation. John had been one of Jesus' disciples, and he was confident that Jesus loved him.

As you read 1 John, look for ways you can follow Jesus' command to show love.

Jesus Christ Is Eternal Life

Christ was alive when the world began, yet I myself have seen him with my own eyes and listened to him speak. I have touched him with my own hands. He is God's message of life. ²This one who is life from God has been shown to us, and we guarantee that we have seen him; I am speaking of Christ, who is eternal Life. He was with the Father and then was shown to us. ³Again I say, we are telling you about what we ourselves have actually seen and heard, so that you may share the fellowship and the joys we have with the Father and with Jesus Christ his son. ⁴And if you do as I say in this letter, then you, too, will be full of joy, and so will we.

⁵This is the message God has given us to pass on to you: that God is Light and in him is no darkness at all. ⁶So if we say we are his friends but go on living in spiritual darkness and sin, we are lying. ⁷But if we are living in the light of God's presence, just as Christ

does, then we have wonderful fellowship and joy with each other, and the blood of Jesus his Son cleanses us from every sin.

⁸If we say that we have no sin, we are only fooling ourselves and refusing to accept the truth. ⁹But if we confess our sins to him, he can be depended on to forgive us and to cleanse us from every wrong. [And it is perfectly proper for God to do this for us because Christ died to wash away our sins.] ¹⁰If we claim we have not sinned, we are lying and calling God a liar, *for he says we have sinned.*

2 Love God, Not This World

My little children, I am telling you this so that you will stay away from sin. But if you sin, there is someone to plead for you before the Father. His name is Jesus Christ, the one who is all that is good and who pleases God completely. ²He is the one who took God's wrath against our sins upon himself and brought us into fellowship with God; and he is the forgiveness for our sins, and not only ours but all the world's.

³And how can we be sure that we belong to him? By looking within ourselves: are we really trying to do what he wants us to?

⁴Someone may say, "I am a Christian; I am on my way to heaven; I belong to Christ." But if he doesn't do what Christ tells him to, he is a liar. ⁵But those who do what Christ tells them to will learn to love God more and more. That is the way to know whether or not you are a Christian. ⁶Anyone who says he is a Christian should live as Christ did.

⁷Dear brothers, I am not writing out a new rule for you to obey, for it is an old one you have always had, right from the start. You have heard it all before. ⁸Yet it is always new, and works for you just as it did for Christ; and as we obey this commandment, *to love one another,* the darkness in our lives disappears and the new light of life in Christ shines in.

⁹Anyone who says he is walking in the light of Christ but dislikes his fellow man is still in darkness. ¹⁰But whoever loves his fellow man is "walking in the light" and can see his way without stumbling around in darkness and sin. ¹¹For he who dislikes his brother is wandering in spiritual darkness and doesn't know where he is going, for the darkness has made him blind so that he cannot see the way.

¹²I am writing these things to all of you, my little children, because your sins have been forgiven in the name of Jesus our Savior. ¹³I am saying these things to you older men because you really know Christ, the one who has been alive from the beginning. And you young men, I am talking to you because you have won your battle with Satan. And I am writing to you younger boys and girls because you, too, have learned to know God our Father.

¹⁴And so I say to you fathers who know the eternal God, and to you young men who are strong with God's Word in your hearts, and have won your struggle against Satan: ¹⁵Stop loving this evil world and all that it offers you, for when you love these things you show that you do not really love God; ¹⁶for all these worldly things, these evil desires—the craze for sex, the ambition to buy everything that appeals to you, and the pride that comes from wealth and importance—these are not from God. They are from this evil world itself. ¹⁷And this world is fading away, and these evil, forbidden things will go with it, but whoever keeps doing the will of God will live forever.

¹⁸Dear children, this world's last hour has come. You have heard about the Antichrist who is coming—the one who is against Christ—and already many such persons have appeared. This makes us all the more certain that the end of the world is near. ¹⁹These "against-Christ" people used to be members of our churches, but they never really belonged with us or else they would have stayed. When they left us it proved that they were not of us at all.

²⁰But you are not like that, for the Holy Spirit has come upon you, and you know the truth. ²¹So I am not writing to you as to those who need to know the truth, but I warn you as those who can discern the difference between true and false.

²²And who is the greatest liar? The one who says that Jesus is not Christ. Such a person is antichrist, for he does not believe in God the Father and in his Son. ²³For a person who doesn't believe in Christ, God's Son, can't have God the Father either. But he who has Christ, God's Son, has God the Father also.

²⁴So keep on believing what you have been taught from the beginning. If you do, you will always be in close fellowship with both God the Father and his Son. ²⁵And he himself has promised us this: *eternal life.*

²⁶These remarks of mine about the Antichrist are pointed at those who would dearly love to blindfold you and lead you astray. ²⁷But you have received the Holy Spirit, and he lives within you, in your hearts, so that you don't need anyone to teach you what is right. For he teaches you all things, and he is the Truth, and no liar; and so, just as he has said, you must live in Christ, never to depart from him.

²⁸And now, my little children, stay in happy fellowship with the Lord so that when he comes you will be sure that all is well and will not have to be ashamed and shrink back from meeting him. ²⁹Since we know that God is always good and does only right, we may rightly assume that all those who do right are his children.

Family Devotions

☐ DEVOTION 355
BECOMING MORE LIKE JESUS

Read 1 John 2:3-10

Becoming More Like Jesus Memory Verse

Let everything you do reflect your love of the truth and the fact that you are in dead earnest about it.
Titus 2:7

As Kevin entered the waiting room, the office nurse smiled at him. "Your father's almost done for the day, Kevin," she said.

Soon Kevin and his father were in their car, headed for home. "Dad, when someone comes for a checkup, how do you tell whether they're sick or not?" Kevin asked.

Dr. Brown grinned at his son. "Well, when a patient comes in for an exam, I first ask if he has any complaints," he explained. "I also check height, weight, blood pressure, and heartbeat. I listen to the lungs, and I look at the ears, eyes, nose, and throat. If I suspect any illness, I sometimes take a blood sample or run some other tests. But normally, if the basic signs are all OK, the patient is healthy."

"That doesn't sound very complicated," exclaimed Kevin. "If that's all there is to a checkup, it must not be very important."

"Oh, but it is!" replied his father. "If everyone would have an examination regularly, many illnesses could be prevented." Then he added, "There's another kind of checkup that's even more important—a spiritual one. And that's one we can give ourselves."

"How do we do that?" asked Kevin.

"By examining the vital signs of our Christian life," said his father. "First, think about your prayer and Scripture reading habits. Have they become irregular? Also consider your church attendance and your general attitude toward spiritual things. If you have bad feelings towards anyone, make up your mind to repair the relationship as soon as possible. Ask God to reveal any areas of sin in your life. Finally, try to remember the last time you witnessed to someone or did any other work for the Lord."

"That doesn't sound too hard," said Kevin thoughtfully. "I think I'll give myself a checkup today."

How About You?
When was the last time you gave yourself a spiritual checkup? You'd be surprised at how often a simple lapse in Bible reading, prayer, or church attendance can lead to big problems. God doesn't want your Christian life to be an unstable, unhappy experience. Be sure to take regular checkups! *S. K.*

• For the next devotional, turn to page 1239.   • To start the next topic, turn to page 41.   • For notes on BECOMING MORE LIKE JESUS, see pages 234, 983, 1105, and 1164.

3 We Are God's Children

See how very much our heavenly Father loves us, for he allows us to be called his children—think of it—and we really *are!* But since most people don't know God, naturally they don't understand that we are his children. ²Yes, dear friends, we are already God's children, right now, and we can't even imagine what it is going to be like later on. But we do know this, that when he comes we will be like him, as a result of seeing him as he really is. ³And everyone who really believes this will try to stay pure because Christ is pure.

⁴But those who keep on sinning are against God, for every sin is done against the will of God. ⁵And you know that he became a man so that he could take away our sins, and that there is no sin in him, no missing of God's will at any time in any way. ⁶So if we stay close to him, obedient to him, we won't be sinning either; but as for those who keep on sinning, they should realize this: They sin because they have never really known him or become his.

⁷Oh, dear children, don't let anyone deceive you about this: if you are constantly doing what is good, it is because you *are* good, even as he is. ⁸But if you keep on sinning, it shows that you belong to Satan, who since he first began to sin has kept steadily at it. But the Son of God came to destroy these works of the devil. ⁹The person who has been born into God's family does not make a practice of sinning because now God's life is in him; so he can't keep on sinning, for this new life has been born into him and controls him—he has been *born again.*

¹⁰So now we can tell who is a child of God and who belongs to Satan. Whoever is living a life of sin and doesn't love his brother shows that he is not in God's family;¹¹for the message to us from the beginning has been that we should love one another.

¹²We are not to be like Cain, who belonged to Satan and killed his brother. Why did he kill him? Because Cain had been doing wrong and he knew very well that his brother's life was better than his. ¹³So don't be surprised, dear friends, if the world hates you.

¹⁴If we love other Christians, it proves that we have been delivered from hell and given eternal life. But a person who doesn't have love for others is headed for eternal death. ¹⁵Anyone who hates his Christian brother is really a murderer at heart; and you know that no one wanting to murder has eternal life within. ¹⁶We know what real love is from Christ's example in dying for us. And so we also ought to lay down our lives for our Christian brothers.

¹⁷But if someone who is supposed to be a Christian has money enough to live well, and sees a brother in need, and won't help him—how can God's love be within *him?* ¹⁸Little children, let us stop just *saying* we love people; let us *really* love them, and *show it* by our *actions.* ¹⁹Then we will know for sure, by our actions, that we are on God's side, and our consciences will be clear, even when we stand before the Lord. ²⁰But if we have bad consciences and feel that we have done wrong, the Lord will surely feel it even more, for he knows everything we do.

²¹But, dearly loved friends, if our consciences are clear, we can come to the Lord with perfect assurance and trust, ²²and get whatever we ask for because we are obeying him and doing the things that please him. ²³And this is what God says we must do: Believe on the name of his Son Jesus Christ, and love one another. ²⁴Those who do what God says—they are living with God and he with them. We know this is true because the Holy Spirit he has given us tells us so.

4 What's True and What's Not?

Dearly loved friends, don't always believe everything you hear just because someone says it is a message from God: test it first to see if it really is. For there are many false teachers around, ²and the way to find out if their message is from the Holy Spirit is to ask: Does it really agree that Jesus Christ, God's Son, actually became man with a human body? If so, then the message is from God. ³If not, the message is not from God but from one who is against Christ, like the "Antichrist" you have heard about who is going to come, and his attitude of enmity against Christ is already abroad in the world.

⁴Dear young friends, you belong to God and have already won your fight with those who are against Christ because there is someone in your hearts who is stronger than any evil teacher in this wicked world. ⁵These men belong to this world, so, quite naturally, they are concerned about worldly affairs and the world pays attention to them. ⁶But we are children of God; that is why only those who have walked and talked with God will listen to us. Others won't. That is another way to know whether a message is really from God; for if it is, the world won't listen to it.

⁷Dear friends, let us practice loving each other, for love comes from God and those who are loving and kind show that they are the children of God, and that they are getting to know him better. ⁸But if a person isn't loving and kind, it shows that he doesn't know God—for God is love.

⁹God showed how much he loved us by sending his only Son into this wicked world to bring

Family Devotions

☐ Devotion 356
Encouraging Others

Read 1 John 4 : 7-12

"What's Beth's problem?" asked Brian as his sister left the room. "She was acting awful gloomy."

"This is the day her friends leave for summer camp," sighed Mom. "Beth was fortunate to get a job, and she can't afford to quit—but she loves camp so much!"

"We ought to do something special for her so she won't be so mopey." Brian wrinkled his brow. Then he snapped his fingers. "Let's have a party—a surprise family party."

"A you're-special-to-us party?" asked Mom. "All right. I'll fix her favorite dinner, and you can decorate the dining room."

"What about presents?" asked Brian.

Mom thought for a minute. "Why don't we make love coupons? I'll make one with a promise to make her bed and clean up her room every day this week. Then she can sleep later. You could wash the dishes when it's her turn," suggested Mom.

Brian groaned. "Let's not get carried away. We do want to make her feel better, but there's a limit!"

Mom laughed and gave him a quick hug. "This is a lovely idea, Son. God says we should show love to one another, and you're doing that today."

When Beth came in from work, she stood in the doorway and stared. On the dining room wall was a big banner—"We love you, Beth." The table was set with the best china, and there were streamers and balloons everywhere.

After dinner, Beth looked around at her family. "I love all of you," she said. Looking at the dirty dishes, she winked at Brian. "Especially you, little brother. I hope you don't get dishpan hands this week!"

Encouraging Others Memory Verse

So encourage each other to build each other up, just as you are already doing.
1 Thessalonians 5:11

How About You?

Does someone in your family need a pick-me-up? As you remember all that God did to show his great love for you, will you, in turn, go out of your way to show love to that downhearted person? Maybe you can plan a party, do more than your share of the chores, or help in some special way. You'll be surprised to find how much it will lift everyone's spirits. *B. W.*

• For the next devotional, turn to page 1245. • To start the next topic, turn to page 141. • For notes on Encouraging Others, see pages 108, 157, 474, 1156, and 1170.

to us eternal life through his death. [10]In this act we see what real love is: it is not our love for God but his love for us when he sent his Son to satisfy God's anger against our sins.

[11]Dear friends, since God loved us as much as that, we surely ought to love each other too. [12]For though we have never yet seen God, when we love each other God lives in us, and his love within us grows ever stronger. [13]And he has put his own Holy Spirit into our hearts as a proof to us that we are living with him and he with us. [14]And furthermore, we have seen with our own eyes and now tell all the world that God sent his Son to be their Savior. [15]Anyone who believes and says that Jesus is the Son of God has God living in him, and he is living with God.

[16]We know how much God loves us because we have felt his love and because we believe him when he tells us that he loves us dearly. God is love, and anyone who lives in love is living with God and God is living in him. [17]And as we live with Christ, our love grows more perfect and complete; so we will not be ashamed and embarrassed at the day of judgment, but can face him with confidence and joy because he loves us and we love him too.

[18]We need have no fear of someone who loves us perfectly; his perfect love for us eliminates all dread of what he might do to us. If we are afraid, it is for fear of what he might do to us and shows that we are not fully convinced that he really loves us. [19]So you see, our love for him comes as a result of his loving us first.

[20]If anyone says "I love God," but keeps on hating his brother, he is a liar; for if he doesn't love his brother who is right there in front of him, how can he love God whom he has never seen? [21]And God himself has said that one must love not only God but his brother too.

5 Love God and Obey Him

If you believe that Jesus is the Christ—that he is God's Son and your Savior—then you are a child of God. And all who love the Father love his children too. [2]So you can find out how much you love God's children—your brothers and sisters in the Lord—by how much you love and obey God. [3]Loving God means doing what he tells us to do, and really, that isn't hard at all; [4]for every child of God can obey him, defeating sin and evil pleasure by trusting Christ to help him.

[5]But who could possibly fight and win this battle except by believing that Jesus is truly the Son of God? [6-8]And we know he is, because God said so with a voice from heaven when Jesus was baptized, and again as he was facing death—yes, not only at his baptism but also as he faced death. And the Holy Spirit, forever truthful, says it too. So we have these three witnesses: the voice of the Holy Spirit in our hearts, the voice from heaven at Christ's baptism, and the voice before he died. And they all say the same thing: that Jesus Christ is the Son of God. [9]We believe men who witness in our courts, and so surely we can believe whatever God declares. And God declares that Jesus is his Son. [10]All who believe this know in their hearts that it is true. If anyone doesn't believe this, he is actually calling God a liar because he doesn't believe what God has said about his Son.

[11]And what is it that God has said? That he has given us eternal life and that this life is in his Son. [12]So whoever has God's Son has life; whoever does not have his Son, does not have life.

[13]I have written this to you who believe in the Son of God so that you may know you have eternal life. [14]And we are sure of this, that he will listen to us whenever we ask him for anything in line with his will. [15]And if we really know he is listening when we talk to him and make our requests, then we can be sure that he will answer us.

[16]If you see a Christian sinning in a way that does not end in death, you should ask God to forgive him, and God will give him life unless he has sinned that one fatal sin. But there is that one sin which ends in death, and if he has done that, there is no use praying for him. [17]Every wrong is a sin, of course. I'm not talking about these ordinary sins; I am speaking of that one that ends in death.

[18]No one who has become part of God's family makes a practice of sinning, for Christ, God's Son, holds him securely, and the devil cannot get his hands on him. [19]We know that we are children of God and that all the rest of the world around us is under Satan's power and control. [20]And we know that Christ, God's Son, has come to help us understand and find the true God. And now we are in God because we are in Jesus Christ his Son, who is the only true God; and he is eternal Life.

[21]Dear children, keep away from anything that might take God's place in your hearts. Amen.

Sincerely, John

RECEIVING CHRIST AS SAVIOR 5:13 Some people *hope* they will be given eternal life. John says we can *know* we have it. Our certainty is based on God's promise that he has given us eternal life through his Son. This is true whether you feel close to God or distant from him. Eternal life is not based on feelings, but on facts. You can know you have eternal life if you believe God's truth. If you lack assurance as to whether you are a Christian, ask yourself if you have honestly committed your life to him as your Savior and Lord. If so, you know by faith that you are indeed a child of God. **To begin the series of devotionals on RECEIVING CHRIST AS SAVIOR, turn to page 235.**

2 John

IN NEW Testament days it was common for teachers to travel from town to town. People in the towns would welcome these teachers by giving them food and a place to stay. Christians enjoyed having traveling teachers come and tell them more about Jesus. But some teachers weren't really teachers. They were just lazy people who wanted free food and a free place to stay. Some other teachers taught lies about Jesus. They didn't teach the truth that Paul, Peter, and other disciples of Jesus wrote about.

People wondered how to show Christian love to these false teachers. John wrote that it doesn't help false teachers to support them in their lies. It also doesn't help non-Christians to see Christians supporting wrong stories about Jesus. Therefore, the best way to help everyone is not to support the false teachers.

Showing Jesus' love can be tricky sometimes. As you read 2 John, think about how you can show God's kind of love.

Beware of False Teachers

From: John, the old Elder of the church.

To: That dear woman Cyria, one of God's very own, and to her children whom I love so much, as does everyone else in the church. ²Since the Truth is in our hearts forever, ³God the Father and Jesus Christ his Son will bless us with great mercy and much peace, and with truth and love.

⁴How happy I am to find some of your children here and to see that they are living as they should, following the Truth, obeying God's command.

⁵And now I want to urgently remind you, dear friends, of the old rule God gave us right from the beginning, that Christians should love one another. ⁶If we love God, we will do whatever he tells us toA. And he has told us from the very first to love each other.

⁷Watch out for the false leaders—and there are many of them around—who don't believe that Jesus Christ came to earth as a human being with a body like ours. Such people are against the truth and against Christ. ⁸Beware of being like them

and losing the prize that you and I have been working so hard to get. See to it that you win your full reward from the Lord. ⁹For if you wander beyond the teaching of Christ, you will leave God behind; while if you are loyal to Christ's teachings, you will have God too. Then you will have both the Father and the Son.

¹⁰If anyone comes to teach you, and he doesn't believe what Christ taught, don't even invite him into your home. Don't encourage him in any way. ¹¹If you do, you will be a partner with him in his wickedness.

¹²Well, I would like to say much more, but I don't want to say it in this letter, for I hope to come to see you soon, and then we can talk over these things together and have a joyous time.

¹³Greetings from the children of your sister—another choice child of God.

Sincerely, John

LOVING OTHERS **1:5-6** The love Christians should have for one another is a recurrent New Testament theme. Yet love for one's neighbor is an old rule first appearing in the third book of Moses (Leviticus 19:18). We can show love in many ways: by avoiding prejudice and discrimination, by accepting people, by listening, helping, giving, serving, and refusing to judge. (See also Matthew 22:37-39 and 1 John 2:7-8.) **To begin the series of devotionals on** *LOVING OTHERS*, **turn to page 313.**

3 John

THE BIBLE teaches that it's good to help Christians who have needs, even people we don't know. How often do you get the chance to help and serve other Christians?

John wrote his third letter to a friend named Gaius to tell him what a great job he was doing in serving others. Gaius belonged to a church far away, but stories of his hospitality had reached John. When traveling teachers, missionaries, and other Christians came into town, Gaius made sure they had a place to stay and everything they needed. Gaius knew that by helping these travelers, he was helping the Good News of Jesus to go farther.

Who are people you can show hospitality to? As you read 3 John, think of ways you can help Christians in your church, your community, and around the world.

Hospitality Pleases God

From: John, the Elder.

To: Dear Gaius, whom I truly love.

²Dear friend, I am praying that all is well with you and that your body is as healthy as I know your soul is. ³Some of the brothers traveling by have made me very happy by telling me that your life stays clean and true and that you are living by the standards of the Gospel. ⁴I could have no greater joy than to hear such things about my children.

⁵Dear friend, you are doing a good work for God in taking care of the traveling teachers and missionaries who are passing through. ⁶They have told the church here of your friendship and your loving deeds. I am glad when you send them on their way with a generous gift. ⁷For they are traveling for the Lord and take neither food, clothing,

shelter, nor money from those who are not Christians, even though they have preached to them. ⁸So we ourselves should take care of them in order that we may become partners with them in the Lord's work.

⁹I sent a brief letter to the church about this, but proud Diotrephes, who loves to push himself forward as the leader of the Christians there, does not admit my authority over him and refuses to listen to me. ¹⁰When I come I will tell you some of the things he is doing and what wicked things he is saying about me and what insulting language he is using. He not only refuses to welcome the missionary travelers himself but tells others not to, and when they do he tries to put them out of the church.

¹¹Dear friend, don't let this bad example influence you. Follow only what is good. Remember that those who do what is right prove that they are God's children; and those who continue in evil prove that they are far from God. ¹²But everyone, including Truth itself, speaks highly of Demetrius. I myself can say the same for him, and you know I speak the truth.

¹³I have much to say, but I don't want to write it, ¹⁴for I hope to see you soon and then we will have much to talk about together. ¹⁵So good-bye for now. Friends here send their love, and please give each of the folks there a special greeting from me.

Sincerely, John

SHOWING KINDNESS 1:5 In the church's early days, traveling prophets, evangelists, and teachers were helped on their way by people like Gaius who housed and fed them. Hospitality—showing kindness to friends or strangers by sharing our home with them—is a lost art in many churches today.

When company arrives at the door, with them comes the promise of soiled floors, dirty dishes, altered schedules, personal expense, and inconvenience. From sharing a meal to providing a bed, hospitality costs us something: time, energy, and money. But how we treat others reflects our true values. Perhaps the most effective way to demonstrate God's values and Christ's love to others is to invite and welcome guests into our home.

We would do well to invite more people for meals—fellow church members, young people, traveling missionaries, those in need, visitors. This is an active and much-appreciated way to show our love. Also look for other creative ways that your family can show kindness to God's workers. It may be in the form of a letter of encouragement, a "care" package, financial support, an open home, or prayer. **To begin the series of devotionals on SHOWING KINDNESS, turn to page 81.**

Family Devotions

☐ **DEVOTION 357**
SERVING GOD WILLINGLY

Read 3 John 1 : 5 - 8

"Oh, no," cried Tanya, "not again! All we ever do is have missionaries stay at our house. If it's not missionaries, it's visiting preachers—or even complete strangers, like when people got stranded in the snowstorm last winter!"

"That's part of our ministry, honey," Dad told her.

"Ministry?" Tanya questioned.

"That's right," her father answered. "Mom and I wanted to go to the mission field, but my health didn't permit it."

"So we decided we would open our home to missionaries whenever we could," finished Mom, "and we also want to use our home as a place to witness to others whenever possible."

Tanya had never thought about entertaining people as a ministry. All she could see was that it meant doing more dishes and often giving up her bedroom to guests. "Does the Bible say you're supposed to have company?" Tanya asked.

Mom smiled. "Well, it does say we should get into the habit of inviting guests home for dinner," she said. It also says . . ." Mom picked up her Bible, opened it, and began to read aloud. "Dear friend, you are doing a good work for God in taking care of the traveling teachers and missionaries who are passing through."

Tanya took a deep breath. "Boy, I didn't know the Bible said anything about having company." Then she added with a smile, "I guess I'd better go clean up my room—it's part of our mission field, after all!"

Serving God Willingly
Memory Verse

Anyone who takes care of a little child like this is caring for me! And whoever cares for me is caring for God who sent me. Your care for others is the measure of your greatness.
Luke 9:48

How About You?
When you have to help prepare a meal, wash extra dishes, or give up your room because your parents are entertaining, do you grumble about it, or do you think of it as sharing what you have with others? God wants you to share. Will you do it cheerfully for him? *R. J.*

• For the next devotional, turn to page 1251. • To start the next topic, turn to page 427. • For notes on *SERVING GOD WILLINGLY*, see pages 49, 319, 890, 920, and 922.

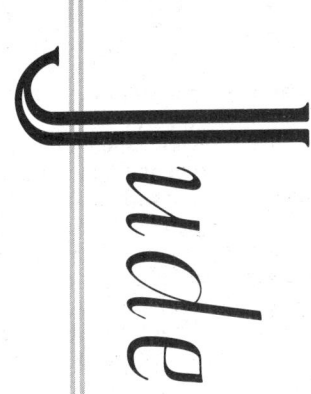

Jude

HOW WELL do you know what you believe? If someone gave you a good argument against Christianity, would you be able to stick to your faith?

When Jude wrote his letter, wrong teachings about Jesus were being brought into the church by people who said they were Christians. But they didn't want to believe the whole gospel—just the parts that sounded good to them. Then they tried to get other Christians to join them in their wrong beliefs.

There will always be a danger of people who say they're Christians spreading wrong teachings about Jesus. It's important to know what we believe so we can stand up against them. As you read Jude, look for reasons it's important to know what you believe.

To Christians Everywhere

From: Jude, a servant of Jesus Christ, and a brother of James.

To: Christians everywhere—beloved of God and chosen by him. ²May you be given more and more of God's kindness, peace, and love.

³Dearly loved friends, I had been planning to write you some thoughts about the salvation God has given us, but now I find I must write of something else instead, urging you to stoutly defend the truth that God gave once for all to his people to keep without change through the years. ⁴I say this because some godless teachers have wormed their way in among you, saying that after we become Christians we can do just as we like without fear of God's punishment. The fate of such people was written long ago, for they have turned against our only Master and Lord, Jesus Christ.

⁵My answer to them is: Remember this fact—which you know already—that the Lord saved a whole nation of people out of the land of Egypt and then killed every one of them who did not

trust and obey him. ⁶And I remind you of those angels who were once pure and holy but turned to a life of sin. Now God has them chained up in prisons of darkness, waiting for the judgment day. ⁷And don't forget the cities of Sodom and Gomorrah and their neighboring towns, all full of lust of every kind, including lust of men for other men. Those cities were destroyed by fire and continue to be a warning to us that there is a hell in which sinners are punished.

⁸Yet these false teachers carelessly go right on living their evil, immoral lives, degrading their bodies and laughing at those in authority over them, even scoffing at the Glorious Ones. ⁹Yet Michael, one of the mightiest of the angels, when he was arguing with Satan about Moses' body, did not dare to accuse even Satan, or jeer at him, but simply said, "The Lord rebuke you." ¹⁰But these men mock and curse at anything they do not understand, and like animals, they do whatever they feel like, thereby ruining their souls.

¹¹Woe upon them! For they follow the example of Cain who killed his brother; and like Balaam, they will do anything for money; and like Korah, they have disobeyed God and will die under his curse.

¹²When these men join you at the love feasts of the church, they are evil smears among you, laughing and carrying on, gorging and stuffing themselves without a thought for others. They are like clouds blowing over dry land without giving rain, promising much, but producing nothing. They are like fruit trees without any fruit at picking time. They are not only dead, but doubly dead, for they have been pulled out, roots and all, to be burned.

¹³All they leave behind them is shame and disgrace like the dirty foam left along the beach by the wild waves. They wander around looking as bright as stars, but ahead of them is the everlasting gloom and darkness that God has prepared for them.

¹⁴Enoch, who lived seven generations after Adam, knew about these men and said this about them: "See, the Lord is coming with millions of his holy ones. ¹⁵He will bring the people of the world before him in judgment, to receive just punishment and to prove the terrible things they have done in rebellion against God, revealing all they have said against him." ¹⁶These men are constant gripers, never satisfied, doing whatever evil they feel like; they are loudmouthed "show-offs," and when they show respect for others, it is only to get something from them in return.

¹⁷Dear friends, remember what the apostles of our Lord Jesus Christ told you, ¹⁸that in the last times there would come these scoffers whose whole purpose in life is to enjoy themselves in every evil way imaginable. ¹⁹They stir up arguments; they love the evil things of the world; they do not have the Holy Spirit living in them.

²⁰But you, dear friends, must build up your lives ever more strongly upon the foundation of our holy faith, learning to pray in the power and strength of the Holy Spirit.

²¹Stay always within the boundaries where God's love can reach and bless you. Wait patiently for the eternal life that our Lord Jesus Christ in his mercy is going to give you. ²²Try to help those who argue against you. Be merciful to those who doubt. ²³Save some by snatching them as from the very flames of hell itself. And as for others, help them to find the Lord by being kind to them, but be careful that you yourselves aren't pulled along into their sins. Hate every trace of their sin while being merciful to them as sinners.

²⁴,²⁵And now—all glory to him who alone is God, who saves us through Jesus Christ our Lord; yes, splendor and majesty, all power and authority are his from the beginning; his they are and his they evermore shall be. And he is able to keep you from slipping and falling away, and to bring you, sinless and perfect, into his glorious presence with mighty shouts of everlasting joy. Amen.

Jude

RESPECTING GOD'S WORD 1:3 Jude emphasizes the important relationship between correct doctrine and true faith. The truth of the Bible must not be compromised because it gives us the real facts about Jesus and salvation. Scripture is inspired by God and should never be twisted or changed; when it is, we become confused over right and wrong and lose sight of the only path that leads to eternal life. **To begin the series of devotionals on RESPECTING GOD'S WORD, turn to page 11.**

Revelation

DO YOU know the difference between thanking and praising? We *thank* Jesus for all the things he's done for us and given us. We *praise* Jesus for who he is and what he is like.

The book of Revelation is a great book of praise. It lets us see more of who Jesus is. It shows us how we will see Jesus at the end of time.

Jesus gave this message to the apostle John in a vision, which included many signs and symbols about what is going to happen in the future. What John saw was impossible for him to describe, so he tried to say what it was *like*. Don't try to understand all the details in Revelation—John didn't! Instead, let John's descriptions show you that Jesus is the glorious, victorious Lord of all. As you read Revelation, look for reasons to praise Jesus.

A Revelation about the Future

This book unveils some of the future activities soon to occur in the life of Jesus Christ. God permitted him to reveal these things to his servant John in a vision; and then an angel was sent from heaven to explain the vision's meaning. ²John wrote it all down—the words of God and Jesus Christ and everything he heard and saw.

³If you read this prophecy aloud to the church, you will receive a special blessing from the Lord. Those who listen to it being read and do what it says will also be blessed. For the time is near when these things will all come true.

⁴*From:* John
To: The seven churches in Turkey.
Dear Friends:

May you have grace and peace from God who is, and was, and is to come; and from the sevenfold Spirit before his throne; ⁵and from Jesus Christ who faithfully reveals all truth to us. He was the first to rise from death, to die no more. He is far greater than any king in all the earth. All praise to him who always loves us and who set us free from our sins by pouring out his lifeblood for us. ⁶He has gathered us into his Kingdom and made us priests of God his Father. Give to him everlasting glory! He rules forever! Amen!

⁷See! He is arriving, surrounded by clouds; and every eye shall see him—yes, and those who pierced him. And the nations will weep in sorrow and in terror when he comes. Yes! Amen! Let it be so!

⁸"I am the A and the Z, the Beginning and the Ending of all things," says God, who is the Lord, the All Powerful One who is, and was, and is coming again!

⁹It is I, your brother John, a fellow sufferer for the Lord's sake, who am writing this letter to you. I, too, have shared the patience Jesus gives, and we shall share his Kingdom!

I was on the island of Patmos, exiled there for preaching the Word of God and for telling what I knew about Jesus Christ. ¹⁰It was the Lord's Day and I was worshiping, when suddenly I heard a loud voice behind me, a voice that sounded like a trumpet blast, ¹¹saying, "I am A and Z, the First and Last!" And then I heard him say, "Write down everything you see, and send your letter to the seven churches in Turkey: to the church in Ephesus, the one in Smyrna, and those in Pergamos, Thyatira, Sardis, Philadelphia, and Laodicea."

¹²When I turned to see who was speaking, there behind me were seven candlesticks of gold. ¹³And standing among them was one who looked like Jesus, who called himself the Son of Man, wearing a long robe circled with a golden band across his chest. ¹⁴His hair was white as wool or snow, and his eyes penetrated like flames of fire. ¹⁵His feet gleamed like burnished bronze, and his voice thundered like the waves against the shore. ¹⁶He held seven stars in his right hand and a sharp, double-bladed sword in his mouth, and his face shone like the power of the sun in unclouded brilliance.

¹⁷,¹⁸When I saw him, I fell at his feet as dead; but he laid his right hand on me and said, "Don't be afraid! Though I am the First and Last, the Living One who died, who is now alive forevermore, who has the keys of hell and death—don't be afraid! ¹⁹Write down what you have just seen and what will soon be shown to you. ²⁰This is the meaning of the seven stars you saw in my right hand and the seven golden candlesticks: The seven stars are the leaders of the seven churches, and the seven candlesticks are the churches themselves.

2 John Writes to Seven Churches

"*Write a letter to the leader of the church at Ephesus and tell him this:*

"I write to inform you of a message from him who walks among the churches and holds their leaders in his right hand.

"He says to you: ²I know how many good things you are doing. I have watched your hard work and your patience; I know you don't tolerate sin among your members, and you have carefully examined the claims of those who say they are apostles but aren't. You have found out how they lie. ³You have patiently suffered for me without quitting.

⁴"Yet there is one thing wrong; you don't love me as at first! ⁵Think about those times of your first love (how different now!) and turn back to me again and work as you did before; or else I will come and remove your candlestick from its place among the churches.

⁶"But there is this about you that is good: You hate the deeds of the licentious Nicolaitans, just as I do.

⁷"Let this message sink into the ears of anyone who listens to what the Spirit is saying to the churches: To everyone who is victorious, I will give fruit from the Tree of Life in the Paradise of God.

⁸"*To the leader of the church in Smyrna write this letter:*

"This message is from him who is the First and Last, who was dead and then came back to life.

⁹"I know how much you suffer for the Lord, and I know all about your poverty (but you have heavenly riches!). I know the slander of those opposing you, who say that they are Jews—the children of God—but they aren't, for they support the cause of Satan. ¹⁰Stop being afraid of what you are about to suffer—for the devil will soon throw some of you into prison to test you. You will be persecuted for 'ten days.' Remain faithful even when facing death and I will give you the crown of life—an unending, glorious future. ¹¹Let everyone who can hear listen to what the Spirit is saying to the churches: He who is victorious shall not be hurt by the Second Death.

¹²"*Write this letter to the leader of the church in Pergamos:*

"This message is from him who wields the sharp and double-bladed sword. ¹³I am fully aware that you live in the city where Satan's throne is, at the center of satanic worship; and yet you have remained loyal to me and refused to deny me even when Antipas, my faithful witness, was martyred among you by Satan's devotees.

¹⁴"And yet I have a few things against you. You tolerate some among you who do as Balaam did when he taught Balak how to ruin the people of Israel by involving them in sexual sin and encouraging them to go to idol feasts. ¹⁵Yes, you have

Family Devotions

☐ **DEVOTION 358**
CULTIVATING GODLY ATTITUDES

Read Revelation 2:19

Cultivating Godly Attitudes
Memory Verse

Whatever you do or say, let it be as a representative of the Lord Jesus, and come with him into the presence of God the Father to give him your thanks.
Colossians 3:17

Brenda was in a bad mood. "I don't see why I have to go to that special service at the nursing home Friday night," she grumbled.

"But you told your youth leader you'd be there," said Mom. "When you joined the choir, you knew it would cost you some of your free time."

"What free time?" grumbled Brenda. "Seems like lately I'm always at the church doing something!" Brenda turned to her little sister Tammy, who had come into the room holding a small box. "Is that your present for Grandma's birthday?"

"Yes—want to see it?" Tammy smiled and lifted the lid off the box. "I hope Grandma likes it."

"Oh, a scarf! That's pretty," Brenda said. "But take off the price tag before you wrap it."

Tammy shook her head. "I'm going to leave it on so Grandma will know it cost a lot!"

"Don't do that, silly," Brenda scolded. "It will seem like you're bragging about how much it cost."

Mom nodded. "I agree with Brenda," she said. "The important thing is not the price of your gift, but the fact that you love Grandma and want to please her."

As Tammy left the room, Brenda laughed. "If Tammy only knew how much Grandma has spent on gifts for her, she wouldn't think what she paid for that scarf was such a big deal." She glanced at Mom. "Why are you looking at me like that?"

"Tammy isn't the only one who leaves her price tag showing," replied Mom. "I just heard you talking about how much you're doing for God and how much it cost you."

Brenda turned red. "You're right," she admitted. "He's done a lot more for me than I could ever do for him. . . . I guess going to sing at the nursing home Friday night is no big deal."

How About You?

Do you think you've made a lot of sacrifices for God? Remember, everything you have was given to you by God. If you truly love him, you'll serve him willingly and cheerfully. He notices all your good deeds—you don't need to brag about them or complain about how much you're giving up for God. Just be thankful for all he has done for you. *S. K.*

• For the next devotional, turn to page 1253.   • To start the next topic, turn to page 15.   • For notes on CULTIVATING GODLY ATTITUDES, see pages 337, 383, 472, 622, and 1216.

some of these very same followers of Balaam among you!

¹⁶"Change your mind and attitude, or else I will come to you suddenly and fight against them with the sword of my mouth.

¹⁷"Let everyone who can hear, listen to what the Spirit is saying to the churches: Everyone who is victorious shall eat of the hidden manna, the secret nourishment from heaven; and I will give to each a white stone, and on the stone will be engraved a new name that no one else knows except the one receiving it.

¹⁸"*Write this letter to the leader of the church in Thyatira:*

"This is a message from the Son of God, whose eyes penetrate like flames of fire, whose feet are like glowing brass.

¹⁹"I am aware of all your good deeds—your kindness to the poor, your gifts and service to them; also I know your love and faith and patience, and I can see your constant improvement in all these things.

²⁰"Yet I have this against you: You are permitting that woman Jezebel, who calls herself a prophetess, to teach my servants that sex sin is not a serious matter; she urges them to practice immorality and to eat meat that has been sacrificed to idols. ²¹I gave her time to change her mind and attitude, but she refused. ²²Pay attention now to what I am saying: I will lay her upon a sickbed of intense affliction, along with all her immoral followers, unless they turn again to me, repenting of their sin with her; ²³and I will strike her children dead. And all the churches shall know that I am he who searches deep within men's hearts, and minds; I will give to each of you whatever you deserve.

²⁴,²⁵"As for the rest of you in Thyatira who have not followed this false teaching ('deeper truths,' as they call them—depths of Satan, really), I will ask nothing further of you; only hold tightly to what you have until I come.

²⁶"To everyone who overcomes—who to the very end keeps on doing things that please me—I will give power over the nations. ²⁷You will rule them with a rod of iron just as my Father gave me the authority to rule them; they will be shattered like a pot of clay that is broken into tiny pieces. ²⁸And I will give you the Morning Star!

²⁹"Let all who can hear listen to what the Spirit says to the churches.

3 *"To the leader of the church in Sardis write this letter:*

"This message is sent to you by the one who has the seven-fold Spirit of God and the seven stars.

"I know your reputation as a live and active church, but you are dead. ²Now wake up! Strengthen what little remains—for even what is left is at the point of death. Your deeds are far from right in the sight of God. ³Go back to what you heard and believed at first; hold to it firmly and turn to me again. Unless you do, I will come suddenly upon you, unexpected as a thief, and punish you.

⁴"Yet even there in Sardis some haven't soiled their garments with the world's filth; they shall walk with me in white, for they are worthy. ⁵Everyone who conquers will be clothed in white, and I will not erase his name from the Book of Life, but I will announce before my Father and his angels that he is mine.

⁶"Let all who can hear listen to what the Spirit is saying to the churches.

⁷"*Write this letter to the leader of the church in Philadelphia.*

"This message is sent to you by the one who is holy and true and has the key of David to open what no one can shut and to shut what no one can open.

⁸"I know you well; you aren't strong, but you have tried to obey and have not denied my Name. Therefore I have opened a door to you that no one can shut.

⁹"Note this: I will force those supporting the causes of Satan while claiming to be mine (but they aren't—they are lying) to fall at your feet and acknowledge that you are the ones I love.

¹⁰"Because you have patiently obeyed me despite the persecution, therefore I will protect you from the time of Great Tribulation and temptation, which will come upon the world to test everyone alive. ¹¹Look, I am coming soon! Hold tightly to the little strength you have—so that no one will take away your crown.

¹²"As for the one who conquers, I will make him a pillar in the temple of my God; he will be secure and will go out no more; and I will write my God's Name on him, and he will be a citizen in the city of my God—the New Jerusalem, coming down from heaven from my God; and he will have my new Name inscribed upon him.

¹³"Let all who can hear listen to what the Spirit is saying to the churches.

¹⁴"*Write this letter to the leader of the church in Laodicea:*

"This message is from the one who stands firm, the faithful and true Witness [of all that is or was or evermore shall be], the primeval source of God's creation:

¹⁵"I know you well—you are neither hot nor cold; I wish you were one or the other! ¹⁶But since you are merely lukewarm, I will spit you out of my mouth!

FAMILY DEVOTIONS

☐ **DEVOTION 359**
OBEDIENCE

Read Revelation 3:7-13

Obedience Memory Verse

Oh, that they would always have such a heart for me, wanting to obey my commandments. Then all would go well with them in the future, and with their children throughout all generations!
Deuteronomy 5:29

"Grandma, it's not fair! Mrs. Moore is just picking on me!" whined Alyssa. She showed her teacher's note to her grandmother. "Mom is gonna be so mad when she gets home and sees this."

"So you don't agree with what your teacher wrote?" asked Grandma, reading the letter. "It says here that your attitude needs work."

"Mrs. Moore just wants to complain about something," said Alyssa. "I do everything I'm supposed to do when I'm supposed to do it."

Grandma was silent for a moment. "Alyssa, I'm wondering how you *act* when you obey your teacher."

Alyssa felt uncomfortable and looked at her feet.

"When Mrs. Moore asks you to do something, do you roll your eyes as you do it?" Grandma asked gently. "Or when you're giving the correct answer to a question—because you did your homework well—do you say it with a sneer because you know you're right? Or you may do what you're told, but do you complain about having to do it?"

"What's the difference, as long as I obey?" asked Alyssa.

"Did you know I used to be known as a grumbler?" asked Grandma.

"*You*, Grandma?" said Alyssa in amazement.

"Yes, and I never did anything wrong either. But everything that I did right I complained about. One day I was reading the Bible and learned that God wants us to love to obey him. I learned that my attitude is as important as my actions."

"So you mean if I want to obey God, I have to do it with my heart, too, and not just with my body," said Alyssa thoughtfully.

Grandma nodded.

"I'm going to make sure Mrs. Moore doesn't have to send any more notes home about me," said Alyssa, smiling.

How About You?
How's your attitude when you do what you're told? It can be hard to get out of a habit of complaining, but Jesus can help you. Today as you obey, look for ways you can do it with your heart and not just your actions. *J. A. G.*

¹⁷"You say, 'I am rich, with everything I want; I don't need a thing!' And you don't realize that spiritually you are wretched and miserable and poor and blind and naked.

¹⁸"My advice to you is to buy pure gold from me, gold purified by fire—only then will you truly be rich. And to purchase from me white garments, clean and pure, so you won't be naked and ashamed; and to get medicine from me to heal your eyes and give you back your sight. ¹⁹I continually discipline and punish everyone I love; so I must punish you unless you turn from your indifference and become enthusiastic about the things of God.

²⁰"Look! I have been standing at the door, and I am constantly knocking. If anyone hears me calling him and opens the door, I will come in and fellowship with him and he with me. ²¹I will let everyone who conquers sit beside me on my throne, just as I took my place with my Father on his throne when I had conquered. ²²Let those who can hear listen to what the Spirit is saying to the churches."

4 The Glorious Throne

Then as I looked, I saw a door standing open in heaven, and the same voice I had heard before, which sounded like a mighty trumpet blast, spoke to me and said, "Come up here and I will show you what must happen in the future!"

²And instantly I was in spirit there in heaven and saw—oh, the glory of it!—a throne and someone sitting on it! ³Great bursts of light flashed forth from him as from a glittering diamond or from a shining ruby, and a rainbow glowing like an emerald encircled his throne. ⁴Twenty-four smaller thrones surrounded his, with twenty-four Elders sitting on them; all were clothed in white, with golden crowns upon their heads. ⁵Lightning and thunder issued from the throne, and there were voices in the thunder. Directly in front of his throne were seven lighted lamps representing the seven-fold Spirit of God. ⁶Spread out before it was a shiny crystal sea. Four Living Beings, dotted front and back with eyes, stood at the throne's four sides. ⁷The first of these Living Beings was in the form of a lion; the second looked like an ox; the third had the face of a man; and the fourth, the form of an eagle, with wings spread out as though in flight. ⁸Each of these Living Beings had six wings, and the central sections of their wings were covered with eyes. Day after day and night after night they kept on saying, "Holy, holy, holy, Lord God Almighty—the one who was, and is, and is to come."

⁹And when the Living Beings gave glory and honor and thanks to the one sitting on the throne, who lives forever and ever, ¹⁰the twenty-four Elders fell down before him and worshiped him, the Eternal Living One, and cast their crowns before the throne, singing, ¹¹"O Lord, you are worthy to receive the glory and the honor and the power, for you have created all things. They were created and called into being by your act of will."

5 The Sealed Scroll and the Lamb

And I saw a scroll in the right hand of the one who was sitting on the throne, a scroll with writing on the inside and on the back, and sealed with seven seals. ²A mighty angel with a loud voice was shouting out this question: "Who is worthy to break the seals on this scroll and to unroll it?" ³But no one in all heaven or earth or from among the dead was permitted to open and read it.

⁴Then I wept with disappointment because no one anywhere was worthy; no one could tell us what it said.

⁵But one of the twenty-four Elders said to me, "Stop crying, for look! The Lion of the tribe of Judah, the Root of David, has conquered, and proved himself worthy to open the scroll and to break its seven seals."

⁶I looked and saw a Lamb standing there before the twenty-four Elders, in front of the throne and the Living Beings, and on the Lamb were wounds that once had caused his death. He had seven horns and seven eyes, which represent the seven-fold Spirit of God, sent out into every part of the world. ⁷He stepped forward and took the scroll from the right hand of the one sitting upon the throne. ⁸And as he took the scroll, the twenty-four Elders fell down before the Lamb, each with a harp and golden vials filled with incense—the prayers of God's people!

⁹They were singing him a new song with these words: "You are worthy to take the scroll and break its seals and open it; for you were slain, and your blood has bought people from every nation as gifts for God. ¹⁰And you have gathered them into a kingdom and made them priests of our God; they shall reign upon the earth."

¹¹Then in my vision I heard the singing of millions of angels surrounding the throne and the Living Beings and the Elders:

ACCEPTING OTHERS 5:9-10 People from every nation are praising God before his throne. The gospel is not limited to a specific culture, race, or country. Anyone who comes in repentance and faith is accepted by God and will be part of his Kingdom. Don't allow prejudice or bias to stop you from sharing Christ with others. Christ welcomes all people into his Kingdom. **To begin the series of devotionals on ACCEPTING OTHERS, turn to page 207.**

Family Devotions

☐ DEVOTION 360
RECEIVING CHRIST AS SAVIOR

Read Revelation 3:20-22

In Sunday school class, Mrs. Tomkins spoke about Paul's experiences with Felix and King Agrippa. "Both men heard the gospel," she said, "but neither made up his mind to accept Christ. I hope none of you put off making such an important decision." Anita thought about talking to Mrs. Tomkins after class and asking her about being saved. But when class was dismissed, she spotted Becky at the door. She hurried over and began to talk about school.

On the way home from church, Anita hummed along as the voices of a choir came over the car radio. "I have decided to follow Jesus. . . ." She considered the words. *I guess I don't really follow Jesus,* she thought. *Mrs. Tomkins made it sound like I needed to make a decision.*

Her thoughts were interrupted by her sister, Joni. "Look at the big sale sign in the store window!" All Anita could think about then was the clothes she wanted to buy.

After dinner that day, Anita put the few leftovers in her dog's dish. She opened the back door and called, "Come, Spunky. I've got something good for you." Spunky looked up. He romped toward the door. Then he hesitated as a bird caught his attention. "Forget the bird. Come on," Anita yelled. Spunky came closer. He put his paw on the threshold. Another dog barked. Spunky was off running around the yard. Anita was frustrated. "Spunky, come on! Aren't you hungry? What are you waiting for?" Spunky sniffed the grass. "Make up your mind," Anita shouted. "Either come in or stay out!"

Suddenly it dawned on Anita that she had been acting just like Spunky. She allowed all sorts of things to take her attention away from the most important decision she had to make. Spunky could take his time, and it really wouldn't matter. But she couldn't linger any longer. It was time for her to trust Christ and to commit herself to him.

Receiving Christ as Savior
Memory Verse

For God loved the world so much that he gave his only Son so that anyone who believes in him shall not perish but have eternal life.
John 3:16

How About You?

Have you made up your mind to accept Jesus as your Savior? If not, don't delay. You might not have another opportunity. Confess your sin and ask Jesus to come into your life today! *J. H.*

• For the next devotional, turn to page 1257.   • For the next devotional on RECEIVING CHRIST AS SAVIOR, turn to page 1257.   • For notes on RECEIVING CHRIST AS SAVIOR, see pages 839, 842, 1146, 1234, and 1240.

¹²"The Lamb is worthy" (loudly they sang it!) "—the Lamb who was slain. He is worthy to receive the power, and the riches, and the wisdom, and the strength, and the honor, and the glory, and the blessing."

¹³And then I heard everyone in heaven and earth, and from the dead beneath the earth and in the sea, exclaiming, "The blessing and the honor and the glory and the power belong to the one sitting on the throne, and to the Lamb forever and ever." ¹⁴And the four Living Beings kept saying, "Amen!" And the twenty-four Elders fell down and worshiped him.

6 Breaking the Seals One by One

As I watched, the Lamb broke the first seal and began to unroll the scroll. Then one of the four Living Beings, with a voice that sounded like thunder, said, "Come!"

²I looked, and there in front of me was a white horse. Its rider carried a bow, and a crown was placed upon his head; he rode out to conquer in many battles and win the war.

³Then he unrolled the scroll to the second seal and broke it open, too. And I heard the second Living Being say, "Come!"

⁴This time a red horse rode out. Its rider was given a long sword and the authority to banish peace and bring anarchy to the earth; war and killing broke out everywhere.

⁵When he had broken the third seal, I heard the third Living Being say, "Come!" And I saw a black horse, with its rider holding a pair of balances in his hand. ⁶And a voice from among the four Living Beings said, "A loaf of bread for $20, or three pounds of barley flour, but there is no olive oil or wine."

⁷And when the fourth seal was broken, I heard the fourth Living Being say, "Come!" ⁸And now I saw a pale horse, and its rider's name was Death. And there followed after him another horse whose rider's name was Hell. They were given control of one-fourth of the earth, to kill with war and famine and disease and wild animals.

⁹And when he broke open the fifth seal, I saw an altar, and underneath it all the souls of those who had been martyred for preaching the Word of God and for being faithful in their witnessing. ¹⁰They called loudly to the Lord and said, "O Sovereign Lord, holy and true, how long will it be before you judge the people of the earth for what they've done to us? When will you avenge our blood against those living on the earth?" ¹¹White robes were given to each of them, and they were told to rest a little longer until their other brothers, fellow servants of Jesus, had been martyred on the earth and joined them.

¹²I watched as he broke the sixth seal, and there was a vast earthquake; and the sun became dark like black cloth, and the moon was blood-red. ¹³Then the stars of heaven appeared to be falling to earth—like green fruit from fig trees buffeted by mighty winds. ¹⁴And the starry heavens disappeared as though rolled up like a scroll and taken away; and every mountain and island shook and shifted. ¹⁵The kings of the earth, and world leaders, and rich men, and high-ranking military officers, and all men great and small, slave and free, hid themselves in the caves and rocks of the mountains, ¹⁶and cried to the mountains to crush them. "Fall on us," they pleaded, "and hide us from the face of the one sitting on the throne, and from the anger of the Lamb, ¹⁷because the great day of their anger has come, and who can survive it?"

7 The 144,000 Chosen by God

Then I saw four angels standing at the four corners of the earth, holding back the four winds from blowing so that not a leaf rustled in the trees, and the ocean became as smooth as glass. ²And I saw another angel coming from the east, carrying the Great Seal of the Living God. And he shouted out to those four angels who had been given power to injure earth and sea, ³"Wait! Don't do anything yet—hurt neither earth nor sea nor trees—until we have placed the Seal of God upon the foreheads of his servants."

⁴⁻⁸How many were given this mark? I heard the number—it was 144,000; out of all twelve tribes of Israel, as listed here:

Judah	12,000	Naphtali	12,000	Issachar	12,000
Reuben	12,000	Manasseh	12,000	Zebulun	12,000
Gad	12,000	Simeon	12,000	Joseph	12,000
Asher	12,000	Levi	12,000	Benjamin	12,000

⁹After this I saw a vast crowd, too great to count, from all nations and provinces and languages, standing in front of the throne and before the Lamb, clothed in white, with palm branches in their hands. ¹⁰And they were shouting with a mighty shout, "Salvation comes from our God upon the throne, and from the Lamb."

¹¹And now all the angels were crowding around the throne and around the Elders and the four Living Beings, and falling face down before the throne and worshiping God. ¹²"Amen!" they said. "Blessing, and glory, and wisdom, and thanksgiving, and honor, and power, and might, be to our God forever and forever. Amen!"

¹³Then one of the twenty-four Elders asked me, "Do you know who these are, who are clothed in white, and where they come from?"

¹⁴"No, sir," I replied. "Please tell me."

Family Devotions

☐ DEVOTION 361
RECEIVING CHRIST AS SAVIOR

Read Revelation 5 : 9-10

Receiving Christ as Savior
Memory Verse

If you tell others with your own mouth that Jesus Christ is your Lord and believe in your own heart that God has raised him from the dead, you will be saved.
Romans 10:9

"I wish I had enough money to buy that new computer game I've been wanting," said Tony to his friend Jacob. "If only there were some way I could make extra cash." Tony thought a minute. "I know! You wanted to buy the tires from my old bike, and Dad said it would be OK. So I'll sell them to you."

"My dad OK'd it, too, so it's a deal," Jacob agreed.

Tony took part of the money he received and bought the game. It was lots of fun, and the boys enjoyed it nearly every day.

When the weather turned sunnier, Tony and Jacob began taking long bike rides—until one day when Tony ran over a broken bottle and slashed his front tire. "Now I wish I had kept those old bike tires I sold to you," he groaned.

"Well, I only used one, so I'll sell the other back to you," offered Jacob.

"It's a deal," agreed Tony. The boys got the tire and went to Tony's house to fix his bike.

"I thought you sold those tires to Jacob," said Tony's dad when he saw the boys at work.

"I bought this one back," Tony explained.

Dad smiled. "You redeemed it."

"*Redeemed* it?" asked Tony. "Isn't that a Bible word?"

Dad nodded. "Yes, it's used many times in the Bible. What you did with the bike tire is a good example of the meaning of the word. *Redeemed* simply means 'bought back.' God wanted to buy us back from the slavery of sin. He knew we were sinful people and that the only way we could be redeemed was for his Son to die. We weren't bought by money, but rather by the blood of the Lord Jesus Christ."

"Wow," said Tony. "Now when I hear that word I'll know what it means."

How About You?
Have you been redeemed? If you are not a Christian, you are a slave to sin. This sin separates you from God. He had to pay the price to buy you out of sin and back to himself. No amount of money can do that. It's only through the precious blood of the Lord Jesus Christ that you can be bought back from sin. Accept what Jesus has done for you. L. M. W.

• For the next devotional, turn to page 1261. • For the next devotional on RECEIVING CHRIST AS SAVIOR, turn to page 1265. • For notes on RECEIVING CHRIST AS SAVIOR, see pages 839, 842, 1146, 1234, and 1240.

"These are the ones coming out of the Great Tribulation," he said; "they washed their robes and whitened them by the blood of the Lamb. ¹⁵That is why they are here before the throne of God, serving him day and night in his temple. The one sitting on the throne will shelter them; ¹⁶they will never be hungry again, nor thirsty, and they will be fully protected from the scorching noontime heat. ¹⁷For the Lamb standing in front of the throne will feed them and be their Shepherd and lead them to the springs of the Water of Life. And God will wipe their tears away."

8 The Seventh Seal Is Broken

When the Lamb had broken the seventh seal, there was silence throughout all heaven for what seemed like half an hour. ²And I saw the seven angels that stand before God, and they were given seven trumpets.

³Then another angel with a golden censer came and stood at the altar; and a great quantity of incense was given to him to mix with the prayers of God's people, to offer upon the golden altar before the throne. ⁴And the perfume of the incense mixed with prayers ascended up to God from the altar where the angel had poured them out.

⁵Then the angel filled the censer with fire from the altar and threw it down upon the earth; and thunder crashed and rumbled, lightning flashed, and there was a terrible earthquake.

⁶Then the seven angels with the seven trumpets prepared to blow their mighty blasts.

⁷The first angel blew his trumpet, and hail and fire mixed with blood were thrown down upon the earth. One-third of the earth was set on fire so that one-third of the trees were burned, and all the green grass.

⁸,⁹Then the second angel blew his trumpet, and what appeared to be a huge burning mountain was thrown into the sea, destroying a third of all the ships; and a third of the sea turned red as blood; and a third of the fish were killed.

¹⁰The third angel blew, and a great flaming star fell from heaven upon a third of the rivers and springs. ¹¹The star was called "Bitterness" because it poisoned a third of all the water on the earth and many people died.

¹²The fourth angel blew his trumpet, and immediately a third of the sun was blighted and darkened, and a third of the moon and the stars so that the daylight was dimmed by a third, and the nighttime darkness deepened. ¹³As I watched, I saw a solitary eagle flying through the heavens crying loudly, "Woe, woe, woe to the people of the earth because of the terrible things that will soon happen when the three remaining angels blow their trumpets."

9

Then the fifth angel blew his trumpet, and I saw one who was fallen to earth from heaven, and to him was given the key to the bottomless pit. ²When he opened it, smoke poured out as though from some huge furnace, and the sun and air were darkened by the smoke.

³Then locusts came from the smoke and descended onto the earth and were given power to sting like scorpions. ⁴They were told not to hurt the grass or plants or trees, but to attack those people who did not have the mark of God on their foreheads. ⁵They were not to kill them, but to torture them for five months with agony like the pain of scorpion stings. ⁶In those days men will try to kill themselves but won't be able to—death will not come. They will long to die—but death will flee away!

⁷The locusts looked like horses armored for battle. They had what looked like golden crowns on their heads, and their faces looked like men's. ⁸Their hair was long like women's, and their teeth were those of lions. ⁹They wore breastplates that seemed to be of iron, and their wings roared like an army of chariots rushing into battle. ¹⁰They had stinging tails like scorpions, and their power to hurt, given to them for five months, was in their tails. ¹¹Their king is the Prince of the bottomless pit whose name in Hebrew is Abaddon, and in Greek, Apollyon [and in English, the Destroyer].

¹²One terror now ends, but there are two more coming!

¹³The sixth angel blew his trumpet, and I heard a voice speaking from the four horns of the golden altar that stands before the throne of God, ¹⁴saying to the sixth angel, "Release the four mighty demons held bound at the great River Euphrates."

¹⁵They had been kept in readiness for that year and month and day and hour, and now they were turned loose to kill a third of all mankind. ¹⁶They led an army of 200,000,000 warriors—I heard an announcement of how many there were.

¹⁷,¹⁸I saw their horses spread out before me in my vision; their riders

---

RESISTING TEMPTATION 9:20-21 These men were so hard-hearted that even plagues did not drive them to God. People don't usually fall into immorality and evil suddenly; they slip into it a little at a time until, hardly realizing what has happened, they are irrevocably mired in their wicked ways. Any person who allows sin to take root in his life can find himself in this predicament. Temptation entertained today becomes sin tomorrow, then a habit the next day, then death and separation from God forever (see James 1:15). To think you could never become this evil is the first step toward a hard heart. **To begin the series of devotionals on *RESISTING TEMPTATION,* turn to page 7.**

wore fiery-red breastplates, though some were sky-blue and others yellow. The horses' heads looked much like lions', and smoke and fire and flaming sulphur billowed from their mouths, killing one-third of all mankind. [19]Their power of death was not only in their mouths, but in their tails as well, for their tails were similar to serpents' heads that struck and bit with fatal wounds.

[20]But the men left alive after these plagues *still refused to worship God!* They would not renounce their demon-worship, nor their idols made of gold and silver, brass, stone, and wood—which neither see nor hear nor walk! [21]Neither did they change their mind and attitude about all their murders and witchcraft, their immorality and theft.

10 An Angel with a Scroll to Eat

Then I saw another mighty angel coming down from heaven, surrounded by a cloud, with a rainbow over his head; his face shone like the sun and his feet flashed with fire. [2]And he held open in his hand a small scroll. He set his right foot on the sea and his left foot on the earth [3]and gave a great shout—it was like the roar of a lion—and the seven thunders crashed their reply.

[4]I was about to write what the thunders said when a voice from heaven called to me, "Don't do it. Their words are not to be revealed."

[5]Then the mighty angel standing on the sea and land lifted his right hand to heaven [6]and swore by him who lives forever and ever, who created heaven and everything in it and the earth and all that it contains and the sea and its inhabitants, that there should be no more delay, [7]but that when the seventh angel blew his trumpet, then God's veiled plan—mysterious through the ages ever since it was announced by his servants the prophets—would be fulfilled.

[8]Then the voice from heaven spoke to me again, "Go and get the unrolled scroll from the mighty angel standing there upon the sea and land."

[9]So I approached him and asked him to give me the scroll. "Yes, take it and eat it," he said. "At first it will taste like honey, but when you swallow it, it will make your stomach sour!" [10]So I took it from his hand, and ate it! And just as he had said, it was sweet in my mouth, but it gave me a stomachache when I swallowed it.

[11]Then he told me, "You must prophesy further about many peoples, nations, tribes, and kings."

11 Two Prophets

Now I was given a measuring stick and told to go and measure the temple of God, including the inner court where the altar stands, and to count the number of worshipers. [2]"But do not measure the outer court," I was told, "for it has been turned over to the nations. They will trample the Holy City for forty-two months. [3]And I will give power to my two witnesses to prophesy 1,260 days clothed in sackcloth."

[4]These two prophets are the two olive trees, and two candlesticks standing before the God of all the earth. [5]Anyone trying to harm them will be killed by bursts of fire shooting from their mouths. [6]They have power to shut the skies so that no rain will fall during the three and a half years they prophesy, and to turn rivers and oceans to blood, and to send every kind of plague upon the earth as often as they wish.

[7]When they complete the three and a half years of their solemn testimony, the tyrant who comes out of the bottomless pit will declare war against them and conquer and kill them; [8,9]and for three and a half days their bodies will be exposed in the streets of Jerusalem (the city fittingly described as "Sodom" or "Egypt")—the very place where their Lord was crucified. No one will be allowed to bury them, and people from many nations will crowd around to gaze at them. [10]And there will be a worldwide holiday—people everywhere will rejoice and give presents to each other and throw parties to celebrate the death of the two prophets who had tormented them so much!

[11]But after three and a half days, the spirit of life from God will enter them, and they will stand up! And great fear will fall on everyone. [12]Then a loud voice will shout from heaven, "Come up!" And they will rise to heaven in a cloud as their enemies watch.

[13]The same hour there will be a terrible earthquake that levels a tenth of the city, leaving 7,000 dead. Then everyone left will, in their terror, give glory to the God of heaven.

[14]The second woe is past, but the third quickly follows:

[15]For just then the seventh angel blew his trumpet, and there were loud voices shouting down from heaven, "The Kingdom of this world now belongs to our Lord, and to his Christ; and he shall reign forever and ever."

[16]And the twenty-four Elders sitting on their thrones before God threw themselves down in worship, saying, [17]"We give thanks, Lord God Almighty, who is and was, for now you have assumed your great power and have begun to reign. [18]The nations were angry with you, but now it is your turn to be angry with them. It is time to judge the dead and reward your servants—prophets and people alike, all who fear your Name, both

great and small—and to destroy those who have caused destruction upon the earth."

¹⁹Then, in heaven, the temple of God was opened and the ark of his covenant could be seen inside. Lightning flashed and thunder crashed and roared, and there was a great hailstorm, and the world was shaken by a mighty earthquake.

12 The Woman and the Dragon

Then a great pageant appeared in heaven, portraying things to come. I saw a woman clothed with the sun, with the moon beneath her feet, and a crown of twelve stars on her head. ²She was pregnant and screamed in the pain of her labor, awaiting her delivery.

³Suddenly a red Dragon appeared, with seven heads and ten horns, and seven crowns on his heads. ⁴His tail drew along behind him a third of the stars, which he plunged to the earth. He stood before the woman as she was about to give birth to her child, ready to eat the baby as soon as it was born.

⁵She gave birth to a boy who was to rule all nations with a heavy hand, and he was caught up to God and to his throne. ⁶The woman fled into the wilderness, where God had prepared a place for her, to take care of her for 1,260 days.

⁷Then there was war in heaven; Michael and the angels under his command fought the Dragon and his hosts of fallen angels. ⁸And the Dragon lost the battle and was forced from heaven. ⁹This great Dragon—the ancient serpent called the devil, or Satan, the one deceiving the whole world—was thrown down onto the earth with all his army.

¹⁰Then I heard a loud voice shouting across the heavens, "It has happened at last! God's salvation and the power and the rule, and the authority of his Christ are finally here; for the Accuser of our brothers has been thrown down from heaven onto earth—he accused them day and night before our God. ¹¹They defeated him by the blood of the Lamb and by their testimony; for they did not love their lives but laid them down for him. ¹²Rejoice, O heavens! You citizens of heaven, rejoice! Be glad! But woe to you people of the world, for the devil has come down to you in great anger, knowing that he has little time."

¹³And when the Dragon found himself cast down to earth, he persecuted the woman who had given birth to the child. ¹⁴But she was given two wings like those of a great eagle, to fly into the wilderness to the place prepared for her, where she was cared for and protected from the Serpent, the Dragon, for three and a half years.

¹⁵And from the Serpent's mouth a vast flood of water gushed out and swept toward the woman in an effort to get rid of her; ¹⁶but the earth helped her by opening its mouth and swallowing the flood! ¹⁷Then the furious Dragon set out to attack the rest of her children—all who were keeping God's commandments and confessing that they belong to Jesus. He stood waiting on an ocean beach.

13 The Two Strange Creatures

And now, in my vision, I saw a strange Creature rising up out of the sea. It had seven heads and ten horns, and ten crowns upon its horns. And written on each head were blasphemous names, each one defying and insulting God. ²This Creature looked like a leopard but had bear's feet and a lion's mouth! And the Dragon gave him his own power and throne and great authority.

³I saw that one of his heads seemed wounded beyond recovery—but the fatal wound was healed! All the world marveled at this miracle and followed the Creature in awe. ⁴They worshiped the Dragon for giving him such power, and they worshiped the strange Creature. "Where is there anyone as great as he?" they exclaimed. "Who is able to fight against him?"

⁵Then the Dragon encouraged the Creature to speak great blasphemies against the Lord; and gave him authority to control the earth for forty-two months. ⁶All that time he blasphemed God's Name and his temple and all those living in heaven. ⁷The Dragon gave him power to fight against God's people and to overcome them, and to rule over all nations and language groups throughout the world. ⁸And all mankind—whose names were not written down before the founding of the world in the slain Lamb's Book of Life—worshiped the evil Creature.

⁹Anyone who can hear, listen carefully: ¹⁰The people of God who are destined for prison will be arrested and taken away; those destined for death will be killed. But do not be dismayed, for here is your opportunity for endurance and confidence.

¹¹Then I saw another strange animal, this one coming up out of the earth, with two little horns like those of a lamb but a fearsome voice like the Dragon's. ¹²He exercised all the authority of the Creature whose death-wound had been healed, whom he required all the world to worship. ¹³He did unbelievable miracles such as making fire flame down to earth from the skies while everyone was watching. ¹⁴By doing these miracles, he was deceiving people everywhere. He could do these marvelous things whenever the first Creature was there to watch him. And he ordered the people of the world to make a great statue of the first Creature, who was fatally wounded and then

Family Devotions

☐ DEVOTION 362
CONTENTMENT

Read Revelation 14:12

Contentment Memory Verse

I know how to live on almost nothing or with everything. I have learned the secret of contentment in every situation, whether it be a full stomach or hunger, plenty or want.
Philippians 4:12

"Nothing's going my way," Tim told his friend Brett, as he kicked a stone on the pavement. "I want to live with my dad, but it's been decided that we kids have to stay with Mom."

"That's too bad," said Brett.

"Dad always took time to do stuff with me," Tim continued. "Y'know—guy stuff. Now I'll only get to be with him every other weekend."

"Well, you can talk to him on the phone, too, can't you?" asked Brett. "You still have a lot to be thankful for."

Tim remembered that ever since he met Brett at the beginning of the school year, he had never seen nor heard anything about Brett's father. "Does your dad live with you?" Tim asked.

Brett shook his head. "My dad died," he said softly.

"Oh," said Tim, not sure what else to say. "Sorry." Tim and Brett walked quietly. "How do you survive without ever seeing your dad?" Tim asked finally.

"It's not easy," Brett said, "but one day when I was trying to make a play guitar with rubber bands and a long box, Mom helped me understand how she deals with it." Brett paused, and Tim looked at him curiously. "Some rubber bands stretched and fit over my box easily, but others were tight and pulled out thin in order to get around the cardboard. A few even snapped," added Brett. He was silent, remembering.

"What does that have to do with making it without your dad?" Tim asked.

"The ones that fit supertight made the best music on my new guitar. And Mom said that as things happen in life, we're stretched, too—like those smaller rubber bands," explained Brett. "We may be uncomfortable, but we can choose to be content and make music, even during the hard times of our lives, or we can give up and snap and be useless. Mom and I decided to trust God to use this hard part of our lives for his good."

How About You?
Have things happened in your life that are hard to accept? God wants you to be content in every situation. With God's help, decide that you'll accept what he has allowed so that even your attitude may be a testimony for him. *N. E. K.*

• For the next devotional, turn to page 1263. • To start the next topic, turn to page 121. • For notes on CONTENTMENT, see pages 542, 547, 902, and 1063.

came back to life. ¹⁵He was permitted to give breath to this statue and even make it speak! Then the statue ordered that anyone refusing to worship it must die!

¹⁶He required everyone—great and small, rich and poor, slave and free—to be tattooed with a certain mark on the right hand or on the forehead. ¹⁷And no one could get a job or even buy in any store without the permit of that mark, which was either the name of the Creature or the code number of his name. ¹⁸Here is a puzzle that calls for careful thought to solve it. Let those who are able, interpret this code: the numerical values of the letters in his name add to 666!

14 The Lamb and a Great Choir

Then I saw a Lamb standing on Mount Zion in Jerusalem, and with him were 144,000 who had his Name and his Father's Name written on their foreheads. ²And I heard a sound from heaven like the roaring of a great waterfall or the rolling of mighty thunder. It was the singing of a choir accompanied by harps.

³This tremendous choir—144,000 strong—sang a wonderful new song in front of the throne of God and before the four Living Beings and the twenty-four Elders; and no one could sing this song except those 144,000 who had been redeemed from the earth. ⁴For they are spiritually undefiled, pure as virgins, following the Lamb wherever he goes. They have been purchased from among the men on the earth as a consecrated offering to God and the Lamb. ⁵No falsehood can be charged against them; they are blameless.

⁶And I saw another angel flying through the heavens, carrying the everlasting Good News to preach to those on earth—to every nation, tribe, language, and people.

⁷"Fear God," he shouted, "and extol his greatness. For the time has come when he will sit as Judge. Worship him who made the heaven and the earth, the sea and all its sources."

⁸Then another angel followed him through the skies, saying, "Babylon is fallen, is fallen—that great city—because she seduced the nations of the world and made them share the wine of her intense impurity and sin."

⁹Then a third angel followed them shouting, "Anyone worshiping the Creature from the sea and his statue, and accepting his mark on the forehead or the hand ¹⁰must drink the wine of the anger of God; it is poured out undiluted into God's cup of wrath. And they will be tormented with fire and burning sulphur in the presence of the holy angels and the Lamb. ¹¹The smoke of their torture rises forever and ever, and they will have no relief day or night, for they have worshiped the Creature and his statue, and have been tattooed with the code of his name. ¹²Let this encourage God's people to endure patiently every trial and persecution, for they are his saints who remain firm to the end in obedience to his commands and trust in Jesus."

¹³And I heard a voice in the heavens above me saying, "Write this down: At last the time has come for his martyrs to enter into their full reward. Yes, says the Spirit, they are blessed indeed, for now they shall rest from all their toils and trials; for their good deeds follow them to heaven!" ¹⁴Then the scene changed, and I saw a white cloud and someone sitting on it who looked like Jesus, who was called "The Son of Man," with a crown of solid gold upon his head and a sharp sickle in his hand.

¹⁵Then an angel came from the temple and called out to him, "Begin to use the sickle, for the time has come for you to reap; the harvest is ripe on the earth." ¹⁶So the one sitting on the cloud swung his sickle over the earth, and the harvest was gathered in. ¹⁷After that another angel came from the temple in heaven, and he also had a sharp sickle.

¹⁸Just then the angel who has power to destroy the world with fire, shouted to the angel with the sickle, "Use your sickle now to cut off the clusters of grapes from the vines of the earth, for they are fully ripe for judgment." ¹⁹So the angel swung his sickle on the earth and loaded the grapes into the great winepress of God's wrath. ²⁰And the grapes were trodden in the winepress outside the city, and blood flowed out in a stream 200 miles long and as high as a horse's bridle.

15

And I saw in heaven another mighty pageant showing things to come: Seven angels were assigned to carry down to earth the seven last plagues—and then at last God's anger will be finished.

²Spread out before me was what seemed to be an ocean of fire and glass, and on it stood all those who had been victorious over the Evil Creature and his statue and his mark and number. All were holding harps of God, ³,⁴and they were singing the song of Moses, the servant of God, and the song of the Lamb:

"Great and marvelous
Are your doings,
Lord God Almighty.
Just and true
Are your ways,
O King of Ages.
Who shall not fear,

FAMILY DEVOTIONS

☐ DEVOTION 363
RESPECTING GOD'S WARNINGS

Read Revelation 20 : 11-15

"If God is so loving, I don't think he would send anybody to hell," said Jerry firmly.

"Well," his friend Don began, praying for the right words to say, "The Bible—" A loud outburst of yelps from his dog interrupted the discussion. The boys rushed to the door just in time to see a boy ride off on Jerry's new bike. They ran after him, but soon realized it would do no good.

Jerry moaned, "Call your dad." Don's father was a police officer.

Don ran to the phone, and soon a squad car pulled up to the curb. Don's father emerged and led a young boy up to the house. Another officer lifted a mangled bike from the trunk. Jerry's jaw sagged as he recognized the bent frame, and he started shouting at the boy. Don's father held up his hand. "Calm down, Jerry," he said. "If that's your bike, this boy will have to pay for the damage."

Later that day, the boys resumed their discussion about whether God would send anyone to hell. When Jerry continued to insist that a loving God wouldn't do that, Don had an idea. "Hey, Jerry," he said, "why should the kid who took your bike today have to be punished for it?"

Jerry stared at him. "Because he stole it and ruined it!"

"But aren't you a loving person?" Don asked.

"Well, sure, but what he did was wrong!" Jerry stopped. He saw where this conversation was going.

Don nodded. "It would be wrong for crime to go unpunished," he agreed. Then he made his point. "God is holy, and he can't ignore crime, either—the crime of sin. If he did, it would be wrong."

"I guess you're right," Jerry said. He knew he'd better give this matter more thought.

Respecting God's Warnings
Memory Verse

If my people will humble themselves and pray, and search for me, and turn from their wicked ways, I will hear them from heaven and forgive their sins and heal their land.
2 Chronicles 7:14

How About You?
Do you find it hard to believe that a loving God could send someone to hell? Do you think that everyone will go to heaven, one way or another? Because God is loving, he provided a way to heaven through the blood of Jesus. Because God is holy, he will not ignore the sin of those who refuse his gift. That need not happen to you. Accept his gift today. *J. B.*

• For the next devotional, turn to page 1265. • To start the next topic, turn to page 11. • For notes on RESPECTING GOD'S WARNINGS, see pages 219, 874, and 1126.

O Lord,
And glorify your Name?
For you alone are holy.
All nations will come
And worship before you,
For your righteous deeds
Have been disclosed."

⁵Then I looked and saw that the Holy of Holies of the temple in heaven was thrown wide open! ⁶The seven angels who were assigned to pour out the seven plagues then came from the temple, clothed in spotlessly white linen, with golden belts across their chests. ⁷And one of the four Living Beings handed each of them a golden flask filled with the terrible wrath of the Living God who lives forever and forever. ⁸The temple was filled with smoke from his glory and power; and no one could enter until the seven angels had completed pouring out the seven plagues.

16 Seven Flasks of Wrath

And I heard a mighty voice shouting from the temple to the seven angels, "Now go your ways and empty out the seven flasks of the wrath of God upon the earth."

²So the first angel left the temple and poured out his flask over the earth, and horrible, malignant sores broke out on everyone who had the mark of the Creature and was worshiping his statue.

³The second angel poured out his flask upon the oceans, and they became like the watery blood of a dead man; and everything in all the oceans died.

⁴The third angel poured out his flask upon the rivers and springs and they became blood. ⁵And I heard this angel of the waters declaring, "You are just in sending this judgment, O Holy One, who is and was, ⁶for your saints and prophets have been martyred and their blood poured out upon the earth; and now, in turn, you have poured out the blood of those who murdered them; it is their just reward."

⁷And I heard the angel of the altar say, "Yes, Lord God Almighty, your punishments are just and true."

⁸Then the fourth angel poured out his flask upon the sun, causing it to scorch all men with its fire. ⁹Everyone was burned by this blast of heat, and they cursed the name of God who sent the plagues—they did not change their mind and attitude to give him glory.

¹⁰Then the fifth angel poured out his flask upon the throne of the Creature from the sea, and his kingdom was plunged into darkness. And his subjects gnawed their tongues in anguish, ¹¹and cursed the God of heaven for their pains and sores, but they refused to repent of all their evil deeds.

¹²The sixth angel poured out his flask upon the great River Euphrates and it dried up so that the kings from the east could march their armies westward without hindrance. ¹³And I saw three evil spirits disguised as frogs leap from the mouth of the Dragon, the Creature, and his False Prophet. ¹⁴These miracle-working demons conferred with all the rulers of the world to gather them for battle against the Lord on that great coming Judgment Day of God Almighty.

¹⁵"Take note: I will come as unexpectedly as a thief! Blessed are all who are awaiting me, who keep their robes in readiness and will not need to walk naked and ashamed."

¹⁶And they gathered all the armies of the world near a place called, in Hebrew, Armageddon—the Mountain of Megiddo.

¹⁷Then the seventh angel poured out his flask into the air; and a mighty shout came from the throne of the temple in heaven, saying, "It is finished!" ¹⁸Then the thunder crashed and rolled, and lightning flashed; and there was a great earthquake of a magnitude unprecedented in human history. ¹⁹The great city of "Babylon" split into three sections, and cities around the world fell in heaps of rubble; and so all of "Babylon's" sins were remembered in God's thoughts, and she was punished to the last drop of anger in the cup of the wine of the fierceness of his wrath. ²⁰And islands vanished, and mountains flattened out, ²¹and there was an incredible hailstorm from heaven; hailstones weighing a hundred pounds fell from the sky onto the people below, and they cursed God because of the terrible hail.

17 A Drunken Woman

One of the seven angels who had poured out the plagues came over and talked with me. "Come with me," he said, "and I will show you what is going to happen to the Notorious Prostitute, who sits upon the many waters of the world. ²The kings of the world have had immoral relations with her, and the people of the earth have been made drunk by the wine of her immorality."

³So the angel took me in spirit into the wilderness. There I saw a woman sitting on a scarlet animal that had seven heads and ten horns, written all over with blasphemies against God. ⁴The woman wore purple and scarlet clothing and beautiful jewelry made of gold and precious gems and pearls, and held in her hand a golden goblet full of obscenities:

⁵A mysterious caption was written on her forehead: "Babylon the Great, Mother of Prostitutes

FAMILY DEVOTIONS

☐ **DEVOTION 364**
RECEIVING CHRIST AS SAVIOR

Read Revelation 21 : 21-27

As Mike cleaned his bike, his father was listening to a preacher on the radio. Mike heard snatches of the message—something about a very important book God keeps, called the Book of Life. The preacher said that only people whose names were written in the book would be allowed into heaven. Mike wanted to be sure his name was there, so he decided he'd be very good.

Mike made a list of the good things he had done that week and showed it to his Sunday school teacher. "Do you think God will write my name in his book now?" he asked.

Miss Lewis put her arm around Mike. "Let me ask you something," she said. "Do you think I should write down your name as one of the winners in our Bible-reading rally because you have done all these good things?"

Mike looked puzzled as he shook his head. "No. I didn't read enough chapters yet," he said.

Miss Lewis nodded. "That's right," she agreed. "You have to meet the requirement to be a winner. The requirement is that you read the assigned chapters, not that you be good. In the same way, you must meet God's requirement to get your name in his book—and it's not by being good either."

"Really?" Mike's spirits fell.

"God's requirement is that you trust Jesus to be your Savior. God knew that no one could ever be good enough to go to heaven," explained Miss Lewis. "We're all sinners, and heaven is a perfect place."

As they talked about it, Mike realized for the first time that he really was not good and that he needed Jesus to take his sins away.

Mike bowed his head right there and told God how sorry he was that he had sinned, and he asked Jesus to come into his life. In his mind's eye, he could see Jesus writing in a big book in heaven: "Mike Roberts."

Receiving Christ as Savior
Memory Verse

For God loved the world so much that he gave his only Son so that anyone who believes in him shall not perish but have eternal life.
John 3:16

How About You?
Is your name written in the Book of Life? If not, receive Jesus as your Savior. Then thank him for writing your name in his book and preparing a place for you in heaven. *M. N.*

• For the next devotional, turn to page 1267. • For the next devotional on *RECEIVING CHRIST AS SAVIOR*, turn to page 1267. • For notes on *RECEIVING CHRIST AS SAVIOR*, see pages 839, 842, 1146, 1234, and 1240.

and of Idol Worship Everywhere around the World."

⁶I could see that she was drunk—drunk with the blood of the martyrs of Jesus she had killed. I stared at her in horror.

⁷"Why are you so surprised?" the angel asked. "I'll tell you who she is and what the animal she is riding represents. ⁸He was alive but isn't now. And yet, soon he will come up out of the bottomless pit and go to eternal destruction; and the people of earth, whose names have not been written in the Book of Life before the world began, will be dumbfounded at his reappearance after being dead.

⁹"And now think hard: his seven heads represent a certain city built on seven hills where this woman has her residence. ¹⁰They also represent seven kings. Five have already fallen, the sixth now reigns, and the seventh is yet to come, but his reign will be brief. ¹¹The scarlet animal that died is the eighth king, having reigned before as one of the seven; after his second reign, he too, will go to his doom. ¹²His ten horns are ten kings who have not yet risen to power; they will be appointed to their kingdoms for one brief moment, to reign with him. ¹³They will all sign a treaty giving their power and strength to him. ¹⁴Together they will wage war against the Lamb, and the Lamb will conquer them; for he is Lord over all lords, and King of kings, and his people are the called and chosen and faithful ones.

¹⁵"The oceans, lakes, and rivers that the woman is sitting on represent masses of people of every race and nation.

¹⁶"The scarlet animal and his ten horns—which represent ten kings who will reign with him—all hate the woman, and will attack her and leave her naked and ravaged by fire. ¹⁷For God will put a plan into their minds, a plan that will carry out his purposes: They will mutually agree to give their authority to the scarlet animal so that the words of God will be fulfilled. ¹⁸And this woman you saw in your vision represents the great city that rules over the kings of the earth."

18 The Fall of Babylon

After all this I saw another angel come down from heaven with great authority, and the earth grew bright with his splendor.

²He gave a mighty shout, "Babylon the Great is fallen, is fallen; she has become a den of demons, a haunt of devils and every kind of evil spirit. ³For all the nations have drunk the fatal wine of her intense immorality. The rulers of earth have enjoyed themselves with her, and businessmen throughout the world have grown rich from all her luxurious living."

⁴Then I heard another voice calling from heaven, "Come away from her, my people; do not take part in her sins, or you will be punished with her. ⁵For her sins are piled as high as heaven, and God is ready to judge her for her crimes. ⁶Do to her as she has done to you, and more—give double penalty for all her evil deeds. She brewed many a cup of woe for others—give twice as much to her. ⁷She has lived in luxury and pleasure—match it now with torments and with sorrows. She boasts, 'I am queen upon my throne. I am no helpless widow. I will not experience sorrow.' ⁸Therefore the sorrows of death and mourning and famine shall overtake her in a single day, and she shall be utterly consumed by fire; for mighty is the Lord who judges her."

⁹And the world leaders who took part in her immoral acts and enjoyed her favors will mourn for her as they see the smoke rising from her charred remains. ¹⁰They will stand far off, trembling with fear and crying out, "Alas, Babylon, that mighty city! In one moment her judgment fell."

¹¹The merchants of the earth will weep and mourn for her, for there is no one left to buy their goods. ¹²She was their biggest customer for gold and silver, precious stones, pearls, finest linens, purple silks, and scarlet; and every kind of perfumed wood, and ivory goods, and most expensive wooden carvings, and brass, and iron, and marble; ¹³and spices, and perfumes, and incense, ointment, and frankincense, wine, olive oil, and fine flour; wheat, cattle, sheep, horses, chariots, and slaves—and even the souls of men.

¹⁴"All the fancy things you loved so much are gone," they cry. "The dainty luxuries and splendor that you prized so much will never be yours again. They are gone forever."

¹⁵And so the merchants who have become wealthy by selling her these things shall stand at a distance, fearing danger to themselves, weeping and crying, ¹⁶"Alas, that great city, so beautiful—like a woman clothed in finest purple and scarlet linens, decked out with gold and precious stones and pearls! ¹⁷In one moment, all the wealth of the city is gone!"

And all the shipowners and captains of the merchant ships and crews will stand a long way off, ¹⁸crying as they watch the smoke ascend, and saying, "Where in all the world is there another city such as this?" ¹⁹And they will throw dust on their heads in their sorrow and say, "Alas, alas, for that great city! She made us all rich from her great wealth. And now in a single hour all is gone...."

²⁰But you, O heaven, rejoice over her fate; and you, O children of God and the prophets and the apostles! For at last God has given judgment against her for you.

Family Devotions

☐ DEVOTION 365
RECEIVING CHRIST AS SAVIOR

Read Revelation 21 : 27

"Chuck can't come over this afternoon," said Ken. "He has to go with his mom on door-to-door visitation and give out church literature and stuff."

"Is that right?" Mom was interested. "Are Chuck and his family Christians?"

Ken shook his head. "I don't think so. They talk about Jesus, but they don't believe he's God. That doesn't make sense to me. They seem to think they have to do a lot of things to be saved—like this calling program. And they think they have to be very faithful in going to church or they won't be saved for sure. I don't understand it. I don't think Chuck does either, but he does whatever he's supposed to—says it can't hurt."

Dad spoke up. "Sounds to me like he needs to drop the oars and catch hold of the rope." he said.

"There's a river with a big waterfall near the town where I grew up," explained Dad. "Just above the falls the water is very wild and dangerous. It's unsafe for boating, and I remember one time when a man in a rowboat got caught in the swift current. It was pulling him closer and closer to the falls. A crowd gathered on the bank, and people called to him to row harder. He tried his best, but we could see he wasn't going to make it. Then someone threw a rope to him. Do you suppose the crowd continued to encourage him to row? Oh no! Then the cry was, 'Drop your oars! Grab the rope!' He did, and they pulled him to shore." Dad paused, still seeing the scene in his mind. "Like the man in the boat, Chuck needs to stop working to save himself. The only way he can be saved is to stop struggling and just trust Jesus to save him."

Receiving Christ as Savior Memory Verse

If you tell others with your own mouth that Jesus Christ is your Lord and believe in your own heart that God has raised him from the dead, you will be saved.
Romans 10:9

How About You?
Are you struggling to save yourself? Do you hope that going to church, praying, giving, or trying to be good will save you from your sins and earn a place for you in heaven? It won't. You will be saved only when you stop trying to save yourself and simply trust Christ. Do that today. H. M.

• For the next devotional, turn to page 1269. • To start the next topic, turn to page 7. • For notes on RECEIVING CHRIST AS SAVIOR, see pages 839, 842, 1146, 1234, and 1240.

²¹Then a mighty angel picked up a boulder shaped like a millstone and threw it into the ocean and shouted, "Babylon, that great city, shall be thrown away as I have thrown away this stone, and she shall disappear forever. ²²Never again will the sound of music be there—no more pianos, saxophones, and trumpets. No industry of any kind will ever again exist there, and there will be no more milling of the grain. ²³Dark, dark will be her nights; not even a lamp in a window will ever be seen again. No more joyous wedding bells and happy voices of the bridegrooms and the brides. Her businessmen were known around the world, and she deceived all nations with her sorceries. ²⁴And she was responsible for the blood of all the martyred prophets and the saints."

19 A Hallelujah Chorus

After this I heard the shouting of a vast crowd in heaven, "Hallelujah! Praise the Lord! Salvation is from our God. Honor and authority belong to him alone; ²for his judgments are just and true. He has punished the Great Prostitute who corrupted the earth with her sin; and he has avenged the murder of his servants."

³Again and again their voices rang, "Praise the Lord! The smoke from her burning ascends forever and forever!"

⁴Then the twenty-four Elders and four Living Beings fell down and worshiped God, who was sitting upon the throne, and said, "Amen! Hallelujah! Praise the Lord!"

⁵And out of the throne came a voice that said, "Praise our God, all you his servants, small and great, who fear him."

⁶Then I heard again what sounded like the shouting of a huge crowd, or like the waves of a hundred oceans crashing on the shore, or like the mighty rolling of great thunder, "Praise the Lord. For the Lord our God, the Almighty, reigns. ⁷Let us be glad and rejoice and honor him; for the time has come for the wedding banquet of the Lamb, and his bride has prepared herself. ⁸She is permitted to wear the cleanest and whitest and finest of linens." (Fine linen represents the good deeds done by the people of God.)

⁹And the angel dictated this sentence to me: "Blessed are those who are invited to the wedding feast of the Lamb." And he added, "God himself has stated this."

¹⁰Then I fell down at his feet to worship him, but he said, "No! Don't! For I am a servant of God just as you are, and as your brother Christians are, who testify of their faith in Jesus. Worship God. The purpose of all prophecy and of all I have shown you is to tell about Jesus."

¹¹Then I saw heaven opened and a white horse standing there; and the one sitting on the horse was named Faithful and True—the one who justly punishes and makes war. ¹²His eyes were like flames, and on his head were many crowns. A name was written on his forehead, and only he knew its meaning. ¹³He was clothed with garments dipped in blood, and his title was "The Word of God." ¹⁴The armies of heaven, dressed in finest linen, white and clean, followed him on white horses.

¹⁵In his mouth he held a sharp sword to strike down the nations; he ruled them with an iron grip; and he trod the winepress of the fierceness of the wrath of Almighty God. ¹⁶On his robe and thigh was written this title: "King of Kings and Lord of Lords."

¹⁷Then I saw an angel standing in the sunshine, shouting loudly to the birds, "Come! Gather together for the supper of the Great God! ¹⁸Come and eat the flesh of kings, and captains, and great generals; of horses and riders; and of all humanity, both great and small, slave and free."

¹⁹Then I saw the Evil Creature gathering the governments of the earth and their armies to fight against the one sitting on the horse and his army. ²⁰And the Evil Creature was captured, and with him the False Prophet, who could do mighty miracles when the Evil Creature was present—miracles that deceived all who had accepted the Evil Creature's mark, and who worshiped his statue. Both of them—the Evil Creature and his False Prophet—were thrown alive into the Lake of Fire that burns with sulphur. ²¹And their entire army was killed with the sharp sword in the mouth of the one riding the white horse, and all the birds of heaven were gorged with their flesh.

20 The 1,000 Years

Then I saw an angel come down from heaven with the key to the bottomless pit and a heavy chain in his hand. ²He seized the Dragon—that old Serpent, the devil, Satan—and bound him in chains for a thousand years, ³and threw him into the bottomless pit, which he then shut and locked so that he could not fool the nations any more until the thousand years were finished. Afterwards he would be released again for a little while.

⁴Then I saw thrones, and sitting on them were those who had been given the right to judge. And I saw the souls of those who had been beheaded for their testimony about Jesus, for proclaiming the Word of God, and who had not worshiped the Creature or his statue, nor accepted his mark on their foreheads or their hands. They had come to life again and now they reigned with Christ for a thousand years.

FAMILY DEVOTIONS

☐ DEVOTION 366
RESPECTING GOD'S WORD

Read Revelation 22 : 18-21

"See what Larry loaned me?" Martin handed a book to his father. "They use it in his church—it's their Bible. It's almost like ours, except there are a few things in it that aren't in ours."

Dad flipped through the pages. "There certainly are."

"But there are lots of things that are the same as our Bible," Martin continued. "It's interesting."

"Yes, but very dangerous," Dad warned.

"Dangerous?" Martin snorted. "How could it be dangerous? It teaches a lot of the same things the Holy Bible teaches—things like loving one another and not stealing or lying. If a person followed all the teachings in this book, he would be a good person."

"Yes, but being a good person won't save anyone," Dad reminded. "There is only one way to heaven—Jesus."

"Well, yeah, but . . ." Martin hesitated. "I still don't see anything so wrong with this book."

Dad explained. "This book is portrayed as God's revelation to man, yet it doesn't acknowledge Jesus as the only way to heaven. When people accept it as the Word of God, they get off course. I remember seeing a chart once that showed what would happen if a rocket fired at the moon were off course by just five degrees. It showed that if the rocket were five degrees off course at blast-off, it would be more than ten thousand miles off target by the time it reached the moon," said Dad. "In fact, it wouldn't reach the moon—it would bypass it completely."

"Wow!" Martin raised his eyebrows.

"Being just a little bit off course on our journey to heaven means missing heaven completely," continued Dad. "The Bible is our chart. We must follow it and not be sidetracked by other so-called bibles that are *almost* right."

Respecting God's Word Memory Verse

Your words are what sustain me; they are food to my hungry soul. They bring joy to my sorrowing heart and delight me. How proud I am to bear your name, O Lord.

Jeremiah 15:16

How About You?

The Bible is the book which will show you the way to heaven. Other books may explain how you can be sure of heaven, but they must always refer to, and agree with, what God says in the Bible. If they don't, you must not believe them. Stay with the Word of God. B. W.

• To start the next topic, turn to page 5.   • For notes on RESPECTING GOD'S WORD, see pages 208, 369, 1188, and 1248.

⁵This is the First Resurrection. (The rest of the dead did not come back to life until the thousand years had ended.) ⁶Blessed and holy are those who share in the First Resurrection. For them the Second Death holds no terrors, for they will be priests of God and of Christ, and shall reign with him a thousand years.

⁷When the thousand years end, Satan will be let out of his prison. ⁸He will go out to deceive the nations of the world and gather them together, with Gog and Magog, for battle—a mighty host, numberless as sand along the shore. ⁹They will go up across the broad plain of the earth and surround God's people and the beloved city of Jerusalem on every side. But fire from God in heaven will flash down on the attacking armies and consume them.

¹⁰Then the devil who had betrayed them will again be thrown into the Lake of Fire burning with sulphur where the Creature and False Prophet are, and they will be tormented day and night forever and ever.

¹¹And I saw a great white throne and the one who sat upon it, from whose face the earth and sky fled away, but they found no place to hide. ¹²I saw the dead, great and small, standing before God; and The Books were opened, including the Book of Life. And the dead were judged according to the things written in The Books, each according to the deeds he had done. ¹³The oceans surrendered the bodies buried in them; and the earth and the underworld gave up the dead in them. Each was judged according to his deeds. ¹⁴And Death and Hell were thrown into the Lake of Fire. This is the Second Death—the Lake of Fire. ¹⁵And if anyone's name was not found recorded in the Book of Life, he was thrown into the Lake of Fire.

21 A New Heaven and New Earth

Then I saw a new earth (with no oceans!) and a new sky, for the present earth and sky had disappeared. ²And I, John, saw the Holy City, the new Jerusalem, coming down from God out of heaven. It was a glorious sight, beautiful as a bride at her wedding.

³I heard a loud shout from the throne saying, "Look, the home of God is now among men, and he will live with them and they will be his people; yes, God himself will be among them. ⁴He will wipe away all tears from their eyes, and there shall be no more death, nor sorrow, nor crying, nor pain. All of that has gone forever."

⁵And the one sitting on the throne said, "See, I am making all things new!" And then he said to me, "Write this down, for what I tell you is trustworthy and true: ⁶It is finished! I am the A and the Z—the Beginning and the End. I will give to the thirsty the springs of the Water of Life—as a gift! ⁷Everyone who conquers will inherit all these blessings, and I will be his God and he will be my son. ⁸But cowards who turn back from following me, and those who are unfaithful to me, and the corrupt, and murderers, and the immoral, and those conversing with demons, and idol worshipers and all liars—their doom is in the Lake that burns with fire and sulphur. This is the Second Death."

⁹Then one of the seven angels who had emptied the flasks containing the seven last plagues came and said to me, "Come with me and I will show you the bride, the Lamb's wife."

¹⁰In a vision he took me to a towering mountain peak, and from there I watched that wondrous city, the holy Jerusalem, descending out of the skies from God. ¹¹It was filled with the glory of God and flashed and glowed like a precious gem, crystal clear like jasper. ¹²Its walls were broad and high, with twelve gates guarded by twelve angels. And the names of the twelve tribes of Israel were written on the gates. ¹³There were three gates on each side—north, south, east, and west. ¹⁴The walls had twelve foundation stones, and on them were written the names of the twelve apostles of the Lamb.

¹⁵The angel held in his hand a golden measuring stick to measure the city and its gates and walls. ¹⁶When he measured it, he found it was a square as wide as it was long; in fact it was in the form of a cube, for its height was exactly the same as its other dimensions—1,500 miles each way. ¹⁷Then he measured the thickness of the walls and found them to be 216 feet across (the angel called out these measurements to me, using standard units).

¹⁸⁻²⁰The city itself was pure, transparent gold like glass! The wall was made of jasper, and was built on twelve layers of foundation stones inlaid with gems: the first layer with jasper; the second with sapphire; the third with chalcedony; the fourth with emerald; the fifth with sardonyx; the sixth layer with sardus; the seventh with chrysolite; the eighth with beryl; the ninth with topaz; the tenth with chrysoprase; the eleventh with jacinth; the twelfth with amethyst.

²¹The twelve gates were made of pearls—each gate from a single pearl! And the main street was pure, transparent gold, like glass.

²²No temple could be seen in the city, for the Lord God Almighty and the Lamb are worshiped in it everywhere. ²³And the city has no need of sun or moon to light it, for the glory of God and of the Lamb illuminate it. ²⁴Its light will light the nations of the earth, and the rulers of the world will come and bring their glory to it. ²⁵Its gates never close; they stay open all day long—and

there is no night! ²⁶And the glory and honor of all the nations shall be brought into it. ²⁷Nothing evil will be permitted in it—no one immoral or dishonest—but only those whose names are written in the Lamb's Book of Life.

22 The River of Life

And he pointed out to me a river of pure Water of Life, clear as crystal, flowing from the throne of God and the Lamb, ²coursing down the center of the main street. On each side of the river grew Trees of Life, bearing twelve crops of fruit, with a fresh crop each month; the leaves were used for medicine to heal the nations.

³There shall be nothing in the city that is evil; for the throne of God and of the Lamb will be there, and his servants will worship him. ⁴And they shall see his face; and his name shall be written on their foreheads. ⁵And there will be no night there—no need for lamps or sun—for the Lord God will be their light; and they shall reign forever and ever.

⁶,⁷Then the angel said to me, "These words are trustworthy and true: 'I am coming soon!' God, who tells his prophets what the future holds, has sent his angel to tell you this will happen soon. Blessed are those who believe it and all else written in the scroll."

⁸I, John, saw and heard all these things, and fell down to worship the angel who showed them to me; ⁹but again he said, "No, don't do anything like that. I, too, am a servant of Jesus as you are, and as your brothers the prophets are, as well as all those who heed the truth stated in this book. Worship God alone."

¹⁰Then he instructed me, "Do not seal up what you have written, for the time of fulfillment is near. ¹¹And when that time comes, all doing wrong will do it more and more; the vile will become more vile; good men will be better; those who are holy will continue on in greater holiness."

¹²"See, I am coming soon, and my reward is with me, to repay everyone according to the deeds he has done. ¹³I am the A and the Z, the Beginning and the End, the First and Last. ¹⁴Blessed forever are all who are washing their robes, to have the right to enter in through the gates of the city and to eat the fruit from the Tree of Life.

¹⁵"Outside the city are those who have strayed away from God, and the sorcerers and the immoral and murderers and idolaters, and all who love to lie, and do so.

¹⁶"I, Jesus, have sent my angel to you to tell the churches all these things. I am both David's Root and his Descendant. I am the bright Morning Star. ¹⁷The Spirit and the bride say, 'Come.' Let each one who hears them say the same, 'Come.' Let the thirsty one come—anyone who wants to; let him come and drink the Water of Life without charge.

¹⁸And I solemnly declare to everyone who reads this book: If anyone adds anything to what is written here, God shall add to him the plagues described in this book. ¹⁹And if anyone subtracts any part of these prophecies, God shall take away his share in the Tree of Life, and in the Holy City just described.

²⁰"He who has said all these things declares: Yes, I am coming soon!"

Amen! Come, Lord Jesus!

²¹The grace of our Lord Jesus Christ be with you all. Amen!

Complete List of Memory Verses

Verse	Topic
Deuteronomy 5:29	*OBEDIENCE*
Joshua 1:9	*SERVING GOD BOLDLY*
1 Chronicles 28:20	*PERSEVERANCE*
2 Chronicles 7:14	*RESPECTING GOD'S WARNINGS*
2 Chronicles 16:9	*STANDING FOR RIGHTEOUSNESS*
Psalm 32:8	*TRUSTING GOD FOR GUIDANCE*
Psalm 46:1	*TRUSTING GOD FOR HELP*
Psalm 51:10	*CONFESSING SIN*
Psalm 119:9	*AVOIDING SIN*
Psalm 133:1	*ACCEPTING OTHERS*
Proverbs 3:6	*PUTTING GOD FIRST*
Proverbs 12:22	*KEEPING YOUR PROMISES*
Isaiah 41:10	*OVERCOMING FEAR*
Isaiah 43:1	*KNOWING YOU'RE SPECIAL TO GOD*
Isaiah 55:8-9	*TRUSTING GOD'S PLAN*
Jeremiah 15:16	*RESPECTING GOD'S WORD*
Jeremiah 29:11	*LEAVING THE FUTURE IN GOD'S HANDS*
Hosea 6:3	*KNOWING GOD*
Micah 6:8	*BECOMING MORE LIKE JESUS*
Malachi 3:10	*GIVING TO GOD*
Luke 9:48	*SERVING GOD WILLINGLY*
Luke 10:27	*RESPECTING OTHERS*
Luke 12:8	*SHARING YOUR FAITH*
Luke 12:31	*MAKING THE BEST CHOICES*
Luke 14:11	*HUMILITY*
John 3:16	*RECEIVING CHRIST AS SAVIOR*
Romans 8:28	*DEALING WITH CHANGE*
Romans 10:9	*RECEIVING CHRIST AS SAVIOR*
2 Corinthians 1:3	*SHOWING COMPASSION*
Galatians 6:9	*SHARING YOUR FAITH*
Galatians 6:10	*SHOWING KINDNESS*
Ephesians 4:25	*HONESTY*
Ephesians 6:1	*RESPECTING AUTHORITY*
Philippians 2:3	*RESPECTING OTHERS*
Philippians 2:5	*CULTIVATING GODLY ATTITUDES*
Philippians 4:4	*TRUE JOY*
Philippians 4:6	*PRAYING AT ALL TIMES*
Philippians 4:8	*OPTIMISM*
Philippians 4:12	*CONTENTMENT*
Colossians 3:13	*FORGIVING OTHERS*

Complete List of Memory Verses

Colossians 3:17 .... *CULTIVATING GODLY ATTITUDES*
1 Thessalonians 5:11 .... *ENCOURAGING OTHERS*
Titus 2:7 .... *BECOMING MORE LIKE JESUS*
Hebrews 2:18 .... *RESISTING TEMPTATION*
Hebrews 10:24 .... *FAITH IN ACTION*
Hebrews 10:25 .... *GOING TO CHURCH*
James 1:19-20 .... *OVERCOMING ANGER*
James 5:7 .... *PATIENCE*
James 5:13 .... *GIVING THANKS*
1 Peter 2:11 .... *AVOIDING SIN*
1 John 1:9 .... *CONFESSING SIN*
1 John 3:18 .... *LOVING OTHERS*

List of Memory Verses by Topic

ACCEPTING OTHERS
Psalm 133:1
How wonderful it is, how pleasant, when brothers live in harmony!

AVOIDING SIN
1 Peter 2:11
Dear brothers, you are only visitors here. Since your real home is in heaven, I beg you to keep away from the evil pleasures of this world; they are not for you, for they fight against your very souls.

Psalm 119:9
How can a young man stay pure? By reading your Word and following its rules.

BECOMING MORE LIKE JESUS
Micah 6:8
No, he has told you what he wants, and this is all it is: *to be fair, just, merciful, and to walk humbly with your God.*

Titus 2:7
Let everything you do reflect your love of the truth and the fact that you are in dead earnest about it.

CONFESSING SIN
1 John 1:9
But if we confess our sins to him, he can be depended on to forgive us and to cleanse us from every wrong. [And it is perfectly proper for God to do this for us because Christ died to wash away our sins.]

Psalm 51:10
Create in me a new, clean heart, O God, filled with clean thoughts and right desires.

CONTENTMENT
Philippians 4:12
I know how to live on almost nothing or with everything. I have learned the secret of contentment in every situation, whether it be a full stomach or hunger, plenty or want.

CULTIVATING GODLY ATTITUDES
Philippians 2:5
Your attitude should be the kind that was shown us by Jesus Christ.

Colossians 3:17
Whatever you do or say, let it be as a representative of the Lord Jesus, and come with him into the presence of God the Father to give him your thanks.

List of Memory Verses by Topic

DEALING WITH CHANGE
Romans 8:28
We know that all that happens to us is working for our good if we love God and are fitting into his plans.

ENCOURAGING OTHERS
1 Thessalonians 5:11
So encourage each other to build each other up, just as you are already doing.

FAITH IN ACTION
Hebrews 10:24
In response to all he has done for us, let us outdo each other in being helpful and kind to each other and in doing good.

FORGIVING OTHERS
Colossians 3:13
Be gentle and ready to forgive; never hold grudges. Remember, the Lord forgave you, so you must forgive others.

GIVING THANKS
James 5:13
Is anyone among you suffering? He should keep on praying about it. And those who have reason to be thankful should continually be singing praises to the Lord.

GIVING TO GOD
Malachi 3:10
Bring all the tithes into the storehouse so that there will be food enough in my Temple; if you do, I will open up the windows of heaven for you and pour out a blessing so great you won't have room enough to take it in! Try it! Let me prove it to you!

GOING TO CHURCH
Hebrews 10:25
Let us not neglect our church meetings, as some people do, but encourage and warn each other, especially now that the day of his coming back again is drawing near.

HONESTY
Ephesians 4:25
Stop lying to each other; tell the truth, for we are parts of each other and when we lie to each other we are hurting ourselves.

HUMILITY
Luke 14:11
For everyone who tries to honor himself shall be humbled; and he who humbles himself shall be honored.

KEEPING YOUR PROMISES
Proverbs 12:22
God delights in those who keep their promises and abhors those who don't.

KNOWING GOD
Hosea 6:3
Oh, that we might know the Lord! Let us press on to know him, and he will respond to us as surely as the coming of dawn or the rain of early spring.

KNOWING YOU'RE SPECIAL TO GOD
Isaiah 43:1
But now the Lord who created you, O Israel, says, Don't be afraid, for I have ransomed you; I have called you by name; you are mine.

LEAVING THE FUTURE IN GOD'S HANDS
Jeremiah 29:11
For I know the plans I have for you, says the Lord. They are plans for good and not for evil, to give you a future and a hope.

LOVING OTHERS
1 John 3:18
Little children, let us stop just *saying* we love people; let us *really* love them, and *show it* by our *actions*.

MAKING THE BEST CHOICES
Luke 12:31
He will always give you all you need from day to day if you will make the Kingdom of God your primary concern.

OBEDIENCE
Deuteronomy 5:29
Oh, that they would always have such a heart for me, wanting to obey my commandments. Then all would go well with them in the future, and with their children throughout all generations!

OPTIMISM
Philippians 4:8
Fix your thoughts on what is true and good and right. Think about things that are pure and lovely, and dwell on the fine, good things in others. Think about all you can praise God for and be glad about.

OVERCOMING ANGER
James 1:19-20
Dear brothers, don't ever forget that it is best to listen much, speak little, and not become angry; for anger doesn't make us good, as God demands that we must be.

OVERCOMING FEAR
Isaiah 41:10
Fear not, for I am with you. Do not be dismayed. I am your God. I will strengthen you; I will help you; I will uphold you with my victorious right hand.

PATIENCE
James 5:7
Now as for you, dear brothers who are waiting for the Lord's return, be patient, like a farmer who waits until the autumn for his precious harvest to ripen.

PERSEVERANCE
1 Chronicles 28:20
Be strong and courageous and get to work. Don't be frightened by the size of the task, for the Lord my God is with you; he will not forsake you. He will see to it that everything is finished correctly.

PRAYING AT ALL TIMES
Philippians 4:6
Don't worry about anything; instead, pray about everything; tell God your needs, and don't forget to thank him for his answers.

PUTTING GOD FIRST
Proverbs 3:6
In everything you do, put God first, and he will direct you and crown your efforts with success.

RECEIVING CHRIST AS SAVIOR
John 3:16
For God loved the world so much that he gave his only Son so that anyone who believes in him shall not perish but have eternal life.

Romans 10:9
If you tell others with your own mouth that Jesus Christ is your Lord and believe in your own heart that God has raised him from the dead, you will be saved.

RESISTING TEMPTATION
Hebrews 2:18
For since he himself has now been through suffering and temptation, he knows what it is like when we suffer and are tempted, and he is wonderfully able to help us.

RESPECTING AUTHORITY
Ephesians 6:1
Children, obey your parents; this is the right thing to do because God has placed them in authority over you.

RESPECTING GOD'S WARNINGS
2 Chronicles 7:14
If my people will humble themselves and pray, and search for me, and turn from their wicked ways, I will hear them from heaven and forgive their sins and heal their land.

RESPECTING GOD'S WORD
Jeremiah 15:16
Your words are what sustain me; they are food to my hungry soul. They bring joy to my sorrowing heart and delight me. How proud I am to bear your name, O Lord.

RESPECTING OTHERS
Philippians 2:3
Don't be selfish; don't live to make a good impression on others. Be humble, thinking of others as better than yourself.

Luke 10:27
You must love the Lord your God with all your heart, and with all your soul, and with all your strength, and with all your mind. And you must love your neighbor just as much as you love yourself.

SERVING GOD BOLDLY
Joshua 1:9
Yes, be bold and strong! Banish fear and doubt! For remember, the Lord your God is with you wherever you go.

SERVING GOD WILLINGLY
Luke 9:48
Anyone who takes care of a little child like this is caring for me! And whoever cares for me is caring for God who sent me. Your care for others is the measure of your greatness.

SHARING YOUR FAITH
Luke 12:8
And I assure you of this: I, the Messiah, will publicly honor you in the presence of God's angels if you publicly acknowledge me here on earth as your Friend.

Galatians 6:9
And let us not get tired of doing what is right, for after a while we will reap a harvest of blessing if we don't get discouraged and give up.

SHOWING COMPASSION
2 Corinthians 1:3
What a wonderful God we have—he is the Father of our Lord Jesus Christ, the source of every mercy, and the one who so wonderfully comforts and strengthens us in our hardships and trials.

SHOWING KINDNESS
Galatians 6:10
That's why whenever we can we should always be kind to everyone, and especially to our Christian brothers.

STANDING FOR RIGHTEOUSNESS
2 Chronicles 16:9
For the eyes of the Lord search back and forth across the whole earth, looking for people whose hearts are perfect toward him, so that he can show his great power in helping them.

TRUE JOY
Philippians 4:4
Always be full of joy in the Lord; I say it again, rejoice!

TRUSTING GOD FOR GUIDANCE
Psalm 32:8
I will instruct you (says the Lord) and guide you along the best pathway for your life; I will advise you and watch your progress.

TRUSTING GOD FOR HELP
Psalm 46:1
God is our refuge and strength, a tested help in times of trouble.

TRUSTING GOD'S PLAN
Isaiah 55:8-9
This plan of mine is not what you would work out, neither are my thoughts the same as yours! For just as the heavens are higher than the earth, so are my ways higher than yours, and my thoughts than yours.

Topical Index

This index locates the devotionals and notes for each of the forty-five topics covered in *The Family Devotions Bible*. Page numbers are provided to make it easy to find all the features listed.

ACCEPTING OTHERS
Devotions
Deuteronomy 16:9-14	207
1 Samuel 1:9-17	289
1 Samuel 10:26-27	299
1 Samuel 16:1-7	305
Isaiah 11:3-5	671
John 17:20-23	1029
Acts 10:25-28	1049

Notes
Judges 11:3	270
Galatians 3:28	1140
Philemon 1:13-16	1196
Revelation 5:9-10	1254

AVOIDING SIN
Devotions
Deuteronomy 5:18	195
Judges 7:1-22	265
2 Kings 5:20-27	387
Proverbs 6:27-28	617
Isaiah 1:16-19	663
Isaiah 33:13-16	687
Ezekiel 36:25-27	805
Daniel 1:8-16	819
Luke 9:57-62	973
Romans 6:20-23	1081
Romans 12:1-2	1087
2 Timothy 2:19-22	1187
1 Peter 1:22–2:3	1225
1 Peter 2:11-16	1227

Notes
Deuteronomy 29:18	220
2 Samuel 11:1ff.	332
2 Kings 10:24	392
Song of Solomon 4:12	657

BECOMING MORE LIKE JESUS
Devotions
Leviticus 19:16	131
Deuteronomy 26:12-13	215
1 Samuel 25:1-31	317
Esther 1:7-8	499
Isaiah 6:5	665
Lamentations 3:40	773
Ezekiel 34:23-31	803
Amos 7:7-8	849

John 13:34-35 1019
Romans 5:1-5 1079
Titus 2:6-8 1193
James 3:5-10 1219
2 Peter 1:5-9 1233
1 John 2:3-10 1237
Notes
Joshua 6:21 234
Luke 14:34 983
1 Corinthians 9:24-27 1105
Colossians 2:20-23 1164

CONFESSING SIN
Devotions
Genesis 35:1-4, 9-12 41
Leviticus 4:13-14, 27-28 117
Numbers 5:5-10 153
Numbers 32:23 185
Judges 17:1-6 277
2 Samuel 12:13-20 335
2 Chronicles 24:17-20 457
Nehemiah 9:28-38 491
Psalm 89:14-18 577
Psalm 130 599
Isaiah 29:15-16 683
Isaiah 57:15-21 711
Romans 2:18-23 1075
1 Timothy 1:12-17 1179
Notes
1 Chronicles 21:8 429
Ezra 10:3-4, 11 479
Hosea 6:1-3 836
Zechariah 3:2-4 881
James 5:9 1220

CONTENTMENT
Devotions
Exodus 20:15-17 89
Numbers 11:4-10 159
Judges 3:30–4:3 263
2 Samuel 16:1-4; 19:24-30 339
Philippians 4:6-13 1159
Hebrews 13:5 1211
Revelation 14:12 1261
Notes
Psalm 23:2-3 542
Psalm 34:9-10 547
Matthew 6:24 902
Acts 20:33 1063

CULTIVATING GODLY ATTITUDES
Devotions
Leviticus 7:11-15, 28-29 121
Leviticus 11:44-45 125
Numbers 14:26-30 163
1 Chronicles 4:9-10 415
2 Chronicles 20:15-26 455

Proverbs 23:22-25 635
Jeremiah 17:7-10 737
Jeremiah 18:1-6 739
John 3:1-8 1005
1 Corinthians 3:10-15 1097
1 Corinthians 6:19-20 1101
Galatians 6:4 1141
Colossians 3:8-15 1163
Revelation 2:19 1251
Notes
2 Samuel 15:14 337
2 Kings 2:9 383
Ezra 1:5 472
Proverbs 13:3 622
James 1:5 1216

DEALING WITH CHANGE
Devotions
Genesis 12:1-5 15
Numbers 9:15-23 155
Deuteronomy 31:6-8 223
Joshua 1:1-5 231
Joshua 3:1-5, 12-17 233
Isaiah 12 673
Romans 8:26-31 1083
Notes
Genesis 46:3-4 56
Numbers 10:21 156
1 Samuel 2:2 288
2 Timothy 1:13-14 1186
Hebrews 2:9 1198

ENCOURAGING OTHERS
Devotions
Isaiah 51:12 705
Luke 22:25-32 995
Romans 14:1-4 1091
Romans 16:3-10 1093
1 Corinthians 8:8-13 1103
James 3:8-10, 13-18 1221
1 John 4:7-12 1239
Notes
Exodus 39:43 108
Numbers 10:29-32 157
Ezra 5:1-2 474
Philippians 1:3-11 1156
1 Thessalonians 5:9-11 1170

FAITH IN ACTION
Devotions
Leviticus 23:22 141
2 Kings 12:15 395
Psalm 15 537
Psalm 51:1-13 557
Matthew 21:28-32 919
James 2:14-20 1217
1 Peter 2:12 1229

Notes
Psalm 99:3 583
Amos 2:6-7 846
Acts 25:11 1068
2 Peter 1:6 1232

FORGIVING OTHERS
Devotions
Genesis 27:41; 33:1-11 39
Genesis 50:14-21 59
Joshua 20:1-6 251
2 Samuel 19:15-23 343
Matthew 18:21-22 917
Ephesians 4:17-32 1147
Colossians 3:12-15 1165
Notes
Judges 15:1ff. 273
1 Kings 1:52-53 356
Psalm 103:12 586
Daniel 4:19 822

GIVING THANKS
Devotions
Numbers 21:4-6 169
1 Samuel 7:7-12 293
1 Chronicles 29:10-20 437
Psalm 57 559
Psalm 68:4-10, 19-20 565
Psalm 150 609
Luke 17:11-19 987
Notes
Psalm 92:1-2 582
Psalms 146–150 608
Hosea 2:12 834

GIVING TO GOD
Devotions
Exodus 35:20-29 105
2 Samuel 24:18-24 349
Proverbs 11:24-28 621
Malachi 3:8-12 891
Acts 9:36-43 1047
2 Corinthians 8:2-15 1127
2 Corinthians 9:6-8 1129
Notes
Numbers 31:28-30 182
1 Chronicles 26:27 433
2 Corinthians 8:10-15 1128

GOING TO CHURCH
Devotions
Deuteronomy 4:9-14 193
Deuteronomy 10:12-13, 17-21 201
Nehemiah 8:1-6 489
Psalm 66 563
2 Corinthians 4:7-10, 16 1125
2 Timothy 2:15; 3:14-17 1189
Hebrews 10:19-25 1205

Notes
Lamentations 2:7 770
Luke 4:16 965
John 2:14-16 1002

HONESTY
Devotions
Genesis 27:1-18, 23-25 33
Genesis 43:19-23 51
Exodus 8:8, 15, 24-32 71
Job 27:3-4 521
Proverbs 12:17-22 623
Proverbs 29:5 639
Acts 24:16 1067
Notes
1 Samuel 15:13-14 304
Ezekiel 45:9-11 813
Micah 7:1-4 863

HUMILITY
Devotions
2 Chronicles 15:7 449
Job 5:8-27 509
Isaiah 29:19 685
Isaiah 42:5-12 695
Daniel 4:28-33 823
Zephaniah 2:3 875
Luke 1:26-33, 46-49 961
Notes
Genesis 49:18 57
2 Kings 8:12-13 390
1 Chronicles 17:16-20 428
Obadiah 1:4 854
1 Peter 5:6 1228

KEEPING YOUR PROMISES
Devotions
Numbers 30:1-2 181
Deuteronomy 23:21-23 213
Ruth 3:18–4:1 283
Proverbs 25:11-15, 19 637
Ecclesiastes 5:1-7 649
Matthew 25:14-23 925
Luke 16:10-12 985
Notes
Numbers 32:16-19 183
Ruth 3:18–4:1 284
Hosea 10:4 838

KNOWING GOD
Devotions
Deuteronomy 6:4-8 197
2 Samuel 12:1-11 333
Psalm 119:43-68 595
Daniel 6:1-10 825
Mark 1:35 935
Acts 17:10-12 1059
1 Timothy 4:7-10 1181

Notes
- Leviticus 16:1-25 129
- Psalm 147:5 610
- Ezekiel 48:35 815
- Hebrews 11:1 1208

KNOWING YOU'RE SPECIAL TO GOD
Devotions
- 1 Samuel 16:4-13 307
- 1 Chronicles 1:1-10 411
- Psalm 8:3-9 535
- Psalm 139:14-18 603
- John 6:1-13 1009
- John 15:16 1027
- 1 Corinthians 12:20-27 1109

Notes
- Judges 3:15-21 260
- Haggai 2:23 878
- Matthew 10:29-31 908
- Luke 1:46-55 960

LEAVING THE FUTURE IN GOD'S HANDS
Devotions
- Exodus 12:1-13 75
- 1 Samuel 28:1-20 321
- 2 Kings 19:9-22, 30-37 403
- Ezra 8:21-23 477
- Isaiah 47:1-14 701
- Jeremiah 29:8-13 747
- Micah 5:10-15 861

Notes
- 2 Kings 21:6 405
- 2 Chronicles 18:22 452
- Daniel 12:13 831
- Acts 19:18-19 1061

LOVING OTHERS
Devotions
- 1 Samuel 18:1-3; 20:12-17 313
- 1 Kings 18:3-4 373
- Job 42:7-10 529
- Matthew 9:18-26 905
- Mark 14:3-9 953
- Luke 10:30-37 975
- 1 Corinthians 13:4-10 1111

Notes
- Song of Solomon 8:6-7 658
- Mark 12:29-31 951
- Luke 6:27 967
- 2 John 1:5-6 1242

MAKING THE BEST CHOICES
Devotions
- Judges 16:1-5, 16-31 275
- 1 Kings 11:1-13 367
- 2 Chronicles 34:14-33 467
- Psalm 90:9-17 579
- Zechariah 8:9-23 885

Mark 6:7-13, 30-31 941
1 Timothy 6:9-18 1183
Notes
1 Kings 3:6-9 358
Ecclesiastes 12:1 652
Mark 8:36-37 944

OBEDIENCE
Devotions
Genesis 22:1-12 25
Exodus 1:15-21 63
Deuteronomy 8:1-10 199
Jeremiah 7:21-26 727
Matthew 28:19-20 931
John 14:15-21 1023
Revelation 3:7-13 1253
Notes
1 Samuel 26:8ff. 319
1 Chronicles 15:13-15 425
Esther 3:2 500
Job 6:29-30 510
Jeremiah 38:9-13 757

OPTIMISM
Devotions
Genesis 17:1-8 19
Genesis 45:4-8; 50:18-20 55
Numbers 13:25-33 161
Psalm 78:17-22 571
Isaiah 54:4-10 707
Jeremiah 17:7-8 735
Acts 16:22-32 1057
Notes
Leviticus 26:40-45 143
Psalm 11:1-4 536
Isaiah 22:13-14 677
Mark 5:36 940

OVERCOMING ANGER
Devotions
Leviticus 19:17-18 133
Proverbs 15:1 625
Ecclesiastes 7:9 651
Jonah 4 857
Matthew 5:21-22 903
2 Corinthians 2:5-11 1123
2 Corinthians 12:20 1133
Notes
Numbers 25:10-11 176
Job 7:11 511
Mark 3:5 936
John 2:15-16 1003

OVERCOMING FEAR
Devotions
Genesis 7:17-20; 8:1; 9:8-17 13
Exodus 14:13-22 79
Psalm 91 581

Isaiah 41:8-10, 13 693
Mark 4:36-41 939
Luke 21:9-19 993
1 Corinthians 15:51-57 1113
Notes
Deuteronomy 3:21-22 191
Nehemiah 2:3 482
Psalm 46:1-3 554
Psalm 112:7-8 592
Matthew 14:28 912

PATIENCE
Devotions
Psalm 37:1-9 549
Ecclesiastes 3:1-11 645
Isaiah 55:6-11 709
Mark 11:22-25 949
Galatians 5:22–6:1 1139
2 Thessalonians 3:5 1175
Hebrews 10:32-38 1207
Notes
Genesis 29:20-28 35
Joshua 11:18 242
2 Samuel 5:4-5 329
Esther 6:10-13 502

PERSEVERANCE
Devotions
Genesis 32:22-29 37
Exodus 5:1-9; 6:1-13 69
Joshua 14:6-14 245
Judges 1:16–2:5 259
Psalm 40:1-3 551
Isaiah 40:25-31 691
Hebrews 12:1-3 1209
Notes
2 Samuel 2:21-23 326
2 Chronicles 29:11 461
Esther 8:15-17 503
Jeremiah 44:9-10 760
2 Thessalonians 1:5 1174

PRAYING AT ALL TIMES
Devotions
Genesis 37:5-9, 18-28 45
Exodus 33:17-18 101
Numbers 21:7 171
Nehemiah 1:4-11 483
Nehemiah 4:7-9 485
Daniel 6:11-28 827
Luke 11:5-8 977
Notes
1 Kings 8:56-61 363
2 Chronicles 6:30 442
Mark 9:23 945
Acts 4:24-30 1040
Acts 12:5 1051

PUTTING GOD FIRST
Devotions
- Leviticus 1:1-4 115
- Deuteronomy 18:9-14 211
- Joshua 24:14-15 253
- 1 Samuel 8:4-22 295
- Psalm 63:1-7 561
- Jeremiah 2:26-32 721
- Jeremiah 31:18-20 749

Notes
- 2 Kings 15:34-35 397
- Nehemiah 10:28ff. 492
- Ecclesiastes 1:8-11 644
- Ezekiel 20:39 791
- Luke 13:30 982

RECEIVING CHRIST AS SAVIOR
Devotions
- Joshua 2:1-15; 6:22-25 235
- 1 Samuel 9:2; 13:1-14 301
- 2 Samuel 22:21-27 347
- Isaiah 49:13-16 703
- Habakkuk 3:18 871
- Luke 18:10-14 989
- John 3:16-21 1007
- John 14:1-6 1021
- John 15:1-8 1025
- Acts 13:26-39 1053
- Revelation 3:20-22 1255
- Revelation 5:9-10 1257
- Revelation 21:21-27 1265
- Revelation 21:27 1267

Notes
- Hosea 14:1-2 839
- Joel 2:12-13 842
- Ephesians 2:3 1146
- 2 Peter 2:19 1234
- 1 John 5:13 1240

RESISTING TEMPTATION
Devotions
- Genesis 3:1-7 7
- Genesis 39:7-23 47
- Exodus 34:10-17 103
- Psalm 1 533
- Jeremiah 4:1-4, 14 723
- Jeremiah 22:1-5 741
- 1 Corinthians 10:12-13 1107

Notes
- Judges 8:31 268
- 2 Chronicles 14:7 448
- Luke 4:3 964
- Revelation 9:20-21 1258

RESPECTING AUTHORITY
Devotions
- Deuteronomy 31:12-13 225
- Joshua 17:14-18:3 247

1 Kings 1:5-8, 43-45	355
1 Kings 2:1-4	357
1 Kings 21:4-10	377
Ecclesiastes 8:5-7	653
Jeremiah 36:1-4, 21-26	755

Notes

1 Samuel 19:1-2	311
1 Chronicles 10:11-12	420
1 Timothy 5:17-18	1182

RESPECTING GOD'S WARNINGS
Devotions

Genesis 19:1, 12-17, 24-26	21
Job 34:16-28	525
Psalm 111:10	591
Ezekiel 33:1-5	801
Nahum 1:1-3, 7-12	867
1 Thessalonians 5:1-11	1171
Revelation 20:11-15	1263

Notes

Deuteronomy 27:15-26	219
Zephaniah 3:2	874
2 Corinthians 7:11	1126

RESPECTING GOD'S WORD
Devotions

Genesis 6:1-21	11
Exodus 24:1-7	93
Exodus 40:16, 21, 23, 32	109
Leviticus 10:8-11	123
Psalm 119:97-105	597
Proverbs 3:1-6; 8:5-16	619
Revelation 22:18-21	1269

Notes

Deuteronomy 17:18-20	208
1 Kings 13:7-31	369
2 Timothy 3:16	1188
Jude 1:3	1248

RESPECTING OTHERS
Devotions

Genesis 1:28-31	5
Exodus 10:16-29	73
Exodus 20:12	87
Exodus 28:33-35, 40-43	97
Leviticus 19:32	135
Numbers 16:1-3, 28-32	165
1 Samuel 24:1-11	315
Job 1:14-22	507
Psalm 133	601
Proverbs 16:31	627
Proverbs 20:20	633
Isaiah 46:3-4	699
Galatians 3:26-29	1137
Ephesians 6:1-4	1151

Notes

1 Samuel 30:11-15	322

2 Kings 1:13-15 382
Romans 12:10 1088
James 2:2-4 1218

SERVING GOD BOLDLY
Devotions
Genesis 14:11-20 17
Exodus 3:1-11; 4:10-12 65
1 Samuel 17:45-51 309
Matthew 5:14-16 901
Matthew 14:23-33 913
Mark 11:1-11 947
1 Thessalonians 2:2-8 1169
Notes
2 Samuel 3:7 327
2 Kings 20:5-6 404
Esther 4:16 501
Jeremiah 1:6-8 720
Jonah 1:3 856

SERVING GOD WILLINGLY
Devotions
1 Samuel 2:18; 3:1-21 291
2 Kings 5:1-5 385
1 Chronicles 11:10-14 421
1 Chronicles 28:8-20 435
Isaiah 6:8 667
Hebrews 6:10-12 1203
3 John 1:5-8 1245
Notes
Genesis 41:38-40 49
1 Chronicles 9:17-18 419
Malachi 1:6-8 890
Matthew 20:27 920
Matthew 23:11-12 922

SHARING YOUR FAITH
Devotions
1 Chronicles 16:23-31 427
Psalm 31:19-24 545
Psalm 145 607
Ezekiel 3:4-11 777
Ezekiel 3:16-17 779
Matthew 4:18-22 897
Matthew 26:69-75 927
Mark 16:15 957
Luke 12:8-12 979
John 7:1-5 1011
Acts 2:41-47 1037
Acts 4:13-20; 5:12-32 1041
Acts 28:16-31 1071
1 Corinthians 4:1-5 1099
Notes
2 Chronicles 30:11 462
Ezekiel 2:6-8 776
John 9:25 1015
Romans 1:5 1074

SHOWING COMPASSION
Devotions
Psalm 71:18-24	569
Proverbs 17:17	629
Isaiah 59:3-8	713
Hosea 6:1-3	837
Zechariah 7:8-10	883
John 11:32-36	1017
2 Corinthians 1:3-7	1121

Notes
Deuteronomy 15:7-11	206
Job 2:13	506
Job 16:1ff.	515
Isaiah 58:1ff.	710
Mark 2:3	934

SHOWING KINDNESS
Devotions
Exodus 16:1-6	81
Exodus 22:21; 23:9	91
Leviticus 19:33-34	137
Psalm 19:12-14	541
Psalm 101:1-2	585
Proverbs 19:22	631
Matthew 5:7	899

Notes
Isaiah 3:16-26	664
Zechariah 2:8	880
Acts 2:44	1038
3 John 1:5	1244

STANDING FOR RIGHTEOUSNESS
Devotions
Leviticus 22:31-32	139
Numbers 25:1-3	175
Joshua 7:1-12	237
Psalm 71:15-17	567
Ezekiel 11:5	783
Acts 5:1-11	1043
Ephesians 5:14-21	1149

Notes
Exodus 2:3ff.	62
1 Samuel 11:6	298
1 Kings 15:30	371
Isaiah 24:4-5	678
Mark 11:14-15	948

TRUE JOY
Devotions
Exodus 16:7-12	83
Deuteronomy 12:18	203
Job 10	513
Psalm 118:24	593
Ecclesiastes 3:12-13, 22	647
Isaiah 61:3-10	715
Philippians 2:14-18	1157

Notes
    Psalm 4:7 532
    John 15:11 1024
    Philippians 4:4 1160

TRUSTING GOD FOR GUIDANCE
Devotions
    Genesis 24:1-9 27
    Exodus 13:17-22 77
    Joshua 9:3-18 239
    2 Chronicles 7:14 445
    Psalm 25:4-10 543
    Psalm 48 555
    John 20:24-29 1031

Notes
    Job 28:13 522
    Psalm 43:3-4 553
    Proverbs 1:7-9 614
    Isaiah 19:14-15 676
    Acts 16:6 1056

TRUSTING GOD FOR HELP
Devotions
    Genesis 25:27-34 29
    Exodus 4:10-15 67
    Psalm 86 575
    Psalm 143:7-12 605
    Isaiah 26:3-4 679
    Ezekiel 18:25-32 789
    Hebrews 4:12-16 1201

Notes
    Joshua 10:25 240
    Joshua 19:47-48 249
    2 Chronicles 32:1ff. 464
    Psalm 18:30 539
    Jeremiah 32:6-12 751

TRUSTING GOD'S PLAN
Devotions
    Genesis 4:6-7 9
    Numbers 3:14-37 149
    Deuteronomy 26:16-18 217
    2 Kings 17:5-14 399
    Job 23:10-12 519
    Psalm 107:1-8 589
    Luke 12:16-21 981
    John 21:17-22 1033

Notes
    Joshua 21:43-45 252
    1 Samuel 9:3ff. 296
    Jeremiah 12:5-6 731
    Habakkuk 2:4 870